August 21–24, 2011
San Diego, California, USA

Association for
Computing Machinery

Advancing Computing as a Science & Profession

KDD'11

Proceedings of the 17th ACM SIGKDD Conference on

Knowledge Discovery and Data Mining

Sponsored by:

ACM SIGKDD and ACM SIGMOD

Association for
Computing Machinery

Advancing Computing as a Science & Profession

The Association for Computing Machinery
2 Penn Plaza, Suite 701
New York, New York 10121-0701

ISBN: 978-1-4503-0934-9 (Digital)

ISBN: 978-1-4503-1256-1 (Print)

Additional copies may be ordered prepaid from:

ACM Order Department
PO Box 30777
New York, NY 10087-0777, USA

Phone: 1-800-342-6626 (USA and Canada)
+1-212-626-0500 (Global)
Fax: +1-212-944-1318
E-mail: acmhelp@acm.org
Hours of Operation: 8:30 am – 4:30 pm ET

Printed in the USA

General Chair's Welcome Message

It is my great honor and pleasure to welcome you to ACM SIGKDD's *17th Annual Conference on Knowledge Discovery and Data Mining, KDD2011,* being held in San Diego, California, from August 21 through August 24, 2011. This year's KDD Conference continues its tradition of being the premier forum for the sharing of leading edge research results and industrial experiences of KDD theory, technology, and applications, among it's multi-disciplinary participants from academia, government, and industry. The KDD2011 organization committee has worked hard to help organize this year's conference, and to ensure that it maintains its pre-eminent position as the top worldwide conference for dissemination of cutting edge technical progress of this community.

The science and business of extracting actionable insights from data has never been more important. We are experiencing an explosion of data, and the consequent interest in analyzing this information in a timely and rigorous fashion. Data and content volumes are expected to grow exponentially in the next decade. Much of the new growth is expected to dominantly come from unstructured content; documents, images, audio and video. These trends are setting up the stage for a fascinating set of new research challenges, and simultaneously driving the need for accelerated deployment of our research advances, ranging from algorithmic advances in core modeling and learning techniques, to scalable methods for parallel and distributed mining of massive scale data, to new paradigms for consumption and delivery of the analytic insights. It is my hope that attendees at this conference will be able to sense and appreciate the impressive progress our community is making in addressing these challenges.

We have made a few changes this year to the traditional KDD conference format, to address the growing interest in this technology. The conference will begin as always with workshops and tutorials on Sunday, and then we have a full 3-day program for the main body of the conference. The extended 3-day main program has allowed us to include additional keynote plenary talks and make space for some exciting new content. We are launching a new track this year, called the Industry Practice Expo. The aim of the IPE track is to bring in eminent practitioners of KDD from industry to share with the participants their in depth experiences on what it means to successfully deploy working instances of high impacting KDD solutions.

You will get to read more details of the technical program in the forewords from our Program Chairs. Industry/Government Application Chairs, and Industry Practice Expo Chairs. I would like to truly thank and appreciate all the hard work put in by the entire organization committee of the conference. In addition, no conference can be run on its own today without the generous support from our industry and government sponsors. I wish to thank them all. Special thanks to ACM and SIGKDD for providing solid support in all matters, organizational and financial. Finally, thanks to all of you, conference attendees and participants, for your continued endorsement of this important venue. Enjoy the conference!

Chid Apte
KDD2011 General Chair
IBM Research, Yorktown Heights, NY, USA

ACM SIGKDD 2011 Program Chairs' Welcome

The KDD conference has come a long way from its origins as an IJCAI workshop in Detroit in 1989, evolving into a full-fledged research conference in 1995, with continued growth since – were it publicly traded it would have been an excellent investment over the years. This year we received a record 714 submissions to the research program, from which 126 papers were accepted, 56 as talks and 70 as posters, for an aggregate acceptance rate of 17.6% (quite similar to recent years). As a comparative example, twelve years ago in 1999, when this conference was also held in San Diego, there were 280 papers submitted to the research program and 52 were accepted as talks or posters.

The success and growth of the KDD conference over the past two decades has paralleled the broader emergence of machine learning and data mining as major areas of research in academia and industry. Among the academic conferences, the KDD conference has typically more of an emphasis on applications when compared to sibling conferences such as NIPS and ICML. Yet it is important to keep in mind that the successes of data mining and machine learning depend not only on successful applications. It is the *synergy* of research and application that drives our field forward - one without the other will wither. This synergy is also what makes our field vibrant and fun – who among us knew while listening to lectures on linear algebra or probability in high-school or college that we would later apply these ideas to discover information from data as diverse as Web pages, medical images, movie ratings, and climate records.

The breadth of topics covered in this year's research program is correspondingly diverse, including social networks, privacy, text mining, predictive modeling, time-series forecasting, spatial data analysis, and more. We are very fortunate to have 4 world-class keynote speakers this year, providing expert overviews of the latest advances in optimization, Web mining, causality, and bioinformatics. If you have not heard these speakers before you have a treat in store – and if you have heard them speak before, then you already know not to miss any of these 4 talks. The panel discussion on Wednesday afternoon on data mining prize competitions is also well worth your attention – participants include several of the world's leading authorities on this topic.

The process of whittling down the initial 714 submissions to the final set of 126 accepted papers required the coordination and time of a large number of willing volunteers. The program committee (PC) consisted of over 350 reviewers (PC members) and 37 senior PC members. In the first phase each submitted paper was automatically assigned to 3 reviewers (after a bidding process) and to a single senior PC member. Once the reviews from each of the 3 reviewers were completed, the senior PC members had the option of initiating a discussion for any of their papers, e.g., if there was significant divergence in scores among reviewers, or if a paper was on the borderline of being accepted. Following the discussion phase, the senior PC members provided a recommendation score for each paper in terms of its suitability for acceptance, and (optionally) a short meta-review. In the final phase, we (the program chairs) analyzed all of this information, starting with the obvious accept and reject decisions, and then gradually focusing in more detail on the papers near the borderline, seeking additional reviews and input from the PC and senior PC members where appropriate. It is quite likely that in hindsight some worthy papers may have been rejected as part of this process – these errors are an unfortunate reality of modern computer science conferences, and hard to avoid when a very large number of decisions have to be made over a short time span based on a subjective reviewing process.

We made a number of changes to the reviewing and decision process this year compared to recent years. For example, we jettisoned the author-response phase – there are certainly some merits to be gained by allowing such a phase, but we felt that the aggregate time and effort spent by authors and reviewers in total often outweighs the specific gains obtained for a relatively small number of individual papers. We also added a conditional accept phase – of the 126 accepted papers, 43 had been identified by 2 or more the reviewers as needing significant improvement in writing (typos, grammar, etc). These papers were duly revised and resubmitted by the authors (in some cases with multiple iterations) until we felt that they were ready for publication in the proceedings. Our decision to include this extra round of revision came from our observation that the quality of writing has deteriorated in recent years at computer science conferences - it is increasingly common to encounter poorly written papers in published proceedings. This reflects poorly on our field and motivated our desire to try to improve the writing quality this year. Our attempts are likely to have been only partly successful, but we nonetheless encourage chairs and authors for future conferences to continue to raise the bar for writing quality.

We conclude with some well-deserved words of thanks to the large supporting cast. We are extremely grateful to the PC members and senior PC members for volunteering their time to help in the reviewing process. Diligent peer review is an essential cornerstone for research progress – we thank you all for the many detailed and conscientious reviews that were generated. Last year's program chairs, Andrew Tomkins and Qiang Yang, were generous in providing us with advice and expertise based on lessons learned in 2010. Professor Jie Tang and his colleagues at Tsinghua volunteered their time and effort to provide valuable rankings of papers for reviewers during the bidding process. We would also like to convey our sincere thanks to the staff who run the Microsoft CMT system – they were more than willing to answer questions and help us at all times during the submission, reviewing, and decision process. And finally we would like to thank all of our colleagues on the KDD 2011 organization committee who were a pleasure to work with and without whom we would not have a conference.

Let the 17th ACM SIGKDD conference begin – we hope you enjoy it!

Joydeep Ghosh and Padhraic Smyth
ACM SIGKDD 2011 Program Chairs

Foreword to the Industrial/Government Track

The 2011 Industrial/Government track continued the revitalization that began in 2010 by clearly focusing on three areas of applied KDD work that are the sources of value to industrial and government organizations: (1) deployed applications, (2) knowledge discoveries, and (3) emerging applications. These areas build on the results of KDD research by applying the results of such research to enable the construction of novel and useful applications, the discovery of novel, interesting and useful knowledge, and the extension and application of research results to specific real world problems of interest. Papers were solicited and reviewed in these three areas:

- Deployed KDD systems that are providing real value to industry, government, or other organizations or professions. These deployed systems could support ongoing knowledge discovery or could be applications that employ discovered knowledge, or some combination of the two.

- Discoveries of knowledge with demonstrable value to industry, government, or other users (e.g., scientific or medical professions). This knowledge must be "externally validated" as interesting and useful; it can not simply be a model that has better performance on some traditional KDD metric such as accuracy or area under the curve.

- Emerging applications and technology that provide insight relevant to the above value propositions. These emerging applications must have clear user interest and support to distinguish them from KDD research papers, or they must provide insight into issues and factors that affect the successful use of KDD technology and methods. Papers that describe infrastructure that enables the large-scale deployment of KDD techniques also are in this area.

Industry/Government track papers not only document and recognize significant accomplishments in these three areas, but also provide feedback to KDD researchers about needs, constraints, and applicability of KDD algorithms, methods and techniques in the real world. Our emphasis was on papers that advance the understanding of practical, applied, or pragmatic issues related to the use of KDD technologies in industry and government settings and highlight new research challenges arising from attempts to create such real KDD applications. We encouraged potential authors to address these issues and challenges in the Call for Papers and the accompanying Author Instructions (see http://www.kdd.org/kdd2011/author_instructions_industry.shtml)

Our review process began with a validation by the reviewers that the authors correctly classified their paper's area – to ensure that the paper was reviewed according to the applicable criteria for that area – and a check that all required elements for that area were addressed in the paper. These required elements were:

- Deployed KDD case studies describe deployed projects with measurable benefits that include KDD technology. These papers must clearly describe the industry or government problem that is solved, the overall architecture of the deployed system, the data sources used, the reasons for the choices of particular KDD technologies, how KDD technologies solved the problem, the particular KDD process embodied by the deployed application, the use and payoff of the application, the costs to develop the application, the maintenance plan, and the number and types of users.

- Papers that describe discoveries of knowledge must clearly state what data sources and background knowledge were used, what data mining algorithms were tried, what overall KDD process was used, what the new discovered knowledge is, how the new knowledge was validated, and what the value to the industry or government is of such newly discovered knowledge. Note that this category is intended for significant discoveries of domain knowledge that were enabled by KDD technologies and processes, and not for reporting of KDD research results.

- Emerging application and technology papers discuss prototype applications, tools for focused domains or tasks, useful techniques or methods, useful system architectures, scalability enablers, tool evaluations, or integration of KDD with other technologies. Such papers must clearly explain the requirements arising from the particular industry or government setting for which the application is being developed and from the particular databases on which the application is based. These papers must also identify how the emerging solution is using KDD technologies to address these requirements, the deployment plan, and the evaluation methodology and metrics for the emerging application. Pragmatic issues and considerations include important practical and research considerations, approaches, and architectures that enable successful applications. This category may include comparative evaluations of different KDD technologies for particular application problems. Preferences will be given to papers whose insights may generalize to other domains or problems. Product advertisements will not be accepted.

Specific review criteria included:

- Value/Payoff: What are the measurable benefits of the deployed application, the value of the newly discovered knowledge, or the generalizable insights from the emerging application?
- Cost: What is the cost/effort of the reported project? (To develop and maintain the application or to discover the new knowledge)
- External Significance: Is there clear evidence that the application problem being addressed and the KDD solution matters to an identified external set of users?
- External Validity: Is the knowledge discovered/used by the application externally validated? (This can be demonstrated by its use by a business, government, or profession; by publication in a peer-reviewed domain journal, or other means)
- Does the paper thoroughly describe the data sources and background knowledge used?
- Does the paper thoroughly describe the selection, use, appropriateness and effectiveness of the KDD technologies and/or data mining algorithms?
- Does the paper describe the KDD process enabled by the application or used to discover knowledge?
- Novelty/Originality: Does the work apply KDD technology to a new problem? Does it develop or apply a new type of KDD technology to an existing problem? Does it apply KDD technology to achieve a better result than with previous technology?

- Technical soundness: Does the paper show an accurate understanding of KDD research and technology? Does it identify relevant past work? Does it appropriately match techniques to problem characteristics?
- Evaluation: Is the reported work carefully evaluated? Is it statistically sound? Are the results compared to appropriate baselines? To other approaches and solutions? To previously reported work? Are its claims supported?
- Deployment/Use: Is there clear evidence that the application is deployed or on a path to deployment, or that the discovered knowledge will be used?
- Clarity: Is the paper written clearly? Is it organized logically? Are there sufficient figures and tables to illustrate its main points? Is it accessible to readers without specialized domain knowledge? Is it accessible to readers from different technical specialties and application domains?
- Does the paper contain insights or results that will generalize or apply to other domains or is it specialized to a particular domain?
- Will the paper be accessible to non-specialists in the particular domain?

Overall, we reviewed 73 papers and accepted 26, of which 9 describe deployed applications, 3 knowledge discoveries, and 14 emerging applications. The application areas cover a broad range, including finance, security, internet, text mining, science, retail, medical, and social, showing the many different fields to which KDD is being applied and adding value.

We hope you find these papers interesting and look forward to continued improvements in the use of KDD techniques to provide real value to industry and government.

Ted Senator and Michael Zeller
Industrial/ Government Track Program Chairs

Foreword to the KDD 2011 Industry Practice Expo

It is our distinct honor to welcome you to the inaugural Industry Practice Expo track at the KDD conference. The Industry Practice Expo features invited talks from leading experts who have developed and deployed successful, large-scale data mining applications and systems in their respective fields. We trust that this opportunity for the KDD community to hear directly from the experts will start a new era of cross-fertilization of ideas in knowledge discovery and data mining from various disciplines.

The field of Knowledge Discovery and Data Mining has matured tremendously over the past 15 years. This advancement in the field is duly reflected in the KDD conference publications describing the leading edge research and industry/government applications. At the planning meeting for KDD 2011, Usama Fayyad, the SIGKDD chairman, proposed starting a new track that would complement the already well-established Research and Industry/Government tracks at the KDD conference and showcase the successes and best-practices of applications and systems of knowledge discovery and data mining in various industries. While the Research and Industry/Government tracks would continue their excellent work featuring the latest advances in the field via peer-reviewed publications, the Industry Practice Expo track would feature invited talks from leading experts who would otherwise not publish in the KDD Research or Industry/Government tracks either because of time-constraints or because they are from industries where their work is publicized in forums other than the KDD conference. Armed with this mandate we started on an almost year long journey to conceive, implement, and present to you the inaugural KDD Industry Practice Expo.

We have kept our ambitions very high right from the beginning and have aspired to bring together a group of leading-experts to deliver a series of technical talks focusing on innovative and leading-edge, large-scale applications and systems of data mining in areas such as finance, health-care, bio-informatics, public policy, infrastructure (transportation, utilities, etc.), telecommunications, social media, and computational advertising. We wanted to select the talks that will inspire and motivate fellow members of our KDD community by spreading awareness of various seminal, innovative, and proven applications of knowledge discovery and data mining, sharing key insights and best-practices, and introducing new problems, challenges, and methodologies. We have been immensely fortunate to have the opportunity of working with an advisory committee for the Industry Practice Expo. The committee comprises of individuals who are luminaries in their own right and have generously devoted their time and energies in guiding us through the process. We are extremely grateful for their advice, constant support and encouragement.

We have selected a great panel of speakers who represent a broad cross-section of KDD applications and systems across multiple industries. In putting together this Industry Practice Expo track we have taken the time and effort to get to know each potential speaker well, carefully reviewed their work to better understand their contributions and ensure that the material they present would be interesting and valuable to the KDD audience. We would like to thank all of our speakers for their time and patience as we went through the vetting process and for graciously accepting our invitation to present their work at the KDD conference.

We warmly welcome you to the inaugural KDD Industry Practice Expo and hope that you will enjoy it and find it useful in your professional endeavors. Your suggestions and comments are very welcome.

Best regards,

Rajesh Parekh and Ying Li
Industry Practice Expo Track co-chairs

Table of Contents

General Chair's Welcome Message ... iii
Chid Apte *(IBM Research)*

ACM SIGKDD 2011 Program Chairs' Welcome ... iv
Joydeep Ghosh *(University of Texas at Austin)*, Padhraic Smyth *(University of California, Irvine)*

Foreword to the Industrial/Government Track ... vi
Ted Senator *(SAIC)*, Michael Zeller *(Zementis)*

Foreword to the KDD 2011 Industry Practice Expo ... ix
Rajesh Parekh *(Groupon)*, Ying Li *(Microsoft)*

ACM SIGKDD 2011 Conference Organization ... xxii

KDD'11 Research Track Program Committees ... xxiii

KDD'11 Industry/Government Program Committee ... xxvii

ACM SIGKDD 2011 Industry Practice Expo Advisory ... xxviii

Kdd'11 Sponsors & Supporters ... xxix

Keynote Address 1

- **Convex Optimization: From Embedded Real-Time to Large-Scale Distributed** ... 1
  Stephen Boyd *(Stanford University)*

Keynote Address 2

- **Internet Scale Data Analysis** ... 2
  Peter Norvig *(Google)*

Keynote Address 3

- **Cancer Genomics** ... 3
  David Haussler *(Univerisity of California, Santa Cruz)*

Keynote Address 4

- **The Mathematics of Causal Inference** ... 5
  Judea Pearl *(University of California, Los Angeles)*

Session A1: Classification

- **CHIRP: A New Classifier Based on Composite Hypercubes on Iterated Random Projections** ... 6
  Leland Wilkinson, Anushka Anand, Dang Nhon Tuan *(University of Illinois at Chicago)*
- **Supervised Learning for Provenance-Similarity of Binaries** ... 15
  Sagar Chaki, Cory Cohen, Arie Gurfinkel *(Carnegie Mellon Software Engineering Institute)*
- **Trading Representability for Scalability: Adaptive Multi-Hyperplane Machine for Nonlinear Classification** ... 24
  Zhuang Wang *(Siemens Corporate Research)*, Nemanja Djuric *(Temple University)*, Koby Crammer *(The Technion)*, Slobodan Vucetic *(Temple University)*
- **An Improved GLMNET for L1-Regularized Logistic Regression** ... 33
  Guo-Xun Yuan, Chia-Hua Ho, Chih-Jen Lin *(National Taiwan University)*

Session A1: Matrix Factorization

- **Integrating Low-Rank and Group-Sparse Structures for Robust Multi-Task Learning** 42
  Jianhui Chen, Jiayu Zhou, Jieping Ye *(Arizona State University)*
- **Model Order Selection for Boolean Matrix Factorization** 51
  Pauli Miettinen *(Max Planck Institute for Informatics)*, Jilles Vreeken *(Universiteit Antwerpen)*
- **Rank Aggregation via Nuclear Norm Minimization** 60
  David F. Gleich *(Sandia National Laboratories)*, Lek-Heng Lim *(University of Chicago)*
- **Large-Scale Matrix Factorization with Distributed Stochastic Gradient Descent** 69
  Rainer Gemulla *(Max-Planck-Institut für Informatik)*,
  Peter J. Haas, Erik Nijkamp, Yannis Sismanis *(IBM Almaden Research Center)*

Session A1: Graph Analysis

- **Diversity in Ranking via Resistive Graph Centers** 78
  Avinava Dubey *(IBM Research India)*, Soumen Chakrabarti *(IIT Bombay)*,
  Chiranjib Bhattacharyya *(IISc Bangalore)*
- **Collective Graph Identification** 87
  Galileo Mark Namata, Stanley Kok, Lise Getoor *(University of Maryland)*
- **Semi-Supervised Ranking on Very Large Graphs with Rich Metadata** 96
  Bin Gao, Tie-Yan Liu *(Microsoft Research Asia)*, Wei Wei *(Huazhong University of Science and Technology)*,
  Taifeng Wang, Hang Li *(Microsoft Research Asia)*
- **Benefits of Bias: Towards Better Characterization of Network Sampling** 105
  Arun S. Maiya, Tanya Y. Berger-Wolf *(University of Illinois at Chicago)*

Session A2: Web User Modeling

- **Scalable Distributed Inference of Dynamic User Interests for Behavioral Targeting** 114
  Amr Ahmed, Yucheng Low *(Carnegie Mellon University)*,
  Mohamed Aly, Vanja Josifovski, Alexander J. Smola *(Yahoo! Research)*
- **Multiple Domain User Personalization** 123
  Yucheng Low *(Carnegie Mellon University)*, Deepak Agarwal, Alexander J. Smola *(Yahoo! Research)*
- **Click Shaping to Optimize Multiple Objectives** 132
  Deepak Agarwal, Bee-Chung Chen, Pradheep Elango, Xuanhui Wang *(Yahoo! Labs)*
- **Response Prediction Using Collaborative Filtering with Hierarchies and Side-Information** 141
  Aditya Krishna Menon *(University of California at San Diego)*, Krishna-Prasad Chitrapura,
  Sachin Garg *(Yahoo! Labs)*, Deepak Agarwal *(Yahoo! Research)*, Nagaraj Kota *(Yahoo! Labs)*

Session A2: User Modeling

- **From Bias to Opinion: A Transfer-Learning Approach to Real-Time Sentiment Analysis** 150
  Pedro H. Calais Guerra, Adriano Veloso, Wagner Meira Jr., Virgílio Almeida *(Universidade Federal de Minas Gerais)*
- **User Reputation in a Comment Rating Environment** 159
  Bee-Chung Chen *(Yahoo! Research)*, Jian Guo *(Harvard University)*, Belle Tseng, Jie Yang *(Yahoo! Labs)*
- **Selecting a Comprehensive Set of Reviews** 168
  Panayiotis Tsaparas *(Microsoft Research)*, Alexandros Ntoulas *(Zynga)*, Evimaria Terzi *(Boston University)*

Session A2: Online Data and Streams

- **Enabling Fast Prediction for Ensemble Models on Data Streams** 177
  Peng Zhang *(Chinese Academy of Sciences & National Engineering Laboratory for Information Content Security)*,
  Jun Li, Peng Wang *(Chinese Academy of Sciences)*, Byron J. Gao *(Texas State University at San Marcos)*,
  Xingquan Zhu *(University of Technology, Sydney)*,
  Li Guo *(Chinese Academy of Sciences & National Engineering Laboratory for Information Content Security)*

- **Online Active Inference and Learning** 186
  Josh Attenberg *(NYU Polytechnic Institute)*, Foster Provost *(New York University)*
- **Unbiased Online Active Learning in Data Streams** 195
  Wei Chu *(Microsoft)*, Martin Zinkevich, Lihong Li, Achint Thomas, Belle Tseng *(Yahoo! Labs)*
- **Learning to Trade Off Between Exploration and Exploitation in Multiclass Bandit Prediction** 204
  Hamed Valizadegan *(University of Pittsburgh)*, Rong Jin *(Michigan State University)*, Shijun Wang *(National Institute of Health)*

Session A3: Deployed 1

- **Linear Scale Semantic Mining Algorithms in Microsoft SQL Server's Semantic Platform** 213
  Kunal Mukerjee, Todd Porter, Sorin Gherman *(Microsoft)*
- **Combining File Content and File Relations for Cloud Based Malware Detection** 222
  Yanfang Ye *(Comodo Security Solutions, Inc.)*, Tao Li *(Florida International University)*, Shenghuo Zhu *(NEC Laboratories America)*, Weiwei Zhuang *(Xiamen University)*, Egemen Tas, Umesh Gupta, Melih Abdulhayoglu *(Comodo Security Solutions, Inc.)*
- **High-Precision Phrase-Based Document Classification on a Modern Scale** 231
  Ron Bekkerman *(LinkedIn Corporation)*, Matan Gavish *(Stanford University)*
- **Activity Analysis Based on Low Sample Rate Smart Meters** 240
  Feng Chen *(Virginia Tech)*, Jing Dai *(IBM T.J. Watson Research Center)*, Bingsheng Wang *(Virginia Tech)*, Sambit Sahu, Milind Naphade *(IBM T.J. Watson Research Center)*, Chang-Tien Lu *(Virginia Tech)*

Session A3: Deployed 2

- **Estimating the Number of Users Behind IP Addresses for Combating Abusive Traffic** 249
  Ahmed Metwally, Matt Paduano *(Google, Inc.)*
- **Data-Driven Multi-Touch Attribution Models** 258
  Xuhui Shao *(Turn, Inc.)*, Lexin Li *(North Carolina State University)*
- **Bid Landscape Forecasting in Online Ad Exchange Marketplace** 265
  Ying Cui, Ruofei Zhang, Wei Li, Jianchang Mao *(Yahoo! Labs)*
- **Detecting Adversarial Advertisements in the Wild** 274
  D. Sculley, Matthew Eric Otey, Michael Pohl, Bridget Spitznagel, John Hainsworth, Yunkai Zhou *(Google, Inc.)*

Session A3: Discovery

- **Applying Data Mining Techniques to Address Disaster Information Management Challenges on Mobile Devices** 283
  Li Zheng, Chao Shen, Liang Tang, Tao Li, Steve Luis, Shu-Ching Chen *(Florida International University)*
- **Enhancing Investment Decisions in P2P Lending: An Investor Composition Perspective** 292
  Chunyu Luo *(Dalian University of Technology & Rutgers University)*, Hui Xiong *(Rutgers University)*, Wenjun Zhou *(University of Tennessee)*, Yanhong Guo, Guishi Deng *(Dalian University of Technology)*
- **From Market Baskets to Mole Rats: Using Data Mining Techniques to Analyze RFID Data Describing Laboratory Animal Behavior** 301
  Dan P. McCloskey, Michael E. Kress, Susan P. Imberman, Igor Kushnir, Susan Briffa-Mirabella *(College of Staten Island)*
- **A Pattern Discovery Approach to Retail Fraud Detection** 307
  Prasad Gabbur, Sharath Pankanti, Quanfu Fan, Hoang Trinh *(IBM Research)*

Session A4: Emerging 1

- **Driving with Knowledge from the Physical World** 316
  Jing Yuan *(University of Science and Technology of China & Microsoft Research Asia)*, Yu Zheng, Xing Xie *(Microsoft Research Asia)*, Guangzhong Sun *(University of Science and Technology of China)*

- **Interactive Learning for Efficiently Detecting Errors in Insurance Claims** 325
  Rayid Ghani, Mohit Kumar *(Accenture Technology Labs)*
- **NIMBLE: A Toolkit for the Implementation of Parallel Data Mining and Machine Learning Algorithms on MapReduce** 334
  Amol Ghoting, Prabhanjan Kambadur, Edwin Pednault, Ramakrishnan Kannan *(IBM T.J. Watson Research Center)*
- **Classification of Proxy Labeled Examples for Marketing Segment Generation** 343
  Dean Cerrato, Rosie Jones, Avinash Gupta *(Akamai Technologies)*
- **Ameliorating Buyer's Remorse** 351
  Rakesh Agrawal, Samuel Ieong *(Microsoft Research)*, Raja Velu *(Syracuse University)*

Session A4: Emerging 2

- **Experiences with Mining Temporal Event Sequences from Electronic Medical Records: Initial Successes and Some Challenges** 360
  Debprakash Patnaik, Patrick Butler, Naren Ramakrishnan *(Virginia Tech)*, Laxmi Parida *(IBM T.J. Watson Research Center)*, Benjamin J. Keller *(Eastern Michigan University)*, David A. Hanauer *(University of Michigan)*
- **Understanding Atrophy Trajectories in Alzheimer's Disease Using Association Rules on MRI Images** 369
  György J. Simon, Peter W. Li, Clifford R. Jack, Jr., Prashanthi Vemuri *(Mayo Clinic)*
- **A Case Study in a Recommender System Based on Purchase Data** 377
  Bruno Pradel *(Université Pierre et Marie Curie)*, Savaneary Sean *(KXEN Europe)*, Julien Delporte *(INSA de Rouen)*, Sébastien Guérif, Céline Rouveirol *(Université Paris-Nord)*, Nicolas Usunier *(Université Pierre et Marie Curie)*, Françoise Fogelman-Soulié *(KXEN Europe)*, Frédéric Dufau-Joel *(La Boîte à Outils)*
- **Detecting Bots via Incremental LS-SVM Learning with Dynamic Feature Adaptation** 386
  Feilong Chen *(Michigan State University)*, Supranamaya Ranjan *(Narus Corporation)*, Pang-Ning Tan *(Michigan State University)*
- **Toward Personalized Care Management of Patients at Risk – The Diabetes Case Study** 395
  Hani Neuvirth, Michal Ozery-Flato, Jonathan Laserson, Michal Rosen-Zvi, Jianying Hu, Martin S. Kohn, Shahram Ebadollahi *(IBM Research)*

Session A4: Emerging 3

- **Matching Unstructured Product Offers to Structured Product Specifications** 404
  Anitha Kannan *(Microsoft Research)*, Inmar E. Givoni *(University of Toronto)*, Rakesh Agrawal, Ariel Fuxman *(Microsoft Research)*
- **Predictive Client-Side Profiles for Personalized Advertising** 413
  Mikhail Bilenko, Matthew Richardson *(Microsoft Research)*
- **Smoothing Techniques for Adaptive Online Language Models: Topic Tracking in Tweet Streams** 422
  Jimmy Lin, Rion Snow, William Morgan *(Twitter)*
- **Democrats, Republicans and Starbucks Afficionados: User Classification in Twitter** 430
  Marco Pennacchiotti, Ana-Maria Popescu *(Yahoo! Labs)*

Session B1: Text Mining 1

- **Beyond Keyword Search: Discovering Relevant Scientific Literature** 439
  Khalid El-Arini, Carlos Guestrin *(Carnegie Mellon University)*
- **Collaborative Topic Modeling for Recommending Scientific Articles** 448
  Chong Wang, David M. Blei *(Princeton University)*
- **Partially Labeled Topic Models for Interpretable Text Mining** 457
  Daniel Ramage, Christopher D. Manning *(Stanford University)*, Susan Dumais *(Microsoft Research)*

Session B1: Text Mining 2

- **Refining Causality: Who Copied from Whom?** 466
  Tristan Snowsill, Nick Fyson, Tijl De Bie, Nello Cristianini *(University of Bristol)*
- **Conditional Topical Coding: An Efficient Topic Model Conditioned on Rich Features** 475
  Jun Zhu, Ni Lao *(Carnegie Mellon University)*, Ning Chen *(Tsinghua University)*,
  Eric P. Xing *(Carnegie Mellon University)*
- **Tracking Trends: Incorporating Term Volume into Temporal Topic Models** 484
  Liangjie Hong, Dawei Yin *(Lehigh University)*, Jian Guo *(University of Michigan)*,
  Brian D. Davison *(Lehigh University)*

Session B1: Privacy

- **Differentially Private Data Release for Data Mining** 493
  Noman Mohammed, Rui Chen, Benjamin C. M. Fung *(Concordia University)*,
  Philip S. Yu *(University of Illinois at Chicago)*
- **k-NN as an Implementation of Situation Testing for Discrimination Discovery and Prevention** 502
  Binh Thanh Luong *(Institute for Advanced Studies)*, Salvatore Ruggieri, Franco Turini *(University of Pisa)*
- **Exploiting Vulnerability to Secure User Privacy on a Social Networking Site** 511
  Pritam Gundecha, Geoffrey Barbier, Huan Liu *(Arizona State University)*

Session B2: Social Networks

- **On the Semantic Annotation of Places in Location-Based Social Networks** 520
  Mao Ye, Dong Shou, Wang-Chien Lee, Peifeng Yin
  (University of California, Santa Barbara & The Pennsylvania State University),
  Krzysztof Janowicz *(University of California)*
- **Sparsification of Influence Networks** 529
  Michael Mathioudakis *(University of Toronto)*, Francesco Bonchi, Carlos Castillo, Aristides Gionis,
  Antti Ukkonen *(Yahoo! Research)*
- **Leveraging Collaborative Tagging for Web Item Design** 538
  Mahashweta Das, Gautam Das *(University of Texas at Arlington)*,
  Vagelis Hristidis *(Florida International University)*

Session B2: Theory

- **Stackelberg Games for Adversarial Prediction Problems** 547
  Michael Brückner, Tobias Scheffer *(University of Potsdam)*
- **Leakage in Data Mining: Formulation, Detection, and Avoidance** 556
  Shachar Kaufman, Saharon Rosset *(Tel-Aviv University)*, Claudia Perlich *(Media6Degrees)*
- **An Information Theoretic Framework for Data Mining** 564
  Tijl De Bie *(University of Bristol)*

Session B2: Frequent Sets

- **Tell Me What I Need to Know: Succinctly Summarizing Data with Itemsets** 573
  Michael Mampaey, Nikolaj Tatti, Jilles Vreeken *(University of Antwerp)*
- **Direct Local Pattern Sampling by Efficient Two-Step Random Procedures** 582
  Mario Boley *(Fraunhofer IAIS and University of Bonn)*, Claudio Lucchese *(I.S.T.I.-C.N.R. Pisa)*,
  Daniel Paurat *(University of Bonn)*, Thomas Gärtner *(Fraunhofer IAIS and University of Bonn)*
- **Mining Frequent Closed Graphs on Evolving Data Streams** 591
  Albert Bifet, Geoff Holmes, Bernhard Pfahringer *(University of Waikato)*,
  Ricard Gavaldà *(UPC-Barcelona Tech)*

Session C1: Text Mining

- **Latent Topic Feedback for Information Retrieval** 600
  David Andrzejewski, David Buttler *(Lawrence Livermore National Laboratory)*
- **Localized Factor Models for Multi-Context Recommendation** 609
  Deepak Agarwal, Bee-Chung Chen, Bo Long *(Yahoo! Labs)*
- **Latent Aspect Rating Analysis without Aspect Keyword Supervision** 618
  Hongning Wang, Yue Lu, ChengXiang Zhai *(University of Illinois at Urbana-Champaign)*

Session C1: Unsupervised Learning

- **Density Estimation Trees** 627
  Parikshit Ram, Alexander G. Gray *(Georgia Institute of Technology)*
- **Unsupervised Clustering of Multidimensional Distributions Using Earth Mover Distance** 636
  David Applegate, Tamraparni Dasu, Shankar Krishnan, Simon Urbanek *(AT&T Labs - Research)*
- **Online Heterogeneous Mixture Modeling with Marginal and Copula Selection** 645
  Ryohei Fujimaki *(NEC Laboratories America)*, Yasuhiro Sogawa *(Osaka University)*,
  Satoshi Morinaga *(NEC Corporation)*

Session C1: Graph Mining

- **Dual Active Feature and Sample Selection for Graph Classification** 654
  Xiangnan Kong *(University of Illinois at Chicago)*, Wei Fan *(IBM T.J. Watson Research Center)*,
  Philip S. Yu *(University of Illinois at Chicago)*
- **It's Who You Know: Graph Mining Using Recursive Structural Features** 663
  Keith Henderson, Brian Gallagher *(Lawrence Livermore National Laboratory)*,
  Lei Li, Leman Akoglu *(Carnegie Mellon University)*, Tina Eliassi-Rad *(Rutgers University)*,
  Hanghang Tong *(IBM T.J. Watson Research Center)*, Christos Faloutsos *(Carnegie Mellon University)*
- **Triangle Listing in Massive Networks and Its Applications** 672
  Shumo Chu, James Cheng *(Nanyang Technological University)*

Session C2: Scalability

- **Fast Clustering Using MapReduce** 681
  Alina Ene, Sungjin Im, Benjamin Moseley *(University of Illinois)*
- **Clustering Very Large Multi-Dimensional Datasets with MapReduce** 690
  Robson L. F. Cordeiro, Caetano Traina, Jr. , Agma J. M. Traina *(University of São Paulo)*,
  Julio López, U Kang, Christos Faloutsos *(Carnegie Mellon University)*
- **Selective Block Minimization for Faster Convergence of Limited Memory Large-Scale Linear Models** 699
  Kai-Wei Chang, Dan Roth *(University of Illinois at Urbana-Champaign)*

Session C2: Predictive Modeling

- **Bounded Coordinate-Descent for Biological Sequence Classification in High Dimensional Predictor Space** 708
  Georgiana Ifrim *(University College Cork)*, Carsten Wiuf *(Bioinformatics Research Centre)*
- **Multi-Source Domain Adaptation and Its Application to Early Detection of Fatigue** 717
  Rita Chattopadhyay, Jieping Ye, Sethuraman Panchanathan *(Arizona State University)*,
  Wei Fan *(IBM T.J. Watson Research Center)*, Ian Davidson *(University of California, Davis)*
- **Two-Locus Association Mapping in Subquadratic Time** 726
  Panagiotis Achlioptas *(University of Crete)*, Bernhard Schölkopf *(Max Planck Institute for Intelligent Systems)*,
  Karsten M. Borgwardt *(Max Planck Institutes Tübingen)*

Demonstration Track

- **A Taxi Business Intelligence System** 735
  Yong Ge, Chuanren Liu, Hui Xiong *(Rutgers University)*, Jian Chen *(Tsinghua University)*
- **Apolo: Interactive Large Graph Sensemaking by Combining Machine Learning and Visualization** 739
  Duen Horng Chau, Aniket Kittur, Jason I. Hong, Christos Faloutsos *(Carnegie Mellon University)*
- **Article Clipper – A System for Web Article Extraction** 743
  Jian Fan *(Hewlett-Packard Labs Palo Alto)*, Ping Luo *(Hewlett-Packard Labs China)*, Suk Hwan Lim, Sam Liu, Parag Joshi, Jerry Liu *(Hewlett-Packard Labs Palo Alto)*
- **Data Intensive Analysis on the Gordon High Performance Data and Compute System** 747
  Robert S. Sinkovits, Pietro Cicotti, Shawn Strande, Mahidhar Tatineni, Paul Rodriguez, Nicole Wolter, Natasha Balac *(University of California, San Diego)*
- **Frontex Real-Time News Event Extraction Framework** 749
  Martin Atkinson *(Joint Research Centre)*, Jakub Piskorski *(Frontex)*
- **LikeMiner: A System for Mining the Power of 'Like' in Social Media Networks** 753
  Xin Jin, Chi Wang *(University of Illinois at Urbana Champaign)*, Jiebo Luo *(Eastman Kodak Company)*, Xiao Yu, Jiawei Han *(University of Illinois at Urbana Champaign)*
- **MIME: A Framework for Interactive Visual Pattern Mining** 757
  Bart Goethals, Sandy Moens, Jilles Vreeken *(ADReM, University of Antwerp)*
- **SIGKDD Demo: Sensors and Software to Allow Computational Entomology, an Emerging Application of Data Mining** 761
  Gustavo Batista, Eamonn Keogh *(University of California, Riverside)*, Agenor Mafra Neto *(ISCA Technologies)*, Edgar Rowton *(Walter Reed Army Institute of Research)*
- **Social Flocks: A Crowd Simulation Framework for Social Network Generation, Community Detection, and Collective Behavior Modeling** 765
  Cheng-Te Li, Shou-De Lin *(National Taiwan University)*
- **Topic-Level Social Network Search** 769
  Jie Tang, Sen Wu, Bo Gao, Yang Wan *(Tsinghua University)*
- **Video Analytics Solution for Tracking Customer Locations in Retail Shopping Malls** 773
  Harikrishna G. N. Rai, Kishore Jonna, P. Radha Krishna *(Infosys Technologies Limited)*

Industrial Practice Expo Track

- **"Which Half Is Wasted?": Controlled Experiments to Measure Online-Advertising Effectiveness** 777
  David Reiley *(Yahoo! Labs)*
- **Accelerating Large-Scale Data Mining Using In-Database Analytics** 778
  Mario E. Inchiosa *(Netezza)*
- **Applications of Data Mining and Machine Learning in Online Customer Care** 779
  Ravi Vijayaraghavan, P V Kannan *(24/7 Customer Innovation Labs)*
- **Broad Scale Predictive Modeling and Marketing Optimization in Retail Sales** 780
  Dan Steinberg *(Salford Systems)*, Felipe Fernandez Martinez *(Interfe)*
- **Knowledge Discovery and Data Mining in Pharmaceutical Cancer Research** 781
  Paul Rejto *(Pfizer)*
- **Operational Security Analytics – Doing More with Less** 782
  Colleen McCue *(GeoEye Analytics)*
- **Real-Time Risk Control System for CNP (Card Not Present)** 783
  Tai Hsu *(Alibaba Group)*
- **The Power of Analysis and Data** 784
  David Norton *(Caesar's Entertainment)*

- **The Practitioner's Viewpoint to Data Mining – Key Lessons Learned in the Trenches and Case Studies** 785
  Richard Boire *(Boire Filler Group)*
- **Thriving as a Data Miner in the Real World** 786
  John F. Elder, IV *(Elder Research, Inc.)*

Poster Session

- **2D-Interval Predictions for Time Series** 787
  Luis Torgo *(University of Porto)*, Orlando Ohashi *(LIAAD-INESC Porto LA)*
- **A Game Theoretic Framework for Heterogeneous Information Network Clustering** 795
  Faris Alqadah *(Johns Hopkins University)*, Raj Bhatnagar *(University of Cincinnati)*
- **A GPU-Tailored Approach for Training Kernelized SVMs** 805
  Andrew Cotter, Nathan Srebro, Joseph Keshet *(Toyota Technological Institute at Chicago)*
- **A Multi-Task Learning Formulation for Predicting Disease Progression** 814
  Jiayu Zhou, Lei Yuan, Jun Liu, Jieping Ye *(Arizona State University)*
- **A Simple Statistical Model and Association Rule Filtering for Classification** 823
  Gyorgy J. Simon *(Mayo Clinic)*, Vipin Kumar *(University of Minnesota)*, Peter W. Li *(Mayo Clinic)*
- **A Time-Dependent Topic Model for Multiple Text Streams** 832
  Liangjie Hong *(Lehigh University)*, Byron Dom, Siva Gurumurthy, Kostas Tsioutsiouliklis *(Yahoo! Labs)*
- **Active Learning for Node Classification in Assortative and Disassortative Networks** 841
  Cristopher Moore, Xiaoran Yan, Yaojia Zhu *(University of New Mexico)*,
  Jean-Baptiste Rouquier *(Rhône-Alpes Complex Systems Institute and ENS Lyon)*,
  Terran Lane *(University of New Mexico)*
- **Active Learning Using On-Line Algorithms** 850
  Chris Mesterharm, Michael J. Pazzani *(Rutgers University)*
- **Algorithms for Speeding Up Distance-Based Outlier Detection** 859
  Kanishka Bhaduri, Bryan L. Matthews *(NASA Ames Research Center)*, Chris R. Giannella *(The MITRE Corp.)*
- **An Effective Evaluation Measure for Clustering on Evolving Data Streams** 868
  Hardy Kremer, Philipp Kranen, Timm Jansen, Thomas Seidl *(RWTH Aachen University)*,
  Albert Bifet, Geoff Holmes, Bernhard Pfahringer *(University of Waikato Hamilton)*
- **An Iterated Graph Laplacian Approach for Ranking on Manifolds** 877
  Xueyuan Zhou *(University of Chicago)*, Mikhail Belkin *(The Ohio State University)*,
  Nathan Srebro *(Toyota Technological Institute at Chicago)*
- **Anomaly Localization for Network Data Streams with Graph Joint Sparse PCA** 886
  Ruoyi Jiang, Hongliang Fei, Jun Huan *(University of Kansas)*
- **Approximate Kernel k-means: Solution to Large Scale Kernel Clustering** 895
  Radha Chitta, Rong Jin, Timothy C. Havens, Anil K. Jain *(Michigan State University)*
- **Ask Me Better Questions: Active Learning Queries Based on Rule Induction** 904
  Parisa Rashidi, Diane J. Cook *(Washington State University)*
- **Automatically Tagging Email by Leveraging Other Users' Folders** 913
  Yehuda Koren, Edo Liberty, Yoelle Maarek, Roman Sandler *(Yahoo! Research)*
- **Axiomatic Ranking of Network Role Similarity** 922
  Ruoming Jin, Victor E. Lee, Hui Hong *(Kent State University)*
- **Brain Effective Connectivity Modeling for Alzheimer's Disease by Sparse Gaussian Bayesian Network** 931
  Shuai Huang, Jing Li, Jieping Ye *(Arizona State University)*,
  Adam Fleisher, Kewei Chen *(Banner Good Samaritan Medical Center)*,
  Teresa Wu *(Arizona State University)*, Eric Reiman *(Banner Good Samaritan Medical Center)*
- **Classification of Functional Magnetic Resonance Imaging Data Using Informative Pattern Features** 940
  Francisco Pereira, Matthew Botvinick *(Princeton University)*

- **Clustering with Relative Constraints** ... 947
  Eric Yi Liu, Zhaojun Zhang, Wei Wang *(University of North Carolina at Chapel Hill)*
- **Common Component Analysis for Multiple Covariance Matrices** ... 956
  Huahua Wang, Arindam Banerjee, Daniel Boley *(University of Minnesota)*
- **Compression of Weighted Graphs** ... 965
  Hannu Toivonen, Fang Zhou, Aleksi Hartikainen, Atte Hinkka *(University of Helsinki)*
- **Content-Driven Trust Propagation Framework** ... 974
  V.G.Vinod Vydiswaran, ChengXiang Zhai, Dan Roth *(University of Illinois)*
- **Cost-Aware Travel Tour Recommendation** ... 983
  Yong Ge *(Rutgers University)*, Qi Liu *(Rutgers University & University of Science and Technology of China)*,
  Hui Xiong *(Rutgers University)*, Alexander Tuzhilin *(New York University)*, Jian Chen *(Tsinghua University)*
- **Discovering Highly Reliable Subgraphs in Uncertain Graphs** ... 992
  Ruoming Jin, Lin Liu *(Kent State University)*, Charu C. Aggarwal *(IBM T. J. Watson Research Center)*
- **Discovering Shakers from Evolving Entities via Cascading Graph Inference** ... 1001
  Xiaoxiao Shi *(University of Illinois at Chicago)*, Wei Fan *(IBM T.J. Watson Research Center)*,
  Jianping Zhang *(Deloitte Financial Advisory Services LLP)*, Philip S. Yu *(University of Illinois at Chicago)*
- **Discovering Spatio-Temporal Causal Interactions in Traffic Data Streams** ... 1010
  Wei Liu *(University of Sydney)*, Yu Zheng *(Microsoft Research Asia)*,
  Sanjay Chawla *(University of Sydney)*, Jing Yuan *(University of Science and Technology of China)*,
  Xie Xing *(Microsoft Research Asia)*
- **Display Advertising Impact: Search Lift and Social Influence** ... 1019
  Panagiotis Papadimitriou, Hector Garcia-Molina *(Stanford University)*,
  Prabhakar Krishnamurthy *(Yahoo! Labs)*, Randall A. Lewis, David H. Reiley *(Yahoo! Research)*
- **Diversified Ranking on Large Graphs: An Optimization Viewpoint** ... 1028
  Hanghang Tong, Jingrui He, Zhen Wen, Ravi Konuru, Ching-Yung Lin *(IBM T.J. Watson Research Center)*
- **Entity Disambiguation with Hierarchical Topic Models** ... 1037
  Saurabh S. Kataria *(The Pennsylvania State University)*, Krishnan S. Kumar, Rajeev Rastogi, Prithviraj Sen,
  Srinivasan H. Sengamedu *(Yahoo! Labs)*
- **Exploiting Place Features in Link Prediction on Location-Based Social Networks** ... 1046
  Salvatore Scellato, Anastasios Noulas, Cecilia Mascolo *(University of Cambridge)*
- **Fast Approximate Similarity Search Based on Degree-Reduced Neighborhood Graphs** ... 1055
  Kazuo Aoyama *(NTT Corporation)*, Kazumi Saito *(University of Shizuoka)*,
  Hiroshi Sawada, Naonori Ueda *(NTT Corporation)*
- **Fast Coordinate Descent Methods with Variable Selection for Non-Negative Matrix Factorization** ... 1064
  Cho-Jui Hsieh, Inderjit S. Dhillon *(University of Texas at Austin)*
- **Fast Locality-Sensitive Hashing** ... 1073
  Anirban Dasgupta, Ravi Kumar, Tamas Sarlós *(Yahoo! Research)*
- **Friendship and Mobility: User Movement in Location-Based Social Networks** ... 1082
  Eunjoon Cho, Seth A. Myers, Jure Leskovec *(Stanford University)*
- **GBASE: A Scalable and General Graph Management System** ... 1091
  U Kang *(Carnegie Mellon University)*, Hanghang Tong, Jimeng Sun,
  Ching-Yung Lin *(IBM T.J. Watson Research Center)*, Christos Faloutsos *(Carnegie Mellon University)*
- **Human Mobility, Social Ties, and Link Prediction** ... 1100
  Dashun Wang *(Northeastern University & Harvard University)*,
  Dino Pedreschi *(Northeastern University & University of Pisa)*,
  Chaoming Song *(Northeastern University & Harvard University)*,
  Fosca Giannotti *(Northeastern University & Istituto di Scienza e Tecnologie dell'Informazione del C.N.R.)*,
  Albert-László Barabási *(Northeastern University & Harvard University & Harvard Medical School)*
- **I Want to Answer; Who Has a Question? Yahoo! Answers Recommender System** ... 1109
  Gideon Dror, Yehuda Koren, Yoelle Maarek, Idan Szpektor *(Yahoo! Research)*

- **Improving Predictions Using Aggregate Information** 1118
  Amit Dhurandhar *(IBM T.J. Watson Research Center)*
- **INCONCO: Interpretable Clustering of Numerical and Categorical Objects** 1127
  Claudia Plant *(Florida State University)*, Christian Böhm *(University of Munich)*
- **Incorporating SAT Solvers into Hierarchical Clustering Algorithms – An Efficient and Flexible Approach** 1136
  Sean Gilpin, Ian Davidson *(University of California, Davis)*
- **Latent Graphical Models for Quantifying and Predicting Patent Quality** 1145
  Yan Liu *(University of Southern California)*, Pei-yun Hseuh, Rick Lawrence, Steve Meliksetian, Claudia Perlich, Alejandro Veen *(IBM T.J. Watson Research Center)*
- **Logical-Shapelets: An Expressive Primitive for Time Series Classification** 1154
  Abdullah Mueen, Eamonn Keogh, Neal Young *(University of California, Riverside)*
- **Meta Optimization and Its Application to Portfolio Selection** 1163
  Puja Das, Arindam Banerjee *(University of Minnesota)*
- **Mining Closed Episodes with Simultaneous Events** 1172
  Nikolaj Tatti, Boris Cule *(University of Antwerp)*
- **Mining Mobility Data to Minimise Travellers' Spending on Public Transport** 1181
  Neal Lathia, Licia Capra *(University College London)*
- **Mining Mobility User Profiles for Car Pooling** 1190
  Roberto Trasarti, Fabio Pinelli, Mirco Nanni, Fosca Giannotti *(ISTI - CNR)*
- **Mining Partially Annotated Images** 1199
  Zhongang Qi, Ming Yang, Zhongfei (Mark) Zhang *(Zhejiang University)*, Zhengyou Zhang *(Microsoft Research)*
- **Multi-View Transfer Learning with a Large Margin Approach** 1208
  Dan Zhang *(Purdue University)*, Jingrui He *(IBM T.J. Watson Research Center)*, Yan Liu *(University of Southern California)*, Luo Si *(Purdue University)*, Richard D. Lawrence *(IBM T.J. Watson Research Center)*
- **MultiRank: Co-Ranking for Objects and Relations in Multi-Relational Data** 1217
  Michaek K. Ng *(Hong Kong Baptist University)*, Xutao Li, Yunming Ye *(Harbin Institute of Technology)*
- **On Dynamic Data-Driven Selection of Sensor Streams** 1226
  Charu C. Aggarwal *(IBM T. J. Watson Research Center)*, Yan Xie, Philip S. Yu *(University of Illinois at Chicago)*
- **On the Privacy of Anonymized Networks** 1235
  Pedram Pedarsani, Matthias Grossglauser *(École Polytechnique Fédérale de Lausanne)*
- **Ontology Enhancement and Concept Granularity Learning: Keeping Yourself Current and Adaptive** 1244
  Shan Jiang *(Peking University)*, Lidong Bing *(The Chinese University of Hong Kong)*, Bai Sun, Yan Zhang *(Peking University)*, Wai Lam *(The Chinese University of Hong Kong)*
- **Personal Privacy vs. Population Privacy: Learning to Attack Anonymization** 1253
  Graham Cormode *(AT&T Labs-Research)*
- **Privacy-Preserving Social Network Publication Against Friendship Attacks** 1262
  Chih-Hua Tai *(National Taiwan University)*, Philip S. Yu *(University of Illinois at Chicago)*, De-Nian Yang, Ming-Syan Chen *(Academia Sinica)*
- **Probabilistic Topic Models with Biased Propagation on Heterogeneous Information Networks** 1271
  Hongbo Deng, Jiawei Han, Bo Zhao, Yintao Yu, Cindy Xide Lin *(University of Illinois at Urbana-Champaign)*
- **Prominent Streak Discovery in Sequence Data** 1280
  Xiao Jiang *(Shanghai Jiao Tong University)*, Chengkai Li *(University of Texas at Arlington)*, Ping Luo, Min Wang *(HP Labs China)*, Yong Yu *(Shanghai Jiao Tong University)*
- **Protecting Location Privacy Using Location Semantics** 1289
  Byoungyoung Lee, Jinoh Oh, Hwanjo Yu, Jong Kim *(Pohang University of Science and Technology)*

- **Ranking-Based Classification of Heterogeneous Information Networks** 1298
  Ming Ji, Jiawei Han, Marina Danilevsky *(University of Illinois at Urbana-Champaign)*
- **Real-Time Bidding Algorithms for Performance-Based Display Ad Allocation** 1307
  Ye Chen, Pavel Berkhin, Bo Anderson *(Microsoft)*, Nikhil R. Devanur *(Microsoft Research)*
- **Revisiting Sequential Pattern Hiding to Enhance Utility** 1316
  Aris Gkoulalas-Divanis *(IBM Research-Zurich)*, Grigorios Loukides *(Vanderbilt University)*
- **Sampling Hidden Objects Using Nearest-Neighbor Oracles** 1325
  Nilesh Dalvi, Ravi Kumar, Ashwin Machanavajjhala, Vibhor Rastogi *(Yahoo! Research)*
- **Scalable kNN Search on Vertically Stored Time Series** 1334
  Shrikant Kashyap *(National University of Singapore)*, Panagiotis Karras *(Rutgers University)*
- **Serendipitous Learning: Learning Beyond the Predefined Label Space** 1343
  Dan Zhang *(Purdue University)*, Yan Liu *(University of Southern California)*, Luo Si *(Purdue University)*
- **Spatially Regularized Logistic Regression for Disease Mapping on Large Moving Populations** 1352
  Vuk Malbasa, Slobodan Vucetic *(Temple University)*
- **Temporal Multi-Hierarchy Smoothing for Estimating Rates of Rare Events** 1361
  Nagaraj Kota *(Yahoo! Labs)*, Deepak Agarwal *(Yahoo! Research)*
- **Thermocast: A Cyber-Physical Forecasting Model for Data Centers** 1370
  Lei Li *(Carnegie Mellon University)*, Chieh-Jan Mike Liang *(Microsoft Research Asia)*,
  Jie Liu, Suman Nath *(Microsoft Research)*, Andreas Terzis *(Johns Hopkins University)*,
  Christos Faloutsos *(Carnegie Mellon University)*
- **Towards Bounding Sequential Patterns** 1379
  Chedy Raïssi *(INRIA)*, Jian Pei *(Simon Fraser University)*
- **User-Click Modeling for Understanding and Predicting Search-Behavior** 1388
  Yuchen Zhang *(Microsoft Research Asia)*,
  Weizhu Chen *(Microsoft Research Asia & Hong Kong University of Science and Technology)*,
  Dong Wang *(Microsoft Research Asia)*, Qiang Yang *(Hong Kong University of Science and Technology)*
- **User-Level Sentiment Analysis Incorporating Social Networks** 1397
  Chenhao Tan, Lillian Lee *(Cornell University)*, Jie Tang *(Tsinghua University)*,
  Long Jiang, Ming Zhou *(Microsoft Corporation)*, Ping Li *(Cornell University)*
- **Web Information Extraction Using Markov Logic Networks** 1406
  Sandeepkumar Satpal *(Microsoft)*, Sahely Bhadra *(Indian Institute of Science)*,
  S. Sundararajan, Rajeev Rastogi, Prithviraj Sen *(Yahoo! Labs)*

Author Index 1415

ACM SIGKDD 2011 Conference Organization

General Chair:	*Chid Apte (IBM Research)*
Program Co-Chairs:	*Joydeep Ghosh (UT Austin)* *Padhraic Smyth (UC Irvine)*
Industry/Government Track Co-Chairs:	*Ted Senator (SAIC)* *Michael Zeller (Zementis)*
Industry Practice Expo Co-Chairs:	*Ying Li (Microsoft)* *Rajesh Parekh (Groupon)*
Sponsorship Chair:	*Balaji Krishnapuram (Siemens)*
Student Awards Chair:	*Jimeng Sun (IBM Research)*
SIGKDD Chair:	*Usama Fayyad (ChoozOn Corporation)*
Tutorials Chair:	*Deepak Agarwal (Yahoo!)*
Workshops Co-Chairs:	*Ian Davidson (UC Davis)* *Jennifer Dy (Northeastern)*
Posters Chair:	*Sofus A. Macskassy (Fetch Technologies)*
Publicity Co-Chairs:	*Rayid Ghani (Accenture)* *Yan Liu (USC)*
Publications Co-Chairs:	*Jie Tang (Tsinghua University)* *Alexandru Niculescu-Mizil (NEC Laboratories America)*
Web Co-Chairs:	*Melissa Carroll (IBM Research)* *David Eis (Princeton University)*
Exhibits and Demos Co-Chairs:	*Natasha Balac (UC San Diego)* *Hui Xiong (Rutgers)*
Local Arrangements Chair:	*Nancy Davis (ION)*
Registrations Chair:	*Claudia Perlich (Media6Degrees)*
Treasurer:	*Vikas Sindhwani (IBM Research)*
KDD Cup Co-Chairs:	*Gideon Dror (Yahoo!)* *Yehuda Koren (Yahoo!)* *Markus Weimer (Yahoo!)*
KDD Awards Chair:	*Osmar Zaiane (Alberta)*
KDD Research Paper Awards Chairs:	*Andrew Tomkins (Google)* *Rich Caruana (Microsoft)*

KDD'11 Research Track Program Committees

Senior Program Committee:

Niall Adams (Imperial College)
Charu Aggarwal (IBM)
Arindam Banerjee (University of Minnesota)
Rich Caruana (Microsoft)
Corinna Cortes (Google)
Gautum Das (University of Texas, Arlington)
Charles Elkan (University of California, San Diego)
Johannes Gehrke (Cornell University)
Aristides Gionis (Yahoo! Barcelona)
Dimtrios Gunopulos (University of Athens)
Jiawei Han (UIUC)
George Karypis (University of Minnesota)
Yehuda Koren (Yahoo! Research)
Jure Leskovec (Stanford University)
David Madigan (Columbia University)
Chris Meek (Microsoft Research)
Katarina Morik (University of Dortmund)
Zoran Obradovic (Temple University)
Srini Parthasarathy (The Ohio State University)
Jian Pei (Simon Fraser University)
Raghu Ramakrishnan (Yahoo! Research)
Matt Richardson (Microsoft)
Saharon Rosset (Tel Aviv University)
Sunita Sarawagi (IIT, Bombay)
Arno Siebes (Utrecht University)
Alex Smola (Yahoo! and ANU)
Ramakrishnan Srikant (Google)
Evimaria Terzi (Boston University)
Andrew Tomkins (Google)
Alex Tuzhilin (New York University)
Wei Wang (University of North Carolina, Chapel Hill)
Stefan Wrobel (Fraunhofer IAIS & University of Bonn)
Eric Xing (Carnegie Mellon University)
Qiang Yang (Hong Kong UST)
Philip Yu (University of Illinois, Chicago)
Mohammed Zaki (RPI)
Zhi-Hua Zhou (Nanjing University)

Program Committee:

Naoki Abe (IBM T.J. Watson Research Center)
James Abello (DIMACS/Rutgers University)
Sreangsu Acharyya (University of Texas, Austin)
Ryan Adams (University of Toronto)
Foto Afrati (National Technical University of Athens)
Eugene Agichtein (Emory University)
Mohammad Al Hasan (IUPUI)
Aijun An (York University)
Aris Anagnostopoulos (Sapienza University of Rome)
Christoforos Anagnostopoulos (University of Cambridge)
Annalisa Appice (University Aldo Moro of Bari)
Arthur Asuncion (Uviversity of California, Irvine)
Sitaram Asur (Hewlett Packard Labs)
Vassilis Athitsos (University of Texas, Arlington)
Amir Atiya (Cairo University)
Lars Backstrom (Cornell University)
Tony Bagnall (University of East Anglia)
James Bailey (University of Melbourne)
Tim Bailey (University of Queensland)
Sugato Basu (Google Research)
Stephen Bay (Deloitte Consulting)
Roberto Bayardo (Google)
Paul Bennett (Microsoft Research)
Bettina Berendt (University of Leuven)
Tanya Berger-Wolf (University of Illinois at Chicago)
Pavel Berkhin (Microsoft)
Michele Berlingerio (KDD Lab, ISTI-CNR, Pisa)
Michael Berthold (University of Konstanz)
Chiru Bhattacharya (IISc)
Mikhail Bilenko (Microsoft Research)
Mustafa Bilgic (Illinois Institute of Technology)
Marina Blanton (University of Notre Dame)
Francesco Bonchi (Yahoo! Research)
Edwin Bonilla (CSIRO)
Karsten Borgwardt (Max Planck Institute)
Henrik Bostrom (Stockholm University)
Ulf Brefeld (Yahoo! Barcelona)
Gavin Brown (University of Manchester)
Wray Buntine (NICTA)
Deng Cai (Zhejiang University)
Rui Cai (Microsoft Research, Beijing)
Toon Calders (Technische Universiteit Eindhoven)
Carlos Castillo (Yahoo!)
Deepayan Chakrabarti (Yahoo! Research)
Ed Chang (Google)
Jonathan Chang (Facebook)

Latifur Khan (University of Texas, Dallas)
Daniel Kifer (The Pennsylvania State University)
Seyoung Kim (Carnegie Mellon University)
Irwin King (The Chinese University of Hong Kong)
Sergey Kirshner (Purdue University)
Masaru Kitsuregawa (University of Tokyo)
Mei Kobayashi (IBM Research Lab, Tokyo)
Ronny Kohavi (Microsoft)
George Kollios (Boston University)
Arnd Konig (Microsoft Research)
Pavel Kordík (CTU in Prague)
Nick Koudas (University of Toronto and Sysomos, Inc)
Stefan Kramer (TU, München)
Ravi Kumar (Yahoo!)
Jérome Kunegis (University of Koblenz)
Laks VS Lakshmanan (University of British Columbia)
Terran Lane (University of New Mexico)
Silvio Lattanzi (University of Rome, Sapienza)
Dongwon Lee (The Pennsylvania State University)
Mong Li Lee (NUS)
Kristina Lerman (ISI/USC)
Chen Li (UC Irvine)
Hang Li (Microsoft)
Ming Li (Nanjing University)
Ping Li (Cornell University)
David Liben-Nowell (Carleton College)
Edo Liberty (Yahoo! Research)
Ee-Peng Lim (Singapore Management University)
Chih-Jen Lin (National Taiwan University)
Ching-Yung Lin (IBM T.J. Watson Research Center)
Jessica Lin (GMU)
Charles Ling (University of Western Ontario)
Bing Liu (University of Illinois, Chicago)
Chao Liu (Microsoft Research)
Huan Liu (Arizona State University)
Jun Liu (Arizona State University)
Stefano Lonardi (University of California, Riverside)
Daniel Lowd (University of Oregon)
Aurelie Lozano (IBM Research)
Chang-Tien Lu (Virginia Tech)
Rich Maclin (University of Minnesota)
Michael Madden (National University of Ireland, Galway)
Michael Mahoney (Stanford University)
Donato Malerba (University of Bari)
Dimitris Margaritas (Iowa State University)
Cecilia Mascolo (University of Cambridge)
Mary McGlohon (Google Pittsburgh)
Vasileios Megalooikonomou (Temple University)
Guy Melancon (LaBRI)
Prem Melville (IBM Research)
Aditya Menon (University of California, San Diego)
Srujana Merugu (IBM IRL)
Donald Metzler (University of Southern California)
George Michailidis (University of Michigan)
Ingo Mierswa (Rapid-I)
David Mimno (Princeton University)
Dunja Mladenic (J., Stefan Institute, Slovenia)
Bamshad Mobasher (De Paul University)
M. Arthur Munson (Sandia National Laboratories)
Brendan Murphy (University College Dublin)
Olfa Nasraoui (University of Louisville)
Gonzalo Navarro (University of Chile)
Jennifer Neville (Purdue University)
David Newman (University of California, Irvine)
Siegfried Nijssen (Katholieke Universityersiteit Leuven)
Gerd Paass (Fraunhofer IAIS)
Rina Panigrahy (Microsoft)
Spiros Papadimitriou (IBM)
Panagiotis Papapetrou (Aalto University, Finland)
Haesun Park (Georgia Tech)
Stott Parker (University of California, Los Angeles)
Nicos Pavlidis (Lancaster University)
Dmitry Pavlov (Yandex)
Dino Pedreschi (KDD Lab, University. Pisa, Italy)
Elzbieta Pekalska (University Manchester, UK)
Bernhard Pfahringer (University of Waikato)
Claudia Plant (Florida State University)
John Platt (Microsoft Research)
Ian Porteous (Google)
Daryl Pregibon (Google)
Kunal Punera (Yahoo! Research)
Padma Raghavan (The Pennsylvania State University)
Daniel Ramage (Stanford University)
Naren Ramakrishnan (Virginia Tech)
Sanjay Ranka (University of Florida)
Marc'Aurelio Ranzato (University of Toronto)
Louiqa Raschid (University of Maryland)
Rajeev Rastogi (Yahoo! Labs)
Chandan Reddy (Wayne State)
Lior Rokach (BGU)
Fabio Roli (University of Cagliari)
Celine Rouveirol (University of Paris13)
Stefan Rueping (Fraunhofer IAIS)
Salvatore Ruggieri (University of Pisa)
Ernestina Ruiz (Menasalvas)
Yvan Saeys (University of Gent)
Lorenza Saitta (Unito, Italy)

Joerg Sander (University of Alberta)
Purnamrita Sarkar (University of California, Berkeley)
Shin'ichi Satoh (National Institute of Informatics)
D. Sculley (Google)
Thomas Seidl (RWTH Aachen University)
Dennis Shasha (NYew York University)
Shashi Shekhar (University of Minnesota)
Dou Shen (Buzzlabs)
Luo Si (Purdue University)
Kevin Small (Tufts University)
Mauro Sozio (Max Planck, Saarbrucken)
Myra Spiliopoulou (Otto-von-Guericke-Universityersitaet Magdeburg)
Suvrit Sra (Max Planck Institute)
Rohini Srihari (University at Buffalo, State University of New York)
Harald Steck (Bell-Labs, Alcatel-Lucent)
Michael Steinbach (University of Minnesota)
David Stern (Microsoft Research Cambridge)
L. Venkata Subramaniam (IBM Research - India)
Masashi Sugiyama (Tokyo Institute of Technology)
Jimeng Sun ((IBM T.J. Watson Research Center)
Neel Sundaresan (eBay Research Labs)
Einoshin Suzuki (Kyushi University)
Pang-Ning Tan (Michigan State University)
Jie Tang (Tsinghua University)
Dacheng Tao (University of Technology, Sydney)
Yufei Tao (Chinese University of Hong Kong)
Dimitris Tasoulis (Winton Capital)
Shirish Tatikonda (IBM Almaden Research Center)
Bo Thiesson (Microsoft Research)
HangHang Tong (IBM T.J. Watson Research Center)
Volker Tresp (Siemens)
Panayiotis Tsaparas (Microsoft Research)
Grigorios Tsoumakas (Aristotle University of Thessaloniki)
Allan Tucker (Brunel University)
Michael Turmon (JPL)
Duygu Ucar (Stanford University)
Naonori Ueda (NTT Communication Science Labs)
Antti Ukkonen (Yahoo!)
Lyle Ungar (University of Pennsylvania)
Jaideep Vaidya (Rutgers University.)
Laurens van der Maarten (University of California, San Diego and TU, Delft)
Michalis Vazirgiannis (Athens University of Economics & Business)
Jean-Philippe Vert (Mines Paris Tech and Curie Institute)
Vassilios Verykios (University. of Thessaly)
Vishy Vishwanathan (Purdue University)
Michalis Vlachos (IBM Research)
Chris Volinsky (AT&T Labs - Research)
Jilles Vreeken (University of Antwerp, Belgium)
Slobodan Vucetic (Temple University)
Haixun Wang (Microsoft Asia)
Xuanhui Wang (Yahoo! Labs)
Charles Ward (Stony Brook University)
Markus Weimer (Yahoo! Research)
Gary Weiss (Fordham University)
Sholom Weiss (IBM Research)
Ran Wolff (University of Haifa)
Raymond Chi-Wing Wong (Hong Kong University of Science and Technology)
Weng-Keen Wong (Oregon State University)
Xindong Wu (University of Vermont)
Yanghua Xiao (Fudan University)
Hui Xiong (Rutgers University)
Guirong Xue (Shanghai Jiaotong University)
Kenji Yamanishi (University of Tokyo)
Jun Yan (Microsoft Research Asia)
Xifeng Yan (University of California, Santa Barbara)
Jieping Ye (Arizona State University)
Dit-Yan Yeung (Hong Kong University of Science and Technology)
Xiaoxin Yin (Microsoft Research)
Jeffrey Xu Yu (Chinese University of Hong Kong)
Lei Yu (Binghamton University)
Shipeng Yu (Siemens Medical Solutions)
Yisong Yue (Carnegie Mellon University)
Bianca Zadrozny (IBM Research Brazil)
Carlo Zaniolo (University of California, Los Angeles
Demetris Zeinalipour (University of Cyprus)
Filip Zelezny (Czech Technical University)
Hongyuan Zha (Georgia Tech)
Aidong Zhang (University at Buffalo)
Kun Zhang (Max Planck Institute)
Min-Ling Zhang (Southeast University)
Nan Zhang (George Wash. U)
Zhongfei (Mark) Zhang (SUNY Binghamton)
Jun Zhu (Carnegie Mellon University)
Xingquan Zhu (University of Technology, Sydney)
Arthur Zimek (LMU Munich)

KDD'11 Industry/Government Program Committee

John Akred (Accenture)
Richardo Baeza-Yates (Yahoo! Research)
Michael Berthold (KNIME)
Kanishka Bhaduri (NASA)
Eric Bloedorn (MITRE - USA)
Rainer Burkhardt (JgenCy)
Deng Cai (Zhejiang University)
Katrina Carter-Journet (NASA)
Hong Cheng (The Chinese University of Hong Kong)
David Duling (SAS)
Marty Ellingsworth (ISO Innovative Analytics)
Nancy Grady (Science Applications International Corporation)
Shawndra Hill (Wharton School of Business)
Steven Hillion (Greenplum/EMC)
Derek Hao Hu (Hong Kong UST)
Jianying Hu (IBM T.J. Watson Research Center)
Sergei Israilev (Jabiru Ventures)
Ron Karidi (Microsoft (Israel Innovation Labs)
Mei Kobayashi (IBM Research Lab, Tokyo)
Christoph Lingenfelder (IBM)
Nathan Nan Liu (Hong Kong UST)
David Lo (Singapore Management University)
Jack Lucas (US Government)
Jamie MacLennan (Predixion Software)
Gideon Mann (Google)
Dawn Martin (NASA)
Gabor Melli (Simon Fraser University)
Theodore Omtzigt (Stillwater Supercomputing)
Sinno JIalin Pan (HKUST)
Wei Peng (Xerox)
Ralf Rantzau (Truviso)
Karl Rexer (Rexer Analytics)
Neal Rothleder (MITRE)
Ramendra Sahoo (Citi)
Ashok Savasere (SAS)
Dawit Seid (SAS)
Nitin Sharma (Groupon)
Ali Shaykhian (NASA)
Dou Shen (BuzzLabs)
Jiaqiang Shen (Pearson Education)
Jian-Tao Sun (Microsoft Research)
AC Surendran (Microsoft)
Arun Swami (Google)
Wayne Thompson (SAS)
Hanghang Tong (Carnegie Mellon University)
Ramasamy Uthurusamy (GM)
Peter Van der Putten (Pegasystems & Leiden University)
Ranga Vatsavai (Oak Ridge National Labs)
Andrew Veal (Government Communications HQ, UK)
Dave Vennergrund (Delta Solutions)
Stefan Weber (Siemens AG)

ACM SIGKDD 2011 Industry Practice Expo Advisory Committee & Additional Reviewers

Industry Practice Expo Advisory Committee:

Chid Apte (IBM Research)
John Elder (Elder Research)
Usama Fayyad (ChoozOn Corporation)
Brendan Kitts (Lucid Commerce)
Gabor Melli (Simon Fraser University)
Gregory Piatetsky-Shapiro (KDNuggets)
Bharat Rao (Siemens)
Ted Senator (SAIC)
Ashok Srivastava (NASA)
Ramasamy Uthurusamy (GM)

Additional Reviewers:

Marina Danilevsky (University of Illinois)
Chris Kaufman (University of Minnesota)
Alexandra Korolova (Stanford)
Akhmed Umyarov (University of Minnesota)
America Chambers (UC Irvine)
Chris DuBois (UC Irvine)
Jimmy Foulds (UC Irvine)
Scott Triglia (UC Irvine)
Priyank Patel (UT Austin)
Nikita Sudan (UT Austin)
Sanmi Koyejo (UT Austin)

ACM SIGKDD KDD 2011 Sponsors & Supporters

Sponsors:

Supporters

Two-Locus Association Mapping in Subquadratic Time

Panagiotis Achlioptas
Department of Computer Science
University of Crete, Greece
achliopt@csd.uoc.gr

Bernhard Schölkopf
Department of Empirical Inference
MPI for Intelligent Systems
Tübingen, Germany
bs@tuebingen.mpg.de

Karsten M. Borgwardt
Machine Learning and Computational Biology Research Group
MPIs Tübingen, Germany
karsten@tuebingen.mpg.de

ABSTRACT

Genome-wide association studies (GWAS) have not been able to discover strong associations between many complex human diseases and single genetic loci. Mapping these phenotypes to pairs of genetic loci is hindered by the huge number of candidates leading to enormous computational and statistical problems. In GWAS on single nucleotide polymorphisms (SNPs), one has to consider in the order of 10^{10} to 10^{14} pairs, which is infeasible in practice. In this article, we give the first algorithm for 2-locus genome-wide association studies that is subquadratic in the number, n, of SNPs. The running time of our algorithm is data-dependent, but large experiments over real genomic data suggest that it scales empirically as $n^{3/2}$. As a result, our algorithm can easily cope with $n \sim 10^7$, i.e., it can efficiently search all pairs of SNPs in the human genome.

Categories and Subject Descriptors

H.2.8 [**Database Applications**]: Data Mining

General Terms

Algorithms, Experimentation, Measurement

Keywords

Epistasis detection, two-locus association mapping, lightbulb algorithm

1. INTRODUCTION

A central question in genetics is whether natural variation in phenotypes can be explained by differences between individuals on the genomic level. Advances in sequencing technology allow us now to study these genomic differences at an unprecedented level of detail. Particularly in humans, millions of single nucleotide polymorphisms (SNPs) have been determined [5], that is positions in the genome where one nucleotide varies between different individuals.

KDD'11, August 21–24, 2011, San Diego, California, USA.

Current genome-wide association studies (GWAS) tend to focus on single loci or single SNPs that are associated with a phenotype. GWAS that do consider groups of loci usually assume an additive effect of these loci. Interactive effects, even between pairs of loci, are typically not searched for. Such an *epistatic* interaction effect occurs if the average phenotypic value of the two-locus genotypes deviates from that expected by summing the allelic effects of the two loci [6]. Such gene × gene interactions are widely believed and acknowledged to be a major factor in many complex traits such as many humans diseases [12]. For instance, the presence of gene × gene interactions has been demonstrated in type 1 diabetes [7], type 2 diabetes [8], inflammatory bowel diseases [4] and prostate and breast cancer [18, 1]. Why does one then not routinely scan for pairs of interacting SNPs? The first, computational reason is that the number of pairs of SNPs is extremely large, in the order of 10^{10} to 10^{14}, and is hence not amenable to a straightforward solution by exhaustive enumeration. Testing each of these pairs for association with the phenotype leads directly to the second, the statistical reason. When performing billions of tests, one has to correct for multiple hypothesis testing, in order to reduce the number of false positives, which in turn may lead to a loss in power.

Our focus in this article is on the first of these two reasons, the computational burden caused by the gigantic number of candidate pairs in two-locus mapping. We present an algorithm for efficiently retrieving the top k scoring pairs among all pairs of SNPs, assuming binary phenotypes and the difference-in-correlation [9] as the association criterion. Unlike earlier approaches to this problem, the runtime of our algorithm is *subquadratic in the number of SNPs*.

There are various ways of defining measures of statistical dependence between a pair of SNPs and a binary phenotype. One common strategy is to use a logistic regression model between an SNP pair and the phenotype and to check whether the interaction term coefficient differs significantly from zero. Another measure is the difference in correlation, that is we search for the SNPs whose correlation maximally differs between cases and controls [9]. The latter strategy is the one for which we develop a subquadratic algorithm here.

Previous algorithms work on two-locus association mapping can be broadly divided into the following four categories.

First, there are approaches that exhaustively consider all SNP pairs, for instance in linear or logistic regression, or multifactorial dimension reduction [15]. Due to the large number of candidate pairs, these studies usually only consider tens to hundreds of SNPs.

Second, one may proceed in a two-step procedure, in which one first performs a one-locus association study, and then performs an exhaustive pairwise search between the most significant SNPs from the one-locus mapping [11, 21].

Third, there are approaches, such as genetic algorithms [13, 17], which efficiently return local optima of the function that scores the importance of SNP pairs, but they are incomplete in the sense that they do not necessarily find the best pairs.

Fourth, there are recently published data mining methods such as FastAnova [20] and TEAM [19], which are able to prune a fraction of the computations, but their running time still scales as $\Omega(n^2 m)$, where n is the number of SNPs and m is the number of individuals in the sample. To the best of our knowledge, our method is the first one which overcomes the runtime bottleneck of 2-Locus GWAS of being quadratic in the number of SNPs.

The remainder of this article is organized as follows. In Section 2, we formalize our optimization problem and give an overview of our strategy. In Section 3, we describe the algorithm of [14] for finding the most correlated pair in a set of binary variables. We then present a similar algorithm for the least correlated pair, and, based on that, an algorithm for the pair of variables with maximum difference in correlation between two different sets of measurements (see Section 5). Next, we describe how to extend this last algorithm to multi-valued variables and to Pearson's correlation coefficient measure (Section 6), and discuss strategies on how to set the parameters of this approach (Sections 7.1 and 7.2). Lastly, we evaluate performance in a series of experiments on synthetic and real-world data (Section 8).

2. PROBLEM STATEMENT

The goal of 2-locus genome-wide association studies (2L-GWAS) is to find *pairs* of Single Nucleotide Polymorphisms (SNPs) that jointly determine a phenotypical trait. As common in clinical genetics, we assume that traits are binary.

We assume that we are given an $(m_1 + m_2) \times n$ matrix D of $m_1 + m_2$ patients with n SNPs, where each SNP takes values in $\{0, 1, 2\}$. This matrix consists of two submatrices A and B, of size $m_1 \times n$ and $m_2 \times n$, respectively. A is the set of m_1 cases with phenotype 1, B the set of m_2 controls with phenotype 0. Each SNP is a $(m_1 + m_2) \times 1$ column vector of D. We seek pairs of SNPs whose statistical dependence with the phenotype is maximally different between cases and controls.

Let $P : \{0,1,2\}^{m_1} \times \{0,1,2\}^{m_1} \rightarrow \mathbb{R}$ be a measure of correlation between two vectors (SNPs). Given a matrix C, let $P_C(i, j)$ denote the value of P with input the columns i, j. Our optimization problem is then to find the pair

$$\arg\max_{i,j} |P_A(i,j) - P_B(i,j)|. \tag{1}$$

Assuming that P can be computed in linear time, as is always the case in practice, the problem can be trivially solved in time $O(n^2(m_1 + m_2))$. Without any assumptions on the function P it is not clear that one can do much better. Unfortunately, such a running time greatly limits the size of SNP collections that can be studied in practice. For example, we had to use a cluster of one thousand CPUs for several days in order to solve the problem for 850K SNPs to achieve a ground truth for our experiments.

Our starting point is the seminal work of Paturi et al. for the "Light Bulb Problem" [14], showing that for binary matrices, i.e., with elements in $\{0, 1\}$, one can find the nearest pair of columns in L_1 distance in time $O(n^{2-\gamma})$, where $\gamma > 0$ depends on the difference in distance between the closest and second closest pairs. We first show that in this same setting it is possible to find the pair described in equation (1), with guarantees on time and recall similar to those of [14]. To do this, we exploit heavily both the fact that the data is binary and the linearity of the L_1-distance. Both of these assumptions, though, are not ideal for SNP data, where data is typically ternary, i.e., the entries of D are in $\{0, 1, 2\}$, and a commonly used P is Pearson's correlation coefficient [9]. To address these issues we employ Locality Sensitive Hashing (LSH) to transform the original SNP data into binary data which preserve the original angles. While this transformation, in the worst case, can somewhat distort the Pearson correlation of two SNPs, we show that a modification of our algorithm completely eliminates this problem, without incurring a significant computational penalty.

3. THE MOST CORRELATED PAIR

We first discuss how to solve the problem captured by (1) when the matrices of interest are binary and the correlation P of two columns in D (that is, of two SNPs) is defined as the fraction of rows in which they take the same value, i.e. it is equal to 1 minus their L_1 distance divided by their dimension. The binary assumption is valid for SNPs in inbred species, as all their SNPs are homozygous and can be represented by a two-state variable, but this definition of correlation, as far as we know, has not been used in biological studies yet.

Given a binary matrix D, let $P_D(i, j)$ denote the correlation of column pair $\{i, j\}$ in D, i.e., the fraction of rows in which columns i and j take the same value. Let p_1 and p_2 denote the highest (greatest) and second highest correlations present across all pairs. In a breakthrough 1989 paper, Paturi, Rajasekaran, and Reif [14] gave a subquadratic algorithm for finding

$$\arg\max_{i,j} P_D(i,j).$$

Specifically, the running time of their algorithm is $\tilde{O}(n^{1+\gamma})$, where $\gamma = \log p_1 / \log p_2 < 1$ and the $\tilde{O}(\cdot)$ notation suppresses $(\log n)^q$ factors for any finite $q > 0$. Since the results of [14] are the starting ground for our work, we begin with a few words about how and why the algorithm in [14] works. To simplify the exposition we assume, for now, that p_1, p_2 are given to us as part of the input. We will later see how this assumption can be removed. The algorithm uses a sample-size parameter $k = k(n, \gamma) = O(\log n)$. The choice of k is discussed later.

Algorithm CO

1. Appropriately set the sample-size parameter k.
2. Let $t = n^\gamma \log n$, where $\gamma = \log p_1 / \log p_2$.
3. To succeed with probability $1 - 1/\text{poly}(n)$, repeat t times:
   (a) Select k distinct rows of D uniformly at random, to form a $k \times n$ matrix R.

(b) Partition the columns of R into (no more than 2^k) equivalence classes $E_1, E_2, \ldots, E_\ell$.

(c) For every pair of columns $\{i, j\}$ that end up in the same equivalence class, increment (after perhaps creating) the corresponding counter C_{ij} by 1.

4. Report the pair of columns with maximum counter.

Intuitively, the parameter k is chosen so that we expect to increase a linear number of counters in each round, i.e.,

$$\mathbb{E}\left[\sum_{i=1}^{\ell}\binom{|E_i|}{2}\right] = \Theta(n) .$$

The parameter t is chosen so as to ensure that with probability $1 - 1/\text{poly}(n)$ after t iterations the most correlated pair has increased its associated counter more times than the second most correlated pair.

4. THE LEAST CORRELATED PAIR

Our first step is to give a subquadratic algorithm for finding

$$\arg\min_{i,j} P_D(i,j). \tag{2}$$

We will need the following definition.

DEFINITION 1. *Given a matrix D, let $\overline{D}$ denote the matrix that results by complementing its elements.*

Given a matrix D with m rows and n columns let p_1 and p_2 denote the lowest (smallest) and second lowest correlations present in D. The running time of our algorithm is $\tilde{O}(n^{1+\gamma})$, where $\gamma = \log(1-p_1)/\log(1-p_2)$. Our algorithm for finding its least correlated pair of columns is

Algorithm AC

1. Let U be the $m \times 2n$ matrix that results by concatenating D and $\overline{D}$ row-wise.
2. Find the most correlated pair of columns in U among those pairs of columns in which exactly one of the two columns comes from each of $D, \overline{D}$.

The correctness of algorithm AC comes from observing that for every pair of columns i, j in U in which one column comes from D and one from $\overline{D}$ we have $P_U(i,j) = 1 - P_D(i,j)$.

The crucial observation that makes the above interesting is the following.

OBSERVATION 1. *Step 2 of AC can be carried out using a small modification of CO. Namely, each time we are about to increment a counter C_{ij} in CO we check whether exactly one of each of i, j come from matrices $D, \overline{D}$.*

5. THE MOST DIFFERENT PAIR

The ideas underlying our algorithm for finding the least correlated pair can be adapted to solve the problem of finding

$$\arg\max_{i,j} |P_A(i,j) - P_B(i,j)| \tag{3}$$

for any two $m \times n$ binary matrices A, B. Note that now the two matrices are required to not only have the same number of columns, but also the same number of rows ($m_1 = m_2 = m$). We later discuss how to avoid this requirement by employing randomization. Our main tool is the following.

LEMMA 1. *For two $m \times n$ matrices A, B let*

$$\{x, y\} = \arg\max_{i,j} P_A(i,j) - P_B(i,j) .$$

Let S be an arbitrary subset of $\{1, 2, \ldots, n\}$ and let B' be the matrix that results by complementing all columns of B that belong in S. Let C be the $2m \times n$ matrix that results by concatenating A and B', column-wise. Let $\mathcal{P} = \mathcal{P}(S)$ consist of those pairs of columns of C that have exactly one element from S. If $\{x, y\} \in \mathcal{P}$, then

$$\{x, y\} = \arg\max_{i,j \in \mathcal{P}} P_C(i,j) .$$

PROOF OF LEMMA 1. We will first do some calculations which allow for matrices A and B to have m_1 and m_2 rows, respectively, where m_1 and m_2 can be different. Consider any two pairs of columns $S, T \in \mathcal{P}$. Assume that the columns in pair S agree on s_1 rows of A and s_2 rows of B. Similarly, assume that the columns in pair T agree on t_1 rows of A and t_2 rows of B.

In C, the correlation of the columns in S is

$$\frac{s_1 + m_2 - s_2}{m_1 + m_2} = \frac{s_1 - s_2}{m_1 + m_2} + \frac{m_2}{m_1 + m_2}$$

while the correlation of the columns in T is

$$\frac{t_1 + m_2 - t_2}{m_1 + m_2} = \frac{t_1 - t_2}{m_1 + m_2} + \frac{m_2}{m_1 + m_2} .$$

If $m_1 = m_2 = m$, we see that ordering the elements of $\mathcal{P}$ by their correlation in matrix C is the same as ordering them by their correlation gap in matrices A, B. In fact, the two are related by an affine transformation. □

In order to ensure that when applying Lemma 1 the sought-after pair of columns $\{x, y\}$ is considered, we could try to take different random samples of columns S from C. Alternatively, we can simply consider a twice as large matrix

$$D = \begin{pmatrix} A & A \\ B & \overline{B} \end{pmatrix}$$

and let $\mathcal{P}$ consist of those pairs of columns in D that have exactly one column from amongst the first n. Then

$$\{x, y\} = \arg\max_{i,j \in \mathcal{P}} P_D(i,j) .$$

Thus, by applying algorithm CO to D we will find the pair maximizing $P_A(i,j) - P_B(i,j)$. Reversing the roles of A, B, i.e., applying CO to the matrix

$$E = \begin{pmatrix} A & \overline{A} \\ B & B \end{pmatrix}$$

we find the pair maximizing $P_B(i,j) - P_A(i,j)$. A single comparison then gives us the maximizer of $|P_A(i,j) - P_B(i,j)|$.

5.1 Unequal size matrices

When the two matrices A, B have $m_1 \neq m_2$ rows, respectively, the proof of Lemma 1 fails. In particular, if $m_1 \gg m_2$ then, complemented or not, the elements of B have small influence in the correlation of columns in C.

To overcome this problem we "enrich" the smaller of the two matrices by repeating some of its rows. Specifically, if $m_1/m_2 > 1$, we append $l = \lfloor m_1/m_2 \rfloor - 1$ identical copies of B and a random sample of $m_1 - (l+1)m_2$ rows of B. If we are lucky and m_1/m_2 is integer, then it is clear that every column pair has exactly the same correlation in the resulting matrix as it did in B. If m_1/m_2 is not integer, correlations are only preserved in expectation. Nevertheless, the associated variance is reasonable as the fraction of random rows in the resulting matrix is always less than $1/2$. Finally, in the more interesting biological setting where we use LSH functions, we show how to completely overcome this issue.

6. NON-BINARY DATA

So far, our algorithm applies to binary data and a correlation measure which is the probability of two binary variables being identical. Next, we will show how these ideas can be expanded to handle arbitrary real-valued vectors and Pearson's correlation coefficient. For this, we need to introduce the Locality Sensitive Hash functions (LSH) of [3].

To hash a collection of vectors in $\mathbb{R}^m$, we choose a spherically random vector $\vec{r} \in \mathbb{R}^m$ (by taking its coordinates to be m independent $N(0,1)$ random variables) and define a hash function $h_{\vec{r}}$ as follows:

$$h_{\vec{r}}(\vec{u}) = \begin{cases} 1 \text{ if } \vec{r}\cdot\vec{u} \geq 0 \\ 0 \text{ if } \vec{r}\cdot\vec{u} < 0 \end{cases} \quad (4)$$

FACT 1. *For any pair of vectors* $\vec{v}, \vec{u}$, $Pr[h_r(\vec{u}) = h_r(\vec{v})] = 1 - \theta(\vec{u},\vec{v})/\pi$, *where* θ *is the angle between the two vectors.*

Fact 1 states that the probability that a uniformly random hyperplane separates two vectors is proportional to their angle. Thus, the smaller the angle, the larger the probability that two vectors will hash to the same value. If we hash our input vectors with s independent random hyperplanes, each input vector becomes a (hash) vector in $\{0,1\}^s$, and the expected L1 distance of two hash vectors is proportional to the angle between the corresponding input vectors. It is clear that as s grows, this (random) L1 distance becomes a better and better estimator of the angle between the original vectors. Therefore, the algorithms developed in the previous sections applied on the hash vectors, are randomized algorithms for finding the pairs with largest, smallest and "most different" angles.

To handle Pearson's correlation coefficient we exploit its close relation with the cosine function and, therefore, with the angle between vector pairs.

6.1 Pearson's correlation coefficient

Pearson's correlation coefficient of two random variables u, v is equal to

$$\rho = \frac{cov(v,u)}{\sigma_v \sigma_u}\ , \quad (5)$$

i.e., their covariance divided by the product of their standard deviations. Given d samples of each random variable, organized as d-dimensional vectors $\vec{u}, \vec{v}$, an equivalent definition (see [16]) is:

$$\rho = \cos(\vec{v} - \bar{v}, \vec{u} - \bar{u}), \quad (6)$$

where $\bar{v} = \mathbf{1}\mu_u$ and $\bar{v} = \mathbf{1}\mu_v$, where μ_u and μ_v are the mean values of $\vec{u}$ and $\vec{v}$, respectively.

In view of (6), we see that when seeking the pair of SNPs that are "most different" in terms of Pearson's correlation coefficient between cases and controls, we are simply seeking the pair of SNP vectors whose cosine is most different. We approximate this cosine by the angle of the vectors $\vec{v} - \bar{v}$ and $\vec{u} - \bar{u}$, i.e., we apply the methods of the previous section to them. The reason this works is as follows.

When a pair of vectors has different cosine between the two data sets it must also have some difference in angle between them. Luckily, the absolute value of the derivative of the arccos function is lower-bounded by 1 and stays close to 1 in most of $[-1,+1]$ (of course, if it equaled 1 throughout, the replacement of cosine by angle would be exact.) In particular, in $[-0.85, 0.85]$ this derivative stays bounded by 2, meaning that for pairs whose cosine in both data sets is in this range, their probability of being placed in different buckets is distorted by no more than a factor of 2.

Of course, a factor of 2 would still be a huge systematic error in our context, but there is a simple remedy. Namely, we change the role of the CO algorithm and its variants: instead of using them as methods to find directly the top-scoring pairs by keeping track of the (biased) associated counters we use them as filtering algorithms that simply propose "potentially interesting" pairs to examine. Specifically, for every pair co-occurrence, instead of incrementing a counter and ultimately evaluate pairs by the value of their counters, we measure and evaluate directly the exact Pearson's correlation coefficient "on the fly". (To speed things up one can use a bit-vector to make sure they only measure each pair at most once. As we will see, this is hardly necessary as the majority of pairs that ever co-occur, do so exactly once.)

Finally, the a priori valid concern regarding pairs of SNPs whose cosine might be very close to ± 1 (and for which, thus, the distortion resulting from replacing cosines by angles could be arbitrary) is not borne out by the data. The reason is that the "most different" pairs end up having a difference in cosine of at least 0.7 which puts their angle difference very well within the near-linear regime of the arccos function.

6.2 Number of hyperplanes used

In order to binarize the SNP data via LSH, we map both the case vectors and the control vectors into $\{0,1\}^s$ using s independent random vectors for each. Clearly, the more hyperplanes we use, the better the approximation of the correlation of the SNPs in our dataset. While, theoretically, $s = \Theta(\log n)$ suffices, in practice the correct number of hyperplanes to use is domain-dependent and has to do with parameters like the initial dimension of the vectors and their distribution. As a rule of thumb in our experiments, since the number of individuals was rather small, we took $s = \max\{m_1, m_2\}$. Note now that since the binarized data for cases and controls are of the same dimension, we do not run into the class-size imbalance problem mentioned in Section 5.1.

7. PRACTICAL CONSIDERATIONS

7.1 Running CO in practice

Since p_1 and p_2 are not known a priori, in order to run the algorithm one must replace γ by an estimate $\hat{\gamma}$. In that case, CO is guaranteed to return a pair with correlation strictly larger than $\kappa = p_1(1 - 1/\hat{\gamma})$. (So, it will return the most correlated pair, when $p_2 \leq \kappa$.) In practice, one can run the algorithm multiple times with $\hat{\gamma}$ and check whether the returned pair changes. If that happens, then the estimate for γ needs to be increased. Note that since the exponent will increase, the running time expended prior to the increase is completely dominated (and can therefore be absorbed) in the new exponent. As we will see in Section 7.2, though, in practice there seem to be much more effective ways to address this issue that avoid estimating γ altogether.

7.2 Running AC in practice

As can be easily seen, the modified version of the CO algorithm from Section 3 is at the heart of our approach. To implement it efficiently, in each iteration, after we partition the columns into equivalence classes (buckets), we further partition the columns in each bucket into two equivalence classes, depending on if they were complemented or not. We then increment the counters of all pairs going across the two partitions. In this way, the additional running time after we partition the columns into buckets E_ℓ is proportional only to the number of counters we actually increment, not $\sum E_\ell^2$.

We now discuss how we choose our row-sample size k and how we choose the number of iterations to run. In short: we don't. That is, while one can use the (analogues of the) theoretical estimates from [14] for setting k and t these turn out to be too conservative in practice. Moreover, to overcome the need to know p_1, p_2 in order to set t, entails an additional burden to the running time as we run multiple iterations of the algorithm, effectively searching for p_1, p_2. Instead, we tune both parameters "on the fly", i.e., in a data-dependent way, using the same underlying logic as [14] but applied in a much more fine-grained manner.

7.2.1 *Row-sample size*

We introduce an adaptive strategy that adjusts k at the end of each iteration i of the algorithm based on the number, C_i, of SNP pairs that were examined during iteration i. In particular, we introduce a parameter called Target=$\Theta(n)$ and we adjust k with the aim that Target$/2 \leq C_i \leq 2$Target. We initialize Target to a sufficiently small value, so as not too risk too many co-occurrences in the first iteration. From then on, if $C_i <$ Target$/2$ we increment k, whereas if $C_i > 2 \cdot$ Target we decrement k.

As for the exact value of Target itself, while in [14], the sample size k corresponds to Target $= n$, in practice we found that setting Target to about one order of magnitude less, achieved the same quality of solutions with significantly fewer computations. We discuss this further in Section 7.3.

7.2.2 *Number of iterations*

When we are interested in reporting the "top-h" pairs we keep track of the top-$2h$ pairs discovered at the end of each iteration of the algorithm. We stop at iteration t if in the last $t/2$ iterations, there was no change in the set of top-$2h$ pairs.

7.2.3 *Returning top h pairs*

In running CO as a subroutine for AC we have it report not just the pair of columns with maximum correlation but in fact the top-h pairs. We then measure the actual Pearson's correlation boost for these pairs and consider whether we should report them. For this, we maintain a heap of size h which we update whenever an unmeasured pair with higher correlation than the current heap minimum is discovered. In our experiments h ranges from 10 to a few thousands, making its maintenance a minor fraction of the overall running time.

7.3 Runtime complexity

After centering the data (an operation linear in the size of the data) we compute for each (centered) column its inner product with $s = O(\log n)$ random vectors. At this point, we have a new binary dataset and the real work of our algorithm begins, proceeding in iterations. The work in each iteration can be partitioned into two parts. In the first part we take a random sample of $k = O(\log n)$ rows (individuals) and place them into buckets depending on their k-bit vector. In the second part, pairs that lie in the same bucket are examined. Therefore, if we examine $t \sim n^{1+\gamma}$ pairs in total during the execution of the algorithm, where $\gamma > 0$, the total number of operations by the algorithm is bounded by $O(n(s^2 + n^\gamma))$. Since, typically, $\gamma \geq 1/2$, we see that the total number of examined pairs is a good proxy for the algorithm's running time. Indeed, in practice, the relationship between the number of discovered pairs and the actual running time is essentially the same across a large span of data sets, data sizes, and recall levels.

8. EXPERIMENTAL RESULTS

We have run experiments on four different data sets. These include both binary and ternary SNPs and both real and synthetic data. All experiments were performed either on a single MacPro OS X 10.6 with 16 GB RAM when this was feasible, or using a cluster of 1,000 CPUs, when we needed to scale appropriately.

8.1 Experimental setting

To avoid unfairness in comparisons that result from implementation, hardware, and programming issues, we have focused in our experiments on the key quantity that determines the asymptotic behavior of all relevant algorithms: the number of pairs whose joint statistical behavior is ever examined. So, for example, for brute force this is $\binom{n}{2}$. In our algorithm we will see that the relevant exponent is often significantly lower and gets to about $n^{3/2}$ for real-life massive data sets.

It is important to point out that the running time of our algorithm is linear in this quantity while, at the same time, as is clear by the algorithm's description, all other sampling, binning, and embedding operations are dwarfed by the step of actually measuring the joint behavior of pairs that fall in the same bucket.

Comparison partners: To quantify the quality of our results both in terms of runtime and accuracy, we compare it to i) a brute-force enumeration of all pairs and ii) a two-stage filtering procedure, in which we employ exhaustive enumeration on the subset of top-scoring SNPs from a one-locus association mapping. In order to be able to compute the brute-force approach, we ran experiments on a cluster of 1,000 CPUs, some of which took several days. This brute-force served as a reference and ground truth for evaluating the quality of the results of our algorithm.

We also evaluate the performance of our algorithm by comparing it to the common *two-stage filtering procedure*, that is applying brute force on a carefully selected subset of the SNPs. To select the SNPs we ranked them based on their correlation with class membership and retain only the top-ranking SNPs, ranging from 10% to 50% (0.1 to 0.5) of all SNPs. Then we run an exhaustive search on all pairs of SNPs from this subset.

Evaluation We compared our novel algorithm to its comparison partners based on the following criteria:

- the **speed up factor**, that is, the total speed up compared to brute force in terms of CPU time.
- the **exponent** $(1+\gamma)$ of the number of pairs our algorithm examined. Our method considers $(n^{(1+\gamma)})$ pairs compared to the n^2 pairs computed in brute-force.
- the **recall** among the top-h pairs (where $h \in \{10, 100, 500, 1k, 10k\}$) returned by our algorithm. This is the percentage of the top pairs found by brute force that were also detected by our algorithm.

8.2 Datasets

In our experiments, we used the following datasets:

Full-genome scale real human data: For 850k SNPs from real human data set (dbGap [10]) and 100 individuals in cases and controls (respectively), we used a cluster of 1000 machines for more than 3 days in order to discover by brute force the top 10k pairs as a reference.

Synthetic human data: This is a human data set (ternary SNPs) generated by the simulator Hapsample (Wright et al., 2007) which is publicly accessible from the website http://www.hapsample.org. It consists of 95k SNPs, with 200 cases and 200 controls.

Besides the original dataset we also created smaller datasets by keeping a random sample of 30k and 50k SNPs, while always maintaining all 200 cases and 200 controls for each SNP. On all these datasets we ran brute force enumeration, and the two-stage filtering approach as well.

Real binary data from USC We do as above, for 50k, 100k and 210k SNPs of the genome of a real inbred organism [2]. While our ground truth is the top 1k pairs for the first two smaller sizes of SNP collections, for the largest one is the top 10k. Here the initial number of individuals in cases and controls is 80 and 86 and we transform them (via hashing with appropriate number of random hyper planes) into matrices with 100 rows each, before we run our method.

Synthetic binary data: We also generated synthetic binary data with 200 cases and 200 controls. We generated one dataset with 10k, 50k and 100k SNPs each. The SNPs were drawn randomly from a uniform Binomial distribution. We refer to these datasets as NOISE datasets.

8.3 Results

Key to experiments: For each input, we run our algorithm with different "allowances" on the total number of pairs to measure. We report this allowance as "Pairs" in the table below. Since pairs can be suggested for measurement multiple times, we also report the total number of such "Measurements" proposed. As one can see, these two numbers are quite close, suggesting that it is probably not worthwhile to try to keep track of which pairs have already been measured. To highlight the *asymptotic* nature of our improvements, we write this number of measurements as n^{β} and report the value of β for each experiment. Finally, the remaining columns are our recall fraction relative to the ground truth as computed by Brute Force.

Comparison to brute force We ran our method on all of these four datasets and report results in the following Tables 1, 2, 4, 5, and 6. Except for the NOISE dataset, our method achieves high recall rates on all three datasets, up to 100%, and a speed up factor of 10 to 1000 compared to brute force. The runtime exponent varies for each dataset and SNP number, but on average it is approximately 3/2, compared to 2 for the brute force approach. Only on the NOISE dataset, our recall rates are low, owing to the fact that due to its random character, the correlation differences are here rather uniform across all pairs. As the performance of our algorithm depends on the discrepancy in score between the top pairs and the other pairs, it performs considerably worse on NOISE.

In making comparisons in this context, it is important to keep in mind that for any given value of h, the task of finding the top-h pairs becomes *relatively* easier as the size of the dataset, n, increases. This is because with h fixed and n increasing, the h-th highest ranked pair is more and more "special" relative to the remaining $\binom{n}{2}$ pairs as n is increased, i.e., it has higher contrast. As a result, the *relative* effort of finding it, expressed as a fraction of $\binom{n}{2}$, goes down. This is very well reflected in our experiments, where for a given recall rate at a given h, the exponent of the number of measured pairs keeps dropping as the size of the dataset increases.

Comparison to two-stage approach When we compare our approach to the common two-stage approach [11] on the hap-sample dataset for 30k, 50k and 95k SNPS (see Table 3), we observe that the recall rates of this filtering approach are lower than ours, while we still achieve a significant speed-up over its runtime.

9. DISCUSSION AND CONCLUSIONS

In this article, we have presented a first subquadratic-runtime algorithm for SNP-SNP interaction detection. It renders epistasis detection even on the whole human genome with order 10^7 SNPs [5] computationally feasible on a single PC.

In the current presentation, we have focused on reducing the computational burden caused by the quadratic number of candidate pairs. The other burden is that of determining statistical significance in multiple hypothesis testing. We can compute p-values for our difference-in-correlation test statistic based on the null distribution described in [9], and correct for multiple hypothesis testing, for instance, by Bonferroni correction. Alternatively, we can perform permutations of the phenotypes and approximate the null distribution empirically. In future work, we will examine how to perform this permutation testing more efficiently than just iteratively applying our current algorithm.

Our plan for future work on the biological side is to apply the here described algorithm to the Wellcome Trust's GWA datasets for various human diseases and to plant phenotypes from rice, maize and *Arabidopsis*. On the engineering side, we will study how to implement the here described algorithm on graphical processing units, to yield an extremely fast implementation. On the algorithmic side, we will study the exciting extension to multi-SNP-interaction detection.

# SNPs	Measurements	Exponent	Speedup	Top 10	Top 100	Top 500	Top 1k	Top 10k
845,814	660,788,168	1.48	542	1.0	0.95	0.93	0.91	0.90
845,814	919,392,776	1.51	390	1.0	0.96	0.93	0.93	0.92
845,814	1,194,631,961	1.53	300	0.9	0.94	0.89	0.88	0.88
845,814	2,052,068,774	1.57	175	1.0	0.97	0.97	0.98	0.97

Table 1: Real human dataset

# SNPs	Measurements	Pairs	Exponent	Speedup	Top 10	Top 100	Top 500	Top 1k
30,000	8,699,003	8,220,128	1.55	51	1.00	1.00	0.99	0.93
30,000	14,560,722	13,982,726	1.60	31	1.00	1.00	1.00	0.97
50,000	25,404,287	25,086,963	1.58	50	1.00	1.00	0.99	0.96
50,000	29,721,852	29,301,074	1.59	43	1.00	1.00	1.00	0.98
50,000	55,311,371	54,005,100	1.65	23	1.00	1.00	1.00	0.98
50,000	67,141,119	65,376,171	1.67	19	1.00	1.00	1.00	0.98
95,173	6,725,792	6,711,455	1.37	674	0.80	0.79	0.87	0.86
95,173	13,567,508	13,526,763	1.43	334	0.90	0.91	0.93	0.90
95,173	31,249,917	31,083,315	1.51	145	1.00	1.00	0.96	0.96
95,173	40,225,617	39,965,897	1.53	113	1.00	0.98	0.96	0.98

Table 2: Synthetic human dataset

# SNPs	Fraction kept	Exponent	Speedup	Top 10	Top 100	Top 500	Top 1k
30,000	0.10	1.49	101	0.80	0.50	0.10	0.05
30,000	0.20	1.62	26	0.80	0.61	0.27	0.14
30,000	0.30	1.70	12	0.90	0.68	0.50	0.31
50,000	0.10	1.52	101	0.90	0.46	0.11	0.06
50,000	0.20	1.64	26	0.90	0.67	0.28	0.15
50,000	0.30	1.72	12	0.90	0.70	0.55	0.36
50,000	0.40	1.77	7	0.90	0.71	0.55	0.36
50,000	0.50	1.81	5	0.90	0.71	0.57	0.48
95,173	0.10	1.54	101	0.40	0.39	0.32	0.16
95,173	0.20	1.66	26	0.40	0.40	0.52	0.38
95,173	0.30	1.73	12	0.40	0.44	0.56	0.52

Table 3: Performance of the two-stage filtering approach on the synthetic human dataset. The second column is the fraction of SNPs retained after filtering. The remaining columns are as in the experiments with our algorithm.

# SNPs	Measurements	Pairs	Exponent	Speedup	Top 10	Top 100	Top 500	Top 1k
10,000	3,102,004	2,944,313	1.62	17	1.00	0.99	0.80	0.60
10,000	3,750,058	3,496,129	1.64	14	1.00	1.00	0.82	0.67
10,000	6,236,283	5,649,158	1.70	9	1.00	1.00	0.90	0.75
50,000	33,507,669	32,325,103	1.60	38	1.00	1.00	1.00	0.99
50,000	22,940,479	22,295,748	1.57	55	1.00	0.99	0.97	0.97
100,000	8,255,645	8,186,657	1.38	606	1.00	0.86	0.82	0.80
100,000	16,556,322	16,372,904	1.44	302	0.90	0.92	0.91	0.90
100,000	39,731,329	39,039,859	1.52	126	1.00	1.00	0.98	0.98
100,000	52,762,001	51,732,700	1.54	95	1.00	1.00	0.99	0.98

Table 4: Random SNP samples from USC dataset

# SNPs	Measurements	Pairs	Exponent	Speedup	Top 10	Top 100	Top 500	Top 1k	Top 10k
210,000	18,202,620	18,062,488	1.36	1212	0.90	0.80	0.71	0.71	0.68
210,000	48,844,947	48,384,057	1.44	452	1.00	0.86	0.87	0.86	0.82
210,000	53,260,691	52,724,216	1.45	414	0.80	0.81	0.89	0.88	0.86
210,000	74,054,023	73,044,942	1.48	298	0.90	0.90	0.93	0.93	0.91
210,000	95,844,600	94,598,677	1.50	231	1.00	0.99	0.95	0.94	0.92

Table 5: Entire USC dataset

# SNPs	Measurements	Pairs	Exponent	Speedup	Top 10	Top 100	Top 500	Top 1k
10,000	3,790,269	3,651,534	1.64	14	0.30	0.26	0.20	0.19
10,000	7,619,321	7,082,458	1.72	7	0.60	0.50	0.38	0.38
50,000	15,079,241	14,960,262	1.53	83	0.10	0.12	0.07	0.07
50,000	55,200,578	53,907,259	1.65	23	0.20	0.19	0.18	0.18
100,000	27,253,865	27,143,127	1.49	184	0.00	0.07	0.05	0.04
100,000	39,759,698	39,540,714	1.52	126	0.00	0.07	0.07	0.06

Table 6: NOISE dataset (each entry is 0 or 1 independently, with equal probability).

10. ACKNOWLEDGMENTS

P.A. was visiting the Max Planck Institutes in Tübingen while this research work was done. The authors would like to thank Oliver Stegle and Nino Shervashidze for their comments on the final text. P.A. would like to thank Dimitris Achlioptas for numerous inspiring conversations.

Funding support for the Genome-Wide Association of Schizophrenia Study was provided by the National Institute of Mental Health (R01 MH67257, R01 MH59588, R01 MH59571, R01 MH59565, R01 MH59587, R01 MH60870, R01 MH59566, R01 MH59586, R01 MH61675, R01 MH60879, R01 MH81800, U01 MH46276, U01 MH46289 U01 MH46318, U01 MH79469, and U01 MH79470) and the genotyping of samples was provided through the Genetic Association Information Network (GAIN). The datasets used for the analyses described in this manuscript were obtained from the database of Genotypes and Phenotypes (dbGaP) found at http://www.ncbi.nlm.nih.gov/gap through dbGaP accession number phs000021.v3.p2. Samples and associated phenotype data for the Genome-Wide Association of Schizophrenia Study were provided by the Molecular Genetics of Schizophrenia Collaboration (PI: Pablo V. Gejman, Evanston Northwestern Healthcare (ENH) and Northwestern University, Evanston, IL, USA.

11. REFERENCES

[1] C. E. Aston, D. A. Ralph, D. P. Lalo, S. Manjeshwar, B. A. Gramling, D. C. DeFreese, A. D. West, D. E. Branam, L. F. Thompson, M. A. Craft, D. S. Mitchell, C. D. Shimasaki, J. J. Mulvihill, and E. R. Jupe. Oligogenic combinations associated with breast cancer risk in women under 53 years of age. *Human Genetics*, 116(3):208–221, Feb. 2005.

[2] S. Atwell, Y. S. Huang, B. J. VilhjÃąlmsson, G. Willems, M. Horton, Y. Li, D. Meng, A. Platt, A. M. Tarone, T. T. Hu, R. Jiang, N. W. Muliyati, X. Zhang, M. A. Amer, I. Baxter, B. Brachi, J. Chory, C. Dean, M. Debieu, J. de Meaux, J. R. Ecker, N. Faure, J. M. Kniskern, J. D. G. Jones, T. Michael, A. Nemri, F. Roux, D. E. Salt, C. Tang, M. Todesco, M. B. Traw, D. Weigel, P. Marjoram, J. O. Borevitz, J. Bergelson, and M. Nordborg. Genome-wide association study of 107 phenotypes in *Arabidopsis thaliana* inbred lines. *Nature*, 465(7298):627–631, Jun 2010.

[3] M. S. Charikar. Similarity estimation techniques from rounding algorithms. In *STOC*, 2002.

[4] J. H. Cho, D. L. Nicolae, L. H. Gold, C. T. Fields, M. C. LaBuda, P. M. Rohal, M. R. Pickles, L. Qin, Y. Fu, J. S. Mann, B. S. Kirschner, E. W. Jabs, J. Weber, S. B. Hanauer, T. M. Bayless, and S. R. Brant. Identification of novel susceptibility loci for inflammatory bowel disease on chromosomes 1p, 3q, and 4q: evidence for epistasis between 1p and IBD1. *Proceedings of the National Academy of Sciences of the United States of America*, 95(13):7502–7507, June 1998.

[5] T. H. Consortium. A second generation human haplotype map of over 3.1 million SNPs. *Nature*, 449(7164):851–61, Oct. 2007.

[6] H. J. Cordell. Epistasis: what it means, what it doesn't mean, and statistical methods to detect it in humans. *Hum. Mol. Genet.*, 11(20):2463–2468, Oct. 2002.

[7] H. J. Cordell. Detecting gene-gene interactions that underlie human diseases. *Nat Rev Genet*, 10(6):392–404, June 2009.

[8] N. J. Cox, M. Frigge, D. L. Nicolae, P. Concannon, C. L. Hanis, G. I. Bell, and A. Kong. Loci on chromosomes 2 (NIDDM1) and 15 interact to increase susceptibility to diabetes in mexican americans. *Nature Genetics*, 21(2):213–215, Feb. 1999.

[9] T. Kam-Thong, D. Czamara, K. Tsuda, K. Borgwardt, C. M. Lewis, A. Erhardt-Lehmann, B. Hemmer, P. Rieckmann, M. Daake, F. Weber, C. Wolf, A. Ziegler, B. Putz, F. Holsboer, B. Scholkopf, and B. Muller-Myhsok. EPIBLASTER-fast exhaustive two-locus epistasis detection strategy using graphical processing units. *Eur J Hum Genet*, Dec. 2010.

[10] M. Mailman, M. Feolo, Y. Jin, M. Kimura, K. Tryka, R. Bagoutdinov, L. Hao, A. Kiang, J. Paschall, L. Phan, N. Popova, S. Pretel, L. Ziyabari, M. Lee, Y. Shao, Z. Wang, K. Sirotkin, M. Ward, M. Kholodov, K. Zbicz, J. Beck, M. Kimelman, S. Shevelev, D. Preuss, E. Yaschenko, A. Graeff, J. Ostell, and S. Sherry. The NCBI dbGaP Database of Genotypes and Phenotypes. *Nature Genetics*, 39(10):1181–6, 2007.

[11] J. Marchini, P. Donnelly, and L. R. Cardon. Genome-wide strategies for detecting multiple loci that influence complex diseases. *Nat Genet*, 37(4):413–417, Apr. 2005.

[12] S. K. Musani, D. Shriner, N. Liu, R. Feng, C. S. Coffey, N. Yi, H. K. Tiwari, and D. B. Allison. Detection of gene x gene interactions in genome-wide association studies of human population data. *Human Heredity*, 63(2):67–84, 2007.

[13] R. Nakamichi, Y. Ukai, and H. Kishino. Detection of closely linked multiple quantitative trait loci using a genetic algorithm. *Genetics*, 158(1):463–475, May 2001.

[14] R. Paturi, S. Rajasekaran, and J. Reif. The light bulb problem. In *Proc. 2nd Annu. Workshop on Comput. Learning Theory*, pages 261 – 268, San Mateo, CA, 1989. Morgan Kaufmann.

[15] M. D. Ritchie, L. W. Hahn, and J. H. Moore. Power of multifactor dimensionality reduction for detecting gene-gene interactions in the presence of genotyping error, missing data, phenocopy, and genetic heterogeneity. *Genetic Epidemiology*, 24(2):150–157, Feb. 2003.

[16] J. L. Rodgers and W. A. Nicewander. Thirteen ways to look at the correlation coefficient. *The American Statistician*, 42, 1988.

[17] Y. Wang, X. Liu, K. Robbins, and R. Rekaya. AntEpiSeeker: detecting epistatic interactions for case-control studies using a two-stage ant colony optimization algorithm. *BMC Bioinformatics*, 3:117–117, 2010.

[18] J. Xu, C. D. Langefeld, S. L. Zheng, E. M. Gillanders, B. Chang, S. D. Isaacs, A. H. Williams, K. E. Wiley, L. Dimitrov, D. A. Meyers, P. C. Walsh, J. M. Trent, and W. B. Isaacs. Interaction effect of PTEN and CDKN1B chromosomal regions on prostate cancer linkage. *Human Genetics*, 115(3):255–262, Aug. 2004.

[19] X. Zhang, S. Huang, F. Zou, and W. Wang. TEAM: efficient two-locus epistasis tests in human genome-wide association study. *Bioinformatics (Oxford, England)*, 26(12):i217–227, June 2010.

[20] X. Zhang, F. Zou, and W. Wang. Fastanova: an efficient algorithm for genome-wide association study. In *Proceeding of the 14th ACM SIGKDD international conference on Knowledge discovery and data mining*, pages 821–829, Las Vegas, Nevada, USA, 2008. ACM.

[21] Y. Zhang and J. S. Liu. Bayesian inference of epistatic interactions in case-control studies. *Nature Genetics*, 39(9):1167–1173, September 2007.

A Taxi Business Intelligence System

Yong Ge[1], Chuanren Liu[1], Hui Xiong[1], Jian Chen[2]
[1]Rutgers Business School, Rutgers University
yongge@pegasus.rutgers.edu, {hxiong, chuanren.liu}@rutgers.edu
[2]Tsinghua University
jchen@mail.tsinghua.edu.cn

ABSTRACT

The increasing availability of large-scale location traces creates unprecedent opportunities to change the paradigm for knowledge discovery in transportation systems. A particularly promising area is to extract useful business intelligence, which can be used as guidance for reducing inefficiencies in energy consumption of transportation sectors, improving customer experiences, and increasing business performances. However, extracting business intelligence from location traces is not a trivial task. Conventional data analytic tools are usually not customized for handling large, complex, dynamic, and distributed nature of location traces. To that end, we develop a taxi business intelligence system to explore the massive taxi location traces from different business perspectives with various data mining functions. Since we implement the system using the real-world taxi GPS data, this demonstration will help taxi companies to improve their business performances by understanding the behaviors of both drivers and customers. In addition, several identified technical challenges also motivate data mining people to develop more sophisticate techniques in the future.

Categories and Subject Descriptors

H.2.8 [**Database Management**]: Database Applications—*Data Mining*

General Terms

Algorithms, Experimentation

Keywords

Business Intelligence, Route Recommendation, Taxi Driving Fraud Detection

1. INTRODUCTION

Advances in sensor, wireless communication, and information infrastructures such as GPS, WiFi and RFID have enabled us to collect large amounts of location traces (trajectory data) of individuals or objects. Such a large number of trajectories provide us unprecedented opportunity to automatically discover useful knowledge, which in turn deliver intelligence for real-time decision making in various fields, such as route recommendations and fraud detection.

In this demonstration, we introduce several interesting applications, which are enabled by both the availability of taxi GPS traces and advanced data mining techniques. First, we exploit the knowledge extracted from taxi location traces and develop a route recommendation function based on business success metrics. The key idea is to leverage the business knowledge from the historical data of successful taxi drivers for helping other taxi drivers to improve their business performances. Specifically, this function is able to recommend a driving route, which is essentially a sequence of pick-up points, to taxi drivers. The suggested optimal route is expected to result in the minimal driving distance before the next pick-up event. Since there are usually hundreds of pick-up points in a city and this is naturally a combinatorial problem, efficient algorithms are required to search the optimal route for online recommendation.

In addition, we understand drivers' behaviors from taxi GPS traces and develop a taxi driving fraud detection function. Indeed, fraudulent taxi drivers often commit driving fraud activities and overcharge passengers by deliberately taking unnecessary detours. To detect taxi driving fraud activities, we need to consider different aspects of taxi driving activities, such as traces, speed, time, distance, and traffic situations, which can be revealed from the GPS traces.

Finally, in the demo system, we also provide a function to illustrate some business insights by exploiting the taxi data. The business insight, such as the tip distribution and the economic potential of pick-up points, can guide taxi drivers to improve their performances.

A screenshots of this online demonstration system[1] is shown in Figure 1. We provide a user-friendly interface, which allows user to operate the different functions easily. Also, most output of functions are visualized using the Google Map API. This helps users better explore the results. Finally, two sets of real-world taxi data are collected and explored in the demo system. One is collected from 500 taxi drivers for about 30 days in the San Francisco Bay Area. Another one is collected from 24 taxi drivers in the New York City area for two year period.

2. DRIVING ROUTE RECOMMENDATION

Consider a scenario that a large number of GPS traces of taxi drivers have been collected for a period of time. In this

[1]http://kdd11demo.appspot.com/app.htm

KDD'11, August 21–24, 2011, San Diego, California, USA.

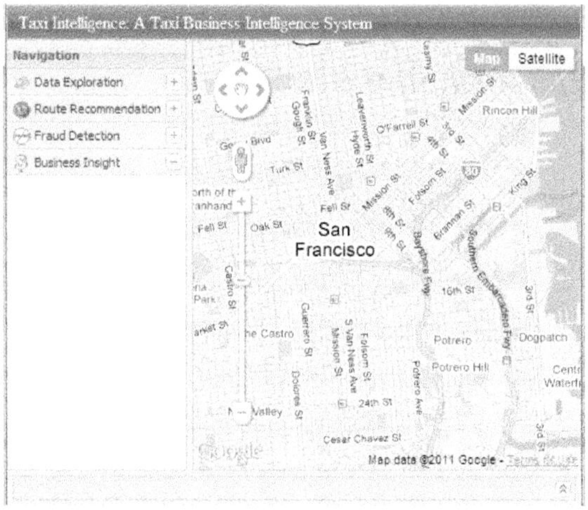

Figure 1: A Screen Shot of the Demo System

collection of location traces, we also have the information about when a cab is available or occupied. In this data set, it is possible to first identify a group of taxi drivers who are very successful in business. Then, we can cluster the pick-up points of these taxi drivers for a certain time period. The centroids of these clusters can be used as the recommended pick-up points with a certain probability of success for new taxi drivers in these areas. Then, a mobile sequential recommendation problem can be described as follows.

Assume that a set of N potential pick-up points, $\mathcal{C}=\{C_1, C_2, \cdots, C_N\}$, is available. Also, the estimated probability that a pick-up event could happen at each pick-up point is known as $P(C_i)$, where $P(C_i)(i = 1, \cdots, N)$ is assumed to be independently distributed. Let $\mathcal{P} = \{P(C_1), P(C_2), \cdots, P(C_N)\}$ denote the probability set. In addition, let $\overrightarrow{\mathcal{R}} = \{\overrightarrow{R_1}, \overrightarrow{R_2}, \cdots, \overrightarrow{R_M}\}$ be the set of all the directed sequences (potential driving routes) generated from $\mathcal{C}$ and $|\overrightarrow{\mathcal{R}}| = M$ is the size of $\overrightarrow{\mathcal{R}}$ - the number of all possible driving routes. Note that the pick-up points in each directed sequence are assumed to be different from each other. Next, let $L_{\overrightarrow{R_i}}$ be the length of route $\overrightarrow{R_i}(1 \leq i \leq M)$, where $1 \leq L_{\overrightarrow{R_i}} \leq N$. Finally, for a directed sequence $\overrightarrow{R_i}$, let $\mathcal{P}_{\overrightarrow{R_i}}$ be the route probability set which includes the probabilities of all pick-up points containing in $\overrightarrow{R_i}$, where $\mathcal{P}_{\overrightarrow{R_i}}$ is a subset of $\mathcal{P}$.

The objective of this MSR problem is to recommend a travel route for a cab driver in a way such that the potential travel distance before having customer is minimized. We defined a function $\mathcal{F}$ to compute the Potential Travel Distance (PTD) before having a customer. The PTD can be denoted as $\mathcal{F}(PoCab, \overrightarrow{\mathcal{R}}, \mathcal{P})$. In other words, the computation of PTD depends on the current position of a cab (PoCab), a suggested sequential pick-up points ($\overrightarrow{\mathcal{R}_\jmath}$), and the corresponding probabilities associated with all recommended pick-up points.

The MSR problem involves the recommendation of a sequence of pick-up points and has combinatorial complexity in nature. We have developed some pruning techniques [4] to efficiently search the optimal route.

2.1 High-Performance Drivers

In real world, there are always high-performance experienced cab drivers, who typically have sufficient driving hours and higher customer occupancy rates - the percentage of driving time with customers. For example, Figure 2 (a) and (b) show the distributions of driving hours and occupancy rates of more than 500 drivers in San Francisco over a period of about 30 days. In the figure, we can clearly see that the drivers have different performances in terms of occupancy rates. Based on this observation, we will first extract a group of high-performance drivers with sufficient driving hours and high occupancy rates. The past pick-up records of these selected drivers will be used for the generation of potential pick-up points for recommendation.

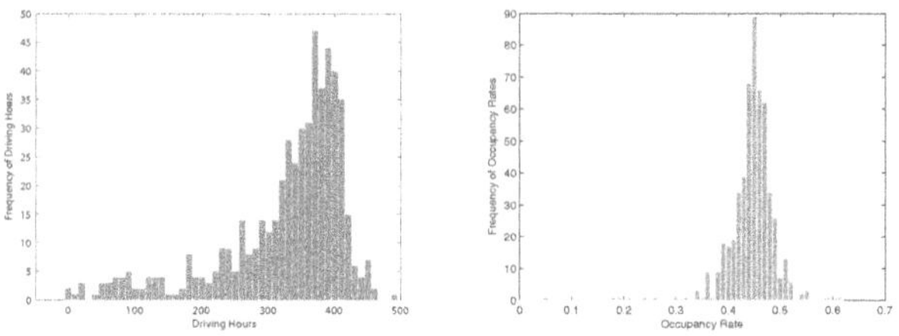

(a) Driving Hours (b) Occupancy Rates

Figure 2: Some Statistics of the Cab Data.

2.2 Clustering Based on Driving Distance

After carefully observing historical pick-up points of high-performance drivers, we notice that there are relative more pick-up events in some places than others. In other words, there are the cluster effect of historical pick-up points. Therefore, we propose to cluster historical pick-up points of high-performance drivers into N clusters. The centroids of these clusters will be used for recommending pick-up points. For this clustering algorithm, we use driving distance rather than Euclidean distance as the distance measure. In this study, we perform clustering based on driving distance during different time periods in order to have recommending pick-up pointers for different time periods. Another benefit of clustering historical pick-up points is to dramatically reduce the computational cost of the MRS problem.

2.3 Probability Calculation

For each recommended pick-up point (the centroid of historical pick-up cluster), the probability of a pick-up event can be computed based on historical pick-up data. The idea is to measure how frequent pick-up events can happen when cabs travel across each pick-up cluster. Specifically, we first obtain the spatial coverage of each cluster. Then, let $\#_T$ denote the number of cabs which have no customer before passing a cluster. For these $\#_T$ empty cabs, the number of pick-up events $\#_P$ is counted in this cluster. Finally, the probability of pick-up event for each cluster (each recommended pick-up point) can be estimated as $P(C_i)_{1 \leq i \leq N} = \frac{\#_P}{\#_T}$, where $\#_P$ and $\#_T$ are recorded for each historical pick-up cluster at different time periods.

2.4 The Recommendation Process

Even though we can find the optimal drive route for a given cab with its current position, it is still a challenging problem about how to make the recommendation for many cabs in the same area. In this section, we address this problem and introduce a strategy for the recommendation process in the real world.

A simple way is to suggest all these empty cabs to follow the same optimal drive route, however there is naturally an

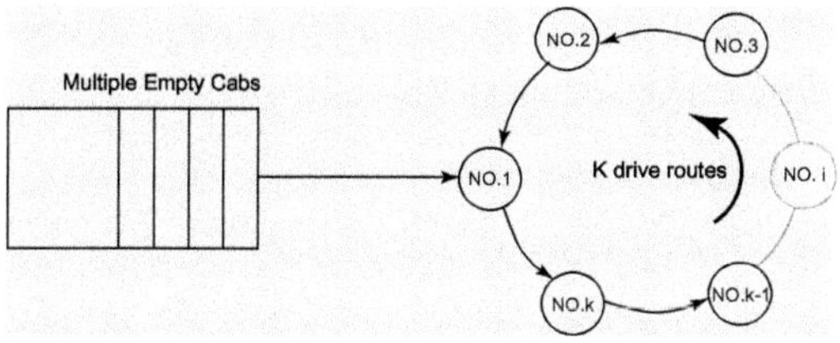

Figure 3: Illustration of the *Circulating Mechanism*.

overload problem, which will degrade the performance of the recommender system. To this end, we employ load balancing techniques [6] to distribute the empty cabs to follow multiple optimal drive routes. The problem of load balancing has been widely used in distributed systems for the purpose of optimizing a given objective through finding allocations of multiple jobs to different computers. For example, the load balancing mechanism distributes requests among web servers in order to minimize the execution time. For the proposed mobile recommendation system, we can treat multiple empty cabs as jobs and multiple optimal drive routes as computers. Then, we can deal with this overload problem by exploiting existing load balancing algorithms. Specifically, in this study, we apply the *circulating mechanism* for the recommender systems by exploiting a Round Robin algorithm [8], which is a static load balancing method.

Under the *circulating mechanism*, to make recommendation for multiple empty cabs, a round robin scheduler alternates the recommendation among multiple optimal drive routes in a circular manner. As shown in Figure 3, we could search k optimal drive routes and recommend the NO.1 route to the first coming empty cab. Then, for the second empty cab, the NO. 2 drive route will be recommended. Assume there are more than k empty cabs, recommendations are repeated from NO. 1 route again after the kth empty cab. In practice, to achieve this, one central dispatch (processor) is needed to maintain the empty cabs and assignments among the top-k driving routes. Note that the load balancing techniques are not the focus of this paper.

3. DRIVING FRAUD DETECTION

Taxi driving frauds are often committed by greedy taxi drivers who overcharge passengers by deliberately taking unnecessary detours. Nowadays, many taxi service complains are related to taxi driving frauds [2, 3, 1]. Therefore, it becomes invaluable for improving taxi services by providing the information about taxi driving frauds. However, it is a challenging issue to detect driving fraud activities committed by experienced and cunning taxi drivers who know how to manipulate the driving routes to commit driving frauds without being disclosed by passengers.

A promising direction to solve this problem is to collect and analyze the GPS traces by taxi drivers. Indeed, GPS tracking devices have been installed in many city taxis and a large amount of GPS traces has been accumulated for the analysis. These GPS traces provide unparallel opportunities for us to develop new ways to uncover taxi driving fraud activities. To that end, in this demonstration, we develop a taxi driving fraud detection function by exploiting GPS traces by taxi drivers.

Even there are already various anomaly detection techniques [5, 7], we are still facing several essential challenges in order to develop a reliable taxi driving fraud detection system. For example, we need to deal with different sets of

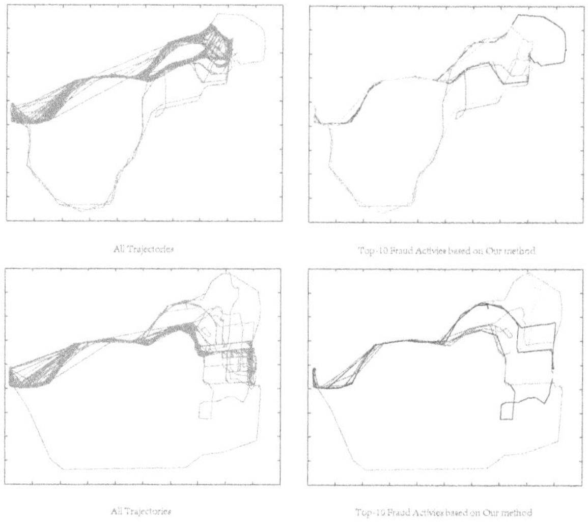

Figure 4: Driving Fraud Activities

trajectories between different pairs of source and end nodes. These trajectories are heterogeneous in nature. Also, we need to distinguish some shortcuts, which are abnormal, from real frauds. In addition, a practical challenge is that some drivers, who commit a driving fraud, may be truly unfamiliar with the local region or may use this as an excuse. Similarly, drivers may argue that they detour due to the traffic situations.

To deal with these practical challenges, we provide different approaches to find two aspects of evidences: travel route evidences and driving distance evidences. Furthermore, these two aspects of evidences are well combined together by using Dempster-Shafer theory. In addition, various customized and suitable techniques are applied to find each evidence. To perform taxi fraud detection, we first identify each pair of source and end nodes, and the trajectories from source to end nodes. For example, in Figure 4, we show some taxi driving fraud activities detected by our approach for two pairs of source and end nodes.

3.1 Regularity of Fraud Activities

After detecting the fraud activities for all pairs of source and end nodes, we are able to count the number of driving fraud activities for each driver. In Figure 5 (a), we show the frequency of driving fraud activities for each driver within about 30 days. We highlight top-3 drivers, who commit the most frauds. To further observe if some drivers habitually commit driving fraud every day, we show the fraud activities day by day for each driver in Figure 5 (b), where each dot represents one fraud activity by a driver in one day. As can be seen, some drivers do have relatively habitual fraud behaviors, such as those top-3 drivers.

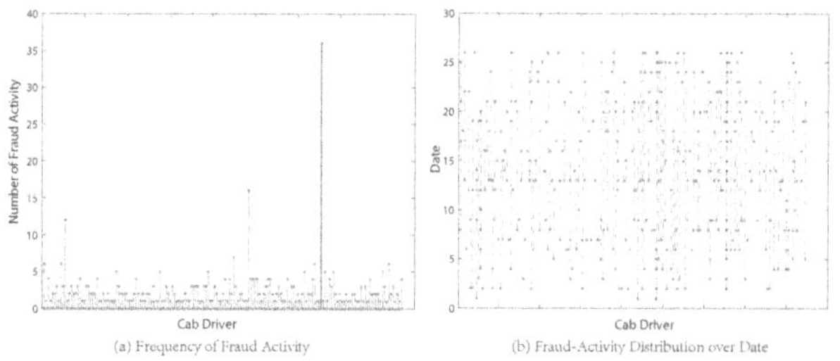

Figure 5: Illustration of Fraud Activities.

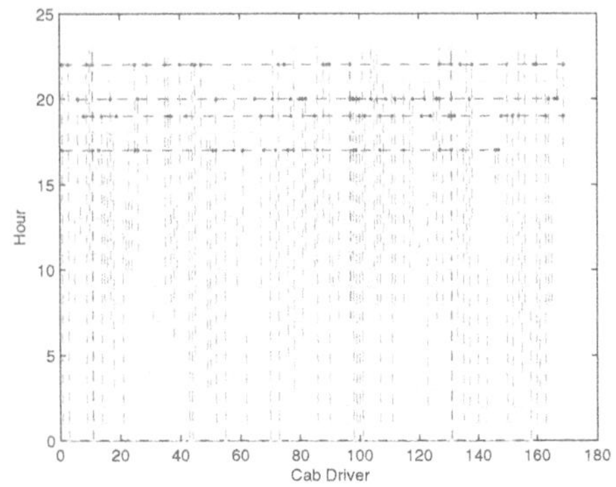

Figure 6: Temporal Distribution of Fraud Activities.

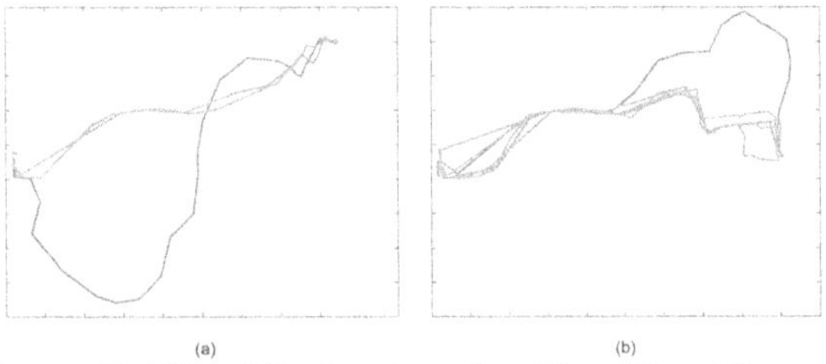

Figure 7: The Mechanism for Handling Excuses.

To further understand the regularity of driving fraud activities, we explore the temporal distribution of all driving fraud activities in Figure 6, where the temporal unit is an hour. In the figure, each dot point represents a driving fraud activity with corresponding driver on x-axis and hour on y-axis. We highlight top-3 drivers with the most fraud activities as vertical blue lines and top-4 time zones (hours) containing most fraud activities as horizontal blue lines. Here, we can observe that more fraud activities are committed around 5PM, 7PM, 8PM and 10PM.

3.2 Mechanism for Possible Excuses

To deal with the possible excuses, we introduce one mechanism to our system. Specifically, after we detect a suspicious driving activity, we recall all previous driving traces of the corresponding driver to check if the driver is familiar with the roads. Meanwhile, to confirm the traffic-related excuse, we recall all driving traces around the same timestamp. For example, in Figure 7 (a), after detecting the driving fraud activity (red one), we recall and plot the drivers' previous driving trajectories (green ones) and can clearly find this driver often operates in this area. Also, in Figure 7 (b), we show all trajectories (green ones) happening within the same minute as the driving fraud activity (red one) and we can see many other drivers did not detour. By this mechanism, we are able to obtain more real-time evidences to deny possible excuses and confirm the fraud behaviors.

4. BUSINESS INSIGHT EXPLORATION

In this section, we briefly introduce the third function, which is designed to exploit taxi data to discover some business insights, which may benefit taxi drivers or companies.

First, we examine the tip geo-distribution. With the taxi data, we are able to obtain the fare and tip information for each transaction, i.e., passenger delivery from a pick-up location to a drop-off location. Considering the different amount of fare for individual transaction, we use relatively tip, which is equal to the ratio of tip to fare, instead of the original tip value. After grouping the transactions, which are spatially neighboring, we obtain the average relative tip in the group and the rough tip geo-distribution across the city. Some examples of geo-distribution are accessible in the online demonstration system.

Also, we introduce the concept of economic potential to evaluate each pick-up point (cluster). The economic potential is expected to take into account not only the probability of pick-up events, but also the expected earnings of transactions (delivery) starting from the pick-up point. Furthermore, the economic potential also contains the "sustainability" information. For example, some pick-up points may usually lead to some very far destinations, where few customers are there. Experienced drivers may be not inclined to take this kind of delivery. Due to the space limitation, we are going to illustrate this economic potential concept in our online demonstration system.

5. CONCLUSION AND FUTURE WORK

In summary, we demonstrated a taxi business intelligence system, which is capable to exploit the knowledge from taxi data for business use. Indeed, the discovered knowledge can be helpful in many different applications, such as improving taxi business performances and passenger experiences. Specifically, in this system, we implemented three functions: route recommendation, fraud detection, and taxi business insight exploration. We developed the system with two sets of real-world taxi data, which were collected from taxis in San Francisco and the New York City. Some preliminary results of three functions are shown in this paper. More results can be explored using the online demo system.

In the future, we plan to improve route recommendation from both efficiency and effectiveness perspectives. Also, more business insights are expected to be mined. In addition, we are communicating with some taxi agents for both more taxi data and exploiting the system in their business.

6. ACKNOWLEDGEMENTS

This research was partially supported by National Natural Science Foundation of China (NSFC) via project numbers 70890082 and 71028002. Also, this work was partly sponsored by WINLAB with industry affiliation program with Panasonic in pursuing data mining to abnormal behavior detection for security and safety applications.

7. REFERENCES

[1] http://www.bustathief.com/taxi-fraud-taxi-scam/.

[2] http://www.consumertraveler.com/today/nyc-taxi-drivers-overcharge-passengers-8-3-millioin/.

[3] http://www.tour-beijing.com/taxi/.

[4] Y. Ge, H. Xiong, A. Tuzhilin, K. Xiao, M. Gruteser, and M. J. Pazzani. An energy-efficient mobile recommender system. In *SIGKDD*, 2010.

[5] Y. Ge, H. Xiong, Z.-H. Zhou, H. Ozdemir, J. Yu, and K. Lee. Top-eye: Top-k evolving trajectory outlier detection. In *ACM CIKM*, Toronto, 2010.

[6] D. Grosu and A. T. Chronopoulos. Algorithmic mechanism design for load balancing in distributed systems. *IEEE TSMC-B*, 34(1):77–84, 2004.

[7] H.-P. Kriegel, M. Schubert, and A. Zimek. Angle-based outlier detection in high-dimensional data. In *SIGKDD*, pages 444–452, Nevada, USA, 2008.

[8] Z. Xu and R. Huang. Performance study of load balancing algorithms in distributed web server systems. In *TR*, CS213 Univ. of California, Riverside.

Apolo: Interactive Large Graph Sensemaking by Combining Machine Learning and Visualization

Duen Horng "Polo" Chau, Aniket Kittur, Jason I. Hong, Christos Faloutsos
School of Computer Science
Carnegie Mellon University
Pittsburgh, PA 15213, USA
{dchau, nkittur, jasonh, christos}@cs.cmu.edu

ABSTRACT

We present APOLO, a system that uses a mixed-initiative approach to help people interactively explore and make sense of large network datasets. It combines visualization, rich user interaction and machine learning to engage the user in bottom-up sensemaking to gradually build up an understanding over time by starting small, rather than starting big and drilling down. APOLO helps users find relevant information by specifying exemplars, and then using a machine learning method called Belief Propagation to infer which other nodes may be of interest.

We demonstrate APOLO's usage and benefits using a Google Scholar citation graph, consisting of 83,000 articles (nodes) and 150,000 citations relationships. A demo video of APOLO is available at `http://www.cs.cmu.edu/~dchau/apolo/apolo.mp4`.

Categories and Subject Descriptors

H.3.3 [**Information Storage and Retrieval**]: Relevance feedback; H.5.2 [**Information Interfaces and Presentation**]: User Interfaces

General Terms

Algorithms, Design, Human Factors

Keywords

Sensemaking, large network, Belief Propagation

1. INTRODUCTION

Extracting useful knowledge from large network datasets has become an increasingly important problem in domains ranging from citation networks of scientific literature; social networks of friends and colleagues; and links between web pages in the World Wide Web. Theories of sensemaking provide a way to characterize and address the challenges faced by people trying to organize and understand large amounts of network-based data. Sensemaking refers to the iterative process of building up a representation or schema of an information space that is useful for achieving the user's goal [13]. For example, a scientist interested in connecting her work to a new domain must build up a mental representation of the existing literature in the new domain to understand and contribute

KDD'11, August 21–24, 2011, San Diego, California, USA.

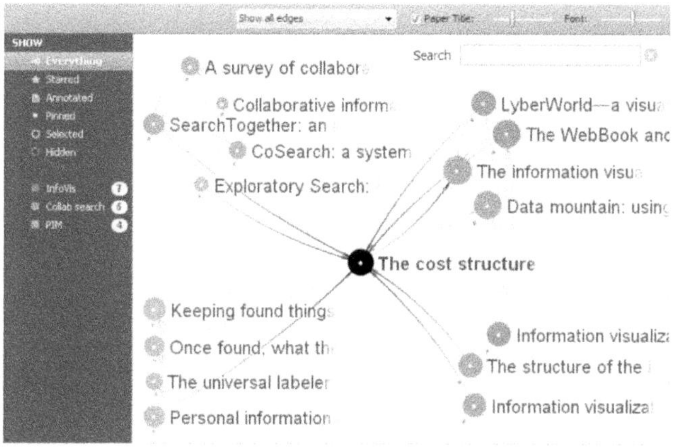

Figure 1: APOLO displaying citation network data around the article *The Cost Structure of Sensemaking*. The user gradually builds up a mental model of the research areas around the article by manually inspecting some neighboring articles in the visualization and specifying them as exemplar articles (with colored dots underneath) for some ad hoc groups, and instructs APOLO to find more articles relevant to them.

to it. Much existing work on graph visualization aims to develop "summary views" of graphs, on the assumption that the user knows nothing or very little about the data. However, such approaches often struggle to work when faced with large networks with millions of nodes and edges. Sometimes, the approaches simply cannot scale up to such data size due to computation or space requirements; sometimes, the views created are too overwhelming, showing too many nodes and edges; and more often, there are simply no good canonical views that can be generated for the graphs (e.g., real, large social networks often do not have well-defined clusters).

We have been investigating a different approach where we help the user start with a small subgraph, then incrementally explore and expand, rather than starting big and drilling down. This style of sensemaking can be found in many real-world scenarios. For example, imagine looking for relevant papers for our own research in a citation network; we would often start with papers that we are familiar with, then look at papers that they have cited or being cited by them. We created the APOLO system [4] (Figure 1) to support this kind of bottom-up sensemaking to help the user gradually build up an understanding over time. Within APOLO, a machine learning algorithm called Belief Propagation (BP) guides the user to explore relevant areas of the graph; in turns, the user specifies the nodes that he is interested in as "exemplars", and BP compute all other nodes' relevance and show the most relevant ones in the visualization. APOLO provides a number of interaction and visualization features that help people develop and evolve externalized represen-

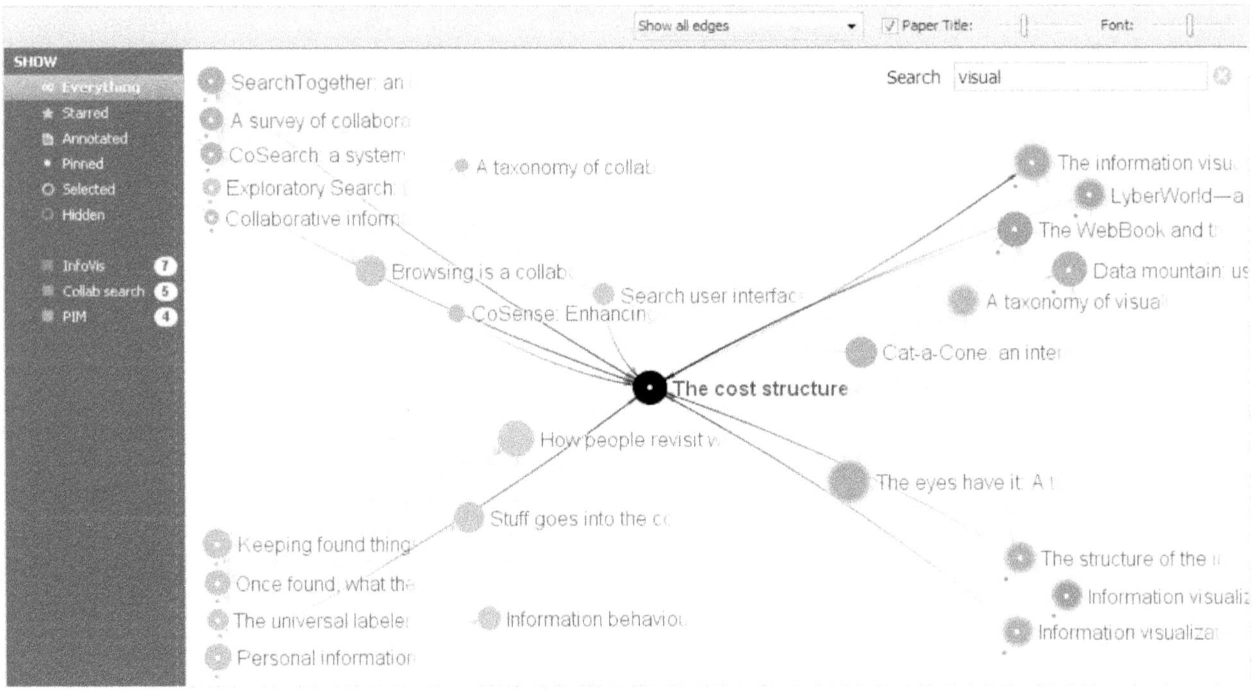

Figure 2: Screenshot of APOLO showing a user exploring the landscape of the related research areas around the article *The Cost Structure of Sensemaking* (highlighted in black). The user gives relevance feedback to APOLO as to which papers he is interested in, as *exemplars* (each with a color dot underneath); and how the exemplars should be categorized (by colors). APOLO incorporates these preferences into BP to find more related nodes, and shows some of the most relevant ones, to avoid overwhelming the user.

tations of their internal mental models to support sensemaking in large network data. For example, APOLO allows the user to (1) create multiple logical groups (via colors); (2) arrange nodes into spatial groups; and (3) sort nodes by their attributes directly within the visualization for quick comparison.

We summarize our main contributions as follows:

- We aptly select, adapt, and integrate work in machine learning and graph visualization in a novel way to help users make sense of large graphs using a mixed-initiative approach. APOLO goes beyond just graph exploration, and enables users to externalize, construct, and evolve their mental models of the graph in a bottom-up manner.
- APOLO offers a novel way of leveraging a complex machine learning algorithm, called Belief Propagation (BP) [15], to intuitively support sensemaking tailored to an individual's goals and experiences; BP was never applied to sensemaking or interactive graph visualization.

2. DEMONSTRATING APOLO

We will demonstrate APOLO's usage, user interaction and fast algorithm through sensemaking scenarios on a Google Scholar citation network dataset, which contains about 83,000 articles (nodes) and 150,000 citations relationships (edges, each represents either a "citing" or "cited-by" relationships).

Scenario. Here, we illustrate one example scenario, where we try to explore and understand the landscape of the related research areas around a seminal article *The Cost Structure of Sensemaking* by Russell et al. (Figure 2 shows final results.) This scenario will touch upon the major features of APOLO. We begin with a single source article highlighted in black in the center of the interface (Figure 4a) and the ten most relevant articles as determined by the built-in BP algorithm. Articles are shown as circles with sizes proportional to their citation count. Citation relationships are represented by directed edges.

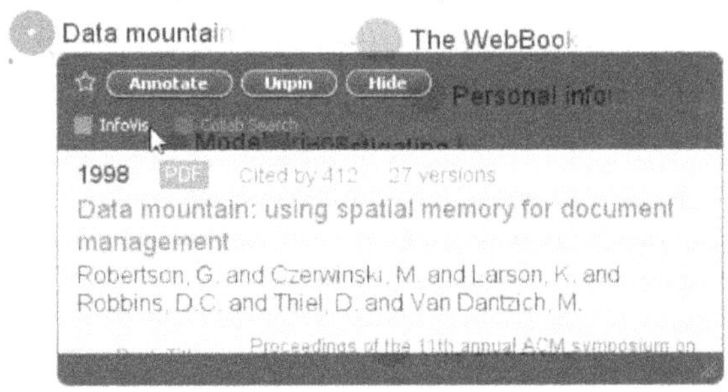

Figure 3: The *Details Panel*, shown when mousing over an article, displays article details obtained from Google Scholar. The user has made the article an *exemplar* the *InfoVis* group by clicking the group's label.

After viewing details of an article by mousing over it (Figure 3), the user moves it to a place on the landscape he thinks appropriate, where it remains pinned (as shown by the white dot at the center). The user can also star, annotate, unpin, or hide the node if so desired. After spatially arranging a few articles the user begins to visually infer the presence of two clusters: articles about *information visualization* (*InfoVis*) and *collaborative search* (*Collab Search*). After creating the labels for these two groups (Figure 4a), the user selects a good example article about *InfoVis* and clicks the *InfoVis* label, as shown in Figure 3, which puts the article into that group. A small blue dot (the group's color) appears below the article to indicate it is now an *exemplar* of that group. Changing an article's group membership causes BP to execute and infer the relevance of all other nodes in the network relative to the exem-

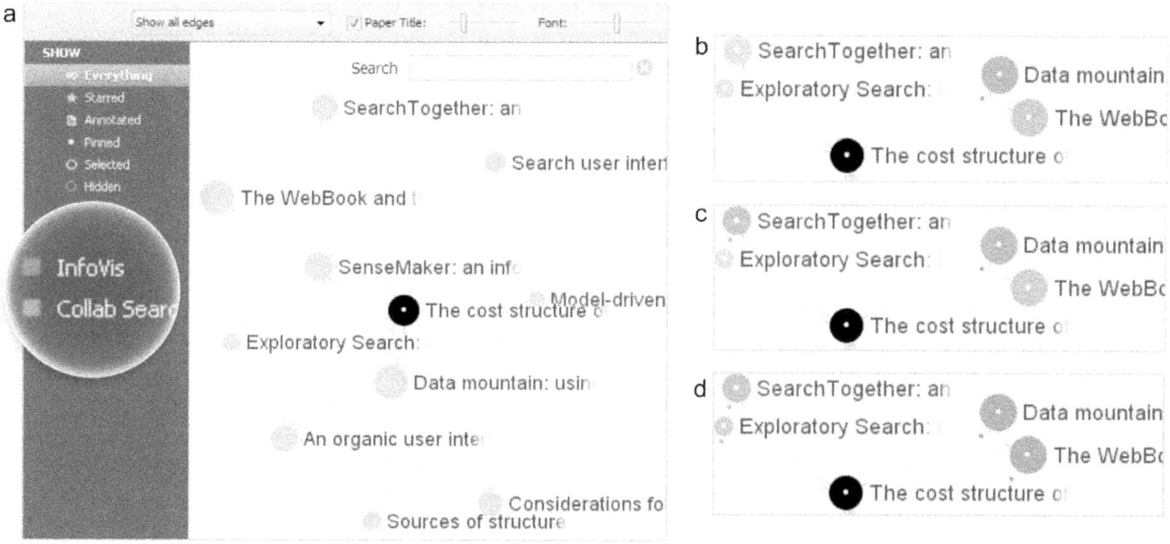

Figure 4: a) In the beginning, the top 10 most relevant articles (in gray) of our starting paper (in black) are shown. Our user has created two groups: *Collab Search* and *InfoVis* (magnified). b-d) Our user first spatially separates the two groups of articles, then assigns them to the groups, making them *exemplars* and causing Apolo to compute the relevance of all other nodes, which is indicated by color saturation; the more saturated the color, the more likely it belongs to the group. The image sequence shows how the node color changes as more exemplars are added.

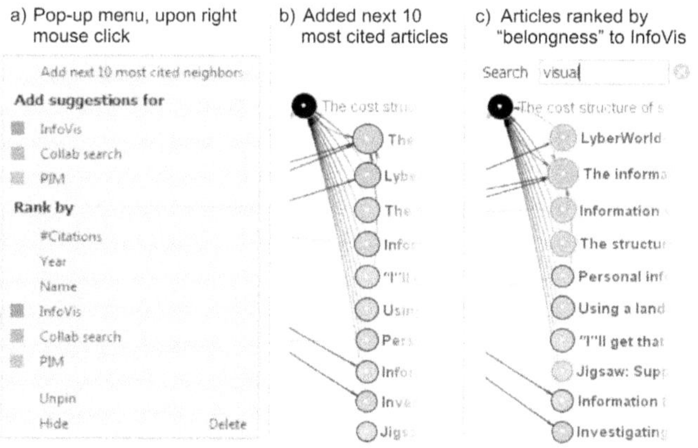

Figure 5: a) Pop-up menu shown upon right click; the user can choose to show more articles, add suggested articles for each group, rank sets of nodes in-place within the visualization, etc. b) Newly added neighboring nodes ranked by citation coun. c) The same nodes, ranked by their "belongness" to the (blue) InfoVis group; articles whose titles contain "visual" are highlighted with yellow halos.

plar(s). A node's relevance is indicated by its color saturation; the more saturated the color, the more likely BP considers the node to belong to the group. Figure 4b-d show how the node color changes as more exemplars are added.

Our user now would like to find more articles for each group to further his understanding of the two research areas. The user right-clicks on the starting paper and selects "Add next 10 most cited neighbors" from the pop-up menu (Figure 5a). By default, new nodes added this way are ranked by citation count (proportional to node size, as shown in Figure 5b) and initially organized in a vertical list to make them easy to identify and process. To see how relevant these new nodes are, he uses Apolo's *rank-in-place* feature to rank articles by their computed relevance to the InfoVis group. To quickly locate the papers about visualization, our user types "visual" in the search box at the top-right corner (Figure 5c) to highlight all articles with "visual" in their titles.

Going further down the list of ranked articles, our users found more InfoVis articles and put them all into that group. Within it, our user further creates two subgroups spatially, as shown in Figure 6, the one on top containing articles about visualization applications (e.g., *Data mountain: using spatial memory for document management*), and the lower subgroup contains articles that seem to provide analytical type of information (e.g., *The structure of the information visualization design space*). Following this work flow, our user can iteratively refine the groups, create new ones, move articles between them, and spatially rearrange nodes in the visualization. The user's landscape of the areas related to Sensemaking following further iterations is shown in Figure 2.

Engaging Our Audience. We will invite our audience to try out APOLO with their own starting set of papers, and collect their feedback on its usability and usefulness. Since we created APOLO to be a general graph sensemaking tool, we will discuss with our audience how APOLO may help with their work in their domains.

3. TECHNICAL DETAILS

The BP algorithm. BP is a fast algorithm; its running time scales linearly with the number of edges in the graph. It has been successfully used in many applications (e.g., error-correcting codes, image de-noising) and domains, but it has never been used for sensemaking. At the high level, BP infers every node's marginal

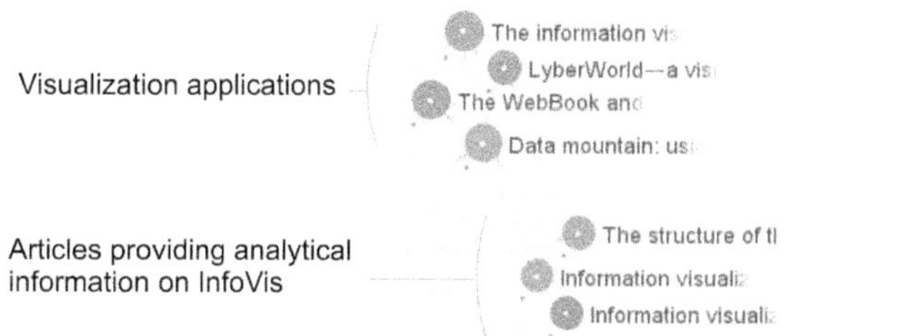

Figure 6: Two spatial subgroups

probabilities being in each of the group created by the user. A group's exemplars have high prior probability being in that group, which BP incorporates to perform inference. We implemented BP as described in [10]. The key settings of the algorithm include: (1) a *node potential* function that represents how likely a node belongs to each group (a value closer to 1 means more likely), e.g., if we have two groups, then we assign (0.99, 0.01) to exemplars of group 1, and (0.5, 0.5) to all other nodes; (2) an *edge potential* function that governs to what extent an exemplar would convert its neighbors into the same group as the exemplar (a value of 1 means immediate conversion; we used 0.58).

Implementation. The APOLO system is written in Java 1.6. It uses the JUNG library [11] for visualizing the network. The network data is stored in an SQLite[1] embedded database, for its cross-platform portability. One of our goals is to offer APOLO as a sensemaking tool that work on a wide range of network data, so we designed the network database schema independently from the APOLO system, so that APOLO can readily be used on different network datasets that follow the schema.

4. RELATED WORK

APOLO builds on a large body of research aimed at understanding and supporting how people can gain insights through visualization [8]. APOLO adopts a bottom-up sensemaking approach [13] aimed at helping users construct their own landscapes of information. APOLO provides several features to help people create flexible, ad-hoc groups as they explore, which fit with the process of how they would learn and represent concepts [2]. This "human in the loop" approach differs from a lot of research in graph mining that studies how to automatically discover clusters (or groupings) in graphs, e.g., Graphcut [9], METIS [6].

Much work has been done on developing methods to compute relevance between two nodes in a network; many of them belong to the class of spreading-activation [1, 7, 3]. Used by APOLO, Belief Propagation [15] is a message passing algorithm over link structures similar to spreading activation, but it is uniquely suited for graph sensemaking because it offers *simultaneous* support for: multiple user-specified exemplars (unlike [14]); any number of groups (unlike [1, 5, 14]); linear scalability with the number of edges (best possible for most graph algorithms); and soft clustering, supporting membership in multiple groups (unlike [9]).

Few tools have integrated graph algorithms to interactively help people make sense of network information [5, 12, 14], and they often only support some of the sensemaking features offered by APOLO, e.g., [14] supports one group and a single exemplar.

5. CONCLUSIONS

We present APOLO, a mixed-initiative system for helping users make sense of large network data. Apolo tightly couples large scale machine learning with rich interaction and visualization features to help people explore graphs through constructing personalized information landscapes.

We will demonstrate APOLO's usage and benefits using a Google Scholar citation graph, consisting of 83,000 articles (nodes) and 150,000 citations relationships. We will invite our audience to try out APOLO, comment on its usability and usefulness, and discuss how APOLO may help with their work.

6. ACKNOWLEDGEMENT

This work is partially supported by an IBM Faculty Award, the National Science Foundation under Grants No. CNS-0721736, IIS0970179, IIS-0968484, OCI-0943148 and under the auspices of the U.S. Department of Energy by Lawrence Livermore National Laboratory under contract No. DE-AC52-07NA27344, and by the Army Research Laboratory under Cooperative Agreement Number W911NF-09-2-0053. The views and conclusions contained in this document are those of the authors and should not be interpreted as representing the official policies, either expressed or implied, of the Army Research Laboratory, the U.S. Government, NSF, or any other funding parties. The U.S. Government is authorized to reproduce and distribute reprints for Government purposes notwithstanding any copyright notation here on.

[1] www.sqlite.org

7. REFERENCES

[1] J. Anderson. A spreading activation theory of memory. *Journal of verbal learning and verbal behavior*, 22(3):261–95, 1983.

[2] L. Barsalou. Ad hoc categories. *Memory & Cognition*, 11(3):211–227, May 1983.

[3] S. Brin and L. Page. The anatomy of a large-scale hypertextual Web search engine* 1. *Computer networks and ISDN systems*, 30(1-7):107–117, 1998.

[4] D. Chau, A. Kittur, J. I. Hong, and C. Faloutsos. Apolo: Making Sense of Large Network Data by Combining Rich User Interaction and Machine Learning. In *Proceeding of the twenty-ninth annual SIGCHI conference on Human factors in computing systems*. ACM, 2011.

[5] Y. Kammerer, R. Nairn, P. Pirolli, and E. H. Chi. Signpost from the masses: learning effects in an exploratory social tag search browser. In *Proc. CHI*, 2009.

[6] G. Karypis and V. Kumar. METIS: Unstructured graph partitioning and sparse matrix ordering system. *The University of Minnesota*, 2.

[7] J. Kleinberg. Authoritative sources in a hyperlinked environment. *Journal of the ACM (JACM)*, 46(5):604–632, 1999.

[8] B. Kules. From keyword search to exploration: How result visualization aids discovery on the web.

[9] V. Kwatra, A. Schodl, I. Essa, G. Turk, and A. Bobick. Graphcut textures: Image and video synthesis using graph cuts. *ACM Transactions on Graphics*, 22(3):277–286, 2003.

[10] M. McGlohon, S. Bay, M. G. Anderle, D. M. Steier, and C. Faloutsos. Snare: a link analytic system for graph labeling and risk detection. In *Proceedings of the 15th ACM SIGKDD international conference on Knowledge discovery and data mining*, KDD '09, pages 1265–1274, New York, NY, USA, 2009. ACM.

[11] J. O'Madadhain, D. Fisher, P. Smyth, S. White, and Y. Boey. Analysis and visualization of network data using JUNG. *Journal of Statistical Software*, 10:1–35, 2005.

[12] A. Perer and B. Shneiderman. Integrating statistics and visualization: case studies of gaining clarity during exploratory data analysis. In *Proc. CHI*, pages 265–274, New York, NY, USA, 2008. ACM.

[13] D. M. Russell, M. J. Stefik, P. Pirolli, and S. K. Card. The cost structure of sensemaking. In *Proc. CHI*, pages 269–276. ACM Press, 1993.

[14] F. van Ham and A. Perer. "Search, Show Context, Expand on Demand": Supporting Large Graph Exploration with Degree-of-Interest. *IEEE TVCG*, 15(6).

[15] J. Yedidia, W. Freeman, and Y. Weiss. Understanding belief propagation and its generalizations. *Exploring artificial intelligence in the new millennium*, 8:236–239, 2003.

Article Clipper- A System for Web Article Extraction

Jian Fan[1], Ping Luo[2], Suk Hwan Lim[1], Sam Liu[1], Parag Joshi[1], Jerry Liu[1]

HP Labs Palo Alto[1]
1501 Page Mill Road
Palo Alto, CA, 94304, USA

HP Labs China[2]
No.1 Zhong Guan Cun East Road
Beijing 100084, China

{jian.fan, ping.luo, suk-hwan.lim, sam.liu, parag.joshi, jerry.liu}@hp.com

ABSTRACT

Many people use the Web as the main source of information in their daily lives. However, most web pages contain non-informative components such as side bars, footers, headers, and advertisements, which are undesirable for certain applications like printing. We demonstrate a system that automatically extracts the informative contents from news- and blog-like web pages. In contrast to many existing methods that are limited to identifying only the text or the bounding rectangular region, our system not only identifies the content but also the structural roles of various content components such as title, paragraphs, images and captions. The structural information enables re-layout of the content in a pleasing way. Besides the article text extraction, our system includes the following components: 1) print-link detection to identify the URL link for printing, and to use it for more reliable analysis and recognition; 2) title detection incorporating both visual cues and HTML tags; 3) image and caption detection utilizing extensive visual cues; 4) multiple-page and next page URL detection. The performance of our system has been thoroughly evaluated using a human labeled ground truth dataset consisting of 2000 web pages from 100 major web sites. We show accurate results using such a dataset.

Categories and Subject Descriptors

H.3.3 [INFORMATION STORAGE AND RETRIEVAL]: Information Search and Retrieval– *Information filtering, Selection process*

General Terms

Algorithms, Experimentation

Keywords

Web article extraction, information extraction, page segmentation.

1. INTRODUCTION

The World Wide Web has become the main source of information for many people. There are many types of web pages, including news, blogs, shopping, maps, financial information, photos, videos, email and more. However, most web pages are designed for on-screen viewing only and may not be suitable for other purposes. Repurposing web content generally requires re-layout of the content. This means that not only the content but also the structural roles of various content components should be recognized. For example, the text of a caption and its associated image must be identified and their spatial proximity must be maintained to ensure a proper new layout.

Extracting informative content from web article pages is a very challenging problem and an active area of research [1][2][3]. Most existing methods only attempt to identify the approximate region of the main body within a web article page. Pasternack and Roth recently presented a method based on the maximum subsequence segmentation, a global optimization over token-level classifiers that generate scores for words using features of trigrams and tags [1]. The article text, as defined by the positions of the first and last tokens, is found by a simple searching algorithm. Wang et al. proposed a template-independent wrapper [2]. Their method is to identify two minimum sub-trees containing title and article body, based on a Support Vector Machine (SVM) using simple content and spatial features. However, as was pointed out by [3], the main body region may also contain some non-informative contents such as advertisements and further identifying them is not trivial. Ping et al. utilized visual features for identifying paragraphs as the basic subsequences for local classifiers and the maximum subsequence algorithm [3]. The use of visual features gives the algorithm the capability to filter out most non-informative elements within the main text region. For extracting the title from an HTML document, Hu et al. proposed a machine learning approach with a large set of features based on both HTML tags and visual attributes [4]. They achieved roughly 70% in both precision and recall. Another important and difficult problem that has not been addressed by most existing methods is the identification of image captions. Rowe and Frew reported a method that relied on placement, format and text content as clues for identifying photographs and captions from semi-randomly selected Web pages [5]. They reported 41% recall with 41% precision for caption identification.

In this demonstration, we show a complete system that identifies both the content and the structural roles of content components from news and blog type web pages. We extract the title, main text body as composed of paragraphs, images and captions, and print links. We also detect and traverse "next page" links for multi-page articles.

2. SYSTEM DESCRIPTION

The system block diagram is shown in Figure 1. Provided as its URL, the article web page is parsed and rendered using a headless Webkit to obtain a complete DOM+visual representation. This is followed by a search for a print link (i.e., printable version) in the web page and uses it for analysis if present. The main article text is detected first and the information is utilized to search for other components. Then, the next page detection module checks to see

KDD'11, August 21–24, 2011, San Diego, California, USA.

if there is a next page in the web page and repeats the process until it traverses to the end of the document. All the pages are concatenated properly after extracting all the relevant content.

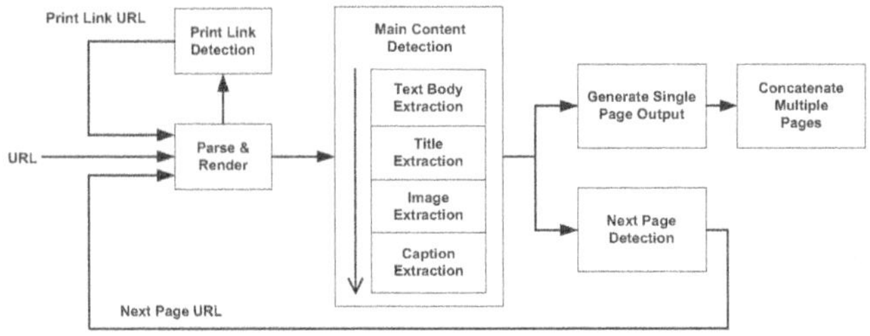

Figure 1. System flowchart.

2.1 Print-link Extraction

Web pages from some web sites provide a hyperlink that leads to a print-friendly web page containing mainly the article itself. Content extraction using these print-friendly pages is generally easier and more reliable. But there are many variations of the print-link representations that made the print link detection a non-trivial problem. First, the link can be text-based, image-based, or both. For text-based links, there is a lexicon of phrases used to represent the print links, such as "print", "print article", "print-friendly version", "print story", etc. For image-based links, in addition to a printer-resembling image icon a print phrase may or may not be present. To complicate the matter further, not all the links contain a valid URL, but instead the pages may be dynamically generated either by the client Javascript or by the server, which are not retrievable using the DOM-based extraction technique since no valid URL is available in the DOM. We observed that almost all print links follow one of the following HTML representations: (1) <a>print phrase</a>, (2) <a><img></a>, (3) <a><img>print phrase</a>, where the <a> and <img> are the HTML hyperlink and image tags, respectively. Note that in cases 2, even though there is no print phrase (only an image icon is used), a print phrase is typically embedded in the attributes of the <img> or <a> tag, such as the "alt" or "title" attribute.

Our approach to the print-link extraction problem takes on two stages: (1) the detection of the print-link, (2) the retrieval of the print-friendly URL from the link attributes. Since a mistake in retrieving the print-friendly URL would cause "catastrophic" failure in the article extraction we aim at achieving a very high precision. This is accomplished by using a print phrase dictionary to find an exact match with the link text content or with the image attribute values. It is important to populate the print phrase dictionary with appropriate phrases since it impacts both the precision and recall. The precision is controlled by using only print phrases encountered in actual web pages, and the recall is maximized by having a comprehensive dictionary.

We estimate that there are roughly 90% of the news article pages have a print link, of which about 35% of them have valid print-friendly URLs. Our solution achieved over 99% precision and over 97% recall.

2.2 Main Article Text Extraction

The detection of the main article text is the cornerstone of the system. Our approach is based on the observation that the article body usually consists of contiguous paragraph blocks occupying the main area of a web page. It includes two steps. First, the consecutive sequence containing the main text body is identified using the Maximum Scoring Subsequence (MSS). Second, discriminative measures based on visual features are applied to purify the main text.

2.2.1 Maximum Scoring Subsequence

Based on the visual attribute of line-break of DOM nodes, we identify the text segments that generally correspond to paragraphs [3]. Among the sequence of text segments $\vec{s} = (s_1, ..., s_n)$ (where s_i is a text segment, indexed in the order that they appear in the HTML file), we aim to identify the sequence of $\vec{s}$ which exactly bounds the text body. Specifically, each segment s_i is assigned a real value $v_i = F(s_i) \cdot Length(s_i)$, where F is a segment level classifier that gives a real value based on the prediction whether the segment belongs to the main text, and *Length(s_i)* is the string length of the text in s_i. The classifier F utilizes the visual features of position, font size, color, number of links and more. Please refer to [3] for more details. Note that the classifier output *F(x)* may be negative. The *MSS* of $\vec{s}$ is identified as $(s_a, ..., s_b)$ corresponding to $(a,b) = \arg\max_{x,y} \sum_{i=x}^{y} v_i$.

2.2.2 Refinement using Other Visual Features

Because *MSS* is limited to selecting a set of consecutive text segments, it may still include some unwanted text content, such as advertisements and link-lists to related stories. It may also include image captions. To remove unwanted text and captions from the article text, we utilize the following visual attributes:

1. Font size. We observed that in most web pages article text has the same font size while captions may have a smaller font size. Therefore the most frequent (in character count) font size is determined and text with smaller font size is pulled from the article text.
2. Horizontal overlap. We observed that text paragraphs belong to an article often overlap significantly in horizontal extent while the unwanted content generally have only a small amount of horizontal overlap with the paragraphs. We leverage this property to further remove those unwanted elements.
3. Horizontal alignment. Some web pages use text alignment (left, center, right) as the sole visual attribute to differentiate captions from others. Similar to the font size, alignment of majority text paragraphs is determined and text with different alignment is removed from the article text.
4. Visual frames. Many web pages use a visible frame to group image and its caption. In order to utilize this property, we detect frames by the border properties as well as background image of HTML elements within the region. Text within a frame will be pulled from article text if two conditions are met: 1) the frame does not contain the whole article text region; 2) text within the frame is not under the node of "blockquote".

2.3 Title Extraction

Title is a unique component of an article. Accordingly, it is often annotated with special html tags (H1-H6) and given visual prominence. Taking these properties into account, our title extraction method includes two steps. In the first step, title candidates are selected according to the following criteria:

1. The horizontal starting position must not exceed the horizontal center position of the main text region, and the top position must not below the top quarter of the main text region.

2. The font size must not be smaller than the font size of the main article text. Text elements with font size equal to that of the main article text are eligible only if they are either tagged with "*H1*" to "*H6*" or they are all bold.

In the second step, we compute a numerical score for each candidate and choose the one with the highest score as the title. The score makes use of the following HTML elements and visual features:

1. Title field. This is a text string delimited by the "<title>" and "</title>" tags in an html file.
2. Header tag "*H1*" to "*H6*". We give higher weight to text elements under a DOM node with the header tags. "*H1*" and "*H6*" have the highest and the lowest weight, respectively.
3. Font size. Title usually has large font size that makes it visually significant.
4. Horizontal alignment with the main text body. Our observation is that most titles are either left or center aligned to the main article text.

For each of the features, a sub score is computed. The matching between a title candidate s and the title field t is measured based on the Levenshtein distance: $m_{s,t} = 1 - \min(d_{s,t}, L_t)/L_t$, where $d_{s,t}$ is the Levenshtein distance between string s and t, and L_t is the string length of the title field t. The sub score $m_{s,t}$ has values in the range of 0 to 1 with 1 representing a perfect match.

The spatial alignment between a title candidate and the main article text region is measured by: $\alpha = 1 - \min(dl, dc)/w_{main}$, where dl and dc are the distance between the lefts and the horizontal centers of the elements and the main article text, respectively, and the w_{main} is the width of the main text region.

The overall score Q for a title candidate s is computed using the formula $Q_s = (m_{s,t} + \lambda) \cdot \beta^{(7-h)} \cdot (0.1 + \alpha)^{\omega} \cdot f_s$, where $m_{s,t}$ is the matching score between the title candidate s and the title field t, α is the spatial alignment score, f_s is the font size in points, h is the header level (h=1 to 6 correspond to *H1* to *H6* tags and h=7 for strings with non-header tags), and parameters $\lambda=0.5$, $\beta=1.15$ and $\omega=2$ are fixed and empirically determined [6].

2.4 Image and Caption Extraction

The goal is to identify images and associated captions that belong to the article. Ultimately this requires image understanding and recognition and is an unsolved problem. Our approach is based on heuristics. Our search of images is limited to the region that encompasses the main text and the title. We rely on simple heuristics based on image dimensions and the presence of the word "advertisement" to eliminate advertisement images. If the image dimension is smaller than a set threshold (e.g., 50 pixels), or the text "advertisement" is found closely above or below the image, the image is deemed as non-informative and excluded.

For each informative image, a search for the corresponding caption is conducted. The primary conditions for a caption candidate are that it must not be part of the article text, its font size must not be larger than the font size of the article text, and it does not consist of all link text. In addition, we search for three spatial image-caption layouts in the following order:

1. Image and caption text are enclosed in a frame. For a given image, we look for a frame containing the image, and then look for qualified text within the same frame. If such text is found, it is annotated as a caption and associated with the image, and the search is called off for that image.
2. Caption below the image. This is the most commonly encountered layout. Additional conditions for qualified captions include: 1) vertical distance to the bottom of the image must be less than two line spaces; 2) must overlap horizontally with the image; 3) must not have a horizontal line or article text in between the caption and the image.
3. Caption on the right side of the image. This is a less common layout. As with layout 2, a search region to the right and similar conditions are imposed.

2.5 Next-page link detection

Many web articles are spread over multiple web pages and require users to click through "next-page" links. An article extraction system is incomplete if it cannot extract a complete article. However, the problem is more difficult than it appears. First, there are many variations of the next-page link, including links with the text of numbers, "next", "next page", the characters ">>", or some combination of these. Second, we must distinguish the next-page link from other kinds of "next" links, including: a) the "next" link for the next article in the same story column, which has a different title and may be totally unrelated to the current article; b) the link for the next page of user comments, which is divided over several pages; c) the "next" link for the next image, which leads only to changing the image.

Our solution to the next-page detection problem takes on four stages:

1. Group all the links in the page into link clusters and rank them in the order as they appear in the HTML file. If the two successive links have the same vertical coordinates, put them into the same link cluster.
2. Identify the link cluster that contains the next-page link. The features we use include: a) the similarity between the link URL and the current page URL; b) the possible number on each link; c) the possible number at the end of the URL (this number is usually the page number of the corresponding page). Given the current page number, denoted by k, if the text on the true next-page link is a number, it must be equal to (k+1); or if the URL of the true next-page link ends with a number, it must be also equal to (k+1).
3. Remove the links to the next-page comment and next image. This is based on our previous works in comment section detection and image caption detection.
4. Compare the current page content with that in the next-page candidate link. The emphasis of the first three steps is on achieving a very high recall. However, in this final step we aim to achieve high precision. More specifically, after we extract the titles and text bodies from the current page and the next-page candidate we compare these results. Only if the two titles are the same and the two text bodies are different, we declare it to be the next-page link.

3. PERFORMANCE EVALUATION

We have built an extensive system to evaluate the performance of our article extraction system automatically. We have collected 2000 web pages from top 50 news web sites and top 50 blog sites such that each site is represented by 20 web pages. All the web pages were saved locally using a Firefox plug-in such that all the contents embedded in the web page are saved properly. In this way, these pages can be accessed in the future even when some of the web pages are either no longer online, or modified. For all the saved 2000 web pages, we had human experts extract and label the informative content of [Title], [Main Body], [Image URL], [Image Caption], [Print Link] and [Next Page Link], and saved the results as text files. These saved text files served as ground truth data to be compared against the generated extraction result.

Performance evaluation was carried out using the saved original web pages. No URL from print-link was used. For quantitative measures, the commonly used precision and recall are computed. For text content (title, article text and caption), we adopt the "bag-of-words" method used in [1] for simplicity. Specifically, for a set of extracted words W_P and a set of labeled (ground truth) words W_L, the precision and recall are defined as $P = |W_P \cap W_L| / |W_P|$ and $R = |W_P \cap W_L| / |W_L|$. For URL-type content (image URL, print-link and next-page-link), we treat each URL as a word and applied the above formula.

Figure 2 shows the average precision and recall of the main text and title and image caption for the 100 web sites. Our main text extraction method achieved very high accuracy across web sites with diverse content and styles. The lowest performance came from ehow.com and answers.com. The title extraction method also preformed very well. The lowest scores were from howtodothings.com and blogspot.com. In comparison, the performance of image caption detection is significantly lower. For several web sites (azcentral.com, gamespot.com, nba.com), we failed to detect most captions. The reasons for the failure includes: 1) image and caption outside the main article region (azcentral.com), 2) caption being link (gamespot.com), 3) captions have the same style as the main text and require semantic understanding (nba.com).

4. CONCLUSION

We have described a system for automatically extracting web article content and key components of the layout. We built an extensive ground truth dataset for performance testing. Our evaluation results show excellent performance across diverse web sites.

We would also like to point out that web article extraction remains to be a challenging problem especially for blog-type pages that may not be professionally designed, and for images and captions that inherently requires semantic understanding. We plan to continue our research in these areas.

5. REFERENCES

[1] J. Pasternack and D. Roth, Extracting article text from the web with maximum subsequence segmentation, WWW, April 20–24, 2009, Madrid, Spain., 971-980. DOI= http://dx.doi.org/10.1145/1526709.1526840

[2] J. Wang, *et al.*, Can we learn a template-independent wrapper for news article extraction from a single training site?, SIGKDD, June 28-July 1, 2009, Paris, France, 1345-1353. DOI= http://dx.doi.org/10.1145/1557019.1557163

[3] P. Luo *et al.*, Web Article Extraction for Web Printing: a DOM+Visual based Approach, DocEng, Sept. 15-18, 2009, Munich, Germany, 66-69.DOI= http://dx.doi.org/10.1145/1600193.1600208

[4] Y. Hu et al., Title Extraction from Bodies of HTML Documents and its Application to Web Page Retrieval, ACM SIGIR, 2005, New York, US, 250-257. DOI= http://dx.doi.org/10.1145/1076034.1076079

[5] Neil C. Rowe, Brian Frew, Automatic caption localization for photographs on World Wide Web pages, Information Processing & Management, Vol. 34, Issue 1, Jan. 1998, 95-107. DOI= http://dx.doi.org/10.1016/S0306-4573(97)00048-4

[6] J. Fan, P. Luo, P. Joshi, Title identification of web article pages using HTML and visual features, Proc. of SPIE-IS&T Electronic Imaging, vol. 7879, 2011. DOI= http://dx.doi.org/10.1117/12.876708

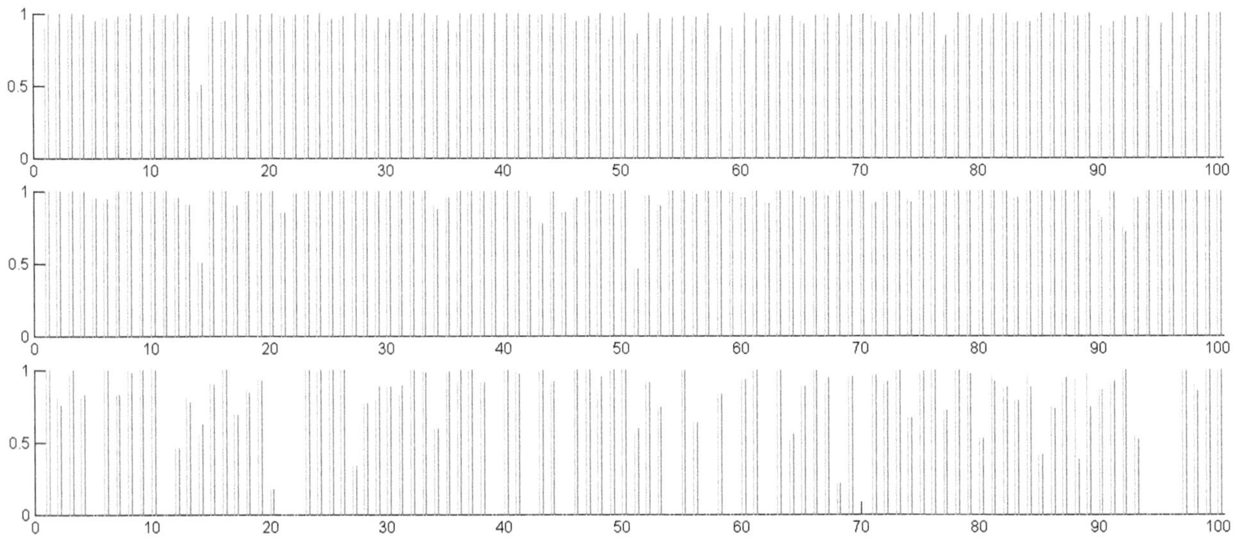

Figure 2. Precision (in red) and recall (in blue) for 100 web sites. (top) Main article text, (middle) title, (bottom) image caption. The missing lines in the bottom plot correspond to sites/pages with no image caption.

Data Intensive Analysis on the Gordon High Performance Data and Compute System

Robert S. Sinkovits, Pietro Cicotti, Shawn Strande, Mahidhar Tatineni, Paul Rodriguez, Nicole Wolter, and Natasha Balac

San Diego Supercomputer Center, University of California, San Diego
[sinkovit, pcicotti, strande, mtatineni, p4rodriguez, nickel, natashab] @sdsc.edu

ABSTRACT
The Gordon data intensive computing system was designed to handle problems with large memory requirements that cannot easily be solved using standard workstations or distributed memory supercomputers. We describe the unique features of Gordon that make it ideally suited for data mining and knowledge discovery applications: memory aggregation using the vSMP software solution from ScaleMP, I/O nodes containing 4 TB of low-latency flash memory, and a high performance parallel file system with 4 PB capacity. We also demonstrate how a number of standard data mining tools (*e.g.* Matlab, WEKA, R) can be used effectively on Dash, an early prototype of the full Gordon system.

General Terms
Algorithms, Measurement, Performance, Design, Reliability, Experimentation, Language

Keywords
Data Mining, Machine Learning, High-performance Computing, Data Intensive Applications, Flash Memory, vSMP

1. INTRODUCTION
Data intensive computing is an important and growing sector of scientific and commercial computing and places unique demands on computer architectures. While the demands are continuing to grow, most present systems, and even planned future systems, don't meet these computing needs very effectively. The majority of the world's most powerful supercomputers are designed for running numerically intensive applications that can make efficient use of distributed memory. Unfortunately, there are a number of factors that limit the utility of these systems for knowledge discovery and data mining. First, the analysis of realistic data sets tends to be limited by I/O performance rather than raw floating-point capability. Second, the underlying algorithms and data structures do not readily lend themselves to parallelization using a message-passing paradigm. Finally, the memory needs for these problems are often much larger than what is available in non-specialized, reasonably priced or readily available hardware.

KDD'11, August 21–24, 2011, San Diego, California, USA.
ACM 978-1-4503-0813-7/11/08.

2. GORDON SYSTEM
The Gordon system [5]and its smaller prototype, Dash, were specifically designed to handle these types of data intensive problems. Their unique architectural features bridge the "missing link" in the memory hierarchy and address the needs of an emerging class of applications whose working sets approach 1 Petabyte in size. Gordon is composed of 32 supernodes, each consisting of 32 compute nodes and two I/O nodes. A compute node contains 64 GB of DDR3 memory and two multi-core Intel Sandy Bridge processors, with each core capable of eight floating-point operations per cycle. The aggregate performance of Gordon is expected to be in excess of 200 TFlops. Groups of 16 compute nodes can access a 4 PB parallel file system through the I/O nodes. Dash and Gordon are available to researchers and educators at U.S. academic or non-profit research institutions through the TeraGrid allocations process. See www.teragrid.org for more details.

While Gordon is well suited for traditional supercomputing workloads, two unique features make it an exceptional resource for data intensive problems. First, each I/O node will have 16 enterprise flash drives with a combined capacity of 4TB. These drives have memory latencies that are roughly two orders of magnitude smaller than those for hard disk and also designed to provide higher sequential read/write bandwidths. Staging large data sets on the flash drives has been shown to lead to greatly reduced run times for a number of data intensive applications [2]. Unlike other systems that make use of flash memory, such as the SDSC Trestles cluster, the configuration of the I/O nodes can be adjusted to best accommodate the workload. In a multi-user production environment, the drives will likely be configured into four software RAID 0 devices to strike a balance between maximizing performance and limiting contention for resources. By contrast, the flash drives in I/O nodes dedicated to a single application can be setup as single large RAID device.

2.1 System Features
The second feature of Gordon that addresses this problem and makes it well suited for data intensive applications is the use of the vSMP software developed by ScaleMP [11] to aggregate memory from across multiple compute nodes to provide access to a large, logical shared memory space. Benchmark studies show that applications with large memory footprints and fairly regular patterns of data access can achieve performances with vSMP comparable to those obtained on much more expensive and specialized hardware [4].

3. DATA INTENSIVE APPLICATIONS

Many scientific and engineering applications operate on enormous data sets and have large memory footprints. When data analytics applications run on the current generation of parallel machines, they spend most of their time simply moving data up and down the memory hierarchy rather than performing useful analytics work. This is due to the fact that gains in processor speeds have far outstripped the corresponding improvements in memory and storage device performance. With every turn of Moore's law, the distance between the CPU and data becomes larger when measured in terms of clock cycles. To use an analogy from astronomy, the processors and the components of the memory sub-system experience a "red shift" where they all recede from each other with each new generation of hardware.

In the meantime, applications are becoming more and more data intensive and therefore make even less optimal use of computational resources. A typical scenario in data mining is for the program to read large amounts of raw data and then build even larger data structures to represent the relationships between the elements before building a predictive model. Examples span many domains and include the analysis and predictive analytics of data from genomics, climate science, astronomy, energy, biomedical informatics and healthcare, social networks and many others.

4. DATA MINING TOOLS

Several modern open-source data mining tools use a visual programming approach that is flexible and user friendly and therefore appealing to data analysts and users with diverse backgrounds. We will accompany our initial analysis with presentation of data analysis tools including more traditional Matlab [6], R [10], WEKA [9], RapidMiner [13] as well as several more recent open source development Map-reduce Phoenix [7], Map-reduce Hadoop [14] tools running a variety of data mining and machine learning algorithms.

WEKA is a widely used data mining suite offering a library of well-documented Java-based functions and classes that can be easily extended. Another popular suite with a somewhat different approach is R [10], which is one of the most widely known open-source statistical and data mining suites. RapidMiner [13], formerly YALE [3] (Yet Another Learning Environment), is an environment for machine learning, data mining, text mining, predictive analytics, and business analytics. It is used for research, education, training, rapid prototyping, application development, and industrial applications.

A popular classification tree induction algorithm implementation C4.5 [1] and J48 [8], matrix factorization, k-means clustering and other algorithms are tested on different hardware configurations (e.g. Dash nodes with hard disk vs. Dash nodes with flash memory, Dash vSMP nodes vs. specialized large-memory ccNUMA nodes). A range of data sets from UCI Machine Learning Repository [12] including sparse collaborative rating data is used for consistent comparison.

5. FUTURE WORK

Future data intensive analysis and data mining investigations will involve the analysis and comparison of data from diverse sources. Metcalfe's law predicts that the possibility of new discoveries grows quadratically with the number of federated databases. For example, one could imagine studying the health of a community using a combination of population demographics, inputs from various environmental sensors, and social science observations such as crime statistics. Another example is to use the ever-increasing quantity of biological data available to assist in the process of drug design. By combining the information in databases containing genome sequences, protein structure and function, and the biomedical literature, researchers can generate more powerful hypotheses since they have all the information relevant to their problem readily at hand. With its large I/O capacity and capability, the Gordon system together with the myriad of predictive analytics software will enable the simultaneous storage of such databases and rapid access to them for accelerated execution of highly complex workflows.

6. ACKNOWLEDGMENTS

This work was supported by NSF Award OCI-0910847 entitled "Gordon: A Data Intensive Supercomputer".

7. REFERENCES

[1] Breiman, L., J. H. Friedman, R. A. Olshen, and C. J. Stone., Classification and Regression Trees, Wadsworth, 1983.

[2] He, J., J. Bennett, and A. Snavely. Dash-IO: an empirical study of flash-based IO for HPC. In *Proceedings of the 2010 TeraGrid Conference (TG '10)*, Pittsburgh, PA, August 2-5, 2010.

[3] Mierswa, I., M. Wurst, R. Klinkenberg, M. Scholz, and T. Euler: *YALE: Rapid Prototyping for Complex Data Mining Tasks*, in *Proceedings of the 12th ACM SIGKDD International Conference on Knowledge Discovery and Data Mining (KDD-06)*, 2006.

[4] Myers, J.A., M. Tatineni, and R.S. Sinkovits. Subset Removal on Massive Data with Dash. In *Proceedings of the 2011 TeraGrid Conference (TG '11)*, Salt Lake City, UT, July 18-21,

[5] Norman, M. and A. Snavely. Accelerating data-intensive science with Gordon and Dash. In Proceedings of the 2010 TeraGrid Conference (TG '10), Pittsburgh, PA, August 2-5, 2010.

[6] Quarteroni, A. and F. Saleri (2006). *Scientific Computing with MATLAB and Octave*. Springer. ISBN 978-3-540-32612-0.

[7] Ranger C., Raghuraman R., Penmetsa A., Bradski G., Kozyrakis C. Evaluating MapReduce for Multi-core and Multiprocessor Systems, *HPCA '07: Proceedings of the 13th International Symposium on High-Performance Computer Architecture.*

[8] Torgo, L. Predicting the Density of Algae Communities using Local Regression Trees in Proceedings of the European Congress on Intelligent Techniques and Soft Computing, EUFIT'99

[9] Utgoff, P. E. ID5: An incremental ID3. Proceedings of the Fifth International Conference on Machine Learning. Ann Arbor, MI: Morgan Kaufmann, pages 107-120, 1988.

[10] "The R Project for Statistical Computing". http://www.gnu.org/software/r/. Retrieved 2011-06-06. "Free Software Directory - GNU R". http://directory.fsf.org/project/gnur/. Retrieved 2011-06-06.

[11] ScaleMP, Inc. http://www.scalemp.com

[12] UCI Machine Learning Repository http://archive.ics.uci.edu/ml/

[13] http://rapid-i.com/

[14] US Patent 7,650,331: "System and method for efficient large-scale data processing

Frontex Real-time News Event Extraction Framework

Martin Atkinson
Joint Research Centre
Via Fermi 2749
21027 Ispra, Italy
Firstname.Lastname@jrc.ec.europa.eu

Jakub Piskorski
Research & Development Unit, Frontex
Rondo ONZ 1
00-124 Warsaw, Poland
Firstname.Lastname@frontex.europa.eu

ABSTRACT

An ever-growing amount of information relevant for early detection of certain threats can be extracted from on-line news. This led to an emergence of news mining tools to help analysts to digest the overflow of information and to extract valuable knowledge from on-line news sources.

This paper gives an overview of the fully operational Real-time News Event Extraction Framework developed for Frontex, the EU Border Agency, to facilitate the process of extracting structured information on border security-related events from on-line news. In particular, a hybrid event extraction system has been constructed, which is applied to the stream of news articles continuously gathered and pre-processed by the Europe Media Monitor—a large-scale multilingual news aggregation engine. The framework consists also of an earth browser, in which events are visualized and an event moderation tool, which allows to access the database of automatically extracted event descriptions and to clean, validate, group, enhance and export them into other knowledge repositories.

Categories and Subject Descriptors

H.3.3 [**Information Systems and Retrieval**]: Text Mining; H.2.8 [**Database Management**]: Database Applications

General Terms

Algorithms, Security, Experimentation

Keywords

Multilingual News Mining, Event Extraction, Visualization

1. INTRODUCTION

On-line news has been considered by various security authorities and organisations around the globe as an important source of information that can be exploited for early detection of certain threats and for situation monitoring during crisis. This is mainly due to the fact that: (a) information on certain security-related events might not be available from any other sources or it might be incomplete (e.g., developments in third countries), (b) there might be a significant delay before such information is made available via official channels, and (c) information from on-line media can be used for cross-checking with information available from other sources. The aforementioned observations together with an ever-growing amount of information transmitted through the Internet led to an emergence of advanced tools that combine techniques from text mining, machine learning, statistical analysis and computational linguistics to help intelligence experts to manage the overflow of information, filter out the relevant from the irrelevant, and to extract valuable and actionable knowledge from on-line sources.

A significant number of approaches to news mining and news exploration systems have been reported recently. The most prevalent way to organize news by such systems is to classify the incoming news into predefined or automatically discovered categories and to group topically simmilar news articles into clusters. However, as has been emphasized in [7], in order to facilitate an in-depth analysis of the news it is essential to extract structured information on the events from the news, i.e., to derive detailed information about them, ideally identifying *who did what to whom, through what methods (instruments), when, where and why* [1]. The current capabilities of news event extraction technology deployed in the security domain are exemplified in [12] (epidemiology) and [6] (armed conflicts), whereas [2] reports on general trends in the field of event extraction.

This paper gives an overview of the Real-time News Event Extraction Framework developed for Frontex[1], to facilitate the process of extracting structured information on border-security related events from on-line media in order to support situation monitoring and intelligence gathering, with a particular focus on incidents related to illegal migration (e.g., illegal entry attempts), cross-border crime (e.g., smuggling), and crisis situations (e.g., violent events, natural disasters, biohazards) at and beyond the EU external borders.

The specific tasks of Frontex impose three requirements on the event extraction tools, in particular, they should: (a) extract information in close to real time, (b) extract as fine-grained event descriptions as possible, (c) process news articles in many different languages, since a significant fraction of relevant events are only reported in non-English, lo-

KDD'11, August 21–24, 2011, San Diego, California, USA.

[1] Frontex - the European Agency for the Management of Operational Cooperation at the External Borders of the Member States of the European Union

cal news. To meet these requirements a hybrid multilingual event extraction engine has been constructed, which is applied to the stream of news articles continuously gathered by a large-scale multilingual news aggregation engine, and is capable to extract event information in 7 languages. It is also equipped with tools for storing, moderation and visualization of the automatically extracted event descriptions.

The event extraction tools presented in this paper are currently being integrated with the pilot version of EUROSUR (an Integrated European Border Surveillance System)[2], that will allow to share information of common interest related to border security between Member States of the European Union. The event extraction tools will be specifically deployed to semi-automatically populate the incident information layer of EUROSUR.

2. FRAMEWORK ARCHITECTURE

The event extraction framework architecture is depicted in Figure 1. First, news articles are gathered by a large-scale news aggregation engine, the Europe Media Monitor (*EMM*)[3] developed at the Joint Research Centre of the European Commission (JRC) [4]. *EMM* retrieves more than 100,000 news articles per day from more than 2500 news feeds in 42 languages. These news articles are geo-located, tagged with meta-data and further filtered (classified) using standard keyword-based techniques in order to select those articles, which potentially refer to security-related incidents and events. In addition, the news articles harvested within a 4-hour window are grouped into clusters in every language individually according to content similarity (using hierarchical agglomerative clustering). The filtering and clustering process is performed every 10 minutes. Figure 2 shows the web interface to EMM.

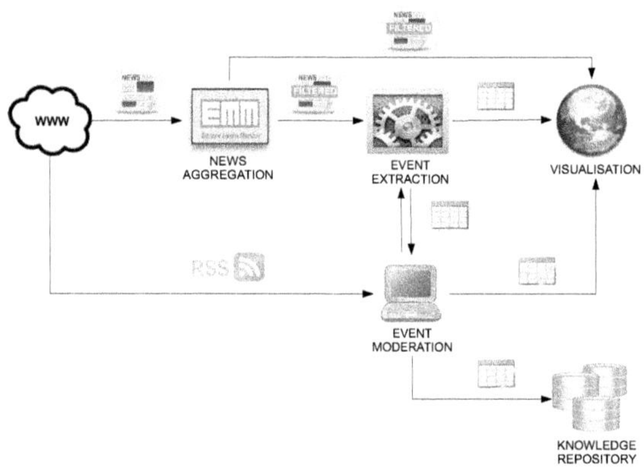

Figure 1: The system architecture.

Next, the stream of filtered news articles and clusters is passed every 10 minutes to the event extraction engine, which consists of two core event extraction systems, namely, *NEXUS*[10, 9], developed at JRC, and *PULS*[5, 12] developed by the University of Helsinki. *NEXUS* follows a shallow cluster-centric approach, which makes it more suitable for extracting information from the entire cluster of topically-related articles, whereas *PULS* follows a non-cluster centric approach and performs a more thorough analysis of the full text of each news article. The main drive behind the deployment of the two aforementioned systems was to: (a) obtain richer coverage wrt. language and event types (both systems have been tuned to detect event types which are not entirely overlapping), and (b) provide a platform to investigate two different approaches to event extraction.

For all event types of interest there is a harmonised event template structure, which includes the following slots: `TYPE`, `SUBTYPE`, `DESCRIPTOR` (free text), `SNIPPET` (text fragment triggering the event), `PUB_DATE`, `DATE`, `LOCATION`, `CONFIDENCE` (system's), `RELEVANCE` (for the user), `SEVERITY`, `SOURCE`, `PERPETRATOR`, `VICTIM`, `ITEM`, `MEANS`, `NUM_AFFECTED`, `NUM_INJURED`, `NUM_KILLED`, `NUM_ARRESTED`, and `WOMEN/MINORS_INVOLVED` (boolean-valued).

The output produced by the core event extraction engine, i.e., a stream of instantiated event templates, is made accessible to the earth browser for visualization of the extracted events on a map. News articles filtered using keyword-based heuristics as potentially relevant to border security domain are also accessible in the earth browser, in a separate layer.

In order to bridge the gap between the automated event extraction phase and an in-depth analysis phase, an event moderation system provides functionality to access the database of automatically extracted event descriptions and to clean, validate, compare, group, filter, enhance and export them. In particular, cleaned and validated event descriptions can be made accessible in a separate 'moderated events' layer in the earth browser and they can be exported into other knowledge repositories. The core event extraction engine can also be applied on any RSS feed on demand.

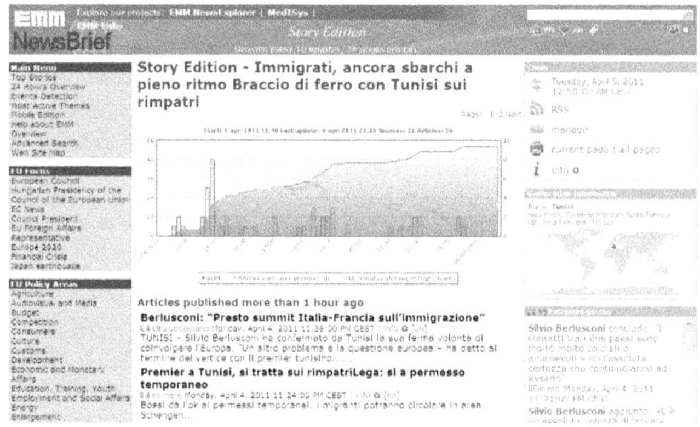

Figure 2: Europe Media Monitor.

3. EVENT EXTRACTION ENGINE

Currently, the core event extraction engine consists of two event extraction systems, namely *NEXUS* and *PULS*.

NEXUS, follows a shallow cluster-centric approach [10, 9]. Each cluster of topically related articles undergoes a shallow linguistic analysis, i.e., fine-grained tokenization, morphological analysis, gazetteer look-up, sentence boundary detection, etc., and a cascade of simple finite-state extraction grammars is applied to each article in the cluster. While the lower-level grammars are used to extract person names (e.g., *Osama bin Laden*), person groups (e.g., *Algerian immigrants*), numerical expressions (e.g., *two hundred*), quantifiers (e.g., *More than*), and other small-scale structures

[2]http://eur-lex.europa.eu/LexUriServ/-LexUriServ.do?uri=COM:2008:0068:FIN:EN:PDF
[3]http://press.jrc.it

(e.g., *small boats*), the top-level grammar consists of 1–2 slot extraction patterns, e.g., `"PER-GROUP <IMMIGRANT> "sbarcati clandestinamente"`, which applied to the text *15 palestinesi sbarcati clandestinamente in Sicilia* would result in assigning the group of 15 Palestinians (*15 palestinesi*) the semantic role `IMMIGRANT`. The grammars are encoded and processed with *ExPRESS*, a highly efficient IE-oriented pattern matching engine [8].

The system processes only initial sentences and the title of each article since: (a) usually the most important parts of the story are placed in the beginning of the article and the least important facts are left toward the end, (b) processing the entire text might involve handling more complex language phenomena (e.g., anaphora, ellipsis and complex syntax), which is hard and requires knowledge-intensive processing[4], (c) if some crucial information has not been captured from one article in the cluster, it might be extracted from other articles in the same cluster.

Since the information about events is scattered over different articles, the last step consists of cross-article cluster-level information fusion in order to produce full-fledged event descriptions, i.e., information extracted locally from each single article in the same cluster is aggregated and validated. This process encompasses mainly three tasks: entity role disambiguation (as a result of extraction pattern application the same entity might be assigned different roles), victim counting and event type classification, all accomplished through heuristics. If the same entity has two roles assigned in the same cluster, preference is given to the role assigned by the most reliable group of patterns, e.g., 2-slot extraction patterns are considered more reliable than 1-slot extraction patterns. It is important to note that *NEXUS* extracts only the main event for each cluster ('one sense per discourse'). See [10, 9] for details on fusion techniques deployed.

NEXUS is capable of processing news in English, Italian, Spanish, French, Portuguese, Russian and Arabic. Due to a linguistically light-weight approach and deployment of weakly supervised methods (bootstrapping techniques) for creating language-specific resources (i.e., domain-specific lexica and extraction patterns), *NEXUS* can be adapted to process texts in a new language in a short time [13, 11]. Although the *NEXUS* architecture is language-independent, the system is quite flexible regarding the grammar design approach that it can implement. In fact, while surface pattern-based grammars proved to be largely effective for English language, to get a comparable performance for Romance languages was obtained through integration of extraction patterns referencing more abstract morphological information due to a number of phenomena within this language family (see [13, 11] for details).

The cluster-centric approach to event extraction described above appeared to work satisfactorily in case of crisis-related events (e.g., man-made and natural disasters, violent events, etc.) [9]. However, extracting information on illegal migration incidents and related cross-border crimes poses additional challenges, e.g., (a) information about incident type is not explicitly encoded in language, (b) such incidents are often reported in local news only, (c) geo-locating is more difficult since there are usually several geo-references in an article[5]. In [3] we address tackling this phenomena in detail.

The *PULS* system[6] is similar in essence to *NEXUS*, but differs in few aspects: (a) it analyzes the entire text of the incoming news articles and performs more in-depth linguistic analysis (e.g., anaphora resolution), which allows us to handle events which may be scattered more widely throughout the article for which not much information has been reported, (b) it is not run on clustered news articles, but attempts to aggregate the extracted facts into groups of related event templates. At the present time, *PULS* analyzes articles in English and French, and is currently being extended to process Russian news.

Both *NEXUS* and *PULS* were evaluated in terms of coverage and precision. As for the border security domain, the precision of slot extraction ranges from 60% to 95% depending on language and slot type, with an average overall slot extraction precision oscillating around 85%. More detailed evaluation figures are given in [3]. In order to improve these figures we are currently exploring the usefulness of cross-lingual information fusion.

4. INFORMATION ACCESS

The main added value to an automated event extraction system is the possibility to clean and combine automatically extracted event descriptions and to visualize them on a map. In order to facilitate this an event moderation component is provided and KML services were set up to visualise the events in earth browsers.

4.1 Event Visualization

For visualisation, events are grouped over time spans, by event classes, source language, and the system that extracted them. This groups events into geo-spacial layers (updated on 10 minute basis) that can then be visualized in tools like Google Earth. The screenshot in Figure 3 shows on the left side the various layers provided from both the automated extraction systems as well as the event moderation system (see 4.2). The events in a given layer are visible on the right side of the window on a map. A selected event (each associated with an icon) shows the instantiated event template in a bubble, with the link to a cluster or single news article from which the information was extracted.

4.2 Event Moderation and Analysis

Event moderation system allows events to be retrieved according to a number of different criteria, including: event type, date of occurrence, language, source (automatically extracted or moderated event), and location. Searches on multiple values are allowed. A screenshot of the user interface to the event moderation system is shown in Figure 4. On the left side 'filtered' events are listed together in different colours according to their source. Selecting an event allows the event template to be visualized (on the right side of the screen) and eventually edited and grouped with other events. The moderation system also provides the possibility to input a new event from say a field report and also

[4]In the context of mining news in different language it is important to note that language-specific processing resources needed to tackle such phenomena might be either non-existing or 'expensive' to obtain.

[5]To event place, country of departure, destination country, places visited on the route, references to countries of origins of the perpetrators, the origin of the means used by authorities, etc.

[6]*http://puls.cs.helsinki.fi*

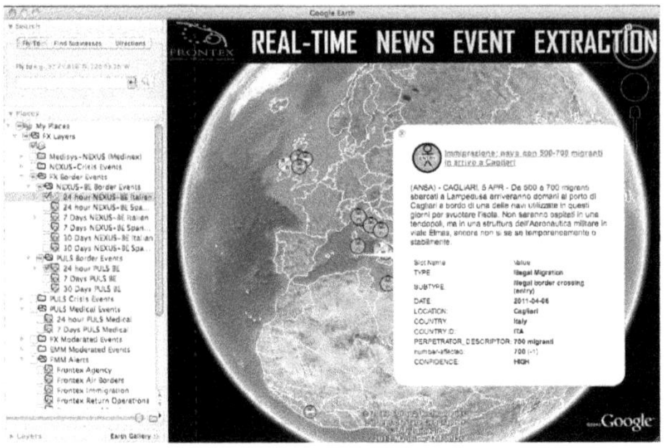

Figure 3: Visualization of events in Google Earth.

to apply event extraction to any RSS data feed. Furthermore, the event moderation tool is equipped with services to translate part of the event template into any of the 27 EU languages. Finally, 'dynamic ontology' allows to define how the extracted events are interpreted and displayed.

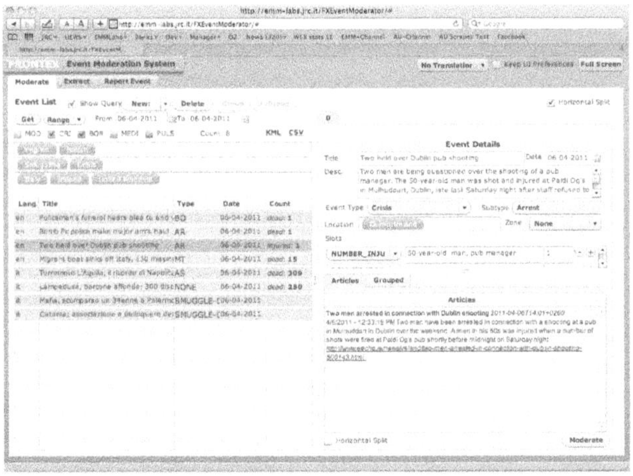

Figure 4: Event moderation: main user interface.

Aggregation of information is the next simple step in a path towards supplying better support to analysts to detect and discover patterns in the pool of gathered information. This is achieved by counting membership of event groups with certain slot values. For instance, grouping by event type, location and time permits the profiling of event type over time and space. An example of this is given in Figure 5, where the aggregation of Civil Unrest and Protest events are shown over time (per week per country since the beginning of 2011 in the Middle East and North Africa - MENA). The foremost peek shows the violence in Egypt followed by Yemen,Bahrain, Libya and finally a high peek from Syria. Clearly this information could be visualized or played over time on a map. A comprehensive description of the event moderation and visualisation can be found in [3].

5. ACKNOWLEDGMENTS

We are greatly indebted to all our colleagues in the OPTIMA action at the Joint Research Centre, who are working on *EMM* and *NEXUS*, and we also would like to the thank our colleagues in the Department of Computer Science of the University of Helsinki, who develop *PULS* system.

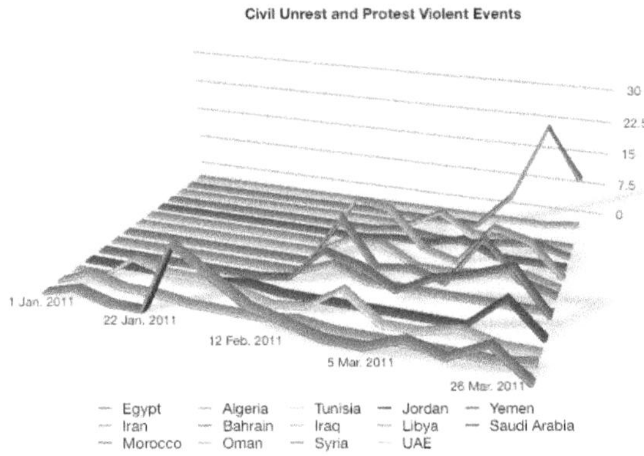

Figure 5: Graph of violent protests in the MENA region (per week basis from the beginning of 2011)

6. REFERENCES

[1] D. Appelt. *Introduction to Information Extraction Technology. Tutorial held at IJCAI-99.*

[2] N. Ashish, D. Appelt, D. Freitag, and D. Zelenko. *Proceedings of the Workshop on Event Extraction and Synthesis.* Held in conjunction with the AAAI 2006.

[3] M. Atkinson, J. Piskorski, R. Yangarber, and E. van der Goot. Multilingual Real-Time Event Extraction for Border Security Intelligence Gathering. In U. K. Wiil, editor, *Open Source Intelligence and Counter-terrorism.* Springer, LNCS, Vol. 2, 2011.

[4] M. Atkinson and E. van der Goot. Near Real Time Information Mining in Multilingual News. In *Proceedings of WWW 2009.*

[5] R. Grishman, S. Huttunen, and R. Yangarber. Real-time Event Extraction for Infectious Disease Outbreaks. In *Proceedings of HLT 2002*, 2002.

[6] G. King and W. Lowe. An Automated Information Extraction Tool For International Conflict Data with Performance as Good as Human Coders. *International Organization*, 57:617–642, 2003.

[7] J. Li, J. Li, and J. Tang. A flexible topic-driven framework for news exploration. In *Proceedings of KDD 2007*, 2007.

[8] J. Piskorski. ExPRESS – Extraction Pattern Recognition Engine and Specification Suite. In *Proceedings of FSMNLP 2007*, 2007.

[9] J. Piskorski, H. Tanev, M. Atkinson, E. van der Goot, and V. Zavarella. Online news event extraction for global crisis surveillance. *Accepted for Transactions on Computational Collective Intelligence*, 2011.

[10] H. Tanev, J. Piskorski, and M. Atkinson. Real-Time News Event Extraction for Global Crisis Monitoring. In *Proceedings of NLDB 2008.*, pages 207–218, 2008.

[11] H. Tanev, V. Zavarella, J. Linge, M. Kabadjov, J. Piskorski, M. Atkinson, and R. Steinberger. Exploiting Machine Learning Techniques to Build an Event Extraction System for Portuguese and Spanish. *Linguamática: Revista para o Processamento Automático das Línguas Ibéricas*, 2:550–566, 2009.

[12] R. Yangarber, L. Jokipii, A. Rauramo, and S. Huttunen. Extracting Information about Outbreaks of Infectious Epidemics. In *Proceedings of the HLT-EMNLP 2005*, Vancouver, Canada, 2005.

[13] V. Zavarella, H. Tanev, and J. Piskorski. Event Extraction for Italian using a Cascade of Finite-State Grammars. In *Proceedings of FSMNLP 2008*, 2008.

LikeMiner: A System for Mining the Power of 'Like' in Social Media Networks

Xin Jin
Dept. of Computer Science
University of Illinois at Urbana-Champaign
201 N. Goodwin Ave.
Urbana, IL USA
xinjin3@illinois.edu

Chi Wang
Dept. of Computer Science
University of Illinois at Urbana-Champaign
201 N. Goodwin Ave.
Urbana, IL USA
chiwang1@illinois.edu

Jiebo Luo
Kodak Research Laboratories
Eastman Kodak Company
1999 Lake Avenue
Rochester, NY USA
jiebo.luo@kodak.com

Xiao Yu
Dept. of Computer Science
University of Illinois at Urbana-Champaign
201 N. Goodwin Ave.
Urbana, IL USA
xiaoyu1@illinois.edu

Jiawei Han
Dept. of Computer Science
University of Illinois at Urbana-Champaign
201 N. Goodwin Ave.
Urbana, IL USA
hanj@cs.uiuc.edu

ABSTRACT

Social media is becoming increasingly ubiquitous and popular on the Internet. Due to the huge popularity of social media websites, such as Facebook, Twitter, YouTube and Flickr, many companies or public figures are now active in maintaining pages on those websites to interact with online users, attracting a large number of fans/followers by posting interesting objects, e.g., (product) photos/videos and text messages. '**Like**' has now become a very popular *social* function by allowing users to express their like of certain objects. It provides an accurate way of estimating user interests and an effective way of sharing/promoting information in social media. In this demo, we propose a system called LikeMiner to mine the power of 'like' in social media networks. We introduce a heterogeneous network model for social media with 'likes', and propose 'like' mining algorithms to estimate representativeness and influence of objects. The implemented prototype system demonstrates the effectiveness of the proposed approach using the large scale Facebook data.

Categories and Subject Descriptors

H.2.8 [**Database Management**]: Database applications –Data Mining; H.3.4 [**Information Storage and Retrieval**]: Systems and Software –Information networks; J.4 [**Computer Applications**]: Social and Behavioral Sciences

KDD'11, August 21–24, 2011, San Diego, California, USA.

General Terms

Algorithms, Design, Experimentation, Human Factors

Keywords

Data mining, social media, information network, like, influence analysis, recommendation, ranking

1. INTRODUCTION

Social media has become one of the most popular web and mobile applications. According to a study[1] from the Nielsen Company, in 2010 the world spent over 110 billion minutes, which equals to 22 percent of all time online, on social-media related websites, such as Facebook, Twitter, YouTube and Flickr. The time spent on these sites by an average visitor increased by 66% over a year ago. Because of the huge popularity and rich personal information available on social media websites, companies or public figures have now being increasingly willing and active in maintaining pages on those websites to interact with online users, attracting a large number of fans/followers by posting interesting (product) photos/videos or text messages.

Figure 1: The like/favorite button for Facebook, YouTube, theAtlantic, Amazon and Flickr, respectively.

'**Like**' has recently become a very popular *social* function on the Internet. Many social media websites, such as Facebook, Twitter, YouTube and Flickr, provide the like/favorite

[1]Nielsen. http://blog.nielsen.com/nielsenwire/global/social-media-accounts-for-22-percent-of-time-online Accessed 2011

button to allow users to express their like of the *objects* (such as text messages, comments, webpages, photos and videos) posted either by personal users or companies and public figures. Many traditional websites now also include the 'like' button, either as a plugin from social media websites or created by themselves, to help promote the webpages. Figure 1 shows the like/favorite buttons used by Facebook, YouTube, theAtlantic, Amazon and Flickr.

If a user clicks 'like' associated with an object, this directly indicates that s/he is highly interested in the object. So the 'like' function provides a more accurate way of estimating user interests than non-direct indicators, such as user-service interaction [20]. Additionally, in some social networks, e.g., Facebook, when a user clicks 'like' to an object, such action will be immediately shared to his/her friends (under allowed privacy setting). So the 'like' function also provides a useful and effective way of sharing or promoting information in social media. Actually, sharing by 'like' may have higher influence because people may pay more attention to the objects *liked* than simply *shared* by friends.

In this demo, we propose a system called LikeMiner to mine the power of 'like' in social media networks. The major contributions are: (a) we introduce a heterogeneous like network model for social media; (b) we propose to construct both visual and textual topic space for social media objects; (c) we propose mining algorithms to estimate representativeness and influence in the social media; and (d) we implement a working system to demonstrate the effectiveness of the proposed approach.

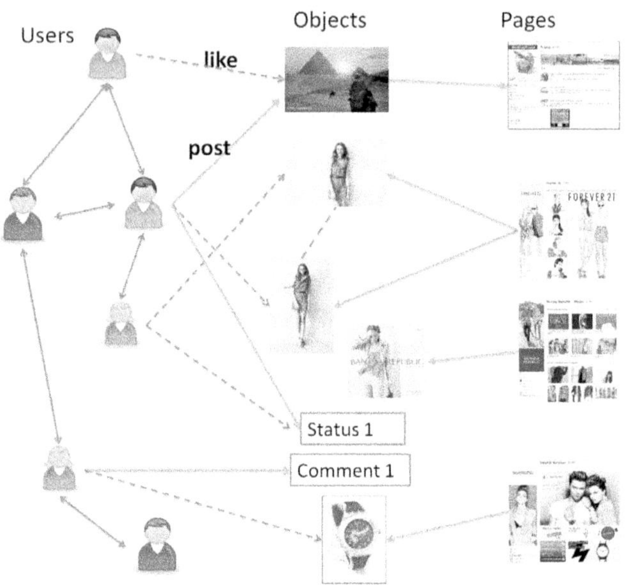

Figure 2: A heterogeneous network model for social media with 'like' function, using Facebook as an example. A blue bidirectional arrow is the friendship link. A red dashed arrow is a *like* action, while a green arrow denotes a *post* action, annotated with the time stamp when it was posted. The dashed blue line shows that the two photos are visually similar.

2. 'LIKE' NETWORK MODEL

We model a social media network with 'like' function as a heterogeneous information network $G = \langle V, E \rangle$. V is the set of nodes from different types, such as users (U), pages (P), and posted objects (O) (such as text messages, comments, photos/videos, accompanied by the posting time). E is the set of directed edges between nodes, including friendship/following links between users, fan links between users and pages, the posting links between users/pages and objects, the like/favorite links between users and the posted objects. Photos are indirectly-linked together by content similarity (dashed lines).

Figure 2 shows an example of such network within Facebook. A user can post an object to his/her wall, or to any company/public-figure pages s/he is a fan. Such object can be liked by his/her friends or non-friends who are also fans of that page. A page can also post its own objects and those interesting ones will be liked by its fans.

3. SYSTEM FRAMEWORK

As shown in Figure 3, the system architecture works as follows. (1) Forming a network model for social media with likes; (2) extracting the topic distribution for the objects, both visual and textual; (3) performing link mining based on the network structure and the object topic distribution; and (4) providing the web interface for browsing, keyword-based topic query and interest-based recommendation, such as recommending product photos or company pages to users who may potentially like them.

3.1 Object Topic Extraction

A *topic space* is a d-dimensional real number space $\mathbb{R}^d$ that encodes some cognitive classification systems such as ontology. Each dimension represents a topic class in the system. For example, in a human-edited Web directory [1] , each category in the directory can be used as a topic class.

A *topic vector* is a vector in the topic space defined above that represents the cognitive property of an object. The component in each dimension indicates how strong the object is associated with the corresponding topic. For example, (Movie:0.5, Soccer:0.3) is a short representation of a sparse topic vector where all the weights are zero except for two topics.

We extract visual topics space for the photos/videos based on the content features, and textual topics space for the textual objects, such as comments and Facebook wall statuses.

3.1.1 Visual Topic Extraction

We can extract different types of image content features [9] [5] [6], such as color histogram, color correlogram [7], texture features [2] [13] [14] [16] [17], Gabor features [15] [18], edge histogram [12] and SIFT [11], to represent the photos from different perspectives. Each type of feature is in a high-dimension space, with the number of dimensions ranging from tens (e.g., color histogram) to hundreds (e.g., SIFT).

Based on the extracted features, we apply our recent algorithm GAD [8] to perform large scale clustering of the photos for each feature space, and treat each cluster as a visual topic. The topic distribution of a photo is based on the similarity of the photo to each cluster center.

3.1.2 Textual Topic Extraction

The task of textual topic extraction is to transform the

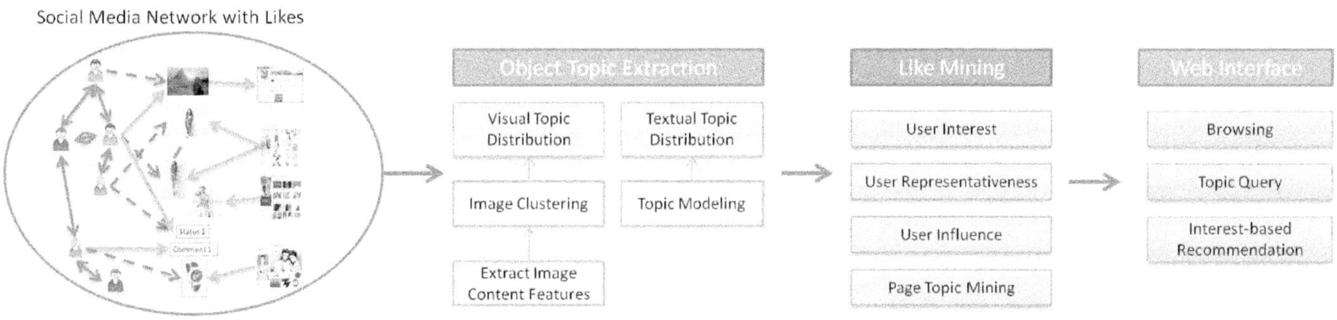

Figure 3: LikeMiner System Architecture.

text associated with a social media object into the most salient topics that occur in the text. A variety of text modeling approaches are possible here, including categorization approaches that classify text into a pre-defined ontology of topics, and topic modeling approaches that automatically find semantically meaningful clusters [3]. For the categorization-based approach, we chose the publicly available DMOZ/ODP hierarchy [1] as our ontology, because of its comprehensive coverage and the availability of labeled webpage data at each hierarchical node.

3.2 User Interest Mining

In this system we use the topic of the objects that a user posted or liked to infer the interest of that user. For every user u, his/her interest is modeled as a linear combination of the topic vector from those objects.

The user topic vector $\mathbf{t}(u)$ may contain some noisy interests. Also, the absolute value in each dimension is highly affected by the number of objects a user liked or posted. We can use smoothing and normalization techniques to transform the user topic vector to accommodate different applications.

3.3 User Representativeness and Influence Mining

Given a specific topic, we mine two kinds of knowledge about users. The first kind is the users who are representative of the opinions among friends in this topic, i.e., the objects s/he likes are also liked by many other users. The second is the influence between users. Some user has strong influence on his/her friends on this specific topic, i.e., the comments, pictures and status about this topic s/he posted are liked by friends.

We mine such knowledge in the following steps. First, we filter the network so that we only keep the users with interest on the given topic and the objects of the corresponding topic. Then, we construct two directional user graphs based on a user-object network and a user-user social network. One is based on co-like relationship, and the other is based on like-post relationship.

We use the co-like graph to mine the representativeness with a PageRank algorithm. We define the random walk probability from one user u to another v according to the co-liked objects and their topics.

The like-post graph is used to perform influence analysis similar to Tang et al. [19]. The difference is that we use directional links based on like-post relationship and we define the weight on every edge from u to v based on the posted and liked objects.

We can further use the result to find a small set of influential users on the network on the given topic based on influence maximization[10]. Scalable algorithms have been developed to solve that problem given the network diffusion model [4]. These algorithms require the network structure and the influence probability as input. We use the influence analysis results r_{uv} to feed the MIA algorithm in [4], and generate the final output of seed users.

3.4 Page Topic and Representativeness Mining

To determine the topic of a page, we aggregate the topic vector from both the objects contained in the page and the users who like the page. Although the topic of one object or one user can be inaccurate, when we collect them together and find the majority, we expect to remedy the sparsity and noises with the help of collective intelligence.

We also mine the topic-specific representativeness of pages in the sense that the more a page has common fans with other pages on the same topic, the more likely this page is a good representative of that topic.

4. DEMONSTRATION

We showcase the LikeMiner prototype system using Facebook as the example application. In addition to 500 million users, there are over 14 million (the number is keep growing) Facebook pages from various categories, such as company, product/service, musician/band, politician, artist, athlete and movie. There are on average 2 million fans for the top 3000 popular pages. The most popular one (Texas Hold'em Poker) has over 40 million fans. Fans not only can see posts submitted by the page, but also can like or post comments/photos/videos to the page. Most Facebook pages are public accessible, we integrate them together to construct a large scale heterogeneous social media network.

Figure 4 shows the web interface of the LikeMiner system. The website is supported by Apache and MySQL. The user interface is supported by PHP and HTML. In this figure, the user submits a topic query "clothing", the system returns the top users (with the user scope option of only friends, friends of friends or everyone) based on interest relevance, representativeness or influence, respectively. The system will also return top relevant photos and pages based on the number of likes, relevance score or representativeness.

In addition, we can calculate the similarity based on the

user topic interest distribution and photo/page topic distribution to recommend photos or pages to the user, which can be used for accurate advertising targeting on social media websites.

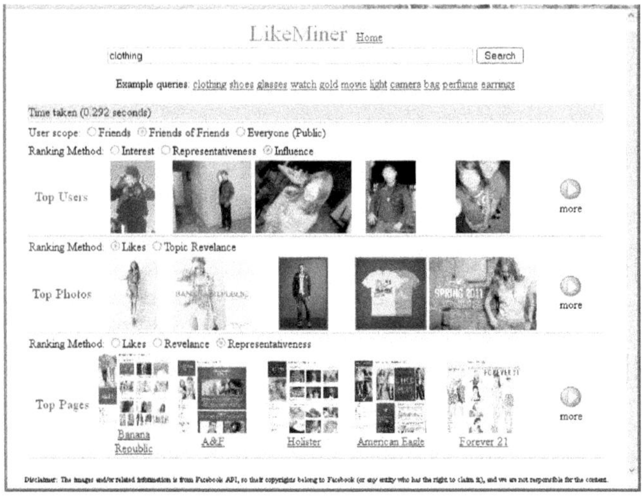

Figure 4: The LikeMiner prototype system. The user profile faces are mosaicked to protect privacy.

Note that this demo uses Facebook as the example since it is currently the most popular social media website. However, the technique proposed can be easily applied/extended to other social media websites, such as Flickr and YouTube. For YouTube, we need to extract the video features to help build the visual topic space.

5. ACKNOWLEDGMENTS

This work was sponsored by Eastman Kodak Company and supported in part by NSF grant IIS-09-05215, MURI award FA9550-08-1-0265 and NS-CTA W911NF-09-2-0053. The views and conclusions contained in this document are those of the authors and should not be interpreted as representing official policies, either expressed or implied, of the sponsors.

6. REFERENCES

[1] *The Open Directory Project (ODP)*, `http://www.dmoz.org`.

[2] S. Aksoy and R. M. Haralick. Textural features for image database retrieval. In *CBAIVL '98: Proceedings of the IEEE Workshop on Content - Based Access of Image and Video Libraries*, page 45, 1998.

[3] D. M. Blei, A. Y. Ng, and M. I. Jordan. Latent dirichlet allocation. *Journal of Machine Learning Research*, 3:993–1022, 2003.

[4] W. Chen, C. Wang, and Y. Wang. Scalable influence maximization for prevalent viral marketing in large-scale social networks. In *KDD'10*, Washington D.C., July 2010.

[5] R. Datta, D. Joshi, J. Li, and J. Z. Wang. Image retrieval: Ideas, influences, and trends of the new age. *ACM Computing Surveys*, 40(2):1–60, April 2008.

[6] T. Deselaers, D. Keysers, and H. Ney. Features for image retrieval: an experimental comparison. *Information Retrieval*, 11(2):77–107, 2008.

[7] J. Huang, S. R. Kumar, M. Mitra, W.-J. Zhu, and R. Zabih. Image indexing using color correlograms. In *Proceedings of the 1997 Conference on Computer Vision and Pattern Recognition (CVPR '97)*, page 762, 1997.

[8] X. Jin, S. Kim, J. Han, L. Kao, and Z. Yin. A general framework for efficient clustering of large datasets based on activity detection. *Statistical Analysis and Data Mining*, 4(1):11–29, 2011.

[9] X. Jin, J. Luo, J. Yu, G. Wang, D. Joshi, and J. Han. iRIN: image retrieval in image-rich information networks. In M. Rappa, P. Jones, J. Freire, and S. Chakrabarti, editors, *WWW*, pages 1261–1264. ACM, 2010.

[10] D. Kempe, J. Kleinberg, and E. Tardos. Maximizing the spread of influence through a social network. In *KDD'03*, pages 137–146, 2003.

[11] D. G. Lowe. Object recognition from local scale-invariant features. In *Proceedings of the International Conference on Computer Vision-Volume 2*, page 1150, 1999.

[12] R. C. Ltd. MINDS's descriptors for still images - spatial edge distribution descriptor. *ISO/IEC/JTC1/SC29/WG11, Lancaster, UK, Feb*, page 109, 1999.

[13] K. Muller and J. R. Ohm. Wavelet-based contour descriptor. *ISO/IEC/JTC1/SC29/WG11, Lancaster, UK, Feb.*, page 567, 1999.

[14] A. V. Nevel. Texture synthesis via matching first and second order statistics of a wavelet frame decomposition. *Image Processing, International Conference on*, 1:72, 1998.

[15] M. Park, J. S. Jin, and L. S. Wilson. Fast content-based image retrieval using quasi-gabor filter and reduction of image feature dimension. In *SSIAI '02: Proceedings of the Fifth IEEE Southwest Symposium on Image Analysis and Interpretation*, page 178, 2002.

[16] A. R. Rao and G. L. Lohse. Towards a texture naming system: identifying relevant dimensions of texture. In *VIS '93: Proceedings of the 4th conference on Visualization '93*, pages 220–227, Washington, DC, USA, 1993. IEEE Computer Society.

[17] Y. M. Ro, S. Y. Kim, K. W. You, M. Kim, and J. Kim. Texture description using atoms of matching pursuits. *ISO/IEC JTC1/SC29/WG11, Lancaster, UK, Feb*, page 612, 1999.

[18] D. M. Squire, W. Muler, H. Muler, and T. Pun. Content-based query of image databases: inspirations from text retrieval. *Pattern Recognition Letters*, 21(13-14):1193–1198, 2000. Selected Papers from The 11th Scandinavian Conference on Image.

[19] J. Tang, J. Sun, C. Wang, and Z. Yang. Social influence analysis in large-scale networks. In *KDD '09*, 2009.

[20] S.-H. Yang, B. Long, A. Smola, N. Sadagopan, Z. Zheng, and H. Zha. Like like alike: joint friendship and interest propagation in social networks. In *Proceedings of the 20th international conference on World wide web*, WWW '11, pages 537–546, 2011.

MIME: A Framework for Interactive Visual Pattern Mining

Bart Goethals
Sandy Moens
Jilles Vreeken
ADReM
University of Antwerp
{first.lastname}@ua.ac.be

ABSTRACT

We present a framework for interactive visual pattern mining. Our system enables the user to browse through the data and patterns easily and intuitively, using a toolbox consisting of interestingness measures, mining algorithms and post-processing algorithms to assist in identifying interesting patterns. By mining interactively, we enable the user to combine their subjective interestingness measure and background knowledge with a wide variety of objective measures to easily and quickly mine the most important and interesting patterns. Basically, we enable the user to become an essential part of the mining algorithm. Our demo[1] currently applies to mining interesting itemsets and association rules, and its extension to episodes and decision trees is ongoing.

Categories and Subject Descriptors

H.2.8 [**Database Applications**]: Data Mining

General Terms

Algorithms, Experimentation

Keywords

MIME, Pattern Exploration, Interactive Visual Mining

1. INTRODUCTION

Data mining is an inherently iterative process; the results of one analysis often lead to new questions, requiring more analysis. In an ideal world, this process is streamlined. That is, data mining is not only iterative, but also interactive: the user can give such feedback immediately, and easily browse the results. In traditional pattern mining, however, algorithms typically produce large amounts of patterns, many of which are not interesting to the user [9], and the results are typically only given in a flat text file, making it hard to analyze the results. By instead providing an iterative and interactive process, the user would be able to explore and refine the discovered patterns on the fly.

KDD'11, August 21–24, 2011, San Diego, California, USA.

In this paper, we present a framework in which we allow the user to interactively mine a database for interesting itemsets and association rules. Our system visualizes all patterns discovered so far, yet, importantly lets the user interactively explore and dynamically modify these in an intuitive manner [2, 10]. By the visualization, users can browse through the mined data more easily and so quickly discover important information. Essentially, in our framework visualization strengthens the interactive mining process, and vice versa.

Basically, our framework, MIME (Making Interactive Mining Easy), draws from user knowledge and interest to improve the collection of patterns discovered by the mining algorithms, by letting the user take control during the mining process, and allowing to adapt the results and so create useful collections of patterns. To assist the user, MIME offers an extensive toolbox of interestingness measures, mining techniques, and visualizations. Using these, the user can easily identify and remove uninteresting or redundant patterns, extend or reduce existing patterns, or apply various post-processing techniques. As such, in our framework the user becomes an essential part of the mining algorithm.

2. DESCRIPTION OF THE SYSTEM

We consider transactional (supermarket) databases $\mathcal{D}$ where each transaction contains a number of items. A pattern is an itemset (a group of items $\{A, B, C\}$ that occur together) or a rule (two groups of items $\{D, E\} \Rightarrow \{F, G, H\}$ where the presence of the first group implies the presence of the second group with a given confidence). The support s of a pattern is the number of transactions in the database in which the pattern is present. The frequency f is the support s relative to the size of the dataset, denoted as $|\mathcal{D}|$. In this setting, frequent itemset mining is defined as the process of finding all patterns in a database that have a frequency f_p higher than or equal to a user-specified threshold f_u.

Most pattern mining techniques produce an amount of output that due to size is difficult to post-process. One could try to reduce the number of results by making the quality thresholds more strict. Unfortunately this does not guarantee the usefulness of the produced patterns. To this end more is required.

MIME combines knowledge of the expert and computational strength of a computer to increase the probability of finding interesting patterns. This is achieved in a visual framework where the expert can create his own pattern collection. In order to evaluate the created/mined patterns,

[1] http://adrem.ua.ac.be/mime

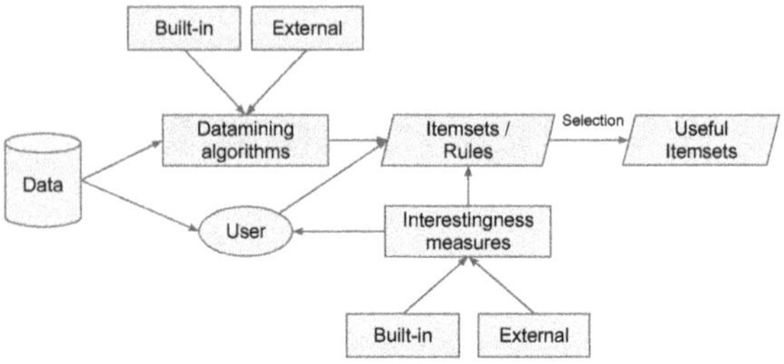

Figure 1: MIME Workflow

MIME implements many interestingness measures. This way the user can select a number of measures that are important for his purpose/domain. The measures improve the knowledge of the user. Our tool also contains a number of standard mining and post-processing algorithms such as Eclat and Apriori. The mining algorithms can be used to construct a starting set of patterns a user can play with and can further construct his collection of useful patterns from.

The overall workflow of MIME is shown in Figure 1. Data is read from a database file and can be used by a user or by mining algorithms to create rules and itemsets. From the created patterns a user can make a decision of which patterns are useful, based on the provided interestingness measures. The user may also apply post-processing algorithms to the created collection of patterns.

All information provided by MIME is computed on-the-fly. When selecting new measures from the toolbox, it computes the corresponding ranks of the discovered patterns and shows them as soon as they are available. Extending or reducing patterns also reflects in an immediate recalculation of the applied measures. The nature of any-time algorithms applies to our framework in the sense that partial information is shown when available.

An important feature is *Best Pattern Extension*. It allows the user to immediately see the individual impact of remaining items on an existing pattern, i.e. a pattern is repeatedly extended by one of the remaining items in the dataset and the ranks (based on the active measure) of the extended patterns are computed and shown in the source dock, using rank decreasing order. Other functionalities for generating patterns based on existing patterns, are the generation of all subsets, subsets of given size, closed supersets, etc. Mining algorithms can also use discovered patterns to filter the mining output. All these features (including mining and post-processing algorithms) provide the user with a toolbox for easy and fast generation of possibly useful patterns.

From the workflow also notice the *External* nodes indicating the use of external/plugin functionality in the tool. In order to provide a widely applicable and easily extensible tool, we have equipped our tool with a plugin system, such that existing mining and post-processing algorithms can be used. The produced patterns are automatically loaded into the MIME framework.

3. MIME

MIME contains a number of different panes a user can interact with. The panes are shown in Figure 2. They are interconnected such that changes in one pane have an effect on one on the other panes. The different panes are:

- *Source Dock*: contains items (the building blocks for rules and itemsets) that are present in the dataset that has been loaded into the framework. All items are automatically sorted in rank decreasing order. The ranks are based on an active interestingness measure and possibly also on a selected pattern. This view also allows grouping of items in the dataset in an item taxonomy. This grouping can be useful in supermarket databases where for instance coke bottles with different sizes represent different items in the data. A limiter has also been added such that the number of visible items can be reduced.

- *Work Dock or Workspace*: shows the constructed and mined patterns. To construct patterns, items can be dragged from the source dock or from already existing patterns. The work dock also shows the interestingness of patterns in two possible manners, using numerical values or using a coloring scheme. An example is shown in Figure 2(b). Also, the number of workspaces is not limited to one; different spaces (collections of patterns) can be created and compared, and information can be sent from one space to another.

- *Toolbox*: shows built-in and plugin measures, mining algorithms and post-processing algorithms that can be used to interact with the data from the source and the work dock. Typically, a user starts by selecting a few measures from the measure bar. The user then runs a mining algorithm or creates a few patterns of its own (possibly based on the output of a mining algorithm) and then runs a post-processing algorithm that is applied to the mined patterns.

- *Global Overview*: an overview of all workspaces is shown here. Information such as the number of items and the number of patterns, are shown by default. Built-in and plugin measures can be used here to compare workspaces. It is thus also possible to compare the outcome of multiple algorithms by applying these algorithms on the same dataset in different workspaces.

4. IMPLEMENTATION

The tool has been implemented in Java using the Qt-Jambi[2]-library for visualization and GUI-purposes.

MIME provides a framework for the exploration of patterns, where a user can create a pattern, see the best pattern extension, add or remove items and so obtain useful patterns. As calculating some measures may be computationally expensive, caching has been used to minimize the number recalculations. Threading has been used to compute as much as possible in the background, not slowing down the user's ability to further explore the dataset. The combination of these two techniques in the tool, creates an environment where interactivity remains high.

A plugin framework has also been used in order to make our tool easily expandable. Plugins can be defined using the configuration file. For the moment there is one constraint on the plugins that can be used: it must contain command-line parameters for an input and output file, which are specified by position of the parameters.

[2]http://qt-jambi.org/

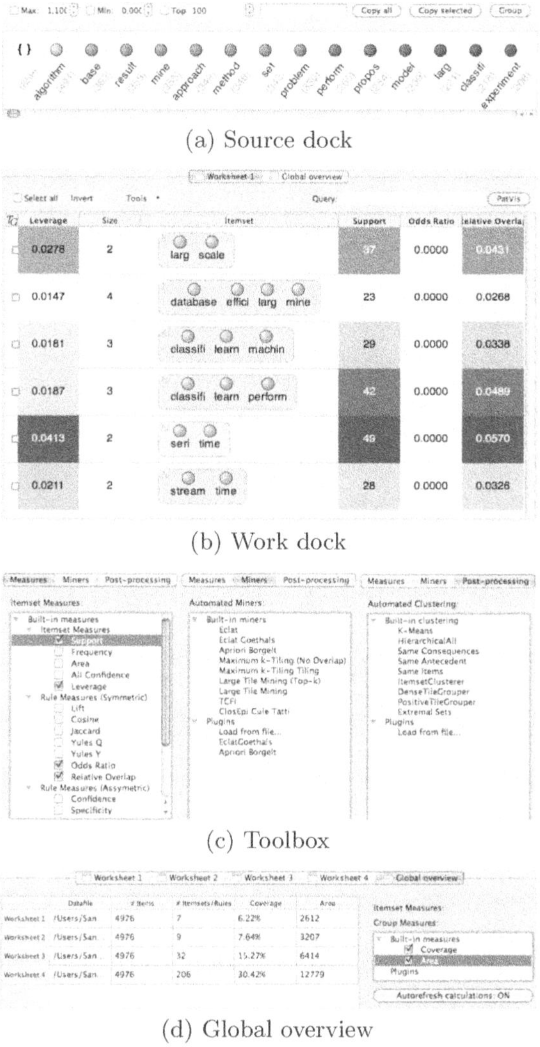

(a) Source dock

(b) Work dock

(c) Toolbox

(d) Global overview

Figure 2: MIME Views

5. ILLUSTRATIVE SCENARIO

In this section we give a demonstration of the capabilities of our tool using the stemmed version of the *ICDM Abstracts* dataset by Tijl De Bie [6]. The database contains 4976 items over 859 transactions. Each transaction represents an abstract of a paper that was published between 2001 and 2008. We start by loading the dataset in memory using the worksheet menu.

Grouping items

In this first step we show how to create item hierarchies. We can select items by clicking on them in the source dock while holding the control modifier. We then use the group button to create a group. For instance grouping together the items

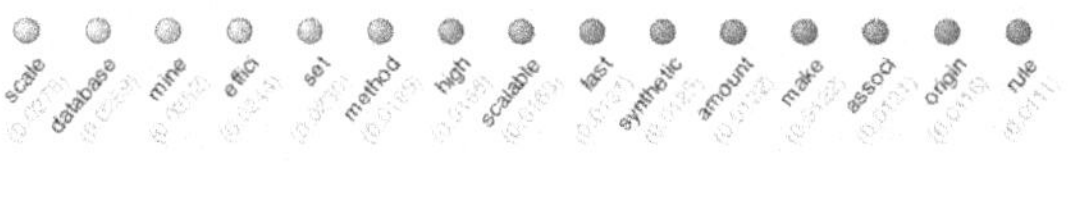

Figure 3: *Best Pattern Extension* {} ⇒{ *larg*}

database (support of 139), *dataset* (70) and *datasets* (132) into a new item called *database-group* (287). The group takes the union of the transactions of the individual items. The new item can now be used as all normal items and is now used when running mining algorithms on the database.

Mining itemsets and rules

To demonstrate how to mine itemsets, we use items with average support (*larg*, *learn* and *time*), and select a few extra measures. We set the leverage measure as primary measure by double clicking.

When selecting the first itemset by clicking on the basket, best pattern extension is activated (Figure 3). This way we can easily see which items are potentially interesting for an existing itemset. For the itemset *larg*, 3 items appear to produce a good ranking (above 0.0250). We select those items and create three new itemsets by dropping the items inside the basket and choosing to create distinct rules. We can then evaluate the remaining patterns in the same fashion, adding new items as long as the quality remains good. The quality is subject to the active measures and to the knowledge of the expert. Figure 2(b) shows a pattern collection that is the result of this process.

We can also apply a mining algorithm to the dataset. We start by selecting a few patterns (this is not mandatory), and use the apriori-implementation by Borgelt[3]. Parameters can be specified and the algorithm can be executed. By selecting patterns from the work dock, the outcome of the algorithm is automatically filtered, i.e. the resulting patterns (if any) are supersets of one of the selected patterns. We may now also apply a post-processing algorithm to the collection of patterns, for instance positive tile clustering.

Rules can be mined in similar fashion, dragging items to the left (resp. right) side of an existing itemset creates a body (resp. head) for this pattern. We can now select the left hand side or the right hand side of the rule to get a reordering of the remaining items in the dataset.

Worksheets and comparing miners

Our tool allows for multiple worksheets. Worksheets can be based on a dataset that is already in use, in which case rules can be copied or moved from one sheet to another. It is also possible to use one of the mining algorithms to construct a collection of patterns, select some of the patterns and copy these to a new worksheet such that we do not lose the original mining results.

When using different worksheets, we can also use the global overview and global measures to compare the results of different mining sessions of the same algorithm, or to compare the results of different mining algorithms.

For the first comparison we create 4 different workspaces using the *Abstracts* database, and run the Apriori miner by Borgelt using 4 different frequency levels (40, 30, 20 and 10%). Figure 2(d) shows the global overview of this setting. Using global information we can adapt the results of the mining algorithms to improve these values.

For the second comparison we can for instance compare the outcome of 4 different tile-based methods with similar thresholds, this way the user can see which miner gives better results for a certain dataset, using information provided by the global overview as reference.

[3]http://www.borgelt.net/apriori.html

Worksheet colors and basket colors

MIME supports graphical and textual (numerical) values for showing ranks. The numerical values can be used to obtain the worksheet coloring shown in Figure 2b. As is the case with the ranking of the items in the source dock, patterns can obtain a coloring scheme depending on the interestingness measure and the other rules in the worksheet. This way the user gets a quick understanding of which measures are similar for patterns without knowing the exact ranks.

Items inside a basket of a pattern can also obtain a coloring scheme based on their personal influence on the pattern. The ranking of the pattern is computed when omitting the specified item and the rank is compared to the current ranking. If the current ranking is better, the item gets a positive coloring (green), and if the current ranking is worse, the item gets a negative coloring (red). If the item does not have an influence it gets a neutral (white) coloring.

6. RELATED WORK

A lot of work has been done comparing and evaluating different objective interestingness measures [8, 11]. The most important outcome is that there is no single measure that can be used for all purposes, and even worse, for some purposes, there exists no measure, and only subjective and semantic criteria based on experience and background knowledge can produce actionable results.

In our tool we have incorporated several objective interestingness measures, but it is the combination of user-knowledge and objective measures enabling subjective interestingness criteria to be applied.

Also in the context of Inductive Databases several interactive constraint-based mining frameworks have been studied [7]. Here, the user typically has the ability to specify all kinds of constraints that are being used during the mining process. In these systems, the visualization and adaptation of the results has not been a major concern. Moreover, our framework could be built on top of such an inductive database implementation [3].

Most similar to the system presented here is the framework for mining decision trees proposed by Ankerst et al. [1]. The user and computer work together in this system such that in each step either the user or the computer can make the decision for a new split. The computer also provides extra computational power by showing the best split, look-ahead information, purity measures, etc. Our approach is similar, but applies to frequent itemsets and association rules, instead of decision trees.

Some methods for visualizing patterns exist [4, 5]. These visualizers present the output of mining algorithms in a compact and graphical format, and allow to further filter the output using queries. They do not provide means to mine the database interactively using subjective criteria and also do not allow to further explore existing patterns.

7. CONCLUSIONS AND FUTURE WORK

MIME is a framework for the interactive mining, exploration, and post-processing of patterns, and allows for easy comparison of different algorithms and pattern collections. It makes the user part of the mining process and so allows for creating patterns and adapting patterns by different mining algorithms and quality measures, as well as personal knowledge and interest. Post-processing algorithms (clustering algorithms for instance) can be applied to the created collection or the user can create hierarchies himself. The tool also contains a plugin system that allows extension of the tool with existing software.

There are still many options for extending MIME that we consider important future work. First, iterative mining algorithms can be incorporated in this system, allowing a speed-up of mining sessions with different quality constraints. Second, caching and pre-computation can be used in this framework by keeping track of user-interactions that are performed most and creating an interaction hierarchy. The system learns about user-interactions and can then decide to pre-compute information. Third, support for mining of decision trees and episodes is in progress. At last, we can also make more use of any-time algorithms, for instance when computing the *Best Pattern Extension*.

8. ACKNOWLEDGMENTS

The authors would like to thank, in alphabetical order, Boris Cule, Koen Smets, for engaging discussions on the topic. Further, the authors would like to thank Andie Similon for his work in programming the pilot-version of MIME.

9. REFERENCES

[1] M. Ankerst, M. Ester, and H.-P. Kriegel. Towards an effective cooperation of the user and the computer for classification. In *Proc. ACM SIGKDD*, pages 179–188, 2000.

[2] E. Bertini and D. Lalanne. Investigating and reflecting on the integration of automatic data analysis and visualization in knowledge discovery. *SIGKDD Explor. Newsl.*, 11:9–18, May 2010.

[3] H. Blockeel, T. Calders, E. Fromont, B. Goethals, A. Prado, and C. Robardet. An inductive database prototype based on virtual mining views. In *Proc. ACM SIGKDD*, pages 1061–1064, 2008.

[4] C. L. Carmichael and C. K.-S. Leung. FpVAT: a visual analytic tool for supporting frequent pattern mining. *SIGKDD Explor. Newsl.*, 11:39–48, May 2010.

[5] A. Datta and K. Techapichetvanich. VisAR : a new technique for visualizing mined association rules. In X. Li, S. Wang, and Z. Dong, editors, *Adv. Data Min. Appl.*, pages 728–728. Springer Berlin / Heidelberg, 2005.

[6] T. De Bie. Maximum entropy models and subjective interestingness: an application to tiles in binary databases. *Data Min. Knowl. Disc.*, In press.

[7] S. Dzeroski, B. Goethals, and P. Panov. *Inductive Databases and Constraint-Based Data Mining.* Springer-Verlag, 2010.

[8] L. Geng and H. J. Hamilton. Interestingness measures for data mining: A survey. *ACM Comput. Surv.*, 38, September 2006.

[9] B. Goethals, N. Tatti, and J. Vreeken. Useful patterns (UP'10) ACM SIGKDD workshop report. *SIGKDD Explor. Newsl.*, 12:56–58, March 2011.

[10] D. A. Keim. Information visualization and visual data mining. *IEEE Trans. Vis. Comp. Graph.*, 8:1–8, January 2002.

[11] V. Kumar, J. Srivastava, and P.-N. Tan. Selecting the right interestingness measure for association patterns. In *Proc. ACM SIGKDD*, pages 32–41, 2002.

SIGKDD Demo: Sensors and Software to Allow Computational Entomology, an Emerging Application of Data Mining

Gustavo Batista
Eamonn Keogh
University of California, Riverside
Riverside, CA, 92521
{gbatista,eamonn}@cs.ucr.edu

Agenor Mafra Neto
ISCA Technologies
Riverside, CA, 92517
president@iscatech.com

Edgar Rowton
Walter Reed Army Institute of Research
Silver Spring, MD, 20910
edgar.rowton@us.army.mil

ABSTRACT
The history of humankind is intimately connected to insects. Insect borne diseases kill a million people and destroy tens of billions of dollars worth of crops annually. However, at the same time, *beneficial* insects pollinate the majority of crop species, and it has been estimated that approximately one third of all food consumed by humans is directly pollinated by bees alone. Given the importance of insects in human affairs, it is somewhat surprising that computer science has not had a larger impact in entomology. We believe that recent advances in sensor technology are beginning change this, and a new field *of Computational Entomology* will emerge. We will demonstrate an inexpensive sensor that allows us to capture data from flying insects, and the software that allows us to analyze the data. Moreover, we will distribute both the sensors and software for *free*, to parties willing to take part in a crowdsourcing project on insect classification.

Categories and Subject Descriptors
H.2.8 [**Database Application**]: Data mining, Scientific database

General Terms
Algorithms, Measurement, Experimentation, Human Factors

Keywords
Agricultural, Spatiotemporal data, Insects, Classification

1. INTRODUCTION
Humankind's history and its destiny are intimately connected to insects. Insect borne diseases kill well over a million people each year, and sicken tens of millions more [16]. Insects also destroy tens of billions of dollars worth of crops and livestock. However, at the same time *beneficial* insects pollinate 75% of crop species, and it has been estimated that 30% of all food consumed by humans is directly pollinated by bees alone [5].

Given the importance of insects to humans, researchers have developed an arsenal of mechanical, chemical, biological, economic and educational tools to help mitigate their harmful effects. Since all such interventions are costly, they depend on knowing the best time and place to intervene. As a group of medical entomologists recently noted just in the context of mosquitoes: "*Accurately georeferenced data are crucial for understanding mosquito biogeography, ecology, and the impact of environmental changes, as well as for species distribution modeling, planning mosquito surveys, and for determining disease risk*" [8]. Such data is currently obtained by having humans inspect mechanical or "sticky" traps. As such, the data are typically sparse, error prone and out of date.

In this demonstration we show simple low-cost sensors we can get accurate counts of flying insects in real time. We believe that these sensors will open up a new area of research, *computational entomology*. We argue that computational entomology is a branch of *data mining* (rather than say, machine learning or biostatistics), because it draws from such traditional data mining techniques as classification, regression, clustering, etc. Furthermore, the classic data mining problems of scalability and dealing with distributed and uncertain data are unavoidable in any task in this domain.

2. OUR INSECT WINGBEAT SENSOR
Incredibly, the idea of classification of insects by sound dates back to the very dawn of computers and commercially available audio recording equipment. In 1945, three researchers at the Cornell University Medical College, Kahn, Celestin and Offenhauser used equipment donated by Oliver E. Buckley (then President of the Bell Telephone Laboratories) to record and analyze mosquito sounds [12].

The authors later wrote "*It is the authors' considered opinion that the intensive application of such apparatus will make possible the precise, rapid, and simple observation of natural phenomena related to the sounds of disease-carrying mosquitoes and should lead to the more effective control of such mosquitoes and of the diseases that they transmit.*" [13]. In retrospect it seems astonishing that more progress on this problem has not been made in the intervening years.

The *logical design* of the sensor is shown in Figure 1. It consists of a side-by-side low-powered laser source/phototransistor. The latter is connected to an electronic board. The laser is pointed at a total internal reflector which returns the slightly scattered light back to the source, with some of it hitting the phototransistor.

KDD'11, August 21–24, 2011, San Diego, CA, USA.

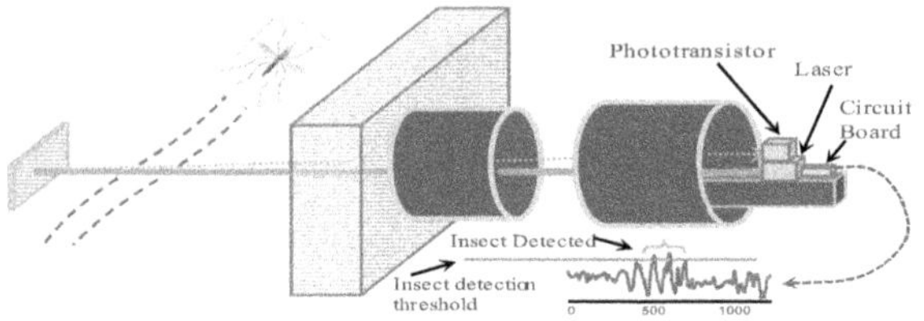

Figure 1: The logical general design of the insect sensor we are developing. It can count insects by recording high-amplitude "bleeps" in the signal, classification takes additional processing. See also Figure 2.

When a *flying insect* crosses the laser beam, its wings partially occlude the light, causing small light fluctuations captured by the phototransistor. This signal is filtered and amplified by a custom designed board, and the output signal is recorded as audio data.

In Figure 2 we show a physical version of the device. Note that the sensor is built into standard PVC pipe fittings. This allows us to add a cheap PVC pipe "portals" to the hundreds of insectaries found in a typical entomological laboratory, and quickly move the sensor between them.

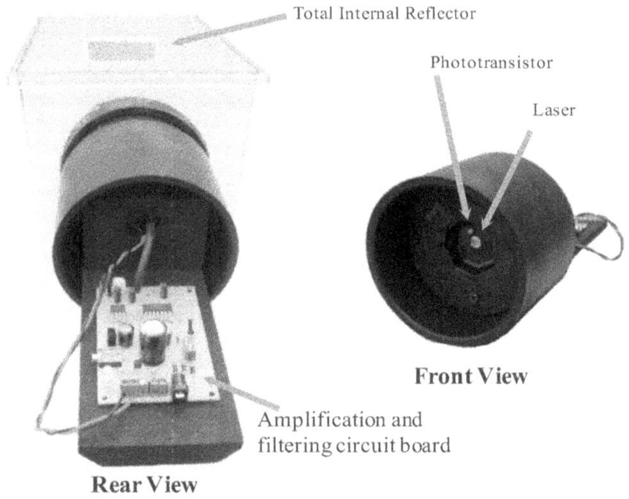

Figure 2: Two views of our insect counting device. The sensor is mounted in standard PVC pipe fittings to allow "plug and play" between different insectaries.

We omit a detailed discussion of the circuitry and logical design of our sensor, other than to say that we are making the circuit design freely available at [14]. The entire system can be made for less than $100, but in bulk, the price can be reduced to less than $10 each.

3. MOTIVATION FOR INSECT CLASSIFICATION

There are at least 3,528 species of mosquitoes [11]. The majority of these are harmless to humans, but a few dozen species transmits disease agents that cause illness and death among humans while depressing economic well-being over large swaths of the globe. *Anopheline* mosquitoes are vectors (living carriers of an infectious agent) of human malaria. *Aedine* mosquitoes transmit arboviruses such as yellow fever, dengue, and dengue hemorrhagic fever. *Culicine* mosquitoes are the primary vectors of various diseases, for example human filariasis, western equine encephalomyelitis, St. Louis encephalitis, and West Nile encephalitis. All these diseases have a serious impact on humans, killing one million people, mostly African children, each year. Despite concerted efforts to control their vectors, most of these mosquito-transmitted diseases are spreading [16].

The first line of defense against vector-borne diseases is *vector control*. Vector control is an umbrella term for any of the dozens of mechanical, chemical, biological methods used to limit or (locally) eradicate a pest. Vector control requires constant surveillance of vector populations. Information about a vector's spatial and temporal distribution is essential in establishing preventive measures. While vector control is an extremely challenging task, control efforts have shown their value in the eradication of other populations of insects of medical importance. Examples of such successful eradications of a harmful insect species from a large region include that of the New World screwworm, Mediterranean fruit flies, and tsetse flies [1].

A complete discussion of possible interventions is beyond the scope of this paper [16]. However current techniques to mitigate mosquitoes deadly effects are myriad, and include:

- The use of insecticidal treated mosquito nets, spraying of insecticides (including controversial chemicals such as DDT);
- The introduction of fish/turtles that eat mosquito larva;
- The introduction of dragonflies which eat adult mosquitoes;
- Attracting, then trapping mosquitoes;
- Habitat reduction by draining ponds and pools;
- Use of chemical films to reduce the surface tension of water (drowning the pupa).

The key to vector control is the development of *predictors* [10][15]. Establishing early and accurate predictors for mosquito population outbreaks and associated risk of epidemics ideally requires compilation of large data sets from individual agencies encompassing data on mosquito populations, landscape ecology, vertebrate hosts, hospital admissions, and data meteorological data including temperature, humidity and wind speed.

Note that most predictors are *surrogates*[1] for the target insect density. For example, meteorological data indirectly tells us of the relative abundance of mosquito breeding grounds, and hospital admission data indirectly and (belatedly) tells us of insect density.

Our work is motivated by the observation that in this domain surrogate variables are always doomed to be inaccurate and/or tardy. If we want to measure insect density, then we should *measure insect density*. As we shall show in the next section, plunging prices for sensors, combined with data mining classification techniques now make this possible.

4. CLASSIFICATION USING WINGBEAT SENSOR DATA

In Figure 1 we showed how a simple threshold on the output of our sensor can detect and *count* insects. However, for the task at hand we need to be able to *classify* the insect species, and in some cases even the insects sex (since only female mosquitoes feed on human blood). Recall that when deployed in the field, more than 99% of

[1] Surrogate is a variable that can be measured (or is easy to measure) that is used in place of one that cannot be measured (or is difficult to measure).

the insects counted may be innocuous or even beneficial. As the reader will have anticipated, we can also use our counting sensor to *classify* insects.

An example of the signal generated by the sensor is presented in Figure 3.*top*. This signal was collected from a bee of the species *Bombus impatiens* (The Common Eastern Bumble Bee) in an insectary. A further analysis of the high amplitude section shows the signal has a peak in the fundamental frequency at 197Hz, and some harmonics in integer multiples of the fundamental frequency, as shown in Figure 3.*bottom*. The first harmonics represents the frequency of interest, i.e., the insect wing-beat frequency.

Whenever possible we do a sanity check to make sure the values returned by our analysis are reasonable. A recent study which measured the wingbeat frequency of this species with a *true* acoustic device found the frequency had a mean of 181 and a min/max of 155/205 respectively [3].

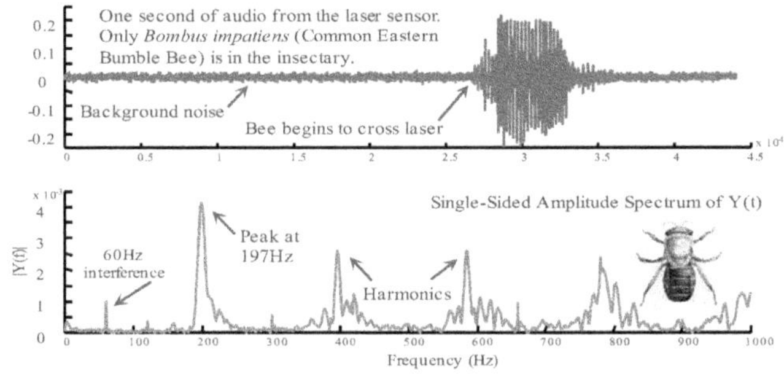

Figure 3: ***top)*** **A one second audio clip recorded by our sensor in insectary containing only** ***Bombus impatiens*** **(Common Eastern Bumble Bee).** ***bottom)*** **An examination of the amplitude section reveals the fundamental frequency at 197Hz, the wingbeat frequency of the bee**

As shown in Figure 3.*top* the raw digital audio signal can be represented by a sequence $S = <s_1, s_2 \ldots s_N>$ where s_i is the signal sampled in the instant i and N is the total number of samples of the signal.

This sequence contains a lot of acoustic information, and features can be extracted from it, including (but not necessarily exclusively) wingbeat frequency. So a feature vector $\bar{X} = <x_1, x_2 \ldots x_D>$ can be generated, where each feature x_j is extracted from S (or some part of it) by an appropriate extraction procedure, defined as a function $X_j : S \rightarrow X_j$, where X_j is the feature domain.

From a set of insect species B we must select the most likely class $\hat{b}$ given the data we have observed. More formally, the intuition behind Bayesian classification is to find the most likely $\hat{b} \in B$, given the feature vector $\bar{X} = X(S)$, that is:

$$\hat{b} = \underset{b \in B}{\operatorname{argmax}} P(b|\bar{X})$$

Where $P(b|\bar{X})$ is the *a posteriori* probability that the signal belongs to a insect of the species b given the features represented by the feature vector $\bar{X}$. Using Bayes rule the equation can be expressed as:

$$\hat{b} = \underset{b \in B}{\operatorname{argmax}} \frac{P(\bar{X}|b)P(b)}{P(\bar{X})}$$

Where $P(\bar{X}|b)$ is the probability of observing the feature vector $\bar{X}$ in class b, $P(b)$ is the a *priori* probability of the species b, that can be estimated from frequencies in the database, and $P(\bar{X})$ is the probability of occurrence of the feature vector $\bar{X}$. This probability is usually unknown, but if the classifier computes the likelihoods of the entire set of species, then $\sum_{b \in B} P(b|\bar{X}) = 1$ and we can obtain the desired probabilities for each likely $b \in B$ with:

$$P(b|\bar{X}) = \frac{P(\bar{X}|b)P(b)}{N_f}$$

Where $N_f = \sum_{b \in B} P(\bar{X}|b)P(b)$, and can be understood as a normalization factor.

Figure 4 shows a wingbeat frequency distribution plot for seven species of insects. We can use these data to predict the insect species, given the wingbeat frequency. For example, suppose we observe an unknown insect with a wingbeat frequency of 500Hz.

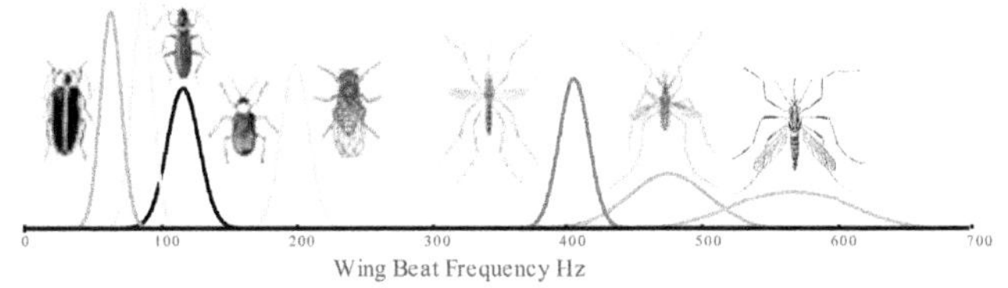

Figure 4: Gaussian curves representing the mean and standard deviation of the wingbeat frequencies of seven species of insects (females only). From left to right, ***Lucidota atra, Chauliognathus marginatus, Oulema melanopus, Drosophila melanogaster, Culex quinquefascitus, Anopheles stephensi, and Aedes aegypti.***

We can calculate the insect's class-conditioned probability of being *Anopheles stephensi* using a Gaussian distribution function, given that we know the mean and standard deviation of the *Anopheles stephensi* wingbeat frequency are 475 and 30 respectively:

$$P(wingbeat = 500|Anopheles) = \frac{1}{\sqrt{2\pi}\,30} e^{-\frac{(500-475)^2}{2\times 30^2}}$$

We can calculate the probabilities for the other classes in a similar manner, and predict our unknown insect as the most likely class. In this example, the unknown insect is about 3.3 times more likely to be an *Anopheles* than *Aedes aegypti* (the second most likely class).

Figure 5 is a plot of the wing-beat frequency histogram for three species captured with our sensor.

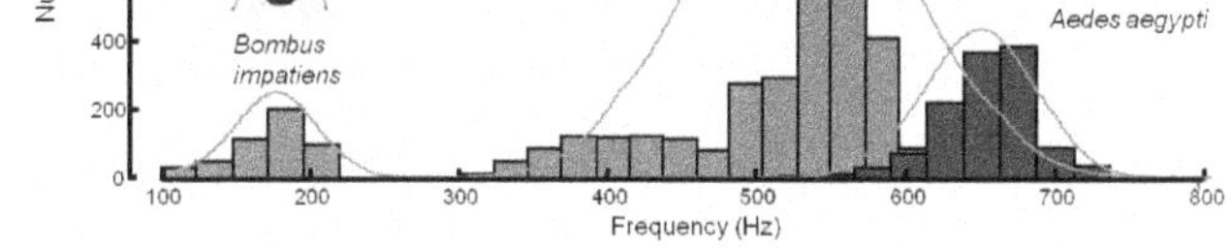

Figure 5: Histogram of one-second fragments for three species: ***Bumble impatiens, Culex quinquefasciatu*** **and** ***Aedes Aegypti***

From Figure 5 we can observe that the distribution for all classes resembles a Gaussian distribution with a long left tail. The Bumblebees wing-beats frequencies are linearly separable from the mosquitoes frequencies, an expected result since the Bumblebees are considerably larger than the mosquitoes, and larger insects usually present lower wingbeat frequencies. Considering the wingbeat frequencies of the mosquitoes alone, *Aedes aegypti* has higher frequency wingbeats than *Culex quinquefasciatu*; however, there is some overlap between the wingbeat frequencies distribution of these two species.

We can use a very simple Bayesian classifier, as discussed above, to categorize the examples into the three classes (species). We assume each class distribution is governed by a Gaussian distribution, with mean and standard deviation, as well as class prior probabilities, $P(b)$. We applied this simple Bayesian classifier to the data and obtained a respectful 96.04% accuracy. The results for each class are summarized in Table 1.

Table 1: Performance summary for each class

		Predicted			Class accuracy
		Bombus	*Culex*	*Aedes*	
Actual	*Bombus*	499	0	0	100.00%
	Culex	0	4139	113	97.34%
	Aedes	0	124	1107	89.92%

Note that the histogram for *Culex quinquefasciatu* in Figure 5 does not appear to be well modeled by a single Gaussian. This is not unexpected; *Culex quinquefasciatu*, like many mosquitoes, is highly sexually dimorphic, the females are larger than the males, and thus have lower wingbeat frequencies. In fact, the data in Figure 5 is suggestive of one Gaussian bump at about 400Hz and another at 550Hz. Ideally we would record training data for each sex separately, however sexing mosquitoes, either as larva or adults is very difficult [7]. We plan to investigate techniques to mitigate this by learning a *mixture model* for the insects [6].

5. COMPUTATIONAL ENTOMOLOGY IS A DATA MINING PROBLEM

We end with a brief discussion as to why the insect classification problem addressed here, and more general computational entomology problems, should be consider a sub-field of *data mining*.

We begin by noting the *scale* of the data considered. A single experiment we did on one species produced more than 200,000 data events. We need to reproduce this experiment at several different times of the year, and at several different latitudes, for at least one-hundred different insect species. We conservatively estimate that we will produce a billion data events in the next year alone. Furthermore, our insect *classification* problem requires contributions from virtually every data mining technique. For example, we use *outlier detection* to throw out spurious events in our audio data, we can use *regression* to predict how the wingbeat frequency of an insect will generalize to new temperatures and altitudes, in the (current) absence of circadian rhythms for all target insects we are using *transfer learning* to fill in missing data [4] by transferring information from an insect in the same genus etc.

Finally, when deploy our sensors in the field, the insect density data we obtain can be used as inputs into several higher-level data mining algorithms, including spatiotemporal analyses [1] and association (rule) discovery. For example, while it has long been known that there is an association between precipitation and mosquito density, the exact nature of this association is still not understood [9]. We have long been able to get minute by minute precipitation data for most of the world, but similarly fine-grained data on insect density has not been available until now.

6. ACKNOWLEDGMENTS

This work was funded by Bill and Melinda Gates Foundation, NSF awards 0803410 and 0808770 and FAPESP award 2009/06349-0. The first author is in leave from the Instituto de Ciências Matemáticas e de Computação, Universidade de São Paulo, Brazil.

The opinions or assertions contained herein are the private views of the authors, and are not to be construed as official, or as reflecting true views of the Department of the Army or the Department of Defense.

7. REFERENCES

[1] G. Andrienko, N. Andrienko, J. Dykes, M. Kraak, and H. Schumann. GeoVA(t) - Geospatial Visual Analytics: Focus on Time. *International Journal of Geographical Information Science*, 24(10): 1453-1457, 2010.

[2] M. Q. Benedict and A. S. Robinson. The first releases of transgenic mosquitoes: an argument for the sterile insect technique. *Trends in Parasitology*, 19: 349–356, 2003.

[3] R. Buchwald and R. Dudley. Limits to vertical force and power production in bumblebees (Hymenoptera: Bombus impatiens). *The Journal of Experimental Biology*, 213: 426-432, 2010.

[4] B. Cao, S. J. Pan, Y. Zhang, D. Yeung, and Q. Yang: Adaptive Transfer Learning. *AAAI 2010 Conference,* 407-412, 2010.

[5] K. W. Dixon. Pollination and Restoration. *Science*, 825, 5940: 571–573. 2009.

[6] M. A. T. Figueiredo and A. K. Jain. Unsupervised Learning of Finite Mixture Models, *IEEE Transactions on Pattern Analysis and Machine Intelligence*, 24: 381-396, 2002.

[7] D. A. Focks. An improved separator for the developmental stages, sexes, and species of mosquitoes (Diptera: Culicidae). *Journal of Medical Entomology*, 17: 567-568, 1980.

[8] D. H. Foley, R. C. Wilkerson, and R. E. Rueda. Importance of the "What", "When" and "Where" of Mosquito Collection Events. *Journal of Medical Entomology,* 46 (4): 717-722, 2009.

[9] H. Gong , A.T. Degaetano, and L. C. Harrington. Climate-based models for west nile culex mosquito vectors in the northeastern US. *International Journal of Biometeorology*, 2010.

[10] M. Grüebler, M. Morand, and B. Naef-Daenzer. A predictive model of the density of airborne insects in agricultural environments. *Agric. Ecosyst. Environ.*, 123 (1-3): 75-80, 2008.

[11] R . Harbach. Mosquito Taxonomic Inventory *mosquito-taxonomic-inventory.info/valid-species-list,* 2011.

[12] M.C. Kahn, W. Celestin, and W. Offenhauser. Recording of sounds produced by certain disease-carrying mosquitoes. *Science* 101: 335–336, 1945.

[13] M. C. Kahn and W. Offenhauser. The identification of certain West African mosquitoes by sound. *American Journal of Tropical Medicine*, 29(5): 827-836, 1949.

[14] Keogh, E. Computational Entomology website. *Online at www.cs.ucr.edu/~eamonn/CE*, 2011.

[15] J.L. Patnaik, L. Juliusson, and R. L. Vogt. Environmental predictors of human West Nile virus infections, Colorado. *Emerg. Infect Dis.*, 13: 1788–1790, 2007.

[16] WHO. World malaria report 2010. Geneva, World Health Organization. *www.who.int/malaria/publications/en/*, 2010.

[17] I. P. Woiwod and C. D. Thomas. Insect Movement: Mechanisms and Consequences. *Royal Entomological Society. CAB International*, 2001.

Social Flocks: A Crowd Simulation Framework for Social Network Generation, Community Detection, and Collective Behavior Modeling

Cheng-Te Li Shou-De Lin
Graduate Institute of Networking and Multimedia,
National Taiwan University, Taipei, Taiwan
{d98944005, sdlin}@csie.ntu.edu.tw

ABSTRACT

This work combines the central ideas from two different areas, crowd simulation and social network analysis, to tackle some existing problems in both areas from a new angle. We present a novel spatio-temporal social crowd simulation framework, *Social Flocks*, to revisit three essential research problems, (a) generation of social networks, (b) community detection in social networks, (c) modeling collective social behaviors in crowd simulation. Our framework produces social networks that satisfy the properties of high clustering coefficient, low average path length, and power-law degree distribution. It can also be exploited as a novel dynamic model for community detection. Finally our framework can be used to produce real-life collective social behaviors over crowds, including community-guided flocking, leader following, and spatio-social information propagation. *Social Flocks* can serve as visualization of simulated crowds for domain experts to explore the dynamic effects of the spatial, temporal, and social factors on social networks. In addition, it provides an experimental platform of collective social behaviors for social gaming and movie animations. *Social Flocks* is at http://mslab.csie.ntu.edu.tw/socialflocks/ .

Categories and Subject Descriptors

H.2.8 [**Database Management**]: Database Applications–*Data mining.*

General Terms

Algorithms, Performance, Design.

Keywords

Social Networks, Crowd Simulation, Flocking, Network Generation, Community Detection, Collective Social Behaviors.

1. INTRODUCTION

It is generally believed that human beings who live and interact in certain geographical area tend to form a social group. In this paper, we present a novel spatio-social simulation framework, *Social Flocks*, to model and exploit such anthropological natures by exploiting the technique of crowd simulation, which is to reveal collective behaviors by simulating the movement process of a number of agents. The central idea of *Social Flocks* is to assume each node as an agent that moves in the space guided by several different kinds of forces. This paper shows that *Social Flocks* can be exploited to solve three major problems in social network analysis and crowd simulation. First, it can be exploited to create networks that satisfy real-world property such as the small-world phenomenon and scale-free properties. Second, given a social network, *Social Flocks* can be utilized to identify network communities. Third, it can be treated as a simulation system that produces three kinds of social-based collective behaviors. The demonstration page of *Social Flocks* is available at http://mslab.csie.ntu.edu.tw/socialflocks/.

Social Network Generation. Social network generation models aim at producing artificial social networks satisfying some well-known properties that have been discovered in real-world social networks [13]. Three of the most essential properties are (a) high *clustering coefficient CC* (nodes are densely-connected to their neighborhood), (b) low *average path length APL* (all pairs of nodes are connected via short paths on average), and (c) *power-law degree distribution.* Watts and Strogatz [18] propose the *random rewiring* model to generate the *small-world* networks with high clustering coefficient. Barabasi and Albert [3] propose the *preferential attachment* mechanism to generate the *scale-free* networks that satisfy both (b) and (c). More advanced generative methods [1][4] have been proposed to model a series of sophisticated network properties as well. However, most of existing generation models ignores the fact that human societies are not formed by random rewiring or preferential attachment. In reality, ancient people migrated to the same geographical regions and gradually interact with each other to form societies. Therefore, in this work, rather than resorting to graph theory or topological composition methods, we exploit the technique of crowd simulation to develop a *CrowdNetGen* component for the generation of realistic social networks. *CrowdNetGen* integrates both spatial and temporal factors when forming a society. In *CrowdNetGen*, we propose two agent-based flocking mechanisms, the *touch* model and the *neighborhood-density* model, to generate social networks by gradually linking nodes that are in contact together. We also demonstrate that our approach is able to generate networks with high CC, low APL, and power-law degree distribution. The generated property values are similar to many empirical studies on real-world complex networks [13]. Though some studies [2][6][7] use the agent-based approach as spatial clues to generate networks, they do not investigate whether the structural properties satisfy those of the real-world.

Finding Communities. Community detection is a well-studied problem in social network mining. Generally it is tackled by first devising an objective function that captures the concept of the community structure (i.e., nodes within a cluster are tightly connected while nodes between communities are loosely connected). Though many methods have been proposed and compared (see Leskovec's review [11]) for community detection, most of them are topology-based approaches that overlook an important fact. Realistically, people form groups not due to the desires to optimize certain objective function, rather they form communities because they interact or contact with each other more frequently [12]. Based on the above insight, we present a new crowd simulation approach, termed *Crowdstering*, to identify communities in a social network.

Simulating Collective Behaviors. Different from *CrowdNetGen* and *Crowdstering* that bring the idea of crowd simulation into a social network mining problem, here we exploit the opposite by bringing the social factors into a crowd simulation framework. Several models have been proposed to simulate crowds to produce collective behaviors, including social force [8], cellular automata [5], and rule-based model [16]. Others use physiological (e.g. locomotion, energy level) and psychological (e.g. impatience, personality attributes) traits of agents to trigger heterogeneous behaviors [15]. However, existing approaches do not consider the social interactions among the agents, thus they are unable to produce social-dependent scenarios. In the third part of this work, we propose to leverage the underlying social network, which captures social relationships among the agents, for crowd simulation. We propose a social network-based crowd simulation, *SocioCrowd*. *SocioCrowd* can simulate three social-based collective crowd behaviors, including *community-guided flocking*, *leader following*, and *spatio-social information propagation*. These real-world social behaviors cannot be correctly modeled using existing methods. The three social-based behaviors can be utilized to create intelligent characters in online gaming and visual effects for the movie industry.

2. *SOCIAL FLOCKS* FRAMEWORK

We first present the *Social Flocks* framework as shown in Figure 1. *Social Flocks* takes advantage of Reynolds' *flocking simulation* model [16] as the backbone, in which we associate each node in a social network with a moving agent to perform the following three tasks. The first part is *CrowdNetGen*. We propose two network generation methods, *touch* and *neighborhood-density* models, to produce networks with properties of high CC, low APL, and power-law degree distribution. Second, given a social network, we propose a new spatio-temporal simulation approach for community detection, *Crowdstering*, by introducing the *acquaintance force* derived from the network into the system. The third part is *SocioCrowd*. By considering the network structure as the social contexts among the agents, we simulate three social-based collective crowd behaviors, including community-guided flocking, leader following, and spatio-social information propagation.

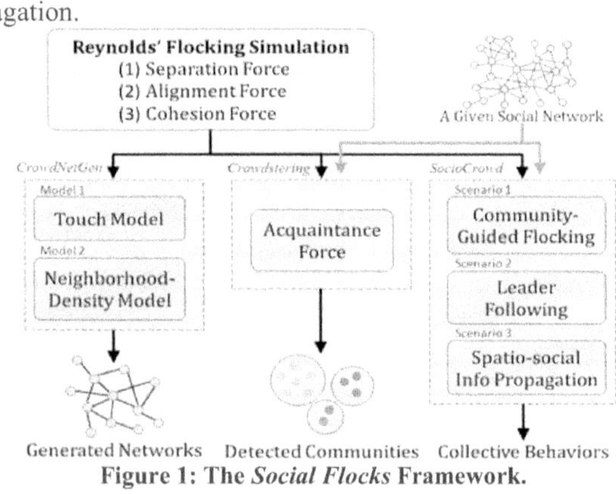

Figure 1: The *Social Flocks* Framework.

Here we briefly introduce Reynolds' flocking model [16]. It is proposed to capture the flocking behavior among artificial agents in a dynamic virtual environment. It consists of three steering rules, (a) *separation force* (f_s) steers each agent to avoid crowding local flockmates, (b) *alignment force* (f_a) steers each agent towards the average heading of local flockmates, and (c) *cohesion force* (f_c) steers each agent to move toward the average position of local flockmates. Besides, each agent is an independent actor and has his own local perception to navigate.

3. SOCIAL NETWORK GENERATION

We exploit a completely different strategy in generating real-world social networks using crowd simulation. The proposed generative model considers each node as an agent. Then as the flocking simulation proceeds, we gradually add edges between nodes based on one of the following models[1].

Touch Model. This model aims to produce a network that reflects the way people in the pre-telecommunication era form groups by physically meeting each other in space. In the touch model, an edge is added to connect agent/node u and v only when u and v have a physical touch during the simulating process. Figure 2 shows that as #round increases from 0 to 1550, the network quickly gathers edges and both CC and APL drastically increase. When the #round reaches 600 to 1000, as highlighted by the orange rectangle, the generated networks possess the small-world properties of high CC≈0.45 and small-world APL≈6. Unfortunately, the touch model does not quite produce the scale-free property. The power-law exponent α is about 1.5, which is smaller than that of many real social networks (α≈2).

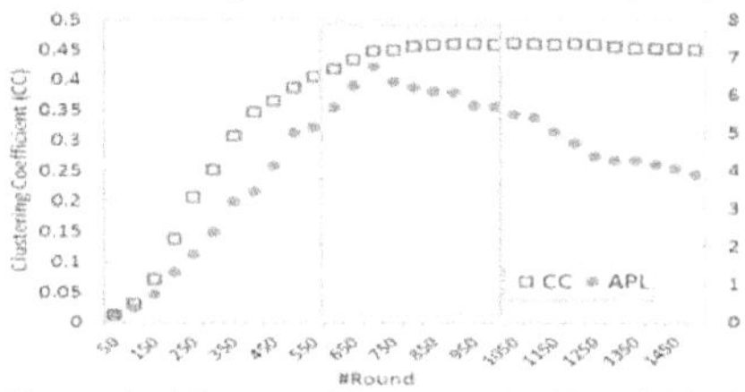

Figure 2: CC and APL under the *Touch* Model.

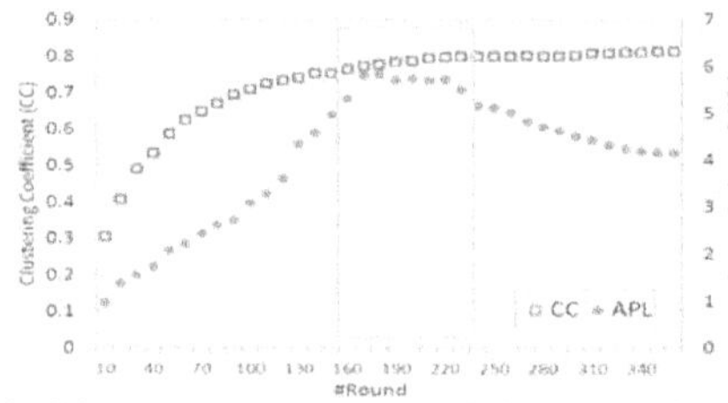

Figure 3: CC and APL under the *neighborhood-density* model.

Neighborhood-Density Model. To satisfy the three real-world properties in the generated networks, we devise the *neighborhood-density* model. The basic intuition is that an agent has higher likelihood to develop connections with others when there are more agents around, and furthermore it is more likely to develop relationship with the leader of a group. For an agent/node v, we define its *neighborhood-density* k_v as the number of neighboring agents within its local perception range ε (set to be 20 pixels here). During the flocking simulation, for each agent/node v, if k_v is larger than a predefined density threshold (set to be 5 in this work), the system adds an edge to connect v to a node u with the highest k_u value in v's local perception (i.e., such node is considered as the leader it perceives. Figure 3 presents the values of CC and APL during the simulation. We can see that as the rounds of simulation increases from 0 to 150, the network quickly gathers edges and both CC and APL increase drastically. The small-world properties emerge with high CC≈0.75 and low APL≈6 between round 150 and 200, as highlighted by the orange rectangle. As #round further increases, more edges are introduced to connect nodes from different flocks, and the APL gradually decreases. CC remains stable because edges are added for all nodes in a neighborhood at the same time (i.e., forming triangles in the network). Note that

[1] In this work, (f_s, f_a, f_c) = (0.5, 0.8, 0.5) for the *touch* model, and (f_s, f_a, f_c) = (0.7, 0.8, 0.5) for the *neighborhood-density* model.

comparing with the touch model, the neighborhood-density model takes fewer rounds to produce high CC and low APL. It is because the touch situations are relatively less likely to happen. In addition, the generated networks under the neighborhood-density model follow the power-law degree distribution. And the power-law exponent α at #round=170 is 1.92. In brief, the neighborhood-density model can produce networks that satisfy the three properties of real-world networks, i.e., high CC, low APL, and power-law degree distribution ($\alpha \approx 2$ in average).

4. FINDING NETWORK COMMUNITIES

In anthropology and evolutionary sciences, the geographic homophily plays a significant role on the formation of different kinds of human societies [12]. People who acquainted with each other usually live and flock in a particular spatial area and have higher potential to interact with one another. We consider such spatio-temporal homophily factor to develop a novel approach, *Crowdstering*, for finding communities in a network. Specifically, given a social network, our goal is to generate flocking groups in a natural way, with each flocking group corresponds to a detected community in the network. The natural way means that except for the steering forces that contributes to the spatio-temporal flocking behavior, our *Crowdstering* is parameter-free with respect to the prior knowledge about the communities, such as the number of communities.

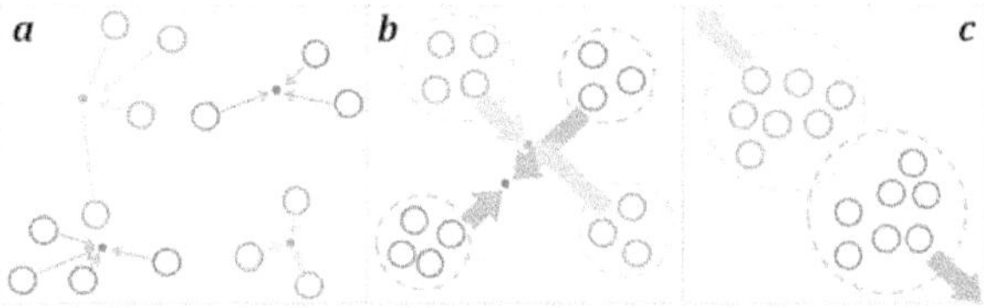

Figure 4: Expected effects of integrating the acquaintance force. (a) Gathering local flocks whose members tend to be acquainted with each other. (b) Attracting and merging local flocks gradually during the simulation. (c) For those far from acquaintances, the repulsions drive them away from one another.

To emerge flocking groups as communities in the simulating space, we introduce the fourth factor, the *acquaintance force* (f_q), into the flocking simulation. While the original three forces are used to produce the flocking behavior by gathering agents that are close enough in the simulating space, the integration of the acquaintance force is expected to emerge the effects: (a) determining the members of each flocking group, (b) steering agents whose corresponding nodes are close enough in the network to flock together, and (c) steering agents whose nodes are far apart in the network to avoid flocking together. An illustration of the idea of acquaintance force is shown in Figure 4. For an agent/node u, the acquaintance force $f_q(u)$ is computed by

$$f_q(u) = \frac{1}{|R_u|}\sum_{v \in R_u} 1 - \frac{Length(u,v)}{\theta},$$

where R_u is the set of agents under the local perception of agent u, $Length(u,v)$ is the length of shortest path between the node u and v in the network, and θ is a constant value that determines the shift border between the attraction and repulsion forces. That says, if $Length(u,v) < \theta$, the agent v will exert an attraction force to u. If $Length(u,v) > \theta$, v will exert an repulsion force to u. And if $Length(u,v) = \theta$, v has no effect on u. In this work, θ is set to be 3.

Here we use an example to show the effectiveness of *Crowdstering*. Given a network with two different sets of detected communities, the simulated outcomes are shown in Figure 5. For Figure 5(a), there are two detected communities, colored yellow and white, and the simulated outcome of our *Crowdstering* is nearly perfect as it emerges two flocking groups. For Figure 5(b), there are three detected communities, colored green, yellow, and white. We find that the previous white community is split into the current white and green communities, while the yellow community remains the same. Though the white and green communities flock together, the acquaintance force is still able to steer agents of each community to be closer in the network and towards two small cohesive flocking subgroups. In addition, we can find some agents who do not form a flock. They could be outliers that are loosely connected to any communities.

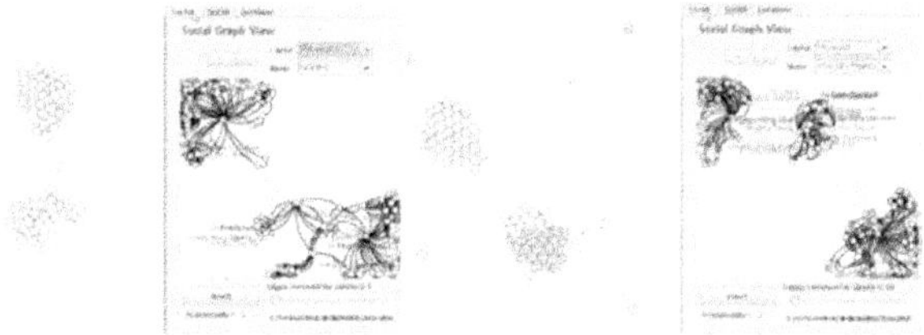

Figure 5: *Crowdstering* for a network with (a) two communities, and (b) three communities.

5. COLLECTIVE SOCIAL BEHAVIORS

Existing crowd simulation studies usually regard each simulation agent as independent (i.e., no social connection between each other). Although general crowd simulation methods can produce the realistic fine-grained human actions, they do not consider any real-life social interactions among the agents. This shortcoming prevents the creation of social-dependent crowd behaviors. Here we aim to leverage the underlying social network, which captures social relationships among agents, to produce collective social behaviors over crowds. The *SocioCrowd* component is developed to simulate three collective behaviors, including community-guided flocking, leader following, and spatio-social information propagation. We collect co-authorships from DBLP to construct the underlying network. An example social subgraph is shown in Figure 6(a).

5.1 Community-Guided Flocking

In the real life, it is assumed that people who are in the same community tend to interact with each other more frequently. We believe it is important that a simulation framework can reproduce such behavior. Therefore, we aim to simulate such common social scenario given a social network with detected communities. Note that in the demo we use the Fast Newman algorithm [14] to find communities community detection. For agents in diverse communities, we use different colors on both network view and 2D view. To integrate communities within the simulation, we design two probabilities, p_c and q_c, to control the possibility of an agent being attracted by others of the same and different community respectively. The simulating results are shown in Figure 6(c), where p_c=1 and q_c=0. It can be observed that agents belonging to the same communities tend to flock. For Figure 6(b), where p_c=0.5 and q_c=1, agents belonging to different communities have higher chance to flock.

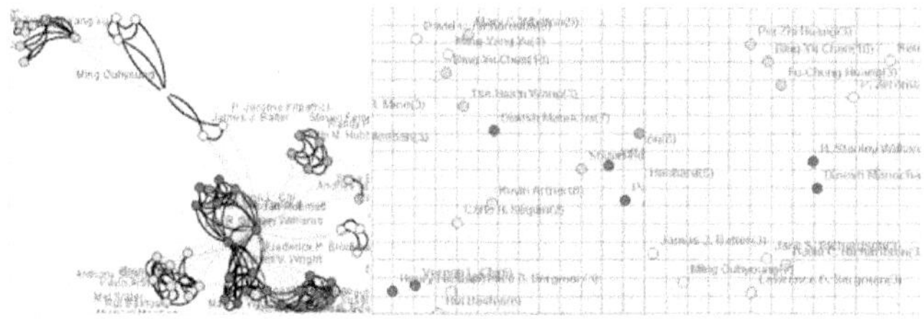

Figure 6: Left to right: (a) Network view with seven detected communities. (b) Simulating behaviors without community effect. (c) Collective behaviors of community-guided flocking.

5.2 Leader Following

A society usually has few leaders who are followed by other ordinary citizens. *SocioCrowd* simulates such social scenario by identifying some central individuals as the leaders in a social network. Three centrality measures (i.e., degree, closeness, and eigenvector) [17] are provided to find central individuals from different viewpoints. During simulation, we design a following probability p_l which allows an individual to follow a leader given the leader appears in the individual's local perception. A higher probability implies the leader attracts more followers. Figure 7 shows the result of leader following behavior, where $p_l = 0.7$.

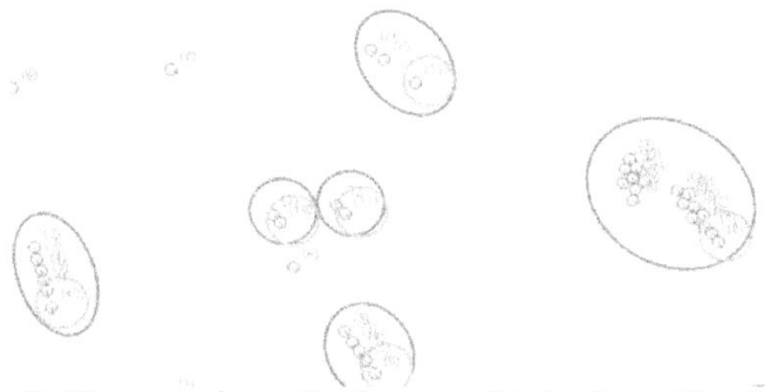

Figure 7: The emerging collective crowd behaviors of leading person following. Each red circled group is a flock and the orange circled ones are the leaders in flocking groups.

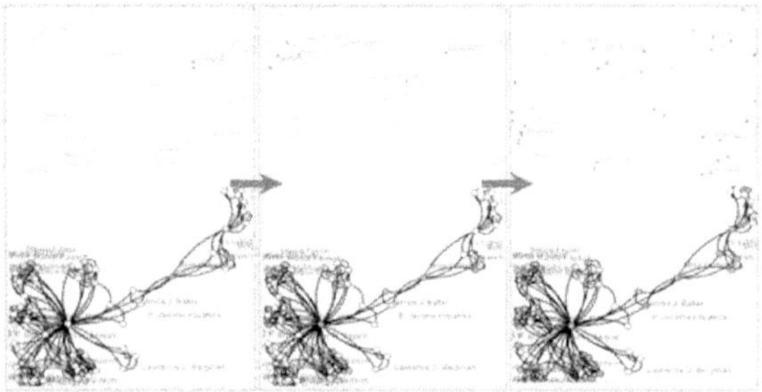

Figure 8: Certain information (purple), is propagated from few to most of the agents shown from left to right. The top is the simulating view while the bottom is the network view.

5.3 Spatio-Social Information Propagation

We simulate how information is propagated among agents. In conventional crowd simulation, agents spread messages only to others who are close to them in space. In real world, however, people do not necessarily communicate with spatially adjacent individuals but rather with socially adjacent ones. With underlying social network, individuals are capable of interacting with their social friends. *SocioCrowd* combines spatial and social clues to perform such information spreading. We adopt the linear threshold model [9] as the spreading strategy, with which an agent is influenced if the summation of the influence levels of its spatial and social neighbors is above a given threshold. A snapshot of influenced agents drawn in red cylinders is shown in Figure 8.

6. CONCLUSIONS

Generally, researchers regard crowd simulation as a sub-area in computer animation, which is not very relevant to the study of social network analysis. This paper, however, discovers a connection between crowd simulation and social network analysis and utilizes such connection to enhance performance on both sides. We first exploit crowd simulation framework to solve two important social network problems, namely generation of a social network that fits the real-world property, and community detection. Comparing with exiting models on network generation and community detection, our solution is able to reflect how ancient people form societies and visualize the dynamics of the generation process. Therefore users can further observe how the social links or communities are generated and utilize dynamic information to pursue further analysis. On the contrary, we also show social networks can benefit the area of crowd simulation. Previous models treat agents as individuals and do not consider the implicit social networks behind them. We have shown that by considering the forces derived from the social connection, it is possible to produce several collective social behaviors, including community-guided flocking, leader following, and spatio-social information propagation. Ongoing work will concentrate on modeling the evolving network properties, such as densification power law and shrinking diameter [10], and producing advanced collective social behaviors, such as riot and evacuation.

7. ACKNOWLEDGMENTS

This work was supported by National Science Council, National Taiwan University and Intel Corporation under Grants NSC99-2911-I-002-201, 99R70600, and 10R70500.

8. REFERENCES

[1] L. Akoglu, and C. Faloutsos. RTG: A Recursive Realistic Graph Generator using Random Typing. *PKDD* 2009.

[2] M. Aoyagi, and A. Namatame. Synchronization in Mobile Agents and Effects of Network Topology. *Agent-Based Social Systems*, 6(3) 31-42, 2009.

[3] A. L. Barabasi, and R. Albert. Emergence of Scaling in Random Networks. *Science* 286(5439), 509-512, 1999.

[4] D. Chakrabarti, and C. Faloutsos. Graph Mining: Laws, Generators, and Algorithms. *ACM Computing Survey*, 38(1), 2006.

[5] S. Chenney. Flow Tiles. *ACM SIGGRAPH/Eurographics Symposium on Computer Animation*. 233-242, 2004.

[6] B. Edmonds. How Are Physical and Social Spaces Related? – Cognitive Agents as the Necessary "Glue", *Agent-based Computational Modeling*, 5:195-214, 2006.

[7] L. Hamill, and N. Gilbert. Social Circles: A Simple Structure for Agent-Based Social Network Models. *Journal of Artificial Societies and Social Simulation*, 12(2), 3, 2009.

[8] D. Helbing, J. Farkas, and T. Vicsek. Simulating Dynamical Features of Escape Panic. *Nature*, 407, 487-490, 2000.

[9] D. Kempe, J. M. Kleinberg, and E. Tardos. Maximizing the Spread of Influence through a Social Network. *ACM SIGKDD*, 137-146, 2003.

[10] J. Leskovec, J. M. Kleinberg, and C. Faloutsos. Graphs over Time: Densification Laws, Shrinking Diameters and Possible Explanations. *ACM SIGKDD*, 177-187, 2005.

[11] J. Leskovec, K. Lang, and M. Mahoney. Empirical Comparison of Algorithms for Network Community Detection. *ACM WWW*, 631-640, 2010.

[12] M. McPherson, L. Smith-Lovin, and J. M. Cook. Birds of a Feather: Homophily in Social Networks. *Annual Review of Sociology*, 27:415-444, 2001.

[13] M. E. J. Newman. The Structure and Function of Complex Networks. *SIAM Review*, 45(2), 2003.

[14] M. E. J. Newman. Fast Algorithm for Detecting Community Structure in Networks. *Physical Review*, E 69, 066133, 2004.

[15] N. Pelechano, J. M. Allbeck, and N. I. Badler. Controlling Individual Agents in High-Density Crowd Simulation. *ACM SIGGRAPH/Eurographics Symposium on Computer Animation*, 99-108, 2007.

[16] C. W. Reynolds. Flocks, Herds and Schools. A Distributed Behavior Model. *ACM SIGGRAPH*, 25-34, 1987.

[17] S. Wasserman, and K. Faust. Social Network Analysis. *Cambridge University Press*, 1994.

[18] D. J. Watts, and S. H. Strogatz. Collective Dynamics of 'Small-world' Networks. *Nature*, 393:440-442, 1998.

Topic-level Social Network Search

Jie Tang, Sen Wu, Bo Gao, and Yang Wan
Department of Computer Science and Technology, Tsinghua University
jietang@tsinghua.edu.cn, gb@keg.cs.tsinghua.edu.cn
{ronaldosen, wy_rdfz}@gmail.com

ABSTRACT

We study the problem of topic-level social network search, which aims to find who are the most influential users in a network on a specific topic and how the influential users connect with each other. We employ a topic model to find topical aspects of each user and a retrieval method to identify influential users by combining the language model and the topic model. An influence maximization algorithm is then presented to find the sub network that closely connects the influential users. Two demonstration systems have been developed and are online available. Empirical analysis based on the user's viewing time and the number of clicks validates the proposed methodologies.

Categories and Subject Descriptors

H.3.3 [**Information Search and Retrieval**]: Text Mining; J.4 [**Social and Behavioral Sciences**]: Miscellaneous

General Terms

Algorithms, Experimentation

Keywords

influence analysis, social networks, topic model, social search

1. INTRODUCTION

With the success of many large-scale online social networks (e.g., Facebook, MySpace, and Twitter), finding people and their connections is becoming one important issue. Given a network, an interesting question is: who are the most influential users on a specific topic? A further question is: how do the influential users connect with each other? Answering the questions can benefit many applications, for example, to understand how research ideas or innovations spread in an academic network. In this paper, the problem is referred to as topic-level social network search.

To quickly grasp the main idea, we give a motivating example in Figure 1 using a coauthor network. The query is "data mining" and the system identifies five major relevant subtopics to the query, including "Data mining/association rule", "Database system", "Data management", "Web database", etc. The user can choose one of the subtopics to search for the most influential authors on the specific topic and to visualize the sub network that connects the influential authors. The colored links between authors indicate different types of relationships. For example, a red-colored link stands for an advisor relationship; while a yellow-colored link indicates an advisee relationship. With such a sub network, we can quickly get an insight of the core community on a specific (queried) topic.

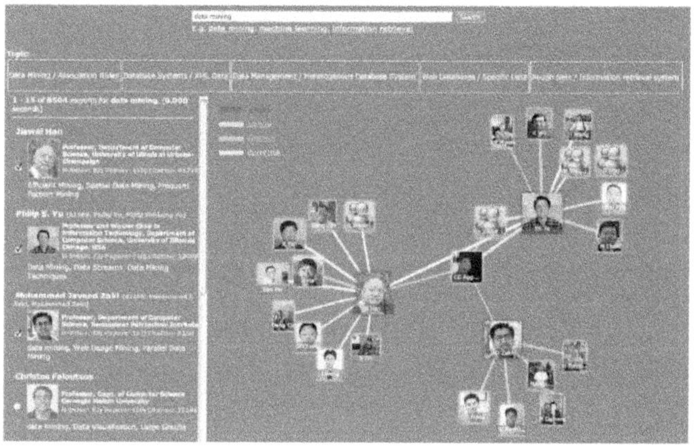

Figure 1: Topic-level social network search in coauthor network.

The problem of topic-level social network search presents a set of challenges:

- First, how to identify the subtopics for a given query?
- Second, how to identify the most influential users on a subtopic?
- Third, how to find the sub network that closely connects the most influential users?

In this paper, employing the coauthor network as the basis in our experiments, we try to conduct a systematic investigation of the problem of topic-level social network search.Specifically, we employ an Author-Conference-Topic (ACT) model [10] to obtain the topic distribution of each author. On each topic, we combine the language model and the topic model to rank authors and select top ranked authors as the most influential authors. Finally, we present

KDD'11, August 21–24, 2011, San Diego, California, USA.

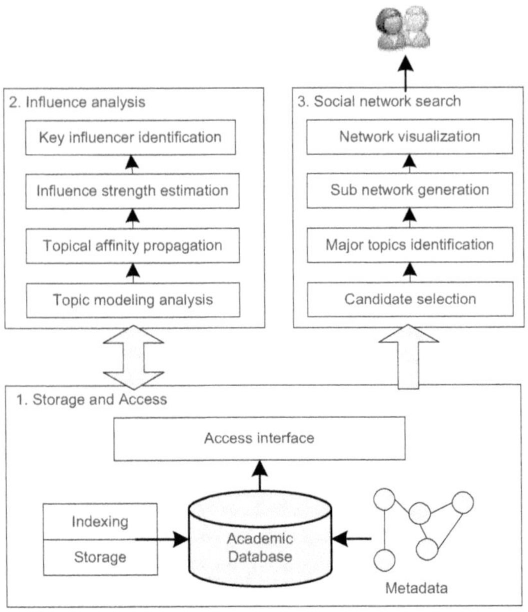

Figure 2: Architecture of topic-level social network search.

an influence maximization-based algorithm to find the sub network that connects the most influential authors for each topic. Based on the proposed approach, we have developed a prototype system[1]. The system has been online for nearly one year and attracted tens of thousands of users. Our empirical evaluation based on the user's viewing time and the number of clicks demonstrates the effectiveness of the proposed methods.

2. TECHNICAL SPECIFICATION

2.1 Architecture

Figure 2 shows the architecture of our approach to the topic-level social network search problem. In general, it consists of the following components:

- *Storage and Access*: it provides storage and indexing for the academic network data. Specifically, the academic database which consists of researcher profiles, publication papers, and conferences is constructed using a combination approach [8]; for storage it employs MySQL; for indexing, it employs the inverted file indexing method.
- *Influence analysis*: it performs an offline topic-based influence analysis. In particular, a topic modeling approach is used to find the topic distribution of all nodes and a topical affinity propagation is performed to quantify the influence between authors [7]; finally the influence strength and the key influencer (the most influential users) are identified based on the learned influence model.
- *Social network search*: Given a query, the system first ranks and retrieves authors as candidate influential authors using a method combining topic model and language model [10]; and then identifies which subtopics are relevant to the query and for each topic, it generates a sub network which centers with the most influential authors.

[1]http://arnetminer.org/association.do?m=home

2.2 Data Preparation

The academic data is located in the distributed Web. For searching and mining the academic network, we need first extract the networking data from the Web.

Some of the academic data can be extracted from structured data sources such as the publication information from DBLP; while other data needs to be extracted from unstructured Web pages such as researchers' homepages. We use a unified approach to extract researcher profiles from the researchers' homepages. We integrate the publication data from online databases. We extract the organization information from Wikipedia using regular expressions.

We employ a unified approach for researcher profiling [8] and a probabilistic approach for dealing with the name disambiguation problem in the integration [5]. The unified approach for research profiling explored in this paper is based on a new Condition Random Field model called Tree-structured Conditional Random Fields(TCRFs) [6].

The extracted/integrated data is stored into an academic network base. With the profiling and integration methods, we have collected 1,483,246 researcher profiles, 2,858,504 publications, 7,042 conferences, and 32,215,473 paper-paper citation relationships, 47,443,857 coauthor relationships, and 14,720,130 paper-published-at relationships. Based on the academic network, we have developed an academic search system, called Arnetminer.org. Services such as expertise search, course search, organization search, and topic browser have been provided. The system is in operation on the internet since 2006 and has attracted millions of users from 202 countries.

2.3 Topic-based Inf uence Analysis

To obtain the topic model for each node, one can use either the conventional topic model (e.g., pLSI or LDA), or a model combining the heterogeneous objects (e.g., ACT), or a model further combining the link information. In this paper, we employ the Author-Conference-Topic (ACT) model [10]. The model simulates the process of writing a scientific paper using a series of probabilistic steps. In essence, the topic model uses a latent topic layer as the bridge to connect the different types of objects. More accurately, for each object it estimates a mixture of topic distribution which represents the probability of the object being associated with every topic. For example, for each author, we have a set of probabilities $\{P(z_i|a)\}$, respectively denoting how likely author a is interested in topic z_i.

We use Gibbs sampling for parameter estimation. During parameter estimation, the algorithm keeps track of a $A \times T$ (author by topic) count matrix, a $T \times V$ (topic by word) count matrix, and a $T \times C$ (topic by conference) count matrix. Given these three count matrices, we can easily estimate the probability of a topic given an author $P(z|a)$, the probability of a word given a topic $P(w|z)$, and the probability of a conference given a topic $P(c|z)$. Interested reader can refer to [10] for more details.

Based on the network and topic distribution on the nodes, we formalize the social influence problem in a topical factor graph model and propose a topical affinity propagation on the factor graph to automatically identify the topic-specific social influence [7]. The main idea is to leverage an affinity propagation at the topic-level for social influence identification. The approach is based on the theory of factor graph [4], in which the observation data are cohesive on both local attributes and relationships. In our setting, the node corresponds to the observation data in the factor graph and the social relationship corresponds to edge between the observation data in the graph.

After topical affinity propagation, we can obtain a pairwise influence score $\{\mu_{st}^z\}$ and the topic distribution $\{\theta_v z\}$, where $\{\mu_{st}^z\}$ indicate the influence of node v_s on node v_t for the topic z and $\{\theta_v z\}$ represents the probability of topic z given node v. Then we can generate the topic-level social influence graphs. Specifically, for each topic z, we first filter out irrelevant nodes, i.e., nodes that have a lower probability than a predefined threshold. An alternative way is to keep only a fixed number (e.g., 1,000) of nodes for each topic-based social influence graph. (This filtering process can be also taken as a preprocessing step of our approach, which is the way we conducted our experiments.) Then, for a pair of nodes (v_s, v_t) that has an edge in the original network G, we create two directed edges between the two nodes and respectively assign the social influence scores μ_{st}^z and μ_{ts}^z. Finally, we obtain a directed social influence graph G_z for the topic z.

2.4 Social Network Search

For a given query, we first retrieve candidate influential users. This can be done using a retrieval method. In this paper, we use a method by combining the language model and ACT model [9]. The relevance score of an author a to the query q is calculated by:

$$P(w|a) = P_{LM}(w|a) \times P_{ACT}(w|a) \quad (1)$$

where $P_{LM}(w|a)$ is the probability of generating word w from author a using the language model and $P_{ACT}(w|d)$ is the generating probability using the ACT model. Then those authors with a higher relevance score (e.g., larger than a threshold) are chosen as candidates.

As the second step, we identify major subtopics for these candidate authors. From the first step, we have a set of candidate authors A_q, and every author has a topic distribution $\{P(z|a)\}_z$. By accumulating the topic distribution of all authors in A_q, we will have a distribution of $\{P(z|A_q)\}z$. Then we rank $P(z|A_q)$ according to the probability and select five topics with the highest probabilities as the major subtopics.

Next, we generate the influence-based sub network. The algorithm is based on the notion of influence maximization [1, 3]. From the previous steps, we obtained a ranked list of candidate influential authors for each topic. The goal of this step is to find a sub network that closely connects the top k influential authors for each topic. The sub network can consist of a number of authors who connect the top k influential authors. This problem has been also studied in [2]. In this work, we formalize the problem as finding a set of authors in the network that maximizes the spread of influence under certain models. The problem is NP-hard, which can be proved by a reduction to the Dominating Set Problem. We utilize an approximate influence maximization-based algorithm [1]. The algorithm uses node's degree as the criterion to select nodes in the social network. To avoid redundant nodes (authors are close with each other in the network), we

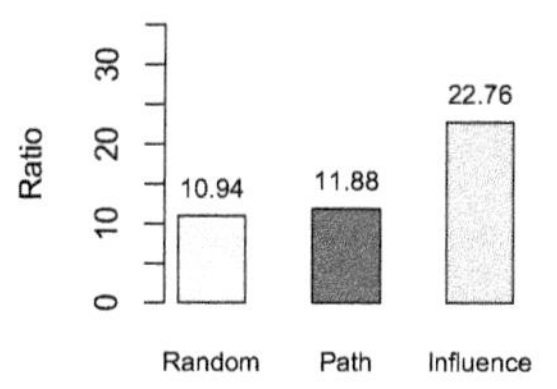

(a) Expand/Remove ratio

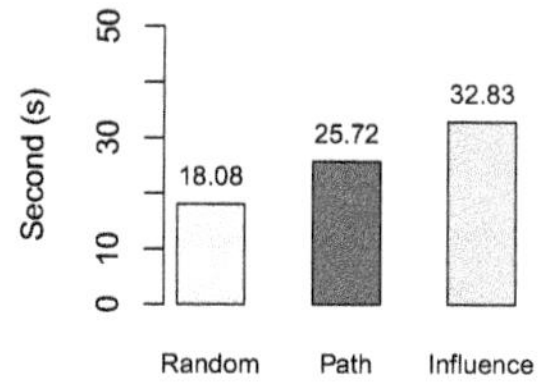

(b) Viewing time (s)

Figure 3: Empirical analysis.

adopt a degree discount method. The idea is as follows: let v and u are neighborhood nodes in the network. If u has been selected in the graph, then when counting the degree of node v, we subtract the edge between u and v. To generalize it, when selecting any new node, we recount the degree of each node by subtracting the number of edges between the new node and any nodes already selected in the social graph.

Finally, we visualize the obtained sub network, which centers with the top k influential authors on the user selected topic.

2.5 Empirical Analysis

We have developed two systems to evaluate the presented algorithms. The first system is deployed in Arnetminer.org, an academic analysis and mining system [10] and the other system is deployed in Tsinghua university centenary celebration system[2].

Evaluation Criteria For evaluation, we consider the average user's viewing time and the average number of clicks. For user's viewing time, we mean when the user submits a query to the system, how much time he will stay on the returned social graph. Staying for a long time means that the user would be more interested in the result than that with a short time. We also design an interactive mechanism, which allows the user to expand an author's detailed social information when she is interested in knowing more about the person or to remove the node from the returned social network when she is not interested in the person. Finally, an Expand/Remove ratio is calculated. A high ratio indicates a better performance.

We compare our influence algorithm with two baseline methods: *Random*, which randomly selects authors to generate the sub network to connect the top k authors; and *Path*, which finds shortest paths between pairwise authors and combines the paths to generate the sub network.

Results Figure 3(a) shows the result of Expand/Remove ratio by different algorithms. It can be seen that our Influence algorithm has the largest ratio, while the Random and the Path algorithm have a lower ratio. Figure 3(b) shows the average viewing time of a user on the returned social graph by the different algorithms. It can be seen again that the Influence algorithm results in the longest viewing time, which confirms the effectiveness of our method. On average, the Influence algorithm almost doubles the ratio of Expand/Remove comparing with the two alternative algorithms; and gains an 27.64%-81.58% increase in terms of viewing time than the two baseline algorithms.

[2]http://alumni.cs.tsinghua.edu.cn/

3. DEMONSTRATION PLAN

We will present our system thoroughly in our demo. Particularly, we will focus on the following aspects.

1. First, we will use a poster to give an overview of the system, including the motivation and major issues addressed in the system. We will introduce the architecture and the main features of the system.
2. Next, we will explain how we conduct the topic-level influence analysis on the heterogeneous academic network. We will describe in detail the principled approaches for quantifying the topic-level influence between users.
3. Then, we will describe the principles for social network search. We will explain how we perform the major topic identification, sub network generation, and network visualization.
4. Finally, we will show statistics of system logs and user feedbacks. We will share our thoughts about the strength and the weakness of the system. We will further discuss the future work of the system.

Finally, please note that this is an ongoing project. Visitors should expect the system to change. We are extracting more researcher profiles and publications and are also developing more practical search services based on feedbacks from users.

3.1 What is New?

The prototype has been integrated into the Arnetminer.org system. In this subsection, we clarify what are new features of this demo, which are also the main contribution of this paper.

1. We present a novel influence analysis problem and introduce how to estimate the topic-level influence strength between nodes in a heterogeneous network. Based on the learned influence model, we identify the key influencer (the most influential nodes) on a specific node from the network. For instance, this demo will show you who are the most influential authors in "data mining", "database", or "machine learning" and who are mainly influenced by these key influencer.
2. We provide a novel social network search function based on the learned influence model. For a given query, the system automatically identifies which topics are the most relevant and which nodes are the relevant to the query and the topic. Then a topic-based sub network is generated according to the learned influence model.
3. We develop a web service interface for the influence-based analysis and search function, based on which the user can retrieve the topic-based sub network for a given query.

4. CONCLUSION AND FUTURE WORK

In this paper, we present a novel system of topic-based social network search. We study this problem on the heterogeneous academic network which consists of authors, conferences, and papers. We design an architecture to perform the influence analysis and topic-based social network search. We employ a topical affinity propagation approach to estimate the influence between nodes in the heterogeneous network and identify the key influencer based on the learned influence model. Further we provide a social network search service based on the output of the topic-level influence analysis. For a given query, the system automatically finds the most relevant topics for each topic, identifies the most influential users on each topic, and generates the sub network that closely connects the most influential users.

The general problem of social network search represents a new and interesting research direction. There are many potential future directions of this work. One interesting issue is to combine the learned influence model with users' behavior to build an more accurate user behavior model. Another issue is to integrate some background knowledge to help identify the most influential users. For example the advisor-advisee relationship can obviously help quantify the influence strength between coauthors. We also consider applying the influence model to some other domains, such as Twitter and flickr, to further validate its effectiveness. Finally, as the scale of the network grows very quickly, how to scale up the approach to handle very large (billions-of-nodes) network is also a challenging problem.

ACKNOWLEDGMENTS

The work is supported by the Natural Science Foundation of China (No. 61073073 , No. 60973102), Chinese National Key Foundation Research (No. 60933013, No.61035004).

5. REFERENCES

[1] W. Chen, Y. Wang, and S. Yang. Efficient influence maximization in social networks. In *KDD'09*, pages 199–207, 2009.

[2] C. Faloutsos, K. S. McCurley, and A. Tomkins. Fast discovery of connection subgraphs. In *KDD'04*, pages 118–127, 2004.

[3] D. Kempe, J. Kleinberg, and E. Tardos. Maximizing the spread of influence through a social network. In *KDD'03*, pages 137–146, 2003.

[4] F. R. Kschischang, B. J. Frey, and H. andrea Loeliger. Factor graphs and the sum-product algorithm. *IEEE TOIT*, 47:498–519, 2001.

[5] J. Tang, A. C. Fong, B. Wang, and J. Zhang. A unified probabilistic framework for name disambiguation in digital library. *IEEE TKDE*, 99(PrePrints), 2011.

[6] J. Tang, M. Hong, J. Li, and B. Liang. Tree-structured conditional random fields for semantic annotation. In *ISWC'06*, pages 640–653, 2006.

[7] J. Tang, J. Sun, C. Wang, and Z. Yang. Social influence analysis in large-scale networks. In *KDD'09*, pages 807–816, 2009.

[8] J. Tang, L. Yao, D. Zhang, and J. Zhang. A combination approach to web user profiling. *ACM TKDD*, 5(1):1–44, 2010.

[9] J. Tang, J. Zhang, R. Jin, Z. Yang, K. Cai, L. Zhang, and Z. Su. Topic level expertise search over heterogeneous networks. *Machine Learning Journal*, 82(2):211–237, 2011.

[10] J. Tang, J. Zhang, L. Yao, J. Li, L. Zhang, and Z. Su. Arnetminer: Extraction and mining of academic social networks. In *KDD'08*, pages 990–998, 2008.

Video Analytics Solution for Tracking Customer Locations in Retail Shopping Malls

Harikrishna G. N. Rai
Infosys Labs
Infosys Technologies Limited
Bangalore, India
+91-80-39135886
harikrishna_rai@infosys.com

Kishore Jonna
Infosys Labs
Infosys Technologies Limited
Hyderabad, India
+91-40-67048044
kishore_jonna@infosys.com

P. Radha Krishna
Infosys Labs
Infosys Technologies Limited
Hyderabad, India
+91-40-67024610
radhakrishna_p@infosys.com

ABSTRACT

Due to increased adoption of digital inclusion in various businesses, location based services are gaining importance to provide value-added services for their customers. In this work, we present a computer vision based system for tracking customer locations by recognizing individual shopping carts inside shopping malls in order to facilitate location based services. We provide an efficient approach for cart recognition that consists of two stages: cart detection and then cart recognition. A binary pattern is placed between two pre-defined color markers and attached to each cart for recognition. The system takes live video feed as input from the cameras mounted on the aisles of the shopping mall and processes frames in real-time. In the cart detection stage, color segmentation, feature extraction and classification are used for detection of binary pattern along with color markers. In recognition stage, segmented binary strip is processed using spatial image processing techniques to decode the cart identification number.

Categories and Subject Descriptors

I.4.8 **[Computing Methodologies]:** Image Processing and Computer Vision – Scene Analysis – *Color, Object recognition, Tracking*

General Terms

Algorithms, Experimentation.

Keywords

Shopping cart detection, Haar-like features, Classification, Color segmentation.

1. INTRODUCTION

Video analytical solutions deal with the extraction of meaningful insights from image frames captured from video cameras. Video cameras are used in various industry segments for the purpose of security, surveillance and tracking. Inferences derived from video analytical systems are of great importance for making critical decisions and predictions in varied industrial application scenarios.

In retail shopping malls, customer tracking technology for responding to in-store promotions is present day need. Retailers are using analytics to exploit how customers behave and analyze their buying patterns. Retailers can analyze data obtained from customer loyalty cards and other programs to determine which stores are being mostly visited by customers, who make inconsistent purchases, jump at coupons or frequently return products. This kind of analysis also help stores to take better decisions about how to tailor sales, coupons and other promotions. There are several solutions in this area which have similar capabilities for providing retailers and suppliers with insights into how consumers react to various displays and merchandising scenarios. These solutions are available for providing retail analytical services by analyzing structured data. However, there is a further need to develop efficient and cost effective solutions that exploits and analyze available unstructured data such as images and videos captured in a shopping mall. One such application area in retail industry is tracking customer movements using the video cameras installed in shopping malls based on the location of cart assigned to customer. A major source of available unstructured data in retail stores is video captured from surveillance camera for security purpose.

Few hardware based solutions which uses Motes, Wireless Sensor Networks (WSN) and Radio Frequency Identification Devices (RFID) exist in the retail industry for the purpose of tracking customer/cart movement and shelf inventory tracking. Wireless transmitters are embedded in shopping carts, throughout the store, and in overhead sensors, creating reams of new data about how shoppers move through stores and where they stop to linger or compare prices; the system can show how much time they spent in front of a display (for instance, newly introduced baby food item). Drawbacks of these dedicated hardware based solution are (i) high cost, (ii) frequent maintenance such as replacing batteries and hardware maintenance, (iii) prone to frequent damage due to mishandling of carts in shopping mall (such as tampering attached device by customers or their kids, sorting of empty carts by back-to-back insertion of one cart to another by shopping mall staff)

To overcome the above limitations, we propose a novel computer vision based approach by using existing surveillance cameras in shopping malls to detect the shopping cart and track

KDD'11, August 21–24, 2011, San Diego, California, USA.

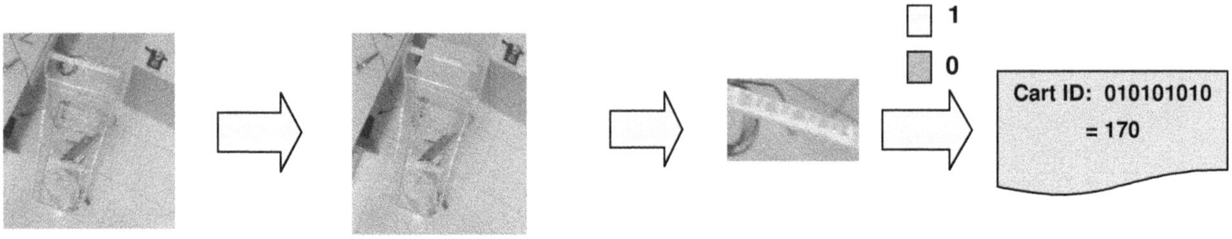

Input frame with cart object | Cart object detection | Cart object recognition | Decoded cart ID

Figure 1. Cart detection and recognition workflow

the customer locations inside retail stores. However there are several challenges in realizing a computer vision based solution for analyzing customer location in retail stores. Low resolution, varied illumination, and non-rigid cart pattern (specifically when lots of object loaded in it) makes it very challenging to detect it with higher accuracy. Also multiple light sources and reflections hamper the quality of captured images. In this work, our focus is to detect multi-view cart using color marker, segment the attached unique binary pattern and to recognize the encoded unique identification number.

2. SYSTEM OVERVIEW

In the proposed system, we process the video frames captured from video cameras mounted at different locations of shopping mall aisles. Further, each frame is processed to detect the carts and recognize their unique identification codes (Cart ID can be in the form of color coded pattern, such as sequence of Bars, where each bar is in White, Black or some color). Initially, unique identification codes are generated using binary bit pattern encoded in black and white bars in the form of strips. We designed two color markers and placed on both sides of the binary pattern on each strip. A strip is attached to a cart body facing the top view of the cart.

We present a computer vision technique to track the shopping cart locations. In our system, video frames are captured from a web camera in real-time. Figure 1 shows the workflow for cart detection and recognition. Each input frame is processed in real-time using novel approaches to analyze the image for shopping cart. First, the strip consisting of binary pattern along with color markers in each frame are detected. Next, the binary bit pattern is segmented and decoded to get the unique cart IDs represented by that pattern. These two stages namely cart detection and cart recognition are detailed in sections 3 and 4 respectively.

In addition to web cam, our proposed system is capable of taking video feed coming from mobile camera or surveillance camera. Also proposed system is not only used for tracking shopping cart, it can be used to track any such similar moving objects in a closed environment where there is a need to track the location of objects under camera surveillance. Shopping cart recognition enables several business applications for Retailers. For instance, sending promotional location based advertisement to retail customers such as latest offers on the products appearing near to them in aisle where they stand in shopping mall.

3. CART DETECTION

Please use a 9-point Times Roman font, or other Roman font with serifs, as close as possible in appearance to Times Roman in which these guidelines have been set. The goal is to have a 9-point text, as you see here. Please use sans-serif or non-proportional fonts only for special purposes, such as distinguishing source code text. If Times Roman is not available, try the font named Computer Modern Roman. On a Macintosh, use the font named Times. Right margins should be justified, not ragged.

Live video streams are processed using various image processing algorithms for cart detection and recognition. Initially frames are preprocessed using smoothening filters and enhancement techniques. This improves the image quality and in-turn helps in improving the accuracy of detection of color marker segment. Object detection [6] is the major requirement for successful recognition of cart-ID in our application. Both camera rotation and cart rotation are two critical factors to detect the cart in real-time. Moreover, loading shopping items having different color, shape and size in the cart, change the cart pattern radically. The role of classifier in our approach is to detect color marker with binary pattern attached to the cart. The classifier will separate the foreground object from the background and detects multiple objects using computer vision based algorithms.

Object detection stage has two steps in our system: (i) color segmentation for initial identification of the region with markers and binary pattern on the cart and (ii) trained classifier for confirming the marker region with pattern. As we assign pre-determined color markers on each side of binary pattern, we use simple color thresholding to segment the color marker regions. In our setup, red color circular objects are used for markers. Scan line operations are performed on image frame to check the pixel intensities with red color (say, in RGB color space, R component in 150 to 255 ranges) and then threshold the region. In this way, we detect two circular red markers and then fit a bounding box to cover these two red markers which encompasses binary pattern. We compute the angle of the bounding box with respect to horizontal axis. The image is

Thresholded strip | Contour extraction | Morphological operations

Figure 2. Recognition steps to decode the binary strip

Figure 3. Cart detection in horizontal direction

Figure 4. Cart detection when it is oriented

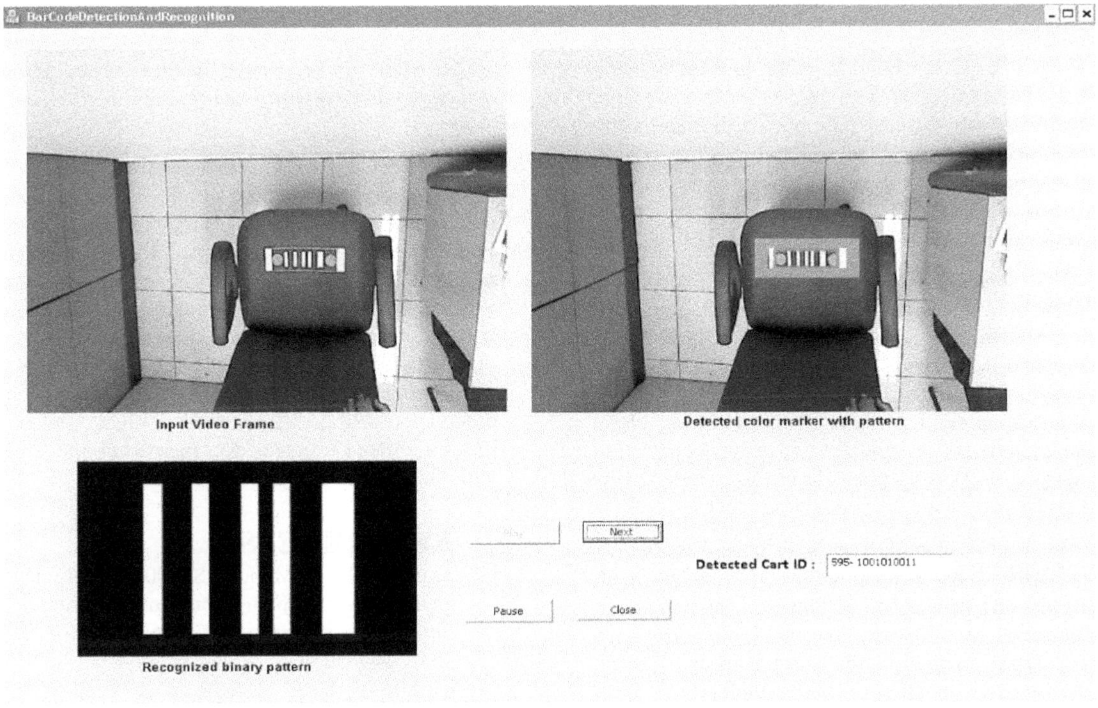

Figure 5. Screenshot of application with moving chair having cart ID 595

rotated so that bounding box is horizontal and these images are given as input for the classifier.

For classifier based detection, low level image features like Histogram of Oriented Gradient (HoG) and Haar-like features are computed. The design of classifier plays a major role in detection of color marker segment. We designed a cascaded classifier using two classifiers namely Ada-boost classifier [1],[,4],[,5] with Haar-like features and Support Vector Machines (SVM) classifier [2],[3] with HoG features to improve the classification performance. The positively detected segments by Ada-boost classifier are given as input to the SVM classifier. False positives as well as the overall detection time are reduced by using the cascaded approach.

4. CART RECOGNITION

Figure 2 shows the steps to decode the binary pattern. In the recognition stage, we threshold the input region so that it generates binary bit sequences depending upon the color chosen for representing 0s and 1s. In our setup we used black and white color bar patterns. Here, white color bar represents 1 and black represents 0. Threshold region is further processed with morphological operations and hole filling process to get better black and white patches. Processed binary segment is analyzed for each scan line to count the number of consecutive 0s and 1s. These counts are stored and the scan line operation is repeated for all rows of processed segment. Depending upon the camera height, width of each binary bit is estimated and final binary value representing cart ID is decoded.

5. EXPERIMENTAL RESULTS

We processed video sequences using a webcam having 2 megapixel resolution that captures video at 30 frames per second. The webcam is integrated to a computer for live streaming purpose. The Webcam was set at 6 feet height (approximately) to cover 5 to 10 meters field of view. Video stream coming out of webcam is processed frame by frame, where each frame size is 640X480 pixels. As cart can come in

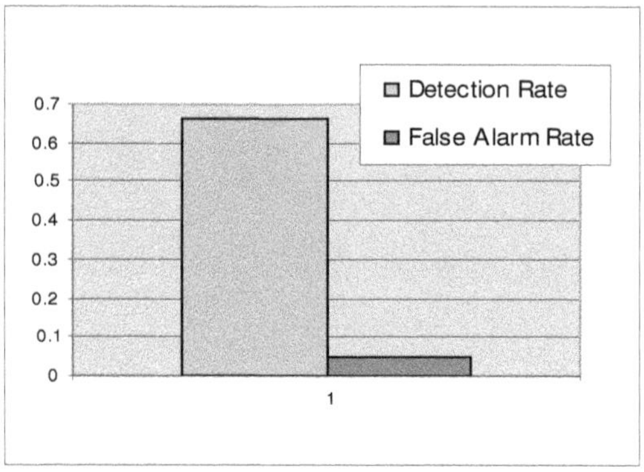

Figure 6. Detection and false alarm rate for horizontal carts

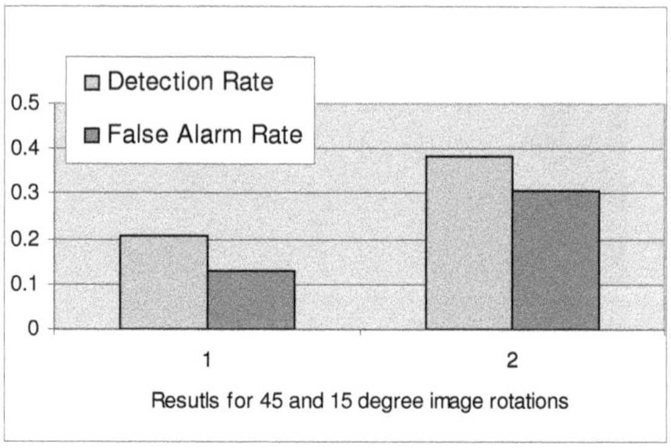

Figure 7. Detection and false alarm rate for rotated carts

any direction with reference to camera field of view, we need to handle cart orientation scenarios to make it rotation invariant in the preprocessing step. If the bounding box generated using color segmentation is horizontal with respect to image plane; segment is directly fed into the classifier module. If there is any change in orientation, the angle at which bounding box is oriented with respect to image plane is measured and image segment is rotated accordingly to make it horizontal before sending to classification module.

Figure 5 shows the screenshot of our application. It shows the input frame taken from a live feed on top left panel. Top right panel shows the detected cart highlighting the red color bounding box around the attached patch with bar codes. Bottom left panel shows the segmented and processed binary pattern. This binary pattern is decoded by the recognition module. Here, we used binary pattern 100 as prefix to all cart identification numbers to indicate the starting point during recognition. Bits following this prefix pattern are decoded into cart ID.

In the experimentation of classifier, we have taken two sample sets to test the performance of the classifier. 1000 images with barcode of different orientations and 500 images with barcode in horizontal orientation. As a first step the two sample sets have been annotated. During annotation, the coordinates and specific location of the barcode on all the 1000 samples have been calculated and collected. First, we applied the classifier on these 1000 images and record the coordinates of the barcode on all the images. Then we compared the classifier output with the annotated data for each image. If the coordinates are overlapping with more than a specified threshold (taken as 60% for this experiment) then the detection in the image is treated as true positive, otherwise it is treated as false positive. The performance of the classifier is computed in terms of Detection Rate (DR) and False Alarm Rate (FAR) as given below:

$$DR = \frac{\text{No. of True Positives}}{\text{Total No. of Objects}} \quad ; \quad FAR = \frac{\text{No. of False Positives}}{\text{Total No. of Images}}$$

Figure 6 shows high detection rate and low false alarm rate for horizontal cart detector. The same process is applied on the classifier from second sample set. In this experiment, image rotation is not required as the barcode is already in horizontal position. Figure 7 shows the results for DR and FAR for rotated binary patterns. Here, as the orientation angle increases the detection rate and false alarm rate decreases. For orientation angle of 15 degrees, number of times image needs to be rotated is 24 (i.e., 360/15). Since the same image is being rotated for more number of times, the detection and false alarm rates are high. For orientation angle of 45 degrees, number of times image needs to be rotated is 8(i.e., 360/45), and hence the detection and false alarm rates are lower.

6. CONCLUSIONS

In this paper, we presented a computer vision based system that is capable of tracking carts in retail shopping malls. Furthermore, we demonstrated detection and recognition of a mobile cart. The proposed system overcomes the limitation of existing hardware based solutions and offers several business benefits such as reduction in cost due to low cost cameras in place of costly hardware devices. This system does not require any frequent maintenance and battery replacements as in WSN based approach. Also this system is highly scalable as it requires installing more cameras for increasing the area of coverage without any changes in the software.

7. REFERENCES

[1] Gavrila, D. and Munder, S. 2007. Multi-cue pedestrian detection and tracking from a moving vehicle. *International Journal of Computer Vision*. 73, 1 (June 2007), 41-59.

[2] Heisele, B., Serre, T., Prentice, S., and Poggio, T. 2003. Hierarchical classification and feature reduction for fast face detection with support vector machines. *Pattern Recognition*. 36, 9 (Sep. 2003), 2007-2017.

[3] Le, D. and Satoh, S. 2006. A multi-stage approach to fast face detection. *IEICE Transactions*. 89-D(7), 2275-2285.

[4] Leibe, B., Leonardis, A. and Schiele. B.2008. Robust object detection with interleaved categorization and segmentation. *International Journal of Computer Vision*. 77, 1-3 (May 2008), 259-289.

[5] Negri, P., Xavier Clady, X. Hanif, S. H. and Prevost L. 2008. A cascade of boosted generative and discriminative classifiers for vehicle detection. *EURASIP Journal on Advances in Signal Processing*. 2008, 2, Article ID 782432, 1-12.

[6] Viola, P. and Jones, M. 2001. Rapid object detection using a boosted cascade of simple features. In *Proceedings of IEEE Conference on Computer Vision and Pattern Recognition* (Kauai, HI, USA, December 8 -14, 2001) 511–518.

Industry Practice Expo Invited Talk

"Which Half is Wasted?": Controlled Experiments to Measure Online-Advertising Effectiveness

David Reiley
Principal Research Scientist
Yahoo! Labs
Santa Clara, CA

reiley@yahoo-inc.com

ABSTRACT

The department-store retailer John Wanamaker famously stated, "Half the money I spend on advertising is wasted—I just don't know which half." Compared with the measurement of advertising effectiveness in traditional media, online advertisers and publishers have considerable data advantages, including individual-level data on advertising exposures, clicks, searches, and other online user behaviors. However, as I shall discuss in this talk, the science of advertising effectiveness requires more than just quantity of data - even more important is the quality of the data. In particular, in many cases, using various statistical techniques with observational data leads to incorrect measurements. To measure the true causal effects, we run controlled experiments that suppress advertising to a control group, much like the placebo in a drug trial. With experiments to determine the ground truth, we can show that in many circumstances, observational-data techniques rely on identifying assumptions that prove to be incorrect, and they produce estimates differing wildly from the truth. Despite increases in data availability, Wanamaker's complaint remains just as true for online advertising as it was for print advertising a century ago.

In this talk, I will discuss recent advances in running randomized experiments online, measuring the impact of online display advertising on consumer behavior. Interesting results include the measurable effects of online advertising on offline transactions, the impact on viewers who do not click the ads, the surprisingly large effects of frequency of exposure, and the heterogeneity of advertising effectiveness across users in different demographic groups or geographic locations. I also show that sample sizes of a million or more customers may be necessary to get enough precision for statistical significance of economically important effects - so we have just reached the cusp of being able to measure effects precisely with present technology. (By comparison, previous controlled experiments using split-cable TV systems, with sample sizes in the mere thousands, have lacked statistical power to measure precise effects for a given campaign.) As I show with several examples that establish the ground truth using controlled experiments, the bias in observational studies can be extremely large, over-or-underestimating the true causal effects by an order of magnitude. I will discuss the (implicit or explicit) modeling assumptions made by researchers using observational data, and identify several reasons why these assumptions are violated in practice. I will also discuss future directions in using experiments to measure advertising effectiveness.

Categories and Subject Descriptors

H.2.8 [**Database Management**]: Data Mining.

General Terms

Algorithms, Experimentation, Human Factors, Management, Measurement.

Keywords

Data Mining, Computational Advertising, Advertising Effectiveness, Experimentation.

Bio

David Reiley is a Principal Research Scientist at Yahoo! Research, where he is using experiments to measure the effects of display advertising. A leader in the field-experiments revolution in economics and the social sciences, he has published experiments on diverse topics, from auction bidding to charitable fundraising, in leading economics journals. Before coming to Yahoo!, Reiley was Arizona Public Service Professor of Economics at the University of Arizona. He has also taught at Vanderbilt University and at the Kellogg School of Management at Northwestern University. Reiley is the Co-Editor for Field Experiments at Economic Inquiry, and a coauthor (with Avinash Dixit and Susan Skeath) of the best-selling game theory textbook Games of Strategy, Third Edition. He holds a bachelor's degree in Astrophysical Sciences from Princeton University, and a PhD in economics from MIT.

KDD'11, August 21–24, 2011, San Diego, California, USA.
ACM 978-1-4503-0813-7/11/08.

Industry Practice Expo Invited Talk

Accelerating Large-Scale Data Mining Using In-Database Analytics

Mario E. Inchiosa
Chief Scientist
Netezza (an IBM Company)
minchiosa@netezza.com

ABSTRACT

In more and more industries, competitive advantage hinges on exploiting the largest quantity of data in the shortest possible time - and doing so cost-effectively. Data volumes are growing exponentially, while businesses are striving to deploy sophisticated and computationally intensive predictive analytics. Often, massive data is stored in a data warehouse running on dedicated parallel hardware, but advanced analytics is performed on a separate compute platform. Moving data from the data warehouse to the compute environment can constitute a significant bottleneck. Organizations resort to considering only a fraction of their data or refreshing their analyses infrequently. To address the data movement bottleneck and take full advantage of parallel data warehouse platforms, vendors are offering new in-database analytics capabilities. They are opening up their platforms, allowing users to run their own user-defined functions and statistical models as well as vendor- and partner-supplied advanced analytics on the database platform, close to the data, in parallel, without transporting the data through a host node or corporate network. In this talk, we will present the need for in-database analytics and discuss a number of the new solutions available, highlighting case studies where solution times have been reduced from hours to minutes or seconds.

Categories and Subject Descriptors

H.2.7 [**Database Administration**]: Data warehouse and repository, H.2.8 [**Database Management**]: Data Mining.

General Terms: Algorithms, Experimentation, Performance, Measurement, Reliability.

Keywords: Large-scale data warehousing, in-database analytics, predictive analytics.

Bio

Dr. Mario E. Inchiosa is U.S. Chief Scientist at Netezza, an IBM Company, where he develops data-intensive high performance computing appliances. His work focuses in particular on the juncture of data warehousing and parallelized advanced analytics and optimization. Dr. Inchiosa received an A.B. in Physics from Harvard College and an A.M. and Ph.D. in Physics from Harvard University. At Harvard, he combined his dual interests in Physics and Computer Science by applying statistical physics to the study of neural network associative memories. He moved on to study the dynamics of neural network associative memories as a post-doc at the Technical University of Munich. Next, he joined SPAWAR Systems Center San Diego, specializing in stochastic non-linear dynamics, signal detection, Monte Carlo simulation, and high performance computing. He was awarded four patents as a result of his research, and he has published over 30 papers, earning Publication of the Year and Technical Publication Excellence awards. In 2001 Dr. Inchiosa joined BiosGroup, a Santa Fe Institute complexity science spin-off (subsequently NuTech Solutions), applying evolutionary algorithms and swarm-like agent based modeling to problems in business and government. He developed pipeline simulation and optimization engines, served as Principal Investigator researching general and geospatial reasoning under uncertainty, and used agent based models to study global market dynamics and co-evolutionary business strategy optimization. As NuTech's Chief Science Officer, Dr. Inchiosa was involved with Netezza's acquisition of NuTech as part of Netezza's strategy to bring advanced analytics capabilities to data warehouse appliances.

KDD'11, August 21–24, 2011, San Diego, California, USA.
ACM 978-1-4503-0813-7/11/08.

Industry Practice Expo Invited Talk

Applications of Data Mining and Machine Learning in Online Customer Care

Ravi Vijayaraghavan
VP, Research
24/7 Customer Innovation Labs
Bangalore, India
ravi@247customer.com

P V Kannan
Founder & CEO
24/7 Customer
Campbell, CA
pvk@247customer.com

ABSTRACT
With the coming of age of web as a mainstream customer service channel, B2C companies have invested substantial resources in enhancing their web presence. Today customers can interact with a company through channels such as phone, chat, email, social media or web self-service. With the availability of web logs, CRM data and text transcripts these online channels are rich with data and they track several aspects of customer behavior and intent. 24/7 Customer Innovation Labs has developed a series of data mining and statistics driven solutions to improve customer experience in each of these online channels.

This talk will focus on solutions to enhance performance of web chat as a customer service channel. 2 stages of customer life-cycle will be considered – new customer acquisition (or sales) and service of existing customers. In customer acquisition the key objective is to maximize "incremental" revenues via chat. While in customer service the objective is to drive up the quality of customer experience (measured by customer satisfaction surveys or mined customer sentiments) through chat. The solution based on machine learning methods involves:

1. Real-time targeting of the right visitors to chat
2. Predicting customer needs
3. Routing customer to the right customer service agent
4. Mining chat transcripts and Social Media Portals to identify key customer issues and customer sentiments
5. Mining agents' responses for performance improvement
6. Feeding back learning from 4 and 5 to 1 (better targeting)

Real-life case studies will be presented to show how that this closed loop solution can quickly improve key metrics.

Categories and Subject Descriptors
H.2.8 [**Database Management**]: Data Mining.

General Terms
Algorithms, Experimentation, Human Factors, Management, Measurement.

Keywords
Data Mining, Predictive systems, CRM, customer acquisition, online customer support.

KDD'11, August 21–24, 2011, San Diego, California, USA.
ACM 978-1-4503-0813-7/11/08.

Bio
Ravi Vijayaraghavan is a Vice-President at 24/7 Customer Innovation Labs where he leads the Analytics and Data Sciences Organization. His team builds data-driven solutions and predictive systems that enable superior customer acquisition and customer service through online and offline channels. Prior to 24/7 Customer, Ravi was at Ford Motor where he focused on the application of large-scale numerical computations for engineering design. Later, he took up a position in the IT Strategy organization and recently led the development of an analytics driven solution to improve the profitability of Ford of Brazil. Ravi was also a Vice President at Mu Sigma Inc., a Chicago based pure-play analytical services company, where he was responsible for client management. Ravi has several refereed and invited publications in major scientific journals and has presented as an invited speaker at several international conferences. He has served in leadership committees in academic societies such as Sigma Xi. In 2004, he was the recipient of a Henry Ford Technology award - the highest technical recognition at Ford Motor Company. Ravi holds a B.Tech degree from Indian Institute of Technology, Madras, a PhD in Engineering from University of Wisconsin-Madison and an MBA (with high distinction) in Strategy and Finance from Ross School of Business, University of Michigan.

PV Kannan co-founded 24/7 Customer in 2000. 24/7 Customer is the first in the industry to provide services across the entire customer lifecycle. 24/7 Customer provides its services to global 1000 companies, round the clock from locations around the world. PV's vision is to make it simple and easy for companies to acquire and retain their customers, and for customers to seek solutions to their queries, anytime and anywhere in the world. PV has been featured as a thought leader in the field of global sourcing, including Tom Friedman's "The World is Flat", "Outsourcing Thought Leaders" by Booz Allen Hamilton, and in Fortune Magazine. He is also a regular speaker at industry events and has been a panelist in Forbes Conference 2006, Academy of 2006 Annual Meeting of the Academy of Management, to name a few. PV's career in on-line and off-line customer sales and service has resulted in a number of U.S. and international patent filings. Prior to 24/7 Customer, PV Kannan was an officer and VP at Kana Software. In 1995, he founded his first company Business Evolution (BEI) based in Princeton, New Jersey, which was acquired by Kana Software in 1999. Prior to Business Evolution, P V worked in the U.S. and Europe in various leadership roles overseeing IT projects.

Industry Practice Expo Invited Talk

Broad Scale Predictive Modeling and Marketing Optimization in Retail Sales

Dan Steinberg
CEO and Founder
Salford Systems
San Diego, CA
dans@salford-systems.com

Felipe Fernandez Martinez
CEO and Partner
Interfe
Brazil
fferna@me.com

ABSTRACT

The challenge of predicting retail sales on a product-by-product basis throughout a network of retail stores has been researched intensively by applied econometricians and statisticians for decades. The principal tools of analysis have been linear regression with Bayesian inspired adjustments to stabilize demand curve estimates. The scale of such analytics can be challenging as retailers often work with more than 100,000 products (SKUs) and typically operate networks of hundreds of brick and mortar stores. Department and grocery stores are excellent examples but fast food restaurants also require such detailed predictive modeling systems. Depending on the objectives of the company, predictions may be required for blocks of time spanning a week or more, or, as in the case of fast food operators, predictions are required for each 15-minute time interval of the operating day. The authors have modernized industry standard approaches to such predictive modeling by leveraging advanced data mining techniques. These techniques are more adept in detecting nonlinear response and accommodating interactions and automatically sifting through hundreds if not thousands of potential factors influencing sales outcomes. Results show that conventional statistical models miss a substantial fraction of the explainable variance while the new methods dominate in terms of performance and speed of model development.

Accurate prediction is required for reliable planning and logistics, and optimization. Optimization with respect to pricing, promotion and assortment can be asked for relative to a variety of objectives (e.g. revenue, profits) and short term and long-term optimization may result in different decisions being taken. A unique challenge for retailers is the large number of constraints to which complex retail organizations are subject. Contracts and special understandings with valued suppliers severely constrain a retailer's flexibility. For example, certain products may not be promotable (or discounted) in isolation, and others (say from competitors) may not be promoted jointly, and the costs of goods sold may well depend on the quantities contracted. We discuss how we have resolved such challenges via a cycle of prediction and simulation to develop a flexible high-speed system for handling arbitrary constraints, arbitrary objectives, and achieve new levels of predictive accuracy and reliability.

KDD'11, August 21–24, 2011, San Diego, California, USA.
ACM 978-1-4503-0813-7/11/08.

Categories and Subject Descriptors

H.2.8 [**Database Management**]: Data Mining.

General Terms

Algorithms, Experimentation, Management, Measurement.

Keywords

Large-scale data mining, predictive analytics, supply-chain optimization, inventory management, smart pricing.

Bio

Dan Steinberg is CEO and founder of Salford Systems, the developer of the CART® decision tree, TreeNet® gradient boosting, and other influential data mining technology. After earning a PhD in Econmometrics at Harvard, Dan began his professional career at Bell Labs, and then as Assistant Professor of Economics at the University of California, San Diego. His consulting experience at Salford Systems has included complex modeling projects for major banks world wide, including CitiBank, Chase, American Express, Credit Suisse, and has included projects in Europe, Australia, New Zealand, Malaysia, Korea, Japan and Brazil. Dan led the teams that won first place awards in the KDDCup 2000, and the 2002 Duke/TeraData Churn modeling competition, and the teams that won awards in the PAKDD competitions of 2006 and 2007. Dan has published papers in economics, econometrics, and computer science journals, and contributes actively to R & D at Salford.

Felipe Fernandez Martinez obtained a degree in Chemical Engineering at the Universidad Michoacana de San Nicolás de Hidalgo in Morelia, México and then completed an MBA at the Instituto Panamericano de Alta Dirección de Empresas (IPADE) and certificates in corporate finance at ESCP Europe and the Instituto Tecnológico Autonomo de México (ITAM). Felipe worked at Carrefour, the world's 2nd largest retailer, for over 12 years. He was Carrefour's Director of Strategic Projects for Latin America with responsibility for Cost optimization, Procurement, Pricing, Supply Chain, and implementation of new analytics tools for Carrefour, Brazil. Prior to joining Carrefour Latin America, Felipe worked for the Carrefour Group in senior level positions in Paris, Italy and Mexico as Cost Optimization Director. Felipe currently is CEO and partner at Interefe, where he advises retailers on projects turning complexity into competitive advantages on three main areas of expertise: Energy efficiency, Analytics and Cost optimization.

Industry Practice Expo Invited Talk

Knowledge Discovery and Data Mining in Pharmaceutical Cancer Research

Paul Rejto
Director, Computational Biology and
Oncology Research
Pfizer
La Jolla, CA
paul.rejto@pfizer.com

ABSTRACT

Biased and unbiased approaches to develop predictive biomarkers of response to drug treatment will be introduced and their utility demonstrated for cell cycle inhibitors. Opportunities to leverage the growing knowledge of tumors characterized by modern methods to measure DNA and RNA will be shown, including the use of appropriate preclinical models and selection of patients. Furthermore, techniques to identify mechanisms of resistance prior to clinical treatment will be discussed. Prospects for systematic data mining and current barriers to the application of precision medicine in cancer will be reviewed along with potential solutions.

Categories and Subject Descriptors

H.2.8 [**Database Management**]: Data Mining.

General Terms

Algorithms, Experimentation, Human Factors, Measurement.

Keywords

Computational Biology, bio-informatics, oncology, micro-arrays, gene sequencing.

Bio

Dr. Rejto is Director of Computational Biology, Oncology Research Unit, Pfizer La Jolla. His research interests include computational methods to support target discovery and validation, animal models, patient selection, resistance modeling and combination therapy. Paul trained in physical and theoretical chemistry (Harvard A.B. magna cum laude; Stanford Ph.D.; UC Berkeley post-doc) and joined Pfizer La Jolla (Agouron) in 1994. During his career, Paul has developed and applied tools for structure-based drug design, led a team that progressed compounds for the treatment of diabetes into the clinic, and built the computational biology group at Pfizer La Jolla. Coaching youth soccer has taught him about leadership.

KDD'11, August 21–24, 2011, San Diego, California, USA.
ACM 978-1-4503-0813-7/11/08.

Industry Practice Expo Invited Talk

Operational Security Analytics - Doing More with Less

Colleen McCue
GeoEye Analytics
McLean, VA
McCue.Colleen@geoeye.com

ABSTRACT

Why just count crime when you can anticipate, prevent and respond more effectively? Companies in the commercial sector have long understood the importance of being able to anticipate or predict future behavior and demand in order to respond efficiently and effectively. Embracing the promise of predictive analytics, the public safety community is moving from a focus on "what happened," to a system that enables the ability to anticipate future events and effectively deploy resources in front of crime; thereby, changing outcomes. While we have become familiar with the use of advanced analytics in support of fraud detection and prevention, techniques similar to those used to support customer loyalty programs and supply chain management have been used to prevent and solve violent crimes, enhance investigative pace and efficacy, support information-based risk and threat assessment, and deploy public safety resources more efficiently. As public safety agencies increasingly are asked to do more with less, the ability to anticipate crime represents a game changing paradigm shift; enabling information-based tactics, strategy and policy in support of prevention and response. Reporting, collecting and compiling data are necessary but not sufficient to increasing public safety. Ultimately, the ability to anticipate, prevent and respond more effectively will enable us to do more with less and change public safety outcomes.

Categories and Subject Descriptors

H.2.8 [**Database Management**]: Data Mining.

General Terms: Algorithms, Experimentation, Human Factors, Management, Measurement, Security.

Keywords

Data Mining, predictive analytics, counter-terrorism, crime prevention, information-based risk assessment, public safety.

Bio

Dr. Colleen McLaughlin McCue, GeoEye Analytics, brings over 18 years of experience in advanced analytics and the development of actionable solutions to complex information processing problems in the applied public safety and national security environment. Her areas of expertise include the application of data mining and predictive analytics to the analysis of crime and intelligence data, with particular emphasis on deployment strategies, surveillance detection, threat and vulnerability assessment, fraud detection, geospatial predictive analytics, and the behavioral analysis of violent crime. Dr. McCue's experience in the applied law enforcement setting and pioneering work in operationally relevant analytical strategies has been used to support a wide array of national security and public safety clients. Dr. McCue has published her research findings in journals and book chapters, and has authored a book on the use of advanced analytics in the applied public safety environment entitled, Data Mining and Predictive Analysis: Intelligence Gathering and Crime Analysis. Dr. McCue earned her undergraduate degree from the University of Illinois at Chicago and Doctorate in Psychology from Dartmouth College. She completed a five-year postdoctoral fellowship in the Department of Pharmacology & Toxicology at the Medical College of Virginia at the Virginia Commonwealth University.

KDD'11, August 21–24, 2011, San Diego, California, USA.
ACM 978-1-4503-0813-7/11/08.

Industry Practice Expo Invited Talk

Real-Time Risk Control System for CNP (Card Not Present)

Tai Hsu
Principal Scientist
Alibaba Group
Santa Clara, CA
taihsu@us.alibaba-inc.com

ABSTRACT

AliExpress is an online e-commerce platform for wholesale products. Credit card is one of its various payment methods. An online transaction using credit cards is called a "card not present" (CNP) transaction where the physical card has not been swiped into a reader. It's also the major type of credit card frauds causing a great overhead of the online operation, sellers, and buyers. To protect customers on our platform, we developed a real-time credit card fraud detection system, using the machine learning technologies which allows us to achieve a precision of 97%, at a recall of 80%. With the system, we can provide the best online shopping experience for our customers, without the high risk of online transactions which always result a high operational cost. We will briefly share our experience and practice in the expo.

Categories and Subject Descriptors

H.2.8 [**Database Management**]: Data Mining.

General Terms

Algorithms, Experimentation, Human Factors, Measurement.

Keywords

Data Mining in e-commerce, fraud detection, financial risk modeling.

Bio

Dr. Tai Hsu's research/specialized areas cover algorithm, artificial intelligence, chemistry, computational biology, cybernetics, data mining, machine learning, robotics, and supercomputing. His work for AliExpress.com significantly reduced the online risk, competitive with Cybersource's. His work in machine 3D vision won the best paper award (European Meeting in on Cybernetics and Systems Research, 2008 and 2006). His research in computational biology won the NLM award (National Library of Medicine, of National Institute of Health, 2001). His work in quantum chemistry won the best paper award (Journal of Chinese Chemical Society, Taiwan). He was named the distinguished employee (2001) of Providian Financial Corporation. Tai is currently a principal scientist of Alibaba Group, as well as the R&D director of Northwestern Polytechnic University. Prior to Alibaba, he worked for several Fortune 500 companies in San Francisco Bay Area. He holds a Ph.D. in CS from Oregon State University, an MBA from Northwestern Polytechnic University, a B.A. in CS plus a minor in math from Wartburg College, and a B.S. in chemistry from National Taiwan University.

KDD'11, August 21–24, 2011, San Diego, California, USA.
ACM 978-1-4503-0813-7/11/08.

Industry Practice Expo Invited Talk

The Power of Analysis and Data

David Norton
Chief Marketing Officer
Caesar's Entertainment
Las Vegas, NV
dnorton@caesars.com

ABSTRACT

Caesars Entertainment, the largest provider of branded casino entertainment, captures a wealth of data for 40 million+ customers through its Total Rewards program. In-depth data analysis has helped Caesars weather the economic downturn by prioritizing marketing spend, expense savings targets and identifying new revenue opportunities. This talk will describe how closed-loop marketing, state-of-the-art user segmentation, and ongoing experimentation via test and control groups have enabled Caesars Entertainment to achieve all-time high customer satisfaction scores and outperform the competition in a challenging economic climate. The lessons learned are generic and apply across multiple industries. Insights will also be provided on the next wave of challenges to be answered analytically.

Categories and Subject Descriptors

H.2.8 [**Database Management**]: Data Mining.

General Terms

Algorithms, Experimentation, Human Factors, Management, Measurement.

Keywords

Large-scale data mining, predictive analytics, market segmentation, revenue optimization.

Bio

David Norton is the Senior Vice President and Chief Marketing Officer at Caesars Entertainment, which operates more than 40 casinos nationwide and 10 others worldwide and has been recognized for its outstanding marketing practices by the Wall St. Journal, Info Week and CIO Magazine. HET's brands include Caesars, Horseshoe, Harrah's, World Series of Poker, Paris, Flamingo and several others. Norton is responsible for the company's direct marketing strategy, Brand Management, Promotions, Alliances, Research, VIP marketing, revenue management, the Total Rewards loyalty program, Internet marketing, multi-cultural marketing, mobile initiatives, Retail, Entertainment, Sales and Travel Services. Prior to joining Harrah's in October of 1998, Norton worked in the credit card industry with American Express, Household International and MBNA. He has a B.S. in Finance from Boston College, an MBA from Loyola College and a Masters in Management of Technology from the University of Pennsylvania and the Wharton School.

KDD'11, August 21–24, 2011, San Diego, California, USA.
ACM 978-1-4503-0813-7/11/08.

Industry Practice Expo Invited Talk

The Practitioner's Viewpoint to Data Mining – Key Lessons Learned in the Trenches and Case Studies

Richard Boire
Co-founder
Boire Filler Group
Canada
RichB@boirefillergroup.com

ABSTRACT

In many data mining exercises, we see information that appears on the surface to demonstrate a particular conclusion. But closer examination of the data reveals that these results are indeed misleading. In this session, we will examine this notion of misleading results in three areas:

- **Statistical Issues**
  Statistical issues such as multicollinearity and outliers can impact results dramatically. We will first outline how these statistical issues can provide misleading results. At the same time, we will demonstrate how the data mining practitioner overcomes these issues through data analysis approaches that provide both more meaningful and non-misleading results to the business community.
- **Overstating of Results**
  From a business standpoint, we will also look at results that appear to be too good to be true. In other words, there appears to be some overstating of results within a given data mining solution. Initially, we will discuss how to identify these situations. Secondly, we will outline what causes this overstatement of results and detail our approach on how we would overcome this predicament.
- **Overfitting**
  Another topic for discussion is overfitting of results. This is particularly the case when building predictive models. In this section of the seminar, we will define what overfitting is and why it is becoming more relevant for understanding by the business community. Once again, analytical approaches will be discussed in terms of how to best handle this issue.

We present two case studies that demonstrate how our principled 4-step approach can be used to solve challenging data mining problems. These 4 steps are as follows:

- How to identify the problem
- How we construct the right data environment to conduct our analytics
- What kind of analytics are employed which include techniques such as *correlation analysis*, *EDA reports*, *logistic regression*, and *gains charts*. More importantly, we discuss how to interpret the output in terms of the actual impact to the business (i.e. increased response rate and ultimately increased ROI.)
- How do we apply the learning to a future initiative and what were the actual results

KDD'11, August 21–24, 2011, San Diego, California, USA.
ACM 978-1-4503-0813-7/11/08.

Categories and Subject Descriptors

H.2.8 [**Database Management**]: Data Mining.

General Terms

Algorithms, Experimentation, Human Factors, Management, Measurement.

Keywords

Data mining, predictive analytics, financial services, ROI optimization, cross-sell and up-sell marketing, segmentation.

Bio

Richard Boire's experience in database marketing and predictive analytics dates back to 1983, when he received an MBA from Concordia University in Finance and Statistics. His initial experience at organizations such as Reader's Digest and American Express allowed him to become a pioneer in the application of predictive modeling technology for all direct marketing programs. Richard formed his own consulting company in 1994 which is now called the Boire Filler Group, a Canadian leader in offering analytical and database services. Richard is a recognized authority and is among the top five experts in this field in Canada. This expertise has evolved into international speaking assignments and workshop seminars in the U.S., England, Eastern Europe, and Southeast Asia. Within Canada, he gives seminars on segmentation and predictive analytics for a variety of marketing organizations. His written articles have appeared in numerous Canadian publications such as Direct Marketing News, Strategy Magazine, and Marketing Magazine. He has taught applied statistics, data mining and database marketing at a variety of institutions across Canada which include University of Toronto, George Brown College, Seneca College, etc. Richard is currently Chair at the CMA's Customer Insight and Analytics Committee and currently sits on the CMA's Board of Directors. He has chaired numerous full day conferences on behalf of the CMA - the 2000 Database and Technology Seminar as well as the 2002 Database and Technology Seminar and the first-ever Customer Profitability Conference in 2005. He has co-authored white papers on the following topics: *'Best Practices in Data Mining'* as well as *'Customer Profitability: The State of Evolution among Canadian Companies'*.

Industry Practice Expo Invited Talk

Thriving as a Data Miner in the Real World

John F. Elder, IV
Elder Research, Inc.
Charlottesville, VA
elder@dataminignlab.com

ABSTRACT

Meaningful work is a deep human need. We all yearn to contribute to something greater than ourselves, be listened to, and work alongside friendly peers. Data mining consulting is a powerful way to use technical skills and gain these great side benefits. The power of analytics and its high return on investment makes one's expertise welcome virtually everywhere. And the variety of projects and domains encountered leads to continual learning as new problems are met and solved. Teaching and writing are possible, and there is great satisfaction in seeing one's work actually implemented and used, potentially touching millions.

Still, in industry, one has the joy and hazards of working closely with other humans, where final success can depend as much on others as oneself, and on social as well as technical issues. In my experience, business risk strongly outweighs technical risk in whether a solution is used. I will share some hard-won lessons learned on how to best succeed, both technically and socially, in the results-oriented world of industry.

Categories and Subject Descriptors

H.2.8 [**Database Management**]: Data Mining.

General Terms

Algorithms, Experimentation, Human Factors, Management, Measurement.

Keywords

Data Mining, Predictive systems, CRM, e-commerce, bio-informatics.

Bio

Dr. John Elder heads a data mining consulting team with offices in Charlottesville Virginia, and Washington, DC (www.datamininglab.com). Founded in 1995, Elder Research, Inc. focuses on investment, commercial and security applications of advanced analytics, including text mining, stock selection, image recognition, process optimization, cross-selling, biometrics, drug efficacy, credit scoring, market timing, and fraud detection.

John obtained a BS and MEE in Electrical Engineering from Rice University, and a PhD in Systems Engineering from the University of Virginia, where he's an adjunct professor teaching Optimization or Data Mining. Prior to 15 years at ERI, he spent 5 years in aerospace defense consulting, 4 heading research at an investment management firm, and 2 in Rice University's Computational & Applied Mathematics department.

Dr. Elder has authored innovative data mining tools, is a frequent keynote speaker, and was co-chair of the 2009 Knowledge Discovery and Data Mining conference, in Paris. John's courses on analysis techniques -- taught at dozens of universities, companies, and government labs -- are noted for their clarity and effectiveness. Dr. Elder was honored to serve for 5 years on a panel appointed by the President to guide technology for National Security. His book with Bob Nisbet and Gary Miner, Handbook of Statistical Analysis & Data Mining Applications, won the PROSE award for Mathematics in 2009. His book with Giovanni Seni, Ensemble Methods in Data Mining: Improving Accuracy through Combining Predictions, was published in February 2010.

John is a follower of Christ and the proud father of 5.

KDD'11, August 21–24, 2011, San Diego, California, USA.
ACM 978-1-4503-0813-7/11/08.

2D-Interval Predictions for Time Series*

Luis Torgo
LIAAD/INESC Porto LA - FC, University of Porto
Rua Campo Alegre, 1021/1055
4169-007 Porto, Portugal
ltorgo@dcc.fc.up.pt

Orlando Ohashi†
LIAAD/INESC Porto LA
Rua Dr. Roberto Frias, 378
4200-465 Porto, Portugal
ohashijr@dcc.fc.up.pt

ABSTRACT

Research on time series forecasting is mostly focused on point predictions - models are obtained to estimate the expected value of the target variable for a certain point in future. However, for several relevant applications this type of forecasts has limited utility (e.g. costumer wallet value estimation, wind and electricity power production, control of water quality, etc.). For these domains it is frequently more important to be able to forecast a range of plausible future values of the target variable. A typical example is wind power production, where it is of high relevance to predict the future wind variability in order to ensure that supply and demand are balanced. This type of predictions will allow timely actions to be taken in order to cope with the expected values of the target variable on a certain future time horizon. In this paper we study this type of predictions - the prediction of a range of expected values for a future time interval. We describe some possible approaches to this task and propose an alternative procedure that our extensive experiments on both artificial and real world domains show to have clear advantages.

Categories and Subject Descriptors

H.4 [**Information Systems Applications**]: Miscellaneous

General Terms

Algorithms

Keywords

Time Series, Forecasting, Prediction

*This work is partially supported by FEDER funds through COMPETE program and by FCT national funds in the context of the project PTDC/EIA/68322/2006.

†The work of Orlando Ohashi is supported by the PhD grant SFRH/BD/61795/2009 from FCT.

KDD'11, August 21–24, 2011, San Diego, California, USA.

1. INTRODUCTION

Time series forecasting is a key modeling technique in many real world applications. One of the goals of developing time series models is to obtain predictions of the future values of the series. The most common form of predictions are the so-called point predictions - at time t try to forecast the value of the series for time $t+h$, where h is the forecasting horizon. However, some applications require a different type of forecasts. Namely, users may be interested in obtaining an interval of plausible values for time $t+h$. Moreover, other applications may even require this type of interval of values for a certain future interval of time $[t+h, t+h+k]$. We will call this latter type of predictions 2D-interval predictions where the goal is to forecast the expected interval of values of the time series for a certain future time interval. How to handle these 2D-interval predictions is the subject of this paper. Figure 1 briefly describes the differences between these three types of forecasts.

Existing work on time series forecasting essentially focus on (i) point predictions (e.g. [6]), (ii) on predicting an interval where the future value is expected to be with a certain probability (e.g. [5]), or even (iii) on generalizing the latter to density forecasts [16]. To the best of our knowledge there is no established method for forecasting an interval of values for an interval of time. Addressing this limitation is the main goal of this paper. The lack of a method to handle these problems is rather surprising given the amount of relevant applications that could benefit from this type of predictions. For instance, any application requiring some form of production planning for a certain demand scenario, will find this type of predictions of high utility. This includes areas like manufacturing in general, energy production, water distribution, etc. For example, in wind power production it is important to predict the future wind variability in order to ensure that supply and demand are balanced [3, 18]. In power production it is common to place bids for the future production. In this context, the forecast of the future wind variability must be accurate not to receive a penalty from any deviation between production and demand. To make optimal decisions, a model that is able to predict the quantiles of the distribution gives much more information than single point predictors [3]. Similar problems are faced in electricity markets, where it is more important to predict the interval of demand than a single value [17]. In inventory management, over-production may lead to inventory costs while under-production may originate unsatisfied demand and lost profits [4]. Other relevant application areas include customer wallet estimation [14] or computer network

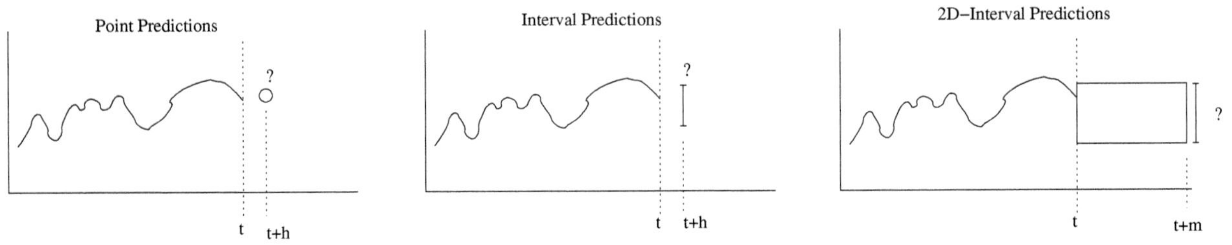

Figure 1: Three types of time series prediction tasks.

traffic analysis [21]. Several investment-related applications (e.g. financial markets) will also find this type of forecasts of great use.

From a theoretical perspective we are talking about forecasting the distribution of the values of the target time series variable for a future time window. The key difference from existing work on density forecasting (e.g. [16]) is the fact that we want to estimate a density for a time interval and not for a single point in time. The applicability to real world scenarios motivates this difference. In this work we restrict this general scenario to the prediction of some descriptive statistics of this distribution. Namely, we will focus on forecasting a kind of interval of "normality" of the values of the series for a certain future time interval. We will represent this interval of normality by the 1st and 3rd quartiles of the variable distribution, though our proposal could be applied to any quantile.

The main contributions of our work are: (1) to increase the awareness of the data mining community to a high-impact task that was not addressed before; and (2) to propose a general method for addressing this class of time series forecasting problems. In the context of the presentation of our proposal we describe an extensive set of experiments that we have carried out to demonstrate the validity of our approach under a wide range of scenarios.

2. PREDICTING 2D-INTERVALS

A 2D-interval is a range where the values of the time series are expected to be included in a future time window with high probability (c.f. Figure 1). The goal of this concept is to provide the user with a plausible range of values of the time series in this future period. It is thus a form of summary statistic of the unknown future distribution of the values of the series for the target forecasting horizon. We will address this general problem by simplifying it into predicting the 1st and 3rd quartiles of this unknown distribution. These two statistics provide us with an interval where a significant number of the values should be contained (assuming a near-normal distribution of the values of the target variable).

2.1 Possible Approaches to the Problem

As mentioned before, we are not aware of any existing approach to the 2D-interval prediction problem. Nevertheless, we can try to apply the existing time series forecasting techniques to obtain this type of forecasts.

Point estimates can be iterated to obtain predictions for more than one point in the future (known as iterated predictions e.g. [6]). At time t we obtain a prediction for time $t+1$. This prediction can be incorporated into the training data available to the model as if it was true, and a new step ahead prediction can be obtained, which in effect would correspond to a prediction for time $t+2$. These iterations can continue until we get a point prediction for all the forecasting interval. Using these predictions we can obtain the statistics we want to have a 2D-interval forecast. This is a simple approach that can be applied to any existing time series modeling technique. The main drawback of this strategy is that by incorporating the one-step ahead predictions into the training data we are potentially amplifying the prediction errors of the models.

Another plausible approach to our problem is to decompose it into several prediction tasks. If we want a 2D-interval for a time window of k steps in the future, then we can transform this into k prediction tasks with each being addressed by a different model designed to obtain a point prediction for $t+i$, where $i \in [1,k]$. Given these k models, to obtain a 2D-interval forecast at time t we use the k models predictions and calculate the necessary statistics to obtain the interval. The main drawback of this approach is the computational cost of obtaining k different models. This may be a critical issue with high-frequency data as it is often the case in time series problems.

Finally, we will also consider a naive approach as a kind of baseline method. A 2D-interval forecast at time t for the interval $[t+1, t+k]$ can be obtained by using the statistics calculated with the known values of the series in the interval $[t-k, t]$. This can be regarded as a kind of random walk approach to our problem and we will expect other alternatives to clearly outperform this baseline method.

2.2 Our Proposal

In order to obtain 2D-interval predictions we propose to directly forecast some summary statistics of the distribution of the time series values for the target future time window. Let Q_α^k and Q_β^k be the α and β unknown quantiles of the time series values for a future time window of length k, respectively. These two values establish an interval where $|\beta - \alpha| \times 100\%$ of the series values are supposed to be included. Assuming a near normal distribution of the values of the target variable the interval between the 1st and 3rd quartiles ($Q_{0.25}$ and $Q_{0.75}$) will contain roughly 50% of the values of the series. We will use the predicted values for these two distribution statistics as the source for obtaining 2D-interval predictions. This means that we will directly forecast these quantile statistics instead of calculating them from predictions of the target time series. Our proposal is thus to define two prediction problems $Q_\alpha^k = f(v_1, \cdots, v_a)$ and $Q_\beta^k = f(v_1, \cdots, v_a)$, where $v_1, \cdots, v_a$ are a set of descriptor variables, and Q_α^k (Q_β^k) is the α (β) quantile of the time series variable for the next k time points, i.e. the estimated quantile for the time interval $[t, t+k]$. In order to be able to obtain models to forecast these quantiles we need to have a set of training data where these values are known. Thus for "preparing" the training sample at time t we will need information on both the selected predictor variables but also on the target time series values in the period $[t+1, t+k]$, where k is the time length of the target 2D-intervals.

The methods presented in Section 2.1 are all based on predicting the value of the target time series for a future time interval. This is done either by iterated predictions or by obtaining several different models. Either way it is based on these predictions that we calculate the summary statistics to obtain the 2D-intervals. In our approach we directly predict these statistics. We claim that this is an easier prediction task as quantile statistics have a distribution that is smoother than the original variables from which they are calculated. In effect, quantiles are known to be robust to a few extreme values, thus smoothing-out these variations on the original time series. This means that the distribution of the quantile variables that we use as targets is clearly more "well behaved" than the distribution of the original series. We expect this to bring an advantage to our proposal, because it should simplify the task of obtaining 2D-intervals. The experiments described in Section 3 are designed to test this hypothesis.

The choice of the predictor variables $v_1, \cdots, v_a$ is not part of our proposal. They should be selected with the goal of trying to optimize the performance of the selected modeling tool in the task of forecasting the target variable. This decision is not different from what is necessary on any other time series prediction task. Our proposal only changes the target variable. In our experiments we will include as predictors recent past values of the time series and also past values of some distribution statistics as we will see in Section 3.

3. EXPERIMENTAL EVALUATION

In this section we evaluate our proposed method for obtaining 2D-interval predictions under a large set of experimental setups. The main goal of these experiments is to check the validity of the hypothesis that directly predicting the quantile statistics is a better method of obtaining intervals of variation of a time series for a future time window. All code, data and extra results not fitting here are provided in a web page[1] associated with this paper, to ensure that our work is replicable.

3.1 Experimental methodology

3.1.1 Models

We have tried to select a wide range of modeling approaches to test our method. The idea is to confirm its validity independently of the technique used to forecast the Q_p^k quantiles. All the used tools are freely available in the R software environment [15], which ensures easy replication of our work. The following is a list of the methods used in our experiments:

Random Walk (RW) - a simple baseline method that uses the quantiles estimated with the last k time series values as predictions for the quantiles of the next k time points;

Regression Trees (RT) - a regression tree (e.g. [1]) based on the R package `rpart` [19]. In our experiments we have used an interface to the `rpart` function provided in package `DMwR` [20] and have tried 4 different variants by using the parameter `se` that controls the level of pruning with values $0, 0.5, 1$ and 1.5.

Support Vector Machines (SVM) - an implementation of SVMs (e.g. [7]) available in the R package `e1071` [8]. We have tried 20 variants by using the parameter *cost* with the values $1, 5, 10, 50, 100$ and the parameter *gamma* with the values $0.001, 0.01, 0.05$ and 0.1.

Random Forest (RF) - an implementation of random forests [2] available in the R package `randomForest` [11]. We have used 3 variants of the parameter *ntree* with the values $500, 1000$ and 1500.

Quantile Regression Forests (QRF) - a random forest variant [12] designed to optimize the prediction of quantiles. We have used the implementation of these models available in the R package `quantregForest` [13]. We have tried 3 variants of the parameter *ntree* with the values $500, 1000$ and 1500.

3.1.2 Evaluation Metrics

There is an extensive literature on evaluation metrics for single point prediction models. Most measures compare the true and predicted values and eventually contrast the performance of the model being evaluated against some baseline. Our prediction task is different as we have mentioned before. We are addressing the prediction of a 2D-interval by means of the 1st and 3rd quartiles, which means there are some similarities with the goals of quantile regression [10]. However, in quantile regression the goal is to obtain point predictions of the quantiles. The evaluation of quantile regression models is usually carried out with the help of Equation 1. It can be easily shown that the value of $L_\alpha(y, \hat{y})$ is optimized by predicting the quantile Q_α (i.e. $\hat{y} = Q_\alpha$).

$$L_\alpha(y, \hat{y}) = \begin{cases} \alpha \cdot (y - \hat{y}) & \text{if} y \geq \hat{y} \\ (1-\alpha) \cdot (\hat{y} - y) & \text{otherwise} \end{cases} \quad (1)$$

In this context, if we want to estimate the values of $Q_{0.25}$ and $Q_{0.75}$ for a certain period of time k we can evaluate the predictions of our models ($\hat{Q}^k_{0.25}$ and $\hat{Q}^k_{0.75}$) using Equation 1, given the true target variable values $y_{t+1}, \cdots, y_{t+k}$. Moreover, if we are given a test set we can calculate the total quantile error (TQE) of our 2D-interval predictions as follows,

$$TQE = \sum_{i=1}^{n} \left[\sum_{j=i}^{i+k} L_{0.25}(y_j, \hat{Q}^k_{0.25,i}) + \sum_{j=i}^{i+k} L_{0.75}(y_j, \hat{Q}^k_{0.75,i}) \right] \quad (2)$$

where $\hat{Q}^k_{\alpha,t}$ is the α quantile prediction for the future k-length interval starting at time t.

We have also compared our alternative models using the mean absolute quantile (MAQ) deviation of the model predictions, i.e.

$$MAQ = \frac{1}{2n} \left[\sum_{i=1}^{n} |Q^k_{0.25,i} - \hat{Q}^k_{0.25,i}| + |Q^k_{0.75,i} - \hat{Q}^k_{0.75,i}| \right] \quad (3)$$

[1] `http://www.dcc.fc.up.pt/~ltorgo/KDD11`

Table 1: Benefit matrix.

	low	*normal*	*high*
$\hat{low}$	2	-1	-2
$\hat{normal}$	-1	1	-1
$\hat{high}$	-2	-1	2

This evaluation metric can be easily obtained by calculating the observed 2D-interval quantiles and comparing these with the predictions of our models. This statistic will measure the average absolute error of our quantile predictions when compared to the true observed quantiles.

The real world applications that we target with this proposal of 2D-interval predictions have some particularities that are not completely captured by the statistics of Equations 2 and 3. Namely, there are usually costs and benefits associated with the predictions of the models. In effect, the predicted intervals are frequently used to carry out some actions (e.g. production planning) that may result in costs or benefits depending on the accuracy of the predictions. We will also evaluate the 2D-interval predictions taking these factors into account. The predicted intervals divide the values in three classes: unusually high or low values, and normal values that are within the intervals. This means that given the predictions $\hat{Q}^k_{0.25}$ and $\hat{Q}^k_{0.75}$ we can discretize the series values into these three classes. Accordingly, we can look at the observed values in the k-length interval and calculate the real $Q^k_{0.25}$ and $Q^k_{0.75}$ values. Using these values we can calculate the true class labels of each value in the k period. Elkan [9] has established the theoretical grounds for cost-sensitive learning. The proposed framework is based on the concept of benefit matrix. This matrix sets the benefits of all accurate predictions, as well as the costs (negative benefits) of the errors. We will also use this setup to evaluate the 2D-interval predictions of our models. We discretize the continuous values of the target time series using the method described above and then calculate the *Utility* of the predictions as the total sum of benefits using the matrix in Table 1.

3.2 Experiments with Artificial Data

The first set of experiments that we will describe involves the use of artificially created data sets. The goal was to test our hypothesis on a diverse range of time series with different dynamic regimes. Figure 2 shows the seven artificial time series we have generated and used in our experiments, each with 3000 values[2]. The gray lines on each graph try to describe the type of regimes in terms of trend and variability that have guided the generation process. As you can observe these series have rather different dynamic regimes in terms of these two important properties.

We have applied the models described in Section 3.1.1 to these 7 problems, using the 3 alternative methods for obtaining 2D-intervals. Our goal is to check which is the best method for obtaining this type of predictions: (i) iterating the model over the k window; (ii) obtaining k different models; or (iii) our proposed method of predicting directly the distribution statistics defining the intervals. For each experimental setup, we have estimated the values of the 3 evaluation metrics (*TQE*, *MAQ* and *Utility*) described in Section 3.1.2 using a Monte Carlo simulation. Namely, we have randomly selected 10 time points within each data set. For each of these 10 points we have used the previous 365 values of the series to obtain the models that were then used to make 2D-interval predictions for the next 90 points using a sliding window approach. At each of these 90 prediction points the goal was to estimate the 2D-interval for a future time window of 10, 20 and 30 time points. The results we present for these 3 different values of k (the time length of the 2D-intervals) are averages over these test sets with 90 points, on the 10 Monte Carlo repetitions (i.e. at randomly selected points of the full time series).

The goal for all alternatives is to obtain an estimate of the 1st and 3rd quartiles for the target time intervals ($k = 10, 20$ and 30). However, depending on the approach followed, these estimates are obtained using a different method as explained in Section 2. Still, all alternatives will use the same predictor variables that were selected with the goal of trying to provide useful information on the recent dynamics of the time series and also past values of k-length descriptive statistics. The used prediction tasks are described by the following general equation,

$$TGT = f(Y_{t-1}, \cdots, Y_{t-10}, Q^{-k}_{0.25,t}, Q^{-k}_{0.75,t}, \bar{Y}^{-k}, \sigma^{-k}_Y) \quad (4)$$

where $Q^{-k}_{\alpha,t}$ is the value of the α quantile calculated using the past k values of the series at time t, $\bar{Y}^{-k}$ is the average time series value on the same past window, σ^{-k}_Y the respective standard deviation, and $Y_{t-1}, \cdots, Y_{t-10}$ are the last 10 values of the series. The target variable (TGT) will be different depending on the approaches. For the iterated predictions this will be the next value of the series, Y_{t+1}. For the k models the targets will be Y_{t+i} where $i \in [1, k]$ for each of the k models. For our proposal there will be two models, one predicting the 1st quartile on the 2D-interval, $Q^k_{0.25,t}$, and the other the 3rd quartile, $Q^k_{0.75,t}$.

All model variants were given exactly the same data in the context of the Monte Carlo simulation, with the exception of the target variable. Given the large set of experimental setups (3 metrics, 7 problems, 3 values for k) we can not afford to present all results given the space restrictions applicable. Nevertheless, we can confirm that in all setups we have observed a similar pattern of results/conclusions. The full experimental results can be checked at the Web page associated with the paper.

Figure 3 shows the results for 3 different setups. We have selected one graph for each series, metric and interval length. The graph on the left shows the TQE scores of all model variants on the first time series when predicting a 2D-interval of length 10. The results of the models are grouped in three batches, one for each different approach we are comparing: the iterated approach ("iterated" on the graphs), the use of several models ("k-models" on the graphs), and our proposal of directly predicting the quantiles ("quantiles" on the graphs). For each of these batches we show the results of all model variants described before. A vertical dashed line marks the best score on each graph and the result of the baseline *RW* model is given as a sub-title of the graphs. The middle graph shows the same type of results this time for the MAQ metric, 4th time series and $k = 20$, while the graph on the right presents the results in terms of *Utility* on the 7th series for $k = 30$. Note that while for the first two metrics lower scores are better, for utility it is the opposite.

[2]The R code used to generate the data sets as well as the data sets themselves, are available at the paper web page.

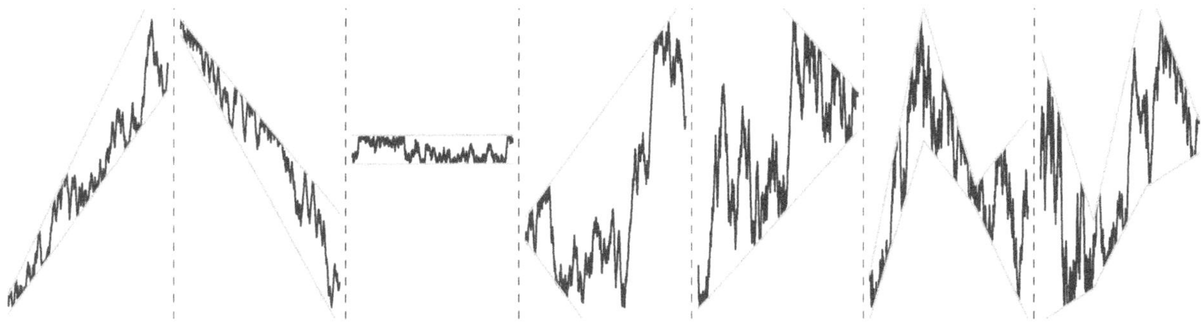

Figure 2: The seven artificial times series problems.

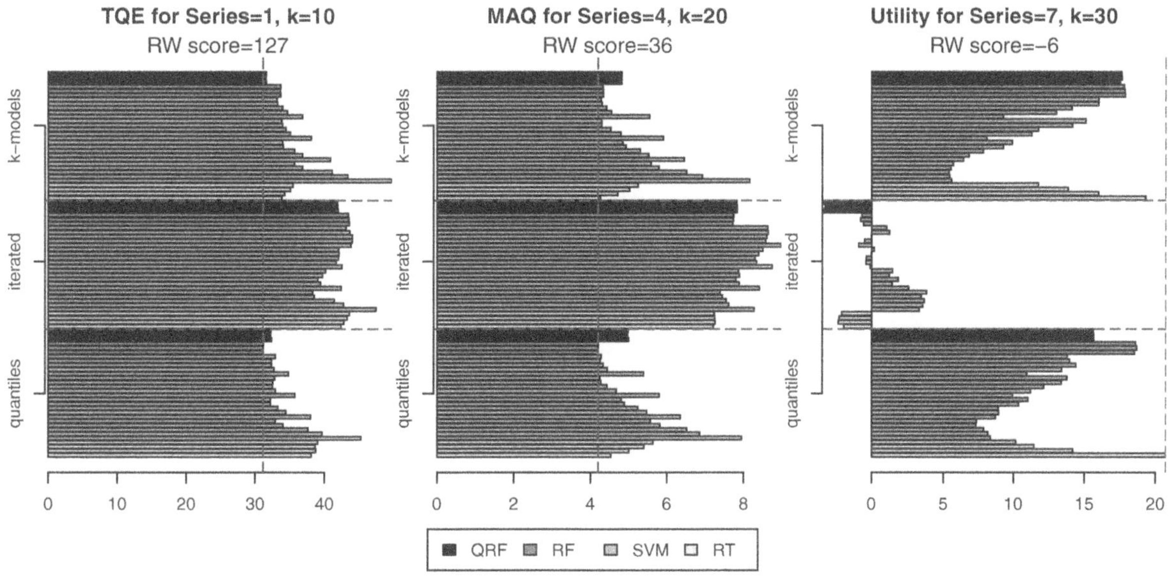

Figure 3: The results on three different experimental setups for the artificial time series.

We have observed that the "k-models" and "quantiles" approaches have rather similar results on these problems. Still, when there is some slight difference this is more frequently favorable to our approach. The "iterated" approach on the contrary is most of the times the worst in terms of scores, although all models typically outperform the baseline *RW* model, as expected. This pattern of results is similar over all experimental setups we have tried with these 7 problems. These results show that the prediction accuracy of our approach is highly competitive with the existing alternatives. Moreover, these scores are obtained with a significant advantage in terms of computational efficiency. In effect, while our approach requires two models to be obtained (one for each quantile), the "k-models" approach requires as many models as the length of the interval, i.e. k models. This is a significant difference as shown in Figure 4. This figure shows the ratio between computation time of "k-models" over our approach. We can observe that, depending on the size of the interval, the "k-models" approach can take from 5 to 30 times more time to be obtained. On dynamic environments where new data is constantly being collected, eventually requiring new models to be obtained, this margin can be rather significant. We do not show the results for the "iterated" approach as they are essentially similar to our proposal.

Summarizing, the experiments on these artificial problems show that our proposal is able to achieve a rather competitive prediction accuracy with a significantly smaller computational cost.

3.3 Experiments with Real World Data

The first real world application of 2D-intervals we describe is related with water quality control in the distribution network of the metropolitan region of Porto, Portugal (serving roughly 1 million people). The company (AdDP) that manages this network has legal limits that must not be reached for several water quality parameters that are monitored. With the goal of avoiding the danger of crossing these limits (and paying the respective high fines) the company internally establishes tighter limits that if broken generate an alarm that leads to several control actions over the network. These actions have associated costs and thus having these internal limits too tight will lead to a high operational cost of the network. However, having wider internal limits, possibly too near the legal ones, will increase the risk of when the alarms are fired being too late for the control actions to have any effect to avoid breaking the legal limits. This means that establishing the intervals of acceptable (normal) values of a large set of water quality parameters is a problem

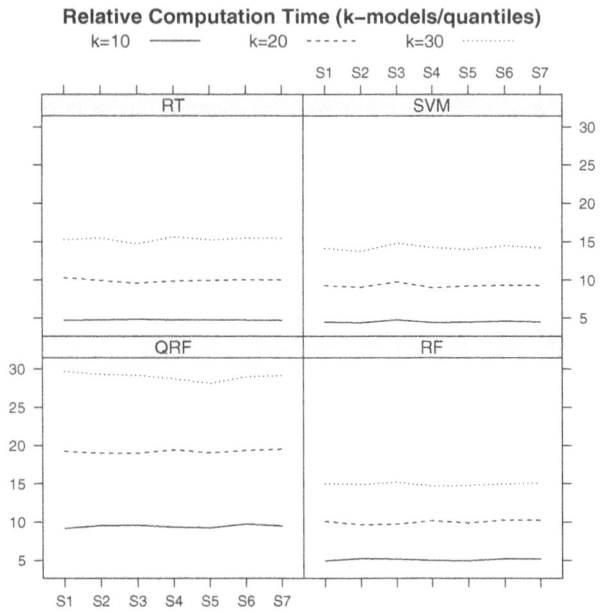

Figure 4: The relative computation times of "k-models" vs "quantiles" on the 7 artificial time series.

with high socio-economical impact for the company and the region. The company is aware of the fact that these intervals that establish a range of normality for each parameter change along the year as the rivers from where the water is collected are very dynamic and change a lot during the seasons of the year. This means that this notion of normal parameter values is dynamic, though the legal limits are fixed.

The AdDP company has provided us daily data concerning a large set of water quality parameters along several years (2000 till 2008). In this paper we focus on the task of trying to forecast a 2D-interval of normal values for a small set of parameters (*pH*, *iron*, *turbidity* and *aluminium*) using this data set. This is a task similar to the ones described in Section 3.3. The interval of "normal" values can again be approximated by the expected 1st and 3rd quartiles on a future time window, i.e. a 2D-interval. We have used exactly the same prediction tasks and predictors as in the artificial problems (c.f. Equation 4). However, following the company requirements, we have only applied our method for a 2D-interval of 30 days (i.e. $k = 30$).

The results we report are again estimates of the 3 evaluation statistics using 10 repetitions of a Monte Carlo simulation. We have used the previous 365 values of each of the four time series and tested the models along a 90 days window, again using a sliding window approach.

Figure 5 shows the results for 3 different setups using the same schema as before. On the left graph we have the TQE scores for the *Iron* time series. The central graph illustrates the results in terms of MAQ for the *pH* parameter, while the right-most graph shows the *Utility* results for *Turbidity*. The overall pattern is similar to the results on the artificial problems. The "iterated" approach is clearly the worst method, while our approach and "k-models" get similar scores. Still, compared to the results on the artificial data, we observe a more marked advantage of our proposal. The exception is the QRF model variants where the "k-models" approach achieves better results whilst not the best overall scores.

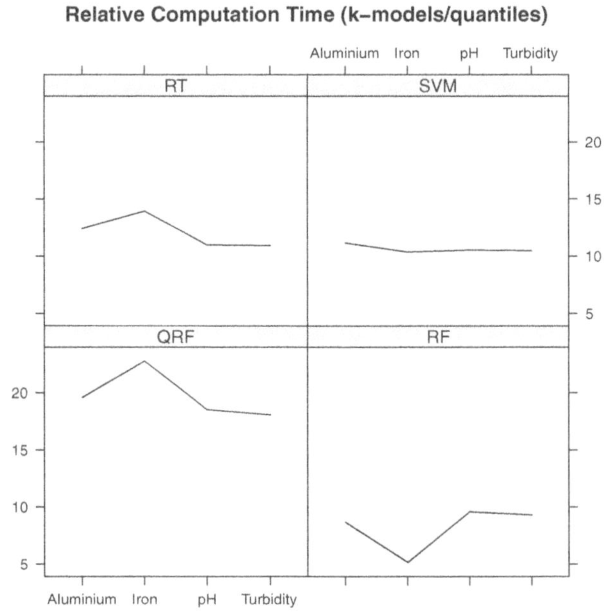

Figure 6: The relative computation times of "k-models" vs "quantiles" on the water quality control problem with $k = 30$.

In terms of computation times the results are show in Figure 6. Again we observe a significant overhead of the "k-models" approach when compared to our proposal.

The second real world problem concerns again a water distribution network, this time in the south of Spain. The problem here is related to production planning in order to face the varying demand in terms of water consumption. We have hourly data concerning the water consumption in a residential area of the water distribution network from Jan, 2005 till Apr, 2005. Our goal is to forecast a 2D-interval for the next 12 and 24 hours (values of k). The distribution of the water demand has very marked seasonal properties not only along the different periods of the day, but also across similar weekdays. Because of this we use a slightly different approach in terms of predictors with the goal of providing the models with information on this weekly seasonal effects. For $k = 12$ we have used the last 6 values of the demand (last 6 hours), the same information as on previous problems regards the quartiles, mean and standard deviation on the past k values, but also the quartiles that we want to forecast measured in the previous week (i.e. on the same weekday/hour) to provide information on this observed weekly seasonality. In the case of $k = 24$ we have increased the number of past values of the series from 6 to 12, while the other predictors stayed the same.

Regards the experiments we have used again 10 random repetitions of a Monte Carlo simulation this time with a training window of 1344 values (8 weeks) and a test window of 336 values (2 weeks), for which predictions were obtained using a sliding window approach. The size of the 2D-intervals (k) was set to 12 and 24 hours.

The results of 3 different setups of these experiments are

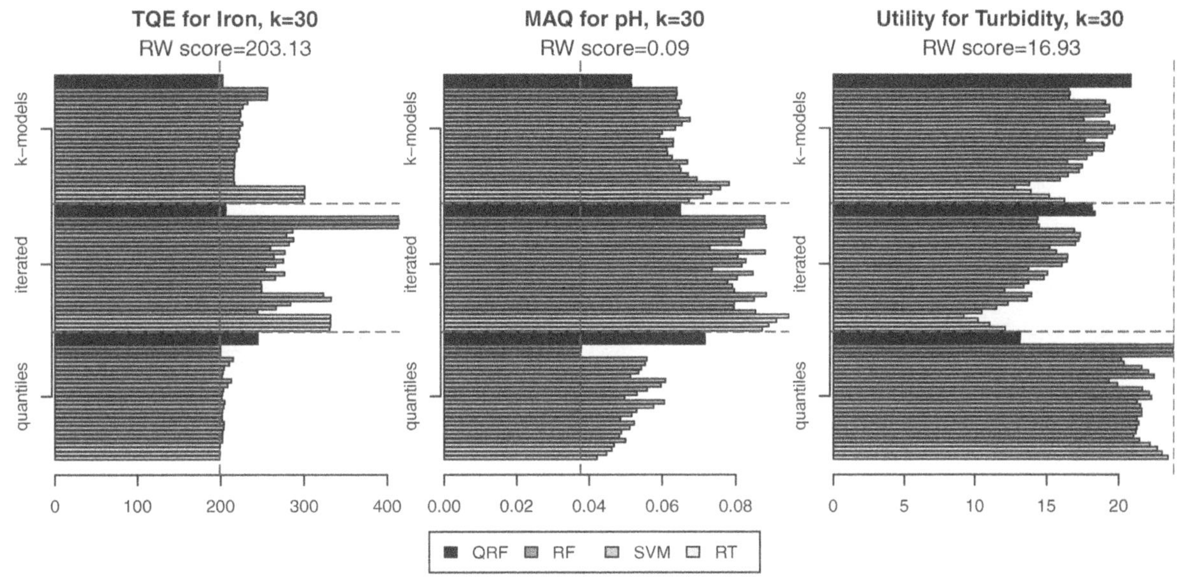

Figure 5: The results on the water quality control problem.

show in Figure 7. The pattern of results is similar to the one observed in the water quality problems. Both "k-models" and our approach have similar results with a slight advantage of our method, while the "iterated" approach clearly lags behind. Once again we have observed that the QRF models achieve better results with the "k-models" approach. We should note that the $Utility$ score is particularly relevant for this type of applications where serious mistakes may have significant financial costs.

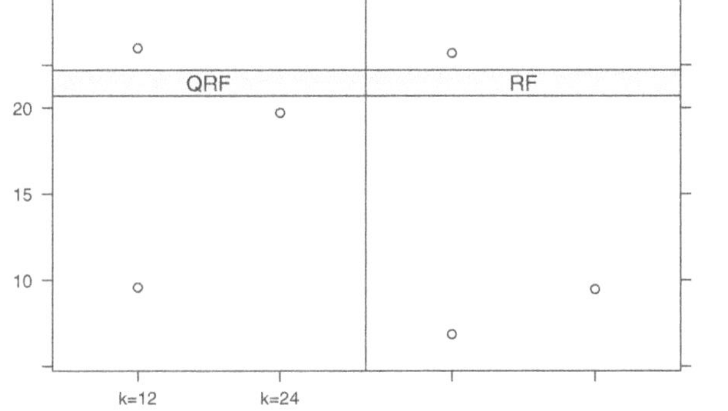

Figure 8: The relative computation times of "k-models" vs "quantiles" on the water consumption problem.

In terms of computation times the scores are shown in Figure 8, and reveal the same type of advantage of our proposal over the "k-models" alternative.

4. CONCLUSIONS

This paper has described 2D-interval predictions, a class of time series tasks with a high relevance for several application domains. To the best of our knowledge there is no established methodology to handle these problems across the several disciplines that address time-dependent data. The main goals of this paper were: (i) to raise the awareness of the data mining community to these relevant problems, and (ii) to propose a new methodology to address these tasks that can be used with any time series modeling technique. The proposal consists in directly predicting the distribution statistics for the target time interval, which allows for instance to obtain a range of plausible values for this period.

We have described our proposal and have carried out an extensive set of experiments designed with the goal of checking the validity of the proposal when compared to existing alternatives. This comparison was carried out from two perspectives: (i) the perspective of prediction accuracy of the 2D-intervals, and (ii) the perspective of the computational cost of the alternatives. This latter issue may be particularly relevant in dynamic contexts where new data arrives at a high pace. The question of the accuracy of the predictions was also addressed from different perspectives trying to capture characteristics that are important to this type of applications (e.g. the costs and benefits of the predictions).

The results of our experiments with several artificial time series and also two real world problems provide clear evidence on the validity of our proposal. It achieves a prediction accuracy that it is highly competitive with the best alternatives in the different experimental setups that were considered, but with a significantly lower computational cost. This makes the proposal particularly adequate for high-frequency time series where 2D-interval predictions may be of use.

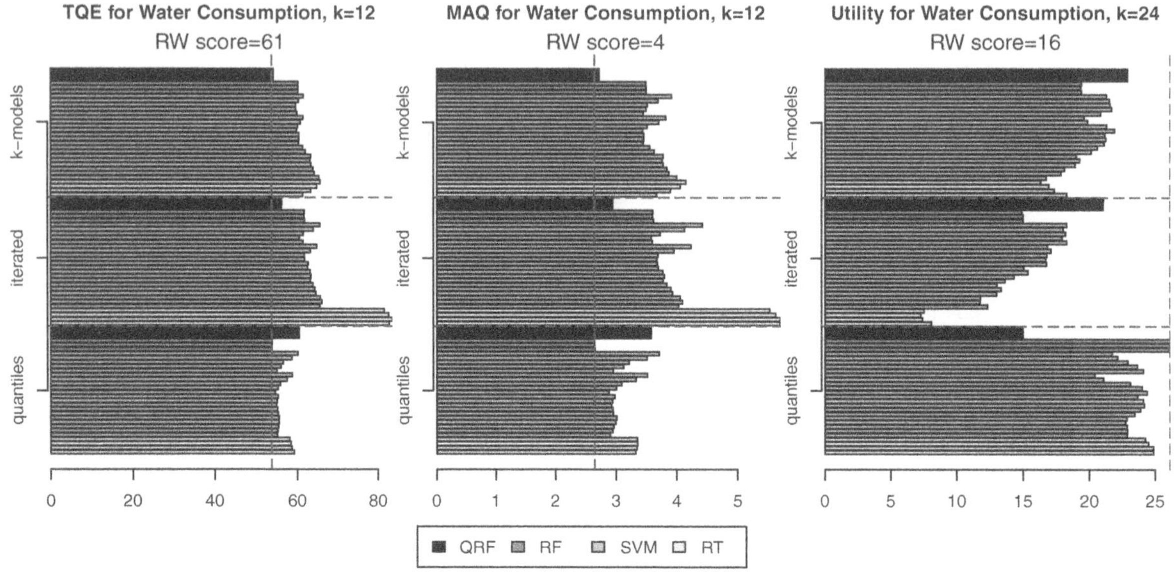

Figure 7: The results on the water consumption problem.

In terms of future work we plan to study our proposal from a more theoretical perspective with the goal of understanding why it achieves these competitive results. Namely, we will try to check the hypothesis that this performance may be caused by the smaller difficulty of the task we address. Predicting these distribution statistics directly, instead of calculating them from the time series predictions, may be easier because distribution statistics (particularly the quantiles we are using) are more stable and not so exposed to the effects of spurious variations on the original time series values.

5. REFERENCES

[1] L. Breiman. *Classification and regression trees.* Chapman & Hall/CRC, 1984.

[2] L. Breiman. Random forests. *Machine learning*, 45(1):5–32, 2001.

[3] J.B. Bremnes. Probabilistic wind power forecasts using local quantile regression. *Wind Energy*, 7(1):47–54, 2004.

[4] C. Chatfield. Prediction intervals. *Journal of Business and Economic Statistics*, 11:121–135, 1993.

[5] C. Chatfield. *Time-Series Forecasting.* Chapman & Hall/CRC, 2001.

[6] C. Chatfield. *The Analysis of Time Series, an introduction.* Chapman & Hall/CRC, 2004.

[7] N. Cristianini and J. Shawe-Taylor. *An introduction to support Vector Machines: and other kernel-based learning methods.* Cambridge Univ Pr, 2000.

[8] E. Dimitriadou, K. Hornik, F. Leisch, D. Meyer, and A. Weingessel. *e1071: Misc Functions of the Department of Statistics (e1071), TU Wien*, 2009. R package version 1.5-22.

[9] C. Elkan. The foundations of cost-sensitive learning. In *International Joint Conference on Artificial Intelligence*, pages 973–978, 2001.

[10] R. Koenker. *Quantile Regression.* Econometric Society Monograph Series. Cambridge University Press, 2005.

[11] A. Liaw and M. Wiener. Classification and regression by randomforest. *R News*, 2(3):18–22, 2002.

[12] N. Meinshausen. Quantile regression forests. *J. Mach. Learn. Res.*, 7:983–999, 2006.

[13] N. Meinshausen. *quantregForest: Quantile Regression Forests*, 2007. R package version 0.2-2.

[14] C. Perlich, S. Rosset, R.D. Lawrence, and B. Zadrozny. High-quantile modeling for customer wallet estimation and other applications. *Proceedings of the 13th ACM SIGKDD international conference on Knowledge discovery and data mining - KDD '07*, pages 977–985, 2007.

[15] R Development Core Team. *R: A Language and Environment for Statistical Computing.* R Foundation for Statistical Computing, 2010.

[16] A. S. Tay and K. F. Wallis. Density forecasting: a survey. *Journal of Forecasting*, 19(4):235–254, 2000.

[17] J.W. Taylor. Density forecasting for the efficient balancing of the generation and consumption of electricity. *International Journal of Forecasting*, 22:707–724, 2006.

[18] J.W. Taylor, P.E. McSharry, and R. Buizza. Wind power density forecasting using ensemble predictions and time series models. *IEEE Transactions on Energy Conversion*, 24:775–782, 2009.

[19] T. M. Therneau and B. Atkinson. R port by B. Ripley. *rpart: Recursive Partitioning*, 2009. R package version 3.1-44.

[20] L. Torgo. *Data Mining with R, learning with case studies.* CRC Press, 2010.

[21] W.B. Wu, Z. Xu, and Y. Wang. Robust prediction of network traffic using quantile regression models. In *2006 IEEE International Conference on Information Reuse and Integration*, pages 220–225, 2006.

A Game Theoretic Framework for Heterogeneous Information Network Clustering

Faris Alqadah*
Johns Hopkins University
733 North Broadway
Baltimore, MD 21205
faris.alqadah@jhu.edu

Raj Bhatnagar
University of Cincinnati
814 Rhodes Hall
Cincinnati, Ohio 45221
raj.bhatnagar@uc.edu

ABSTRACT

Heterogeneous information networks are pervasive in applications ranging from bioinformatics to e-commerce. As a result, unsupervised learning and clustering methods pertaining to such networks have gained significant attention recently. Nodes in a heterogeneous information network are regarded as objects derived from distinct domains such as 'authors' and 'papers'. In many cases, feature sets characterizing the objects are not available, hence, clustering of the objects depends solely on the links and relationships amongst objects. Although several previous studies have addressed information network clustering, shortcomings remain. First, the definition of what constitutes an information network cluster varies drastically from study to study. Second, previous algorithms have generally focused on non-overlapping clusters, while many algorithms are also limited to specific network topologies.

In this paper we introduce a game theoretic framework (GHIN) for defining and mining clusters in heterogeneous information networks. The clustering problem is modeled as a game wherein each domain represents a player and clusters are defined as the Nash equilibrium points of the game. Adopting the abstraction of Nash equilibrium points as clusters allows for flexible definition of reward functions that characterize clusters without any modification to the underlying algorithm. We prove that well-established definitions of clusters in 2-domain information networks such as formal concepts, maximal bi-cliques, and noisy binary tiles can always be represented as Nash equilibrium points. Moreover, experimental results employing a variety of reward functions and several real world information networks illustrate that the GHIN framework produces more accurate and informative clusters than the recently proposed NetClus and state of the art MDC algorithms.

Categories and Subject Descriptors

H.2.8 [**Database Applications**]: Data Mining

*Portions of work were completed while author was attending the University of Cincinnati

General Terms

Algorithms

1. INTRODUCTION

Heterogeneous information networks (HINs) are pervasive in applications ranging from bioinformatics to e-commerce. The nodes of a HIN are regarded as objects derived from distinct domains while the topology of the network is defined by how the domains are related. In many cases, feature sets characterizing the objects are not available, hence, clustering of the objects depends solely on the links and relationships amongst objects. For example, consider the domains of *users*, *websites*, *posts*, and *terms* as illustrated in figure 1. The topology of the network is defined by edges between the domains (figure 1(a)); each edge represents a relation table relating the objects between the pair of domains. In the example, the $websites\_users$ relation captures clicking patterns of users, the $users\_posts$ table specifies which users made postings on different blogs, and the $posts\_terms$ table is a document-terms dataset relating terms to postings. Clustering the nodes of a HIN advances knowledge discovery in two manners. First, hidden associations between objects from differing domains are unveiled; this leads to a better understanding of the hidden structure of the entire network. Second, local clusters within a domain are sharpened and put into greater context, resulting in more accurate local clustering. Consider the HIN in figure 1(b) once again. While no information is available relating websites to blog posts, the fact that $u1$ clusters with both $\{p1, p2\}$ and $\{w1, w2\}$ may suggest a hidden similarity between $\{p1, p2\}$ and $\{w1, w2\}$. Clustering *users* exclusively on clicking patterns leads to the cluster $\{u2, u3\}$; however, when considering the $users\_posts$ relation a strong case can also be made for the clustering $\{u1, u2\}$. Consequently, beyond inference of hidden links between objects, information network clustering revises and puts local clustering of objects within a domain into context. In addition to illustrating the benefits of information network clustering, the above example exposes the need to consider overlapping clusters. How does an algorithm decide between the $\{u1, u2\}$ and $\{u2, u3\}$ clusterings? Considering all the different relations, strong cases can be made for both groupings. This scenario occurs frequently in real world applications such as bioinformatics and text mining where a gene may encompass several functional groups or a document may relate to multiple categories such as "Politics" and "Religion".

1.1 Related Work

Few works have approached the task of clustering data in game theoretic terms. Most notably in [8] the authors propose a game theoretic approach to hypergraph clustering. This work is simi-

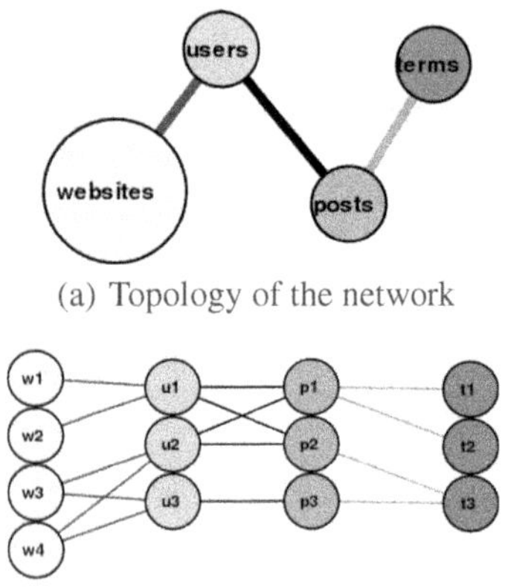

(a) Topology of the network

(b) The Full HIN

Figure 1: A tree-shaped heterogeneous information network with four domains

lar in philosophy to the GHIN framework proposed here; both approaches define clusters in terms of Nash equilibrium points and cultivate algorithms to enumerate these points. The works differ in the type of clustering problem addressed. The hypergraph clustering problem consists of homogeneous objects paired with similarity scores between objects that are known a-priori (although these similarities need not be pairwise and can be of higher order). As a result, the hypergraph clustering game and subsequent rewards are naturally defined only in terms of the given object similarities. In the HIN-clustering problem only relational information between heterogeneous objects is available; hence, in addition to determining a framework to define HIN clusters, appropriate relational reward functions must also be developed. Moreover, although the authors of [8] point out that a game-theoretic framework has the potential to mine overlapping clusters, the final adapted algorithm does not.

HIN-clustering has been addressed in the literature as "multi-way" [18, 17, 5, 6], "information-network" [26, 27], and "relational clustering" [7, 29, 30]. Additionally, bi-clustering [9, 19] algorithms may be viewed as information network clustering algorithms specified for single edge information networks. Nonetheless, the definition of an information network cluster varies from study to study. Multi-way clustering algorithms generalize bi-clustering approaches, hence adopting and generalizing the definition of the respective bi-clustering approach. The definition of a bi-cluster has varied significantly and includes: vertex cuts [12], maximal cliques [16, 28, 32], maximal sub-matrices that minimize variance [10, 15, 11], and maximal sub-matrices that maximize mutual information with respect to a pre-specified number of clusters [13]. Relational and information network clustering approaches utilize similarity measures such as PageRank, SimRank and other ranking measures defined over the information network to perform clustering [30, 26]. The premise of these similarity measures is the recursive definition that similarity between two objects depends on the similarities between the objects linked with them. Recently, NetClus was introduced [27] utilizing similarity measures and the assumption that "every net-cluster is corresponding to a generative model, according to which generative probabilities of every target object in each cluster can be calculated".

Additionally, the majority of algorithms in the literature do not allow for overlapping clusters, require a pre-specified number of clusters, and are limited by the topology of the information network. For example, multi-way clustering algorithms operate on any given topology, but are limited to non-overlapping clusters and require a pre-specified number of clusters. NetClus and other ranking-based approaches are only suited for star shaped networks and still require the number of clusters as a parameter.

1.2 Contributions

The principal contributions of this paper are two fold. First, the GHIN framework, based on game theory, is introduced as a general scheme for defining and mining clusters in HINs. The abstraction of a Nash equilibrium point in a game is employed to define a HIN-cluster while mining the clusters consists of enumerating the Nash equilibrium points. The premise of the framework is that a HIN-cluster constitutes an equilibrium among several possible competing local clusterings of objects in each domain. This idea was inspired by the observation in [24] (expanded upon in [1] to star shaped information networks) that a subspace cluster constitutes a trade-off between the number of data points and attributes admitted. The more objects a subspace cluster encompasses the fewer attributes it will admit and vice-versa. This observation naturally extends to a relational setting. Consider the HIN in figure 1 once again. The more $users$ included in a cluster naturally implies fewer $websites$ jointly visited by those users and fewer $posts$ collectively blogged on. Accordingly, a trade-off exists among objects included in a HIN-cluster based on the topology of the network. Moreover, as the discussion in the previous section depicted, different relations may influence the formation of clusters within a domain in a seemingly contradictory manner. Hence, a cluster that incorporates data from the entire information network should be viewed as an equilibrium point between competing clustering influences. This notion is captured precisely as the Nash equilibrium solution concept of a game involving two or more players. A game is in Nash equilibrium if each player has chosen a strategy and no player has anything to gain by changing only his own strategy unilaterally. In terms of HINs, we define a cluster as a collection of nodes from each domain in which the quality criterion or reward function in each domain cannot be improved by unilaterally changing the clustering of that domain.

The second primary contribution of the paper is the development of specific reward functions in conjunction with GHIN. These reward functions yield effective HIN-clustering algorithms as evidenced by an empirical study. In the sequel we formally introduce the GHIN framework by modeling the HIN-clustering problem as a game and defining the clusters as the Nash equilibrium points of that game. Section 3 establishes the framework for a single edge information network (bi-clustering) and shows that this approach encompasses well-established bi-clustering frameworks. In section 4 the GHIN framework is defined for a general tree-shaped HIN while section 5 proposes two reward functions to be used in conjunction with GHIN. Section 6 displays experimental results and section 7 offers concluding remarks and possible extensions.

2. PRELIMINARIES

We formulate the HIN-clustering problem in the vocabulary of Formal Concept Analysis (FCA). The field of FCA serves as a theoretical basis for association rule analysis, closed itemset mining [31], and bi-clustering [16][2]. Next, the basic terminology and conceptions of game theory are presented and related to HIN-clustering in section 3.

2.1 Heterogeneous Information Networks and FCA

A **context** $\mathbb{K}_{ij} = (G_i, G_j, I_{ij})$ consists of two sets G_i, G_j and a relation I_{ij} between them. We refer to the sets G_i and G_j as

domains. We refer to the elements of each domain G_i, G_j as **objects** and denote them as $g_i^1, \ldots, g_i^{|G_i|}$. A context may be depicted as a $|G_i| \times |G_j|$ binary matrix, denoted as $mat(\mathbb{K}_{ij})$, where $mat(\mathbb{K}_{ij})_{mn} = 1$ if $g_i^m I_{ij} g_j^n$ and 0 otherwise. Moreover, $\mathbb{K}_{ij}$ may also be viewed as a bipartite graph, denoted $grph(\mathbb{K}_{ij})$, with vertex set $G_i \cup G_j$, and edge set I_{ij}. Therefore, $mat(\mathbb{K}_{ij})$ is the adjacency matrix of $grph(\mathbb{K}_{ij})$. A **heterogeneous information network** (HIN) is a graph $\mathbb{G}_n = (\mathbf{V}, \mathbf{E})$ where $\mathbf{V}$ is a set of domains $\{G_1, \ldots, G_n\}$ and $(G_i, G_j) \in \mathbf{E}$ iff $\exists \mathbb{K}_{ij}$. A **subspace** of an information network $\mathbb{G}_n$ is an n-tuple of **object-sets** $(A_1 \subseteq G_1, \ldots, A_n \subseteq G_n)$. In general, the HIN clustering problem is to identify a set of subspaces that maximizes a quality criterion **Q** subject to a set of constraints **C**. Clustering of a single edge HIN amounts to clustering in a singleton context; in this case FCA has been well established as a theoretical base. For object-set A_i define

$$\psi^j(A_i) = \begin{cases} \{g_j \in G_j | g_j I_{ij} g_i \quad \forall g_i \in A_i\} & \text{if } (G_i, G_j) \in \mathbf{E}, \\ \emptyset & \text{otherwise.} \end{cases}$$

In words, $\psi^j(A_i)$ identifies the objects of G_j common to the objects in A_i. If $(G_i, G_j) \in \mathbf{E}$ then generally $\psi^j(A_i)$ maybe computed as $\bigcap_{g \in A_i} \psi^j(g)$.

DEFINITION 1. *A **concept** of the context (G_i, G_j, I_{ij}) is a subspace (A_i, A_j) such that $\psi^j(A_i) = A_j$ and $\psi^i(A_j) = A_i$.*

The above definition can be shown to yield two closure systems on G_i and G_j which are dually isomorphic to each other [14]. For any object-set $A_i \subseteq G_i$, then$(\psi^i(\psi^j(A_i)), \psi^j(A_i))$ is always a concept. A **semi-concept** of a $\mathbb{K}_{ij}$ is a subspace (A_i, A_j) such that $\psi^j(A_i) = A_j$ or $\psi^i(A_j) = A_i$ and constitutes a relaxation on the stricter definition of a concept. Utilizing the binary matrix representation, a concept can be represented by a *maximal* sub-matrix of 1's under suitable permutations of the rows and columns. The term maximal indicates that no row or column can be added to the sub-matrix without the introduction of at least one zero. Concepts can also be thought of as the maximal bi-cliques of $grph(\mathbb{K}_{ij})$ [16]. This is important as it was illustrated in [16] that the maximal bi-cliques of a dataset correspond exactly to the bi-clusters (subspace clusters, co-clusters, projected clusters, closed patterns) of a binary dataset; thus, the bi-clustering problem is modeled by FCA. A natural approach to solving the HIN-clustering problem is to extend FCA-conceptions to the general case of a HIN. In section 3 it is proven that Nash-equilibrium points for a suitably defined game encapsulate the FCA definition of a bi-cluster.

2.2 Game Theory

A game consists of a set of players, positions, moves, and a reward function. The moves are defined by a set of rules and dictate how players may move between different positions. The situation at the start of the game is called the **initial** position. At each position, the rules indicate which player (or players) make a move from that position and what the allowable moves are. For every position p, there must be a sequence of moves from the initial position to p. Some positions are designated as **terminal** positions, and no moves are allowed from such a position, hence, the game ends when a terminal position is reached. A play of the game consists of a sequence of moves starting at the initial position and ending at a terminal position. Every terminal position determines a reward or pay-off to each of the players. A central notion of game theory is **strategy**. A strategy for a player is a specification that tells the player what to do in every situation that might arise during a game. Notice that once a strategy is chosen the player's moves are completely determined.

	Player 2 chooses 0	Player 2 chooses 1	Player 2 chooses 2
Player 1 chooses 0	(0,0)	(1,0)	(2,-2)
Player 1 chooses 1	(0,1)	(1,1)	(3,-2)
Player 1 chooses 2	(-2,2)	(-2,3)	(2,2)

Figure 2: Game displayed in normal form, with Nash equilibrium points highlighted

DEFINITION 2. *A finite, n-player, normal form game, $\mathcal{G}$, is a triple $\langle N, (M_i), (r_i) \rangle$ where*

- *$N = \{1, \ldots, n\}$ is the set of players*
- *$M_i = \{m_i^1, \ldots, m_i^{l_i}\}$ is the set of moves available to player i and l_i is the number of available moves for that player.*
- *$r_i : M_1 \times \cdots \times M_n \to \Re$ is the reward function for each player i. It maps a profile of moves to a value.*

Each player i selects a strategy from the set of all available strategies $\mathbb{P}_i = \{p_i : M_i \to [0, 1]\}$. The primary solution concept for a normal form game is that of a **Nash equilibrium**: a strategy profile in which no player has an incentive to unilaterally deviate [21, 20]. In other words, if each player has chosen a strategy and no player can benefit by unilaterally changing his or her strategy (assuming other players keep theirs unchanged) then the current set of strategy choices and the corresponding payoffs constitute a Nash equilibrium.

DEFINITION 3. *A strategy profile $p^* \in \mathbb{P}$ is a **Nash equilibrium** if :*

$$\forall i \in N, p_i \in \mathbb{P}_i \quad : \quad r_i(p_1^*, \ldots, p_{i-1}^*, p_i, \ldots, p_n^*) \leq r_i(p_1^*, \ldots, p_n^*)$$

A fundamental theorem of game theory is that every finite game in which the players have perfect information has a Nash equilibrium [21, 20]. Normal form games maybe represented by an n-dimensional array of n-vectors by tabulating the function $r(p_1, \ldots, p_n) = (r_1(p_1, \ldots, p_n), \ldots, r_n(p_1, \ldots, p_n))$. In the case of a two-player game, this representation reduces to a matrix whose elements are pairs of real numbers. Figure 2 illustrates the matrix representation of a two-player normal form game in which two players simultaneously select an integer between 0 and 2. If the two players select the same integer the reward is the value of the selected integer. If one player selects a larger number then they give up that many points to the other player and the player with the smaller number is rewarded the value of their own number. The Nash equilibrium points of the game are highlighted in yellow.

3. THE BI-CLUSTERING GAME

The bi-clustering problem can be viewed as a game. Consider two party planners, P_1 and P_2, whose goal is to plan a party by inviting guests on their client lists. Each party planner is responsible for disjoint sets of clients, G_1 and G_2, and can only send out invitations to clients in their set. The party planners receive compensation based on the overall satisfaction of their clients. Party-goers from each set of clients only interact with party-goers of the other set and satisfaction of each individual party-goer is based on the amount of interaction at the party. Additionally, if party goers encounter guests that they do not care for then their satisfaction is negatively impacted. Both P_1 and P_2 are good at their jobs and know whose company each client enjoys and whose company they

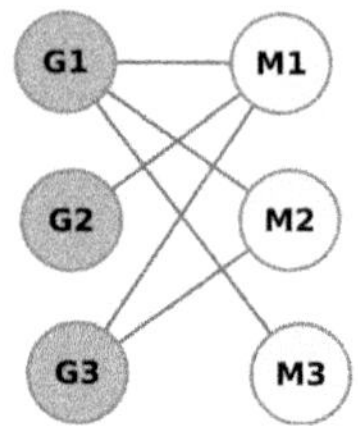

(a) Client Preferences

	$M1$	$M1, M2$	$M1, M2, M3$	$M1, M3$	$M2$	$M2, M3$	$M3$
$G1$	(1,1)	(1,2)	(1,3)	(1,2)	(1,1)	(1,2)	(1,1)
$G1, G2$	(2,1)	(-1,-1)	(-2,-3)	(-1,-1)	(-4,-2)	(-4,-4)	(-4,-2)
$G1, G2, G3$	(3,1)	(0,0)	(-3,-3)	(-3,-2)	(-3,-1)	(-6,-4)	(-9,-3)
$G1, G3$	(2,1)	(2,2)	(0,0)	(-1,-1)	(2,1)	(-1,-1)	(-4,-2)
$G2$	(1,1)	(-2,-4)	(-3,-9)	(-2,-4)	(-5,-5)	(-5,-10)	(-5,-5)
$G2, G3$	(2,1)	(-1,-1)	(-4,-6)	(-4,-4)	(-4,-2)	(-7,-7)	(-10,-5)
$G3$	(1,1)	(1,2)	(-1,-3)	(-2,-4)	(1,1)	(-2,-4)	(-5,-5)

(b) Normal form of the game, w=5

Figure 3: The bi-clustering (party planning) game

don't. Moreover, we assume that P_1 and P_2 do not cooperate but are privy to the guest list of the other at any given point. Thus, the game is for P_1 and P_2 to create guest lists for each party such that they maximize their compensation. It is randomly selected who begins and players alternate selecting individual clients to add or remove from their invitation lists. The game ends when both party planners have completed creating their lists or after a finite time interval. In the subsequent sections we will refer to the game described above as the party planners game or bi-clustering game interchangeably.

Clearly, all subsets $A_1 \subseteq G_1$ and $A_2 \subseteq G_2$ may constitute the terminal nodes of the bi-clustering game. Let the context $\mathbb{K}_{ij} = (G_i, G_j, I_{ij})$ represent the preferences of clients, then, any subspace (A_1, A_2) represents a party and can also be thought of as a strategy profile (p_1, p_2). In order to maximize compensation, each party planner certainly must attempt to invite clients with similar preferences in relation to the clients of the opposing party planner. The bi-clustering game is a finite game in which players have perfect information, therefore, Nash equilibrium points do exist and constitute the primary solution to the game.

DEFINITION 4. *Given $\mathbb{K}_{12} = (G_1, G_2, I_{12})$, then the bi-clustering game is defined as the normal form game*

$$\mathcal{G}_{bicluster} = \langle \{1, 2\}, \{\mathcal{P}(G_1), \mathcal{P}(G_2)\}, \{r_1, r_2\} \rangle \tag{1}$$

where $\mathcal{P}$ denotes the power-set, and r_i is a user selected reward function measuring the subsequent pay-off to the party planner for a given party.

Definition 4 represents the bi-clustering game in its most general form. Additional rules may explicitly be appended to the game (such as minimum bounds on the size of parties) or implicitly enforced through the appropriate selection of reward functions.

DEFINITION 5. *Given $\mathbb{K}_{12} = (G_1, G_2, I_{12})$, then the bi-clusters of $\mathbb{K}$ are defined as the Nash equilibrium pairs (A_1, A_2) of $\mathcal{G}_{bicluster}$.*

Below, it is illustrated that with the use of an intuitive and simple reward function the definition of a bi-cluster in a context is encapsulated by definitions 4 and 5.

3.1 Concepts as Nash Equilibrium Points

As specified by the party-planning game, the reward of P_1 and P_2 is a function of the satisfaction of party-goers. Intuitively, the more friends a party-goer encounters, the greater their satisfaction. On the other hand, as party-goers encounter people they do not care for their satisfaction is negatively impacted. Hence, for a single party-goer $g_1 \in G_1$ (dually $g_2 \in G_2$) attending party (A_1, A_2), define the satisfaction of g_1 as

$$sat_1(g_1, A_2) = \frac{|\psi^2(g_1) \cap A_2| - w * |A_2 \setminus \psi^2(g_1)|}{|A_2|} \tag{2}$$

where w represents the weight of a non interaction. Once again we assume P_1 and P_2 are good at their jobs and the value of w is known to them. The reward of each party planner is then the average satisfaction of all clients magnified by the number of clients:

$$r_i^{sat}(A_i, A_j) = \sum_{g_i \in A_i} sat_i(g_i, A_j) \tag{3}$$

Letting $w = 0$, then r_i^{sat} is exactly the sum of node degrees of all g_i in the subspace A_j normalized by $|A_j|$; hence, node degree is a special case of this reward function. Figure 3 illustrates a sample instance of the bi-clustering game utilizing the r_i^{sat} reward function. Specifically, figure 3(a) represents the context as a bipartite graph, while 3(b) exhibits the normal-form of the game played with $w = 5$ along with Nash equilibrium points. Notice that in this case the Nash equilibrium points correspond exactly to the maximal bi-cliques or bi-clusters of the network. In general, as w grows the fewer negative interactions party planners will tolerate when attempting to maximize r_i^{sat}.

THEOREM 1. *For any instance of $\mathcal{G}_{bicluster}$ in which r_i^{sat} is the selected reward function there exists w^* such that: $\forall w \geq w^*$ if (A_1^*, A_2^*) is a concept of $\mathbb{K} = (G_1, G_2, I_{12})$ then (A_1^*, A_2^*) is a Nash equilibrium point of $\mathcal{G}_{bicluster}$.*

PROOF. *Let (A_1^*, A_2^*) be a concept and*

$$w = \max\{\max_{g_1 \in G_1} \{|\psi^2(g_1)|\}, \max_{g_2 \in G_2} \{|\psi^1(g_2)|\}\}$$

Assume that (A_1^*, A_2^*) is not a Nash equilibrium; then w.l.o.g there must exist (A_1, A_2) such that $r_1^{sat}(A_1, A_2^*) > r_1^{sat}(A_1^*, A_2^*)$. Two cases arise:

1. *(A_1, A_2^*) is a semi-concept. Then*

$$\begin{aligned} \sum_{g_1 \in A_1} sat_1(g_1, A_2^*) &> \sum_{g_1^* \in A_1^*} sat_1(g_1^*, A_2^*) \\ \frac{|A_1| * |A_2^*|}{|A_2^*|} &> \frac{|A_1^*| * |A_2^*|}{|A_2^*|} \\ |A_1| &> |A_1^*| \end{aligned}$$

   By the maximality of concepts, this is a contradiction.

2. *(A_1, A_2^*) is not a semi-concept, then two sub-cases arise:*

   (a) *$A_1 \supseteq A_1^*$. In this case $|A_1| = |A_1^* \cap A_1| + |A_1 \setminus A_1^*|$. Let $d_1 = |A_1 \setminus A_1^*|$ and $d_2 = |A_1^* \cap A_1|$, then by definition of a concept*

$$\begin{aligned} |\psi^2(a_1) \cap A_2^*| &\leq |A_2^*| - 1 \\ |A_2^* \setminus \psi^2(a_1)| &\geq 1 \end{aligned}$$

   for any $a_1 \in A_1 \setminus A_1^*$. Furthermore,

$$w \geq |A_2^*|$$

Hence

$$
\begin{aligned}
r_1^{sat}(A_1, A_2^*) &\geq r_1^{sat}(A_1^*, A_2^*) \\
\frac{d_1(|A_2^*|-1) + d_2|A_2^*| - w * d_1}{|A_2^*|} &\geq \frac{|A_1^*| * |A_2^*|}{|A_2^*|} \\
d_1(|A_2^*|-1) + d_2|A_2^*| - w * d_1 &> |A_1^*| * |A_2^*| \\
d_1(|A_2^*|-1) + d_2|A_2^*| - |A_2^*|d_1 &> |A_1^*| * |A_2^*| \\
d_2|A_2^*| - d_1 &> |A_1^*| * |A_2^*|
\end{aligned}
$$

which is a contracdiction by the property of set difference.

(b) $A_1 \not\supseteq A_1^*$. *Let* $d_1' = |A_1 \setminus A_1^*|$ *and* $d_2' = |A_1^* \cap A_1|$. *In this case, the argument is the same as above, with the distinction that* $d_2 > d_2'$ *and* $d_1 \leq d_1'$.

□

Theorem 1 establishes that definition 5 paired with an intuitive reward function encompasses several previous approaches to bi-clustering in binary relations. Simply varying the value of w leads to FCA [14], fault-tolerant FCA [22], and quasi-biclique [25] approaches.

4. GAME THEORETIC FRAMEWORK

The HIN-clustering problem can be viewed as a multi-player version of $\mathcal{G}_{bicluster}$.

DEFINITION 6. *Given HIN* $\mathbb{G}_n$, *then the HIN-clustering game is defined as the normal form game*

$$\mathcal{G}_{hin} = \langle \{1, \ldots, n\}, \{\mathcal{P}(G_1), \ldots, \mathcal{P}(G_n)\}, \{r_1, \ldots, r_n\} \rangle \quad (4)$$

In the HIN-clustering game, n party planners attempt to plan a party to maximize their individual rewards. Party-goers from each set of clients only interact with clients of other sets specified by $\mathbf{E} \in \mathbb{G}_n$. The multi-player game proceeds exactly as the two-player game and each planner is privy to the guest lists of all other party planners. The terminal nodes of the multi-player party planner game constitutes all subspaces $(A_1, \ldots, A_n)$ of $\mathbb{G}_n$.

DEFINITION 7. *Given a HIN,* $\mathbb{G}_n$, *then the HIN-clusters of* $\mathbb{G}_n$ *are defined as the Nash equilibrium points of* $\mathcal{G}_{hin}$.

Adopting definition 7, the problem of enumerating HIN clusters is equivalent to that of finding Nash equilibrium points in a normal form game. This problem is notorious and has been described as "the most fundamental problem" at the interface of computer science and game theory; however, recent efficient algorithms have been proposed [23]. In particular, the algorithm presented in [23] makes use of a simple search strategy and simple heuristics but has been shown to be quite effective. Thus, in general, these algorithms may be used in conjunction with definition 7 to enumerate HIN clusters with any given reward function. In this paper, however, we propose a more specialized framework tailored to the party planner game due to the fact that we have a deeper understanding of the structure of the problem.

Consider a two player normal form game, then a simple labeling technique for locating all Nash equilibria is [20]:

1. Mark all second components that are maximal among all second components in each row.
2. Mark all first components that are maximal among all first components in each column.
3. Any cell in the matrix that has both components marked is then in a state of Nash equilibrium.

Clearly, the drawback of the labeling technique is the assumption that the game matrix is pre-computed. However, it is infeasible to compute the entire game matrix for the party planners game; in the worst case this would involve enumerating at least $2^{\max(|G_1|,|G_2|)}$ cells in the game matrix. As a result, GHIN is engineered utilizing the labeling technique augmented with heuristics.

4.1 n-Clusters as Candidates

In order to condense the search space for locating a Nash equilibrium, we propose a heuristic to identify initial candidate subspaces. The premise of the argument is that any reward function, $r_i(A_1, \ldots, A_n)$, must be a function of the count and distribution of the edges or interactions in the subspace. Using the notation that $\{-i\}$ denotes the integers $1, \ldots, i-1, i+1, \ldots, n$, each party planner i wishes to maximize the edge count of domain i given the current selection of all other players $\{-i\}$. Hence, we conclude that it is advantageous to all players to start with a party in which all party-goers know each other and is maximal.

HEURISTIC 1. *Given* $\mathbb{G}_n$, *all Nash equilibrium points of* $\mathcal{G}_{hin}$ *are supersets of the* ***n-clusters*** *of* $\mathbb{G}_n$. *An* n*-cluster is a subspace* $(A_1, \ldots, A_n)$ *such that the following conditions hold:*

1. $\forall i, j$ *s.t.* $(G_i, G_j) \in \mathbf{E}$, $(A_i \subseteq G_i, A_j \subseteq G_j)$ *is a semi-concept.*
2. $\forall i$ *there does not exist* g_i *s.t. for* $(A_{-i}, A_i \cup g_i)$ *condition 1 still holds.*

The game theoretic framework for mining HIN-clusters, GHIN, is presented as algorithm 1. The framework sacrifices completeness in order to overcome the computational cost of enumerating Nash equilibrium points. On the other hand, GHIN attempts to maximize coverage of all objects by striving to form the initial n-cluster candidates from each object in the HIN. The set R is utilized to keep track of these 'seed' objects to form the initial candidates. Lines 4-5 entail generating an initial candidate n-cluster C; such subspaces may be computed utilizing the algorithm presented in [1]. Notice on line 5 that only n-clusters that contain objects in R will be formed as candidates; this step attempts to maximize the diversity of the clusters enumerated while overlapping clusters may still be formed through the refinement phase on lines 7-16. Following heuristic 1 and the labeling technique described earlier, GHIN attempts to locate a Nash-equilibrium point by holding all object-sets A_{-i} as fixed points while maximizing the reward for player i (lines 8-11). After each iteration of the *for* loop, C is updated with all the added objects for domain i. Clearly, the entire *repeat* loop is guaranteed to terminate since objects are only being added. The next refinement phase (lines 12-15) is analogous to the previous one except that GHIN attempts to remove objects whose removal increases the reward for player i. The entire refinement process iterates until no change is possible or a user-defined maximum number of iterations, max, is reached. By definition, C constitutes a Nash equilibrium if the refinement phase loop terminates prior to reaching max. Finally, in the case that C is a cluster, then R is updated by removing all objects found in C. The algorithm terminates when no more objects are left in R to form candidates with.

4.2 Computational Complexity

The running time complexity of GHIN depends on the complexity of computing r_i for a given subspace. In general, the worst

Input: $\mathbb{G}_n$, Reward functions: $(r_1, \ldots, r_n)$
Data: Maximum number of iterations to find Nash equilibrium max

begin
  $R \leftarrow \bigcup_{i=1}^{n} G_i \in \mathbf{V}$;
  repeat
    $i \leftarrow$ Randomly select i from $1 \ldots n$;
    $C = (A_1, \ldots, A_n) \leftarrow$ form n-cluster starting from G_i that only encompasses objects in R;
    $R \leftarrow R \setminus \bigcup_{i=1}^{n} A_i \in C$;
    repeat
      repeat
        for $i \leftarrow 1$ **to** n *in random order* **do**
          Add all $g_i \in G_i$ to A_i s.t. $r_i(A_i \cup g_i) > r_i(A_i)$;
      until *No change in* C ;
      repeat
        for $i \leftarrow 1$ **to** n*, in random order* **do**
          Remove all $g_i \in A_i$ from A_i s.t. $r_i(A_i \setminus g_i) > r_i(A_i)$;
      until *No change in* C ;
    until *No change in* C *or* max *reached* ;
    if *Nash equilibrium found* **then**
      Print C as a HIN-cluster ;
      $R \leftarrow R \setminus \bigcup_{i=1}^{n} A_i \in C$;
  until $|R| < 1$;
end

Algorithm 1: Game Theoretic Framework (GHIN) for HIN-clustering

case occurs when all objects in $\mathbb{G}_n$ are utilized to form candidates and the refinement phase executes max number of times. Forming a single candidate with the algorithm proposed in [1] runs in $O(|G_i|)$ time; therefore, the worst case complexity of GHIN is $O(|G_i| * max * |G_i| * n * O(r_i))$. $O(r_i)$ is the computational complexity of computing r_i for a subspace and G_i is the largest domain in $\mathbb{G}_n$. Considering max and n as small constants and assuming $O(r_i)$ is linear with respect to G_i (as is the case with the two reward functions presented next), a more realistic running-time complexity is $O(|G_i|^3)$. On the other hand, our experimental results indicate that even this running time is rarely encountered as the set R tends to die down fairly quickly (see experimental section).

5. REWARD FUNCTIONS

The advantage of GHIN is the fact that any reward function that is primarily based on edge-counts and their distribution may be utilized without any change to the algorithm. Here we present two reward functions with which we implemented GHIN.

5.1 Satisfaction

Extending the satisfaction reward function presented in section 3 to a HIN yields

$$sat_i(g_i, A_{-i}) = \sum_{A_j \subseteq G_j, (G_i, G_j) \in \mathbf{E}} sat_i(g_i, A_j)$$

$$r_i^{sat}(A_i, A_{-i}) = \sum_{g \in A_i} sat_i(g_i, A_{-i})$$

This reward function is a direct generalization of the one presented in section 3. This intuitive reward function is simple to implement and experimental results indicate that it works well in information networks that have approximately equivalent density levels in all contexts. On the other hand, if the contexts of $\mathbb{G}_n$ have significantly different density levels then r_i^{sat} is biased towards objects from those domains that have higher density due to the high node degree of such objects.

5.2 Expected Satisfaction

To address the bias of r_i^{sat} we develop r_i^{esat} in which the satisfaction of a client is based on the expected number of positive interactions and not on the pure count. Given $\mathbb{G}_n$, assume each $g_i \in G_i$ is independent. For a given subspace $(A_1, \ldots, A_n)$ the expected number of positive interactions for $g_i \in A_i$ is the number of success in a sequence of $|A_j|$ draws from a finite population of $|G_j|$ objects without replacement. Hence, the expected number of success is the expected value of a hypergeometrically distributed random variable. For object g_i and object-set A_j in subspace $(A_1, \ldots, A_j, \ldots, A_n)$, let $exp_{ij}(g_i, A_j)$ denote the expected number of positive interactions between g_i and objects in A_j and $var_{ij}(g_i, A_j)$ denote the variance:

$$exp_{ij}(g_i, A_j) = \frac{|A_j| * |\psi^j(g_i)|}{|G_j|}$$

$$var_{ij}(g_i, A_j) = \frac{|A_j| * |\psi^j(g_i)| * (|G_j| - |A_j|) * (|G_j| - |\psi^j(g_i)|}{|G_j|^2 * (|G_j| - 1)}$$

Define satisfaction of a client g_i at a party as the difference between the actual number of positive interactions and the expected number of positive interactions; this can be captured as the z-score:

$$esat(g_i, A_j) = \frac{|\psi^j(g_i) \cap A_j| - exp_{ij}(g_i, A_j)}{\sqrt{var_{ij}(g_i, A_j)}} - w$$

$$esat(g_i, A_{-i}) = \sum_{A_j \subseteq G_j, (G_i, G_j) \in \mathbf{E}} esat(g_i, G_j)$$

$$r_i^{esat}(A_i, A_{-i}) = \sum_{g_i \in A_i} esat(g_i, A_{-i})$$

In the above formulation w is a user-defined parameter which determines how large the standardized score must be to make a positive contribution to the overall reward. The reward for party planner i is simply the sum of the expected satisfaction of each client.

5.3 Tiring Party-Goers

A common problem with overlapping clustering techniques is that the number of clusters enumerated may be quite large [2]. This problem may be overcome in the GHIN framework by incorporating an additional 'tiring' factor into any reward function r_i. The more times party-goer g_i appears in a cluster the less likely g_i is to appear in future clusters. Let $c(g_i)$ denote the number of clusters g_i has appeared in upto the current time-step, then let

$$t = f(c(g_i))$$

where

$$f : \mathbb{N} \rightarrow (0, 1]$$

and f is anti-monotonic. For example:

$$f(x) = \frac{1}{x^2}$$

$$f(x) = \frac{1}{e^x}$$

HIN name	Description	Num domains	Num classes	Total num objects
MER	Newsgroup, Middle East politics and Religion	3	2	24,783
REC	Newsgroup, recreation	3	2	26,225
SCI	Newsgroup, science	3	4	37,413
PC	Newsgroup, pc and software	3	5	35,186
PCR	Newsgroup, politics and Christianity	3	2	24,485
FOUR_AREAS	DBLP subset of database, data mining, AI, and IR papers	4	4	70,517

Figure 4: Real-world HINs

HIN	Algorithm	F_1	$F_{0.5}$	F_2
MER	GHIN expsat	**0.627051**	**0.736396**	**0.622735**
	GHIN sat	0.553790	0.649559	0.569664
	NetClus	0.3759	0.4512	0.322
	MDC	0.3661	0.4533	0.3070
REC	GHIN expsat	**0.544189**	**0.633362**	**0.508778**
	GHIN sat	0.434367	0.485025	0.451840
	NetClus	0.2784	0.2870	0.2704
	MDC	0.2845	0.2953	0.2746
SCI	GHIN expsat	**0.484068**	**0.589704**	**0.530239**
	GHIN sat	0.402306	0.481798	0.462886
	NetClus	0.2609	0.2583	0.2635
	MDC	0.2532	0.2529	0.2535
PC	GHIN expsat	**0.334827**	**0.520472**	0.302943
	GHIN sat	0.306503	0.432229	**0.345382**
	NetClus	0.2254	0.2068	0.2477
	MDC	0.2282	0.2116	0.2476
PCR	GHIN expsat	**0.640894**	**0.793399**	0.508778
	GHIN sat	0.541986	0.574588	**0.530971**
	NetClus	0.3642	0.4396	0.3109
	MDC	0.3440	0.4268	0.2810
FOUR_AREAS	GHIN expsat	**0.623117**	**0.598877**	**0.650079**
	GHIN sat	0.5315	0.506687	0.5588
	NetClus	0.3612	0.36655	0.3560
	MDC	0.5085	0.5162	0.5010

(a) B^3 F-scores

Algorithm	Class	C1	C2	C3	C4
GHIN expsat	DB	0.0601266	**0.93633**	0.0133188	0.0512748
	DM	0.028481	0.0363608	0.0106007	**0.850142**
	IR	**0.882911**	0.0204432	0.133188	0.0339943
	AI	0.028481	0.00686642	**0.842892**	0.0645892
NetClus	DB	0.0553833	**0.450802**	**0.500074**	0.0955971
	DM	0.163934	0.15815	0.128535	0.304584
	IR	0.179553	0.0512035	0.242707	0.112786
	AI	**0.60113**	0.339844	0.128684	**0.487033**
MDC	DB	0.186681	0.232455	**0.803727**	0.000000
	DM	0.261844	0.000000	0.128592	0.161790
	IR	0.003183	0.278748	0.000000	**0.75888**
	AI	**0.548292**	**0.488797**	0.067680	0.079323

(b) Cluster purity of FOUR_AREAS

Figure 5: Extrinsic verification of GHIN compared with NetClus and MDC

Incorporating the tiring factor into the two previously described reward functions :

$$sat(g_i, A_j) = \frac{t * |\psi^i(g_i) \cap A_j| - w * |A_j \setminus \psi^j(g_i)|}{|A_j|}$$

$$esat(g_i, A_j) = t * \frac{|\psi^j(g_i) \cap A_j| - exp_{ij}(g_i, A_j)}{\sqrt{var_{ij}(g_i, A_j)}} - w$$

6. EXPERIMENTAL RESULTS

Six real-world information networks summarized in figure 4 were utilized in the experimental study. Five of the datasets were derived from the 20NewsGroups dataset [4] containing the domains of documents, subject-lines, and all-terms. The FOUR_AREAS network was previously used in [27] and is a subset of the DBLP dataset containing the domains of papers, authors, abstracts, and conferences. All six networks contain class labels: Newsgroup datasets use the usenet group of a document as a class label, while the FOUR_AREAS dataset labels papers according to their research area as data mining, machine learning, database, or information retrieval. All code, data, and experimental setup are publicly available at `http://homepages.uc.edu/~alqadaf`.

6.1 Extrinsic Verification

The clusters produced by `GHIN` using both r_i^{sat} and r_i^{expsat} were compared with the clusters mined by `NetClus` [27] and

Terms	Authors	Conferences
data	Surajit Chaudhuri	VLDB
database	Divesh Srivastava	SIGMOD
queries	H. V. Jagadish	ICDE
databases	Jeffrey F. Naughton	PODS
querys	Michael J. Carey	EDBT
xml	Raghu Ramakrishnan	
mining	Jiawei Han	KDD
learning	Christos Faloutsos	PAKDD
data	Wei Wang	ICDM
frequent	Heikki Mannila	SDM
association	Srinivasan Parthasarathy	PKDD
patterns	Ke Wang	ICML

(a) Sample clusters from FOUR_AREAS

Abstract terms	All terms
israel	israelis
israelis	arabs
apartheid	palestinian
terrorism	occupied
jerusalem	zionist

(b) Sample clusters from MER

Figure 6: Sample clusters mined with GHIN

`MDC` [6]. The `NetClus` algorithm was shown to outperform both `RankClus` [26] and `PLSA` [33], while `MDC` is a generalization and improvement of the seminal information-theoretic co-clustering algorithm introduced by Dhillon [13].

Cluster validity of each clustering was determined via the F_1, $F_{0.5}$, and F_2 measures of the B^3-Precision and B^3-Recall extrinsic cluster validity metrics [3]. These measures were selected to ensure a fair comparison of overlapping and non-overlapping clustering [3]; in addition, it was proven that the B^3 measures retain the desirable properties of cluster homogeneity, cluster completeness, rag bag, and cluster size vs quantity, while many popular extrinsic clustering measures such as precision, recall, mutual information and entropy do not. Let $C(g)$ and $L(g)$ denote the cluster and class label that object g belongs to respectively. Then the precision and recall of any pair of objects g and g' is given as

$$Prec(g, g') = \frac{\min(|C(g) \cap C(g')|, |L(e) \cap L(g')|)}{|C(g) \cap C(g')|} \quad (5)$$

$$Rcl(g, g') = \frac{\min(|C(g) \cap C(g')|, |L(g) \cap L(g')|)}{|L(g) \cap L(g')|} \quad (6)$$

Note that equation 5 is only defined when g and g' share a cluster and equation 6 is only defined when g and g' share a class label. Intuitively, $Prec$ grows if there is a matching category for each clusters where two items co-occur; Rcl grows when we add a shared cluster for each class shared by two items. Thus if we have fewer shared clusters than needed, we loose recall; if we have fewer classes than clusters we lose precision. From these measures B^3-precision and recall are derived:

$$B^3 Prec = Avg_g \left[Avg_{g', C(g) \cap C(g') \neq \emptyset} \left[Prec(g, g') \right] \right] \quad (7)$$

$$B^3 Rcl = Avg_g \left[Avg_{g', L(g) \cap L(g') \neq \emptyset} \left[Rcl(g, g') \right] \right] \quad (8)$$

The $F_{0.5}$ measure weighs precision twice as high as recall while

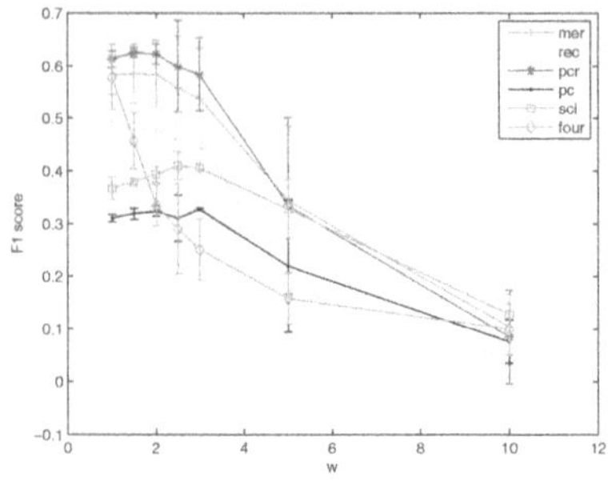

(a) F1 measure

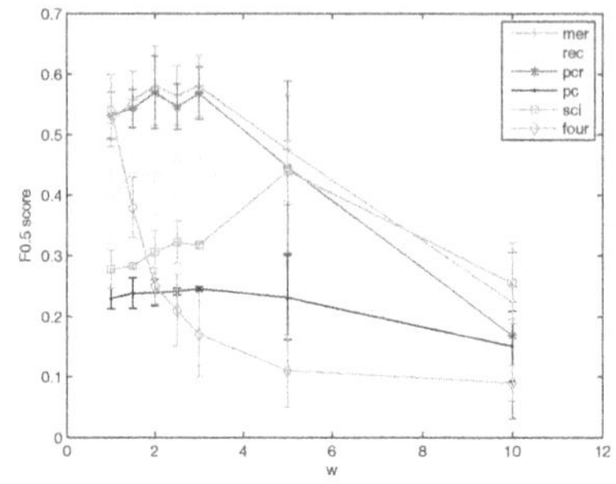

(b) F0.5 measure

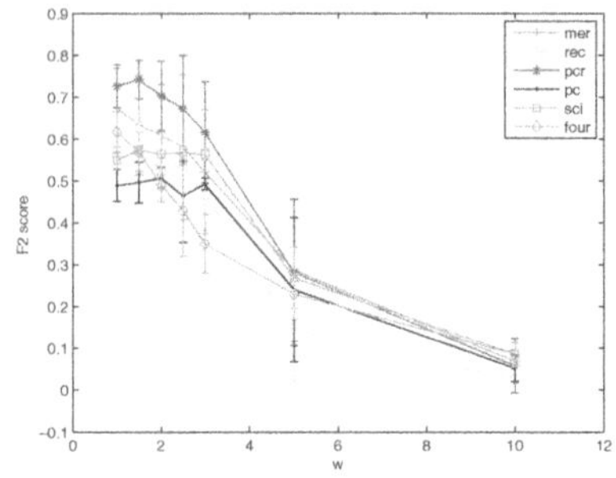

(c) F2 measure

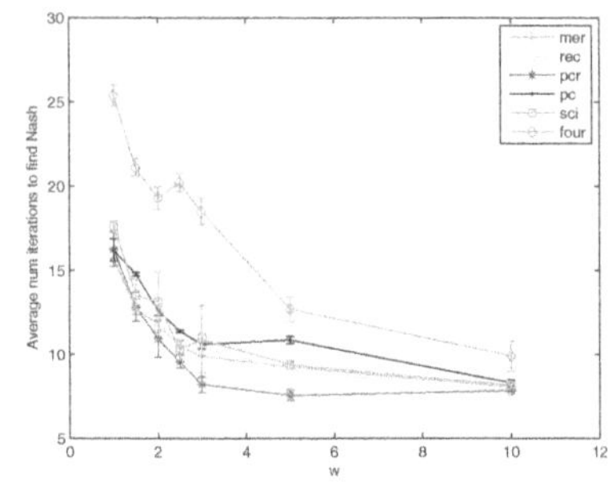

(d) Average number of iterations to find Nash equilibrium

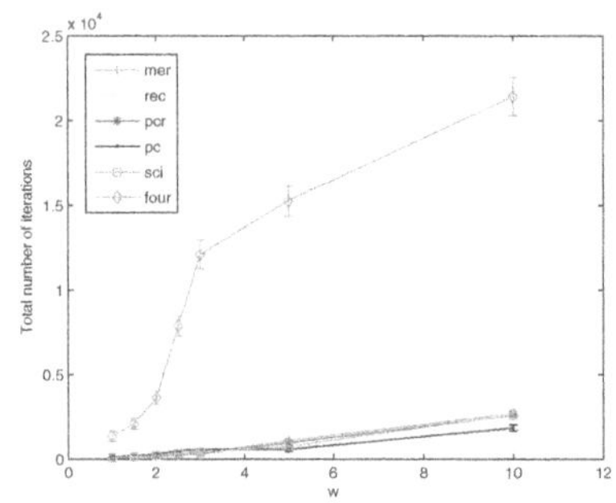

(e) Total number of iterations

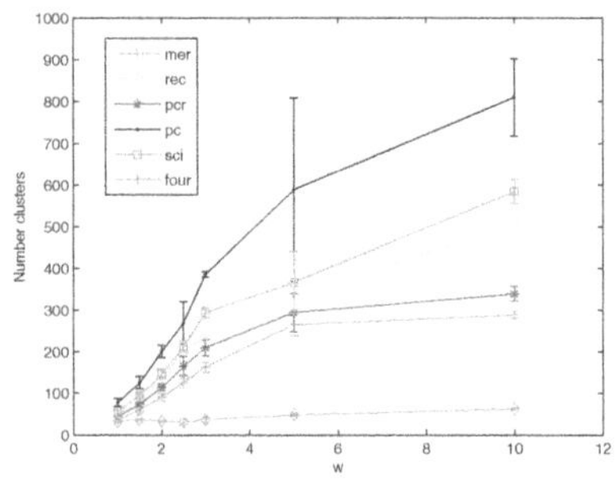

(f) Number of clusters

Figure 7: Parameter study on cluster quality with r_i^{esat}

F_2 weighs recall twice as much as precision and F_1 weighs them equally.

Both NetClus and MDC require the k parameter to indicate the number of desired clusters; this parameter was varied as 2, 4, 8, 16, 32, 64. The max value in GHIN was set to 50 along with tiring factor $f(x) = \frac{1}{x^{3/2}}$ for all experiments; w was varied as illustrated in the parameter study section. For NetClus, the cluster label is obtained according to the largest posterior probability. Each algorithm was run on every HIN with each parameter selection 20 times; the best F-measures are displayed in figure 5(a). As can be seen, GHIN consistently produces higher quality clusters in every information network. Comparing the average and median scores of all runs yielded very similar results. MDC and NetClus consistently produced the best results when $k = 4$ closely matching the number of "true" classes for all F measures; the quality of the clustering decreased significantly as k was increased. GHIN produced between 50 and 200 clusters depending on the setting of w (see parameter section). While the number of clusters is significantly higher than the "true" number of clusters, the clusters produced by GHIN represent very precise, fine-grain and nuanced clusters as opposed to the very broad and global approach NetClus and MDC employ. For example, while the number of categories in MER is only 2, clearly, finer delineations and sub-categories of news posts exist within the categories of Religion and Middle East politics. As seen in figure 6(b), GHIN produced a cluster with terms specifically related to the Israeli-Palestinian conflict; the cluster contained 71 posts all dealing with topic. The trend of smaller more focused clusters was consistently repeated for all datasets. Investigating the purity of clusters further emphasizes this point; figure 5(b) displays the distributions of the objects in the top four clusters (ranked by accuracy of the objects) in the FOUR_AREAS network. Once again, the topical nature of the clusters is evident. On the other hand, MDC and NetClus are hindered by the k parameter; small values of k obstruct precision while large k detracts from recall due to non-overlapping clusters.

6.2 Sample Clusters

Figure 6 displays clusters mined by GHIN from the various information networks. In all cases not the entire cluster is displayed but only the top 5-6 objects ranked by their individual satisfaction score. The clusters from FOUR_AREAS clearly correspond to the documents in the field of databases and data mining; as an added bonus we see that the satisfaction score ($esat$ in this case) does a good job of ranking the objects. Furthermore, the terms in the MER cluster are distinctly linked to the most commonly discussed issue in Middle Eastern politics: the Arab-Israeli conflict.

6.3 Parameter Study

Experiments were performed to study the effects of the w parameter with r_i^{esat}. The overall goal was to observe how cluster quality was effected by parameter selection in addition to examining the effect of w on the algorithmic characteristics of GHIN. We expect larger values of w to yield more precise and accurate clusters at the cost of recall. As can be observed in figures 7(b)-7(c) this trend is clearly visible. The $F_{0.5}$ measure tends to increase with larger values of w until a breaking point (generally where $w = 5$) at which the low recall values dominate the increasing precision. This trend is reiterated by the F_2 measure which continually decreases as w grows larger. While the number of clusters grows (figure 7(f)) with w, fewer objects are clustered overall. This trend is explained by the fact that as stricter criterion on cluster formation is imposed, fewer iterations of the refinement phase are executed and the original candidates form the clusters (figure 7(d)). In these cases the fact that GHIN is an incomplete algorithm leads to less stable results as evidenced by the larger standard deviations in the number of clusters formed (figure 7(f)). As a result, we recommend utilizing values of w between 1.5 and 3. Finally, figure 7(e) highlights the fact that the set R tends to die down pretty quickly resulting in far fewer iterations than objects in the HIN. Hence, for the recommended range of w values, GHIN tends to run in $O(|G_i|^2)$ time. Actual running times on an AMD Atholon 64 X2 Dual Core with 6 GiB of ram did not exceed 200 seconds for all Newsgroup HINs. The execution time maxed out at 500 seconds on FOUR_AREAS utilizing the recommended range of w and exceeded 2 hours at values of $w \geq 5$.

7. CONCLUSION

In this paper a novel game-theoretic framework for heterogeneous information network clustering (GHIN) was presented. Modeling the clustering problem as a game in which players attempt to maximize their reward, clusters are defined as the Nash equilibrium solution concepts. This framework presents a unifying definition of a HIN-cluster. Furthermore, specific domain knowledge may be incorporated via specifying the rules of the game and developing differing reward functions. Utilizing an intuitive reward function we illustrated that the framework encompasses previous well-established formulations of bi-clustering. Additionally, two reward functions were developed in concert with GHIN. Experimental results on several real world information networks demonstrated that GHIN was especially advantageous in mining precise, fine-grain and nuanced clusters.

In depth algorithmic issues related to GHIN were not addressed and further studies are needed in this direction. Specifically, a generalized and efficient systematic approach for enumerating Nash equilibrium points within the confines of the clustering game should be developed as the randomization in the current scheme is a potentially destabilizing factor. Moreover, future work should focus on establishing more effective and efficient reward functions along with suitable heuristics.

8. REFERENCES

[1] F. Alqadah and R. Bhatnagar. An effective algorithm for mining 3-clusters in vertically partitioned data. In *CIKM '08*, 2008.

[2] F. Alqadah and R. Bhatnagar. Discovering substantial distinctions among incremental bi-clusters. In *SDM'09*, 2009.

[3] E. Amigó, J. Gonzalo, J. Artiles, and F. Verdejo. A comparison of extrinsic clustering evaluation metrics based on formal constraints. *Information Retrieval*, 12 (4):461–486, 2009.

[4] A. Asuncion and D. Newman. UCI machine learning repository, 2007.

[5] A. Banerjee, S. Basu, and S. Merugu. Multi-way clustering on relation graphs. In *SDM'07*, 2007.

[6] R. Bekkerman, R. El-Yaniv, and A. McCallum. Multi-way distributional clustering via pairwise interactions. In *ICML '05*, pages 41–48, 2005.

[7] I. Bhattacharya and L. Getoor. Relational clustering for multi-type entity resolution. In *MRDM '05*, 2005.

[8] S. R. Bulo' and M. Pelillo. A game-theoretic approach to hypegraph clustering. In *NIPS2009*, 1571-1579, 2009.

[9] S. Busygin, O. Prokopyev, and P. M. Pardalos. Biclustering in data mining. *Comput. Oper. Res.*, 35(9):2964–2987, 2008.

[10] Y. Cheng and G. Church. Biclustering of expression data. In *ISMB '00*, 2000.

[11] H. Cho, I. Dhillon, Y. Guan, and S. Sra. Minimum sum squared residue co-clustering of gene expression data. In *SDM '04*, 2004.

[12] I. S. Dhillon. Co-clustering documents and words using bipartite spectral graph partitioning. In *KDD '01*, 2001.

[13] I. S. Dhillon, S. Mallela, and D. S. Modha. Information-theoretic co-clustering. In *KDD '03*, pages 89–98, 2003.

[14] B. Gamter and R. Wille. *Formal Concept Analysis: Mathematical Foundations*. Springer-Verlag, Berlin, 1999.

[15] J. Hartigan. Direct clustering of a data matrix. *Journal of the American Statistical Association*, 67, No. 337:123–129, 1972.

[16] J. Li, G. Liu, H. Li, and L. Wong. Maximal biclique subgraphs and closed pattern pairs of the adjacency matrix: A one-to-one correspondence and mining algorithms. *IEEE Trans. Knowl. Data Eng.*, 19(12):1625–1637, 2007.

[17] B. Long, X. Wu, Z. M. Zhang, and P. S. Yu. Unsupervised learning on k-partite graphs. In *KDD '06*, pages 317–326, 2006.

[18] B. Long, Z. M. Zhang, X. Wu, and P. S. Yu. Spectral clustering for multi-type relational data. In *ICML '06*, pages 585–592, 2006.

[19] S. C. Madeira and A. L. Oliveira. Biclustering algorithms for biological data analysis: A survey. *IEEE/ACM Transactions on Computational Biology and Bioinformatics*, 1 (1):24–45, 2004.

[20] E. Mendelson. *Introducing Game Theory and Its Applications*. Chapman & Hall / CRC, 2004.

[21] G. Owen. *Game Theory*. Academic Press, 1995.

[22] R. Pensa and J. Boulicaut. Towards fault-tolerant formal concept analysis. *Congress of the Italian Association for Artificial Intelligence AI* IA*, 3673:21–23, 2005.

[23] R. Porter, E. Nudelman, and Y. Shoham. Simple search methods for finding a nash equilibrium. In *Games and Economic Behavior*, pages 664–669, 2004.

[24] C. M. Procopiuc, M. Jones, P. K. Agarwal, and T. Murali. A monte carlo algorithm for fast projective clustering. In *SIGMOD '02*, pages 418–427, 2002.

[25] K. Sim, J. Li, V. Gopalkrishnan, and G. Liu. Mining maximal quasi-bicliques to co-cluster stocks and financial ratios for value investment. In *ICDM '06*, pages 1059–1063, 2006.

[26] Y. Sun, J. Han, P. Zhao, Z. Yin, H. Cheng, and T. Wu. Rankclus: Integrating clustering with ranking for heterogeneous information network analysis. In *EDBT'09*, 2009.

[27] Y. Sun, Y. Yu, and J. Han. Ranking-based clustering of heterogeneous information networks with star network schema. In *KDD'09*, 2009.

[28] A. Tanay, R. Sharan, and R. Shamir. Discovering statistically significant biclusters in gene expression data. In *ISMB 2002*, 2002.

[29] X. Yin, J. Han, and P. S. Yu. Cross-relational clustering with user's guidance. In *KDD '05*, 2005.

[30] X. Yin, J. Han, and P. S. Yu. Linkclus: efficient clustering via heterogeneous semantic links. In *VLDB '06*, 2006.

[31] M. J. Zaki and M. Ogihara. Theoretical foundations of association rules. In *SIGMOD-DMKD '98*, 1998.

[32] M. J. Zaki, M. Peters, I. Assent, and T. Seidl. Clicks: An effective algorithm for mining subspace clusters in categorical datasets. *Data and Knowledge Engineering special issue on Intelligent Data Mining*, 60 (2):51–70, 2007.

[33] C. Zhai, A. Velivelli, and B. Yu. A cross-collection mixture model for comparative text mining. In *KDD '04*, 2004.

A GPU-Tailored Approach for Training Kernelized SVMs

Andrew Cotter
Toyota Technological Institute at Chicago
6045 S. Kenwood Ave.
Chicago, Illinois 60637
cotter@ttic.edu

Nathan Srebro
Toyota Technological Institute at Chicago
6045 S. Kenwood Ave.
Chicago, Illinois 60637
nati@ttic.edu

Joseph Keshet
Toyota Technological Institute at Chicago
6045 S. Kenwood Ave.
Chicago, Illinois 60637
jkeshet@ttic.edu

ABSTRACT

We present a method for efficiently training binary and multiclass kernelized SVMs on a Graphics Processing Unit (GPU). Our methods apply to a broad range of kernels, including the popular Gaussian kernel, on datasets as large as the amount of available memory on the graphics card. Our approach is distinguished from earlier work in that it cleanly and efficiently handles sparse datasets through the use of a novel clustering technique. Our optimization algorithm is also specifically designed to take advantage of the graphics hardware. This leads to different algorithmic choices then those preferred in serial implementations. Our easy-to-use library is orders of magnitude faster then existing CPU libraries, and several times faster than prior GPU approaches.

Categories and Subject Descriptors

D.1.3 [**Programming Techniques**]: Concurrent Programming

General Terms

Design, Experimentation, Performance, GPGPU

1. INTRODUCTION

Support Vector Machines (SVMs) are among the most popular general purpose learning methods in use today. SVM learning amounts to learning a linear predictor, with regularization (corresponding to a "large margin") ensuring good generalization even in very high dimensions. This predictor need not be linear in the input representation: it is possible to learn a linear predictor in some extremely high dimensional space specified implicitly through a *kernel function*. SVMs were originally suggested in the context of binary classification, but more recently variants following the same principles have also been developed and successfully applied to more complex prediction tasks such as multiclass classification and prediction of structured outputs such as sequences.

Training an SVM amounts to solving a quadratic programming problem (see Section 2). Although general-purpose quadratic programming solvers can only handle fairly small SVM instances, much effort has been made in the past two decades to design special-purpose solvers that can handle large-scale SVM instances. This effort resulted in widely-used packages that can solve both "linear" SVMs (i.e. where the prediction is linear in the input representation) and "kernelized" SVMs (where a non-linear kernel defines the linear prediction space). For linear SVMs, stochastic methods such as PEGASOS [13] and Stochastic Dual Coordinate Ascent [8] have recently been established as being effective at solving extremely large SVM instances, typically in less time than that which is required to read the data into memory. For kernel SVMs, most leading solvers are based on decomposing the dual optimization problem into small subproblems [11, 9, 4, 1, and see also Section 3]. Such approaches can indeed handle fairly large problems, provided that the data fits in memory, but it is not uncommon for training to require many hours or days, even using state-of-the-art optimizers. There is therefore still a strong need for faster training of kernel SVMs.

One attractive possibility for enabling faster SVM training is to leverage the power of Graphical Processing Units (GPUs). GPUs are highly parallel, structured, computational engines and are now available relatively inexpensively and are found in many modern computers. In this paper we discuss how SVM training can be efficiently implemented on a GPU, and present such an implementation for both binary and multiclass SVMs.

Several authors have recently proposed using GPUs for kernelized SVM training [3, 2] and related problems [6]. These previous approaches, however, primarily focused on pointing out the advantages of implementing standard algorithms on graphics hardware, typically using GPU matrix-multiplication libraries, and not on how these algorithms can be modified to better take advantage of the GPU architecture. We study various algorithmic choices for SVM training in the context of GPUs, discuss how the optimal choices and algorithms on a GPU are different than those for a serial implementation, and arrive at an implementation specifically designed for graphics hardware. As with many previous approaches, we assume that the dataset fits in memory, and focus mostly on the Gaussian kernel, although our implementation can handle any kernel function which can be written in the form $K(x, y) = f(\|x\|, \|y\|, \langle x, y\rangle)$ (see Section 5.2), and our ideas apply even more broadly to any kernel which is an aggregation of element-wise operations.

One particularly significant drawback of other GPU SVM solvers is their lack of support for sparse datasets. On the CPU, taking advantage of sparsity is a simple matter, and sparse datasets are encountered frequently enough that many widely-used SVM solvers treat all input vectors as sparse, by default [9, 4, 1]. On the GPU, however, maximum performance is only achieved if memory accesses follow certain fairly-restrictive patterns, which are difficult

KDD'11, August 21–24, 2011, San Diego, California, USA.

to ensure with sparse data. In contrast to other GPU SVM solvers, our implementation does take advantage of sparsity in the training set through a novel "sparsity clustering" approach (Section 5.3).

Overall, our implementation is orders of magnitudes faster then existing CPU implementations, and several times faster on sparse datasets then prior GPU implementations of SVM training.

2. SUPPORT VECTOR MACHINES

We will briefly review the optimization problems that need to be solved in order to train binary and multiclass Support Vector Machine (SVM) classifiers. For a complete description of Support Vector Machines, motivating these optimization problems, we refer the reader to, e.g., Schölkopf and Smola [12].

2.1 Binary classification

We consider training a kernel SVM with an unregularized bias term. Let $(x_1, y_1), \ldots, (x_n, y_n)$, with $x_i \in \mathbb{R}^d$ and $y_i \in \{\pm 1\}$, be a training set of n labeled examples, and let $K : \mathbb{R}^d \times \mathbb{R}^d \to \mathbb{R}$ be a (positive semi-definite) kernel. Here, we focus mostly on the Gaussian kernel $K(x_1, x_2) = e^{-\gamma \|x_1 - x_2\|_2^2}$, parametrized by a scale parameter $\gamma \in \mathbb{R}$, although the methods we present are applicable to a wide range of kernels (see Section 5.2). Given a regularization trade-off parameter $C \in \mathbb{R}$, training an SVM classifier amounts to solving the following optimization problem:

$$\underset{\alpha \in \mathbb{R}^n,\, b \in \mathbb{R}}{\text{minimize}} : \frac{1}{2}\alpha^T Q \alpha + C \sum_{i=1}^{n} \max\left(0, 1 - y_i\left(b + c_i\right)\right) \quad (1)$$

where here and throughout we denote $c_i \overset{def}{=} \sum_{j=1}^{n} \alpha_j y_j K(x_i, x_j)$, which we will call the "responses", and $Q \in \mathbb{R}^{n \times n}$ is a matrix with entries $Q_{ij} \overset{def}{=} y_i y_j K(x_i, x_j)$. The first term in (1) is a regularization term (corresponding to a norm in an implied Hilbert space) and the second term is the empirical loss. After training, the label of an input vector $x \in \mathbb{R}^d$ is given by $\text{sign}(b + \sum_{j=1}^{n} \alpha_j y_j K(x, x_j))$.

As is commonly done, we instead solve the dual of (1):

$$\begin{aligned} \underset{\alpha \in \mathbb{R}^n}{\text{maximize}} &: \mathbf{1}^T \alpha - \frac{1}{2}\alpha^T Q \alpha \\ \text{subject to} &: \forall i \left(0 \le \alpha_i \le C\right) \\ &: \sum_{i=1}^{n} y_i \alpha_i = 0 \end{aligned} \quad (2)$$

An optimum of (2) is also an optimum of (1), with $b = y_i - c_i$ for any i such that $0 < \alpha_i < C$. The goal of this paper is to suggest an efficient method for solving (2) on a GPU.

2.2 Multiclass Classification

For problems where the labels take on more then two possible values, $y_i \in \{1, \ldots, m\}$, we follow the multiclass SVM formulation of Crammer and Singer [5]. In this formulation, each class label y is associated with a coefficient vector $\alpha^{(y)} \in \mathbb{R}^n$, and no unregularized bias is allowed. Training amounts to solving the following optimization problem:

$$\begin{aligned} \underset{\alpha^{(1)}, \ldots, \alpha^{(m)} \in \mathbb{R}^n}{\text{minimize}} &: \frac{1}{2}\sum_{y=1}^{m} \left(\alpha^{(y)}\right)^T K \alpha^{(y)} \\ &+ C \sum_{i=1}^{n} \max_{y \in \{1, \ldots, m\}} \left(1 - \delta_{y, y_i} - c_i^{(y_i)} + c_i^{(y)}\right) \end{aligned} \quad (3)$$

where we denote $c_i^{(y)} \overset{def}{=} \sum_{j=1}^{n} \alpha_j^{(y)} K(x_i, x_j)$, $K \in \mathbb{R}^{n \times n}$, $K_{ij} = K(x_i, x_j)$ is the Gram matrix and δ is the Kronecker delta function. Again, the first term is a regularization term (this time, the sum of the norms of the predictors for each class) and the second is again the empirical loss (a multiclass hinge loss—see Crammer and Singer for further details). After training, the label of an input vector $x \in \mathbb{R}^d$ is given by $\underset{y}{\text{argmax}} (\sum_{j=1}^{n} \alpha_j^{(y)} K(x, x_j))$.

We will again solve the dual, which is given by:

$$\begin{aligned} \underset{\alpha^{(1)}, \ldots, \alpha^{(m)} \in \mathbb{R}^n}{\text{maximize}} &: \sum_{i=1}^{n} \alpha_i^{(y_i)} - \frac{1}{2}\sum_{y=1}^{m} \left(\alpha^{(y)}\right)^T K \alpha^{(y)} \\ \text{subject to} &: \forall i \forall y \left(\alpha_i^{(y)} \le C \delta_{y, y_i}\right) \\ &: \forall i \left(\sum_{y=1}^{m} \alpha_i^{(y)} = 0\right) \end{aligned} \quad (4)$$

3. OPTIMIZATION IN THE DUAL

Efficient kernel SVM optimizers tend to work on the dual formulation (2). For most datasets, the kernel matrix is much too large to fit in memory. Therefore, optimization is typically done by iteratively choosing a subset of the dual variables, which we will call a *working set*, and updating the coefficients α_i corresponding to this set. While the early "chunking" algorithm [10] relied on choosing a *large* working set, subsequent work has tended to show that performing many computationally inexpensive updates on small working sets leads to faster convergence than performing fewer relatively expensive ones. Variants of the popular SMO algorithm take these working sets to be as small as possible (two with an unregularized bias, one without) [11, 7], while SVM-Light, by default, uses working sets of size 10 [9].

The subproblem of optimizing the coefficients corresponding to a given working set is again a quadratic program (though a smaller one). For a binary classification problem, let $\mathcal{I}$ to be the working set of indices to optimize (while holding the remainder fixed). We assume the current set of dual variables α satisfies the constraints, and consider as optimization variables the values Δ_i to *add* to each $\alpha_i : i \in \mathcal{I}$. The subproblem is then given by:

$$\begin{aligned} \underset{\Delta_i \in \mathbb{R} : i \in \mathcal{I}}{\text{maximize}} &: \mathbf{1}^T \Delta - \sum_{i \in \mathcal{I}} \Delta_i y_i c_i - \frac{1}{2} \sum_{i,j \in \mathcal{I}} \Delta_i \Delta_j Q_{i,j} \\ \text{subject to} &: \forall i \in \mathcal{I} \left(-\alpha_i \le \Delta_i \le C - \alpha_i\right) \\ &: \sum_{i \in \mathcal{I}} y_i \Delta_i = 0 \end{aligned} \quad (5)$$

The submatrix $Q_{i,j} : i, j \in \mathcal{I}$ may be found by evaluating only $\frac{1}{2}|\mathcal{I}|\left(|\mathcal{I}| + 1\right)$ kernel inner products, so for small working sets it is reasonable to calculate it on-demand. Calculating each of the responses $c_i : i \in \mathcal{I}$, however, requires the evaluation of n kernel inner products.

This cost cannot be entirely avoided. However, instead of calculating the responses at each iteration, we can alternatively keep a complete set of up-to-date responses on-hand, and merely *update* them after each iteration:

$$c_i' = c_i + \sum_{j \in \mathcal{I}} \Delta_j y_j K(x_i, x_j) \quad (6)$$

The computational cost of such an update is the same as that of calculating the needed responses ($c_i : i \in \mathcal{I}$) afresh at each iteration. However, we may benefit from having all responses available to us, because they are useful in *working set selection*. In recent years, it has been found that when optimizing linear SVMs without an unregularized bias, the cost of choosing a working set in some "smart" way is not justified–doing so randomly leads to far better performance [13, 8]. For kernel SVMs, however, the cost of each update is sufficiently high that it is often worthwhile to choose the working set intelligently, even if this necessitates examining all values c_i at each iteration [14]. SVM optimizers differ in the heuristics used to choose the working set. We discuss this issue in detail in Section 5.

Training a multiclass SVM in the dual poses similar challenges, except that the situation is complicated by the fact that each example is associated with m dual variables, subject to inequality and equality constraints. This makes choosing the working set a more constrained, and thus more difficult, problem.

4. THE GPU ARCHITECTURE

Optimizing the dual problem (2) on a serial architecture is fairly well understood, and many successful implementations are available. In order to illustrate the different considerations involved in optimizing (2) on a highly parallel Graphics Processing Unit (GPU), we briefly discuss the relevant aspects of this specialized hardware. We make no attempt to provide a full description of the graphics hardware, and only highlight those aspects that most influence the different design decisions in a GPU versus CPU based implementation of kernel SVM training. We implemented our optimizer on a NVIDIA GPU using the Compute Unified Device Architecture (CUDA) tools, and refer here specifically to this hardware, although the high-level design considerations are also relevant for other graphics processors.

While one might simplistically think of a GPU as a massively-parallel execution environment for a large number of independent threads, full utilization of the graphics hardware is only possible if the operations performed by concurrently-executing threads are, in a sense, "compatible". In this regard, a GPU shares many aspects of Single-Instruction-Multiple-Data computers.

On the coarsest level, a CUDA program is executed by running the same code on some number of threads, which are distributed among the GPU's processors. The threads possess a small amount of fast local memory which is shared among blocks of threads (see below), but must copy data back and forth between this small fast local memory and the higher latency main memory.

In the problem which we are considering, the most important efficiency consideration is, overwhelmingly, access to main memory ("global memory"). This memory is relatively high bandwidth, but is also high latency. The graphics card performs automatic "latency hiding", in which a thread waiting on a memory access is swapped out for one which is not. This is helpful, but does not fully solve the problem—waiting for memory accesses can still often dominate the runtime of a GPU program. An important programming technique for improving the memory-access patterns of a GPU program is called "coalescing": whenever aligned blocks of 16 consecutive threads (with consecutive thread identifiers) access aligned blocks of 16 consecutive memory locations, these accesses will be "coalesced" into a single memory access, resulting in a significant speedup.

The threads involved in a computation are organized into "blocks" of some number of threads (256 in our application). Each such block has an associated pool of "shared memory", which is much faster than global memory, but slower then registers, and may be accessed by all of the threads in the block. The fact that shared memory is so much faster than global memory may be exploited through a technique known as "staging", in which blocks of global memory are copied into shared memory using coalesced reads, manipulated (not necessarily in a coalesced fashion) by the threads in a block, and then (possibly) staged back into global memory using coalesced writes.

In applications such as ours, where a moderate amount of computation is performed on a large amount of data, taking full advantage of coalescing (often via staging) is of the highest importance. Hence, we will focus primarily on this issue for the remainder of the paper.

5. OUR IMPLEMENTATION

We are now ready to describe the approach we take in optimizing the SVM training problems (2) and (4) on a GPU. Our optimizer closely follows the sketch of Section 3. Computation is divided between the CPU and GPU, with large parallel computations being performed on the graphics hardware, and lightweight serial tasks on the host processor. The vectors α are stored in both the host machine's main memory, and the graphics card's global memory. These two copies must be kept in sync throughout the optimization. The response vectors c are stored in the graphics card's global memory, with only the working set values (i.e. for $i \in \mathcal{I}$) passed to the CPU at each iteration. The cost of these memory transfers is negligible. We begin by initializing $\alpha = 0$ and $c = 0$, and then proceed iteratively, performing the following steps:

1. On the GPU, choose a working set $\mathcal{I}$
2. On the CPU, calculate the Gram matrix restricted to the working set $\mathcal{I}$, and optimize the subproblem (5). This results in updates to the values α_i for $i \in \mathcal{I}$.
3. On the GPU, update all elements of c in response to the change in α_i for $i \in \mathcal{I}$ as in (6).

For the subproblem size that we use, the cost of step (2), performed on the CPU, is insignificant, relative to the GPU portions of the algorithm. For multiclass problems we follow a similar approach, at each iteration optimizing over $\alpha_i^{(y)}$ for $i \in \mathcal{I}$ and all $y \in \{1, \ldots, m\}$.

While it is possible to use working sets as small as two, we use larger working sets, optimizing larger subproblems. This choice is motivated by the observation (Section 4) that the primary efficiency constraint, on the GPU, is not *computation*, but is rather *memory accesses*. We may calculate the kernel matrix rows corresponding to a sufficiently small working set in only one pass over the training data. Hence, in order to extract the maximal utility from each such pass, one would like to use working sets which are as large as is feasible. Conversely, one will often experience diminishing returns (in terms of the amount of "progress" made per iteration) as the size of the working set grows. We found the use of size 16 working sets to be most convenient.

For a sparse dataset, ensuring that memory accesses are coalesced is more difficult than it is for a dense dataset, since if "adjacent" threads are accessing training vectors with different sparsity patterns, then they will not be accessing adjacent memory addresses. We resolve this by first observing that, on sparse machine learning datasets, certain features may occur more frequently than others, or certain sets of features might tend to co-occur, resulting in distinct training vectors often having similar sparsity patterns. We therefore propose clustering the dataset by sparsity pattern, using a simple greedy heuristic, about which more will be said in Section 5.3. Our implementation is structured in such a way that every element of each thread block is always working on the same cluster, i.e. on vectors with the same sparsity pattern, permitting memory accesses to be coalesced.

In the following sections, we discuss the heuristic procedure used to choose the working set, and its GPU implementation (Step 1, discussed in Section 5.1), updating of the c_is (Step 3, discussed in Section 5.2), how sparsity is handled via clustering (Section 5.3), and finally, we briefly mention how labels are predicted for new examples following training (Section 5.4).

5.1 Heuristics

The intuition behind the heuristics which we use to select the working set $\mathcal{I}$ is the same for both binary classification and multiclass: we wish to select the working set which will result in the largest increase in the dual objective function value. We use "first-order" heuristics, in the sense that we estimate the quality of a working set by looking only at the first derivatives of the dual objective. Second-order heuristics have been found to outperform first-order heuristics for binary classification problems with an unregularized bias, when the working set is of size 2 [7]. However, it is not clear how to efficiently generalize such heuristics to either the larger working sets which we must use in order to minimize the number of memory accesses, or to the multiclass objective.

For binary classification problems, we use the same heuristic as SVM-Light [9]. The goal of this heuristic is to choose those elements with respect to which the partial derivatives of the dual objective are large, and to do so in such a way that the set of chosen indices allows for large-magnitude changes which satisfy the constraints. The partial derivatives of the dual objective for binary classification (2) are:

$$\frac{\partial g_b}{\partial \alpha_i} = 1 - y_i c_i$$

Due to the equality constraint $\sum_i y_i \alpha_i = 0$, any increase in $y_i \alpha_i$ for one index i must be matched by corresponding decreases for others. As a result, our size-16 working set will be chosen to contain 8 elements maximizing y_i times the corresponding partial derivative, and 8 minimizing it. We must also respect the inequality constraints $0 \leq \alpha_i \leq C$, so cannot increase any $\alpha_i = C$, nor decrease any $\alpha_i = 0$. Hence, indices i with $\alpha_i = C$ are not considered as candidates for increase during working set selection, with the $\alpha_i = 0$ case being handled analogously.

For multiclass problems, our heuristic is taken from Crammer and Singer [5]. The intuition behind this heuristic is the same as for binary classification, although there are additional complications, due to the fact that there are multiple dual variables corresponding to each element of the training set. The partial derivatives of the multiclass dual objective (4) are:

$$\frac{\partial g_m}{\partial \alpha_i^{(y)}} = \delta_{y,y_i} - c_i^{(y)}$$

Here, δ is the Kronecker delta function. Ideally, we would choose those indices i which maximize the magnitude of the "row gradient" $\{\alpha_i^{(y)} : y \in \{1, \ldots, m\}\}$. However, this simple choice ignores the equality constraints. The ideal solution would be to project these row gradients onto the constraints, but doing so is itself a nontrivial optimization problem, and inappropriate as a component of a "simple" heuristic. Instead, we will approximate these projected row gradients by identifying, for each i, the pair of labels y_+ and y_- for which increasing the dual variable corresponding to the first while decreasing that corresponding to the second by the same amount (thus respecting the constraint $\sum_y \alpha_i^{(y)} = 0$) results in the largest first-order improvement in the dual objective:

$$y_+ = \underset{y:\alpha_i^{(y)} < C}{\operatorname{argmax}} \frac{\partial g_m}{\partial \alpha_i^{(y)}}$$

$$y_- = \underset{y}{\operatorname{argmin}} \frac{\partial g_m}{\partial \alpha_i^{(y)}}$$

Defining $v_i = \partial g_m / \partial \alpha_i^{(y_+)} - \partial g_m / \partial \alpha_i^{(y_-)}$ as the magnitude of the gradient in the direction induced by y_+ and y_- gives the heuristic value for the index i. One can see that this heuristic value lower-bounds the magnitude which would result from properly projecting the row gradient onto the constraints, and furthermore that it must be positive if a nonzero improvement is possible. The working set $\mathcal{I}$ will be composed of the 16 indices i maximizing maximizing v_i.

Both of these heuristics are implemented on the GPU. Calculation of the heuristic values themselves is computationally inexpensive, and may be performed independently for each training example. Hence, distributing this task among the graphics card's threads is straightforward. Finding the maximum (equivalently, minimum) values of these heuristics is a parallel max-reduction, which requires some care to implement efficiently. Our implementation uses a "chunking-and-sorting" procedure, which begins by breaking up the list of heuristic values into chunks, each of which is sorted in parallel using bitonic sort. Then, the maximum values of each chunk are copied into a new list, and we repeat until the total number of elements is below some threshold value. At this point, there are few enough values that parallelization on the GPU is no longer cost-effective, so the remaining heuristic values are copied to the CPU, and the maxima located.

This reduction step is computationally expensive—on our experimental datasets, performing it occupies a significant proportion of the runtime. For smaller working sets (say, size 2, rather than size 16), a similar heuristic, or even a superior second-order heuristic, could be implemented far more efficiently. We have found, however, that the benefits of using large working sets outweigh the extra time spent in the heuristic.

5.2 Updates

The final step in an iteration, and the "heart" of the optimization procedure, is updating the responses c in response to the changes in the dual variables α. Our general approach could theoretically support any kernel which may be written in terms of element-wise operations on the vectors, but our implementation currently only supports kernel functions which can be written in the form $K(x, y) = f(\|x\|, \|y\|, \langle x, y \rangle)$, a representation which supports several popular kernels, including the Gaussian, sigmoid and polynomial kernels. Efficient evaluation of kernel inner products is accomplished by precalculating $\|x\|$ for every training vector, and then calculating $\langle x, y \rangle$ by iterating over those vector elements which are nonzero in both x and y, taking the product of each such pair, and summing the results. The calculation of these inner products amounts to matrix multiplication, which is efficiently implementable on a GPU.

The primary difficulty in the calculation of these kernel elements is in ensuring that memory accesses are coalesced. If the training vectors are dense, then one natural approach would be to make the $16 \cdot i + j$th thread responsible for calculating the kernel inner product of the ith training vector with the jth working set element, by first copying the 16 elements of the working set into a separate buffer (so that they may be read out 16 elements at a time), and then having blocks of 256 threads cooperatively stage in 16×16 chunks of the training and working sets, before calculating their product. This approach would ensure coalesced memory accesses, and is popular in matrix-multiplication implementations.

As is illustrated in the left-hand side of Figure 1, if the training vectors are sparse, then this simple strategy fails, because the differing sparsity patterns of the training vectors cause memory accesses of the working set to be uncoalesced. Our solution, illustrated in the right-hand side of the same figure, is to cluster the training vectors by sparsity pattern. This causes blocks of sequentially-numbered threads to access training vectors with the same sparsity pattern,

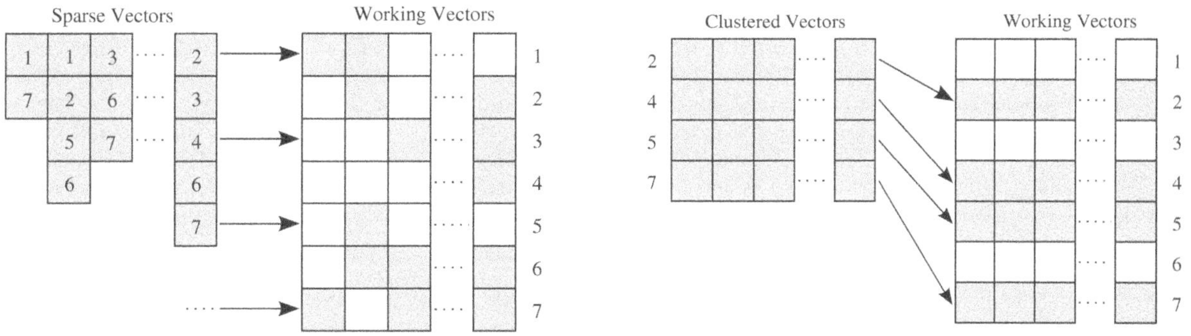

Figure 1: Illustration of memory-access patterns when the training data is sparse (left), or clustered by sparsity pattern (right). The "sparse vectors" are a set of vectors with different sparsity patterns, with the index of each nonzero element being the number contained within the corresponding box. The "clustered vectors" represent a sequence of consecutive training vectors which all have the same sparsity pattern, with the nonzero indices being the numbers to the left. The "working vectors" are dense copies of the 16 elements of the working set $\mathcal{I}$. Note that, in the right-hand diagram, the memory locations which must be accessed lie in the same rows, illustrating that they may be read as aligned 16-element chunks.

ensuring that their accesses to the working set will be coalesced. This comes at the cost of requiring that additional elements occasionally be introduced into the training vectors, in order to ensure that all elements of each cluster have the same sparsity pattern.

Algorithm 1 contains pseudocode for updating the "responses" $c_i = \sum_{j=1}^{n} \alpha_j y_j K(x_i, x_j)$ for all i, in response to a change in 16 αs. As before, the working set vectors are copied out of the training set into a temporary dense matrix, before the call to the update routine. Within the update, the kth training vector is assigned to the kth thread, which calculates the kernel inner products of this vector with all 16 elements of the working set. Each block of 256 threads repeatedly stages in 16×16 chunks of the working set. After each such chunk has been staged in, each thread steps through it, updating the inner products for which it is responsible. Note that in the key inner-loop of the psuedocode, only registers and shared memory are accessed, and these chunks of shared memory are staged in using coalesced reads, thanks to the clustering of the training data.

5.3 Clustering

Clustering by sparsity pattern will result in the greatest improvement in runtime if the clusters S_i are chosen to minimize:

$$\sum_i |\{j : \exists x \in S_i \, (x_j \neq 0)\}|$$

However, it would be counterproductive to perform an extremely high-quality clustering if the resulting savings in optimization runtime were to be less than the amount of time spent finding the clusters. Hence, we wish only to find a coarse clustering quickly. The solution which we propose is to find the clusters greedily, in a single pass over the training data, on the CPU. We define the nonzero elements of a cluster to be the union of the nonzero elements of the vectors assigned to that cluster. If we assign a new training vector x to cluster S, then the sparsity patterns of both S and x will be changed, via the addition of new elements, in order to bring them into correspondence. Algorithm 2 simply iterates over the training set, greedily assigning each x to the cluster which results in the insertion of the fewest new elements.

There is one additional parameter to this algorithm which remains to be explained: the maximum number of "active clusters" k, denoting the number of candidate clusters which will be considered for each training vector. If $k = \infty$, then all clusters are active from the start, resulting in a runtime which is quadratic in n. When k is smaller, a training vector can only be assigned to those clusters which are active at the time it is considered, which improves the runtime from $O(n^2)$ to $O(nk)$. Empirically, we have found that by decreasing k, clustering times can be improved dramatically, with little degradation in quality.

5.4 Classification

It is also important that it be possible to rapidly classify testing vectors using a learned classifier. Recall that we must calculate, for each testing vector x:

$$\text{sign}\left(b + \sum_{i=1}^{n} \alpha_i y_i K(x, x_i)\right) \tag{7}$$

Our classification routine is extremely similar to the update routine of Algorithm 1. The testing set is first broken up into pseudo-"working sets" of size 16. Kernel inner products are calculated in the same fashion as before, after which the sums in equation 7 are computed using a parallel sum-reduction. The key difference is that, during classification, we need only consider those elements of the training set which have nonzero coefficients α_i in equation 7. As a result, before classification, we "finalize" the learned classifier by discarding all of the training vectors with zero coefficients, and re-clustering the remaining vectors.

5.5 Other Approaches

The design choices which we have thus far described have the side-effect of making it difficult for our algorithm to incorporate certain optimizations which are popular in other implementations.

Most SVM optimizers keep a "cache" of recently-computed rows of the kernel matrix, based on the intuition that the same elements of the training set will be repeatedly chosen by the heuristic, particularly when the algorithm is close to convergence. If the kernel matrix rows corresponding to these elements are on-hand, then significant computational effort may be saved. On the GPU, keeping a cache of kernel matrix rows comes at a high cost. As it stands, our algorithm never explicitly stores individual elements of the kernel matrix, and global memory accesses are sufficiently expensive that the performance impact of doing so would be non-negligible. This cost might be justified in some cases, particularly on those datasets containing a small number of training examples, for which cache elements are likely to be accessed frequently. Our GPU implementation, however, is deliberately targeted towards datasets containing

Algorithm 1 GPU algorithm which, for the binary classification objective, updates the responses $c_i = \sum_{j=1}^{n} \alpha_j y_j K(x_i, x_j)$ based on changes of the dual variables α_i to $\alpha_i + \Delta_i$ for $i \in \mathcal{I}$, where $\mathcal{I}$ is the working set. This pseudocode should be read as if it were executing in lockstep on all threads, although in practice synchronization must be performed in order to guarantee that the threads within each block do not fall out of sync. The training vectors for the working set are stored (as dense vectors) in u, while the nonzeros of the current cluster are stored in x, with $\mathcal{J}$ being the indices of these nonzeros.

```
// Thread t ∈ {0, ..., 255} working on cluster C
input u[i][j]: ith element of jth vector of working set
input y[i]: label of ith vector of working set
input Δ[i]: change in α for ith vector of working set
input J[i]: index of ith nonzero of C
input x[i][j]: ith nonzero of jth vector of C
in/out c[i]: response for ith vector of C
// Calculate inner products a[i] = ⟨x[···][t], u[···][i]⟩
let a[i] := 0 for i ∈ {0, ..., 15}
for i = 0 to |J| step 16
    let i' := min {i + 15, |J|}
    Stage u[J[i], ..., J[i']][0, ..., 15] into shared memory
    for j = i to i'
        Copy x[j][t] into a register
        for k = 0 to 15
            let a[k] := a[k] + x[j][t] · u[J[j]][k]
// Update classification c[t]
let b := 0
for i = 0 to 15
    let k := K (||x[···][t]||, ||u[···][i]||, a[i])
    let b := b + Δ[i] · y[i] · k
let c[t] := c[t] + b
```

Algorithm 2 Algorithm for greedily clustering a dataset by sparsity pattern. The algorithm passes once through the dataset, assigning each vector to the cluster to which its addition results in the introduction of the smallest number of nonzero elements. The number of "active clusters" is the total number of candidate clusters which are available at a given time. Choosing this number to be smaller than the total number of clusters dramatically improves runtime, at the cost of a very slight penalty to clustering performance.

```
input n: number of training vectors
input k: number of active clusters
input ℓ: maximum cluster size
input x[i][j]: jth element of ith training vector
output S[i]: ith cluster
let S[i] := ∅ for i ∈ {0, ..., ⌈n/ℓ⌉ − 1}
// a[i] will be 1 for "active" clusters, 0 otherwise
let m := max (k, ⌈n/ℓ⌉)
let a[i] := 1 for i ∈ {0, ..., m − 1}
let a[i] := 0 for i ∈ {m, ..., ⌈n/ℓ⌉ − 1}
for i = 1 to n in random order
    // calculate costs c[j] for active clusters j
    let J_x := {k : x[i][k] ≠ 0}
    for all j : a[j] = 1
        let J_S := {k : ∃x' ∈ S[j] (x'[k] ≠ 0)}
        let c[j] := |S_j| |J_x \ J_S| + |J_S \ J_x|
    // insert x[i] into the lowest-cost cluster
    let j' := argmin_{j:a[j]=1} c[j]
    let S[j'] := S[j'] ∪ {x[i]}
    // activate a new cluster, if necessary
    if |S[j']| = ℓ
      let a[j'] := 0
      if m < ⌈n/ℓ⌉
        let a[m] := 1
        let m := m + 1
```

a relatively large number of high dimensional sparse examples, for which it is unlikely that the use of a cache would prove to be cost-effective.

Bordes et al. [1] propose an elegant compromise between the use of a heuristic, and choosing working sets randomly. Their approach is to maintain a relatively large "active set" of training vectors, for which the responses c are kept up-to-date, and from which elements of the working set are selected using a heuristic. Less useful elements of the active set are periodically removed, and replaced with new elements, selected randomly from the complement of the active set. This reduces the number of elements of c which must be kept up-to-date, thus making both the heuristic, and the c-updates, less expensive. Unfortunately, it is difficult to reconcile this optimization with our clustering-based solution to handling sparsity, since it would be necessary to re-cluster the entire active set after every addition or removal of elements.

Another popular optimization is the use of a "shrinking" heuristic. This heuristic is based on the observation that it may be the case that, during optimization, some correctly-classified training examples will stray so far from the decision surface that they are unlikely to ultimately make any contribution to the optimal classifier. Hence, it is safe to remove these vectors, provided that a check is performed, once optimization completes, to ensure that these removed examples are still correctly-classified, and are outside the margin. Because our clustering-based approach makes it difficult to remove individual elements from the training set during optimization, we do not make use of this optimization.

6. PERFORMANCE COMPARISON

We compared the runtime of our GPU-based SVM training implementation to the fastest CPU-based implementations of which we are aware, as well as to a previous GPU-based implementation. We use these experiments to study the efficiency of specific aspects of our implementation. We tested all implementations on the same machine, which contains an Intel Core i7 920 CPU, and 12G of memory, as well as a pair of NVIDIA Tesla C1060 graphics cards with 4G of memory. The tested GPU implementations use only a single graphics card, so the other is left idle.

Our testing datasets are listed in Figure 1. The Adult and MNIST datasets were downloaded from Léon Bottou's LASVM web page[1]. Cov1 is the covertype-1 dataset of Blackard & Dean. TIMIT is a phonetically transcribed corpus of speech spoken by North American speakers. We use MFCC features extracted from every 10ms frame of a subset of this dataset, along with their first two derivatives, for framewise classification of the stop consonants. Both the MNIST and TIMIT datasets are multiclass, but we also used them in testing binary classification experiments by taking the digit 8 and phoneme `/k/` to be the positive classes, respectively, and the union of all other labels to be the negative class. The regularization and Gaussian kernel parameters for the Adult dataset are taken from Platt [11], while those for MNIST and Cov1 are taken from Bordes et al. [1], except that the regularization parameter on MNIST was

[1] `http://leon.bottou.org/projects/lasvm`

DATA SET	TRAINING SIZE	TESTING SIZE	DIMENSION	CLASSES	BINARY C	γ
ADULT	31562	16282	123	2	1	0.05
COV1	522911	58101	54	2	3	1
MNIST	60000	10000	768	10	1	0.02
TIMIT	63881	22257	39	6	1	0.025

Table 1: Dataset properties and parameters. The "binary C" column contains the regularization trade-off parameter used for binary classification on each dataset. For multiclass, we choose C to be half as large.

	CRAMMER & SINGER		OURS	
DATA SET	TIME	SPEEDUP	TIME	SPEEDUP
MNIST	40M	1×	25S	97×
TIMIT	26M	1×	13S	121×

Table 4: Performance comparison of our multiclass GPU implementation to the CPU implementation of Crammer and Singer [5]. As in Table 3, the reported runtimes do not include time spent during initialization (or clustering).

decreased from 1000 to 1, which we have observed to improve the rate of convergence, with nearly no impact on classification performance.

We instrumented all of the tested implementations to periodically output trace points containing the current program state and the total elapsed time. The time spent inside this instrumentation code was subtracted from this running total. We then used these traces to find the first time at which the relative duality gap, $2(p-d)/(p+d)$, where p is the primal objective value and d the dual, dropped below the threshold $\epsilon = 0.01$.

6.1 Clustering

We first investigate the efficiency of our simple clustering algorithm at creating "good" clusters, i.e. where the sparsity patterns of all data points in each cluster are similar. We investigate the effect of the parameter k controlling the number of active clusters under consideration (see Section 5.3) on both the runtime, and on the quality of the resulting clustering. Table 2 displays the time required to cluster each of the sparse datasets into clusters of size 256, using a varying number of active clusters (including keeping all clusters "active"). We see that by choosing a relatively small number of active clusters, we can achieve fast clustering, with nearly the same quality as we would have with all clusters active. Hence, our implementation defaults to using 64 active clusters.

We also see from Table 2 that the clustering is effective at creating sparse clusters, with the number of non-zeros per cluster being well below the overall dimension of the data. However, on the highly sparse Adult and MNIST data sets, the average number of non-zeros per cluster is still well above the average number of non-zeros per data vector, showing that we do access many extra elements, although far fewer then we would if the data were treated as dense, as it is in other GPU implementations. We have found that the exploitation of sparsity has a concrete impact on performance: on the three sparse datasets on which we experimented, it alone was responsible for roughly a 1.5× speedup.

6.2 Training Runtime

In Table 3 we report the actual training runtimes, and speedups relative to the CPU implementation, for training binary classifiers using the various GPU and CPU implementations[2]. We compare to the following:

- LIBSVM [4], a CPU-based implementation using SMO with the second-order heuristic of Fan et al. [7]. This is, for these datasets, the fastest CPU-based implementation of which we are aware.
- GPUSVM [3], which is a GPU-based implementation of essentially the algorithm used by LIBSVM.

We can see that our method efficiently utilized the GPU, taking between one and two orders of magnitude less time then the best CPU implementation (this of course depends on the specific CPU and GPU used). Our method also outperforms the previous GPU implementation on all datasets, even the dense TIMIT dataset (on which our implementation does not enjoy the benefit of sparsity), and Cov1, which contains a very small number of nonzeros per vector, on average, causing constant per-vector costs (such as evaluating the heuristic) to have a greater impact on the performance than those which depend on the dimensionality of the data (such as kernel evaluations). Our implementation is particularly effective on relatively high-dimensional sparse data sets, such as MNIST, where more time is spent performing kernel evaluations. On lower dimensional data sets, the cost of the chunking-and-sorting procedure by which we select our working set (see Section 5.1) becomes more significant, and the gain relative to Catanzaro et al. is smaller. Even on datasets such as TIMIT and Cov1, the benefits of using larger working sets, and the better handling of sparsity, outweigh the cost of chunking-and-sorting, and we still observe performance gains over Catanzaro et al.

In Table 4, we report runtimes for training multiclass SVMs, comparing with Koby Crammer's CPU-based implementation [5]. We are not aware of any previously published GPU implementation for multiclass SVMs. We see a roughly 100-fold speedup over the CPU implementation.

Finally, we measured proportions of training runtime spent within various components of the optimization routine. The results are plotted in Figure 2. On all datasets except for Cov1, the "update" step takes the majority of the runtime (on Cov1 it takes roughly 43%). This update code utilizes the GPU very efficiently, as all memory accesses are coalesced, indicating that we cannot expect to improve our runtime much by more careful coding. The time spent choosing the working set, and in particular performing the

[2]We are aware of two other GPU SVM implementations. Carpenter [2] is algorithmically very similar to GPUSVM, and reports roughly the same speedups on the Adult, Cov1 and MNIST datasets, relative to LIBSVM, as we observed for GPUSVM (albeit with different values of the parameters C and γ). This is a Windows-only implementation, so we could not experiment with it on our test machine. The other, recently made available at `http://mklab.iti.gr/project/GPU-LIBSVM`, will be presented in the upcoming WIAMIS'11 conference, and is based on precomputing the full Gram matrix on the GPU. Such an approach is only applicable when there are few enough training examples that this matrix can be stored in memory.

DATA SET	AVG. NZ	16 ACTIVE AVG. NZ	16 ACTIVE TIME	64 ACTIVE AVG. NZ	64 ACTIVE TIME	MAX. ACTIVE AVG. NZ	MAX. ACTIVE TIME
ADULT	13.9	57.5	0.042S	48.6	0.13S	45.7	0.24S
COV1	12.0	15.9	0.44S	12.8	1.3S	12.2	20S
MNIST	150	406	0.43S	357	1.5S	345	4.6S

Table 2: Time spent clustering each of the datasets of Table 1 into clusters of size 256, and the resulting average number of nonzeros per vector (see Table 1 for the dataset dimensions). TIMIT is a dense dataset, and is therefore not included.

DATA SET	LIBSVM TIME	LIBSVM SPEEDUP	GPUSVM TIME	GPUSVM SPEEDUP	OURS TIME	OURS SPEEDUP
ADULT	61S	1×	4.5S	14×	1.2S	52×
MNIST	4.4M	1×	11S	23×	3.9S	68×
TIMIT	4.6M	1×	4.9S	56×	3.5S	78×
COV1	4.5H	1×	11M	26×	7.2M	38×

Table 3: Performance comparison of our GPU implementation to the CPU implementation LIBSVM [4] and GPU implementation GPUSVM [3]. All three implementations used the termination criterion $2(p-d)/(p+d) < 0.01$, where p is the primal objective, and d the dual. The reported runtimes do not include time spent loading the dataset, during initialization, or (for our implementation) clustering the training set by sparsity pattern.

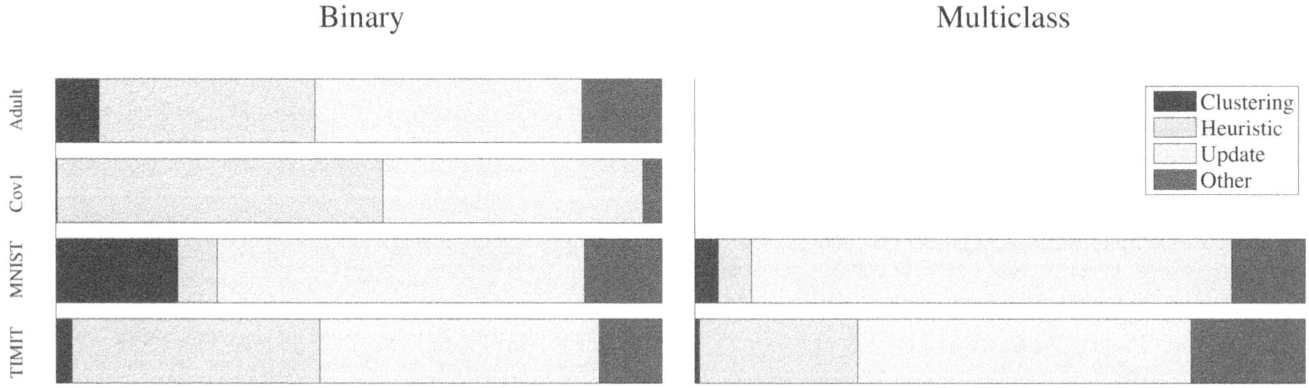

Figure 2: Illustration of the how runtime is distributed among the various parts of the optimization routine. Unlike in Tables 3 and 4, time spent clustering *is* included in these plots. The "heuristic" portion includes the time spent evaluating the heuristic and finding its maximum values. The "other" portion is mostly occupied by copying data between the CPU and GPU, optimizing subproblems on the CPU, and evaluating and testing the termination criterion.

chunking-and-sorting procedure, consumes a significant, but not dominant, portion of the runtime. This seems to be a good tradeoff in terms of the time spent choosing the working set, versus the effectiveness of this choice. As discussed in Section 5, neither clustering the data by sparsity pattern, nor optimizing the subproblems (both performed on the CPU), require a significant amount of time.

7. SUMMARY

We presented a method for efficiently training binary and multiclass kernel SVMs using a GPU. We discussed various design considerations, which are often different than they would be for a serial CPU-based implementation, and also presented a novel approach for handling sparse data on the GPU. The result is an implementation of SVM training that is orders of magnitude faster then CPU implementations, and several times faster than previous GPU implementations. It is also the first GPU implementation we are aware of that handles multiclass classification.

Our implementation is freely available[3] and easy to set up and use. It includes not only a command-line interface, which is similar to those of other popular SVM solvers, but also C library and Matlab interfaces, all of which have full support for multiclass classification, sparse datasets, and all implemented kernels.

[3] `http://nagoya.uchicago.edu/~cotter/projects/gtsvm`

References

[1] A. Bordes, S. Ertekin, J. Weston, and L. Bottou. Fast kernel classifiers with online and active learning. *JMLR*, 6: 1579–1619, September 2005.

[2] A. Carpenter. CUSVM: A CUDA implementation of support vector classification and regression. `http://patternsonascreen.net/cuSVM.html`, 2009.

[3] B. Catanzaro, N. Sundaram, and K. Keutzer. Fast support vector machine training and classification on graphics processors. In *ICML'08*, pages 104–111, 2008.

[4] C.-C. Chang and C.-J. Lin. *LIBSVM: a library for support vector machines*, 2001. Software available at `http://www.csie.ntu.edu.tw/~cjlin/libsvm`.

[5] K. Crammer and Y. Singer. On the algorithmic implementation of multiclass kernel-based vector machines. *JMLR*, 2:265–292, March 2002. ISSN 1532-4435.

[6] T.-N. Do, V.-H. Nguyen, and F. Poulet. Speed up SVM algorithm for massive classification tasks. In *ADMA'08*, pages 147–157, Berlin, Heidelberg, 2008. Springer-Verlag.

[7] R.-E. Fan, P.-S. Chen, and C.-J. Lin. Working set selection using second order information for training support vector machines. *JMLR*, 6:1889–1918, 2005.

[8] C.-J. Hsieh, K.-W. Chang, C.-J. Lin, S. S. Keerthi, and S. Sundararajan. A dual coordinate descent method for large-scale linear SVM. In *ICML'08*, pages 408–415, 2008.

[9] T. Joachims. Making large-scale support vector machine learning practical. In B. Schölkopf, C. Burges, and A. Smola, editors, *Advances in Kernel Methods - Support Vector Learning*. MIT Press, 1998.

[10] E. Osuna, R. Freund, and F. Girosi. Training support vector machines: an application to face detection. In *CVPR'97*, June 1997.

[11] J. C. Platt. Fast training of support vector machines using Sequential Minimal Optimization. In B. Schölkopf, C. Burges, and A. Smola, editors, *Advances in Kernel Methods - Support Vector Learning*. MIT Press, 1998.

[12] B. Schölkopf and A. J. Smola. *Learning with Kernels: Support Vector Machines, Regularization, Optimization, and Beyond.* MIT Press, Cambridge, MA, USA, 2001. ISBN 0262194759.

[13] S. Shalev-Shwartz, Y. Singer, and N. Srebro. Pegasos: Primal Estimated sub-GrAdient SOlver for SVM. In *ICML'07*, pages 807–814, 2007.

[14] S. Shalev-Shwartz, Y. Singer, N. Srebro, and A. Cotter. Pegasos: Primal Estimated sub-GrAdient SOlver for SVM. *Mathematical Programming*, pages 1–34, October 2010.

A Multi-Task Learning Formulation for Predicting Disease Progression

Jiayu Zhou, Lei Yuan, Jun Liu, Jieping Ye
Computer Science and Engineering, Center for Evolutionary Medicine and Informatics, The Biodesign Institute, Arizona State University, Tempe, AZ 85287
{Jiayu.Zhou, Lei.Yuan, Jun.Liu, Jieping.Ye}@asu.edu

ABSTRACT

Alzheimer's Disease (AD), the most common type of dementia, is a severe neurodegenerative disorder. Identifying markers that can track the progress of the disease has recently received increasing attentions in AD research. A definitive diagnosis of AD requires autopsy confirmation, thus many clinical/cognitive measures including Mini Mental State Examination (MMSE) and Alzheimer's Disease Assessment Scale cognitive subscale (ADAS-Cog) have been designed to evaluate the cognitive status of the patients and used as important criteria for clinical diagnosis of probable AD. In this paper, we propose a multi-task learning formulation for predicting the disease progression measured by the cognitive scores and selecting markers predictive of the progression. Specifically, we formulate the prediction problem as a multi-task regression problem by considering the prediction at each time point as a task. We capture the intrinsic relatedness among different tasks by a temporal group Lasso regularizer. The regularizer consists of two components including an $\ell_{2,1}$-norm penalty on the regression weight vectors, which ensures that a small subset of features will be selected for the regression models at all time points, and a temporal smoothness term which ensures a small deviation between two regression models at successive time points. We have performed extensive evaluations using various types of data at the baseline from the Alzheimer's Disease Neuroimaging Initiative (ADNI) database for predicting the future MMSE and ADAS-Cog scores. Our experimental studies demonstrate the effectiveness of the proposed algorithm for capturing the progression trend and the cross-sectional group differences of AD severity. Results also show that most markers selected by the proposed algorithm are consistent with findings from existing cross-sectional studies.

Categories and Subject Descriptors

H.2.8 [**Database Management**]: Database Applications—*Data Mining*; J.3 [**Life and Medical Sciences**]: Health, Medical information systems

General Terms

Algorithms

Keywords

Alzheimer's Disease, regression, multi-task learning, group Lasso, stability selection, cognitive score

1. INTRODUCTION

Alzheimer's disease (AD), the most common type of dementia, is characterized by the progressive impairment of neurons and their connections resulting in loss of cognitive function and ultimately death [20]. AD currently affects about 5.3 million individuals in United States and more than 30 million worldwide with a significant increase predicted in the near future [5]. Alzheimer's disease has been not only the substantial financial burden to the health care system but also the psychological and emotional burden to patients and their families. As the research on developing promising new treatments to slow or prevent AD progressing, the need for markers that can track the progress of the disease and identify it early becomes increasingly urgent.

A definitive diagnosis of AD can only be made through an analysis of brain tissue during a brain biopsy or autopsy [18]. Many clinical/cognitive measures have been designed to evaluate the cognitive status of the patients and used as important criteria for clinical diagnosis of probable AD, such as Mini Mental State Examination (MMSE) and Alzheimer's Disease Assessment Scale cognitive subscale (ADAS-Cog) [25]. MMSE has been shown to be correlated with the underlying AD pathology and progressive deterioration of functional ability [18]. ADAS-Cog is the gold standard in AD drug trial for cognitive function assessment [31]. Since neurodegeneration of AD proceeds years before the onset of the disease and the therapeutic intervention is more effective in the early stage of the disease, there is thus an urgent need to address two major research questions: (1) how can we predict the progression of the disease measured by cognitive scores, e.g., MMSE and ADAS-Cog? (2) what is the smallest set of features (measurements) most predictive of the progression? The prime candidate markers for tracking disease progression include neuroimages such as magnetic resonance imaging (MRI), cerebrospinal fluid (CSF), and baseline clinical assessments [12].

The relationship between the cognitive scores and possible risk factors such as age, APOE gene, years of education and gender has been previously studied [36, 17]. Many existing works analyzed the relationship between cognitive scores and imaging markers based on MRI such as gray matter volumes, density and loss [3, 8, 15, 16, 33], shape of ventricles [14, 34] and hippocampal [34] by correlating these features with baseline MMSE scores. In [13], the intensity and volume of medial temporal lobe altogether with other risk factors and the gray matter were shown to be correlated with the 6-month MMSE score, which allowed us to predict near-future clinical scores of patients. Relations between 6-month atrophy patterns in medial temporal region and memory declination in terms of clinical scores had also been examined in [27]. To predict the longitudinal response to Alzheimer's Disease progression, Ashford and Schmitt built a model with horologic function using "time-index" to measure the rate of dementia progression [4]. In [10], the so-called SPARE-AD index was proposed based on spatial patterns of brain atrophy and its linear effect against MMSE was reported. In a more recent study by Ito *et al.*, the progression rate of cognitive scores was modeled using power functions [17].

Most existing work employed either the regression model [13, 33] or the survival model [37] for modeling the disease progression. The correlation between the ground truth and the prediction is used to evaluate the model [13, 33]. When the size of covariates is small, each covariate can be individually added to the model to examine its effectiveness for predicting the target [17, 38], or univariate analysis is performed individually on all covariates and those who exceed a certain significance threshold are included in the model [27]. When the number of covariates is large and significant correlations among covariates exist, these approaches are suboptimal. To deal with the curse of dimensionality, dimension reduction techniques are commonly employed. Duchesne *et al.* used principle components analysis (PCA) to build a low dimensional feature space from image data [13]. An obvious disadvantage of dimension reduction techniques such as PCA is that the model is no longer interpretable, since all features are involved. Stonnington *et al.* used relevance vector regression (RVR), which integrated feature selection in the training stage [33]. These approaches only predict clinical scores at a single time point and their performances are far from satisfactory to be clinically useful for AD prognosis.

In this paper, we propose a multi-task learning formulation for predicting the progression of the disease measured by the clinical scores at multiple time points and simultaneously selecting markers predictive of the progression. Specifically, we formulate the prediction of clinical scores at a sequence of time points as a multi-task regression problem, where each task concerns the prediction of a clinical score at one time point. Multi-task learning aims at improving the generalization performance by learning multiple related tasks simultaneously. The key of multi-task learning is to exploit the intrinsic relatedness among the tasks. For the disease progression considered in this paper, it is reasonable to assume that a small subset of features is predictive of the progression, and the multiple regression models from different time points satisfy the smoothness property, that is, the difference of the cognitive scores between two successive time points is small. To this end, we develop a novel multi-task learning formulation based on a temporal group Lasso regularizer. The regularizer consists of two components including an $\ell_{2,1}$-norm penalty [39] on the regression weight vectors, which ensures that a small subset of features will be selected for the regression models at all time points, and a temporal smoothness term, which ensures a small deviation between two regression models at successive time points.

We have performed extensive experimental studies to evaluate the effectiveness of the proposed algorithm. We use various types of data from the Alzheimer's Disease Neuroimaging Initiative (ADNI) database including MRI scans, CSF, and clinical scores at the baseline to predict the MMSE and ADAS-Cog scores for the next three years. Our experimental studies show that the proposed algorithm better captures the progression trend and the cross-sectional group differences of AD severity than existing methods. Results also show that most markers selected by the proposed algorithm are consistent with findings from existing cross-sectional studies.

2. PROPOSED MULTI-TASK REGRESSION FORMULATION

In the longitudinal AD study, we measure the cognitive scores of selected patients repeatedly at multiple time points. By considering the prediction of cognitive scores at a single time point as a regression task, we formulate the progression of clinical scores as a multi-task regression problem. We employ the multi-task regression formulation instead of solving a set of independent regression problems since the intrinsic temporal smoothness information among different tasks can be incorporated into the model as prior knowledge.

Consider a multi-task regression problem of t time points with n training samples of d features. Let $\{x_1, x_2, \cdots, x_n\}$ be the input data at the baseline, and $\{y_1, y_2, \cdots, y_n\}$ be the targets, where each $x_i \in \mathbb{R}^d$ represents a sample (patient), and $y_i \in \mathbb{R}^t$ is the corresponding targets (clinical scores) at different time points. In this paper we employ linear models for the prediction. Specifically, the prediction model for the ith time point is given by $f^i(x) = x^T w^i$, where w^i is the weight vector of the model. Let $X = [x_1, \cdots, x_n]^T \in \mathbb{R}^{n\times d}$ be the data matrix, $Y = [y_1, \cdots, y_n]^T \in \mathbb{R}^{n\times t}$ be the target matrix, and $W = [w^1, w^2, ..., w^t] \in \mathbb{R}^{d\times t}$ be the weight matrix. One simple approach is to estimate W by minimizing the following objective function:

$$\min_W \|XW - Y\|_F^2 + \theta_1 \|W\|_F^2, \tag{1}$$

where the first term measures the empirical error on the training data, the second (penalty) term controls the generalization error, $\theta_1 > 0$ is a regularization parameter, and $\|.\|_F$ is the Frobenius norm of a matrix. The regression method above is known as the *ridge regression* and it admits an analytical solution given by:

$$W = (X^T X + \theta_1 I)^{-1} X^T Y. \tag{2}$$

One major limitation of the regression model above is that the tasks at different time points are assumed to be independent with each other, which is not the case in the longitudinal AD study considered in this paper.

2.1 Temporal Smoothness Prior

To capture the temporal smoothness of the cognitive scores at different time points, we introduce a regularization term in the regression model that penalizes large deviations of predictions at neighboring time points, resulting in the following formulation:

$$\min_{W} \|XW - Y\|_F^2 + \theta_1 \|W\|_F^2 + \theta_2 \sum_{i=1}^{t-1} \left\|w^i - w^{i+1}\right\|_2^2, \quad (3)$$

where $\theta_2 \geq 0$ is a regularization parameter controlling the temporal smoothness. This temporal smoothness term can be expressed as:

$$\sum_{i=1}^{t-1} \left\|w^i - w^{i+1}\right\|_F^2 = \|WH\|_F^2,$$

where $H \in \mathbb{R}^{t\times(t-1)}$ is defined as follows: $H_{ij} = 1$ if $i = j$, $H_{ij} = -1$ if $i = j+1$, and $H_{ij} = 0$ otherwise. The formulation in Eq.(3) becomes:

$$\min_{W} \|XW - Y\|_F^2 + \theta_1 \|W\|_F^2 + \theta_2 \|WH\|_F^2. \quad (4)$$

The optimization problem in Eq.(4) admits an analytical solution, as shown below. First, we take the derivative of Eq.(4) with respect to W and set it to zero:

$$X^TXW - X^TY + \theta_1 W + \theta_2 WHH^T = 0, \quad (5)$$

$$\left(X^TX + \theta_1 I_d\right) W + W\left(\theta_2 HH^T\right) = X^TY, \quad (6)$$

where I_d is the identity matrix of size d by d. Since both matrices $(X^TX+\theta_1 I_d)$ and $\theta_2 HH^T$ are symmetric, we write the eigen-decomposition of these two matrices by $Q_1\Lambda_1Q_1^T$ and $Q_2\Lambda_2Q_2^T$, where $\Lambda_1 = diag(\lambda_1^{(1)}, \lambda_1^{(2)}, \ldots, \lambda_1^{(d)})$ and $\Lambda_2 = diag(\lambda_2^{(1)}, \lambda_2^{(2)}, \ldots, \lambda_2^{(d)})$, are their eigenvalues, and Q_1 and Q_2 are orthogonal. Plugging them into Eq. (6) we get:

$$Q_1\Lambda_1Q_1^TW + WQ_2\Lambda_2Q_2^T = X^TY, \quad (7)$$

$$\Lambda_1Q_1^TWQ_2 + Q_1^TWQ_2\Lambda_2 = Q_1^TX^TYQ_2. \quad (8)$$

Denote $\hat{W} = Q_1^TWQ_2$ and $D = Q_1^TX^TYQ_2$. Eq.(8) becomes $\Lambda_1\hat{W} + \hat{W}\Lambda_2 = D$. Thus $\hat{W}$ is given by:

$$\hat{W}_{i,j} = \frac{D_{i,j}}{\lambda_1^{(i)} + \lambda_2^{(j)}}. \quad (9)$$

The optimal weight matrix is then given by $W^* = Q_1\hat{W}Q_2^T$.

2.2 Dealing with Incomplete Data

The clinical scores for many patients are missing at some time points, i.e., the target vector $y_i \in \mathbb{R}^t$ may not be complete. A simple strategy is to remove all patients with missing target values, which, however, significantly reduces the number of samples. We consider to extend the formulation in Eq.(4) with missing target values in the training process. In this case, the analytical solution to Eq.(4) no longer exists. We show how the algorithm above can be adapted to deal with missing target values.

We use a matrix $S \in \mathbb{R}^{n\times t}$ to indicate missing target values, where $S_{i,j} = 0$ if the target value of sample i is missing at the jth time point, and $S_{i,j} = 1$ otherwise. We use the componentwise operator $\odot$ as follows: $Z = A \odot B$ denotes $z_{i,j} = a_{i,j}b_{i,j}$, for all i, j. The formulation in Eq.(4) can be extended to the case with missing target values as:

$$\min_{W} \|S \odot (XW - Y)\|_F^2 + \theta_1 \|W\|_F^2 + \theta_2 \|WH\|_F^2. \quad (10)$$

Denote $\mathcal{P}_r(.)$ as the row selection operator parameterized by a selection vector r. The resulting matrix of $\mathcal{P}_r(A)$ includes only A_i such that $r_i \neq 0$, where A_i is the ith row of A. Let S^i be the ith column of S. We therefore denote $X_{(i)} = \mathcal{P}_{S^i}(X) \in \mathbb{R}^{n_i\times d}$ as the input data matrix of the ith task, and $y_{(i)} = \mathcal{P}_{S^i}(Y^i) \in \mathbb{R}^{n_i\times 1}$ as the corresponding target vector, where n_i is number of samples from the ith task.

Similar to the case without missing target values considered in Section 2.1, we take the derivative of Eq.(10) with respect to w^i $(2 \leq i \leq t-1)$ and set it to zero:

$$Aw^{i-1} + M_iw^i + Aw^{i+1} = T_i, \quad (11)$$

where A, M_i, and T_i are defined as follows:

$$A = -\theta_2 I_d,$$

$$M_i = X_{(i)}^TX_{(i)} + \theta_1 I_d + 2\theta_2 I_d,$$

$$T_i = X_{(i)}^Ty_{(i)}.$$

For the special case $i = 1$, the term $\left\|w^{i-1} - w^i\right\|_2^2$ does not exist, nor is the term $\left\|w^i - w^{i+1}\right\|_2^2$ for $i = t$. We combine the equations for all tasks $(1 \leq i \leq t)$, which can be represented as a block tridiagonal linear system:

$$\begin{pmatrix} M_1 & A & & & 0 \\ A & M_2 & A & & \\ & & \ddots & & \\ & & A & M_{t-1} & A \\ 0 & & & A & M_t \end{pmatrix} \begin{pmatrix} w^1 \\ w^2 \\ \vdots \\ w^{t-1} \\ w^t \end{pmatrix} = \begin{pmatrix} T_1 \\ T_2 \\ \vdots \\ T_{t-1} \\ T_t \end{pmatrix} \quad (12)$$

For a general linear system of size td, it can be solved using Gaussian elimination with a time complexity of $O((td)^3)$. For our block tridiagonal system, the complexity is reduced to $O(d^3t)$ using block Gaussian elimination. For large-scale linear systems, the LSQR algorithm [30], a popular iterative method for the solution of large linear systems of equations, can be employed with a time complexity of $O(Ntd^2)$, where N, the number of iterations, is typically small.

2.3 Temporal Group Lasso Regularization

Because of the limited availability of subjects in the longitudinal AD study and a relatively large number of features at ADNI including MRI features, the prediction model suffers from the so called "curse of dimensionality". In addition, many patients drop out from the longitudinal study after a certain period of time, which reduces the effective number of samples. One effective approach is to reduce the dimensionality of the data. However, traditional dimension reduction techniques such as PCA are not desirable since the resulting model is not interpretable, and traditional feature selection algorithms are not suitable for multi-task regression with missing target values. In the proposed formulation, we employ the group Lasso regularization based on the $\ell_{2,1}$-norm penalty for feature selection [39], which assumes that a small set of features are predictive of the progression. The group Lasso regularization ensures that all regression models at different time points share a common set of features. Together with the temporal smoothness penalty, we obtain the following formulation:

$$\min_{W} \|S\odot(XW - Y)\|_F^2 + \theta_1\|W\|_F^2 + \theta_2\|WH\|_F^2 + \delta\|W\|_{2,1} \quad (13)$$

where $\|W\|_{2,1} = \sum_{i=1}^d \sqrt{\sum_{j=1}^t W_{ij}^2}$, and δ is a regularization parameter. When there is only one task, i.e., $t = 1$, the above formulation reduces to Lasso [35]. When $t > 1$, the weights of one feature over all tasks are grouped using the

ℓ_2-norm, and all features are further grouped using the ℓ_1-norm. Thus, the $\ell_{2,1}$-norm penalty tends to select features based on the strength of the feature over all t tasks.

The objective in Eq.(13) can be considered as a combination of a smooth term and a non-smooth term. The gradient descent or accelerated gradient method (AGM) [29, 28] can be applied to solve the optimization. One of the key steps in AGM is the computation of the proximal operator associated with the $\ell_{2,1}$-norm regularization. We employ the algorithm in the SLEP package [22], which computes the proximal operator associated with the general ℓ_1/ℓ_q-norm efficiently.

2.3.1 Longitudinal Stability Selection

An important issue in the practical application of the proposed formulation is the selection of an appropriate amount of regularization, known as model selection. Cross validation is commonly used for model selection, however it tends to select more features than needed [26]. In this paper, we adapt stability selection to perform model selection for the proposed multi-task regression. Stability selection is a method recently proposed to address the problem of proper regularization using subsampling/bootstrapping [26]. It should be noted that in our formulation we find in our experiments that the list of top features selected by stability selection is not sensitive to the regularization parameters θ_1 and θ_2. We thus focus on the selection of δ, which controls the sparsity of the model, in stability selection.

Let K be the index set of features, i.e., $k \in K$ denotes a feature. Given a set of regularization parameter values Δ and an iteration number γ, longitudinal stability selection works as follows. Let $B_{(j)} = \{B^X_{(j)}, B^Y_{(j)}\}$ be a random subsample from $\{X, Y\}$ of size $\lfloor n/2 \rfloor$ without replacement. For a given $\delta > 0$, let $\tilde{W}^{(j)}$ be the optimal solution of Eq.(13) on $B_{(j)}$. Denote $U^\delta(B_{(j)}) = \{k : \tilde{W}^{(j)}_k \neq 0\}$ as the set of features selected by the model $\tilde{W}^{(j)}$. This process is repeated for γ times and selection probability $\hat{\Pi}^\delta_k$ of each feature k is given by $\sum_{j=1}^{\gamma} I(k \in U^\delta(B_{(j)}))/\gamma$, where $I(.)$ is the indicator function defined as follows: $I(c) = 1$ if c is true and $I(c) = 0$ otherwise. It is clear that $\hat{\Pi}^\delta_k$ computes the fraction of bootstrap experiments for which the feature k is selected. Repeat the above procedure for all $\delta \in \Delta$, and we define the stability score for each feature k by $\mathcal{S}(k) = \max_{\delta \in \Delta}(\hat{\Pi}^\delta_k)$. To find a suitable size of stable feature set $\hat{U}^{\text{stable}}$ we can either use top η stable features:

$$\hat{U}^{\text{stable}} = \{k : \mathcal{S}(k) \text{ ranks among top } \eta \text{ in } K\},$$

or use threshold π_{thr} on the stability score:

$$\hat{U}^{\text{stable}} = \{k : \mathcal{S}(k) \geq \pi_{thr}\}.$$

In our application we choose the top η features. Indeed, cross validation can be performed to determine how many features are needed. However, our empirical results show that using top $\eta = 20$ features is sufficient in most cases of our application.

2.4 Proposed Algorithm

One undesired property of sparse learning methods such as Lasso is that the coefficients corresponding to relevant features are shrunk towards zero [40]. This shrinkage effect would lead to sub-optimal performance. To resolve this problem, existing methods apply adaptive regularization [42], multiple thresholding procedures [41], or multi-stage methods [23, 40]. In this paper, we employ a standard two-stage procedure. In the first stage the algorithm selects features using longitudinal stability selection, resulting in a subset of features $\hat{U}^{stable}$. In the second stage the algorithm performs temporal smoothness regularized regression using selected features. We summarize the proposed algorithm in Algorithm 1.

Algorithm 1 Temporal Group Lasso Multi-Task Regression (TGL)

Input: S, X, Y, θ_1, θ_2 Δ, γ, η
Output: W^*, $\hat{U}^{\text{stable}}$

Stage 1: longitudinal stability selection
Set $K = \{\text{the feature set in } X\}$
for $\delta \in \Delta$ **do**
  for $j = 1$ to γ **do**
    Subsample $B_{(j)} = \{B^X_{(j)}, B^Y_{(j)}\}$ from $\{X, Y\}$
    Compute $\tilde{W}^{(j)}$ by solving Eq.(13) with δ, $B_{(j)}$
    Set $U^\delta(B_{(j)}) = \{k : \tilde{W}^{(j)} \neq 0\}$
  end for
  Calculate $\hat{\Pi}^\delta_k = \sum_{j=1}^{\gamma} I(k \in U^\delta(B_{(j)}))/\gamma$, $\forall k \in K$
end for
Calculate $\mathcal{S}(k) = \max_{\delta \in \Delta}(\hat{\Pi}^\delta_k)$, $\forall k \in K$
Set $\hat{U}^{\text{stable}} = \{k$: $\mathcal{S}(k)$ ranks among top η in $K\}$
Stage 2: temporal smoothness regularized regression
Set $\hat{X} = X$ restricted to the features from $\hat{U}^{\text{stable}}$
if $\exists p, q$ such that $S_{p,q} = 0$ **then**
  Set t = number of tasks, $d = |\hat{U}^{\text{stable}}|$, $A = -\theta_2 I_d$
  for $i = 1$ to t **do**
    $X_{(i)} = \mathcal{P}^i_S(\hat{X})$, $y_{(i)} = \mathcal{P}^i_S(Y^i)$
    $M_i = X^T_{(i)} X_{(i)} + \theta_1 I_d + 2\theta_2 I_d$, $T_i = X^T_{(i)} y_{(i)}$
  end for
  Obtain W^* by solving Eq.(12) with $\{M_i\}, \{T_i\}$.
else
  Compute the analytical solution W^* as in Section 2.1.
end if

3. EXPERIMENTS

In this section we evaluate the proposed algorithm on the ADNI database[1]. The source codes are available online [1].

3.1 Experimental Setup

In the ADNI project, MRI scans, CSF measurements, and clinical scores from selected patients are obtained repeatedly over a 6-month or 1-year interval. We denote each time point by the duration starting from the baseline when the patient came to the hospital for screening. For instance, M06 indicates 6 months after the baseline. We use different combinations of MRI (M), CSF (C), and META (M) (see Table 1) at baseline to predict MMSE and ADAS-Cog scores at four time points: M06, M12, M24, and M36.

For MRI, we download 1.5T MRI data of 675 patients preprocessed by UCSF using FreeSurfer. MRI features can be grouped into 5 categories: cortical thickness average (CTA), cortical thickness standard deviation (CTStd), volume of cortical parcellation (Vol. Cort.), volume of white matter parcellation (Vol. WM.), and surface area (Surf. A.). There are 313 MRI features in total. We remove all samples which fail the MRI quality controls. For other feature

[1] `www.loni.ucla.edu/ADNI/`

Table 1: Features included in the META dataset. Note that the cognitive scores at the baseline are used to predict the future cognitive scores. A detailed explanation of each cognitive score and lab test can be found at [1].

Type	Details
Demographic	age, yrs. of education, gender
Genetic	ApoE-ε4 information
Cognitive scores	MMSE, ADAS-Cog, ADAS-MOD, ADAS sub-scores, CDR, FAQ, GDS, Hachinski, Neuropsychological Battery, WMS-R Logical Memory
Lab tests	RCT1, RCT11, RCT12, RCT13, RCT14, RCT1407, RCT1408, RCT183, RCT19, RCT20, RCT29, RCT3, RCT392, RCT4, RCT5, RCT6, RCT8

sets, we remove samples with missing entries. Each feature combination includes the intersection of available samples, that is the combined dataset has no missing values. Because changes of MMSE and ADAS-Cog are both found to be closely correlated with the baseline MMSE score [17], we include the baseline MMSE score in all feature combinations. With the pre-processing procedure described above, the number of samples available for MMSE and ADAS-Cog at different time points are described in Table 2.

Table 2: The first column of the table indicates the different combinations of three datasets. The numbers of samples for different combinations available for both MMSE and ADAS-Cog at different time points are shown in the table together with the data dimensionality (Dim). C, E, and M refer to CSF, META, and MRI, respectively.

	MMSE				ADAS-Cog				Dim
	M06	M12	M24	M36	M06	M12	M24	M36	
C	332	331	295	198	332	328	294	194	6
E	648	641	567	387	646	636	563	377	52
CE	332	331	295	198	332	328	294	194	57
M	648	641	567	387	646	636	563	377	306
EM	648	641	567	387	646	636	563	377	357
CM	332	331	295	198	332	328	294	194	311
CEM	332	331	295	198	332	328	294	194	362

3.2 Prediction Performance

In this experiment, we compare our proposed approach with ridge regression on the prediction of MMSE and ADAS-Cog using various types of data combinations. We report the results based on the leave-one-out scheme due to the small sample size. 5-fold cross validation is used to select model parameters (θ_1, θ_2 in our approach and θ_1 in ridge regression) in the training data (between 10^{-3} and 10^3). To compare with related works [33, 13], we use correlation coefficient (R-value) given by the correlation between the predicted values and the ground truth, and its correlation significance (P-value) as the evaluation criteria. P-value is given by testing the hypothesis of no correlation [2]. A good prediction model has a high R-value and low P-value (less than 0.0001 for example). The overall performance of the prediction is averaged across all time points weighted by the sample size.

The results for MMSE and ADAS-Cog are summarized in Tables 3 and 4, respectively. Overall, the proposed approach significantly outperforms ridge regression. This is especially the case when the feature space is large and the sample size is small, e.g., CM and CEM (see Table 2). Note that multi-task learning effectively increases the number of samples by learning multiple related tasks simultaneously, while ridge regression treats all tasks independently. Our results verify the effectiveness of multi-task learning for disease progression.

Table 3: Comparison of our proposed approach (TGL) and ridge regression (RidR) on longitudinal MMSE prediction using different data combinations measured by R-value and average P-value. Performance at each time point is reported in terms of R-value. Weighted averages of R-values and P-values across all time points are also given.

		M06	M12	M24	M36	AvgR	P-Val
C	TGL	0.74	0.72	0.71	0.65	0.71	3.3e-026
	RidR	0.74	0.72	0.71	0.65	0.71	3.3e-026
E	TGL	0.83	0.84	0.84	0.78	0.82	7.4e-080
	RidR	0.82	0.83	0.84	0.76	0.82	2.8e-075
CE	TGL	0.80	0.82	0.82	0.72	0.80	7.2e-034
	RidR	0.77	0.80	0.79	0.71	0.77	7.8e-033
M	TGL	0.77	0.75	0.77	0.70	0.75	2.7e-059
	RidR	0.68	0.67	0.71	0.63	0.68	1.2e-045
EM	TGL	0.83	0.84	0.85	0.80	0.83	3.8e-088
	RidR	0.71	0.71	0.74	0.54	0.69	7.1e-032
CM	TGL	0.73	0.73	0.76	0.69	0.73	1.3e-030
	RidR	0.25	0.34	0.36	0.48	0.35	1.0e-006
CEM	TGL	0.80	0.83	0.83	0.72	0.80	8.4e-034
	RidR	0.29	0.36	0.59	0.56	0.43	2.4e-008

Table 4: Comparison of our proposed approach (TGL) and ridge regression (RidR) on longitudinal ADAS-Cog prediction using different data combinations measured by R-value and average P-value.

		M06	M12	M24	M36	AvgR	P-Val
C	TGL	0.70	0.71	0.71	0.66	0.70	1.7e-026
	RidR	0.70	0.71	0.70	0.66	0.70	1.5e-026
E	TGL	0.87	0.87	0.86	0.83	0.86	2.6e-099
	RidR	0.87	0.86	0.86	0.83	0.86	4.1e-097
CE	TGL	0.86	0.85	0.86	0.80	0.85	1.7e-044
	RidR	0.86	0.84	0.85	0.74	0.83	2.7e-035
M	TGL	0.75	0.78	0.76	0.74	0.76	4.4e-066
	RidR	0.66	0.71	0.67	0.61	0.67	4.9e-041
EM	TGL	0.87	0.87	0.86	0.84	0.86	3.2e-104
	RidR	0.80	0.81	0.80	0.70	0.79	2.4e-058
CM	TGL	0.75	0.77	0.75	0.74	0.76	2.5e-035
	RidR	0.55	0.60	0.62	0.53	0.58	5.4e-016
CEM	TGL	0.87	0.86	0.87	0.81	0.86	1.9e-046
	RidR	0.69	0.66	0.63	0.40	0.62	8.6e-010

In Table 5 we compare our approach with three closely related works. In [13], PCA was employed to reduce the dimensionality of the MRI data. Since only limited samples were used, the proposed method resulted in low prediction performance. To the best of our knowledge, the work in [13] is the only one that tried to predict cognitive scores at future time points and reported R/P-Value for comparison. The other two works used the ADNI database as in our study. Stonnington's work predicted baseline cognitive scores using relevance vector regression (RVR) which enforced sparsity in the model [33]. Their regression results were better than those reported in [13]. However their prediction performance is much lower than ours. This is possibly due to the use of different prediction models. Specifically, the model in [33] did not utilize rich temporal smoothness information as in the proposed approach. In [17], very limited risk factors were manually included and tested in their progression model. No actual prediction on the test data was performed. Instead, a visual comparison of the proposed model for different groups was provided, which was similar to our cross-sectional analysis in Section 3.3. It is hard to directly compare their approach with ours, since no prediction measures were reported in [17].

3.3 Cross-Sectional Progression

In this experiment, we study the cross-sectional progression patterns. We predict the progression of different patient groups using models built by ridge regression and our proposed approach on the CEM dataset. The predicted progressions for different groups including AD, MCI, and NL[2] are visualized in a cross-sectional fashion with the mean values of prediction by different methods and the group truth provided. The results are summarized in Figure 1 and Figure 2. For MMSE, the target progression in probable AD patients shows a significant declination pattern, with an annual declination of 3.167 ± 0.40. For MCI patients we observe a slight annual declination of 0.919 ± 0.188. For normal controls, the MMSE scores are very stable with an annual declination of 0.032 ± 0.025. A similar pattern can be observed for ADAS-Cog. Probable AD patients have an annual growth on ADAS-Cog of 7.066 ± 2.257, while for the MCI group the annual growth is 1.558 ± 0.401. In normal controls, we observe a very small annual change (0.007 ± 0.565).

We can also observe from Figure 1 and Figure 2 that the proposed approach can better capture the characteristics of the disease progression measured by clinical scores for different groups of patients. The proposed method performs significantly better than ridge regression for the probable AD group and the MCI group at M36 where the number of training samples is small. The result further verifies the effectiveness of multi-task learning for disease progression especially for small sample size problems.

3.4 Feature Evaluation

In this experiment we evaluate the relevance of features selected by longitudinal stability selection on different feature combinations. Given the range of regularization parameter values Δ, the set of selected features is a function of input data X and target Y, thus for the same data set X but different targets (clinical scores) Y, the algorithm may select different features. Indeed, although different clinical scores are used to measure the cognition status, they may emphasize different aspects of the AD pathology.

The top MRI markers selected by longitudinal stability selection are shown in Figure 3. We observe that volume of left hippocampus, CTA of middle temporal gyri and CTA of left and right entorhinal are among the most stable features for both MMSE and ADAS-Cog scores. These findings agree with the known knowledge that in the pathological pathway of AD, medial temporal lobe (hippocampus and entorhinal cortex) is firstly affected, followed by progressive neocortical damage [7, 11]. Evidence of a significant atrophy of middle temporal gyri in AD patients has also been observed in previous studies [9, 19, 3]. Besides hippocampus and middle temporal, we also find isthmus cingulate a very stable feature for MMSE. The atrophy of isthmus cingulate is considered high in AD patients [24]. In addition, CTA of left inferior parietal and volume of right inferior parietal are also found to be stable. This agrees with evidence from the previous study that includes pathological confirmation of the diagnosis [21], which shows that parietal atrophy contributes to predictive values for diagnosing AD.

[2]AD, MCI, and NL refer to Alzheimer's Disease patients, Mild Cognitive Impairment patients, and normal controls, respectively.

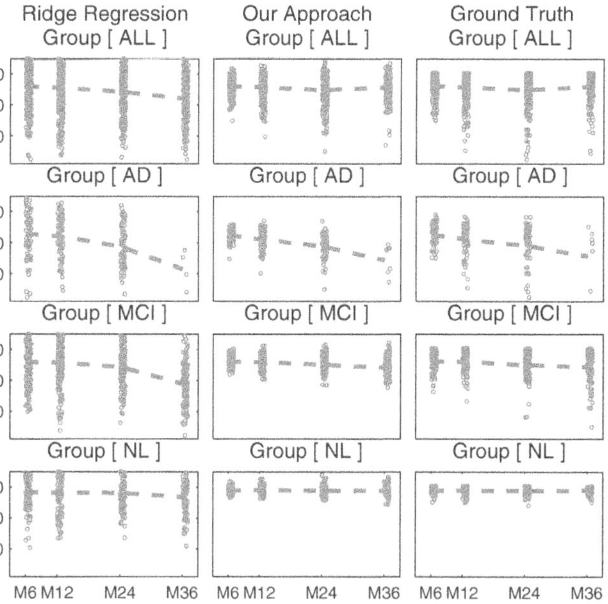

Figure 1: Visual predictive comparison for MMSE on the CEM dataset. The first, second, third, and fourth rows show the results for the complete dataset (ALL), the AD group (AD), the MCI group (MCI), and the NL group (NL), respectively. The left column shows ridge regression results. The middle column shows the results using our proposed approach. The ground truth values are plotted in the right column. The red line connects the mean values of each time point.

To access the effectiveness of CSF features, we perform longitudinal stability selection on the data combining CSF and MRI (Figure 4). In CSF, we use 3 simple features ($A\beta$-42, t-tau and p-tau) and 2 ratio features (t-tau/$A\beta$-42 and p-tau/$A\beta$-42). We observe that $A\beta$-42 and p-tau are among the top three markers, whereas t-tau is not selected in both targets.

Figure 5 shows the stability results of META features (see Table 1). Baseline clinical test scores (MMSE, ADAS-MOD, ADAS-Cog, ADAS-Cog subscores, CDR) and neuropsychological test scores (TRAASCORE, GATVEGESC) are found to be important features for both scores. Among ADAS-Cog subscores, *Word Recall* (subscore 1) and *Orientation* (subscore 7) are found to be important. These findings agree with recent itemized ADAS-Cog analysis, where orientation was found to be the most sensitive item in cross-sectional study of cognitive impairment [32]. The results of stability selection after adding META to MRI are shown in Figure 6. Many MRI features have low stability scores. A possible explanation is that some clinical tests included in META

Table 5: Comparison of the proposed approach with three related works in the literature. AD, MCI, and NL refer to Alzheimer's Disease patients, Mild Cognitive Impairment patients, and normal controls, respectively.

Method	Target	Subjects	Feature	Result
Duchesne *et al.* [13]	M06 MMSE	75 NL, 49 MCI, 75 AD	Baseline MRI, age, gender, years of education	MMSE: 0.31 (p=0.03)
Stonnington *et al.* [33]	baseline MMSE and ADAS-Cog	Set1: 73 AD, 91 NL Set2 (ADNI): 113 AD, 351 MCI, 122 NL	Baseline MRI, CSF	MMSE: Set1: 0.7 (p<10e-5) Set2: 0.48 (p<10e-5) ADAS-Cog: Set2: 0.57 (p<10e-5)
Ito *et al.* [17]	M06-M36 ADAS-Cog	ADNI: 186 AD, 402 MCI, 229 NL	Age, APOE4, gender, family history, years of education	Only visual check. R/P value not report
Our approach	M06-M36 MMSE and ADAS-Cog	ADNI: 133 AD, 304 MCI, 188 NL	Baseline MRI, CSF, and META (see Table 1 for details)	Avg MMSE: 0.83 (p=3.8e-88) Avg ADAS-Cog: 0.86 (p=3.2e-104)

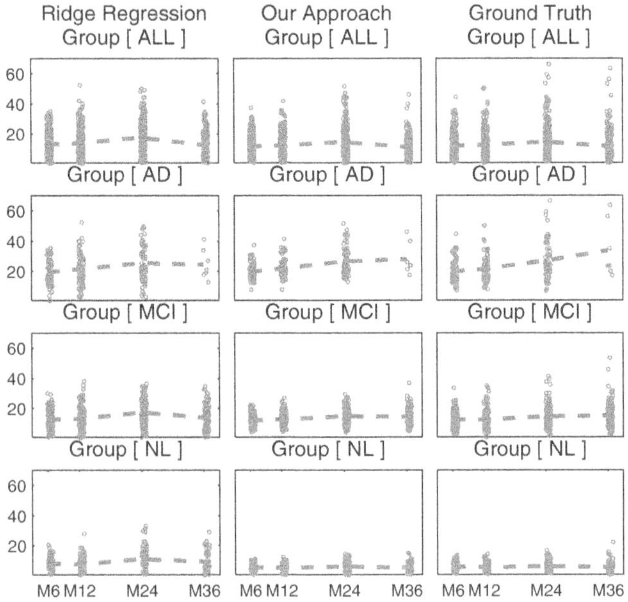

Figure 2: Visual predictive comparison for ADAS-Cog on the CEM dataset.

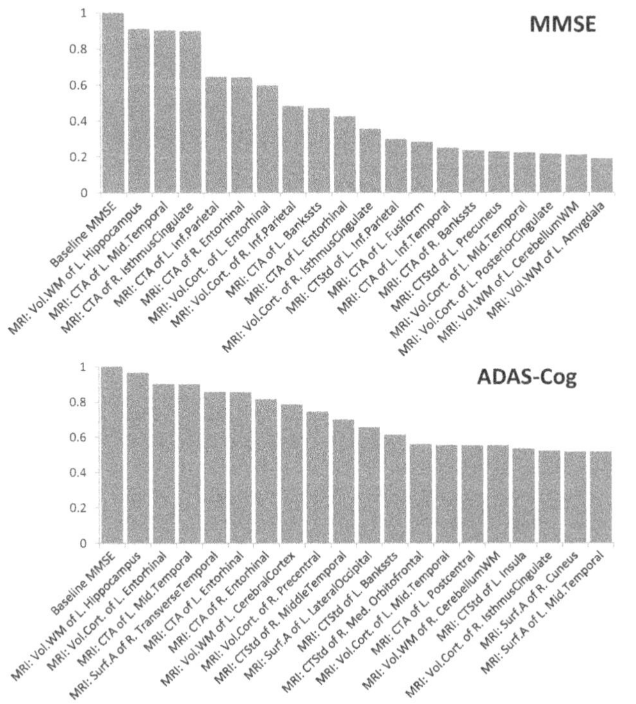

Figure 3: Longitudinal stability selection results for MMSE and ADAS-Cog on MRI data.

features reflect white matter and/or gray matter changes, as discussed in [6].

Next we perform stability selection by adding all three types of features together. Results are shown in Figure 7. We can observe from the figure that there are many features in common for both targets: baseline ADAS-Cog, ADAS-MOD and MMSE; baseline ADAS-Cog subscores 1 and 7; Logic LIMMTOTAL; APOE and DIGITSCOR.

4. CONCLUSION

In this paper, we study the feasibility of predicting AD progression measured by cognitive scores based on baseline measurements. Specifically, we formulate the progression prediction as a multi-task regression problem by considering the prediction of cognitive scores at each time point as a task. To capture the intrinsic relatedness among different tasks at different time points, we propose a temporal group Lasso regularizer, which ensures a small deviation between two regression models at successive time points based on a small subset of features. The effectiveness of the proposed approach in predicting disease progression and feature selection is evaluated by extensive experimental studies on the ADNI database. Results show that the proposed approach can better capture the progression trends than existing methods. Results also show that most features selected by the proposed approach are consistent with findings from existing cross-sectional studies. Our experimental studies demonstrate the promise of multi-task learning for predicting disease progression.

Our proposed formulation for AD progression prediction and feature selection is able to deal with missing values in the target matrix. Missing values in the input matrix, however, cannot be handled. Recent advances on matrix completion have allowed us to complete matrices with many missing values under certain conditions. We will explore such techniques for dealing with missing values in the input data. In addition, in this study we only focus on linear models; we plan to explore non-linear models in the future.

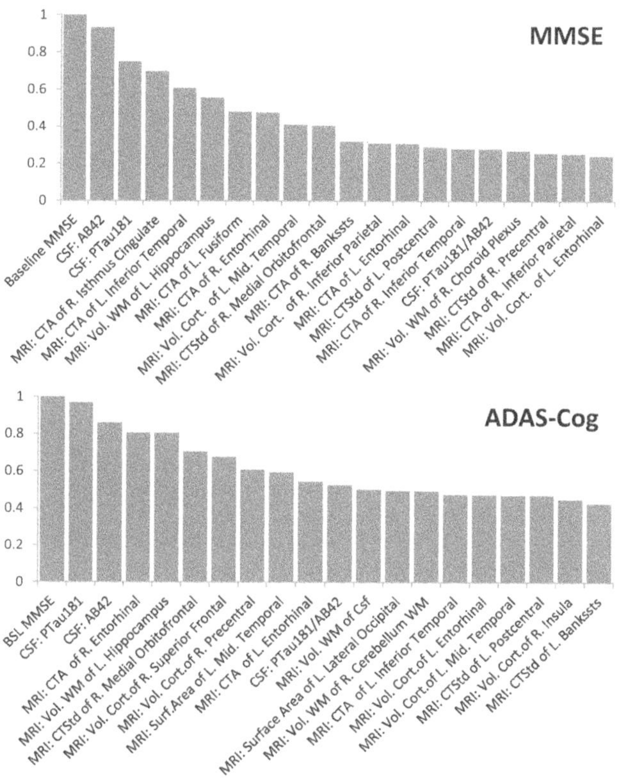

Figure 4: Longitudinal stability selection results for MMSE and ADAS-Cog on MRI+CSF data.

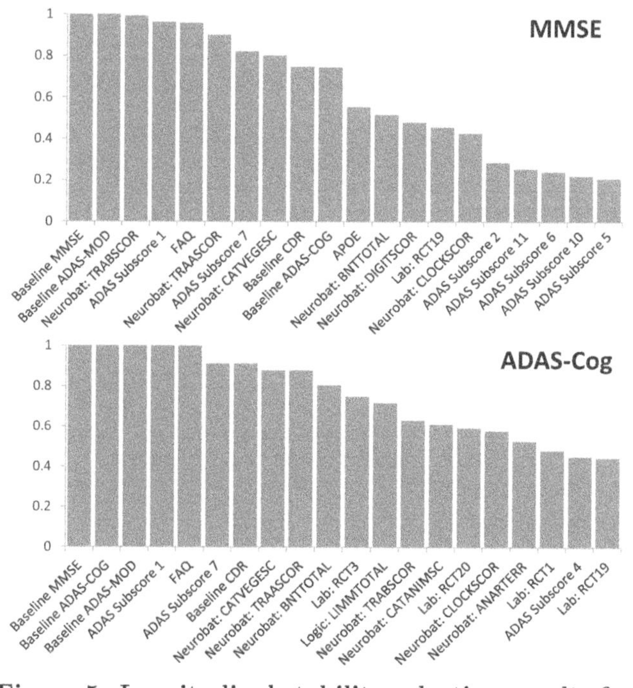

Figure 5: Longitudinal stability selection results for MMSE and ADAS-Cog on META data.

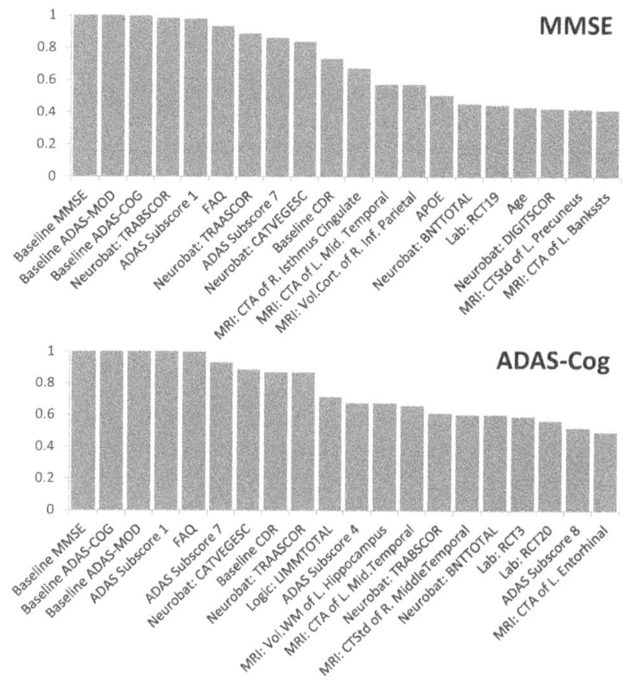

Figure 6: Longitudinal stability selection results for MMSE and ADAS-Cog on MRI+META data.

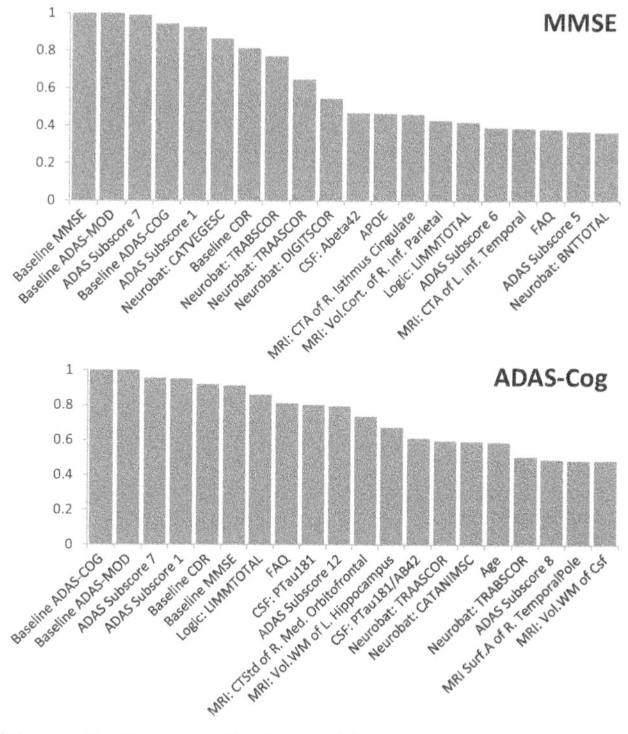

Figure 7: Longitudinal stability selection results for MMSE and ADAS-Cog on MRI+META+CSF data.

Acknowledgments

This research is sponsored in part by NSF IIS-0953662 and NSF CCF-1025177.

5. REFERENCES

[1] www.public.asu.edu/~jye02/AD-Progression.

[2] T. Anderson. *An introduction to multivariate statistical analysis*, volume 374. Wiley New York, 1958.

[3] L. Apostolova et al. 3D mapping of mini-mental state examination performance in clinical and preclinical Alzheimer disease. *Alzheimer Disease & Associated Disorders*, 20(4):224, 2006.

[4] J. Ashford and F. Schmitt. Modeling the time-course of Alzheimer dementia. *Current Psychiatry Reports*, 3(1):20–28, 2001.

[5] A. Association. 2010 alzheimer's disease facts and figures. *Alzheimer's & Dementia*, 6:158–194, 2010.

[6] L. Baxter et al. Relationship of cognitive measures and gray and white matter in Alzheimer's disease. *Journal of Alzheimer's Disease*, 9(3):253–260, 2006.

[7] H. Braak and E. Braak. Neuropathological stageing of Alzheimer-related changes. *Acta neuropathologica*, 82(4):239–259, 1991.

[8] G. Chetelat and J. Baron. Early diagnosis of Alzheimer's disease: contribution of structural neuroimaging. *Neuroimage*, 18(2):525–541, 2003.

[9] A. Convit et al. Atrophy of the medial occipitotemporal, inferior, and middle temporal gyri in non-demented elderly predict decline to Alzheimer's disease. *Neurobiology of aging*, 21(1):19–26, 2000.

[10] C. Davatzikos, F. Xu, Y. An, Y. Fan, and S. Resnick. Longitudinal progression of Alzheimer's-like patterns of atrophy in normal older adults: the SPARE-AD index. *Brain*, 132(8):2026, 2009.

[11] A. Delacourte et al. The biochemical pathway of neurofibrillary degeneration in aging and Alzheimer's disease. *Neurology*, 52(6):1158, 1999.

[12] B. Dubois et al. Research criteria for the diagnosis of Alzheimer's disease: revising the NINCDS-ADRDA criteria. *The Lancet Neurology*, 6(8):734–746, 2007.

[13] S. Duchesne, A. Caroli, C. Geroldi, D. Collins, and G. Frisoni. Relating one-year cognitive change in mild cognitive impairment to baseline MRI features. *NeuroImage*, 47(4):1363–1370, 2009.

[14] L. Ferrarini et al. MMSE scores correlate with local ventricular enlargement in the spectrum from cognitively normal to Alzheimer disease. *Neuroimage*, 39(4):1832–1838, 2008.

[15] G. Frisoni et al. Detection of grey matter loss in mild Alzheimer's disease with voxel based morphometry. *Journal of Neurology, Neurosurgery & Psychiatry*, 73(6):657, 2002.

[16] G. Frisoni, N. Fox, C. Jack, P. Scheltens, and P. Thompson. The clinical use of structural MRI in Alzheimer disease. *Nature Reviews Neurology*, 6(2):67–77, 2010.

[17] K. Ito et al. Disease progression model for cognitive deterioration from Alzheimer's Disease Neuroimaging Initiative database. *Alzheimer's and Dementia*, 6(1):39–53, 2010.

[18] R. P. Jeffrey, R. E. Coleman, and P. M. Doraiswamy. Neuroimaging and early diagnosis of alzheimer disease : A look to the future. *Radiology*, 226:315–336, 2003.

[19] V. Julkunen et al. Cortical Thickness Analysis to Detect Progressive Mild Cognitive Impairment: A Reference to Alzheimer's Disease. *Dementia and geriatric cognitive disorders*, 28(5):404–412, 2009.

[20] Z. Khachaturian. Diagnosis of Alzheimer's disease. *Archives of Neurology*, 42(11):1097, 1985.

[21] M. Likeman et al. Visual assessment of atrophy on magnetic resonance imaging in the diagnosis of pathologically confirmed young-onset dementias. *Archives of neurology*, 62(9):1410, 2005.

[22] J. Liu, S. Ji, and J. Ye. *SLEP: Sparse Learning with Efficient Projections*. Arizona State University, 2009.

[23] J. Liu, P. Wonka, and J. Ye. Multi-stage dantzig selector. In *Advances in Neural Information Processing Systems 23*, pages 1450–1458. 2010.

[24] L. McEvoy et al. Alzheimer Disease: Quantitative Structural Neuroimaging for Detection and Prediction of Clinical and Structural Changes in Mild Cognitive Impairment1. *Radiology*, 251(1):195, 2009.

[25] G. McKhann, D. Drachman, M. Folstein, R. Katzman, D. Price, and E. Stadlan. Clinical diagnosis of Alzheimer's disease: report of the NINCDS-ADRDA Work Group under the auspices of Department of Health and Human Services Task Force on Alzheimer's Disease. *Neurology*, 34:939–44, 1984.

[26] N. Meinshausen and P. Bühlmann. Stability selection. *Journal of the Royal Statistical Society: Series B*, 72(4):417–473, 2010.

[27] E. Murphy et al. Six-month atrophy in MTL structures is associated with subsequent memory decline in elderly controls. *NeuroImage*, 2010.

[28] A. Nemirovski. Efficient methods in convex programming. 2005.

[29] Y. Nesterov. *Introductory lectures on convex optimization: A basic course*. Springer Netherlands, 2004.

[30] C. Paige and M. Saunders. LSQR: An algorithm for sparse linear equations and sparse least squares. *ACM Transactions on Mathematical Software (TOMS)*, 8(1):43–71, 1982.

[31] W. Rosen, R. Mohs, and K. Davis. A new rating scale for Alzheimer's disease. *American Journal of Psychiatry*, 141(11):1356, 1984.

[32] J. Sevigny, Y. Peng, L. Liu, and C. Lines. Item analysis of ADAS-Cog: effect of baseline cognitive impairment in a clinical AD trial. *Am J Alzheimers Dis Other Demen*, 25(2):119–24, 2010.

[33] C. Stonnington, C. Chu, S. Klöppel, C. Jack Jr, J. Ashburner, and R. Frackowiak. Predicting clinical scores from magnetic resonance scans in Alzheimer's disease. *NeuroImage*, 51(4):1405–1413, 2010.

[34] P. Thompson et al. Mapping hippocampal and ventricular change in Alzheimer disease. *Neuroimage*, 22(4):1754–1766, 2004.

[35] R. Tibshirani. Regression shrinkage and selection via the lasso. *Journal of the Royal Statistical Society. Series B (Methodological)*, pages 267–288, 1996.

[36] T. Tombaugh. Test-retest reliable coefficients and 5-year change scores for the MMSE and 3MS. *Archives of clinical neuropsychology*, 20(4):485–503, 2005.

[37] P. Vemuri et al. MRI and CSF biomarkers in normal, MCI, and AD subjects: predicting future clinical change. *Neurology*, 73(4):294, 2009.

[38] K. Walhovd et al. Combining MR imaging, positron-emission tomography, and CSF biomarkers in the diagnosis and prognosis of Alzheimer disease. *American Journal of Neuroradiology*, 31(2):347, 2010.

[39] M. Yuan and Y. Lin. Model selection and estimation in regression with grouped variables. *Journal of the Royal Statistical Society: Series B (Statistical Methodology)*, 68(1):49–67, 2006.

[40] T. Zhang. Some sharp performance bounds for least squares regression with L1 regularization. *Annals of Statistics*, 37(5A):2109–2144, 2009.

[41] S. Zhou. Thresholding procedures for high dimensional variable selection and statistical estimation. *Advances in Neural Information Processing Systems*, 22, 2009.

[42] H. Zou. The adaptive lasso and its oracle properties. *Journal of the American Statistical Association*, 101(476):1418–1429, 2006.

A Simple Statistical Model and Association Rule Filtering for Classification

György J. Simon
Dept. of Health Sciences Research
Mayo Clinic, Rochester, MN
simon.gyorgy@mayo.edu

Vipin Kumar
Dept. of Computer Science
University of Minnesota,
Minneapolis, MN
kumar@cs.umn.edu

Peter W. Li
Dept. of Health Sciences Research
Mayo Clinic, Rochester, MN
li.peter@mayo.edu

ABSTRACT

Associative classification is a predictive modeling technique that constructs a classifier based on class association rules (also known as predictive association rules; PARs). PARs are association rules where the consequence of the rule is a class label. Associative classification has gained substantial research attention because it successfully joins the benefits of association rule mining with classification. These benefits include the inherent ability of association rule mining to extract high-order interactions among the predictors–an ability that many modern classifiers lack–and also the natural interpretability of the individual PARs.

Associative classification is not without its caveats. Association rule mining often discovers a combinatorially large number of association rules, eroding the interpretability of the rule set. Extensive effort has been directed towards developing interestingness measures, which filter (predictive) association rules after they have been generated. These interestingness measures, albeit very successful at selecting interesting rules, lack two features that are highly valuable in the context of classification. First, only few of the interestingness measures are rooted in a statistical model. Given the distinction between a *training* and a *test* data set in the classification setting, the ability to make statistical inferences about the performance of the predictive classification rules on the *test* set is highly desirable. Second, the unfiltered set of predictive assocation rules (PARs) are often redundant, we can prove that certain PARs will not be used to construct a classification model given the presence of other PARs.

In this paper, we propose a simple statistical model towards making inferences on the *test* set about the various performance metrics of predictive association rules. We also derive three filtering criteria based on hypothesis testing, which are very selective (reduce the number of PARs to be considered by the classifier by several orders of magnitude), yet do not effect the performance of the classification adversely. In the case, where the classification model is constructed as a logistic model on top of the PARs, we can mathematically prove, that the filtering criteria do not significantly effect the classifier's performance. We also demonstrate empirically on three publicly available data sets that the vast reduction in the number of PARs indeed did not come at the cost of reducing the predictive performance.

KDD'11, August 21–24, 2011, San Diego, California, USA.

Categories and Subject Descriptors

H.2.8 [**Information Systems**]: Data Mining;
General Terms: Algorithms.

1. INTRODUCTION

Association rule mining [3] is the problem of discovering associations in a large database efficiently. Association rules are rules representing logical implications. Consider, for example, the rule `glucose>125` $\rightarrow$ `diabetes=Yes`. This rule states that people with fasting glucose level exceeding 125 have diabetes with a specific probability, which is called the *precision* of the rule. The left hand side of the rule is its *antecedent* and the right hand side is its *consequent*.

Assume we have a database of patients with some descriptive statistics (which we call *variables*) and an *outcome*, presence or absence of diabetes. Further assume that the variables are binarized (e.g. `glucose>125`). Association rules that contain the outcome (`diabetes=Yes` or `diabetes=No`) as their consequent are *predictive association rules* (PARs). *Associative classification* [21] is the problem of enumerating all PARs in a data set and constructing the classification model with these PARs as predictors of the outcome.

Associative classification has received much research attential over the years (e.g. [21, 20, 29, 30]), which is partly due to the ease of interpretation of the individual rules and partly due its good performance. Associative classification is less greedy than most other rule-based classifiers, because associative classification enumerates *all* PARs, while rule-based classifiers [7] or trees [4] consider only a subset of the PARs. Linear models (e.g. linear discriminant analysis [17] and regression models [15, Chapter 3]) tend to produce interpretable models, but they–with the notable exception of regression trees [5]–lack an inherent ability to discover interactions among the variables. Since PARs can be viewed as (potentially) high-order interactions, the use of PARs is especially beneficial in domains such as genomics [14] and biomedical informatics [28], where discovering interactions among the variables (genes, disease) is the focus of the study.

While the individual PARs are easily interpretable, association rule mining often discover a combinatorial set of rules. To help human users interpret these rule sets, a large number of interestingness measures have been proposed. After discovering association rules, these measures can be applied and the rules can be ranked. Section 6.7 of [25] provides an extensive survey of these measures.

The interestingness measures previously proposed, although successful at selecting interesting rules, fall short for the purpose of classification in two important ways.

First, most interestingness measure (perhaps with exception of the *lift* [6]) are not rooted in a statistical model. In the typical classification setting, the PARs are extracted from a *training* data set, a model is constructed on a *training* data set and the model is applied to a previously unseen *test* data set. Without a statistical model underlying the filtering criterion (or interestingness measure), statistical inference cannot be made about the performance of the criterion on the *test* set.

Second, filtering criteria for classification should take the classifier's characteristics into account and only discard rules that cannot improve the classification performance.

In this paper, we develop a simple statistical model based on sampling theory that allows us to make inferences about the various aspects of PARs on a test set given a training set. Based on this model, we develop three filtering criteria that take the characteristics of the classifier into account. We show mathematically and also demonstrate empirically that our filtering criteria, albeit very selective, only discard rules that would not be utilized by the classifier.

Our paper assumes familiarity with formal hypothesis testing; [8] presents a clear deposition of the topic.

Specifically, our contributions are as follows.

- We develop a simple statistical framework for making inferences about measures related to association rules.
- Based on the statistical model, we derive three filtering criteria with the explicit purpose of only discarding rules that are uninteresting to the classifier. Two of these criteria, *closed itemsets* [31] and *predictive significance* [6, known as *lift*] already exist, our contribution is to derive them from the perspective of the classification under the assumptions of our statistical model. The third criterion is proposed here for the first time.
- We formally demonstrate via hypothesis testing that the above criteria indeed only discard PARs that do not significantly (with respect to a user-specified significance level) impact the classifier's performance. We also provide empirical evidence on three publicly available large data sets.

2. BACKGROUND AND RELATED WORKS

Let an **item** be a predicate of a single term (a logical statement that evaluates to *true* or *false* and does not contain logical OR or AND). For example, `glucose>125` is such a predicate. A **k−itemset** is a set of k items. An itemset is also a predicate evaluating to the conjunction (logical AND) of the predicates corresponding to all k constituent items. For example { `glucose>125`, `diabetes=Yes` } is a 2-itemset. Each item is also an itemset, a 1-itemset. We denote itemsets as a concatenation of their items: e.g. the 3-itemset $\{a, b, c\}$, will be denoted as abc.

A **transaction** is a set of items representing an observation in an experiment. The **transaction database** $\mathcal{T}$ is a collection of transactions.

A transaction T is said to **support** an itemset I, if $T \wedge I = I$: the predicates corresponding to all items in I evaluate to *true* in the transaction. We define the **count** of an itemset as the *number* of transactions in $\mathcal{T}$ that support it; and the **support** of an itemset as the *fraction* of transactions that support it. An itemset is **frequent** if its *support* exceeds a user-specified minimum support threshold. The minimum support threshold is related to the significance of the itemset.

An **association rule** is of from $A \to B$, where A and B are disjoint itemsets. An association rule can be thought of as a logical implication, with A being the **antecedent**, and B being the **consequent** of the rule (implication). We define an association rule to evaluate to *true* only if both A and B are true. Association rules differ from the logical implications in this respect: if A is *false*, a logical implication evaluates to *true* while an association rule does not. The support of an association rule is the support of the itemset AB and the **confidence** of the association rule is

$$\text{confidence}(A \to B) = \frac{\text{s}(AB)}{\text{s}(A)},$$

where $\text{s}(A)$ denotes the support of A. In the context of predictive association rules, the confidence coincides with the predictive precision of the rule, hence we will refer to it as **precision**, too. An association rule is frequent, if its support exceeds the minimum support threshold.

An **associative classification rule**, also known as a **predictive association rule** (PAR), is an association rule, whose consequent is an outcome (or class label). The goal of *associative classification* is to build a classifier from frequent PARs.

Associative classification was first presented by Liu et al. [21]. They invented a technique called Classification Based on Association (**CBA**), where a classifier is constructed from a collection of PARs by classifying each observation by the most precise PAR supported by the observation. The rule is added to the model and the observation is removed from the database. The model construction concludes when no more observations or applicable rules are left.

Motivated by CBA, a number of techniques have been proposed for constructing better classification models on top of PARs. For example, Li et al [20] proposed using multiple PARs for making a prediction for each observation leading to the Multiple Class Association Rules (CMAR) technique. Another improvement, Classification based on Predictive Association Rules (CPAR), assigns weights to the observations and upon correct classification, the weight of the observation is reduced [29]. CPAR can be viewed as a precursor to boosting PARs into a classifier model, which was proposed by Yoon et al. [30]. Ozgur et al [22] proposed a procedure similar to growing decision trees on association rules for regression problems and Wang et al. [27] grew decision trees on PARs with minimum support of 0. Emerging patterns – patterns whose support differs substantially between classes – have also been applied [10, 19].

The underlying theme for the above methods is to transform the classification problem. They transform the data set such that the predictors are the PARs instead of the original data variables. The PARs are presumed more predictive than the original data variables.

The use of PARs as predictors is advantageous for the following reasons. First, it allows for building a less-greedy model. For example, decision trees heuristically prune the search-space of conjunctions of the original predictors, while modeling on top of PARs readily offers the complete set of predictive conjunctions of the original variables. Second, the PARs are rules and hence they are individually easy to interpret. In contrast, SVM models are inherently difficult to interpret and even trees–as close as they are to rules–can get cumbersome to interpret due to the subtree replication problem (see Chapter 4.3.7 in [25]). Third, additive models (including regression models) often have no ability to automatically discover interaction terms. PARs are in essence high order interaction terms–readily available to modeling.

These advantages make PARs complementary to logistic regression, making logistic regression a natural choice for combining PARs into a classification model. Logistic regression analysis is a mature technique for classification problems that has enjoyed significant research effort to make model fitting possible and efficient under a wide variety of unfavorable conditions.

One such adverse condition arises when the number of predictors exceeds the number of observations. Given that association rule mining generally returns a very large number of predictors, such conditions can occur frequently. There are two specific techniques to address this issue. The first one is penalized logistic regression, more specifically Lasso regression [26], which has built-in predictor-selection capability and the second one is stage-wise regression [15] or boosting [13]. It has been shown that under some conditions, boosting and Lasso generate the same model [11].

Logistic regression on top of PARs is closely related to logic regression [24]. A logic regression model is a logistic regression model, whose predictors are logical expressions of the predictors in the original data set. Logic regression aims to discover these logical expressions via simulated annealing. Logistic regression on top of PARs differs from logic regression in that (i) logic regression enumerates only a (not-necessarily optimal) subset of PARs and (ii) logic regression allows for disjunctions as well as conjunctions.

3. METHOD

We begin by describing the computational framework in which we envision our proposed filtering techniques will be applied. In this framework, first, PARs are discovered. A wide range of algorithms can be used towards this end: the original *apriori* algorithm [3], algorithms that discover closed itemsets [31], discriminating or emerging patterns [10]. Second, the discovered patterns are filtered through one or more of the proposed criteria. For maximal efficiency we suggest the following order: Predictive Significance, Closed Itemsets and Component Independence. Third, a logistic regression model is built whose predictors are the filtered PARs.

In the following subsections, we first briefly describe the logistic regression analysis framework. Next, we present our statistical model for association rule mining and we conclude this section by describing our filtering criteria.

3.1 Logistic Regression

Let X be an $N \times p$ binary observation matrix, whose columns are the p PARs and rows are the N observations. Let Y be a vector denoting the outcomes of each observation and C be the outcome of interest (*target outcome*). Further let y_i be a binary response defined as $y_i = 1$ if $Y_i = C$; $y_i = 0$, otherwise.

The logistic regression model is then

$$\text{logit}(Y = C) = \log\left(\frac{\Pr(Y = C)}{\Pr(Y \neq C)}\right) = Xb + c, \qquad (1)$$

where b is the vector of p regression weights, one for each PAR; and c is the weight of the constant term. Once the regression weights have been computed, prediction can be made for an instance x_i

$$\widehat{\Pr(Y_i = C)} = \frac{\exp(x_i b + c)}{1 + \exp(x_i b + c)}. \qquad (2)$$

Models can be fit via minimizing the binomial log likelihood (in b and c)

$$-L = -\left[\sum_{i=1}^{N} y_i \log \Pr(Y_i = C) + (1 - y_i) \log \Pr(Y_i \neq C)\right]. \qquad (3)$$

A Lasso-penalized logistic regression model is fit using *regularized* negative log likelihood: a Lasso-penalty term is added to L (Equation 3)

$$-\left[\sum_{i=1}^{N} y_i \log \Pr(Y_i = C) + (1 - y_i) \log \Pr(y_i \neq C)\right] + \lambda \sum_j |b_j|, \qquad (4)$$

where b_j is the regression weight of the jth PAR and λ is the regularization parameter. The above maximization problem can be solved efficiently using coordinate-wise optimization as described in [12].

3.2 Statistical Model

Our statistical model is based on sampling theory. We assume that both the *training* and *test* data sets are random samples from a population of practically infinite transactions. Our goal is to estimate measures (e.g. support or precision) related to the PARs *in the population* from the training sample. The population measures allow us to make inferences about these measures in a *test* sample. Therefore, for each measure, we distinguish between the population and sample version.

To make this idea more concrete, let us consider the measure of support: the **sample support** of an itemset I is the fraction of items in the *sample* that support I; the **population support** of an item is the fraction of transactions in the *population* that support I. Only the sample support can be observed, the population support needs to be estimated.

We consider the population support a random variable. We can compute a point estimate for the population support as the plug-in estimate

$$\hat{s}(I) = \frac{\text{cnt}(I)}{N},$$

where $\hat{s}$ is the estimate of the population support, $\text{cnt}(\cdot)$ is the count of I in the *sample* and N is the sample size (number of transactions in the training set).

We can also compute a confidence interval using a binomial sampling distribution. Sampling from an infinite population can be viewed as a Bernoulli process, where transactions are selected at random, each supporting I with s(I) (population support) probability. The count of I in the sample is then a binomial random variable

$$\mathrm{cnt}(I) \sim \mathrm{Binom}(N, \mathrm{s}(I)).$$

The $(1-\alpha/2)$ confidence interval of the population support is thus

$$\hat{\mathrm{s}}(I) \pm z_\alpha \sqrt{\hat{\mathrm{s}}(I)\,(1-\hat{s}(I))\,N^{-1}}, \qquad (5)$$

where z_α is the standard normal quantile of $1-\alpha/2$. Note, that the population support is a probability, hence we will use $\mathrm{s}(I)$ and $\Pr(I)$ interchangeably.

Inference about the precision is more complex. Consider the predictive association rule (PAR) $A \to B$, A and B are itemsets. The population precision of the PAR is

$$\mathrm{prec}(A \to B) = \frac{\mathrm{s}(AB)}{\mathrm{s}(A)}. \qquad (6)$$

The limiting distributions of $\mathrm{s}(AB)$ and $\mathrm{s}(A)$ are both normal, so the distribution of precision can be considered a correlated quotient normal distribution. The formulae in [16] can be used to compute the quantiles of this distribution. Alternatively, if the covariance of $\mathrm{s}(A)$ and $\mathrm{s}(AB)$ is known, Fieller's theorem [1] can be applied to obtain a confidence interval for $\mathrm{prec}(A \to B)$.

In some cases, it is useful to instantiate $\mathrm{s}(A)$ by fixing its value to the plug-in estimate (the sample support). By doing so, we reduce precision to a binomial random variable whose point estimate is

$$\widehat{\mathrm{prec}}(A \to B) = \frac{\mathrm{cnt}(AB)}{\mathrm{cnt}(A)}$$

and its confidence interval can be computed as

$$\frac{1}{\mathrm{s}(A)}\left[\hat{\mathrm{s}}(AB) \pm z_\alpha \sqrt{\hat{\mathrm{s}}(AB)\,(1-\hat{s}(AB))\,N^{-1}}\right]. \qquad (7)$$

(Note that $\mathrm{s}(A)$ is instantiated, so it does not need the hat.)

We can use the above confidence intervals to test hypotheses about the supports of itemsets and about the precisions of PARs (given the population support of their antecedents). In the following sections, we derive three filtering criteria, two of which make use of hypothesis testing.

3.3 Filtering

In this section, we present three filtering methods that discard association rules that would not be meaningfully utilized by the logistic regression modeling. The *Closed Itemsets* criterion discards PARs that are synonyms of others; the *Predictive Significance* criterion discards PARs that only appear predictive in the sample but are not predictive in the population and the *Component-independence criterion* discards PARs that are expected to receive 0 regression weight.

3.3.1 Closed Itemsets

Consider an itemset A and all its possible extensions X.

Definition 1 (Closed Itemset). *Itemset A is* ***closed*** *if for all X, $\mathrm{s}(AX) < \mathrm{s}(A)$.*

Intuitively, we only need closed itemsets for classification. Consider the predictive association rule $A \to C$, where C is a class. If the itemset AC is not closed, a super-itemset AXC of AC exists with the same population support as AC. Because every transaction that supports AC must also support AXC, the association rules $A \to C$ and $AX \to C$ evaluate to true for the exact same transactions. In the context of logistic regression, $AX \to C$ and $A \to C$ are perfectly correlated, so they are essentially synonyms.

Population vs. sample closed itemsets. For illustrations below, we will use itemset A, its super-itemset AX and itemset $A\bar{X}$, which contains all items from A but no item from X. While $A\bar{X}$ and A look identical, their supports are not the same. In fact, $\mathrm{s}(A) = \mathrm{s}(AX) + \mathrm{s}(A\bar{X})$.

Lemma 1. *If an itemset is closed in the sample, it is also closed in the population.*

If itemset A is closed in the sample, then for all X, $\hat{\mathrm{s}}(A\bar{X}) > 0$ and hence $\mathrm{s}(A\bar{X}) > 0$. The converse is not true: an itemset that is closed in the population may appear not closed in the sample.

Convention 1. *If an itemset is closed in the sample, we will consider it closed in the population.*

This convention errs on the exclusive side: if the significance is set too high, we may discard some itemsets that are not closed in the sample but are closed in the population.

3.3.2 Predictive Significance

It is very intuitive (and has been proven in the context of boosting) that a PAR is only meaningful in a model if it has non-random predictive capability. If a PAR with target class C classifies observations at random, we expect its precision to be $\Pr(C)$. To ensure that the predictive capability of a PAR is non-random, we need to show that the confidence interval of its population precision does not contain $\Pr(C)$.

Definition 2 (Predictive). *An association rule $X \to C$ is predictive of a target C, if the* population *precision* $\mathrm{prec}(X \to C) > \Pr(C)$.

The precision of rule $X \to C$ is $\Pr(C|X)$. For a random rule, C and X are independent, and hence $\Pr(C|X) = \Pr(C)$, which is the prevalence of the class in the population.

We wish to test whether

$$\mathrm{prec}(X \to C) = \Pr(C|X) = \frac{\mathrm{s}(XC)}{\mathrm{s}(X)} \quad > \quad \Pr(C).$$

By instantiating $s(X)$ (fixing its value to the sample support), substituting $\Pr(C) = \mathrm{s}(C)$ and preserving $s(XC)$ as a random variable, we obtain the hypothesis testing problem of

$$H_0: \ \mathrm{s}(XC) = \mathrm{s}(C)\mathrm{s}(X)$$
$$H_A: \ \mathrm{s}(XC) > \mathrm{s}(C)\mathrm{s}(X).$$

One way to perform this test is through the χ^2-test of independence, which was used by Brin et al.[6]. The drawback of the χ^2-test is that it considers C and X associated if $\neg C$[1] and $\neg X$ are strongly associated even if C and X themselves are not associated. This statistical notion of association is inconsistent with the asymmetric notion of association used in association rule mining.

Alternatively, we can use the confidence interval of precision (Equation 7), which strictly examines the association

[1]For itemset A, $\neg A$ denotes that A evaluates to false.

between C and X (without explicitly examining $\neg C$ and $\neg X$). The rejection region is

$$s(C) < \frac{N}{\text{cnt}(X)}\left[\hat{s}(XC) + z_\alpha\sqrt{\hat{s}(XC)\,(1-\hat{s}(XC))\,N^{-1}}\right],$$

where $\frac{N}{\text{cnt}(X)}$ is $s(X)^{-1}$. Here we assumed that the population support of X is $\text{cnt}(X)/N$.

Illustrative Example. Let us illustrate Predictive Significance through an example. On an 80% training set of the prostate cancer data set that we will describe in detail in the Evaluation section, we selected 3 "signal genes" (genes with 65% precision and maximal support) as well as 27 "noise genes" (genes with 50% precision and minimal support to ensure that these genes indeed represent noise).

At the minimum support threshold of 4% (support count of 3), we discovered 4,167 rules. The predictive significance criterion (at significance level .1) discarded all but 4 rules. These 4 rules had precisions between 68% and 72% on the training set and did not contain any "noise genes".

On the other hand, 3,454 of the 4,167 rules had precision 1 on the training set. A CBA model was constructed using all rules–regardless of significance. The model consisted of 8 rules, naturally all having precision 1. Only two of these 8 rules contained any "signal genes" and all 8 rules contained "noise genes".

Of the 8 rules, only 1 rule classified any instances as positive on the test set, mostly incorrectly (with precision of 33%). The overall test accuracy of the CBA model was 43%. The significant rules, however, had precisions between 62.5% and 66.7% on the test set and upon building a CBA model using only these rules, we attained a test accuracy of 62%.

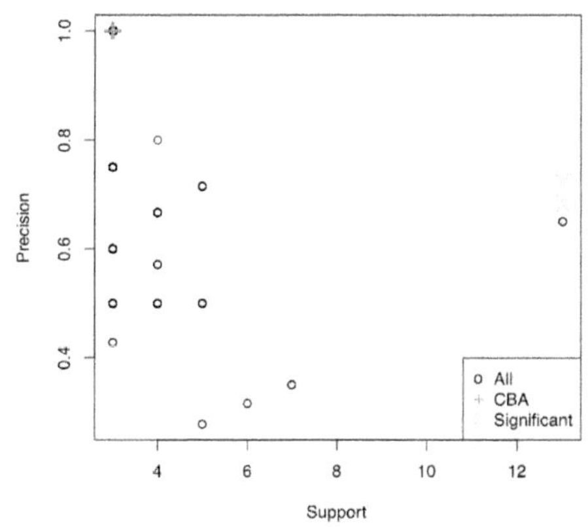

Figure 1: The precision and supports of 30 genes on the prostate cancer. The genes selected by CBA (marked by '+') fail to classify test instances reasonably, while the Significant genes (marked by '×') did.

Figure 1 depicts the 4,167 rules in terms of their supports and precisions on the training set. The rules marked '+' (red) are the rules selected by CBA. The significant rules are marked by green '×'. The figure underscores that precision–even when sorted on support–only tells half of the story; Predictive Significance completes the story.

3.3.3 Component Independence

Let us study a two-class problem with classes C_p and C_n. Let a predictive association rule be $AB \to C$, where C is one of C_p or C_n. The antecedent of the association rule is composed of two *component* itemsets A and B. We consider the independence of these component itemsets conditioned on C_p and C_n.

DEFINITION 3 (COMPONENT INDEPENDENCE). *An association rule $X \to C$ is component independent in A and B, if itemsets A and B exist such that*

$$\begin{aligned} X &= A \cup B, \\ s(ABC_p) &= s(AC_p)s(BC_p) \quad \text{and} \\ s(ABC_n) &= s(AC_n)s(BC_n). \end{aligned}$$

Component independence checking is the following hypothesis testing problem.

$$\begin{aligned} H_0: \quad s(ABC_p) &= s(AC_p)s(BC_p) \quad \text{and} \\ s(ABC_n) &= s(AC_n)s(BC_n) \\ H_A: \quad s(ABC_p) &> s(AC_p)s(BC_p) \quad \text{or} \\ s(ABC_n) &> s(AC_n)s(BC_n) \end{aligned}$$

The hypothesis testing can be carried out using the binomial confidence interval as it was used to test the Predictive Significance. Random variables $s(AC_p)$, $s(AC_n)$, $s(BC_p)$ and $s(BC_n)$ can be instantiated (by fixing their values to the sample estimates) and the confidence interval of the population support for $s(ABC_p)$ and $s(ABC_n)$ can be computed using Equation 5. The rejection region for the first part of the hypothesis is

$$\begin{aligned} \hat{s}(AC_p)\hat{s}(BC_p) \;>\; & \frac{1}{N}\text{cnt}(ABC_p) \\ & + z_\alpha\sqrt{\hat{s}(ABC_p)\,(1-\hat{s}(ABC_p))\,N^{-1}}, \end{aligned}$$

where $\hat{s}(I)$ is the sample estimate of the support of itemset I, computed as $\frac{\text{cnt}(I)}{N}$ with N being the sample size. The rejection region of the second part (component independence with respect to C_n) can be derived analogously.

THEOREM 1. *Logistic regression would assign 0 weight to predictive association rules that are component independent.*

Assume, we have built a logistic regression model

$$\log\left(\frac{\Pr(C_p|x)}{\Pr(C_n|x)}\right) = aI_{A\subset x} + bI_{B\subset x} + cI_{AB\subset x},$$

where x is a transaction; a, b and c are the regression weights; and I_p is the index function that returns 1 if its predicate p evaluates to true and returns 0 otherwise. To simplify the expressions, we omit the constant term.

If x supports A but not B, that is $A \subset x$ but $B \not\subset x$ and $AB \not\subset x$, then

$$\log\left(\frac{\Pr(C_p|x)}{\Pr(C_n|x)}\right) = a. \tag{8}$$

The quantity on the right is the log odds of C_p given that x supports only A, which we denote as $\log O_{C_p|A}$.

Similarly, if x supports B but not A, then

$$\log\left(O_{C_p|B}\right) = b, \tag{9}$$

and if x supports both A and B, we obtain

$$\log O_{C_p|AB} = a + b + c. \tag{10}$$

Inserting Equations 8 and 9 into Equation 10 leads to

$$\log O_{C_p|AB} = \log O_{C_p|A} + \log O_{C_p|B} + c = \log\left(O_{C_p|A}\, O_{C_p|B}\, e^c\right). \tag{11}$$

The regression weight c is 0 if the odds of C_p given A and given B are independent

$$O_{C_p|AB} = O_{C_p|A} O_{C_p|B},$$

or after expanding the definition of odds

$$\frac{\Pr(C_p|AB)}{\Pr(C_n|AB)} = \frac{\Pr(C_p|A)}{\Pr(C_n|A)} \frac{\Pr(C_p|B)}{\Pr(C_n|B)} \tag{12}$$

leading to

$$\frac{s(ABC_p)}{s(ABC_n)} = \frac{s(AC_p)}{s(AC_n)} \frac{s(BC_p)}{s(BC_n)}. \tag{13}$$

Accepting the null hypothesis is a sufficient condition for Equation 13 to hold. Q.E.D.

In practice, we apply Conditional Independence as the last filter. Its computation cost is $O(n^2)$, with n being the number of PARs. Consider itemsets I and its subitemsets A and $(I - A)$, all three of which have passed all previous filters. For all such itemsets, we check whether A and $(I - A)$ are independent.

4. RESULTS

The filtering methods were evaluated on three publicly available data sets. The first one is a genotype data set representing a difficult classification problem (state-of-the-art classifiers can achieve only approximately 65% accuracy); the second one is a gene expression data with 6,000 genes, where modern classifiers (like SVM) can achieve approximately 85% accuracy; and the third data set is very wide gene expression data set–it has 200 times as many predictors as observations,–but very clean: predictive accuracy is in the high 90% range. Table 1 contains a summary description of these data sets.

Name	# of Samples		# of Predictors		Available
	Cases	Controls	Original	Items	
Alzheimer	1237	1254	600,000	100	[2]
Prostate	52	50	6,033	12,066	[9]
Lung	58	49	22,283	44,566	[18]

Table 1: Description of the data sets

Evaluation Method. We consider two classifiers: logistic regression (Lasso-penalized) and CBA. Each classifier was evaluated using various filtering criteria. The filtering criteria are denoted with a string of three letters: C for Closed Itemsets, P for Predictive Significance and I for Component-Independece. A dash signifies the lack of a particular filtering. For example, 'C-I' denotes filtering based on Closed Itemsets and Component Independence (and no filtering based on Predictive Significance). Since the data sets have balanced class distribution, we use *predictive accuracy* as the evaluation metric. Predictive accuracy is the fraction of test instances that were classified correctly.

The classifiers were evaluated using 10-fold cross validation (CV). In case of 10-fold CV, the data set is divided evenly into 10 partitions. The evaluation is performed in 10 iterations. In iteration i, partition i is left out as test set and the remaining 9 partitions are used for constructing the model. After completing the 10 iterations, we obtain 10 accuracy estimates. We report the mean and standard deviation of these 10 accuracies and on occasion, we report the individual measurements.

Lasso has the regularization parameter λ we need to tune. Towards this end, in each iteration, we further divide the 9 partitions 80/20 into a training and validation set. The training set was used for building the classifiers with various settings of the parameter, the validation set was used for selecting the optimal model (optimal parameter setting) and the test set was used for evaluating the model. [2]

4.1 Alzheimer's

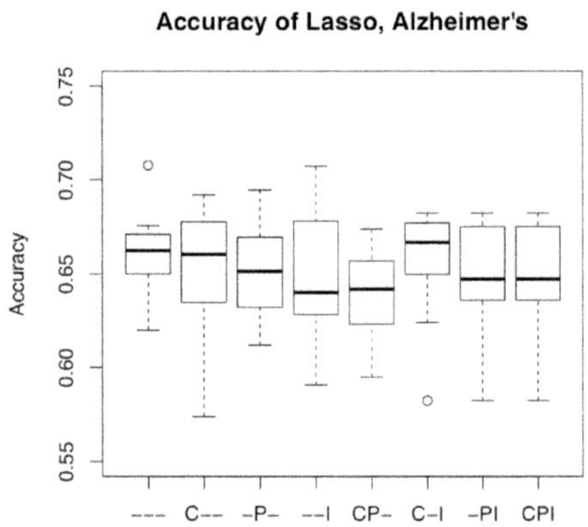

Figure 2: Accuracies (across the 10 folds) for the Logistic model using various filtering criteria

The Alzheimer's data set is the National Institute of Drug Abuse (NIDA) Joint Addiction, Aging and Mental Health (JAAMH) Alzheimer's Disease (AD) genotype data set available from dbGap [2]. The data set is a genotype data set with 600,000 Single Nucleotide Polymorphisms (SNP) as predictors. The data set was preprocessed using the default settings of the genotype data analysis tool `plink` [23]. SNPs can take three different values based on the number of minor alleles the genotype may contain: 0, 1 or 2. SNPs were discretized as 'having at least 1 minor allele'. Our goal was to discover high-order interactions among SNPs, so we selected the 100 most predictive SNPs. Using only 100 SNPs allowed us to lower the minimum support threshold to 180/2491. At this threshold, we discovered approximately 270,000 PARs, some of the PARs having antecedent with over 10 SNPs.

Table 2 depicts the number of PARs remaining after filtering based on various combinations of the proposed criteria. With the exception of the Closed Itemset criterion, the proposed criteria resulted in 1 to 3 orders of magnitude reduction.

[2]In the case, when no filters are applied, we were unable to run the R implementation of Lasso due to insufficient memory. We are using a home-grown boosted logistic model (with efficient memory management) instead. Boosted logistic models and Lasso are known to produce the same results [11] but runtimes in our case are not comparable.

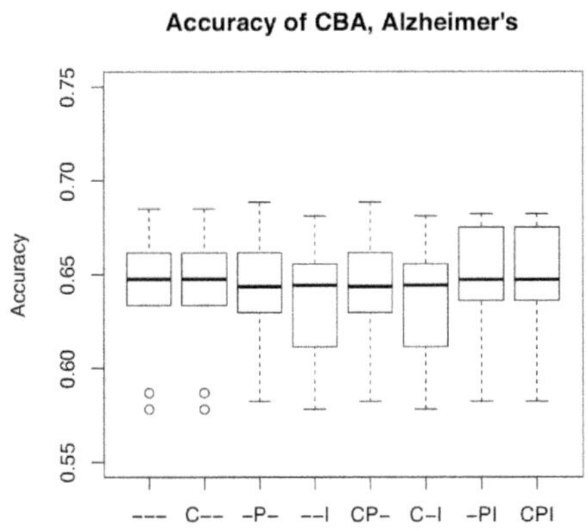

Figure 3: Accuracies (across the 10 folds) for the CBA algorithm

Filter	mean	sd
—	271,822.40	7,033.02
-P-	11,035.50	1,070.18
–I	271.60	1.17
-PI	4.50	.97
C–	202,592.50	5,142.45
CP-	9,270.00	850.20
C-I	217.60	1.71
CPI	4.50	.97

Table 2: Average number of Predictive Association Rules on the Alzheimer's data set for various filtering criteria. ($\alpha = .1$; Bonferroni corrected)

4.1.1 *Effect of filtering on the accuracy*

In this section, we test the main hypothesis of the paper: while the proposed filtering methods aggressively reduce the number of PARs to be considered, they do not effect the classification performance adversely.

We first consider the logistic model. In Figure 2, we present the accuracies obtained under the various filtering criteria. To gain insight into the variability of the accuracy across the 10 folds, the 10 measurements for each filtering criterion are presented as a boxplot. The accuracies across the filtering criteria are only insignificantly different.

4.1.2 *Model size*

One advantage of the proposed filtering is that the number of PARs to consider is reduced which leads to improved interpretability. In many cases, users interpret the actual models rather than the PARs that were discovered. In this section, we consider the model sizes under the various filtering criteria.

We define the model size in the context of logistic regression as the number of PARs with non-zero regression weights. Figure 4 depicts the model sizes under various filtering criteria.

With the exception of the most restrictive filtering criteria, the median model sizes do not change significantly; the 75-th percentiles, however, mirror the patterns seen in the total number of PARs after filtering.

The models built under the two most restrictive criteria contain 2 SNPs, one on the TOMM40 gene and one on the

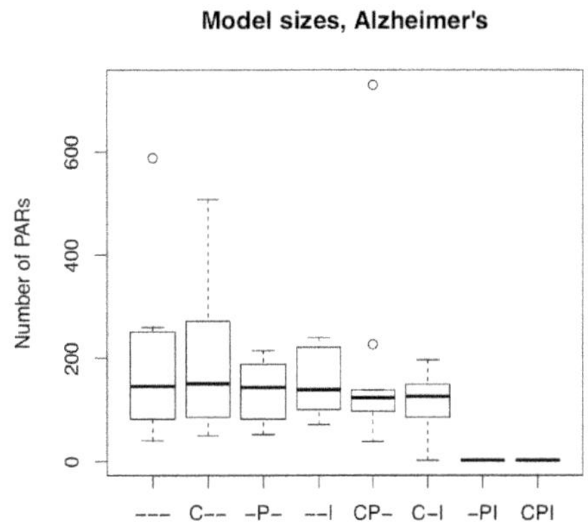

Figure 4: Model sizes (across the 10 folds) for the logistic model using various filtering criteria

APOE4 gene. These SNPs are known to be significantly involved in Alzheimer's disease, and no other SNP in our data set showed significant involvement in the disease (using the `plink` tool [23]; detailed results not shown). Given that only these two SNPs (and other SNPs in linkage disequilibrium with these SNPs) are desired to be present in PARs, the -PI and CPI filtering criteria appear clearly beneficial.

4.1.3 *Comparison Using CBA*

For the sake of completeness, we also compare the effect of filtering on CBA. While we do not expect that filtering based on Closed Itemsets and Predictive Significance would adversely effect CBA's performance, filtering based on Component Independence may have an effect on it. Essentially, Component Independence removes spurious interaction terms; however these interaction terms may have real predictive capability and can have higher precision than the component itemsets (or more precisely, the corresponding PARs).

Figure 3, depicts the accuracies for the CBA algorithm. The figure is analogous to Figure 2 and the conclusion is identical: the accuracies across the filtering criteria are only insignificantly different despite the aggressive filtering that some of the criteria represent.

4.1.4 *Type-I / Type-II error tradeoff*

The Closed Itemsets criterion removes "synonyms", Predictive Significance removes PARs that are not predictive and Component Independence removes PARs that would receive 0 weight. We claim that discarding these PARs does not effect the performance of the classifier, yet differences in performance exist.

First, our experimental evaluation has a random variability, since the data set is randomly partitioned and also the training partition of each fold is randomly partitioned further. Therefore, the models are not built on the exact same training set and random (statistically insignificant) differences between the performances of these models are expected.

Second, during hypothesis testing that determines which PARs are discarded, there are type-I and type-II errors. *Type-I error* occurs when the null hypothesis is incorrectly rejected, that is a spurious PAR is included. Including unnecessary PARs rarely leads to decrease in performance, it only make interpretation more difficult and model construction more costly. *Type-II error* occurs when the null hypothesis is erroneously accepted, that is when a potentially important PAR is discarded. Discarding important PARs can decrease the classification performance.

Through the confidence level α, we can only control the type-I error. We would prefer to directly control the type-II error, but in the absence of a more concrete alternative hypothesis, it is not possible.

It is known, however, that a tradeoff exists between the type-I and the type-II error rates. If we allow the type-I error to increase, we know that the type-II error decreases. This is the reason, why we use relatively high type-I error rates (e.g. in our experiments, we used $\alpha = .1$ instead of the more common choice of .05 or .01). In all practical hypothesis testing situations type-II errors exist and they have the potential to introduce differences in the classification performance.

4.2 Gene Expression Data Sets

4.2.1 Prostate Cancer

The prostate cancer data set is available in a pre-processed form from `http://stat.ethz.ch/~ dettling/`. The data contains the gene expression values for 6,033 genes. Each gene was transformed into two new items signifying whether the gene was over- or under-expressed. The threshold for over- and under-expression was set at 0.5 standard deviations from the mean. All resulting 12,066 items were used.

Henceforth, for brevity, we only focus on the main hypothesis, namely, we report the filtering capability of the various criteria and their impact on the classification accuracy. We also limit our discussion to logistic regression.

Table 3 contains the number of PARs remaining after applying the various combinations of the filtering criteria. A PAR was discarded if the null hypothesis of the filtering criteria was rejected at 0.1 significance level. The variance in the number of PARs across the 10 folds is large. With only 100 instances, the differences between the sample and population distributions can be substantial. This large variance did not translate into equally high variance in the classification accuracy.

Figure 5 depicts the predictive accuracy of the logistic model under the various filtering criteria. To illustrate the variability of accuracy across the 10 folds, the 10 measurements for each filtering criterion are summarized into a boxplot. The classification performance across the various filtering criteria are only insignificantly different.

Filter	mean	sd
—	20,056.10	21,828.25
-P-	6,650.10	7,130.56
–I	401.80	95.66
-PI	29.80	11.89
C–	1,852.50	1,197.17
CP-	548.20	315.34
C-I	328.40	65.49
CPI	28.00	11.36

Table 3: Prostate Data Set. Number of PARs remaining after applying various filtering criteria. Mean and standard deviation across the 10 folds.

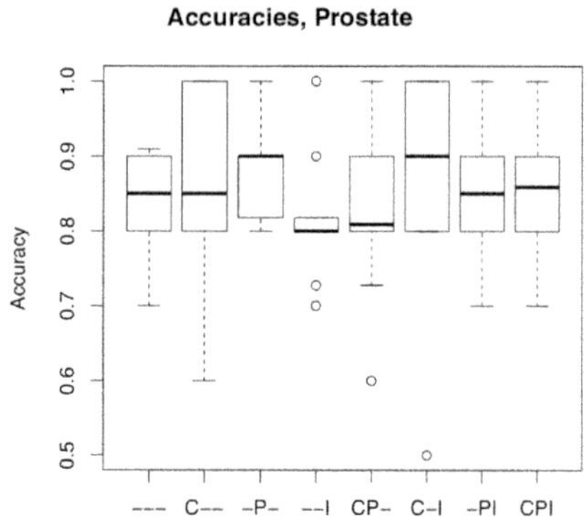

Figure 5: Average accuracy (across the 10 folds) for the logistic model on Prostate using various filtering criteria

4.2.2 EAGLE Lung Cancer

The EAGLE Lung Cancer data set features the expressions of 20,283 genes measures across 107 patients. Analogously to the Prostate data set, each gene were converted into two items, indicating whether the gene is over- or under-expressed, resulting in 44,566 items. All items were used.

Table 4 presents the number of PARs remaining after filtering based on the various criteria. Given that the data set contains only 107 patients, the variability of the number of PARs is high across the 10 folds. Once again, the selectivity of the criteria are substantial[3].

Figure 6 depicts the accuracy of the logistic models under the various filtering criteria. The 10 accuracy measurements across the 10 folds are summarized into a boxplot for each filtering criterion. The conclusion is consistent with the other data sets: there is only insignificant differences in performance.

Filter	mean	sd
—	13,451.00	8,824.40
-P-	13,451.00	8,824.40
–I	127.30	24.96
-PI	127.30	24.96
C–	922.60	593.00
CP-	922.60	593.00
C-I	65.50	21.17
CPI	65.50	21.17

Table 4: Lung Cancer Data Set. Number of PARs remaining after applying various filtering criteria. Mean and standard deviation across the 10 folds.

5. SUMMARY AND CONCLUSION

In this paper, we introduced a simple statistical model based on sampling theory, which allowed us to make inferences about the population versions of performance metrics of predictive association rules (PARs). The population estimates of these metrics, in turn, lead to the ability to test hypotheses on the *test* set. Based on the hypothesis testing framework, we developed or re-derived three filtering criteria

[3]Due to the pronounced differences between the classes, our setting of a high minimum support threshold resulted in the discovery of only predictive significant PARs.

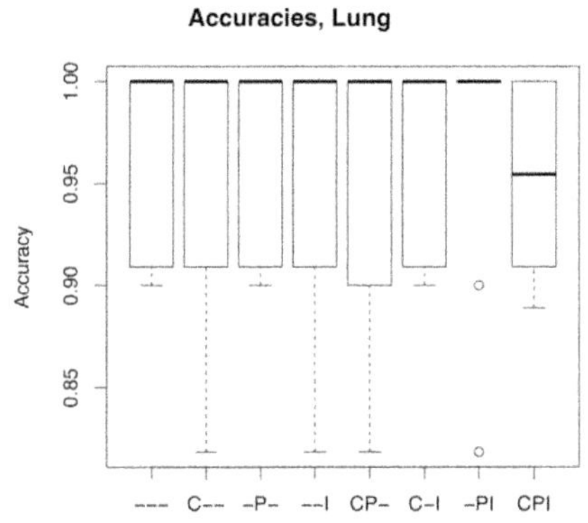

Figure 6: Average accuracy (across the 10 folds) for the logistic model on Lung using various filtering criteria

that vastly reduced the number of PARs to be considered by the subsequent classifier without significantly effecting its performance. We gave a mathematical proof for the case when the classification model was logistic regression. We also demonstrated on three publicly available data sets that the vast reduction in the number of PARs indeed did not come at the cost of reducing the classification performance.

We believe that our statistical model generalizes to other association rule mining problems in a straightforward manner. We foresee that the same methodology can be applied to many flavors of association rule mining, including sequence mining, error-tolerant association rules, spatio-temporal associations, just to name a few.

6. REFERENCES

[1] Fieller's theorem. `http://en.wikipedia.org/wiki/Fieller%27s_theorem`.

[2] National institute on drug abuse (NIDA) joint aging, addiction and mental health (JAAMH) late-onset alzheimer's disease data set. Avaiable from DbGap `http://www.ncbi.nlm.nih.gov/gap`.

[3] Rakesh Agrawal and Ramakrishnan Srikant. Fast algorithms for mining association rules. In *VLDB Conference*, 1994.

[4] Leo Breiman. Random forests. *Machine Learning*, 45(1), 2001.

[5] Leo Breiman, Jerome Friedman, Charles J. Stone, and R.A. Olshen. *Classification and Regression Trees*. CRC Press Reprint, 1998.

[6] Sergey Brin, Rajeev Motvani, and Craig Silverstein. Beyond market baskets: Generalizing association rules to correlations. In *ACM International Conference on Managment of Data (SIGMOD)*, 1997.

[7] William Cohen and Yoram Singer. A simple, fast and efficient rule learner. In *American Association for Artificial Intelligence (AAAI)*, 1999.

[8] Morris H. DeGroon and Mark J. Schervish. *Probability and Statistics*. Addison Wesley, 2010.

[9] Marcel Dettling and Peter Bühlmann. Supervised clustering of genes. *Genome Biology*, 3(12), 2002.

[10] Guozhu Dong, Xiuzhen Zhang, Limsoon Wong, and Jinyan Li. CAEP: Classification by aggregating emerging patterns. *Discovery Science*, 99, 1999.

[11] Jerome Friedman, Trevor Hastie, Sharon Rosset, Robert Tibshirani, and Ji Zhu. Discussion of boosting papers. 2003.

[12] Jerome Friedman, Trevor Hastie, and Robert Tibshirani. Regularization paths for generalized linear models via coordinate descent. *Journal of Statistical Software*, 33(1), 2010.

[13] Jerome H. Friedman. Greedy function approximation: A gradient boosting machine. *Annals of Statistics*, 29:1180, 2001.

[14] Rohit Gupta, Smita Agrawal, Navneet Rao, Ze Tian, Rui Kuang, and Vipin Kumar. Integrative biomarker discovery for breast cancer metastasis from gene expression and protein interaction data using error-tolerant pattern mining. In *International Conference on Bioinformatics and Computational Biology (BICoB)*, 2010.

[15] Trevor Hastie, Robert Tibshirani, and Jerome Friedman. *The Elements of Statistical Learning*. Springer, 2nd edition, 2009.

[16] D. Hinkley. On the ratio of two correlated normal random variables. *Biometrika*, 56(3), 1969.

[17] Richard A. Johnson and Dean W. Wichern. *Applied Multivariate Statistical Analysis*. Prentice Hall, 2002.

[18] Maria Teresa Landi, Tatiana Dracheva, Melissa Rotunno, et al. Gene expression signature of cigaratte smoking and its role in lung adenocarcinoma development and survival. *PLoS ONE*, 3(2), 2008.

[19] Jinyan Li, Guozhu Dong, and Kotagiri Ramamohanarao. Instance-based classification by emerging patterns. In *Practice of Knowledge Discovery in Databases PKDD*, 2000.

[20] Wenmin Li, Jiawei Han, and Jian Pei. CMAR: Accurate and efficient classification based on multiple class-association rules. In *IEEE International Conference on Data Mining*, 2001.

[21] Bing Liu, Wynne Hsu, and Yiming Ma. Integrating classification and association rule mining. In *ACM International Conference on Knowledge Discovery and Data Mining (KDD)*, 1998.

[22] Aysel Ozgur, Pang-Ning Tan, and Vipin Kumar. RBA: An integrated framework for regression based on association rules. In *SIAM International Conference on Data Mining (SDM)*, 2004.

[23] S. Purcell, B. Neale, K. Todd-Brown, L. Thomas, M.A.R. Ferreira, D. Bender, J. Maller, P. Sklar, P.C. de Bakker, M. Daly, and P. Sham. PLINK: a toolset for whole-genome association and population-based linkage analysis. *American Journal of Human Genetics*, 81, 2007.

[24] Ingo Ruczinski, Charles Kooperberg, and Michael LeBlanc. Logic regression. *Journal of Computational and Graphical Statistics*, 12(3), 2003.

[25] Pang-Ning Tan, Michael Steinbach, and Vipin Kumar. *Introduction to Data Mining*. Addison Wesley, 2005.

[26] Robert Tibshirani. Regression shrinkage and selection via the lasso. *Journal of the Royal Statistical Society B*, 58(1), 1996.

[27] Ke Wang, Senqiang Zhou, and Yu He. Growing decision trees on support-less association rules. In *ACM International Conference on Knowledge Discovery and Data Mining (KDD)*, 2000.

[28] Adam Wright, Elizabeth S Chen, and Francine L Maloney. An automated technique for identifying associations between medications, laboratory results and problems. *J Biomed Inform*, 43(6):891–901, Dec 2010.

[29] Xiaoxin Yin and Jiawei Han. CPAR: Classification based on predictive association rules. In *SIAM International Conference on Data Mining (SDM)*, 2003.

[30] Yongwook Yoon and Gary G. Lee. Text categorization based on boosting association rules. In *IEEE International Conference on Semantic Computing*, 2008.

[31] Mohammed Zaki and Ching-Jui Hsiao. Efficient algorithms for mining closed itemsets and their lattice structure. *IEEE Transactions on Knowledge and Data Engineering*, 17(4), 2005.

A Time-Dependent Topic Model for Multiple Text Streams

Liangjie Hong[*] †, Byron Dom §, Siva Gurumurthy, § Kostas Tsioutsiouliklis §
† Dept. of Computer Science and Engineering, Lehigh University, Bethlehem, PA, USA
§ Yahoo! Labs, Sunnyvale, CA, USA
hongliangjie@lehigh.edu, byron_dom@yahoo.com, {shiiva,kostas}@yahoo-inc.com

ABSTRACT

In recent years social media have become indispensable tools for information dissemination, operating in tandem with traditional media outlets such as newspapers, and it has become critical to understand the interaction between the new and old sources of news. Although social media as well as traditional media have attracted attention from several research communities, most of the prior work has been limited to a single medium. In addition temporal analysis of these sources can provide an understanding of how information spreads and evolves. Modeling temporal dynamics while considering multiple sources is a challenging research problem. In this paper we address the problem of modeling text streams from two news sources - Twitter and Yahoo! News. Our analysis addresses both their individual properties (including temporal dynamics) and their inter-relationships. This work extends standard topic models by allowing each text stream to have both local topics and shared topics. For temporal modeling we associate each topic with a time-dependent function that characterizes its popularity over time. By integrating the two models, we effectively model the temporal dynamics of multiple correlated text streams in a unified framework. We evaluate our model on a large-scale dataset, consisting of text streams from both Twitter and news feeds from Yahoo! News. Besides overcoming the limitations of existing models, we show that our work achieves better perplexity on unseen data and identifies more coherent topics. We also provide analysis of finding real-world events from the topics obtained by our model.

Categories and Subject Descriptors

H.4 [**Information Systems Applications**]: Miscellaneous; H.3.3 [**Information Storage and Retrieval**]: Information Search and Retrieval—*clustering*

General Terms

Algorithms, Experimentation, Theory

[*]This work was done when the first author was on a summer internship at Yahoo! Labs.

Keywords

Topic models, Text streams, Temporal dynamics, News, Twitter

1. INTRODUCTION

Social-networking tools such as Facebook, LinkedIn and Twitter, have become the communication tools of choice for a large number of online users. Such tools are increasingly used for disseminating breaking news and eyewitness accounts, and even for organizing flash mobs and protest groups. For instance, Twitter was heavily used in a number of international events, such as the Iran election in 2009, the Haiti earthquakes in 2010, and the tsunami in Japan in 2011. More recently, social networking services were instrumental in facilitating the political upheavals in the Middle East. Social media as well as the on-line publishing of more established media (e.g., newspapers, magazines and televison) have attracted a lot of attention from both researchers and product developers.

This increasing use of social media has resulted in a refocusing of research activities onto related problems, many of which are new. For example, there exists an argument as to whether social media have influenced traditional media sources and in what sense, or vice versa. In addition, people are wondering whether the topics that are shared and discussed on social media significantly differ from traditional information sources and how these topics are transferred from one source to another. Moreover, questions about the differences between various types of social media (e.g., blogs, community-based questions-and-answer portals and microblogging services) have been raised continuously both in research communities and industry. Effectively addressing these issues requires the ability to analyze multiple types of information sources over time.

Problems similar to these have been attacked from various perspectives. For modeling the temporal dynamics of information Kleinberg et al. [14, 15] proposed methods to track the volume of a single term over time. Their later work (e.g., [16]) attempts to monitor the temporal dynamics of "memes" by which the authors mean sentence fragments representing concepts. In addition work has been done to study the dynamics of blogs [9], of online knowledge sharing communities [2], of news articles and stories [16], and of microblog services [13]. While most of the above-mentioned works focused on a single media source, some authors [31, 27, 28] modified Probabilistic Latent Semantic Analysis (PLSA) [11] to simultaneously model documents from different text streams. There is also some recent work in comparing social and traditional media. Zhao et al. [33] tried to obtain latent topics from Twitter and New York Times (NYT) news articles by using topic models. Two different topic models were used to learn the topics from the two sources separately and heuristics were then applied to obtain both common and local topics. Attempts have been made to extend topic models to incorporate temporal dynamics and topic evolution (e.g., [4, 26]). In addition to research projects, commercial products also provide tools to search and browse the dynamics of queries[1], news articles and web traffic[2], and microblogging updates[3].

While existing research offers different methods to monitor and track correlated information sources over time, many of the proposed approaches suffer from significant drawbacks. For instance most of the work on tracking information sources primarily focuses on only one type of source. Given the multiplicity of media channels however, it is potentially more useful to understand multiple information sources simultaneously. Also, tracking a single word or a meme can be quite limiting. Further, most models that consider multiple text collections either have model parameters requiring manual adjustment or have theoretical limitations (see our discussion in Section 2). In addition temporal factors are either not incorporated in the models or are heuristically embedded. For temporal topic models most approaches adopt a Markovian assumption that may not be suitable for social media. Indeed, none of them utilize recent research findings of temporal variations of information in social media [16, 30].

In this paper we address the problem of modeling multiple text streams, including their temporal dynamics, in a principled manner. Our work builds on recent work in both information dynamics and topic models. More specifically, we extend topic models by allowing each text stream to have both local and shared topics. For temporal modeling, we associate each topic with a time-dependent function that characterizes its popularity over time. By combining the two models, we effectively model temporal dynamics of multiple correlated text streams in a unified framework. To summarize the contributions of this paper, the work we describe includes:

- a topic model that discovers common and uncommon topics from multiple text collections
- a temporal model that characterizes the dynamic of topics over time
- a simple and potentially scalable algorithm for mining temporal topics
- interesting results from Yahoo! News and Twitter obtained by applying our model.

The remainder of this paper is organized as follows. Section 2 provides the background and related work. In Section 3 and Section 4, we discuss our model in detail. Section 5 provides experimental results on real-world datasets. We conclude our paper with Section 6, which discusses both conclusions and future work.

2. RELATED WORK

Mining common topics and their temporal dynamics from multiple text streams can be loosely decomposed into the two independent tasks of (1) recovering topics and (2) characterizing their temporal dynamics. We review these two lines of related work.

Based on PLSA, Wang et al. [27] introduced an observed-timestamp variable into the generative model to incorporate temporal dynamics. In addition several heuristics were applied to smooth topics in consecutive time periods. Later, Wang et al. [28] followed a similar idea and used an artificial time-synchronization optimization process in their model to re-organize the time stamps of all documents so that documents with the same time stamp would share similar topics. We argue that the constraint imposed by this synchronization is unrealistic. Note that these two papers do not differentiate between common topics and topics that only occur in a single text stream. Moreover, since both models are based on PLSA, they have the tendency to overfit the data. Furthermore, both models are not well-defined generative models [5] and no assumptions on how topic distributions and per-document topic-proportion distributions change over time were made in these models. In a recent paper, Zhang et al. [32], in addressing the same problem, proposed a non-parametric model in which a Markovian assumption is made regarding the temporal dynamics of document-topic distributions. As mentioned in the previous section, however, according to recent results on information propagation and temporal variations [16, 30], this assumption may not be appropriate for social media.

Independent of temporal factors, two basic approaches to topic discovery from correlated text streams exist in the topic modeling literature. Zhai et al. [31] proposed two variants of the same idea to tackle the problem of modeling multiple text streams. One variant assumes that each document in a text stream is generated by a background language model and a set of topics. Both the background language model and topics are multinomial distributions over words shared across multiple text streams. Since they are shared across all streams, common topics are difficult to identify. The second variant also assumes that each document in a text stream is generated by a background language model and a set of topics. Once a term is chosen to be generated by topics, a topic index is first selected followed by a second-level decision regarding whether the word is generated by a common or a local topic. The model can then explicitly handle common and local topics among multiple streams. Common and local topics are aligned under the same set of indices however, forcing the total number of topics to be the same for all streams. In addition the background language is the same across all text streams, which is too inflexible for the joint modeling of disparate sources such as Twitter and Yahoo! News. Also, per-document topic-proportion parameters must be manually tuned in experiments, which is impractical for real applications. The first variant inspired models introduced in [27, 28] and the second variant was extended to a fully Bayesian formulation by Paul et al. [22, 23], in which the topic proportion parameters were automatically estimated from the inference algorithm but local topics among different text streams were forcibly put under the same set of indices. It is therefore possible that unrelated topics will be brought together under the same topic index due to this constraint.

We briefly review some of the recent extensive work on modeling temporal dynamics in topic models. Early work on incorporating temporal evolution usually made a Markovian assumption by using either a state-space model (e.g., [4, 25]) or a linear model (e.g., [24]). Besides the Markovian assumption, Wang et al. [26] introduced a beta distribution over timestamps using a non-Markovian topic model. Nallapati et al. [20] and Iwata et al. [12] focused on the problem of modeling topics spread on a timeline with multiple resolutions, namely how topics are organized in a hierarchy and how they evolve over time. Ahmed and Xing [1] proposed a non-parametric model to address the birth and death of topics over a timeline using a Markovian assumption. The datasets used in these papers are several orders of magnitude smaller than the one we used in this paper.

3. CORRELATED TEXT STREAMS

3.1 Model Description

Our correlated-text-stream model (`Collection Model`) is an extension of Latent Dirichlet Allocation [5] (LDA). In our

[1]http://www.google.com/insights/search/
[2]http://www.google.com/trends
[3]http://www.google.com

Collection Model, we have a set S of n text streams. Associated with each stream $s \in S$ is a set T_s of *local* topics and associated with all streams is a set T_c of *common* topics. Thus the total number of topics in the model is $(\sum_s |T_s|)+|T_c|$. As in LDA, each topic k is defined as a multinomial distribution over a fixed vocabulary V, denoted as ϕ_k. Local topics $\phi^{(s)}$ are drawn from stream-dependent Dirichlet distributions $\text{Dir}(\beta^{(c)})$ while common topics $\phi^{(c)}$ are drawn from a stream-independent Dirichlet distribution $\text{Dir}(\beta^{(c)})$. Each document d in a stream s, has an associated Bernoulli distribution with parameter $\eta_{d,s} \sim \text{Beta}(\gamma_s^{(s)}, \gamma_s^{(c)})$, indicating how likely the document is to choose local rather than common topics. For convenience we let $\eta_{d,c}$ (where $\eta_{d,c} = 1 - \eta_{d,s}$) represent how likely a document d is to choose common topics. The random variable $x_{d,i} \sim \text{Bernoulli}(\eta_{d,s})$ takes on one of the two values "local" or "common" for each word position i in document d. In addition, each document has two multinomial distributions with parameter vectors $\theta_d^{(s)} \sim \text{Dir}(\alpha_s)$ and $\theta_d^{(c)} \sim \text{Dir}(\alpha_c)$ over T_s and T_c respectively, where α_s and α_c represent the two Dirichlet parameter vectors. The document generation process associated with this model is as follows:

1. For all common topics T_c, draw $\phi^{(c)} \sim \text{Dir}(\beta^{(c)})$
2. For a particular stream s
   (a) For all local topics T_s, draw $\phi^{(s)} \sim \text{Dir}(\beta^{(s)})$
   (b) For each document d in s
      i. Draw Bernoulli parameter $\eta_{s,d} \sim \text{Beta}(\gamma_s^{(s)}, \gamma_s^{(c)})$
      ii. Draw $\theta_d^{(s)} \sim \text{Dir}(\alpha_s)$
      iii. Draw $\theta_d^{(c)} \sim \text{Dir}(\alpha_c)$
      For each word position i in document d
         A. Draw $x_{di} \sim \text{Bernoulli}(\eta_{s,d})$
         B. Draw a topic $z_{di} \sim \text{Multinomial}(\theta_d^{(x_{di})})$
         C. Draw a word $w_{di} \sim \text{Multinomial }(\phi_{z_{di}}^{(x_{di})})$

3.2 Inference via Collapsed Gibbs Sampling

In order to estimate the hidden parameters in the model, we apply collapsed Gibbs sampling using the following updating rules:

$$p(x_{di} = s, z_{di} = t) \propto$$
$$\frac{c_{d,s-i} + \gamma_s^{(s)}}{N_d + \gamma_s^{(s)} + \gamma_s^{(c)} - 1} \frac{m_{d,z-i} + \alpha_z}{\sum_{z \in T_s} m_{d,z-i} + \alpha_z} \frac{n_{z,w-i} + \beta_w^{(s)}}{\sum_w^V n_{z,w-i} + \beta_w^{(s)}}$$
$$p(x_{di} = c, z_{di} = t) \propto$$
$$\frac{c_{d,c-i} + \gamma_s^{(c)}}{N_d + \gamma_s^{(s)} + \gamma_s^{(c)} - 1} \frac{m_{d,z-i} + \alpha_z}{\sum_{z \in T_c} m_{d,z-i} + \alpha_z} \frac{n_{z,w-i} + \beta_w^{(c)}}{\sum_w^V n_{z,w-i} + \beta_w^{(c)}} \tag{1}$$

where $c_{d,s-i}$ is the number of words in document d assigned to local topics (excluding w_{di}), $m_{d,z-i}$ is the number of words in document d assigned to topic z (excluding the current one) and $n_{z,w-i}$ is the number of occurrences of term w assigned to topic z (excluding the current one). By using the samples from Gibbs sampling, parameters $\{\theta_d^{(s)}, \theta_d^{(c)}\}$, $\{\phi_s, \phi_c\}$ and $\{\eta_{d,s}, \eta_{d,c}\}$ can be effectively estimated as follows:

$$\theta_{d,z}^{(x)} = \frac{m_{d,z} + \alpha_z}{\sum_{z \in T_x} m_{d,z} + \alpha_z} \quad , x \in \{s, c\} \tag{2}$$

$$\phi_{z,w}^{(x)} = \frac{n_{z,w} + \beta_w}{\sum_{z \in T_x} n_{z,w} + \beta_w} \quad , x \in \{s, c\} \tag{3}$$

$$\eta_{d,x} = \frac{c_{d,x} + \gamma_s^{(x)}}{N_d + \gamma_s^{(s)} + \gamma_s^{(c)}} \quad , x \in \{s, c\} \tag{4}$$

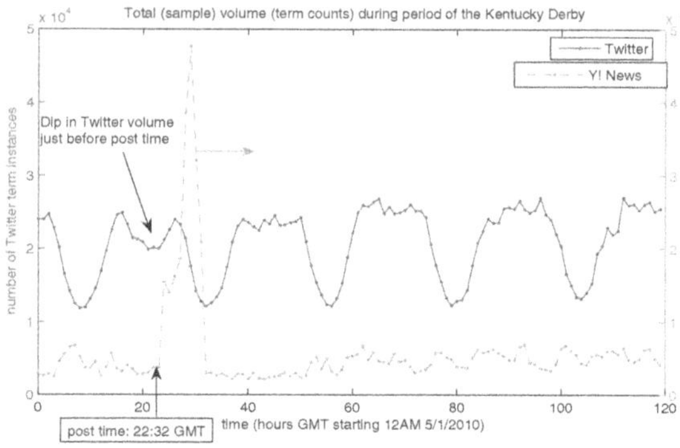

Figure 1: This figure shows the total volume (term instance counts) of Twitter and Yahoo! News as functions of time over the first 120 hours (GMT) of May 2010.

The formalism of our model resembles in spirit that of Chemudugunta et al. [6] where each term is "split" into corpus-level "background" topics, document-level "special" topics and normal topics. However, their work is only for a single corpus while our model fits multiple collections. Hyper-parameters like β, α and γ can be estimated using standard methods introduced by Minka [19].

4. MODELING TEMPORAL DYNAMICS

4.1 Temporal Dynamics for Topics

In this section we review a temporal model for news articles, introduced in [16] and present an alternate derivation. Before proceeding however, it bears pointing out that, as stated in [16], "rigorous analysis of the proposed model appears to be quite complex." The referred-to model embodies two driving forces for news-article publishing which the authors refer to as *imitation* and *recency*. The authors assert that this pair constitutes a minimum set for the purpose of explaining the temporal dynamics $n(t)$ of news-article publishing, but that the real situation is undoubtedly more complicated. We agree that there are factors beyond just these two. For example consider the Twitter and Yahoo! News total-volume data plotted in Figure 1. Note the enormous surge in the volume of news articles beginning after the Kentucky Derby[4], the premier American thoroughbred-horse race, and continuing for several hours. This clearly demonstrates significant elasticity in the volume capacity of the various sources contributing to Yahoo! News.

We start by assuming the following setting, which is a response that looks like a *proportional controller*[5] except that the "control point" n_{max} is not a constant.

$$\frac{dn}{dt} = \lambda [n_{\text{max}} - n(t)], \tag{5}$$

where n_{max} is a function of both t and n. The form (5) captures the *saturation* effect mentioned above. The saturation value n_{max} varies with both n and t, however. We assume that it is the product of a term $(\zeta n(t))$ embodying the *imitation* effect mentioned above and a term (νt^{-1}) embodying the *recency* effect, where ζ and ν are adjustable parameters. Substituting the resulting expression for n_{max} into (5), we obtain:

$$\frac{dn}{dt} = \lambda n(t) [\zeta \nu t^{-1} - 1] \tag{6}$$

[4] http://en.wikipedia.org/wiki/Kentucky_Derby
[5] See http://en.wikipedia.org/wiki/Proportional_control.

Figure 2: Overall Algorithm

```
Initialize Gibbs Sampler
while Not Converging do
    E-step
    For all documents in all text streams, update topic assignments using (1)
    M-step
    Update α, β and γ values through the method introduced in [19]
    for Each local and common topic do
        1) Fit gaussian function to α values
        2) Fit "temporal gamma" function by using the parameters from the previous step
        3) Re-calculate α values for topic k by using fitted function
    end for
end while
```

Next we solve this differential equation, assuming that the event occurs at $t = 0$ for convenience. For an event occurring at time t_0 let $t \to t - t_0$. We must also ensure that our solution satisfies the following boundary conditions.

1. $n(t) = 0$ for $t \le 0$.
2. $n(t) \ge 0$ for $t > 0$.
3. $n(t) \to 0$ as $t \to \infty$.

The solution of (6) proceeds in the following steps.

$$\begin{aligned} \frac{1}{n}\frac{dn}{dt} &= \lambda\,[\zeta\nu t^{-1} - 1], \\ \int_1^t \frac{1}{n}\frac{dn}{dt}\,dt &= \lambda\zeta\nu \int_1^t t^{-1}\,dt - \lambda \int_1^t dt, \\ \ln n(t) &= \ln n(t=1) + \lambda\zeta\nu \ln t - \lambda t + \lambda, \\ \ln n(t) &= \ln A + q \ln t - \lambda t, \\ n(t) &= A\,t^q\,e^{-\lambda t}, \end{aligned} \tag{7}$$

where $A := n(t = 1)\,e^{\lambda}$ and $q := \lambda\zeta\nu$. Next we apply our boundary conditions to the solution given in (7). First, to enforce condition 1 we multiply the solution of (7) by the Heaviside unit step function $u(t)$, which equals 0 for $t < 0$ and 1 for $t > 0$. Thus, we have

$$n(t) = u(t)\,A\,t^q\,e^{-\lambda t}. \tag{8}$$

Condition 2 requires that $A > 0$ and Condition 3 requires that $\lambda > 0$. The form of (8) has been demonstrated to capture spikes of news articles and social-media blogs [16, 30].

4.2 Incorporating Temporal Dynamics

In this section we describe how to incorporate the temporal model described above into our `Collection Model` and then introduce the inference approach to estimate the parameters in the model. We assume that the temporal dynamics of each topic are independent of each other. In other words, the popularity of one topic does not affect that of the other topics. We realize that this is a simplified assumption. The basic intuition behind embeding temporal dynamics into the model is to allow certain topics to have a higher probability of being selected. For example, during the Soccer World Cup in June and July of 2010, news articles and Twitter messages may naturally be more likely to talk about the World Cup, rather than politics. We encode this notion by associating the Dirichlet parameters for each topic with a time-dependent function. This function governs the variation of those parameters and thus indirectly controls the popularity of the associated topics. More specifically, for all common topics (with parameters α_c) and local topics (with parameters α_s), we let each dimension α_k in Dirichlet parameters α to be associated with the following time-dependent function.

$$\alpha_k(t) = f_k(t) = A_k t^{q_k} e^{-\lambda_k t} \tag{9}$$

where $f_k(t)$ is the temporal model described in Section 4.1. However, if we naïvely associate α_k with f_k, the model may face difficult problems since the temporal model unrealistically assumes that the starting point of the time t for all topics is time stamp 0. In other words, different topics should have different starting times t_0. Thus, we modify it into the following form:

$$f_k(t) = C_k + u(t - t_0^k)(A_k|t - t_0^k|^{q_k} \exp(-\lambda_k|t - t_0^k|)) \tag{10}$$

where t_0 is the starting time stamp of the topic, A_k controls the height of the prior knowledge, q_k indicates how quickly the topic would rise to the peak, λ_k controls the rate of decay and C_k is the "noise" level of the topic. We refer to the right hand side of (10) as the "temporal gamma function".

The absolute-value function guarantees that the time-dependent part is only active when t is larger than t_0. Additionally, $u(t - t_0)$ is a step function that is 1 for $t \ge t_0$ and 0 otherwise. In our implementation, a "soft" version of the step function as $u(t - t_0^{(k)}) = 1/(1 + \exp(-(t - t_0^{(k)}))$ is used. Intuitively, this equation states that the prior knowledge of each topic is fixed over time (by the "noise" level C_k) until a starting point t_0 and from that point on it follows a temporal gamma function controlled by three parameters, A_k, q_k and λ_k. The crux of the problem is to estimate the values of these five parameters from the data.

The absolute-value function and the parameter t_0 in (10) present challenges to model fitting (parameter estimation). To address this, rather than directly fitting $f_k(t)$, we use the following heuristic similar to that used in [18]. We first fit the following Gaussian function:

$$\alpha_k(t) \approx g_k(t) = C_k' + A_k' \exp(-(t - \mu_k)^2/2\sigma_k^2), \tag{11}$$

where μ_k is the mean and σ_k^2 is the variance. The resulting parameter values are then used to obtain initial parameter values for fitting the temporal gamma function of (10). This Gaussian function is straightforward to fit and its symmetric form allows us to obtain t_0 easily. We set the initial values of C_k and A_k in (10) to those obtained by fitting the Gaussian function and we fix $t_0^{(k)} = \mu_k - \sigma_k$. This process simplifies our inference algorithm. Note that the Gaussian approximation is only used to find initial values of the parameters including t_0. In our later experiments we find that this approximation gives reasonable initial values.

The outline of our inference algorithm is shown in Figure 2. Overall, we incorporate the functional optimization problem with Gibbs sampling into a stochastic EM framework (e.g., similar to [7]). In the E-step we gather topic assignments and useful counts by Gibbs sampling through (1). In the M-step we optimize the proposed objective functions to obtain the updated hyper-parameters for the next iteration. More specifically, the first step is to estimate the Dirichlet parameters α from counts obtained from Gibbs Sampling. This can be done in several ways [19]. We use Newton's method in this step. The second step is to use these α values to fit the Gaussian function (11) and then, using the parameters from the fitted Gaussian function as initial values, to fit our temporal gamma function (10). For both problems we minimize the following objective functions:

$$\operatorname*{argmin}_{g_k} G_k = \frac{1}{2}\sum_t \Big(\alpha_k(t) - g_k(t)\Big)^2 \tag{12}$$

$$\operatorname*{argmin}_{f_k} F_k = \frac{1}{2}\sum_t \Big(\alpha_k(t) - f_k(t)\Big)^2 \tag{13}$$

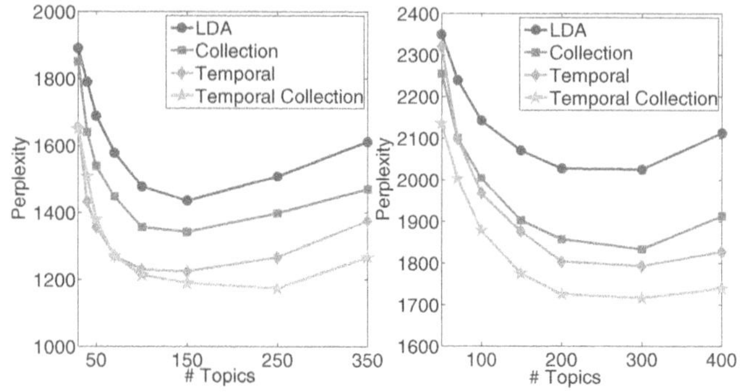

Figure 3: Perplexity Comparison Between Multiple Models. Left-hand plot: random 80%/20% train/test split; Right-hand plot: past/future 20-days/10-days train/test split.

We use the L-BFGS algorithm[17] implemented in GNU/GSL Library[8], which only requires the first-order gradients to obtain the optimal values for the parameters in both functions. Note that the method proposed here is potentially scaleable to very large datasets. For example LDA-style Gibbs sampling has been scaled to very large dataset sizes by [21], which is particularly useful for our E-step. For our M-step a stochastic gradient descent can be used instead of the usual Newton's method. We denote the whole algorithm as the `Temporal Collection` model.

5. EVALUATION

We utilize a real-world dataset consisting of Yahoo! News and Twitter messages from May 2010 to evaluate our method. Since the original dataset is quite large, we sample news articles and Tweets proportional to the total volume of each hour in May, resulting in 233,488 news articles and 1,736,350 Twitter messages in total. We use each hour as a time unit, which starts from 0, the first hour of May 1, 2010 to 720, the last hour of May 30, 2010. All the experiments are based on this dataset. The models used are (1) Latent Dirichlet Allocation (`LDA`), (2) Correlated Stream Model (`Collection`), introduced in Section 3, (3) Temporal Dynamics Topic Model (`Temporal`), introduced in Section 4.2 but ignoring multiple collection effects, and (4) Correlated Collection Model with Temporal Dynamics (`Temporal Collection`), introduced in Section 4.2. For `Collection` and `Temporal Collection`, we set the number of common topics to 20 $\sim$ 50 (depending on the total number of topics) and equally divide the remaining topics into all other streams, as local topics. We do not compare with other similar methods because `Collection` and `Temporal Collection` can essentially represent the two major directions of previous work discussed in Section 2.

5.1 Perplexity Evaluation

Following common practice for comparing topic models, we use *perplexity* of the held-out test data as our goodness-of-fit measure. Perplexity is defined as $\exp\left(-\frac{\sum_{d=1}^{D}\sum_{i=1}^{N_d}\log p(w_{d,i}|\text{M})}{\sum_{d=1}^{D}N_d}\right)$ where $w_{d,i}$ represents the ith term in document d, M is the model and N_d is the number of words in document d. First, we randomly sample 80% of the data as the training data and use the remaining 20% as the test data. Although this is a common evaluation procedure for topic models, it may not reflect real-world scenarios for temporal text collections because it may give additional undesirable advantages to models knowing the "future." All models are trained on the same training set and evaluated using the same test set. In the training phase we obtain topic distributions ϕ and all other hyper-parameters. In the testing phase we fix them and perform 100 Gibbs-sampling iterations for each document in the test set, obtaining θ_d. Using these newly estimated θ_d, we calculate $p(w_{d,i}|\text{M}) = \sum_z^K \phi_{k,w}\theta_{d,k}$ and then compute perplexity. The result is shown on the left-hand side in Figure 3. The second setting we choose is closer to real-world scenarios. We train all models on the first 20 days in May and test the perplexity on the remaining 10 days, shown on the right-hand side in Figure 3. As is evident in the figure, the perplexity exhibits a minimum with respect to the number of topics in both settings. As the number of topics is increased beyond that minimum, overfitting appears to set in, as was also observed in [10]. For both settings `Temporal Collection` significantly outperforms the others.

5.2 Common Topics and Local Topics

Here we manually compare the topics obtained by `Temporal Collection` and by `LDA` to determine which topics are meaningful and to see if any interesting patterns are discovered by the model. As we described previously, the advantage of `Temporal Collection` is to identify common topics among multiple text collections in a principled manner. Since `LDA` does not provide any mechanism for retrieving common topics explicitly, we use the following heuristic ranking method to indicate the prevalence of a topic T on both News and Twitter: $\frac{1}{2}\left[\frac{n(z_T,\text{News})}{\sum_{T'} n(z_{T'},\text{News})} + \frac{n(z_T,\text{Twitter})}{\sum_{T'} n(z_{T'},\text{Twitter})}\right]$ where $n(z_T, \text{News})$ is the number of tokens assigned to topic T in News and $n(z_T, \text{Twitter})$ is the number of tokens assigned to the same topic in Twitter. Basically, this simple heuristic measures how likely a topic is to be assigned to a token in both News and Twitter on average. The higher this value is, the more likely this topic will appear, on average. We rank all the topics obtained by `LDA` through this method and show the top 5 on the left top part of Table 1. For `Temporal Collection`, since common topics are identified automatically, we just need to rank all common topics and extract the top ones, by the following criterion: $\frac{1}{2}\left(\mathbb{E}[\theta_i^{\text{News}}]+\mathbb{E}[\theta_i^{\text{Twitter}}]\right)$ where $\mathbb{E}[\theta_i^{\text{News}}]$ is the expected value of θ_i for common topic t_i on news and similarly for Twitter. This equation can be interpreted as the average of the expected value of topic k appearing in a document on both collections. The quantity $\mathbb{E}[\theta_i]$ can be easily computed by $\frac{\alpha_i}{\sum_k \alpha_k}$ and normalized across all time epochs. The top 5 common topics are listed on the right top part of the same table.

The first column and the third column of the Table 1 show the *title* of the topics, a label given by the authors for easier interpretation. All topics (the second and the fourth column) are represented by the top ranked terms by $\phi_{z,w}$. Note that all these models are fit in an unsupervised manner in which no explicit human labels are available beforehand. From the results it is clear that both methods rank some potential common topics highly, such as "Oil Spill" and "Financial Crisis". However, it is also noticeable that simple ranking heuristics may not give appropriate scores to the topics. For instance the ranking scheme may prefer the topics from a collection that is significantly larger than the other, even if a topic only appears in one collection. For example, the two "junk" topics shown on the left are examples of this situation. In addition, if two topics are common to both data collections but one is popular among a lot of short documents (e.g., Twitter messages) and the other is prevalent in a relative small number of long documents (e.g., news articles), some sort of normalization schemes is clearly needed. Although there exist some sophisticated ranking heuristics

Table 1: Example Topics from Our Dataset

Comparison of Top Ranked Common Topics between LDA (Left) and Temporal Collection (Right)			
Title	**Top Terms**	**Title**	**Top Terms**
"finance"	percent billion bank market greece financial banks debt	"finance"	percent billion bank greece financial debt banks euro crisis
"crime"	police car times vehicle found york square street bomb	"oil spill"	oil gulf spill coast drilling mexico water louisiana
"junk"	link cont via #jobs #fb album super live wii #tcot #news	"world cup"	world cup team league final players south season club
"oil spill'	oil gulf spill coast mexico gas drilling sea water	"health care"	health medical care cancer hospital patients study research
"junk"	dont people cant thats youre bad look tell talk	"UK election"	minister party prime cameron political leader president

Comparison of Local Topics between News (Left) and Twitter (Right)			
News		Twitter	
Title	**Top Terms**	**Title**	**Top Terms**
"crime"	police car times vehicle found york square street	"social media"	blog video post check news via twitter online facebook
"US election"	election party law president vote political campaign	"hash tags"	#fb info #quote #fail #ge #lol #ff #twibbon cont
"China"	minister china south india north chinese korea indian	"non-English"	les pas pour sur une cest est qui avec bien suis tout faire
"jobs"	budget tax million money pay bill federal increase cuts	"junk"	cant this wait watch next believe gonna watching just
"education"	school students schools board education district college	"junk"	that would have could never were wish there

[3], we argue that our model can handle these issues in a more principled way by modeling common topics explicitly. For instance the α values for common topics can shed light on how popular these topics are, either in one of the data collections or in all of them.

Since similar ranking heuristics do not work well for LDA to provide local topics for Twitter and news, we only report the local topics found by our method, shown in the lower part of Table 1. On the left-hand side top ranked local topics on news are presented while on the right hand side top local topics found on Twitter are shown. Interesting observations can be made based upon these results. First, news articles tend to have more "formal" topics, such as politics, education and economy, whereas a large fraction of the Twitter stream consists of personal chat and opinions. Therefore, besides the common topics (e.g., Table 1) in both news and Twitter, local topics for Twitter seem less understandable and coherent. Indeed, throughout several experiments conducted on May's data and on other months as well, we observe that most of the local topics on Twitter are not very interesting. On the other hand, based on our experiments, some local topics (e.g "Crime") are on news but seldom picked up on Twitter. Many different kinds of criminal incidents are reported on a variety of news sources but not many of them really trigger interest on Twitter. Note that we understand that these results are preliminary and more thorough experiments are required. Nevertheless, our method provides a tool to investigate these interesting phenomena which are difficult or were impossible to be examined before [33].

5.3 Case Study on A Common Topic

Besides finding common and local topics on news and Twitter, our model also provides information about the temporal dynamics of these topics. Here we take a topic related to "Kentucky Derby" as an example to show the usefulness of our method. The Kentucky Derby[6] is the premier annual American horse race and has a significant international following. In 2010 it took place on May 1st. We try to identify the topics related to this event from the results obtained by our model. Remember that topics are only distributions over words. In order to find potential topics, we check the ranking positions of a list of terms which are known to be related to the event (e.g., "horse", "race", "kentucky", "derby"). If these terms are ranked highly in a particular topic, we consider that topic to be about the Kentucky Derby. We list the top 5 ranked terms of the topic we found by this simple heuristic just described: "derby", "race", "borel", "kentucky" and "horse". The topic we matched is a **common** topic and therefore it has the same distribution over words for both News and Twitter, meaning that once an article in News or a message in Twitter refers to this topic, the same word distribution is used to generate words, which is guaranteed by the model. However, the difference between News and Twitter on how this topic would be selected in a document is controlled by a stream-specific prior $\sim \text{Dir}(\alpha_t^{(c)})$ and further governed by a stream-dependent temporal gamma function.

In order to show the time series of the topic on news and Twitter, we transform the counts into a valid distribution by calculating a $p(t|z) = \frac{p(z|t)p(t)}{\sum_{t'} p(z|t')p(t')}$ where t is a time epoch. Then, $p(z|t)$ is estimated by the number of tokens assigned to topic z in time epoch t divided by the total number of tokens in time epoch t and $p(t)$ is estimated by the total number of tokens in time t divided by the overall number of tokens across all time epochs. Basically, the probability $p(t|z)$ tells us how likely the topic would appear in time epoch t. The results are shown in Figure 4. We first show the topic on the whole timeline (720 hours in May) on the top and show the first 120 hours at the bottom of the figure. The first observation is that the topic has two major peaks on both news and Twitter, shown in the upper part. This may reflect that "Kentucky Derby" is indeed a popular sports event. From the first 120-hour view of the topic, it is interesting to see that the topic first exhibited a peak on News and exhibited another peak on Twitter several hours later. This is a concrete example demonstrating the potential usage of our model to analyze common topics on multiple text streams in the timeline. A similar kind of analysis is conducted in [33] using sophisticated heuristics to find common topics and to view the timelines of topics.

5.4 Case Study on Hashtags

Hashtags, a type of community convention[7] which starts with a "#" sign, have been heavily used as annotations to represent events and topics on Twitter. We select several hashtags that can act as indicators for certain events where each hashtag is clearly associated to some events in May, 2010. More specifically, we choose #mothersday for "Mothers Day", #memorialday for "Memorial Day", #bp for "Oil Spill",#kentuckyderby for "Kentucky Derby", #gaga for "Lady Gaga" and #justinbieber for "Justin Bieber". We wish to see whether these events can be discovered by different models and how well these topics can be presented. We believe these hashtags represent a large range of social events and therefore are representative. In order to make a fair comparison, we

[6]http://en.wikipedia.org/wiki/Kentucky_Derby

[7]http://twitter.pbworks.com/Hashtags

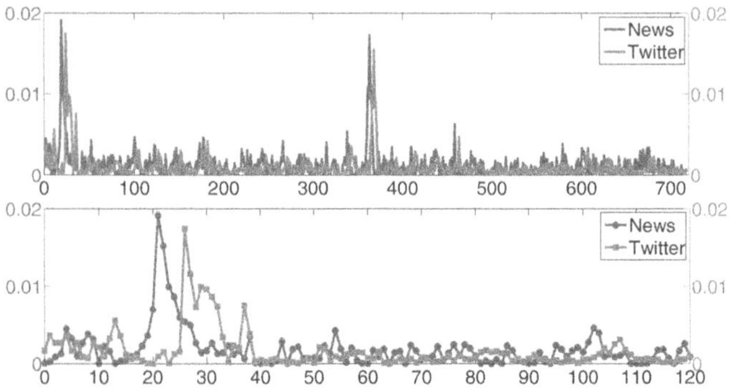

Figure 4: Temporal dynamics of "Kentucky Derby" on News and Twitter (X-axis is the hours in May, 2010. Y-axis is $p(t|z)$).

Table 2: Hashtag-to-Topic Mappings

Hashtag	Top Terms of Mapped Topic
[a] Hashtag Mapping for LDA model	
#mothersday	family home life children mother son friends
#memorialday	event june call center community club park
#bp	oil gulf spill coast mexico gas drilling
#kentuckyderby	race car track kentucky win top cars
#gaga & #justinbieber	justin lady super try bieber ider rio gaga jonas
[b] Hashtag Mapping for Temporal Collection model	
#mothersday	family children day home life church mother
#memorialday	memorial event day june community center
#bp	oil gulf spill coast drilling mexico water louisiana
#kentuckyderby	derby race borel kentucky horse super
#gaga & #justinbieber	bieber music video song gaga album lady

[c] KL Divergence between Hashtags and Matched Topics	
Hashtag	LDA vs. Temporal Collection
#mothersday	1.1911 / 0.7714
#memorialday	1.4331 / 0.9365
#bp	0.3958 / 0.1577
#kentuckyderby	1.9924 / 0.8183
#gaga & #justinbieber	2.2391 / 1.1754

transform the volume of these hashtags over time into distributions by using a technique similar to those introduced above. The first question we want to ask is whether the models can identify topics that reflect the events behind these hashtags. We map hashtags onto the topics obtained by the models and top ranked terms in these topics are examined to see whether these terms have any relationships with the underlying events. To map the hashtags, we calculate the following probability $p(z|w) = \frac{p(w|z)p(z)}{\sum_{z'} p(w|z')p(z')}$ where $p(w|z)$ is exactly $\phi_{z,w}$, provided by the trained models and $p(z)$ can be easily estimated by the counts. Intuitively, this probability tells us how likely a topic is to be selected, given the term. For the Temporal Collection model, all topics (including common topics and local topics) are treated as candidates to be matched. We map hashtags to topics for both LDA and our model, shown in the upper part of Table 2. Both models map #gaga and #justinbieber together onto a single topic, indicating that topics obtained by these models do not strictly correspond to real world events. Although some top ranked terms are similar for both models, the results from the Temporal Collection model are arguably better, in terms of *interpretation* of these terms. For instance, the Temporal Collection model explicitly ranks terms "memorial" and "day" highly in the list, implying this topic has much closer relationship with "Memorial Day", while LDA only has terms with broader connections with this kind of event. Similarly, the Temporal Collection model ranks more specific terms highly for 'Kentucky Derby" (e.g., "borel", "horse", "pletcher") while the topic obtained by LDA is essentially related to many races including "car races" and "horse races".

Table 3: Evaluation on Retrieval Performance

Method	MAP
TF-IDF	0.673
TF-IDF + Plain LDA	0.685
TF-IDF + Collection	0.703
TF-IDF + Temporal Collection	0.732

We can also compare the time-series of topics and hashtags to determine whether they are similar. The assumption is that, if they behave similarly on the timeline, the topics might be good choices for *explaining* the underlying events. Note that we are **not** seeking the **exact** match here since the topics have many more terms rather than a single hashtag and it may explain multiple events. Again, we transform the volumes into probabilities. We plot the time series of selected hashtags and the time series of selected topics in the same plots, shown in Figure 5. For each hashtag we compare its time series, obtained using LDA, with those obtained from our model. Although top ranked terms may look similar, the time series of these topics behave significantly differently. For LDA, because of the fixed Dirichlet hyper-parameter α over time, the models may give inappropriate "pseudo counts" for certain topics in the timeline. Indeed, one property of Dirichlet distribution can shed some lights on the observation: $\mathbb{E}[\theta_k] = \frac{\alpha_k}{\sum_{k'} \alpha_{k'}}$ where the expected value of θ_k, the proportion of topic k represented in a document, is the ratio of the Dirichlet parameter α_k over the sum of all α values. Since α values are fixed over time, this expected value will also be constant over time, leading to the fact that the topic assignments fluctuate around a certain value, though with variance, which is exactly shown in our experiments. This drawback of LDA may lead to difficulty in identifying the peaks of these topics. On the other hand, in our model, since the hyper-parameters α are controlled by the temporal gamma functions, the rise and fall of these values may give good hints for the model to assign topics to words, yielding better modeling temporal dynamics. Also, from the results, our models can better match the peaks of hashtags, indicating that the method can better reflect real events.

We can further compare these time series quantitatively. Since these time series are valid distributions over time, KL divergence is employed to measure their "distance" as follows: $\sum_t p(t|w_1) \log \frac{p(t|w_1)}{p(t|w_2)}$. KL divergence is non-negative and the smaller the value is, the more similar two distributions are. We calculate the KL divergence between hashtag time series and topic time series for both LDA and our model. The results are shown in the bottom part of Table 2. From the results it is obvious that the time series of topics obtained by the Temporal Collection model better match the corresponding hashtag time series, yielding lower KL divergence scores. This also validates the visual evidence from Figure 5.

5.5 Performance on Retrieval

As a further demonstration of the utility and effectiveness of our model, we apply it in a toy application that uses it as part of an information-retrieval relevance measure. For a query q and document d, the idea is to use the probability $p(q|d)$ that q was generated by d's generating model as a measure of the relevance of d to q. In a scheme similar to that used in [29] we use a relevance measure $S(d|q)$ that is a linear combination of $p(q|d)$ and a simple TF-IDF-

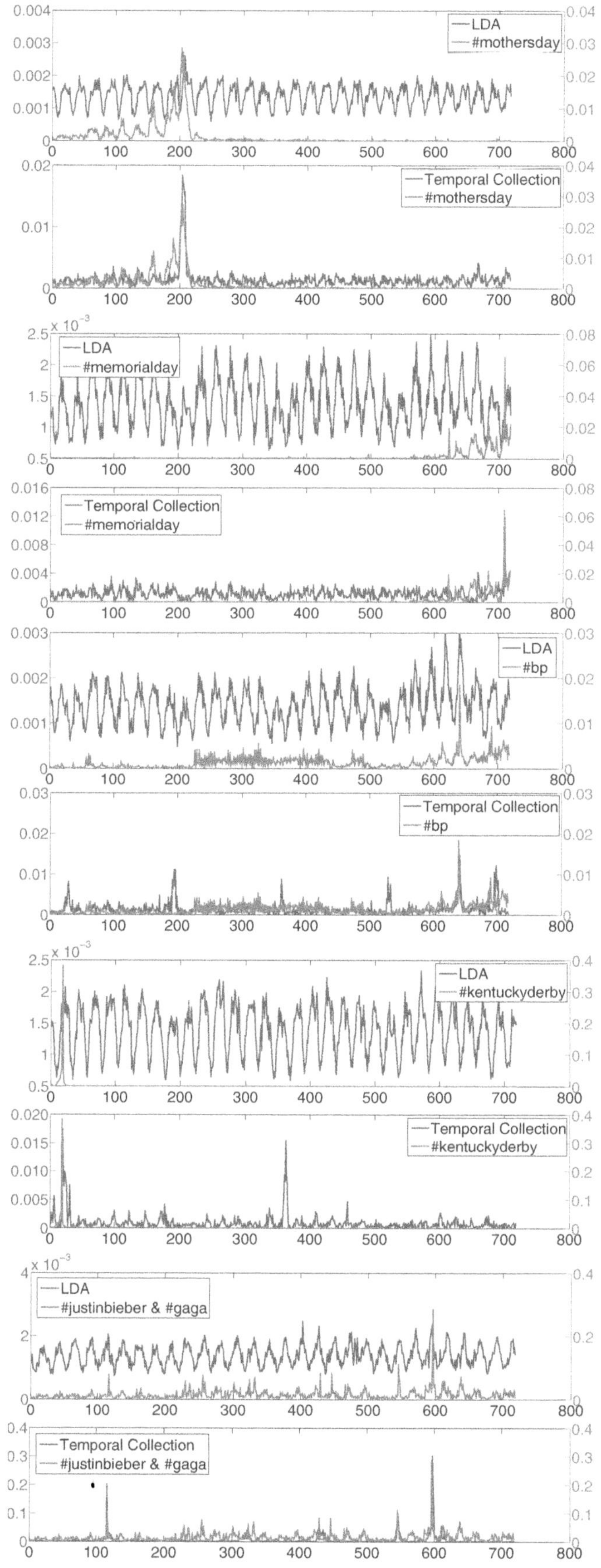

Figure 5: The distributions $p(t|z)$ of mapped topics in May. X-axis is the hour number. Y-axis is the probability.

based cosine-similarity score $\tau(d, q)$. That is

$$S(d|q) = \lambda \tau(d,q) + (1-\lambda)\, p(q|d). \qquad (14)$$

For our experiment we select the top 20 queries from `GoogleInsights` in the time period of May 2010, corresponding to our datasets. To select retrieval candidates we compute $\tau(d, q)$ for all tweet-query pairs (d, q) and use these scores to rank the tweets for all queries. We then select the top 50 tweets from that ranking for each query. These tweets and queries are then submitted to Amazon Mechanical Turk for manual relevance judgements, which we use as ground truth. These judgements are assigned using a three-level scale consisting of "relevant", "neutral" and "non-relevant." For each pair (d, q) three judges are assigned to assess the relevance and only the pairs on which at least two workers agree are kept, leaving a total of 922 tweets.

Mean Average Precision (MAP) for the top 20 positions is used for retrieval-accuracy characterization. These top-20 MAP scores are computed for each of four combinations of the TF-IDF measure $\tau(d, q)$ and a topic model. For each combination the parameter λ of (14) is varried over the range $[0, 1]$ and the optimal (highest MAP) value is determined. The corresponding MAP values are shown in Table 3. From these results we see that the choice of topic model used affects retrieval accuracy, with the highest retrieval accuracy being associated with the combination of TF-IDF and `Temporal Collection` scores.

6. CONCLUSION & FUTURE WORK

Modeling the temporal dynamics of topics is still a challenge, especially on multiple data collections. In this paper we propose a model for use in automatically analyzing multiple correlated text streams with their temporal behavior in a principled way. Our method bridges the recent advances in topic-modeling and information cascading in social media. We extend topic models by allowing each text stream to have local topics and shared topics, overcoming several theoretical problems of previously proposed models for similar problems. For temporal modeling we associate each topic with a time-dependent function that characterizes its popularity over time. By combining the two models, we can effectively model the temporal dynamics of multiple correlated text streams in a unified framework. Compared to related work our method is easy to implement and can potentially scale to large datasets. Additionally our method provides a new tool for browsing and mining a variety of types of social media simultaneously. For future work it will be interesting to utilize Bayesian non-parametric techniques to automatically learn the number of topics from the dataset. This is especially valuable for our model where the number of common topics and local topics must be manually assigned in current settings. In addition in order to better reflect real events, topics can be linked with named entities such that each topic is forced to contain a certain number of entities. It is also interesting to see hierarchical modeling of topics with temporal dynamics, which permits users to "zoom in" and "zoom out" on large topics (e.g. "oil spill") and track their evolution over time.

Acknowledgements

We thank Suju Rajan and Brian D. Davison for helping to improve the quality of the paper.

7. REFERENCES

[1] A. Ahmed and E. P. Xing. Timeline: A dynamic hierarchical Dirichlet process model for recovering birth/death and evolution of topics in text stream. In *Proceedings of the 26th*

International Conference on Conference on Uncertainty in Artificial Intelligence (UAI), pages 20–29, 2010.

[2] A. Aji and E. Agichtein. Deconstructing interaction dynamics in knowledge sharing communities. In *International Conference on Social Computing, Behavioral Modeling, and Prediction*, pages 273–281, 2010.

[3] L. Alsumait, D. Barbará, J. Gentle, and C. Domeniconi. Topic significance ranking of LDA generative models. In *Proceedings of the European Conference on Machine Learning and Knowledge Discovery in Databases (ECML/PKDD)*, pages 67–82, 2009.

[4] D. M. Blei and J. D. Lafferty. Dynamic topic models. In *Proceedings of the 23rd International Conference on Machine Learning (ICML)*, pages 113–120, 2006.

[5] D. M. Blei, A. Y. Ng, and M. I. Jordan. Latent Dirichlet Allocation. *The Journal of Machine Learning Research*, 3:993–1022, 2003.

[6] C. Chemudugunta, P. Smyth, and M. Steyvers. Modeling general and specific aspects of documents with a probabilistic topic model. In *NIPS*, pages 241–248, 2006.

[7] G. Doyle and C. Elkan. Accounting for burstiness in topic models. In *Proceedings of the 26th Annual International Conference on Machine Learning (ICML)*, pages 281–288, 2009.

[8] M. Galassi, J. Davies, J. Theiler, B. Gough, G. Jungman, P. Alken, M. Booth, and F. Rossi. *GNU Scientific Library Reference Manual - Third Edition (v1.12)*. Network Theory Ltd., 2009. `http://www.gnu.org/software/gsl/`.

[9] M. Goetz, J. Leskovec, M. McGlohon, and C. Faloutsos. Modeling blog dynamics. In *International AAAI Conference on Weblogs and Social Media (ICWSM)*, 2009.

[10] T. L. Griffiths and M. Steyvers. Finding scientific topics. *Proceedings of the National Academy of Sciences of the United States of America*, pages 5228–5235, 2004.

[11] T. Hofmann. Unsupervised learning by probabilistic latent semantic analysis. *Machine Learning*, 42:177–196, 2001.

[12] T. Iwata, T. Yamada, Y. Sakurai, and N. Ueda. Online multiscale dynamic topic models. In *Proceedings of the 16th ACM SIGKDD International Conference on Knowledge Discovery and Data Mining*, pages 663–672, 2010.

[13] A. Java, X. Song, T. Finin, and B. Tseng. Why we Twitter: Understanding microblogging usage and communities. In *Proceedings of the 9th WebKDD*, pages 56–65, 2007.

[14] J. Kleinberg. Bursty and hierarchical structure in streams. *Journal Data Mining and Knowledge Discovery*, 7(4):373–397, 2003.

[15] J. Kleinberg. Temporal dynamics of on-line information streams. In *Data Stream Management: Processing High-Speed Data Streams*, 2005.

[16] J. Leskovec, L. Backstrom, and J. Kleinberg. Meme-tracking and the dynamics of the news cycle. In *Proceedings of the 15th ACM SIGKDD International Conference on Knowledge Discovery and Data Mining*, pages 497–506, 2009.

[17] D. C. Liu and J. Nocedal. On the limited memory BFGS method for large scale optimization. *Mathematical Programming*, 45(3):503–528, 1989.

[18] T. Masada, D. Fukagawa, A. Takasu, T. Hamada, Y. Shibata, and K. Oguri. Dynamic hyperparameter optimization for Bayesian topical trend analysis. In *Proceeding of the 18th ACM Conference on Information and Knowledge Management (CIKM)*, pages 1831–1834, 2009.

[19] T. P. Minka. Estimating a Dirichlet distribution. Technical report, 2009. `http://research.microsoft.com/en-us/um/people/minka/papers/dirichlet/`.

[20] R. M. Nallapati, S. Ditmore, J. D. Lafferty, and K. Ung. Multiscale topic tomography. In *Proceedings of the 13th ACM SIGKDD International Conference on Knowledge Discovery and Data Mining*, pages 520–529, 2007.

[21] D. Newman, A. Asuncion, P. Smyth, and M. Welling. Distributed algorithms for topic models. *The Journal of Machine Learning Research*, 10:1801–1828, 2009.

[22] M. Paul. Cross-collection topic models: Automatically comparing and contrasting text. Master's thesis, UIUC, 2009.

[23] M. Paul and R. Girju. Cross-cultural analysis of blogs and forums with mixed-collection topic models. In *Proceedings of the 2009 Conference on Empirical Methods in Natural Language Processing (EMNLP)*, pages 1408–1417. Association for Computational Linguistics, 2009.

[24] I. Pruteanu-Malinici, L. Ren, J. Paisley, E. Wang, and L. Carin. Hierarchical Bayesian modeling of topics in time-stamped documents. *IEEE Transactions on Pattern Analysis and Machine Intelligence*, 32:996–1011, June 2010.

[25] C. Wang, D. M. Blei, and D. Heckerman. Continuous time dynamic topic models. In *Proceedings of the 24th Conference in Uncertainty in Artificial Intelligence (UAI)*, pages 579–586, 2008.

[26] X. Wang and A. McCallum. Topics over time: A non-Markov continuous-time model of topical trends. In *Proceedings of the 12th ACM SIGKDD International Conference on Knowledge Discovery and Data Mining*, pages 424–433, 2006.

[27] X. Wang, C. Zhai, X. Hu, and R. Sproat. Mining correlated bursty topic patterns from coordinated text streams. In *Proceedings of the 13th ACM SIGKDD International Conference on Knowledge Discovery and Data Mining*, pages 784–793, 2007.

[28] X. Wang, K. Zhang, X. Jin, and D. Shen. Mining common topics from multiple asynchronous text streams. In *Proceedings of the Second ACM International Conference on Web Search and Data Mining (WSDM)*, pages 192–201, 2009.

[29] X. Wei and W. B. Croft. LDA-based document models for ad-hoc retrieval. In *Proceedings of the 29th annual international ACM SIGIR Conference on Research and Development in Information Retrieval*, pages 178–185, 2006.

[30] J. Yang and J. Leskovec. Patterns of temporal variation in online media. In *Proceedings of the fourth ACM International Conference on Web search and Data Mining (WSDM)*, pages 177–186, 2011.

[31] C. Zhai, A. Velivelli, and B. Yu. A cross-collection mixture model for comparative text mining. In *Proceedings of the 10th ACM SIGKDD International Conference on Knowledge Discovery and Data Mining*, pages 743–748, 2004.

[32] J. Zhang, Y. Song, C. Zhang, and S. Liu. Evolutionary hierarchical Dirichlet processes for multiple correlated time-varying corpora. In *Proceedings of the 16th ACM SIGKDD International Conference on Knowledge Discovery and Data Mining*, pages 1079–1088, 2010.

[33] W. X. Zhao, J. Jiang, J. Weng, J. He, E.-P. Lim, H. Yan, and X. Li. Comparing Twitter and traditional media using topic models. In *ECIR*, pages 338–349, 2011.

Active Learning for Node Classification in Assortative and Disassortative Networks

Cristopher Moore*
Computer Science Dept.
University of New Mexico
Albuquerque NM 87131 USA
and Santa Fe Institute
moore@cs.unm.edu

Xiaoran Yan
Computer Science Dept.
University of New Mexico
Albuquerque NM 87131 USA
everyxt@gmail.com

Yaojia Zhu
Computer Science Dept.
University of New Mexico
Albuquerque NM 87131 USA
yaojia.zhu@gmail.com

Jean-Baptiste Rouquier
Complex Systems Institute
Rhône-Alpes
ENS Lyon, France
jrouquie@gmail.com

Terran Lane
Computer Science Dept.
University of New Mexico
Albuquerque NM 87131 USA
terran@cs.unm.edu

ABSTRACT

In many real-world networks, nodes have class labels, attributes, or variables that affect the network's topology. If the topology of the network is known but the labels of the nodes are hidden, we would like to select a small subset of nodes such that, if we knew their labels, we could accurately predict the labels of all the other nodes. We develop an active learning algorithm for this problem which uses information-theoretic techniques to choose which nodes to explore. We test our algorithm on networks from three different domains: a social network, a network of English words that appear adjacently in a novel, and a marine food web. Our algorithm makes no initial assumptions about how the groups connect, and performs well even when faced with quite general types of network structure. In particular, we do not assume that nodes of the same class are more likely to be connected to each other—only that they connect to the rest of the network in similar ways.

Categories and Subject Descriptors:
I.2.6 [**Artificial Intelligence**]: Learning
G.2.2 [**Discrete Mathematics**]: Graph theory

General Terms: Algorithms, Experimentation, Theory

Keywords: complex networks, structure and function, community detection, information theory, active learning, collective classification, transductive graph labeling

1. INTRODUCTION

In many social, biological, and technological networks, nodes have underlying attributes or variables that are correlated with the network's topology. Blogs tend to link to other blogs with similar political views [1]. In vertebrate food webs, predators tend to eat prey whose mass is smaller, but not too much smaller, than their own [11]. Networks of word adjacencies are correlated with those words' parts of speech [30]. In the Internet, different types of service providers form different kinds of links based on their capacities and business relationships [3, 13]—and so on.

There has been a great deal of work on efficient algorithms for community detection in networks (see [12, 32] for reviews). However, most of this work defines a "community" as a group of nodes with high density of connections within the group and a low density of connections to the rest of the network. While this type of *assortative* community structure is common in social networks, we are interested in a more general definition of *functional* community—a group of nodes that connect to the rest of the network in similar ways. A set of predators might form a functional group in a food web, not because they eat each other, but because they eat similar prey. In English, nouns often follow adjectives, but seldom follow other nouns. Even some social networks have *disassortative* structure where pairs of nodes are more likely to be connected if they are from different classes. For example, some human societies are divided into moieties, and only allow marriages between different moieties [21].

We consider a setting where the topology of the network is known, but the class labels of the nodes are not. This could be the case, for instance, if we have a network of blogs and hyperlinks between them (like citations, trackbacks, blogrolls, etc.) and we are trying to classify the blogs according to their political leanings. Another possible application is in online social networks, where friendships are known and we are trying to infer hidden demographic variables. This problem is sometimes referred to as collective classification [35]. However, in that work the focus is on classification of individual nodes. In contrast, our focus is on the discovery of functional communities in the network, and our underlying generative model is designed around the assumption of that these communities exist.

We make no initial assumptions about the structure of the network—for instance, whether its groups are assortative, disassortative, or some mixture of the two. We assume that

*This work was supported by the McDonnell Foundation.

KDD'11, August 21–24, 2011, San Diego, California, USA.

we can learn the label of any given node, but at a cost, say in terms of work in the field or laboratory. Our goal is to identify a small subset of nodes such that, once we explore them and learn their labels, we can accurately predict the labels of all the others.

We present a general approach to this problem. Our algorithm uses information-theoretic measures to decide which node to explore next—that is, which one will give us the most information about the rest of the network. We start with a probabilistic generative model of the network, called a *stochastic block model* [20, 38], in which groups connect to each other according to a matrix of probabilities. This model allows an arbitrary mixture of assortative and disassortative structure, as well as directed links from one group to another, and has been used to model networks in many fields (e.g. [4, 19, 33]).

We stress, however, that our approach could be applied equally well to many other probabilistic models, such as those where nodes belong to a mixture of classes [2], a hierarchy of classes and subclasses [10], locations in a latent geographical or social space [17], or niches in a food web [39]. It could also be applied to degree-corrected block models such as those in [23, 26, 31], which treat the nodes' degrees as parameters rather than data to be predicted.

At each stage of the learning process, some of the nodes' labels are already known and we need to decide which node to explore next. We do this by estimating, for each node, the mutual information between its label and the joint distribution of all the others' labels, conditioned on the labels of the nodes that are known so far. We obtain this estimate by Gibbs sampling, giving each classification of nodes a probability integrated over the parameters of the block model. We then explore the node for which this mutual information is largest.

A key fact about the mutual information, which we argue is essential to our algorithm's performance, is that it is not just a measure of uncertainty: it is a combination of uncertainty about a node's label and the extent to which it is correlated with the labels of other nodes. Thus the algorithm explores nodes which maximize the expected amount of information it will gain about the entire network. It skips nodes whose labels seem obvious to it, or which are uncertain but have little effect on other nodes. In an assortative network, for instance, it starts by exploring nodes which are central to their communities, and then explores nodes along the boundaries between them, without being told in advance to pursue this strategy.

We also present an alternate approach which maximizes a quantity we call the *average agreement*. For each node v, this is the average number of nodes at which two independent samples of the Gibbs distribution agree, conditioned on the event that they agree at v. Like mutual information, average agreement is high for nodes that are highly correlated with the rest of the network. A similar idea (but not applied to networks) is present in [34].

We test our algorithm on three real-world networks: the social network of a karate club, a network of common adjacent words in a Charles Dickens novel, and a marine food web of species in the Antarctic. Each of these networks is curated in the sense that we possess the correct node labels, such as the faction of the social network each individual belongs to, the part of speech of each word, or the part of the habitat each species lives in. We judge our algorithm according to how accurately it predicts the labels of the unexplored nodes, as a function of the number of nodes it has explored so far. We also compare our algorithm with several simple heuristics, such as exploring nodes based on their degree or betweenness centrality, and find that it significantly outperforms them.

2. RELATED WORK

The idea of designing experiments by maximizing the mutual information between the variable we learn next and the joint distribution of the other variables, or equivalently the expected amount of information we gain about the joint distribution, has a long history in statistics, artificial intelligence, and machine learning, e.g. Mackay [25] and Guo and Greiner [16]. Indeed, it goes back to the work of Lindley [24] in the 1950s. However, to our knowledge this is the first time it has been coupled with a generative model to discover hidden variables in networks.

In recent work, Zhu, Lafferty, and Ghahramani [41] study active learning of node labels using Gaussian fields and harmonic functions defined using the graph Laplacian. However, this technique only applies to networks where neighboring nodes are likely to be in the same class—that is, networks with assortative community structure. In contrast, our techniques are capable of learning about much more general types of network structure, including disassortative and directed relationships between functional communities.

Another approach to active learning of node labels is found in the work of Bilgic and Getoor [6] and Bilgic, Mihalkova, and Getoor [7], who use collective vector-based classifiers. By properly defining the collective relationships between nodes, both assortative or disassortative communities can be learned in this framework. However, our technique differs from theirs by using mutual information as the active learning criterion, which takes into account not just uncertainty, but correlations as well.

Additional works by Goldberg, Zhu, and Wright [14] and Tong and Jin [36] also perform semi-supervised learning on graphs, and handle the disassortative case. But they work in a setting where they know, for each link, if the ends should have the same or different labels, such as if one writer quotes another with pejorative words. In contrast, we work in a setting where we have no such information: only the topology is available to us, and there are no signs on the edges telling us whether we should propagate similar or dissimilar labels.

3. MODEL AND METHODS

We represent our network as a directed graph $G = (V, E)$ with n nodes. We assume that there are k classes of nodes, so that each node v has a class label $t(v) \in \{1, \ldots, k\}$. We are given the graph G, and our goal is to learn the labels $t(v)$. To do this, we assume that G is generated by a probabilistic model, in which its topology is correlated with these labels.

The simplest such model, although by no means the only one to which our methods could be applied, is a stochastic block model [20, 38]. It assumes that for each pair of nodes u, v, there is an edge from u to v with a probability $p_{t(u),t(v)}$ that depends only on their labels, and that these events are independent. Given a classification, i.e., a function $t : V \to \{1, \ldots, k\}$ assigning a label to each node, the probability of generating a given graph G in this model is

$$P(G\,|\,t,p) = \left(\prod_{(u,v)\in E} p_{t(u),t(v)} \right) \left(\prod_{(u,v)\notin E} (1 - p_{t(u),t(v)}) \right)$$
$$= \prod_{i,j=1}^{k} p_{ij}^{e_{ij}} (1-p_{ij})^{n_i n_j - e_{ij}} . \qquad (1)$$

Here $n_i = |\{v \in V : t(v) = i\}|$ is the number of nodes of class i, and $e_{ij} = |\{(u,v) \in E : t(u) = i, t(v) = j\}|$ is the number of edges from nodes of class i to nodes of class j. If we wish to focus on undirected graphs, we can modify this expression by restricting the product over pairs of classes with $i \le j$. We can also forbid self-loops, if we wish, by replacing n_i^2 in the term $i = j$ with $n_i(n_i - 1)$ or $\binom{n_i}{2}$ in the directed or undirected case respectively.

This kind of stochastic block model is well-known in the machine learning, statistics, and network communities [5, 37, 15, 18, 19, 33] and has also been used in ecology to identify groups of species in food webs [4]. Unlike e.g. [37, 18, 19], we do not assume that p_{ij} takes one value when $i = j$ and a smaller value when $i \neq j$. In other words, we do not assume an assortative community structure, where nodes are more likely to be connected to other nodes of the same class. Nor do we require in general that $p_{ij} = p_{ji}$, since the directed nature of the edges may be important—for instance, in a food web or word adjacency network.

If all classifications t are equally likely *a priori*, then Bayes' rule implies that the Gibbs distribution on the classifications, i.e., the probability of t given G, is proportional to the probability of G given t:

$$P(t\,|\,G) \propto P(G\,|\,t) . \qquad (2)$$

In order to define $P(G\,|\,t)$, we need to integrate $P(G\,|\,t,p)$ over some prior probability distribution on p. If we assume that the p_{ij} are independent, then this integral factors over the product (1). In particular, if each p_{ij} follows a beta prior, we have the Bayesian estimate of edge probabilities

$$P(G\,|\,t) = \iiint_0^1 \mathrm{d}\{p_{ij}\}\, P(G\,|\,t,p)$$
$$= \prod_{i,j=1}^{k} \int_0^1 \mathrm{d}p_{ij}\, \mathrm{Beta}(p_{ij}|\alpha,\beta)\, p_{ij}^{e_{ij}} (1-p_{ij})^{n_i n_j - e_{ij}}$$
$$= \prod_{i,j=1}^{k} \frac{\Gamma(\alpha+\beta)}{\Gamma(\alpha)\Gamma(\beta)} \int_0^1 \mathrm{d}p_{ij}\, p_{ij}^{e_{ij}+\alpha-1} (1-p_{ij})^{n_i n_j - e_{ij}+\beta-1}$$
$$= \prod_{i,j=1}^{k} \frac{\Gamma(\alpha+\beta)}{\Gamma(\alpha)\,\Gamma(\beta)} \frac{\Gamma(e_{ij}+\alpha)\,\Gamma(n_i n_j - e_{ij} + \beta)}{\Gamma(n_i n_j + \alpha + \beta)} . \qquad (3)$$

For reasonable choices of the hyperparameters α and β, the prior dominates only in small data cases, such as very small networks or sparsely populated classes. For such small data cases, the beta prior allows the user to input some domain knowledge about, say, the (dis)assortativity of the target network's community structure. In the limit of large data, the prior will wash out and the data-driven community structure will dominate.

If the user wishes to remain agnostic, however, he or she can specify a uniform prior ($\alpha = \beta = 1$) and allow the learning algorithm to estimate the degree of assortativity, disassortativity, directedness, and so on entirely from the data. We take this approach in this paper, in which case

$$P(G\,|\,t) = \prod_{i,j=1}^{k} \frac{1}{(n_i n_j + 1)\binom{n_i n_j}{e_{ij}}} . \qquad (4)$$

An even simpler approach is to assume that the p_{ij} take their maximum likelihood values

$$\hat{p}_{ij} = \operatorname*{argmax}_p P(G\,|\,t,p) = e_{ij}/n_i n_j , \qquad (5)$$

and set $P(G\,|\,t) = P(G\,|\,t,\hat{p})$. This approach was used, for instance, for a hierarchical block model in [10]. When k is fixed and the n_i are large, this will give results similar to (4), since the integral over p is tightly peaked around $\hat{p}$. However, for any particular finite graph it makes more sense, at least to a Bayesian, to integrate over the p_{ij}, since they obey a posterior distribution rather than taking a fixed value. Moreover, averaging over the parameters as in (4) discourages overfitting, since the average likelihood goes down when we increase k and hence the volume of the parameter space. This gives us a principled way to determine k automatically, although in this paper we set k by hand. Other methods to determine k include minimum description length (MDL) techniques [33] and the Akaike information criterion [4]

4. ACTIVE LEARNING

In the active learning setting, the algorithm can learn the class label of any given node, but at a cost—say, by devoting resources in the laboratory or the field. Since these resources are limited, it has to decide which node to explore. Its goal is to explore a small set of nodes and use their labels to guess the labels of the remaining nodes.

One natural approach is to explore the node v with the largest mutual information (MI) between its label $t(v)$ and the labels $t(G \setminus v)$ of the other nodes according to the Gibbs distribution (2). We can write this as the difference between the entropy of $t(G \setminus v)$ and its conditional entropy given $t(v)$,

$$\mathrm{MI}(v) = I(v; G \setminus v) = H(G \setminus v) - H(G \setminus v\,|\,v) . \qquad (6)$$

Here $H(G \setminus v\,|\,v)$ is the entropy, averaged over $t(v)$ according to the marginal of $t(v)$ in the Gibbs distribution, of the joint distribution of $t(G \setminus v)$ conditioned on $t(v)$. In other words, $\mathrm{MI}(v)$ is the expected amount of information we will gain about $t(G \setminus v)$, or equivalently the expected decrease in the entropy, that will result from learning $t(v)$.

Since the mutual information is symmetric, we also have

$$\mathrm{MI}(v) = I(v; G \setminus v) = H(v) - H(v\,|\,G \setminus v) , \qquad (7)$$

where $H(v)$ is the entropy of the marginal distribution of $t(v)$, and $H(v\,|\,G \setminus v)$ is the entropy, on average, of the distribution of $t(v)$ conditioned on the labels of the other nodes. Thus $\mathrm{MI}(v)$ is large if (i) we are uncertain about v, so that $H(v)$ is large, and (ii) v is strongly correlated with the other nodes, so that $H(v\,|\,G \setminus v)$ is small.

We estimate these entropies by sampling from the space of classifications t according to the Gibbs distribution. Specifically, we use a single-site heat-bath Markov chain. At each step, it chooses a node v uniformly from among the unexplored nodes, and chooses its label $t(v)$ according to the conditional distribution proportional to $P(G \mid t)$, assuming that the labels of all other nodes stay fixed. In addition to exploring the space, this allows us to collect a sample of the conditional distribution of the chosen node v and its entropy. Since $H(v \mid G \setminus v)$ is the average of the conditional entropy, and since $H(v)$ is the entropy of the average conditional distribution, we can write

$$I(v; G \setminus v) = -\sum_{i=1}^{k} \langle P_i \rangle \ln \langle P_i \rangle + \left\langle \sum_{i=1}^{k} P_i \ln P_i \right\rangle , \quad (8)$$

where P_i is the probability that $t(v) = i$ and $\langle \cdot \rangle$ denotes the average, according to the Gibbs distribution, over the labels of the other nodes.

We offer no theoretical guarantees about the mixing time of this Markov chain, and it is easy to see that there are families of graphs and values of k for which it it takes exponential time. However, for the real-world networks we have tried so far, it appears to converge to equilibrium in a reasonable amount of time. We test for equilibrium by measuring whether the marginals change noticeably when the number of updates is increased by a factor of 2. We improve our estimates by averaging over many runs, each one starting from an independently random initial state.

We say that the algorithm is in *stage* j if it has already explored j nodes. In that stage, it estimates $\mathrm{MI}(v)$ for each unexplored node v, using the Markov chain to sample from the Gibbs distribution conditioned on the labels of the nodes explored so far. It then explores the node v with the largest MI. We provide it with the correct value of $t(v)$ from the curated network, and it moves on to the next stage.

The mutual information is not the only quantity we might use to identify which node to explore. Another is the *average agreement*, which we define as follows. Given two classifications t_1, t_2, define their *agreement* as the number of nodes on whose labels they agree,

$$|t_1 \cap t_2| = |\{v : t_1(v) = t_2(v)\}| \ . \quad (9)$$

Since our goal is to label as many nodes correctly as possible, we wish we could maximize the agreement between an classification t_1, drawn from the Gibbs distribution, and the correct classification t_2. However, the algorithm doesn't know t_2, so it assumes that it is drawn from the Gibbs distribution as well. Exploring v projects onto the part of the joint distribution of (t_1, t_2) where $t_1(v) = t_2(v)$. So, we define $\mathrm{AA}(v)$ as the expected agreement between two classifications t_1, t_2 drawn independently from the Gibbs distribution, conditioned on the event that they agree at v:

$$\mathrm{AA}(v) = \frac{\sum_{t_1,t_2:t_1(v)=t_2(v)} P(t_1)P(t_2)\,|t_1 \cap t_2|}{\sum_{t_1,t_2:t_1(v)=t_2(v)} P(t_1)P(t_2)} \ . \quad (10)$$

We estimate the numerator and denominator of $\mathrm{AA}(v)$ using the same heat-bath Gibbs sampler as for $\mathrm{MI}(v)$, except that we sample independent pairs of classifications (t_1, t_2) by starting the Markov chain at two independently random initial states.

5. RESULTS AND DISCUSSION

We tested our algorithms on three different networks from three different fields. The first is Zachary's Karate Club [40]. As shown in Fig. 1, this is a social network consisting of 34 members of a karate club, where undirected edges represent friendships. The club split into two factions, indicated by diamonds and circles respectively. One of them centered around the instructor (node 1) and the other around the club president (node 34), each of which formed their own club. Shaded nodes are more peripheral, and have weaker ties to their communities. This network is highly assortative, with a high density of edges within each faction and a low density of edges between them.

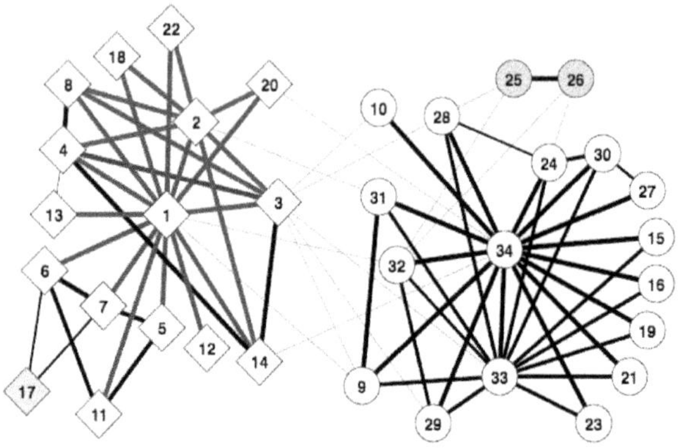

Figure 1: Zachary's Karate Club.

We judge the performance of each algorithm by asking, at each stage and for each node, with what probability the Gibbs distribution assigns it the correct label. In each stage we sampled the Gibbs distribution using 100 independently chosen initial conditions, doing 2×10^4 steps of the heat-bath Markov chain for each one, and computing averages using the last 10^4 steps. Increasing the number of Markov chain steps to 10^5 per stage produced only marginal improvements in performance. Fig. 2 shows what fraction of the unexplored nodes are assigned the correct label with probability at least q, for various thresholds $q = 0.1, 0.3, 0.5, 0.7, 0.9$, as a function of the stage j.

After exploring just four or five nodes, both of our algorithms succeed in correctly predicting the labels of most of the remaining nodes—i.e., to which faction they belong—with high accuracy. The AA algorithm performs slightly better than MI, achieving an accuracy close to 100% after exploring nine nodes. Of course, the Karate Club network is quite small, and there are many community-finding algorithms that classify the two factions with perfect or near-perfect accuracy [32, 12].

Perhaps more interesting is the *order* in which our algorithms choose to explore the nodes. In Fig. 3, we sort the nodes in order of the median stage at which they are explored. Error bars show 90% confidence intervals over 100 independent runs of each algorithm. Some nodes show a large variance in the stage in which they are explored, while others are consistently explored at the beginning or end of the process. Both algorithms start by exploring nodes 1 and 34, which are central to their respective communities. Note that these nodes are chosen, as we argued above, not just because their labels are uncertain, but because they are highly correlated with the labels of other nodes.

After learning that nodes 1 and 34 are in class 1 and 2 respectively, the algorithms "know" that the network consists of two assortative communities. They they explore nodes such as 3, 9, and 10 which lie at the boundary between

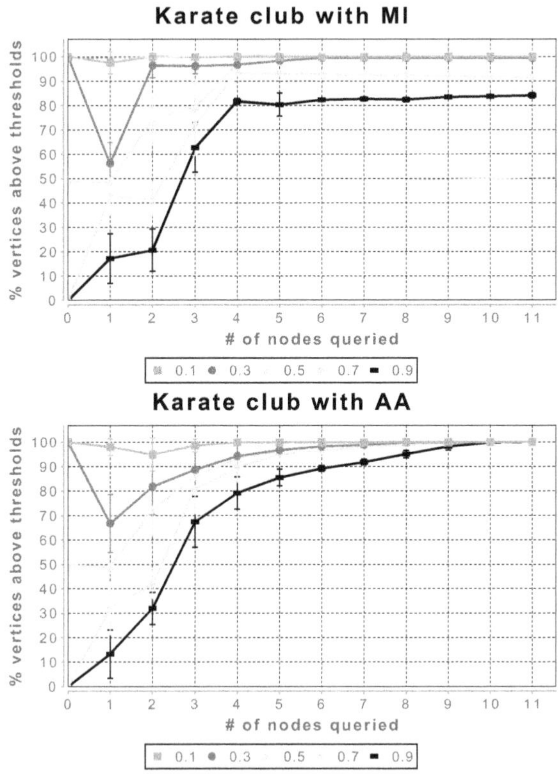

Figure 2: Results of the active learning algorithms on Zachary's Karate Club network.

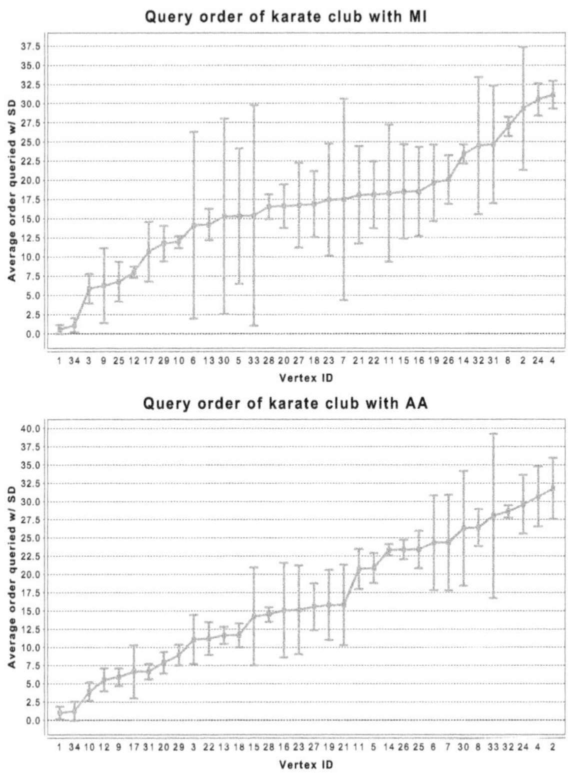

Figure 3: The order in which the active learning algorithms explore nodes in Zachary's Karate Club.

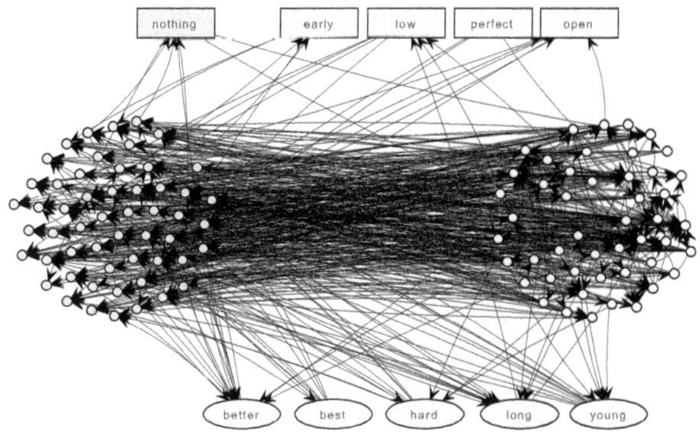

Figure 4: The order in which the active learning algorithm MI explores nodes in word adjacency network from the novel *David Copperfield*.

these communities. Once the boundary is clear, they can easily predict the labels of the remaining nodes. The last nodes to be explored are those such as 2, 4, and 24, which lie so deep inside their communities that their labels are not in doubt.

The second network consists of the 60 most commonly occurring nouns and the 60 most commonly occurring adjectives in Charles Dickens' novel *David Copperfield*. A directed edge connects any pair of words that appear adjacently in the text, pointing from the preceding word to the following one. Excluding eight words which are disconnected from the rest leaves a network with 112 nodes [29]. Unlike Zachary's Karate Club, this network is both directed and highly disassortative. Of the 1494 edges, 1123 of them point from adjectives to nouns. This lets us classify most nodes early on, simply by labeling a node as an adjective or noun if its out-degree or in-degree is large.

Accordingly, our algorithms focus their attention on words about which they are uncertain, like "early," "low," and "nothing," whose out-degrees and in-degrees in the text are roughly equal, and words like "perfect" that precede words of both classes (see Fig. 4, where green and yellow nodes represent nouns and adjectives respectively; rectangular nodes are explored first, and elliptical ones last). Once these nodes are resolved, both algorithms achieve high accuracy—80% accuracy after exploring 20 nodes and close to 100% after exploring 65 nodes (see Fig. 5).

In each stage we sampled the Gibbs distribution using 100 independently chosen initial conditions, doing 5×10^4 steps of the heat-bath Markov chain for each one, and computing averages using the last 2.5×10^4 steps. Increasing the number of Markov chain steps to 10^5 per stage produced only marginal improvements in performance. As in Fig. 2, the y-axis shows the fraction of unexplored nodes which are labeled correctly by the conditional Gibbs distribution with probability at least q, for $q = 0.1, 0.3, 0.5, 0.7, 0.9$. The performance of the two algorithms is similar in the later stages, but unlike the Karate Club, here MI performs noticeably better than AA in the early stages.

The third network is a food web of 488 species in the Weddell Sea in the Antarctic [11, 9, 22], with edges pointing to each predator from its prey. This data set is very rich,

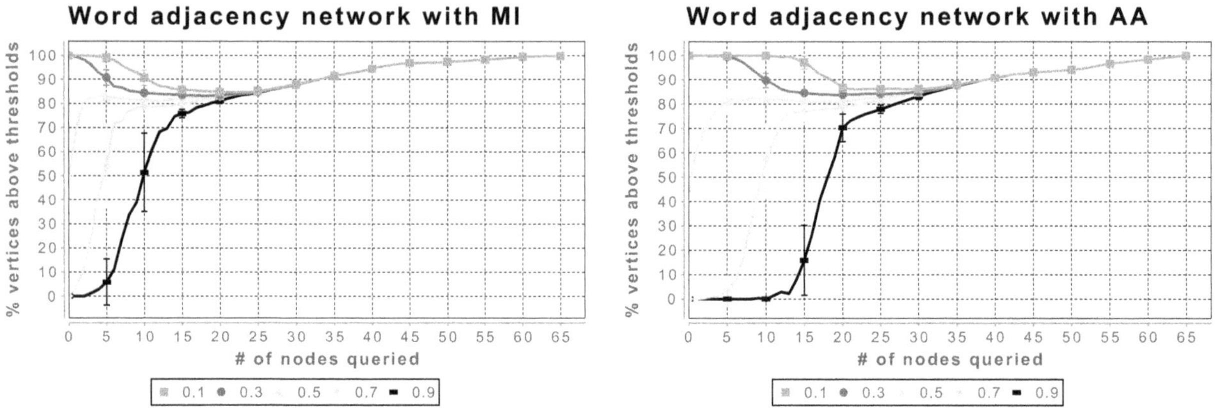

Figure 5: Results of the active learning algorithms on word adjacency network in the novel *David Copperfield* by Charles Dickens.

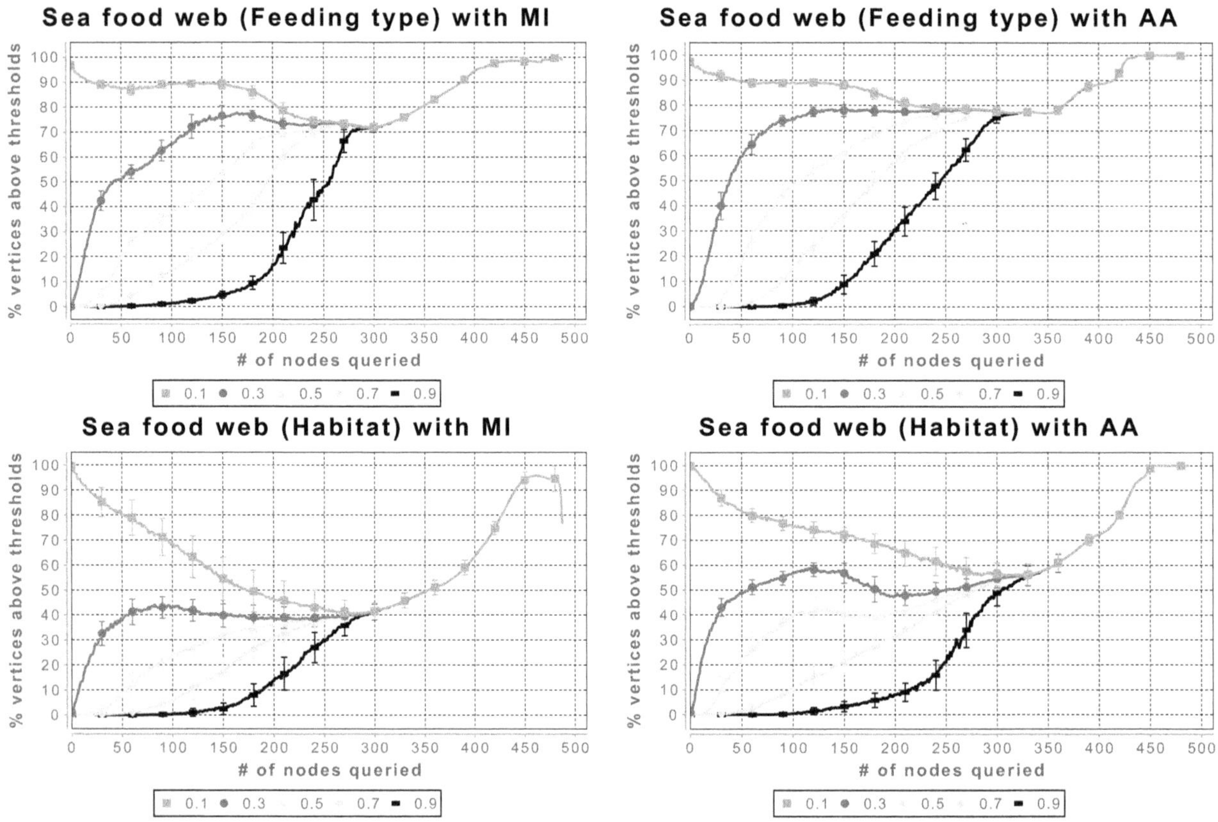

Figure 6: Results for the Weddell Sea food web.

but we focus on two particular variables—the feeding type and the habitat in which the species lives. The feeding type takes $k = 6$ values, namely primary producer, omnivorous, herbivorous/detrivorous, carnivorous, detrivorous, and carnivorous/necrovorous. The habitat variable takes $k = 5$ values, namely pelagic, benthic, benthopelagic, demersal, and land-based.

We show results of our algorithms for both variables in Fig. 6. The results are averaged over 100 runs of each algorithm. In each stage we sampled the Gibbs distribution using 100 independently chosen initial conditions, doing 5×10^4 steps of the heat-bath Markov chain for each one, and computing averages using the last 2.5×10^4 steps. For the feeding type, after exploring half the nodes, both algorithms correctly label about 75% of the remaining nodes. For the habitat variable, both algorithms are less accurate, although AA performs somewhat better than MI. Note that the accuracy only includes the unexplored nodes, not the nodes we have already explored. Thus it can decrease if we explore easily-classified nodes early on, so that hard-to-classify nodes form a larger fraction of the remaining ones.

Fig. 6 shows that both algorithms get to a state where they are confident, but wrong, about many of the unexplored nodes. For the feeding type variable, for instance, after the AA algorithm has explored 300 species, it labels 75% of the remaining nodes correctly with probability 90%, but it labels the other 25% correctly with probability less than 10%. In other words, it has a high degree of confidence about all the nodes, but is wrong about many of them. Its accuracy improves as it explores more nodes, but it doesn't achieve high accuracy on all the unexplored nodes until there are only about 60 of them left.

Why is this? We argue that the fault lies, not with our learning algorithms and the order in which they explore the nodes, but with the stochastic block model and its ability to model the data. For example, for the habitat variable, these algorithms perform well on pelagic, demersal, and land-based species. But the benthic habitat, which is the largest and most diverse, includes species with many feeding types and trophic levels.

These additional variables have a large effect on the topology, but they are not taken into account by the block model. As a result, more than half the benthic species are mislabeled by the block model in the following sense: even if we condition on the correct habitats of *all* the other species, the species' most likely habitat is pelagic, benthopelagic, demersal, or land-based. Specifically, 219 of the 488 species are mislabeled by the most likely block model, 94% of them with confidence over 0.9.

Of course, we can also regard our algorithms' mistakes as evidence that these habitat classifications are not cut and dried. Indeed, ecologists recognize that there are "connector species" that connect one habitat to another, and belong to some extent to both.

To test our hypothesis that it is the block model's inability to model the data that causes some nodes to be misclassified, we artificially modified the data set to make it consistent with the block model. Starting with the nodes' original class labels, we updated the habitat of each species to its most likely value according to the block model, given the habitats of all the other species. After iterating this process six times, we reached a fixed point where each species' habitat is consistent with the block model's predictions. On this synthetic data set both of our learning algorithms perform perfectly, predicting the habitat of every species with close to 100% accuracy after exploring just 18% of them.

More generally, it is important to remember that the topology of the network is only imperfectly correlated with the nodes' types. Zachary [40] relates that one of members of the Karate Club joined the instructor's faction even though the network's topology suggests that he was more strongly connected to the president. The reason is that he was only three weeks away from a test for his black belt when the split occurred. He had already invested four years learning the instructor's style of karate, and if he had joined the president's club he would have had to start over with a white belt. In any real-world network, there is information of this kind that is not reflected in the topology and which is hidden from our algorithm. If a node is of a given class for idiosyncratic reasons like these, we cannot expect any algorithm based solely on topology and the other nodes' class labels—no matter how sophisticated a probabilistic model we use—to correctly classify it.

6. COMPARISON WITH SIMPLE HEURISTICS

We compared our active learning algorithms with several simple heuristics. These include exploring the node with the highest degree in the subgraph of unexplored nodes, exploring the node with the highest betweenness centrality (the fraction of shortest paths that go through it, see [8, 27, 28]) in the subgraph of unexplored nodes, and exploring a node chosen uniformly at random from the unexplored ones. We judge the performance of these heuristics using the same Gibbs sampling process as for MI and AA.

In Fig. 7, we show the results of these heuristics at the 0.9 accuracy threshold on all three networks, including both the habitat and feeding type variables in the food web. On Zachary's Karate Club (left) our algorithms outperform these heuristics consistently. In the *David Copperfield* network (right), the highest-degree and highest-betweenness heuristics enjoy an early lead, but quickly hit a ceiling and are surpassed by MI and AA.

For the Weddell Sea food web (bottom), the highest-degree and highest-betweenness heuristics perform poorly throughout the learning process. One reason for this is that many nodes with high degree or high betweenness are easy to classify from the labels of their neighbors. By exploring these nodes first, these heuristics leave themselves mainly with hard-to-classify nodes. The random-node heuristic performs surprisingly well early on, but all three heuristics are worse than MI or AA once they have explored half the nodes.

7. CONCLUSION

Active learning, using mutual information or average agreement coupled with a generative model, offers a new approach to analyzing networks where the topology is known, but knowledge of class labels is incomplete and costly to obtain. We have shown for three networks, one social, one lexical, and one biological, that our algorithms do a good job of predicting the labels of unexplored nodes after exploring a relatively small fraction of the network, correctly recognizing both assortative and disassortative functional communities. Certainly not all networks are well-described by the simple block model we use here, but our approach can be general-

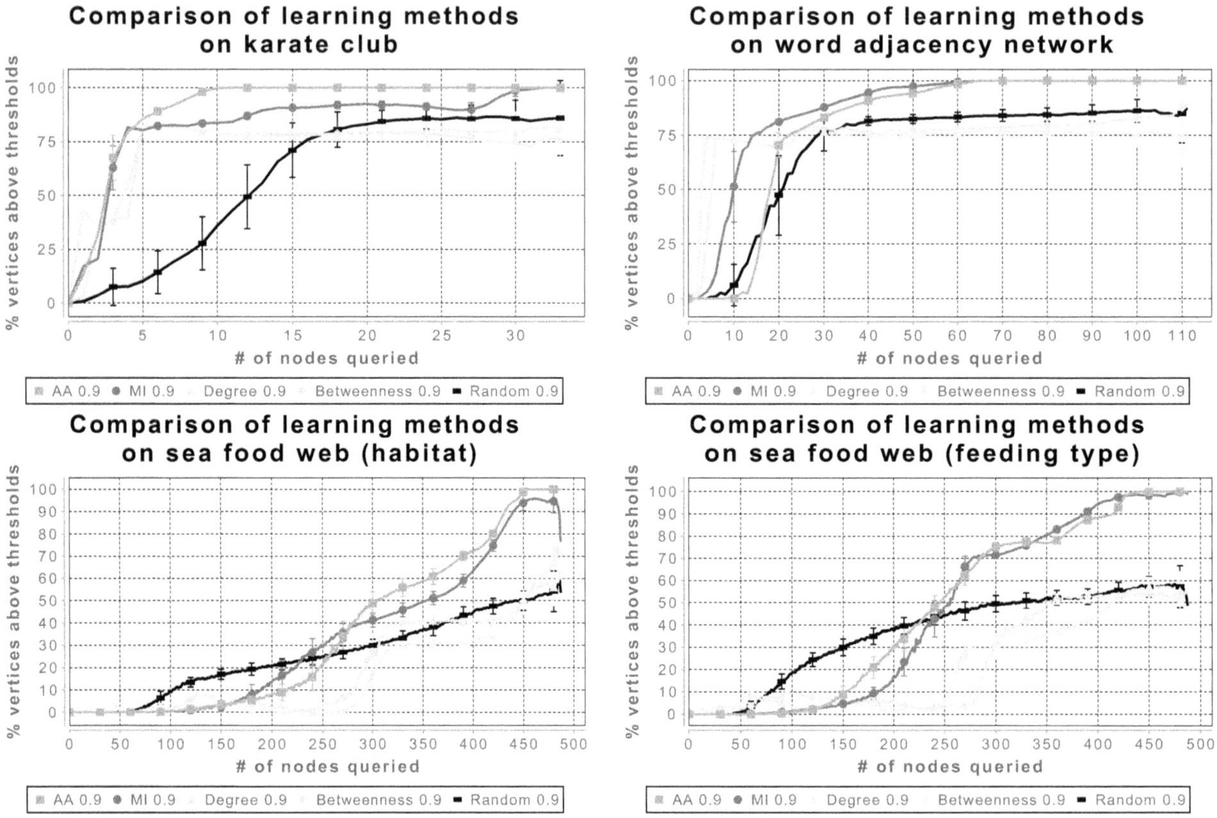

Figure 7: A comparison of the MI and AA learning algorithms with three simple heuristics.

ized to probabilistic network models which take information on the nodes' locations or degrees into account.

Acknowledgments. We are grateful to Joel Bader, Aaron Clauset, Jennifer Dunne, Nathan Eagle, Brian Karrer, Jon Kleinberg, Mark Newman, Cosma Shalizi, and Jerry Zhu for helpful conversations, and to Ute Jacob for the Weddell Sea food web data. J.-B. R. is also grateful to the Santa Fe Institute for their hospitality. This work was supported by the McDonnell Foundation.

8. REFERENCES

[1] L. Adamic and N. Glance. The political blogosphere and the 2004 US election: Divided they blog. In *Proc 3rd Intl Workshop on Link Discovery.*, 2005.

[2] E. M. Airoldi, D. M. Blei, S. E. Fienberg, and E. P. Xing. Mixed membership stochastic blockmodels. *J. Machine Learning Research*, 9:1981–2014, 2008.

[3] D. Alderson, L. Li, W. Willinger, and J. C. Doyle. Understanding internet topology: principles, models, and validation. *IEEE/ACM Trans. Networks*, 13(6):1205–1218, 2005.

[4] S. Allesina and M. Pascual. Food web models: a plea for groups. *Ecology Letters*, 12:652–662, 2009.

[5] P. J. Bickel and A. Chen. A nonparametric view of network models and newman-girvan and other modularities. *Proc. Natl. Acad. Sci.*, 106:21068–21073, 2009.

[6] M. Bilgic and L. Getoor. Link-based active learning. In *NIPS Workshop on Analyzing Networks and Learning with Graphs*, 2009.

[7] M. Bilgic, L. Mihalkova, and L. Getoor. Active learning for networked data. In *Proc. Intl. Conf. on Machine Learning*, 2010.

[8] U. Brandes. A faster algorithm for betweenness centrality. *Journal of Mathematical Sociology*, 25(2):163–177, 2001.

[9] U. Brose, L. Cushing, E. L. Berlow, T. Jonsson, C. Banasek-Richter, L. F. Bersier, J. L. Blanchard, T. Brey, S. R. Carpenter, M. F. Blandenier, et al. Body sizes of consumers and their resources. *Ecology*, 86(9):2545–2545, 2005.

[10] A. Clauset, C. Moore, and M. E. J. Newman. Hierarchical structure and the prediction of missing links in networks. *Nature*, 453(7191):98–101, 2008.

[11] U. B. et al. Consumer-resource body-size relationships in natural food webs. *Ecology*, 87(10):2411–2417, 2006.

[12] S. Fortunato. Community detection in graphs. *Physics Reports*, 2009.

[13] L. Gao and J. Rexford. Stable internet routing without global coordination. *IEEE/ACM Trans. Networks*, 9(6):681–692, 2001.

[14] A. B. Goldberg, X. Zhu, and S. Wright. Dissimilarity in graph-based semi-supervised classification. *J. Machine Learning Research W&P*, 2:155–162, 2007.

[15] R. Guimera and M. Sales-Pardo. Missing and spurious interactions and the reconstruction of complex

networks. *Proc. Natl. Acad. Sci.*, 106:22073–22078, 2009.

[16] Y. Guo and R. Greiner. Optimistic active learning using mutual information. In *Proc. Intl. Joint Conf. on Artificial Intelligence*, 2007.

[17] M. S. Handcock, A. E. Raftery, and J. M. Tantrum. Model-based clustering for social networks. *J. Royal Statist. Soc. A*, 170(2):1–22, 2007.

[18] M. B. Hastings. Community detection as an inference problem. *Physical Review E*, 74(3):035102, 2006.

[19] J. M. Hofman and C. H. Wiggins. Bayesian approach to network modularity. *Physical Review Letters*, 100(25):258701, 2008.

[20] P. W. Holland, K. B. Laskey, and S. Leinhardt. Stochastic blockmodels: first steps. *Social networks*, 5:109–137, 1983.

[21] M. Houseman and D. R. White. *Taking Sides: Marriage Networks and Dravidian Kinship in Lowland South America*, pages 214–243. Transformations of Kinship. Smithsonian Institution Press, 1998.

[22] U. Jacob. *Trophic Dynamics of Antarctic Shelf Ecosystems, Food Webs and Energy Flow Budgets.* PhD thesis, University of Bremen, 2005.

[23] B. Karrer and M. E. J. Newman. Stochastic blockmodels and community structure in networks, 2010. Preprint, arXiv:1008.3926v1.

[24] D. V. Lindley. On a measure of the information provided by an experiment. *Ann. Math. Statist.*, 27(4):986–1005, 1956.

[25] D. J. MacKay. Information-based objective functions for active data selection. *Neural Computation*, 4(4):590–604, 1992.

[26] M. Mørup and L. K. Hansen. Learning latent structure in complex networks. In *NIPS Workshop on Analyzing Networks and Learning with Graphs*, 2009.

[27] M. Newman. Scientific collaboration networks. II. shortest paths, weighted networks, and centrality. *Physical Review E*, 64(1), 2001.

[28] M. E. J. Newman. A measure of betweenness centrality based on random walks. *Social Networks*, 27(1):39–54, 2005.

[29] M. E. J. Newman. Finding community structure in networks using the eigenvectors of matrices. *Physical Review E*, 74(3):36104, 2006.

[30] M. E. J. Newman and E. A. Leicht. Mixture models and exploratory analysis in networks. *Proc. Natl. Acad. Sci.*, 104:9564–9569, 2006.

[31] A. S. Patterson, Y. Park, and J. S. Bader. Degree-corrected block models. Manuscript.

[32] M. A. Porter, J. P. Onnela, and P. J. Mucha. Communities in networks. *Notices of the American Mathematical Society*, 56(9):1082–1097, 2009.

[33] M. Rosvall and C. T. Bergstrom. An information-theoretic framework for resolving community structure in complex networks. *Proc. Natl. Acad. Sci.*, 104(18):7327, 2007.

[34] N. Roy and A. McCallum. Toward optimal active learning through sampling estimation of error reduction. In *Proc. 18th Intl. Conf. on Machine Learning*, pages 441–448, 2001.

[35] P. Sen, G. M. Namata, M. Bilgic, L. Getoor, B. Gallagher, and T. Eliassi-Rad. Collective classification in network data. *AI Magazine*, 29(3):93–106, 2008.

[36] W. Tong and R. Jin. Semi-supervised learning by mixed label propagation. In *Proc. 22nd Intl. Conf. on Artificial intelligence*, volume 1, pages 651–656, 2007.

[37] J. Čopič, M. O. Jackson, and A. Kirman. Identifying community structures from network data. *B.E. Press Journal of Theoretical Economics*, 9(1):Article 30, 2009.

[38] Y. J. Wang and G. Y. Wong. Stochastic blockmodels for directed graphs. *J. American Statistical Assn.*, 82(397):8–19, 1987.

[39] R. J. Williams, A. Anandanadesan, and D. Purves. The probabilistic niche model reveals the niche structure and role of body size in a complex food web. *PLoS One*, 5(8):e1209, 2010.

[40] W. W. Zachary. An information flow model for conflict and fission in small groups. *J. Anthropological Research*, 33(4):452–473, 1977.

[41] X. Zhu, J. Lafferty, and Z. Ghahramani. Combining active learning and semi-supervised learning using gaussian fields and harmonic functions. In *Proc. ICML-2003 Workshop on the Continuum from Labeled to Unlabeled Data*, 2003.

Active Learning using On-line Algorithms

Chris Mesterharm
Rutgers Computer Science Department
110 Frelinghuysen Road
Piscataway, NJ 08854, USA
mesterha@cs.rutgers.edu

Michael J. Pazzani
Rutgers Computer Science Department
110 Frelinghuysen Road
Piscataway, NJ 08854, USA
pazzani@rutgers.edu

ABSTRACT

This paper describes a new technique and analysis for using on-line learning algorithms to solve active learning problems. Our algorithm is called Active Vote, and it works by actively selecting instances that force several perturbed copies of an on-line algorithm to make mistakes. The main intuition for our result is based on the fact that the number of mistakes made by the optimal on-line algorithm is a lower bound on the number of labels needed for active learning. We provide performance bounds for Active Vote in both a batch and on-line model of active learning. These performance bounds depend on the algorithm having a set of unlabeled instances in which the various perturbed on-line algorithms disagree. The motivating application for Active Vote is an Internet advertisement rating program. We conduct experiments using data collected for this advertisement problem along with experiments using standard datasets. We show Active Vote can achieve an order of magnitude decrease in the number of labeled instances over various passive learning algorithms such as Support Vector Machines.

Categories and Subject Descriptors

I.2.6 [**Artificial Intelligence**]: Learning—*Induction*

General Terms

Algorithms, Design, Performance, Theory

1. INTRODUCTION

In this paper, we study a type of inductive learning called active learning [28]. The model of induction we use is based on a set of instances X where each instance $x \in X$ is given a label $y \in \{0, 1\}$. Our goal is to learn a function that correctly assigns labels to a large number of instances in X using a small number of labeled instances. In active learning, we get labeled instances by selecting from a set $\hat{X} \subset X$. The labels for these selected instances can be determined by various procedures such as consulting a human expert. We assume there is a cost for each label.

We propose an active learning algorithm that works by combining several copies of an on-line learning algorithm. Our modification works with any on-line learning algorithm, but it benefits most by using an on-line algorithm that has a worst-case upper-bound on the number of mistakes. The main intuition of our algorithm is to actively select instances to force the on-line algorithms to make mistakes. If we can force enough mistakes then the on-line algorithms must learn the concept. What is more likely is that the algorithm will reach a point where it can no longer guarantee mistakes. In practice, at this point the algorithm is close to a good concept, but either way, the algorithm reverts to passive learning and does not suffer a penalty.

Previous inexpensive active learning algorithms such as uncertainty sampling with a probabilistic classifier [21] and Active Majority [22] often show an order of magnitude decrease in the number of labels required over passive learning but lack strong theoretical justification. More recent work has focused on strengthening the theory of active learning [11, 3, 12, 6, 18]. While these results are encouraging, the algorithms are often expensive and they do not have the dramatic decreases in label costs seen on practical problems by earlier algorithms. In this paper, we start with an efficient well-performing algorithm and attempt to better understand why it works in order to improve its performance and theoretical justification.

Our algorithm is strongly related to the Active Majority technique of Liere and Tadapalli [22]. In this paper, we present a new analysis that explains why Active Majority works, and based on that understanding, we present refinements to improve its performance. We call this new technique Active Vote. Active Vote can modify any on-line algorithm for active learning.

The motivating application for this research is to provide a content owner more control over the advertisements served on their website. These advertisements are typically served by an ad network such as Google's Adsense for content. While these ad networks have proven to be profitable, they sometimes place ads that the content owners believe their readers might find inappropriate. In this paper, we present an application that allows a content owner to provide feedback on the ads that appear on their website and uses that information to learn a classifier that is used to block ads that are deemed inappropriate. Active learning is important for this problem because most content owners will not take the time to provide feedback on thousands of ads.

KDD'11, August 21–24, 2011, San Diego, California, USA.

The paper is organized as follows. The next section defines different types of active learning. Section 2 motivates the use of on-line algorithms for active learning by describing how they relate in an exact model of learning. The main motivation is based on the fact that the number of mistakes made by the optimal on-line learning is a lower-bound for the number of label requests needed by any active learning algorithm. Section 4 describes our active learning technique, Active Vote, and Section 5 gives performance bounds for Active Vote. In Section 6, we give information on our Internet advertisement application, and Section 7 gives our experimental results. We perform experiments on four datasets including the previously mentioned Internet advertisement domain.

2. ACTIVE LEARNING MODELS

In this section, we explain several different types of active learning. We divide active learning models into two groups: batch learning and on-line learning. This section also reviews information on batch and on-line learning.

2.1 Batch Models

The most common type of active learning deals with batch learning. Batch active learning assumes that the learning algorithm has access to a large set of unlabeled instances. The algorithm requests labels for some small subset of these instances and uses this information to learn a hypothesis. The goal is that this hypothesis predicts the correct label for future instances. To make this problem solvable, one typically assumes that all the instances are drawn from the same distribution and that there are some restrictions on the form of this distribution. The goal of the algorithm is to maximize the accuracy of the learned hypothesis.

A common restriction on active batch learning is that the learning algorithm is presented the instances in a stream. To keep the algorithm efficient, the algorithm must decide as soon as it sees the instance whether or not it wants to request the label. If it does not request the label, then the instance is skipped. This means the algorithm does not have to keep track of large numbers of unlabeled instances. We instead focus on the situation where the algorithm is allowed to select the best instance from the set of instances, $\hat{X}$. In this way the algorithm can further optimize its choice. If there is a limit to the number of instances the algorithm can store or process, then one can easily convert to a stream algorithm by selecting the best instance in some fixed number of observed instances.

Another possible active batch model is based on transduction. This is the same as the previous active batch models except that the algorithm is evaluated on the remaining instances in $\hat{X}$. This is an interesting active learning model when $\hat{X}$ is finite because the learning algorithm is motivated to find difficult instances not just to learn the concept but also to remove them from evaluation. While we feel our techniques are applicable to this problem, we do not directly address transduction in this paper.

2.2 On-line Models

On-line learning is best understood by viewing the learning problem as a sequence of instances. The learning algorithm is presented an instance and the algorithm must predict the label. Soon after prediction, the algorithm receives the label and uses this information to update its prediction hypothesis. The goal of the algorithm is to minimize the number of incorrect predictions. Many on-line learning problems are based on predicting the future. For example, with the stock market the label is readily available after the market has closed.

For on-line active learning, we consider two possible models. The first model is based on bootstrapping. By this we mean that we have an early phase of learning where we try to learn as much as possible and we do not care about mistakes. Afterward we switch to on-line learning where we are penalized for mistakes. As an example, consider preallocation of resources for computer program scheduling. We don't know the resources until after executing the program, but we could set up a bootstrap period in which we test several programs. It would be useful to use active learning during the bootstrap to maximize how much we learn. Later, we shift to traditional on-line learning where we want to minimize mistakes. This is the on-line model that we consider in this paper.

The second model assumes that all labels have some cost. Therefore, the on-line algorithm must request labels to perform updates. To minimize costs the algorithm can actively learn by not requesting every label. However, the algorithm is always penalized for mistakes even if it does not request the label [9]. We do not consider this model in this paper because we are primarily interested in cases where we are not penalized for mistakes during active learning. However, this model can be extended to benefit from a bootstrap procedure as previously explained.

3. EXACT LEARNING

The main idea of this paper is to take an on-line algorithm and to convert it into an active algorithm by attempting to select instances that cause mistakes. In order to motivate this idea, we use the exact model of learning to show how on-line learning and active learning are related.

Exact learning assumes there is a finite set of hypotheses H such that one hypothesis $h_{\text{opt}} \in H$ predicts all the instances in X correctly. The hypotheses in H are all distinct with respect to the instances in X. For on-line learning, an adversary selects the instances, and the goal of the algorithm is to minimize the number of mistakes it makes on this sequence of instances. For active learning the algorithm is allowed to ask for the label of any instance in X, and the goal of the algorithm is to find h_{opt} using a minimal number of label requests. In this framework, the label requests are called membership queries [1].

Let $M(O)$ be the worst-case number of mistakes made by any on-line algorithm O on all possible sequences, and let O_{opt} be the optimal algorithm. Let Q be any deterministic membership query algorithm that never queries the same instance more than once and returns when only a single hypothesis is consistent with all previous queries. Let $L(Q)$ be the maximum number of membership queries made by Q. Lastly, let $VC(H)$ be the VC dimension of the set of concepts [29]. The following bound gives a relation between active and on-line learning in the exact model [1].

$$VC(H) \leq M(O_{\text{opt}}) \leq \lg(|H|) \leq L(A) \leq |\hat{X}|. \quad (1)$$

While dealing with the limited exact learning model, the previous bounds capture the main intuition of this paper. If we have a good on-line algorithm and we can force it to make mistakes on a significant number of the actively selected instances, then this procedure should be effective for active learning.

Unfortunately, this will not always work. The easiest example is the singleton set [23, 1]. For this set of concepts, only a single instance in X is labeled 1. The optimal on-line algorithm always predicts 0 until it gets the singleton instance. The algorithm might see a large number of instances, but it can only make one mistake. The membership query algorithm is allowed to request the instances, but it has no idea where to look. It makes $|X|$ label requests in the worst case.

Singleton sets are one of the reasons membership query learning is difficult. In essence, if only a small, arbitrary portion of the space has a specific label value, then the algorithm must, in the worst case, get labels for most of the instances to find a few instances. It is a needle in a haystack problem. We will return to this problem in Section 5.3.

4. ACTIVE LEARNING ALGORITHM

A large motivation for early research in active learning is the Query by Committee algorithm [16]. This algorithm keeps track of the version space of all consistent hypotheses. The Query by Committee algorithm samples two hypotheses from the version space and requests the label for any instance where the hypotheses do not agree. It then updates the version space based on the requested label.

Various authors have expanded on this research with the goal of making the algorithm more tractable. Our algorithm is most similar to the algorithm Active Majority [22]. Instead of storing the whole hypothesis space, Active Majority stores k copies of an on-line algorithm. The algorithm receives a stream of unlabeled instances. For each instance, the algorithm randomly selects two of the hypotheses and requests the label if the hypotheses disagree. All k algorithms use this labeled instance to update their hypothesis. After training, the algorithm makes predictions by taking the majority vote of the k hypotheses.

We take a very similar approach but with a different motivation. The k hypotheses stored by Active Majority do not approximate the version space. Instead they hold k hypotheses that are hopefully converging to the optimal hypothesis in different ways. If those hypotheses make different predictions on some of the unlabeled instances, then we can use those instances to force mistakes. As long as the on-line algorithms do not depend on distributional assumptions for learning, they can learn even when the instances do not come from a distribution but are instead actively queried. This lack of distributional dependence is common for many on-line algorithms because they are designed to perform well even when an adversary is generating instances [25].

Just like Active Majority, our algorithm Active Vote can modify any on-line algorithm to the active setting. We give the on-line algorithm the prefix Active Voting (AV) to denote that the modification is being used. The pseudo code for the modification is given in Figure 1.

There are three main differences between Active Vote and Active Majority. When there is a disagreement between some of the k hypotheses, Active Vote always uses an instance that it can guarantee causes the most mistakes. The best case is when $\lfloor k/2 \rfloor$ of the hypotheses predict one label. We call the set of instances that correspond to this best case the confusion set. The motivation for the algorithm is that anytime the label is requested for an element

Active Vote(A, k, u, r, B, R)
  Initialization
    Algorithm A predicts labels in $\{-1, 1\}$
    Create copies A_1 to A_k of algorithm A.
    Perturb each copy with u random updates.
    The integer r partially controls random queries.
    Instances in B are for active queries.
    Instances in R are for random queries.
    Set $t \leftarrow 0$.
  Active Learning
    Select Instance
      If t mod r is 0 then
        Select and remove x from R.
      Else let $x' = \arg\min_{x \in B} D(x) = |\sum_{i=1}^{k} A_i(x)|$.
        If $D(x') = k$ then
          Select and remove x from R.
        Else let $x \leftarrow x'$
          Select and remove x from B.
      Request label y for x.
    Update
      Update $A_1(x, y)$ to $A_k(x, y)$.
      $t \leftarrow t + 1$.

Figure 1: Pseudo-code for Active Vote.

of the confusion set, a mistake must occur in at least $\lfloor k/2 \rfloor$ of the k hypotheses. Active Majority is different because the instances it selects are not guaranteed to maximize the number of mistakes.

The second difference is based on what happens when there are no more unlabeled instances that are guaranteed to cause mistakes. The Active Majority algorithm does not consider this situation most likely because it is specified as an instance stream algorithm. This can cause problems for highly label skewed problems because it might take some time to converge on the area of the input space where the concept is located. Early in the learning, all the hypotheses might converge to predicting the majority label, and Active Majority will not request any additional labels.

Active Vote is designed to select unlabeled instances from a pool; however, if all the hypotheses agree, we do not want to randomly select instances from this same pool. The remaining instances are biased and are no longer a random sample. Therefore we keep an active pool, B, for active instances and a random pool, R, for random instances. After we query an instance, we permanently remove it. If we know ahead of time that the label budget is c labels, then we can randomly select c instances for the random pool. Furthermore, if we find at some point we cannot use all the instances in the random pool, we can move them to the active pool.

There are advantages to sometimes using random queries even when there are unlabeled instances that would cause mistakes. It is difficult for a user of the active learning program to have confidence in the results without some type of feedback. A small random sample might not give high statistical confidence of the accuracy, but it can give enough information to show the user that the algorithm is achieving useful accuracy. It is also possible that the user might require a better accuracy estimate. While this can cost the algorithm a large number of labels, it can still be significantly less than the number of labels needed for passive learning. We discuss this issue in Section 5. Parameter r is used to control these random queries. The algorithm performs a random query once every r queries.

In order for Active Majority or Active Vote to work, the initial hypotheses of the k algorithms must be different. Active Majority uses a technique that randomizes the weights of hyperplanes at the start of learning. We randomize in a more general way that can be applied to any on-line algorithm that is tolerant to noise. We force the algorithm to update on a small number of randomly generated instances. Since these can be considered noisy instances, the random updates do not have a large effect on the mistake bound.

The final difference is based on what the algorithms return after the active learning is complete. Active Majority just returns the k hypotheses that are used in a batch setting to make predictions with a majority vote. Active Vote does not specify what it returns as it depends on the problem. In principal, it returns the k algorithms and their history of hypotheses and instances; however, typically the algorithm does not need to store all that information. Section 5 and Section 7 give some specific examples.

Lastly, we want to address the cost of Active Vote. Let C be the confusion set. A straightforward search of the active pool, B, to find the next instance to query would take $k(|B| - |C|)$ predictions. As long as C is not too small, this can be significantly improved by a simple randomized search. If C is empty, then the algorithm must make $k|B|$ predictions to find the next instance. However, if after a query from the random pool, R, none of the hypotheses has changed, then Active Vote can just proceed to take another query from R. This is typical on many problems because by the time the confusion set is empty the algorithm's k hypotheses all have high accuracy. The cost of the predictions and the updates of the k hypotheses depend on the choice of the on-line algorithm. The on-line algorithm that we consider in this paper is optimal in that its predictions and updates asymptotically take no more time than the time needed to read an instance. We discuss our choice for the on-line algorithm in Section 7.1. We also give information on features and modifications that combine beneficially with Active Vote.

5. BOUNDS

In this section, we give bounds on the performance of Active Vote. All of these bounds depend on keeping the confusion set non-empty. We start with a simple way to bound the number of mistakes made by at least one of the basic algorithm copies used by Active Vote. Let S be the sequence of previous instance queries. Let I_C be the subsequence of indexes that are queried from the confusion set, let I_O be the other active indexes, and let I_R be the subsequence of indexes sampled from the random pool. For example, if Active Vote performs the following sequence of queries: random, confusion, random, other, confusion, random, then $I_C = (2, 5)$, $I_O = (4)$, and $I_R = (1, 3, 6)$.

Lemma 1. The *AV-A* algorithm has at least one basic algorithm A_i that makes at least $\lfloor \frac{k}{2} \rfloor \frac{|I_C|}{k}$ mistakes.

PROOF. Assume each of the basic algorithms makes less than $\lfloor \frac{k}{2} \rfloor \frac{|I_C|}{k}$ mistakes. Since there are k basic algorithms there must be less than $|I_C| \lfloor \frac{k}{2} \rfloor$ total mistakes summed over all basic algorithms. This is a contradiction because every update from the confusion set causes at least $\lfloor \frac{k}{2} \rfloor$ basic algorithm mistakes and there are $|I_C|$ confusion set updates. □

5.1 On-line Bootstrap

Our next result applies to using Active Vote for the online bootstrapping problem. The Active Vote algorithm is only used during the bootstrap phase of learning. After the bootstrap is finished, we return the basic algorithm that has made the most mistakes. This algorithm is used for the remaining on-line trials. The idea behind this result is to simply subtract the mistakes during the bootstrap phase of learning from total mistakes the algorithm can make. See Section 2.2 for a description of the on-line bootstrap problem.

Theorem 1. When using Active Vote for bootstrap on-line learning, during the on-line phase of learning, the number of mistakes is at most $M(A) - \lfloor \frac{k}{2} \rfloor \frac{|I_C|}{k}$.

PROOF. Based on Lemma 1, at least $\lfloor \frac{k}{2} \rfloor \frac{|I_C|}{k}$ mistakes occur during the bootstrap. This leaves $M(A) - \lfloor \frac{k}{2} \rfloor \frac{|I_C|}{k}$ mistakes to occur during the on-line trials. □

The optimal bound for this theorem is achieved by any even k value. Choosing a specific value of k will depend on the learning problem. This requires giving a more precise definition of the bootstrap model. For example, when dealing with an adversary, how should one model the set of bootstrap instances? We plan to address this issue in future research.

5.2 Batch

For batch data, we assume the instances are independently sampled from a fixed distribution. First, we give a slight modification of a result by Cesa-Bianci *et al.* that bounds the average accuracy of the hypotheses an on-line algorithm learns when instances are sampled from a fixed distribution.

Notice that we are not bounding the accuracy of the final hypothesis. We are bounding the average accuracy of a sequence of hypotheses. This is often necessary when using on-line algorithms. Just because an on-line algorithm has a good upper-bound on mistakes does not guarantee that the final hypotheses of the algorithm will have a low error rate. Theoretically and practically, if one wants to use an on-line algorithm in a batch setting, it is important to use a technique that generates accurate hypothesis [24, 8]. We will give more details on this issue in the experimental section of the paper.

In this lemma, we introduce some new notation. Let $M(A, S, I)$ represent the number of mistakes algorithm A makes when run on sequence S if we only count mistakes for instances indexed by index set I.

Lemma 2. When running algorithm A with instance sequence S, for any $\delta \in (0, 1]$,

$$\Pr\left(\sum_{i \in I_R} \frac{err_D(h_i)}{|I_R|} \geq \frac{M(A, S, I_R)}{|I_R|} + \sqrt{\frac{2\ln\left(\frac{1}{\delta}\right)}{|I_R|}}\right) \leq \delta.$$

PROOF. We use a result of Cesa-Bianci *et al.* [8] but apply it to a subsequence of the hypotheses instead of all the hypotheses. The original result is an application of the Hoeffding-Azuma inequality. □

Next we apply Lemma 2 to upper-bound the average error of certain hypotheses used in Active Vote. The hypotheses we bound are from the basic algorithm that has made the most mistakes during the previous trials. We only bound the hypotheses queried from the random pool, R.

Theorem 2. When running *AV-A*, let h_i be the hypotheses generated by the basic algorithm that has made the most mistakes during random queries. For any $\delta \in (0, 1]$,

$$\Pr\left(\sum_{i \in I_R} \frac{err_D(h_i)}{|I_R|} \geq \frac{M(A) - \lfloor \frac{k}{2} \rfloor \frac{|I_C|}{k}}{|I_R|} + \sqrt{\frac{2\ln\left(\frac{k}{\delta}\right)}{|I_R|}}\right) \leq \delta.$$

PROOF. We apply Lemma 2 with $\delta' = \delta/k$ to all k algorithms run by *AV-A*. Using a union bound guarantees that the bound holds on all k algorithms with probability δ. Next, we use Lemma 1 to show that $M(A, S, I_R) \leq M(A) - \lfloor k/2 \rfloor |I_C|/k$ for the basic algorithm that made the most mistakes. □

Because we rarely know enough about the learning problem to generate upper-bounds on mistakes, the bound in Theorem 2 is more for guidance. Constraints on the learning problem can lead to choices for the algorithm to use with Active Vote. For actual feedback on performance, we can use the data dependent bound from Lemma 2. The data dependent bounds also motivate a change in the algorithm. As long as there are sufficient random samples, Active Vote should return the basic algorithm that made the fewest mistakes on instances selected from the random pool. The bound in Lemma 2 can be used to determine what constitutes sufficient.

5.3 Confusion Set

All the bounds in this section rely on keeping instances in the confusion set. Unfortunately, it is not always possible to keep the confusion set non-empty. As mentioned in Section 3, there are sets of concepts, such as the singleton in exact learning, that have small upper-bounds on mistakes yet require membership queries to request labels for every instance. If we could keep the confusion set non-empty for a constant fraction of the label queries, then we would break these lower-bounds.

When dealing with active learning and a distribution, things are not much better. In this setting, the goal is to create an algorithm that with $1 - \delta$ probability returns a hypothesis that is ϵ close to the best hypothesis the algorithm can represent. The lower bounds for active learning and passive learning are essentially the same for both of these problems [5]. Therefore, in the worst-case active learning cannot help.

However, in practice, active learning is often effective. Many practical problems have a reasonable label split that removes the need to worry about the singleton set. In cases with large label skew, techniques to actively search for the minority label can be effective [2]. Also, as pointed out in [4], the lower-bounds on active learning for many concept classes are non-uniform in that they depend on changing the concept as ϵ goes to zero. A more careful analysis gives a much more favorable result for many popular concept classes.

The essence of the confusion set is to have a small number of algorithms that all converge in different ways to the target concept. As long as their disagreement contains unlabeled instances, then, on average, the algorithms can make rapid progress to the target function. However, one of the advantages of this active learning technique is that it does not degrade if the confusion set is empty. Instead it just reverts to random queries. Therefore, if one does encounter a difficult active learning problem, then, just as the active learning lower-bounds imply, the algorithm has an upper-bound based on passive learning.

6. INTERNET AD APPLICATION

Our motivation for researching active learning is an application for improving Internet advertisement. We are interested in the advertisements content owners (newspapers, blogs, etc...) place on their websites using an advertising network such Google's AdWords. While these ad networks have proven to be profitable, they sometimes place ads that the content owners might find inappropriate. Examples of inappropriate ads we have seen include the following.

- A web site for children's pet rabbits featuring an ad for the Rabbit personal massager.
- An advertisement for a product to get rid of woodpeckers on a bird watching site.
- An ad selling home tanning beds on a news web site discussing tanning beds as a cause of skin cancer.

To give an illustrative example, new-jersey-birds.com is a web site devoted to bird watching in new jersey and includes information and photographs of many birds, including woodpeckers. Due to simple keyword matching and bidding [14], ads might appear on the website such that describe products to get rid of woodpeckers while the web site is intended for those more interested in attracting woodpeckers. We worked with the owners of new-jersey-birds.com to alternate between two text ads. One ad read "Get Rid of Woodpeckers, Products, reviews and info on getting rid of woodpeckers. Free shipping at amazon.com." The other was identical but replaced "Get Rid of" with "Attract". Out of 4235 impression to get rid of woodpeckers only 2 were clicked while out of 4188 impressions to attract woodpeckers, 27 were clicked.

To analyze the extent of the problem, we wrote a program to download Google Ads placed on this website on a page featuring photos of a cute baby goose. 5.4% were about bird watching, 29.9% about hunting, 21.8% about removing geese. The remaining ads were more general ads or ads about other topics (e.g., New Jersey). While many ad networks do give some limited amount of control for the content owner, it normally requires the domain owner to block particular ads or high-level categories without fine-grained control.

While one of our research tracks is looking at a general semantic solution to inappropriate ads, in this paper, we explore allowing the content owner to create a classifier that blocks such ads using active learning. We have designed an application that uses active learning to learn a classifier from examples labeled by the content owner that can automatically block inappropriate ads. There are two motivations for blocking such ads. First, content owners might believe their readers will finds the ads offensive. Second, the content owner may have prior knowledge which leads him believe that his readers would prefer certain ads over others.

Our ad blocking application has several components. We use a daemon to collect ad information such as the ad URL, ad text, and the ad landing page HTML. Another component displays ads to the content owner and records feedback for a subset of the ads. See Figure 2 for a picture of the

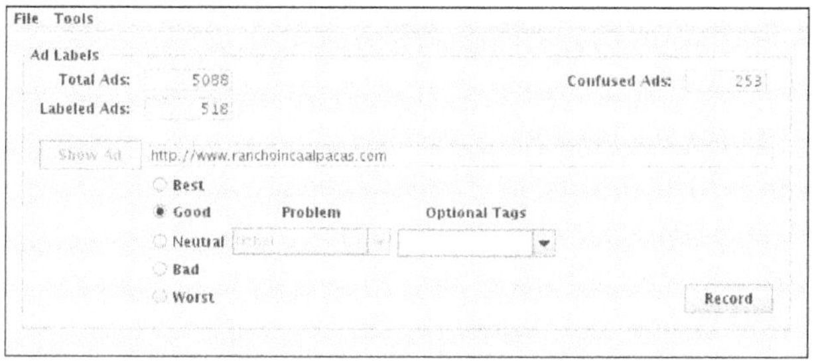

Figure 2: Ad Labeling Interface

ad labeling interface. This component uses active learning to decide which ads to display for labeling. A final component classifies unlabeled ads, and if the ad is labeled as inappropriate, it is removed as a candidate for presentation.

For this problem, we need an algorithm that quickly converges to a good concept because we want to reduce the number of ad labels that a content owner must provide. Ideally, we want an algorithm that can learn a fairly accurate classifier with as few as ten labeled instances; however, at this stage of our research, our goal is an algorithm that reduces the number of required labels by a significant fraction over passive learning. We also need an algorithm that can select in real time which instances to label. It defeats the purpose of using active learning if the user of the application must wait several minutes to receive the next instance, particularly when each instance only requires seconds to label. Active Vote is easily able to fulfill these requirements on standard inexpensive personal computers.

7. EXPERIMENTS

In this section, we provide the results of our active learning algorithm on various datasets. We use four datasets for our experiments: the Reuters corpus dataset, our own dataset for Internet advertisement, the KDDCUP 99 network intrusion dataset, and the MNIST handwritten digit dataset. The experiments are focused exclusively on testing the batch performance of various algorithms.

7.1 Basic On-line Algorithm

The on-line algorithm we use for our experiments is a version of Alma_2 [17]. The algorithm represents its current hypothesis as a hyperplane. Let n be the number of attributes and let m be the maximum number of non-zero attributes in any instance. Alma_2 requires $O(n)$ storage but can be implemented to perform predictions and updates in $O(m)$ time [27]. Alma_2 is similar to the Perceptron algorithm [7], but Alma_2 adjusts its updates as it learns in a way that tends to improve generalization performance. We use a version of Alma_2 that only updates its hypothesis on mistakes, as this form of the algorithm does not require any problem specific tuning of parameters. This is important for active learning since any type of validation is difficult given the biased sample of instances generated by sampling from $\hat{X}$.[1]

A useful modification for on-line algorithm is instance recycling [27]. This technique saves a window of recent labeled instances. A parameter controls the maximum number of times an instance can be used in an update. In our experiments, we set the maximum update for an instance to be four to limit overfitting. After the algorithm makes a mistake, it loops over the recent instances looking for mistakes. Any mistake causes an additional update and increases the counter associated with that instance. The trial is over when all instances in the window that are below their maximum update count are predicted correctly.

For Active Vote, we make two modifications to instance recycling to help keep instances in the confusion set. First, we randomly perturb the maximum update count for the instances. This is implemented by flipping a fair coin for each newly labeled instance to decide whether to increase the maximum use count by one. The second modification randomizes the instance recycling iteration. When the algorithm starts to recycle over the old instances, the algorithm randomly selects a starting instance from the window. Both of these modifications are used to force the on-line algorithms to make slightly different updates with the goal of keeping the confusion set non-empty. We use the prefix RR to any on-line algorithm that has been modified to use this randomized recycling procedure.

7.2 Experimental Setup

Each experiment is averaged over 50 permutations of a training set. We use permutations instead of cross-validation to make it easier to adjust the size of the training set for learning curve experiments. For each experiment, we use a standard t-test to give 95% confidence intervals.

We compare the active learning algorithms to the Support Vector Machine $\text{SVM}^{\text{light}}$ [10, 20] and various passive forms of the Alma_2 algorithm. As explained in Section 5.2, the final hypothesis of Alma_2 can have a high variance in accuracy. To stabilize and improve performance, we use a slight modification of a hypothesis averaging technique given by Schapire *et al.* In [15], they predict with a hyperplane that is an average over all the previous hyperplanes. We find performance improves by taking a weighted average where the hypothesis from query t has weight t. Intuitively, this is sensible because an effective learning algorithm is converging on the target concept and therefore the later hypotheses should be more accurate. We add the prefix W to any on-line algorithm that is modified with this averaging technique.

For all of the experiments, we give the results for the active learning algorithms AV-RR-Alma_2 and AM-Alma_2. We set $k = 7$ for both algorithms following the choice for Active Majority found in [22]. The random recycling saves the most recent 500 instances and has a maximum update count for each instance of either 3 or 4. Note that instance recycling is independent for each of the k algorithms. The update count of an instance for one algorithm is unrelated to the update count for the other algorithms. We modify Active Majority slightly by using our initial hypotheses randomization procedure. For both active algorithms, we initialize the hyperplanes with five random instances. Last, we make all predictions for both algorithms using the majority vote of the $k = 7$ hypotheses. This is the procedure used by Active Majority in Lierc and Tadepalli [22], and we find that Active Voting with instance recycling is stable enough that it does not need anything more complicated.

The last parameter for Active Vote is r, which controls the frequency of forced random queries. We set $r = \infty$ and do not perform any forced random queries. Random queries are

[1] Another advantage of the Alma is that it allows kernel functions to expand its feature space. This could be important for active learning problems that need non-linear spaces.

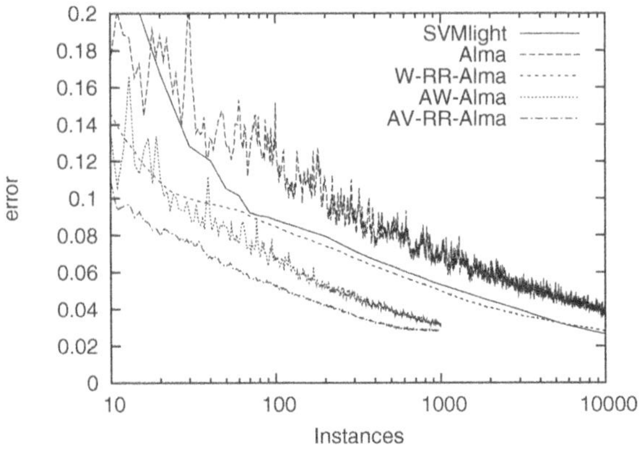

Figure 3: Error rates for the Reuters earn concept

useful to gauge performance or identify accurate hypotheses, but they tend to slow the learning. For our experiments, we use a test set to evaluate the algorithms and therefore do not need to use this feature.

7.3 Reuters

We use the Reuters-21578, Distribution 1.0 text collection [13]. We only use documents that either have topics specified or have no topics but which have a TOPICS tag value of yes. This latter group is defined to have no relevant topic. From this we create binary concepts based on the ten most frequent topics. Each document is represented as a bag of words with stemming [19] applied to each word. This gives a total of 13484 documents with 37086 words.

We train the algorithms using 10000 documents and test with the remaining 3484. We repeat this procedure using 50 permutations of the data. Active Vote divides its 10000 training examples into an active pool of size 9000 and a random pool of size 1000; therefore, we limit the algorithm to 1000 active queries. We also stop Active Majority after 1000 queries. Because it does not use a random pool, anytime all seven hypotheses agree on all remaining unlabeled instances, we just take a random query from all the instances. We include previously labeled instances in this random query because the remaining unlabeled instances might be biased based on the instances removed by the active queries.[2]

In Figure 3, we give the results for the most frequent concept, earn. Notice the high variability of Alma_2. The algorithm does tend to stabilize as the number of instances increases presumably because $Alma_2$ decreases the size of its updates as it learns. When we add instance recycling and weight averaging with the W-RR-Alma_2 algorithm, we see a large decrease in error rate and an improvement in stability. Again, it is important to use these or similar techniques when using these types of on-line algorithms in a batch setting. We see that the performance of W-RR-Alma_2 is comparable to $\mathrm{SVM}^{\mathrm{light}}$ for most of the plot.

During the early label queries, $\mathrm{SVM}^{\mathrm{light}}$ has the worst performance. This is a result of using the default parameters. While the default parameters tend to work well for a large number of instances, during the early queries it is preferable for $\mathrm{SVM}^{\mathrm{light}}$ to learn a concept that perfectly separates the data. Unfortunately, the optimal parameter choice for a small number of instances can give poor performance for larger training sizes. Since we are mostly interested in the performance of $\mathrm{SVM}^{\mathrm{light}}$ with all the training instances, we always use the default parameter.

For a small number of labeled instances, the two best performing algorithms are the active algorithms. However, one problem with AM-Alma_2 is that it has an intrinsic instability similar to the basic algorithm Alma_2. AV-RR-Alma_2 is much more stable because the instance recycling adds stability. We also see that Active Vote has more than a 20% reduction in error for most queries up to query 600. This is the point at which, on average, the algorithm starts to make a large number of queries from the random pool of instances. In practice, it can be useful to use this as a stopping criteria for the active learning because the rate of learning has slowed substantially. This is intuitive. Once an on-line algorithm has, on average, a high accuracy hypothesis, sampling from the problem distribution will require the algorithm to see many labeled instances before it makes a mistake and changes its hypothesis.

In Table 1, we give results for the first seven most frequent concepts.[3] In the heading for each column, we include the name of the label and the percentage of documents that contain that label. It is interesting that the performance of WR-Alma_2 at 10000 passive queries is almost identical to the performance of AV-RR-Alma_2 at 1000 active queries. This gives Active Voting an order of magnitude improvement in the number of labeled instances over a reasonably optimized version of Alma_2. In truth, the performance is actually better since AV-RR-Alma_2 starts making most of its queries from the random pool between 200 to 700 instances depending on the concept. After that point the improvement in accuracy is minimal.

The Support Vector Machine is consistently doing the best at 10000 queries, however, in many cases its improvement is not statistically significant over AV-RR-Alma. $\mathrm{SVM}^{\mathrm{light}}$ is more frequently statically tied with WR-alma_2 because WR-alma_2 has a confidence interval that is almost ten times larger than AV-RR-Alma_2. This large variability is also seen in Active Majority.

When dealing with a smaller number of queries, the active learning algorithms always perform best. Unfortunately at 100 queries, it is difficult to evaluate AM-Alma_2 because it has such a large confidence interval. This can occur with an on-line algorithm that uses its final hypothesis for batch learning. Even a majority vote with $k = 7$ hypotheses is not enough to add significant stability. However, the mean of AV-RR-Alma_2 is always lower after 100 queries.

At 1000 queries, either AV-RR-Alma_2 has a smaller mean or it is very similar to AM-Alma_2. In general, AV-RR-Alma_2 converges faster and with less variance than AM-Alma_2, but they appear to be converging to a similar accuracy. We do find it somewhat surprising that Active Majority does so well after 1000 queries. We also performed artificial data experiments with label noise as high as 10% where AM-Alma_2 has much greater problems with stability, while AV-RR-Alma_2 is able to quickly converge to a hypothesis that is close to optimal.

7.4 Internet Ads

The experiments we perform are based on ads found on

[2]This will slightly reduce the number of true label queries required by the algorithm.

[3]We removed the remaining three concepts because of space limitations. Their results are similar.

Table 1: Reuters error rates

Alg	earn(.296)	acq(.182)	money(.059)	grain(.047)	crude(.047)	trade(.041)	interest(.038)
100 queries							
W-RR-Alma	.0847±.0136	.1309±.0490	.0558±.0097	.0448±.0081	.0465±.0072	.0406±.0073	.0370±.0066
AM-Alma	.0677±.0333	.0994±.0630	.0484±.0410	.0403±.0930	.0377±.0403	.0417±.0426	.0403±.0672
AV-RR-Alma	.0522±.0098	.0733±.0165	.0397±.0103	.0252±.0075	.0272±.0090	.0281±.0083	.0279±.0083
1000 queries							
W-RR-Alma	.0499±.0090	.0628±.0115	.0380±.0074	.0308±.0101	.0323±.0102	.0307±.0082	.0295±.0069
AM-Alma	.0314±.0091	.0443±.0092	.0244±.0056	.0142±.0049	.0189±.0050	.0197±.0051	.0199±.0051
AV-RR-Alma	.0282±.0049	.0374±.0063	.0237±.0047	.0134±.0041	.0186±.0035	.0197±.0048	.0204±.0043
10000 queries							
W-RR-Alma	.0282±.0052	.0382±.0063	.0246±.0046	.0144±.0038	.0191±.0041	.0195±.0041	.0205±.0050
SVM	.0265±.0007	.0352±.0008	.0227±.0007	.0132±.0006	.0181±.0006	.0191±.0007	.0186±.0006

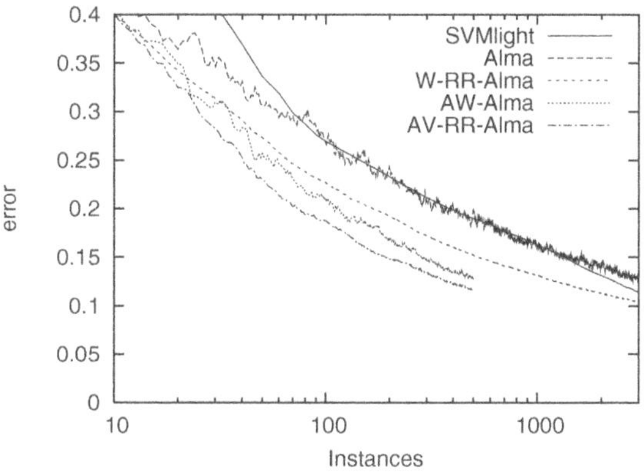

Figure 4: Error rates for Internet ad experiments

twelve websites that deal with various farm animal related topics.[4] We allow the content owner to specify one of five ratings for an ad. For these experiments, any ad that is rated below neutral is considered an inappropriate ad. The ads are represented based on the text of the ad and the text on the ad landing page. We use a bag of words representation with stemming on all words [19]. We also added extra attributes for words that appear in the ad and words in the titles and headers of the landing page.

In Figure 4, we include a plot of our results. The experiment is identical the experiment performed with the Reuters data except that we only have 4143 instances. We use 3000 of the instances for training and 1143 instances for the test set. The active experiments are limited to 500 queries. As can be seen, the results are similar with the *AV-RR*-Alma$_2$ algorithm giving the best performance with fewest label queries. While the active to passive label ratio is only 1/4, we speculate this is because we are on parts of the learning curve that have higher error rates compared to the Reuters data. We plan to explore this in future research.

7.5 KDDCUP and MNIST

The primary purpose for these two datasets is to compare against the active learning algorithm of Beygelzimer *et al* [6]. We believe this is an interesting comparison given the strong theoretical motivation behind this recent algorithm. However, we want to stress that the comparison is more of a qualitative comparison because the experiments performed

[4]The data will be made publicly available on a the UCI Machine Learning repository [13].

Table 2: KDDCUP99 Error rates

Alg	100	500	1000	10000
AA-J48	.032	.0065		
J48	.052	.012	.012	
AM-Alma	.0115	.00882	.00705	
AV-RR-Alma	**.00861**	**.00582**	**.00388**	
W-RR-Alma	.0253	.0137	.01026	**.00339**
SVM	.0202	.0124	.0115	.00574

in [6] uses a decision tree, J48, as their basic algorithm and use PCA to reduce both problems to 25 attributes. For these experiments, we do not report statistical significance because of space constraints; however, we follow a similar procedure as the previous experiments, using 50 permutations to compute the average performance. The statistical significance is similar to the Reuters experiments.

The KDDCUP99 dataset is a large set of network intrusion data from a previous KDDCUP competition. Each instance consists of 41 symbolic or continuous attributes. To improve performance when learning with a hyperplane, we expand the attribute space by using a binning technique on the continuous attributes. This technique breaks the attribute up into at most 30 intervals and creates a new attribute for each of these intervals. A binning attribute has a value of 1 if the original continuous attribute has a value greater than the end point of the interval, otherwise the binning attribute has a value of 0. This allows the algorithm to learn concepts that represent a range of values using only two binning attributes [26].

The results for 100, 500, 1000, and 10000 label queries are reported in Table 2. We use the notation *AA*-J48 to refer to the learning algorithm of Beygelzimer *et al.* when applied to the J48 decision tree algorithm. The results show that at 100 queries *AV-RR*-Alma$_2$ has roughly 1/3 the error rate of *W-RR*-Alma$_2$, and that for some error rates, *W-RR*-Alma$_2$ uses over ten times as many labels as Active Vote. While the improvement of *AA*-J48 is not as dramatic, it still gives a large decrease in error rate with roughly 50% of the error rate of J48 at 500 queries.

The MNIST dataset is a dataset of handwritten digits with 256 bit grayscale information for a grid of 28 by 28 pixels. Since this dataset already has a large number of attributes, we just use the 728 continuous values normalized to the [0,1] interval. The results are reported in Table 3. While the results are not as good as the KDDCUP99 experiment, we still see that *AV-RR*-Alma$_2$ has close to half the error rate of *W-RR*-Alma$_2$ at 100 queries. The results for *AA*-J48 show minimal improvement. In [6], the authors speculate

Table 3: MNIST Error rates

Alg	100	500	1000	10000
AA-J48	.18	.107	.082	
J48	.18	.107	.093	
AM-Alma	.104	.0549	.0477	
AV-RR-Alma	**.0633**	**.0421**	**.0408**	
W-RR-Alma	.108	.0580	.0497	**.0373**
SVM	.0818	.0501	.0452	.0374

that the large amount of noise in the MNIST dataset causes the poor performance of *AA*-J48. This might also explain the somewhat poor performance of *AM*-Alma_2.

8. CONCLUSION

This paper revisits some of the previous research in active learning. which showed promise because the algorithms are computationally efficient and the results gave dramatic decreases in label queries on practical problems. We provide a new way to understand one of these algorithms in terms of on-line learning, and we show how to take this new understanding to give a more effective way to convert on-line algorithms into active learning algorithms.

While not a focus of the paper, our results naturally apply to a new type of active learning problem that is based on bootstrapping an on-line problem so that it can maximize its learning. We plan to expand our understanding of this framework in future research.

Another area that requires more research is the confusion set. While we did not have a problem keeping elements in the confusion set, we are interested in algorithms/problems in which we can prove that the confusion set will be nonempty until the algorithm achieves an accurate hypothesis. This might require changes such as selecting instances for labeling based on how they affect the next confusion set.

9. REFERENCES

[1] D. Angluin. Queries revisited. *Theor. Comput. Sci.*, 313:175–194, February 2004.

[2] J. Attenberg and F. Provost. Why label when you can search? In *KDD*, 2010.

[3] M. F. Balcan, A. Beygelzimer, and J. Langford. Agnostic active learning. In *ICML*, 2006.

[4] M. F. Balcan, S. Hanneke, and J. W. Vaughan. The true sample complexity of active learning. *Machine Learning*, 80(2-3):111–139, 2010.

[5] A. Beygelzimer, S. Dasgupta, and J. Langford. Importance weighted active learning. In *ICML*, 2009.

[6] A. Beygelzimer, D. Hsu, J. Langford, and T. Zhang. Agnostic active learning without constraints. In *NIPS*, 2010.

[7] H. D. Block. The perceptron: A model for brain functioning. *Reviews of Modern Physics*, 34(1):123–135, 1962.

[8] N. Cesa-Bianchi, A. Conconi, and C. Gentile. On the generalization ability of on-line learning algorithms. *IEEE Transactions on Information Theory*, 50(9):2050–2057, 2004.

[9] N. Cesa-Bianchi, C. Gentile, and L. Zaniboni. Worst-case analysis of selective sampling for linear classification. *Journal of Machine Learning Research*, 7:1205–1230, 2006.

[10] C. Cortes and V. Vapnik. Support-vector networks. *Machine Learning*, 20(3):273–297, 1995.

[11] S. Dasgupta. Coarse sample complexity bounds for active learning. In Y. Weiss, B. Schölkopf, and J. Platt, editors, *NIPS*, pages 235–242, Cambridge, MA, 2006. MIT Press.

[12] S. Dasgupta, D. Hsu, and C. Monteleoni. A general agnostic active learning algorithm. In *NIPS*, 2007.

[13] C. B. D.J. Newman, S. Hettich and C. Merz. UCI repository of machine learning databases, 1998; http://archive.ics.uci.edu/ml/.

[14] B. Edelman, M. Ostrovsky, and M. Schwarz. Internet advertising and the generalized second-price auction *American Economic Review*, 97(1):242–259, 2007.

[15] Y. Freund and R. E. Schapire. Large margin classification using the perceptron algorithm. In *COLT*, 1998.

[16] Y. Freund, H. S. Seung, E. Shamir, and N. Tishby. Selective sampling using the query by committee algorithm. *Machine Learning*, 28:133–1680, 1997.

[17] C. Gentile. A new approximate maximal margin classification algorithm. *Machine Learning*, 2:213–242, 2001.

[18] S. Hanneke. Rates of convergence in active learning. *The Annals of Statistics*, 39(1):333–361, 2011.

[19] M.-C. Jenkins and D. Smith. Conservative stemming for search and indexing. In *SIGIR*, 2005.

[20] T. Joachims. Making large-scale support vector machine learning practical. In A. S. B. Schölkopf, C. Burges, editor, *Advances in Kernel Methods: Support Vector Machines*. MIT Press, Cambridge, MA, 1999.

[21] D. D. Lewis and W. A. Gale. A sequential algorithm for training text classifiers. In *SIGIR*, pages 3–12. Springer-Verlag, 1994.

[22] R. Liere and P. Tadepalli. Active learning with committees for text categorization. In *AAAI*, pages 591–596, 1997.

[23] N. Littlestone. Learning quickly when irrelevant attributes abound: A new linear-threshold algorithm. *Machine Learning*, 2:285–318, 1988.

[24] N. Littlestone. From on-line to batch learning. In *COLT*, pages 269–284, 1989.

[25] N. Littlestone. *Mistake Bounds and Linear-threshold Learning Algorithms*. PhD thesis, Computer Science, University of California, Santa Cruz, 1989. Technical Report UCSC-CRL-89-11.

[26] W. Maass and M. K. Warmuth. Efficient learning with virtual threshold gates. *Information and Computation*, 141:378–386, 1997.

[27] C. Mesterharm. *Improving On-line Learning*. PhD thesis, Computer Science, Rutgers, The State University of New Jersey, 2007.

[28] B. Settles. Active learning literature survey. Computer Sciences Technical Report 1648, University of Wisconsin–Madison, 2009.

[29] V. Vapnik and A. Chervonenkis. On the uniform convergence of relative frequencies of events to their probabilities. *Theory of Probability and its Applications*, 16:264–280, 1971.

Algorithms for Speeding up Distance-Based Outlier Detection

Kanishka Bhaduri
MCT Inc., NASA Ames Research Center
Moffett Field, CA 94035 USA
Kanishka.Bhaduri-1@nasa.gov

Bryan L. Matthews
SGT Inc., NASA Ames Research Center
Moffett Field, CA 94035 USA
Bryan.L.Matthews@nasa.gov

Chris R. Giannella
The MITRE Corp.
300 Sentinel Dr., Suite 600
Annapolis Junction, MD 20701 USA
cgiannel@acm.org

ABSTRACT

The problem of distance-based outlier detection is difficult to solve efficiently in very large datasets because of potential quadratic time complexity. We address this problem and develop sequential and distributed algorithms that are significantly more efficient than state-of-the-art methods while still guaranteeing the same outliers. By combining simple but effective indexing and disk block accessing techniques, we have developed a sequential algorithm *iOrca* that is up to an order-of-magnitude faster than the state-of-the-art. The indexing scheme is based on sorting the data points in order of increasing distance from a fixed reference point and then accessing those points based on this sorted order. To speed up the basic outlier detection technique, we develop two distributed algorithms (*DOoR* and *iDOoR*) for modern distributed multi-core clusters of machines, connected on a ring topology. The first algorithm passes data blocks from each machine around the ring, incrementally updating the nearest neighbors of the points passed. By maintaining a cutoff threshold, it is able to prune a large number of points in a distributed fashion. The second distributed algorithm extends this basic idea with the indexing scheme discussed earlier. In our experiments, both distributed algorithms exhibit significant improvements compared to the state-of-the-art distributed method [13].

Categories and Subject Descriptors

H.2.8 [**Database Management**]: Database applications—*Data Mining*

General Terms

Algorithms, Experimentation, Performance

Keywords

Outlier detection, Distributed computing, Nearest neighbor

KDD'11, August 21–24, 2011, San Diego, California, USA.
Copyright 2011 ACM 978-1-4503-0813-7/11/08 ...$10.00.

1. INTRODUCTION

Unsupervised outlier detection is an important and well-studied problem in the data mining, machine learning, and statistics literature. Given the broad array of meanings that may be sensibly ascribed to the term "outlier", many variations of the problem have been developed and addressed. One commonly used definition in the literature involves defining points as outliers if their nearest neighbors are sufficiently distant (distance-based outliers). A specific form of the problem along these lines can be stated by first defining an *outlier score* for each point x in dataset D as the distance to the kth nearest neighbor of x in D [3] or, similarly, the sum or average of the distances of the k nearest neighbors of x in D [15]. Then the outlier detection problem is as follows: given parameters t and k, find the top t points in D in terms of their outlier scores[1]. This definition has been used in many domains to find anomalies such as Earth sciences, astronomy, space applications and more [8].

The naive nested loop algorithm requires $O(n^2)$ (with $n = |D|$) computation time which is infeasible for large datasets. A key idea for improvement, developed by Bay and Schwabacher [4] (the *Orca* algorithm), is to maintain the t-th largest outlier score and use it as a *cutoff threshold*. When considering a point x, if the distance to the k-th nearest neighbor found thus far is less than the threshold, then x can be immediately pruned. A key to making this idea work even better is considering the points in D in an order such that the outliers are considered as early as possible. Doing so allows the cutoff threshold to be set as high as possible, as early as possible in the algorithm. One of the key contributions of our work is a simple and quick-to-build index that allows the points to be considered in an order that significantly improves upon the random ordering of Orca [4]. The index is a list of two-tuples consisting of IDs of data points ordered by decreasing distance to a randomly chosen reference point and the respective distances. For a given test point x, we search on the index for finding its k nearest neighbors by gradually "spiraling out" along the index. Based on a new termination criterion that we develop, the

[1]All of our algorithms can be used with either of these two definitions of outlier score. For simplicity, henceforth we will work with the k nearest neighbor definition. A closely related version of the problem we study was developed in [12]: given parameters r and k, find all points in D whose outlier score is less than r. However, [15] argue that r can be difficult to set and is dataset dependent. We do not consider the "r-version" of the problem further in this paper.

algorithm can terminate without having to scan the entire dataset. These contributions combine to form *iOrca*, a new outlier detection algorithm.

We also develop two distributed algorithms both on top of a ring overlay network leveraging the modern multi-core cluster of machines. The first algorithm passes data blocks around the ring allowing the computation of k nearest neighbors to proceed in a parallel. Along the way, the cutoff threshold is updated and distributed across all nodes. As such, data points can be pruned at any node without central coordination. This idea allows the cutoff threshold to be utilized fully and efficiently and offers a significant improvement over the distributed parallel Bay's algorithm (PBay) [13]. The second distributed algorithm extends this basic idea with the indexing scheme discussed earlier.

Our main contributions: (1) We develop a new outlier detection algorithm, *iOrca*, which improves upon the Orca algorithm [4] by means of a novel indexing scheme. The index allows for greater pruning of data points based on the cutoff threshold and also allows for more efficient computation of the k nearest neighbors of any given datapoint. Furthermore, it allows us to terminate the algorithm much earlier, without even looking at all the data points for outliers, thereby saving both I/O cost and runtime. (2) We develop two new distributed outlier detection algorithms based on a ring computation which allows the cutoff threshold to be exploited efficiently in a distributed fashion. To the best of the authors' knowledge, this paper shows for the first time how indexing can be used in conjunction with distributed processing to speed up distance-based outlier detection technique. (3) We experimentally demonstrate that our sequential and distributed algorithms are significantly more efficient than the respective state-of-the-art methods.

2. RELATED WORK

The naive approach of distance-based outlier detection takes quadratic time with respect to the number of points in the dataset by comparing each point with the rest. Such a technique has been proposed by Knorr and Ng [12]. Their first algorithm is a block nested loop algorithm which scales as $O(n^2d)$, where n is the size and d is the dimensionality of the dataset. Their second algorithm partitions the dataset into cells that are hyper-rectangles. By efficiently pruning the unpromising rectangles early, their second algorithm executes in time linear in n but exponential in d. Hence, both these algorithms do not work well for large datasets.

Spatial database indexing methods such as KD-tree [5], R-tree [10] or X-tree [6] can be used for speeding up nearest neighbor search. The main idea is to query the k-nearest neighbors of each point in the index structure. This method works extremely well for low dimensional datasets, often scaling as $O(n \log n)$. However, they scale poorly with the dimension of the data, making them inefficient for dimension greater than 10 [7].

Ordering the data often helps in the nearest neighbor search for outlier detection. Knorr and Ng [12] present an idea in which the data is first split into multiple cells (hyper rectangles) and only the corners of the minimum bounding rectangles (MBRs) are stored. For any test point, all those MBRs are pruned which cannot contain the nearest neighbors of the test point. One major drawback of this approach is that the complexity of these hyper rectangles increases exponentially with the dimension of the dataset, rendering them ineffective for high dimensional datasets. Similar problems with R-tree based indexing schemes have also been reported by Ramaswamy *et al.* [15].

Orca proposed by Bay and Schwabacher [4] shows how distance-based outlier detection can be made efficient using a simple pruning strategy and randomization of the dataset. We describe it in more detail in Section 3.3 since this forms a baseline for our comparison. To speed up Orca, Ghoting *et al.* [9] have proposed the Recursive Binning and Re-Projection (RBRP) method. In their method, the data is first clustered and then, for any test point x_t, the nearest neighbors of x_t are first searched in the cluster in which x_t belongs to and then in the next closest cluster and so on. The authors empirically show that this method speeds up Orca. However, this method needs to load the entire dataset in memory during the clustering phase which can be a serious drawback for large and high dimensional datasets. Also, for each test point, RBRP needs to go through the data in a particular order, leading to an excessive number of disk I/O. Furthermore, RBRP does not reorder the test data points and so the growth in the cutoff rate is much slower compared to *iOrca*. Another technique for improving Orca is the Dolphin algorithm proposed by Angiulli and Fassetti [2]. In their method, using a pivot-based index, they only need two sequential scans of the dataset, leading to an improved running time with respect to Orca. However, the authors use the "r" definition of outliers and hence do not find the same outliers as Orca or *iOrca*. Moreover, [2] does not demonstrate the accuracy of their method compared to Orca or RBRP.

There exist some approaches to speeding up distance-based outlier detection methods using parallel/distributed computing. In the PBay algorithm by Lozano and Acuna [13], a master node first splits the data into separate chunks for each processor. Then the master node loads each block of test data and broadcasts it to each of the worker nodes. Each worker node then executes Orca using its local database and the test block. The nearest neighbors of the test points from all the workers are aggregated at the master node to find the global set of nearest neighbors for those test points. All points whose score is less than the cutoff are dropped and the cutoff is updated accordingly. The cutoff is broadcast back to all the worker nodes along with the next block of test data. The algorithm that we propose in this paper distributes workload among the nodes more efficiently and does not require the master node to do all the aggregation of the nearest neighbors; as a result both of our distributed algorithms are much faster. Hung and Cheung [11] present a parallel version of the basic nested loop algorithm which is not suitable for distributed computation since it requires all the dataset to be exchanged among all the nodes. Otey *et al.* [14] present a distributed algorithm in which the definition of outlier is completely different than the one presented here. In order to process mixed attributes, their definition is based on support. In their work, outlier score function is defined by taking into account the dependencies among all the attributes in the dataset and outliers are those points which contradict these dependencies. Angiulli *et al.* [1] present a distributed distance-based outlier detection algorithm based on the concept of *solving set* which can be viewed as a compact representation of the original dataset. The solving set is such that by comparing any data point to only the elements of the solving set, it can be concluded if the point is an outlier or not. This solving set is itself updated as more and more points are processed such that it at least contains the correct scores of the top t requested outliers. They demonstrated the performance of their algorithm on only two real datasets which shows linear scalability (wrt number of nodes). Our algorithm combines both distributed processing and indexing, thereby giving us better speedup.

3. BACKGROUND

3.1 Notations

Let $t, k > 0$ be fixed (user-defined) parameters. Let D be a finite subset of $\mathbb{R}^d$ having n points such that $|D| \geq \max\{t, k\}$. Given $x \in D$, let $N_k(x, D)$ denote the set of k nearest neighbors from $\{D \setminus \{x\}\}$ to x (with respect to Euclidean distance with ties broken according to some arbitrary but fixed total ordering $\prec$).

Let $\delta_k(x, D)$ denote the maximum distance between x and all the points in $N_k(x, D)$ *i.e.* the distance between x and its k-nearest neighbors in D. $\delta_k(x, D)$ can be viewed as an *outlier ranking function.* Let $O_{t,k}(D)$ denote the top t points (outliers) in D according to $\delta_k(., D)$. In the rest of the description, for simplicity, we rewrite $N_k(b, D)$, $\delta_k(b, D)$ and $O_{t,k}(D)$ as $N_k(b)$, $\delta_k(b)$ and O_k.

DEFINITION 3.1 (CENTRALIZED PROBLEM DEFINITION). *Given integers $t, k > 0$, and dataset D, the goal of outlier detection algorithm is to compute the outliers O_k in D as quickly as possible.*

3.2 Distributed problem definition

In the distributed setup, there are p machines $P_1, \ldots, P_p$ connected to each other in a ring $\mathcal{G}$, such that P_i's neighbor Γ_i is known to P_i. Each P_i holds a dataset D_i such that size of $|D_i| \geq \{t, k\}$. We assume that the datasets are disjoint *i.e.* $D_i \cap D_j = \emptyset, \forall i \neq j$.

DEFINITION 3.2 (DISTRIBUTED PROBLEM DEFINITION). *Given integers $t, k > 0$, and dataset D_i at each node P_i, the goal of outlier detection algorithm is to compute the outliers O_k (in D) as quickly as possible, where $D = \bigcup_{i=1}^{p} D_i$.*

In the above definition, we have assumed that the distributed outlier detection algorithm produces the same set of outliers as Orca [4]. The algorithms that we have proposed in this paper all guarantee that the set of outliers are the same as Orca, therefore, we drop the issue of accuracy from our problem definition.

3.3 Distance-based outlier detection with pruning: Orca

In this section we describe Orca [4] in detail since it forms our baseline for comparison. Orca achieves a near-linear runtime for many datasets by using a simple pruning rule and randomization. It is disk-based and processes the data in blocks instead of reading in all the data at once from memory. The pseudo-code of the algorithm is shown in Alg. 1. The inputs are k, t, the block size b, and the dataset D. The basic idea of the algorithm is very simple. Let cutoff c denote the score of the t-th largest outlier (or 0 if less than t points have been processed). It reads in a block of data from the memory (call it the test block) and then computes the nearest neighbors of each point in the test block by looking at all the other points. During this computation it keeps track of the nearest neighbors found so far for each test point. As soon as the outlier score (*e.g.* the distance to the k-th nearest neighbor) drops below c, that point is pruned since it can no longer be an outlier. If any outlier is found for this block, both the outlier list and the cutoff are updated. As more points are processed, c increases, and the algorithm achieves a better prune rate.

In Orca, the number of disk access is $O(n/b * n)$ where $n = |D|$. Also, as shown in [4], the expected number of distance computations to prune a non-outlier point x is $1/\rho_x$, where ρ_x is the probability that a point chosen at random lies within the cutoff threshold. Since this is independent of n, it achieves a near linear time performance on the entire dataset. However, to achieve this, ρ_x needs to be a constant. This does not hold for many datasets as we demonstrate later. Our indexing technique described in the next section helps to alleviate this problem by ensuring that the cutoff grows faster, the nearest neighbors of a test point are found quicker and the algorithm terminates earlier without having to scan the entire database.

Input: k, t, b, D
Output: O_k, the set of top t outliers in D
Initialization: $c \leftarrow 0$, $O \leftarrow \emptyset$
while $B \leftarrow$ *get_next_block*$(D, b) <> \emptyset$ **do**
  forall the $b \in B$ **do** $N_k(b) \leftarrow \emptyset$;
  forall the $i = 1$ *to* $|D|$ **do**
    $x =$ **getFromfile**(i, D);
    forall the $b \in B, b \neq x$ **do**
      if $|N_k(b)| < k$ *or dist*$(b, x) <$ *maxdist*$(b, N_k(b))$ **then**
        $N_k(b) \leftarrow$ Update_nbors$(N_k(b), x, k)$;
        $\delta_k(b) \leftarrow \max\{\|b - y\| : y \in N_k(b)\}$;
        if $\delta_k(b) < c$ **then** $B \leftarrow B \setminus b$;
      end
    end
  end
  for b=*1 to* B **do**
    newO $\leftarrow$ *newO* $\bigcup [b;\ \delta_k(b);\ N_k(b)]$;
  end
  $O_k \leftarrow$ Find_Top_t$(newO \cup O_k, t)$;
  $c \leftarrow \min\{\delta_k(y, D) : y \in O\}$;
end

Algorithm 1: Orca by Bay and Schwabacher [4].

4. FAST OUTLIER DETECTION USING INDEXING: IORCA

In Orca, one of the factors that affects the prune rate is the cutoff threshold. If the cutoff grows very slowly, it does many redundant comparisons for inliers. To alleviate this problem, we need to develop a method such that: (1) the cutoff is updated faster, (2) the data is rearranged such that for every point, the nearest neighbors are found quickly, (3) it does not perform unnecessary disk accesses in order to achieve (1) and (2), and (4) the index is fast to build and does not require the entire data to be loaded in memory. In the remainder of this section we show how our indexing method addresses each of these problems elegantly.

In order to update the cutoff faster, we need to process the outliers as early as possible. In our indexing method, we first select a random point R from D as a reference point

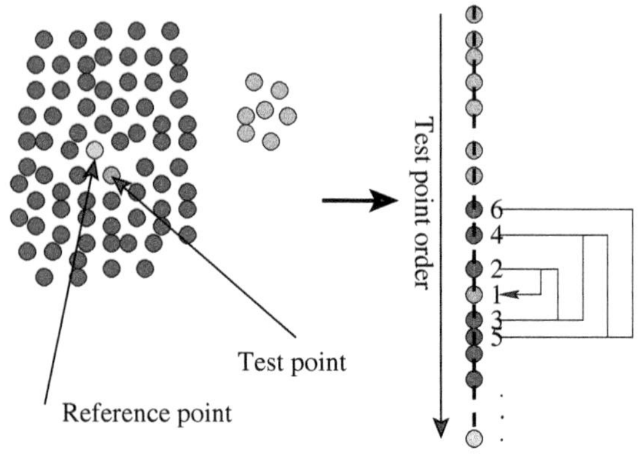

Figure 1: Description of the index. Left figure shows a dataset with normal points in blue, outliers in red and the reference and test point. The right figure shows the order in which the test points are processed with the points farthest from the reference point being processed first.

and then calculate the distance of all the other points in D from R. Then the points in the database are reordered with increasing distance from R. Fig. 1 shows the index for a dataset. The left part shows the original dataset. The blue circles represent the inlier points while the red ones denote the outliers. The green circle at the center is the randomly chosen reference point. The right part of the figure shows the index. The index is simply a one dimensional list of ordered points where the ordering is determined by the distance of all the points in the database from the reference point (highest to lowest). Instead of traversing through the data in the original order (or random order [4]), we test the points along this index order. The rationale for this traversal is as follows. Since we choose R at random, it is likely that R will be one of the inlier points if there are more inliers than outliers. Therefore, the points farthest from R will be more likely be the outliers. Since we process the points in decreasing distance to R, it is very likely that the outliers will be processed first, leading to a faster increase in the cutoff threshold. This approach would therefore, satisfy challenge (1) as stated above.

Re-ordering the database for testing has another advantage. If the points are processed in this order, it can be shown that *iOrca* can stop the processing and terminate much early compared to other state of the art methods by using the following termination criterion.

LEMMA 4.1. *[Stopping rule] Let L be the index as described in this section. Let R be the reference point used to build L. Let x_t be any test point currently being tested by iOrca. If*

$$\|x_t - R\| + \|R - x_{n-k+1}\| < c,$$

then iOrca can terminate the execution immediately, where c is the current cutoff threshold, x_{n-k+1} is the true k-th nearest neighbor of R and $\|\cdot\|$ is the 2-norm of a vector.

PROOF. By applying triangle inequality for every point x_j, where $n-k+1 \leq j \leq n$, it follows that,

$$\|x_t - x_j\| < \|x_t - R\| + \|R - x_j\| < c$$

i.e. there exist at least k points between x_{n-k+1} and x_n whose distance to x_t is less than c. This implies that the distance between x_t and its k-th nearest neighbor is less than c, in which case it can be pruned. Surprisingly, the entire execution of the algorithm can be terminated at this point since, for any other test point x'_t closer to y than x^t (and hence not yet tested), we can show that,

$$\begin{aligned} \|x'_t - x_{n-k+1}\| &< \|x'_t - y\| + \|x_{n-k+1} - y\| \\ &< \|x_t - y\| + \|x_{n-k+1} - y\| < c \end{aligned}$$

This shows that if the result holds for any test point, it will hold for all subsequent test points and so the algorithm can stop without further testing of any other point. □

Note that these distances are pre-computed and available in memory. Therefore, checking if the condition holds is extremely fast and causes very little overhead.

In order to quickly find the nearest neighbors of a test point, we again apply our index. Instead of starting the search from the beginning of the database for every test point, we start the search from the location it lies along the index and then gradually "spiraling" out. Figure 1 shows one of the test points T (magenta color) in the dataset. It also shows where T lies along the index. Now the search for the nearest neighbor spirals out from T by first looking at the nearest two points (top and bottom) and then continuing further until the score of that point drops below the threshold (in which case the point is pruned) or the test point has a score higher than the t-th largest outlier (in which case the outlier list and the cutoff are updated). Since the index prescribes a total ordering of the points projected along one dimension, it is likely that, for a test point x_t, if x_i is closer to x_t than x_j along the index, then it will be so when the actual distances are also computed *i.e.* if

$$\|x_t - y\| > \|x_i - y\| > \|x_j - y\|$$

then it is expected that

$$\|x_t - x_i\| < \|x_t - x_j\|.$$

As a result, we can find the nearest neighbors very fast as demonstrated by our extensive experimental study.

The above technique prescribes a way of testing each point by traversing the database points in a spiral order. Loading the entire database for testing each point one by one is I/O expensive; instead, we process the test points in blocks such that they can be tested simultaneously by creating a spiral search order for that entire test block. Our index allows us to do this by loading a block of index distances (they are the distances of the test points to y), computing the average distance and then starting the spiral search from the location where this average lies along the index. Since after ordering, the test blocks are expected to be similar, testing them using the same spiral order helps speed up the search as well.

Finally, our index is simple and cheap to compute. It can be entirely loaded in memory at runtime since it only consists of n floating point numbers and the associate integer indices.

Putting these building blocks together, we develop a novel indexed version of Orca (*iOrca*) which is upto an order of magnitude faster than Orca and costs less disk I/O. The pseudo-code of *iOrca* is shown in Alg. 2. Note that the choice of R is critical in determining the effectiveness of the pruning. However, discussion on a proper choice of R is beyond the scope of this paper.

Input: k, t, b, D
Output: O_k, the set of top t outliers in D
Initialization: $c \leftarrow 0$, $O_k \leftarrow \emptyset$, $L =$ **BuildIndex**(D);
while $B \leftarrow$ *get_next_block*$(D, b, L) <> \emptyset$ **do**
    // process points as specified in $L.id$
    if *(Lemma 4.1 holds for* $B(1)$*)* **then** Terminate;
    else
        $\mu =$ **findAvg**$(L(B))$;
        $startID =$ **find**$(L >= \mu)$;
        $order =$ **spiralOrder**$(L.id, startID)$;
        forall the $b \in B$ **do** $N_k(b) \leftarrow \emptyset$;
        forall the $i = 1$ *to* $|D|$ **do**
            $x =$ **getFromfile**$(order(i), D)$;
            forall the $b \in B, b \neq x$ **do**
                if $|N_k(b)| < k$ *or* $dist(b, x) < maxdist(b, N_k(b))$ **then**
                    $N_k(b) \leftarrow$ Update_nbors$(N_k(b), x, k)$;
                    $\delta_k(b) \leftarrow \max\{\|b - y\| : y \in N_k(b)\}$;
                    if $\delta_k(b) < c$ **then** $B \leftarrow B \setminus b$;
                end
            end
        end
        for b=1 *to* B **do**
            $newO \leftarrow newO \bigcup [b; \quad \delta_k(b); \quad N_k(b)]$;
        end
        $O_k \leftarrow$ Find_Top_t$(newO \cup O_k, t)$;
        $c \leftarrow \min\{\delta_k(y, D) : y \in O\}$;
    end
end

Algorithm 2: Indexed Orca (*iOrca*)

Complexity analysis: For building the index, n distance computations are needed, each taking $O(d)$ time. Also, the sorting takes $O(n \log n)$ time, giving a total running time of $O(n \log n + nd)$. n floating point numbers are required to be stored as the index, so the space requirement is $O(n)$. Since we block both the test points and the reference points using a block size of b, the number of disk accesses is $O(n/b * n/b)$ in the worst case, unless the algorithm can terminate early.

5. DISTRIBUTED OUTLIER DETECTION ALGORITHM: DOOR

In this section we describe two distributed algorithms for distance-based outlier detection (*DOoR*). The algorithms are disk-aware, and substantially faster than the state of the art methods while still guaranteeing correct results.

In our distributed setup, we assume that there is a central node which does the reporting of all the outliers. We also assume that all nodes $P_1, \ldots, P_n$ in $\mathcal{G}$ form a ring (except the leader node P_0) *i.e.* any node P_i can communicate with nodes P_i+1 and P_i-1, $1 \leq i < p$. It is further assumed that the leader has access to all the data; splits the dataset into n partitions and ships them to the nodes, while still maintaining a copy for itself to be used as the test points. Each P_i has access to its own data block D_i; the test blocks are supplied either by the leader or read from the disk. P_0 maintains the current list of outliers O_k, of at most t points which currently have the largest $\delta_k(, D)$. Initially O_k is empty and accumulates more points as their k-nearest neighbors w.r.t D are computed by other machines. The leader also maintains a cutoff threshold, $c = \min\{\delta_k(x, D) : x \in O\}$, with $c = -\infty$ initially. Whenever this threshold is changed, it is broadcast to all nodes for more efficient pruning of points.

Input: k, t, b, D_i
while $B \leftarrow$ *get_next_block*$(D_i, b) \neq \emptyset$ **do**
    forall the $b \in B$ **do** $\mathcal{L}_k(b) \leftarrow \emptyset$;
    forall the $\ell = 1$ *to* $|D_i|$ **do**
        $x =$ **getFromfile**(ℓ, D_i);
        forall the $b \in B, b \neq x$ **do**
            if $|\mathcal{L}_k(b)| < k$ *or* $dist(b, x) < maxdist(b, \mathcal{L}_k(b))$ **then**
                $\mathcal{L}_k(b) \leftarrow$ Update_nbors$(\mathcal{L}_k(b), x, k)$;
                $r_b \leftarrow \max\{\|b - y\| : y \in \mathcal{L}_k(b)\}$;
                if $r_b < c_i$ **then** $B \leftarrow B \setminus b$; $\tau_i \leftarrow \tau_i + 1$;
            end
        end
    end
    forall the $b \in B$ **do**
        Send $(b, \mathcal{L}_k(b), r_b)$ to machine $(i+1) \mod p$;
    end
    CheckMsg();
    CheckThreshold();
end
Procedure CheckMsg()
begin
    while *(received buffer* $\neq \emptyset$*)* **do**
        Extract $(x, \mathcal{L}_k(x), r_x)$ from *received buffer*;
        $\mathcal{L}_k(x) \leftarrow N_k(x, D_i) \cup \mathcal{L}_k(x)$;
        $r_x \leftarrow \max\{\|x - y\| : y \in \mathcal{L}_k(x)\}$;
        if $r_x > c_i$ **then**
            if *x originated in machine* P_i **then**
                Send $(x, r_x, \mathcal{L}_k(x))$ (a potential outlier message) to the leader machine (P_0);
            end
            else Send $(x, \mathcal{L}_k(x), r_x)$ to machine $(i+1) \mod p$ (put it in received buffer of machine $(i+1) \mod p$);
        end
        else $\tau_i \leftarrow \tau_i + 1$;
    end
end
On receiving a new threshold c: $c_i \leftarrow c$;

Algorithm 3: *DOoR* at any worker node P_i.

Each worker node works in a *push-pull* mode. Description of the worker node for *DOoR* is given in Fig. 2 and Alg. 3. The inputs to each worker are k, t, size of the block b, and the local dataset D_i. Machine P_i maintains a threshold c_i it has received from the leader. Initially $c_i = -\infty$. For each point b in the test data block B, machine P_i also maintains:

- $\mathcal{L}_k(b)$— the k-nearest neighbors found thus far for b
- $r_b = \max\{\|b - y\| : y \in \mathcal{L}_k(b)\}$

Initially, $\mathcal{L}_k(b) \leftarrow \emptyset$ and $r_b = 0$ for each point $b \in B$. In the *push* mode, for each point $b \in B$, the algorithm checks to see if there exist a set of neighbors in $\mathcal{L}_k(b)$ such that the current score of b is below c_i *i.e.* if $r_b < c_i$. If this is true, then the point is no longer tested and pruned; otherwise b along with its nearest neighbors found so far $\mathcal{L}_k(b)$ and r_b are forwarded (*pushed*) to the next node P_{i+1} for validation.

The other phase of *DOoR* is the *pull* phase in which P_i first checks to see if there are any messages in the received buffer (RB) from node P_{i-1}. If RB is not empty, P_i needs to validate all the received points against its local data D_i. It does so by first extracting the points from RB and then checking, for every point x in RB, if there are any neighbors in D_i which are closer than the ones in $\mathcal{L}_x$ (which contains the current closest neighbors as received from P_{i-1}). The neighbor list and the value of r_x are updated accordingly. As a result, if r_x becomes less than c_i, then x is pruned. Otherwise, if x originated in P_i itself, it has survived the pruning of all the nodes and is sent to the leader node P_0 (since it can be a potential outlier data point). If x did not originate on P_i, is forwarded to P_{i+1} with the updated nearest neighbors. Node P_i then goes back to the push mode and begins testing the new set of points. In any step of the execution, if any node gets a new cutoff threshold c, it immediately sets $c_i \leftarrow c$ and resumes the processing.

Alg. 4 shows the tasks executed by the leader node in *DOoR*. It initializes the outlier list O_k to null. Whenever it receives a new potential outlier x, it adds x to O_k if the outlier list contains less than t points. If it contains t points, the outlier in O_k with the smallest score is replaced by x. If due to either of these computations, the outlier list becomes full, the cutoff is set to the score of the smallest outlier and it is then broadcast to all the nodes.

Finally, we discuss the assignment of test points to the worker nodes. There are several ways this can be done. In our implementation, we choose a simple but effective approach. This is shown in Fig. 2. Instead of testing all the test blocks in parallel at all nodes, we assign the test blocks in a round robin fashion: the first test block (red) is assigned to the top left node, the second to the top right and the third goes to the bottom node. These points are then tested in parallel at the nodes. Some of the test points are locally pruned, and the remaining ones are then validated at the other nodes by passing them through the ring topology formed by the nodes. The next set of blocks are then read and this process continues until all the test points are exhausted. Unlike the Parallel Bay's algorithm (PBay) [13], our method is expected to be faster since we do not evaluate the same test block in parallel at all the nodes. For a set of test points, we leverage the nearest neighbors found at one node to continue the search on the next node, instead of starting from scratch at all the nodes for that test block. As a result, the size of the test block keeps diminishing as it moves around the ring from one node to the other.

One critical component of any distributed algorithm is the termination criterion. In our algorithm this can be implemented in one of two ways. Each node P_i keeps track of τ_i, the total number of points that it has pruned, and the leader machine keeps track of ρ, the total number of points it received as potential outliers. Periodically the leader polls the workers for their values of τ_i's. Whenever $\sum_{i=1}^{n} \tau_i + \rho = |D|$, the leader sends a terminate message to all the nodes. Alternatively, each node can send a termination signal to the leader when the remaining test block size becomes zero.

The second distributed algorithm that we describe in this paper combines the index developed for *iOrca* and the distributed processing of *DOoR*. We call this the indexed distributed outlier detection algorithm or *iDOoR*. The leader node first reorders the data based on a randomly chosen reference point. This is to ensure that the points which have the highest distance to the reference point (the potential outliers) are processed first. Then it broadcasts the reference

```
Input: D_i, n, k
Output: O_k, the set of outliers
Initialization: O_k ← ∅;
if (x, r_x, L_k(x)) is received then
    ρ ← ρ + 1;
    if |O_k| ≤ t − 2 then O_k ← O_k ∪ [x;  r_x;  L_k(x)];
    if |O_k| = t − 1 then
        O_k ← O_k ∪ [x;  r_x;  L_k(x)];
        c ← min{δ_k(y, D) : y ∈ O_k};
        Broadcast c to all nodes;
    end
    if |O_k| ≥ t then
        if r_x > min{δ_k(y, D) : y ∈ O_k} then
            Drop y ∈ O_k with minimum δ_k, add x to O_k;
            c ← min{δ_k(y, D) : y ∈ O_k};
            Broadcast c to all nodes;
        end
    end
end
```

Algorithm 4: Distributed outlier detection at master node

point to all the worker nodes and splits the data amongst all the nodes as before. Any worker node on receiving the reference point builds its own index on its local dataset D_i. The rest of the algorithm is similar to *DOoR*. On receiving a block of test points, any worker node executes the spiral search based on the index built on D_i for the entire block. To reduce the number of messages exchanged between the master node and the worker nodes, before every new test block is sent out, the master node checks to see if Lemma 4.1 holds for the test block. Since the index is stored in memory, these computations do not require any extra disk access. If this condition holds for any test block, *iDOoR* can terminate. We omit the pseudo code here due to shortage of space.

It is fairly easy to argue the correctness of *DOoR* or *iDOoR*. First note that if the cutoff $c = 0$, we pass all the data points through all the nodes, thereby ensuring that the nearest neighbors of all the points are correctly found. In the presence of cutoff, the latter is only updated by the leader. At any point during the execution of the algorithm $c_i < c$, guaranteeing no false dismissals.

6. EXPERIMENTS

6.1 Setup

We have implemented our algorithms in Java. The centralized experiments have been run on a 64-bit 2.33 GHz quad core Dell precision 690 desktop running Red Hat Enterprise Linux version 5.4 having 18GB of physical memory. For the distributed experiments, we have used a mid-range linux cluster comprised of 16 slave nodes each containing two, quad-core 2.66GHz CPU totaling 128 cores and 256GB Ram (2Gb/Core). It is controlled by two master nodes and has 30Tb storage. The distributed Java code uses the Java RMI (remote method invocation) framework to mange the worker nodes with a central client handling communication between the distributed threads. In all the experiments, we report the wall time to include both the CPU and I/O time. Note that we do not report accuracy, because our method is guaranteed to produce the same outliers as Orca. We have

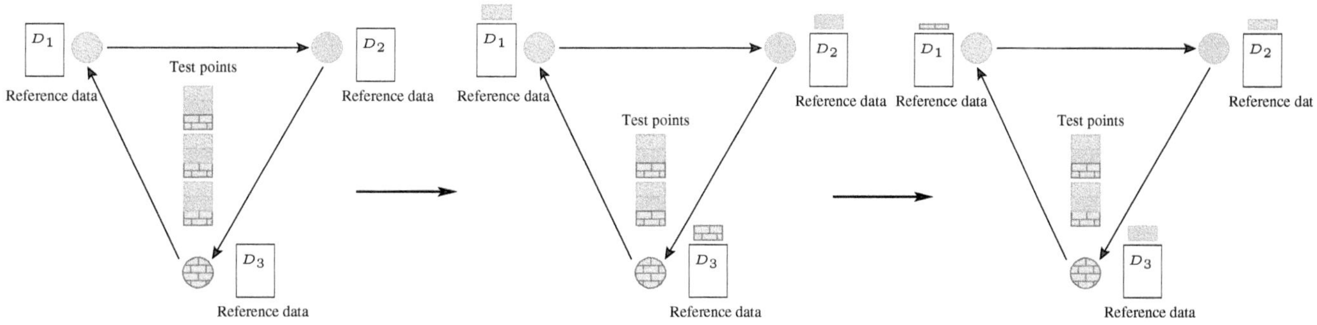

Figure 2: Execution of distributed algorithm. The leftmost picture shows the setup: the test points are color coded to show which block is assigned to which node. Second picture shows that assignment. Third figure shows how the non-pruned points are tested at the other nodes.

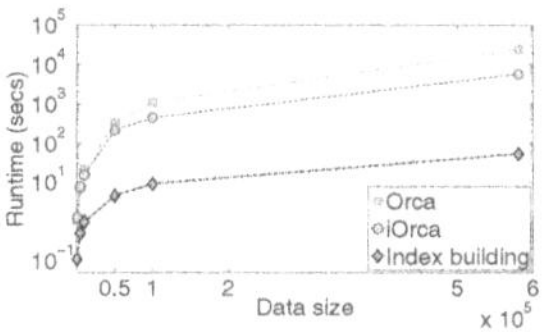

(a) Runtime for Covtype

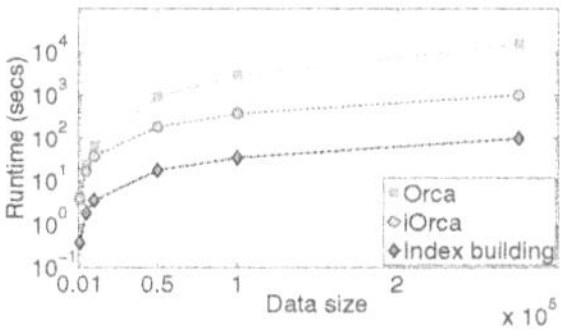

(b) Runtime for Landsat

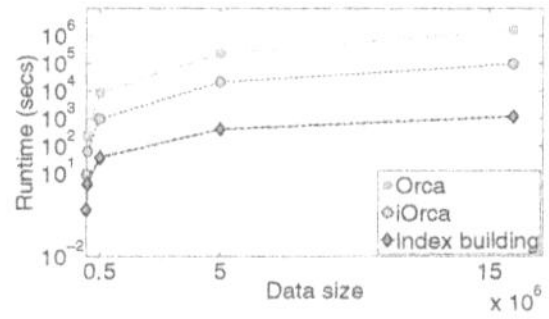

(c) Runtime for MODIS

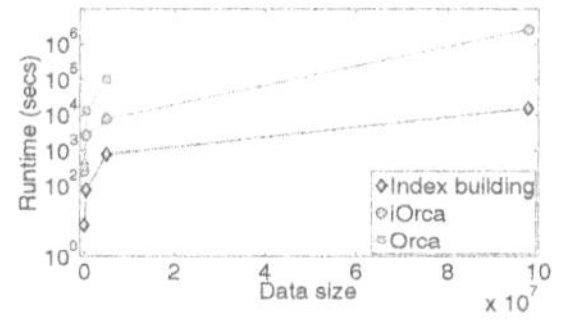

(d) Runtime for CarrierX

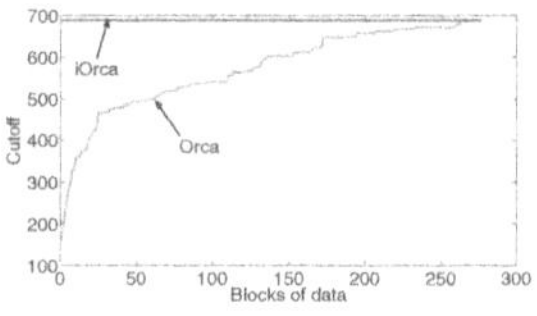

(e) Cutoff for Landsat

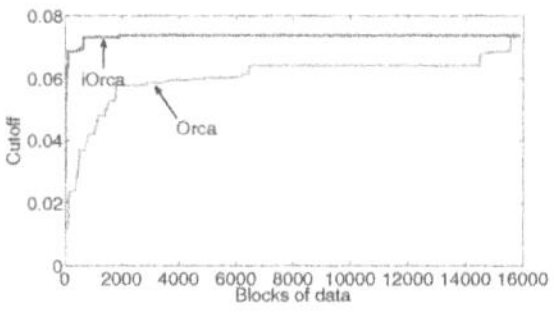

(f) Cutoff for MODIS

Figure 3: Figure showing running time for the 4 datasets ((a) - (d)). As clearly shown for each dataset, *iOrca* beats Orca in running time. This happens because the cutoff increases at faster rate compared to Orca ((e) and (f)).

tested our algorithms on the following real datasets[2]:

1. *Covertype*: contains 581,012 instances and 10 features
2. *Landsat*: contains 275,465 instances and 60 features
3. *MODIS*: contains 15,900,968 instances and 7 features
4. *CarrierX*: contains 97,814,864 instances and 19 features

Unless otherwise stated, we have used the following default values for the parameters: block size, $b = 1000$, $t = 30$ and $k = 5$.

[2]The first 2 datasets are available at `http://archive.ics.uci.edu/ml/index.html`. MODIS is available at `http://modis.gsfc.nasa.gov/data/dataprod/dataproducts.php?MOD_NUMBER=09`. The last is a proprietary dataset from a partner airline.

6.2 Centralized results: *iOrca*

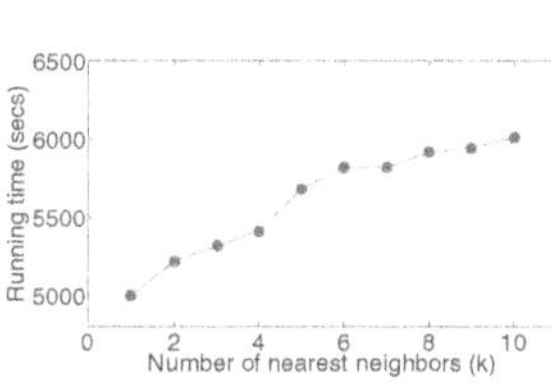

(a) Time vs. k for Covtype

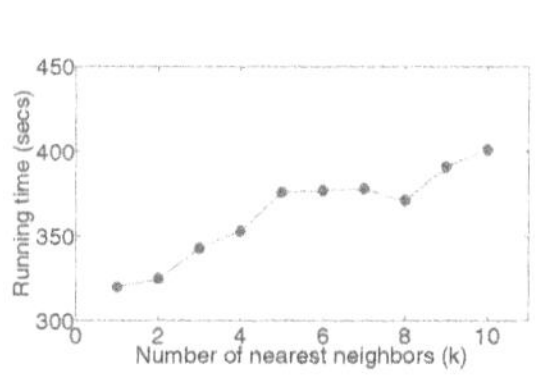

(b) Time vs. k for Landsat

Figure 4: Running time vs. k for *iOrca*.

Our first set of experiments demonstrates the benefits of our indexing method in speeding up Orca in a purely centralized setting. Fig. 3 ((a)–(d)) shows the results for the 4 datasets. Each of the Figures (a) - (d) shows the running time (in log scale) along the y-axis for Orca (red squares), *iOrca* (blue circles) and the index building phase of *iOrca* (black diamond). The x-axis are random samples from these datasets. As clearly shown, *iOrca* beats Orca; the decrease in running time is from 2 to 17 times compared to Orca. The decrease in runtime occurs because of the following. (1) The indexing method orders the points in such a manner that those which are farthest from a common reference point are processed first. Since these points are the potential outliers, the cutoff increases much faster (compared to Orca), leading to faster pruning of inliers. (2) The spiral search helps to find the nearest neighbors for each test point much faster than going through the data in the original order. (3) The early stopping criterion helps to avoid testing all the data points. For the Landsat dataset, there are 276 blocks of test data and iOrca only needs to process the first 6 blocks before the early stopping condition signals termination. Similarly, for the MODIS dataset, there are 16,000 blocks of test data and *iOrca* only evaluates the first 13,000 leading to significant savings in both I/O and runtime.

Note that for the CarrierX dataset, we could not plot the runtime of Orca on the entire dataset since it has not finished in more than 8 days. The last two plots (e) and (f) of Fig. 3 compares how the cutoff grows for both Orca and *iOrca* for Landsat and MODIS datasets as each test block is processed.

The next set of figures (Fig. 4) demonstrates the impact on runtime of varying the number of nearest neighbors k for he Covtype and Landsat datasets. As shown, the runtime

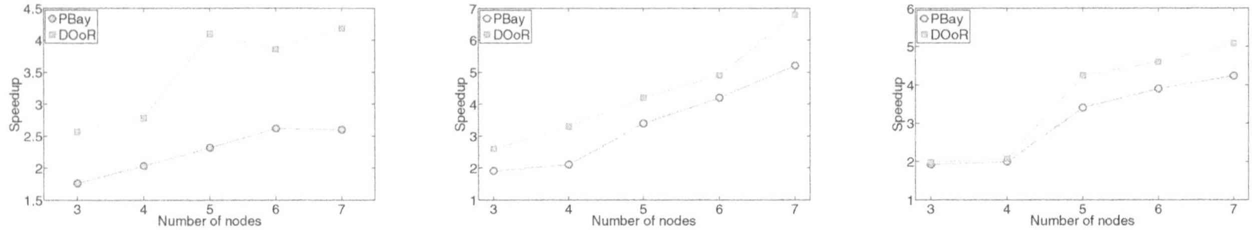

(a) Scalability for Covtype (b) Scalability for MODIS (c) Scalability for CarrierX

Figure 5: Speedup of *DOoR* vs PBay [13] algorithm with Orca as the baseline.

increases very slowly as k is increased. This shows that for both these datasets, the spiral search technique is able to find the nearest neighbors of a test point in very little time, leading to a very slow growth in runtime.

Comparison to other methods:

We have compared our algorithm with the RBRP algorithm [9]. Unfortunately, the source code made available by the authors was in C and so we re-implemented it in Java. Overall we found it to be much slower than *iOrca* because of primarily two reasons: (1) the number of clusters produced is roughly of the order of 1000 for most of the datasets; moreover, finding the nearest clusters for each cluster is, in itself, a quadratic time computation with respect to the number of clusters, and (2) as described in Section 2, processing each test point one by one leads to an unacceptably large number ($O(n^2)$) of disk I/O, thereby slowing down the performance dramatically.

6.3 Distributed results: *DOoR* and *iDOoR*

Fig. 5 shows the performance results for *DOoR*. The red curve shows the speedup (ratio of the runtimes) that is obtained by running *DOoR* on 3 to 7 distributed machines when compared against a centralized Orca. The blue curve shows the speedup of obtained by PBay [13] vs. Orca. As shown, the speedup of *DOoR* is much greater compared to that of PBay for all the datasets. For Covertype and MODIS, the speedup is almost linear for *DOoR*. This shows that our distributed algorithm *DOoR* is more efficient in finding outliers compared to PBay. The primary reason for this is that *DOoR* can better utilize the cutoff by assigning different test blocks to different nodes at the beginning, unlike PBay which assigns the same test block to all the nodes. As a result in *DOoR*, each test block keeps shrinking in size as it travels through the ring for validation. Moreover, *DOoR* can leverage the nearest neighbors of the test points found at one node to speed up the search at the successive node in the ring. In contrast, PBay tests all the blocks in parallel at all the nodes, leading to more computations.

Finally, we present the speedup results for *iDOoR* in Fig. 6. In this case, our baseline is the *iOrca* algorithm. We are interested in answering the following question: *Does distributed processing help in reducing the runtime of iOrca?* As shown in the figure, for most cases, *iDOoR* is faster than *iOrca* (speedup > 1 indicates this). The x-axis shows the number of machines used while the y-axis shows the speedup obtained. Each experiment is run for three datasets shown by the three colored bars. Note that in this case, the speedup is less than linear. Due to the index, the cutoff in *iOrca* increases very fast; as a result, most of the outliers are found

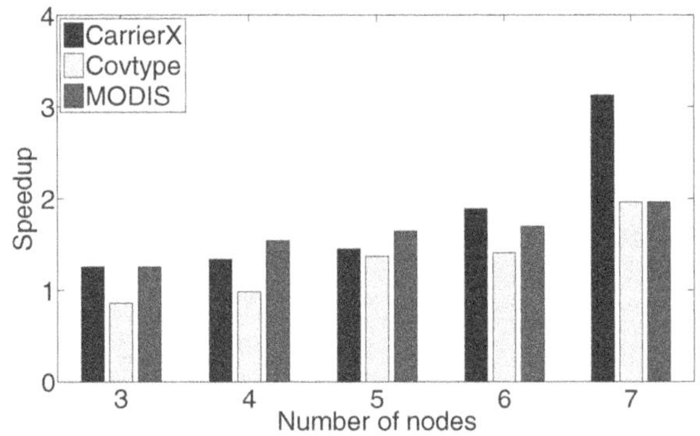

Figure 6: Speedup of *iDOoR* vs. *iOrca*.

in the first 20% of the blocks and the algorithm can process the rest of the data very fast. *iDOoR* helps to speed up the first 20% of the execution, but for the later 80%, of the execution the overhead of message passing is more than the single threaded *iOrca*. This is the prime reason why we do not find a linear increase in speedup when the number of machines is increased. Currently, we are working on a hybrid method whereby we can switch between these two modes on the fly.

7. CONCLUSION

In this paper we have developed both sequential and distributed outlier detection methods that are significantly more efficient than existing methods while still guaranteeing the exact same outliers. Using a simple, but effective indexing and disk block accessing techniques, our sequential algorithm *iOrca* is up to an order-of-magnitude more efficient than the state-of-the-art. By allowing the algorithm to stop early, *iOrca* can terminate even before looking at all the test points. We further propose two distributed algorithms for outlier detection (*DOoR*) and *iDOoR* that can be run on multi-core cluster of machines connected on a ring topology. By combining the index scheme along with distributed processing, our distributed algorithm is much faster than [13] as validated on large public datasets.

Acknowledgments

This research is supported by the NASA SSAT project under NASA Aeronautics Mission Directorate. This work has been approved for public release by The MITRE Corporation, case 11-2367, distribution unlimited. The author's affiliation with The MITRE Corporation is provided for identification purposes only, and is not intended to convey or imply MITRE's concurrence with, or support for, the positions, opinions or viewpoints expressed by the author.

8. REFERENCES

[1] F. Angiulli, S. Basta, S. Lodi, and C. Sartori. A Distributed Approach to Detect Outliers in Very Large Data Sets. In *Proocedings of Euro-Par'10*, pages 329–340, 2010.

[2] F. Angiulli and F. Fassetti. DOLPHIN: An Efficient Algorithm for Mining Distance-based Outliers in Very Large Datasets. *ACM TKDD*, 3:4:1–4:57, 2009.

[3] F. Angiulli and C. Pizzuti. Fast Outlier Detection in High Dimensional Spaces. In *Proceedings of PKDD'02*, pages 15–26, 2002.

[4] S. Bay and M. Schwabacher. Mining distance-based outliers in near linear time with randomization and a simple pruning rule. In *Proceedings of SIGKDD'03*, pages 29–38, 2003.

[5] J. Bentley. Multidimensional binary search trees used for associative searching. *Commun. ACM*, 18:509–517, 1975.

[6] S. Berchtold, D. Keim, and H. Kriegel. The X-tree : An Index Structure for High-Dimensional Data. In *Proceedings of VLDB'96*, pages 28–39, 1996.

[7] M. Breunig, H. Kriegel, R. Ng, and J. Sander. LOF: Identifying Density-based Local Outliers. In *Proceedings of SIGMOD'00*, pages 93–104, 2000.

[8] V. Chandola, A. Banerjee, and V. Kumar. Anomaly Detection: A Survey. *ACM Computing Surveys*, 41:15:1–15:58, 2009.

[9] A. Ghoting, S. Parthasarathy, and M. Otey. Fast mining of distance-based outliers in high-dimensional datasets. *DMKD*, 16:349–364, 2008.

[10] A. Guttman. R-Trees: A Dynamic Index Structure for Spatial Searching. In *Proceedings of SIGMOD'84*, pages 47–57, 1984.

[11] E. Hung and D. Cheung. Parallel Mining of Outliers in Large Database. *Distrib. Parallel Databases*, 12:5–26, 2002.

[12] E. Knorr and R. Ng. Algorithms for Mining Distance-Based Outliers in Large Datasets. In *Proceedings of VLDB'98*, pages 392–403, 1998.

[13] E. Lozano and E. Acuna. Parallel Algorithms for Distance-Based and Density-Based Outliers. In *Proceedings of ICDM'05*, pages 729–732, 2005.

[14] M. Otey, A. Ghoting, and S. Parthasarathy. Fast Distributed Outlier Detection in Mixed-Attribute Data Sets. *DMKD*, 12:203–228, 2006.

[15] S. Ramaswamy, R. Rastogi, and K. Shim. Efficient Algorithms for Mining Outliers from Large Data Sets. In *Proceedings of SIGMOD'00*, pages 427–438, 2000.

An Effective Evaluation Measure for Clustering on Evolving Data Streams

Hardy Kremer, Philipp Kranen,
Timm Jansen, Thomas Seidl
RWTH Aachen University, Germany
lastname@cs.rwth-aachen.de

Albert Bifet, Geoff Holmes,
Bernhard Pfahringer
University of Waikato Hamilton, New Zealand
{abifet,geoff,bernhard}@cs.waikato.ac.nz

ABSTRACT

Due to the ever growing presence of data streams, there has been a considerable amount of research on stream mining algorithms. While many algorithms have been introduced that tackle the problem of clustering on evolving data streams, hardly any attention has been paid to appropriate evaluation measures. Measures developed for static scenarios, namely structural measures and ground-truth-based measures, cannot correctly reflect errors attributable to emerging, splitting, or moving clusters. These situations are inherent to the streaming context due to the dynamic changes in the data distribution.

In this paper we develop a novel evaluation measure for stream clustering called Cluster Mapping Measure (CMM). CMM effectively indicates different types of errors by taking the important properties of evolving data streams into account. We show in extensive experiments on real and synthetic data that CMM is a robust measure for stream clustering evaluation.

Categories and Subject Descriptors

H.2.8 [**Database Management**]: Database Applications—*Data Mining*; I.5.3 [**Pattern Recognition**]: Clustering

General Terms

Measurement, Experimentation

1. INTRODUCTION

Mining patterns from data streams is constantly gaining importance in many applications. Streams consist of data tuples that need to be processed as they arrive, and mining these streams is challenging since the data distribution underlying a stream can evolve significantly over time. Stream mining tasks are, for example, classification [4], association rule mining [30], or clustering [1, 8, 23]. In stream clustering, a clustering is constantly adapted to reflect changes in the observed stream. Besides dealing with evolving distributions, stream clustering algorithms have to meet several technical requirements, including limited time, limited memory, and processing the stream in a single pass. A multitude of stream clustering algorithms has been proposed in the literature that satisfy these requirements.

Of major importance is the quality of the resulting clusterings, which can be measured by evaluation measures, also termed criteria, indices, validation measures, or validation indices. Research on evaluation measures for static datasets, i.e. traditional clustering without the streaming context, looks back at a history of more than thirty years. While clustering itself is commonly accepted as a difficult and subjective task [21], the validation of clustering results is even described as the most difficult and frustrating part of cluster analysis [20]. This holds for evaluation no matter whether or not a ground truth is available against which to compare the clustering result. The usage of a ground truth can strictly categorize the proposed measures into internal and external measures [7, 25, 38, 41]: Internal measures consider only the structure and properties of the clusters, e.g. their compactness or the distance between them. External measures compare the resulting clustering against a ground truth, e.g. punishing an algorithm for putting objects from different ground truth clusters into a single cluster.

The MOA Framework [5, 24, 29] is an open source benchmarking software for data stream mining, which contains a set of stream clustering algorithms from the literature as well as an extensive collection of evaluation measures. The experience from implementing and using MOA showed two major disadvantages of existing evaluation measures: First, none can properly handle the peculiarities of evolving data streams such as overlapping due to merging or drifting clusters or noisy data streams. As a consequence the measures cannot effectively reflect the occurring errors. Second, the vast majority of evaluation measures achieve suboptimal results even if the ground truth clustering is tested. The Cluster Mapping Measure (CMM) proposed in this paper overcomes these shortcomings and enables effective evaluation of clustering results on evolving streams.

2. RELATED WORK

We first review existing work on evaluation measures for clustering on static data sets. After that we discuss related work on stream clustering algorithms and identify the evaluation measures employed in the individual approaches.

As mentioned in Sec. 1, evaluation measures can be categorized into internal and external measures, depending on whether or not they employ a ground truth clustering for comparison. A different categorization additionally identifies so called relative measures, comparing the single partitions within a clustering result. However, this group is less recognized and solutions are often specialized to a specific domain [36, 42]; we focus on internal and external measures. Table 1 lists (without claiming completeness) a collection of internal and external measures from the literature with references to formulae and more detailed description. Apart from these, other measures exist that deal with fuzzy clustering [6] or focus on finding the best number of clusters [37, 40]. For readability and space reasons we reduced the amount of measures used in our experiments to the ones highlighted in gray. Our choice of internal measures is based on a study of thirty measures in [28]; the external measures resulted as best choices in three recent studies [7, 38, 41].

Internal measures	External measures
Gamma [2]	Rand statistic [41, 32]
C Index [18]	Jaccard coefficient [12]
Point-Biserial [27]	Folkes and Mallow Index [12]
Log Likelihood [16]	Hubert Γ statistics [17]
Dunn's Index [11]	Minkowski score [7]
Tau [34]	Purity [43]
Tau $\underline{A}$ [18]	van Dongen criterion [39]
Tau $\underline{C}$ [18]	V-measure [35]
CDbw [14]	Completeness [35]
Ratio of Repetition [18]	Homogeneity [35]
Sum squared dists SSQ [15]	Variation of information [26]
Adj. Ratio of Clustering [18]	Mutual information [10]
Fagan's Index [18]	Class-based entropy [38]
Deviation Index [18]	Cluster-based entropy [43]
$\underline{Z}$-Score Index [18]	Precision [33]
$\underline{D}$ Index [18]	Recall [33]
Silhouette coefficient [22]	F-measure [33]

Table 1: Internal and external evaluation measures.

Stream clustering algorithms can be categorized from different perspectives, e.g. whether convex or arbitrary shapes are found. Convex stream clustering approaches are based on a k-center clustering [1, 23, 31]. Approaches for arbitrary shaped clusters use kernels [19], fractal dimensions [3], or density based methods [8, 9]. In the evaluation of these papers, the used measures are those for static data sets, most often Entropy (Purity), Precision, or the F-measure. In convex approaches, which are the most prevalent in the literature, often also the sum of squared distances is used (e.g., [1, 31]), i.e. the compactness of spherical clusters is measured, which does not testify the quality of a clustering.

Most stream clustering algorithms use an internal representation, called *micro clustering*, that is constantly updated. Only when required, the output (macro) clusterings are generated by an offline component, e.g. k-means.

In summary, we find that despite the amount of work on developing evaluation measures as well as developing stream clustering algorithms, no attempt has been made to meet the requirements of both tasks.

3. PRELIMINARIES

In this section we provide formal definitions used throughout the paper. We concentrate on spherical clusters, which constitute the most prevalent model. It is e.g. also used in the online components of density based algorithm [9].

An object arriving on a data stream is represented by a tuple of attribute values. We define a stream as follows:

DEFINITION 1. ***Stream.*** *A stream $\mathcal{S} = \{o_1, o_2, \ldots\}$ is an infinite sequence of objects o_i, where each object is a d-dim. tuple of attribute values $o_i = (o_{i1}, \ldots, o_{id})$ with $o_{ij} \in \mathbb{R}$.*

In order to give more influence to recent data, objects are assigned an age-depending weight. We exemplarily define the weight using an exponential decay function as in [1]. Other weighting functions assign a binary weight (sliding window) using either the age or the cardinality for thresholding.

DEFINITION 2. ***Weight.*** *Let t_{now} be the current time and t_o the arrival time of object o with $t_o \leq t_{now}$. Then the weight of o is $w(o) = \beta^{-\lambda \cdot (t_{now} - t_o)}$.*

The parameters β and λ control the form of the aging function, e.g. if $\beta = 2$ then $1/\lambda$ is the half life of o. Apart from the complete stream $\mathcal{S}$ we often only consider a subset of the most recent objects that we call horizon.

DEFINITION 3. ***Horizon.*** *The horizon $\mathcal{H}$ for a stream $\mathcal{S}$ and threshold ξ is defined as $\mathcal{H} = \{o \in \mathcal{S} | w(o) \geq \xi\}$.*

To employ a consistent terminology we also formally define clustering and ground truth.

DEFINITION 4. ***Clustering.*** *A clustering algorithm takes a set $\mathcal{O} = \{o_1, \ldots, o_n\}$ of objects as input and returns a cluster set $\mathcal{C} = \{C_1, \ldots, C_k, C_\emptyset\}$. $o \in C_i$ implies that o lies within the cluster boundary of C_i and $C_\emptyset$ contains all unassigned objects. Objects may fall into several clusters.*

DEFINITION 5. ***Ground truth.*** *For a given object set $\mathcal{O} = \{o_1, \ldots, o_n\}$ a ground truth $\mathcal{CL} = \{Cl_1, \ldots, Cl_l\}$ is a partitioning of $\mathcal{O}$ with $\forall i \neq j : Cl_i \cap Cl_j = \emptyset$ and $\bigcup_{i=1}^{l} Cl_i = \mathcal{O}$. The partitions Cl_i are called classes and $Cl(o)$ is the class of o. In the presence of noise Cl_{noise} is the noise class, $\mathcal{CL}^+ = \mathcal{CL} \cup \{Cl_{noise}\}$ and $\mathcal{O}^+ = \mathcal{O} \cup Cl_{noise}$.*
We define the ground truth cluster Cl_i° as the smallest cluster that contains all objects from Cl_i within its boundary: $\forall o \in Cl_i$: $o \in Cl_i^\circ$.

The ground truth cluster resulting from a class may contain points from other classes as well, i.e. $Cl_i^\circ \supseteq Cl_i$, and two clusters resulting from two different ground truth classes can overlap, i.e. they are not necessarily disjoint since objects may fall into the boundaries of other classes.

4. CLUSTER MAPPING MEASURE

In stream processing, data mining algorithms have to take the special properties of the scenario into account. Likewise, for a reasonable comparison of the algorithms, evaluation measures should also consider these special circumstances:

1. **Aging / decay** Dealing with this property is probably the simplest task, because faults caused by a clustering algorithm can be weighted by the influence of the corresponding points (cf. Def. 2).

2. **Missed points** Moving clusters yield errors for missed points. These errors should reflect the seriousness, e.g. how close the point is to its actual cluster.

3. **Misplaced points** Evolution, merging, and splitting of clusters yield overlapping clusters and thereby easily misplaced points. A measure that punishes these misplaced points equally to misplaced points laying outside of any overlapping region does not account for the special circumstances of evolving streams.

4. **Noise** Including noise in a found cluster is often inevitable in the model of the clustering algorithm and should be accounted for by an effective measure.

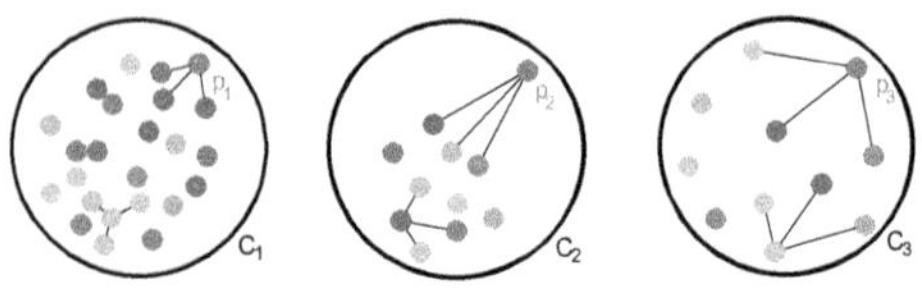

Figure 1: Point connectivity in clusters. p_1 and p_3 have stronger connections to their clusters than p_2.

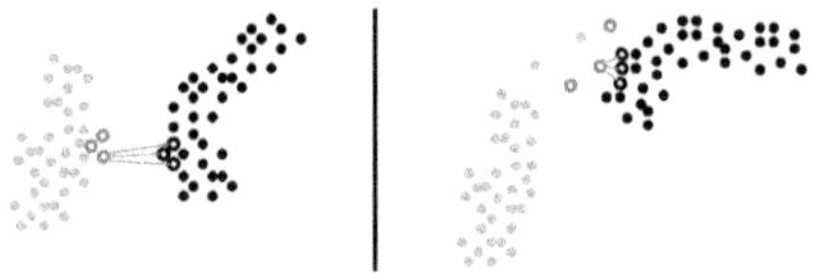

Figure 2: The errors due to misplaced points (blue circles) is less severe in the right example.

Summarizing these properties, three fault cases can be identified that have to be considered in depth, namely missed points, misplaced points, and noise inclusion. The penalty for such errors of stream clustering algorithms should reflect their seriousness and take the age of the points as well as the clustering model into account. CMM is a normalized sum of the penalties for occurring errors that accounts for all aspects mentioned above. Two important prerequisites for the computation are a notion of how well an object fits into a cluster and a mapping from found clusters to ground truth classes. We introduce these prerequisites and CMM in the following section and analyze its behavior in the fault scenarios in Sec. 5.

4.1 Connectivity

A central concept used throughout CMM is the connectivity between points and clusters. This connectivity states how well the point is connected to the cluster, i.e. how it fits the distribution of the cluster in comparison to the other points. We define the connectivity as a distance based concept that ranges from 0 to 1, where 0 indicates no connectivity and 1 indicates a strong connectivity. As a prerequisite we define the average k-neighborhood distance for points and clusters. k is a locality parameter, and we show in Sec. 6 that it has only marginal influence on CMM effectiveness.

DEFINITION 6. ***average k-neighborhood distance.*** *The k-neighborhood (knh) of a point p in a cluster C_i are the k closest points, i.e. $knh(p, C_i) \subseteq C_i \setminus p$ with $|knh(p, C_i)| \leq k$, and for objects $o_{in} \in knh(p, C_i)$ and $o_{out} \in C_i \setminus knh(p, C_i)$ it holds $\forall o_{in} \forall o_{out} : dist(p, o_{out}) \geq dist(p, o_{in})$. The average distance of p to its k neighbors in C_i is then*

$$knhDist(p, C_i) = \frac{1}{k} \sum_{o \in knh(p, C_i)} dist(p, o)$$

and the average distance for a Cluster C_i is

$$knhDist(C_i) = \frac{1}{|C_i|} \sum_{p \in C_i} knhDist(p, C_i)$$

Based on this distance we define connectivity as follows:

DEFINITION 7. ***Point connectivity.*** *The connectivity of a point p to a Cluster C_i is defined as*

$$con(p, C_i) = \begin{cases} 1 & \text{if } knhDist(p, C_i) < knhDist(C_i) \\ 0 & \text{if } C_i = \emptyset \\ \frac{knhDist(C_i)}{knhDist(p, C_i)} & \text{else} \end{cases}$$

Fig. 1 shows examples for connectivity scenarios for spherical clusters using $k = 3$. In the left case the points are densely and rather equally distributed within the cluster. Point p_1 has a strong connectivity to cluster C_1, since its average neighborhood distance is similar to that of C_1. In C_2, the points are not equally distributed. Point p_2 is not strongly connected, since its average neighborhood distance is larger than the average of C_2. In the right example, p_3 also has a comparably large average neighborhood distance, but it is still strongly connected to C_3, because C_3 is less dense.

Fig. 2 illustrates the connectivity of points from the gray cluster (blue circles) to the black cluster. Misplacing gray points in the black cluster seems more severe in the left example, since they are strongly connected to their own (gray) cluster and hardly connected to the black cluster (cf. blue circles). In contrast, on the right they have a stronger connection to the black cluster making the misplacement error intuitively less severe.

4.2 Cluster mapping

To decide whether a point is misplaced we need a mapping from the clusters returned by a stream clustering algorithm to ground truth classes. Before we give a formal definition of the employed mapping we will discuss an example.

As described in Sec. 3 clusters Cl_j° resulting from the ground truth classes (cf. Def. 5) may overlap. Fig. 3(a) shows an example. The gray points belong to class Cl_1, the black points to class Cl_2. The solid circles are the cluster boundaries resulting from a spherical clustering model, i.e. Cl_1° and Cl_2°, and there are black points that fall into the boundary of the gray cluster and vice versa. The figure demonstrates that on evolving data streams a simple majority voting for mapping found clusters to ground truth clusters is not feasible. The core problem are clusters of different densities, frequently occurring in streaming scenarios due to novelty or disappearance of clusters. In the figure, the black cluster is dense and the gray cluster is still emerging, i.e. there are only 10 objects present in the gray concept. The overlapping due to the convex model yields a majority of the black class even in the ground truth cluster Cl_1° of the gray class, i.e. a majority voting would map both C_1 and Cl_1° to the wrong (black) class due to the dominance of the black objects. A majority voting cannot obtain a correct mapping in these scenarios because its decision is based on a single class's objects in a cluster, ignoring the other classes' information that often indicate novel or fading clusters.

To solve this issue we map clusters C_i to ground truth classes Cl_j according to the similarity of C_i's and Cl_j°'s class distributions, i.e. we take the clustering model into account. We define these distributions of classes inside a cluster as frequency histograms.

DEFINITION 8. ***Class distribution.*** *For a given clustering $\mathcal{C} = \{C_1, \ldots, C_k\}$ and ground truth $\mathcal{CL} = \{Cl_1, \ldots, Cl_l\}$, the histogram of the class distribution in cluster C_i is*

$$\rho(C_i) = (|C_i \cap Cl_1|, \ldots, |C_i \cap Cl_l|)$$

$\rho(C_i)_a$ is the a-th component of $\rho(C_i)$ representing the frequency of class Cl_a in cluster C_i.

Def. 8 analogously applies to ground truth clusters Cl_j° that result from classes Cl_j. The right part of Fig. 3 illustrates the class distributions for the shown clusters.

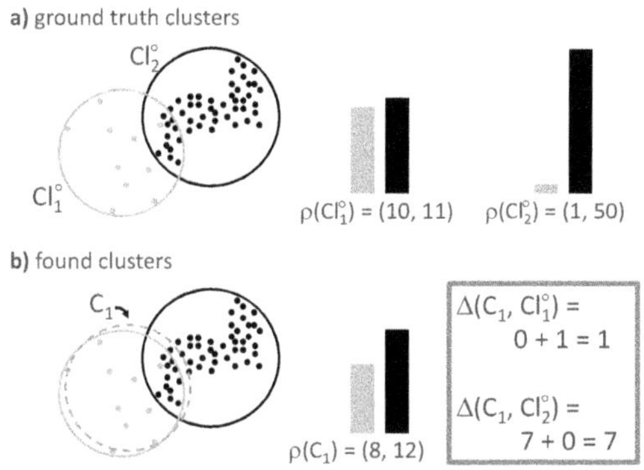

Figure 3: Mapping from found clusters to ground truth clusters is based on class distributions. Mapping clusters based on majority voting cannot recognize emerging or disappearing clusters.

We map clusters based on class distribution similarity. Concretely, we map a cluster C_i to the ground truth class Cl_j, whose ground truth cluster Cl_j° covers the majority of C_i's class frequencies.

DEFINITION 9. ***Cluster mapping.*** *For a given clustering* $\mathcal{C} = \{C_1, \ldots, C_k, C_\emptyset\}$ *and ground truth* $\mathcal{CL} = \{Cl_1, \ldots, Cl_l\}$,

$$\Delta(C_i, Cl_j^\circ) = \sum_{a=1}^{l} \max\{0, \rho(C_i)_a - \rho(Cl_j^\circ)_a\}$$

is the total surplus of objects from classes $Cl_1, \ldots, Cl_l$ *in* C_i *compared to* Cl_j°, *where the surplus is the number of class objects from* Cl_i *not covered by the class distribution of the ground truth cluster* Cl_j°. C_i *is then mapped to the class*

$$map(C_i) = \begin{cases} \underset{Cl_j \in \mathcal{CL}}{\text{argmin}} \{\Delta(C_i, Cl_j^\circ)\} & \text{if } \forall Cl_j : \Delta(C_i, Cl_j^\circ) > 0 \\ \emptyset & \text{if } C_i = C_\emptyset \\ \underset{\substack{Cl_j \in \mathcal{CL} \\ \Delta(C_i, Cl_j^\circ) = 0}}{\text{argmax}} \{|C_i \cap Cl_j^\circ|\} & \text{else} \end{cases}$$

The first and most important case ensures that for a set of ground truth clusters, C_i is mapped to the ground truth class that induces the least surplus on class frequencies. If we would also consider negative differences, as e.g. in L_p-norms, micro clusters would always be mapped to the smallest ground truth class. Employing a majority voting is not generally feasible in the streaming context as explained above. The second case ensures that the unassigned object set $C_\emptyset$ is not mapped to any class, enabling a correct penalty for missed non-noise points (cf. the analysis in Sec. 5.1). The third case arises if C_i completely fits into one or more ground truth clusters; in this special case, a majority voting is applied. If a ground truth cluster Cl_i° falls completely into another cluster Cl_j°, i.e. $\forall a : \rho(Cl_i^\circ)_a \leq \rho(Cl_j^\circ)_a$, C_i is mapped to the larger cluster's class; such clusters are inseparable, as we discuss in Sec. 5.3. If we use this mapping in Fig. 3, the found cluster C_1 in (b) as well as the ground truth clusters Cl_i° in (a) are correctly mapped.

4.3 Cluster Mapping Measure

With the mapping from found clusters to ground truth classes, we can now determine the set $\mathcal{F} \subseteq \mathcal{O}^+$ of points that cause *faults*, i.e. missed points, misplaced points, or included noise points.

DEFINITION 10. ***Fault set.*** *For* $\mathcal{O}^+ = \mathcal{O} \cup Cl_{noise}$, $\mathcal{CL}^+ = \mathcal{CL} \cup \{Cl_{noise}\}$, *and* $\mathcal{C} = \{C_1, \ldots, C_k, C_\emptyset\}$, *the set of objects mapped to a false class is*

$$\mathcal{F} = \{o \in \mathcal{O}^+ | \exists C_i : o \in C_i \wedge map(C_i) \neq Cl(o)\}$$

Obviously, a single point o can cause several faults. The set of clusters in which o causes a fault is

$$faultClu(o) = \{C_i \in \mathcal{C} | o \in C_i \wedge map(C_i) \neq Cl(o)\}$$

The penalty for a fault point depends on the connectivity to both its true class and the assigned class.

DEFINITION 11. ***Penalty.*** *Let o be an object from the fault set and* $C_i \in faultClu(o)$. *The penalty for o is*

$$pen(o, C_i) = con(o, Cl(o)) \cdot (1 - con(o, map(C_i)))$$

The ***overall penalty*** *for a fault point o w.r.t. all found clusters* $C_i \in \mathcal{C}$ *is defined as*

$$pen(o, \mathcal{C}) = \max_{C_i \in faultClu(o)} \{pen(o, C_i)\}$$

The single penalty function can handle all three fault types, and we detail on this in Sec. 5.1. To sustain comparability between points, we only count a fault point's most serious fault in the overall penalty.

Now we can define the CMM, which indicates how different a given clustering is from a given ground truth. CMM is a normalized sum of the penalties: if no fault occurs CMM will be 1 and 0 indicates maximal error.

DEFINITION 12. ***CMM.*** *Given an object set* $\mathcal{O}^+ = \mathcal{O} \cup Cl_{noise}$, *a ground truth* $\mathcal{CL}^+ = \mathcal{CL} \cup \{Cl_{noise}\}$, *a clustering* $\mathcal{C} = \{C_1, \ldots, C_k, C_\emptyset\}$, *and the fault set* $\mathcal{F} \subseteq \mathcal{O}^+$, *the* ***Cluster Mapping Measure*** *between* $\mathcal{C}$ *and* $\mathcal{CL}^+$ *is defined using the point weight* $w(o)$ *and the overall penalty from Def. 11 as*

$$CMM(\mathcal{C}, \mathcal{CL}) = 1 - \frac{\sum_{o \in \mathcal{F}} w(o) \cdot pen(o, \mathcal{C})}{\sum_{o \in \mathcal{F}} w(o) \cdot con(o, Cl(o))}$$

and if $\mathcal{F} = \emptyset$, *then* $CMM(\mathcal{C}, \mathcal{CL}) = 1$.

5. ANALYSIS & REFINEMENT

In this section we first analyze how CMM handles different fault types caused by evolving streams. In Sec. 5.2 we refine CMM such that it is robust against errors occurring due to the clustering model and that it can measure how well a clustering reflects the ground truth's main concepts. Sec. 5.3 introduces a structure analysis for data sets.

5.1 Missed, Misplaced, and Noise inclusion

In this section we discuss how the penalties differ for the three fault types and why these faults are correctly reflected.

An object $o \in \mathcal{CL}$ is missed if it is unassigned and is not a noise object, i.e. $o \in C_\emptyset \wedge o \notin CL_{noise}$. The set of these objects is called $\mathcal{F}_{missed}$. The connectivity of o to its class $Cl(o)$ gives an idea of how severe it is if an algorithm excludes o from a cluster mapped to $Cl(o)$. More precisely, if o is hardly connected to $Cl(o)$ then the exclusion of o is not as severe as an exclusion of a highly connected object. This is expressed by the first term in the penalty definition. The second term equals to 1 according to Def. 7, i.e.

$$o \in \mathcal{F}_{missed} \Rightarrow pen(o, C_\emptyset) = con(o, Cl(o)) \cdot \underbrace{(1 - con(o, \emptyset))}_{=1}$$

If a noise object o_{noise} is assigned to a cluster C_i, this noise inclusion is considered a fault, and the corresponding set is called $\mathcal{F}_{noise}$. We want to penalize noise inclusion according to the connection between o_{noise} and $map(C_i)$, i.e. if $con(o_{noise}, map(C_i))$ has a high value then we want to assign a low error and vice versa. This is expressed by the second term in the penalty definition, the first term is close to 1 due the random distribution of noise, i.e. $o \in \mathcal{F}_{noise} \Rightarrow$

$$pen(o, C_i) = \underbrace{con(o, Cl_{noise})}_{\approx 1 \text{ for noise}} \cdot (1 - con(o, map(C_i)))$$

For a misplacement error assume an object o from class $Cl(o)$ is assigned to cluster C_i and C_i is mapped to another class, i.e. $map(C_i) \neq Cl(o)$. Misplaced objects are summarized in $\mathcal{F}_{misplaced}$. In this case we want to consider both the connection of o to its true class $Cl(o)$ and its connection to the wrongly assigned class $map(C_i)$. More precisely, a high value for $con(o, Cl(o))$ yields a high error and a low value for $con(o, map(C_i))$ yields a high error as well. The penalty in CMM combines both aspects by multiplication.

A better understanding of clusterings and their evaluation can be achieved by constraining CMM (cf. Def. 12) to one of the subsets $\mathcal{F}_{missed}$, $\mathcal{F}_{noise}$, or $\mathcal{F}_{misplaced}$ (cf. Sec. 6).

5.2 Model error and concept detection

If one wants to evaluate the goodness of a given clustering algorithm, the corresponding approach, i.e. its underlying clustering model, is of importance. For example, given the data sets from Fig. 2 or 3, a spherical clustering algorithm can never reach a perfect result, since even the ground truth clusters contain objects from different classes yielding misplacement errors. How meaningful is a measure that tells you an algorithm has 70% performance if you don't know whether it's model even allows it to perform better?

CMM shall measure how well an algorithm solved the clustering task with respect to its approach. To this end it is checked for each object, whether it causes an error in the corresponding ground truth clusters Cl_j° (cf. Def. 5). If an error occurs also in the ground truth, it is called an error by model and the object is added to the set $\mathcal{F}_{model}$. These errors by model are then excluded in the CMM computation. This way the ground truth always yields a perfect result and so can an algorithm.

Any stream clustering algorithm has to adhere to memory constraints for its internal representation, i.e. the total number of clusters or micro clusters is limited. Due to aging of objects, drifting clusters, and newly emerging clusters the algorithm constantly has to update its representation and decide on the position and size of its clusters. It is more important to reflect the main concepts of the current data distribution rather than spending limited resources to represent some concepts very detailed and missing other concepts in exchange. In other words, for two given clusterings with equally many missed objects, the one that better covers the concepts is preferable (cf. Fig. 4). To operationalize this aspect we decrease the penalty for missed points with respect to the severity of the fault. Formally, we redefine the overall penalty for this fault type. For an object $o \in \mathcal{F}_{missed}$ we test for all clusters C_i with $map(C_i) = Cl(o)$ the relative distance of o to the cluster boundary of C_i, i.e. $o \in \mathcal{F}_{missed} \Rightarrow$

$$pen(o, \mathcal{C}) = con(o, Cl(o)) \cdot \max_{\substack{C_i \in \mathcal{C} \\ map(C_i) = Cl(o)}} \{1 - e^{-\frac{minDist(o, C_i)}{maxDist(o, C_i)}}\}$$

The second term simplifies to $1 - e^{-\frac{d-r}{d+r}}$ for spherical clusters, where d is the distance of o to C_i's center and r its radius.

Figure 4: The concept is better recognized on the left.

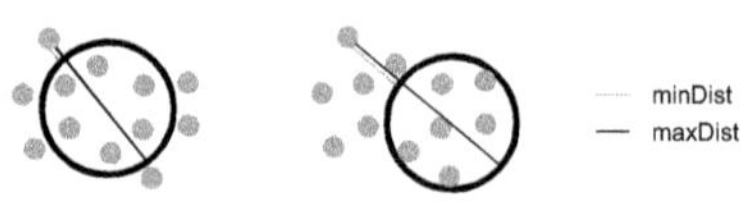

5.3 Structure analysis

To analyze the structure of a given data set, we define the connectivity between two classes, which is based on the same concept as Def. 7. Intuitively, the connection from class Cl_i to class Cl_j is high, if several points that have a strong connection within Cl_i show a strong connection to Cl_j at the same time. The definition below uses the same locality parameter k as Def. 6.

DEFINITION 13. ***Class connectivity.*** *For a locality parameter k the connectivity from class Cl_i to class Cl_j is*

$$con_{Cl_i \to Cl_j} = \max_{\substack{KM \subseteq Cl_i \\ |KM| = k}} \left\{ \frac{1}{k} \sum_{p \in KM} con(p, Cl_i) \cdot con(p, Cl_j) \right\}.$$

The symmetric connectivity between two classes is then $con(Cl_i, Cl_j) = \min\{con_{Cl_i \to Cl_j}, con_{Cl_j \to Cl_i}\}$

The above definition considers the k points within Cl_i that maximize the product of connectivity to both classes. The blue objects in Fig. 2 illustrate the connectivity between the two classes gray and black. In both cases the two classes are not strongly connected.

If two ground truth classes have a strong connectivity, the two classes are difficult to separate from each other. To avoid misplacement penalties between such classes, we merge classes who's connectivity according to Def. 13 exceeds a threshold τ and assign their points the same label. Analyzing the structure of a given ground truth $\mathcal{CL} = \{Cl_1, \ldots, Cl_l\}$ hence yields a reduced set of classes $\mathcal{CL}' = \{Cl'_1, \ldots, Cl'_h\}$ with $h \leq l$. As an indicator of how well the classes in a given ground truth $\mathcal{CL}^+$ are separable we define:

$$Separability(\mathcal{CL}^+) = h/l$$

In Fig. 5 we demonstrate for different horizons how the Separability is influenced by different τ values.

Figure 5: Evaluation of different τ values.

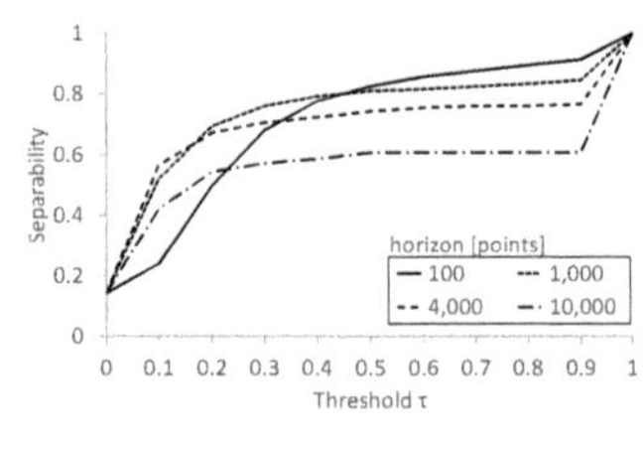

For the structure analysis in the experiments in Sec. 6, we use $\tau = 0.5$. To complete the structure analysis we define a second indicator, counting the percentage of objects represented redundantly, i.e. covered by several ground truth clusters Cl_i°:

$$Red(\mathcal{CL}^+) = |\{o \in \mathcal{O}^+ | o \in Cl_i^\circ \wedge o \in Cl_j^\circ \wedge i \neq j\}| / |\mathcal{O}^+|$$

This indicator allows for a more in depth analysis of the different measures' behavior in the empirical evaluation.

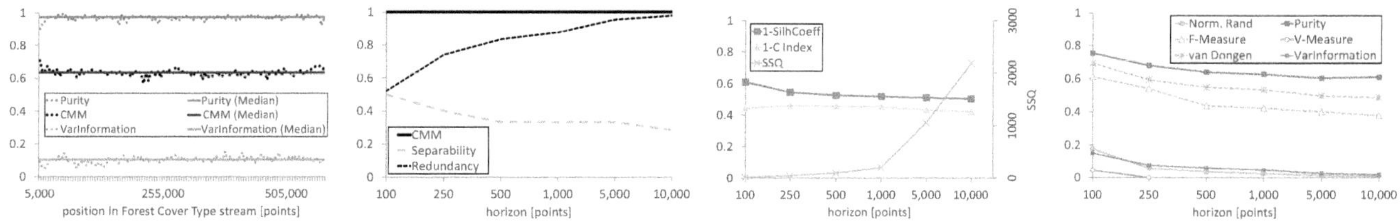

(a) CluStream clustering (b) CMM & structure analysis (c) internal measures (d) external measures

Figure 6: 10-dim. *Forest Cover Type* stream: (a): Illustration of the individual evaluations for a real stream clustering and the resulting medians. (b-d): Varying horizon on ground truth clusterings.

6. EXPERIMENTS

We evaluate CMM in comparison to evaluation measures introduced in Sec. 2. For repeatability, we integrated CMM into MOA (cf. Sec. 7). First of all, we describe our evaluation framework.

Stream generator. The generator's output is a stream of data points that have class labels and weights reflecting a point's age, depending on the used horizon. Since clusters move, a larger horizon yields more tail-like clusters; a small horizon yields more sphere-like clusters. Technically, the data points are obtained by generating clusters, which have a center and a maximal radius and which move through a unit cube ($[0,1]^d$) into a random direction. At the cube boundaries, the clusters bounce off. At specific intervals all cluster centers are shifted by 0.01 in their corresponding direction and points are equally drawn from each generating cluster. On average, the number of points in each cluster is equal. Our stream generator has the following parameters: the number of clusters moving through the dataspace, the number of generated points, the shift interval, the cluster radius, the dimensionality, and the noise degree.

Real world data streams. We use the 10 continuous attributes of *Forest Cover Type*[1], consisting of 581,012 objects and 7 classes, and we use the 34 continuous attributes of *Network Intrusion*[2], consisting of 4,898,431 objects and 5 classes. This variant was also used in [1, 8].

Cluster generator. We evaluate measures in specific clustering error scenarios, which are obtained by generating clusterings out of the synthetic stream that reflect a desired error level. We create cluster join, radius decrease, and cluster remove errors and the cluster boundaries are determined by a technique from [13]. The cluster join error simulates that two classes are covered by a single cluster by joining pairs of nearby, non-overlapping clusters; e.g., an error level of 0.4 indicates that all pairwise clusters are joint whose minimal boundary distance is below 40% of the minimum of their cluster radii. By this, we achieve a more realistic scenario without joining of far apart clusters. The radius decrease error states that the generated clusters have a radius that is smaller than the radius of the corresponding ground truth cluster. An error level of 1 states that the radius of the error cluster is 0; for an error level of 0 the two radii are equal. The cluster remove error denotes how many clusters are missed by a clustering; for an error level of 0.4, 40% of the clusters are removed from the error-free clustering.

Setup. We compare CMM and its variants (cf. Sec. 5.1) with internal and external measures from the literature (cf. Sec. 2). In selected experiments, we provide the structural measures Separability and Redundancy (cf. Sec. 5.3). All measures, besides the Sum of Squared distances (SSQ), are normalized to $[0, 1]$. For some measures the best value corresponds to 0; we reverse them and indicate this by "1-" in the plots. The values of SSQ are plotted on a secondary y-axis. By using clusterings from the cluster generator, we ensure an evaluation unbiased by possible incorrect outcomes of stream clustering algorithms. Moreover, we evaluate real clusterings of CluStream [1] and DenStream [8] using CMM. The CMM parameter k was preliminary fixed to 2; the choice of k only has marginal influence on CMM effectiveness, as we will later illustrate. Synthetic data is generated with the following settings: the dimensionality is 2, the number of points is $200,000$, the cluster number is 6, the cluster radius is 0.075, the shift interval is 100 points, and noise is equally distributed and fixed at 10%.

The horizon is defined by the number of included points, i.e. $h = |\mathcal{H}|$, and the evaluation frequency is the horizon. The values in all plots are the medians over all evaluations of the analyzed stream, as illustrated in Fig. 6(a) for three measures on CluStream clusterings of Forest Cover Type.

Varying horizon on real data. Fig. 6 shows experiments where we analyze the robustness of the measures under a varying horizon. We use error-free Forest Cover Type clusterings, i.e. the ground truth. By a varying horizon this ground truth changes; with greater horizons the cluster tails become longer, increasing the probability of overlapping clusters. This is confirmed by the two structural measures in Fig. 6(b): Redundancy rises while Separability (of clusters) drops. The comparison of CMM with the competing measures shows a clear picture: CMM (in Fig. 6(b)) achieves perfect quality that is stable over all settings. In contrast, both internal (Fig. 6(c)) and external measures (Fig. 6(d)) degrade with increasing horizons, showing that they cannot cope with higher redundancy and the worsened separability that occurs with larger horizons. More surprisingly, however, is that they also deliver low qualities for small horizons, indicating their general inability to express that the analyzed clusterings are error-free.

Error level. We analyze how good the measures can reflect the errors in generated clusterings.

We start with the internal measures in Fig. 7, where each graph corresponds to one error type. Comparing an external measure like CMM with internal measures is inherently unfair; however, since internal measures are often used in practice, we think a general overview of their performance in error scenarios is of interest. From the three plots, we can conclude the following: The C Index shows nearly no reaction; only extreme cases ($error \to 1$) for radius decrease and cluster remove errors are indicated through quality drops. The Silhouette Coefficient reflects the cluster join error, but can-

[1]http://archive.ics.uci.edu/ml/datasets/Covertype
[2]http://kdd.ics.uci.edu/databases/kddcup99/kddcup99.html

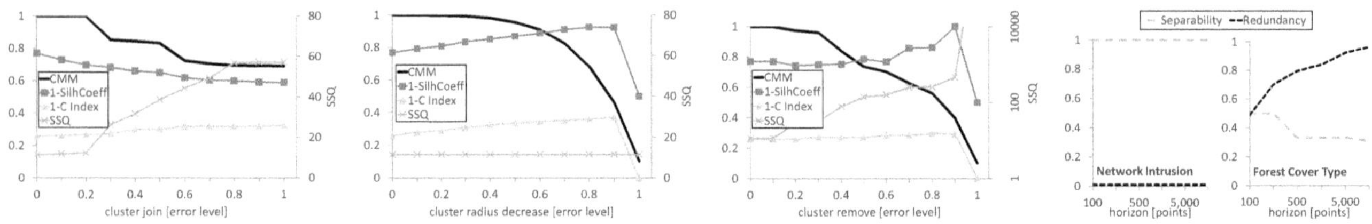

(a) Cluster Join Error (b) Radius Decrease Error (c) Cluster Remove Error (d) Structure analysis

Figure 7: (a-c): CMM & internal measures under different error types with $h = 5,000$; (d): Structure analysis.

not reflect the other errors, where the corresponding values even rise. The SSQ, which is used in many stream clustering publications [1, 9], shows a good reaction on the cluster join and the cluster remove error; however, if we look at the corresponding maximal values (60 and 10,000) a practical use is questionable due to its unnormalized nature. CMM shows a very good performance on all scenarios, and a deeper analysis will be included in the next paragraph.

In Fig. 9 we compare CMM with the external measures using horizons of 5,000 and 10,000. We start with cluster join errors. Note that due to the technique used for creating this error (only nearby clusters are joined), the error level 1 does not indicate that all clusters are joined into a single cluster. Fig. 9(a) and 9(b) show that CMM reflects this error well, i.e. with an increasing number of joined clusters the quality constantly drops. We expect this to be caused by misplaced points, i.e. points that are assigned to wrong clusters, which is confirmed by $\text{CMM}_{misplaced}$. CMM_{noise} illustrates that when clusters are joined the resulting clusters tend to absorb noise points due to their larger sizes. The external measures in Fig. 9(c) also reflect the errors. However, a general problem of these measures are error-free settings (error=0) in which they show lower qualities (0.8-0.6). We suspect this to be caused by cluster overlap and it worsens with a larger horizon, as illustrated in Fig. 9(d). Considering that these measures are normalized to $[0, 1]$, this is a severe problem. In contrast, CMM shows maximal quality in error-free settings for both horizons and this also holds for the other error types in Fig. 9. The cluster radius decrease error is analyzed for CMM in Fig. 9(e) and 9(f). This error mostly results in missed points, which is shown by CMM_{missed} and thus by CMM. Here we also demonstrate the influence of the CMM refinement that better measures how well the main concepts of the data are reflected by a clustering (cf. Sec. 5.2). The figure shows that at lower error levels, CMM does not decrease as rapidly as the variants without refinement (green lines). This is intended, since the main concepts of the data are well represented at this stage and only close points are missed. From the six measures in Fig. 9(g), four can basically reflect the error; however, for lower error levels (≤ 0.4) three of the measures go up and the negative effects of larger horizons on all competing measures are again obvious in Fig. 9(h). Especially the bad performance of Purity is mentionable, a measure which is the main evaluation method in many stream clustering publications [8, 19]. The cluster remove error is analyzed in Fig. 9(i)-9(l). This error corresponds to removal of complete clusters and thus concepts; accordingly and in contrast to the radius decrease error this loss of concepts should be reflected by a constant decrease of the measured quality. This is achieved by CMM. A comparison to its variant without refinement shows that for this error type the refinement has no undesired effects; this refinement only affects the measurement of radius decrease errors. The external measures show a similar behavior as for the radius decrease error: only three reflect the error at all and their expressiveness strongly decreases for larger horizons.

Summarized, CMM can precisely reflect all errors. Most of the internal measures cannot reflect the errors at all, while some of the external measures reflect the errors but have serious problems in settings without errors or larger horizons.

CMM locality parameter k. In Fig. 8 we analyze the influence of k (cf. Sec. 4.1). We simulate a more realistic evaluation scenario by using synthetic clusterings with embedded errors (error level=0.5). For each error type, we tried 10 different ks ($k \in \{1, .., 10\}$) with 4 different horizons. On the left we plot the standard deviation of the CMM results w.r.t. the choice of k: CMM values for two of the error types are influenced by k for very small horizons; however, considering the value range of the CMM and the small standard deviations (< 0.009), these effects are negligible. This is also illustrated on the right, where we plot the exact CMM values with a horizon of $10,000$ for the individual ks on the range $[0.8, 0.98]$. Both figures show that k has only marginal influence for very small horizons and does not affect CMM for larger horizons.

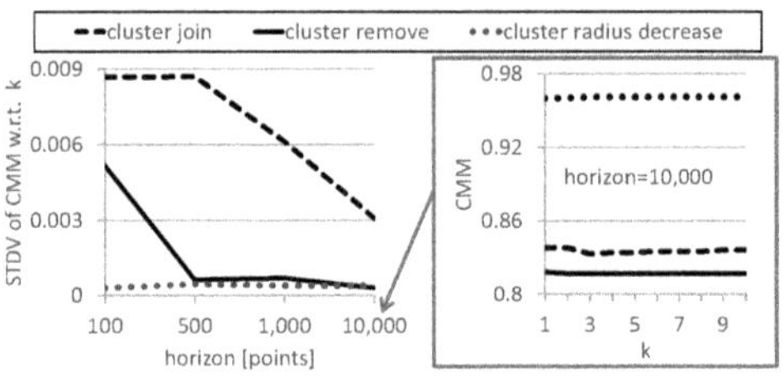

Figure 8: Marginal effects (std. deviation < 0.009) of varying k.

Real data and stream clustering algorithms. Finally, we analyze the measures in real application scenarios, in which real world data streams are clustered by actual stream clustering algorithms, as in this case CluStream [1] and DenStream [8]. In Fig. 10, we distinguish between macro clusterings, i.e. the output of the algorithms, and micro clusterings, i.e. the underlying internal representations constantly adapted by the algorithms. The macro clusterings are produced from the micro clusterings by an offline component. Comparability is ensured by using CluStream's offline component in CluStream and DenStream. We apply an horizon of 1,000. A structure analysis of the real world streams is shown in Fig. 7(d): Forest Cover Type has high redundancy and low separability; Network Intrusion has no redundancy and high separability, making the clusters easier to find.

We start with Network Intrusion. The results obtained by DenStream for the macro clustering in Fig 10(a) confirm

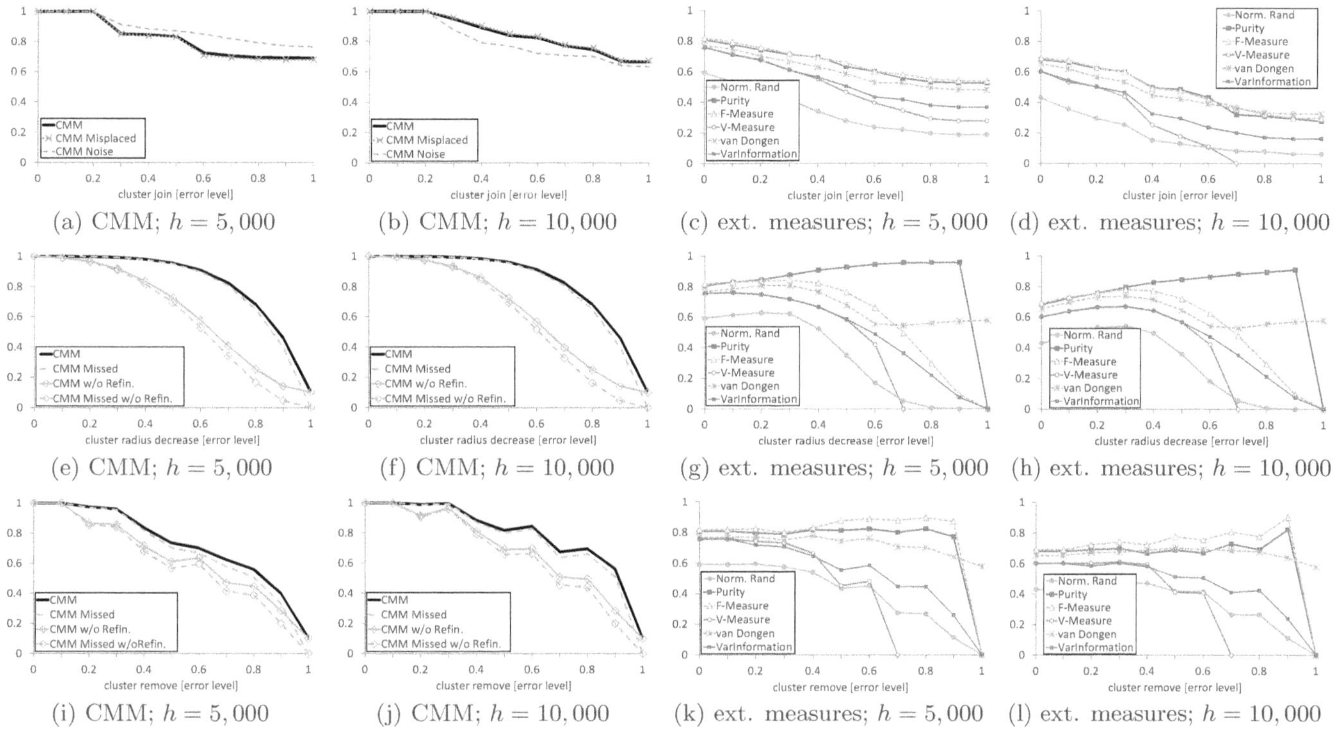

(a) CMM; $h = 5,000$ (b) CMM; $h = 10,000$ (c) ext. measures; $h = 5,000$ (d) ext. measures; $h = 10,000$

(e) CMM; $h = 5,000$ (f) CMM; $h = 10,000$ (g) ext. measures; $h = 5,000$ (h) ext. measures; $h = 10,000$

(i) CMM; $h = 5,000$ (j) CMM; $h = 10,000$ (k) ext. measures; $h = 5,000$ (l) ext. measures; $h = 10,000$

Figure 9: Evaluating CMM and external measures under different error types.

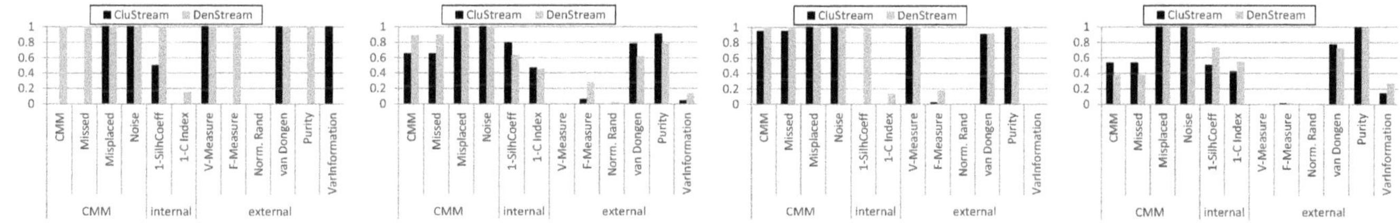

(a) Macro clusterings of *Network Intrusion* data. (b) Macro clusterings of *Forest Cover Type* data. (c) Micro clusterings of *Network Intrusion* data. (d) Micro clusterings of *Forest Cover Type* data.

Figure 10: Evaluation of *CluStream* and *DenStream* on real world data streams.

the conclusions from the structural analysis: nearly all evaluation measures indicate that high quality clusterings are generated. For CluStream, however, we can make a surprising conclusion. CMM and most of the other measures indicate that the found clusterings are of low quality. This is mostly caused by missed points, as CMM_{Missed} shows. In contrast, the evaluation of micro clusterings used by CluStream in Fig. 10(c) shows another picture: the micro clusterings are of high quality. We can conclude that CluStream correctly identifies the concepts in the data, but the used offline method that generates the macro clusters from the micro clusters is ineffective for this data type.

For Forest Cover Type in Fig. 10(b) and 10(d), we can conclude by CMM_{Missed} that DenStream covers nearly all of the concepts in the macro clusterings. CluStream, however, seems to miss more concepts of the data. For this dataset, the macro clusterings of both CluStream and DenStream are of higher quality than the micro clusterings.

Summarized, CMM is an effective measure for evaluation on real data streams and clusterings generated by stream clustering algorithms, and its variants help in understanding why an analyzed clustering is of a specific quality.

7. CONCLUSION

Evaluation of clustering results on static data sets received a lot of research attention for several decades. Many recent publications deal with the important task of clustering on evolving data streams. However, despite the amount of work on evaluation measures and on stream clustering algorithms, no effort has been made to meet the requirements of both tasks. In this paper we proposed a novel and effective evaluation measure for clustering on evolving data streams called CMM. It is the first measure that takes the important properties of the streaming context into account. It is based on a novel mapping component that can handle emerging and disappearing clusters correctly. We included CMM into the open source MOA framework [29] and showed in extensive experiments on real and synthetic data that it is a robust measure precisely reflecting errors in data stream scenarios.

Acknowledgments. This work has been supported by the UMIC Research Centre, RWTH Aachen University, Germany. Special thanks go to Marc Wichterich for his valuable comments and thorough reviewing of the paper.

8. REFERENCES

[1] C. C. Aggarwal, J. Han, J. Wang, and P. S. Yu. A framework for clustering evolving data streams. In *VLDB*, pages 81–92, 2003.

[2] F. B. Baker and L. J. Hubert. Measuring the power of hierarchical cluster analysis. *Journal of the American Statistical Association (JASA)*, 70(349):31–38, 1975.

[3] D. Barbará and P. Chen. Using the fractal dimension to cluster datasets. In *ACM SIGKDD*, pages 260–264, 2000.

[4] A. Bifet, G. Holmes, B. Pfahringer, R. Kirkby, and R. Gavaldà. New ensemble methods for evolving data streams. In *ACM SIGKDD*, pages 139–148, 2009.

[5] A. Bifet, G. Holmes, B. Pfahringer, P. Kranen, H. Kremer, T. Jansen, and T. Seidl. MOA: Massive online analysis, a framework for stream classification and clustering. In *JMLR*, 2010.

[6] M. Bouguessa, S. Wang, and H. Sun. An objective approach to cluster validation. *Pattern Recognition Letters*, 27(13):1419–1430, 2006.

[7] M. Brun, C. Sima, J. Hua, J. Lowey, B. Carroll, E. Suh, and E. R. Dougherty. Model-based evaluation of clustering validation measures. *Pattern Recognition*, 40(3):807–824, 2007.

[8] F. Cao, M. Ester, W. Qian, and A. Zhou. Density-based clustering over an evolving data stream with noise. In *SIAM SDM*, pages 328–339, 2006.

[9] Y. Chen and L. Tu. Density-based clustering for real-time stream data. In *ACM SIGKDD*, pages 133–142, 2007.

[10] T. Cover and J. Thomas. *Elements of Information Theory (2nd Edition)*. Wiley-Interscience, 2006.

[11] J. Dunn. Well separated clusters and optimal fuzzy partitions. *Journal of Cybernetics*, 4:95–104, 1974.

[12] E. Folkes and C. Mallows. A method for comparing two hierarchical clusterings. *JASA*, 78:553–569, 1983.

[13] B. Gartner. Fast and robust smallest enclosing balls. In *ESA*, pages 325–338. Springer, 1999.

[14] M. Halkidi and M. Vazirgiannis. A density-based cluster validity approach using multi-representatives. *Pattern Recognition Letters*, 29(6):773–786, 2008.

[15] J. Han and M. Kamber. *Data Mining: Concepts and Techniques*. Morgan Kaufmann, 2001.

[16] J. A. Hartigan. *Clustering Algorithms*. Wiley, 1975.

[17] L. Hubert and P. Arabie. Comparing partitions. *Journal of Classification*, 2:193–218, 1985.

[18] L. J. Hubert and J. R. Levin. A general statistical framework for assessing categorical clustering in free recall. *Psychological Bulletin*, 83(6):1072–1080, 1976.

[19] A. Jain, Z. Zhang, and E. Y. Chang. Adaptive non-linear clustering in data streams. In *ACM CIKM*, pages 122–131, 2006.

[20] A. K. Jain and R. C. Dubes. *Algorithms for Clustering Data*. Prentice-Hall, 1988.

[21] A. K. Jain, M. N. Murty, and P. J. Flynn. Data clustering: A review. *ACM CS*, 31(3):264–323, 1999.

[22] L. Kaufmann and P. Rousseeuw. *Finding Groups in Data: an Introduct. to Cluster Analysis*. Wiley, 1990.

[23] P. Kranen, I. Assent, C. Baldauf, and T. Seidl. Self-adaptive anytime stream clustering. In *IEEE ICDM*, pages 249–258, 2009.

[24] P. Kranen, H. Kremer, T. Jansen, T. Seidl, A. Bifet, G. Holmes, and B. Pfahringer. Clustering performance on evolving data streams: Assessing algorithms and evaluation measures within MOA. In *IEEE ICDMW*, pages 1400–1403, 2010.

[25] Y. Liu, Z. Li, H. Xiong, X. Gao, and J. Wu. Understanding of internal clustering validation measures. In *IEEE ICDM*, pages 911–916, 2010.

[26] M. Meila. Comparing clusterings: an axiomatic view. In *ICML*, pages 577–584, 2005.

[27] G. W. Milligan. An examination of the effect of six types of error perturbation on fifteen clustering algorithms. *Psychometrika*, 45(3):325–342, 1980.

[28] G. W. Milligan. A monte carlo study of thirty internal criterion measures for cluster analysis. *Psychometrika*, 46(2):187–199, 1981.

[29] MOA project. http://moa.cs.waikato.ac.nz.

[30] S. G. Mojaveri, E. Mirzaeian, Z. Bornaee, and S. Ayat. New approach in data stream association rule mining based on graph structure. In *IEEE ICDM*, pages 158–164, 2010.

[31] L. O'Callaghan, A. Meyerson, R. Motwani, N. Mishra, and S. Guha. Streaming-data algorithms for high-quality clustering. In *ICDE*, pages 685–694, 2002.

[32] W. Rand. Objective criteria for the evaluation of clustering methods. *JASA*, 66:846–850, 1971.

[33] C. Rijsbergen. *Information Retrieval (2nd Edition)*. Butterworths, London, 1979.

[34] F. J. Rohlf. Methods for comparing classifications. *Annual Review of Ecology and Sys.*, 5:101–113, 1974.

[35] A. Rosenberg and J. Hirschberg. V-measure: A conditional entropy-based external cluster evaluation measure. In *EMNLP-CoNLL*, pages 410–420, 2007.

[36] V. Roth, M. L. Braun, T. Lange, and J. M. Buhmann. Stability-based model order selection in clustering with applications to gene expression data. In *ICANN*, pages 633–640. Springer, 2002.

[37] S. Saitta, B. Raphael, and I. F. C. Smith. A comprehensive validity index for clustering. *Intell. Data Anal. (IDA)*, 12(6):529–548, 2008.

[38] M. J. Song and L. Zhang. Comparison of cluster representations from partial second- to full fourth-order cross moments for data stream clustering. In *IEEE ICDM*, pages 560–569, 2008.

[39] S. Van Dongen. Performance criteria for graph clustering and markov cluster experiments. *Report-Information systems*, (12):1–36, 2000.

[40] L. Wang, U. T. V. Nguyen, J. C. Bezdek, C. Leckie, and K. Ramamohanarao. iVAT and aVAT: Enhanced visual analysis for cluster tendency assessment. In *PAKDD (1)*, pages 16–27. Springer, 2010.

[41] J. Wu, H. Xiong, and J. Chen. Adapting the right measures for k-means clustering. In *ACM SIGKDD*, pages 877–886, 2009.

[42] K. Y. Yeung, D. R. Haynor, and W. L. Ruzzo. Validating clustering for gene expression data. *Bioinformatics*, 17(4):309–318, 2001.

[43] Y. Zhao and G. Karypis. Empirical and theoretical comparisons of selected criterion functions for document clustering. *ML*, 55(3):311–331, 2004.

An Iterated Graph Laplacian Approach for Ranking on Manifolds

Xueyuan Zhou
Department of Computer Science
University of Chicago
Chicago, IL
zhouxy@cs.uchicago.edu

Mikhail Belkin
Department of Computer Science and Engineering
The Ohio State University
Columbus, OH
mbelkin@cse.ohio-state.edu

Nathan Srebro
Toyota Technological Institute at Chicago
Chicago, IL
nati@uchicago.edu

ABSTRACT

Ranking is one of the key problems in information retrieval. Recently, there has been significant interest in a class of ranking algorithms based on the assumption that data is sampled from a low dimensional manifold embedded in a higher dimensional Euclidean space.

In this paper, we study a popular graph Laplacian based ranking algorithm [23] using an analytical method, which provides theoretical insights into the ranking algorithm going beyond the intuitive idea of "diffusion." Our analysis shows that the algorithm is sensitive to a commonly used parameter due to the use of symmetric normalized graph Laplacian. We also show that the ranking function may diverge to infinity at the query point in the limit of infinite samples. To address these issues, we propose an improved ranking algorithm on manifolds using Green's function of an iterated unnormalized graph Laplacian, which is more robust and density adaptive, as well as pointwise continuous in the limit of infinite samples.

We also for the first time in the ranking literature empirically explore two variants from a family of twice normalized graph Laplacians. Experimental results on text and image data support our analysis, which also suggest the potential value of twice normalized graph Laplacians in practice.

Categories and Subject Descriptors

H.3.3 [**INFORMATION STORAGE AND RETRIEV**]: Information Search and Retrieval—*Retrieval models*

General Terms

Theory

Keywords

Iterated graph Laplacian, Green's function

1. INTRODUCTION

Information retrieval is becoming progressively more important with the fast growing amounts of digital data, and as Internet search engines become necessary tools for finding useful information among huge amounts of data on the Web. In retrieval, ranking is a key step to provide a "relevance" score for the search results so that the most "relevant" results are presented to users first.

In recent years, the graph Laplacian has become an important object in manifold related machine learning and data mining [5, 26, 1, 23]. The ranking on manifolds algorithm in [23] estimates a real-valued function on the whole data set by "diffusion" based on a graph Laplacian, which can be used as a density adaptive ranking score for all data points. One key advantage of this family of graph Laplacian based ranking algorithms is that they are density adaptive, combining local information encoded in the local neighborhood graph and global information from the graph Laplacian into a final ranking function.

Given the success of Laplacian based methods in machine learning and data mining, there is still relatively little analytical analysis of these algorithms. One example is [13], which contains a surprising finding for a family of popular graph Laplacian based semi-supervised learning methods. It turns out that when labeled data is fixed and unlabeled data increases, the estimator on unlabeled points degenerates to a constant. The essential cause of this degenerate behavior is that the solution space is too rich, which leads to overfitting. See [24] for more discussions and a solution based on iterated Laplacians.

The semi-supervised problem setting is related to the ranking problem in [23], which motivates the analysis of these algorithms from a functional analysis point of view to obtain new theoretical insights going beyond the intuitive "diffusion" analogy. For instance, we can ask the following questions about ranking: what is the ranking function space? what are its properties? and, what should the ranking function be in the limit of infinite data? These questions are not just basic theoretical foundations of ranking, but are also crucial to the applications of ranking algorithms in practice.

In this paper, we try to answer these questions. Our contributions are as follows: first, we study a graph Laplacian based ranking on manifolds algorithm [23] from a functional analysis point of view. We show that the algorithm is sensitive to a commonly used parameter due to its use of the symmetric normalized graph Laplacian. This is not the case when the unnormalized graph Laplacian is used. This observation is different from the case of spectral clustering considered in [21], where the normalized graph Laplacian turns out to have better theoretical properties.

We also show that the ranking function diverges to infinity at the query point in the limit of infinite samples in higher dimensions. A close relation between the Green's function and the reproducing kernel based on the graph Laplacians is discussed, which connects the graph Laplacian based ranking algorithms to kernel methods.

Second, we propose an approach based on the iterated graph Laplacian, using unnormalized graph Laplacians. Compared to the existing method [23], our method has several preferable properties: it is more robust, more density adaptive, and behaves well as the amount of unlabeled data increases.

Finally, we test two interesting variants from a family of twice normalized graph Laplacians, which also give competitive results on ranking and suggest their potential values in practice. To the best of our knowledge, this is the first time they are used in ranking.

We review the graph Laplacian in section (2), including the finite sample case and their continuous limits. Then in section (3), we study an existing graph Laplacian based ranking on manifolds algorithm [23]. Based on the analysis, we suggest using an iterated unnormalized graph Laplacian for ranking in section (4). We provide experimental results on text and image benchmarks.

1.1 Problem Setup

Given a random sample set $X = \{x_1, x_2, \cdots, x_n\}$, where x_i is a random vector, drawn i.i.d. from a fixed unknown smooth probability distribution $p(x)$ $(0 < a \leqslant p(x) \leqslant b < +\infty)$. We assume the density is supported on Ω, which is either a compact subset of $\mathbb{R}^d$ or a d-dimensional Riemannian submanifold of $\mathbb{R}^N$. The problem of ranking considered in this paper is to find a ranking score function $f(x) : x \mapsto \mathbb{R}$, providing a "similarity" measure between the query point x_i and all other points $x_j \in X/\{x_i\}$, such that the smaller the value $|f(x_i) - f(x_j)|$ is, the more similar x_i and x_j are. Let the initial query be x_1, and the ranking function value at x_1, i.e., $f(x_1)$ be known, which is typically set as $f(x_1) = +1$. The analysis in this paper also applies to multiple query points. By a convenient abuse of notation, $f(x)$ means both the continuous function value at x in the limit of infinite points and the xth element of the column vector f such that $f_x = f(x)$ in the case of finite X.

2. GRAPH LAPLACIAN

In this section, we review two graph Laplacians that will be used later, including both their discrete forms and their continuous limits.

2.1 Graph Laplacians

Given the sample set X, we can build an undirected weighted graph $G(V, E)$ such that x_i is mapped to the vertex v_i, and the edge weight $w(e_{ij}) = w_{ij}$ is a similarity measure between x_i and x_j. In this paper, we use a symmetric k nearest neighbor (k-NN) graph [12] as $G(V, E)$. A common weight function is

$$w_{ij} = K\left(\frac{\|x_i - x_j\|^2}{t}\right) = e^{-\frac{\|x_i - x_j\|^2}{t}} \quad (1)$$

Denote the connection weight matrix on graph G as W, and let D be a diagonal matrix with $D_{ii} = D(x_i) = \sum_j w_{ij}$. There are several ways of defining a graph Laplacian [20]. We first introduce the unnormalized and symmetric normalized graph Laplacians L_u and L_s, which are closed related to the ranking algorithm we will study. Other interesting graph Laplacians will be introduced later in section (4.2).

$$\begin{aligned} L_u = &\quad D - W \\ L_s = &\quad D^{-1/2} L_u D^{-1/2} = I - D^{-1/2} W D^{-1/2} \end{aligned} \quad (2)$$

Both L_u and L_s are real symmetric and semi-definite matrices. We order the eigenvalues of all graph Laplacians in this paper in an increasing order $\lambda_1 \leqslant \lambda_2 \leqslant \cdots \leqslant \lambda_n$. For L_u and L_s, the smallest eigenvalues are both zero. This means L_u and L_s are not full rank. From norm point of view, it means $f^T L_u f$ and $f^T L_s f$ are semi-norms with null spaces spanned by their first eigenvectors. The first eigenvector of L_u is constant,

$$v_1 = \left(\frac{1}{\sqrt{n}}, \frac{1}{\sqrt{n}}, \cdots, \frac{1}{\sqrt{n}}\right)^T \quad (3)$$

while for L_s, a non-constant vector

$$v_1 = \left(\sqrt{D(x_1)}, \sqrt{D(x_2)}, \cdots, \sqrt{D(x_n)}\right)^T \quad (4)$$

where $D(x_i)$ is the degree for vertex x_i in graph G.

2.2 Limits of Graph Laplacians

As we obtain more sample points, the parameter t needs to be decreased in order to let the graph Laplacian to better capture local information. Therefore, the limit analysis of a graph Laplacian involves two limits, the number of data points, $n \to \infty$, and the kernel width, $t \to 0$. See [3, 7, 11] for more on limit analysis of graph Laplacians. On finite sample set X,

$$\frac{1}{n} L_u f(x_i) = \frac{1}{n} \sum_{j=1}^{n} K\left(\frac{\|x_i - x_j\|^2}{t}\right)(f(x_i) - f(x_j)) \quad (5)$$

where $f(x_i)$ is the ith element of vector f.

In the limit as $n \to \infty$ and $t \to 0$ at a proper rate (see [3, 11]), for a smooth function $f(x) \in C^2$, the limit of $L_u f(x)$ is

$$\frac{1}{nt^{d/2+1}} L_u f(x) \xrightarrow{\text{a.s.}} -p(x)\Delta_{p^2} f(x) \quad (6)$$

where $\Delta_{p^2} f(x) = \frac{1}{p^2(x)} \text{div}[p^2(x) \text{grad} f(x)]$ is called the *weighted Laplacian*, see e.g., [9]. In the limit, the degree function $D(x)$ converges to the underlying density $p(x)$ up to a constant coefficient, see e.g., [10, Chapter 2].

However, the limit of L_s is not a weighted Laplacian of $f(x)$, as shown in [11]

$$\frac{1}{t^{d/2+1}} L_s f(x) \xrightarrow{\text{a.s.}} -\sqrt{p(x)}\Delta_{p^2}[\frac{f(x)}{\sqrt{p(x)}}] \quad (7)$$

where $1/n$ is canceled by the normalization. This means if we use L_s as an empirical Laplacian in an algorithm, it is not a strictly "diffusion" based algorithm. If we let $F(x) = f(x)/\sqrt{D(x)}$, then the limit is a weighted Laplacian for function $F(x)$, but not $f(x)$. We will see later in section (3.2), this delicate detail has a great influence on ranking.

From the finite sample and infinite limit analyses of the graph Laplacians, it is easy to see that the null space of L_u is spanned by a constant vector, and in the limit it is spanned by a constant function. While for L_s, the difference is a weight: the null space is spanned by vector $\sqrt{D(x)}$ as in equation (4) in discrete case, and by function $\sqrt{p(x)}$ in the continuous limit. See [2] for the convergence of graph Laplacian eigenvectors to weighted Laplacian eigenfunctions.

3. ANALYSIS OF RANKING ON MANIFOLDS

In [23], the authors proposed a ranking function (column vector) as

$$f = (I - \alpha S)^{-1} y \tag{8}$$

where y is a column vector with the query element y_1 set as 1, and 0 on all other points, $S = D^{-1/2} W D^{-1/2}$, I is an identity matrix, and $\alpha \in [0, 1)$ is a tuning parameter. This algorithm is based on the intuition of "information diffusion." The idea is to propagate the query "information" along the data manifold in a density adaptive way.

Next, we show that it can be rewritten using the symmetric normalized graph Laplacian L_s. By splitting the identity matrix into $(1-\alpha)I + \alpha I$, we can rewrite f as

$$f = \alpha \left[(\frac{1-\alpha}{\alpha}) I + L_s \right]^{-1} y = \alpha(\beta I + L_s)^{-1} y \tag{9}$$

where $\beta = \frac{1-\alpha}{\alpha} > 0$. In ranking, we can drop the global constant α without changing the result. Then the ranking function is equivalent to $f = (\beta I + L_s)^{-1} y$.

A closer look at this problem can reveal that it is also the solution of two other equivalent problems (up to constant coefficients): a discrete Laplace equation and a discrete potential energy minimization problem. See [23] for more details, and see [16] for more on boundary value problems. Next, we further study the ranking function $(\beta I + L_s)^{-1} y$.

3.1 Green's Function and Reproducing Kernel in Ranking

Consider the ranking function $(\beta I + L_s)^{-1} y$. Since only one element of y is nonzero, the ranking function f (column vector) is, in fact, the first column of matrix $(\beta I + L_s)^{-1}$, i.e., the column corresponding to the query point. Thus, this inverse matrix is the key object for the ranking problem.

Reproducing Kernel of Reproducing Kernel Hilbert Space: The function space equipped with a (semi-)norm of the form $f^T Q f$ with a (semi-)definite matrix Q is a reproducing kernel Hilbert space (RKHS)[1], and its reproducing kernel matrix is the pseudoinverse of Q, denoted as Q^+, see e.g., [4, Chapter 6] and [17]. Let $Q = (\beta I + L_s)$, which is positive definite since $\beta > 0$, and its inverse exists. Ranking function f then is just a kernel function centered at query point x_1, i.e., $f(x) = K(x_1, x)$, where $K = (\beta I + L_s)^{-1}$ is the reproducing kernel matrix. We denote $K(x, y)$ as the (x, y) element of the matrix K in discrete case.

The additional term βI is used to complete the semi-norm $f^T L_s f$ to a norm, since L_s is not full rank. If we remove βI ($\beta = 0$), and use the pseudoinverse of L_s, we can still obtain a ranking function f as a kernel function, but it is in the subspace that is orthogonal to the first eigenvector of L_s.

The Green's Function: We know the Green's function of a Laplace operator can be seen as the inverse of a Laplacian, which implies $G_s = (\beta I + L_s)^{-1}$. See [6] for more on discrete Green's function on graphs. By eigenvector expansion we have

$$G_s(x, y) = \sum_{k=1}^{n} \frac{1}{\lambda_k + \beta} v_k(x) v_k(y) = K(x, y) \tag{10}$$

where λ_k is the kth eigenvalue of L_s and v_k is the associated eigenvector. This is the same as kernel function $K(x, y)$ since $K = (\beta I + L_s)^{-1}$. Notice that if we restrict the graph Laplacian to a subgraph, then it has full rank and is invertible. We consider the Green's function over the whole graph, which is used in [23].

3.2 Null Space Effect

For the ranking function $f = (\beta I + L_s)^{-1} y$, parameter β plays an important role in this problem. On one hand, from a numerical computation point of view, βI makes $L_s + \beta I$ invertable since L_s is not full rank. On the other hand it "kills" the null space of L_s, which is spanned by the first eigenvector of L_s. The ranking function (the kernel/Green's function) can be written as follows since $\lambda_1 = 0$.

$$G_s(x, y) = \frac{1}{\beta} v_1(x) v_1(y) + \sum_{i=2}^{n} \frac{1}{\lambda_i + \beta} v_i(x) v_i(y) \tag{11}$$

This means if β is too small such that $\frac{1}{\beta} >> \frac{1}{\lambda_i + \beta}$, the behavior of the ranking function might be determined by $v_1(x)$ alone. In ranking, if $v_1(x)$ is a function that is unrelated to the relevance ordering of samples, we will have an uninformative ranking function. This is the case for L_s when the density $p(x)$ is not uniform, since $v_1(x)$ is non-constant and determined by the denisty. For query x_1, by dropping a constant coefficient $v_1(x_1)$, the ranking function then becomes

$$f(x) = G_s(x_1, x) \approx \frac{v_1(x)}{\beta} \tag{12}$$

This means the ranking function $f = (\beta I + L_s)^{-1} y$ is very sensitive to β. Recall that for L_s, we have $v_1(x) = \sqrt{D(x)}$, where $D(x)$ is the degree function for vertex x on the graph. In this case,

$$f(x) \approx \frac{\sqrt{D(x)}}{\beta} \tag{13}$$

This also implies that, for small β, the ranking on graph G is influenced by methods used to construct G. For instance, parameter k in kNN graphs directly varies degree function $D(x)$. Likewise $D(x)$ is affected by the decision to build either a symmetric or asymmetric kNN graph. These are important issues in practice. From the original "diffusion" based iterative algorithm [23], it is difficult to discover these issues.

When $v_1(x)$ is constant, which is the case for L_u, $v_1(x)/\beta$ will not change the ranking since we only need an ordering. In this case, we can safely drop the constant shift $v_1(x)/\beta$, then the second term in equation (11) determines the ranking. This means L_u will be more robust than L_s in terms of parameter β. This problem is less important in regression since the task there is to estimate a real-valued function, while in ranking, we ultimately need an ordering. Notice that other than the null space effect, β also influences the ranking in "spectra shift" $1/(\lambda_i + \beta)$.

One simple solution is to use L_u instead of L_s. Another solution is to modify the ranking function when using L_s.

[1]When there exists a null space, we mean the subspace orthogonal to its null is an RKHS.

Since this problem is caused by the first eigenvector, associated with the zero eigenvalue, one straightforward solution is to remove the first eigenvector. Then the ranking function becomes

$$f(x) = \sum_{i=2}^{n} \frac{1}{\lambda_i + \beta} v_i(x_1) v_i(x) \tag{14}$$

Function $f(x)$ lives in the subspace that is orthogonal to the first eigenvector, since all the eigenvectors of L_s are orthogonal. This can be implemented by computing the pseudoinverse of L_s, which removes the first eigenvector[2]. Notice that even we remove v_1, the ranking functions using L_s and L_u are still different due to the differences between their eigenvectors.

Therefore, β should not be set to any fixed value for different data sets in practice when using L_s. Instead, β should be chosen by validation. When training data is not available or not enough for validation, β should be set to zero and the pseudoinverse should be used to compute the ranking function. We will test how parameter β changes the ranking results in the experiments.

3.3 Diverging Ranking Function

Since the ranking function can be rewritten as a Green's function of a Laplacian, then it is possible that it is not a pointwise well-defined continuous function in the limit of infinite samples. Instead of an analysis involving generalized functions and Sobolev spaces, we use a simple example to show how this Green's function diverges to infinity at the query point in spaces having dimensions greater than one ($d \geqslant 2$).

Assume we remove the first eigenvector and ignore the density, then the ranking function is the Green's function of a regular Laplacian Δ. In $\mathbb{R}^3$ or higher dimensions, the Green's function of a regular Laplacian is

$$G(x, y) = \frac{1}{\|x - y\|_{\mathbb{R}^d}} \tag{15}$$

where $|G(x,x)| = \infty$. In our case, $G_s(x,x) = K(x,x) = \infty$ means if we enforce $y_1 = 1 = G_s(x_1, x_1)$, the diverging $G_s(x_1, x_1)$ will cause the ranking function to be 0 at all other points by a normalization as the following.

$$f(x) = \frac{G_s(x_1, x)}{G_s(x_1, x_1)} = \begin{cases} 1, \text{when } x = x_1 \\ 0, \text{when } x \neq x_1 \end{cases} \tag{16}$$

In $\mathbb{R}^2$, we also have $|G(x,x)| = \infty$, but the Green's function has a different form. Thus, this problem happens for graph Laplacians in spaces having dimensions greater than one[3]. More importantly, this problem happens to all versions of graph Laplacians, including L_u, L_s and all the graph Laplacians that will be introduced later. For L_s, the bounded density weight will not change this fact.

One trivial solution to this problem is that there is no need to maintain $f(x_1) = y_1 = 1$, since we only need an ordering, instead of a real-valued function $f(x)$ as in regression. In the finite sample case, it is possible to obtain a real-valued ranking function (vector) since $G_s(x,x)$ will always be finite. However, due to the sharp increase of $G_s(x,x)$ in high dimensions as we have more and more samples, the random noise might easily damage the ranking.

In order to solve the diverging problem of the ranking function in the limit of infinite samples, we need to find the Green's function of a "higher order" Laplacian, in a higher order Sobolev space, see e.g., [19]. This idea can be implemented by the Green's function of an iterated graph Laplacian defined as the following,

$$L_u^m = \sum_{k=1}^{n} \lambda_k^m v_k v_k^T$$

where λ_k and v_k are the eigenpair of L_u and $m \geqslant 0$. Similarly, we can also define the corresponding iterated graph Laplacian for L_s and other version of graph Laplacians. Since L_u is real and symmetric, for integer m, L_u^m is exactly the power of matrix L_u.

4. RANKING BY GREEN'S FUNCTION

Based on previous analyses, the null space effect of L_s suggests that we should use a graph Laplacian that has a constant first eigenvector, or remove the first eigenvector of L_s in the ranking function. The diverging ranking function problem suggests to use the Green's function of an iterated graph Laplacian. In this section, we use L_u as an example to show an improved solution, then discuss the improved method on a Gaussian mixture, and at last we introduce several other interesting graph Laplacians.

The Green's function of the iterated Laplacian L_u^m, with a possible additional term βI but allowing $\beta = 0$ (meaning we remove the first eigenvector by pseudoinverse) is defined as [4]

$$G_u^m(x, y) = \sum_{i=1}^{n} \left(\frac{1}{\lambda_i + \beta} \right)^m v_i(x) v_i(y) \tag{17}$$

When $\beta = 0$, the pseudoinverse should be used to remove $v_1(x)$. It is easy to see that in matrix form $G_u^m = [(\beta I + L_u)^{-1}]^m$. In the limit of infinite samples, as long as $2m > d$, $f(x) = G_u^m(x_1, x)$ is a continuous function by the Sobolev embedding theory. See e.g. [19] for more on Laplacians and Sobolev spaces. The ranking function then becomes the following.

$$f = \left[(\beta I + L_u)^{-1}\right]^m y, \quad \beta \geqslant 0. \tag{18}$$

Besides β, the other important parameter is m, which defines a spectra transform of the form $g(\lambda) = \lambda^m$ on L_u. For a weighted Laplacian, the smaller λ_i is the smoother v_i will be. This means the eigenvectors are in decreasing smoothness order when we order λ_i in an increasing order. For the Green's function, eigenvalues are $1/\lambda_k^m$ when $\beta = 0$. Then the power transform of the spectra acts as a low pass filter, smoothing the Green's function as m increases. This idea can be quantitatively described by Sobolev norms, see [19, Chapter 5].

Overall, the two parameters $\beta \geqslant 0$ and $m \geqslant 0$ act as a spectra transform to the Green's function, where m acts as a scaling between different "frequency" levels, while β acts as a shift along a fixed "frequency" level. This effect is similar to the Fourier analysis and multiple resolution analysis, since the eigenvectors of a graph Laplacian not only form

[2]This can be implemented by pseudoinverse "pinv" of L_s in Matlab by setting a small threshold for eigenvalue cutoff.

[3]Intrinsic dimension $d \geqslant 2$ on manifolds.

[4]It is also possible to define $G_u^m(x, y) = \sum_{i=1}^{n} 1/(\lambda_i^m + \beta) v_i(x) v_i(y)$.

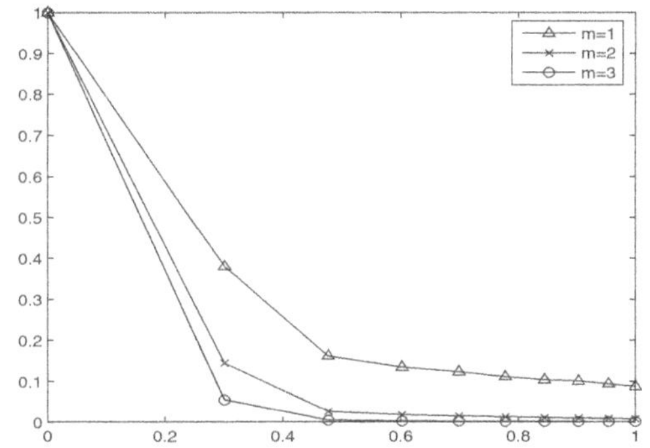

Figure 1: Low-pass filter effect: re-scaled top 10 eigenvalues (λ_i^{-m}) of G_u^m on a mixture of two Gaussians in 2D (without $\lambda_1 = 0$). Horizontal axis is $\log_{10}(i)$, vertical axis is λ_i^{-m}, and $\beta = 0$.

an orthonormal basis, but also have an intrinsic smoothness ordering. The Green's function of an iterated graph Laplacian also has a similar spectral density as the Matérn model [18] in a Gaussian process.

4.1 Empirical Study on Gaussian Mixture

In order to have an intuitive understanding of the effect of m and β, we generate an artificial data set and plot the transformed spectra and ranking function in Figure (1), Figure (2) and Figure (3). The data set includes a mixture of two Gaussians of unit variance on $\mathbb{R}^2$ centered at $(\pm 1.5, 0)$, and an additional uniform over $[-3, 3] \times [-3, 3]$ to avoid empty regions. The query point is at $(-2, -1.8)$.

In Figure (1), we re-scale the eigenvalues of G_u^m to make the spectra of different m values are comparable. As m increases, we can see that the low frequency components (eigenvectors with smaller indices) have larger and larger weights in the final ranking function. This makes the ranking function smoother and smoother, but still in a data dependent way. This low-pass filter effect has a different behavior from that in [7], where a Markov random walk explanation applies. The eigenvalues here connect closely to the Sobolev spaces [19] and decrease much faster.

For a good ranking function, the top of the ranking list should be points that are, on one hand near the query point in terms of the Euclidean distance in the chosen feature space. On the other hand, points on the top of the list should shift towards the nearby high density regions in order to obtain more relevant results on average. In Figure (2), the contour lines of the Green's function using both L_u and L_s and the top 100 ranked points are shown, where we can see two distinct features.

First, the null space effect for L_s is clear. In the upper row of Figure (2), different β values change the behavior of L_s-based ranking function dramatically. When $\beta = 10^{-4}$, the Green's function using L_s is almost the same as eigenvector v_1 of L_s, which is the square root of the density of a mixture of two Gaussians. The top 100 ranked points are those on the same contour lines, which is completely uninformative for ranking. For "pinv" ($\beta = 0$), the pseudoinverse of L_s does not include v_1, so the Green's function is density adaptive and the top 100 ranked points are reasonable neighbors in $\mathbb{R}^2$. When $\beta = 1$, the Green's function acts as a Gaussian in $\mathbb{R}^2$, capturing no density information. When $\beta = 0.01$, the results are reasonable and similar to "pinv" case. This problem does not happen to L_u (lower row), since its first eigenvector is constant. The results are much stable for different β values. In the contour plot for L_u when $\beta = 10^{-4}$, even the Green's function is almost flat as a constant (indicated by its contour line values), but a reasonable ordering can still be recovered. Any constant shift will not change the ordering, which is essential for ranking. Although L_s can still be useful with a proper β value, in practice choosing a sensitive parameter can be difficult.

Notice that the slight difference of the ranking functions for different β using L_u is caused by the weight $1/(\lambda_i + \beta)$. Overall, the effect of β is twofold: β not only plays an important role in the first eigenvector as in $1/\beta$, but also changes other eigenvector components as in $1/(\lambda_i + \beta)$.

Second, as m increases, the top 100 ranked points are shifted towards the nearby high density regions, as shown in Figure (3). This will increase the relevant results on average in practice. Results using L_u also have a similar behavior.

4.2 Different Graph Laplacians

In the experiments, we also tested several other interesting versions of graph Laplacians, which are introduced here. Given the weight matrix W constructed from the sample set X, there are three empirical graph Laplacians associated with W: L_u, L_s, and L_r. We introduced L_u and L_s in section (2), and $L_r = D^{-1}L_u = I - D^{-1}W$. It is easy to see that L_r is a weighted version of L_u. Since L_r is not symmetric, above analyses will not apply directly to L_r. Therefore, we only test it empirically in the experiments.

There exists another way of defining graph Laplacians, which involves a normalization of W using a parameter $\alpha \in \mathbb{R}$ [7]. First, the weight matrix W is normalized to another weight matrix

$$\tilde{W}_\alpha = D^{-\alpha} W D^{-\alpha} \tag{19}$$

Then we can define the associated degree matrix $\tilde{D}_\alpha$ for $\tilde{W}_\alpha$, and define each graph Laplacian accordingly as before. For each α, again there are three empirical graph Laplacian $\tilde{L}_u^\alpha$, $\tilde{L}_s^\alpha$ and $\tilde{L}_r^\alpha$. When $\alpha = 1/2$, denote $\tilde{L}_u^{1/2}$ as L_p[5], and when $\alpha = 1$, denote $\tilde{L}_u^1$ as L_g. In the limit of infinite samples [10, Corollary 2.40]

$$\frac{1}{nt^{d/2+1}} L_p f(x) \xrightarrow{\text{a.s.}} -\frac{1}{p(x)} \text{div}[p(x)\text{grad} f(x)] \tag{20}$$

In this case, the measure hidden inside of the weighted Laplacian is $p(x)$, instead of $p^2(x)$ as for L_u. This graph Laplacian might be preferred in practice since the random samples are drawn from $p(x)$ instead of $p^2(x)$. For L_g, we have

$$\frac{1}{nt^{d/2+1}} L_g f(x) \xrightarrow{\text{a.s.}} -\frac{1}{p(x)} \Delta f(x) \tag{21}$$

In this case, the limit has no density drifting term, but with a density outside of the Laplace operator. We will test the empirical performances of these two graph Laplacians in the experiments.

[5]Notice that $f^T L_p f$ is different from $f^T L_s f$, since $f^T L_p f = \frac{1}{2}\sum_{i,j} w_{ij}/\sqrt{D(x_i)D(x_j)}(f(x_i) - f(x_j))^2$ and $f^T L_s f = \frac{1}{2}\sum_{i,j} w_{ij}(f(x_i)/\sqrt{D(x_i)} - f(x_j)/\sqrt{D(x_j)})^2$.

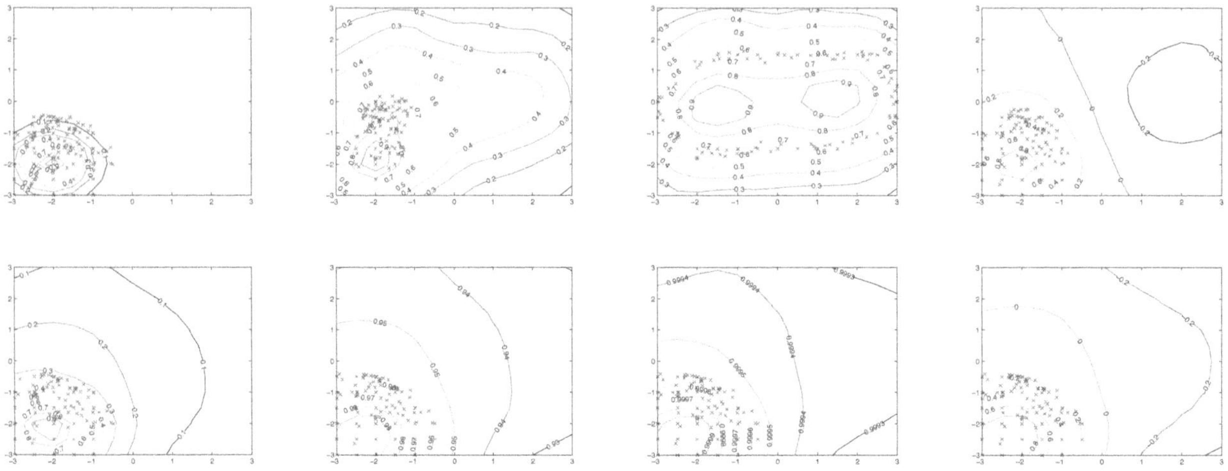

Figure 2: Sensitivity of β on L_s(top row) and L_u(lower row): Green's function at $(-2, -1.8)$ over a mixture of two Gaussians at $(\pm 1.5, 0)$ with $m = 1$. Left to right: $\beta = 1$, $\beta = 10^{-2}$, $\beta = 10^{-4}$, pinv ($\beta = 0$).

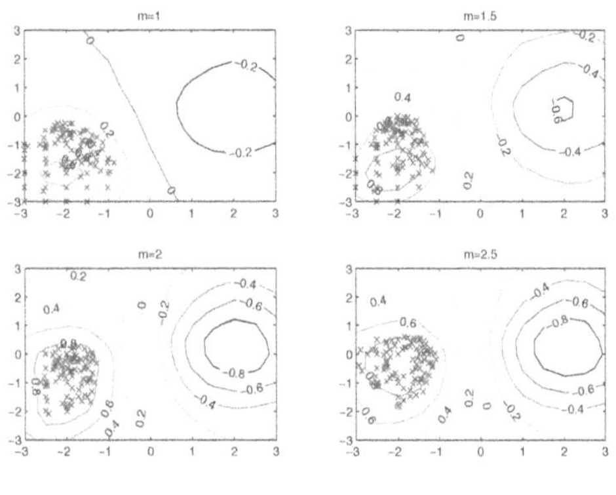

Figure 3: Green's function with different m values using L_s.

5. EMPIRICAL STUDY

In this section, we test the ranking function based on the iterated graph Laplacians on several text and image benchmarks.

5.1 Experiment Setup

Data Sets: Benchmarks include COIL20 images[6] [14], MNIST image digits[7], 20 Newsgroups text data[8], and Scene image data set used in [15].

The COIL20 data set contains 20 objects. The images of each object were taken 5 degrees apart as the object is rotated on a turntable and each object has 72 images. The total number of the images in this data set is 1440, and the size of each image used in this paper is 32×32 pixels, with 256 grey levels per pixel. Thus, each image is represented by a 1024-dimensional raw pixel vector. The MNIST digits image data set consists of 10 handwritten digits, and each image is represented by a 784-dimensional raw pixel vector. In this paper, we use a subset of 2000 images of the original data set, with 200 images for each digit. The 20 Newsgroups data set includes documents of 20 different classes, and each document is represented as a 61188-dimensional TFIDF vector. A subset of 2000 documents is used, with 100 from each group. The Scene data set contains 8 outdoor scene categories. A subset of 2000 images is used, with 125 from each category. After computing the Gist descriptor for each image using online code[9] with 4×4 blocks, each image is represented as a 512-dimensional vector. For COIL20, MNIST, and Scene data sets, the Gaussian weight is used to compute the weight on weighted graphs, while for 20 Newsgroups, the Cosine weight is used.

Evaluation Criteria: The main evaluation criteria in this paper is mean average precision (mAP). The average precision (AP) is the area below the recall-precision curves. The AP is a number between 0 and 1 with 1 meaning the first M returned points are all the relevant data in the whole data set. The mean AP is the average of AP for a set of queries. In this paper, we use each sample point of the data set as a query, then take the average over all the AP scores. We also use the precision-scope curves to show the performance on the top of the ranked list on Scene data. Since in image retrieval, results on the top of the returned list are much more important than others to users.

5.2 Experimental Results

There are four parameters for ranking using the iterated graph Laplacians: k and t for the graph construction, and β and m for the ranking function. For graph Laplacian based machine learning and data mining methods, graph construction related parameter k in kNN graphs and t in Gaussian weights have been studied both theoretically and empirically, see e.g., [26] and the reference therein. In order to capture the local information of the underlying manifold, both k and t should work together to generate a good graph. For example, a small k with a wide range of t, or a large k

[6]http://www.cs.columbia.edu/CAVE/software/softlib/coil-20.php

[7]http://yann.lecun.com/exdb/mnist/

[8]http://www.zjucadcg.cn/dengcai/Data/TextData.html

[9]http://people.csail.mit.edu/torralba/code/spatialenvelope/

Table 1: **mAP on different data sets, with different β values. "pinv" corresponds to results from ranking functions with the first eigenvector removed, as in (14).**

β	10^{-5}	10^{-4}	10^{-3}	$\mathbf{10^{-2}}$	10^{-1}	1	pinv	10^{-5}	10^{-4}	10^{-3}	$\mathbf{10^{-2}}$	10^{-1}	1	pinv
	MNIST, $k = 10$, $t = 10^6$, $m = 1$							COIL20, $k = 10$, $t = 10$, $m = 1$						
L_u	0.57	0.57	0.57	**0.57**	0.56	0.51	0.57	0.80	0.80	0.80	**0.81**	0.81	0.77	0.66
L_s	0.11	0.12	0.18	**0.50**	0.54	0.48	0.57	0.36	0.48	0.78	**0.80**	0.78	0.75	0.65
	20News, $k = 10$, $m = 1$							Scene, $k = 10$, $t = 0.10$, $m = 1$						
L_u	0.47	0.47	0.47	**0.46**	0.44	0.39	0.47	0.57	0.57	0.57	**0.57**	0.56	0.52	0.57
L_s	0.07	0.07	0.10	**0.33**	0.43	0.38	0.47	0.14	0.14	0.18	**0.45**	0.54	0.50	0.56

but with a relatively small t. In this paper, we focus on β and m.

Parameter β: We first compare the original ranking algorithm in [23] using L_s as in equation (18) with different values of β and $m = 1$, to the algorithm using other graph Laplacians. The mAP scores for L_s and L_u with different β values are reported in Table (1). We can see that the ranking algorithm using L_s is very sensitive to parameter β. This confirms our null space effect analysis in section (3.2). The commonly used value of β, which is approximately 0.01, is far from being a good choice for L_s (except the special data set COIL20). Contrary to L_s, ranking results using L_u are much more stable on β.

One interesting observation is that, when we do not have enough training data to choose β by validation, using the pseudoinverse by setting $\beta = 0$ also gives competitive results. This is true for both L_u and L_s, as shown in "pinv" column in Table (1).

We also tested L_r, L_p and L_g, the results of which are not reported here due to the limited space. The performance of L_r is even worse than L_s, which is potentially due to the asymmetric normalization. The ranking performance of L_p and L_g is comparable to that of L_u when other parameters are chosen as in Table (1).

Parameter m: How parameter m changes the ranking function depends on the underlying density as shown in Figure (2), and also depends on how we normalize the graph Laplacian. In Table (2), mAP on different data sets with different m values is reported, where 5-fold cross validation is used to choose parameter k, t, and β. We choose $k \in \{5, 10, 50, 100, 500, 1000, |X|\}$, with $|X|$ meaning complete graphs, $\beta \in \{10^{-5}, 10^{-4}, 10^{-3}, 10^{-2}, 10^{-1}, 10^0, 10^1\}$, on MNIST $t \in \{10^0, 10^1, 10^2, 10^3, 10^4, 10^5\} \times 10^5$, and on Scene $t \in \{10^{-2}, 10^{-1}, 10^0, 10^1, 10^2, 10^3\}$.

We can see that results with $m > 1$ on the three data sets can be better than ranking with $m = 1$, which is particularly clear for L_u, and also generally true for L_p and L_g, except L_p on MNIST. But most values of $m > 1$ are not helpful for L_s and L_r. This is probably due to the fact that the normalization step complicates the corresponding iterated Laplacians, which is particularly true considering that the limit of L_s is not a weighted Laplacian.

Notice that the results in Table (2) are obtained by choosing the best parameters by validation, including β. This means we already eliminated the null space effect in Table (2). In large scale computing, validation might not be available.

Different Graph Laplacians: Among different versions of graph Laplacians, we find that the results of three "unnormalized" graph Laplacians (L_u, L_p, and L_g) are roughly comparable, as shown in Table (2). To the best of our knowledge, this is the first time that L_p and L_g are tested in ranking. One interesting result is that on MNIST, the ranking using L_p with $m = 1$ is much better than all other graph Laplacians. Based on Table (2), if we have to choose one graph Laplacian to use, then L_p is the best choice. The overall performance of L_p suggests the potential value of L_p and the family of twice normalized graph Laplacian $\tilde{L}^u_\alpha$. This is interesting since among all the weighed graph Laplacians $\tilde{L}^u_\alpha$, L_p is the only "natural" one (see e.g. [25]), whose weight corresponds to the probability density $p(x)$, i.e., $\int_\Omega p(x)dx = 1$. Notice that for L_u, the weight is $p^2(x)$ and $\int_\Omega p^2(x)dx \neq 1$ generally.

Table 2: mAP on different data sets, with different m values. Results in bold are the best for each graph Laplacian, choosing the smallest m in case of a tie.

m		1	2	4	8	16	32
MNIST	L_u	0.63	**0.65**	0.65	0.65	0.62	0.59
	L_s	**0.65**	0.65	0.64	0.59	0.63	0.62
	L_r	**0.65**	0.62	0.58	0.58	0.61	0.54
	L_p	**0.69**	0.68	0.64	0.66	0.65	0.65
	L_g	0.62	**0.65**	0.65	0.63	0.64	0.63
20News	L_u	0.45	0.49	0.51	0.49	**0.52**	0.47
	L_s	0.47	**0.50**	0.44	0.47	0.46	0.37
	L_r	0.47	**0.49**	0.41	0.43	0.40	0.24
	L_p	0.44	0.48	**0.51**	0.47	0.51	0.48
	L_g	0.43	0.47	**0.50**	0.47	0.50	0.47
Scene	L_u	0.56	0.58	**0.59**	0.57	0.57	0.57
	L_s	**0.57**	0.55	0.53	0.55	0.56	0.47
	L_r	**0.55**	0.51	0.52	0.52	0.47	0.45
	L_p	0.56	0.58	**0.59**	0.56	0.59	0.59
	L_g	0.56	0.57	**0.59**	0.57	0.59	0.58

Content Based Image Retrieval: A natural application of ranking is content based image retrieval. We test different graph Laplacians on Scene image data set, and the precision-scope curves for L_u, L_s and L_r are shown in Figure (4). Due to the limited space, we only report one typical result with a fixed parameter setting. However, results of several different k and t combinations follow a similar pattern: L_u is better than L_s, and L_s is better than L_r.

Study on COIL20: The construction of COIL20 can be seen as an idealization of a real world scenario. Consider all the images of the same object on the Internet, for instance the Eiffel Tower. It is likely different visitors take the photo

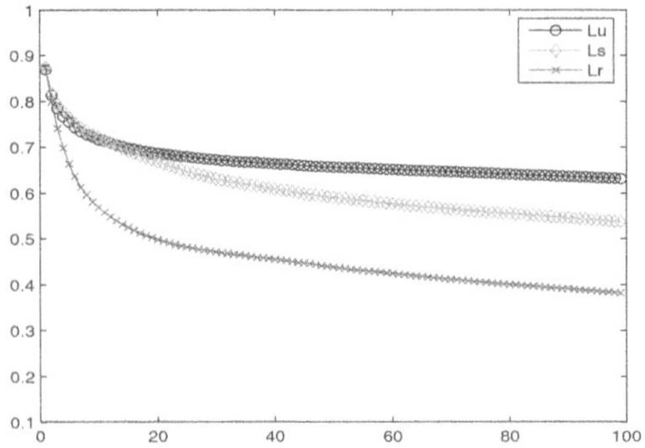

Figure 4: Typical precision-scope curves on Scene images using different graph Laplacians ($k = 10$, $\beta = 0.01$, $m = 1$, and $t = 0.1$).

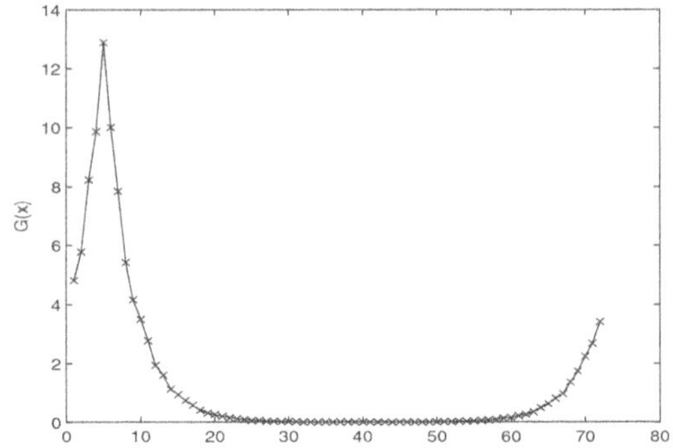

Figure 5: Green's function at $i = 5$ over the first class of COIL20.

of the tower from different angles. Then this is a similar setting as COIL20. Compared to the equal angle rotation and fixed shooting radius in COIL20, the main differences are random angle rotations and radiuses in real world. Therefore, we report more detailed experiment results on COIL20.

When $k = 1000$, $t = 1$, $\beta = 0.01$, and $m = 1$, we can obtain a perfect mAP on COIL20 data set, using either L_s or L_u. This setting is a little different from what is usually used in practice, i.e., k is small to capture the local manifold structure. On one hand a large k and a small t still can capture the local information, on the other hand, we believe a large k is helpful to the numerical stability by capturing global information in this case[10].

The Green's function with $k = 1000$, $t = 1$, $m = 1$ and $\beta = 0$ for class $Y = 1$ is shown in Figure (5)[11], where x axis is the index of the first class in COIL20. If we see it as a periodic function by connecting two ends of the interval (x axis), the Green's function or reproducing kernel function at index 5 is very similar to the reproducing kernel function over a 1D circle, e.g., [22, Chapter 2]. This empirically shows that each class of COIL20 is likely distributed on an intrinsic 1D circle. If we order the images according to this Green's function, the original rotation order can be recovered correctly. Notice that $G(x_1, x)$ on images of other classes are several order smaller, so we omit that part of the ranking function in the figure.

Numerical Issues: One key numerical issue in computing the Green's function of an iterated graph Laplacian is that we should compute the Green's function matrix G_u of L_u first, then raise the power of G_u to obtain G_u^m, instead of computing the inverse of L_u^m directly. This is due to the fact that the first several eigenvalues of L_u is very small, therefore, raising the power of L_u can easily make those eigenvalues much smaller, which increases the condition number of L_u^m dramatically.

The most expensive step to compute the Green's function of a graph Laplacian is to invert a $n \times n$ matrix, which costs $O(n^3)$. However, it is possible to take advantage of the sparsity of the problem to obtain a lower cost. Consider the ranking function of the form $f = [(\beta I + L_u)^{-1}]^m y$. For $\beta > 0$, since $(\beta I + L_u)$ is sparse when m is small, solving $(\beta I + L_u)^m f = y$ can cost as low as $O(kn)$, where k is the sparsity of the coefficient matrix. For $\beta = 0$, we need to compute L_u^{-1} (pseudoinverse), which can be rewritten as $[D(I - P)]^{-1} = (I - P)^{-1} D^{-1}$, where $P = D^{-1}W$, and $(I - P)^{-1} = \sum_{i=1}^{\infty} P^i$ can be potentially compressed and computed efficiently, see e.g., [8, Section 6.2].

[10]Notice that on other data sets a smaller k is preferred.

[11]This is the first class of COIL20, the toy duck.

6. SUMMARY

In this paper, we analyzed a popular graph Laplacian based ranking algorithm introduced in [23] from a functional analysis point of view. From the theoretical analyses and experimental results, our findings for ranking on manifolds are as follows:

1. The ranking algorithm based on L_s is sensitive to the commonly used parameter β. However, this is not the case for the unnormalized Laplacian L_u.

2. When choosing β by validation is not feasible, the pseudoinverse of the graph Laplacian ($\beta = 0$) can also give competitive results.

3. Using iterated graph Laplacian has a solid theoretical foundation and can improve ranking results in practice.

4. L_p gives competitive results, which suggests the potential value of using the "unnormalized" twice normalized graph Laplacian $\tilde{L}_u^{\alpha}$ in practice.

7. ACKNOWLEDGMENTS

We thank the anonymous reviewers for helping to improve the paper.

8. REFERENCES

[1] M. Belkin and P. Niyogi. Laplacian Eigenmaps for Dimensionality Reduction and Data Representation. *Neural Comp*, 15(6):1373–1396, 2003.

[2] M. Belkin and P. Niyogi. Convergence of Laplacian Eigenmaps. In B. Schölkopf, J. Platt, and T. Hoffman, editors, *Advances in Neural Information Processing Systems 19*, pages 129–136. MIT Press, Cambridge, MA, 2007.

[3] M. Belkin and P. Niyogi. Towards a Theoretical Foundation for Laplacian-Based Manifold Methods. *Journal of Computer and System Sciences*, 74(8):1289–1308, 2008.

[4] A. Berlinet and C. Thomas-Agnan. *Reproducing Kernel Hilbert Spaces in Probability and Statistics*. Kluwer Academic Publishers, 2003.

[5] O. Chapelle, B. Schölkopf, and A. Zien, editors. *Semi-Supervised Learning*. MIT Press, Cambridge, MA, 2006.

[6] F. Chung and S.-T. Yau. Discrete Green's functions. *J. Combinatorial Theory (A)*, 91:191–214, 2000.

[7] R. R. Coifman and S. Lafon. Diffusion maps. *Applied and Computational Harmonic Analysis*, 21(1):5–30, 2006.

[8] R. R. Coifman and M. Maggioni. Diffusion wavelets. *Applied and Computational Harmonic Analysis*, 21(1):53–94, 2006.

[9] A. Grigor'yan. Heat kernels on weighted manifolds and applications. *Cont. Math.*, 398:93–191, 2006.

[10] M. Hein. *Geometrical aspects of statistical learning theory*. PhD thesis, Wissenschaftlicher Mitarbeiter am Max-Planck-Institut für biologische Kybernetik in Tübingen in der Abteilung, 2005.

[11] M. Hein, J.-Y. Audibert, and U. V. Luxburg. Graph Laplacians and their Convergence on Random Neighborhood Graphs. *Journal of Machine Learning Research*, 8:1325–1368, 2007.

[12] M. Maier, M. Hein, and U. von Luxburg. Optimal construction of k-nearest-neighbor graphs for identifying noisy clusters. *Theoretical Computer Science*, 410(19):1749–1764, 2009.

[13] B. Nadler, N. Srebro, and X. Zhou. Semi-Supervised Learning with the Graph Laplacian: The Limit of Infinite Unlabelled Data. In *Twenty-Third Annual Conference on Neural Information Processing Systems*, 2009.

[14] S. A. Nene, S. K. Nayar, and H. Murase. Columbia Object Image Library (COIL-20). Technical Report CUCS-005-96, February 1996.

[15] A. Oliva and A. Torralba. Modeling the shape of the scene: a holistic representation of the spatial envelope. *International Journal of Computer Vision*, 42(3):145–175, 2001.

[16] B. D. Reddy. *Introductory Function Analysis, with Applications to Boundary Value Problems and Finite Elements*. Springer, 1997.

[17] A. Smola and R. Kondor. Kernels and regularization on graphs. In *16th Annual Conference on Learning Theory and 7th Kernel Workshop*. Springer Verlag, 2003.

[18] M. L. Stein. *Interpolation of Spatial Data: Some Theory for Kriging*. Springer, New York., 1999.

[19] M. E. Taylor. *Partial Differential Equations I: Basic Theory*. Springer, New York, 1996.

[20] U. von Luxburg. A Tutorial on Spectral Clustering. *Statistics and Computing*, 17(4):395–416, 2007.

[21] U. von Luxburg, M. Belkin, and O. Bousquet. Consistency of spectral clustering. *Ann. Statist.*, 36(2):555–586, 2008.

[22] G. Wahba. *Spline Models for Observational Data.* Volume 59 of CBMS-NSF Regional Conference Series in Applied Mathematics, Philadelphia: SIAM, 1990.

[23] D. Zhou, J. Weston, A. Gretton, O. Bousquet, and B. Schölkopf. Ranking on Data Manifolds. In *Advances in Neural Information Processing Systems (NIPS) 16*, pages 169–176. MIT Press, 2004.

[24] X. Zhou and M. Belkin. Semi-supervised Learning by Higher Order Regularization. In G. Gordon, D. Dunson, and M. Dudík, editors, *The 14th International Conference on Artificial Intelligence and Statistics*, 2011.

[25] X. Zhou and N. Srebro. Error Analysis of Laplacian Eigenmaps for Semi-supervised Learning. In G. Gordon, D. Dunson, and M. Dudík, editors, *The 14th International Conference on Artificial Intelligence and Statistics*, 2011.

[26] X. Zhu. Semi-Supervised Learning Literature Survey. Technical report, 2008. University of Wisconsin Madison, Computer Sciences TR 1530.

Anomaly Localization for Network Data Streams with Graph Joint Sparse PCA

Ruoyi Jiang, Hongliang Fei, Jun Huan
Department of Electrical Engineering and Computer Science
University of Kansas
Lawrence, KS 66047, USA
{jiangruoyi, hfei, jhuan}@ittc.ku.edu

ABSTRACT

Determining anomalies in data streams that are collected and transformed from various types of networks has recently attracted significant research interest. Principal Component Analysis (PCA) has been extensively applied to detecting anomalies in network data streams. However, none of existing PCA based approaches addresses the problem of identifying the sources that contribute most to the observed anomaly, or anomaly localization. In this paper, we propose novel sparse PCA methods to perform anomaly detection and localization for network data streams. Our key observation is that we can localize anomalies by identifying a sparse low dimensional space that captures the abnormal events in data streams. To better capture the sources of anomalies, we incorporate the structure information of the network stream data in our anomaly localization framework. We have performed comprehensive experimental studies of the proposed methods, and have compared our methods with the state-of-the-art using three real-world data sets from different application domains. Our experimental studies demonstrate the utility of the proposed methods.

Categories and Subject Descriptors

H.2.8 [**Database Management**]: Database Applications-Data Mining

General Terms

Algorithms, Experimentation

Keywords

Network Data Streams, Anomaly Localization, PCA, Sparse Learning

1. INTRODUCTION

Determining anomalies in data streams that are collected and transformed from various types of networks has recently attracted significant research interest in the data mining community [4, 15, 29, 32]. Applications of the work could be found in network traffic data [32], sensor network streams [4], social networks [29], and finance networks [15] among others.

The common limitation of aforementioned methods is that they are incapable of identifying the sources that contribute most to the observed anomalies, or anomaly localization. With fast-accumulating stream data, an outstanding data analysis issue is *anomaly localization*, where we aim to discover the specific sources that contribute most to the observed anomalies. Anomaly localization in network data streams is apparently critical to many applications, including monitoring the state of buildings [31], or locating the sites for flooding and forest fires [9]. In the stock market, pinpointing the change points in a set of stock price time series is critical for making intelligent trading decisions [25]. For network security, localizing the sources of the most serious threats in computer networks helps ensure security in networks [21].

Principal Component Analysis (PCA) is arguably the most widely applied unsupervised anomaly detection technique for network data streams [12, 21, 22]. However, a fundamental problem of PCA, as claimed in [28], is that the current PCA based anomaly detection methods can not be applied to anomaly localization. Our key observation is that the major obstacle for extending the PCA technique to anomaly localization lies in the high dimensionality of the abnormal space. If we manage to identify a low dimensional approximation of the high dimensional abnormal subspace using a few sources, we "localize" the abnormal sources. The starting point of our investigation hence is the recently studied sparse PCA framework [33] where PCA is formalized in a sparse regression problem where each principle component (PC) is a sparse linear combination of the original sources. However, sparse PCA does not fit directly into our problems in that sparse PCA enforces sparsity randomly in the normal and abnormal subspaces. In this paper, we explore two directions in improving sparse PCA for anomaly detection and localization.

First, we develop a new regularization scheme to simultaneously calculate the normal subspace and the sparse abnormal subspace. In the normal subspace, we do not add any regularization but use the same normal subspace as ordinary PCA for anomaly detection. In the abnormal subspace, we enforce that different PCs share the same sparse structure hence it is able to do anomaly localization. We call this method *joint space PCA* (JSPCA). Second, we observe that abnormal streams are usually correlated to each other. For example in stock market, index changes in differ-

KDD'11, August 21–24, 2011, San Diego, California, USA.

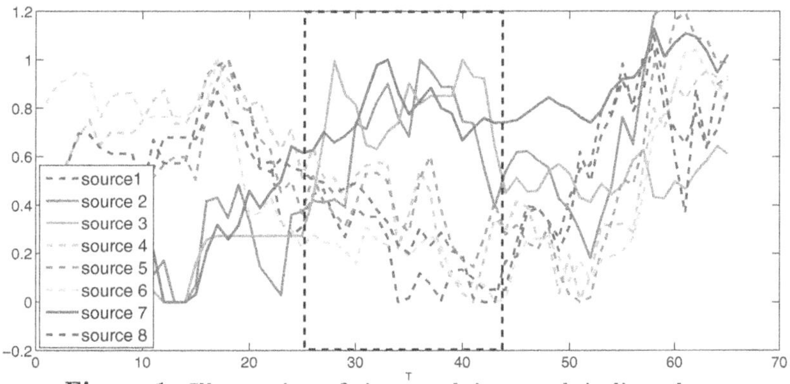

Figure 1: Illustration of time-evolving stock indices data

ent countries are often correlated. For incorporating stream correlation in anomaly localization we design a *graph guided sparse PCA* (GJSPCA) technique. Our experimental studies demonstrate the effectiveness of the proposed approaches on three real-world data sets from financial markets, wireless sensor networks, and machinery operating condition studies.

As an example of anomaly detection and anomaly localization in network data streams, we show the normalized stock index streams of eight countries over a period of three months in Figure 1. We notice an anomaly in the marked window between time stamps 25 and 42. In that window sources 1, 4, 5, 6, 8 (denoted by dotted lines) are normal sources. Sources 2, 3, 7 (denoted by solid lines) are abnormal ones since they have a different trend from that of the other sources. In the marked window, the three abnormal sources clearly share the same increasing trend while the rest share a decreasing trend.

The remainder of the paper is organized as follows. In section 2 we present related work of anomaly localization. In section 3, we discuss the challenge of applying PCA to anomaly localization. In section 4 we introduce the formulation of JSPCA and GJSPCA and the related optimization algorithm. We present our experimental study in section 5 and conclude in section 6.

2. RELATED WORK

Existing work on anomaly localization from network data streams could be roughly divided into two categories: those at the source level and those at the network level. The source level anomaly localization approaches embed detection algorithm at each stream source, resulting in a fully distributed anomaly detection system [10, 23]. The major problem of these approaches is that source level anomalies may not be indicative of network level anomalies due to the ignorance of the rest of the network [12].

To improve source level anomaly localization methods, several algorithms have been recently proposed to localize anomaly at the network level. Brauckhoff [3] applied association rule mining to network traffic data to extract abnormal flows from the large set of candidate flows. Their work is based on the assumption that anomalies often result in many flows with similar characteristics. Such an assumption holds in network traffic data streams but may not be true in other data streams such as finance data. Keogh *et al.* [20] proposed a nearest neighbor based approach to identify abnormal subsequences within univariate time series data by sliding windows. They extracted all possible subsequences and located the one with the largest Euclidean distance from its closest non-overlapping subsequences. However, the method only works for univariate time series generated from a single source. In addition, if the data is distributed on a non-Euclidean manifold, two subsequences may appear deceptively close as measured by their Euclidean distance [30]. L. Fong *et al.* developed a nonparametric change-point test based on U-statistics to detect and localize change-points in high-dimensional network traffic data [26]. The limitation is that the method is specifically designed for the Denial of Service (DOS) attack in communication networks and cannot be generalized to other types of network data streams easily.

Most related to our work, Ide *et al.* [13, 14] measured the change of neighborhood graph for each source to perform anomaly localization and developed a method called Stochastic Nearest Neighbor (SNN). Hirose *et al.* [11] designed an algorithm named Eigen Equation Compression (EEC) to localize anomalies by measuring the deviation of covariance matrix of neighborhood sources. In these two studies, we have to build a neighborhood graph for each source for each time interval, which is unlikely to scale to a large number of sources. In [18], we proposed a two step approach that first computed normal subspace from ordinary PCA and then derived a sparse abnormal subspace on the residual data subtracted from the original data.

In this paper, we design a unified approach to jointly learn normal subspace for anomaly detection and sparse abnormal subspace for anomaly localization, in which we derive a low dimensional approximation of the abnormal subspace by enforcing the loadings of normal sources to vanish across the PCs that span the abnormal subspace. Using three real world data sets across several domains, our experimental studies demonstrate the effectiveness of the proposed method over the state-of-the-art.

3. PRELIMINARIES

We introduce the notations used in this paper and background information regarding PCA and sparse PCA.

3.1 Notation

We use capital letters such as X to denote a matrix and bold lowercase letters such as $\mathbf{x}$ to denote a vector. Greek letters such as λ_1, λ_2 are Lagrangian multipliers. $\langle A, B\rangle$ represents the matrix inner product defined as $\langle A, B\rangle = tr(A^T B)$ where tr represents the matrix trace. Given a matrix X we use x_{ij} to denote the entry of X at the ith row and jth column. We use $x^{(i)}$ to represent the ith entry of a vector $\mathbf{x}$. $||\mathbf{x}||_p = (\sum_{i=1}^{n} |x_i|^p)^{\frac{1}{p}}$ denotes the l_p norm of the vector $\mathbf{x} \in \mathbb{R}^n$. Given a matrix $A \in \mathbb{R}^{p\times k}$, $\|A\|_{1,q} = \sum_{i=1}^{p} \|\tilde{\mathbf{a}}_i\|_q =$ is the l_1/l_q norm of the matrix A, where $\tilde{\mathbf{a}}_i$ is the ith row of A. Unless stated otherwise, all vectors are column vectors.

3.2 Network Data Streams

Our work focuses on data streams that are collected from multiple sources. We call the set of data stream sources together as a network since we often have information regarding the structure of the sources.

Following [7], *Network Data Streams* are multi-variate time series $\mathcal{Z}$ from p sources where $\mathcal{Z} = \{Z_i(t)\}$ and $i \in [1, p]$. p is the dimensionality of the network data streams. Each function $Z_i : \mathbb{R} \to \mathbb{R}$ is a *source*. A source is also called a "node" in the communication network community and a "feature" in the data mining and machine learning community.

Typically we focus on time series sampled at (synchronized) discrete time stamps $\{t_1, t_2, \ldots, t_n\}$. In such cases, the network data streams are represented as a matrix $X = (x_{i,j})$ where $i \in [1, n]$, $j \in [1, p]$ and $x_{i,j}$ is the reading of the stream source j at the time sample t_i.

3.3 Applying PCA for Anomaly Localization

Our goal is to explore a Principal Component Analysis (PCA) based method for performing anomaly detection and localization simultaneously. PCA based anomaly detection technique has been widely investigated in [12, 21, 22]. In applying PCA to anomaly detection, one first constructs the normal subspace $\mathbf{V}_1$ by the top k PCs and the abnormal subspace $\mathbf{V}_2$ by the remaining PCs, then projects the original data on $\mathbf{V}_1$ and $\mathbf{V}_2$ as:

$$X = X\mathbf{V}_1\mathbf{V}_1^T + X\mathbf{V}_2\mathbf{V}_2^T = X_n + X_a \quad (1)$$

where $X \in \mathbb{R}^{n \times p}$ is the data matrix with n time stamps from p data sources, X_n and X_a are the projections of X on normal subspace and abnormal subspace respectively. The underlying assumption of PCA based anomaly detection is that X_n corresponds to the regular trends and X_a captures the abnormal behaviors in the data streams. By performing statistical testing on the squared prediction error $SPE = tr(X_a^T X_a)$, one determines whether an anomaly happens [12, 21]. The larger SPE is, the more likely an anomaly exists.

Although PCA has been widely studied for anomaly detection, it is not applicable for anomaly localization. The fundamental problem, as claimed in [28], lies in the fact that there is no direct mapping between two subspaces $\mathbf{V}_1$, $\mathbf{V}_2$ and the data sources. Specifically, let $\mathbf{V}_2 = [\mathbf{v}_{k+1}, \cdots, \mathbf{v}_p]$ be the abnormal subspace spanned by the last $p-k$ PCs, X_a is essentially an aggregated operation that performs linear combination of all the data sources, as follows:

$$\begin{aligned} X_a &= X\mathbf{V}_2\mathbf{V}_2^T \\ &= \left[\sum_{j=1}^{p} \mathbf{x}_j \tilde{\mathbf{v}}_j \tilde{\mathbf{v}}_1^T, \cdots, \sum_{j=1}^{p} \mathbf{x}_j \tilde{\mathbf{v}}_j \tilde{\mathbf{v}}_i^T, \cdots, \sum_{j=1}^{p} \mathbf{x}_j \tilde{\mathbf{v}}_j \tilde{\mathbf{v}}_{p-k}^T\right] \end{aligned} \quad (2)$$

where $\mathbf{x}_j$ is the data from the jth source and $\tilde{\mathbf{v}}_j$ is the jth row of $\mathbf{V}_2$. Considering the ith column of X_a with the value $\sum_{j=1}^{p} \mathbf{x}_j \tilde{\mathbf{v}}_j \tilde{\mathbf{v}}_i^T$, there is no correspondence between the original ith column of X and ith column of X_a. Such an aggregation makes PCA difficult to identify the particular sources that are responsible for the observed anomalies.

Although all the previous works claim PCA based anomaly detection methods *cannot* do localization, we solve the problem of anomaly localization in a reverse way. Instead of locating the anomalies directly, we filter normal sources to identify anomalies by employing the fact that normal subspace captures the general trend of data and normal sources have little or no projection on abnormal subspace. The following theorem provides a necessary condition for data sources to have no projection on abnormal subspace.

THEOREM 3.1. *Suppose $\mathbb{Z} = \{i | \tilde{v}_i = \mathbf{0}^T\}$ is the set that contains all the indices for the zero rows of $\mathbf{V}_2$, then $\forall t \in \mathbb{Z}$, $\mathbf{x}_t$ has no projection on the abnormal subspace. In other words, these sources have no contribution to the abnormal behavior.*

PROOF. Consider the squared prediction error $SPE = tr(X_a^T X_a)$ and plug equation 2 in:

$$\begin{aligned} tr(X_a^T X_a) &= tr(X_a X_a^T) \\ &= tr(\mathbf{V}_2^T X^T X \mathbf{V}_2) \\ &= tr((\textstyle\sum_{j=1}^{p} \mathbf{x}_j \tilde{\mathbf{v}}_j)^T (\sum_{j=1}^{p} \mathbf{x}_j \tilde{\mathbf{v}}_j)) \\ &= \sum_{i=1}^{p} \sum_{j=1}^{p} tr(\tilde{\mathbf{v}}_i^T \mathbf{x}_i^T \mathbf{x}_j \tilde{\mathbf{v}}_j) \\ &= \sum_{i \notin \mathbb{Z}} \sum_{j \notin \mathbb{Z}} (\mathbf{x}_i^T \mathbf{x}_j \tilde{\mathbf{v}}_j \tilde{\mathbf{v}}_i^T) \end{aligned} \quad (3)$$

From equation (3), it is clear that $\forall i \in \mathbb{Z}$, the data $\mathbf{x}_i$ from source i has no projection on abnormal subspace and hence would be excluded from the statistics used for anomaly detection. We call such a pattern with an entire row with zeros *"joint sparsity"*. □

Unfortunately ordinary PCA does not guarantee any sparsity in PCs. Sparse PCA is a recently developed algorithms where each PC is a sparse linear combination of the original sources [33]. However existing sparse PCA method has no guarantee that different PCs share the same sparse representation and hence has no guarantee for the joint sparsity. To illustrate the point, we plotted the entries of each PC for ordinary PCA (figure 2(a)) and for sparse PCA (figure 2(b)) for the stock data set shown in figure 1. White blocks indicate zero entries and the darker color indicates a larger absolute loading. Sparse PCA produces sparse entries but that alone does not indicate sources that contribute most to the observed anomaly.

Below we present our extensions of PCA that enable us to perform anomaly localization efficiently.

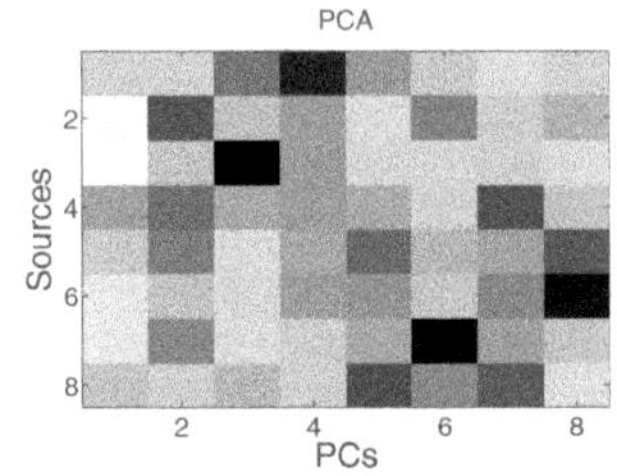

(a) PCA

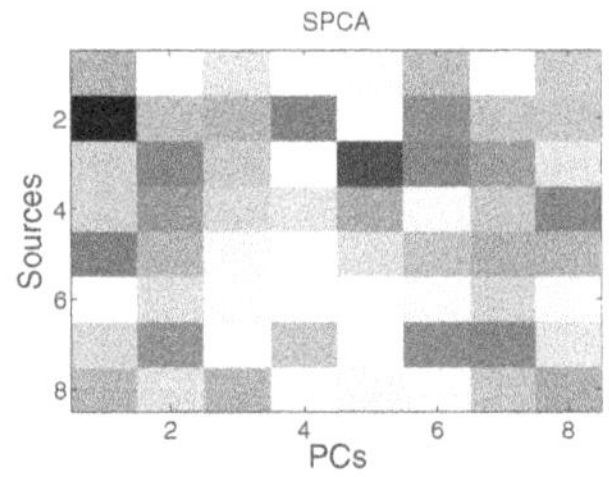

(b) SPCA

Figure 2: Comparing PCA and Sparse PCA.

4. METHODOLOGY

In this section, we propose a novel regularization framework called joint sparse PCA (JSPCA) to enforce joint sparsity in PCs in the abnormal space while preserving the PCs in the normal subspace so that we can perform simultaneous anomaly detection and anomaly localization. Then we consider the network topology in the original data and incorporate such topology into JSPCA and develop an approach named Graph JSPCA (GJSPCA).

4.1 Joint Sparse PCA

Our objective here is to derive a set of PCs $\mathbf{V} = [\mathbf{V}_1, \mathbf{V}_3]$ such that $\mathbf{V}_1$ is exactly the ordinary normal subspace and $\mathbf{V}_3$ is a sparse approximation of the ordinary abnormal subspace with the joint sparsity. The following regularization framework guarantees the two properties simultaneously.

$$\begin{array}{ll} \min\limits_{\mathbf{V}_1,\mathbf{V}_3} & \frac{1}{2}||\mathbf{X} - \mathbf{X}\mathbf{V}_1\mathbf{V}_1^T - \mathbf{X}\mathbf{V}_3\mathbf{V}_3^T||_F^2 + \lambda||\mathbf{V}_3||_{1,2} \\ \text{s.t.} & \mathbf{V}^T\mathbf{V} = I_{p\times p} \end{array} \tag{4}$$

Equation (4) can be simplified with one variable $\mathbf{V}$:

$$\begin{array}{ll} \min\limits_{\mathbf{V}} & \frac{1}{2}||\mathbf{X} - \mathbf{X}\mathbf{V}\mathbf{V}^T||_F^2 + \lambda||\mathbf{W} \circ \mathbf{V}||_{1,2} \\ \text{s.t.} & \mathbf{V}^T\mathbf{V} = I_{p\times p} \end{array} \tag{5}$$

Here $\circ$ is the *Hadamard product* operator (entry-wise product), λ is a scalar controlling the balance between sparse and fitness, $W = [\tilde{\mathbf{w}}_1, \cdots, \tilde{\mathbf{w}}_p]^T$ with jth row vector:

$$\tilde{\mathbf{w}}_j = [\underbrace{0, \cdots, 0}_{k}, \underbrace{1, \cdots, 1}_{p-k}]^T, \quad j = 1, \cdots, p \tag{6}$$

The regularization term $||W \circ V||_{1,2}$ is a L_1/L_2 penalty which enforces joint sparsity for each source across in the abnormal subspace spanned by the remaining $p - k$ principal components.

The major disadvantage of equation (5) is that it poses a difficult optimization problem since the first term (the trace norm) is concave and the second term (the L_1/L_2 norm) is convex. Motivated by the formalization of sparse PCA using two variables and an alternative optimization algorithm in [33], we consider a relaxed version:

$$\begin{array}{ll} \min\limits_{A,B} & \frac{1}{2}||X - XBA^T||_F^2 + \lambda||\mathbf{W} \circ \mathbf{B}||_{1,2} \\ \text{s.t.} & A^TA = I_{p\times p} \end{array} \tag{7}$$

and with the vector form:

$$\begin{array}{ll} \min\limits_{A,B} & \frac{1}{2}\sum_{i=1}^{n}||\tilde{\mathbf{x}}_i - AB^T\tilde{\mathbf{x}}_i||_2^2 + \lambda\sum_{j=1}^{p}||\tilde{\mathbf{w}}_j \circ \tilde{\mathbf{b}}_j||_2 \\ \text{s.t.} & A^TA = I_{p\times p} \end{array} \tag{8}$$

where $\tilde{\mathbf{x}}_i$ is the ith row of X, $A, B \in \mathbb{R}^{p\times p}$ and $\tilde{\mathbf{b}}_j$ is the jth row of B. The advantage of the new formalization is two folds: first, equation (8) is convex to each subproblem when fixing one variable and optimizing the other. As asserted in [33] disregarding the Lasso penalty, the solution of equation (8) corresponds to exact PCA; second, we only impose penalty on the remaining $p - k$ PCs and preserve the top k PCs representing the normal subspace from ordinary PCA. Such a formalization will guarantee that we have the ordinary normal subspace for anomaly detection and the sparse abnormal subspace for anomaly localization. Note that Jenatton *et al.* recently proposed a structured sparse PCA [16], which is similar to our formalization. But their structure is defined on groups and cannot be directly applied for anomaly localization.

Figure 4(a) demonstrates the principal components generated from JSPCA for the stock market data shown in figure 1. Joint sparsity across the PCs in abnormal subspace pinpoints the abnormal sources 2,3,7 by filtering out normal sources 1, 4, 5, 6, 8. Such result matches the truth in figure 1.

4.2 Graph Guided Joint Sparse PCA

In many real-world applications, the sources generating the data streams may have structure, which may or may not change with time. As the example mentioned in figure 1, stock indices from source 2, 3 and 7 are closely correlated over a long time interval. If source 2 and 3 are anomalies as demonstrated in Figure 4(a), it is very likely that source 7 is an anomaly as well. This observation motivates us to develop a regularization framework that enforce smoothness across features. In particular, we model the structure among sources with an undirected graph, where each node represents a source and each edge encodes a possible structure relationship. We hypothesize that by incorporating structure information of sources we can build a more accurate and reliable anomaly localization model. Below, we introduce the graph guided *joint sparse* PCA, which effectively encodes the structure information in the anomaly localization framework.

To achieve the goal of smoothness of features, we add an extended l_2 (Tikhonov) regularization factor on the graph laplacian regularized matrix norm of the $p - k$ PCs. This is an extension of the l_2 norm regularized Laplacian on a single vector in [8]. With this addition, we obtain the following optimization problem:

$$\begin{array}{ll} \min\limits_{A,B} & \frac{1}{2}\sum_{i=1}^{n}||\tilde{\mathbf{x}}_i - AB^T\tilde{\mathbf{x}}_i||_2^2 + \lambda_1\sum_{j=1}^{p}||\tilde{\mathbf{w}}_j \circ \tilde{\mathbf{b}}_j||_2 + \\ & \frac{1}{2}\lambda_2 \sum_{i=k+1}^{p} \mathbf{b}_i^T L \mathbf{b}_i \\ \text{s.t.} & A^TA = I_{p\times p} \end{array} \tag{9}$$

where $\mathbf{b}_i$ is the ith column of matrix B, $\tilde{\mathbf{w}}_j$ is defined in (6) and L is the *Laplacian* of a graph that captures the correlation structure of sources [8].

By introducing W matrix defined in (6), we simplify the second regularization term with a matrix format:

$$\begin{array}{ll} \min\limits_{A,B} & \frac{1}{2}\sum_{i=1}^{n}||\tilde{\mathbf{x}}_i - AB^T\tilde{\mathbf{x}}_i||_2^2 + \lambda_1\sum_{j=1}^{p}||\tilde{\mathbf{w}}_j \circ \tilde{\mathbf{b}}_j||_2 + \\ & \frac{1}{2}\lambda_2 tr((W \circ B)^T L (W \circ B)) \\ \text{s.t.} & A^TA = I_{p\times p} \end{array} \tag{10}$$

In figure 4 we show the comparison of applying JSPCA and GJSPCA on the data shown in figure 1. Both JSPCA and GJSPCA correctly localize the abnormal sources 2,3,7. Comparing JSPCA and GJSPCA, we observe that in GJSPCA the entry values corresponding to the three abnormal sources 2,3,7 are closer (a.k.a. smoothness in the feature space). In the raw data, we observe that sources 2,3,7 share an increasing trend. The smoothness is the reflection of the shared trend and helps highlight the abnormal source 7. As evaluated in our experimental study, GJSPCA outperforms JSPCA. We believe that the additional structure information utilized in GJSPCA helps.

4.3 Anomaly Scoring

To quantitatively measure the degree of anomalies for each source, we define anomaly score and normalized anomaly score as following.

DEFINITION 4.1. *Given p sources, the normal subspace $V_1 = [\mathbf{v}_1, \cdots, \mathbf{v}_k]$ and the abnormal subspace $V_3 = [\mathbf{v}_{k+1}, \cdots, \mathbf{v}_n]$, the anomaly score for source i, $i = 1 \cdots p$ is defined on the*

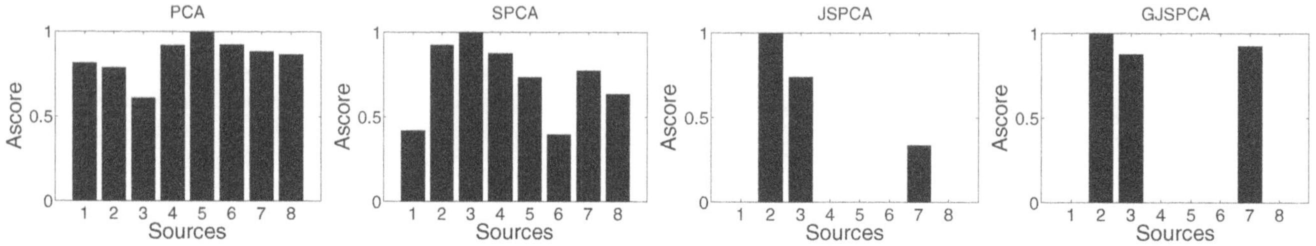

Figure 3: Comparing different anomaly localization methods. From left to right: PCA, sparse PCA, JSPCA, and GJSPCA.

L_1 norm of the ith row of V_3, divided by the size of the row:

$$\zeta_i = \frac{||\tilde{v}_i||_1}{p-k} \tag{11}$$

where $\tilde{v}_i$ is the ith row of V_3. For each input data matrix X, (11) results in a vector $\zeta = [\zeta_1, \cdots, \zeta_p]^T$ of anomaly scores. The normalized score for source i is defined as:

$$\tilde{\zeta}_i = \zeta_i / \max\{\zeta_i, i = 1, \cdots p\}$$

A higher score indicates a higher probability that a source is abnormal. We show the anomaly scores obtained from PCA, SPCA, JSPCA and GJSPCA for the stock data in figure 3. JSPCA and GJSPCA both succeed to localize three anomalies by assigning nonzero scores to anomalous sources and zero to normal ones, while PCA and SPCA both fail. Comparing JSPCA and GJSPCA we find that JSPCA assigns higher anomaly scores to source 2 and 3 but a lower score to source 7, and GJSPCA has smooth effect on the abnormal scores. It assigns similar scores for the three sources. The similar scores demonstrate the effect of smooth regularization term induced by the graph Laplacian. The smoothness also sheds light on the reason why GJSPCA outperforms JSPCA a little in anomaly localization in our detailed experimental evaluation.

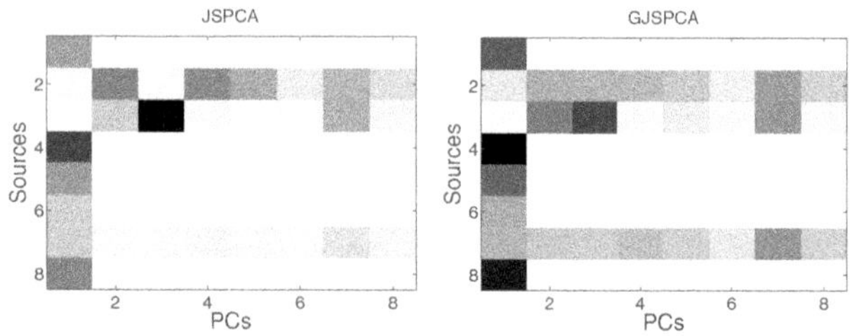

(a) JSPCA (b) GJSPCA

Figure 4: Comparing *joint sparse PCA* (JSPCA) and *graph joint sparse PCA* (GJSPCA).

4.4 Optimization Algorithms

We present our optimization technique to solve equations (8) and (10) based on accelerated gradient descent [27] and projected gradient scheme [2]. Although equations (8) and (10) are not joint convex for A and B, they are convex for A and B individually. The algorithm solves A, B iteratively and achieves a local optimum.

A **given** B: If B is fixed, we obtain the optimal A analytically. Ignoring the regularization part, equation (8) and equation (10) degenerate to

$$\begin{array}{ll} \min\limits_{A} & \frac{1}{2}||X - XBA^T||_F^2 \\ \text{s.t.} & A^TA = I_{p\times p} \end{array} \tag{12}$$

The solution is obtained by a reduced rank form of the Procrustes Rotation. We compute the SVD of GB to obtain the solution where $G = X^TX$ is the gram matrix.

$$\begin{array}{rcl} GB & = & UDV^T \\ \hat{A} & = & UV^T \end{array} \tag{13}$$

Solution in the form of Procrustes Rotation is widely discussed, see [33] for example for a detailed discussion.

B **given** A: If A is fixed, we consider equation (10) only since equation (8) is a special case of equation (10) when $\lambda_2 = 0$, Now the optimization problem becomes:

$$\begin{array}{ll} \min\limits_{A,B} & \frac{1}{2}\sum_{i=1}^{n}||\tilde{\mathbf{x}}_i - AB^T\tilde{\mathbf{x}}_i||_2^2 + \lambda_1 \sum_{j=1}^{p}||\tilde{\mathbf{w}}_j \circ \tilde{\mathbf{b}}_j||_2 + \\ & \frac{1}{2}\lambda_2 tr((W\circ B)^T L (W \circ B)) \end{array} \tag{14}$$

Equation (14) can be rewritten as $\min\limits_{B} \quad F(B) \stackrel{\text{def}}{=} f(B) + R(B)$, where $f(B)$ takes the smooth part of equation(14)

$$f(B) = \frac{1}{2}\sum_{i=1}^{n}||\tilde{\mathbf{x}}_i - AB^T\tilde{\mathbf{x}}_i||_2^2 + \frac{1}{2}\lambda_2 tr((W\circ B)^T L(W\circ B)) \tag{15}$$

and $R(B)$ takes the nonsmooth part, $R(B) = \lambda_1 \sum_{j=1}^{p} ||\tilde{\mathbf{w}}_j \circ \tilde{\mathbf{b}}_j||_2$. It is easy to verify that (15) is a convex and smooth function over B with Lipschitz continuous gradient and the gradient of f is: $\nabla f(B) = G(B - A) + \lambda_2 L(W \circ B)$.

Considering the minimization problem of the smooth function $f(B)$ using the first order gradient descent method, it is well known that the gradient step has the following update at step $i+1$ with step size $1/L_i$:

$$B_{i+1} = B_i - \frac{1}{L_i}\nabla f(B_i) \tag{16}$$

In [1, 27], it has shown that the gradient step equation (16) can be reformulated as a linear approximation of the function f at point B_i regularized by a quadratic proximal term as $B_i = \operatorname*{argmin}_B f_{L_i}(B, B_i)$, where

$$f_{L_i}(B, B_i) = f(B_i) + \langle B - B_i, \nabla f(B_i)\rangle + \frac{L_i}{2}||B - B_i||_F^2 \tag{17}$$

Based on the relationship, we combine equations (17) and $R(B)$ together to formalize the *generalized gradient update step*:

$$\begin{array}{rcl} Q_{L_i}(B, B_i) & = & f_{L_i}(B, B_i) + \lambda_1 ||W \circ B||_{1,2} \\ q_{L_i}(B_i) & = & \operatorname*{argmin}\limits_{B} Q_{L_i}(B, B_i) \end{array} \tag{18}$$

The insight of such a formalization is that by exploring the structure of regularization $R(.)$ we can easily solve the optimization in equation (18), then the convergence rate is the same as that of gradient decent method. Rewriting the optimization problem in equation(18) and ignoring terms that do not depend on B, the objective can be expressed as:

$$q_{L_i}(B_i) = \underset{B \in \mathcal{M}}{\operatorname{argmin}} \left(\frac{1}{2}||B-(B_i-\frac{1}{L_i}\nabla f(B_i))||_F^2+\frac{\lambda_1}{L_i}||W \circ B||_{1,2}\right) \tag{19}$$

With ordinary first order gradient method for smooth problems, the convergence rate is $O(1/\sqrt{\epsilon})$ [27] where ϵ is the desired accuracy. In order to have a better convergence rate, we apply the Nestrerov accelerated gradient descent method [27] with $O(1/\sqrt{\epsilon})$ convergence rate, and solve the *generalized gradient update step* in equation (18) for each gradient update step. Such a procedure has demonstrated scalability and fast convergence in solving various sparse learning formulations [6, 17, 24]. Below we present the accelerated projected gradient algorithm. The stopping criterion is that the change of the objective values in two successive steps is less than a predefined threshold (e.g. 10^{-5}).

Algorithm 1 Accelerated Projected Gradient Descent

```
Input: B_0, W ∈ R^{p×p}, L_1 > 0, F(.), Q_L(.,.) and max-iter.
Output: B.
Initialize B_1 := B_0, t_{-1} := 0, t_0 := 1;
for i = 1 to max-iter do
    α_i := (t_{i-2} - 1)/t_{i-1};
    S := B_i + α_i(B_i - B_{i-1});
    while (true) do
        Compute q_{L_i}(S) in Eq. (19);
        if F(q_{L_i}(S)) > Q_{L_i}(q_{L_i}(S), S) then
            L_i := 2 × L_i;
        else
            break;
        end if
    end while
    B_{i+1} := q_{L_i}(S), L_{i+1} := L_i;
    t_i := 1/2 (1 + sqrt(1 + 4 t_{i-1}^2));
    if (Convergence) then
        B := B_{i+1}, break;
    end if
end for
return B;
```

Now we focus on how to solve the generalized gradient update in equation (19). Let $C = B_i - \frac{1}{L_i}\nabla f(B_i)$ and $\tilde{\lambda} = \lambda_1/L_i$, equation (19) can be represented as:

$$\begin{aligned} q_{L_i}(B_i) &= \underset{B}{\operatorname{argmin}}(\tfrac{1}{2}||B-C||_F^2 + \tilde{\lambda}||W \circ B||_{1,2}) \\ &= \underset{\tilde{\mathbf{b}}_1,\cdots,\tilde{\mathbf{b}}_p}{\operatorname{argmin}} \textstyle\sum_{j=1}^{p}(\tfrac{1}{2}||\tilde{\mathbf{b}}_j - \tilde{\mathbf{c}}_j||_2^2 + \tilde{\lambda}||\tilde{\mathbf{w}}_j \circ \tilde{\mathbf{b}}_j||_2) \end{aligned} \tag{20}$$

where $\tilde{\mathbf{b}}_j^T, \tilde{\mathbf{c}}_j^T$ and $\tilde{\mathbf{w}}_j^T \in \mathbb{R}^p$ are row vectors denoting the jth row of matrices B, C and W. By the additivity of equation (20), we decompose equation (20) into p subproblems. For each subproblem, we ignore the row index j:

$$\min_{\mathbf{b}} \frac{1}{2}||\mathbf{b}-\mathbf{c}||_2^2 + \tilde{\lambda}||\mathbf{w} \circ \mathbf{b}||_2 \tag{21}$$

For simplicity, we assume $\mathbf{b}, \mathbf{c}$ and $\mathbf{w}$ are row vectors here. The following theorem provides the analytical solution of equation (21).

THEOREM 4.1. *Given $\tilde{\lambda}, \mathbf{w} = [\mathbf{0}_{1\times k}, \mathbf{1}_{1\times(p-k)}]$ and $\mathbf{c} = [\mathbf{c}_1, \mathbf{c}_2]$ where $\mathbf{c}_1 = [c_1, \cdots, c_k]$, $\mathbf{c}_2 = [c_{k+1}, \cdots, c_p]$ and k is the number of PCs representing the normal subspace, the optimal solution for (21) $\mathbf{b}^* = [\mathbf{b}_1^*, \mathbf{b}_2^*]$ is given by:*

$$\mathbf{b}_1^* = \mathbf{c}_1$$

and

$$\mathbf{b}_2^* = \begin{cases} (1 - \frac{\tilde{\lambda}}{||\mathbf{c}_2||_2})\mathbf{c}_2 & ||\mathbf{c}_2||_2 > \tilde{\lambda} \\ 0 & \textit{otherwise} \end{cases} \tag{22}$$

PROOF. By the definition of the l_2 norm, the equation (21) can be rewritten as:

$$\min_{\mathbf{b}_1,\mathbf{b}_2} \frac{1}{2}||\mathbf{b}_1 - \mathbf{c}_1||_2^2 + \frac{1}{2}||\mathbf{b}_2 - \mathbf{c}_2||_2^2 + \tilde{\lambda}||\mathbf{b}_2||_2 \tag{23}$$

where $\mathbf{b} = [\mathbf{b}_1, \mathbf{b}_2]$. The solution can be found by decomposing (23) into two subproblems and solving one ordinary least square problem and one least square problem with l_2 norm regularization. Since there is no regularization on $\mathbf{b}_1$ and the two subproblems are independent, the optimal solution of the ordinary least square problem is $\mathbf{b}_1^* = \mathbf{c}_1$. With optimal $\mathbf{b}_1^*$, (23) degenerates to

$$\min_{\mathbf{b}_2} \frac{1}{2}||\mathbf{b}_2 - \mathbf{c}_2||_2^2 + \tilde{\lambda}||\mathbf{b}_2||_2 \tag{24}$$

The analytical solution of equation (24) is given in equation (22) and can be found by forming Lagrangian dual. A detailed proof can be found in [24]. □

We summarize what is briefly discussed previously for GJSPCA in the algorithm below. Note that JSPCA is a special case of GJSPCA, we obtain the algorithm for JSPCA by setting $\lambda_2 = 0$. Given data matrix $X \in \mathbb{R}^{n\times p}$ and the number of PCs representing normal subspace k and regularization parameters λ_1, λ_2, GJSPCA optimizes two matrix variables alternatively and returns the matrix B composed of ordinary PCs representing normal subspace and joint sparse PCs representing the abnormal subspace.

Algorithm 2 Graph Joint Sparse PCA (GJSPCA)

```
Input: X, k, λ_1, λ_2 and max_iter.
Output: B.
A := I_{p×p}, G := X^T X;
for iter = 1 to max_iter do
    Compute B given A using Algorithm 1;
    Compute A given B via (13);
    if (Converge) then
        break;
    end if
end for
return B;
```

5. EXPERIMENTAL STUDIES

We have conducted extensive experiments with three real-world data sets to evaluate the performances of JSPCA and GJSPCA on anomaly localization. We implemented our version of two anomaly localization methods at the network level: stochastic nearest neighbor (SNN) [14] and eigen equation compression (EEC) [11] since no executables were provided by the original authors. We implemented all four methods with Matlab and performed all experiments on a desktop machine with 6 GB memory and a Intel core i7 2.66 GHz CPU.

5.1 Data Sets

We used three real-world data sets from different application domains. For each data set, we singled out several intervals with anomalies. The anomalies are either labeled by the original data provided or manually labeled by ourselves when no labeling is provided. Note that we are only interested in the intervals where anomalies really exist since we focus on localizing anomalies. We used a sliding window with fixed size L and offset $L/2$ to create multiple data windows from the given intervals. The sliding window moves forward with the offset $L/2$ until it reaches the end of the intervals. We run all four methods on each data window to evaluate and compare their performances.

To run GJSPCA we calculated the pair-wise correlation between any two sources within the window. We produced a correlation graph for the data streams with a correlation threshold δ in that if the correlation between two sources is greater than δ, we connect the two sources with an edge. This construction is meaningful because for highly correlated data, streams influence each other and such influence has been shown critical for better anomaly localization, as evaluated in our experimental studies.

Below we briefly discuss the data collection and data preprocessing procedures for the three data sets. In Table 1, we list the intervals that we selected, the dimensionality of the network data streams, the sliding window size L, and the total number of data windows W for each data set.

Table 1: Characteristics of Data Sets. D: Data sets. D1: Stock Indices, D2: Sensor, D3: MotorCurrent. T: total number of time stamps, p: dimensionality of the network data streams, I: total number of intervals, *Indices*: starting point and ending point of the intervals, W: total number of data windows, L: sliding window size.

D	T	p	I	*Indices*	W	L
D1	2396	8	4	[261-300], [361- 400] [761-800], [1631-1670]	12	20
D2	11000	7	4	[2371-2530],[3346-3550] [7191-7215], [8841-8870]	37	20
D3	1500	20	1	[1-1500]	29	50

The Stock Indices Data Set: The stock indices data set includes 8 stock market index streams from 8 countries: Brazil (Brazil Bovespa), Mexico (Bolsa IPC), Argentina (MERVAL), USA (S&P 500 Composite), Canada (S&P TSX Composite), HK (Heng Seng), China (SSE Composite), and Japan (NIKKEI 225). Each stock market index stream contains 2396 stamps recording the daily stock price indices from January 1st 2001 to March 5th 2010.

Since this data set has no ground truth, we manually labeled all the daily indices for the selected intervals. In our labeling we followed the criteria list in [5] where small turbulence and co-movements of most markets are considered as normal, dramatic price changes or significance deviation from the co-movements (e.g. one index goes up while the others in the market drop down) are considered as abnormal.

The Sun Spot Sensor Data Set: We collected a sensor data set in a car trial for transport chain security validation using seven wireless Sun Small Programmable Object Technologies (SPOTs). Each SPOT contains a 3-axis accelerometer sensor. In our data collection, seven Sun SPOTs were fixed in the separated boxes and were loaded on the back seat of a car. Each Sun SPOTs recorded the magnitude of accelerations along x, y, z axis with a sample rate of 390ms. We simulated a few abnormal events including box removal and replacement, rotation and flipping. The overall acceleration $\sqrt{(x^2+y^2+z^2)}$ was used to detect the designed anomalous events.

The Motor Current Data Set: The Motor Current Data is the current observation generated by the state space simulations available at UCR Time Series Archive [19]. The anomalies are the simulated machinery failure in different components of a machine. The current value was observed from 21 different motor operating conditions, including one healthy operating mode and 20 faulty modes. For each motor operating condition, 20 time series were recorded with a length of 1,500 samples. Therefore, there are 20 normal time series and 400 abnormal time series altogether.

In our evaluation, we randomly extracted 20 time series out of 420 with the length 1500. 10 time series are from normal series and the rest are from abnormal series.

5.2 Model Evaluation

For evaluation, since our focus is anomaly localization, we did not evaluate anomaly detection although our methods are able to do both. We used the standard ROC curves and area under ROC curve (AUC) to evaluate the anomaly localization performance. Below we introduce the details regarding the construction of ROC curves.

As defined in equation 11, a higher abnormal score indicates a higher probability the source is abnormal, which is the same as that of the baseline methods [11, 14] for comparison. To have a fair comparison, we compared the normalized abnormal score among each method. The reason for normalization is that the anomaly scores generated by the baseline methods have different orders of magnitude. We used the term "anomaly score" to refer to the normalized abnormal score in the following analysis.

For each data window, the abnormal score vector $\tilde{\zeta} = [\tilde{\zeta}_1, \cdots, \tilde{\zeta}_p]^T$ was generated and compared with a cut-off threshold between $[0, 1]$ to separate abnormal sources and innocent sources. We performed the same procedure for all the data windows and finally we obtained a prediction matrix with size w by p, such that w is the number of data window and p is the number of sources. Each entry in the prediction matrix is 0 or 1 to indicate whether the source is normal or abnormal. Comparing the prediction matrix with the ground truth resulted in a pair of true positive rate (TPR) and false positive rate (FPR), where TPR is the total number of true detected abnormal sources over the total number of abnormal sources, and FPR is the total number of incorrect detected abnormal sources over the total number of normal sources in W windows. By changing the threshold, we obtained the ROC curve and the AUC value.

5.3 Anomaly Localization Performance

We have two parameters to tune in JSPCA: λ_1: controlling the sparsity, and k: the dimension of normal subspace. GJSPCA has two more parameters: λ_2: controlling the smoothness, and δ, the correlation threshold to construct the correlation graph. For the other two methods, we need to select the number of neighbors k for SSN and the number of clusters c for EEC. We first performed a grid search for each method to identify the optimal parameters and then

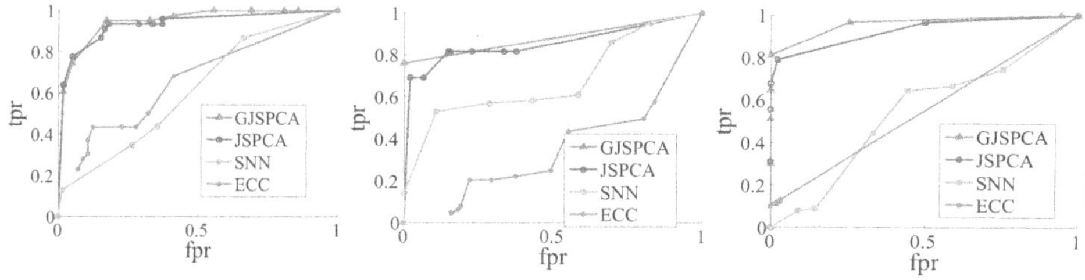

Dataset \ Method (AUC)	SNN	ECC	JSPCA	GJSPCA
Stock Indices	0.6119	0.6510	0.9316	0.9457
Sensor	0.6783	0.3491	0.8527	0.8798
MotorCurrent	0.5444	0.5515	0.9273	0.9601

Figure 5: ROC curves and AUC for different methods on three data sets. From left to right: ROC for the stock indices data, ROC for the sensor data, ROC curve for MotorCurrent data, AUC for the three ROC plots

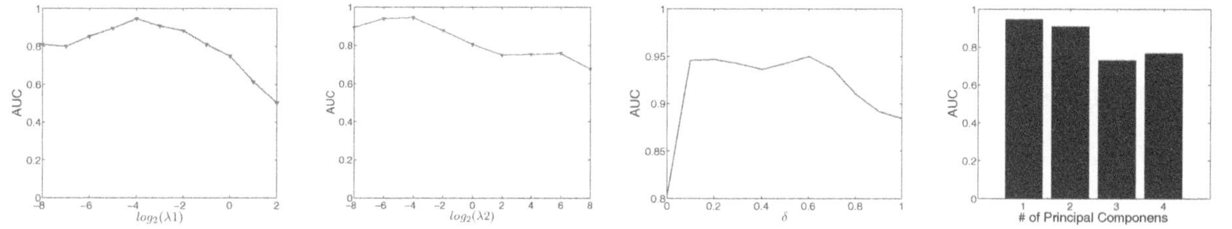

Figure 6: From left to right, sensitivity analysis on λ_1, λ_2, δ, and the dimension of the normal subspace.

compared the performances. The performances of different methods depend on the parameter selection. We evaluated the sensitivity of our results in the next selection.

For each data set, we tuned λ_1, λ_2 within $\{2^{-8}, 2^{-7}, \cdots, 2^8\}$ and δ from 0.1 to 0.9. k was tuned from 1 to 4 for the stock market and sensor data, and from 2 to 7 for the motor current data. All the ranges were set by empirical knowledge. Our empirical study showed that the performances did not change significantly as the parameters vary in a wide range, which reduced the parameter search space significantly.

Table 2 lists the best parameter combination for JSPCA and GJSPCA. For SNN, we tuned the number of neighbors k in the range $2 \sim 6$ (for stock index data set and sensor data) and in the range $2 \sim 10$ (for motorcurrent data) respectively. For EEC method, the number of clusters c was tuned between $2 \sim 4$.

In Figure 5, we show the performances for the four methods on three different data sets. JSPCA and GJSPCA clearly outperform the other two methods. The AUC value of JSPCA and GJSPCA are both above 0.85 on three data sets, while that of EEC and SNN are around $[0.5 \sim 0.6]$. Compared with JSPCA, GJSPCA is slightly better, which supports our hypothesis on the importance of incorporating the structure information of network data streams into anomaly localization. SNN clearly outperforms EEC on Sensor data, and is comparable with EEC for the other two data sets.

5.4 Parameter Selection

In this section, we evaluated the sensitivity of our methods to different modeling parameters. In order to do so, we selected one parameter at a time, systematically changed its value while fixing the others at their optimal values. Although our approaches have more parameters than the other two methods, the sensitivity analysis shows that performances of our methods are remarkably stable over a wide range of parameters. Next we show the sensitivity study on the stock indices data set for the parameters λ_1 and λ_2, δ, k. Similar results are observed on the other two data sets.

Table 2: Optimal parameters combinations on three data sets. J*:JSPCA, GJ*: GJSPCA.

	λ_1		k		λ_2	δ
Data set	J*	GJ*	J*	GJ*	GJ*	GJ*
Stock Indices	2^{-3}	2^{-4}	1	1	2^{-4}	0.6
Sensor	2^{-7}	2^{-5}	1	1	2^{-6}	0.6
MotorCurrent	2^{-2}	2^{-2}	5	5	2^{-8}	0.5

In Figure 6, we show the stability by changing λ_1. We observe that AUC is quite stable over a wide range of λ_1. A similar phenomenon is also observed when changing λ_2. In the middle part of figure 6, we performed sensitivity analysis on parameter δ. We observe that AUC remains stable for $\delta \in [0.15, 0.6]$. When $\delta = 0$, the graph is a complete graph and the smoothness regularization will penalize the loadings of each source across the PCs to be similar to each other. Hence very low δ leads to a worse performance. On the other hand, when $\delta = 1$, the graph is just a set of isolated sources. The structure information is missing, therefore the performance is not optimal.

An important parameter in PCA based anomaly detection is k, the number of PCs spanning the normal subspace. In [28], Ringberg *et al.* claimed that the anomaly detection performance was very sensitive to k. We demonstrate in the right part of figure 6 that our methods achieve a relatively stable performance as the dimension of normal subspace changes from 1 to 4. More specifically, the overall AUC gradually decreases from 0.96 to 0.72 as k changes from 1 to 3 and then increases to 0.77 at $k = 4$. However even in the worst case $k = 3$ it still has a good performance with AUC$= 0.73$. This study demonstrates that our model is not sensitive to k.

6. CONCLUSIONS AND FUTURE WORK

Previous work on PCA based anomaly detection claimed that PCA cannot be used for anomaly localization. We propose two novel approaches, *joint sparse PCA* (JSPCA) and *graph joint sparse PCA* (GJSPCA), for anomaly detection and localization in network data streams. By enforcing joint sparsity on the PCs representing the abnormal subspace and incorporating the structure information of network via regularization, we significantly extend the applicability of PCA based technique for localization. Our experimental studies on three real world data sets demonstrate the effectiveness of our approach. Our future works will focus on three directions: (a) how to select the number of principal components that best interpret the normal subspace, and (b) how to extend our approach to kernel PCA, and (c) how to develop alternative optimization techniques to improve the scalability.

Acknowledgments

The work is partially supported by the NSF award IIS 0845951 and the Office of Naval Research N00014-07-1-1042.

7. REFERENCES

[1] D. P. Bertsekas. *Nonlinear programming.* Athena Scientific. 2nd edition., 1999.

[2] S. Boyd and L. Vandenberghe. *Convex Optimization.* Cambridge University Press, 2004.

[3] D. Brauckhoff, X. Dimitropoulos, A. Wagner, and K. Salamatian. Anomaly extraction in backbone networks using association rules. In *Proceedings of the 9th ACM SIGCOMM conference on Internet measurement conference*, IMC '09, pages 28–34, New York, NY, USA, 2009. ACM.

[4] S. Budhaditya, D.-S. Pham, M. Lazarescu, and S. Venkatesh. Effective anomaly detection in sensor networks data streams. *IEEE International Conference on Data Mining, ICDM2009*, 0:722–727, 2009.

[5] V. Chandola, A. Banerjee, and V. Kumar. Anomaly detection: A survey. *ACM Comput. Surv.*, 41(3), 2009.

[6] X. Chen, W. Pan, J. T. Kwok, and J. G. Carbonell. Accelerated gradient method for multi-task sparse learning problem. In *ICDM*, pages 746–751, 2009.

[7] P. H. dos Santos Teixeira and R. L. Milidiú. Data stream anomaly detection through principal subspace tracking. In *SAC '10: Proceedings of the 2010 ACM Symposium on Applied Computing*, pages 1609–1616, New York, NY, USA, 2010. ACM.

[8] H. Fei and J. Huan. Boosting with structure information in the functional space: an application to graph classification. In *Proceedings of the ACM SIGKDD International Conference on Knowledge Discovery and Data Mining (SIGKDD)*, 2010.

[9] C. Franke and M. Gertz. Orden: outlier region detection and exploration in sensor networks. In *SIGMOD Conference*, pages 1075–1078, 2009.

[10] X. Gu and H. Wang. Online anomaly prediction for robust cluster systems. In *ICDE*, pages 1000–1011, 2009.

[11] S. Hirose, K. Yamanishi, T. Nakata, and R. Fujimaki. Network anomaly detection based on eigen equation compression. In *KDD '09: Proceedings of the 15th ACM SIGKDD international conference on Knowledge discovery and data mining*, pages 1185–1194, New York, NY, USA, 2009. ACM.

[12] L. Huang, M. I. Jordan, A. Joseph, M. Garofalakis, and N. Taft. In-network pca and anomaly detection. In *In NIPS*, pages 617–624, 2006.

[13] T. Idé, A. C. Lozano, N. Abe, and Y. Liu. Proximity-based anomaly detection using sparse structure learning. In *SDM*, pages 97–108, 2009.

[14] T. Idé, S. Papadimitriou, and M. Vlachos. Computing correlation anomaly scores using stochastic nearest neighbors. In *ICDM '07: Proceedings of the 2007 Seventh IEEE International Conference on Data Mining*, pages 523–528, Washington, DC, USA, 2007. IEEE Computer Society.

[15] M. Isaac, B. Raul, E. Gerard, and G. Moisès. On-line fault diagnosis based on the identification of transient stages. In *in Proc. of 20th European Symposium on Computer Aided Process Engineering ÍC ESCAPE20.* Elsevier B.V., 2010.

[16] R. Jenatton, G. Obozinski, and F. Bach. Structured sparse principal component analysis. In *Proceedings of the 13th International Conference on Artificial Intelligence and Statistics (AISTATS) 2010*, 2010.

[17] S. Ji and J. Ye. An accelerated gradient method for trace norm minimization. In *ICML '09: Proceedings of the 26th Annual International Conference on Machine Learning*, pages 457–464, New York, NY, USA, 2009. ACM.

[18] R. Jiang, H. Fei, and J. Huan. Anomaly localization by joint sparse pca in wireless sensor networks. In *Proceedings of the The 4th International Workshop on Knowledge Discovery from Sensor Data (SensorKDD-2010)*, 2010.

[19] E. Keogh and T. Folias. The ucr time series data mining archive. Website, 2002. `http://www.cs.ucr.edu/eamonn/TSDMA/index.html`.

[20] E. Keogh, J. Lin, and A. Fu. Hot sax: Efficiently finding the most unusual time series subsequence. In *Proceedings of the Fifth IEEE International Conference on Data Mining*, ICDM '05, pages 226–233, Washington, DC, USA, 2005.

[21] A. Lakhina, M. Crovella, and C. Diot. Diagnosing network-wide traffic anomalies. In *In ACM SIGCOMM*, pages 219–230, 2004.

[22] A. Lakhina, M. Crovella, and C. Diot. Mining anomalies using traffic feature distributions. In *In ACM SIGCOMM*, pages 217–228, 2005.

[23] J.-G. Lee, J. Han, and X. Li. Trajectory outlier detection: A partition-and-detect framework. In *ICDE*, pages 140–149, 2008.

[24] J. Liu, S. Ji, and J. Ye. Multi-task feature learning via efficient l2,1-norm minimization. In *Conference on Uncertainty in Artificial Intelligence (UAI) 2009*, 2009.

[25] X. Liu, X. Wu, H. Wang, R. Z. 0003, J. Bailey, and K. Ramamohanarao. Mining distribution change in stock order streams. In *ICDE*, pages 105–108, 2010.

[26] A. Lung-Yut-Fong, C. Lévy-Leduc, and O. Cappé. Distributed detection/localization of change-points in high-dimensional network traffic data. *CoRR*, abs/0909.5524, 2009.

[27] Y. Nesterov. Introductory lectures on convex optimization: A basic course. 2003.

[28] H. Ringberg, A. Soule, J. Rexford, and C. Diot. Sensitivity of pca for traffic anomaly detection. In *SIGMETRICS '07: Proceedings of the 2007 ACM SIGMETRICS international conference on Measurement and modeling of computer systems*, pages 109–120, New York, NY, USA, 2007. ACM.

[29] J. Silva and R. Willett. Detection of anomalous meetings in a social network. In *42nd Annual Conference on Information Sciences and Systems, 2008. CISS 2008.*, pages 636 –641, 2008.

[30] J. B. Tenenbaum, V. de Silva, and J. C. Langford. A Global Geometric Framework for Nonlinear Dimensionality Reduction. *Science*, 290(5500):2319 – 2323, 2000.

[31] N. Xu, S. Rangwala, and *et al.* . A wireless sensor network for structural monitoring. In *IN SENSYS*, pages 13–24, 2004.

[32] J. Zhang, Q. Gao, and H. Wang. Anomaly detection in high-dimensional network data streams: A case study. In *IEEE International Conference on Intelligence and Security Informatics, 2008. ISI 2008.*, pages 251 –253, June 2008.

[33] H. Zou, T. Hastie, and R. Tibshirani. Sparse principal component analysis. *Journal of Computational and Graphical Statistics*, 15(2):265–286, 2006.

Approximate Kernel k-means: Solution to Large Scale Kernel Clustering

Radha Chitta, Rong Jin, Timothy C. Havens, Anil K. Jain
Dept. of Computer Science and Engineering
Michigan State University
East Lansing, MI, 48824, USA
chittara@msu.edu, rongjin@cse.msu.edu, havenst@gmail.com, jain@cse.msu.edu

ABSTRACT

Digital data explosion mandates the development of scalable tools to organize the data in a meaningful and easily accessible form. Clustering is a commonly used tool for data organization. However, many clustering algorithms designed to handle large data sets assume linear separability of data and hence do not perform well on real world data sets. While kernel-based clustering algorithms can capture the non-linear structure in data, they do not scale well in terms of speed and memory requirements when the number of objects to be clustered exceeds tens of thousands. We propose an approximation scheme for kernel k-means, termed **approximate kernel k-means**, that reduces both the computational complexity and the memory requirements by employing a randomized approach. We show both analytically and empirically that the performance of approximate kernel k-means is similar to that of the kernel k-means algorithm, but with dramatically reduced run-time complexity and memory requirements.

Categories and Subject Descriptors

H.3.3 [**Information Search and Retrieval**]: Clustering; I.5.3 [**Pattern Recognition**]: Clustering—*Algorithms*

General Terms

Performance

Keywords

Large-scale clustering, Kernel clustering, k-means

1. INTRODUCTION

Advances in data collection and storage technologies over the past few years have resulted in data explosion in every scientific domain. A study by IDC and EMC Corp [1] predicted the creation of 35 trillion gigabytes of digital data by the year 2020. Much of this data (text, images and videos) is generated through online services like e-mail, social networks and blogs. Large-scale clustering is one of the principal tools to efficiently organize the massive amount of data and to enable convenient access by users. Clustering has found use in various applications such as web search, image retrieval, gene expression analysis, recommendation systems and market research based on transaction data [8, 24].

Most large-scale clustering techniques reported in the literature focus on grouping based on the Euclidean distance with the inherent assumption that all the data points lie in a Euclidean geometry. Kernel-based clustering methods overcome this limitation by embedding the data points into a high-dimensional non-linear manifold and defining their similarity using a nonlinear kernel distance function [27]. A number of kernel-based clustering methods such as spectral clustering [34, 41], non-negative matrix factorization (NMF) [44], kernel Self-Organizing Maps (SOM) [23, 32] and kernel neural gas [36] have been proposed. In this study, we focus on kernel k-means [17, 39, 40] due to its simplicity and efficiency. For instance, unlike spectral clustering, kernel k-means does not require the computation of the top eigenvectors of the kernel matrix, whose time complexity is cubic in the number of data points. In addition, several studies [12, 13, 45] have established the equivalence of kernel k-means and other kernel-based clustering methods, suggesting that most kernel-based clustering methods yield similar results.

Kernel k-means is a nonlinear extension of the classical k-means algorithm. It replaces the Euclidean distance function $d^2(x_a, x_b) = \|x_a - x_b\|^2$ employed in the k-means algorithm with a non-linear kernel distance function defined as

$$d_\kappa^2(x_a, x_b) = \kappa(x_a, x_a) + \kappa(x_b, x_b) - 2\kappa(x_a, x_b),$$

where $x_a \in \Re^d$ and $x_b \in \Re^d$ are two data points and $\kappa(.,.) : \Re^d \times \Re^d \to \Re$ is the kernel function. While the kernel distance function enables the clustering algorithm to capture the nonlinear structure in data, it requires computation and storage of an $n \times n$ kernel matrix in memory, rendering it non-scalable to large data sets. In this paper, we address the challenge posed by the large kernel matrix.

Note that the full kernel matrix is required in kernel k-means because the cluster centers are represented as a linear combination of *all* the data points, in accordance with the representer theorem [38]. In other words, the cluster centers lie in the subspace spanned by all the data points to be clustered. We can avoid computing the full kernel matrix by restricting the cluster centers to a smaller subspace. We randomly select a small number of data points, and approximate the cluster centers using vectors in the subspace spanned by this subset. This approximation requires the

KDD'11, August 21–24, 2011, San Diego, California, USA.

computation and storage of only a small portion of the full kernel matrix, leading to a significant speedup of kernel k-means. We demonstrate, both theoretically and empirically, that the approximate kernel k-means yields similar clustering performance as the kernel k-means using the full kernel matrix.

The rest of the paper is organized as follows. Section 2 outlines the related work on large scale clustering and the kernel k-means algorithm. We present the approximate kernel k-means algorithm in Section 3 and its analysis in Section 4. Section 5 summarizes the results of our empirical studies, and Section 6 concludes this study with future work.

2. RELATED WORK

We first review the related work on large scale clustering and kernel based clustering, and then describe the kernel k-means algorithm.

2.1 Large scale clustering

A number of methods have been developed to efficiently cluster large data sets. Incremental clustering [5, 6] and divide-and-conquer based clustering algorithms [3, 18] were designed to operate in a single pass over the data points, thereby reducing the time required for clustering. Sampling based methods, such as CLARA [26] and CURE [19], reduce the computation time by finding the cluster centers based on a small number of randomly selected data points. The coreset algorithms [21] apply a similar idea except that the cluster centers are found based on a small set of representative, instead of randomly selected data points. Clustering algorithms, such as BIRCH [47], CLARANS [35], improve the clustering efficiency by summarizing the data set into data structures like trees and graphs for efficient data access.

With the evolution of cloud computing, parallel processing techniques for clustering [7, 9, 10, 15, 25, 33] are gaining popularity. These techniques speedup the clustering process by first dividing the task into a number of independent sub-tasks that can be performed simultaneously, and then efficiently merging these solutions into the final solution.

2.2 Kernel based clustering

Most of the existing methods for large scale clustering are based on the Euclidean distance, and are therefore, unable to deal with the data sets that are not linearly separable. Kernel based clustering techniques address this limitation by introducing a kernel distance function to capture the nonlinear structure in data [27]. Various kernel based clustering algorithms have been developed, including kernel k-means [39, 40], spectral clustering [34, 41], NMF [44], kernel SOM [23, 32] and kernel neural gas [36]. A key challenge faced by all the kernel-based algorithms is scalability as they require computing the full kernel matrix whose size is quadratic in the number of data points. Sampling methods, such as the Nystrom method [20, 43], have been employed to address this challenge [16, 31]. The key idea is to obtain a low rank approximation of the kernel matrix by sampling a number of columns of the kernel matrix and performing clustering using the approximate kernel matrix. A variety of sampling techniques are proposed in [4, 14, 28] and it has been shown that uniform sampling yields the best performance when compared to the other sampling techniques [28]. Finally, in [37], random projection is used along with the sampling method to further improve the clustering efficiency.

2.3 Kernel k-means

Let $X = \{x_1, x_2, ..., x_n\}$ be the input data set consisting of n data points, where $x_i \in \Re^d$, C be the number of clusters and $K \in \Re^{n\times n}$ be the kernel matrix with $K_{ij} = \kappa(x_i, x_j)$, where $\kappa(\cdot,\cdot)$ is the kernel function. Let $\mathcal{H}_\kappa$ be the Reproducing Kernel Hilbert Space (RKHS) endowed by the kernel function $\kappa(\cdot,\cdot)$, and $|\cdot|_{\mathcal{H}_\kappa}$ be the functional norm for $\mathcal{H}_\kappa$. The objective of kernel k-means is to minimize the *clustering error*, defined as the sum of squared distances between the data points and the center of the cluster to which the point is assigned. Hence, the kernel k-means problem can be cast as the following optimization problem:

$$\min_{U\in\mathcal{P}} \max_{\{c_k(\cdot)\in\mathcal{H}_\kappa\}_{k=1}^C} \sum_{k=1}^{C}\sum_{i=1}^{n} U_{ki}|c_k(\cdot) - \kappa(x_i,\cdot)|^2_{\mathcal{H}_\kappa}, \tag{1}$$

where $U = (\mathbf{u}_1, \ldots, \mathbf{u}_C)^\top$ is the cluster membership matrix, $c_k(\cdot) \in \mathcal{H}_\kappa, k \in [C]$ are the cluster centers, and domain $\mathcal{P} = \{U \in \{0,1\}^{C\times n} : U^\top\mathbf{1} = \mathbf{1}\}$, where $\mathbf{1}$ is a vector of all ones. For convenience of presentation, we introduce two normalized versions of U. Let $n_k = \mathbf{u}_k^\top\mathbf{1}$ be the number of data points assigned to the kth cluster. We denote by

$$\begin{aligned}\widehat{U} &= (\widehat{\mathbf{u}}_1, \ldots, \widehat{\mathbf{u}}_C)^\top = [\text{diag}(n_1, \ldots, n_C)]^{-1}U,\\ \widetilde{U} &= (\widetilde{\mathbf{u}}_1, \ldots, \widetilde{\mathbf{u}}_C)^\top = [\text{diag}(\sqrt{n_1}, \ldots, \sqrt{n_C})]^{-1}U,\end{aligned}$$

the ℓ_1 and ℓ_2 normalized membership matrices, respectively.

It is easy to verify that given the cluster membership matrix U, the optimal solution for cluster centers is

$$c_k(\cdot) = \sum_{i=1}^{n} \widehat{U}_{ki}\kappa(x_i,\cdot), k \in [C]. \tag{2}$$

As a result, we can formulate (1) as an optimization problem over U:

$$\min_U \text{tr}(K) - \text{tr}(\widetilde{U}K\widetilde{U}^\top). \tag{3}$$

As indicated in (3), a naive implementation of kernel k-means requires computation and storage of the full $n \times n$ kernel matrix K, rendering it unsuitable for data sets with n greater than a few ten thousands. To the best of our knowledge, only a few attempts have been made to scale kernel k-means for large data sets. In [46], the memory requirement is reduced by dividing kernel matrix into blocks and using one block of the kernel matrix at a time. Although this technique handles the memory complexity, it still requires the computation of the full kernel matrix. The objective of our work is to reduce both the computational complexity and the memory requirements of kernel k-means.

3. APPROXIMATE KERNEL K-MEANS

A simple and naive approach for reducing the complexity of kernel k-means is to randomly sample m points from the data set to be clustered, and find the optimal cluster centers based only on the sampled points; then assign every unsampled data point to the cluster whose center is nearest. We refer to this 2-step process as the **two-step kernel k-means**, detailed in Algorithm 1. Though this approach has reduced run-time complexity and memory requirements, its performance does not match that of the full kernel k-means, unless it is provided with a sufficiently large sample of data points.

We propose a superior approach for reducing the complexity of kernel k-means based on a simple but important observation. Kernel k-means requires the computation of the full kernel matrix K as the cluster centers $\{c_k(\cdot), k \in [C]\}$ are linear combinations of *all* the data points to be clustered, in accordance with (2). In other words, the cluster centers lie in the subspace spanned by all the data points, i.e., $c_k(\cdot) \in \mathcal{H}_a = \text{span}(\kappa(x_1, \cdot), \ldots, \kappa(x_n, \cdot)), k \in [C]$. We can avoid computing the full kernel matrix if we restrict the solution for the cluster centers to a smaller subspace $\mathcal{H}_b \subset \mathcal{H}_a$. $\mathcal{H}_b$ should be constructed such that (i) $\mathcal{H}_b$ is small enough to allow efficient computation, and (ii) $\mathcal{H}_b$ is rich enough to yield similar clustering results as those using $\mathcal{H}_a$. We employ a simple randomized approach for constructing $\mathcal{H}_b$: we randomly sample m data points ($m \ll n$), denoted by $\widehat{X} = \{\widehat{x}_1, \ldots, \widehat{x}_m\}$, and construct the subspace $\mathcal{H}_b = \text{span}(\widehat{x}_1, \ldots, \widehat{x}_m)$. Given the subspace $\mathcal{H}_b$, we modify (1) as

$$\min_{U \in \mathcal{P}} \max_{\{c_k(\cdot) \in \mathcal{H}_b\}_{k=1}^C} \sum_{k=1}^{C} \sum_{i=1}^{n} U_{ki} |c_k(\cdot) - \kappa(x_i, \cdot)|^2_{\mathcal{H}_\kappa}. \quad (4)$$

Let $K_B \in \Re^{n \times m}$ represent the kernel similarity matrix between data points in X and the sampled data points $\widehat{X}$, and $\widehat{K} \in \Re^{m \times m}$ represent the kernel similarity between the sampled data points. The following lemma allows us to reduce (4) to an optimization problem involving only the cluster membership matrix U.

LEMMA 1. *Given the cluster membership matrix U, the optimal cluster centers to (4) are given by*

$$c_k(\cdot) = \sum_{i=1}^{m} \alpha_{ki} \kappa(\widehat{x}_i, \cdot), \quad (5)$$

where $\alpha = \widehat{U} K_B \widehat{K}^{-1}$. The optimization problem for U is given by

$$\min_U tr(K) - tr(\widetilde{U} K_B \widehat{K}^{-1} K_B^\top \widetilde{U}^\top). \quad (6)$$

PROOF. Let $\varphi_i = (\kappa(x_i, \widehat{x}_1), \ldots, \kappa(x_i, \widehat{x}_m))$ and $\alpha_i = (\alpha_{i1}, \ldots, \alpha_{im})$ be the i-th rows of matrices K_B and α respectively. As $c_k(\cdot) \in \mathcal{H}_b = \text{span}(\widehat{x}_1, \ldots, \widehat{x}_m)$, we can write $c_k(\cdot)$ as

$$c_k(\cdot) = \sum_{i=1}^{m} \alpha_{ki} \kappa(\widehat{x}_i, \cdot).$$

and write the objective function in (4) as

$$\sum_{k=1}^{C} \sum_{i=1}^{n} U_{ki} |c_k(\cdot) - \kappa(x_i, \cdot)|^2_{\mathcal{H}_\kappa}$$

$$= \text{tr}(K) + \sum_{k=1}^{C} \left(n_k \alpha_k^\top \widehat{K} \alpha_k - 2\mathbf{u}_k^\top K_B \alpha_k \right). \quad (7)$$

By minimizing over α_k, we have

$$\alpha_k = \widehat{K}^{-1} K_B^\top \widehat{\mathbf{u}}_k, k \in [C]$$

and therefore, $\alpha = \widehat{U} K_B \widehat{K}^{-1}$. We complete the proof by substituting the expression for α into (7). □

As indicated by Lemma 1, we need to compute only K_B [1] for finding the cluster memberships. When $m \ll n$, this computational cost would be significantly smaller than that of computing the full matrix. Note that the problem in (6) can also be viewed as approximating the kernel matrix K in (4) by $K_B \widehat{K}^{-1} K_B^\top$, which is equivalent to the Nystrom method for low rank matrix approximation. We refer to the proposed algorithm as **Approximate Kernel *k*-means**, outlined in Algorithm 2. Figure 1 illustrates and compares this algorithm with the two-step kernel k-means on a 2-dimensional synthetic data set.

Algorithm 1 Two-step Kernel k-means

1: **Input**:
- $X = (x_1, \ldots, x_n)$: the set of n data points to be clustered
- $\kappa(\cdot, \cdot) : \Re^d \times \Re^d \mapsto \Re$: kernel function
- m: the number of randomly sampled data points ($m \ll n$)
- C: the number of clusters

2: Randomly select m data points from X, denoted by $\widehat{X} = (\widehat{x}_1, \ldots, \widehat{x}_m)$.
3: *// Step 1*
4: Compute the cluster centers, denoted by $c_k(\cdot), k \in [C]$, by applying the standard kernel k-means to $\widehat{X}$.
5: *// Step 2*
6: **for** $i = 1, \ldots, n$ **do**
7: Find the closest cluster center k_* for x_i by

$$k_* = \arg\min_{k \in [C]} |c_k(\cdot) - \kappa(x_i, \cdot)|_{\mathcal{H}_\kappa}$$

8: Update the ith column of U by $U_{ki} = 1$ for $k = k_*$ and zero otherwise.
9: **end for**

4. ANALYSIS

In this section, we first analyze the computational complexity of the proposed approximate kernel k-means algorithm, and then examine the quality of the data partitions generated by the proposed algorithm.

4.1 Computational Complexity

The most expensive operation in the proposed algorithm is the matrix inversion $\widehat{K}^{-1}$ and calculation of $T = K_B \widehat{K}^{-1}$, which has a computational cost of $O(m^3 + m^2 n)$. The computational cost of computing α and updating the membership matrix U is $O(mnCl)$, where l is the number of iterations needed for convergence. Hence, the overall computational cost is $O(m^3 + m^2 n + mnCl)$. We can further reduce the computational complexity by avoiding the matrix inversion $\widehat{K}^{-1}$ and formulating the calculation of $\alpha = \widehat{U} T = \widehat{U} K_B \widehat{K}^{-1}$ as the following optimization problem:

$$\min_{\alpha \in \Re^{C \times m}} \frac{1}{2} \text{tr}(\alpha \widehat{K} \alpha) - \text{tr}(\widehat{U} K_B \alpha^\top) \quad (8)$$

If $\widehat{K}$ is well conditioned (i.e., the minimum eigen value of $\widehat{K}$ is significantly larger than zero), we can solve the optimization problem in (8) by a simple gradient descent method

[1] Note that $\widehat{K}$ is part of K_B and therefore does not need to be computed separately.

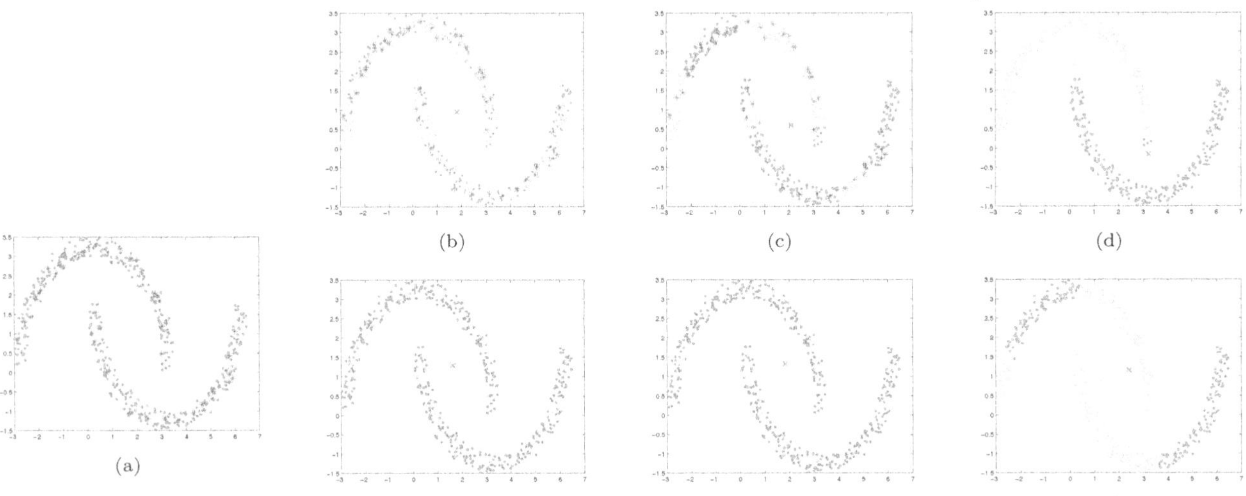

Figure 1: Illustration of the approximate kernel k-means algorithm and the two-step kernel k-means algorithm on a 2-D data set. Figure (a) shows all the data points (in red) and the sampled points (in blue). Figures (b)-(d) and (e)-(g) show the process of discovery of the two clusters in the data set and their centers (represented by x) by the proposed algorithm and the two-step algorithm, respectively. The approximate kernel k-means algorithm assigns labels to all the data points during each iteration while constraining the centers to the subspace spanned by the sampled points. The two-step algorithm clusters only the sampled points and assigns labels to the remaining points in the final phase.

Algorithm 2 Approximate Kernel k-means

```
Input:
  • X = (x_1, ..., x_n): the set of n data points to be clustered
  • κ(·,·) : ℜ^d × ℜ^d ↦ ℜ: kernel function
  • m: the number of randomly sampled data points (m ≪ n)
  • C: the number of clusters
  • MAXITER: maximum number of iterations
Randomly sample m data points from X, denoted by X̂ = (x̂_1, ..., x̂_m).
Compute K_B = [κ(x_i, x̂_j)]_{n×m} and K̂ = [κ(x̂_i, x̂_j)]_{m×m}.
Compute T = K_B K̂^{-1}.
Randomly initialize the membership matrix U.
Set t = 0.
repeat
  Set t = t + 1.
  Compute the ℓ_1 normalized membership matrix Û by Û = [diag(U1)]^{-1} U.
  Calculate α = ÛT.
  for i = 1, ..., n do
    Find the closest cluster center k_* for x_i by
        k_* = arg min_{k∈[C]} α_k^T K̂ α_k − 2φ_k^T α_k
    where α_k and φ_k are the kth rows of matrix α and K_B, respectively.
    Update the ith column of U by U_{ki} = 1 for k = k_* and zero otherwise.
  end for
until the membership matrix U does not change or t > MAXITER
```

with a convergence rate of $O(\log(1/\varepsilon))$, where ε is the desired accuracy. As the computational cost of each step in the gradient descent method is $O(m^2C)$, the overall computational cost is only $O(m^2Cl\log(1/\varepsilon)) \ll O(m^3)$ when $Cl \ll m$. Using this trick, we reduce the overall computational cost to $O(m^2Cl + mnCl + m^2n)$. As the largest matrix that needs to be stored in memory in Algorithm 2 is K_B, the memory requirement is only $O(mn)$. This is a dramatic decrease in the run-time and memory requirements for large data sets when compared to the $O(n^2)$ complexity of classical kernel k-means.

4.2 Error Bound

In this section, we compare the clustering error of our algorithm with that of kernel k-means run using the full kernel. As the proposed algorithm differs from the standard kernel k-means algorithm only by the restriction of the cluster centers to a smaller subspace $\mathcal{H}_b$, constructed using the sampled data points, our analysis will be focused on bounding the expected error due to this constraint.

We introduce binary random variables $\xi = (\xi_1, \xi_2, ..., \xi_n)^\top \in \{0,1\}^n$ to represent the random sampling process, where $\xi_i = 1$ if x_i is selected for constructing the subspace and zero otherwise. The following proposition allows us to write the clustering error in terms of random variable ξ.

Proposition 1. *Given the cluster membership matrix $U = (\mathbf{u}_1, \ldots, \mathbf{u}_C)^\top$, the clustering error can be expressed in ξ as*

$$\mathcal{L}(U, \xi) = tr(K) + \sum_{k=1}^{C} \mathcal{L}_k(U, \xi), \tag{9}$$

where $\mathcal{L}_k(U, \xi)$ is

$$\mathcal{L}_k(U, \xi) = \min_{\alpha_k \in \Re^n} -2\mathbf{u}_k^\top K(\alpha_k \circ \xi) + n_k(\alpha_k \circ \xi)^\top K(\alpha_k \circ \xi).$$

Note that $\xi = \mathbf{1}$, where $\mathbf{1}$ is a vector of all ones, implies that all the data points are chosen for constructing the subspace $\mathcal{H}_b$, which is equivalent to kernel k-means using the full kernel matrix. As a result, $\mathcal{L}(U, \mathbf{1})$ is the clustering error of the standard kernel k-means algorithm.

The following lemma bounds the expectation of the clustering error.

LEMMA 2. *Given the membership matrix U, we have the expectation of $\mathcal{L}(U, \xi)$ bounded as follows*

$$\mathrm{E}_\xi[\mathcal{L}(U,\xi)] \leq \mathcal{L}(U,\mathbf{1}) + tr\left(\widetilde{U}\left[K^{-1} + \frac{m}{n}[diag(K)]^{-1}\right]^{-1}\widetilde{U}^\top\right),$$

where $\mathcal{L}(U,\mathbf{1}) = tr(K) - tr(\widetilde{U}K\widetilde{U}^\top)$.

PROOF. We first bound $\mathrm{E}_\xi[\mathcal{L}_k(U,\xi)]$ as

$$\begin{aligned}
&\frac{1}{n_k}\mathrm{E}_\xi[\mathcal{L}_k(U,\xi)]\\
=\ & \mathrm{E}_\xi\left[\min_\alpha -2\widehat{\mathbf{u}}_k^\top K(\alpha\circ\xi) + (\alpha\circ\xi)^\top K(\alpha\circ\xi)\right]\\
\leq\ & \min_\alpha \mathrm{E}_\xi\left[-2\widehat{\mathbf{u}}_k^\top K(\alpha\circ\xi) + (\alpha\circ\xi)^\top K(\alpha\circ\xi)\right]\\
=\ & \min_\alpha -2\frac{m}{n}\widehat{\mathbf{u}}_k^\top K\alpha + \frac{m^2}{n^2}\alpha^\top K\alpha + \frac{m}{n}\left(1-\frac{m}{n}\right)\alpha^\top \mathrm{diag}(K)\alpha\\
\leq\ & \min_\alpha -2\frac{m}{n}\widehat{\mathbf{u}}_k^\top K\alpha + \frac{m}{n}\alpha^\top\left(\frac{m}{n}K + \mathrm{diag}(K)\right)\alpha.
\end{aligned}$$

By minimizing over α, we obtain

$$\alpha_* = \left(\frac{m}{n}K + \mathrm{diag}(K)\right)^{-1} K\widehat{\mathbf{u}}_k.$$

Thus, $\mathrm{E}_\xi[\mathcal{L}_k(U,\xi)]$ is bounded as

$$\begin{aligned}
&\mathrm{E}_\xi[\mathcal{L}_k(U,\xi)] + n_k\widehat{\mathbf{u}}_k^\top K\widehat{\mathbf{u}}_k\\
\leq\ & n_k\widehat{\mathbf{u}}_k^\top\left(K - K\left[K + \frac{n}{m}\mathrm{diag}(K)\right]^{-1}K\right)\widehat{\mathbf{u}}_k\\
=\ & \widetilde{\mathbf{u}}_k^\top\left(K^{-1} + \frac{m}{n}[\mathrm{diag}(K)]^{-1}\right)^{-1}\widetilde{\mathbf{u}}_k.
\end{aligned}$$

We complete the proof by adding up $\mathrm{E}_\xi[\mathcal{L}_k(U,\xi)]$ and using the fact that

$$\mathcal{L}_k(U,\mathbf{1}) = \min_\alpha -2\mathbf{u}_k^\top K\alpha + n_k\alpha^\top K\alpha = -\widetilde{\mathbf{u}}_k^\top K\widetilde{\mathbf{u}}_k.$$

□

COROLLARY 1. *Assume $\kappa(x,x) \leq 1$ for any x. Let $\lambda_1 \geq \lambda_2 \geq \ldots \geq \lambda_n \geq 0$ be the eigen values of matrix K. Given the membership matrix U, we have*

$$\begin{aligned}
\frac{\mathrm{E}_\xi[\mathcal{L}(U,\xi)]}{\mathcal{L}(U,\mathbf{1})} &\leq 1 + \frac{\sum_{i=1}^C \lambda_i/[1+\lambda_i m/n]}{tr(K) - \sum_{i=1}^C \lambda_i}\\
&\leq 1 + \frac{C/m}{\sum_{i=C+1}^n \lambda_i/n}.
\end{aligned}$$

PROOF. As $\kappa(x,x) \leq 1$ for any x, we have $\mathrm{diag}(K) \preceq I$, where I is an identity matrix. As $\widetilde{U}$ is an ℓ_2 normalized matrix, we have

$$\begin{aligned}
&\mathrm{tr}\left(\widetilde{U}\left[K^{-1} + \frac{m}{n}[\mathrm{diag}(K)]^{-1}\right]^{-1}\widetilde{U}^\top\right)\\
\leq\ & \mathrm{tr}\left(\widetilde{U}\left[K^{-1} + \frac{m}{n}I\right]^{-1}\widetilde{U}^\top\right)\\
\leq\ & \sum_{i=1}^C \frac{\lambda_i}{1+m\lambda_i/n} \leq \frac{Cn}{m}
\end{aligned}$$

and

$$\mathcal{L}(U,\mathbf{1}) = \mathrm{tr}(K - UKU^\top) \geq \mathrm{tr}(K) - \sum_{i=1}^C \lambda_i.$$

We complete the proof by combining the above inequalities. □

To illustrate the result of Corollary 1, consider a special kernel matrix K that has its first a eigen values equal n/a and the remaining eigen values equal zero; i.e. $\lambda_1 = \ldots = \lambda_a = n/a$ and $\lambda_{a+1} = \ldots = \lambda_n = 0$. We further assume $a > 2C$; i.e., the number of non-zero eigen values of K is larger than twice the number of clusters. Then, according to Corollary 1, we have

$$\frac{\mathrm{E}_\xi[\mathcal{L}(U,\xi)] - \mathcal{L}(U,\mathbf{1})}{\mathcal{L}(U,\mathbf{1})} \leq 1 + \frac{Ca}{m(a-C)} \leq 1 + \frac{2C}{m},$$

indicating that when the number of non-zero eigen values of K is significantly larger than the number of the clusters, the difference in the clustering errors between the standard kernel k-means and our approximation scheme will decrease at the rate of $O(1/m)$.

5. EXPERIMENTS

In this section, we demonstrate empirically that the proposed algorithm is not only more efficient than kernel k-means in terms of run-time complexity and memory, its performance in terms of clustering error and prediction accuracy is on par with that of the kernel k-means. We have evaluated our algorithm on two popular image data sets: Imagenet and MNIST. We first execute our algorithm on small and medium-sized data sets and compare its performance with that of the full kernel k-means, and then assess its performance on a large data set, for which computing the full kernel is infeasible. All algorithms were implemented in MATLAB and run on an Intel Xeon 2.8GHz processor with 140GB RAM.

5.1 Data sets

- **Small Imagenet:** The Imagenet data set [11] consists of over 1.2 million images that are organized according to the WordNet hierarchy. Each node in this hierarchy represents a concept (known as the "synset"). In order to perform preliminary analysis, we chose 20,000 images from 12 synsets (odometer, geyser, manhole cover, rapeseed, cliff dwelling, door, monarch butterfly, mountain, daily paper, shoji, villa and website) at the leaf nodes in the hierarchy. We call this data set the *small Imagenet data set.* Figure 2 shows a few examples of the images from the synsets used to form this data set. We extracted keypoints from each image using the VLFeat library [42] and represented each keypoint as a 128 dimensional SIFT descriptor; an average of 3,055 keypoints were extracted from each image. We employed the spatial pyramid kernel [30] to calculate the pairwise similarity with the number of pyramid levels set to be 4, which has been shown to be effective for object recognition and image retrieval.
- **MNIST:** The MNIST data set [2] is a subset of the database of handwritten digits available from NIST. It contains a total of 70,000 784-dimensional binary images from 10 digit classes. Two types of kernel functions were used for this data set, as suggested in [46]: the neural kernel defined as $\kappa(x,y) = tanh(ax^\top y + b)$, and the normalized polynomial kernel defined by $\kappa(x,y) = (x^\top y + 1)^d$. We set the parameters a, b and d to 0.0045, 0.11 and 5, respectively, according to [46].

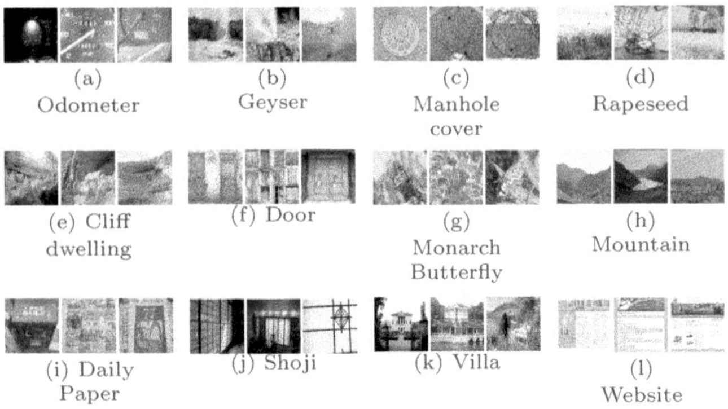

(a) Odometer (b) Geyser (c) Manhole cover (d) Rapeseed
(e) Cliff dwelling (f) Door (g) Monarch Butterfly (h) Mountain
(i) Daily Paper (j) Shoji (k) Villa (l) Website

Figure 2: Imagenet Data set

- **Full Imagenet:** To evaluate the performance of our algorithm on very large data sets, we tested it on the full Imagenet data set containing 1,262,102 images. The images are organized to form a synset tree with 1000 leaf nodes, each leaf node representing a class of images. We merged the leaves of this synset tree based on their similarity to form a 164-class data set. The SIFT descriptors were computed using the VLFeat library [42] and a random subset of 10 million SIFT features were clustered to form a visual vocabulary. Each SIFT descriptor was then quantized into a visual word using the nearest cluster center.[2] We obtain a 900-dimensional vector representation for each image, which is then normalized to lie in the range $[0, 1]$. We employed the RBF kernel, with the parameter σ set to 0.1, to compute their pairwise similarity.

5.2 Baseline and evaluation metrics

For the small Imagenet and MNIST data sets, we compare the proposed approximate kernel k-means algorithm with the full kernel k-means and the two-step kernel k-means algorithms using the same randomly initialized membership matrix. For the full Imagenet data set, it is currently infeasible to compute and store the full kernel on a single system due to memory constraints. We compare the performance of our algorithm on this data set with that of the two-step kernel k-means algorithm.

We evaluate the efficiency of the proposed algorithm for different sample sizes ranging from 50 to 10,000. We measure the time taken for computing the kernel matrix and clustering the data points. We measure the clustering performance using the *error reduction*, defined as the ratio of the difference between the initial clustering error (on random initialization) and the final clustering error (after running the clustering algorithm) to the initial clustering error. Larger the error reduction, greater is the cluster compactness. To evaluate the difference in the clustering results of our algorithm and the full kernel k-means, we calculate the *Adjusted Rand Index* (ARI) [22], a measure of similarity between two data partitions. The adjusted Rand index value lies in $[0, 1]$. A value close to 1 indicates better matching between the two partitions than a value close to 0. We finally examine the prediction accuracy of our algorithm by calculating the Normalized Mutual Information (NMI) [29] with respect to the true class distribution. Analogous to the adjusted Rand index, an NMI value of 1 indicates perfect matching with the true class distribution whereas 0 indicates perfect mismatch.

[2]This data set can be downloaded from `http://image-net.org/download-features`.

Table 1: Results for the small Imagenet data set

$C = 12$	Preprocessing time: 24,236.22 seconds				
Sample size	Running time (seconds)			ARI	
	Kernel calculation	Approx Kernel k-means	Two-step Kernel k-means	Approx vs Full kernel	Two-step vs Full kernel
Full	33,132.06	81.23 (±43.66)		-	
1000	1564.26 (±63.66)	34.56 (±4.20)	1.05 (±0.28)	0.77 (±0.18)	0.58 (±0.06)
500	810.03 (±24.36)	10.81 (±2.31)	0.01 (±0.001)	0.75 (±0.11)	0.51 (±0.04)
100	203.65 (±20.87)	4.33 (±1.32)	0.02 (±0.005)	0.71 (±0.05)	0.28 (±0.06)
50	79.88 (±4.61)	3.99 (±1.61)	0.01 (±0.001)	0.68 (±0.05)	0.26 (±0.13)

5.3 Experimental results

Small Imagenet: Table 1, and Figures 3(a) and 4(a) compare the performance of the proposed algorithm on the small Imagenet data set with full kernel k-means and the two-step kernel k-means. Table 1 lists the running time of the algorithms and the ARI values. Figures 3(a) and 4(a) show the error reduction and NMI achieved by the the three algorithms, respectively. All the results are averaged over 10 runs.

In order to make the comparison meaningful, we divide the running time into three categories: the preprocessing time, needed for constructing the multi-resolution histogram and the spatial pyramid from the SIFT descriptors, the time for computing the kernel matrix, and the time for clustering. Note that the preprocessing time is shared by all the clustering algorithms. We observe that a significant speedup (over 90%) is achieved by both the proposed algorithm and the two-step algorithm in kernel computation when compared to the full kernel k-means. When we compare the clustering time of our algorithm with that of the two-step algorithm for the same sample sizes, the two-step algorithm seems more efficient. This is due to the fact that our algorithm needs to compute the inverse matrix $\widehat{K}^{-1}$. However, when the two algorithms are compared with the requirement that they yield the same clustering performance, we observe from the ARI, error reduction and NMI values that our algorithm is more efficient. With just 50 samples, our algorithm significantly outperforms the two-step algorithm provided with 1000 samples.

We also observe that our algorithm is able to achieve clustering performance equivalent to that of the full kernel k-means. The two-step kernel k-means algorithm yields a much lower error reduction and NMI. This observation indicates that it is insufficient to estimate the cluster centers using only the randomly sampled data points and further justifies the design of the proposed algorithm.

MNIST: Tables 2 and 3 show the results for the MNIST data set using the neural and polynomial kernels, respectively. Compared to the full kernel k-means, we observe that a significant amount of time was saved by the proposed clustering algorithm as well as by the two-step algorithm in clustering the data.

As seen in Figures 3(b) and 3(c), equal amount of error reduction is achieved by both the full kernel k-means and the

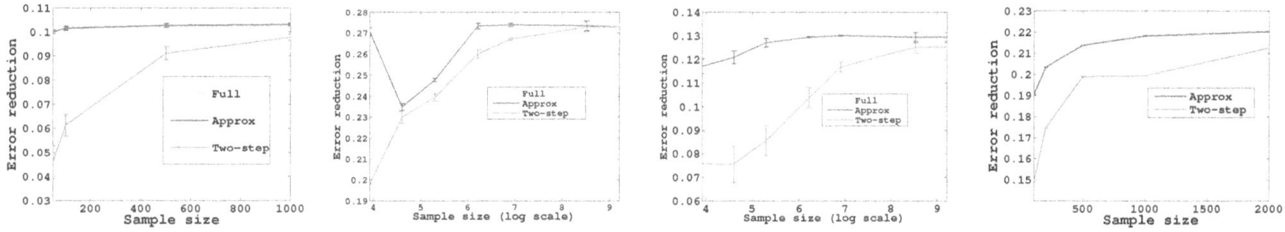

(a) Small Imagenet(20k) (b) MNIST using the neural kernel (c) MNIST using the polynomial kernel (d) Full Imagenet

Figure 3: Clustering error reduction

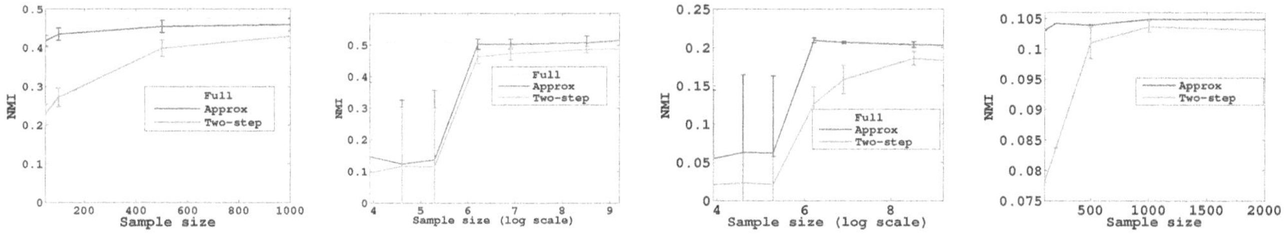

(a) Small Imagenet(20k) (b) MNIST using the neural kernel (c) MNIST using the polynomial kernel (d) Full Imagenet

Figure 4: Normalized Mutual Information with respect to the true class labels

Table 2: Results for the MNIST data set using the neural kernel

C = 10	Kernel parameters: a=0.0045 b=0.11				
Sample size	Running time (seconds)			ARI	
	Kernel calculation	Approx Kernel k-means	Two-step Kernel k-means	Approx vs Full kernel	Two-step vs Full kernel
Full	514.54	3953.62 (±2157.69)		-	
10000	107.58 (±41.38)	13759.05 (±6273.2)	75.93 (±0.01)	0.71 (±0.13)	0.71 (±0.08)
5000	41.07 (±5.12)	1478.85 (±178.97)	14.63 (±6.58)	0.71 (±0.12)	0.70 (±0.12)
1000	7.88 (±0.18)	75.26 (±22.42)	0.59 (±0.08)	0.70 (±0.12)	0.58 (±0.09)
500	5.37 (±0.53)	72.24 (±29.44)	0.25 (±0.02)	0.69 (±0.11)	0.48 (±0.07)
200	5.34 (±0.33)	53.48 (±30.17)	0.18 (±0.03)	0.61 (±0.24)	0.36 (±0.05)
100	2.02 (±0.09)	22.7 (±13.30)	0.06 (±0.002)	0.47 (±0.14)	0.37 (±0.05)
50	1.46 (±0.14)	12.11 (±8.42)	0.05 (±0.002)	0.40 (±0.10)	0.25 (±0.03)

Table 3: Results for the MNIST data set using the polynomial kernel

C = 10	Kernel parameter: degree=5				
Sample size	Running time (seconds)			ARI	
	Kernel calculation	Approx Kernel k-means	Two-step Kernel k-means	Approx vs Full kernel	Two-step vs Full kernel
Full	472.19	2027.68 (±570.63)		-	
10000	119.71 (±38.09)	14407.35 (±7161.1)	47.72 (±0.10)	0.95 (±0.05)	0.87 (±0.03)
5000	47.72 (±5.88)	1449.33 (±229.83)	6.25 (±1.29)	0.90 (±0.06)	0.81 (±0.04)
1000	9.13 (±0.07)	51.54 (±13.23)	0.54 (±0.09)	0.91 (±0.06)	0.72 (±0.07)
500	5.49 (±0.38)	45.59 (±18.40)	0.24 (±0.02)	0.90 (±0.03)	0.65 (±0.08)
200	5.21 (±0.82)	43.03 (±15.47)	0.16 (±0.05)	0.84 (±0.03)	0.33 (±0.05)
100	2.27 (±0.6)	21.55 (±5.60)	0.09 (±0.002)	0.68 (±0.03)	0.41 (±0.03)
50	1.84 (±0.48)	13.16 (±4.32)	0.05 (±0.002)	0.62 (±0.06)	0.32 (±0.16)

Table 4: Results for the full Imagenet data set using the RBF kernel

C = 20	Kernel parameter: $\sigma = 0.1$		
Sample size	Running time (seconds)		
	Kernel calculation	Approx Kernel k-means	Two-step Kernel k-means
2000	344.39 (±3.77)	22890.79 (±1987.79)	24.06 (±1.97)
1000	181.93 (±11.95)	11406.77 (±1170.08)	11.81 (±1.36)
500	168.83 (±0.27)	2649.13 (±12.15)	5.44 (±0.02)
200	68.15 (±0.16)	1912.05 (±8.98)	2.36 (±0.02)
100	47.29 (±1.12)	1119.33 (±43.25)	1.34 (±0.01)

proposed algorithm for $m \geq 500$. For $m < 500$, we observed that the algorithm does not always converge to the optimal solution owing to the relatively small sample size, leading to significant variations in the error reduction. Figures 4(b) and 4(c) show the NMI plots for the neural and polynomial kernels, respectively. We again observe that the performance of the proposed algorithm is significantly better than that of the two-step kernel k-means and comparable to that of the full kernel k-means.

Full Imagenet: Over 6.4TB of memory is required to store the full kernel matrix for this data set. Hence, it is currently infeasible to store the full kernel and execute the full kernel k-means on a single system. The proposed approximate scheme alleviates this issue as it does not require the computation of the full kernel. Table 4 compares the running time of our algorithm with that of the two-step kernel k-means algorithm for different sample sizes with the RBF kernel parameter σ set to 0.1. We observe that although the time taken for clustering the points by the our method is considerably greater than that of the two-step method, our algorithm performs significantly better than the two-step algorithm, in terms of both error reduction and NMI, as seen in Figures 3(d) and 4(d). These results demonstrate that our algorithm is more effective than the two-step algorithm for clustering large data sets.

6. CONCLUSIONS

We have proposed an efficient approximation for the kernel k-means algorithm, suitable for large data sets. The key idea is to avoid computing the full kernel matrix by restricting the cluster centers to a small subspace spanned by a set of randomly sampled data points. We show theoretically and empirically that the proposed algorithm is (i) efficient in both computational complexity and memory requirement, and (ii) is able to yield similar clustering results as the kernel k-means algorithm using the full kernel matrix. In the future, we plan to analytically investigate the sample complexity of the proposed algorithm, i.e. the minimum number of samples required to yield similar clustering results as the full kernel K-mean algorithm. We also plan to further enhance the efficiency of the proposed algorithm through ensemble and semi-supervised clustering techniques.

Acknowledgements

This research was partially supported by the Office of Naval Research (ONR Grant N00014-11-1-0100). Timothy Havens is supported by the National Science Foundation under Grant 1019343 to the Computing Research Association for the CI Fellows Project. Part of Anil Jain's research was also supported by WCU (World Class University) program funded by the Ministry of Education, Science and Technology through the National Research Foundation of Korea (R31-10008). Anil Jain is also affiliated with Korea University, Anam-Dong, Seoul, S. Korea.

7. REFERENCES

[1] http://gigaom.files.wordpress.com/2010/05/2010-digital-universe-iview_5-4-10.pdf.

[2] http://yann.lecun.com/exdb/mnist.

[3] C.C. Aggarwal, J. Han, J. Wang, and P.S. Yu. A framework for clustering evolving data streams. In *Proceedings of the International Conference on Very Large Databases*, pages 81–92, 2003.

[4] M.A. Belabbas and P.J. Wolfe. Spectral methods in machine learning and new strategies for very large datasets. *Proceedings of the National Academy of Sciences*, 106(2):369–374, 2009.

[5] F. Can. Incremental clustering for dynamic information processing. *ACM Transactions on Information Systems*, 11(2):143–164, 1993.

[6] F. Can, E.A. Fox, C.D. Snavely, and R.K. France. Incremental clustering for very large document databases: Initial MARIAN experience. *Information Sciences*, 84(1-2):101–114, 1995.

[7] C.T. Chu, S.K. Kim, Y.A. Lin, Y.Y. Yu, G. Bradski, A.Y. Ng, and K. Olukotun. Map-reduce for machine learning on multicore. In *Advances in Neural Information Processing Systems 19*, pages 281–288, 2007.

[8] S. Daruru, N.M. Marin, M. Walker, and J. Ghosh. Pervasive parallelism in data mining: dataflow solution to co-clustering large and sparse netflix data. In *Proceedings of the SIGKDD conference on Knowledge Discovery and Data mining*, pages 1115–1124, 2009.

[9] A.S. Das, M. Datar, A. Garg, and S. Rajaram. Google news personalization: scalable online collaborative filtering. In *Proceedings of the International Conference on World Wide Web*, pages 271–280, 2007.

[10] S. Datta, C. Giannella, and H. Kargupta. K-means clustering over a large, dynamic network. In *Proceedings of the SIAM Data Mining Conference*, pages 153–164, 2006.

[11] J. Deng, W. Dong, R. Socher, L.J. Li, K. Li, and L. Fei-Fei. Imagenet: A large-scale hierarchical image database. In *Proceedings of the IEEE Conference on Computer Vision and Pattern Recognition*, 2009.

[12] I. Dhillon, Y. Guan, and B. Kulis. A unified view of kernel k-means, spectral clustering and graph cuts. Technical report, University of Texas at Austin, 2004. (Tech. rep. TR-04-25).

[13] C. Ding, X. He, and H.D. Simon. On the equivalence of nonnegative matrix factorization and spectral clustering. In *Proceedings of the SIAM Data Mining Conference*, pages 606–610, 2005.

[14] P. Drineas and M.W. Mahoney. On the Nystrom method for approximating a Gram matrix for improved kernel-based learning. *The Journal of Machine Learning Research*, 6:2153–2175, 2005.

[15] D. Foti, D. Lipari, C. Pizzuti, and D. Talia. Scalable parallel clustering for data mining on multicomputers. *Parallel and Distributed Processing*, pages 390–398, 2000.

[16] C. Fowlkes, S. Belongie, F. Chung, and J. Malik. Spectral grouping using the Nystrom method. *IEEE Transactions on Pattern Analysis and Machine Intelligence*, pages 214–225, 2004.

[17] M. Girolami. Mercer kernel-based clustering in feature space. *IEEE Transactions on Neural Networks*, 13(3):780–784, 2002.

[18] S. Guha, A. Meyerson, N. Mishra, R. Motwani, and L. O'Callaghan. Clustering data streams: Theory and practice. *IEEE Transactions on Knowledge and Data Engineering*, pages 515–528, 2003.

[19] S. Guha, R. Rastogi, and K. Shim. Cure: an efficient clustering algorithm for large databases. *Information Systems*, 26(1):35–58, 2001.

[20] W. Hackbusch. *Integral equations: Theory and Numerical treatment*. Birkhauser, 1995.

[21] S. Har-Peled and S. Mazumdar. On coresets for k-means and k-median clustering. In *Proceedings of the ACM Symposium on Theory of Computing*, pages 291–300, 2004.

[22] L. Hubert and P. Arabie. Comparing partitions. *Journal of classification*, 2(1):193–218, 1985.

[23] R. Inokuchi and S. Miyamoto. LVQ clustering and SOM using a kernel function. In *IEEE International Conference on Fuzzy Systems*, volume 3, pages 1497–1500, 2005.

[24] D. Jiang, C. Tang, and A. Zhang. Cluster analysis for gene expression data: A survey. *IEEE Transactions on Knowledge and Data Engineering*, 16(11):1370–1386, 2004.

[25] D. Judd, P.K. McKinley, and A.K. Jain. Large-scale parallel data clustering. *IEEE Transactions on*

Pattern Analysis and Machine Intelligence, 20(8):871–876, 1998.

[26] L. Kaufman and P.J. Rousseeuw. *Finding Groups in Data: An Introduction to Cluster Analysis.* Wiley Blackwell, 2005.

[27] D.W. Kim, K.Y. Lee, D. Lee, and K.H. Lee. Evaluation of the performance of clustering algorithms in kernel-induced feature space. *Pattern Recognition*, 38(4):607–611, 2005.

[28] S. Kumar, M. Mohri, and A. Talwalkar. Sampling techniques for the Nystrom method. In *Proceedings of the Conference on Artificial Intelligence and Statistics*, pages 304–311, 2009.

[29] T.O. Kvalseth. Entropy and correlation: Some comments. *IEEE Transactions on Systems, Man and Cybernetics*, 17(3):517–519, 1987.

[30] S. Lazebnik, C. Schmid, and J. Ponce. Beyond bags of features: Spatial pyramid matching for recognizing natural scene categories. In *Proceedings of the IEEE Conference on Computer Vision and Pattern Recognition*, volume 2, pages 2169–2178, 2006.

[31] L.L. Liu, X.B. Wen, and X.X. Gao. Segmentation for SAR Image Based on a New Spectral Clustering Algorithm. *Life System Modeling and Intelligent Computing*, pages 635–643, 2010.

[32] D. MacDonald and C. Fyfe. The kernel self-organising map. In *Proceedings of the International Conference on Knowledge-Based Intelligent Engineering Systems and Allied Technologies*, volume 1, pages 317–320, 2002.

[33] D. Newman, A. Asuncion, P. Smyth, and M. Welling. Distributed inference for latent dirichlet allocation. In *Advances in Neural Information Processing Systems*, volume 20, pages 17–24, 2007.

[34] A. Ng, M. Jordan, and Y. Weiss. On spectral clustering: Analysis and an algorithm. In *Advances in Neural Information Processing Systems 14*, pages 849–856, 2001.

[35] R.T. Ng and J. Han. CLARANS: A method for clustering objects for spatial data mining. *IEEE Transactions on Knowledge and Data Engineering*, pages 1003–1016, 2002.

[36] A. K. Qinand and P. N. Suganthan. Kernel neural gas algorithms with application to cluster analysis. *Pattern Recognition*, 4:617–620, 2004.

[37] T. Sakai and A. Imiya. Fast spectral clustering with random projection and sampling. *Machine Learning and Data Mining in Pattern Recognition*, pages 372–384, 2009.

[38] B. Scholkopf, R. Herbrich, and A. Smola. A generalized representer theorem. In *Proceedings of Computational Learning Theory*, pages 416–426, 2001.

[39] B. Scholkopf, A. Smola, and K.R. Muller. Nonlinear component analysis as a kernel eigenvalue problem. *Neural Computation*, 10(5):1299–1314, 1996.

[40] J. Shawe-Taylor and N. Cristianini. *Kernel Methods for Pattern Analysis.* Cambridge University Press, 2004.

[41] J. Shi and J. Malik. Normalized cuts and image segmentation. *IEEE Transactions on Pattern Analysis and Machine Intelligence*, 22(8):888–905, 2002.

[42] A. Vedaldi and B. Fulkerson. Vlfeat: An open and portable library of computer vision algorithms. `http://www.vlfeat.org`, 2008.

[43] C. Williams and M. Seeger. Using the Nystrom method to speed up kernel machines. In *Advances in Neural Information Processing Systems 13*, pages 682–688, 2001.

[44] W. Xu, X. Liu, and Y. Gong. Document clustering based on non-negative matrix factorization. In *Proceedings of the ACM SIGIR Conference*, pages 267–273, 2003.

[45] H. Zha, X. He, C. Ding, M. Gu, and H. Simon. Spectral relaxation for k-means clustering. In *Advances in Neural Information Processing Systems*, volume 2, pages 1057–1064, 2002.

[46] R. Zhang and A.I. Rudnicky. A large scale clustering scheme for kernel k-means. In *Proceedings of the International Conference on Pattern Recognition*, pages 289–292, 2002.

[47] T. Zhang, R. Ramakrishnan, and M. Livny. BIRCH: an efficient data clustering method for very large databases. *ACM SIGMOD Record*, 25(2):103–114, 1996.

Ask Me Better Questions: Active Learning Queries Based on Rule Induction

Parisa Rashidi
Washington State University
Pullman, Washington
prashidi@eecs.wsu.edu

Diane J. Cook
Washington State University
Pullman, Washington
cook@eecs.wsu.edu

ABSTRACT

Active learning methods are used to improve the classification accuracy when little labeled data is available. Most traditional active learning methods pose a very specific query to the oracle, i.e. they ask for the label of an unlabeled example. This paper proposes a novel active learning method called RIQY (**R**ule **I**nduced active learning **Q**uer**Y**). It can construct generic active learning queries based on rule induction from multiple unlabeled instances. These queries are shorter and more readable for the oracle and encompass many similar cases. Also the learning algorithm can achieve higher accuracy rates by asking fewer queries. We evaluate our algorithm on 12 different real datasets. Our results show that we can achieve higher accuracy rates using fewer queries compared to the traditional active learning methods.

Categories and Subject Descriptors

I.2.6 [**Computing Methodologies**]: ARTIFICIAL INTELLIGENCE—*Learning*; I.5.1 [**Computing Methodologies**]: Pattern Recognition—*Models*; H.2.8 [**Information Systems**]: DATABASE MANAGEMENT—*Data mining*

General Terms

Algorithms, Design, Performance, Human Factors

Keywords

active learning, machine learning

1. INTRODUCTION

In recent years, a variety of active learning methods have been proposed [26, 29] and it has been used in various application domains such as drug discovery [31], text classification [19], media retrieval [3] and medical image classification [15]. Active learning is primarily used when little labeled data is available, but unlabeled data is abundant. Its goal is to minimize the human annotation efforts via posing targeted queries to an oracle, instead of labeling the whole dataset. Active learning methods usually select an informative unlabeled instance and ask the oracle for the label of the instance. The oracle, mainly a human oracle, provides the correct label of the instance and then the newly labeled instance is added to the training dataset.

Despite enormous progress in the active learning field in recent years, there are still some shortcomings that need to be addressed. Traditional active learning methods usually ask for the label of a specific unlabeled instance. Though this might result in some accuracy improvement, however it might not be very easy for an oracle to label a very specific case. This can be especially true if the query contains many features, and if those features represent high precision numeric data. Also some features might be irrelevant for a certain query and eliminating those features can result in a shorter and more readable query. This can also prevent the oracle's confusion.

For example in the real world, a medical domain expert prefers to be presented with a generic diabetes query which (1) embodies similar patient cases together, (2) only includes relevant symptoms and (3) involves range values instead of very specific exact values for the lab test results. Such a query will be shorter, less confusing and more intuitive. Besides the domain expert will be able to answer more queries in less time and the learning algorithm can achieve higher accuracy rates by posing fewer queries.

We present a novel method for constructing generic active learning queries based on rule induction. We call our method RIQY, standing for **R**ule **I**nduced active learning **Q**uer**Y** method. Our method exploits the underlying density distribution to find an informative instance as well as its most similar cases. Then by using a rule induction classifier to infer rules for separating those similar cases from the rest of data, we construct a generic query. We evaluate our algorithm on two different sets of data. The first set of data consists of various real world datasets from the UCI repository [11]. The second set of data includes several human activity recognition datasets from the WSU repository [6]. Our results on both sets of data show that our method is able to achieve higher accuracy rates using fewer queries compared to the traditional active learning methods. Our method is also relatively easy to implement as it employs the well known machine learning components.

The remainder of this paper is organized as follows. First we will provide a brief overview of the active learning and rule induction literature in Section 2. Next, in Section 3 we will present a motivational example. In Section 4, we

KDD'11, August 21–24, 2011, San Diego, California, USA.

explain our approach and its details. We then present the results of our experiments in Section 5. Finally we bring up our conclusions and discussion of future work in section 6.

2. RELATED WORK

A variety of active learning approaches have been proposed during the past decade [26, 29]. The simplest form of active learning is the uncertainty sampling method which was introduced by Lewis and Gale [18]. Uncertainty sampling first labels all the unlabeled instances using a classifier. Then it chooses the most uncertain instance and asks the oracle for its label. Other researchers have extended this method to multi-class classification problems by using uncertainty measures such as the entropy measure [16]. It should be noted that the uncertainty sampling method can select the outliers, as it ignores the underlying distribution and the outliers as isolated points can be highly uncertain.

Another type of active learning method is the committee based active learning method. It constructs a committee of classifiers and selects an unlabeled example that causes the maximum disagreement among the classifiers [28, 12, 19]. Similar to the committee based method is the co-testing method which trains two classifiers on two uncorrelated views of data [22]. Version space reduction methods also discard areas of the hypothesis space that have no direct effect on the error rate [30].

More recently, density weighted methods have been proposed [33, 23, 32, 27]. Density weighted methods balance the uncertainty of a sample with its representativeness according to the underlying data distribution. These methods ask for the label of an uncertain instance which is also similar to the other unlabeled instances. As density weighted methods sample from the maximal density regions, they perform well with minimally labeled data. They are also better able to deal with the outlier problem [8]. Settles and Craven [27] have shown that if the proximities are pre-computed and cached, then the computational complexity of those methods is no different than the traditional active learning methods.

We use a weighted density method for selecting the initial informative instance. As we are adding many instances at a time, selecting the non-outlier instances can be quite vital to avoid the accumulating errors. Using a density weighted method allows us to avoid selecting such outliers.

There are a number of active learning frameworks that resemble our work. Batch mode active learning [1, 14] generates queries in groups instead of a single instance at a time. However batch mode active learning still requires the oracle to label "all" of the instances in a batch and does not reduce the set of similar queries to a generic query.

The multiple instance active learning method also groups several instances together [7, 27]. The group is labeled negative if the oracle labels all the instances in the group as negative, but it is labeled positive if at least one of the instances is marked positive. Again the oracle has to label all the instances instead of a generic query.

Druck et al [9] proposed a feature labeling method where a single feature is queried for its label. For example, in a baseball vs. hockey text classification problem, the presence of the word "puck" is a strong indicator of hockey. As this method is selecting one feature at a time, it can be said that it is a specific case of our method. Note that we exploit both instances and features.

Du et al. [10] also recently proposed a method for grouping several instances together. Their method does not take into account the actual data distribution as they are grouping synthetic data points together. They randomly generate a fixed number of synthetic data points around an informative instance selected by an uncertainty sampling method. As pointed out by others [17], synthetic data points might not exactly reflect the actual data distribution and taking this approach might in fact result in adding the outliers.

In contrast to the above methods, our RIQY method aggregates multiple actual instances into a single generic query and it takes into account the actual data distribution. It avoids selecting the outliers by employing a density weighted method. Our method is also easy to implement as it uses the well known machine learning components.

We employ rule induction for forming generic active learning queries. Rule based classifiers have a long history and many rule based classifiers have proposed in the literature. A number of such methods include CN2 [4], Ripper [5], AQ [20] and C4.5 decision tree rules [25]. Rule induction classifiers try to identify the sets of highly predictive features as a rule. They usually prune redundant or noisy rules in order to achieve better prediction accuracies. Rules offer the advantage of having a natural expression that is quite easy for humans to understand. We use a C4.5 classifier [25] to induce generic active learning queries based on a number of similar instances.

3. MOTIVATIONAL EXAMPLE

We show by an example how our RIQY method can pose shorter and more meaningful queries to the oracle and how such queries can aggregate multiple similar cases together. Figure 1 better highlights the differences between a traditional active learning method versus our RIQY method.

For example consider a heart disease dataset. We assume that it has 20+ features and the classification task is to predict whether a patient has heart disease or not. An example query will be as following.

"*What is the class label if (sex= female) and (age =39) and (chest pain type = 3) and (serum cholesterol = 150.2 mg/dL) and (fasting blood sugar = 150 mg/dL) ... and (electrocardiographic result = 1) and (maximum heart rate achieved = 126) and (exercise induced angina = 90) and (heart old peak = 2.3) and (number of major vessels colored by fluoroscopy = 3)?*"

Note that for the sake of brevity here we only show a number of features. But in reality all the features are included in the query to be presented to the oracle. From this example query, one can clearly see how such a long and overly specific query with so many features can be difficult to be answered by a domain expert. Besides, a similar case would require another query to be posed to the oracle, without taking advantage of the previous cases. Also many features might be indeed irrelevant to the query at hand.

Although one can apply a feature selection method as a preprocessing step here, but it should be noted that it would discard the features in a global manner. In contrast, we are looking at the problem of discarding a "locally" irrelevant feature for a number of similar instances. For example, "exercise induced angina" feature might be relevant for the whole dataset, but it might not very discriminating for a group of patients whose "age > 65".

In the real world, a domain expert usually expects queries in a shorter and more intuitive form, with range values in-

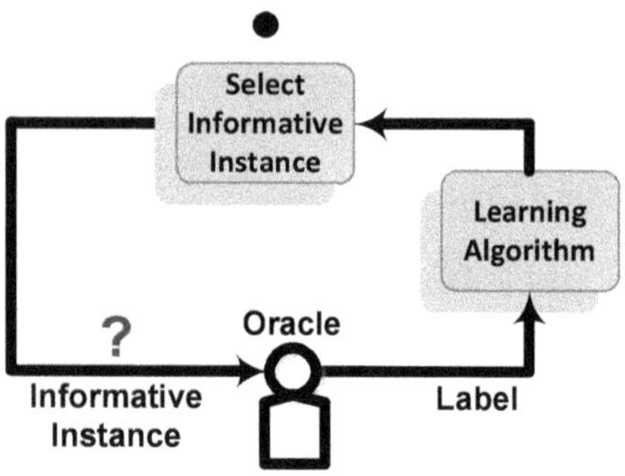

(a) Traditional active learning.

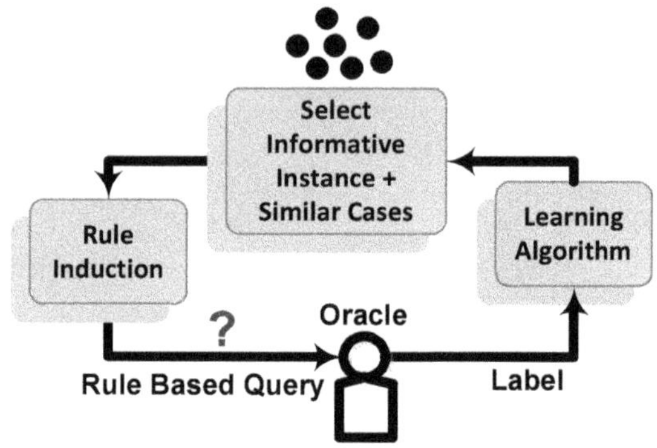

(b) Our RIQY active learning method.

Figure 1: Traditional active learning methods versus our RIQY active learning method.

stead of exact values and with similar cases aggregated together as a generic case. One such example is:

"*What is the class label if (age > 65) and (chest pain type = 3) and (serum cholesterol > 240 mg/dL) ?*"

In the following sections, we show how we can construct such generic queries as a form of rule induction.

4. MODEL

Our input data is an n-dimensional feature vector which is denoted by $x = \langle x_1, x_2, \cdots, x_n \rangle$. Each labeled instance x is assigned a class $y_j \in y$. The function that measures the informativeness of an instance x is denoted by $\Phi(x)$ and the most informative instance is denoted by x^*. We assume that each dataset is composed of a small labeled dataset $\mathcal{L}$, a large unlabeled dataset $\mathcal{U}$ and a test dataset $\mathcal{T}$ which is set aside for the evaluation purposes only.

We also assume that the oracle is able to answer our queries and to provide us with a label l and a confidence value c. There is a proximity matrix M that shows the similarity between each two data points in our dataset. The proximity matrix is used to identify the nearest neighbors of x^*. All the proximities are cached and pre-computed as mixed Euclidean distances. For a more efficient nearest neighbor search, one can employ methods such as kd-tree [24] or locality sensitive hashing (LSH) [13]. If the original dataset contains a large number of features, one can perform conventional feature selection methods to obtain a more representative dataset. But as we mentioned before, a preprocessing feature selection step is quite different than the local feature selection process during rule induction, as the locally relevant features can vary from query to query.

In summary our method works as following. First we train a classifier $\mathcal{C}$ on a small labeled dataset $\mathcal{L}$ to identify the potential informative instances. This step is similar to most of the traditional active learning methods. Our informativeness measure is a variation of density weighted method that also takes into account the dissimilarity to the previously labeled data in order to achieve a more efficient method.

After identifying the most informative instance, we select its nearest neighbors as well as its enemies. The enemies set is obtained through random sampling of the rest of the unlabeled data. The nearest neighbors and the enemies are combined together into a single dataset. The nearest neighbors are assigned a label of 0, while the enemies are assigned a label of 1, regardless of their original labels. By separating the nearest neighbors from the enemies using a rule induction classifier, we can obtain the essential discriminating features. Rules naturally have an expressive format which is quite suitable for human oracle. Next, we present the induced rules to the oracle and update the labeled dataset. This is repeated until a maximum number of queries is posed or until a specified accuracy improvement is achieved.

Figure 2 shows the main components of our method. In the next subsection, we will explain our method in more detail.

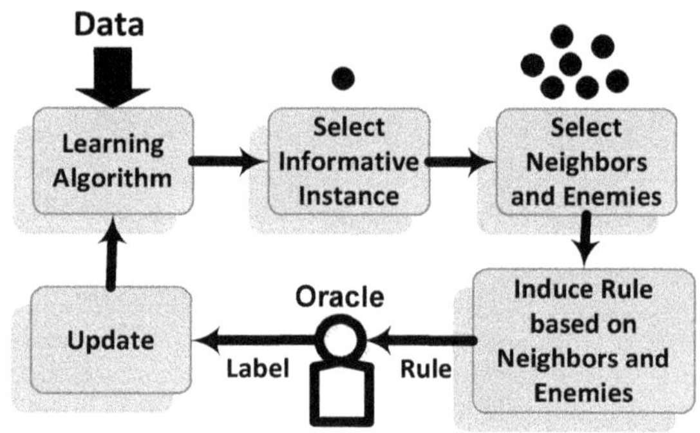

Figure 2: The main components of our method.

4.1 Model Details

The first step in our method is to select the most informative instance x^* among the pool of unlabeled instances. As mentioned before, we use a variation of density weighted method for measuring the informativeness of an instance x. Our measure considers the similarity of x to the other unlabeled instances, as well as its dissimilarity to the previously labeled instances. Considering similarity to the other unlabeled instances allows us to select an instance that is representative of many other similar cases. Considering its dissimilarity to the previously labeled instances allows us to avoid querying similar instances repetitively, thus leading to a more effective method. Equation 1 shows our method for selecting the most informative instance x^*.

$$x^* = \arg\max_x \left[(1-\alpha) * \Phi(x) + \alpha * \frac{|\mathcal{L}| * \sum_{u=1}^{|\mathcal{U}|} M[x, x_u]}{|\mathcal{U}| * \sum_{l=1}^{|\mathcal{L}|} M[x, x_l]} \right] \quad (1)$$

In Equation 1, parameter α balances the contribution of density versus the base informativeness measure $\Phi(x)$. Here the second term shows the contribution of density with respect to both labeled and unlabeled data. The first term, $\Phi(x)$, refers to a base informativeness measure. The base informativeness measure here is an entropy measure as in Equation 2. But it can be replaced by any other base informativeness measure. Here y_i ranges over all possible label values.

$$\Phi(x) = -\sum_i P_\theta(y_i|x) \log P_\theta(y_i|x) \quad (2)$$

After an informative instance has been selected, a generic query is constructed based on the informative instance and its similar instances. Algorithm 1 outlines further details of our RIQY method.

Algorithm 1 RIQY Active Learning method

1: **procedure** FINDRULEBASEDQUERY($\mathcal{L}$, $\mathcal{U}$, M)
2:     **while** stopping criteria is not met **do**
3:         Train a classifier $\mathcal{C}$ using $\mathcal{L}$
4:         Use $\mathcal{C}$ to compute $p(y|x)$ $\forall x \in \mathcal{U}$
5:         Find x^* using Equation 1
6:         Find $\mathcal{N}_{x^*}$
7:         Sample $\{\mathcal{U} - \mathcal{N}_{x^*}\}$ to get $\mathcal{E}_{x^*}$
8:         $\Delta = \mathcal{N}^+_{x^*} \bigcup \mathcal{E}^-_{x^*}$
9:         Form rule set $\mathcal{R}$ from Δ
10:         Select $\acute{\mathcal{R}}$ from $\mathcal{R}$ based on γ and a
11:         $c, l \leftarrow$ askOracle($\acute{\mathcal{R}}$)
12:         **for all** $x_j \in \Delta$ **do**
13:             **if** x_j is covered by some $r_k \in \acute{\mathcal{R}}$ **then**
14:                 Update w_j as in Equation 3
15:                 **if** $w_j > \theta$ **then**
16:                     Add x_j to $\mathcal{L}$ with label l_k
17:                 **end if**
18:             **end if**
19:         **end for**
20:     **end while**
21: **end procedure**

Lines 3−4 trains a classifier $\mathcal{C}$ based on the available training data $\mathcal{L}$, and computes the class probabilities for each unlabeled instance $x \in \mathcal{U}$. In line 5, based on the obtained class probabilities and the underlying distribution, we select the most informative instance x^* according to Equation 1.

Next, we find x^* similar instances and form a generic query based on those instances. We first select the nearest neighbors of x^* in line 6. The size of neighborhood (or the enemy vicinity) is a fixed fraction ϵ of the unlabeled dataset $\mathcal{U}$. In other words, $|\mathcal{N}_{x^*}| = |\mathcal{U}| * \epsilon$. To get the enemies set $\mathcal{E}_{x^*}$, we sample from $\mathcal{U} - \mathcal{N}_{x^*}$. The size of the enemies set is the same as the neighbors set, i.e. $|\mathcal{E}_{x^*}| = |\mathcal{U}| * \epsilon$. We chose them to be of the same size to avoid any class imbalance problems. As over time the unlabeled dataset gets smaller and as more labeled data becomes available, the neighborhood size as well as the enemy vicinity becomes smaller. This allows us to pose more focused queries over time.

Next in line 8, we combine the nearest neighbors $\mathcal{N}_{x^*}$ and the enemies $\mathcal{E}_{x^*}$ into a single set Δ. Each instance of the nearest neighbors is assigned a label of 0 in Δ, while each instance belonging to the enemies is assigned a label of 1 in Δ, regardless of their original labels. We denote the relabeled sets by $\mathcal{N}^+_{x^*}$ and $\mathcal{E}^-_{x^*}$.

Then a rule induction classifier such as C4.5 [25] is used to generate a number of rules $\mathcal{R}$ from Δ in line 9. Through separation of the nearest neighbors of x^* from its enemies by using a rule induction classifier, we can obtain the essential features for discriminating x^* and its similar cases from the rest of data in form of rules. Note that each rule $r \in \mathcal{R}$ is accompanied by its coverage value γ and its accuracy a. The coverage value shows how many instances are covered by a certain rule and the accuracy shows the discriminative power of a rule for distinguishing between positive and negative instances. We select the rules with a minimum accuracy $a_{\min}$ in order to avoid adding the incorrect instances. The rules are then sorted according to their coverage values and the top N rules with the highest coverage value are selected as $\acute{\mathcal{R}}$ in line 10. Note that normally we set N to 1 to present one rule a time to the oracle. But it is also possible to present several rules at a time in a batch mode.

Line 11 poses the rule set $\acute{\mathcal{R}}$ to the oracle and receives the corresponding labels l_i and confidences c_i for each rule $r_i \in \acute{\mathcal{R}}$. Lines 12-19 update each unlabeled instance $x_j \in \Delta$ that is covered by some rule $r_k \in \acute{\mathcal{R}}$, according to Equation 3.

$$w_j = c_k * \frac{1}{|X_{r_k}|} \sum_{k}^{|X_{r_k}|} M[j, k] \quad (3)$$

Here w_j shows the weight of instance x_j in our dataset. The set of all instances that are covered by a certain rule r_k is denoted by X_{r_k}. The instance's weight increases proportionately with its similarity to the query neighborhood and the oracle's confidence about query's label.

At the end, those instances covered by some rule and with a weight above the weight threshold θ are added to the labeled dataset $\mathcal{L}$. This process continues until we reach the stopping criteria. The stopping criteria can be either reaching a maximum number of queries or reaching a certain minimum classification accuracy improvement.

5. EXPERIMENTS

We perform a number of experiments on two sets of real world data in order to evaluate our RIQY active learning algorithm. The data in our experiments consists of 6 real world datasets from the UCI repository [11] and 6 human activity recognition datasets from the WSU repository [6].

5.1 Experiment Setup

The first set of data includes 6 real world datasets from the UCI repository [11]. These datasets include the Germany credit approval dataset, the Wisconsin breast cancer dataset, the heart disease dataset, the wine dataset, the ionosphere dataset and the chess dataset. All the datasets are binary classification problems, except for the wine dataset. Further details of those datasets is shown in Table 1.

Dataset	Number of Features	Attributes Type	Number of Examples
Credit approval	20	Numeric-Nominal	1000
Ionosphere	34	Numeric	351
Wine	13	Numeric	178
Heart Disease	13	Numeric-Nominal	270
Breast Cancer	9	Nominal	699
Chess	36	Nominal	3196

Table 1: The UCI datasets.

The activity recognition datasets consists of data collected from 6 different smart apartments [6]. We will refer to those datasets as B3, C, K4, M, T1 and T2. Each smart apartment is equipped with different types of sensors such as infrared motion sensors installed on ceilings and walls, water sensors installed on faucets, contact switch sensors installed on doors and cabinets, and item sensors on the key items. All the datasets are collected during normal day-to-day life of residents without any experimental settings. The annotated activities in those datasets are shown in Table 2.

	B3	C	K4	M	T1	T2
Hygiene	✓		✓	✓		
Leave Home	✓	✓	✓	✓	✓	✓
Cook	✓		✓	✓	✓	✓
Relax	✓		✓	✓	✓	✓
Take Med	✓	✓		✓		
Eat	✓	✓	✓	✓	✓	✓
Sleep	✓	✓	✓	✓		
Bathing	✓		✓			
Bed to toilet	✓	✓	✓	✓		
Work	✓	✓	✓	✓		

Table 2: The annotated activities in each dataset.

All the activity datasets represent multi-class classification problems. Each activity instance is represented by features composed of sensor locations and activity duration. Further information about these datasets is shown in Table 3.

We split each dataset into three disjoint parts: a small labeled dataset $\mathcal{L}$ (about 1%-2% of data), a test dataset $\mathcal{T}$ (about 25% of data) and an unlabeled dataset $\mathcal{U}$ (the rest of data). All the results are averaged over 3 runs in order to reduce the experiment variation. The initial classification step is performed using a support vector machine from the LibSVM library [2]. Using a cross validation method, we found the following values for our parameters: $\alpha = 0.5$, $\theta = 0.5$, $a_{\min} = 0.85$ and $\epsilon = 0.2$ for the UCI dataset and $\epsilon = 0.01$ for the WSU activity recognition datasets. A C4.5 decision tree from the RapidMiner tool was used for constructing rules [21]. We set the minimal information gain to 0.1. We confined the depth of the tree to a maximum of 10 attributes to prevent very long queries, though in most cases the generated query is shorter.

To simulate the effect of a human oracle in determining the label of a specific rule, we consider all the instances that are covered by a specific rule. The label of the rule is then reported as the majority label and the confidence is reported as the majority fraction. It should be noted that our datasets as real world datasets contain noisy examples, which can lead to lower confidences. Similarly, the noisy examples can also confuse a domain expert in the real world. Though by infusing many similar cases together into a generic query, the effect of noisy examples is reduced, still in some cases this might lead to a lower confidence.

5.2 Experiment Results

After performing the initial preprocessing steps such as proximity computation, we ran our algorithm on both sets of UCI and WSU datasets.

First we show two example queries from the wine dataset and the B3 activity dataset. In the B3 query, the actual sensor numbers have been replaced by their location.

Wine query "*What is the alcohol type if alcohol percentage is* 12–14 *and Proanthocyanidins is* 0.4–1.2 *and color intensity is* 1.2–7.1 ?"

B3 query "*What is the activity label if duration is* 5–101 *minutes and* 78%–100% *of the sensors are work area sensors and* 1%–2% *of the activated sensors are bedroom sensors* ?"

The first query reduces the number of features by 76.9% and it aggregates a total of 13 instances. The second query reduces the number of features by 80% and it aggregates a total of 113 instances. One can clearly see how our method results in shorter and more intuitive queries.

Next, we computed the classification accuracy of our method. We set the number of selected rules N to 1. In order to compare our method to a traditional active learning method, we also performed the same experiments using an uncertainty sampling method. The results of our experiments on UCI datasets can be seen in Figure 3. Similarly, the results on the WSU datasets are shown in Figure 4. We can see that our method outperforms the uncertainty sampling method in most cases by reaching higher accuracy rates with fewer queries. This can be attributed to utilizing the actual underlying distribution of data and avoiding querying the outliers.

It should be noted that the results of applying our RIQY method might vary from dataset to dataset, depending on the type of data and whether it can be generalized easily or not. Also the noisy instances and the regularity of the dataset can play a role in determining the classification accuracy. For example, dataset T2 represents a smart apartment

Dataset	Number of Features	Number of Activities	Number of Examples	Data Type
B3	15	10	3361	Numeric
C	10	6	511	Numeric
K4	14	9	746	Numeric
M	13	9	2270	Numeric
T1	10	4	1431	Numeric
T2	11	4	163	Numeric

Table 3: The WSU datasets.

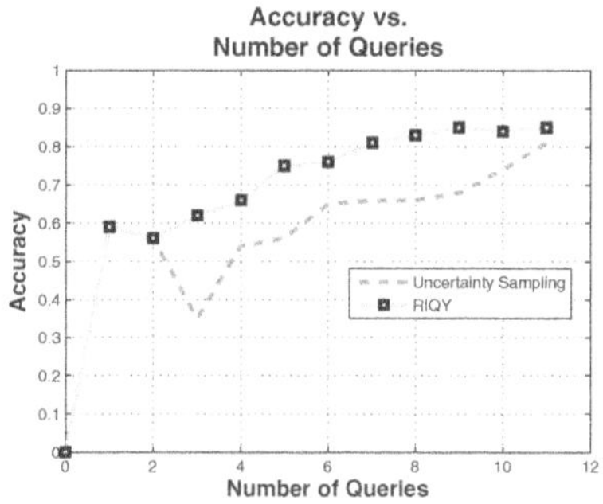

(a) Heart disease dataset.

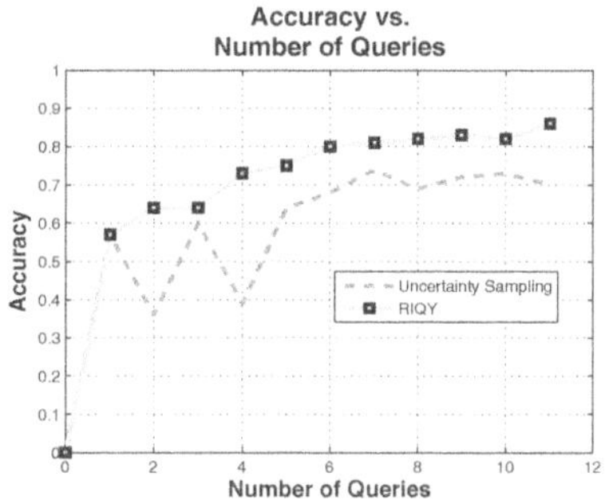

(b) Ionosphere dataset.

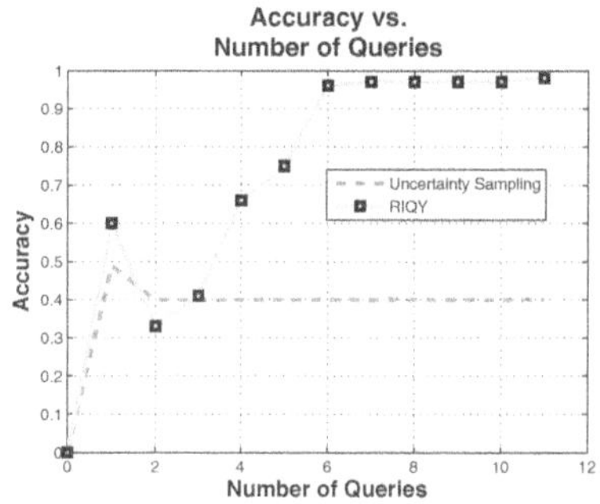

(c) Wine dataset.

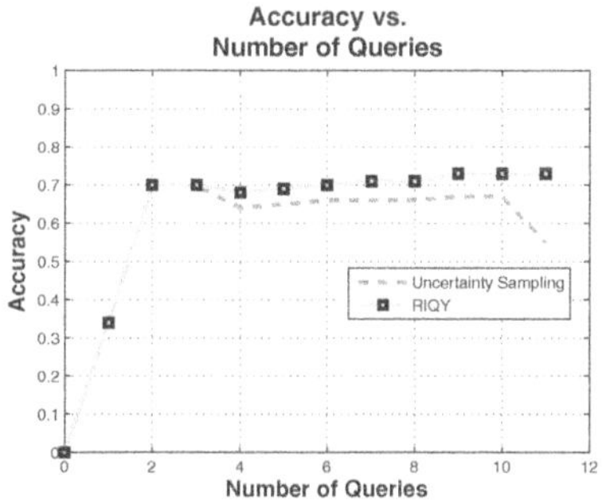

(d) German credit approval dataset.

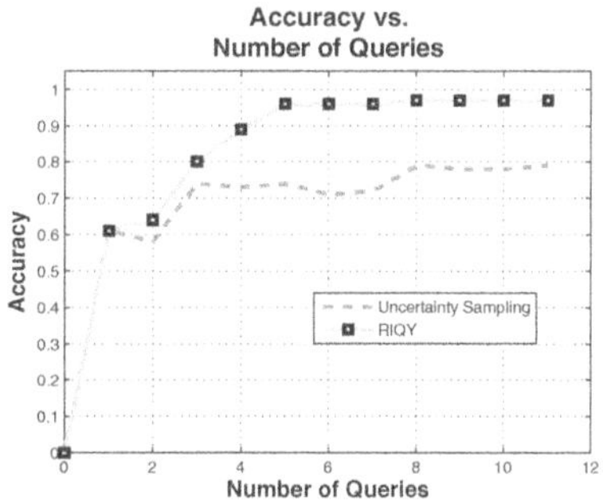

(e) Wisconsin breast cancer dataset.

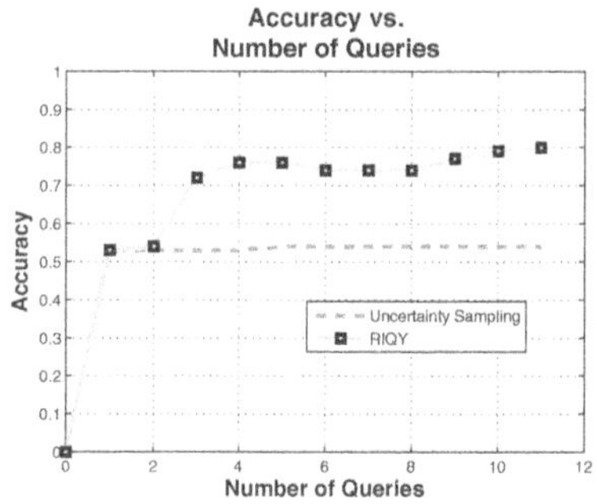

(f) Chess dataset.

Figure 3: Accuracy for different UCI datasets vs. the number of queries.

where the residents did not have a regular schedule. Therefore, the algorithm is not able to take much advantage of the similarities between various instances of the same activity. Despite all these, we still can see that in most cases our method offers a higher accuracy rate by using fewer and shorter queries.

Table 4 and Table 5 show the average feature reduction, the average oracle confidence and the average number of added instances for the UCI and WSU datasets. Note that the average number of added instances is 1 for the uncertainty sampling method. From these tables we can see how in average the number of features is reduced by our RIQY method. This makes it possible to pose shorter queries.

In another experiment, we explored the effect of increasing the number of posed rules (N) to the oracle. Figure 5 shows the results of our experiment on two example datasets: the Wisconsin breast cancer dataset and the T2 dataset. We can see that increasing the number of posed rules to the oracle can lead to higher accuracy rates. Note that as we add the rules in the order of descending coverage, posing the last rule might not have the same effect as posing the first rule. Also though increasing the number of posed rules to the oracle increases the total number of queries, however many irrelevant features are not included in each rule. Therefore despite posing more queries, the total number of features to be handled by the oracle is still small.

In summary, the above results show how we can construct more generic active learning queries based on rule induction. Our results confirm that such a method can lead to higher classification accuracy rates with fewer and shorter queries.

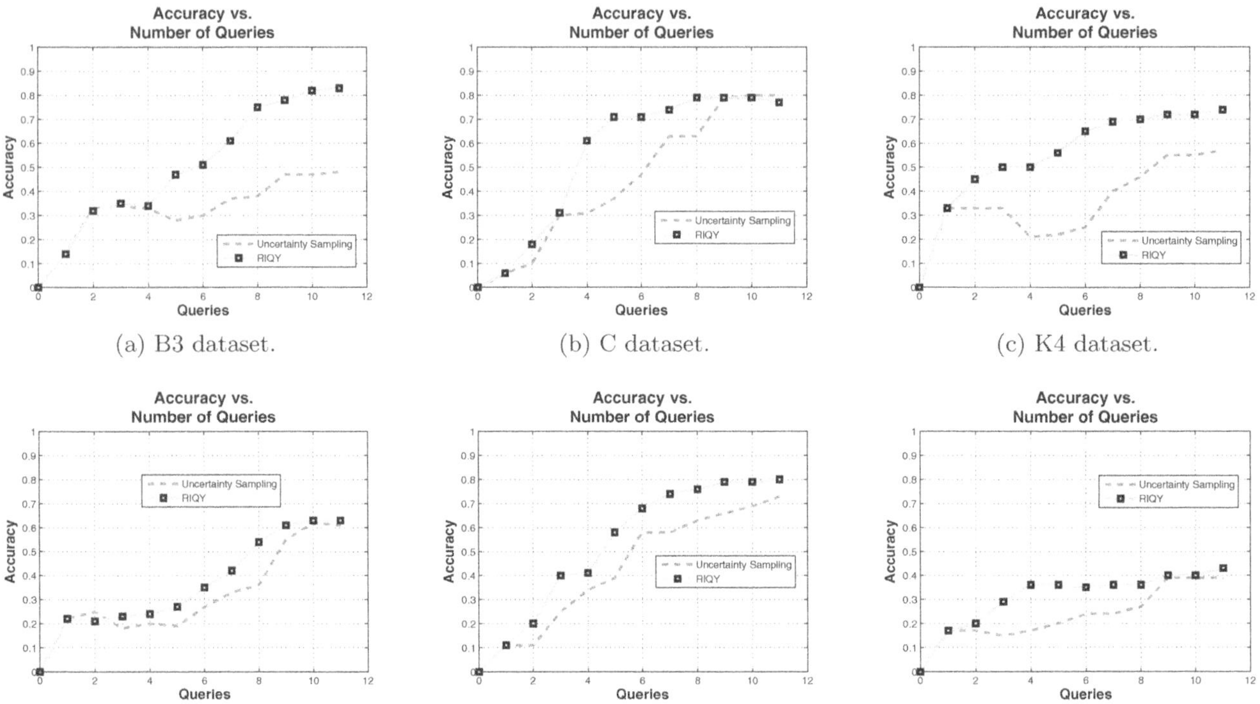

(a) B3 dataset. (b) C dataset. (c) K4 dataset.

(d) M dataset. (e) T1 dataset. (f) T2 dataset.

Figure 4: Accuracy for different WSU datasets vs. the number of queries.

Dataset	Avg. Features Reduction	Avg. Oracle Confidence	Avg. Added Instances
Credit approval	84.5%	74.4%	51
Ionosphere	90.8%	76.4%	23
Wine	77.6%	75.0%	10
Heart Disease	76.9%	77.6%	14
Breast Cancer	68.8%%	94.5%	34
Chess	88.6%	88.0%	200

Table 4: Some statistics based on our RIQY active learning method for UCI datasets.

Dataset	Avg. Features Reduction	Avg. Oracle Confidence	Avg. Added Instances
B3	88.0%	64.6%	66
C	85.0%	74.9%	12
K4	86.0%	71.1%	16
M	81.0%	64.9%	44
T1	73.6%%	88.9%	40
T2	90.3%	46.4%	2

Table 5: Some statistics based on our RIQY active learning method for WSU datasets.

6. CONCLUSION AND FUTURE WORK

We showed a method called RIQY for constructing generic active learning queries based on rule induction. RIQY is able to construct shorter and more intuitive queries that are easier for a human oracle to answer, allowing us to better utilize our human resources. Our method also allows the learning algorithm to achieve a higher accuracy rate using fewer queries. RIQY is easy to implement as it employs the well known machine learning components.

In the future, we intend to employ our method on more sophisticated data types, such as graphs and sequences. We also intend to explore the effects of a noisy oracle and to pro-

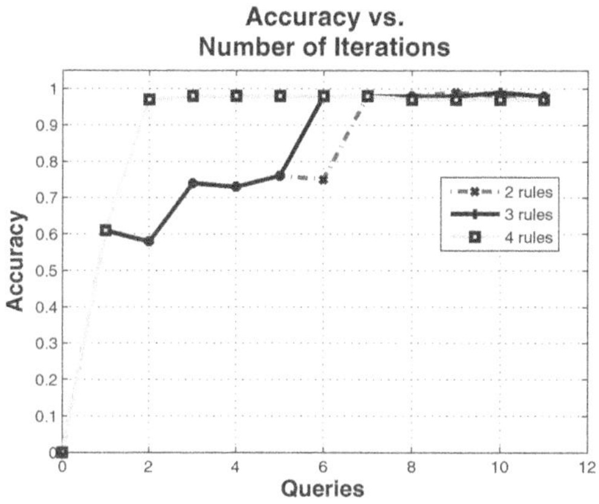

(a) Wisconsin breast cancer dataset.

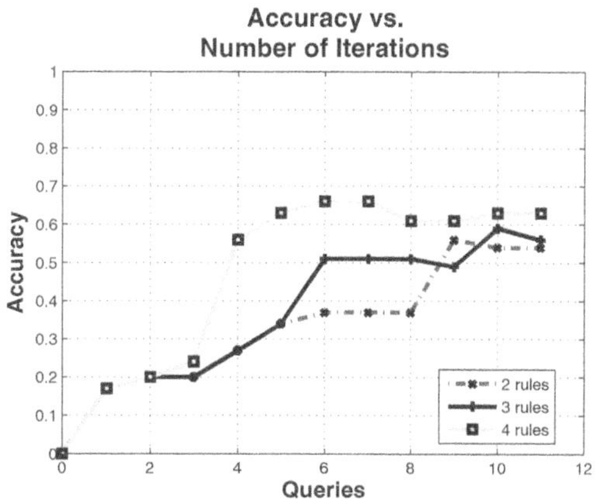

(b) T2 dataset.

Figure 5: Accuracy vs. number of posed rules.

pose methods for preventing the resulting accuracy degradation. It is also part of our future plan to perform actual user studies with human oracles to further explore the advantages of using our method over similar traditional active learning methods.

7. REFERENCES

[1] K. Brinker. Incorporating diversity in active learning with support vector machines. In *International Conference on Machine Learning*, pages 59–66, 2003.

[2] C.-C. Chang and C.-J. Lin. *LIBSVM: a library for support vector machines*, 2001. Software available at http://www.csie.ntu.edu.tw/~cjlin/libsvm.

[3] M.-y. Chen, M. Christel, A. Hauptmann, and H. Wactlar. Putting active learning into multimedia applications: dynamic definition and refinement of concept classifiers. In *13th annual ACM international conference on Multimedia*, MultiMedia 2005, pages 902–911, New York, NY, USA, 2005. ACM.

[4] P. Clark and T. Niblett. The cn2 induction algorithm. *Mach. Learn.*, 3:261–283, March 1989.

[5] W. W. Cohen. Fast effective rule induction. In *International Conference on Machine Learning*, ICML'95, pages 115–123, 1995.

[6] D. Cook, L. Holder, B. Shirazi, and M. Schmitter-Edgecombe. *WSU CASAS Smart Home Project*, 2010. At http://ailab.eecs.wsu.edu/casas/datasets.html.

[7] T. G. Dietterich, R. H. Lathrop, and T. Lozano-Pérez. Solving the multiple instance problem with axis-parallel rectangles. *Artificial Intelligence*, 89:31–71, January 1997.

[8] P. Donmez, J. G. Carbonell, and P. N. Bennett. Dual strategy active learning. In *Proceedings of the 18th European conference on Machine Learning*, ECML '07, pages 116–127, Berlin, Heidelberg, 2007. Springer-Verlag.

[9] G. Druck, G. Mann, and A. McCallum. Learning from labeled features using generalized expectation criteria. In *Proceedings of the 31st annual international ACM SIGIR conference on Research and development in information retrieval*, SIGIR '08, pages 595–602, New York, NY, USA, 2008. ACM.

[10] J. Du and C. X. Ling. Asking generalized queries to domain experts to improve learning. *IEEE Transactions on Knowledge and Data Engineering*, 22:812–825, 2010.

[11] A. Frank and A. Asuncion. UCI machine learning repository, 2010.

[12] Y. Freund, H. S. Seung, E. Shamir, and N. Tishby. Selective sampling using the query by committee algorithm. *Mach. Learn.*, 28:133–168, September 1997.

[13] A. Gionis, P. Indyk, and R. Motwani. Similarity search in high dimensions via hashing. In *Proceedings of the 25th International Conference on Very Large Data Bases*, VLDB '99, pages 518–529, San Francisco, CA, USA, 1999. Morgan Kaufmann Publishers Inc.

[14] Y. Guo and D. Schuurmans. Discriminative Batch Mode Active Learning. In *Advances in Neural Information Processing Systems*, volume 20, pages 593–600, 2008.

[15] S. C. H. Hoi, R. Jin, J. Zhu, and M. R. Lyu. Batch mode active learning and its application to medical image classification. In *23rd international conference on Machine learning*, ICML 2006, pages 417–424, New York, NY, USA, 2006. ACM.

[16] R. Hwa. Sample selection for statistical parsing. *Computational Linguistics*, 30:253–276, September 2004.

[17] K. Lang. NewsWeeder: learning to filter netnews. In *International Conference on Machine Learning*, pages 331–339, 1995.

[18] D. D. Lewis and W. A. Gale. A sequential algorithm for training text classifiers. In *Information Retrieval*, pages 3–12, 1994.

[19] A. McCallum and K. Nigam. Employing em and pool-based active learning for text classification. In *International Conference on Machine Learning*, ICML 1998, pages 350–358, 1998.

[20] R. S. Michalski, I. Mozetic, J. Hong, and N. Lavrac. The multi-purpose incremental learning system aq15

and its testing application to three medical domains. In *AAAI'86*, pages 1041–1047, 1986.

[21] I. Mierswa, M. Wurst, R. Klinkenberg, M. Scholz, and T. Euler. Yale: Rapid prototyping for complex data mining tasks. In L. Ungar, M. Craven, D. Gunopulos, and T. Eliassi-Rad, editors, *KDD '06: Proceedings of the 12th ACM SIGKDD international conference on Knowledge discovery and data mining*, pages 935–940, New York, NY, USA, August 2006. ACM.

[22] I. Muslea, S. Minton, and C. A. Knoblock. Selective sampling with redundant views. In *17th National Conference on Artificial Intelligence and 12th Conference on Innovative Applications of Artificial Intelligence*, AAAI 2000, pages 621–626. AAAI Press, 2000.

[23] H. T. Nguyen and A. Smeulders. Active learning using preclustering. In *International Conference on Machine Learning*, pages 79–89, 2004.

[24] R. Panigrahy. An improved algorithm finding nearest neighbor using kd-trees. In *Proceedings of the 8th Latin American conference on Theoretical informatics*, LATIN'08, pages 387–398, Berlin, Heidelberg, 2008. Springer-Verlag.

[25] J. R. Quinlan. *C4.5: programs for machine learning.* Morgan Kaufmann Publishers Inc., San Francisco, CA, USA, 1993.

[26] B. Settles. Active Learning Literature Survey. Technical Report 1648, University of Wisconsin–Madison, 2009.

[27] B. Settles and M. Craven. An analysis of active learning strategies for sequence labeling tasks. In *Empirical Methods in Natural Language Processing*, pages 1070–1079, 2008.

[28] H. S. Seung, M. Opper, and H. Sompolinsky. Query by committee. In *Proceedings of the fifth annual workshop on Computational learning theory*, COLT '92, pages 287–294, New York, NY, USA, 1992. ACM.

[29] K. Tomanek and F. Olsson. A web survey on the use of active learning to support annotation of text data. In *Workshop on Active Learning for Natural Language Processing*, NAACL HLT 2009, pages 45–48, Stroudsburg, PA, USA, 2009. Association for Computational Linguistics.

[30] S. Tong and D. Koller. Support vector machine active learning with application sto text classification. In *Proceedings of the Seventeenth International Conference on Machine Learning*, ICML '00, pages 999–1006, 2000.

[31] M. K. Warmuth, J. Liao, G. Rätsch, M. Mathieson, S. Putta, and C. Lemmen. Active learning with support vector machines in the drug discovery process. *Journal of Chemical Information and Computer Sciences*, 43, 2003.

[32] Z. Xu, R. Akella, and Y. Zhang. Incorporating diversity and density in active learning for relevance feedback. In *European conference on IR research*, ECIR'07, pages 246–257, 2007.

[33] Z. Xu, K. Yu, V. Tresp, X. Xu, and J. Wang. Representative sampling for text classification using support vector machines. In *European Conference on IR research*, ECIR'03, pages 393–407, 2003.

Automatically Tagging Email by Leveraging Other Users' Folders

Yehuda Koren, Edo Liberty, Yoelle Maarek, and Roman Sandler
Yahoo! Research
Haifa 31905, ISRAEL
{yehuda, edo.liberty, yoelle, romats}@ymail.com

ABSTRACT

Most email applications devote a significant part of their real estate to organization mechanisms such as folders. Yet, we verified on the Yahoo! Mail service that 70% of email users have never defined a single folder. This implies that one of the most well known email features is underexploited. We propose here to revive the feature by providing a method for generating a lighter form of folders, or tags, benefiting even the most passive users. The method automatically associates, whenever possible, an appropriate semantic tag with a given email. This gives rise to an alternate mechanism for organizing and searching email.

We advocate a novel modeling approach that exploits the overall population of users, thereby learning from the wisdom-of-crowds how to categorize messages. Given our massive user base, it is enough to learn from a minority of the users who label certain messages in order to label that kind of messages for the general population. We design a novel cascade classification approach, which copes with the severe scalability and accuracy constraints we are facing. Significant efficiency gains are achieved by working within a low dimensional latent space, and by using a novel hierarchical classifier. Precision level is controlled by separating the task into a two-phase classification process.

We performed an extensive empirical study covering three different time periods, over 100 million messages, and thousands of candidate tags per message. The results are encouraging and compare favorably with alternative approaches. Our method successfully tags 72% of incoming email traffic. Performance-wise, the computational overhead, even on surge large traffic, is sufficiently low for our approach to be applicable in production on any large Web mail service.

Categories and Subject Descriptors

H.2.8 [**Database Applications**]: Data Mining

General Terms

Algorithms

Keywords

email classification, automatic foldering, multiclass classification, multi-label classification, hierarchical classifier

1. INTRODUCTION

Mail products and services from the early Lotus Notes and Thunderbird applications to more recent Web-based email services such as Hotmail, Yahoo! Mail and Gmail, all offer organization features such as folders or labels to help users browse their email. While there has been much heated discussion on which mechanism is most suitable when organizing personal information in general, in the so-called "folders vs labels war"[1], two pre-requisites for either mechanism are that users need to (1) manually define and maintain such folders or labels and (2) manually move messages into folders or label these messages as appropriate. It turns out however that most users do not take the pain to do this. Indeed, we have verified on the Yahoo! Mail service, one of the top 3 mail services in terms of active number of users, that 70% of email users have never defined even a single folder. We can safely assume that other mail clients or services do not fare better in spite of the prime real estate space folders and labels use on the mail interface.

We propose here to revive this underexploited feature by devising a mechanism for automatically associating "tags" with email messages. Note we are not taking sides in the folders vs labels debate as each has its pros and cons as demonstrated by Civan et al [8]. Instead we focus on a general mechanism that can be used to support the automation of either labels or folders assignment. More specifically, we want to associate with any email message a ranked list of tags when appropriate. These tags can then be directly mapped into user-customizable labels or into disjoint folders (or even a hierarchy of folders if tags are appropriately clustered).

One unique aspect of our proposed solution is that unlike previous approaches, we propose to first look "horizontally" at the overall population of folders' users, rather than immediately personalizing for each individual user's inbox. Given that Yahoo! Mail counts several hundred millions active users, even only 30% of the population gives a wealth of data for us to learn from.

In order to check whether such an approach is realistic, we first needed to verify that folder users expose enough of a common behavior for us to extrapolate to the rest of the population. So as a prologue to this work, we examined the distribution of folder names on a large sample of Yahoo! Mail users. We observed that many users share the same "head" folders for similar needs. Figure 1 shows the existence and frequency of these head folders. These include expected head folders such as "travel","jobs", "friends", "family",

[1]http://www.cloudave.com/1912/google-gmail-finally-ends-the-folder-vs-label-war-what-next-find-the-answer-here/

"bills", "shopping", folders exposing new Web habits and behaviors such as "facebook", or more surprising ones like "recipes". This preliminary study gave us the motivation for this work, namely as users do seem to have common needs, we can hope to define a classification model that would generate popular tags. This would allow us to automate stage 1 of the email organization (the naming of folders/labels) as well as the associated stage 2, the actual labeling of any incoming message with a popular tag when appropriate. Note that we do not attempt to support here a full classification model for rare needs. We could indeed observe that like in Web search and commerce [12], many folder users expose "extraordinary" long tail tastes and generated rare if not unique folders. Yet, we argue that providing even common tags for "ordinary" needs to this majority of users who never organize email is already extremely valuable.

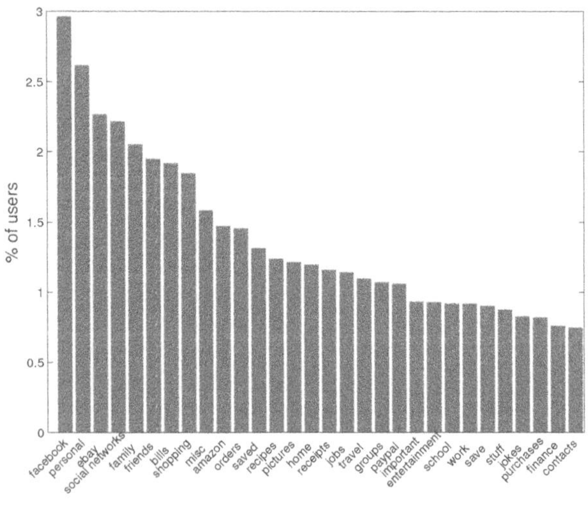

Figure 1: Most popular folders

Devising such an automated tagging system in the context of a real-life huge mail system however poses multiple challenges:

1. **Scalability:** As we are dealing with a huge number of users and even a larger number of incoming messages. Given today's latency expectations, is critical to meet tight performance requirements, and devise highly scalable techniques, raising questions such as whether all messages need to be processed? can we afford to parse and utilize each message full-text body? The resulting system must examine thousands of potential tags for billions of messages per day. Moreover, this must be performed in the time-critical email delivery pipeline.
2. **Precision:** False classification must be kept to a minimum as users are in a passive role where they are presented tags by default. Users are quick to judge when dealing with personal content they are extremely familiar with and will tolerate only minimal irrelevant results. Techniques need to be devised to control and tune precision as needed, as we strive to a close to perfect precision (even at the cost of lowering recall).

Note that there exist multiple additional challenges on the product side in order to ensure a smooth user experience and eventual adoption. This requires answering questions such as: do tags need to be exposed by default and removed upon demand? can they be renamed? how do they live side by side with existing folders? etc. We are not addressing these here and we will keep them for future work. We focus here on these scalability and precision requirements, and propose to use a two-phase cascade classification process in order to address them. For the first phase, we introduce a novel multi-class classifier, referred to as the *tag-vs-tag classifier*, whose role is to pick the most appropriate tags for each message and return them as a short ranked list. For the second phase, we use a *tag-vs-notag classifier*, which separately verifies for each of the candidate tags whether it should or should not be presented.

Using this two-phase-process allows our system to perform well on both scalability and precision requirements. In terms of scalability, the novel design of the presented tag-vs-tag classifier outputs $O(1)$ top tags for a message in time that scales logarithmically with the overall number of tags. For a typical message in our implementation, this requires less than 2 microseconds. This process is described in Sec. 4. In terms of precision, correct thresholds for the *tag-vs-notag classifiers* (Sec. 5) filter out tags that do not meet the prescribed precision requirements. Since this phase only examines $O(1)$ candidate tags, it cannot hurt our overall performance guarantee. Setting these thresholds is made significantly harder due to the fact that a single message might receive multiple valid labels. For example, "bills", "shopping" and "amazon" (tags that are derived from the popular folders shown in Figure 1) might all correctly describe different aspects of a single message. Overcoming these difficulties is explained in Sec. 5.

The key contributions of this paper are the following:

- A new "horizontal" view of the email classification challenge that allows to leverage the wisdom of crowds for tagging messages.
- A novel cascade classification model specifically designed for performance and scalability. This model selects the appropriate tag out thousands of options under harsh performance requirements.
- A new estimator for the presence of each tag within the (unlabeled) Inbox. This facilitates quality control via the automatic setting of precision cutoffs per tag.
- An analysis of email corpus much larger than previously reported.

2. RELATED WORK

The task of automatically assigning email messages into folders, commonly referred to as "foldering", is usually considered a special case of text categorization. Since we cannot hope to survey the entire field of text categorization we focus here only on those efforts aimed directly at email foldering. As in most domains, application of standard text based methods require special accommodations; please see, e.g., [4, 9] for good comparative studies.

All reported works classify messages of a single user (or maillist [2]). The approaches include rule-based systems (e.g., [9, 18]), IR methods: k-NN [6] and tf-idf, and machine learning methods: naïve Bayes (NB), decision trees, support vector machines(SVM), maximum entropy (MaxEnt) and neural networks (NN) [1, 4, 10, 14]. Another common approach is to consider additional properties of email messages and utilize structural features, e.g., [2, 15]. Results for these methods are commonly given for the Enron and SRI datasets [4, 6, 7, 15].

A significant aspect differentiating our work is considering many users simultaneously. In previous works, each user's emails and foldering habits were learned separately. In this work we share information between users and learn the foldering habits of the entire population. This is crucial for being able to service passive (non-foldering) users, which are the majority of the population. This global approach, however, significantly raises the computational challenges. Instead of the few tags used by a single user, here we must consider for each message thousands of possible tags used by the entire population. Moreover, it is quite likely that multiple different tags are appropriate for a single message.

In addition, our performance requirements are much tighter, as we need to scale to a large production email system. Hence, we must resort to fastest methods, while many of the previously reported approaches would not be practical. This includes severe limitations on the message features available to us at delivery time. As a side note, the largest publicly available dataset (Enron), contains 500 times fewer messages than the corpora we employ here,

3. BASIC NOTIONS AND CONVENTIONS

This work deals with *email messages* (or simply, *messages*). Each message is viewed as a set of *features*. The used message features are unigrams and bigrams from the subject line and sender details. The features are binary (either exist or not, with no associated count or weight). Some messages are labeled with *tags*. In practice, the tags are the folder names to which users assign their messages. Hence, in our training data at most one tag is associated with any message. Typically, we deal with a few thousand different tags, assigned to many millions of messages.

We index individual tags by x and y and their number by n. Messages are indexed by i and j. The set of features associated with message i is denoted by F_i. We work with four message sets: a set of labeled training messages $\mathcal{T}$, labeled test messages $\hat{\mathcal{T}}$, unlabeled training messages $\mathcal{I}$ and unlabeled test messages $\hat{\mathcal{I}}$. Unlabeled messages are sampled from non-foldered inbox messages.

4. PHASE 1: PICK A TAG

As explained in the introduction, our process begins with efficiently searching for the most appropriate tags for each message. In this section we describe three classifiers that are built to scale to a large number of tags and messages. While the first two models are adequately fast to train offline, their online prediction performance is still too slow to be practical. The third exhibits also efficient online prediction. Common to all these methods is the need for a low dimensional representation of messages and tags.

4.1 Latent factor representation

A key component underlying our models is a mapping of both messages and tags into a joint low dimensional space of dimension ℓ, to which we refer as the latent factor representation, as follows:

- Each tag x is mapped into a vector $p_x \in \mathbb{R}^\ell$
- Each feature f is mapped into a vector $v_f \in \mathbb{R}^\ell$
- Each message i is mapped to a vector $q_i \in \mathbb{R}^\ell$, defined by the message features to be: $q_i = \frac{1}{|F_i|}\sum_{f\in F_i} v_f$

In addition, we introduce biases for tags, such that the bias of tag x is denoted by b_x. The latent space representation strives to capture the semantics of the tags and messages, such that affinities in the latent space reflect semantic relations. Working in low-dimensional space is extremely beneficial. It allows us to design efficient multiclass classifiers, with low dimensional dense representation leading to memory locality and a small number of used parameters. In our setting, we use a latent space dimensionality of $\ell = 50$, which gives a good tradeoff between time and accuracy.

Given such a latent space representation and a message i, tags are ranked by their affinity to the message defined for each tag x as

$$r_{ix} \stackrel{\text{def}}{=} b_x + q_i^T p_x = b_x + \frac{1}{|F_i|}\sum_{f\in F_i} v_f^T p_x. \qquad (1)$$

Thus, the learning task is learning the latent factor representation. We will offer two alternative ways to learn such a mapping. As explained earlier, the major challenge would be making such a process computationally efficient.

4.2 A max-likelihood approach

Given a message i, the tags are assumed to follow the multinomial distribution

$$p(x|i;\Theta) = \frac{\exp(r_{ix})}{\sum_y \exp(r_{iy})} \qquad (2)$$

where Θ denotes set of model parameters.

We seek to assign tags to all messages in a way that maximizes the log likelihood of the training data

$$L(\mathcal{T};\Theta) \stackrel{\text{def}}{=} \sum_{(i,x)\in\mathcal{T}} \log p(x|i;\Theta). \qquad (3)$$

Note that this model is a latent space analogous to multinomial logistic regression [13] and to MaxEnt [4].

Learning proceeds by stochastic gradient ascent. Given a training example (i, x) we update each parameter θ by

$$\Delta\theta = \eta\frac{\partial \log p(x|i;\Theta)}{\partial\theta} = \eta\left(\frac{\partial r_{ix}}{\partial\theta} - \sum_y p(y|i)\frac{\partial r_{iy}}{\partial\theta}\right) \qquad (4)$$

where η is the learning rate.

However, such a training scheme is too slow to be practical, as each of its update rules requires summing over the n tags. Thus, we resort to a sampling approach of the weighted sum in (4). We adopt the importance sampling trick by Bengio and Senécal [5].

Let $p(x|\mathcal{T})$ denote the empirical probability of tag x in the labeled training set $\mathcal{T}$. This is the distribution from which we sample tags into a set $\mathcal{J}$. Thus, the expensive-to-compute $p(y|i)$ probabilities appearing in (4) are replaced with the weighting scheme

$$w(x|i) = \frac{\exp(r_{ix})/p(x|\mathcal{T})}{\sum_{y\in\mathcal{J}}\exp(r_{iy})/p(y|\mathcal{T})} \qquad (5)$$

Accordingly, the approximated gradient ascent step given training example (i, x) is

$$\Delta\theta = \eta\left(\frac{\partial r_{ix}}{\partial\theta} - \sum_{y\in\mathcal{J}} w(y|i)\frac{\partial r_{iy}}{\partial\theta}\right) \qquad (6)$$

The set $\mathcal{J}$ is sampled with replacement based on $p(x|\mathcal{T})$. To do so, we randomly sample a (i, x) pair from the training set, and add the tag x to $\mathcal{J}$. As mentioned in [5], the size of set $\mathcal{J}$ should grow as the training process proceeds, because at later training phases more delicate parameter adjustments need to be made. We devise a simple rule for controlling the sample size based on the fitness of the current estimate. Given a training example (i, x), we first sample a fixed fraction of the tags population (in our implementation, $n/32$ tags). Then, we keep sampling tags into $\mathcal{J}$ till satisfying:

$$\sum_{y\in\mathcal{J}} p(y|i) > c\cdot p(x|i) \Leftrightarrow \sum_{y\in\mathcal{J}}\exp(r_{iy}) > c\cdot\exp(r_{ix}) \qquad (7)$$

We use $c = 2$ and a maximal sample size of n. This adaptive sampling automatically increases the sample size as parameters converge to their final values and the correct tags receive relatively high probability. We refer to this method as *FlatLikelihood*.

4.3 A normalized hinge loss approach

Here we adapt a learning to rank approach, originated by Weston et al. [19]. We try to minimize the number of misclassified messages by noticing that message i is misclassified if it is tagged x and for some other tag y we have $r_{ix} \leqslant r_{iy}$. Our error function is therefore defined by

$$E(\mathcal{T}) = \sum_{(i,x)\in\mathcal{T}} I(\exists_y : r_{ix} \leqslant r_{iy}) . \quad (8)$$

Let us denote the number of tags violating example (x, i) by

$$\#violations(x, i) = |\{y | r_{ix} \leqslant r_{iy}\}|. \quad (9)$$

Using this notation, we rewrite (8) in an equivalent form

$$E(\mathcal{T}) = \sum_{(i,x)\in\mathcal{T}} \frac{\sum_y I(r_{ix} \leqslant r_{iy})}{\#violations(x, i)} \quad (10)$$

where 0/0 is taken as 0 [19]. Replacing the indicator function with a continuous hinge loss with a margin, to get the loss function

$$E^1(\mathcal{T}) = \sum_{(i,x)\in\mathcal{T}} \frac{\sum_y |1 - r_{ix} + r_{iy}|_+}{\#violations^1(x, i)} \quad (11)$$

where $|x|_+ = x$ if $x > 0$ or zero otherwise. In addition the margin-aware $\#violations^1(x, i)$ is defined as $|\{y | r_{ix} \leqslant r_{iy} + 1\}|$.

Minimizing (11) is costly due to the requirement to sum over all potential tags. Hence, much like in the max-likelihood case, a sampling approach is used. To make things easier, now the sum is not weighted by an expensive-to-compute probability, so we can get its unbiased estimate by uniformly drawing tags with replacement into a set $\mathcal{J}$. This way, an unbiased estimator of $E^1(\mathcal{T})$ would be

$$\hat{E}^1(\mathcal{T}) = \sum_{(i,x)\in\mathcal{T}} \frac{\sum_{y\in\mathcal{J}} |1 - r_{ix} + r_{iy}|_+}{\#violations^1(\mathcal{J}, x, i)} \quad (12)$$

where $\#violations^1(\mathcal{J}, x, i) \stackrel{def}{=} |\{y \in \mathcal{J} | r_{ix} \leqslant r_{iy} + 1\}|$.

Learning is done by a stochastic gradient descent on $\hat{E}^1$. Given a training example (i, x), we sample into $\mathcal{J}$ $n/32$ tags, and keep on sampling till $\#violations^1(\mathcal{J}, x, i) \geqslant 1$ or till hitting n samples. We refer to this method as *FlatNormalizedHinge*.

In our experimental study, both FlatLikelihood and FlatNormalizedHinge produce better results than several known baselines. However, they still suffer from poor online computational efficiency. Indeed, for each new message, we must evaluate all possible tags. Thus, the main use of these two models is in constructing a tree hierarchy of the tags, as described in the next section.

4.4 Hierarchical classifier

We stick to the principles of the latent factor models developed in the previous section. However, in order to let their prediction performance scale to a large number of tags and messages, we draw inspiration from works on language modeling, where words are modeled within a hierarchy, thereby enabling prediction of the next word out of a large vocabulary [16, 17].

The first step is embedding all tags as leaves of a binary hierarchical structure by recursively partitioning the tags into balanced groups. To this end, we represent each tag x by its latent space mapping p_x, as computed by either FlatLikelihood or FlatNormalizedHinge. Then we apply a k-means clustering (the variant by [3]) with $k = 2$ to the tags' representations. We create two equally sized clusters by sorting the tags according to their distance from the two means, and splitting at the middle point. Then, we continue recursively until reaching singletons. Hence, the n tags are identified with leafs of a binary tree (hierarchy) of depth $O(\log n)$.[2]

Each internal tree node a is associated with a hyperplane $b_a + z^T p_a = 0$ for $p_a, z \in \mathbb{R}^\ell$. For a given message i, along with its latent factor representation q_i, we traverse the tree according to half spaces q_i is in (with respect to the internal nodes' hyperplanes). More precisely, we employ the following traversal rule: at internal node a, proceed to the left child if $b_a + q_i^T p_a > 0$, otherwise proceed to the right child. Hence, given a message and a trained tree, one can traverse the root-to-leaf path in $O(\log n)$ steps.

We still need to devise ways for learning the parameters of the model, i.e., the internal nodes' hyperplanes and the messages' representation. Intuitively, a classifier trained on the formed hierarchy should encourage training examples to follow the paths leading to their true tags. More precisely, define $d_{ax} = 1$ if the leaf corresponding to x is a left offspring of a and $d_{ax} = -1$ if x is a right offspring of a.[3] If message i is tagged by x we strive to have $sign(b_a + q_i^T p_a) = d_{ax}$. If this is true for all internal nodes leading from the root to x, then message i will be correctly classified. Learning the parameters (b_a, p_a, q_i) can be based on either the max likelihood principle or on the normalized hinge loss. We first show the derivation for the normalized hinge loss.

Given a hierarchy T, and a training example (i, x), we define the set of violating nodes as

$$\#violations^1(T, x, i) = |\{a \in \text{path}_x | (b_a + q_i^T p_a) d_{ax} \leqslant 1\}|.$$

Here path_x stands for the set of internal nodes on the path from the root of the tree to x. Then, the normalized hinge loss associated with the training set, given hierarchy T is defined as

$$\hat{E}^1(\mathcal{T}; T) = \sum_{(i,x)\in\mathcal{T}} \frac{\sum_{a\in\text{path}_x} |1 - (b_a + q_i^T p_a) d_{ax}|_+}{\#violations^1(T, x, i)} \quad (13)$$

Optimizing is done by stochastic gradient descent. Each training example requires traversing only a $O(\log n)$-long path, which compares favorably with the $O(n)$ tag comparisons required by the FlatNormalizedHinge (even after sampling). The impact of this structure for online prediction is even more significant at stated above. Henceforth, we dub this method as *HierNormalizedHinge*.

The derivation for maximizing the log likelihood is analogous. For a message i, at a tree node a we define the probability to proceed to the left child using the logistic function as $\sigma(a, i) = (1 + \exp(-b_a - q_i^T p_a))^{-1}$. Learning is done by stochastic gradient ascent on the training set log likelihood

$$L(\mathcal{T}; T) = \sum_{(i,x)\in\mathcal{T}} \sum_{a\in\text{path}_x} \frac{1}{2}(1 + d_{ax}) \log \sigma(a, i) + \frac{1}{2}(1 - d_{ax}) \log(1 - \sigma(a, i)) \quad (14)$$

Henceforth, this method is referred to as *HierLikelihood*.

Hierarchical classifiers are natural for suggesting a single tag per message. In case more than one tag suggestion is required, we use an empirical confusion matrix. For each tag we record the tags it most commonly confused with. This way a single leaf outputs a list of multiple ranked tag suggestions. We elaborate more on this, and on performance evaluation in the empirical study (Sec. 6).

[2] We have tried several other clustering methods. Our experiments showed that performing k-means clustering on normalized vectors (whereas tag x is mapped to $p_x/\|p_x\|$) slightly improves subsequent classifier performance.

[3] A leaf x is a left(right) offspring of a if the left(right) child of a is on the path from the root node to x.

5. PHASE 2: TO TAG OR NOT TO TAG?

In the second phase we get a message together with a short list of suggested tags produced by the first phase. For each of the suggested tags, we decide whether we should keep it or filter it out. This is achieved by applying a binary classifier to each message and suggested tag independently.

For each tag we train a binary classifier by comparing messages labeled by the tag to unlabeled messages. Unlike in the first phase, the measure of success here is hard to evaluate. This is because each tag has a different presence within the set of unlabeled messages. For example, the tag "generic stuff" is rarely used (thus being associated with only a few labeled messages), and still a relatively large number of unlabeled messages could justifiably receive this tag. Moreover, different kinds of messages have different probabilities of being labelled. This makes the distribution of labeled messages different than the distribution of unlabeled one, e.g., travel related messages are much more likely to be tagged than promotions. Addressing this issue is the main challenge faced by the second phase. We first address the general problem and then discuss it for our case.

From this point on we view this problem as a one-tag-problem: either tag or not tag. We are required to construct a high precision classifier f for tag x. We make the crucial assumption that each message which justifies tag x is actually labeled x with probability $prob_x$ independently of the message content. In other words, the probability of a message being labeled x is independent of its content *conditioned* on x justifying tag x.

We denote by $\hat{\mathcal{T}}_x$ the set of messages labeled by x in $\hat{\mathcal{T}}$ and by $\hat{\mathcal{I}}_x$ the set of unlabeled messages in $\hat{\mathcal{I}}$ which justify tag x. In order to argue against the precision of f we must estimate the size of $\hat{\mathcal{I}}_x$. This can be performed with the help of a picky-classifier g whose precision is (almost) perfect but whose recall might be very low. We assume such g exists. Let $g(\hat{\mathcal{T}}_x)$ denote the set of messages g identifies as labeled by x in $\hat{\mathcal{T}}_x$. From our assumption, the content distribution in $\hat{\mathcal{T}}_x$ and $\hat{\mathcal{I}}_x$ is identical. This means that g should exhibit the same recall on both sets which gives $|g(\hat{\mathcal{I}}_x)|/|\hat{\mathcal{I}}_x| \approx |g(\hat{\mathcal{T}}_x)|/|\hat{\mathcal{T}}_x|$. Moreover, since g's precision is almost perfect we have that $|g(\hat{\mathcal{I}}_x)| \approx |g(\hat{\mathcal{I}})|$. We therefore get that

$$|\hat{\mathcal{I}}_x| \approx |g(\hat{\mathcal{I}})| \cdot |\hat{\mathcal{T}}_x|/|g(\hat{\mathcal{T}}_x)|. \quad (15)$$

Having approximated the size of $\hat{\mathcal{I}}_x$ we return to estimating the precision of our classifier f. Again by our independent tagging probability assumption, we have that the recall of f on $\hat{\mathcal{T}}_x$ approximates its recall on $\hat{\mathcal{I}}_x$, i.e., $|f(\hat{\mathcal{I}}_x)|/|\hat{\mathcal{I}}_x| \approx |f(\hat{\mathcal{T}}_x)|/|\hat{\mathcal{T}}_x|$. Moreover, $f(\hat{\mathcal{I}}_x)$ is exactly the set of unlabeled messages which are *correctly* classified by f. Dividing this by the overall number of labeled messages $f(\hat{\mathcal{I}})$ we get the precision of f.

$$precision(f) = \frac{|f(\hat{\mathcal{I}}_x)|}{|f(\hat{\mathcal{I}})|} \approx \frac{|f(\hat{\mathcal{T}}_x)|}{|g(\hat{\mathcal{T}}_x)|} \cdot \frac{|g(\hat{\mathcal{I}})|}{|f(\hat{\mathcal{I}})|}. \quad (16)$$

We now discuss our specific choices of classifiers. For g we use a Naïve Bayes classifier [13] trained to separate messages tagged x in $\mathcal{T}$ from all messages of $\mathcal{I}$. The reason for using the Naïve Bayes classifier here is a relative comfort in setting a uniformly sufficiently high cutoff value for achieving our close-to-perfect precision demands. Consequently, we set the cutoff to $\exp(10)$. It is worth noting that the choice of the Naïve Bayes classifier is somewhat arbitrary. Many other binary classifiers could be used with appropriate thresholds to the same effect.

For f, several binary classifiers were tried, including Naïve-Bayes, hinge loss-based, and logistic regression-based. The best empirical results were achieved with the method described in the following.

We keep using the mapping of messages and tags into a low dimensional space as described in Sec. 4.1. The mapping here is not identical to the ones computed in Sec. 4.1 but, for the sake of clarity, we keep using the same symbols. Moreover, for computational reasons the mapping of messages to the latent space, q_i, is shared between all tags. An individual tag classification is carried out by thresholding on $r_{ix} = b_x + q_i^T p_x$.

We follow a logistic-regression strategy, implemented in the low dimensional latent space. For a message i, we define its probability of it being labeled x as:

$$p(x|i) = (1 + \exp(-r_{ix}))^{-1} \quad (17)$$

Hence, $1 - p(x|i)$ is the probability that message i is not labeled by x. We maximize the log-likelihood of the combined training set

$$\sum_{(i,x)\in\mathcal{T}} \log p(x|i) + \sum_{i\in\mathcal{I}} \sum_{x} \log(1 - p(x|i)) \quad (18)$$

Learning is done by stochastic gradient ascent. Training time is potentially long due to the second summation which runs over all unclassified messages and tags. This can be controlled by limiting the relative size of $|\mathcal{I}|$ to be comparable to the number of messages belonging to a single tag. In terms of classifier accuracy such a limitation is reasonable.

We set each classifier f_x such that $f_x(i)$ returns true if $r_{ix} \geq \gamma_x$. The thresholds γ_x are chosen such that the precision of f_x is high enough according to Equation 16. More details are given in the empirical study (Sec. 6).

6. EMPIRICAL STUDY

6.1 Dataset description

We experimented with email data gathered from anonymized Yahoo! Mail users. Performance and privacy requirements limited us to analyzing only the subject and sender fields of each message. Overall we collected close to 200 million foldered messages. The messages were partitioned into three different datasets by arrival month that we refer to as T1, T2, and T3. Within each dataset, we split the messages into train and test sets by arrival time.

We limited ourselves to popular user-defined folders defined by a large enough number of users and directly mapped them into a raw list of 6,000 tags. We then ran the FlatLikelihood model of Sec. 4.2 on the T1 corpus. The resulting embedding of the tags within the low dimensional space allowed us to identify synonymous tags, by clustering tags by their low dimensional embeddings' cosine similarity. For each of the 819 non-singleton clusters a representative tag was selected. Namely, the one most frequently used. For example, for the cluster *{facebook, fb, facebook stuff, face book,... }* the tag *facebook* was retained and all other tags/folders merged. Similarly *fun* was retained for *{fun, jokes, humor, keepers, fun stuff, funny, funnies, jokes etc, funny stuff, funnys, joke,... }*, and *recipes* for *{recipes, recipies, food, receipes, cooking, food recipes, recopies, allrecipes, all recipes,... }*. In addition, some tags were removed, based on signals indicating they were hard to classify. They typically were of three types: (1) Ambiguous tags such as *{a, b, c, d, anything, stuff, just stuff, emails, everything, everything else, misc,... }*, which in any case would not bring any value to users; (2) Personal names, which mean something else to each user, do not fit our global learning task and most of all would endanger privacy; (3) Offensive or inappropriate tags. Note also that we focused on a single language for consistency purposes so all non-English tags were removed as well. The cleaning and relabeling process reduced the number of tags from 6,000 to 2,000, and eliminated about 50%

Corpus title	size before cleaning	size after cleaning
T1 Train	64,944,551	35,682,312
T1 Test	6,870,011	3,975,829
T2 Train	26,699,484	7,374,012
T2 Test	3,444,248	1,779,385
T3 Train	71,237,679	37,783,613
T3 Test	26,699,484	14,300,864
Total	199,895,457	100,896,015

Table 1: Three foldered messages datasets, gathered over 3 different periods, each split into train- and test-set

Corpus title	size
T4 Untagged Train	8,330,355
T4 Untagged Test	8,329,492
T5 Untagged Train	20,134,623
T5 Untagged Test	20,139,110
Total	56,933,580

Table 2: Two non-foldered message datasets, gathered at different periods, each split into train- and test-set

of the messages. Note that in a deployed product, in addition to the automated process, which is key to regular updates and applicability to other geos, we believe that quality control should also be conducted by a human editor in order to formally approve the final list of tags before exposing to users. We do not expect this process to be too tedious given the relatively short size and generality of the final list. It would also clearly respect the terms and conditions of most mail services as it would only be applied in the final stage on massively aggregated and thus anonymized data.

The description of the datasets is given in Table 1. A histogram of the number of messages in each folder for the T3 Train dataset is given in Fig. 2. In addition, the left column in Table 4 lists the most populated folders in the dataset by messages (as opposed to by users as depicted in Fig. 1).

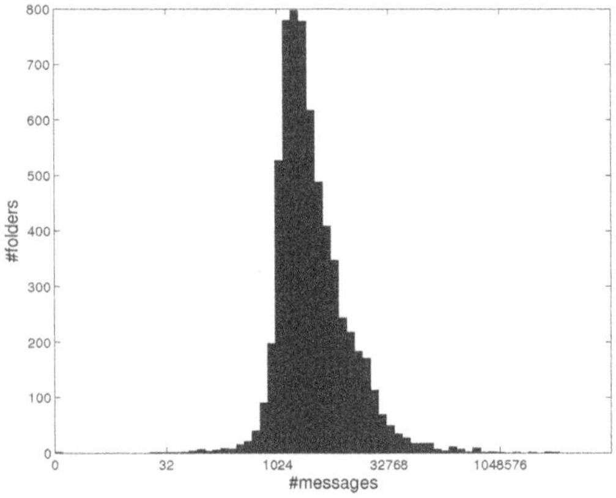

Figure 2: Histograms of number of messages per folder in the T3 train set (mode: 1,167, median: 2,438, mean: 20,773)

In order to enable the second phase of the our method, we sampled two datasets of non-foldered messages. Each dataset was split into train and test sets. These datasets are described in Table 2.

Each message is represented as a set of 70 features at most, with an average of 15. A feature can be a unigram (single word) or a bigram (adjacent words) extracted after tokenizing the subject and sender fields, or a full sender domain. Thus, for a message from ancestry.com (a genealogy service), the full domain feature is *ancestry.com*, a sender feature is *ancestry*, and subject features include *{family, family tree, your family}*.

Feature selection was performed as follows. We computed the information gain of each feature with respect to each folder (a standard procedure in text feature selection, see e.g., [11]). Information gain tends to grow with folder size and accordingly would favor larger folders. Hence, to ensure a minimal representation for each folder, we retained the 20 features with the highest information gain per folder. Beyond this, we ranked all features by their maximal information gain value, and kept the top features. The process reduced the number of features to 2^{16}, which allowed us to represent each feature using a short integer.

6.2 Evaluating Phase 1 "tag-vs-tag" classification

Accuracy comparison: The tag-vs-tag classifier used in the first phase of our approach was evaluated on the three datasets of foldered messages. For each message, all 2000 tags were considered. We computed the accuracy rate as the fraction of messages for which we suggested the tag that was originally assigned by the user. Note that such an accuracy metric underestimates the true performance of the method. This is because a suggested tag which is different from the one the user chose might also fit the message. We compared our methods to several baseline models, which we now describe.

First, we used a nearest-neighbors approach, whose variants were used in the past for foldering messages. We view each folder as a long document containing all its messages. A standard vector space (aka tf-idf) representation is used for the resulting document corpus and for each test message. Then, we assign each message to the folder most similar to it based on cosine similarity. Results of such an approach significantly lagged behind the rest. For the T3 test set it could correctly assign 32.70% of messages into their given tags. The main issue with this naive Information Retrieval approach is that it fails to distinguish well populated folders from scarcer ones. Hence a quick fix would be to augment each cosine value with the popularity of the tag, that is, the number of messages belonging the respective folder. Our experiments showed best results when multiplying the cosine with the square root of tag popularity. Consequently, accuracy on the T3 data grew to 51.07%.

Next we applied a Naïve Bayes classifier (NB) [13], which typically performs decently in text classification and was previously used for email classification. In order for NB to produce suitable results, one needs to smooth both feature counts and folder sizes. That is, in order to estimate the probability of observing feature f at tag (or, folder) x, we count: (1) n_x – the number of messages belonging to folder x; (2) $n_{x,f}$ – the number of messages with feature f at folder x. Then we define a smoothed conditional probability

$$p(f|x) = \frac{n_{x,f} + \kappa_1}{n_x + \kappa_2} \qquad (19)$$

The feature count smoother, κ_1, is standard with NB, and we set its value to 1. Of a much greater importance was the folder count smoother, κ_2, which penalizes small folders. We set its value to 10^4. The rest of NB derivation follows as usual. The fitness of tag x for message i is taken to be $p(x)\prod_{f\in F_i} p(f|x)$. The NB classifier could classify 55.47% of T3 messages into their given tags, which is an improvement over the nearest neighbors classifier.

Next we report on the accuracy of the FlatLikelihood classifier described in Sec. 4.2. Note that this classifier can be viewed as a scalable version of Logistic Regression (or the equivalent MaxEnt), allowing it to deal with thousands of labels through a latent space mapping and importance sampling. FlatLikelihood could classify 57.68% of T3 test messages to their exact given tags, exceeding the accuracy of NB.

HierLikelihood, the hierarchical version of FlatLikelihood, surprised us by meaningfully exceeding the accuracy of FlatLikelihood, thereby yielding a 61.58% accuracy rate. This shows that constraining the classifier to a strict hierarchical tag structure, did not harm but rather improved performance. The same phenomenon was observed on the T1 and T2 datasets. We speculate that the rigid hierarchical structure could serve as regularizer contributing to the generalization power of the classifier.

Finally, let us mention the normalized hinge classifiers, which yield best accuracy in our tests. The flat version (FlatNormalizedHinge) achieved an accuracy rate of 62.78%, whereas the much faster hierarchical version (HierNormalizedHinge) got a slightly lower accuracy of 62.38%. Since these margin-based classifiers share resemblance with SVM, their superior results bode well with the findings by Bekkerman et al. [4], which stated that the SVM classifier produces best results in a related email classification task.

The results we have described for T3 follow the same trend also on the T1 and T2 test sets. Full results are described in Fig. 3.

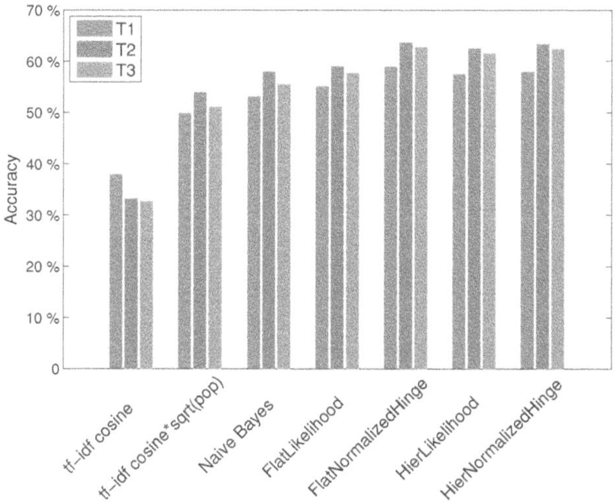

Figure 3: Accuracy of different tag-vs-tag classifiers

These classifiers can output more than a single label. Hence, we let FlatLikelihood and FlatNormalizedHinge list for each message the top-K tags of highest scores. Following the same procedure with the hierarchical classifiers would badly affect their computational speed advantage. Hence, as previously explained, we employed an approximated approach for the hierarchical classifiers. We stored for each tree leaf an ordered list of the folders most frequently leading to the leaf, and returned the top-K head elements of that list. Accordingly, recall-at-K results are depicted in Fig. 4. The approximated approach makes the hierarchical methods lag behind the flat ones as K grows. Still, for all the four methods recall@10 already exceeds 80%.

Run times: We trained the classifiers with stochastic gradient descent (or ascent), while looping over the dataset with a decaying learning rate. When visiting the l-th example the decayed learning rate was set to $10^6/(5 \cdot 10^6 + l)$. Regularization (weight decay) was found counter-productive and hence is not employed. Training stops after visiting 2^{28} examples, a point where observed accuracy of the process converges for all tried methods. We report times

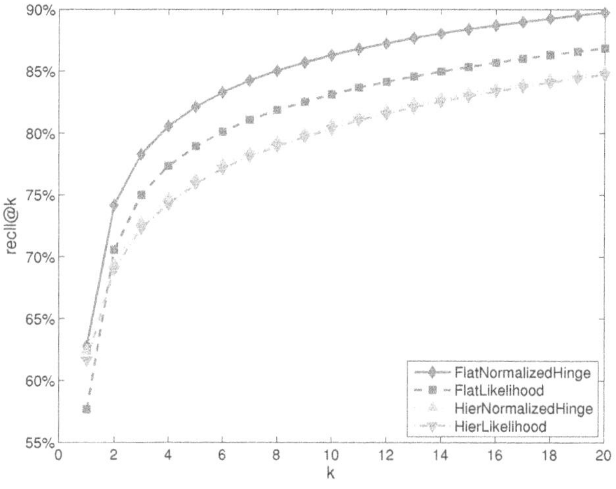

Figure 4: Recall-at-K for different tag-vs-tag classifiers on T3

measured on a HP DL160 G6, 2xXeon X5650 2.67GHz system (with single threaded processes). Training times differ dramatically between the hierarchical and the flat classifiers, as depicted in Fig. 5. The fastest one, HierNormalizedHinge, takes 1017 seconds to complete training. HierLikelihood closely follows with a run time of 3440 seconds. The flat classifiers took much longer to complete: 30,679 seconds for FlatNormalizedHinge and 41,126 seconds for FlatLikelihood.

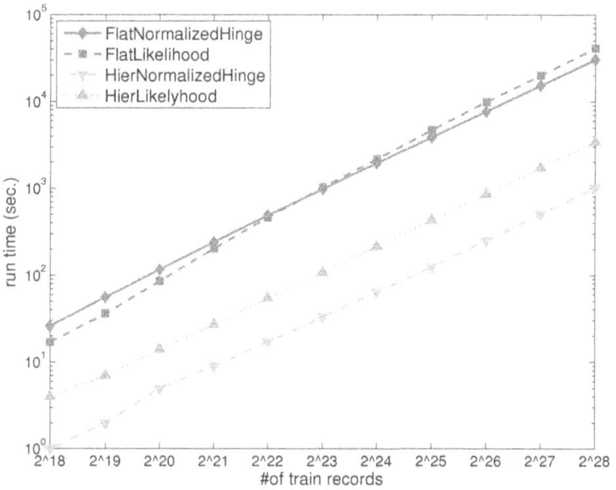

Figure 5: Training times of the tag-vs-tag classifiers

Much more important than the offline train time are the online prediction times. We measure the cumulative time required to predict the 20,056,078 records within the three test sets. Results are shown in Table 3. Here the train-free NB and the nearest neighbors classifiers, were proved to be slowest, taking 54 hours to label 1 billion messages. Assisted with their memory-local low-dimensional representation, FlatLikelihood and FlatNormalizedHinge could accomplish the same task in half the time – 27 hours, which is still way too slow for our system requirements. Note that while the FlatLikelihood and FlatNormalizedHinge differ in training, at test time they use the same linear function and hence take the same computation time. Finally, as expected, the hierarchical classifiers are significantly faster, requiring less than half an hour to label 1 billion

method	prediction time	records/sec	hours/ GigaRecord
tf-idf cosine	3920 sec	5116.35	54.29
tf-idf cosine*sqrt(pop)	4642 sec	4320.57	64.29
Naïve Bayes	3885 sec	5162.44	53.81
FlatLikelihood	1961 sec	10227.47	27.16
FlatNormalizedHinge	1968 sec	10191.10	27.26
HierLikelihood	35 sec	573030.8	0.48
HierNormalizedHinge	35 sec	573030.8	0.48

Table 3: Prediction running times of the various classifers on the total 20,056,078 test messages (the three test sets combined). We also report the throughput of each method in records/sec, and the time (in hours) to process 10^9 records.

messages. In other words, HierNormalizedHinge and HierLikelihood took less than 2 microseconds to label a message, satisfying our performance requirements. As a conclusion, HierNormalized-Hinge clearly proves as our chosen method for Phase 1.

6.3 Evaluating Phase 2 "tag-vs-notag" classification

The tag-vs-notag classifier was applied to the results screened by the first phase HierNormalizedHinge. The first task at this stage consisted in evaluating the fraction of inbox messages that can be labeled with each of the tags. We followed the estimation process described in Sec. 5. The 20 most covering tags are described in the second column of Table 4. Note the striking difference between the tags actually employed by users (first column of the table) and the tags fitting most messages (second column of the table), which we find quite illuminating. For example, a tag like "advertisement" was found to be related to over 32% of (non-spam) inbox messages. Not surprisingly, such a tag was nowhere to be found among the top tags actually used by users. This in short tells the difference between the objectives of two phases of the system. The first phase attempts at suggesting the tags that actual users are expected to pick, and in case of multiple appropriate tags it will follow the wisdom of crowds. Hence, it will prioritize tags in a way resembling the first column in the table. On the other hand, the second phase evaluates the fit between each tag and a message, thereby favoring some rather generic tags such as those at the top of the second column of the table.

In order to assess the quality of the tag-vs-notag classifier, we computed its precision-recall curve on the T5 Untagged test set. Such a curve is necessarily approximate, where we employ the methods described in Sec. 5 for estimating precision and recall. In addition, since the second phase considers a separate classifier per tag, we averaged results over all tags. The results are depicted in Fig. 6. We decided to set the classifiers' thresholds in order to achieve an estimated 100% precision level for each of the tags. At this level, the expected average recall would be 75.5%.

An ultimate test of our system consists of evaluating coverage as the fraction of total Inbox messages it can tag, or, the fraction of messages "surviving" the two-phase screening. When the first phase generates only the single top tag for each message, the second phase retains 67.74% of the suggested tags, leaving 67.74% of the inbox messages tagged. This fraction slowly improves when we allow the first phase suggest more tags. For example, when the first phase suggests 10 (20) tags per message, 71.26% (72.61%) of the Inbox get eventually tagged. These numbers indicate that our tagging system would be not only discoverable but clearly visible

Most used	Most Inbox coverage	Most suggested
facebook 13.89%	advertisement 32.19%	facebook 17.67%
groups 9.22%	facebook 26.22%	groups 13.38%
friends and family 4.55%	promotions 20.96%	stores 5.19%
ebay and paypal 4.30%	stores 15.94%	friends and family 3.19%
jobs 3.55%	groups 15.16%	jobs 1.59%
orders 3.40%	videos 13.84%	advertisement 1.17%
travel 1.96%	spam 12.16%	work 1.17%
pictures 1.95%	adult 11.62%	tagged 1.14%
recipes 1.89%	attachments 10.87%	videos 1.00%
bills 1.87%	movies 9.60%	travel 0.86%
fun 1.71%	shopping 8.19%	spiritual 0.78%
school 1.61%	stories 7.54%	ebay and paypal 0.76%
finance 1.37%	newsletters 7.38%	health and fitness 0.59%
amazon 1.23%	work 7.34%	shopping 0.55%
news 1.09%	sales 6.90%	news 0.55%
shopping 1.07%	clothes 6.60%	newsletters 0.54%
work 1.01%	friends and family 5.93%	yahoo 0.51%
stores 0.84%	array 5.33%	orders 0.49%
health and fitness 0.82%	entertainment 5.13%	friendster 0.47%
tagged 0.81%	business 5.08%	amazon 0.46%

Table 4: List of 20-top tags in terms of: (a) number of messages inserted by user population to the corresponding folders; (b) number of messages passing the tag's classifier (here shown percentages exceed 100%, as a single message can agree with multiple tags); (c) number of messages our method assigned the tag.

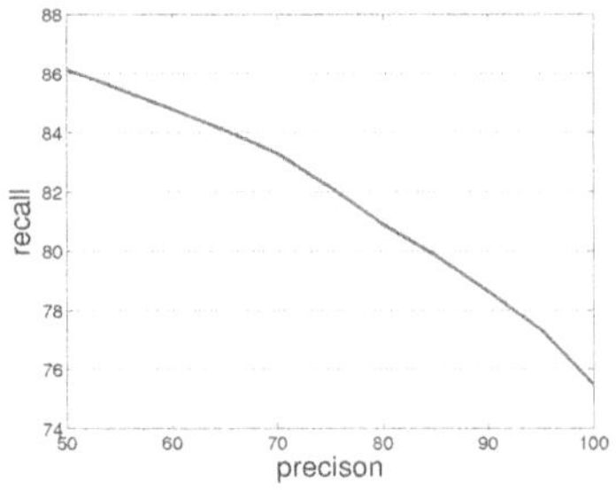

Figure 6: Precision recall curve averaged over tag-vs-notag classifiers. Since we are interested in high precision, we zoom-in on the higher precision half of the curve.

to most users. The rightmost column of Table 4 lists the tags most often suggested by the whole process on the T5 Untagged test set.

In spite of the fact that during the first phase multiple tags can be suggested, we found out that most of those besides the first one are rejected by the second phase. For example, when the first phase suggests 10 tags per message, then at the 71.26% of messages actually keeping at least one tag, an average of just 2.22 tags per message survive. Similarly, when the first phase is allowed to suggest 20 tags, then an average of 2.54 tags survive for messages actually keeping at least one tag. We view this positively, as we would not want a single message carry too many tags.

7. CONCLUSIONS

We have described here a system for labeling email messages at a very large scale. The system is based on leveraging the folders of relatively few users in order to get a tagging coverage of over 70% of the Yahoo! Mail incoming messages.

Given the scale and system integration constraints we faced, we designed highly efficient classifiers that cope with thousands of considered tags per each incoming message. All our methods share the property of mapping the messages into a low dimensional latent space, thereby enabling a more compact and efficient representation. Furthermore, we borrowed two of the most successful email classification approaches (Logistic Regression and Margin-based) and showed how their training and predictions can be made faster by using sampling and hierarchical classification techniques. The speed-up was substantial enough to satisfy our performance needs, classifying a message in less than 2 microseconds.

An end-user facing classifier, which assumes almost no user intervention or interaction, must obey very strict precision goals. Hence, after deciding on a shortlist of ranked tags per message, each suggested tag has to pass another filter deciding whether it is worth triggering or not. The major challenge here was estimating the true coverage a tag has on the population of untagged messages, which would enable us to decide at which distinct certainty level we can trigger each tag. We devised a novel method for achieving such estimations.

A classifier is as good as its underlying features. While our system inhibits us from time expensive analysis of email body, there are numerous other features that we would like to consider in the future. These include the number of recipients in To: and Cc: fields, the length of a message, the number and names of file attachments, style (html/plain) signals, and more sophisticated subject tokenization techniques.

Acknowledgments

We would like to thank the Yahoo! mail engineering team for their great help in facilitating this research and pushing it into production, with special thanks to Woody Anderson, Vishwanath Ramarao, and Andrew Sloane. In addition we thank Vinod Nair for his most valuable advice. Final thanks go to Andrei Broder for the product definition and many other insights.

8. REFERENCES

[1] D. Aberdeen, O. Pacovsky, and A. Slater. The learning behind gmail priority inbox. In *LCCC : NIPS 2010 Workshop on Learning on Cores, Clusters and Clouds*.

[2] M. Aery and S. Chakravarthy. emailsift: Email classification based on structure and content. In *ICDM*, pages 18–25, 2005.

[3] D. Arthur and S. Vassilvitskii. k-means++: the advantages of careful seeding. In *Proc. 18th ACM-SIAM Symposium on Discrete Algorithms (SODA'07)*, pages 1027–1035. SIAM, 2007.

[4] R. Bekkerman, A. Mccallum, and G. Huang. Automatic categorization of email into folders: Benchmark experiments on Enron and SRI corpora. In *In Technical Report, Computer Science department, IR-418*, pages 4–6.

[5] Y. Bengio and J.-S. Senécal. Quick training of probabilistic neural nets by sampling. In *Proc. 9th International Workshop on Artificial Intelligence and Statistics (AISTATS'03)*, 2003.

[6] P. Bermejo, J. A. Gámez, and J. M. Puerta. Improving the performance of naïve bayes multinomial in e-mail foldering by introducing distribution-based balance of datasets. *Expert Syst. Appl.*, 38:2072–2080, March 2011.

[7] S. Chakravarthy, A. Venkatachalam, and A. Telang. A graph-based approach for multi-folder email classification. In *ICDM*, pages 78–87, 2010.

[8] A. Civan, W. Jones, P. Klasnja, and H. Bruce. Better to organize personal information by folders or by tags?: The devil is in the details. *Proc. American Society for Information Science and Technology*, 45(1):1–13, 2008.

[9] W. Cohen. Learning rules that classify e-mail. In *In Papers from the AAAI Spring Symposium on Machine Learning in Information Access*, pages 18–25. AAAI Press.

[10] Y. Diao, H. Lu, and D. Wu. A comparative study of classification based personal e-mail filtering. In *PAKDD*, pages 408–419, 2000.

[11] G. Forman. An extensive empirical study of feature selection metrics for text classification. *Journal of Machine Learning Research*, 3:1289–1305, March 2003.

[12] S. Goel, A. Broder, E. Gabrilovich, and B. Pang. Anatomy of the long tail: Ordinary people with extraordinary tastes. In *WSDM*, 2010.

[13] T. Hastie, R. Tibshirani, and J. Friedman. *The elements of statistical learning: data mining, inference and prediction (2nd edition)*. Springer, 2008.

[14] S. Kiritchenko and S. Matwin. Email classification with co-training. In *CASCON*, page 8, 2001.

[15] B. Klimt and Y. Yang. The Enron corpus: A new dataset for email classification research. In *In ECML*, pages 217–226, 2004.

[16] A. Mnih and G. E. Hinton. A scalable hierarchical distributed language model. In *NIPS*, pages 1081–1088, 2008.

[17] F. Morin and Y. Bengio. Hierarchical probabilistic neural network language model. In *Proc. 11th International Workshop on Artificial Intelligence and Statistics (AISTATS'05)*, pages 246–252, 2005.

[18] R. B. Segal and J. O. Kephart. Incremental learning in swiftfile. In *In Proc. Seventh International Conference on Machine Learning*, pages 863–870. Morgan Kaufmann, 2000.

[19] J. Weston, S. Bengio, and N. Usunier. Large scale image annotation: Learning to rank with joint word-image embeddings. *Machine Learning Journal*, 81:21–35, 2010.

Axiomatic Ranking of Network Role Similarity*

Ruoming Jin Victor E. Lee Hui Hong
Department of Computer Science
Kent State University, Kent, OH, 44242, USA
{jin,vlee,hhong}@cs.kent.edu

ABSTRACT

A key task in analyzing social networks and other complex networks is role analysis: describing and categorizing nodes by how they interact with other nodes. Two nodes have the same role if they interact with *equivalent* sets of neighbors. The most fundamental role equivalence is automorphic equivalence. Unfortunately, the fastest algorithm known for graph automorphism is nonpolynomial. Moreover, since exact equivalence is rare, a more meaningful task is measuring the role *similarity* between any two nodes. This task is closely related to the link-based similarity problem that SimRank addresses. However, SimRank and other existing simliarity measures are not sufficient because they do not guarantee to recognize automorphically or structurally equivalent nodes. This paper makes two contributions. First, we present and justify several axiomatic properties necessary for a role similarity measure or metric. Second, we present RoleSim, a role similarity metric which satisfies these axioms and which can be computed with a simple iterative algorithm. We rigorously prove that RoleSim satisfies all the axiomatic properties and demonstrate its superior interpretative power on both synthetic and real datasets.

Categories and Subject Descriptors

E.1 [**Data Structures**]: Graphs and Networks; H.2.8 [**Database Management**]: Database Applications—*Data Mining*

General Terms

Theory, Algorithms, Measurement, Experimentation

Keywords

Complex network, Social network, Vertex similarity, Role similarity, Ranking, Automorphic equivalence

1. INTRODUCTION

In social science, it is well-established that individual agents tend to play roles or assume positions within their interaction network. For instance, in a university, each individual can be classified into the position of faculty member, administrator, staff, or student. Indeed, role discovery in is a major research subject in classical social science [40]. rwInterestingly, recent studies have found not only do roles appear in other types of networks, including food webs [26], world trade [15], and even software systems [8], but also roles can help to predict node functionality. For instance, in a protein interaction network, proteins with similar roles tend to serve similar metabolic functions. Thus, if we know the function of one protein, we can predict that all other proteins having a similar role would also have similar function [17]. In other cases, such as online social networks, there are no *a priori* role categories. The classifications must be learned based on the interaction patterns.

A central question in studying the roles in a network system is how to define *role similarity*. In particular, how can we rank two nodes' role similarity in terms of their interaction patterns? Despite its vital importance for network analysis and decades of work by social scientists, joined recently by computer scientists, no satisfactory metric for role similarity has yet emerged. A key issue is the encapsulation of graph automorphism into a role similarity metric: *if two nodes are automorphically equivalent, then they should share the same role and their role similarity should be maximal*. From a network topology viewpoint, automorphic nodes have equivalent surroundings. Figure 1 illustrates a graph with nodes $S1$ and $J1$ being automorphically equivalent. Automorphism can be further generalized in terms of *coloration*: assuming each node is assigned a color, then two nodes are equivalent if their neighborhoods consist of the same color spectrum [11].

The traditional social science approach for role analysis has been to define suitable mathematical equivalence relations for nodes so they can be partitioned into equivalence classes (roles). An essential property of these equivalences is that they should positively confirm automorphic equivalence, i.e., if any two nodes are automorphic, then they are role-equivalent. (The converse is not necessarily true.) Confirming automorphism is verifying a solution, which is often algorithmically less complex than discovering a solution. Thus though there is no known polynomial-time algorithm for discovering graph automorphism,[1] role equivalence algorithms [3, 5, 35] can still guarantee to satisfy the aforementioned automorphism confirmation property. These equivalence rules also directly correspond to the aforementioned coloration.

However, by relying on strict equivalence rules, these role modeling schemes can produce only binary similarity metrics: two nodes are either equivalent (similarity = 1) or not (similarity = 0). In real-world networks, usually only a very small portion of the node-pairs would satisfy an equivalence criteria [27] and among

*This work was supported in part by a NSF CAREER grant (IIS-0953950).

[1]The computational complexity of graph isomorphism and automorphism are still unproven to be either P or $NP - Complete$.

Equivalence	Neigh. Rule	Non-singleton Classes
Structural	exactly same	{S3,S4},{J3,J4}, {L3,L4,L5}
Automorphic, Equit. Part.	same number per class	{S1,J1},{S2,J2}, {S3,S4,J3,J4}, {L3,L4,L5}
Regular	same class	{S1,J1,L1},{S2,J2,L2}, {S3,S4,J3,J4,L3,L4,L5}

Table 1: Equivalence Classes for Figure 1

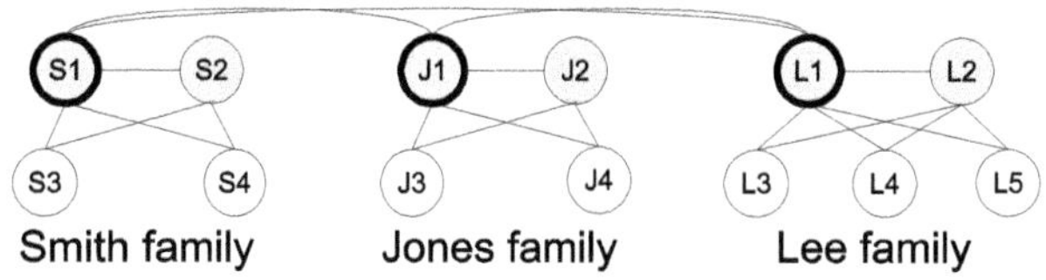

Figure 1: Example Graph for Equivalence Classes.

those, many are simply trivially equivalent (such as singletons or children of the same parent). In addition, strict rule-based equivalence is not robust with respect to network noise, such as false-positive or false-negative interactions. Thus, it is desirable in many real world applications to rank node-pairs by their degree of similarity or provide a real-valued node similarity *metric*.

Recent research works have proposed various measures of node similarity based on similarity of interactions. Leicht [21] defines a to be similar to b if a's neighbor is similar to b. This definition does not fit the class-based concept of roles. Jeh's SimRank [18] is based on the following principle: "two nodes are similar if they link to similar nodes". Mathematically, for any two different nodes x and y, SimRank computes their similarity recursively according to the average similarity of all the neighbor pairs (a neighbor of x paired with a neighbor of y). A single node has self-similarity value 1. This is equivalent to the probability that two simultanous random walkers, starting at x and y, will eventually meet. Most other node structural similarity measures [1, 12, 22, 43, 44, 45] are variants of SimRank. Though SimRank seems to capture the intuition of the above recursive structural similarity, its random walk matching does not satisfy the basic graph automorphism condition. For example, in Figure 1, though $S1$ and $J1$ are automorphically equivalent, SimRank assigns them a value of 0.226. We discuss this further in Section 3.2. To our best knowledge, there is no available real-valued structural similarity measure satisfying the automorphic equivalence requirement. Since automorphic equivalence is a pivotal characteristic of the notion of role, its lack disqualifies these existing measures from serving as authentic role similarity measures.

Thus we have an open problem: *Can we derive a real-valued role similarity measure or ranking which complies with the automorphic equivalence requirement?* In this paper, we develop the first real-valued similarity measure to solve this problem. In addition, our measure is also a metric, i.e., it satisfies the triangle inequality. The key feature of our role similarity measure is a weighted generalization of the *Jaccard coefficient* to measure the neighborhood similarity between two nodes. Unlike SimRank, which considers the average similarity among all possible pairings of neighbors, our measure counts only those pairs in the matching of the two neighbor sets which maximizes the targeted similarity function.

2. ROLE EQUIVALENCE

In social network analysis, the traditional approach for discovering role groups is to define a equivalence relation and to partition the actors into equivalence classes. Actors who fulfill the same role are equivalent. Over the years, four definitions have stood out. These four, in decreasing order of strictness, are structural equivalence, automorphic equivalence, equitable partition, and regular equivalence. Figure 1 shows how these different definitions generate different roles from the same network.

Let $G = (V, E)$ be a graph with vertex set $V = \{v_1, ..., v_n\}$ and edge set E. For any node $v \in V$, let $N(v)$ be the neighbors of v and N_v be the degree of v.

• **Structural Equivalence:** Two actors are *structurally equivalent* if they interact with the *same* set of others [24]. Mathematically, u and v are structurally equivalent if and only if $N(u) = N(v)$. For example, consider the extended family shown in Figure 1. $S1$, $J1$, and $L1$ are siblings, $S2$, $J2$, and $L2$ are spouses, and the remaining nodes are their children. Each family's children, $\{S3, S4\}$, $\{J3, J4\}$, and $\{L3, L4, L5\}$, form a nontrivial equivalence class. However, none of the parents can be grouped together via structural equivalence. This model is too strict to be useful for simplifying a large network and to discover meaningful roles.

• **Automorphic Equivalence:** Two actors (nodes) u and v are *automorphically equivalent* if there is an automorphism σ of G where $v = \sigma(u)$ [4]. An automorphism σ of a graph G is a permutation of vertex set V such that for any two nodes u and v, $(u, v) \in E$ iff $(\sigma(u), \sigma(v)) \in E$. In social terms, u and v can swap names, along with possibly some other name swaps, while preserving all the actor-actor relationships. Let $\Gamma(G)$ be the group of all automorphisms of graph G. For any two nodes u and v in G, $u \equiv v$ if $u = \sigma(v)$ for some $\sigma \in \Gamma(G)$. Note that $\equiv$ is an equivalence relation on V; if $u \equiv v$ we say that u is automorphically equivalent to v. The equivalence classes generated under $\Gamma(G)$ (or $\equiv$) are called orbits. The equivalence class for vertex $v \in V$ is called the orbit of v, and denoted as $\Delta(v) = \{\sigma(v) \in V, \sigma \in \Gamma(G)\} = \{u|u \equiv v\}$. Each orbit corresponds to a role in the automorphic equivalence. Understanding the importance of automorphic equivalence and applying it to role modeling was a major breakthrough in classical social network research. In our example Figure 1, from the topology alone, we cannot distinguish between the Smith family and the Jones family. The Lee family is distinct, because it has three children instead of two. Therefore, the equivalence classes are $\{S1, J1\}, \{S2, J2\}, \{S3, S4, J3, J4\}, \{L1\}, \{L2\}$, and $\{L3, L4, L5\}$. Interestingly, automorphically equivalent classes must have equivalent indirect relations as well, such as equivalent in-laws and cousins. However, automorphic equivalence is hard to compute and still very strict.

• **Exact Coloration (Equitable Partition):** An *exact coloration* of graph G assigns a color to each node, such that any two nodes share the same color iff they have the same number of neighbors of each color [10]. Nodes of the same color form an equivalence class. An exact coloration is also referred to as equitable partition [14] and graph divisor [7] and is often applied in the vertex classification/refinement for canonical labeling in a graph isomorphism test [32, 29]. A graph may have several exact colorations; in general we seek the fewest colors. In our example, structural equivalence and automorphic equivalance offer two different exact colorations. Exact coloration relaxes automorphism by considering only immediate neighborhood equivalence, yet it still embodies a recursive aspect to role modeling.

• **Regular Equivalence (Bisimulation):** Two actors are *regularly equivalent* if they interact with the same variety of role classes, where class is recursively defined by regular equivalence [41]. Unlike automorphic equivalence and exact coloration, regular equivalence does not care about the cardinality of neighbor relationships, only whether they are nonzero. For example, using regular equivalence, all three families are now equivalent. There are only three equivalence classes: $sibling - parent\{S1, J1, L1\}$, $spouse - parent\{S2, J2, L2\}$, and $child$. Note that under regular equivalence, any two automorphically equivalent nodes may be merged into the same regular equivalence class. In computer science, the regular equivalence is often referred to as the bisimulation, which is widely used in automata and modal logic [28].

3. AXIOMATIC ROLE SIMILARITY

An equivalence relation, however, tells us nothing about non-equivalent items. The real-world need is for a measure that not only recognizes automorphic equivalence, such as Smith child/spouse/parent to Jones child/spouse/parent (Figure 1), but also tells us that a Lee child/spouse/parent has strong similarity to a Lee or Smith child/spouse/parent. Over the years, several methods have been developed for addressing various link-based similarity problems (co-citation [34], coupling [20], SimRank [18]). Recently, several researchers have tried to apply these measurements to role modeling [17, 45]. However, none of these encompass the aforementioned automorphic equivalence property and thus are inadequate for measuring role similarity. To deal with this shortcoming and to clarify the problem, we first identify a list of axiomatic properties that all role similarity measures should obey.

DEFINITION 1. (**Axiomatic Role Similarity Properties**) *Given a graph $G = (V, E)$, any $sim(a, b)$ that measures the neighbor-based role similarity between vertices a and b in V should satisfy properties P1 to P5:*

- *P1) Range: $0 \leq sim(a, b) \leq 1$, for all a and b.*
- *P2) Symmetry: $sim(a, b) = sim(b, a)$.*
- *P3) Automorphism confirmation: If $a \equiv b$, $sim(a, b) = 1$.*
- *P4) Transitive similarity: If $a \equiv b$, $c \equiv d$, then $sim(a, c) = sim(a, d) = sim(b, c) = sim(b, d)$.*
- *P5) Triangle inequality: $d(a, c) \leq d(a, b) + d(b, c)$, where distance $d(a, c)$ is defined as $1 - sim(a, c)$.*

Any node similarity measure satisfying the first four conditions (without triangle inequality) is called an **admissible role similarity measure**. *Any node similarity measure satisfying all five conditions is an* **admissible role similarity *metric***.

Property 1 describes the standard normalization where 1 means fully similar and 0 means completely dissimilar (i.e., the two neighborhoods have nothing in common). Property 2 indicates that similarity, like distance, must be symmetric. Property 3 expresses our idea that fully similar means automorphically equivalent. Property 4 claims that the similarity between two nodes is equal to the similarity between equivalent members of the first two node's respective equivalence classes. In other words, we can simply define the similarity for the orbits, i.e., $sim(\Delta(u), \Delta(v)) = sim(u, v)$. This guarantees consistency of values at an orbit-level. Property 5 assumes the measure is metric-like, i.e., satisfying the triangle inequality. This is much stronger than transitivity, enforcing an *ordering* of values.

Note that Property 5 implies Property 4. However, since most similarity measures do not necessarily satisfy the triangle inequality, we specify Property 4 separately. Further, Property 3 is an essential criterion which distinguishes the role similarity measure from other existing measures. As we discussed earlier, the automorphic equivalence can be relaxed to exact coloration or regular equivalence. In this case, we may replace Property 3 accordingly. Our work will focus on the automorphic equivalence though it can handle its generalization as well.

THEOREM 1. (**Generalized Transitive Similarity**) *For any two pairs of nodes $a, b \in V$, $c, d \in V$, if $sim(a, b) = 1$ and $sim(c, d) = 1$, then, their cross similarities are all equal, i.e., $sim(a, c) = sim(a, d) = sim(b, c) = sim(b, d)$.*

Proof: From the triangle inequality, we have $d(a, c) \leq d(a, b) + d(b, c) \leq d(b, c)$ and $d(b, c) \leq d(b, a) + d(a, c) \leq d(a, c)$ $(d(a, b) = 0)$. Thus, $d(a, c) = d(b, c)$. Similarly, $d(a, d) = b(b, d)$, $d(c, a) = d(d, a)$, and $d(d, a) = d(d, b)$. Put together, we have $sim(a, c) = sim(a, d) = sim(b, c) = sim(b, d)$. □

Thus, if we partition the nodes into equivalence classes where similarity equals 1, we can simply record the similarity values between equivalent classes. Let $\Delta(x)$ and $\Delta(y)$ be the equivalence classes for node x and y, respectively. Then, we can define $sim(\Delta(x), \Delta(y)) = sim(x, y)$.

3.1 Binary-Valued Role Similarity Measures

THEOREM 2. (**Binary Admissibility**) *Given any equivalence relation that also satisfies automorphism confirmation (P3), its binary indicator function is an admissible similarity* metric.

The proof of the Theorem is omitted due to lack of space and can be found in [19]. Note that automorphic equivalence, regular equivalence, and exact coloration all satisfy P3, so they are admissible metrics. Though these similarity measures are admissible, binary-valued measures do not help us to understand the degree of similarity or dissimilarity. We would like a real-valued measure that ranks the degree of role similarity.

Before presenting our proposed real-valued role similarity metric for network roles, we first examine some similarity measures proposed in earlier works.

3.2 SimRank is Not Admissible

The SimRank [18] similarity between nodes u and v is the average similarity between u's neighbors and v's neighbors:

$$SR(u, v) = \frac{(1 - \beta)}{|N(u)||N(v)|} \sum_{x \in N(u)} \sum_{y \in N(v)} SR(x, y), \text{for } u \neq v,$$
$$SR(v, v) = 1,$$

where β is a decay factor, $0 < \beta < 1$, so that the influence of neighbors decreases with distance. The original SimRank measure is for directed graphs. Here, we focus on its undirected version, though our comments also hold for the directed version. SimRank values can be computed iteratively, with successively iterations approaching a unique solution, much as PageRank [31] does.

THEOREM 3. *SimRank is not an admissible role similarity measure.*

Proof: We give examples where property 3 (automorphic equivalence) does not hold. In Figure 2(a), a and b have the same neighbors. By even the strictest definition (structural equivalence), a and b have the same role. However, since SimRank's initial assumption is that there is no similarity among c, d, and e, when it computes the average similarity of a and b's neighbors, it does not discover that a and b have equivalent neighborhoods. Assuming the best case where c, d, and e are in fact equivalent and using $\beta = 0.15$, $SR(a, b)$ converges to only 0.667. If the neighbors are not equivalent, a to b should still be equivalent, but SimRank gives an even lower value. SimRank has an another problem (Figure 2(b)) when

(a) Structural equivalence (b) Odd Distance

Figure 2: Problematic configurations for SimRank

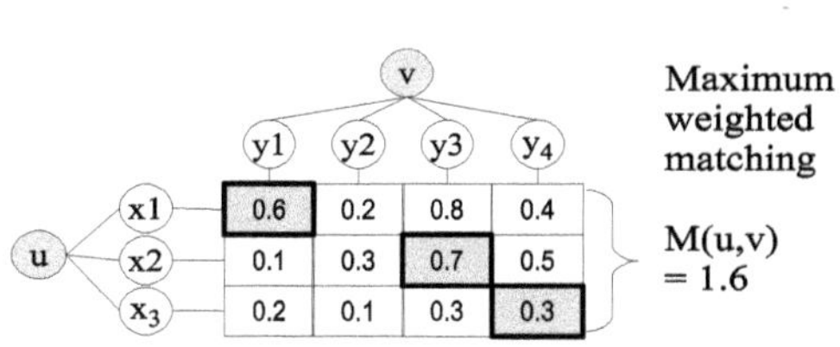

Figure 3: RoleSim(a,b) based on similarity of their neighbors

there is an odd distance between two nodes. Nodes u and v are automorphically equivalent, but because there are no nodes that are an equal distance from both u and v, $SimRank(u, v) = 0$!

We note that other variants of SimRank [1, 12, 22, 43, 44, 45] also do not meet the automorphic equivalence property for to similar reasons. More discussion of these variants can be found in [19].

4. ROLESIM: A REAL-VALUED ADMISSIBLE ROLE SIMILARITY

To produce an admissible real-valued role similarity measure, we face two key challenges: First, it is computationally difficult to verify the automorphic equivalence property. Though not proven to be NP-complete, the graph automorphism problem has no known polynomial algorithm [13]. Second, all the existing real-valued role similarity measures have problems dealing with even simple conditions such as structural equivalence (Subsection 3.2). To meet these challenges, we take the following approach: Given an initial simplistic but admissible role similarity measurement for each pair of nodes, refine the measurement by expressing similarity in terms of neighboring values, while maintaining the automorphic and structural equivalence properties. Next, we formally introduce RoleSim, the first admissible real-valued role similarity measure (metric) and its associated properties.

4.1 RoleSim Definition

Given a graph $G = (V, E)$, the RoleSim measure realizes the recursive node structural similarity principle "two nodes are similar if they relate to similar objects" as follows.

DEFINITION 2. **(RoleSim metric)** *Given two vertices u and v, where $N(u)$ and $N(v)$ denote their respective neighbohoods and N_u and N_v denote their respective degrees, then $RoleSim(u, v) =$*

$$(1-\beta)\max_{M(u,v)} \frac{\sum_{(x,y)\in M(u,v)} RoleSim(x,y)}{N_u + N_v - |M(u,v)|} + \beta \qquad (1)$$

where $x \in N(u)$, $y \in N(v)$, and $M(u, v)$ is a **matching** *between $N(u)$ and $N(v)$, i.e., $M(u,v) = \{(x,y) | x \in N(u), y \in N(v)$, and no other$(x', y') \in M(u,v)$, s.t. $, x = x'$ or $y = y'\}$. The parameter β is a decay factor, $0 < \beta < 1$.*

The decay factor, similar to the one used in PageRank [31], both dampens the recursive effect and guarantees a minimal RoleSim score of β. We will sometimes abbreviate $RoleSim(u, v)$ as $R(u, v)$. **R** refers to the entire matrix of values. Figure 3 illustrates the matching process. The (x, y) grid is the subset of the RoleSim matrix of values corresponding to the pairings of neighbors of these two vertices. A matching selects one cell per row and column. If the number of rows differs from the number of columns, then the matching size is limited to $|M(u, v)| = min(N_u, N_v)$. A maximal matching is a matching where the total value of selected cells is maximum. In contrast, SimRank computes the average of every cell in the neighbor grid.

4.1.1 Relation to Jaccard Coefficient

RoleSim employs a generalization of the Jaccard coefficient, which measures the commonality between two sets A and B as $J(A, B) = \frac{|A\cap B|}{|A\cup B|}$. Previous works [12] have used this index to compare node neighborhoods; several variants exist [30]. Our denominator is similar to that of the Tanimoto coefficient [37], which measures simlarity between multisets or between vectors. In our generalization, however, sets A and B are not vectors and need not share any common elements; instead, there is a weighted matching M between *similar* elements in A and B, i.e., $(a, b) \in M, a \in A, b \in B$. Let $r(a, b) \in [0, 1]$ record the similarity between a and b.

DEFINITION 3. **(Generalized Jaccard Coefficient)** *The generalized Jaccard coefficient measures the similarity between two sets A and B under matching M, defined as*

$$J(A, B|M) = \frac{\sum_{(a,b)\in M} r(a,b)}{|A| + |B| - |M|} \qquad (2)$$

The original Jaccard coefficient is a special case which uses the following matching M: Let $r(x, y) = 1$ if $x = y$; otherwise 0. Then define $M = \{r(x,x) | x \in A, x \in B\}$. Thus, the generalized Jaccard coefficient $J(A, B|M)$ reduces to $J(A, B)$. Comparing Eq. (1) and (2), we see that the heart of $RoleSim(u, v)$ is equivalent to the maximum of the generalized Jaccard coefficient between $N(u)$ and $N(v)$, among all matchings $M(u, v)$. Then, $RoleSim(u, v) =$

$$(1-\beta)\max_{M(u,v)} J(N(u), N(v)|M(u,v)) + \beta \qquad (3)$$

4.1.2 Relation to Weighted Matching

The definition and significance of the RoleSim for any node pair (u, v) is closely related to *maximal weighted matching*. For any nodes u and v in graph G, define a weighted bipartite graph $(N(u) \cup N(v), N(u) \times N(v))$, with each edge $(x, y) \in N(u) \times N(v)$ having weight $RoleSim(x, y)$. Let the total weight of neighbor matching $M(u, v)$ between u and v be $w(M(u, v)) = \sum_{(x,y)\in M(u,v)} RoleSim(x, y)$. Let $\mathcal{M}$ be the maximal weighted matching for $(N(u) \cup N(v), N(u) \times N(v))$. It is clear that

$$w(\mathcal{M}) = \max_{M(u,v)} w(M(u,v)). \qquad (4)$$

Using this, we can represent $RoleSim(u, v)$ in terms of maximal weighted matching $\mathcal{M}$. In Figure 3, the shaded cells represent the maximal matching: $0.7 + 0.6 + 0.3 = 1.6$.

THEOREM 4. **(Maximal Weighted Matching)** *The RoleSim between nodes u and v corresponds linearly to the maximal weighted matching $\mathcal{M}$ for the bipartite graph $(N(u) \cup N(v), N(u) \times N(v))$, with each edge $(x, y) \in N(u) \times N(v)$ having the weight $RoleSim(x, y)$:*

$$RoleSim(u,v) = (1-\beta)\frac{w(\mathcal{M})}{\max(N_u, N_v)} + \beta \qquad (5)$$

Proof: We need to show that Equations (1) and (5) are equivalent. Without loss of generality, let $N_u \geq N_v$. First, we show that *the cardinality of the maximal weighted matching* $|\mathcal{M}| = \min(N_u, N_v) = N_v$. It cannot be greater, because there are insufficient elements in N_v. It cannot be smaller, because if it were, there must exist an available edge between an uncovered node in N_u with one in N_v. Adding this edge would increase the matching (every edge has weight $\geq \beta$). If $|\mathcal{M}| = \min(N_u, N_v)$, it follows that $N_u + N_v - |M| = \max(N_u, N_v)$. Thus, the denominators in Equations (1) and (5) are constant and identical. It is then a trivial observation that the numerators are in fact the same. Therefore, the maximal value fo the entire Equation (1) is the same as the value in (5). □

Theorem 4 not only shows the key equilibrium of role similarities between pairs of nodes in a graph G, but shows that RoleSim may be computed using existing maximal matching algorithms.

4.2 RoleSim Computation

RoleSim values can be computed iteratively and are guaranteed to converge, just as in PageRank and SimRank. First we outline the procedure. In the next section, we prove that the calculated values comprise an admissible role similarity metric.

Step 1: Let the initial matrix of RoleSim scores be $\mathbf{R^0}$, estimated but admissible scores between any pair of nodes in G.

Step 2: Compute the kth iteration $\mathbf{R^k}$ scores from the $(k-1)^{th}$ iteration's values, $\mathbf{R^{k-1}}$. Specifically, for any nodes u and v,

$$\mathbf{R^k}(u,v) = (1-\beta) \max_{M(u,v)} \frac{\sum_{(x,y)\in M(u,v)} \mathbf{R^{k-1}}(x,y)}{N_u + N_v - |M(u,v)|} + \beta \quad (6)$$

Based on Theorem 4, we compute Equation (6) by finding the maximal weighted matching in the weighted bipartite graph $(N(u) \cup N(v), N(u) \times N(v))$ with each edge $(x,y) \in N(u) \times N(v)$ having weight $\mathbf{R^{k-1}}(x,y)$).

Step 3: Repeat Step 2 until $\mathbf{R}$ values converge for each pair of nodes in G.

THEOREM 5. **(Convergence)** *For any admissible set of RoleSim scores* $RoleSim^0$, *the iterative computational procedure for RoleSim converges, i.e., for any* (u,v) *pair,*

$$\lim_{k\to\infty} RoleSim^k(u,v) = RoleSim(u,v) \quad (7)$$

This can be proven by showing that the maximum absolute difference between any $\mathbf{R^k}(u,v)$ and $\mathbf{R^{k+1}}(u,v)$ is monotonically decreasing. The proof can be found in [19].

Unlike PageRank and SimRank which converge to values independent of the initialization, the convergent RoleSim score is sensitive to the initialization. Rather than being a disadvantage, this sensitivity provides the necessary relaxation to compute automorphic role similarity in polynomial time, by utilizing the initialization as prior knowledge.

4.3 Admissibility of RoleSim

Here, we present one of the key contributions of this paper: the axiomatic admissibility of RoleSim. If the initial computation is admissible, and because the iterative computation of Equation (5) maintains admissibility (i.e., is an invariant transform of the axiomatic properties), then the final measure is admissible.

THEOREM 6. **(Invariant Transformation)** *If the* k^{th} *iteration* $RoleSim^k$ *is an admissible role similarity metric, then so is* $RoleSim^{k+1}$.

For each axiomatic property P, we must show "If the kth iteration $RoleSim^k$ satisfies Axiom P, then so does $RoleSim^{k+1}$." Properties 1 (Range) and 2 (Symmetry) are trivially invariant, so we will focus on the other three.

Automorphism Confirmation Invariance Proof: For nodes $u \equiv v$, there is a permutation σ of vertex set V, such that $\sigma(u) = v$, and any edge $(u,x) \in E$ iff $(v, \sigma(x)) \in E$. This indicates that σ provides a one-to-one equivalence between nodes in $N(u)$ and $N(v)$. Also, u and v have the same number of neighbors, i.e., $N_u = N_v$. So, it is clear that the maximal weighted matching $\mathcal{M}$ in the bipartite graph $(N(u) \cup N(v), N(u) \times N(v))$ selects $N_u = N_v$ pairs of weight 1 each. Thus, $RoleSim^{k+1}(u,v) = (1-\beta)\frac{w(\mathcal{M})}{\max(N_u,N_v)} + \beta = 1$. □

Transitive Similarity Invariance Proof: Assume for any $a \equiv b$, $c \equiv d$, $RoleSim^k(a,c) = RoleSim^k(b,d)$. Denote the maximal weighted matching between $N(a)$ and $N(c)$ as $\mathcal{M}$. Since there is a one-to-one equivalence correspondence σ between $N(a)$ and $N(b)$ and a one-to-one equivalence correspondence σ' between $N(c)$ and $N(d)$, we can construct a matching $\mathcal{M}'$ between $N(b)$ and $N(d)$ as follows: $\mathcal{M}' = \{(\sigma(x), \sigma'(y)) | (x,y) \in \mathcal{M}\}$. Since transitive similarity holds for $RoleSim^k$, we have $RoleSim^k(x,y) = RoleSim^k(\sigma(x), \sigma'(y))$. Thus, $w(\mathcal{M}') = w(\mathcal{M})$, and

$$(1-\beta)\frac{w(\mathcal{M})}{\max(N_a,N_c)} + \beta = (1-\beta)\frac{w(\mathcal{M}')}{\max(N_b,N_d)} + \beta$$
$$RoleSim^{k+1}(a,c) = RoleSim^{k+1}(b,d). \quad \square$$

Triangle Inequality Invariance Proof: For iteration k, for any nodes a, b, and c, $d^k(a,c) \leq d^k(a,b) + d^k(b,c)$, where $d^k(a,b) = 1 - RoleSim^k(a,b)$. We must prove that this inequality still holds for the next iteration: $d^{k+1}(a,c) \leq d^{k+1}(a,b) + d^{k+1}(b,c)$.

Observation: *if there is a matching M between $N(a)$ and $N(c)$ which satisfies* $1 - ((1-\beta)\frac{w(M)}{N_c} + \beta) \leq d^{k+1}(a,b) + d^{k+1}(b,c)$, *then* $d^{k+1}(a,c) \leq d^{k+1}(a,b) + d^{k+1}(b,c)$. This is because $\frac{w(M)}{N_c} \leq \frac{w(\mathcal{M})}{N_c}$, where $\mathcal{M}$ is the maximal weighted matching between $N(a)$ and $N(c)$, and thus, $1 - ((1-\beta)\frac{w(M)}{N_c} + \beta) \geq 1 - ((1-\beta)\frac{w(\mathcal{M})}{N_c} + \beta) = d^{k+1}(a,c)$.

We break down the proof into three cases:
Case 1. $(N_b \leq N_a \leq N_c)$, Case 2. $(N_a \leq N_b \leq N_c)$, and
Case 3. $(N_a \leq N_c \leq N_b)$.

Case 1: Since N_b is smallest, $|\mathcal{M}(a,b)| = |\mathcal{M}(b,c)| = N_b$. Define matching M between $N(a)$ and $N(c)$ as $M = \{(x,z) | (x,y) \in \mathcal{M}(a,b) \wedge (y,z) \in \mathcal{M}(b,c)\}$. Then using our observation above:

$$d^{k+1}(a,b) + d^{k+1}(b,c) - (1 - (1-\beta)\frac{w(M)}{N_c} - \beta)$$
$$= (1-\beta)[-\frac{w(\mathcal{M}(a,b))}{N_a} - \frac{w(\mathcal{M}(b,c))}{N_c} + \frac{w(M)}{N_c}] + 1 - \beta$$
$$= (1-\beta)[\frac{N_b - w(\mathcal{M}(a,b))}{N_a} - \frac{N_b}{N_a} + \frac{N_b - w(\mathcal{M}(b,c))}{N_c}$$
$$- \frac{N_b}{N_c} - \frac{N_b - w(M)}{N_c} + \frac{N_b}{N_c}] + 1 - \beta$$
$$\geq (1-\beta)[1 - \frac{N_b}{N_a} + \frac{\sum_{(x,y)\in\mathcal{M}(a,b)}(1 - R^k(x,y))}{N_c}$$
$$+ \frac{\sum_{(y,z)\in\mathcal{M}(b,c)}(1 - R^k(y,z))}{N_c} - \frac{\sum_{(x,z)\in M}(1 - R^k(x,z))}{N_c}]$$
$$\geq (1-\beta)[\frac{\sum_{(x,y,z)}(d^k(x,y) + d^k(y,z) - d^k(x,z))}{N_c}] \geq 0$$

(x,y,z) means $(x,y) \in \mathcal{M}(a,b)$, $(y,z) \in \mathcal{M}(b,c)$, $(x,z) \in M$ □

Cases 2 and 3 can be proven by a similar technique; the details are in [19].

By combining the admissible initial configurations given in Sec 4.4 with Theorem 6 on invariance, we have shown that the iterative RoleSim computation generates a real-valued, admissible role similarity measure.

THEOREM 7. (**Admissibility**) *If the initial $RoleSim^0$ is an admissible role similarity measure, then at each k-th iteration, $RoleSim^k$ is also admissible. When RoleSim computation converges, the final measure $\lim_{k\to\infty} RoleSim^k$ is admissible.*

4.4 Initialization

According to Theorem 7, an initial admissible RoleSim measurement $\mathbf{R^0} = I(\cdot)$ is needed to generate the desired real-valued role similarity ranking. What initial admissible measures or prior knowledge should we use? We consider three schemes:

1. **ALL-1** : $I(u, v) = 1$ for all u, v.
2. **Degree-Binary (DB)**: If two nodes have the same degree ($N_u = N_v$), then $I(u, v) = 1$; otherwise, 0.
3. **Degree-Ratio (DR)**: $I(u, v) = (1 - \beta)\frac{min(N_u,N_v)}{max(N_u,N_v)} + \beta$.

These schemes come from the following observation: *nodes that are automorphically equivalent have the same degree.* Basically, equal degree is a necessary but not sufficient condition for automorphism. This observation is key to RoleSim: degree affects both the size of a maximal matching set and the denominator of the Jaccard Coefficient.

THEOREM 8. (**Admissible Initialization**) *ALL-1, Degree-Binary, and Degree-Ratio are all admissible role similarity measures. Moreover, Degree-Binary and ALL-1 are admissible role similarity* metrics.

Its proof is omitted due to lack of space and can be found in [19]. Note that SimRank's initialization ($SimRank^0(u, v) = 1$ iff $u = v$) is NOT admissible, because it does exactly the wrong thing: setting the initial value of any potentially equivalent nodes to 0. SimRank iterations try to build up from zero. However, due to its problems with structural equivalence and odd-length paths that we noted, SimRank will never increase the value enough to discover equivalent pairs that were neglected at the start.

In addition, we make the following interesting observation (based on the definition of RoleSim formula): *Let $\mathbf{R^1}(ALL-1)$ be the matrix of RoleSim values at the first iteration after $\mathbf{R^0} = \mathbf{1}$ (All-1 initialization); and let $\mathbf{R^0}(DR)$ be the matrix of RoleSim initialized by the Degree-Ratio (DR) scheme. Then, $\mathbf{R^1}(ALL - 1) = \mathbf{R^0}(DR)$.* Basically, the Degree-Ratio (DR) is exactly equal to the RoleSim state one iteration after ALL-1 initialization. Thus, ALL-1 and DR generate the same final results. The simple formula for DR is much faster than neighbor matching, so DR is essentially one iteration faster. On the other hand, we may consider the simple ALL-1 scheme to be sufficient, since it works as well as the more sophisticated DR. Especially, after the simple initialization, RoleSim's maximal matching process automatically discriminates between nodes of different degree and continues to learn differences among neighbors as it iterates. In our experiments, we will further empirically study these initialization schemes.

4.5 Computational Complexity

Given n nodes, we have $O(n^2)$ node-pair similarity values to update for each iteration. For each node-pair, we must perform a maximal weighted matching. For weighted bipartite graph ($N(u) \cup N(v), N(u) \times N(v)$), the fastest algorithm based on augmenting paths (Hungarian method) can compute the maximal weighted matching in $O(x(x \log x + y))$, where $x = |N(u) \cup N(v)|$ and $y = |N(u)| \times |N(v)|$.

A fast greedy algorithm offers a $\frac{1}{2}$-approximation of the globally optimal matching in $O(y \log y)$ time [2]. If an equivalence matching exists (i.e., $w(\mathcal{M}) = \max(N_u, N_v)$), the greedy method will find it. This is important, because it means that a greedy RoleSim computation still generates an admissible measure. Using greedy neighbor matching, the time complexity of RoleSim is $O(kn^2d')$, for k iterations, where d' is the average of $y \log y$ over all vertex-pair bipartite graphs in G. The space complexity is $O(n^2)$. We note that in order to handle very large graphs, in [19], we introduce an interesting *iceberg RoleSim* computation algorithm which can discover high RoleSim pairs without full materializing the entire RoleSim matrix. It is beyond the scope of this paper and we omit its further discussion.

5. EXPERIMENTAL EVALUATION

In this section we experimentally investigate the ranking ability and performance of the RoleSim algorithm for computing role similarity metric values. We analyze the effect of different initialization schemes, and compare RoleSim to several state-of-the-art node similarity algorithms Specifically, we focus on the following:

1. How do different initialization schemes perform in terms of their final RoleSim score and computational efficiency?
2. Do node-pairs with high RoleSim scores have similar network roles, and for any two nodes known to have similar network roles, do they have high RoleSim scores?

Clearly, the ideal validation study requires an explicit role model and role similarity measure, which often do not exist. In the following study, we utilize a well-known role-related random graph model and external measures of real datasets which provide strong role indication for these evaluations.

We set $\beta = 0.1$ for both RoleSim and SimRank, defining convergence to be when values change by less than 1% of their previous values. We ran several RoleSim tests with both exact matching and greedy matching. The results were nearly identical (> 90% of cells have no difference; maximum difference was small), so we focus on greedy matching from here on. We implemented the algorithms in C++ and ran all large tests on a 2.0GHz Linux machine with dual-core Opteron CPU and 4.0GB RAM.

For our tests, we use three types of graphs:

• **BL**: probabilistic block-model [39], where each block is generally considered to be corresponding to a role [42]. Here, nodes are partitioned into blocks. Each node in block i has probability p_{ij} of linking to each node in block j. Thus, the underlying block-model may serve as the ground-truth for testing role similarity.

• **SF**: Large Scale-Free random graphs [2] offer another model of large social or complex networks.

• Real-world networks, with a measureable feature similar to social role, are used for validating RoleSim performance.

5.1 Comparing Initialization

In Section 4.4 we saw that Degree-Ratio generates the same results as ALL-1 by shortcutting the first iteration. This reduces computation time by roughly 10%. Now we ask: Does Degree-Binary initialization (DB, binary indicator which equals 1 when degrees $N_u = N_v$) give similar results, quickly?

[2]http://pywebgraph.sourceforge.net/

Relative to All-1 Initialization	Degree-Binary Min	Degree-Binary Avg.	Degree-Binary Max	Degree-Ratio
Diff. in percentile rank	0.14%	0.38%	11.17%	none
Pearson correl. coeff.	0.9994	0.9998	0.9999	1
Relative execution time	0.32	0.52	0.80	≈ 0.9
Relative # iterations	0.38	0.58	0.88	1 fewer

Table 2: Comparison of Initialization Methods

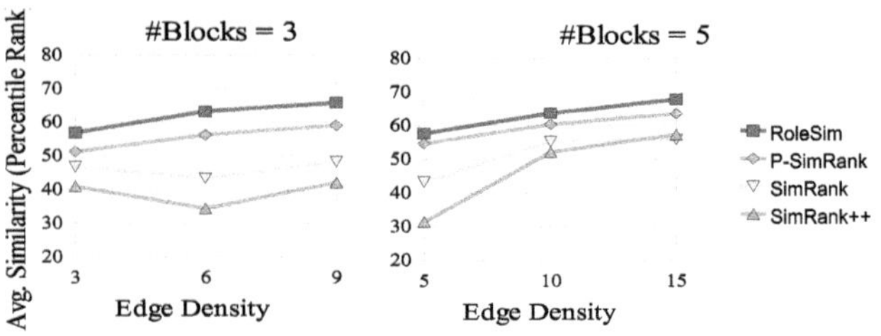

Figure 4: Avg. similarity ranking for nodes in the same block

We ran RoleSim using both ALL-1 and DB on 12 graphs, some scale-free and some block-model, having 500 to 10,000 nodes, and edge densities from 1 to 10. We then converted values to percentile ranking, where 100% means the highest value and 50% is the median value. Test results are summarized in Table 2. The high correlation coefficient means the rankings are virtually identical, so the rankings are not very sensitive to the initialization method. Moreover, DB took 20% from 68% less time to converge. Overall, DB seems to be the preferred initialization scheme in terms of computational efficiency. Thus, we adopt it for the rest of the experiments.

5.2 General Role Detection

How well does RoleSim discover roles in complex graphs? Specifically, given a ground truth knowledge of roles, do nodes having similar roles have high scores? To answer this, we generated probabilistic block-model graphs, where blocks behave like "noisy" roles, due to sampling variance. We generated graphs with $N = 1000$ nodes and either 3 or 5 blocks. We varied the edge density $\frac{|E|}{|V|}$, with higher densities for graphs with more blocks. The size of each block and the p_{ij} values were randomized; we generated 3 random instances for each graph class. We compared RoleSim to the state-of-the-art SimRank, SimRank++ [1], and P-SimRank [12] measures.

For each measure and trial, we ranked its similarity scores. This normalizes the scoring among the four measures. Next, for each graph, we computed the average rank of all pairs of nodes within the same block, then averaged the three trials for each graph class.

Our results (Figure 4) show that RoleSim outperforms all other algorithms across all the tested conditions. None of the algorithms score perfectly, due to the inherent edge distribution variance of the probabilistic model. P-SimRank is better than SimRank, perhaps because it uses Jaccard Coefficient weighting, a step towards our RoleSim approach. Accuracy takes time. SimRank and SimRank++ run at the same speed. P-SimRank is about twice as slow, taking 184s to complete the most dense graph. RoleSim took 948s to complete the same graph.

5.3 Real Dataset: Co-author Network

We applied RoleSim and the best alternative measure, P-SimRank, to a real-world network having an external role measure. Our first dataset [36] is a co-author network of 2000 database researchers. Two authors are linked if they co-authored a paper from

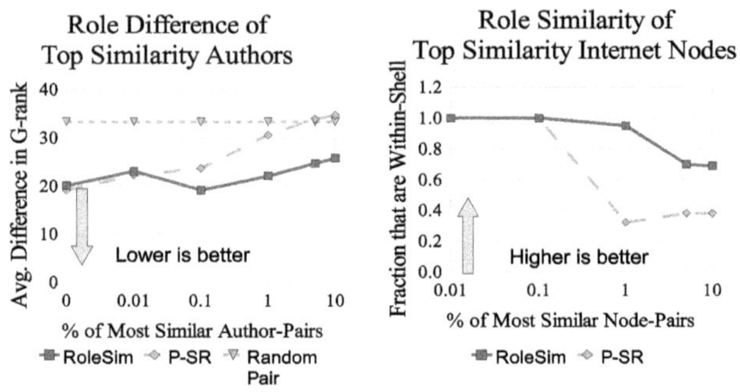

(a) Top Coauthors (b) Top Internet nodes

Figure 5: Similarity of Nodes for Top Ranked Node-Pairs

2003 to 2008. We pruned the network to the largest connected component (1543 nodes, 15483 edges). An author's role depends recursively on the number of connections to other authors, and the roles of those others. Hence, it measures collaboration. We use the G-index as a proxy measure for co-author role (H-index provides similar results and is omitted here). The G-index measures the influence of a scientific author's publications, its value being the largest integer G such that the G most cited publications have at least G^2 citations. While G-index and co-author role are not precisely the same, G-index score is influenced strongly by the underlying role. High impact authors tend to be highly connected, especially with other high impact authors. If a paper is highly cited, this boosts the score of every co-author. Thus, we expect that if two authors have similar G-index scores, their node-pair is likely to have a high role simlarity value. To normalize RoleSim, P-SimRank, and G-index values, we converted each raw value to a percentile rank.

Figure 5(a) addresses our second validation question (high rank$\rightarrow$ similar roles?). For the top ranked 0.01% of author-pairs, the average difference in G-index ranking is 20 points, for both RoleSim and P-SimRank, well below the random-pair difference of 33. A below-average difference confirms that the authors are relatively similar. However, as we expand the search towards 10%, RoleSim continues to detect authors with similar authorship performance, while P-SimRank converges to random scoring.

To validate $role \rightarrow rank$ performance, we binned the authors into 10 roles based on G-index value (bottom 10%, next 10%, etc.). For every pair of authors within the same role decile, we looked up role similarity rank and computed an average per bin. We also computed averages for pairs of authors not in the same bin (dissimilar roles). Figure 6(a) shows our results. The average within-bin RoleSim value is consistently between 55% and 60%, better than the random-pair score of 50, and independent of whether the G-index is high or low. It performs equally well for all roles. P-SimRank within-bin scores (dashed line), however, are inconsistent. Performance of P-SimRank is worse than random for low G-scores, perhaps due to low density of links in the network. For the cross-bin data, the X-axis is the difference in decile bins for the two authors in a pair. The falling line of RoleSim indicates that role similarity correctly decreases as G-index scores become less similar. For P-SimRank, however, the cross-bin scores (dashed line) hover around 50, equivalent to random scoring.

5.4 Real Dataset: Internet Network

Our second dataset is a snapshot of the Internet at the level of autonomous systems (22963 nodes and 48436 edges), as generated

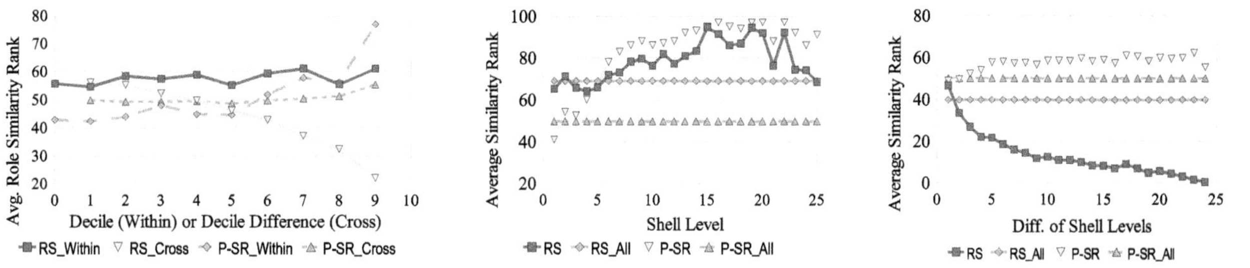

(a) Similarity of Authors Binned by K-index (b) Internet Graph Intra-Shell Similarity (c) Internet Graph Cross-Shell Similarity

Figure 6: Similarity Rank for Nodes Grouped by External Role Measure

by Newman[3]. Several studies have confirmed that the Internet is hierarchically organized, with a densely connected core and stubs (singly-connected nodes) at the periphery [38, 6]. A node's position within the network (proximity to the core) and its relation to others affects its efficiency for routing and its robustness. Inspired by [6], we use K-shells to delineate roles.

The K-core of a graph is the induced subgraph where every node connects to at least K other nodes in the subgraph. If $K' > K$, then the K'-core must be an induced subgraph of the K-core. The K-shell is defined as the 'ring' of nodes that are included in a graph's $(K-1)$-core but not its K-core. Thus we can decompose a graph into a set of nested rings, becoming denser as we move inward.

Using K-shells as our roles, we perform tests and analyses similar to those of the coauthor network. In Figure 5(b) we see that both measures do well for the top 0.1%, but P-SimRank's falters significantly when the range is expanded to the top 1%.

Next, we treat K-shells the same way that we treated G-index decile bins in the previous test. See Figures 6(b) and 6(c). Unlike decile bins, the shells do not have equal sizes. K-shells 1, 2, and 3 together contain 92% of all nodes. To clarify how these three shells dominate, we also show horizontal lines representing the combined weighted average rank of all within-shell comparisons. RoleSim's within-shell values are consistently high, averaging 70%. Conversely, P-SimRank finds strong above-average similarity for the small high-K shells, but nearly random similarity for shells 1 to 3, pulling its overall performance down to 50%.

In cross-shell analysis, RoleSim is able to distinguish different shells very well: RoleSim approaches zero as shell difference approaches maximum. On the other hand, P-SimRank shows almost no correlation to shell difference. Many of its scores are above-average when they should be below-average (dissimilar). On the whole, it seems that P-SimRank is not detecting role, but something related to connectedness and density.

In all these experiments, we can see that RoleSim provides positive answer to the role similarity ranking: 1) node-pairs with similar roles have higher RoleSim ranking than node-pairs with dissimilar roles, and 2) high RoleSim ranking indicates that nodes have similar roles. P-SimRank scores, however, do not correlate with network role similarity.

6. RELATED WORK

The role similarity problem is a distinct special case of the more general structural or link similarity problems, which find applications in co-citation and bibliographic networks [25], recommender systems, [1] and Web search [16]. Link similarity means that two objects accrue similarity if they have similar links.

[3]Internet dataset, http://www-personal.umich.edu/ mejn/netdata/

Formal definitions of role, which define exactly what is being measured, arose from the social science community [24, 33, 9]. Block partitioning can be used to group nodes directly into roles [42]. However, this does not produce individual node-pair similarities, so it is not useful as a ranking method.

SimRank [18] is the best known algorithm to implement a recursive definition of object similarity: two objects are similar if they relate to similar objects. SimRank has an elegant random walk interpretation: $SimRank(a, b)$ is the probability that two independent simultaneous random walkers, beginning at a and b, will eventually meet at some node. However, the more neighbors that a and b have in common, the less likely that they will both randomly choose the same neighbor. This then explains SimRank's problem with structural equivalence. Recently, Zhao [45] has pointed out that in-neighbor and out-neighbor SimRank can be used as a univeral framework to describe co-citation (common in-neighbors), bibliographic coupling (commnon out-neighbors), or a weighted combination of the two. The number of iterations reflects the search radius for discovering similarity. As we note in Section-3.2, SimRank has an undesirable trait: its values decrease when the number of common neighbors increases. Several works have tried to address this problem. SimRank++ [1] adds an *evidence* weight which partially compensates for the neighbor matching cardinality problem. In [12], the two walkers are not fully independent. Instead, the overall probability of a meeting b is weighted to be Jaccard coefficient $\frac{|N(u) \cap N(v)|}{|N(u) \cup N(v)|}$. Recently, MatchSim [23] has also used maximal matching of neighbors to address problems with SimRank's scoring. However, our formulations have important differences. Because they retained SimRank's initialization, their work does not guarantee automorphic equivalence in the final results. Also, their work is intuition-based, without a theory of correctness. They provide one specific formulation, while we define a theoretical framework for *any* admissible measure or metric. Because RoleSim satisfies the triangle inequality, it is a true metric.

7. CONCLUSION

We have developed RoleSim, the first real-valued role similarity measure that confirms automorphic equivalence. We have also presented a set of axioms which can test any future measure to see if it is an admissible measure or metric. Our experimental tests demonstrate RoleSim's correctness and usefulness on real world data, opening up exciting possibilities for scientific and business applications. At the same time, we see that other well-known measures, while suitable for other tasks, are not suitable for role similarity. This axiomatic approach may prove useful for developing and validating solutions to other related tasks.

8. REFERENCES

[1] Ioannis Antonellis, Hector Garcia-Molina, and Chi-Chao Chang. Simrank++: query rewriting through link analysis of the clickgraph (poster). In *WWW'08*, pages 1177–1178, 2008.

[2] D. Avis. A survey of heuristics for the weighted matching problem. *Network*, 13:475–493, 1983.

[3] Vladimir Batagelj, Patrick Doreian, and Anuška Ferligoj. An optimizational approach to regular equivalence. *Social Networks*, 14:121–135, 1992.

[4] Stephen P. Borgatti and Martin G. Everett. Notions of position in social network analysis. *Sociological Methodology*, 22:1–35, 1992.

[5] Stephen P. Borgatti and Martin G. Everett. Two algorithms for computing regular equivalence. *Social Networks*, 15:361–376, 1993.

[6] Shai Carmi, Shlomo Havlin, Scott Kirkpatrick, Yuval Shavitt, and Eran Shir. A model of internet topology using k-shell decomposition. *PNAS*, 104(27):11150–11154, July 2007.

[7] Dragos M. Cvetkovíc, Michael Doob, and Horst Sachs. *Spectra of Graphs: Theory and Applications, 3rd Revised and Enlarged Edition*. Wiley, 1998.

[8] Natalia Dragan, Michael L. Collard, and Jonathan I. Maletic. Using method stereotype distribution as a signature descriptor for software systems. In *ICSM*, pages 567–570, 2009.

[9] Martin G. Everett. Role similarity and complexity in social networks. *Social Networks*, 7:353–359, 1985.

[10] Martin G. Everett and Stephen P. Borgatti. Exact colorations of graphs and digraphs. *Social Networks*, 18:319–331, 1996.

[11] M.G. Everett and S. P. Borgatti. Regular equivalence: General theory. *J. Mathematical Sociology*, 19:29–52, 1994.

[12] Dániel Fogaras and Balázs Rácz. Scaling link-based similarity search. In *WWW'05*, pages 641–650, 2005.

[13] Scott Fortin. The graph isomorphism problem. Technical Report TR 96-20, Dept. Computer Science, Univ. of Alberta, Edmonton, Alberta, Canada, July 1996.

[14] C. Godsil and G. Royle. *Algebraic Graph Theory*. Springer-Verlag, New York, 2001.

[15] E.M. Hafner-Burton, M. Kahler, and A.H. Montgomery. Network analysis for international relations. *International Organization*, 63(03):559–592, 2009.

[16] Taher H. Haveliwala. Topic-sensitive pagerank: A context-sensitive ranking algorithm for web search. *IEEE Trans. on Knowl. and Data Eng.*, 15(4):784–796, 2003.

[17] Petter Holme and Mikael Huss. Role-similarity based functional prediction in networked systems: application to the yeast proteome. *J. R. Soc. Interface*, 2(4):327–33, 2005.

[18] Glen Jeh and Jennifer Widom. Simrank: a measure of structural-context similarity. In *KDD'02*, pages 538–543, 2002.

[19] Ruoming Jin, Victor E. Lee, and Hui Hong. Axiomatic ranking of network role similarity. Technical Report arXiv:1102.3937, http://arXiv.org, 2011.

[20] M. M. Kessler. Bibliographic coupling between scientific papers. *American Documentation*, 14(1):10–25, 1963.

[21] E. A. Leicht, Petter Holme, and M. E. J. Newman. Vertex similarity in networks. *Phys. Rev. E*, 73:026120, 2005.

[22] Pei Li, Yuanzhe Cai, Hongyan Liu, Jun He, and Xiaoyong Du. Exploiting the block structure of link graph for efficient similarity computation. In *PAKDD'09*, pages 389–400, 2009.

[23] Zhenjiang Lin, Michael R. Lyu, and Irwin King. Matchsim: a novel neighbor-based similarity measure with maximum neighborhood matching. In *CIKM'09*, pages 1613–1616, 2009.

[24] F. P. Lorrain and H. C. White. Structural equivalence of individuals in networks. *J. Math. Sociology*, 1:49–80, 1971.

[25] Wangzhong Lu, Jeannette Janssen, Evangelos Milios, and Nathalie Japkowicz. Node similarity in networked information spaces. In *CASCON'01*, pages 11–25, 2001.

[26] J. J. Luczkovich, S.P. Borgatti, J.C. Johnson, and M.G. Everett. Defining and measuring trophic role similarity in food webs using regular coloration. *J. Theoretical Biology*, 220:303–321, 2003.

[27] Ben D. MacArthur, Rubén J. Sánchez-García, and James W. Anderson. Note: Symmetry in complex networks. *Discrete Appl. Math.*, 156(18):3525–3531, 2008.

[28] Maarten Marx and Michael Masuch. Regular equivalence and dynamic logic. *Social Networks*, 25(1):51–65, 2003.

[29] B.D. McKay. Practical graph isomorphism. *Congressus Numerantium*, 30:45–87, 1981.

[30] Guy Melançon and Arnaud Sallaberry. Edge metrics for visual graph analytics: A comparative study. In *Proc. 12th Int'l Conf. Inform. Visual.*, pages 610–615, 2008.

[31] Lawrence Page, Sergey Brin, Rajeev Motwani, and Terry Winograd. The pagerank citation ranking: Bringing order to the web. Technical Report SIDL-WP-1999-0120, Stanford Univ., 1999.

[32] Ronald Read and Derek Corneil. The graph isomorphism disease. *J. Graph Theory*, 1:339–363, 1977.

[33] Lee Douglas Sailer. Structure equivalence: meaning and definition, computation and application. *Social Networks*, 1:73–80, 1978.

[34] Henry Small. Co-citation in the scientific literature: A new measure of the relationship between two documents. *J. Amer. Soc. Information Sci.*, 24:265–269, 1973.

[35] Malcolm K. Sparrow. A linear algorithm for computing automorphic equivalence classes: the numerical signatures approach. *Social Networks*, 15(2):151–170, 1993.

[36] Jie Tang, Jing Zhang, Limin Yao, and Juanzi Li. Extraction and mining of an academic social network. In *WWW'08*, pages 1193–1194, New York, 2008. ACM.

[37] T. T. Tanimoto. An elementary mathematical theory of classification and prediction. *IBM Taxonomy Application M. and A.6*, 3, Nov. 1958.

[38] Sudhir L. Tauro, Georgos Siganos, C. Palmer, and Michalis Faloutsos. A simple conceptual model for the internet topology. In *Proc. IEEE Global Telecomm. Conf.*, pages 1667–1671, 2001.

[39] Y.J. Wang and G.Y. Wong. Stochastic blockmodels for directed graphs. *J. Amer.Stat. Assoc.*, 82(397):8–19, 1987.

[40] Stanley Wasserman and Katherine Faust. *Social network analysis: methods and applications*. Cambridge University Press, 1994.

[41] Douglas R. White and Karl P. Reitz. Graph and semigroup homomorphisms on networks of relations. *Social Networks*, 5:193–234, 1983.

[42] Harrison White, Scott Boorman, and Ronald Breiger. Social structure from multiple networks. i: Blockmodels of roles and positions. *Am. J. Sociology*, 81:730–780, 1976.

[43] Wensi Xi, Edward A. Fox, Weiguo Fan, Benyu Zhang, Zheng Chen, Jun Yan, and Dong Zhuang. Simfusion: measuring similarity using unified relationship matrix. In *SIGIR'05*, pages 130–137, 2005.

[44] Xiaoxin Yin, Jiawei Han, and Philip S. Yu. Linkclus: efficient clustering via heterogeneous semantic links. In *VLDB'06*, pages 427–438, 2006.

[45] Peixiang Zhao, Jiawei Han, and Yizhou Sun. P-rank: a comprehensive structural similarity measure over information networks. In *CIKM'09*, pages 553–562, 2009.

Brain Effective Connectivity Modeling for Alzheimer's Disease by Sparse Gaussian Bayesian Network

Shuai Huang[1], Jing Li[1], Jieping Ye[1], Adam Fleisher[2], Kewei Chen[2], Teresa Wu[1], Eric Reiman[2]

[1]School of Computing, Informatics, and Decisions Systems Engineering, Arizona State University, Tempe, AZ, 85287

[2]Banner Alzheimer's Institute, Banner Good Samaritan Medical Center, Phoenix, AZ, 85006

ABSTRACT

Recent studies have shown that Alzheimer's disease (AD) is related to alteration in brain connectivity networks. One type of connectivity, called effective connectivity, defined as the directional relationship between brain regions, is essential to brain function. However, there have been few studies on modeling the effective connectivity of AD and characterizing its difference from normal controls (NC). In this paper, we investigate the sparse Bayesian Network (BN) for effective connectivity modeling. Specifically, we propose a novel formulation for the structure learning of BNs, which involves one L1-norm penalty term to impose sparsity and another penalty to ensure the learned BN to be a directed acyclic graph – a required property of BNs. We show, through both theoretical analysis and extensive experiments on eleven moderate and large benchmark networks with various sample sizes, that the proposed method has much improved learning accuracy and scalability compared with ten competing algorithms. We apply the proposed method to FDG-PET images of 42 AD and 67 NC subjects, and identify the effective connectivity models for AD and NC, respectively. Our study reveals that the effective connectivity of AD is different from that of NC in many ways, including the global-scale effective connectivity, intra-lobe, inter-lobe, and inter-hemispheric effective connectivity distributions, as well as the effective connectivity associated with specific brain regions. These findings are consistent with known pathology and clinical progression of AD, and will contribute to AD knowledge discovery.

Categories and Subject Descriptors

H.2.8 [**Database Management**]: Database Applications – Data Mining; J.3 [**Life and Medical Sciences**]: Health, Medical information systems

General Terms

Algorithms

Keywords

Brain network, Alzheimer's disease, neuroimaging, FDG-PET, Bayesian network, sparse learning

1. INTRODUCTION

Alzheimer's disease (AD) is the most common cause of dementia and the fifth leading cause of death in people over 65 in the US. The current annual cost of AD care in the U.S. is more than $100 billion, which will continue to grow fast. The existing knowledge about the cause of AD is very limited. Clinical diagnosis is imprecise with a definite diagnosis only possible by autopsy. Also, there is currently no cure for AD, while most drugs only modestly alleviate symptoms. To tackle these challenging issues in AD studies, fast advancing neuroimaging techniques hold great promise. Recent studies have shown that neuroimaging can provide sensitive and reliable measures of AD onset and progression, which can complement the conventional clinical-based assessments and cognitive measures.

In neuroimaging-based AD research, one important area is brain connectivity modeling, i.e., identification of how different brain regions interact to produce a cognitive function in AD, compared with normal aging. Research in this area can substantially promote AD knowledge discovery and identification of novel connectivity-based AD biomarkers to be used in clinical practice. There are two types of connectivity being studied: *functional connectivity* refers to the covarying pattern of different brain regions; *effective connectivity* refers to the directional relationship between regions [1].

A vast majority of the existing research focuses on functional connectivity modeling. Various methods have been adopted such as correlation analysis [2], Principal Component Analysis (PCA) [3], PCA-based Scaled Subprofile Model [4], Independent Component Analysis [5], and Partial Least Squares [6]. Recently, sparse models have also been introduced, such as sparse multivariate or vector autoregressions [7] and sparse inverse covariance estimation [8]. Sparse models have shown great effectiveness because neuroimaging datasets are featured by "small n large p", i.e., the number of AD patients (n) can be close to or less than the number of brain regions modeled (p). Also, many past studies based on anatomical brain databases have shown that the true brain network is indeed sparse [9].

Compared with functional connectivity modeling, effective connectivity modeling has the advantage of helping identify the pathway/mechanism whereby distinct brain regions communicate with each other. However, the existing research in effective connectivity modeling is much less extensive. Models that have been adopted include structural equation models [10] and dynamic causal models [11]. The limitations of these models include (i) they are confirmative, rather than explanatory, i.e., they require a prior model of connectivity to start with; (ii) they require a substantially larger sample size than the number of regions modeled; a typical number of regions included is less than 10 given the sample size limit. These limitations make them inappropriate for AD connectivity modeling, because there is little prior knowledge of which regions should be included and how they are connected.

We propose sparse Bayesian Networks (BN) for effective connectivity modeling. A BN is an explanatory model and the sparse estimation makes it possible to include a large number of brain regions. In a BN representation of effective connectivity, the nodes are brain regions. A directed arc from node X_i to X_j (X_i is called a parent of X_j) indicates a direct influence from X_i to X_j. Sparsity consideration has been common in the BN learning literature. For example, some early work used score functions, such as BIC and MDL, to measure the goodness-of-fit of a BN, in which a penalty term on the model complexity is usually included in the score [12]. Recently, driven by modern applications such as genetics, learning of large-scale BNs has been very popular, in which sparsity consideration is indispensible. The Sparse Candidate (SC) algorithm [13], one of the first BN structure learning algorithms to be applied to a large number of variables, assumes that the maximum number of parents for each node is limited to a small constant. The L1MB-DAG algorithm developed in [14] uses LASSO [15] to identify a small set of potential parents for each variable. Some other algorithms, such as the Max-Min Hill-Climbing (MMHC) [16], Grow-Shrink [17], TC and TC_bw [18], all follow the same line. Most of these existing algorithms employ a two-stage approach: Stage 1 is to identify the potential parents of each variable; Stage 2 usually applies some heuristic search algorithms (e.g., hill-climbing) or orientation methods (e.g., Meek's rules [19]) to identify the parents out of the potential parent set. An apparent weakness of the two-stage approach is that if a true parent is missed in Stage 1, it will never be recovered in Stage 2. Another weakness of the existing algorithms is computational efficiency, i.e., it may take hours or days to learn a large-scale BN such as one with 500 nodes.

In this paper, we propose a new sparse BN learning algorithm, which is called SBN. It is a one-stage approach that identifies the parents of all variables directly. The main contributions of this paper include:

- We propose a novel sparse BN learning algorithm, i.e., SBN, using one L1-norm penalty term to impose sparsity and another penalty term to ensure the learned BN is a directed acyclic graph (DAG).
- We present theoretical guidance on how to select the regularization parameter associated with the second penalty.
- We perform theoretical analysis to reason why the two-stage approach popularly adopted in the existing literature has a high risk of failing to identify the true parents. Also, we conduct extensive experiments on synthetic data to compare SBN and the existing algorithms in terms of the learning accuracy and scalability.
- We apply SBN to FDG-PET data of 42 AD patients and 67 normal controls (NC) subjects enrolled in the ADNI (Alzheimer's Disease Neuroimaging Initiative) project, and identify the effective connectivity models for AD and NC.

Our study reveals that the effective connectivity of AD is different from NC in many ways, including the global-scale effective connectivity, intra-lobe, inter-lobe, and inter-hemisphere effective connectivity distributions, as well as the effective connectivity associated with specific brain regions. The findings are consistent with known pathology and clinical progression of AD.

2. BAYESIAN NETWORK: KEY DEFINITIONS AND CONCEPTS

This section introduces the key definitions and concepts of BNs that are relevant to this paper:

A BN is composed of a structure and a set of parameters. The structure (Fig. 1) is a DAG that consists of p nodes $[X_1, ..., X_p]$ and directed arcs between some nodes; no cycle is allowed in a DAG. Each node represents a random variable. If there is a directed arc from X_i to X_j, X_i is called a *parent* of X_j and X_j is called a *child* of X_i. Two nodes are called *spouses* if they share a common child. If there is a *directed path* from X_i to X_j, i.e., $X_i \rightarrow \cdots \rightarrow X_j$, X_i is called an *ancestor* of X_j. A directed arc is also a directed path and a parent is also an ancestor according to this definition. The *Markov Blanket (MB)* of X_j is a set of variables given which X_j will be independent of all other variables. The MB includes the parents, children, and spouses of X_j.

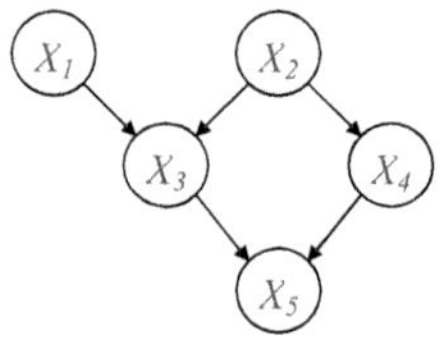

Figure 1. A BN structure

In this paper, we use the following notations with respect to a BN structure: Denote the structure by a $p \times p$ matrix $\mathbf{G}$, with entry $\mathbf{G}_{ij} = 1$ representing a directed arc from X_i to X_j. The set of parents of a node X_i is denoted by $\mathbf{PA}(X_i) = [X_{i_1}, ..., X_{i_k}]^T$. In addition, we define a $p \times p$ matrix, $\mathbf{P}$, which records all the directed paths in the structure, i.e., if there is a directed path from X_i to X_j, entry $\mathbf{P}_{ij} = 1$; otherwise, $\mathbf{P}_{ij} = 0$.

In addition to the structure, other important components of a BN are the parameters. The parameters are the conditional probability distribution of each node given its parents. Specifically, when the nodes follow a multivariate Gaussian distribution, a regression-type parameterization can be adopted, i.e., $X_i = \boldsymbol{\beta}_i{}^T \mathbf{PA}(X_i) + \varepsilon_i$ with $\varepsilon_i \sim N(0, \sigma_i{}^2)$ and $\boldsymbol{\beta}_i = [\beta_{i_1 i}, \cdots, \beta_{i_k i}]^T$. Then, the parameters of a BN are $\mathbf{B} = [\boldsymbol{\beta}_1, ..., \boldsymbol{\beta}_p]$. Without loss of generality, we assume that the nodes are standardized, i.e., each with a zero mean and unit variance. This means, if using $\boldsymbol{x}_i = [x_{i1}, ..., x_{in}]$ to denote the sample vector for X_i, and n to denote the sample size, we have $\sum_{j=1}^{n} x_{ij} = 0$ and $\boldsymbol{x}_i \boldsymbol{x}_i^T = n - 1$.

3. THE PROPOSED SPARSE BN STRUCTURE LEARNING ALGORITHM

One of the challenging issues in BN structure learning is to ensure that the learned structure must be a DAG, i.e., no cycle is present. To achieve this, we first identify a sufficient and necessary condition for a DAG, which is given as Lemma 1 below.

Lemma 1. *A sufficient and necessary condition for a DAG is* $\beta_{ji} \times \mathbf{P}_{ij} = 0$ *for every pair of nodes* X_i *and* X_j.

Proof. To prove the necessary condition, suppose that a BN structure,

$\mathbf{G}$, is a DAG. Let's assume that $\beta_{ji} \times \mathbf{P}_{ij} \neq 0$ for a pair of nodes X_i and X_j. Then, there exists a directed path from X_j to X_i and a directed path from X_i to X_j, i.e., there is a cycle in $\mathbf{G}$, which is a contradiction to our presumption that $\mathbf{G}$ is a DAG. To prove the sufficient condition, suppose that $\beta_{ji} \times \mathbf{P}_{ij} = 0$ for every pair of nodes X_i and X_j. If $\mathbf{G}$ is not a DAG, i.e., there is a cycle, it means that there exist two variables, X_i and X_j, with a directed arc from X_j to X_i ($\beta_{ji} \neq 0$) and a directed path from X_i to X_j ($\mathbf{P}_{ij} = 1$). This contradicts with our assumption that $\beta_{ji} \times \mathbf{P}_{ij} = 0$ for every pair of nodes X_i and X_j. □

Based on Lemma 1, we further present our formulation of the sparse BN structure learning. It is an optimization problem with the objective function and constraints given by:

$$\widehat{\mathbf{B}} = min_{\mathbf{B}} \sum_{i=1}^{p} \left\{ \begin{matrix} (\boldsymbol{x}_i - \boldsymbol{\beta}_i{}^T \boldsymbol{x}_{/i})(\boldsymbol{x}_i - \boldsymbol{\beta}_i{}^T \boldsymbol{x}_{/i})^T \\ + \lambda_1 \|\boldsymbol{\beta}_i\|_1 \end{matrix} \right\} \quad (1)$$
$$s.t. \quad \beta_{ji} \times \mathbf{P}_{ij} = 0, \; i, j = 1, \ldots, p, i \neq j.$$

The notations are explained as follows: $\boldsymbol{x}_i = [x_{i1}, \ldots, x_{in}]$ denotes the sample vector for X_i, where n is the sample size. $\boldsymbol{x}_{/i}$ denotes the sample matrix for all the variables except X_i .The first term in the objective function, $\sum_{i=1}^{p} \{(\boldsymbol{x}_i - \boldsymbol{\beta}_i{}^T \boldsymbol{x}_{/i})(\boldsymbol{x}_i - \boldsymbol{\beta}_i{}^T \boldsymbol{x}_{/i})^T\}$, is a profile likelihood to measure the model fit. The second term, $\|\boldsymbol{\beta}_i\|_1$, is the sum of the absolute values of the elements in $\boldsymbol{\beta}_i$ and thus is the so-called L1-norm penalty [15]. The regularization parameter, λ_1, controls the number of nonzero elements in the solution to $\boldsymbol{\beta}_i$, $\widehat{\boldsymbol{\beta}}_i$; larger λ_1, less nonzero elements. Because less nonzero elements in $\widehat{\boldsymbol{\beta}}_i$ correspond to fewer arcs in the learned BN structure, a larger λ_1 results in a sparser structure. In addition, the constraints are to assure that the learned BN is a DAG (see Lemma 1 and Theorem 1 below). We remark that these constraints are functions of $\mathbf{B}$ only, since $\mathbf{P} = \text{expm}(\mathbf{G})$ [20]. Here, $\text{expm}(\mathbf{G})$ is the matrix exponential of $\mathbf{G}$.

Solving the constrained optimization in (1) is difficult. Therefore, the penalty method [21] is employed to transform it into an unconstrained optimization problem, through adding an extra L1-norm penalty into the original objective function, i.e.,

$$\widehat{\mathbf{B}}_{ap} = \min_{\mathbf{B}} \sum_{i=1}^{p} f_i(\boldsymbol{\beta}_i) =$$
$$min_{\mathbf{B}} \sum_{i=1}^{p} \left\{ \begin{matrix} (\boldsymbol{x}_i - \boldsymbol{\beta}_i{}^T \boldsymbol{x}_{/i})(\boldsymbol{x}_i - \boldsymbol{\beta}_i{}^T \boldsymbol{x}_{/i})^T \\ + \lambda_1 \|\boldsymbol{\beta}_i\|_1 + \lambda_2 \sum_{j \in X_{/i}} |\beta_{ji} \times \mathbf{P}_{ij}| \end{matrix} \right\}, \quad (2)$$

where $j \in X_{/i}$ denotes that the variable indexed by j, i.e., X_j is a variable different from X_i. Here, $\lambda_2 \sum_{j \in X_{/i}} |\beta_{ji} \times \mathbf{P}_{ij}|$ is to push $\beta_{ji} \times \mathbf{P}_{ij}$ to become zero. Under some mild conditions, there exists a λ_2^* such that for all $\lambda_2 \geq \lambda_2^*$, $\widehat{\mathbf{B}}_{ap}$ is also a minimizer for (1) [21]. Theorem 1 gives a practical estimation for λ_2^*.

Theorem 1. *Any $\lambda_2 > (n-1)^2 p/\lambda_1 - \lambda_1$ will guarantee $\widehat{\mathbf{B}}_{ap}$ to be a DAG.*

Proof. To prove this we first need to show that with a certain value of λ_1 and any value of λ_2, $\widehat{\mathbf{B}}_{\text{ap}}$ is bounded. This can be seen from $\lambda_1 \|\widehat{\boldsymbol{\beta}}_i\|_1 \leq (\boldsymbol{x}_i - \widehat{\boldsymbol{\beta}}_i{}^T \boldsymbol{x}_{/i})(\boldsymbol{x}_i - \widehat{\boldsymbol{\beta}}_i{}^T \boldsymbol{x}_{/i})^T + \lambda_1 \|\widehat{\boldsymbol{\beta}}_i\|_1 + \lambda_2 \sum_{j \in X_{/i}} |\hat{\beta}_{ji} \times \mathbf{P}_{ij}| \leq \boldsymbol{x}_i \boldsymbol{x}_i^T = n - 1$, for each $\widehat{\boldsymbol{\beta}}_i$. The last inequality holds because $\boldsymbol{x}_i \boldsymbol{x}_i^T$ is the value of the function on the left hand side with $\boldsymbol{\beta}_i = 0$, which is obviously larger than the function value with $\boldsymbol{\beta}_i = \widehat{\boldsymbol{\beta}}_i$. The last equality holds since we have standardized all the variables. Thus, we know that $\max_{k \in \mathbf{PA}(X_i)} |\hat{\beta}_{ki}| \leq (n-1)/\lambda_1$. Now, we use proof-by-contradiction to show that, with any $\lambda_2 > (n-1)^2 p/\lambda_1 - \lambda_1$, we will get a DAG. Suppose that such a λ_2 doesn't guarantee a DAG. Then, there must be at least a pair of variables X_i and X_j with $\beta_{ji} \times \mathbf{P}_{ij} \neq 0$, i.e., $\beta_{ji} \neq 0$ and $\mathbf{P}_{ij} = 1$. Based on the first order optimality condition, $\beta_{ji} \neq 0$ i.f.f. $|(\boldsymbol{x}_i - \widehat{\boldsymbol{\beta}}_{i/j}^T \boldsymbol{x}_{/(i,j)})\boldsymbol{x}_j^T| - (\lambda_1 + \lambda_2 |\mathbf{P}_{ij}|) > 0$. Here, $\widehat{\boldsymbol{\beta}}_{i/j}^T$ denotes the elements in $\widehat{\boldsymbol{\beta}}_i$ without $\hat{\beta}_{ji}$, and $\boldsymbol{x}_{/(i,j)}$ denotes the sample matrix for all the variables except X_i and X_j. However, we have

$$|(\boldsymbol{x}_i - \widehat{\boldsymbol{\beta}}_{i/j}^T \boldsymbol{x}_{/(i,j)})\boldsymbol{x}_j^T| \leq |\boldsymbol{x}_i \boldsymbol{x}_j^T| + \sum_{k \in X_{/(i,j)}} |\hat{\beta}_{ki} \boldsymbol{x}_k \boldsymbol{x}_j^T| <$$
$$(n-1)p \max_{k \in X_{/i}} \hat{\beta}_{ki} < (n-1)^2 p/\lambda_1,$$

which results in $|(\boldsymbol{x}_i - \widehat{\boldsymbol{\beta}}_{i/j}^T \boldsymbol{x}_{/(i,j)})\boldsymbol{x}_j^T| - (\lambda_1 + \lambda_2 |\mathbf{P}_{ij}|) < 0$.□

Theorem 1 implies that if we specify any $\lambda_2 > (n-1)^2 p/\lambda_1 - \lambda_1$, we will get a minimizer of (1) through solving (2). However, in practice, directly solving (2) by specifying a large λ_2 may converge slowly. This is because that the unconstrained problem in (2) may be ill-conditioned with a too large value for λ_2 [40]. To avoid this, the "warm start" method [21] can be used, which works in the following way: first, it specifies a series of values for λ_2, i.e., $\lambda_2^0 < \lambda_2^1 < \lambda_2^2 < \cdots < \lambda_2^M$, where λ_2^0 is small and $\lambda_2^M > (n-1)^2 p/\lambda_1 - \lambda_1$; next, it optimizes (2) with $\lambda_2 = \lambda_2^0$ to get a minimizer $\widehat{\mathbf{B}}_{ap}^0$, using an arbitrary initial value; then, it optimizes (2) with $\lambda_2 = \lambda_2^1$, using $\widehat{\mathbf{B}}_{ap}^0$ as an initial value; this process iterates, until it optimizes (2) with $\lambda_2 = \lambda_2^M$. With the last minimizer as the initial value for the next optimization problem, this method can be quite efficient.

Given λ_1 and λ_2, the BCD algorithm [22] can be employed to solve (2). The BCD algorithm updates each $\boldsymbol{\beta}_i$ iteratively, assuming that all other parameters are fixed. In our situation, this is equivalent to optimizing $f_i(\boldsymbol{\beta}_i)$ iteratively and the algorithm will terminate when some convergence conditions are satisfied. We remark that $f_i(\boldsymbol{\beta}_i)$, after some transformation, is similar to LASSO [15], i.e.,

$$f_i(\boldsymbol{\beta}_i) = (\boldsymbol{x}_i - \boldsymbol{\beta}_i{}^T \boldsymbol{x}_{/i})(\boldsymbol{x}_i - \boldsymbol{\beta}_i{}^T \boldsymbol{x}_{/i})^T$$
$$+ \sum_{j \in X_{/i}} (\lambda_1 + \lambda_2 |\mathbf{P}_{ij}|) |\beta_{ji}|. \quad (3)$$

As a result, the shooting algorithm [23] for LASSO may be used to optimize $f_i(\boldsymbol{\beta}_i)$ in each iteration. Note that at each iteration for optimizing $f_i(\boldsymbol{\beta}_i)$, we also need to calculate $\mathbf{P}_{ij}$ for $j \in X_{/i}$. This can be done by a Breadth-first search on $\mathbf{G}$ with X_i being the root node. A more detailed description of the BCD algorithm used to solve (2) is given in Figure 2.

Input: sample matrix, $\mathbf{X}$; $\{\lambda_i\}_{i=1,2}$; initial $\mathbf{B}^0$;
Initialize: Let $t = 0$;
Repeat
  For $i = 1, 2, \ldots, p$
    A Breadth-first search on $\mathbf{G}$ with X_i being the root node to calculate $\mathbf{P}_{ij}$ for $j = 1, \ldots, p$.
    Use the shooting algorithm to optimize $f_i(\boldsymbol{\beta}_i)$ and get $\boldsymbol{\beta}_i^{t+1}$;
  End for
Until converge

Figure 2. The BCD algorithm used for solving (2)

Finally, we want to mention that the L2-norm penalty, $\lambda_2 \sum_{j \in X_{/i}} (\beta_{ji} \times \mathbf{P}_{ij})^2$, might also be used in (2). The advantage is that it is a differentiable function of β_{ji}. Also, as shown in [21],

$\beta_{ji} \times \mathbf{P}_{ij} \to 0$ when $\lambda_2 \to \infty$. However, the limitation of the L2-norm penalty, compared with the L1-norm penalty, is that there is no guarantee that a finite λ_2 exists to assure $\beta_{ji} \times \mathbf{P}_{ij} = 0$ for all pairs of X_i and X_j.

Time complexity analysis of the proposed algorithm: Each iteration of the BCD algorithm consists of two operations: a shooting algorithm and a Breadth-first search on $\mathbf{G}$. These two operations cost $O(pn)$ [24] and $O(p + |\mathbf{G}|)$, respectively. Here $|\mathbf{G}|$ is the number of nonzero elements in $\mathbf{G}$. If $\mathbf{G}$ is sparse, i.e., $|\mathbf{G}| = Cp$ with a small constant C, $O(p + |\mathbf{G}|) = O(p)$. Thus, the computational cost at each iteration is only $O(pn)$. Furthermore, each sweep through all columns of $\mathbf{B}$ costs $O(p^2n)$. Our simulation study shows that it usually takes no more than 5 sweeps to converge.

4. THEORETICAL ANALYSIS OF THE COMPETITIVE ADVANTAGE OF THE PROPOSED SBN ALGORITHM

Simulation studies in Sec. 5 will show that SBN is more accurate than various existing algorithms that employ a two-stage approach. This section aims to provide some theoretical insights about why it is so. Recall that Stage 1 of the two-stage approach is to identify potential parents of each variable X_i. The existing algorithms achieve this by identifying the MB of X_i. A typical way is variable selection based on regression, i.e., to build a regression of X_i on all other variables and consider the variables selected to be the MB. The key differences between various algorithms are the type of regression used and the method in variable selection. For example, the TC algorithm [18] uses ordinary regression and a t-test for variable selection; the L1MB-DAG algorithm [14] uses LASSO.

In the regression of X_i, the coefficients for the variables that are not in the MB will be small (theoretically zero due to the definition of MB). However, the coefficients for the parents may also be very small due to the correlation between the parents and children. As a result, some parents may not be selected in the variable selection, i.e., they will be missed in Stage 1 of the two-stage approach, leading to greater BN learning errors. In contrast, the SBN may not suffer from this, because it is a one-stage approach that identifies the parents directly.

To further illustrate this point, we analyze one two-stage algorithm, the TC algorithm. TC does variable selection using a t-test. To determine whether a variable should be selected, a t-test uses the statistic $\hat{\beta}/se(\hat{\beta})$, where $\hat{\beta}$ is the estimate for the regression coefficient of this variable and $se(\hat{\beta})$ is the standard error. The larger the $\hat{\beta}/se(\hat{\beta})$, the higher chance the variable will be selected. Theorems 2 and 3 below show that even though the value of $\hat{\beta}/se(\hat{\beta})$ corresponding to a parent of X_i is large in the true BN, its value may decrease drastically in the regression of X_i on all other variables. Theorem 2 focuses on a specific type of BNs, a general tree, in which all variables have one common ancestor and there is at most one directed path between two variables. Theorem 3 focuses on a general inverse tree, which becomes a general tree if all the arcs are reversed. The proof of Theorem 2 can be found in the Appendix. The proof of Theorem 3 is not shown here due to space limitations.

Theorem 2. Consider a general tree with $m + 2$ variables, whose structure and parameters are given by $X_1 = e_1$, $X_2 = \beta_{12}X_1 + e_2$, $X_i = \beta_{2i}X_2 + e_i$, $i = 3,4,\dots,m$. All the variables have unit variance. If X_2 is regressed on all other variables in Stage 1 of TC, i.e., $X_2 = \beta_{12}^{MB}X_1 + \beta_{23}^{MB}X_3 + \cdots + \beta_{2m}^{MB}X_n + e_2^{MB}$, the coefficient for X_2's parent, X_1, is:

$$\beta_{12}^{MB} = \beta_{12}\frac{\prod_{i=3}^{m}(1-\beta_{2i}^2)}{\prod_{i=3}^{m}(1-\beta_{2i}^2)+\sum_{i=3}^{m}\left[\beta_{2i}^2\prod_{j=3,j\neq i}^{m}(1-\beta_{2i}^2)\right]} < \beta_{12}, \text{ and}$$

$$\frac{\beta_{12}^{MB}}{se(\beta_{12}^{MB})} = \frac{\beta_{12}}{se(\beta_{12})}\sqrt{\frac{\prod_{i=3}^{m}(1-\beta_{2i}^2)}{\prod_{i=4}^{m}(1-\beta_{2i}^2)+\sum_{i=4}^{m}\left[\beta_{2i}^2\prod_{j=3,j\neq i}^{m}\left(1-\beta_{2j}^2\right)\right]}} < \frac{\beta_{12}}{se(\beta_{12})}.$$

Theorem 3. Consider a general inverse tree with $m + l + 2$ variables, whose structure and parameters are given by $X_i = e_i$, $i = 1,2,\dots,l,l+3,\dots,l+m$, $X_{l+1} = \sum_{i=1}^{l}\beta_{i,l+1}X_i + e_{l+1}$, $X_{l+2} = \beta_{l+1,l+2}X_{l+1} + \sum_{i=3}^{m}\beta_{l+i,l+2}X_{l+i} + e_{l+2}$. All the variables have unit variance. If X_{l+1} is regressed on all other variables, i.e., $X_{l+1} = \sum_{i=1}^{l}\beta_{i,l+1}^{MB}X_i + \beta_{l+1,l+2}^{MB}X_{l+2} + \sum_{i=3}^{m}\beta_{l+i,l+2}^{MB}X_{l+i} + e_{l+1}^{MB}$, the coefficients for X_{l+1}'s parent, X_k $(k = 1,2,\dots,l)$, are:

$$\beta_{k,l+1}^{MB} = \beta_{k,l+1}\frac{1-\sum_{i=1}^{m}\beta_{l+2+i,l+2}^2-\beta_{l+1,l+2}^2}{1-\sum_{i=1}^{m}\beta_{l+2+i,l+2}^2-\beta_{l+1,l+2}^2\sum_{i=1}^{m}\beta_{i,l+1}^2} < \beta_{k,l+1}, \text{ and}$$

$$\frac{\beta_{k,l+1}^{MB}}{se(\beta_{k,l+1}^{MB})} = \frac{\beta_{k,l+1}}{se(\beta_{k,l+1})}\frac{1-\sum_{i=1}^{m}\beta_{l+2+i,l+2}^2-\beta_{l+1,l+2}^2}{1-\sum_{i=1}^{m}\beta_{l+2+i,l+2}^2-\beta_{l+1,l+2}^2\sum_{i=1}^{m}\beta_{i,l+1}^2}$$

$$\times\sqrt{\frac{\left(1-\sum_{i=1}^{m}\beta_{i,l+1}^2\right)\left(1-\sum_{i=1}^{m}\beta_{l+2+i,l+2}^2-\beta_{l+1,l+2}^2\sum_{i=1}^{m}\beta_{i,l+1}^2\right)}{\left(1-\sum_{i=1}^{m}\beta_{l+2+i,l+2}^2-\beta_{l+1,l+2}^2\sum_{i=1,i\neq k}^{m}\beta_{i,l+1}^2\right)}}$$

$$\times\sqrt{\frac{1-\sum_{i=1}^{m}\beta_{i,l+1}^2\left(1-\sum_{i=1}^{m}\beta_{l+2+i,l+2}^2-\beta_{l+1,l+2}^2\right)}{1-\sum_{i=1,i\neq k}^{m}\beta_{i,l+1}^2\left(1-\sum_{i=1}^{m}\beta_{l+2+i,l+2}^2-\beta_{l+1,l+2}^2\right)}} < \frac{\beta_{12}}{se(\beta_{12})}.$$

For example, consider a general tree with $\beta_{12} = 0.3$, $\beta_{2i} = 0.8$, $m = 8$. Based on Theorem 2, $\beta_{12}^{MB} = 0.028 \ll \beta_{12}$ and $\beta_{12}^{MB}/se(\beta_{12}^{MB}) = 0.092\sqrt{n-1} \ll \beta_{12}/se(\beta_{12}) = 0.3144\sqrt{n-1}$.

Consider a general inverse tree with seven variables: $X_i, i = 1,\cdots,5$, are parents of X_6 which is a parent of X_7;

$[\beta_{16},\cdots,\beta_{56}] = [0.24, 0.325, 0.256, 0.304, 0.216]$; $\beta_{67} = 0.3$. Based on Theorem 3,

$[\beta_{16}^{MB},\cdots,\beta_{56}^{MB}] = [0.036, 0.053, 0.038, 0.045, 0.032] \ll [\beta_{16},\cdots,\beta_{56}]$ and $[\beta_{16}^{MB}/se(\beta_{16}^{MB}),\cdots,\beta_{56}^{MB}/se(\beta_{56}^{MB})]$ is equal to $[0.1142, 0.1672, 0.1216, 0.1444, 0.1026] \times \sqrt{(n-1)}$

which is less than $[\beta_{16}/se(\beta_{16}),\cdots,\beta_{56}/se(\beta_{56})]$ since the later one is equal to

$[0.306, 0.4491, 0.3266, 0.3878, 0.2785] \times \sqrt{(n-1)}$.

Note that these theorems derive the relationship between β^{MB} ($\beta^{MB}/se(\beta^{MB})$) and β ($\beta/se(\beta)$) at the population-level (i.e., sampling error is not considered), so they use the notation "β" not "$\hat{\beta}$".

5. SIMULATION STUDIES ON SYNTHETIC DATA

We show four sets of simulations. The first one is to show that, on a general tree, the existing algorithms based on the two-stage approach may miss some true parents with high probabilities, while the proposed SBN performs well. The second simulation is to compare the structure learning accuracy of SBN with other competing algorithms, on benchmark networks. The third and fourth simulations are to investigate the scalability of SBN and compare it with other competing algorithms.

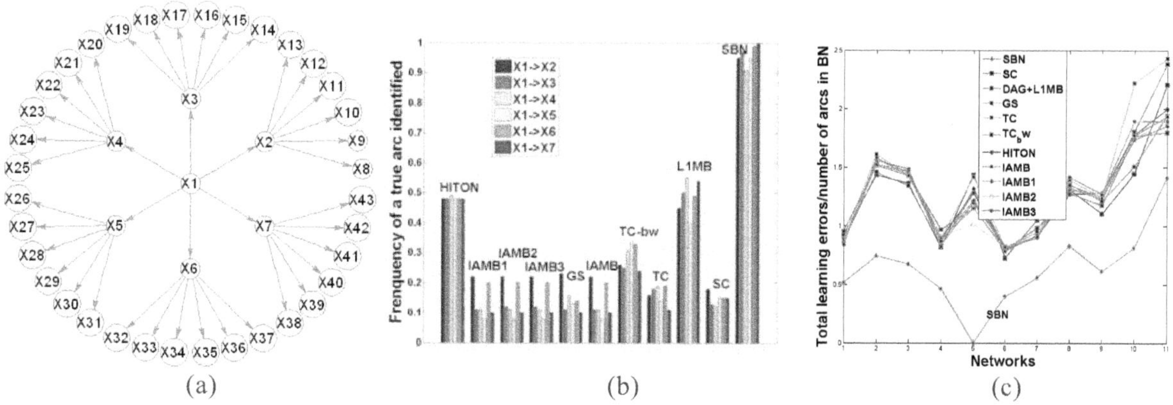

(a) (b) (c)

Figure 3. (a): The general tree in Sec. 5.1 (regression coefficients are 0.3 for arcs between X_1 and X_i, $i = 2, \cdots, 7$, and 0.8 for others); (b) Simulation results for the general tree; (c) Simulation results for 11 benchmark networks.

5.1 Learning accuracy for general tree

Ten existing algorithms are selected: HITON-PC [25], IAMB and three of its variants [26], GS [17], SC [13], TC and its advanced version TC-bw [18], and L1MB [14]. We simulate data from the general tree in Figure 3(a) with a sample size of 200.

We apply the selected algorithms on the simulated data; the parameters of each algorithm are selected in the way that the authors have suggested in their papers, respectively. In applying the proposed SBN, λ_1 is selected by BIC; λ_2 is set to be $10[(n-1)^2 p/\lambda_1 - \lambda_1]$ which empirically guarantees a DAG to be learned. The initial value of SBN is the output of L1MB which uses LASSO in Stage 1 to identify the MB for each variable. We treat the identified MB by L1MB as parents and use the resulting "BN" (not necessarily a DAG) as the initial value for SBN. The results over 100 repetitions are shown in Figure 3(b). The X-axis records the 10 selected algorithms and the proposed SBN (the last one). The Y-axis records the frequency of a true arc being identified. Each color bar corresponds to a true arc indicated in the legend. Six true arcs are shown, i.e., the arcs between X_1 and X_i, $i = 2, \cdots, 7$. Because X_1 is the parent of X_i, the Y-axis actually shows how well the parent of X_i can be identified by each of the algorithms. Figure 3 (b) shows that, SBN performs much better than all others. This can be explained by Theorem 1. Specifically, the MB of X_i includes X_1 and six children. Although the coefficient linking X_1 to X_i is as high as 0.3, this coefficient in the regression that regresses X_1 on its MB reduces to 0.028, due to the inclusion of the children in the regression. As a result, X_1 will have a high probability of being excluded from the MB identified in Stage 1 of the existing algorithms.

5.2 Learning accuracy for Benchmark networks

We select seven moderately large networks from BNR [27]. We also use the tiling technique to produce two large BNs, alarm2 and hailfinder2. Two other networks with specific structures, factor and chain, are also considered. The 11 networks are: (number of nodes/edges): 1. factors (27/68), 2. alarm (37/46), 3. barley (48/84), 4. carpo (61/74), 5. chain(7/6), 6. hailfinder (56/66), 7. insurance (27/52), 8. mildew (35/46), 9. water (32/66), 10. alarm2 (296/410), 11. hailfinder2 (280/390). To specify the parameters of a network, i.e., to specify the regression coefficients of each variable on its parents, we randomly sample from $\pm 1 + N(0,1/16)$. Then, we simulate data from the networks with sample size 100, and apply the 10 algorithms to learn the BN structures. The results over 100 repetitions are shown in Figure 3(c). The X-axis records the 11 networks. The Y-axis records the ratio of the total learning error (false positives plus false negatives) to the number of arcs in the true BN. Each curve corresponds to one of the 11 algorithms under comparison. We can observe that the lowest curve (i.e., best performance) is SBN.

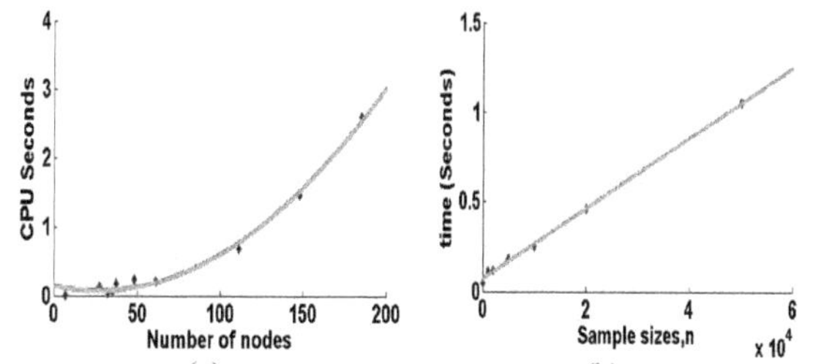

(a) (b)

Figure 4. Scalability of SBN with respect to (a) the number of variables in a BN, p, and (b) the sample size, n, on a computer with Intel Core 2, 2.2 G Hz, 4G

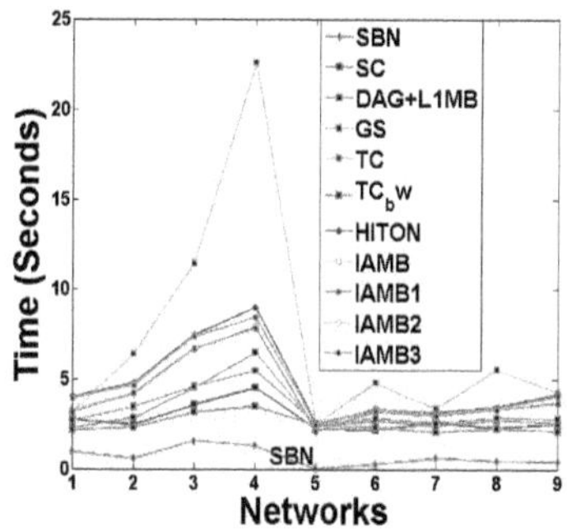

Figure 5. Comparison of SBN with competing algorithms on the CPU time in structure learning of the other nine benchmark networks

5.3 Scalability

We study two aspects of scalability for SBN: the scalability with respect to the number of variables in a BN, p, and the scalability with respect to the sample size, n. We use the CPU time for each sweep through all the columns of **B** as the parameter for measurement. Specifically, we fix n =1000, and vary p by using the 11 benchmark networks. Also, we fix p=37 (the Alarm network). The results over 100 repetitions are shown in Figure 4 (a) and (b), respectively. It can be seen that the computational cost is linear in n and quadratic in p, which confirms our theoretical time complexity analysis in Section 3.

Table 2. Names of the AVOIs for effective connectivity modeling (L = left hemisphere, R = right hemisphere)

	Frontal lobe		Parietal lobe		Occipital lobe		Temporal lobe
1	Frontal_Sup_L	13	Parietal_Sup_L	21	Occipital_Sup_L	27	Temporal_Sup_L
2	Frontal_Sup_R	14	Parietal_Sup_R	22	Occipital_Sup_R	28	Temporal_Sup_R
3	Frontal_Mid_L	15	Parietal_Inf_L	23	Occipital_Mid_L	29	Temporal_Pole_Sup_L
4	Frontal_Mid_R	16	Parietal_Inf_R	24	Occipital_Mid_R	30	Temporal_Pole_Sup_R
5	Frontal_Sup_Medial_L	17	Precuneus_L	25	Occipital_Inf_L	31	Temporal_Mid_L
6	Frontal_Sup_Medial_R	18	Precuneus_R	26	Occipital_Inf_R	32	Temporal_Mid_R
7	Frontal_Mid_Orb_L	19	Cingulum_Post_L			33	Temporal_Pole_Mid_L
8	Frontal_Mid_Orb_R	20	Cingulum_Post_R			34	Temporal_Pole_Mid_R
9	Rectus_L					35	Temporal_Inf_L 8301
10	Rectus_R					36	Temporal_Inf_R 8302
11	Cingulum_Ant_L					37	Fusiform_L
12	Cingulum_Ant_R					38	Fusiform_R
						39	Hippocampus_L
						40	Hippocampus_R
						41	ParaHippocampal_L
						42	ParaHippocampal_R

6. BRAIN EFFECTIVE CONNECTIVITY MODELING OF AD BY SBN

FDG-PET baseline images of 49 AD and 67 normal control (NC) subjects from the ADNI project (www.loni.ucla.edu/ADNI) were used in this study. After spatially normalizing the images to the Montreal Neurological Institute (MNI) template coordinate space, average PET counts were extracted from the 116 brain anatomical regions of interest (AVOIs) defined by the Automated Anatomical Labeling [28] technique. We then selected 42 AVOIs that are considered to be potentially relevant to AD, as reported in the literature. Each of the 42 AVOIs became a node in the SBN. Please see Table 2 for the name of each AVOI brain region. These regions are distributed in the four major neocortical lobes of the brain, i.e., the frontal, parietal, occipital, and temporal lobes.

We apply SBN to learn a BN for AD and another one for NC, to represent their respective effective connectivity models. In the learning of an AD (or NC) effective connectivity model, the value for λ_1 needs to be selected. In this paper, we adopt two criteria in selecting λ_1: one is to minimize the prediction error of the model and the other is to minimize the BIC. Both criteria have been popularly adopted in sparse learning [12,14,15]. The two criteria lead to similar findings discovered from the effective connectivity models, so only the results based on the minimum prediction error are shown in this section. Specifically, Figure 6 shows the effective connectivity models for AD and NC. Each model is represented by a "matrix". Each row/column is one AVOI, X_j. A black cell at the i-th row and j-th column of the matrix represents that X_i is a parent of X_j. On each matrix, four red squares are used to highlight the four lobes, i.e., the frontal, parietal, occipital, and temporal lobes, from top-left to bottom-right. The black cells inside each red square reflect intra-lobe effective connectivity, whereas the black cells outside the squares reflect inter-lobe effective connectivity. The following interesting observations can be drawn from the effective connectivity models:

Global-scale effective connectivity:

The total number of arcs in a BN connectivity model, equal to the number of black cells in a matrix plot in Figure 6, represents the amount of effective connectivity (i.e., the amount of directional information flow) in the whole brain. This number is 285 and 329 for AD and NC, respectively. In other words, AD has 13.4% less effective connectivity than NC. Loss of connectivity in AD has been widely reported in the literature [34, 38-40].

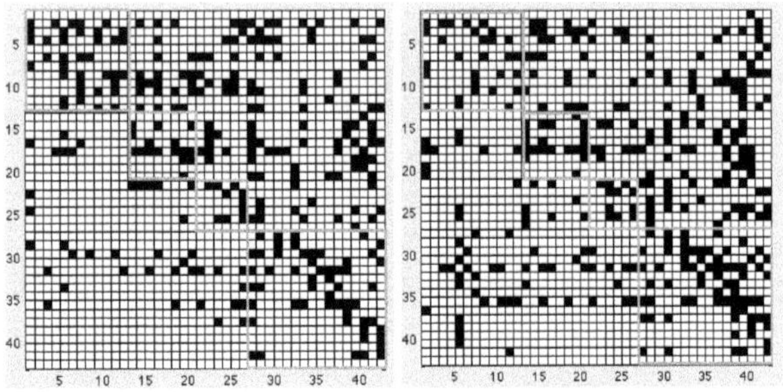

(a) (b)

Figure 6. Brain effective connectivity models by SBN. (a) AD. (b) NC.

Intra-/inter-lobe effective connectivity distribution:

Aside from having different amounts of effective connectivity at the global scale, AD may also have a different distribution pattern of connectivity across the brain from NC. Therefore, we count the number of arcs in each of the four lobes and between each pair of lobes in the AD and NC effective connectivity models. The results are summarized in Table 3. It can be seen that the temporal lobe of AD has 22.9% less effective connectivity than NC. The decrease in connectivity in the temporal lobe of AD has been extensively reported in the literature [29, 2, 30]. The interpretation may be that AD is featured by a dramatic cognitive decline and the temporal lobe is responsible for delivering memory and other cognitive functions. As a result, the temporal lobe is affected early and severely by AD and the connectivity network in this lobe is severely disrupted. On the other hand, the frontal lobe of AD has 27.6% more connectivity than NC. This has been interpreted as compensatory reallocation or recruitment of cognitive resources [29-32]. Because the regions in the frontal lobe are typically affected later in the course of AD (our data are mild to moderate AD), the increased connectivity in the frontal lobe may help preserve some cognitive functions in AD patients. In addition, AD shows a decrease in the amount of effective connectivity in the parietal lobe which has also been reported to be affected by AD. There is no significant difference between AD and NC in the occipital lobe. This is reasonable because the occipital lobe is primarily involved in the brain's visual function which is not affected by AD.

Table 3. Intra – and inter – lobe effective connectivity amounts

(a) AD

	Frontal	Parietal	Occipital	Temporal
Frontal	37	28	18	43
Parietal		16	14	42
Occipital			10	23
Temporal				54

(b) NC

	Frontal	Parietal	Occipital	Temporal
Frontal	29	32	12	61
Parietal		20	16	42
Occipital			11	36
Temporal				70

Furthermore, the most significant reduction in inter-lobe connectivity in AD is found between the frontal and temporal lobes, i.e., AD has 29.5% less effective connectivity than NC. This may be attributed to the temporal lobe disruption of the default mode network in AD [34].

Direction of local effective connectivity:

One advantage of BNs over undirected graphical models in brain connectivity modeling is that the directed arcs in a BN reflect directional effect of one region over another, i.e., the effective connectivity. Specifically, if there is a directed arc from brain regions X_i to X_j, it indicates that X_i takes a dominant role in the communication with X_j. The connectivity modes in Figure 6 reveal a number of interesting findings in this regard:

(i) There are substantially fewer black cells in the area defined by rows 27-42 and columns 1-26 in AD than NC. Recall that rows 27-42 correspond to regions in the temporal lobe. Thus, this pattern indicates a substantial reduction in arcs pointing from temporal regions to the other regions in the AD brain, i.e., temporal regions lose their dominating roles in communicating information with the other regions as a result of AD. The loss is most severe in the communication from temporal to frontal regions.

(ii) Rows 31 and 35, corresponding to brain regions "Temporal_Mid_L" and "Temporal_Inf_L", respectively, are among the rows with the largest number of black cells in NC, i.e., these two regions take a significantly dominant role in communicating with other regions in normal brains. However, the dominancy of the two regions is substantially reduced by 34.8% and 36.8%, respectively, in AD. A possible interpretation is that these are neocortical regions associated with amyloid deposition and early FDG hypometabolism in AD [34-37, 41-42].

(iii) Columns 39 and 40 correspond to regions "Hippocampus_L" and "Hippocampus_R", respectively. There are a total of 33 black cells in these two columns in NC, i.e., 33 other regions dominantly communicate information with the hippocampus. However, this number reduces to 22 (33.3% reduction) in AD. The reduction is more severe in Hippocampus_L (50%). The hippocampus is well known to play a prominent role in making new memories and in recall. It has been widely reported that the hippocampus is affected early in the course of AD, leading to memory loss – the most common symptom of AD.

(iv) There are a total of 93 arcs pointing from the left hemisphere to the right hemisphere of the brain in NC; this number reduces to 71 (23.7% reduction) in AD. The number of arcs from the right hemisphere to the left hemisphere in AD is close to that in NC. This provides evidence that AD may be associated with inter-hemispheric disconnection and the disconnection is mostly unilateral, which has also been reported by some other papers [43-44].

7. CONCLUSION

In this paper, we proposed a BN structure learning algorithm, called SBN, for identifying effective connectivity of AD from FDG-PET data. SBN adopted a novel formulation that involves one L1-norm penalty term to impose sparsity on the learning and another penalty to ensure the learned BN to be a DAG. We performed theoretical analysis on the competitive advantage of SBN over the existing algorithms in terms of learning accuracy. Our analysis showed that the existing algorithms employ a two-stage approach in BN structure identification, which makes them have a high risk of failing to identify the parents of each variable. Also, we performed theoretical analysis on the time complexity of SBN, which showed that it is linear in the sample size and quadratic in the number of variables. Furthermore, we conducted experiments to compare SBN with 10 competing algorithms and found that SBN has significantly better performance in learning accuracy.

We applied SBN to identify the effective connectivity models of AD and NC from PDG-PET data, and found that the effective connectivity of AD is different from NC in many ways. Clinically, our findings may provide an additional tool for monitoring disease progress, evaluating treatment effects, and enabling early detection of network disconnection in prodromal AD. Future studies may be conducted to verify the statistical significance of the identified effective connectivity difference between AD and NC, and estimate the strength of the directed arcs identified by SBN to help improve the sensitivity and specificity of the effective connectivity models. Finally, although this paper focuses on the structure learning of Gaussian BNs, the same formulation can be adopted to discrete BNs, which will be explored in our future research.

Appendix A

There are some notation changes as follows for the convenience of the derivation: we use $b_0 = \beta_{12}$, $b_1 = \beta_{23}$, $b_2 = \beta_{24}$, ..., $b_n = \beta_{2m}$, $Y_1 = X_3$, $Y_2 = X_4$, ... , $Y_n = X_m$.

Based on Wright's second decomposition rule [33], the covariance matrix of all the variables, T_n, can be represented as a function of the parameters of the BN, $b_0, \cdots, b_n$, i.e.,

$$\mathrm{T_n} = cov(X_2, X_1, Y_1, \cdots, Y_n) = \begin{bmatrix} 1 & b_0 & b_1 & b_2 & \cdots & b_n \\ b_0 & 1 & b_0 b_1 & b_0 b_2 & \cdots & b_0 b_n \\ b_1 & b_0 b_1 & 1 & b_1 b_2 & \cdots & b_1 b_n \\ b_2 & b_0 b_2 & b_1 b_2 & 1 & \cdots & b_2 b_n \\ \cdots & \cdots & \cdots & \cdots & \cdots & \cdots \\ b_n & b_0 b_n & b_1 b_n & b_2 b_n & \cdots & 1 \end{bmatrix} \quad \text{(A-1)}$$

Now, consider the regression of X_2 on all other variables, i.e., $X_2 = b_0^{MB} X_1 + b_1^{MB} Y_1 + \cdots + b_n^{MB} Y_n + e_2^{MB}$. According to the Least Square criterion, the regression coefficients,

$$[b_0^{MB}, \cdots, b_n^{MB}]^T = C_n^{-1}[b_0, \cdots, b_n]^T, \quad \text{(A-2)}$$

where C_n is a sub-matrix of $\mathrm{T_n}$ by deleting the 1st column and 1st row from T_n. Denote $\mathrm{C_n^{-1}}$ by $\mathrm{A_n} = (a_{ij})$. Then,

$$b_0^{MB} = a_{11}b_0 + a_{12}b_1 + a_{13}b_2 + \cdots + a_{1n+1}b_n. \quad \text{(A-3)}$$

Our final objective is to express b_0^{MB} by the parameters of the BN. This can be achieved if we can express $a_{11}, a_{12}, a_{13}, \cdots, a_{1\,n+1}$ by the parameters of the BN, which is the goal of the following derivation.

It is known that

$$a_{1j} = (-1)^{1+j} \frac{\det(C_{ij,n})}{\det(C_n)}, \quad \text{(A-4)}$$

where $C_{1j,n}$ is a matrix by deleting the 1st row and the jth column from C_n. So, the problem becomes calculation of $\det(C_n)$ and $\det(C_{1j,n})$.

(i) Calculation of $\det(C_n)$: We first show the result:

$$\det(C_n) = \prod_{i=1}^{n}(1 - b_i^2) + \sum_{i=1}^{n}\left(b_i^2 \prod_{j=0,j\neq i}^{n}(1 - b_j^2)\right) \quad \text{(A-5)}$$

Next, we will use the induction method in 1)-2) below to prove (A-5):

1) When $n = 1$, it is easy to see that (A-5) holds.

2) Assume that (A-5) holds for $n - 1$, i.e.,

$$\det(C_{n-1}) = \prod_{i=1}^{n-1}(1 - b_i^2) + \sum_{i=1}^{n-1}\left(b_i^2 \prod_{j=0,j\neq i}^{n-1}(1 - b_j^2)\right).$$

Then we need prove that (A-5) holds for n. Based on the definition of a determinant,

$$\det(C_n) = \sum_{j=1}^{n+1}(-1)^{1+j} c_{1j} \det(C_{1j,n}), \quad \text{(A-6)}$$

where c_{1j} is the entry at the 1st row and jth column of C_n.

Now we need to derive $\det(C_{1j,n})$ (only results are shown below due to page limits):

When $j = 1$,

$\det(C_{1j,n}) = \prod_{i=2}^{n}(1-b_i^2) + \sum_{i=2}^{n}\left(b_i^2 \prod_{j=1,j\neq i}^{n}(1-b_j^2)\right)$, (A-7)

When $j \neq 1$,

$\det(C_{1j,n}) = (-1)^{1+j+1} b_0 b_j \prod_{k=1,k\neq j}^{n}(1-b_k^2)$. (A-8)

Then, insert (A-7), (A-8), and $c_{11} = 1$, $c_{12} = b_0 b_1$, ..., $c_{1n+1} = b_0 b_n$ into (A-6):

$$\det(C_n) = \prod_{i=2}^{n}(1-b_i^2) + \sum_{i=2}^{n}(b_i^2 \prod_{\substack{j\neq i \\ j=1}}^{n}(1-b_j^2)) + \sum_{j=1}^{n} -b_0^2 b_j^2 \prod_{\substack{k=1 \\ k\neq j}}^{n}(1-b_k^2)$$

$$= \prod_{j=1}^{n}(1-b_j^2) + \sum_{j=1}^{n} b_j^2 \prod_{\substack{k=0 \\ k\neq j}}^{n}(1-b_k^2)$$

This completes the proof for (A-5).

(ii) Calculation of $\det(C_{1j,n})$: $\det(C_{1j,n})$has been obtained by (A-7) and (A-8). Inserting (A-5), (A-7), and (A-8) into (A-4), we get:

$$a_{11} = \frac{\prod_{j=2}^{n}(1-b_j^2) + \sum_{j=2}^{n}(b_j^2 \prod_{\substack{k\neq j \\ k=1}}^{n}(1-b_k^2))}{\prod_{i=1}^{n}(1-b_i^2) + \sum_{i=1}^{n}(b_i^2 \prod_{\substack{k\neq i \\ k=0}}^{n}(1-b_k^2))}$$

Furthermore, $a_{11} + a_{12}b_0b_1 + a_{13}b_0b_2 + \cdots + a_{1n+1}b_0b_n = 1$. Inserting this into (A-3), we get $b_0^{MB} = a_{11}\left(1-(1-b_0^2)\right)/b_0$. Plugging in the a_{11} above, we can get:

$$b_0^{MB} = b_0 \frac{\prod_{j=1}^{n}(1-b_j^2)}{\prod_{i=1}^{n}(1-b_i^2) + \sum_{i=1}^{n}(b_i^2 \prod_{\substack{k\neq i \\ k=0}}^{n}(1-b_k^2))} \quad \text{(A-9)}$$

Obviously, the fraction at the right-hand side is between 0 and 1. Therefore, $|b_0^{MB}| < |b_0|$.

Next we derive the formula for $b_0^{MB}/se(b_0^{MB})$. It is known that $se^2(b_0^{MB}) = a_{11}/[(n-1)(T_n^{-1})_{11}]$. Since $(T_n^{-1})_{11} = \det(C_n)\,/\det(T_n) = \det(C_n)\,/\prod_{i=0}^{n}(1-b_i^2)$ and $\det(C_n)$ is given in (A-5), we can get:

$$se^2\left(b_0^{MB}\right) = \frac{1}{n-1}\frac{\prod_{i=0}^{n}(1-b_i^2)}{\prod_{i=1}^{n}(1-b_i^2) + \sum_{i=1}^{n}(b_i^2 \prod_{\substack{k\neq i \\ k=0}}^{n}(1-b_k^2))} \quad \text{(A-10)}$$

$$\times \frac{\prod_{j=2}^{n}(1-b_j^2) + \sum_{j=2}^{n}(b_j^2 \prod_{\substack{k\neq j \\ k=1}}^{n}(1-b_k^2))}{\prod_{i=1}^{n}(1-b_i^2) + \sum_{i=1}^{n}(b_i^2 \prod_{\substack{k\neq i \\ k=0}}^{n}(1-b_k^2))}$$

Also, $se^2(b_0) = (1-b_0^2)/(n-1)$. Putting this together with (A-9) and (A-10), we can get:

$$\frac{b_0^{MB}}{se\left(b_0^{MB}\right)} = \frac{b_0}{se\left(b_0\right)} \times \sqrt{\frac{\prod_{i=1}^{n}(1-b_i^2)}{\prod_{j=2}^{n}(1-b_j^2) + \sum_{j=2}^{n}(b_j^2 \prod_{\substack{k\neq j \\ k=1}}^{n}(1-b_k^2))}}$$

It is obvious that the part in the "{ }" is less than one. Therefore, $b_0^{MB}/se(b_0^{MB}) < b_0\,/se(b_0\,)$. □

Acknowledgments

This research is sponsored in part by NSF IIS-0953662 and NSF MCB-1026710.

8. REFERENCES

[1] Horwitz, B. 2003. The Elusive Concept of Brain Connectivity, *Neuroimage* 19, 466-470.

[2] Azari, N., Rapoport, S. 1992. Patterns of Interregional Correlations of Cerebral Glucose Metabolic Rates in Patients with Dementia of the Alzheimer Type. *Neurodegeneration* 1: 101–111.

[3] Friston, K.J. 1994. Functional and Effective Connectivity in Neuroimaging: A Synthesis. *Human Brain Mapping* 2, 56-78.

[4] Alexander, G., Moeller, J. 1994. Application of the Scaled Subprofile Model to Functional Imaging in Neuropsychiatric Disorders: A Principal Component Approach to Modeling Brain Function in Disease. *Human Brain Mapping* 2, 79-94.

[5] Calhoun, V., Adali, T., Pearison, G. and Pekar, J. 2001. Spatial and Temporal Independent Component Analysis of Functional MRI Data Containing a Pair of Task-Related Waveforms. *HumanBrain Mapping* 13, 43-53.

[6] McIntosh, A., Bookstein, F., Haxby, J. and Grady, C. 1996. Spatial Pattern Analysis of Functional Brain Images Using Partial Least Squares. *Neuroimage* 3, 143-157.

[7] Chiang, J., Wang, Z., and McKeown, M.J. 2009. Sparse Multivariate Autoregressive (mAR)-based Partial Directed Coherence (PDC) for EEG Analysis. *Proceedings of the 2009 IEEE International Conference on Acoustics, Speech and Signal Processing*: 457-460.

[8] Huang, S., Li, J., Sun, L., Ye, J., Fleisher, A., Wu, T., Chen, K. and Reiman, E. 2010. Learning Brain Connectivity of Alzheimer's Disease by Sparse Inverse Covariance Estimation, *NeuroImage*, 50, 935-949.

[9] Hilgetag, C., Kotter, R., Stephan, K.E. and Sporns, O. 2002. *Computational Methods for the Analysis of Brain Connectivity*. In: Ascoli, G.A. (Ed.), Computational Neuroanatomy. Humana Press, Totowa, NJ.

[10] Bullmore, E., Horwitz, B., Honey, G., Brammer, M., Williams, S. and Sharma, T. 2000. How Good is Good Enough in Path Analysis of fMRI? *Neuroimage* 11, 289–301.

[11] Friston, K.J., Harrison, L. and Penny, W. 2003. Dynamic Causal Modeling. *Neuroimage* 19, 1273-1302.

[12] Lam, W. and Bacchus, F. 1994. Learning Bayesian Belief Networks: an Approach based on the MDL Principle, *Computational Intelligence* 10, p.269–293.

[13] Friedman, N., Nachman, I. and Pe'er, D. 1999. Learning Bayesian Network Structure from Massive Datasets: The "Sparse Candidate" Algorithm, *UAI 1999*.

[14] Schmidt, M., Niculescu-Mizil, A. and Murphy, K. 2007. A. Learning Graphical Model Structures using L1-Regularization Paths, *AAAI 2007*.

[15] Tibshirani, R. 1996. Regression Shrinkage and Selection via the Lasso, *Journal of Royal Statistical Society, Series B*, 58(1):267–288.

[16] Tsamardinos, I., Brown, L. and Aliferis, C. 2006. The Max-Min Hill-Climbing Bayesian Network Structure Learning Algorithm, *Machine Learning*, 65(1), 31-78.

[17] Margaritis, D. and Thrun, S. 1999. Bayesian Network induction via local neighborhoods. *NIPS* 1999.

[18] Pellet, J. and Elisseeff, A. 2008. Using Markov Blankets for Causal Structure Learning, *JMLR* 9, 1295-1342.

[19] Meek, C. 1995. Causal inference and causal explanation with background knowledge. *UAI 1995*.

[20] Estrada, E. and Naomichi, H. 2008. Communicability in Complex Networks. *Phys. Rev. E* 77 036111.

[21] Gill, P.E. *Class Notes for Math 271ABC: Numerical Optimization*. Department of Mathematics, UCSD.

[22] BERTSEKAS, D. 1999. *Nonlinear Programming, 2nd Edition*, Athena Scientific, Belmont.

[23] Fu, W. 1998. Penalized Regressions: the Bridge versus the Lasso, *Computational and Graphical Statistics*, 7 (3), 397-416.

[24] Friedman, J.; Hastie, T.; Hofling, H. and Tibshirani, R. 2007. Pathwise Coordinate Optimization, *The Annals of Applied Statistics* 2, 302-332.

[25] Aliferis, C., Tsamardinos, I. and Statnikov, A. 2003. HITON, a Novel Markov Blanket Algorithm for Optimal Variable Selection. *AMIA 2003*, 21-25.

[26] Tsamardinos, I. and Aliferis, C. 2003. Towards Principled Feature Selection: Relevancy, Filters and Wrappers. *AISTAT 2003*.

[27] http://www.cs.huji.ac.il/labs/compbio/Repository.

[28] Tzourio-Mazoyer, N., Landeau, B., Papathanassiou, D., Crivello, F., Etard, O., Delcroix, N., Mazoyer, B. and Joliot, M. 2002. Automated Anatomical Labeling of Activations in SPM using a Macroscopic Anatomical Parcellation of the MNI MRI Single-Subject Brain. *Neuroimage*,15:273-289.

[29] Supekar, K., Menon, V., Rubin, D., Musen, M and Grecius, M. 2008. Network Analysis of Intrinsic Functional Brain Connectivity in AD. *PLoS Comput Biol* 4(6) 1-11.

[30] Wang, K., Liang, M., Wang, L., Tian, L., Zhang, X., Li, K. and Jiang, T. 2007. Altered Functional Connectivity in Early AD: A Resting-State fMRI Study. *Human Brain Mapping* 28, 967-978.

[31] Gould, R., Arroyo, B. Brown, R., Owen, A., Bullmore, E and Howard, R. 2006. Brain Mechanisms of Successful Compensation during Learning in AD, *Neurology* 67 (6), 1011-1017.

[32] Stern, Y. 2006. Cognitive Reserve and Alzheimer Disease, *Alzheimer Disease Associated Disorder* 20, 69-74.

[33] Korb, K.B. and Nicholson, A.E. 2003. *Bayesian Artificial Intelligence*. Chapman & Hall/CRC, London, UK.

[34] Greicius, M., Srivastava, G., Reiss, A. and Menon, V. 2004. Default-mode Network Activity Distinguishes AD from Healthy Aging: Evidence from Functional MRI, *PNAS*. 101, 4637–4642.

[35] Alexander, G.E., Chen, K., Pietrini, P., Rapoport S. and Reiman, E. 2002. Longitudinal PET Evaluation of Cerebral Metabolic Decline in Dementia: A Potential Outcome Measure in AD Treatment Studies. *Am.J.Psychiatry* 159, 738-745.

[36] Braak, H., Braak, E., 1996. Evolution of the Neuropathology of Alzheimer's Disease. *Acta Neurol Scand Suppl* 165, 3-12.

[37] Braak, H., Braak, E., Bohl, J., 1993. Staging of Alzheimer-Related Cortical Destruction. *Eur Neurol* 33, 403-408.

[38] Hedden, T., Van Dijk, K. Becker, J., Mehta, A., Sperling, R., Johnson, K. and Buckner, R. 2009. Disruption of Functional Connectivity in Clinically Normal Older Adults Harboring Amyloid Burden. *J. Neurosci.* 29, 12686–12694.

[39] Andrews-Hanna, J., Snyder, A., Vincent, J., Lustig, C., Head, D., Raichle, M and Buckner, R. 2007. Disruption of Large-Scale Brain Systems in advanced Aging, *Neuron* 56, 924–935.

[40] Wu, X., Li, R. Fleisher, A.S., Reiman, E., Guan, X., Zhang, Y., Chen, K. and Yao, L. 2011. Altered Default Mode Network Connectivity in Alzheimer's Disease - A Resting Functional MRI and BN Study, *Human Brain Mapping*, in press.

[41] Ikonomovic, M., Klunk, W. Abrahamson, E. Mathis, C. Price, J., Tsopelas, N., Lopresti, B. et al. 2008. Post-mortem Correlates of in vivo PiB-PET Amyloid Imaging in a Typical Case of Alzheimer's Disease. *Brain* 131, 1630-1645.

[42] Klunk, W., Engler, H., Nordberg, A. et al. 2004. Imaging brain amyloid in Alzheimer's disease with Pittsburgh Compound-B. *Ann Neurol*. 55, 306-319.

[43] Reuter-Lorenz, P. and Mikels, J. 2005. A Split-Brain Model of Alzheimer's Disease? Behavioral Evidence for Comparable intra and interhemispheric Decline. *Neuropscyhologia* 43, 1307-1317.

[44] Lipton, A., Benavides, R., Hynan, L.S., Bonte, F.J., Harris, T.S., White, C.L. 3rd, Bigio, E.G. 2004. Lateralization on Neuroimaging does not Differentiate Frontotemporal Lobar Degeneration from Alzheimer's Disease. *Dement Geriatr Cogn Disord* 17(4), 324-327.

Classification of Functional Magnetic Resonance Imaging Data using Informative Pattern Features

Francisco Pereira and Matthew Botvinick
Princeton Neuroscience Institute and Psychology Department
Princeton University, Princeton NJ 08542
{fpereira,matthewb}@princeton.edu

ABSTRACT

The canonical technique for analyzing functional magnetic resonance imaging (fMRI) data, statistical parametric mapping, produces maps of brain locations that are more active during performance of a task than during a control condition. In recent years, there has been increasing awareness of the fact that there is information in the entire pattern of brain activation and not just in saliently active locations. Classifiers have been the tool of choice for capturing this information and used to make predictions ranging from what kind of object a subject is thinking about to what decision they will make. Such classifiers are usually trained on a selection of voxels from the 3D grid that makes up the activation pattern; often this means the best accuracy is obtained using few voxels, from all across the brain, and that different voxels will be chosen in different cross-validation folds, making the classifiers hard to interpret. The increasing commonality of datasets with tens to hundreds of classes makes this problem even more acute. In this paper we introduce a method for identifying informative subsets of adjacent voxels, corresponding to brain patches that distinguish subsets of classes. These patches can then be used to train classifiers for the distinctions they support and used as "pattern features" for a meta-classifier. We show that this method permits classification at a higher accuracy than that obtained with traditional voxel selection, and that the sets of voxels used are more reproducible across cross-validation folds than those identified with voxel selection, and lie in plausible brain locations.

Categories and Subject Descriptors

I.5 [**Computing Methodologies**]: Pattern Recognition

General Terms

Algorithms, Experimentation

Keywords

functional MRI, classification, feature synthesis, clustering, neuroscience

1. INTRODUCTION

Functional Magnetic Resonance Imaging (fMRI) is a technique used in psychological experiments to measure the blood oxygenation level throughout the brain, which is a proxy for neural activity; this measurement is called *brain activation*. The data resulting from such an experiment is a 3D grid of cells named *voxels* covering the brain (on the order of tens of thousands, usually), measured over time as tasks are performed and thus yielding one time series per voxel (collected every 1-2 seconds and yielding hundreds to thousands of points).

Traditionally, this has been used to contrast brain activation during a task of interest, e.g. reading words, with activation during a related control condition, e.g. reading nonsense words, with the goal of identifying brain locations where the two differ. The most common analysis technique for doing this – statistical parametric mapping [3] – tests each voxel individually by regressing its time series on a predicted time series determined by the task contrast of interest. This fit is scored and thresholded at a given statistical significance level to yield a brain image with clusters of voxels that respond differently to the two tasks (colloquially, these are the images that show parts of the brain that "light up"). Note also that, in tandem with this task-contrasting activation, there are many other processes taking place in the brain that will happen for both tasks : visual processing to read the words, attentional processing due to task demands, etc. The output of this process for a given experiment is a set of 3D coordinates of all the voxel clusters that appear reliably across all the subjects in a study. This result is easy to interpret, since there is a lot of information about what processes each brain area may be involved in. The coordinates are comparable across studies, and thus result reproduciblity is also an expectation.

In recent years, there has been increasing awareness of the fact that there is information in the entire pattern of brain activation and not just in saliently active locations. Classifiers have been the tool of choice for capturing this information and used to make predictions ranging from what stimulus a subject is seeing, what kind of object they are thinking about or what decision they will make [11] [13] [7]. Such classifiers are usually trained on a selection of voxels from the 3D grid that makes up the activation pattern; often this means the best accuracy is obtained using few voxels, from all across the brain, and that different voxels will be chosen in different cross-validation folds. Domain experts will generally raise two types of concern in face of this. The first is that the classifiers can be hard to interpret, e.g. does weight placed in a voxel in one area mean that that area is used? The second is the lack of reproducibility in face of the choice of different voxels in different folds. Even though there might be redundant information which would explain this, the results can still be perceived as dubious.

One approach to this problem is to try and regularize classifiers so that they include as many informative voxels as possible [1], thus identifying localizable clusters of voxels that may overlap across folds. A different approach is to cross-validate classifiers over small sections of the grid covering the brain, known as *searchlights* [10] [14]. This can be used to produce a map of the accuracy in the searchlight around each voxel, taking advantage of the pattern of activation across all the voxels contained in it. Such a map can then be thresholded to leave only locations where accuracy is significantly above chance.

A different issue that affects both of these approaches stems from the increasing commonality of datasets with tens to hundreds of tasks or stimuli. Knowing the location of a voxel does not suffice to interpret what it is doing, as it could be very different from stimulus to stimulus (rather than just active or not, as in the two task situation). It's also possible for neighbouring voxels to be doing different things relatex to the same task, thus barring any attempt to cluster them by their time series. Few brain locations will differentiate between all possible stimuli, say, at the spatial resolution of fMRI, and hence defining a searchlight size or shape is a trade-off between including voxels and making it harder to learn a classifier and excluding voxels and thus the number of distinctions that can be made.

Our goal is to attempt to address all of these issues by building a classifier that works in terms of *the presence or absence of patterns of activation across certain regions*, rather than the level of activation in individual voxels. The procedure we will describe involves building searchlights of various sizes and shapes in a data-driven manner, and learning pattern detectors operating over those searchlights. The outputs of these can then be used as the inputs to the classifier.

2. DATA AND METHODS

2.1 Data

As we described earlier, the grid covering the brain contains on the order of tens of thousands voxels, measured over time as tasks are performed, every 1-2 seconds, yielding hundreds to thousands of 3D images per experiment. During an experiment a given task is performed a certain number of times – trials – and often the images collected during one trial are collapsed or averaged together, giving us one 3D image that can be clearly labelled with what happened in that trial, e.g. what stimulus was being seen or what decision a subject made. Although the grid covers the entire head, only a fraction of its voxels contain cortex in a typical subject; hence we only consider these voxels as features.

A *searchlight* is a small section of the 3D grid [10], in our case a $27 = 3 \times 3 \times 3$ voxel cube. Analyses using searchlights generally entail computing a statistic [10] or cross-validating a classifier over the dataset containing just those voxels [14], and do so for the searchlights centered around each voxel in the brain. The intuition for this is that individual voxels are very noisy features, and an effect observed across a group of voxels is more trustworthy.

In the experiment performed to obtain our dataset [1] [12], subjects observed a word and a line drawing of an item, displayed on a screen for 3 seconds and followed by 8 seconds of a blank screen. The items named/depicted belonged to one of 12 categories: animals, body parts, buildings, building parts, clothing, furniture, insects, kitchen, man-made objects, tools, vegetables and vehicles. The task was to think about the item and its properties while it was displayed. There were 5 different exemplars of each of the 12 categories and 6 experimental epochs. In each epoch all 60 exemplars were shown in random order without repetition, and all epochs had the same exemplars. During an experiment the task repeated a total of 360 times, and a 3D image of the fMRI-measured brain activation acquired every second. Each example for classification purposes was the average image during a 4 second span while the subject was thinking about the item shown a few seconds earlier (a period which contains the peak of the signal during the trial); *the dataset thus contains 360 examples*, as many as trial tasks. The voxel size was $3 \times 3 \times 5$ mm, with the number of voxels being between 20000 and 21000 depending on which of the 9 subjects is considered.

2.2 Algorithm

This section describes the entire procedure that takes place given a training set and test set, which would appear in the context of cross-validation. In our experiments this is performed by using even or odd epochs as the two folds, with 180 examples in each. We do this – rather than a leave-one-epoch-out, for instance – because we are interested in estimating the reproducibility of models learned on two datasets from the same subject, and using training sets with overlapping examples would give an inflated estimate of this. The procedure has two parts, described separately for clarity.

2.2.1 Identifying informative voxel sets

The first goal is to identify different kinds of information present throughout the brain. Ultimately, we would like to understand how a certain semantic category is represented throughout the brain (e.g. do "Insects" and "Animals" share part of their representation because both kinds of things are alive?). Intuitively, there is information in a given location if at least two categories can be distinguished looking at their respective patterns of activation there (or otherwise the pattern of activation is noise or common to all categories). A natural starting point is to consider whether each pair of categories can be distinguished in each of the thousands of searchlights covering the brain, and to do this for all pairs.

The second goal is to assemble as large a region as possible containing one kind of information. Examining each small searchlight makes sense if we consider that, a priori, we don't know where the information is or how big a pattern of activation would have to be considered (with some exceptions, notably areas that respond to faces, houses or body parts see [8] for a review). That said, if the same categories are distinguishable in two adjacent searchlights (which overlap) then it is reasonable to assume that all their voxels put together would still be able to make the same distinctions.

[1]The data were kindly shared with us by Tom Mitchell and Marcel Just, from Carnegie Mellon University.

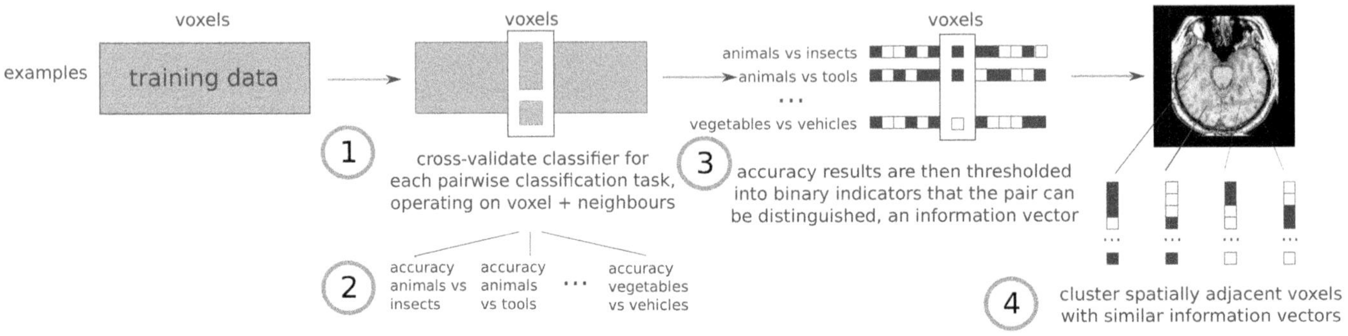

Figure 1: Identifying informative voxel sets

Doing this repeatedly allows us to find a kind of natural searchlight, not bound by shape or size assumptions, which we call an *informative voxel set.*

Figure 1 depicts the steps in the procedure to identify informative voxel sets. Within a training set, and for each pairwise classification task (e.g. animals-vs-insects, tools-vs-buildings, etc):

1. Cross-validate a classifier in the searchlight centered around each voxel and obtain an accuracy value.
2. Assign that value to the voxel at the center of the searchlight, yielding an accuracy brain image.
3. Transform the accuracy brain image into a p-value brain image (of obtaining accuracy as high or higher under the null hypothesis that the classes are not distinguishable, see Section 2.2.4 for details). Threshold this at 0.01 (uncorrected) to get a binary brain image with candidate locations for whether this class distinction can be made.

After these steps we have as many binary images as there are pairs of classes (66 pairs total). These can also be seen as a new dataset, with *#pairs* examples and *#voxels* features, where each voxel has a *#pairs information vector* summarizing what distinctions can be made inside its searchlight. We can now use agglomerative clustering of adjacent voxels with similar information vectors to build informative voxel sets (step 4 in Figure 1, see Section 2.2.4 for details of the clustering algorithm). The final result is an assignment of each voxel to a cluster, and an information vectors for each cluster. Note that there are typically only a few tens of clusters with 2 or more voxels.

We do not correct for multiple comparisons at the binary brain image stage because we want to retain as many reasonable, low p-value candidate voxels as possible. In our experience noise voxels that have low p-values don't have too many neighbours with low p-values as well, so they should be eliminated during the clustering stage.

2.2.2 *Constructing pattern features for classification*

The goal of the second part of the procedure is use the informative voxel sets to create features that correspond to indicators of a certain pattern being present in each set, and convert train and test examples into this new feature space. Given the informative sets identified in the training data in the first part, Figure 2 shows the steps taken:

1. For each informative set, train as many classifiers as there are class distinctions in the corresponding information vector (the classifier is trained on all the voxels in the informative set). Any classifier will do, as long as it can be trained to output the probability of one of the two classes given an example.
2. For each informative set, apply the classifiers learned to the voxels in the set across *all* examples of the training data. The output of a classifier over all the examples becomes a new *pattern feature*, taking values in the $[0, 1]$ range; extreme values mean that the classifier detects the pattern corresponding to one of the two classes. Each set gives rise to as many pattern features are there distinctions in its information vector. Note that each classifier will be applied to examples of classes other than the two used to train it; this is deliberate, as the classifier is being used solely as pattern detector.
3. The same feature construction process is done for the test set, applying the classifiers learned on the training set.

2.2.3 *Learn a classifier over pattern features*

After the construction of training and test pattern feature datasets, a classifier can be trained and tested, as shown in step 4 in Figure 2. There is no need to use the same kind of classifier as that used for pattern feature construction; in our case, we need only a classifier that is interpretable in the sense that we can ascertain the sensitivity of its predictions to each of the features.

2.2.4 *Further Details*

Classifiers on searchlights.

The classifier cross-validated in each searchlight, for each pair of classes, was LDA (Linear Discriminant Analys, [5]) with a shrinkage estimator of the covariance matrix that sets the shrinkage parameter automatically [16]. We used it because it could capture the covariance structure of the voxels inside a searchlight, given there were at most 27 voxels in it. The cross-validation was done inside the training set (3 epochs, containing 180 examples belonging to 12 classes), leaving one epoch out. There were thus 10 examples of each class for each pairwise discrimination. The resulting accuracy for each pairwise discrimination was converted into a p-value, by computing the probability of classifying that many

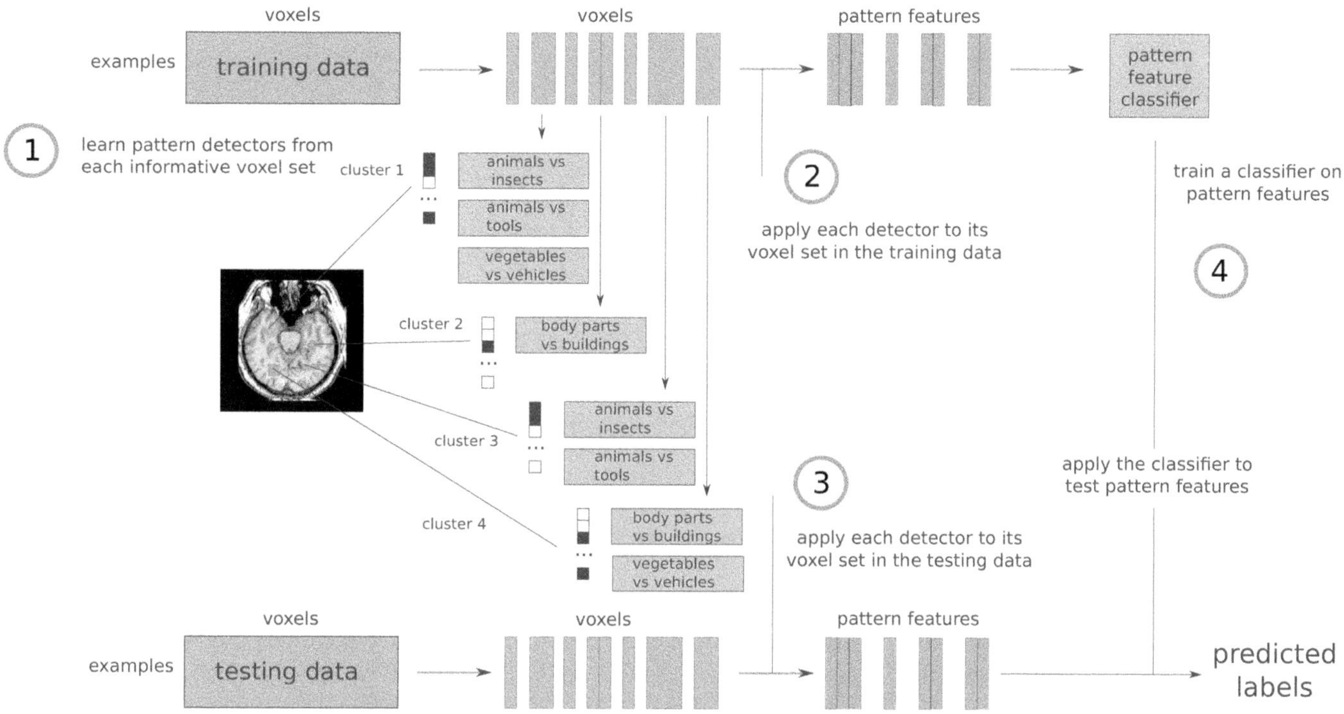

Figure 2: Constructing pattern features

or more examples correctly if the classifier were performing at chance level. Under the null hypothesis the number of correctly labelled examples has a binomial distribution with $p = 0.5$ and $n = \#examples$. For more details see [15].

Clustering of information vectors.

At the start of the agglomerative clustering process, each voxel is a cluster by itself and has an associated binary information vector with 66 entries corresponding to which pairs of classes can be distinguished in its surrounding searchlight. For each voxel we compute the similarity of its information vector with those of all its neighbours, which takes a few tens of seconds.

The similarity measure between two vectors $\mathbf{v}_i$ and $\mathbf{v}_j$ is obtained by computing the number of 1-entries present in both vectors, $\sum_{pairs} \texttt{AND}(\mathbf{v}_i, \mathbf{v}_j)$, the number of 1-entries present in only one of them, $\sum_{pairs} \texttt{XOR}(\mathbf{v}_i, \mathbf{v}_j)$ and then the measure

$$\text{similarity}(\mathbf{v}_i, \mathbf{v}_j) = \frac{\sum_{pairs} \texttt{AND}(\mathbf{v}_i, \mathbf{v}_j) - \frac{\sum_{pairs} \texttt{XOR}(\mathbf{v}_i, \mathbf{v}_j)}{2}}{\sum_{pairs} \texttt{AND}(\mathbf{v}_i, \mathbf{v}_j)}$$

The measure was chosen with several properties in mind. The first is that it peaks at 1 if the two vectors match exactly, and decreases – possibly into negative values – if there are mismatches; it will tolerate more mismatches if there are more distinctions being made. The second is that it will cluster sparse vectors as readily as dense vectors, as long as there are vew few mismatches. The number of entries present in only one is divided by 2 so that the differences do not get twice the weight of the similarities.

We then iterate the following steps:

1. find the two adjacent clusters (voxels, in the first iteration) whose information vectors are the most similar
2. merge the clusters, obtaining a new information vector that will represent the cluster (this is obtained by computing a soft-AND function of the initial information vectors of all voxels in both clusters, which makes an entry 1 if 90% of voxels have it)
3. update the similarity between that cluster and all its neigbours (a very small fraction of the number of similarities computed during initialization)

stopping when similarity drops below very conservative threshold for the measure (0.9, ensures that only voxels with almost identical profiles get merged). The soft-AND appears to produce reasonable results for the amount of noise present, in that it is robust to small differences (e.g. if a single voxel in a large cluster has 0 entry in which all others have a 1, then the cluster prototype should still have a 1 there, and vice versa). This runs in a few minutes for all our subjects.

Generation of pattern features from informative sets.

After clustering stops there are typically several thousand clusters left, given the high similarity threshold we use, hence we have to select which ones will give rise to pattern features. For each cluster, we know the number of voxels in it and also its information vector, which is an indication of how many class pairs can be distinguished there. Regardless of size, we use clusters that support at least 6 distinctions ($\frac{1}{2}$ of the number of classes), as we are interested in clusters that encode semantic representations and thus are likely to have patterns shared across several classes.

This is the main parameter of the algorithm. It could be set to a value we know we want a priori or be chosen by cross-validation inside the training set if accuracy is the main goal. We report the results for various settings to examine the sensitivity of results – both qualitatively and quantitatively – to this setting.

For each cluster selected we then train as many classifiers as there are distinctions in its information vector, and use their output when applied to train and test data to produce pattern features, as described earlier. We use a linear SVM (LIBSVM [2], $\lambda = 1$) for this purpose.

Classifier on pattern features.

The final step in the procedure is to train a classifier on the pattern features produced from the training set. This classifier can be chosen so as to produce a model relating pattern features to class labels in a manner is intuitive to a domain expert. One example might be a decision tree where the first decision would depend on the presence of a certain pattern in a particular voxel cluster. Presence would indicate the subject was thinking of a living thing, whereas a different pattern would be present for inanimate objects. Expanding further would essentially provide a representation for examples of a particular category composed of the presence and absence of a combination of patterns. For our experiments we use a linear SVM (LIBSVM [2], λ=1), as our primary interest is determining how the method performs as gauged by a number of quantitative measures.

3. EXPERIMENTS

3.1 Baseline

We will contrast experimental results obtained with our method with a baseline of classification using voxel selection. The scoring criterion for each voxel is the accuracy of a LDA searchlight classifier doing 12 way classification. The number of voxels to use was selected by nested cross-validation inside the training set [2]. The results are shown in the first line of Table 1. Whereas the accuracy is above chance (0.08) for all subjects, it is rather low for some. There are at least two factors responsible for this. The first is that some classes give rise to very similar patterns of activation (e.g. "buildings" and "building parts"), and hence examples in these classes are confusable (confusion matrices bear this out). The second factor is that subjects vary in their ability to stay focused on the task and avoid stray thoughts or remembering other parts of the experiment, hence examples may not belong to the class corresponding to the label or even any class at all. [12] also points out that accuracy is correlated with a subject's ability to stay still during the experiment.

3.2 Results

Table 1 shows the classification accuracy results obtained with our method, varying the threshold used for determining which clusters to draw pattern features from. Highlighted in bold is the threshold we would like to use, since we would like to have clusters that distinguish at least a few classes from others, but do not wish to overly restrict the choice to clusters that distinguish several. The results indicate that the threshold choice might not make much difference for any but the subjects where classification performance was worse (P5 and P9, where voxel selection did not improve results relative to using the whole brain).

The results also show that there is no loss of information in switching from using voxels to using pattern detectors as features. Depending on the subject and set of results, there are generally thousands of voxel clusters being used, *each of which gives rise to as many pattern detector features as there are class distinctions supported by that cluster.* Hence we typically have many thousands of features and yet the accuracy is comparable or better than that obtained with voxel selection; one possible explanation for this is the existence of many correlated detector features.

Note that classification happens in a 2-fold cross-validation procedure, and that that the total number of examples is 360. This is the reason why we opted not to include error bars on classification results or perform paired t-tests to compare pairs of them. Instead, we performed sign tests that look at whether our method outperformed the baseline voxel selection method for each subject, yielding a p-value < 0.01 at the various thresholds.

The vast majority of the clusters are just single voxels and their searchlights. Given this, it's legitimate to ask to what extent our method suffers from the lack of overlap in voxels used in the two halves of the dataset that tends to affect voxel selection. Table 2 shows the overlap, computed as $\frac{\#\text{voxels selected in both folds}}{\#\text{voxels selected in either fold}}$. In the baseline case the overlap is between selected voxel subsets, for our method it's between the voxels that belong to sets used to produce patern detectors. As expected, overlap decreases as we raise the threshold for using clusters to produce pattern detectors. The ranges of numbers of clusters used are given in the last column of the table, and the lower and upper limits correspond to the worst and best subject in terms of accuracy. Regardless of threshold choice, our procedure for identifying informative voxel sets using pairwise classification profiles seems to also provide more reliable voxel selection (considering the number of single searchlight clusters). The results suggest that, for this dataset, most searchlights support at least 9-12 category distinctions.

Finally, we can examine the locations of the clusters identified, as the dataset has been annotated with anatomical labels for each voxel [17]. For the various subjects, the overwhelming majority of clusters lie in various locations inside either occipital cortex (the various visual cortices, where visual representations are assembled, see for instance [9]) or temporal cortex (e.g. the various temporal gyri, the fusiform gyrus, the lingual gyrus, and other locations connected with representations of semantic information [6], [4], [12]).

4. CONCLUSIONS AND FURTHER WORK

We have introduced a method to synthesize features corresponding to the presence/absence of certain patterns of activation across small brain regions, identified in a data-driven way. Such features appear to preserve or enhance the information contained in the levels of activation in individual voxels. We conclude this from results showing that they permit classification at a higher accuracy than that obtained with a classifier working over voxels selected using a competitive method. Moreover, the sets of voxels used are more reproducible across cross-validation folds than those identified with voxel selection, and lie in plausible brain locations.

[2]Possible choices were 50, 100, 200, 400, 800, 1200, 1600, 2000, 4000, 8000, 16000 or all voxels.

We are continuing to develop this method, with the next stage being identifying correlated pattern feature detectors and use that to further condense small clusters into larger ones, if possible, or non-contiguous units. The ultimate goal is to be able to robustly identify the various types of information present in a pattern of brain activation, as defined by the ability to distinguish some subset of the classes from another subset. Given this, it will be feasible to try and related such distinctions to existing theories about how semantic information is represented across the brain. A second reason for doing this is to reduce the number of clusters considered in the final classifier. The desired outcome is one where the pattern of brain activation for a given class can be succintly described in terms of cluster subpatterns being present or absent, and classes related by which subpatterns they share.

5. REFERENCES

[1] M. K. Carroll, G. a. Cecchi, I. Rish, R. Garg, and a. R. Rao. Prediction and interpretation of distributed neural activity with sparse models. *NeuroImage*, 44(1):112–22, Jan. 2009.

[2] C. Chang and C. Lin. LIBSVM: a library for support vector machines. Technical report, 2001.

[3] K. J. Friston, J. Ashburner, S. J. Kiebel, T. E. Nichols, and W. D. Penny. *Statistical Parametric Mapping: The Analysis of Functional Brain Images.* Academic Press, 2006.

[4] S. J. Hanson, T. Matsuka, and J. V. Haxby. Combinatorial codes in ventral temporal lobe for object recognition: Haxby (2001) revisited: is there a "face" area? *NeuroImage*, 23(1):156–66, 2004.

[5] T. Hastie, R. Tibshirani, and J. Friedman. *The elements of statistical learning: data mining, inference and prediction.* Springer-Verlag, 2001.

[6] J. Haxby, M. Gobbini, M. Furey, A. Ishai, J. Schouten, and P. Pietrini. Distributed and overlapping representations of faces and objects in ventral temporal cortex. *Science*, 293(5539):2425, 2001.

[7] J. Haynes and G. Rees. Decoding mental states from brain activity in humans. *Nature Reviews Neuroscience*, 7(7):523–34, 2006.

[8] M. A. Just, V. L. Cherkassky, S. Aryal, and T. M. Mitchell. A neurosemantic theory of concrete noun representation based on the underlying brain codes. *PloS one*, 5(1):e8622, 2010.

[9] K. N. Kay, T. Naselaris, R. J. Prenger, and J. L. Gallant. Identifying natural images from human brain activity. *Nature*, 452(7185):352–5, 2008.

[10] N. Kriegeskorte, R. Goebel, and P. Bandettini. Information-based functional brain mapping. *Proceedings of the National Academy of Sciences*, 103(10):3863, 2006.

[11] T. M. Mitchell, R. Hutchinson, R. S. Niculescu, F. Pereira, X. Wang, M. Just, and S. Newman. Learning to Decode Cognitive States from Brain Images. *Machine Learning*, 57(1/2):145–175, Oct. 2004.

[12] T. M. Mitchell, S. V. Shinkareva, A. Carlson, K. Chang, V. L. Malave, R. A. Mason, and M. A. Just. Predicting human brain activity associated with the meanings of nouns. *Science (New York, N.Y.)*, 320(5880):1191–5, 2008.

[13] K. A. Norman, S. M. Polyn, G. J. Detre, and J. V. Haxby. Beyond mind-reading: multi-voxel pattern analysis of fMRI data. *Trends in cognitive sciences*, 10(9):424–30, 2006.

[14] F. Pereira and M. Botvinick. Information mapping with pattern classifiers: a comparative study. *NeuroImage (to appear)*, 2010.

[15] F. Pereira, T. M. Mitchell, and M. Botvinick. Machine learning classifiers and fMRI: a tutorial overview. *NeuroImage*, 45(1 Suppl):S199–209, Mar. 2009.

[16] J. Schäfer and K. Strimmer. A shrinkage approach to large-scale covariance matrix estimation and implications for functional genomics. *Statistical applications in genetics and molecular biology*, 4:Article32, Jan. 2005.

[17] N. Tzourio-Mazoyer, B. Landeau, D. Papathanassiou, F. Crivello, O. Etard, N. Delcroix, B. Mazoyer, and M. Joliot. Automated anatomical labeling of activations in SPM using a macroscopic anatomical parcellation of the MNI MRI single-subject brain. *NeuroImage*, 15(1):273–89, 2002.

Table 1: Classification accuracy for the 9 subjects. The p-value of the sign-test for the number of subjects where our method outperforms voxel selection is < 0.01 for the various thresholds.

	P1	P2	P3	P4	P5	P6	P7	P8	P9
baseline (using all voxels)	0.31	0.21	0.19	0.27	0.13	0.09	0.14	0.13	0.15
baseline (voxel selection)	0.53	0.33	0.24	0.34	0.14	0.16	0.21	0.20	0.15
#voxels selected (fold 1)	1200	400	200	1600	800	800	800	400	2000
#voxels selected (fold 2)	800	200	100	800	50	8000	100	1200	100
inclusion threshold 3	0.57	0.34	0.33	0.42	0.16	0.21	0.24	0.16	0.18
inclusion threshold 6	**0.57**	**0.34**	**0.33**	**0.42**	**0.17**	**0.28**	**0.23**	**0.20**	**0.17**
inclusion threshold 9	0.58	0.34	0.33	0.43	0.16	0.31	0.22	0.20	0.19
inclusion threshold 12	0.56	0.36	0.35	0.41	0.17	0.30	0.21	0.16	0.14

Table 2: Cross-fold overlap in voxels used for the 9 subjects.

	P1	P2	P3	P4	P5	P6	P7	P8	P9	#clusters used
baseline (voxel selection)	0.24	0.12	0.05	0.08	0.01	0.06	0.02	0.04	0.01	-
inclusion threshold 3	0.29	0.22	0.24	0.35	0.44	0.46	0.45	0.43	0.43	approx. 3000-8500
inclusion threshold 6	**0.29**	**0.22**	**0.24**	**0.35**	**0.17**	**0.20**	**0.19**	**0.17**	**0.16**	approx. 1000-4500
inclusion threshold 9	0.26	0.15	0.19	0.23	0.07	0.13	0.11	0.09	0.06	approx. 250-2500
inclusion threshold 12	0.30	0.15	0.19	0.21	0.05	0.13	0.12	0.05	0.03	approx. 50-1500

Clustering with Relative Constraints

Eric Yi Liu
liuyi@cs.unc.edu

Zhaojun Zhang
zzj@cs.unc.edu

Wei Wang
weiwang@cs.unc.edu

Department of Computer Science
University of North Carolina at Chapel Hill
Chapel Hill, NC 27599-3175 USA

ABSTRACT

Recent studies [26, 22] have suggested using relative distance comparisons as constraints to represent domain knowledge. A natural extension to relative comparisons is the combination of two comparisons defined on the same set of three instances. Constraints in this form, termed *Relative Constraints*, provide a unified knowledge representation for both partitional and hierarchical clusterings. But many key properties of *relative constraints* remain unknown.

In this paper, we answer the following important questions that enable the broader application of *relative constraints* in general clustering problems:

- **Feasibility**: Does there exist a clustering that satisfies a given set of *relative constraints*? (consistency of constraints)
- **Completeness**: Given a set of consistent *relative constraints*, how can one derive a complete clustering without running into dead-ends?
- **Informativeness**: How can one extract the most informative *relative constraints* from given knowledge sources?

We show that any hierarchical domain knowledge can be easily represented by *relative constraints*. We further present a hierarchical algorithm that finds a clustering satisfying all given constraints in polynomial time. Experiments showed that our algorithm achieves significantly higher accuracy than the existing metric learning approach based on relative comparisons.

Categories and Subject Descriptors

H.2.8 [**Database Management**]: Database Applications —*Data mining*; I.5.3 [**Pattern Recognition**]: Clustering— *Algorithms*

General Terms

Algorithms,Experimentation

Keywords

Relative constraints, constrained clustering, hierarchical clustering

1. INTRODUCTION

Clustering is traditionally considered an unsupervised learning task, but side information is available in many applications which may provide extra guidance to the clustering procedure. In recent years, many papers on semi-supervised clustering or constrained clustering investigated the effect of incorporating such domain knowledge into traditional unsupervised clustering algorithms (see for survey, [8]). In these studies, domain knowledge usually appears as constraints, typically in the form of pairwise relations [30, 31]. The must-link (ML) and cannot-link (CL) constraints indicate that two data instances must or cannot belong to the same cluster. Clustering with both types of pairwise constraints has been proven to have an intractable feasibility problem: determining the existence of any partition of data instances into a given number of clusters that satisfies all the constraints is **NP**-complete [14]. Therefore, an efficient clustering algorithm that satisfies all constraints for all datasets does not exist unless **P**=**NP** [14].

Recent studies [26, 22] have suggested using relative distance comparisons to represent domain knowledge: a is closer to b than to c, or equivalently $d(a,b) < d(a,c)$ where $d(...)$ is the distance function. The rationale behind relative comparisons is as follows: a domain expert usually has some general sense of closeness (similarity) among a subset of data instances. Such knowledge of closeness may be vague and only in a relative sense, that is, we can only determine, between two instances, which one is closer to a given third instance, but we cannot determine an absolute closeness measure. Several metric learning approaches [26, 22] were developed to redefine the distance function based on input relative comparisons.

A natural extension to relative comparisons is to consider, among three data instances, which two form the closest pair. Given three instances a, b, c, we use $ab|c$ to denote that (a, b) is the closest pair. This is equivalent to two relative comparisons defined on a, b, c: $d(a,b) < d(a,c)$ and $d(a,b) < d(b,c)$. We use the term "*relative constraint*" to denote constraints in this form. *Relative constraint* is a natural extension to relative comparison and can often be used in applications of relative comparisons. This is because, when a relative comparison is used, other comparisons regarding the same three instances are often available (or attainable at low cost).

The advantage of *relative constraints* over existing constraint models is that it unifies instance-level constraints with structure-level knowledge. Traditionally, instance-level constraints fit well into partitional clustering schemes (such as *K-Means*) while their use in hierarchical clustering is unintuitive[1]. Each *relative constraint*, as a natural extension to instance-level relative comparisons, represents a local hierarchy where the closest pair are merged before the more distant instance being merged with either instance of the pair (Fig.1(b)). This local hierarchical information can be naturally exploited in a hierarchical setting. Thus, *relative constraints* provide a unified knowledge representation for both partitional and hierarchical clustering frameworks. The use of *relative constraints* also greatly expands the possible sources of domain knowledge: besides existing sources for relative comparisons, *relative constraints* can be obtained from structural knowledge such as ontology and taxonomy databases.

In [5], the authors demonstrated the potential usefulness of *relative constraints* in hierarchical text clustering (under the term *Must-Link-Before constraints*). However, unlike pairwise constraints, many important properties of *relative constraints* remain unexplored and this hinders the application of *relative constraints*. In this paper, we answer the following important questions and thus facilitate the use of *relative constraints* in general clustering problems:

- **Feasibility**: Does there exist a clustering hierarchy (and partition) that satisfies a given set of relative constraints? (consistency of constraints) Unlike pairwise constraints, we show that the feasibility problem of *relative constraints* can be solved in polynomial time. This implies the possibility of a polynomial-time clustering algorithm that satisfies all given consistent *relative constraints*.

- **Completeness**: Given a set of consistent relative constraints, how can one derive a complete clustering hierarchy (and partition) without running into dead-ends? We found that, given a set of consistent constraints, a naive hierarchical approach which does not violate any constraint in any step can still run into dead-ends. This is the scenario where the hierarchy is developed incompletely because no pair of clusters could be further merged, though other merging sequences may produce a much more complete hierarchy. This suggests that the first algorithm (iHAC) presented in [5] does not guarantee a complete hierarchy if all constraints are enforced. A similar problem has been reported for pairwise constraints [15].

- **Informativeness**: How can one extract the most informative *relative constraints* from given knowledge sources? We show that any domain knowledge in the form of tree-like hierarchies can be conveniently decomposed into *relative constraints*. When the degree of any internal node is bounded by a constant, the $O(n)$ most informative constraints can be selected, which represent the complete hierarchical knowledge of n instances. This property is particularly useful in applications such as data analysis with constraints from ontology databases (Gene Ontology [2], DBLP [23], etc.). Other examples include the topic class hierarchy in [5].

[1]In [15], the authors discussed the problems with pairwise constrains in hierarchical clustering. For relative comparisons, existing work focuses on partitional clustering.

In this paper, we propose a hierarchical algorithm named *ReCon* that finds a complete hierarchy or k-partition satisfying all given constraints whenever possible. We validated our model and algorithm with real-world datasets. Experiments with randomly generated constraints showed that our algorithm significantly outperforms the existing metric learning approach based on relative comparisons. With informative constraints that are selected systematically from existing hierarchical knowledge, the existing metric learning approach does not achieve noticeable performance gains. Our algorithm *ReCon*, on the contrary, exhibits substantial accuracy improvements.

2. RELATED WORK

2.1 Pairwise Constraints

The pairwise must-link and cannot-link constraints were first introduced in [30, 31]. Since then, many studies have been done to exploit the pairwise constraints in clustering problems. Existing methods generally fall into two categories: directly enforcing constraints in modified clustering algorithms or learning a new metric from constraints. In the first category, Wagstaff et al. proposed a variant of the widely used K-Means algorithm that can enforce constraints in cluster assignments at each iteration [31]. In [6], Basu et al. used constraints to initialize the K-Means algorithm instead of random seeding. A density-based method that incorporates pairwise constraints is given in [25]. Recently, an agglomerative hierarchical approach is proposed in [15] by Davidson and Ravi. In the second category, pairwise constraints are used in defining optimization criteria for a desired metric. Klein et al. [21] used constraints to adjust Euclidean distance by shortest-path algorithm. Xing and collaborators [32] attempted to learn Mahalanobis distance using convex optimization. The HMRF-KMeans algorithm proposed in [7] combines both constraint satisfaction and metric learning into a single probabilistic framework. MPCK-Means [9] learns an individual metric for each cluster and allows violation of constraints by imposing penalties.

2.2 Relative Distance Comparisons and Relative Constraints

Existing studies on relative comparisons focus on metric learning. In [26], an SVM-like approach is proposed to learn a weighted distance function from relative comparisons. Kumar et al. [22] proposed to learn an SVaD measure from relative comparisons. Note that existing work on relative comparisons can be used to solve clustering problems with *relative constraints* (since each relative constraint is equivalent to two relative comparisons). In [4, 5], *Relative constraints* have been investigated under the term *Must-Link-Before constraints* with a focus on text clustering. Its important properties such as feasibility and informativeness however remain largely unknown.

3. RELATIVE CONSTRAINTS

3.1 Definition of Relative Constraints

We consider, among three data instances, which two form the closest pair. Given three data instances a, b, c, we write $ab|c$ if (a, b) is the closest pair. In other words, $ab|c$ represents $d(a,b) < d(a,c)$ and $d(a,b) < d(b,c)$ where $d(...)$ is the distance function. Hence, each *relative constraint* equals two relative comparisons defined on the same set of three instances.

The *relative constraints* also unambiguously represent the knowledge of conditional cluster assignments: given $ab|c$, if a, c or b, c belong to the same cluster, then a, b, c must all belong to the same cluster. Note that the three involved instances can be arbitrarily chosen from the whole set of data instances. A constraint in the conditional form does not prevent three involved instances from being selected from the same cluster or three different clusters. In addition, the closest pair is unordered, i.e., $ab|c$ equals $ba|c$.

3.2 Relative Constraints as Rooted Triplets

The relative closeness of data instances can be represented by a rooted and unordered tree or hierarchy. In the hierarchy, each leaf represents a data instance and each internal node represents a group of instances that are similar at certain level. Instances with higher similarity are grouped at a lower level, before instances that are more distant merge into bigger groups. In this paper, we use the terms "tree" and "hierarchy" interchangeably to refer to such structure.

The local hierarchy of each *relative constraint* $ab|c$ is a rooted binary tree with three leaves as shown in Fig.1(b). In this tree, the closest pair a, b are merged first before they are merged with c. A rooted binary tree with three leaves is called a *rooted triplet*. *Rooted triplet* is an important concept first introduced in modeling phylogenies (which represent evolutionary relatedness among organisms). Representing *relative constraints* using *rooted triplets* enables us to leverage the theories and algorithms developed in phylogenetic tree studies.

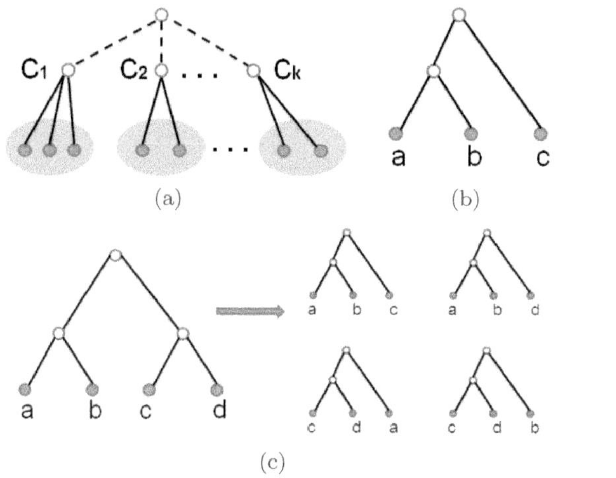

Figure 1: (a) The hierarchical representation of non-hierarchically labeled classes or partitional clustering (b) The rooted triplet representing the local hierarchy of constraint $ab|c$ (c) An exemplar hierarchy of four data instances can be decomposed into a set of rooted triplets

3.2.1 Inducing Rooted Triplets From Bigger Hierarchy

Here we introduce the "induce" operation for *rooted triplets*. To induce a *rooted triplet* from a bigger hierarchy, we first find the minimum subtree connecting the three involved instances. Then we contract edges whose both end-nodes are of degree two. Consider the example in Fig.1(c). We can induce the following *rooted triplets*: $ab|c$, $ab|d$, $cd|a$, $cd|b$ from the given hierarchy. If the hierarchy is not binary, it is possible to induce a subtree in which all three instances are direct children of the root. In this case, we say the three instances are unconstrained since their relative closeness is unspecified.

4. INCORPORATING RELATIVE CONSTRAINTS IN CLUSTERING

Most of existing clustering algorithms fall into two types: partitional clustering generates a k-partition of data where k is either given or automatically found; hierarchical algorithms create a global hierarchy or dendrogram from which a k-partition can be obtained. Recall that a relative constraint can be viewed as a conditional cluster assignment or a *rooted triplet*. We now define the satisfaction of relative constraints for both hierarchy and k-partition of data instances.

Definition 4.1 A hierarchy of data instances satisfies all constraints if all the corresponding *rooted triplets* can be induced from the hierarchy. If there exists at least one hierarchy that satisfies all constraints, we say that the constraints are consistent.

Definition 4.2 A k-partition satisfies all constraints if all the equivalent conditional cluster assignments are satisfied. i.e., for each constraint in the form of $ab|c$, if a, c or b, c belong to the same cluster, then a, b, c must all belong to the same cluster.

In this section, we discuss how to incorporate *relative constraints* into a hierarchical clustering framework. Our algorithm generates a hierarchy of data instances that satisfies all constraints as long as the given constraints are consistent. Given any k, a k-partition that satisfies all the constraints can then be generated by cutting the resulting hierarchy at the appropriate level.

4.1 Feasibility Under Relative Constraints

We first examine the feasibility problem for hierarchical clustering under *relative constraints*. To be more specific, given a set of data instances, does there exist a clustering hierarchy of instances that satisfies all given *relative constraints*?

4.1.1 Existence of Hierarchy

Since *relative constraints* can be represented by *rooted triplets*, the above problem is equivalent to the problem of determining the existence of a supertree: given a set of *rooted triplets*, is there a tree from which all *rooted triplets* can be induced? We denote the set of data instances by D. The set of constraints is denoted by C. The set of instances involved in constraints is denoted by D_C. Obviously, we only need to determine whether there is a supertree T for D_C that satisfies all *relative constraints* in C. Data instances not involved in any constraints can be arbitrarily added as leaves in T without violating any constraints.

The existence problem of supertree can be solved by the *OneTree* algorithm initially given in [1]. Several variants of *OneTree* algorithm have been proposed [24, 10]. Below is a simplified version of the *OneTree* algorithm presented in [24]. The algorithm operates by transforming all constraints into a graph representation: a vertex is created for each instance; an edge connects two vertices a, b if there is any constraint of the form $ab|*$. It then tests the connectivity of the graph: if the graph is disconnected, then, for each connected component, it finds the subset of instances in the component and the subset of constraints defined only on these instances. These subsets of instances and constraints are then tested by a recursive call of the algorithm. This recursive procedure is based on the property that a set of constraints is consistent if and only if any sub-graph defined on more than two instances is disconnected. The algorithm returns a hierarchy that satisfies all constraints if any such hierarchy exists. The complexity of the algorithm is $O(|D_C| \times |C|)$. The algorithm does not exhaust all possible hierarchies that satisfy C.

1. **Function** ***OneTree***(C,D)
2. Input: set $C = \{r_1, ..., r_m\}$ of relative constraints,
3. set $D = \{d_1, ..., d_n\}$ of data instances
4. Output: a hierarchy T of D that satisfies C
5. If $|D| = 1$, return a single node labelled by d_1
6. If $|D| = 2$, return a tree with two leaves d_1 and d_2
7. Create sets $D_i = \{d_i\}$, $i = 1..n$
8. For each constraint $(ab|c) \in C$, merge the sets D_i, D_j containing a, b.
9. If there is only one set left, return fail
10. For each remaining set D_i do
11. Let C_i be the set of constraints of which all three instances are in D_i
12. If *OneTree*(C_i,D_i) returns a tree then call it T_i else return fail
13. Construct a tree T by connecting the roots of all T_i to a new root
14. Return T

4.1.2 *k-partition by Cutting Hierarchy*

Given any clustering hierarchy satisfying all constraints, we can always cut the hierarchy to form a k-partition. The cutting starts from the root level and goes down following the recursion levels in *OneTree* algorithm. The resulting k-partition always satisfies all constraints. Due to its simplicity, we omit the proof here.

4.2 A Clustering Algorithm That Generates A Complete Hierarchy

The above *OneTree* algorithm only ensures the satisfaction of constraints. It does not consider instance attributes or incorporate any metric function in generating hierarchy. The hierarchy returned is determined only by the graph representation of constraints. Hence, the *OneTree* algorithm cannot be used as a hierarchical clustering algorithm.

We now present our modified hierarchical agglomerative algorithm that incorporates *relative constraints* in the clustering procedure. Given a set of n instances, the traditional agglomerative algorithm starts with n clusters where each cluster contains only one instance. At each round, two closest clusters are merged. The algorithm completes when there is only one cluster left. Now with *relative constraints* incorporated, we want to ensure that: (1) we do not violate any constraint (2) we generate a complete hierarchy as long as the constraints are consistent.

The first condition can be easily satisfied: at each round, for any constraints in the form of $ab|c$, if a, b do not belong to the same cluster, we do not merge the clusters containing b, c or a, c. The satisfaction of the second condition is however obscure: if we do not violate any constraint in each round, do we always get a complete hierarchy? The answer is unfortunately no. It is possible that, though given constraints are not violated at any previous round, the hierarchical clustering algorithm runs into a dead-end where any further merging violates some given constraint. A simple example consists of four data instances a, b, c, d and two constraints $ab|c$, $cd|a$. There exists a complete hierarchy as in Fig.1(c). If b, d are merged according to some metric in the first round, there is no possible merging move in the second round.

In the above example, the constraint $ab|d$ can actually be inferred from the two given constraints. With $ab|d$ inferred, merging b, d in the first round becomes an invalid choice. One may think of pre-computing all inferable constraints to determine the eligible merging choices at each round. The set of all constraints that can be inferred is called the *closure* of the given constraints. Unlike pairwise constraints, the closure of *relative constraints* cannot be trivially computed. To be more specific, we cannot repeatedly apply low-order inference rules to derive the complete closure. This is due to the existence of irreducible inference rules for *rooted triplets* [10]: for any $n > 3$, there are inference rules of order n that cannot be derived from rules involving fewer than n *rooted triplets*. The property prevents us from quickly pre-computing all eligible merging steps at each round.

To avoid running into dead-ends, we resort back to the *OneTree* algorithm which tests the existence of any complete hierarchy. At each round, before merging two clusters, we test whether there still exists a solution if the two are merged. A merging step is compatible with constraints only if it does not change the existence of a complete solution. Our complete algorithm *ReCon* is presented below.

1. **Algorithm** ***ReCon***
2. Input: set $C = \{r_1, ..., r_m\}$ of relative constraints,
3. set $D = \{d_1, ..., d_n\}$ of data instances
4. If *OneTree*(C,D_C) returns fail then return fail
5. Create clusters $CL_i = \{d_i\}$, $i = 1..n$
6. While number_of_clusters > 1 do
7. Let $S = \{i : CL_i \ remains\}$
8. Find the closest pair of clusters CL_i, CL_j s.t.
9. Neither $(i * |j)$ or $(j * |i)$ is in C
10. and
11. *TestCompatibility*(C, S, i, j) is true
12. Merge CL_i, CL_j into CL_i
13. *UpdateConstraints*$(\ i, j\ )$

1. **Function** ***UpdateConstraints***(i,j)
2. Input: i, j are the two clusters merged
3. For each constraint $(ab|c) \in C$ do
4. If any of a, b, c is equal to j then update it to be i
5. If $a = b$ then remove this constraint

1. **Function** ***TestCompatibility***(C',S,i,j)
2. Input: set C' of relative constraints,
3. set S of cluster indices
4. i, j are the two clusters to merge
5. Output: *true* if merging i, j is compatible with C'
6. If $|S| = 2$, return true
7. Create sets $S_e = \{e\}$ for each $e \in S$
8. Merge S_i and S_j
9. For each constraint $(ab|c) \in C'$ do
10. Merge the sets S_e, S_f containing a, b.
11. If there is only one set left then return false
12. Let S_e be the set containing i, j

13. Let C_e be the set of constraints of which all three instances are in S_e
14. Return *TestCompatibility*(C_e,S_e,i,j)

The *TestCompatibility* function is modified from the *OneTree* algorithm to allow more efficient tests. Note that the worst-case complexity of our *TestCompatibility* function is the same as that of *OneTree* ($O(|D_C| \times |C|)$). But generally *TestCompatibility* can finish much faster (at each level, it only examines one connected component of the graph representation of constraints). The actual complexity of our algorithm depends on the specific choice of merging strategy and other implementation choices. In this paper, we adopt the centroid-based hierarchical clustering based on a priority queue implementation. The overall worst-case complexity of our algorithm is $O(|D|^2 log|D| + |D| \times |D_C|^3 \times |C|)$. This is based on the extreme assumption that any pair of clusters that are both involved in constraints always have shorter distance measures (than that of any other pairs). In real applications, this worst-case scenario is very unlikely to happen and our algorithm can efficiently handle large datasets with thousands of constraints(Sec.5.3). If more efficient component tracking techniques are adopted [17, 18], the worst-case complexities of *TestCompatibility* and the whole algorithm can be further reduced to $O(|D_C| log^2|C|)$ [19] and $O(|D|^2 log|D| + |D| \times |D_C|^3 log^2|C|)$, respectively.

4.2.1 Handling Outliers in Getting k-partitions

Although the resulting binary-hierarchy embeds all given constraints, it does not guarantees a perfect k-cutting in the presence of outliers. The outliers do not merge with their expected clusters before real clusters get merged. This can potentially be solved by using more appropriate metric functions and placing constraints on the branch size. In this work, we adopt a simple branch-size threshold in cutting the hierarchy: branches with size smaller than a given threshold are considered outliers and are first ignored in the k-cutting process. After k clusters are obtained, outlier branchs are merged with their nearest clusters.

4.3 Informative Constraints from Hierarchical Knowledge

As discussed in previous sections, the use of *relative constraints* greatly expands the possible sources of knowledge. Besides existing instance-level sources for relative comparisons (such as manually labeled classes and relations), *relative constraints* as local hierarchies can be extracted from structural knowledge. Examples of such structural knowledge include ontology/taxonomy databases such as Gene Ontology [2] and DBLP [23]. Other examples include the topic class hierarchy in [5]. These knowledge resources are often in the form of tree-like hierarchies defined on a partially overlapping set of data instances. (Non-hierarchically labeled classes can also be represented by a two-level hierarchy by adding a dummy root (Fig.1(a)).) In this section, we discuss how to extract the most informative constraints from a given hierarchical knowledge.

Traditionally, constraints are generated at the instance level. Given a hierarchy of instances or a set of labeled instances, one can enumerate all possible triple-wise combinations and induce the corresponding relative constraints. This straightforward approach leads to an extraordinarily large constraint space. If the given hierarchical knowledge involves n data instances of interests, one would get $O(n^3)$ constraints. A randomly sampled subset of constraints could contain limited information due to redundancy in information. In [5], the authors noted this problem and tried to address this by first grouping similar instances before generating constraints. However, a significant amount of information can be lost in this preprocessing step. Also, parameters and metrics need to be defined for specific tasks.

Since each *relative constraint* can be represented by a *rooted triplet*, we can leverage the existing theories and algorithms in phylogenetic tree studies. It is possible to use a much smaller set of informative constraints to represent the whole set of constraints (equivalently, the whole set can be inferred from the smaller subset). For binary hierarchies, it can be shown that $n-2$ constraints are enough to capture all information. A linear-time algorithm for finding the minimum set of *rooted triplets* from a binary hierarchy is given in [13]. The most informative *relative constraints* can thus be generated accordingly. For general hierarchies, the polynomial-time algorithm given in [24] can be easily modified to decompose a general hierarchy into $O(n)$ constraints if the degree of all internal nodes are bounded. Due to space limitations, we omit the details of the decomposition algorithm here.

5. EXPERIMENTS

In this section, we show the effect of our model and algorithm on datasets of various sizes from the UCI repository [3]. Note that our algorithm does not assume any specific metric function or merging strategy. For the evaluations presented, we explored both Euclidean distance and a learned metric based on [26]. In our implementation, we used the centroid-based hierarchical clustering. Any other merging strategies and distance measures can be incorporated as well (e.g., the inverse of sample covariance when the data is assumed to be Gaussian). The clustering accuracies in experiments are reported in the pairwise F-measure:

$$Precision = \frac{\#PairsCorrectlyPredictedInSameCluster}{\#TotalPairsPredictedInSameCluster}$$

$$Recall = \frac{\#PairsCorrectlyPredictedInSameCluster}{\#TotalPairsInSameCluster}$$

$$F\text{-}Measure = \frac{2 \times Precision \times Recall}{Precision + Recall}$$

We give results for six real-world datasets from the UCI repository [3]. Table 1 lists the number of instances, dimensions and clusters of these datasets. The *Digits-389* and *Letters-IJLT* datasets are subsets from the original *Digits* and *Letters* handwritten character recognition datasets. The two subsets contain the character classes that are considered difficult to distinguish. We evaluated our algorithm with both randomly selected constraints and informative constraints derived from a knowledge hierarchy.

Dataset	#instances	#dimensions	#clusters
Iris	150	4	3
Wine	178	13	3
Ionosphere	351	34	2
Transfusion	748	5	2
Digits-389	3165	16	3
Letters-IJLT	3059	16	4

Table 1: The datasets used in the experiments

We compared our method with an existing metric learning method [26][2]. Each relative constraint can be viewed as two relative distance comparisons. A new metric function was learned from these comparisons by optimizing an SVM-like quadratic function. We set the regularization parameter C to be 1 and $A = I$ following the examples in [26]. We then solved the optimization problem using SVM-light [20]. We refer to the learned metric as "*SVM-Metric*". For each dataset, we compared the following clustering schemes:

- *ReCon + Euclidean Metric*
- *ReCon + SVM-Metric*
- *K-Means + SVM-Metric* (use learned metric alone)

We also included two unsupervised clustering schemes as baselines:

- *Hierarchical + Euclidean Metric*
- *K-Means + Euclidean Metric*

The first unsupervised approach serves as the baseline for *ReCon*. The second provides baseline for *K-Means + SVM-Metric*.

5.1 Randomly Sampled Constraints

In our experiments with randomly sampled constraints, the number of constraints ranges from 0 to $|D|$ where $|D|$ is the number of data instances. For these non-hierarchical datasets with known cluster labels, we do not know the true metric that separates the clusters (or if such metric exists). Thus, we randomly sampled constraints in the form of $ab|c$ where a, b are from the same cluster and c is from a different cluster. Our algorithm does not take this as must-link or cannot-link information and only consider this as a, b being closer than b, c and a, c. For each setting, we took the average of 50 runs of different random constraints. Fig.2 shows the accuracies measured with the five clustering schemes.

In most experiments, incorporating *SVM-Metric* in *K-Means* performed significantly better than its baseline (*K-Means + Euclidean Metric*). This proves that the learned *SVM-Metric* is very useful in representing domain knowledge. We notice that the accuracy curves of *K-Means + SVM-Metric* are relatively flat. This indicates that using *SVM-Metric* alone can get "saturated" soon and the performance does not improve with increasing numbers of constraints fed. We conjecture that this is due to its SVM-like optimization: the few support vectors representing the metric remained mostly unchanged unless there was a big change in the distribution of training data.

Our algorithm *ReCon*, incorporating either of the metrics, outperformed *K-Means + SVM-Metric* by large margins in all but one experiments. The only exception is *Iris*. This is probably because, being a relatively clean dataset, *Iris* can be well described by a metric defined on few dimensions. The advantage of our method on the remaining five datasets was generally obvious with a small amount of constraints regardless of the baseline accuracies (without constraints). It is interesting that *ReCon + Euclidean Metric* generally performed better than *ReCon + SVM-Metric*. We speculate that this is because the learned *SVM-metric* was optimized from a boundary supported by major data distribution but violating some of the constraints fed. Thus, when *ReCon* tried to enforce all given constraints, it led to conflicts and lowered the overall clustering performance.

We also notice that, despite the significant average improvement, the clustering quality in individual runs could vary considerably when applying different sets of randomly sampled relative constraints. An example is shown in Fig.3 where the min, max and average accuracies of *ReCon + Euclidean Metric* on *Digits-389* and *Letters-IJLT* are included. Similar phenomena have been observed in applying pairwise constraints using various existing approaches [16]. Note that the variance of using *SVM-Metric* alone is lower due to its "saturation" behavior. But this is at the cost of having much lower overall accuracy.

In real-world problems, it is thus important to quantify the potential benefit of given relative constraints. Davidson et al. proposed two measures, *informativeness and coherence*, to capture the potential benefit brought by pairwise constraints to a given algorithm/metric [29]. The measures are intuitive and easy to compute. But they are still insufficient in explaining the complicated behavior of constrained clustering. For example, the information redundancy of different constraints is not modeled and the coherence model in metric space is oversimplified. The situation gets more complicated with *relative constraints* where triple-wise relations are used. In the next section, we show that the benefit of constraints can be maximized when informative constraints are extracted from existing hierarchical knowledge.

5.2 Informative Constraints from a Given Hierarchy

The above experiments are based on randomly generated constraints of which the informativeness is difficult to quantify. But, as discussed in Sec.4.3, existing domain knowledge in the form of hierarchy can be effectively decomposed into a small set of constraints. Thus, given a hierarchy involving n instances, we can always find the most informative constraints that capture all topological information in the hierarchy.

To demonstrate the effectiveness of this property, we consider the two-level hierarchy formed using true cluster labels (Fig.1(a)). We used a simple method to generate $(k-1) \times |D|$ constraints that represents the two-level hierarchy. The number of clusters, k, in our experiment is between 2 and 4. Other general hierarchies can be decomposed based on the method in [24] as discussed in Sec.4.3.

Function ***GenerateConstraints***(C, D)
Input: a set of clusters CL_1 ... CL_k
each cluster $CL_i = \{d_1^i, ..., d_n^i\}$ where d_j^i is a data instance in this cluster
Output: set C of relative constraints
For each cluster CL_i
For each data instance d_j^i in CL_i
For each cluster CL_l other than CL_i
Add $(d_1^i d_j^i | d_1^l)$ into C
Return C

Fig.4 shows the results of applying these informative constraints. As in previous experiments, each accuracy curve is an average of multiple runs. When applying random subsets of the selected constraints, we observed stable and consistent improvements with *ReCon*. Similar to our previous experiments, *ReCon* showed significant improvements over

[2]We did not include [5] in comparison due to its focus on text clustering.

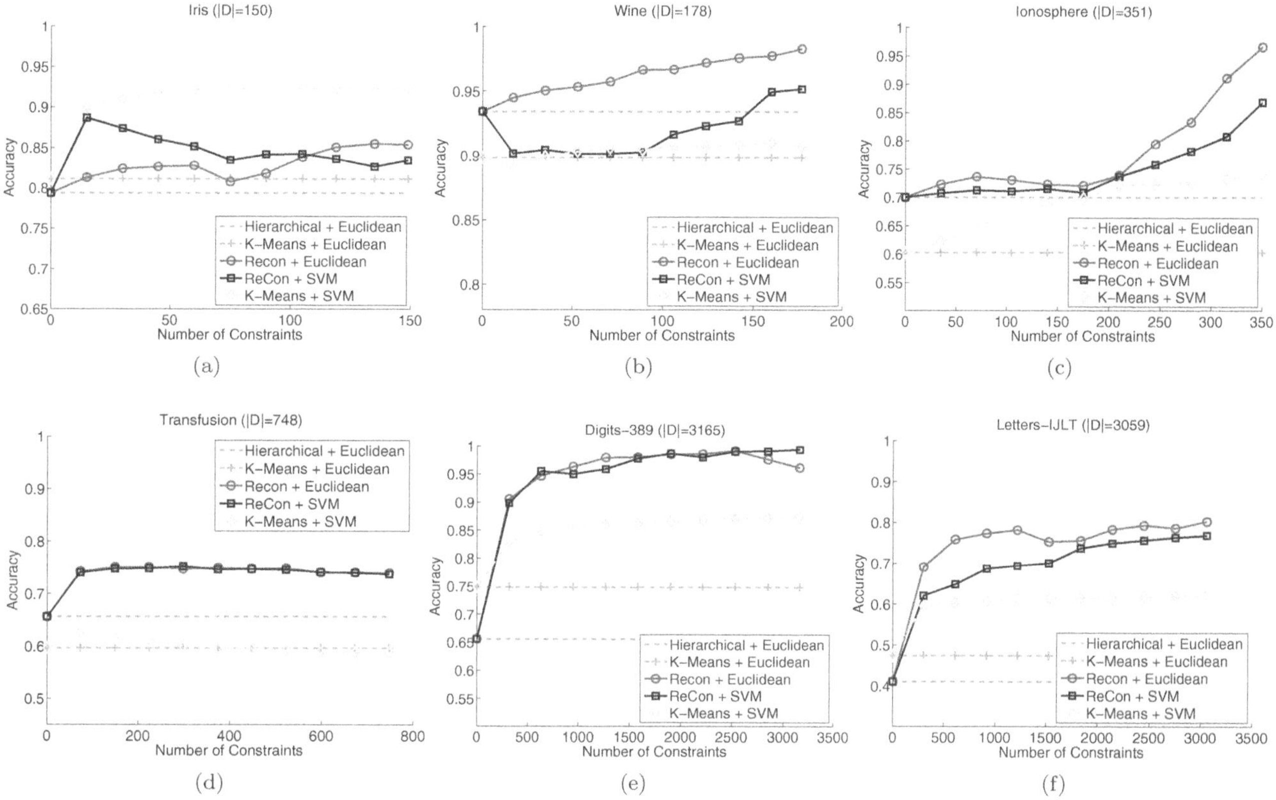

Figure 2: The clustering accuracy for 6 UCI datasets with randomly generated relative constraints. For each dataset, the number of constraints ranges from 0 to the number of instances in the dataset.

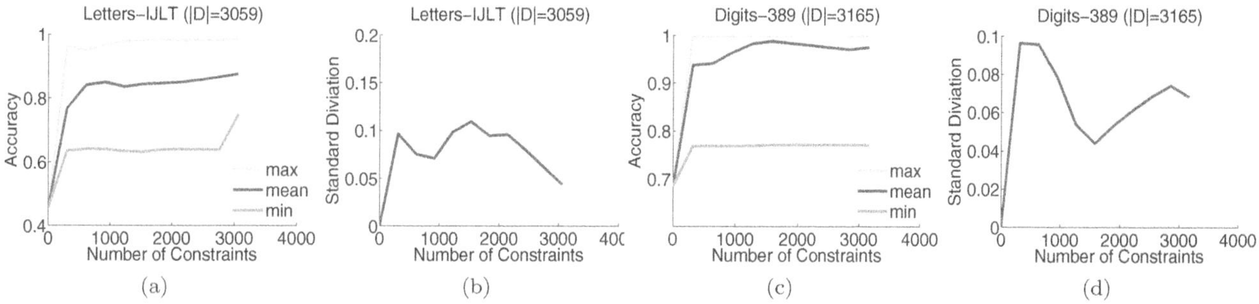

Figure 3: The variance of accuracy of 50 different runs of *Letters-IJLT* and *Digits-389*. Randomly generated constraints are applied with *ReCon + Euclidean Metric* in each run: (a) Min, max and average accuracy of *Letters-IJLT* (b) Standard deviation of *Letters-IJLT* (c) Min, max and average accuracy of *Digits-389* (d) Standard deviation of *Digits-389*

using *SVM-Metric* alone in all experiments (including *Iris* this time). With all the constraints incorporated, *ReCon* always created a binary-hierarchy that embeds the original two-level hierarchy. In the resulting k-partition, we achieved 100% accuracy on all six datasets. In comparing with using randomly generated constraints of the same amount, *ReCon* attained significantly higher accuracy with informative constraints. The variance of the performance gain was also much smaller which indicates the steady informativeness of these constraints. The effect of informative constraints is however uncertain with the metric learning approach: *K-Means + SVM-Metric* tended to reach its "saturation" with fewer constraints in *Iris* and *Digits-389*. It also achieved higher accuracy in *Transfusion*. But the overall accuracy gain in all experiments was very limited and the clustering results became worse in *Ionosphere*.

In real-world problems, the true class labels or cluster assignments are apparently unavailable. But, if there exists reliable hierarchical knowledge of a subset of instances, we demonstrate a promising way to select the most informative relative constraints. Such informative set of constraints can be fully utilized in our algorithm while the metric learning approach does not benefit from this informativeness.

5.3 Running Time

Fig.5(a) and Fig.5(b) show the running time of *ReCon + Euclidean Metric* on *Letters-IJLT* and *Digits-389*. Both datasets have more than 3,000 instances and the number

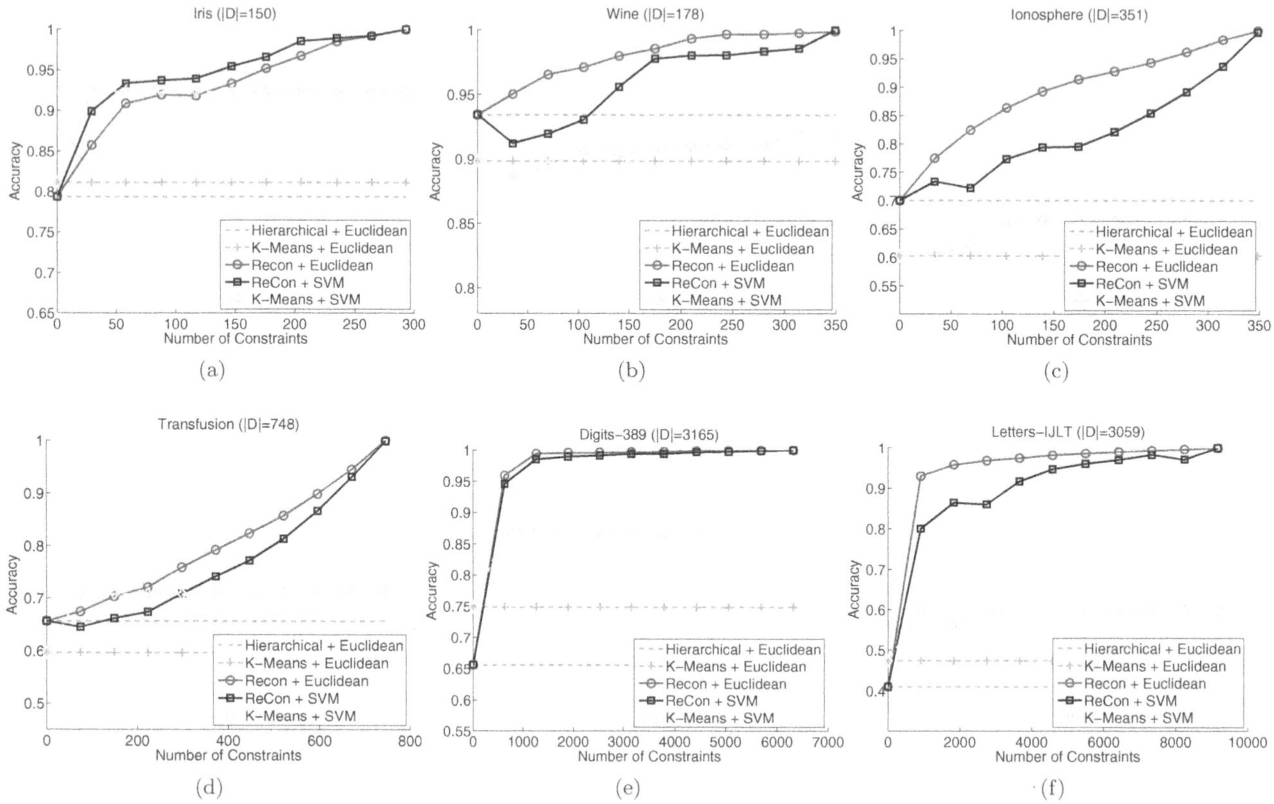

Figure 4: The clustering accuracy for 6 UCI datasets with informative constraints. For each dataset, $(k-1)\times|D|$ constraints are selected where k is the number of clusters and $|D|$ is the number of instances in the dataset. We evaluate the clustering accuracy with random subsets and complete set of the selected constraints.

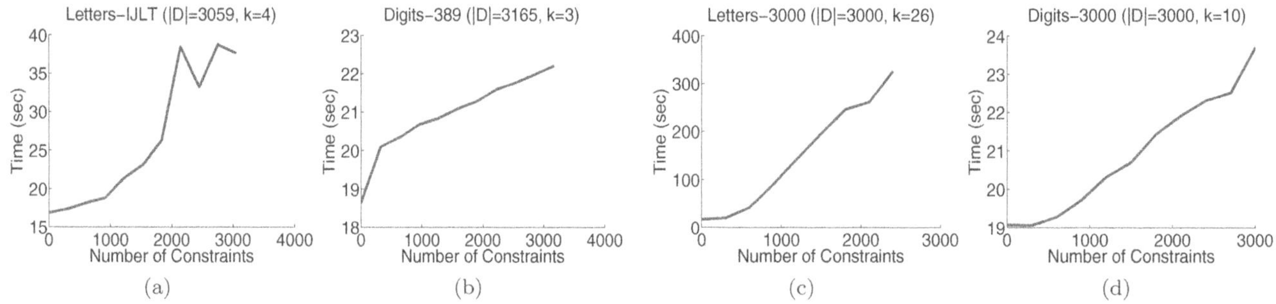

Figure 5: The running time of *ReCon + Euclidean Metric* on *Letters-IJLT*, *Digits-389*, *Letters-3000* and *Digits-3000*.

of constraints applied ranges from 0 to 3,000. Experiments were conducted on a PC with 2.6GHz Intel CPU and 8G RAM. The time plotted is the average of 50 runs of independently sampled constraint sets. The running time largely depends on the distribution of the data and the constraints selected. For comparison, we include two plots of datasets of large number of clusters (Fig.5(c) and 5(d)). *Letters-3000* has 3,000 instances randomly sampled from all 26 classes in the original Letters dataset. *Digits-3000* is sampled from all 10 classes in Digits dataset. In most experiments we conducted with the UCI datasets, our algorithm completed clustering within a few minutes.

6. CONCLUSIONS

In this paper, we investigated the important properties of *relative constraints*, an extension to relative comparisons to represent domain knowledge. Each *relative constraint* describes the local hierarchy of three instances. Besides existing instance-level knowledge sources, informative constraints can be systematically obtained from hierarchical knowledge resources such as Gene Ontology [2] and DBLP [23]. This property is desirable in making constrained clustering practical. We also present an efficient hierarchical algorithm that finds a complete hierarchy (and its corresponding partition) satisfying all given *relative constraints*. Experiments on real-world data showed promising results of applying *relative constraints*. Our algorithm significantly outperforms the metric learning approach based on relative comparisons. In addition, our algorithm exhibits unique advantage in utilizing informative constraints that are systematically extracted.

In the future work we plan to investigate how to integrate *relative constraints* with other existing constraint models. For example, pairwise constraints can be present together with *relative constraints* in many problems.

Handling Noisy Constraints

In this paper, we assume a reliable source of consistent constraints and focus on the hard-satisfaction of all given constraints. In reality, domain knowledge may contain errors and the obtained constraints can be noisy (or even become inconsistent). Hence, handling noisy/inconsistent constraints is an important step in applying *relative constraints*. If all constraints are of equal weight, one obvious approach to address inconsistency is to derive a maximum subset of consistent constraints from the given inconsistent constraints. This reduces to the Maximum Triplet Consistency problem [11] and its approximations [27, 28, 12]. Also, metric learning approaches can be used as a subroutine to filter noisy constraints. We plan to explore a more effective way to combine our framework with existing metric learning studies.

Acknowledgments

The authors would like to thank the reviewers for their valuable comments. This work was partially supported by NSF grants IIS-0812464 and IIS-0448392.

7. REFERENCES

[1] A. V. Aho, Y. Sagiv, T. G. Szymanski, and J. D. Ullman. Inferring a tree from lowest common ancestors with an application to the optimization of relational expressions. *SIAM Journal on Computing*, 10(3):405–421, 1981.

[2] M. Ashburner and et. al. Gene ontology: tool for the unification of biology. the gene ontology consortium. *Nature genetics*, 25(1):25–29, May 2000.

[3] A. Asuncion and D. Newman. UCI machine learning repository, 2007.

[4] K. Bade and A. Nurnberger. Personalized hierarchical clustering. In *WI '06*, pages 181–187, 2006.

[5] K. Bade and A. Nurnberger. Creating a cluster hierarchy under constraints of a partially known hierarchy abstract. In *SDM '08*, pages 13–24, 2008.

[6] S. Basu, A. Banerjee, and R. Mooney. Semi-supervised clustering by seeding. In *ICML '02*, pages 19–26, 2002.

[7] S. Basu, M. Bilenko, and R. J. Mooney. A probabilistic framework for semi-supervised clustering. In *KDD '04*, pages 59–68, 2004.

[8] S. Basu, I. Davidson, and K. L. Wagstaff. *Constrained clustering: advances in algorithms, theory, and applications*. Chapman and Hall/CRC, 2008.

[9] M. Bilenko, S. Basu, and R. J. Mooney. Integrating constraints and metric learning in semi-supervised clustering. In *ICML '04*, page 11, 2004.

[10] D. Bryant and M. Steel. Extension operations on sets of leaf-labelled trees. *Advances in Applied Mathematics*, 16(4):425–453, 1995.

[11] J. Byrka, S. Guillemot, and J. Jansson. New results on optimizing rooted triplets consistency. In *ISAAC '08*, 2008.

[12] D. Chen, O. Eulenstein, D. Fernandez-Baca, and M. Sanderson. Minimum-flip supertrees: complexity and algorithms. *IEEE/ACM transactions on computational biology and bioinformatics*, 3(2):165–73, 2006.

[13] M. Constantinescu and D. Sankoff. An efficient algorithm for supertrees. *Journal of Classification*, 12(1):101–112, 1995.

[14] I. Davidson and S. Ravi. Clustering with constraints: Feasibility issues and the k-means algorithm. *In SDM '05*, page 138, 2005.

[15] I. Davidson and S. Ravi. Using instance-level constraints in agglomerative hierarchical clustering: theoretical and empirical results. *Data Mining and Knowledge Discovery*, 18(2):257–282, 2008.

[16] I. Davidson, K. Wagstaff, and S. Basu. Measuring constraint-set utility for partitional clustering algorithms. *LNAI*, 4213:115–126, 2006.

[17] M. R. Henzinger, V. King, and T. Warnow. Constructing a tree from homeomorphic subtrees, with applications to computational evolutionary biology. *Algorithmica*, 24(1):1–13, 1999.

[18] J. Holm, K. de Lichtenberg, and M. Thorup. Poly-logarithmic deterministic fully-dynamic algorithms for connectivity, minimum spanning tree, 2-edge, and biconnectivity. *Journal of the ACM*, 48(4):723–760, 2001.

[19] J. Jansson, J. H. Ng, K. Sadakane, and W. K. Sung. Rooted maximum agreement supertrees. *Algorithmica*, 43(4):293–307, 2005.

[20] T. Joachims. Making large-scale support vector machine learning practical. *Advances in kernel methods: support vector learning*, pages 169–184, 1999.

[21] D. Klein, S. Kamvar, and C. Manning. From instance-level constraints to space-level constraints: Making the most of prior knowledge in data clustering. In *ICML '02*, pages 307–314, 2002.

[22] N. Kumar and K. Kummamuru. Semisupervised clustering with metric learning using relative comparisons. *IEEE Transactions on Knowledge and Data Engineering*, 20(4):496–503, 2008.

[23] M. Ley. The DBLP computer science bibliography: Evolution, research issues, perspectives. In *SPIRE '02*, pages 1–10, 2002.

[24] P. Meei and N. Wormald. Reconstruction of rooted trees from subtrees. *Discrete Applied Mathematics*, 69(1):19–31, 1996.

[25] C. Ruiz, M. Spiliopoulou, and E. Menasalvas. C-dbscan: Density-based clustering with constraints. In *RSFDGrC '07*, pages 216–223, 2007.

[26] M. Schultz and T. Joachims. Learning a distance metric from relative comparisons. In *NIPS '04*, 2004.

[27] C. Semple and M. Steel. A supertree method for rooted trees. *Discrete Applied Mathematics*, 105(1-31-3):147–158, 2000.

[28] S. Snir and S. Rao. Using max cut to enhance rooted trees consistency. *IEEE/ACM transactions on computational biology and bioinformatics*, 3(4):323–33, 2006.

[29] K. Wagstaff, S. Basu, and I. Davidson. When is constrained clustering beneficial, and why? In *AAAI '06*, pages 59–60, 2006.

[30] K. Wagstaff and C. Cardie. Clustering with instance-level constraints. In *ICML '00*, pages 1103–1110, 2000.

[31] K. Wagstaff, C. Cardie, S. Rogers, and S. Schrödl. Constrained k-means clustering with background knowledge. In *ICML '01*, pages 577–584, 2001.

[32] E. Xing, A. Ng, M. Jordan, and S. Russell. Distance metric learning with application to clustering with side-information. In *NIPS '02*, pages 505–512, 2002.

Common Component Analysis for Multiple Covariance Matrices

Huahua Wang
Computer Science & Engg
Univ of Minnesota, Twin Cities
huwang@cs.umn.edu

Arindam Banerjee
Computer Science & Engg
Univ of Minnesota, Twin Cities
banerjee@cs.umn.edu

Daniel Boley
Computer Science & Engg
Univ of Minnesota, Twin Cities
boley@cs.umn.edu

ABSTRACT

We consider the problem of finding a suitable common low dimensional subspace for accurately representing a given set of covariance matrices. With one covariance matrix, this is principal component analysis (PCA). For multiple covariance matrices, we term the problem *Common Component Analysis* (CCA). While CCA can be posed as a tensor decomposition problem, standard approaches to tensor decompositions have two critical issues: (i) tensor decomposition methods are iterative and rely on the initialization; (ii) for a given level of approximation error, it is difficult to choose a suitable low dimensionality. In this paper, we present a detailed analysis of CCA that yields an effective initialization and iterative algorithms for the problem. The proposed methodology has provable approximation guarantees w.r.t. the global maximum and also allows one to choose the dimensionality for a given level of approximation error. We also establish conditions under which the methodology will achieve the global maximum. We illustrate the effectiveness of the proposed method through extensive experiments on synthetic data as well as on two real stock market datasets, where major financial events can be visualized in low dimensions.

Categories and Subject Descriptors: H.2.8 [**Database Management**]: Database applications – Data mining

General Terms: Algorithms

Keywords: PCA, Dimensionality Reduction, Tensor Decompositions, PARAFAC, TUCKER

1. INTRODUCTION

In recent years, simultaneous analysis of multiple high dimensional covariance matrices is becoming increasingly important in diverse application domains ranging from finance to climate and environmental sciences [30, 31, 32, 11, 34]. The traditional approach for finding an accurate low-dimensional approximation to a high-dimensional covariance matrix is principal component analysis (PCA) [14, 4]. In particular, PCA finds an orthogonal projection of a single covariance matrix to a low-dimensional space while preserving as much of the "energy" or variance as possible. The problem can be solved by performing the eigenvalue decomposition (EVD) on the single covariance matrix under consideration.

KDD'11, August 21–24, 2011, San Diego, California, USA.

Given multiple covariance matrices, we consider the problem of finding a suitable common low-dimensional subspace for accurately representing all the covariance matrices. We term the problem *Common Component Analysis* (CCA). PCA is not suitable for finding such a subspace for multiple covariance matrices, particularly if the covariance matrices span different subspaces. Examples include stock market data where financial shocks and volatility arise from different sources, and yield stock return covariance matrices in different subspaces. The low-dimensional covariance representation of the high-dimensional covariance matrices can take two possible forms: diagonal or full. Existing models where diagonal low rank matrices are considered, such as PARAFAC/ CANDECOMP [16, 17, 24, 22] and common principal components (CPC) [12, 13], do not allow interactions among low-dimensional components and essentially assume that underlying factors are uncorrelated. Moreover, multiple matrices can be simultaneously diagonalized with an orthogonal transformation if and only if they commute [19], which need not be true in general. Consequently, in this paper, we consider the case where the low-dimensional covariance matrices are full matrices. Such decompositions have been widely studied under different names, such as the Tucker2 model [35, 16, 24, 25, 22], tensor PCA [6], 2DSVD [9], GLRAM [37], and tensor decompositions [21, 22, 26, 33]. Variance correlation [11] and Cholesky decomposition [3, 31] have also been used to simultaneously model multiple covariance matrices in low dimensions.

While CCA can be posed as a tensor decomposition problem, unlike PCA, standard approaches to tensor decompositions have two critical issues: (i) tensor decomposition methods are iterative and rely on the initialization; (ii) for a given level of approximation error, efficiently choosing a suitable low dimensionality is difficult in general. In this paper, we present a detailed analysis that alleviates the two issues in the context of CCA. We start by showing that our problem is equivalent to maximizing (not minimizing) a convex function over a compact but non-convex set. As a result, finding the global maximum is difficult in general. With an analysis using a simpler variant of CCA, we derive lower and upper bounds for the CCA objective for any orthonormal matrix. The bounds naturally lead to corresponding lower and upper bounds for the global maximum of CCA. We also give sufficient conditions under which the global maximum will be achieved. In [9], similar bounds were established for a local maximum of a related problem, but the closeness of the bounds w.r.t. the global maximum was not explicitly investigated. Using our bounds, an effective initialization is proposed. It has been observed that a similar initialization often leads to the global maximum [37, 9], particularly for rank-1 approximations [27, 20]. Our analysis shows that instead of starting with a given low dimensionality, one can start with an approximation error bound, and appropriately choose a sufficient dimensionality for CCA satisfying the given error bound. We present two algorithms to iteratively improve the objective for CCA starting from the proposed initialization. One algorithm adopts an existing idea from tensor decompositions [24, 25, 6, 9, 37]. In each iteration, the update in the standard tensor decomposition algorithm requires computing the EVD of an $n \times n$ matrix, where n is the dimensionality of the observed high-dimensional covariance matrices. We also propose a novel algorithm based on an auxiliary function [28, 29]. In each iteration, the update in the novel algorithm only requires performing the singular value decomposition (SVD) of an $r \times n$ matrix, where r is the dimensionality of the latent low-dimensional covariance matrices. When $r \ll n$, the auxiliary-function-based algorithm is substantially more efficient than the standard tensor decomposition algorithm.

The remainder of this paper is organized as follows. We formulate the common component analysis (CCA) problem in Section 2. In Section 3, we analyze the problem, establish lower and upper bounds for the global maximum, introduce the initialization and its optimality properties, establish sufficient conditions under which the global maximum will be achieved, and also discuss the connections to related work. In Section 4, we present two algorithms for CCA given a suitable initialization, which can work with a given dimensionality or a given approximation error bound. We report experimental results on synthetic data as well as two stock market datasets to illustrate the performance of the proposed ideas in Section 5, and conclude in Section 6.

Notation: Matrices are denoted by uppercase bold letters, e.g., $\mathbf{X}, \mathbf{U}$, etc. The diagonal entries in a diagonal matrix are generally assumed to be in non-decreasing order, especially if arising from the EVD or SVD. $\mathbb{I}_r$ (with r an integer) denotes a $r \times r$ identity matrix.

2. PROBLEM FORMULATION

Assume we have a set of high-dimensional covariance matrices $\mathbf{X}_t \in \mathbb{R}^{n \times n}, 1 \le t \le T$. The key hypothesis driving our analysis is that the high-dimensional covariance matrices are indeed linearly transformed versions of a set of low-dimensional covariance matrices $\mathbf{Y}_t \in \mathbb{R}^{r \times r}, 1 \le t \le T$. While the linear transformation $\mathbf{U} \in \mathbb{R}^{n \times r}$ as well as the low-dimensional covariance matrices $\mathbf{Y}_t, 1 \le t \le T$, are unknown, each $\mathbf{X}_t$ is assumed to be well approximated by $\mathbf{U}\mathbf{Y}_t\mathbf{U}^T$. In particular,

$$\mathbf{X}_t = \mathbf{U}\mathbf{Y}_t\mathbf{U}^T + \mathbf{E}_t \, , \tag{1}$$

where $\mathbf{E}_t$ is the residual matrix. Without loss of generality, $\mathbf{U}$ is assumed to be orthonormal, i.e., $\mathbf{U}^T\mathbf{U} = \mathbb{I}_r$. The goal is to find $\mathbf{U}$ and $\mathbf{Y}_t, 1 \le t \le T$ such that the sum of squares of the Frobenius norms of all the residual matrices is minimized. The problem can be formally stated as follows:

$$\min_{\substack{\mathbf{U},\mathbf{Y}_t \\ \mathbf{U}^T\mathbf{U}=\mathbb{I}_r}} \sum_{t=1}^{T} \|\mathbf{X}_t - \mathbf{U}\mathbf{Y}_t\mathbf{U}^T\|_F^2 \, . \tag{2}$$

Since $\mathbf{U}$ determines a common subspace for all the covariance matrices, we call the above formulation *Common Component Analysis* (CCA). There are several appealing properties for the choices of orthonormal matrix $\mathbf{U}$ and non-diagonal matrix $\mathbf{Y}_t$. First, since $\mathbf{U}$ is orthonormal, the formulation allows one to visualize covariance matrices in the low-dimensional subspaces (see Figure 4 in Section 5.2). With non-orthonormal $\mathbf{U}$, such low-dimensional covariance matrices can be difficult to interpret. Second, it turns out that the choices can reduce CCA to a maximization problem over $\mathbf{U}$ (see Lemma 1) by dropping out $\mathbf{Y}_t$, thus facilitating a theoretical analysis. Further, the full matrix $\mathbf{Y}_t$ allows interactions among components and leads to substantially lower approximation errors (see Section 5.1 and 5.2).

We make a few observations before continuing with our analysis. If there is only one covariance matrix $\mathbf{X}_1$ under consideration, then the model reduces to standard PCA. If $\mathbf{X}_t$ is not a covariance matrix, i.e., $\mathbf{X}_t \in \mathbb{R}^{m \times n}$, it is modeled as $\mathbf{X}_t = \mathbf{U}\mathbf{Y}_t\mathbf{V}^T + \mathbf{E}_t$, where $\mathbf{U} \in \mathbb{R}^{m \times r}, \mathbf{Y}_t \in \mathbb{R}^{r \times s}, \mathbf{V} \in \mathbb{R}^{s \times n}$, and the existing literature on tensor decompositions is relevant [24, 26, 22, 21, 6, 9, 37, 16, 17, 35]. Assuming $r = s$ and restricting $\mathbf{Y}_t$ to be diagonal leads to the PARAFAC/CANDECOMP models [24, 22]. When such restrictions are not imposed, one gets the Tucker2 model [24, 22]. Iterative algorithms and data mining applications of such decompositions have been studied in the literature [24, 22, 23, 9, 37]. Unlike most existing settings, in our model each $\mathbf{X}_t$ is a positive semi-definite matrix, and $\mathbf{Y}_t$ is also positive semi-definite. In particular, CCA is different from CPC [12, 13]. While CPC aims to simultaneously diagonalize a set of strictly positive definite covariance matrices using a maximum likelihood approach [13], CCA is discussed in a least squares setting. We discuss technical relationships of our analysis to existing models in Section 3.5.

We start the analysis with the following two results. Space does not permit us to include the proofs, which can be found in [36].

Lemma 1 *The optimum $\mathbf{Y}_t$ in (2) satisfies $\mathbf{Y}_t = \mathbf{U}^T\mathbf{X}_t\mathbf{U}$. Further, the optimal $\mathbf{U}$ in (2) is the solution to the following problem:*

$$\max_{\mathbf{U}^T\mathbf{U}=\mathbb{I}_r} f(\mathbf{U}) = \max_{\mathbf{U}^T\mathbf{U}=\mathbb{I}_r} \operatorname{Tr}(\mathbf{U}^T M(\mathbf{U})\mathbf{U}) \, , \tag{3}$$

where

$$M(\mathbf{U}) = \sum_{t=1}^{T} \mathbf{X}_t\mathbf{U}\mathbf{U}^T\mathbf{X}_t \, . \tag{4}$$

Lemma 2 *For $\mathbf{U} \in \mathbb{R}^{n \times r}$ (not necessarily orthonormal), $f(\mathbf{U})$ is a convex function.*

Unfortunately, the fact that $f(\mathbf{U})$ is convex does not help us because we are *maximizing* $f(\mathbf{U})$ in (3) instead of minimizing it. Further, the constraint set $\mathbf{U}^T\mathbf{U} = \mathbb{I}_r$ is not convex. As a result, the problem in (3) is not convex. In fact, the problem is one of maximizing a convex function over a bounded non-convex feasible set. As a result, there may be several local maxima. If starting from an initial guess, the standard approaches to tensor decompositions will likely get stuck in a local maximum. Furthermore, it is difficult to characterize the proximity of such solutions in terms of the function value achieved with respect to the global maximum. In the next two sections, we develop a simple way to initialize $\mathbf{U}$ along with algorithms for iterative updates with guarantees relative to the global maximum.

3. ANALYSIS

In this section, we analyze CCA in terms of a simpler model called common component analysis 1 (CCA1). We show that CCA1 is a PCA-style problem and can be solved using the EVD. More importantly, the solution to CCA1 leads to lower and upper bounds on the global maximum of CCA and suggests a good initialization for any iterative algorithm for CCA. We also show how to choose a suitable dimensionality sufficient to satisfy a given approximation error bound. In addition, sufficient conditions for a global maximum and the connections to related work are considered.

Table 1: CCA and CCA1

CCA	CCA1
$\mathbf{X}_t = \mathbf{U}\mathbf{Y}_t\mathbf{U} + \mathbf{E}_t$	$\mathbf{X}_t = \mathbf{U}\mathbf{Z}_t + \mathbf{E}_t$
$M(\mathbf{U}) = \sum_t \mathbf{X}_t\mathbf{U}\mathbf{U}^T\mathbf{X}_t$	$M(\mathbb{I}_n) = \sum_t \mathbf{X}_t^2$
$f(\mathbf{U}) = \text{Tr}(\mathbf{U}^T M(\mathbf{U})\mathbf{U})$	$f_1(\mathbf{U}) = \text{Tr}(\mathbf{U}^T M(\mathbb{I}_n)\mathbf{U})$

3.1 A Simpler Model: CCA1

Instead of the original problem in (2), we consider a simpler decomposition given by

$$\mathbf{X}_t = \mathbf{U}\mathbf{Z}_t + \mathbf{E}_t \,, \tag{5}$$

where $\mathbf{U} \in \mathbb{R}^{n \times r}$ and $\mathbf{Z}_t \in \mathbb{R}^{r \times n}$. Assuming the residual norms to be small, the problem of finding $\mathbf{U}, \mathbf{Z}_t$ can be posed as follows:

$$\min_{\substack{\mathbf{U},\mathbf{Z}_t \\ \mathbf{U}^T\mathbf{U}=\mathbb{I}_r}} \sum_{t=1}^{T} \|\mathbf{X}_t - \mathbf{U}\mathbf{Z}_t\|_F^2 \,. \tag{6}$$

We call the above problem CCA1 since it only considers a one-sided projection compared to the two-sided projection in CCA. Similar to CCA, the simplified problem CCA1 allows an alternative characterization as follows:

Lemma 3 *The optimal $\mathbf{Z}_t$ in (6) satisfies $\mathbf{Z}_t = \mathbf{U}^T\mathbf{X}_t$. Furthermore, the optimal $\mathbf{U}$ in (5) is the solution to the following problem:*

$$\max_{\mathbf{U}^T\mathbf{U}=\mathbb{I}_r} f_1(\mathbf{U}) = \max_{\mathbf{U}^T\mathbf{U}=\mathbb{I}_r} \text{Tr}(\mathbf{U}^T M(\mathbb{I}_n)\mathbf{U}) \,, \tag{7}$$

where $\mathbb{I}_n$ is an identity matrix of size n and

$$M(\mathbb{I}_n) = \sum_{t=1}^{T} \mathbf{X}_t^2 \,. \tag{8}$$

Note that CCA1 in (7) is a PCA problem on $M(\mathbb{I}_n)$, which can be solved using the EVD. Table 1 shows a relative comparison between CCA and CCA1.

3.2 Lower and Upper Bounds

The solution of CCA1 helps significantly in characterizing the solution to CCA. We focus on developing lower and upper bounds on the global maximum of CCA based on the solution of CCA1. Since CCA1 is essentially the PCA problem over $M(\mathbb{I}_n) = \sum_t \mathbf{X}_t^2$, if $\mathbf{U}_0$ denotes the top r eigenvectors of $M(\mathbb{I}_n) = \sum_{t=1}^T \mathbf{X}_t^2$, then $\mathbf{U}_0$ is the solution to (7). Let $f_1^{\max} = f_1(\mathbf{U}_0)$ be the maximum value of $f_1(\mathbf{U})$, and let $M_T = \text{Tr}(M(\mathbb{I}_n)) = \text{Tr}\left(\sum_t \mathbf{X}_t^2\right)$. With this notation, we have the following result:

Theorem 1 *Let $M_T = \text{Tr}(\sum_t \mathbf{X}_t^2)$. Then, with $f_1(\mathbf{U})$ and $f(\mathbf{U})$ denoting the objective functions for CCA1 and CCA respectively as in (7) and (3), for any $\mathbf{U}$ with $\mathbf{U}^T\mathbf{U} = \mathbb{I}_r$, we have*

$$\frac{f_1^2(\mathbf{U})}{M_T} \leq f(\mathbf{U}) \leq f_1(\mathbf{U}) \,. \tag{9}$$

Definition 1 Let p_1 denote the fraction of 'energy' in $\sum_t \mathbf{X}_t^2$ captured by the rank-r PCA solution $\mathbf{U}_0$. In particular,

$$p_1 = \frac{f_1^{\max}}{M_T} = \frac{\text{Tr}\left(\mathbf{U}_0^T\left(\sum_t \mathbf{X}_t^2\right)\mathbf{U}_0\right)}{\text{Tr}\left(\sum_t \mathbf{X}_t^2\right)} \,, \tag{10}$$

so that $0 \leq p_1 \leq 1$.

Using this definition and Theorem 1, we have the following result bounding the value of the global maximum of CCA.

Corollary 1 *Let $f_1^{\max}$ and $f^{\max}$ be the global maximum of CCA1 and CCA, respectively, over $\mathbf{U}^T\mathbf{U} = \mathbb{I}_r$, and let p_1 be defined in Definition 1. Then, we have*

$$p_1 f_1^{\max} \leq f^{\max} \leq f_1^{\max} \,. \tag{11}$$

Recall that the solution to CCA1 is $\mathbf{U}_0$, the top-r eigenvectors of $\sum_t \mathbf{X}_t^2$. Thus, it is easy to compute $f_1^{\max} = f_1(\mathbf{U}_0)$ and $p_1 = f_1^{\max}/M_T$. From Theorem 1, it follows that $p_1 f_1^{\max} \leq f(\mathbf{U}_0) \leq f_1^{\max}$. According to Corollary 1, the relative error of $f(\mathbf{U}_0)$ w.r.t. the global maximum is

$$\frac{f^{\max} - f(\mathbf{U}_0)}{f^{\max}} \leq 1 - p_1 \,. \tag{12}$$

Now if $\mathbf{U}_0$ is chosen as the initialization, the iterative updates for $f(\mathbf{U})$ converge to $\mathbf{U}_0^*$ (see Section 4) and $f(\mathbf{U}_0^*)$ satisfies

$$p_1 f_1^{\max} \leq f(\mathbf{U}_0) \leq f(\mathbf{U}_0^*) \leq f^{\max} \leq f_1^{\max} \,. \tag{13}$$

As a result, we have the following theoretical bound for the relative error of $f(\mathbf{U}_0^*)$ w.r.t. the global maximum.

Corollary 2 *Let $\mathbf{U}_0$ be the r leading principal eigenvectors of $M(\mathbb{I}_n) = \sum_t \mathbf{X}_t^2$, and $f(\mathbf{U}_0^*)$ be the solution to CCA with the initialization $\mathbf{U}_0$. Then, the relative error of $f(\mathbf{U}_0^*)$ with respect to $f^{\max}$ satisfies*

$$\frac{f^{\max} - f(\mathbf{U}_0^*)}{f^{\max}} \leq 1 - p_1 \,. \tag{14}$$

It is interesting to note that p_1 governs the closeness of the local maximum w.r.t. the global maximum. In PCA, the fraction p_1 depends on the choice of dimension r. Empirical studies show that the upper bound $1 - p_1$ becomes fairly small for the first r leading components (see Figure 3 in Section 5.2). On the other hand, if p_1 is small ($1 - p_1$ is large), r should be increased so that a reasonable fraction (say, $p_1 = 0.9$) of energy can be preserved. The choice of r according to p_1 in CCA will be discussed in Section 3.3.

Once $f(\mathbf{U}_0^*)$ is found, the empirical bound of the relative error of $f(\mathbf{U}_0^*)$ w.r.t. the global maximum becomes

$$\frac{f^{\max} - f(\mathbf{U}_0^*)}{f^{\max}} \leq 1 - \frac{f(\mathbf{U}_0^*)}{f_1^{\max}} \,. \tag{15}$$

3.3 Approximate Relative Error and Rank

In certain applications, one may have to pick a suitable rank r to preserve a certain fraction of the observed covariance structure. The goal is to find the lowest rank r sufficient to explain a given fraction of the observed covariance, or equivalently to keep the approximation error below a given threshold. In PCA, since its solution based on the EVD has a nested structure, one can simply keep appending principal components until the desired error is reached. However, such a nested approximation structure is not present in CCA and more generally in the case of tensor decompositions. In particular, if the rank $(r-1)$ solution is insufficient, the computation must be carried out from scratch to obtain the rank r solution. In this section, we show that such elaborate calculations can be avoided by using the bounds relative to the CCA1 problem.

We start by defining the *Approximate Relative Error* (ARE) as a measure of quality of the the approximation obtained by CCA. For any $\mathbf{U}$, we have

$$ARE(\mathbf{U}) = \frac{\sum_{t=1}^T \|\mathbf{X}_t - \mathbf{U}\mathbf{Y}_t\mathbf{U}^T\|_F^2}{\sum_{t=1}^T \|\mathbf{X}_t\|_F^2} \,. \tag{16}$$

We define the cumulative percentage of energy captured by the solution to CCA as follows:

Definition 2 Let $M_T = \text{Tr}(M(\mathbb{I}_n))$, and let $f(\mathbf{U}_0^*)$ be the maximum of CCA obtained by an iterative algorithm with the initialization $\mathbf{U}_0$ (see Section 4). The cumulative percent of energy p captured by $\mathbf{U}_0^*$ is defined as

$$p = \frac{f(\mathbf{U}_0^*)}{M_T}, \tag{17}$$

so that $0 \leq p \leq 1$.

For our problem, p defines how much energy over all the covariances is preserved by their corresponding latent covariances. Dividing inequality (13) by M_T and plugging in $p_1 = f_1{}^{\max}/M_T$ yield lower and upper bounds for p:

$$p_1^2 \leq p \leq p_1 . \tag{18}$$

In CCA1 (essentially PCA), given a p_1, the corresponding rank r is easy to obtain. Using the bounds for p, one can also develop a simple way to obtain a suitable rank r for CCA. To do this, we first relate p to the approximate relative error $ARE(\mathbf{U}_0^*)$.

Proposition 1 *Let $\mathbf{U}_0^*$ be the solution of CCA. Then $ARE(\mathbf{U}_0^*) = 1 - p$.*

Plugging $ARE(\mathbf{U}_0^*)$ into inequality (18), it is easy to derive the following lower and upper bounds for $ARE(\mathbf{U}_0^*)$:

$$1 - p_1 \leq ARE(\mathbf{U}_0^*) \leq 1 - p_1^2 . \tag{19}$$

Given an upper bound δ for $ARE(\mathbf{U}_0^*)$, we now show how to obtain a suitable rank r for $\mathbf{U}_0^*$ in CCA. Since $ARE(\mathbf{U}_0^*) \leq 1 - p_1^2$, it is sufficient to ensure $1 - p_1^2 \leq \delta \Rightarrow p_1 \geq \sqrt{1-\delta}$. Since p_1 corresponds to $\mathbf{U}_0$ in a PCA setting, one can easily obtain a rank-r $\mathbf{U}_0$ such that $p_1 \geq \sqrt{1-\delta}$. Initializing the iterations for CCA with $\mathbf{U}_0$ will lead to a $\mathbf{U}_0^*$ satisfying $ARE(\mathbf{U}_0^*) \leq \delta$. Note that since the construction is based on a bound, there may be a lower-rank $\mathbf{U}_0^*$ satisfying the constraint.

3.4 Conditions for Global Maximum

We now analyze a condition under which a global maximum of CCA is achieved for a given rank r. The particular case under consideration is when equality holds in (13), i.e., $f(\mathbf{U}_0^*) = f_1^{\max}$, where $f(\mathbf{U}_0^*)$ is a local maximum, implying $f(\mathbf{U}_0^*) = f^{\max}$.

Let $\mathbf{U}_0$ be the initialization consisting of the r principal eigenvectors of $M(\mathbb{I})$, we have the following result:

Theorem 2 *Let $\mathbf{U}_0$ be the r principal eigenvectors of $M(\mathbb{I}_n)$ associated with the nonzero r largest eigenvalues, then $\text{rank}(M(\mathbf{U}_0)) \geq r$, where $M(\mathbf{U}_0)$ is defined in Lemma 1.*

Based on Theorem 2, we now show that $\text{rank}(M(\mathbf{U}_0)) = r$ is a necessary and sufficient condition that $f(\mathbf{U}_0^*) = f_1^{\max}$, thereby implying that $\mathbf{U}_0^*$ achieves the global optimum. Moreover, in this situation, the solution achieving the global maximum is the initialization $\mathbf{U}_0$ itself.

Theorem 3 *Let $\mathbf{U}_0$ be the solution to CCA1, i.e., the r principal eigenvectors of $M(\mathbb{I})$, and let $\mathbf{U}_0^*$ be the solution found in Algorithm 1 with the initialization $\mathbf{U}_0$. Then, $\text{rank}(M(\mathbf{U}_0)) = r$ is a necessary and sufficient condition for $f(\mathbf{U}_0^*) = f_1^{\max}$. Moreover, $\mathbf{U}_0$ is the solution achieving the global maximum for CCA.*

A special case of the result occurs when $\text{rank}(M(\mathbb{I})) = r$. When $\text{rank}(M(\mathbb{I})) = r$, $\text{rank}(M(\mathbf{U}_0)) \leq \text{rank}(M(\mathbb{I})) = r$. By Theorem 2, $\text{rank}(M(\mathbf{U}_0)) \geq r$, implying $\text{rank}(M(\mathbf{U}_0)) = r$. Thus $\mathbf{U}_0$ achieves the global maximum. In this case, since all the eigenvectors are kept, the fraction of energy $p_1 = 1$. The global optimality then follows in a straightforward manner from the bounds discussed in Section 3.3.

3.5 Connections to Related Work

Given a set of rectangular matrices $\mathbf{X}_t \in \mathbb{R}^{m \times n}, 1 \leq t \leq T$, the Tucker2 model [35, 16, 24, 22], 2DSVD [9], GLRAM [37], etc., aim to find common components $\mathbf{U} \in \mathbb{R}^{m \times r}$ and $\mathbf{V} \in \mathbb{R}^{n \times s}$ such that

$$\mathbf{X}_t = \mathbf{U}\mathbf{Y}_t\mathbf{V}^T + \mathbf{E}_t , \tag{20}$$

where $\mathbf{Y}_t \in \mathbb{R}^{r \times s}$, $\mathbf{U}$ and $\mathbf{V}$ are orthonormal matrices, and $\mathbf{E}_t$ is the residual. $\mathbf{U}$ and $\mathbf{V}$ can be obtained by performing the EVD iteratively on matrices $M_1(\mathbf{V}) = \sum_t \mathbf{X}_t\mathbf{V}\mathbf{V}^T\mathbf{X}_t^T \in \mathbb{R}^{m \times m}$ and $M_2(\mathbf{U}) = \sum_t \mathbf{X}_t^T\mathbf{U}\mathbf{U}^T\mathbf{X}_t \in \mathbb{R}^{n \times n}$ respectively. An initialization similar to the one proposed for CCA is usually used in these methods, e.g., initializing $\mathbf{U}$ with the EVD of $\sum_t \mathbf{X}_t\mathbf{X}_t^T$ or $\mathbf{V}$ with the EVD of $\sum_t \mathbf{X}_t^T\mathbf{X}_t$. It has been observed empirically that such an initialization usually leads to the good solutions [37, 9], particularly in rank-1 approximation experiments [27, 20]. When a locally optimal solution is found, say $(\mathbf{U}^*, \mathbf{V}^*)$, Ding et al. [9] established lower and upper bounds for a local maximum based on the eigenvalues of $M_1(\mathbf{V}^*)$ and $M_2(\mathbf{U}^*)$, but the bounds w.r.t. the global maximum were not explicitly given.

In (20), if $r = s$ and $\mathbf{Y}_t$ is diagonal, it becomes PARAFAC / CANDECOMP with orthonormal constraints [16, 17, 24, 22], referred to as PARAFAC in the sequel. If PARAFAC is applied to the covariance matrices in our case, $\mathbf{U}$ and $\mathbf{V}$ are the same. In this case, PARAFAC has the same formula as CCA except that $\mathbf{Y}_t$ is a diagonal matrix in PARAFAC but is a full matrix in CCA. In contrast to the least squares approach in PARAFAC, CPC [12, 13] simultaneously diagonalizes the positive definite matrices using a maximum likelihood approach [13]. Since the off-diagonal elements are zero in $\mathbf{Y}_t$, PARAFAC and CPC do not allow interactions among components in $\mathbf{U}$ and $\mathbf{V}$. On the other hand, if covariance matrices are simultaneously diagonalizable with an orthonormal transformation [19], it turns out that $\mathbf{Y}_t$ in CCA is also diagonal. A similar result has also been noted in the context of CPC [12, 13].

Proposition 2 *If covariance matrices $\mathbf{X}_t$ are simultaneously diagonalizable with an orthonormal transformation, the low dimensional covariance matrices $\mathbf{Y}_t$ in CCA are diagonal.*

4. ALGORITHMS

In this section, we present algorithms for solving CCA for a given dimensionality or a given approximation error bound. For a given dimensionality, we present two algorithms that iteratively improve a given initial solution. For a given approximation error bound, we show how to determine a sufficient dimensionality, reducing the problem to the first case.

4.1 CCA for a Given Dimensionality

Iterative EVD based CCA: For a given dimensionality, EVD can be used to solve for $\mathbf{U}$ in CCA1 in (7). However, CCA in (3) has four $\mathbf{U}$'s, which cannot be found using the same approach, since this problem does not correspond to an EVD problem. Instead, we perform the EVD iteratively by fixing the two inner $\mathbf{U}$'s to the current iterate $\mathbf{U}_k$. Recall that CCA involves maximizing $f(\mathbf{U}) = \text{Tr}(\mathbf{U}^T M(\mathbf{U})\mathbf{U})$ where $M(\mathbf{U}) = \sum_{t=1}^T \mathbf{X}_t\mathbf{U}\mathbf{U}^T\mathbf{X}_t$ is of size $n \times n$. If $\mathbf{U}_k$ is the current iterate, then we compute $M(\mathbf{U}_k)$ and solve the following surrogate problem to obtain $\mathbf{U}_{k+1}$:

$$\max_{\mathbf{U}^T\mathbf{U}=\mathbb{I}_r} \text{Tr}(\mathbf{U}^T M(\mathbf{U}_k)\mathbf{U}) . \tag{21}$$

Algorithm 1 Iterative EVD (IEVD) Algorithm for CCA

1: Input: $\mathbf{X}_t, 1 \leq t \leq T$, initialization $\mathbf{U}_0 \in \mathbb{R}^{n \times r}$
2: Output: $\mathbf{U}, \mathbf{Y}_t, 1 \leq t \leq T$
3: **repeat**
4: Perform the EVD on $M(\mathbf{U}_k) = \sum_t \mathbf{X}_t \mathbf{U}_k \mathbf{U}_k^T \mathbf{X}_t$
5: Choose the leading r eigenvectors $\mathbf{U}_{k+1}$
6: Compute $\mathbf{Y}_t = \mathbf{U}_{k+1}^T \mathbf{X}_t \mathbf{U}_{k+1}$
7: **until** $\left| \frac{f(\mathbf{U}_{k+1}) - f(\mathbf{U}_k)}{f(\mathbf{U}_k)} \right| \leq \varepsilon$

Clearly, $\mathbf{U}_{k+1}$ can be obtained by applying a rank-r EVD on $M(\mathbf{U}_k)$. The idea behind such an update has been explored in the literature on tensor decompositions [24, 25, 9, 37]. As the following result shows, such an update will improve the objective function, i.e., $f(\mathbf{U}_{k+1}) \geq f(\mathbf{U}_k)$.

Theorem 4 *Let $\mathbf{U}_{k+1}$ be the r principal eigenvectors of $M(\mathbf{U}_k)$, then $f(\mathbf{U}_{k+1}) \geq \mathrm{Tr}(\mathbf{U}_{k+1}^T M(\mathbf{U}_k)\mathbf{U}_{k+1}) \geq f(\mathbf{U}_k)$. Equality holds when $\mathbf{U}_{k+1}$ and $\mathbf{U}_k$ span the same subspace.*

Algorithm 1 presents the corresponding algorithm for a given dimension r as input. The objective function increases at every step until a certain stopping criterion is satisfied. If $\mathbf{U}_0^*$ is the final solution, from the analysis of Section 3.3, we know that $f(\mathbf{U}_0^*) \geq p_1 f^{\max}$, and the approximate relative error satisfies $1 - p_1 \leq ARE(\mathbf{U}_0^*) \leq 1 - p_1^2$.

Auxiliary Function based CCA: In the iterative EVD method, the update has to repeatedly calculate the EVD of an $n \times n$ matrix. If n is large, the update becomes a bottleneck. In this section, we present an efficient update that only calculates the SVD of an $r \times n$ matrix. To introduce the new update, we first define an auxiliary function $g(\mathbf{U}, \mathbf{V})$ as follows:

$$g(\mathbf{U}, \mathbf{V}) = \mathrm{Tr}\left(\sum_t^T (\mathbf{U}^T \mathbf{X}_t \mathbf{U})(\mathbf{V}^T \mathbf{X}_t \mathbf{V})\right) . \qquad (22)$$

where $\mathbf{U}^T\mathbf{U} = \mathbb{I}_r$ and $\mathbf{V}^T\mathbf{V} = \mathbb{I}_r$. Clearly, $g(\mathbf{U}, \mathbf{U}) = f(\mathbf{U})$.

Given $\mathbf{U}_k$, if we can find a $\mathbf{U}_{k+1}$ satisfying $g(\mathbf{U}_k, \mathbf{U}_{k+1}) \geq g(\mathbf{U}_k, \mathbf{U}_k)$, the auxiliary function increases. Theorem 5 shows that $\mathbf{U}_{k+1}$ can be obtained by performing the SVD on an $r \times n$ matrix $\sum_t^T \mathbf{Y}_t^k \mathbf{V}^T \mathbf{X}_t$, where $\mathbf{Y}_t^k = \mathbf{U}_k^T \mathbf{X}_t \mathbf{U}_k$. Such a $\mathbf{U}_{k+1}$ increases $f(\mathbf{U})$.

Theorem 5 *Let $\mathbf{U}_{k+1} = \mathbf{Q}\mathbf{P}^T$, where $\mathbf{P}$ and $\mathbf{Q}$ are respectively the left and right r singular vectors of $\sum_t^T \mathbf{Y}_t^k \mathbf{U}_k^T \mathbf{X}_t$, where $\mathbf{Y}_t^k = \mathbf{U}_k^T \mathbf{X}_t \mathbf{U}_k$, then*

$$f(\mathbf{U}_k) \leq g(\mathbf{U}_k, \mathbf{U}_{k+1}) \leq f(\mathbf{U}_{k+1}) .$$

Equality holds when $\mathbf{U}_k$ and $\mathbf{U}_{k+1}$ span the same subspace.

Based on Theorem 5, we propose Algorithm 2 using the auxiliary function, yielding a solution satisfying the bounds of Section 3.3.

Time Complexity: In both algorithms, the most expensive steps are the iterative updates. In Algorithm 1, step 4 takes $O(Tn^2r)$ time to compute $M(\mathbf{U}_k)$ and $O(n^3)$ time for the EVD, and step 6 takes $O(Tn^2r)$. Overall, the cost of the updating steps in Algorithm 1 is $O(Tn^2r + n^3)$. In Algorithm 2, step 5 takes $O(Tn^2r)$ to compute the matrix $\sum_t \mathbf{Y}_t^k \mathbf{U}_k^T \mathbf{X}_t$ and $O(r^2n)$ for the SVD, and steps 6 and 7 require $O(nr^2)$ and $O(Tn^2r)$ respectively. Assuming $r \ll n$, the overall cost of the updating steps in Algorithm 2 is $O(Tn^2r)$.

Algorithm 2 Auxiliary Function (AF) Algorithm for CCA

1: Input: $\mathbf{X}_t, 1 \leq t \leq T$, initialization $\mathbf{U}_0 \in \mathbb{R}^{n \times r}$
2: Output: $\mathbf{U}, \mathbf{Y}_t, 1 \leq t \leq T$
3: Compute $\mathbf{Y}_t^0 = \mathbf{U}_0^T \mathbf{X}_t \mathbf{U}_0$
4: **repeat**
5: Perform the SVD on matrix $\sum_t \mathbf{Y}_t^k \mathbf{U}_k^T \mathbf{X}_t = \mathbf{P}\mathbf{D}\mathbf{Q}^T$
6: Compute $\mathbf{U}_{k+1} = \mathbf{Q}\mathbf{P}^T$
7: Compute $\mathbf{Y}_t^{k+1} = \mathbf{U}_{k+1}^T \mathbf{X}_t \mathbf{U}_{k+1}$
8: **until** $\left| \frac{g(\mathbf{U}_{k+1}, \mathbf{U}_{k+1}) - g(\mathbf{U}_k, \mathbf{U}_k)}{g(\mathbf{U}_k, \mathbf{U}_k)} \right| \leq \varepsilon$

4.2 CCA for a Given Approximation Error

We consider a setting where instead of the dimension r, an upper bound δ on the approximate relative error (ARE) is given. In such a setting, one can choose a sufficient dimension r and a corresponding initialization $\mathbf{U}_0$ based on our analysis in Section 3.3, and use any of the algorithms in Section 4.1 to obtain a $\mathbf{U}$ guaranteeing the error bound. In particular, it is sufficient to choose the dimension r of the initialization $\mathbf{U}_0$ such that the fraction of energy captured in CCA1 given by $p_1 = \frac{\mathrm{Tr}(\mathbf{U}_0^T M(\mathbb{I})\mathbf{U}_0)}{\mathrm{Tr}(M(\mathbb{I}))}$ satisfies $p_1 \geq \sqrt{1-\delta}$, as discussed in Section 3.3. Since $M(\mathbb{I})$ is fixed, and CCA1 is an EVD problem, choosing a suitable dimension r such that $p_1 \geq \sqrt{1-\delta}$ is straightforward due to the nested structure in the EVD. If such a $\mathbf{U}_0$ is used to initialize the algorithms in Section 4.1, the final solution $\mathbf{U}_0^*$ will satisfy $f(\mathbf{U}_0^*) \geq \sqrt{1-\delta} f^{max}$ and $ARE(\mathbf{U}_0^*) \leq \delta$, which is the prescribed bound on the approximation error.

5. EXPERIMENTAL RESULTS

In this section, the performance of CCA is evaluated on both artificial datasets and two real-world stock market datasets, one spanning 21 years from 1990-2010, and the other 14 years from 1971-1984. Evaluation is done in terms of the *Approximate Relative Error* (ARE) (16) for all datasets, and also the ability to track volatility in low-dimensions for the stock market datasets. The performance of CCA is compared with PARAFAC with orthonormal constraints, PCA, and Random Projection (RP) [8, 1]. While CCA and PARAFAC are computed on the entire set of covariance matrices, PCA is computed based on the single aggregated covariance. For RP, $\mathbf{U}$ is generated as follows: (i) each entry of $\mathbf{U}$ is generated via an i.i.d. normal distribution; and (ii) $\mathbf{U}$ is normalized via the classical Gram-Schmidt orthogonalization [15] and normalization.

5.1 Artificial Data

Artificial data were generated following the model in (1). In particular, $\mathbf{Y}_t$ and $\mathbf{U}$ were generated first, then $\mathbf{X}_t$ was calculated by adding noise to $\mathbf{U}\mathbf{Y}_t\mathbf{U}^T$. $\mathbf{Y}_t$ was generated as the covariance matrix of a set of randomly generated samples. The samples were generated from the following four Gaussian distributions with means

$$m1 = [0, 0], m2 = [5, 0], m3 = [0, 5], m4 = [5, 5] ,$$

and covariances

$$[\boldsymbol{\Sigma}_1 | \boldsymbol{\Sigma}_2 | \boldsymbol{\Sigma}_3 | \boldsymbol{\Sigma}_4] = \left[\begin{array}{cc|cc|cc|cc} 4 & 0 & 4 & 0 & 0.01 & 0 & 1 & 0 \\ 0 & 1 & 0 & 0.01 & 0 & 2 & 0 & 2 \end{array}\right] .$$

Instead of using a fixed $\mathbf{U}$, it was mildly perturbed as follows:

$$\mathbf{U}_{t+1} \leftarrow QR(\mathbf{U}_t + \gamma E_t) , \qquad (23)$$

where γ is a small constant, $E_t \in \mathbb{R}^{n \times r}$ where $E_{ij} \sim N(0, 1)$, and $\mathbf{U}_{t+1}$ is obtained from the QR factorization of $(\mathbf{U}_t + \gamma E_t)$. In (23), $\mathbf{U}_1$ was randomly generated, $r = 2$, and we considered two values of the high-dimensionality $n = 5, 10$. The experiment was

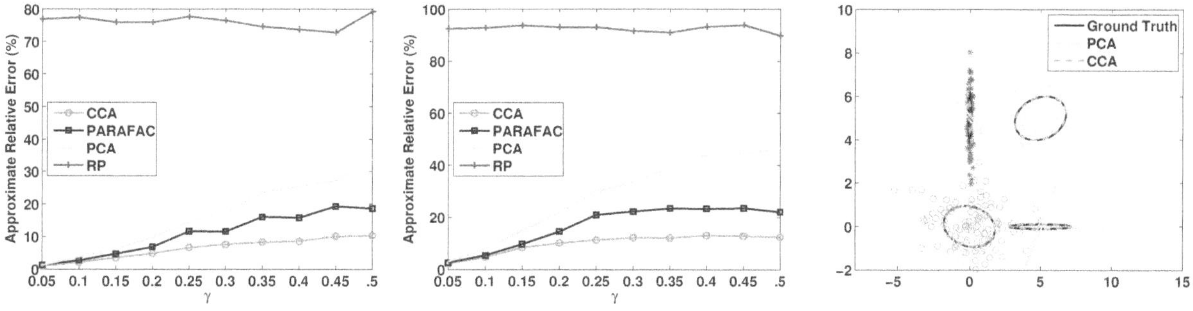

(a) $n = 5$ (b) $n = 10$ (c) Latent Covariances in 2D

Figure 1: (a)-(b) Approximation Relative Error (ARE) on artificial data in different dimensions r and increasing noise level γ. CCA outperforms PARAFAC, PCA and RP, especially with high noise levels. (c) 2D latent covariances. CCA tracks the true covariance better than PCA.

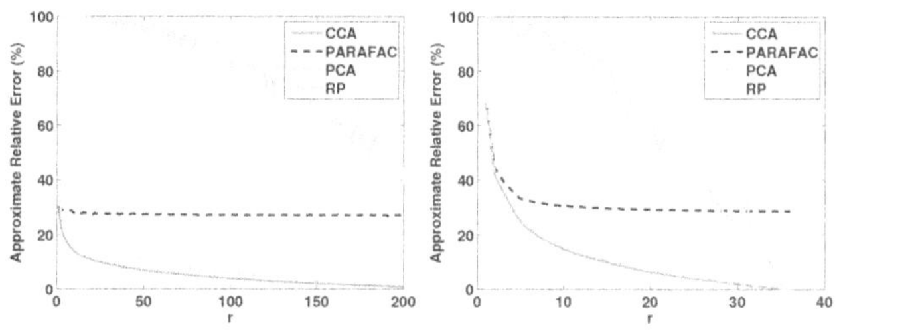

(a) S&P500 (b) NYSE

Figure 2: Approximation Relative Error (ARE) on S&P 500 and NYSE in different dimensions r. CCA outperforms PARAFAC, PCA and RP.

repeated 50 times, and the final results reported were the average over the 50 runs.

Results: Figure 1 (a)-(b) shows the comparative performance of CCA, PARAFAC, PCA, and RP in terms of the ARE (lower is better) across different noise levels γ for fixed low-dimensionality $r = 2$. As the figures show, CCA outperforms PARAFAC and PCA, and significantly outperforms RP. The improvement of CCA over other methods is more pronounced for high noise levels (high γ). For low noise levels, CCA and PARAFAC are competitive since all the covariance matrices are nearly diagonal. Due to the structure of the covariance matrices (nearly diagonal but different), PARAFAC outperforms PCA which maximizes the total covariance instead.

Figure 1(c) shows the shape of 2-dimensional covariances when $n = 10, \gamma = 0.1$. For each Gaussian distribution, covariance of the samples is its ground truth, which is plotted in black. The latent covariances for CCA and PCA, shown respectively in magenta and cyan, are calculated based on the leading 2 components. Since the black ellipses are entirely overlapped by the red ones, the ground truth is not visible. While CCA is able to recover the ground truth, PCA seems to find a subspace that maximizes the total covariance but is not suitable for separate covariances.

5.2 Stocks Data

We considered two real world stock market datasets. The first dataset, S&P500, is based on daily closing prices of the 263 stocks in the current S&P500 index from 1990 to 2010. The second dataset, NYSE, is a widely used dataset of daily closing prices of 36 stocks at daily resolution spanning from 1971 to 1984 [18, 2, 7].

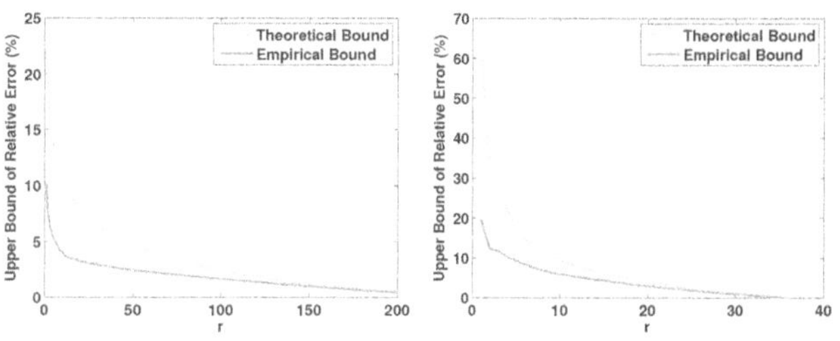

(a) S&P500 (b) NYSE

Figure 3: The upper bound of the relative error of the CCA results w.r.t. the global maximum on S&P 500 and NYSE in different dimensions r. The theoretical bound in (14) and empirical bound in (15) are in green and red, respectively. The upper bounds are very small for the first r principal components.

Methodology: For the experiments, the covariance of the daily log-return was considered for both datasets, where $\text{return}_t = \log \frac{x_t}{x_{t-1}} \times 100\%$, x_t is the daily closing stock price. For each dataset, we constructed the monthly average of the daily covariances, and each average monthly covariance was considered as an observed covariance matrix $\mathbf{X}_t$. For S&P500, there are $21 \times 12 = 252$ observed covariance matrices $\mathbf{X}_t \in \mathbb{R}^{263\times 263}$. For NYSE, there are $14 \times 12 = 168$ covariance matrices $\mathbf{X}_t \in \mathbb{R}^{36\times 36}$.

ARE: The performance of the four methods is evaluated in terms of the ARE on S&P500 and NYSE, as shown in Figure 2. On both datasets, CCA outperforms PARAFAC and PCA, and significantly outperforms RP. Interestingly, the performance of PARAFAC does not improve with increasing r (dimensionality) possibly because the covariances cannot be simultaneously diagonalized. PCA performs much better than PARAFAC, which is in direct contrast with the observed results for the artificial dataset. Note that CCA performs the best on both types of data, which illustrates the flexibility of the model. PCA is competitive with CCA on NYSE but worse on S&P500, especially for low dimensions. There are two possible explanations: NYSE is a low-dimensional dataset with $n = 36$, whereas S&P500 is a relatively high-dimensional dataset with $n = 263$; and the stock market has been more volatile in the 1990-2010 range (S&P500) as compared to the 1971-1984 range (NYSE).

Quality of CCA Solution: Figure 3 shows the upper bounds of the relative error of CCA results w.r.t. the global maximum value. The

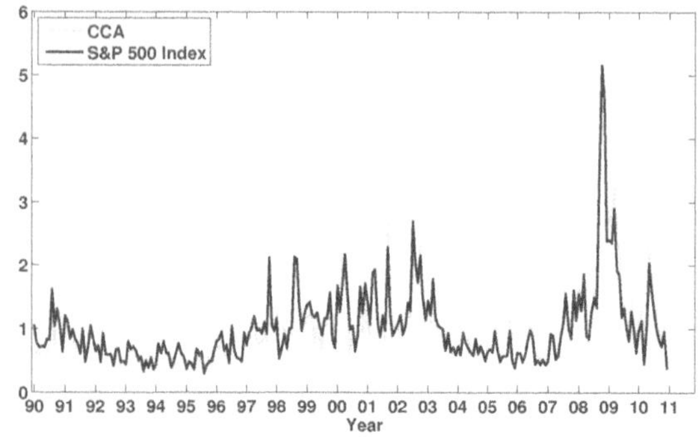

(a) 1D Latent Covariances S&P 500

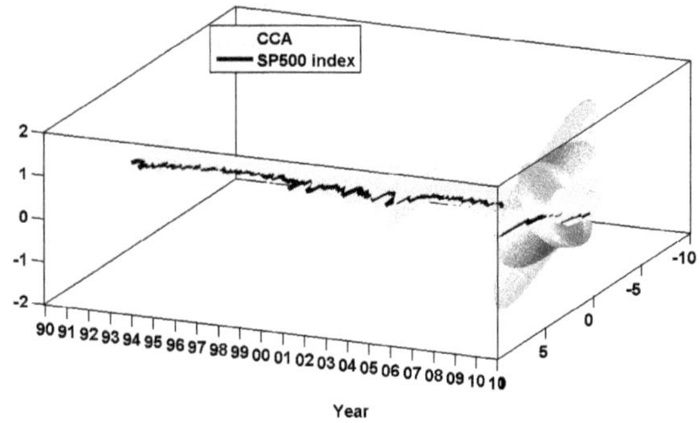

(b) 2D Latent Covariances S&P 500

Figure 4: Latent Covariances over time for S&P500 from 1990 to 2010. The two financial meltdowns in 2001 and 2008 are prominently captured in the latent low-dimensional space.

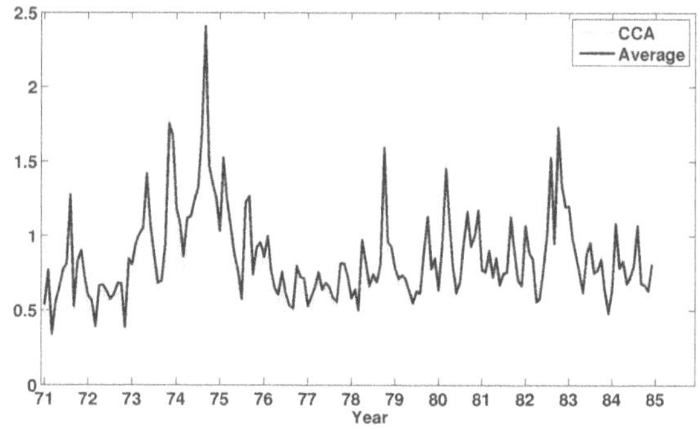

(a) 1D Latent Covariances NYSE

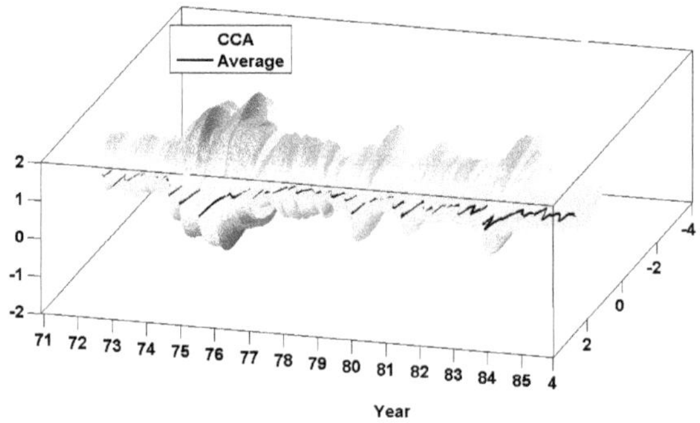

(b) 2D Latent Covariances NYSE

Figure 5: Latent Covariances over time for NYSE from 1970 to 1984. The stock market crash of 1974 is captured in the latent low-dimensional space.

green curve is the theoretical upper bound $1 - p_1$ in (14), which depends on the choice of dimensionality r and the dataset. When $r = 1$, the theoretical bound is fairly good on S&P500 but bad on NYSE. However, as r increases, the bounds decrease rapidly. When $r = 10$, the theoretical upper bounds are already approximately 10% on both datasets. After a local maximum $f(\mathbf{U}_0^*)$ is found, the empirical upper bound in (15) is plotted in red. On both datasets, the empirical upper bounds provide significant improvements over the theoretical upper bounds, especially for low values of r. For example, the empirical upper bound on NYSE decrease to 20% when $r = 1$. When $r = 10$, the empirical bounds further decrease to 5% on both datasets.

Volatility: In Figures 4 and 5 we plot the latent covariance matrices (level sets) obtained from CCA in dimensions $r = 1, 2$ for S&P500 and NYSE, and compare them to the volatilities [5, 11, 10] of their proxies. The proxy of the S&P 500 dataset is the S&P500 index, while the proxy of NYSE is the average of 36 stocks. The reason we expect $\mathbf{Y}_t$ to track volatility well is as follows: For n stocks, the trace of the covariance $\mathbf{X}_t$ is equal to $n\sigma^2$, where σ is the volatility (standard deviation) of the proxy. If $\mathbf{Y}_t$ approximates $\mathbf{X}_t$ well, the trace of $\sqrt{\mathbf{Y}_t/n}$ should approximate σ. In both datasets, for 1D ($r = 1$), $\sqrt{\mathbf{Y}_t/n}$ tracks the volatility almost exactly. For 2D ($r = 2$), $\sqrt{\mathbf{Y}_t/n}$ are ellipses that change shape/size over time, and the volatility (black curve) is always on the circumference of the ellipses. It is interesting to note that the latent covariances for S&P 500 (Figure 4) seem to capture the two major financial meltdowns, viz the dot-com bubble around 2001 and the major financial crisis around 2008, even in such a low dimensionality. The crisis in 2008 looks significantly worse, and the ellipses in the 2D plot have different shapes possibly indicating different market segments being more adversely affected. Similarly, the latent covariances for NYSE (Figure 5) capture the stock market crash around 1973-1974 resulting from the collapse of the Bretton Woods system along with the 'Nixon Shock' and the devaluation of the US dollar. Such interpretable results show the potential of CCA in high-dimensional real world problems.

Choose r given ARE: We also evaluated our method in choosing the dimensionality r given an ARE upper bound. The results on the S&P 500 dataset are shown in Table 2. The first row is the given ARE upper bound δ, the second row shows the sufficient r computed as in Section 4.2 and the corresponding ARE, and the third row shows the smallest r that would have satisfied the bound and the corresponding ARE. The chosen r satisfies the bound, but can be conservative at times especially when the ARE decreases rapidly with increasing r.

$\delta(\%)$	30	20	10	5
Chosen r (ARE)	3(21.50)	10(14.18)	45(7.58)	97(4.20)
Smallest r (ARE)	2(24.67)	4(19.70)	26(9.88)	81(5.00)

Table 2: Choosing r given an ARE upper bound on S&P 500.

Running Time: Figure 6 compares the running times (in seconds) of Algorithm 1 and Algorithm 2 on the S&P 500 dataset. The experiments were run in Matlab 7.1 on an Intel P8600 2.4GHz PC with 2G memory. When r is small, i.e., low-dimensional projections, Algorithm 2 is much faster than Algorithm 1. As r increases, Algorithm 2 possibly spends more time on the SVD step, and probably requires more steps to converge, so the superiority in running time decreases.

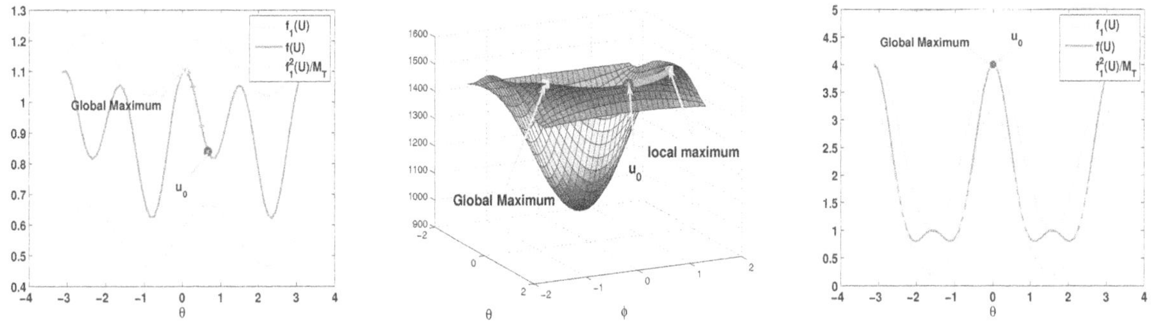

(a) A global maximum is found with the proposed initialization (b) A local maximum is found with the proposed initialization (c) A global maximum is the initialization

Figure 7: Optimizing $f(\mathbf{U})$ in CCA based on CCA1 initialization and iterative updates. Objective $f(\mathbf{U})$ for CCA is shown in red; the lower and upper bounds based on $f_1(\mathbf{U})$ for CCA1 are shown in green and cyan respectively. Three scenarios are shown: (a) iterations converge to a global maximum, (b) iterations converge to a local maximum, and (c) initialization is a global maximum.

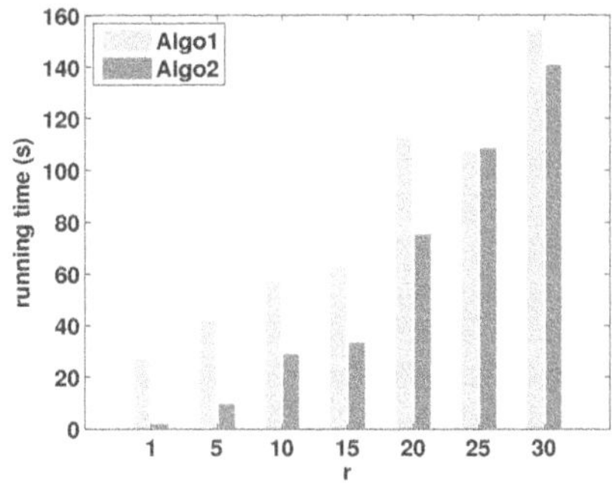

Figure 6: Running times of Algorithm 1 and Algorithm 2 on S&P 500 in different dimensions r. The auxiliary function based method (Algorithm 2) is distinctly faster for low-dimensional projections.

5.3 Additional Numerical Simulations

We study CCA (Algorithm 1) on low-dimensional problems to better understand the proposed ideas, including cases where the approach can and cannot find the global maximum of $f(\mathbf{U})$. It is important to recall that while $f(\mathbf{U})$ is a convex function for unconstrained $\mathbf{U}$, the model requires maximizing $f(\mathbf{U})$ on the domain of $\mathbf{U}$ determined by $\mathbf{U}^T\mathbf{U} = \mathbb{I}_r$, and the problem may thus have multiple local maxima.

We illustrate different scenarios for using Algorithm 1 to solve CCA in Figure 7. In Figure 7(a), we consider 3 time steps for a 2-dimensional covariance matrix, with

$$\mathbf{X} = [\mathbf{X}_1|\mathbf{X}_2|\mathbf{X}_3] = \left[\begin{array}{cc|cc|cc} 1 & 0 & 0 & 0 & 0.22 & 0.22 \\ 0 & 0.25 & 0 & 1 & 0.22 & 0.22 \end{array}\right].$$

The vector $\mathbf{u}$ is parameterized as $\mathbf{u} = [\sin(\theta), \cos(\theta)]^T$, and the x-axis denotes θ. Note that $f(\mathbf{u})$ is convex in $\mathbf{u}$ but not θ, which explains the nonconvex plot of the objective (in red). Further, the domain of θ is in $[-\pi, \pi]$, and the function is periodic beyond that domain. Algorithm 1 is used to find the best rank-1 approximation $\mathbf{u}$. In particular, the initialization $\mathbf{u}_0$ is the optimal solution of $f_1(\mathbf{u})$, denoted by a small blue circle $\circ$. The searching trajectory is denoted by magenta +, and the optimal solution of $f(\mathbf{u})$ by a green $\square$. The upper and lower bounds are plotted in cyan and green respectively. For this scenario, with the proposed initialization, a global maximum can be found, as illustrated in Figure 7(a). However, the initialization does not always lead to a global maximum as shown in Figure 7(b). In Figure 7(b), we consider

$$\mathbf{X}_1 = \begin{bmatrix} 29.7995 & 2.5707 & 1.7377 \\ 2.5707 & 30.1445 & -0.0292 \\ 1.7377 & -0.0292 & 24.1799 \end{bmatrix},$$
$$\mathbf{X}_2 = \begin{bmatrix} 21.8515 & -2.2068 & 2.0377 \\ -2.2068 & 22.8371 & 0.0490 \\ 2.0377 & 0.0490 & 21.1336 \end{bmatrix},$$
$$\mathbf{X}_3 = \begin{bmatrix} 8.5273 & -2.5322 & 1.1011 \\ -2.5322 & 9.6724 & -0.9796 \\ 1.1011 & -0.9796 & 6.4754 \end{bmatrix},$$

and the vector $\mathbf{u}$ is parameterized as $\mathbf{u} = [\sin(\theta), \cos(\theta)\sin(\phi), \cos(\theta)\cos(\phi)]^T$. In Figure 7(b), θ and ϕ are the x-axis and y-axis respectively, and $f(\mathbf{u})$ is shown in the z-axis. For this scenario, the final solution is a good local maximum but is not a global maximum, which is also marked in the figure. Finally, Figure 7(c) shows a case where the initialization itself achieves a global maximum of CCA. In Figure 7(c), we consider

$$\mathbf{X} = [\mathbf{X}_1|\mathbf{X}_2] = \left[\begin{array}{cc|cc} 1 & 0 & 0 & 0 \\ 0 & 0 & 0 & 1 \end{array}\right],$$

and $\mathbf{u}$ is parameterized as in Figure 7(a). For this scenario, if $\mathbf{u}_0$ denotes the initialization obtained from CCA1, we see that $f_1^{\max} = f_1(\mathbf{u}_0) = f(\mathbf{u}_0)$, implying $f(\mathbf{u}_0) = f^{\max}$.

6. CONCLUSIONS

In this paper, we introduced a framework called CCA for simultaneously modeling multiple covariance matrices in low dimensions. While the framework has similarities with existing approaches to tensor decompositions, we presented a novel and unique analysis of CCA in terms of a more tractable PCA framework called CCA1, which provides lower and upper bounds for the global maximum for CCA. The bounds also lead to an effective initialization scheme so that the results of CCA have clear approximation guarantees w.r.t. the global maximum. We also discussed non-trivial conditions under which the global maximum will be achieved. We proposed two algorithms: a standard tensor decomposition algorithm and an efficient auxiliary function based algorithm. They can work with either a fixed dimensionality or an approximate relative error. We illustrated the effectiveness of our approaches on synthetic data and on two real world stock market datasets.

While CCA can be considered as a special case of classical tensor decomposition methods, the analysis presented in this paper discusses two important issues encountered in the general case. Such an analysis can potentially be extended to more general settings considered in the tensor decomposition literature, and will be considered in future work. In the present analysis, all covariance matrices were assumed to be available. In real life domains such as finance and climate sciences, the observed covariance matrices become available over time. We plan to investigate extensions of the CCA framework to the online setting where the observed matrices become available over time.

Acknowledgment

This research was supported in part by NSF grants IIS-0916750, IIS-0812183, IIS-0534286, NSF CAREER grant IIS-0953274 and NASA grant NNX08AC36A.

7. REFERENCES

[1] D. Achlioptas. Database-friendly random projections. In *ACM SIGMOD-SIGACT-SIGART symposium on Principles of database systems*, pages 274–281, 2001.

[2] A. Agarwal, E. Hazan, S. Kale, and R. E. Schapire. Algorithms for portfolio management based on the Newton method. In *Proceedings of the 23rd International Conference on Machine Learning (ICML)*, 2006.

[3] T. Anderson. *An Introduction to Multivariate Statistics, 3rd ed.* John Wiley, 2003.

[4] C. M. Bishop. *Pattern Recognition and Machine Learning*. Springer, 2007.

[5] T. Bollerslev, J. Russell, and M. Watson. *Volatility and Time Series Econometrics: Essays in Honor of Robert Engle*. 2010.

[6] D. Cai, X. He, and J. Han. Subspace learning based on tensor analysis. In *Technical Report UIUCDCS-R-2005-2572*, 2005.

[7] T. M. Cover. Universal portfolios. *Mathematical Finance*, 1(1):1–29, 1991.

[8] S. Dasgupta. Experiments with random projection. In *Proceedings of the 16th Conference on Uncertainty in Artificial Intelligence (UAI)*, pages 143–151, 2000.

[9] C. Ding and J. Ye. Two-dimensional singular value decomposition (2DSVD) for 2D maps and images. In *Proceedings of the 5th SIAM International Conference on Data Mining (SDM)*, pages 32–43, 2005.

[10] R. Engle. Autoregressive conditional heteroskedasticity with estimates of the variance of UK inflation. *Econometrica*, 50:987–1008, 1982.

[11] R. Engle. Dynamic conditional correlation: A simple class of multivariate generalized autoregressive conditional heteroscedasticity models. *Journal of Business and Economic Statistics*, 20:339–350, 2002.

[12] B. N. Flury. Common principal components in k groups. *Journal of American Statistical Association*, 79(388):892–898, 1984.

[13] B. N. Flury. *Common Principal Components and Related Multivariate Models*. John Wiley, 1988.

[14] K. Fukunaga. *Introduction to Statistical Pattern Recognition, 2nd edition*. Academic Press, 1990.

[15] G. H. Golub and C. V. Loan. *Matrix Computations,3rd ed.* Johns Hopkins University Press, 1996.

[16] R. A. Harshman. Foundations of the PARAFAC procedure: Models and conditions for an explanatory multimodal factor analysis. *UCLA Working Papers in Phonetics*, 16:1–84, 1970.

[17] R. A. Harshman. PARAFAC. Tutorial and applications. *Chemometrics and Intelligent Laboratory Systems*, 38(2):149–171, 1997.

[18] D. Helmbold, R. Schapire, Y. Singer, and M. Warmuth. Online portfolio setection using multiplicative weights. *Mathematical Finance*, 8(4):325–347, 1998.

[19] R. A. Horn and C. R. Johnson. *Matrix Analysis*. Cambridge University Press, 1985.

[20] E. Kofidis and P. A. Regalia. On the best rank-1 approximation of higher-order supersymmetric tensors. *SIAM Journal on Matrix Analysis and Applications*, 23(3):863–884, 2000.

[21] T. G. Kolda. Orthogonal tensor decompositions. *SIAM Journal on Matrix Analysis and Applications*, 23(1):243–255, 2001.

[22] T. G. Kolda and B. W. Bader. Tensor decompositions and applications. *SIAM Review*, 51(3):455–500, 2009.

[23] T. G. Kolda, B. W. Bader, and J. P. Kenny. Higher- order web link analysis using multilinear algebra. In *Proceedings of the fifth IEEE International Conference on Data Mining (ICDM)*, pages 242–249, 2005.

[24] P. M. Kroonenberg. *Applied Multiway Data Analysis*. Wiley, 2008.

[25] P. M. Kroonenberg and J. de Leeuw. Principal component analysis of three-mode data by means of alternating least squares algorithms. *Psychometrika*, 45(1):69–97, 1980.

[26] L. D. Lathauwer, B. D. Moor, J. Vandewalle, and J. V. A multilinear singular value decomposition. *SIAM Journal on Matrix Analysis and Applications*, 21(4):1253–1278, 2000.

[27] L. D. Lathauwer, B. D. Moor, J. Vandewalle, and J. V. On the best rank-1 and rank-$(r_1, r_2, ..., r_n)$ approximation of higher-order tensors. *SIAM Journal on Matrix Analysis and Applications*, 21(4):1324–1342, 2000.

[28] D. D. Lee and H. S. Seung. Algorithms for non-negative matrix factorization. In *Advances in Neural Information Processing Systems (NIPS)*, pages 556–562, 2001.

[29] J. D. Leeuw and G. Michaildis. Majorization methods in statistics. *Biostatistics*, 9(3):432–441, 2008.

[30] J. A. Patz, D. Campdell-Lendrum, T. Holloway, and J. A. Foley. Impact of regional climate change on human health. *Nature*, 438:310–317, 2005.

[31] M. Pourahmadi, M. J. Daniels, and T. Park. Simultaneous modelling of the Cholesky decomposition of several covariance matrices. *Journal of Multivariate Analysis*, 98:568–587, 2006.

[32] J. T. Scruggs and P. Glabadanidis. Risk premia and the dynamic covariance between stock and bond returns. *Journal of finance and quantitative analysis*, 38(2):295–316, 2003.

[33] J. Sun, D. Tao, and C. Faloutsos. Beyond streams and graphs: Dynamic tensor analysis. In *Proceedings of the 12th ACM SIGKDD International Conference on Knowledge Discovery and Data Mining (KDD)*, pages 374–383, 2006.

[34] S. Tadjudin and D. A. Landgrebe. Covariance estimation with limited training samples. *IEEE Transactions on Geoscience and Remote Sensing*, 37(4), 1999.

[35] L. R. Tucker. Some mathematical notes on three-mode factor analysis. *Psychometrika*, 31:279–311, 1966.

[36] H. Wang, A. Banerjee, and D. Boley. Common component analysis for multiple covariance matrices. *Technical Report, TR-10-017, University of Minnesota, Twin Cities*, 2010. `http://www.cs.umn.edu/tech_reports_upload/tr2010/10-017.pdf`.

[37] J. Ye. Generalized low rank approximations of matrices. *Machine Learning Journal*, 61:167–191, 2005.

Compression of Weighted Graphs

Hannu Toivonen
Department of Computer Science and HIIT
University of Helsinki, Finland
hannu.toivonen@cs.helsinki.fi

Fang Zhou
Department of Computer Science and HIIT
University of Helsinki, Finland
fang.zhou@cs.helsinki.fi

Aleksi Hartikainen
Department of Computer Science and HIIT
University of Helsinki, Finland
aleksi.hartikainen@helsinki.fi

Atte Hinkka
Department of Computer Science and HIIT
University of Helsinki, Finland
atte.hinkka@cs.helsinki.fi

ABSTRACT

We propose to compress weighted graphs (networks), motivated by the observation that large networks of social, biological, or other relations can be complex to handle and visualize. In the process also known as graph simplification, nodes and (unweighted) edges are grouped to supernodes and superedges, respectively, to obtain a smaller graph. We propose models and algorithms for weighted graphs. The interpretation (i.e. decompression) of a compressed, weighted graph is that a pair of original nodes is connected by an edge if their supernodes are connected by one, and that the weight of an edge is approximated to be the weight of the superedge. The compression problem now consists of choosing supernodes, superedges, and superedge weights so that the approximation error is minimized while the amount of compression is maximized.

In this paper, we formulate this task as the 'simple weighted graph compression problem'. We then propose a much wider class of tasks under the name of 'generalized weighted graph compression problem'. The generalized task extends the optimization to preserve longer-range connectivities between nodes, not just individual edge weights. We study the properties of these problems and propose a range of algorithms to solve them, with different balances between complexity and quality of the result. We evaluate the problems and algorithms experimentally on real networks. The results indicate that weighted graphs can be compressed efficiently with relatively little compression error.

Categories and Subject Descriptors

E.1 [**Data Structures**]: Graphs and Networks; H.2.8 [**Database Applications**]: Data Mining; H.4 [**Information Systems Applications**]: Miscellaneous

KDD'11, August 21–24, 2011, San Diego, California, USA.

General Terms

Algorithm, Experimentation, Performance

Keywords

Weighted Graph, Network, Compression, Graph Mining

1. INTRODUCTION

Graphs and networks are used in numerous applications to describe relationships between entities, such as social relations between persons, links between web pages, flow of traffic, or interactions between proteins. In many applications, relationships have weights that are central to any use or analysis of graphs: how frequently do two persons communicate or how much do they influence each other's opinions; how much web traffic flows from one page to another or how many cars drive from one crossing to another; or how strongly does one protein regulate the other one?

We propose models and methods for the compression of weighted graphs into smaller graphs that contain approximately the same information. In this process, also known as graph simplification in the context of unweighted graphs [12, 14], nodes are grouped to supernodes, and edges are grouped to superedges between supernodes. A superedge then represents all possible edges between the pairs of nodes in the adjacent supernodes.

This problem is different from graph clustering or partitioning where the aim is to find groups of strongly related nodes. In graph compression, nodes are grouped based on the similarity of their relationships to other nodes, not by their (direct) mutual relations.

As a small example, consider the co-authorship social network in Figure 1a. It contains an excerpt from the DBLP Computer Science Bibliography[1], a subgraph containing Jiawei Han and Philip S. Yu and a dozen related authors. Nodes in this graph represent authors and edges represent co-authorships. Edges are weighted by the number of co-authored articles.

Compressing this graph just by about 30% gives a simpler graph that highlights some of the inherent structure or roles in the original graph (Figure 1b). For instance, Ke Wang and Jianyong Wang have identical sets of co-authors (in this excerpt from DBLP) and have been grouped together. This is also an example of a group that would not be found by

[1] http://dblp.uni-trier.de/

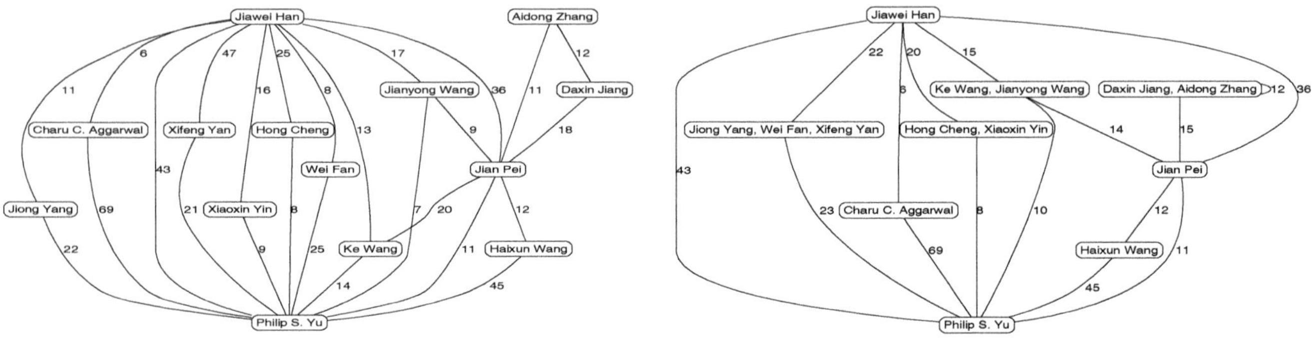

(a) Before compression (14 nodes, 26 edges)

(b) After some compression (9 nodes, 16 edges)

Figure 1: A neighborhood graph of Jiawei Han in the DBLP bibliography.

traditional graph clustering methods, since the two nodes grouped together are not directly connected. Daxin Jiang and Aidong Zhang have been grouped, but additionally the self-edge of their supernode indicates that they have also authored papers together.

Groups that could not be obtained by the existing compression algorithms of [12, 14] can be observed among the six authors that (in this excerpt) only connect to Jiawei Han and Philip S. Yu. Instead of being all grouped together as structurally equivalent nodes, we have three groups that have different weight profiles. Charu C. Aggarwal is a group by himself, very strongly connected with Philip S. Yu. A second group includes Jiong Yang, Wei Fan, and Xifeng Yan, who are roughly equally strongly connected to both Jiawei Han and Philip S. Yu. The third group, Hong Cheng and Xiaoxin Yin, are more strongly connected to Jiawei Han. Such groups are not found with methods for unweighted graphs [12, 14].

In what we define as the *simple weighted graph compression problem*, the approximation error of the compressed graph with respect to original edge weights is minimized by assigning each superedge the mean weight of all edges it represents. For many applications on weighted graphs it is, however, important to preserve relationships between faraway nodes, too, not just individual edge weights. Motivated by this, we also introduce the *generalized weighted graph compression problem* where the goal is to produce a compressed graph that maintains connectivities across the graph: the best path between any two nodes should be approximately equally good in the compressed graph as it is in the original graph, but the path does not have to be the same.

Compressed weighted graphs can be utilized in a number of ways. Graph algorithms can run more efficiently on a compressed graph, either by considering just the smaller graph consisting of supernodes and superedges, or by decompressing parts of it on the fly when needed. An interesting possibility is to provide an interactive visualization of a graph where the user can adjust the abstraction level of the graph on the fly.

The main contributions of this paper are the following.

1. We present the simple and generalized weighted graph compression problems. The compressed graphs can be decompressed easily, or they can be used without a separate decompression by many graph algorithms.

2. We analyze the problem and derive successive bounds for the distances between graphs.

3. We present several algorithms for the weighted graph compression problems. The algorithms exhibit different time/quality trade-offs.

4. We give extensive experimental results on real weighted graphs. The experiments show that weighted graphs can be compressed effectively and efficiently, and that compression can have surprisingly little effect on clustering.

The rest of this paper is organized as follows. We formulate and analyze the weighted graph compression problems in Section 2. Related work is briefly reviewed in Section 3. We give algorithms for the weighted graph compression problems in Section 4 and evaluate them experimentally in Section 5. Section 6 contains concluding remarks.

2. PROBLEM DEFINITION

The goal is to compress a given weighted graph into a smaller one. We address two variants of this problem. In the first one, the simple weighted graph compression problem, the goal is to produce a compressed graph that can be decompressed into a graph similar to the original one. In the second variant, the generalized weighted graph compression problem, the decompressed graph should approximately preserve the strengths of connections between all nodes.

2.1 Weighted and compressed graphs

We start by defining concepts and notations common to both problem variants of weighted graph compression.

Definition A *weighted graph* is a triple $G = (V, E, w)$, where V is a set of vertices (or nodes), $E \subset V \times V$ is a set of edges, and $w : E \to \mathbb{R}^+$ assigns a (non-negative) weight to each edge $e \in E$. For notational convenience, we define $w(u, v) = 0$ if $(u, v) \notin E$.

In this paper, we actually assume that graphs and edges are undirected, and in the sequel use notations such as $\{u, v\} \in V \times V$ in the obvious way. The definitions and algorithms can, however, be easily adapted for the directed case. In the compressed graph we also use self-edges, i.e., an edge from a node back to itself. The following definition of a compressed graph largely follows the definition of graph summarization for the unweighted case [12]. The essential role of weights will be defined after that.

Definition A weighted graph $S = (V', E', w')$ is a *compressed representation (or compressed graph) of* G if $V' = \{v'_1, \ldots, v'_n\}$ is a partition of V (i.e., $v'_i \subset V$ for all i, $\cup_i v'_i = V$, and $v'_i \cap v'_j = \emptyset$ for all $i \neq j$). The nodes $v' \in V'$ are also called *supernodes*, and edges $e' \in E'$ are also called *superedges*.

We use the notation $com : V \to V'$ to map original nodes to the corresponding supernodes: $com(u) = v'$ if and only if $u \in v' \in V'$.

The idea is that a supernode represents all original nodes within it, and that a single superedge represents all possible edges between the corresponding original nodes, whether they exist in G or not. Apparently, this may cause structural errors of two types: a superedge may represent edges that do not exist in the original graph, or edges in the original graph are not represented by any superedge. (Our algorithms only commit the first kind of errors, i.e., they will not miss any edges, but they may introduce new ones.) In addition, edge weights may have changed in compression. We will next formalize these issues using the concepts of decompressed graphs and graph dissimilarity.

Definition Given G and S as above, the *decompressed graph* $dec(S)$ *of* S is a weighted graph $dec(S) = (V, E'', w'')$ such that $E'' = \{\{u, v\} \in V \times V \mid \{com(u), com(v)\} \in E'\}$ and $w''(\{u, v\}) = w'(\{com(u), com(v)\})$. (By the definition of compressed representation, $V = \cup_{i=1}^{n} V'_i$.)

In other words, a decompressed graph has the original set of nodes V, and there is an edge between two nodes exactly when there is a superedge between the corresponding supernodes. The weight of an edge equals the weight of the corresponding superedge.

Definition Given G and S as above, the *compression ratio* of S (with respect to the original graph G) is defined as $cr(S) = \frac{|E'|}{|E|}$.

The compression ratio measures how much smaller the compressed graph is. The number of supernodes vs. original nodes is not included in the definition since nodes are actually not compressed, in the sense that their identities are preserved in the supernodes and hence no space is saved. They are also always completely recovered in decompression.

2.2 Simple weighted graph compression

Compression ratio does not consider the amount of errors introduced in edges and their weights. This issue is addressed by a measure of dissimilarity between graphs. We first present a simple distance measure that leads to the simple weighted graph compression problem.

Definition The *simple distance* between two graphs $G_a = (V, E_a, w_a)$ and $G_b = (V, E_b, w_b)$, with an identical set of nodes V, is

$$dist_1(G_a, G_b) = \sqrt{\sum_{\{u,v\} \in V \times V} (w_a(\{u, v\}) - w_b(\{u, v\}))^2}. \tag{1}$$

This distance measure has an interpretation as the Euclidean distance between G_a and G_b in a space where each pair of nodes $\{u, v\} \in V \times V$ has its own dimension. Given the distance definition, the dissimilarity between a graph G and its compressed representation S can then be defined simply as $dist_1(G, dec(S))$. The distance can be seen as the cost of compression, whereas the compression ratio represents the savings. Our goal is to produce a compressed graph which optimizes the balance between these two. In particular, we will consider the following form of the problem.

Definition Given a weighted graph G and a compression ratio $cr, 0 < cr < 1$, the *simple weighted graph compression problem* is to produce a compressed representation S of G with $cr(S) \leq cr$ such that $dist_1(G, dec(S))$ is minimized.

Other forms can be just as useful. One obvious choice would be to give a maximum distance as parameter, and then seek for a minimum compression ratio. In either case, the problem is complex, as the search space consists of all partitions of V. However, the compression ratio is non-increasing and graph distance non-decreasing when nodes are merged to supernodes, and this observation can be used to devise heuristic algorithms for the problem, as we do in Section 4.

2.3 Generalized weighted graph compression

We next generalize the weighted graph compression problem. In many applications, it is not the individual edge weights but the overall connectivity between nodes that matters, and we propose a model that takes this into account. The model is based on measuring the best paths between nodes, and trying to preserve these qualities. We start with some preliminary definitions and notations.

Definition Given a graph $G = (V, E, w)$, a *path* P is a set of edges $P = \{\{u_1, u_2\}, \{u_2, u_3\}, \ldots, \{u_{k-1}, u_k\}\} \subset E$. We use the notation $u_1 \overset{P}{\rightsquigarrow} u_k$ to say that P is a path between u_1 and u_k, and that u_1 and u_k are the endnodes of P.

The definition of how good a path is and which is the best one depends on the kind of graph and the application. For the sake of generality, we parameterize our formulation by a path quality function q. For example, in a flow graph where edge weights are capacities of edges, path quality q can be defined as the maximum flow through the path (i.e., as the minimum edge weight on the path). In a probabilistic or uncertain graph where edge weights are probabilities that the edge exists, q often is defined as the probability that the path exists (i.e., as the product of the edge weights). Without loss of generality, we assume that the value of any path quality function is positive, and that a larger value of q indicates better quality. We also parameterize the generalized definition by a maximum path length λ. The goal of generalized weighted graph compression will be to preserve all pairwise connectivities of length at most λ.

Definition Given a weighted graph $G = (V, E, w)$, a path quality function q, and a positive integer λ, the λ*-connection* between a pair of nodes u and v is defined as

$$Q_\lambda(u, v; G) = \begin{cases} \max_{P \subset E : u \overset{P}{\rightsquigarrow} v, |P| \leq \lambda} q(P) & \text{if such } P \text{ exists} \\ 0 & \text{otherwise,} \end{cases}$$

i.e., as the quality of the best path, of length at most λ, between u and v. If G is obvious in the context, we simply write $Q_\lambda(u, v)$.

Definition Let G_a and G_b be weighted graphs with an identical set V of nodes, and let λ be a positive integer and q a path quality function as defined above. The *generalized distance between G_a and G_b (with respect to λ and q)* is

$$dist_\lambda(G_a, G_b) = \sqrt{\sum_{\{u,v\} \in V \times V} (Q_\lambda(u, v; G_a) - Q_\lambda(u, v; G_b))^2}. \tag{2}$$

Definition Given a weighted graph G and a compression ratio $cr, 0 < cr < 1$, the *generalized weighted graph compression problem* is to produce a compressed representation S of G with $cr(S) \leq cr$ such that $dist_\lambda(G, dec(S))$ is minimized.

The simple weighted graph compression problem defined earlier is an instance of this generalized problem with $\lambda = 1$ and $q(\{e\}) = w(e)$. In this paper, we will only consider the two extreme cases with $\lambda = 1$ and $\lambda = \infty$. For notational convenience, we often write $dist(\cdot)$ instead of $dist_\lambda(\cdot)$ if the value of λ is not significant.

Algorithm 1 merge(u, v, S)

Input: Nodes u and v, and a compressed graph $S = (V, E, w)$ s.t. $u, v \in V$
Output: A compressed graph S' obtained by merging u and v in S

1: $S' \leftarrow S$ {i.e., $(V', E', w') \leftarrow (V, E, w)$}
2: $z \leftarrow \{u \cup v\}$
3: $V' \leftarrow V' \setminus \{u, v\} \cup \{z\}$
4: **for all** $x \in V$ s.t. $u \neq x \neq v$, and $\{u, x\}$ or $\{v, x\} \in E$ **do**
5: $\quad w'(\{z, x\}) = \frac{|u| Q_\lambda(\{u,x\};S) + |v| Q_\lambda(\{v,x\};S)}{|u|+|v|}$
6: $w'(\{z, z\}) = \frac{W(u,u) + W(v,v) + W(u,v)}{|z|(|z|-1)/2}$
7: **return** S'

8: **function** $W(x, y)$:
9: **if** $x \neq y$ **then**
10: $\quad$ **return** $Q_\lambda(\{x, y\}; S)|x||y|$
11: **else**
12: $\quad$ **return** $Q_\lambda(\{x, x\}; S)|x|(|x| - 1)/2$

2.4 Optimal superedge weights and mergers

Given a compressed graph structure, it is easy to set the weights of superedges to optimize the simple distance measure $dist_1(\cdot)$. Each pair $\{u, v\} \in V \times V$ of original nodes is represented by exactly one pair $\{u', v'\} \in V' \times V'$ of supernodes, including the cases $u = v$ and $u' = v'$. In order to minimize Equation 1, given the supernodes V', we need to minimize for each pair $\{u', v'\}$ of supernodes the sum $\sum_{\{u,v\} \in u' \times v'} (w(\{u, v\}) - w'(\{u'v'\}))^2$. This sum is minimized when the superedge weight is the mean of the original edge weights (including "zero-weight edges" for those pairs of nodes that are not connected by an edge):

$$w'(\{u', v'\}) = \frac{\sum_{\{u,v\} \in u' \times v'} w(\{u, v\})}{|u'|\,|v'|}, \tag{3}$$

where $|x|$ is the number of original nodes in supernode x.

The compression algorithms that we propose below work in an incremental, often greedy fashion, merging two supernodes at a time into a new supernode (following the ideas of references [12, 14]). The merge operation that these algorithms use is specified in Algorithm 1. It takes a graph and its two nodes as parameters, and it returns a graph where the given nodes are merged into one and the edge weights of the new supernode are set according to Equation 3. Line 6 of the merge operation sets the weight of the self-edge for the supernode. When $\lambda = 1$, function $W(x, y)$ returns the sum of weights of all original edges between x and y using their mean weight $Q_1(\{x, y\}; S)$. The weight of the self-edge is then zero and the edge non-existent if neither u or v has a self-edge and if there is no edge between u and v.

Setting superedge weights optimally is much more complicated for the generalized distance (Equation 2) when $\lambda > 1$: edge weights contribute to best paths and therefore distances up to λ hops away, so the distance cannot be optimized in general by setting each superedge weight independently. We use the merge operation of Algorithm 1 as an efficient, approximate solution also in these cases, and leave more optimal solutions for future work.

2.5 Bounds for distances between graphs

Our algorithms for the compression problem produce the compressed graph S by a sequence of merge operations, i.e., as a sequence $S_0 = G, S_1, \ldots, S_n = S$ of increasingly compressed graphs. Since the distance function $dist(\cdot)$ is a metric and satisfies the triangle inequality (recall its interpretation as Euclidian distance), the distance of the final compressed graph S from the original graph G can be upper-bounded by

$$dist(G, dec(S)) \leq \sum_{i=1}^{n} dist(dec(S_{i-1}), dec(S_i)).$$

An upper bound for the distance between two graphs can be obtained by considering only the biggest distance over all pairs of nodes. Let G_a and G_b be weighted graphs with an identical set V of nodes, and denote the maximum distance for any pair of nodes by $d_{\max}(G_1, G_2) = \max_{\{u,v\} \in V \times V} |(Q_\lambda(u, v; G_a) - Q_\lambda(u, v; G_b))|$. We now have the following bound:

$$\begin{aligned} dist(G_1, G_2) &\leq \sqrt{\textstyle\sum_{\{u,v\} \in V \times V} d_{\max}(G_1, G_2)^2} \\ &\propto d_{\max}(G_1, G_2). \end{aligned} \tag{4}$$

This result can be used by compression algorithms to bound the effects of potential merge operations.

2.6 A bound on distances between nodes

We now derive an upper bound for $d_{\max}(S, S')$ above when $S' = \text{merge}(u, v, S)$ for some nodes u and v in V (cf. Algorithm 1). Let $d_{\max}(u, v; S)$ be the maximum difference of weights between any two edges merged together as the result of merging u and v:

$$\begin{aligned} d_{\max}(u, v; S) = \\ \max\{ &\max_{x:\{u,x\} \text{ or } \{v,x\} \in E} (|Q_\lambda(u, x; S) - Q_\lambda(v, x; S)|), \\ &|Q_\lambda(u, u; S) - Q_\lambda(v, v; S)|, \\ &|Q_\lambda(u, u; S) - Q_\lambda(u, v; S)|, \\ &|Q_\lambda(v, v; S) - Q_\lambda(u, v; S)| \ \}. \end{aligned} \tag{5}$$

The first element is the maximum over all edges to neighboring nodes x, and the rest are the differences between edges that are merged into the self-edge.

For $\lambda = 1$ it is fairly obvious that we have the bound

$$d_{\max}(S, \text{merge}(u, v, S)) \leq d_{\max}(u, v; S), \tag{6}$$

since all effects of merge operations are completely local to the edges adjacent to the merged nodes. The situation is more complicated for $\lambda = \infty$ since a merger can also affect arbitrary edges. Luckily, many natural path quality functions q have the property that a change in the weight of an edge (from $w(e)$ to $w'(e)$) changes the quality of the whole path (from $q(P)$ to $q'(P)$) at most as much as it changes the edge itself:

$$\frac{|q(P) - q'(P)|}{q(P)} \leq \frac{|w(e) - w'(e)|}{w(e)}.$$

Path quality functions q that have this property include the sum of edge weights (e.g., path length), product of edge weights (e.g., path probability), minimum edge weight (e.g., maximum flow), maximum edge weight, and average edge weight. Based on this property, we can infer that the biggest distance after merging u and v will be seen on the edges connecting u, v and their neighbors, i.e., that the bound of Equation 6 holds also for $\lambda = \infty$ for many usual path quality functions.

Based on Equations 4 and 6, we have a fast way to bound the effect of merging any two nodes. We will use this bound in some of our algorithms.

3. RELATED WORK

Graph compression as presented in this paper is based on merging nodes that have similar relationships to other entities i.e., that are structurally most equivalent — a classic concept in social network analysis [11]. Structural equivalence and many other types of relations between (super)nodes have been considered in social networks under block modeling (see, e.g., [3]), where the goal is both to identify supernodes and to choose among the different possible types of connections between them. Our approach (as well as that of references [12, 14], see below) uses only two types: "null" (no edges) and "complete" (all pairs are connected), as these seem to be best suited for compression.

Graph compression has recently attracted new interest. The work most closely related to ours is by Navlakha et al. [12] and Tian et al. [14], who independently proposed to construct graph summaries of unweighed graphs by grouping nodes and edges to supernodes and superedges. We generalize these approaches in two important and related directions: to weighted graphs, and to long-range, indirect (weighted) connections between nodes.

Both above-mentioned papers also address issues we do not consider here. Navlakha et al. [12] propose a representation which has two parts: one is a graph summary (in our terminology, an unweighted compressed graph), the other one is a set of edge corrections to fix the errors introduced by mergers of nodes and edges to superedges. Tian et al. [14] consider labeled graphs with categorical node and edge attributes, and the goal is to find relatively homogeneous supernodes and superedges. This approach has been generalized by Zhang et al. [17] to numerical node attributes which are then automatically categorized. They also addressed interactive drill-down and roll-up operations on graphs. Tian et al. used both top-down (divisive) and bottom-up (agglomerative) algorithms, and concluded that top-down methods are more practical in their problem [14], whereas Navlakha et al. had the opposite experience [12]. This difference is likely due to different use of node and edge labels. The methods we propose work bottom-up since we have no categorical attributes to guide a divisive approach like Tian et al. had.

Unweighted graph compression techniques have been used to simplify graph storage and manipulation. For example, Chen et al. [4] successfully applied a graph compression method to reduce the number of embeddings when searching frequent subgraphs in a large graph. Navlakha et al. [13] revealed biological modules with the help of compressed graphs. Furthermore, Chen et al. [5] incorporated the compressed graph notion with a generic topological OLAP framework to realize online graph analysis.

There are many related but subtly different problems. Graph partitioning methods (e.g. [8, 6]) aim to find groups of nodes that are more strongly connected to each other than to nodes in other groups. Extraction of a subgraph, whether based on a user query (e.g. [7, 10]) or not (e.g., [16, 9, 15]) produces a smaller graph by just throwing out edges and nodes. Web graph compression algorithms aim to produce as compact a representation of a graph as possible, in different formats (e.g., [1, 2]). For more related work, we refer to the good overviews given in references [12, 14].

4. ALGORITHMS

We next propose a series of algorithms for the weighted graph compression problem. All of the proposed algorithms work more or less in a greedy fashion, merging two (super)nodes and their edges at a time until the specified compression rate is achieved. All these algorithms have the following input and output:

Input: weighted graph $G = (V, E, w)$, compression ratio cr $(0 < cr < 1)$, path quality function q, and maximum path length $\lambda \in \mathbb{N}$.

Output: compressed weighted graph $S = (V', E', w')$ with $cr(S) \leq cr$, such that $dist(G, dec(S))$ is minimized.

Brute-force greedy algorithm. The brute-force greedy method (Algorithm 2) computes the effects of all possible pairwise mergers (Line 4) and then performs the best merger (Line 5), and repeats this until the requested compression rate is achieved. The algorithm generalizes the greedy algorithm of Navlakha et al. [12] to distance functions $dist_\lambda(\cdot)$ that take the maximum path length λ and the path quality function q as parameters.

Algorithm 2 Brute-force greedy search

1: $S \leftarrow G$ {i.e., $(V', E', w') \leftarrow (V, E, w)$}
2: **while** $cr(S) > cr$ **do**
3:   **for all** pairs $\{u, v\} \in V' \times V'$ **do** {(*)}
4:     $d_{\{u,v\}} \leftarrow dist(G, dec(merge(u, v, S)))$
5:   $S \leftarrow merge(\arg\min_{\{u,v\}} d_{\{u,v\}}, S)$
6: **return** S

(*) 2-hop optimization can be used, see text.

The worst-case time complexity for simple weighted graph compression is $O(|V|^4)$, and for generalized compression $O(|V|^3|E| \log |V|)$. We omit the details for brevity.

2-hop optimization. The brute-force method, as well as all other methods we present here, can be improved by the 2-hop optimization. Instead of arbitrary pairs of nodes, the 2-hop optimized version only considers u and v for a potential merger if they are exactly two hops from each other. Since

2-hop neighbors have a shared neighbor that can be linked to the merged supernode with a single superedge, some compression may result. The 2-hop optimization is safe in the sense that any merger by Algorithm 1 that compresses the graph involves 2-hop neighbors.

The time saving by 2-hop optimization can be significant: for the brute-force method, for instance, there are approximately $O(deg\,|E|)$ feasible node pairs with the optimization, where deg is the average degree, instead of the $O(|V|^2)$ pairs in the unoptimized algorithm.

For the randomized methods below, a straight-forward implementation of 2-hop optimization by random walk has a nice property. Assume that one node has been chosen, then find a random pair for it by taking two consequtive random hops starting from the first node. Now 2-hop neighbors with many shared neighbors are more likely to get picked, since there are several 2-hop paths to them. Such pairs, with many shared neighbors, lead to better compression. A uniform selection among all 2-hop neighbors does not have this property.

Thresholded algorithm. We next propose a more practical algorithmic alternative, the thresholded method (Algorithm 3). It iterates over all pairs of nodes and merges all pairs (u, v) such that $d_{\max}(u, v; S) \leq T_i$ (Lines 5–6). The threshold value T_i is increased iteratively in a heuristic manner whenever no mergers can be done with the current threshold (Lines 2 and 4).

Algorithm 3 Thresholded algorithm

1: **for all** $0 \leq i \leq K$ **do**
2: $\quad T_i \leftarrow 2^{-K+i}$
3: $S \leftarrow G$ {i.e., $(V', E', w') \leftarrow (V, E, w)$}
4: **for all** $i = 0, \ldots, K$ **do**
5: $\quad$ **while** there exists a pair $\{u, v\} \in V' \times V'$ such that $d_{\max}(u, v; S) \leq T_i$ **do** {(*)}
6: $\quad\quad S \leftarrow merge(u, v, S)$
7: $\quad\quad$ **if** $cr(S) \leq cr$ **then**
8: $\quad\quad\quad$ **return** S

(*) 2-hop optimization can be used, see text.

Different schemes for setting the thresholds would give different results and time complexity. The heuristic we have used has $K = 20$ exponentially growing steps and aims to produce relatively high-quality results faster than the brute-force method. Increasing the threshold in larger steps would give a faster method, but eventually a random compression (cf. Algorithm 5 below). We will give better informed, faster methods below.

The time complexity is $O(|V|^4)$ for the simple and $O(|V|^4 + |V|^2|E| \log |V|)$ for the generalized problem. These are upper bounds for highly improbable worst cases, and in practice the algorithm is much faster. See experiments in Section 5 for details on real world performance.

Randomized semi-greedy algorithm. The next algorithm is half random, half greedy (Algorithm 4). In each iteration, it first picks a node v at random (Line 3). Then it chooses node u so that the merge of u and v is optimal with respect to $d_{\max}(u, v; S)$ (Line 6). With 2-hop optimization, this algorithm is a generalized version of the randomized algorithm of Navlakha et al. [12].

The worst-case time complexity of the algorithm is

Algorithm 4 Randomized semi-greedy algorithm

1: $S \leftarrow G$ {i.e., $(V', E', w') \leftarrow (V, E, w)$}
2: **while** $cr(S) > cr$ **do**
3: $\quad$ randomly choose $v \in V'$
4: $\quad$ **for all** nodes $u \in V'$ **do** {(*)}
5: $\quad\quad d_u \leftarrow d_{\max}(v, u; S)$
6: $\quad S \leftarrow merge(\arg\min_u d_u, v, S)$
7: **return** S

(*) 2-hop optimization can be used, see text.

$O(|V|^3)$ for the simple and $O(|V|^2|E| \log |V|)$ for the generalized problem.

Random pairwise compression. Finally, we present a naive, random method which simply merges pairs of nodes at random without any aim to produce a good compression (Algorithm 5). The uninformed random method provides a baseline for the quality or other methods that make informed decisions about mergers.

Algorithm 5 Random pairwise compression

$S \leftarrow G$ {i.e., $(V', E', w') \leftarrow (V, E, w)$}
while $cr(S) > cr$ **do**
$\quad$ randomly choose $\{u, v\} \in V' \times V'$ {(*)}
$\quad S \leftarrow merge(u, v, S)$
return S

(*) 2-hop optimization can be used, see text.

The time complexity of the random algorithm is $O(|V|^2)$ for the simple and $O(|V||E| \log |V|)$ for the generalized problem. The random algorithm is essentially the fastest possible compression algorithm that uses pairwise mergers. It therefore provides a baseline (lower bound) also for runtime comparisons.

Interactive compression. Thanks to the simple agglomerative structure of the methods, all of them lend themselves to interactive visualization of graphs where the abstraction level can be adjusted dynamically. This simply requires that the merge operations save the hierarchical composition of the supernodes produced. A drill-down operation then corresponds to backtracking merge operations, and a roll-up operation corresponds to mergers.

5. EXPERIMENTS

We next present experimental results on the weighted graph compression problem using algorithms introduced in the previous section and real data sets. With these experiments we aim to address the following questions. (1) How well can weighted graphs be compressed: what is the trade-off between compression (lower number of edges) and distance to the original graph? (2) How do the different algorithms fare in this task: how good are the results they produce? (3) What are the running times of the algorithms? And, finally: (4) How does compression affect the use of the graph in clustering?

5.1 Experimental setup

We extracted test graphs from the biological Biomine database[2] and from a co-authorship graph compiled from

[2]http://biomine.cs.helsinki.fi

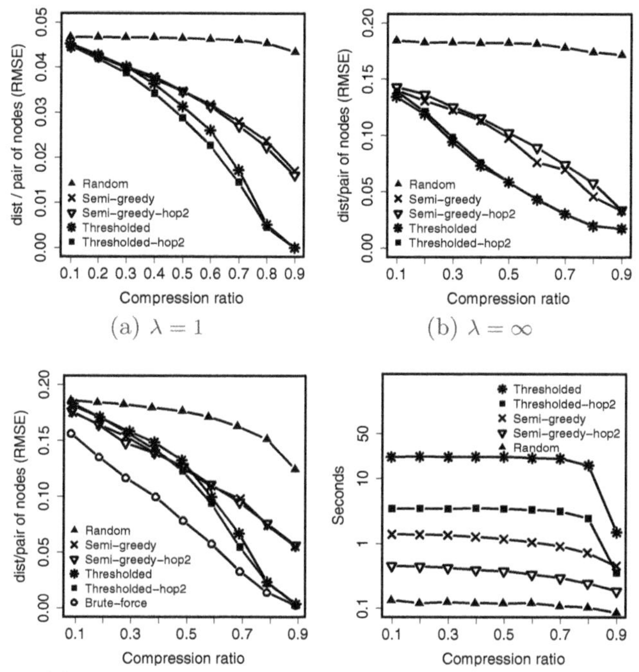

(a) $\lambda = 1$ (b) $\lambda = \infty$

(c) Small graphs, $\lambda = 1$ (d) $\lambda = 1$

Figure 2: (a)-(c): Distance between the compressed and the original graph as a function of compression ratio. (d): Running times of algorithms.

the DBLP computer science bibliography. Edge weights are in $[0, 1]$, and the path quality function is the product of weights of the edges in the path. Below we briefly describe how the datasets were obtained.

A set of 30 connection graphs, each consisting of around 1000 nodes and 2411 to 3802 edges (median 2987 edges; average node degree 2.94) was used in most of the tests. These graphs were obtained as connection graphs between three sets of related genes (different gene sets for each of the 30 replicates) so that they contain some non-trivial structure. We mostly report mean results over all 30 graphs.

A set of 30 smaller graphs was used for tests with the time-consuming brute-force method. These graphs have 50 nodes each and 76 to 132 edges (median 117 edges; average node degree 2.16).

Two series of increasingly larger graphs were used to compare the scalability of the methods. The sizes in one series range from 1000 to 5000 nodes and from 2000 to 17000 edges, and in the other series from 10 000 to 200 000 nodes and about 12 000 to 400 000 edges.

The algorithms were implemented in Java, and all the experiments were run on a standard PC with 4 GB of main memory and an Intel Core 2 Duo 3.16 GHz processor.

5.2 Results

Compressibility of weighted graphs. Figures 2a and 2b give the distance between the compressed and original graphs as a function of the compression ratio. For better interpretability, the distance is represented as the root mean square error (RMSE) over all pairs of nodes. Overall, the distances are small. Compression to half of the original size can be achieved with errors of 0.03 ($\lambda = 1$) or 0.06 ($\lambda = \infty$) per node pair. Especially for $\lambda = \infty$ graphs compress very nicely.

Comparison of algorithms. Figure 2c complements the comparison with results for the smaller graphs, and now including the brute-force method ($\lambda = 1$). The brute-force method clearly produces the best results (but is very slow as we will see shortly). Note also how small graphs are relatively harder to compress and the distances are larger than for the standard set of larger graphs.

The thresholded method is almost as good for compression ratios 0.8-0.9 but the gap grows a bit for smaller compression ratios. The semi-greedy version, on the other hand, is not as good with the larger compression ratios, but has a relatively good performance with smaller compression ratios. The random method is consistently the worst. A few early bad mergers already raise the distance for high compression ratios. Experiments on larger graphs could not be run with the brute force methods.

Efficiency of algorithms. Mean running times of the algorithms (except brute-force, see below) over the 30 standard graphs are shown in Figure 2d. The differences in the running times are big between the methods, more than two orders of magnitude between the extremes.

The 2-hop-optimized versions are an order of magnitude faster than the unoptimized versions while the results were equally good (cf. Figure 2c). 2-hop optimization thus very clearly pays off.

The brute-force method is very slow compared to the other methods (results not shown). Its running times for the small graphs were 1.5–5 seconds with $\lambda = 1$ where all other methods always finished within 0.4 seconds. With $\lambda = \infty$, the brute-force method spent 20–80 seconds whereas all other methods used less than 0.5 second.

Running times with $\lambda = \infty$ are larger than with $\lambda = 1$ by an order of magnitude, for the semi-greedy versions by two orders of magnitude (not shown).

We evaluated the effect of graph size on running times of the three fastest algorithm, using the series of increasingly large graphs and a fixed compression ratio 0.8 (Figures 3a and 3b). For $\lambda = 1$ the random method should be linear (and deviations are likely due to random effects). The thresholded method seems in practice approximately quadratic as is to be expected: for any value of λ, it will iterate over all pairs of nodes. The semi-greedy algorithm has a much more graceful behavior, even if slightly superlinear. Relative results are similar for $\lambda = \infty$.

Additional scalability experiments were run with larger graphs from both biological and co-authorship domains, using the semi-greedy algorithm with 2-hop optimization, compression ratio $cr = 0.8$, and $\lambda = 1$ (Figures 3c and 3d). The algorithm compressed graphs of upto 400000 edges in less than 10 minutes (biology) or in less than 3 minutes (co-authorship). The biological graphs contain nodes with high degrees, and this makes the compression algorithms slower.

Effect of compression on node clustering results. We next study how errors introduced by weighted graph compression affect methods that work on graphs. As a case study, we consider node clustering and measure the difference of clusters in the original graph vs. clusters in (the decompressed version of) the compressed graph.

We applied the k-medoids clustering algorithm on the 30 standard graphs. We set $k = 3$, corresponding to the three gene groups used to obtain the graphs. The proximity be-

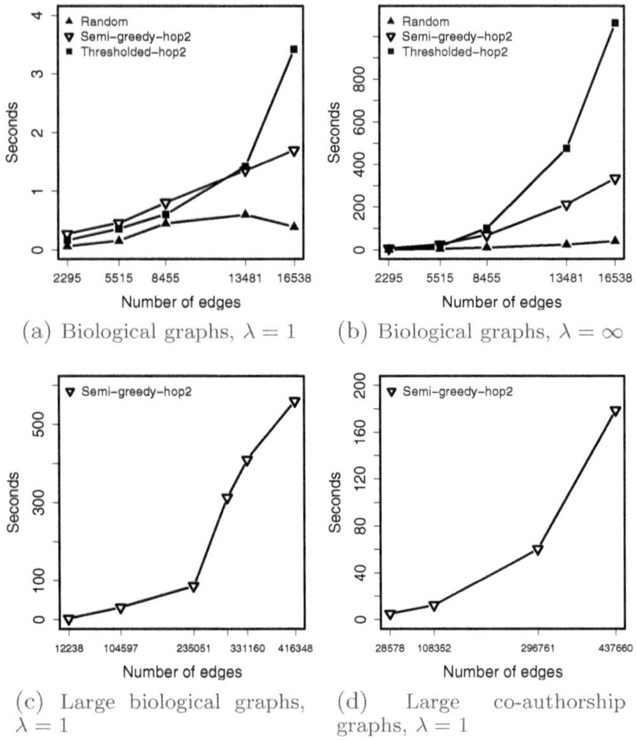

(a) Biological graphs, $\lambda = 1$ (b) Biological graphs, $\lambda = \infty$

(c) Large biological graphs, $\lambda = 1$ (d) Large co-authorship graphs, $\lambda = 1$

Figure 3: Running times of weighted graph compression algorithms on graphs of various sizes from different sources.

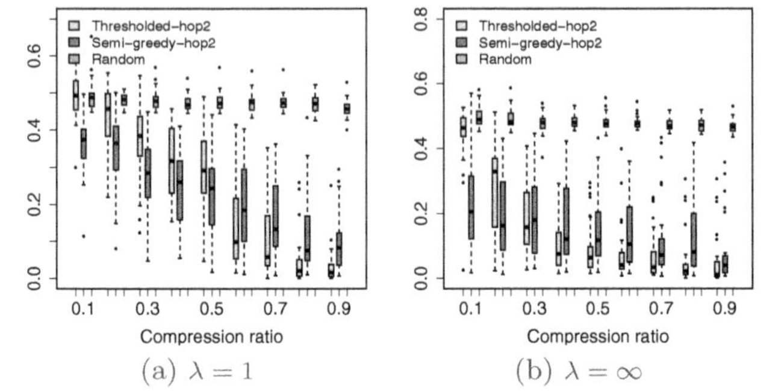

(a) $\lambda = 1$ (b) $\lambda = \infty$

Figure 4: Effect of compression on node clustering. Y-axis is the fraction of node pairs clustered inconsistently in the original and the compressed graph.

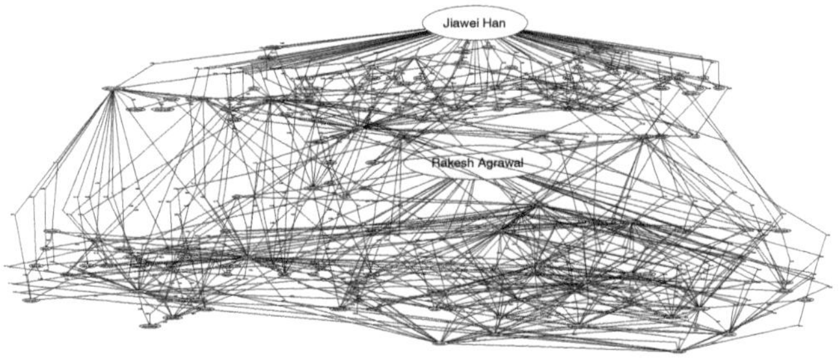

(a) G, 150 nodes, 613 edges

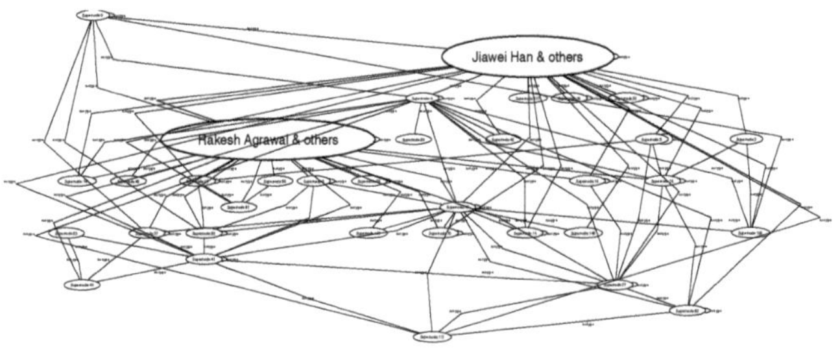

(b) S, $cr = 0.2$, 34 nodes, 114 edges

Figure 5: A joint DBLP co-authorship neighborbood graph G of Jiawei Han and Rakesh Agrawal and its compressed version S ($\lambda = \infty$).

tween two nodes was computed as the product of weights (probabilities) of edges on the best path. We measure the difference between clusterings by the fraction of node pairs that are clustered inconsistently in the clusterings, i.e., assigned to the same cluster in one graph and to different clusters in the other graph.

According to the results, the thresholded and semi-greedy compression methods can compress a weighted graph with little effect on node clustering (Figure 4). The effect is small especially when $\lambda = \infty$, where the inconsistency ratio is less than 0.1 (the thresholded method) or 0.3 (the semi-greedy method) for a wide range of compression ratios. The effects of the thresholded and semi-greedy versions are larger for $\lambda = 1$, especially when the compression ratio cr becomes smaller. This is because a clustering based solely on immediate neighborhoods is more sensitive to individual edge weights, whereas $Q_\infty(\cdot)$ can find a new best path elsewhere if an edge on the current best path is strongly changed.

Surprisingly, the semi-greedy method performs best in this comparison with compression ratio $cr \leq 0.2$. With $\lambda = \infty$ even an aggressive compression introduced relatively little changes to node clustering. In the other extreme, clusters found in randomly compressed graphs are quite—but not completely—different from the clusters found in the original graph. Close to 50% of pairs are clustered inconsistently, whereas a random clustering of three equally sized clusters would have about $2/3$ inconsistency.

Examples on compressed co-authorship graphs. As a final, rough illustration of weighted graph compression on real graphs, Figure 5 shows weighted graph compression on a co-authorship graph. The graph has been extracted from the DBLP computer science bibliography and contains the union of the co-authorship neighborhoods of Jiawei Han and Ragesh Agrawal. The number of jointly authored articles is used as the edge weight.

Even if details are not visible, compression clearly helps to bring out the structures of the social network. For instance, different roles of co-authors with respect to other authors in the network can be seen. Many supernodes have self-edges to indicate the average strength of connection between authors within the supernode. An interactive graphical display of the compressed graphs, with a possibility to explore the graph and its different abstraction levels, would be a valuable tool for a better understanding of the structure of the social networks.

6. CONCLUSIONS

We presented the problem of weighted graph compression, derived bounds for it, and gave algorithms and experimental results on real datasets. We proposed two forms of the problem: a simple one, where the compressed graph should preserve edge weights, and a generalized one, where the compressed graph should preserve strengths of connections of upto λ hops. The generalized form may be valuable especially for graph analysis algorithms that rely more on strengths of connections than individual edge weights.

The results indicate the following. (1) Weighted graphs can be compressed quite a lot with little loss of information. (2) The generalized weighted graph compression problem is promising as a pre-processing step for computationally complex graph analysis algorithms: clustering of nodes was affected very little by generalized compression. (3) Weighted graphs can be compressed efficiently. E.g., the semi-greedy method processed a 16 000 edge graph in 2 seconds.

An additional good property of the proposed methods, built in to the problem definition, is that compressed graphs are graphs, too. This gives two benefits. First, some graph algorithms can be applied directly on the compressed graph with reduced running times. Second, representing graphs as graphs is user-friendly. The user can easily tune the abstraction level by adjusting the compression ratio (or the maximum distance between the compressed and the original graph). This can also be done interactively to support visual inspection of a graph.

There are several directions in which this work can be developed further. Different merge operations may be considered, also ones that remove edges. More efficient algorithms can be developed for even better scalability to large graphs. It could be useful to modify the methods to guarantee a bounded edge-wise or node pair-wise error, or to also accommodate categorical labels.

7. ACKNOWLEDGMENTS

This work has been supported by the Algorithmic Data Analysis (Algodan) Centre of Excellence of the Academy of Finland (Grant 118653) and by the European Commission under the 7th Framework Programme FP7-ICT-2007-C FET-Open, contract no. BISON-211898.

8. REFERENCES

[1] M. Adler and M. Mitzenmacher. Towards compressing web graphs. In *Data Compression Conference*, pages 203–212, 2001.

[2] P. Boldi and S. Vigna. The webgraph framework I: compression techniques. In *WWW '04: Proceedings of the 13th international conference on World Wide Web*, pages 595–602, New York, NY, USA, 2004. ACM.

[3] S. P. Borgatti and M. G. Everett. Regular blockmodels of multiway, multimode matrices. *Social Networks*, 14:91–120, 1992.

[4] C. Chen, C. Lin, M. Fredrikson, M. Christodorescu, X. Yan, and J. Han. Mining graph patterns efficiently via randomized summaries. In *2009 Int. Conf. on Very Large Data Bases*, pages 742–753, Lyon, France, August 2009. VLDB Endowment.

[5] C. Chen, X. Yan, F. Zhu, J. Han, and P. Yu. Graph OLAP: Towards online analytical processing on graphs. In *ICDM '08: Proceedings of the 2008 Eighth IEEE International Conference on Data Mining*, pages 103–112, Washington, DC, USA, 2008. IEEE Computer Society.

[6] U. Elsner. Graph partitioning - a survey. Technical Report SFB393/97-27, Technische Universität Chemnitz, 1997.

[7] C. Faloutsos, K. S. McCurley, and A. Tomkins. Fast discovery of connection subgraphs. In *KDD '04: Proceedings of the tenth ACM SIGKDD international conference on Knowledge discovery and data mining*, pages 118–127, New York, NY, USA, 2004. ACM.

[8] P.-O. Fjällström. Algorithms for graph partitioning: A Survey. In *Linköping Electronic Atricles in Computer and Information Science, 3*, 1998.

[9] S. Hauguel, C. Zhai, and J. Han. Parallel PathFinder Algorithms for Mining Structures from Graphs. In *2009 Ninth IEEE International Conference on Data Mining*, pages 812–817. IEEE, 2009.

[10] P. Hintsanen and H. Toivonen. Finding reliable subgraphs from large probabilistic graphs. *Data Mining and Knowledge Discovery*, 17:3–23, 2008.

[11] F. Lorrain and H. C. White. Structural equivalence of individuals in social networks. *Journal of Mathematical Sociology*, 1:49–80, 1971.

[12] S. Navlakha, R. Rastogi, and N. Shrivastava. Graph summarization with bounded error. In *SIGMOD '08: Proceedings of the 2008 ACM SIGMOD international conference on Management of data*, pages 419–432, New York, NY, USA, 2008. ACM.

[13] S. Navlakha, M. Schatz, and C. Kingsford. Revealing Biological Modules via Graph Summarization. *Presented at the RECOMB Systems Biology Satellite Conference. J. Comp. Bio.*, 16:253–264, 2009.

[14] Y. Tian, R. Hankins, and J. Patel. Efficient aggregation for graph summarization. In *SIGMOD '08: Proceedings of the 2008 ACM SIGMOD international conference on Management of data*, pages 567–580, New York, NY, USA, 2008. ACM.

[15] H. Toivonen, S. Mahler, and F. Zhou. A framework for path-oriented network simplification. In *Advances in Intelligent Data Analysis IX*, volume 6065/2010, pages 220–231, Berlin/Heidelberg, May 2010. Springer-Verlag.

[16] G. T. Toussaint. The relative neighbourhood graph of a finite planar set. *Pattern Recognition*, 12(4):261–268, 1980.

[17] N. Zhang, Y. Tian, and J. Patel. Discovery-driven graph summarization. In *Data Engineering (ICDE), 2010 IEEE 26th International Conference on*, pages 880–891. IEEE, 2010.

Content-driven Trust Propagation Framework

V.G.Vinod Vydiswaran
University of Illinois
Urbana, IL
vgvinodv@illinois.edu

ChengXiang Zhai
University of Illinois
Urbana, IL
czhai@cs.uiuc.edu

Dan Roth
University of Illinois
Urbana, IL
danr@illinois.edu

ABSTRACT

Existing fact-finding models assume availability of structured data or accurate information extraction. However, as online data gets more unstructured, these assumptions are no longer valid. To overcome this, we propose a novel, content-based, trust propagation framework that relies on signals from the textual content to ascertain veracity of free-text claims and compute trustworthiness of their sources. We incorporate the quality of relevant content into the framework and present an iterative algorithm for propagation of trust scores. We show that existing fact finders on structured data can be modeled as specific instances of this framework. Using a retrieval-based approach to find relevant articles, we instantiate the framework to compute trustworthiness of news sources and articles. We show that the proposed framework helps ascertain trustworthiness of sources better. We also show that ranking news articles based on trustworthiness learned from the content-driven framework is significantly better than baselines that ignore either the content quality or the trust framework.

Categories and Subject Descriptors

H.3.3 [**Information Storage and Retrieval**]: Information Search and Retrieval—*Information filtering*; I.2 [**Computing Methodologies**]: Artificial Intelligence

General Terms

Design, Algorithms, Measurement, Experimentation

Keywords

Trust models, credibility, graph algorithms, fact-finders

1. INTRODUCTION

As online content grows exponentially, reliance on the Web content is also growing in many domains. Surveys show that more people, independent of age, now rely on online content for news, opinion, social networking, and other aspects of personal well-being, including health. An early-2009 poll [3] found that 62% of Americans got their information about HIV and AIDS through media sources, including news websites and the Internet, as compared to only 13% who received the information from their doctors. Similarly, while the readership of traditional newspapers is declining, accessing news online has steadily increased over the past few years. In a March 2010 survey of US Internet users [1] on the primary source used to find news, it was found that the Web/Internet is, by far, the most popular source (49%) as compared to television (32%) and newspapers (9%).

The relative ease of publishing online, however, has led to a significant impact on the overall quality of information accessible to the consumers. A user searching online for news would not be able to easily distinguish a trustworthy news article from another that is biased or nonfactual. In such a scenario, users would like to know whether a claim or an article they find online is indeed trustworthy and which sources are more trustworthy than others.

To address this problem, in this paper, we study how to predict trustworthiness of textual claims. We propose a novel, content-driven, trust propagation framework that helps ascertain the veracity of free-text claims and compute trustworthiness of their sources based on the quality of evidence. As a specific instance of such a framework, we measure the trustworthiness of news sources and stories. Given a collection of news text articles from multiple sources, we would like to ascertain relevant, trustworthy news articles and sources to help users gauge the veracity of given claims.

Although trustworthiness frameworks have been studied earlier, they were mainly focused on structured "facts" (claims) and the underlying information network. There are two major lines of previous work: the first is TruthFinder [24] that aims at computing the veracity of "facts" and trustworthiness of sources, utilizing the relationship between source and claims and the interaction between claims. The second relevant framework is proposed by Pasternack and Roth [19], who extend the fact-finding models by incorporating prior knowledge about claims into an existing fact-finding algorithm and formulate it as a linear program. Both have assumed structured data, i.e., they assume that there exists explicit correspondence between sources and claims.

The problem setup addressed in this work, however, is significantly different. We postulate that sources do not necessarily state the claims they make explicitly, making it difficult for information extraction algorithms to extract them accurately. Instead, sources give certain evidence in favor of or against claims, which are in free-text form. Existing trust models do not handle such scenarios. We propose that trust computation frameworks should assimilate the relevance of evidence content found for a claim, uncertainty in quality of these evidence artifacts, and the information network structure to compute trustworthiness. This paper presents such a "content-driven" framework for computing trust, which is an enhancement to previous fact-finding models.

The key contributions of this paper are as follows: (i) we propose a novel, content-driven, trust computation framework (Sec. 3) and describe factors that affect computation of trustworthiness; (ii) we present approaches to address uncertainty of evidence and similarity between evidence documents (Sec. 4); and (iii) we instantiate a model to compute trustworthiness of news sources (Sec. 5.1), utilizing trust scores assigned to news stories by humans. Our experiments show that the instantiated model helps assess trustworthiness of news sources better and that ranking news articles based on our model is significantly better than baselines that ignore either the evidence quality or the trust framework.

2. PROBLEM DEFINITION

The overall goal is to estimate the veracity of textual claims. A **claim** is a statement, topic, or a document whose veracity is unknown. It can be a "fact" (alternatively, "true claim") or a "hoax" (alternatively, "false claim"). Previous literature have sometimes called these "facts", but we prefer a more unbiased nomenclature.

In a typical instantiation of the problem, the claim is input to the system and the framework would estimate the veracity of the claim. One of the key factors in determining the veracity is the characteristics of the sources that support the claim. A **source** gives evidence for (or "expresses") a claim. Trustworthy sources support true claims or contradict false claims, while untrustworthy sources support false claims or contradict true claims. In addition, a piece of **evidence** is a passage, document, or artifact that supports or contradicts a claim. "Good" (trusted) evidence boosts the source's trustworthiness and the claim's veracity.

An overall judgment on the veracity of the claim is made based on the trustworthiness of the sources giving evidence for the claim and the relevance and nature of evidence found. Instead of classifying claims as true or false, the proposed framework assigns confidence scores to claims and ranks evidence and sources based on trustworthiness, to help users decide the claims' veracity for themselves. The typical questions that the framework helps answer are:

- **Veracity of claims:** How truthful is this claim?
- **Source trustworthiness:** What are the trusted sources for this claim?
- **Evidence trustworthiness:** Which pieces of evidence are more trustworthy than others for this claim?

2.1 Sample instantiation of the problem

As a specific instance of the problem, consider the need to judge the trustworthiness of news available online. We can find many news articles on a topic from various sources, but they are not equally trustworthy. The news articles may be written by biased media sources or may be opinion articles that are more biased than, say, news reports. Our overall goal is to assign veracity of reporting on a given topic, in addition to inferring which sources and news articles are more trustworthy than others.

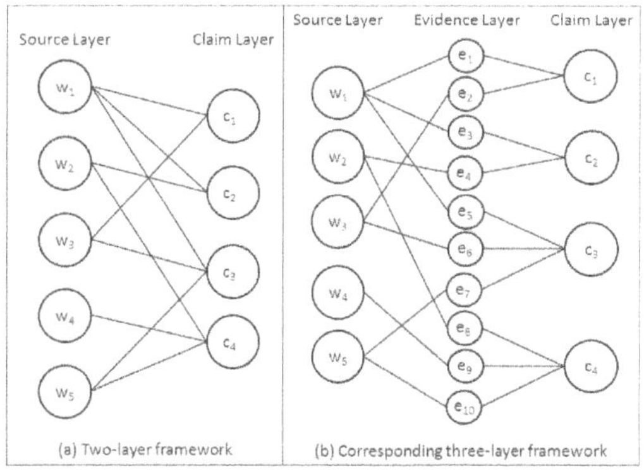

Figure 1: Two-layer trust framework and its corresponding three-layer representation

3. CONTENT-DRIVEN TRUST FRAMEWORK

3.1 Modeling trustworthiness

As mentioned in Sec. 1, the trust frameworks proposed so far are built on structured data and assume accurate information extraction. Previous work on computing trustworthiness [24, 19] are based on a bi-partite graph structure, consisting of the source layer and the claim layer (Fig. 1(a)). The nodes in the claim layer are linked to all the source nodes that express the claim. Typically, the claim score depends solely on the score of the sources linked to the claim, and conversely, the source score depends only on the score of the claims the source is linked to. A source is assumed to contribute uniformly to all the claims it expresses.

The two-layer architecture ignores the content and the context in which the source expresses the claim. To overcome this limitation, we propose a framework that includes content nodes as an intermediate layer. The framework, hence, is a three-tier graph consisting of source, evidence (content), and claim layers (see Fig. 1(b)). Each content node represents the evidence given by a source for a claim, and links to one source node and one claim node. This allows the trust framework to explicitly capture the textual context in which a source provides evidence to a claim.

Formally, let $\mathcal{W} = \{w_1, w_2, \ldots, w_M\}$ be the set of M source websites. Each website w is assigned a trustworthiness score $\tau(w) \in [0,1]$. If a source is completely trusted, its trustworthiness score $\tau(w) = 1$. Let $\mathcal{C} = \{c_1, c_2, \ldots, c_N\}$ be the N claims in the dataset. Each claim c has an overall veracity score, $\sigma(c) \in [0,1]$. $\sigma(c) = 1$ for facts and 0 for hoaxes. The veracity score may also be interpreted as the confidence of classifying a claim as true.

A claim c_i is associated with p pieces of evidence, $\mathcal{E}(c_i) = \{e_{i1}, e_{i2}, \ldots, e_{ip}\}$. A piece of evidence, e, links one source website, $w(e) \in \mathcal{W}$, to one claim, $c(e) \in \mathcal{C}$, and has a confidence score, $\psi(e) \in [0,1]$. $\psi(e)$ represents the confidence in the evidence's trustworthiness. Finally, let $\mathcal{C}(w_i) = \{c \in \mathcal{C} | \exists e \in \mathcal{E} : (c(e) = c) \wedge (w(e) = w_i)\}$ denote the claims for which the source w_i gives some evidence.

In addition to the nodes, the framework also consists of interaction edges between the graph nodes. There are three main types of interactions in the proposed framework:

1. Evidence - Claim interaction (or **Content Relevance**): The evidence - claim edges represent the relevance

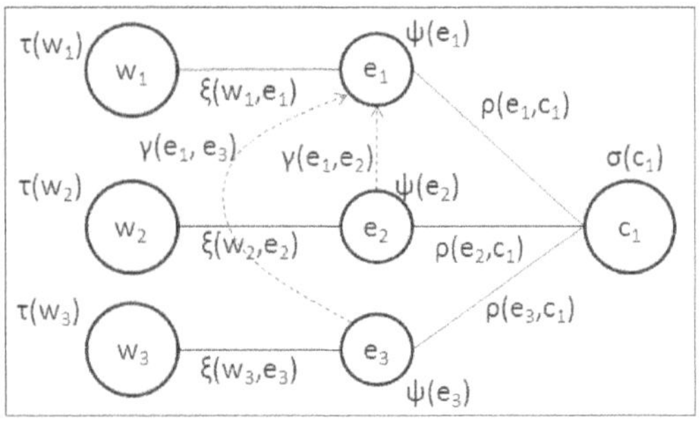

Figure 2: Factors influencing trustworthiness of claims and sources. Inter-evidence interactions are shown only with respect to evidence e_1 for clarity.

of evidence for a claim. Let $\rho(e, c)$ measure the extent of relevance of a piece of evidence e to claim c. The measure allows for highly relevant pieces of evidence to be weighted more than other evidence artifacts.

2. Evidence - Evidence interaction (or **Content Equivalence**): Evidence artifacts are not independent of each other. In fact, multiple sources may give very similar evidence for a claim. We define $\gamma(e_1, e_2)$ to be a measure of influence on evidence e_i due to evidence e_j. This may be either symmetric or asymmetric. Adding this measure of influence constrains the framework to make similar evidence artifacts get similar trustworthiness score, even though they may come from different sources that are not equally trustable.

3. Source - Evidence interaction: Another measure that affects the trustworthiness of claims is the confidence of the source w on a piece of evidence e, and by extension on the claim. Let $\xi(w, e)$ denote this measure. This is especially useful to model the confidence of extraction module (in the structured setup). Note that this has a different interpretation than $\tau(w)$, the trustworthiness of the source. $\tau(w)$ denotes how trustworthy are the claims made by the source: "is w a reliable source?" On the other hand, $\xi(w, e)$ denotes how confident is the fact that source w gave evidence e for the claim, and hence it can be different for different pieces of evidence given by the same source w.

Fig. 2 summarizes the factors influencing trustworthiness of claims. It shows the various parameters affecting $\sigma(c_1)$, and inter-evidence influence with respect to evidence e_1.

3.2 Computing trust scores over framework

Next, we present techniques to compute the trustworthiness scores over the trust framework. We start with the evidence confidence scores, $\psi(e)$, which are initialized solely based on features from the evidence artifacts. Let $\psi^{(0)}(e)$ denote this initial estimate of the quality of evidence. Next, we assume uniform initial trustworthiness, $\tau^{(0)}(w)$, for all sources. If there is some prior knowledge on source trustworthiness, i.e. if some sources are "preferred" over others, then this information can be used to estimate $\tau^{(0)}(w)$. Once these nodes are initialized, the scores for nodes in other layers are computed iteratively as follows, until convergence.

Eq. 1 computes the average estimate of the claim veracity score based on the pieces of evidence relevant to the claim and the current estimate of the trustworthiness of their sources. Then, Eq. 2 re-estimates the source trustworthiness, based on new claim veracity scores. Finally, the evidence score is recomputed (Eq. 3) as a linear interpolation of the previous and new estimates of source trustworthiness:

$$\sigma^{(n+1)}(c_i) = \frac{\sum_{e_j \in \mathcal{E}(c_i)} \left[\psi^{(n)}(e_j) \times \tau^{(n)}(w(e_j))\right]}{|\mathcal{E}(c_i)|} \quad (1)$$

$$\tau^{(n+1)}(w_i) = \frac{\sum_{c_j \in \mathcal{C}(w_i)} \sigma^{(n+1)}(c_j)}{|\mathcal{C}(w_i)|} \quad (2)$$

$$\psi^{(n+1)}(e_i) = \mu\, \psi^{(n)}(e_i) + (1-\mu)\, \tau^{(n+1)}(w(e_i)) \quad (3)$$

where μ denotes the interpolation parameter to control the bias of prior knowledge of $\psi(e)$ on future estimates. Once the algorithm converges, $\sigma(c)$ gives an estimate of the veracity of claim c, $\tau(w)$ shows the trustworthiness of source w, and $\psi(e)$ gives a goodness score for the piece of evidence e.

3.3 Modeling inter-evidence influence on trust scores

In addition to the source and other intrinsic properties of the evidence artifact, other pieces of evidence similar to an evidence artifact also influence its trustworthiness. To capture this effect, we introduce a similarity metric, $\gamma(e_i, e_j)$ as a measure of influence on e_i due to e_j. It may be either symmetric or asymmetric. Typical examples of $\gamma(e_i, e_j)$ between textual pieces of evidence include cosine and TF-IDF similarity, and advanced similarity metrics such as topic-sensitive similarity based on LDA [5]. Specific domain-level knowledge can also be incorporated into this function, such as rule-based named entity similarity or using thesauri for finding similarity between medical treatments.

The inter-evidence similarity $\gamma(e_i, e_j)$ can be incorporated to improve the estimate of $\psi(e_i)$ (Eq. 3), as follows:

$$\tilde{\psi}^{(n+1)}(e_i) = \lambda \left(\frac{\sum_{\substack{e_j \in \mathcal{E}(c(e_i)) \\ e_j \neq e_i}} \left[\psi^{(n)}(e_j) \times \gamma(e_i, e_j)\right]}{|\mathcal{E}(c(e_i))| - 1} \right) + (1-\lambda)\, \psi^{(n+1)}(e_i) \quad (4)$$

where e_j spans over all pieces of evidence except e_i, that give evidence for claim $c(e_i)$. λ denotes the interpolation parameter that controls the effect of inter-evidence similarity in estimating $\psi(e)$. Such a formulation allows us to vary λ to model existing trust formulations. For example, setting $\lambda = 0$ effectively ignores the effect of evidence on each other, mirroring fact-finding algorithms such as Sums [19].

3.4 Modeling relevance of evidence

The formulation explained so far simplistically assumes all evidence artifacts are uniformly relevant to the given claim. However, an evidence may either strongly assert a claim or refer to it only in passing. In such scenarios, it may be prudent to weight the claim veracity score towards more relevant pieces of evidence. This factor is incorporated in the computation of claim veracity (Eq. 1) by adding the factor $\rho(e, c)$, as follows:

$$\tilde{\sigma}^{(n+1)}(c_i) = \frac{\sum_{e_j \in \mathcal{E}(c_i)} \phi\left(\psi^{(n)}(e_j), \tau^{(n)}(w(e_j)), \rho(e_j, c_i)\right)}{|\mathcal{E}(c_i)|}$$

In this work, we have formulated the combination function ϕ as a product of the factors:

$$\tilde{\sigma}^{(n+1)}(c_i) = \frac{\sum_{e_j \in \mathcal{E}(c_i)} \left[\psi^{(n)}(e_j) \times \tau^{(n)}(w(e_j)) \times \rho(e_j, c_i)\right]}{|\mathcal{E}(c_i)|} \quad (5)$$

3.5 Modeling source-evidence interaction

As described in Sec. 3.1, the source-evidence interaction parameters, $\xi(w,e)$, are useful to model extraction accuracy in a structured domain instantiation. In trust propagation computation, the contribution of the trust score for a piece of evidence e from its source w is given by $\tau(w) \times \xi(w,e)$.

4. INSTANTIATING TRUST FRAMEWORK

Now that the details of the framework have been described, we can instantiate the framework for computing trustworthiness of claims. This requires the following steps:

1. Collecting relevant evidence for claims, and defining $\rho(e,c)$ and $\xi(w,e)$.
2. Assigning evidence scores, $\psi(e)$.
3. Defining similarity between evidence documents, $\gamma(e_i,e_j)$.

4.1 Collecting evidence for claims

When a claim is input to the system, relevant pieces of evidence are identified from a collection of documents. First, a text corpus of documents is collected and a retrieval index is built over these potential evidence artifacts. Then, for every claim c, the index is used to retrieve relevant pieces of evidence, which are then used to instantiate the evidence layer of the framework. For each retrieved document e, the retrieval score is normalized to $[0,1]$ scale and used as $\rho(e,c)$.

For the sample instantiation to compute news trustworthiness (described in Sec. 2.1), the index is built over a collection of news stories. In this domain, since we do not have any extraction module, we uniformly set $\xi(w,e)$ to 1.

4.2 Assigning evidence scores

The initial evidence scores can be assigned in multiple ways, as follows:

1. **Uniform weight**: All pieces of evidence are set to a uniform weight, $\psi^{(0)}(e)$. If $\psi^{(0)}(e)=1$, the framework reduces to the two-layer trust framework. $\psi^{(0)}(e)<1$ denotes all evidence artifacts are uniformly, but not fully trusted.
2. **Assign weights based on retrieval score**: When the pieces of evidence are retrieved for a claim, they can be scored based on the rank and retrieval score given by the retrieval system such that top ranked artifacts get higher weight. In the experiments presented in this paper (Sec. 6), this represents the ranking baseline where sources and pieces of evidence are ranked based on a retrieval system, rather than the trust framework.
3. **Assign weights based on weak supervision**: It may be possible to assign non-uniform weights to the pieces of evidence based on human judgments, as humans may be able to review the artifacts to decide if they are trustworthy.
4. **Learn weights**: The evidence scores can be learned based on features from the evidence artifact, such as attribution of claims, style of writing, and reference to other articles that are trusted.

In this work, we will use the first three variants of assigning evidence scores. Our dataset consists of human-rated articles, where annotators judged stories in a stand-alone mode without looking at the source features. Hence, instead of learning the weights, we use these judgments as good signals for the score we want to learn. Learning scores using features from the evidence artifact is not considered in this paper, and is an interesting future direction to explore, especially for corpora where supervision is not available.

4.3 Finding similarity between documents

The effect of pieces of evidence on each other is captured in a similarity metric $\gamma(e_i,e_j)$, as follows:

1. **Strict similarity**: The strictest form of similarity between pieces of evidence is duplicate matching, where $\gamma(e_i,e_j)=1$ only if $e_i=e_j$ and 0 otherwise. This may be required, for instance, to link up duplicate nodes if an evidence document is repeated as multiple nodes in the framework.

2. **Vector similarity**: The baseline similarity measure for text documents is the cosine similarity between documents, where the documents are represented as a binary vector of words and cosine similarity is given by the dot product of the two vectors. Another option is to use TF-IDF similarity, where a word's frequency is weighted by the word's IDF. If v_i and v_j are vector representations of the two documents, such that $v_i[w]$ is the product of frequency of word w in e_i and the IDF of w, then TF-IDF similarity is given by:

$$\text{TF-IDFsim}(v_i,v_j)=\frac{\sum_{w\in V}(v_i[w]\times v_j[w])}{\sqrt{\sum_{w\in V}(v_i[w])^2}\sqrt{\sum_{w\in V}(v_j[w])^2}}$$

3. **Topic-based similarity**: The similarity of documents can also be measured based on the topical similarity between them. A probabilistic mixture model is learned on the evidence documents for a claim, and documents are assigned to clusters based on the learned model. The details of the model are given in Sec. 4.3.1. Two documents that are clustered together have higher similarity than those from different clusters.

In the current work, these similarity factors were combined in the following formula:

$$\gamma(e_i,e_j)=\begin{cases}1 & \text{if } e_i=e_j\\ \text{TF-IDFsim}(v_i,v_j) & \text{if } e_i\neq e_j \wedge e_j\in g(e_i)\\ \alpha\times\text{TF-IDFsim}(v_i,v_j) & \text{otherwise}\end{cases}\quad(6)$$

where v_i, v_j are TF-IDF vector representations of e_i, e_j, respectively, $g(e)$ is the cluster to which e belongs, and α is the average-length cluster similarity between $g(e_i)$ and $g(e_j)$.

4.3.1 *Clustering evidence documents*

Once the evidence documents are retrieved for a claim, we cluster them based on common aspects in the evidence text after learning a probabilistic mixture model. We used the PLSA model [13] with a background component [25]. Formally, let $\theta_1,\theta_2,\ldots,\theta_k$ be k aspect-based unigram language models and θ_B be the background language model. A document d is generated word-by-word from the following mixture model:

$$p_d(w)=\lambda_B p(w|\theta_B)+(1-\lambda_B)\sum_{j=1}^{k}[\pi_{d,j}p(w|\theta_j)]$$

where w is a word, $\pi_{d,j}$ is document-specific weight for the jth aspect and $\sum_{j=1}^{k}\pi_{d,j}=1$. λ_B is the mixture weight for the background model θ_B, and is set to a large value (typically, 0.95). The model parameters, $\Theta=(\theta_j,\pi_{d,j})_{j=1}^{k}$, can be estimated using Expectation Maximization [8] (details are omitted due to space limitation).

Once the model parameters are learned, the documents are clustered in one of k clusters based on which topic model best explains the document. A document d is assigned to cluster $j'=\arg\max_{j\in[1,n]}\pi_{d,j}$. As explained above, documents belonging to one cluster are considered more similar to each other than to documents from different clusters.

5. EXAMPLE INSTANTIATIONS

We outline how the proposed trust framework can be instantiated in different scenarios to demonstrate applicability of the framework across both structured and unstructured domains. We present sample instantiations in three domains, viz., news, books, and health forums. However, we will evaluate the framework only in the news domain.

5.1 Trusting Online News

Our first instantiation uses the proposed trust framework to capture the trustworthiness of news online (see Sec. 2.1). The objective is to check veracity of claims of the form: "News coverage on ⟨a given topic⟩ is fair and unbiased." The input is, hence, in the form of topics (keyword queries). The framework outputs the veracity scores for claims and identifies most trusted news sources and stories. Here, the claim layer consists of topics of interest or genres of news that are given as input. For each topic/genre of interest, the evidence layer consists of news stories for the given topic. We define two models depending on the type of sources, such that the source layer consists of either the websites where the news was published ("*Source model*"), or the reporters writing the news story ("*Author model*"). To clarify, the *Source model* is modeled with ⟨source, evidence, claim⟩ layers, while the *Author model* is modeled with ⟨author, evidence, claim⟩ layers. As described in Sec. 4, the other parameters are set as follows: $\rho(e, c)$ is set based on retrieval score, normalized to $[0, 1]$; $\xi(w, e) = 1$ uniformly; $\psi^{(0)}(e)$ is computed based on user ratings; and $\gamma(e_i, e_j)$ is set according to Eq. 6. Clustering of news articles is done using a simple mixture model as described in Sec. 4.3.1, with $k = 4$.

The two models compute the veracity of news: how trustworthy is the news covering a particular topic of interest, or how trustworthy a news genre is, when compared to other news genres. It must be noted that trustworthiness in this domain signifies if the reporting of news is unbiased and fair, and if facts expressed in news stories are accurate with good coverage. This notably differs from finding trustworthiness of extracted numeric facts such as "Shakespeare was born in 1564." or "The height of Mt. Everest is 8848 meters."

5.2 Trusting Author lists on Online Bookstores

To show how the framework can be used to model trustworthiness in structured data, we present the framework with respect to the Books dataset used by Yin et al. [24]. The dataset consists of books with four extracted fields, viz., the source, the book title, ISBN, and the author list as given by the source.

To instantiate a model based on this dataset, the bookstores are the sources, and the claims are candidate lists of authors for a particular book. The evidence layer consists of the author lists given by a source for a particular book. The aim is to identify the most "trusted" candidate author list. To achieve this, the model loads the data for all books and builds the trust network. $\psi^{(0)}(e)$, $\tau^{(0)}(w)$, and $\xi(w, e)$ are set to 1. Content relevance and equivalence functions, $\rho(e, c)$ and $\gamma(e_i, e_j)$, show similarity of lists of author names, and can be built using person name similarity metrics [7]. In fact, by allowing the original text to appear in the model, our framework allows a source to support multiple claims to varying degrees, not committing to one (possibly faulty) person name normalization. This leads to a voting strategy that is more robust to data cleaning or extraction errors.

News Genre	# Stories	Avg. Rating
News Report	7,881	3.65
Opinion	6,611	3.69
News Analysis	2,634	3.73
Special Report	2,177	3.83
News	816	3.54
Editorial	634	3.73
Interview	583	3.87
Poll	301	3.73
Investigative Report	276	4.10
Review	169	3.71
Comment	141	3.67
Breaking News	124	3.66
Comedy News	114	3.75
Press Release	92	3.83
Advocacy	76	3.91
Speech	55	3.90
Statement	43	3.82
Research	34	3.96
Entertainment	17	3.39
Cartoon	12	3.74
Advertisement	3	2.43
Dramatization	2	3.48
Miscellaneous	369	3.52
Total	23,164	3.70

Table 1: News genres in the dataset, sorted by number of stories in each genre. The average rating for each genre is also shown.

5.3 Trusting Treatments from Health Forums

The framework can be also used in domains where relation extraction is needed, such as in question answering over the Web. Consider the scenario of trusting medical claims given in health forum posts. If a known disease-treatment pair is given as a relation query (the *claim*), the structured query is used to find relevant posts (the *evidence*) from medical forums and message boards (the *source*). The aim is to verify if the claims expressed in health forums are trustable, and if certain health forums are more trustable than others.

To achieve this, we can set up the framework by issuing a relation query [20] on an index over forum posts. The posts are rated on the sentiment expressed about the effectiveness of the query treatment (the *confidence in evidence*, $\psi(e)$). $\rho(e, c)$ is set depending on how strongly the treatment relation is expressed in the post, that is if the post is specifically about the treatment claim or talks about the treatment in passing. $\gamma(e_i, e_j)$ is set based on similarity of content between posts or grouping based on post authors.

6. EXPERIMENTS

The key research questions we want to evaluate are:
1. Does the trust framework help in identifying trustworthiness of claims and the most trusted sources for a claim?
2. Does the addition of content nodes in the proposed trust framework help users rank highly trusted evidence documents before other relevant, but not-as-trusted documents?
3. What is the effect of the evidence scoring strategy used? Specifically, how does evidence scoring strategy affect the overall trustworthiness of sources?
4. What is the effect of clustering articles? Specifically, does the source trustworthiness change with news genres?

6.1 Dataset characteristics

We instantiate and evaluate the framework in the news domain, as described in Sec. 5.1. News data was collected from a community-driven news review website, NewsTrust[1]. NewsTrust allows members to analyze news articles on various tenets of good journalism. Members can rate stories on accuracy of facts, fairness and bias in reporting, style, depth

[1] `http://www.newstrust.net/`

Topic	(1) Health care	(2) Obama administration	(3) Bush administration	(4) Democratic policy	(5) Republican policy
Trust score	**0.538**	**0.558**	**0.646**	**0.462**	**0.443**
Trusted Sources	OurFuture.org	Democracy Now	Democracy Now	Common Dreams	Consortium News
	TruthOut	Consortium News	TruthOut	Consortium News	Salon
	PolitiFact	Common Dreams	Consortium News	Democracy Now	Women's eNews
	FactCheck	TruthOut	Salon	FAIR	FactCheck
	AlterNet	Salon	Common Dreams	Salon	New Republic
	Media Matters	FactCheck	McClatchy	New Republic	Washington Post
	Huffington Post	Washington Independent	Huffington Post	San Francisco Chronicle	New York Times
	New York Times	Huffington Post	Boston Globe	FactCheck	Wall Street Journal
	New Republic	Washington Post	Washington Post	New York Times	Boston Globe
	CNN	New York Times	New York Times	Washington Post	The Guardian
	NPR	The Guardian	The Guardian	Women's eNews	Congressional Quarterly
	Washington Post	Los Angeles Times	AlterNet	The Guardian	Huffington Post
	Associated Press	The Hill	The Politico	Wall Street Journal	Bloomberg
	Time	The Politico	Newsweek	American Prospect	Christian Science Monitor
	The Politico	Newsweek	The Hill	Los Angeles Times	The Hill

Topic	(6) Immigration	(7) Gay rights	(8) Corruption	(9) Election reform	(10) WikiLeaks
Trust score	**0.508**	**0.499**	**0.544**	**0.514**	**0.605**
Trusted Sources	Democracy Now	Washington Post	Democracy Now	TruthOut	Democracy Now
	AlterNet	Slate	Consortium News	Consortium News	AlterNet
	NPR	New York Times	TruthOut	Huffington Post	McClatchy
	New York Times	Women's eNews	Seattle Times	Journalism.org	The Nation
	San Francisco Chronicle	Mother Jones	Common Dreams	AlterNet	New York Times
	Washington Post	Los Angeles Times	Talking Points Memo	New York Times	Salon
	Washington Independent	Salon	Inter Press Service	Washington Post	Wired
	Huffington Post	Huffington Post	Huffington Post	Los Angeles Times	Christian Science Monitor
	Associated Press	San Francisco Chronicle	Washington Post	Congressional Quarterly	The Guardian
	The Hill	Media Matters	Salon	Washington Independent	Economist
	Los Angeles Times	Washington Independent	New York Times	Think Progress	New Republic
	New America Media	Associated Press	Wall Street Journal	The Politico	Reuters
	CNN	The Politico	Mother Jones	Associated Press	Pajamas Media

Table 2: Variation of most trusted sources and overall trust score for various politics news topics. For each topic, only sources that contribute at least 10 articles for that topic are shown.

of coverage, attribution of quotes to sources, and other qualitative aspects of news. In addition, other popularity-based factors such as viewing, sharing, "liking", and discussing a story are recorded. NewsTrust combines these ratings from multiple reviewers and assigns an overall score to each story. The scores are in the range of $[1, 5]$ and are considered as "gold-standard" during evaluation. Further analysis showed that the scores were biased towards higher values (i.e., news stories were generally rated as trustworthy) and they followed a Gaussian distribution with mean 3.7 and standard deviation 0.59.

We crawled all the stories under "Politics" section from the NewsTrust website in October 2010, and identified the source (website), author, and genre for the news story. In total, we collected 24,388 stories from 23 news genres. After removing stories for which no reviews were posted, we had a set of 23,164 stories. Table 1 gives the distribution of number of stories and average rating per genre. Each story belongs to one genre, and is written by one or more authors and is posted on one or more websites, based on the authors' affiliations. In all, we had 8,603 unique authors and 1,960 unique sources in the dataset. We built a search index over the news stories using the Lemur toolkit[2].

In the collected dataset, since a news story might link to multiple sources (multiple reporters working on a story, say), we could not directly treat each story as evidence when instantiating our trust framework. Instead, we duplicated the news stories such that each story links to exactly one source. Further, these duplicates were tied together with inter-evidence similarity, $\gamma(e_i, e_j) = 1$. As we observed that the scores followed a Gaussian distribution, with $\mu = 3.7$ and $\sigma = 0.59$, we normalized the scores to the range $[0, 1]$ using a probabilistic interpretation of cumulative distribution function of the Gaussian distribution. Stating mathematically, if $\mathcal{D}$ is a data corpus and x is the original score, the new score $\widetilde{x}$ is given by $\widetilde{x} = \Pr(\text{score}(d) < x \mid d \in \mathcal{D})$.

[2]`http://www.lemurproject.org/`

#	Topic	Retrieval	Two-stage model	Our model
1	Health care	0.886	0.895	**0.932**
2	Obama administration	0.852	0.876	**0.927**
3	Bush administration	0.931	0.921	**0.971**
4	Democratic policy	0.894	0.769	**0.922**
5	Republican policy	0.774	0.848	**0.936**
6	Immigration	0.820	0.952	**0.983**
7	Gay rights	0.832	**0.864**	0.807
8	Corruption	0.874	0.841	**0.941**
9	Election reform	0.864	0.889	**0.908**
10	WikiLeaks	**0.886**	0.860	0.825
	Average	0.861	0.869	**0.915**

Table 3: NDCG values for ten news topics in politics. The improvement of the ranking using our *Trust model* is significant at $p = 0.05$ using Wilcoxon's signed rank test, over both the *Retrieval* and *Two-stage model* runs.

6.2 Evaluating veracity of claims

We first verify if the framework can be used to judge if the claim is trustworthy or not. To evaluate this, we collected a set of ten political news topics and retrieved evidence documents for these topics from the dataset. Then, we initialized the *Source model* with these pieces of evidence, and ran the model to rate the trustworthiness of the claim topics.

Table 2 shows the overall trust score and top trusted sources for each political topic. We see that, according to the model, the news coverage of topics such as "Bush administration" and "WikiLeaks" are fairly trustworthy. In contrast, coverage on "Republican policy" and "Democratic policy" is not as trustworthy. It is also interesting to see that although the coverage of current and past presidential administration is fairly trustworthy overall, the articles on "Obama administration" are significantly less trustworthy than the coverage of "Bush administration". For most topics, fact verifying websites such as PolitiFact and FactCheck are among the top trusted sources.

6.3 Evaluating ranking of evidence documents

To quantitatively evaluate performance, we measure how well the proposed news trust model ranks documents on

Retrieval		Two-stage model		Our Trust model		Ideal	
The Politico	3.28	AlterNet	3.95	Dem. Now	3.97	NPR	4.14
Wash. Indep.	3.30	NYT	3.97	AlterNet	3.95	Dem. Now	3.97
Huff. Post	3.38	Wash. Post	3.38	NPR	4.14	NYT	3.97
AP	3.97	LA Times	3.66	NYT	3.97	AP	3.97
NYT	3.97	Wash. Indep.	3.30	SFO Chron.	3.73	AlterNet	3.95

Table 4: Top five results for a sample topic, "Immigration", for *Retrieval*, *Two-stage model*, our proposed *Trust model*, and *Ideal* runs. Instead of docID, the document source is shown, along with the trust score. Some names have been abbreviated.

trustworthiness. Consider a use-case scenario where a user searches for a topic. Ideally, we would want to show more trusted documents higher in the ranked list. Traditional search algorithms rank documents on relevance rather than trustworthiness. When the user searches for news on a particular topic, a ranked list of relevant news stories is retrieved. Let us call this the *Retrieval* run. Using the trust model we learned, we can rerank these documents based on the trustworthiness of the source, to obtained a new document ranking (the *Trust model* run). We also rerank these document using an instantiation that mimics existing two-layer trust models (the *Two-stage model* run). Note that in the *Two-stage model* run, the graph structure is similar to that of the *Trust model*, except that all pieces of evidence get uniform weight and are not allowed to change across iterations. Using the gold-standard document scores as weights, we compute the normalized discounted cumulative gain (NDCG) measure for all three runs. NDCG [14], a ranking performance measure, computes the ratio of discounted cumulative gain of a run (where the weight of a relevant document is discounted by its rank) to the *ideal* discounted cumulative gain (assuming documents are ranked in decreasing order of their weights). NDCG values are in $[0, 1]$ and higher numbers are preferred.

Table 3 shows the NDCG values for ten news topics in politics. We see that the *Trust model* run has the highest NDCG value for eight of the ten topics. The improvement is statistically significant at $p = 0.05$ level using Wilcoxon's signed rank test, compared to both the *Retrieval* run and the *Two-stage model* run. Table 4 shows a sample comparison of ranking in the *Retrieval*, *Two-stage model*, *Trust model*, and *ideal* runs for the topic "Immigration". For each run, the source name of the document and the document's rating is shown. We see that the *Trust model* based ranking is significantly better than ranking based on either the *Retrieval* run or the *Two-stage model*, and has ranked documents from more trusted sources higher. It is not surprising that our method outperforms the *Retrieval* run as the latter doesn't model trustworthiness. However, the fact that our method also outperforms the *Two-stage model* significantly shows that incorporating content information into the trust framework is beneficial.

6.4 Effect of varying evidence scoring scheme

In prior research on trust models, the trustworthiness of claims is based on trustworthiness of sources, and the links between sources and claims are assumed to be ideal (completely trustworthy). In contrast, we propose a framework where the links (representing evidence for a claim from a source) are assumed to have a non-uniform trust rating.

To evaluate the effect of using evidence-based scoring, we set up two model variants – one in which all pieces of evidence have a uniform score (of 1.0), while in the other, the scores are based on the trust scores based on reviews given by users of NewsTrust. The former corresponds to previous fact-finding models, such as TruthFinder [24] and Sums [19], where the evidence layer is essentially ignored.

Table 6(a) shows the effect of variation of evidence scoring scheme for the *Source model*. The first column shows the results when all pieces of evidence get the same weight and the sources are ranked by popularity. The second column shows results when pieces of evidence get non-uniform scores, but the sources are ranked on the average of trust-rating score of pieces of evidence from the source (without using the trust framework). The third column shows how the ranking varies when the trust rating is used to score evidence artifacts in the *Source model* and the model is let to iterate. We observe that when the model is allowed to converge[3], more well-known sources tend to come up higher in the ranked list and relatively unknown sources that have few, but trusted, stories are pushed further down the list.

Unfortunately, we do not have gold labeling of true trustworthiness of sources to give a complete quantitative evaluation. Instead, we found the results of a 2010 poll [2] that asked participants which TV news sources are "mostly fair" (as compared to "liberal" or "conservative"). Based on this partial ranking, we find that our trust framework gives a Kendall's rank correlation measure[4], $\tau = 0.714$ when compared to the "ideal" ranking given by user polls, better than using voting or average rating ($\tau = 0.143$ for both).

Table 6(b) shows the results for a similar setup for the *Author model* and we see that the top results from the *Author model* (column 3) are all award-winning investigative reporters, unlike in the other two variants.

Voting (Popularity)	Average rating	Our Trust model
News Report	Investigative Report	Speech
Opinion	Research	Investigative Report
News Analysis	Advocacy	Interview
Special Report	Speech	Press Release
News	Interview	Poll
Editorial	Press Release	Statement
Interview	Special Report	Opinion
Poll	Statement	Research
Investigative Report	Comedy News	Comedy News
Review	Cartoon	Review

Table 5: Top ten news genres based on different scoring schemes, viz. (i) voting (popularity), (ii) average rating, and (iii) our trust model.

6.5 Effect of trust scores on news genres

We now try to understand how the proposed framework using trust-based evidence scores affects the rating of news genres in general. We use the *Source model* to rate news genres based on trustworthiness of news articles in that genre.

[3]Empirically, the model converges in 3–5 iterations.

[4]Kendall's rank correlation measure [16] compares two ranked lists, L_1 and L_2, by computing the following:

$$\text{Kendall's } \tau = \frac{\#(\text{concordant pairs}) - \#(\text{discordant pairs})}{\#(\text{total pairs}) = \binom{n}{2}}$$

where a pair of entries (o_1, o_2) are said to be concordant if o_1 appears either before or after o_2 in both lists L_1 and L_2, and is called a discordant pair if the order of the pair (o_1, o_2) is reversed from L_1 to L_2. The value of τ ranges from -1 for reversed lists (fully discordant) to $+1$ for concordant lists.

(a) Top News Sources (using *Source model*)		
Voting (Popularity)	Average rating	Our Trust model
New York Times	3BlueDudes	ABC News
Washington Post	Democracy Now	CNN
Huffington Post	Consortium News	Wall Street Journal
Associated Press	Media Matters	Reuters
Los Angeles Times	TruthOut	Associated Press
The Politico	Common Dreams	San Francisco Chronicle
Wall Street Journal	The Nation	The Hill
AlterNet	FactCheck	Newsweek
Democracy Now	AlterNet	Seattle Times
Salon	Salon	Seattle Post Intelligencer
TruthOut	Seattle Post Intelligencer	The Politico
Seattle Post Intelligencer	New Yorker	Huffington Post
The Guardian	Mother Jones	MSNBC
Consortium News	McClatchy	Atlantic Monthly
Reuters	Huffington Post	BBC News
The Nation	The Guardian	NPR
CNN	Seattle Times	The Independent
McClatchy	New York Times	New Republic
Newsweek	Washington Post	Time

(b) Top News Reporters (using *Author model*)		
Voting (Popularity)	Average rating	Our Trust model
Amy Goodman	Jim Hightower	Juan Gonzalez
Glenn Greenwald	Sharif Abdel Kouddous	Robert Parry
Paul Krugman	Juan Gonzalez	Amy Goodman
Robert Parry	Ray McGovern	Jason Leopold
Sam Stein	Robert Parry	Glenn Greenwald
Juan Gonzalez	Amy Goodman	Paul Krugman
Jonathan Weisman	Jason Leopold	Frank Rich
Dan Balz	Glenn Greenwald	Dan Froomkin
Jason Leopold	Bill Moyers	John Nichols
Shailagh Murray	Greg Palast	Jon Stewart
Adam Nagourney	Paul Krugman	Paul Kane
Dan Eggen	Scott Horton	Dan Eggen
Paul Kane	Matt Taibbi	Juliet Eilperin
Peter Baker	Robert Reich	Michael D. Shear
Michael D. Shear	Lori Robertson	Arianna Huffington
Jeff Zeleny	Frank Rich	Sam Stein
Frank Rich	Michael Winship	Peter Baker
Jon Stewart	David Sirota	Jason Linkins
Ed Morrissey	Dan Froomkin	Shailagh Murray

Table 6: Top news sources and reporters as computed by three scoring schemes, viz., (i) voting (popularity), (ii) average rating, and (iii) our *Trust model* with evidence influence; after filtering out sources with less than 100 (or reporters with less than 30) stories each in the dataset.

Overall	News Report	Opinion	News Analysis	Special Report	Editorial	Interview
ABC News	Washington Times	Weekly Standard	Associated Press	Newsweek	Wall Street Journal	Huffington Post
CNN	ABC News	The Moderate Voice	Wall Street Journal	The Politico	Economist	Washington Post
Wall Street Journal	Seattle Post Intelligencer	Think Progress	Los Angeles Times	Associated Press	The Nation	PBS
Reuters	Agence France-Presse	Wall Street Journal	Huffington Post	Los Angeles Times	Washington Post	Bill Moyers Journal
Associated Press	CBS News	Daily Kos	AlterNet	New York Times	Seattle Post Intelligencer	MSNBC
San Francisco Chronicle	San Francisco Chronicle	Op Ed News	Time	Washington Post	New York Times	Democracy Now

Table 7: Variation of most trusted sources for different genres of news. For each genre, only sources that contribute at least 30 articles for that genre are included in the analysis.

We varied the scoring scheme, similar to those explained in Sec. 6.4, and Table 5 summarizes the findings.

We see that although "News Report" and "Opinion" are the most popular news genres, the stories in those genres do not tend to be highly trustworthy, and are not in top 10 news genres based on average rating of news stories. In contrast, "Investigative Reports" and "Press Releases" are more trustworthy genres. It was interesting to observe that "News Analysis" rates quite poorly, even lower than "Comedy News" in the ratings given by NewsTrust members and in our trust model results.

6.6 Effect of genre on source trustworthiness

Next, we wanted to analyze if the trusted sources tend to remain the same or vary across genres. Do some news sources specialize in specific genres and are more trusted than others for these specific genres? We compared the top news sources for different genres of news to study the pattern and Table 7 summarizes the results for six genres.

We find that the top-ranked sources per genre vary significantly across genres. For example, in the "Interview" genre, *PBS* and *Bill Moyers Journal* that specialize in this genre are rated high on trust scores. Similarly, *Wall Street Journal* and *Economist* are most trusted in the "Editorial" genre, while they do not occur in top trusted sources for "News Report" and "Special Report" genres. Interestingly, for the "Opinion" genre, the most trusted sources are primarily online news magazines and blogs.

7. RELATED WORK

In recent years, researchers have worked on different notions of trust for specific scenarios. Similar to the work on trust models introduced earlier, most of the research has focused on structured domain. Dong et al. [9, 10] propose models to detect copying of information and aggregate information from multiple sources to detect true value of a data item. Wu and Marian [23] find most suitable numeric answers by corroborating evidence from multiple sources. In contrast, our work proposes a general framework that uses content to estimate trustworthiness of claims, and can be extended to find most suitable answer (claim) by comparing claim trustworthiness as a post-processing step. In other works, Gallard et al. [11] incorporate the "hardness" of facts in the trust model, such that knowing easy facts earns less trust than knowing hard facts. WikiTrust [4] measures trustworthiness of Wikipedia pages based on revision history.

There has been some work in measuring quality of text in community-generated data. Shah and Pomerantz [21] measure the "quality" of answers in community QA setting using machine learning approaches. The definition of quality is, however, akin to popularity rather than trust. Su et al. [22] try to detect trustworthiness of community QA in terms of textual and linguistic features alone.

Formulating trust frameworks as iterative algorithms is not new. Search engines learn "quality" of a website based on reputation-based models such as PageRank [6] and HITS [17] using similar computation on the Web graph. In HITS, for instance, each website has a hub score and an authority score. The hub score of a webpage is computed using the authority scores of neighboring pages, and vice versa. Topic-specific extensions have been proposed to compute PageRank over websites per topic [12].

Researchers in other fields, including social scientists, have studied the theoretical and social aspects of trust. Lankes [18] studied how the advent of Internet has shifted the user's perception of credibility from authoritative figures, such as librarians, to reliable entities, such as Web search engines. Kelton et al. [15] developed principles of trust by integrating behavioral and social science studies and research on information quality. Our work proposes a computational framework to facilitate such an integration.

8. CONCLUSION AND FUTURE WORK

In this paper, we proposed a content-driven trust computation framework that incorporates the quality of evidence content to compute the trustworthiness of sources and determine the veracity of free-text claims. We instantiated the framework in the news domain using human ratings as supervision for determining quality of evidence. We showed that incorporating evidence into the trust computation not only allows modeling trustworthiness in unstructured domain, but also improves the performance of the framework to find trustworthy sources. Reranking news articles based on trustworthiness computed by the proposed framework shows statistically significant improvement over retrieval-based ranking that ignores trustworthiness of sources and over trust models that ignore variation in evidence quality.

The current instantiation of the framework utilizes weak supervision at the evidence level in the form of human judgment on the trustworthiness of news articles. However, such supervision may not be available in other domains or for all news articles. In future, we plan to learn the weights in a supervised setting. We also plan to apply the trust framework on other domains with claims in any free-text sentence form, and use linguistic resources to compute content similarity.

Acknowledgments

The survey results reported in this paper were obtained from searches of the iPOLL Databank and other resources provided by the Roper Center for Public Opinion Research, University of Connecticut. This research was supported by the Multimodal Information Access and Synthesis Center at UIUC, part of CCICADA, a DHS Science and Technology Center of Excellence and the Army Research Laboratory under agreement W911NF-09-2-0053. Any opinions, findings, conclusions, or recommendations are those of the authors and do not necessarily reflect the view of the sponsors.

9. REFERENCES

[1] Gather: The Changing Face of News Media, May 25th, 2010. `http://www.emarketer.com/`.

[2] Polls: PBS Most Trusted News Source. TVNewsCheck, Feb 18th, 2010 (Retrieved Feb 16th, 2011). `http://www.tvnewscheck.com/`.

[3] Survey by Henry J. Kaiser Family Foundation, January 26-March 8, 2009.

[4] B. T. Adler and L. de Alfaro. A Content-driven Reputation System for the Wikipedia. In *Proc. of World Wide Web (WWW)*, pages 261–270, 2007.

[5] D. M. Blei, A. Y. Ng, and M. I. Jordan. Latent Dirichlet Allocation. *Journal of Machine Learning Research*, 3:993–1022, 2003.

[6] S. Brin and L. Page. The Anatomy of a Large-Scale Hypertextual Web Search Engine. *Computer Networks*, 30(1–7):107–117, 1998.

[7] W. W. Cohen, P. Ravikumar, and S. E. Fienberg. A Comparison of String Distance Metrics for Name-Matching Tasks. In *IJCAI Workshop on Information Integration on the Web*, 2003.

[8] A. P. Dempster, N. M. Laird, and D. B. Rubin. Maximum likelihood from incomplete data via the EM algorithm. *Journal of Royal Statistical Society, Series B*, 39(1):1–38, 1977.

[9] X. L. Dong, L. Berti-Equille, Y. Hu, and D. Srivastava. Global Detection of Complex Copying Relationships Between Sources. *Proc. of VLDB Endowment (PVLDB)*, 3(1):1358–1369, 2010.

[10] X. L. Dong, L. Berti-Equille, and D. Srivastava. Truth Discovery and Copying Detection in a Dynamic World. *Proc. of VLDB Endowment (PVLDB)*, 2(1):562–573, 2009.

[11] A. Galland, S. Abiteboul, A. Marian, and P. Senellart. Corroborating Information from Disagreeing Views. In *Proc. of WSDM*, pages 131–140, 2010.

[12] T. H. Haveliwala. Topic-sensitive PageRank. In *Proc. of 11th Intl. Conf. on World Wide Web (WWW)*, pages 517–526, 2002.

[13] T. Hofmann. Probabilistic Latent Semantic Indexing. In *Proc. of* 22nd *Intl. ACM Conf. on Research and development in Information Retrieval (SIGIR)*, pages 50–57, 1999.

[14] K. Järvelin and J. Kekäläinen. Cumulated Gain-based Evaluation of IR Techniques. *ACM Transactions on Information Systems*, 20(4):422–446, 2002.

[15] K. Kelton, K. R. Fleischmann, and W. A. Wallace. Trust in Digital Information. *Journal of the American Society for Infromation Science and Technology*, 59(3):363–374, 2008.

[16] M. G. Kendall. A New Measure of Rank Correlation. *Biometrika*, 30:81–89, 1938.

[17] J. M. Kleinberg. Authoritative Sources in a Hyperlinked Environment. *Journal of ACM*, 46(5):604–632, 1999.

[18] R. D. Lankes. Credibility on the Internet: Shifting from Authority to Reliability. *Journal of Documentation*, 64(5):667–686, 2007.

[19] J. Pasternack and D. Roth. Knowing what to believe (when you already know something). In *Proc. of Intl. Conf. on Computational Linguistics (COLING)*, pages 877–885, 2010.

[20] D. Roth, M. Sammons, and V. Vydiswaran. A Framework for Entailed Relation Recognition. In *Proc. of* 47th *Annual Meeting of the Association for Computational Linguistics (ACL)*, pages 57–60, 2009.

[21] C. Shah and J. Pomerantz. Evaluating and Predicting Answer Quality in Community QA. In *Proc. of* 33rd *Intl. ACM SIGIR Conf. on Research and development in Information Retrieval*, pages 411–418, 2010.

[22] Q. Su, C.-R. Huang, and H. K. yun Chen. Evidentiality for Text Trustworthiness Detection. In *Proc. of the Workshop on NLP and Linguistics: Finding the Common Ground*, pages 10–17, 2010.

[23] M. Wu and A. Marian. Corroborating Answers from Multiple Web Sources. In *Proc. of the 10th Intl. Workshop on Web and Databases (WebDB)*, pages 1–6, 2007.

[24] X. Yin, J. Han, and P. S. Yu. Truth Discovery with Multiple Conflicting Information Providers on the Web. *IEEE Transactions on Knowledge and Data Engineering*, 20(6):796–808, 2008.

[25] C. Zhai, A. Velivelli, and B. Yu. A Cross-Collection Mixture Model for Comparative Text Mining. In *Proc. of Intl. Conf. on Knowledge Discovery and Data Mining (KDD)*, pages 743–748, 2004.

Cost-aware Travel Tour Recommendation

Yong Ge[1], Qi Liu[1,2], Hui Xiong[1], Alexander Tuzhilin[3], Jian Chen[4]
[1] Rutgers Business School, Rutgers University
hxiong@rutgers.edu, yongge@pegasus.rutgers.edu
[2] University of Science and Technology of China, feiniaol@mail.ustc.edu.cn
[3] Leonard N. Stern School of Business, New York University, atuzhili@stern.nyu.edu
[4] Tsinghua University, jchen@mail.tsinghua.edu.cn

ABSTRACT

Advances in tourism economics have enabled us to collect massive amounts of travel tour data. If properly analyzed, this data can be a source of rich intelligence for providing real-time decision making and for the provision of travel tour recommendations. However, tour recommendation is quite different from traditional recommendations, because the tourist's choice is directly affected by the travel cost, which includes the financial cost and the time. To that end, in this paper, we provide a focused study of cost-aware tour recommendation. Along this line, we develop two cost-aware latent factor models to recommend travel packages by considering both the travel cost and the tourist's interests. Specifically, we first design a cPMF model, which models the tourist's cost with a 2-dimensional vector. Also, in this cPMF model, the tourist's interests and the travel cost are learnt by exploring travel tour data. Furthermore, in order to model the uncertainty in the travel cost, we further introduce a Gaussian prior into the cPMF model and develop the GcPMF model, where the Gaussian prior is used to express the uncertainty of the travel cost. Finally, experiments on real-world travel tour data show that the cost-aware recommendation models outperform state-of-the-art latent factor models with a significant margin. Also, the GcPMF model with the Gaussian prior can better capture the impact of the uncertainty of the travel cost, and thus performs better than the cPMF model.

Categories and Subject Descriptors

H.2.8 [**Database Management**]: Database Applications—*Data Mining*

General Terms

Algorithms, Experimentation

Keywords

Cost-aware Recommendation, Matrix Factorization

1. INTRODUCTION

Recent years have witnessed a revolution in digital strategy for travel industry. As a result, massive amounts of travel data have been accumulated, and thus provide unparallel opportunities for people to understand user behaviors and generate useful knowledge, which in turn deliver intelligence for real-time decision making in various fields, including that of travel tour recommendation.

Recommender systems address the information overloaded problem by identifying user interests and providing personalized suggestions. In general, there are three ways to develop recommender systems[2]. The first one is content-based. It suggests items which are similar to those a given user has liked in the past. The second way is based on collaborative filtering[16, 20, 17, 5]. In other words, recommendations are made according to the tastes of other users that are similar to the target user. Finally, a third way is to combine the above and have a hybrid solution [6]. However, the development of recommender systems for travel tour recommendation is significantly different from developing recommender systems for traditional domains, since the tourist's choice is directly affected by the travel cost which includes both the financial cost and various other types of costs, such as time and opportunity costs.

Indeed, there are some unique characteristics of travel tour data, which distinguish the tour recommendation from the traditional recommendation, such as movie recommendation. First, the prices of travel packages can vary a lot. For example, by examining the real-world tour logs collected by a travel company, we can find that the prices of packages can range from $50 to $10000. Second, the time cost of packages also varies very much. For instance, while some travel packages take less than 3 day, other packages may take more than 10 days. In traditional recommender systems, the cost for taking a recommended item, such as a movie, is usually not a concern for the customers. However, the tourists usually have the financial and time constraints for selecting a travel package. In fact, Figure 1 shows the cost distributions of some tourists. In the figure, each point corresponds to one user. As can be seen, both the financial and time costs vary a lot among different tourists. Therefore, for the traditional recommendation models, which do not consider the cost of travel packages, it is difficult to provide the right tour recommendation for the right tourists. For example, traditional recommender systems might recommender a travel package to a tourist who cannot afford it because of the price.

To address this challenge, in this paper, we propose a cost-aware recommender system, which aims to mine the

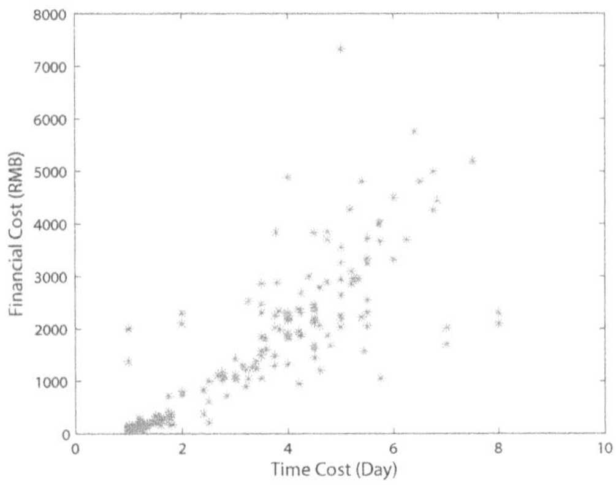

Figure 1: The Cost Distribution.

cost preferences and user interests simultaneously from the large scale of tour logs. The proposed recommender system is based on the latent factor model, which is one of the most popular approaches for collaborative filtering. In addition to the latent space features U_i and V_j that are widely used in latent factor models for recommender systems, such as the PMF model [24], we also introduce two types of costs into our model. The first type of costs refers to the observable costs of a tour package, defined in terms of the financial cost of the package and the time cost associated with the duration of the trip. For example, if a person goes on a trip to Cambodia for 7 days and pays \$2000 for travel package j, then the observed package costs are denoted as a vector $C_{V_j} = (2000, 7)$. The second type of cost refers to unobserved costs associated with the user, which is denoted as a 2-dimensional latent cost vector C_{U_i}. Here, C_{U_i} is introduced to model user i's preference to the two aspects of cost.

The response of an active user to one specific item (tour package) is modeled as: $S(C_{U_i}, C_{V_j}) \cdot U_i^T \cdot V_j$, where S is the similarity function to measure the match of user and item cost. We denote this method as the cPMF model. In addition to the unknown latent features, such as U_i and V_j, user *cost vector* C_{U_i} also needs to be learned under the given loss function.

Furthermore, since there is still some uncertainty about the expense and the time cost that a user can afford, we further introduce a Gaussian priori $\mathcal{G}(C_{U_i})$, instead of using the *cost vector* C_{U_i}, on user cost to express the uncertainty. This Gaussian priori leads to an enhanced prediction model, denoted as the GcPMF model, which is trained by maximizing the posterior over the latent features and the parameters of Gaussian prior with observed data. In addition, efficient algorithms are developed to solve the optimization problems.

Finally, experiments on real-world tour logs show that both cPMF and GcPMF models outperform benchmark latent factor models with a significant margin. Moreover, the GcPMF model with the Gaussian priori leads to better performances than the cPMF model with the *cost vector*.

2. RELATED WORK

Two types of collaborative filtering models have been intensively studied recently (particularly with the incentive of NetFlix prize): memory-based and model-based approaches. Memory-based algorithms[10, 16, 5] essentially make rating prediction via using the rating of some other neighboring ratings. In the model-based approaches, training datasets are used to train a predefined model. Different approaches [14, 25, 29, 23]vary due to different statistical models assumed for the data. In particular, various matrix factorization (MF)[26, 24, 18, 3] methods have been proposed for collaborative filtering. Most MF approaches focus on fitting the user-item rating matrix using low rank approximation and use the learned latent user/item features to make predictions for unknown rating. In [24], PMF model was proposed by introducing Gaussian noise to observed rating. Under the Gaussian assumption, maximizing the posterior probability over latent features is equal to minimizing the square error, which is the objective function of most MF methods. More recently, more complex methods are proposed to consider user/item side information[1, 12], social influence[22], temporal information[19] and spatio-temporal context[21]. However, most of the above methods were developed for recommendation of movie, article, book or webpage, for which expense and time cost are usually not essential to the recommendation results. Including the latent item/user features, our cPMF and GcPMF models also explicitly address the two types of cost for travel recommendation.

Travel-related recommendation has been studied before. For instance, in [13], one probabilistic topic model was proposed to mine two types of topics, i.e.,local topics (e.g.,lava, coastline) and global topics(e.g.,hotel, airport) from travelogue on the website. Travel recommendation is performed by recommending destination, which is similar to a given location or relevant to a given travel intention, to a user. [7] presents UbiquiTO tourist guide for intelligent content adaptation. UbiquiTO uses a rule-based approach to adapt the content of the provided recommendation. [30] also deploys content adaptation approach for presenting tourist-related information. Both content and presentation recommendations are tailored to particular mobile devices and network capabilities. They use content-based, rule based and Bayesian classification methods to provide tourism-related mobile recommendations. [4] presents a method to recommend various places of interest for tourists using physical, social and modal types of contextual information (including mobile location-based contextual information). The recommendation algorithm is based on the Factor Model that is extended to model the impact of the selected contextual conditions on the predicted rating.

Also some works [15, 9, 8, 11]related to profit/cost-based recommender systems have been done. For instance, [15] studies the impact of firm's profit incentives on the design of recommender systems and identifies the conditions under which a profit-maximizing recommender recommends the item with highest margins and those under which it recommends the most relevant item. It also explores the mismatch between consumer and firm incentives and determines the social costs associated with this mismatch. The paper [9] studies the question of how a vendor can directly incorporate profitability of items into the recommendation process so as to maximize the expected profit while still providing accurate recommendations. The proposed approach takes the output of a traditional recommender system and adjusts it according to item profitability.

However, most of these prior travel-related and cost-related work did not explicitly consider the expense and time cost for travel recommendation. Also our travel tour recommendation specifically consider travel package recommendation by using large amount of users' travel logs collected from a travel agent.

3. COST-AWARE LATENT FACTOR MODELS

In this section, we first introduce a *cost-aware* probabilistic matrix factorization model, named cPMF. Then, we further exploit Gaussian prior on user costs and develop an *enhanced* cost-aware probabilistic matrix factorization model, called GcPMF. For both cPMF and GcPMF models, we derive the objective functions and develop effective solutions for the optimization problems.

3.1 The cPMF Model

cPMF is a cost-aware probabilistic matrix factorization model which represents user/item costs with 2-dimensional vectors as shown in Figure 2 (b). Suppose we have N users and M packages. Let R_{ij} be the rating of user i for package j, U_i and V_j represent D-dimensional user-specific and package-specific latent feature vectors respectively (both U_i and V_j are column vectors in this paper). Also, let C_{U_i} and C_{V_j} represent 2-dimensional cost vectors for user U_i and package V_j respectively. In addition, C_U and C_V simply denote the sets of all the user costs and all the package costs respectively. The conditional distribution over the observed ratings $R \in \mathbb{R}^{N\times M}$ is:

$$p(R|U,V,C_U,C_V,\sigma^2) = \prod_{i=1}^{N}\prod_{j=1}^{M}[\mathcal{N}(R_{ij}|f(U_i,V_j,C_{U_i},C_{V_j}),\sigma^2)]^{I_{ij}} \tag{1}$$

where $\mathcal{N}(x|\mu,\sigma^2)$ is the probability density function of the Gaussian distribution with mean μ and variance σ^2, and I_{ij} is the indicator variable that is equal to 1 if user i rated item j and is equal to 0 otherwise. The function $f(x)$ is to approximate the rating for item j by user i. Considering the cost preference for tour recommendation, we define $f(x)$ as:

$$f(U_i,V_j,C_{U_i},C_{V_j}) = S(C_{U_i},C_{V_j})\cdot U_i^TV_j \tag{2}$$

where $S(C_{U_i},C_{V_j})$ is a similarity function to measure the similarity between user-cost vector and item-cost vector. Several existing similarity/distance functions can be used here to perform this calculation, such as Pearson coefficient, the cosine similarity or Euclidean distance. C_V can be considered to be known in this paper because we can directly obtain the cost information for tour packages from the tour logs. C_U is the user cost vector which is going to be estimated. Moreover, we also exploit zero-mean spherical Gaussian prior[24] on user and item latent feature vectors:

$$p(U|\sigma_U^2) = \prod_{i=1}^{N}\mathcal{N}(U_i|0,\sigma_U^2\mathbf{I}),$$
$$p(V|\sigma_V^2) = \prod_{j=1}^{M}\mathcal{N}(V_j|0,\sigma_V^2\mathbf{I}) \tag{3}$$

As shown in Figure 2, in addition to user and item latent factor features, we also need to learn user cost vector simultaneously. Thus, by a Bayesian inference, we have

$$\begin{aligned} & p(U,V,C_U|R,C_V,\sigma^2,\sigma_U^2,\sigma_V^2) \\ & \quad\propto\ p(R|U,V,C_U,C_V,\sigma^2)p(U|\sigma_U^2)p(V|\sigma_V^2) \\ & \quad=\ \prod_{i=1}^{N}\prod_{j=1}^{M}[\mathcal{N}(R_{ij}|f(U_i,V_j,C_{U_i},C_{V_j}),\sigma^2)]^{I_{ij}} \\ & \qquad\times\prod_{i=1}^{M}\mathcal{N}(U_i|0,\sigma_U^2\mathbf{I})\times\prod_{j=1}^{N}\mathcal{N}(V_j|0,\sigma_V^2\mathbf{I}) \end{aligned} \tag{4}$$

U,V and C_U can be learned by maximizing this posterior or log-posterior over user-cost vectors, user and item features with hyperparameters (i.e. the observation noise variance and prior variance) being fixed. By Equation (4) or Figure 2, we can find that cPMF is actually an enhanced general model of PMF by taking the cost into consideration. In other words, if we limit $S(C_{U_i},C_{V_j})$ as 1 for all pairs of user and item, cPMF will be a PMF model.

The log of the posterior distribution in Equation (4) is:

$$\begin{aligned} & \ln p(U,V,C_U|R,C_V,\sigma^2,\sigma_U^2,\sigma_V^2) = \\ & -\tfrac{1}{2\sigma^2}\sum_{i=1}^{N}\sum_{j=1}^{M}I_{ij}(R_{ij}-f(U_i,V_j,C_{U_i},C_{V_j}))^2 \\ & -\tfrac{1}{2\sigma_U^2}\sum_{i=1}^{N}U_i^TU_i-\frac{1}{2\sigma_V^2}\sum_{j=1}^{M}V_j^TV_j-\frac{1}{2}[(\sum_{i=1}^{N} \\ & \sum_{j=1}^{M}I_{ij})\ln\sigma^2+ND\ln\sigma_U^2+MD\ln\sigma_V^2]+C, \end{aligned} \tag{5}$$

where C is a constant that does not depend on the parameters. Maximizing the log-posterior over user-cost vectors, user and item features is equivalent to minimize the sum-of-squared-errors objective function with respect to U, V and $C_U = (C_{U_1}, C_{U_2}, \cdots, C_{U_N})$:

$$\begin{aligned} E = & \frac{1}{2}\sum_{i=1}^{N}\sum_{j=1}^{M}I_{ij}(R_{ij}-S(C_{U_i},C_{V_j})\cdot U_i^TV_j)^2 \\ & +\tfrac{\lambda_U}{2}\sum_{i=1}^{N}||U_i||_F^2+\frac{\lambda_V}{2}\sum_{j=1}^{M}||V_j||_F^2, \end{aligned} \tag{6}$$

where $\lambda_U = \sigma^2/\sigma_U^2$, $\lambda_V = \sigma^2/\sigma_V^2$, and $||\cdot||_F^2$ denotes the Frobenius norm.

Since the dimension of cost vectors is small [27], we use the Euclidean distance for the similarity function as $S(C_{U_i},C_{V_j}) = 1-||C_{U_i}-C_{V_j}||^2$. Since two attributes of the cost vector have significantly different levels of scale, we utilize the Min-Max Normalization technique to preprocess all cost vectors of items. Then the value of attribute of cost vectors is scaled to fit in a specific range $[0,1]$. Subsequently, the value of the learned user cost vector and the similarity value also locate in the similar range. A local minimum of the objective function given by Equation (6) can be obtained by performing gradient descent in U_i, V_j and C_{U_i} as:

$$\begin{aligned} \frac{\partial E}{\partial U_i} &= \sum_{j=1}^{M}I_{ij}\left(S\left(C_{U_i},C_{V_j}\right)\cdot U_i^TV_j-R_{ij}\right) \\ &\quad\cdot S\left(C_{U_i},C_{V_j}\right)V_j+\lambda_U U_i \\ \frac{\partial E}{\partial V_j} &= \sum_{i=1}^{N}I_{ij}\left(S\left(C_{U_i},C_{V_j}\right)\cdot U_i^TV_j-R_{ij}\right) \\ &\quad\cdot S\left(C_{U_i},C_{V_j}\right)U_i^T+\lambda_V V_j \\ \frac{\partial E}{\partial C_{U_i}} &= \sum_{j=1}^{M}I_{ij}\left(S\left(C_{U_i},C_{V_j}\right)U_i^TV_j-R_{ij}\right) \\ &\quad\cdot U_i^TV_jS'\left(C_{U_i},C_{V_j}\right), \end{aligned} \tag{7}$$

where $S'\left(C_{U_i},C_{V_j}\right)$ is the derivative with respect to C_{U_i}. From this training process based on gradient descent, C_U can be eventually learned to express the user's cost.

3.2 The GcPMF Model

In real-world, the user expectation on the financial cost and the time of travel packages usually varies around certain values. Also, as shown in Equation (6), overfitting can happen if we perform the optimization with respect to C_{U_i} ($i = 1 \cdots N$). These two observations suggest that it might be better if we could use a distribution to mode the user cost instead of representing it as a fixed 2-dimension vector. Therefore, we propose to use 2-dimensional Gaussian distribution to model the user cost in the GcPMF model as:

$$p(C_{U_i}|\mu_{C_{U_i}}, \sigma^2_{C_U}) = \mathcal{N}(C_{U_i}|\mu_{C_{U_i}}, \sigma^2_{C_U}\mathbf{I}). \quad (8)$$

In Equation (8), $\mu_{C_{U_i}}$ is the mean of the Gaussian distribution for the cost of user U_i. Also, $\mu_{C_{U_i}}$ is a 2-dimensional column vector. $\sigma^2_{C_U}$ is assumed to be the same for all the users for simplicity.

In the GcPMF model, since we use a 2-dimensional Gaussian distribution, instead of a 2-dimensional vector, to represent the user cost, we need to change the function to measure the similarity/match between the user's cost and the package cost [28]. Considering each package's cost is represented by a constant vector and the user's cost is characterized via a distribution, we can naturally measure the similarity between the user's cost and the package's cost as:

$$S_G(C_{V_j}, \mathcal{G}(C_{U_i})) = \mathcal{N}(C_{V_j}|\mu_{C_{U_i}}, \sigma^2_{C_U}\mathbf{I}), \quad (9)$$

where we simply use $\mathcal{G}(C_{U_i})$ to represent the cost distribution of user U_i. Please note that for the GcPMF model, C_{U_i} represents the variable of the user cost distribution $\mathcal{G}(C_{U_i})$, instead of a user cost vector. Furthermore, the function to approximate the rating for item j by user i is defined as:

$$\begin{aligned} f_G(U_i, V_j, \mathcal{G}(C_{U_i}), C_{V_j}) &= S_G(C_{V_j}, \mathcal{G}(C_{U_i})) \cdot U_i^T V_j \\ &= \mathcal{N}(C_{V_j}|\mu_{C_{U_i}}, \sigma^2_{C_U}\mathbf{I}) \cdot U_i^T V_j \quad (10) \end{aligned}$$

With this user cost representation and the similarity function, a similar Bayesian inference as Equation (4) is:

$$\begin{aligned} & p(U, V, \mu_{C_U}|R, C_V, \sigma^2, \sigma^2_U, \sigma^2_V, \sigma^2_{C_U}) \\ & \propto p(R|U, V, \mu_{C_U}, C_V, \sigma^2, \sigma^2_{C_U}) p(C_V|\mu_{C_U}, \sigma^2_{C_U}) p(U|\sigma^2_U) p(V|\sigma^2_V) \\ & = \prod_{i=1}^{N}\prod_{j=1}^{M} \left(\mathcal{N}\left(R_{ij}|f_G\left(U_i, V_j, \mathcal{G}(C_{U_i}), C_{V_j}\right), \sigma^2\right)\right)^{I_{ij}} \\ & \quad \times \prod_{i=1}^{N}\prod_{j=1}^{M} \mathcal{N}(C_{V_j}|\mu_{C_{U_i}}, \sigma^2_{C_U}\mathbf{I})^{I_{ij}} \\ & \quad \times \prod_{i=1}^{N} \mathcal{N}(U_i|0, \sigma^2_U\mathbf{I}) \times \prod_{j=1}^{M} \mathcal{N}(V_j|0, \sigma^2_V\mathbf{I}), \quad (11) \end{aligned}$$

where $\mu_{C_U} = (\mu_{C_{U_1}}, \mu_{C_{U_2}}, \cdots, \mu_{C_{U_N}})$, which denotes the set of means of all users' cost distribution. $p(C_V|\mu_{C_U}, \sigma^2_{C_U})$ is the likelihood given the parameters of user cost distribution. Given the known ratings of each user, the cost of packages rated by this user can actually be treated as observations of each user's cost. This is why we represent the likelihood over C_V, i.e. the set of package's cost. Then we are able to derive the likelihood as $\prod_{i=1}^{N}\prod_{j=1}^{M} \mathcal{N}(C_{V_j}|\mu_{C_{U_i}}, \sigma^2_{C_U}\mathbf{I})I_{ij}$.

The log of the posterior distribution in Equation (11) can be derived as:

$$\begin{aligned} & \ln p(U, V, \mu_{C_U}|R, C_V, \sigma^2, \sigma^2_U, \sigma^2_V, \sigma^2_{C_U}) = \\ & -\tfrac{1}{2\sigma^2}\sum_{i=1}^{N}\sum_{j=1}^{M} I_{ij}(R_{ij} - f_G\left(U_i, V_j, \mathcal{G}(C_{U_i}), C_{V_j}\right))^2 \\ & -\tfrac{1}{2\sigma^2_{C_U}}\sum_{i=1}^{N}\sum_{j=1}^{M} I_{ij}(C_{V_j} - \mu_{C_{U_i}})^T(C_{V_j} - \mu_{C_{U_i}}) - \\ & \tfrac{1}{2\sigma^2_U}\sum_{i=1}^{N} U_i^T U_i - \frac{1}{2\sigma^2_V}\sum_{j=1}^{M} V_j^T V_j - \frac{1}{2}[(\sum_{i=1}^{N}\sum_{j=1}^{M} I_{ij})\ln\sigma^2 \\ & +(\sum_{i=1}^{N}\sum_{j=1}^{M} I_{ij})\ln\sigma^2_{C_U} + ND\ln\sigma^2_U + MD\ln\sigma^2_V] + C, \quad (12) \end{aligned}$$

where C is also a constant. Maximizing this log-posterior over user-cost means, user and item features is equivalent to minimize the sum-of-squared-errors objective function with respect to U, V and $\mu_{C_U} = (\mu_{C_{U_1}}, \mu_{C_{U_2}}, \cdots, \mu_{C_{U_N}})$:

$$\begin{aligned} E = & \frac{1}{2}\sum_{i=1}^{N}\sum_{j=1}^{M} I_{ij}\left(R_{ij} - \mathcal{N}(C_{V_j}|\mu_{C_{U_i}}, \sigma^2_{C_U}\mathbf{I}) \cdot U_i^T V_j\right)^2 \\ & + \tfrac{\lambda_U}{2}\sum_{i=1}^{N} ||U_i||^2_F + \frac{\lambda_V}{2}\sum_{j=1}^{M} ||V_j||^2_F \\ & + \tfrac{\lambda_{C_U}}{2}\sum_{i=1}^{N}\sum_{j=1}^{M} I_{ij}||C_{V_j} - \mu_{C_{U_i}}||^2, \quad (13) \end{aligned}$$

where $\lambda_{C_U} = \sigma^2/\sigma^2_{C_U}$, $\lambda_U = \sigma^2/\sigma^2_U$, $\lambda_V = \sigma^2/\sigma^2_V$. As we can see from Equation (13), the Gaussian prior introduced on user's cost leads to one more regularization term to the objective function, thus easing the over-fitting. The GcPMF model is also the enhanced general model of PMF, since the objective function (13) reduces to that of PMF if $\sigma^2_{C_U}$ is limited to be infinite. A local minimum of the objective function given by Equation (13) can be identified by performing gradient descent in U_i, V_j and $\mu_{C_{U_i}}$ as:

$$\begin{aligned} \frac{\partial E}{\partial U_i} &= \sum_{j=1}^{M} I_{ij}\left(\mathcal{N}(C_{V_j}|\mu_{C_{U_i}}, \sigma^2_{C_U}\mathbf{I}) \cdot U_i^T V_j - R_{ij}\right) \\ & \quad \cdot\mathcal{N}(C_{V_j}|\mu_{C_{U_i}}, \sigma^2_{C_U}\mathbf{I})V_j + \lambda_U U_i \\ \frac{\partial E}{\partial V_j} &= \sum_{i=1}^{N} I_{ij}\left(\mathcal{N}(C_{V_j}|\mu_{C_{U_i}}, \sigma^2_{C_U}\mathbf{I}) \cdot U_i^T V_j - R_{ij}\right) \\ & \quad \cdot\mathcal{N}(C_{V_j}|\mu_{C_{U_i}}, \sigma^2_{C_U}\mathbf{I})U_i^T + \lambda_V V_j \\ \frac{\partial E}{\partial \mu_{C_{U_i}}} &= \sum_{j=1}^{M} I_{ij}\left(\mathcal{N}(C_{V_j}|\mu_{C_{U_i}}, \sigma^2_{C_U}\mathbf{I})U_i^T V_j - R_{ij}\right) \cdot \\ & U_i^T V_j \mathcal{N}'(C_{V_j}|\mu_{C_{U_i}}, \sigma^2_{C_U}\mathbf{I}) + \lambda_{C_U}\sum_{j=1}^{M} I_{ij}(\mu_{C_{U_i}} - C_{V_j}), \quad (14) \end{aligned}$$

where $\mathcal{N}'(C_{V_j}|\mu_{C_{U_i}}, \sigma^2_{C_U}\mathbf{I})$ is the derivative with respect to $\mu_{C_{U_i}}$. For the same reason, we also utilize the Min-Max Normalization to preprocess all the cost vectors of item before training the model.

In the experiments, instead of using Equation (2) and Equation (10), which may have predictions out of the valid rating range, the results of Equation (2) and Equation (10) are thus further passed through the logistic function $g(x) = 1/(1 + exp(-x))$, which bounds the range of predictions as $[0, 1]$. Also, we map the ratings $1, \cdots, K$ (K is the maximum rating value) to the interval $[0, 1]$ using the function

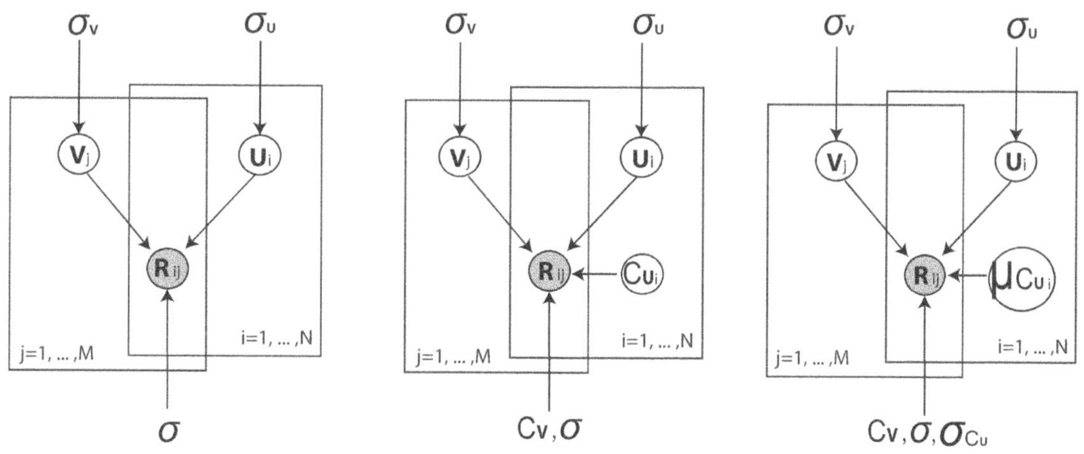

Figure 2: Graphical Models.

$t(x) = (x-1)/(K-1)$, thus the valid rating range matches the range of predictions by our models.

3.3 Discussion of the Model Efficiency

The main computation of gradient methods is to evaluate the object function and its gradients against variables. Because of the sparseness of matrices R, the computational complexity of evaluating the object function (6) is $\mathcal{O}(\eta f)$, where η is the number of nonzero entries in R and f is the number of latent factors. The computational complexity for gradients $\frac{\partial E}{\partial U}$, $\frac{\partial E}{\partial V}$ and $\frac{\partial E}{\partial C_U}$ in Equation (7) is also $\mathcal{O}(\eta f)$. Thus, for each iteration, the total computational complexity is $\mathcal{O}(\eta f)$. Thus, the computational cost of the cPMF model is linear with respect to the number of observed ratings in the sparse matrix R. Similarly, we can analyze and obtain the overall computational complexity of the GcPMF model is also $\mathcal{O}(\eta f)$ because the only difference between GcPMF and cPMF is that we need to compute the probability of the Gaussian distribution as the cost similarity instead of the Euclidean distance involved in cPMF. This complexity analysis shows that the proposed models are efficient and can scale to very large data. In addition, to speed-up training, instead of performing batch learning, we divide the training set into sub-batches and update the feature vectors and cost vectors/parameters after each sub-batch.

4. EXPERIMENTAL RESULTS

Here, we provide an empirical evaluation of the performances of cPMF and GcPMF on real-world travel tour data.

4.1 Travel Tour Data Description

The travel tour data set used in this paper is provided by a travel company. In the data set, there are more than 200,000 expense records starting from the beginning of 2000 to October 2010. In addition to the Customer ID and Package ID, there are many other attributes for each record, such as the start date, the travel days, the package name and some short descriptions of the package, and the cost of the package. Also, the data set includes some information about the customers, such as age and gender. From these records, we are able to obtain the information about users (tourists), items (packages) and user ratings. Instead of using explicit rating (i.e. scores from 1 to 5), we use the number of visits as the implicit rating. This is similar to the use of the number of clicks for measuring the user interests in Web pages. Moreover, we are able to know the financial and time cost for each package from these tour logs. Finally, the tourism data is much sparser than the movie data. For instance, a user can usually watch more than 12 movies each year, while there are not many people who will travel more than 12 times every year. In fact, many tourists only have one or two travel records in the data set.

To reduce the challenge of sparseness, we simply ignore users, who have traveled less than 4 times, as well as packages which have been used for less than 4 times. After this preprocessing, we have 34007 pairs of ratings with 1384 packages and 5724 users. However, the sparseness is still quite low, i.e. 0.4293%, which is much lower than the famous Movielens data set [1] with sparseness as 4.25% and Eachmovie [2] with sparseness as 2.29%. Actually, in the Movielens data set, all users have rated at least 20 movies, while in our travel data, 85.66% users have available ratings less than 10. For our travel log data, instead of using explicit rating, we use implicit rating; that is, the number of travels. Since a user may purchase the same package multiple times for her/his family members, and many local travel packages are even visited multiple times by the same user. There are still a lot of implicit ratings larger than 1, though over 50% of implicit ratings are 1. Some statistics of the item-user rating matrix are summarized in Table 1. From the total pairs of ratings, we randomly select 5% pairs of ratings as the test data for evaluation.

Table 1: Some Characteristics of Travel Data

Statistics	User	Package
Min Number of Rating	4	4
Max Number of Rating	62	1976
Average Number of Rating	5.94	24.57

4.2 Evaluation Metrics

The Root Mean Square Error (RMSE) is used to measure the prediction quality in comparison with benchmark collaborative filtering methods. The RMSE is defined as:

$$RMSE = \sqrt{\frac{\sum_{ij}(r_{ij} - \hat{r}_{ij})^2}{N}}, \tag{15}$$

[1] http://www.cs.umn.edu/Research/GroupLens.
[2] HP retired the EachMovie dataset

where r_{ij} denotes the rating of item j by user i, $\hat{r}_{ij}$ denotes the corresponding rating predicted by the model, and N denotes the number of tested ratings.

In addition to RMSE, the Cumulative Distribution (CD) [16] is also applied for evaluating the performances of different models. Essentially, CD is designed to measure the qualify of top-K recommendations. The CD measurement could explicitly guide people to specify K in order to contain the most interesting items in the suggested top-K set with certain probability. In the following, we briefly introduce how to compute CD with the testing set(more details about this validation method can be found in [16]). First, all highest ratings in the testing set are selected. Assume that we have $\mathcal{M}$ ratings with the highest rating. For each item i with the highest rating by user u, we randomly select $\mathcal{C}$ additional items and predict the ratings by u for i and other $\mathcal{C}$ items. Then, we order these $\mathcal{C}+1$ items based on their predicted ratings in a decreasing order. There are $\mathcal{C}+1$ different possible ranks for item i, ranging from the best case where none(0%) of the random $\mathcal{C}$ items appearing before item i, to the worst case where all (100%) of the random $\mathcal{C}$ items appearing before item i. For each of those $\mathcal{M}$ ratings, we independently draw the $\mathcal{C}$ additional items, predict the associated ratings, and derive a relative ranking (RR) between 0% and 100%. Finally, we analyze the distribution of overall $\mathcal{M}$ RR observations, and estimate the cumulative distribution (CD). In our experiments, we specify $\mathcal{C} = 200$ and obtain 761 RR observations in total.

4.3 The Details of Training

Here, we introduce the training details for the comparison of SVD, PMF [24], cPMF, and GcPMF models. The SVD model was trained to minimize the sum-squared error only to the observed entries of the target matrix. The feature vectors of the SVD model were not regularized in any way. For the PMF model, we empirically specified the parameters as: $\lambda_U = 0.05$ and $\lambda_V = 0.005$. For cPMF and GcPMF models, we used the same values for λ_U and λ_V, together with $\lambda_{C_U} = 0.2$ for the GcPMF model. Also, we specified $\sigma^2_{C_U} = 0.09$ for the GcPMF model in the following. Moreover, we initialized the cost vector of each user or the Gaussian mean vector with the average cost of all items rated by this user u, while user/item latent feature vectors were initialized randomly. Finally, we simply removed the global effect [20] by subtracting the average rating of the training set from each rating before performing collaborative filtering. All the models were compared with the test set.

4.4 Performance Comparisons

First, a performance comparison of all the models with 10-dimensional latent features in terms of RMSE is shown in Figure 3. As can be seen, both cPMF and GcPMF outperform PMF or SVD with significant margins, since the RMSE values achieved by cPMF or GcPMF are much lower than those achieved by PMF or SVD. Also, the performances of GcPMF are consistently better than that of cPMF. In addition, given the same parameters and the initialization setting, both cPMF and GcPMF lead to faster convergence than PMF and SVD. Towards the end of training, SVD has the serious overfitting issues. The above results suggest that it is essential to consider the travel cost for travel tour recommendation and the proposed two cost-aware models can

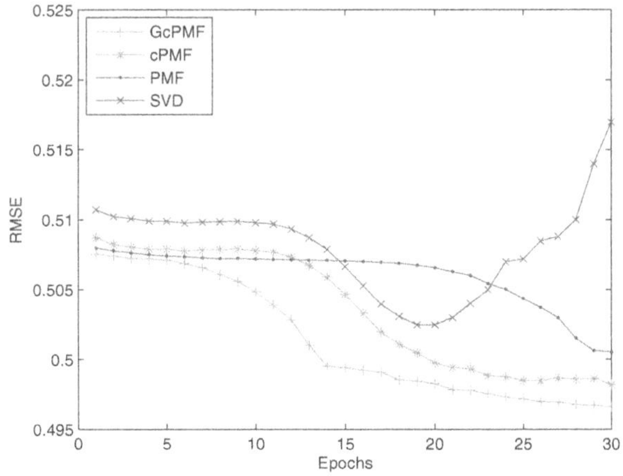

Figure 3: A Performance Comparison in terms of RMSE (10D Latent Features).

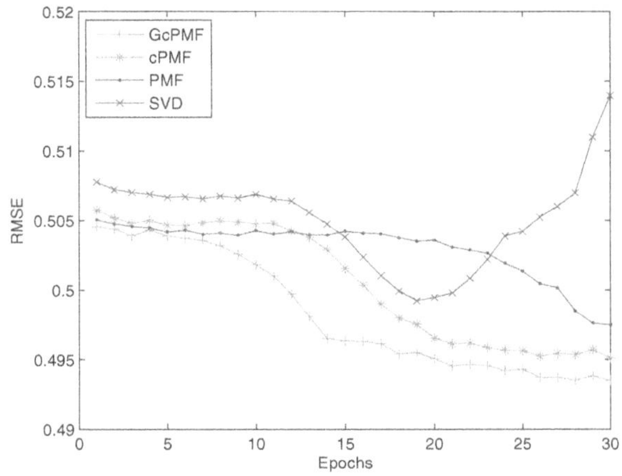

Figure 4: A Performance Comparison in terms of RMSE (30D Latent Features).

capture the cost effect well. Finally, in Figure 4, similar results can also be observed for 30-dimensional latent features.

Second, we compared the performances of all the models using the CD measure introduced in Subsection 4.2. Figure 5, shows the cumulative distribution of the computed percentile ranks for the four models over all 761 RR observations. Note that we used 10-dimensional latent features in Figure 5. As can be seen, both cPMF and GcPMF models outperform the competing models. For example, considering the point of 0.1 on x-axis, the CD value for GcPMF at this point suggests that, if we recommend top-20 from random 201 packages to users, approximately at least one package matches user interest and cost-expectation with probability as 53%. Since people usually are more interested in top-5 or even top-3, out of 201 packages, we zoom in on the head of the x-axis, which represent top-K recommendation in a more detailed way. As shown in Figure 6, a more clear difference can be observed. For example, GcPMF model has a probability of almost 0.5 to suggest a highest-rated package before other random 198 packages. In other words, if we use GcPMF to recommend top-2 packages out of 201 packages, we can match user's needs with probability of 0.5. This outperforms PMF and SVD with over 60% percentage and around 20% percentage respectively. Also, cPMF leads to

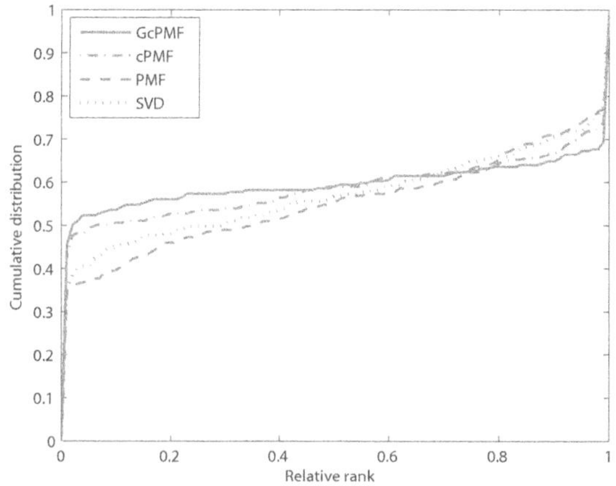

Figure 5: A Performance Comparison in terms of CD (10D Latent Features).

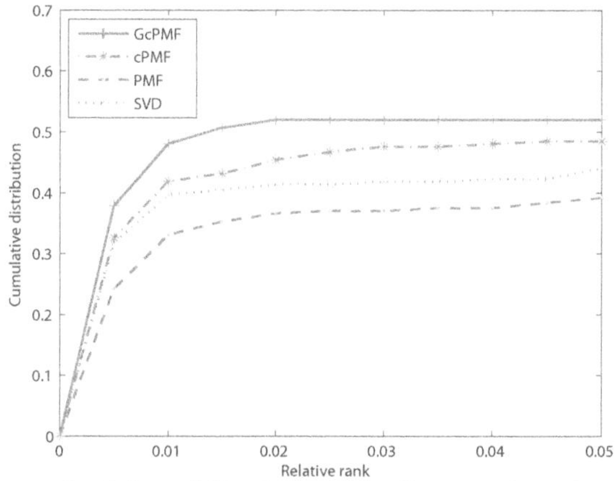

Figure 6: A Local Performance Comparison in terms of CD (10D Latent Features).

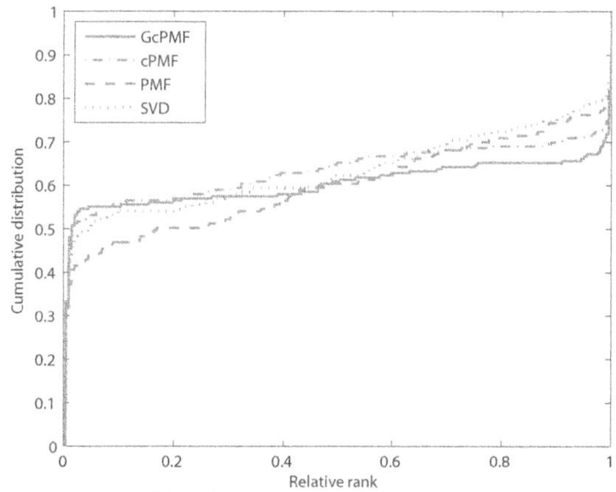

Figure 7: A Performance Comparison in terms of CD (30D Latent Features).

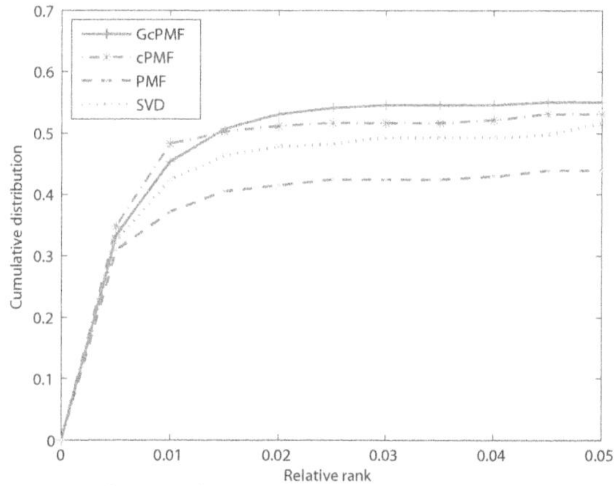

Figure 8: A Local Performance Comparison in terms of CD (30D Latent Features).

slight better performance than SVD and much better performance than PMF. In addition, we show more comparisons in Figures 7 and 8 with 30-dimensional latent features, where a similar trend can be observed.

4.5 Cost Visualization

In this subsection, we illustrate the user cost learned by our models. These learned user cost features could help travel companies for customer profiling. Since we normalized the package cost vectors into [0, 1] before feeding into our models, the learned user cost features (C_U and μ_{C_U}) via our models have the similar scale as normalized package cost vectors. To visualize the learned C_U, we first restored the scale of user cost features (C_U and μ_{C_U}) by using the inverse transformation of MinMax normalization. Figure 9 shows the financial cost feature of C_U for randomly-selected 40 users, where each user corresponds to a column of vertically-distributed points. Neighboring users are differentiated with different colors. For example, for the right vertical blue points, *star* represents the learned user financial cost feature and *dot* represents the financial cost of packages, which are rated by this specific user in the training set. As we can see, the learned user financial cost feature is relatively representative. However, there is still obvious variance among the package cost features by some users. That is why we apply Gaussian distribution to model user cost. To illustrate the effectiveness of Gaussian assumption for user cost, in Figure 10, we visualize the learned μ_{C_U} for randomly-selected 12 users. For each subfigure of Figure 10, we directly plot the learned 2-dimension μ_{C_U} (without inverse transformation) for individual user and all normalized 2-dimension cost vectors of packages, which are rated by the user in the training set. And μ_{C_U} is represented as *star* and *dot* represents package cost vector.

4.6 Performances on Different Users

For the four competing models, the prediction performances for users with different number of observed ratings usually vary a lot, because the user feature vectors are updated differently during the training process. The user cost vector of cPMF or the Gaussian distribution of GcPMF play as an effective constraint to limit the prediction via the similarity weight. Thus, the performance of cPMF and GcPMF on users with few observed ratings are expected to be better than the competing models. Figure 11 shows this effect by comparing RMSE on different users for the four models. In this experiment, we used 10-dimensional latent factors, and the users were grouped by the number of observed ratings in the training set. Also, we used the RMSE value of final epoch for all models. As we can see, even for users with less than 6 observed ratings, cPMF and GcPMF lead to better performances in terms of RMSE.

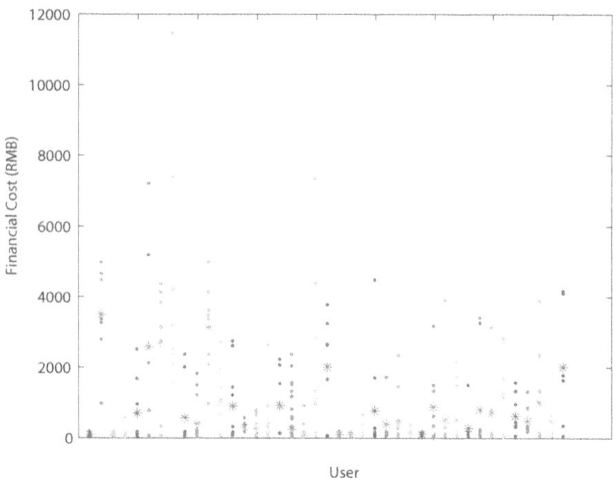

Figure 9: An Illustration of User Financial Cost.

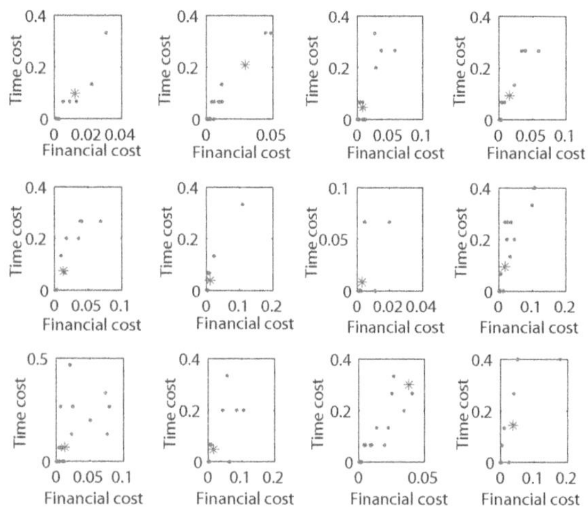

Figure 10: An Illustration of Gaussian Parameters of User Cost.

4.7 The Model Efficiency

In this subsection, we compare the efficiency of four models. Table 2 shows the training time of GcPMF, cPMF, PMF and SVD models. Here, we used the same 10-dimensional latent features. Since there is some additional cost for computing the similarity function in GcPMF and cPMF, a little more time is required for each updating in GcPMF and cPMF than the competing models, such as PMF and SVD. In addition, the computing of Gaussian distribution in GcPMF is more time-consuming than the computing of Frobenius norm in cPMF. However, the computing time of GcPMF is still linearly increasing as the number of training pairs increases as discussed in Subsection 3.3.

Table 2: A Comparison of the Model Efficiency

Models	Training Time (Second)
SVD	3.623112
PMF	3.411250
cPMF	4.894951
GcPMF	10.878244

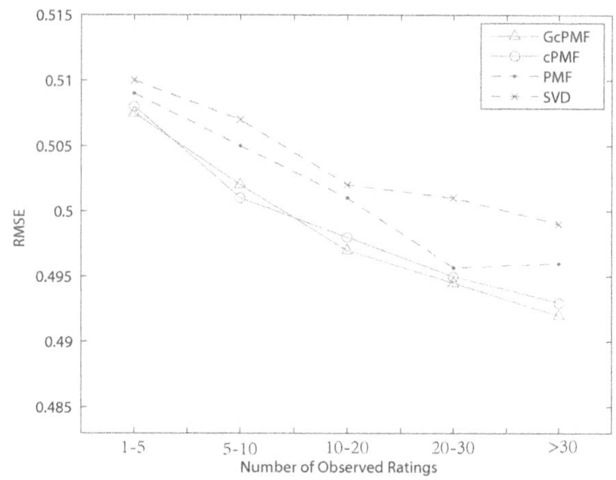

Figure 11: Performances on Different Users.

5. CONCLUSION AND DISCUSSION

In this paper, we studied the problem of travel tour recommendation by analyzing a large amount of travel logs collected from a travel agent company. One unique characteristic of tour recommendation is that there are different financial and time costs associated with each travel package. Different tourists usually have different levels of "affordability" for these two aspects of cost. Thus, we explicitly incorporated observable and unobservable cost factors into the recommendation model; that is, we used a latent factor model to represent unobserved cost factors together with other types of latent variables to model additional latent factors.

Specifically, we developed a cost-aware latent factor model, called cPMF, to learn the user/item latent features and user cost preferences simultaneously. In cPMF, we model unobserved user's cost with a 2-dimensional vector and learn the user cost vector and latent features. In addition, considering that there is usually some variance for the user cost preference, we further model user's cost with a Gaussian distribution and propose the enhanced GcPMF model. Experimental results on real-world travel logs showed that both cPMF and GcPMF models led to better learning performances than benchmark methods, such as PMF and SVD, while the learning performance of GcPMF is slightly better than that of cPMF. Furthermore, we illustrated the learned user cost preferences, which are helpful for travel companies to profile their customers.

Finally, we would like to point out that, although we have focused on incorporating costs into the travel-related applications in this paper, our approach is more general and goes well beyond travel-related applications. In particular, our approach can be applicable to a broad range of other applications in which some costs are observable and explicitly defined, while others are unobservable and need to be modeled using latent variables. For instance, let us consider an electronic product recommendation scenario, such as recommending a digital camera at Amazon.com. Different users can usually afford different prices. To provide better personalized recommendation to different users, it is expected to apply cost-aware collaborative filtering models to learn the customer's cost preference and other interests. The prediction of rating can be decided by the learned latent features and user cost preference. This will most likely lead to better performance for recommendation than traditional models without considering the cost context. We would like to explore these issues further as a part of our future research of cost-aware recommender systems.

6. ACKNOWLEDGEMENTS

This research was partially supported by National Science Foundation (NSF) via grant number CCF-1018151, and National Natural Science Foundation of China (NSFC) via project numbers 70890082 and 71028002. Please contact Professor Hui Xiong for any comments.

7. REFERENCES

[1] R. P. Adams, G. E. Dahl, and I. Murray. Incorporating side information in probabilistic matrix factorization with gaussian processes. In *Computing Research Repository - CORR*, 2010.

[2] G. Adomavicius and A. Tuzhilin. Towards the next generation of recommender systems: A survey of the state-of-the art and possible extensions. *TKDE, 2005*, 2005.

[3] D. Agarwal and B. C. Chen. Regression-based latent factor models. In *In KDD '09: Proceedings of the 15th ACM SIGKDD international conference on Knowledge discovery and data mining*, pages 19–28, 2009.

[4] L. Baltrunas, F. Ricci, and B. Ludwig. Context relevance assessment for recommender systems. In *Proceedings of the 2011 International Conference on Intelligent User Interfaces, 13-16 February 2011, Palo Alto, CA, USA*, 2011.

[5] R. M. Bell and Y. Koren. Scalable collaborative filtering with jointly derived neighborhood interpolation weights. In *IEEE ICDM 2007*, pages 43–52, 2007.

[6] R. D. Burke. Hybrid web recommender systems. *Lecture Notes in Computer Science*, 4321:377–408, 2007.

[7] F. Cena, L. Console, C. Gena, A. Goy, G. Levi, S. Modeo, and I. Torre. Integrating heterogeneous adaptation techniques to build a flexible and usable mobile tourist guide. *AI Communication*, 19(4):369–384, 2006.

[8] L.-S. Chen, F.-H. Hsu, M.-C. Chen, and Y.-C. Hsu. Developing recommender systems with the consideration of product profitability for sellers. *Information Sciences*, 178(4):1032–1048, 2008.

[9] A. Das, C. Mathieu, and D. Ricketts. Maximizing profit using recommender systems. In *WWW*, 2010.

[10] M. Deshpande and G. Karypis. Item-based top-n recommendation. In *ACM Transactions on Information Systems*, pages 22(1):143–177, 2004.

[11] Y. Ge, H. Xiong, A. Tuzhilin, K. Xiao, M. Gruteser, and M. J. Pazzani. An energy-efficient mobile recommender system. In *KDD 2010.*

[12] Q. Gu, J. Zhou, and C. H. Q. Ding. Collaborative filtering weighted nonnegative matrix factorization incorporating user and item graphs. In *SIAM SDM*, pages 199–210, 2010.

[13] Q. Hao, R. Cai, C. Wang, R. Xiao, J.-M. Yang, Y. Pang, and L. Zhang. Equip tourists with knowledge mined from travelogues. In *the 19th International World Wide Web Conference*, 2010.

[14] T. Hofmann. Latent semantic models for collaborative filtering. *ACM Transactions on Information Systems - TOIS*, 22(1):89–115, 2004.

[15] K. Hosanagar, R. Krishnan, and L. Ma. Recommended for you: The impact of profit incentives on the relevance of online recommendations. In *Proceedings of the International Conference on Information Systems*, 2008.

[16] Y. Koren. Factorization meets the neighborhood: a multifaceted collaborative filtering model. In *KDD 2008*, pages 426–434, 2008.

[17] Y. Koren. Collaborative filtering with temporal dynamics. In *KDD 2009*, pages 447–456, 2009.

[18] Y. Koren, R. M. Bell, and C. Volinsky. Matrix factorization techniques for recommender systems. *IEEE Computer - COMPUTER*, 42(8):30–37, 2009.

[19] T.-K. H. J. S. J. G. C. Liang Xiong, Xi Chen. Temporal collaborative filtering with bayesian probabilistic tensor factorization. In *SIAM International Conference on Data Mining*, pages 211–222, 2010.

[20] Q. Liu, E. Chen, H. Xiong, and C. H. Q. Ding. Exploiting user interests for collaborative filtering: interests expansion via personalized ranking. In *ACM CIKM*, pages 1697–1700, Toronto, Canada, 2010.

[21] Z. Lu, D. Agarwal, and I. S. Dhillon. A spatio-temporal approach to collaborative filtering. In *Conference on Recommender Systems - RecSys*, pages 13–20, 2009.

[22] H. Ma, I. King, and M. R. Lyu. Learning to recommend with social trust ensemble. In *Research and Development in Information Retrieval*, pages 203–210, 2009.

[23] B. Marlin. Modeling user rating profiles for collaborative filtering. In *In NIPS*. MIT Press, 2003.

[24] R. Salakhutdinov and A. Mnih. Probabilistic matrix factorization. In *Neural Information Processing Systems 21 (NIPS 2008)*, 2008.

[25] B. M. Sarwar, G. Karypis, J. A. Konstan, and J. T. Riedl. Application of dimensionality reduction in recommender system - a case study. In *In ACM WebKDD Workshop*, 2000.

[26] N. Srebro, J. Rennie, and T. Jaakkola. Maximum margin matrix factorizations. In *Advances in Neural Information Processing Systems (NIPS) 17, 2005.*

[27] M. Wang, X.-S. Hua, J. Tang, and R. Hong. Beyond distance measurement: Constructing neighborhood similarity for video annotation. In *IEEE Transactions on Multimedia*, volume 11, 2009.

[28] M. Wang, X.-S. Hua, J. Tang, and R. Hong. Unified video annotation via multi-graph learning. In *IEEE Transactions on Circuits and Systems for Video Technology*, volume 19, 2009.

[29] G. Xue, C. Lin, Q. Yang, W. Xi, H. Zeng, Y. Yu, and Z. Chen. Scalable collaborative filtering using cluster-based smoothing. In *In Proc. of SIGIR*, pages 114–121, 2005.

[30] Z. Yu, X. Zhou, D. Zhang, C.-Y. Chin, X. Wang, and J. Men. Supporting context-aware media recommendations for smart phones. *IEEE Pervasive Computing*, 5(3):68–75, July 2006.

Discovering Highly Reliable Subgraphs in Uncertain Graphs *

Ruoming Jin
Kent State University
Kent, OH, USA
jin@cs.kent.edu

Lin Liu
Kent State University
Kent, OH, USA
lliu@cs.kent.edu

Charu C. Aggarwal
IBM T. J. Watson Research Ctr
Hawthorne, NY, USA
charu@us.ibm.com

ABSTRACT

In this paper, we investigate the *highly reliable subgraph* problem, which arises in the context of uncertain graphs. This problem attempts to identify all induced subgraphs for which the probability of connectivity being maintained under uncertainty is higher than a given threshold. This problem arises in a wide range of network applications, such as protein-complex discovery, network routing, and social network analysis. Since exact discovery may be computationally intractable, we introduce a novel sampling scheme which enables approximate discovery of highly reliable subgraphs with high probability. Furthermore, we transform the core mining task into a new *frequent cohesive set problem* in deterministic graphs. Such transformation enables the development of an efficient two-stage approach which combines novel *peeling techniques* for maximal set discovery with depth-first search for further enumeration. We demonstrate the effectiveness and efficiency of the proposed algorithms on real and synthetic data sets.

Categories and Subject Descriptors

H.2.8 [**Database Management**]: Database Applications—*Data Mining*

General Terms

Algorithms, Theory

Keywords

Uncertain graph, Reliable subgraph, Frequent cohesive set

1. INTRODUCTION

Networks have evolved into a unified conceptual abstract to model both natural and man-made complex systems such as the web, social networks, and cellular systems. Such networks often have inherent uncertainty. In a telecommunication or electrical network, a link can be unreliable and may fail with certain probability [11, 31]. In a protein interaction network, the pairwise interaction is derived from (approximate) statistical models [4, 3, 21]; in a social network, trust and influence issues may impact the likelihood of social interactions [12, 26, 1]. The *uncertain graph model* is a convenient framework to address such scenarios [30, 38, 41, 40, 39] in a unified way. In this model, each edge is associated with an *edge existence probability* to quantify the likelihood that this edge exists in the graph. An uncertain graph is also referred to as a *probabilistic graph* [2, 17].

It is evident that the connectivity of the network is a complex probabilistic function of the network topology and edge uncertainty. Such problems are notoriously difficult [34, 5] because of the combinatorially large number of possible instantiations of an uncertain graph. For example, even the simple problem of pairwise vertex reachability, which can be easily computed in linear time in deterministic graphs, becomes a $\#P$-complete problem in the uncertain scenario [5]. The *network reliability problem* [10] is a generalization of pairwise reachability, in which the goal is to determine the probability that *all pairs of nodes* are reachable from one another. In other words, network reliability measures the probability that the entire graph remains connected under uncertainty. The basic reachability problem is also referred to as *two-terminal network reliability* and the latter problem is referred to as *all-terminal network reliability*, which is also $\#P$-complete [5]. As we will see, the reliable subgraph problem addressed in this paper is an even further generalization of these problems, as it relates to subgraph **discovery** satisfying the reliability property. Network reliability algorithms have numerous applications in communication networks [11, 31], biological networks [3], and social networks [33, 35].

This paper uses a pattern mining approach towards reliable subgraph discovery, which is independent of specific sets of vertices. We address the problem of determining all *highly reliable sets of vertices* for which the induced subgraphs have network reliability above a user-specified threshold. The problem of discovering all highly reliable subgraphs can be found in a wide range of network applications. In a protein-protein interaction network, the highly reliable subgraphs can be used for identifying the core of protein complexes [3]. In a telecommunication network, the highly reliable subgraphs can serve as the basic constructs to help connect a source and a destination [29]. In social networks with edge uncertainty, highly reliable subgraphs can help discover cohesive groups [35]. The highly reliable subgraph problem on uncertain networks can be considered analogous to dense component mining in the deterministic scenario [28]. However, the combination of network topology and edge probabilities make this problem much more challenging, because a structurally dense component with low probability edges may not be reliable, and vice versa. In general, the subtle effects of different levels of uncertainty in different structural portions of the network need to be addressed by any algorithm for reliable sub-

*R. Jin and L. Liu were partially supported by the National Science Foundation, under CAREER grant IIS-0953950.

KDD'11, August 21–24, 2011, San Diego, California, USA.

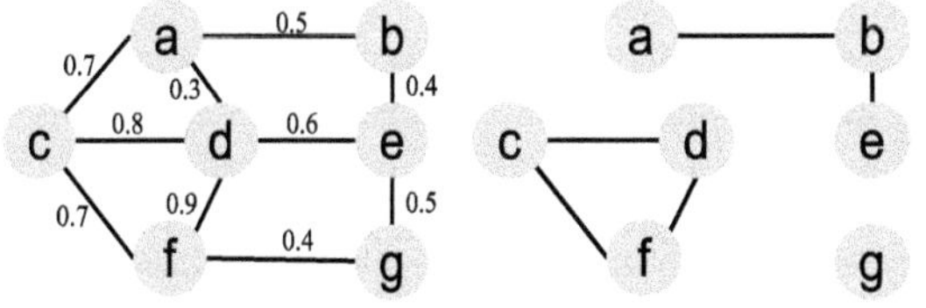

(a) Uncertain Graph $\mathcal{G}$ (b) G_1 with 0.00254016

Figure 1: Running Example

graph mining. In order to address these goals, we make the following contributions in this paper:

1. We introduce and formally define the problem of discovering all highly reliable subgraphs in uncertain graphs (Section 2).
2. We propose a sampling scheme, which enables approximate discovery of highly reliable subgraphs with guaranteed probabilistic accuracy. We transform the uncertain graph mining problem into a new *frequent cohesive set discovery* problem in deterministic graphs (Section 3).
3. We present a two-stage approach to discover all frequent cohesive sets. The algorithm combines an efficient top-down *peeling* approach in the first stage (to discover all *maximal* frequent cohesive sets) with a fast depth-first-search (DFS) mining procedure to discover the remaining non-maximal frequent cohesive sets (Section 4).
4. We demonstrate the effectiveness and efficiency of the proposed algorithms on real and synthetic data sets (Section 5).

2. PROBLEM FORMULATION

We denote an *uncertain directed graph* by $\mathcal{G} = (V, E, P)$, where V is a set of vertices, E is a set of edges, and $P : E \rightarrow (0, 1]$ is a function that determines the probability of existence of edge e in the graph. It is assumed that the uncertainty variables of different edges are independent of one another, though our approach also applies in principle to the *conditional probability model* [30], as long as a computational method for generating appropriate samples of the uncertain graph is available.

A *possible graph* $G = (V_G, E_G)$ of an uncertain graph $\mathcal{G}$ is a deterministic graph which is a possible *outcome* of the random variables representing the edges of the probabilistic graph $\mathcal{G}$. We denote the possible graph by $G \sqsubseteq \mathcal{G}$. The graph G contains a subset of edges of $\mathcal{G}$. In other words, we have $E_G \subseteq \mathcal{G}$. The total number of such possible graphs is $2^{|E|}$, because for each edge, we have two cases as to whether or not that edge is present in the graph. The probability of sampling the graph G from the random variables representing the uncertain graph $\mathcal{G}$ is given by the following sampling or realization probability $\mathbf{Pr}[G]$:

$$\mathbf{Pr}[G] = \prod_{e \in E_G} p(e) \prod_{e \in E \setminus E_G} (1 - p(e)).$$

We present an example of an uncertain graph $\mathcal{G}$ and its possible realization G_1 in Figure 1. The uncertain graph $\mathcal{G}$ has 2^{10} possible outcomes, and the sampling probability of G_1 is defined as follows:

$$\mathbf{Pr}[G_1] = p(a,b)p(b,e)p(c,d)p(c,f)p(d,f)(1 - p(a,c)) \times (1 - p(a,d))(1 - p(d,e))(1 - p(e,g))(1 - p(f,g)) = 0.00254016$$

The network reliability [10] measures the likelihood that the entire graph is connected and can be formally defined as follows:

DEFINITION 1. **(Network Reliability)** *Given an uncertain graph $\mathcal{G} = (V, E, P)$, its network reliability $\mathbf{R}[\mathcal{G}]$ is defined as the probability that its sampled realizations remain connected. This probability can be mathematically quantified as follows:*

$$\mathbf{R}[\mathcal{G}] = \sum_{G \sqsubseteq \mathcal{G}} \mathbf{I}(G) \cdot \mathbf{Pr}[G], \text{ where } \mathbf{I}(G) \text{ is an indicator function,}$$

$$\mathbf{I}(G) = \begin{cases} 1, & \text{if } G \text{ is connected;} \\ 0, & \text{otherwise} \end{cases}$$

The definition can be easily generalized to the induced subgraph $\mathcal{G}[V_s]$ for a subset of vertices $V_s \subseteq V$:

$$\mathbf{R}[\mathcal{G}[V_s]] = \sum_{G \sqsubseteq \mathcal{G}} \mathbf{I}(G[V_s]) \cdot \mathbf{Pr}[G], \text{ where } G[V_s] \text{ is the induced}$$

subgraph of V_s. For simplicity, we also refer to $\mathbf{R}[\mathcal{G}[V_s]]$ as the *subgraph reliability* with respect to V_s.

Next, we introduce the problem of discovering all highly reliable subgraphs in an uncertain graph:

DEFINITION 2. **(Highly Reliable Subgraph (HRS) Problem)** *Given an uncertain graph $\mathcal{G} = (V, E, P)$ and a reliability threshold $\alpha \in [0, 1]$, determine all induced subgraphs whose network reliability is at least α.*

In other words, we have $\mathbf{R}[\mathcal{G}[V_s]] \geq \alpha$. The resulting set is denoted by $\mathcal{S}_\alpha$. We make the important observation that the *downward closure property* does *not* hold for reliable subgraphs:

LEMMA 1. *Given an uncertain graph $\mathcal{G}$ and two subsets V_s and V'_s where $V_s \supset V'_s$, we cannot claim either $\mathbf{R}[\mathcal{G}[V_s]] \geq \mathbf{R}[\mathcal{G}[V'_s]]$ or $\mathbf{R}[\mathcal{G}[V_s]] \leq \mathbf{R}[\mathcal{G}[V'_s]]$.*

For instance, in the uncertain graph $\mathcal{G}$ depicted in Figure 1, $\mathbf{R}[\mathcal{G}[\{c,d,f\}]] = 0.902 > \mathbf{R}[\mathcal{G}[\{d,f\}]] = 0.9$ and we have $\mathbf{R}[\mathcal{G}[\{b,e,g\}]] = 0.2 < \mathbf{R}[\mathcal{G}[\{e,g\}]] = 0.5$. The lack of downward closure creates a challenge from an algorithmic perspective.

In addition, we can use a simple property of the uncertain graph in order to preprocess it and drop some of the edges in order to reduce computational complexity. This property is as follows: *Given an uncertain graph $\mathcal{G} = (V, E, P)$ and a reliability threshold α, for an induced subgraph $\mathcal{G}[V_s]$ of $\mathcal{G}$, if there is an edge cut $C \subseteq E(\mathcal{G}[V_s])$ in $\mathcal{G}[V_s]$ (removing all edges in C makes $\mathcal{G}[V_s]$ disconnected), such that $p(C) = \sum_{e \in C} p(e) < \alpha$, then $\mathbf{R}[\mathcal{G}[V_s]] < \alpha$.* Given this, we can further observe the following:

LEMMA 2. **(Edge-Cut Lemma)** *Given an uncertain graph $\mathcal{G} = (V, E, P)$ and a reliability threshold α, for any edge cut C in $\mathcal{G}$, $C \subseteq E$ which breaks the uncertain graph into two parts $\mathcal{G}[V_1]$ and $\mathcal{G}[V_2]$ ($V_1 \cup V_2 = V$ and $C \subseteq V_1 \times V_2$), then if $p(C) = \sum_{e \in C} p(e)$, then, for any high reliable subgraph (HRS) $\mathcal{G}[V_s]$, either we have $V_s \subseteq V_1$ or $V_s \subseteq V_2$. In other words, there is no HRS $\mathcal{G}[V_s]$ with $V_s \cap V_1 \neq \emptyset$ and $V_s \cap V_2 \neq \emptyset$.*

The implication of this lemma is that if for any cut C in uncertain graph $\mathcal{G}$ with $p(C) < \alpha$, then, we can safely drop all the edges in C without missing any HRS. Clearly, this reduces the number of candidate sets. However, finding all such cuts with value at most α is computationally prohibitive. In this work, we apply a simple linear min-cut algorithm [32] starting from each vertex in the uncertain graph in order to drop edges. This algorithm starts from an arbitrary vertex (a single vertex set) in a graph, and then iteratively selects a vertex most tightly connected to the current set of vertices and add it into the set until we find a cut C with $p(C)$ less than α. At this point, we drop all the edges in the cut. We utilize this procedure to preprocess the uncertain graph $\mathcal{G}$ by repeating the procedure for all vertices.

We note that all singleton vertex sets are always highly reliable, and a pair of vertices is a highly reliable set if and only if they are connected by an edge with probability at least α. Therefore, we will focus on the interesting case of finding all highly reliable vertex sets in $\mathcal{S}_\alpha$ with set size no less than 3. Finally, since each induced subgraph is uniquely determined by its vertex set, we report only vertex sets in $\mathcal{S}_\alpha$, and interchangeably use the terms "vertex sets" and "induced subgraphs" in this paper.

3. SAMPLING APPROXIMATION SCHEME

Since the network reliability problem is #P-complete, the generalized problem studied in this paper is at least as intractable. The methods available for exact determination of subgraph reliability are designed for cases where graphs are very small (tens of vertices at most) [31]. We note that the problem of subgraph reliability estimation and subgraph pattern discovery have different levels of difficulty in terms of solvability. The former problem can of course be partially addressed by allowing approximate estimation through Monte-Carlo sampling; however we will see that it continues to be a challenge to avoid uncontrolled false positives or negatives in the pattern discovery version of the problem. The sampling approach for subgraph reliability estimation is as follows:
(1) We first sample N possible graphs, $G_1, G_2, \cdots, G_N$ of $\mathcal{G}$ according to edge probability function P; and (2) for any subset of vertices V_s, we compute the indicator function $\mathbf{I}(G_i[V_s])$ (whether the induced subgraph $G_i[V_s]$ itself is a connected component) for each sample graph G_i. Given this, the sampling estimator ($\widehat{\mathbf{R}}[\mathcal{G}[V_s]]$) of the subgraph reliability is as follows:

$$\mathbf{R}[\mathcal{G}[V_s]] \approx \widehat{\mathbf{R}}[\mathcal{G}[V_s]] = \frac{\sum_{i=1}^{N} \mathbf{I}(G_i[V_s])}{N}$$

The sampling estimator $\widehat{\mathbf{R}}[\mathcal{G}[V_s]]$ is an *unbiased* estimator of the subgraph reliability, i.e., $E(\widehat{\mathbf{R}}[\mathcal{G}[V_s]]) = \mathbf{R}[\mathcal{G}[V_s]]$. More importantly, by applying the Chernoff-Hoeffding Bound [9, 19], we can determine whether an induced subgraph is highly reliable with high probability:

LEMMA 3. *With sample size $N \geq \frac{2}{\epsilon^2}\ln\frac{2}{\delta}$, for any subset of vertices V_s, $Pr(|\widehat{\mathbf{R}}[\mathcal{G}[V_s]] - \mathbf{R}[\mathcal{G}[V_s]]| \geq \epsilon) \leq \delta$.*

We would naturally like to use this approach for determining the highly reliable set $\mathcal{S}_\alpha$. However, from a set mining perspective, it is hard to probabilistically control the number of false positives or negatives. This is because the use of sampling to determine the reliability of an induced subgraph is a multiple hypothesis test, and it is inherently difficult to provide guarantees in such cases [6, 7]. Some recent results have shown how to effectively use multiple hypothesis tests for the special case of the frequent pattern mining problem [15, 27], but these methods cannot be used to provide guarantees for our problem.

To deal with this challenge, we utilize two sets to approximate $\mathcal{S}_\alpha$: *(a) the first set $\overline{S}$ which tries to maximize the recall of discovering highly reliable subgraphs; (b) the second set $\underline{S}$ which tries to maximize the precision of discovery.* These two sets provide flexible and complementary choices for different applications. In cases where we do not wish to miss any highly reliable subgraphs (false negatives), the first set can be used, and then false positives can be filtered out. If the application is designed for discovering some of the very highly reliable subgraphs, the second set is more helpful. When the two sets are similar, it is evident that it is possible to achieve both high precision and recall. We will design an approach which achieves this goal.

Sampling-based Approach for Highly Reliable Set Discovery: Our sampling-based approach utilizes additional parameters ϵ and δ for controlling the discovery results. The approach consists of two steps:
Step 1: *Sample $N_1 = \frac{2}{\epsilon^2}\ln\frac{2}{\delta}$ possible graphs of $\mathcal{G}$, denoted as dataset D_1, discovering all induced subgraphs $\mathcal{G}[V_s]$ with reliability $\widehat{\mathbf{R}}[\mathcal{G}[V_s]] \geq \alpha - \epsilon$ using N_1 sampled graphs:*

$$\overline{S} = \{\mathcal{G}[V_s] | \widehat{\mathbf{R}}[\mathcal{G}[V_s]] \geq \alpha - \epsilon\}$$

Step 2: *Sample $N_2 = \frac{2}{\epsilon^2}\ln\frac{2|\overline{S}|}{\delta}$ possible graphs of $\mathcal{G}$, denoted as dataset D_2, discovering all induced subgraphs $\mathcal{G}[V_s]$ with reliability $\widehat{\mathbf{R}}[\mathcal{G}[V_s]] \geq \alpha + \epsilon$ using N_2 sampled graphs and $\mathcal{G}[V_s] \in \overline{S}$:*

$$\underline{S} = \{\mathcal{G}[V_s] | \widehat{\mathbf{R}}[\mathcal{G}[V_s]] \geq \alpha + \epsilon\} \cap \overline{S}$$

We make the following observations about this approach.

THEOREM 1. *(**Precision and Recall**) The sets $\overline{S}$ and $\underline{S}$ produced by the sampling procedure have the following properties:*

1. *The expected fraction of missed highly reliable subgraphs is at most δ. In other words, we have $E(\frac{|\mathcal{S}_\alpha \setminus \overline{S}|}{|\mathcal{S}_\alpha|}) \leq \delta$;*
2. *With probability at least $1-\delta$, all induced subgraph in $\underline{S}$ are highly reliable subgraphs: $Pr(\forall \mathcal{G}[V_s] \in \underline{S}, \mathbf{R}[\mathcal{G}[V_s]] \geq \alpha) \geq 1-\delta$ and $Pr(|\underline{S} \cap \mathcal{S}_\alpha|/|\underline{S}| = 1) \geq 1-\delta$;*
3. *With probability at least $1-\delta$, the precision of $\overline{S}$ is no less than $\beta = \frac{|\underline{S}|}{|\overline{S}|}$ ($\underline{S} \subseteq \overline{S}$): $Pr(|\mathcal{S}_\alpha \cap \overline{S}|/|\overline{S}| \geq \beta) \geq 1-\delta$. When β is close to 1, the two sets become similar and the precision increases;*
4. *The expected fraction of missed highly reliable subgraphs in $\underline{S}$ is no higher than $\delta + 1 - \beta + \delta\beta/|\overline{S}| \approx \delta + 1 - \beta$: $E(\frac{|\mathcal{S}_\alpha \setminus \underline{S}|}{|\mathcal{S}_\alpha|}) \leq \delta + 1 - \beta + \delta\beta/|\overline{S}| \approx \delta + 1 - \beta$. When β is close to 1, the expected false negative rate is small.*

We omit the detailed proofs since these are direct applications of the Chernoff-Hoeffding bounds. It is evident from Theorem 1 that δ is directly responsible for controlling the precision and recall of the reliable subgraph discovery algorithm. The parameter ϵ needs further explanation. Though it does not directly appear in the precision and recall formulas, it helps to control the difference between $\overline{S}$ and $\underline{S}$. In other words, when ϵ decreases, β tends to increase. However, since the required sample sizes N_1 and N_2 are inversely related to the square of ϵ, it may be important to balance between computational cost and approximation quality. We will examine these tradeoffs in detail in the experimental section.

An important observation is that the precision and recall are controlled in this approach by different probabilistic criteria. Specifically, in order to control recall, the expected false negative rate is applied instead of the standard Bonferroni correction for multiple comparison [15]. This is because of the difficulty in determining the size of the result set $\mathcal{S}_\alpha$. To deal with this problem, we simply employ the expected false negative rate in the first step. Once we have a candidate set $\overline{S}$, we are able to utilize a more strict Bonferroni correction approach [15] in the second step for controlling precision. It is important to remember that the approach (and the corresponding theoretical results) can be applied to an uncertain graph in which edge probabilities are not independent, as long as appropriate samples of the graph can be generated. For this purpose, an independent set of possible graphs can be generated from the uncertain graph by a Gibbs sampler or a Markov Chain Monte Carlo technique [30].

Discovering Frequent Cohesive Sets: The aforementioned sampling approximation scheme results in a new graph mining problem, which we call the *Frequent Cohesive Set* (FCS) problem:

DEFINITION 3. ***(Frequent Cohesive Set Problem)*** *Given a graph G and a subset of vertices $V_s \subseteq V[G]$, if its induced subgraph $G[V_s]$ forms one connected component, then V_s is referred to as a* **cohesive set** *in G. Given a set of graphs $D = \{G_1, G_2, \cdots, G_N\}$ with vertices $V(G_1) = V(G_2) = \cdots = V(G_N) = V$ and a minimal support threshold θ, a frequent cohesive set (FSC) is any subset of vertices $V_s \subseteq V$ that is a cohesive set in at least $\theta \cdot N$ graphs.*

In order to be consistent with the problem of highly reliable subgraph discovery, we denote the frequency of V_s being cohesive as $\widehat{\mathbf{R}}[V_s]$. In addition, the **maximal frequent cohesive set (MFCS)** problem identifies all frequent cohesive sets in D, for which none of their supersets are cohesive. In the aforementioned sampling approach, the first step is the key, and it is needed to solve the MFCS problem. Specifically, the dataset D_1 consists of N_1 graphs (Step 1 in the sampling approach), and the generation of the approximate set $\overline{S}$ corresponds to the discovery of all frequent cohesive sets in D_1 with minimum support $\theta = \alpha - \epsilon$. Once we have determined $\overline{S}$, we only need to determine whether each of the vertex sets is frequently cohesive in the new sampling dataset D_2 (Step 2). Since connectivity can be checked for each induced subgraph in linear time [20], this can be done rather quickly. Due to the simplicity of the second step, we omit further discussion and focus on the first step of discovering all frequent cohesive sets in a graph database.

Interestingly, to the best of our knowledge, this problem has not been studied before. The closest is Yan *et al.*'s work [36] on mining closed frequent subgraphs with connectivity constraints. The main difference is that in our problem, there is no isomorphism requirement on the induced subgraphs, a fact which can be leveraged towards more efficient algorithm design. In the next section, we will introduce an efficient method for mining all the FCS in a large graph database. Finally, we note that it is possible to generalize the cohesive set with additional connectivity constraints, in a manner similar to [36]. For instance, each induced subgraph may not only be connected, but k-connected as well. Our algorithm can be generalized to handle such constraints as well. However, this is beyond the scope of the present work.

4. MINING FREQUENT COHESIVE SETS

The frequent cohesive set problem is similar to the highly reliable subgraph problem, in that it also lacks the downward closure property (Lemma 1). This creates an algorithmic challenge for the pattern mining process. In order to address this challenge, we develop a novel two-stage mining algorithm. In the first stage, a novel top-down *peeling* process is employed to iteratively refine patterns to make them converge into maximal frequent cohesive sets (MFCS) (Subsections 4.1 and 4.2). In the second stage, we perform a DFS mining process which utilizes the MFCS as the boundary to prune the search space for discovering all the non-maximal frequent cohesive sets (Subsection 4.3). We will now describe these different stages.

4.1 Peeling Algorithm for MFCS

In this subsection, we describe a novel and efficient algorithm for mining the maximal frequent cohesive sets (MFCS). We refer to our approach as the *peeling* algorithm, because we work from *supersets to subsets* during pattern discovery, as patterns are being iteratively refined (or peeled). Clearly, a successful peeling approach requires two main properties: **(a)** We need to dicover the initial patterns containing all the MFCS. **(b)** We need an effective peeling approach in order to converge to the correct MFCS. In the following, we address these two key issues and provide details of the peeling algorithm.

Relaxation Approach: In order to discover the initial patterns which contain all the maximal frequent cohesive sets (MFCS), we relax the *cohesive* condition on a vertex set by allowing connectivity through vertices outside the set. This relaxed problem also turns out to be easier to solve because it satisfies the downward closure property. Specifically, we introduce the *maximal frequent linked sets* (MFLS) problem, which allows connectivity of a vertex set not just through the induced subgraph itself, but other vertices as well.

DEFINITION 4. ***(Maximal Frequent Linked Set Problem)*** *A subset of vertices $V_s \subseteq V[G]$ in graph G is said to be a* **linked set** *if it belongs to a connected component in G. Given a graph database $D = \{G_1, G_2, \cdots, G_N\}$ with $V(G_1) = V(G_2) = \cdots = V(G_N) = V$ and a minimum support threshold θ, a subset of vertices $V_s \subseteq V$ is referred to as a* **frequent linked set**, *if it is a linked set in at least $\theta \cdot N$ graphs.*

The frequency of V_s being linked in D is denoted as $\widehat{\mathbf{R}}_L[V_s]$. The **maximal frequent linked set** problem tries to identify all the frequent linked sets in D, such that any superset of these sets is not frequently linked. A frequent linked set relaxes the cohesive constraint by not requiring the set to be connected only through the vertices (and edges) of the induced subgraph. It is easy to see that any frequent cohesive set must be a frequent linked set, though the reverse is not necessarily true. Consequently, *if V_s is a maximal frequent cohesive set (MFCS), then there must be a maximal frequent linked set (MFLS) V_s', such that $V_s' \supseteq V_s$*. Thus, the set of all MFLS can naturally serve as the initial pattern set which forms an "upper bound" on all MFCS. Furthermore, unlike the FCS problem, the relaxed MFLS problem has the *down-closure property*, which allows efficient discovery.

Discovering all MFLS is surprisingly simple, because we can reduce it to the classical maximal frequent itemset problem [14], for which many efficient algorithms are available. Specifically, the *transformation* procedure which converts the graph database D into a transactional database T is as follows:
For each graph $G_i \in D$, find all its connected components, i.e., $G_i = C_{i1} \cup C_{i2} \cup \cdots \cup C_{ik}$. Output the vertex set of each connected component as an independent transaction, i.e., $T = T \cup \{V[C_{i1}], V[C_{i2}], \cdots, V[C_{ik}]\}$ ($T = \emptyset$ initially).

LEMMA 4. *The set of all maximal frequent itemsets (MFI) in T with minimum support θ is equivalent to maximal frequent linked sets (MFLS) in D with the same minimum support level.*

Note that the transformation process can be achieved very quickly [20], since it has linear computational complexity with respect to the size of the graph database. Thus, the question is how we can refine these MFLS to produce the final set of all maximal frequent cohesive itemsets (MFCS). Next, we discuss how this initial set can be peeled.

Naïve Peeling: The basic idea of peeling is as follows. For each initially discovered maximal frequent linked set (MFLS) m in D, we keep refining it in order to convert it to a (maximal) frequent cohesive set (FCS). Specifically, if m is not a frequent cohesive set, we first effectively peel the graph database so that it contains only vertices in m. In other words, to refine m, we only work on the partial graph database $D[m] = \{G_1[m], G_2[m], \cdots, G_N[m]\}$, which contains only the induced subgraph of m for each graph in D. Note that once we peel the graphs so that they contain only vertex set m, they may become disconnected (since they are likely to be linked through other vertices in the graph). Then, we can discover all the maximal frequent linked sets (MFLS) on the partial graph database $D[m]$ using the earlier method. Thus, we can recursively perform this process until all maximal frequent linked sets (MFLS) converge into the frequent cohesive sets.

Algorithm 1 Peeling$(D, mfls, MFCS)$

Parameter: D: the graph database $D = \{G_1, G_2 \cdots, G_N\}$;
Parameter: $mfls$: the intermediate maximal frequent linked sets;
Parameter: $MFCS$: the final maximal frequent cohesive sets;
1: **for each** $m \in mfls$ **do**
2:   **if** $\widehat{\mathbf{R}}[m|D[m]] \geq \theta$ {if m is a frequent cohesive set} **then**
3:     **if** $\nexists m' \in MFCS \wedge m' \supseteq m$ **then**
4:       $MFCS \leftarrow prune(MFCS \cup \{m\})$; {maximal patterns}
5:     **end if**
6:   **else**
7:     $T \leftarrow transform(D[m])$ {transform graph database to transactional database};
8:     $mfls' \leftarrow MFI(T, \theta)$ {maximal frequent itemsets};
9:     **Peeling**$(D, mfls', MFCS)$;
10:   **end if**
11: **end for**

Algorithm 1 sketches the peeling process. The input is the initial MFLS discovered using the aforementioned MFI mining approach. Then, we invoke the *peeling* algorithm. In the loop (Lines 1 to 13), we iteratively visit each maximal frequent linked set m in $mfls$. If m is indeed a frequent cohesive set ($\widehat{\mathbf{R}}[m|D[m]] \geq \theta$), we try to add it in the result set $MFCS$ (Lines 3 to 5) where the *prune* procedure enforces the maximal constraint. If not, we perform the refinement process described in lines $8 - 10$. In other words, we discover the maximal frequent linked sets in $D[m]$. We recursively perform peeling for all newly discovered MFLS (Line 11).

THEOREM 2. *(***Correctness of Peeling***) The* **Peeling** *algorithm (Algorithm 1) can discover all maximal frequent cohesive sets from graph database D with minimum support θ.*

The proof of the theorem is omitted for simplicity. Note that the peeling process requires us to recursively invoke the pattern discovery algorithm on smaller sets. It is important to remember that later invocations of the MFI procedure are typically on transactions of *much* smaller length. This is therefore typically very fast at lower levels of the recursion. Furthermore, the cost to compute $\widehat{\mathbf{R}}[m|D[m]]$ and transform a graph database to a transactional database requires a simple DFS scan of $D[m]$ [20], which is a comparatively very small overhead to MFI mining. Nevertheless, the naïve peeling algorithm may redundantly re-examine the same intermediate frequent linked sets (MFLS) multiple times. For example, when two MFLS overlap along a large number of vertices, then their individual peeling processes may produce the same intermediate MFLS. The recursion could then create a combinational explosion, the bulk of which is redundant processing. This needs to be controlled in order to enable more efficient and practical pattern discovery. In the following, we will present a number of elegant methods to avoid duplicate work, and significantly speed up the peeling algorithm.

4.2 Fast Peeling Algorithm

In order to speed up vertex pattern generation, we use the methods of *layered peeling* and *transaction reduction*. We discuss them below.

Layered Peeling: This technique focuses on reducing the processing of redundant intermediate patterns. The basic idea is that instead of performing the recursive peeling of each individual intermediate pattern, we employ a *layered peeling* strategy. For an initial set of patterns in the first layer, we peel them all together to produce another set of intermediate patterns in the second layer. We then perform the same peeling process for the new set of intermediate patterns. If the new patterns (frequent linked sets) are frequent cohesive sets, we remove them from the new layer. More importantly, *each layer is composed of only maximal patterns*. This is based on the following observation:

LEMMA 5. *Given two frequent linked sets m and m', if $m \subseteq m'$, then the maximal frequent cohesive sets (MFCS) contained by m, denoted as $MFCS(m)$, must be contained in $MFCS(m')$. Furthermore, assuming a pattern T is already known to be a FCS, then in the new layer, if it contains an intermediate pattern which is the subset of T, then, the intermediate pattern can be pruned without missing any MFCS.*

This property ensures that it is sufficient to work only with maximal linked sets without losing information. This allows each unique intermediate pattern to be peeled only once when it is necessary for new maximal frequent cohesive set discovery. In addition, for the latter statement, if m is such an intermediate pattern $m \subseteq T$, then m cannot produce any new MFCS. Using our running example in Figure 1 with 100 sampling graphs and $\theta = 0.5$, we need three layers to discover all the MFCS. In the first layer which includes all the initial MFLS in G, we have four: $\{a, b, c, d, f\}$, $\{a, c, d, f, g\}$, $\{c, d, e, f, g\}$, and $\{a, c, d, f, e\}$. Then, in the second layer, we have three MFCS $\{c, d, e, f\}$, $\{a, c, d, f\}$, and $\{a, b\}$, and two intermediate patterns (MFLS) $\{d, e, f, g\}$ and $\{c, d, f, g\}$. Finally, in the third layer, from the last two intermediate patterns, we found one MFCS $\{e, g\}$ and two new intermediate patterns $\{c, d, f\}$ and $\{d, e, f\}$. Since we already knew $\{a, c, d, f\}$ is a MFCS, we can prune $\{c, d, f\}$ from the new layer. Similarly, we can prune $\{d, e, f\}$ because of $\{d, e, f, g\}$. Thus, the third layer becomes empty and we already have found all the MFLS.

Transaction Reduction: In the method discussed above, we ensure that patterns in a given layer do not contain one another. However, this does not account for the fact that patterns which are produced in lower layers may be subsets of those produced in earlier layers. Therefore, in order to further speed up the peeling algorithm, we would like to prevent such non-maximal patterns from being generated in the first place. The following lemma provides an important tool for achieving this.

LEMMA 6. *Let us assume that the patterns in the current layer L are visited sequentially. Let $P \subseteq L$ include those patterns which have already been visited (peeled) at any given time point. Let V_{ij} be the vertex set of a connected component C_{ij} in $G_i[m]$, where $m \in L$ has not been peeled. If there is another pattern (frequent linked sets) m' which has been processed (peeled) ($m' \in P$) and $V_{ij} \subseteq m$, then we can safely drop V_{ij} in the transactional database transformed from $D[m]$ without losing any potential maximal frequent cohesive sets in D.*

The same dropping condition can be applied for any discovered (maximal) frequent cohesive sets in D. If any transaction is a subset of a (maximal) frequent cohesive set in D, we can also safely drop it. This is because transactions such as V_{ij} cannot contribute to any new MFCS, and can only help generate patterns which are subsets of patterns which have already been visited. Thus, dropping such transactions in the first place can help prevent the generation of unnecessary patterns. In addition, such transaction reduction can also help reduce the computational cost, because it results in a smaller database for MFI.

Overall Algorithm: Algorithm 2 depicts the fast peeling process. Initially, L contains all the maximal frequent linked sets in D (Line

1). Then we iteratively visit each element m of L in decreasing order of pattern size. This order is chosen in order to maximize the efficiency of search space pruning. This is based on Lemma 6. We try to add those frequent cohesive patterns into the result set $MFCS$ (line 6 to 10), where *prune* maintains the maximal constraint for $MFCS$. For those that are not frequent cohesive sets, *transReduc* produces and reduces the transactions which are contained by patterns in P or $MFCS$ (Line 11) according to Lemma 6. This reduced database T is used to generate the intermediate patterns $mfls'$ (Line 13). These are merged into L' by the *prune* procedure to maintain the maximal constraint(Line 14). Finally, the new layer will be processed (Line 17) until there are no new patterns to be generated.

Algorithm 2 FastPeeling(D))

Parameter: D: the graph database $D = \{G_1, G_2 \cdots, G_N\}$; {Step 1: generating initial patterns}
1: $L \leftarrow MFI(transform[D], \theta)$ {L: existing layer};
2: $L' \leftarrow \emptyset$ {L': new layer}; $MFCS \leftarrow \emptyset$ {the result set};
3: **while** $L \neq \emptyset$ **do**
4: $P \leftarrow \emptyset$ {already peeled patterns in L}
5: **for each** $m \in L$ {decreasing order of the pattern size} **do**
6: **if** $\widehat{\mathbf{R}}[m|D[m]] \geq \theta$ {if m is a frequent cohesive set} **then**
7: **if** $\nexists m' \in MFCS \wedge m' \supseteq m$ **then**
8: $MFCS \leftarrow prune(MFCS \cup \{m\})$;
9: **end if**
10: **else**
11: $T \leftarrow$ **transReduce**$(D[m], P \cup MFCS)$ {Lemma 6}
12: $mfls' \leftarrow MFI(T, \theta)$ {maximal frequent itemsets};
13: $L' \leftarrow prune(L' \cup mfls')$; {Lemma 5: maximal patterns}
14: **end if**
15: $P \leftarrow P \cup \{m\}$;
16: **end for**
17: $L \leftarrow prune(L' \cup MFCS) \setminus MFCS$ {Lemma 5: pruning using FCS}; $L' \leftarrow \emptyset$;
18: **end while**

The computational complexity of our algorithm is dominated by the cost of mining Maximal Frequent Itemsets (MFI). Let the cost of mining MFI in the transformed transactional database from the entire graph database D be $O(MFI_D)$ (Line 1). For i-th layer L, we can break it into the minimal number c_i of batches, such that the patterns are all disjoint with one another in each batch. Thus, we can see the overall cost of each layer is bounded by $O(c_i MFI_D)$. If there are a total of k layers, then the total computational complexity is $O((\sum_{i=1}^{k} c_i) MFI_D)$. However, since the transactional database in each batch is typically much smaller than the first transactional database (Line 1), the total cost of mining MFI for all layers is generally even smaller than the cost of MFI mining once at the start (Line 1). We note the number of total layers is typically quite small in practice. For example, in all our experiments, this number was less than 5. Therefore, the total computational complexity of the peeling approach is proportional to a single execution of MFI_D (or $O(MFI_D)$). As we will show from the experimental results in Section 5, the overall computational time of peeling is no higher than 2 times that of mining MFI in the first round.

4.3 DFS Mining for Non-Maximal FCS

While the previous section provides a way to discover maximal patterns, we also need to discover all non-maximal frequent cohesive sets. A naïve approach would be to directly apply the peeling algorithm to further discover the remaining sets. To do that, we can explicitly remove each vertex from the (maximal) frequent cohesive set to produce the intermediate patterns for further peeling. For instance, for a (maximal) pattern $\{a, b, c, d\}$, we can generate new intermediate patterns $\{b, c, d\}$, $\{a, c, d\}$, $\{a, b, d\}$, and $\{a, b, c\}$. Clearly, this may significantly increase the number of times we need to scan the graphs, and invoke the maximal frequent itemset mining algorithm. The speedup techniques of Lemma 5 and 6 are also not directly applicable in this case. The key question is whether we can leverage our knowledge of the maximal frequent cohesive sets in order to enable discovery of the non-maximal ones. In the following, we provide a positive answer to this question by amortizing the discovery across different maximal patterns.

The basic idea of our mining algorithm is that we perform a DFS traversal on $\mathcal{G}$ to enumerate any *connected vertex sets* in V which are contained by at least one MFCS being covered in the peeling algorithm. Then, for each of these vertex sets, we perform an efficient test to determine whether they are frequently cohesive. Since there is a standard method for enumerating connected vertex sets along the lines of enumerating cliques [23, 8], the main issue is how we can efficiently control the enumeration boundary. Clearly, we may simply test whether each discovered vertex set is contained by a MFCS, but such a test can be rather costly [37]. Therefore, we next discuss how to speed up this test.

Fast Subset Checking: Each MFCS is assigned a unique ID, and each vertex in the uncertain graph is associated with a list that records the IDs of each MFCS containing it. Furthermore, each enumerating vertex set maintains a list which is the intersection of the lists from its individual vertices. In other words, the list records all the MFCS which contain the vertex set. Importantly, this list can be maintained in an incremental fashion. We also note that when the list for a vertex set is empty, it is implied that no MFCS contains it.

Fast Connectivity Test: In order to test whether a vertex set V_s is frequently cohesive, the straightforward method would be to directly check the connectivity of each induced subgraph $G_1[V_s]$, $G_2[V_s]$, $\cdots$, $G_N[V_s]$. An observation which enables convenient speedup is as follows: *For a fully connected induced subgraph, if a new vertex is added and it is adjacent to at least one vertex in the subgraph, then the new subgraph is also connected.*

This implies that we can use a binary vector to record whether each induced subgraph of the current vertex set is connected, and then we can apply it to test whether its immediate expansion by one vertex is connected. It is only when the induced subgraph is not fully connected that we need to traverse its immediate expansion in order to determine its connectivity.

Algorithm Description: Algorithm 3 describes a DFS mining procedure in order to discover all non-maximal frequent cohesive sets. First, we note that parameters v, V_s, N and Ex are the standard parameters for enumerating the connected vertex sets in a graph [23, 8]: v is the newly expanded vertex in the current connected vertex set V_s in uncertain graph $\mathcal{G}$; N records all the neighbors of V_s, which can be possibly added into V_s; and Ex is the exclusion list of vertices which should not be added into V_s (a basic mechanism to avoid the redundant enumeration of the same connected vertex set in a graph). Ex typically records those vertices visited earlier in the DFS enumeration order. The parameter ID is for the aforementioned boundary test and vector Con is for the fast connectivity test.

For each newly expanded vertex set V_s (to which vertex v was newly added), Algorithm 3 first checks whether it is a FCS using the *fast connectivity test* (Lines 1 to 10). Then, no matter whether the vertex set is a FCS or not, each of its neighbors except those in the exclusion list (avoid redundant enumeration) will be visited (Line 11). This is a typical way for recursively enumerating the connected vertex set. Specifically, ID' is the list recording all the IDs of those MFCS containing $V_s \cup \{w\}$ and it is maintained incrementally (Line 12). Once a vertex w is visited, we put it immedi-

Algorithm 3 **MiningNonMaximal**(v, V_s, ID, Con, N, Ex)

Parameter: v {the newly added edge-vertex in V_s}
Parameter: V_s {the current vertex sets}
Parameter: ID {the IDs of maximal cohesive sets containing V_s}
Parameter: Con {the binary vector for connectivity}
Parameter: N {the neighbors of V_s}
Parameter: Ex {exclusion list of vertices (already expanded)}
1: **for each** $G_i \in D$ **do**
2:   **if** $Con[i]$ **then**
3:     $Con'[i] \leftarrow (Neighbor(v|G_i) \cap V_s) \neq \emptyset$;
4:   **else**
5:     $Con'[i] \leftarrow Connected(G_i[V_s])$;
6:   **end if**
7: **end for**
8: **if** $\widehat{\mathbf{R}}[V_s] \geq \theta$ {using Con' to compute} **then**
9:   $FCS \leftarrow FCS \cup \{V_s\}$ {non-maximal frequent cohesive sets}
10: **end if**
11: **for each** $w \in N \backslash Ex$ **do**
12:   $ID' \leftarrow ID \cap ID[w]$; {MFCS containing V_s}
13:   $Ex \leftarrow Ex \cup \{w\}$;
14:   **if** $|ID'| > 1 \vee (|ID'| = 1 \wedge V_s \cup \{v\} \neq$ MFCS in $ID')$ **then**
15:     **MiningNonMaximal**$(w, V_s \cup \{v\}, ID', Con', Neighbor(w|\mathcal{G}) \cup N, Ex)$;
16:   **end if**
17: **end for**

Procedure Main
1: $Ex \leftarrow \emptyset$;
2: **for each** $w \in V \backslash Ex$ **do**
3:   $Ex \leftarrow Ex \cup \{w\}$;
4:   **MiningNonMaximal**$(w, \{w\}, ID[w], \mathbf{0}, \mathbf{Neighbor(w|\mathcal{G}), Ex})$;
5: **end for**

ately in the exclusion list so that the latter iteration will not visit it again (Line 13). For each newly expanded vertex set, when either its list ID' is contained by at least two MFCS or is a strict subset of the only MFCS ($|ID'| = 1$), we know it has not reached the boundary yet and cannot be considered a candidate for non-maximal FCS (Lines 14 – 15).

Note that the worst case computational complexity of this algorithm is determined by the total number of connected vertex subsets which are bounded by MFCS. For each connected vertex set, we need to traverse each of its induced subgraphs in the graph database. This has linear cost.

5. EXPERIMENTAL EVALUATION

In this section, we present experimental results studying the accuracy and efficiency of our method. Specifically, we are interested in the following two questions:

1. Accuracy: How well does the sampling approach approximate the set of highly reliable subgraphs S_α? Recall that we utilize two sets $\overline{S}$ and $\underline{S}$ ($\overline{S} \supseteq \underline{S}$) to approximate S_α, and these two sets are designed to measure recall and precision respectively. When the two sets are similar, they can provide accurate estimation of the S_α according to Theorem 1. In such cases, the precision and recall are both high. It is easy to see that the fraction $\beta = \frac{|\underline{S}|}{|\overline{S}|}$ provides a good indicator for the accuracy of the sampling approach for experimental evaluation.

2. Efficiency: What is the performance in terms of overall running time? As we mentioned before, the sampling approach consists of two steps for (1) sampling dataset D_1 and for (2) sampling dataset D_2.

In step (1), we need to discover all frequent cohesive sets (FCS) from D_1. Specifically, step (1) contains two stages: in the first stage, we apply peeling (naïve or fast) algorithms to discover all maximal frequent cohesive set (MFCS); and in the second stage, we utilize a DFS mining process using MFCS to discover all the remaining Non-Maximal FCS. Given this, we would like to understand how the computational time is distributed between Steps (1) and (2), and a quantification of the efficiency advantage of fast peeling over the naïve approach. Step (2) can be implemented much more efficiently, because it requires us to only check membership on D_2.

All algorithms were implemented using C++ and the Standard Template Library (STL), and were conducted on a 2.0GHz Dual Core AMD Opteron CPU with 4.0GB RAM running Linux.

Table 1: β(%) vs varying ϵ ($\delta = 0.01, \alpha = 0.99$)

	ϵ =0.030	ϵ =0.035	ϵ =0.040	ϵ =0.045	ϵ =0.050
Yeast	55.92	54.26	53.63	53.55	49.54
Fly	57.86	56.90	52.40	52.57	52.62
Mouse	98.65	99.10	99.10	99.10	99.10
Rat	100.00	100.00	100.00	100.00	100.00
DBLP	73.90	70.28	70.01	68.60	65.11

Table 2: β(%) vs varying δ ($\epsilon = 0.05, \alpha = 0.99$)

	δ=0.01	δ=0.008	δ=0.006	δ=0.004	δ=0.002
Yeast	46.78	46.72	49.66	49.30	48.76
Fly	50.76	51.46	51.46	52.23	52.91
Mouse	99.10	99.10	99.10	99.10	99.10
Rat	100.00	100.00	100.00	100.00	100.00
DBLP	65.49	66.73	67.42	65.32	66.23

5.1 Experimental Results on Real Datasets

In this subsection, we report our experimental results on five real datasets: four protein-protein interaction (PPI) uncertain graphs and one coauthor graph. The PPI datasets are integrated from BioGRID database and STRING databases, and are provided by the author in [39]. The coauthorship network is derived from DBLP, and is extracted from the dataset provided by the author in [30]. The summary of those datasets are listed in Figure 2, where the last column $avg(p_e)$ indicates the average edge probability in the uncertain graph.

In the first three groups of experiments, we focus on studying how the accuracy indicator β is affected by the three user-defined parameters, the reliability threshold α, the confidence level δ, and ϵ which directly relates to β (Section 3).

Varying ϵ: In this experiment, we fix the reliability threshold α and the confidence level δ with $\alpha = 0.99$ and $\delta = 0.01$ (99% confidence), and we vary the ϵ from 0.03 to 0.05. Table 1 reports the variation of the accuracy indicator β with ϵ on each dataset. First, it is evident that β is always at least 50%, and in 3 out of 5 datasets (Mouse, Rat, and DBLP), β is generally much higher than 65%. The lowest values of β were obtained for the Yeast and Fly data sets, but were still above or very close to 50%. Taking $\overline{S}$ as the example, this simply suggests that at least half of the discovered subgraphs in $\overline{S}$ are guaranteed to be highly reliable ($\geq \alpha = 0.99$), and the expected fraction of HRS being missed by $\overline{S}$ is no more than 1%. The best performance was obtained on Mouse and Rat, for which β was very close to 1. A detailed analysis shows that most of the subgraphs discovered from these two datasets are very small and their number is also small. They also seem to form a

Table 3: β(%) vs varying α ($\epsilon = 0.05, \delta = 0.01$)

	α=0.99	α=0.97	α=0.95	α=0.93	α=0.90
Yeast	48.64	9.25	5.25	52.94	80.92
Fly	51.27	41.87	30.92	52.77	63.69
Mouse	99.10	92.36	86.42	94.24	96.04
Rat	100.00	100.00	100.00	98.00	97.13
DBLP	65.51	53.82	45.64	68.13	83.84

	$\|V\|$	$\|E\|$	$agv(p_e)$
Yeast	162	300	0.148
Fly	3751	7384	0.456
Mouse	199	286	0.413
Rat	130	178	0.374
DBLP	1000	2356	0.560

Figure 2: datasets summary

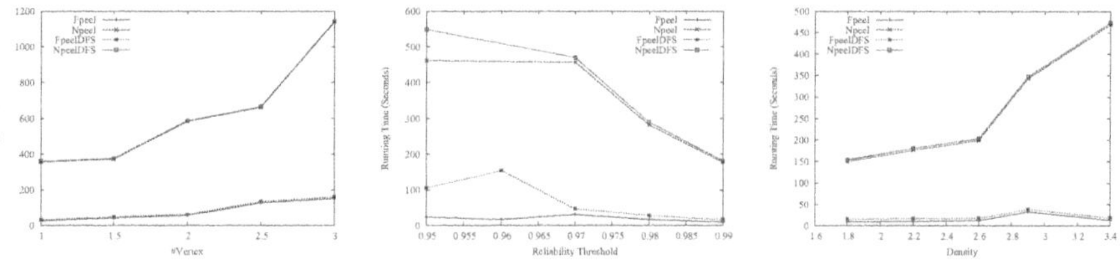

(a) Time vs. $|V|$ (b) Time vs. α (c) Time vs. Density

Figure 3: Running Time vs. Random Block Model Graphs

Table 4: Execution time(seconds) for real datasets (ϵ = 0.05, δ = 0.01, α = 0.99)

	NpeelDFS			FpeelDFS		
	Step 1-p	Step 1-d	Step 2	Step 1-p	Step 1-d	Step 2
Yeast	30.03	3.05	47.23	0.99	2.88	44.71
Fly	437.08	22.76	209.90	23.28	19.22	180.95
Mouse	28.79	0.05	0.86	0.75	0.05	0.84
Rat	8.67	0.02	0.44	0.39	0.02	0.40
DBLP	368.67	63.60	26.64	26.58	61.77	28.52

few small components. Thus, these small components are highly reliable and are easily discovered without too many false positives. Second, it is evident that β increases for lower values of ϵ. This is because reduced values of ϵ lead to higher sample sizes, and also because smaller ϵ would result in more accurate thresholds for the hypothesis test. In other words, $\alpha-\epsilon$ increases and $\alpha+\epsilon$ decreases. Thus, $\overline{S}$ tends to reduce and $\underline{S}$ tends to increase as ϵ reduces.

Varying δ: In this experiment, we fix the reliability threshold α and parameter ϵ ($\alpha = 0.99$ and $\epsilon = 0.05$), and we vary δ from 0.01 to 0.002, which correspond to very high levels of confidence. Table 2 reports the accuracy indicator β with respect to different values of δ on each dataset. First, we can see that the overall accuracy indicator β is consistent with the first experiment, because it is usually larger than 50%. Second, we observe that as δ decreases (confidence level $1-\delta$ increases), β also tends to increase. However, the margin of increase is relatively small. This is because the influence of δ on sample size is proportional to $\ln(1/\delta)$, whereas the influence of ϵ on sample size is proportional to $1/\epsilon^2$. Therefore, δ has a much smaller influence on the sample size. This also suggests that the overall recall rate of $\overline{S}$ is quite consistent, because of our earlier observation that the expected false negative rate is δ.

Varying α: In this experiment, we fix the confidence parameter δ and parameter ϵ ($\delta = 0.01$ and $\epsilon = 0.05$), and we vary the reliability threshold α from 0.99 to 0.90. Table 3 reports the accuracy indicator β with respect to the different α on each dataset. Interestingly, we note that when α reduces, β first decreases and then increases. This reduction in β is particularly noticeable for the Yeast data set, though it is moderate for all other data sets. The reason for the decreasing-increasing trend seems related to the distribution of highly reliable subgraphs. When α is very high ($\alpha = 0.99$), both $\underline{S}$ and $\overline{S}$ are quite small and also close. As α slightly decreases, $\overline{S}$ (defined by threshold $\alpha+\epsilon$) remains relatively stable, but $\overline{S}$ (with threshold $\alpha-\epsilon$) can grow rather quickly. This results in a decrease in β. However, when α further decreases, the set $\overline{S}$ grows faster than $\underline{S}$. Therefore, the difference between them becomes smaller.

Execution Time: In this experiment, we study the computational time of Steps 1 and 2, and compare the performance of naïve peeling and fast peeling. Specifically, we fix the parameters α, δ and ϵ, and report the peeling time (discovering MFCS in Step 1), the DFS mining time (discovering Non-maximal FCS in Step 1), and the time in Step 2. We denote NpeelDFS to be the algorithm utilizing the naïve peeling (Algorithm 1) and FpeelDFS (Algorithm 2) to the algorithm utilizing the fast peeling. We can see that in most of the cases, the peeling stage requires most of the computational time in NpeelDFS. The FpeelDFS algorithm is faster than the naïve peeling approach by more than one order of magnitude. Furthermore, we observe that the overall computational times of Steps 1 and Step 2 become comparable in the case of the fast peeling approach. Since the processing in Step 2 is rather straightforward (checking whether a given subgraph is a FCS on the larger dataset D_2), we do not consider further optimization of this step here.

5.2 Experimental Results on Synthetic Datasets

Here, we focus on studying the running time of our mining approach on synthetic datasets. Specifically, we utilize the block-random graph model [24], which can generate both the Erdös-Rényi random graph and Scale-free random graph, along with a specified community structure. The edge existence probability is uniformly generated between 0 and 1. We report the overall running time of NpeelDFS and FpeelDFS, and their respective peeling time (Npeel and Fpeel) in Step 1. The default parameters are $\alpha = 0.99$, $\delta = 0.01$, and $\epsilon = 0.05$. Figure 3(a) reports the running time with respect to the graph size as the the number of vertices change from 1000 to 3000 with the average edge density fixed at 1.5. Figure 3(b) reports the running time with respect to the reliability threshold varying from 0.95 to 0.99 on an uncertain graph with 1000 nodes and edge density fixed to 1.5. Figure 3(c) reports the running time with respect to the edge density varying from 1.8 to 3.5 on an uncertain graph with 1000 nodes. Here, we can see that throughout these experiments, the overall running time of the fast peeling based approach FpeelDFS is much faster than that of the naïve peeling approach NpeelDFS. In addition, in most of the cases, it seems the peeling time (discovering MFCS) is also a major component of the overall running time.

6. RELATED WORK

The work closest to ours is the most reliable subgraph problem [16, 17, 25, 18]. Given a set of vertices, this problem tries to remove K edges from the original graph so that the remaining subgraph can maximize the probability of these vertices belonging to one connected component. Thus, the highly reliable subgraph (HRS) problem can be viewed as a generalization of the most reliable subgraph problem, because no initial set of vertices is specified. Furthermore, HRS also puts more constraints on vertex set reliability, because it requires all vertices in each subgraph to be fully connected, whereas the most reliable problem only requires the targeted set of vertices in the subgraph to be connected. Because of these differences, the methods developed for most reliable subgraph mining cannot be generalized to this new problem.

Mining uncertain graphs has recently attracted much attention in the data mining and database research communities [30, 38, 39, 40]. Specifically, Zou *et al.* study mining frequent subgraphs [39] and top k-cliques [40] in a single uncertain graph. Potamias *et al.* study the k-Nearest Neighbor problem in uncertain graphs [30]. Yuan *et al.* study a new variant of the shortest path problem in an uncertain graph [38], and Jin *et al.* study the distance-constraint reachability problem, a generalization of the classic two-terminal reliability problem [22].

The frequent cohesive set (FCS) discovery problem studied in this work is closely related to frequent pattern mining [13]. This broad subfield has been extensively studied since its inception in the early nineties. However, the frequent cohesive set (FCS) problem has not been studied before. Furthermore, we deviate from natural pattern mining approaches which focus on bottom-up strategies (level-wise or pattern-growth). Here, we introduce a novel peeling approach which enables top-down pattern discovery.

7. CONCLUSIONS AND SUMMARY

In this paper, we present a method for mining reliable subgraph patterns in uncertain graphs. Such problems are extremely challenging in the uncertain scenario and tend to be $\#P$-complete. We present a probabilistic method for mining such reliable graphs which retains efficiency and also provides probabilistic bounds for accuracy. A novel peeling approach reduces the computational complexity by carefully pruning of large portions of the massive search space during the pattern discovery and exploration process. We present experimental results illustrating the effectiveness and efficiency of the method.

8. REFERENCES

[1] E. Adar and C. Re. Managing uncertainty in social networks. *IEEE Data Eng. Bull.*, 30(2):15–22, 2007.

[2] C. C. Aggarwal, editor. *Managing and Mining Uncertain Data*. Advances in Database Systems. Springer, 2009.

[3] S. Asthana, O. D. King, F. D. Gibbons, and F. P. Roth. Predicting protein complex membership using probabilistic network reliability. *Genome Res*, 14(6):1170–1175, June 2004.

[4] J. S. Bader, A. Chaudhuri, J. M. Rothberg, and J. Chant. Gaining confidence in high-throughput protein interaction networks. *Nature Biotechnology*, 22(1):78–85, December 2003.

[5] M. O. Ball. Computational complexity of network reliability analysis: An overview. *IEEE Transactions on Reliability*, 35:230–239, 1986.

[6] Y. Benjamini and Y. Hochberg. Controlling the false discovery rate: A practical and powerful approach to multiple testing. *Journal of the Royal Statistical Society. Series B (Methodological)*, 57(1):289–300, 1995.

[7] Y. Benjamini and D. Yekutieli. The Control of the False Discovery Rate in Multiple Testing under Dependency. *The Annals of Statistics*, 29(4):1165–1188, 2001.

[8] C. Chen, X. Yan, F. Zhu, and J. Han. gapprox: Mining frequent approximate patterns from a massive network. In *ICDM*, pages 445–450, 2007.

[9] H. Chernoff. A measure of asymptotic efficiency for tests of a hypothesis based on the sum of observations. *The Annals of Mathematical Statistics*, 23(4):493–507, 1952.

[10] C. J. Colbourn. *The Combinatorics of Network Reliability*. Oxford University Press, Inc., 1987.

[11] J. Ghosh, H. Q. Ngo, S. Yoon, and C. Qiao. On a Routing Problem Within Probabilistic Graphs and its Application to Intermittently Connected Networks. In *INFOCOM'07*, pages 1721–1729, 2007.

[12] R. Guha, R. Kumar, P. Raghavan, and A. Tomkins. Propagation of trust and distrust. In *WWW'04*, pages 403–412, 2004.

[13] J. Han, H. Cheng, D. Xin, and X. Yan. Frequent Pattern Mining: Current Status and Future Directions. *Data Mining and Knowledge Discovery*, 14(1), 2007.

[14] J. Han, M. Kamber, and J. Pei. *Data Mining: Concepts and Techniques, Second Edition (The Morgan Kaufmann Series in Data Management Systems)*. Morgan Kaufmann, 2nd edition, 2006.

[15] S. Hanhijärvi, K. Puolamäki, and G. C. Garriga. Multiple hypothesis testing in pattern discovery, 2009. arXiv:0906.5263v1 [stat.ML].

[16] P. Hintsanen. The most reliable subgraph problem. In *PKDD*, pages 471–478, 2007.

[17] P. Hintsanen and H. Toivonen. Finding reliable subgraphs from large probabilistic graphs. *Data Min. Knowl. Discov.*, 17(1):3–23, 2008.

[18] P. Hintsanen, H. Toivonen, and P. Sevon. Fast discovery of reliable subnetworks. In *ASONAM*, pages 104–111, 2010.

[19] W. Hoeffding. Probability inequalities for sums of bounded random variables. *Journal of the American Statistical Association*, 58(301):13–30, 1963.

[20] J. Hopcroft and R. Tarjan. Algorithm 447: efficient algorithms for graph manipulation. *Commun. ACM*, 16:372–378, June 1973.

[21] R. Jiang, Z. Tu, T. Chen, and F. Sun. Network motif identification in stochastic networks. *PNAS*, 103(25):9404–9409, June 2006.

[22] R. Jin, L. Liu, B. Ding, and H. Wang. Distance-constraint reachability computation in uncertain graphs. In *Proceedings of the VLDB Endowment*, volume 4, 2011.

[23] R. Jin, S. McCallen, and E. Almaas. Trend motif: A graph mining approach for analysis of dynamic complex networks. In *ICDM*, pages 541–546, 2007.

[24] B. Karrer and M. E. J. Newman. Stochastic blockmodels and community structure in networks. *Phys. Rev. E*, 83(1):016107, Jan 2011.

[25] M. Kasari, H. Toivonen, and P. Hintsanen. Fast discovery of reliable *k*-terminal subgraphs. In *PAKDD (2)*, pages 168–177, 2010.

[26] D. Kempe, J. M. Kleinberg, and É. Tardos. Maximizing the spread of influence through a social network. In *KDD*, pages 137–146, 2003.

[27] A. Kirsch, M. Mitzenmacher, A. Pietracaprina, G. Pucci, E. Upfal, and F. Vandin. An efficient rigorous approach for identifying statistically significant frequent itemsets. In *PODS'09*, pages 117–126, 2009.

[28] V. E. Lee, N. Ruan, R. Jin, and C. Aggarwal. A survey of algorithms for dense subgraph discovery. In Charu C. Aggarwal and Haixun Wang, editors, *Managing and Mining Graph Data*, pages 303–336. Springer US, 2010.

[29] V. Manfredi, R. Hancock, and J. Kurose. Robust routing in dynamic manets. In *Annual Conference of the International Technology Alliance (ACITA)*, 2008.

[30] M. Potamias, F. Bonchi, A. Gionis, and G. Kollios. k-nearest neighbors in uncertain graphs. *PVLDB*, 3(1):997–1008, 2010.

[31] G. Rubino. Network reliability evaluation. In *Network performance modeling and simulation*, pages 275–302. 1999.

[32] M. Stoer and F. Wagner. A simple min-cut algorithm. *J. ACM*, 44:585–591, July 1997.

[33] G. Swamynathan, C. Wilson, B. Boe, K. Almeroth, and B. Y. Zhao. Do social networks improve e-commerce?: a study on social marketplaces. In *WOSP '08: Proceedings of the first workshop on Online social networks*, pages 1–6, 2008.

[34] L. G. Valiant. The complexity of enumeration and reliability problems. *SIAM Journal on Computing*, 8(3):410–421, 1979.

[35] D. R. White and F. Harary. The cohesiveness of blocks in social networks: Node connectivity and conditional density. *Sociological Methodology*, 31:305–359, 2001.

[36] X. Yan, X. J. Zhou, and J. Han. Mining closed relational graphs with connectivity constraints. In *KDD '05*, 2005.

[37] D. M. Yellin. An algorithm for dynamic subset and intersection testing. *Theoretical Computer Science*, 129(2):397–406, 1994.

[38] Y. Yuan, L. Chen, and G. Wang. Efficiently answering probability threshold-based shortest path queries over uncertain graphs. In *DASFAA*, pages 155–170, 2010.

[39] Z. Zou, H. Gao, and J. Li. Discovering frequent subgraphs over uncertain graph databases under probabilistic semantics. In *KDD*, pages 633–642, 2010.

[40] Z. Zou, J. Li, H. Gao, and S. Zhang. Finding top-k maximal cliques in an uncertain graph. In *ICDE*, pages 649–652, 2010.

[41] Z. Zou, J. Li, H. Gao, and S. Zhang. Mining frequent subgraph patterns from uncertain graph data. *IEEE Trans. on Knowl. and Data Eng.*, 22(9), 2010.

Discovering Shakers from Evolving Entities via Cascading Graph Inference

Xiaoxiao Shi[†], Wei Fan[‡], Jianping Zhang[*], and Philip S. Yu[†]
[†]Department of Computer Science, University of Illinois at Chicago
[‡]IBM T.J.Watson Research Center
[*]Analytic & Forensic Technology , Deloitte Financial Advisory Services LLP
{xiaoxiao,psyu}@cs.uic.edu, weifan@us.ibm.com, jianpzhang@deloitte.com

ABSTRACT

In an interconnected and dynamic world, the evolution of one entity may cause a series of significant value changes for some others. For example, the currency inflation of Thailand caused the currency slump of other Asian countries, which eventually led to the financial crisis of 1997. We call such high impact entities *shakers*. To discover shakers, we first introduce the concept of a *cascading graph* to capture the causality relationships among evolving entities over some period of time, and then infer shakers from the graph. In a cascading graph, nodes represent entities and weighted links represent the causality effects. In order to find hidden shakers in such a graph, two scoring functions are proposed, each of which estimates how much the target entity can affect the values of some others. The idea is to artificially inject a significant change on the target entity, and estimate its direct and indirect influence on the others, by following an inference rule under the Markovian assumption. Both scoring functions are proven to be only dependent on the structure of a cascading graph and can be calculated in polynomial time. Experiments included three datasets in social sciences. Without directly applicable previous methods, we modified three graphical models as baselines. The two proposed scoring functions can effectively capture those high impact entities. For example, in the experiment to discover stock market shakers, the proposed models outperform the three baselines by as much as 50% in accuracy with the ground truth obtained from Yahoo! Finance.

Categories and Subject Descriptors

H.2.8 [**Database Management**]: Database applications-Data mining

*This research was conducted at MITRE Corporation prior to the author's joining Deloitte Financial Advisory Services LLP.

KDD'11, August 21–24, 2011, San Diego, California, USA.

General Terms

Algorithms

Keywords

Cascading Graph, Shakers, Dynamic Entity

1. INTRODUCTION

In an interconnected and dynamic world, the evolution of one entity may cause a series of significant value changes for some others. Examples include the volatile and intercorrelated financial markets, or the climate changes of neighboring areas. This is typically called the domino or butterfly effect. A famous case is the currency inflation of Thailand, which caused the financial crisis of 1997. We call such high impact entities *shakers* and our objective is to find the shakers in a set of evolving entities. It is important to mention that shakers are different from the influential nodes studied in [12, 33] and the effectors in [15]. One of the key differences is that the former two studies investigate entities with only one of two possible states (active and inactive), while shakers allow entities with numerical attributes and continuous changes (*e.g.*, stock prices), which is more general and more complicated. In addition, shaker formulation allows for different types of effects (*e.g.*, positive effect and negative effect introduced in Section 2). With the general problem setting, the following two challenges need to be addressed:

- C1: Given the set of evolving entities with continuously changing numerical attributes, how to determine who affects whom?
- C2: After determining the causalities among the entities (by solving C1), how to detect hidden shakers?

To solve C1, we use evolving data (*e.g.*, time series, streaming, sensory) to model the entity evolutions and detect the latent entity causalities by measuring and capturing the similarity of the evolution trends. The intuition is that if an entity A affects entity B, then: (1) the changes in A occurs prior to the changes in B, and (2) they will have similar trends.

For example, Fig. 1(a) plots the price evolutions of two stocks over time. One is Amazon.com and the other is its business partner, a cargo transportation company. It is clear that the evolutions of the two stocks are almost the same but the change in Amazon.com takes the lead. Hence, we say that Amazon.com affects its business partner in the stock market. This is the major assumption of our research to find causalities via these temporal correlations. Note that

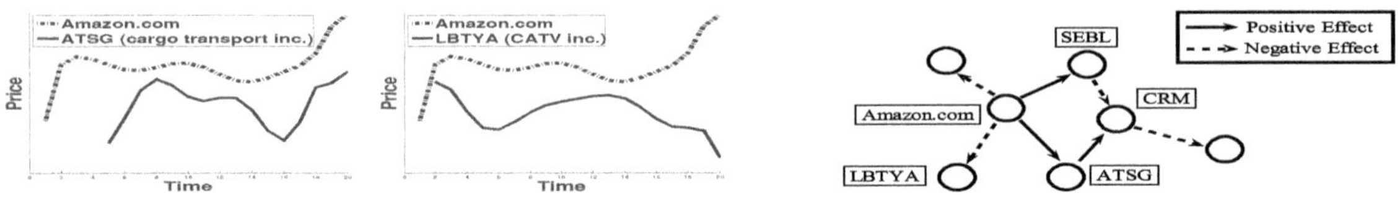

(a) Positive effect (b) Negative effect (c) Fraction of the cascading graph with positive and negative edges (effects)

Figure 1: Example of the cascading graph on stock data learned from the algorithm

although the two concepts are not exactly the same, yet the existence of some correlations can lead us to induce, under some fairly broad conditions, the existence of certain causal relations. This assumption is broadly used in other fields such as Philosophy [29], Bioinformatics [32] and Economics (*e.g.*, the 2003 Nobel Prize winning work in economic time series analysis [9]). By detecting such causalities between each entity pair, we construct a cascading graph as follows:

DEFINITION 1 (CASCADING GRAPH). *A cascading graph is a weighted directed graph $\mathcal{G} = (\mathcal{V}, \mathbf{E}, \mathcal{A})$ where*

- *$\mathcal{V}$ represents the set of entities. $\forall v \in \mathcal{V}$, $a_v(\tau) \in \mathcal{A}$ is its attribute that evolves over time τ. For simplicity, $\mathcal{A} \subseteq \mathbb{R}$ is a set of real numbers.*
- *$\mathbf{E} \in \mathbb{R}^{|\mathcal{V}|\times|\mathcal{V}|}$ is called the* cascading matrix *such that $\mathbf{E}(i, j) = e$ is the causality effect from entity v_i to entity v_j. And $|e|$ determines the strength or confidence of the causality. Furthermore, $e < 0$ if it is a* negative effect *such that the value increase of one entity causes the value decrease of another as in Fig. 1(b); $e > 0$ if it is a* positive effect *as in Fig. 1(a).*

An example of a cascading graph on stock data is illustrated in Fig. 1(c) where solid lines represent edges with positive effects ($e > 0$, or as in Fig. 1(a)) and dotted lines represent negative effects ($e < 0$, or as in Fig. 1(b)). It is important to note that the introduction of negative effect provides an advantage not found in other graphical models (*e.g.*, [10, 4]). It extends the expressive power to model a wide range of networks that naturally contain opposite correlations among the nodes. Examples include the cooperation and competition networks of the business institutions, stock correlation networks, *etc.* However, with previously proposed methods, it is not obvious how to discover 1 in such a graph:

1. Graphical Models: In a cascading graph, since it allows for negative effects (edges), the adjacency matrix, or the cascading matrix $\mathbf{E}$ is not stochastic. Hence, as far as we know, there is no graphical model (*e.g.*, [10, 4, 14]) that can be directly applied to mine the latent shakers.
2. Influence Propagation Models: Most of the previous methods (*e.g.*, [1, 33, 12] and the IC model [13]) investigate the graph with positive edges. However, given the cascading graph with negative edges, the influence propagation becomes more complicated, because some of them may be reduced or canceled. As in Fig. 1(c), "Amazon.com" has two inference propagation paths to "CRM". One is "Amazon $\rightarrow$ ATSG$\rightarrow$CRM" that can increase the value of CRM, but the other is the negative effect "Amazon $\rightarrow$SEBL $\rightarrow$CRM" that decreases its value. Hence, with the negative effect canceling the positive effect, "Amazon.com" may finally cause no value change (no influence) on "CRM". Traditional influence propagation models do not consider such situations.

Since previous models are not directly applicable, in this paper, two scoring functions are proposed to find the shakers by evaluating each node's accumulated influence and maximal influence. The key idea is to artificially inject a significant value change in the target node, and estimate its direct and indirect influence on other nodes by following a graph inference rule under the Markovian assumption. Using linear algebra to perform a transformation, the two scoring functions are proven to be (a) only dependent on the structure of the cascading graph, and (b) they can be calculated in polynomial time.

We conducted three sets of experiments. These experiments focused on the following problems in social sciences: finding the economy shakers of countries, finding the most influential economy indicators, and finding the NASDAQ stock market shakers. Without directly applicable methods, three previous graphical models are modified as baselines. It is observed that the two proposed scoring functions can effectively capture the shakers. For example, in the experiment of finding stock market shakers, the proposed models outperform the three baselines by as much as 50% in accuracy, with the ground truth coming from Yahoo! Finance. Moreover, one of the shakers, AAPL (Apple Inc.), is successfully captured; it later leads to a big drop of the NASDAQ stocks in January 2011 despite the good news of most other stocks.

2. PROBLEM FORMULATION

Given a set of evolving entities, the objective is to find shakers whose value changes can significantly affect the values of many other entities. The following provides a more formal definition of the related concepts.

DEFINITION 2 (EVOLVING ENTITY). *Denote $v \in \mathcal{V}$ as an entity, $a_v(\tau) \in \mathcal{A} \subseteq \mathbb{R}$ as the attribute of v that evolves over the time variable τ. In this paper, the time variable is considered to be discrete, and we use $a_v(t)$ to denote the attribute value of entity v at time step t.*

The evolving attributes are used to detect causality relationships among the entities. The general idea is that $\forall v, w \in \mathcal{V}$, if the trend of $a_v(\tau)$ is similar to that of $a_w(\tau)$ and one is prior to the other as in Fig. 1(a), then v and w have a causality relationship. More details can be found in Section 3. Note that once the causality relationships are determined, the present values of the entities (*i.e.*, $a_v(\tau), a_w(\tau)$, *etc.*) are no longer important. Instead, to find the shakers, we are more interested in their value changes and the entities causing those changes. As such, we use a $1 \times |\mathcal{V}|$ vector $\mathbf{C}_t$ to denote the value changes of the entities at time t such that

$$\mathbf{C}_t(i) = a_{v_i}(t) - a_{v_i}(t-1)$$

is the value change of node v_i at time t. Then, shaker is defined as follows

DEFINITION 3 (SHAKER). *Given an entity $v \in \mathcal{V}$, assume its value significantly changes, say, at the beginning where $t = 0$. By following the influence propagation path, if the values of other entities significantly change afterwards where $t = 1, 2, \cdots$, we call the entity v a* shaker.

This is a general definition of shaker and the key intuition here is to estimate whether the target entity v can cause significant changes of many others afterwards ($t > 0$).

Cascading Graph

The key step to find shakers is to capture and summarize the complicated causality relationships among the entities, and unveil the shakers by inferring how the causality effect is propagated. To do so, we propose to use cascading graph $G = (\mathcal{V}, \mathbf{E}, \mathcal{A})$. A cascading graph is a graph, in which nodes in $\mathcal{V}$ are entities and weighted directed edges in $\mathbf{E}$ represent causalities. In Section 3, we show how to extract a cascading matrix $\mathbf{E}$ from evolving entities. An example of a cascading graph is shown in Fig. 2, where v_1, v_2 and v_3 have some effects on the entity v_4. The main advantage of cascading graph, not found in traditional graph models, is its flexibility to model negative effects. These are formulated as negative edges, *e.g.*, edge (v_1, v_4) in Fig. 2. One challenge is that negative effects may cancel the influence of positive effects in later influence propagation. Thus, the temporal correlation detected at the initial state may disappear in later inferences. More details can be found in Eq. 1. Hence, in addition to shaker discovery, cascading graphs can be used in a wide range of applications where entities have opposite relationships. Traditional stochastic graphical models, however, are not able to model such complicated relationships because the adjacency matrix is non-stochastic. We next define an inference rule for cascading graphs.

Inference on Cascading Graph. Similar to first order Markov process, we make the Markovian assumption that the attribute value changes $\mathbf{C}_t$ at time t only depend on those at time $t-1$:

$$\mathbf{C}_t(i) = \sum_{j=1}^{|\mathcal{V}|} \mathbf{C}_{t-1}(j)\mathbf{E}(j,i) \tag{1}$$

where $\mathbf{E}(j,i)$ is the causality effect from entity v_j to entity v_i such that $\sum_{j=1}^{|\mathcal{V}|} |\mathbf{E}(j,i)| = 1$. Hence, $\mathbf{E}(j,i)$ can also be interpreted as the weight of the "ingredient" of the mixture effects to v_i. For instance, in Fig. 2, 50% of the effects to v_4 are from v_1, 20% are from the entity v_2 and the rest are from the entity v_3 such that:

$$\mathbf{C}_t(4) = -0.5\mathbf{C}_{t-1}(1) + 0.2\mathbf{C}_{t-1}(2) + 0.3\mathbf{C}_{t-1}(3)$$

Note that $\mathbf{E}(1,4) = -0.5 < 0$ is a negative effect. Hence, when the node v_1's value increases at time $t-1$, v_4's value tends to decrease at time t, since $\mathbf{C}_t(4) \propto -0.5\mathbf{C}_{t-1}(1)$. As such, negative effect (edge) tends to lead the value to change in an opposite direction, while positive effect makes the value moving in the same direction. In matrix form, the

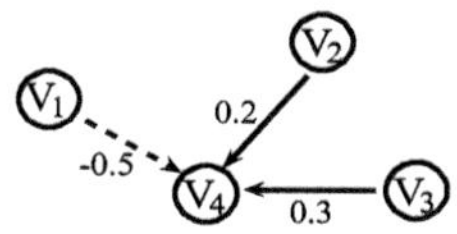

Figure 2: Inference on cascading graph

inference rule in Eq. 1 can be written as:

$$\mathbf{C}_t = \mathbf{C}_{t-1}\mathbf{E} = \mathbf{C}_{t-2}\mathbf{E}^2 = \cdots = \mathbf{C}_0\mathbf{E}^t \tag{2}$$

It is interesting to mention that the cascading matrix $\mathbf{E}$ is similar to a transition probability matrix in Markov process, and $\mathbf{C}_t$ is similar to a state vector at time t. However, unlike a transition probability matrix, the cascading matrix $\mathbf{E}$ allows for negative values and hence it is not stochastic. In Section 4, we provide an analysis on how traditional graphical models do not perform well in this case.

Model Formulation for Shaker Discovery

To evaluate the influence of the target node v_i, we artificially change its value at time $t = 0$, and then infer its effect on other entities during $0 < t < T$, where T is the time span we are interested in. In other words, we do not care about the changes after time T, which is a user-specified parameter studied in the experiment section. To find shakers, the following steps are performed:

1. Artificially change the value: Define a new vector $\mathbf{C}_0^{(v_i)}$ such that $\forall j \neq i, \mathbf{C}_0^{(v_i)}(j) = \mathbf{C}_0(j)$, but $|\mathbf{C}_0^{(v_i)}(i)| \gg |\mathbf{C}_0(i)|$. In other words, $\mathbf{C}_0^{(v_i)}$ is different from $\mathbf{C}_0$ only in the target node v_i.

2. Influence inference: Define vector $\mathbf{C}_t^{(v_i)}$ as the estimated value changes at time t with $\mathbf{C}_0^{(v_i)}$ as the initial state, or $\mathbf{C}_t^{(v_i)} = \mathbf{C}_0^{(v_i)}\mathbf{E}^t$ with the influence rule in Eq. 2.

Note that the vector $\mathbf{C}_t^{(v_i)}$ is derived after the value of the target entity v_i suffers a big jump ($|\mathbf{C}_0^{(v_i)}(i)| \gg |\mathbf{C}_0(i)|$). Hence, we want to study the difference between the two vectors $\mathbf{C}_t^{(v_i)}$ and $\mathbf{C}_t$ to investigate how the jumping value affects others. Two scoring functions are defined.

DEFINITION 4 (ACCUMULATED INFLUENCE). *Given an entity v_i, the accumulated influence $\mathbf{AI}(v_i)$ is defined as the accumulated relative difference between the two vectors*

$$\mathbf{AI}(v_i) = \sum_{t=1}^{T} \frac{\partial \mathbf{C}_t^{(v_i)}}{\partial \mathbf{C}_0^{(v_i)}} \tag{3}$$

where $\partial \mathbf{C}_t^{(v_i)} = \|\mathbf{C}_t^{(v_i)} - \mathbf{C}_t\|$ and $\| * \|$ is the L-2 norm that summarizes the difference.

It is interesting to note that $\partial \mathbf{C}_t^{(v_i)} / \partial \mathbf{C}_0^{(v_i)}$ has a similar form as function derivative $\frac{\partial f(x)}{\partial x}$ that evaluates how fast a function changes at a certain direction. We use it to capture how effectively the influence can be propagated through node v_i. However, it is not easy to obtain $\partial \mathbf{C}_t^{(v_i)} / \partial \mathbf{C}_0^{(v_i)}$. It is not known how to determine $\mathbf{C}_0^{(v_i)}$, since we only know $|\mathbf{C}_0^{(v_i)}(i)| \gg |\mathbf{C}_0(i)|$ without any specific value. In the next section, we prove that $\mathbf{AI}(v_i)$ is actually independent of $\mathbf{C}_t$, $\mathbf{C}_t^{(v_i)}$ and $\mathbf{C}_0^{(v_i)}$, and it can be efficiently calculated only with a cascading matrix $\mathbf{E}$, or the topology of the cascading graph. Similarly, we define maximal influence as follows:

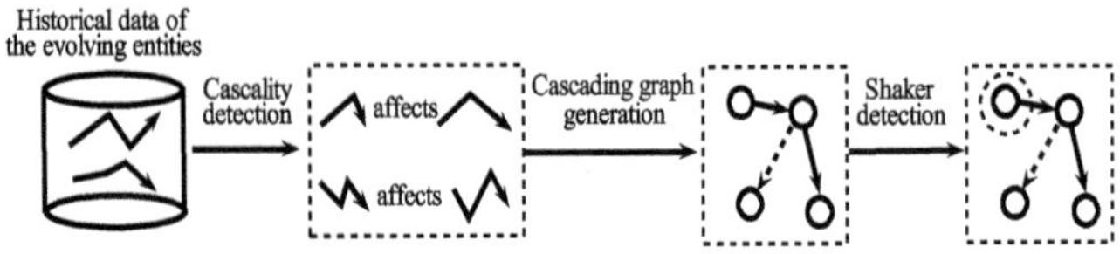

Figure 3: Algorithm flow

DEFINITION 5 (MAXIMAL INFLUENCE). *Given an entity v_i, we define the maximal influence as*

$$\mathbf{MI}(v_i) = \max_{t=1,2,\ldots,T} \frac{\partial \mathbf{C}_t^{(v_i)}}{\partial \mathbf{C}_0^{(v_i)}} \tag{4}$$

Unlike accumulated influence, maximal influence only considers the moment when the target entity exerts the most influence on others despite the effect potentially disappearing later. In the next section, we introduce how to construct the cascading graph and how to calculate the two scoring functions in polynomial time.

3. PROPOSED ALGORITHM

The algorithm flow is sketched in Fig. 3, which contains two main parts. The first is to examine the entity causalities and generate the cascading graph by evaluating the similarities of their evolution trends. The second is to infer shakers in the static cascading graph.

Cascading graph construction

To construct a cascading graph, or equivalently, to fill out all the entries of the cascading matrix $\mathbf{E}$, we need to determine the causality $\mathbf{E}(i,j)$ between each entity pair $\forall v_i, v_j \in \mathcal{V}$. If they have similar evolution trends and one follows another, we say that they have strong causality relationship. To do so, we first fit each evolution trend of $\forall v_i \in \mathcal{V}$ by a function $f_i(t)$. Then we utilize basic function transformations (such as scaling, shifting, *etc.*) to match the two functions and find their similarity. In particular, the following optimization problem is devised

$$\min_{\hat{h},\hat{u},\hat{t},\hat{s}} \epsilon(i,j) = \sum_{t=0}^{L} \left(f_i(t) - (\hat{h} f_j(\hat{u}t + \hat{t}) + \hat{s})\right)^2 \tag{5}$$

where L is the time span determined by the data itself, $\hat{t}$ is the shifting along the time variable whereas $\hat{s}$ is the shifting along the output, $\hat{h}$ is the constant to change the scale of the output and $\hat{u}$ is the constant to allow dynamic time warping [25]. The optimization function thus matches the two evolution functions with the above four types of algebra transformations. If the two entities have very similar evolving trends, they will be almost perfectly matched by Eq. 5. In this case, $\epsilon(i,j)$ will be small and we say that they have strong causality relationship; otherwise we say they have weak causality relationship. Hence, we define the strength of a causality as $e^{-\frac{\epsilon(i,j)}{\sigma}}$, which is similar to the similarity function in normalized cut [28]. Furthermore, the solved values of $\hat{h}$ and $\hat{t}$ encode the properties of the causality

- if $\hat{h} > 0$, it is a positive effect as in Fig. 1(a); if $\hat{h} < 0$, it means the value increase of one entity causes the value decrease of another; we call it a negative effect.
- if $\hat{t} > 0$, it means $f_i(t)$ leads the trend, or v_i affects v_j.

We define

$$\mathbf{E}(i,j) = \frac{\hat{h}}{|\hat{h}|} e^{-\frac{\epsilon(i,j)}{\sigma}}, \ \mathbf{E}(j,i) = 0 \tag{6}$$

If $\hat{t} < 0$, it means v_j affects v_i

$$\mathbf{E}(i,j) = 0, \ \mathbf{E}(j,i) = \frac{\hat{h}}{|\hat{h}|} e^{-\frac{\epsilon(j,i)}{\sigma}} \tag{7}$$

If $\hat{t} = 0$, neither v_i nor v_j takes the lead. Hence $\mathbf{E}(i,j) = \mathbf{E}(j,i) = 0$.

In the above formula, the constant σ is a normalization term to ensure $\sum_{i=1}^{|\mathcal{V}|} |\mathbf{E}(i,j)| = 1$, and the sign of $\mathbf{E}$ is determined by $\hat{h}$. As such, the cascading matrix $\mathbf{E}$ is determined and we assume that it is static and that it does not change over the duration of the study. To solve Eq. 5, we assume that the evolution of each entity v_i is determined by an n-degree polynomial function such that $f_i(t) = \sum_{r=0}^{n} k_r t^r$ where k_rs are the polynomial coefficients. Choosing a polynomial function has several advantages: (1) It can fit both linear and nonlinear (*e.g.*, [30, 18]) evolution functions perfectly. (2) It can effectively capture the turns of the evolving trends, which is an important clue in determining causality. Hence, we denote the evolution functions of v_i and v_j as $f_i(t) = \sum_{r=0}^{n} k_r t^r$ and $f_j(t) = \sum_{r=0}^{n} \hat{k}_r t^r$ where n is the degree discussed in Section 4. We then substitute them into Eq. 5 and use coordinate descent to solve the optimization problem. The general idea is to solve one variable at a time by fixing the values of the others. To be specific, we first solve $\hat{h}$ by setting $\frac{\partial \epsilon(v,w)}{\partial \hat{h}} = 0$ with $\hat{u}$, $\hat{t}$ and $\hat{s}$ set as the initial values.

$$\hat{h} = \sum_{t=0}^{L}(\sum_{r=0}^{n} k_r t^r - \hat{s}) / \sum_{t=0}^{L}\sum_{r=0}^{n} \hat{k}_r(\hat{u}t + \hat{t})^r \tag{8}$$

We solve $\hat{t}$, $\hat{u}$ and $\hat{s}$ similarly, and then solve $\hat{h}$ again with the new values of $\hat{t}$, $\hat{u}$ and $\hat{s}$. The process is performed iteratively C times to approach the optimal solution; the convergence rate is discussed in Section 4. We then use the optimal solution $\epsilon(i,j)$ of each entity pair v_i and v_j to determine each entry of the cascading matrix $\mathbf{E}$.

Shaker detection by computing accumulated influence and maximal influence

Recall that we define the accumulated influence (Eq. 3) and maximal influence (Eq. 4) to capture the shakers. However, both scoring functions involve some undetermined variables such as $\mathbf{C}_t^{(v_i)}$. As a result, the two functions seem to be not computable with the unknown variables. We next prove that both scoring functions actually only depend on the cascading matrix $\mathbf{E}$ or the topology of the graph.

THEOREM 1. *The value of the accumulated influence $\mathbf{AI}(v_i)$ only depends on the cascading matrix $\mathbf{E}$.*

PROOF. We can rewrite the accumulated influence as

$$\begin{aligned}\mathbf{AI}(v_i) &= \sum_{t=1}^{T} \frac{\partial \mathbf{C}_t^{(v_i)}}{\partial \mathbf{C}_0^{(v_i)}} = \sum_{t=1}^{T} \frac{\|\mathbf{C}_t^{(v_i)} - \mathbf{C}_t\|}{\|\mathbf{C}_0^{(v_i)} - \mathbf{C}_0\|} \\ &= \sum_{t=1}^{T} \frac{tr\left((\mathbf{E}^t)^T \cdot (\mathbf{C}_0^{(v_i)} - \mathbf{C}_0)^T (\mathbf{C}_0^{(v_i)} - \mathbf{C}_0) \cdot \mathbf{E}^t\right)}{tr\left((\mathbf{C}_0^{(v_i)} - \mathbf{C}_0)^T (\mathbf{C}_0^{(v_i)} - \mathbf{C}_0)\right)}\end{aligned} \tag{9}$$

Input: $\mathcal{V}$:the set of evolving entities; n (default 9) : the degree of the polynomial functions used to fit the data; C (default 3) : the number of iterations in the optimization; T (default 6) : parameter to control the time span;

Output: R_A=Ranking according to $\mathbf{AI}(v)$ and R_M=Ranking according to $\mathbf{MI}(v)$ for $\forall v \in \mathcal{V}$

/* Construct the cascading graph */

1 **for** $\forall v_i \in \mathcal{V}$ **do**

2   **for** $\forall v_j \in \mathcal{V}$ **do**

3   Solve $\min_{\hat{h},\hat{u},\hat{t}} \epsilon(i,j)$ in Eq. 5 with n and C;

4   Determine $\mathbf{E}(i,j)$ and $\mathbf{E}(j,i)$ as Eq. 6 and 7.

5   **end**

6 **end**

/* Shaker detection */

7 Calculate $\mathbf{E}^t$ for $t = 1, \cdots, T$

8 **for** $\forall v_i \in \mathcal{V}$ **do**

9   $\mathbf{AI}(v_i) = \sum_{t=1}^{T} \sum_{j=1}^{|\mathcal{V}|} \mathbf{E}^t(i,j)^2$

10   $\mathbf{MI}(v_i) = \max\{\sum_{j=1}^{|\mathcal{V}|} \mathbf{E}^t(i,j)^2\}$

11 **end**

12 $R_A \leftarrow$Rank $v \in \mathcal{V}$ according to $\mathbf{AI}(v)$ (descending)

13 $R_M \leftarrow$Rank $v \in \mathcal{V}$ according to $\mathbf{MI}(v)$ (descending)

Algorithm 1: Shaker Detection via Cascading Graph

Denote $\Delta\mathbf{C} = \mathbf{C}_0^{(v_i)} - \mathbf{C}_0$, and it is important to note that $\Delta\mathbf{C}(i) \neq 0$ and $\forall j \neq i, \Delta\mathbf{C}(j) = 0$ since only the target entity v_i is changed in $\mathbf{C}_0^{(v_i)}$. As such, $(\Delta\mathbf{C})^T\Delta\mathbf{C}$ is a $|\mathcal{V}| \times |\mathcal{V}|$ matrix with only the (i,i)-th entry being non-zero. We denote the value as q. Hence, it is not difficult to get that

$$tr\Big((\mathbf{E}^t)^T \cdot (\mathbf{C}_0^{(v_i)} - \mathbf{C}_0)^T(\mathbf{C}_0^{(v_i)} - \mathbf{C}_0) \cdot \mathbf{E}^t)\Big) = \sum_{j=1}^{|\mathcal{V}|} q\mathbf{E}^t(i,j)^2 \tag{10}$$

And therefore

$$\mathbf{AI}(v_i) = \sum_{t=1}^{T} \frac{\sum_{j=1}^{|\mathcal{V}|} q\mathbf{E}^t(i,j)^2}{q} = \sum_{t=1}^{T}\sum_{j=1}^{|\mathcal{V}|} \mathbf{E}^t(i,j)^2 \tag{11}$$

Hence, $\mathbf{AI}(v_i)$ only depends on the cascading matrix $\mathbf{E}$. □

Similarly, we have the following theorem.

THEOREM 2. *The maximal influence* $\mathbf{MI}(v_i)$ *only depends on the cascading matrix* $\mathbf{E}$ *where*

$$\mathbf{MI}(v_i) = \max_{t=1,\cdots,T}\{\sum_{j=1}^{|\mathcal{V}|} \mathbf{E}^t(i,j)^2\} \tag{12}$$

It is necessary to mention again that both Theorem 1 and Theorem 2 are very important, since they provide methods to calculate the two scoring functions that are superficially not computable. Furthermore, it is not difficult to see that the computations of the two scoring functions are now linear to the cardinality of the entity set $|\mathcal{V}|$ with T as a relatively small number (discussed in Section 4).

Algorithm complexity analysis

The complete algorithm is presented in Algorithm 1, which contains two main parts: cascading graph generation and shaker detection. The algorithm complexity from Step 1 to Step 6 is $O(C \cdot n \cdot L \cdot |\mathcal{V}|^2)$ where n is the degree of the polynomial function, L is the time span of the data, and C is the number of iterations of the coordinate descent in Step 3. With n and C being relatively small numbers (discussed in Section 4), the complexity is $O(L|\mathcal{V}|^2)$. The most expensive step of the second part is to calculate the matrix power (Step 7), whose complexity is $O(T|\mathcal{V}|^{2.4})$ with divide and conquer strategy. As a result, the complexity of the whole algorithm is $O(|\mathcal{V}|^{2.4})$ and the space complexity is $O(|\mathcal{V}|^2)$, given that T is a small constant as discussed in Section 4.4.

4. EXPERIMENTS

Recall that the proposed model contains two main parts: one is to generate the cascading graph from the evolving entities; the second is to find the shakers in the graph. We consider the steps together and focus on the evaluation of the shakers discovered at the end. Also note that the output (Algorithm 1) is the ranking of the entities according to their estimated influence scores; the entities rank at the top are the shakers. Hence, we evaluate the methods with both classification and ranking related criteria. Three methods are chosen for comparison. It is important to note that since these comparison methods are not designed to handle negative edges and mine shakers, some modifications (as outlined below) are necessary:

1. The first method to compare is the weighted PageRank [4], a state-of-the-art algorithm to rank influential websites. It is used in [34] to find influential nodes in a network, and we adopt the same mechanism to find the shakers. Note that PageRank does not work on the network with negative edges. Hence, we treat all negative and positive edges the same by setting the edge weights as their absolute values, in order to run PageRank on the dataset without getting errors.

2. The second comparison method is based on the Independent Cascade (IC) model [15, 11] that is widely used as an information propagation framework on network. We use the weighted IC model in [33] as a comparison model to find the top-k nodes that maximize the influence. Similar to PageRank, we modify the cascading graph by setting the edge weights as their absolute values in order to make the model work.

3. The last comparison method is the Linear Threshold (LT) model used in [11, 13]. It is also a popular network influence propagation model, and we use the influential node selection algorithm in [11] as the third comparison model. As the previous two, in order to make the model work on the dataset, we set the edge weights as their absolute values.

It is important to emphasize again that it is a necessary step to treat all positive and negative edges the same by setting edge weights as their absolute values. This strategy is considered to induce the least information loss in order to make the comparison models work, without getting a software error.

Three datasets (Table 1) from social sciences are used to evaluate the algorithms. The economic dataset contains the historical data of 967 economic indicators of the United States covering a 30 year period. The GDP dataset is the

Table 1: Summary of experimental datasets and the number of edges of their cascading graphs.

	# Entities	Time Span	# Edges	Meaning of the Entities	Meaning of the Shakers
Economic dataset	967	30	80,195	Economic indicators	Key economic indicators
GDP dataset	150	50	5,823	Countries with GDP	High impact countries in economy
Stock dataset	2730	260 (52 weeks)	2,793,323	Stocks	Stock leaders

historical GDP data for 150 countries, and the Stock dataset contains the historical daily prices of 2730 stocks. We treat the economic indicators, countries and the stocks as entities respectively; their historical data are used as the evolving attributes, as described in Table 1 . The physical meanings of the shakers in the three datasets are also shown in Table 1. Note that we adopt a pruning step to set $\mathbf{E}(i, j) = 0$ if its value is less than 10^{-4} to reduce noise.

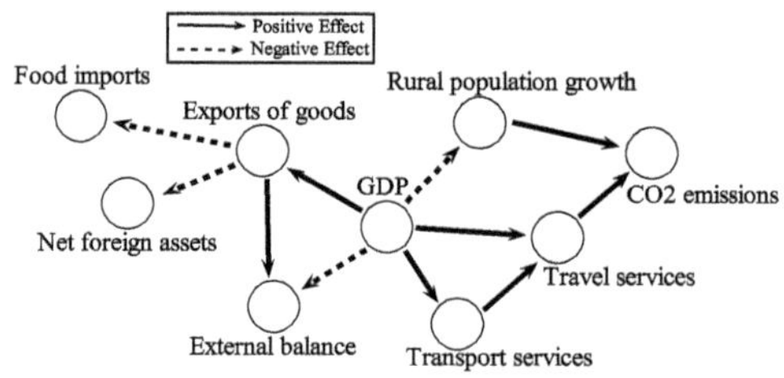

Figure 4: A fraction of the cascading graph of economic indicators

4.1 Finding the most important economic indicators

The first experiment is to find the shakers in 967 economic indicators (*e.g.*, consumer expenditure, interest rate, *etc.*). The data was downloaded from the World Bank [2]. Each of the economic indicators is regarded as an entity and the objective is to find the shakers who contribute the most to the value changes of other indicators. Recall that we use the evolution trend similarity between each entity pair to detect the causalities, which are then summarized into the cascading graph. A fraction of the generated cascading graph is shown in Fig. 4. As it can be observed, it is a complicated network. For example, the increase of GDP has a positive effect on the number of travel services, but negative effect on the rural population growth rate. Moreover, both the rural population and travel services will then increase the CO_2 emissions. Hence, it is not obvious to derive whether GDP has a positive, negative or even no effect (effect cancellation) on CO_2 emissions. With such a complicated network, we aim at finding the shakers who will contribute the most to the value changes of other entities. The top-5 shakers found by the proposed models as well as the three comparison methods are presented in Table 2. As pointed out in [31, 19], some of the widely accepted important economic indicators are the GDP, Gross National Income (GNI), Purchasing Power Parity (PPP), the GDP derived from PPP, and the GNI derived from PPP. Note that all of these indicators are discovered by the two proposed scoring functions. But in the comparison methods, only the Independent Cascade (IC) model discovers one such indicator (GNI), while missing the rest. The most important reason for the poor performances is that the comparison models are not designed to handle a cascading graph that has a more general but more complicated influence propagation schema. Hence, the two scoring functions offer more advantages to find the shakers.

4.2 Finding country-level economy shakers

We downloaded the gross domestic product (GDP) historical data for 150 countries covering a 50 year period (1960-2009) from the World Bank [2]. Each country is modeled as an entity. The objective is to find the top-10 economy shakers according to the development of their GDPs. We use the economy ranking of countries in 2010 as the ground truth [24]. Note that we only consider the countries with complete GDP data for all 50 years in the World Bank and hence some important countries such as Russia, Germany, *etc.*, do not appear in the data and ground truth. The top-10 countries from the ground truth are the United States, China, Japan, France, United Kingdom, Italy, Brazil, Canada, India and Spain. If the found shaker belongs to the top-10 countries regardless of its rank, then we consider it as a correct prediction; otherwise, it is a false prediction.

The results are presented in Table 3, with the accuracy summarized in the last row. It can be observed that the two proposed scoring functions effectively capture the high impact countries in economy, while the comparison models have poor performances. For example, in the economics textbook [31], it is not surprising that United States, United Kingdom and Japan have had strong impacts on the world during the past 50 years. It is also reasonable that countries like Brazil and China are becoming more and more important in recent years [3]. All of these countries were found by the two scoring functions just by tracing the GDP value changes but without any other information. On the contrary, the comparison model LT misses "United States" and IC misses "United Kingdom". Note that between the two proposed scoring functions, the accumulated influence criterion performs a little better (90% accuracy) on this dataset. But it is important to mention again that the two scoring functions have their own statistical meanings and one should choose from them based on different needs of interpretations. For instance, if one only cares about the entities' maximal impact regardless of the impact disappearing later, then the maximal influence criterion should be chosen.

4.3 Stock market shaker detection

We downloaded the historical daily price data for 2730 stocks from Yahoo! Finance [6]. All the 2730 stocks are from NASDAQ in a single year period (from 11/30/2009 to 11/30/2010) and we aimed at finding the stock market shakers who affect the market the most. It is important to mention that we also generated the ground truth from Yahoo! Finance. More specifically, we can find the stock industry leadership rankings [7] with various criteria such as market capitalization, PEG ratio, *etc.* For example, Google Inc. (GOOG) ranks first among the 85 stocks of the same industry according to its market capitalization, and ranks 15th according to its PEG ratio. We then re-rank the stocks according to their average rankings across all criteria in ascending order. For example, the average ranking score of

Table 2: Top 5 Shakers of Economic Indicators

PageRank	IC	LT	Accumulated	Maximal
Net current transfers	GNI	Arable land	GNI	GNI
Merchandise imports	Workers' remittances	Agricultural machinery	GDP	GDP
Current account balance	Export volume index	Net income from abroad	GDP, PPP	GNI, PPP
Export volume index	Changes in inventories	Net bilateral aid flows	GNI, PPP	GDP, PPP
Net trade in goods and services	Net current transfers	Changes in inventories	PPP	PPP

Table 3: Top 10 Economy Shakers (only consider the countries with complete GDP data in World Bank)

PageRank	IC	LT	Accumulated Influence	Maximal Influence
Zimbabwe	Japan ✓	Austria	United States ✓	United States ✓
United States ✓	United States ✓	Andorra	Japan ✓	United Kingdom ✓
United Kingdom ✓	Zimbabwe	Israel	United Kingdom ✓	Japan✓
Belgium	Andorra	Serbia	France ✓	France✓
Switzerland	Namibia	Timor-Leste	China ✓	Brazil ✓
Japan ✓	Vietnam	Guinea-Bissau	Brazil ✓	Italy ✓
France✓	Italy ✓	Malta	Italy ✓	Spain ✓
Sweden	Angola	Hungary	Spain ✓	Sweden
Brazil ✓	Lithuania	Australia	Mexico	China ✓
Italy ✓	Fiji	Chile	Canada ✓	Mexico
Accuracy: 60%	Accuracy: 30%	Accuracy: 0%	**Accuracy: 90%**	Accuracy: 80%

GOOG is $(1+15)/2 = 8$ if we only consider the two criteria, and it ranks first if the average scores of other stocks are larger than 8. As such, the top 20% of stocks in each industry are considered to be the true market shakers. We then conduct three sets of experiments in this dataset to evaluate the models

1. Finding stock market shakers in each of the 7 sectors classified in Yahoo! Finance: consumer goods, basic materials, industrial goods, services, healthcare, technology and financial.
2. Finding stock market shakers in the overall market.
3. Case study to see how the stock market shakers affect the market after the studied period (after 11/30/2010).

Result analysis By tracing the evolutions of stock prices, we generate 7 cascading graphs for the 7 different sectors and analyze their stock market shakers respectively. Recall that the final output (Algorithm 1) is the rankings of the entities with respect to their influence scores, with the top ranked ones being the shakers. We evaluated the accuracies of the top 10% of the rankings (50 such stocks in each sector on average) and the results are presented in Fig. 5. It is clear that the two proposed scoring functions outperform the comparison models. For example, in the healthcare sector, the accuracies of the three comparison methods are just around 35%, while those of the proposed models are over 70%. Again, the reason is that the comparison methods are not suitable to handle networks such as a cascading graph with opposite correlations. The aim of the second experiment was to find the stock market shakers in all of the 2730 stocks. In this case, only one cascading graph is generated to summarize the causality relationships among all stocks to find the global market shakers. The lift curves are plotted in Fig. 6, where we can clearly observe that the two proposed models beat the comparison methods. We also present the top 10 stock market shakers in Table 4, in which the two proposed scoring functions clearly outperform the comparison models by as much as 50% in accuracy. Note that the Apple Inc. (AAPL) is identified by both proposed functions. More interestingly, AAPL suffers a big slide on

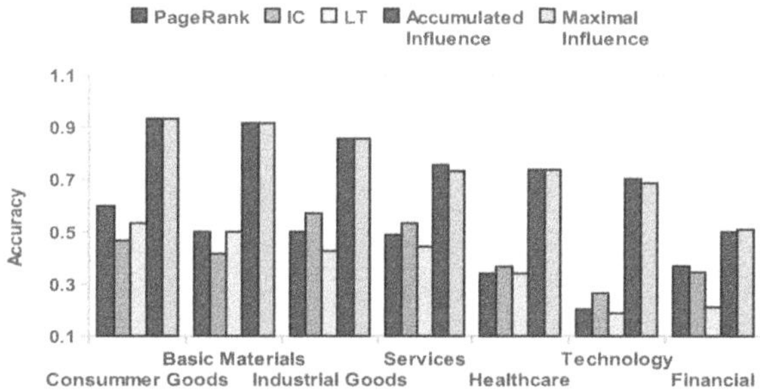

Figure 5: Accuracy of the top 10% of rankings

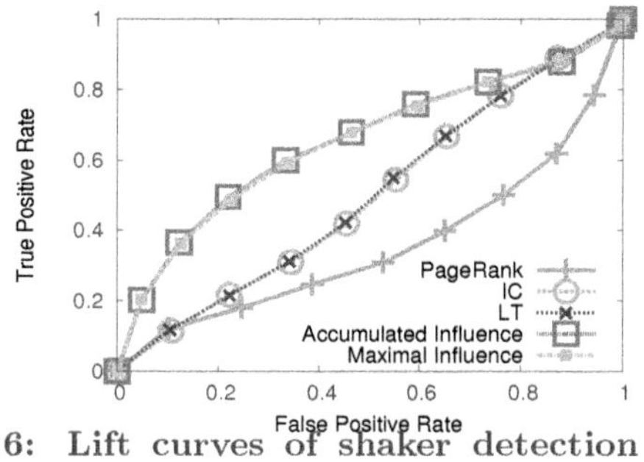

Figure 6: Lift curves of shaker detection in 2730 NASDAQ stocks

January 18th, 2011 following the news release of its CEO Steve Jobs taking a medical leave. The NASDAQ 100 index ($NDX) follows its big loss the next day [26] even though there are strong earning reports from companies like IBM and despite the rally of the Asian market. Note that the internal market mechanism may be very complicated and there may be other reasons for the market slide in addition to AAPL, but the market shaker does reveal the risk ahead.

4.4 Parameter Sensitivity

There are three parameters in the proposed model. We choose the "Basic materials" sector of the stock data to analyze the three parameters, and choose the accumulated influence as the scoring function since the maximal influence criterion has similar performances. The first parameter is

Table 4: **Top 10 Stock Shakers in NASDAQ**

PageRank	IC	LT	Accumulated Influence	Maximal Influence
AACOU ✓	VCLT ✓	AAPL ✓	ACGL ×	ACGL ×
CAPS ✓	FITBP ✓	RDWR ×	MICC ✓	MICC ✓
TWER ×	WGOV ×	ABBC ×	HBANP ✓	HBANP ✓
JSDA ×	TLCR ✓	LCUT ✓	SHPGY ✓	SHPGY ✓
EVBS ×	VYFC ✓	AKAM ×	VGIT ✓	VGIT ✓
ZANE ×	BTFG ×	ADTN ✓	ATRI ×	ATRI ×
AUTH ×	ALOG ✓	AFSI ×	VCLT ✓	VCLT ✓
PFBC ×	ABCD ×	ACXM ✓	COST ✓	COST ✓
IBNK ×	ZUMZ ×	AAWW ✓	AAPL ✓	AAPL ✓
IMOS ×	AACC ×	DNDN ×	PNRA ✓	PNRA ✓
Accuracy: 20%	Accuracy: 50%	Accuracy: 50%	**Accuracy: 80%**	**Accuracy: 80%**

the degree n of the polynomial function, which is used to fit the data; the result is shown in Fig. 7(a). It can be observed that the result tends to be stable when the degree is larger than 8. This is because even if we set the degree larger, the coefficients of the high degree terms tend to be zero in order to minimize the ridge loss with regularization term. In practice, one can choose the degree n to be a median number (*e.g.*, $n = 10$), or adaptively choose n according to the fitting loss with regularization. The second parameter is the number of iterations of the coordinate descent to solve the optimization in Eq. 5. As in Fig. 7(b), the objective function actually converges very fast since the four variables have closed-form solutions in each iteration. The last parameter is the time span T across which the influence is estimated. In other words, we only consider the influence of the target nodes within T step. It can be observed from Fig. 7(c) that the performance is stable after $T > 5$. It means that the effects are propagated efficiently. In the experiment, we set $n = 9, C = 3$ and $T = 6$.

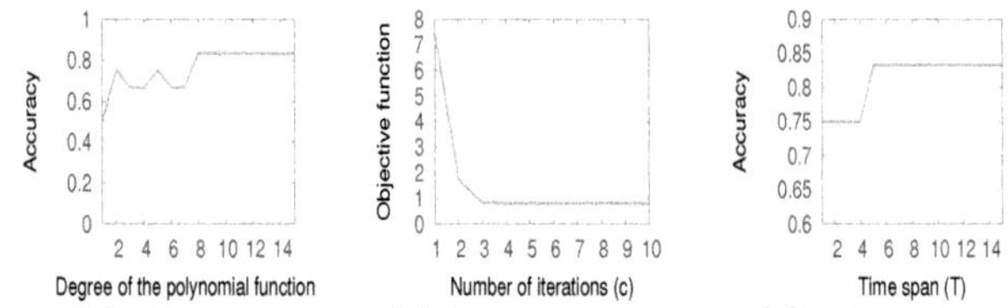

(a) Degree (b) Convergence (c) Time span

Figure 7: Parameter sensitivity analysis

5. RELATED WORK

There are several areas of work that we build upon. First of all, causality has attracted intensive interest in artificial intelligence. An increasing number of works are proposed to model the causality among discrete and countable events by using their frequency of co-occurrences (*e.g.*, [27, 10, 23]). In reality, however, on the one hand, there may be a huge number of observed events; on the other hand, there is usually a time latency between the cause and the effect. Hence, it is generally very difficult to detect the underlying causality of the entities just by observing their co-occurrence. The present work investigates the transformations of the entity evolution trends instead of the co-occurrence to detect causality. In one of the steps of the proposed model, we borrow the idea of time series (*e.g.*, [22, 35]), although it is not the focus of the paper. We fit the evolving data with polynomial functions and detect the similarity among the function transformations. There may be other time series techniques that can be used to find the causalities, such as using some discrete transformations ([20, 21]). But the most important advantage of polynomial fitting is that it can give us closed form solutions in each iteration that leads to the efficient computation (Fig. 7(b)).

Information diffusion and influence maximization is another area of related work. It has attracted considerable attention (*e.g.*, [8, 16, 34]) in recent years. The general idea is to trace the information propagation on a given network by various models, and find the top influential nodes or effectors that can best explain the phenomenon (*e.g.*, [1, 17, 15, 13]). Usually, the entities have only one of only two states (active or inactive) and the found influential nodes usually have wide spreads. With a different objective, the proposed model allows numerical attributes of the entities and considers whether the target nodes cause attribute value changes for some others, which are not necessarily the ones with large spreads. Furthermore, the proposed model allows for negative edges in the network where the influence diffusion becomes more complicated. Extensive experiments show that it is better to handle the entities that naturally contain opposite correlations. Another area of related work is data mining in economics. For example, in [5], a network based approach is applied to find similarities/communities among time-series foreign exchanges, but it does not consider influence cancellation between negative effects and positive effects.

6. CONCLUSION

Given a set of evolving entities with complex, latent and dynamic relationships, this paper investigates the problem of mining shakers or entities that can cause significant value changes for others. An example is the stock market shakers that significantly affect the prices of other stocks. We address the problem by proposing a cascading graph that summarizes the causalities among the entities by capturing the similarities of their evolving trends. More importantly, two scoring functions (accumulated and maximal effects) are formulated in order to capture the degree or efficiency on how the target entity affects others. To do so, we artificially inject a significant change on the target entity where its effects propagate throughout the network, and then estimate its influence on other nodes for a given period of time. Although the two scoring functions seem unsolvable because of several undetermined variables, we formally prove that the unknown variables can be canceled with the inference rule derived from Markovian assumption, and the two scoring functions are actually only dependent on the structure of the cascading graph. The proposed model is evaluated on three real world datasets from social sciences: an economic indicator dataset, a country GDP development dataset and the stock market dataset. It is observed that the proposed model outperforms the three comparison methods substantially. For example, in the stock market dataset, the accuracies of the three comparison methods are just around 35% while those of the proposed models are over 70% in the healthcare sector.

Acknowledgement The authors would like to thank the MITRE Corporation for their support to this work. They would also like to express their gratitude to Dr. Ali Hadjarian for his proofreading of the paper.

7. REFERENCES

[1] N. Agarwal, H. Liu, L. Tang, and P. S. Yu. Identifying the influential bloggers in a community. In *WSDM*, pages 207–218, 2008.

[2] World bank dataset. http://data.worldbank.org/.

[3] BRIC. http://en.wikipedia.org/wiki/bric.

[4] S. Brin and L. Page. The anatomy of a large-scale hypertextual web search engine. In *WWW*, pages 107–117, 1998.

[5] D.J. Fenn, M.A. Porter, P.J. Mucha, M. McDonald, S.Williams, N.F. Johnson, and N.S. Jones. Dynamical clustering of exchange rates. *preprint (2010) arXiv:0905.4912v2*, 2010.

[6] Yahoo! finance. http://finance.yahoo.com/.

[7] Yahoo! finance industry ranking. http://finance.yahoo.com/q/in?s=aapl+industry.

[8] M. Gomez-Rodriguez, J. Leskovec, and A. Krause. Inferring networks of diffusion and influence. In *KDD*, pages 1019–1028, 2010.

[9] C. W. J. Granger. Investigating causal relations by econometric models and cross-spectral methods. *Econometrica*, 37(3):424–438, 1969.

[10] D. Heckerman, D. Geiger, and D. M. Chickering. Learning bayesian networks: The combination of knowledge and statistical data. *Machine Learning*, 20(3):197–243, 1995.

[11] D. Kempe, J. Kleinberg, and É. Tardos. Influential nodes in a diffusion model for social networks. In *IN ICALP*, pages 1127–1138, 2005.

[12] D. Kempe, J. M. Kleinberg, and É. Tardos. Maximizing the spread of influence through a social network. In *KDD*, pages 137–146, 2003.

[13] M. Kimura, K. Saito, and R. Nakano. Extracting influential nodes for information diffusion on a social network. In *AAAI*, pages 1371–1376, 2007.

[14] J. M. Kleinberg, R. Kumar, P. Raghavan, S. Rajagopalan, and A. S. Tomkins. The web as a graph: measurements, models, and methods. In *COCOON*, pages 1–17, 1999.

[15] T. Lappas, E. Terzi, D. Gunopulos, and H. Mannila. Finding effectors in social networks. In *KDD*, pages 1059–1068, 2010.

[16] J. Leskovec, L. A. Adamic, and B. A. Huberman. The dynamics of viral marketing. In *EC*, pages 228–237, 2006.

[17] J. Leskovec, M. McGlohon, C. Faloutsos, N. S. Glance, and M. Hurst. Patterns of cascading behavior in large blog graphs. In *SDM*, pages 551–556, 2007.

[18] D. Li, J. Shen, and J. Xie. Study on representation of time series based on subsection polynomial fitting. In *FSKD*, pages 1371–1376, 2007.

[19] D. Miles and A. Scott. *Macroeconomics: understanding the wealth of nations*. John Wiley and Sons., 2nd edition, 2005.

[20] A. Mueen and E. J. Keogh. Online discovery and maintenance of time series motifs. In *KDD*, pages 1089–1098, 2010.

[21] A. Mueen, E. J. Keogh, Q. Zhu, S. Cash, and M. B. Westover. Exact discovery of time series motifs. In *SDM*, pages 473–484, 2009.

[22] S. Papadimitriou, J. Sun, and C. Faloutsos. Streaming pattern discovery in multiple time-series. In *VLDB*, pages 697–708, 2005.

[23] J. Pearl. Causal inference in statistics: an overview. *Statistics Surveys*, 3:96–146, 2009.

[24] Country ranking in GDP. http://en.wikipedia.org/wiki/list-of-countries-by-gdp-(nominal).

[25] C. A. Ratanamahatana, J. Lin, D. Gunopulos, E. J. Keogh, M. Vlachos, and G. Das. Mining time series data. In *Data Mining and Knowledge Discovery Handbook*, pages 1049–1077. 2010.

[26] Market reaction on AAPL. http://www.finanzen.net/nachricht/aktien/market-snapshot-stocks-mostly-down-after-apple-goldman-results-1012909.

[27] G. Shafer. Causal logic. In *ECAI*, pages 711–720, 1998.

[28] J. Shi and J. Malik. Normalized cuts and image segmentation. *IEEE Trans. Pattern Anal. Mach. Intell.*, 22(8):888–905, 2000.

[29] Q. Smith. Causation and the logical impossibility of a divine cause. *Philosophical Topics*, 21(1):169–191, 1996.

[30] Y. Sun, Q. Meng, Z. Chen, and Y. Zhang. Normalizing the polynomial match for the nonlinear signal in transducers. *Sensors and Actuators*, 125:76–83, 2005.

[31] T. D. Tregarthen and L. Rittenberg. *Macroeconomics*. Worth Publishers, 2nd edition, 2000.

[32] Ioannis Tsamardinos. Causal data mining in bioinformatics. *ERCIM News*, 2007(69), 2007.

[33] Y. Wang, G. Cong, G. Song, and K. Xie. Community-based greedy algorithm for mining top-k influential nodes in mobile social networks. In *KDD*, pages 1039–1048, 2010.

[34] D. Wu, Y. Ke, J. X. Yu, P. S. Yu, and L. Chen. Detecting leaders from correlated time series. In *DASFAA*, pages 352–367, 2010.

[35] B. Yi, N. Sidiropoulos, T. Johnson, H. V. Jagadish, C. Faloutsos, and A. Biliris. Online data mining for co-evolving time sequences. In *ICDE*, pages 13–22, 2000.

Discovering Spatio-Temporal Causal Interactions in Traffic Data Streams

Wei Liu
University of Sydney,
Sydney, Australia
wei.liu@sydney.edu.au

Yu Zheng
Microsoft Research Asia,
Beijing, China
yuzheng@microsoft.com

Sanjay Chawla
University of Sydney,
Sydney, Australia
sanjay.chawla@sydney.edu.au

Jing Yuan
University of Science and
Technology of China
yuanjing@mail.ustc.edu.cn

Xing Xie
Microsoft Research Asia,
Beijing, China
xingx@microsoft.com

ABSTRACT

The detection of outliers in spatio-temporal traffic data is an important research problem in the data mining and knowledge discovery community. However to the best of our knowledge, the discovery of relationships, especially causal interactions, among detected traffic outliers has not been investigated before. In this paper we propose algorithms which construct outlier causality trees based on temporal and spatial properties of detected outliers. Frequent substructures of these causality trees reveal not only recurring interactions among spatio-temporal outliers, but potential flaws in the design of existing traffic networks. The effectiveness and strength of our algorithms are validated by experiments on a very large volume of real taxi trajectories in an urban road network.

Categories and Subject Descriptors

H.2.8 [**Database Applications**]: Data mining

General Terms

Algorithms

Keywords

Spatio-temporal outliers; outlier causalities; frequent substructures; urban computing and planning;

1. INTRODUCTION

The increasing availability of location-acquisition technologies including GPS and WIFI have resulted in huge volumes of spatio-temporal data, especially in the form of trajectories [2, 5, 7, 15, 14, 19, 17]. Unusual patterns of moving objects' trajectories generally reflect abnormal traffic streams on road networks, which could be caused by aperiodic events including celebrations, parades, large-scale business promotions, protests, traffic control and traffic jams. Therefore, the detection of outliers/anomalies from trajectory data can help in sensing abnormal events and plan for their impact on the smooth flow of traffic. In this study, we treat both known (planned) and unknown (unplanned) events that behave differently from daily network traffics as anomalies.

Challenges and Contributions

In order to successfully detect outliers and causal interactions among them, the following challenges need to be addressed: (i) Heterogeneous traffic patterns: the traffic patterns on roads vary across days of a week and hours of a day. Different road segments have often distinct time-variant traffic patterns. It is difficult to use one model to detect outliers across the road network at different time periods. (ii) Data sparseness and distribution skewness: even though we could have a large number of sensors (taxis) probing the traffic on roads, there are many roads that have only a small number of samples given a large size of road networks in a major city. Moreover, a few road segments are traveled by thousands of vehicles in a few hours, while some segments may be only driven on a few times in a day. These two properties together result in unique challenges in detecting outliers from traffic data. (iii) Causality among outliers: we not only need to discover outliers from the traffic, but also infer causal relationships and interactions among them, especially given the large number of outliers that could be identified. So a challenge is how to detect the appearance, growth, disappearance and transformation of outliers by time (e.g., propagation of a traffic jam).

In this paper we design several steps to address the above challenges and propose solutions to the problem of detecting spatio-temporal outliers and causal relationships among them from traffic data streams. We use contexts of road networks in this study, however, algorithms proposed in this paper can be generally applied to domains of networking [12,

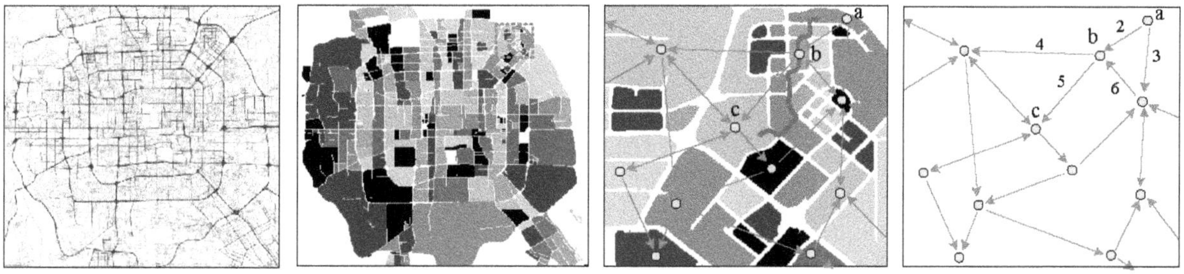

(a) Road network of Beijing (b) Partitioned regions (c)Example of traffic among regions (d) A graph of regions

Figure 1: An example using traffic networks in the city of Beijing. Based on major roads in the traffic network, the entire city (subfigure (a)) is partitioned into regions (subfigure (b)). Trajectories of moving objects (such as a moving taxi shown by a blue trajectory in subfigure (c)) connect neighboring regions, based on which we create the notion of links (subfigure (d)).

13] and climate change [18, 23, 8] etc. More specifically, the **contributions** we make in this paper are:

1. *City-wide traffic modeling*: we partition the urban area of a city into regions using the framework of the city's road network. Then we build a region graph where a node is a region and a link captures the traffic flow among two regions. We formulate the outlier detection problem as identifying the most outlying "links" from the region graph in terms of the spatio-temporal properties of a link.

2. *Outlier tree construction*: we propose the `STOTree` algorithm based on both spatial and temporal properties of detected outliers (which are certain "links" in a time frame) to construct outlier trees, which uncover causal relationships among these outliers.

3. *Frequent outlier subtree discovery*: we propose the `freqentSubtree` algorithm, inspired by association rule mining, which generates the most frequent sub-structure (subtree) from all discovered outlier trees. These frequent subtrees reveal recurrent abnormalities in the data and suggest inherent problems in existing road networks.

The rest of the paper is structured as follows. In Section 3 we introduce the overall framework of our model, including preliminary concepts and notations that we use in this paper. In Section 4 we propose algorithms for discovering spatio-temporal outliers and causal relationships. Experiments and their analysis are reported in Section 5. We conclude in Section 6 with directions for future work.

2. RELATED WORK

To the best of our knowledge this is the first paper that proposes the problem of discovering casual relationships among spatio-temporal outliers. However, there have been a number of efforts on detecting only outliers from spatially and temporally distributed data. For example, principle component analysis (PCA) has been used for network-wide anomaly detection [13, 26, 20, 1]. However, PCA results (as we will show) cannot capture volume heterogeneity and are also very sensitive to parameter settings which are highly data dependent. Under certain circumstances, large anomalies in turn can effect the PCA computation leading to both false positives and false negatives [20].

The problem of outlier monitoring has also been studied in [2] which builds local clusters on trajectory streams and monitors outliers that are defined by a "trajectory" (instead of a spatial link as ours). Another method is Sun *et al.* [22] where a measure, spatial local outlier measure (SLOM), is proposed to capture the local behavior of datum in their spatial neighborhood. This measure takes into account the local stability around a data point and suppresses the reporting of outliers in highly unstable areas. A generalized local statistical (GLS) framework is proposed in [6] which studies the performance of local based methods on detecting outliers in geo-statistical data with either linear or nonlinear trends, and compares them against global based methods. Wu *et al.* [23] design algorithms detecting the most abnormal discrepancy regions in precipitation data, where they use four sweep lines to form grids which are treated as regions. However, none of these approaches model and capture temporal relations (causalities) among detected outlying regions. Lee *et al.* [15, 14] have designed a "partition-and-group" framework for clustering and detecting trajectory outliers. In their approach, they first partition the trajectories into small segments and then use both distance and density to detect abnormal sub-trajectories. This is different from our work as we detect abnormal regions and links of the entire traffic network (instead of objects moving in the network).

Moving objects are usually associated with periodic behavioral patterns, and there have been several methods proposed to address the problem of detecting such periodic movements [3, 4, 10, 9, 16]. Cao *et al.* [3, 4] proposed abbreviated list tables (ALT) to find subsequences that appear periodically and frequently in data sequences, but the periodic patterns they detect are very sensitive to parameter settings. Similarly, Elfeky *et. al.* [9] have proposed specific definitions of periodicities and algorithms for identifying the periodic patterns.

3. OVERVIEW

In this section, we introduce our notations, definitions and the main structure of the proposed model.

3.1 Preliminary Concepts

The overall traffic map is partitioned into regions (*Rgn*) bounded by high level (i.e. major) roads, each of which may consist of a number of road segments. Figure 1(a) and 1(b) demonstrate an example of region formations.

DEFINITION 1. Trajectory*: A trajectory Tr is a trace cre-*

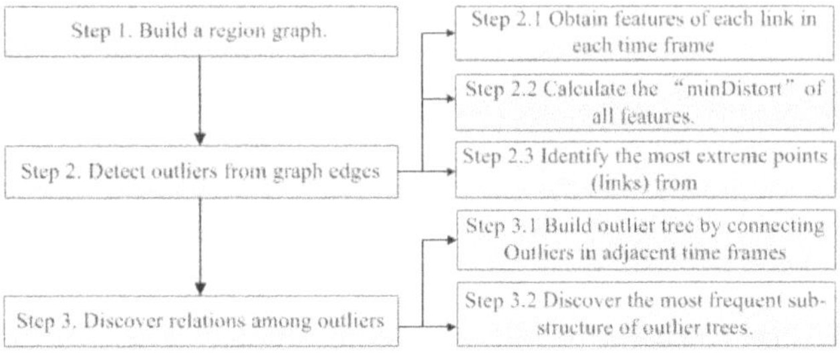

Figure 2: The overall structure of our model for detecting spatio-temporal outliers and their inter-causalities.

ated by a moving object in geographical space. A Tr is represented by of a set of time-ordered points, e.g. $Tr : p_1 \rightarrow p_2 \rightarrow ... \rightarrow p_n$, where each point consists of a geospatial coordinate set and a timestamp, i.e. p = (longitude, latitude, timestamp).

DEFINITION 2. Transition*: Given a trajectory $Tr : p_1 \rightarrow p_2 \rightarrow ... \rightarrow p_n$, there exists a transition S between Rgn_1 and Rgn_2, if there exists adjacent points p_i and p_{i+1} ($1 \leq i \leq n+1$) such that p_i is in Rgn_1 and p_{i+1} is in Rgn_2, and Rgn_1 is not the same to Rgn_2. A transition is associated with a leaving time (timestamp of p_i) and an arriving time (timestamp of p_{i+1}).*

DEFINITION 3. Link*: A link (Lnk) is comprised of a pair of regions ($<Rgn^o, Rgn^d>$) indicating a virtual spatial connection between the origin region and the destination region. There exists a link from one region (Rgn^o) to another (Rgn^d) if and only if there exists at least one object moving from Rgn^o at timestamp ts_i to Rgn^d at ts_{i+1}. Figure 1(c) and 1(d) give examples of links.*

DEFINITION 4. Time frame*: A time frame (tf) is a set of consecutive time intervals[1]. Figure 3(a) shows an example of a time frame.*

DEFINITION 5. Spatio-temporal outlier*: A spatio- temporal outlier (STO) is a link whose non-spatial and non-temporal attribute values are very different from the values of its spatio-temporal neighbors. Spatio-temporal neighbors of a link Lnk_i are the links whose locations and timestamps are close to those of Lnk_i.*

DEFINITION 6. Outlier causality*: STO_2 (with a region pair $<Rgn_2^o, Rgn_2^d>$ and a time frame tf_2) is caused by STO_1 (containing a region pair $<Rgn_1^o, Rgn_1^d>$ and a time frame tf_1) if and only if the following conditions hold true: (i) The destination of STO_1 is the same as the origin of STO_2 (i.e. $Rgn_1^d = Rgn_2^o$); (ii) Time frames tf_1 and tf_2 are consecutive to each other and tf_1 is ahead of tf_2.*

During the construction of an outlier tree, an outlier STO_i is a a child of another outlier STO_j if STO_i is caused by STO_j.

3.2 Framework

The main structure of our model is illustrated in Figure 2. The three main steps are preprocessing traffic data to build a region graph, detecting outliers and finally discover causal relationships between the discovered outliers. The second and the third step have three and two sub-steps respectively. Details of these (sub-)steps are described in the following section.

[1] We call a "time interval" a "timebin" in the rest of the paper.

4. METHODOLOGY

In this section, we provide details of our model as shown in Figure 2. Specifically, we focus on the detection of spatio-temporal outliers based on each link's "distort", construct outlier causality trees based on these outliers, and discover the most frequent causal trees which are indicative of recurrent traffic abnormalities.

4.1 Building the Graph of Regions

In our study, we assume the map of traffic network, the set of major roads, and the trajectories of objects are all known. Although it is more straightforward to apply a simple "$n \times m$" grid on maps to define regions, cells of a grid are equal-sized and do not reflect natural differences of regions in a traffic network. So instead of using equal-sized grids, we define regions of a traffic network by road segments as illustrated in Figure 1. In detail, we build a graph of regions according to the following three steps.

1. *Region Partitioning*: As shown in Figure 1(a) and Figure 1(b), we partition a city into dis-jointed regions using the major roads of the city. Here we employ Connected Components Labeling (an image segment method) [21] to partition a map into regions effectively and efficiently, since the problem of subdivisions in a polygonal region is known to be NP-complete [11].

2. *Formulating transitions*: By scanning the trajectory data set, we transfer each trajectory into a sequence of transitions between pairs of regions in terms of definition 2. As demonstrated in Figure 1(c), a trajectory passing three regions a, b, and c results in two transitions: $a \Rightarrow b$, and $b \Rightarrow c$.

3. *Generating links*: If there is a transition generated between two regions, we connect the two regions with a link (refer to Definition 3). In timebin j, a link i ($Lnk_i = <Rgn^o, Rgn^d>$) is associated with a feature vector of three properties $\vec{f}_{i,j} \equiv <\#Obj, Pct_o, Pct_d>$:

   (a) $\#Obj$: Total number of objects on the links (i.e. objects moving from Rgn^o to Rgn^d in this timebin);

   (b) Pct_o: The proportion of $\#Obj$ among all objects moving out of Rgn^o in this timebin;

   (c) Pct_d: The proportion of $\#Obj$ among all objects moving into Rgn^d in this timebin;

   Then, using Figure 1(d) as an example (where the number shown on each link is the number of transitions pertaining to the link), the property of link $a \Rightarrow b$ is $\vec{f}_{i,j} = <\#Obj{=}2, Pct_o{=}\frac{2}{2+3}{=}0.4, Pct_d = \frac{2}{2+6}{=}0.25>$.

4.2 Detecting Outliers from Graph Links

Assume each time frame is comprised of a fixed number of q timebins. Given a time frame tf_j, we denote the sequence of feature values of a link Lnk_i in this time frame by:

$$F_{i,j} = < \vec{f}_{i,j-q+1}, \vec{f}_{i,j-q+2}, ..., \vec{f}_{i,j} > . \quad (1)$$

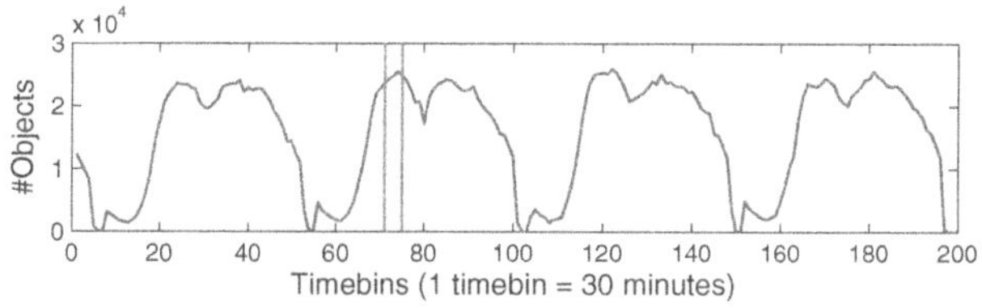

(a) An example of time frame defined by the segment between two vertical (green) lines.

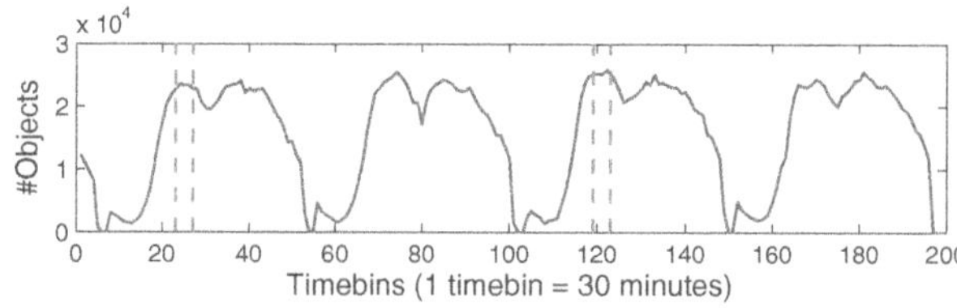

(b) Time frames to be compared with the one in (a)

Figure 3: An example of the number of taxis on a certain link in four adjacent days. Gaps between green vertical lines represent time frames, each of which is comprised of several timebins. One unit of timebin in x-axis represents 30 minutes (i.e. 48 timebins comprise a day). The value of *minDistort* of the time frame in subfigure (a) is obtained by calculating the smallest difference between the time frame in (a) and the ones at the same time in adjacent days as shown in subfigure (b).

For each link (Lnk_i) in each time frame tf_j, we calculate the distortion between two time frames (denoted by $minDistort_{i,j}$) by searching for the minimum difference between tf_j and the same time frames of the same days on consecutive weeks. With this approach *minDistort* is capable of capturing the special pattern of traffic data that similar behaviors are observed during the same time of different days or the same day of different weeks etc.

Algorithm 1 shows the procedure of calculating distorts. In line 7 of the algorithm, we obtain the difference between two time frames of a link by computing their Euclidean distance:

$$Distance(tf_j, tf_t, Lnk_i) = \sqrt{\sum_{k=0}^{q-1} \|\vec{f}_{i,j-k} - \vec{f}_{i,t-k}\|^2} \quad (2)$$

We use $minDistort_{i,j}$ obtained from Algorithm 1 as the "non-spatial and non-temporal attributes" (see Definition 5) of each link in each time frame. Extreme values among *minDistort* of all links are identified as temporal outliers. By subtracting the *min* and dividing by the *max* the feature values of the links are in the range of [0,1]. The normalization removes the effect of different regions and volume sizes. Another advantage of using *minDistort* is that it prevents the examination of many repeating patterns (where $minDistort \approx 0$).

Then *for each time frame*, there is a corresponding three dimensional vector (formed by features <#Obj, Pct_o, Pct_d>) shown in Figure 4. As each point represents a link, we identify the most extreme points as outliers in that time frame. To normalize the effect of variances along different directions, we use the Mahalanobis distance (instead of Euclidean distance) to measure the the extremeness of data points. We

Algorithm 1 `minDistort`: calculating minimum distort of time sequences

Input: Lnk_i: a link; tf_j: a time frame; t: number of adjacent weeks to check
Output: $minDistort_{i,j}$: the degree of distort for link Lnk_i in time frame tf_j

```
1: minDist ← +Infinity;
2: T ← tf_{j±u weeks, u ∈ {−t, ..., t}}
3: for All time frames tf_t in T do
4:    if tf_t overlap with tf_j then
5:       Continue;
6:    end if
7:    currentDist ← Distance(tf_j, tf_t, Lnk_i);
8:    if currentDist < minDist then
9:       minDist ← currentDist;
10:   end if
11: end for
12: Return minDist;
```

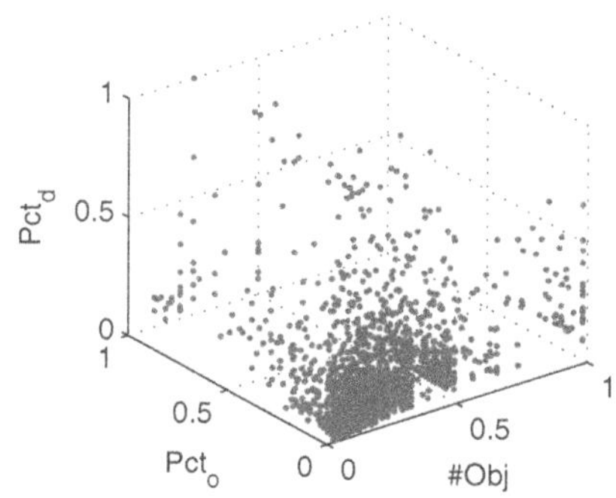

Figure 4: An illustration of the three-dimensional unit cube formed by three features <#Obj, Pct_o, Pct_d> before normalization for computing the Mahalanobis distance. We label the most "extreme" points among all points as outliers. For example, outlier points are the ones whose distance are the farthest to the center of the data cluster.

use the Mahalanobis distance here in order to normalize the distance by the variance in different directions.

In this way, **the outliers detected are links whose features have the largest difference from both their temporal neighbors (for using "*minDistort*") and spatial neighbors (for being detected "among all links")** – so they are *spatio-temporal* outliers (STOs). Another advantage of identifying "extreme points" as outliers is that it can detect abnormal links with either too low volumes or too high volumes since extremeness of points are based on their Mahalanobis distances.

Now each STO is a spatial **link** associated with a time frame. We represent a STO by its link Lnk_i (containing an original region and a destination region) and its time frame tf_j, i.e., $STO_{i,j} = < Rgn_{i,o}, Rgn_{i,d}, tf_j >$.

4.3 Constructing Outlier Trees

We propose an algorithm named `STOTree` that finds outlier dependencies by looking at the relationship of outliers from the earliest time frame through the last. **The main insight of `STOTree` is that an outlier STO_1 is a parent of another outlier STO_2 if STO_1 occurred before STO_2 in time and they are spatially correlated.** Al-

Algorithm 2 `STOTree`: constructing all outlier trees

Input: $STOutlier$: a set of spatial-temporal outliers of size $t \times k$ where t is the number of time frames, and k is the number of outliers to examine in a time frame.
Output: $STOTrees$: a list of roots of spatial-temporal trees.

1: $STOTrees \leftarrow$ an empty set $\{\}$;
2: **for** Each time frame i ($i \in (1, ..., t)$) **do**
3:   **for** Each outlier j ($j \in (1, ..., k)$) in time frame i **do**
4:     $STORoot_{i,j} \leftarrow$ `FindAllChildren`($STOutlier_{i,j}$, i);
5:     $STOTrees \leftarrow STOTrees \cup STORoot_{i,j}$;
6:   **end for**
7: **end for**
8: Return $STOTrees$;

Subroutine: `FindAllChildren`($STOutlier_{i,j}$, i)
9: **if** Time frame i is the last time frame **then**
10:   Return $STOutlier_{i,j}$;
11: **end if**
12: $STOutlier_{i,j}.subnodes \leftarrow$ an empty set$\{\}$;
13: **for** Each outlier u ($u \in (1, ..., k)$) in time frame $i+1$ **do**
14:   **if** $STOTrees$ contains $STOutlier_{i+1,u}$ **then**
15:     continue;
16:   **end if**
17:   **if** $STOutlier_{i,j}.Rgn^d == STOutlier_{i+1,u}.Rgn^o$ **then**
18:     $STOutlier_{i,j}.subnodes \leftarrow STOutlier_{i,j}.subnodes \cup FindAllChildren(STOutlier_{i+1,u}, i+1)$;
19:   **end if**
20: **end for**
21: Return $STOutlier_{i,j}$;

gorithm 2 demonstrates the process of constructing outlier trees from discovered outliers. Note the algorithm results in a collection of trees (a forest). The subroutine (Line 9 to 21) is a recursive function used to retrieve all possible descendants of a node. For each time frame, this recursive function is called on each outlier of the current time frame to compare with each outlier of next time frame, unless the "current" outlier tree already contains outliers of next time frame (Line 14 to 16). So the overall time complexity of the outlier tree construction process on each time frame is upper bounded by $O(k^2)$, where k is the number of outliers in a time frame.

We do not place a restriction on the maximum size of outlier trees in the `STOTree` algorithm, under the assumption that abnormal events caused by one single accident are not expected to last for a long time and the size outlier trees should not grow infinitely. In Section 5.3 we provide empirical evidence that confirms the maximum size of trees is usually small.

Now we give an example by using Figure 5 to demonstrate the process of Algorithm 2 for building outlier trees. Figure 5 uses top 3 outliers in three consecutive time frames, so the input parameters in Algorithm 2 in this case are $k = 3$ and $t = 3$. The algorithm starts from time frame 1 (Line 2 of Algorithm 2), and for each of the top three outlying links (Line 3 to 6), i.e., $A \Rightarrow B$, $C \Rightarrow D$ and $E \Rightarrow F$, the algorithm searches in time frame 2 (Line 13 to 20) and checks whether there is any following link that can be a child of a previous link (Line 17 to 19). This allows the algorithm to find outlying links $B \Rightarrow G$ and $B \Rightarrow E$ as children of $A \Rightarrow B$; and similarly it identifies link $H \Rightarrow K$ in time frame 3 as a child of $J \Rightarrow H$ in time frame 2. Therefore two outlier trees are built up as shown in the right side of Figure 5. In this way, Algorithm 2 scans through all time frames of traffic data we have, and builds a forest of various outlier trees.

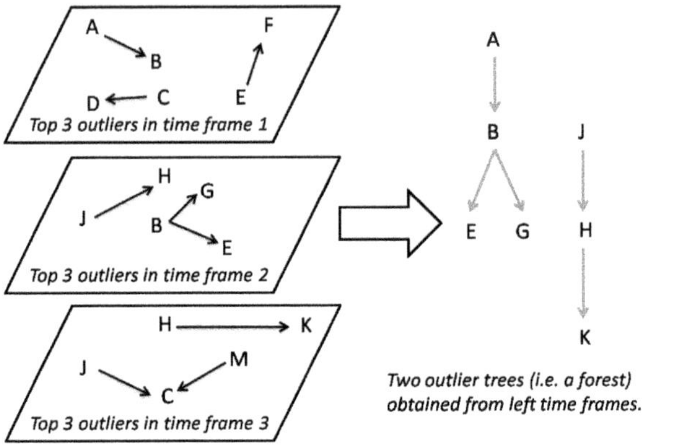

Figure 5: A synthetic example for demonstrating the process of building a forest of two outlier trees. The subfigure on the left illustrates top 3 outlying links in three consecutive time frames, and the one on the right shows two outlier trees obtained from these time frames.

4.4 Causal Outlier Detection

Denote by T the forest containing all outlier trees. The most significant and recurring causal relationships correspond to the most frequent subtrees of T. The mechanism of discovering frequent subtrees from all outlier trees is inspired by the process of mining frequent item sets, except that we design our own strategy to generate frequent subtree candidates (through node insertion on trees).

The process of discovering frequent substructures from constructed outlier trees is shown in Algorithm 3. Given a predefined support threshold ϵ, we first find all single nodes whose supports exceed ϵ (Line 3 of the algorithm), then we use this set of frequent single nodes to form candidates of frequent subtrees. The "while" iteration (Line 6 to 30) first generates candidates of subtrees (Line 9 to 15), and then checks the support of each candidate and performs filtering (Line 18 to 29) according to ϵ.

When generating subtree candidates, new subtrees (whose sizes are increased by one) are created by inserting a frequent single node into previous frequent subtrees. This node insertion process is given in Algorithm 4. The single node to be inserted is first compared with the root of the tree, and is inserted as a subnode of the root (Line 1 to 3 of Algorithm 4) if the root can be a parent of the single node and its existing children do not contain the single node. Otherwise, the single node is compared and checked whether it can be inserted into branches below the root (i.e. a recursive process shown in Line 8 to 12). When counting the support of a candidate subtree, we increase the frequency of the candidate by one if all nodes (with their immediate subnodes) of the candidate have an exact match with a discovered outlier tree (Line 21 to 23).

The effectiveness and strengths of our algorithms, `STOTree` and `frequentSubtree`, are evaluated in the next section.

5. EXPERIMENTS AND ANALYSIS

In this section we report on the experiments carried out on taxi trajectory data on the road network of Beijing city. Our experiments are conducted on a 64 bit server with 3.2 GHz CPU and 8 GB memory. We note that although we are using road traffic data, our methods and algorithms can be

Algorithm 3 `frequentSubtree`: discovering frequent subtrees from STOutlier trees

Input: *STOTrees*: a list of roots of spatial-temporal trees; ϵ: a support threshold for frequent substructure selection.
Output: *freqentSubtrees*: a list of roots of frequent spatial-temporal subtrees.

```
// Form a list of frequent nodes (i.e. frequent trees of size 1).
numTrees ← number of roots in STOTrees;
frequentNodes ← unique nodes appearing at least
    numTrees × ε times in STOTrees.
mergeTarget ← frequentNodes
freqentSubtrees ← an empty set{};
while size(mergeTarge) > 0 do
    // Form candidates of frequent subtrees;
    subtreeCandidates ← an empty set {};
    for Each node singleton_i in mergeTarge do
        for Each root root_j in mergeTarget do
            if nodeInsertion(root_j, singleton_i) then
                subtreeCandidates ← subtreeCandidates ∪ root_j;
            end if
        end for
    end for
    // Filer subtree candidates by threshold of support ε;
    Clear mergeTarget;
    for Each candidate candidate_i in subtreeCandidates do
        count ← 0;
        for Each root root_j in mergeTarget do
            if root_j contains candidate_i then
                count ← count + 1;
            end if
        end for
        if count > ε × numTrees then
            freqentSubtrees ← freqentTrees ∪ candidate_i;
            mergeTarget ← mergeTarget ∪ candidate_i;
        end if
    end for
end while
Return freqentSubtrees;
```

Table 1: Statistics of regions and links in the graph built from road network traffics.

#Regions	#Links	Avg. #Obj	Avg. Pct_o	Avg. Pct_d
396	10109	742.48	27.07	27.7702

easily adapted into other domains such as finding anomalies in the internet traffic data and even climate data.

5.1 Data and Parameters

Data: We test our algorithms based on a real GPS trajectory dataset generated by 33,000 taxis in a period of 6 months (from 01/03/2009 to 31/08/2009) [25, 24] . The total distance traveled by the taxis is more than 800 million kilometers and the total number of GPS points is nearly 1.5 billion. The average sampling interval and average distance of between two consecutive points are around 3.1 minutes and 300 meters respectively.

We define ten minutes as a timebin, and six timebins as a time frame (hence one time frame represents an hour). We check two adjacent weeks in *minDistort* calculations (i.e. the parameter t in Algorithm 1).

Road Network: We perform evaluations based on the road network of Beijing, which contains 106,579 road nodes and 141,380 road segments.

Algorithm 4 `nodeInsertion`: inserting a node to an outlier tree

Input: *Root*: a root of an outlier tree; *Singleton*: a node to be inserted.
Output: *true/false*: whether or not the node insertion is successful.

```
if Root.Rgn_d equals singlton.Rng_o && Root.subnodes does
    not contain singlton then
    Root.subnodes ← Root.subnodes ∪ singlton;
    Return true;
else
    if size(Root.subnodes) == 0) then
        Return false;
    else
        for Root of each subnode subRoot in Root.subnodes do
            if InsertNode(subRoot, Singleton) then
                Return true;
            end if
        end for
    end if
end if
Return false;
```

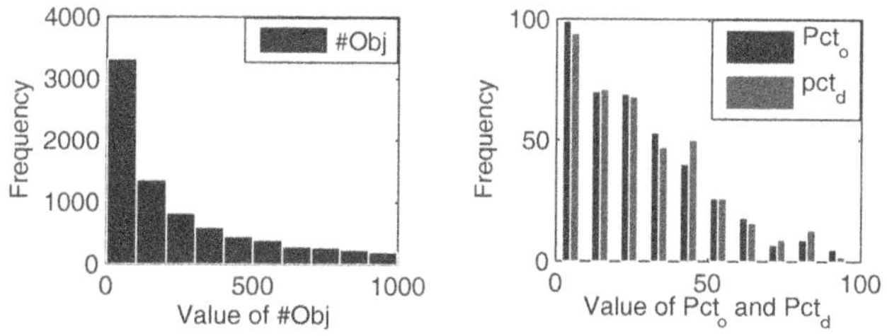

Figure 6: Histograms of the three features (i.e. <*#Obj*, Pct_o, Pct_d>) of all links in the region graph we obtained.

5.2 Results from Building Graphs

The statistics (e.g. number of regions and links) of the graph built are presented in Table 1. We note that in our evaluations, the number of links built by using 1 month, 2 months, ..., until all 6 months of taxi trajectories remains constant at 10109. This observation implies that although the links are *dynamic*[2] (dependent of traffic data), the model we have built does not miss any links even if one uses only a small fraction of taxi trajectories to build the underlying traffic graph. The distribution of the three features of links are presented in Figure 6.

5.3 Evaluations on Outlier Trees

In this experiment, we bound the value of k (i.e. number of outliers to be identified in each time frame) between 1 and 99, and report its effects on constructing outlier trees (shown as in Figure 7 and 8).

We set the minimum size of a tree (i.e. total number of nodes) to 2, and hence ignore singles nodes (trees of size 1) in counting final outlier trees. What we observe from Figure 7 is that, although the total number of trees constructed by detected outliers increase substantially when k increases (left subfigure), the maximum size of all trees has a smoothly increasing trend (right subfigure). This observation validates our earlier belief that abnormal events caused

[2]By contrast, regions are always *static* (independent of traffic data).

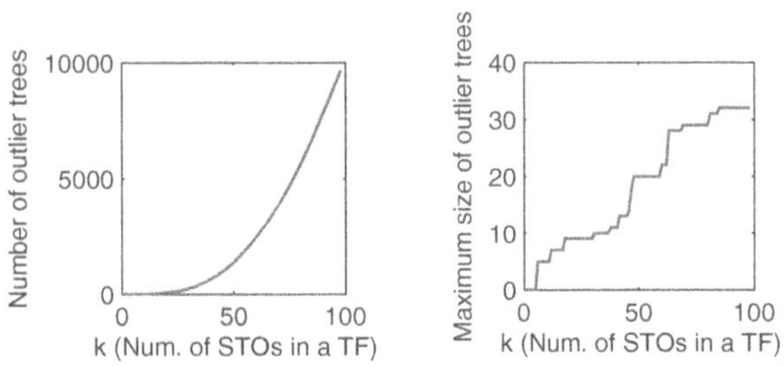

Figure 7: Total number of outlier trees and the maximum size of trees under different settings of k (the number of outliers in a time frame to construct outlier trees). "TF" in the label of x-axis is short for "time frame". While the number of trees increases dramatically when k increases, the maximum size of trees grows relatively smoothly.

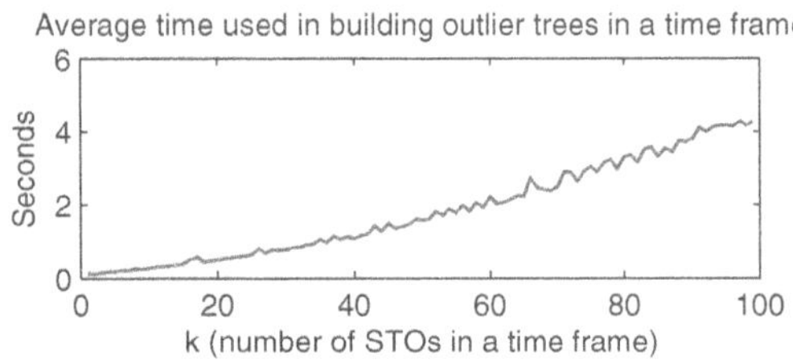

Figure 8: Average time (in seconds) used for constructing outlier trees under different settings of k (the number of outliers in a time frame to construct outlier trees). When k increases, the average time grows almost linearly.

by one single accident normally do not last very long, and that the maximum size of trees is usually small.

In Section 4.3 we have explained that the time complexity of our outlier tree construction algorithm `STOTree` is in the worst case (i.e. upper bounded by) $O(k^2)$. Here we present empirical results that illustrate `STOTree` runs much faster than $O(k^2)$ in practice. From Figure 8 we can observe that the average time used for building trees in a time frame increases almost linearly (instead of quadratically) with k. This indicates `STOTree` can potentially be used in an online setting, and can detect outlier causalities on the fly.

Moreover, the spatio-temporal outliers and their causal interactions detected by our algorithms all coincide with known abnormal events. The following are two prominent examples of known events:

Known event 1. The Bejing–HongKong highway was under traffic control for building viaducts of a Beijing light rail (i.e. the light rail of Fangshan line[3]) at midnight of the May 5th, 2009;

Known event 2. The entry fee into Olympic sports center was waived during day time on 7th August, 2009.

By using our model, the above two known outliers are successfully detected as shown in Figure 9(a) and 9(b) respectively. However, they are not detected by PCA based techniques as in [13]. As Figure 10 shows, the links of these two known abnormal events are among other points and are undistinguishable in the coordinate framework formed by the first two principle components from PCA.

[3] `http://en.wikipedia.org/wiki/Fangshan_Line,_Beijing_Subway`

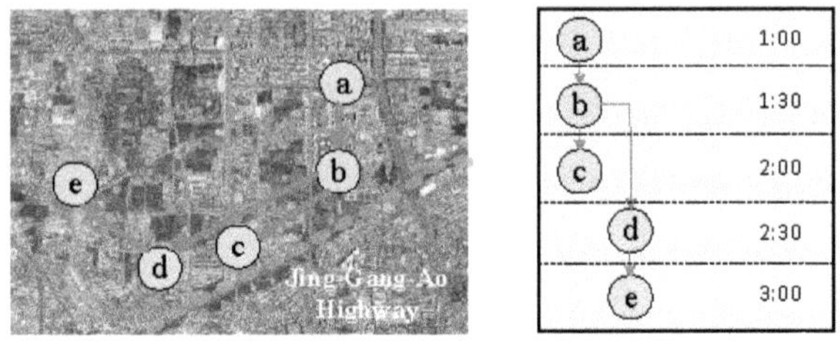

(a) An outlier tree besides Beijing–HongKong (Jing-Gang-Ao) highway between 4th and 5th ring road in time frames of 1:00am to 4:00am, on May 5th, 2009.

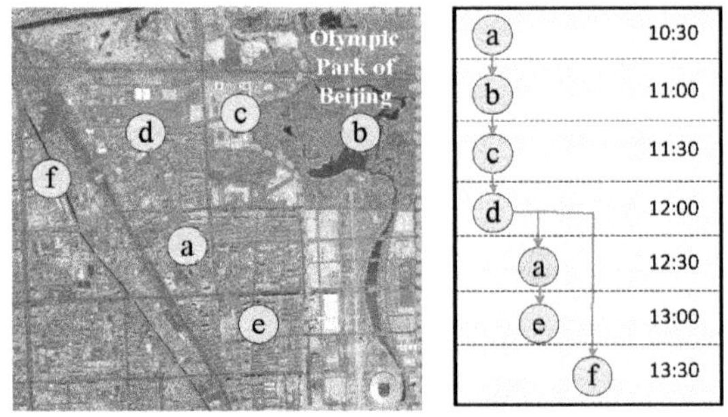

(b) An outlier tree around Olympic sports center of time frames from 10:00am to 2:30pm, on August 07, 2009. Note that there exists a loop in this tree, where region a firstly showed up as an origin of an outlying link $a \Rightarrow b$, and then later became a destination of another outlying link $d \Rightarrow a$.

Figure 9: Examples of two outlier trees. These outlier trees coincide with the events that (a) Bejing–HongKong highway was under traffic control for constructing viaducts in the midnight of May 5th, 2009; (b) the Olympic sports center was free of charge to visit at August 7th, 2009.

A major reason for the failure of PCA is that the first known outlier (event *1*) occurred in the *off-peak hour* of most links, and the second known outlier (event *2*) happened in the *peak hour* of most links – in other words, they are captured by the smallest principle components (*PC*s) and the largest *PC*s respectively. The difficulty of choosing appropriate *PC*s makes it hard to use PCA to detect both of these two traffic events.

5.4 Evaluations on Frequent Subtrees

In this experiment, we control the value of support threshold ϵ, and report its effects on discovering frequent outlier subtrees in terms of the number of subtrees passing through ϵ and their maximum support. We test the properties of frequent subtrees on five sets of support threshold: $\epsilon \in \{0.01, 0.05, 0.1, 0.15, 0.2\}$. We ignore values of ϵ higher than 0.2, since the total number of frequent subtrees is already considerably small when $\epsilon = 0.2$ (as shown in Figure 11(a)). However, as long as the number of subtrees is higher than zero, the `freqentSubtree` algorithm can still identify the most frequent subtree that has the highest support (as shown in Figure 11(b) on $\epsilon = 0.15$). This observation illustrates the *completeness* of the frequent subtrees generated by the `freqentSubtree` algorithm.

Recall that regions indicated by the most frequent (i.e. with highest support) subtrees are the ones that have strategic design drawbacks from the perspective of urban road

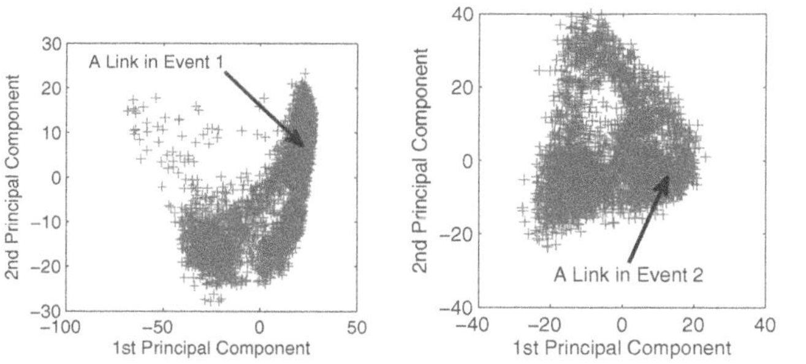

(a) Coordinate formed by top two principle components in time frames of known event 1. (b) Coordinate formed by top two principle components in time frames of known event 2.

Figure 10: Data points in terms of links in the coordinate formed by top two principle components from PCA. The two known abnormal events detected by our model can not be identified by PCA approaches.

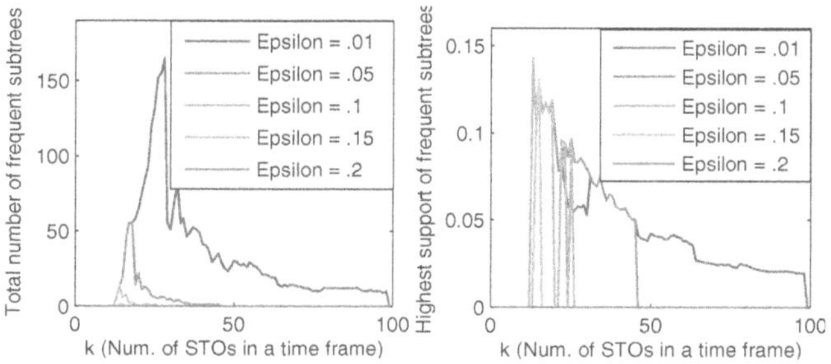

(a) (b)

Figure 11: Total number of frequent subtrees and the highest support among them under different settings of k and support threshold ϵ. The number of discovered trees becomes significantly small when the support threshold is high (e.g. $\epsilon = 0.2$ in subfigure (a)). However, as long as the number of subtrees is higher than zero, the frequent subtrees that have the highest support can still be identified by our algorithms (e.g. $\epsilon = 0.15$ in subfigure (b)).

network planning. For example, when $k = 7$, the top two frequent subtrees fall in the suburb of "Wangjing" and "Laoshan" respectively, shown in Figure 12. These subtrees indicate that both of the two suburbs are much more frequently overloaded with vehicles than other suburbs, and are in need of public transportation systems (e.g. subways) passing through them to reduce the need of commutations on ground. Such indications coincide with the future subway construction plan[4] of Beijing city: (*i*) New subway lines of Line 14 and Line 15 will be launched to travel through the suburb of "Wangjing" in year 2011 and 2013 respectively; (*ii*) Subway Line 10 (second construction stage) to be put into use by year 2012 will be centered at the suburb of "Laoshan".

These relationships between the official subway construction plans and our frequent subtrees validate the correctness of the `frequentSubtree` algorithm, and demonstrate the capability of our model in detecting design flaws in existing road networks.

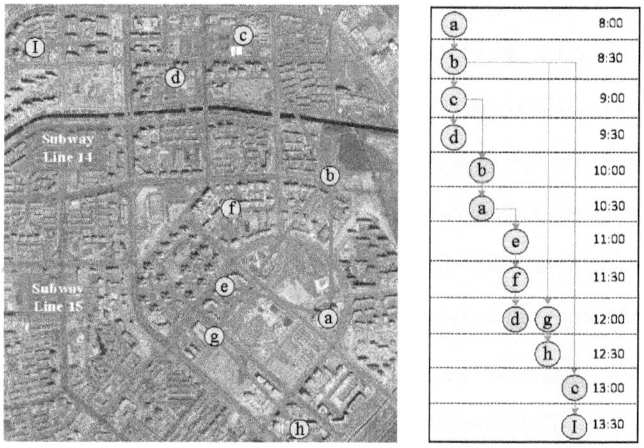

(a) The most frequent subtree with support 12.5% covering the suburb of "Wangjing". Note that there are several loops appearing in this tree, which indicates circular causalities among certain regions.

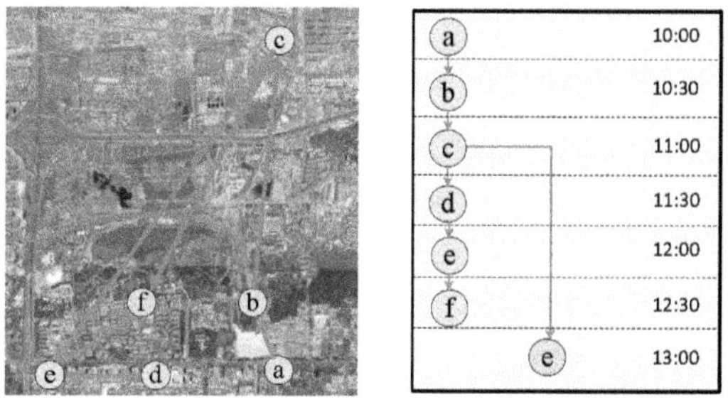

(b) The second most frequent subtree with support 11.3% covering the suburb of "Laoshan".

Figure 12: Top two frequent substrees and suburbs they cover ("Wangjing" and "Laoshan") when $k = 7$. These two subtrees suggest that there are potential design flaws in the current road networks spanning the two suburbs. These results coincide with (and hence are validated by) future construction plan of Beijing subways.

6. CONCLUSIONS AND FUTURE WORK

In this paper we have studied the problem of detecting spatio-temporal outlier and their causal interactions from traffic data streams. We have proposed `STOTree`, an algorithm for discovering spatio-temporal outliers and causal relationships between them. While the worst-case time complexity of `STOTree` is quadratic (in the number of outliers in each time frame), empirical evidence strongly suggests that the complexity is closer to linear time.

We have also proposed a `frequentSubtree` algorithm which can be used to reveal recurrent anomalies in the road network. Based on the `STOTree` and `frequentSubtree` algorithm we were able to identify real and valid instances of anomalies in Beijing traffic data. This suggests that our approach has the potential of contributing to a new data driven approach towards road traffic analysis.

In future our plan is to apply and extend the use of our algorithms in the domain of internet traffics etc.

[4]`http://en.wikipedia.org/wiki/Beijing_Subway`

7. REFERENCES

[1] D. Brauckhoff, K. Salamatian, and M. May. Applying PCA for traffic anomaly detection: Problems and solutions. In *Proceedings of the 28th IEEE International Conference on Computer Communications (INFOCOM'09)*, pages 2866–2870, 2009.

[2] Y. Bu, L. Chen, A. Fu, and D. Liu. Efficient anomaly monitoring over moving object trajectory streams. In *Proceedings of the 15th SIGKDD Conference on Knowledge Discovery and Data Mining (KDD'09)*, pages 159–168, 2009.

[3] H. Cao, D. Cheung, and N. Mamoulis. Discovering partial periodic patterns in discrete data sequences. *Advances in Knowledge Discovery and Data Mining (PAKDD 2004)*, pages 653–658, 2004.

[4] H. Cao, N. Mamoulis, and D. Cheung. Discovery of periodic patterns in spatiotemporal sequences. *Knowledge and Data Engineering, IEEE Transactions on*, 19(4):453–467.

[5] H. Cao, N. Mamoulis, and D. Cheung. Mining frequent spatio-temporal sequential patterns. In *Proceedings of the 5th IEEE International Conference on Data Mining (ICDM'05)*, pages 82–89, 2005.

[6] F. Chen, C.-T. Lu, and A. P. Boedihardjo. Gls-sod: a generalized local statistical approach for spatial outlier detection. In *Proceedings of the 16th ACM SIGKDD international conference on Knowledge discovery and data mining (KDD'10)*, pages 1069–1078, 2010.

[7] L. Chen, M. Ozsu, and V. Oria. Robust and fast similarity search for moving object trajectories. In *Proceedings of the 24th ACM SIGMOD International Conference on Management of Data (SIGMOD'05)*, pages 491–502, 2005.

[8] M. Das and S. Parthasarathy. Anomaly detection and spatio-temporal analysis of global climate system. In *Proc. of the Third International Workshop on Knowledge Discovery from Sensor Data*, pages 142–150, 2009.

[9] M. Elfeky, W. Aref, and A. Elmagarmid. Periodicity detection in time series databases. *IEEE Transactions on Knowledge and Data Engineering*, pages 875–887, 2005.

[10] M. Elfeky, W. Aref, and A. Elmagarmid. WARP: time warping for periodicity detection. In *Fifth IEEE International Conference on Data Mining (ICDM'05)*, pages 8–17, 2005.

[11] R. Estkowski. No Steiner point subdivision simplification is NP-Complete. In *Proceedings of the 10th Canadian Conference on Computational Geometry*, pages 11–20, 1998.

[12] S. Hirose, K. Yamanishi, T. Nakata, and R. Fujimaki. Network anomaly detection based on eigen equation compression. In *Proceedings of the 15th SIGKDD Conference on Knowledge Discovery and Data Mining (KDD'09)*, pages 1185–1194, 2009.

[13] A. Lakhina, M. Crovella, and C. Diot. Diagnosing network-wide traffic anomalies. In *Proceedings of the ACM SIGCOMM Conference on Applications, Technologies, Architectures, and Protocols for Computer Communication (SIGCOMM'04)*, pages 219–230, 2004.

[14] J. Lee, J. Han, and X. Li. Trajectory outlier detection: A partition-and-detect framework. In *Proceedings of the 24th International Conference on Data Engineering (ICDE'08)*, pages 140–149, 2008.

[15] J. Lee, J. Han, and K. Whang. Trajectory clustering: a partition-and-group framework. In *Proceedings of the 26th ACM SIGMOD International Conference on Management of Data (SIGMOD'07)*, pages 593–604, 2007.

[16] Z. Li, B. Ding, J. Han, R. Kays, and P. Nye. Mining periodic behaviors for moving objects. In *Proceedings of the 16th ACM SIGKDD international conference on Knowledge discovery and data mining (KDD'10)*, pages 1099–1108, 2010.

[17] M. Lippi, M. Bertini, and P. Frasconi. Collective Traffic Forecasting. *Proceedings of the European Conference on Machine Learning and Principles and Practice of Knowledge Discovery in Databases (ECML PKDD 2010)*, pages 259–273, 2010.

[18] A. C. Lozano, H. Li, A. Niculescu-Mizil, Y. Liu, C. Perlich, J. Hosking, and N. Abe. Spatial-temporal causal modeling for climate change attribution. In *Proceedings of the 15th SIGKDD Conference on Knowledge Discovery and Data Mining (KDD'09)*, pages 587–596, 2009.

[19] N. Pelekis, I. Kopanakis, C. Panagiotakis, and Y. Theodoridis. Unsupervised Trajectory Sampling. *Proceedings of the European Conference on Machine Learning and Principles and Practice of Knowledge Discovery in Databases (ECML PKDD 2010)*, pages 17–33, 2010.

[20] H. Ringberg, A. Soule, J. Rexford, and C. Diot. Sensitivity of PCA for traffic anomaly detection. In *Proceedings of the 2007 ACM SIGMETRICS International Conference on Measurement and Modeling of Computer Systems (SIGMETRICS'07)*, pages 109–120, 2007.

[21] A. Rosenfeld. Connectivity in digital pictures. *Journal of the ACM (JACM)*, 17(1):160, 1970.

[22] P. Sun and S. Chawla. On local spatial outliers. In *Proceedings of the Fourth IEEE International Conference on Data Mining (ICDM'04)*, pages 209–216, 2004.

[23] E. Wu, W. Liu, and S. Chawla. Spatio-temporal outlier detection in precipitation data. *Knowledge Discovery from Sensor Data*, pages 115–133, 2010.

[24] J. Yuan, Y. Zheng, X. Xie, and G. Sun. Driving with knowledge from the physical world. In *Proceedings of the 17th ACM SIGKDD Conference on Knowledge Discovery and Data Mining (KDD'11)*, 2011.

[25] J. Yuan, Y. Zheng, C. Zhang, W. Xie, X. Xie, G. Sun, and Y. Huang. T-drive: Driving directions based on taxi trajectories. In *Proceedings of the 18th ACM SIGSPATIAL International Conference on Advances in Geographic Information Systems (ACM SIGSPATIAL GIS 2010)*, 2010.

[26] Y. Zhang, Z. Ge, A. Greenberg, and M. Roughan. Network anomography. In *Proceedings of the 5th ACM SIGCOMM conference on Internet Measurement*, pages 30–42, 2005.

Display Advertising Impact: Search Lift and Social Influence

Panagiotis Papadimitriou
Stanford University
Stanford, CA, USA
papadimitriou@stanford.edu

Hector Garcia-Molina
Stanford University
Stanford, CA, USA
hector@cs.stanford.edu

Prabhakar Krishnamurthy
Yahoo! Labs
Santa Clara, CA, USA
pkmurthy@yahoo-inc.com

Randall A. Lewis
Yahoo! Research
Santa Clara, CA, USA
ralewis@yahoo-inc.com

David H. Reiley
Yahoo! Research
Santa Clara, CA, USA
reiley@yahoo-inc.com

ABSTRACT

We study the impact of display advertising on user search behavior using a field experiment. In such an experiment, the treatment group users are exposed to some display advertising campaign, while the control group users are not. During the campaign and the post-campaign period we monitor the user search queries and we label them as relevant or irrelevant to the campaign using techniques that leverage the bipartite query-URL click graph. Our results indicate that users who are exposed to the advertising campaign submit 5% to 25% more queries that are relevant to it compared to the unexposed users.

Using the social graph of the experiment users, we also explore how users are affected by their friends who are exposed to ads. Our results indicate that a user with exposed friends is more likely to submit queries relevant to the campaign, as compared to a user without exposed friends. The result is surprising given that the display advertising campaign that we study does not include any incentive for social action, e.g., discount for recommending friends.

Categories and Subject Descriptors

H.2.8 [**Database Management**]: Database Applications—*Data Mining*; G.3 [**Mathematics of Computing**]: Probability and Statistics—*Experimental Design*

General Terms

Experimentation, Measurement

Keywords

advertising impact, ad effectivenes, display ads, search lift, social influence, field experiment

KDD'11, August 21–24, 2011, San Diego, California, USA.

1. INTRODUCTION

Display advertising - showing graphical, often interactive, advertisements (ads) on regular web pages - is approximately a $9 billion business in US [17]. In the simplest form of display advertising an *advertiser* purchases *ad impressions* on a *publisher*'s web page. An ad impression occurs each time a *user* loads the publisher's web page and sees the advertiser's ad as part of the page. To assess the success of display advertising campaigns, advertisers need metrics to estimate the user response. One such metric is the *search lift*, i.e., the ratio of the proportions of search queries related to a campaign submitted by users who were *exposed* as opposed to users who were not exposed to the campaign ads. Apart from direct user response, advertisers also expect their campaigns to impact users through *social influence*. That is, a user who is exposed to the campaign may make other users who were not directly exposed interested in the advertised products, e.g., through word-of-mouth spreading of the ad message. Thus, to get a full picture one needs to measure the response of exposed users as well as the response of friends of the exposed users.

Without reliable estimates of the display advertising impact, it is hard to assess the value of display advertising and set fair prices for both advertisers and publishers (web page owners). For example, if the advertisers over-estimate the possible social influence of their campaigns, they may purchase overpriced ad impressions and lose money. On the contrary, if the advertisers under-estimate the impact of display advertising, then the publishers may lose money by selling under-priced ad impressions. Taking into account the impact on friends also helps advertisers assess the value of an ad impression on a per user basis. For example, if 1 out of 10 friends of an exposed user responds to a display advertising campaign, a single ad impression is expected to have the same impact as an impression to two users without friends.

The key challenge for evaluating the influence of an ad campaign is in linking an exposed user to the desired actions of that or other users. For example, say Alice is exposed to an ad for the online retailer Zappos.com offering a discount on Nike shoes. The ad is displayed while Alice is browsing a Yahoo.com site. After seeing the ad, Alice communicates with Bob say via email, and then Bob performs an action related to the campaign. Ideally, we would like Bob to purchase Nike shoes at Zappos, but having Bob buy anything else at Zappos would be good, or having Bob buy Nike shoes elsewhere would also be good. The problem is that Bob's purchase will probably be made at a site unrelated to the Yahoo! site that displayed the ad, so it is very hard to connect Bob's purchase with

Alice's identity in order to "credit" the ad displayed to Alice for influencing the purchase.

For these reasons, it is very hard to use a traditional metric like *purchase lift*, which measures the increase in actual product purchases due to a campaign. Another traditional metric is the click-through rate (CTR) of clickable ads. In this case, the desired action is that a user clicks on the URL presented in the ad. Here again, it is very difficult to connect a click through by Bob to the original ad seen by Alice. Bob is unlikely to see the ad for Nike shoes at Zappos even if he logged on to a Yahoo! site.

For search lift it is possible, though still challenging, to connect Alice's ad impression with Bob's submission of a search query related to Nike or Zappos. To make the connections, Alice and Bob's actions must be performed on systems that have consistent user identities. For instance, we must know that the user submitting the query related to the ad is the same user who communicates via email with Alice, who in turn is the user who saw the ad in the first place. Fortunately, for our work we are able to use "traces" of displayed ads, submitted search queries, and user relationships with consistent user identities, which makes the evaluation of search lift feasible. Of course, our results will be "conservative", in the sense that Alice may influence other users that we do not know about.

As we will discuss, another challenge is the actual definition of search lift due to social influence. In particular, Bob may have several friends or connections. Some of the friends, like Alice, may have been exposed to an ad from the campaign, and others may not have. If Bob has 4 friends, two which have seen the ad, how do we account for influence? Is this case the same as if Bob has 4 exposed friends out of a total of 8? And how long after Alice saw an ad, do we credit that ad for actions taken by Bob? We address such questions as we develop our evaluation metrics.

Previous works have studied the impact of display advertising on exposed users [12] and independently studied influence (not related to ads) in social networks [2]. To the best of our knowledge our work is the first study of social influence effects of display advertising. There are also several works (e.g., [4]) that study social influence for viral marketing. However in most of these works social influence is the result of some explicit and observable social action, e.g., sending a movie suggestion to 5 friends. In our case the social influence is implicit and, consequently, it is sparse and harder to observe. Despite of the sparsity, such a study is possible nowadays because of the large amount of data that is available to advertising networks.

In this paper we study search lift and social influence in display advertising using a controlled experiment. In such an experiment, real users that visit a publisher's web site are randomly partitioned into a group that is exposed to an ad campaign (treatment group) and a group that is not exposed (control group), and we compare the search behavior of users in the two groups. Prior to measuring search lift, we describe how to determine the queries related to a given advertising campaign. Our methods leverage user clicks in the search results and they yield queries that are relevant to different aspects of the campaign, so that we can measure different aspects of the campaign impact. In our social influence study we compare the search behavior of users in the control group with a varying number of friends in the treatment group. Our results show that the more user friends that are exposed to ads, the more likely the user is to submit queries related to the ad.

The rest of the paper is organized as follows: in Section 2 we present some notation. In Section 3 we present our approach to estimating the search lift in the context of a field experiment. In Section 4 we present our approach to estimating the social influence in the context of a field experiment. In Section 5 we show how to determine which queries are related to a given advertising campaign. In Section 6 we present the experimental results, in Section 7 we present the related work and we conclude in Section 8.

2. NOTATION

A display advertisement (ad) a is typically a static or an interactive image that conveys some advertiser message.

An ad *impression* $V(u, a, w, t)$ is the event that the *user* u views the ad a as part of the web page w at time t.

A *search event* $S(u, q, t)$ denotes that user u submits query q to a search engine at time t.

A *display advertising campaign* is defined as $D = (A, U, W, P)$: a set of ads A, a set of targeted users U, a set of serving web pages W and a campaign period P. Sets U, W and the period P reflect the advertiser's preferences with respect to the impressions of the campaign ads. For example, the advertiser's preferences for the "buy Nike shoes at Zappos" campaign with $A = \{a\}$ can be:

- U: set of all users located in US;
- W: set of web pages under shopping.yahoo.com domain; and
- P: hours 9am-5pm during the days Dec 13 through Dec 17.

Given a campaign D an ad impression $V(u, a, w, t)$ may occur when a user $u \in U$ visits a web page $w \in W$ at time $t \in P$.

3. SEARCH LIFT

In this section we present our approach to the calculation of search lift as the result of a display advertising campaign. In Section 3.1 we briefly discuss the setup of a field experiment. In Section 3.2 we discuss what the queries of interest are for users that participate in the field experiment. Then, we define the *search lift* in Section 3.3 and we discuss some variations in Section 3.4.

3.1 Field experiment

We study the impact of a campaign D on users using a *field experiment*. In such an experiment we partition the targeted users of the campaign U into a *control* group C and a *treatment* group T and we substitute campaign D with the following two campaigns:

- the treatment campaign $D_T = (A, T, W, P)$ that we obtain from D by replacing the targeted users U with T; and
- the control campaign $D_C = (A_C, C, W, P)$ that we obtain from D by replacing the targeted U with C and the campaign ads A with A_C. Each ad $a \in A_C$ should convey no advertiser message, so that it has negligible impact on the users who view it. For example, such an ad on a shopping.yahoo.com web page could have a message about the web page itself.

Then we measure the impact of ads A by comparing the search behaviors of users in the control group C as opposed to users in the treatment group T.

Note that the exposure to display ads is only one of the factors that affect a user's search behavior. Other factors may include the web pages the user browses, the email messages he reads or even the discussions he has with his friends. However, the impact of such factors should be identical (in expectation) on the users of the two groups, because the users are allocated to the control and the treatment group at random. The only difference between the users of the two groups is the exogenous exposure to different display ads and this difference may have an impact on the users' search behaviors.

3.2 Susceptible Queries

We focus on user queries that are submitted within some period δ after an ad impression. We refer to the parameter δ as the *influence period* and to the queries the are submitted in the time interval $(t, t+\delta]$ after an ad impression $V(u, a, w, t)$ as the *susceptible queries*.

The influence period δ captures the fact that the impact of an ad impression diminishes as time elapses. In our experiments we present results for different values of δ that range from 10 minutes up to 2 weeks.

Given the influence period δ and the ad impressions of a user u we define the boolean function:

$$\text{susc}\left(S(u,q,t),\delta,D\right)=\begin{cases} true & \exists t',a,w: a\in A\wedge \\ & w\in W\wedge V(u,a,w,t')\wedge \\ & t\in(t',t'+\delta] \\ false & \text{otherwise.}\end{cases} \tag{1}$$

The query q is susceptible if there is at least one ad impression $V(u, a, w, t')$ such that the query q is submitted within time δ after the time t'.

Given the susc function we let

$$B(u,\delta,D)=\{q: S(u,q,t)\wedge \text{susc}\left(S(u,q,t),\delta,D\right)\} \tag{2}$$

denote the *bag*[1] containing all of u's susceptible queries. We denote the bag of queries submitted by any C user as $B(C, \delta, D) = \bigcup_{u\in C} B(u, \delta, D)$ and the bag of queries submitted by any T user as $B(T, \delta, D)$.

Note that the definition of susceptible queries is the same for both the treatment and the control group users. Although the control group users do not see ads from campaign D, we still use Eq. 2 to determine the influenced queries, so that we do not introduce any bias in the selection of queries for the two groups.

3.3 Search Lift Definition

We estimate the impact of a campaign D by comparing the queries in the bag $B(C, \delta, D)$ with the queries in the bag $B(T, \delta, D)$. To perform such a comparison we introduce the notion of query relevance to a given advertising campaign. Then we extend the relevance notion to bags of queries and we finally use this notion to compare the two bags.

For each query q the value of function $\text{rel}(q, D) \in [0, 1]$ shows the relevance of q to the campaign D. If the query is irrelevant then $\text{rel}(q, D) = 0$. To illustrate, in the example of the "buy Nike shoes at Zappos" campaign, the query "zappos nike shoes" may have relevance score 1, the query "shoes" may have relevance 0.5 and the query "news" may have relevance 0. Later in Section 5 we present an algorithm for calculating the values of the rel function.

Using the rel function as a parameter we define the *effective proportion* of a query bag B that is relevant to the campaign D as:

$$\text{eff}\left(B,D;\text{rel}\right)=\frac{\sum_{q\in B}\text{rel}\left(q,D\right)}{|B|}. \tag{3}$$

If all of the B queries are relevant to D, then $\text{eff}(B, D; rel) = 1$. If half of the B queries are relevant to D then $\text{eff}(B, D; rel) = 0.5$.

Finally, we compare the relevance of queries submitted by C and T users using the *search lift* metric that is defined as follows:

$$\text{lift}\left(C,T,\delta,D;\text{rel}\right)=\frac{\text{eff}\left(B(T,\delta,D),D;\text{rel}\right)}{\text{eff}\left(B(C,\delta,D),D;\text{rel}\right)}. \tag{4}$$

[1] A *bag* or *multiset* is an object collection whose members need not be distinct (unlike a set, whose members are distinct).

In other words, the search lift is the ratio of the proportion of the campaign related queries submitted by T users to the proportion of campaign related queries submitted by C users. The lift is expected to be greater than 1, since the T users are expected to submit more queries relevant to the campaign than the C users.

To draw any statistically significant conclusions about the search lift on real data, it is critical to estimate reliable confidence intervals. We elaborate on this issue in Section 6.3.1 of the experiments.

3.4 Impact of Different Campaign Aspects

Campaign ads may convey more than one message to the users. For example, most retail display advertisements include a certain *brand* product or a series of brand products that are available from some *retailer*. Examples of such ads are "buy Nike shoes at Zappos" or "buy Seagate hard drive at Newegg." The advertiser in such cases can be either the brand company or the retailer company or both. In case of the first ad, three possible user searches after an ad view are the following: "nike shoes zappos" or "nike shoes" or "zappos". Note that the second query implies some user intent that will not probably benefit the retailer, while the last query implies some intent that will not probably benefit the brand. Measuring campaign impact with respect to either of the parties is important, since it allows a fair allocation of the campaign cost or it can provide the advertiser with useful insight to improve the campaign. For example, if the advertiser is Zappos and the advertising campaign seems to raise interest mostly in Nike shoes rather than the Zappos itself, then Zappos can redesign the ads of the campaign to decrease the emphasis on Nike shoes.

Since search queries provide rich information about the user intent, search lift can be used to estimate the impact of different aspects of a campaign. Without loss of generality, in this paper we focus on retail advertising. Thus, we define three different types of search lift using different rel function definitions to measure the impact of the different aspects of a campaign:

- *Brand lift* measures the search lift between groups C and T with respect to queries that are relevant to the campaign brand, e.g., Nike or Seagate. In this case rel quantifies how relevant the query is to the brand.
- *Retailer lift* measures the search lift between groups C and T with respect to queries that are relevant to the campaign retailer, e.g., Zappos or Newegg. Similarly, the rel function quantifies how relevant the query is to the retailer.
- *Total lift* measures the search lift between groups C and T with respect to queries that are relevant either to the campaign brand or the campaign retailer. Here the rel function quantifies how relevant the query is to the either the brand or the retailer.

Note that it is hard to define analogous types for other display advertising impact metrics such as the CTR or purchase lift. CTR measures only views of the ad landing page and ignores views of the brand web site or views of retailer pages beyond the landing page. Moreover, metrics like the purchase lift would require monitoring user purchases not only in the campaign retailer store, but also in all retailer stores that carry products of the advertised brand. The cost of such monitoring would be high.

4. SOCIAL INFLUENCE

We study the impact of display advertising taking into account that users are part of a social network. We represent the social network with an undirected graph $G = (U, E)$. Each node $u \in U$ represents a user and each edge $e = (u, u')$ represents that users u and u' are friends. Our goal is to study how user search queries

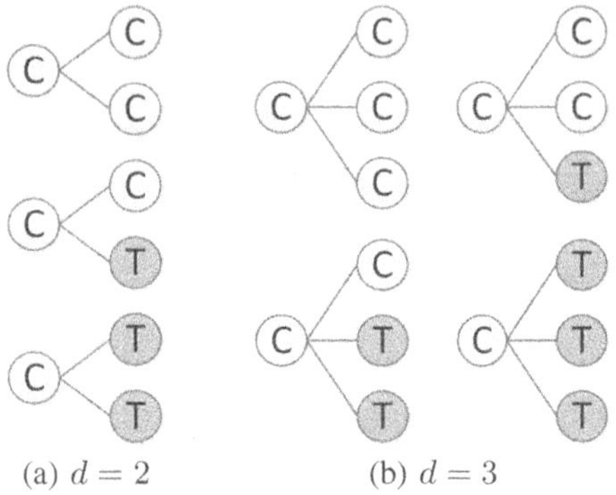

Figure 1: Control user subgroups

vary depending on the number of friends that have seen ads from campaign D. The motivation for this study is that users may convey advertisement messages to their friends. For example, say that Alice sees ads about Zappos and she thinks of buying a pair of shoes from the online store. Alice may ask the opinion of her friend Bob about the potential purchase and Bob will end up searching online for Zappos and browsing the online catalog to find items of interest.

To quantify the influence by friends exposed to ads we define the *social search lift* similarly to the search lift in Section 4.2. Prior to this definition we redefine the notion of susceptible queries in the context of social influence in Section 4.1

4.1 Susceptible Queries under Social Influence

In case of social influence, we focus on the queries of user u after his friends have been exposed to ads and within some influence period δ. Thus, if u' is a friend of u and there is an ad impression $V(u', a, w, t)$, then we refer to the queries of u during the time interval $(t, t+\delta]$ as the *susceptible queries under social influence* or simply as the susceptible queries. Similarly to Eq. 1, we define a boolean function that determines whether a query is susceptible:

$$\text{susc}_s\left(S(u,q,t),\delta,D,G\right) = \begin{cases} true & \exists t', a, w, u' : a \in A \wedge \\ & w \in W \wedge \\ & u' \in U \wedge (u,u') \in E \wedge \\ & V(u',a,w,t') \wedge \\ & t \in (t', t'+\delta] \\ false & \text{otherwise} \end{cases} \tag{5}$$

The subscript in susc_s denotes that this definition is used in the context of social influence.

Thus, in case of social influence the bag that contains all of the susceptible queries of user u is defined as:

$$B_s(u,\delta,D,G) = \{q : S(u,q,t) \wedge \text{susc}_s\left(S(u,q,t),\delta,D,G\right)\} \tag{6}$$

similarly to Eq. 2 (See Section 4.3 for a discussion of why chose these particular definitions).

4.2 Social Search Lift

In the case of social search lift we focus on users of the control group and divide them into subgroups based on their total number of friends and the number of friends that belong to the treatment group. We denote with $C(d_T/d)$ the set of users who have d_T friends in the treatment group out of a total of d friends:

$$C(d_T/d) = \{u \in C : d_T = |\{(u,u') \in E \wedge u' \in T\}|, \quad d = |\{(u,u') \in E\}|\} \tag{7}$$

For example, in Figure 1(a) we show three different control group users (the users on the left of each connected triple) that have two friends. The user on top belongs to $C(0/2)$, because he has two friends belonging to the control group. The user in the middle belongs to the $C(1/2)$ group, because he has one friend in the control and one in the treatment group. Finally, the user at the bottom belongs to $C(2/2)$, because both of his friends belong to the treatment group. Similarly, in Figure 1(b) we present examples of the user subgroups with users that have 3 friends in total.

As we argue in the Section 4.3, in this setting it is interesting to study user searches among groups with the same total of d friends, but a varying number d_T of treatment friends. In particular, we compare the queries of groups with $d_T > 0$ with the queries of users with $d_T = 0$. The social search lift is defined as follows:

$$\text{lift}_s\left(C(d_T/d), C(0,d), \delta, D; \text{rel}\right) = \frac{\text{eff}\left(B_s(C(d_T/d),.), D; \text{rel}\right)}{\text{eff}\left(B_s(C(0/d),.), D; \text{rel}\right)}, \tag{8}$$

where $B_s(C(d_T/d),.) = B_s(C(d_T/d),\delta,D,G)$ is the bag that contains the susceptible queries of all users in the $C(d_T/d)$ group.

4.3 Discussion

In this section we discuss our choices for the definition of the social search lift and discuss the reasoning behind them.

Why do we compare users with the same number of friends? Considering users with the same number of friends d is important to avoid introducing any bias in the selection of groups that we compare. For example, if we compare users with no friends in T versus users that have at least one friend in T, then we end up comparing users that may have zero friends total versus users with at least one friend. Users in such groups are different, and if we observe different search behavior, we cannot attribute these differences only to advertising.

Why are susceptible queries under social influence defined as in Eq. 5? What are the shortcomings of alternative options? We use the following examples to illustrate the alternatives and discuss their shortcomings.

EXAMPLE 1. *Say that D is a campaign with a two-day period $P = \{Sunday, Monday\}$, and we wish to calculate the social search lift* lift_s *between $C(0/1) = \{Alice\}$ and $C(1/1) = \{Bob\}$ with $\delta = 1$ day. Alice's only friend X is in the control group, while Bob's only friend Y is in the treatment group. Say that Y sees a treatment ad on Monday morning and, consequently, Bob's Monday queries are considered susceptible. Say also that X sees a control ad Monday morning at the same time as Y. Which of Alice's queries should we consider susceptible? Those that we designate as susceptible will be compared with Bob's susceptible queries to obtain the* lift_s*. Since Alice's friend does not see any treatment ads that may have an impact on her, one option would be to consider all of Alice's queries during P as suceptible. However, this way will compare Bob's Monday queries with Alice's Sunday and Monday queries. The differences between such bags cannot be attributed solely to D, because Sunday queries are different from Monday queries. For instance, the Sunday queries may be more shopping related compared to the Monday queries. So, with such a definition we would get a biased estimate of the social influence. However, if we use the definition of Eq. 5, we will only consider Alice's Monday queries as susceptible, since they follow X's control ad impression. That comparison will reflect the impact of D.*

Note that in a real scenario Alice's and Bob's friends do not see ads exactly at the same time. However, this example illustrates the comparison we will make in our analysis knowing that, in expectation, ad delivery patterns should be statistically identical for randomly assigned control and treatment groups.

In [15] we present similar examples that justify our definitions for users with friends in both the treatment and the control group.

5. QUERY RELEVANCE FUNCTION

Calculating search lift requires defining the relevance function rel. Different definitions of this function are required to measure the impact of different aspects of a campaign. There are different ways to define such a function, and in our preliminary experiments we tried some alternative approaches that all yielded similar results. In the following subsections we present a method that leverages user query logs and uses the the random walk algorithm ARW that was introduced by Fuxman et al. [6] for keyword generation in sponsored search. We picked this method because it requires minimum domain specific knowledge for the campaign that we study.

ARW Algorithm. The method uses the *click graph* $G_c(Q, W, E_c)$ which is a bipartite graph whose vertexes are user queries Q and web URLs W. The click graph has an edge (q, w) if there is at least one user who submitted query q and clicked URL w in the search results. The weight $\beta(q, w)$ of every edge is equal to the total number of clicks to w by the users that submitted q.

In addition to the bipartite click graph G_c, a seed of URLs S is required as input to the ARW algorithm. In our case, these URLs must be relevant to the search lift type that we wish to calculate. For example, in our case measuring retailer lift, the seed set may consist of all URLs in the retailer's online domain. The algorithm's output is a vector containing the probability that each query is relevant to the seed set S. We consider the value of $\text{rel}\,(q, D)$ as equal to the corresponding output probability for the query node q.

At a high level, $\text{rel}\,(q, D)$ is the probability that a random walker that starts from q in the click graph will end up at a URL in S, assuming that the S URLs are absorbing states in the walk. To prevent long walks, the algorithm assumes that there is a transition probability α that the random walker jumps to an absorbing *null* node from any node in the graph. Finally, the algorithm uses a threshold parameter γ to set all the node probabilities to zero if they are below γ.

Binarization. In Section 6.3.1 we show how we can obtain confidence intervals for the lift, assuming that the rel function is binary. To obtain a binary relevance function $\text{rel}_\theta(q, D) \in \{0, 1\}$ we can use a relevance threshold θ as follows:

$$\text{rel}_\theta(q, D) = \begin{cases} 1, & \text{if rel}\,(q, D) \geq \theta \\ 0, & \text{otherwise.} \end{cases} \tag{9}$$

6. EXPERIMENTS

In this section we evaluate the impact of display ads on real users using the methodology we have presented so far. The goals of the experiments are the following:

- To illustrate the queries that are relevant to a campaign as returned by the algorithm of Section 5,
- To quantify the search lift between the control and the treatment group,
- To understand how the search lift decreases as the time δ from the ad impressions increases, and
- To quantify the social search lift between users in the control group that have different numbers of friends in the treatment group.

We address these goals in Sections 6.2 to 6.4, after we present the experimental setup in Section 6.1.

6.1 Experimental Setup

6.1.1 *Field Experiment*

Our data comes from a field experiment with two display advertising campaigns D_1 and D_2 that ran on Yahoo! web pages. We withhold the names of the advertiser, brands, and products in compliance with contractual agreements. The unnamed advertiser in both campaigns is the same popular department store chain; we refer to it as the Retailer. Campaign D_1 advertises clothes and shoes from a luxury brand Brand1 and campaign D_2 advertises clothes and shoes from a popular designer brand Brand2. Both campaigns' advertisements look similar and feature models wearing the advertised clothes along with a message such as "Buy Brand1 clothes at the Retailer" occupying one quadrant of the ad. Campaign D_1 has 12 distinct ads and campaign D_2 has 4 distinct ads. The campaign period P_1 for D_1 was a week of Spring in 2010, and the campaign period P_2 for D_2 was the following week. The sets of serving pages, W_1 and W_2, for both campaigns were identical and they and spanned the Yahoo! network, with a supermajority of the impressions being shown on Yahoo! Mail. Finally, user sets U_1 and U_2 targeted by the ads were also identical and they composed of the same 3 million users.

For each of the two campaigns, we created a control group campaign using *house ads* with a call to action to try one of Yahoo!'s products. The house ads and the retailer's ads were identical in other respects such ad size, position on page, a call-to-action message.

We divided the set of 3 million users into three subsets with 1 million users each: the control group C, the 1st treatment group $T1$, and the 2nd treatment group $T2$. The users in the control group C saw only the house ads in both of the campaigns. The users in the first treatment group $T1$ saw only the retailer ads in both of the campaigns. Finally, users in the second treatment group $T2$ saw the same number of ads as the other two groups, but this group's ads were split evenly between house ads and the retailer's in both campaigns. In the search lift experiments, we only focus on groups C and $T1$. In the social search lift experiments, we focus on the control group C and we study how the search behavior of C users is affected as the number of friends in the treatment groups $T1$ and $T2$ varies.

6.1.2 *User Logs and Social Graph*

For all of the 3 million targeted users we have 70,435,009 click-log records that span a period of 8 weeks, starting 3 weeks before the beginning of D_1 and ending 3 weeks after the end of campaign D_2. We refer to each of these 8 weeks as the 1st week, the 2nd week and so on. Campaign D_1 took place during the 4th week, and campaign D_2 took place during the 5th week. Each log record corresponds to one search event $S(u, q, t)$. We also have 62,042,992 impression-log records that span the two weeks of the campaigns

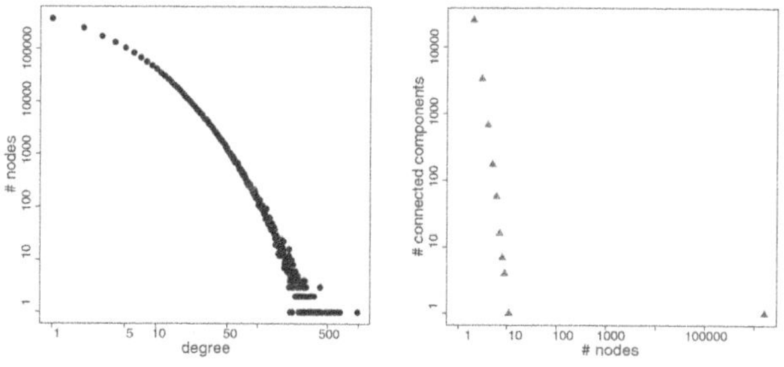

(a) Degree (b) Conn. Components

Figure 2: Social graph distributions.

D_1 and D_2. Each impression-log record corresponds to an ad-view event $V(u, a, w, t)$.

We constructed a social graph for the 3 million users based on explicit connections that users created via Yahoo!'s social applications such as:

- Messenger, which allows users to exchange Instant Messages with their friends;
- Pulse, which allows users to share their current status and view the status of their friends; and
- Digu, which allows users to post blogs, likes, videos, pictures, etc.

The graph also contains implicit connections between pairs of users that have exchanged email messages through Yahoo! Mail.

The constructed graph has 1,600,962 nodes with at least one connection and 6,694,245 edges in total. The degree distribution follows a power law distribution as shown in the double logarithmic plot in Figure 2(a). The median degree in the graph is 4. The graph is not connected and has 29,793 connected components after removing the singleton nodes. In Figure 2(b) we present the distribution of nodes in these components. Note that despite the big number of components, there is a giant component that contains approximately 3/4 of the graph nodes.

Note that joining the ad impression logs, the query logs and the social graph is possible, because all 3 million users have Yahoo! accounts. If such a user is logged in at some Yahoo! property such as Yahoo! Mail, then a user identifier is passed to Yahoo! servers along with any request for a page from a Yahoo! property. This is a common practice for the web sites[2] with multiple properties and authenticated users. In this way we can record the queries and the ad impression of a particular user. We can also join these records with the social graph, since users participate in the Yahoo! social properties with their Yahoo! accounts.

6.1.3 *Implementation*

We implemented the ARW algorithm and function eff in Python. In the eff implementation, we first read the ad impression log and we maintain in memory the time intervals for every user when a susceptible query may occur. Then, we read the query log and keep counters for the relevant susceptible queries and all susceptible queries of every user group. The running time of our implementation was dominated by the time to read the log files. We ran our experiments on a Linux Server with Intel Xeon Quad Core with 16 GB RAM.

6.2 Relevant queries

We use the algorithm that we presented in Section 5 to determine the queries that are relevant to Brand1, Brand2 and the Retailer. The algorithm input consists of all of the click log records and a seed of relevant URLs for each of the two brands and the retailer. To create these seed for Brand1, we just selected all the URLs under the Brand1 domain. We selected the seeds for Brand2 and the Retailer in a similar fashion. After experimenting with several values, we set the transition probability to the null node $a = 0.01$ and the threshold $\gamma = 0.01$. A manual inspection of the relevance scores computed for the search queries showed that these parameter values provided the most informative results.

In Figure 3 we plot the histograms of query relevance scores with respect to Brand1 (Figure 3(a)), Brand2 (Figure 3(b)) and Retailer (Figure 3(c)). In all of the three figures we have omitted the count of queries with rel $(q, D) = 0$. In each plot the total area of the bars

[2]E.g., google.com, bing.com, aol.com

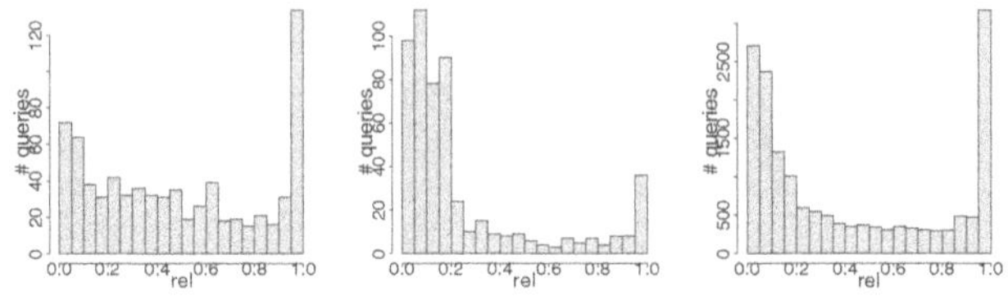

(a) Brand1 (b) Brand2 (c) Retailer

Figure 3: Relevance score histograms

shows the total number of queries that are relevant to the campaign, i.e., their relevance scores are greater than zero. There are 751 queries that are relevant to Brand1, 541 queries that are relevant to Brand2 and 16,549 queries that are relevant to Retailer.

Note that in all of the plots the number of queries that have relevance probability higher than 0.95 is high. These queries are mostly rare queries that appear once or twice in the click log and have clicks only to the brand or the retailer URLs. Most of the queries that have a relevance score higher that 0.3 usually include a URL from the retailer or the brand web site as the their top result.

In case of brands, the queries with relevance scores that are smaller than 0.2 refer to popular brand products that are carried by many online retailers such as amazon.com or macys.com. The users that search for these products first see the search listings for these retailers and rarely click on the listings for the brand web site. There are more such queries for Brand2, since Brand1 is a luxury brand and few retailers carry its products. In case of the retailer, the queries with relevance scores below 0.2 are not usually strongly related to the retailer. For example, some of these queries were related to products carried by many different stores, including the Retailer.

Based on these results we set the value of θ for the binary version of the relevance function that we introduced in Section 5. In particular we set $\theta = 0^+$ for the relevance functions of the two brands and $\theta = 0.2$ for the relevance function of the retailer. The relevance function for the total lift in either of the campaigns is the maximum of the two corresponding brand and retailer relevance function values. Although we use fixed θ values throughout the remainder of the paper, additional results in [15] show that our estimates are robust for a wide range of θ values.

6.3 Search Lift

We evaluate the search lift of the two campaigns using the relevance functions that we presented in Section 6.2. In Section 6.3.1 we present a formula for computing the confidence interval of the search lift. We use this formula throughout the experiments section. In Section 6.3.2 we compare the search behavior of the control and treatment in the pre-campaign weeks to confirm that the the two groups are similar. In Section 6.3.3 we evaluate the different types of lift for the two campaigns and present how the lift changes as the time δ increases. Throughout this section, we refer to group C as the control group and to group $T1$ as the treatment group.

6.3.1 *Confidence Intervals*

We defined the search lift in Eq. 4 as the ratio of the proportions eff $(B(T, \delta, D), D; \text{rel})$ and eff $(B(C, \delta, D), D; \text{rel})$. Search lift is defined similarly to the *relative risk* which is used in statistics and in mathematical epidemiology to assess the risk of an event (or of developing a disease) relative to some exposure. The advantage of such a definition is that we can use the approaches developed for the relative risk to obtain a confidence interval for the search lift.

In this paper we use the formula presented in Altman et al. [1], where they show that log(lift $(C, T, \delta, D; \text{rel})$) approximately follows a normal distribution. This formula requires that we use the binary relevance function rel_θ that we discussed in Section 5. If $n_T = |\{q : q \in B(T, \delta, D) \wedge \text{rel}_\theta(q, D) = 1\}|$ is the number of relevant queries in the treatment group bag and n_C is similarly the number of relevant queries in the control group bag, then the standard error of the lift logarithm is:

$$SE = \sqrt{\frac{1}{n_T} - \frac{1}{|B(T,\delta,D)|} + \frac{1}{n_C} - \frac{1}{|B(C,\delta,D)|}}.$$

Thus, the $100(1-\alpha)\%$ confidence interval for the lift is:

$$[e^{\log(\text{lift}(C,T,\delta,D)) - z^* SE}, e^{\log(\text{lift}(C,T,\delta,D)) + z^* SE}] =$$

$$[\text{lift}\,(C,T,\delta,D))e^{-z^* SE}, \text{lift}\,(C,T,\delta,D))e^{+z^* SE}], \qquad (10)$$

where z^* is the upper $(1-\alpha)/2$ critical value for the standard normal distribution. In the rest of the experiments, we use $\alpha = 0.05$ to obtain 95% confidence intervals.

6.3.2 Pre-campaign Searches

In this section we explore the search behavior of the control and the treatment group prior to the beginning of the ad campaigns. For this study we use the relevance function for the total search lift that we discussed in Section 6.2. Note that the presented proportions are calculated with respect to all queries, since during the pre-campaign period there are no susceptible queries (there are no ad impressions from D_1 and D_2).

In Figure 4 we present the percentage of relevant queries submitted by both the control and the treatment group during the two weeks before the beginning of the first campaign. The plot on the left focuses on queries that are relevant to the first campaign, i.e., queries relevant to Brand1 and the Retailer, while the plot on the right focuses on queries that are relevant to the second campaign, i.e., queries that are relevant to Brand2 and the Retailer. The red bars in the plots represent the control group and the blue bars represent the treatment group. The bars are indexed by the week (x-axis), and the height of each bar shows the percentage of queries that are relevant to the campaign. For example, the left-most red bar on the left plot shows that approximately 0.32% of the queries submitted during the 3rd week by control-group users were relevant to either Brand1 or the Retailer. In each bar we have plotted the 95% confidence interval.

Note that the percentages of the relevant queries submitted by both groups at the same week are very similar and the corresponding 95% confidence intervals significantly overlap. Difference-in-means t-tests fail to reject for each comparison, validating that the randomization of users into the treatment and control groups was successful. This fact shows that in the absence of an advertising campaign the search behavior of the two groups would be similar.

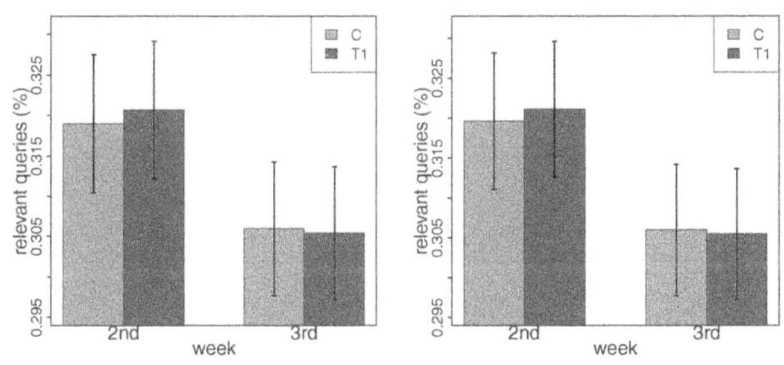

(a) Campaign D_1 (b) Campaign D_2

Figure 4: Pre-campaign searches (D_1 and D_2 took place in the 4th and 5th week, respectively).

6.3.3 Campaign Effect

In this section we study the search lift as a function of the influence time δ. Our study has two goals: (a) to help estimate the advertising impact by studying the actual values of the search lift and (b) to show the persistence of the advertising effects as the time from the ad impressions grows.

We calculated the search lift for campaigns D_1 and D_2 using the following values for the parameter δ: 1 hour, 12 hours, 1 day, 2 days, 3 days, 1 week and 2 weeks. To calculate the brand lift, the retailer lift and the total lift we used the binary relevance functions that we presented in Section 6.2. In Figure 5(a) we plot the total lift, in Figure 5(b) we plot the brand lift and in Figure 5(c) we plot the retailer lift. There are two lines in each plot, one for each campaign. The x-axis in each plot shows the value of δ. The y-axis shows the lift. The error bars in the plots show the 95% confidence intervals. For example, the right-most point in the solid line of the Figure 5(a) shows that for queries submitted within 14 days after a D_1 ad impression, the total lift is approximately 1.07, i.e., the users in the treatment group $T1$ submitted 7% more queries related to D_1 compared to the users in the control group C. In general, a point that is above the line lift $= 1$ indicates that the advertising campaign has a positive impact on the treatment group.

Let us focus first on the lifts of campaign D_2. Note that all of the three lift curves (total lift, brand lift and retailer lift) are decreasing. This trend was expected since the impact of the advertising campaign should diminish over time. Note also that all of the three curves are convex which means that the lift decrease becomes slower as δ increases. The total lift is as high as 1.25, if we focus on user queries within the first hour and remains above 1 with confidence 95% even whithin a week (7 days). The brand lift drops from 2.3 in the first hour to 1.3 in the first three days. After three days the lift is not greater than 1 with 95% confidence. Finally, the retailer lift drops from 1.12 in the first hour to 1.05 in the first week. In all three cases note that confidence intervals for small δ values are wide because for such values the number of examined queries is small.

Regarding campaign D_1, the results are similar to those for D_2, but there are some interesting differences. While the D_1 brand lift curve is decreasing and convex, similar to the D_2 curves, there is an uptick in the total lift and retailer lift curves at $\delta = 3$ days. This uptick is due to the fact that the retailer is the same in both campaigns, and there is an overlap of the D_1 post campaign period with the D_2 campaign period. Thus, the susceptible queries that correspond to D_1 ad impressions at the end of the 4th week contain retailer-related queries that are submitted after D_2 ad impressions at the beginning of the 5th week. In these plots, it is noteworthy that the uptick appears only in the total and the retailer lift curves, while the brand lift curve is smooth. This fact confirms that the lift breakdown into retailer and brand lift can successfully illustrate different aspects of the campaign impact.

To compare the two campaigns we can focus on $\delta = 2$ days where the overlap between the campaign influence periods is small. Note that the total lifts have similar values, while the D_1 retailer lift is slightly smaller and the Brand1 lift is higher than the Brand2 lift. The brand lift difference becomes more statistically significant as δ increases and has confidence higher than 95% for $\delta = 2$ weeks (when both campaigns are over). Given that the ads for both the campaigns were very similar, these differences are surprising. However, they clearly indicate that in the context of these campaigns a luxury brand such as Brand1 could raise more user interest compared to a popular brand such as Brand2. Thus, if the advertiser is the retailer, these results can help him choose the brand products that he is going to illustrate in his campaign.

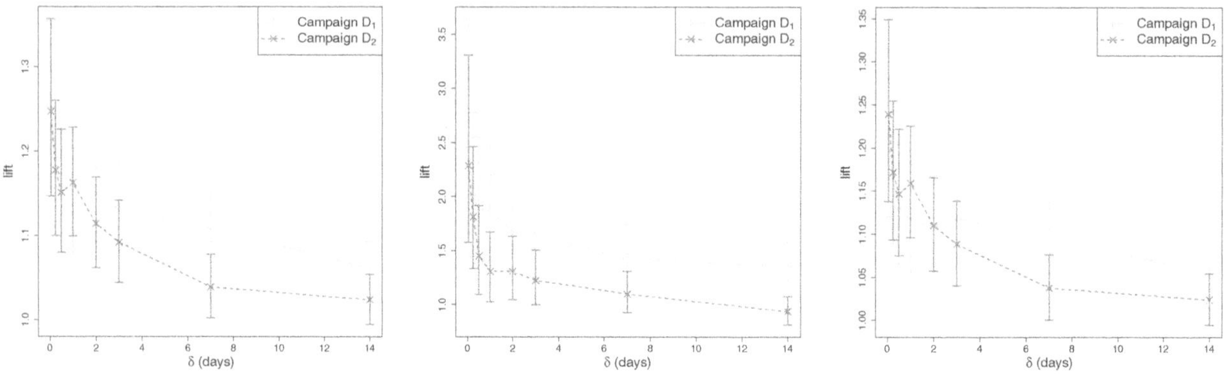

(a) Total lift

(b) Brand lift

(c) Retailer lift

Figure 5: Lift as a function of δ.

To summarize, our results show that the display advertising campaigns have a statistically significant impact on user search behavior. The impact decreases as the time from the last ad impression increases. Finally, the different lift types may provide interesting insights about the impact of display advertising.

6.4 Social Influence

In this section we study the social search lift between groups of users in the control group. To compute the social search lift, recall that we need to compare the queries of the groups $C(d_T/d)$ and $C(0/d)$. The users in these groups have the same number of friends d, but the users in $C(d_T/d)$ have d_T friends in the treatment group, while the the users $C(0/d)$ have no friends in the treatment group.

Because of the power-law degree distribution of the social graph, we can obtain reliable estimates of the social search lift only for small values of d such as 1,2 and 3. As d increases, not only does the number of nodes that have degree d decrease, but also these nodes are further divided into $d + 1$ groups with different number of friends d_T in the treatment group. Thus, $C(d_T/d)$ for larger d values is too small to obtain a tight confidence interval. However, note that due to the power law the the users with 1,2 and 3 friends account for more than half of total number of users.

In the results that we present below we refer to users that belong to both $T1$ and $T2$ as the treatment group users. Recall that the users in $T2$ are exposed to the retailer ads, but they see on average half of the retailer ads that the $T1$ users see. Unlike our study on the plain search lift, in this section we study interactions between users in the social graph and we cannot ignore the impact of $T2$ users on their friends.

We calculate the social lift using Eq. 4.2 and the binary relevance functions presented in Section 6.2. In Figure 6 we present the social search lift results for campaigns D_1 (Figure 6(a)) and D_2 (Figure 6(b)) using $\delta = 1$ day as the influence period. In each plot there are three curves and each curve looks at a different number d of total friends. The x-axis show the number of friends in the treatment group as a percentage of the total friends and the y-axis shows the value of the social search lift. The error bars in the curves show the 95% confidence intervals. For example, in Figure 6(a) the middle point of the $d = 2$ line shows that the social search lift is approximately 1.2. In other words, users in the $C(1/2)$ group submit 20% more queries relevant to the campaign compared to $C(0/2)$ users.

Since the confidence intervals are wide in all of the cases, we will not try to interpret the absolute values of the plot, but we will focus instead on some qualitative observations. Note that all curves are increasing. This shows that the number of friends in the treatment group is positively correlated with the percentage of queries that are relevant to the ad campaign. This result becomes more statistically significant as the number of friends in the treatment group increases. For example, the confidence intervals for the social search lift of $C(2/2)$ lies above the lift $= 1$ line in both plots. Note also that, as we discussed above, the confidence intervals become wider as the number of total friends increases.

In other experiments that we do not report in this paper, we estimated the social search lift for varying values of δ. In many cases, the results indicate that the social search lift reaches its maximum for $\delta = 12$ hours, before it starts decreasing. Although this result follows intuition, the evidence that we have from the data is not statistically significant. Thus, this claim requires further exploration.

7. RELATED WORK

Work on advertising effectiveness has blossomed with the advent of internet marketing. Recent work has made use of randomized field experiments [12, 13, 11, 7]. Much of the work has focused on measuring the impact of display advertising on clicks [11], account sign-ups [11, 13] and sales [12] using large-scale field experiments. Goldgard et al. [7] focus on identifying ad properties that increase advertising impact through traditional user surveys.

Unlike previous works [3, 5], in our efforts to measure the impact of display advertising on online search behavior, we have made use of a randomized field experiment in order to avoid spurious conclusions caused by activity bias. Fulgoni et al. [5] present data about the search lift and purchase lift as collected by Comscore[3]. However, their observations should be treated with caution, since they are using observational data to simulate a field experiment. Chan et al. [3] use search lift to estimate the advertising impact, but their

[3]http://www.comscore.com

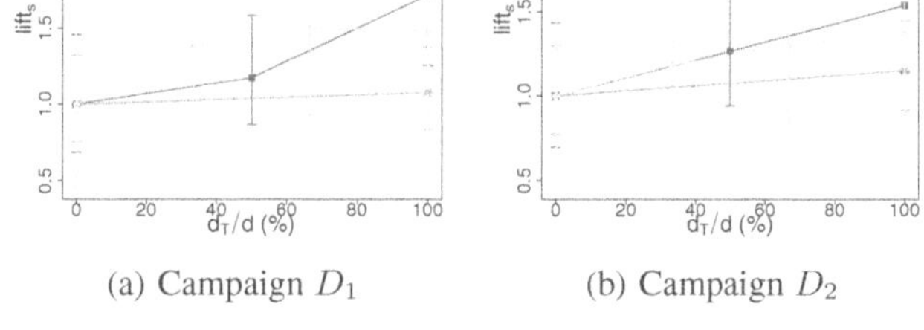

(a) Campaign D_1

(b) Campaign D_2

Figure 6: Social search lift vs T friends percentage ($\delta = 1$ day).

focus is on how to use observational data coupled with statistical modeling to simulate field experiments. While Lewis et al. [14] show the impact of a display advertising campaign on search in one of their examples in the context of a field experiment, their analysis was limited to the overall impact of a single-day campaign on a list of advertiser-selected, brand-relevant keywords. Their estimate of a 6% search lift is similar to our estimates (in this limited setting).

We have advanced the aforementioned literature in search lift [3, 5, 14] by introducing a computational method of determining search query relevance in combination with ad effectiveness. The contributions of the method are found in its following abilities: (a) it can assess relevancy, even for queries in the long tail generated in response to exposure to an advertiser's campaign, (b) it can assess instantaneous or persistent effects of display advertising through the influence period δ, and (c) it can identify different aspects of the advertising impact. Additionally, this paper represents a first step in measuring the social influence of display advertising. As such, this paper represents a unique contribution to the advertising effectiveness literature regarding the impact of display advertising on retail consumer search.

Finally, our study on display advertising social impact differs also unique compared to studies of social influence in other application domains [4, 9, 16, 10, 8], since in the case of display advertising there is not an obervable user action that can trigger social influence.

8. CONCLUSIONS

Our study of display advertising and search lift shows that ad impressions do influence user search behavior. The impact is stronger during the first hour after an ad impression and it diminishes as time elapses. However, even a week after an ad impression exposed users search more about the advertised products compared to unexposed users.

Search lift proved also very effective in identifying the impact of different aspects of the campaign. Using search lift we were able to identify that in two very similar retail advertising campaigns there were different aspects that elicited user interest. In particular, in the first campaign users showed more interest in the advertised products brand, while in the second campaign users got more interested in the retailer store that carries the advertised products. Such insights about the performance of display advertising are very important for the design and the evaluation of advertising campaigns.

Finally, our results show that exposed users do convey advertising messages to their friends who end up submitting queries related to the display ads. This result can help advertisers and publishers to obtain a more thorough picture about the impact of display advertising.

A promising direction for future work is the design of a system that delivers ad impressions taking into account the social influence. In such a system ads will be more likely to be shown to users that do not have exposed friends rather than users who may have already been influenced by their social contacts. Given that publishers typically have a budget for ad impressions, such a system could improve the effectiveness of display advertising.

9. REFERENCES

[1] D. Altman, D. Machin, T. Bryant, and S. Gardner. *Statistics with Confidence: Confidence Intervals and Statistical Guidelines*. BMJ Books, 2nd edition edition, 2000.

[2] A. Bagherjeiran and R. Parekh. Combining behavioral and social network data for online advertising. In *ICDM Workshops*, pages 837–846, 2008.

[3] D. Chan, R. Ge, O. Gershony, T. Hesterberg, and D. Lambert. Evaluating online ad campaigns in a pipeline: causal models at scale. In *Proceedings of the 16th ACM SIGKDD international conference on Knowledge discovery and data mining*, KDD '10, pages 7–16, New York, NY, USA, 2010. ACM.

[4] P. Domingos and M. Richardson. Mining the network value of customers. In *KDD '01: Proceedings of the seventh ACM SIGKDD international conference on Knowledge discovery and data mining*, pages 57–66, New York, NY, USA, 2001. ACM.

[5] G. M. Fulgoni and M. P. Morn. How online advertising works: Whither the click?, 2008. Online report.

[6] A. Fuxman, P. Tsaparas, K. Achan, and R. Agrawal. Using the wisdom of the crowds for keyword generation. In *WWW*, pages 61–70, 2008.

[7] A. Goldfarb and C. Tucker. Online display advertising: Targeting and obtrusiveness. *To appear in MARKETING SCIENCE*, 2011.

[8] S. Guo, M. Wang, and J. Leskovec. The role of social networks in online shopping: information passing, price of trust, and consumer choice. In *Proceedings of the 12th ACM conference on Electronic commerce*, EC '11, pages 157–166, New York, NY, USA, 2011. ACM.

[9] D. Kempe, J. Kleinberg, and E. Tardos. Maximizing the spread of influence through a social network. In *KDD '03: Proceedings of the ninth ACM SIGKDD international conference on Knowledge discovery and data mining*, pages 137–146, New York, NY, USA, 2003. ACM.

[10] J. Leskovec, L. A. Adamic, and B. A. Huberman. The dynamics of viral marketing. *ACM Trans. Web*, 1, May 2007.

[11] R. Lewis. *Where's the "Wear-Out?": Online Display Ads and the Impact of Frequency*. PhD thesis, MIT Dept of Economics, 2010.

[12] R. Lewis and D. Reiley. Does retail advertising work: Measuring the effects of advertising on sales via a controlled experiment on Yahoo!, 2010. Working paper.

[13] R. Lewis and T. Schreiner. *Can Online Display Advertising Attract New Customers?* PhD thesis, MIT Dept of Economics, 2010.

[14] R. A. Lewis, J. M. Rao, and D. H. Reiley. Here, there, and everywhere: correlated online behaviors can lead to overestimates of the effects of advertising. In *Proceedings of the 20th international conference on World wide web*, WWW '11, pages 157–166, New York, NY, USA, 2011. ACM.

[15] P. Papadimitriou, P. Krishnamurthy, R. Lewis, D. Reiley, and H. Garcia-Molina. Display advertising impact: Search lift and social influence. Technical report, Stanford University, 2011.

[16] J. E. Phelps, R. Lewis, L. Mobilio, D. Perry, and N. Raman. Viral marketing or electronic word-of-mouth advertising: Examining consumer responses and motivations to pass along email. *Journal of Advertising Research*, 44(04):333–348, 2004.

[17] D. Silverman. Internet advertising revenue report: 2010 first half-year results, 2010.

Diversified Ranking on Large Graphs: An Optimization Viewpoint

Hanghang Tong Jingrui He Zhen Wen Ravi Konuru Ching-Yung Lin
IBM T.J. Watson Research Center
Hawthorne, NY, USA
{htong, jingruhe, zhenwen, rkonuru, chingyung}@us.ibm.com

ABSTRACT

Diversified ranking on graphs is a fundamental mining task and has a variety of high-impact applications. There are two important open questions here. The first challenge is the *measure* - how to quantify the goodness of a given top-k ranking list that captures both the relevance and the diversity? The second challenge lies in the *algorithmic* aspect - how to find an optimal, or near-optimal, top-k ranking list that maximizes the measure we defined in a scalable way?

In this paper, we address these challenges from an optimization point of view. Firstly, we propose a goodness measure for a given top-k ranking list. The proposed goodness measure intuitively captures both (a) the relevance between each individual node in the ranking list and the query; and (b) the diversity among different nodes in the ranking list. Moreover, we propose a *scalable* algorithm (*linear* wrt the size of the graph) that generates a *provably near-optimal* solution. The experimental evaluations on real graphs demonstrate its effectiveness and efficiency.

Categories and Subject Descriptors

H.2.8 [**Database Management**]: Database Applications – Data Mining

General Terms

Algorithm, experimentation

Keywords

Diversity, ranking, scalability, graph mining

1. INTRODUCTION

Given an author-paper network, how to find the top-k most related conferences for a given author? How to diversify the ranking list so that it captures the whole spectrum of the given author's research interest? It is now widely realized that diversity is a key factor to address the uncertainty and ambiguity in an information need; and to cover the different aspects of the information need [32]. Diversity is also positively associated with personnel performance and job retention rate in a large organization [38].

Despite their own success of the previous works (See Section 6 for a review), two important questions remain open in diversified ranking on large graphs. The first challenge is the *measure* - for a given top-k ranking list, how can we quantify its goodness? Intuitively, a good top-k ranking list should capture both the relevance and the diversity. For example, given a task which typically requires a set of different skills, if we want to form a team of experts, not only should the people in the team have relevant skills, but also they should somehow be 'different' from each other so that the whole team can benefit from the diversified, complementary knowledge and social capital. However, there does not exist such a goodness measure for the graph data in the literature. Most of the existing works for diversified ranking on graphs are based on some heuristics. The only exception is [27], where the authors made an important step towards this goal by providing some optimization explanations, which is achieved by defining a *time-varying* objective function at each iteration. But still, it is not clear what *overall* objective function the algorithm tries to optimize.

The second challenge lies in the *algorithmic* aspect - how can we find an optimal, or near-optimal, top-k ranking list that maximizes the goodness measure? Bringing diversity into the design objective implies that we need to optimize on the set level. In other words, the objective function for a subset of nodes is usually not equal to the sum of objective functions of each individual nodes. It is usually very hard to perform such set-level optimization. For instance, a straight-forward method would need exponential enumerations to find the exact optimal solution, which is infeasible even for medium size graphs. This, together with the fact that real graphs are often of large size, reaching billions of nodes and edges, poses the challenge for the optimization algorithm - how can we find a near-optimal solution in a scalable way?

In this paper, we address these challenges from an optimization point of view. We propose a goodness measure which intuitively captures both (a) the relevance between each individual nodes in the ranking list and the query node; and (b) the diversity among different nodes in the ranking list. We further propose a *scalable* algorithm (*linear* wrt the size of the graph) that generates a *provably near-optimal* top-k ranking list. To the best of our knowledge, this is the first work for diversified ranking on large graphs that (1) has a clear optimization formulation; (2) finds a provably near-optimal solution; and (3) enjoys the linearly scalability. The main contributions of the paper are summarized as follows:

- *A measure* to quantify goodness for a top-k ranking list that captures both relevance and diversity;
- *An algorithm* to find a diversified top-k ranking list from large graphs;

KDD'11, August 21–24, 2011, San Diego, CA, USA.

Table 1: Symbols

Symbol	Definition and Description
$\mathbf{A}, \mathbf{B}, \ldots$	matrices (bold upper case)
$\mathbf{A}(i,j)$	the element at the ith row and j^{th} column of $\mathbf{A}$
$\mathbf{A}(i,:)$	the ith row of matrix $\mathbf{A}$
$\mathbf{A}(:,j)$	the jth column of matrix $\mathbf{A}$
$\mathbf{A}'$	transpose of matrix $\mathbf{A}$
$\mathbf{a}, \mathbf{b}, \ldots$	vectors
$\mathcal{I}, \mathcal{J}, \ldots$	sets (calligraphic)
$\otimes$	element-wise Hadamard product
$\mathbf{r}$	an $n \times 1$ ranking vector
$\mathbf{p}$	an $n \times 1$ query vector ($\mathbf{p}(i) \geq 0, \sum_{i=1}^{n} \mathbf{p}(i) = 1$)
$\mathbf{I}$	an identity matrix
$\mathbf{1}$	a vector/matrix with all elements set to 1s
$\mathbf{0}$	a vector/matrix with all elements set to 0s
n, m	the number of the nodes and edges in the graph
k	the budget (i.e., the length of the ranking list)
c	the damping factor $0 < c < 1$

- *Proofs and complexity analysis*, showing that our method is *provably near-optimal* in terms of optimization quality with *linear* scalability;
- *Extensive experimental evaluations*, demonstrating the effectiveness and efficiency of our method.

The rest of the paper is organized as follows. We introduce notation and formally define the problems in Section 2. We present and analyze the proposed measure and algorithm in Section 3 and Section 4, respectively. We provide experimental evaluation in Section 5. We review the related work in Section 6 and conclude in Section 7.

2. PROBLEM DEFINITIONS

Table 1 lists the main symbols we use throughout the paper. In this paper, we consider the most general case of directed, weighted, irreducible unipartite graphs. We represent a general graph by its adjacency matrix[1]. Following the standard notation, we use bold upper-case for matrices (e.g., $\mathbf{A}$), bold lower-case for vectors (e.g., $\mathbf{a}$), and calligraphic fonts for sets (e.g., $\mathcal{I}$). We denote the transpose with a prime (i.e., $\mathbf{A}'$ is the transpose of $\mathbf{A}$). For a bipartite graph with adjacency matrix $\mathbf{W}$, we can convert it to the equivalent unipartite graph: $\mathbf{A} = \begin{pmatrix} \mathbf{0} & \mathbf{W} \\ \mathbf{W} & \mathbf{0} \end{pmatrix}$. We use subscripts to denote the size of matrices/vectors (e.g., $\mathbf{A}_{n\times n}$ means a matrix of size $n \times n$). When the size of matrices/vectors are clear from the context, we omit such subscripts for brevity. Also, we represent the elements in a matrix using a convention similar to Matlab, e.g., $\mathbf{A}(i,j)$ is the element at the ith row and j^{th} column of the matrix $\mathbf{A}$, and $\mathbf{A}(:,j)$ is the jth column of $\mathbf{A}$, etc. With this notation, we can represent a sub-matrix of $\mathbf{A}$ as $\mathbf{A}(\mathcal{I},\mathcal{I})$, which is a block of matrix $\mathbf{A}$ that corresponds to the rows/columns of $\mathbf{A}$ indexed by the set $\mathcal{I}$.

In this paper, we focus on personalized PageRank [30, 11] since it is one of the most fundamental ranking methods on graphs, and has shown its success in many different application domains in the past decade. Formally, it can be defined as follows:

$$\mathbf{r} = c\mathbf{A}'\mathbf{r} + (1-c)\mathbf{p} \tag{1}$$

where $\mathbf{p}$ is an $n \times 1$ personalized vector ($\mathbf{p}(i) \geq 0, \sum_{i=1}^{n} \mathbf{p}(i) = 1$). Sometimes, we also refer to $\mathbf{p}$ as the query vector. c ($0 < c < 1$) is a damping factor; $\mathbf{A}$ is the row-normalized adjacency matrix of the graph (i.e., $\sum_{j=1}^{n} \mathbf{A}(i,j) = 1$ $(i = 1, ..., n)$; and $\mathbf{r}$ is the $n\times 1$ resulting ranking vector. Note that if $\mathbf{p}(i) = 1/n(i = 1, ..., n)$, it is reduced to the standard PageRank [30]; if $\mathbf{p}(i) = 1$ and $\mathbf{p}(j) = 0 (j \neq i)$, the resulting ranking vector $\mathbf{r}$ gives the proximity scores from node i to all the other nodes in the graph [37].

[1]In practice, we store these matrices using an adjacency list representation, since real graphs are often very sparse.

In order to simplify the description of our upcoming method, we also introduce the so-called 'Google matrix' $\mathbf{B}$:

$$\mathbf{B} = c\mathbf{A}' + (1-c)\mathbf{p}\mathbf{1}_{1\times n} \tag{2}$$

where $\mathbf{1}_{1\times n}$ is a $1 \times n$ row vector with all elements set to 1s. Intuitively, the 'Google matrix' $\mathbf{B}$ can be viewed as the personalized adjacency matrix that is biased towards the query vector $\mathbf{p}$. It turns out that the ranking vector $\mathbf{r}$ defined in eq. (1) satisfies $\mathbf{r} = \mathbf{B}\mathbf{r}$. In other words, the ranking vector $\mathbf{r}$ is the right eigenvector of the $\mathbf{B}$ matrix with the eigenvalue 1. It can be verified that $\mathbf{B}$ is a column-wise stochastic matrix (i.e., each column of $\mathbf{B}$ sums up to 1). By Perron-Frobenius theorem [10], it can be shown that 1 is the largest (in module) simple eigenvalue of the matrix $\mathbf{B}$; and the ranking vector $\mathbf{r}$ is unique with all non-negative elements since the graph is irreducible.

Our goal is two-fold: (1) we want a goodness measure to quantify the quality of a given top-*k* ranking list that captures both the relevance and the diversity; and (2) given the goodness measure, we want an optimal or near-optimal algorithm to find a top-*k* ranking list that maximizes such goodness measure in a scalable way. With the above notations and assumptions, our problems can be formally defined as follows:

PROBLEM 1. **(Goodness Measure.)**

Given: *A large graph $\mathbf{A}_{n\times n}$, the query vector $\mathbf{p}$, the damping factor c, and a subset of k nodes $\mathcal{S}$;*

Output: *A goodness score $f(\mathcal{S})$ of the subset of nodes $\mathcal{S}$, which measures (a) the relevance of each node in $\mathcal{S}$ wrt the query vector $\mathbf{p}$, and (b) the diversity among all the nodes in the subset $\mathcal{S}$.*

PROBLEM 2. **(Diversified Top-*k* Ranking Algorithm.)**

Given: *A large graph $\mathbf{A}_{n\times n}$, the query vector $\mathbf{p}$, the damping factor c, and the budget k;*

Find: *A subset of k nodes $\mathcal{S}$ that maximizes the goodness measure $f(\mathcal{S})$.*

In the next two sections, we present our solutions for these two problems respectively.

3. THE PROPOSED GOODNESS MEASURE

In this section, we address Problem 1. Our goal is to define a goodness measure to quantify the quality of a given top-*k* ranking list that captures both the relevance and the diversity. We first discuss some design objectives of such a goodness measure; and then present our solution followed by some theoretical analysis.

3.1 Design Objectives

As said before, a good diversified top-*k* ranking list should balance between the relevance and the diversity. The notion of relevance is clear for personalized PageRank, - larger value in the ranking vector $\mathbf{r}$ means more relevant wrt the query vector $\mathbf{p}$. On the other hand, the notion of diversity is more challenging. Intuitively, a diversified subset of nodes should be *dis-similar* with each other. Take the query *'Find the top-k conferences for Philip Yu from the author-conference network'* as an example. Dr. *Philip*

Yu is a professor at University of Illinois at Chicago. His recent major research interest lies in databases and data mining. He also has broad interests in several related domains, including systems, parallel and distributed processing, web applications, and performance modeling, etc. A top-k ranking list for this query would have high relevance if it consists of all the conferences from databases and data mining community (e.g., *SIGMOD, VLDB, KDD*, etc) since all these conferences are closely related to his major research interest. However, such a list has low diversity since these conferences are too similar with each other (e.g., having a large overlap of contributing authors, etc). Therefore, if we replace a few databases and data mining conferences by some representative conferences in his other research domains (e.g., *ICDCS* for distributed computing systems, *WWW* for web applications, etc), it would make the whole ranking list more diverse (e.g., the conferences in the list are more dis-similar with each other).

Furthermore, if we go through the ranking list from top down, we would like to see the most relevant conferences to appear first in the ranking list. For example, a ranking list in the order of *'SIGMOD', 'ICDCS', 'WWW'* is better than *'ICDCS', 'WWW', 'SIGMOD'* since databases (*SIGMOD*) is a more relevant research interest for Dr. *Philip Yu*, compared with distributed computing systems (*ICDCS*), or web applications (*WWW*). In this way, the user can capture Dr. *Philip Yu*'s main research interest by just inspecting a few top-ranked conferences/nodes. This suggests the so-called *diminishing returns property* of the goodness measure - it would help the user to know better about Dr. *Philip Yu*'s whole research interest if we return more conferences/nodes in the ranking list; but the *marginal benefit* becomes smaller and smaller as we go down the ranking list.

Another implicit design objective lies in the algorithmic aspect. The proposed goodness measure should also allow us to develop an effective and scalable algorithm to find an optimal (or at least near-optimal) top-k ranking list from large graphs. We will discuss and address this issue in the next section.

To summarize, for a given top-k ranking list, we aim to provide a single goodness score that (1) measures the *relevance* between each individual node in the list and the query vector $\mathbf{p}$; (2) measures the *similarity (or dis-similarity)* among all the nodes in the ranking list; (3) exhibits some diminishing returns property wrt the size of the ranking list; and (4) enables some effective and scalable algorithm to find an optimal (or near-optimal) top-k ranking list.

3.2 The Proposed Measure

Let $\mathbf{A}$ be the row-normalized adjacency matrix of the graph, $\mathbf{B}$ be the 'Google matrix' defined in eq (2), $\mathbf{p}$ be the personalized vector and $\mathbf{r}$ be the ranking vector. For a given ranking list $\mathcal{S}$ (i.e., $\mathcal{S}$ gives the indices of the nodes in the ranking list; and $|\mathcal{S}| = k$.), the proposed goodness measure is formally defined as follows:

Goodness Measure:

$$\mathrm{f}(\mathcal{S}) = 2\sum_{i\in\mathcal{S}} \mathbf{r}(i) - \sum_{i,j\in\mathcal{S}} \mathbf{B}(i,j)\mathbf{r}(j) \quad (3)$$

We can also represent $\mathrm{f}(\mathcal{S})$ by using the matrix $\mathbf{A}$ instead:

$$\mathrm{f}(\mathcal{S}) = 2\sum_{i\in\mathcal{S}} \mathbf{r}(i) - c\sum_{i,j\in\mathcal{S}} \mathbf{A}(j,i)\mathbf{r}(j) - (1-c)\sum_{j\in\mathcal{S}} \mathbf{r}(j)\sum_{i\in\mathcal{S}} \mathbf{p}(i)$$

where c is the damping factor in personalized PageRank, and $\mathbf{1}_{1\times|\mathcal{S}|}$ is a row vector of length $|\mathcal{S}|$ with all the elements set to 1s. It can be shown that it is equivalent to eq. (3).

Notice that the goodness measure in eq (3) is independent on the ordering of the different nodes in the subset $\mathcal{S}$. If we simply change the ordering of the nodes for the same subset $\mathcal{S}$, it does not affect the goodness score. However, as we will show in Section 4, we can still output an *ordered* subset based on the diminishing returns need when the user is seeking for a diverse top-k ranking list.

3.3 Proofs and Analysis

Let us analyze how the proposed goodness measure meets our design objectives in subsection 3.1.

There are two terms in eq (3), the first term is twice the sum of the ranking scores in the ranking list. For the second term, recall that $\mathbf{B}$ can be viewed as the personalized adjacency matrix wrt the query vector $\mathbf{p}$, where $\mathbf{B}(i,j)$ indicates the similarity (i.e., the strength of the connection) between nodes i and j. In other words, the second term in eq (3) is the sum of all the similarity scores between any two nodes $i, j (i, j \in \mathcal{S})$ in the ranking list (weighted by $\mathbf{r}(j)$). Therefore, the proposed goodness measure captures both the relevance and the diversity. The more relevant (higher $\mathbf{r}(i)$) each individual node is, the higher the goodness measure $\mathrm{f}(\mathcal{S})$. At the same time, it encourages the diversity within the ranking list by penalizing the (weighted) similarity between any two nodes in $\mathcal{S}$.

The proposed measure $\mathrm{f}(\mathcal{S})$ also exhibits the diminishing returns property, which is summarized in Theorem 1. The intuitions of Theorem 1 are as follows: (1) by P1, it means that the utility of an empty ranking list is always zero; (2) by P2, if we add more nodes into the ranking list, the overall utility of the ranking list does not decrease; and (3) by P3, the marginal utility of adding new nodes is relatively small if we already have a large ranking list.

THEOREM 1. **Diminishing Returns Property of $\mathbf{f}(\mathcal{S})$.** *Let Φ be an empty set; $\mathcal{I}, \mathcal{J}, \mathcal{R}$ be three sets s.t., $\mathcal{I} \subseteq \mathcal{J}$, and $\mathcal{R} \cap \mathcal{J} = \Phi$. The following facts hold for $f(\mathcal{S})$:*
P1: $f(\Phi) = 0$;
P2: $f(\mathcal{S})$ is monotonically non-decreasing, i.e., $f(\mathcal{I}) \leq f(\mathcal{J})$;
P3: $f(\mathcal{S})$ is submodular, i.e., $f(\mathcal{I}\cup\mathcal{R}) - f(\mathcal{I}) \geq f(\mathcal{J}\cup\mathcal{R}) - f(\mathcal{J})$.

PROOF of *P1*. It is obviously held by the definition of $\mathrm{f}(\mathcal{S})$. □

PROOF of *P2*. Let $\mathcal{T} = \mathcal{J} \setminus \mathcal{I}$. Substituting eq (3) into $\mathrm{f}(\mathcal{J}) - \mathrm{f}(\mathcal{I})$ and canceling the common terms, we have

$$\begin{aligned} & \mathrm{f}(\mathcal{J}) - \mathrm{f}(\mathcal{I}) \\ = & \; 2\sum_{i\in\mathcal{T}} \mathbf{r}(i) - \sum_{i\in\mathcal{I}}\sum_{j\in\mathcal{T}} \mathbf{B}(i,j)\mathbf{r}(j) - \sum_{i\in\mathcal{T}}\sum_{j\in\mathcal{J}} \mathbf{B}(i,j)\mathbf{r}(j) \\ = & \; (\sum_{j\in\mathcal{T}} \mathbf{r}(j) - \sum_{j\in\mathcal{T}}\sum_{i\in\mathcal{I}} \mathbf{B}(i,j)\mathbf{r}(j)) \\ & + (\sum_{i\in\mathcal{T}} \mathbf{r}(i) - \sum_{i\in\mathcal{T}}\sum_{j\in\mathcal{J}} \mathbf{B}(i,j)\mathbf{r}(j)) \end{aligned} \quad (4)$$

Recall that the matrix $\mathbf{B}$ is a column-wise stochastic matrix (i.e., each column of $\mathbf{B}$ sums up to 1). The first half of eq (4) satisfies

$$\begin{aligned} & (\sum_{j\in\mathcal{T}} \mathbf{r}(j) - \sum_{j\in\mathcal{T}}\sum_{i\in\mathcal{I}} \mathbf{B}(i,j)\mathbf{r}(j)) \\ = & \sum_{j\in\mathcal{T}} \mathbf{r}(j)(1 - \sum_{i\in\mathcal{I}} \mathbf{B}(i,j)) \\ = & \sum_{j\in\mathcal{T}} \mathbf{r}(j) \sum_{i\notin\mathcal{I}} \mathbf{B}(i,j) \geq 0 \end{aligned} \quad (5)$$

For the second half of eq (4), we have that

$$\begin{aligned} & (\sum_{i\in\mathcal{T}} \mathbf{r}(i) - \sum_{i\in\mathcal{T}}\sum_{j\in\mathcal{J}} \mathbf{B}(i,j)\mathbf{r}(j)) \\ = & \sum_{i\in\mathcal{T}} (\mathbf{r}(i) - \sum_{j\in\mathcal{J}} \mathbf{B}(i,j)\mathbf{r}(j)) \\ = & \sum_{i\in\mathcal{T}}\sum_{j\notin\mathcal{J}} \mathbf{B}(i,j)\mathbf{r}(j) \geq 0 \end{aligned} \quad (6)$$

The last equality in eq (6) is due to the fact that $\mathbf{r} = \mathbf{B}\mathbf{r}$, and each element in $\mathbf{r}$ is non-negative.

Putting eq (4)-(6) together, we have that $f(\mathcal{J}) \geq f(\mathcal{I})$, which completes the proof of P2. □

PROOF of *P3*. Again, let $\mathcal{T} = \mathcal{J} \setminus \mathcal{I}$. Substituting eq (4) into $(f(\mathcal{I} \cup \mathcal{R}) - f(\mathcal{I})) - (f(\mathcal{J} \cup \mathcal{R}) - f(\mathcal{J}))$ and canceling the common terms, we have

$$\begin{aligned} & (f(\mathcal{I} \cup \mathcal{R}) - f(\mathcal{I})) - (f(\mathcal{J} \cup \mathcal{R}) - f(\mathcal{J})) \\ = & (\sum_{i \in \mathcal{J}} \sum_{j \in \mathcal{R}} \mathbf{B}(i,j)\mathbf{r}(j) - \sum_{i \in \mathcal{I}} \sum_{j \in \mathcal{R}} \mathbf{B}(i,j)\mathbf{r}(j)) \\ + & (\sum_{i \in \mathcal{R}} \sum_{j \in \mathcal{J} \cup \mathcal{R}} \mathbf{B}(i,j)\mathbf{r}(j) - \sum_{i \in \mathcal{R}} \sum_{j \in \mathcal{I} \cup \mathcal{R}} \mathbf{B}(i,j)\mathbf{r}(j)) \\ = & \sum_{j \in \mathcal{R}} \sum_{i \in \mathcal{T}} \mathbf{B}(i,j)\mathbf{r}(j) + \sum_{i \in \mathcal{R}} \sum_{j \in \mathcal{T}} \mathbf{B}(i,j)\mathbf{r}(j) \geq 0 \end{aligned}$$

Therefore, we have that $f(\mathcal{I} \cup \mathcal{R}) - f(\mathcal{I}) \geq f(\mathcal{J} \cup \mathcal{R}) - f(\mathcal{J})$, which completes the proof of P3. □

4. THE PROPOSED ALGORITHM

In this section, we address Problem 2. Here, given the initial query vector $\mathbf{p}$ and the budget k, we want to find a subset of k nodes that maximizes the goodness measure defined in eq (3). We first analyze the main challenges in optimizing eq (3); and then present the proposed algorithm DRAGON, followed by some theoretical analysis and discussion.

4.1 Challenges

Problem 2 is essentially a subset selection problem to find the optimal k nodes that maximize eq (3). Theorem 1 indicates that it is not easy to find the exact optimal solution of Problem 2 - it is *NP-hard* to maximize a monotonic submodular function if the function value is 0 for an empty set [18]. For instance, a straight-forward method would take exponential enumerations $\binom{n}{k}$ to find the exact optimal k nodes, which is not feasible in computation even for a medium size graph (e.g., with a few hundred nodes).

We can also formulate Problem 2 as a binary quadratic programming problem. Let $\mathbf{x}_{n \times 1}$ be a binary indicator vector ($\mathbf{x}(i) = 1$ means node i is selected in the subset $\mathcal{S}$, and 0 means it is not selected). Problem 2 can be expressed as the following binary quadratic programming problem:

$$\begin{aligned} \min \quad & \mathbf{x}'\mathbf{D}\mathbf{x} \\ \text{Subject to:} \quad & \mathbf{x}(i) \in \{0,1\} (i = 1, ..., n) \\ & \sum_{i=1}^{n} \mathbf{x}(i) = k \end{aligned} \tag{7}$$

where $\mathbf{D} = (\mathbf{B} - 2\mathbf{I}_{n \times n})\text{diag}(\mathbf{r})$, $\mathbf{I}_{n \times n}$ is an identity matrix of size $n \times n$, and $\text{diag}(\mathbf{r})$ is a diagonal matrix with $\mathbf{r}(i,i) (i = 1, ..., n)$ being the diagonal elements.

Eq. (7) is still not easy to solve due to (1) the binary constrains on the variable $\mathbf{x}$ and (2) the quadratic term in the objective function. If we relax the binary constrain on $\mathbf{x}$ as $0 \leq \mathbf{x}(i) \leq 1 (i = 1, ..., n)$, we can solve the relaxed problem by standard quadratic programming packages. We refer to this strategy as 'Lin-QP'. However, there are two major limitations of this method. First of all, we do not know what the gap is between eq. (7) and its relaxed version. Therefore, it is not clear how good the final solution is in terms of maximizing the original goodness measure (eq (3)) even if we can solve the relaxed problem optimally[2]. Second, most, if not all, of the existing quadratic programming packages require *polynomial* complexity in computation. This makes this strategy very slow, or even infeasible, for a graph with more than a few thousand nodes.

Another possible solution for eq. (7) is to remove the quadratic term in the objective function as follows. Starting from some initial indicator vector $\hat{\mathbf{x}}$, we iterate between the following two steps: (1) approximate the objective function in eq. (7) by its first order Taylor expansion around $\hat{\mathbf{x}}$; and (2) update $\hat{\mathbf{x}}$ by solving a binary integer programming problem for the approximated objective function, which is linear wrt $\mathbf{x}$. We refer to this strategy as 'Ite-BIP'. However, the two main issues still exist: (1) it is not clear how such approximation will downgrade the overall optimization performance; (2) the binary integer programming itself, again, requires *polynomial* time, which does not scale to large graphs.

4.2 The Proposed DRAGON Algorithm

Our proposed DRAGON algorithm is presented in Alg. 1. In step 1, we compute the ranking vector $\mathbf{r}$ (e.g., by the power method, etc). Then after some initializations (steps 2-5), we select k nodes one-by-one as follows. At each time, we compute the score vector $\mathbf{s}$ in step 7. Then, we select one node with the highest score in the vector $\mathbf{s}$ and add it to the subset $\mathcal{S}$ (steps 8-9). After that, we use the selected node to update the two reference vectors $\mathbf{u}$ and $\mathbf{v}$ (steps 10-11). Note that '$\otimes$' denote the element-wise product between two matrices/vectors. Intuitively, the score vector $\mathbf{s}$ keeps the *marginal* contribution of each node for the goodness measure given the current selected subset $\mathcal{S}$. From step 7, it can be seen that at each iteration, the values of such marginal contribution either keeps unchanged or decreases. This is consistent with P3 of Theorem 1 - as there are more and more nodes in the subset $\mathcal{S}$, the marginal contribution of each node is monotonically non-increasing. It is worth pointing out that we use the original normalized adjacency matrix $\mathbf{A}$, instead of the 'Google matrix' $\mathbf{B}$ in Alg. 1. This is because for many real graphs, the matrix $\mathbf{A}$ is often very sparse, whereas the matrix $\mathbf{B}$ might not be[3]. In the case $\mathbf{B}$ is dense, it is not efficient in either time or space to use $\mathbf{B}$ in Alg. 1.

In Alg. 1, although we try to optimize a goodness measure that is not affected by the ordering of different nodes in the subset, we can still output an ordered list to the user based on in which iteration these nodes are selected - earlier selected nodes in Alg. 1 are placed at the top of the resulting top-*k* ranking list. This ordering naturally meets the diminishing returns need when the user is seeking for a diverse top-*k* ranking list as we analyzed in subsection 3.1.

4.3 Proofs and Analysis

Here, we analyze the *optimality* as well as the *complexity* of the proposed algorithm. We show that our DRAGON leads to a *near-optimal* solution, and at the same time it enjoys *linear scalability* in both time and space.

Optimality. The optimality of the proposed DRAGON is given in Lemma 1. According to Lemma 1, our DRAGON is *near-optimal* - its solution is within a fixed fraction ($1 - 1/e \approx 0.63$) from the global optimal one. Given the hardness of Problem 2, such near-optimality is acceptable in terms of optimization quality.

LEMMA 1. **Near-Optimality of DRAGON.** *Let $\mathcal{S}$ be the subset found by* DRAGON*; $|\mathcal{S}| = k$; and $\mathcal{S}^* = argmax_{|\mathcal{S}|=k} f(\mathcal{S})$. We have that $f(\mathcal{S}) \geq (1 - 1/e) f(\mathcal{S}^*)$, where e is the base of the natural logarithm.*

PROOF. Omitted for Brevity □

[2] It is worth pointing out that it is not even easy to find an optimal solution for the relaxed problem by quadratic programming because the matrix $\mathbf{D}$ (1) might be asymmetric and (2) is not always semi-positive definite.

[3] To see this, notice that $\mathbf{B}$ is a full matrix if $\mathbf{p}$ is uniform.

Algorithm 1 DRAGON for Problem 2

Input: The row-normalized adjacency matrix $\mathbf{A}$ of the graph, the damping factor c, the query vector $\mathbf{p}$, and the budget k;
Output: A subset of k nodes $\mathcal{S}$.

1: Compute the ranking vector $\mathbf{r}$: $\mathbf{r} = c\mathbf{A}'\mathbf{r} + (1-c)\mathbf{p}$;
2: Initialize $\mathcal{S}$ as the empty set; set $\mathbf{u} = \mathbf{v} = \mathbf{0}_{n\times 1}$;
3: **for** $i = 1 : n$ **do**
4: Initialize $\hat{\mathbf{s}}(i) = (2 - c\mathbf{A}(i,i) - (1-c)\mathbf{p}(i))\mathbf{r}(i)$;
5: **end for**
6: **for** iter $= 1 : k$ **do**
7: Compute the score vector $\mathbf{s} = \hat{\mathbf{s}} - \mathbf{u} \otimes \mathbf{r} - \mathbf{v}$;
8: Find $i = \text{argmax}_j \mathbf{s}(j)(j = 1, ..., n; j \notin \mathcal{S})$;
9: Add node i into $\mathcal{S}$;
10: Update $\mathbf{u} \leftarrow \mathbf{u} + c\mathbf{A}(:,i) + (1-c)\mathbf{p}(i)\mathbf{1}_{n\times 1}$;
11: Update $\mathbf{v} \leftarrow \mathbf{v} + c\mathbf{A}'(:,i)\mathbf{r}(i) + (1-c)\mathbf{r}(i)\mathbf{p}$;
12: **end for**
13: Return the subset $\mathcal{S}$

Time Complexity. The time complexity of the proposed DRAGON is given in Lemma 2. According to Lemma 2, our DRAGON has *linear* time complexity wrt the size of the graph. Therefore it is scalable to large graphs in terms of computational time.

LEMMA 2. **Time Complexity of DRAGON.** *The time complexity of Alg. 1 is $O(m + nk)$.*

PROOF. Omitted for brevity. □

We would like to point out that the proposed DRAGON can be further sped up. Firstly, notice that the $O(m)$ term in Lemma 2 comes from computing the ranking vector $\mathbf{r}$ (step 1) by the most commonly used power method. There are a lot of fast methods for computing $\mathbf{r}$, either by effective approximation (e.g., [37]), or by parallelism (e.g. [13]). These methods can be naturally plugged in our DRAGON, which might lead to further computational savings. Secondly, the $O(nk)$ term in Lemma 2 comes from the greedy selection step in steps 6-12. Thanks to the monotonicity of $\text{f}(\mathcal{S})$ as we show in Theorem 1, we can use the similar lazy evaluation strategy as [20] to speed up this process, without sacrificing the optimization quality.

Space Complexity. The space complexity of the proposed DRAGON is given in Lemma 3. According to Lemma 3, our DRAGON has *linear* space complexity wrt the size of the graph. Therefore it is also scalable to large graphs in terms of space cost.

LEMMA 3. **Space Complexity of DRAGON.** *The space complexity of Alg. 1 is $O(m + n + k)$.*

PROOF. Omitted for brevity. □

4.4 Discussion - Comparisons

In literature, there exist two other methods to encourage diversity in the top-*k* ranking list for personalized PageRank. Here, we make a comparison in terms of *optimality, convergence,* and *scalability* of different methods. ARW [42] is based on an intuitive heuristic by greedily selecting the highest ranked node and setting it as the absorbing state. From theoretical point of view, it is not clear what ARW [42] tries to optimize. And also, it requires a matrix inverse of the same size of the graph, which is not scalable to large graphs. RRW [27] is based on vertex reinforced random walk [31]. Compared with ARW [42], it makes an important step forward by providing some optimization explanations via defining a *time-varying* objective function that changes at each iteration step. However, it is still not clear what overall metric it tries to measure; and how good its optimization solution is. Moreover, RRW [27] introduced some modifications and approximation techniques to the original vertex reinforced random walk, and it is not clear how the modified vertex reinforcement random walk converges[4].

Table 2: Comparison of different methods. Our proposed DRAGON is the only method that leads to a near-optimal solution with linear scalability.

Method	Measure	Optimality	Scalability	Convergence
ARW [42]	NA	NA	No	Yes
RRW [27]	Partial	NA	Yes	NA
DRAGON	Yes	Near-optimal	Yes	Yes

5. EXPERIMENTAL EVALUATIONS

In this section, we provide empirical evaluations for the proposed DRAGON. Our evaluations mainly focus on (1) the effectiveness and (2) efficiency of the proposed DRAGON.

5.1 Experimental Setup

Data sets. We use the DBLP publication data[5] to construct a co-authorship network, where each node is an author and the edge weight is the number of the co-authored papers between the two corresponding persons. Overall, we have $n = 418,236$ nodes and $m = 2,753,798$ edges. We also construct much smaller co-authorship networks, using the authors from only one conference (e.g., *KDD, SIGIR, SIGMOD*, etc.). For example, *KDD* is the co-authorship network for the authors in the 'KDD' conference. These smaller co-authorship networks typically have a few thousand nodes and up to a few tens of thousands edges. We also construct the co-authorship networks, using the authors from multiple conferences (e.g., *KDD+SIGIR*). For these graphs, we denote them as *Sub(n,m)*, where n and m are the numbers of nodes and edges in the graph, respectively.

Machine configurations. For the computational cost and scalability, we report the wall-clock time. All the experiments ran on the same machine with four 2.4GHz AMD CPUs and 48GB memory, running Linux (2.6 kernel). For all the quantitative results, we randomly generate a query vector $\mathbf{p}$ and feed it into different methods for a top-*k* ranking list with the same length. We repeat it 100 times and report the average.

Evaluation criteria. To the best of our knowledge, there is no universally accepted measure for diversity. In [27], the authors suggested an intuitive notion based on the density of the induced subgraph from the original graph $\mathbf{A}$ by the subset $\mathcal{S}$. The intuition is as follows: the lower the density (i.e., the less 1-step neighbors) of the induced subgraph, the more diverse the subset $\mathcal{S}$. Here, we generalize this notion to the t-step graph in order to also take into account the effect of those in-direct neighbors. Let Sign(.) be a binary function operated element-wise on a matrix, i.e., $\mathbf{Y} = \text{Sign}(\mathbf{X})$, where $\mathbf{Y}$ is a matrix of the same size as $\mathbf{X}$, $\mathbf{Y}(i,j) = 1$ if $\mathbf{X}(i,j) > 0$, $\mathbf{Y}(i,j) = 0$ otherwise. We define the t-step connectivity matrix $\mathbf{C}^t$ as $\mathbf{C}^t = \text{Sign}(\sum_{i=1}^{t} \mathbf{A}^i)$. That is, $\mathbf{C}^t(i,j) = 1$ (0) means that node i can (cannot) reach node j on the graph $\mathbf{A}$ within t-steps/hops. With this $\mathbf{C}^t$ matrix, we define the diversity of a given subset $\mathcal{S}$ as eq (8). Here, the value of $\text{Div}(t)$ is always between 0.5 and 1 - higher means more diverse. If all the nodes in $\mathcal{S}$ are reachable from each other within t-steps, we say that the subset $\mathcal{S}$

[4]Even if it converges, its stationary state might not be unique according to [31].

[5]http://www.informatik.uni-trier.de/~ley/db/

is the least diverse ($\text{Div}(t) = 0.5$). On the other extreme, If all the nodes in $\mathcal{S}$ cannot reach each other within t-steps, the subset $\mathcal{S}$ is the most diverse ($\text{Div}(t) = 1$).

$$\text{Div}(t) = \frac{1}{1 + \sum_{i,j \in \mathcal{S}, i \neq j} \mathbf{C}^t(i,j)/(|\mathcal{S}| \cdot (|\mathcal{S}| - 1))} \quad (8)$$

For the task of top-k ranking, the notion of diversity alone, though important, might not be enough for the information need. For example, if we simply randomly select k nodes as the top-k ranking list, these k nodes might not connected with each other at all given that the length of the ranking list k is usually much smaller than the number of nodes n in the graph. Therefore, it has a high diversity. However, it is unlikely that such a ranking list can well fit the user's information need since each of them might have very low relevance score. In other words, a diversified top-k ranking list should also have high relevance. That said, we will mainly focus on evaluating how different methods balance between the diversity and the relevance.

Notice that the relevance score for each individual node is often very small on large graphs (since the L_1 norm of the ranking vector is 1). To make the two quantities (diversity vs. relevance) comparable with each other, we need to normalize the relevance scores. Let $\hat{\mathcal{S}}$ be the top-k ranking list by the original personalized PageRank, we define the normalized relevance score for a given subset $\mathcal{S}(|\mathcal{S}| = k)$ as eq (9). Since the personalized PageRank always gives the k most relevant nodes, the Rel defined in eq (9) is always between 0 and 1 - higher means more relevant.

$$\text{Rel} = \frac{\sum_{i \in \mathcal{S}} \mathbf{r}(i)}{\sum_{i \in \hat{\mathcal{S}}} \mathbf{r}(i)} \quad (9)$$

5.2 Effectiveness of DRAGON: Case Studies

Let us start with an illustrative example to gain some visual intuitions. In Fig. 1, we show a fictitious co-authorship network, where each node corresponds to an author (e.g., *John, Smith, etc*), and the edge weight is the number of the co-authored papers. There are three communities in this network (e.g., *DM, DB* and *IR*). From Fig. 1, we can see that node 1 has very strong connections to the *DM* community. In other words, *DM* might be his/her major research interest. In addition, s/he also has some connections to the *IR* and *DB* communities. Given the budge $k = 3$, personalized PageRank returns all the three nodes (nodes 2, 3 and 5) from *DM* community which is consistent with the intuition since personalized PageRank solely focuses on the relevance. In contrast, the proposed DRAGON returns nodes 2, 6, and 10, each of which is still relevant enough to the query node 1. At the same time, they are diversified from each other, covering the whole spectrum of his/her research interest (*DM, DB,* and *IR*).

We also conduct cast studies on real graphs. We construct a co-authorship networks from *SIGIR* (the major conference on information retrieval) and *ICML* (the major conference on machine learning). We issue a query to find the top-*10* co-authors for Prof. *Yiming Yang*. The results are shown in Fig. 2. We compare it with the original personalized PageRank. *Yiming Yang* is a professor from Carnegie Mellon University; and she has broad interest in information retrieval and machine learning. From Fig. 2, we have the following observations. Firstly, both DRAGON and personalized PageRank share the same authors for the top-*3* returned authors, indicating that DRAGON also captures those highly relevant authors wrt the querying author. Secondly, our DRAGON returns a more diverse list of authors. For example, although *ChengXiang Zhai* is not a co-author of *Yiming Yang*, they shares a lot of research interest in information retrieval, and has a lot of indirect connections through other *IR* people. In contrast, the existence of some

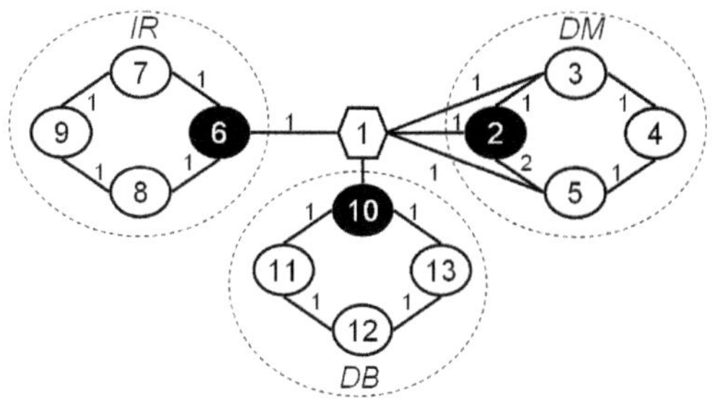

Figure 1: An illustrative example of a co-authorship network with three communities. Given the query node 1 and the budget $k = 3$, the proposed DRAGON returns three relevant and diversified nodes (2, 6, and 10, in black). In contrast, personalized PageRank returns nodes 2, 3 and 5 (all from the *DM* community).

authors in the ranking list by personalized PageRank is somehow redundant, in terms of helping the user to understand Prof. *Yiming Yang*'s whole collaboration network. For example, Prof. *Alex G. Hauptmann* is also from Carnegie Mellon University. Although, he has a lot of co-authored papers with *Yiming Yang*, they are also co-authored with *Jian Zhang* and *Rong Jin*. Therefore, given that *Jian Zhang* and *Rong Jin* are already in the ranking list, his existence does not provide much marginal information about *Yiming Yang*'s collaboration network. As a quantitative indicator, the average degree of the induced subgraph by DRAGON is only *2.8*, which is much lower (i.e., more diverse) than that by personalized PageRank (*4.3*). Finally, notice that for some authors, although they show up in both lists, their positions in the ranking list are different. For example, *Jian-Yun Nie* shows at the 4th and the 8th positions in the two ranking lists, respectively. This is because *Jian-Yun Nie* makes the top-*4* authors more diverse compared with *Thomas Pierce*, although its individual relevance score is lower than the latter.

5.3 Comparison with Alternative Methods for Diversified Ranking on Graphs

We compare the proposed DRAGON with ARW [42] and RRW [27], both of which also aim to improve the diversity of personalized PageRank. We skip the comparison with MMR [6] for brevity since [27] shows that its performance is not as good as RRW for the graph-type data. For RRW [27], it has two variants based on different approximation methods it actually uses: the one based on the cumulative estimation (referred to as 'RRW-a') and the other one based on the pointwise estimation (referred to as 'RRW-b').

First, let us compare how different methods balance between the relevance and the diversity. Fig. 3 shows the results on the *NIPS* co-authorship network. We test with different budgets ($k = 10, 20, 30, 40, 50, 100$). In Fig. 3, $\text{Div}(1)$ means that we only consider 1-step neighbors to measure the diversity (i.e., setting $t = 1$ in eq (8)). $\text{Div}(2)$ means that we consider both 1-step and 2-step neighbors (i.e., setting $t = 2$ in eq (8)). We only present the results by RRW-a since RRW-b gives similar results. From Fig. 3, we can see that all the three methods are effective to improve the diversity. The proposed DRAGON achieves a better balance between the relevance and the diversity. For ARW, although it gives the highest diversity score, its (normalized) relevance score is too low - only about half of the other two methods. This is because in ARW, *only* the first node is selected according to the relevance;

(a) Dragon	(b) Personalized PageRank
Jian Zhang	Jian Zhang
Rong Jin	Bryan Kisiel
Bryan Kisiel	Rong Jin
Jian-Yun Nie	Thomas Pierce
Wei-Ying Ma	Monica Rogati
Thomas Pierce	Tom Ault
Jan O. Pedersen	Alex G. Hauptmann
Ni Lao	Jian-Yun Nie
Jaime G. Carbonell	Ni Lao
ChengXiang Zhai	Abhimanyu Lad

Figure 2: Top-10 authors for Prof. Yiming Yang. Our DRAGON return a relevant, but more diverse list of authors. The difference between the two lists is highlighted in black.

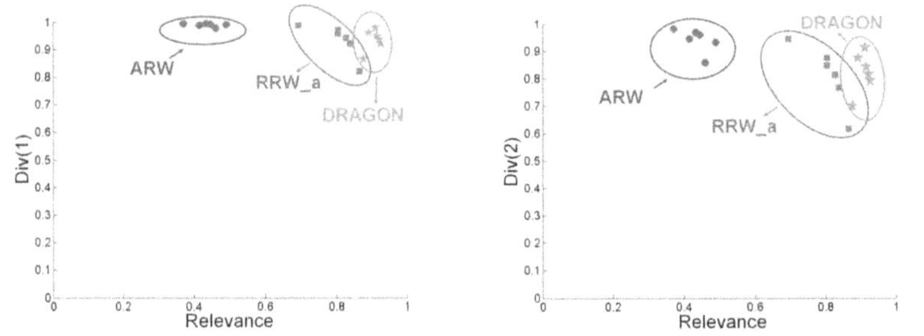

(a) Diversity by 1-step neighbors (b) Diversity by 1- and 2-step neighbors

Figure 3: Diversity and Relevance trade-off of different methods.

and all the remaining *(k-1)* are selected by diversity. As for RRW-a, both its relevance and diversity scores are lower than the proposed DRAGON. It is interesting to notice from Fig. 3(b) that the diversity of RRW-a drops a lot when it is measured by within 2-step neighbors (i.e., Div(2)). This is consistent with the intuition of RRW. In RRW (both RRW-a and RRW-b), it achieves the diversity by encouraging 1-step neighboring nodes to compete with each other. Consequently, the density of its within 1-step induced subgraph might low (i.e., high diversity), it is not necessary the case for the within t-step ($t \geq 2$) induced subgraph.

In order to test how the overall performance of different methods vary across different data sets, we take the average between relevance and diversity scores. The results are presented in Fig. 4, using four different co-authorship networks (*SIGMOD, NIPS, SIGIR, SIGGRAPH*). For the space limitation, we omit the results when the diversity is measured by within 1-steps neighbors, which is similar as the results by within 2-steps neighbors. It can be seen that the proposed DRAGON consistently performs the best.

5.4 Comparison with Alternative Optimization Methods

Here, we evaluate the effectiveness and the efficiency of the proposed DRAGON in terms of maximizing the goodness measure $f(\mathcal{S})$. We compared it with the two methods we introduced in subsection 4.1. We also compare it with two other heuristics. The first method (referred to as 'Heuristic1') starts with generating a candidate pool (e.g., the top $10 \times k$ most relevant nodes), picks one seed node, and then repeatedly adds the most dis-similar (measured by **A**) node into the ranking list from the candidate pool. The second method (referred to as 'Heuristic2') also starts with generating a candidate pool, puts all the nodes from candidate pool in the list, and then repeatedly drops a most similar (measured by **A**) node from the list.

First, let us evaluate how the different methods balance between the optimization quality (measured by $f(\mathcal{S})$) and the speed (measured by wall-clock time). Fig. 5 shows the results from the co-authorship network of *NIPS* and *KDD* conferences with the budget $k = 20$, where $f(\mathcal{S})$ is normalized by the highest one among different methods. It can be seen that the proposed DRAGON is the best - it leads to the highest optimization quality (i.e., highest $f(\mathcal{S})$) with the least amount of wall-clock time. Notice that the y-axis is in logarithm scale.

We also conduct experiments on the co-authorship network constructed from multiple conferences. Fig. 6 shows the results on these data sets with the budget $k = 20$. Here *Sub(n,m)* means a co-authorship network with n nodes and m edges. We stop the program if it takes more than 100,000 seconds (i.e., more than 10 days). It can be seen from Fig. 6 that the proposed DRAGON is consistently best across all the different data sets - it leads to highest optimization quality (i.e., highest $f(\mathcal{S})$) with least amount of wall-clock time. The normalized $f(\mathcal{S})$ for 'Lin-QP' is missing for *Sub(24K,114K)* because it fails to finish within 100,000 seconds. This indicates that it is not feasible for large graphs. For the smaller graphs, 'Lin-QP' leads to slightly lower $f(\mathcal{S})$ than the proposed DRAGON; but it requires 3-5 orders of magnitude wall-clock time. For all the other comparative methods, they lead to worse optimization quality with longer wall-clock time.

5.5 Scalability

We also evaluate the scalability of DRAGON. When we evaluate the scalability wrt the number of the nodes in the graph, we fix the number of edges and vice versa. The results in Fig. 7 are consistent with the complexity analysis in subsection 4.3 - the proposed DRAGON scales linearly wrt both n and m, which means that it is suitable for large graphs.

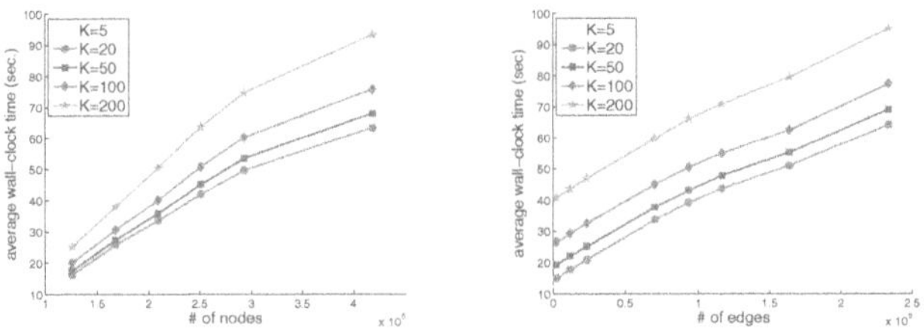

(a) Time vs. # of nodes (b) Time vs. # of edges

Figure 7: Scalability of DRAGON. The proposed DRAGON scales linearly wrt the size of the graph.

6. RELATED WORK

In this section, we review the related work, which can be categorized into four parts: ranking on graphs, diversity, set-level optimization for data mining and general graph mining.

Ranking on Graphs. Personalized PageRank is one of the most fundamental and most widely used ranking methods on graphs. It has been successfully applied to many high-impact applications [30, 11].Many other ranking methods on graphs are built upon, and/or share the similar ideas as personalized PageRank, such as RalationalRank [9, 3], random walk with restart [37], SimRank [22], etc. Because of its generality and wide applicability, we choose Personalized PageRank as the starting point of our method. Other ranking methods on graphs include HITS [15], electricity-based methods [17], etc. There also exist a lot of work to speed-up the computation of personalized PageRank, such as [37, 33, 13]. It is worth pointing out that all these fast algorithms can be naturally plugged into the proposed DRAGON to gain further savings in computational time.

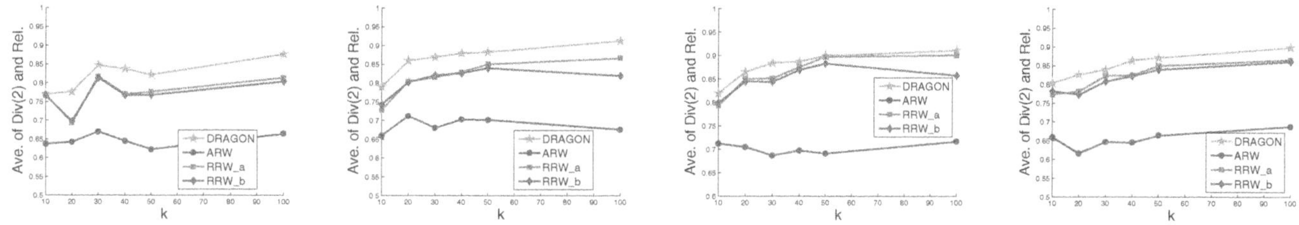

(a) *SIGMOD* (b) *NIPS* (c) *SIGIR* (d) *SIGGRAPH*

Figure 4: Comparison with alternative methods for diversified ranking on graphs. The average of the relevance and the diversity vs. the budget k (larger is better). The proposed DRAGON(red star) consistently performs the best.

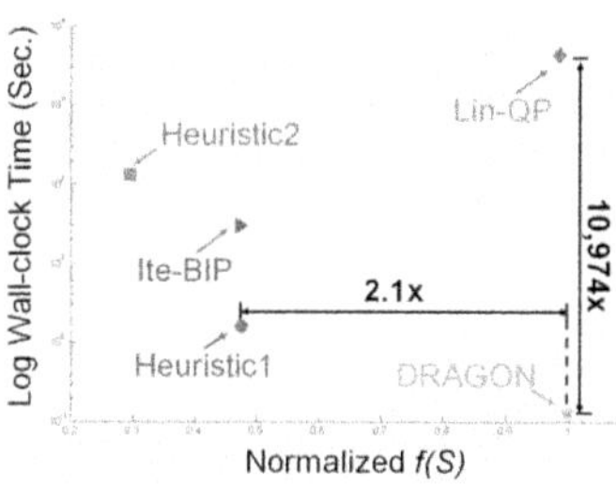

Figure 5: Wall-clock time vs. quality on the *NIPS+KDD* co-authorship Network. The y-axis is in logarithm scale. The proposed DRAGON is the best. It has the highest f($\mathcal{S}$) with the least amount of time.

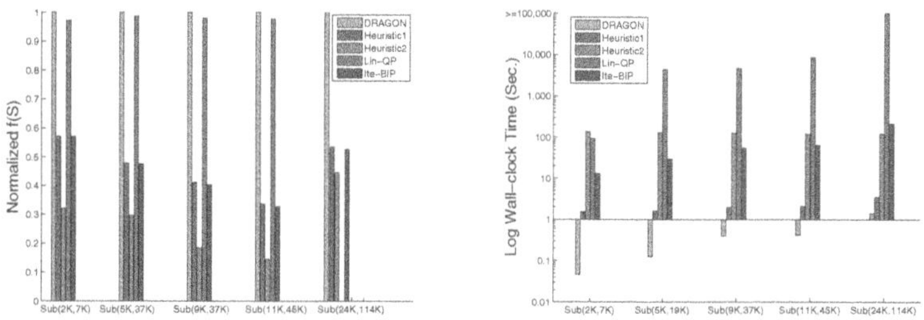

(a) Comparison on the normalized f($\mathcal{S}$) (higher is better)

Comparison on wall-clock time (lower is better)

Figure 6: Comparison of different optimization methods. Our DRAGON(the left most one) always leads to the highest f($\mathcal{S}$), with the least amount of time. Best viewed in color.

Diversity. It is now widely recognized that diversity is a highly desired property in many data mining tasks, such as expertise and legal search [32], recommendation system [43], blog filtering [7], document summarization [6], etc. It is a powerful tool to address the uncertainty and ambiguity; and/or to cover the different aspects of an information need [32]. For the graph-type data, [42] was among the first to address the diversified ranking on graphs. [27] proposed to balance between the relevance and diversity based on the vertex reinforcement random walk on graphs . However, they suffer from some important subtle issues as we show in subsection 4.4. There are also a lot of algorithms to improve the diversity for other types of data (e.g., document, etc), including [6, 41, 21], etc.

Set-level Optimization for Data Mining. In the recent years, set-level optimizationhas been playing a very important role in many data mining tasks. Many set-level optimization problems are NP-hard. Therefore, it is difficult, if not impossible, to find the global optimal solutions. However, if the function is monotonic sub-modular with 0 function value for the empty set, a greedy strategy can lead to a provably near-optimal solution [18]. This powerful strategy has been recurring in many different settings, e.g., immunization, outbreak detection, blog filtering, sensor placement, influence maximization, structure learning, etc. (See [18] for a comprehensive review). In this paper, we introduce a new type of submodular function tailored for diversified ranking on large graphs.

General Graph Mining. There is a lot of work on graph mining. Representative works include pattern and law mining [5], frequent substructure discovery [39], compression [26], fraud and anomaly detection [29], community mining and graph partition [14, 34, 25, 40], social action tracking [36], user click-through modeling [1, 2], collaborative filtering [16, 8, 35, 12], term formation [19], network classification [28], link prediction [23, 24, 4], etc.

7. CONCLUSION

In this paper, we address the diversified ranking on large graphs from an optimization point of view. To the best of our knowledge, this is the first work for diversified ranking on large graphs that (1) has a clear optimization formulation (see eq. (3)); (2) finds provably near-optimal solutions (see Theorem 1 and Lemma 1); and (3) enjoys the linear scalability (see Lemma 2 and Lemma 3). Our experimental evaluations on real graphs validate that our method is (1) indeed effective to balance the relevance and the diversity in top-k ranking; and (2) scalable to large graphs.

8. ACKNOWLEDGEMENT

Research was sponsored by the Army Research Laboratory and was accomplished under Cooperative Agreement Number W911NF-09-2-0053. The views and conclusions contained in this document are those of the authors and should not be interpreted as representing the official policies, either expressed or implied, of the Army Research Laboratory or the U.S. Government. The U.S. Government is authorized to reproduce and distribute reprints for Government purposes notwithstanding any copyright notation here on.

9. REFERENCES

[1] C. L. 0001, F. Guo, and C. Faloutsos. Bbm: bayesian browsing model from petabyte-scale data. In *KDD*, pages 537–546, 2009.

[2] D. Agarwal, A. Z. Broder, D. Chakrabarti, D. Diklic, V. Josifovski, and M. Sayyadian. Estimating rates of rare events at multiple resolutions. In *KDD*, pages 16–25, 2007.

[3] A. Angel, S. Chaudhuri, G. Das, and N. Koudas. Ranking objects based on relationships and fixed associations. In *EDBT'09*, pages 910–921, 2009.

[4] L. Backstrom and J. Leskovec. Supervised random walks: predicting and recommending links in social networks. In *WSDM*, pages 635–644, 2011.

[5] A. Broder, R. Kumar, F. Maghoul1, P. Raghavan, S. Rajagopalan, R. Stata, A. Tomkins, and J. Wiener. Graph structure in the web: experiments and models. In *WWW Conf.*, 2000.

[6] J. G. Carbonell and J. Goldstein. The use of mmr, diversity-based reranking for reordering documents and producing summaries. In *SIGIR*, pages 335–336, 1998.

[7] K. El-Arini, G. Veda, D. Shahaf, and C. Guestrin. Turning down the noise in the blogosphere. In *KDD*, pages 289–298, 2009.

[8] Y. Ge, H. Xiong, A. Tuzhilin, K. Xiao, M. Gruteser, and M. J. Pazzani. An energy-efficient mobile recommender system. In *KDD*, pages 899–908, 2010.

[9] F. Geerts, H. Mannila, and E. Terzi. Relational link-based ranking. In *VLDB*, pages 552–563, 2004.

[10] G. H. Golub and C. F. V. Loan. *Matrix Perturbation Theory*. The Johns Hopkins University Press, 1996.

[11] T. H. Haveliwala. Topic-sensitive pagerank. *WWW*, pages 517–526, 2002.

[12] D. Heckerman, D. M. Chickering, C. Meek, R. Rounthwaite, and C. M. Kadie. Dependency networks for collaborative filtering and data visualization. In *UAI*, pages 264–273, 2000.

[13] U. Kang, C. E. Tsourakakis, and C. Faloutsos. Pegasus: A peta-scale graph mining system. In *ICDM*, pages 229–238, 2009.

[14] G. Karypis and V. Kumar. Multilevel -way hypergraph partitioning. In *DAC*, pages 343–348, 1999.

[15] J. M. Kleinberg. Authoritative sources in a hyperlinked environment. *J. ACM*, 46(5):604–632, 1999.

[16] Y. Koren. Collaborative filtering with temporal dynamics. In *KDD*, pages 447–456, 2009.

[17] Y. Koren, S. C. North, and C. Volinsky. Measuring and extracting proximity in networks. In *KDD*, pages 245–255, 2006.

[18] A. Krause and C. Guestrin. Beyond convexity - submodularity in machine learning. In *ICML*, 2008.

[19] T. Lappas, K. Liu, and E. Terzi. Finding a team of experts in social networks. In *KDD*, pages 467–476, 2009.

[20] J. Leskovec, A. Krause, C. Guestrin, C. Faloutsos, J. M. VanBriesen, and N. S. Glance. Cost-effective outbreak detection in networks. In *KDD*, pages 420–429, 2007.

[21] L. Li, K. Zhou, G.-R. Xue, H. Zha, and Y. Yu. Enhancing diversity, coverage and balance for summarization through structure learning. In *WWW*, pages 71–80, 2009.

[22] P. Li, H. Liu, J. X. Yu, J. He, and X. Du. Fast single-pair simrank computation. In *SDM*, pages 571–582, 2010.

[23] D. Liben-Nowell and J. Kleinberg. The link prediction problem for social networks. In *Proc. CIKM*, 2003.

[24] R. Lichtenwalter, J. T. Lussier, and N. V. Chawla. New perspectives and methods in link prediction. In *KDD*, pages 243–252, 2010.

[25] A. S. Maiya and T. Y. Berger-Wolf. Sampling community structure. In *WWW*, pages 701–710, 2010.

[26] H. Maserrat and J. Pei. Neighbor query friendly compression of social networks. In *KDD*, pages 533–542, 2010.

[27] Q. Mei, J. Guo, and D. R. Radev. Divrank: the interplay of prestige and diversity in information networks. In *KDD*, pages 1009–1018, 2010.

[28] J. Neville, B. Gallagher, and T. Eliassi-Rad. Evaluating statistical tests for within-network classifiers of relational data. In *ICDM*, pages 397–406, 2009.

[29] C. C. Noble and D. J. Cook. Graph-based anomaly detection. In *KDD*, pages 631–636, 2003.

[30] L. Page, S. Brin, R. Motwani, and T. Winograd. The PageRank citation ranking: Bringing order to the web. Technical report, Stanford Digital Library Technologies Project, 1998. Paper SIDL-WP-1999-0120 (version of 11/11/1999).

[31] R. Pemantle. Vertex reinforced random walk. *Prob. Th. and Rel. Fields*, pages 117–136, 1992.

[32] F. Radlinski, P. N. Bennett, B. Carterette, and T. Joachims. Redundancy, diversity and interdependent document relevance. *SIGIR Forum*, 43(2):46–52, 2009.

[33] P. Sarkar and A. W. Moore. Fast nearest-neighbor search in disk-resident graphs. In *KDD*, pages 513–522, 2010.

[34] V. Satuluri and S. Parthasarathy. Scalable graph clustering using stochastic flows: applications to community discovery. In *KDD*, pages 737–746, 2009.

[35] H. Shan and A. Banerjee. Generalized probabilistic matrix factorizations for collaborative filtering. In *ICDM*, pages 1025–1030, 2010.

[36] C. Tan, J. Tang, J. Sun, Q. Lin, and F. Wang. Social action tracking via noise tolerant time-varying factor graphs. In *KDD*, pages 1049–1058, 2010.

[37] H. Tong, C. Faloutsos, and J.-Y. Pan. Fast random walk with restart and its applications. In *ICDM*, pages 613–622, 2006.

[38] L. Wu. Social network effects on performance and layoffs: Evidence from the adoption of a social networking tool. *Job Market Paper*, 2011.

[39] D. Xin, J. Han, X. Yan, and H. Cheng. Mining compressed frequent-pattern sets. In *VLDB*, pages 709–720, 2005.

[40] X. Yin, J. Han, and P. S. Yu. Cross-relational clustering with user's guidance. In *KDD*, pages 344–353, 2005.

[41] Y. Yue and T. Joachims. Predicting diverse subsets using structural svms. In *ICML*, pages 1224–1231, 2008.

[42] X. Zhu, A. B. Goldberg, J. V. Gael, and D. Andrzejewski. Improving diversity in ranking using absorbing random walks. In *HLT-NAACL*, pages 97–104, 2007.

[43] C.-N. Ziegler, S. M. McNee, J. A. Konstan, and G. Lausen. Improving recommendation lists through topic diversification. In *WWW*, pages 22–32, 2005.

Entity Disambiguation with Hierarchical Topic Models

Saurabh S. Kataria*
Pennsylvania State U.
State College, PA
skataria@ist.psu.edu

Krishnan S. Kumar
Yahoo! Labs
Bangalore, India
krishsk@yahoo-inc.com

Rajeev Rastogi
Yahoo! Labs
Bangalore, India
rrastogi@yahoo-inc.com

Prithviraj Sen
Yahoo! Labs
Bangalore, India
sen@yahoo-inc.com

Srinivasan H Sengamedu
Yahoo! Labs
Bangalore, India
shs@yahoo-inc.com

ABSTRACT

Disambiguating entity references by annotating them with unique ids from a catalog is a critical step in the enrichment of unstructured content. In this paper, we show that topic models, such as *Latent Dirichlet Allocation* (LDA) and its hierarchical variants, form a natural class of models for learning accurate entity disambiguation models from crowd-sourced knowledge bases such as Wikipedia. Our main contribution is a *semi-supervised* hierarchical model called *Wikipedia-based Pachinko Allocation Model* (WPAM) that exploits: (1) All words in the Wikipedia corpus to learn word-entity associations (unlike existing approaches that only use words in a small fixed window around annotated entity references in Wikipedia pages), (2) Wikipedia annotations to appropriately bias the assignment of entity labels to annotated (and co-occurring unannotated) words during model learning, and (3) Wikipedia's category hierarchy to capture co-occurrence patterns among entities. We also propose a scheme for pruning spurious nodes from Wikipedia's crowd-sourced category hierarchy. In our experiments with multiple real-life datasets, we show that WPAM outperforms state-of-the-art baselines by as much as 16% in terms of disambiguation accuracy.

Categories and Subject Descriptors

H.2.8 [**Database applications**]: Data mining

General Terms

Algorithms, Theory, Performance

*Work done while first author was interning at Yahoo!Labs.

KDD'11, August 21–24, 2011, San Diego, California, USA.

Keywords

Entity Resolution, Disambiguation, Topic Models

1. INTRODUCTION

Even though the world wide web is a veritable knowledge base for everything under the sun, a large chunk of it still exists in the form of unstructured text generated with little or no curation. One important step to instilling structure into such free-form text is to collect all references to entities within it and annotate them with ids from an existing catalog of entities. Doing this will not only enable merge operations with other pieces of similarly annotated text but also promises to aid semantic search, information extraction and integration, document classification, and a host of other applications. For instance, if we know that a user is browsing a page about Michael Jordan the basketball player, then we can show the user additional articles related to only Michael Jordan the sportsperson and not Michael I. Jordan the machine learning researcher.

The crucial task in annotating entity references is to decide which entity from the catalog a particular reference is associated with. In this paper, we refer to this problem as the *entity disambiguation* problem.

1.1 Leveraging Wikipedia for Entity Disambiguation

With over 3.4 million crowd-sourced entities, Wikipedia [2] is clearly a formidable resource, one that can serve as a comprehensive reference catalog for large-scale entity disambiguation. Each Wikipedia entity has a separate page, and a vast network of internal links annotate words in the body of pages with entities that they refer to. The copious annotations constitute valuable training data, and prior work [9, 17, 11, 19, 14] has used them to learn models for disambiguating entities at scale. Thus, Wikipedia has enabled a paradigm of *weak supervision* where freely available annotations are used to train machine-learned models.

One way to broadly categorize the various entity disambiguation approaches proposed in the literature is based on the sources of evidence that they utilize. The *local context* of a reference forms one major source of evidence used in previous work [9, 17, 11, 14]. For instance, there exist a number of Columbus's, e.g., explorer, film director, etc., but if the words "ocean" or "ship" appear in the vicinity, then that should increase our belief that the reference is to the explorer. Existing approaches use local context evidence for entity disambiguation in two steps. First, they learn the context for each entity from the local context of annotated references to the entity (embedded in other Wikipedia pages). Subsequently, to resolve a reference, they compare the local context of the reference with the (learned) context for each candidate entity to determine their compatibility.

Co-occurrence patterns form yet another major source of evidence used in prior work [11, 19, 14] where the hypothesis is that certain entities often appear together and disambiguating one reference should help to decide which entities the other references within the same document are referring to. For example, there are eight Michael Jordan's (basketball player, researcher, actor, etc.) and three Charles Barkley's (basketball player, politician, etc.) in Wikipedia. But if a document contains mentions of both Michael Jordan and Charles Barkley, then we can be fairly certain that both references are to basketball players.

1.2 Shortcomings of Existing Approaches

Prior research works [9, 17, 14], when computing local context compatibility, have used a range of window sizes (e.g., 55 words in [9] and 7 words in [17]) around each reference for determining the words that are a part of its local context. Finding a single optimal value for the window size parameter is a non-trivial task – a window size that is too small can cause important words to be excluded from the local context while irrelevant words may become part of the context with too large a window size.

Furthermore, even though freely available knowledge bases such as Wikipedia contain a large number of annotations, they are still at best, only *partially* annotated datasets. (Usually, only the first occurrence of a relevant reference on a page is annotated as advocated by Wikipedia's manual of style [4].) Existing disambiguation methods completely ignore un-annotated references to an entity in a Wikipedia page, and so the local context of these references is not included in the context for the entity.

1.3 Problem Definition

We denote the set of all Wikipedia entity pages by $\mathcal{W}$. Consider an arbitrary set of documents $\mathcal{D}$. These can be news articles, product or restaurant reviews, blog posts, or crawled web pages. The entity disambiguation problem is to label the entity references in documents from $\mathcal{D}$ with Wikipedia entities in $\mathcal{W}$. In this paper, we assume that entity references are given to us. Thus, we do not address the problem of identifying entity references in text which is a separate problem that can be handled using named-entity recognizers as described in [11], dictionary lookups, etc.

1.4 Our Contributions

Our main contribution is a *weakly semi-supervised hierarchical topic model* for entity disambiguation called *Wikipedia-based Pachinko Allocation Model* (WPAM). WPAM is a hierarchical variant of the popular *Latent Dirichlet Allocation* (LDA) [7] topic model, and is inspired by the *Pachinko Allocation Model* (PAM) recently proposed in [16]. However, unlike PAM which is completely unsupervised, WPAM is semi-supervised. WPAM extensively leverages Wikipedia pages, annotations, and category information to provide a form of weak supervision when training models. To the best of our knowledge, our work is the first to apply topic models in conjunction with Wikipedia for large-scale entity disambiguation. There is a body of work [5, 8, 25] that employs topic models for entity resolution but, like PAM, these are also unsupervised and do not exploit Wikipedia resources.

Topic models associate a latent topic with each word in a document. One of our key ideas is to associate a distinct topic with each Wikipedia entity. Thus, using topic models to label words with entity-specific topics provides us with a principled approach to entity disambiguation. Unlike existing disambiguation schemes (described earlier), topic models are oblivious to window size settings – their internal machinery naturally selects words that frequently co-occur with each entity (across the entire document corpus) to learn word-entity mappings. The selected words can be from anywhere within a document including the neighborhood of un-annotated references. Thus, topic models circumvent the issue of setting a window size and still learn high-quality word-entity associations, and this can boost disambiguation accuracy. Early topic models like LDA relied primarily on co-occurrences at the word level for labeling. Subsequent *hierarchical* versions such as PAM are capable of capturing not only word-entity associations but also co-occurrence patterns among entities using a topic hierarchy.

WPAM uses Wikipedia's category hierarchy [3] as the topic hierarchy to disambiguate entities with hierarchical topic models. Wikipedia's category hierarchy contains entities as leaves and each entity is assigned to (one or more) parent categories. Furthermore, semantically related entities (that are likely to occur together in documents) are grouped under one or more relevant categories. For instance, Michael Jordan and Charles Barkley are both assigned to the category "African American basketball players" (among a number of others) which is a sub-category of "American basketball players" and "African-American sportspeople". Thus, WPAM uses a flexible, semantically rich topic hierarchy that captures entity correlations much better compared to the rigid hierarchies with a fixed number of levels used by different PAM variants (e.g., four-level PAM [16]).

With millions of fine-grained topics, one per entity, the space of possible word-topic assignments is enormous and this can confound PAM. Thus, a key challenge here is to be able to guide the topic models so that they annotate words with the correct entities. To this end, we develop *weakly semi-supervised* techniques that exploit Wikipedia's crowd-sourced annotations for WPAM model learning. During learning, when selecting an entity to label a word, our techniques introduce a bias in favor of entities that frequently appear in annotations for either the word or the document containing it. This bias originating from annotated words also spreads to co-occurring un-annotated words, and recursively through them to more words. Thus, since un-annotated portions of documents also play a role in propagating entity labels, WPAM's learning techniques are semi-supervised.

Finally, due to the lack of curation and the crowd-sourced manner in which it is produced, the Wikipedia hierarchy contains some spurious categories that can mislead our WPAM model. For example, Michael Jordan is listed under the categories "Living People" and "1963 Births". We develop techniques to prune such irrelevant categories containing uncorrelated entities which co-occur infrequently.

To gauge the effectiveness of our topic model-based entity disambiguation approach, we conduct an extensive experimental study using two real-life datasets: (1) Held-out subset of annotated Wikipedia data, and (2) Pre-annotated news articles from New York Times (NYT). Our experimental results indicate that our WPAM model is able to achieve an impressive disambiguation accuracy of 70% compared to 54% for the current state-of-the-art method of [14].

The rest of the paper is organized as follows. In Section 2, we develop weakly semi-supervised techniques for LDA and use Wikipedia annotations to learn accurate disambiguation models based on entity context alone. In Section 3, we develop weakly semi-supervised techniques for our WPAM hierarchical topic model that exploits both Wikipedia annotations and its category hierarchy to learn accurate models of disambiguation based on both entity context and co-occurrence. In Section 4, we experiment with real-life Wikipedia and NYT datasets to demonstrate the efficacy of our proposed techniques. We take a closer look at relevant related work in Section 5, and Section 6 concludes the paper.

2. WEAKLY SEMI-SUPERVISED TOPIC MODELS

Topic models represent documents as mixtures of (latent) topics, where each topic is a probability distribution over words. The document-topic and topic-word distributions are learned automatically from the data in an unsupervised manner with no human labeling or prior knowledge required.

Our entity disambiguation models build upon the popular LDA model which has been extensively used for classification of short text segments [23], unsupervised entity resolution [5, 8, 25], prediction of movie ratings from reviews [6], and extraction of ratable aspects of objects from online reviews [27]. In this section, we first show how to use LDA to assign entity labels to document words by mapping each entity to a separate topic. We then present techniques that leverage Wikipedia annotations to bias prior document-topic and topic-word distributions. The result is a semi-supervised version of LDA which is different from the unsupervised models previously used for entity resolution [5, 8, 25].

2.1 Latent Dirichlet Allocation

LDA is a probabilistic generative model that assumes Dirichlet priors on document-topic and topic-word distributions. Consider a collection of M documents containing words from the vocabulary of terms $\{1, \ldots, T\}$, and let $\{1, \ldots, K\}$ be a set of topics. The LDA model is defined by two parameters: (1) the multinomial distribution $\vec{\theta}_m = P(z|d = m)$ over topics for each document m, and (2) the multinomial distribution $\vec{\phi}_k = P(w|z = k)$ over words for each topic k. LDA's document generation process is as follows:

- For each topic k, sample word distribution $\vec{\phi}_k \sim \text{Dir}(\vec{\beta})$.
- For each document m
  - Sample topic distribution $\vec{\theta}_m \sim \text{Dir}(\vec{\alpha})$.
  - For each word w_i in document m
    - Sample a topic $z_i \sim \text{Mult}(\vec{\theta}_m)$.
    - Sample a word $w_i \sim \text{Mult}(\vec{\phi}_{z_i})$.

Above, $\text{Dir}(\vec{\alpha})$ and $\text{Dir}(\vec{\beta})$ are Dirichlet distributions with hyper-parameters $\vec{\alpha}$ and $\vec{\beta}$, respectively. And $\text{Mult}(\vec{\theta}_m)$ and $\text{Mult}(\vec{\phi}_{z_i})$ are multinomial distributions. In the following subsections, we will use $\vec{w}$ to denote the vector of words contained in the documents, and $\vec{z}$ to denote the corresponding topics for the words.

2.2 Inference Using Gibbs Sampling

The problem of statistical inference involves estimating the probability distribution $\vec{\phi}_k$ over words associated with each topic k, the distribution over topics $\vec{\theta}_m$ for each document m, and often, the topic responsible for generating each word. Instead of directly estimating $\vec{\phi}_k$ and $\vec{\theta}_m$, we use the approach of [12] that first constructs the posterior distribution $P(\vec{z}|\vec{w})$ and then estimates $\vec{\phi}_k$ and $\vec{\theta}_m$ from this posterior distribution.

To efficiently estimate the posterior distribution, [12] uses Gibbs sampling which is a simple and widely applicable *Markov chain Monte Carlo* (MCMC) algorithm for sampling from complex high-dimensional distributions. Starting with a random topic assignment $\vec{z}$, the Gibbs sampling algorithm iterates through each word in the document corpus. In each step, the algorithm samples a topic assignment for a word w_i conditioned on the topic assignments of all other words. More formally, in each Gibbs sampling step, the algorithm replaces z_i by a topic drawn from the distribution $P(z_i|\vec{z}_{-i}, \vec{w})$, where $\vec{z}_{-i}$ is $\vec{z}$ without the ith component.

For a word $w_i = t$ in document m, the conditional probability that $z_i = k$ is given by (a detailed derivation of the formula below can be found in [13]):

$$P(z_i = k|\vec{z}_{-i}, \vec{w}, \vec{\alpha}, \vec{\beta}) \propto \frac{n_{t,-i}^{(k)} + \beta_t}{\sum_{t'=1}^{T}(n_{t',-i}^{(k)} + \beta_{t'})} \cdot \frac{n_{k,-i}^{(m)} + \alpha_k}{\sum_{k'=1}^{K}(n_{k',-i}^{(m)} + \alpha_{k'})} \quad (1)$$

Above, $n_{t,-i}^{(k)}$ is the number of times term t is assigned topic k excluding the current assignment; similarly, $n_{k,-i}^{(m)}$ is the number of words in document m that are assigned topic k excluding the current assignment. The Gibbs sampling equation (1) is fairly intuitive – the first term is the probability of term t under topic k and the second term is the probability of topic k in document m. Observe that due to the second term, the topic assignment for a word is heavily influenced by the topic assignments for the remaining words in the document. Therefore, co-occurring words do influence each other's topic assignments and will very likely be assigned the same topic by the Gibbs sampling algorithm.

The sequence of samples obtained from Gibbs sampling form a Markov chain that converges to the posterior distribution $P(\vec{z}|\vec{w})$. Thus, after an initial burn-in period, we can get a representative set of samples from the distribution by collecting Gibbs samples at regularly spaced intervals. These can then be used to estimate the distributions $\vec{\phi}_k$ and $\vec{\theta}_m$ as described in [12, 13].

In our implementation, we estimate the $\vec{\alpha}$ and $\vec{\beta}$ Dirichlet hyper-parameters using Minka's fixed-point iteration [21].

2.3 Using LDA for Entity Disambiguation

We use LDA to develop an unsupervised algorithm for disambiguating the entity references in document set $\mathcal{D}$. Essentially, our disambiguation algorithm runs Gibbs sampling with a separate topic per Wikipedia entity. Thus, Gibbs sampling assigns entity labels to all the words in the documents, effectively disambiguating all the entity references.

Our disambiguation algorithm has two phases: *training* and *labeling*. In the training phase, we run Gibbs sampling only on the collection of Wikipedia pages $\mathcal{W}$. Let $\vec{z}_{\mathcal{W}}$ denote the topic assignments for words in $\mathcal{W}$ at the end of the training phase. Next, in the labeling phase, we run an *incremental* Gibbs sampling algorithm on $\mathcal{W} \cup \mathcal{D}$ that only samples topics for words in $\mathcal{D}$ while keeping the topics for words in $\mathcal{W}$ fixed at $\vec{z}_{\mathcal{W}}$. Let $\vec{z}_{\mathcal{D}}$ be the topic assignments for words in $\mathcal{D}$. Then, in each incremental Gibbs sampling step during the labeling phase, only $\vec{z}_{\mathcal{D}}$ changes but $\vec{z}_{\mathcal{W}}$ stays constant. A topic for word w_i in $\mathcal{D}$ is sampled according to the Gibbs sampling equation (1). Note that the count $n_{t,-i}^{(k)}$ in the equation is the total number of times term t is assigned topic k across $\vec{z}_{\mathcal{D}}$ and $\vec{z}_{\mathcal{W}}$.

A major scalability challenge is that with a separate topic per Wikipedia entity, the number of topics K is equal to the number of entities in Wikipedia which can be quite large. As a result, in each Gibbs sampling step, the cost of sampling a topic assignment for w_i from its conditional distribution can be prohibitive since we need to compute the conditional probabilities for all K topics according to Equation (1). The key observation we make here is that in general only a few entities are relevant to each document. And these are typically entities with a surface form that matches a keyword in the document. (The surface forms for an entity are the anchor text appearing within links to the entity embedded in Wikipedia pages.) Thus, for each document, we identify the entities with matches, and only consider topics corresponding to these entities when sampling a topic assignment for a word in the document. This simple optimization results in a substantial speedup, enabling us to scale to lots of topics.

2.4 Weakly Semi-Supervised LDA

The standard LDA topic model is completely unsupervised, and determines topics for words entirely based on the co-occurrence patterns of words across documents. However, with millions of fine-grained topics, the space of topic assignments to words is vast, and this makes the task of finding a "good" topic assignment extremely challenging.

In this section, we leverage the prior Wikipedia annotations of words with entities to provide a form of weak supervision to the basic LDA model with the objective of improving its labeling accuracy. Let $\mathcal{A}$ denote the portions of Wikipedia pages containing only annotated words along with their entity labels. The key idea underlying our approach is to bias the topic-word distributions $\vec{\phi}_k$ in favor of words that are frequently annotated with (the entity corresponding to) topic k in $\mathcal{A}$, and the document-topic distributions $\vec{\theta}_m$ in favor of topics (corresponding to entities) that frequently occur in document m's annotations in $\mathcal{A}$.

We consider the Wikipedia annotations $\mathcal{A}$ as multinomial observations that bias the distributions of parameters $\vec{\theta}_m$ and $\vec{\phi}_k$. Recall that $\vec{\theta}_m$ and $\vec{\phi}_k$ have Dirichlet priors with hyper-parameters $\vec{\alpha}$ and $\vec{\beta}$, respectively. $P(\vec{\phi}_k|\vec{\beta}, \mathcal{A})$, the posterior distribution of $\vec{\phi}_k$ conditioned on annotations $\mathcal{A}$, can be shown to be $\mathrm{Dir}(\vec{\phi}_k|\vec{\beta} + \vec{\delta}^{(k)})$. Here, $\delta_t^{(k)}$ is the number of times term t is assigned topic k in $\mathcal{A}$. Similarly, we can show that $\vec{\theta}_m$ has a Dirichlet posterior with hyper-parameters $\vec{\alpha} + \vec{\delta}^{(m)}$ where $\delta_k^{(m)}$ is the number of annotated words in document m that are assigned topic k in $\mathcal{A}$.

We finally get the conditional probability that $z_i = k$ (for word $w_i = t$ in document m) given the observed Wikipedia annotations $\mathcal{A}$ as:

$$P(z_i = k|\vec{z}_{-i}, \vec{w}, \vec{\alpha}, \vec{\beta}, \mathcal{A}) \tag{2}$$
$$\propto \frac{n_{t,-i}^{(k)} + \beta_t + \delta_t^{(k)}}{\sum_{t'=1}^{T}(n_{t',-i}^{(k)} + \beta_{t'} + \delta_{t'}^{(k)})} \cdot \frac{n_{k,-i}^{(m)} + \alpha_k + \delta_k^{(m)}}{\sum_{k'=1}^{K}(n_{k',-i}^{(m)} + \alpha_{k'} + \delta_{k'}^{(m)})}$$

Thus, we incorporate knowledge of Wikipedia annotations in the new Gibbs sampling equation (2) above by adding the prior counts $\delta_t^{(k)}$ and $\delta_k^{(m)}$ observed in $\mathcal{A}$ to the counts $n_{t,-i}^{(k)}$ and $n_{k,-i}^{(m)}$, respectively. This has the effect of biasing the topic assignment for a word (in each Gibbs sampling step) in favor of topics that frequently appear in annotations $\mathcal{A}$ for either the word or the document containing it. Furthermore, this topic bias spreads to other occurrences of the word in the document corpus as well as to co-occurring words, and recursively through them to more words. These words that propagate topic assignment biases can be un-annotated words not contained in $\mathcal{A}$, and hence our LDA model with biased $\vec{\phi}_k$ and $\vec{\theta}_m$ distributions is semi-supervised. Note that this bias propagation can be quite powerful in practice; in fact, previous research on semi-supervised learning [18, 22] has shown that if we can avail of large amounts of unlabeled data and combine that with the labeled training data then the accuracy of machine-learned models can be dramatically improved. Our experimental results corroborate this with semi-supervised LDA improving disambiguation accuracy by as much as 30.2% over standard LDA.

3. WEAKLY SEMI-SUPERVISED HIERARCHICAL TOPIC MODEL

LDA selects topics based on correlations among words, but it does not explicitly model correlations among topics. However, real-world documents are generally topically coherent, and so a model that can capture topic correlations as well can lead to higher disambiguation accuracy. As pointed out in Section 1, exploiting topic correlations can help to resolve an ambiguous Michael Jordan reference to the basketball player (as opposed to the researcher) if the document also contains a reference to Charles Barkley the basketball player. LDA may have difficulty disambiguating such references because it can combine arbitrary sets of topics.

Hierarchical topic models extend LDA to capture both word and topic correlations in a single unified framework. A hierarchical topic model takes as input a topic hierarchy which can be an arbitrary DAG over topics with interior nodes representing a correlation among child topics. It assigns each word a root-to-leaf topic path with a preference for annotating a document's words with overlapping paths that share subpaths starting at the root. Thus, the topics for each document are close by in the topic hierarchy, and therefore highly correlated.

In Section 3.1, we describe our *weakly semi-supervised hierarchical topic model* which we call *Wikipedia-based Pachinko Allocation Model* (WPAM). WPAM builds on the *Pachinko Allocation Model* (PAM) proposed in [16] but differs from [16] in two important respects. First, [16] focuses on a fixed four-level topic hierarchy – a problem with such a rigid structure is that it may not accurately model real-world topic correlations. In contrast, WPAM leverages the Wikipedia category hierarchy that has a flexible DAG structure with a different number of levels in different regions of the hierarchy. The Wikipedia hierarchy groups semantically related entities (and categories) under one or more relevant categories – thus, it is quite effective at capturing topic correlations. A second key difference between PAM and WPAM is that PAM is unsupervised. WPAM, on the other hand, is a weakly semi-supervised model that uses Wikipedia annotations as training data to bias topic assignments.

The Wikipedia hierarchy contains over 0.34 million categories and is generated by human volunteers. Consequently, it is not perfect and contains irrelevant categories such as "Living People", "People with Year of Birth Missing", etc. In Section 3.2, we describe a scheme for cleansing the hierarchy of extraneous category nodes.

3.1 Wikipedia-based Pachinko Allocation Model

WPAM uses Wikipedia's category hierarchy as the topic hierarchy which we denote by H. Non-leaf topics in H are Wikipedia categories, and leaf topics correspond to Wikipedia entities. We denote the set of children of a non-leaf topic k by $c(k)$. WPAM assigns a root-to-leaf path $z_i = \langle z_{i1}, z_{i2}, \ldots, z_{il_i} \rangle$ from H to each word w_i in the document corpus. Here, z_{i1} is always the root, and topic $z_{i(j+1)}$ is a child of z_{ij}. The WPAM model is defined by the following parameters: (1) For each document m and non-leaf topic k, a multinomial distribution $\vec{\theta}_{mk}$ over k's children $c(k)$, and (2) For each leaf topic k, a multinomial distribution $\vec{\phi}_k$ over words.

The model parameters $\vec{\theta}_{mk}$ have a Dirichlet prior with hyper-parameters $\vec{\alpha}_k$, and the parameters $\vec{\phi}_k$ have a Dirichlet prior with hyper-parameters $\vec{\beta}$. As shown in Section 2.4, with the Wikipedia annotations $\mathcal{A}$, $\vec{\phi}_k$ has a Dirichlet posterior with hyper-parameters $\vec{\beta} + \vec{\delta}^{(k)}$ which we denote by $\vec{\beta}^{(k)}$ (recall that $\delta_t^{(k)}$ is the number of times term t is assigned topic k in $\mathcal{A}$). Similarly, if $\delta_{kk'}^{(m)}$ is the number of topic paths in document m in $\mathcal{A}$ containing k' as a subtopic of k, then $\vec{\theta}_{mk}$ can be shown to have a Dirichlet posterior with hyper-parameters $\vec{\alpha}_k + \vec{\delta}_k^{(m)}$ which we denote by $\vec{\alpha}_k^{(m)}$.

A slight problem we face here is that Wikipedia annotations only specify entities and not paths in the topic hierarchy H. Furthermore, since H is a DAG, there can be multiple paths in H from the root to the leaf topic corresponding to an entity. This makes it difficult to obtain exact $\delta_{kk'}^{(m)}$ counts for topic, subtopic pair occurrences in $\mathcal{A}$. So we approximate $\delta_{kk'}^{(m)}$ as follows. First, for each annotation $a \in \mathcal{A}$ in document m, we compute the fraction of paths in H from the root to the entity specified in a that pass through topic k and its subtopic k'. The fraction essentially represents the probability that a topic path for annotation a passes through the topic, subtopic pair (k, k'). Our $\delta_{kk'}^{(m)}$ estimate is then the sum of the fraction values for all the annotations in document m. Note that we can compute the number of paths between any two nodes of a DAG efficiently using dynamic programming, and this can be used to calculate the path fraction value for each annotation.

WPAM uses the Dirichlet posterior distribution for each $\vec{\phi}_k$ and $\vec{\theta}_{mk}$ to generate documents, and so it is a semi-supervised model. The generative process for a document collection under WPAM is as follows:

- For each leaf topic k, sample word distribution $\vec{\phi}_k \sim \text{Dir}(\vec{\beta}^{(k)})$. Here, $\vec{\beta}^{(k)} = \vec{\beta} + \vec{\delta}^{(k)}$.
- For each document m
  - For each non-leaf topic k, sample topic distribution $\vec{\theta}_{mk} \sim \text{Dir}(\vec{\alpha}_k^{(m)})$. Here, $\vec{\alpha}_k^{(m)} = \vec{\alpha}_k + \vec{\delta}_k^{(m)}$.
  - For each word w_i in document m
    * Sample a root-to-leaf path $z_i = \langle z_{i1}, z_{i2}, \ldots, z_{il_i} \rangle$ of length l_i from the topic hierarchy H. For each topic z_{ij} in the topic path, sample child $z_{i(j+1)} \sim \text{Mult}(\vec{\theta}_{mz_{ij}})$.
    * Sample a word $w_i \sim \text{Mult}(\vec{\phi}_{z_{il_i}})$.

As before, we can use Gibbs sampling to compute the topic path assignments $\vec{z}$ for document words in $\vec{w}$. Essentially, Gibbs sampling draws samples from the posterior distribution $P(\vec{z}|\vec{w})$ by sequentially sampling topic paths for each z_i from $P(z_i|\vec{z}_{-i}, \vec{w})$. For a word $w_i = t$ in document m, the conditional probability that $z_i = \langle k_1, k_2, \ldots, k_l \rangle$ is given by:

$$P(z_i = \langle k_1, k_2, \ldots, k_l \rangle | \vec{z}_{-i}, \vec{w}, \{\vec{\alpha}_k\}, \vec{\beta}, \mathcal{A}) \tag{3}$$

$$\propto \frac{n_{t,-i}^{(k_l)} + \beta_t^{(k_l)}}{\sum_{t'=1}^{T} (n_{t',-i}^{(k_l)} + \beta_{t'}^{(k_l)})} \cdot \prod_{j=1}^{l-1} \frac{n_{k_j k_{j+1},-i}^{(m)} + \alpha_{k_j k_{j+1}}^{(m)}}{\sum_{k' \in c(k_j)} (n_{k_j k',-i}^{(m)} + \alpha_{k_j k'}^{(m)})}$$

Above, $n_{t,-i}^{(k_l)}$ is the number of occurrences of term t with leaf topic k_l excluding the current assignment, and $n_{k_j,k',-i}^{(m)}$ is the number of times topic k' appears as a subtopic of topic k_j in a topic path of document m excluding the current assignment. In Equation (3) above, the first term is the probability of term t under leaf topic k_l and the second term is the probability of path $\langle k_1, k_2, \ldots, k_l \rangle$ in document m. Observe that the second term induces a clustering effect among the topic paths of a document with a preference for paths with common subpaths from the root. Thus, words in a document are assigned entity labels that are close by in H, and hence correlated.

Our entity disambiguation algorithm first runs WPAM's Gibbs sampling on the collection of Wikipedia documents $\mathcal{W}$. In the labeling phase, it disambiguates each reference in $\mathcal{D}$ by running incremental Gibbs sampling on $\mathcal{W} \cup \mathcal{D}$. Each reference is finally labeled with the entity at the leaf of the topic path assigned to it. Note that, as in Section 2.3, we can significantly speed up our sampling algorithm by only considering the restriction of H to topics and entities mentioned in the document. In our experiments, we found that exploiting the Wikipedia category hierarchy enables WPAM to achieve up to 26.1% higher disambiguation accuracy.

3.2 Pruning Noisy Categories from Hierarchy

As mentioned earlier, due to the crowd-sourced manner in which it is produced, the Wikipedia hierarchy contains some spurious categories. These categories can cause WPAM to incorrectly infer topic correlations, and assign wrong entity labels to words. In this subsection, we propose a scheme to detect such spurious non-leaf topics, and prune them from the topic hierarchy H.

Now, good topics are the ones whose child topics are correlated and frequently co-occur in documents. Thus, our scheme for detecting spurious topics defines a goodness measure for each topic based on the co-occurrence of its children, and then deletes the topics with low goodness scores. A natural candidate for the goodness measure is *entropy* since it increases with the number of subtopics per document and as the co-occurrence among subtopics grows. Consider the set of Wikipedia pages $\mathcal{W}$. Let $\vec{z}$ be the topic paths in H assigned to words in $\mathcal{W}$ by WPAM's Gibbs sampling algorithm when training the WPAM model on $\mathcal{W}$. Then, for a non-leaf topic k, we define the entropy $E(k)$ as:

$$E(k) = -\sum_{m \in \mathcal{W}} \sum_{k' \in c(k)} \frac{n_{kk'}^{(m)}}{\sum_{k' \in c(k)} n_{kk'}^{(m)}} \log \frac{n_{kk'}^{(m)}}{\sum_{k' \in c(k)} n_{kk'}^{(m)}} \quad (4)$$

(Recall that $n_{kk'}^{(m)}$ is the number of times topic k' appears as a subtopic of topic k in a topic path of document m.) It is easy to see that if each document contains very few of topic k's children, then the value of $E(k)$ is low. In fact, in the extreme case, when only one subtopic of k appears per document, k's entropy is 0. On the other hand, if many of k's subtopics appear in each document, then the value of $E(k)$ is higher. The maximum value of course is $|\mathcal{W}| \cdot \log |c(k)|$ when all of k's subtopics are uniformly distributed within each document. Thus, the entropy $E(k)$ is effective at capturing subtopic co-occurrence counts for topic k, and so we use it as the goodness measure for topics.

Our scheme for pruning spurious topics from the Wikipedia hierarchy H iteratively deletes topics k with the lowest entropy scores $E(k)$. During each iteration, it breaks ties between topics with identical entropy scores by selecting the topic k that occurs most frequently in topic paths. The rationale here is that frequent topics have higher confidence levels. A topic k is deleted from hierarchy H by performing the following two modifications: (1) For every child k' of k, new edges are added from the parents of k to k' (thus parents of k become parents of k's children), and (2) Topic k and all the edges incident on k are deleted.

The stopping criterion for deleting topics from H is once the disambiguation accuracy of models trained with the new hierarchy (after a deletion) starts to decrease. In our experiments, we measure the disambiguation accuracy for a hierarchy H by first learning on a training dataset and then testing the learned model on a validation set.

4. EXPERIMENTAL RESULTS

In this section, we show that our WPAM model performs better than the state-of-the-art baselines proposed in [14] on real-life datasets. More specifically, we show that WPAM improves disambiguation accuracy by as much as 16% compared to [14]. We also show that our semi-supervised LDA model has 30.2% higher accuracy compared to standard LDA, and our WPAM model outperforms the best performing and standard LDA models by as much as 26.1% and 43%, respectively. We finally show that hierarchy pruning improves disambiguation performance by 6%.

4.1 Experimental Setup

Datasets: We created two datasets – one from Wikipedia and another from the New York Times corpus. The first dataset (called **WIKI**) is an extract of Wikipedia containing people belonging to seven categories – tennis, basketball, football and baseball players along with actors, musicians, and scholars. This dataset contains 58,577 people, each with an entity page, 627,370 intra-Wikipedia links/annotations and 13,035,881 tokens (after stop word removal). The second dataset is a subset of the New York Times annotated corpus [1]. The full corpus contains 1,855,658 annotated articles published in the New York Times, with 2,372,244 annotations. In some of our experiments, we train on WIKI and test on a subset of the New York Times corpus containing entities that occur in WIKI too. To do this, we first need to match the entity names that occur in the WIKI dataset with those that occur in the New York Times corpus. We use exact string matching to identify matching entity names. The subset of the New York Times corpus that contains references to these matched entities is what we use to perform our experiments and we refer to this extract as NYT in the sequel. NYT contains 9151 unique person names, 65,012 references, 47,581 documents, and 23,283,125 tokens after stopword removal.

The experiments are performed on the above datasets in unlabeled and held-out modes. In the "unlabeled" mode, we present the dataset to the algorithms after hiding a subset of the annotations present in the dataset. Subsequently, we estimate performance based on the predictions on the hidden references. In the "held-out" mode, all references in the test data are unannotated. The datasets are called WIKI-U, WIKI-H, and NYT-H.

WIKI-U: In WIKI-U (WIKI data in the unlabeled mode), the training data consists of 4 splits each containing 75% of the pages in WIKI. In the remaining 25%, we hide 30% of the annotations. 100% of the data is used for training and precision is computed on the references with hidden annotations. We report the average precision over the 4 splits.

WIKI-H: In WIKI-H (WIKI data in held-out mode), the splits are the same as WIKI-U. The hidden portions of the pages (that is, 30% of 25% of the pages) are treated as separate held-out test pages. In other words, these parts are not used for training and are used only to evaluate performance.

NYT-H: In this case, WIKI is used for training and NYT is used for testing.

Performance Metrics: In our experiments, we use precision as the primary metric of comparison: precision is the fraction of entity references that are annotated correctly. In some applications, instead of the best matching entity, a (short) ranked list of entities is used to capture the correct entity. The metric used in these cases is "Precision@k" which is defined as the fraction of references for which the correct entity appears in the *top-k* candidate list for that reference. In our experiments, following prior work [14], we compare words appearing in the text with surface forms of entities in Wikipedia and choose the longest match to identify references.

Outline of Experiments: We perform the following experiments.

- Baseline, LDA variants, PAM, and WPAM on WIKI-U and WIKI-H.
- Baseline, LDA variants, PAM, and WPAM on NYT-H.
- Hierarchy pruning.
- Train and test execution times.

Baselines: We use the following two baselines from [14]. Local Context (LC): Given a local context window around a reference and an entity, LC first builds a feature vector by comparing the window with the entity's textual metadata (extracted from Wikipedia) using string similarity metrics. The feature vector is then input to a support vector machine (SVM) and the entity with the highest SVM score is the disambiguation result.

Collective Disambiguation (CD): CD uses all the local contextual windows for references in a document and attempts to assign an entity to each reference such that the sum of

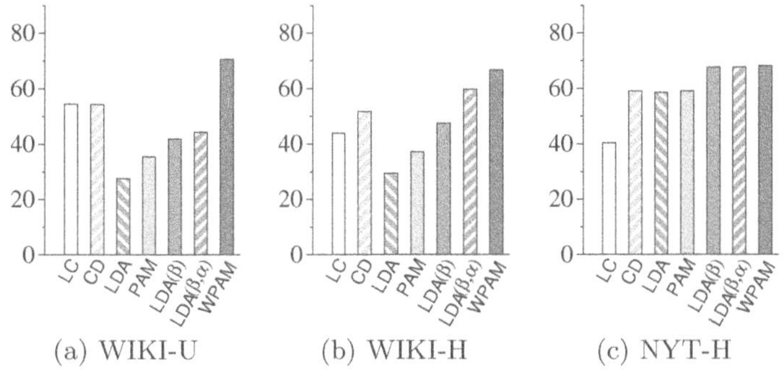

Figure 1: Precision of baselines, LDA variants, PAM, and WPAM.

the average SVM scores and the average *relatedness scores* [19] among pairs of assigned entities is maximized. For this optimization, in addition to the greedy hill climbing implemented in [14], we also use more sophisticated inference algorithms such as *loopy belief propagation* (LBP) [28]. The results we report were obtained using max-product LBP (using exponentiated relatedness as entries in clique potentials).

LDA variants: Section 2.4 introduced weakly semi-supervised LDA models. To estimate the gains in performance achieved by biasing the distributions of parameters $\vec{\theta}_m$ and $\vec{\phi}_k$, we experiment with two variants of weakly semi-supervised LDAs. Recall that semi-supervised learning was achieved by adding precounts $\vec{\delta}^{(k)}$ and $\vec{\delta}^{(m)}$ to Dirichlet hyperparameters $\vec{\beta}$ and $\vec{\alpha}$, respectively. We refer to LDA with only precounts in $\vec{\beta}$ as LDA(β), and with precounts in both $\vec{\alpha}$ and $\vec{\beta}$ as LDA(β, α).

For WPAM, we found that instead of initializing the Gibbs sampling algorithm with a random topic assignment, initializing word topics in a document with more frequently occurring candidate entities gives better performance. We report results with the latter initialization scheme.

Platform: The experiments were run on a Linux system with 32GB main memory and 8 64-bit 1.87GHz 4-core Intel Xeon processors each with 4MB cache.

4.2 Performance Comparison

Figure 1 shows the results of testing on WIKI-U, WIKI-H, and NYT-H. On all three datasets, WPAM outperforms all the remaining models. Furthermore, LDA, PAM, LDA(β), LDA(β, α), and WPAM show a steady progression of improving performance demonstrating the benefits of increasing levels of supervision and exploitation of the category hierarchy.

On the WIKI-U, WIKI-H, and NYT-H datasets, WPAM shows 16%, 15%, and 9% improvements, respectively, over CD. In fact, on the NYT-H dataset, all three proposed topic models, LDA(β), LDA(β, α) and WPAM, perform significantly better than the LC and CD baselines. This is because LC and CD use only limited local context for disambiguation compared to topic models. Furthermore, the superior performance of WPAM can be attributed to (1) the use of semi-supervised learning enabled by Wikipedia annotations, and (2) the Wikipedia hierarchy to capture entity co-occurrence patterns. We investigate the individual benefits due to each of these two aspects next.

To gauge the gains due to semi-supervision, we compare the precision of LDA(β, α) and the standard LDA models. LDA(β, α) outperforms standard LDA on WIKI-U, WIKI-H, and NYT-H by 16.8%, 30.2%, and 9.1%, respectively. Similar gains are achieved by WPAM compared to PAM. This clearly demonstrates that unsupervised topic models have difficulty handling a large number of fine-grained topics, and semi-supervised learning techniques that combine unlabeled and labeled data are required.

To measure the efficacy of hierarchical models, we compare the precision of WPAM with the best performing LDA model, LDA(β, α). The difference in precision between WPAM and LDA(β, α) on WIKI-U and WIKI-H are 26.1% and 7.1%, respectively. A possible reason for LDA(β, α) doing almost as well as WPAM on NYT-H could be the smaller number of references contained in an NYT document. On an average, an NYT document contains 1.38 references whereas the corresponding number for a WIKI document is 20.83. This implies that there is less entity co-occurrence to be exploited in NYT. The precision gains are even more striking when we compare WPAM to standard LDA – on WIKI-U, WIKI-H, and NYT-H, WPAM outperforms standard LDA by 43%, 37.2%, and 9.6%, respectively.

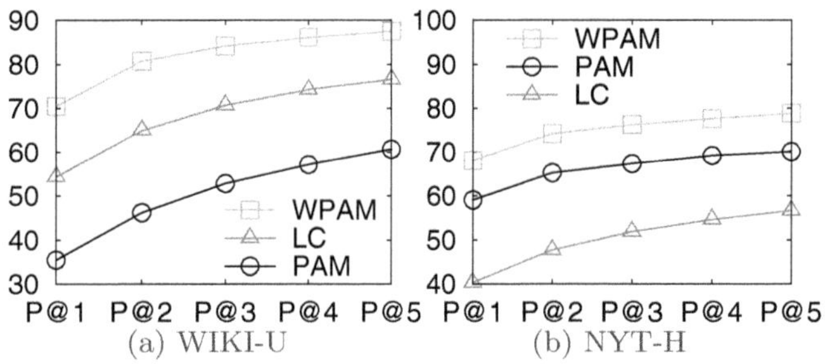

Figure 2: Precision@k results for WPAM, PAM, and LC.

Figure 2 shows Precision@k results, for $k = 1, \cdots, 5$, for WPAM, PAM, and LC. We use SVM scores and likelihoods to rank for LC and WPAM, respectively. Figure 2(a) shows that P@5 can reach as high as 87.5%, which is achieved by WPAM on WIKI-U. Also, P@5 for WPAM is almost 17.1% and 1.9% more than that for LDA(β, α) on WIKI-U and NYT-H, respectively (data not shown).

4.3 Hierarchy Pruning

The default Wikipedia hierarchy for all the entities in our dataset consists of 1225 non-leaf nodes, 58577 leaves, and 75910 paths. As mentioned in Section 3.2, not all of the nodes help WPAM, and hence it is necessary to prune the hierarchy. The pruning is done using the entropy-based method as described in Section 3, which not only uses the topic path assignments for document words, but also the performance of the learned WPAM model on a held-out dataset.

We performed pruning with three datasets, each being a 10% random extract of WIKI. Figure 3 depicts the variation of precision with number of nodes deleted from the hierarchy averaged across the splits. The performance of pruning reaches a maximum when the optimal hierarchy is reached, and then drops drastically upon further pruning. Since the performance does not increase monotonically towards the maximum, we use this steep drop as the stopping criterion for pruning.

The reason the performance reaches a maximum at the last stages of pruning is due to the nature of the Wikipedia

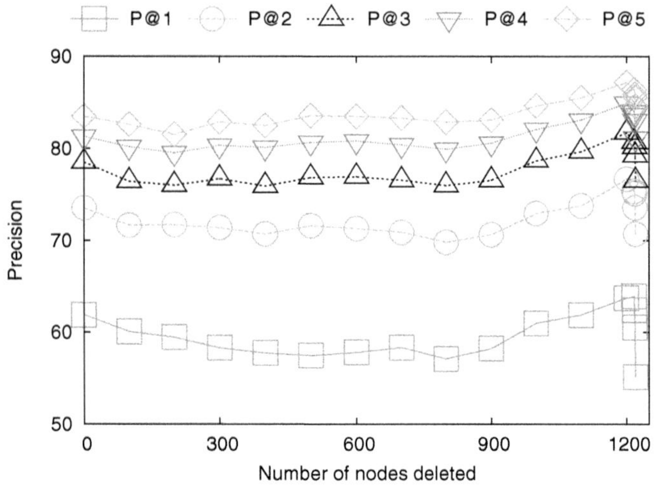

Figure 3: Variation of precision with pruning.

corpus and its corresponding hierarchy. The final pruned hierarchy consists of one root with 8 non-leaf nodes as children thus forming a three-level hierarchy (along with the entities forming the leaves). Hence, dynamic pruning deletes most of the non-leaf nodes (more than 1200) in the hierarchy to obtain optimal performance. Observe that the final pruned hierarchy has 6% higher precision compared to the original hierarchy.

4.4 Training and Test Times

Topic models are known to require excessive amounts of training time. Our code on full WIKI takes two and a half days to train. For a mid-to-large scale application such as ours, this issue exists with the baseline algorithms too. For example, [14] points out that it is not difficult to generate SVM learning problems for LC with millions of constraints. The number of constraints is a function of the number of annotations and entities in the training set. Training an SVM on full WIKI has 6,241,263 constraints even after we restrict the number of candidates per reference to 10 and takes almost a day (using the libsvm [10] JAVA implementation).

Labeling with WPAM's Gibbs sampling algorithm, however, is much faster compared to the baseline. For our experiments, the labeling time of WPAM is roughly of the order of few tens of milliseconds per reference. In contrast, testing with the baseline models may require comparing each window with each entity in the extreme case costing around 0.2 sec of disambiguation time per reference. Hence labeling using topic models is approximately 10 times faster.

5. RELATED WORK

Due to its scale and coverage, Wikipedia has been the knowledge base of choice for most of the large-scale entity disambiguation approaches proposed in the literature [9, 11, 17, 19, 14]. The early Wikipedia-based disambiguation schemes [9, 17] resolved one reference at a time using only local context information. Subsequent works [11, 19, 14] propose to disambiguate all the references in a page collectively taking into account the relatedness of entities. Of these, [19] performs a limited form of collective disambiguation based on entity co-occurrence patterns – the entities selected to disambiguate the ambiguous references in a page are the ones that co-occur frequently with (entities for) the unambiguous references in the page.

Unlike [19], [11] performs full-fledged collective disambiguation by also including ambiguous references in each disambiguation decision. It represents each entity as a feature vector consisting of local context information and categories for the entity. It then disambiguates a reference in a page with the entity whose feature vector matches best with the aggregated feature vector for the page (over all possible entity disambiguations for all references in the page). Clearly, a problem with the scheme of [11] is that the aggregate vector for a page may include irrelevant entities.

[14] formulates entity disambiguation as a joint optimization problem that seeks to collectively annotate all the references within a document so that the compatibility of each entity's context with the local context of its reference and the co-occurrence between entity pairs is maximized. The optimization problem is NP-hard, and the authors resort to a hill-climbing strategy that greedily annotates references with entities that maximize the objective function.

We pointed out the shortcomings of the above-mentioned approaches in Section 1.2 – these include using a fixed-size window around a reference to define its local context (with no consensus on the best window size), and ignoring words that appear in the vicinity of un-annotated references when computing the context for an entity.

Our WPAM entity disambiguation model does not suffer from any of the above-mentioned problems since it is based on hierarchical topic models. Hierarchical models allow diverse sources of evidence like word-entity associations and entity co-occurrence patterns to be combined in a single unified framework for entity disambiguation. Moreover, topic models do not need to use difficult-to-set window parameters – their internal machinery can naturally use words from anywhere in the document, including the vicinity of un-annotated references, to learn high-quality word-entity mappings. WPAM differs from previously proposed hierarchical models like PAM [16] in two aspects: (1) WPAM uses the Wikipedia category hierarchy, and (2) Learning in WPAM is weakly semi-supervised with Wikipedia annotations serving as training data.

Word sense disambiguation and entity resolution are two related areas of research that bear close connections to entity disambiguation. Topic models have been used in both of these areas previously [5, 8, 25]. The main differentiating factor between entity disambiguation and such related fields is the assumption of the presence of a catalog of entities. Word sense disambiguation and entity resolution usually do not assume the presence of any such catalog and researchers in these fields have devoted most of their efforts to developing unsupervised algorithms. Thus, none of [5, 8] or [25] consider including prior annotations/labels for weakly semi-supervised learning the way we do in this paper.

Recently, there have been attempts to incorporate document labels into topic models [6, 15, 24]. Since our aim is to annotate words instead of documents, these approaches are quite different from the topic models we develop in this paper. [27] proposes the Multi-grain LDA topic model that uses local topics at the sentence level to capture ratable aspects like sound quality, battery life, etc. in user reviews. The Multi-grain LDA model is orthogonal to hierarchical topic models that instead model semantic relationships between topics typically at the document level. Similar to us,

[23] runs LDA on Wikipedia pages to discover hidden topics that are then used as additional features to classify short text segments. However, [23] only considers a few hundred coarse-grained topics, and does not exploit Wikipedia's annotations or category hierarchy for topic inference.

6. CONCLUSION

In this paper, we proposed the weakly semi-supervised hierarchical topic model WPAM for disambiguating entities. WPAM uses all the words in a document, including those in the vicinity of un-annotated references, to learn high-quality word-entity associations. It leverages Wikipedia annotations to appropriately bias the assignment of entity labels to annotated words (and un-annotated words co-occurring with them), and the Wikipedia category hierarchy to capture entity context and co-occurrence patterns in a single unified disambiguation framework. We devised a scheme for pruning spurious categories with poorly correlated subcategories in the hierarchy. In large-scale experiments with both held out subsets of Wikipedia and the NYT corpus, our WPAM model achieved over 70% disambiguation accuracy compared to about 54% for the existing state-of-the-art baselines. Promising directions for future work include exploring the use of other hierarchical topic models (e.g., hPAM [20]) for entity disambiguation, and learning good topic hierarchies from Wikipedia using non-parametric priors (e.g., hierarchical Dirichlet processes [26]).

7. REFERENCES

[1] New York Times dataset. `http://www.ldc.upenn.edu/Catalog/`.

[2] Wikipedia. `http://www.wikipedia.org`.

[3] Wikipedia category hierarchy. `http://en.wikipedia.org/wiki/Special:Categories`.

[4] Wikipedia manual of style. `http://en.wikipedia.org/wiki/Wikipedia:Manual_of_Style`.

[5] I. Bhattacharya and L. Getoor. A latent dirichlet model for unsupervised entity resolution. In *SDM*, 2006.

[6] D. Blei and J. McAuliffe. Supervised topic models. In *NIPS*, 2007.

[7] D. Blei, A. Ng, and M. Jordan. Latent dirichlet allocation. *JMLR*, 2003.

[8] J. Boyd-Graber, D. Blei, and X. Zhu. A topic model for word sense disambiguation. In *EMNLP*, 2007.

[9] R. Bunescu and M. Pasca. Using encyclopedic knowledge for named entity disambiguation. In *European Association for Computational Linguistics*, 2006.

[10] C.-C. Chang and C.-J. Lin. LIBSVM – A Library for Support Vector Machines. `http://www.csie.ntu.edu.tw/~cjlin/libsvm/`.

[11] S. Cucerzan. Large-scale named entity disambiguation based on Wikipedia data. In *EMNLP*, 2007.

[12] T. Griffiths and M. Steyvers. Finding scientific topics. In *Proceedings of the National Academy of Sciences*, 2004.

[13] G. Heinrich. Parameter estimation for text analysis. Technical report, 2005.

[14] S. Kulkarni, A. Singh, G. Ramakrishnan, and S. Chakrabarti. Collective annotation of wikipedia entities in web text. In *KDD*, 2009.

[15] S. Lacoste-Julien, F. Sha, and M. I. Jordan. DiscLDA: Discriminative learning for dimensionality reduction and classification. In *NIPS*, 2008.

[16] W. Li and A. McCallum. Pachinko allocation: DAG-structured mixture models of topic correlations. In *ICML*, 2006.

[17] R. Mihalcea and A. Csomai. Wikify! linking documents to encyclopedic knowledge. In *CIKM*, 2007.

[18] D. J. Miller and H. S. Uyar. A mixture of experts classifier with learning based on both labelled and unlabelled data. In *NIPS*, 1997.

[19] D. Milne and I. Witten. Learning to link with Wikipedia. In *CIKM*, 2008.

[20] D. Mimno, W. Li, and A. McCallum. Mixtures of hierarchical topics with pachinko allocation. In *ICML*, 2007.

[21] T. P. Minka. Estimating a dirichlet distribution. Technical report, Microsoft Research, 2003.

[22] K. Nigam, A. McCallum, S. Thrun, and T. Mitchell. Learning to classify text from labeled and unlabeled documents. In *AAAI*, 1998.

[23] X.-H. Phan, L.-M. Nguyen, and S. Horiguchi. Learning to classify short and sparse text & web with hidden topics from large-scale data collections. In *WWW*, 2008.

[24] D. Ramage, D. Hall, R. Nallapati, and C. D. Manning. Labeled LDA: A supervised topic model for credit attribution in multi-labeled corpora. In *EMNLP*, 2009.

[25] L. Shu, B. Long, and W. Meng. A latent topic model for complete entity resolution. In *ICDE*, 2009.

[26] Y. Teh, M. Jordan, M. Beal, and D. Blei. Hierarchical dirichlet processes. *J. of the American Statistical Association*, 2005.

[27] I. Titov and R. McDonald. Modeling online reviews with multi-grain topic models. In *WWW*, 2008.

[28] J. Yedidia, W. Freeman, and Y. Weiss. Generalized belief propagation. In *NIPS*, 2000.

Exploiting Place Features in Link Prediction on Location-based Social Networks

Salvatore Scellato
Computer Laboratory
University of Cambridge
ss824@cam.ac.uk

Anastasios Noulas
Computer Laboratory
University of Cambridge
an346@cam.ac.uk

Cecilia Mascolo
Computer Laboratory
University of Cambridge
cm542@cam.ac.uk

ABSTRACT

Link prediction systems have been largely adopted to recommend new friends in online social networks using data about social interactions. With the soaring adoption of location-based social services it becomes possible to take advantage of an additional source of information: the places people visit.

In this paper we study the problem of designing a link prediction system for online location-based social networks. We have gathered extensive data about one of these services, Gowalla, with periodic snapshots to capture its temporal evolution. We study the link prediction space, finding that about 30% of new links are added among "place-friends", i.e., among users who visit the same places. We show how this prediction space can be made 15 times smaller, while still 66% of future connections can be discovered. Thus, we define new prediction features based on the properties of the places visited by users which are able to discriminate potential future links among them.

Building on these findings, we describe a supervised learning framework which exploits these prediction features to predict new links among friends-of-friends and place-friends. Our evaluation shows how the inclusion of information about places and related user activity offers high link prediction performance. These results open new directions for real-world link recommendation systems on location-based social networks.

Categories and Subject Descriptors

H.2.8 [**Database Management**]: Database Applications—*Data mining*

General Terms

Experimentation, Measurement

Keywords

link prediction, location-based services, social networks

1. INTRODUCTION

Location-based online social networks have seen soaring popularity, attracting millions of users [12]. People are increasingly sharing their location with their friends: such *check-ins* can be broadcasted to friends, while messages, tips or other information related to a place can be generated and shared. As many other online social services, location-based networks may greatly benefit from link recommendation, since as users add more and more friends their engagement with the service increases [15].

An inherent characteristic of these social networks is that they may have millions of nodes, but, at the same time, they are often quite sparse, with low density of links among these nodes. As a result, the link prediction space is so huge and highly imbalanced that real approaches merely focus on finding friends in the the 2-hop social neighborhood, i.e., friends-of-friends of a user [8]. Extending prediction efforts to the 3-hop neighborhood, or even further, may likely result in an exponentially larger set of increasingly less likely candidates. As a consequence, the link prediction problem appears so heavily influenced by network distance between users that each social neighborhood should be treated as a separate prediction problem [17].

Nonetheless, in location-based social networks there is an unprecedented source of potential promising candidates for link prediction: the places visited by each user. Data about the venues where users check-in can be exploited to find and predict future connections. Therefore, the question we tackle in this work is: *how do we design a link prediction system which exploits data about user check-ins?*

To investigate the practical feasibility of such approach we have collected extensive longitudinal data about an online location-based service, Gowalla, with hundreds of thousands of users and more than one million different venues. We have acquired complete data about places, users, their friends and their check-ins for 4 consecutive monthly snapshots (Section 2). We analyze the link prediction space by investigating how new friendship connections are created over time: we discover that *about 30% of all new links appear among users that check-in at the same places*. Thus, these "place-friends" represent disconnected users that can become direct connections (Section 3).

We argue that effective link prediction on location-based services can greatly benefit from focusing only on the friends-of-friends and on the place-friends of a user. This design choice makes the prediction space about 15 times smaller than the entire set of candidates and, yet, it covers about 66% of new social ties. In addition, this reduced prediction set offers a better balance between the number of new links and its total size. As a result, practical implementation of link prediction systems can become more feasible, since for each user only a much smaller set of potential friends has to be explored to compute predictions.

The challenge is then how to exploit the information given by the check-ins of two users, who do not share any friends but who visit the same places, to predict whether they will become direct connections. In fact, activity and interaction revolving around physical places can result in social ties emerging among individuals and correlated to the properties of the place itself, as the sociological "focus theory" suggests [9]. Hence, we define prediction features which quantify users that are likely to become friends considering the places they visit and the properties of these places. Our prediction features are based on user check-ins and on the concept of "place entropy" [5], which is used to discriminate venues that are more or less likely to foster social connections (Section 4).

We finally describe how such prediction features, combined with other measures, can be used in a supervised learning framework to predict future links in a realistic deployment (Section 5) [17]. Our evaluation shows the effectiveness of our design choices, with AUC values of up to 0.96 when predicting links between users who visits the same places but have no friends in common (Section 6). Our approach can be adopted in any scenario where users of a social service disclose data about their visits to places. We conclude the paper with an overview of related results (Section 7) and with a discussion of future works (Section 8).

2. DATASET

In this section we briefly describe Gowalla and the collection procedure we used to acquire our dataset, presenting some of its basic properties.

2.1 Data collection

Gowalla is a location-based social networking service created in 2008 that allows users to add friends and share their location with them. The friendship relationship is mutual, requiring each user to accept friendship requests to allow location sharing.

We have downloaded four monthly snapshots of Gowalla data between May and August 2010: we were able to exhaustively query all user accounts, downloading information regarding their profiles, their friends and their past check-ins. We also gathered the geographic location of each place. This dataset represents a sequence of *complete* snapshots of a large-scale online service: this will allow us to study how links are created over time and to evaluate how a link prediction system would perform in a real scenario.

t	Users	Active users	Places	Check-ins
1	252,020	148,234	958,823	7,475,401
2	291,812	168,925	1,104,771	9,073,157
3	325,025	189,512	1,226,847	10,537,516
4	382,750	216,734	1,421,262	12,846,151

Table 1: Properties of our Gowalla dataset across the different temporal snapshots: total number of registered users and active users, total number of different places, total number of check-ins.

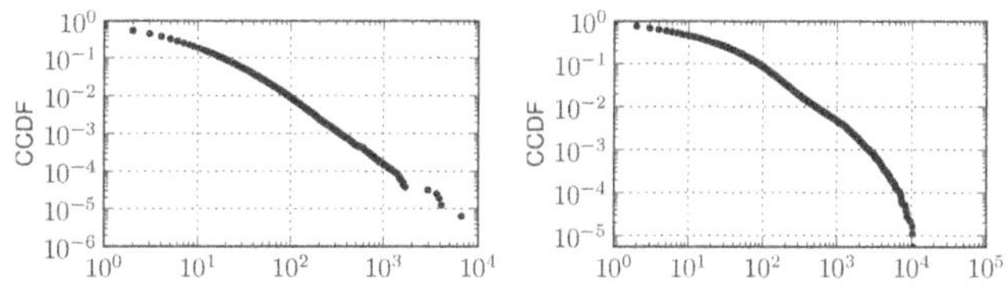

(a) Friends per user (b) Places per user

Figure 1: Complementary Cumulative Distribution (CCDF) of the number of friends (a) and of the number of places (b) per user for the last snapshot of the dataset (Month 4). The probability distributions do not change significantly across different snaphots.

t	N	K	G_C	$\langle k \rangle$
1	109,045	476,409	102,951 (94.4%)	8.73
2	124,190	559,901	117,868 (94.7%)	9.01
3	138,387	630,045	131,711 (95.1%)	9.10
4	159,391	736,778	152,011 (95.3%)	9.24

Table 2: Properties of the social graphs at each snapshot: number of nodes N and edges K, number of nodes G_C (and their proportion) in the giant connected component and average node degree $\langle k \rangle$.

2.2 Dataset properties

In the 4 consecutive monthly snapshots Gowalla increased its total number of registered users from about 250 thousands to about 380 thousands, as shown in Table 1, constantly exhibiting about 56% of active users, that is users with at least one friend or one check-in.

As reported in Table 2, each snapshot of our dataset results in a social graph with a subset of the active users: each graph exhibits a large giant connected component, always containing more than 94% of all the nodes. The average number of friends per user grows from 8.73 to 9.24: moreover, as described in Figure 1(a), the degree distribution shows a heavy tail, with only 1% of users having more than 100 friends. Overall the social network is sparse, making link prediction challenging because of the scarcity of social ties. User check-in activity also presents a heavy-tailed distribution: 90% of users with check-ins have visited less than 100 different venues, as detailed by Figure 1(b). Even though users might visit only few places, users who visit the same places are still more likely to become friends than what would be expected on average, as we will see later.

Finally, we note that while many users might have social connections and no check-ins, there are also many accounts with check-ins but no friends at all. On average, *only 57% of active users have both some friends and some check-ins, while 26% have no friends and 17% have no check-ins.* This partition is approximately constant across our temporal snapshots of Gowalla.

3. PREDICTION SPACE ANALYSIS

In this section we study how new friendship connections are created by Gowalla users, exploring how the prediction space can be divided to improve link prediction performance. We will introduce the concept of *place-friends* and show how the search for new social ties can be greatly simplified.

t	U_t	E_t^{NEW}	S_t^{NEW}	P_t^{NEW}	$S_t^{NEW} \cap P_t^{NEW}$	$S_t^{NEW} \cup P_t^{NEW}$
1	148,234	43,812 (100.00%)	24,174 (56.41%)	13,150 (30.01%)	7,677 (17.52%)	30,187 (68.90%)
2	168,925	40,643 (100.00%)	21,118 (51.96%)	12,572 (30.93%)	7,131 (17.54%)	26,559 (65.35%)
3	189,512	58,238 (100.00%)	30,581 (51.51%)	20,107 (34.52%)	10,935 (18.78%)	39,753 (68.26%)

Table 3: Link formation: for each monthly network snapshot we report the total number of active users U_t, the total number of new links appearing among them in the next snapshot E_t^{NEW} and the breakdown of this quantity among new links appearing among friends-of-friends S_t^{NEW} and among place-friends P_t^{NEW}, including the intersection and union of these two latter sets. Percentages are computed with respect to the total number of new links.

3.1 Definition and notation

Formally, we represent each snapshot of our dataset as an undirected graph $G_t = (V_t, E_t)$ for $t = 1, 2, 3, 4$, where t indicates the different snapshots in time of the dataset. The set of nodes $V_t = \{u_1, u_2, \ldots, u_{N_t}\}$ is composed of N_t users and the set of edges E_t is composed of pairs of users that are present in each other's friend lists in snapshot t. We define Γ_i^t as the set of users connected to user u_i in graph G_t, so that $k_i^t = |\Gamma_i^t|$ is the number of friends of u_i in snapshot t. In addition, there are L_t different places $M_t = \{m_1, m_2, \ldots, m_{L_t}\}$ where users have checked-in at and c_{ij}^t represents the number of check-ins that user u_i has ever done at place m_j until time t, with the number of check-ins of a user in a place able only to increase with time. All the check-ins of user u_i until time t can also be represented as a vector $\vec{c_i^t} = (c_{i1}^t, c_{i2}^t, \ldots c_{iL_t}^t)$. Then, Φ_j^t is the set of all users who have checked-in at place m_j and Θ_i^t is the set of all places where user u_i has checked-in at, both until snapshot t. Finally, $A_t = \bigcup_{j=1}^{L_t} \Phi_j^t$ is the set of all users with at least one check-in at snapshot t, while $U_t = V_t \cup A_t$ is the set of all users present at snapshot t with at least one friend or one check-in.

3.2 Dividing prediction space

Users do not add friendship connections at random with all other users but, instead, tend to prefer other users that are "close" to them, either in social sense or along other dimensions such as geographic proximity or topic interest [15, 1, 6, 19]. For instance, many links do appear between individuals at closer social distance from each other, with the 2-hop neighborhood of single nodes being the largest source of new ties [17]. This seems to hold also in Gowalla: as shown in Figure 2(a), the number of new links appearing between users which are d hops away exponentially decreases with d. Moreover, the likelihood that a couple of users at network distance d will have a link in the next snapshot of our dataset decreases sharply with d, as described by Figure 2(b): the probability that two users with at least one friend in common, thus being at distance $d = 2$, will become friends is above 10^{-4}, but this value quickly tumbles down below 10^{-5} and to 10^{-6} at distance $d = 3$ and $d = 4$ respectively. Hence, pairs of users at larger distances give a weaker contribution to link formation, both in terms of absolute number of new links and likelihood of a new social tie [14].

Nonetheless, in a location-based social network the social dimension is not the only one to be exploited and investigated. Instead, in our context there is an additional source of information about social ties: the places where users check-in. In particular, users may add a new connection not because of a shared friend but because of a shared place.

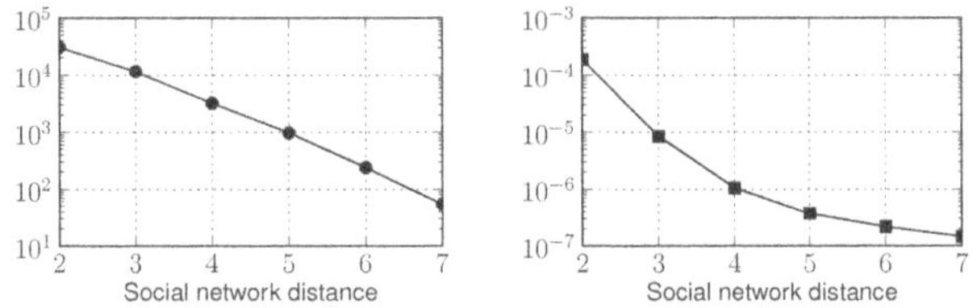

(a) New links (b) Probability of a new link

Figure 2: Number of new links appearing among pairs of nodes at different values of social distance (a) and their relative probability of appearance (b). Pairs of users at closer distance are both generating a larger number of social links and more likely to turn into social links.

In order to quantify how users seek and add new friends, for each snapshot and for each user u_i we define two sets of potential friend couples:

Friends-of-friends

$$S_i^t = \{(u_i, u) : u \in \Big(\bigcup_{u_k \in \Gamma_i^t} \Gamma_k^t\Big) \setminus \Gamma_i^t\}$$

Place-friends

$$P_i^t = \{(u_i, u) : u \in \Big(\bigcup_{m_k \in \Theta_i^t} \Phi_k^t\Big) \setminus \Gamma_i^t\}$$

While friends-of-friends are all those users that share at least one friend without being directly connected, place-friends are all those users that have checked-in at least in one common place but are not connected to each other. These two sets may not be disjoint for a given user u_i. Finally, we define two sets containing all the potential pairs of nodes that are either friends-of-friends or place-friends in a given snapshot: $S_t = \bigcup_{u_i} S_i^t$ and $P_t = \bigcup_{u_i} P_i^t$.

The monthly snapshots of our dataset make it possible to quantify how many new social links appear within these two sets. For every network snapshot $G_t = (V_t, E_t)$ we define $E_t^{NEW} = E_{t+1} \cap ((U_t \times U_t) \setminus E_t)$ as the set of all new links appearing in the next network snapshot $t+1$ among all users already present at snapshot t. In Table 3 new links appearing between temporal snapshots are classified according to their origin: $S_t^{NEW} = E_t^{NEW} \cap S_t$ and $P_t^{NEW} = E_t^{NEW} \cap P_t$ are, respectively, the set of new links among friends-of-friends and the set of new links among place-friends.

About two-thirds of all new links appear within $S_t \cup P_t$. In particular, while about 50% of new links appear among friends-of-friends, more than 30% of new friends are added among place-friends that check-in at the same venues. Fi-

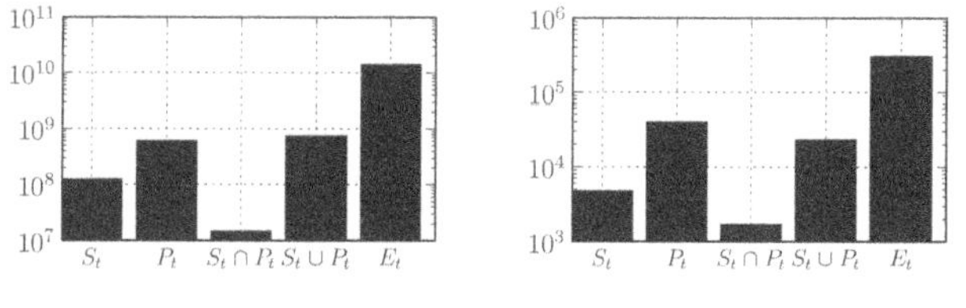

(a) Prediction space size (b) Imbalance ratio

Figure 3: Number of potential friends (a) and imbalance ratio (b) for each class of potential new links: for social potential neighbors S_t, for place potential neighbors P_t, for their intersection and union and for the entire set of users E_t. Results averaged over all temporal snapshots.

nally, about 13% of new links appear between users without any friends in common but who are place-friends.

3.3 Reducing prediction space

In addition to the absolute number of new links appearing among friends-of-friends and place-friends, it is also important to study how link prediction feasibility can vary across these prediction spaces. In a prediction space there are both couples of users that will become connected and couples that will not: the performance of prediction approaches depends on the total number of these potential couples and on the relative proportion of these two classes. Exhaustive approaches would scale with the total number of potential links, which can become prohibitively large for real-world online social networks with millions of users. Also, the two classes can present an extremely skewed distribution, with new links being greatly outnumbered by couples of users that will never create a social tie. This problem is worsened by the fact that these new links are actually the occurrences of greater interest, yet they are difficult to find.

In Figure 3(a) we report the prediction space size for the friends-of-friends set S_t and the place-friends set P_t, including also their intersection and union, along with the size of the overall prediction space for the entire dataset. While there are more than 11 billions couples of users, there are about 700 million place-friends (P_t) and about 100 million friends-of-friends (S_t), with their intersection reducing the prediction space to about 20 million entities. Thus, by focusing prediction efforts only on place-friends or friend-of-friends the prediction space can be reduced by about 15 times, while still covering two-thirds of all new links.

Then, we study the *imbalance ratio* of a prediction set, which is the ratio between the total number of items and the actual number of new links that will appear within it. Imbalance ratios are key indicators of link prediction systems performance: they express how many real instances should be considered and analyzed, on average, before a prediction can be successfully done. Place-friends and friends-of-friends offer lower imbalance ratios than the overall prediction space, as presented in Figure 3(b): hence, not only they offer a smaller prediction space, but also the likelihood that new links will be found is about 20 times higher than the average.

However, discovering friends between users who check-in at the same places appears challenging. Not all places have the same importance for different users and, thus, not all

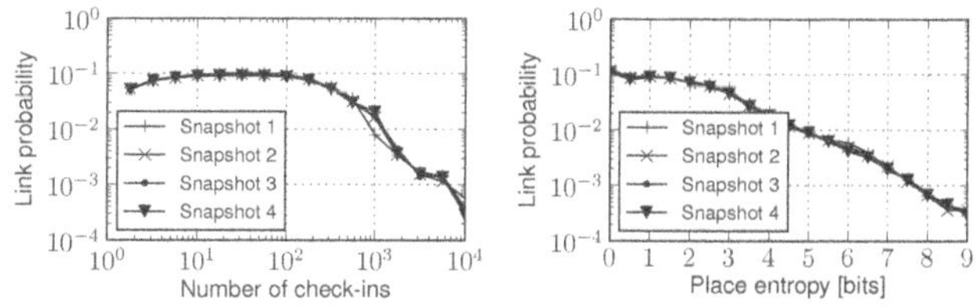

(a) (b)

Figure 4: Average probability that two users who have checked-in at a place are friends as a function of the number of check-ins in that place (a) and as a function of place entropy (b).

places are equally likely to foster new social ties among individuals who visit them. The key idea is then to take advantage of the properties of a place to predict new links.

4. PREDICTION FEATURES

In this section we will describe how place properties can be exploited in link prediction systems and we will introduce the prediction features we adopt in our model.

4.1 Place Properties

Places can be characterized by taking into account users check-in: in fact, the average probability that two users who have checked-in at the same place are friends exhibits a decreasing trend as the place has more check-ins, as shown in Figure 4(a). Yet, there is not much difference when a place has less than 100 check-ins.

However, a place where only a small number of users regularly check-in is likely to be a place with a significant importance for them, such as private houses, gyms, offices. Conversely, a place with a similar total number of check-ins but made by several users is likely to be a public place without considerable significance to its visitors, such as touristic places, airports, train stations and so on.

Hence, a more suitable measure of how much a venue promotes social connections among its visitors should take into account both the number of users that check-in and their number of check-ins. A feasible combination is to exploit information theory and define an entropy-based measure to assess the importance of place for social link creation. *Place entropy* has been used in ecology to measure place biodiversity [5]: the underlying assumption is that a uniform distribution of species in a given physical environment is much more diverse than a skewed distribution, where only a few species are overwhelmingly present.

Let C_k^P be the total number of check-ins all users have at place m_k and $q_{ik} = c_{ik}/C_k^P$ the fraction of check-ins that user u_i has at location m_k with respect to the total number of check-ins at place m_k. Then $\{q_{1k}, \dots, q_{Nk}\}$ is a discrete probability distribution that describes how likely a check-in at m_k was made by a certain user. Thus, we define E_k as the entropy of place m_k:

$$E_k = - \sum_{u_i \in \Phi_k} q_{ik} \log q_{ik} \quad (1)$$

Venues visited by several casual users are less likely to foster the creation of social links between them. Hence, places with higher entropy might result in less social links among their visitors than venues with lower values. This is confirmed by Figure 4(b): the average probability that two users who have checked-in at the same place are friends decreases as the entropy of the place itself increases. Place entropy seems to offer a strong discriminative power: as we will see, it is a successful indicator of whether a certain place is likely to result in social ties between its visitors.

4.2 Feature definition

Link prediction methods are based on numeric scores computed for pairs of users. These values tend to capture proximity of two users across different dimensions, with the underlying assumption that couples of users that are similar or close are likely to develop a social connection between them.

We will consider *social features*, which can be computed for friends-of-friends, *place features* which can be computed for place-friends, and *global features*, that can be computed for any couple of users even, if they do not share any friend or place. All features are described in Table 4 and discussed in the following paragraphs.

4.2.1 Place features

When two users check-in at the same places they might have many chances to be in contact with each other and, therefore, to create a new connection between them. The two features `common_p` and `overlap_p` denote respectively the number and the fraction of common places between two users, while `w_common_p` takes into account the number of check-ins of both users and `w_overlap_p` is given by the cosine similarity of the two check-in vectors.

Then, we define two features based on the entropy of the places that two users share: `min_ent`, the minimum place entropy across all the shared venues, and `aa_ent`, the sum of the inverse of each place entropy value, a measure inspired by the Adamic-Adar similarity score [1]. Similarly, we define corresponding features considering the number of check-ins, `aa_p` and `min_p`: in this case the relevance of a shared place is higher if it has only a few check-ins.

4.2.2 Social features

Several link prediction features are based on the assumption that two users that share many common neighbors are more likely to create a direct connection. Thus, given two users we define `common_n` as their number of common neighbors and `overlap_n` as their Jaccard coefficient [21]. In addition, `aa_n` is their Adamic-Adar measure based on the degrees of the shared neighbors [1].

4.2.3 Global features

Finally, we define measures that can be adopted for any pair of users, as they are based on their individual properties.

An approach to link prediction is to consider the geographic distance between two users, since geographic proximity is related to higher chances of social connection [16, 2, 19, 4]. We define m_{l_i} as the "home-location" where user u_i has most check-ins: given two users, we compute `geodist` as the geographic distance between their home locations. At the same time, `w_geodist` is the same distance divided by the product of the number of check-ins each user has done in their home location.

Another method to define global features is to consider how many friends users have added or how many places they have visited. We define `pa` as the preferential attachment score of two users [3], whereas `pp`, or *place-product*, is given by the product between the number of places that each user has visited. These two features tend to capture more active users that tend to visit many places or add many friends.

Place features	
`common_p`	$\|\Phi_i \cap \Phi_j\|$
`overlap_p`	$\frac{\|\Phi_i \cap \Phi_j\|}{\|\Phi_i \cup \Phi_j\|}$
`w_common_p`	$\vec{c_i}\vec{c_j}$
`w_overlap_p`	$\vec{c_i}\vec{c_j}/\sqrt{\vec{c_i}^2\vec{c_j}^2}$
`aa_ent`	$\sum_{m_k \in \Phi_i \cap \Phi_j} \frac{1}{E_k}$
`min_ent`	$\min(E_k : m_k \in \Phi_i \cap \Phi_j)$
`aa_p`	$\sum_{m_k \in \Phi_i \cap \Phi_j} \frac{1}{\log C_k^P}$
`min_p`	$\min(C_k^P : m_k \in \Phi_i \cap \Phi_j)$
Social features	
`common_n`	$\|\Gamma_i \cap \Gamma_j\|$
`overlap_n`	$\frac{\|\Gamma_i \cap \Gamma_j\|}{\|\Gamma_i \cup \Gamma_j\|}$
`aa_n`	$\sum_{z \in \Gamma_i \cap \Gamma_j} \frac{1}{\log(\|\Gamma_z\|)}$
Global features	
`geodist`	$\mathrm{dist}(m_{l_i}, m_{l_j})$
`w_geodist`	$\mathrm{dist}(m_{l_i}, m_{l_j})/c_{il_i}c_{jl_j}$
`pa`	$\|\Gamma_i\|\|\Gamma_j\|$
`pp`	$\|\Phi_i\|\|\Phi_j\|$

Table 4: List of prediction features.

5. LINK PREDICTION

In this section we describe our link prediction framework. Our proposal builds on two key choices:

- reducing the prediction space by focusing only on friends-of-friends and place-friends;
- exploiting prediction features based on the places visited by users.

We propose a *supervised learning approach* to link prediction, modelling it as a binary classification problem which adopts the prediction features previously described.

5.1 Prediction candidates

Let us consider a dataset snapshot, with U_t being the set of all users and $G_t = (V_t, E_t)$ the relative social network (as defined in Section 3.1). The link prediction problem can be formulated as: given the dataset snapshot at time t as input, compute and return a set of pairs of users $E_t^{PRED} \subset (U_t \times U_t) \setminus E_t$ that are predicted to appear in E_{t+1}

The entire prediction space $(U_t \times U_t) \setminus E_t$ contains all the potential couples between users that are not yet connected by a link. Exploiting the findings of our previous analysis of this prediction space in Gowalla, we select three disjoint prediction sets:

i) **Social**: links appearing among couples that are friends-of-friends but not place-friends (the set $S_t \setminus P_t$);

ii) **Place**: links appearing among users that are place-friends but not friends-of-friends (the set $P_t \setminus S_t$);

iii) **Place-social**: links appearing among users that are both friends-of-friends and place-friends (the set $S_t \cap P_t$).

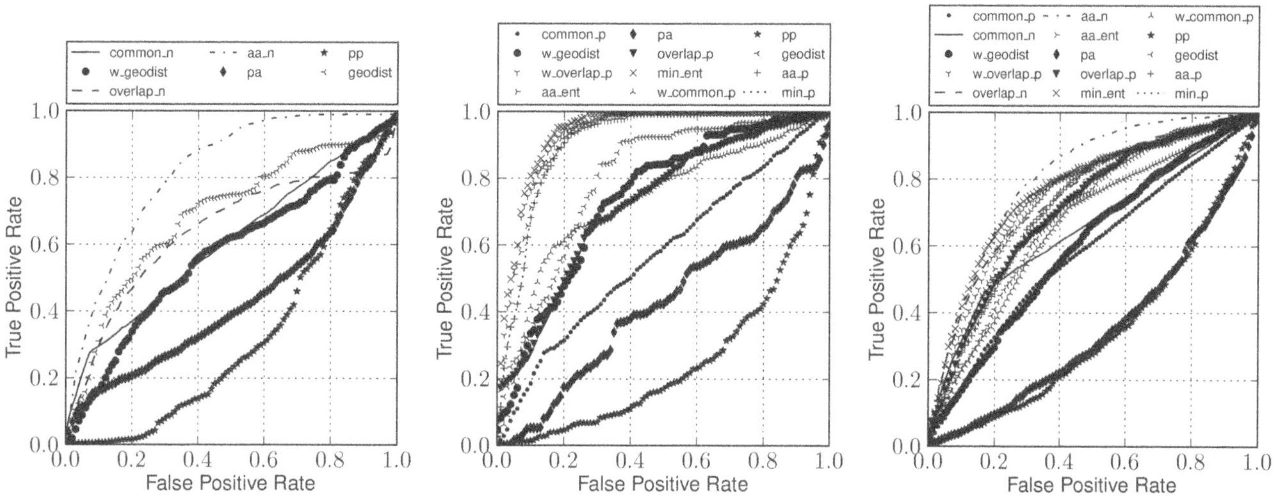

(a) Social (b) Place (c) Place-social

Figure 5: ROC curves for individual features used as unsupervised prediction methods on the three different prediction sets.

Our choice is motivated by the fact that combining these three prediction sets results in a set of candidates about 15 times smaller than the entire prediction space while still allowing us to predict two-thirds of new social ties, as discussed in Section 3.3.

5.2 Prediction algorithm

We adopt a supervised learning approach: for every snapshot t, we compute features at time t for couples of disconnected users and we assign a positive label to each couple if they become connected with a link at $t+1$, or a negative label otherwise. Thus, training and test sets are built so that features from a given time interval are mapped to class labels in a future time interval. Hence, given our 4 snapshots, we can create 3 learning sets, each one with labels drawn from the next snapshot.

Classifiers can then be trained to build models and recognize positive and negative items from their features. As motivated by recent results [17], the choice of a supervised learning formulation to address the link prediction problem stems from the heavily skewed distribution of class labels. Unlike unsupervised methods, class distributions are learned by supervised algorithms, allowing a more effective discovery of inter-class boundaries and hence better classification performance.

6. EXPERIMENTAL EVALUATION

We now present the experimental evaluation of our method: this section includes an investigation of the predictive power of each similarity feature and then an analysis about different supervised classifiers which use these features. Our results show how link prediction systems based on our proposal may be feasibly deployed on similar services with high accuracy.

6.1 Evaluation strategy

For each snapshot t and for each prediction set we sample disjoint training and test datasets: these datasets are always sampled to maintain the original unbalanced distribution of positive and negative items in the real data. Finally, for every item we compute all available prediction features: the only limitations are that in the Social prediction set *place features* are not defined and in the Place prediction set *social features* are not defined. All our evaluation tests have been performed with the WEKA framework, which implements several machine learning algorithms, using default parameters (unless otherwise specified) [25].

We adopt Receiver-Operating-Characteristic (ROC) curves as the main tool to evaluate prediction performance [18]. ROC curves describe how the fraction of true positives over all the positive cases changes as a function of the fraction of true negatives over all the negative cases when the decision threshold varies. A ROC plot is a monotonic non-decreasing plot of true positive rate as a function of false positive rate. A random classifier will result, on average, in the curve $y = x$, while better classifiers will result in curves closer to the upper left corner. ROC curves are particularly able to assess classification performance for highly imbalanced datasets, as in our case. The area under the ROC curve (AUC) is often adopted as a scalar measure of the overall performance.

6.2 Individual features evaluation

We study the predictive power of each individual feature: we compute predictive scores for every pair of disconnected users in the test set and then we numerically rank these candidates according to their score. Given a decision threshold, new links are predicted for all the candidates with scores higher (or lower, depending on the directionality) than the threshold. As we vary the decision threshold we get true and false positives, generating a ROC curve: these curves are then presented in Figure 5 for each prediction set.

In the Social prediction space, as shown in Figure 5(a), the best feature is `aa_n`, which dominates the other ones. Interestingly, we observe how the global features `pa` and `pp` perform worse than a random predictor. This denotes how

Algorithm	Set	Precision	Recall	AUC
Model trees	S	0.79	0.28	**0.87**
	P	0.87	0.34	**0.96**
	PS	0.92	0.62	**0.95**
Random forests	S	0.92	0.39	**0.85**
	P	0.95	0.72	**0.87**
	PS	0.98	0.84	**0.92**
J48	S	0.63	0.04	0.62
	P	0.86	0.34	0.90
	PS	0.90	0.64	0.91
Naïve Bayes	S	0.01	0.16	0.74
	P	0.01	0.36	0.92
	PS	0.04	0.22	0.82

Table 5: Precision and recall on the positive items and overall AUC for different supervised classifiers on the three different prediction sets Social (S), Place (P) and Place-social (PS). Results obtained through 10-fold cross validation and averaged over 20 different random training sets from snapshot $t = 1$.

in the social neighborhood of a given user global indicators are not as useful as measures based on common friends: this may denote how users do not have access to a global view of the network. Instead, global features `geodist` and `w_geodist` perform better, with the former more accurate than the latter. Overall, `aa_n`, `overlap_n` and `geodist` give the best performance, with AUC values between 0.73 and 0.82.

In the Place prediction space, as reported in Figure 5(b), `min_ent`, `w_overlap_p` and `min_p` show the best results, followed by `aa_ent` and `aa_p`. Sharing places with low entropy values or with a few check-ins seems an important indicator of potential friendship, as well as having a large overlap of visited places. These features achieve high AUC values between 0.88 and 0.93. The other features perform slightly worse, with `geodist` doing better than the other ones. Global features `pa` and `pp` show again inverted performance as in the Social case.

Finally, in the Place-social prediction space, as shown in Figure 5(c), all prediction features can be evaluated. As `aa_n` dominates in Social and `min_ent` dominates in Place, they also achieve the best results in this case, with the former having a larger AUC (0.80 against 0.76).

In general, prediction performance is higher in the Place set, while prediction within the other two sets achieves lower AUC values. It is seems easier to predict links among place-friends than among friends-of-friends: this may be due to the fact that more information is available when two users share visited places. However, the prediction space size is much larger in the Place set than in the other two sets, representing an interesting trade-off between prediction effectiveness and search complexity. In essence, the Social set provides good candidates for new links, given its lower imbalance ratio, but then it is difficult to discriminate between them because there is no other information except global features and shared friends. Instead, even if the Place set has higher imbalance ratios, the properties of the places where users check-in provide useful information to discover new friendship connections.

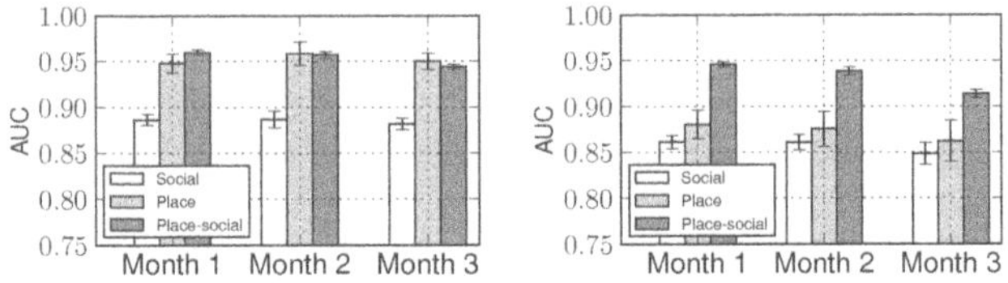

(a) Model trees (b) Random forests

Figure 6: Prediction performance in terms of AUC of model trees (a) and random forests (b) on the three separate Social, Place and Place-social prediction sets, in each temporal snapshots. Results averaged over 20 random datasets, error bars show standard deviation.

6.3 Supervised learning evaluation

We assess whether our prediction features can be combined to characterize a model of link formation across the three prediction sets. Our aim is to achieve at least the same predictive power of the best individual features with a supervised algorithm. We compare the performance of the following classifiers: J48 (equivalent to C4.5[20]), Naïve Bayes, model trees with linear regression on the leaves [10], and random forests (10 trees, 4 random features each) [24]. We run 10-fold cross validation over 20 different training set sampled over each prediction dataset and we consider the AUC value as an overall performance metric [22]. In addition, we also consider two additional metrics computed over positive items: the average *precision*, that is the fraction of positive predictions that are correct, and the average *recall*, that is the fraction of real links that are correctly predicted.

We present our results in Table 5. There is variability across different classifiers: the best performance in terms of AUC are given by random forests and model trees, which are the only two methods that outperform individual features across the three prediction sets (the only exception being random forests underperforming on the Place set). Nonetheless, random forests present higher values of precision and recall than model trees.

As random forests and model trees outperform the other methods, we choose these two classifiers for the next part of this evaluation, where we consider prediction performance across consecutive temporal snapshots of Gowalla. In this case, for every snapshot and for each prediction set we sample disjoint training and test sets of equal size and we compute predictions, averaging results over 20 randomly sampled datasets. As seen in Figures 6, model trees achieve better AUC values on the three prediction sets and across temporal snapshots. Altogether, the two algorithms have lower performance in the Social prediction set, with AUC values between 0.84 and 0.89, whereas Place and Place-social present higher values. Model trees offer slightly better performance than random forests: in particular, the latter algorithm performs worse than individual features on the Place prediction set. A potential explanation for this behavior is that random forests tend to perform poorly when faced with a large heterogeneous set of features, since randomly chosen features are more likely to include less relevant information [11]. This may be the case for the Place set, while this is not the case for Social set, where there are less features, nor for the Place-social set, where there are more fea-

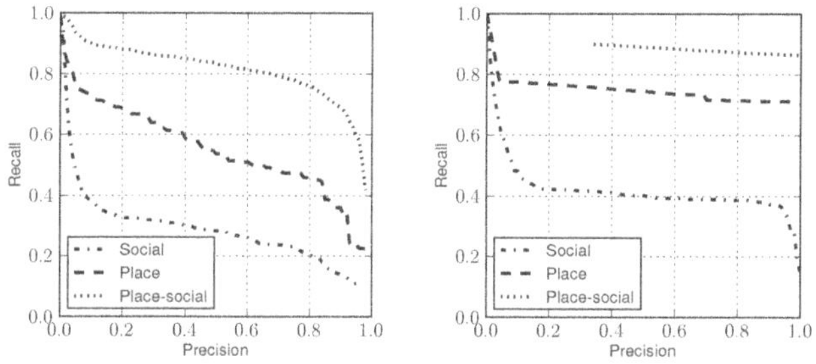

(a) Model trees (b) Random forests

Figure 7: Precision-recall curve for model trees (a) and random forests (b) obtained on the three separate prediction sets, averaged across the three temporal snapshots.

tures but their prediction performance is more homogeneous. However, investigating the precision-recall trade-off offers a different insight on the prediction performance. Given the same level of precision, random forests consistently achieve higher values of recall than model trees, as described in Figure 7. In summary, our prediction framework exhibit high effectiveness with both methods, since they are able to leverage the information contained in our prediction features.

Finally, to understand to which extent different feature classes are contributing to prediction performance we focus only on the Place-social prediction set, where all features are used to build the prediction model, and we test what prediction performance can be achieved by using only one feature class with respect to the full model. As described by Table 6, social features alone provide the worst performance, while both place and global features achieve AUC values closer to the full model. Hence, these two latter classes are mainly contributing to the overall performance, as they exploit information about place check-ins (Place features) and geographic distance between users (Global features). Again, this provides evidence that the choice of including data coming from location-based activity in the prediction model leads to better performance than in purely social-based methods.

6.4 Discussion and implications

Our results are grounded on two main important design choices: focusing link prediction only on a reduced set of candidate pairs of users and exploiting location-based user activity to define successful prediction features. These two simple ideas are able to improve overall performance of link prediction systems: as a consequence, real-world systems can be deployed, making use of predicted links to suggest friends to users and engage them more with the service. In addition, recommending friends among users who check-in in the same places may seem more important in location-based services, since users can directly interact with them when checking-in at these common places.

Our framework enables the prediction of new social ties even for users who do not yet have any friendship connection, provided that they visit and check-in at places. Standard link prediction methods based on social features are of no use in this scenario, since it is impossible to compute prediction features for these isolated users [13]. In some sense, this is

Algorithm	Full model	Social	Place	Global
Model trees	0.95	0.90	0.92	0.92
Random forests	0.93	0.88	0.92	0.92

Table 6: AUC for model trees and random forests on the Place-social prediction set when the full set of prediction features is used and when only a single set of prediction features is used. Results averaged the three snapshots and over 20 different random training and test sets.

a scenario which represents new users of the service: they have signed up, they have checked-in in some places but they are not engaging with other users. Thus, predicting their future links might be extremely important to make them more active participants.

Potentially, our proposal to exploit location-based activity to predict new friends could result in improving prediction performance even further by accessing additional information, such as fine-grained temporal information of user activity or direct interaction among users. For instance, users that check-in at the same place and *at the same time* can be much more likely to become friends [4].

7. RELATED WORKS

The link prediction problem in social networks has been under scrutiny for many years. The seminal work by Liben-Nowell and Kleinberg addresses the problem from an algorithmic point of view, investigating how different proximity features can be exploited to predict the occurrence of new ties in a social network [15]. They adopt an unsupervised approach, where scores are computed for all potential candidates and then ranked to obtain the most likely predictions.

More recently, researchers have advocated supervised approaches to link prediction, given the possibility of modelling the task as a binary classification problem. In particular, Lichtenwalter et al. have presented a detailed analysis of challenges in link prediction systems, discussing imbalance problems and proposing to treat prediction separately for different classes of potential friends [17]. While we also adopt a supervised approach, we additionally consider how link prediction can be performed when additional information not arising from social ties is available.

A related approach to find online social ties among mobile users has been presented by Cranshaw et al. [5]: they track a small number of mobile users in the physical world to discover their connections on online social networks. While focusing as well on information-based measures, our approach considers a much larger set of users and studies their activity on a location-based service. Eagle et al. have considered how interactions between people over mobile phones can accurately predict relations among them [7]. Conversely, we do not consider direct interaction nor communication between users to predict social links. A recent work by Crandall et al. [4] shows how temporal and spatial co-occurences between people help to infer social ties among them: while their main goal is to put forward a generative model which explains empirical data, our study has a different aim, that is, designing a link prediction system to be used on real-world location-based services. Furthermore, our work deals with a different type of data: since we exploit check-ins at well-defined venues, we can infer that two individuals visited exactly the same place without dealing with generic geographic coordinates. As a consequence, our prediction system achieves higher precision while being more feasible for a real-world deployment.

Another thread of research has been addressing the geographic properties of social networks. Liben-Nowell et al. described how the probability of friendship between two individuals can be related to the geographic distance between them [16]. Furthermore, some users on online social networks also exhibit more friendship connections over short geographic distances, with many clusters of friends living nearby [23]. We take advantage of these findings and we explicitly include prediction features based on geographic distance in our prediction framework.

8. CONCLUSION AND FUTURE WORK

In this paper we have described and evaluated a link prediction model based on place properties of a location-based social network. We have studied a large real-world service, Gowalla, finding that the link prediction space can be reduced about 15 times by focusing on place-friends and friends-of-friends only, while still discovering about 66% of all new links. Then, we have described how the properties of the venues visited by users can be used to define prediction features with high predictive power. Building on these findings, we have shown how real link prediction systems can achieve high precision in a prediction space smaller than exhaustive approaches.

Among the future directions of our work we envisage the definition of systems that infer social tie strength from location-based activity and the design of a link recommender system which exploits temporal information about user check-ins.

Acknowledgments

We would like to thank Ilias Leontiadis and Charalampos Rotsos for many useful comments and discussions.

9. REFERENCES

[1] L. A. Adamic and E. Adar. Friends and neighbors on the Web. *Social Networks*, 25(3):211–230, July 2003.

[2] L. Backstrom, E. Sun, and C. Marlow. Find me if you can: improving geographical prediction with social and spatial proximity. In *Proceedings of WWW '10*, pages 61–70, New York, NY, USA, 2010. ACM.

[3] A. Barabási, H. Jeong, Z. Neda, E. Ravasz, A. Schubert, and T. Vicsek. Evolution of the social network of scientific collaborations. *Physica A*, 311(3-4):590–614, August 2002.

[4] D. J. Crandall, L. Backstrom, D. Cosley, S. Suri, D. Huttenlocher, and J. M. Kleinberg. Inferring social ties from geographic coincidences. *PNAS*, 107(52):22436–22441, 2010.

[5] J. Cranshaw, E. Toch, J. Hong, A. Kittur, and N. Sadeh. Bridging the Gap Between Physical Location and Online Social Networks. In *Proceedings of UBICOMP '10*, pages 119–128, New York, NY, USA, 2010. ACM.

[6] N. Eagle and A. S. Pentland. Reality mining: sensing complex social systems. *Personal and Ubiquitous Computing*, 10(4):255–268, March 2006.

[7] N. Eagle, A. S. Pentland, and D. Lazer. Inferring friendship network structure by using mobile phone data. *PNAS*, 106(36):15274–15278, September 2009.

[8] Facebook. People You May Know. `http://blog.facebook.com/blog.php?post=15610312130`.

[9] S. L. Feld. The Focused Organization of Social Ties. *The American Journal of Sociology*, 86(5):1015–1035, 1981.

[10] E. Frank, Y. Wang, S. Inglis, G. Holmes, and I. H. Witten. Using model trees for classification. *Machine Learning*, 32:63–76, July 1998.

[11] M. Gashler, C. Giraud-Carrier, and T. Martinez. Decision Tree Ensemble: Small Heterogeneous Is Better Than Large Homogeneous. In *Proceedings of ICMLA '08*, pages 900–905. IEEE, December 2008.

[12] GigaOM. Foursquare Hits 4 Million Users. `http://gigaom.com/2010/10/21/foursquare-hits-4-million-users/`.

[13] V. Leroy, B. B. Cambazoglu, and F. Bonchi. Cold start link prediction. In *Proceedings of KDD'10*, pages 393–402, New York, NY, USA, 2010. ACM.

[14] J. Leskovec, L. Backstrom, R. Kumar, and A. Tomkins. Microscopic evolution of social networks. In *Proceeding of KDD' 08*, pages 462–470, New York, NY, USA, 2008. ACM.

[15] D. Liben-Nowell and J. Kleinberg. The link prediction problem for social networks. In *Proceedings of CIKM '03*, pages 556–559, New York, NY, USA, 2003. ACM.

[16] D. Liben-Nowell, J. Novak, R. Kumar, P. Raghavan, and A. Tomkins. Geographic routing in social networks. *PNAS*, 102(33):11623–11628, August 2005.

[17] R. N. Lichtenwalter, J. T. Lussier, and N. V. Chawla. New perspectives and methods in link prediction. In *Proceedings of KDD '10*, pages 243–252, New York, NY, USA, 2010. ACM.

[18] F. J. Provost, T. Fawcett, and R. Kohavi. The Case against Accuracy Estimation for Comparing Induction Algorithms. In *Proceedings of ICML '98*, ICML '98, pages 445–453, San Francisco, CA, USA, 1998. Morgan Kaufmann Publishers Inc.

[19] D. Quercia and L. Capra. Friendsensing: recommending friends using mobile phones. In *Proceedings of RecSys '09*, RecSys '09, pages 273–276, New York, NY, USA, 2009. ACM.

[20] J. R. Quinlan. *C4.5: programs for machine learning*. Morgan Kaufmann Publishers Inc., San Francisco, CA, USA, 1993.

[21] G. Salton. *Introduction to Modern Information Retrieval*. McGraw-Hill Companies, September 1983.

[22] S. L. Salzberg. On comparing classifiers: Pitfalls to avoid and a recommended approach. *Data Mining and Knowledge Discovery*, 1:317–327, 1997.

[23] S. Scellato, C. Mascolo, M. Musolesi, and V. Latora. Distance Matters: Geo-social Metrics for Online Social Networks. In *Proceedings of WOSN' 10*, June 2010.

[24] L. B. Statistics and L. Breiman. Random Forests. In *Machine Learning*, pages 5–32, 2001.

[25] I. H. Witten and E. Frank. *Data Mining: Practical Machine Learning Tools and Techniques*. Morgan Kaufmann Series in Data Management Systems. Morgan Kaufmann, second edition, June 2005.

Fast Approximate Similarity Search Based on Degree-Reduced Neighborhood Graphs

Kazuo Aoyama
NTT Communication Science Laboratories, NTT Corporation
2-4, Hikaridai, Seika-cho, Soraku-gun, Kyoto, 619-0237, Japan
aoyama.kazuo@lab.ntt.co.jp

Kazumi Saito
University of Shizuoka
52-1, Yada, Suruga-ku, Shizuoka, Shizuoka, 422-8526, Japan
k-saito@u-shizuoka-ken.ac.jp

Hiroshi Sawada
NTT Communication Science Laboratories, NTT Corporation
2-4, Hikaridai, Seika-cho, Soraku-gun, Kyoto, 619-0237, Japan
sawada.hiroshi@lab.ntt.co.jp

Naonori Ueda
NTT Communication Science Laboratories, NTT Corporation
2-4, Hikaridai, Seika-cho, Soraku-gun, Kyoto, 619-0237, Japan
ueda.naonori@lab.ntt.co.jp

ABSTRACT

This paper presents a fast approximate similarity search method for finding the most similar object to a given query object from an object set with a dissimilarity with a success probability exceeding a given value. As a search index, the proposed method utilizes a degree-reduced k-nearest neighbor (k-DR) graph constructed from the object set with the dissimilarity, and explores the k-DR graph along its edges using a greedy search (GS) algorithm starting from multiple initial vertices with parallel processing. In the graph-construction stage, the structural parameter k of the k-DR graph is determined so that the probability with which at least one search trial of those with multiple initial vertices succeeds is more than the given success probability. To estimate the greedy-search success probability, we introduce the concept of a basin in the k-DR graph. The experimental results on a real data set verify the approximation scheme and high search performance of the proposed method and demonstrate that it is superior to E^2LSH in terms of the expected search cost.

Categories and Subject Descriptors

I.2 [**Artificial Intelligence**]: Problem Solving, Control Methods, and Search—*graph and tree search strategies*; H.3 [**Information Storage and Retrieval**]: Information Search and Retrieval—*search process*

General Terms

Algorithms, Performance, Theory

KDD'11, August 21–24, 2011, San Diego, California, USA.

Keywords

Similarity search, Index structure, Neighborhood graph, Approximate algorithm

1. INTRODUCTION

A similarity search that finds valid objects similar to a given query object has been a fundamental technique for many applications in a variety of fields such as data mining, pattern recognition, computational geometry, computational biology, and statistics [5, 9]. In these fields, some applications require to obtain a solution quickly, even if it is not always exact, rather than an exact solution after a long computation time. An exact similarity search, in particular, is often a time-consuming task when employing a large-scale data set with medium to high *intrinsic* dimensionality estimated based on certain definitions [5, 12, 14]. In such cases, an approximate similarity search is a promising approach to improving search efficiency, although this comes at the expense of degrading the quality of the search result.

Of the many approaches to achieving an approximate similarity search, we focus on a class that gives probabilistic guarantees of the quality of the search results. A representative approach from this class is the locality-sensitive hashing (LSH) scheme [1, 2, 10, 21]. The LSH scheme performs a fast similarity search with a given success probability by reducing the search space. More specifically, the neighborhoods of a query object in an original space are embedded in *buckets* represented by an identical sequence of hash values obtained by a set of hash functions such that the collision probability is much higher for objects that are close to each other than for those that are far apart. A small set of *buckets* with hash values identical to those of the query object corresponds to the search space. The LSH scheme is an efficient technique, but it is only applicable to limited metric spaces such as a Euclidean space with a limited distance measure.

There is a graph-based approach [8, 11, 17, 20] for similarity searches, which is applicable to various types of spaces because it employs a graph representation of a given data set with a dissimilarity. Experimental results obtained with this approach have been reported for large-scale document data sets with high *intrinsic* dimensionality [3], high-dimensional image data sets [19], and a non-metric space consisting of a Gaussian mixture model set and a Kullback-Leibler divergence as a dissimilarity [4]. However, the graph-based approach has two problems. First, the task of constructing a graph as a search index from a given data set with a dissimilarity incurs a high computational cost. For instance, the computational complexity of constructing a k-nearest neighbor (k-*NN*) graph is $\mathcal{O}(n^2)$ with a brute-force approach, where n denotes the number of objects in the data set. The second major problem is that the accuracy of the search result is unclear because a graph-based approach is heuristic. The former problem of constructing a k-*NN* graph is equivalent to the *all-k-nearest-neighbor* problem, to which considerable research efforts have been devoted [6, 18]. We can utilize their results for constructing the graph index. The latter problem has not really been studied. To improve the availability of the graph-based approach, we tackle the problem of how to control the search accuracy.

This paper presents a fast approximate similarity search method based on a neighborhood-graph index. The proposed method has two main algorithms: one is for constructing a graph as a search index and the other for searching on the graph. The graph-construction algorithm builds a special neighborhood graph, which is called a *degree-reduced k-nearest neighbor* (k-*DR*) graph, from a given data set with a dissimilarity. As the search algorithm, we adopt a greedy search (*GS*) algorithm that efficiently finds the vertex *closest from* a query vertex by exploring the k-*DR* graph along its edges. We determine the graph structural parameter k in the graph-construction stage so that the *GS* algorithm succeeds with a success probability exceeding a given value. To estimate the greedy-search (*GS*) success probability, we introduce the concept of a *basin* in the graph.

The remainder of this paper consists of seven sections. Section 2 formulates the problem we attempt to overcome. Section 3 provides preliminaries regarding graph-based similarity search. Section 4 describes the key concept of a *basin* in a graph, and explains the relationship between the basin and the success probability of a greedy search on the graph. Section 5 details our proposed approximate approach, in particular, a new graph-construction algorithm and a parallel greedy search algorithm. Section 6 describes an extension of the proposed method to a range query. Section 7 shows our experimental settings and reports our results. The final section offers our conclusions.

2. PROBLEM FORMULATION

Let $\mathcal{X}$ be a space consisting of valid objects, where dissimilarity $D(x,y)$, $x,y \in \mathcal{X}$ from object x to another y is defined. We solve an approximate nearest neighbor problem as follows. Given object set $X \subset \mathcal{X}$ and query object $q \in \mathcal{X}$, efficiently find target object $x^*(q)$ *closest from* q, that is,

$$x^*(q) = \arg\min_{x \in X}\{D(q,x)\} \tag{1}$$

with a probability of at least $1-\delta$, where δ is the failure probability with which the search algorithm fails to find $x^*(q)$. Note that the object whose dissimilarity from q is minimal among all the objects in X is referred to as the object *closest from* q instead of the object *closest to* q.

3. PRELIMINARIES

We deal with a similarity search problem as a graph-search problem. The graph-search problem is to efficiently find the vertex closest from a given query, by exploring a graph along its edges from an initial vertex with a search algorithm. In our problem, the graph is not given in advance but it is constructed from a given object set with a dissimilarity between the objects. This section reviews the graph representations of a given object set X based on a dissimilarity $D(q,x)$, where $q \in \mathcal{X}$ and $x \in X$, followed by a search algorithm on the constructed graph Γ. Henceforth, we use identical symbols for corresponding elements in the original space and the graph unless otherwise stated. For instance, each object $x \in X$ in the original space corresponds to vertex x on Γ constructed from X, and query object q is treated as an isolated vertex q if $q \notin X$.

3.1 k-NN and k-DR Graphs

We construct a degree-reduced undirected k-nearest neighbor (k-*DR*) graph denoted by $\Gamma_{(k)DR}$ from X based on a dissimilarity, and utilize $\Gamma_{(k)DR}$ as an index for a search algorithm. We describe the structure and properties of $\Gamma_{(k)DR}$, compared with an undirected k-nearest neighbor (k-*NN*) graph denoted by $\Gamma_{(k)NN}$ as a baseline. Graph-construction algorithms for these graphs are detailed in Section 5.1.

Let $N_k(x)$ denote a set of k nearest neighbors of x measured with a dissimilarity. $\Gamma_{(k)NN}$ is constructed by the connection of each x and its $N_k(x)$ with undirected edges. Let $V_{(k)NN}(x)$ denote an adjacent vertex set of x, which is expressed by $N_k(x) \cup \{y : x \in N_k(y)\}$. Let $E_{(k)NN}(x)$ denote a set of undirected edges joining x and elements of $V_{(k)NN}$, which is represented as $E_{(k)NN}(x) = \{e\{x,y\} : y \in V_{(k)NN}(x)\}$, where $e\{x,y\}$ is the undirected edge between x and y. Then $\Gamma_{(k)NN} = (X, \cup_{x \in X} E_{(k)NN}(x))$.

$\Gamma_{(k)DR}$ differs from $\Gamma_{(k)NN}$ in not having an edge between x and $y \in N_k(x)$, without which a greedy search (*GS*) algorithm can reach x from y along the existing edges. Then $\Gamma_{(k)DR}$ has a smaller average degree than $\Gamma_{(k)NN}$. Moreover, $\Gamma_{(k)DR}$ has *small-world* properties [22]: homophily, which is the tendency of *like to associate with like* [16] and an extremely small average shortest path length. These properties enable a search algorithm using only local information to find a target vertex on the graph efficiently. In this paper, we use $\Gamma_{(k)DR}$ as an index because it has the foregoing features, which make it suitable for a similarity search. The symbols for $\Gamma_{(k)NN}$ are also used for $\Gamma_{(k)DR}$. We summarize the notations and definitions we have used in "**Object and Dissimilarity**" and "**Graph**" in **Table 1**.

Example 1. Figure 1 shows k-*NN* and k-*DR* graphs for $k = 1, 2$, which are constructed from the ten given vertices depicted as circles. The 1-*NN* graph $\Gamma_{(1)NN}$ and the 1-*DR* graph $\Gamma_{(1)DR}$ are identical as shown in Fig. 1(a). $\Gamma_{(2)NN}$ and $\Gamma_{(2)DR}$ are shown in Fig. 1(b) and (c), respectively. $\Gamma_{(2)DR}$ has a smaller average degree than $\Gamma_{(2)NN}$. These average degrees are proportional to the numbers of edges of $|E_{(2)DR}| = 10$ and $|E_{(2)NN}| = 13$.

3.2 Greedy Search on Graphs

We use a greedy search (*GS*) algorithm to explore graph $\Gamma_{(k)DR}$. Given query vertex q and initial vertex x_0, the *GS* algorithm first evaluates the dissimilarity from q to x_0, $D(q, x_0)$, and then evaluates the dissimilarities from q to

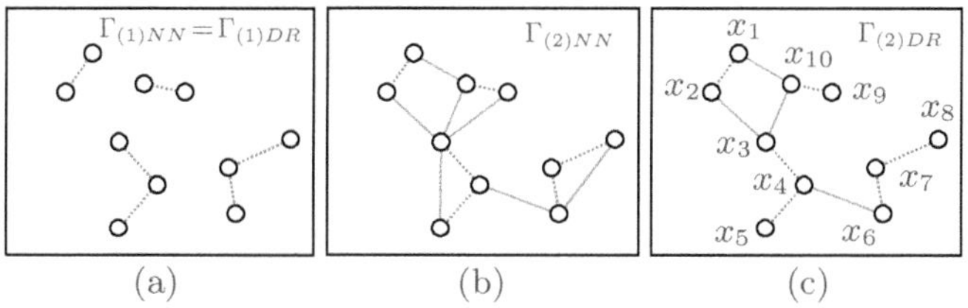

Figure 1: Graphs constructed from 10 given vertices depicted as circles: (a) 1-*NN* graph or 1-*DR* graph with 6 undirected edges denoted as dashed lines, (b) 2-*NN* graph with 7 added edges denoted as solid lines, (c) 2-*DR* graph with 4 added edges.

Table 1: Notations and Definitions

Notation	Description and Definition
Object and Dissimilarity	
$\mathcal{X}$	Given space with a dissimilarity
X	Object (vertex) set or a data set; $X \subset \mathcal{X}$
n	The number of objects (vertices) in X; $\|X\|$
q	Query object (vertex)
$D(x,y)$	Dissimilarity from x to y, $x, y \in \mathcal{X}$
$x^*(q)$	Target object (vertex) that is the vertex closest from q; $\arg\min_{x \in X}\{D(q,x)\}$
$N_k(x)$	Set of k nearest neighbors of x
Graph	
Γ	Graph
$\Gamma_{(k)NN}$	Undirected k-nearest neighbor graph
$\Gamma_{(k)DR}$	Degree-reduced k-nearest neighbor graph
$V_{(k)NN}(x)$	Adjacent vertex set of x on $\Gamma_{(k)NN}$
$V_{(k)DR}(x)$	Adjacent vertex set of x on $\Gamma_{(k)DR}$
$e\{x,y\}$	Undirected edge between x and y
$E_{(k)NN}(x)$	$\{e\{x,y\} : y \in V_{(k)NN}(x)\}$
$E_{(k)DR}(x)$	$\{e\{x,y\} : y \in V_{(k)DR}(x)\}$
Search	
GS, *PGS*	Greedy search, Parallel greedy search
δ	Search failure probability
$c(q;\Gamma)$	Search cost for q when given Γ
$C_{[i]}(q;\Gamma)$	Set of vertices whose dissimilarities from q are evaluated in the ith parallel process
$D_{min[i]}(q;\Gamma)$	The minimum dissimilarity from q in the ith parallel process
$R(q)$	Set of objects within dissimilarity r from q
Basin and Search Success Probability	
$Basin(q;\Gamma)$	Set of vertices on given Γ, from which a *GS* algorithm finds $x^*(q)$
Q', q'	Quasi-query vertex set $Q' \subset \mathcal{X}$; $q' \in Q'$
Q	Query vertex set; $q \in Q$
S	Test-vertex set for the Monte Carlo method
T	Target vertex set for Q' or Q
L	The number of search trials for each query q or the number of initial vertices for each q
$p(Success\|q;\Gamma)$	*GS* success probability finding $x^*(q)$ on Γ
$\tilde{p}(Success\|q,S;\Gamma)$	*GS* success probability for q estimated with the Monte Carlo method using S
$\hat{p}(Success\|q;L,\Gamma)$	Probability that at least one search trial in L trials for identical q succeeds on Γ
$\langle\hat{p}(Success;L,\Gamma)\rangle$	Ensemble average of a probability $\hat{p}(Success\|q;L,\Gamma)$

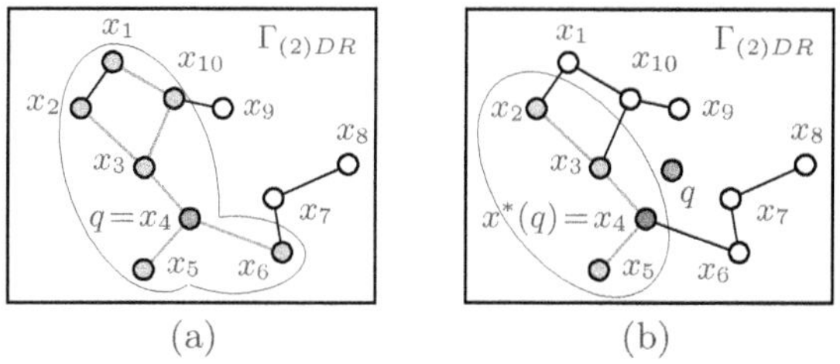

Figure 2: Basins in the 2-*DR* graph with 10 vertices: (a) Basin of q=x4 denoted as filled circles, (b) Basin of isolated q whose x*(q) is x4.

all the vertices in an adjacent vertex set of x_0, $V_{(k)DR}(x_0)$. Let us call x_0 an expanded vertex whose adjacent vertices are evaluated in terms of their dissimilarities from q. If $D(q,x_0) > D(q,x)$, where $x = \text{argmin}_{y \in V_{(k)DR}(x_0)}\{D(q,y)\}$, the *GS* algorithm sets x at the next expanded vertex and repeats this operation. Conversely, the *GS* algorithm terminates if $D(q,x_0) \leq D(q,x)$. Suppose that $\Gamma_{(2)DR}$ shown in Fig. 1(c) is provided and x_4 is set as query vertex q. The *GS* algorithm starting from x_2 first evaluates $D(x_4,x_2)$ and then compares it with the minimum dissimilarity $D(x_4,x_3)$ in $\{D(x_4,x_1), D(x_4,x_3)\}$. Since $D(x_4,x_3) < D(x_4,x_2)$, the *GS* algorithm sets x_3 as the next expanded vertex and repeats this operation. Finally, the *GS* algorithm reaches x_4, and terminates. Note that when Γ and q are given, *a set of initial vertices* from which q is reachable with the *GS* algorithm is uniquely specified. This fact leads us to the concept of a *basin* in a graph, detailed in the next Section.

4. BASINS IN GRAPHS

We first define the basin of query vertex $q \in \mathcal{X}$ in *Definition 1*, which is a key concept for understanding the proposed approximate approach, and then explain the relationship between the basin of q and the success probability of a greedy search (*GS*) algorithm that finds the target vertex $x^*(q)$ closest from q, starting from an initial vertex chosen uniformly at random from all the vertices in X in graph Γ.

Definition 1. Given graph Γ constructed from object set $X \subset \mathcal{X}$ based on a dissimilarity and query vertex $q \in \mathcal{X}$, a basin of q denoted as $Basin(q;\Gamma)$ is defined by a set of vertices on Γ from which a greedy search (*GS*) algorithm can find the target vertex $x^*(q)$ closest from q along the edges of Γ. Let $GS(x_0,q;\Gamma)$ denote a function that returns the closest vertex from q exactly when a *GS* algorithm with initial vertex x_0 on Γ terminates. Then $Basin(q;\Gamma)$ is expressed as

$$Basin(q;\Gamma) = \{x_0 \in X : x^*(q) = GS(x_0,q;\Gamma)\} \ . \quad (2)$$

Example 2. To provide an intuitive understanding of the basin of a vertex, we show examples in Figs. 2(a) and (b), where each q is given for the 2-*DR* graph constructed from a set of 10 vertices X. In Fig. 2(a) where $q \in X$ and $q = x^*(q) = x_4$, the basin of $q = x_4$ denoted by $Basin(q;\Gamma_{(2)DR})$ is $\{x_4, x_1, x_2, x_3, x_5, x_6, x_{10}\}$ and the ratio of the number of the basin's elements to $|X| = 10$ is 0.7. In Fig. 2(b) where q is an isolated vertex, i.e., $q \notin X$ and $x^*(q) = x_4$, the basin of q, $Basin(q;\Gamma_{(2)DR})$, is $\{x_4, x_2, x_3, x_5\}$ and the ratio is 0.4. In spite of the identical target vertex $x^*(q) = x_4$ in these two cases, the basins have different numbers of elements. This arises from q's position, namely whether $q \in X$ or $q \notin X$.

In the latter case, for instance, the *GS* algorithm starting from x_{10} does not select x_3 as the next expanded vertex but selects x_9 because $D(q,x_9) < D(q,x_3)$. Therefore, $x_{10} \notin \mathit{Basin}(q;\Gamma_{(2)DR})$. Thus the position of q affects its basin.

From *Definition 1*, we note that the success probability of the *GS* algorithm coincides with the ratio of the number of vertices in the basin of q to that of all the vertices $n = |X|$. The *GS* success probability $p(\mathit{Success}|q;\Gamma)$ is expressed by

$$p(\mathit{Success}|q;\Gamma) = \frac{1}{n}\sum_{x_0\in X} I\left(x_0 \in \mathit{Basin}(q;\Gamma)\right) = \frac{|\mathit{Basin}(q;\Gamma)|}{n}, \tag{3}$$

where $I(\cdot)$ is the indicator function that returns one only if the condition holds, and $|\mathit{Basin}(q;\Gamma)|$ denotes the number of elements the basin contains, which is called *basin size*.

Suppose that L search trials on Γ for an identical q are performed independently with the *GS* algorithm, and initial vertex $x_{0[i]}$ $(i = 1, 2, \cdots, L)$ in multiset X_0 chosen uniformly at random from X is employed in a distinct search trial among the L trials. Consider the exact probability that at least one search trial succeeds in finding $x^*(q)$. Then the probability $\hat{p}(\mathit{Success}|q;L,\Gamma)$ with which at least one of the L search trials for query q succeeds is expressed by

$$\hat{p}(\mathit{Success}|q;L,\Gamma) = 1 - \left(1 - p(\mathit{Success}|q;\Gamma)\right)^L. \tag{4}$$

In the ideal case, the probability $\hat{p}(\mathit{Success};L,\Gamma)$ is expressed as

$$\hat{p}(\mathit{Success};L,\Gamma) = \sum_{\forall q} \hat{p}(\mathit{Success}|q;L,\Gamma)\cdot p(q), \tag{5}$$

where $p(q)$ denotes the probability mass function of q. In practice, it is difficult to calculate the probability in Eq. (5) because $p(q)$ is unknown or the calculation of exact $\hat{p}(\mathit{Success}|q;L,\Gamma)$ requires a high computational cost even if $p(q)$ were given in advance.

Instead of the exact calculation of $\hat{p}(\mathit{Success};L,\Gamma)$, we first approximate $p(q)$ with an empirical distribution function of quasi-query vertex $q'_{[j]} \in Q'$ $(j = 1, 2, \cdots, |Q'|)$, which is chosen from $\mathcal{X}$ by simple random sampling. Then $\hat{p}(\mathit{Success};L,\Gamma)$ is approximated by

$$\langle\hat{p}(\mathit{Success};L,\Gamma)\rangle \simeq \frac{1}{|Q'|}\sum_{q'\in Q'} \hat{p}(\mathit{Success}|q';L,\Gamma), \tag{6}$$

where $\langle\star\rangle$ denotes an ensemble average of $\star$. Moreover, we make practical use of the Monte Carlo method for calculating $\hat{p}(\mathit{Success}|q';L,\Gamma)$. The Monte Carlo method uses a set of test vertices chosen from X by simple random sampling, which works as a set of initial vertices for a *GS* algorithm and which is denoted by $S_{[j]}$, consisting of $s_{[j][h]} \in S_{[j]}$ $(h = 1, 2, \cdots, |S_{[j]}| \ll n)$. Then we can estimate the ensemble average of the probability as

$$\begin{aligned}
&\langle\hat{p}(\mathit{Success};L,\Gamma)\rangle \\
&\simeq \frac{1}{|Q'|}\sum_{j=1}^{|Q'|}\left\{1 - \left(1 - \frac{1}{|S_{[j]}|}\sum_{h=1}^{|S_{[j]}|} I(s_{[j][h]} \in \mathit{Basin}(q'_{[j]};\Gamma))\right)^L\right\} \\
&= \frac{1}{|Q'|}\sum_{q'_{[j]}\in Q'}\left\{1 - \left(1 - \tilde{p}(\mathit{Success}|q'_{[j]};\Gamma)\right)^L\right\},
\end{aligned} \tag{7}$$

where $\tilde{p}(\mathit{Success}|q'_{[j]};\Gamma)$ denotes the *GS* success probability estimated by the Monte Carlo method using the test-vertex set $S_{[j]}$ corresponding to each $q'_{[j]}$.

5. PROPOSED GRAPH-BASED METHOD

This section details the graph-based approximate similarity search method. This method consists of two main algorithms: one for building an index and the other for searching based on the index. We construct $\Gamma_{(k)DR}$ as the index and use a *GS* algorithm for traversing the $\Gamma_{(k)DR}$ along its edges with parallel processing using multiple initial vertices.

5.1 Graph-Construction Algorithm

We begin by clarifying the construction of a simple *k-NN* graph $\Gamma_{(k)NN}$. A parameter k of $\Gamma_{(k)NN}$, which is provided in advance, indicates the number of out-edges for each vertex, i.e., an out-degree. Given object set $X \subset \mathcal{X}$, k and rank list $\mathit{List}(X, k_{max})$, $k_{max} > k$, where the k_{max} nearest neighbors of each object in X are listed in ascending order of dissimilarity, we construct $\Gamma_{(k)NN} = (X, \cup_{x\in X} E_{(k)NN}(x))$ by connecting each vertex x and $y \in N_k(x)$ with undirected edges $E_{(k)NN}(x)$ with reference to the $\mathit{List}(X, k_{max})$. We adopt an incremental procedure on k, that is, we construct $\Gamma_{(1)NN}$ for $k' = 1$, then construct $\Gamma_{(2)NN}$ by incrementing k' by one, and we repeat this procedure until $k' = k$.

Next, let us consider the construction of $\Gamma_{(k)DR}$ on the assumption that the parameter k is provided in advance. $\Gamma_{(k)DR}$ is constructed with the incremental procedure on k in the same way as $\Gamma_{(k)NN}$. However, unlike the construction algorithm for $\Gamma_{(k)NN}$, that for $\Gamma_{(k)DR}$ generates an undirected edge between x and its k'th nearest neighbor vertex y only if the *GS* algorithm starting from y cannot find x along the already existing edges on $\Gamma_{(k')DR}$. This operation reduces the number of edges of each vertex, i.e., the degree, compared with that in $\Gamma_{(k')NN}$, maintaining a path through which x is reachable from y with the *GS* algorithm.

Finally, consider the construction of $\Gamma_{(k)DR}$ on the assumption that the parameter k is *not* provided in advance so that $\Gamma_{(k)DR}$ enables the *GS* algorithm to find the nearest neighbor of query vertex q with a given success probability. Given X, $\mathit{List}(X, k_{max})$, failure probability δ, a set Q' of quasi-queries $q_{[j]} \in \mathcal{X}$, $j = 1, 2, \cdots, |Q'|$, a target vertex set of the $x^*(q_{[j]}) \in X$ denoted by T, a test-vertex set $S_{[j]} = S \subset X$ for estimation of a basin size, and the number of initial vertices L for each query for a *GS* algorithm, $\Gamma_{(k)DR}$ is constructed by **Algorithm 1**. A novel procedure in this algorithm is the judgment of whether it increments k', $(k' \le k)$, shown on **Line 2** in **Algorithm 1**. Once the algorithm constructs $\Gamma_{(k')DR}$ at the k'th stage, it compares the given search success probability $1-\delta$ with $\langle\hat{p}(\mathit{Success};L,\Gamma_{(k')DR})\rangle$. The $\langle\hat{p}(\mathit{Success};L,\Gamma_{(k')DR})\rangle$ monotonically increases with k' because the basin size $|\mathit{Basin}(q'_{[j]}, S;\Gamma_{(k')DR})|$ monotonically increases. Note that we appropriately replace the variables in Eqs. (3) and (7) with the above-mentioned variables, for instance, Γ and q are replaced with $\Gamma_{(k')DR}$ and $q'_{[j]}$, respectively. In addition, S independent of j is introduced instead of $S_{[j]}$. Using the monotonic increase of $\langle\hat{p}(\mathit{Success};L,\Gamma_{(k')DR})\rangle$ with k', the algorithm terminates only precisely when the following inequality holds.

$$\begin{aligned}
1-\delta &< \frac{1}{|Q'|}\sum_{q'_{[j]}\in Q'}\left\{1 - \left(1 - \tilde{p}(q'_{[j]};\Gamma_{(k')DR})\right)^L\right\} \\
&= \langle\hat{p}(\mathit{Success};L,\Gamma_{(k')DR})\rangle
\end{aligned} \tag{8}$$

This algorithm is characterized by two procedures: the termination condition in inequality (8) shown on **Line 2** in **Algorithm 1** and the degree-reduction procedure shown on **Lines 6–8**, where x and y are mutually added to the set of their adjacent vertices, only if the *greedy-reachability checking* (*GRC*) algorithm shown in **Algorithm 2** returns **FALSE**. The proposed graph-construction algorithm completes $\Gamma_{(k)DR}$ by controlling k so that the ensemble average of the probability is greater than $1-\delta$ that at least one of the L search trials succeeds.

Algorithm 1 *Graph-Construction Algorithm* $GC(X, List(X, k_{max}), \delta, Q', T, S, L)$

Input: X, $List(X, k_{max})$, δ, Q', T, S, L
Output: $\Gamma_{(k)DR}$
1. Define $\Gamma_{(0)DR} = (X, \emptyset)$ at $k' = 0$, and Set $k' \leftarrow 0$
2. **while** $1-\delta \geq \langle \hat{p}(Success; L, \Gamma_{(k')DR}) \rangle$ **do**
3. Set $k' \leftarrow k' + 1$
   Set $\Gamma_{(k')DR} \leftarrow \Gamma_{(k'-1)DR}$
4. **for all** $x \in X$ **do**
5. Set $\{y\} \leftarrow N_{k'}(x) \setminus N_{(k'-1)}(x)$
6. **if** $\boldsymbol{GRC}(x, y; \Gamma_{(k')DR})$ = **FALSE then**
7. Set $V_{(k')DR}(x) \leftarrow V_{(k')DR}(x) \cup \{y\}$
   Set $V_{(k')DR}(y) \leftarrow V_{(k')DR}(y) \cup \{x\}$
8. **end if**
9. **end for**
10. **end while**
11. Set $k \leftarrow k'$
12. Set $\Gamma_{(k)DR} \leftarrow (X, \cup_{x \in X} E_{(k)DR}(x))$,
    where $E_{(k)DR}(x) = \{e\{x, y\} : y \in V_{(k)DR}(x)\}$
13. **return** $\Gamma_{(k)DR}$

Algorithm 2 *Greedy-Reachability Checking Algorithm* $GRC(x, y; \Gamma_{(k')DR})$

Input: $x,\ y \in X$, $\Gamma_{(k')DR}$
Output: **TRUE** or **FALSE**
Set $z \leftarrow \arg\min_{z' \in V_{(k')DR}(y)}\{D(x, z')\}$
if $D(x, z) \leq D(x, y)$ **then**
  return TRUE
else
  return FALSE
end if

5.2 Search Algorithm on Graphs

The proposed approximate similarity search method employs L search trials for each query for the estimation of the *GS* success probability. Since these search trials are completely independent of each other, we perform the L search trials with L parallel processes using the simple parallel greedy search (*PGS*) algorithm shown in **Algorithm 3**. In practice, the L search trials may be partitioned into any combinations of serial and parallel processes.

Given $\Gamma_{(k)DR}$, $q \in \mathcal{X}$, and a set $X_0(q)$ of initial vertices $x_{0[i]}(q)$ ($i = 1, 2, \cdots, L$: i denotes the identification number of processes in parallel.), the *PGS* algorithm returns both the closest vertex z from q among those found by the L search trials, and search cost $c(q)$ defined by the maximum number of dissimilarity calculations among those performed by the L search trials until each trial terminates. In **Algorithm 3**, $D_{min[i]}(q; \Gamma_{(k)DR})$ and $C_{[i]}(q; \Gamma_{(k)DR})$ denote the minimum dissimilarity from q in the search process so far and a set of vertices whose dissimilarity from q are evaluated, respectively. Moreover, $x_{[i]}$ is the vertex closest from q in the adjacent vertices of the currently expanded vertex, and $z_{[i]}$ is the vertex closest from q in the expanded vertices.

Algorithm 3 *Parallel Greedy Search Algorithm* $PGS(q, X_0(q); \Gamma_{(k)DR})$

Input: $\Gamma_{(k)DR}$, $q \in \mathcal{X}$,
  $X_0 = (x_{0[1]}, x_{0[2]}, \cdots, x_{0[L]})$, $x_{0[i]} \in X$
Output: (z, c)
for each initial vertex $x_{0[i](q)}$ **in parallel do**
  Set $z_{[i]} \leftarrow x_{0[i]}(q)$, $x_{[i]} \leftarrow x_{0[i]}(q)$,
  $D_{min[i]} \leftarrow D(q, z_{[i]})$, $C_{[i]} \leftarrow \{z_{[i]}\}$
  while $z_{[i]} = x_{[i]}$ **do**
    Set $x_{[i]} \leftarrow \arg\min_{y_{[i]} \in V_{(k)DR}(z_{[i]})}\{D(q, y_{[i]})\}$,
    $C_{[i]} \leftarrow C_{[i]} \cup V_{(k)DR}(z_{[i]})$
    if $D(q, x_{[i]}) < D(q, z_{[i]})$ **then**
      Set $D_{min[i]} \leftarrow D(q, x_{[i]})$, $z_{[i]} \leftarrow x_{[i]}$
    end if
  end while
end for
Set $z \leftarrow \arg\min_{i=1,\cdots,L}\{D_{min[i]}\}$,
  $c \leftarrow \arg\max_{i=1,\cdots,L}\{|C_{[i]}|\}$
return (z, c)

---

6. EXTENSIONS

The proposed method can be easily extended to one for a range query to be answered by E^{2}LSH. This problem is formulated as follows.

Problem. Suppose that the same space $\mathcal{X}$ as that described in Section 2 is given. Given object set $x \in X \subset \mathcal{X}$, query object $q \in \mathcal{X}$, and a dissimilarity from q denoted by r, report a set of objects $R(q)$ within r from q with greater than or equal to a given *recall*. $R(q)$ and the *recall* for q denoted by $Recall(q)$ are defined as follows.

$$R(q) = \{x : D(q, x) < r\}\ . \tag{9}$$

$$Recall(q) = |\tilde{R}(q) \cap R(q)| \,/\, |R(q)|\ , \tag{10}$$

where $\tilde{R}(q)$ denotes a set of reported objects.

The *PGS* algorithm in **Algorithm 3** is modified so that the search algorithm collects the vertices within a given dissimilarity (or radius) r from q. We assume that $|R(q)| < |Basin(q; \Gamma_{(k)DR})|$. This assumption guarantees that the *GS* algorithm for q always finds target vertex $x^*(q)$ once it reaches a vertex within the radius $R(q)$. It is also experimentally shown in Section 7.2 that this assumption is reasonable since the expected basin size in $\Gamma_{(k)DR}$ reaches over 6,000 when $|X| = 60,000$, even if $k = 10$, while we rarely need such a large number of vertices as an answer. The modified search algorithm differs from a simple *GS* algorithm in its use of stack storing vertices within $R(q)$. The search algorithm pushes the vertices, which are evaluated in terms of their dissimilarities from q but are not expanded, into the stack. The stack plays a similar role to the *open list* in the A^* or the Frontier search algorithm [7, 13]. However, the proposed search algorithm pops a vertex from the stack and employs it as the next expanded vertex only after a greedy search part in the search algorithm terminates. This procedure is repeated until the stack is empty. The modified *PGS* algorithm for range queries is detailed in **Appendix A**.

7. EXPERIMENTS

This section shows our experimental settings and results. We first describe data sets and then show the properties of basins in $\Gamma_{(k)DR}$. Finally, we demonstrate the search performance of the proposed similarity search method, compared with E^{2}LSH.

Table 2: Average normalized basin size on $\Gamma_{(k)DR}$; $(1/|\mathbf{Y}|)\sum_{y\in Y}(|Basin(y;\Gamma_{(k)DR})|/n)$.

Position of vertex y	k				
$y \in Y \subset \mathcal{X}$	10	20	40	60	100
$y \in Y = Q'$, $(Q' \cap X = \emptyset)$	0.12	0.26	0.39	0.45	0.50
$y \in Y = X$	0.23	0.47	0.69	0.78	0.86

7.1 Data sets

To demonstrate the effectiveness and efficiency of the proposed approximate similarity search method, we prepared an image data set, the MNIST database of handwritten digits [15]. We used 60,000, 4,850, and 4,841 images from the MNIST database for object set X, query set Q, and quasi-query set Q', which were disjoint from each other, respectively. In particular, quasi-query set Q' was used for graph construction and query set Q was used to evaluate search performance. For evaluation only, the two target-vertex sets that correspond to the quasi-query set and the query set were prepared in advance. A feature vector extracted from the image was represented as a point on the unit hypersphere in a 784-dimensional Euclidean space. A dissimilarity, which is a distance in this case, between a pair of points was measured by the Euclidean distance.

7.2 Basin properties

We analyzed the properties of basins in $\Gamma_{(k)DR}$ constructed from the object set X to verify that the basin size of $\Gamma_{(k)DR}$ monotonically increases with k, i.e., GS success probability $p(Success|q;\Gamma_{(k)DR})$ monotonically increases with k, and the Monte Carlo method works effectively, maintaining the accuracy of search results.

First, we calculated the exact basin sizes in $\Gamma_{(k)DR}s$ with various k values, $k=10,20,40,60,100$, for vertex y in two distinct vertex sets Y, i.e., $Y=Q'$ $(Y\cap X=\emptyset)$ and $Y=X$. Note that y is an isolated vertex that is not connected to $\Gamma_{(k)DR}$ when $Y=Q'$. Table 2 shows the average basin sizes in $\Gamma_{(k)DR}s$, which are normalized by $n=|X|$. The average basin size increased with k for both $Y=Q'$ and $Y=X$. In particular, the average normalized basin size in $\Gamma_{(100)DR}$ at $k=100$ reaches a very large value of 0.50, which corresponds to half of all the vertices in X, even if y does not exist in $\Gamma_{(100)DR}$, i.e., $Y=Q'$, although $\Gamma_{(100)DR}$ is constructed to guarantee that each vertex is reachable only from the vertices within its 100th nearest neighbor by the GS algorithm. In addition to this property of the average normalized basin size, we experimentally confirmed that basin-size distributions for $\Gamma_{(k)DR}$ shifted from a small to a large basin-size region with an increase in k. These properties allow us to utilize inequality (8) as the termination condition in the graph-construction algorithm.

Next, we show the effectiveness of the Monte Carlo method in comparison with the approach using all the vertices in X as the test vertices that work as initial vertices for the GS algorithm in the graph-construction stage. We calculated the ensemble average of $\hat{p}(Success;L,\Gamma_{kDR})$ for the following various settings. For each quasi-query $q'_{[j]}\in Q'$ $(|Q'|=4,841)$, we prepared three test-vertex sets $S_{[j]}$ with a different number of elements: the first is $|X|=n$ denoted by "All," the second is 160, and the last is 40. The size of each test-vertex set is denoted by $|\bar{S}|$ $(|\bar{S}|=|S_{[j]}|)$. In addition, $\Gamma_{(k)DR}s$ with various k values $(10\le k\le 100)$ were employed, and three different L values, $L=4,8,16$, were adopted. Figure 3 shows comparison results for ensemble averages of the probabilities with which at least one of the L search trials succeeds. Surprisingly, the ensemble average, shown by the lines labeled $|\bar{S}|/n\simeq 0.07\%$, closely coincided with those of the exact average for any k and L, even though the number of test vertices was only 40 corresponding to less than 0.07% of all the vertices in X.

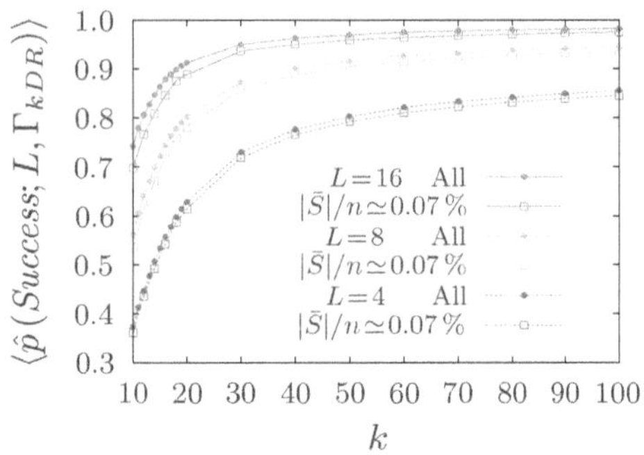

Figure 3: Comparison of two types of ensemble averages of the probability where at least one of L search trials succeeds for $\Gamma_{(k)DR}$. One type was calculated using all the vertices in X and the other was estimated by the Monte Carlo method using 40 test vertices corresponding to less than 0.07 % of $n=|X|$.

Table 3: Values of k of $\Gamma_{(k)DR}s$ constructed by using test-vertex sets with three distinct sizes when $L=16$.

Basin size calculation method	$1-\delta$			
	0.95	0.90	0.85	0.80
Exact, $\bar{S}=X$ (All)	31	19	15	12
Monte Carlo, $|\bar{S}|=160$ (0.27 %)	33	20	15	13
Monte Carlo, $|\bar{S}|=40$ (0.07 %)	40	22	17	14

Given $\Gamma_{(k)DR}$, the value of $\hat{p}(Success;L,\Gamma_{(k)DR})$ estimated by the Monte Carlo method using the small set was always smaller than that exactly calculated using X as $\bar{S}$, $\bar{S}=X$. This finding implies that a k value of $\Gamma_{(k)DR}$ obtained with the graph-construction algorithm that uses the Monte Carlo method for the estimation of $\hat{p}(Success;L,\Gamma_{(k)DR})$ was larger than or equal to that obtained with the graph-construction algorithm using the exactly calculated $\hat{p}(Success;L,\Gamma_{(k)DR})$, as shown in Table 3. Then the GS algorithm on the $\Gamma_{(k)DR}$ constructed based on the termination condition shown as inequality (8) using $\hat{p}(Success;L,\Gamma_{(k)DR})$ estimated by the Monte Carlo method succeeds with more than the given success probability. Consequently, we can adopt the Monte Carlo method to reduce the computational cost of estimating the basin size.

7.3 Graph construction

This section confirms that tuple (k,L) is feasible for the given failure probability δ, that is, $k\ll n$ and L is an appropriate value for the degree of parallelism in a practical search task. The computational complexity of graph construction is also discussed.

We have a degree of the freedom in the selection of k and L to achieve an identical search success probability $1-\delta$ although L is fixed at a certain value in Section 5.1. When δ and the estimated basin sizes are given and either k or L is fixed, the lower bound on the remaining parameter is derived

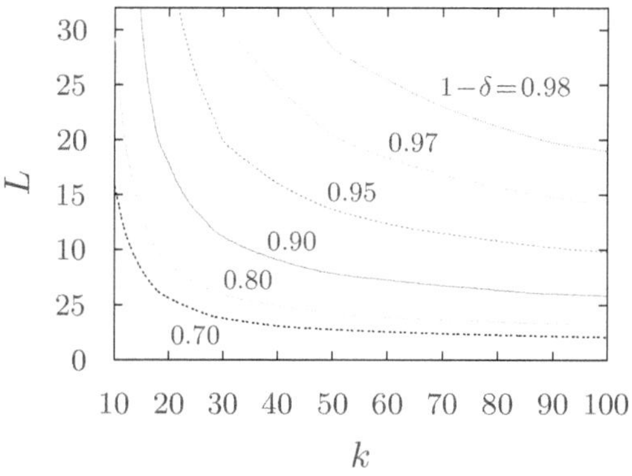

Figure 4: Contour plot of search success probability 1−δ versus k and L, evaluated with basin sizes estimated by the Monte Carlo method using 40 test vertices.

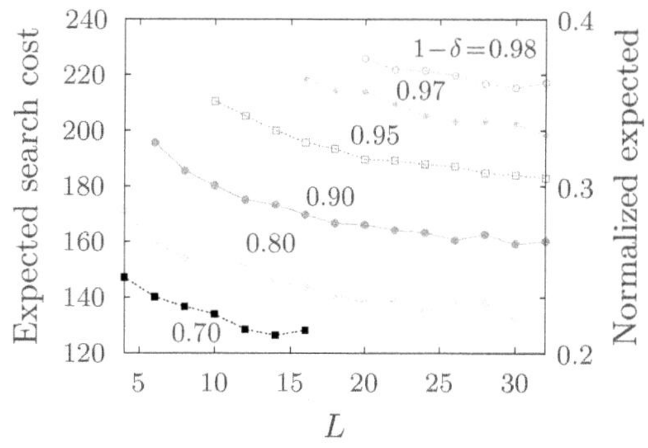

Figure 5: Expected search cost against L. Levels for achieving success probabilities of $1-\delta = 0.98, 0.97, 0.95, 0.90, 0.80, 0.70$ are given in the graph-construction stage. Although k is omitted, it is uniquely determined from δ and L.

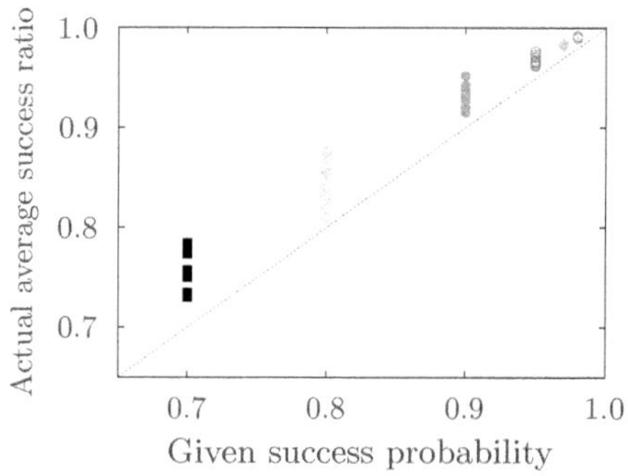

Figure 6: Relationship between given success probability and actual average success ratio obtained by a search using the constructed graph.

from inequality (8). We employed vertex set X with 60,000 vertices, quasi-query set Q' with 4,841 vertices, target-vertex set T where a target vertex for each quasi-query was calculated in advance, and test-vertex set S with 40 vertices chosen from X by simple random sampling. The basin size for each quasi-query was estimated as a GS success probability by the Monte Carlo method using test-vertex set S. Figure 4 shows feasible solutions on tuple (k, L) for the given $1-\delta$, which were obtained by applying the estimated basin sizes to inequality (8). When the search success probability $1-\delta$ was given, L decreased monotonically with k. In contrast, when a large L was given, $1-\delta$ increased with k, because generally the basin size of a vertex increases with k, i.e., the GS success probability increases with k.

Next, we discuss the computational cost evaluated by the number of dissimilarity calculations (or distance calculations for the MNIST database). The proposed graph-construction algorithm needs $List(X, k_{max})$, where $k_{max} \ll n$, e.g., $k_{max} = 200$, is determined in advance. The computational cost for making the $List(X, k_{max})$ is $\mathcal{O}(n^2)$ with the brute-force approach. Moreover, the space complexity is $\mathcal{O}(n)$. Although the graph-construction algorithm in **Algorithm 1** seems to perform time-consuming basin-size calculations every time k' is updated, the Monte Carlo method successfully reduces the computational cost, while maintaining the accuracy of the search results as shown in Fig. 3 and Table 3. The basin-size calculations do not have any effect on the computational complexity.

7.4 Search performance

We evaluated the search performance with the expected search cost. Given $\Gamma_{(k)DR}$, a set of query vertices $q \in Q \subset \mathcal{X}$, and the number of search trials L per query, the expected search cost $E[c(\Gamma_{(k)DR})]$ is defined by

$$E[c(\Gamma_{(k)DR})] = \frac{1}{|Q|} \sum_{q \in Q} \max_{i=1,\cdots,L} \{|C_{[i]}(q; \Gamma_{(k)DR})|\} \ , \quad (11)$$

where $|C_{[i]}(q; \Gamma_{(k)DR})|$ denotes the search cost of the ith search trial for q on $\Gamma_{(k)DR}$. Figure 5 shows the expected search costs that will be incurred in achieving the given success probability $1-\delta$. For the various success probabilities, we employed $\Gamma_{(k)DR}$ constructed with L and the corresponding k shown in Section 7.3.

The proposed method performed a similarity search at an extremely low cost but with a high search success probability. For instance, when the method employed the $\Gamma_{(22)DR}$ constructed by **Algorithm 1** under the condition of $1-\delta = 0.90$ and $L = 16$, the expected search cost was only 169.25, corresponding to around 0.28% of n, which is indicated by the point at $L = 16$ on line $1-\delta = 0.90$ in Fig. 5. Moreover, the actual search success ratio was 0.93, which was higher than the given success probability $1-\delta = 0.90$. The expected search cost had a tendency to decrease with L when $\Gamma_{(k)DR}$s were applied, which were constructed under the condition of an identical search success probability and various Ls. This is because the GS algorithm on the $\Gamma_{(k)DR}$ with a smaller k value terminates with a lower search cost independent of search success or failure. Thus, we should construct $\Gamma_{(k)DR}$ using as large an L value as possible.

Figure 6 shows the relationship between a given success probability for the graph construction and an actual average success ratio obtained with an actual search using the constructed graph. The actual average success ratios always exceeded the corresponding given success probabilities.

7.5 Comparison with E²LSH

We compared the proposed method extended for a range query as described in Section 6 with the E^2LSH reported in [1], although it is difficult to compare the two methods directly due to the differences in their operating principles. The range query problem for the comparison is to report a set of points $R(\mathbf{q})$ within r from $\mathbf{q}$, given a set of points $\mathbf{x} \in X$ in a Euclidean space $\mathbb{R}^d$ with the Euclidean distance, query point $\mathbf{q} \in \mathbb{R}^d$, and distance (or radius) r from $\mathbf{q}$. We evaluated the *recall* and the search cost defined for each method.

For a fair and simple comparison, we adopted *serial processing* for the proposed method's search algorithm instead of the *parallel processing* in **Algorithm 4**. The search algorithm executed L search trials for each query in series, where each trial started from the corresponding initial vertex. During the successive L trials, once the distance between a query and a vertex was calculated, it was cached and not calculated twice. The search cost of the proposed method was evaluated by the number of distance calculations.

We briefly review the E^{2}LSH to better understand its search cost. The E^{2}LSH builds an index using a set of hash functions that maps a point into a sequence of integers. The hash function $h_{\mathbf{a},b}(\mathbf{x})$ is expressed by

$$h_{\mathbf{a},b}(\mathbf{x}) = \lfloor (\mathbf{a} \cdot \mathbf{x} + b) / w \rfloor \ , \quad (12)$$

where b and w are real parameters and $\mathbf{a}$ is a random projection vector whose entries are chosen from a Gaussian distribution. By using $\mathcal{L}$ sets each consisting of κ random projection vectors, a point is represented by distinct $\mathcal{L}$ sequences, i.e., buckets each consisting of κ hash values derived from Eq. (12). To identify $\mathcal{L}$ buckets for a point, we need $\kappa \cdot \mathcal{L}$ inner-product calculations.

In the search stage, the $\mathcal{L}$ buckets for $\mathbf{q}$ are identified by the $\kappa \cdot \mathcal{L}$ inner-product calculations. Then a union of the sets of buckets identical to those used for $\mathbf{q}$ is made. E^{2}LSH answers the range query from the exact distance evaluation of the points in the union of the sets. The parameters κ and $\mathcal{L}$ are determined by a given failure probability δ and the collision probability $p(\mathcal{D}(\mathbf{x}, \mathbf{y}); w)$ of a pair of points $(\mathbf{x}, \mathbf{y})$ on a random projection vector, where $\mathcal{D}(\mathbf{x}, \mathbf{y})$ denotes a Euclidean distance between $\mathbf{x}$ and $\mathbf{y}$. For the range query problem, given radius r from $\mathbf{q}$, the probability p that $\mathbf{q}$ collides with $\mathbf{x}$ within r in at least one bucket in $\mathcal{L}$ is expressed by $1-(1-p^{\kappa})^{\mathcal{L}}$. Then κ and $\mathcal{L}$ are set at values such that the following inequality is fulfilled.

$$1 - \delta \le 1 - (1 - p^{\kappa})^{\mathcal{L}} \quad (13)$$

The search cost of E^{2}LSH was measured by the sum of two costs: one is the product $\kappa \cdot \mathcal{L}$ corresponding to the number of inner-product calculations for identifying the $\mathcal{L}$ buckets for $\mathbf{q}$ and the other is the number of distinct points encountered in the $\mathcal{L}$ buckets for selecting the points within r from $\mathbf{q}$ by the exact distance calculation.

We used object set X with 60,000 points and query set Q with 4,850 points. E^{2}LSH set the parameters r and w at 0.65 and 4.0,respectively, as in [1], and employed tuple $(\kappa, \mathcal{L})$ to minimize the expected search cost. In contrast, the proposed method employed L initial vertices per query and the same r as E^{2}LSH, evaluated the *Recall*$(\mathbf{q})$ for each $\mathbf{q}$, and obtained the *average recall* by $(1/Q)\sum_{\mathbf{q}\in Q} Recall(\mathbf{q})$, where *Recall*$(\mathbf{q})$ is expressed by Eq. (14) in **Appendix** A. The expected search costs of the two methods were obtained by $(1/Q)\sum_{\mathbf{q}\in Q} c(\mathbf{q})$, where $c(\mathbf{q})$ denotes the search cost for each $\mathbf{q}$. Figure 7 shows the expected search costs of both methods on a logarithmic scale against the actual *average recall*. The expected search cost of the proposed method with $(k, L) = (10, 16)$ at an *average recall* of 0.91 was around one-sixth that of E^{2}LSH, and at only 1655.1 corresponding to 2.76% of $|X|$. Moreover, the proposed method with $L=8$ reduced the expected search costs from those where $L=16$. Thus the proposed method efficiently performed a similarity search even for a range query.

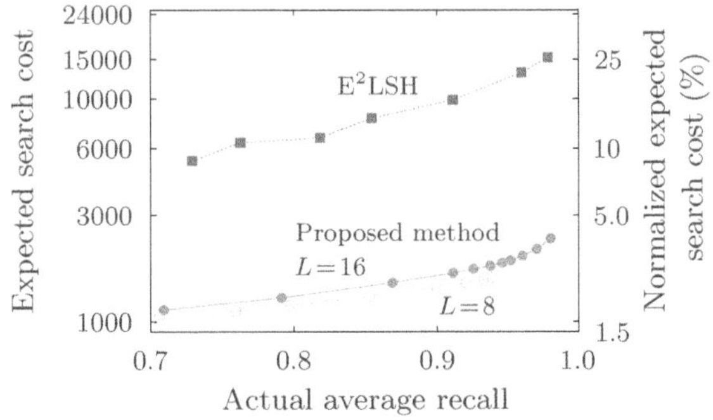

Figure 7: Expected search costs of proposed method and E^{2}LSH on a logarithmic scale against actual average recall. The expected search cost of the proposed method (L = 16) was around one-sixth that of E^{2}LSH when the actual average recall was 0.91.

8. CONCLUSION

We presented a fast approximate similarity search method that utilized a degree-reduced k-nearest neighbor graph (k-*DR* graph) with a controlled k value as a search index, and explored the k-*DR* graph along its edges by using a greedy search (*GS*) algorithm starting from multiple initial vertices with parallel processing. In the graph-construction stage, we determined the k value so that the *GS* algorithm on the k-*DR* graph with parallel processing succeeds with at least a given success probability, by using an ensemble average of the greedy-search success probability estimated based on *basins* in the k-*DR* graph. Furthermore, we extended the proposed method for a nearest-neighbor query to that for a range query. Compared with E^{2}LSH for the MNIST database, the experimental results demonstrated that the extended method was superior to E^{2}LSH in terms of the expected search cost for achieving a given recall.

9. ACKNOWLEDGMENTS

This work is partially supported by KAKENHI (20500109) and the FIRST program of JSPS.

10. REFERENCES

[1] A. Andoni, M. Datar, N. Immorlica, P. Indyk, and V. Mirrokni. *Nearest-neighbor methods in learning and vision; theory and practice*, chapter 3: Locality-sensitive hashing using stable distributions. The MIT Press, Cambridge, Massachusetts, 2005.

[2] A. Andoni and P. Indyk. Near-optimal algorithms for approximate nearest neighbor in high dimensions. In *Proc. IEEE Symp. Foundations of Computer Science*, pages 459–468, October 2006.

[3] K. Aoyama, K. Saito, T. Yamada, and N. Ueda. Fast similarity search in small-world networks. In R. M. et al., editor, *Complex Networks: Int. Workshop on Complex Networks*, pages 185–196. Springer, 2009.

[4] K. Aoyama, S. Watanabe, H. Sawada, Y. Minami, N. Ueda, and K. Saito. Fast similarity search on a large speech data set with neighborhood graph

indexing. In *Proc. Int. Conf. Acoustics, Speech, Signal Process.*, pages 5358–5361, March 2010.

[5] E. Chávez, G. Navarro, R. Baeza-Yates, and J. L. Marroquín. Searching in metric spaces. *ACM Comp. Surveys*, 33(3):273–321, September 2001.

[6] J. Chen, H.-R. Fang, and Y. Saad. Fast approximate *kNN* graph construction for high dimensional data via recursive Lanczos bisection. *The Journal of Machine Learning Research*, 10:1989–2012, 2009.

[7] R. Dechter and J. Pearl. Generalized best-first search strategies and the optimality of A*. *Journal of the ACM*, 32(3):505–536, July 1985.

[8] H. Hacid and T. Yoshida. Neighborhood graphs for indexing and retrieving multi-dimensional data. *J. Intelligent Information Systems*, 34:93–111, 2010.

[9] G. R. Hjaltason and H. Samet. Index-driven similarity search in metric spaces. *ACM Trans. Database System*, 28(4):517–580, December 2003.

[10] P. Indyk and R. Motwani. Approximate nearest neighbors: Towards removing the curse of dimensionality. In *Proc. ACM Symp. Theory of Computing*, pages 604–613, May 1998.

[11] J. W. Jaromczyk and G. T. Toussaint. Relative neighborhood graphs and their relatives. *Proc. IEEE*, 80(9):1502–1516, September 1992.

[12] D. R. Karger and M. Ruhl. Finding nearest neighbors in growth-restricted metrics. In *Proc. ACM Symp. on Theory of Computing*, pages 741–750, May 2002.

[13] R. E. Korf, W. Zhang, I. T. Thayer, and H. Hohwald. Frontier search. *Journal of the ACM*, 52(5):715–748, September 2005.

[14] R. Krauthgamer and J. R. Lee. Navigating nets: Simple algorithms for proximity search. In *Proc. ACM-SIAM Symp. Discrete Algorithms*, pages 798–807. SIAM/SIGACT, January 2004.

[15] Y. LeCun, L. Bottou, Y. Bengio, and P. Haffner. Gradient-based learning applied to document recognition. *Proc. IEEE*, 86(11):2278–2324, 1998.

[16] Ö. Şimşek and D. Jensen. Decentralized search in networks using homophily and degree disparity. In *Proc. Int. Joint Conf. Artificial Intelligence*, pages 304–310, July 2005.

[17] M. T. Orchard. A fast nearest-neighbor search algorithm. In *Proc. Int. Conf. Acoustics, Speech, Signal Process.*, volume 4, pages 2297–2300, 1991.

[18] P. Ram, D. Lee, W. B. March, and A. G. Gray. Linear-time algorithms for pairwise statistical problems. In *Advances in Neural Information Processing Systems 22 (Dec 2009)*. MIT Press, 2010.

[19] J. Sakagaito and T. Wada. Nearest first traversing graph for simultaneous object tracking and recognition. In *Proc. IEEE Conf. Computer Vision and Pattern Recognition*, pages 1–7, June 2007.

[20] T. B. Sebastian and B. B. Kimia. Metric-based shape retrieval in large databases. In *Proc. Int. Conf. Pattern Recognition*, volume 3, pages 291–296, 2002.

[21] Y. Tao, K. Yi, C. Sheng, and P. Kalnis. Quality and efficiency in high dimensional nearest neighbor search. In *Proc. SIGMOD*, pages 563–575, June 2009.

[22] D. J. Watts and S. H. Strogatz. Collective dynamics of 'small-world' networks. *Nature*, 393:440–442, 1998.

APPENDIX

A. PARALLEL GREEDY SEARCH ALGORITHM FOR RANGE QUERIES

A parallel greedy search algorithm for range queries (*PGSR*) is shown as a pseudo-code in **Algorithm 4**. The symbols in the pseudo-code have the same meaning in **Algorithm 3**. Given $\Gamma_{(k)DR}$, query q, a set of initial vertices $X_0(q)$, and radius r from q, the *PGSR* begins to traverse $\Gamma_{(k)DR}$ from the initial vertex $x_{0[i]}$ with the *GS* algorithm in parallel after initialization on **Lines 2–7**. When the current expanded vertex $z_{[i]}$ is within the radius, the *PGSR* pushes $z_{[i]}$'s adjacent vertex $y_{[i]}$, whose dissimilarity from q is less than r, into the stack $W_{[i]}$, and simultaneously adds $y_{[i]}$ to the set $\tilde{R}_{[i]}$, as shown on **Lines 11–15**. The *PGSR* pops a vertex from $W_{[i]}$ and sets it at the next expanded vertex $z_{[i]}$ exactly when the *GS* algorithm terminates, as shown on **Line 21**. The *PGSR* continues to explore $\Gamma_{(k)DR}$, collecting the vertices within the radius until stack $W_{[i]}$ is empty as shown on **Line 22**. Finally, the L sets, $\tilde{R}_{[i]}(q)$, of the vertices within the radius are merged into $\tilde{R}(q)$, and the *recall* of the search result with the *PGSR* is evaluated by

$$Recall(q) = \frac{|\bigcup_{i=1,\cdots,L} \tilde{R}_{[i]}(q;\Gamma_{kDR}) \bigcap R(q)|}{|R(q)|}. \quad (14)$$

Algorithm 4 *Parallel Greedy Search Algorithm for Range Query*; $PGSR(q, X_0(q); r, \Gamma_{(k)DR})$

Input: $\Gamma_{(k)DR}$, r, $q \in \mathcal{X}$,
$X_0 = (x_{0[1]}, x_{0[2]}, \cdots, x_{0[L]})$, $x_{0[i]} \in X$
Output: $(\tilde{R}(q), c)$
1. **for** each initial vertex $x_{0[i]}$ **in parallel do**
2. Set $z_{[i]} \leftarrow x_{0[i]}$, $x_{[i]} \leftarrow z_{[i]}$, $D_{min[i]} \leftarrow D(q, z_{[i]})$, $C_{[i]} \leftarrow \{z_{[i]}\}$
3. **if** $D(q, z_{[i]}) < r$ **then**
4. Set $\tilde{R}_{[i]}(q) \leftarrow \{z_{[i]}\}$, $W_{[i]} \leftarrow \{z_{[i]}\}$
5. **else**
6. Set $\tilde{R}_{[i]}(q) \leftarrow \emptyset$, $W_{[i]} \leftarrow \emptyset$
7. **end if**
8. **repeat**
9. **while** $z_{[i]} = x_{[i]}$ **do**
10. Set $x_{[i]} \leftarrow \arg\min_{y_{[i]} \in V_{(k)DR}(z_{[i]})}\{D(q, y_{[i]})\}$
11. **for all** $y \in V_{(k)DR}(z_{[i]})$ **do**
12. **if** $(D(q, y_{[i]}) < r) \wedge (y_{[i]} \notin C_{[i]})$ **then**
13. Set $\tilde{R}_{[i]}(q) \leftarrow \tilde{R}_{[i]}(q) \cup \{y_{[i]}\}$, push$(W_{[i]}, y_{[i]})$
14. **end if**
15. **end for**
16. Set $C_{[i]} \leftarrow C_{[i]} \cup V_{(k)DR}(z_{[i]})$
17. **if** $D(q, x_{[i]}) < D(q, z_{[i]})$ **then**
18. Set $D_{min[i]} \leftarrow D(q, x_{[i]})$, $z_{[i]} \leftarrow x_{[i]}$
19. **end if**
20. **end while**
21. Set $z_{[i]} \leftarrow$ pop$(W_{[i]})$, $x_{[i]} \leftarrow z_{[i]}$
22. **until** $W_{[i]} = \emptyset$
23. **end for**
24. Set $\tilde{R}(q) \leftarrow \bigcup_{i=1,\cdots,L} \tilde{R}_{[i]}(q)$, $c \leftarrow \arg\max_{i=1,\cdots,L}\{|C_{[i]}|\}$
25. **return** $(\tilde{R}(q), c)$

Fast Coordinate Descent Methods with Variable Selection for Non-negative Matrix Factorization

Cho-Jui Hsieh
Dept. of Computer Science
University of Texas at Austin
Austin, TX 78712-1188, USA
cjhsieh@cs.utexas.edu

Inderjit S. Dhillon
Dept. of Computer Science
University of Texas at Austin
Austin, TX 78712-1188, USA
inderjit@cs.utexas.edu

ABSTRACT

Nonnegative Matrix Factorization (NMF) is an effective dimension reduction method for non-negative dyadic data, and has proven to be useful in many areas, such as text mining, bioinformatics and image processing. NMF is usually formulated as a constrained non-convex optimization problem, and many algorithms have been developed for solving it. Recently, a coordinate descent method, called FastHals [3], has been proposed to solve least squares NMF and is regarded as one of the state-of-the-art techniques for the problem. In this paper, we first show that FastHals has an inefficiency in that it uses a cyclic coordinate descent scheme and thus, performs unneeded descent steps on unimportant variables. We then present a variable selection scheme that uses the gradient of the objective function to arrive at a new coordinate descent method. Our new method is considerably faster in practice and we show that it has theoretical convergence guarantees. Moreover when the solution is sparse, as is often the case in real applications, our new method benefits by selecting important variables to update more often, thus resulting in higher speed. As an example, on a text dataset RCV1, our method is 7 times faster than FastHals, and more than 15 times faster when the sparsity is increased by adding an L1 penalty. We also develop new coordinate descent methods when error in NMF is measured by KL-divergence by applying the Newton method to solve the one-variable sub-problems. Experiments indicate that our algorithm for minimizing the KL-divergence is faster than the Lee & Seung multiplicative rule by a factor of 10 on the CBCL image dataset.

Categories and Subject Descriptors

I.2.6 [**Artificial Intelligence**]: Learning; G.1.6 [**Numerical Analysis**]: Optimization

General Terms

Algorithms, Performance, Experimentation

1. INTRODUCTION

Non-negative matrix factorization (NMF) ([20, 14]) is a popular matrix decomposition method for finding non-negative representations of data. NMF has proved useful in dimension reduction of image, text, and signal data. Given a matrix $V \in \mathbb{R}^{m\times n}$, $V \geq 0$, and a specified positive integer k, NMF seeks to approximate V by the product of two non-negative matrices $W \in \mathbb{R}^{m\times k}$ and $H \in \mathbb{R}^{k\times n}$. Suppose each column of V is an input data vector, the main idea behind NMF is to approximate these input vectors by nonnegative linear combinations of nonnegative "basis" vectors (columns of W) with the coefficients stored in columns of H.

The distance between V and WH can be measured by various distortion functions — the most commonly used is the Frobenius norm, which leads to the following minimization problem:

$$\min_{W,H\geq 0} f(W,H) \equiv \frac{1}{2}\|V-WH\|_F^2 = \frac{1}{2}\sum_{i,j}(V_{ij}-(WH)_{ij})^2 \quad (1)$$

To achieve better sparsity, researchers ([7, 22]) have proposed adding regularization terms, on W and H, to (1). For example, an L1-norm penalty on W and H can achieve a more sparse solution:

$$\min_{W,H\geq 0} \frac{1}{2}\|V-WH\|_F^2 + \rho_1 \sum_{i,r} W_{ir} + \rho_2 \sum_{r,j} H_{rj}. \quad (2)$$

One can also replace $\sum_{i,r} W_{ir}$ and $\sum_{r,j} H_{rj}$ by Frobenius norm of W and H. Note that usually $m \gg k$ and $n \gg k$. Since f is non-convex, we can only hope to find a stationary point of f. Many algorithms ([15, 5, 1, 23]) have been proposed for this purpose. Among them, Lee & Seung's multiplicative-update algorithm [15] has been the most common method. Recent methods follow the Alternating Nonnegative Least Squares (ANLS) framework suggested by [20]. This framework has been proved to converge to stationary points by [6] as long as one can solve each nonnegative least square sub-problem exactly. Among existing methods, [18] proposes a projected gradient method, [11] uses an active set method, [10] applies a projected Newton method, and [12] suggests a modified active set method called BlockPivot for solving the non-negative least squares sub-problem. Very recently, [19] developed a parallel NMF solver for large-scale web data. This shows a practical need for further scaling up NMF solvers, especially when the matrix V is sparse, as is the case for text data or web recommendation data.

Coordinate descent methods, which update one variable at a time, are efficient at finding a reasonable solution efficiently, a property that has made these methods successful in large scale classification/regression problems. Recently, a coordinate descent method, called FastHals [3], has been proposed to solve the least squares NMF problem (1). Compared to methods using the ANLS framework which spend significant time in finding an exact solution for each subproblem, a coordinate descent method can efficiently give a reasonably good solution for each sub-problem and switch to the next round. Despite being a state-of-the-art method, FastHals has an inefficiency in that it uses a cyclic coordinate descent scheme and thus, may perform unneeded descent steps on unimportant variables. In this paper, we present a variable selection scheme that uses the gradient of the objective function to arrive at a new coordinate descent method. Our method is considerably faster in practice and we show that it has theoretical convergence guarantees, which was not addressed in [3]. We conduct experiments on large sparse datasets, and show that our method generally performs 2-3 times faster than FastHals. Moreover when the solution is sparse, as is often the case in real applications, our new method benefits by selecting important variables to update more often, thus resulting in higher speed. As an example, on a text dataset RCV1, our method is 7 times faster than FastHals, and more than 15 times faster when the sparsity is increased by adding an L1 penalty.

Another popular distortion measure to minimize is the KL-divergence between V and WH:

$$\min_{W,H\geq 0} L(W,H) = \sum_{i,j} V_{ij}\log(\frac{V_{ij}}{(WH)_{ij}}) - V_{ij} + (WH)_{ij} \quad (3)$$

The above problem has been shown to be connected to Probabilistic Latent Semantic Analysis (PLSA) [4]. As we will point out in Section 3, problem (3) is more complicated than (1) and algorithms in the ANLS framework cannot be easily extended to solve (3). For this problem, [3] proposes to solve by a sequence of local loss functions — however, a drawback of the method in [3] is that it will not converge to a stationary point of (3). In this paper we propose a cyclic coordinate descent method for solving (3). Our new algorithm applies the Newton method to get a better solution for each variable, which is better compared to working on the auxiliary function as used in the multiplicative algorithm of [15]. As a result, our cyclic coordinate descent method converges much faster than the multiplicative algorithm. We further provide theoretical convergence guarantees for cyclic coordinate descent methods under certain conditions.

The paper is organized as follows. In Section 2, we describe our coordinate descent method for least squares NMF (1). The modification for the coordinate descent method for solving KL-NMF (3) is proposed in Section 3. Section 4 discusses the relationship between our methods and other optimization techniques for NMF, and Section 5 points out some important implementation issues. The experiment results are given in Section 6. The results show that our methods are more efficient than other state-of-art methods.

2. COORDINATE DESCENT METHOD FOR LEAST SQUARES NMF

2.1 Basic update rule for one element

The coordinate descent method updates one variable at a time until convergence. We first show that a closed form update can be performed in $O(1)$ time for least squares NMF if certain quantities have been pre-computed. Note that in this section we focus on the update rule for variables in W — the update rule for variables in H can be derived similarly.

Coordinate descent methods aim to conduct the following one variable updates:

$$(W,H) \leftarrow (W + sE_{ir}, H)$$

where E_{ir} is a $m \times k$ matrix with all elements zero except the (i,r) element which equals one. Coordinate descent solves the following one-variable subproblem of (1) to get s:

$$\min_{s:W_{ir}+s\geq 0} g_{ir}^W(s) \equiv f(W + sE_{ir}, H). \quad (4)$$

We can rewrite $g_{ir}^W(s)$ as

$$g_{ir}^W(s) = \frac{1}{2}\sum_j (V_{ij} - (WH)_{ij} - sH_{rj})^2$$

$$= g_{ir}^W(0) + (g_{ir}^W)'(0)s + \frac{1}{2}(g_{ir}^W)''(0)s^2. \quad (5)$$

For convenience we define

$$G^W \equiv \nabla_W f(W,H) = WHH^T - VH^T. \quad (6)$$

$$\text{and } G^H \equiv \nabla_H f(W,H) = W^TWH - W^TV. \quad (7)$$

Then we have

$$(g_{ir}^W)'(0) = (G^W)_{ir} = (WHH^T - VH^T)_{ir}$$

$$\text{and } (g_{ir}^W)''(0) = (HH^T)_{rr}.$$

Since (5) is a one-variable quadratic function with the constraint $W_{ir} + s \geq 0$, we can solve it in closed form:

$$s^* = \max\Big(0, W_{ir} - (WHH^T - VH^T)_{ir}/(HH^T)_{rr}\Big) - W_{ir}. \quad (8)$$

Coordinate descent algorithms then update W_{ir} to

$$W_{ir} \leftarrow W_{ir} + s^*. \quad (9)$$

The above one variable update rule can be easily extended to NMF problems with regularization as long as the gradient and second order derivative of sub-problems can be easily computed. For instance, with the L1 penalty on both W and H as in (2), the one variable sub-problem is

$$\bar{g}_{ir}^W(s) = \Big((WHH^T - VH^T)_{ir} + \rho_1\Big)s + \frac{1}{2}(HH^T)_{rr}s^2 + \bar{g}_{ir}^W(0),$$

and thus the one variable update becomes

$$W_{ir} \leftarrow \max\Big(0, W_{ir} - ((WHH^T - VH^T)_{ir} + \rho_1)/(HH^T)_{rr}\Big).$$

Compared to (8), the new W_{ir} is shifted left to zero by the factor $\frac{\rho_1}{(HH^T)_{rr}}$, so the resulting W_{ir} generally has more zeros.

A state-of-the-art cyclic coordinate descent method called FastHals is proposed in [3], which uses the above one variable update rules.

2.2 Variable selection strategy

With the one variable update rule, FastHals [3] conducts a cyclic coordinate descent. It first updates all variables in W in cyclic order, and then updates variables in H, and so on. Thus the number of updates performed for each variable is exactly the same. However, an efficient coordinate descent method should update variables with frequency proportional to their "importance". In this paper, we exhibit a carefully chosen variable selection scheme (with not too much overhead) to obtain a new coordinate descent algorithm that has the ability to select variables according to their "importance", thus leading to significant speedups. Similar strategies has been employed in Lasso or feature selection problems [17, 21]. To illustrate the idea, we take a text dataset

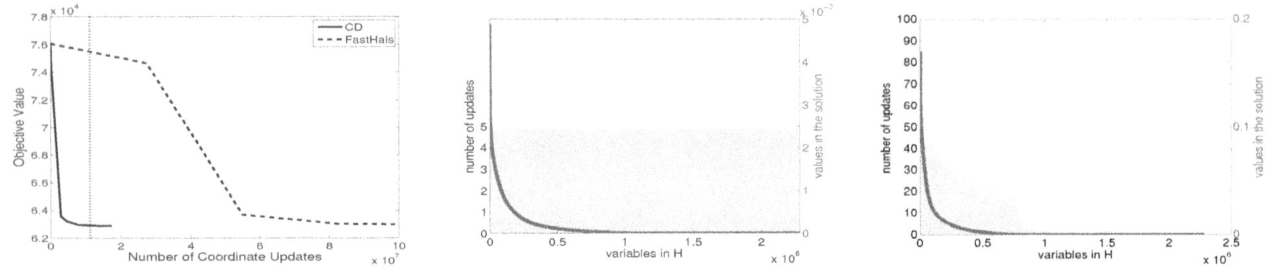

(a) Coordinate updates versus objective value

(b) The behavior of FastHals

(c) The behavior of GCD

Figure 1: Illustration of our variable selection scheme. Figure 1(a) shows that our method GCD reduces the objective value more quickly than FastHals. With the same number of coordinate updates (as specified by the vertical dotted line in Figure 1(a)), we further compare the distribution of their coordinate updates. In Figure 1(b) and 1(c), the X-axis is the variables of H listed by descending order of their final values. The solid line gives their final values, and the light blue bars indicate the number of times they are chosen. The figures indicate that FastHals updates all variables uniformly, while the number of updates for GCD is proportional to their final values, which helps GCD to converge faster.

RCV1 with L1 penalty as an example. In Figures 1(b) and 1(c) the variables of the final solution H are listed on the X-axis — note that the solution is sparse as most of the variables are 0. Figure 1(b) shows the behavior of FastHals, which clearly shows that each variable is chosen uniformly. In contrast, as shown in Figure 1(c), by applying our new coordinate descent method, the number of updates for the variable is roughly proportional to their final values. For most variables with final value 0, our algorithm will never pick them to update. Therefore our new method focuses on nonzero variables and reduces the objective value more efficiently. Figure 1(a) shows that we can attain a 10-fold speedup by applying our variable selection scheme.

We now show that with an appropriate data structure, we can select variables that lead to maximum decrease of objective function in $O(k+\log m)$ time with a pre-computed gradient. However, $O(\log m)$ can be expensive in practice, so we further provide an alternate efficient row-based variable selection scheme that needs $O(k)$ time per update.

Before presenting our variable selection method, we first introduce our framework. Similar to FastHals, our algorithm switches between W and H in the outer iterations:

$$(W^0, H^0) \rightarrow (W^1, H^0) \rightarrow (W^1, H^1) \rightarrow \cdots \quad (10)$$

Between each outer iteration are the following inner updates:

$$(W^i, H^i) \rightarrow (W^{i,1}, H^i) \rightarrow (W^{i,2}, H^i) \cdots. \quad (11)$$

Later we will discuss the reason why we have to focus on W or H for a sequence of updates.

Suppose we want to choose variables to update in W. If W_{ir} is selected, as discussed in Section 2.1, the optimal update will be (8), and the function value will be decreased by

$$D^W_{ir} \equiv g^W_{ir}(0) - g^W_{ir}(s^*) = -G^W_{ir}s^* - \frac{1}{2}(HH^T)_{rr}(s^*)^2. \quad (12)$$

D^W_{ir} measures how much we can reduce the objective value by choosing the coordinate W_{ir}. Therefore, if D^W can be maintained, we can greedily choose variables according to it. If we have G^W, we can compute s^* by (8) and compute D^W by (12), and so an element of D^W can be computed in $O(1)$ time. At the beginning of a sequence of W's updates, we can precompute G^W. The details will be provided in Section 2.3. Now assume we already have G^W, and W_{ir} is updated to $W_{ir}+s^*$. Then G^W will remain the same except for the ith row, which will be replaced by

$$G^W_{ij} \leftarrow G^W_{ij} + s^*(HH^T)_{rj} \quad \forall j = 1, \ldots, k. \quad (13)$$

Using (13), we can maintain G^W in $O(k)$ time after each variable update of W. Thus D^W can also be maintained in $O(k)$ time.

However, maintaining G^H at each inner update of W is more expensive. From (7), when each element of W is changed, the whole matrix G^H will be changed, thus every element of D^H may also change. So the time cost for maintaining D^H is at least $O(kn)$, which is too much compared to $O(k)$ for maintaining D^W. This is the reason that we follow the alternative minimization scheme and restrict ourselves to either W or H for a sequence of inner updates.

After the i-th row of G^W is updated, we can immediately maintain the i-th row of D^W by (12). To select the next variable-to-update, we want to select the index (i^*, r^*) that satisfies $(i^*, r^*) = \arg\max_{i,r} D^W_{ir}$. However, a brute force search through the whole matrix D^W will require $O(mk)$ time. To overcome this, we can store the largest value v_i and index q_i for each row of D^W, i.e.,

$$q_i = \arg\max_j D^W_{ij}, \; v_i = D^W_{i,q_i}. \quad (14)$$

As in (13), when W_{ir} is updated, only the ith row of G^W and D^W will change. Therefore the vector $\boldsymbol{q}$ will remain the same except for one component q_i. Since the ith row of D^W contains k elements and each element can be computed in constant time, we can recalculate q_i in $O(k)$ time. Each time we only change the largest value in $\{q_i \mid i = 1, \ldots, m\}$, therefore we can store these values using a heap data structure so that each retrieval and re-calculation of the largest value can be done in $O(\log m)$ time. This way the total cost for one update will be $O(k + \log m)$.

A stopping condition is needed for a sequence of updates. At the beginning of updates to W, we can store

$$p^{\text{init}} = \max_{i,j} D^W_{ij}. \quad (15)$$

Our algorithm then iteratively chooses variables to update until the following stopping condition is met:

$$\max_{i,j} D^W_{ij} < \epsilon p^{\text{init}}, \quad (16)$$

where ϵ is a small positive constant. Note that (16) will be satisfied in a finite number of iterations as $f(W, H)$ is lower bounded, and so the minimum for $f(W, H)$ with fixed H is achievable. A small ϵ value indicates each sub-problem is solved to high accuracy, while a larger ϵ value means our algorithm switches more often between W and H. We choose $\epsilon = 0.001$ in our experiments.

In practice, this method can work when k is large. However, when $k \ll m$, the $\log m$ term in the update cost will dominate. Moreover, each heap operation costs more time than a simple floating point operation. Thus we further design a more efficient row-based variable selection strategy.

First, we have an observation that when one W_{ir} is updated, only the ith row of D^W will be changed. Therefore if we update variables in the ith row and there is a variable in the jth row with larger potential decrease D^W_{jr}, we will not change D^W_{jr}. Choosing the largest D^W value in one row costs $O(k)$, which is cheaper than $O(\log m)$ when k small. Therefore we can iteratively update variables in the ith row (that lead to maximum decrease in objective function) until the inner stopping condition is met:

$$\max_j D^W_{ij} < \epsilon p^{\text{init}}. \tag{17}$$

Our algorithm then update variables in the $(i+1)$-st row, and so on. Since changes in other rows will not affect the D^W values in the ith row, after our algorithm sweeps through row 1 to row m, (17) will be met for each row, thus the stopping condition (16) will also be met for the whole W.

2.3 Time complexity analysis

Algorithm 1 GCD for least squares NMF

- Given: V, k, ϵ (typically, $\epsilon = 0.001$)
- Output: W, H
- Compute $P^{VH} = VH^T$, $P^{HH} = HH^T$, $P^{WV} = W^TV$, $P^{WW} = W^TW$
- Initialize $H^{\text{new}} \leftarrow 0$
- While (not converged)
  1. Compute $P^{VH} \leftarrow P^{VH} + V(H^{\text{new}})^T$ according to the sparsity of H^{new}
  2. $W^{\text{new}} \leftarrow 0$
  3. $G^W \leftarrow WP^{HH} - P^{VH}$
  4. $S^W_{ir} \leftarrow \max(W_{ir} - \frac{G^W_{ir}}{P^{HH}_{rr}}, 0) - W_{ir}$ for all i, r.
  5. $D^W_{ir} \leftarrow -G^W_{ir}S^W_{ir} - \frac{1}{2}P^{HH}_{rr}(S^W_{ir})^2$ for all i, r.
  6. $q_i \leftarrow \arg\max_j D^W_{ij}$ for all $i = 1, \ldots, m$, and $p^{\text{init}} \leftarrow \max_i D^W_{i,q_i}$
  7. For $i = 1, 2, \ldots, m$
     - While $D^W_{i,q_i} < \epsilon p^{\text{init}}$
       - 7.1. $s^* \leftarrow S^W_{i,q_i}$
       - 7.2. $P^{WW}_{q_i,:} \leftarrow P^{WW}_{q_i,:} + s^* W_{q_i,:}$ (Also do a symmetric update for $P^{WW}_{:,q_i}$)
       - 7.3. $W^{\text{new}}_{i,q_i} \leftarrow W^{\text{new}}_{i,q_i} + s^*$
       - 7.4. $G^W_{i,:} \leftarrow G^W_{i,:} + s^* P^{HH}_{q_i,:}$
       - 7.5. $S^W_{ir} \leftarrow \max(W_{ir} - \frac{G^W_{ir}}{P^{HH}_{rr}}, 0) - W_{ir}$ for all $r = 1, \ldots, k$.
       - 7.6. $D^W_{ir} \leftarrow -G^W_{ir}S^W_{ir} - \frac{1}{2}P^{HH}_{rr}(S^W_{ir})^2$ for all $r = 1, \ldots, k$.
       - 7.7. $q_i \leftarrow \arg\max_j D^W_{ij}$.
  8. $W \leftarrow W + W^{\text{new}}$
  9. For updates to H, repeats analogues steps to Step 1 through Step 8.

Our coordinate descent method with variable selection strategy can be summarized in Algorithm 1. We call our new coordinate descent algorithm GCD– Greedy Coordinate Descent since we take a greedy step of maximum decrease in objective function. The one-variable update and variable selection strategy are in the inner loop (step 7) of Algorithm 1. Before the inner loop, we have to initialize the gradient G^W and objective function decrease matrix D^W. G^W in (6) has two terms WHH^T and VH^T (in Algorithm 1, we use P^{VH}, P^{HH}, P^{WV} and P^{WW} to store matrices VH^T, HH^T, W^TV and W^TW). For the first term, since HH^T is maintained in an analogous way to step 7.2), computing $W(HH^T)$ costs $O(mk^2)$ time. For the second term VH^T, we can also store the updates in H^{new} so that $H^{\text{new}} = H^{i+1} - H^i$, and then updates VH^T by step 1. Assume that, on average, step 7 has t coordinate updates, then the number of nonzeros in H^{new} is at most t. With sparse matrix multiplication, step 1 costs $O(mt)$. However, when H^{new} is dense, we should use a dense matrix multiplication for step 1, which costs $O(nmk)$ and is independent of t.

Table 1: Time complexity analysis for Algorithm 1. We focus on time cost for one complete update of W. Here t is average number of inner updates, and s is number of nonzeros in V.

	dense V	sparse V
Compute matrix VH^T (Step 1)	$\min(O(mt), O(nmk))$	$\min(O(\frac{st}{n}), O(sk))$
Initialize gradient/decreasing matrix (Steps 3 to 6)	$O(mk^2)$	$O(mk^2)$
Update inner product (Steps 7.2)	$O(tk)$	$O(tk)$
Update gradient and decreasing matrix (Step 7.4 to 7.7)	$O(tk)$	$O(tk)$

Table 1 summarizes the cost of one outer iteration (step 1 to 9). To get the amortized cost per coordinate update, we can divide the numbers by t. We first consider when V is dense. When $t < k^2$, $O(mk^2)$ will dominate the complexity. When $k^2 \le t \le nk$, computational time for computing VH^T dominates the complexity and the time cost per coordinate update is $O(m)$. In this case, time cost per update is the same as FastHals. When t is larger than nk, the time cost per update will decrease. We summarize the amortized cost per update as below:

$$\begin{cases} O(\frac{mk^2}{t}) & \text{if } k^2 > t \\ O(m) & \text{if } nk > t \ge k^2 \\ O(\frac{nmk}{t}) & \text{if } nm > t \ge nk \\ O(k) & \text{if } t > nm \end{cases}$$

When V is sparse, assume there are s nonzero elements in V, the complexity for the computing VH^T is modified while others remain the same.

3. COORDINATE DESCENT METHOD FOR NMF WITH KL-DIVERGENCE

To apply coordinate descent for solving NMF with KL-divergence (3), we consider the one-variable sub-problem:

$$\begin{aligned} h_{ir}(s) &= L(W + sE_{ir}, H) \\ &= \sum_{j=1}^{n} -V_{ij}\log\Big((WH)_{ij} + sH_{rj}\Big) + sH_{rj} + \text{constant}. \end{aligned} \tag{18}$$

Here we discuss the updates to W, the update rules for H can be derived similarly. Unlike the one-variable subproblem of least squares NMF (5), minimizing $h_{ir}(s)$ has no closed form solution. Thus FastHals fails to derive a coordinate descent method for KL-divergence. Instead of solving the one-variable sub-problem $h_{ir}(s)$, FastHals in [3] minimizes the following one-variable problem for each update:

$$\bar{h}_{ir}(s) = \sum_j -(V_{ij} - \sum_{t \neq r} W_{it}H_{tj}) \log(sH_{rj}) + sH_{rj}.$$

The above problem has a closed form solution, but the solution is different from the one-variable sub-problem (18), thus FastHals solves a different problem and may converge to a different final solution. Therefore we can say that application of coordinate descent to solve NMF with KL-divergence has not been studied before.

In this section, we propose the use of Newton's method to solve the sub-problems. Since h_{ir} is twice differentiable, we can iteratively update s by Newton direction:

$$s \leftarrow \max(-W_{ir}, s - h'_{ir}(s)/h''_{ir}(s)), \quad (19)$$

where the first term comes from the non-negativity constraint. The first derivative $h'_{ir}(s)$ and the second derivative $h''_{ir}(s)$ can be written as

$$h'_{ir}(s) = \sum_{j=1}^{n} H_{rj}\left(1 - \frac{V_{ij}}{(WH)_{ij} + sH_{rj}}\right). \quad (20)$$

$$h''_{ir}(s) = \sum_{j=1}^{n} \frac{V_{ij}H_{rj}^2}{((WH)_{ij} + sH_{rj})^2}. \quad (21)$$

For KL-divergence, we need to take care of the behavior when $V_{ij} = 0$ or $(WH)_{ij} = 0$. For $V_{ij} = 0$, by analysing the asymptotic behavior, $V_{ij}\log((WH)_{ij}) = 0$ for all positive values of $(WH)_{ij}$, thus we can ignore those entries. Also, we do not consider the case that one row of V is entirely zero, which can be removed by preprocessing. When $(WH)_{ij} + sH_{rj} = 0$ for some j, the Newton direction $-h'_{ir}(s)/h''_{ir}(s)$ should be infinity. In this situation we reset s so that $W_{ir}+s$ is a small positive value and restart the Newton method. When $H_{rj} = 0$ for all $j = 1, \ldots, n$, the second derivative (21) is zero. In this case $h_{ir}(s)$ is constant, thus we do not need to change W_{ir}.

To execute Newton updates, each evaluation of $h'_{ir}(s)$ and $h''_{ir}(s)$ takes $O(n)$ time for the summation. For general functions, we often need a line search procedure to check sufficient decrease from each Newton iteration. However, as we now deal with the special function (18), we prove the following theorem to show that Newton method without line search converges to the optimum of each sub-problem:

Theorem 1

If a function $f(x)$ with domain $x \geq 0$ can be written in the following form

$$f(x) = -c_i \sum_{i=1}^{l} \log(a_i + b_i x) + \sum_j b_i x,$$

where $a_i > 0, b_i, c_i \geq 0\ \forall i$, then the Newton method without line search converges to the global minimum of $f(x)$.

The proof based on the strict convexity of log function is in the Appendix of our technical report [9]. By the above Theorem, we can iteratively apply (19) until convergence. In practice, we design the following stopping condition for Newton method:

$$|s^{t+1} - s^t| < \epsilon|W_{ir} + s^t| \text{ for some } \epsilon > 0,$$

where s^t is the current solution and s^{t+1} is obtained by (19).

As discussed earlier, variable selection is an important issue for coordinate descent methods. After each inner update $W_{ir} \leftarrow W_{ir} + s^*$, the gradient for $h_{it}(s)$ will change for all $t = 1, \ldots, k$. As mentioned in Section 2, for NMF with square loss we can update the gradient for one row of W in $O(k)$ time. However, there is no easy way to update the values together for KL-divergence. To maintain the gradient, we need to update $(WH)_{ij}$ for all $j = 1, \ldots, n$ by

$$(WH)_{ij} = (WH)_{ij} + s^* H_{rj} \quad \forall j, \quad (22)$$

and then recompute $h'_{it}(0)$ for all $t = 1, \ldots, k$ by (20). Therefore maintaining $h'_{it}(0)$ will take $O(kn)$ time. This is expensive compared to the time cost $O(n)$ for updating one variable, so we just update variables in a cyclic order. Thus our method for KL-divergence is a Cyclic Coordinate Descent (CCD). Notice that to distinguish our method for KL-divergence with FastHals (cyclic coordinate descent for least squares NMF), through this paper CCD indicates our method for KL-divergence.

In summary, our algorithm chooses each variable in W once in a cyclic order, minimizing the corresponding one-variable sub-problem, and then switches to H. Each Newton update takes $O(n)$ time, so each coordinate update costs $O(n\bar{d})$ time where $\bar{d}$ is the average number of Newton iterations. Algorithm 2 summarizes the details.

Algorithm 2 CCD for NMF with KL-divergence

1. Given: V, k, W, H, ϵ (typically, $\epsilon = 0.5$)
2. Output: W, H
3. $P^{WH} \leftarrow WH$.
4. While (not converged)
    - 4.0.1. For $i = 1, \ldots, m$ (updates in W)
        - For $r = 1, \ldots, k$
            - While 1
                - Compute s by (19).
                - $w^{\text{old}} = W_{ir}$.
                - $W_{ir} \leftarrow W_{ir} + s$.
                - Maintain $(WH)_{i,:}$ by (22).
                - If $|s| < \epsilon w^{\text{old}}$, Break
    - 4.0.2. For updates to H, repeats steps analogous to Step 4.0.1

4. CONVERGENCE PROPERTIES AND RELATIONS WITH OTHER METHODS

4.1 Methods for Least Squares NMF

For NMF, $f(W, H)$ is convex in W or H but not simultaneously convex in both W and H, so it is natural to apply alternating minimization, which iteratively minimizes the following two problems

$$\min_{W \geq 0} f(W, H) \text{ and } \min_{H \geq 0} f(W, H) \quad (23)$$

until convergence. As mentioned in [10], we can categorize NMF solvers into two groups: exact methods and inexact methods. Exact methods are guaranteed to achieve optimum for each sub-problem (23), while inexact methods only guarantee decrease in function value. Each sub-problem for least squares NMF can be decomposed into a sequence of non-negative least square (NNLS) problems. For example, minimization with respect to H can be decomposed into $\min_{h_i \geq 0} \|V - Wh_i\|^2$, where h_i is the ith column of H. Since the convergence property for exact methods has been proved in [6], any NNLS solver can be applied to solve NMF in an alternating fashion. However, as mentioned before, very recently an inexact method FastHals has been proposed proposed [3]. The success of FastHals shows that exactly solving sub-problems may slow down convergence. This makes sense because when (W, H) is still far from optimum, there is no reason in paying too much effort for solving sub-problems exactly. Since GCD does not solve sub-problems exactly, it can avoid paying too much effort for each sub-problem. On the other hand, unlike most inexact methods, GCD guarantees the quality of each updates by setting a stopping condition and, thus converges faster than inexact methods.

Moreover, most inexact methods do not have a theoretically convergence proof, thus the performance may not be stable. In contrast, we prove that GCD converges to a stationary point by the following theorem:

Theorem 2
For least squares NMF, if a sequence $\{(W_i, H_i)\}$ is generated by GCD, then every limit point of this sequence is a stationary point.

The proof can be found in the appendix of our technical report [9]. This convergence result holds for any inner stopping condition $\epsilon < 1$, thus it is different from the proof for exact methods, which assumes that each sub-problem is solved exactly. It is easy to extend the convergence result for GCD to regularized least squares NMF.

4.2 Methods for NMF with KL divergence

NMF with KL divergence is harder to solve compared to square loss. Assume an algorithm applies an iterative method to solve $\min_{W \geq 0} f(W, H)$, and needs to compute the gradient at each iteration. After computing the gradient (6) at the beginning, least squares NMF solvers can maintain the gradient in $O(mk^2)$ time when W is updated. So it can do many inner updates for W with comparatively less effort $O(mk^2) \ll O(nmk)$. Almost all least squares NMF solvers take advantage of this fact. However, for KL-divergence, the gradient (20) cannot be maintained within $O(nmk)$ time after each update of W, so the cost for each sub-problem is $O(nmkt)$ where t is the number of inner iterations, which is large compared to $O(nmk)$ for square loss.

Our algorithm (CCD) spends $O(nmk\bar{d})$ time where $\bar{d}$ is the average number of Newton iterations, while the multiplicative algorithm spends $O(nmk)$ time. However, CCD has a better solution for each variable because we use a second order approximation of the actual function, which is better compared to working on the auxiliary function as used in multiplicative algorithm proposed by [15]. Experiments in Section 6 show CCD is much faster.

In addition to the practical comparison, the following theorem proves CCD converges to a stationary point under certain condition. FastHals for least squares NMF can also be covered by this theorem because it is also a cyclic coordinate descent method.

Theorem 3
For any limit points (W^*, H^*) of CCD (or FastHals), assume w_r^* is the rth column of W^* and h_r^* is the rth row of H^*, if

$$\|w_r^*\| > 0, \|h_r^*\| > 0 \;\; \forall r = 1, \ldots, k, \tag{24}$$

then (W^*, H^*) is a stationary point of (3) (or (1)).

With the condition (24), the one-variable sub-problems for the convergence subsequence are strictly convex. Then the proof follows the proof of Proposition 3.3.9 in [2]. For KL-NMF, (24) is violated only when corresponding row/columns of V are all zero (otherwise the objective value will be infinity). Therefore, zero row/columns of V can be removed by preprocessing to ensure the convergence of CCD. For least squares NMF, usually (24) holds in practice so that FastHals also converges to a stationary point.

For CCD with regularization on both W and H, each one-variable sub-problem becomes strictly quasiconvex, thus we can apply Proposition 5 in [6] to prove the following theorem:

Theorem 4
Any limit point (W^*, H^*) of CCD (or FastHals) is a stationary point of (3) (or (1)) with L1 or L2 regularization on both W and H.

5. IMPLEMENTATION ISSUES

5.1 Implementation with MATLAB and C

It is well known that MATLAB is very slow in loop operations and thus, to implement GCD, the "for loop" in Step 7 of Algorithm 1 is slow in MATLAB. To have an efficient implementation, we transfer three matrices W, G^W, HH^T to C by MATLAB-C interface in Step 7. At the end of the loop, our C code returns W^{new} back to the main MATLAB program. Although this implementation gives an overhead to transfer $O(nk + mk)$ size matrices, our algorithm still outperforms other methods in experiments. In the future, it is possible to directly use BLAS3 library to have a faster implementation in C.

5.2 Stopping Condition

The stopping condition is important for NMF solvers. Here, we adopt projected gradient as stopping condition as in [18]. The projected gradient for $f(W, H)$, i.e., $\nabla^P f(W, H)$ has two parts including $\nabla^P_W f(W, H)$ and $\nabla^P_H f(W, H)$, where

$$\nabla^P_W f(W, H)_{ir} \equiv \begin{cases} \frac{\partial}{\partial W_{ir}} f(W, H) & \text{if } W_{ir} > 0, \\ \min(0, \frac{\partial}{\partial W_{ir}} f(W, H)) & \text{if } W_{ir} = 0. \end{cases} \tag{25}$$

$\nabla^P_W f(W, H)$ can be defined in a similar way. According to the KKT condition, (W^*, H^*) is a stationary point if and only if $\nabla^P f(W^*, H^*) = 0$, thus we can use $\nabla^P f(W^*, H^*)$ to measure how close we are to a stationary point. We stop the algorithm after the norm of projected gradient satisfies the following stopping condition:

$$\|\nabla^P f(W, H)\|_F^2 \leq \epsilon \|\nabla^P f(W^0, H^0)\|_F^2,$$

where W^0 and H^0 are initial points.

6. EXPERIMENTS

In this section, we compare the performance of our algorithms with other NMF solvers. All sources used for our comparisons are available at `http://www.cs.utexas.edu/~cjhsieh/nmf`. All the experiments were executed on 2.83 GHz Xeon X5440 machines with 32G RAM and Linux OS.

6.1 Comparison on dense datasets

For least squares NMF, we compare GCD with three other state-of-the-art solvers:

1. ProjGrad: the projected gradient method in [18]. We use the MATLAB source code at `http://www.csie.ntu.edu.tw/~cjlin/nmf/`.
2. BlockPivot: the block-pivot method in [12]. We use the MATLAB source code at `http://www.cc.gatech.edu/~hpark/nmfsoftware.php`.

Table 2: The comparisons for least squares NMF solvers on dense datasets. For each method we present time/FLOPs (number of floating point operations) cost to achieve the specified relative error. The method with the shortest running time is boldfaced. The results indicate that GCD is most efficient both in time and FLOPs.

dataset	m	n	k	relative error	Time (in seconds)/FLOPs			
					GCD	FastHals	ProjGrad	BlockPivot
Synth03	500	1,000	10	10^{-4}	**0.6/0.7G**	2.3/2.9G	2.1/1.4G	1.7/1.1G
			30	10^{-4}	**4.0/5.0G**	9.3/16.1G	26.6/23.5G	12.4/8.7G
Synth08	500	1,000	10	10^{-4}	**0.21/0.11G**	0.43/0.38G	0.53/0.41G	0.56/0.35G
			30	10^{-4}	**0.43/0.46G**	0.77/1.71G	2.54/2.70G	2.86/1.43G
CBCL	361	2,429	49	0.0410	**2.3/2.3G**	4.0/10.2G	13.5/14.4G	10.6/8.1G
				0.0376	**8.9/8.8G**	18.0/46.8G	45.6/49.4G	30.9/29.8G
				0.0373	**14.6/14.5G**	29.0/75.7G	84.6/91.2G	51.5/53.8G
ORL	10,304	400	25	0.0365	**1.8/2.7G**	6.5/14.5G	9.0/9.1G	7.4/5.4G
				0.0335	**14.1/20.1G**	30.3/66.9G	98.6/67.7G	33.9/38.2G
				0.0332	**33.0/51.5G**	63.3/139.0G	256.8/193.5G	76.5/82.4G

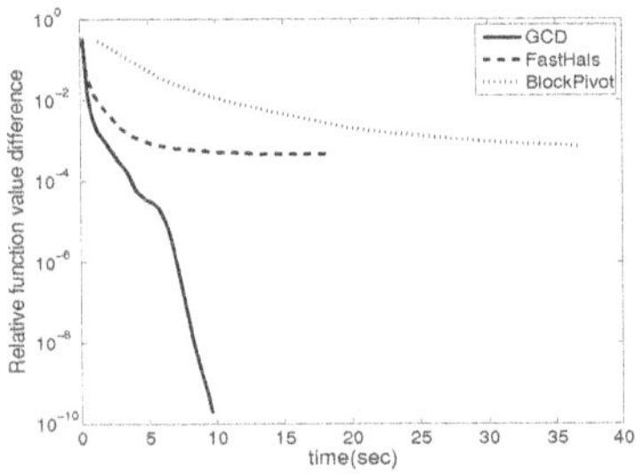

(a) Objective value for Yahoo-News dataset

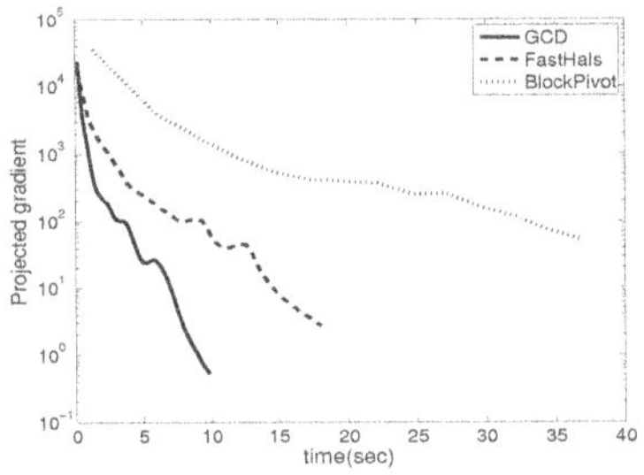

(b) Project gradient for Yahoo-News dataset

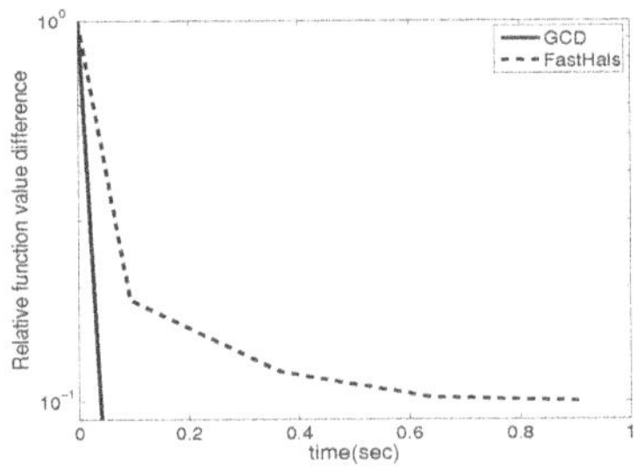

(c) L1 regularized objective value for Yahoo-News dataset, with $\rho_1 = 10$, $\rho_2 = 20$

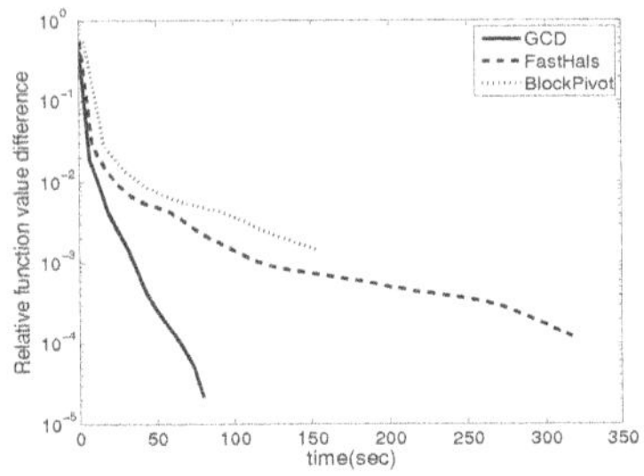

(d) Objective value for MNIST dataset

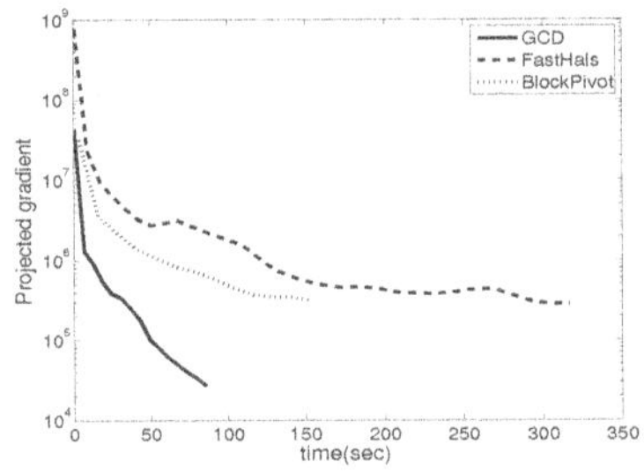

(e) Projected gradient for MNIST dataset

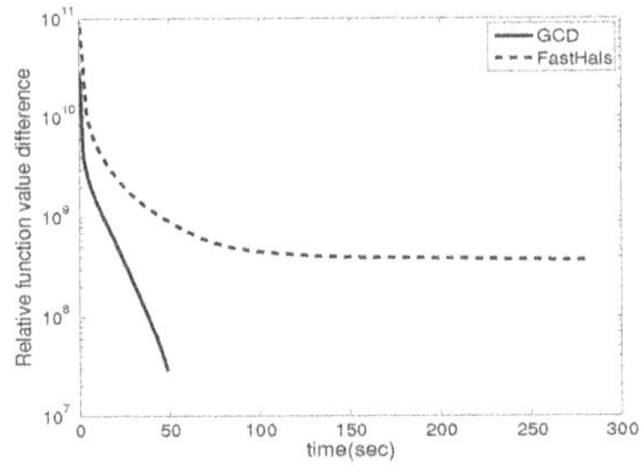

(f) L1 regularized objective value for NMIST dataset with $\rho_1 = 50,000$, $\rho_2 = 100,000$

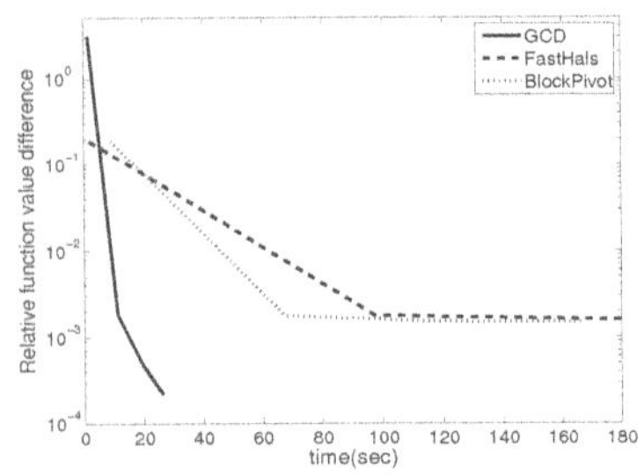

(g) Objective value for RCV1 dataset

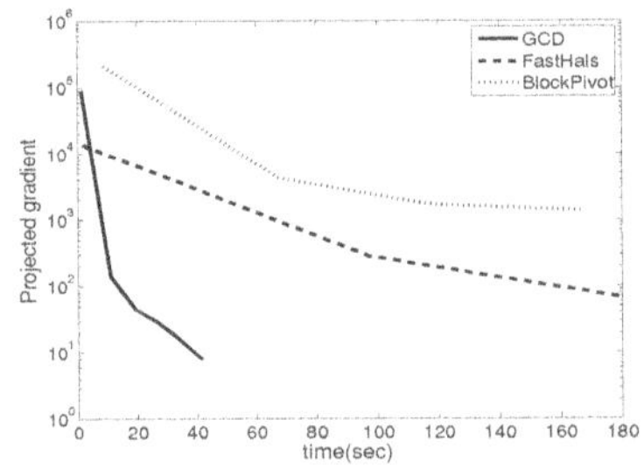

(h) Projected gradient for RCV1 dataset

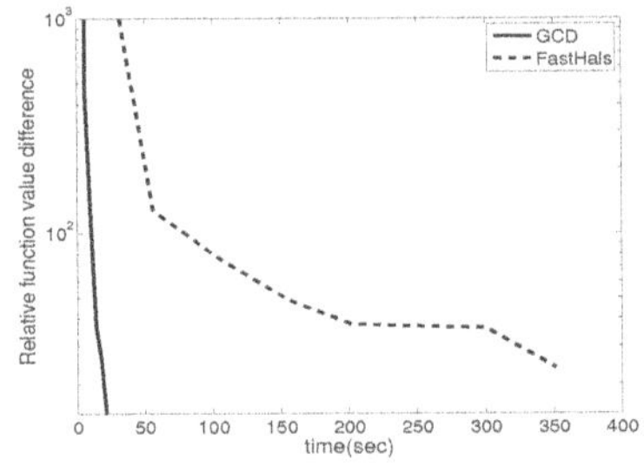

(i) L1 regularized objective value for RCV1 dataset with $\rho_1 = 0.005$, $\rho_2 = 0.05$

Figure 2: Time comparison for large sparse datasets. The result indicate that GCD is both faster and converges to better solutions.

3. FastHals: Cyclic coordinate descent method in [3]. We implemented the algorithm in MATLAB.

For GCD, we set the inner stopping condition ϵ to be 0.001. We test the performance on the following dense datasets:

1. Synthetic dataset: Following the process in [12], we generate the data by first randomly creating W and H, and then compute $V = WH$. We generate two datasets Synth03 and Synth08, the suffix numbers indicate 30% or 80% variables in solutions are zeros.
2. CBCL image dataset: `http://cbcl.mit.edu/cbcl/software-datasets/FaceData2.html`
3. ORL image dataset: `http://www.cl.cam.ac.uk/research/dtg/attarchive/facedatabase.html`

We follow the same setting as in [8] for CBCL and ORL datasets. The size of the datasets are summarized in Table 2. To ensure a fair comparison, all experimental results in this paper are the average of 10 random initial points.

Table 2 compares the CPU time for each solver to achieve the specified relative error defined by $\|V - WH\|_F^2/\|V\|_F^2$. For synthetic dataset, since the exact factorization exists, all the methods can achieve very low objective function value. From Table 2, we can conclude that GCD is two to three times faster than BlockPivot and FastHals on dense datasets.

As mentioned in Section 5, we implement part of GCD in C. To have a fair comparison, the FLOPs (number of Floating Point Operations) is listed in Table 2. FastHals is competitive in time but slow in FLOPs. This is because it fully utilizes dense matrix-multiplication operations, which is efficient in MATLAB.

For NMF with KL divergence, we compare the performance of our cyclic coordinate descent method (CCD) with the multiplicative update algorithm (Multiplicative) proposed in [15]. As mentioned in Section 3, the method proposed in [3] solves a different formulation, so we do not include it in our comparisons. Table 3 shows the runtime for CCD and Multiplicative to achieve the specified relative error. For KL-divergence, we define the relative error to be the objective value $L(W, H)$ in (3) divided by $\sum_{i,j} V_{ij} \log(\frac{V_{ij}}{(\sum_j V_{ij})/n})$, which is the distance between V_{ij} and the uniform distribution for each row. We implement CCD in C and Multiplicative in MATLAB, so we also list the FLOPs in Table 3. Table 3 shows that CCD is 2 to 3 times faster than Multiplicative at the beginning, and can be 10 times faster to get a more accurate solution. If we consider FLOPs, CCD is even better.

6.2 Comparison on sparse datasets

In Section 6.1, BlockPivot, FastHals, and GCD are the three most competitive methods. To test their scalability, we further compare their performances on large sparse datasets. We use the following sparse datasets:

1. Yahoo-News (K-Series): A news articles dataset.
2. RCV1 [16]: An archive of newswire stories from Reuters Ltd. The original dataset has 781,265 documents and 47,236 features. Following the preprocessing in [18], we choose data from 15 random categories and eliminate unused features. However, our data is much larger than the one used in [18].
3. MNIST [13]: A collection of hand-written digits.

The statistics of the datasets are summarized in Table 4. We set k according to the number of categories for each datasets. We run GCD and FastHals with our C implementations with sparse matrix operations, and for BlockPivot we use the author's code in MATLAB with sparse V as input.

Table 3: Time comparison results for KL divergence. * indicates the specified objective value is not achievable. The results indicate CCD outperforms Multiplicative

dataset	k	relative error	Time (in seconds)/FLOPs	
			CCD	Multiplicative
Synth03	10	10^{-3}	**11.4/5.2G**	34.0/68.1G
		10^{-5}	**14.8/6.8G**	144.2/240.6G
	30	10^{-3}	**121.1/58.7G**	749.5/2057.4G
		10^{-5}	**184.32/89.3G**	7092.3/18787.8G
Synth08	10	10^{-2}	**2.5/1.7G**	30.3/71.6G
		10^{-5}	**13.0/8.8G**	*
	30	10^{-2}	**22.6/11.2G**	46.0/93.9G
		10^{-5}	**56.8/27.7G**	*
CBCL	49	0.1202	38.2/**18.2G**	**21.2**/64.1G
		0.1103	**123.2/58.4G**	562.6/781.3G
		0.1093	**166.0/78.7G**	3266.9/2705.4G
ORL	25	0.3370	**73.7/35.0G**	165.2/336.3G
		0.3095	**253.6/117.0G**	902.2/1323.0G
		0.3067	**370.2/177.5G**	1631.9/3280.2G

Table 4: Statistics of data sets. k is the value of reduced dimension we use in the experiments.

Data set	m	n	#nz	k
Yahoo-News	21,839	2,340	349,792	20
MNIST	7,80	60,000	8,994,156	10
RCV1(subset)	31,025	152,120	7,817,031	15

In Figure 2(a), 2(d), 2(g), we show the CPU time for the 3 methods to reduce the objective value of least squares NMF, versus with logarithmically decreasing values of $(f(W, H) - f^*)/f^*$, where f^* denote the lowest average objective value, for 10 initial points, of the 3 methods.

Compared to FastHals and BlockPivot, GCD converges to a local optimum with lower objective value. This is important for nonconvex optimization problems because we can find a better local optimum. To further compare the speed of convergence to local optimums, we check the projected gradient $\nabla^P f(W, H)$, which measures the distance between current solution and stationary points. The results are in Figure 2(b), 2(e) and 2(h). The figures indicate that GCD converges to the stationary point in lesser CPU time.

We further add L1 penalty terms as in (2). We only include GCD and FastHals in the comparison because BlockPivot does not provide the same regularized form in their package. Figures 2(c), 2(f) and 2(i) compare the methods for reducing the objective value of (2). For this comparison we choose the parameters λ_1 and λ_2 so that on average more than half the variables in the solution of W and H are zero. The figures indicate that GCD achieves lower objective function value than FastHals in MNIST, and for Yahoo-News and RCV1, GCD is more than 10 times faster. This is because GCD can focus on nonzero variables while FastHals updates all the variables at each iteration.

7. DISCUSSION AND CONCLUSIONS

In summary, we propose coordinate descent methods that do variable selection for solving least squares NMF and KL-NMF. Our methods have theoretical guarantees and are efficient on real-life data. The significant speedups on sparse data show a potential to apply NMF to larger problems. In the future, our method can be extended to solve NMF with missing values or other matrix completion problems.

8. REFERENCES

[1] M. Berry, M. Browne, A. Langville, P. Pauca, and R. Plemmon. Algorithms and applications for approximate nonnegative matrix factorization. *Computational Statistics and Data Analysis*, 2007. Submitted.

[2] D. Bersekas and J. Tsitsiklis. Parallel and distributed computation. *Prentice-Hall*, 1989.

[3] A. Cichocki and A.-H. Phan. Fast local algorithms for large scale nonnegative matrix and tensor factorizations. *IEICE Transaction on Fundamentals*, E92-A(3):708–721, 2009.

[4] E. Gaussier and C. Goutte. Relation between PLSA and NMF and implications. *28th Annual International ACM SIGIR Conference*, 2005.

[5] E. F. Gonzales and Y. Zhang. Accelerating the Lee-Seung algorithm for non-negative matrix factorization. Technical report, Department of Computational and Applied Mathematics, Rice University, 2005.

[6] L. Grippo and M. Sciandrone. On the convergence of the block nonlinear Gauss-Seidel method under convex constraints. *Operations Research Letters*, 26:127–136, 2000.

[7] P. O. Hoyer. Non-negative sparse coding. In *Proceedings of IEEE Workshop on Neural Networks for Signal Processing*, pages 557–565, 2002.

[8] P. O. Hoyer. Non-negative matrix factorization with sparseness constraints. *Journal of Machine Learning Research*, 5:1457–1469, 2004.

[9] C.-J. Hsieh and I. S. Dhillon. Fast coordinate descent methods with variable selection for non-negative matrix factorization. *Department of Computer Science TR-11-06, University of Texas at Austin*, 2011.

[10] D. Kim, S. Sra, and I. S. Dhillon. Fast Newton-type methods for the least squares nonnegative matrix appoximation problem. *Proceedings of the Sixth SIAM International Conference on Data Mining*, pages 343–354, 2007.

[11] J. Kim and H. Park. Non-negative matrix factorization based on alternating non-negativity constrained least squares and active set method. *SIAM Journal on Matrix Analysis and Applications*, 30(2):713–730, 2008.

[12] J. Kim and H. Park. Toward faster nonnegative matrix factorization: A new algorithm and comparisons. *Proceedings of the IEEE International Conference on Data Mining*, pages 353–362, 2008.

[13] Y. LeCun, L. Bottou, Y. Bengio, and P. Haffner. Gradient-based learning applied to document recognition. *Proceedings of the IEEE*, 86(11):2278–2324, November 1998. MNIST database available at `http://yann.lecun.com/exdb/mnist/`.

[14] D. D. Lee and H. S. Seung. Learning the parts of objects by non-negative matrix factorization. *Nature*, 401:788–791, 1999.

[15] D. D. Lee and H. S. Seung. Algorithms for non-negative matrix factorization. In T. K. Leen, T. G. Dietterich, and V. Tresp, editors, *Advances in Neural Information Processing Systems 13*, pages 556–562. MIT Press, 2001.

[16] D. D. Lewis, Y. Yang, T. G. Rose, and F. Li. RCV1: A new benchmark collection for text categorization research. *Journal of Machine Learning Research*, 5:361–397, 2004.

[17] Y. Li and S. Osher. Coordinate descent optimization for l1 minimization with application to compressed sensing; a greedy algorithm. *Inverse Probl. Imaging*, 3(3):487–503, 2009.

[18] C.-J. Lin. Projected gradient methods for non-negative matrix factorization. *Neural Computation*, 19:2756–2779, 2007.

[19] C. Liu, H. chih Yang, J. Fan, L.-W. He, and Y.-M. Wang. *Distributed Non-negative Matrix Factorization for Web-Scale Dyadic Data Analysis on MapReduce.* 2010.

[20] P. Paatero and U. Tapper. Positive matrix factorization: A non-negative factor model with optimal utilization of error. *Environmetrics*, 5:111–126, 1994.

[21] S. Perkins, K. Lacker, and J. Theiler. Grafting: Fast, incremental feature selection by gradient descent in function space. *Journal of Machine Learning Research*, 3:1333–1356, 2003.

[22] J. Piper, P. Pauca, R. Plemmons, and M. Giffin. Object characterization from spectral data using nonnegative factorization and information theory. In *Proceedings of AMOS Technical Conference*, 2004.

[23] R. Zdunek and A. Cichocki. Non-negative matrix factorization with quasi-newton optimization. *Eighth International Conference on Artificial Intelligence and Soft Computing, ICAISC*, pages 870–879, 2006.

Fast Locality-Sensitive Hashing

Anirban Dasgupta Ravi Kumar Tamás Sarlós
Yahoo! Research
701 First Avenue
Sunnyvale, CA 94089
{anirban,ravikumar,stamas}@yahoo-inc.com

ABSTRACT

Locality-sensitive hashing (LSH) is a basic primitive in several large-scale data processing applications, including nearest-neighbor search, de-duplication, clustering, etc. In this paper we propose a new and simple method to speed up the widely-used Euclidean realization of LSH. At the heart of our method is a fast way to estimate the Euclidean distance between two d-dimensional vectors; this is achieved by the use of randomized Hadamard transforms in a non-linear setting. This decreases the running time of a (k, L)-parameterized LSH from $O(dkL)$ to $O(d \log d + kL)$. Our experiments show that using the new LSH in nearest-neighbor applications can improve their running times by significant amounts. To the best of our knowledge, this is the first running time improvement to LSH that is both provable *and* practical.

Categories and Subject Descriptors. H.3.3 [**Information Storage and Retrieval**]: Information Search and Retrieval; H.4.m [**Information Systems Applications**]: Miscellaneous; G.3 [**Mathematics of Computing**]: Probability and Statistics—*Probabilistic algorithms*

General Terms. Algorithms, Experimentation, Performance, Theory

Keywords. Nearest neighbor search, Locality-sensitive hashing, Hadamard transform, Dimension reduction

1. INTRODUCTION

Locality sensitive hashing (LSH) is a basic primitive in large-scale data processing algorithms that are designed to operate on objects (with features) in high dimensions. The idea behind LSH [23, 22] is the following: construct a family of functions that hash objects into buckets such that objects that are similar will be hashed to the same bucket with high probability. Here, the type of the objects and the notion of similarity between them determine the particular hash function family. Typical instances include the Jaccard coefficient as similarity when the underlying objects are sets and the ℓ_2 norm as distance (i.e., dissimilarity) or the cosine/angle as similarity when the underlying objects are vectors.

KDD'11, August 21–24, 2011, San Diego, California, USA.

With such a powerful primitive, many large-scale data processing problems that previously suffered from the "curse of dimensionality" suddenly become tractable. For instance, in conjunction with standard indexing techniques, it becomes possible to search for nearest-neighbors efficiently [16]: given a query, hash the query into a bucket, use the objects in the bucket as candidates for near neighbors, and rank them according to their similarity to the query. Likewise, popular operations such as near-duplicate detection [7, 28, 19], all-pairs similarity [6], similarity join/record-linkage [25], temporal correlation [10], are made easier.

In this paper objects are vectors and the distance between vectors is the Euclidean (ℓ_2) norm. This choice is motivated by many applications in text processing, image/video indexing/retrieval, natural language processing, etc. When the similarity measure between vectors is their angle, Charikar [9] gave a very simple LSH called SIMHASH: the hash of an input vector is the sign of its inner product with a random unit vector. It can be shown that the probability that the hashes of two vectors agree is a function of the angle between the underlying vectors [17]. Datar et al. [12] present constructions based on stable distributions for the ℓ_p norm; their construct is almost identical to Charikar's in the ℓ_2 case. Since then, there have been efforts to make these LSH constructions more efficient and practical [27, 13, 5]. Each of these LSH constructions works by first using a randomized estimator of the similarity measure, pasting multiple such constructions to create one hash function with an appropriately small collision rate, and then using multiple such hash functions to get the right tradeoff between the collision rate and recall.

Main results. In this paper we obtain algorithmic improvements to the query time of the basic LSH in the ℓ_2 setting. At a high level, we improve the query time of the LSH for estimating ℓ_2 for d-dimensional vectors from $O(dkL)$ to $O(d \log d + kL)$, where roughly, each hash function maps into a vector of k bits and L different hash functions are used. Experiments on different, large, and high-dimensional datasets show that these theoretical gains translate to a typical improvement of 20% or more in the LSH query time. We also extend our results to the angle-based similarity, where we improve the query-time to ϵ-approximate the angle between two d-dimensional vectors from $O(d/\epsilon^2)$ to $O(d \log 1/\epsilon + 1/\epsilon^2)$; we postpone the details of this result to the full version of the paper. To the best of our knowledge, this is the first query-time improvement to LSH that is both provable and practical.

Our improvement consists of two new algorithms. The first algorithm, called `ACHash`, works by computing the following sequence applied to the input vector: randomly flip the signs of each coordinate of the vector, apply the Hadamard transform, and compute the inner product with a sparse Gaussian vector. This particular sequence of operations is directly inspired by the fast Johnson–

Lindenstrauss transform proposed by Ailon and Chazelle [1] for dimension reduction. The second algorithm, called DHHash, works by computing the following sequence applied to the input vector: randomly flip the signs of each coordinate of the vector, apply the Hadamard transform, multiply each coordinate by independent unit Gaussians, and apply another Hadamard transform. DHHash, even though it has only comparable theoretical guarantees to ACHash, performs much better in practice. The use of a Gaussian operator sandwiched by Hadamard transforms is a novel step in DHHash.

Clearly, both the algorithms exploit the computational advantages of the Hadamard transform and that is where we gain the improved query time. The space requirements of naive LSH lie between ACHash and DHHash whereas, the latter has a better query time than the former. Notice that our algorithms are extremely simple in practice; they have been implemented on top of a publicly available LSH package. A bulk of our contribution lies in proving that these algorithms do not compromise the basic LSH guarantees. The main technical difficulty we encounter is in the non-linear but inevitable operation of bucketizing the projection (or taking the sign). The proof of ACHash is relatively simple and relies on an application of the Bernstein's concentration bound. The proof of DHHash is intricate, since in addition we need to deal with dependent Gaussian random variables; it uses a novel analysis method based on matrix perturbation. The techniques we develop for the analysis may be of independent interest.

2. RELATED WORK

The related work falls into three main categories: the vast literature on data structures and indexing for similarity search, the extensive work on LSH and related methods, and the use of FFT-like methods in dimension reduction.

There have been several indexing data structures proposed for nearest-neighbor search and approximate nearest-neighbor search, such as the R-tree, the K-D tree, the SR-tree, etc. Unfortunately, these index structures do not scale well with the dimension of the data [32] and this is precisely where LSH-like techniques kick in. We do not delve into the myriad of searching and indexing techniques for similarity joins: the readers can refer to the survey [15] and the tutorial [25].

LSH was first articulated in a series of papers by Indyk et al. [23] and Indyk and Motwani [22]. Since then, it has become the state-of-the-art technique for similarity search in high dimensions. Charikar [9] developed an LSH for angles (called SIMHASH) and thus cosine similarities in Euclidean space. Datar et al. [12] presented LSH schemes based on stable distribution for ℓ_p norms.

Panigrahy [30] proposed the entropy-based LSH to (provably) reduce the space requirements of SIMHASH. In this scheme, in addition to considering the bucket corresponding to the query, buckets corresponding to perturbed versions of the query also considered. Unfortunately, while the space requirements are reduced, the query time is considerably increased. Lv et al. [27] designed a careful probing heuristic to look up multiple buckets that have a high probability of containing the nearest neighbors of a query. They obtain both space and query time improvements, but are not able to offer any provable guarantees of performance. Broder et al. [8] developed an LSH based on min-wise independent permutations for the Jaccard similarity for sets. There have been several followup work to LSH, improving its performance both theoretically (e.g., [30]) and practically (e.g., [27, 18]). Our results are mostly complementary and can be combined with these variants. We refer to the recent thesis of Andoni [3] and the survey by Andoni and Indyk [4] for further background.

Ailon and Chazelle [1] pioneered the use of FFT in dimensionality reduction; their main application was to obtain a fast version of the Johnson–Lindenstrauss transform. Our first algorithm is directly inspired by their work. Eshghi and Rajaram [13] proposed a class of LSH for angles based on the theory of concomitants from statistics; they use DFT as a heuristic to speed up their computations and do not offer any theoretical guarantees of correctness. Concurrently and independently of our work, Vybiral [31] obtained a version of the Johnson–Lindenstrauss theorem using circulant matrices and Gaussian random variables. His proof uses the fact that circulant matrices can be diagonalized using the discrete Fourier transform. Even though this appears syntactically close to our use of the double Hadamard transform, it is unclear if his analysis can be adapted either to the Hadamard transform setting or to the angle setting (as opposed to the distance setting in Johnson–Lindenstrauss theorem). Recently, Bachrach and Porat [5] and Feigenblat et al. [14] presented constructions that speed up the computation of the LSH for Jaccard similarity, namely, min-wise independent fingerprints, by an exponential factor.

3. BACKGROUND

First, we set up some notation that will be used throughout the paper. Let X denote the set of input vectors in $\Re^d$ and let $|X| = n$. Let $x \in X$ denote an input vector and let $y \in \Re^d$ denote the query vector. Let $\|x\| = \|x\|_2$ denote the Euclidean norm of vector x unless otherwise noted and let $\|A\|_F$ be the Frobenius norm of matrix A. Let $[k]$ denote the set $\{1, \ldots, k\}$.

Let $N(0, \sigma)$ be the zero-mean Gaussian distribution with variance σ^2 and let $N(0, C)$ be the zero-mean multidimensional Gaussian distribution with covariance C. Let G be a $d \times d$ diagonal matrix where each diagonal entry is independently $N(0, 1)$. Let D be a $d \times d$ diagonal matrix where each diagonal entry is an independent Bernoulli random variable, i.e., D_{ii} is ± 1 equiprobably. Let M be a random permutation matrix of order d.

Hadamard matrices. We will use the following family of Hadamard matrices in our algorithms. Let $H_d \in \Re^{d \times d}$ denote the Hadamard matrix of order d, defined as follows: $H_2 = \begin{pmatrix} 1 & 1 \\ 1 & -1 \end{pmatrix}$ and $H_{2^k} = H_2 \otimes H_{2^{k-1}}$, where $\otimes$ denotes the tensor product. For Hadamard matrices of order d, using an FFT-like algorithm, matrix-vector multiplication can be done in $O(d \log d)$ time; this fact will be important for our running time analysis. Since it will be clear from the context, we will drop the subscript d from H_d. Let D_{H_i} denote a $d \times d$ diagonal matrix such that $(D_{H_i})_{jj} = H_{ij}$. (For more background on Hadamard matrices and their properties, the readers are referred to standard CS undergraduate textbooks.)

An overview of LSH. We give a brief description of a basic LSH for ℓ_2 [12, 3]; we refer to this as the *naive* LSH. Let $X \subseteq \Re^d$ be the set of input points and let q be a query point. Given a distance parameter R and a recall parameter δ, our aim is to create a data structure to efficiently return at least $1 - \delta$ fraction of the neighbors of each query point that are at most a distance R (in ℓ_2 norm) from it. Let k, L, and w be parameters that we will choose later. Let A be a $k \times d$ random matrix where each A_{ij} is a random variable drawn independently from $N(0, 1)$ and let A_i denote the ith row of A. Let $b \in \Re^d$ be a random vector such that each b_i is chosen uniformly in $[w]$. For each $i \in [k]$, define $h_i(x) = \lfloor \frac{A_i \cdot x + b_i}{w} \rfloor$ to be the ith hash value for x. For $u = \|x - y\|$, let $p(u)$ be the (*collision*) probability that $h_i(x) = h_i(y)$ for any i. If $f(\cdot)$ denotes the density function of $N(0, 1)$, a simple argument in [12] shows that

$$p(u) = \int_0^w \frac{1}{u} f\left(\frac{t}{u}\right)\left(1 - \frac{t}{w}\right) dt,$$

which monotonically decreases with u.

Define $g(x) = (h_1(x), \ldots, h_k(x))$, i.e., a concatenation of the k hash values. The probability that $g(x) = g(y)$ is then $p^k(u)$. We then create L independent copies of $g(\cdot)$ as $g_1(x), \ldots, g_L(x)$. At preprocessing time, each point in the database is stored in each of the hash buckets $g_1(x), \ldots, g_L(x)$. During query time, for a given query point y, we compute $g_1(y), \ldots, g_L(y)$, and search all these L buckets to get a set of candidates. This candidate set may then be pruned based on whether we desire only the exact R-near neighbors. Following our previous calculation, the expected fraction of R-neighbors of the query point y that we get as candidates is at least $1-(1-p^k(R))^L$. We thus want this quantity to be at least $1-\delta$, the targeted recall. This theoretically determines the values of the parameters k and L. In practice, as well as in our experiments, these parameters are determined by doing a grid search over the nearby k and L values using a sample of input points. The value of w is chosen to be 4, as suggested in [12]. The space used by the LSH data structure scales with L, the number of hash tables constructed. The time needed to find out the exact R-near neighbors of a query point consists of both the projection time and the time taken to prune the candidate set.

4. ALGORITHM ACHash

In this section we present the first LSH algorithm that we call ACHash. This algorithm is essentially a modification of the fast Johnson–Lindenstrauss transform (FJLT) of Ailon and Chazelle [1], with suitable rounding and thresholding steps for obtaining the hashing buckets. We first present ACHash and then argue that the collision probabilities of ACHash are very close to that of the naive LSH scheme.

We first recap FJLT whose goal is to obtain a faster version of the celebrated Johnson–Lindenstrauss transform. Given an input vector, FJLT first pre-conditions the vector so that it becomes dense while its length is unchanged. This is accomplished by using a random diagonal matrix and a Hadamard transform; this amounts to a random length-preserving rotation of the vector. As we mentioned earlier, the Hadamard transform can be computed in $O(d \log d)$ time. Once the input vector is densified, FJLT then projects the vector to a smaller dimension. The key observation is that given that the input vector has been densified, a very sparse Gaussian matrix is sufficient.

In ACHash, the steps are similar. We first pre-condition the input vector using a random diagonal matrix and a Hadamard transform, then apply a sparse Gaussian matrix followed by a rounding. We now proceed to a more formal description of ACHash (Algorithm 1). Let k and L be the parameters of LSH. Let $q = \min\left(\Theta\left(\frac{\log 1/\delta}{\epsilon^2}\frac{\log(d/\delta)}{d}\right), 1\right)$ and let P be a $k \times d$ matrix where $P_{ij} = 0$ with probability $1-q$ and is $N(0, 1/q)$ with probability q. Note that the pre-conditioning needs to be computed only once. The time necessary to compute all the LSH buckets for one query point is thus $O(d \log d + kL \log^2 d)$.

We now proceed with the proof that the above method works. We first state the following key property of the pre-conditioning step shown in [1], which says that the vector $\hat{x}$ (Step 1) is sufficiently dense.

LEMMA 1 ([1]). *Let $x \in \Re^d$ be such that $\|x\| = 1$. Then, $\|HDx\|_\infty = O(\sqrt{\frac{\log(d/\delta)}{d}})$, with probability at least $1-\delta$.*

Next we show a technical statement that guarantees that the subsampling using the matrix P preserves the Euclidean distances. For each $i \in [k]$, let S_i denote the set of coordinates such P_{ij} was chosen to be sampled from $N(0, 1/q)$. For a vector z, let z_{S_i} denote its restriction to the coordinate set S_i.

Algorithm 1 ACHash(x)

1: Compute $\hat{x} = HDx$.
2: **for** $i = 1, \ldots, L$ **do**
3: Generate $P \in \Re^{k \times d}$ where each P_{ij} is independently $N(0, 1/q)$ with probability q and 0 otherwise.
4: Generate $b \in \Re^k$ where each b_i is independently and uniformly in $[w]$.
5: Store

$$\texttt{ACHash}_i(x) = \left\lfloor \frac{P\hat{x} + b}{w} \right\rfloor$$

as the ith hash of x.

LEMMA 2. *Let $v \in \Re^d$ be such that $\|v\|_\infty = O(\sqrt{\frac{\log(d/\delta)}{d}})$ and $\|v\| = 1$. For all $\epsilon, \delta \in (0,1)$, if $q = \Omega\left(\frac{\log(1/\delta)}{\epsilon^2}\frac{\log(d/\delta)}{d}\right)$, then*

$$\Pr\left[\left|\sum_{j \in S_i} v_j^2 - q\right| > \epsilon q\right] \le \delta.$$

PROOF. Let us define random variables $\delta_j = 1$ if $j \in S_i$, and apply Bernstein's inequality [29, Theorem 2.7] to the random variables $w_j = \delta_j v_j^2$. Note that

$$\sum_j E[w_j^2] = \sum_j q v_j^4 \le q\|v\|_\infty^2 \|v\|^2 = q\|v\|_\infty^2 = O\left(\frac{q\log(d/\delta)}{d}\right).$$

Therefore we have that

$$\begin{aligned}\Pr\left[|\sum_j w_j - q| > t\right] &\le \exp\left(-\frac{t^2/2}{\sum_j E[w_j^2] + \|w\|_\infty t/3}\right)\\ &\le \exp\left(-\frac{t^2/2}{O(q\log(d/\delta)/d + t\log(d/\delta)/(3d))}\right)\\ &\le \delta,\end{aligned}$$

for $t = \epsilon q$ and $q = \Omega\left(\frac{2}{\epsilon^2}\log(\frac{1}{\delta})\left(1+\frac{\epsilon}{3}\right)\frac{\log(d/\delta)}{d}\right)$. □

The next theorem shows that the collision probabilities of ACHash are very similar to that of the naive LSH. Let $u = \|x - y\|$ and let

$$p_{\mathrm{AC}}(u) = \Pr[\texttt{ACHash}_i(x) = \texttt{ACHash}_i(y)]$$

denote the probability that all k hash values of ACHash agree for a generic $i \in [L]$.

THEOREM 3. *For all $\epsilon, \delta \in (0,1)$, we have*

$$-(k+1)\delta + p^k((1+\epsilon)u) \le p_{\mathrm{AC}}(u) \le p^k((1-\epsilon)u) + (k+1)\delta.$$

PROOF. Let $\hat{x} = HDx$, $\hat{y} = HDy$, and $z = \hat{x} - \hat{y}$. Since HD is a unitary transformation, we have $\|z\| = u$. Using Lemma 1 we have that $\|\hat{x}\|_\infty, \|\hat{y}\|_\infty = O(\sqrt{\frac{\log(d/\delta)}{d}})$. By Lemma 2, we have that for all $i \in [k]$, with probability at least $1 - k\delta$,

$$(1-\epsilon)u \le \sum_{j \in S_i} z_j^2/q \le (1+\epsilon)u.$$

Thus each z_{S_i} preserves the distance u to within a factor of $1 \pm \epsilon$. Multiplying $\hat{x}_{S_i}$ by the Gaussian random variables (from P) and the bucketization performed in steps 4 and 5 corresponds to doing a naive LSH on each of $\hat{x}_{S_i}$ and $\hat{y}_{S_i}$ vectors. Since the random variables are all independent, we get the corresponding guarantees from the naive LSH and the proof is complete by taking a union bound over all the bad events. □

5. ALGORITHM DHHash

In this section we present an improved hashing algorithm. While this algorithm is somewhat motivated by ACHash, it has two applications of the Hadamard transform and hence we call it DHHash. As before, we present the steps involved in computing the hash and then argue that the collision probabilities of DHHash are very close to that of the naive LSH scheme.

The first step is to pre-condition the input vector by applying a random diagonal matrix followed by a Hadamard transform. While this is the same as before, the rest of the steps are different. The next step is to apply a random permutation, followed by a random diagonal Gaussian matrix, and an another Hadamard transform. This will give us a vector from which k entries are sampled without replacement to give a particular hash bucket; the sampling step is then repeated L times independently. The formal description is given below (Algorithm 2). The time taken by DHHash to compute the buckets for a given query is thus $O(d \log d + kL)$, which is an improvement over ACHash.

The intuition behind the sequence of transformations used in DHHash is as follows.The first random diagonal matrix-Hadamard transform combination smoothens the input vectors so that the maximum coordinate is bounded w.h.p. For such smoothened vectors, the subsequent combination of the random *Gaussian* diagonal matrix and Hadamard transform simulates the multiplication of the input vectors by an i.i.d. Gaussian matrix – this is the key novelty in designing this transform. The final sampling then gives the indices of the hash buckets.

The crucial point to note in DHHash is that the vector itself is computed only once and kL indices are sampled with replacement from the resulting vector. This introduces dependence among the L hash buckets, but as our experiments will show, this dependence does not adversely affect the LSH performance. Note that it is possible to get a set of L independent buckets in $O(Ld \log k)$ time by repeatedly invoking a $O(d \log k)$ subroutine [2, 26] for computing k elements out of the randomized Hadamard transform. Recall the definitions of G, M and b from Section 3.

Algorithm 2 DHHash(x)

1: Compute

$$\zeta = \left\lfloor \frac{HGMHDx + b}{w} \right\rfloor.$$

2: **for** $i = 1, \ldots, L$ **do**

3: Store k entries sampled without replacement from ζ as DHHash$_i(x)$, the ith hash of x.

For ease of notation, let us recall the steps of the hashing operation as follows. For input vectors x and y, let $\hat{x}$ and $\hat{y}$ be their pre-conditioned and permuted versions, i.e., $\hat{x} = MHDx, \hat{y} = MHDy$. Let $g = \text{diag}(G)$ and let $g_i = (D_{H_i})\, g$. Observe that

$$\zeta_i(x) = \left\lfloor \frac{g_i^T \hat{x} + b_i}{w} \right\rfloor$$

is precisely the ith coordinate of vector ζ computed in Step 1 of Algorithm 2.

In what follows, we will show a bound on the collision probability of DHHash. Our guarantees will only be for a set of k indices sampled without replacement from ζ. Note that in the actual algorithm, we repeat this construction L times; while this seems to work well in practice, we do not have any theoretical guarantees on the joint distribution of the L choices.

Let S be a subset of k coordinates chosen at random without replacement, and without loss of generality we can assume $S = [k]$. Let $p_S(u)$ denote the probability that the hash bucket generated using these coordinates are the same for both x and y, where $u = \|\hat{x} - \hat{y}\| = \|x - y\|$. Since the b_i are i.i.d. uniform, observe that $p_S(u)$ can be written as

$$p_S(u) = \int_{\forall i, t_i = 0}^{t_i = w} f(t_1, \ldots, t_k) \prod_i \left(1 - \frac{t_i}{w}\right) dt_1 \ldots dt_k, \quad (1)$$

where $f(\cdot)$ denotes the joint pdf of the random variables τ_i where $\tau_i = g_i^T(\hat{x} - \hat{y})$.

Note that the distribution of $(\tau_1, \ldots, \tau_k)$ is a multidimensional Gaussian since each of $\tau_i = g^T D_{H_i}(\hat{x} - \hat{y})$ is a linear transformation of the Gaussian random variable g. If the Gaussian random vectors g_i were all independent, then we would have $p_S(u) = p^k(u)$. In our case the $g_i = D_{H_i} g$ are *not* independent. Nevertheless, we show strong lower and upper bounds on $p_S(u)$.

At a high level, our proof consists of two key steps. First we observe that the covariance of $(\tau_1, \ldots, \tau_k)$ depends on the "smoothness" of the vector $\hat{x} - \hat{y}$; ensuring this smoothness is precisely the role of the pre-conditioner. Second, we show that if the τ_i's are nearly uncorrelated, then $p_S(u)$ is close to $p^k(u)$. Let $c = O\left(\frac{\log d}{d}\right)$ and $\gamma = \sqrt{2c \log(d/\delta)}$ for the remainder of the proof.

LEMMA 4. *Let $\hat{x}$ and $\hat{y}$ be vectors in $\Re^d$ such that $\|\hat{x}\| = \|\hat{y}\| = 1$ and $\|\hat{x}\|_\infty \leq \sqrt{c}$ and $\|\hat{y}\|_\infty \leq \sqrt{c}$. Also, assume that $d > \log(d/\delta) \log(d)$ holds for a small fixed constant $\delta \in (0, 1)$. Then with probability $1 - \delta$, it holds that for all $i \neq j \in [d]$*

$$|\langle D_{H_i}\hat{x}, D_{H_j}\hat{y} \rangle| < \gamma.$$

PROOF. Consider a fixed i and j and let T be the set of coordinates t where $H_{it} = H_{jt}$. Since M is a random permutation, we can consider T as a random set of $d/2$ coordinates. Let $\delta_t = 1$ if $t \in T$ and 0 otherwise. Then,

$$\langle D_{H_i}\hat{x}, D_{H_j}\hat{y} \rangle = \sum_{t \in T} \hat{x}_t \hat{y}_t - \sum_{t \notin T} \hat{x}_t \hat{y}_t = 2 \sum_{t \in T} \hat{x}_t \hat{y}_t - \hat{x}^T \hat{y}.$$

Over the random choice of T, we have that

$$E\left[\sum_{t \in T} \hat{x}_t \hat{y}_t\right] = \hat{x}^T \hat{y}/2.$$

For $t \in [d]$ let $X_t = \delta_t \hat{x}_t \hat{y}_t - \hat{x}_t \hat{y}_t / 2$. Note that the events $t \in T$ are not independent. However, since we can regard T as a set of $d/2$ coordinates sampled without replacement, we can employ the same form of Bernstein's inequality that is applicable to the independent case [20]. Note that

$$E[X_t^2] \leq \hat{x}_t^2 \hat{y}_t^2 / 4 \leq c\hat{x}_t^2 / 4,$$

and thus $\sum_t E[X_t^2] \leq c/4$. Also observe that $|X_t| \leq c$. Therefore, from Bernstein's inequality it follows that

$$\Pr\left[\left|\sum_{t \in T} \hat{x}_t \hat{y}_t - \frac{\hat{x}^T \hat{y}}{2}\right| > u\right] \leq 2 \exp\left(-\frac{u^2}{\sum_t EX_t^2 + cu/3}\right)$$

$$\leq 2 \exp\left(-\frac{u^2}{c/4 + cu/3}\right).$$

By choosing $u = \gamma$, we have that $u < 1$ and $c/4 + cu/3 < 2c/3$. Thus it holds with probability $1 - 2(\delta/d)^3$ that

$$\left| \sum_{t \in T} \hat{x}_t \hat{y}_t - \frac{\hat{x}^T \hat{y}}{2} \right| \leq \gamma,$$

which means that for this i, j pair,

$$\left| \langle D_{H_i} \hat{x}, D_{H_j} \hat{y} \rangle - \frac{\hat{x}^T \hat{y}}{2} \right| = \left| 2 \sum_{t \in T} \hat{x}_t \hat{y}_t - \hat{x}^T \hat{y} \right| = \gamma.$$

Taking a union bound over all $i \neq j$ pairs, the statement of the lemma holds with probability at least $1 - O(\delta^3/d)$. □

We are now ready to state our main technical theorem. Observe that for a small enough γ, i.e., a large enough input dimension d, and for $k \ll d$ in Theorem 5, we have $u', u'' \approx u$ and $A_{k,\gamma}, B_{k,\gamma} \approx 1$ and therefore $p_S(u) \approx p^k(u)$.

THEOREM 5. *Assume that* $\gamma = o(k^{-2})$. *Let* $u' = u\sqrt{\frac{1-k\gamma}{1-2k\gamma}}$, $u'' = u(1-k\gamma)^{1/2}$, *and* $A_{k,\gamma} = 1 + O(k^2\gamma)$ *and* $B_{k,\gamma} = 1 - \Theta(k^2\gamma)$ *be constants depending on* k *and* γ. *Then,*

$$-2\delta + B_{k,\gamma} p^k(u'') \leq p_S(u) \leq A_{k,\gamma} p^k(u') + 2\delta.$$

PROOF. We give lower and upper bounds for the probability density function of the projections $f(\tau_1, \ldots, \tau_k)$ defined in (1).

Define the covariance matrix $C \in \Re^{k \times k}$ as $C_{ij} = E[\tau_i \tau_j]$. Thus, for all $i, j \in [1, k]$ we have that

$$\begin{aligned} C_{ij} &= (\hat{x} - \hat{y})^T D_{H_i} E[gg^T] D_{H_j} (\hat{x} - \hat{y}) \\ &= (\hat{x} - \hat{y})^T D_{H_i} D_{H_j} (\hat{x} - \hat{y}). \end{aligned}$$

It follows that $C_{ii} = u^2$. Using Lemma 1 with the vector $z = (1/u)(\hat{x} - \hat{y})$, we have that $\|z\|_\infty \leq \|x\|_\infty + \|y\|_\infty \leq 2\sqrt{c}$ with probability at least $1 - \delta$. Conditioning on this event, from Lemma 4 it follows that with probability at least $1 - \delta$, $|C_{ij}| \leq \gamma u^2$ for all $i \neq j$. Let $\Sigma = u^2 I_k$. Therefore C can be written as $C = \Sigma + u^2 E = u^2(I + E)$, where $|E_{ij}| \leq \gamma$ and $E_{ii} = 0$ and hence

$$\|E\| \leq \|E\|_F \leq k\gamma. \tag{2}$$

Now let

$$f_V(v) = \frac{1}{(2\pi)^{k/2}\sqrt{\det V}} \exp\left(-\frac{1}{2} v^T V^{-1} v\right)$$

denote the pdf of the k-dimensional Gaussian $N(0, V)$.

Using the perturbation result about the determinant [24, Corollary 2.14], we have that

$$\frac{|\det I - \det \frac{C}{u^2}|}{\det I} \leq \left(1 + \left\| I - \frac{C}{u^2} \right\|\right)^k - 1 \leq (1 + k\gamma)^k - 1,$$

and therefore

$$2 - (1 + k\gamma)^k \leq \det \frac{C}{u^2} \leq (1 + k\gamma)^k.$$

Also, for any vector v,

$$-v^T C^{-1} v + v^T \Sigma^{-1} v = v^T(-(I + E)^{-1} + I)v/u^2. \tag{3}$$

Using the standard matrix inverse perturbation bound [21, Section 5.8], we have that

$$\|(I + E)^{-1} - I\| \leq \frac{\|E\|}{1 - \|E\|}.$$

Therefore from (in)equalities (2) and (3),

$$\begin{aligned} v^T(-(I + E)^{-1} + I)v &\leq v^T v \|(I + E)^{-1} - I\| \\ &\leq v^T v \frac{\|E\|}{1 - \|E\|} \leq v^T v \frac{k\gamma}{1 - k\gamma}. \end{aligned}$$

Thus,

$$\begin{aligned} -v^T C^{-1} v &= -v^T \Sigma^{-1} v + v^T(\Sigma^{-1} - C^{-1})v \\ &\leq -u^{-2} v^T v + u^{-2} \frac{v^T v k\gamma}{1 - k\gamma} \\ &= -v^T v u'^{-2} = -v^T \Sigma'^{-1} v, \end{aligned}$$

where $u' = u/\sqrt{1 - \frac{k\gamma}{1-k\gamma}} = u\sqrt{\frac{1-k\gamma}{1-2k\gamma}}$ and $\Sigma' = u'^2 I$. Similarly,

$$\begin{aligned} -v^T C^{-1} v &\geq -u^{-2} v^T v - u^{-2} \frac{v^T v k\gamma}{1 - k\gamma} \\ &\geq -u^{-2} v^T v (1 - k\gamma)^{-1} = -v^T v u''^{-2} = -v^T \Sigma''^{-1} v, \end{aligned}$$

where $u'' = u(1 - k\gamma)^{1/2}$ and $\Sigma'' = u''^2 I$.

Now,

$$\begin{aligned} f(v) &= \frac{\exp(-v^T C^{-1} v/2)}{(2\pi)^{k/2}\sqrt{\det C}} \\ &\leq \frac{\exp(-v^T \Sigma'^{-1} v/2)}{(2\pi)^{k/2}\sqrt{\det \Sigma'}} \frac{\sqrt{\det \Sigma'}}{\sqrt{\det C}} \\ &\leq f_{\Sigma'}(v) \frac{(1 - k\gamma)^{k/2}}{(1 - 2k\gamma)^{k/2}\sqrt{2 - (1 + k\gamma)^k}} = f_{\Sigma'}(v) A_{k,\gamma}, \end{aligned}$$

where $A_{k,\gamma} := \frac{(1-k\gamma)^{k/2}}{(1-2k\gamma)^{k/2}\sqrt{2-(1+k\gamma)^k}}$. Similarly, using the lower bounds,

$$\begin{aligned} f(v) &\geq \frac{\exp(-v^T \Sigma''^{-1} v/2)}{(2\pi)^{k/2}\sqrt{\det \Sigma''}} \frac{\sqrt{\det \Sigma''}}{\sqrt{\det C}} \\ &\geq f_{\Sigma''}(v) \sqrt{\frac{(1 - k\gamma)^k}{(1 + k\gamma)^k}} = f_{\Sigma''}(v) B_{k,\gamma}, \end{aligned}$$

where we set $B_{k,\gamma} := \sqrt{\frac{(1-k\gamma)^k}{(1+k\gamma)^k}}$.

Using the above bounds for $f(\cdot)$ in (1), we have the main claim of the theorem. Observe that for $\gamma = o(k^{-2})$, we have $(1 + k\gamma)^{-k/2} = 1 - \Theta(k^2\gamma)$, $(1 - k\gamma)^{k/2} = 1 - \Theta(k^2\gamma)$, and $(1 - 2k\gamma)^{-k/2} = 1 + O(k^2\gamma)$. Substituting these into the definitions of $A_{k,\gamma}$ and $B_{k,\gamma}$ above, we obtain $A_{k,\gamma} = 1 + O(k^2\gamma)$ and $B_{k,\gamma} = 1 - \Theta(k^2\gamma)$. □

6. EXTENSIONS TO ANGLE SIMILARITY

In this section we sketch how to apply our methods to the setting when the similarity of two vectors is given by the angle between them. Along with the fast projection techniques of Sections 4 and 5, the idea is to use the signs of the projections [9]. Due to lack of space, we only provide a high-level description and omit the proofs.

To extend `ACHash` to the angle setting, we set the ith hash of the input vector x to be $\mathrm{sgn}(PHDx)$. Provided that the angles are not very close to zero, we can show that the above hashing method has low bias in estimating the actual angle and that the estimates are correct with high probability. The mild technical condition of the angles not being to close to zero is easy to satisfy, say, by randomly perturbing all input vectors.

Name	# points	dimensions	# queries
FLICKR	1 million	1024	10k
QUERIES	1 million	376	10k
MNIST	60k	784	10k
P53	14.6k	5408	2k

Figure 1: Description of datasets.

To extend DHHash to the angle setting, we now compute $\zeta = \text{sgn}(\frac{HGMHDx+b}{w})$ instead; the rest of the steps are as before. Once again, we can show that this yields an LSH for the angle-based similarity of the input vectors.

7. EXPERIMENTS

In this section we describe the experimental results obtained by running our algorithms, compared against a standard LSH implementation as the baseline. We start by describing the datasets, at least two of which are publicly available for repeatability purposes.

We performed experiments in the R-near-neighbor setting. Given an input dataset and a query point, the goal is to return the set of points that lie within distance R of the query point.

7.1 Datasets

The experiments were performed on the following four datasets: FLICKR, QUERIES, MNIST, and P53. The basic statistics of the datasets are summarized in Figure 7.1.

The FLICKR dataset consists of images represented as dense vectors of dimension 1024 computed by a convolutional neural network. Out of these images, we sampled one million images in order to create the input dataset, and another 10,000 images to create the query set. When creating the query set, we ensured that the same image (according to the identifier present in the dataset) does not belong to both the input dataset and the query set. The QUERIES dataset was created by following the description given in [10], where the authors use an analogous dataset to demonstrate how temporal correlation of search queries is indicative of semantic similarity. In creating the QUERIES dataset, we calculated the frequencies of queries submitted to a major search-engine for 376 consecutive days. Each query q is then represented as a vector X_q of length 376, where the entry X_{qi} is the frequency of query q on the ith day. We kept only the 1.01 million most frequent queries, and again partitioned and sampled the set to obtain 1 million input vectors and 10,000 query vectors. Each of the input vectors and query vectors were also normalized using the mean and standard deviation as $\tilde{X}_{qi} = (X_{qi} - \mu(X_q))/\sigma(X_q)$, as described in [10].

For the sake of repeatability, we also perform the experiments on two smaller, publicly available datasets, namely, MNIST[1] and P53 [11][2]. The MNIST dataset consists of byte representations of images of handwritten digits that have been size normalized and pre-partitioned into training and test sets. We used this data set as-is, the 60k training images as the input points and 10k test images as query points. The P53 dataset consists of feature vectors that are each of size 5409, where each dimension indicates a feature value extracted from a biophysical model of the P53 protein. For this dataset, we removed all the data points that have missing entries, reducing the size of the dataset from 16.7k to 16.6k. These points were then partitioned randomly into 2k query points and 14.6k input points.

[1] yann.lecun.com/exdb/mnist/
[2] archive.ics.uci.edu/ml/datasets/p53+Mutants

7.2 Experimental method

We based our LSH implementation on the *Exact* Euclidean LSH (E^2LSH) implementation of Andoni et al.[3] E^2LSH implements R-near neighbor by first constructing a set of candidates using the LSH hash-buckets that the query point falls into, and then pruning the set of candidate by comparing each of them to the query point. The total query time is thus dependent on both the time taken to compute the LSH buckets and on the number of candidates returned by the LSH buckets.

E^2LSH also applies a pairing "trick" to speed up the LSH computation.[3] This reduces the time to compute all the probe locations in the LSH tables from $O(dkL)$ to $O(dk\sqrt{L})$. For any even k, L is set to $m(m-1)$. For a data point x, first it computes the $k/2$-wide LSH values $\{u^{(i)}(x) : i = 1, \ldots, m\}$ and then obtains L LSH values from these as $h^{(i,j)}(x) = (u^{(i)}(x), u^{(j)}(x))$, where $i \neq j$. Although the h values are not independent any more, the resulting scheme is still provably correct if L is set to slightly higher than in the fully independent case.

We compared four different algorithms, namely, DHHash, naive LSH (Naive), and two variants ACHash50 and ACHash25, where the sparsity parameter q of Algorithm 1 is set to 0.5 and 0.25 respectively. We ran E^2LSH with the pairing trick and modified the code to use each of these algorithms to compute the above described $u^{(i)}$ functions.

7.3 Metrics

For each dataset, we chose four different radii R, and these were chosen such that the average numbers of R-near neighbors are approximately 10, 25, 50, and 100. We present four different metrics for each dataset, for each radius:

- the average recall, i.e., fraction of R-near neighbors that are actually returned,
- the average query time per query measured in seconds elapsed,
- the time taken to compute the LSH indices,
- the space usage as measured by the number of hash tables constructed, L,
- the average number of nearest neighbor candidates that the E^2LSH algorithm had to sift through.

Note that E^2LSH filters set of candidates by computing the exact distances, it never reports false R-neighbors, i.e., its precision is always 1 irrespective of the LSH function used.

In order to be able to compare the query times of the different LSH for various algorithms, we fixed the targeted recall at 0.9. Since the performance of LSH schemes is sensitive to the parameters k and $L = m(m-1)$, we iterated over a range of parameters k and m and selected the parameter tuple that had the minimum average query time while having a macro-averaged recall over 0.9. Ideally, we would like to fix the recall of all the candidates exactly at 0.9 to be able to compare the query times. However, because of the small discrete jumps in the average recall in each of the LSH techniques, we were able to only approximately align the recall numbers of different algorithms. E^2LSH provides a functionality to estimate the optimal parameter set for a given recall and a given radius. We used this initial estimation to guide the construction of the grid of parameters that we searched over for each method.

7.4 Results

We demonstrate the efficiency of our algorithms by carefully studying multiple metrics and datasets.

[3] www.mit.edu/~andoni/LSH/

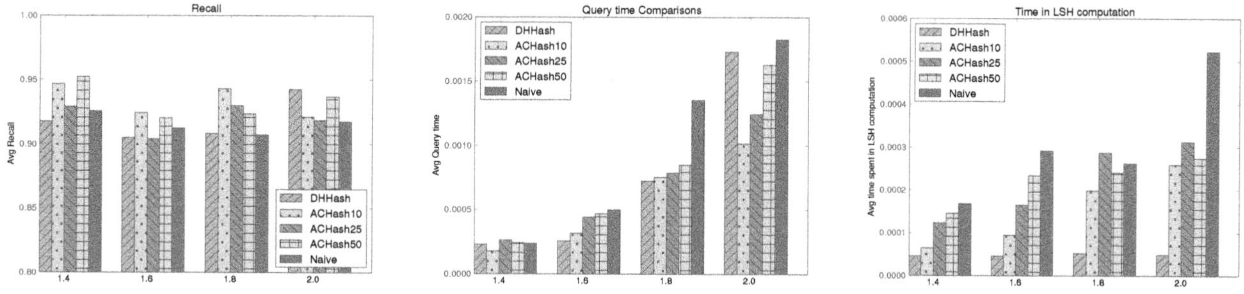

(a) Recall, LSH query time, and LSH computation time for FLICKR.

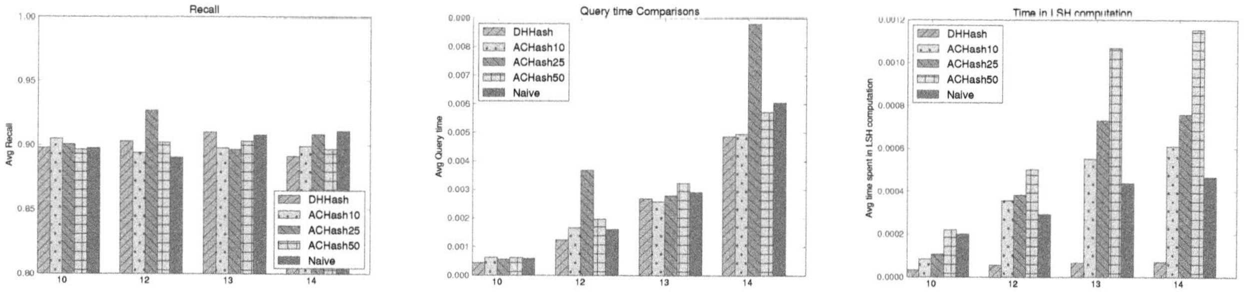

(b) Recall, LSH query time, and LSH computation time for QUERIES.

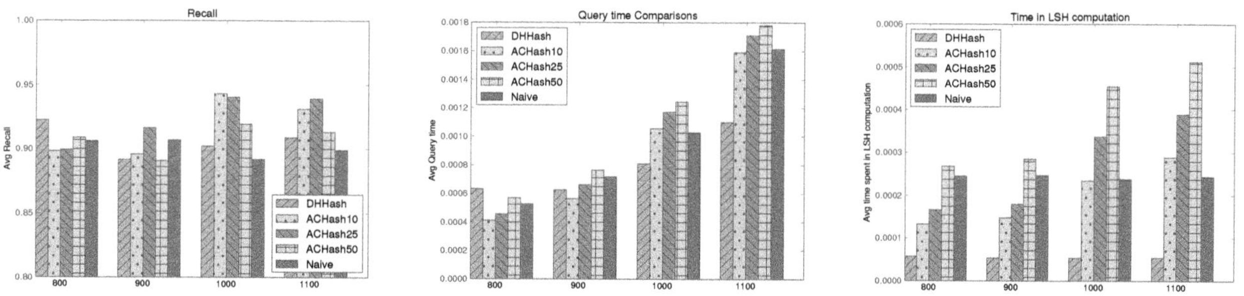

(c) Recall, LSH query time, and LSH computation time for MNIST.

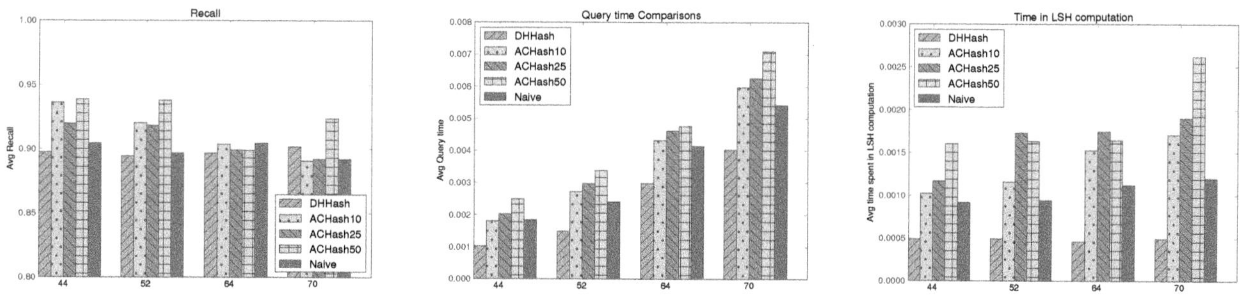

(d) Recall, LSH query time, and LSH computation time for P53.

Figure 2: Recall, query times and LSH computation time for all four datasets

Recall. The first column in Figure 2 shows the recall levels achieved at the chosen parameter tuples for each of the radius values. As discussed above, the recall values are very close to each other, but are not aligned perfectly. The differences are at most a few percentage points. We observe that the recall for `DHHash` is almost always more than that of `Naive` at the chosen parameter tuple, thus making our claims of query time improvements justified.

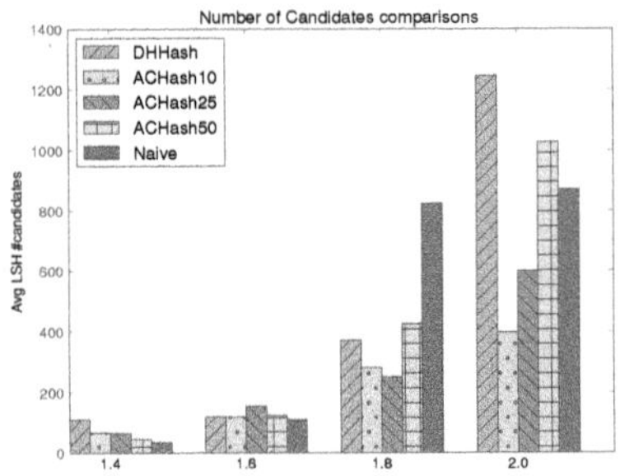

(a) FLICKR LSH candidates.

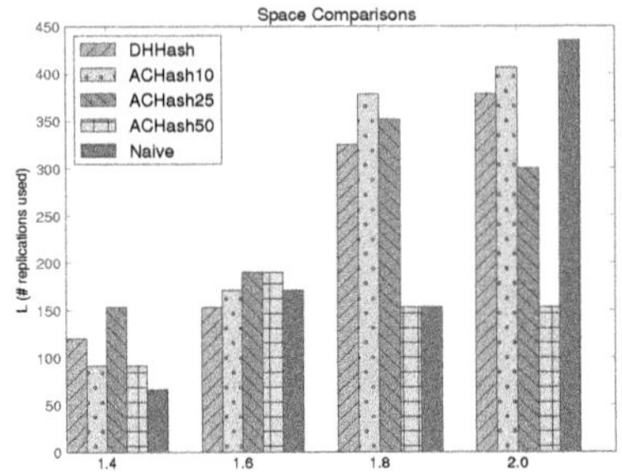

(b) FLICKR space usage.

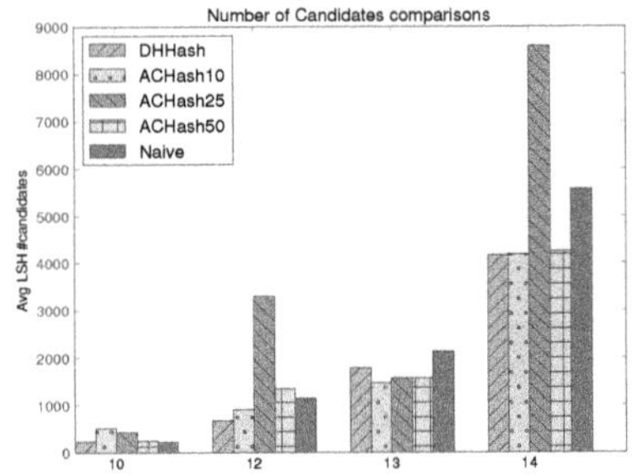

(c) QUERIES LSH candidates.

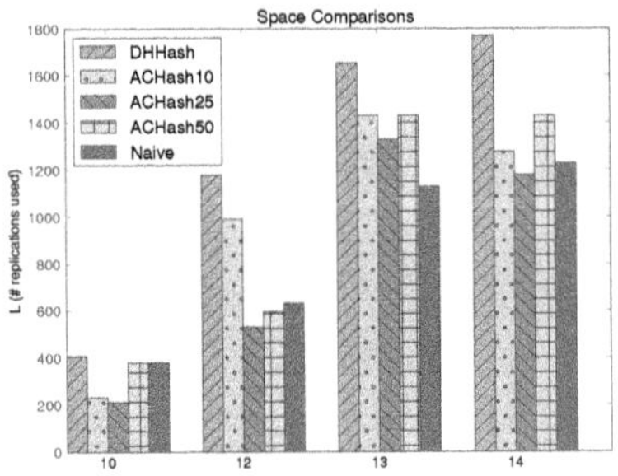

(d) QUERIES space usage.

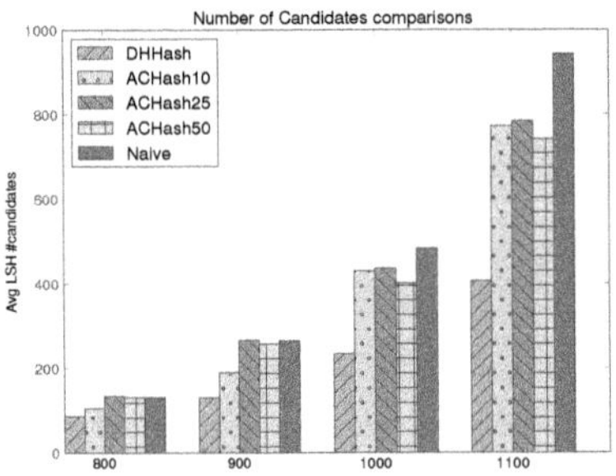

(e) MNIST LSH candidates.

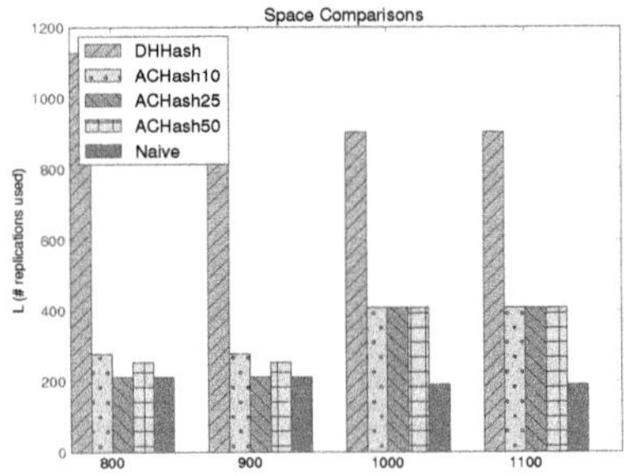

(f) MNIST space usage.

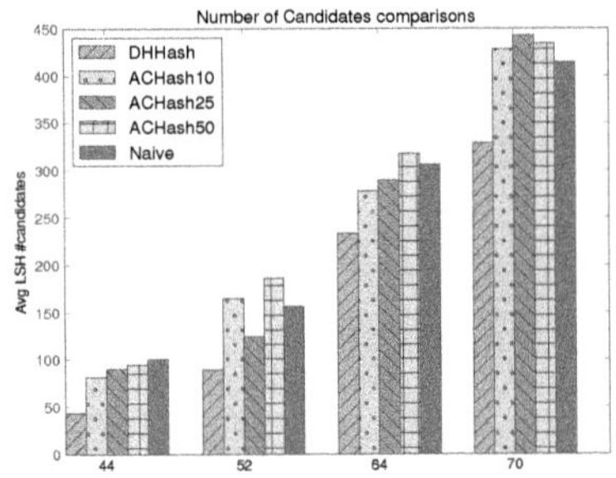

(g) P53 LSH candidates.

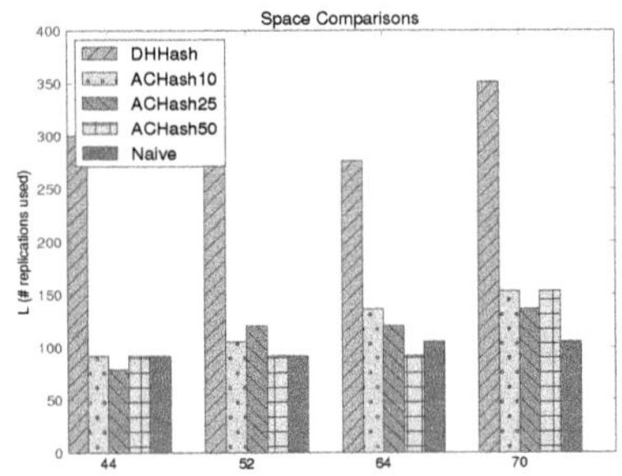

(h) P53 space usage.

Figure 3: Number of LSH candidates and space usage for all four datasets.

Query time. The middle column in Figure 2 depicts the average query times obtained with the parameters that gave the aforementioned recalls. Overall, we see about a 15-20% improvement in most cases (and up to 50% maximum) by using `DHHash` over `Naive`. Using the two different variants of `ACHash`, however, does not always provide a uniform improvement in query time over `Naive`. Even at comparable (or lesser) recalls, we see `ACHash` variants performing slightly worse than `Naive`. We however, have not experimented with the sparsity settings of `ACHash` exhaustively. Overall this underlines the benefits of `DHHash` being parameter free.

LSH computation. The last column in Figure 2 shows the time taken in the computation of the LSH index for the average query point. As predicted by theory, `DHHash` is always an order of magnitude faster than `Naive`. `ACHash`, however, is not always faster than `Naive`, which is a result of two effects: at the sparsity setting we used, it still needs to compute an almost dense matrix-vector product, and the number of replications L needed for `ACHash` (and for `DHHash`) is typically more than that required for `Naive`.

Candidate set size. Figures 3(a), 3(c), 3(e), 3(g) illustrate the number of candidates that the LSH index returned as hits and the actual pairwise distance computed for by E^2LSH. The results are mostly correlated with the respective query times, except for the rare cases where in spite of having generated more candidates, `DHHash` runs faster as an effect of having computed the LSH functions much more efficiently.

Space usage. Finally, figures 3(b), 3(d), 3(f) and 3(h) show the space used by the chosen parameter settings, measured by the value of L, the number of replications performed. Except for FLICKR, `DHHash` has been able to improve runtime only at the expense of using more space than `Naive`.

Overall, we observe that due to the pairing "trick" described earlier, `Naive` spends the majority of time in filtering the candidates. Compared to `Naive`, `DHHash` achieves greater improvements in query time than those possible by speeding up the LSH computation only for the same L and k. Its optimal k and L are larger, resulting in an increase in the number of cheap LSH operations performed and a decrease in the more expensive distance computations during filtering.

8. CONCLUSIONS

In this paper we proposed two new algorithms to speed up LSH for the Euclidean distance. Our algorithms exploit the property of being able to compute Hadamard transforms fast and consequently are able to reduce the hash index construction time to $O(d \log d + kL)$. While our algorithms are simple and easy to implement in practice, most of the difficulty is in showing provable guarantees on their performance. We develop novel analysis methods to this end. Our extensive experiments on four large datasets show that our algorithms achieve more than 20% improvement in query time over standard `DHHash` implementations.

Since LSH is so fundamental, our algorithms open up a wide possibility for their use in diverse settings. Interesting future directions include using our algorithms for applications such as deduplication, clustering, similarity joins, all-pair similarity search, etc.

9. REFERENCES

[1] N. Ailon and B. Chazelle. The fast Johnson–Lindenstrauss transform and approximate nearest neighbors. *SIAM J. Comput.*, 39(1):302–322, 2009.

[2] N. Ailon and E. Liberty. Fast dimension reduction using Rademacher series on dual BCH codes. *Discrete and Computational Geometry*, 42(4):615–630, 2009.

[3] A. Andoni. *Nearest Neighbor Search: the Old, the New, and the Impossible*. PhD thesis, MIT, 2009.

[4] A. Andoni and P. Indyk. Near-optimal hashing algorithms for approximate nearest neighbor in high dimensions. *Commun. ACM*, 51(1):117–122, 2008.

[5] Y. Bachrach and E. Porat. Fast pseudo-random fingerprints. *Arxiv preprint arXiv:1009.5791*, 2010.

[6] R. J. Bayardo, Y. Ma, and R. Srikant. Scaling up all pairs similarity search. In *Proc. 16th WWW*, pages 131–140, 2007.

[7] A. Broder, S. C. Glassman, M. S. Manasse, and G. Zweig. Syntactic clustering of the web. In *Proc. 6th WWW*, pages 391–404, 1997.

[8] A. Z. Broder, M. Charikar, A. M. Frieze, and M. Mitzenmacher. Min-wise independent permutations. *J. Comput. Syst. Sci.*, 60(3):630–659, 2000.

[9] M. S. Charikar. Similarity estimation techniques from rounding algorithms. In *Proc. 34th STOC*, pages 380–388, 2002.

[10] S. Chien and N. Immorlica. Semantic similarity between search engine queries using temporal correlation. In *Proc. 14th WWW*, pages 2–11, 2005.

[11] S. Danziger, J. Zeng, Y. Wang, R. Brachmann, and R. Lathrop. Choosing where to look next in a mutation sequence space: Active Learning of informative p53 cancer rescue mutants. *Bioinformatics*, 23(13):i104, 2007.

[12] M. Datar, N. Immorlica, P. Indyk, and V. Mirrokni. Locality-sensitive hashing scheme based on p-stable distributions. In *Proc. 20th SOCG*, pages 253–262, 2004.

[13] K. Eshghi and S. Rajaram. Locality sensitive hash functions based on concomitant rank order statistics. In *Proc. 14th KDD*, pages 221–229, 2008.

[14] G. Feigenblat, E. Porat, and A. Shiftan. Even better framework for min-wise based algorithms. *Arxiv preprint arXiv:1102.3537*, 2011.

[15] I. K. Fodor. A survey of dimension reduction techniques. Technical Report UCRL-ID-148494, Lawrence Livermore National Laboratory, 2002.

[16] A. Gionis, P. Indyk, and R. Motwani. Similarity search in high dimensions via hashing. In *Proc. 25th VLDB*, pages 518–529, 1999.

[17] M. X. Goemans and D. P. Williamson. Improved approximation algorithms for maximum cut and satisfiability problems using semidefinite programming. *J. ACM*, 42(6):1115–1145, 1995.

[18] J. He, W. Liu, and S. Chang. Scalable similarity search with optimized kernel hashing. In *Proc. 16th KDD*, pages 1129–1138, 2010.

[19] M. R. Henzinger. Finding near-duplicate web pages: A large-scale evaluation of algorithms. In *Proc. 29th SIGIR*, pages 284–291, 2006.

[20] W. Hoeffding. Probability inequalities for sums of bounded random variables. *J. ASA*, 58(301):13–30, 1963.

[21] R. Horn and C. Johnson. *Matrix analysis*. Cambridge Univ Press, 1990.

[22] P. Indyk and R. Motwani. Approximate nearest neighbors: Towards removing the curse of dimensionality. In *Proc. 30th STOC*, pages 604–613, 1998.

[23] P. Indyk, R. Motwani, P. Raghavan, and S. Vempala. Locality-preserving hashing in multidimensional spaces. In *Proc. 29th STOC*, pages 618–625, 1997.

[24] I. Ipsen and R. Rehman. Perturbation bounds for determinants and characteristic polynomials. *SIAM J. Matrix Analysis and Applications*, 30(2):762–776, 2008.

[25] N. Koudas and D. Srivatsava. Approximate joins: Concepts and techniques. In *Proc. 31st VLDB*, page 1363, 2005.

[26] E. Liberty, N. Ailon, and A. Singer. Dense fast random projections and lean Walsh transforms. In *Proc. 12th RANDOM*, pages 512–522, 2008.

[27] Q. Lv, W. Josephson, Z. Wang, M. Charikar, and K. Li. Multi-probe LSH: Efficient indexing for high-dimensional similarity search. In *Proc. VLDB*, pages 950–961, 2007.

[28] G. S. Manku, A. Jain, and A. D. Sarma. Detecting near-duplicates for web crawling. In *Proc. 16th WWW*, pages 141–150, 2007.

[29] C. McDiarmid. Concentration. In M. Habib, C. McDiarmid, J. Ramirez-Alfonsin, and B. Reed, editors, *Probabilistic Methods for Algorithmic Discrete Mathematics*, volume 16, pages 195–248. Springer, 1998.

[30] R. Panigrahy. Entropy-based nearest neighbor search in high dimensions. In *Proc. 17th SODA*, pages 1186–1195, 2006.

[31] J. Vybiral. A variant of the Johnson–Lindenstrauss lemma for circulant matrices. *J. Functional Analysis*, 260(4):1096–1105, 2011.

[32] R. Weber, H. Schek, and S. Blott. A quantitative analysis and performance study for similarity search methods in high dimensional spaces. In *Proc. 24th VLDB*, pages 194–205, 1998.

Friendship and Mobility: User Movement in Location-Based Social Networks

Eunjoon Cho *
Stanford University
ejcho@stanford.edu

Seth A. Myers *
Stanford University
samyers@stanford.edu

Jure Leskovec
Stanford University
jure@cs.stanford.edu

ABSTRACT

Even though human movement and mobility patterns have a high degree of freedom and variation, they also exhibit structural patterns due to geographic and social constraints. Using cell phone location data, as well as data from two online location-based social networks, we aim to understand what basic laws govern human motion and dynamics. We find that humans experience a combination of periodic movement that is geographically limited and seemingly random jumps correlated with their social networks. Short-ranged travel is periodic both spatially and temporally and not effected by the social network structure, while long-distance travel is more influenced by social network ties. We show that social relationships can explain about 10% to 30% of all human movement, while periodic behavior explains 50% to 70%. Based on our findings, we develop a model of human mobility that combines periodic short range movements with travel due to the social network structure. We show that our model reliably predicts the locations and dynamics of future human movement and gives an order of magnitude better performance than present models of human mobility.

Categories and Subject Descriptors: H.2.8 [**Database Management**]: Database Applications – *Data mining*
General Terms: Algorithms, theory, experimentation.
Keywords: Human mobility, Communication networks, Social networks.

1. INTRODUCTION

While we would like to believe that our movement and mobility patterns have a high degree of freedom and variation, at a global scale human mobility exhibits structural patterns subject to geographic and social constraints. One would expect that people exhibit strong periodic behavior in their movement as they move back and forth between their homes and workplaces [7, 23]. Mobility is probably also constrained geographically by the distance one can travel within a day [12]. Moreover, mobility may further be shaped by our social relationships [11, 26] as we may be more likely to visit places that our friends and people similar to us visited in the past.

*Authors contributed equally to this work.

KDD'11, August 21–24, 2011, San Diego, California, USA.

Even though the above are some of the most fundamental questions and hypotheses about the dynamics of human mobility, answers to them remain largely unknown mostly due to the fact that reliable large scale human mobility data has been hard to obtain. Recently, however, location-based online social networking applications have emerged, where users share their current location by *checking-in* on websites such as Foursquare, Facebook, Gowalla, etc. While traditionally records of calls made by cell phones have been used to track the location of the cell phone towers associated with the calls [12, 17, 30], location-based social networks [15, 29, 28] provide an important new dimension in understanding human mobility. In particular, while cell phone data provides coarse location accuracy, location-based social networks provide location-specific data, as one can distinguish between a check-in to the office on the 2nd floor and a check-in to a coffee shop on the 1st floor of the same building. On the other hand, check-ins to location-based social networks are usually sporadic [28] while cell phone data provides better temporal resolution as a user "checks-in" whenever she makes or receives a call. Both types of data also contain network information. Location-based social networks maintain explicit friendship networks, while in mobile phones the network can be inferred from the communication network [8].

This data allows for studying the three main aspects of human mobility: geographic movement (where do we move?), temporal dynamics (how often do we move?) and the social network (how do social ties interact with movement?). Previous studies have mostly focused on at most two out of these three aspects. For example, research has focused on building models of human movement and dynamics [2, 12, 30], understanding the role of geographic distance and social interaction [1, 11, 24, 26, 31] and the change of our perception of (media) space [15, 4]. Studies have also explored how social networks are embed into the underlying geography [22, 19, 29], and how geo-data can be used to infer social ties [5, 8, 6]. In contrast, we study the interaction of all three aspects of human mobility to devise a coherent model of human movement and dynamics.

In the broader context, understanding and modeling human mobility has many applications and consequences. Knowledge of users' locations can help improve large scale systems, such as cloud computing, content-based delivery networks [21], and location-based recommendations [13, 32, 33]. More broadly, accurate models of human mobility are essential for urban planning [10], understanding human migration patterns [14], and spread of diseases [9].

Present work. We study the relation between human geographic movement, its temporal dynamics, and the ties of the social network. In particular, we analyze the role of geography and daily routine on human mobility patterns as well as the effect of social ties, i.e., friends that one travels to meet. We seek to identify the fundamental factors that govern human mobility and aim to answer questions, such as, how likely is a person going to a place because she has a friend there? How likely is a person to make a new friend by going to a place? How does this probability increase or decrease when she travels long distances from home?

Overview of results: Empirical findings. We use the data from two popular online location-based social networks, Gowalla and Brightkite, as well as a trace of 2 million mobile phone users from a European country. We observe that people generally move periodically within a bounded region but occasionally travel long distance. People are generally more likely to visit a distant place if it is in proximity of an existing friend. Thus, perhaps surprisingly, the short-ranged travel is less impacted by the social network structure, while if a person travels a long distance then they are more likely to travel near an existing friend. Overall, we find that the influence of friendship on one's mobility is two times stronger than the influence of mobility on creating new friendships. We also note strong agreement and robustness of the patterns of human mobility between the cell phone and the location-based social network check-in data.

Generally, there are both benefits and limits to using mobility of friends to predict an individual's location. We find that users are most likely to check-in right after a friend has checked-in to the same place, and the probability drops off following a power law as the time difference increases. We show that a similarity of movement trajectories is a strong indication of a tie in the social network. Despite strong correlation between friendship and mobility, there are limits in using friendship alone to predict mobility. For example, 84% of the people have less than 20% of their check-ins visited by a friend prior to their own check-in. Overall, social relationships can explain about 10% of human movement in cell phone data and up to 30% of movement in location-based social networks, while periodic movement behavior explains about 50% to 70%.

Overview of results: The mobility model. Building on our empirical findings we develop a *Periodic & Social Mobility Model* for predicting mobility of individuals. In particular, we build on the observation that people show strong periodic behavior throughout certain periods of the day alternating between primary (e.g., "home") and secondary (e.g., "work") locations on weekdays, and "home" and social network driven locations on weekends. Our model has three components: (1) a model of spatial locations that a user regularly visits, (2) a model of temporal movement between these locations, and (3) a model of movement that is influenced by the ties of the social network (i.e., meeting friends). We capture the temporal dynamics of transitioning between these locations with a day-specific periodic transition model. We model user locations with a mixture of Gaussians centered at "home" and "work" locations. On top of this we use a model of "social" movement that governs user behavior over the weekends and weeknights.

We develop an expectation-maximization based parameter estimation method and evaluate the predictive power of the *Periodic & Social Mobility Model* using three evaluation metrics. Experiments show that our model outperforms current mobility models for more than a factor of two on all three metrics. In particular, our model predicts the exact user location at any time with 40% accuracy, with an average relative distance error of 0.23% for cell phone locations, and 2.7% for social check-ins. We observe strong robustness of the model and agreement of results between the cell phone and the location-based social network check-in data.

Further related work. Models of human mobility consider movement either as a diffusive process [2], or a stochastic process centered about a single fixed point [12]. Our model considers human mobility as a time-varying stochastic process around several fixed points. This additional flexibility of our model leads to a factor of two better predictive accuracy. More specialized mobility models have also been considered for wireless networks to model user transition between wireless access points [18, 27]. Similarly, there have also been attempts to capture the periodicity of human mobility using GPS position traces [20, 33] which are mostly governed by the physical embedding of road networks [16]. While GPS and wireless networking data allow for constantly tracing the user location, such studies have been limited to a relatively small number of users and small geographic areas (e.g., university campus). In contrast, our cell phone data covers two million users of a large country and check-ins from location-based social networks span the entire planet.

2. CHARACTERISTICS OF CHECK-INS

We use three different datasets that capture human mobility. First we consider two online location-based social networks. We collected all the public check-in data between Feb. 2009 and Oct. 2010 for Gowalla and Apr. 2008 to Oct. 2010 for Brightkite. The total number of check-ins for Gowalla is 6.4 million and 4.5 million for Brightkite. Gowalla and Brightkite also contain an explicit social network. In Gowalla the friendships are undirected and in Brightkite they are directed. For simplicity, we consider Brightkite as an undirected friendship network by only considering bi-directional edges. There are 196,591 nodes, 950,327 edges in Gowalla and 58,228 nodes, 214,078 edges in Brightkite.

To ensure that our observations on human movement are not specific to data based on check-ins from location-based social networks, we also include a dataset of cell phone location trace data. The cell phone dataset comes from a major cell phone service provider in Europe, and consists of nearly two million users and 450 million phone calls users over the course of 455 days. For each call, the nearest cell phone tower of both the person making and receiving the call was recorded. Overall, this means we have nearly 900 million "check-ins" with a spatial accuracy of about 3km. We only consider check-ins that happened within the country, and we create social network ties between pairs of people that have both called each other at least five times (10 calls total), yielding a network on 2 million nodes and 4.5 million edges.

In the remainder of the paper we will use word "check-in" to refer to an event when the time and the location of a particular user is recorded. For location-based social networks, this means that a user checked-in to a specific location using the online social network website/application, and for cell phone data this means a user either initiated or received a phone call. In all our plots we show Brightkite data in blue, Gowalla in red, and cell phone data in green.

Check-in behavior of users. In the following sections we analyze spatial and social characteristics of user check-ins. We are interested in understanding how far from their homes people tend to travel and how likely are they to meet social network friends at locations that they travel to. As user home locations are not explicitly given, we infer them by discretizing the world into 25 by 25km cells and defining the home location as the average position of check-ins in the cell with the most check-ins [29]. Manual inspection shows that this infers home locations with 85% accuracy.

First, we measure how far from their homes users tend to travel. Figure 1 plots the number of check-ins as a function of the distance from home for Brightkite, Gowalla and the cell phones. We observe that the distributions follow a power law with exponential cutoff in which there is an interesting kink at around 100km. The distribution decays faster for the travel of less than 100km and then flattens out for long distance jumps. We fit the power law parameters using

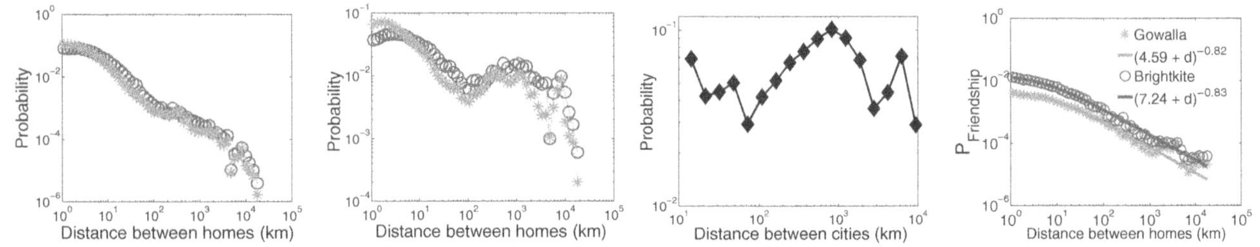

(a) Friends (b) All users (c) 200 largest cities (d) Probability of friendship

Figure 2: Distribution of home distances between (a) friends and (b) all users. (c) Distance between 200 world's largest cities. (d) Probability of friendship as a function of distance when one accounts for non-uniform population density.

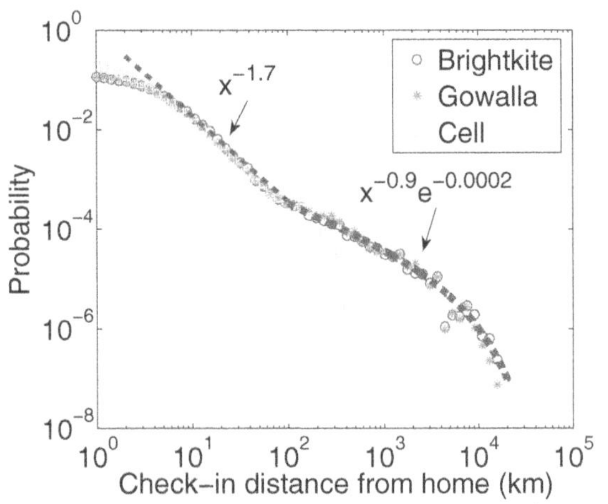

Figure 1: Fraction of check-ins as a function of distance traveled from home. Note the change in slope at around 100km.

maximum likelihood [3] and note a clear distinction in the power law exponents (1.7 vs 0.9) at around the 100km mark. Another interesting observation is that the distributions are extremely similar for all datasets. While Brightkite and Gowalla include check-ins from the whole world, cell phone data drops off quicker due to the small size of the country.

The distinct change of the distribution at the 100km mark can be explained by the non-uniform population density. We calculate the distribution of distances between the homes of friends in Fig. 2(a) and observe a similar kink at around 100km, which shows that the probability of two friends living a certain distance away decreases quickly at first but then slows down after the distance between the homes increases above 100km. Moreover, if we examine the distribution of distances between homes of random pairs of users in Fig. 2(b) we note an even stronger change around the 100km mark. As the number of pairs of people living closer than 100km decreases quickly with the distance, the distribution increases/flattens after the 100km mark. This abrupt change at 100km can be explained by the fact that users are geographically non-uniformly spread over the Earth and that humans cluster in cities. Interestingly, this suggests that around 100km is the typical human radius of "reach" [26] as it takes about 1 to 2 hours to drive such distance. For example, Fig. 2(c) shows distribution of distances between 200 of the world's largest cities. The distribution of city distances follows a qualitatively similar pattern as the distances between pairs of users. We correct for this geographic non-uniformity and calculate the probability that a user has a friend at particular distance in Fig. 2(d). Now the kink at 100km disappears and the probability of friendship drops as a power law with an exponent of around 0.85 [1, 24]. This is interesting as it demonstrates that the kink at 100km is not due to some inherent property of our social interactions but is rather the effect of non-uniform population density, where human population clusters in circles that are more than 100km apart.

3. FRIENDSHIP AND MOBILITY

So far, we examined how far from their homes people tend to travel and investigated the presence of the kink at the 100km mark. Now, we focus on the interaction of the person's social network structure and their mobility.

Moving close to a friend's home. We begin by investigating the sociability of human movement by measuring how likely is person A to travel close to the home of her friend B. We aim to understand how the location of A's friend B affects movement of A. We examine the fraction of check-ins that are in the vicinity of B's home. Intuitively we expect that people are more likely to move to a place in which they have friends, and that this likelihood decreases as the distance of travel increases. So far we saw that most of our friends live geographically close to us, and thus we would expect that they impact our movement the most. However, as we will see later, this is not the case.

To quantify this effect we proceed as follows. We say that user A "visits" her friend B if A checks-in within radius r of B's home, and we aim to compute $P_{data}(d)$, which measures the probability that A visits a friend given that A travels distance d from home. Quantity $P_{data}(d)$ is simply the fraction of A's check-ins at distance d from her home that occur in radius r (we set $r = 25km$) of one of A's friends. We experimented with various values of r and observed consistent behaviors.

Solid lines in Figure 3(a) plot $P_{data}(d)$, the fraction of friend visiting check-ins as a function of the distance traveled from home. Notice that both Gowalla and Brightkite exhibit similar behavior in that the probability of visiting a friend's home levels off to a value of 0.3 after the 100km mark. This means that if a user travels more than 100km from her home, then there is a 30% chance that they will jump close to an existing friend's home. Moreover, we observe that the probability of visiting a friend's home remains constant after the 100km mark. The number of possible locations one can visit increases with the distance, and the number of friends decreases with the distance as well. This suggests that the probability of visiting a friend would decrease with the distance traveled (more possible locations to visit and less friends, and thus smaller probability of visiting a friend). Interestingly, we observe that the probability of visiting a friend remains constant as a function of distance traveled. We consider this surprising as it suggests that the effect friends have on the our movement grows with their distance from us. To more precisely establish this we next compare the effect of friends on our movement to a null model that ignores the social network structure, and we then establish a causal relationship between the social network and mobility.

We compare the fraction of friend visiting check-ins $P_{data}(d)$ to a null model, $P_{null}(d)$, which quantifies the probability that a

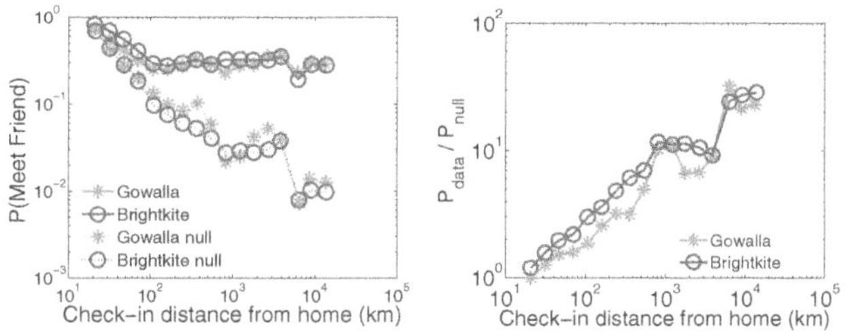

(a) (b)

Figure 3: (a) Probability that a user will travel to friend's home as a function of distance traveled. (b) Influence of a friend relative to the null model.

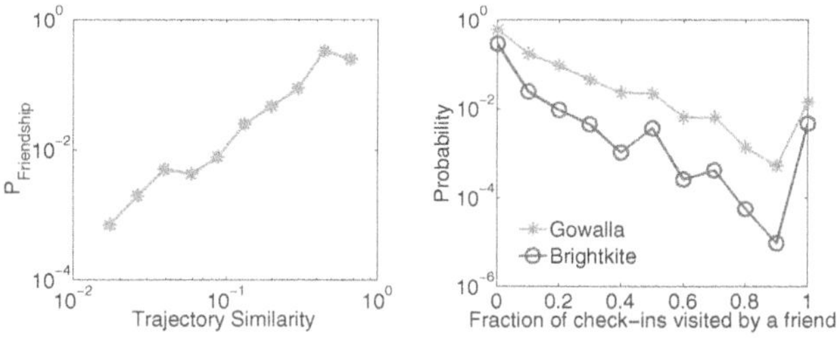

(a) (b)

Figure 4: (a) Check-in similarity and probability of friendship. (b) Fraction of check-ins that were visited by a friend before a user checked-in at that same location.

friend will be within the vicinity of a user if the user would travel "randomly". We consider the case where the user moves randomly with respect to the overall population density and measure the probability that a user travels to the vicinity of her friend's home. We plot $P_{null}(d)$ in Figure 3(a) using dashed lines, and (as expected) we observe a strong monotonic decrease. This means if people traveled independent of the network structure (but according to the overall population density) then the farther away they move from home the less likely they are to visit a friend's home. Additionally, in Fig. 3(b) we compare the real data with the null model to quantify the relative effect of friends on a user's movement. We observe that the actual influence of a friend on a user making a long distance jump increases with the distance. For example, the relative influence of a friend who lives 1,000km away is 10 times greater than the influence of a friend who lives 40km away. We also considered a version of the null model where users travel the exact same distance from home as in the real data but in a random direction. In this case we observe an even stronger effect of the social network on human mobility.

Influence of friends on an individual's mobility. We just observed a surprising increase of the effect of distant friends on an individual's mobility. However, so far we can only conclude that the relative correlation between one's travels and locations of her friends' homes increases with the distance traveled. Since friendships could have been created before or after the movement of a user, there are two possible explanations for this phenomena. If friendships are created first, then the explanation is that friendships influence where people travel. However, if movement precedes tie creation then it is traveling that influences/creates our social networks.

To distinguish between an existing friendship causing a user to move to a certain location and a movement to a certain place that then causes a formation of a new friendship, we obtained the Gowalla social network at two different time points t_1 and t_2 approximately three months apart. Comparing the network structure and check-ins between times t_1 and t_2 allows us to measure the degree of causality in each direction. We measure the effect of a user's existing friendship on her mobility by examining a set of check-ins C_a that occurred one day after time t_1. Using check-ins in C_a we then measure what fraction of them occurred within the vicinity of friend's home, i.e., in radius $r = 25$ from one of the existing friends' homes. Since the network only contains edges created before time t_1 this quantifies the degree of influence of existing social network ties on future movement of a user. Similarly, we also examine the influence of mobility on creating new social network ties by examining a set of check-ins C_b on a day before time t_1. We then count what fraction of check-ins in C_b led to creation of new friendships in the next three month period. We consider the mobility of user A to cause formation of a friendship (A, B) if at least one of A's check-ins in the set C_b occurred within radius r ($r = 25km$) of B's home. Since the check-in preceded the formation of the social network tie we can consider this as the influence of movement on social network tie creation.

Performing the experiment on Gowalla we find that on average there is a 61% probability that a user will visit a home of an existing friend. However, the probability that a check-in will lead to a new formation of a new friendship is 24%. Basically, the influence of friendship on individual's mobility is about 2.5 times greater than the influence of mobility on creating friendships. We also performed a similar experiment using the cell phone data and consistently observed very similar behavior. We considered pairs of people living more than 100km apart and found that the probability of meeting an existing friend at a particular location is 70% higher than the probability of mobility creating new network ties.

Moving to where a friend has checked-in before. So far we examined the movement of A while we kept the locations of her friends B fixed, i.e., we only considered A going close to B's home. Now we extend the setting and consider the case where both A and her friends B are simultaneously moving and we are interested in various aspects of the probability that they meet. Social check-in data gives us the exact location (e.g., the name of the coffee shop) a user has visited. We perform a similar set of experiments as before and examine the fraction of the user's check-ins have been visited by at least one of her friends prior to the user's first check-in to that specific place. We also devise a null model and make very similar observations as before. We find that the farther away a user travels the more likely that movement is influenced by a friend. The amount that friendship influences movement when traveling long distances (longer than 1,000km) is an order of magnitude higher than the influence when traveling short distances (shorter than 25km). Again, we also observe that for movement farther than 100km from home the probability of checking-in at the exact same location as a friend has checked-in in the past remains constant at around 10%. (We omit the plots due to brevity.)

Limits of using friendship for predicting mobility. Although we have shown the increasing influence of friends on one's mobility, only 9.6% of all check-ins in Gowalla and 4.1% of all check-ins in Brightkite were first visited by a friend and then by the user. To further explore this we now study the limits of using friendship for predicting human mobility. We observe strong correspondence between the trajectory similarity of users and probability of friendship. However, we also show that in general only a small fraction of users have a high overlap in check-ins with their friends.

Here, we explore the connection between trajectory similarly of a pair of users and the probability that they are connected in the social network. For each user we create a trajectory vector where the i-th component counts the number of times the user checked-in to location i. We then define trajectory similarity between a pair

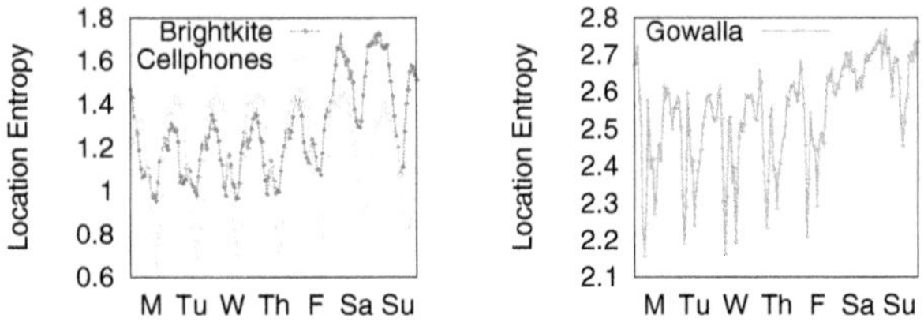

(a) Brightkite and Cellphones (b) Gowalla

Figure 5: Average entropy of check-in locations over time. Notice periodicity and low location entropy in the mornings.

of users as the cosine similarity between corresponding trajectory vectors. Fig. 4(a) shows the probability of friendship as a function of trajectory similarity. We observe strong dependency between the two quantities, e.g., when a pair of users has more than 40% of check-ins in common then the friendship probability is above 0.3. We consider this a strong presence of social and geographical homophily [25].

Although we have shown a strong correlation between trajectory similarity and friendship, users have to have a certain amount of check-in overlap in order for the trajectory similarity to be meaningful. To investigate this we compute the fraction of each user's check-in locations that were previously visited by a friend and then plot the distribution of this quantity in Fig. 4(b). We observe that the majority of the users have zero check-ins that were previously checked-in by a friend. In Gowalla, 84% of users have less than 20% of their check-ins that were previously visited by a friend, and 52% of the users have zero check-ins that were previously visited by a friend. This means that for about 50% of the users there is basically no information about their mobility that could be inferred from their social network.

Temporal and geographic periodicity of human movement. Our investigations of the effects of social network on human mobility so far have given mixed results. On one hand we found that social network influences long distance travel more than short distance travel, while on the other hand, we also observed that a relatively small fraction of user check-ins were previously checked-in by a friend. We now turn our attention to the non-social factors of human mobility. In particular, we explore periodicity (both temporal and geographical) of human mobility. Intuitively we expect that certain types of locations, such as home and work, are visited regularly, and often during the same times of the day.

One way to quantify the periodicity is to measure the fraction of user check-ins that are visits to previously already visited locations. We observe that 53% of all check-ins in Brightkite (31% in Gowalla) have been previously visited by the same user. This means that if a user checks-in into a place for the first time, there is 53% chance she might return and check-in again. On the other hand, the effect of the social network is about 5 times smaller, i.e., as we have shown before there is only a 10% chance that a user will check-in to a place where a friend has checked-in before.

Last, we also explore the connection between geographic and temporal periodicity. Figure 5 plots the average Shannon entropy of check-in locations for each hour of the week. The lower the entropy, the lower the variability of check-ins during that time period. We observe the periodicity on both the 24 hour and the 7 day scale. For all days, the early morning hours have the lowest location entropy (i.e., most people are at home). Location entropy increases when people are commuting during the rush hour and in the evening when they might be out socializing. During the work week entropy is lower compared to that of the weekend (at least for the Brightkite and Gowalla data). This suggests that people are commuting to and from work at roughly the same time during the work week, as opposed to the weekend when peoples' travel and schedules are less predictable.

4. MODEL OF HUMAN MOBILITY

In the following section we develop a model of human mobility that can accurately predict future movements of an individual. Our results so far have given strong evidence of geographic (returning to the same places) and temporal (traveling at regular times of the day) periodicity as well as the increasing relative effect of the social network structure on an individual's mobility. We proceed by formulating a coherent model that incorporates the three essential ingredients of human mobility: temporally and geographically periodic movement with the social network structure. First, we present the *Periodic Mobility Model* (*PMM*) that we later extend to *Periodic & Social Mobility Model* (*PSMM*) to also account for the mobility due to the social network structure.

***Periodic Mobility Model* (*PMM*)**. We build on the intuition that the majority of human movement is based on periodic movement between a small set of latent states (locations). For simplicity we introduce the model using just two latent states (even though our model can handle an arbitrary number of them). One can simply think of the two latent states as "work" and "home". Depending on the time of the day, an individual's movements will either be centered around home, work, or somewhere in between the two locations as they "commute" in between them.[1] Fig. 6 illustrates the model: (a) for each user we infer the centers of geographic locations of two latent states and model them with a gaussian distribution; (b) we model the probability of whether the user is in the home/work state as a function of the time of day. Fig. 6(a) shows a user in San Francisco that lives in the Mission (red crosses) and works in the Financial district (blue circles). For each check-in, we infer whether it was generated while in the home or work state, and the squares denote the geographic center of home/work check-ins. Fig. 6(b) illustrates the temporal model of how the user transitions between the two states with the distance from the center of the circle being proportional to the probability that a user resides in that state (user stays at "home" overnight (blue) and at "work" (red) during the day).

We can also think of our model in a generative way. A user determines the location of her check-in in the following way: given the time of the day, the user first samples whether she is in the "home" or "work" state (Fig. 6(b)). Then, depending on the state the user samples the geographic position of her check-in from the appropriate home/work location distribution (Fig. 6(a)).

We now proceed by formally introducing the *PMM* model. Let t be the current time of the day and let $x_u(t)$ denote the geographic position of user u at time t. Let $c_u(t)$ be the "state" at time t, where $c_u(t) = H$ denotes that the user is in the "home" state at time t, and $c_u(t) = W$ indicates the user is in the "work" state. The spatial location of user's check-ins is then governed by the appropriate home/work check-in location distribution $P\left[x(t) = x | c_u(t)\right]$. The probability distribution over the locations of a user at time t is simply the mixture of "home" and "work" location distributions where mixing coefficients are governed by the temporal model (belief over the current state of the user):

$$\begin{aligned} P\left[x(t) = x\right] =& P\left[x_u(t) = x | c_u(t) = H\right] \cdot P\left[c_u(t) = H\right] \\ &+ P\left[x_u(t) = x | c_u(t) = W\right] \cdot P\left[c_u(t) = W\right]. \end{aligned}$$

[1]Note that geographic locations of latent states are unknown and we have to infer them. Also, the latent states simply correspond to latent positions around which most check-ins are centered. We name the states "home" and "work" for easier exposition.

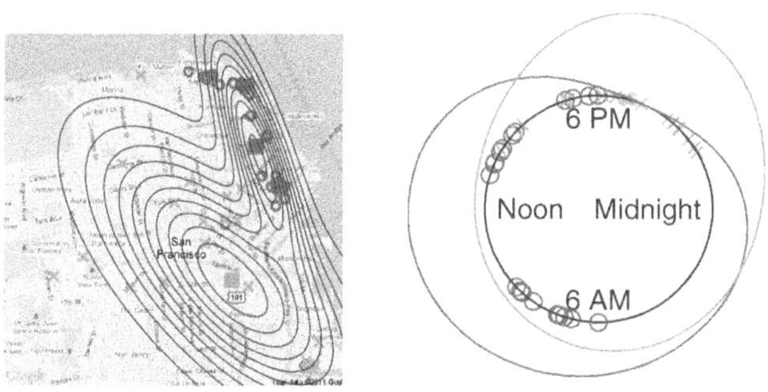

(a) Spatial model (b) Temporal model

Figure 6: (a) Check-ins of a user in San Francisco: geographic distribution of check-ins when in home/work state. (b) Temporal model: distance to the red/blue line from the center is proportional the prob. of user being in home/work state.

This means that at any point in time a user is either in "home" or "work" state and $P\left[c_u(t)\right]$ models the probability distribution over the state of the user over time. We then maintain the distribution over possible check-in locations independently for both states.

Temporal component of the *PMM* model. We model $P\left[c_u(t)\right]$, the probability distribution over the state of the user, with a truncated Gaussian distribution parameterized by the time of the day:

$$N_H(t) = \frac{P_{c_H}}{\sqrt{2\pi\sigma_H^2}} \exp\left[-\left(\frac{\pi}{12}\right)^2 \frac{(t-\tau_H)^2}{2\sigma_H^2}\right]$$

$$N_W(t) = \frac{P_{c_W}}{\sqrt{2\pi\sigma_W^2}} \exp\left[-\left(\frac{\pi}{12}\right)^2 \frac{(t-\tau_W)^2}{2\sigma_W^2}\right]$$

and then

$$P\left[c_u(t) = H\right] = \frac{N_H(t)}{N_H(t) + N_W(t)}$$

$$P\left[c_u(t) = W\right] = \frac{N_W(t)}{N_H(t) + N_W(t)}$$

where τ_H is the average time of the day when a user is in the "home" state, σ_H is the variance in time of day, and P_{c_H} is the time-independent probability that any given check-in was generated by the "home" state. It should be noted that special consideration is needed when calculating τ_H because we are treating the time of day as cyclical, i.e., 11:59pm and 12:01am are only two minutes apart. Therefore, τ_H and τ_W are calculated in the same manner as an average of angles about a circle. For example, Figure 7(b) shows the probability distribution over the state (blue:home, red:work) of the user as a function of the time of the day.

Spatial component of the *PMM* model. Many previous papers [12, 2] have used normal distributions to model human movement around a particular point. We adopt this by modeling the movement when a user is in the home/work state using a 2-dimensional time-independent Gaussian distribution:

$$P\left[x_u(t) = x_i | c_u(t)\right] = \begin{cases} \sim \mathcal{N}(\mu_H, \Sigma_H) & \text{if } c_u(t) = H \\ \sim \mathcal{N}(\mu_W, \Sigma_W) & \text{if } c_u(t) = W \end{cases}$$

where Σ_H, Σ_W are the "home", "work" check-in position covariance matrices. μ_H and μ_W are the means of user's check-in locations when she is in home and work state, respectively.

Our model is effectively a two-state mixture of Gaussians with a time-dependent state prior. This means that our model classifies each of the user's check-ins as either being generated by the "home" or "work" state. The temporal part of the model governs the transition between home/work states and then depending on the state geographic location of the check-in is generated the time-varying mixture of two time-invariant 2-dimensional Gaussian distributions. Figure 8 shows distribution of user location over time.

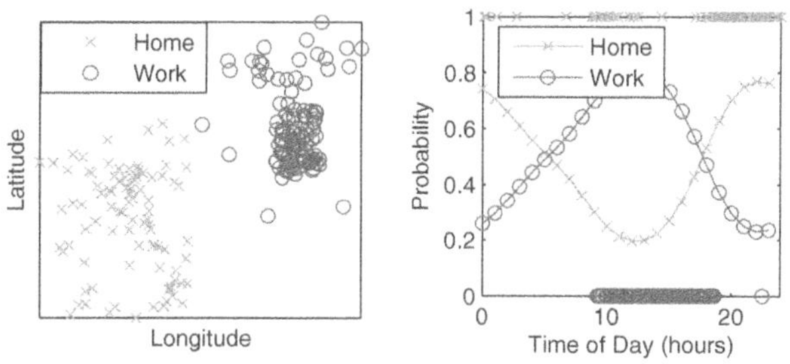

(a) Location of user check-ins (b) Home/work state

Figure 7: *Periodic Mobility Model.* (a) Check-in locations generated by home/work state. (b) State distribution over time.

***Periodic & Social Mobility Model* (*PSMM*)**. Next, we extend the *Periodic Mobility Model* with social network-driven mobility. We refer to the new model as *Periodic & Social Mobility Model* (*PSMM*). To include the social network information to the model, we introduce another check-in classification $z_u(t)$, where $z_u(t) = 1$ implies the check-in is social (non-periodic) and $z_u(t) = 0$ implies that it is periodic. The *PSMM* mobility model then becomes:

$$\begin{aligned} P_u[x(t) = x] = &P[x(t) = x | z_u(t) = 1] \cdot P[z_u(t) = 1] \\ &+ P[x(t) = x | z_u(t) = 0] \cdot P[z_u(t) = 0] \end{aligned}$$

where $P[x(t) = x | z_u(t) = 0]$ is the *Periodic Mobility Model*.

Given that user u makes a social check-in (i.e., social network influenced check-in), the probability that u will check-in at a certain place x_i is determined by two factors: how long since a friend, say w, has checked in, and the distance of w's check-in to x_i. We model this as follows:

$$P[x_u(t) = x_i | z(t) = 1] \sim \sum_{(t_j, x_j) \in J_u} |t_j - t|^{-\alpha} \cdot ||x_i - x_j||^{-\beta}$$

where J_u is the set of check-ins by user u's friends made on the same day. t_j denotes the time and x_j is the location of the j-th checkin by u's friends. The particular power-law parametric forms are motivated by the following observations: the probability user u checking-in Δt time units after w has checked-in decays as power-law (Fig. 9(a)) and Fig. 9(b) shows that the distribution of the distance between two friends at the time of a cell phone call also decays as power law. From the modeling perspective this means that if user u performs a social check-in then it will more likely be close in space and in time to one of her friend's check-ins.

Fitting *PMM* and *PSMM* models. First, we describe how to fit the parameters of the *PMM* independent of the social network and then consider the fitting of social check-ins. The parameters of the model are fitted using Expectation-Maximization (EM). To begin, each check-in is randomly labeled as either a "home" or "work" check-in. At each iteration, first the model parameters μ, Σ, τ, and σ are fitted by the current labeling using maximum likelihood estimation. This parameter fitting is known as the "E-step." All of these parameters MLE's have closed-form solutions, making this step very efficient. Once the model parameters have been fitted, the check-ins are reassigned to the state (home/work) according to the new model density function. This labeling reassignment is known as the "M-step". With this new check-in labeling, the "E-step" is once again performed, and iterations continue until convergence. Since EM is known to only converge to local optima, we re-run the algorithm using several different random initial assignment of check-in labels and take the fit with the highest likelihood.

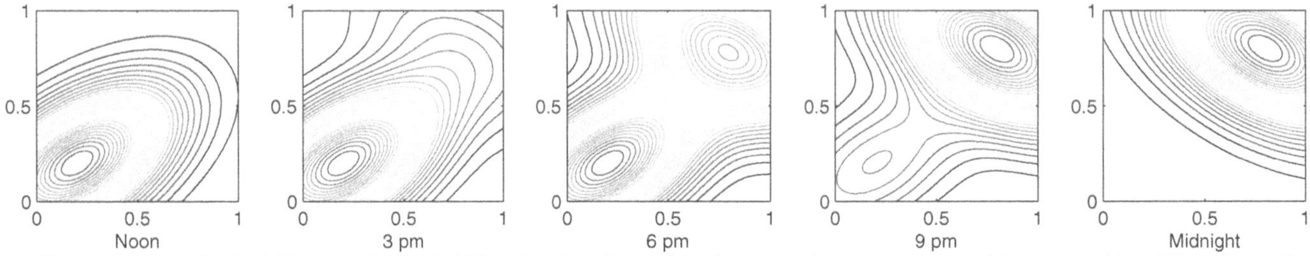

Figure 8: *Periodic Mobility Model*: Probability density of user location over time as user transitions from "work" to "home".

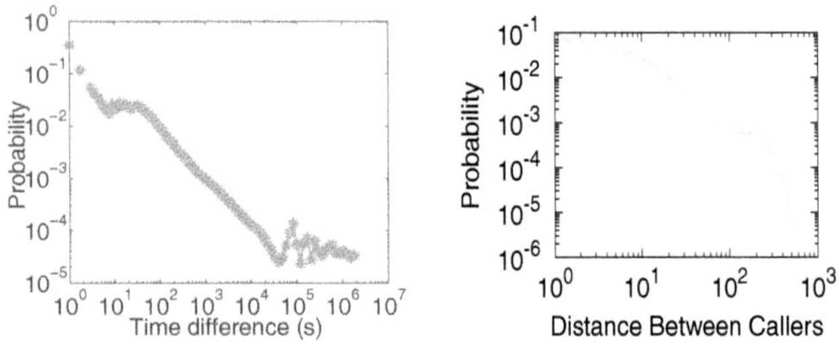

(a) Time decay (b) Distance decay

Figure 9: Temporal and spatial properties of check-ins: (a) Time since last friend has checked-in to the same place. (b) Distance between two users at the time of a call.

PMM has 18 parameters: 4 parameters for temporal model (mean and variance of time when the home/work state occurs), 12 for the spatial model (two 2-d means and corresponding covariance matrices) and 2 parameters for the social model (time and distance decay). In order to prevent overfitting we use several regularizations: we impose a minimum singular value of 10^{-7} on Σ (usually, this value is naturally several orders of magnitude larger), and we bound the temporal variance σ to be above 10^{-4}.

We fit *PSMM* as follows. We train the original *PMM* model where we allow a check-in to be classified as "home", "work" or "outlier" (i.e., social) check-in. Thus we assume that check-ins that are not fit well with the periodic model are the result of social activity. We then fit the social model to these "outlier" check-ins. Overall, 10%-30% of all check-ins are classified as social check-ins. The relabeling of the social check-ins and the fitting of the model parameters α and β is done for each user through EM.

5. EXPERIMENTAL EVALUATION

In the following section, we evaluate the proposed *PMM* and *PSMM* models on all three datasets. In particular, we are interested in the predictive performance of the models, i.e., given the time of the day we aim to as accurately as possible predict the geographic location of the user. We consider three evaluation metrics and three strong baseline location prediction methods for comparison.

Evaluation metrics. To compare different mobility models, we use the following evaluation metrics. First, we consider the average log-likelihood of the check-ins in the unseen test set. This measures how well the test set fits the model. The second metric we consider is predictive accuracy, i.e., given the time of day of a check-in in the test set, how accurately can each model predict the exact location of the check-in. For example, accuracy of 0.5 means that 50% of the time the model correctly predicts the exact check-in location (out of all known locations). Accuracy is a very harsh metric. For example, if a model would always predict the true location with exactly 1 meter error, the accuracy of such model would be zero. The third performance metric we consider is the Expected Distance Error, which can be considered a soft version of accuracy in that it does not insist on predicting the exact location, and it takes into account the spatial proximity of predictions to actual check-ins. We define Expected Distance Error as follows. For a given check-in in the test set, we measure expected distance between the check-in and a check-in generated from the model's probability distribution:

$$d(P) = \frac{1}{|C_{te}|} \sum_{c \in C_{te}} E_{P(x)} [||x_c - x||] = \frac{1}{|C_{te}|} \sum_{c \in C_{te}} \int_x ||x_c - x|| \cdot P(x) dx.$$

Since it is computationally infeasible to calculate the exact expected distance error across each point on the entire globe, we compute the error over all locations ever checked-in by the user.

One issue with this metric is that it does not consider the typical distance a user travels. Thus, using the expected error distance metric to compare the performance of a model across two different users is uninformative if the two users travel on different scales. For example, if user typically travels 1,000km then an average distance error of 10km is much more acceptable than the same error for someone who typically travels only 20km. To correct for this we normalize the error by the radius of gyration [12], which is the average distance a user travels on a particular day. For the expected distance error of each user, we divide it by the user's radius of gyration for that particular day of the week, creating the *relative* expected distance error.

Baseline models. We also consider three non-trivial baseline models for comparison. The first baseline, which we refer to as the *Most Frequented Location Model* (*MF*) assigns the probability of a user checking-in at a location x_c during a given hour of the day h_c as the fraction of previous check-ins during that hour h_c that were at location x_c. More precisely, let C_u be the set of all check-ins of user u, then the Most Frequented Location Model is

$$P_M[x_u(t) = x | t \in h] = \frac{|\{c | c \in C_u, x_c = x, h_c = h\}|}{|\{c | c \in C_u, h_c = h\}|}.$$

Despite its simplicity, this model is a very strong baseline. For every hour of the day the *MF* predicts the most likely (most often checked-in) location of a particular user. The model is also very intuitive as it imitates the following reasoning: Assume that you are asked to guess the location of a friend at 2pm on a Wednesday. If you knew their place of work, you would be able to pin point them with a high level of certainty. Similarly, if you knew the location of your friend's most frequented happy hour spot, locating them at 6pm on a Friday would be easy as well. In fact, if a user is perfectly periodic, then as $|C_u| \to \infty$, P_M will converge to the true underlying model. What this model lacks (and what our model corrects) is that it does not consider distance or the spatial proximity of locations.

The second baseline, the *Gaussian Model* (*G*), has been proposed by Gonzales et al. [12]. It models human movement as a stochastic process centered around a single point. For a given day of the week, let μ_x be the mean location of check-ins that occurred on that day of the week, and let Σ_x be the covariance matrix:

$$P_M[x_u(t) = x] \sim \mathcal{N}(\mu_x, \Sigma_x).$$

Note that this model is static in time and captures the scale of a user's movements more than anything else.

Lastly, we also consider a model that could potentially have very good performance. The *RW* model always predicts the next location of a user to be the location of her last known check-in location.

Experimental setup. In all our experiments we only consider users that had at least 10 check-ins on each day of the week. We put 80% of their check-ins in the training set and the remaining 20% in the test set. This means that we evaluate the models on 6,233 Brightkite, 10,997 Gowalla, and 853,812 Cellphone users. For each user we build 7 models, one for each day of the week. Overall, this means that at minimum we use only 8 check-ins (on a particular day) to build a model and remaining 2 to test the model.

Predicting mobility. First, we compare the performance of the periodic *PMM* model with the performance of the baselines. For brevity we only discuss results for Brightkite and Cellphones.

Figure 10(a) shows the accuracy for all four models for Brightkite. The Gaussian model (*G*), proposed by Gonzalez [12], performs worst with an average accuracy of 19.7%, predicting last known location of the user (*RW*) gives 22.7% accuracy, while the most frequent location model (*MF*) scores 32.5%. Our model gives an 83.1% improvement over the Gaussian model and 11.0% relative improvement over the *MF* model. Furthermore, *PMM* can determine the *exact* location of a check-in up to 40% of the time. Considering how much noise is in the data and the large number of different locations a user visits, we consider this a remarkable result. Interestingly we also observe that all models exhibit better performance on weekdays while predicting user location is harder on the weekends.

Similarly, Fig. 10(b) shows the accuracy for the Cellphones. We make similar observations. Again, *PMM* does 110.9% and 44.3% better than the *G* and *RW* models, respectively, with overall accuracy of 42%. However, the difference between *PMM* and *MF* is smaller. This is due to the coarser spatial resolution of the cellphone data: mobility is captured in coarser detail and thus less location "smoothing" is needed.

Figures 10(c) and 10(d) give results for test data log-likelihood evaluation metric. The Gaussian model (*G*) performs far the worst, with the *PMM* outperforming the two baselines on both datasets. (*RW* is not included because it has no density function.)

Last, Figures 10(e) and 10(f) display the Relative Expected Distance Error for the four models. Average relative distance error of *PMM* is 2.9% on Brightkite and 0.27% on cellphones. Overall, this is 55.6% better than Gaussian model, 28.9% better than last location model (RW) and 27.4% better than most-frequent location model (MF). In absolute terms, the average absolute location error of *PMM* is about 10km on Cellphones and 90km on Brightkite.

Predictive performance of the social model. For both average log-likelihood and the relative expected distance error, *PSMM* provides considerable improvement over *PMM* for both Brightkite and Cellphones — about a 10% relative improvement for the relative expected distance error and about a 25% relative improvement for log-likelihood. We expect that with denser data sets (more check-in data), the occurrence of two friends checking-in at the exact same place will become more frequent, and then *PSMM* will yield even higher improvement over the periodic model.

Similarity of daily mobility patterns. We also quantify how similar are mobility patterns during different days of the week. We establish this using the following model "similarity" metric: Let

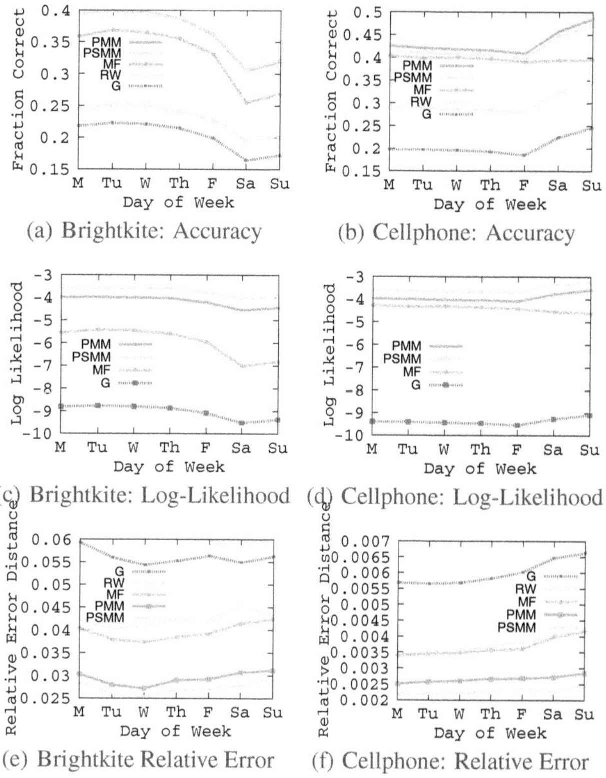

(a) Brightkite: Accuracy (b) Cellphone: Accuracy (c) Brightkite: Log-Likelihood (d) Cellphone: Log-Likelihood (e) Brightkite Relative Error (f) Cellphone: Relative Error

Figure 10: Performance of the *Periodic Mobility Model* (*PMM*) and the *Periodic & Social Mobility Model* (*PSMM*), compared to three baseline models. (a,b) Accuracy of check-in location prediction; (c,d) Log-likelihood of check-ins in the test set; (e,f) Expected Distance Error of predicted check-in location.

C_1 and C_2 represent two different sets of check-ins, and let P_1 and P_2 be the *PMM* fitted to these two sets. Then we define

$$S(P_1, P_2) = \frac{\sum_{c \in C_1 \cup C_2} P_1(c) \cdot P_2(c)}{\sqrt{\sum_{c \in C_1 \cup C_2} P_1(c)^2}\sqrt{\sum_{c \in C_1 \cup C_2} P_2(c)^2}}.$$

S measure is analogous to covariance sampled at a subset of points. S measure can compare any two *PMM* models, whether they are models for different days of the week for one user, or the same day of the week for two different users. $S(P_1, P_2) = 1$ if $P_1 = P_2$.

Figure 11 represents the average S between the models for each day of the week for high volume users of (a) Brightkite and (b) Cellphones. The work days show strong correlation with each other, but less correlation with the weekend days. Similarly, the weekend days (Saturday and Sunday) show a stronger correlation with each other than they do with the other days. This implies that even in the absence of a commute to and from work, there is still periodic structure to human movement.

Number of latent states. So far we only considered the model with two latent states ("home" and "work") but it seems very natural to consider richer models with additional latent states. Indeed, when 3, 4, etc. latent states are used (each latent state with its own spacial Gaussian and temporal periodic prior) the accuracy of the model increases. For each latent state that is added, however, the returns are diminishing. Even the performance gained by adding the third latent state to the model is minor compared to the difference between the two state model and a single state model. For example, the average accuracy across all days of the week for Brightkite is 19.7% using a single state model, whereas the two state model

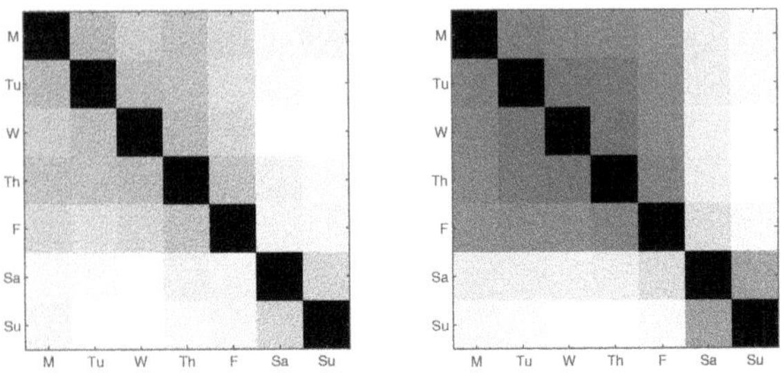

(a) Brightkite (b) Cellphones

Figure 11: Average cross-similarity between a user's periodic models constructed for each day of the week. The darker the square, the stronger the similarity. Note that the work days are more similar to each other than to the weekend days.

has an accuracy of 36.1%, which is a 83.1% relative improvement. Using a three state model only increases performance by another 3.3%. Thus we conclude that the two state "home" and "work" model is rich enough to capture the human mobility.

6. CONCLUSION

We investigated patterns of human mobility on three large but very different datasets: two sets of location-based social network check-in data spanning the whole planet and also cellphone location data. Even though location-based social networking services are very different from cell phone tower location data, we found many common patterns of human mobility across the datasets. Most surprisingly, we found that humans experience a combination of strong short range spatially and temporally periodic movement that is not impacted by the social network structure, while long-distance travel is more influenced by the social network ties.

We also developed a model of human mobility dynamics. The model combines the periodic day-to-day movement patterns with the social movement effects coming from the friendship network. Our model reliably captures and predicts human mobility patterns and outperforms current mobility models by a factor of two.

Acknowledgements

Research was in-part supported by NSF CNS-1010921, NSF IIS-1016909, Microsoft Faculty Fellowship, Albert Yu & Mary Bechmann Foundation, Intel, IBM, Lightspeed and Yahoo. Eunjoon Cho was supported by the Samsung Scholarship.

7. REFERENCES

[1] L. Backstrom, E. Sun, and C. Marlow. Find me if you can: Improving geographical prediction with social and spatial proximity. In *WWW '10*, pages 61–70, 2010.

[2] D. Brockmann, L. Hufnagel, and T. Geisel. The scaling laws of human travel. *Nature*, 2006.

[3] A. Clauset, C. R. Shalizi, and M. E. J. Newman. Power-law distributions in empirical data. *SIAM Review*, 2009.

[4] N. Couldry and A. Mccarthy. *Mediaspace: Place, Scale and Culture in a Media Age (Comedia)*. Routledge, Nov. 2003.

[5] D. Crandall, L. Backstrom, D. Cosley, S. Suri, D. Huttenlocher, and J. Kleinberg. Inferring social ties from geographic coincidences. *PNAS*, 2010.

[6] J. Cranshaw, E. Toch, J. I. Hong, A. Kittur, and N. Sadeh. Bridging the gap between physical location and online social networks. In *UbiComp*, pages 119–128, 2010.

[7] N. Eagle and A. Pentland. Eigenbehaviors: Identifying structure in routine. *Behavioral Ecology and Soc.*, 2009.

[8] N. Eagle, A. Pentland, and D. Lazer. Inferring friendship network structure by using mobile phone data. *PNAS*, 2009.

[9] S. Eubank, H. Guclu, V. S. Anil Kumar, M. V. Marathe, A. Srinivasan, Z. Toroczkai, and N. Wang. Modelling disease outbreaks in realistic urban social networks. *Nature*, 2004.

[10] E. Glaeser and M. Kahn. Sprawl and urban growth. *Handbook of regional and urban economics*, 2004.

[11] J. Goldenberg and M. Levy. Distance is not dead: Social interaction and geographical distance in the internet era. *Arxiv*, abs/0906.3202, 2009.

[12] M. C. Gonzalez, C. A. Hidalgo, and A.-L. Barabasi. Understanding individual human mobility patterns. *Nature*, 453(7196):779–782, 2008.

[13] Q. Hao, R. Cai, C. Wang, R. Xiao, J.-M. Yang, Y. Pang, and L. Zhang. Equip tourists with knowledge mined from travelogues. In *WWW '10*, pages 401–410, 2010.

[14] T. J. Hatton and J. G. Williamson. Global Migration and the World Economy: Two Centuries of Policy and Performance. The MIT Press, 2008.

[15] L. Humphreys. Mobile social networks and social practice: A case study of dodgeball. *Journal of Computer-Mediated Communication*, 2008.

[16] B. Jiang, J. Yin, and S. Zhao. Characterizing the human mobility pattern in a large street network. *Physical Review E*, 80(2):021136, Aug. 2009.

[17] A. Kapoor, N. Eagle, and E. Horvitz. People, quakes, and communications: Inferences from call dynamics about a seismic event and its influences on a population. In *AAAI Spring Symposiumg*, 2010.

[18] M. Kim, D. Kotz, and S. Kim. Extracting a mobility model from real user traces. *INFOCOM '06*, 2006.

[19] R. Lambiotte, V. Blondel, C. Dekerchove, E. Huens, C. Prieur, Z. Smoreda, and P. Vandooren. Geographical dispersal of mobile communication networks. *Physica A*, 387(21):5317–5325, Sept. 2008.

[20] K. Lee, S. Hong, S. J. Kim, I. Rhee, and S. Chong. SLAW: A new mobility model for human walks. In *INFOCOM '09*, pages 855–863, 2009.

[21] T. Leighton. Improving performance on the internet. *Queue*, 6:20–29, 2008.

[22] J. Leskovec and E. Horvitz. Planetary-scale views on a large instant-messaging network. In *WWW '08*, 2008.

[23] Z. Li, B. Ding, J. Han, R. Kays, and P. Nye. Mining periodic behaviors for moving objects. *KDD '10*, 2010.

[24] D. Liben-Nowell, J. Novak, R. Kumar, P. Raghavan, and A. Tomkins. Geographic routing in social networks. *PNAS*, 2005.

[25] M. McPherson, L. Smith-Lovin, and J. M. Cook. Birds of a feather: Homophily in social networks. *Annual Review of Sociology*, 27(1):415–444, 2001.

[26] D. Mok, B. Wellman, and J. Carrasco. Does distance matter in the age of the internet? *Urban Studies*, 47(13), 2010.

[27] A. J. Nicholson and B. D. Noble. Breadcrumbs: Forecasting mobile connectivity. In *MOBICOM '08*, pages 46–57, 2008.

[28] A. Noulas, S. Scellato, C. Mascolo, and M. Pontil. An empirical study of geographic user activity patterns in foursquare. In *ICWSM '11*, 2011.

[29] S. Scellato, A. Noulas, R. Lambiotte, and C. Mascolo. Socio-spatial properties of online location-based social networks. In *ICWSM '11*, 2011.

[30] C. Song, Z. Qu, N. Blumm, and A. Barabási. Limits of predictability in human mobility. *Science*, 2010.

[31] B. Wellman and K. Hampton. Living networked on and off line. *Contemporary Sociology*, 28(6):648–654, Nov. 1999.

[32] V. W. Zheng, Y. Zheng, X. Xie, and Q. Yang. Collaborative location and activity recommendations with GPS history data. In *WWW '10*, pages 1029–1038, 2010.

[33] Y. Zheng, L. Zhang, X. Xie, and W.-Y. Ma. Mining interesting locations and travel sequences from GPS trajectories. In *WWW '09*, pages 791–800, 2009.

GBASE: A Scalable and General Graph Management System

U Kang
Carnegie Mellon University
ukang@cs.cmu.edu

Hanghang Tong
IBM T.J. Watson
htong@us.ibm.com

Jimeng Sun
IBM T.J. Watson
jimeng@us.ibm.com

Ching-Yung Lin
IBM T.J. Watson
chingyung@us.ibm.com

Christos Faloutsos
Carnegie Mellon University
christos@cs.cmu.edu

ABSTRACT

Graphs appear in numerous applications including cyber-security, the Internet, social networks, protein networks, recommendation systems, and many more. Graphs with millions or even billions of nodes and edges are common-place. How to store such large graphs efficiently? What are the core operations/queries on those graph? How to answer the graph queries quickly? We propose GBASE, a scalable and general graph management and mining system. The key novelties lie in 1) our storage and compression scheme for a parallel setting and 2) the carefully chosen graph operations and their efficient implementation. We designed and implemented an instance of GBASE using MAPREDUCE/HADOOP. GBASE provides a parallel indexing mechanism for graph mining operations that both saves storage space, as well as accelerates queries. We ran numerous experiments on real graphs, spanning *billions* of nodes and edges, and we show that our proposed GBASE is indeed fast, scalable and nimble, with significant savings in space and time.

Categories and Subject Descriptors

H.2.8 [**Database Management**]: Database Applications—*Data Mining*

General Terms

Design, Experimentation, Algorithms

Keywords

Graph, Indexing, Compression, Distributed Computing

1. INTRODUCTION

Graphs have been receiving increasing research attention, being applicable in a wide variety of high impact applications, like social networks, cyber-security, recommendation systems, fraud/anomaly detection, protein-protein interaction networks, to name a few. In fact, *any* many-to-many database relationship can be easily treated as a graph, with myriads of additional applications (patients and symptoms; customers and locations they have been to; documents and terms in IR, etc). To add to the challenge of graph mining, even the volume of such graphs is unprecedented, reaching and exceeding billions of nodes and edges.

KDD'11, August 21–24, 2011, San Diego, California, USA.

Problem Definitions.
Our goal is to build a general graph management system in parallel, distributed settings to support billion-scale graphs for various applications. For the goal, we address the following problems:

1. *Storage.* How can we efficiently store and manage such huge graphs in parallel, distributed settings to answer graph queries efficiently? How should we split the edges into smaller units? How should we group the units into files?
2. *Algorithms.* How can we define common, core algorithms to satisfy various graph applications?
3. *Query Optimization.* How can we exploit the efficient storage and general algorithms to execute queries efficiently?

For all the problems, *scalability* is a major challenge. The size of graphs has been experiencing an unprecedented growth. For example, one of the graphs we use here, the *Yahoo Web graph* from 2002, has more than 1 *billion* nodes and almost *7 billion* edges. Similar size, or even larger graphs, exist: the Twitter graph spans several Terabytes; click-streams are reported to reach Petabyte scale [25]. Such large graphs violate the assumption that the graph can be fit in main memory or at least the disk of a single workstation, on which most of existing graph algorithms have been built. Thus, we need to re-think those algorithms, and to develop scalable, parallel ones, to manage graphs that span Tera-bytes and beyond.

Our Contributions.
We propose GBASE, a scalable and general graph management system, to address the above challenges. The main contributions are the following:

1. *Storage.* We propose a novel graph storage method called 'block compression' to efficiently store homogeneous regions of graphs. We also propose a grid based method to efficiently place blocks into files. We run our algorithm on billion-scale graphs and show that the block compression method leads up to $50\times$ less storage and faster running time. Our block compression method is agnostic to the underlying storage mechanism, which can be applied to distributed file systems as well as relational databases.
2. *Algorithms.* We identify a core graph operation, and use it to formulate *seven* different types of graph queries in-

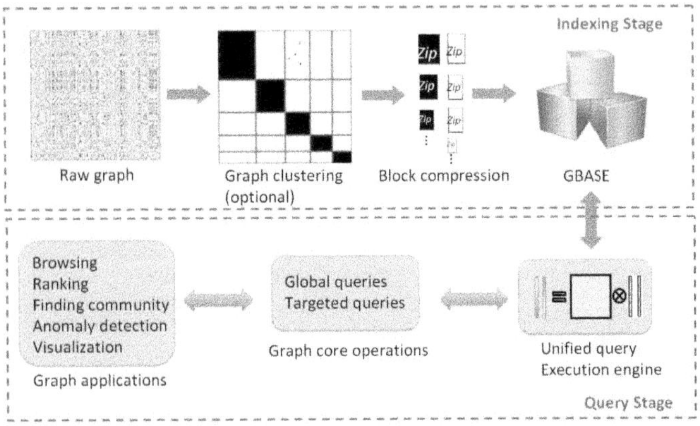

Figure 1: Overall framework of GBASE. 1. Indexing Stage: raw graph is clustered and divided into compressed blocks. 2. Query Stage: global and targeted queries from various graph applications are handled by a unified query execution engine.

cluding neighborhood, induced subgraph, egonet, K-core, and cross-edges. The novelty is in formulating edge-based queries(induced subgraph) as well as node-based queries(neighborhoods) using a unified framework.

3. *Query Optimization.* We propose a grid selection strategy to minimize disk accesses and answer queries quickly. We also propose a MAPREDUCE algorithm to support incidence matrix based queries using the original adjacency matrix, without explicitly building the incidence matrix.

The rest of this paper is organized as follows. We first present the overall framework in Section 2. We describe the storage and indexing method in Section 3, and then the query execution in Section 4. We provide experimental evaluations and comparisons in Section 5. After reviewing the related work in Section 6, we conclude in Section 7.

2. OVERALL FRAMEWORK

The overall framework of our GBASE is summarized in Figure 1. The design objective is to balance storage efficiency and query performance on large graphs. It comprises of two components: the indexing stage and the query stage. In this Section, we give a high level overview of each stage; and we will give more details in Section 3 and 4, respectively.

In the indexing stage, given the original raw graph which is stored as a big edge file, GBASE first partitions it into several homogeneous blocks. Second, according to the partition results, we reshuffle the nodes so that the nodes belonging to the same partition are put nearby. Third, we compress all non-empty block through standard compression such as GZip. Finally, we store the compressed blocks, together with some meta information (e.g., the block row id and column id, and all the encoded node ids), into the graph databases. For many real graphs, such homogeneous blocks, community-like structure, do exist. Therefore, after partition and reshuffling, the resulting blocks are either relatively dense (e.g., the diagonal blocks in Figure 1) or very sparse (e.g., the off-diagonal blocks in Figure 1). Both cases are space efficient for compression (i.e., the compression ratio is high). In the extreme case that a given block is empty, we do not store it at all. Our experiments (See Section 5) show that in some cases, we only need less than 2% storage space of the original after the indexing stage.

In the query stage, our goal is to provide a set of core operations that will be sufficient to support a diverse set of graph applications, e.g., ranking, community detection, anomaly detection, and etc. The key of the on-line query stage is the query execution engine, which unifies the different types of inputs as query vectors. It also unifies the (seemingly) different types of operations on the graph by a unified matrix-vector multiplication which we will introduce in Section 4. By doing so, GBASE is able to support multiple different types of queries simultaneously. Table 1 summarizes the queries (the first column) that are supported by GBASE. These queries construct the main building blocks for a variety of important graph applications (Table 1). For example, the diversity of RWR(Random Walk with Restart [35]) scores among the neighborhood of a given edge/node is a strong indicator of abnormality of that node/edge [34]. The ratio between the number of edges (or the summation of edge weights) and number of nodes within the egonet can help find abnormal nodes on weighted graphs [6]. The K-cores and cross-edges can be used for visualization and finding communities in large graphs.

Query \ Applications	Browsing	Ranking	Finding Community	Anomaly Detection	Visualization
Connected Comp.			✓	✓	
Radius				✓	✓
PageRank, RWR	✓	✓		✓	
Induced Subgraph	✓		✓		✓
(K)-Neighborhood	✓		✓		✓
(K)-Egonet	✓		✓	✓	✓
K-core			✓		✓
Cross-edges				✓	✓

Table 1: Applications of GBASE. Notice that GBASE answers wide range of both global(top 3 rows) and targeted queries(bottom 5 rows with bold fonts) with applications in browsing[29, 35, 24], ranking[29, 35], finding communities[20, 24], anomaly detection[34, 20, 19, 6], and visualization[24, 7].

Symbol	Definition
$\mathcal{G}$	Graph.
A	Adjacency matrix of the graph $\mathcal{G}$.
B	Incidence matrix of the graph $\mathcal{G}$.
n	Number of nodes.
m	Number of edges.
k	Number of partitions.
p, q	Partition indices, $1 \leq p, q \leq k$.
$I^{(p)}$	Set of nodes belonging to the p-th partition.
$l^{(p)}$	Partition size, $l^{(p)} \equiv \|I^{(p)}\|, 1 \leq p \leq k$.
$\mathcal{G}^{(p,q)}$	Subgraphs induced by p-th and q-th partitions.
$m^{(p,q)}$	Number of edges in $\mathcal{G}^{(p,q)}$.
$H(.)$	Shannon entropy function.

Table 2: Definitions of symbols

3. GRAPH STORAGE AND INDEXING

In this section, we describe in details the indexing and storage stage of GBASE. We use the symbols in Table 2.

3.1 Baseline Storage Scheme

A typical way to store the raw graph is to use the adjacency list format: for each node, it saves all the out-neighbors adjacent from the node. The adjacency list format is simple and might be good for answering out-neighbor queries. However, it is not efficient format for answering general queries including in-neighbor queries and ego-net queries as we will see in Section 4. For the reason, we instead use the sparse adjacency matrix format, where we save each edge by a (source,destination) pair. The advantage of the sparse adjacency matrix format is its generality and flexibility to enable efficient storage and indexing techniques as we will see later in this and the next sections.

The storage system should be designed to be efficient in both storage cost and on-line query response. To this end, we propose to index and store the graph on the homogeneous block, community-like structure, levels. Next, we will describe how to *form*, *compress* and *store/place* such blocks.

3.2 Block Formulation

The first step is to partition the graph, i.e., re-order the rows and columns, and make homogeneous regions into blocks. Partitioning algorithms form an active research area, and finding optimal partitions is orthogonal to our work. Any partition algorithms, e.g., METIS [22], Disco [30], etc, can be naturally plugged into GBASE.

Graph partitioning can be formally defined as follows. The input is the original raw graph denoted by $\mathcal{G}$. Given a graph $\mathcal{G}$, we partition the nodes into k groups. The set of nodes that are assigned into the p-th partition for $1 \leq p \leq k$ is denoted by $I^{(p)}$. The subgraph or block induced by p-th source partition and q-th destination partition is denoted as $\mathcal{G}^{(p,q)}$. The sets $I^{(p)}$ partition the nodes, in the sense that $I^{(p)} \cap I^{(p')} = \emptyset$ for $p \neq p'$, while $\bigcup_p I^{(p)} = \{1, \ldots, n\}$. In terms of storage, the objective is to find the optimal k partitions which lead to smallest total storage cost of all blocks/subgraphs $\mathcal{G}^{(p,q)}$ where $1 \leq p, q \leq k$. Intuitively, we want the induced subgraphs to be homogeneous (meaning the subgraphs are either very dense or very sparse), which captures not only community structure but also leads to small storage cost.

For many real graphs, the community/clustering structure can be naturally identified. For instance, in Web graphs, the lexicographic ordering of the URL can be used as an indicator of community [10] since there are usually more intra-domain links compared with the inter-domain links. For authorship network, the research interest is often a good indicator to find communities since authors with the same or similar research interest tend to have more collaborations. For patient-doctor graph, the patient information (e.g., geography, disease type, etc) can be used to find the communities (patients with similar disease and living in the same neighborhood have higher chance to visit the same doctor).

3.3 Block Compression

The homogeneous block representation provides a more compact representation of the original graph. It enables us to encode the graph in a more efficient way. The encoding of a block $\mathcal{G}^{(p,q)}$ consists of the following information:

- source and destination partition ID p and q;
- the set of sources $I^{(p)}$and the set of destinations $I^{(q)}$.
- the payload, the bit string of subgraph $\mathcal{G}^{(p,q)}$.

A naive way of encoding a block is *raw block encoding* which only stores the coordinates of the non-zero entries in the block. Although this method saves the storage space since the nonzero elements within the block can be encoded with a smaller number of bits ($log(\max(l^{(p)}, l^{(q)})$) than the original, the savings are not great.

To achieve better compression, we propose *zip block encoding* which converts the adjacency matrix of the subgraph into a binary string and stores the compressed string as the payload. Compared

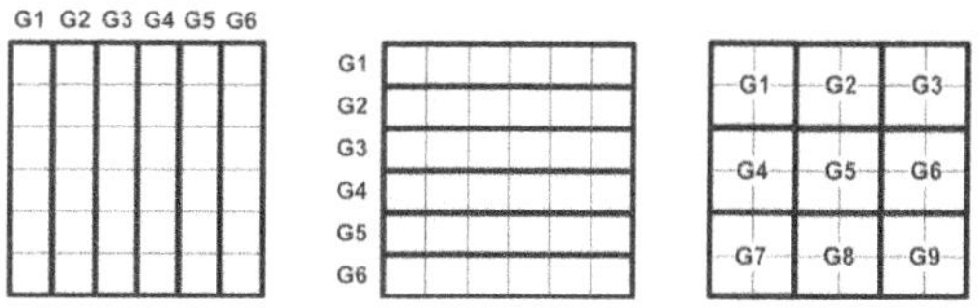

(a) Vertical Placement (b) Horizontal Placement (c) Grid Placement

Figure 2: Adjacency matrices showing possible placement of blocks into files in HADOOP. The smallest rectangle represents a block in the adjacency matrix. The placement strategy determines which of the blocks are grouped into files G1 to G6 or G9. Vertical placement in (a) is good for in-neighbor queries, but inefficient for out-neighbor or egonet queries. Horizontal placement in (b) is good for out-neighbor queries, but inefficient for in-neighbor or egonet queries. GBASE uses the grid placement, shown in (c), which is efficient for all types of queries.

to the raw block encoding, the zip block encoding requires more cpu time to zip and unzip blocks. However, the storage savings and the reduced data transfer size help to improve performance of GBASE as we will see in Section 5.

For example, we have the following adjacency matrix of a graph:

$$\mathcal{G} = \begin{pmatrix} 1 & 0 & 0 \\ 1 & 0 & 0 \\ 0 & 1 & 1 \end{pmatrix} \qquad (1)$$

raw block encoding will just store the non-zero coordinates $(0,0)$, $(1,0)$, $(2,1)$, and $(2,2)$ as the payload. Zip block encoding will converts the matrix into a binary string $110, 001, 001$ (in the column major order) and then use the compression of this string as the payload.

Storage Estimation. The storage needed for raw block encoding is $2 * m^{(p,q)} * log(max(l^{(p)}, l^{(q)}))$. The storage needed for zip block encoding is $l^{(p)} l^{(q)} H(d)$, where $d = \frac{m^{(p,q)}}{l^{(p)} l^{(q)}}$ is the density of $\mathcal{G}^{(p,q)}$. $H(\cdot)$ is the Shannon entropy function: $H(X) = -\sum_x p(x) \log p(x)$ where $p(x)$ is the probability that $X = x$. Note that the number of bits to encode an edge in zip block encoding decreases as d increases, while it is constant in raw block encoding.

3.4 Block Placement

After we compress the blocks, we need to store/place them in the file system (e.g., HDFS of HADOOP, relational DB). Here, the main idea is to place several blocks together into a file, and select only relevant files as inputs in the query stage. The question is, how do we place blocks into files? A typical approach is to use vertical placement to place the vertical blocks in a file as shown in Figure 2(a). The other alternative is to use horizontal placement to place the horizontal blocks in a file as shown in Figure 2(b). However, both of the placement techniques are good only for one type of query: for example, horizontal and vertical placement is good for out-neighbor and in-neighbor queries, respectively.

To solve the problem, GBASE uses the grid placement as shown in Figure 2(c). The advantage of the grid placement is that it can answer various types of queries efficiently as we will see in Section 4. Suppose we store all the compressed blocks in K files. With vertical/horizontal placement, we need $O(K)$ file accesses to find the in- and out-neighbors of a given query node. In contrast, we only need $O(\sqrt{K})$ files accesses with grid placement.

4. HANDLING GRAPH QUERIES

In this section, we describe query execution in GBASE. GBASE supports both "global" queries, as well as "targeted" queries for one or a few specific nodes. The answer to global queries requires traversal of the whole graph, like, e.g., diameter estimation. In contrast, "targeted" queries need to access only parts of the graph. GBASE supports seven different queries including neighborhoods, induced subgraphs, egonets, K-core, and cross-edges.

4.1 Global Queries

Global queries are performed by repeated joins of edge blocks and vector blocks. GBASE supports the following graph queries: degree distribution, PageRank, RWR("Random Walk with Restart"), radius estimations, and discovery of connected components. Our contribution here is that our proposed storage and compression scheme reduce the graph storage significantly, and enable faster running time as shown in Figure 5. The global queries also serve as primitives for targeted queries(see 'T6: K-core' in Section 4.2), enabling a variety of applications as shown in Table 1.

4.2 Targeted Queries

Many graph mining operations can be unified as matrix-vector multiplication. Here that matrix is either the adjacency matrix A of size $n \times n$ or the incidence matrix B of size $m \times n$ where n and m are the number of nodes and edges in the graph, respectively. Each row of the incidence matrix corresponds to an edge, and it has two non-zeros whose column ids are the node ids of the edge.

The matrix-vector multiplication observation has the extra benefit that it corresponds to an SQL join. Thus, graph mining could use all the highly optimized join algorithms in the literature (hash join, indexed join etc), while still leverages the proposed block compression storage scheme.

In fact, for each of the upcoming primitives, we shall first give the matrix-vector details, and then the SQL code.

T1: 1-step neighbors.

The first query is to find 1-step in-neighbors and out-neighbors of a query node v.

Matrix-Vector version

Given a query node v, its 1-step in-neighbors can be found by the following matrix-vector multiplication:

$$in^1(v) = A \times e_v, \tag{2}$$

where the matrix is the adjacency matrix of the graph A and the vector is the 'indicator vector' e_v which is the n-vector whose v-th element is 1, and all other elements are 0s. The 1-step in-neighbors of the query node v are those nodes whose corresponding values in $in^1(v)$ are 1s.

The 1-step out-neighbors can be obtained in the similar way by replacing A with its transpose A^T.

SQL version

We can also find 1-step in-neighbors and out-neighbors by the standard SQL. Assume we have a table `E(src, dst)` storing the edges, with attributes 'source' (`src`) and 'destination' (`dst`). The 1-step out-neighbors of a query node 'q' are given by

```
SELECT dst
FROM E
WHERE src='q'
```

without even requiring a join. 1-step in-neighbor can be answered in a similar way.

T2: K-step neighbors.

The next query is to find 'within k-step' neighbors. Let us only consider the k-step in-neighbors. k-step out-neighbors can be found in similar way - we only need to replace the matrix A by its transpose A^T in the matrix-vector multiplication version; and switch `src` and `dst` in the SQL version.

Matrix-Vector version

The k-step in-neighbors $nh^k(v)$ of the query node v is defined recursively by $(k-1)$-step neighbors $nh^{k-1}(v)$ in terms of matrix-vector multiplication as follows:

$$nh^k(v) = A \times nh^{k-1}(v), \tag{3}$$

where the 0-step in-neighbors $nh^0(v)$ is just the indicator vector e_v. After the k multiplications, the k-step in-neighbors are those nodes whose corresponding values in $nh^k(v)$ or $nh^{k-1}(v)$ are 1s.

SQL version

As before, assume we have a table `E` with attributes `src` and `dst`. The k-step in-neighbors can also be found by SQL join. In general, the k-step in-neighbors is a $(k-1)$-way join. For example, the 2-step in-neighbors of a query node 'q' is given by the following SQL join:

```
SELECT E2.src
FROM E as E1, E as E2
WHERE E1.dst='q'
   AND E1.src = E2.dst
```

T3: Induced subgraph.

Given a set of nodes V_q in a graph $\mathcal{G}$, the induced subgraph is defined to be a graph whose nodes are V_q and an edge between two nodes v_1 and v_2 exist if they are adjacent in $\mathcal{G}$.

Matrix-Vector version

Let B be the $m \times n$ incidence matrix where m and n are the number of edges and nodes of the graph, respectively. Let e_{vq} be the n-vector, whose corresponding elements for V_q are 1s, and 0s otherwise.

Then, the induced subgraph $S(V_q)$ from V_q is expressed by the following matrix-vector multiplication:

$$S(V_q) = B \times e_{vq}, \tag{4}$$

where the resulting vector $S(V_q)$ is m-vector and the elements in $S(V_q)$ have values of 0, 1, or 2. The induced subgraph is given by those edges whose corresponding values in $S(V_q)$ are 2s since it means that the incident nodes (both the source and the target) of the edges are in V_q.

SQL version

Assume we have an incidence matrix as table B, with attributes *eid*, *srcid*, and *dstid*, representing the edge id, the source node id, and the destination id of a row in the incident matrix, respectively. Also assume we have a query vector table Q with an attribute *nodeid*. Then the induced subgraph is given by the following join:

```
SELECT B.eid, B.srcid, B.dstid
FROM B, Q as Q1, Q as Q2
WHERE B.srcid=Q1.nodeid
   AND B2.dstid=Q2.nodeid
```

T4: 1-step egonet.

Informally, the 1-step-away egonet (or just 'egonet') of a node v is its 1-step-away vicinity. Formally, it is defined as the induced subgraph that includes v and its 1-step neighbors. Extracting the egonet of a query node v is a special case of extracting induced subgraph. That is, the set of nodes V_q is defined to be the v and its 1-step in-neighbors and out-neighbors.

The details are omitted, since we can combine earlier expressions (for both the matrix-vector case, as well as for the SQL case).

T5: K-step egonet.

K-step egonet of a node v is defined to be the induced subgraph from v and its within-k step neighbors. Extracting the k-step egonet of a query node v is also a special case of extracting induced subgraph. That is, the set of nodes V_q is defined to be the v and its within-k step neighbors. Thus, the same expression for the k-step neighbors and the induced subgraph can be used for extracting k-step egonet.

T6: K-core.

K-core of a graph is a maximal connected subgraph in which all vertices have degree at least K [7]. K-core is useful for finding communities and visualizing graphs. Although it seems complicated at first, all K-cores of a large graph can be enumerated by GBASE using primitives defined before:

1. Compute degrees of all nodes. Let C be the set of nodes with degree >= K.
2. Compute induced subgraph G' using C.
3. Find connected components of G'. The resulting components are the K-core.

T7: Cross-edges.

Given two disjoint sets V_1 and V_2 of nodes, how can we find the cross edges connecting the two sets? Cross-edges are useful for visualizing the interaction of two distinct sets of nodes, as well as anomaly detection (e.g., a set of nodes having few edges to the rest of the world are suspicious). Cross-edges can be computed by GBASE using induced subgraph queries:

1. Computed induced subgraphs $S(V_1)$, $S(V_2)$, $S(V_1 \cup V_2)$ using nodes in V_1, V_2, and $(V_1 \cup V_2)$, respectively.
2. Let E_1, E_2, and E_{12} be the set of edges in $S(V_1)$, $S(V_2)$, and $S(V_1 \cup V_2)$, respectively. The cross edges are exactly the edges in $E_{12} - E_1 - E_2$.

4.3 Query Execution Engine

We describe the query execution engine of GBASE built on the top of HADOOP, an open source implementation of MAPREDUCE which is a distributed large scale data processing platform.

Overview.

As described in previous sections, the main operation of GBASE is the matrix-vector multiplication. GBASE handles queries by executing appropriate block matrix-vector multiplication modules. The global queries are typically handled by multiple matrix-vector multiplications since the answer to the queries is often a fixed point of the multiplication(e.g., the first eigenvector in case of PageRank). The local queries require one or few multiplications.

Most of the operations require the adjacency matrix of the graph. Thus, GBASE uses the adjacency matrix directly as its input. However, some operations including the induced subgraph require the incidence matrix which is different from the adjacency matrix. We will see how to handle the queries requiring incidence matrix efficiently at the end of this subsection.

Grid Selection.

Before running the matrix-vector multiplication, GBASE selects the grids containing the blocks relevant to the queries. Only the files corresponding to the grids are fed into HADOOP jobs that GBASE executes. For global queries, we need to select all the grids since all the blocks are relevant. For targeted queries, however, we can select only relevant grids. For in-neighbor queries, we select grids whose column range contains the query node as shown in Figure 3(a). For out-neighbor queries, we select grids whose row range contains the query node as shown in Figure 3(b). For egonet queries, we select grids whose row or column range contains the query. As we will see in Section 5, this grid selection has advantages of decreasing the running time.

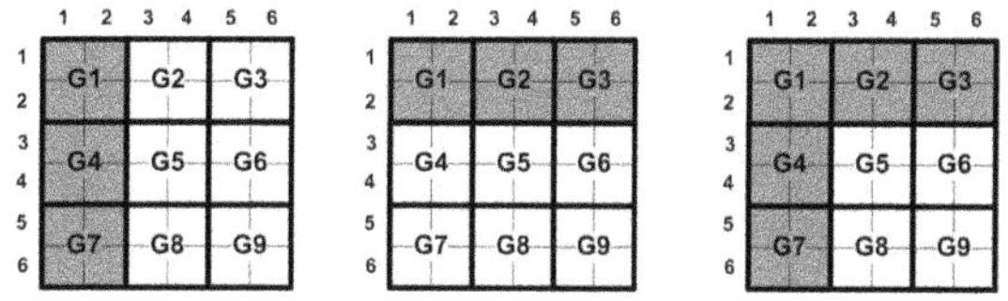

(a) 1-step in-neighbors　(b) 1-step out-neighbors　(c) 1-step in- and out-neighbors

Figure 3: Grid selection in 6 by 6 blocks where the query node belongs to the second block. The smallest rectangle corresponds to a block, and a bigger rectangle containing 4 blocks is a grid which is saved in a file. Notice that GBASE selects different grids based on the type of the query and the query node id. For example, GBASE selects G1, G4, and G7, instead of all the grids for in-neighbors query. This reduced input size results in the decreased running time.

Handling Incidence Matrix Queries.

While the majority of operations use the adjacency matrix, the induced subgraph queries use the incidence matrix. Thus, GBASE need to access the incidence matrix to support the queries. A naive approach is to build the incidence matrix $B^{m \times n}$ by numbering edges sequentially. However, it requires the storage to save B which is twice the size of the original adjacency matrix. The question is, can we answer incidence matrix queries efficiently without the additional storage?

Our proposed main idea is to derive the incidence matrix from the original adjacency matrix as required. That is, an adjacency matrix element (src, dst) can be interpreted as $([src, dst], src)$ and $([src, dst], dst)$ of the incidence matrix where $[src, dst]$ is the edge id. Thus, the query execution algorithm for handling incidence matrix can work on the original adjacency matrix by treating each adjacency matrix element as two incidence matrix elements.

The HADOOP algorithm for the induced subgraph, which reflect the main idea, is shown in Algorithm 1. The algorithm is composed of two stages. In the first stage, the elements in the incidence matrix and the query vector are grouped together to generate partial results. Notice that two incidence matrix elements are generated (line 6,7 of Algorithm 1) for an adjacency matrix element. In the second stage, the partial results are summed to get the final result. Note that only edges having the sum 2 are included in the egonet since it means that the two incidence nodes of the edges are contained in the query node set.

5. EXPERIMENTS

To evaluate our GBASE system, we perform experiments to answer the following questions:

Q1 How much does our zip block encoding reduce the data size?

Q2 How do our algorithms scale up with the graph sizes and the number of machines?

Q3 How do our indexing and query execution methods save query response time?

Datasets. We use large graph datasets summarized in Table 3 . The YahooWeb dataset is a web graph from Yahoo! with 1.4 billion

Algorithm 1: HADOOP algorithm for Induced Subgraph

```
Input  : Edge E = {(src, dst)} of a graph G = (V, E),
         Query Node Set V_q = {nodeid}
Output: Edges belonging to the subgraph induced from V_q

InducedSubgraph-Map1(Key k, Value v);
begin
    if (k, v) is of type E then
        (src, dst) <- (k, v);
        // Emit incidence matrix elements
        Output(src, [src, dst]);
        Output(dst, [src, dst]);
    else if (k, v) is of type V_q then
        (nodeid) <- (k, v);
        Output(nodeid,'1');
    end
end
InducedSubgraph-Reduce1(Key k, Value
v[1..r]);
begin
    if v[] contains '1' then
        Remove '1' from v[];
        foreach p ∈ v[1..r − 1] do
            [src, dst] <- p;
            // Emit partial multiplication result
            Output([src, dst], 1);
        end
    end
end
InducedSubgraph-Map2(Key k, Value v);
begin
    Output(k, v); // Identity Mapper
end
InducedSubgraph-Reduce2(Key k, Value
v[1..r]);
begin
    sum <- 0;
    foreach num ∈ v[1..r] do
        sum = sum + num;
    end
    // Select edges whose incident nodes belong to the query
    node set
    if sum=2 then
        [src, dst] <- k;
        Output(src, dst);
    end
end
```

nodes, 6.6 billion edges, and 120GB in space. YahooWeb is one of the largest real graph which helps us test the scalability of our GBASE system on real workload. In order to show the performance across different data scales, we use two synthetic data generators: Kronecker [23] and Erdős-Rényi [14] to generate multiple realistic graphs with different sizes.

Storage Schemes. We use the following notations to distinguish different storage and indexing methods:

- GBASE RAW(original RAW encoding): raw encoding which is the original adjacency matrix format.
- GBASE NNB(No clustering, No compression, Blocking): raw block encoding without compression and clustering.

Graph	Nodes	Edges	File Size
YahooWeb	1,413 M	6,636 M	0.12 TB
Kronecker	177 K	1,977 M	25 GB
	120 K	1,145M	13.9 GB
	59 K	282 M	3.3 GB
	20 K	6 M	439 MB
Erdős-Rényi	177 K	1,977 M	25 GB
	120 K	1,145M	13.9 GB
	59 K	282 M	3.3 GB
	20 K	6 M	439 MB

Table 3: Order and size of networks. M: millon. YahooWeb: http://webscope.sandbox.yahoo.com Kronecker, Erdős-Rényi: http://www.cs.cmu.edu/~ukang/dataset

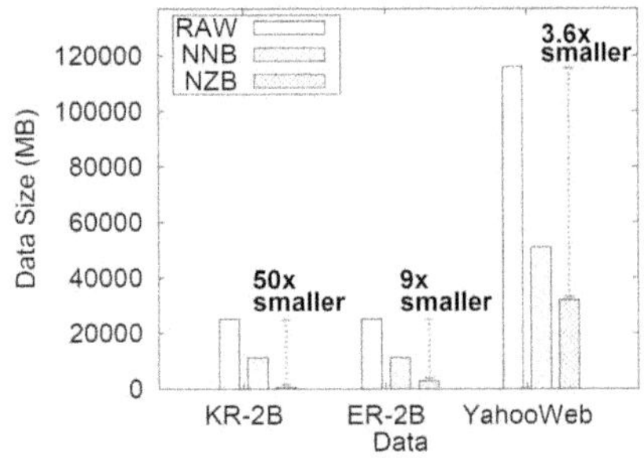

Figure 4: Effect of different encoding methods for GBASE. KR-2B: Kronecker graph with 2 billion edges. ER-2B: Erdős-Rényi random graph with 2 billion edges. Notice our proposed zip block encoding(NZB) decreases the input sizes significantly, reducing to 50× smaller than the original(RAW). The Kronecker and the Erdős-Rényi graphs have better performance gain than the YahooWeb graph since the first two are denser than the last and thus take advantage of the compression. The Kronecker graph has better compression than the Erdős-Rényi graph since it has a block-like structure from the construction.

- GBASE NZB(No clustering, Zip compression, Blocking): zip block encoding without clustering.
- GBASE CZB(Clustering, Zip compression, Blocking): zip block encoding with clustering.
- GBASE CZB+GS(CZB with Grid Selection): grid selection as described in Section 4.3.

We deploy our GBASE HADOOP implementation onto the M45 HADOOP cluster by Yahoo!. The cluster has total 480 machines with 1.5 Petabyte total storage and 3.5 Terabyte memory.

5.1 Space Efficiency Comparison

We show the data size over three different graphs across different storage schemes in Figure 4: 1) KR-2B is a graph of 177K nodes and about 2 billion edges generated using Kronecker generator; 2) ER-2B is of the same size as KR-2B but generated by Erdős-Rényi generator; 3) YahooWeb is the real Yahoo web graph of 1.4 billion nodes and 6.6 billion edges. We have the following observations:

Size Reduction. The zip block encoding(NZB) reduces the raw data size significantly (50×, 9×, and 3.6× smaller than the original(RAW) size for Kronecker, Erdős-Rényi, and YahooWeb graphs, respectively). In contrast, the raw block encoding(NNB) decrease the size at most 2.3× smaller than the original(RAW).

Density and Compression. The zip block encoding compression ratio is better for the dense graphs(Kronecker and Erdős-Rényi) than the sparse YahooWeb graph. The reason is that the

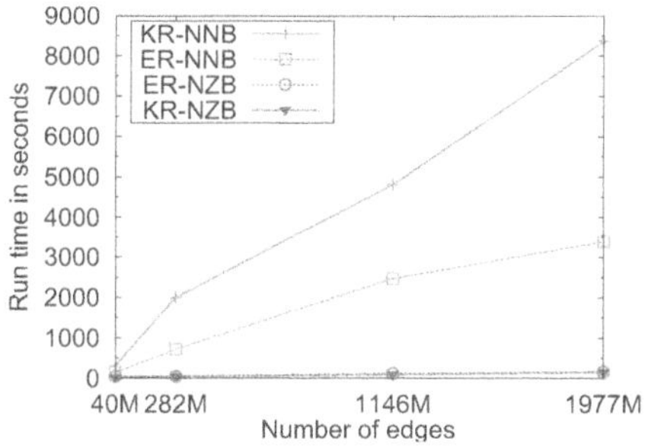

Figure 5: Scalability of indexing in GBASE. KR-NNB: Kronecker graph with raw block encoding. ER-NNB: Erdős-Rényi graph with raw block encoding. ER-NZB: Erdős-Rényi graph with zip block encoding. KR-NZB: Kronecker graph with zip block encoding. Notice that the indexing time is linear on the number of edges. Also notice that the zip block encoding(NZB) takes 50× smaller time than the raw block encoding(NNB), since the output size is smaller.

number of nonzero blocks is much smaller in the dense graphs and thus it results in more storage savings by compression.

Block Structure and Compression. The Kronecker graph has more than 5× better compression ratio than the Erdős-Rényi graph. The reason is that the Kronecker graph is block structured from the construction, and thus it benefits the compression algorithm better than its random counterpart.

To summarize, zip block encoding has shown great space savings across all datasets, which confirms the design objective of GBASE.

5.2 Indexing Time Comparison

So far, we have compared the resulting space efficiency of different methods. Next, we evaluate the indexing time required by each methods. In Figure 5, we show the running time of GBASE indexing process vs. the number of edges for graphs generated by both Kronecker(KR) and Erdős-Rényi(ER) generators.

Running Time. Seemingly to our surprise, zip block encoding(NZB) requires much less time compared to raw block encoding(NNB), despite the additional compression step: NZB performs 50× faster than NNB for 1977M edges. The reason is because the resulting compressed block is much smaller than straightforward block encoding without compression. Thus, the running time for writing the compressed blocks to disks is much smaller than the uncompressed block.

Linear Scalability. The indexing times for both zip (NZB) and raw block encoding (NNB) increase linearly as the number of edges for both Kronecker and Erdős-Rényi graphs. This confirms the scalability of our encoding schemes.

Thanks to the great storage benefit, additional compression step of zip block encoding(NZB) is worthwhile. In YahooWeb graph, we observe a similar trend as Kronecker and Erdős-Rényi graphs.

5.3 Global Query Time

So far, we confirmed the scalability and efficiency of the indexing phase. Next we evaluate the performance of different schemes on the query phase. Here, we show the scalability of GBASE global queries in Figure 6(a,b). We run the PageRank queries on Kronecker and Erdős-Rényi graphs. All the experiments except NZB are performed on Kronecker graphs. We use the zip blocked Kronecker graphs for the CZB experiment since the Kronecker graphs are block structured from its construction. For NZB experiment, we use the zip blocked Erdős-Rényi graph with the same number of nodes and edges since the Erdős-Rényi graph has nonzeros randomly distributed in the adjacency matrix.

Running Time. We see that CZB, which combines the clustering and the zip block encoding, performs the best. It outperforms RAW, NNB, NZB by 14×, 4.6×, and 2.6×, respectively, for 10 machines. The main reason of the better performance is the decreased I/O time due to reduced storage.

Machine Scalability. All the methods scale up near-linearly with the number of machines as we see in Figure 6(a).

Edge Scalability. The methods also scale up near-linearly with the number of edges as we see in Figure 6(b).

5.4 Targeted Query Time

We show the performance on targeted queries in Figure 6(c). Since the targeted queries are often against a small subset of the data, increasing the number of machines does not matter here for improving an individual query. Therefore, we only demonstrate the result with fixing the number of machines to 100. All the experiments report the average running time of 5 randomly selected query nodes. The node ids in the YahooWeb graph is encoded in a clustered manner since all the pages in a domain are numbered sequentially. Thus, we use the zip blocked YahooWeb graph for the CZB experiment.

Grid Selection. We see that GBASE CZB+GS, which combined the clustering, the zip block encoding, and the grid selection, works the best for all the targeted queries. Especially, it works the best for 1-neighborhood query outperforming all other competitors from 1.6× to 4×. The reason is that the grid selection method works better if the portion of the relevant grids is small. For 1-neighborhood query, the portion is the smallest($\sqrt{K}$ for total K grids), while other queries can have many relevant grids depending on the number of neighbors of the query node.

Effect of Zip Block Encoding. The clustered zip block encoding(CZB) performs slightly better than the raw block encoding(NNB) for 1-neighborhood and egonet queries, while it worked slightly worse than NNB for the 2-neighborhood query. The reason is that the size gain of the zip block encoding in CZB is not big enough to overshadow the increased running time for the zip compression. However, the performance of zip block encoding will continuously increase as better clustering algorithm is developed, as shown in the well clustered graph results of Figure 6(a,b). Moreover, the zip block encoding enjoys additional benefits of less storage and indexing time.

6. RELATED WORK

In this section, we review the related work, which can be categorized into four parts: (1) graph indexing techniques, (2) graph queries, (3) column store and (4) parallel data management.

Graph Indexing. Graph indexing is very active in both databases community as well as data mining community in the recent years. To name a few, Trißl et al [36] proposed to index the graph using pre- and postorder number to answer the reachability queries. Chierichetti et al [12] explored link reciprocity for adjacency queries. Aggarwal et al [5] proposed using edge sampling to handle graph connectivity queries. Sarkar et al [32] explored the clustering properties to proximity queries on graphs. Maserra et al [27] proposed a Eulerian data structure for neighborhood queries.

Despite of their success, there are two major limitations of these work. First, all the indexing techniques are designed for *one* particular type of queries. Therefore, their performance might be highly optimized for that particular type of query, but they are far sub-optimal for the remaining, vast majority types of queries. Second, they are implicitly designed for the centralized computa-

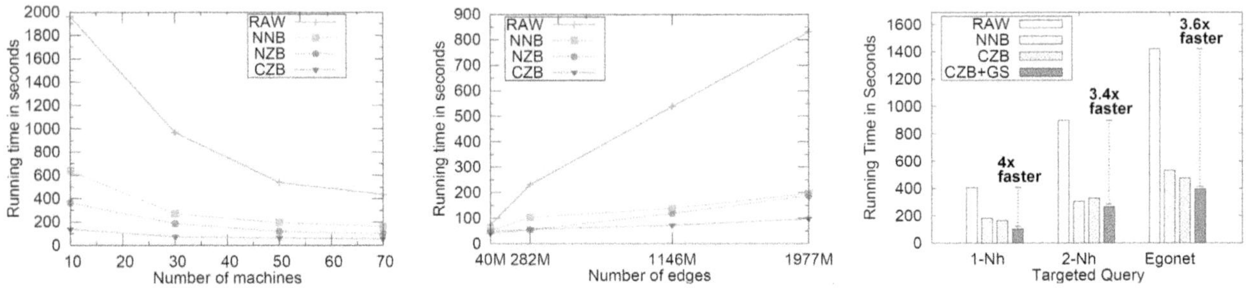

(a) Global query: machine scalability (b) Global query: edge scalability (c) Targeted query: running time

Figure 6: (a,b): Running time and scalability in one iteration of global queries in GBASE on Kronecker and Erdős-Rényi graphs. The CZB method which combines the clustering and the zip block encoding outperforms the RAW method by 14$\times$. Notice also that all the methods scale up near-linearly on the number of machines and edges. (c): Running time of targeted queries over different storage and indexing methods, on YahooWeb graph. K-Nh denotes K step neighborhood query. Note that the CZB+GS(grid selection method combined with the clustered zip block encoding) outperforms the others by 4$\times$ at maximum.

tional mode, which limits the size of the graph such indexing techniques can support. These limitations are carefully addressed in the GBASE, which supports multiple different types of queries simultaneously and is naturally applicable to the distributed computing environment.

Finally, there are works on indexing *many small* graphs using frequent subgraph [37, 39] or significant graph patterns [38], which is quite different from our setting where we have *one large* graph.

Graph Queries. There are numerous different queries on graphs. To name a few, graph-level queries answer some global statistics of the whole graph, e.g., estimating diameters [19], counting connected components [20], etc. Node-level queries, on the other hand, focus on the relationship among individual nodes. Representative queries include neighborhood [27], proximity [35], PageRank [29], centrality [9], etc. Between the graph-level and individual node-level, there are also queries on the sub-graph level, e.g., community detection [21, 8], finding induced subgraph [4], etc. GBASE covers a wide range of queries, including the global and the node-level ones, by a unified matrix-vector multiplication framework.

Column Store. Column-oriented DBMS has gained its popularity in the recent years, due to (among other merits) its excellent I/O efficiency for read-extensive analytical workloads. From research community, some representative works include [33, 3, 2, 18, 16]. A notable work of column store database from industrial side is HBase(http://hbase.apache.org/). HBase is designed for large sparse data, built on the top of HADOOP core. Different from HBase, our GBASE partitions the data in two dimensions (both columns and rows) and it is tailored for large real graphs. By leveraging the block and community-like property which exists in many real graphs, GBASE enjoys the advantages of both row-oriented and column-oriented storages.

Parallel Data Management. Parallel data processing has attracted a lot of industrial attention recently due to the success of MAPREDUCE, a parallel programming framework [13], and its open source version HADOOP [1]. Due to its excellent scalability, ease of use, and cost advantage, MAPREDUCE and MAPREDUCE-like systems have been extensively explored for various data processing. Representative work include Pregel [26], PEGASUS [20], SCOPE [11], Dryad [17], PIG Latin [28], Sphere [15], and Sawzall [31], etc. Among them, both PEGASUS and Pregel focus on large graph querying/mining and are most related to our work. The proposed GBASE provides an even lower-level support in terms of storage cost by indexing the graph on the homogeneous block levels, which are ignored in either PEGASUS or Pregel. In addition, both PEGASUS and Pregel essentially perform node/vertex-centralized computation. Our GBASE is more flexible in the sense that it also supports edge-centralized processing (e.g., induced subgraphs, ego-net, etc) in addition to node-centralized processing.

7. CONCLUSION

In this paper, we propose GBASE, a scalable and general graph management system. The main contributions are the followings.

1. *Storage.* We carefully design GBASE to efficiently store homogeneous regions of graphs in distributed settings using a novel 'block compression'. Experiments on billion-scale graphs show that the storage and running time reduced up to 50$\times$ of the original.
2. *Algorithms.* We unify node-based and edge-based queries using matrix-vector multiplications on the adjacency and the incidence matrices. As a result, we get *seven* different types of versatile graph queries supporting various applications.
3. *Query Optimization.* We propose a fast graph query execution algorithm using a grid selection. Also, we provide a efficient MAPREDUCE algorithm to support incidence matrix based queries using the original adjacency matrix, without explicitly building the incidence matrix.

Researches on large graph mining can benefit significantly from GBASE's efficient storage, widely applicable primitive operations, and fast query execution engine. Future research directions include query optimization for multiple, heterogeneous queries, and better support for time evolving graphs.

Acknowledgement

This material is based upon work supported by the National Science Foundation under Grants No. IIS-0705359 and IIS0808661, by the Defense Threat Reduction Agency under contract No. HDTRA1-10-1-0120, and by the Army Research Laboratory and was accomplished under Cooperative Agreement Number W911NF-09-2-0053. This work is also partially supported by an IBM Faculty Award, and the Gordon and Betty Moore Foundation, in the eScience project. The views and conclusions contained in this document are those of the authors and should not be interpreted as representing the official policies, either expressed or implied, of the Army Research Laboratory, the U.S. Government, or the National Science Foundation. The U.S. Government is authorized to reproduce and distribute reprints for Government purposes notwithstanding any copyright notation here on.

8. REFERENCES

[1] Hadoop information. http://hadoop.apache.org/.

[2] Daniel J. Abadi, Peter A. Boncz, and Stavros Harizopoulos. Column oriented database systems. *PVLDB*, 2009.

[3] Daniel J. Abadi, Samuel Madden, and Nabil Hachem. Column-stores vs. row-stores: how different are they really? In *SIGMOD Conference*, pages 967–980, 2008.

[4] Louigi Addario-Berry, W. Sean Kennedy, Andrew D. King, Zhentao Li, and Bruce A. Reed. Finding a maximum-weight induced k-partite subgraph of an i-triangulated graph. *Discrete Applied Mathematics*, 158(7):765–770, 2010.

[5] Charu C. Aggarwal, Yan Xie, and Philip S. Yu. Gconnect: A connectivity index for massive disk-resident graphs. *PVLDB*, 2(1):862–873, 2009.

[6] Leman Akoglu, Mary McGlohon, and Christos Faloutsos. oddball: Spotting anomalies in weighted graphs. In *PAKDD (2)*, pages 410–421, 2010.

[7] I. Alvarez-Hamelin, L. Dall'Asta, A. Barrat, and A. Vespignani. k-core decompositions: A tool for the visualization of large scale networks. *http://arxiv.org/abs/cs.NI/0504107*.

[8] Periklis Andritsos, Renée J. Miller, and Panayiotis Tsaparas. Information-theoretic tools for mining database structure from large data sets. In *SIGMOD*, 2004.

[9] David A. Bader, Shiva Kintali, Kamesh Madduri, and Milena Mihail. Approximating betweenness centrality. *WAW*, 2007.

[10] Paolo Boldi and Sebastiano Vigna. The webgraph framework i: compression techniques. In *WWW*, 2004.

[11] Ronnie Chaiken, Bob Jenkins, Per-Ake Larson, Bill Ramsey, Darren Shakib, Simon Weaver, and Jingren Zhou. Scope: easy and efficient parallel processing of massive data sets. *VLDB*, 2008.

[12] Flavio Chierichetti, Ravi Kumar, Silvio Lattanzi, Michael Mitzenmacher, Alessandro Panconesi, and Prabhakar Raghavan. On compressing social networks. In *KDD*, 2009.

[13] Jeffrey Dean and Sanjay Ghemawat. Mapreduce: Simplified data processing on large clusters. *OSDI'04*, December 2004.

[14] P. Erdős and A. Rényi. On random graphs. *Publicationes Mathematicae*, 6:290–297, 1959.

[15] Robert L. Grossman and Yunhong Gu. Data mining using high performance data clouds: experimental studies using sector and sphere. *KDD*, 2008.

[16] Sándor Héman, Marcin Zukowski, Niels J. Nes, Lefteris Sidirourgos, and Peter A. Boncz. Positional update handling in column stores. In *SIGMOD*, 2010.

[17] Michael Isard and Yuan Yu. Distributed data-parallel computing using a high-level programming language. In *SIGMOD Conference*, pages 987–994, 2009.

[18] Milena Ivanova, Martin L. Kersten, Niels J. Nes, and Romulo Goncalves. An architecture for recycling intermediates in a column-store. In *SIGMOD*, 2009.

[19] U Kang, C.E Tsourakakis, Ana Paula Appel, C Faloutsos, and Jure Leskovec. Radius plots for mining tera-byte scale graphs: Algorithms, patterns, and observations. *SIAM International Conference on Data Mining*, 2010.

[20] U Kang, C.E Tsourakakis, and C. Faloutsos. Pegasus: A peta-scale graph mining system - implementation and observations. *ICDM*, 2009.

[21] G. Karypis and V. Kumar. Parallel multilevel k-way partitioning for irregular graphs. *SIAM Review*, 41(2):278–300, 1999.

[22] George Karypis and Vipin Kumar. Multilevel -way hypergraph partitioning. In *DAC*, pages 343–348, 1999.

[23] Jure Leskovec, Deepayan Chakrabarti, Jon M. Kleinberg, and Christos Faloutsos. Realistic, mathematically tractable graph generation and evolution, using kronecker multiplication. *PKDD*, pages 133–145, 2005.

[24] Ching-Yung Lin, Nan Cao, Shixia Liu, Spiros Papadimitriou, Jimeng Sun, and Xifeng Yan. Smallblue: Social network analysis for expertise search and collective intelligence. In *ICDE*, pages 1483–1486, 2009.

[25] Chao Liu, Fan Guo, and Christos Faloutsos. Bbm: bayesian browsing model from petabyte-scale data. In *KDD*, 2009.

[26] Grzegorz Malewicz, Matthew H. Austern, Aart J. C. Bik, James C. Dehnert, Ilan Horn, Naty Leiser, and Grzegorz Czajkowski. Pregel: a system for large-scale graph processing. In *SIGMOD Conference*, pages 135–146, 2010.

[27] Hossein Maserrat and Jian Pei. Neighbor query friendly compression of social networks. In *KDD*, 2010.

[28] Christopher Olston, Benjamin Reed, Utkarsh Srivastava, Ravi Kumar, and Andrew Tomkins. Pig latin: a not-so-foreign language for data processing. In *SIGMOD '08*, pages 1099–1110, 2008.

[29] Lawrence Page, Sergey Brin, Rajeev Motwani, and Terry Winograd. The PageRank citation ranking: Bringing order to the web. Technical report, Stanford Digital Library Technologies Project, 1998.

[30] Spiros Papadimitriou and Jimeng Sun. Disco: Distributed co-clustering with map-reduce. *ICDM*, 2008.

[31] Rob Pike, Sean Dorward, Robert Griesemer, and Sean Quinlan. Interpreting the data: Parallel analysis with sawzall. *Scientific Programming Journal*, 2005.

[32] Purnamrita Sarkar and Andrew W. Moore. Fast nearest-neighbor search in disk-resident graphs. In *KDD*, pages 513–522, 2010.

[33] Michael Stonebraker, Daniel J. Abadi, Adam Batkin, Xuedong Chen, Mitch Cherniack, Miguel Ferreira, Edmond Lau, Amerson Lin, Samuel Madden, Elizabeth J. O'Neil, Patrick E. O'Neil, Alex Rasin, Nga Tran, and Stanley B. Zdonik. C-store: A column-oriented dbms. In *VLDB*, 2005.

[34] Jimeng Sun, Huiming Qu, Deepayan Chakrabarti, and Christos Faloutsos. Neighborhood formation and anomaly detection in bipartite graphs. In *ICDM*, pages 418–425, 2005.

[35] Hanghang Tong, Christos Faloutsos, and Jia-Yu Pan. Fast random walk with restart and its applications. In *ICDM*, pages 613–622, 2006.

[36] Silke Trißl and Ulf Leser. Fast and practical indexing and querying of very large graphs. In *SIGMOD*, 2007.

[37] D. Xin, J. Han, X. Yan, and H. Cheng. Mining compressed frequent-pattern sets. In *VLDB*, pages 709–720, 2005.

[38] Xifeng Yan, Hong Cheng, Jiawei Han, and Philip S. Yu. Mining significant graph patterns by leap search. In *SIGMOD Conference*, pages 433–444, 2008.

[39] Peixiang Zhao, Jeffrey Xu Yu, and Philip S. Yu. Graph indexing: Tree + delta >= graph. In *VLDB*, 2007.

Human Mobility, Social Ties, and Link Prediction

Dashun Wang[1,2] Dino Pedreschi[1,3] Chaoming Song[1,2] Fosca Giannotti[1,4] Albert-László Barabási[1,2,5]

[1]CCNR, Dept. of Physics and Computer Science, Northeastern University, Boston, MA 02115, USA
[2]CCSB, Dana-Farber Cancer Institute, Harvard University, Boston, MA 02115, USA
[3]KDD Lab, Dipartimento di Informatica, Università di Pisa, 56127 Pisa, Italy
[4]KDD Lab, ISTI-CNR, Istituto di Scienza e Tecnologie dell'Informazione del C.N.R., 56124 Pisa, Italy
[5]Dept. of Medicine, Brigham and Women's Hospital, Harvard Medical School, Boston, MA 02115, USA
{dashunwang, dino.pedreschi, chaoming.song, fosca.giannotti, barabasi}@gmail.com

ABSTRACT

Our understanding of how individual mobility patterns shape and impact the social network is limited, but is essential for a deeper understanding of network dynamics and evolution. This question is largely unexplored, partly due to the difficulty in obtaining large-scale society-wide data that simultaneously capture the dynamical information on individual movements and social interactions. Here we address this challenge for the first time by tracking the trajectories and communication records of 6 Million mobile phone users. We find that the similarity between two individuals' movements strongly correlates with their proximity in the social network. We further investigate how the predictive power hidden in such correlations can be exploited to address a challenging problem: which new links will develop in a social network. We show that mobility measures alone yield surprising predictive power, comparable to traditional network-based measures. Furthermore, the prediction accuracy can be significantly improved by learning a supervised classifier based on combined mobility and network measures. We believe our findings on the interplay of mobility patterns and social ties offer new perspectives on not only link prediction but also network dynamics.

Categories and Subject Descriptors

H.2.8 [**Database Management**]: Database Applications—*Data mining*

General Terms

Measurement, Performance

Keywords

Human Mobility, Link Prediction, Social Network

1. INTRODUCTION

Social networks have attracted particular interest in recent years, largely because of their critical role in various applications [11, 5]. Despite the recent explosion of research in this area, the bulk of work has focused on the social space only, leaving an important question of to what extent individual mobility patterns shape and impact the social network, largely unexplored. Indeed, social links are often driven by spatial proximity, from job- and family-imposed programs to joint involvement in various social activities [28]. These shared social foci and face-to-face interactions, represented as overlap in individuals' trajectories, are expected to have significant impact on the structure of social networks, from the maintenance of long-lasting friendships to the formation of new links.

Our knowledge of the interplay between individual mobility and social network is limited, partly due to the difficulty in collecting large-scale data that record, simultaneously, dynamical traces of individual movements and social interactions. This situation is changing rapidly, however, thanks to the pervasive use of mobile phones. Indeed, the records of mobile communications collected by telecommunication carriers provide extensive proxy of individual trajectories and social relationships, by keeping track of each phone call between any two parties and the localization in space and time of the party that initiates the call. The high penetration of mobile phones implies that such data captures a large fraction of the population of an entire country. The availability of these massive CDRs (Call Detail Record) has made possible, for instance, the empirical validation in a large-scale setting of traditional social network hypotheses such as Granovetter's strength of weak ties [27], the development of a first generation of realistic models of human mobility [14, 29] and its predictability [30]. Indeed, despite the inhomogeneous spatial resolution (the uneven reception area of mobile phone towers) and sampling rates (the timing of calls), the large volume of CDR data allows us to reconstruct many salient aspects of individual daily routines, such as the most frequently visited locations, and the time and periodicity of such visits. Therefore, these data serve as an unprecedented social microscope helping us scrutinize the mobility patterns together with social structure and the intensity of social interactions.

In this work, we follow the trajectories and communication patterns of approximately 6 Million users over three months, by using CDR data from an anonymous country, aiming to measure for any pair of users u and v:

- *How similar is the movement of u and v.* For this purpose, we introduce a series of *co-location* measures quantifying the similarity between their movement routines, prompting us to call them the *mobile homophily* between u and v.

- *How connected are u and v in the social network.* For this purpose, we adopt several well-established measures of network proximity, based on the common neighbors or the structure of the paths connecting u and v in the who-calls-whom network.

- *How intense is the interaction between u and v.* For this purpose we use the number of calls between u and v as a measure of the strength of their tie.

Our analysis offers empirical evidence that these three facets, co-location, network proximity and tie strength, are positively correlated with each other. In particular, we find that the higher the mobile homophily of u and v, the higher the chance that u and v are strongly connected in the social network, and that they have intense direct interactions. These findings uncover how the social network, made of numerous explicit who-calls-whom ties, is embedded into an underlying mobility network, made with the implicit ties dictated by the mobile homophily.

The emergence of such surprising three-fold correlation hints that it is conceivable, to some extent, to predict one of the three aspects given the other two. Indeed, we demonstrate in this study how the predictive power hidden in these correlations can be exploited to identify new ties that are about to develop in a social network. Specifically, we study the influence of co-location and mobile homophily in link prediction problems, asking: what is the performance of mobility-based measures in predicting new links, and can we predict more precisely whether two users u and v (that did not call each other in the past) will call each other in the future, by combining the measurements of their network proximity *and* mobile homophily? Our key findings are summarized as follows:

- The mobility measures on their own carry remarkably high predictive power, comparable to that of network proximity measures.

- By combining both mobility and network measures, we manage to significantly boost the predictive performance in supervised classification, detecting interesting niches of new links very precisely. For example, by considering a subset of potential links (pairs of users) with high network proximity and mobile homophily, we are able to learn a decision-tree classifier with a precision of 73.5% and a recall of 66.1% on the positive class. In other words, only approximately one fourth of the predicted new links were false positives, and only one third of the actual new links were missed by the predictor.

To the best of our knowledge, this work presents the first assessment of the extent individuals' daily routines as a determinant of social ties, from empirical analysis to prediction models. With recent proliferating advances on human mobility and social networks, we believe our findings are of fundamental importance in our understanding of human behavior, provide significant insights towards not only link prediction problems but also the evolution and dynamics of networks, and could potentially impact a wide array of areas, from privacy implications to urban planning and epidemic prevention.

2. MOBILE PHONE DATA

Currently the most comprehensive data that contains simultaneously both human mobility and social interactions across a large segment of the population is collected by mobile phone companies. Indeed, mobile phones are carried by their owners during their daily routines. As mobile carriers record for billing purposes the closest mobile tower each time the user uses his phone, the data capture in detail individual movements. With almost 100% penetration of mobile phones in industrial countries, the mobile phone network is the most comprehensive proxy of a large-scale social network currently in existence. We exploit in this study a massive CDR dataset of approximately 6 Million users, which, to the best of our knowledge, is the largest dataset analyzed to date containing both human trajectories and social interactions. We focused on 50k individuals selected as the most active users (identical to those that were studied in [30]), following not only their trajectories but also their communication records during 14 successive weeks in 2007[1].

The resulting dataset contains around 90M communication records among the individuals, and over 10k distinct locations covering a radius of more than 1000 km. Each record, for our purposes, is represented as 4-tuple $\langle x, y, t, l\rangle$, where user x is the caller, user y is the callee, t is the time of the call, and l is the location of the tower that routed the call. The temporal granularity used in this study is the hour, justified by the findings in [14, 30, 29]. Let V denotes the set of users. For each user $x \in V$, the total number of calls initiated by x is denoted as $n(x)$. For x's i-th communication, where $1 \le i \le n(x)$, the time stamp, location, and the contacted user are denoted as $T_i(x)$, $L_i(x)$ and $N_i(x)$, respectively. Given a time interval between t_0 and t_1, the set of communications between pairs of users occurred within the interval is denoted as $E[t_0, t_1] \equiv \{(x, y)|x, y \in V, \exists i, 1 \le i \le n(x), t_0 \le T_i(x) < t_1, N_i(x) = y\}$. In other words, we add an edge (x, y) if there has been at least one communication between x and y in the interval. Therefore, $G[t_0, t_1] \equiv \{V, E[t_0, t_1]\}$ is the resulting social network within the time interval.

To prepare for the link prediction experiments, we further separate our data into 2 parts: first 9 weeks for constructing the old network and the rest 5 weeks for the new network. For each link $e \in E$, we classify it according to its time stamp $t(e)$. $E_t \equiv \{e|e \in E, t \le t(e) < t + 1\}$ is defined as the set of edges of the resulting network after aggregating the communications in the t-th week. The "past" and "future" sets are therefore denoted as $E_{old} = \bigcup_{t=1}^{9} E_t$ and $E_{new} = \bigcup_{t=10}^{14} E_t$. In our study, we focus on nodes in the largest connected component $G_{old} = \{V_{old}, E_{old}\}$, where we observe in total $|V_{old}| = 34,034$ users and $|E_{old}| = 51,951$ links.

3. NETWORK PROXIMITY

General approaches in link prediction tasks have been focused on defining effective network based "proximity" measures, so that two nodes that are close enough on the graph

[1]Unfortunately, we cannot make this dataset available due to NDA.

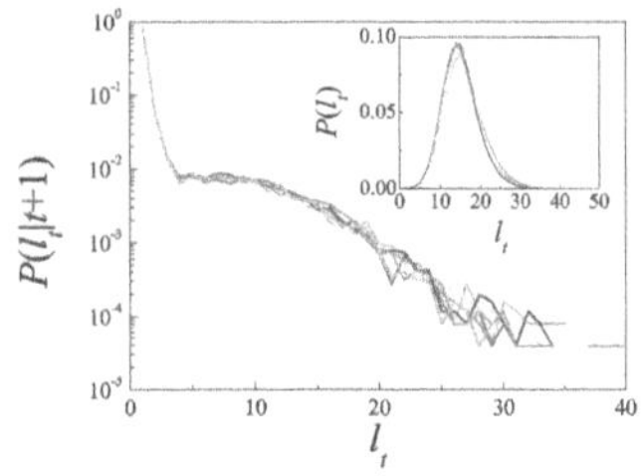

Figure 1: The probability density function $P(l_t|t+1)$ that a new link has chemical distance l in previous week. Inset: the probability density function of chemical $P(l_t)$ for different weeks.

but not yet connected may have a better likelihood of becoming connected in the future. As the main focus of the paper is to explore the predictive power of mobility compared and combined with topological predictors, we selected four representative quantities which have been proven to perform reasonably well in previous studies (for more details of the quantities and their performance on citation networks, see [21].)

- *Common neighbors.* The number of neighbors that nodes x and y have in common. That is, $CN(x,y) \equiv |\Gamma(x) \cap \Gamma(y)|$, where $\Gamma(x) \equiv \{y|y \in V, (x,y) \in E\}$ is the set of neighbors of x.
- *Adamic-Adar* [1]. A refinement of $CN(x,y)$ by weighting common neighbors based on their degrees, instead of simple counting. Therefore the contribution from hubs to common neighbors is penalized by the inverse logarithm of their degree. $AA(x,y) \equiv \sum_{z \in \Gamma(x) \cap \Gamma(y)} \frac{1}{\log |\Gamma(z)|}$.
- *Jaccard's coefficient.* Defined as the size of the intersection of the neighbors of two nodes, $\Gamma(x)$ and $\Gamma(y)$, divided by the size of their union, characterizing the similarity between their sets of neighbors. $J(x,y) \equiv |\Gamma(x) \cap \Gamma(y)| / |\Gamma(x) \cup \Gamma(y)|$.
- *Katz* [17]. Summation over all possible paths from x to y with exponential damping by length to weight short paths more heavily. $K(x,y) \equiv \sum_{l=1}^{\infty} \beta^l \cdot |paths^l_{x,y}|$, where $paths^l_{x,y}$ is the set of all paths with length l from x to y (damping factor β is typically set to 0.05.)

Most network proximity measures are related to the chemical distance on the graph, under the natural assumption that new links are more likely to occur between nodes that are within a small distance on the graph. The *chemical distance* $l(x,y|E)$ is defined as the length of the shortest path between two nodes x and y. $l(x,y|E) = 1$ implies that nodes x and y are connected, or $(x,y) \in E$. The role of chemical distance on tie formation can be tested directly by measuring the probability $P(l_t|t+1)$ for a new link $e \equiv (x,y) \in E_{t+1}$ to have a chemical distance l_t measured at previous week t. That is, $P(l_t|t+1) \equiv |\{e|e \equiv (x,y) \in E_{t+1}, l(x,y|E_t) = l_t\}| / |E_{t+1}|$. This distribution is shown in Fig. 1, different colors indicating different time windows t. We find, first of all, $P(l_t|t+1)$ is stable over different weeks (1 through 14), indicating that the aggregation process we adopted to construct the network is robust, and that $P(l_t|t+1)$ is largely independent wrt the time windows. Second, $P(l_t|t+1)$ decays rapidly as l_t increases, consistent with previous studies [20] on other data sets. This implies that the majority of new links are between nodes within two hops from each other, i.e., nodes with common neighbors. Third, the Poisson distribution of the chemical distance for arbitrary pairs (inset of Fig. 1) suggests that the most probable distance for two users to form a link at random is around 12, while it is only 2 for pairs that do form new links.

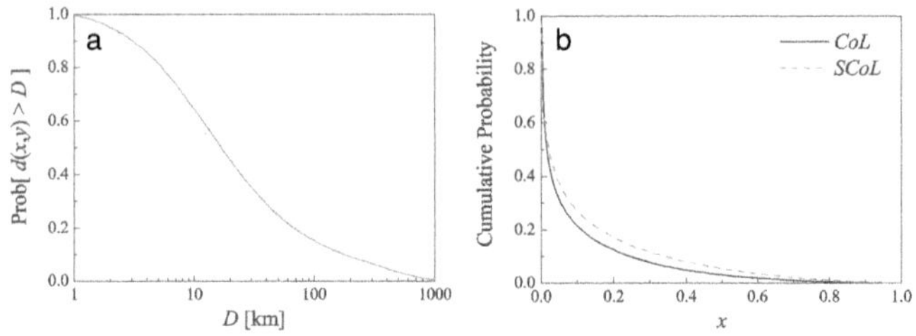

Figure 2: a) The probability two users i and j have distance $d(i,j) > D$. b) The probability two users i and j have Co-Location $CoL(i,j)$ (solid) and Spatial Co-Location $SCoL(i;j)$ (dashed) greater than x.

4. MOBILE HOMOPHILY

Similar to the graph-based approaches, a natural strategy to predict new links by leveraging mobility information is to look for quantities that capture some degree of closeness in physical space between two individuals. Indeed, people who share high degree of overlap in their trajectories are expected to have a better likelihood of forming new links [28]. Therefore, we explored a series of quantities aiming to define the similarity in mobility patterns of two individuals.

- *Distance.* Let
$$ML(x) \equiv \text{argmax}_{l \in Loc} PV(x,l)$$
be the most likely location of user x, where Loc is the set of all locations (cell phone towers), and
$$PV(x,l) \equiv \sum_{i=1}^{n(x)} \delta(l, L_i(x)) / n(x)$$
is the probability that user x visits location l^2. We define $d(x,y) \equiv \text{dist}(ML(x), ML(y))$ as the distance between two users x and y, representing the physical distance between their most frequented locations.
- *Spatial Co-Location Rate.* The probability that users x and y visit at the same location, not necessarily at the same time. Assuming that the probability of visits for any two users are independent, we define:
$$SCoL(x,y) \equiv \sum_{l \in Loc} PV(x,l) \times PV(y,l)$$
- *Spatial Cosine Similarity.* The cosine similarity of user x and y's trajectories, capturing how similar their visitation frequencies are, assigned by the cosine of the angle between the two vectors of number of visits at each location for x and y.
$$SCos(x,y) \equiv \sum_{l \in Loc} \frac{PV(x,l) \times PV(y,l)}{\|PV(x,l)\| \times \|PV(y,l)\|}$$

[2]Here $\delta(a,b) = 1$ if $a = b$, 0 otherwise.

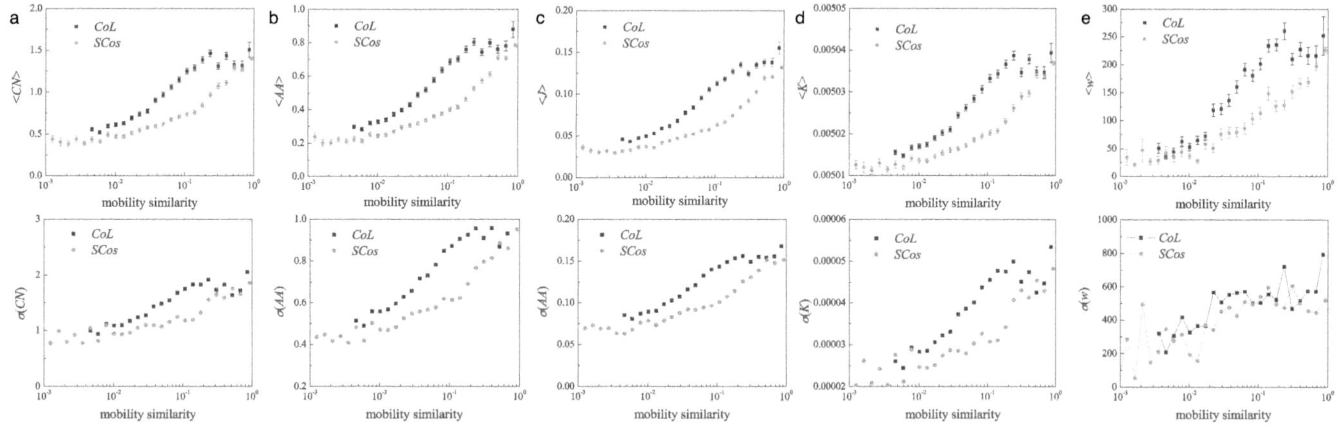

Figure 3: Correlations between mobility measures (CoL and $SCos$) and a) Common Neighbor, b) Adamic Adar, c) Jaccard Coefficient, d) Katz, and e) link weight. The upper panels show the mean values, whereas the lower panels show the standard deviations

- *Weighted Spatial Cosine Similarity.* The *tf-idf* version of cosine similarity of the visitation frequencies of users x and y, where the contribution of each location l is inversely proportional to the (log of) its overall population in l. Coherent with the *tf-idf* idea in information retrieval, this measure promotes co-location in low-density areas, while penalizes co-location in populated places.

- *Co-Location Rate.* The probability for users x and y to appear at the same location during the same time frame (hour):

$$CoL \equiv \frac{\sum_{i=1}^{n(x)} \sum_{j=1}^{n(y)} \Theta\left(\Delta T - |T_i(x) - T_j(y)|\right) \delta\left(L_i(x), L_j(y)\right)}{\sum_{i=1}^{n(x)} \sum_{j=1}^{n(y)} \Theta\left(\Delta T - |T_i(x) - T_j(y)|\right)}$$

where $\Theta(x)$ is the Heaviside step function, and ΔT is set to 1 hour. This quantity takes into account the simultaneous visits of two users at the same location, i.e., both spatial and temporal proximity, normalized by the number of times they are both observed at the same time frame.

- *Weighted Co-Location Rate.* The *tf-idf* version of CoL, i.e., the probability for two users x and y to co-locate during the same hour, normalized by the (log of) population density of the co-location at that hour.

- *Extra-role Co-Location Rate.* The probability for two users x and y to co-locate in the same hour at night or during weekends. As shown in [10], close proximity of two individuals during off-hours may serve as a powerful predictor for symmetric friendships.

The quantities listed above either aim at measuring the geographical closeness or the degree of trajectory overlap of two individuals, characterizing their mobile homophily. It should be noted that it is not obvious whether the spatiotemporal co-location measures, e.g., CoL, would yield better estimates of the probability of face-to-face interactions than spatial only measures, e.g., $SCoL$. Indeed, on one hand, CoL quantifies the co-presence of two users in the same place around the same moments, corresponding to a high likelihood of meeting face-to-face. Yet there are circumstances where two users do co-locate but are not captured by the data if any one of them did not place any phone calls. And this latter case is captured to some extent by $SCoL$, as the necessary condition for two individuals to meet is the spatial overlap of their trajectories.

We now explore the distributions of the various measures over the linked pairs of individuals $(x, y) \in E_{old}$. In Fig. 2a we show the complementary cumulative distribution function (CCDF) of geographical distances $d(x, y)$. We find that $d(x, y)$ follows a fat-tailed distribution, consistent with previous studies [19, 18, 22], meaning that while most friends live close to each other, there are also friends who are far apart. The CCDF plots of CoL and $SCoL$ are shown in Fig. 2b as solid and dashed line, respectively. $SCoL$ measures the probability for two users to appear at the same location, capturing, spatially, the degree of trajectory overlapping. CoL quantifies the probability of appearing at the same place around the same time, characterizing the spatiotemporal overlap of trajectories. We find that "friends" typically do co-locate, in that most pairs $(x, y) \in E_{old}$ exhibit non-zero spatial or spatio-temporal overlap in their trajectories, and such overlap decays very fast.

5. CORRELATION BETWEEN MOBILE HOMOPHILY AND NETWORK PROXIMITY

We explore a series of connections between similarity in individual mobility patterns and social proximity in the call graph, by measuring the correlation between the proposed mobility and network quantities, using again the edges in G_{old}. We also consider the strength of the ties in the network, quantified by the number of calls placed between any two users (during the first 9 weeks of our observation period.) In Fig. 3, we plot the mean values and the standard deviations of Common neighbors, Adamic-Adar, Jaccard's coefficient, Katz, and the strength of social ties for different values of Co-Location and Spatial Cosine Similarity, discretized by logarithmic binning. We find that the quantities that characterize the proximity in the social graph systematically correlate with mobility measures. The more similar two users' mobility patterns are, the higher is the chance

Table 1: Pearson Coefficients

	CoL	$SCos$	J	CN	AA	K	w	dML
CoL	1	0.76286	0.25359	0.19618	0.2251	0.18952	0.14521	-0.17894
$SCos$	0.76286	1	0.30789	0.25657	0.28679	0.24933	0.14402	-0.24938
J	0.25359	0.30789	1	0.82384	0.88147	0.81108	0.11348	-0.10136
CN	0.19618	0.25657	0.82384	1	0.94437	0.99939	0.05989	-0.098562
AA	0.2251	0.28679	0.88147	0.94437	1	0.93806	0.086881	-0.10126
K	0.18952	0.24933	0.81108	0.99939	0.93806	1	0.053842	-0.095631
w	0.14521	0.14402	0.11348	0.05989	0.086881	0.053842	1	-0.029339
dML	-0.17894	-0.24938	-0.10136	-0.098562	-0.10126	-0.095631	-0.029339	1

that they have close proximity in the social network, as well as the higher is the intensity of their interactions. Furthermore, Fig. 4 demonstrates that the geographical distance between two individuals decays logarithmically with mobility measures. We omit the plots where the network proximity measures and the tie strength are on the x-axis, due to space limitations, but we observe a qualitatively similar trend in all cases. The Pearson coefficients of each pairs of variables are reported in Table 1. It is interesting to observe that tie strength, although conceived as a network measure, is more strongly correlated with mobile homophily than with network proximity measures.

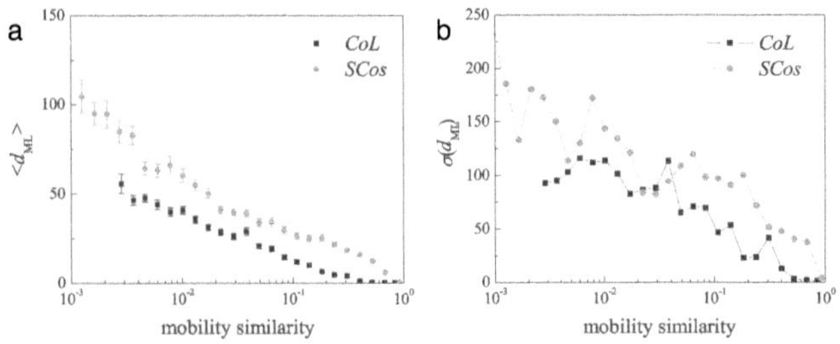

Figure 4: Correlations between mobility measures (CoL and $SCos$) and distance between two individuals. (a) mean values and (b) standard deviations.

Taken together, our results indicate that mobile homophily, network proximity and tie strength strongly correlate with each other. This fact implies that mobile homophily is a viable alternate candidate to predict network structures, and motivates the investigation of a novel approach to link prediction that takes into account both mobility and network measures. Moreover, we find that the standard deviation for the correlation plots are not small, hinting that there are extra degrees of freedom which allow us to further improve our predictive power by using supervised classification methods combining the mobility and network dimensions together.

6. LINK PREDICTION

6.1 Design of the link prediction experiment

We now study the link prediction problem in the context of our mobile social network. Link prediction is a classification problem, aimed at detecting, among all possible pairs of users that did not call each other in the past, those that will communicate in the future. We define a *potential link* any pair of users (u, v) such that $(u, v) \notin E_{old}$, i.e., users u and v did not call each other from week 1 through 9, and a *new link* any potential link (u, v) such that $(u, v) \in E_{new}$, i.e., users u and v did not call each other from week 1 through week 9, but did call each other (at least once) from week 10 through week 14. Finally, we define a *missing link* any potential link which is not a new link, i.e., a pair of users that did not call each other in the entire period from week 1 through week 14. For any potential link (u, v), let $NL(u, v)$ be a binary variable with value 1 if (u, v) is a new link, and 0 if (u, v) is a missing link.

In this setting, link prediction is formalized as a binary classification problem over the set of all potential links, where the class label is specified by the NL variable, and the predictive variables are the network and mobility quantities introduced in Sec. 3 and 4, measured over the first period from week 1 through week 9. According to this formulation, we aim to predict whether a potential link becomes a new link in the "future" based on the observation of its "past" network connectedness and mobile homophily.

Our dataset consists of $n = 34,034$ users and $m = 51,951$ links, resulting in $(n(n-1)/2) - m = 579,087,610$ potential links. Yet the actual new links are only 12,484 – about 2 new links every 10^5 potential links! The significant number of potential links creates obvious computational challenges, both in terms of memory and time. Moreover, the huge disproportion between new links and missing links implies an extreme unbalance between the positive and negative class, which makes the classification task prohibitive. To cope with both difficulties, we followed two complementary strategies for selecting subsets of potential links: *i*) *progressive sampling*: we consider increasingly large samples of missing links, up to some manageable size, and *ii*) *links with common neighbors*: we concentrate on the interesting case of pairs of nodes that are two hops away in the network, i.e., nodes with common neighbors, and consider the entire population of potential links between such nodes. We report below the results obtained in our link prediction analysis in both cases.

Another dimension of our study is the kind of classification used. Adhering to the machine learning terminology [23], we consider both *unsupervised* and *supervised* link prediction:

- The unsupervised method, originally proposed in [21], consists in ranking the set of potential links using one of the available network or mobility quantities, and then classifying as new links the k top-ranked potential links, where k is the expected number of new links (as measured in the dataset.) The rest are classified as missing links.

- The supervised method consists in learning a classifier, e.g., a decision tree, using a training set of new links and missing links, and then classifying each pair as a new or missing link according to the class assigned by the learned classifier.

Different unsupervised classifiers are obtained by considering the various network and mobility measures, and different supervised classifiers are obtained by considering different combinations of the same quantities as predictive variables. We systematically constructed the complete repertoire of classifiers, based either on network quantities, or mobility quantities, or the combination of the two. We then compared their quality and predictive power. To this extent, we put particular attention on the metric used to assess a classifier, given that simple accuracy (over either the training or test set) is a misleading measure for classifiers learned over highly unbalanced datasets. Indeed, recall that in our case the trivial classifier that labels each potential link as missing has a 99.998% accuracy. The real challenge in link prediction is achieving high *precision* and *recall* over positive cases (new links), defined in terms of the confusion matrix of a classifier (see Table 2): *precision* $= \frac{TP}{TP+FP}$, and *recall* $= \frac{TP}{TP+FN}$. Traditionally, precision and recall are combined into their harmonic mean, the F-measure. However, we put more emphasis on precision, as the most challenging task is to classify some potential links as new links with high probability, even at the price of a non negligible number of false negatives. We also use lift and gain charts to compare the precision of the various classifiers over the percentiles of the examined test cases.

6.2 Progressive sampling of missing links

In our first set of experiments we created various unsupervised and supervised classifiers over the complete dataset of positive cases, i.e., 12,484 new links, augmented with up to 51M negative cases of missing links. We assess the precision achieved by each classifier when used with all 12,484 new links and increasing fractions of missing links, i.e., to 1%, 25%, 50%, 75% and 100% of the total 51M missing links sampled. Figure 5 summarizes our findings for unsupervised classifiers. For each network/mobility quantity Q and each dataset with increasing samples of missing links, we rank the potential links in the dataset for decreasing values of Q, and the top ranked 12,484 links are predicted as new links. Each line in Fig. 5 describes how the precision for different quantities decays with the size of missing links. On the positive side, all unsupervised classifiers are significantly better than random guessing, and the decay of their precision tends to stabilize. Nevertheless, as these 51M links are only about 10% of the total missing links, we conclude that all quantities exhibit modest predictive power. The most surprising finding is that the co-location measures have a comparable precision to network measures: slightly worse than best network predictors (Katz, Adamic-Adar), but better than Common Neighbors. Moreover, mobility measures have a slower decay than network measures over increasing negative sample size. The observation that the two classes of measures have approximately similar predictive power offer further evidence that social connectedness is strongly correlated with mobile homophily.

	predicted class = 0	predicted class = 1
actual class = 0	TN (true neg.)	FP (false pos.)
actual class = 1	FN (false neg.)	TP (true pos.)

Table 2: Confusion matrix of a binary classifier

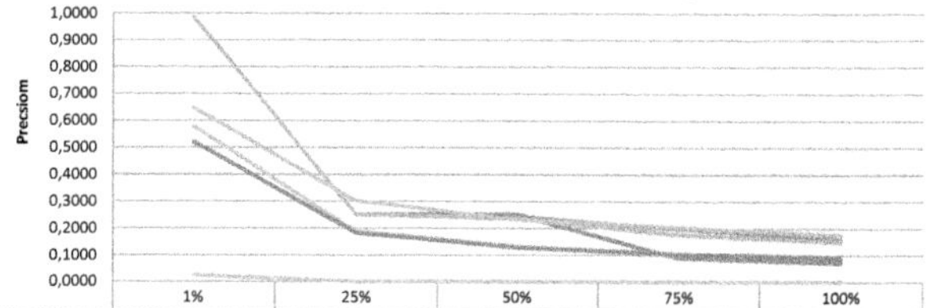

	1%	25%	50%	75%	100%
Adamic Adar	0,9841	0,2507	0,2441	0,1988	0,1602
Common Neighbors	0,9829	0,2507	0,2507	0,0895	0,0715
Cosine Colocation	0,5794	0,1871	0,1325	0,1069	0,0906
ST Colocation	0,5203	0,1817	0,1295	0,1049	0,0884
Jaccard	0,9833	0,2507	0,2363	0,1777	0,1505
Katz	0,6451	0,3014	0,2333	0,2047	0,1762
Random	0,0237	0,0010	0,0005	0,0003	0,0002

Figure 5: Precision of unsupervised classifiers over increasing fractions of missing links (1%, 25%, 50%, 75% and 100% of the total 51M missing links sampled). Ranking is obtained using the various network and mobility measure. Precision refers to the fraction of new links among the top-ranked 12,484 potential links. The precision of the random classifier is shown as baseline.

Figure 6 illustrates the supervised case: we consider the best classifiers obtained using network and mobility measures, both in isolation and combined together. Once again, we consider negative samples of increasing size, up to 51M missing links, and measure the decay of precision as in the unsupervised case. We considered a vast repertoire of classification algorithms (decision trees, random forests, SVM, logistic regression) under diverse parameter settings, and report in the chart the most robust classifiers, evaluated with cross validation, with strongest evidence against overfitting. In the chart we also compare the precision of the supervised methods (evaluated on an independent test set) with that of the best unsupervised predictor (Katz). We observe that the precision of the supervised classifiers is about double of their unsupervised counterpart, and mobility measures once again achieve comparable predictive powers to the traditional network measures. The best precision, around 30% in the 51M case, is obtained using the network and mobility measures combined together. Therefore, using network measures in combination with co-location measures yields a sensible improvement. Indeed, the probability of correctly predicting a new link is 1500+ times larger than random guessing.

6.3 Potential links with common neighbors

To get better insight, we concentrate on the nodes that are two hops away from each other in E_{old}, i.e., all potential links (u, v) of mobile users in our complete network such that u and v have at least one common neighbor during the first two months. The motivations behind this approach are two-fold. First, most new links that do form belong to this category (Fig. 1), and we hope to boost our prediction models by focusing on this most promising set of links. Second, by focusing on these links, the total number of potential links becomes computationally manageable, which enables us to assess the asymptotic behavior of prediction accuracy.

There are 266,750 potential links in this case, of which 3,130 (1.17%) formed a new link. Note that, different from

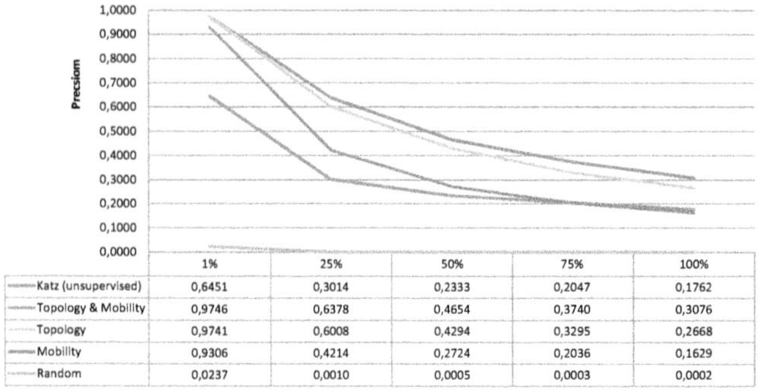

Figure 6: Precision of the best supervised classifiers found over increasing fractions of missing links (1%, 25%, 50%, 75% and 100% of the total 51M missing links sampled), using only network measures, only mobility measures, and combination of both. Precision of best unsupervised classifier (K) and random classifier is shown as baseline.

the previous case, we now consider the entire population of missing links. We study the precision of the unsupervised and supervised methods in this case. In the unsupervised case, the precision for the different measures is computed by considering the fraction of new links in the top-ranked 3,130 cases in the list ordered by the precision of each measure in descending order:

Measure	Precision
Katz	9.1%
Adamic-Adar	7.8%
Spatial Cosine Similarity	5.6%
Weighted Spatial Cosine Similarity	5.6%
Extra-role Co-Location Rate	5.1%
Weighted Co-Location Rate	5.1%
Common Neighbors	5.1%
Co-Location Rate	5.0%
Jaccard	3.0%

As we now have a complete set of negative cases, we corroborate our findings in Sec. 6.2 that mobility measures indeed yield remarkably high predictive power in the unsupervised setting, comparable to network measures in the link prediction literature. Furthermore, various mobility measures have very similar performance, indicating these measures all adequately capture the similarity in mobility patterns.

In the supervised case, after systematic, yet heuristic, exploration of a large space of classification methods with different parameters, we construct a decision-tree using Quinlan's C4.5 classification over the combined network and mobility measures, with cross validation to control over-fitting, applied to the subset of potential links with common neighbors under the further constraint $AA > 0.5$ and $SCoL > 0.7$. Our tree has the following confusion matrix over an independent test set (1 = new link), implying a precision of 73.5% and a recall of 66.1%.

	pred. class = 0	pred. class = 1
actual class = 0	6,627	82
actual class = 1	117	228

Both precision and recall are one order of magnitude larger than all previous figures. The lift chart (Fig. 7) for this classifier shows how, e.g., 86.4% of new links are found by considering only the top 10% positive cases, as ranked by the classifier in descending order of their probability of being new links. Interestingly, we find that the classifier obtained with the procedure discussed above, but using network measures only, has precision 36.2% and recall 6.1%, suggesting that the combination of topology and mobility measures is crucial to achieve high precision and recall. In other words, learning a supervised classifier based on combined network and mobility measures significantly boosts the precision and recall of predicted new links. The price to pay is that we need to focus on a niche of promising potential links with high AA and $SCos$ coefficients, concentrating on a relatively small number of candidates, yet for those we gain a very high probability of guessing the correct new links. While stressing the use of specific classification techniques, e.g., ad-hoc link prediction methods optimized for highly-unbalanced data, such as HPLP [23, 6], to achieve better precision is beyond our goals here, it is indeed an interesting open question for future research.

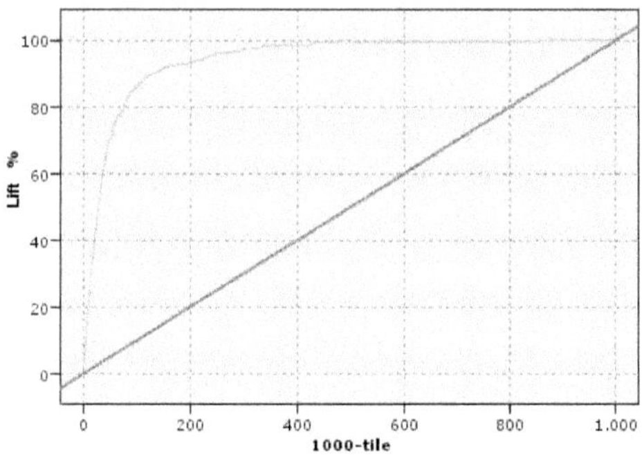

Figure 7: Lift chart of the best decision tree found in the dataset of potential links with common neighbors; the x-axis represents the percentiles of the potential links in the test set ranked by decreasing probability of being new links, as specified by the learned classifier. A point (x, y) in the blue curve represents the fact that y% of the actual new links are found when considering the top-ranked x% potential links predicted as positive. The red straight line is the lift of the random classifier. In our classifier, more than 85% new links are found considering only the 10% most probable positive potential links.

7. RELATED WORK

In this section, we review three categories of related work: studies on human mobility patterns, link prediction in social networks, and interplay between physical space and network structure.

7.1 Human Mobility

In the past few years, the availability of large-scale datasets, such as mobile-phone records and global-positioning-system (GPS) data, has offered researchers from various disciplines access to detailed patterns of human behavior, greatly enhancing our understanding of human mobility.

From statistical physics perspective, significant efforts have been made to understand the patterns of human mobility. Brockmann et al. [4] tested human movements using half a million dollar bills, finding that the dispersal of bills is best modeled by continuous-time random walk (CTRW) models. González et al. [14] then showed that each individual is characterized by a time-independent travel distance and a significant probability to re-visit previous locations, by using mobile phone data of 100,000 individuals. Song et al. [29] then proposed a statistically self-consistent microscopic model for individual mobility. Researchers have also found individuals' daily routines are highly predictable, by using principal component analysis [9] and measuring mobility entropy [30].

From data mining perspective, there have been a number of studies mining frequent patterns on human movements. General approaches are based on frequent patterns and association rules, and build predictive models for future locations. To name a few, Morzy used a modified version of Apriori [25] and Prefixspan [26] algorithms to generate association rules. Jeung et al. [16] developed a hybrid approach by combining predefined motion functions with the movement patterns of the object, extracted by a modified version of the Apriori algorithm. Yavas et al. [32] predicted user movements in a mobile computing system. Furthermore, Giannotti et al. [12, 13] developed trajectory pattern mining, and applied it to predict the next location at a certain level of accuracy by using GPS data [24].

7.2 Link prediction in social networks

Link prediction has attracted much interest in recent years after the seminal work of Liben-Nowell and Kleinberg [21]. It is a significant challenge in machine learning due to the inherent extreme disproportion of positive and negative cases. Existing approaches have focused on defining various proximity measures on network topology, to serve as predictors of new links in both supervised [2, 31, 23, 15] and unsupervised [21] frameworks. Most of the empirical analyses are based on co-authorship networks, and the domain-dependent features developed in certain studies (see, e.g., [2]) are tailored to this particular data set. The supervised high-performance link prediction method HPLP in [23, 15] has also been applied to a large phone dataset, using only network proximity measures.

The fundamental difference of our study from this literature is that we focus on the impact of human mobility, an intrinsic property of human behavior, on link prediction. Indeed, we have designed a broad range of mobile homophily measures and explored their power in predicting new links. Our research is orthogonal to the above line of research, in the sense that any general link prediction method can be used in combination with our mobility features, e.g., the machine learning techniques for extremely unbalanced classes.

7.3 Interplay between physical space and network structure

Although it is in general difficult to obtain data that contain simultaneously the geographical and network information, there have been a few interesting attempts to assess the interplay between the two. For example, there is empirical evidence [19, 18, 22] showing that the probability of forming a social tie decays with distance as a power law. Based on this fact, Backstrom, et al. [3] introduced an algorithm that predicts the location of an individual. A few recent studies focused either on small populations of volunteers, whose whereabouts and social ties were monitored at fine detail using ad-hoc smart-phone applications [10] and location-sharing services [8], or on large but specific online communities such as Flickr [7]. Although none of these data could provide a society-wide picture of either social interactions or individuals' daily routines, these studies indeed indicate that the strong correlation between physical space and network structures emerges in many diverse settings.

8. CONCLUSIONS AND FUTURE WORK

Recent advances on human mobility and social networks have turned the fundamental question, to what extent do individual mobility patterns shape and impact the social network, into a crucial missing chapter in our understanding of human behavior. In this work, by following daily trajectories and communication records of 6 Million mobile phone subscribers, we address this problem for the first time, through both empirical analysis and predictive models. We find the similarity between individuals' movements, their social connectedness and the strength of interactions between them are strongly correlated with each other. Human mobility could indeed serve as a good predictor for the formation of new links, yielding comparable predictive power to traditional network-based measures. Furthermore, by combining both mobility and network measures, we show that the prediction accuracy can be significantly improved in supervised learning.

We believe our findings on the interplay of mobility patterns and social ties offer new perspectives on not only link prediction but also network dynamics. At the same time, they also have important privacy implications. Indeed, the surprising power of mobility patterns in predicting social ties indicates potential information leakage from individuals' movements to their friendship relations, posing a new challenge in privacy protection. Furthermore, we believe our results could impact a wide array of phenomena driven by human movements and social networks, from urban planning to epidemic prevention.

The results presented in this paper also open up many interesting directions for future research. The first is to search for improvement in link prediction tasks by judiciously mixing mobility and network measures. For example, we find that adding co-location measures into Adamic-Adar could yield a precision of 9.6% in unsupervised classification, overtaking any traditional measures listed in the paper. While exhaustively searching for such quantities is beyond our goals here, further work in this direction would be very important. The second direction is to study this problem in a more systematic manner by using more users and different datasets from multiple countries. Indeed, in this paper, we mostly focused on 50k active users from one single country. This approach inevitably introduced some sampling bias, impacts of which are not yet fully-understood. It is therefore important to adapt current frameworks to more users in the dataset and similar datasets from different countries. Another interesting direction is to look at the inverse problem with respect to this work. Indeed, upon uncovering the strong correlations between mobility similarity and social connectedness and predicting links based on mobility patterns, the question thereafter is can we gain more insights about individuals' whereabouts by leveraging our knowledge of their social ties and activity patterns? In sum, the increasing availability of mobile phone data and the emergence of location-based social networking websites has the power to revolutionize our understanding of the interplay between mobility and social networks, making this field particularly fallow for new results.

Acknowledgement. The authors wish to thank members of CCNR in Boston and KDD Lab in Pisa for many useful discussions, and anonymous reviewers for many insightful suggestions. This work was supported by Google Research Award; the *Mobility, Data Mining and Privacy* (MODAP) EU FET OPEN Coord. Action; the NSCTA sponsored by the U.S. ARL under Agreement Number W911NF-09-2-0053; the James S. McDonnell Foundation 21st Century Initiative in Studying Complex Systems; the U.S. ONR under Agreement Number N000141010968; the DTRA awards WMD BRBAA07-J-2-0035 and BRBAA08-Per4-C-2-0033; the NSF within the Information Technology Research (DMR-0426737), and IIS-0513650 programs.

9. REFERENCES

[1] L. Adamic and E. Adar. Friends and neighbors on the web. *Social Networks*, 25(3):211–230, 2003.

[2] M. Al Hasan, V. Chaoji, S. Salem, and M. Zaki. Link prediction using supervised learning. In *SDM: Workshop on Link Analysis, Counter-terrorism and Security*, 2006.

[3] L. Backstrom, E. Sun, and C. Marlow. Find me if you can: improving geographical prediction with social and spatial proximity. In *WWW*, pages 61–70, 2010.

[4] D. Brockmann, L. Hufnagel, and T. Geisel. The scaling laws of human travel. *Nature*, 439(7075):462–465, 2006.

[5] G. Caldarelli. *Scale-free networks: complex webs in nature and technology*. Oxford University Press, 2007.

[6] D. A. Cieslak and N. V. Chawla. Learning decision trees for unbalanced data. In *ECML/PKDD*, pages 241–256, 2008.

[7] D. Crandall, L. Backstrom, D. Cosley, S. Suri, D. Huttenlocher, and J. Kleinberg. Inferring social ties from geographic coincidences. *Proceedings of the National Academy of Sciences*, 107(52):22436, 2010.

[8] J. Cranshaw, E. Toch, J. Hong, A. Kittur, and N. Sadeh. Bridging the gap between physical location and online social networks. In *Ubicomp*, pages 119–128, New York, NY, USA, 2010. ACM.

[9] N. Eagle and A. Pentland. Eigenbehaviors: Identifying structure in routine. *Behavioral Ecology and Sociobiology*, 63(7):1057–1066, 2009.

[10] N. Eagle, A. Pentland, and D. Lazer. Inferring friendship network structure by using mobile phone data. *Proceedings of the National Academy of Sciences*, 106(36):15274, 2009.

[11] D. Easley and J. Kleinberg. *Networks, crowds, and markets: Reasoning about a highly connected world*. Cambridge University Press, 2010.

[12] F. Giannotti, M. Nanni, and D. Pedreschi. Efficient mining of temporally annotated sequences. In *SDM*, 2006.

[13] F. Giannotti, M. Nanni, F. Pinelli, and D. Pedreschi. Trajectory pattern mining. In *KDD*, pages 330–339, 2007.

[14] M. González, C. Hidalgo, and A.-L. Barabási. Understanding individual human mobility patterns. *Nature*, 453(7196):779–782, 2008.

[15] Z. Huang, X. Li, and H. Chen. Link prediction approach to collaborative filtering. In *JCDL*, pages 141–142. ACM, 2005.

[16] H. Jeung, Q. Liu, H. T. Shen, and X. Zhou. A hybrid prediction model for moving objects. In *ICDE*, pages 70–79, 2008.

[17] L. Katz. A new status index derived from sociometric analysis. *Psychometrika*, 18(1):39–43, 1953.

[18] G. Krings, F. Calabrese, C. Ratti, and V. Blondel. Urban gravity: a model for inter-city telecommunication flows. *J. Stat. Mech.-Theor. Exp.*, page L07003, 2009.

[19] R. Lambiotte, V. Blondel, C. De Kerchove, E. Huens, C. Prieur, Z. Smoreda, and P. Van Dooren. Geographical dispersal of mobile communication networks. *Physica A: Statistical Mechanics and its Applications*, 387(21):5317–5325, 2008.

[20] J. Leskovec, L. Backstrom, R. Kumar, and A. Tomkins. Microscopic evolution of social networks. In *KDD*, pages 462–470, 2008.

[21] D. Liben-Nowell and J. M. Kleinberg. The link prediction problem for social networks. In *CIKM*, pages 556–559, 2003.

[22] D. Liben-Nowell, J. Novak, R. Kumar, P. Raghavan, and A. Tomkins. Geographic routing in social networks. *Proceedings of the National Academy of Sciences*, 102(33):11623, 2005.

[23] R. Lichtenwalter, J. T. Lussier, and N. V. Chawla. New perspectives and methods in link prediction. In *KDD*, pages 243–252, 2010.

[24] A. Monreale, F. Pinelli, R. Trasarti, and F. Giannotti. Wherenext: a location predictor on trajectory pattern mining. In *KDD*, pages 637–646, 2009.

[25] M. Morzy. Prediction of moving object location based on frequent trajectories. In *ISCIS*, pages 583–592, 2006.

[26] M. Morzy. Mining frequent trajectories of moving objects for location prediction. In *MLDM*, pages 667–680, 2007.

[27] J. P. Onnela, J. Saramaki, J. Hyvonen, G. Szabo, D. Lazer, K. Kaski, J. Kertesz, and A.-L. Barabasi. Structure and tie strengths in mobile communication networks. *Proceedings of the National Academy of Sciences*, 104(18):7332–7336, 2007.

[28] M. Rivera, S. Soderstrom, and B. Uzzi. Dynamics of Dyads in Social Networks: Assortative, Relational, and Proximity Mechanisms. *Annual Review of Sociology*, 36:91–115, 2010.

[29] C. Song, T. Koren, P. Wang, and A.-L. Barabási. Modelling the scaling properties of human mobility. *Nature Physics*, 2010.

[30] C. Song, Z. Qu, N. Blumm, and A.-L. Barabasi. Limits of predictability in human mobility. *Science*, 327(5968):1018, 2010.

[31] C. Wang, V. Satuluri, and S. Parthasarathy. Local probabilistic models for link prediction. In *ICDM*, pages 322–331, 2007.

[32] G. Yavas, D. Katsaros, Ö. Ulusoy, and Y. Manolopoulos. A data mining approach for location prediction in mobile environments. *Data Knowl. Eng.*, 54(2):121–146, 2005.

I Want to Answer, Who Has a Question? Yahoo! Answers Recommender System

Gideon Dror, Yehuda Koren, Yoelle Maarek and Idan Szpektor
Yahoo! Research
Haifa 31905, Israel
{gideon.dror,yehudako,yoelle.maarek,idan_szpektor}@yahoo.com

ABSTRACT

Yahoo! Answers is currently one of the most popular question answering systems. We claim however that its user experience could be significantly improved if it could route the "right question" to the "right user." Indeed, while some users would rush answering a question such as "what should I wear at the prom?," others would be upset simply being exposed to it. We argue here that Community Question Answering sites in general and Yahoo! Answers in particular, need a mechanism that would expose users to questions they can relate to and possibly answer.

We propose here to address this need via a multi-channel recommender system technology for associating questions with potential answerers on Yahoo! Answers. One novel aspect of our approach is exploiting a wide variety of content and social signals users regularly provide to the system and organizing them into channels. Content signals relate mostly to the text and categories of questions and associated answers, while social signals capture the various user interactions with questions, such as asking, answering, voting, etc. We fuse and generalize known recommendation approaches within a single symmetric framework, which incorporates and properly balances multiple types of signals according to channels. Tested on a large scale dataset, our model exhibits good performance, clearly outperforming standard baselines.

Categories and Subject Descriptors

H.2.8 [**Database Management**]: Database Apps—*Data Mining*

General Terms

Algorithms

Keywords

Recommender systems, User models, Yahoo! Answers

1. INTRODUCTION

In spite of the continuous progress of Web search engines in the last 20 years, many users' needs still remain unanswered. Two common reasons for queries not being satisfied are (1) the intent behind the query not being well expressed, and (2) the absence of relevant content. Query assistance tools such as query auto-completion or related queries cannot, as of today, deal with complex, heterogeneous needs. In addition, there will always exist ill-defined, subjective or narrow needs for which content has little chance to have been authored prior to the query being issued. As humorously written by Alexia Tsotsis[1] *"Just Because Google Exists Doesn't Mean You Should Stop Asking People Things."*

Community Question Answering (CQA) sites have been precisely devised to answer these different needs. Examples include Yahoo! Answers, Baidu Zhidao, Naver Ji-Sik-In, WikiAnswers, or more recent ones such as Aardvark, Quora and Facebook Questions. While CQA sites can feature factoid questions, their primary goal is to satisfy needs such as opinion seeking (*"What do you think about my song lyrics?"*), recommendation (*"We are a family of five, what's a good travel destination in Europe?"*), open-ended questions, (*"I would like to study in France next year, what should I do if I don't master the language?"*) or problem solving (*"How do I solve this Poisson distribution problem?"*).

In this work, we focus on Yahoo! Answers, one of the largest CQA sites with 30 millions questions and answers a month and 2.4 asked questions per second [19]. One important characteristic of Yahoo! Answers, as compared to WikiAnswers for instance, is that its primary goal is to satisfy the asker's needs, even if the majority of users would have preferred other answers. In addition, unlike more recent players such as Facebook Questions, Yahoo! Answers users broadcast their questions to potentially all users of the site.

Searching for questions to answer is a different challenge than regular Web search, as users are driven by more than content similarity or page popularity. In practice, users of Yahoo! Answers find it hard to search for questions they would like to answer. When in an "answering mood," they mainly skim through long and dynamic lists of open questions. Figure 1 shows a snapshot of a list of recent questions at a given time, demonstrating the difficulty of finding questions to answer on the front page of Yahoo! Answers. Browsing by category only slightly corrects this issue.

We propose to address the "answering mood" need by suggesting the "right questions" to potential answerers via a novel multi-channel recommender (MCR) system approach. The key challenge here is to adequately define the subjective notion of "right." In addition, unlike typical recommendation tasks, such as book recommendation, which aims to satisfy the user (*e.g.*, the buyer is the target as well as the judge of quality), in our task, while the target user is the answerer, the quality of the answer is judged by others, namely the asker or the community of voters.

Potential answerers are driven by multiple factors, ranging from

KDD'11, August 21–24, 2011, San Diego, California, USA.

[1] http://techcrunch.com/2010/10/23/google-vs-humans/

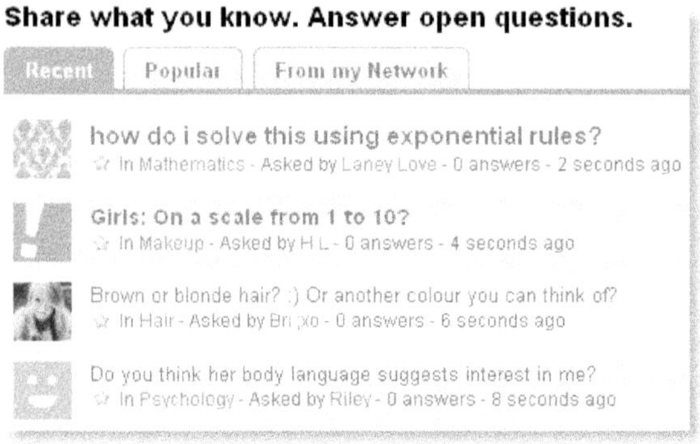

Figure 1: A snapshot of the most recent questions in Yahoo! Answers, showing the diversity of questions.

personal expertise to social reward and game experience. They might pick questions according to their domain of interest, to the number of previous answers (targeting those with only a few answers for better chance to get a best answer), to the users involved or for simple entertainment purpose. Consequently, we present a novel recommender system approach that combines a broad mix of signals available within the system, integrating different recommender system disciplines.

Our key contribution is a novel multi-channel recommendation model, which accounts for the multiple dimensions of the data. Our model combines multiple types of textual features, following the *content analysis* school of recommender systems. These features originate from fields of different importance levels, and their respective weights are automatically determined. At the same time, in a fully symmetric manner, the model weighs together different types of user actions and social features thus following a *collaborative filtering* approach. The model was designed for the special needs of question routing in Yahoo! Answers, but we expect it to fit other scenarios where multiple types of features, with varying importance levels, need to be integrated together in order to fully describe user behavior.

2. RELATED WORK AND BACKGROUND

2.1 Yahoo! Answers

With more than a billion posted answers[2], Yahoo! Answers is currently the largest existing CQA site. The system is question-centric, rather than user-centric as in more recent systems such as Quora. In addition to asking and answering questions, users can "star" an interesting question, vote for a best answer, and rate answers with "thumbs up" or "thumbs down." They can also "trace" questions to receive activity updates, and follow the activity of other users becoming their "fans."

A question thread starts by a user asking a question and assigning it to a category out of a list of predefined categories. The question remains "open" for four days with an option for extension, or for less if the asker chose a best answer within this period. If after this time period no best answer is chosen, its status changes into "in-voting", and any user can then vote for a best answer until a clear winner arises. Only then is the question considered "resolved."

One of the main problems in Yahoo! Answers is a high variance in perceived question and answer quality. This problem was the object of numerous research studies in recent years. Some studies attempted to assess the quality of answers [2, 21, 24], or questions [22, 23], and rank them accordingly. Others looked at active users, scoring their "reliability" as an indicator of quality for answers or votes [5, 15], identifying spammers [16], or predicting whether the asker of a question will be satisfied with the received answers [3].

All of these prior efforts focus on evaluating content quality *after the fact*, *i.e.*, after questions have been resolved. Our research focuses on a complementary task: matching questions to users *before answers are written*. Our goal is not only to increase the flow of answers and the chance for answerers to achieve a best answer rating, but also in the long run to improve the overall quality of Yahoo! Answers. To the best of our knowledge, only the recent work of Horowitz and Kamvar [12], addresses this task in CQA. We next review it within the larger scope of recommender systems.

2.2 Recommender Systems

We argue here that the problem at hand is a natural fit for a recommender system approach. Indeed, recommender systems attempt to profile user preferences and model the interaction between users and products [13] and are increasingly excelling at dealing with huge collections. In our case, the items to be recommended to users are simply questions.

Recommender systems are based on two different strategies: *collaborative filtering* (CF) and *content analysis* (CA) [9]. The CF approach relies on analyzing relationships between users and interdependencies among products in order to identify new user-item matches. The only required information is the past behavior of users, such as their previous transactions or product ratings. The two primary schools of CF are (1) latent factor models, which explain ratings by characterizing both items and users on factors inferred from rating patterns, *e.g.*, by matrix factorization [14] and (2) neighborhood methods. The original neighborhood methods (user-user) compute the relationships among users, estimating unknown ratings based on recorded ratings of like minded users [11]. An analogous alternative is the item-item approach that estimates ratings by exploiting previous ratings made by the same user on similar items [17, 20]. In Yahoo! Answers the items (*e.g.*, the questions) are volatile, with new questions arriving every second, while the user population is more constant. Hence, user-user methods are more relevant to our task.

While CF has enjoyed much success recently, it is still facing severe difficulties in the so-called *cold-start* scenarios, in which items to recommend are new to the system and have experienced very few (if at all) user actions. We must consider such scenarios as well, since the most interesting questions are often those that did not attract mass user interactions and have not yet been answered in a satisfactory manner. Hence, we also resort to the other class of recommender systems techniques, namely, content analysis. These techniques create a characterizing profile for each user or product. The resulting profiles allow programs to associate users with matching products. Our method introduces a novel, symmetric integration of CF with CA approaches that allows exploiting behavioral signals together with user- and question-attributes.

Some prior works also addressed the need to combine CA with CF, sometimes known as *hybrid recommenders*. Among the more recent notable works are [1, 10], which are both based on latent factor models, where the factors are initialized and centered on item and user attributes. Our approach is different. We chose not to rely on latent factor modeling for two key reasons. First, learning such a model is non-trivial when dealing with volatile questions and relatively new users. Second, as justified later, we would like to use a multi-channel approach. Such an approach, while being critical to success, renders the known factor models less usable, hence the need to develop an alternate methodology.

[2]http://yanswersblog.com/index.php/archives/2010/05/03/1-billion-answers-served/

A recent study [12], discussed the related problem of routing questions to users of the social service Aardvark. The proposed system is centered around external sources of social relations between users, and on assignment of questions and users into predefined topics. Our setup requires a different treatment: external social relations are not available, but we need to differentiate between a rich variety of user-question interaction signals accessible within Yahoo! Answers. Our approach is very different from expert search tasks such as [18, 4] that try to identify an authoritative answer that would satisfy most; in our context the key objective is to satisfy the sole asker, in a variety of questions, some factoid but many being subjective where the notion of expertise is irrelevant.

Finally, an interesting related work deals with Google news recommendation [6]. The problem there is similar to ours in terms of scalability and volatility of items with a high churn rate. The authors use a blend of three separate CF methods in a highly scalable fashion. We follow a different direction, in combining CA with CF, and in addressing separate types of user feedback.

3. PROBLEM CHARACTERIZATION

Recommender systems face multiple recognized challenges, such as non-uniform data patterns (each user interacting with a different set of items), data sparseness, noisy user input, and scalability. Beyond these, the task of recommending questions brings additional, less well addressed challenges, which induce the unique design criteria for our model. We believe that such challenges are and will continue being typical in other recommendation scenarios, especially those involving user generated content.

The first factor to consider is that different families of item descriptors need to be exploited. A question may be described by textual attributes, which come from the question itself and from its answers. Another question descriptor may be its category, as selected by the asker. Finally, following a common approach in collaborative-filtering systems, a question may be annotated with social attributes: the set of users that showed interest in it. It seems that incorporating different kinds of signals somehow compensates for the severe sparseness of the data. A major challenge arising here is finding a smooth and natural way of integrating these different attribute types, while expressing the different significance level of each. This becomes even more challenging when considering the multiple channels through which users can interact with a question, as detailed below.

A second factor comes from the need to account for the multiple kinds of interactions of different intensities between users and questions. These interactions range from more explicit/active expressions of interest like asking or answering a question, to more passive ones such as emailing a question to a contact. When data per user and item is scarce, exploiting these diverse types of user-item interactions is vital. Yet, care should be taken when integrating different signals together, since some types of interactions should be more indicative than others. For example, we would expect that answering be a more meaningful interaction than mailing. Our approach induces hundreds of interactions, so we must rely on an automated procedure for combining them together effectively.

Finally, we have a major interest in new questions, which are those requiring solicitation of answerers. This represents a significant departure from the common recommender system setup, where the item-set is close to static. Such a setup usually dedicates distinct parameters for each item, *e.g.*, item-item similarity weights or item factor vectors. Yet, our approach for modeling questions should be different, since only scarce information is usually available for fresh questions. Thus, we refrain from directly modeling specific questions via associated parameters. Instead, questions are treated and parameterized through their attributes, which are shared among all questions. This decision also greatly benefits the computational complexity of our model. With millions of questions in our inventory, and several new questions arriving each second, both time and space complexities become easier to manage when not modeling each question in isolation.

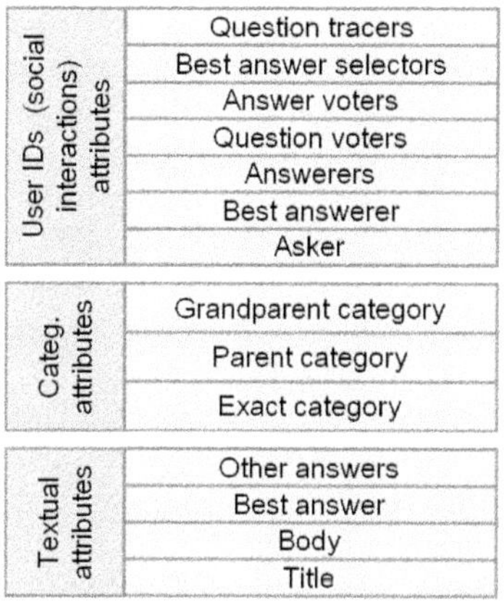

Figure 2: Three families of question attributes

We note that the very nature of our data blurs the distinction between social and content-based signals as the the textual content annotating a question is the result of a social interaction. Conversely, user feedback, or "ratings," also represent a form of content. Hence, a cornerstone of our modeling choice is to smoothly merge social-based collaborative filtering with attribute-based content analysis.

4. A MULTI-CHANNEL RECOMMENDER SYSTEM MODEL

In this section we introduce a Multi-Channel Recommender system model (MCR) for assessing the match between a user and a question. We first explain how questions and users are mapped into their *attribute representation*, then how multiple *features* are derived from the multi-channel attributes of the users and questions and finally how user and question-specific features are incorporated into MCR and how the model is trained.

4.1 Question Attributes

Question attributes are split into three *families* according to their source: textual, categories and user IDs, as illustrated in Figure 2.

4.1.1 Textual Family

The first family of attributes encodes textual information and takes text tokens as values. These tokens are extracted from the various textual fields associated with the question. For each text block, our tokenizer annotates each word with its part-of-speech (POS) tag and lemma. The output of this process consists of a list of lemmatized terms (words or multi-word expressions), together with their POS tags.

As previously mentioned, question fields are of varying importance. Hence, the extracted terms are counted separately within each field, producing four sets of $(term, count)$ as values of four attributes: the question *title*, the question *body*, the *best answer* and finally *other answers*.

Following a common information retrieval approach, we filter out non-representative terms (trivial examples being stop words). This is done in two steps. First, for every question, we retain only terms that are either nouns, verbs or adjectives, based on their POS tags. Then, each term t is ranked by its "usefulness" $L(t)$. We define "usefulness" as the entropy of the (smoothed) distribution of categories given t, where the distribution is over the number of occurrences of t in each category. Entropy plays here the same role as *idf* in the vector space model used in information retrieval.

$$L(t) = H_C(t) = -\sum_{c \in C} \Pr(c|t)\log(\Pr(c|t))$$

$$\Pr(c|t) = \frac{\#_c(t) + \alpha}{\sum_{c' \in C}[\#_{c'}(t) + \alpha]}$$

where C is the set of all categories in Yahoo! Answers, $\#_c(t)$ is the number of times term t appeared in text fields within category c, and $\alpha = \frac{100}{|C|}$. Note that $H_C(t)$ is a principled way to perform a *tf-idf* style ranking, where categories are playing the role of documents. We chose categories instead of questions as the "documents" since a question is typically very short while a category typically contains a lot of text that is related to a specific topic. Note that we keep only the N best terms of lowest $L(t)$ value. We verified that by setting N to $65,000$, 99% of questions kept at least one textual attribute. As an illustration, consider the question "*Would the introduction of new technology ruin the tension in football? If so: why?*." Table 1 shows examples of its textual attributes: "football" appears once in the title, once in the best answer, 20 times in other answers, "technology" appears once in the title, 33 times in other answers, etc.

4.1.2 Category Family

Another family of attributes reflects the category of the question that the user has to select, from a predefined taxonomy, when posting question. We obviously select the user-selected category as a direct attribute, but we also add parent and grand-parent categories, when available, in order to inherit semantic similarities. Indeed, the shared parent category, "Internet", between "YouTube" and "Flickr" makes questions posted in "YouTube" closer to those posted in "Flickr" than in "Dogs". We limit ourselves to direct, parent and grand-parent as this is the current maximal depth in Yahoo! Answers. An instance of direct, parent and grand-parent category attributes for the previously mentioned example question, which was posted in the category "*Sports >Football (Soccer) > UEFA Champions League*", is shown in Table 1.

4.1.3 User IDs Family

The third family of attributes relates to the identity of the users who interacted with a question. Users can interact with a question in various ways, each deserving a different treatment. Therefore, we maintain a distinct attribute for each type of role, and count separately the number of interactions for a given role. We thus have seven attributes for seven roles, each taking as value a set of $(user\_id, count)$:

- *asker:* the user asking the question
- *best answerer:* the user who provided the best answer
- *answerers:* other users who answered the question
- *question voters:* users who starred the question as interesting
- *answer voters:* users who voted on the quality of individual answers (by "thumb up/down" votes)
- *best answer selectors:* users who participated in the best answer voting process

Table 1: Example of attributes for "*Would the introduction of new technology ruin the tension in football? If so: why?*"

Attribute	Value
title	{(football,1),(technology,1),...}
best answer	{(football,1),(ref,1),...}
other answers	{(football,20),(technology,33),(ref,6),...}
category	UEFA Champions League
parent category	Football (Soccer)
grand parent category	Sports
asker	id(Patrick Viera)
best answerer	id(Dazman)
tracers	{u9, u20, u100}

- *question tracers:* users who requested to receive updates on the question

This model is flexible as it is easy to add more types of interaction as they become available. Some signals that we have not leveraged yet and plan to consider in the future relate to passive interactions, such as clicks on a specific question. While these signals may be weak at the individual question level, they remain the main signals for non signed-in or very new users, and could potentially bring value when aggregated over the large population of Yahoo! Answers anonymous visitors. Table 1 lists user ids attributes for our same example question. As per their values, we see that the question was asked by Patrick Viera, user 'Dazman' got the best answer, and 3 users, identified by their ids, u9, u20, u100, traced it.

4.1.4 Formal question attributes model

Let us now define a formal notation for question attributes. A question q is described by an attribute matrix $Q_q \in \mathbb{R}^{d_2 \times d_1}$. The d_1 columns of the matrix correspond to each individual textual token, category and user. The d_2 rows correspond to the attributes. $Q_q[i][j]$ holds the count for term j of attribute i. In the example in Table 1, $Q_q[title][football] = 1$. In our current implementation $d_2 = 14$, as follows. The first four rows of the matrix, $Q_q[1 \dots 4, :]$, correspond to the textual attributes. The next three rows correspond to the categories family. Finally, $Q_q[8 \dots 14, :]$ correspond to the user attribute family. The matrix is saved in a sparse representation.

4.2 User attributes

User properties are mainly derived from the properties of questions with which the respective user has interacted. Hence, they borrow much of the basic structure of the question attributes, following the three-family, multi-attribute structure. Additionally, users may explicitly pick their preferences over attributes within each of the attribute families. We next describe these two types of attribute sources and their formal modeling.

4.2.1 Question-driven attributes

In our model, users adopt many of their properties from the questions and answers they interact with in separate ways. We do not want to arbitrarily weigh the relative importance of each of these interaction types. Hence, we keep them separate by adding another dimension to the user repository, called *channels*. This dimension has no parallel in the question repository. In Section 4.5, we learn the relative importance of each channel.

In our implementation, depicted in Figure 3, we use the following channels that qualify the user interaction with the questions: (1) asked, (2) best answered, (3) answered, (4) voted on question, (5) voted on an associated answer, (6) voted on best answer, (7) traced the question. Note that these seven channels are exactly those that were used for the social attributes annotating a question. However,

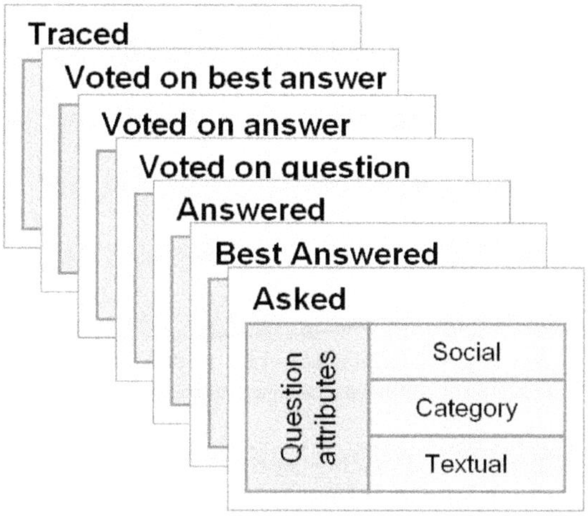

Figure 3: Seven channels

here they serve a different purpose: associating a user with questions (rather than annotating a question with users). Each channel, in a complete separation from the other channels, aggregates properties from the questions corresponding to a certain kind of interaction. Importantly, this aggregation still preserves the multi-family representation of the aggregated question attributes.

For example, for the 'best answered' channel, all question attributes for which the user gave the best answer are aggregated. Thus, textual attributes have their values aggregated across these questions, with a separate summation of term counts for each attribute. Similarly for user-ID attributes, we aggregate all other users who interacted with questions for which the target user gave best answer. This gives rise to multiple modes of user-user relations, on which we elaborate next.

The model describes 49 kinds of user-user interaction. Those are generated by the Cartesian product of the two identical 7-tuples {*asked, best answered, answered, voted on question, voted on answer, voted on best answer, traced*}. Here, for example, relations such as (*best answered, asked*) correspond to users who asked questions for which the target user gave the best answer. These explicitly stored user-user interactions are analogous to traditional user-user collaborative filtering models, with one main distinction: we do not list a single type of user-user relation, but rather 49 different such relations. Furthermore, our model addresses additional kinds of *implicit* social relations. All textual information entered by a user for a question is being added to the attributes of all other users interacting with the same question. The resulting hybrid of textual and social features is a key to the success of the model by alleviating the sparseness problem of textual attributes.

Using multiple channels of interaction is not as prohibitive in terms of scale as it might seem. Indeed, a classifier can easily handle and weigh them together such a number of possibilities as discussed in Section 4.3. The benefit of using multiple types of interaction lies in the flexibility to weigh each such interaction appropriately in a data-driven learning, without worrying about a dilution effect caused by adding less important interactions. This enables us to consider all available modes of interactions, thereby exploiting all available signals and lessening the sparseness problem.

4.2.2 *Explicit user attributes*

Beyond the so-far discussed channels, which capture indirect, question-derived user attributes, we allocate one more channel for expressing direct user preferences. For example, a user can explicitly specify which keywords and categories he is interested in, or which other users s/he would like to follow. All these are stored within an additional channel that we refer to as the *explicit relations* channel. In Yahoo! Answers, the only explicit relation currently available is which users are followed by the modeled user. So the textual and category families within the explicit relations channel remain empty.

4.2.3 *Formal user attributes model*

Formally, a user u is represented by a 3-dimensional tensor (or, a "cube") $U_u \in \mathbb{R}^{d_3 \times d_2 \times d_1}$. The first dimension of the tensor corresponds to the channels of interaction ($d_3 = 8$ in our implementation). The other two dimensions correspond to attributes and values, in analogy to the question representation. For all channels except the last one, we derive attributes from corresponding question attributes. This is accomplished in the following manner. Let $c \in \{1$ (=asked), 2 (=best answered), 3 (=answered), 4 (=voted on question), 5 (=voted on answer), 6 (=voted on best answer), 7 (=traced)$\}$ be a channel. We denote by $Q^c(u)$ the set of questions with which user u interacted through channel c. Then, the corresponding part of the user attributes is defined as:

$$U_u[c, :, :] = \sum_{q \in Q^c(u)} Q_q$$

Two remarks are in place:

1. While we chose to aggregate by summation, an alternative implementation could have been averaging:

$$U_u[c, :, :] = \frac{\sum_{q \in Q^c(u)} Q_q}{|Q^c(u)|}$$

However, such an averaging loses the relative support of the channel, which dictates its relative importance compared to other channels. For example, one user may have "asked" much more than "voted," whereas another user mostly "traced," but rarely "asked" or "voted." Clearly, these two users deserve different treatments when combining their channels.

2. Typical user-user models store only nearest neighbors user-user relations reflecting the strongest user-user relations. We currently do not employ this option, as our data is already sparse enough and do not require any further sparsification.

4.3 Interaction features

Our goal is to predict which users will answer a question. To this end, given a user and a question, their respective attributes are compared, generating *interaction features*. These features are used by a classifier to evaluate the match between the user and the question.

Pairing each question attribute with each user attribute creates multiple features. Since attributes of different families share no overlap (*e.g.*, a textual attribute has nothing in common with a social attribute, which contain users rather than words), we concentrate only on attribute pairs within the same family. For each question and user attributes of the same family, we create a distinct interaction feature by measuring the (modified) cosine similarity between their corresponding attribute vectors, which is a common way of measuring interaction. Note that the user attribute is a composite index, consisting of a channel and a question attribute.

Formally, let t be one of the question attributes, and s be one of the user attributes under channel c, such that s and t belong to the same family. Then, the interaction feature resulting by matching s and t under c is the inner product:

$$\frac{Q_q[t]^T}{\|Q_q[t]^T\|} \cdot \frac{U_u[c, s]}{\|\sum_{c'} U_u[c', s]\|}$$

We modify the cosine, by normalizing the second multiplier by $\|\sum_{c'} U_u[c', s]\|$. As mentioned earlier, the usual $\|U_u[c, s]\|$ normalizer would be unwise, as it wipes out all information on the relative strength of various channels for the specific user.

In our data, the textual family consists of four attributes: title, body, best answer, and other answers. In the user model, these attributes are multiplied by the seven aforementioned channels. Therefore, four question-attributes interact with 28 user attributes, thus producing 112 separate interaction features. Similarly the three attributes of the category family on the question side interact with 21 user-side category attributes, yielding 63 interaction features. Finally, the 7 social attributes of a question interact with the 50 social attributes of a user (including the added attribute from the explicit relations channel), adding 350 social interaction features. In total, the number of interaction features employed is 525.

4.4 Bias features

The so far mentioned interaction features explain the match between a user and a question. However, one can observe additional activities in the system that do relate to the matching of a particular user to a certain question. For example, some users are simply more active than others and sometimes answer questions unrelated to their field of interest, seemingly just for the sake of it. Similarly, some questions that already received several answers are less attractive to users who shoot for best answer votes.

We address these intuitions by adding 5 user-specific and question-specific biases as features to each question-user pair. For users, we add the number of best answers and the number of other answers they provided in the last 4 months, which is the time period used to build the user models in our experiments. For questions, we add the current number of answers, stars and votes at the engagement time of the matched user with the question.

4.5 Learning to route questions

The level of fit between a user and a question is learned from their respective features. Given a user, we employ a binary classifier that distinguishes between questions that meet the user's preferences and skills, and questions that do not. In order to train the classifier, we create a training set of user-question pairs, with positive and negative examples. More details on the construction of the training set and a corresponding test-set are provided in Section 5.1, while the choice of a classifier for optimal performance on these datasets is detailed in Section 5.2.

5. EMPIRICAL STUDY

5.1 Experimental Setup

In our approach, user profiles (or rather their attributes) are rather static, while question profiles are highly dynamic. Hence, in the following experiments, we built user profiles based on past user activity, and then, at test time, we match these users to new questions. User profiles were constructed from four consecutive months of Yahoo! Answers activity logs. New questions were then taken from the following fifth month.

In order to train and test our model for the task of question-routing, we need a dataset containing both positive and negative examples of question-user pairs. Here, positive examples are pairs for which it is known that the user can answer well the question. They can be comfortably generated by picking users and questions for which they provided best answers.

Generating negative examples is trickier, as the data does not provide any explicit indication as to which questions do not fit a user. We are thus confronted to a one class problem, which requires

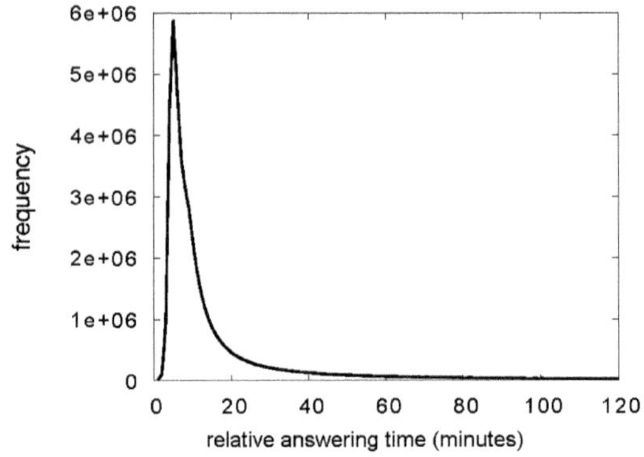

Figure 4: Frequency of answering time relative to question creation time over a 4 month period

from us to generate negative examples that are close to the true classification boundary.

A simple approach for generating negative examples is by randomly sampling from the Cartesian product of users and questions, assuming that almost all pairs are negatives. Yet, the vast majority of these pairs have no shared value, and thus all interaction features are null. As an example, it would be trivial to identify that a question posted at *Beauty & Style* will probably not be answered by a user whose activity is centered about *Video & Online Games* category. Hence, while a classifier trained on such data would perform almost perfectly in distinguishing positive from negative examples, the learned classifier would not be helpful in the more interesting and delicate cases. Thus, aiming at a better negative example set, we randomly sampled negative examples as user-question pairs such that the question's category is among the categories the user previously interacted with (posted a question, answered etc.). The task at hand is therefore more difficult problem, as the model is now required to identify user's propensity and tastes at a finer level of granularity, within a category.

As already discussed, user engagement time may have a substantial effect on user-question matching, since at the information available for the tested question, and thus the feature-set presented to the classifier, varies with time. In this, work we considered typical user behavior in the system. For positive examples, engagement time was taken as the time the user actually answered the question. For each negative example, engagement time was sampled according to answer time distribution in Yahoo! Answers (Figure 4). Notice that almost all answers are given within 60 minutes of the question creation time. Our final dataset consisted of $1,256,262$ examples with an equal number of positive and negative examples. The set had $169,392$ unique users, and each user was associated with an identical number of positive and negative examples. In the following, we use a $80\% : 20\%$ split between training and test sets respectively, so that the sets are user disjoint.

5.2 Model Training

We conducted extensive preliminary experimentation, training the MCR model using several linear and non-linear classifiers. Since the feature space is not very large (530 features), we could afford using complex classifiers. The best results were achieved by Gradient Boosted Decision Trees (GBDT) [7, 8]. The GBDT classifier robustly estimated our complex model thanks to our compact representation of only several hundred features, together with the large number of examples (see Section 5.1).

There are four parameters controlling GBDT: (1) number of trees,

(2) size of each tree, (3) shrinkage (or, "learning rate"), and (4) sampling rate. Our experiments did not show much sensitivity to any of these parameters. In our setup the parameter settings are: #trees=100, tree-size=20, shrinkage=1, and sampling-rate=0.5. As we position our problem as a classification problem, we trained the GBDT classifier using logistic loss.

5.3 Baseline Models

We used a flat representation of overlapping features as baseline models. In this representation, each textual term, category id and user id is a feature with an associated weight. The weight of each feature is the sum, over all channels and attributes, of the multiplication of the feature weight in the question and in the user models. Formally, using the notation introduced in Sections 4.1.4 and 4.2.3, the baseline representation of a user-question example is described by a feature vector, where the weight of feature f is:

$$\sum_c \sum_s \sum_t w_c \cdot Q_q[t, f] \cdot U_u[c, s, f]$$

where c are all the possible channels; s and t are all the possible user and question attributes, respectively. Finally, w_c are manually set channel weights, following a common practice of using *ad hoc* weights when dealing with multi-channel data. Note that, while information is lost once all channels and attributes are aggregated together, the baseline models have the power to set a different weight for each specific basic feature (textual term, user id, etc), which is not possible in the MCR model.

We constructed two baselines: the *simple baseline* model assumes all channels are equally informative ($w_c = 1$), whereas the *weighted baseline* assumes some interactions of the user with the system are more informative. Specifically, for the weighted baseline, we manually chose $w_c = 1$ for *asking, answering* and *best-answering* and $w_c = \frac{1}{2}$ for the remaining channels.

In this setup, the dimensionality of the feature space of the baseline models is very high $(122, 564)$. This prevents us from training a complex classifier such as GBDT. Yet, it has been established that linear classifiers are among the best performers when dealing with high-dimensional classification [25]. Accordingly, the baseline models were trained using Stochastic Gradient Decent with a logistic loss, efficiently implemented by Vowpal Wabbit [3]. We trained both baseline models with learning rate decreasing as $\eta_t \simeq t^{-1}$ and set the number of epochs to 15, as further training had no significant effect on results.

It turned out that such feature weights are not suitable for gradient-based classifiers. This is due to the fact that different features have different scales and that the norms of feature vectors for different users differ by several orders of magnitude. We examined several ways to modify the feature distribution: (1) *standardization*: each feature is scaled so that its variance is 1, (2) *logarithm transformation*: $x_i \leftarrow \log(1 + x_i)$ and (3) *normalization*: the features of each feature family (category, text, user-ids) are scaled to have a squared norm 1. Table 2 shows that the weighted baseline with normalization provided best results and thus can be used for comparison with the MCR model. Note that this normalization is similar to the one applied to the features in Section 4.3.

Table 2: Baseline accuracy using various weight preprocessing

	original	standardized	log	normalized
Simple Baseline	0.538	0.537	0.559	0.590
Weighted Baseline	0.544	0.539	0.563	0.593

[3]http://hunch.net/~vw/

Table 3: Performance of MCR vs baseline

	Accuracy	AUC
Weighted Baseline	0.593	0.637
MCR	0.741	0.824

Table 4: Top eight intersection features for the MCR model

Channel	Question attribute	User attribute	Importance
best-answerer	category	category	100.00
other-answerer	category	category	37.26
admin	asker	fan	32.16
other-answerer	title	title	22.54
best-answerer	title	title	21.07
best-answerer	asker	asker	15.60
other-answerer	gpcategory†	gpcategory†	15.30
best-answer-voter	title	title	14.53

†'gpcategory' stands for 'grandparent category'

Table 5: Ablation tests on different feature-subsets

Feat. Families	No. features	Accuracy	AUC
social	350	0.593	0.642
text	112	0.718	0.728
social + text	462	0.721	0.725
category	63	0.729	0.804
social + category	413	0.731	0.802
text + category	175	0.738	0.813
all	530	0.741	0.824

5.4 Results

We evaluated the performance of MCR and the baseline by calculating the *accuracy* and the *Area Under ROC Curve (AUC)* on test examples. Accuracy is a standard metric for classifiers performance, measuring the fraction of correctly classified examples. The AUC metric measures the probability that a positive example is scored higher than a negative example. Unlike accuracy, AUC does not depend on a choice of threshold for segregating test examples into positives and negatives.

Table 3 details the results for the two models. Although considerable work was invested in improving the baseline, the MCR model performance turned out to be significantly better with no tuning whatsoever. This result shows the advantage of the MCR model, integrating various recommendation signals via different interaction channels, while automatically setting their relative importance.

To gain some insight on our model's performance, we inspected the most important features, as ranked by GBDT. Table 4 details the eight most important features, whose importance is normalized such that the top ranking feature has importance score of 100. Each feature in the table is composed of the channel, question and user attributes involved in generating it. From the table we see that the top features are quite evenly distributed between textual attributes (title), category attributes (category) and social (user) attributes (fan, asker), showing the importance of utilizing each of these families. In addition, while the dominating channels are mostly related to answers, one of the highest ranked features come from the 'best-answer-vote' channel, and not from directly answering a question, indicating a strong correlation between users who participate in best-answer voting and those who could actually answer well the target question. This also shows the importance of splitting the attribute space into multiple channels, as otherwise this signal would have been lost.

To further analyze the MCR model, we conducted ablation tests on the different attribute families utilized in our approach: textual, category and user social attributes. Table 5 describes the results of testing the classifier with the possible feature-subsets, as well as the number of features in each subset. The results show that direct social features between users play only a marginal role in the dis-

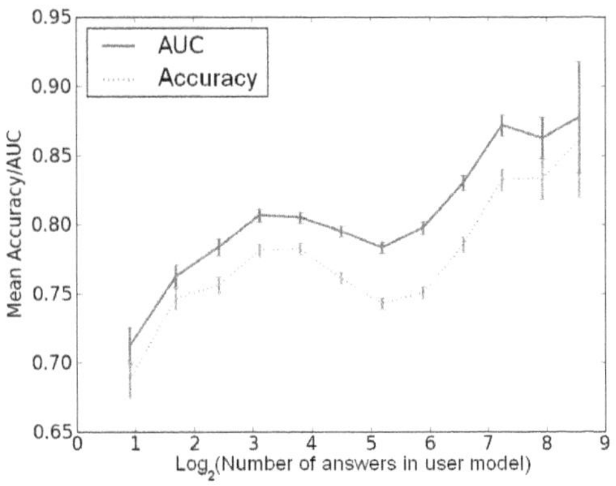

Figure 5: Mean accuracy and AUC vs. past number of answers by user (error bars represent standard deviation)

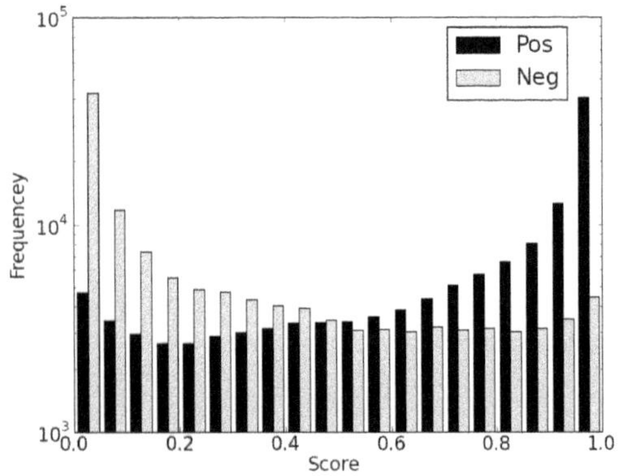

Figure 6: Frequencies of positive (black) and negative (gray) test examples as a function of their MCR scores

covery of promising user-question pairs. This is an opposite result to the successful utilization of social features in other recommender system setups (see Section 2.2). Yet, we would like to re-emphasize that social relations are also utilized by our model implicitly. For example, an answer entered by a user for a question is also added to the profiles of all other users interacting with this question.

Finally, we expect the MCR model to be more precise when recommending questions to users who interact more with the system. In order to verify this point, we divided the users into 12 disjoint bins on a logarithmic scale, according to the number of answered questions in the user model. Figure 5 depicts the mean accuracy and AUC for each set of users. The overall increase in performance is evident, confirming that our model significantly improves its recommendations for more active users.

5.5 Error Analysis

The distribution of the scores assigned by the MCR model to the test examples exhibits an interesting phenomenon: the distributions of the negative examples and the positive examples are bimodal. In the case of negative examples, a significant fraction of false positives, *e.g.*, examples incorrected classified as positive, is scored very high, as high as the best positive examples. Similarly, a significant fraction of false negatives is scored very low, as low as low scored negative examples. This bi-modality phenomenon is clearly visible in Figure 6, which depicts these distributions using a logarithmically scaled vertical axis.

We also qualitatively analyzed a random sample of 50 false negatives with scores smaller than 0.1 and 50 false positives with scores greater than 0.9. The analysis of the false negatives shows that about 33% of these errors are due to users who decided to sporadically answer a question outside their typical domains of interest. For example, a user usually answering in domains such as movies and baby-names decided to answer a question in biology. These misses are difficult to avoid, since it seems that no signal could be used to identify them based on user's history only.

Analyzing the false positives showed that about half of the them are actually not erroneous matches as far as we can tell. These pairs, selected as part of our automatic sampling procedure for generating negative examples, actually capture a user who would probably answer well the paired question, based on the user's profile, even if the user did not answer it in practice, possibly because s/he was not exposed to it. For instance, a user highly active in the 'Singles & Dating' category, and specifically in answering to "flirting/courting" questions, would probably answer well the paired question *"Is it wrong to talk about other girls to a girl that likes you?."* Such pairs should have been counted as correct classifications instead of errors, if we could properly identify them.

6. CONCLUSIONS

This paper introduced a novel multi-channel recommender system approach for suggesting questions to potential answerers in Yahoo! Answers. The primary goal of our work was to improve user engagement by exposing users to "irresistible questions" they will want to answer. We hope that an additional important benefit of our system will be the improvement in the quality (or perception of quality) of Yahoo! Answers content in the long run, with potential benefits to other question-answering systems in general.

Exploiting all available signals has been shown to be central to improving recommenders quality. This was a key driver of our approach, which uses a multi-channel model to easily support the expression of any available signal. We considered multiple types of relations between a user and a question, between a question and a token, and between users and categories. Yet, we did not aggregate heterogeneous attributes at the data generation stage but rather took advantage of their large number and of the even larger number of their combinations and organized them into a multi-channel representation. Eventually, all these attributes are combined together by a learning algorithm that accounts for their inter-relations and varying importance levels. The MCR model enabled us to take advantage of various types of signals, in full symmetry, without worrying about which should be emphasized, or which would dilute others. We follow the user-user modeling paradigm that learns to recommend by borrowing actions of other similar users. We extended it by separating hundreds of user-user relations and smoothly fusing a content-based recommender.

Our experiments showed that learning to combine many signals significantly improves the baseline. Our analysis discovered that direct social relations are not as important as content signals. Additionally, learning to combine the many signal types revealed interesting insights on user behavior within Yahoo! Answers, *e.g.*, that content related to users' votes is also indicative of their answering preferences.

In this work, our goal was to assess the match between user-question pairs independently from each other. In future work, we plan to tackle the global matching problem between all users and all open questions under two constraints: (1) diversity to keep users engaged and (2) question coverage so that as many questions as possible be answered.

7. REFERENCES

[1] D. Agarwal and B.-C. Chen. Regression based latent factor models. In *Proc. Conference on Knowledge Discovery and Data Mining (KDD'09)*, pages 19–28, 2009.

[2] E. Agichtein, C. Castillo, D. Donato, A. Gionis, and G. Mishne. Finding high quality content in social media, with an application to community-based question answering. In *Proc. international conference on Web search and web data mining (WSDM'10)*, pages 183–194, 2008.

[3] E. Agichtein, Y. Liu, and J. Bian. Modeling information-seeker satisfaction in community question answering. *ACM Transactions on Knowledge Discovery from Data (TKDD)*, 3(2), 2009.

[4] S. Bao, H. Duan, Q. Zhou, M. Xiong, Y. Yu, and Y. Cao. Research on expert search at enterprise track of trec 2006. In E. M. Voorhees and L. P. Buckland, editors, *Proceedings of the Fifteenth Text REtrieval Conference*, 2006.

[5] J. Bian, Y. Liu, D. Zhou, E. Agichtein, and H. Zha. Learning to recognize reliable users and content in social media with coupled mutual reinforcement. In *Proc. international conference on World wide web (WWW'09)*, pages 51–60, 2009.

[6] A. S. Das, M. Datar, A. Garg, and S. Rajaram. Google news personalization: Scalable online collaborative filtering. In *Proc. international conference on World Wide Web (WWW'07)*, pages 271–280, 2007.

[7] J. H. Friedman. Greedy function approximation: A gradient boosting machine. *The Annals of Statistics*, 29:1189–1232, 2001.

[8] J. H. Friedman. Stochastic gradient boosting. *Computational Statistics & Data Analysis*, 38:367–378, 2002.

[9] D. Goldberg, D. A. Nichols, B. M. Oki, and D. B. Terry. Using collaborative filtering to weave an information tapestry. *Commun. ACM*, 35(12):61–70, 1992.

[10] A. Gunawardana and C. Meek. A unified approach to building hybrid recommender systems. In *Proc. conference on Recommender systems (RecSys'09)*, pages 117–124, 2009.

[11] J. L. Herlocker, J. A. Konstan, A. Borchers, and J. Riedl. An algorithmic framework for performing collaborative filtering. In *Proc. conference on Research and development in information retrieval (SIGIR'99)*, pages 230–237, 1999.

[12] D. Horowitz and S. Kamvar. The anatomy of a large-scale social search engine. In *Proc. International World Wide Web Conference (WWW'10)*, 2010.

[13] P. Kantor, F. Ricci, L. Rokach, and B. Shapira, editors. *Recommender Systems Handbook: A Complete Guide for Research Scientists and Practitioners*. Springer, 2010.

[14] Y. Koren, R. M. Bell, and C. Volinsky. Matrix factorization techniques for recommender systems. *IEEE Computer*, 42(8):30–37, 2009.

[15] C. T. Lee, E. M. Rodrigues, G. Kazai, N. Milic-Frayling, and A. Ignjatovic. Model for voter scoring and best answer selection in community Q&A services. In *Web Intelligence*, pages 116–123, 2009.

[16] K. Lee, J. Caverlee, and S. Webb. Uncovering social spammers: social honeypots + machine learning. In *Proc. conference on Research and development in information retrieval (SIGIR'10)*, pages 435–442, 2010.

[17] G. Linden, B. Smith, and J. York. Amazon.com recommendations: Item-to-item collaborative filtering. *IEEE Internet Computing*, 07(1):76–80, 2003.

[18] C. Macdonald and I. Ounis. Voting for candidates: adapting data fusion techniques for an expert search task. In *Proceedings of the 15th ACM international conference on Information and knowledge management*, CIKM '06, pages 387–396, New York, NY, USA, 2006. ACM.

[19] L. Rao. Yahoo mail and im users update their status 800 million times a month. TechCrunch, Oct 28 2009. http://techcrunch.com/2009/10/28/yahoo-mail-and-im-users-update-their-status-800-million-times-a-month/.

[20] B. M. Sarwar, G. Karypis, J. A. Konstan, and J. Riedl. Item-based collaborative filtering recommendation algorithms. In *Proc. International World Wide Web Conference (WWW'01)*, pages 285–295, 2001.

[21] C. Shah and J. Pomerantz. Evaluating and predicting answer quality in community qa. In *Proc. conference on Research and development in information retrieval (SIGIR'10)*, pages 411–418, 2010.

[22] Y.-I. Song, C.-Y. Lin, Y. Cao, and H.-C. Rim. Question utility: A novel static ranking of question search. In *Proce. conference on artificial intelligence (AAAI'08)*, pages 1231–1236, 2008.

[23] K. Sun, Y. Cao, X. Song, Y.-I. Song, X. Wang, and C.-Y. Lin. Learning to recommend questions based on user ratings. In *Proc. conference on Information and knowledge management (CIKM'09)*, pages 751–758, 2009.

[24] M. Surdeanu, M. Ciaramita, and H. Zaragoza. Learning to rank answers on large online qa collections. In *ACL*, pages 719–727, 2008.

[25] Y. Yang and X. Liu. A re-examination of text categorization methods. In *Proc. conference on Research and development in information retrieval (SIGIR'99)*, pages 42–49, 1999.

Improving Predictions using Aggregate Information

Amit Dhurandhar
adhuran@us.ibm.com
Mathematical Sciences Dept.
IBM T.J. Watson
1101 Kitchawan Road
Yorktown Heights, USA

ABSTRACT

In domains such as consumer products or manufacturing amongst others, we have problems that warrant the prediction of a continuous target. Besides the usual set of explanatory attributes we may also have exact (or approximate) estimates of *aggregated targets*, which are the sums of disjoint sets of individual targets that we are trying to predict. Hence, the question now becomes can we use these aggregated targets, which are a coarser piece of information, to improve the quality of predictions of the individual targets? In this paper, we provide a simple yet provable way of accomplishing this. In particular, given predictions from any regression model of the target on the test data, we elucidate a provable method for improving these predictions in terms of mean squared error, given exact (or accurate enough) information of the aggregated targets. These estimates of the aggregated targets may be readily available or obtained – through multilevel regression – at different levels of granularity. Based on the proof of our method we suggest a criterion for choosing the appropriate level. Moreover, in addition to estimates of the aggregated targets, if we have exact (or approximate) estimates of the mean and variance of the target distribution, then based on our general strategy we provide an optimal way of incorporating this information so as to further improve the quality of predictions of the individual targets. We then validate the results and our claims by conducting experiments on synthetic and real industrial data obtained from diverse domains.

Categories and Subject Descriptors

H.2.8 [**Database Management**]: Data Mining

General Terms

Algorithms

Keywords

Regression,Hierarchical,Coarse to fine

KDD'11, August 21–24, 2011, San Diego, California, USA.

1. INTRODUCTION

In many industries such as consumer products, manufacturing where we have a supply chain consisting of a manufacturer who produces and sends goods to various distribution centers (DC) who further redistribute the goods amongst the stores, we observe a certain delay from the time that the goods are produced to the stores finally receiving them. As time goes by, finer and finer pieces of information become available. From a strategic point of view, however, the manufacturer may want to know initially how his goods are going to be distributed among the various DCs and stores with as much accuracy as possible. Based on his past experience, he may be able to come up with predictions of how much each store or DC might order. However, the question we ask is the following: is it at all possible to improve the quality of these predictions knowing the total amount of goods that are going to be distributed for the current time period? In this paper, we answer this question affirmatively, that is, we provide a simple method to provably improve predictions obtained based on past observations, by using estimates or actual values of the target at a coarser level of granularity for the current time period.

It is easy to see that if we have the true values (or accurate estimates) at a particular level of granularity, we can sum them up to get estimates at a coarser level of granularity. For example, if we have predictions for a coarser level of granularity and true values at a finer level, we can improve the predictive accuracy at the coarser level by aggregating the finer estimates and using them as predictions. This is seen in figure 1a. However, if we have the converse problem then the solution is not obvious. What we mean by this is that, if we knew coarser values and were trying to improve the quality of our predictions at a finer level, it's not clear if there is in fact a provable way of improving the accuracy. In other words, given predictions of the target for the current time period based on past experience – this could be the output of a regression model or something else – we improve (more precisely never worsen) the quality of these predictions using *aggregated target* information, i.e. using information about the sums of different sets of targets we are trying to predict. This will become clearer if we consider figure 1b, where we have predictions for the three datapoints (denoted by circles). The sum of the true targets is 9 and the method we suggest in this paper uses this value 9 to improve the accuracy of the predictions. In fact, as you will see, even if the value 9 is not the exact sum of the targets but an "accurate enough" estimate, our method still guar-

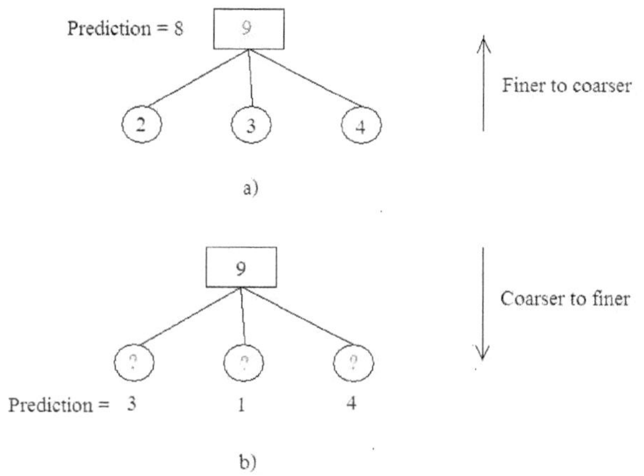

Figure 1: a) Using finer estimates to improve coarser predictions. b) Using coarser estimates to improve finer predictions.

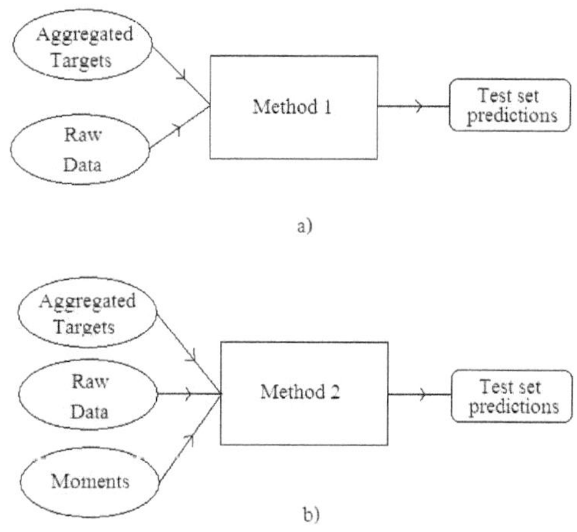

Figure 2: The basic method in this paper represented in a) takes as input the raw data and the aggregated targets (exact or estimates) at a single or multiple levels and outputs the test predictions. The enhanced method represented in b) takes in addition the moment information of the target distribution to give further improved predictions.

antees that the new predictions obtained by its application will be no less accurate than the old predictions.

Such a method can be used not only for supply chain kind of problems but in any problem where good quality aggregate information is available and we want to predict at a finer level of granularity. A good example of this may be census data where information at a national or state level may be more reliable than data at a city or county level where there might be missing data since some people may not turn in the survey. Predicting the missing values can be done more effectively knowing the aggregate information. If aggregate information is available at multiple levels of granularity with varying accuracy, choosing the right level of granularity so as to maximize the improvement in predictions is not obvious. In this paper, we provide a criterion for choosing this optimal level of granularity.

Information at a coarser level of granularity may not always be available as is the case in standard machine learning settings. In this case, we could build regression models on the historical data by aggregating it at various levels of granularity and use the "best" model to give us estimates of the aggregated targets at that level of granularity. These estimates can then be used in conjunction with our method to improve the predictions at the finest level of granularity which we care about. The "best" model is not necessarily the most accurate model amongst those built at the various coarser levels of granularity since, as we will see later, the amount of improvement in predictive accuracy at the finest level by using our method is a function of both the accuracy of the models and the level of granularity they are built at. Consequently, we provide an algorithm for choosing the model that is most likely to elevate the accuracy of the predictions. In the trivial case, the best model might be the model at the finest level, which would suggest that aggregating the data isn't too helpful. An algorithm of this nature however, can be used for a wide variety of machine learning tasks such as predicting time series data where the aggregate models would predict the potential drift, if any, over time and this drift if accurately captured can assist in improving individual predictions [6, 1, 2]. Another example is microarray data which is sparse and hence aggregating it can help predictive accuracy [8].

In addition to this, we enhance our method of using aggregated targets to improve finer predictions to be able to use distribution information of the target if available. In particular, we find the optimal weighting based on the mean and variance of the distribution of the target that will maximize the impact on the quality of the predictions in expectation. If this information is not available one may estimate these moments from the data, if deemed appropriate. The input-output of the original method and the enhanced method are pictorially depicted in figure 2.

Using coarser information to improve predictions has been of some interest lately [9, 7, 10, 4, 11, 5]. In [9, 7, 4, 11] the authors employ this philosophy to improve performance of models in certain computer vision tasks (viz. pose estimation, face recognition, etc.). In [10] however, the idea is used to improve the performance of NLP models. The primary difference between this past literature and our work is that the results in this paper are for the regression setting while the past literature mainly considers the classification and the structured prediction setting. In the regression setting, there has been some work [5] related to using aggregate information, but this is with respect to a specific problem of identifying socio-economic factors that may lead to hospital admissions for heart and circulatory diseases. Our method in contrast is not necessarily restricted to any particular domain. In fact, as we will see in the experimental section, it is applicable in multiple diverse domains. Moreover, in this paper, we explicitly provide a provable method to improve predictions at a finer level of granularity using aggregate information.

The rest of the paper is organized as follows: In the next section, we first describe our method. We then formally state this through lemmas and theorems (proofs in appendix) that show that our method in fact works. We then show that the predictions can be further improved if the mean and variance of the target are accurately known. Based on the proofs of these previous results, in cases where we may have estimates at multiple (coarser) levels of granularity, we provide a criterion that chooses a level that using our method is most likely to maximize the improvement in the quality of predictions at the finer level of granularity. In traditional settings where these estimates may not be available apriori, we suggest an algorithm where we build regression models at multiple levels of granularity on the training set in order to obtain the corresponding estimates. We then using our criterion decide on the level and hence, the regression model to be used to improve the quality of predictions obtained from a regression model built at the (finer) level of granularity that we care about. In Section 3, we present results of experiments performed on synthetic and real datasets and empirically validate the efficacy of our method. In Section 4, we discuss further extensions and summarize the major findings in this paper.

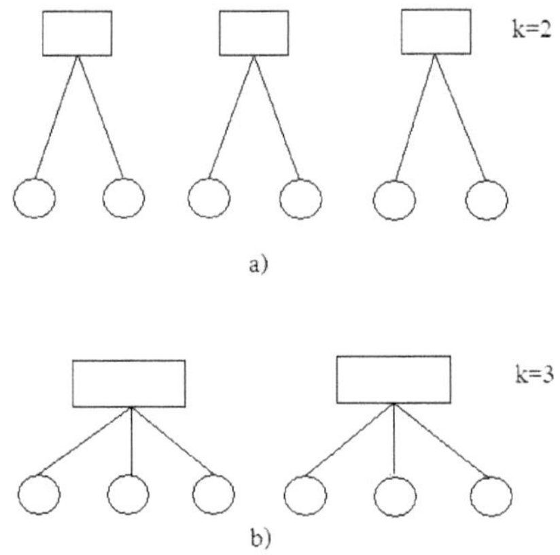

Figure 3: a) Aggregation granularity is 2. b) Aggregation granularity 3.

2. TRICKLING DOWN AGGREGATES

In this section we first describe a simple method to trickle down aggregate information in order to improve finer predictions. We formally state the relevant results with proofs provided in the appendix. If estimates of the aggregated target are available at multiple (coarser) levels of granularity, we then based on our proofs for the previous results, suggest a criterion to choose the level that using our method is most likely to maximize the improvement in the quality of predictions at the (finest) level of granularity we want to predict. If these estimates are not available, we suggest an algorithm for obtaining them and using the criterion to decide the appropriate level.

Before we start formally describing our results we define a couple of terms.

Aggregation granularity: We define aggregation granularity k as the number of values at the finest level of granularity (i.e. at the level of the original dataset) summed together to form coarser estimates. For example, in figure 3a, the aggregation granularity is 2 since, if the circles represent datapoints at the finest level then the rectangles which denote coarser estimates are sums of pairs of these circles. Similarly, in figure 3b, the aggregation granularity is 3, since the rectangles are sums of triplets of the circles.

Aggregated targets: These are sums of the individual targets in each set, where the sets form a partitioning of the individual targets in the dataset. Note that the rectangles in figure 3 would denote aggregated targets if the circles denoted individual target values.

2.1 Method and Results

An informal description of our method where the aggregation granularity is k is as follows. We first sum up the various sets of k predictions corresponding to the aggregated targets which are already available or obtained by techniques described before. With this we have each of the aggregated targets associated with its own sum of k predictions. We now subtract each of these sums from the corresponding aggregated targets which gives us the corresponding differences. We then divide each of these differences by k and uniformly add them to the corresponding k predictions. Thus, in figure 1b, where 9 is the aggregated target with 3, 1 and 4 being the predictions, we would first add 3, 1 and 4 which gives us 8, then subtract 8 from 9 which gives us 1 and then finally add $\frac{1}{3}$ to the original predictions which would give us $\frac{10}{3}$, $\frac{4}{3}$ and $\frac{13}{3}$ as the new predictions. If additional information regarding the distribution (mean and variance) of the target is available, then rather than distributing the differences uniformly amongst the predictions an optimal convex weighting scheme is derived.

With this, we now present four results which includes a formal description of the method we described above.

- In Lemma 1 we show that knowing the *true or exact* values of the aggregated targets and predictions of the individual targets, our method can produce new modified predictions that are never worse in terms of mean squared error (MSE) than the original predictions.
- In Theorem 1 we show that knowing *approximate* values (within a certain error bound) of the aggregated targets and predictions of the individual targets, our method can produce new modified predictions that are never worse in terms of MSE than the original predictions.
- Lemma 2 shows that even if we know the exact values of the aggregated targets and have predictions of the individual targets, and if we alter our method slightly where we distribute the differences non-uniformly amongst the predictions, then the claim made in 1 no longer holds. In other words, the MSE of the new predictions might be greater than the old predictions if all the differences are not distributed uniformly.
- Lastly, in lemma 3 we show that in addition to knowing the aggregated targets and having predictions of

the individual targets, if we also know the mean and variance of the target distribution then we can derive optimal weights for distributing the differences which may be non-uniform.

Lemma 1. *Consider two sets of N real numbers* $X = \{x_1, x_2, ..., x_N\}$ *and* $\bar{X} = \{\bar{x_1}, \bar{x_2}, ..., \bar{x_N}\}$ *(estimates). Let* $A = \{a_1, ..., a_m\}$ *and* $\bar{A} = \{\bar{a_1}, ..., \bar{a_m}\}$ *such that if, k is the aggregation granularity,* $l_i = min(ik, N) - (i-1)k$, $m = \lceil \frac{N}{k} \rceil$, *then* $a_i = \sum_{j=(i-1)k+1}^{min(ik,N)} x_j$ *and* $\bar{a_i} = \sum_{j=(i-1)k+1}^{min(ik,N)} \bar{x_j}$*. If* $\epsilon_i = a_i - \bar{a_i}$ *then,*

$$\sum_{j=1}^{N}(x_j - \bar{x_j})^2 \geq \sum_{j=1}^{N}(x_j - \hat{x_j})^2$$

where $\hat{x_j} = \bar{x_j} + \frac{\epsilon_{\lceil \frac{j}{k} \rceil}}{l_{\lceil \frac{j}{k} \rceil}}$

The result below shows that even if the values at the coarser level of granularity are not known exactly but with "some" error, they still can be used to enhance accuracy.

Theorem 1. *Consider two sets of N real numbers* $X = \{x_1, x_2, ..., x_N\}$ *and* $\bar{X} = \{\bar{x_1}, \bar{x_2}, ..., \bar{x_N}\}$ *(estimates). Let* $A = \{a_1, ..., a_m\}$ *and* $\bar{A} = \{\bar{a_1}, ..., \bar{a_m}\}$ *where if k is the aggregation granularity, then* $l_i = min(ik, N) - (i-1)k$, $m = \lceil \frac{N}{k} \rceil$, $a_i = \sum_{j=(i-1)k+1}^{min(ik,N)} x_j$ *and* $\bar{a_i} = \sum_{j=(i-1)k+1}^{min(ik,N)} \bar{x_j}$*. If* $\epsilon_i = a_i - \bar{a_i}$ *and* $\delta_i \in [0, 2\epsilon_i]$ *then,*

$$\sum_{j=1}^{N}(x_j - \bar{x_j})^2 \geq \sum_{j=1}^{N}(x_j - \hat{x_j})^2$$

where $\hat{x_j} = \bar{x_j} + \frac{\delta_{\lceil \frac{j}{k} \rceil}}{l_{\lceil \frac{j}{k} \rceil}}$

Lemma 2. *Consider two sets of N real numbers* $X = \{x_1, x_2, ..., x_N\}$ *and* $\bar{X} = \{\bar{x_1}, \bar{x_2}, ..., \bar{x_N}\}$ *(estimates). Let* $A = \{a_1, ..., a_m\}$ *and* $\bar{A} = \{\bar{a_1}, ..., \bar{a_m}\}$ *where if k is the aggregation granularity,* $l_i = min(ik, N) - (i-1)k$, $m = \lceil \frac{N}{k} \rceil$, *then* $a_i = \sum_{j=(i-1)k+1}^{min(ik,N)} x_j$ *and* $\bar{a_i} = \sum_{j=(i-1)k+1}^{min(ik,N)} \bar{x_j}$*. If* $\epsilon_i = a_i - \bar{a_i}$ *and* $\forall i \sum_{j=(i-1)k+1}^{min(ik,N)} \alpha_j = 1$ *where* $\forall j\ \alpha_j \geq 0$ *with all* α_j *(for any i) not being equal then there always exists a* X *and* $\bar{X}$ *such that,*

$$\sum_{j=1}^{N}(x_j - \bar{x_j})^2 \leq \sum_{j=1}^{N}(x_j - \hat{x_j})^2$$

where $\hat{x_j} = \bar{x_j} + \alpha_j \epsilon_{\lceil \frac{j}{k} \rceil}$

Lemma 3. *Consider two sets of N real numbers* $X = \{x_1, x_2, ..., x_N\}$ *and* $\bar{X} = \{\bar{x_1}, \bar{x_2}, ..., \bar{x_N}\}$ *(estimates). Let* $A = \{a_1, ..., a_m\}$ *and* $\bar{A} = \{\bar{a_1}, ..., \bar{a_m}\}$ *where if k is the aggregation granularity,* $l_i = min(ik, N) - (i-1)k$, $m = \lceil \frac{N}{k} \rceil$, *then* $a_i = \sum_{j=(i-1)k+1}^{min(ik,N)} x_j$ *and* $\bar{a_i} = \sum_{j=(i-1)k+1}^{min(ik,N)} \bar{x_j}$*. If* $\epsilon_i = a_i - \bar{a_i}$ *and it is known that* $X \sim D$ *where* μ *is the mean of the distribution D (i.e.* $E[X]$*) and* σ^2 *is the variance then,*

$$E[\sum_{j=1}^{N}(x_j - \bar{x_j})^2] \geq E[\sum_{j=1}^{N}(x_j - \hat{x_j})^2] \qquad (1)$$

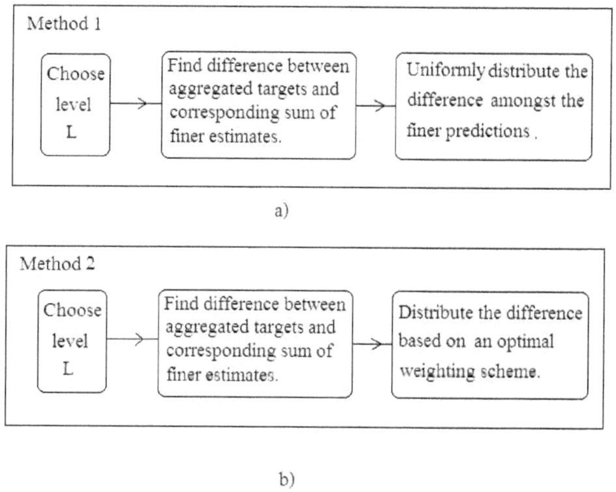

Figure 4: The two methods represented in figure 2 are illustrated above. The first one evenly distributes the differences while the second one distributes the differences based on a convex weighting scheme.

where $\hat{x_j} = \bar{x_j} + \alpha_{\lceil \frac{j}{k} \rceil}^{(j \bmod l_{\lceil \frac{j}{k} \rceil}+1)} \epsilon_{\lceil \frac{j}{k} \rceil}$, $\alpha_{\lceil \frac{j}{k} \rceil}^{(j \bmod l_{\lceil \frac{j}{k} \rceil}+1)} \geq 0$ *and* $\sum_{i=1}^{l_p} \alpha_p^{(i)} = 1\ \forall p \in \{1, ..., \lceil \frac{N}{k} \rceil\}$*. The optimal alphas that minimize the expectation on the right side of the inequality in equation 1 are given by,*

$$\alpha_p^{(i)} = \frac{1}{l_p \epsilon_p^2}[l_p \epsilon_p(\mu - \bar{x}_{i+k(p-1)}) - (2l_p - 1)(\sigma^2 + \mu^2)]; i \neq l_p$$

$$\alpha_p^{(l_p)} = \frac{1}{l_p \epsilon_p^2}[(2l_p - 1)(l_p - 1)(\sigma^2 + \mu^2) - l_p \epsilon_p((l_p - 1)\mu + \bar{x}_{i+k(p-1)} - a_p)]$$

A high level description of the methods formally described in lemma 1 and in lemma 3 are shown in figure 4.

2.2 Choosing between Multiple levels

Based on the proofs (in the appendix) of the results in the previous subsection, we observe that the reduction in MSE by applying our method is a function of the aggregation granularity and the accuracy of the estimates of the aggregated targets. In particular, the smaller the aggregation granularity and the lower the error the more significant the improvement. However, if we have estimates of the aggregated targets at multiple levels of granularity with varying accuracy, in the general case, it is not clear as to which level will lead to the most improvement. For example, at $k = 2$ we might have an error of 0.2 and at $k = 3$ we might have an error of 0.15. In this case, it is not clear whether to use the estimates of the aggregated target at level 2 or level 3. Note that if the error at level 3 was more than that at level 2 then the choice is obvious and we would choose level 2. Hence, we see that in choosing the appropriate level there is a trade-off between the aggregation granularity and the error of the estimates of the aggregated targets.

Criterion: If k is the aggregation granularity and MSE_k

denotes the mean squared error of the aggregated targets at aggregation granularity k then the level that is most likely to lead to maximum improvement in the predictions of the target is given by,

$$L = \min_k \operatorname*{argmin}_k kMSE_k \qquad (2)$$

Hence, if there are multiple k values with the same value of the objective we choose the minimum k. If $L = 1$ is the answer then that means that the aggregated targets at coarser levels will most likely not help in improving the predictive accuracy.

One may ask what the thought process is in using the estimates of the aggregated targets if one is able to compute the MSE at that level which implies one knows true values of the aggregated targets. The point of this exercise is to come up with a criterion that in a traditional machine learning setting can be used to choose a regression model at a certain level of aggregation based on the training set followed by using this model to estimate aggregated targets on the test set, which then can be used to improve predictions of the target on the test set. An algorithm for the same is described below.

Algorithm for choosing level/model in traditional settings: In a standard machine learning setting where we have a training and a test set, we can train M models one for each of the M levels of aggregation on the training set and use the criterion mentioned in equation 2 to decide the best level and the corresponding model to be used to improve the predictions on the test set (i.e. of a model built at $k = 1$). If the test set size is N, potentially M could be N, however it makes little sense to build models beyond a certain level for mainly two reasons: 1) the corresponding dataset sizes (due to aggregation) at or beyond that level or aggregation granularity may be insufficient to train a model and 2) beyond a certain aggregation granularity even if we knew the exact values of the aggregated targets at those levels, the enhancement they produce in the quality of predictions is minuscule. As we will witness in the experimental section building models beyond $k = 10$ is quite unnecessary.

A flowchart describing the algorithm to decide the level and model is given in figure 5. As per the flowchart, we end up using the model R_L to predict aggregated targets on the test set. The estimates produced by R_L can then be used to improve the predictions of the model built to predict the target by using the strategy we outlined before. Note that the strategy changes depending on if in addition to these estimates we also use the estimates (or actuals if available) of the moments of the target distribution.

3. EXPERIMENTS

In this section we evaluate our proposed solutions on synthetic data as well as on 3 real industrial datasets obtained from diverse domains. In all the reported experiments we use ridge regression – which is a commonly used regression technique – as our baseline technique that will be used to predict the target as well as the aggregated targets (if not available). Moreover, whenever the algorithm in figure 5 is used, we build models till M is the test set size. However, we see that in each of the cases the optimal level L chosen by our algorithm is always < 10.

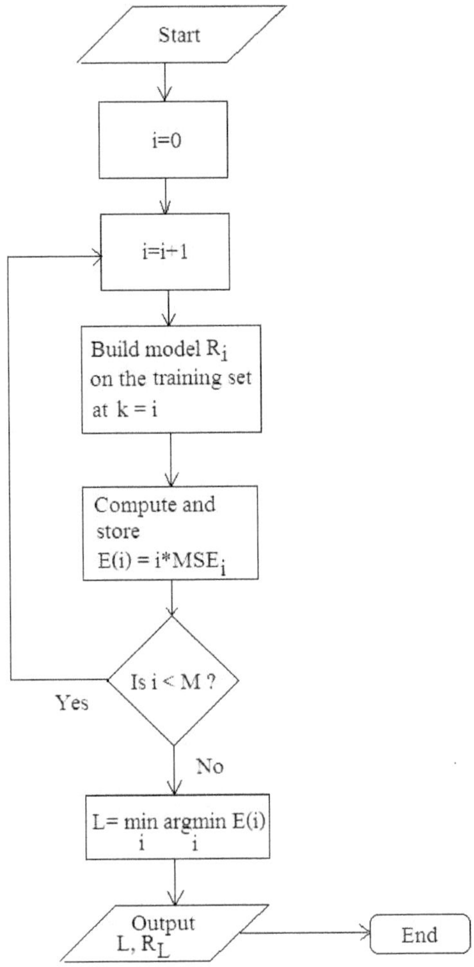

Figure 5: Algorithm for choosing the appropriate level and the corresponding regression function given that models are built at M levels i.e from $k = 1$ to $k = M$.

3.1 Synthetic Data Experiments

Setup: We generate synthetic datasets from an 11 dimensional Gaussian distribution, of which 10 are explanatory attributes and the last one is the target. We set the mean of this Gaussian to be the origin while the correlation matrix takes different values so as to generate different types of datasets. The general form of this correlation matrix is fixed however, in that all entries corresponding to correlation between two different explanatory attributes are set to zero – this is implied since we want independent explanatory attributes – while the standard deviation of all of the 11 attributes is set to σ and the correlation between the explanatory attributes and target is set to ρ. In order to generate datasets with different amounts of correlation between the explanatory attributes and target we vary ρ while to generate datasets with different variances of the individual attributes we vary σ. Moreover, to observe the behavior of our method on different dataset sizes, we create

$\sigma\downarrow,\rho\rightarrow$	0.8	0.6	0.4	0.2
0.8	0.15,0.27	0.09,0.23	0.11,0.33	0.31,0.42
0.6	0.19,0.20	**0.04**,0.13	**0.03**,0.33	0.52,0.47
0.4	0.16,0.22	**0.03**,0.12	**0.01**,0.16	0.31,0.45
0.2	0.27,0.41	0.18,0.32	0.37,0.36	0.48,0.61

Table 1: For dataset of size 100 we see above the $p-values$ of the paired t-test. The entries before the comma are $p-values$ for testing hypothesis H_0 and entries following the comma are $p-values$ for testing the hypothesis T_0. The entries in bold are cases where the corresponding null hypothesis are rejected.

$\sigma\downarrow,\rho\rightarrow$	0.8	0.6	0.4	0.2
0.8	0.23,0.26	0.08,0.09	0.10,0.27	0.24,0.39
0.6	0.16,0.13	**0.03,0.04**	**0.02,0.03**	0.43,0.46
0.4	0.17, 0.21	**0.03,0.02**	**0.02,0.01**	0.28,0.41
0.2	0.34,0.32	0.17,0.25	0.33,0.41	0.42,0.53

Table 2: For dataset of size 1000 we see above the $p-values$ of the paired t-test. The entries before the comma are $p-values$ for testing hypothesis H_0 and entries following the comma are $p-values$ for testing the hypothesis T_0. The entries in bold are cases where the corresponding null hypothesis are rejected.

datasets of size 100 and 1000 for each ρ and σ combination that we consider. In particular, we create datasets for $\rho = \{0.8, 0.6, 0.4, 0.2\} \times \sigma = \{0.8, 0.6, 0.4, 0.2\}$ as seen in tables 1 (dataset size = 100) and 2 (dataset size = 1000). For each of the combinations of these parameters we sample 100 datasets.

Each dataset that is obtained which is of a particular size and sampled with particular ρ and σ, is randomly split into train (70%) and test sets (30%). This is done 50 times to generate 50 different train and test splits on the same dataset. On each training dataset we first learn a model using just ridge regression (R), then we learn using ridge regression alongwith our algorithm in figure 5 (R+A) and finally we learn using ridge regression alongwith our algorithm and moment information (R+A+M) estimated from the training set which gives us an estimate of the optimal weights as per lemma 3. On the corresponding test sets we compute the MSE of each of these three techniques in predicting the target. Thus, for each combination of parameters we now get 50×100=5000 MSE values for the three techniques. The aggregates are formed using consecutive samples produced by the sampling process.

Using these MSE values we primarily want to decipher the parameter settings when R is worse than R+A and R+A is worse than R+A+M. To arrive at these conclusions in a statistically sound manner, we use the paired t-test [3] to confirm that the reductions in MSE from R to R+A and R+A to R+A+M are statistically significant. Hence, we carry out two hypothesis tests. The first one to see if the differences in MSE between R and R+A are significant and second one to see if the differences in MSE between R+A and R+A+M are significant. The null hypothesis in the first case is,

H_0 : The models R and R+A are equivalent.

The null hypothesis in the second case is,

T_0 : The models R+A and R+A+M are equivalent.

Observations: From the results in tables 1 and 2 we see that the hypothesis H_0 is rejected (i.e. $p-value < 0.05$) when the correlation between explanatory attributes and the target is neither too high nor too low and when the standard deviation of the attributes is moderate. A possible reason for this to happen is as follows: At high correlations the explanatory attributes are excellent predictors of the target and hence, a simple method is sufficient to be able to predict the target accurately. At low correlations the explanatory attributes contain very little information that can be used to predict the target irrespective of the modelling method used. At moderate correlations the explanatory attributes are reasonable predictors of the target. In this case however, when the variance of the target is high, aggregating using algorithm in figure 5 does not reduce the variance sufficiently until we have aggregated by more than a few levels and as mentioned before, higher the aggregation granularity lesser the improvement. When the variance of the target is low, further aggregating keeps the variance in the same regime which is low and hence the predictive power of the attributes does not change significantly at lower levels. At mid variances however, aggregation causes the variances to fall in the low regime and hence, at even low levels of aggregation we predict accurately which then enhances the performance of the model predicting the target.

From the results in tables 1 and 2 we see that the hypothesis T_0 is rejected when the dataset size is large and the other conditions are the same as that for hypothesis H_0 to be rejected. For R+A+M to work well it is required that R+A works at least reasonably since, if our estimates of the aggregated targets using algorithm in figure 5 are not accurate then irrespective of how we distribute these estimates the prediction quality will not improve by much. When R+A works really well there isn't much room for improvement. Moreover, a larger dataset size aids in obtaining more accurate estimates of the moments. Hence, the scenarios where R+A+M shows improvement over R+A is a subset of the cases where R+A shows improvement over R.

3.2 Real Data Experiments

We now test the efficacy of our approach on 3 real industrial datasets obtained from varied domains. Since, the records in each of these datasets are ordered by time, we respect this time ordering and use the first 70% of the records for training and the remaining 30% (i.e. most recent 30%) records for testing. We then report the MSE on the test set as a measure of evaluation for the different techniques with the results shown in figure 6.

Supply Chain Dataset: This dataset is obtained from an actual manufacturer and contains data at two levels namely; at the (finer) distribution center (DC) level and at the (coarser) manufacturer level. The goal is to predict the inventory position at a DC given past inventory positions and other attributes such as age of the inventory and product type (viz.

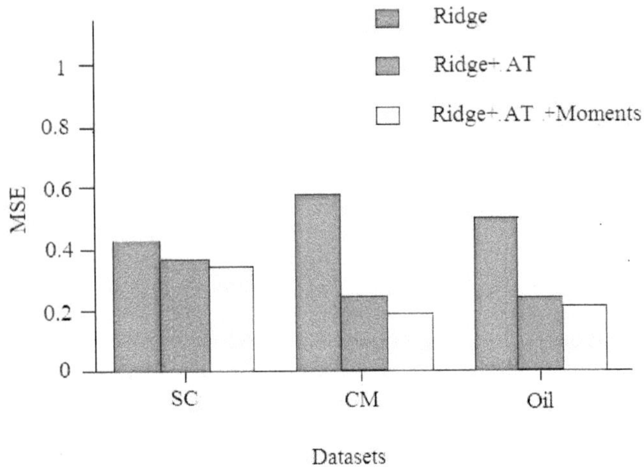

Figure 6: Comparison of three variants on three real datasets is shown above. SC stands for a Supply Chain dataset, CM stands for a chip manufacturing dataset and Oil stands for an Oil production dataset. AT implies aggregated target information.

egg beaters, pasta etc.). In addition, to this we also have information about the total amount shipped (aggregate information) from the manufacurer to meet the demands of the DC. Hence, in this case we do not need to use algorithm in figure 5 since, we already have aggregate information. We just need to use results in lemma 1 and lemma 3 (estimating the moments from the data). In our dataset there are 7 distribution centers and the data was collected daily for about a year (dataset size is 357).

Chip Manufacturing Dataset: In the chip manufacturing industry predicting speed of the wafers (collections of chips) accurately ahead of time can be crucial in choosing the appropriate set of wafers to send forward for further processing. Eliminating faulty wafers can save the industry a huge amount of resources in terms of time and money.

This dataset has 175 features where, the wafer speed is one of them. The other features are a combination of physical measurements and electrical measurements made on the wafer. The dataset size is 2361. In this case, aggregate information is unavailable and hence, we use the algorithm in figure 5 to estimate the aggregated targets, which can be viewed as estimating drift in the time series.

Oil Production Dataset: Oil companies periodically launch production logging campaigns to get an idea of the overall performance as well as to assess their individual performance at particular oil wells and reservoirs. These campaigns are usually expensive and laden with danger for the people involved in the campaign. Automated monitoring of oil production equipment is an efficient, risk free and economical alternative to the above solution.

The dataset we perform experiments on, is obtained from a major oil corporation. There are a total of 9 attributes in the dataset. These attributes are obtained from the sensors of a 3-stage separator which separates oil, water and gas. The 9 attributes are composed of 2 measured levels of the oil water interface at each of the 3 stages and 3 overall attributes. Our target is Daily production which indicates the amount of oil produced every day at the well. The dataset size is 992. In this case too, aggregate information is unavailable and hence, we use the algorithm in figure 5 to estimate the aggregated targets.

Observations: In figure 6, we observe the behavior of the three variants, namely: 1) ridge regression (R), 2) ridge regression using (actual or estimated) aggregated targets (R+A) and 3) ridge regression using (actual or estimated) aggregated targets alongwith estimated moments (R+A+M), on the three datasets. First we see that the performance improves consistently as we go from R to R+A and from R+A to R+A+M. However, the extent of the improvement differs in the 3 cases. A possible reason for the improvement from R+A to R+A+M being more significant on CM than on the other datasets could be that the larger dataset size leads to more accurate estimates of the moments as compared to the other datasets. The improvement from R to R+A is more pronounced on CM and Oil than on SC since, the L returned by algorithm in figure 5 is much lower than 7 – which is the aggregation granularity for SC – and the inaccuracies in the estimates of the aggregated targets for these two cases are only slight.

4. DISCUSSION

In this paper, we proposed a provable way of improving prediction quality with the help of accurate aggregate or coarser information. In cases where we may have (estimates of) aggregated targets at multiple levels we provided a way of choosing the optimal level so as to maximize the improvement in prediction quality. We have provided an algorithm for the same, in standard machine learning settings where aggregate information may not be available from an independent source. Moreover, using estimates of the moments of the target distribution, we have provided a way of better distributing the aggregate information so as to further enhance the predictive accuracy.

In the future, it may be desirable to choose multiple levels rather than just a single level and in some provable manner use the corresponding aggregated targets in an attempt to obtain results superior to the ones in this paper. Moreover, when the data is unordered one could first cluster the data and then apply the suggested algorithms to further enhance the predictive power. A method that encapsulates these ideas might be of some interest. In any case, we believe that we have laid the basic groundwork for the creation of advanced methods such as these.

Acknowledgement

I would like to thank Jayant Kalagnanam for providing data and exposing me to such problems. I would like to thank Naoki Abe and Aurelie Lozano for helpful discussions. I would also like to thank Brian White and Katherine Turner for proofreading the paper.

APPENDIX

Proof of Lemma 1

PROOF. Consider two sets of N real numbers $X = \{x_1, x_2, ..., x$ and $\bar{X} = \{\bar{x_1}, \bar{x_2}, ..., \bar{x_N}\}$ (estimates). Let $A = \{a_1, ..., a_m\}$

and $\bar{A} = \{\bar{a_1}, ..., \bar{a_m}\}$ where if k is the aggregation granularity, $l_i = min(ik, N) - (i-1)k - 1$, $m = \lceil \frac{N}{k} \rceil$, then $a_i = \sum_{j=(i-1)k+1}^{min(ik,N)} x_j$ and $\bar{a_i} = \sum_{j=(i-1)k+1}^{min(ik,N)} \bar{x_j}$. Let $\epsilon_i = a_i - \bar{a_i}$ and $\hat{x_j} = \bar{x_j} + \frac{\epsilon_{\lceil \frac{j}{k} \rceil}}{l_{\lceil \frac{j}{k} \rceil}}$.

Let the mean squared error based on the original estimates i.e. $(\bar{x_i})$ be given by,

$$MSE_{old} = \frac{1}{N}\sum_{i=1}^{N}(x_i - \bar{x_i})^2 \tag{3}$$

Hence, the mean squared error based on new estimates i.e. $(\hat{x_i})$ is given by,

$$\begin{aligned} &MSE_{new} \\ &= \frac{1}{N}\sum_{i=1}^{N}(x_i - \hat{x_i})^2 = \frac{1}{N}\sum_{i=1}^{N}((x_i - \bar{x_i}) - \frac{\epsilon_{\lceil \frac{i}{k} \rceil}}{l_{\lceil \frac{i}{k} \rceil}})^2 \\ &= \frac{1}{N}\sum_{i=1}^{N}(x_i - \bar{x_i})^2 - \frac{1}{N}[\sum_{i=1}^{N}(\frac{2}{l_{\lceil \frac{i}{k} \rceil}}(x_i - \bar{x_i})\epsilon_{\lceil \frac{i}{k} \rceil} - \frac{1}{l^2_{\lceil \frac{i}{k} \rceil}}(\epsilon_{\lceil \frac{i}{k} \rceil})^2)] \\ &= MSE_{old} - \frac{1}{N}A \end{aligned} \tag{4}$$

where $A = \sum_{i=1}^{N}(\frac{2}{l_{\lceil \frac{i}{k} \rceil}}(x_i - \bar{x_i})\epsilon_{\lceil \frac{i}{k} \rceil} - \frac{1}{l^2_{\lceil \frac{i}{k} \rceil}}(\epsilon_{\lceil \frac{i}{k} \rceil})^2)$. Now to prove our result we have to show that $A \geq 0$.

$$\begin{aligned} A &= \sum_{i=1}^{N}(\frac{2}{l_{\lceil \frac{i}{k} \rceil}}(x_i - \bar{x_i})\epsilon_{\lceil \frac{i}{k} \rceil} - \frac{1}{l^2_{\lceil \frac{i}{k} \rceil}}(\epsilon_{\lceil \frac{i}{k} \rceil})^2) \\ &= \sum_{p=1}^{\lceil \frac{N}{k} \rceil}(\frac{2}{l_p}(\sum_{i=(p-1)k+1}^{min(pk,N)} x_i - \sum_{i=(p-1)k+1}^{min(pk,N)} \bar{x_i})\epsilon_p - \frac{1}{l_p^2}l_p\epsilon_p^2) \quad (5) \\ &= \sum_{p=1}^{\lceil \frac{N}{k} \rceil}(\frac{2}{l_p}\epsilon_p^2 - \frac{1}{l_p}\epsilon_p^2) = \sum_{p=1}^{\lceil \frac{N}{k} \rceil}\frac{1}{l_p}\epsilon_p^2 \geq 0 \end{aligned}$$

Proof of Theorem 1

PROOF. The proof of the theorem follows from the proof of lemma 1 where we substitute ϵ_i with $\delta_i \in [0, 2\epsilon_i]$ in equation 4. With this we have,

$$MSE_{new} = MSE_{old} - \frac{1}{N}B \tag{6}$$

where $B = \sum_{i=1}^{N}(\frac{2}{l_{\lceil \frac{i}{k} \rceil}}(x_i - \bar{x_i})\delta_{\lceil \frac{i}{k} \rceil} - \frac{1}{l^2_{\lceil \frac{i}{k} \rceil}}(\delta_{\lceil \frac{i}{k} \rceil})^2)$. Now to prove our result we have to show that $B \geq 0$.

$$\begin{aligned} B &= \sum_{i=1}^{N}(\frac{2}{l_{\lceil \frac{i}{k} \rceil}}(x_i - \bar{x_i})\delta_{\lceil \frac{i}{k} \rceil} - \frac{1}{l^2_{\lceil \frac{i}{k} \rceil}}(\delta_{\lceil \frac{i}{k} \rceil})^2) \\ &= \sum_{p=1}^{\lceil \frac{N}{k} \rceil}(\frac{2}{l_p}(\sum_{i=(p-1)k+1}^{min(pk,N)} x_i - \sum_{i=(p-1)k+1}^{min(pk,N)} \bar{x_i})\delta_p - \frac{1}{l_p^2}l_p\delta_p^2) \quad (7) \\ &= \sum_{p=1}^{\lceil \frac{N}{k} \rceil}(\frac{2}{l_p}\delta_p\epsilon_p - \frac{1}{l_p}\delta_p^2) = \sum_{p=1}^{\lceil \frac{N}{k} \rceil}\frac{-1}{l_p}\delta_p(\delta_p - 2\epsilon_p) \end{aligned}$$

The above quadratic equation has 2 roots $\delta_p = 0$ and $\delta_p = 2\epsilon_p$ and we already know that $B \geq 0$ when $\delta_p = \epsilon_p$. Since, $\epsilon_p \in [0, 2\epsilon_p]$ and the function is a quadratic in δ_p we have $B \geq 0 \; \forall \delta_p \in [0, 2\epsilon_p]$.

Proof of Lemma 2

PROOF. In equation 5 substituting the alphas we have,

$$A = \sum_{p=1}^{\lceil \frac{N}{k} \rceil} 2\epsilon_p \sum_{i=(p-1)k+1}^{min(pk,N)} [(x_i - \bar{x_i})\alpha_i - \frac{\epsilon_p}{2}\alpha_i^2] \tag{8}$$

We thus have to show that when all alphas for a particular p are not equal then there always exist X and $\bar{X}$ such that $A < 0$. We can show this by proving that there always exist $\{x_{(p-1)k+1}, ..., x_{min(pk,N)}\}$ and $\{\bar{x}_{(p-1)k+1}, ..., \bar{x}_{min(pk,N)}\}$ such that the above equation for any particular p is less than zero and hence, if we replicate this case for all p then their sum is less than zero which implies $A < 0$. With this we have to show that for any p (in our setting), $2\epsilon_p \sum_{i=(p-1)k+1}^{min(pk,N)}[(x_i - \bar{x_i})\alpha_i - \frac{\epsilon_p}{2}\alpha_i^2] \leq 0$.

Without loss of generality (w.l.o.g.) we will prove the above result for $p = 1$ and the proof should be valid for all p. Hence, we will show that when all alphas for $p = 1$ are not equal then there always exist $\{x_1, ..., x_k\}$ and $\{\bar{x_1}, ..., \bar{x_k}\}$ such that, $2\epsilon_1 \sum_{i=1}^{k}[(x_i - \bar{x_i})\alpha_i - \frac{\epsilon_1}{2}\alpha_i^2] \leq 0$.

Since all alphas are not equal, w.l.o.g. assume that $\alpha_1 > \alpha_2$ where $\alpha_1 \geq \alpha_i \; \forall i \in \{1, ..., k\}$ and $\alpha_2 \leq \alpha_i \; \forall i \in \{1, ..., k\}$. We will prove the result by dividing it into 2 cases. Case 1 is $\epsilon_1 \geq 0$ and case 2 is $\epsilon_1 \leq 0$. Notice that we have freedom to choose values for X and $\bar{X}$ to prove our result.

Case 1: We choose x_i and $\bar{x_i}$ such that $x_i = \bar{x_i} \; \forall i \in \{3, ..., k\}$ and $x_2 - \bar{x_2} \geq \bar{x_1} - x_1 \geq 0$. This forces $\epsilon_1 \geq 0$ as desired. Hence, for the previous equation to be true, a sufficient condition is, $\alpha_1(x_1 - \bar{x_1}) + \alpha_2(x_2 - \bar{x_2}) \leq 0$ which implies $\bar{x_1} - x_1 \geq \frac{\alpha_2}{\alpha_1}(x_2 - \bar{x_2})$. We can always find $x_1, \bar{x_1}, x_2$ and $\bar{x_2}$ such that $x_2 - \bar{x_2} \geq \bar{x_1} - x_1 \geq \frac{\alpha_2}{\alpha_1}(x_2 - \bar{x_2}) \geq 0 \; \forall \alpha_i$ where $i \in \{1, ..., k\}$.

Case 2: This is analogous to case 1. All the inequalities in case 1 can be reversed and hence, we need to find $x_1, \bar{x_1}, x_2$ and $\bar{x_2}$ such that $x_2 - \bar{x_2} \leq \bar{x_1} - x_1 \leq \frac{\alpha_2}{\alpha_1}(x_2 - \bar{x_2}) \leq 0 \; \forall \alpha_i$ where $i \in \{1, ..., k\}$, which is definitely possible.

Proof of Lemma 3

PROOF. Since we take expectations with respect to the underlying distribution for the result of this lemma the objective we have to maximize to get the optimal alphas is the expected value of equation 8 given a_p and $\bar{a_p}$, i.e. $E[A|a_p, \bar{a_p}]$. This function is concave in the alphas and hence by forming the lagrangian and maximizing the objective given the constraints on the alphas we get, $\alpha_p^{(i)} = \frac{1}{2\epsilon_p^2}[2\epsilon_p(\mu - \bar{x}_{i+k(p-1)} + \lambda)]; i \neq l_p$ and $\lambda = \frac{-2}{l_p}(2l_p - 1)(\sigma^2 + \mu^2)$, where λ is the lagrange parameter. Notice that $\alpha_p^{(l_p)}$ is uniquely defined since the alphas sum to 1. With this the optimal alphas are given by, $\alpha_p^{(i)} = \frac{1}{l_p\epsilon_p^2}[l_p\epsilon_p(\mu - \bar{x}_{i+k(p-1)}) - (2l_p - 1)(\sigma^2 + \mu^2)]; i \neq l_p$ and $\alpha_p^{(l_p)} = \frac{1}{l_p\epsilon_p^2}[(2l_p - 1)(l_p - 1)(\sigma^2 + \mu^2) - l_p\epsilon_p((l_p - 1)\mu + \bar{x}_{i+k(p-1)} - a_p)]$

A. REFERENCES

[1] A. Arnold, Y. Liu, and N. Abe. Temporal causal

modeling with graphical granger methods. In *KDD*. ACM, 2007.

[2] A. Dhurandhar. Multistep time series prediction in complex instrumented domains. In *Large-scale Analytics for Complex Instrumented Systems workshop, ICDM*. IEEE, 2010.

[3] T. Dietterich. Approximate statistical tests for comparing supervised classification learning algorithms. *Neural Computation*, 10:1895–1923, 1998.

[4] F. Fleuret and D. Geman. Coarse-to-fine face detection. *Int. J. Comput. Vision*, 41:85–107, 2001.

[5] C. Jackson, N. Best, and S. Richardson. Hierarchical related regression for combining aggregate and individual data in studies of socio-economic disease risk factors. *Journal Of The Royal Statistical Society Series A*, 171(1):159–178, 2008.

[6] Y. Liu, J. Kalagnanam, and O. Johnsen. Learning dynamic temporal graphs for oil-production equipment monitoring system. In *KDD*, pages 1225–1234. ACM, 2009.

[7] D. Munoz, J. Bagnell, and M. Hebert. Stacked hierarchical labeling. In *ECCV*, 2010.

[8] M. Park, T. Hastie, and R. Tibshirani. Averaged gene expressions for regression. *Biostatistics*, pages 212–227, 2007.

[9] B. Sapp, A. Toshev, and B. Taskar. Cascaded models for articulated pose estimation. In *ECCV*, 2010.

[10] P. Slav. Coarse-to-fine natural language processing. Phd Thesis UC Berkeley, 2009.

[11] D. Weiss and B. Taskar. Structured prediction cascades. In *Proc. AISTATS*, 2010.

INCONCO: Interpretable Clustering of Numerical and Categorical Objects

Claudia Plant
Florida State University
cplant@fsu.edu

Christian Böhm
University of Munich
boehm@dbs.ifi.lmu.de

ABSTRACT

The integrative mining of heterogeneous data and the interpretability of the data mining result are two of the most important challenges of today's data mining. It is commonly agreed in the community that, particularly in the research area of clustering, both challenges have not yet received the due attention. Only few approaches for clustering of objects with mixed-type attributes exist and those few approaches do not consider cluster-specific dependencies between numerical and categorical attributes. Likewise, only a few clustering papers address the problem of interpretability: to explain why a certain set of objects have been grouped into a cluster and what a particular cluster distinguishes from another. In this paper, we approach both challenges by constructing a relationship to the concept of data compression using the Minimum Description Length principle: a detected cluster structure is the better the more efficient it can be exploited for data compression. Following this idea, we can learn, during the run of a clustering algorithm, the optimal trade-off for attribute weights and distinguish relevant attribute dependencies from coincidental ones. We extend the efficient Cholesky decomposition to model dependencies in heterogeneous data and to ensure interpretability. Our proposed algorithm, INCONCO, successfully finds clusters in mixed type data sets, identifies the relevant attribute dependencies, and explains them using linear models and case-by-case analysis. Thereby, it outperforms existing approaches in effectiveness, as our extensive experimental evaluation demonstrates.

Categories and Subject Descriptors

H.2.8 [**Database Applications**]: Data mining; E.4 [**Coding and Information Theory**]: Data compactification and compression

General Terms

Algorithms

1. MOTIVATION

With multiple books, surveys, and papers, the research area of *clustering* has already gained a high level of maturity. Nevertheless, we address in this paper two challenges for the clustering problem, which are of high practical importance but have received too little attention until now. The first of these two challenges is the **interpretability** of the result. Most of the current algorithms for clustering merely assign objects to groups without making any attempt to further explain, *why* a certain set of objects has been selected to build a cluster and *what* distinguishes one cluster from another. In this paper, we represent clusters by model formulas, involving case-by-case analysis of categorical attributes and linear combinations of numerical attributes. For the interpretability of a clustering result involving a medium to high number of attributes, it is essential to avoid overly complex model formulas. Therefore, our algorithm searches specifically for a natural balance between a good fit of the data to the model and suitable reduction of the model complexity (also leading to *generalization*). The most important goal of data mining in general is to gain actionable knowledge from data (or colloquially speaking, to stop starving for knowledge while drowning in data). The objective of interpretability is mission-critical for a successful application of clustering in the whole knowledge discovery process.

The second big challenge which is addressed in this paper are **mixed-type attributes**. The overwhelming majority of previous clustering algorithms is restricted to numerical objects, like vectors, metric objects, or nodes in a weighted or unweighted graph. There are also some approaches for categorical objects like K-modes [8] but there is a severe lack of solutions which can handle objects having both numerical *and* categorical attributes. Most of the few existing approaches like the algorithm K-Prototypes [17] typically use two different optimization goals, one for the numerical and another for the categorical data, see also Section 6. Whenever these two goals disagree, a manually chosen weighting factor has to decide how to resolve this tie situation. The weighting factor solution, however, is not completely satisfactory because it is difficult to select and it is not allowed to vary between different clusters or change over time (while the clusters evolve). Moreover, such approaches implicitly assume the independence between attributes of different types. In contrast, our solution considers the task of learning weighting factors and detecting dependencies between attributes (of the same or different type) as part of the overall clustering process. It is commonly agreed in the data mining community that there is a severe lack of knowledge discovery methods for mixed-type attributes. In panel discussions [25] and position papers [29] this has been identified as one of the 10 most important challenges in data mining for the next decade. Our method gives a comprehensive answer to the two challenges of mixed-type attributes and interpretability in clustering.

Contributions

We propose a principled approach to informative clustering of objects represented by mixed categorical and numerical data. The optimization goal is defined in Section 3 and our algorithm IN-

KDD'11, August 21–24, 2011, San Diego, California, USA.

CONCO based on this optimization goal in Section 4. The major benefits of our algorithm INCONCO (for **IN**terpretable **C**lustering of **N**umerical and **C**ategorical **O**bjects) can be summarized as follows:

- Relying on the principle of Minimum Description Length (MDL), INCONCO seamlessly integrates numerical and categorical information in clustering.
- INCONCO clusters by revealing dependency patterns among the mixed-type attributes by an extended Cholesky decomposition.
- Attribute dependency patterns are formalized by conditional probabilities which yield interpretable formulas concisely describing the cluster content.
- The practical applicability of our algorithm guaranteed since INCONCO does not require input parameters and is scalable.

2. EXTENDED CHOLESKY

In previous approaches to numerical subspace and correlation clustering like EM-clustering [19], ORCLUS [2] and 4C [7], the dependencies between attributes are usually detected and managed by the Eigenvalue decomposition of the covariance matrix of a cluster, called Principal Component Analysis (PCA). Assuming Gaussianity, PCA is searching for the directions of maximum variance in the data space and transforms the original, dependent attributes into new, uncorrelated (and possibly fewer) attributes, which are defined by the Eigenvectors corresponding to the large Eigenvalues. However, the interpretation of this model is difficult because (1) the Eigenvectors do not describe directly how the original attributes depend from each other but instead the indirect dependency from the new, Eigenvector based attributes, and (2) the dependencies are not restricted to the most relevant ones: reported is always a complete model defining in an $(n \times m)$-matrix how the original n attributes determine the m new ones. The only gain w.r.t. interpretability is the dimensionality reduction if $m < n$.

In this paper, we handle and represent dependencies by a decomposition which is inspired from the Cholesky decomposition [13]. The advantages of the original Cholesky decomposition over PCA are: (1) Cholesky much more efficient than PCA, approximately by a factor of 10, see e.g. [23]. (2) Its result directly interrelates the original attributes to each other for a higher degree of interpretability. (3) Using suitable pivoting strategies [9] the number of reported attribute dependencies can be considerably further reduced over the PCA result. Our decomposition extends the original Cholesky decomposition in two additional aspects yielding further major advantages over PCA: (4) Categorical attributes are considered in a seamless way and (5) of all observable dependencies only a subset of relevant ones are considered (where relevance is decided by MDL). *We base our cluster notion on this extended Cholesky decomposition which captures mixed-type attribute dependencies in descriptive formulas. This powerful cluster model serves as an optimization goal for an efficient top-down clustering strategy.*

Notation. We assume a database $\mathcal{DB}$ consisting of a number $n = |\mathcal{DB}|$ of objects, each consisting of c categorical and d numerical attributes $\mathcal{A} = \{A, B, C, ...\}, \mathcal{X} = \{x, y, z, ...\}$ with $|\mathcal{A}| = c$ and $|\mathcal{X}| = d$. The task of our clustering algorithm is to decompose $\mathcal{DB}$ into disjoint clusters $\{\mathcal{C}_1, ..., \mathcal{C}_k\}$ where k is eventually not an input parameter but determined by the overall clustering method. Each cluster is described by its *weight* $w_i = \frac{|\mathcal{C}_i|}{n}$ and a probability distribution for every categorical and numerical attribute. Every categorical attribute $A \in \mathcal{A}$ consists of $m_A = |A|$ distinct values $\{a_1, ..., a_{m_A}\}$. The probability of each attribute value in a cluster is denoted by $P(A = a_i)$. If categorical attributes A and B are dependent, we consider the joint probability

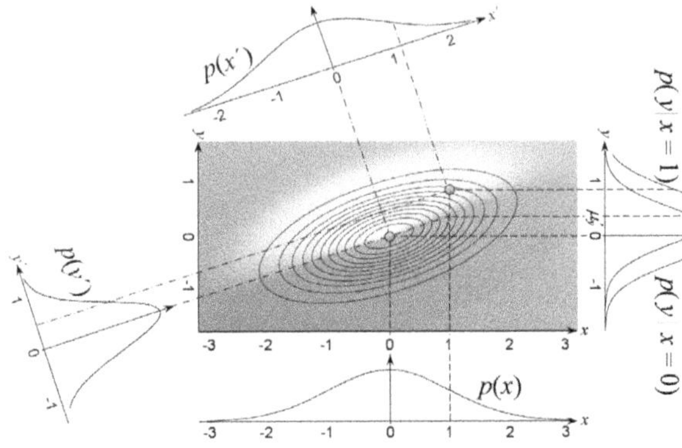

Figure 1: PCA vs. the Conditional Cholesky Sequence.

of the form $P(A = a_i, B = b_j, ...)$ (where we consider A and B typically as a joint attribute $C = (AB)$ having the distinct values $\{(a_1, b_1), (a_1, b_2), ...\}$) and the conditional probability of the form $P(A = a_i | B = b_j, ...)$. Whenever it is clear to what attribute or what value we relate, we write only $P(A|B), p(a_1)$, etc. The probability density function of the numerical attributes is described by a Gaussian, defined by mean μ and $(d \times d)$-covariance matrix Σ:

$$p(x_1, ..., x_d) = N_{\mu,\Sigma}(x) = \frac{1}{\sqrt{(2\pi)^d |\Sigma|}} \cdot \mathbf{e}^{-\frac{1}{2}(x-\mu)^T \Sigma^{-1}(x-\mu)}.$$

The joint probability of one (or more) categorical and one (or more) numerical attributes is modeled by a case-by-case analysis, associating to each categorical value an individual Gaussian:

$$p(A, x) = \begin{cases} P(A = a_1) \cdot N_{\mu_1,\Sigma_1}(x) \text{ if } A = a_1, \\ P(A = a_2) \cdot N_{\mu_2,\Sigma_2}(x) \text{ if } A = a_2, \\ \dots \end{cases} \quad (1)$$

The categorical attribute A may actually be composed of several attributes $A = \{A_{i_1}, A_{i_2}, ...\}$, and likewise, the numerical attribute from several numerical attributes $x = (x_{j_1}, x_{j_2}, ...)^T$. An attribute which may be composed from one or more original attributes of the same or different type is called a *super-attribute* $S \subseteq A \cup X$ having a dimension d_S and a number of categorical attributes c_S with $0 \leq d_S \leq d$ and $0 \leq c_S \leq c$. Our method described in Section 3 will find for each cluster a disjoint partitioning of the attributes into super-attributes. Thereby, we consider the super-attributes as independent from each other. This is not a limitation since it is also possible to group all original attributes into one super-attribute to regard every pair of original attributes as dependent.

Original Cholesky Decomposition

We consider a d-dimensional mean and a $(d \times d)$ covariance matrix Σ. The Cholesky decomposition generates from $\Sigma = [\sigma_{i,j}]$ a lower triangular matrix $L = [l_{i,j}]$ with $j \geq i$ such that $\Sigma = L \cdot L^T$, $\Sigma^{-1} = (L^{-1})^T L^{-1}$, $|\Sigma| = |L|^2 = \prod_i l_{i,i}^2$. L can be determined and inverted ($L^{-1} =: [\bar{l}_{i,j}]$) in $\frac{1}{6}d^3$ steps:

$$l_{i,i} = \Big(\sigma_{i,i} - \sum_{1 \leq k < i} l_{i,k}^2\Big)^{1/2}, l_{j,i} = \frac{1}{l_{i,i}}\Big(\sigma_{i,j} - \sum_{1 \leq k < i} l_{j,k} \cdot l_{i,k}\Big).$$

Creating a Sequence of Conditional Probabilities

It is possible to rewrite the Gaussian probability density function using the Cholesky decomposition to gain a sequence of conditional probabilities which can be multiplied using Bayes' theorem:

$$N_{\mu,\Sigma}(x) = \frac{1}{\sqrt{(2\pi)^d |L|^2}} \cdot \mathbf{e}^{-\frac{1}{2}(x-\mu)^T \cdot (L^{-1})^T \cdot L^{-1} \cdot (x-\mu)}.$$

By a substitution of a new series of variables $\mu' = (\mu'_1, \dots, \mu'_{d'})^T$,

$$\mu'_1 = \mu_1; \quad \mu'_i := \mu_i - \frac{1}{\bar{l}_{i,i}} \sum_{1 \leq j < i} \bar{l}_{i,j}(x_j - \mu_j) \quad \forall i \geq 2. \quad (2)$$

we obtain $N_{\mu,\Sigma}(x) = \prod_i \frac{1}{\sqrt{2\pi l_{i,i}^2}} \cdot \mathbf{e}^{-\frac{(x_i-\mu_i')^2}{2\cdot l_{i,i}^2}} = \prod_{1\le i\le d} N_{\mu_i',l_{i,i}^2}(x_i)$.
The last formula can be interpreted as a sequence of conditional PDFs, because the first factor of the product formula uses the original mean $\mu_1' = \mu_1$ and variance $l_{1,1}^2 = \sigma_1^2$. The second factor represents a Gaussian which has been shifted from the original μ_2 using a linear term involving x_1, the third factor a Gaussian shifted by x_1 and x_2, and so on. Together, we can say that

$$N_{\mu,\Sigma}(x) \quad = \quad p(x_1) \cdot p(x_2|x_1) \cdot p(x_3|x_1,x_2) \cdot \ldots$$

The intuition of this sequence of conditional probabilities and the relationship to PCA is visualized in Figure 1. PCA handles the dependency by rotating the Gaussian until it is axis-parallel (by multiplication with the Eigenvector matrix). The resulting attributes (x' and y'), depicted above and left from the multivariate Gaussian, are independent but also less interpretable than the original coordinates. In contrast, Cholesky first evaluates the original x-dimension, as depicted below the multivariate Gaussian. Depending on the value of the x-coordinate (for the two marked points, $x = 0$ and $x = 1$), two different Gaussians for the y-coordinate are valid (determined by μ_y'). Of course, the product of the two PCA probabilities always agrees with the conditional sequence: $p(x') \cdot p(y') = p(x) \cdot p(y|x)$, because Cholesky and PCA are just two different methods to factorize the multivariate Gaussian.

Nevertheless, Cholesky has many advantages over PCA. Apart from being by a constant (but high) factor faster than PCA, the model is also much more interpretable for the following two reasons: (1) The original variables are maintained, and all projections are orthogonal to the original coordinates. Equation (2) can be effectively used to present the attribute dependencies in a formal but also intuitive way. (2) Typically even many of the triangular entries in the resulting matrix L are zero, if the original covariance matrix is not fully occupied. Therefore, the model formulas generated by Cholesky are much simpler, particularly if the corresponding numerical attributes are reordered prior to the actual Cholesky decomposition. For reordering, several different pivoting algorithms such as AMD, MMD and SYMMMD [9] are available. In contrast, the Eigenvector matrices of PCA are often fully occupied, and even if a row-echelon form is gained from that, a fully occupied triangular matrix is typically obtained. In Section 3, we develop a strategy to exploit and enhance this effect by an MDL-based criterion. In the next section, we show how categorical attributes can be inserted at appropriate positions in the sequence of conditional probabilities.

Considering Categorical Attributes

If a numerical and a categorical attribute are not independent from each other, this dependency can also be handled by a conditional probability in either direction. The simplest case is that the numerical attribute is conditionally dependent on the categorical attribute, $p(x|A)$. According to the definition in Equation (1), we have:

$$p(x|A) = \begin{cases} N_{\mu_1,\Sigma_1}(x) \text{ if } A = a_1, \\ N_{\mu_2,\Sigma_2}(x) \text{ if } A = a_2, \\ \ldots \end{cases}$$

This works also if A and/or x are composed from more than one categorical/numerical attribute. Also the other way round $P(A|x)$ can be easily determined by exploiting Bayes' theorem:

$$P(A|x) = P(A) \cdot p(x|A)/p(x).$$

If a given super-attribute contains both numerical and categorical attributes, then the probabilities of the categorical attributes can be inserted into the conditional chain at the beginning. If two or more categorical variables A, B, C are dependent from each other, we insert at the beginning a chain like $P(A) \cdot P(B|A) \cdot P(C|A,B)$. For every numerical attribute x which is dependent on one or more categorical attributes A, B (maybe in addition to a dependency from a combination of numerical attributes y, z which is already considered in the conditional sequence by the Cholesky decomposition), we simply replace the corresponding original expression $p(x|y,z)$ in the chain by $p(x|A,B,y,z)$. Note that this term is a shortcut for the interpretable formula:

$$x = \begin{cases} \alpha_{1,1}y + \beta_{1,1}z + \epsilon_{1,1} \text{ if } A = a_1 \wedge B = b_1, \\ \alpha_{1,2}y + \beta_{1,2}z + \epsilon_{1,2} \text{ if } A = a_1 \wedge B = b_2, \\ \ldots \end{cases}$$

where $\alpha_{i,j}$ and $\beta_{i,j}$ are constants and $\epsilon_{i,j} \sim N_{\mu,\sigma^2}$ is a normally distributed error term. Obviously, such formulas are the better interpretable the fewer attributes are present in a super-attribute. We will show in the next section how to decide which attribute combinations should be regarded as independent in order to improve the overall clustering result and obtain a good trade-off between data fit and interpretability.

3. MINIMUM DESCRIPTION LENGTH

The principle of Minimum Description Length (MDL) is a well established technique to evaluate and compare different competing statistical models for the description of data, and for tuning the parameters of these models [26]. MDL optimizes for a good fit of the data to the model, formalized by the entropy of the data given the model while punishing the model complexity. This is done by relating the problem of model selection to that of data compression: By Huffman coding, objects are coded with short codewords if they are, according to the model, in more likely areas of the (discrete or continuous) data space. In contrast, less likely objects are coded by longer codewords which results in an average length of the code words which is equivalent to the entropy of the data. If the model has parameters such as probabilities, mean vectors, covariance matrices, these parameters have to be included to the compression cost as a "code book", required to be able to decompress the coded data again.

MDL for Data Compression

The coding costs for a categorical attribute A are provided by the entropy $H(A)$, and a for a numerical attribute x by the differential entropy $h(x)$:

$$H(A) \quad = \quad -\sum_{a\in A} P(A=a)\log(P(A=a)), \tag{3}$$

$$h(x) \quad = \quad -\int_{\mathcal{R}^d} p(x)\log_2 p(x)\mathbf{d}x \quad = \tag{4}$$

$$\quad = \quad \frac{1}{2}\log_2\left((2\pi\mathbf{e})^d|\Sigma|\right) \quad \text{for } p(x) = N_{\mu,\Sigma}(x). \tag{5}$$

Both equations are also valid if a super-attribute is actually composed from two or more single categorical or numerical attributes, respectively. The summation of Eq. (3) is in this case over all combinations of values of the respective attributes. If the statistical model consists of clusters, each represented by a separate, complex model, then the MDL consists of the entropy of the cluster assignment ($-\sum_{1\le i\le k} w_i \cdot \log_2 w_i$, also called the cluster-ID-cost of the model), followed by the average of the entropies and differential entropies of all clusters, weighted by $w_i = \frac{|C_i|}{n}$.

Every parameter of the model is usually accounted by $\frac{1}{2}\log_2 n$. Here, the number of bits is dependent on the overall number of objects to be described by the model. This corresponds to the observation that parameters should be coded with higher accuracy if a higher number of objects is coded. For fewer objects a less accurate knowledge of the parameters is sufficient. The term $\frac{1}{2}\log_2 n$ represents again an optimal balance of coding accuracy and data fit.

MDL for Dependent Mixed Attributes

Lets now consider a super-attribute S composed of one or more numerical attributes $x = (x_{i_1}, x_{i_2}, ..., x_{i_{d'}})^T$ and one or more categorical attributes $A = (A_{j_1}, A_{j_2}, ..., A_{j_{c'}})$ where c' is the number of categorical attributes and d' the number of numerical attributes (the dimension) in S. It is natural to consider the differential entropy of the common probability according to Equation (1):

$$h(A,x) = -\sum_{a\in A}\int_{\mathcal{R}^{d'}} p(A,x)\log_2 p(A,x)\mathbf{d}x =$$

$$= -\sum_{a\in A}\int_{\mathcal{R}^{d'}} P(a)\cdot N_{\mu,\Sigma}(x)\cdot \log_2\left(P(a)\cdot N_{\mu,\Sigma}(x)\right)\mathbf{d}x =$$

$$= -\sum_{a\in A}\left(P(a)\log_2 P(a) - \frac{1}{2}P(a)\log_2\left((2\pi\mathbf{e})^{d'}|\Sigma|\right)\right). \quad (6)$$

The entropy of every super-attribute can be determined using Equation (6). The number of parameters of a super-variable having c' categorical attributes $A = \{A_{i_1}, ..., A_{i_{c'}}\}$ and d' numerical attributes is determined as follows: First, the overall number of possible combinations of categories of this super-attribute must be determined by $m = |A| = \prod_{1\le j\le c'} m_{i_j}$. If the super-attribute has *no* categorical attributes, we set by default $m = 1$. For each of these combinations, the probability must be stored as one parameter. In addition, for each of the category-combinations, one separate d'-variate Gaussian must be stored with d' components of the mean vector μ and potentially $\frac{1}{2}d'\cdot(d'+1)$ entries of the decomposed covariance matrix L. The overall number of parameters therefore sums up to $m\cdot(1+d'+\frac{1}{2}d'\cdot(d'+1))$. The number of bits required for one cluster including code book and data coding corresponds to:

$$MDL(S) = |\mathcal{C}_i|\cdot h(A,x) + \frac{1}{2}\left(1+d'+\frac{1}{2}d'\cdot(d'+1)\right)m\log_2 n.$$

Grouping Attributes into Super-attributes

Our algorithm starts with a number $(c+d)$ of trivial super-attributes, each consisting of one attribute and then merges in each step the best pair of old super-attributes into a new one. This is repeated until no more improvement is possible. Technically, we store during the run of the algorithm one vector of super-attributes representing the current state and one matrix containing all possible pairs of super-attributes to be formed from the current state. For each of the entries of the current state vector and the future state matrix, we store the value $MDL(S)$. In each step of the algorithm, the pair (S,T) of super-attributes is merged which yields the maximum cost saving, i.e. for which $MDL(S\cup T) - MDL(S) - MDL(T)$ is maximal. Then, the entries corresponding to S and T in the current state vector and the corresponding rows and columns in the future state matrix are deleted, and the element $(S\cup T)$ is moved from the future state matrix to the current state vector. Finally, a new column (and row) of the symmetric future state matrix is determined by tentatively merging the new super-attribute with every other super-attribute in the current state vector. The whole procedure is repeated until no more MDL improvement is possible. The example in Figure 2 starts on the left side with trivial super-attributes, each consisting of a single numerical or categorical attribute. The current state vector is $\{(A),(B),(x),(y),(z)\}$. All 2-combinations of these attributes are tentatively formed and stored in the upper triangular *future matrix*, as indicated in the diagram. In Figure 2 it is assumed that merging of B and y (the marked entry of the future matrix) pays off best, and therefore, in the next step, the corresponding rows and columns are removed, and instead a new row and column with super-attribute (By) is appended, and the corresponding new row and column is computed using tentative mergers into possible super-attributes $\{(ABy),(Bxy),(Byz)\}$. This is repeated until no more improvement is possible or all attributes are grouped into a common super-attribute.

Optimization Goal for Clustering

For each cluster $\mathcal{C}_i, 1\le i\le k$, an individual grouping $\mathcal{S}_i = \{S_{i,1}, S_{i,2}, ...\}$ of attributes into super-attributes is determined according to the algorithm proposed in the previous paragraph. The overall MDL of Cluster $\mathcal{C}_i$ corresponds to:

$$MDL(\mathcal{C}_i) = n\cdot w_i\log_2(w_i) + \sum_{S_{i,j}\in\mathcal{S}_i} MDL(S_{i,j}). \quad (7)$$

The complete database requires the following code-length:

$$MDL(\mathcal{DB}) = \sum_{1\le i\le k} MDL(\mathcal{C}_i).$$

The overall optimization goal of our clustering method is the minimization of $MDL(\mathcal{DB})$, that means find a complete and disjoint partitioning of $\mathcal{DB}$ into a set of clusters $\{\mathcal{C}_1, ..., \mathcal{C}_k\}$ with $\mathcal{DB} = \mathcal{C}_1\cup ...\cup\mathcal{C}_k$ and $\mathcal{C}_i\cap\mathcal{C}_j = \emptyset\ \forall i\ne j$ such that

$$\{\mathcal{C}_1, ..., \mathcal{C}_k\} = \underset{k\in\mathcal{N},\mathcal{C}_1,...,\mathcal{C}_k\subseteq\mathcal{DB}}{\text{argmin}}\left(\sum_{1\le i\le k} MDL(\mathcal{C}_i)\right), \quad (8)$$

where k is usually not a user-provided parameter but, instead also part of the optimization process. If the user intentionally wants to perform the clustering method with a certain, pre-selected number of clusters k, this is possible as well.

4. THE ALGORITHM INCONCO

The extended Cholesky decomposition proposed in Section 2 and 3 to enhance interpretability and to handle mixed-type attributes (including the conditional sequences and grouping of attributes into super-attributes) can in principle be used as a stand-alone technique to analyze heterogeneous data (without clustering or as a postprocessing step after clustering). However, we integrated the extended Cholesky decomposition tightly into a clustering algorithm to perform a targeted search for *interpretable* mixed-type clusters. Our bisecting top-down paradigm is fully automatic and guarantees runtime efficiency. We first describe the algorithm k-INCONCO in which the number k of clusters to be searched for is a parameter. Later this algorithm will be merely used as a building block for the more general algorithm INCONCO which repeatedly applies k-INCONCO with $k = 2$ in a bisecting fashion. The algorithm k-INCONCO is an iterative algorithm performing the two steps *assignment* of points to clusters and *model-computation* interchanging until convergence. The model-computation is essentially the grouping of attributes into super-attributes, as described in Section 3. During the attribute grouping, our extended Cholesky decomposition of the covariance matrix is computed, and the model is determined in form of a sequence of conditional probabilities including numerical and categorical terms. The initialization is done by sampling of k objects $\in\mathcal{DB}$, and then a first assignment of the database objects to the cluster representatives using all attributes as singleton super-attributes. From the obtained clusters, the super-attributes are determined as described in Section 3.

In the assignment step, the models of each cluster are evaluated for every object $o\in\mathcal{DB}$. The object o is assigned to that cluster in which it has the least MDL-cost, i.e. for which it has the

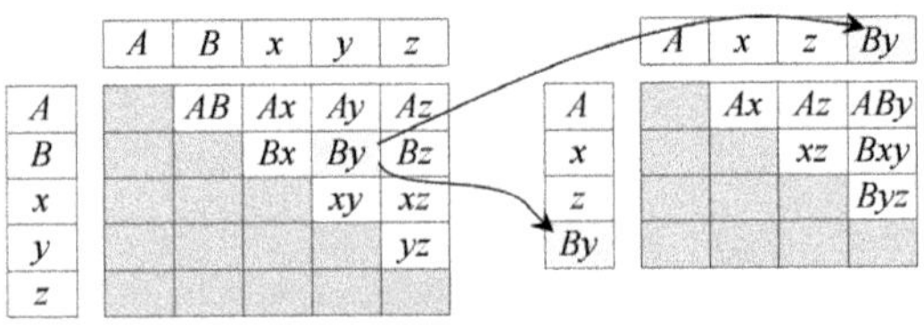

Figure 2: Grouping of Super-attributes.

```
algorithm INCONCO (): set of clusters
  Cluster C_S := k-INCONCO (1);
  return PARTITION-REC (C_R) ;
algorithm k-INCONCO (k): set of k clusters
  {C_1, ..., C_k} := INITIALIZATION (k);
  repeat
    assign every object to C_i with minimum coding cost;
    determine the super-attributes according to Section 3;
  until convergence;
  return {C_1, ..., C_k};
procedure INITIALIZATION (k): set of k clusters
  resultMDL := ∞;
  for i := 1 to 10 do
    select k different objects from DB;
    assign the remaining objects according to MDL;
    determine the super-attributes according to Section 3;
    re-assign the objects according to the super-attributes;
    if MDL(DB) ≤ resultMDL then
      resultMDL := MDL(DB);
      store clusters and super-attributes in {C_1, ..., C_k};
  return {C_1, ..., C_k};
procedure PARTITION-REC (Cluster C): set of clusters
  {C_L, C_R} := k-INCONCO (2);
  if MDL(C_L) + MDL(C_R) ≥ MDL(C) then
    return {C};
  else
    return PARTITION-REC (C_L)∪ PARTITION-REC (C_R);
```

Figure 3: The Algorithm INCONCO.

highest log-likelihood. Thus, also in the assignment step, possible dependencies between numerical and categorical attributes are considered. Therefore, the algorithm performs a targeted search for clusters exhibiting interpretable dependencies between attributes of the same or different kind. The pseudocode of k-INCONCO is defined in Figure 3. INCONCO (a top-down partitioning algorithm) is a version of our method which does not require to specify the number k of clusters to be searched for in advance, and is thus fully automatic. INCONCO starts by assuming the complete database in one cluster. Then, iteratively one cluster is selected and split up into two using the algorithm k-INCONCO with $k = 2$. Our method always selects that cluster for which the overall MDL profits most. INCONCO is also defined in Figure 3.

INCONCO clusters the data set in a bisecting style starting with the complete data set, and repeatedly partitioning it by calling the method k-INCONCO (with $k = 2$). Being an iterative method, we have to ensure that k-INCONCO converges and finds at least a local optimum of Eq. (7).

LEMMA 1 (MONOTONICITY OF MDL).
In the iterations of k-INCONCO, Eq. (7) is a monotonically non-increasing function.

PROOF. *k-INCONCO inherits from k-Means the property that both the re-assignment of objects to clusters and the re-determination of the cluster model can never increase the MDL. This is obvious in the re-assignment step because an object is assigned to that cluster in which it has least cost. It is also true for the re-determination of the model: The previous model (i.e. the set of super-attributes determined in the last iteration of k-INCONCO) of a certain cluster is always part of the solution space. If no better set of super-attributes can be found in the current iteration, we use the same super-attributes as in the last iteration. Of course, the contingency table(s) of the categorical attributes and the means and variances of the numerical attributes may be updated, but like in K-means, these updates can never decrease the log-likelihood and thus can never increase the MDL. If a better set of super-attributes can be found (with lower MDL cost), then the MDL has been decreased as well. Since both steps are monotonic, Eq. (7) is also a monotonically non-increasing function.* □

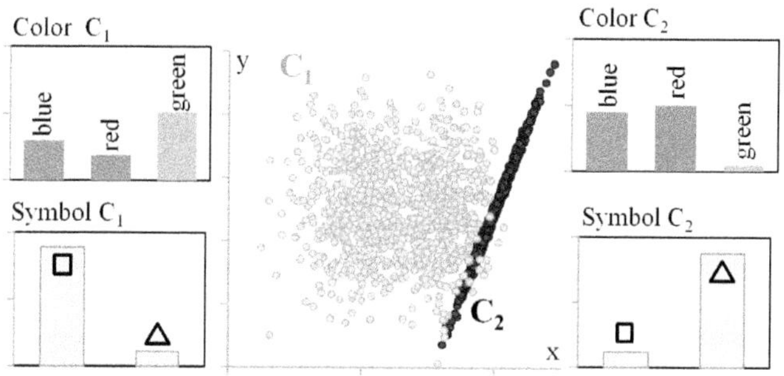

Figure 4: Mixed-type Data Set consisting of two clusters represented by two numerical (x, y) and two categorical attributes (*color* = {*blue, red, green*}; *symbol* = $\{\square, \triangle\}$).

From the strictly decrease of the MDL criterion it follows that (1) the algorithm converges (as stated in the following lemma, and (2) that the algorithm performs a steepest descent towards a local minimum of the cost function. Like in K-means and many similar clustering algorithms it cannot be guaranteed that the local optimum corresponds also to the global optimum. As usual, we perform a number of runs of the overall algorithm (i.e. INCONCO) with different initializations in order to explore different parts of the solution space. We can easily decide according to the MDL criterion which of the runs has the best overall performance.

LEMMA 2 (CONVERGENCE OF k-INCONCO).
The algorithm k-INCONCO converges after a finite number of iterations.

PROOF. *From Lemma 1 it follows that (1) the MDL-criterion is monotonically non-increasing. Being a compression-based criterion, it is obvious that (2) there exists a lower limit of the MDL since no infinite compression ratio is possible. Taking (1) and (2) together, k-INCONCO must converge after a finite number of steps.* □

5. EXPERIMENTS

In this section, we provide an extensive experimental evaluation comparing INCONCO to K-means [14], K-modes [8] and K-means-mixed [3]. K-means and K-modes serve as a baseline and K-means-mixed is a state-of-the-art technique for mixed data clustering. All experiments have been performed on a workstation equipped with a 2.4 GHz CPU and 3 GB of main memory. We obtained the Java code of K-means-mixed from the authors and implemented all other algorithms in Java. For comparison in effectiveness, we report the Normalized Mutual Information (NMI) between class labels and cluster-IDs [28]. NMI scales between 0 and 1, where NMI = 1 represents the perfect clustering and NMI = 0 means a completely random clustering, i.e. no dependency between cluster-IDs assigned by the algorithm and the ground truth. Moreover, we report precision and recall. We report the best result of 10 random initializations. With MDL, INCONCO provides an internal clustering quality measure which is part of our method. Therefore, selecting the best result is easy. In all experiments, we selected the result of INCONCO providing the best data compression which is the result with the smallest MDL. For the comparison methods, on synthetic data we selected the result having the highest NMI with the ground truth.

Proof of Concept

To provide an objective comparison in effectiveness, we constructed a synthetic example data set consisting of numerical and categorical attributes with cluster-specific patterns of attribute dependencies. The data set displayed in Figure 4 is composed of two clusters

C_1, C_2, each consisting of 1,000 objects. Especially the categorical attribute *symbol* seems to be very useful for cluster separation: In cluster C_1 we observe 89% $\Box$ and only 11% $\triangle$, conversely, in C_2 88% of the objects have the symbol $\triangle$, and there are only 12% $\Box$ (cf. left and right panel of Figure 4). Moreover, the distribution of the numerical attributes support the fact that both clusters have been generated by different mechanisms (cf. Figure 4 (middle)).

However, considering each attribute separately reveals only parts of the ground truth. For each cluster, we generated a unique pattern of attribute dependencies illustrated in Figure 5. Especially, in cluster C_1 the values of both categorical attributes depend on the numerical x-coordinate, see Figure 5(a).

Table 1 summarizes the results of INCONCO and the comparison methods. As the only technique supporting mixed-type attribute dependencies, INCONCO perfectly clusters this data set. Only one of the 2,000 objects is wrongly clustered. This clustering has an NMI of 0.99 and precision and recall above 99% for both clusters. Besides partitioning the objects into clusters, the result of INCONCO includes a model for each cluster concisely describing the attribute dependencies using case-by-case analysis. In cluster C_1 the attributes *symbol, color* and x are grouped into a common super-attribute and the complex three-fold dependency is modeled by the following case-by-case analysis:

$$\mu(x) = \begin{cases} 35.0 & \text{if } symbol = \Box \text{ and } color = blue, \\ 37.9 & \text{if } symbol = \Box \text{ and } color = red, \\ 41.0 & \text{if } symbol = \Box \text{ and } color = green, \\ 30.7 & \text{if } symbol = \triangle \text{ and } color = blue, \\ 33.6 & \text{if } symbol = \triangle \text{ and } color = red, \\ 36.0 & \text{if } symbol = \triangle \text{ and } color = green. \end{cases}$$

In cluster C_2 the numerical attributes x and y are grouped into a common super-attribute and their strong linear dependency is discovered as follows: $\mu(x) = 0.9 \cdot y$.

Although the detected attribute dependencies are very valuable for interpretation, one might wonder if this synthetic data set really requires such a complex algorithm since the clusters seem to be separable using the categorical information alone. K-modes successfully detects the differences in probability for the symbols and boxes in the two clusters: All *green* and *blue boxes* are assigned to one cluster. All remaining objects are assigned to the other cluster. In total 209 objects are wrongly clustered which corresponds to an NMI of 0.52 Without considering the information of the numerical features, it is not possible to successfully cluster this example data set. Approaching the problem from the numerical side, we ran K-means on the numerical coordinates since the clusters seem to be well separable in the x-coordinate. In total, 348 objects are

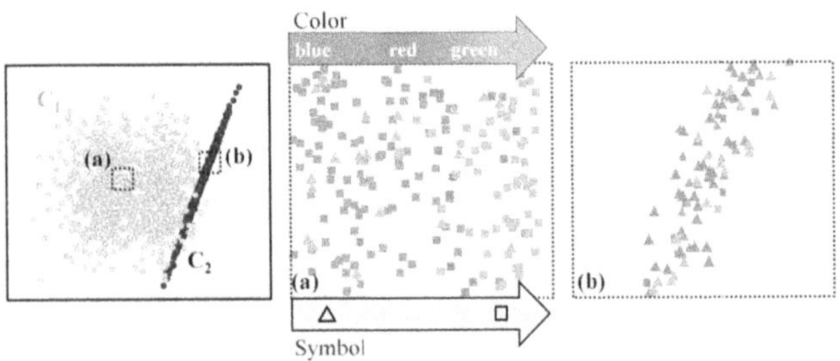

Figure 5: Detailed View of Attribute Dependency Patterns. (a) In cluster C_1 the categorical attributes *symbol* and *color* depend on the numerical x-coordinate: The larger x, the more likely we observe $\Box$ and the colors change from *blue* over *red* to *green* with increasing x. **(b)** In cluster C_2, the numerical coordinates are strongly correlated but we do not observe any further dependencies. INCONCO is the only technique which exploits mixed-type attribute dependencies for clustering.

	wrongly clustered	Prec. C_1%	Rec. C_1%	Prec. C_2%	Rec. C_2%	NMI
INCONCO	**1**	**100**	**99.9**	**99.9**	**100**	**0.99**
K-modes	209	93.9	84.6	85.9	94.5	0.52
discretized	661	70.5	57.8	64.3	76.1	0.1
K-means	348	**100**	65.2	74.2	**100**	0.44
binerized	326	93.3	84.6	85.9	94.5	0.37
K-means-mixed	225	89	88.4	88.4	89.1	0.49

Table 1: Results on Synthetic Data.

wrongly clustered, resulting in an NMI of 0.44. Let us note that some specialized algorithms for detecting linear and non-linear correlation clusters on numerical data have been proposed, e.g. 4C [7], ORCLUS [2] and CURLER [27]. However, these approaches are designed for numerical data only and none of them is suitable for detecting mixed-type attribute dependencies.

When mining mixed-type data, a frequently chosen option is transforming all attributes to a common type. To illustrate this, we re-ran K-Modes and K-Means after discretizing the numerical and binarizing the categorical attributes. This feature transformation does not improve the results of K-means and K-modes. Choosing a suitable resolution for discretization is a non-trivial task. We report the result obtained with 10 equi-width bins, which was the best choice among several trials. Since the attributes in our example are nominal, they have no natural order. Therefore, we binarized the attributes. After binarization the categorical information has with five attributes more weight than the two numerical features. This weighting is artificially introduced by the feature transformation not justified by the ground truth. Since these experiments illustrates the severe difficulties associated with feature transformation, we do not consider this option in the real data experiments.

Recently, some methods for integrative clustering of mixed-type data have been proposed, e.g. K-prototypes [17], CFIKP [30], CAVE [16] and K-means-mixed [3], see also Section 6. We selected to compare to K-means-mixed which is a state-of-the-art technique performing metric learning to find a suitable weighting of the relative importance of numerical and categorical data in clustering. K-means-mixed assigns 225 objects to the wrong cluster which results in an NMI of 0.49. Interestingly, K-means-mixed only clusters the data according the attribute *symbol* which is the most relevant single attribute for clustering, cf. Figure 4. To summarize, integrating numerical and categorical information as performed by K-means-mixed is not sufficient for successfully clustering our example data set. INCONCO performs best by exploiting mixed-type attribute dependencies.

Eigenvalue vs. Cholesky Decomposition

The major reason for basing our technique on the Cholesky decomposition is to enhance the interpretability of the attribute dependencies. We illustrate this on a synthetic data set of 1,000 objects and 10 numerical attributes which exhibits a strong correlation among two pairs of attributes. Figure 6(a) depicts the color-coded Eigenvectors resulting from PCA. Each attribute is expressed by a linear combination of all other attributes. Thus, the Eigenvector matrix is fully occupied and many entries differ much from zero (coded

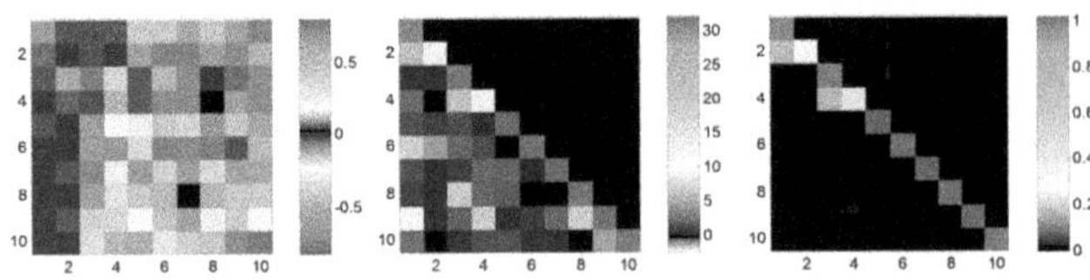

(a) Eigenvectors (b) Row-echelon Form (c) INCONCO

Figure 6: Comparison of PCA, Cholesky Decomposition and INCONCO's Super-attribute Grouping in Interpretability.

in black color). Figure 6(b) depicts the triangular matrix resulting from Cholesky decomposition. The interpretability is improved since also in the occupied part of the matrix many entries are relatively close to zero. Finally, Figure 6(c) displays the result after attribute grouping into super-attributes. Only the relevant two pairs of truly existing attribute dependencies have non-zero values. This fact is automatically transformed into an understandable formula and reported as part of the result by INCONCO.

Mixed-type Attribute Dependencies in Real Data

Dermatology Data. The dermatology data on erythemato-squamous diseases (http://archive.ics.uci.edu/ml/datasets/Dermatology) with 358 instances contains clinical and histopathological information measured by 33 categorical attributes and the age of the subject as a numerical attribute. INCONCO detects meaningful class-pure clusters in this data set and reveals interesting attribute dependencies. The result of INCONCO with an NMI of 0.93 consists of 6 clusters, each of which representing a certain disease with high precision and recall, see Table 2.

The largest cluster consists of 112 subjects and represents the group of subjects suffering from psoriasis (class 1 in Table 2) with precision of 99.1% and recall of 100%. In this cluster, INCONCO reveals an interesting dependency between the categorical attributes *itching* and *Koebner Phenomenon*, both having 4 categories representing the intensity of the symptom. The Koebner Phenomenon is a reaction to skin injury often seen in psoriasis patients and it perfectly makes sense that its intensity is strongly related to the intensity of itching. This dependency can only be observed for the psoriasis cluster.

Another interesting attribute dependency is observed in a cluster with 20 objects representing the disease pityriasis rubra pilaris (class with precision and recall of 100%. In this cluster, the categorical attribute *family history* and the numerical attribute *age* depend on each other:

$$\mu(age) = \begin{cases} 9.3 & \text{if } \textit{family history} = \textit{true}, \\ 11.2 & \text{if } \textit{family history} = \textit{false}. \end{cases}$$

The binary attribute family history indicates whether the disease has been observed in the family. In this cluster, patients with family history are in average two years younger than patients without a family history. Probably, the disease is diagnosed earlier in young patients with a family history since they are sent to medical care by their parents. Also this dependency is cluster-specific.

Parameterized to find K = 6 clusters, K-modes and K-means do not perform well on this data set. The best result of K-means has an NMI of only 0.08. This is not surprising, since we have only one numerical attribute. K-modes performs slightly better with an NMI of 0.24. With an NMI of 0.86 K-means-mixed is the best comparison method. Interestingly, although the attribute *age* is the only numerical attribute, integrating numerical and categorical information is beneficial. As INCONCO, K-means-mixed perfectly identifies the diseases lichen planus (class 3) and pityriasis rubra pilaris (class 6) by creating class-pure clusters. However, the diseases seboreic dermatitis (class 2) and pityriasis rosea (class 4) are assigned to a common cluster resulting an a low precision for these classes, cf. Table 2. INCONCO creates own clusters for these diseases, and assigns most objects correctly (precision and recall for classes 2 and 4 are above 75%). Moreover, INCONCO much better identifies the largest group of psoriasis (precision and recall of class 1 above 99%). To summarize, INCONCO automatically detects the true number of clusters in this data set, reveals interesting novel information on cluster-specific attribute dependencies and outperforms the comparison methods in clustering accuracy.

Algorithm / Class	1	2	3	4	5	6
INCONCO						
Precision %	**99.1**	**97.8**	**100.0**	**78.3**	**100.0**	**100.0**
Recall %	**100.0**	**76.7**	**100.0**	**97.9**	**100.0**	**100.0**
K-means						
Precision %	30.3	21.3	31.3	18.9	13.9	40.4
Recall %	21.6	26.7	28.2	31.2	22.9	95.0
K-modes						
Precision %	100.0	20.6	29.7	17.7	34.8	1.0
Recall %	52.7	59.0	72.2	63.2	28.8	85.0
K-means-mixed						
Precision %	100.0	55.5	**100.0**	44.4	94.1	**100.0**
Recall %	67.6	100.0	**100.0**	100.0	100.0	**100.0**

Table 2: Results on Dermatology Data. The classes correspond to: 1 psoriasis, 2 seboreic dermatitis, 3 lichen planus, 4 pityriasis rosea, 5 cronic dermatitis, 6 pityriasis rubra pilaris.

Automobile Data. The automobile data set (http://archive.ics.uci.edu/ml/datasets/Automobile) consists of 193 instances which are described by 15 numerical and 10 categorical attributes. The numerical attribute *normalized-losses* and 7 instances have been removed from the original data set due to too many missing values. The result of INCONCO consists of 7 clusters each characterized by a unique pattern of attribute dependencies.

The clusters capture well the different segments of the automotive market. Cluster 1 is composed of 20 large relatively cheap cars mostly manufactured by Nissan and Toyota (scaled average price: 0.37). Cluster 2 is composed of 25 cheap small cars, 22 of which have 2 doors only (average price: 0.18). Cluster 3 is composed of 24 expensive very large cars mostly from the brands Mercedes and Volvo (average price 0.88). Cluster 4 consists of 22 high quality small cars, manufactured e.g. by Audi and Saab. 15 of these 22 cars have only two doors but are relatively expensive in comparison to cluster 2 (average price 0.84). Cluster 5 represents 24 upper middle class cars (average price 0.74). Cluster 6 represents 52 middle class cars of medium size and price. As indicated by positive values in the attribute *symboling*, these cars tend to best preserve their value over time. Cluster 7 represents 16 premium cars manufactured by BMW, Porsche, Jaguar and Mercedes (average price: 0.97).

Figure 7 visualizes the pair-wise attribute dependencies of each cluster. Pairwise dependencies among numerical, categorical and mixed (i.e. numerical-categorical) attributes are displayed in different colors (in the same order of attributes for each cluster). We can observe that (1) INCONCO detects unique cluster-specific attribute dependency patterns; (2) many interesting dependencies involving mixed types are detected; and (3) the dependency patterns are sparse which is essential for interpretability. Let us focus on cluster 5 exhibiting a variety of attribute dependencies of all types. Note that Figure 7 displays the pair-wise dependencies only and does not visualize the grouping of attributes into super-attributes. In cluster 5 consisting of 24 data objects, 6 non-trivial super-attributes consisting of more than one attribute have been detected. One of the super-attributes describes a dependency between the numerical attributes *engine size*, *horsepower* and the binary attribute *aspiration*. INCONCO describes the well known fact that with turbo aspiration larger horsepower is possible with a smaller engine size by the following formula:

$$\mu(\textit{engine size}) = \begin{cases} 0.86 \cdot \textit{horsepower} \text{ if } \textit{aspiration} = \textit{standard}, \\ 0.77 \cdot \textit{horsepower} \text{ if } \textit{aspiration} = \textit{turbo}. \end{cases}$$

Another 3-fold dependency is detected between the binary attribute *fuel type* and the numerical attributes *compression ratio* and *peak-rpm*:

$$\mu(\textit{peak-rpm}) = \begin{cases} 0.58 \cdot \textit{compression ratio} \text{ if } \textit{fuel type} = \textit{diesel}, \\ 2.45 \cdot \textit{compression ratio} \text{ if } \textit{fuel type} = \textit{gas}. \end{cases}$$

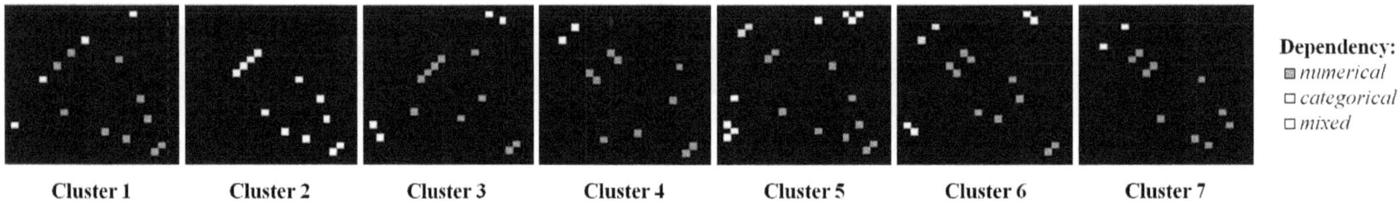

Figure 7: INCONCO Clustering of Automobile Data: Cluster-specific Attribute Dependency Patterns.

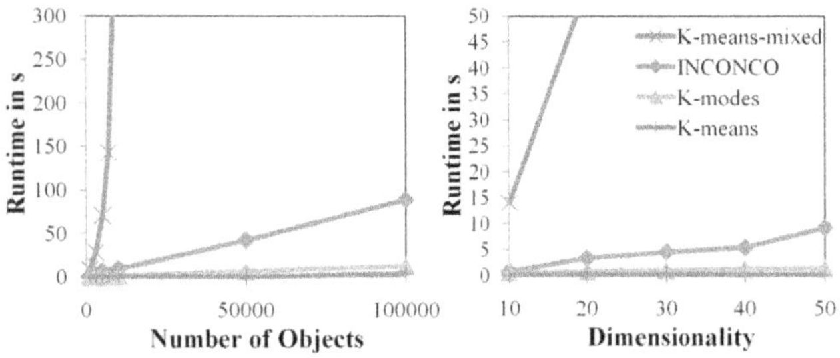

Figure 8: Scalability.

Diesel engines usually have much higher compression rates than gasoline engines, and tend to have a lower number of resolutions per minute compared to gas engines in the same price segment. The result of the comparison methods strongly depends on the choice of the number of clusters K. Moreover, none of the comparison methods provide an internal clustering quality measure like INCONCO with MDL, and no other method can detect attribute dependencies.

Efficiency

To evaluate the efficiency, we generated synthetic data sets as described in Section 5 with varying numbers of objects ranging from 1,000 to 100,000, cf. Figure 8 (left). All comparison methods have been parameterized with the correct K. INCONCO automatically finds the correct number of clusters which causes some runtime overhead. However, INCONCO is still highly efficient. K-means-mixed is the slowest technique among the comparison methods. Already clustering the smallest data set with 1,000 points requires over 2 minutes with K-means-mixed. INCONCO processes 1,000 points in 9 seconds. Processing 7,000 points requires 40 minutes with K-means-mixed and 30 seconds with INCONCO. In average, INCONCO is by a factor of 31 faster than K-means-mixed. To assess the scalability w.r.t. the dimensionality, we created synthetic data sets of various dimensionality ranging from 10 to 50. Each data set is composed of 50% categorical and 50% numerical dimensions for INCONCO and K-means-mixed. K-means-mixed scales worst in the dimensionality. Using efficient Cholesky decomposition and clustering of attributes into super-attributes, INCONCO is in average by a factor 16 faster than K-means-mixed.

6. RELATED WORK AND DISCUSSION

The vast majority of the clustering literature has been focussing on clustering numerical data. This field is very mature with a large volume of research papers , e.g. the fundamental approach K-means [14], BIRCH [32] and DBSCAN [11], to mention a few. Recently, the areas of correlation clustering or generalized subspace clustering have attracted lots of attention. Prominent algorithms include, e.g., ORCLUS [2], 4C [7] and CURLER [27]. These algorithms combine local PCA with clustering to detect clusters exhibiting unique linear or non-linear attribute dependencies in high-dimensional vector data. Recently, also some effort has been made towards a better interpretability of vector clustering e.g., by avoiding redundancy in the results [20, 21] or providing interactive visualization tools [22]. Achtert et al. [1] propose a post-processing technique to derive quantitative models from the result of correlation clustering algorithms. A system of linear equations describing the cluster-specific attribute correlations is obtained by transforming the Eigenvector matrix into row-echelon form. Also related to our approach are the research topics of feature selection for clustering, projected and subspace clustering, for a survey see [18]. These approaches focus on finding axis-parallel clusters in high-dimensional numerical data. Approaches to co-clustering or bi-clustering such as [10] simultaneously cluster columns and rows of contingency tables. One major benefit shared by axis-parallel subspace clustering and co-clustering is the interpretability: The resulting subspace clusters or co-clusters are represented by subsets of the original features, and not by arbitrarily complex linear combinations of the features as in correlation clustering. INCONCO combines the flexibility of correlation clustering without loosing the interpretability of subspace and co-clustering by identifying only those attribute dependency patterns which are truly relevant to model a cluster. Another recent line of research focusses on avoiding restrictive parameter settings and assumptions in clustering, e.g. X-Means [24] and OCI [5]. These approaches relate vector clustering to data compression and derive clustering objective functions based on the Minimum Description Length principle [26]. However, all these techniques are only applicable to numerical data.

Compared to the huge volume of literature on clustering numerical data, only relatively few papers focus on clustering categorical data, e.g. K-modes [8], STIRR [12], LIMBO [4] and CLICKS [31]. The algorithm K-modes extends the K-means clustering algorithm for categorical data. LIMBO is a hierarchical clustering of categorical data based on the Information Bottleneck Principle. Recently, the algorithm CLICKS has been proposed for detecting subspace clusters in categorical data. However, to the best of our knowledge, no algorithm explicitly searches for cluster-specific attribute dependencies in categorical data.

Some approaches for clustering mixed-type data have recently been proposed, e.g. K-prototypes [17], CFIKP [30], CAVE [16], CEBMDC [15], INTEGRATE [6] and K-means-mixed [3]. Most of these algorithms rely on the basic algorithmic paradigm of K-means. Besides the number of clusters K, for most approaches the relative importance of numerical and categorical information needs to be specified by input parameters. Some algorithms propose strategies for balancing numerical and categorical information in clustering: The framework CEBMDC integrates separately generated numerical and categorical clusterings with a cluster ensemble approach; INTEGRATE and CAVE apply ideas from information theory. We selected for comparison the algorithm K-means-mixed. The clustering objective function of this algorithm explicitly considers the significance of each single attribute for clustering. The definition of significance is based on the idea that attributes which distinguish among instances in the mixed data space should have more importance in the clustering process. By iteratively optimizing the objective function, the attribute significance is dynamically adjusted.

Discovering attribute dependency patterns in clustering mixed-type data is a research question which has not been addressed so far. Our approach INCONCO is a solution inspired by ideas for interpretable correlation clustering [1] and clustering by data compression [26].

7. CONCLUSION

Our algorithm INCONCO addresses major challenges in clustering: INCONCO clusters *mixed-type data* consisting of numerical and categorical attributes. INCONCO clusters by *revealing cluster-specific dependency patterns* among the attributes. Dependency patterns are discovered by integrating several numerical and categorical attributes into super-attributes which represent the semantic concepts of the cluster. To *facilitate interpretation* of the clustering result, we express dependency patterns by conditional probabilities of the original attributes. To further facilitate the practical application and interpretability, we base the clustering objective function of INCONCO on the Minimum Description Length principle relating clustering to data compression. Supported by MDL, INCONCO detects the truly relevant clusters and attribute dependency patterns in the data.

8. REFERENCES

[1] E. Achtert, C. Böhm, H.-P. Kriegel, P. Kröger, and A. Zimek. Deriving quantitative models for correlation clusters. In *KDD Conference*, pages 4–13, 2006.

[2] C. C. Aggarwal and P. S. Yu. Finding generalized projected clusters in high dimensional spaces. In *SIGMOD Conference*, pages 70–81, 2000.

[3] A. Ahmad and L. Dey. A k-mean clustering algorithm for mixed numeric and categorical data. *Data Knowl. Eng.*, 63(2):503–527, 2007.

[4] P. Andritsos, P. Tsaparas, R. J. Miller, and K. C. Sevcik. Limbo: Scalable clustering of categorical data. In *EDBT Conference*, pages 123–146, 2004.

[5] C. Böhm, C. Faloutsos, and C. Plant. Outlier-robust clustering using independent components. In *SIGMOD Conference*, pages 185–198, 2008.

[6] C. Böhm, S. Goebl, A. Oswald, C. Plant, M. Plavinski, and B. Wackersreuther. Integrative parameter-free clustering of data with mixed type attributes. In *PAKDD*, pages 38–47, 2010.

[7] C. Böhm, K. Kailing, P. Kröger, and A. Zimek. Computing clusters of correlation connected objects. In *SIGMOD Conference*, pages 455–466, 2004.

[8] A. Chaturvedi, P. E. Green, and J. D. Caroll. K-modes clustering. *Journal of Classification*, 18(1).

[9] T. A. Davis. *Direct Methods for Sparse Linear Systems*. Society for Industrial and Applied Mathematics, 1996.

[10] I. S. Dhillon, S. Mallela, and D. S. Modha. Information-theoretic co-clustering. In *In KDD Conference*, pages 89–98. ACM Press, 2003.

[11] M. Ester, H.-P. Kriegel, J. Sander, and X. Xu. A density-based algorithm for discovering clusters in large spatial databases with noise. In *KDD Conference*, 1996.

[12] D. Gibson, J. Kleinberg, and P. Raghavan. Clustering categorical data: an approach based on dynamical systems. *The VLDB Journal*, 8(3-4):222–236, 2000.

[13] G. H. Golub and C. F. V. Loan. *Matrix Computations*. The Johns Hopkins University Press, 3rd edition, 1996.

[14] J. A. Hartigan. *Clustering Algorithms*. John Wiley & Sons, 1975.

[15] Z. He, X. Xu, and S. Deng. Clustering mixed numeric and categorical data: A cluster ensemble approach. *CoRR*, abs/cs/0509011, 2005.

[16] C.-C. Hsu and Y.-C. Chen. Mining of mixed data with application to catalog marketing. *Expert Syst. Appl.*, 32(1):12–23, 2007.

[17] Z. Huang. Extensions to the k-means algorithm for clustering large data sets with categorical values. *Data Min. Knowl. Discov.*, 2(3):283–304, 1998.

[18] H.-P. Kriegel, P. Kröger, and A. Zimek. Clustering high-dimensional data: A survey on subspace clustering, pattern-based clustering, and correlation clustering. *ACM Trans. Knowl. Discov. Data*, 3:1:1–1:58, March 2009.

[19] J. B. Macqueen. Some methods of classification and analysis of multivariate observations. In *Proceedings of the Fifth Berkeley Symposium on Mathematical Statistics and Probability*, pages 281–297, 1967.

[20] G. Moise and J. Sander. Finding non-redundant, statistically significant regions in high dimensional data: a novel approach to projected and subspace clustering. In *KDD Conference*, pages 533–541, 2008.

[21] E. Müller, I. Assent, S. Günnemann, R. Krieger, and T. Seidl. Relevant subspace clustering: Mining the most interesting non-redundant concepts in high dimensional data. In *ICDM Conference*, pages 377–386, 2009.

[22] E. Müller, I. Assent, R. Krieger, T. Jansen, and T. Seidl. Morpheus: interactive exploration of subspace clustering. In *KDD Conference*, pages 1089–1092, 2008.

[23] Y. Okiyama, T. Nakano, K. Yamashita, Y. Mochizuki, N. Taguchi, and S. Tanaka. Acceleration of fragment molecular orbital calculations with cholesky decomposition approach. *Chemical Physics Letters*, 490(1-3):84 – 89, 2010.

[24] D. Pelleg and A. Moore. X-means: Extending K-means with efficient estimation of the number of clusters. In *ICML Conference*, pages 727–734, 2000.

[25] G. Piatetsky-Shapiro, C. Djeraba, L. Getoor, R. Grossman, R. Feldman, and M. J. Zaki. What are the grand challenges for data mining? *KDD 2006 panel report. SIGKDD Explorations*, 8(2):70–77, 2006.

[26] J. Rissanen. *Information and Complexity in Statistical Modeling*. Springer, 2007.

[27] A. K. Tung, X. Xu, and B. C. Ooi. CURLER: Finding and visualizing nonlinear correlation clusters. In *SIGMOD Conference*, pages 467–478, 2005.

[28] N. X. Vinh, J. Epps, and J. Bailey. Information theoretic measures for clusterings comparison: is a correction for chance necessary? In *ICML Conference*, pages 1073–1080, 2009.

[29] Q. Yang and X. Wu. 10 challenging problems in data mining research. *IJITDM*, 5(4):597–604, 2006.

[30] J. Yin and Z. Tan. Clustering mixed type attributes in large dataset. In *ISPA Conference*, pages 655–661, 2005.

[31] M. J. Zaki, M. Peters, I. Assent, and T. Seidl. Clicks: An effective algorithm for mining subspace clusters in categorical datasets. *Data Knowl. Eng.*, 60(1):51–70, 2007.

[32] T. Zhang, R. Ramakrishnan, and M. Livny. Birch: An efficient data clustering method for very large databases. In *SIGMOD Conference*, pages 103–114, 1996.

Incorporating SAT Solvers into Hierarchical Clustering Algorithms - An Efficient and Flexible Approach

Sean Gilpin
Department of Computer Science
University of California, Davis
Davis, CA 95616
sagilpin@ucdavis.edu

Ian Davidson
Department of Computer Science
University of California, Davis
Davis, CA 95616
indavidson@ucdavis.edu

ABSTRACT

The area of constrained clustering has been actively pursued for the last decade. A more recent extension that will be the focus of this paper is constrained hierarchical clustering which allows building user-constrained dendrograms/trees. Like all forms of constrained clustering, previous work on hierarchical constrained clustering uses simple constraints that are typically implemented in a procedural language. However, there exists mature results and packages in the fields of constraint satisfaction languages and solvers that the constrained clustering field has yet to explore. This work marks the first steps towards introducing constraints satisfaction languages/solvers into hierarchical constrained clustering. We make several significant contributions. We show how many existing and new constraints for hierarchical clustering, can be modeled as a Horn-SAT problem that is easily solvable in polynomial time and which allows their implementation in any number of declarative languages or efficient solvers. We implement our own solver for efficiency reasons. We then show how to formulate constrained hierarchical clustering in a flexible manner so that any number of algorithms, whose output is a dendrogram, can make use of the constraints.

Categories and Subject Descriptors

H.2.8 [**Database Applications**]: Data Mining

General Terms

Algorithms, Experimentation

1. INTRODUCTION AND MOTIVATION

The area of clustering with constraints was introduced to the machine learning and data mining fields by Wagstaff and Cardie [18] a decade ago. During the past ten years much research has occurred in the field with the seminal paper [18] obtaining over five hundred citations and a recent collected edition [4] describes many innovative applications. Despite the great attention given to constrained clustering two noticeable "gaps" in the research have occurred. Firstly, despite an extensive survey [13] of application journals in domains such as biology, chemistry and physics showing that **hierarchical, not non-hierarchical, clustering** is the most prevalent clustering approach, little effort has looked at constrained hierarchical clustering. Secondly, the connection with the closely related computer science fields of constraint programming languages, declarative languages, and constraint satisfaction solvers has received little attention.

The first gap/limitation described above greatly limits the use of constrained clustering algorithms since in that survey it was found that over 50% of applications of clustering were to create hierarchies. This is not too surprising given that hierarchies are of more use to practitioners since they offer a more comprehensive summary of the data and can model temporal relationships such as evolution. The introduction of constrained hierarchies offers even more benefits since hierarchical techniques tend to be used in areas where considerable domain expertise already exists and hence should provide a ready source of constraints if they are rich enough to model the concepts in these fields.

The second gap/limitation is perhaps the most startling given the aim of constrained clustering is to find clusterings consistent with a given set of constraints. Modeling constraints in a procedural language is greatly limiting and gave rise to declarative languages with built-in constraint satisfaction techniques such as resolution thereby freeing the programmer to model the constraints rather than designing algorithms to solve them. A severe limitation to introducing more complex constraints beyond the seminal constraints `must-link` and `cannot-link` is that determining if they can be efficiently satisfied, and how to satisfy them becomes a difficult issue. **Our first order logic formulation, can be propositionalized into a set of Horn-SAT constraints allowing us to check the consistency of the constraints and find dendrograms that satisfy all of the supplied constraints in polynomial time.**

We make the first steps to combining hierarchical constrained clustering and constraint programming languages and solvers. Our previous work [8] explored using constraint satisfaction techniques and 2-SAT for non-hierarchical clustering in a limited setting ($k = 2$). The direction we take in this paper has many immediate and long term benefits to the field, some of which we now list.

- The domain-expert/user can specify a collection of **different types of constraints**. Previous work has focused on only one type of instance-level constraint.
- The constraints are capable of expressing hierarchical information including partial dendrograms.
- The domain-expert/user can specify a large collection of constraints and they can be efficiently checked for inconsistencies and satisfaction unlike the non-hierarchical case which is in general NP-Complete [7].

- Extensive complexity and algorithm design results have created a rich literature of which normal forms of clauses are efficiently solvable and algorithms exist to solve large collections of clauses. For example, in this paper we make use of the fact that clauses in Horn-form are efficiently solvable and base our own solver on the work of Dowling and Gallier [9].
- The user and algorithm designer are free to focus on data mining algorithms and not how to model or satisfy constraints.
- By separating out the constraint satisfaction part of the algorithm and formally modeling it, we create a reusable framework that can be used with a variety of algorithms that build hierarchies.

We begin this paper by describing previous work, which is limited to just six papers, in Section 2. In Section 3 we describe our first order logic language to model constraints. Section 4 shows how an agglomerative clustering algorithm can use our formalism to find solutions to constrained hierarchical clustering problems. The description of our experiments and results can be found in Section 5.

2. PREVIOUS WORK

Despite the popularity of applying hierarchical clustering algorithms, little work has focused on hierarchical constrained clustering. Previous work has explored using instance level constraints for hierarchical clustering. Davidson and Ravi use `must-link` (ML) and `cannot-link` (CL) constraints previously used for non-hierarchical clustering and demonstrated their use for hierarchical clustering [6, 7]. Kestler and Kraus showed the limitations of using ML and CL constraints with hierarchical clustering and proposed a method to limit the scope of the constraints [12]. They used `must-link` and `cannot-link` constraints for their problem, but because of their application, needed different sets of constraints for the top half of their dendrogram than for the bottom half. They created an algorithm to do so and conjectured that their work could be extended so that constraints could be specified at more than the two levels. Bade and Nürnberger proposed a new type of constraint for hierarchical clustering, `must-link-before` (`MLB`), a trinary relationship that specifies that two points should be joined together before either are joined to a specified third point in the resulting hierarchy [2, 3]. We show these and other constraints can be naturally modeled in our framework.

Recently there has also been work by Davidson, Ravi, and Shamis which showed how 2-SAT solvers can be used as a basis to form non-hierarchical clustering algorithm's objective functions [8]. This paper instead looks at modeling complex constraints (not the objective function) in hierarchical clustering and using Horn-SAT.

3. A FORMULATION FOR CONSTRAINED HIERARCHICAL CLUSTERING

In this section we outline at a high level how to build a knowledge base that can both model a dendrogram and the constraints the dendrogram must satisfy. The implementation of our constraint solver propositionalizes the knowledge base, so we only add sentences that will propositionalize into Horn clauses. We first define the trinary relationship `together(x,y,i)` which will express that instances x and y must be in the same cluster at level i in the dendrogram. We will then show in the next section four properties that a dendrogram must satisfy and define them using the `together` relationship.

DEFINITION 1. ***together* Relation.** *`together(x,y,i)` which if true* **requires** *points x and y to be in the same cluster at level i.*

Our work in this section can be summarized as follows.

- We give a definition of dendrogram using the `together` relationship that requires the following properties to be satisfied: `Transitivity`, `Symmetry`, `Inter-level link` and `Full-tree` (see Section 3.1).
- Each of four properties can be expressed in Horn form (see Section 3.3).
- The definition of dendrogram we use is quite broad and includes dendrograms where no, one, or multiple merges occur at each level in the tree.
- We show that all types of existing constraints can be easily modeled using the `together` relationship and expressed as Horn sentences (see Section 3.2).
- Our formulation lends itself to both new global and local types of constraints.

Once we have created a set of sentences (a knowledge base) to represent our problem and the constraints, a SAT solver will try to find a model that satisfies all of the sentences and thus can be interpreted as a dendrogram that satisfies the user constraints. If it is unable to do so then the set of sentences is unsatisfiable, which would manifest itself in a contradiction. **Our knowledge base is in first order logic but we propositionalize it and use an efficient solver.**

3.1 How to Model a Dendrogram

We now describe a logic formulation for hierarchical clustering that allows us to express each of the previously described constraints in the literature (global, `must-link-before`, level specific) and new variations. The definition of **dendrogram** we use is a sequence of clusterings where each clustering is derived from the previous clustering in the sequence through zero or more merge operations[1]. A **complete dendrogram** is defined as a dendrogram that has only one cluster in the final clustering in that sequence. Throughout this paper, we refer to the "leaf end" of a tree as the first level of a dendrogram, and the root of the tree as the top level of a dendrogram.

We first constrain `together` to reflect a clustering for each value of i by requiring it to respect the equivalence relation properties of transitivity, symmetry, and reflexivity. We then force each clustering at different levels of i to be related through merges by enforcing the inter-level link property. Finally we ensure the relationship will represent a complete dendrogram by enforcing the full-tree dendrogram property. These properties are described formally below. By adding sentences that enforce these properties to our formalism, any satisfying model will be interpretable as a full dendrogram. We will then be able to add our own domain or problem specific constraints to find hierarchical clusterings that satisfy those constraints as well (assuming they are consistent).

Reflexivity.

Every instance is always in the same cluster as itself.

DEFINITION 2. ***Reflexivity Property***

$$\forall i, x[\mathtt{together}(x,x,i)]$$

[1]Requiring one or more merges per level, although a more natural formulation, leads to an NP-Hard constraint satisfaction problem.

Symmetry.

If instance a is in the same cluster as instance b at a particular level i, then a is also in the same cluster as b at that level.

DEFINITION 3. ***Symmetry Property.***

$$\forall i, x, y[\texttt{together(x,y,i)} \rightarrow \texttt{together(y,x,i)}]$$

Transitivity.

If instance a and instance b are in the same cluster (`together(a,b,i)`) and instance b and instance c are in the same cluster (`together(b,c,i)`) then instance a and instance c are in the same cluster (`together(a,c,i)`).

DEFINITION 4. ***Transitivity Property.***

$$\forall i, x, y, z[\texttt{together(x,y,i)} \wedge \texttt{together(y,z,i)} \rightarrow \texttt{together(x,z,i)}]$$

Implied Inter-Level Links.

Due to the nature of hierarchical clustering, if two instances are in the same cluster at a given level, they will also be in the same cluster at higher levels in the hierarchy. Another way of putting this, is that once two instances have been merged into the same cluster, they can never be unmerged.

DEFINITION 5. ***Implied Inter-level Links***

$$\forall i, x, y[\texttt{together(x,y,i)} \rightarrow \texttt{together(x,y,i+1)}]$$

Complete Dendrograms.

If our resulting dendrograms are to form a complete tree, then the top level of the hierarchy must contain just one cluster containing all instances.

DEFINITION 6. ***Complete Dendrogram Property***

$$\forall x, y[\texttt{together(x,y,top)}]$$

3.2 Modeling User Constraints

The power of using a logic formulation for hierarchical clustering is that many different types of user constraints can be easily added. All of the constraint types described in previous work (instance constraints [7], level specific instance constraints [12], `must-link-before` [3]) can be formulated using only Horn clauses of our core relation (see Definition 1). We also show how the expressiveness of logic allows us to easily extend the `must-link-before` constraints to encode a notion of distance.

Global constraints.

In previous work Davidson and Ravi explore using `must-link` and `cannot-link` constraints for hierarchical clustering. The `must-link` and `cannot-link` constraints were originally formulated for use with non-hierarchical clustering [7]. Since each level of a dendrogram effectively corresponds to a different non-hierarchical clustering, an obvious interpretation of the constraints is that they must hold in each and every level of the dendrogram. We refer to such unconditional `must-link` and `cannot-link` constraints as global constraints since they apply to each level of the dendrogram. Note that a single `cannot-link` constraint prevents a full dendrogram from being constructed. Therefore the use of the global `cannot-link` constraint cannot be used without removing the full dendrogram requirement.

A global constraint can easily be specified in our framework by replicating the constraint at each level in the dendrogram.

OBSERVATION 1. ***Encoding Global Must/Cannot-Link Constraints [7]***

$$ML(a,b) \equiv \forall i \quad \texttt{together(a,b,i)}$$

$$CL(a,b) \equiv \forall i \quad \neg\texttt{together(a,b,i)}$$

Must Link Before Constraints.

The `must-link-before` constraints formulated and explored in the work of Bade and Nürnberger, are important because they are created specifically for use with hierarchical clustering and are simple to create in practice. `must-link-before` is a trinary relationship that specifies that two instances, a and b, are more similar to each other than either is to a third instance, c. Hence any satisfying dendrogram must have a and b in the same cluster before either is in the same cluster as c. A key observation is that the `must-link-before` constraint is logically equivalent to the claim that if either of a or b are in the same cluster as c, then a and b must already be in the same cluster at the previous level (higher levels are closer to the dendrogram root).

OBSERVATION 2. ***Encoding Must-Link-Before Constraint [3]***

$$\texttt{must-link-before(a,b,c)} \equiv$$

$$\forall i \quad \texttt{together(a,c,i+1)} \rightarrow \texttt{together(a,b,i)}$$

$$\forall i \quad \texttt{together(b,c,i+1)} \rightarrow \texttt{together(a,b,i)}$$

$$\neg\texttt{together(b,c,1)}$$

$$\neg\texttt{together(a,c,1)}$$

The last two sentences are necessary to handle boundary conditions and simply state that the distant point cannot be linked with either of the close points in the first merge.

Level Specific Constraints.

The constraints specified by Kestler and Kraus allowed sets of ML and CL constraints to be specified at different levels of the hierarchy. The $together_i$ relation maps directly to that notion as we can specify ML constraints at a specific level i. To specify cannot links we can use a negated $together_i$ relation which is also in Horn form (because a sentence consisting of a single negative literal meets the definition of a Horn clause, see Definition 7). These constraints have previously been used successfully in specific applications but in general they are not easily generated because domain knowledge of the form that two instances should be together or apart at specific levels in the dendrogram is rare. However, if such information is available it can be both useful and complex to satisfy. Consider if the domain expert states that x and y should be together at level i, a and b together at level $i+1$, and x and a should be apart at level $i+2$. Due to entailment this will generate a range of additional constraints at level $i+2$ namely cannot-links between (x,b), (y,a), (y,b). If the domain expert were to inadvertently state any of these pairs should be together this would create an inconsistency. The benefit of our approach at modeling constraints in a logic and using solvers is that such inconsistency can be easily checked in polynomial time.

Other Constraints.

Our underlying core relation (see Definition 1) can be used to model a variety of constraints. For example, it is easy to extend the MLB constraint to take into account distances between merges. For example, while a constraint $MLB(a, b, c)$ specifies that instance a and b must be merged together before a and c or b and c, it does not say how soon before they should be merged. We may wish to specify that a and b should be merged together much sooner before a or b are merged with c. This may be the case if we believe a and b share a close common ancestor but are only remotely related to c. Consider the situation where a and b should not be merged with c until d merges/time-steps. This can be formulated very similarly to how `must-link-before` constraints are.

OBSERVATION 3. ***Encoding MLB-After-d***

$$must - link - before_d(a, b, c) \equiv$$

$\forall i$ `together(a,c,i+d)` $\rightarrow$ `together(a,b,i)`

$\forall i$ `together(b,c,i+d)` $\rightarrow$ `together(a,b,i)`

$\neg$`together(b,c,1)`

$\vdots$

$\neg$`together(b,c,d)`

$\neg$`together(a,c,1)`

$\vdots$

$\neg$`together(a,c,d)`

The interpretation of this constraint relies on how merges are performed, which is algorithm dependent. If exactly one merge occurs per level then it will be the case that a and b will be together d merges before either are merged with c. This extended MLB then can be considered as a strong suggestion as to the distance between the triple. In the case when d=1, this definition reduces to the `must-link-before` constraint.

3.3 Propositionalization

Russel and Norvig give a general method for creating a set of set of propositional sentences (CNF) from any first order knowledge base [16]. A satisfying truth assignment for the propositional sentences can be translated into a model satisfying the first order knowledge base. All of the first order logic sentences we used to define a dendrogram (reflexivity, symmetry, transitivity, implied inter-level link) and all user constraints described in this paper can be propositionalized into Horn clauses.

DEFINITION 7. *[Horn Clause] A Horn clause is a disjunction of literals (propositions or negated propositions) in which at most one of the literals is not negated. A Horn clause is logically equivalent to a sentence in which the conjunction of the variables from the negative literals, imply the variable from the only positive literal. For example* $\neg P \vee \neg Q \vee R \equiv (P \wedge Q) \rightarrow R$

The naive approach of model-checking [16] exhaustively tries all combinations of propositional values (true or false) but will take exponential time. The SAT problem is famously known to be NP-complete and therefore no general-purpose polynomial time algorithm is capable of exactly solving it (assuming P$\neq$ NP)[5, 11].

If instead of allowing general logical sentences, we restrict the sentences to be composed only of Horn clauses, then there are efficient algorithms that can solve the satisfiability problem. In this paper we use the algorithm presented by Dowling and Gallier which can either find a minimal satisfying truth assignment, or determine that the sentences are inconsistent in linear time with respect to the total number of literals in all of the Horn clauses [9]. When a satisfying truth assignment is found, it can be used to construct a dendrogram that will satisfy all of the user constraints.

4. ALGORITHMS

In this section we describe our algorithm for incorporating constraint solvers into agglomerative algorithms. As shall be seen, our work is algorithm independent and we experimentally show its performance using single and complete linkage algorithms. It is worthwhile discussing at a high level how our work can be incorporated into the agglomerative algorithm. This is shown in Figure 1.

Algorithm Generate Constrained Dendrogram
Input: $C_{dendrogram}$: The clauses that model the properties of a dendrogram (see section 3.1).
C_{user}: The clauses representing the different types of given user constraints (see section 3.2).
X: A set of data points to build a dendrogram from.
Output: D: a dendrogram that at each level satisfies all constraints.

1. Let $KB = C_{dendrogram} \cup C_{user}$
2. **if** $(RequiredJoins = Solver(KB))$ *fails* **then**
   exit // the user constraints are contradictory

   // Note $RequiredJoins$ is a list of triples $< x, y, i >$.
   // Each triple states that these two points must be
   // joined at this level. These are points that must be joined
   // to satisfy the constraints in KB.

3. **while** (Agglomerative-Algorithm Not Converged)
   a) Join = Agglomerative-Algorithm(RequiredJoins,X)
   // The agglomerative algorithm choose the best legal join
   b) KB = $KB \cup$ Join
   c) RequiredJoins = Inc-Solver(RequiredJoins, KB)
   end
4. Construct D from RequiredJoins

Figure 1: Our Algorithm Used in the Experimental Settings.

Firstly, in Line 1, the clauses representing the user constraints and the dendrogram properties are added to form the core knowledge base. This knowledge base is fed into our solver in Line 2. If the solver fails then the constraints are inconsistent and should be modified (future work will explore using MAXSAT and other formulations to determine which constraints to repair). If the solver succeeds it returns a list of required joins at given levels to satisfy the constraints. Line 3 applies any agglomerative algorithm to select appropriate joins. The solver is called at each level in the dendrogram because the interaction between the joins the algorithm chooses, and the user constraints, may produce additional constraints. In Sections 4.2 and 4.3 we will give the details of our constraint solver. We will give the full details of how the solver fits into a hierarchical clustering algorithm in Section 4.1.

4.1 Full Constrained Hierarchical Clustering Algorithm

Our propositional constraints along with a Horn-SAT solver can be used by any agglomerative hierarchical clustering algorithm. Agglomerative algorithms typically work by finding closest points, merging them, and then updating the distance matrix for the new clusters. This same procedure can be used with our constraint solver to solve constrained hierarchical clustering. When an agglomerative algorithm choses two closest points a and b to be merged, this can be turned into a constraint `together(a,b,i)` where i is the current step the agglomerative algorithm is on. This constraint can be added to the set of logic sentences specifying the constrained problem (the knowledge base). Solving the SAT problem will determine if the merge violates the constraints. If it does violate the constraints, the sentences will be unsatisfiable and the algorithm will need to pick the next closest pair of points until it finds a pair that does not violate the constraints of the problem.

In the case that adding the constraint does not cause the knowledge base to become inconsistent, the Horn-SAT solver will produce a variable assignment which will include the results of merging the two points. In this case the SAT solver need not be restarted, and more merges can continue to be processed without restarting the solver. Merging two clusters may have logical consequences that causes other unrelated clusters to merge together. For example if a constraint `MLB(a,b,c)` is specified, and the merge chosen by the algorithm causes b and c to be put in the same cluster before a and b are in the same cluster, then a logical consequence is that a and b will be merged at a lower level. Therefore, when updating the distance functions, it is generally necessary to check the details of the resulting variable assignment rather that just updating based on the points that were explicitly merged together.

4.2 Horn-SAT

Our Horn-SAT solver determines if a set of Horn clauses is satisfiable, and if so, produces a minimal satisfying truth assignment. A minimal truth assignment will have the fewest number of variables set to true as possible. There are three types of Horn clauses: (1) those consisting only of a positive literal, (2) those with negative literals and a positive literal, (3) and those with only negative literals. In the case when there are no clauses consisting solely of a single positive literal, the clauses are always satisfiable by assigning every variable the value false. When there are no clauses that only have negative literals, then the set of clauses can always be satisfied by assigning every variable the value true. Therefore, the single positive literal clauses are what initially drive the process of requiring variables to be assigned the value true. Setting a variable to true can lead to simplification in the remaining clauses. If all of the negative literals in a clause are set to true, then any positive literal in the clause must be set to true. If such a clause has no positive literal, then the clause has been simplified to the unsatisfiable `false`, and the set of clauses is unsatisfiable.

The Horn-SAT algorithms proposed by Dowling and Gallier [9] works by starting with an all false variable assignment and only assigning a variable the value true if necessary (clauses with only a positive literal, or have been simplified to have only a positive literal). Once a variable is assigned the value true, the variable is added to a queue of variables that will be used to further simplify the remaining clauses. A mapping between each variable and a list of all clauses containing the variable as a negative literal is maintained. If the simplification leads to a clause with a single positive literal, then the variable from the positive literal is added to the queue. The simplification can also lead to the unsatisfiable sentence `false` in which case the set of clauses is unsatisfiable. The algorithm finishes when all variables in the queue have been processed and has a linear runtime with respect to the total number of literals in all of the clauses whose satisfiability is being tested.

4.3 Horn-SAT With Equivalence Relation

The Horn-SAT solver described in the previous section will work for our purposes but will require us to create a large number of propositional sentences to model the properties used to define a dendrogram. The modifications to the solver outlined in this section allow the dendrogram properties to be modeled implicitly, leaving propositional sentences only for use in expressing the user constraints. Our custom Horn-SAT solver takes advantage of our propositions being based on the `together` relationship. Given a constant i, the `together(x,y,i)` relationship satisfies reflexivity, symmetry, and transitivity, making it an equivalence relation. For each possible level in the hierarchy we maintain a disjoint set data structure which can be used to manipulate an equivalence relation. A disjoint set data structure is initialized so that each point is in its own set and the operation of the disjoint set data structure are `merge(x,y)`, which merges the sets that contain x and y, and `find(x)` which returns the name of the set x belongs to. Using the disjoint set data structure, we can set the value of a proposition `together(x,y,i)` to true by selecting the ith disjoint set data structure and executing `merge(x,y)`. Furthermore we can test the value of the same proposition by evaluating `find(x)==find(y)`. Each disjoint set data structure will naturally assure all of the equivalence relation properties of our dendrogram definition are enforced. To ensure that the inter-level link property is enforced, any time a proposition `together(x,y,i)` is set to true the solver will also set `together(x,y,k)` to true for all $k > i$. To enforce the full dendrogram property all of the instances in the top level disjoint-set data structure must be merged into one cluster on initialization.

Our algorithm processes variables in the queue as normal, except whenever a variable needs to be set to true, we simply perform a `merge` operation. However such merges lead to many propositions becoming true (assuming either set has more than one instance). To avoid tracking those propositions that become true during merges, we do not end the algorithm after the positive variable queue becomes empty. Instead, every time the queue becomes empty we scan through the list of variables that are still contained as negative literals in some clause. We check the truth values of such variables, and if they are true, we add them to the queue.

4.4 Runtime Analysis

In this section we give a brief analysis of the general Horn-SAT algorithm, then an analysis of the runtime of our custom solver. For those who initially wish to skip the analysis, the overall runtime to initialize and solve the satisfaction problem with our custom solver is $O({l_n}^2 + n^2)$, where l_n is the total number of negative literals contained in the propositional Horn clauses, and n is the number of instances being clustered. Additional constraints can be added to the knowledge base and incrementally solved for in $O({l_{nr}}^2)$ time where l_{nr} is the number of negative literals in the remaining Horn clauses (calls to the solver generally leads to simplification of the Horn clauses leading to fewer negative literals).

In the general Horn-SAT solver, each variable that must be set to true is put on the queue once. When processing that variable we check which Horn clauses are affected by setting the variable true. Only the clauses that have negative literals that use the same variable as the variable being set to true are affected. Each variable that shows up as a positive literal in any of the clauses, has an associated list of clauses, where each clause on the list is a clause that will be affected if the variable is set to true. When a variable is set to true all negative literals using that variable are removed from their clauses (and implicitly replaced by a false constant). If any of the clauses are left with only a positive literal that has not already been set to true, then that variable is added to the queue.

Adding variables to the queue takes constant time. Removing a negative literal takes constant time. Processing a variable from the queue requires removing some negative literals and possibly adding some more variables to the queue. Each variable can only be added to the queue once. Therefore the total worst case running time is $O(l_n + l_p + i_o)$ where l_n is the number of negative literals, l_p is the number of positive literals, and i_o the time needed to initialize the necessary data-structures. Dowling and Gallier show that $O(l_n + l_p + i_o) = O(l_n + l_p)$ and details of the correctness and running time of their algorithm can be found in their paper [9].

Our custom solver does extra work when processing each variable in the queue. When a proposition `together(x,y,i)` is set to true we merge the points x, y in the disjoint set data structures corresponding to level i and above. A disjoint set data structure can represent multiple disjoint sets and perform find and join operations that for practical purposes run in constant time [17] (actually uses $O(\alpha(n))$ where $\alpha(n)$ is the inverse of the Ackerman function which grows very slowly, e.g. $\alpha(9876!) = 5$). A dendrogram can have at most n levels so a there are at most n constant time merges performed to process a propositional variable in the positive literal queue. Additionally, each disjoint set data structure can be initialized in linear time with respect to the number of instances, leading to an additional $O(n^2)$ initialization runtime cost.

The custom solver also does extra work every time the positive literal queue is emptied. Every time the queue empties, it is necessary to scan through all negative literals still contained in a Horn clause and check if any of the associated variables have become true. In the worst case only one negative literal will be removed from the clause list each time the queue is emptied. In this case the total amount of work added by the necessity to check those variables is $O({l_n}^2\alpha(n)) \approx O({l_n}^2)$. So the total runtime for our custom Horn-SAT algorithm to take into account this extra work is $O((l_n + l_p + {l_n}^2)\alpha(n) + n^2) \approx O({l_n}^2 + n^2)$. After initially solving the satisfaction problem for a set of constraints, adding an additional variable to the positive literal queue to create additional merges as described in Section 4.1, will take $O({l_{nr}}^2\alpha(n)) \approx O({l_{nr}}^2)$ time, where l_{nr} is the number of remaining negative literals.

5. EXPERIMENTS

Previous work has shown that constraints can be advantageous in increasing the quality of clusterings [3, 2, 7, 6, 12]. Therefore in our experimental results we focus on two different questions:

- Does our method of incorporating constraints into hierarchical algorithms (see Figure 1) produce undesirable results?

- Can the more complex constraints such as those that allow incorporating partial dendrograms produce better results?

The first question we wanted our experiments to answer is how adding constraints using our algorithm would increase the quality of the resulting dendrogram. This is an important question, because we would like users to be able to add this functionality into their clustering algorithms and immediately see better results without having to understand the internals of the constraint solver. We therefore devised experiments to see if this approach would yield good results.

The second question is most important and attempts to address how the quality of resulting dendrograms would be affected by using new constraints that our formulation allows, such as the distance encoded `must-link-before`. On the surface our extension to the `must-link-before` constraint certainly appears stronger, but if it does not lead to better results, then the added complexity is not worthwhile. We created some experiments that would directly compare the results of using `must-link-before` constraints, and our extension to `must-link-before` on the same data sets, to determine whether there is a significant difference between the two in terms of dendrogram quality.

5.1 Simulated User Driven Constraints

Previous work in constrained hierarchical clustering has focused on evaluating sets of randomly generated constraints. In some scenarios that makes sense, but we wanted to create constraints that a user might make after finding unacceptable results in an already attempted hierarchical clustering. We generate these by first creating a dendrogram using our hierarchical clustering algorithm with no constraints, and comparing the output to the known hierarchical structure. We find a set of points that are merged together too soon and create a MLB-After-d constraint to enforce the correct merge order. We then continue the process by rerunning the clustering algorithm with the new constraint, finding the next error, and generating a new constraint based on it.

5.2 Measurements

We used two measurements to calculate the quality of our hierarchical clustering results: F-score and H-Correlation. F-score measure the trade-off between precision and recall and relies only on the labels of each instance. To obtain the F-score we assign each cluster a class based on the majority class membership in the cluster. Each cluster has its F-score calculated and weighted by the number of instances in the cluster. Finally the average F-score over all of the clusters in the hierarchy is used to represent the quality of hierarchical clustering.

H-Correlation is a measurement devised specifically for hierarchical clustering [1]. Rather than using the instance labels, the hierarchical structure is used to measure the quality of the results. Therefore the true hierarchical structure of the data is needed to use this measurement. The measurement iterates over all triples (a,b,c) in the data set and counts the number of times the triples satisfy $MLB(a, b, c)$ in the true hierarchy S_t, the learned hierarchy S_l, and both simultaneously S_b. A higher H-Correlation is desirable and is calculated using:

$$H = \frac{S_b}{S_t + S_l}$$

5.3 Data

Artificial Data Set.

We created a method to artificially generate hierarchical data sets. The data sets generated each have 8 classes whose instances are normally distributed with a mean and variance specific to the class. The method with which those Gaussian parameters are specified is what causes the data to have a hierarchical structure. An initial mean corresponding to the root of the hierarchy is used to calculate two new means which correspond to the two clusters at the next lower level in the tree. Recursively, each of those means is used to randomly generate two new means until there are a total of 8 leaves in the tree. The variance at the root node starts at 1 and is reduced by half at each lower level in the tree. This creates a hierarchy with 5 levels. The first level is the root and has 1 cluster, the second level has 2 clusters, the third 4, the fourth 8, and the last level has as many clusters as there are instances. Each of the data sets were created with a total of 120 five dimensional instances (15 instances per class).

Newsgroup Data Set.
To test our algorithms on a real world data set we utilized the 20 Newsgroups data set [15]. This is a collection of around 20,000 documents from 20 different newsgroups. A freely available version of this data set has already already been processed into a document-term matrix using the lexing capabilities of Rainbow [14]. The number of terms in the document-term matrix is over 60,000 so we used PCA to reduce the number of dimensions to 100. This data has a natural hierarchical structure based on the way the topics were originally organized. In figure 5.3 the hierarchical relationship between the newsgroups is displayed. The class we used for each document when calculating the F-score is the name of the newsgroup the document was posted in.

- **Computers**
  - ○ Hardware
    - * comp.os.mswindows.misc
    - * comp.windows.x
    - * comp.graphics
  - ○ Software
    - * comp.sys.ibm.pc.hardware
    - * comp.sys.mac.hardware
- **Recreation**
  - ○ Automobiles
    - * rec.autos
    - * rec.motorcycles
  - ○ Sports
    - * rec.sport.baseball
    - * rec.sport.hockey
- **Sale**
  - * misc.forsale
- **Science**
  - * sci.med
  - ○ Technology
    - * sci.crypt
    - * sci.electronics
    - * sci.space
- **Politics**
  - * talk.politics.guns
  - ○ International
    - * talk.politics.mideast
    - * talk.politics.misc
- **Philosophy/Religion**
  - * alt.atheism
  - ○ Theism
    - * talk.religion.misc
    - * soc.religion.christian

Figure 2: Hierarchical structure of the 20 Newsgroup data set.

5.4 Experimental Setup

The experiments we ran attempted to simulate the process users might use to incrementally create constraints for their problems. In our experiments we first perform unconstrained hierarchical clustering and then find triples of instances that were merged in the wrong order in relationship to the known true hierarchy. We take one such triple, create a constraint that will correct it, and run our constrained hierarchical clustering algorithm with the new constraint. We then continue the process, always creating one new constraint based on an erroneous merge order in the previous clustering, and then add the constraint to those from the previous steps and re-cluster. We use standard agglomerative hierarchical clustering algorithms and use the Horn-SAT solver to ensure that the constraints are satisfied. We used both single linkage and complete linkage distance update steps in order to compare how they each behave in a constrained clustering environment.

In order to show the significance of our results we repeated each experiment 10 times. For the artificial data set each independent run of experiments started by randomly generating a new data set. The Newsgroup data set was not randomly generated, but is sufficiently large so that we were able to randomly sample the instances so that each set of experiments had a sample of 200 instances with equal number of instances in each class. After creating the data set, each experiment was executed using the same data set, so the different methods could be compared on the same data. We performed a full combinatorial experiment on: choice of data set, type of constraints and distance function. The results of each of these experiments averaged over all 10 experimental runs are plotted below.

5.5 Results

Our results answered our questions fairly conclusively. We first wanted to determine if using our Horn-SAT solver with standard agglomerative clustering algorithms would improve the quality of our results. The left most measurement on each graph in our results is the measurement taken for unconstrained hierarchical clustering. By adding our `MLB-after-d` constraints we saw improved performance as the number of constraints increased. The improvement is significantly larger than global constraints presented in our earlier work [7] given the constraint is more expressive and capable of encoding a partial dendrogram.

Secondly we wanted to determine if there were advantages to being able to formulate new types of constraints using logic. The F-score measurements in all of the experiments suggest that this is the case since the `MLB-after-d` constraints all outperformed the original `must-link-before` constraints. The H-correlation measurement was created by the inventors of the `must-link-before` constraint and centrally uses that constraint. It is therefore quite encouraging to see that in our experiments using H-correlation, that the MLB After-d constraints were often able to perform better than the `must-link-before` constraint which the measure is based on.

6. CONCLUSION

In this work we attempted to create a constraint solver that would allow any agglomerative hierarchical clustering algorithm to become a *constrained* hierarchical clustering algorithm, through declarative means, rather than procedurally. Logic is a good choice for constraint specification, because it is formal, yet widely understood and studied. There are also many algorithms for solving the satisfiability/consistency problem that can be utilized by a constraint solver.

We showed how logic can be used to model dendrograms and user constraints in such a way that the satisfiability could be tested in polynomial time. All of the constraint types in previous work on constrained hierarchical clustering are expressible in Horn form, as are the logical sentences needed to model a dendrogram. This ensures that we can find solutions that satisfy the constraints efficiently. A still unexplored direction for our framework is maximizing the number of constraints satisfied in the case of an inconsistent set of constraints.

We implemented our solver and integrated it into an agglomerative hierarchical clustering algorithm, with as little extra work as possible. We have also made our solver and experiment code available on-line[10]. Our experiments show that taking just that simple step can lead to a well performing constrained hierarchical clustering algorithm. There are other ways this solver could be used to perform hierarchical clustering, but it was more interesting to us to see how it could be used by existing clustering algorithms with no additional work.

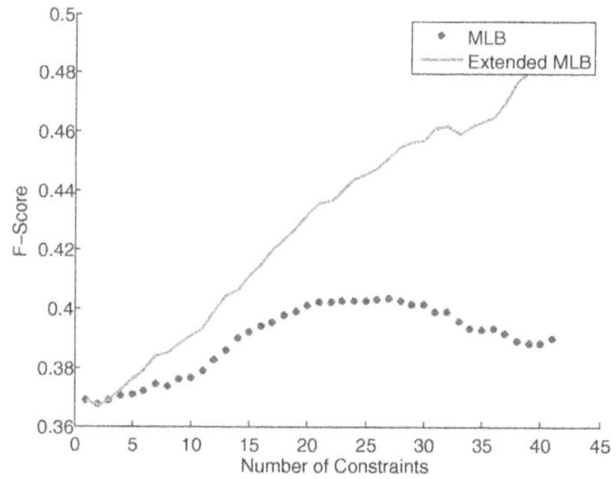

(a) Single linkage, F-score.

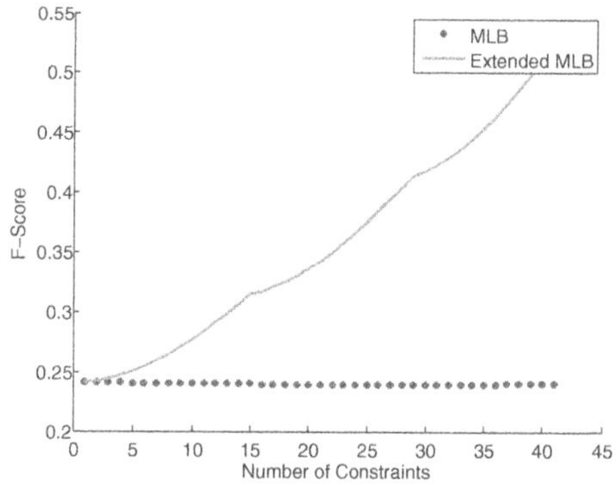

(b) Complete linkage, F-score.

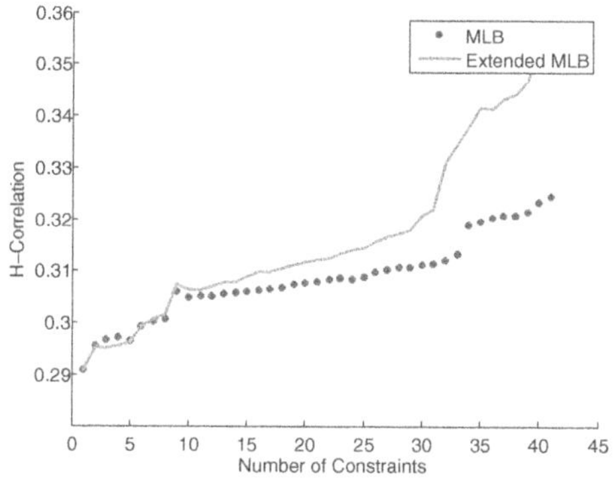

(c) Single linkage, H-correlation

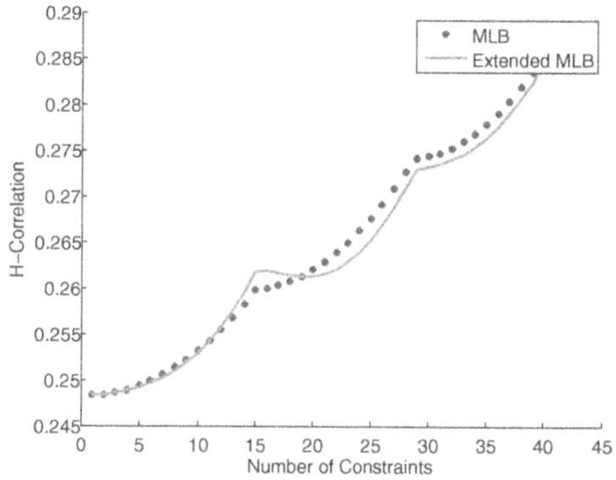

(d) Complete linkage, H-correlation

Figure 3: Artificial data set results.

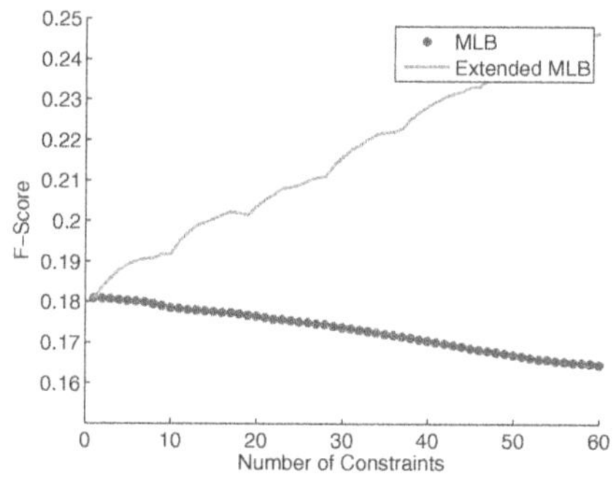

(a) Single linkage, F-score.

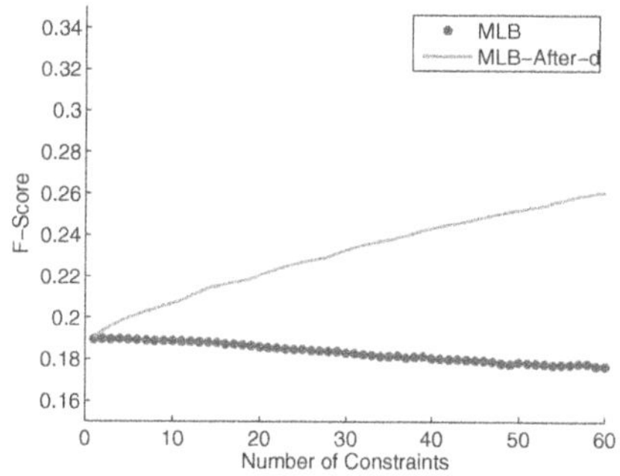

(b) Complete linkage, F-score.

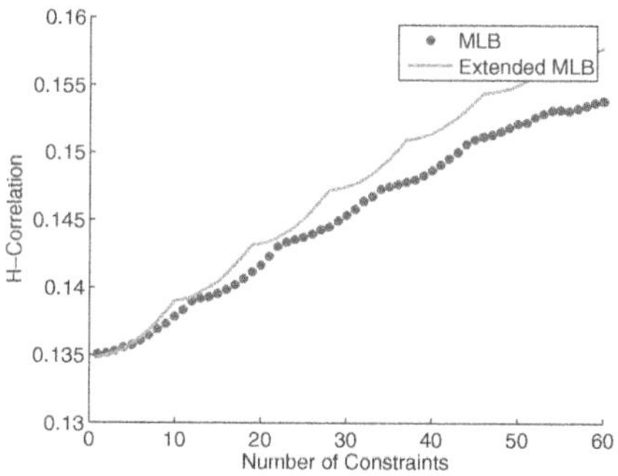

(c) Single linkage, H-correlation

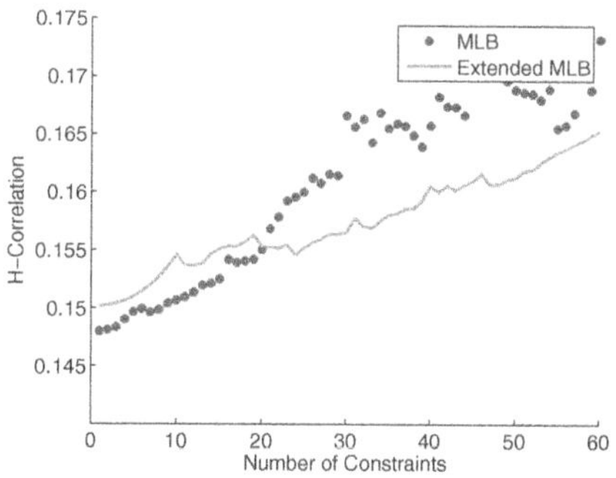

(d) Complete linkage, H-correlation

Figure 4: 20 Newsgroups data set results.

7. REFERENCES

[1] K. Bade and D. Benz. Evaluation strategies for learning algorithms of hierarchies. In *Proceedings of the 32nd Annual Conference of the German Classification Society (GfKl'08)*, 2009.

[2] K. Bade and A. Nürnberger. Personalized hierarchical clustering. In *WI '06: Proceedings of the 2006 IEEE/WIC/ACM International Conference on Web Intelligence*, pages 181–187, Washington, DC, USA, 2006. IEEE Computer Society.

[3] K. Bade and A. Nürnberger. Creating a cluster hierarchy under constraints of a partially known hierarchy. In *Proceedings of the SIAM International Conference on Data Mining, SDM 2008*, pages 13–24, 2008.

[4] S. Baso, I. Davidson, and K. L. Wagstaff, editors. *Constrained Clustering: Advances in Algorithms, Theory, and Applications*. CRC Press, 2009.

[5] S. A. Cook. The complexity of theorem-proving procedures. In *STOC '71: Proceedings of the third annual ACM symposium on Theory of computing*, pages 151–158, New York, NY, USA, 1971. ACM.

[6] I. Davidson and S. S. Ravi. Agglomerative hierarchical clustering with constraints: Theoretical and empirical results. In *Knowledge Discovery in Databases: PKDD 2005, 9th European Conference on Principles and Practice of Knowledge Discovery in Databases*, pages 59–70, 2005.

[7] I. Davidson and S. S. Ravi. Using instance-level constraints in agglomerative hierarchical clustering: theoretical and empirical results. *Data Min. Knowl. Discov.*, 18(2):257–282, 2009.

[8] S. Davidson, Ravi. A sat-based framework for efficient constrained clustering. In *Siam Data Mining (SDM)*, 2010.

[9] W. F. Dowling and J. J. Gallier. Linear-time algorithms for testing the satisfiability of propositional horn formulae. *J. Logic Programming*, 3:267–284, 1984.

[10] S. Gilpin. Code for algorithms in this paper. `http://csiflabs.cs.ucdavis.edu/~sagilpin/`.

[11] R. Karp. Reducibility among combinatorial problems. In R. Miller and J. Thatcher, editors, *Complexity of Computer Computations*, pages 85–103. Plenum Press, 1972.

[12] H. A. Kestler, J. M. Kraus, G. Palm, and F. Schwenker. On the effects of constraints in semi-supervised hierarchical clustering. In *Artificial Neural Networks in Pattern Recognition, Second IAPR Workshop, ANNPR 2006*, pages 57–66, 2006.

[13] J. R. Kettenring. A perspective on cluster analysis. *Stat. Anal. Data Min.*, 1(1):52–53, 2008.

[14] A. K. McCallum. Bow: A toolkit for statistical language modeling, text retrieval, classification and clustering. `http://www.cs.cmu.edu/~mccallum/bow`, 1996.

[15] J. Rennie. 20 newsgroups data set.

[16] S. J. Russell and P. Norvig. *Artificial Intelligence a Modern Approach*. Prentice Hall, Upper Saddle River, N.J., 2nd international edition edition, 2003.

[17] R. E. Tarjan. Efficiency of a good but not linear set union algorithm. *J. ACM*, 22(2):215–225, 1975.

[18] K. Wagstaff and C. Cardie. Clustering with instance-level constraints. In *Proceedings of the Seventeenth International Conference on Machine Learning (ICML 2000)*, pages 1103–1110, 2000.

Latent Graphical Models for Quantifying and Predicting Patent Quality

Yan Liu[1], Pei-yun Hseuh[2], Rick Lawrence[2], Steve Meliksetian[2], Claudia Perlich[2], Alejandro Veen[2]
[1] Computer Science Department, University of Southern California, Los Angeles, CA 90089
[2] IBM T. J. Watson Research, Yorktown Heights, NY 10598

ABSTRACT

The number of patents filed each year has increased dramatically in recent years, raising concerns that patents of questionable validity are restricting the issuance of truly innovative patents. For this reason, there is a strong demand to develop an objective model to quantify patent quality and characterize the attributes that lead to higher-quality patents. In this paper, we develop a latent graphical model to infer patent quality from related measurements. In addition, we extract advanced lexical features via natural language processing techniques to capture the quality measures such as clarity of claims, originality, and importance of cited prior art. We demonstrate the effectiveness of our approach by validating its predictions with previous court decisions of litigated patents.

Categories and Subject Descriptors

H.2.8 [**Database Applications**]: Data Mining

General Terms

Algorithms, Design, Experimentation

Keywords

Graphical models, Text Mining, Measurement Models

1. INTRODUCTION

Technological advances and broadening innovation have led to a dramatic increase in the number of patents filed each year. The resulting patent backlog is staggering: at the end of 2008, there were 1.2M patent applications pending at the US patent office, an increase by a factor of 4.3 over the number outstanding at the end of 1997 [3]. This backlog creates huge challenges to current patenting systems because more and more patent applications of dubious value are entering the pipeline, diverting the attention of critical resources (e.g. patent examiners) needed to ensure that high-quality patents are issued in a timely manner.

From a legal perspective, patent quality is a measure of whether a patent is written in a manner such that it could withstand rigorous examination were it to be challenged in a court of law. In other words, a high-quality patent should be clearly written and its prior art (in patents as well as other publications) is well researched and referenced. Note that the patent quality is different from the economic value of the patent in that the latter is largely determined by the demand in the market for the underlying technology covered in the claims of the application. Patent experts agree that higher-quality patents are more likely to cite relevant (and higher-quality) prior art and include claims that are clearly differentiated with respect to the prior art. The objective of this work is to build a machine learning model to understand and characterize patent quality based on the input from legal experts. If successful, such a model could eventually provide actionable insight to inventors, examiners, and attorneys on the quality of a patent at any point in the patent lifecycle.

An immediate challenge in building a supervised model for patent quality is obtaining a sufficient number of labeled training examples. A landmark study [10] in the intellectual property (IP) law community addresses the issue by associating patent quality with validity as ruled by a court of law. Specifically, a set of labeled examples has been collected [10] by examining all Federal Circuit cases between 2003 and 2009 in which the court ruled on the validity of an issued patent. This labor-intensive process yielded 250 cases adjudicating the validity of 351 patents, 104 of which were ruled valid (some court cases deal with more than one patent at once). While court decisions are an accepted indicator of patent quality, the number of patents that reach the Federal Circuit is limited to a number far smaller than what is needed to train a robust high-dimensional model for prediction. Hiring legal experts to examine and label a large number of patents is neither sufficiently scalable nor likely to result in a consistent dataset.

In this paper, we introduce a latent graphical framework in which patent quality is a latent (hidden) variable and its value can be estimated from other correlated measurements which can be easily obtained for a large number of patents. This idea of measurement modeling was first introduced in [9]. The measurement model is a Bayesian framework in exponential families to estimate the unobserved target from one or more functions (called measurements) of the target. The motivation behind the model is simple: available measurements, such as partial labels, general constraints, and structured label constraints on the model, provide a glimpse of the hidden target variable, thus providing partial infor-

KDD'11, August 21–24, 2011, San Diego, California, USA.

mation about the underlying model. Although the measurement model in [9] provides a general and powerful framework, there remain at least two challenges in applying this methodology to the problem of estimating patent quality:

1. *What are the most effective measurements for estimating patent quality and how are they correlated with quality?*

2. *What are relevant lexical features of a patent that can help predict its quality?*

To answer the first question, we rely on domain experts and existing literature in the IP law community. In patent law, the number of *forward references* (i.e. the number of times a patent is cited by other patents after it is issued) has been identified as an indicator of the economic value of a patent [5] and could carry information on the quality of the patent. In addition, *court ruling* is considered as the most authoritative measurement of quality because patents upheld by the court are likely to be of higher quality than those rejected. Addressing the second question, we explore advanced natural language processing techniques to extract quality-related lexical features. These include straightforward structural characteristics of the patent (e.g. the number of independent claims) as well as text-based features to capture key attributes, such as novelty of the claims, alignment of the claims with the body of application, and other metrics suggested by patent experts.

In recent years, many studies have been conducted to model citation and influence in scientific publications via statistical models in the machine learning community [?, ?, ?]. However, our work is significantly different from existing work from several perspectives: (1) our task focuses on quality analysis, which is related to individual parameters, such as citation or influence, but is more general and difficult to quantify; (2) in our task, the value of our target variable is unobserved. As a result, specific latent models have to be developed and the evaluation is more challenging; (3) our proposed approach not only utilizes machine learning models to estimate patent quality, but also extracts domain-specific features via natural language processing techniques.

The rest of the paper is organized as follows. Section 2 describes the patent data used in our analysis. Section 3 discusses our modeling approaches, and Section 4 provides an overview of the lexical features used in the models. Section 5 summarizes the experiment results, illustrating both the performance of our broader methodology and its application to quantifying patent quality. Section 6 compares our approach with existing work in the area of modeling patent quality.

2. BACKGROUND

An internal patent database is hosted at IBM to store and organize the USPTO's (United States Patent and Trademark Office) weekly data feed with bibliographic information for patent grants and published patent applications [6]. Each week, the data feed provides approximately 3000 newly granted U.S. utility patents and an even larger number of published U.S. patent applications.

For the work described in this paper, we only deal with granted patents. This results in a collection of approximately 4 millions patents from 1975 to 2010. The "raw" data is an electronic (XML) version of the patent certificate, including patent number, title, filing and issue date, inventor and assignee information, the classes the patent is categorized under both the U.S. and the IPC (International Patent Classification) systems, lists of the referenced U.S. and foreign patents, a list of referenced non-patent publications (often academic articles), and the names of the primary and assistant examiners. It also includes unstructured texts such as the patent abstract, description, claims, and even some (limited) information on the drawings. This raw data feed is processed and organized into several tables, which make it easily accessible and analyzable. For instance, it provides fields that list the number of claims as well as the number of domestic, foreign, and non-patent references. In addition, the patent database is supplemented by data from additional sources, for instance, assignee information (assignee code and address). We also generate the citation network, i.e., a graph linking each patent with the patents it cites (namely, backward references in IP law terms) as well as all subsequent patents that cite this patent (namely, forward references).

3. LATENT GRAPHICAL MODELS

The main challenge we face in the task of quantifying patent quality is the lack of ground truth. Since some indirect measure of quality is abundant and relatively easier to obtain, we might be able to develop machine learning models to estimate the value of target variables. In this section, we first review the measurement model and then describe our proposed latent graphical models to quantify patent quality.

3.1 Review of Measurement Models

In [9], a Bayesian approach is developed for measurement modeling. Here we describe the model with a frequentist point of view. More specifically, suppose we are given observations $x_1, \ldots, x_n$ and our goal is to estimate the response variables $Y_1, \ldots, Y_n$. Unlike classical supervised learning, we do not observe the labels of Y directly, but are provided a list of measurements τ_σ that reveals some information about Y, i.e. $W = \tau_\sigma(Y, x)$. We can define the joint probability of response variable Y and measurements W as follows:

$$P(Y, W|\sigma, \theta, x) = P(Y|x, \theta)P(W|Y, x, \sigma). \qquad (1)$$

For computational convenience, we can define the probability distributions $P(Y|x, \theta)$ and $P(W|Y, x, \sigma)$ to be in exponential families. For example, we can have

$$P(Y|\theta, x) = \exp(-h(\varphi_\theta(x, Y)) + \text{const}),$$
$$P(W|Y, x, \sigma) = \exp(-g(W - \tau_\sigma(x, Y)) + \text{const}),$$

where h and g are log-concave functions, and $\varphi_\theta(x, Y)$ is the feature defined over x and Y. By estimating the values of θ, we can estimate the posterior probability of Y given the observations X. One major advantage of the measurement model is its capability to incorporate any type of measurement to help predict Y.

Given the model defined in eq(1), a natural question is whether we are able to achieve globally optimal solutions. The question was not answered in [9], but with some simple derivations, we can show that if the conditional distributions $P(Y|x, \theta)$ and $P(W|Y, x, \sigma)$ correspond to generalized linear models with matching link functions, the incomplete log-likelihood $L(\theta, \sigma)$ is a concave function of parameter θ and

σ in a convex domain, thus resulting in globally optimal solutions.

3.2 Measurement Model for Quantifying Patent Quality

The measurement model provides a flexible framework of estimating the response variable by integrating different measurements. However, in real applications, it is more important to identify relevant measurements, as well as the generating functions from the target variable to the identified measurements (such as h and g), so that accurate estimates of the target variable can be obtained.

In our specific application to patent quality, several measurements have been identified by domain experts:

1. The number of forward citations: it is believed to be determined at least in part by quality;
2. Court decisions: patents ruled as "valid" by courts are expected to be of higher quality than those ruled as "invalid";
3. Reexamination records: reexamination is a process in which a third party or an inventor can request patent examiners to verify that the subject matter in the claim is patentable. A patent that passes the reexamination tends to have a higher likelihood of being high-quality.

In this paper, we demonstrate our solution using the first two measurements, namely forward citations and court decisions. We choose these two measurements not only because they are most related to patent quality, but also because they represent two common types of measurements in many applications. For example, in evaluating the quality of scientific publications, the number of citations and publishing venues are usually considered as important measures.

3.2.1 *Prerequisites*

We begin by introducing the notation. Given patent observations, $x_1, \ldots, x_n$, we are interested in estimating their quality $Q_1, \ldots, Q_n$, which are unobserved. We are provided with two measurements of Q, i.e. forward citation count C and court decision D. Notice that the court decision is available only for a limited number of patents. We set the value of D to 0 if its value is not available.

Given observations x, we need to extract meaningful features relevant to Q, which we later refer to as F_q. This task itself is very challenging in natural language processing and text mining. Our solution to this problem is discussed in Section 4. Furthermore, we need to define the linking functions between forward citation C and quality Q. We resort to the Poisson distribution since the citation count of a patent or a paper within one time period (e.g. 10 years) is usually modeled via Poisson [14]. In addition to quality, the number of citations can be also determined by many other factors, such as filing year, filing classes, venue/journal, inventors, and so on. These features do not necessarily directly contribute to the quality of a patent (given the content of the patent), so we conceptually separate them from quality-related features and denote them as F_c. Notice that our model allows any types of overlap between quality-related features F_q and citation-related features F_c. Here we only separate them for the convenience of illustrating ideas.

3.2.2 *Latent Graphical Models for Quantifying Patent Quality*

Next we formally define the proposed latent graphical models (LGM).

Measurement on Forward Citation: The forward citations include three components: self-citations, examiner-added citations, and citations provided by the patent authors which are not self-citations. To remove the noise and potential bias added by authors citing their own work and by examiner intervention, we use only the final category of citations. Moreover, we limit the count to the one within 10 years after a patent is filed since it takes at least four to five years for a patent to be well-accepted and cited. We model the number of citations C of each patent as a Poisson distribution whose mean is determined by a linear combination of control features F_c and its quality Q. In other words, we have

$$C \sim \text{Poisson}(\lambda), \quad \log \lambda = \beta_C^T F_c + \log Q, \qquad (2)$$

where β_C is the coefficient of feature F_c.

Measurement on Court Ruling: Court decisions can provide the constraint that valid patents have higher quality than invalid patents. To model these constraints, we can maximize the difference of quality value between the valid patents Q_i and invalid patents Q_j. Suppose d_i and d_j are the labels of court decisions, which are equal to 1 if valid and -1 if invalid. Then we can model the posterior probability of P(d|Q) as follows:

$$P(d|Q) = \frac{1}{Z}\prod_{(i,j)} \exp(Q_i - Q_j) = \frac{1}{Z}\exp\sum_{(i,j)}(d_i Q_i + d_j Q_j),$$

where i, j are any pair of valid and invalid patents. We can further derive the model as follows:

$$P(d|Q) = \frac{1}{Z}\prod_i \exp(w(d_i) d_i Q_i),$$

$w(d_i)$ is equal to the number of negative examples if d_i is 1 and equal to the number of positive examples if d_i is -1.

Distribution of Target Variable: Given quality-related features F_q, we model the quality Q as a Gamma distribution:

$$Q \sim \text{Gamma}(a, b), \quad \log b = \beta_q F_q.$$

The choice of the Gamma distribution has two advantages: it is conjugate to the Poisson distribution, which leads to mathematical convenience, and its shape is highly flexible.

Proposed Model: Putting everything together (see Figure 1), we can define the joint distribution of measurement C and D as well as hidden variable Q as follows:

$$P(c, d, Q) = P(c|Q)P(d|Q)P(Q) = \\ [\frac{1}{c!}e^{c(\beta_C F_c)}Q^c e^{-\exp(\beta_C F_c)Q}] \times [\frac{1}{Z}\prod_i \exp(w(d_i)d_i Q_i)] \\ \times [\frac{\exp(\beta_q F_q)^a}{\Gamma(a)} Q^{a-1} e^{-\exp(\beta_q F_q)Q}].$$

To estimate the value of D, we can resort to the EM algorithm [?]. Since there is no closed form for $P(Q|c, d)$, variational methods have to be applied [?]. That is, we assume

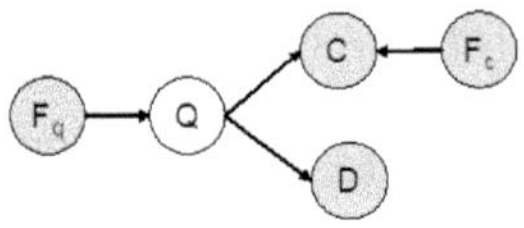

Figure 1: Latent Graphical Models for Patent Quality Estimation

that $P(Q_i|c_i, d_i)$ has the following simple form:

$$q(Q_i|c_i, d_i) = \prod_i P(Q_i|c_i, d_i), \; Q_i|c_i, d_i \sim \text{Gamma}(a_i^0, b_i^0),$$

where a_i^0 and b_i^0 are variational parameters to be estimated. By minimizing the KL-divergence between q and p, we have

$$\begin{aligned} KL(q||p) &= \int_q q \log \frac{q}{p} \\ &= \sum_i (a_0^i \log \beta_0^i - \log \Gamma(a_0^i) + (a_0^i - 1)E[\log Q_i] - b_0^i E[Q_i]) \\ &- \sum_i (-\log c_i + c_i \beta_C F_c^i + c_i E[\log Q_i'] - \exp(\beta_C F_c^i) E[Q_i'] \\ &+ a(\beta_q F_q^i) - \log \Gamma(a) + (a-1)E[\log Q_i'] - \exp(\beta_q F_q^i) E[Q_i'] \\ &- \log Z + \sum_i w(d_i) d_i E[Q_i]). \end{aligned} \quad (3)$$

E-step: Taking the derivative of eq(3) and setting them to zero, we have the following solution to a_0^i and b_0^i:

$$a_0^i = a + c_i, \quad b_0^i = \exp(\beta_C F_c^i) + \exp(\beta_q F_q^i) - w(d_i) d_i.$$

M-step: Taking the derivative of Q with respect to β_C, β_q and a, we have the following updating equations:

$$\begin{aligned} \frac{\partial Q}{\partial \beta_C} &= \sum_i (c_i F_c^i - F_c^i \hat{a}_0^i \exp(\beta_C F_c^i)/\hat{b}_0^i), \\ \frac{\partial Q}{\partial \beta_q} &= \sum_i (a F_q^i - F_q^i \hat{a}_0^i \exp(\beta_q F_q^i)/\hat{b}_0^i), \\ \frac{\partial Q}{\partial a} &= \sum_i (\beta_q F_q^i + \Psi(\hat{a}_0^i) - \log \hat{b}_0^i) - N\Psi(a), \end{aligned}$$

where Ψ is the digamma function.

3.3 Discussion

Measurement modeling is a powerful framework which integrates different measurements into one model. However, there are some alternatives to utilizing individual measurement and estimating the value of target variables. In this section, we examine some simpler solutions, including the EM algorithm, regression residual analysis, and constrained regression.

Expectation-maximization: If we only consider the measurement of forward citations, a simple approach could be modeling the quality of a patent Q by the following generation process:

$$C \sim \text{Poisson}(\exp(\beta_C F_c) Q); \quad Q \sim \text{Gamma}(a, b).$$

Since the Gamma distribution is conjugate to the Poisson distribution, the posterior probability of Q also follows a Gamma distribution, i.e.

$$Q|c, \beta_C, F_c, a, b \sim \text{Gamma}(c + a, \exp(\beta_C F_c) + b).$$

We can easily derive the EM-algorithm and therefore omit the details. This approach can be seen as the simplest version of the measurement model.

Regression Residual Analysis: An alternative to latent models is regression analysis. That is, we assume that the citation count C within a time period is generated from a Poisson distribution whose parameter λ is a linear combination of F_c:

$$C \sim Poisson(\lambda), \quad \log(\lambda) = \beta^T F_c.$$

It can be seen easily that the control features F_c cannot fully explain the citation count. Borrowing the idea of residual analysis in statistics, we can think of the residuals of the Poisson regression, i.e. $R = C - \exp(\beta^T F_c)$, as features strongly correlated with patent quality Q.

Constrained Regression: Given additional measurement on court ruling, we can extend the model of residual analysis and improve the estimation of patent quality via constrained regression. In other words, we can use the court decisions as additional constraints in the objective function of Poisson regression so that valid patents have a higher residual than invalid patents. In the end, we have the following constrained optimization problem:

$$\max_\beta \sum_i c_i(\beta^T F_c^i) - \exp(\beta^T F_c^i)$$
$$\text{s.t.} \quad c_n - \exp(\beta^T F_c^n) <= c_p - \exp(\beta^T F_c^p) + \xi_k, \quad \xi_k >= 0,$$

where p and n are the indexes of any pair of positive and negative examples, and ξ_k is the slack variable to allow noise in court ruling. The solution to the optimization function above can be obtained by similar technique used in ranking logistic regression [7]. We omit further discussion.

These simple solutions provide reasonable alternatives to measurement models. However, we can see easily that for each specific measurement, we have to develop a model accordingly. In contrast, measurement models provide a unified framework that can easily incorporate different types of measurements.

4. EXTRACTING QUALITY-RELATED FEATURES

Similar to many other machine learning applications, the success of modeling patent quality depends heavily on whether we can extract the most appropriate features. In general, the features can be extracted directly from the patent itself, as well as from the examination history after the patent is filed with the patent office. Since our objective is to characterize quality at any point in the patent process, we focus on features that are available at the time of filing. They only only include simple numerical features, such as the number of inventors and the number of independent claims, but also could be much more sophisticated lexical features that capture specific concepts in patent law.

Our approach to lexical feature extraction is motivated by the following five questions: (1) How well does the language used in the claims and the abstract align with that used in the body (specification) of the patent? (2) What is the importance of the invention inferred from the cited prior art? (3) How complex is the patent and how broad is the patent coverage? (4) How relevant is the invention to the technology covered within the patent field or class? (5) How original is the invention when compared with prior art?

While the first three groups of features characterize the applicants' effort in application writing and prior art search, the latter two, i.e., relevance and originality, can measure the technology impact. Note that we did not make any assumptions on the orthogonality of the five groups. In fact, we expect some groups to be complimentary or contradictory to each other. For example, relevance and originality seem to be contradictory at first sight, but the interplay between them is unclear and our learning models could potentially provide some interesting insight.

4.1 Written Description Alignment

Patent experts point regularly to the degree of alignment of the claims and the patent body as an important quality component [10]. Therefore, we analyze the texts of a patent to capture the degree of alignment between various parts of the patent. For example, we can calculate content similarity e.g., Euclidean distance (Euc), between pairs of word vectors representing different parts of the patents, such as abstract-claims (A-C), abstract-description (A-D), and claims-description (C-D). Because this measure is a distance, it increases if the claims and description are poorly aligned. Accordingly, we would expect this measure to correlate inversely with validity.

4.2 Citation Quality

The number of backward citations to the prior art has been studied as both an indicator of economic value [12] and patent quality [13]. An obvious reason for this observation is that better patents (as measured either by ultimate value or intrinsic quality) are more likely to reference the relevant prior art [13]. Since we focus on features that are available at the time of filing, we can extract features that capture the average age of cited patents, i.e., the time since the referenced patent was issued. It is likely that some measure of the quality (or "authority") of the cited prior art is more meaningful than a simple count of backward references. Hence, we compute the mean PageRank score [?] of all the citations by a patent, which indicates the authority level of the cited prior art. This is done by constructing a citation network from all domestic patents by the time of filing and then applying the standard PageRank algorithm to this time-sensitive network.

4.3 Complexity and Reported Coverage

Patent complexity and breadth have been reported as an important indicator of patent value in previous research. For example, Reitzig [12] has studied the number of independent and dependent claims and the number of words describing the state of the art. In addition to these simple measures, we also include the number of classes the applicants have tagged as an initial step to characterizing patent breadth. We count both the number of reported classes under the US classification and International Patent Classification (IPC) scheme.

4.4 Technology Relevance

To measure how relevant an invention could be to other patents in the same field or class, we apply information theoretic measures to calculate the similarity between the target patent and the background (i.e., all patents filed in the same year or from the same class). In short, we represent each patent as a word vector, and calculate the average similarity score (e.g. cosine similarity or KL-divergence), between the query and all patents in the background. Some examples include: *1. avgCosine-pyear*: average cosine similarity score between the target patent and all patents filed in the same year in the same class; *2. avgConsine-all*: average cosine similarity score between the target patent and all patents filed till current year in the same class; *3. avgPKL*: average point-wise KL-divergence between the target patent and all patents patents filed till current year in the same class.

4.5 Claim Originality

It is known that a patent cannot be filed if the subject matter would have been obvious to a person with ordinary skills in the area at the time of filing. The hypothesis is that higher-quality patents describe technologies that are more recently developed (more likely to be novel) and are not commonplace (less likely to be obvious). To measure these concepts, we construct n-gram vectors to represent the technology space of each patent. Two types of features are then calculated to reflect claim originality and commonality. Claim originality features are calculated based on the age of n-grams, i.e. how long (in years) a technology (represented by an n-gram) has been in the field since its first introduction. Claim commonality is computed based on the n-gram usage, i.e. how many times a technology has been mentioned up to the current filing year.

We address claim originality first. Given the earliest occurring year of words and the number of word occurrences at each time point, it is straightforward to compute the age of n-grams (words) [1]. If a word has first appeared in this patent, the word will have its age as 0, tagged as a "nascent word". If a word appears for the first time within the last year, the word will have an age smaller than one year, tagged as a "recent word". Similar ideas have also been explored recently in [6]. Consistent with the hypothesis above, we expect a higher-quality patent will have a higher proportion of nascent and recent words. For example, consider the two patents listed in Figure 2. While the patent on the left (US6306383) uses many recent words to describe its invention, the one on the right (US6605646) has a very equal distribution over word age. In fact, when brought to court, the Federal Circuit court has ruled US6306383 as valid and US6605646 as invalid. Notice that the range of the originality scores as defined here could vary significantly in different fields. For example, there might be more jargon terms in biology than in others, which translates to very different statistics for new words across domains. This problem could be solved by normalization so that the scores of patents in different fields could be comparable.

For commonality, it is straightforward to compute the usage of words by counting the number of times a word has been mentioned prior to the filing date. If a word has appeared more than a pre-determined threshold, the word will be tagged as a heavily-used word. As older words are expected to be mentioned more, we also compute word contribution, i.e., the accumulated rate of word occurrences (average word usage per day). If a word has accumulated faster than a pre-determined threshold, the word will be tagged as a high-contribution word. A higher-quality patent is expected to use less common language, and thus have lower proportions of heavily-used and high-contribution words.

[1] For simplicity, the features here are computed on unigrams (words).

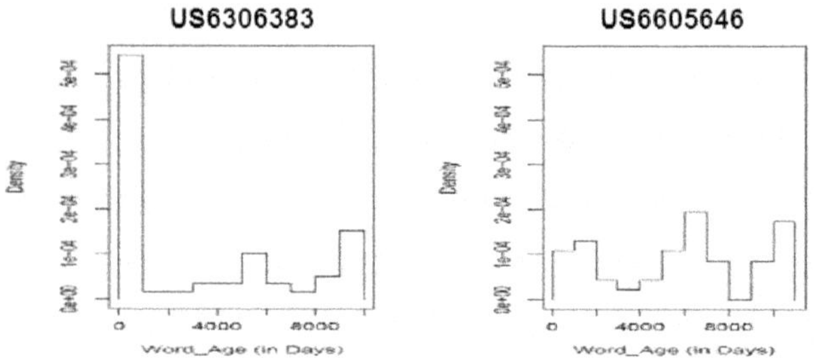

Figure 2: The distributions of word age features of a valid patent (US6306383: Method for topical treatment of scars with protein kinase C inhibitors) and an invalid patent (US6605646: Vitamin supplement composition).

Here is a list of lexical features we have extracted: 1. *NascentWordProp*: the proportion of nascent words in the claims; 2. *RecentWordProp*: the proportion of recent words in the claims; 3. *HeavyUseWordProp*: the proportion of heavily used words in the claims; 4. *HighContrWordProp*: the proportion of fast accumulated words in the claims; 5. *AvgWordAge*: the average age of words in the claims; 6. *AvgWordUsage*: the average usage of words in the claims; 7. *AvgWordContr*: the average accumulation rate of words in the claims.

5. EXPERIMENT RESULTS

To fairly evaluate the performance of different methods, one needs to have the ground truth of target variables. Unfortunately, these are not directly available in our application. Therefore we generate a simulation dataset to mimic the properties of our application data while holding the ground truth for evaluation. The experiments on simulation data are essential since it is the only way to directly verify the effectiveness of our algorithm. In the actual application, we have no choice but to validate the results indirectly, i.e. by comparing the agreement of predictions with the outcomes of court decisions, which are believed to be strongly correlated with patent quality. The desired output in our application is a ranked list of patents based on their patent quality scores – therefore only the ranking order matters. We use Kendall's τ rank correlation coefficient [8] and AUC (area under curve) as the evaluation measures. In this section, we describe our results on both simulation data and application data respectively.

5.1 Simulation Data

Our objective here is to evaluate different methods on a simulation dataset with properties similar as the one in our application. We sample data points from the distribution with underlying model shown in Figure 1. Specifically, we assume that the input features for forward citation F_c and and features for quality F_q are generated from multivariate Gaussian distributions with 5 features and 10 features respectively. The parameters β_C and β_q are generated uniformly from [0, 1], and the ground truth of hidden variable Q (i.e. our desired labels) comes from a Gamma distribution. Unlike traditional supervised learning, we are also provided with two measurements: forward citations (positive discrete value) from a Poisson distribution and court decisions D (binary value) from Bernoulli distributions. To fully understand the performance of our model, we investigate two learning scenarios: (1) we are given the observations of all relevant features, i.e. F_c, F_q; (2) we are given the observations of partial features only.

Complete Feature Observations: We conduct experiments on three versions of the latent graphical models (LGM), by varying the inputs as follows: (1) $C + F_c$: measurement C and its associated features F_c; (2) $C + F_c + F_q$: the input of $C + F_c$ plus the quality-associated features F_q; (3) $C + F_c + F_q + D$: the input of $C + F_c + F_q$ plus court ruling D. To examine the learning behavior of different algorithms, we vary the number of input examples from 20 to 100 by a step size of 20, run each experiments 30 times, and report the averaged correlation coefficients between the predicted value and the ground truth (see Figure 3(a)). We can see that when the number of training examples is limited (e.g. 20), the algorithm with the most input and measurements $C + F_c + F_q + D$ performs the best. However, when we increase the number of examples, the three algorithms perform comparably. Note that the algorithm $C + F_c + F_q$ performs even better than $F_c + F_q + D$ when the number of examples is large (e.g. 100). This seems to indicate that the use of unreliable measurements may deteriorate the performance, even with a sufficient number of examples.

Partial Feature Observations: In many applications, we can work on smart feature engineering and extract as many useful features as possible. But it is still unlikely that we are able to identify all of the relevant features. Therefore we are interested in answering the following question: how much will partial features affect the performance of our model? In Figure 3(b), we show the performance of different algorithms by fixing the number of examples to 100, but varying the percentage of observable features (including both F_c and F_q). We can see that when there are only 20% feature observations, the algorithm $C + F_c + F_q + D$ still performs comparably to those with complete set of features. However, as expected, this advantage diminishes when the percentage of features is increased to around 80%.

Comparison With Other Baselines: Finally, we compare our approach with other baselines. Figure 3(c) shows the results on 100 training examples by different methods. The first two bars show simple dummy predictors in which we simply use the value of measurements C or D directly as the prediction. The next two bars show results by residual analysis discussed in Section 3.3. More specifically, we use logistic regression for measurement D, and Poisson regression for measurement C. The final three bars show the results of our LGM model, which clearly outperforms other baseline methods.

5.2 Application on Analyzing Patent Quality

In our application to patent quality, we use forward citations and court decisions as the measurements to build our model. We define forward citations as the number of cites within ten years after the patent is filed – this is available for all patents before 2000 (since the data for this study were collected in 2010). In contrast, there are a limited number of patents, which were litigated by Federal Circuit. Therefore we create two datasets: one is a set of randomly selected

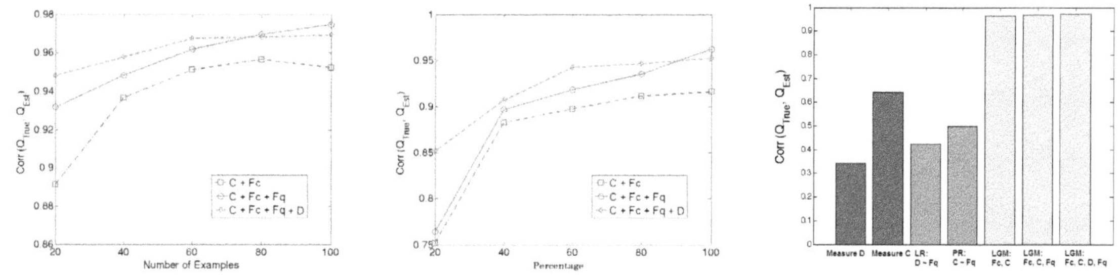

(a) Complete Feature Observation (b) Partial Feature Observation (c) Comparison of Different Methods

Figure 3: Experiment results on simulation data: (a) Correlation scores with complete observations of features; (b) Correlation scores with partial observation of features; (c) Comparison with alternative solutions: measure D and measure C refers to the dummy predictor which simply uses court decision D or citation C to estimate quality; LR and PR refer to residual analysis using logistic regression and Poisson regression; LGM refers to our latent graphical models.

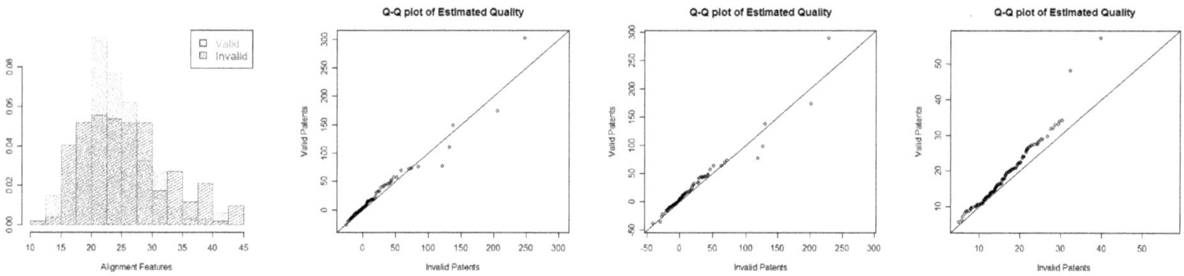

(a) Alignment Features (b) Linear Regression (c) Poisson Regression (d) LGM

Figure 4: (a) Demonstration of alignment features for differentiating valid and invalid patents. (b-d) Q-Q Plot of Predicted Value by Different Methods (Input: $C + F_c$) of Valid and Invalid Patents. (b) Linear regression; (c) Poisson regression; (d) Latent graphical models (LGM)

12K examples from all patents filed before 2000 (referred to as dataset I), and the other is a subset of the data used in [10], which consists of 351 patents (filed before 2000) with decisions by the Federal Circuit Court (referred to as dataset II).

Evaluation of Feature Extraction. Before discussing the modeling results, we first examine the effectiveness of feature extraction. To avoid topic drift, we will not discuss the detailed results on all lexical features (the content of which might justify another paper), but highlight some interesting observations. First, we demonstrate in Figure 4(a) how the alignment scores can help differentiate valid and invalid patents ruled by the court. Table 1 shows the list of lexical features used as input (i.e. feature F_q) in our model, as well as their p-value scores of statistical significant tests (the null assumption is that the feature value of valid patents has the same distribution as invalid patents). Note that the alignment features are the most significant ones among all the lexical features.

Another challenge in feature extraction is to identify informative features associated with forward citations, i.e. F_c. Recall that we extract these features because they contribute to forward references, but are not directly related to patent quality. Based on domain knowledge, we use filing year, patent classification, and the number of claims for F_c.

Evaluation of Patent Quality. Unlike simulation data, the ground truth of patent quality is not available. Therefore we have no choice but to indirectly evaluate the results. Here we use the agreement between estimated quality and court ruling decisions (which are believed to be the closest observations of patent quality). In some models, we also need to include the court decision as measurements to estimate patent quality. Therefore, it is not legitimate to include this type of information during training and then validate its performance on the same information (since the accuracy of such an in-sample analysis would be overly optimistic). Therefore we use 5-fold cross-validation, i.e. we split dataset II into 5 subsets, and withhold one subset for testing while training our model on a combined set of dataset I and the other 4 subsets (i.e. excluding the court ruling information of the patents in the test set). To estimate the quality of a patent in the test set, we simply compute its expectation, i.e. $E[Q] = a/(\exp(F_c\beta_c) + \exp(F_q\beta_q))$, which does not require the knowledge of court decisions.

We first examine the effectiveness of forward citations as a measurement. Since this measure is available for both

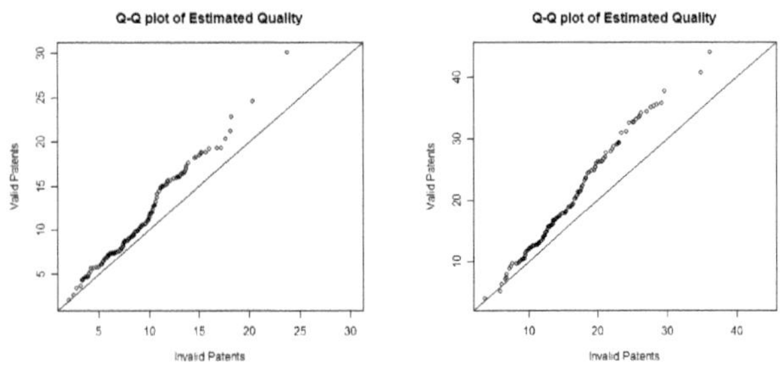

(a) LGM: $C + F_c + F_q$ (b) LGM: $C + F_c + F_q + D$

Figure 5: Q-Q Plot of Predicted Value by (a) LGM (Input: $C+F_c+F_q$) of Valid and Invalid Patents and (b) LGM (Input: $C+F_c+F_q+D$) of Valid and Invalid Patents

Table 1: Validation of extracted lexical features for differentiating court ruling (P-value). * means the statistically significant. + (or −) means positive (or negative) coefficient in a single-variable logistic regression.

Group	Feature	P-value	+/−
Alignment	A-D (Euc)	0.027*	+
	A-C (Euc)	0.043*	+
	D-C (Euc)	0.022*	+
Citation Quality	Page rank	0.650	+
	Num. of Reference	0.002*	+
Complexity	Claim length	0.001*	−
	Count of unique content words	0.017*	+
Relevance	AvgCosineall	0.304	+
Originality	Avg Age	0.107	+
	Recent Word Prop	0.207	+
Commonality	Avg Usage	0.040*	−
	Avg Contribution	0.233	−

datasets, we run experiments on a combined set of datasets I and II. We compare the performance of our method with alternative approaches, including regression residual analysis using linear regression and Poisson regression (discussed in Section 3.3). Figure 4 shows a Q-Q plot of the predicted quality for valid and invalid patents in dataset II. We can see that our LGM approach can yield a comparably better distinction (see Table 2(a) for p-values). Next, we examine whether including quality-related features F_q helps to improve the performance. Figure 5(a) shows a Q-Q plot of predicted quality for valid and invalid patents on the 351 examples. We can clearly see a better distinction compared to using the forward citation measurement alone (see Figure 4(d)). Finally, we examine whether additional constraint measurement, i.e. court decisions, can help improve our prediction. The Q-Q plot in Figure 5(b) suggests that our LGM approach with more measurements achieves the best performance of all methods.

Prediction of Court Ruling Decisions. Another approach to indirectly evaluate the effectiveness of our approach is to build a binary classifier (e.g. logistic regression) to predict the court ruling decisions using the output of LGM. As we can see in Table 2, our LGM model outperforms the logistic regression model specifically built to predict court ruling (with an AUC score of 0.625 compared to 0.618). In addition, by including the predicted value of patent quality $\hat{Q}$ as an additional input feature to the logistic regression model, we can achieve an AUC score as high as 0.734. These results are important, because it indicates that our LGM approach is an effective means to estimate patent quality, and it could extract significant information complementary to known features related to patent quality and citation.

Table 2: Performance of patent quality predictions by different methods. (a). The results are reported based on 5-fold cross-validation by evaluating the agreement between the predicted patent quality and the court ruling decision. Evaluation measures include P-value (the result of significance test with the null assumption that estimated quality of valid patents has the same distribution with invalid patents), Kendall's τ rank correlation (Corr) between predicted quality and court ruling, and AUC (area under curve of using predicted quality to rank probability of being valid in court ruling). (b). $^{\triangle}$ represents results from a classifier to predict the court ruling decision directly, instead of patent quality estimation models as previous rows. The input features in the classifier (logistic regression) include citation features F_c, quality features F_q and estimated patent quality $\hat{Q}$ from latent graphical models (LGM).

(a). Experiment Results of Patent Quality Prediction				
Input	Method	P-value	Corr	AUC
$C + F_c$	LinReg	3.73e-1	0.048	0.504
	PosReg	2.42e-1	0.053	0.508
	LGM	1.15e-2	0.109	0.543
$C + F_c + F_q$	LGM	5.75e-3	0.198	0.574
$C + D^- + F_c + F_q$	LGM	1.32e-5	0.245	0.625
(b). Experiment Results of Court Ruling Classifier				
$C + F_c + F_q$	LogReg $^{\triangle}$	-	-	0.618
$C + F_c + F_q + \hat{Q}$	LogReg $^{\triangle}$	-	-	0.734

6. DISCUSSION AND CONCLUSION

In this paper, we develop advanced machine learning and text mining techniques to address a key problem in patent law, namely providing objective measures of the quality of a patent at any stage in the patent lifecycle. A major challenge is the limited availability of reliable labels for quality. We address this limitation by introducing a latent graphical model, an extension of the measurement model, to infer quality from available measurements related to patent quality. These choice of measurements are guided by domain knoweldge, and we use the number of forward references and court decisions. In addition, we extract a number of lexical features to capture quality-related features via natural language processing techniques. The output from latent graphical models, when combined with other text-based features, achieves an AUC score close to 0.74 for predicting court decisions.

Our work is the first attempt to apply rigorous machine learning methods with lexical-based features to the problem of characterizing patent quality. A number of papers [1, 5, 13, 2] have modeled patent citation behavior in an effort to understand patent quality. Our approach is fundamentally different in several respects:

1. We model patent quality as a hidden variable that partially determines forward references since the number of forward references depends on both economic value and the quality.
2. We represent a patent using both structured features and text-based features in order to capture a broader set of expert-specified characteristics;
3. We validate our model against a "gold standard", namely court decisions on the validity of 351 patents.

We note that other recent work, e.g. [6], have used sophisticated text-based features to represent the novelty of patent claims, but they have not used such features in a supervised model for quality. Finally, our broad methodology could be applied to many other applications, such as analyzing the quality of scientific publications and microblogging data.

7. REFERENCES

[1] J. Allison and M. Lemley. How federal circuit judges vote in patent validity cases. *Florida State University Law Review*, 27:745–766, 2000.

[2] G. Csardi, J. Tobochnik, P. Erdi, L. Zalanyi, and K. J. Strandburg. Patent citation networks revisited: Signs of a twenty-first century change? *North Carolina Law Review*, 87, 2009.

[3] M. Ehrlich. Taking the pulse of patents. *Scientific American*, 2009.

[4] A. V. et. al. A model for court decisions on patent validity. *To be submitted*, 2010.

[5] B. H. Hall, A. Jaffe, and M. Trajtenberg. Market value and patent citations. *RAND Journal of Economics*, 36(1):16–38, 2005.

[6] M. A. Hasan, W. S. Spangler, T. D. Griffin, and A. Alba. Coa: Finding novel patents through text analysis. In *Proceedings of KDD*, 2009.

[7] E. Hüllermeier, J. Fürnkranz, W. Cheng, and K. Brinker. Label ranking by learning pairwise preferences. *Artif. Intell.*, 172:1897–1916, 2008.

[8] M. Kendall. *Rank Correlation Methods.* Charles Griffin & Company Limited, 1948.

[9] P. Liang, M. I. Jordan, and D. Klein. Learning from measurements in exponential families. In *ICML*, page 81, 2009.

[10] R. J. Mann and M. Underweiser. A new look at patent quality. *To be submitted*, 2010.

[11] S. Merugu, S. Rosset, and C. Perlich. A new multi-view regression approach with an application to customer wallet estimation. In *KDD*, pages 656–661, 2006.

[12] M. Reitzig and J. T. Paper. Improving patent valuation methods for management validating new indicators by understanding patenting strategies. *Research Policy*, 33 (6-7):939–=957, 2004.

[13] B. Sampat. Determinants of patent quality: An empirical analysis. working paper, 2005. Mailman School of Public Health and School of International and Public Affairs, Columbia University.

[14] M. L. Wallace, V. Larivièrea, and Y. Gingrasa. Modeling a century of citation distributions. *Journal of Informetrics*, 3:296–303, 2009.

Logical-Shapelets: An Expressive Primitive for Time Series Classification

Abdullah Mueen
UC Riverside
mueen@cs.ucr.edu

Eamonn Keogh
UC Riverside
eamonn@cs.ucr.edu

Neal Young
UC Riverside
neal@cs.ucr.edu

ABSTRACT

Time series shapelets are small, local patterns in a time series that are highly predictive of a class and are thus very useful features for building classifiers and for certain visualization and summarization tasks. While shapelets were introduced only recently, they have already seen significant adoption and extension in the community.

Despite their immense potential as a data mining primitive, there are two important limitations of shapelets. First, their expressiveness is limited to simple binary presence/absence questions. Second, even though shapelets are computed offline, the time taken to compute them is significant.

In this work, we address the latter problem by introducing a novel algorithm that finds shapelets in less time than current methods by an order of magnitude. Our algorithm is based on intelligent caching and reuse of computations, and the admissible pruning of the search space. Because our algorithm is so fast, it creates an opportunity to consider more expressive shapelet queries. In particular, we show for the first time an augmented shapelet representation that distinguishes the data based on conjunctions or disjunctions of shapelets. We call our novel representation *Logical-Shapelets*. We demonstrate the efficiency of our approach on the classic benchmark datasets used for these problems, and show several case studies where logical shapelets significantly outperform the original shapelet representation and other time series classification techniques. We demonstrate the utility of our ideas in domains as diverse as gesture recognition, robotics, and biometrics.

Categories and Subject Descriptors

H.2.8 [**Database Management**]: Database Applications—*Data Mining*

General Terms

Algorithm

Keywords

Time Series, Classification, Information Gain, Logic Expression

1. INTRODUCTION

Time series shapelets were introduced in 2009 as a primitive for time series data mining [19]. Shapelets are small sequences that separate the time series into two classes by asking the question *"Does this unknown object have a subsequence that is within T of this shapelet?"* Where there are three or more classes, repeated application of shapelets can be used (i.e. a decision tree-like structure) to predict the class label. Figure 1 shows examples of shapelets found in a dataset of accelerometer signals [11]. Every time series in the dataset corresponds to one of two hand motions performed by an actor tracing a *circular* or *rectangular* path through the air with an input device. The shapelet denoted by P in the figure is the one that maximally separates the two classes when used with a suitable threshold. In essence, the shapelet P captures the sinusoidal acceleration pattern of the circular motion along the Z-axis.

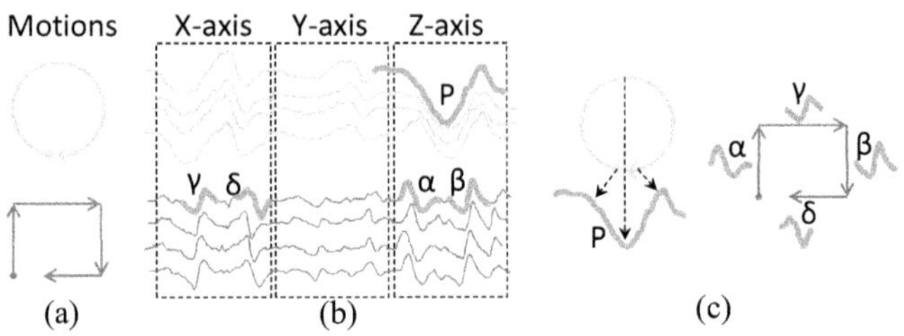

Figure 1: (a) Idealized motions performed with a Wii remote. (b) The concatenated accelerometer signals from recordings of actors performing the motions (c) Examples of Shapelets that describe each of the motions.

Time series shapelets are generating increasing interest among researchers [5] [13] [18] for at least two reasons. First, in many cases time series shapelets can learn the inherent structure of the data in a manner that allows intuitive interpretation. For example, beyond classifying, say, normal/abnormal heartbeats, shapelets could tell a cardiologist that the distinguishing feature is at the beginning of the dicrotic pulse. Second, shapelets are usually much shorter than the original time series, and unlike instance based methods that require comparison to the entire dataset, we only need one shapelet at classification time. Therefore, shapelets create a very compact representation of the class concept, and this compactness means that the time and space required for classification can be significantly reduced, often by at least two orders of magnitude. This is a particularly desirable property in resource limited systems such as sensor nodes, cell phones, mobile robots, smart toys, etc.

Despite the above promising features of time series shapelets, the current algorithm [19] for discovering them is still relatively lethargic and, therefore, does not scale up to use on real-world datasets, which are often characterized by being noisy, long, and nonuniformly sampled. In addition, the current definition of shapelets is not expressive enough to represent certain concepts that seem quite common in the real world (examples appear later in this work). In particular, the expressiveness of shapelets is limited to simple binary presence/absence questions. While recursive application of these binary questions can form a decision tree-like structure, it is important to recognize that the full expressive power of a classic, machine-learning decision tree is not achieved (recall a decision tree represents the concept space of disjunction of conjunctions). For example, differentiating classes by using only binary questions is not possible if, the classes differ only in the *number* of occurrences of a specific pattern rather than presence/absence of a pattern.

In this work, we address the problem of scalability and show how this allows us to define a more expressive shapelet representation. We introduce two novel techniques to speedup search for shapelets. First, we precompute sufficient statistics [16] to compute the distance (i.e. similarity) between a shapelet and a subsequence of a time series in amortized constant time. In essence, we trade time for space, finding that a relativity small increase in the space required can help us greatly decrease the time required. Second, we use a novel admissible pruning technique to skip the costly computation of entropy (i.e. the goodness measure) for the vast majority of candidate shapelets. We have achieved up to 27× speedup over the current algorithm experimentally. We further show that we can combine multiple shapelets in logic expressions such that complex concepts can be described. For example, in the dataset shown in figure 1, there are discontinuities in the rectangular motion. It will not be possible to describe the rectangular class using one shapelet if there are variable pause times at the corners in different instances. In such cases, we can express the rectangular class by the logical shapelet "α **and** β **and** γ **and** δ." Here, each literal corresponds to one of the straight line motions as shown in figure 1(c). In addition, our algorithm is able to increase the gap/margin between classes even if they are already separated. This allows for more robust generalization from the training to test data. We have successfully used our algorithm to find interesting combinations of shapelets in accelerometer signals, pen-based biometrics, and accelerometer signals from a mobile robot.

It is important to note that there is essentially zero-cost for the expressiveness of logical shapelets. If we apply them to a dataset that does not need their increased representational power, they simply degenerate to classic shapelets, which are a special case. Thus, our work complements and further enables the growing interest in shapelets as a data mining tool. For example, [18] uses shapelets on streaming data as "early predictors" of a class, [13] uses an extension of shapelets in an application in severe weather prediction, [6] uses shapelets to find representative prototypes in a dataset, and [5] use shapelets to do gesture recognition from accelerometer data. However, none of these works have considered the logical combinations of shapelets we consider here or have obtained an significant speedup over the original algorithm.

2. DEFINITION AND BACKGROUND

In this section, we define shapelets and the other notations used in the paper.

Definition 1. A *Time Series* T is a sequence of real numbers $t_1, t_2, \ldots, t_m$. A time series *subsequence* $S_{i,l} = t_i, t_{i+1}, \ldots, t_{i+l-1}$ is a continuous subsequence of T starting at position i and length l.

A time series of length m can have $\frac{m(m+1)}{2}$ subsequences of all possible lengths from one to m.

If we are given two time series X and Y of same length m, we can use the euclidean norm of their difference (i.e. $X - Y$) as a distance measure. To achieve scale and offset invariance, we must normalize the individual time series using *z-normalization* before the actual distance is computed. This is a critical step; even tiny differences in scale and offset rapidly swamp any similarity in shape [8]. In addition, we normalize the distances by dividing with the length of the time series. This allows comparability of distances for pairs of time series of various lengths. We call this *length-normalization*.

The normalized euclidean distance is generally computed by the formula $\sqrt{\frac{1}{m}\sum_{i=1}^{m}(x_i - y_i)^2}$. Thus, computing a distance value requires time linear on the length of the time series. In contrast, we compute the normalized eucledian distance between X and Y using five numbers derived from X and Y. These numbers are denoted as sufficient statistics in [16]. The numbers are $\sum x$, $\sum y$, $\sum x^2$, $\sum y^2$ and $\sum xy$. It may appear that we are doing more work than necessary; however, as we make clear in section 3.1, computing the distance in this manner enables us to reuse computations and reduce the amortized time complexity from *linear* to *constant*.

The sample mean and standard deviation can be computed from these statistics as $\mu_x = \frac{1}{m}\sum x$ and $\sigma_x^2 = \frac{1}{m}\sum x^2 - \mu_x^2$, respectively. The positive correlation and the normalized euclidean distance between X and Y can then be expressed as below [14].

$$C(x, y) = \frac{\sum xy - m\mu_x\mu_y}{m\sigma_x\sigma_y} \tag{1}$$

$$dist(x, y) = \sqrt{2(1 - C(x, y))} \tag{2}$$

Many time series data mining algorithms (1-NN classification, clustering, density estimation, etc.) require only the comparison of time series that are of equal lengths. In contrast, time series shapelets require us to test if a short time series (the shapelet) is contained within a certain threshold somewhere inside a much longer time series. To achieve this, the shorter time series is slid against the longer one to find the best possible alignment between them. We call this distance measurement the *subsequence distance* and define it as $sdist(x, y) = \sqrt{2(1 - C_s(x, y))}$ where x and y are the two time series with lengths m and n, respectively, and for $m \leq n$

$$C_s(x, y) = \min_{0 \leq l \leq n-m} \frac{\sum_{i=1}^{m} x_i y_{i+l} - m\mu_x\mu_y}{m\sigma_x\sigma_y} \tag{3}$$

In the above definition μ_y and σ_y denote the mean and standard deviation of m consecutive values from y starting at position $l + 1$. Note that, $sdist$ is not symmetric.

Assume that we have a dataset D of N time series from C different classes. Let us also assume, every class i ($i = 1, 2, \ldots, C$) has n_i ($\sum_i n_i = N$) labeled instances in the dataset. An instance time series in D is also denoted by D_i for $i = 1, 2, \ldots, N$.

Definition 2. The *entropy* of a dataset D is defined as $E(D) = -\sum_{i=1}^{C} \frac{n_i}{N} log(\frac{n_i}{N})$.

If the smallest time series in D is of length m, there are at least $N\frac{m(m+1)}{2}$ subsequences in D that are shorter than every time series in D. We define a *split* as a tuple (s, τ) where s is a subsequence and τ is a distance threshold. A split divides the dataset D into two disjoint subsets or partitions $D_{left} = \{x : x \in D, sdist(s, x) \leq \tau\}$ and $D_{right} = \{x : x \in D, sdist(s, x) > \tau\}$. We define the cardinality of each partition by $N_1 = |D_{left}|$ and

Algorithm 1 $Shapelet\_Discovery(D)$

Require: A dataset D of time series
Ensure: Return the shapelet
1: $m \leftarrow$ minimum length of a time series in D
2: $maxGain \leftarrow 0, maxGap \leftarrow 0$
3: **for** $j \leftarrow 1$ to $|D|$ **do** {every time series in D}
4: $S \leftarrow D_j$
5: **for** $l \leftarrow 1$ to m **do** {every possible length}
6: **for** $i \leftarrow 1$ to $|S| - l + 1$ **do** {every start position}
7: **for** $k \leftarrow 1$ to $|D|$ **do** {compute distances of every time series to the candidate shapelet $S_{i,l}$}
8: $L_k \leftarrow sdist(S_{i,l}, D_k)$
9: $sort(L)$
10: $(\tau, updated) \leftarrow bestIG(L, maxGain, maxGap)$
11: **if** $updated$ **then** {gain and/or gap are changed}
12: $bestS \leftarrow S_{i,l}$,$best\tau \leftarrow \tau$,$bestL \leftarrow L$
13: **return** $(bestS, best\tau, bestL, maxGain, maxGap)$

Algorithm 2 $sdist(x, y)$

Require: Two time series x and y. Assume $|x| \leq |y|$.
Ensure: Return the normalized distance between x and y
1: $minSum \leftarrow \infty$
2: $x \leftarrow zNorm(x)$
3: **for** $j \leftarrow 1$ to $|y| - |x| + 1$ **do** {every start position on y}
4: $sum \leftarrow 0$
5: $z \leftarrow zNorm(y_{j,|x|})$
6: **for** $i \leftarrow 1$ to $|x|$ **do** {compute the eucledian distance}
7: $sum \leftarrow sum + (z_i - x_i)^2$
8: $minSum \leftarrow min(minSum, sum)$
9: **return** $\sqrt{minSum/|x|}$

$N_2 = |D_{right}|$. We use two quantities to measure the goodness of a split: *information gain* and *separation gap*.

Definition 3. The *information gain* of a split is $I(s, \tau) = E(D) - \frac{N_1}{N}E(D_{left}) - \frac{N_2}{N}E(D_{right})$.

Definition 4. The *separation gap* of a split is $G(s, \tau) = \frac{1}{N_2}\sum_{x \in D_{right}} sdist(s, x) - \frac{1}{N_1}\sum_{x \in D_{left}} sdist(s, x)$.

Now we are in position to define time series shapelets.

Definition 5. The *shapelet* for a dataset D is a tuple of a subsequence of an instance within D and a distance threshold (i.e. a split) that has the maximum information gain while breaking ties by maximizing the separation gap.

2.1 Brute-force Algorithm

In order to properly frame our contributions, we begin by explaining the brute-force algorithm for finding shapelets in a dataset D (algorithm 1). Dataset D contains multiple time series of two or more classes and possibly of different lengths.

Since time series can be considered to be points in high dimensional space, we will denote D as a database of points. The algorithm generates a candidate subsequence $S_{i,l}$ in the three loops in lines 3, 5, and 6 of algorithm 1, which essentially generates all possible subsequences of all possible lengths from D. In lines 7-9, an array L is created which holds the points in D in the sorted order of their distance from the shapelet candidate. A schematic view of this array is illustrated in figure 2. We call this schematic line an *orderline*. Intuitively, the ideal shapelet is the one that orders the

Algorithm 3 $bestIG(L, magGain, maxGap)$

Require: An order line L and current best gain and gap.
Ensure: Update the best information gain and separation gap and return the split point τ
1: **for** $k \leftarrow 1$ to $|D| - 1$ **do**
2: $\tau \leftarrow (L_k + L_{k+1})/2$
3: Count $n_{1,i}$ and $n_{2,i}$ for $i = 1, 2, \ldots, C$.
4: Count N_1 and N_2 for both the partitions.
5: $I \leftarrow$ Information gain computed by definition 3
6: $G \leftarrow$ Separation gap computed by definition 4
7: **if** $(I > maxGain$ **or** $(I = maxGain \bigwedge G > maxGap))$ **then**
8: $maxGain \leftarrow I, maxGap \leftarrow G, max\tau \leftarrow \tau$
9: $updated \leftarrow$ **true**
10: **return** $(max\tau, updated)$

data as such all instances of one class are near the origin, and all instances of the other classes are to the far right, with no interleaving of the classes.

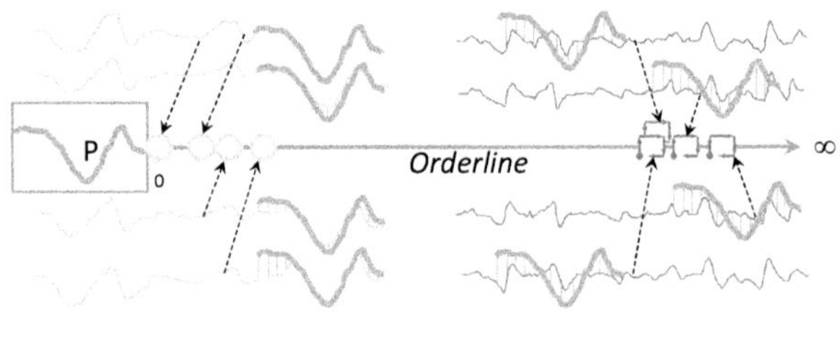

Figure 2: Orderline for the shapelet P. Each time series is placed on the orderline based on the $sdist$ from P. Note that, the time series that carries P is placed at position 0 on the orderline. Also note that, P aligns at different positions on different time series.

Distance values are computed by algorithm 2. Both of the normalizations – z-normalization and length-normalization (before and after the computation of euclidean distance, respectively) – are performed here. Note that repeatedly performing normalization before computing distances is expensive because the same sequences are normalized multiple times. Our novel caching mechanism in section 3.1 will remove this difficulty.

Given the orderline, the computation of information gain is linear in the dataset size. Algorithm 3 describes the method of finding the best split point paired with the current candidate sequence. At line 2, we selected the mid points between two consecutive points on the orderline as split (τ) points. Although there are infinite possible split points, there are at most $|D| - 1$ distinct splits that can result in different information gains. Therefore, it is sufficient to try only these $|D| - 1$ splits. Computing the information gain from the orderline requires $O(N)$ time, which includes counting statistics per class for the three sets (i.e. D, D_{left}, D_{right}) in line 3 and 4. The rest of the computation can be done in $O(C)$ time in line 5 and 6. Finally, the current best gain and gap are updated if appropriate.

The time complexity of the algorithm, assuming no additional memory usage (i.e. linear space cost), is clearly untenable. There are at least $N\frac{m(m+1)}{2}$ shapelet candidates (i.e. the number of iterations through loops in line 3, 5, and 6). For each of the candidates, we need to compute distances to each of the N time series in D (i.e. line 8). Every distance computation takes $O(m^2)$ time. In total, we need $O(N^2m^4)$ arithmetic operations. Such a huge computational cost makes the brute-force algorithm infeasible for real applications. Since N is usually small as being the size of a labeled dataset, and m is large to make the search for local features meaningful, we focus on reducing factors of m from the cost.

3. SPEEDUP TECHNIQUES

The original shapelet work introduced by Ye, *et al.* [19] showed an admissible technique for abandoning some unfruitful entropy computations early. However, this does not improve the worst case complexity. In this work, we reduce the worst case complexity by caching distance computations for future use. In addition, we describe a very efficient pruning strategy resulting in an order of magnitude speedup over the method of Ye *et al.*.

3.1 Efficient Distance Computation

In algorithm 1, any subsequence of D_j with any length and starting at any position is a potential shapelet candidate. Such a candidate needs to be compared against every subsequence of D_k with the same length, starting at any position. The visual intuition of the situation is illustrated by figure 3. For any two instances D_j and D_k in D, we need to consider all possible parallelograms like the ones shown in the figure. For each parallelogram, we need to scan the subsequences to sum up the squared errors while computing the distance. Clearly there is a huge redundancy of calculations between successive and overlapping parallelograms.

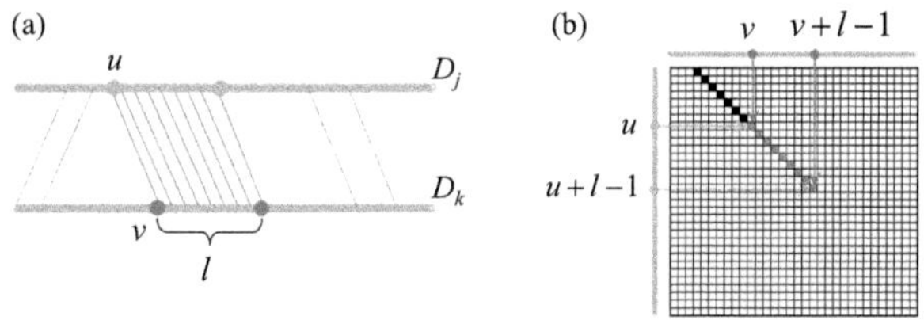

Figure 3: (a) Illustration of a distance computation required between a pair of subsequences starting at positions u and v, respectively, and of length l. Dashed lines show other possible distance computations. (b) The matrix $\mathbb{M}$ for computing the sum of products of the subsequences in (a).

Euclidean distance computation for subsequences can be made faster by reusing overlapping computation. However, reusing computations of z-normalized distances for overlapping subsequences needs at least quadratic space and, therefore, is not tenable for most applications. When we need all possible pairwise distances among the subsequences, as we do in finding shapelets, spending the quadratic space saves a whole order of magnitude of computation time.

For every pair of points (D_j, D_k) we compute five arrays. We represent these arrays as $Stats_{x,y}$ in the algorithms. Two of the arrays (i.e. $\mathbb{S}_x$ and $\mathbb{S}_y$) store the cumulative sum of the individual time series x and y. Another two (i.e. $\mathbb{S}_{x^2}$ and $\mathbb{S}_{y^2}$) store the cumulative sum of squared values. The final one (i.e. $\mathbb{M}$) is a 2D array that stores the sum of products for different subsequences of x and y. The arrays are defined mathematically below. All of the arrays have left margin of zero values indexed by 0. More precisely, $\mathbb{S}_x[0], \mathbb{S}_y[0], \mathbb{S}_{x^2}[0], \mathbb{S}_{y^2}[0], \mathbb{M}[0,0], \mathbb{M}[u,0]$ for $u = 1, 2, \ldots, |x|$, and $\mathbb{M}[0,v]$ for $v = 1, 2, \ldots, |y|$ are all zeros.

$$\mathbb{S}_x[u] = \sum_{i=0}^{u} x_i\,, \qquad \mathbb{S}_y[v] = \sum_{i=0}^{v} y_i,$$
$$\mathbb{S}_{x^2}[u] = \sum_{i=0}^{u} x_i^2\,, \qquad \mathbb{S}_{y^2}[v] = \sum_{i=0}^{v} y_i^2$$
$$\mathbb{M}[u,v] = \begin{cases} \sum_{i=0}^{v} x_{i+t} y_i & \text{if } u > v, \\ \sum_{i=0}^{u} x_i y_{i+t} & \text{if } u \leq v \end{cases}$$

Algorithm 4 $sdist\_new(u, l, Stats_{x,y})$

Require: start position u and length l and the sufficient statistics for x and y.
Ensure: Return the subsequence distance between $x_{u,l}$ and y

```
minSum ← ∞
{M, S_x, S_y, S_x2, S_y2} ← Stats_x,y
for v ← 1 to |y| − |x| + 1 do
    d ← distance computed by (1) and (2) in constant time
    if d < minSum then
        minSum ← d
return √minSum
```

where $t = abs(u - v)$.

Given that we have computed these arrays, the mean, variance, and the sum of products for any pair of subsequences of the same length can be computed as below.

$$\mu_x = \frac{\mathbb{S}_x[u+l-1] - \mathbb{S}_x[u-1]}{l},\ \mu_y = \frac{\mathbb{S}_y[v+l-1] - \mathbb{S}_y[v-1]}{l}$$
$$\sigma_x = \frac{\mathbb{S}_{x^2}[u+l-1] - \mathbb{S}_{x^2}[u-1]}{l} - \mu_x^2,\ \sigma_y = \frac{\mathbb{S}_{y^2}[v+l-1] - \mathbb{S}_{y^2}[v-1]}{l} - \mu_y^2$$

$$\sum_{i=0}^{l-1} x_{u+i} y_{v+i} = \mathbb{M}[u+l-1, v+l-1] - \mathbb{M}[u-1, v-1].$$

This in turn means that the normalized euclidean distance (the information we actually want) between any two subsequences $x_{u,l}$ and $y_{v,l}$ of any length l can now be computed using equations 1 and 2 in constant time. The algorithm 4 describes the steps. The algorithm takes as input the starting position u and the length l of the subsequence of x. It also takes the precomputed $Stats_{x,y}$ carrying the sufficient statistics. The algorithm iterates for all possible start positions v of y and returns the minimum distance. Thus we can see that the procedure $sdist\_new$ saves at least an $O(m)$ inner loop computation from procedure $sditst$.

3.2 Candidate Pruning

The constant time approach for distance computation introduced in the previous section helps reduce the total cost of shapelet discovery by a factor of m. Our next goal is to reduce the number of iterations that occur in the **for** loop at line 6 in the algorithm 1. The core idea behind our attack on this problem is the following observation: If we know (s, τ) is a poor shapelet (i.e. it has low information gain) then any similar subsequence to s must also result in a low information gain and, therefore, a costly evaluation (computing all the distances) can be safely skipped. Assume we have observed a good best-so-far shapelet at some point in the algorithm. Let us denote this shapelet (S_p, τ_p) and its information gain I_p. Imagine we now test $(S_{i,l}, \tau)$, and it has very poor information gain $I_{i,l} < I_p$. Let us consider the next subsequence $S_{i+1,l}$. Here is our fundamental question. Is it possible to use the relationship (the Euclidean distance) between $S_{i,l}$ and $S_{i+1,l}$, to prune $S_{i+1,l}$?

To develop our intuition, let us first imagine a pathological case. Suppose that $dist(S_{i,l}, S_{i+1,l}) = 0$; in other words, $S_{i+1,l}$ is the exact same shape as $S_{i,l}$. In that case we can obviously prune $S_{i+1,l}$, since its information gain must also be $I_{i,l}$. Suppose, however, in the more realistic case, that $S_{i,l}$ and $S_{i+1,l}$ are similar, but not identical. We may still be able to prune $S_{i+1,l}$. The trick is to ask, "how good could $S_{i+1,l}$ be?" , or a little more formally, "What is an upper bound on the information gain of $S_{i+1,l}$". It turns out that it is simple to calculate this bound!

Let the distance between $S_{i,l}$ and $S_{i+1,l}$ be R. By triangular inequality, $sdist(S_{i+1,l}, D_k)$ can be as low as $sdist(S_{i,l}, D_k) - R$ and as high as $sdist(S_{i,l}, D_k) + R$ regardless of the alignment of

$S_{i+1,l}$ on D_k. Thus, every point on the orderline of $S_{i,l}$ has a "mobility" in the range $[-R, R]$ from its current position. Given this mobility, our goal is to find the best configuration of the points that gives maximum information gain when split into two partitions. The points that lie outside $[\tau - R, \tau + R]$ can have no effect on the information gain for candidate $(S_{i+1,l}, \tau)$. For the points inside $[\tau - R, \tau + R]$ we can shift them optimistically in either direction to increase the information gain.

Every class $c \in C$ has n_c instances in the database which are divided into two partitions by a split. Let $n_{c,1}$ and $n_{c,2}$ be the number of instances of class c in partition D_{left} and D_{right}, respectively. A class is weighted to the left (or simply called *left-major/right-minor*) if $\frac{n_{c,1}}{N_1} > \frac{n_{c,2}}{N_2}$. Similarly, a class is called *right-major/left-minor* if $\frac{n_{c,1}}{N_1} \leq \frac{n_{c,2}}{N_2}$. The following lemma describes the optimal choice for a single point. We relegate the proof to Appendix to enhance the flow of the paper.

THEOREM 1. *Shifting a point from its minor partition to its major partition always increases information gain.*

If we shift a point from the minor partition to the major partition, the major/minor partitions of the class remain the same as before shifting, simply because, if $\frac{n_{c,1}}{N_1} > \frac{n_{c,2}}{N_2}$ then $\frac{n_{c,1}+1}{N_1+1} > \frac{n_{c,2}-1}{N_2-1}$. Therefore, shifting all the minor points of a class to its major partition increases the information gain monotonically, and thus, this can be treated as an atomic operation. We denote such a sequence of shifts as a "*transfer*". Transferring a class may change the major-minor partitions of other classes and, consequently, the transfer direction for that class. Therefore, if we transfer every class based on the major-minor partitions in the initial orderline, it does not necessarily guarantee the maximum information gain.

In the case of two-class datasets, there is always one left-major and one-right major class. Therefore, shifting all of the points in $[\tau - R, \tau + R]$ to their major partition will not change the major-minor partitions of either of the classes; thus, this guarantees the optimization (i.e. the upper bound) even if the initial transfer directions are used.

For a case of more than two-classes, almost all of the time initial major-minor partitions hold after all of the transfers are done. Unfortunately, it is possible to *construct* counter examples, even if we rarely confront them on real data. To obtain the optimal bound we need to try all possible transfer directions for all of the classes resulting in 2^C trials. Fortunately, many classification problems deal with a small number of classes. For example, 60% of the UCR time series datasets have four or less classes. Given this fact, having the 2^C constant in the complexity expression will not be an issue for many problems.

Algorithm 5 describes the computation of the upper bound. The algorithm loops through all distinct split positions (line 2-3). For every split position, the algorithm transfers all of the classes to their major partition based on the initial orderline (line 5-6) and computes the information gain to find the upper bound. Note that line 4 is "commented out" in the algorithm which is a **for** loop that checks all of the 2^C combinations of transfer directions. For exact bound in the case of many-class datasets, this line should be uncommented.

To summarize, for the two-class case we have an exact and admissible pruning technique. In the multi-class case we have a powerful heuristic that empirically gives answers that are essentially indistinguishable from the optimal answer.

3.3 The Fast Shapelet Discovery Algorithm

With the speedup techniques described in the previous section, we are now ready to plug them into algorithm 1 and build a faster version as shown in algorithm 6.

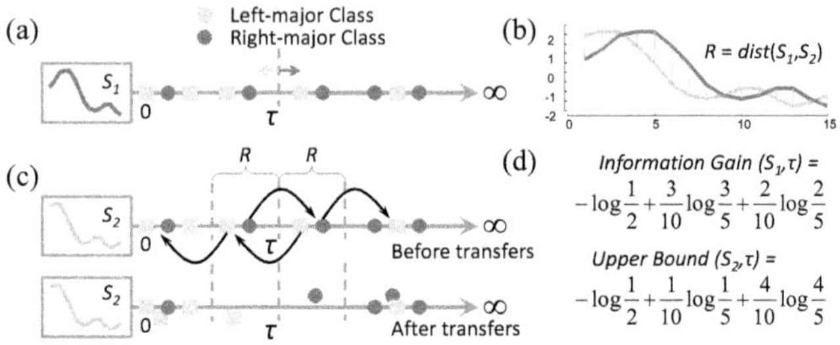

Figure 4: (a) A sequence S_1 and its orderline. (b) Distance between the sequences S_1 and S_2 is R. (c) The points on the orderline within $[\tau - R, \tau + R]$ are transferred to their majority partition. (d) The computation of the information gain for (S_1, τ) and upper bound for (S_2, τ).

Algorithm 5 $upperIG(L, R)$

Require: An order line L and the candidate distance R.
Ensure: Return an upper bound of information gain.

```
1: maxI ← 0
2: for k ← 1 to |D| − 1 except j do
3:     τ ← (L_k + L_{k+1})/2
4:     //for all 2^C combinations of transfer directions do
5:         for all points p ∈ [τ − R, τ + R]
6:             move p to its majority end.
7:         Count n_{1,i} and n_{2,i} for i = 1, 2, ..., C.
8:         Count N_1 and N_2 for both the partitions.
9:         I ← information gain computed by definition 3
10:        maxI ← max(maxI, I)
11: return maxI
```

In lines 5-7, the sufficient statistics are computed for the current time series D_j paired with every other time series D_k.

The algorithm maintains a set of orderlines in the history H. For every candidate $S_{i,l}$, before committing to the expensive computation of the orderline, the algorithm quickly computes upper bounds using the orderlines in the history (line 14). If *any* of the upper bounds is smaller than the maximum gain achieved so far we can safely abandon the candidate (line 15).

Since the upper bound computation is based upon the triangular inequality, we are only allowed to use the previous orderlines computed for sequences of the same length as the current candidate [1]. Therefore, once the search moves on to the next length the algorithm clears the history H and starts building it up for the new length (line 9).

The size of the history H is a user-defined value and the algorithm is insensitive to this value once it is set to at least five. To prevent our history cache in line 22 growing without bound, we need to have a replacement policy. The oldest-first (LIFO) policy is the most suitable for this algorithm. This is because the recent subsequences tend to be correlated with the current candidate and, therefore, have small distances from the candidate. Note that, we do not add all orderlines to the history. We only add the orderlines that have less information gain (i.e. orderlines for poor shapelet candidate) than the current $maxGain$. Because only poor candi-

[1]The reader may wonder why we cannot create a bound between a sequence and a shorter sequence that is its prefix. Such bounds cannot be created because we are normalizing *all* sequences, and after normalizing the distances may increase *or* decrease.

Algorithm 6 $Fast\_Shapelet\_Discovery(D)$

Require: A dataset D of time series

Ensure: Return the shapelet

$m \leftarrow$ minimum length of a time series in D

$maxGain \leftarrow 0, maxGap \leftarrow 0$

for $j \leftarrow 1$ to $|D|$ **do** {every time series in D}

  $S \leftarrow j$th time series of D

  for $k \leftarrow 1$ to $|D|$ **do** {compute statistics for S and D_k}

    $x \leftarrow S, y \leftarrow D_k$

    $Stats_{x,y} \leftarrow \{\mathbb{M}, \mathbb{S}_x, \mathbb{S}_y, \mathbb{S}_{x^2}, \mathbb{S}_{y^2}\}$

  for $l \leftarrow 1$ to m **do** {every possible length}

    clear H

    for $i \leftarrow 1$ to $|S|$ **do** {every start position}

      for $w \leftarrow 1$ to $|H|$ **do** {every candidate in H}

        $(L', S') \leftarrow H[w]$

        $R \leftarrow sdist(S_{i,l}, S')$

        if $upperIG(L', R) < maxGain$ **then** {prune this candidate}

          continue with next i

      for $k \leftarrow 1$ to $|D|$ **do** {since not pruned; compute distances of every time series to the candidate $S_{i,l}$}

        $L_k \leftarrow sdist\_new(i, l, Stats_{x,y})$

      $sort(L)$

      $(\tau, updated) \leftarrow bestIG(L, maxGain, maxGap)$

      if $updated$ **then** {gain and/or gap are changed}

        $bestS \leftarrow S_{i,l}, best\tau \leftarrow \tau, bestL \leftarrow L$

      add $(L, S_{i,l})$ to H if $maxGain$ is not changed

return $(bestS, best\tau, bestL, maxGain, maxGap)$

dates have the power of pruning similar candidates by predicting their low information gain.

4. LOGICAL SHAPELET

A shapelet is a tuple consisting of a subsequence and a split point (threshold) that attempts to separate the classes in exactly two different groups. However, it is easy to imagine situations where it may not be sufficient to use only one shapelet to achieve separation of classes, but a *combination* of shapelets. To demonstrate this, we show a simple example. In Figure 5(a), we have a two-class problem where each class has two time series. The square class contains two sinusoidal patterns with both positive and negative peaks, while the circle class has only one positive *or* one negative peak. If we attempt to use the classic shapelet definition to separate these classes, we find there is no way to do so. Classic shapelets simply do not have the expressiveness to represent this concept. The reason is that every single distinct pattern appears in both of the classes, or in only one of the time series of one of the classes. For example, in 5(b) three different unary shapelets and their orderlines are illustrated, and none of them achieved a separation between the classes.

To overcome this problem, we propose using multiple shapelets which allow distinctions based on logical combinations of the shapelets. For example, if we use the first two shapelets in figure 5(b) then we can say that (S_1, τ_1) **and** (S_2, τ_2) separate the classes best. From now on, we use standard logic symbols $\bigwedge$ and $\bigvee$ for **and** and **or** operations. For a new instance x, if $sdist(S_1, x) < \tau_1$ $\bigwedge$ $sdist(S_2, x) < \tau_2$ is true, then we can classify x as a member of the square class, or otherwise the circle class. When using multiple shapelets in such a way, chaining of logical combinations among the shapelets is possible; for example, $(S_1, \tau_1) \bigwedge (S_2, \tau_2) \bigvee (S_3, \tau_3)$. However, for the sake of simplicity and to guard against over fitting with too complex a model [4], we only consider two cases, only $\bigwedge$, and only $\bigvee$ combinations. We further guard against overfitting with too flexible a model by allowing only just a single threshold for both shapelets.

We have already seen how to create an orderline for classic shapelets, how do we define an orderline for conjunctive or disjunctive shapelets? To combine the orderlines for such cases, we adopt a very simple approach. For $\bigwedge$ operation, the *maximum* of the distances from the literal shapelets is considered as the distance on the new orderline, and for $\bigvee$ the *minimum* is considered. Apart from these minor changes, the computation of the entropy and information gain are unchanged.

For example, in figure 5(d) the combined orderline for $(S_1 \bigwedge S_2, \tau)$ is shown. The two classes are now separable because both the shapelets occur *together* in the square class and do not both occur together in individual instances of the circle class.

Given these minor changes to allow logical shapelets, we can still avail ourselves of the speedup techniques proposed in section 3. The original shapelet algorithm just needs to be modified to run multiple times, and some minor additional bookkeeping must be done. When the first shapelet is found by the algorithm 6, we now test to see if there is any class whose instances are in both the partitions of the optimal split. We call such a class "broken" (We could say "non-linearly separable," however, our situation has a slightly different interpretation). If there is a broken class, we continue to search for a new shapelet on the same dataset that can merge the parts of the broken class. However, this time we *must* make sure that new shapelet does not have a match with a subsequence in D_k that overlaps with the matching subsequence of an already discovered shapelet. After finding the new shapelet, we combine the orderlines and the threshold based on the appropriate logic operation. Finally, we are in position to measure the information gain to see if it is better than our best-so-far. If the gain improves, we test for a broken class again and continue as before. Once there is no broken class or the gain does not increase, we recursively find shapelet(s) in the left and right partitions.

The above approach is susceptible to overfitting. It can degenerate into $(S_1, \tau_1) \bigvee (S_2, \tau_2) \bigvee \ldots \bigvee (S_{n_i}, \tau_n)$ where n_i is the number of instances in the class i and each S_j for $j = 1, 2, \ldots, n_i$ is a subsequence of different instances of class i in the dataset D. In this case, all of the instances of class i would be in the left side with zero distances. To avoid overfitting, we can have a hard bound on the number of literals in the logic expression. In this work, the bound is hard coded to four, however, for a very large dataset we could slowly increase this number, if we carefully check to guard against overfitting. Note that the situation here is almost perfectly analogous to the problem of overfitting in decision trees, and we expect that similar solutions could work here.

5. EVALUATION

We begin by noting that we have taken extraordinary lengths to make all our experiments reproducible. As such, all code and data are available at [2], and will be maintained there in perpetuity. Moreover, while our proposed algorithm is not sensitive to the few parameters required as inputs, we explicitly state all parameters for every dataset at [2].

We wish to demonstrate two major points with our experiments. First, our novel speedup techniques can be used to find both classic and logical shapelets significantly faster. Second, there exist real-world problems for which logical shapelets are significantly more accurate than classic shapelets or other state-of-the-art techniques (see section 6).

To demonstrate the speedup, we have taken 24 datasets from the

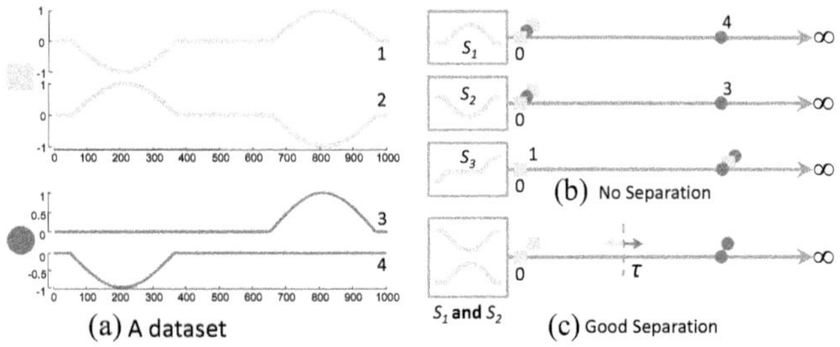

Figure 5: (a) Two classes of synthetic time series. (b) Examples of single shapelets that cannot separate the classes. Any other single shapelet would fail similarly. (c) Two shapelets connected by an *and* operation can separate the classes.

UCR time series archive [9]. For brevity the names and properties of these datasets and *tables* of time taken for running *the* shapelet algorithms on these datasets can be found at [2]. Here we content ourselves with a visual summary. In figure 6*(left)*, we show the speedups over the original algorithm. Our algorithm obtained *some* speedup for all of the datasets with a maximum of 27.2.

The two speedup methods described in section 3 are not independent of each other. Therefore, we also measure the *individual* speedups for each of the techniques while deactivating the other. The individual speedup factors for both the techniques are plotted in figure 6*(right)*. There is no speedup for two of the datasets (shown by stars) when only the candidate pruning method is active. The reason is that the amount of pruning achieved for these datasets cannot surpass the overhead costs of computing the upper bounds for every candidate. However, when the technique of efficient distance computation is active, speedups are achieved for *all* of the datasets including these two.

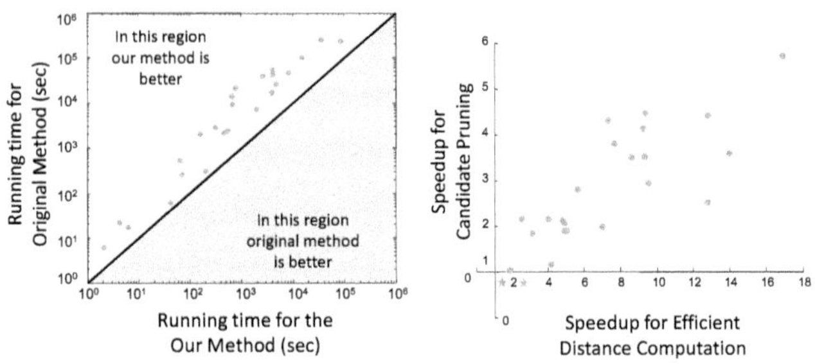

Figure 6: *(left)* Comparison of running times between our method and the original shapelet algorithm. Note the log scale on both axes. *(right)* The individual speedup factors for both of our proposed techniques: Candidate Pruning and Efficient Distance Computation.

It is critical to note that our improvements in speed are not due to trivial differences in hardware or to simple implementation optimizations, but reflect the utility of the two original techniques introduced in section 3. In particular, all experiments were done on exactly the same environment and on the same input data files. The code for the original shapelet discovery algorithm was graciously donated by Dr. Ye who also confirmed that we are using her code in the best possible manner. Since our technique reduced the worst case complexity by a factor of m and has an admissible pruning technique which is not present in the original code, we can be sure that the speedup is valid.

As described in section 3.2, our linear time upper bound is not admissible for the many-class cases. Among the 24 datasets we used for scalability experiments, 13 datasets have more than two classes. For these 13 datasets, the average rate of computing false upper bound is just 1.56% with a standard deviation of 2.86%. In reality, the impact of false bounds on the final result is inconsequential because of the massive search space for shapelet. Our algorithm rarely misses the optimal information gain in that space and has not missed in *any* of the above 13 many-class datasets.

6. CASE STUDIES

In this section we show three case studies in three different domains. In all the case studies we demonstrate that logical combinations of shapelets can describe the difference between the classes very robustly. We compare our algorithm to the 1-NN classifier using Dynamic Time Warping (DTW) because a recent extensive comparison of dozens of time series classification algorithms, on dozens of datasets, strongly suggests that 1-NN DTW is exceptionally difficult to beat [3]. Note that the 1-NN classifier using DTW is less amenable for realtime classification of time series since it requires an $O(m^2)$ distance measure to be computed for every instance in the dataset. In contrast, classification with shapelets requires just a single $O(n(m-n))$ calculation (n is the length of the shapelet). Thus, classification with time series shapelets is typically thousands of times faster than 1-NN DTW. We do not experimentally show this here, since it was amply demonstrated in the original shapelet paper [19].

6.1 Cricket: Automatic Scorer

In the game of cricket (a very popular game in British Commonwealth countries), an umpire signals different events in the game to a distant scorer/book-keeper. Typically, the signals involve particular motions of the hands. For example, the umpire stretches up both the hands above the head to signal a score of "six." A complete list of signals can be found in [1]. Researchers have recently begun to attempt to classify these signals automatically to ease/remove the task of a scorer [10].

In [10], a dataset was collected in which two accelerometers have been placed on both wrists of four different umpires. The umpires performed twelve different signals used in the game of cricket at least ten times. For simplicity of presentation, we select only two classes from the dataset that has a unique possibility of confusion. The two classes are "No Ball" and "Wide Ball." To signal "No Ball," the umpire must raise *one* of his hands to the shoulder-height and keep his hand horizontal until the scorer confirms the record. To signal "Wide Ball," the umpire stretches both of the hands horizontally at shoulder-height (see figure 7).

Each accelerometer has three synchronous and independent measurements for three axes (X,Y, and Z). For every signal performed, the six channels are concatenated to form one time series. We append low variance white noise to each example in the dataset to make them of length 308. The training set has nine examples as shown in figure 7. The test set has 98 examples. Note that the examples for "No Ball" are only right hand signals. This is true for the test set also. To cover the left handed case and also to include examples of different lengths, we have generated another test set using the accelerometer on a standard smart phone. This test set contains 64 examples of length 600. Each class has an equal number of examples in both of the training sets.

On this dataset, we performed 1-NN classification using Euclidean distance and Dynamic Time Warping (DTW) as distance measures. We also considered DTW with the Sakoe-Chiba band [15], as it has been shown to outperform classic DTW on many

Algorithms	Original Test set	New Test set
1-NN Euclidean distance	94.89%	56.25%
1-NN Dynamic Time Warping	**98.98%**	87.50%
1-NN DTW-Sakoe-Chiba	94.89%	75.00%
Shapelet	44.89%	48.43%
Logical Shapelet	95.91%	**89.06%**

Table 1: The accuracies of different algorithms on the two test sets.

datasets [7]. The results are shown in table 1. It is interesting to consider why Logical Shapelets generalize the new data the best. We conjecture that it is the ability of Logical Shapelets to extract just the meaningful part of the signal. In contrast, DTW and Euclidean distance must account for the entire time series, including sections that may be unique to individual umpires idiosyncratic motion, but not predictive of the concept.

The Computationally expensive 1-NN DTW performs well in both of the cases, but not suitable for real-time applications. The original shapelet algorithm fails to capture the fact that the inherent difference between the classes is in the number of occurrences of the shapelet. Our logical shapelet algorithm captures the sharp rises in the Z-axes for "Wide Ball" from the original training set. No such "No Ball" signal can have two such rises in the Z-axes, and therefore, classification accuracy does not decrease significantly for the new test set.

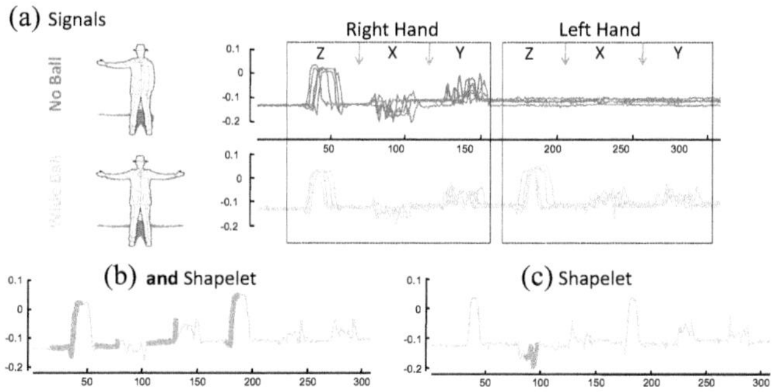

Figure 7: (a)The training set of the cricket dataset by concatenating signals from every axis of the accelerometer. (b) The two signs an umpire performs to declare two types of illegal delivery. (c) Shapelets found by our algorithm and the original algorithm.

6.2 Sony AIBO Robot: Surface Detection

The SONY AIBO Robot is a small, dog-shaped, quadruped robot that comes equipped with multiple sensors, including a tri-axial accelerometer. We consider a dataset created by [17] where measurements of the accelerometer are collected. In the experimental setting, the robot walked on two different surfaces: carpet and cement. For simplicity we consider only the X-axis readings. A snap shot of the data is shown in figure 8(a). Each time series represents one walk cycle. Cemented floors are hard compared to carpets and, therefore, offer more reactive force than carpets. As such, there are clear and sharp changes in the acceleration on the cemented floor. In addition, there is a much larger variability when the robot walks on cement.

The test set has 20 instances of walk cycles on the two types of floors. The training set has 601 instances. A walk cycle is of length 70 at 125 hertz. We have experimented on this dataset and found a pair of shapelets shown in figure 8(b). The shapelets are connected by $\bigwedge$ and come from the two different shifts-of-weight in the walk cycle on the carpet floor. The pair of shapelets has a significantly higher classification accuracy compared to classic nearest neighbor algorithms (see table 2).

Algorithms	Surface Detection	Passgraphs
1-NN Euclidean distance	69.55%	63.36%
1-NN Dynamic Time Warping	72.55%	71.76%
1-NN DTW-Sakoe-Chiba	69.55%	**74.05%**
Shapelet	93.34%	60.31%
Logical Shapelet	**96.34%**	70.23%

Table 2: The accuracies of different algorithms on the passgraph trajectories and accelerometer signals from SONY AIBO robot.

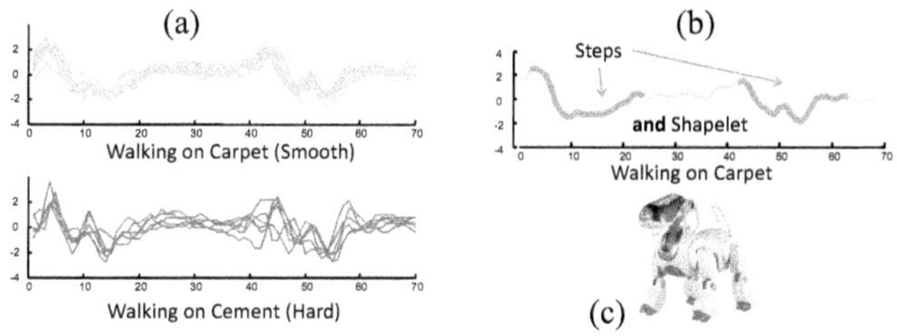

Figure 8: (a) Two classes of time series from the SONY AIBO accelerometer. (b) The *and*-shapelets from the walk cycle on carpet. (c) The Sony AIBO Robot.

6.3 Passgraphs: Preventing Shoulder-Surfers

Passgraphs are a recently proposed biometric system used to authenticate a person and allow her access to some resource. A grid of dots is presented to the user and she is tasked to connect some of the dots in the grid in some specific order as a password. In contrast to text-based passwords where the user can shield the the entered text (at an ATM for example), Passgraphs are vulnerable to "shoulder-surfing" as it is easy for a miscreant to see and memorize the connection sequence over the shoulder of the user. To prevent the shoulder-surfing attack, [12] has proposed methods involving pen-pressure. There are also methods based on other pen properties such as friction, acceleration, etc.

In this case study, we use the data from [12] to see if logical shapelets can classify between the same pen sequences performed by different users. We selected x-axis trajectories of two different users drawing the same passgraph. The logical shapelet shown in figure 9 consists of tiny fragments of the three turns (peaks in the time series) in the passgraph connected by $\bigvee$ operations. These shapelets have better accuracies than 1-NN classifier and are promising enough to use in a real authentication system. This is because the shapelets can be learned at training time when the user sets the password, and it is not possible for the shoulder surfer to mimic the idiosyncratic pen path of the real user when attempting to impersonate her. Note that, $\bigwedge$ operations in this case would have imposed a harder rule for the user to produce *all* instead of *some* of the shapelets exactly to get authenticated.

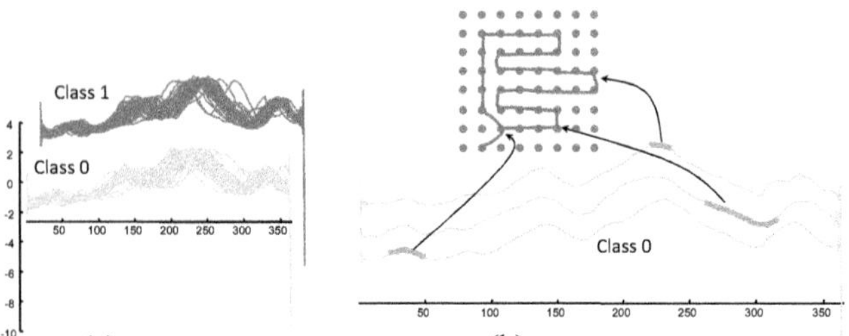

(a) Two Classes (b) or Shapelet

Figure 9: (a) Two classes of X-axis trajectories drawn by different users. (b) The *or*-shapelets from three different examples of class 0 showing three turns in the passgraphs.

7. CONCLUSIONS

In this paper, we introduce logical shapelets: a new time series classification primitive with more expressiveness than classic shapelets. We have demonstrated the existence of logical concepts in time series datasets, and the utility of logical shapelets in domains as diverse as gesture recognition, robotics and user authentication. We further describe novel techniques to efficiently find both classic and logical shapelets. Our approach is significantly faster for every one of the twenty-four datasets we tested.

Acknowledgements: Thanks to all the donars of the datasets. This work was funded by NSF awards 0803410 and 0808770.

8. APPENDIX: PROOF OF THEOREM 1

PROOF. Lets assume c is a left-major class. So $\frac{n_{c,1}}{N_1} > \frac{n_{c,2}}{N_2}$. If we move one point of class c from the right partition to the left partition, for $i = 1, 2, \ldots, C$ the change in information gain is ΔI.

$$\Delta I = \sum_i \frac{n_{i,1}}{N} \log \frac{n_{i,1}}{N_1} + \sum_i \frac{n_{i,2}}{N} \log \frac{n_{i,2}}{N_2} - \sum_{i \neq c} \frac{n_{i,1}}{N} \log \frac{n_{i,1}}{N_1+1} - \sum_{i \neq c} \frac{n_{i,2}}{N} \log \frac{n_{i,2}}{N_2-1} - \frac{n_{c,1}+1}{N} \log \frac{n_{c,1}+1}{N_1+1} - \frac{n_{c,2}-1}{N} \log \frac{n_{c,2}-1}{N_2-1}$$

Using $\sum_{i \neq c} n_{i,1} = N_1 - n_{c,1}$ and $\sum_{i \neq c} n_{i,2} = N_2 - n_{c,2}$, we can simplify the above as below.

$$N.\Delta I = N_1 \log N_1 - n_{c,1} \log n_{c,1} + (n_{c,1}+1) \log(n_{c,1}+1) + N_2 \log N_2 - n_{c,2} \log n_{c,2} + (n_{c,2}-1) \log(n_{c,2}-1) - (N_1+1) \log(N_1+1) - (N_2-1) \log(N_2-1)$$

Since, $\frac{n_{c,1}}{N_1} > \frac{n_{c,2}}{N_2}$ for $t \in [0, 1]$ the following is also true $\frac{n_{c,1}+1-t}{N_1+1-t} > \frac{n_{c,2}-t}{N_2-t}$. In addition, $n_{c,1}, N_1, n_{c,2}, N_2$ are all positive integers; therefore, we can take log on both side and integrate from 0 to 1.

$\int_0^1 \log \frac{n_{c,1}+1-t}{N_1+1-t} dt - \int_0^1 \log \frac{n_{c,2}-t}{N_2-t} dt > 0$. If we evaluate the integral, it becomes the right-side part of the above equation for $N.\Delta I$. Therefore, $\Delta I > 0$. □

9. REFERENCES

[1] *BBC SPORT | Cricket | Laws & Equipment.* http://news.bbc.co.uk/sport2/hi/cricket/rules_and_equipment.

[2] *Supporting webpage containing code, data, excel sheet and slides.* http://www.cs.ucr.edu/~mueen/LogicalShapelet.

[3] H. Ding, G. Trajcevski, P. Scheuermann, X. Wang, and E. Keogh. Querying and mining of time series data: experimental comparison of representations and distance measures. *Proc. VLDB Endow.*, 1:1542–1552, 2008.

[4] P. Domingos. Process-oriented estimation of generalization error. In *Proceedings of the Sixteenth International Joint Conference on Artificial Intelligence*, pages 714–719, 1999.

[5] B. Hartmann and N. Link. Gesture recognition with inertial sensors and optimized dtw prototypes. In *IEEE International Conference on Systems Man and Cybernetics (SMC)*, pages 2102 –2109, 2010.

[6] B. Hartmann, I. Schwab, and N. Link. Prototype optimization for temporarily and spatially distorted time series. In *the AAAI Spring Symposia*, 2010.

[7] E. Keogh. Exact indexing of dynamic time warping. In *Proceedings of the 28th international conference on Very Large Data Bases*, VLDB '02, pages 406–417, 2002.

[8] E. Keogh and S. Kasetty. On the Need for Time Series Data Mining Benchmarks: A Survey and Empirical Demonstration. *Data Mining and Knowledge Discovery*, 7(4):349–371, 2003.

[9] E. Keogh, X. Xi, W. L., and C. A. Ratanamahatana. *The UCR Time Series Classification/Clustering Homepage:.* www.cs.ucr.edu/~eamonn/time_series_data/.

[10] M. H. Ko, G. West, S. Venkatesh, and M. Kumar. Online context recognition in multisensor systems using dynamic time warping. In *Intelligent Sensors, Sensor Networks and Information Processing Conference, 2005.*, pages 283 – 288, 2005.

[11] J. Liu, L. Zhong, J. Wickramasuriya, and V. Vasudevan. uwave: Accelerometer-based personalized gesture recognition and its applications. *Pervasive and Mobile Computing*, 5(6):657–675, 2009.

[12] B. Malek, M. Orozco, and A. E. Saddik. Novel shoulder-surfing resistant haptic-based graphical password. In *In the Proceedings of the EuroHaptics conference*, 2006.

[13] A. McGovern, D. Rosendahl, R. Brown, and K. Droegemeier. Identifying predictive multi-dimensional time series motifs: an application to severe weather prediction. *Data Mining and Knowledge Discovery*, 22:232–258, 2011.

[14] A. Mueen, S. Nath, and J. Liu. Fast approximate correlation for massive time-series data. In *SIGMOD Conference*, pages 171–182, 2010.

[15] H. Sakoe and S. Chiba. Dynamic programming algorithm optimization for spoken word recognition. *Acoustics, Speech and Signal Processing, IEEE Transactions on*, 26(1):43 – 49, 1978.

[16] Y. Sakurai, S. Papadimitriou, and C. Faloutsos. Braid: Stream mining through group lag correlations. In *SIGMOD Conference*, pages 599–610, 2005.

[17] D. Vail and M. Veloso. Learning from accelerometer data on a legged robot. In *In Proceedings of the 5th IFAC/EURON Symposium on Intelligent Autonomous Vehicles*, 2004.

[18] Z. Xing, J. Pei, P. Yu, and K. Wang. Extracting interpretable features for early classification on time series. In *the Proceedings of SDM*, 2011.

[19] L. Ye and E. Keogh. Time series shapelets: a new primitive for data mining. In *Proceedings of the 15th ACM SIGKDD international conference on Knowledge discovery and data mining*, KDD, pages 947–956, 2009.

Meta Optimization and its Application to Portfolio Selection

Puja Das
Dept of Computer Science & Engg
Univ of Minnesota, Twin Cities
pdas@cs.umn.edu

Arindam Banerjee
Dept of Computer Science & Engg
Univ of Minnesota, Twin Cities
banerjee@cs.umn.edu

ABSTRACT

Several data mining algorithms use iterative optimization methods for learning predictive models. It is not easy to determine upfront which optimization method will perform best or converge fast for such tasks. In this paper, we analyze Meta Algorithms (MAs) which work by adaptively combining iterates from a pool of base optimization algorithms. We show that the performance of MAs are competitive with the best convex combination of the iterates from the base algorithms for online as well as batch convex optimization problems. We illustrate the effectiveness of MAs on the problem of portfolio selection in the stock market and use several existing ideas for portfolio selection as base algorithms. Using daily S&P500 data for the past 21 years and a benchmark NYSE dataset, we show that MAs outperform existing portfolio selection algorithms with provable guarantees by several orders of magnitude, and match the performance of the best heuristics in the pool.

Categories and Subject Descriptors

H.2.8 [**Database Management**]: Database Applications—*Data mining*

General Terms

Algorithms, Theory

Keywords

Meta Optimization, Online Learning, Portfolio Selection

1. INTRODUCTION

Several data mining algorithms use iterative update methods for learning predictive models. Typically, there are several choices for iterative update methods including gradient based or Newton step based optimization routines, stochastic gradient descent algorithms, domain specific methods, evolutionary and genetic algorithms, or plain heuristics. It is not easy to determine upfront which method will converge fast or perform the best.

While multiple iterative update methods can be run in an embarrassingly parallel manner, it is unclear if iterates from multiple algorithms for the same problem can be meaningfully combined to guarantee good optimization performance. Ideally, one would like the combined iterates to outperform the best algorithm in the pool, noting that the best algorithm may be different for different problem settings and domains. Such a desideratum is related to ensemble methods for prediction problems, where one expects the ensemble prediction to outperform the single best predictor in the pool [13, 6, 7]. In this paper, we investigate a related question in the contest of iterative optimization: Can iterates from multiple iterative update algorithms for the same problem be combined in a way so as to outperform the single best algorithm in the pool in terms of optimization performance? Related questions have been investigated in certain other contexts, including online learning [9, 22] and genetic programming [24, 27].

The setting we consider is fairly general: Given a canonical convex optimization problem $\min_{x\in P} \phi(x)$ and a set of k different base algorithms which generate an iterate $x_{t,h} \in P, 1 \leq h \leq k$ in every iteration, can we form an adaptive convex combination of the iterates $x_t^{w_t} = \sum_{h=1}^{k} w_{t,h}x_{t,h}$ whose performance is at least as good as the best single algorithm. There is no requirement from the base algorithms other than producing a feasible $x_{t,h} \in P$ in every iteration. In particular, the base algorithms need not guarantee monotonic improvements in the objective function, and may be based on a heuristic without any guarantees. To make our analysis general, we even allow the convex function to change over time. Using advances in online learning and online convex optimization [8, 22, 20, 9, 15], we develop two algorithms for adaptively combining iterates which are guaranteed to be as good as the best convex combination of iterates, and hence the best algorithm.

We extensively evaluate the proposed methodology in an important problem in financial data mining—portfolio selection [23, 10, 16, 1]. The goal is to adaptively update a portfolio over a set of stocks so that the returns over time are maximized. The problem can be posed as an online convex optimization problem, where the convex function gets determined by market movements on each day [1, 16, 10]. Due to its importance, the portfolio selection problem has been widely studied for six decades [23, 19, 10, 9], and numerous algorithms and heuristics exist on how to pick the next days portfolio which forms the iterate $x_{t,h}$ in our setting. We use a pool of these existing algorithms for portfolio selection, and focus on creating a portfolio by adaptively combining the portfolios suggested by the base algorithms. Through our analysis and algorithms, we establish theoretical results and illustrate strong empirical performance. In particular, we show that the meta algorithms for portfolio selection will be universal, i.e., competitive with the best constant rebalanced portfolio (CRP) chosen in hindsight [10, 18, 4], if any base algorithm in the pool is universal. Note that universal portfolios are guaranteed to be as good as the best stock

KDD'11, August 21–24, 2011, San Diego, California, USA.

even in adversarial settings. Our experiments show that the meta algorithms outperform all existing universal algorithms by orders of magnitude, by suitably leveraging good heuristics in the pool. For example, trading on S&P500 stocks over the past 21 years (1990-2010), the meta algorithms multiply the starting wealth by 10^3 times even with two major financial meltdowns. Further, the proposed meta algorithms clearly outperform other simplistic approaches to combining portfolios.

The rest of the paper is organized as follows. We present a general framework and two algorithms for meta optimization in Section 2. In Section 3, we specialize the analysis and algorithms to the problem of portfolio selection. We present comprehensive experimental results in Section 4, and conclude in Section 5.

2. ONLINE META OPTIMIZATION

Consider the following generic convex optimization problem which shows up while building models for a variety of data mining tasks [25]:

$$\min_{x \in P} \phi(x) , \tag{1}$$

where ϕ is a convex function and $P \in \mathbb{R}^d$ determines the convex feasible set. For the meta-optimization setting, we assume access to k different iterative algorithms $A_1, \ldots, A_k$, referred to as *base algorithms*, which attempt to solve the above problem. In particular, A_h is assumed to generate a feasible $x_{t,h} \in P$ at every iteration. The analysis we present does not depend on any other properties of the base algorithms or the iterates. The iterates may be coming from a iterative convex optimization routines based on gradient or Newton methods, from domain specific heuristics, or even entirely arbitrary guesses. The proposed meta-algorithm picks a suitable iterate from the convex hull of the iterates at any time, given by:

$$\text{Co}(X_t) = \left\{ X_t w = \sum_{h=1}^{k} w_h x_{t,h} \middle| \sum_{h=1}^{k} w_h = 1, w_h \geq 0 \right\} ,$$

where $X_t = [x_{t,1} \cdots x_{t,k}] \in \mathbb{R}^{d \times k}$ is the matrix of iterates. Let Δ_k denote the k-dimensional simplex. Then, it is easy to see that the best point $x_t^w = X_t w = \sum_h w_h x_{t,h} \in \text{Co}(X_t)$ will always achieve a lower (better) objective function value than any of the individual iterates, i.e.,

$$\min_{w \in \Delta_k} \phi\left(\sum_{h=1}^{k} w_h x_{t,h}\right) \leq \phi(x_{t,h}), \ \forall h .$$

Figure 1 shows examples to illustrate the above point. In Figure 1(a), the best point in the convex hull of the iterates achieves the global minimum of the function; in Figure 1(b), it is nearest to the global minimum; and in Figure 1(c), the best point in the convex hull is an iterate itself, i.e., a corner of the hull.

In general, the best point $x_t^w = X_t w \in \text{Co}(X_t)$ inside the convex hull or equivalently the best convex combination $w \in \Delta_k$ cannot be obtained in closed form. One can design optimization algorithms to find the best point inside the convex hull. Note that such computations have to be repeated at every iteration, since corners of the hull, determined by X_t, changes in every iteration. In this section, we develop algorithms which adaptively pick $w_t \in \Delta_k$ based on X_{t-1}, and show that the iterates $x_t^{w_t} = X_t w_t = \sum_h w_{t,h} x_{t,h}$ of the meta-algorithm are competitive with any fixed convex combination $w \in \Delta_k$ used over iterations, i.e., $\forall w \in \Delta_k$ we have

$$\sum_{t=1}^{T} \phi(X_t w_t) \leq \sum_{t=1}^{T} \phi(X_t w) + o(T) . \tag{2}$$

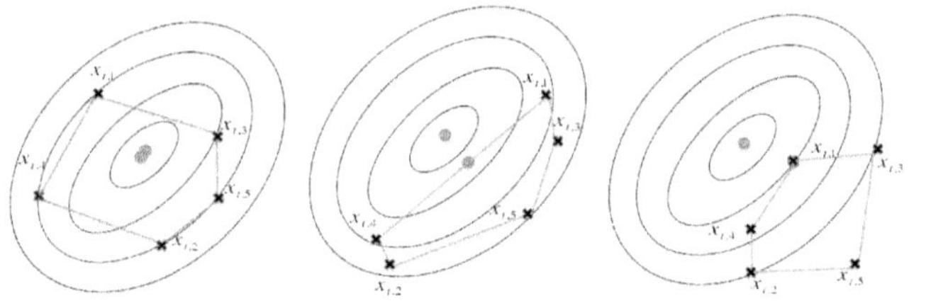

(a) (b) (c)

Figure 1: The best convex combination x_t^w of the iterates from the base algorithms is always better than individual iterates $x_{t,h}$(the red dot is the global minimum and the green dot is the best point in the convex hull of iterates): (a) x_t^w achieves the global minimum, (b) x_t^w is on an edge of the hull, and (c) x_t^w overlaps with the best iterate.

In particular, if any $w^* \in \Delta_k$ achieves the global minimum, the adaptive approach will find the global minimum as well. Indeed, instead of simply being competitive with the single best iterate, the adaptive $x_t^{w_t}$ will be competitive with any convex combinations of them (Figure 1). To present our analysis in its full generality, we consider the online convex optimization (OCO) setting [28], where the convex function itself can change over time. We denote the convex function at time t to be ϕ_t. Note that we can recover the batch case analysis for a fixed ϕ as a special case by simply setting $\phi_t = \phi, \forall t$. In the OCO setting, we intend to get a set of adaptive iterates $x_t^{w_t}$ such that the following form of *regret bounds* are satisfied:

$$\sum_{t=1}^{T} \phi_t(X_t w_t) \leq \min_{w \in \Delta_k} \sum_{t=1}^{T} \phi_t(X_t w_t) + o(T) . \tag{3}$$

2.1 Online Gradient Updates

Our meta algorithm and analysis for Online Gradient Updates (OGU) involves suitably reducing the Online Meta Optimization (OMO) problem to an online learning problem over k experts [22, 9], where each expert corresponds to a corner for meta-optimization. We start by recalling a standard result from the online learning literature [22, 12, 3]:

Lemma 1 *Let $\ell_t \in [0,1]^k, t = 1, \ldots, T$, be an arbitrary sequence of loss vectors over the k experts. If one maintains an adaptive distribution over the experts using multiplicative updates given by $p_{t+1}(h) = p_t(h) \exp(-\eta \ell_t(h))/Z_t$, where $\eta > 0$ and Z_t is the partition function, then for any $w \in \Delta_k$, the following inequality holds:*

$$\sum_{t=1}^{T} p_t^T \ell_t \leq \frac{\eta \sum_{t=1}^{T} w^T \ell_t + \log k}{1 - \exp(-\eta)} . \tag{4}$$

Variants of the above result form the basis of much work in online learning, boosting, game theory, and numerous other developments in the past two decades [22, 12, 11, 2, 3, 9]. We now outline a transformation of the OMO problem to the above online learning setting.

For our analysis, we assume that the sequence of convex functions ϕ_t can be arbitrary, but satisfies $\|\nabla \phi_t(x)\|_\infty \leq g_\infty$ for $x \in P$. Further, we assume $x \in P$ satisfies $\|x\|_1 \leq c$. For the portfolio selection application in Section 3, we will obtain specific values for g_∞ and c. Let

$$f_t(w) = \phi_t(X_t w) . \tag{5}$$

Algorithm 1 Online Gradient Update (OGU) for Meta Optimization

Initialize $w_{1,h} = \frac{1}{k}, h = 1, \ldots, k$
For $t = 1, \ldots, T$
  Receive $X_t = [x_{t,1} \cdots x_{t,k}]$ from base algorithms
  Compute $x_t^{w_t} = \sum_{h=1}^{k} w_{t,h} x_{t,h}$
  Receive convex function ϕ_t from nature
  Update distribution

$$w_{t+1,h} = w_{t,h} \exp(-\eta \ell_t(h))/Z_t$$

where $\ell_t(h)$ is as in (6) and Z_t is the partition function.

Since $\phi_t : P \mapsto \mathbb{R}$, where $P \subseteq \mathbb{R}^d$, is a convex function, the function $f_t : \Delta_k \mapsto \mathbb{R}$ is also convex. To see this, first note that the Hessian $\nabla^2 f_t(w) = X_t^T \nabla^2 \phi_t(X_t w) X_t$. Since ϕ_t is convex, $\nabla^2 \phi(X_t w)$ is positive semi-definite. Hence, $\nabla^2 f_t(w)$ is positive semi-definite, implying convexity of f_t. Define loss vector

$$\ell_t = \frac{1}{2}\left(\frac{\nabla f_t(w_t)}{c g_\infty} + e\right) \in \mathbb{R}^k , \tag{6}$$

where e is the all ones vector. Based on this definition of loss, Algorithm 1 presents an adaptive algorithm for Online gradient update for meta optimization. We establish the following regret bound for OGO for this algorithm:

Theorem 1 *For any sequence of convex functions ϕ_t such that $\|\nabla \phi_t(x)\|_\infty \leq g_\infty$, and any sequence of iterates $X_t = [x_{t,1} \cdots$ $\cdots x_{t,k}]$ such that $\|x_{t,h}\|_1 \leq c$, for $\eta = \log\left(1 + \sqrt{\frac{2\log k}{T}}\right)$ in Algorithm 1, we have*

$$\sum_{t=1}^{T} f_t(w_t) - \min_{w \in \Delta_k} \sum_{t=1}^{T} f_t(w) \leq 2 c g_\infty \left(\sqrt{2T \log k} + \log k\right) . \tag{7}$$

PROOF. Since $\nabla f_t(w_t) = X_t^T \nabla \phi_t(X_t w_t)$, $\|\nabla f_t(w_t)\|_\infty = \max_h |x_{t,h}^T \nabla \phi_t(x_t^{w_t})|$. From Hölder's inequality [26, 14, 21],

$$|x_{t,h}^T \nabla \phi_t(X_t w_t)| \leq \|x_{t,h}\|_1 \|\nabla \phi_t(X_t w_t)\|_\infty \leq c g_\infty .$$

Hence $\frac{\nabla f_t(w_t)}{c g_\infty} \in [-1, 1]^k$, so that $\ell_t \in [0, 1]^k$. From Lemma 1, Algorithm 1 will satisfy (4). Let $\epsilon = 1 - \exp(-\eta)$ so that from Lemma 1 we have

$$\sum_{t=1}^{T} w_t^T \ell_t - \sum_{t=1}^{T} w^T \ell_t \leq \epsilon T + \frac{1}{\epsilon} \log k ,$$

where we have used $\sum_{t=1}^{t} w^T \ell_t \leq T$. Choosing $\epsilon = \frac{\sqrt{2 \log k}}{\sqrt{2 \log k} + \sqrt{T}}$, a direct calculation shows

$$\sum_{t=1}^{T} \ell_t^T (w_t - w) \leq \sqrt{2T \log k} + \log k . \tag{8}$$

Now, since f_t is convex, we have

$$f_t(w_t) - f_t(w) \leq \nabla f_t(w_t)^T (w_t - w) = 2 c g_\infty \ell_t^T (w_t - w) ,$$

where the last equality follows since $e^T(w_t - w) = 0$ as $w_t, w \in \Delta_k$. Adding over all t and using (8), we have

$$\begin{aligned}\sum_{t=1}^{T} f_t(w_t) - \sum_{t=1}^{T} f_t(w) &\leq 2 c g_\infty \sum_{t=1}^{T} \ell_t^T (w_t - w) \\ &\leq 2 c g_\infty \left(\sqrt{2T \log k} + \log k\right) .\end{aligned}$$

Noting that the above inequality holds for any $w \in \Delta_k$ completes the proof. □

Since $2 c g_\infty \left(\sqrt{2T \log k} + \log k\right) = o(T)$, we have a desired form of the bound. Further, assuming $\phi_t = \phi$ gives the corresponding bound for the batch optimization case.

Algorithm 2 Online Newton Update (ONU) for Meta Optimization

Initialize $w_1 \in \Delta_k$
Let $\beta = \min\left\{\frac{1}{8 c g_\infty}, \alpha\right\}$
For $t = 1, \ldots, T$
  Receive $X_t = [x_{t,1} \cdots x_{t,k}]$ from base algorithms
  Compute $x_t^{w_t} = \sum_{h=1}^{k} w_{t,h} x_{t,h}$
  Receive convex function ϕ_t from nature
  Update distribution

$$w_{t+1,h} = \prod_{\Delta_k}^{A_t} \left(w_t - \frac{2}{\beta} A_t^{-1} \nabla f_t\right) ,$$

where A_t and $\prod_{\Delta_k}^{A_t}$ are as in (9) and (10).

2.2 Online Newton Updates

Our analysis for Online Newton Updates (ONU) build on recent advances in Online Convex Optimization (OCO) [15, 1]. The analysis of ONU differs from the standard analysis of online Newton step [15] due to two reasons: first, our analysis focuses on the derived convex function $f_t : \Delta_k \mapsto \mathbb{R}$ instead of the original convex function $\phi_t : P \mapsto \mathbb{R}$, and second, our bounds are based on the L_∞ norm of ϕ_t instead of the L_2 norm, which can be substantially larger for high-dimensional problems.

Following [15], we consider convex functions ϕ_t which satisfy the α-exp-concavity property: there is a $\alpha > 0$ such that for $x \in P$, $\exp(-\alpha \phi_t(x))$ is a concave function . Note that α-exp-concave functions ϕ_t are more general than ones which have bounded gradients and Hessians which are strictly bounded away from 0, i.e., $\nabla^2 \phi_t \succeq H\mathbb{I}$ for some constant $H > 0$. As before, we assume that L_∞ norm of the gradient of ϕ_t are bounded above, i.e., $\|\nabla \phi_t\|_\infty \leq g_\infty$.

With these assumptions, Algorithm 2 presents the Online Newton Update (ONU) algorithm for Online Meta Optimization [15]. In essence, the algorithm takes a Newton-like step from the current iterate w_t, and then projects the vector to the feasible set Δ_k to obtain w_{t+1}. Note that the algorithm does not use the actual Hessian of f_t, but a matrix based on the outer product of the gradients defined as:

$$A_t = \sum_{\tau=1}^{t} \nabla f_t \nabla f_t^T + \epsilon \mathbb{I} , \tag{9}$$

where $\epsilon = \frac{k}{\beta^2 c^2}$. Further $\prod_{\Delta_k}^{A_t}$ is the projection onto Δ_k using the Mahalanobis distance induced by A_t, i.e.,

$$\prod_{\Delta_k}^{A_t} (\tilde{w}) = \underset{w \in \Delta_k}{\operatorname{argmin}} \, (w - \tilde{w})^T A_t^{-1} (w - \tilde{w}) . \tag{10}$$

We start our analysis by showing that if ϕ_t is α-exp-concave for $x \in P$, then f_t is α-exp-concave for $w \in \Delta_k$ for the same (set of) α.

Lemma 2 *If ϕ_t is α-exp-concave for some $\alpha > 0$, then f_t as defined in (5) is also α-exp-concave.*

PROOF. Let $h_t(w) = \exp(-\alpha f_t(w))$. The Hessian is given by

$$\begin{aligned}\nabla^2 h_t(w) &= [\alpha^2(\nabla f_t)(\nabla f_t)^T - \alpha\nabla^2 f_t]h_t(w)\\ &= X_t^T[\alpha^2(\nabla\phi_t)(\nabla\phi_t)^T - \alpha\nabla^2\phi_t]X_t h_t(w)\end{aligned}$$

Let $\psi_t(x) = \exp(-\alpha\phi_t(x))$. Since ϕ_t is α-exp-concave, the Hessian $\nabla^2\psi_t \preceq 0$, so that

$$[\alpha^2(\nabla\phi_t)(\nabla\phi_t)^T - \alpha\nabla^2\phi_t]\psi_t(x) \preceq 0 \,.$$

Let $B_t = [\alpha^2(\nabla\phi_t)(\nabla\phi_t)^T - \alpha\nabla^2\phi_t]$. Since $\psi_t(x) \geq 0$, we have

$$B_t \preceq 0 \quad \Rightarrow \quad X_t^T B_t X_t \preceq 0 \,,$$

so that $\nabla^2 h_t \preceq 0$ since $h_t(w) \geq 0$, implying h_t is α-exp-concave. □

We now establish a result, similar to Lemma 3 in [15], but using the L_∞ bound g_∞ and the fact that $\|x\|_1 \leq c$ for $x \in P$.

Lemma 3 *For $\beta \leq \min\{\frac{1}{8cg_\infty}, \alpha\}$, for any $w, w_t \in \Delta_k$, we have*

$$\begin{aligned}f_t(w) \geq{}& f_t(w_t) + \nabla f_t(w_t)^T(w - w_t)\\ &+ \frac{\beta}{4}(w - w_t)^T\nabla f_t(w_t)\nabla f_t(w_t)^T(w - w_t) \,.\end{aligned} \tag{11}$$

PROOF. Since $\beta \leq \alpha$, following the proof of Lemma 3 in [15] we have

$$f_t(w) \geq f_t(w_t) - \frac{1}{\beta}\log[1 - \beta\nabla f_t(w_t)^T(w - w_t)] \,.$$

Now, by Hölder's inequality,

$$|\beta\nabla f_t(w_t)^T(w - w_t)| \leq \beta\|\nabla f_t(w_t)\|_\infty\|w - w_t\|_1 \leq 2\beta c g_\infty \leq \frac{1}{4} \,.$$

Since $-\log(1-z) \geq z + \frac{1}{4}z^2$ for $|z| \leq \frac{1}{4}$, using it for $z = \beta\nabla f_t(w_t)^T(w - w_t)$ completes the proof. □

We now present the main result for ONU:

Theorem 2 *For any sequence of α-exp-concave functions ϕ_t such that $\|\nabla\phi_t\|_\infty \leq g_\infty$ for $x \in P$ where $\|x\|_1 \leq c$, for $T \geq 2a$ where $a = \frac{32 g_\infty}{c^2}$, we have the following regret bound:*

$$\sum_{t=1}^T f_t(w_t) - \min_{w\in\Delta_k}\sum_{t=1}^T f_t(w) \leq k\left(8cg_\infty + \frac{1}{\alpha}\right)\log\frac{eT}{a} \,. \tag{12}$$

PROOF. Using Lemma 3 and using the proof of Theorem 2 in [15], we have

$$\sum_{t=1}^T R_t \leq \frac{1}{\beta}\sum_{t=1}^T \nabla_t^T A_t^{-1}\nabla_t + \frac{\beta}{4}(w_t - w)^T(A_1 - \nabla_1\nabla_1^T)(w_1 - w) \,,$$

where $R_t = f_t(w_t) - f_t(w)$ for any $w \in \Delta_k$, $\nabla_t = \nabla f_t$, and $A_t = \sum_{\tau=1}^t \nabla_\tau\nabla_\tau^T + \epsilon\mathbb{I}$ as in (9). Since $A_1 - \nabla_1\nabla_1^T = \epsilon\mathbb{I}$, $\|w_1 - w\|_2^2 \leq 4c^2$, and $\epsilon = \frac{k}{\beta^2 c^2}$, we have

$$\begin{aligned}\sum_{t=1}^T R_t &\leq \frac{1}{\beta}\sum_{t=1}^T \nabla_t^T A_t^{-1}\nabla_t + \frac{\beta}{4}\epsilon\|w_1 - w\|_2^2\\ &\leq \frac{1}{\beta}\sum_{t=1}^T \nabla_t^T A_t^{-1}\nabla_t + \frac{k}{\beta} \,.\end{aligned}$$

Since $\|\nabla f_t\| \leq \sqrt{k}\|\nabla f_t\|_\infty \leq \sqrt{k}cg_\infty$, from Lemma 11 in [15], we have

$$\sum_{t=1}^T \nabla_t^T A_t^{-1}\nabla_t \leq k\log\left(\frac{kc^2 g_\infty^2 T}{\epsilon} + 1\right) \leq k\log\left(\frac{T}{2a} + 1\right) ,$$

where we have used $\epsilon = \frac{k}{\beta^2 c^2}$, $\beta \leq \frac{1}{8cg_\infty}$, and $a = \frac{32 g_\infty}{c^2}$. For $T \geq 2a$, $\frac{T}{2a} + 1 \leq \frac{T}{a}$. Plugging everything back, we have

$$\sum_{t=1}^T R_t \leq \frac{k}{\beta}\left(\log\frac{T}{a} + 1\right) = \frac{k}{\beta}\log\frac{eT}{a} \,.$$

Since $\beta = \min\{\frac{1}{8cg_\infty}, \alpha\}$, we have

$$\frac{1}{\beta} = \max\left\{8cg_\infty, \frac{1}{\alpha}\right\} \leq 8cg_\infty + \frac{1}{\alpha} \,.$$

Plugging this upper bound back completes the proof. □

3. META OPTIMIZATION FOR PORTFOLIO SELECTION

We consider a stock market consisting of n stocks $\{s_1, \ldots, s_n\}$ over a span of T periods. For ease of exposition, we will consider a period to be a day, but the analysis presented in the paper holds for any valid definition of a 'period,' such as an hour or a month. Let $r_t(i)$ denote the *price relative* of stock s_i in day t, i.e., the multiplicative factor by which the price of s_i changes in day t. Hence, $r_t(i) > 1$ implies a gain, $r_t(i) < 1$ implies a loss, and $r_t(i) = 1$ implies the price remained unchanged. We assume $r_t(i) > 0$ for all i, t. Let $r_t = \langle r_t(1), \ldots, r_t(n)\rangle$ denote the vector of price relatives for day t, and let $r_{1:t}$ denote the collection of such price relative vectors upto and including day t. A portfolio $x_t = \langle x_t(1), \ldots, x_t(n)\rangle$ on day t can be viewed as a probability distribution over the stocks that prescribes investing $x_t(i)$ fraction of the current wealth in stock $s_t(i)$. Note that the portfolio x_t has to be decided before knowing r_t which will be revealed only at the end of the day. The multiplicative gain in wealth at the end of day t, is then simply $r_t^T x_t = \sum_{i=1}^n r_t(i)x_t(i)$. Given a sequence of price relatives $r_{1:t-1} = \{r_1, \ldots, r_{t-1}\}$ upto day $(t-1)$, the sequential portfolio selection problem in day t is to determine a portfolio x_t based on past performance of the stocks. At the end of day t, r_t is revealed and the actual performance of x_t gets determined by $r_t^T x_t$. Over a period of T days, for a sequence of portfolios $x_{1:T} = \{x_1, \ldots, x_t\}$, the multiplicative gain in wealth is then

$$S(x_{1:T}, r_{1:T}) = \prod_{t=1}^T\left(r_t^T x_t\right) \,. \tag{13}$$

The above problem can be viewed as an Online Convex Optimization (OCO), where the convex function $\phi_t(x_t) = -\log(r_t^T x_t)$, and the cumulative loss over T iterations is

$$\sum_{t=1}^T \phi_t(x_t) = -\sum_{t=1}^T \log(r_t^T x_t) = -\log S(x_{1:T}, r_{1:T}) \,. \tag{14}$$

There are numerous algorithms in the literature for picking the portfolio x_t on a given day based on past information $r_{1:(t-1)}$ [10, 16, 9, 1, 5]. Instead of proposing new algorithms for the task, we focus on meta optimization to combine the portfolios from a pool of base algorithms from the literature. We now specialize the general case results and algorithms of Section 2 to the task of portfolio selection.

Consider k base algorithms $\{A_1, \ldots, A_k\}$ for portfolio selection where algorithm A_h generates a portfolio $x_{t,h} \in \Delta_n$ based on the past information $r_{1:(t-1)}$. Recall that our analysis does not impose any other constraints on the base algorithms and so they can be based on theoretically well grounded ideas [10, 16, 1] or good heuristics [5]. Given the set of base portfolios $X_t = [x_{t,1} \cdots x_{t,k}]$, the goal of the meta algorithm is to choose $w_t \in \Delta_k$ to construct the portfolio $x_t^{w_t} = X_t w_t$ and subsequently incur loss $f_t(w_t) = \phi_t(x_t^{w_t}) = -\log(r_t^T x_t^{w_t}) = -\log(r_t^T X_t w_t)$. Since a portfolio $x \in \Delta_n$, we have $c = \|x\|_1 = 1$. Among all price relatives over all stocks, let $r_{\min} = \min_{i,t} r_t(i) > 0$ and let $r_{\max} = \max_{i,t} r_t(i)$. Since $\nabla\phi_t(x) = -\frac{r_t}{r_t^T x}$, $\|\nabla\phi_t(x)\|_\infty \leq \frac{r_{\max}}{r_{\min}} = g_\infty$. For convenience, we use $\bar{u} = \frac{r_{\max}}{r_{\min}}$. For our subsequent analysis, we note that

$$\nabla f_t(w_t) = -\frac{X_t^T r_t}{r_t^T X_t w_t} . \tag{15}$$

Gradient Updates: Since $\nabla\phi_t(x)$ for portfolio selection is a positive vector, one can define the loss vector for OGU in Algorithm 1 as follows:

$$\ell_t = \frac{\nabla f_t(w_t)}{c g_\infty} = -\frac{1}{2\bar{u}} \frac{X_t^T r_t}{r_t^T X_t w_t} + e . \tag{16}$$

With this modification, the OGU in Algorithm 1 has the following guarantee:

Corollary 1 *For any sequence of price relatives $r_{1:T}$ and any sequence of base portfolios $X_{1:T}$, the log-wealth accumulated by Algorithm 1 choosing adaptive w_t satisfies the following regret bound:*

$$\max_{w \in \Delta_k} \sum_{t=1}^{T} \log(r_t^T X_t w) - \sum_{t=1}^{T} \log(r_t^T X_t w_t) \leq \bar{u}\left(\sqrt{2T \log k} + \log k\right) . \tag{17}$$

The proof follows from a direct application of Theorem 1. We briefly discuss the implication of the fact that the wealth accumulated by the adaptive meta algorithm will be competitive with any fixed combination strategy chosen in hindsight. If one of the base algorithms is *universal* [10, 16, 4, 17, 9], i.e., competitive with best constant rebalanced portfolio (CRP) [10, 4] in hindsight so that

$$\max_{x \in \Delta_n} \sum_{t=1}^{T} \log(r_t^T x) - \sum_{t=1}^{T} \log(r_t^T x_t) = o(T) , \tag{18}$$

then our meta algorithm will also be universal. Also, since the best CRP would outperform the best stock, having an universal algorithm in the pool is sufficient to ensure the meta algorithm will be competitive with the single best stock in hindsight. More generally, the meta algorithm will be competitive with the best convex combination of the base algorithms, which is guaranteed to be better than the best base algorithm in the pool (Figure 1).

Newton Updates: We start our analysis with the following result:

Lemma 4 *$\phi_t(x) = -\log(r_t^T x)$ is a α-exp-concave function for $\alpha \in (0, 1]$.*

PROOF. Let $\psi_t(x) = \exp(-\alpha\phi_t(x)) = (r_t^T x)^\alpha$. A direct calculation shows the Hessian to be

$$\nabla^2\psi_t(x) = \alpha(\alpha - 1)\frac{r_t r_t^T}{r_t^T x}\psi_t(x) ,$$

which is negative semi-definite for $\alpha > 0$ if $\alpha \in (0, 1]$. □

As a result, Algorithm 2 can be applied as a meta algorithm for the portfolio selection problem. As before, $c = 1, g_\infty = \bar{u}$. Choosing $\alpha = 1$, $\beta = \min\{\frac{1}{8\bar{u}}, \alpha\} = \frac{1}{8\bar{u}}$ since $\bar{u} = \frac{r_{\max}}{r_{\min}} \geq 1$. Hence, $\frac{1}{\beta} = 8\bar{u}$. Further, $a = \frac{32 g_\infty}{c^2} = 32\bar{u}$, so that $\frac{a}{e} \leq 12\bar{u}$. Using the above values in Algorithm 2, from Theorem 2 we have the following result:

Corollary 2 *For any sequence of price relatives $r_{1:T}$ and any sequence of base portfolios $X_{1:t}$, the log-wealth accumulated by Algorithm 2 choosing adaptive w_t satisfies the following regret bound:*

$$\max_{w \in \Delta_k} \sum_{t=1}^{T} \log(r_t^T X_t w) - \sum_{t=1}^{T} \log(r_t^T X_t w_t) \leq 8k\bar{u} \log \frac{T}{12\bar{u}} . \tag{19}$$

As before, the proof follows from a direct application of Theorem 2. The bound has the same optimality properties as discussed in the context of OGU above. In fact, the worst case regret of ONU grows as $O(\log T)$ as opposed to $O(\sqrt{T})$ for OGU. The bound for OGU can in fact be sharpened in this setting by suitably modifying the OGU algorithm and analysis using the fact that the Hessian $\nabla^2 f_t$ is bounded away from 0 under the assumption $\min_{i,t} r_{i,t} > 0$.

4. EXPERIMENTAL RESULTS

We conducted extensive experiments on two financial data-sets to establish how effective Online Meta Optimization can be carried out by OGU and ONU. In this section, we describe the datasets that were chosen for the experiments, the algorithms, the parameter choices and most importantly the results of our experiments.

Datasets: The experiments were conducted on two major datasets: the New York Stock Exchange dataset (NYSE) [10] and a Standard & Poor's 500 (S&P 500) dataset. The NYSE dataset consists of 36 stocks with data accumulated over a period of 22 years from July 3, 1962 to Dec 31 1984. The dataset captures the bear market that lasted between January 1973 and December 1974. However, all of the 36 stocks increase in value in the 22-year run.

The S&P500 dataset that we used for our experiments consists of 263 stocks which were present in the S&P500 index in December 2010 and were alive since January 1990. This period of 21 years from 1990 to 2010 covers bear and bull markets of recent times.

Methodology: We ran a pool of base portfolio selection algorithms and the Meta Algorithms on the datasets (NYSE and S&P500). For our experiments, this pool included universal and non-universal algorithms. We start by briefly describing the base algorithms and the Meta Algorithms.

4.1 Base Algorithms

Of the base algorithms that we used for our experiments UP, EG and ONS are *universal* while Anticor and its variant are heuristics.

Universal Portfolios (UP): The key idea behind Cover's [10] UP is to maintain a distribution over all Constant Rebalanced Portfolios (CRPs) and perform a Bayesian update after observing every r_t. Each CRP q is a distribution over n stocks and hence lies in the n-simplex, one uses a distribution $\mu(q)$ over the n-simplex. The universal portfolio x_t is defined as:

$$x_t(i) = \frac{\int_q q(i) S_{t-1}(q, r_{1:t-1})\mu(q)dq}{\int_q S_{t-1}(q, r_{1:t-1})\mu(q)dq} . \tag{20}$$

UP has a regret of $O(\log T)$ with respect to the best CRP in hindsight. However, the updates for UP are computationally prohibitive.

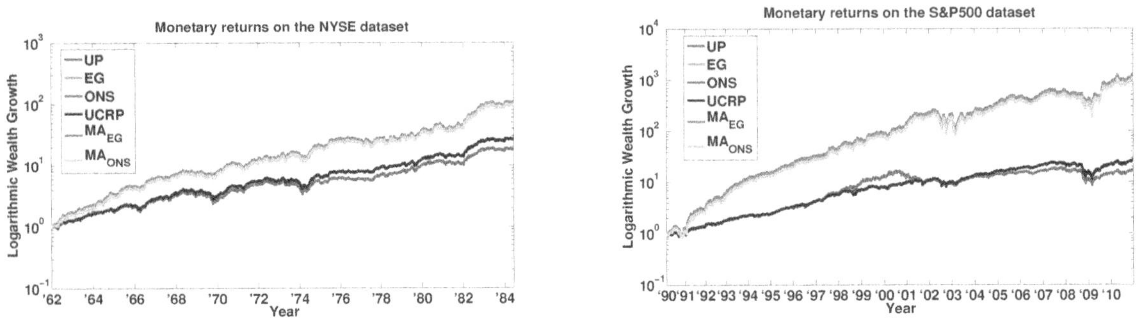

(a) Monetary returns on NYSE. (b) Monetary returns on S&P500.

Figure 2: Monetary returns of the Meta Algorithms, MA $_{EG}$ and MA $_{ONS}$ for \$1 investment, is competitive with the best performing base algorithm ONS in this case(best viewed in color).

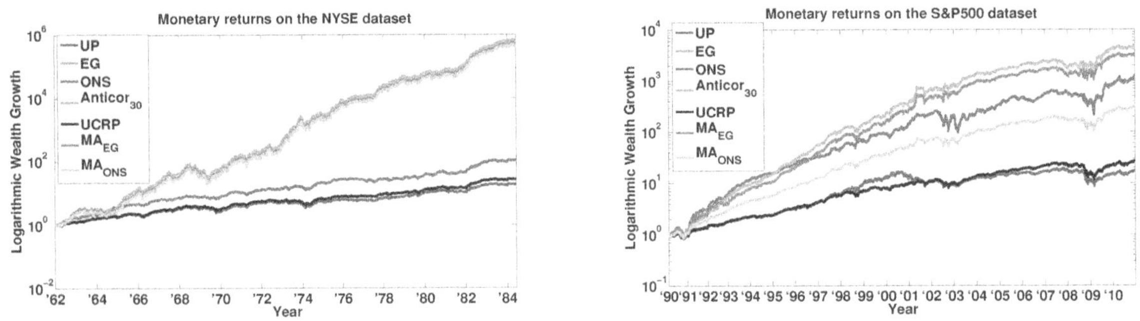

(a) Monetary returns on NYSE. (b) Monetary returns on S&P500.

Figure 3: Monetary returns of the meta algorithms(MA$_{EG}$, MA$_{ONS}$) when Anticor$_{30}$ is added to the pool of base algorithms. Anticor$_{30}$ performs best and particularly MA$_{EG}$ is able to track Anticor$_{30}$ (best viewed in color).

Exponentiated Gradient (EG): Exponentiated Gradient (EG) [16] scales linearly with the number of stocks but is weaker in regret than UP. The EG investment strategy was introduced and analyzed by [16]. At the start of day t, the algorithm computes its new portfolio vector x_t such that it stays close to x_{t-1} and does well on the price relatives r_{t-1} for the previous day. The updated portfolio turns out to be

$$x_t(i) = \frac{x_{t-1}(i)\exp(\eta r_{t-1}(i)/x_{t-1}^T r_{t-1})}{\sum_{i'=1}^{n} x_{t-1}(i')\exp(\eta r_{t-1}(i')/x_{t-1}^T r_{t-1})}. \tag{21}$$

where $\eta > 0$ is a parameter called the learning rate.

Online Newton Step (ONS): ONS uses a Newton step based method to compute the portfolio for the next iteration [1]. The Online Newton Step method can be shown to achieve sublinear regret and hence is an universal strategy.

The ONS algorithm uses following portfolio update method for round $t > 1$:

$$x_t = \prod_{\Delta_n}^{\mathbf{A_{t-1}}} \left(x_{t-1} - \frac{1}{\beta}\mathbf{A}_{t-1}^{-1}\nabla_{t-1} \right) \tag{22}$$

where $\nabla_t = \nabla[\log(x_t \cdot r_t)]$, $\mathbf{A}_t = \sum_{\tau=1}^{t} \nabla_\tau \nabla_\tau + \mathbb{I}$, β is a non-negative constant, and $\prod_{\Delta_n}^{\mathbf{A_{t-1}}}$ is the projection onto the n-simplex Δ_n.

Anticor: Anticor is a heuristic based method which does not confirm to the *universal* property for portfolio selection algorithms [5]. Here learning the best stocks (to invest money in) is done by exploiting the volatility of the market and the statistical relationship between the stocks. It implements the 'reversal to the mean' market phenomenon rather aggressively. One of the most important parameters for Anticor is the window length win. The version of Anticor implemented, works with two most recent windows of length win. The strategy is to move money from a stock i to stock j if the growth rate of stock i is greater than the growth rate of j in the most recent window. An additional condition that requires to be satisfied is the existence of a positive correlation between stock i in the second last window and stock j in the last window. For more details on the Anticor algorithm please refer to [5]. The experiments with different variations of the Anticor algorithm in [5], brought to the fore the exceptional empirical performance improvement that this heuristic-based approach can achieve over theoretically motivated approaches.

The performance of Anticor is sensitive to the window size win [5]. One way to address this issue is to adaptively learn the weights and invest in a weighted version of all Anticor$_{win}$s where $win \leqslant W$. We consider a variant BAH(Anticor$_W$), which maintains a uniform buy-and-hold investment on the Anticor$_{win}$, $win \in [2, W]$.

4.2 Meta Algorithms

Meta Algorithms (MAs) are constructed by combining a pool of base algorithms. Meta algorithm MA$_{EG}$ uses the gradient updates and this follows from OGU in Algorithm 1 and Meta Algorithm MA$_{ONS}$ uses Newton updates and follows from ONU in Algorithm 2. Meta Algorithms MA$_{EG}$ and MA$_{ONS}$ are universal if at least one of the base algorithms in their pool is universal.

Additionaly, we used two other versions of Meta Algorithms for our experiments: MA$_{Anticor}$ and MA$_{BAH}$. MA$_{Anticor}$ is a Meta Algorithm version of Anticor. Like Anticor it works with differ-

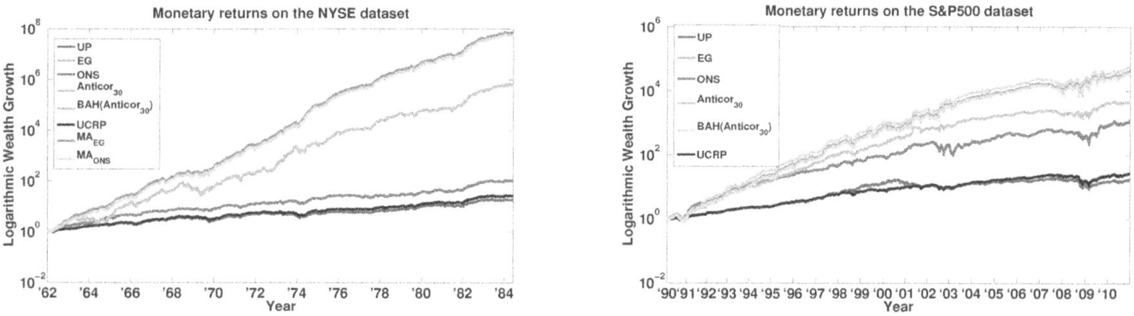

(a) Monetary returns on NYSE.

(b) Monetary returns on S&P500.

Figure 4: Monetary returns of the meta algorithms(MA$_{EG}$, MA$_{ONS}$). BAH(Anticor$_{30}$)is added to the pool of base algorithms. The Meta Algorithms continue to track the best algorithm in the pool.(best viewed in color).

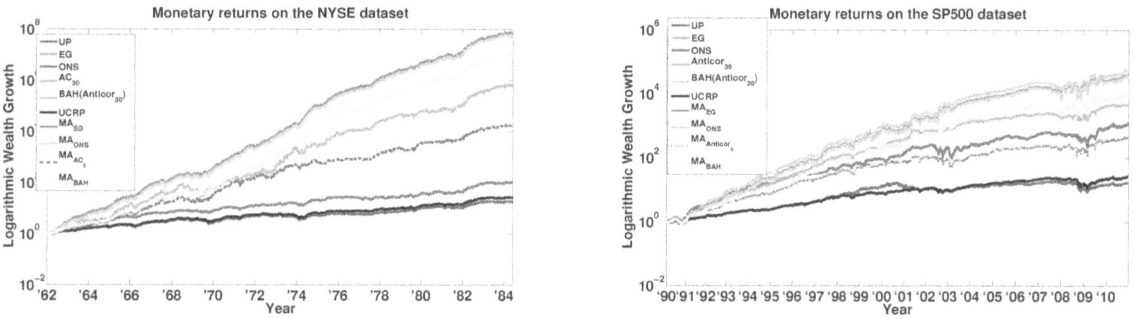

(a) Monetary returns on NYSE.

(b) Monetary returns on S&P500.

Figure 5: Monetary returns of the meta algorithms(MA$_{EG}$, MA$_{ONS}$, MA$_{Anticor}$, MA$_{BAH}$). MA$_{EG}$ performs best while MA$_{Anticor}$ doesn't fare well.(best viewed in color).

ent window lengths over the pool of base algorithms. MA$_{BAH}$ does a uniform buy-and-hold over the base algorithms and does not move money between the algorithms. Unlike MA$_{EG}$ and MA$_{ONS}$, MA$_{Anticor}$ and MA$_{BAH}$ have no performance guarantees.

4.3 Results

The experimental setup can be broadly categorized into three subcategories: (a) Universal Pool, (b) Mixed Pool 1 and (c) Mixed Pool 2 based on the pool of base algorithms that were used by the MAs.

Universal Pool: In the Universal Pool setup, the MAs worked with universal base algorithms UP, EG, and ONS. Figure 2 shows the wealth accumulated by the universal base algorithms on the NYSE and S&P500 datasets. We see that ONS performs best, followed by EG and UP. Figure 2 also shows that the two Meta Algorithms MA$_{EG}$ and MA$_{ONS}$ are able to catch up with the performance of ONS, the best performing algorithm in the pool.

Mixed Pool 1: The Mixed Pool 1 is formed by adding Anticor to the Universal Pool of base algorithms. In Figure 3, we see that there is a stark difference in the wealth garnered by Anticor as compared to the Universal Pool of base algorithms. While for the NYSE dataset, Anticor's wealth is of the order of 10^6 (almost 10^4 times the wealth gathered by ONS), for S&P500, the wealth reaches the order of 10^3. MA$_{EG}$ is able to catch up with the performance of Anticor for both the datasets. MA$_{ONS}$ is very slightly behind Anticor and MA$_{EG}$ on the NYSE dataset. On S&P500, the base algorithm ONS outperforms MA$_{ONS}$ (which is still better than UP and EG by a sybstantial margin).

Mixed Pool 2: To further emphasize the strength of the MAs we formed Mixed Pool 2 of base algorithms by adding BAH(Anticor$_W$) to Mixed Pool 1. BAH(Anticor$_W$) outperforms Anticor$_{win}$ (for $win \leqslant W$), EG, UP, and ONS. Figure 4 shows that the wealth achieved by MA$_{EG}$ and MA$_{ONS}$ with BAH(Anticor$_W$) in the pool, is almost as much as BAH(Anticor$_W$) itself. Thus we see that Meta Algorithms, MA$_{EG}$ and MA$_{ONS}$ are competitive with the best base algorithm in all the three experimental setups.

Figure 5, shows the performance of MA$_{Anticor}$ and MA$_{BAH}$ with the Mixed Pool 2 of base algorithms. The performance of the MA$_{Anticor}$ is inferior than both MA$_{EG}$ and MA$_{ONS}$. We could attribute this inferior performance to the inherent nature of Anticor which will tend to move money away from the base algorithms which are performing well. With a buy-and-hold version of MA called MA$_{BAH}$, the wealth gained is more than Anticor$_w$, but less than that of BAH(Anticor$_W$) and MA$_{EG}$ and MA$_{ONS}$.

Parameter choices: Parameter choices had to be made for the universal as well as non-universal base algorithms. For EG, we experimented with different learning rate (η) values and found $\eta = 0.05$ to be a good choice, validating the observations in [16]. For ONS, β value was chosen as 1. This gave better results than when β was chosen as a function of the market-variability (refer to [1] for details).

The window size w for Anticor$_{win}$ was taken to be 30. The performance of Anticor$_{win}$ is a function of win as demonstrated in [5]. BAH(Anticor$_W$) combines multiple Anticor$_{win}$ algorithms, $win \in [2, W]$ to harness the strength of these different versions. We choose $W = 30$ for our experiments which might not be the optimal value for the NYSE and S&P500 datasets. Hoever, it is observed that BAH(Anticor$_{30}$) surpasses all the base universal algo-

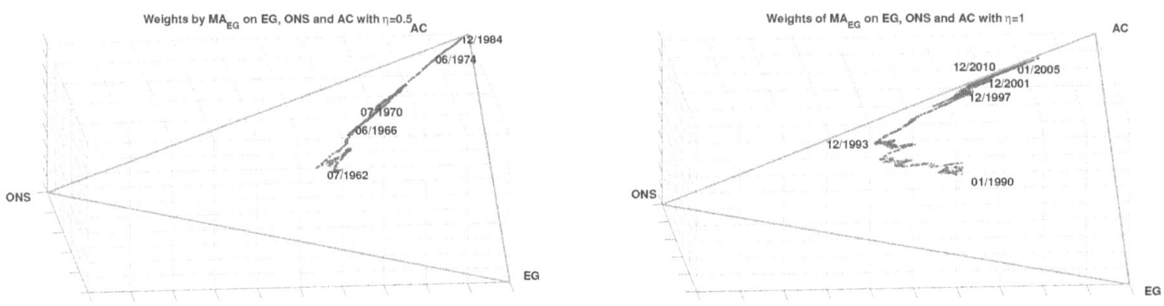

(a) NYSE: weights of MA_{EG} with η=0.5.

(b) S&P500: weights of MA_{EG} with η=1.

Figure 6: Traces the weights maintained by MA_{EG} on the base algorithms EG, ONS and AC for NYSE and S&P500 with η values 0.5 and 1 respectively(best viewed in color).

rithms and Anticor_{30} in terms of empirical performance and helps us establish that MA_{EG} and MA_{ONS} can always manage to track the best strategy even if it is a heuristic.

The rate at which MA_{EG} caught up with Anticor in terms of wealth increased as we increased the value of η. However, for very high values of η ($\eta \geqslant 50$), the increase in the wealth gathered by MA_{EG} changed by a small amount. For MA_{ONS}, the β value was chosen according to Lemma 3. $MA_{Anticor}$ was run with different window lengths. We plotted the results with a window length of 5, as this version was observed to perform reasonably well. It was observed that the performance of $MA_{Anticor}$ decreased as the window length was increased beyond 10 days.

APY and Volatility: Table 1 presents the monetary returns in dollars, APY and volatility of the universal and non-universal algorithms on the two datasets.

The wealth for the algorithms has been expressed as the final return on an initial investment of $1. The values given for MA_{EG} and MA_{ONS} are with Mixed Pool 2 of base algorithms. The top three final returns appear in bold-face.

APY: The Annual Percentage Yield (APY) of the algorithms were calculated based on the following formula:

$$\mathbf{APY} = \left[(\mathbf{Final/Initial})^{\frac{1}{\mathbf{T_{years}}}} - 1 \right] \times 100$$

where **Final** and **Initial** are the final return and initial investment respectively for $\mathbf{T_{years}}$. BAH(Anticor_{30}, MA_{EG} and MA_{ONS} have the top three (in the order mentioned) APY for both the datasets.

Volatility: Volatility of the Algorithms were calculated by taking the standard deviation of the sequence of daily wealth relatives (${x_t}^T r_t$) over $\mathbf{T_{years}}$. Anticor_{30} and BAH(Anticor_{30}) have more than twice the volatility of the base universal algorithms. MA_{EG} and MA_{ONS} have almost the same volatility as BAH(Anticor_{30}). This could be explained by the fact that the MAs try to track BAH(Anticor_{30}).

Figure 6 renders the path traced by MA_{EG} as a weighted combination of EG, ONS, and Anticor. Our experiments show that Anticor outperforms EG and ONS in terms of accumulated wealth by an overwhelming margin. Hence, we see that MA_{EG} converges towards the Anticor corner and the rate of convergence depends on the learning rate η. We also conducted experiments where we interchanged the weights of AC and ONS (switched corners) once every t' days. The value of t' was taken to be 500, 1000 and 2000 days for our experiments. Even after switching, MA_{EG} quickly learned that Anticor is the best performing strategy. This led MA_{EG} to automatically adjust its weight distribution over the base algoothms. MA_{EG} is sensitive to the volatility. Our experiments show that

Table 1: Monetary returns in dollars (per $1 investment), APY and volatility of universal and non-universal algorithms

Algorithm		NYSE	SP500
UP	wealth	18.56	17.42
	APY	14.20	15.36
	volatility	0.0089	0.0139
EG	wealth	27.10	26.83
	APY	16.18	17.88
	volatility	0.0085	0.0116
ONS	wealth	109.17	1217.39
	APY	23.78	42.65
	volatility	0.0113	0.0201
Anticor_{30}	wealth	617754.61	4769.39
	APY	83.32	52.73
	volatility	0.0284	0.0191
BAH(Anticor_{30})	wealth	**77626129.46**	**58591.86**
	APY	**128.37**	**73.14**
	volatility	0.0195	0.03296
MA_{EG}	wealth	**68381688.71**	**41678.69**
	APY	**127.06**	**70.21**
	volatility	0.0194	0.0287
MA_{ONS}	wealth	**61119978.64**	**37667.41**
	APY	**125.90**	**69.36**
	volatility	0.0194	0.0286

MA_{EG} might prefer ONS earlier on due to its low volatility (See Figure 6 (b)). But as the wealth accumulated by Anticor increases, it shifts its weight from ONS to Anticor.

5. CONCLUSIONS

In this paper, we have presented the idea of designing new Meta Algorithms which work with a pool of base algorithms for optimization. We have shown that solutions from multiple iterative algorithms can be combined by Meta Algorithms to outperform the single best base algorithm. We demonstrate the efficacy of the Meta Algorithms in the domain of Online Portfolio Selection. Detailed experiments over the NYSE and S&P500 datasets show that the Meta Algorithms MA_{EG} and MA_{ONS} beat the universal algorithms in terms of empirical performance but are still competitive with the best CRP in hindsight.

Although, the Meta Algorithms have exceptional performance,

they do not take into account the commission one has to pay while trading. This is also a shortcoming with the existing universal and non-universal portfolio selection algorithms [10] [16] [1] [5]. Most of these algorithms trade every stock every day which is not practical as one can incur huge amount of commission costs. As part of our future work, we would like to investigate if a sparse version of the meta algorithm can take care of commissions and yet achieve good empirical performance. Also, the current models for on-line portfolio selection do not model risk. Modeling risk and taking account of volatility of stocks is an interesting direction for our future work.

Acknowledgements: The research was supported by NSF CAREER award IIS-0953274, and NSF grants IIS-0916750, IIS-0812183, IIS-1029711, and NetSE-1017647. The authors also wish to thank Huahua Wang and Padmanabhan Balasubramanian for their help.

6. REFERENCES

[1] A. Agarwal, E. Hazan, S. Kale, and R. Schapire. Algorithms for portfolio management based on the newton method. *Proceedings of the 23rd International Conference on Machine Learning*, pages 9–16, 2006.

[2] S. Arora, E. Hazan, and S. Kale. The multiplicative update algorithm: A meta algorithm and applications. Technical report, Dept of Computer Science, Princeton University, 2005.

[3] A. Banerjee. On Bayesian bounds. In *Proceedings of the 23rd International Conference on Machine Learning*, 2006.

[4] A. Blum and A. Kalai. Universal portfolios with and without transaction costs. In *Proceedings of the 10th Annual Conference on Learning Theory*, 1997.

[5] A. Borodin, R. El-Yaniv, and V. Gogan. Can we learn to beat the best stock. *Journal of Artificial Intelligence Research*, 21:579–594, 2004.

[6] L. Breiman. Bagging predictors. *Machine Learning*, 24:123–140, 1996.

[7] L. Breiman. Random forests. *Machine Learning*, 45:5–32, 2001.

[8] N. Cesa-Bianchi, Y. Freund, D. P. Helmbold, D. Haussler, R. Schapire, and M. K. Warmuth. How to use expert advice. *Journal of the ACM*, 44(3):427–485, 1997.

[9] N. Cesa-Bianchi and G. Lugosi. *Prediction, Learning, and Games*. Cambridge University Press, 2006.

[10] T. Cover. Universal portfolios. *Mathematical Finance*, 1:1–29, 1991.

[11] Y. Freund and R. Schapire. Adaptive game playing using multiplicative weights. *Games and Economic Behavior*, 29:79–103, 1999.

[12] Y. Freund and R. E. Schapire. A decision-theoretic generalization of on-line learning and an application to boosting. *Journal of Computer and System Sciences*, 55(1):119–139, 1997.

[13] J. Friedman, T. Hastie, and R. Tibshirani. Additive logistic regression: A statistical view of boosting. *Annals of Statistics*, 2000.

[14] B. Fristedt and L. Gray. *A Modern Approach to Probability Theory*. Birkhauser Verlag, 1997.

[15] E. Hazan, A. Agarwal, and S. Kale. Logarithmic regret algorithms for online convex optimization. *Machine Learning*, 69(2-3):169–192, 2007.

[16] D. Helmbold, E. Scahpire, Y. Singer, and M. Warmuth. Online portfolio setection using multiplicative weights. *Mathematical Finance*, 8(4):325–347, 1998.

[17] A. Kalai and S. Vempala. Efficient algorithms for universal portfolios. *Journal of Machine Learning Research*, 3(3):423–440, 2002.

[18] A. Kalai and S. Vempala. Efficient algorithms for on-line optimization. *Journal of Computer and System Sciences*, 713:291–307, 2005.

[19] J. L. Kelly. A new interpretation of information rate. *Bell Systems Technical Journal*, 35:917–926, 1956.

[20] J. Kivinen and M. Warmuth. Exponentiated gradient versus gradient descent for linear predictors. *Information and Computation*, 132(1):1–64, 1997.

[21] O. Knill. Probability. Course notes from Caltech, 1994.

[22] N. Littlestone and M. Warmuth. The weighted majority algorithm. *Information and Computation*, 108:212–261, 1994.

[23] H. Markowitz. Portfolio selection. *Journal of Finance*, 7:77–91, 1952.

[24] T. Soule. Voting teams: A cooperative approach to non-typical problems. *Proceedings of the Genetic and Evolutionary Computation Conference*, pages 916–922, 1999.

[25] P. Tan, M. Steinbach, and V. Kumar. *Introduction to Data Mining, (First Edition)*. 2005.

[26] D. Williams. *Probability with Martingales*. Cambridge University Press, 1991.

[27] W. Yan, M. Sewell, and C. D. Clack. Learning to optimize profits beats predicting returns – comparing techniques for financial portfolio optimisation. *Proceedings of the Genetic and Evolutionary Computation Conference*, pages 1681–1688, 2008.

[28] Martin Zinkevich. Online convex programming and generalized infinitesimal gradient ascent. *Proceedings of the 20th International Conference on Machine Learning*, 2003.

Mining Closed Episodes with Simultaneous Events

Nikolaj Tatti, Boris Cule
ADReM, University of Antwerp, Antwerpen, Belgium
firstname.lastname@ua.ac.be

ABSTRACT

Sequential pattern discovery is a well-studied field in data mining. Episodes are sequential patterns describing events that often occur in the vicinity of each other. Episodes can impose restrictions to the order of the events, which makes them a versatile technique for describing complex patterns in the sequence. Most of the research on episodes deals with special cases such as serial, parallel, and injective episodes, while discovering general episodes is understudied.

In this paper we extend the definition of an episode in order to be able to represent cases where events often occur simultaneously. We present an efficient and novel miner for discovering frequent and closed general episodes. Such a task presents unique challenges. Firstly, we cannot define closure based on frequency. We solve this by computing a more conservative closure that we use to reduce the search space and discover the closed episodes as a postprocessing step. Secondly, episodes are traditionally presented as directed acyclic graphs. We argue that this representation has drawbacks leading to redundancy in the output. We solve these drawbacks by defining a subset relationship in such a way that allows us to remove the redundant episodes. We demonstrate the efficiency of our algorithm and the need for using closed episodes empirically on synthetic and real-world datasets.

Categories and Subject Descriptors

H.2.8 [**Database management**]: Database applications—Data mining; G.2.2 [**Discrete mathematics**]: Graph theory

General Terms

Algorithms, Theory

Keywords

Frequent episodes, Closed episodes, Depth-first search

1. INTRODUCTION

Discovering interesting patterns in data sequences is a popular aspect of data mining. An episode is a sequential pattern representing a set of events that reoccur in a sequence [14]. In its most general form, an episode also imposes a partial order on the events. This allows great flexibility in describing complex interactions between the events in the sequence.

Existing research in episode mining is dominated by two special cases: parallel episodes, patterns where the order of the events does not matter, and serial episodes, requiring that the events must occur in one given order. Proposals have been made (see Section 2) for discovering episodes with partial orders, but these approaches impose various limitations on the events. In fact, to our knowledge, there is no published work giving an explicit description of a miner for general episodes.

We believe that there are two main reasons why general episodes have attracted less interest: Firstly, implementing a miner is surprisingly difficult: testing whether an episode occurs in the sequence is an **NP**-complete problem. Secondly, the fact that episodes are such a rich pattern type leads to a severe pattern explosion.

Another limitation of episodes is that they do not properly address simultaneous events. However, sequences containing such events are frequently encountered, in cases such as, for example, sequential data generated by multiple sensors and then collected into one stream. In such a setting, if two events, say a and b, often occur simultaneously, existing approaches will depict this pattern as a parallel episode $\{a, b\}$, which will only tell the user that these two events often occur near each other, in no particular order. This is a major limitation, since the actual pattern contains much more information.

In this paper we propose a novel and practical algorithm for mining frequent closed episodes that properly handles simultaneous events. Such a task poses several challenges.

Firstly, we can impose four different relationships between two events a and b: (1) the order of a and b does not matter, (2) events a and b should occur at the same time, (3) b should occur after a, and (4) b should occur after or at the same time as a. We extend the definition of an episode to handle all these cases. In further text, we consider events simultaneous only if they occur exactly at the same time. However, we can easily adjust our framework to consider events simultaneous if they occur within a chosen time interval.

Secondly, a standard approach for representing a partial order of the events is by using a directed acyclic graph

(DAG). The mining algorithm would then discover episodes by adding nodes and edges. However, we point out that such a representation has drawbacks. One episode may be represented by several graphs and the subset relationship based on the graphs is not optimal. This ultimately leads to outputting redundant patterns. We will address this problem.

Thirdly, we attack the problem of pattern explosion by using closed patterns. There are two particular challenges with closed episodes. Firstly, we point out that we cannot define a unique closure for an episode, that is, an episode may have several maximal episodes with the same frequency. Secondly, the definition of a closure requires a subset relationship, and computing the subset relationship between episodes is **NP**-hard.

We mine patterns using a depth-first search. An episode is represented by a DAG and we explore the patterns by adding nodes and edges. To reduce the search space we use the *instance-closure* of episodes. While it is not guaranteed that an instance-closed episode is actually closed, using such episodes will greatly trim the pattern space. Finally, the actual filtering for closed episodes is done in a post-processing step. We introduce techniques for computing the subset relationship, distinguishing the cases where we can do a simple test from the cases where we have to resort to recursive enumeration. This filtering will remove all redundancies resulting from using DAGs for representing episodes.

The rest of the paper is organised as follows: In Section 2, we discuss the most relevant related work. In Section 3, we present the main notations and concepts. Section 4 introduces the notion of closure in the context of episodes. Our algorithm is presented in detail in Sections 5, 6 and 7. In Section 8 we present the results of our experiments, before presenting our conclusions in Section 9. The proofs of the theorems can be found in the Appendix[1] and the code of the algorithm is available online[2].

2. RELATED WORK

The first attempt at discovering frequent subsequences, or serial episodes, was made by Wang et al. [22]. The dataset consisted of a number of sequences, and a pattern was considered interesting if it was long enough and could be found in a sufficient number of sequences. A complete solution to a more general problem was later provided by Agrawal and Srikant [2] using an APRIORI-style algorithm [1].

Looking for frequent general episodes in a single event sequence was first proposed by Mannila et al. [14]. The WINEPI algorithm finds all episodes that occur in a sufficient number of windows of fixed length. Specific algorithms were given for the case of parallel and serial episodes. However, no algorithm for detecting general episodes was provided.

Some research has gone into outputting only closed subsequences, where a sequence is considered closed if it is not properly contained in any other sequence which has the same frequency. Yan et al. [23], Tzvetkov et al. [20], and Wang and Han [21] proposed methods for mining such closed patterns, while Garriga [5] further reduced the output by post-processing it and representing the patterns using partial orders.[3] Harms et al. [12], meanwhile, experiment with closed serial episodes. In another attempt to trim the output, Garofalakis et al. [8] proposed a family of algorithms called SPIRIT which allow the user to define regular expressions that specify the language that the discovered patterns must belong to.

Pei et al. [17], and Tatti and Cule [19] considered restricted versions of our problem setup. The former approach assumes a dataset of sequences where the same label can occur only once. Hence, an episode can contain only unique labels. The latter pointed out the problem of defining a proper subset relationship between general episodes and tackled it by considering only episodes where two nodes having the same label had to be connected. In our work, we impose no restrictions on the labels of events making up the episodes.

In this paper we use frequency based on a sliding window as it is defined for WINEPI. However, we can easily adopt our approach for other monotonically decreasing measures, as well as to a setup where the data consists of many (short) sequences instead of a single long one. Mannila et al. propose MINEPI [14], an alternative interestingness measure for an episode, where the support is defined as the number of minimal windows. Unfortunately, this measure is not monotonically decreasing. However, the issue can be fixed by defining support as the maximal number of non-overlapping minimal windows [13, 18]. Zhou et al. [24] proposed mining closed serial episodes based on the MINEPI method. However, the paper did not address the non-monotonicity issue of MINEPI.

Alternative interestingness measures, either statistically motivated or aimed to remove bias towards smaller episodes, were made by Garriga [4], Méger and Rigotti [15], Gwadera et al. [9, 10], Calders et al. [3], Cule et al. [7], and Tatti [18].

Using episodes to discover simultaneous events has, to our knowledge, not been done yet. However, this work is somewhat related to efforts made in discovering sequential patterns in multiple streams [6, 11, 16]. Here, it is possible to discover a pattern wherein two events occur simultaneously, as long as they occur in separate streams.

3. EPISODES WITH SIMULTANEOUS EVENTS

We begin this section by introducing the basic concepts that we will use throughout the paper. First we will describe our dataset.

DEFINITION 1 A *sequence event* $e = (id(e), lab(e), ts(e))$ is a tuple consisting of three entries, a unique id number $id(e)$, a label $lab(e)$, and a time stamp integer $ts(e)$. We will assume that if $id(e) > id(f)$, then $ts(e) \geq ts(f)$. A *sequence* is a collection of sequence events ordered by their ids.

Note that we are allowing multiple events to have the same time stamp even when their labels are equivalent. For the sake of simplicity, we will use the notation $s_1 \cdots s_N$ to mean a sequence $((1, s_1, 1), \ldots, (N, s_N, N))$. We will also write $s_1 \cdots (s_i s_{i+1}) \cdots s_N$ to mean the sequence

$$((1, s_1, 1), \ldots, (i, s_i, i), (i + 1, s_{i+1}, i), \ldots, (N, s_N, N - 1)).$$

This means that s_i and s_{i+1} have equal time stamps.

Our next step is to define patterns we are interested in.

DEFINITION 2 An *episode event* e is a tuple consisting of two entries, a unique id number $id(e)$ and a label $lab(e)$.

[1] http://adrem.ua.ac.be/publications

[2] http://adrem.ua.ac.be/implementations

[3] Despite their name, the partial orders discovered by Garriga are different from general episodes.

An *episode graph* G is a directed acyclic graph (DAG). The graph may have two types of edges: *weak edges* $WE(G)$ and *proper edges* $PE(G)$.

An *episode* consists of a collection of episode events, an episode graph, and a surjective mapping from episode events to the nodes of the graph which we will denote by $nd(e)$. A proper edge from node v to node w in the episode graph implies that the events of v must occur before the events of w, while a weak edge from v to w implies that the events of w may occur either at the same time as those of v or later.

We will assume that the nodes of G are indexed and we will use the notation $nd(G, i)$ to refer to the ith node in G.

When there is no danger of confusion, we will use the same letter to denote an episode and its graph. Note that we are allowing multiple episode events to share the same node even if these events have the same labels.

Definition 3 Given an episode G and a node n, we define $lab(n) = \{lab(e) \mid nd(e) = n\}$ to be the multiset of labels associated with the node. Given two multisets of labels X and Y we write $X \leq_{lex} Y$ if X is lexicographically smaller than or equal to Y. We also define $lab(G)$ to be the multiset of all labels in G.

Definition 4 A node n in an episode graph is a *descendant* of a node m if there is a path from m to n. If there is a path containing a proper edge we will call n a *proper descendant* of m. We similarly define a *(proper) ancestor*. A node n is a *source* if it has no ancestors. A node n is a *proper source* if it has no proper ancestors. We denote all sources of an episode G by $src(G)$.

We are now ready to give a precise definition of an occurrence of a pattern in a sequence.

Definition 5 Given a sequence s and an episode G, we say that s covers G if there exists an *injective* mapping m from the episode events to the sequence events such that

1. labels are respected, $lab(m(e)) = lab(e)$,
2. events sharing a same node map to events with the same time stamp, in other words, $nd(e) = nd(f)$ implies $ts(m(e)) = ts(m(f))$,
3. weak edges are respected, if $nd(e)$ is a descendant of $nd(f)$, then $ts(m(e)) \geq ts(m(f))$,
4. proper edges are respected, if $nd(e)$ is a proper descendant of $nd(f)$, then $ts(m(e)) > ts(m(f))$.

Note that this definition allows us to abuse notation and map graph nodes directly to time stamps, that is, given a graph node n we define $ts(m(n)) = ts(m(e))$, where $nd(e) = n$.

Consider the first three episodes in Figure 1. A sequence $ab(cd)$ covers G_1 and G_3 but not G_2 (proper edge (c, d) is violated). A sequence $(ab)cd$ covers G_1 and G_2 but not G_3.

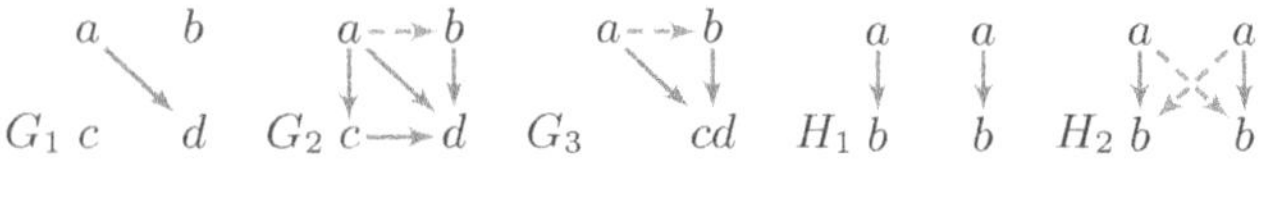

Figure 1: Toy episodes. Proper edges are drawn solid. Weak edges are drawn dashed.

Finally, we are ready to define support of an episode based on fixed windows. This definition corresponds to the definition used in Winepi [14]. The support is monotonically decreasing which allows us to do effective pruning while discovering frequent episodes.

Definition 6 Given a sequence s and two integers i and j we define a *subsequence*

$$s[i, j] = \{e \in s \mid i \leq ts(e) \leq j\}$$

containing all events occurring between i and j.

Definition 7 Given a window size ρ and an episode s, we define the *support* of an episode G in s, denoted $fr(G; s)$, to be the number of windows of size ρ in s covering the episode,

$$fr(G; s) = |\{s[i, i + \rho - 1] \mid s[i, i + \rho - 1] \text{ covers } G\}|.$$

We will use $fr(G)$ whenever s is clear from the context. An episode is *σ-frequent* (or simply *frequent*) if its support is higher or equal than some given threshold σ.

Consider a sequence *abcdacbd* and set the window size $\rho = 4$. There are 2 windows covering episode G_1 (given in Figure 1), namely $s[1, 4]$ and $s[5, 8]$. Hence $fr(G_1) = 2$.

Theorem 8 *Testing whether a sequence s covers an episode G is an **NP**-complete problem, even if s does not contain simultaneous events.*

4. SUBEPISODE RELATIONSHIP

In practice, episodes are represented by DAGs and are mined by adding nodes and edges. However, such a representation has drawbacks [19]. To see this, consider episodes H_1 and H_2 in Figure 1. Even though these episodes have different graphs, they are essentially the same — both episodes are covered by exactly the same sequences, namely all sequences containing *abab*, *a*(*ab*)*b*, (*aa*)(*bb*), *aa*(*bb*), (*aa*)*bb*, or *aabb*. In other words, essentially the same episode may be represented by several graphs. Moreover, using the graph subset relationship to determine subset relationships between episodes will ultimately lead to less efficient algorithms and redundancy in the final output. To counter these problems we introduce a subset relationship based on coverage.

Definition 9 Given two episodes G and H, we say that G is a *subepisode* of H, denoted $G \preceq H$, if any sequence covering H also covers G. If $G \preceq H$ and $H \preceq G$, we say that G and H are *similar* in which case we will write $G \sim H$.

This definition gives us the optimal definition for a subset relationship in the following sense: if $G \npreceq H$, then there exists a sequence s such that $fr(G; s) < fr(H; s)$.

Consider the episodes given in Figure 1. It follows from the definition that $H_1 \sim H_2$, $G_1 \preceq G_2$, and $G_1 \preceq G_3$. Episodes G_2 and G_3 are not comparable.

Theorem 10 *Testing $G \preceq H$ is an **NP**-hard problem.*

Proof. The hardness follows immediately from Theorem 8 as we can represent sequence s as a serial episode H. Then s covers G if and only if $G \preceq H$. □

As mentioned in the introduction, pattern explosion is *the* problem with discovering general episodes. We tackle this by mining only closed episodes.

Definition 11 An episode G is closed if there is no $H \succ G$ with $fr(G) = fr(H)$.

We should point out that, unlike with itemsets, an episode may have several maximal superepisodes having the same frequency. Consider G_1, G_3, and G_4 in Figure 2, sequence *abcbdacbcd* and window size $\rho = 5$. The support of episodes G_1, G_3 and G_4 is 2. Moreover, there is no superepisode of G_3 or G_4 that has the same support. Hence, G_3 and G_4 are both maximal superepisodes having the same support as G_1. This implies that we cannot define a closure operator based on frequency. However, we will see in the next section that we can define a closure based on instances. This closure, while not removing all redundant episodes, will prune the search space dramatically. The final pruning will then be done in a post-processing step.

Figure 2: Toy episodes demonstrating closure.

Our final step is to define transitively closed episodes that we will use along with the instance-closure (defined in the next section) in order to reduce the pattern space.

DEFINITION 12 Let G be an episode. A *transitive closure*, $tcl(G)$, is obtained by adding edges from a node to each of its descendants making the edge proper if the descendant is proper, and weak otherwise. If $G = tcl(G)$ we say that G is transitively closed.

It is trivial to see that given an episode G, we have $G \sim tcl(G)$. Thus we can safely ignore all episodes that are not transitively closed. From now on, unless we state otherwise, all episodes are assumed to be transitively closed.

5. HANDLING EPISODE INSTANCES

The reason why depth-first search is efficient for itemsets is that at each step we only need to handle the current projected dataset. In our setup we have only one sequence so we need to transport the sequence into a more efficient structure.

DEFINITION 13 Given an input sequence s and an episode G, an *instance* i is a valid mapping from G to s such that for each $e \in range(i)$ there is no $f \in s - range(i)$ such that $lab(e) = lab(f)$, $ts(e) = ts(f)$ and $id(f) < id(e)$. We define $first(i) = \min ts(i(n))$ to be the smallest time stamp and $last(i) = \max ts(i(n))$ to be the largest time stamp in i. We require that $last(i) - first(i) \leq \rho - 1$, where ρ is the size of the sliding window. An *instance set* of an episode G, defined as $inst(G)$ is a set of all instances ordered by $first(i)$.

The condition in the definition allows us to ignore some redundant mappings whenever we have two sequence events, say e and f, with $lab(e) = lab(f)$ and $ts(e) = ts(f)$. If an instance i uses only e, then we can obtain i' from i by replacing e with f. However, i and i' are essentially the same for our purposes, so we can ignore either i or i'. We require the instance set to be ordered so that we can compute the support efficiently. This order is not necessarily unique.

Consider sequence *abcbdacbcd* and G_1 in Figure 2. Then $inst(G_1) = ((1,2,3,5),(1,4,3,5),(6,7,8,10),(6,9,8,10))$[4].

[4]For simplicity, we write mappings as tuples

Using instances gives us several advantages. Adding new events and edges to episodes becomes easy. For example, adding a proper edge (n, m) is equivalent to keeping instances with $ts(i(n)) < ts(i(m))$. We will also compute support and closure efficiently. We should point out that $inst(G)$ may contain an exponential number of instances, otherwise Theorem 8 would imply that $\mathbf{P} = \mathbf{NP}$. However, this is not a problem in practice.

The depth-first search described in Section 6 adds events to the episodes. Our next goal is to define algorithms for computing the resulting instance set whenever we add an episode event, say f, to an episode G. Given an instance i of G and a sequence event e we will write $i + e$ to mean an expanded instance by setting $i(f) = e$.

Let G be an episode and let $I = inst(G)$ be the instance set. Assume a node $n \in V(G)$ and a label l. Let H be the episode obtained from G by adding an episode event with label l to node n. We can compute $inst(H)$ from $inst(G)$ using the AUGMENTEQUAL algorithm given in Alg. 1.

Algorithm 1: AUGMENTEQUAL(I, n, l), augments I

input : $I = inst(G)$, a node n, a label l
output: $inst(G$ with n augmented with $l)$

return $\left\{ i + e \mid \begin{array}{l} i \in I, e \in s, lab(e) = l, \\ ts(n) = ts(e), i + e \text{ is an instance} \end{array} \right\}$;

The second augmentation algorithm deals with the case where we are adding a new node with an single event labelled as l to a parallel episode. Algorithm AUGMENT, given in Alg. 2, computes the new instance set. The algorithm can be further optimised by doing augmentation with a type of merge sort so that post-sorting is not needed.

Algorithm 2: AUGMENT(I, l), augments instances

input : $I = inst(G)$, label l of the new event
output: $inst(G$ with a new node labelled with $l)$

$E \leftarrow \{e \in s \mid lab(e) = l\}$;
$J \leftarrow \{i + e \mid i \in I, e \in E, i + e \text{ is an instance}\}$;
Sort J by $first(i)$;
return J;

Our next step is to compute the support of an episode G from $inst(G)$. We do this with the SUPPORT algorithm, given in Alg. 3. The algorithm is based on the observation that there are $\rho - (last(i) - first(i))$ windows that contain the instance i. However, some windows may contain more than one instance and we need to compensate for this.

THEOREM 14 SUPPORT$(inst(G))$ *computes* $fr(G)$.

PROOF. Since I is ordered by $first(i)$, the first for loop of the algorithm removes any instance for which there is an instance j such that $first(i) \leq first(j) \leq last(j) \leq last(i)$. In other words, any window that contains i will also contain j. We will show that the next for loop counts the number of windows containing at least one instance from W, this will imply the theorem.

To that end, let $i_n \in J$ be the nth instance in J and define S_n to be the set of windows of size ρ containing i_n. It follows that $|S_n| = \rho - (last(i_n) - first(i_n))$ and that the first window of S_n starts at $a_n = 1 + last(i_n) - \rho$. Let

Algorithm 3: SUPPORT(I), computes support

input : $I = inst(G)$
output: $fr(G)$
1 $J \leftarrow \emptyset$; $l \leftarrow \infty$;
2 **foreach** $i \in I$ in reverse order **do**
3   **if** $last(i) < l$ **then**
4   Add i to J;
5         $l \leftarrow last(i)$;
6 $l \leftarrow -\infty$; $f \leftarrow 0$;
7 **foreach** $i \in J$ **do**
8     $d \leftarrow \rho - (last(i) - first(i))$;
9     $a \leftarrow 1 + last(i) - \rho$;
10     $d \leftarrow d - \max(0, 1 + l - a)$;
11     $f \leftarrow f + d$;
12     $l \leftarrow first(i)$;
13 **return** f;

$C_n = \bigcup_{m=1}^{n} S_m$. Note that because of the pruning we have $a_{n-1} < a_n$, this implies that $C_{n-1} \cap S_n = S_{n-1} \cap S_n$. We know that $|S_{n-1} \cap S_n| = \max(0, 1 + first(i_{n-1}) - a_n)$. This implies that on Line 10 we have $d = |S_n - S_{n-1}|$ and since $|C_n| = |C_{n-1}| + d$, this proves the theorem. □

Finally, we define a closure episode of an instance set.

DEFINITION 15 Let $I = inst(G)$ be a set of instances. We define an *instance-closure*, $H = icl(I)$ to be the episode having the same nodes and events as G. We define the edges

$$PE(H) = \{(a, b) \mid ts(i(a)) < ts(i(b))\ \forall i \in I\} \text{ and}$$
$$WE(H) = \{(a, b) \mid ts(i(a)) \leq ts(i(b))\ \forall i \in I\} - PE(H).$$

If $G = icl(I)$ we say that G is i-closed.

Consider sequence *abcbdacbcd* and episodes given in Figure 2. Since events b and c always occur between a and d in $inst(G_1)$, the instance closure is $icl(inst(G_1)) = G_2$. Note that G_2 is not closed because G_3 and G_4 are both superepisodes of G_2 with the same support. However, instance-closure reduces the search space dramatically because we do not have to iterate the edges implied by the closure. Note that the closure may produce cycles with weak edges. However, we will later show that we can ignore such episodes.

6. DISCOVERING EPISODES

We are now ready to describe the mining algorithm. Our approach is a straightforward depth-first search. The algorithm works on three different levels.

The first level, consisting of MINE (Alg. 4), and MINEPARALLEL (Alg. 5), adds episode events. MINE is only used for creating singleton episodes while MINEPARALLEL provides the actual search. The algorithm adds events so that the labels of the nodes are decreasing, $lab(nd(G, i + 1)) \leq_{lex} lab(nd(G, i))$. The search space is traversed by either adding an event to the last node or by creating a node with a single event. Episodes $G_1, \ldots, G_5$ in Figure 3 are created by the first level. The edge in G_5 is augmented by the closure.

The second level, MINEWEAK, given in Alg. 6, adds weak edges to the episode, while the third level, MINEPROPER, given in Alg. 7, turns weak edges into proper edges. Both algorithms add only those edges which keep the episode transitively closed. The algorithms keep a list of forbidden weak edges W and forbidden proper edges P. These lists guarantee that each episode is visited only once.

G_6 and G_7 in Figure 3 are discovered by MINEWEAK, however, the weak edges are converted into proper edges by the instance-closure.

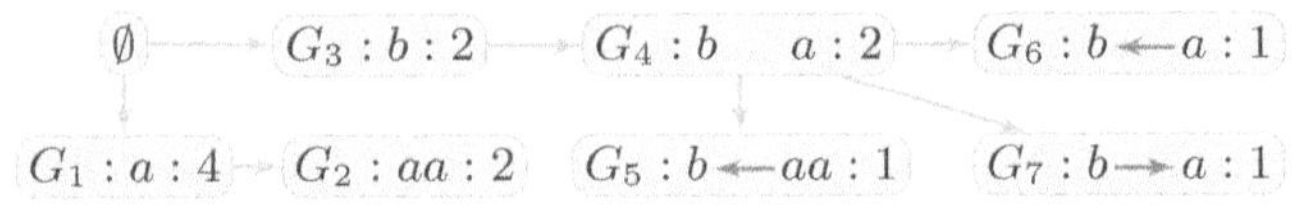

Figure 3: Search space for a sequence $(aa)ba$, window size $\rho = 2$, and support threshold $\sigma = 2$. Each state shows the corresponding episode and its support.

Algorithm 4: MINE, discovers frequent closed episodes

for $x \in \Sigma$ **do**
    $I \leftarrow inst$(singleton episode with the label x);
    $G \leftarrow$ TESTEPISODE($I, \emptyset, \emptyset$);
    if $G \neq$ **null then** MINEPARALLEL(I, G);

Algorithm 5: MINEPARALLEL(I, G), recursive routine adding episode events

input : episode G, $I = inst(G)$
MINEWEAK($I, G, \emptyset$);
$M \leftarrow |V(G)|$;
$n \leftarrow nd(G, M)$;
for $x \in \Sigma, x \geq \max lab(n)$ **do**
    if $M = 1$ **or** $lab(n) \cup \{x\} \leq_{lex} lab(nd(G, M - 1))$ **then**
        $J \leftarrow$ AUGMENTEQUAL(I, n, x);
        $H \leftarrow$ TESTEPISODE($J, \emptyset, \emptyset$);
        if $H \neq$ **null then**
            MINEPARALLEL(J, H);
for $x \in \Sigma, x \leq \min lab(n)$ **do**
    $J \leftarrow$ AUGMENT(I, x);
    $H \leftarrow$ TESTEPISODE($J, \emptyset, \emptyset$);
    if $H \neq$ **null then**
        MINEPARALLEL(J, H);

Algorithm 6: MINEWEAK(I, G, W), recursive routine adding weak edges

input : ep. G, $I = inst(G)$, forbidden weak edges W
$A \leftarrow \{(a, b) \mid a, b \in V(G), (a, b) \notin E(G)\}$;
MINEPROPER($I, G, A, \emptyset$);
for $(a, b) \notin E(G) \cup W$ **do**
    if $G + (a, b)$ is transitively closed **then**
        $J \leftarrow \{i \in I \mid ts(i(a)) \leq ts(i(b))\}$;
        $H \leftarrow$ TESTEPISODE($J, W, \emptyset$);
        if $H \neq$ **null then**
            MINEWEAK(J, H, W);
        Add (a, b) to W;

At each step, we call TESTEPISODE. This routine, given a set of instances I, will compute the instance-closure $icl(I)$ and test it. If the episode passes all the tests, the algorithm

Algorithm 7: MINEPROPER(I, G, W, P), recursive routine adding proper edges

input : episode G, $I = inst(G)$, forbidden weak edges W, forbidden proper edges P

for $(a, b) \in WE(G) - P$ **do**
  if $G+$ proper edge (a, b) is transitively closed **then**
    $J \leftarrow \{i \in I \mid ts(i(a)) < ts(i(b))\}$;
    $H \leftarrow$ TESTEPISODE(J, W, P);
    if $H \neq$ **null then**
      MINEPROPER(J, H, W, P);
    Add (a, b) to P;

will return the episode and the search is continued, otherwise the branch is terminated. There are four different tests. The first test checks whether the episode is frequent. If we pass this test, we compute the instance-closure $H = icl(I)$. The second test checks whether H contains cycles. Let G be an episode such that $I = inst(G)$. In order for H to have cycles we must have two nodes, say n and m, such that $ts(i(n)) = ts(i(m))$ for all $i \in I$. Let G' be an episode obtained from G by merging nodes in n and m together. We have $G \preceq G'$ and $fr(G) = fr(G')$. This holds for any subsequent episode discovered in the branch allowing us to ignore the whole branch.

If the closure introduces into H any edge that has been explored in the previous branches, then that implies that H has already been discovered. Hence, we can reject H if any such edge is introduced. The final condition is that during MINEPROPER no weak edges should be added into H by the closure. If a weak edge is added, we can reject H because it can be reached via an alternative route, by letting MINEWEAK add the additional edges and then calling MINEPROPER.

The algorithm keeps a list $\mathcal{C}$ of all discovered episodes that are closed. If all four tests are passed, the algorithm tests whether there are subepisodes of G in $\mathcal{C}$ having the same frequency, and deletes them. On the other hand, if there is a superepisode of G in $\mathcal{C}$, then G is not added into $\mathcal{C}$.

7. TESTING SUBEPISODES

In this section we will describe the technique for computing $G \preceq H$. In general, this problem is difficult to solve as pointed out by Theorem 10. Fortunately, in practice, a major part of the comparisons are easy to do. The following theorem says that if the labels of G are unique in H, then we can easily compare G and H.

THEOREM 16 *Assume two episodes G and H. Assume that $lab(G) \subset lab(H)$ and for each event e in G only one event occurs in H with the same label. Let π be the unique mapping from episode events in G to episode events in H honouring the labels. Then $G \preceq H$ if and only if*

1. *$nd(e) = nd(f)$ implies that $nd(\pi(e)) = nd(\pi(f))$,*
2. *$nd(e)$ is a proper child of $nd(f)$ implies that $nd(\pi(e))$ is a proper child of $nd(\pi(f))$,*
3. *$nd(e)$ is a child of $nd(f)$ implies that $nd(\pi(e))$ is a child of $nd(\pi(f))$ or $nd(\pi(e)) = nd(\pi(f))$,*

for any two events e and f in G.

Algorithm 8: TESTEPISODE(I, W, P), tests the episode $icl(I)$ and updates $\mathcal{C}$, the list of discovered episodes

input : $I = inst(G)$, forbidden weak edges W, forbidden proper edges P

output: $icl(I)$, if $icl(I)$ passes the tests, **null** otherwise

$f \leftarrow$ SUPPORT(I);
if $f < \sigma$ **then return null**;
$G \leftarrow icl(I)$;
if there are cycles in G **then**
  return null;
if $WE(G) \cap W \neq \emptyset$ **or** $PE(G) \cap P \neq \emptyset$ **then**
  return null;
$fr(G) \leftarrow f$;
foreach $H \in \mathcal{C}, lab(H) \cap lab(G) \neq \emptyset$ **do**
  if $fr(G) = fr(H)$ **and** $G \preceq H$ **then**
    return G;
  if $fr(G) = fr(H)$ **and** $H \preceq G$ **then**
    Delete H from $\mathcal{C}$;
Add G to $\mathcal{C}$;
return G;

If the condition in Theorem 16 does not hold we will have to resort to enumerating the sequences covering H. In order to do that, we need to extend the definition of coverage and subset relationship to the set of episodes.

DEFINITION 17 A sequence s covers an episode set $\mathcal{G}$ if there is an episode $G \in \mathcal{G}$ such that s covers G. Given two episode sets $\mathcal{G}$ and $\mathcal{H}$ we define $\mathcal{G} \preceq \mathcal{H}$ if every sequence that covers $\mathcal{H}$ also covers $\mathcal{G}$.

We also need a definition of a prefix subgraph.

DEFINITION 18 Given a graph G, a *prefix subgraph* is a non-empty induced subgraph of G with *no* proper edges such that if a node n is included then the parents of n are also included. Given a multiset of labels L and an episode G we define $pre(G, L)$ to be the set of all maximal prefix subgraphs such that $lab(V) \subseteq L$ for each $V \in pre(G, L)$. We define $tail(G, L) = \{G - V \mid V \in pre(G, L)\}$ to be the episodes with the remaining nodes. Finally, given an episode set $\mathcal{G}$ we define $tail(\mathcal{G}, L) = \bigcup_{G \in \mathcal{G}} tail(G, L)$.

EXAMPLE 19 Consider episodes given in Figure 4. We have $tail(G, ab) = \{H_1, H_2, H_3\}$ and $tail(G, a) = \{H_1\}$.

Figure 4: Toy episodes demonstrating $tail(G, ab)$.

The main motivation for our recursion is given in the following theorem.

THEOREM 20 *Given an episode set $\mathcal{G}$ and an episode H, $\mathcal{G} \preceq H$ if and only if for each prefix subgraph V of H, we have $tail(\mathcal{G}, lab(V)) \preceq H - V$.*

We focus for the rest of this section on implementing the recursion in Theorem 20. We begin by an algorithm, GENERATE, given in Alg. 9, that, given a graph without proper edges, discovers all prefix subgraphs.

Algorithm 9: GENERATE(G, V), recursive routine for iterating the nodes of all prefix subgraphs of G

input : graph G, nodes V discovered so far
output: list of nodes of all prefix subgraphs

$\mathcal{O} \leftarrow \emptyset$;
foreach $n \in src(G)$ **do**
    $\mathcal{O} \leftarrow \mathcal{O} \cup \{V + n\} \cup$ GENERATE$(G - n, V + n)$;
    Remove n and its descendants from G;
return $\mathcal{O}$;

Given a prefix subgraph V of H, our next step is to discover all maximal prefix subgraphs of G whose label sets are subsets of $L = lab(V)$. The algorithm, CONSUME, creating this list, is given in Alg. 10. CONSUME enumerates over all sources. For each source n such that $lab(n) \subseteq L$, the algorithm tests if there is another node sharing a label with n. If so, the algorithm creates an episode without n and its descendants and calls itself. This call produces a list of prefix graphs $\mathcal{W}$ not containing node n. The algorithm removes all graphs from $\mathcal{W}$ that can be augmented with n (since in that case they are not maximal). Finally, CONSUME adds n to the current prefix subgraph, removes n from G, and removes $lab(n)$ from L.

Algorithm 10: CONSUME(G, L, V), recursive routine for iterating the nodes of all prefix subgraphs of G whose labels are contained in L

input : graph G, nodes V discovered so far, L label set
output: list of nodes of all maximal prefix subgraphs

$\mathcal{O} \leftarrow \emptyset$;
while $src(G) \neq \emptyset$ **do**
    $n \leftarrow$ a node from $src(G)$;
    if $lab(n) \not\subseteq L$ **then**
        Remove n and its descendants from G;
        continue;
    if there is $m \in V(G)$ s.t. $lab(n) \cap lab(m) \neq \emptyset$ **then**
        $H \leftarrow G$ with n and its descendants removed;
        $\mathcal{W} \leftarrow$ CONSUME(H, L, V);
        $\mathcal{O} \leftarrow \mathcal{O} \cup \{W \in \mathcal{W} \mid lab(W) \cup lab(n) \not\subseteq L\}$;
    $V \leftarrow V + n$; $L \leftarrow L - lab(n)$;
    Remove n from G;
return $\mathcal{O} \cup \{V\}$;

We are now ready to describe the recursion step of Theorem 20 for testing the subset relationship. The algorithm, STEP, is given in Alg. 11. Given an episode set $\mathcal{G}$ and a graph H, the algorithm computes $\mathcal{G} \preceq H$. First, it tests whether we can apply Theorem 16. If this is not possible, then the algorithm first removes all nodes from H not carrying a label from $lab(G)$ for $G \in \mathcal{G}$. This is allowed because of the following lemma.

LEMMA 21 *Let G and H be two episodes. Let $n \in V(H)$ be a node such that $lab(n) \cap lab(G) = \emptyset$. Let H' be the episode obtained from H by removing n. Then $G \preceq H$ if and only if $G \preceq H'$.*

STEP continues by creating a subgraph Y of H containing only proper sources. The algorithm generates all prefix subgraphs $\mathcal{V}$ of Y and tests each one. For each sub-

Algorithm 11: STEP$(\mathcal{G}, H)$, recursion solving $\mathcal{G} \preceq H$

input : episode set $\mathcal{G}$ and an episode H
output: $\mathcal{G} \preceq H$

foreach $G \in \mathcal{G}$ **do**
    if Theorem 16 guarantees that $G \preceq H$ **then**
        return true;
    if Theorem 16 states that $G \not\preceq H$ **and** $|\mathcal{G}| = 1$ **then**
        return false;
$V(H) \leftarrow \{n \in V(H) \mid lab(n) \cap lab(G) \neq \emptyset, G \in \mathcal{G}\}$;
$Y \leftarrow$ subgraph of H with only proper sources;
$\mathcal{V} \leftarrow$ GENERATE$(Y, \emptyset)$;
foreach $V \in \mathcal{V}$ **do**
    $F \leftarrow H - V$; $\mathcal{T} \leftarrow \emptyset$;
    foreach $G \in \mathcal{G}$ **do**
        $X \leftarrow$ subgraph of G with only proper sources;
        $\mathcal{W} \leftarrow$ CONSUME$(X, lab(V), \emptyset)$;
        $\mathcal{T} \leftarrow \mathcal{T} \cup \{G - W \mid W \in \mathcal{W}\}$;
    if STEP$(\mathcal{T}, F)$ = **false then**
        return false;
return true;

graph $V \in \mathcal{V}$, STEP calls CONSUME and builds an episode set $\mathcal{T} = tail(\mathcal{G}, lab(V))$. The algorithm then calls itself recursively with STEP$(\mathcal{T}, H - V)$. If at least one of these calls fails, then we know that $\mathcal{G} \not\preceq H$, otherwise $\mathcal{G} \preceq H$.

Finally, to compute $G \preceq H$, we simply call STEP$(\{G\}, H)$.

8. EXPERIMENTS

We begin our experiments with a synthetic dataset. Our goal is to demonstrate the need for using the closure. In order to do that we created sequences with a planted pattern $(s_1 s_2)(s_3 s_4) \cdots (s_{2N-1} s_{2N})$. We added this pattern 100 times 50 time units apart from each other. We added 500 noise events uniformly spreading over the whole sequence. We sampled the labels for the noise events uniformly from 900 different labels. The labels for the noise and the labels of the pattern were mutually exclusive. We varied N from 1 to 7. We ran our miner using a window size of $\rho = 10$ and varied the support threshold σ. The results are given in Table 1.

When we are using a support threshold of 100, the only closed frequent patterns are the planted pattern and its subpatterns of form $(s_i s_{i+1}) \cdots (s_j s_{j+1})$, since the frequency of these subpatterns is slightly higher than the frequency of the whole pattern. The number of instance-closed episodes (given in the 4th column of Table 1) grows more rapidly. The reason for this is that the instance-closure focuses on the edges and does not add any new nodes. However, this ratio becomes a bottleneck only when we are dealing with extremely large serial episodes, and for our real-world datasets this ratio is relatively small.

The need for instance-closure becomes apparent when the number of instance-closed episodes is compared to the number of all possible general subepisodes (including those that are not tranistively closed) of a planted pattern, given in the 5th column of Table 1. We see that had we not used instance-closure, a single pattern having 6 nodes and 12 events renders pattern discovery infeasible.

Table 1: **Results from synthetic sequences with a planted episode P. The columns show the number of nodes in P, the support threshold, the size of the final output, the number of instance-closed episodes, the number of subepisodes of P, and the number of sequence scans, respectively.**

$\lvert V(P)\rvert$	σ	$\lvert\mathcal{C}\rvert$	i-closed	frequent	scans
1	100	1	3	3	46
2	100	3	15	27	200
3	100	6	63	729	744
4	100	10	255	59 049	3 964
5	100	15	1 023	14 348 907	11 123
6	100	21	4 095	$\approx 10^{10}$	48 237
7	100	28	16 383	$\approx 2 \times 10^{13}$	191 277
7	50	29	16 384	$> 2 \times 10^{13}$	191 243
7	40	32	16 387	$> 2 \times 10^{13}$	191 298
7	30	39	16 394	$> 2 \times 10^{13}$	191 463
7	20	127	16 488	$> 2 \times 10^{13}$	197 773
7	10	684	52 297	$> 2 \times 10^{13}$	480 517

As we lower the threshold, the number of instance-closed episodes and closed episodes increases, however the ratio between instance-closed and closed episodes improves. The reason for this is that the output contains episodes other than our planted episode, and those mostly contain a small number of nodes.

We also measured the number of sequence scans, namely the number of calls made to SUPPORT, to demonstrate how fast the negative border is growing. Since our miner is a depth-first search and the computation of frequency is based on instances, a single scan is fast, since we do not have to scan the whole sequence.

Our second set of experiments was conducted on real-world data. The dataset consists of alarms generated in a factory, and contains 514 502 events of 9 595 different types, stretching over 18 months. An entry in the dataset consists of a time stamp and an event type. Once again, we tested our algorithm at various thresholds, varying the window size from 3 to 15 minutes. Here, too, as shown in Table 2, we can see that the number of i-closed episodes does not explode to the level of all frequent episodes, demonstrating the need for using the i-closure as an intermediate step. Furthermore, we see that in a realistic setting, the number of i-closed episodes stays closer to the number of closed episodes than in the above-mentioned synthetic dataset. This is no surprise, since real datasets tend to have a lot of patterns containing a small number of events.

As the discovery of all frequent episodes is infeasible, we estimated their number as follows. An episode G has $a(G) = 3^{|PE(G)|}2^{|WE(G)|}$ subepisodes (including those that are not transitively closed) with the same events and nodes. From the discovered i-closed episodes we selected a subset $\mathcal{G}$ such that each $G \in \mathcal{G}$ has a unique set of events and a maximal $a(G)$. Then the lower bound for the total number of frequent episodes is $\sum_{G\in\mathcal{G}} a(G)$. Using such a lower bound is more than enough to confirm that the number of frequent episodes explodes much faster than the number of closed and i-closed episodes, as can be seen in Table 2.

Furthermore, our output contained a considerable number of episodes with simultaneous events — patterns that no existing method would have discovered. The runtimes ranged from just under 2 seconds to 90 seconds for the lowest reported thresholds.

Table 2: Results from the alarms dataset.

win (s)	$\sigma/10^3$	$\lvert\mathcal{C}\rvert$	i-closed	freq.(est)	scans
180	500	6	6	6	194
180	400	8	8	8	220
180	300	12	12	12	282
180	240	23	26	26	792
600	2 000	4	4	4	128
600	1 000	24	27	39	374
600	500	90	137	493	1 196
600	280	422	698	2 321	8 758
900	2 000	24	26	40	350
900	1 000	52	58	94	745
900	500	280	426	1 997	4 604
900	350	1 845	9 484	190 990	63 735

Our third dataset consisted of trains delayed at a single railway station in Belgium. The dataset consists of actual departure times of delayed trains, coupled with train numbers, and contains 10 115 events involving 1 280 different train IDs, stretching over a period of one month. A window of 30 minutes was chosen by a domain expert. The time stamps were expressed in seconds, so a single train being delayed on a particular day would be found in 1800 windows. Therefore, the frequency threshold for interesting patterns had to be set relatively high. The results are shown in Table 3, and were similar to those of the alarm dataset. The runtimes ranged from a few milliseconds to 55 minutes for the lowest reported threshold. The largest discovered pattern was of size 10, and the total number of frequent episodes at the lowest threshold was at least 33 million, once again demonstrating the need for both outputting only closed episodes and using instance-closure.

Table 3: Results from the trains dataset.

σ	$\lvert\mathcal{C}\rvert$	i-closed	freq.(est)	scans
30 000	141	141	141	9 575
20 000	1 994	1 995	2 593	219 931
17 000	8 352	8 416	22 542	812 363
15 000	26 170	26 838	172 067	2 231 360
13 000	94 789	101 882	3 552 104	6 865 877
12 000	189 280	211 636	33 660 094	12 966 895

9. CONCLUSIONS

In this paper we introduce a new type of sequential pattern, a general episode that takes into account simultaneous events, and provide an efficient depth-first search algorithm for mining such patterns.

This problem setup has two major challenges. The first challenge is the pattern explosion which we tackle by discovering only closed episodes. Interestingly enough, we cannot define closure based on frequency, hence we define closure based on instances. While it holds that frequency-closed episodes are instance-closed, the opposite is not true. However, in practice, instance-closure reduces search space dramatically so we can mine all instance-closed episodes and discover frequency-closed episodes as a post-processing step.

The second challenge is to correctly compute the subset relationship between two episodes. We argue that using a subset relationship based on graphs is not optimal and will lead to redundant output. We define a subset relationship based on coverage and argue that this is the correct definition. This definition turns out to be **NP**-hard. However, this is not a problem since in practice most of the comparisons can be done efficiently.

10. ACKNOWLEDGMENTS

Nikolaj Tatti is supported by a Post-doctoral Fellowship of the Research Foundation – Flanders (FWO).

The authors wish to thank Toon Calders for providing the proof that checking whether a sequence covers an episode is **NP**-hard on a small piece of paper.

11. REFERENCES

[1] R. Agrawal and R. Srikant. Fast algorithms for mining association rules. In *Proceedings of the 20th International Conference on Very Large Data Bases (VLDB 1994)*, pages 487–499, 1994.

[2] R. Agrawal and R. Srikant. Mining sequential patterns. *11th International Conference on Data Engineering (ICDE 1995)*, 0:3–14, 1995.

[3] T. Calders, N. Dexters, and B. Goethals. Mining frequent itemsets in a stream. In *Proceedings of the 7th IEEE International Conference on Data Mining (ICDM 2007)*, pages 83–92, 2007.

[4] G. Casas-Garriga. Discovering unbounded episodes in sequential data. In *Knowledge Discovery in Databases: PKDD 2003, 7th European Conference on Principles and Practice of Knowledge Discovery in Databases*, pages 83–94, 2003.

[5] G. Casas-Garriga. Summarizing sequential data with closed partial orders. In *Proceedings of the SIAM International Conference on Data Mining (SDM 2005)*, pages 380–391, 2005.

[6] G. Chen, X. Wu, and X. Zhu. Sequential pattern mining in multiple streams. In *Proceedings of the 5th IEEE International Conference on Data Mining (ICDM 2005)*, pages 585–588, 2005.

[7] B. Cule, B. Goethals, and C. Robardet. A new constraint for mining sets in sequences. In *Proceedings of the SIAM International Conference on Data Mining (SDM 2009)*, pages 317–328, 2009.

[8] M. Garofalakis, R. Rastogi, and K. Shim. Mining sequential patterns with regular expression constraints. *IEEE Transactions on Knowledge and Data Engineering*, 14(3):530–552, 2002.

[9] R. Gwadera, M. J. Atallah, and W. Szpankowski. Markov models for identification of significant episodes. In *Proceedings of the SIAM International Conference on Data Mining (SDM 2005)*, pages 404–414, 2005.

[10] R. Gwadera, M. J. Atallah, and W. Szpankowski. Reliable detection of episodes in event sequences. *Knowledge and Information Systems*, 7(4):415–437, 2005.

[11] R. Gwadera and F. Crestani. Discovering significant patterns in multi-stream sequences. In *Proceedings of the 8th IEEE International Conference on Data Mining (ICDM 2008)*, pages 827–832, 2008.

[12] S. K. Harms, J. S. Deogun, J. Saquer, and T. Tadesse. Discovering representative episodal association rules from event sequences using frequent closed episode sets and event constraints. In *Proceedings of the IEEE International Conference on Data Mining (ICDM 2001)*, pages 603–606, 2001.

[13] S. Laxman, P. S. Sastry, and K. P. Unnikrishnan. A fast algorithm for finding frequent episodes in event streams. In *Proceedings of the 13th ACM SIGKDD international conference on Knowledge discovery and data mining (KDD 2007)*, pages 410–419, 2007.

[14] H. Mannila, H. Toivonen, and A. I. Verkamo. Discovery of frequent episodes in event sequences. *Data Mining and Knowledge Discovery*, 1(3):259–289, 1997.

[15] N. Méger and C. Rigotti. Constraint-based mining of episode rules and optimal window sizes. In *Knowledge Discovery in Databases: PKDD 2004, 8th European Conference on Principles and Practice of Knowledge Discovery in Databases*, pages 313–324, 2004.

[16] T. Oates and P. R. Cohen. Searching for structure in multiple streams data. In *Proceedings of the 13th International Conference on Machine Learning (ICML 1996)*, pages 346–354, 1996.

[17] J. Pei, H. Wang, J. Liu, K. Wang, J. Wang, and P. S. Yu. Discovering frequent closed partial orders from strings. *IEEE Transactions on Knowledge and Data Engineering*, 18(11):1467–1481, 2006.

[18] N. Tatti. Significance of episodes based on minimal windows. In *Proceedings of the 9th IEEE International Conference on Data Mining (ICDM 2009)*, pages 513–522, 2009.

[19] N. Tatti and B. Cule. Mining closed strict episodes. In *Proceedings of the 10th IEEE International Conference on Data Mining (ICDM 2010)*, 2010.

[20] P. Tzvetkov, X. Yan, and J. Han. Tsp: Mining top-k closed sequential patterns. In *Proceedings of the 3rd IEEE International Conference on Data Mining (ICDM 2003)*, pages 347–354, 2003.

[21] J. Wang and J. Han. Bide: Efficient mining of frequent closed sequences. *20th International Conference on Data Engineering (ICDE 2004)*, 0:79, 2004.

[22] J. T.-L. Wang, G.-W. Chirn, T. G. Marr, B. Shapiro, D. Shasha, and K. Zhang. Combinatorial pattern discovery for scientific data: some preliminary results. *ACM SIGMOD Record*, 23(2):115–125, 1994.

[23] X. Yan, J. Han, and R. Afshar. Clospan: Mining closed sequential patterns in large datasets. In *Proceedings of the SIAM International Conference on Data Mining (SDM 2003)*, pages 166–177, 2003.

[24] W. Zhou, H. Liu, and H. Cheng. Mining closed episodes from event sequences efficiently. In *Proceedings of the 14th Pacific-Asia Conference on Knowledge Discovery and Data Mining(1)*, pages 310–318, 2010.

Mining Mobility Data to Minimise Travellers' Spending on Public Transport

Neal Lathia, Licia Capra
Department of Computer Science
University College London
Gower Street, London, WC1E 6BT, UK
n.lathia, l.capra@cs.ucl.ac.uk

ABSTRACT

As the public transport infrastructure of large cities expands, transport operators are diversifying the range and prices of tickets that can be purchased for travel. However, selecting the best fare for each individual traveller's needs is a complex process that is left almost completely unaided. By examining the relation between urban mobility and fare purchasing habits in large datasets from London, England's public transport network, we estimate that travellers in the city cumulatively spend, per year, up to approximately GBP 200 million more than they need to, as a result of purchasing the incorrect fares.

We propose to address these incorrect purchases by leveraging the huge volumes of data that travellers create as they move about the city, by providing, to each of them, personalised ticket *recommendations* based on their estimated future travel patterns. In this work, we explore the viability of building a fare-recommendation system for public transport networks by (a) formalising the problem as two separate prediction problems and (b) evaluating a number of algorithms that aim to match travellers to the best fare. We find that applying data mining techniques to public transport data has the potential to provide travellers with substantial savings.

Categories and Subject Descriptors: H.3.3 [Information Search and Retrieval]: Information Filtering

General Terms: Algorithms

Keywords: Mobility, Public Transport, Filtering, Recommender Systems

1. INTRODUCTION

At face value, the problem of buying a ticket for travel on an urban public transport system seems simple and mundane. However, this is only the case for cities where there is only one fare or ticket type available for purchase. Increasingly, various metropolises around the world are diversifying the fares that they offer, in order to cater for the different needs of the city's residents: they may offer single, multi-trip, and tourist (or visitor) tickets, as well as tickets that restrict travellers to specific transport modalities (e.g., a bus or train-only ticket). Invariably, all of these tickets are offered at different prices. Travellers are now faced with the problem of having to purchase a ticket from a large list of candidate fares, by first estimating their own future travel needs, and then selecting the one that seems to cater for their needs best.

The public transport network in London, UK is a prime example of this scenario. The rich pricing scheme operated by Transport for London (TfL) introduces a variety of ticket options that range in price, transport modality, temporal validity *and* geographical boundaries. In fact, the optimal ticket for each of the city's travellers will depend on *who* they are (which determines which discounts they are eligible for) and three factors that directly affect cost: *where* they travel to and from (i.e., their geographic requirements), *when* they travel (e.g., rush-hour or day time) and *how frequently* they move between places, over time periods that span from single days to an entire year. While these multiple behavioural dimensions influence what the cheapest travel option will be, the current ticket sales process has no transparent link between usage and pricing: the decision of the best ticket is left unaided to each individual traveller. As a result, travellers are never informed as to whether they are indeed making the best decisions for themselves. TfL itself estimates that over GBP 300,000 is wasted *per day* by passengers buying paper tickets instead of opting for the electronic equivalent[1], and other investigations have revealed that approximately GBP 30 million of travel credit is sitting in the system, idle and unused[2]. These vast sums of wasted money all point to the fact that making the correct decision at the point of purchase is not only uninformed and lacking in transparency, but also incredibly difficult for travellers to reason about, in order to purchase the cheapest fare for themselves.

There are two significant obstacles confronting this complex decision: first, travellers need to *understand* the relationship between mobility and fares. To that end, we describe London's current pricing system in Section 2, which includes 7 temporal, 9 geographical, and 12 user categories, with the various conditions that influence the suitability of certain tickets for travellers. Second, each traveller needs to rely on her own memory and anticipated mobility patterns in order to decide what the best ticket will be. This is where the greatest opportunity for data mining lies: London's RFID-based Oyster card, much like Seattle's Orca

KDD'11, August 21–24, 2011, San Diego, California, USA.

[1] http://golondon.about.com/od/londontransport/qt/oyster_card.htm
[2] http://www.bbc.co.uk/news/10162991

card or the Tokyo Metro system's tickets (based on near-field mobile phone communication) is a uniform payment system that produces a digital record every time a trip is made and a ticket is purchased. Mining the travel data that is created as travellers enter and exit stations can be used to aide them when purchasing tickets. In this work, we propose and evaluate recommendation algorithms that aim to leverage each traveller's mobility patterns in order to determine what the best fare is for each unique individual. In particular, we make the following contributions:

- We present an extensive analysis of anonymised ticket purchasing behaviour and public transport usage datasets (Section 3); we link the two datasets in order to examine the relation between mobility and purchase habits and quantify the extent that London travellers waste money by buying the incorrect fares: our data shows that travellers overspend by approximately GBP 200 million per year by buying the incorrect fares.
- We compliment this analysis with the results of a survey (Section 3.3) that explores the heuristics and methods that travellers currently adopt when selecting the best fare for themselves.
- We design and evaluate (Section 4) algorithms that provide personalised ticket-purchase recommendations to travellers with an available travel history. We do so by splitting the problem into two: predicting future travel habits and matching travel habits to fares. We evaluate our proposals with accuracy metrics and by quantifying how much money travellers in our datasets could have saved (had they followed our recommendations).

We recognise that our contributions may reduce the gross income of travel operators. However, these systems can be used to encourage the adoption of public transport by promoting the cost-effectiveness of travel.

2. BACKGROUND

The services and pricing structures adopted by public transport authorities around the world are not uniform. However, in general, all systems will have an inherent relation between usage and pricing. In this work, we focus on London, England, due to the availability of data (although we note that our techniques could easily be adapted to other systems). The TfL public transport infrastructure is a vast, multi-modal network of underground trains (11 interconnected lines with 270 stations), overground trains (5 lines with 78 stations) and buses (about 8,000 buses serving 19,000 stops) as well as trams, river services, and other specialised services. At the broadest level, travellers must opt to either use a single, contact-less smart card (the Oyster card) to pay for their journeys or buy paper-based tickets. In order to encourage the use of the Oyster card, facilities are in place for travellers to automatically add credit to their card (*auto top-up*) and buy or renew travel passes online and using machines in each station; the ease of purchase of all fares on the Oyster card is roughly similar. However, use of an Oyster card does not determine what fares travellers should buy. In particular, there are a number of factors that must be considered when selecting tickets:

1. User Categories. There are 12 user categories, ranging from full fare-paying adults, to students, children of varying age ranges, disability/60+"freedom" passes (which entitle bearers to free travel), war veterans, bus discounts, groups and school parties. If any of these users also have one of many different additional cards (e.g., a National Rail membership card), they are entitled to further discounts.

2. Modality Restrictions. There are some tickets that are for exclusive use on the bus network, while others do not limit the transport modality that the traveller opts for.

3. Geographic and Routing Restrictions. The TfL rail network is subdivided into nine concentric zones. Zone 1 covers central London and higher-numbered zones are progressively further away from city centre. The cost of travel by train is influenced by the number of zones that are traversed; for example, a rush-hour single fare from Zone 6 to Zone 2 that goes via Zone 1 costs GBP 4.50, while the fare for a trip between the same zones, *without* going via Zone 1 costs GBP 2.50. There are particular cases where the actual route that is taken will change the cost. For example, a rush-hour single between Zones 1 and 2 (e.g., Goodge St to Archway) costs GBP 2.50, but if mobility is restricted to the Euston-Watford Junction train line (e.g., Euston to South Hampstead), the fare is GBP 2.00.

4. Travel Cards or Pay As You Go. Travellers can opt to pay for their trips on a per-trip basis (using *"pay as you go"*, PAYG, fares), or use 7-day, monthly, or annual passes, also called *travel cards*, which allow for unlimited travel within purchased zones. It is important to note that PAYG and *travel card* use is not mutually exclusive. Travellers can opt for combinations of the two; for example, they can buy a Zone 1 to 2 travel card and then use *pay as you go* for any travel that goes beyond these Zones (both tickets are stored within the same physical Oyster card). In this case, they will be charged a mixed fare, which corresponds to the PAYG cost for a single fare in the zones that are not covered by their travel card.

5. Temporal Categories. TfL has defined two distinct travel times: *peak* times, 6:30-9:30AM and 4:00-7:00PM Monday to Friday (reflecting the rush-hour commuting travellers) and *off-peak*, 9:30AM-4:00PM and after 7PM during week days and all of weekends and public holidays. PAYG as well as day-only travel card prices tend to, but do not always, differ in price between these times (note that the weekly/monthly/annual travel cards do not differentiate between peak and off-peak travel).

6. Additional Conditions. TfL has also implemented a *price capping* system for Oyster cards to limit the amount of PAYG credit that any one traveller can use in a single day. If a traveller has so many trips in one day such that it would have been cheaper to travel with a day pass, then the fare that will be charged will be the price-cap limit, which is the same as the day travel card ticket price (although there are separate peak and off-peak limits). Unfortunately, the capping does not transfer daily cards to further time periods (e.g., weekly, monthly), regardless of whether the latter would have been cheaper or not.

All the above conditions and related fare prices are subject to an annual review and continuous changes. Inextricably, a number of sub-optimal choices can easily be made: for example, using PAYG will be more expensive than travel cards for high frequency travellers. In this work, we will focus on full-fare paying adult tickets. How do travellers make purchases in this environment? In the following section, we examine the relation between mobility and purchase deci-

(%)	Type
	Pay As You Go
49.8	≤ GBP 5
24.2	GBP 5.01 - GBP 10
15.5	GBP 10.01 - GBP 20
7.7	GBP 20.01 - GBP 30
	Travel Cards
70.8	7-day travel card
15.8	1-month travel card
11.6	7-day bus/tram pass
1.9	1-month bus/tram pass

(a) Top-4 Purchase Types

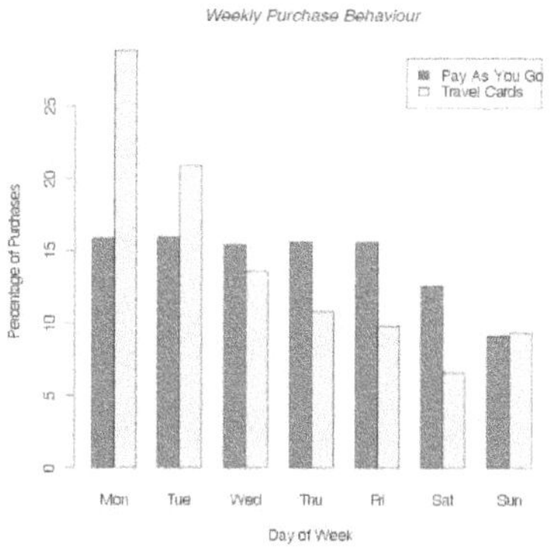

(b) Weekly Purchase Distribution

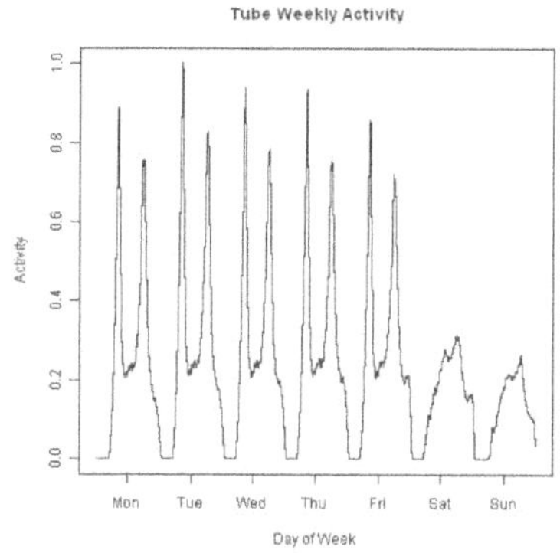

(c) Week Ongoing Journeys

Figure 1: Fare Purchases: (a) the most frequently bought travel cards and top-up amounts, (b) *when* people purchase over a cumulative week, and (c) the cumulative ongoing (rail) journeys across a week.

Name	Users	Rail/Tube Trips	Bus Trips
D1	264,304	4,350,039	5,014,664
D2	267,357	4,315,821	4,734,435

Table 1: Two 83-day Travel history datasets of a 5% sample of TfL travellers. D1 is May-July 2009, D2 is October 2009-January 2010.

Name	Number of Purchases	
	PAYG	TravelCards
P1	1,646,987	134,721
P2	1,732,583	125,704

Table 2: Ticket purchase datasets from the same users and date ranges as Table 1.

sions by analysing two large datasets of London trips and fare purchases.

3. MOBILITY AND TICKET PURCHASES

In this section, we first analyse anonymised purchase and travel behaviour data from TfL (Section 3.1), highlighting emerging trends and consistencies in both travellers' movements and purchases. We then quantify how much travellers overspend, by computing the cheapest fares for the trips they took (Section 3.2). Finally, we investigate the heuristics that travellers adopt to support purchase decisions, by reporting the results of an online survey (Section 3.3).

3.1 Dataset Analysis

In this analysis, we use two pairs of datasets of Oyster card usage from different 83-day periods (May-July 2009 and October 2009-January 2010). Each dataset is a 5% sub-sample of all users who were recorded during the two periods. The *mobility* datasets (D1 and D2), contain the travel history of the sampled users: an anonymised, unique user id, the modality, origin, destination, the journey's start and end times in minutes, and the travel ticket type as recorded by the user's Oyster card (note that, as travellers are not required to use their card to exit buses, we only have origin and start time for these trips; this does not affect pricing as bus fares do not depend on the trip destination). The purchase history datasets (P1 and P2) contain both PAYG credit and travel card purchases during the same time frame, along with where (which station), when (which day), and how much credit/what type of travel card (temporal and geographical boundaries) was purchased. Together, the two datasets sum to traveller spending of over GBP 500 million.

We took a number of steps to clean the data. First, the datasets suffer from the *edge effect*: some users will be making trips with travel cards that were purchased prior to the purchase history date range that we observe. Second, the purchase data has *missing entries*, potentially due to lost data from ticket sales done through authorised retailers. Note that, since PAYG fares are paid on a per-journey basis, these entries do not have this problem. To compensate for the edge effect, we pruned the profiles of those travellers who use travel cards until the date of the first (observed) purchase. If there was no observed purchase, or the traveller was using an annual card, we removed them from the dataset; we lost approximately 20% of the users. We then pruned any inconsistent or erroneous entries (trips with the same origin and destination, with end times prior to start times, or with unknown tickets), and then sampled all adult Oyster cards to produce the final datasets; an overview of these is provided in Tables 1 and 2. In this section, we analyse the combined datasets in order to examine the relation between purchase behaviour and mobility.

1. Ticket Purchases: travellers buy credit in small increments. Figure 1(a) shows the top-4 most popular travel card purchases (grouped by temporal validity) and PAYG credit amounts (grouped in GBP5 increments); these account for, respectively, 95.5% and 98.6% of all the purchases. This clearly shows that travellers tend to opt to *buy credit in small increments*: half of the credit purchases are less than GBP 5 and 74% are less than GBP 20, which indicates that credit is bought on an as-required basis. 7-day long passes are the most popular travel card purchase. We inspected this further by looking at the use of travel cards and PAYG by individual travellers. Overall, a majority of travellers do not use travel cards: 75.9% and 77% of the users in D1 and D2 respectively never make a trip with a travel card. However, travel cards are used more often than PAYG on bus trips (70% of trips are made with travel cards); having a travel card is an incentive to use the bus. This trend

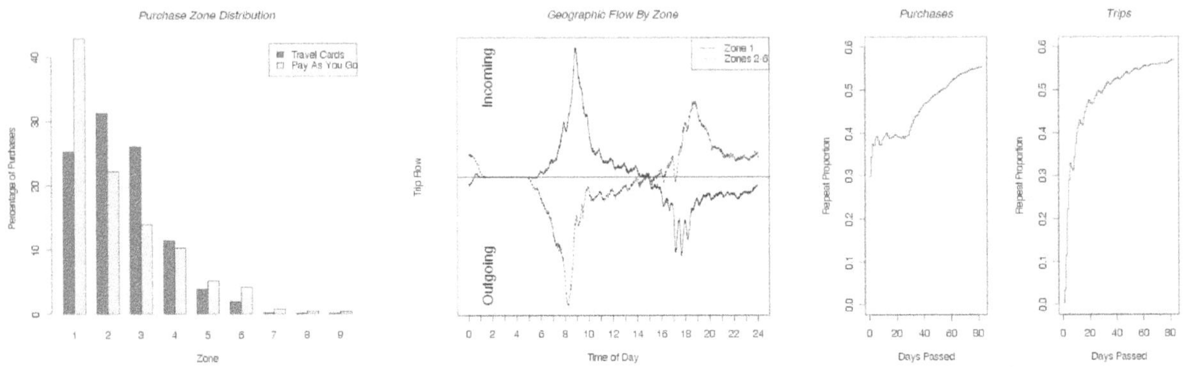

(a) Zone Purchase Distribution (b) Geographic Flow by Zone (c) Repeat Trips and Purchases

Figure 2: *Pay As You Go* Credit and Travel Cards: (a) the geographic purchase distribution, by zone, (b) the cumulative number of entries and exits (flow) into Zone 1 and outside Zone 1, and (c) the average proportion of repeat trips and purchases in the datasets over time.

flips for rail trips (38.2% travel card, 59.4% PAYG), with the remaining fraction being mixed fares.

2. Temporal Distribution: travel cards are bought on Mondays. Figure 1(b) shows the temporal distribution of purchases in a week: while credit purchases tend to remain constant throughout the week, travel cards are mostly bought in the early days of the week. Again, travellers are viewing the system on a weekly-basis, and may thus be discounting the potential benefit of month/year passes. Figure 1(c) shows the the cumulative number of ongoing trips over 7 days; the commuting majority dominate over the week day patterns.

3. Geographical Distribution: PAYG travellers do not plan ahead. Figure 2(a) plots the geographic distribution of purchases, split by fare zone (recall that Zone 1 is central London, with higher zones being concentric circles around it). The majority of PAYG purchases occur within Zone 1, while there are more travel cards bought in Zones 2 and 3 than central London. A potential explanation for this comes from the aggregate trip data. After clustering the stations by fare zone, we can count arrivals (+1) and departures (−1) from each zone and sum these two together. At any given time period, a zone's flow is positive if there are more arrivals than departures, and negative if there are more departures than arrivals. The resulting data is shown in Figure 2(b). The only zone to be positive in the morning (arrivals) and negative in the afternoon (departures) is Zone 1; all other zones, which have been grouped in Figure 2(b), each *individually* show departure trips in the morning and arrival trips in the afternoon/evening. Relating purchase behaviour to traveller flow indicates that PAYG credit, must be mainly purchased between commuter's outbound and return journey, while travel cards are more frequently bought before or after the day's travel.

4. Repeat Behaviours: travellers do the same thing again and again. To what extent are travellers making the same trips and buying the same fares repeatedly? We examined this question by defining a repeat trip made by an individual as a *train* trip with the same origin and destination as a previously taken trip (we do not include bus trips since we do not know where travellers alighted). Similarly, we defined a repeat purchase as either a PAYG credit purchase with *exactly* the same amount as has been purchased before, or a travel card that has been bought before. After the 83 days of each dataset, we find that over half of all the trips *and* purchases have been seen before, as shown in Figure 2(c): travellers are highly regular in both their movements and purchases.

Based on the above analysis, two facts emerge: (1) there exists high *regularity* (and thus predictability) of both travel behaviour (Figures 1(a) 1(b) 1(c)) and of purchase behaviour (Figures 1(a) 2(c)); (2) there exists a strong correlation between travel behaviour (e.g., what travel zones are crossed) and purchase behaviour (e.g,. what ticket type, PAYG versus travel card are purchased) (Figures 2(a) 2(c)). However, a question arises as to whether this *repeated correlation* between travel and purchase behaviours is optimal, or whether travellers are wasting their money instead. In the following section, we quantify how much people overspend by computing the optimal fares for each traveller.

3.2 Potential Savings

In this section, we look at what travellers *could have* saved, had they made the optimal purchase decisions for all their travel habits, that is, had they known, a priori, exactly what trips they were going to make and purchased the cheapest sequence of fares. We first encoded the tube network structure and implemented Floyd's algorithm [1] to find the shortest path between any origin and destination (by number of hops). This way, we can infer which zones each trip should traverse and thus which PAYG, travel card, and mixed fares are applicable. Although our data is from 2009, we used 2011 fares since historical fares are not currently available; this does not affect our results since (a) we are using the same fares to compute both the "actual" and optimal trip costs and (b) the relative benefit of one fare over another is the same.

We then compute, for each individual, a sequence of optimal fares by building a tree, where each node is a ticket and a chain of linked nodes denotes a sequence of purchase decisions. Tickets have two corresponding costs: the initial cost (which is zero for PAYG and non-zero for travel cards), and any additional charges that a traveller is subject to while using that ticket (e.g., mixed-fare trips). The nodes also have a geographic validity (i.e., zones) and expiry date: single fares expire immediately, while travel cards expire a

Spending	Cumulative	Trip Avg	User Avg
D1 Actual	13,797,168.10	1.47	52.20
D1 Optimal	11,395,244.90	1.22	43.11
Difference	**2,401,923.20**	**0.25**	**9.09**
D2 Actual	13,393,208.20	1.47	50.09
D2 Optimal	11,196,687.40	1.24	41.88
Difference	**2,196,520.80**	**0.23**	**8.21**

Table 3: Results (GBP) for D1 (May - July 2009) and D2 (Oct 2009 - Jan 2010) with the actual and optimal spending, quantified as cumulative, trip average, and user average spend.

number of days after purchase. For each trip that a traveller makes, the leaves of the tree that are expired or not valid are expanded by adding child nodes representing the tickets that the traveller could select from. The cheapest fare is computed with a depth-first search on the tree. Brute-force exhaustive search on this tree would have a space complexity of $O(b^d)$, where the branching factor b is the number of available fares and the depth d is the number of trips taken by the user. The resulting computational cost is prohibitive for all users who have taken more than a handful of trips in the 83-day periods covered by our datasets. We have thus adopted a number of heuristic expansion and pruning rules that reduce this search space [2], as we describe next.

Expansion Constraints. First, we implemented TfL's price "capping" system that prevents a traveller's daily PAYG cost from exceeding that of the relevant travel card. Second, we consider the *geographical* requirements of all the user's trips. For example, if a traveller will only commute between Zone 3 to Zone 4, then fares and travel cards that do not include these areas (e.g., a Zone 1-2 travel card) are not amongst the available options to expand the leaves. When expanding the tree, we further reduced the number of candidate child nodes by taking transport modality into consideration; for example, if we are expanding based on a rail trip, then bus-only fares are not included.

Pruning Rules. We also defined a *pruning* function that, as the tree grows, removes the subtrees with ticket sets that are already more expensive than those in other subtrees. More formally, let us define $expire(X)$ as the expiry date of the cheapest fare sequence starting from a generic node X, and $cost(X)$ as the total cost of the cheapest fare sequence from node X. Given two sibling nodes X and Y, we prune X's branch if the following holds:

$$(expire(X) \leq expire(Y)) \wedge (cost(X) > cost(Y)) \quad (1)$$

In other words, if a ticket has a shorter temporal validity than another and is already more expensive, then it can be pruned. Similarly, if a node with a smaller geographic range is already more expensive than another with a larger range, then this is due to the extra incurred cost of mixed-fare trips and the node can be pruned. For example, a ticket for Zone 3 to 4 is "smaller" than Zone 3 to 5, and any trips between Zone 3 and 5 using it will be charged at a mixed-fare rate.

The potential savings are shown in Table 3. Overall, we find that this 5% sample of travellers are spending just under GBP 2.5 million more than they need to. Overall, each user in D1, on average, overspends by GBP 10. Two points to note are: (a) using this sample of people to approximate the entire population would mean multiplying these figures by 20 and (b) both datasets only cover an 83 day period. In other words, we estimate that travellers cumulatively spend up to approximately GBP 200 million per year more than they need to, by simply buying the incorrect fares.

In the following section, we aim to answer this question by uncovering the heuristics used by travellers to guide their purchase choices; we will then propose algorithms that can provide travellers with cost-saving ticket recommendations.

3.3 Purchase Decision Survey

There are a number of aspects relating to purchase decisions that the datasets do not reveal; the datasets cannot tell us *why* people opt for the fares that they buy and any biases that they may be subject to. To explore this space, we designed an online survey. The survey was divided into three sections: (a) questions about *travel habits*: travel times, typical trip origins/destinations, and transport modes that are most often used; (b) questions about *purchasing habits*: typical top-up amounts and travel cards bought and why they are purchased; and lastly (c) open-ended questions about their impressions of cost-saving and fare selection. The survey was disseminated online (via twitter and mailing lists) and completed by 119 travellers (30% students).

The origin/destination pairs reported show that 92% of respondents travel into Zone 1 during a typical week day, much like the results we found in Figure 2(b). While self-reported travel behaviour broadly correlates to that observed in the two large datasets, we found significant differences in terms of habits: only 7% of respondents claimed to top-up by less than GBP 5, which does not match the proportion of these transactions (49.5%) we found in the datasets. Furthermore, a large proportion of respondents stated that they never buy travel cards (46%), although this falls short of the proportion of users in the larger datasets who also exhibited this behaviour. Only 18% of respondents claimed that they typically buy a 7-day travel card, although we had previously found this to be the most popular purchase choice.

These differences between self-reported and observed purchasing data can be explained in two ways: they may be due to the demographic biases in this sample of survey respondents (even though their self-reported travel behaviour did match that observed in our datasets), or they may be a consequence of the divergence between travellers's perceived versus actual purchase behaviour (e.g., they may be unaware of the high volume and cumulative effect of small transactions that they carry out). We explored the misalignment between travellers' perceived and actual behaviour further, by asking *why* they opt for the fares they buy. PAYG was preferred when users expected their travel to be irregular (38.8% of the total votes), and when they believed this was the cheapest option for them (with 32.2% of the votes). Travel cards were preferred for convenience (39.4%), and again because it was thought to be cost-saving (44.9%). However, despite money-saving being a top priority overall, our previous analysis demonstrates massive amounts of money is actually being wasted by the travellers. We also asked respondents about *when* they top up their PAYG credit versus when they purchase a travel-card, and the majority of them (77%) reported that they only top up when they have insufficient credit to enter the system, demonstrating no element of planning whatsoever in this behaviour.

In the following section, we show how data mining tech-

		Avg Trips/Day	Geography		Travel Time		Travel Modality	
Method	**Span**	**MAE**	**Precision**	**Recall**	**Precision**	**Recall**	**Precision**	**Recall**
Last Profile	1	0.72	0.9974	0.9976	0.8774	0.8313	0.9198	0.9161
	7	0.41	0.9939	0.9940	0.8532	0.8509	0.9049	0.9050
	30	0.30	0.9891	0.9899	0.8955	0.9172	0.9303	0.9298
Avg Profile	1	0.76	0.9996	0.9693	0.7267	0.7881	0.8239	0.8935
	7	0.38	0.9978	0.9759	0.8607	0.8214	0.9123	0.8722
	30	0.29	0.9916	0.9845	0.9156	0.9149	0.9444	0.9231
Moving Avg	1	0.69	0.9979	0.9963	0.5570	0.8285	0.7181	0.9443
	7	0.37	0.9956	0.9908	0.8096	0.8689	0.8866	0.9131
	30	0.29	0.9916	0.9844	0.9039	0.9192	0.9389	0.9314

Table 4: Averaged Results for D1 and D2 when predicting users' travel profiles: How many trips per day will they take? What zones will they travel between? Will they only travel off-peak? Lastly, will they only take bus trips?

niques can be applied to aide travellers by providing fare recommendations based on their trip history.

4. RECOMMENDING TICKETS

We formalise the ticket recommendation problem as follows. If we consider the factors that influence travel cost (as outlined in Section 2), we can conclude that knowing a traveller's *detailed* future trips, as origin-destination pairs, is not strictly necessary in order to recommend the best fare. This is due to the zone structure of the stations: the fact that a user went from Leicester Square to Heathrow Airport is not needed to determine cost (all that is required is that a trip was taken from Zone 1 to Zone 6). Instead, a number of features shared by these trips are more relevant. Determining the appropriate fare can be based on an estimate of the broad aspects of a traveller's habits, such as frequency and geographic areas of travel. More formally, given a sequence of T(u) trips by user u, a traveller's habits between time t and $(t+\Delta)$ can be summarised as:

$$P_u(t, t+\Delta) = \{d, f, b, r, pt, ot, G\} \quad (2)$$

where d is the number of trips, f is the average trips per day, b and r represent the proportion of trips that were taken with buses and by rail respectively, pt and op are the proportion of peak and off-peak trips, and G is an N×N matrix, with N = the number of zones in London, and each $G_{i,j}$ is the frequency count of trips between these two areas. We assume that, for other cities, a similar profile could be designed with a basic understanding of the public transport fare structure.

Given this set up, the task of recommending the next suitable fare(s) can be decomposed into two prediction problems. The first is predicting a user's *future mobility patterns* $P_u(t, t+\Delta)$, given a sequence of P_u from prior to t. The second problem is to fit the appropriate fare to a profile of mobility requirements (i.e., predicting a ticket given a travel profile). In the following sections, we look at and evaluate each of these prediction problems individually.

4.1 Predicting Future Travel Habits

The first step in determining the best fares for a traveller is forecasting their travel habits, in order to understand their needs. As above, each user's trips over a particular period can be condensed into a *profile* of values representing their geographical, temporal, and modality requirements. The objective here is therefore to predict these values, given a history of profiles. We applied a number of baseline algorithms to this problem.

1. **Last Profile:** assumes that travel habits are constant; a future profile between time t and $(t+\Delta)$ is predicted to be the same as the profile between $(t-\Delta)$ and t.

2. **Cumulative/Average Profile:** leverages more historical data than the last value; the modality, temporal and geographic features are simply sums of past behaviour (e.g., we predict that a user will travel in Zone 1-2 if that traveller has trips between these zones in the past). If we define H as the *set* of profiles, each of span Δ, that come before t:

$$H = [P(t_0, t_0+\Delta), ..., P(t-\Delta, t)] \quad (3)$$

Then the future profile trip frequency is defined the average of the past ones:

$$P_u(t, t+\Delta) = \frac{1}{|H|}\sum_{i \in H} H_i \quad (4)$$

3. **Moving Average Profile.** Lastly, we define a moving average profile, which gives additional weight to more recent profiles. At each time interval $(t, t+\Delta)$, the trip frequency f is defined as:

$$f_{t,t+\Delta} = \alpha \cdot f_{t-\Delta,t} + (1-\alpha) \cdot f_{t-2\Delta,t-\Delta} \quad (5)$$

All members of the traveller's profile are similarly updated, with the same scaling factor α.

Our experiments proceed as follows: given each user's trips, we can form a set of n profiles for a given time length (e.g., Δ =1-day profiles). We then use the historical profiles $[0, 1, ..., n-1]$ in order to predict the nth profile: Δ remains fixed. We repeat this process for all users and varying time lengths. Our evaluation metrics focus on the aspects of these predictions that will directly affect cost: we first estimate the average trips per day for a given user, and measure error with the mean absolute error (MAE); we then measure precision and recall of classifying travel within each pair of geographic zones, whether a user will *solely* take bus trips, and whether a user will *only* travel during off-peak times.

All the results are shown in Table 4. We found that users' travel habits are easily estimated with these baselines: for example, precision and recall are consistently above 98% across all methods, when predicting what zones each user will travel in. A number of interesting trends also appear: for example, estimating average trips per day becomes more accurate over longer time spans. Classifying whether travellers will solely travel in off-peak times and whether they will only take bus trips is estimated slightly less accurately, although precision and recall values are still very high (91-94%). To explain these highly accurate results, it is important to reinforce that we are predicting habits over very coarse features (zones rather than stations): at this granularity of geography, travellers are incredibly consistent.

Note that each of the algorithms we used views the components of travellers' profiles as independent from one another (which is not the case); there are a number of models that could leverage inter-dependencies between profile features in order to improve predictions. However, since we found that even these simple baselines produce highly accurate results, we leave an examination of more complex models [4] as future work.

Note that, in the above approach, each algorithm was computing predictions over a pre-defined prediction window Δ. In practice, in order to recommend tickets to travellers, multiple windows of different length will need to be considered simultaneously ($t + \Delta$, $t + \Delta'$, $t + \Delta''$, etc.), in order to be able to recommend what the best next purchase is, between tickets of different time validity (PAYG, week, and month travel cards), which we leave as future work.

4.2 Predicting the Next Cheapest Fare

The next problem we need to solve is matching travel habits to the cheapest fares; this setting heavily relies on an accurate forecast of each user's travel profile. In this work we assume that these were predicted accurately. In future work, we plan on investigating the effect of prediction errors in users' travel profile on the ticket recommendations they receive. We regard this as a generic classification problem: given a vector of values representing trip habits, we need to select from a set of categorical labels representing tickets. Classification has been widely addressed in the literature and there are a range of algorithms that are readily applicable to this scenario. Our evaluation proceeds as follows: given the trip data described above, we first compute the travel profiles and optimal fares for each user (as per Section 3.2). We thus produce a dataset of profile instances of *varying lengths* Δ, each with the corresponding label. We then randomly split this data into training (80% of the users) and test (20% of the users) sets. We split by user so that we could quantify how much these users would save with our algorithms; we also measure the accuracy of classifying the instances in the test set as the number of correctly classified instances over the total number of instances. The techniques we evaluated on our data include:

1. **Baseline**. This classifier simply returns the most frequent class in our training set (PAYG). Inherently, we expect this classifier to do relatively well; by (correctly) predicting the fares for those users who should travel on PAYG, it corrects the cases of users who bought travel cards without needing to do so.

2. **Naïve Bayes**. This classifier, based on Bayes' theorem, assumes that each feature of the users' profiles is independent from the others. Given a profile with n features $P_u = \{F_1, F_2, ..., F_n\}$, the probability that the best fare is ticket C is estimated as:

$$p(C|P_u) = p(C)\prod_{i=1}^{n} p(F_i|C) \qquad (6)$$

The best ticket is then selected as the class with the highest probability. For all features that do not relate to geographic requirements (i.e., all except feature G above), the posterior probability that feature F_i in class C has value v is estimated with a Gaussian distribution that is parameterised with the mean, μ_C, and variance, σ_C^2, of the feature F_i in class C:

$$P(F_i = v|C) = \frac{1}{\sqrt{2\pi\sigma_C^2}} e^{-\frac{(v-\mu_C)^2}{2\sigma_C^2}} \qquad (7)$$

The geographic features, instead, are transposed into binary variables, and the posterior is estimated as the proportion of instances in class C where F_i is non zero.

3. **k-Nearest Neighbours**. This technique operates by finding, for each test profile, the k most similar profiles; the predicted class is the most frequent class that appears in the neighbour set. We first defined similarity as the absolute difference between two profiles (thus, smaller values indicate higher similarity). We also introduced two small modifications: we gave higher weight to the average trips per day and days of travel (by using the squared difference) than to the proportion of bus trips (by ignoring the similarity between pairs of profiles where one only rides the bus and the other does not).

4. **Decision Trees**. The C4.5 algorithm [5] is a statistical classifier that generates a decision tree which can be used to classify test instances. It does so by recursively partitioning the data on a single attribute, according to the measured information gain of each split, where gain is defined relative to the *entropy* $E(S)$ of each group S:

$$E(S) = -\sum_{i=1}^{n} p(x_i)\log_b p(x_i) \ , \qquad (8)$$

where n is the number of classes (i.e., tickets) and $p(x_i)$ is the proportion of S belonging to class i. In this work, we used the open-source implementation of C4.5 from the WEKA project [6].

	Accuracy (%)		Savings (GBP)	
Method	D1	D2	D1	D2
Baseline	74.99	76.91	326,447.95	306,145.85
Naïve Bayes	77.46	80.71	393,585.81	369,232.24
k-NN (5)	96.74	97.09	465,822.17	426,375.85
C4.5	98.01	98.29	473,918.38	434,082.81
Oracle	100.0	100.0	479,583.91	438,923.30

Table 5: Ten-fold cross validated classification accuracy for each dataset and average cumulative savings if travellers used each algorithm's recommendation.

We measure each classifier's performance with the proportion of correctly classified test instances (which we denote as accuracy); a summary of the ten-fold cross validated results is shown in Table 5. The accuracy of the baseline is due to the large proportion of users in our datasets who have very few trips (thus making PAYG their cheapest fare). However, all the algorithms were able to outperform the baseline by varying amounts: the C4.5 decision tree produced the most accurate results, at over 96% and 98% for D1 and D2 respectively. We also quantified the savings that our travellers could have cumulatively achieved, had they followed each algorithm's recommendation, along with the maximum possible savings computed with the tree-based method described in Section 3.2 (denoted "oracle"). The total amount of possible savings, for both datasets, were over GBP 400 thousand. In both cases, the savings obtained by the C4.5 decision tree were less than 5 thousand pounds away from the optimal: over 99% of the potential savings were obtained by this algorithm's classifications. Interestingly, the baseline also provides modest savings: it seems from this that a large waste is generated by people buying travel cards that they then do not use.

5. RELATED WORK

By combining data from public transport and fare purchases, this study has a wide range of related research. At the broadest level, we categorise these into two different groups: understanding *mobility*, which has been studied using a variety of different data sources, and investigating and mining *decision making* contexts, by building recommender systems.

5.1 Mining and Modeling Mobility

Insight into human mobility is recognised as the key to understanding a variety complex phenomena, such as the spread of disease and traffic pattern forecasting [7], as well as giving an understanding into urban design and flow. It has been studied using mobile phone data [7, 8], travel data [3], and bank note dispersal patterns [9]. Fare collection data provides an alternative data source into people's commuting habits and mobility; the analysis in Section 3 highlighted a range of behaviours, ranging from aggregate, city-wide flows to individual modality choices.

These works examine mobility in isolation. Richer scenarios have also been researched: for example, Graham and Glaister [10] developed models to test the influence of traffic pricing on congestion and travel times. More generally, many transport-related projects are dedicated toward understanding mobility and building advanced traveller information systems (for example, [11, 12]). These systems all aim to help people travel, but rarely factor in the cost of doing so; we found that, in the context of public transport, there have been no efforts dedicated to helping commuters buy cost-saving fares.

5.2 Decision Making

Decision making is also at the forefront of research and popular literature [13]. In the field of data mining, there are two questions that arise: the first is *when* to make a decision in a volatile environment. For example, Etzioni *et al.* [14] mine airfare data in order to predict when the best time to buy a plane ticket is; in this case, airfare prices vary over time according to hidden variables (such as seat availability). Much like algorithmic trading, the basis of the decision is to predict the minimum of a time-varying price. The methods developed by these researchers do not apply to the problem of public transport fare selection, as prices will not vary at such heightened frequencies. Instead, our context relates to decision making in the face of an abundance of options. In general, the solution for the information overload problem [15] in web settings (e-commerce, movie rentals and music) is building online recommender systems [16]. As the web becomes evermore mobile, the breadth of contexts addressed by recommender systems is also growing to include urban navigation [17]. While personalisation and recommender systems have been widely adopted in online environments, there still exists a broad variety of contexts where users need to make complex decisions without the aide of these technologies. One area where recommender systems have little to no presence is the domain of the *individual, off-line* financial transactions and purchase decisions that people need to regularly make. This paper considers one such example: the problem of selecting which public transport ticket is best suited to a particular traveller.

6. CONCLUSION

In this paper, we investigated the financial benefits that can be offered to travellers after mining their mobility data. At face value, our proposals may be seen as detrimental to business, since they lower the gross income of the transport authority. However, by offering a service that enables travellers to understand and improve their spending habits, the adoption and use of public transport may actually rise, as travellers know that they are being given the best fare.

The details of this study are location-specific: we focus on the fare and public transport network structure in London, and also on the data that is available from the AFC system adopted by TfL. The applicability of these techniques to other cities will rely on the data collection and fare structures in place; for example, the fare scheme in Seoul, Korea, also factors in distance [18]. However, an overriding conclusion is that the *availability* and *mining* of AFC data presents many opportunities for personalised, dynamic services that cater for individual travellers [19].

We first evaluated baseline algorithms for estimating traveller mobility patterns, and found them to be highly consistent. We then evaluated algorithms that, given a travel profile, can predict what the best fare will be. Both prediction problems remain considerate of each traveller's privacy: they do not require the full trip history of each user to be stored, but only a less fine grained summary profile.

The evaluation metrics that we used focused on *accuracy*, *precision*, *recall*, and *potential savings*. In practice, rank-based metrics may also be helpful, since a deployed system would not want to recommend a single ticket for purchase, but rather present the most appropriate set of fares to each traveller, allowing them to make their own decisions. However, a useful side-effect of the classification algorithms that we evaluated is that they also pave the way for *explanations* to be given to travellers (e.g., we recommend the week pass since you tend to travel x times per week but only y times per month). In fact, a key role of this system would be to simplify the ticket purchase decision process, by decreasing the number of fare options offered to each traveller, so that they are aligned with their travel behaviour; as a consequence of the *informed* choices being made, users may then adapt their behaviour based on the fares they have purchased.

We conclude by noting how similar techniques could be applied to a myriad of scenarios: wherever traces of human behaviour can be collected, data mining can be used to complement the daily decisions that people make. Examples include recommending telephone contracts (or call plans) based on mobile phone usage or recommending investment and saving plans based on bank account data.

Acknowledgements. The authors would like to thank Angela Sasse and Philip Inglesant for help with the survey and Tamas Jambor, Joachim Neumann and Xavier Amatriain for their comments. The research leading to these results has received funding from the European Community's Seventh Framework Programme (FP7-SST-2008-RTD-1) under Grant Agreement n. 234239.

7. REFERENCES

[1] R. W. Floyd. Algorithm 97: Shortest Path. *Communications of the ACM*, 5(6), June 1962.

[2] R. Zhou and E. A. Hansen. Breadth-First Heuristic Search. *Artificial Intelligence*, 170, April 2006.

[3] C. Roth, S.M. Kang, M. Batty, and M. Barthelemy. Structure of Urban Movements: Polycentric Activity and Entangled Hierarchical Flows. *PLOS ONE*, 6.

[4] T. W. Anderson. *The Statistical Analysis of Time Series*. Wiley-Interscience, 1994.

[5] J. R. Quinlan. Improved Use of Continuous Attributes in C4.5. *Journal of Artificial Intelligence Research*, 4:77–90, 1996.

[6] M. Hall, E. Frank, G. Holmes, B. Pfahringer, and P. Reutemann. The WEKA Data Mining Software. *SIGKDD Explorations*, 11, 2009.

[7] M. C. Gonzalez, C. A. Hidalgo, and A-L Barabasi. Understanding Individual Human Mobility Patterns. *Nature*, 453:779–782, June 2008.

[8] C. Ratti, R.M. Pulselli, S. Williams, and D. Frenchman. Mobile Landscapes: Using Location Data from Cell Phones for Urban Analysis. *Environment and Planning B*, 33(5):727–748, 2006.

[9] D. Brockmann, L. Hufnagel, and T. Geisel. The Scaling Laws of Human Travel. *Nature*, 439, January 2006.

[10] D. J. Graham and S. Glaister. Spatial Implications of Transport Pricing. *Journal of Transport Economics and Policy (JTEP)*, 40(2), May 2006.

[11] B. Ferris, K. Watkins, and A. Borning. OneBusAway: Results from Providing Real-Time Arrival Information for Public Transit. In *ACM CHI*, Atlanta, GA, 2010.

[12] J.L. Ambite, G. Barish, C.A. Knoblock, M. Muslea, J. Oh, and S. Minton. Getting from Here to There: Interactive Planning and Agent Execution for Optimizing Travel. In *14th Conference on Innovative Applications of Artificial Intelligence (IAAI)*, pages 862–869, Menlo Park, California, 2002.

[13] B. Schwartz. *The Paradox of Choice: Why More is Less*. Harper Perennial, 2004.

[14] O. Etzioni, C. A. Knoblock, R. Tuchinda, and A. Yates. To Buy or Not to Buy: Mining Airfare Data to Minimize Ticket Purchase Price. In *ACM KDD*, Washington DC, USA, 2003.

[15] A. Borchers, J. Herlocker, J. Konstan, and J. Riedl. Ganging up on Information Overload. *IEEE Computer*, 31:106–108, 1998.

[16] F. Ricci, L. Rokach, B. Shapira, and P. Kantor, editors. *Recommender System Handbook*. Springer, 2010.

[17] D. Quercia, N. Lathia, F. Calabrese, G. Di Lorenzo, and J. Crowcroft. Recommending Social Events from Mobile Phone Location Data. In *IEEE ICDM*, Sydney, Australia, December 2010.

[18] W. Jang. Travel Time and Transfer Analysis Using Transit Smart Card Data. *Transportation Research Board*, 2010.

[19] H. Bryan and P. Blythe. Understanding Behaviour Through Smartcard Data Analysis. *Proceedings of the Institution of Civil Engineers: Transport*, 160(4), 2007.

Mining Mobility User Profiles for Car Pooling

Roberto Trasarti
Fabio Pinelli
Mirco Nanni
Fosca Giannotti

KDD Lab, ISTI, CNR
email: name.surname @ isti.cnr.it

ABSTRACT

In this paper we introduce a methodology for extracting mobility profiles of individuals from raw digital traces (in particular, GPS traces), and study criteria to match individuals based on profiles. We instantiate the profile matching problem to a specific application context, namely proactive car pooling services, and therefore develop a matching criterion that satisfies various basic constraints obtained from the background knowledge of the application domain. In order to evaluate the impact and robustness of the methods introduced, two experiments are reported, which were performed on a massive dataset containing GPS traces of private cars: (i) the impact of the car pooling application based on profile matching is measured, in terms of percentage shareable traffic; (ii) the approach is adapted to coarser-grained mobility data sources that are nowadays commonly available from telecom operators. In addition the ensuing loss in precision and coverage of profile matches is measured.

Categories and Subject Descriptors

H.3.4 [**Systems and Software**]: User profiles and alert services; H.2.8 [**Database Applications**]: Data mining

General Terms

Algorithms

Keywords

Trajectory patterns, Spatio-temporal data mining

1. INTRODUCTION

The analysis of movement data has been recently fostered by the widespread diffusion of new techniques and systems for monitoring, collecting and storing location-aware data, generated by a wealth of technological infrastructures, such as GPS positioning and wireless networks [7]. These have made massive repositories of spatio-temporal data available that record human mobile activities, such as data location from mobile phones, and GPS tracks from mobile devices.

There are many potential opportunities, and movement data have already been recognized by private and public institutions as a valuable source of information to assess the lifestyle, habits and demands of citizens in terms of mobility.

The traditional use of mobility data, for instance in the context of urban traffic monitoring and transportation planning, mainly focuses on inferring simple measurements and aggregations, such as density of traffic, and car flows on road segments. Recent research in mobility analysis has been extended in order to identify the behaviors that people (taken as a whole group, rather than as individuals) consistently follow, such as groups of trajectories with a common route [2] or popular itineraries [6]. This can also be extended to problems that need to link different geographical areas. This is because we can now infer information in terms of origin-destination pairs of areas that exchange traffic, as well as the routes along which the exchange occurs.

Despite the great attention that this area has attracted, current work on mobility analysis largely neglects a key element that lies in between single trajectories and a whole population, i.e. the individual person, with his/her regularities and habits, that can be differed from the population. In fact, analysing individuals (rather than just large groups) provides the basis for an understanding of systematic mobility, as opposed to occasional movements, which is fundamental in some mobility planning applications, e.g. public transport. This paper proposes a framework that accommodates a "middle level element", providing a two-phase process: first an individual-centered mobility model extraction; then a population-wide analysis based on the individual models. Our framework can be seen as a new approach in the learning paradigm since it provides a local-to-global analysis.

The main contributions of this paper are: (i) we introduce the concept of the *mobility profile* of a user as the set of his/her *routine trips*, and define a general method based on trajectory clustering to extract such profiles; (ii) we show an instantiation of the method on the GPS data of vehicles with a *route similarity* function. We perform an empirical evaluation of the effects of the different parameter settings of the method; (iii) we propose a car pooling service on the basis of the GPS-based profiling method; (iv) we study the robustness of the general method w.r.t. the downgrading of the spatio-temporal richness of the data. We thus generated a synthetic GSM-like dataset out of the GPS data, and instantiated the method on these data. The final comparison

KDD'11, August 21–24, 2011, San Diego, California, USA.

confirms the goodness of the method for profile extraction, in the sense that comparable profiles are extracted for each user. In contrast, the car pooling service does not appear to be well supported by the second scenario.

The rest of the paper is organised as follows. In Sec.2 we present the background on mobility data mining, in Sec.3 we present the methodology for the mobility profile extraction in terms of GPS-equipped vehicles. In Sec.4 we define the match between a pair of profiles and its application to a car pooling service. In Sec.5 a downgrading quality precision process is presented and its impact on the mobility profile extraction and matching is investigated in detail. Section 6 highlights the most promising future lines of research.

2. BACKGROUND AND RELATED WORK

The core contribution of this paper consists in a methodology for mobility analysis, aimed in particular to match users based on their individual mobility behaviours. While mobility data mining [7] as a whole is a recent research field, a significant amount of works with similar objectives already exists.

A close body of research can be found in the mobility clustering literature, aimed at finding sets of trajectories that are similar. The standard approach adapts classical distance-based algorithms and defines ad hoc distances for trajectory data [10], possibly with limited ad hoc refinements [2]. Alternative, ad hoc solutions include variants of model-based clustering [5], collective movements detection methods [9], and others. Based on similar solutions a recommendation system is proposed in [14,15] where the user trajectories are translated into sequence of regions of interest and then compared. As opposed to existing solutions, in our proposal the evaluation of similarity between individuals is not realized as a direct comparison of trajectories. Instead, a two-phase analysis is performed, that first finds typical behaviours for each single user (and this task clearly falls within the scope of trajectory clustering), and then compares pairs of users through a comparison between their corresponding sets of behaviours. The research in analyzing the mobility data is increasing; most works try either to infer simple movement aggregates (average speed, etc.) in local areas, with an emphasis to real-time applications, or to discover macro-level laws of human mobility, such as the law governing the distribution of traveled distances [8, 11], with applications to high-level evaluations of predictability of human mobility [12]. The analysis framework proposed in this paper can adapt to different mobility data types, and indeed a comparative study is performed on several of them, which provides insights on how spatial granularity (GPS precise points vs. GSM large cells) and sampling rate (continuous vs. phone call rates) affect the process.

3. MOBILITY PROFILES EXTRACTION

The daily mobility of each user can be essentially summarized by a set of single trips that the user performs during the day. When trying to extract a *mobility profile* of users, our interest is in the trips that are part of their habits, therefore neglecting occasional variations that divert from their typical behavior. Therefore in order to identify the individual mobility profiles of users from their GPS traces, the following steps will be performed - see Figure 1:

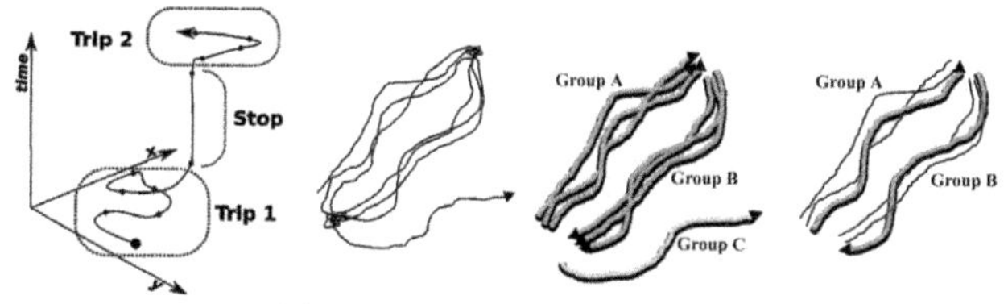

(a) (b) (c)

Figure 1: Mobility profile extraction process: (a) trip identification; (b) group detection/outlier removal; (c) selection of representative mobility profiles.

1. divide the whole history of the user into trips (Figure 1(a))
2. group trips that are similar, discarding the outliers (Figure 1(b))
3. from each group, extract a set of representative trips, to be used as mobility profiles (Figure 1(c)).

3.1 Mobility profile definitions

Trips. The history of a user is represented by the set of points in space and time recorded by their mobility device:

DEFINITION 1 (USER HISTORY). *The user history is defined as an ordered sequence of spatio-temporal points* $H = \langle p_1 \dots p_n \rangle$ *where* $p_i = (x, y, t)$ *and* x, y *are spatial coordinates and* t *is an absolute timepoint.*

This continuous stream of information contains different trips made by the user, therefore in order to distinguish between them we need to detect when a user stops for a while in a place. This point in the stream will correspond to the end of a trip and the beginning of the next one. In literature there are two main approaches: clustering-based [3] and heuristic-based [14]. In this paper we adopt the latter for computational efficiency reasons. Thus we look for points that change only in time; i.e. they keep the same spatial position for a certain amount of time quantified by the temporal threshold $th^{stop}_{temporal}$. Specularly, a spatial threshold $th^{stop}_{spatial}$ is used to remove both the noise introduced by the imprecision of the device and the small movements that are of no interest for a particular analysis.

DEFINITION 2 (POTENTIAL STOPS). *Given the history* H *of a user and the thresholds* $th^{stop}_{spatial}$ *and* $th^{stop}_{temporal}$, *a* potential stop *is defined as a maximal subsequence* S *of the user's history* H *where the points remain within a spatial area for a certain period of time:* $S = \langle p_m \dots p_k \rangle \,|0 < m \leq k \leq n \wedge \forall_{m \leq i \leq k} Dist(p_m, p_i) \leq th^{stop}_{spatial} \wedge Dur(p_m, p_k) \geq th^{stop}_{temporal}$.

where $Dist$ is the Euclidean distance function defined between the spatial coordinates of the points, and Dur is the difference in the temporal coordinates of the points. Potential stops can overlap with each other (yet, none of them can completely contain the other, for the maximality condition), making it difficult to use them as a basis for further analysis. In order to avoid this, a criterion of *early selection* is adopted to remove any overlaps:

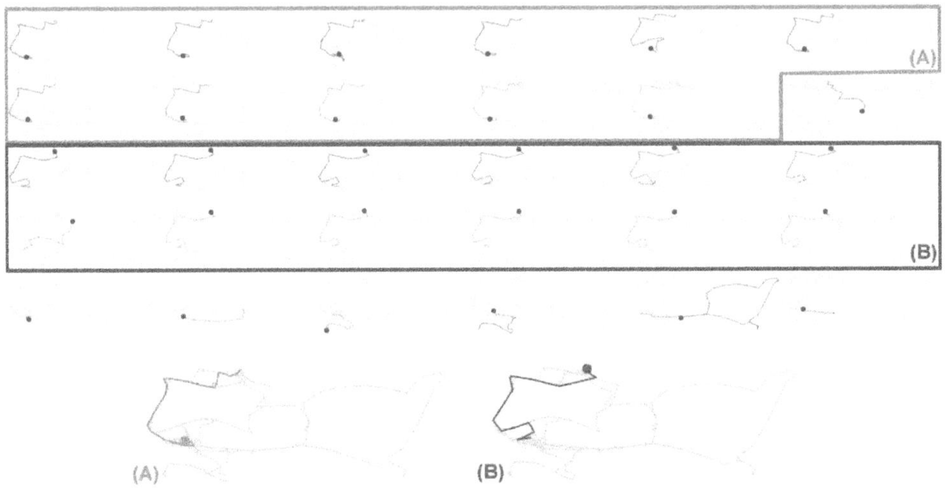

Figure 2: Trajectories of a user and the corresponding groups and routines extracted (A and B). Of the 30 trips, 11 are part of group A, and 12 of group B, while the remaining 7 are noise. The two routines are spatially similar, yet move in opposite directions (points represent the end of trips), i.e., south (A) vs. north (B).

DEFINITION 3 (ACTUAL STOPS). *Given a sequence of potential stops $S_{set} = \langle S_1, \ldots, S_N \rangle$, sorted by starting time (i.e., $S \leq S' \Leftrightarrow S = \langle (x, y, t), \ldots \rangle \wedge S' = \langle (x', y', t'), \ldots \rangle \wedge t \leq t'$), the corresponding sequence of* actual stops *$ActS$ is defined as the minimal sequence of potential stops such that:*

1. $S_1 \in ActS$
2. *if* $S_i \in ActS \wedge k = \min\{j | j > i \wedge S_j \cap S_i = \emptyset\} < \infty \Rightarrow S_k \in ActS$

We indicate with $\overline{S} = \langle S_1 \ldots S_t \rangle$ the set of all actual stops over H. Once we have found the stops in the users history we can identify the trips:

DEFINITION 4 (TRIP). *A trip is defined as a subsequence T of the user's history H between two consecutive actual stops in the ordered set $\overline{S}$ or between an actual stop and the first/last point of H (i.e., p_1 or p_n):*

- $T = \langle p_m, \ldots, p_k \rangle \,|0 < m \leq k \leq n \wedge \exists i(S_i = \langle \ldots, p_m \rangle \wedge S_{i+1} = \langle p_k, \ldots \rangle)$, *or*
- $T = \langle p_1, \ldots, p_m \rangle \,|0 < m \leq n \wedge \exists i(S_i = \langle p_m, \ldots \rangle)$, *or*
- $T = \langle p_k, \ldots, p_n \rangle \,|0 < k \leq n \wedge \exists i(S_i = \langle \ldots, p_k \rangle)$.

The set of extracted trips $\overline{T} = \langle T_1 \ldots T_c \rangle$ in Fig. 1(a), are the basic steps to create the user mobility profile. Notice that the thresholds $th^{stop}_{spatial}$ and $th^{stop}_{temporal}$ are the knobs for expressing specific analytical requirements.

Trip groups. Our objective is to use the set of trips of an individual user to find his/her routine behaviors. We do this by grouping together similar trips based on concepts of spatial distance and temporal alignment, with corresponding thresholds for both the spatial and temporal components of the trips. In order to be defined as *routine*, a behavior needs to be supported by a significant number of similar trips. The above ideas are formalized as follows:

DEFINITION 5 (TRIP GROUP). *Given a set of trips $\overline{T}$, spatial and temporal thresholds $th^{group}_{spatial}$ and $th^{group}_{temporal}$, a spatial distance function $\delta : \overline{T}^2 \rightarrow \mathcal{R}$ and a temporal alignment constraint $\alpha : \overline{T}^2 \times \mathcal{R} \rightarrow \mathcal{B}$ between pairs of trips, and a minimum support threshold $th^{group}_{support}$, a* trip group *for $\overline{T}$ is defined as a subset of trips $g \subseteq \overline{T}$ such that:*

1. $\forall t_1, t_2 \in g. \delta(t_1, t_2) \leq th^{group}_{spatial} \wedge \alpha(t_1, t_2, th^{group}_{temporal})$;
2. $|g| \geq th^{group}_{support}$.

Condition 1 requires that the trips in a group are approximately co-located, both in space and time, while condition 2 requires that the group is sufficiently large. Again, the thresholds are the knobs that the analyst will progressively tune the extraction process with.

Mobility Profile. Each group obtained in the previous step represents the typical mobility habit of a user, i.e., one of his/her routine movements. Here we summarize the whole group by choosing the central element of such a group:

DEFINITION 6 (ROUTINE). *Given a trip group g and the distance function δ used to compute it, its* routine *is defined as the medoid of the set, i.e.:*

$$routine(g,\delta) = \arg\min_{t \in g} \sum_{t' \in g \setminus \{t\}} \delta(t, t')$$

Notice that the temporal alignment is always satisfied over each pair of trips in a group, therefore the alignment relation α does not appear in the definition. Now we are ready to define the users mobility profile.

DEFINITION 7 (MOBILITY PROFILE). *Given a set of trip groups G of a user and the distance function δ used to compute them, the user's* mobility profile *is defined as his/her corresponding set of routines:*

$$profile(G,\delta) = \{routine(g,\delta) \mid g \in G\}$$

Algorithm 1: *Mobility profile construction*

INPUT:
User's Observations D
Spatial distance measure δ
Temporal alignment relation α
Set of Thresholds $th^{stop}_{spatial}$, $th^{stop}_{temporal}$, $th^{group}_{spatial}$, $th^{group}_{temporal}$, $th^{group}_{support}$

OUTPUT:
Mobility profile of the user P

BEGIN
$H = OrderByTime(D)$;
$\overline{T} = BuildTrips(H, th^{stop}_{spatial}, th^{stop}_{temporal})$;
$C = SelectGroups(\overline{T}, \delta, \alpha, th^{group}_{spatial}, th^{group}_{temporal}, th^{group}_{support})$;
$P = \emptyset$;
FOR EACH $c \in C$ DO
    IF $size(c) > th^{group}_{support}$ THEN
        $P = P \cup \{routine(c,\delta)\}$;
END;

Mobility profile construction. The whole mobility profile extraction – from the initial user history to the final mobility profiles – is summarized in Algorithm 1. The definitions provided in the previous section were kept generic w.r.t. the distance function δ. Different choices can satisfy different needs, possibly both conceptually (which criteria define a good group/routine assignment) and pragmatically (for instance, simpler criteria might be preferred for the sake of scalability). Obviously, the results obtained by different instantiations can vary greatly. Hence w.r.t. Algorithm 1 the crucial point is the *SelectGroup* procedure. Our proposal is to use a clustering method to carry out this task. We choose the clustering algorithm for trajectories proposed in [2], consisting of two steps. First, a density-based clustering is performed, thus removing noisy elements and producing dense – yet, possibly extensive – clusters. Secondly, each cluster is split through a bisection k-medoid procedure. Such method splits the dataset into two parts through k-medoid (a variant of k-means) with $k = 2$, then the same splitting process is recursively applied to each sub-group. Recursion stops when each resulting sub-cluster is compact enough to fit within a distance threshold of its medoid, by removing sub-clusters that are too small. The bisection k-medoid procedure guarantees that requirements 1 and 2 of Definition 5 are satisfied. The clustering method adopted is parametric w.r.t. a repertoire of similarity functions, that includes: *Ends* and *Starts* functions, comparing trajectories by considering only their last (respecively, first) points; *Route similarity*, comparing the paths followed by trajectories from a purely spatial viewpoint (time is not considered); *Synchronized route similarity*, similar to Route similarity but considering also time.

3.2 Profiling GPS-equipped vehicles

In this section we present the results of our method applied to a real dataset of GPS observations of 2,107 real car users in Tuscany in a time period of 12 days covering different kind of territories such as urban and suburban areas. This is a sample of data obtained by a private company employed specifically as a service for insurance companies and other clients called *octotelematics* [1]. The process is implemented using the data mining query language provided by the M-Atlas system [13]. We processed this dataset of observations using the *mobility profile construction* algorithm, with the following parameters:

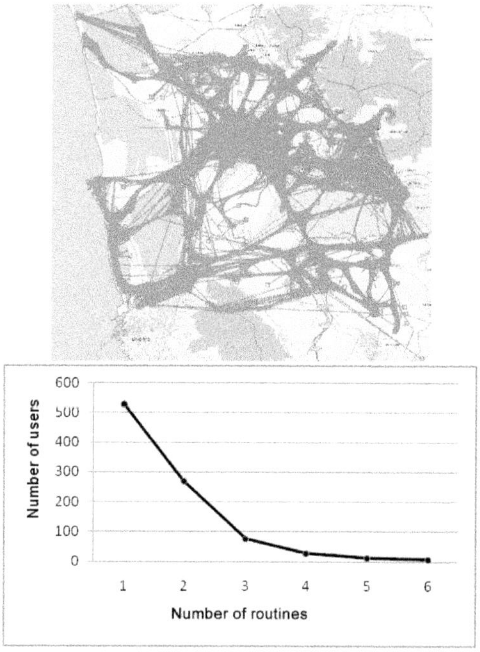

Figure 3: The set of trips extracted from the user observations (top) and the distribution of routines by the users (bottom).

δ **and** α : we adopted the *route similarity* function described in [2] as spatial distance function (δ). The route similarity function performs an alignment between points of the trajectories (trips) that are going to be compared, and then computes the sum of distances between corresponding points. In addition, we adopted a temporal alignment constraint (α) which simply computes the temporal distance between the starting points of the two trips, and compares it against the temporal threshold.

$th^{stop}_{spatial}$ **and** $th^{stop}_{temporal}$: 50 meters and 1 hour, this means that we consider a stop when a user stays with his/her car in an area of 50 m^2 for at least one hour. Single trips of a user are thus the movements between these stops.

$th^{group}_{spatial}$ **and** $th^{group}_{temporal}$: 250 meters and 1 hour, we want to group trips which are *similar* considering a maximum of 250 meters and a temporal alignment of 1 hour.

$th^{group}_{support}$: 4 trips, only the groups with at least 4 trips survive the pruning process, the others are not considered interesting enough for the mobility profiles.

An example of how the *mobility profile construction* works is shown in Fig.2. As can be seen, two main routes are frequently repeated, each time with small variations. In addition, they appear to represent symmetric trips, such as home-to-work and work-to-home routine movements. The

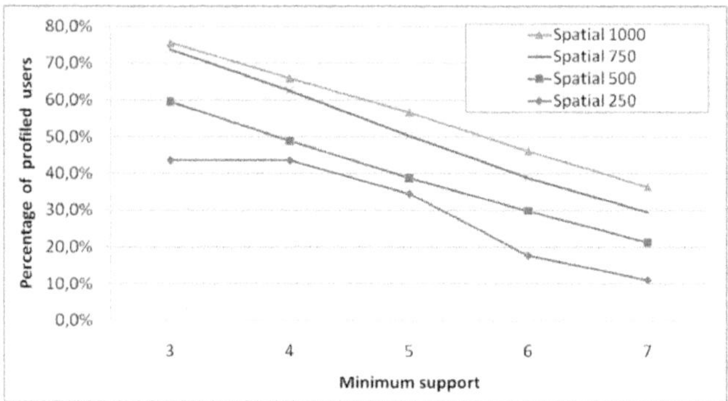

Figure 4: Different settings of parameters lead to a different mobility profile extraction.

corresponding mobility profiles are depicted at the bottom of the figure. Notice that seven user trips were occasional trips that did not fit any consistent habit, and therefore were (correctly) filtered out by our algorithm.

Globally during the execution of the algorithm, a set of 46,163 trips is generated (Fig.3(top)) and the result of the mobility profile construction is a set of 1,504 routines that form 919 mobility profiles (i.e., for 43.6% of the 2,107 users a profile was extracted). Figure 3 (bottom) shows the distribution of the number of routines per user, with almost every user having one or two routines, which usually correspond to the commute to (and from) work (not always at the same time).

To understand how the process is affected by the parameters, using different configurations we analyzed the percentage of users with a mobility profile. The results are shown in Fig.4. They confirm that by using loose constraints, a profile can be built for almost 77% of users. Such percentage decreases to 12% when a strict set of constraints is applied. When looking at the results obtained with a low spatial constraint, we must consider that the clustering method groups together fewer trips and thus pruning using the support threshold becomes more effective. Finally the temporal threshold for the *mobility profile construction* does not seem to have much influence. In fact we discovered that the results significantly change only with a very high threshold. This is simply because we mixed together trips in different periods of the day, thus for clarity's sake, we only show the threshold equal to one hour.

The purpose of the following analysis is to show to what degree the mobility profiles remain persistent and stable considering two time windows: *days 1-6* and *days 7-12*. Figure 5(top) presents the number of profiles extracted in the two time windows and the number of common profiles. It is important to note that the percentage of users profiled in both periods is around 50%, which means that their behavior is *persistent* in time. However although they are profiled in both periods, we want to understand if their routines are similar considering the same spatial threshold used for the grouping phase. In other words, if a routine extracted in the first period remains in the same hypothetical group. The results in Fig.5(bottom) show that for the same experiment we have a percentage of 74% of routines remaining stable.

The thresholds used in the rest of the paper correspond to the ones presented at the beginning of this section. There are two reasons why we chose this configuration: (i) from Fig.4

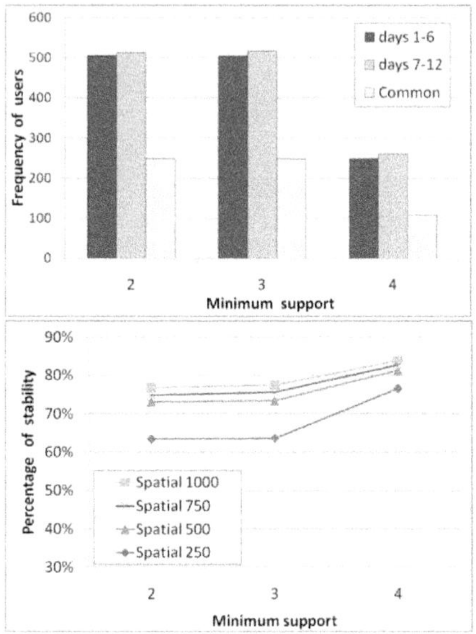

Figure 5: The process is performed on two different time windows and then compared to show how many mobility profiles are persistent (top) and stable (bottom).

it seems that the process reaches a critical point before the decay in performance, and (ii) we want to maintain a critical point of view in order to discover the real capability of the process.

4. MOBILITY PROFILE MATCHING

In this paper we focus on a *car pooling* application aimed at identifying pairs of users that could most likely share their vehicle for one or more of their routine trips. The service might be deployed as a system that provides pro-active suggestions to facilitate the matching process, without the need for the user to explicitly describe (and update) the trips of interest. The starting point of this analysis is the set of representative trips which make up the user mobility profiles. These mobility profiles represent their different typical behaviors, and by comparing them, we can understand if a user can be *served* by another user.

DEFINITION 8 (ROUTINE CONTAINMENT). *Given two mobility routines* $T_1 = \langle p_1^1 \dots p_n^1 \rangle$ *and* $T_2 = \langle p_1^2 \dots p_m^2 \rangle$, *and thresholds* $th_{distance}^{walking}$ *and* $th_{time}^{wasting}$, *we say that* T_1 is contained in T_2, *denoted* $contained(T_1, T_2, th_{distance}^{walking}, th_{time}^{wasting})$

$$\text{iff: } contained(T_1, T_2, th_{distance}^{walking}, th_{time}^{wasting}) \equiv \exists i, j \in \mathcal{N} \mid 0 < i \leq j \leq m \wedge Dist(p_1^1, p_i^2) + Dist(p_n^1, p_j^2) \leq th_{distance}^{walking} \wedge Dur(p_1^1, p_i^2) + Dur(p_n^1, p_j^2) \leq th_{time}^{wasting}$$

Thresholds $th_{distance}^{walking}$ and $th_{time}^{wasting}$ represent the total spatial and temporal distances allowed between the two routines in space and time, in other words:

$th_{distance}^{walking}$: represents the maximum distance the user which *is served* could walk to reach the meeting point and then to reach their final destination at the end of the trip.

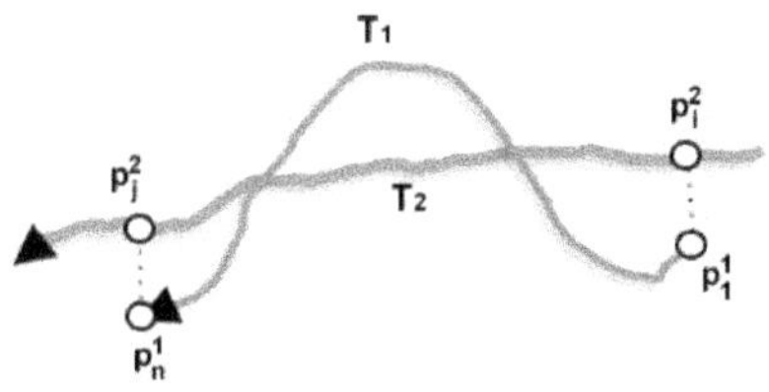

Figure 6: Example of routine containment test for Definition 8: the start point and end point of T_1 are considered and matched against their corresponding nearest points in T_2.

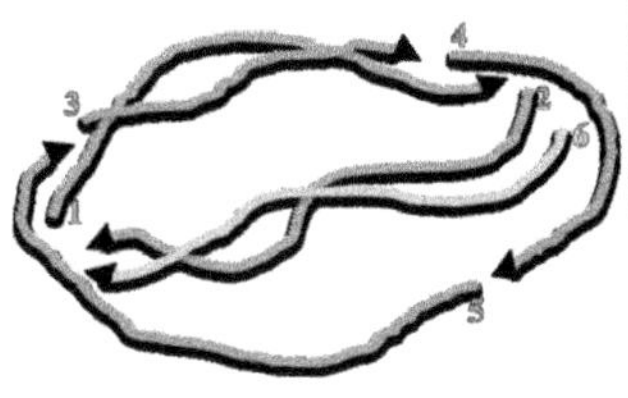

	1	2	3	4	5	6
1	-	-	F	F	F	F
2	-	-	F	F	F	T
3	T	F	-	-	-	F
4	F	F	-	-	-	F
5	F	F	-	-	-	F
6	F	T	F	F	F	-

	-	0	1/2
	1/3	-	0
	1	0	-

Figure 7: Example of the mobility profile matching process: the routines of the same color belong to the same mobility profile. On the right the matrix of containment between routines (top) and the matrix of the profile share-ability (bottom) with instantiated values.

$th_{time}^{wasting}$: represents the maximum delay the user which *is served* allows, considering the departure and the arrival time.

It is important to note that the *contains* relation is not reflexive because one trip can include the other but not vice versa. This is a basic requirement in the car pooling application because the destinations of the user which *serves* the other can be very far from the destination of the one who is *served* (Fig.6). Extending the definition to the mobility profiles of the users, we can compute the share-ability level of each pair of users:

DEFINITION 9 (MOBILITY PROFILE SHARE-ABILITY). *Given two mobility profiles $\tilde{T}_1$ and $\tilde{T}_2$, and thresholds $th_{distance}^{walking}$ and $th_{time}^{wasting}$, the* Mobility profile share-ability *measure between $\tilde{T}_1$ and $\tilde{T}_2$ is defined as the fraction of routines in $\tilde{T}_1$ which are contained in at least one routine in $\tilde{T}_2$:*

$$profileShare(\tilde{T}_1, \tilde{T}_2, th_{distance}^{walking}, th_{time}^{wasting}) = \frac{\left| \left\{ p \in \tilde{T}_1 \mid \exists q \in \tilde{T}_2 . Share(p, q, th_{distance}^{walking}, th_{time}^{wasting}) \right\} \right|}{\mid \tilde{T}_1 \mid}$$

By applying this definition to all possible pairs of users (i.e., to their corresponding profiles) we can build a matrix of share-ability, thus expressing how good the match of each pair is. The process is presented in Algorithm 2, where first a *routine containment matrix* is built over single mobility routines, then the results corresponding to each pair of users are collapsed to form a mobility profile share-ability matrix, by applying the Definition 9. In the algorithm, $\hat{P}$ represents the set of all routines of all users, while function $get\_user(p)$ returns the user that owns routine p (identical routines generated by different users are distinguished, here). A visual example of the result is shown in Fig.7.

Algorithm 2: *Matching matrices*

INPUT:
Set of Users U
Users' routines $\hat{P}$
Set of Thresholds $th_{distance}^{walking}, th_{time}^{wasting}$
OUTPUT:
Routine containment matrix $M : \hat{P}^2 \rightarrow Bool$
Mobility profile share-ability matrix $C : U^2 \rightarrow Real$

BEGIN
FOR EACH $(p, q) \in \hat{P}^2$ DO
  IF $get\_user(p) \neq get\_user(q)$ THEN
    $M(p, q) := contains(p, q, th_{distance}^{walking}, th_{time}^{wasting})$;
FOR EACH $(u, v) \in U^2$ DO
  IF $u \neq v$ THEN
    $\forall x \in \{u, v\} . \hat{P}_x := \{p \in \hat{P} | get\_user(p) = x\}$;
    $C(u, v) = profileShare(\hat{P}_u, \hat{P}_v, th_{distance}^{walking}, th_{time}^{wasting})$;
END;

4.1 The car pooling service with GPS data

We used Algorithm 2 to perform the matching process on our data with different parameter settings. The results in Figure 9 show how the performances are affected, in terms of percentage routines and mobility profiles that have at least one match. Note that by allowing a *walking distance* of 5 km and a *wasting time* of 1 hour, 89% of profiled users have (at least) one match, which decreases to 66% if the *wasting time* becomes half an hour. Figure 8 shows two examples of matching between two users. The red user can be served by the violet user on the basis of the routines shown. In the two examples it is interesting to see that in the first case (A), the starts and ends of the routines are quite close, therefore these users can both serve or be served by each other; in the second case (B) the relation is unidirectional, since the red routine ends much earlier than the other, and therefore the *contain* relation does not hold in the opposite direction.

Considering a hypothetical car pooling service built on top of the proposed method, using a *walking distance* of 2.5 km and a *wasting time* of 1 hour, we can calculate some statistics regarding the potential impact of the service. In fact 684 users, corresponding to 32.4% of participants, receive at least one indication of a possible host for one of their routines. This means that if everybody takes the opportunity of sharing a / their car using this system, traffic could be decreased significantly. As previously mentioned, one advantage of the system is that users do not need to manually declare their common trips (indeed, routines are automatically detected), which is a major flaw of current car pooling systems, and probably contributes substantially to their failure. As shown in section 3.2, the system can keep reasonably up-to-date routines and profiles by executing the profiling process once every two weeks (or more), using a temporal sliding window on the data.

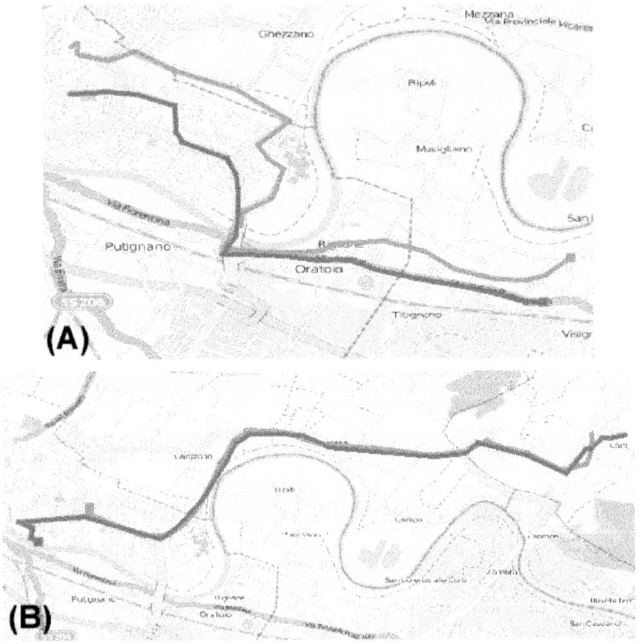

Figure 8: Examples of routine containment: red routines are contained in the violet ones.

5. DOWNGRADING DATA PRECISION

User profiles can also be extracted and compared on the basis of mobile phone network traces that are commonly (and massively) available from telecom operators. It is therefore natural to wonder whether the loss in spatial and temporal precision and completeness that characterizes this kind of data can compromise the current usability of our methodology. The general methodology introduced so far in this paper can be directly applied to this kind of data and enables us to perform exactly the same kind of analysis on both GPS and GSM data and compare the results. In this section we discuss three issues, how to: (i) set up a test to compare profile extractions over different spatio temporal granularities of the same dataset; (ii) instantiate the profile extraction method w.r.t. different spatio temporal granularities; and (iii) compare and interpret the profiles of the same user extracted at different spatio temporal granularities.

5.1 GSM data simulation

In the context of GSM technology there are two different forms of data collection: in the first, named *Handset-based*, the mobile device collects the history of its positions as the sequence of the towers that it traversed. In the second, named *Network-based*, the network collects the sequence of towers that serve a calling device.

Handset-based simulation. In order to simulate a *Handset-based* localization system we apply a transformation on GPS data named *GPS generalization* defined as follows:

DEFINITION 10 (GSM GENERALIZATION). *Given a user GPS history $H = \langle p_1, \ldots p_n, \rangle$ and a set of GSM cells C, let functions $tower : C \to \mathcal{R}^2$ and $cover : C \to 2^{\mathcal{R}}$ denote, for each cell, the position of its tower and its spatial coverage, respectively. Then, the GSM generalization of H is defined as the sequence $H_{GSM} = \langle g_1, \ldots g_n \rangle$ such that $\forall_{0<i\leq n}.g_i = (x^*, y^*, t) \wedge p_i = (x, y, t) \in H \wedge \exists c \in C.tower(c) = (x^*, y^*) \wedge (x, y) \in cover(c)$.*

The result is a sequence of points with timestamps, each point represents the tower (and therefore the cell it covers) that captures a corresponding point in the GPS traces of the original dataset.

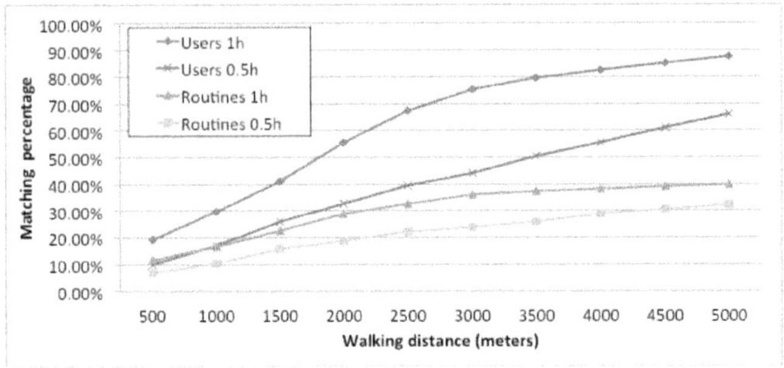

Figure 9: Matching percentages of users (upper curves) and routines (lower curves) for different settings of the spatial and temporal thresholds.

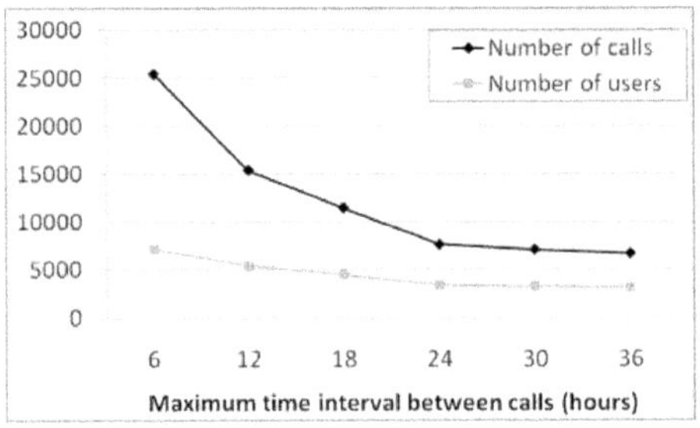

Figure 10: Number of users and number of calls in the Network-based simulation

Network-based simulation. The particular feature of the *CDR* data is the fact that they are collected only when the user is calling. Therefore to simulate such data starting from the GPS traces, we need to insert holes corresponding to the missing data due to the not-calling status of the user. We therefore use two different probability functions:

- Pr_{call}: To determine when a user starts a call, we use an exponential distribution specifying the maximum time interval Int in which the user performs at least one call.
- $Pr_{duration}$: In [4], the authors present a study of the distribution of durations, which determines a way to define the probability of a call duration. They define a function called TLAC which simulates over 96% of the duration of a user's call. We use this function in order to simulate when a call terminates.

With the definition of probabilities Pr_{call} and $Pr_{duration}$, we can use different values for the maximum time interval Int to obtain different scenarios. In the following, we denote each of these datasets as H^{Int}. Figure 10 shows some basic statistics of six different datasets obtained with a time interval $Int \in \{6; 12; 18; 24; 30; 36\ hours\}$.

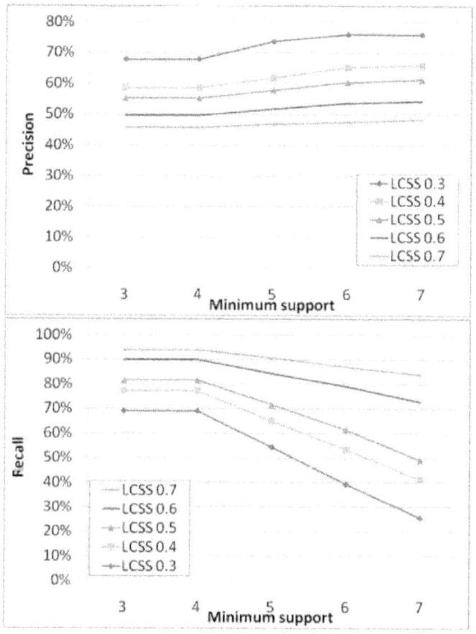

Figure 11: *Precision* and *recall* of the profile construction in GSM_H data

5.2 Profiling users with GSM data

The particular features of the GSM context require only two small changes w.r.t. the GPS in order to adapt the method: the first is related to the spatial granularity of stops to construct the trips and the second is the similarity function adopted.

- In computing stops and trips we set the spatial threshold $th^{stop}_{spatial} = 0$. This is because each location in the history of the user already represents an area, namely the coverage area of the tower serving the device.
- The route similarity adopted in the case of GPS traces is replaced with the *Longest Common Sub-Sequence* (LCSS) distance. We adopt this distance function in order to measure the longest sequence of towers crossed by two users.

To summarize the effect of spatial downgrading we used the following elements:

GPS is the set of profiles extracted with the GPS profile extraction method

GSM_H is the set of profiles extracted with the GSM-profile extraction method on the handset-based data.

GSM_{CDR} is the set of profiles extracted with the GSM-profile extraction method on the network-based data.

We use *precision* and *recall* measures to compare the quality of GPS versus GSM_H profiles and GPS versus GSM_{CDR} profiles. The idea, in both cases, is to use the GPS profiles as a ground truth against which to verify the GSM profiles.

Handset-based. Fig. 11(top) shows the *precision* of the GSM_H profiles considering different support values and varying the minimum $LCSS$ distance. Note that a greater value of the minimum support threshold corresponds to an increase in *precision*. In addition, using a smaller minimum distance leads to a more precise set of mobility profiles. This means that the mobility profiles extracted from

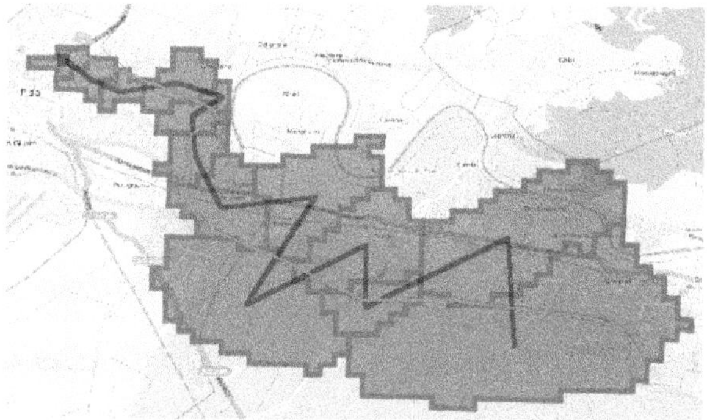

Figure 12: The red line represents the GPS routine, the blue areas connected through the black line indicate the GSM routine.

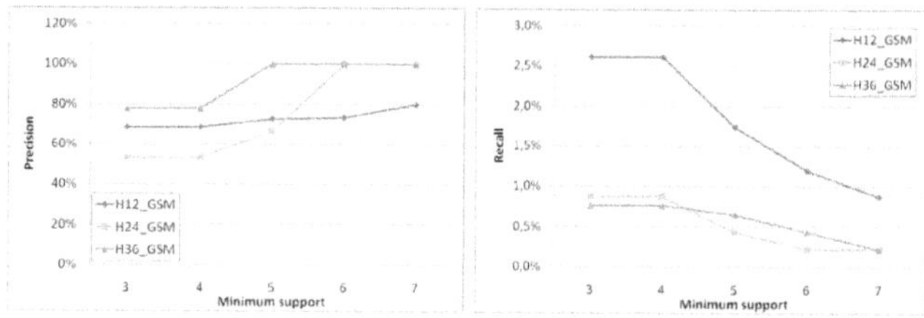

Figure 13: *Precision* and *recall* of the profile construction in GSM_{CDR} data considering a time interval $Int \in 12, 24, 36$

GSM_H data correspond, in most cases, to the profiles obtained with the GPS data. The *recall* measure is depicted in Fig. 11(bottom), where it can be seen that with a greater support threshold, the *recall* measure decreases. Furthermore, the decreasing behavior is enforced using a more restrictive distance value. It is worth highlighting that for some configurations, we are able to obtain a precision close to 60% and a *recall* greater than 70%. Figure 12 shows the results of selecting the same user in the GPS and GSM_H datasets and performing the profile construction in both cases, where the precise correspondence between the GPS routine and the GSM routine is clear.

Network-based. The effect of the loss of spatial precision and temporal completeness becomes more remarkable considering GSM_{CDR} data. In fact, on this kind of data the process is only able to build a profile for few users. This is clearly reflected in Fig.13 where we obtain high values of *precision* but a very low level of *recall* for all configurations of the input parameters. This is because the process constructs few mobility profiles on this data, which often correspond to the profiles contained on the GPS ones.

5.3 The car pooling service with GSM data

In this case the spatial distance constraint is included in the spatial approximation introduced with the GSM generalization of each point. Therefore, the matching between two users is computed by means of the same $Contains$ and $ProfileShare$ functions defined in Section 4, setting the threshold $th^{walking}_{distance} = 0$. To investigate the impact of the downgrading process on the mobility profile matching, again we study the trend of *precision* and *recall* measures w.r.t. the mobility profile share-ability matrix discussed in Sec. 4.1.

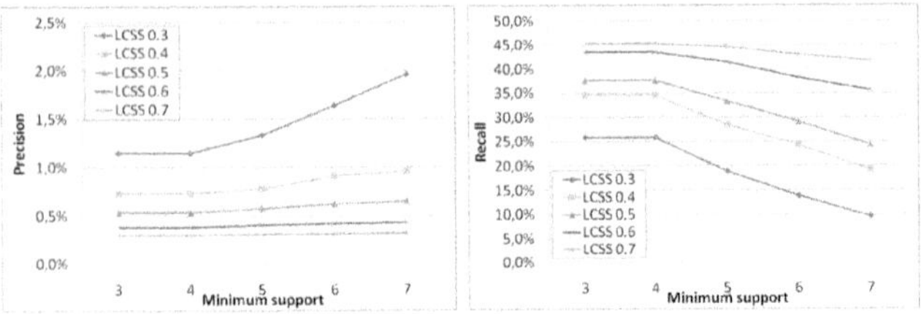

Figure 14: *Precision* and *recall* of the matching in GSM_H data

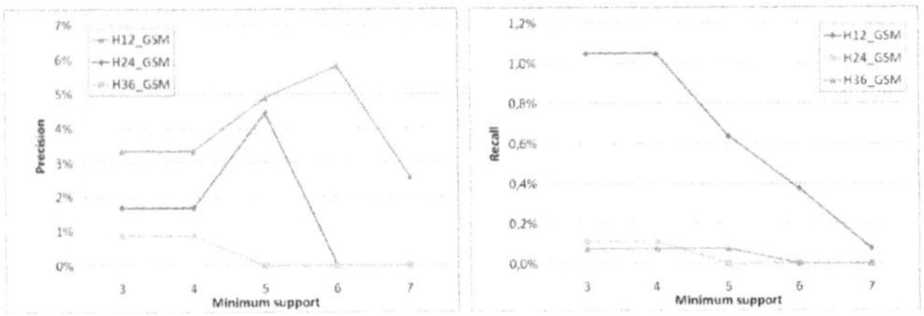

Figure 15: *Precision* and *recall* of the matching in GSM_H data considering a time interval $Int \in 12, 24, 36$

The influence of the spatial degradation introduced with the GSM generalization is substantial as shown in Fig. 14 where the *precision* reaches low values and the *recall* measure shows a decreasing trend but maintains considerable stability. In fact, the spatial generalization enables the GSM_H mobility profile matching process to verify the share relation between a pair of users in several more cases, by producing a bigger share-ability matrix w.r.t. the one obtained with the GPS data. Concerning an evaluation of the matching process on GSM_{CDR} data, shown in Fig.15, we obtain low results both for *precision* and *recall*. This is due to the fact that the generalization data does not allow any matching between a pair of mobility profile users.

6. CONCLUSIONS

In this paper we proposed an analysis aimed at discovering and matching mobility profiles, then we showed as it may foster an intelligent car pooling service. We applied the proposed analytical framework to two different scenarios: GPS vehicular data and (simulated) GSM mobile phone data.

Future developments include a wide empirical evaluation of the persistence of user profiles, as well as their tolerance to transient changes in mobility habits (caused by road works, extraordinary events, etc.) and their reaction times to steady changes. Also, alternative profile matching schema will be explored, in order to deal with the loss of performance with less rich forms of data, and a method to automatically suggest the parameters in all the steps involved in the process will be investigated to increase the applicability in real scenarios. Finally, more complex and realistic simulations of GSM and CDR data might be considered, moving from the static tower assignment used in this work, based on shortest distance, to a dynamic one that better models the non-deterministic and noisy nature of actual assignments.

7. REFERENCES

[1] *Octotelematics*. http://www.octotelematics.com/.

[2] G. Andrienko, N. Andrienko, S. Rinzivillo, M. Nanni, D. Pedreschi, and F. Giannotti. *Interactive Visual Clustering of Large Collections of Trajectories*. VAST: Symposium on Visual Analytics Science and Technology, 2009.

[3] V. Bogorny, C. A. Heuser, and L. O. Alvares. A conceptual data model for trajectory data mining. In *GIScience*, pages 1–15, 2010.

[4] P. O. V. de Melo, L. Akoglu, C. Faloutsos, and A. A. Loureiro. *Surprising Patterns for the Call Duration Distribution of Mobile Phone Users*. ECML PKDD: European Conference on Machine Learning and Principles and Practice of Knowledge Discovery in Databases, 2010.

[5] S. Gaffney and P. Smyth. Trajectory clustering with mixture of regression models. In *Proceedings of the 5th International Conference on Knowledge Discovery and Data Mining (KDD'99)*, pages 63–72. ACM, 1999.

[6] F. Giannotti, M. Nanni, F. Pinelli, and D. Pedreschi. Trajectory pattern mining. In *KDD*, pages 330–339, 2007.

[7] F. Giannotti and D. Pedreschi, editors. *Mobility, Data Mining and Privacy - Geographic Knowledge Discovery*. Springer, 2008.

[8] M. Gonzalez, C. A. Hidalgo, and A.-L. Barabási. Understanding individual human mobility patterns. *Nature*, 453:779–782, 2008.

[9] P. Kalnis, N. Mamoulis, and S. Bakiras. On discovering moving clusters in spatio-temporal data. In *Proceedings of 9th International Symposium on Spatial and Temporal Databases (SSTD'05)*, pages 364–381. Springer, 2005.

[10] N. Pelekis, I. Kopanakis, I. Ntoutsi, G. Marketos, and Y. Theodoridis. Mining trajectory databases via a suite of distance operators. In *ICDE Workshops*, pages 575–584, 2007.

[11] C. Song, T. Koren, P. Wang, and A.-L. Barabási. Modelling the scaling properties of human mobility. *Nature Physics*, 7:713–, 2010.

[12] C. Song, Z. Qu, N. Blumm, and A.-L. Barabási. Limits of predictability in human mobility. *Science*, 327:1018–1021, 2010.

[13] R. Trasarti, F. Giannotti, M. Nanni, D. Pedreschi, and C. Renso. *A Query Language for Mobility Data Mining*. IJDWM: International Journal of Data Warehousing and Mining., 2010.

[14] X. Xiao, Y. Zheng, Q. Luo, and X. Xie. Finding similar users using category-based location history. In *Proceedings of the 18th SIGSPATIAL International Conference on Advances in Geographic Information Systems*, 2010.

[15] H. Yoon, Y. Zheng, X. Xie, and W. Woo. Smart itinerary recommendation based on user-generated gps trajectories. In *Proceedings of the 7th international conference on Ubiquitous intelligence and computing*, 2010.

Mining Partially Annotated Images

Zhongang Qi, Ming Yang, and Zhongfei (Mark) Zhang
Zhejiang Provincial Key Lab of Information Network Technology
Dept. of ISEE, Zhejiang University, China
{zhongangqi, cauchym, zhongfei}@zju.edu.cn

Zhengyou Zhang
Microsoft Research
One Microsoft Way, Redmond, WA, USA
zhang@microsoft.com

ABSTRACT

In this paper, we study the problem of mining partially annotated images. We first define what the problem of mining partially annotated images is, and argue that in many real-world applications annotated images are typically partially annotated and thus that the problem of mining partially annotated images exists in many situations. We then propose an effective solution to this problem based on a statistical model we have developed called the Semi-Supervised Correspondence Hierarchical Dirichlet Process (SSC-HDP). The main idea of this model lies in exploiting the information pertaining to partially annotated images or even unannotated images to achieve semi-supervised learning under the HDP structure. We apply this model to completing the annotations appropriately for partially annotated images in the training data and then to predicting the annotations appropriately and completely for all the unannotated images either in the training data or in any unseen data beyond the training process. Experiments show that SSC-HDP is superior to the peer models from the recent literature when they are applied to solving the problem of mining partially annotated images.

Categories and Subject Descriptors

H.2.8 [**Database Management**]: Database Applications—*Data mining, Image databases*; H.3.3 [**Information Storage and Retrieval**]: Information Search and Retrieval—*Retrieval models*; I.5.1 [**Pattern Recognition**]: Models—*Structural*

General Terms

Algorithms, experimentation

Keywords

Semi-supervised learning, Partially annotated training set, Image annotation completion and prediction

1. INTRODUCTION

With the development of technologies to acquire, store, and transmit massive amounts of data, recent years have witnessed an explosive growth in the size of digital image collections. Efficient methods for image classification and retrieval play an important role in discovering useful information from large-scale and diverse image collections. It is noted that the majority of the existing image annotation methods, based on either supervised learning or semi-supervised learning, assume that either the images in the training data are completely annotated appropriately or the given annotations in the training data can be updated through transductive learning. We argue that in reality it is difficult, if not impossible, and also unnecessary and impractical to have this assumption. Figure 1 is a typical example of a given annotated image in the training data in the literature of image annotation. Here the given ground truth annotations of this image are just *person*, *bottle*, and *TVmonitor* whereas it is clear that there are many other objects in this image that should also be given as part of the ground truth annotation labels such as the microphone, sofa, door, telephone, and books but they are actually not included in the ground truth annotation labels. In many existing image annotation methods, the given annotation label set is presumably assumed to be appropriate and complete. However, it is clear from this example that the given annotation labeling is typically far away from being actually complete in many such applications in the real-world. It is well understood that while image annotation is laborious and time-consuming, completely annotated images are hard to acquire. Even with the laborious effort of manually annotating images, labels may still be missing due to the subjectivity, different foci, lack of patience to complete the annotations to every detail or even ignorance of certain details for human perception. In this case, these annotated images are actually partially annotated instead of completely annotated and the assumption that the given annotations are complete would certainly mislead the learning. While there are label propagation learning methods proposed in the recent literature to update the given annotations to a certain degree during the learning process, all these methods are transductive learning in the sense that they are unable to predict the appropriate and complete annotation labels for any out-of-sample images after the learning.

Consequently, we argue that partially annotated or completely unannotated images typically exist in many situations. This paper thus studies this practical problem — mining partially annotated images, in which we develop a solution to complete the given partial annotations of the images in the training dataset and to generate and complete the annotations for all unannotated images in the testing dataset. We have the following two assumptions for the partially annotated image training set: 1) Every label of an image in the training set is correct and appropriate; 2) Whether or not an image in the training set is annotated completely is unknown, which means that there may exist images lacking appropriate labels, or even images completely unannotated at all.

KDD'11, August 21–24, 2011, San Diego, California, USA

Figure 1: An example of an annotated image with the given ground truth annotations as *person*, *bottle*, and *TVmonitor* while many other objects in the image are not labeled at all.

We highlight the contributions of this work as follows.

- We argue that the partially annotated images exist in many applications and thus it is necessary and desirable to study the problem of mining partially annotated images.
- We develop an effective solution to the problem of mining partially annotated images based on a statistical model we have developed called the Semi-Supervised Correspondence Hierarchical Dirichlet Process (SSC-HDP).
- We demonstrate through extensive evaluations utilizing real datasets that the SSC-HDP model performs well in comparison with the peer methods in the literature as an effective and promising solution to the problem of mining partially annotated images.

This paper is organized as follows. Section 2 briefly reviews the related work in the area of image annotation and retrieval. Section 3 describes the data representation and symbols used in this work. In Section 4, we introduce the proposed SSC-HDP model, and present an efficient algorithm to estimate the parameters of the model. We present experimental results for SSC-HDP, and compare them with those of the peer methods in the literature in Section 5. Finally, we conclude this study in Section 6.

2. RELATED WORK

Various approaches have been proposed in the area of image annotation and retrieval in the past years [7]. Basically, these approaches can be classified into various categories from different views. One way of the classification is to reduce the problem into "one-vs-all" (OVA) mode, or to introduce a set of bridge variables. The image annotation and retrieval problem has been cast as a multi-label learning problem. In semantic scene classification [5] , an image is considered as one instance, which may belong to more than one conceptual class. Boutell et al. [5] introduce several transformation methods that map the multi-label learning problem into the single-label classification problem. A more complicated situation is when an image is represented as a bag of instances, and belongs to a bag of classes. Hence, the original annotation problem becomes a multi-instance and multi-label learning problem. Zhou and Zhang [29] solve this problem by mapping it into a single-instance and multi-label learning problem. All of the above methods are finally reduced to the solution of training several binary classifiers in the OVA mode, each of which is used for one class.

Different from the above approaches, another paradigm for image annotation is to introduce a set of latent variables as a bridge,

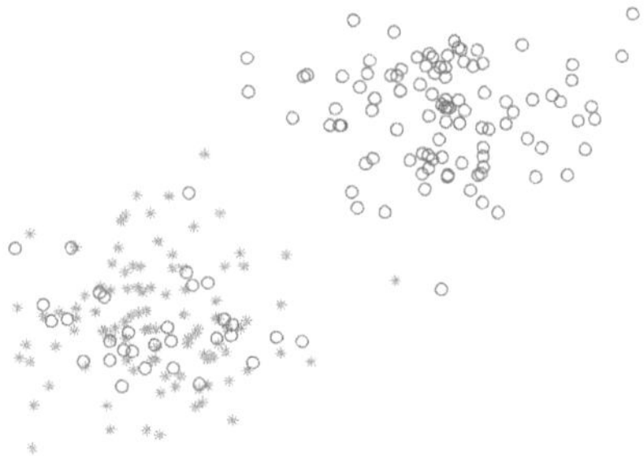

Figure 2: Example of Positive and Unlabeled Data. The asterisks are labeled data from the positive class, while the circles are unlabeled data from both classes.

where each variable has joint distributions not only with the semantic labels, but also with the image feature descriptors. Barnard et al. [2] propose two classes of models, the multi-modal hierarchical aspect models using clusters as the bridge variables and the mixture of multi-modal LDA (MoM-LDA) model extending the Latent Dirichlet Allocation (LDA) [4] to learning the joint distribution of words and images. Compared with MoM-LDA, Blei and Jordan [3] propose the correspondence LDA (Corr-LDA) model under which each label shares a latent variable with a randomly selected image feature descriptor in one image. In [9, 12, 13], the annotated images in the training set are used as the connection variables to compute the joint probability of labels and image regions. Zhang et al. [28] propose a probabilistic semantic model using a hidden concept layer to exploit the synergy among the modalities. Li and Fei-Fei [14] propose an integrative model, somewhat similar to MoM-LDA, to classify the types of the events and object components of images. In order to adapt to the number of the latent variables based on the training data, the multi-modal HDP (MoM-HDP) model based on a Hierarchical Dirichlet Process (HDP) [25] is proposed by Yakhnenko and Honavar [26]. Yang et al. [27] propose a generative model, called Dirichlet-Bernoulli Alignment, to describe the multi-class multi-label multi-instance corpora.

From the aspect of the type of the training set, the approaches in this area can also be categorized into supervised learning and semi-supervised learning. Most of the previous work uses datasets of completely annotated images as the training set. There has been work on semi-supervised image annotation by adding a large amount of additional unannotated images into the training set. In [15, 23], the co-training framework is applied to utilize the unlabeled data to improve the performance of the algorithm. Loeff et al. [19] use manifold regularization to incorporate the information from the unlabeled data. The work in [19, 24] is the most relevant to ours in the sense that they can also formulate the problem we proposed as an inductive learning problem, though their methods are completely different from ours.

This problem of mining partially annotated images, which is demonstrated as the Weak Label problem in [24], is also related to the graph label propagation problem, specifically the graph label propagation problem in the context of image annotation. Solutions are developed [16] to iteratively update the given annotation labels in the training data and to predict the annotation labels for the initially unlabeled images in the dataset. However, all these methods for the graph label propagation problem are transductive learning in nature and consequently, are unable to predict the annotation labels for any new, out-of-sample images after the learning.

In this paper, we introduce the Semi-Supervised Correspondence Hierarchical Dirichlet Process (SSC-HDP), a statistical model using partially annotated images as the training set. Compared with

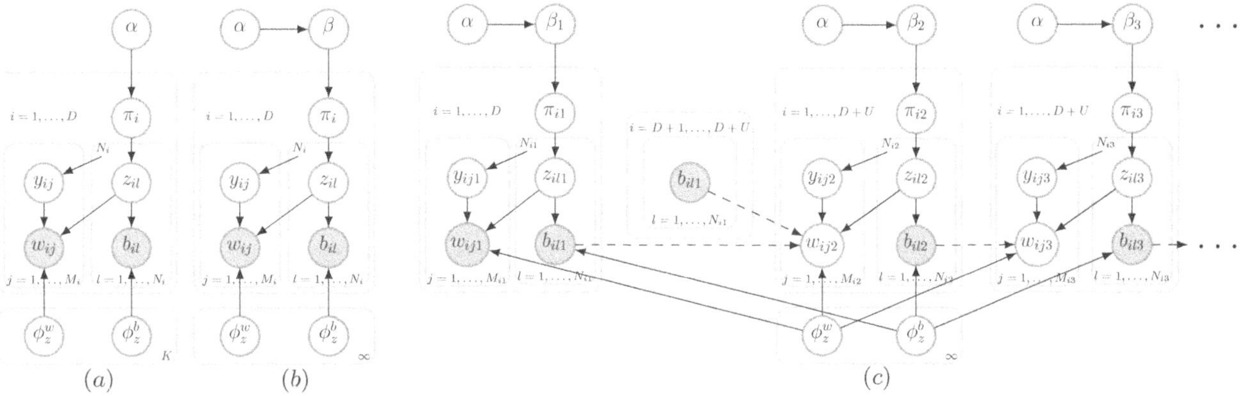

Figure 3: Graphical Model for (a) Corr-LDA, (b) Corr-HDP, and (c) SSC-HDP (The dashed line indicates the initial assignment).

MoM-HDP, SSC-HDP considers the correspondence between the latent variables which respectively generate the image descriptors and their labels in each image. Compared with Corr-LDA, SSC-HDP adapts to the number of latent variables based on the training set. More importantly, the major difference between SSC-HDP and MoM-HDP, Corr-LDA, as well as other image annotation models, is that SSC-HDP can train partially annotated images, and complete the annotation for partially annotated images through the training process. In addition, as an inductive learning approach, new unannotated images can be predicted with appropriate annotation labels and can be added seamlessly as part of the training data to further improve the performance of the SSC-HDP model.

3. DATA REPRESENTATION AND SYMBOLS

We denote an image set as $\mathcal{I}$, the visual word vocabulary as $\mathcal{V}$, and the label vocabulary as $\mathcal{L}$. We follow the notations in a bag-of-words representation for both images and annotations. For each image $I_i \in \mathcal{I}$, let an N-dimensional vector $\mathbf{b}_i = (b_{i,1}, b_{i,2}, \ldots, b_{i,N})'$ be the visual word representation for I_i, where $b_{i,j}$ is the count of the jth visual word $V_j \in \mathcal{V}$ appeared in I_i. Let an M-dimensional vector $\mathbf{w}_i = (w_{i,1}, w_{i,2}, \ldots, w_{i,M})'$ be the label representation for I_i, where $w_{i,j} \in \{0, 1\}, 0 \leq j \leq M$ represents the occurrence of the jth label $L_j \in \mathcal{L}$. If I_i is fully annotated or partially annotated, I_i is represented as a pair $(\mathbf{b}_i, \mathbf{w}_i)$. Otherwise, I_i is unannotated and represented as $\mathbf{b}_i$. Consequently, a partially annotated training set of D images is denoted as $\mathscr{D} = \{I_d\}_{d=1}^{D} = \{(\mathbf{b}_d, \mathbf{w}_d)\}_{d=1}^{D}$, and an unannotated set of U images is denoted as $\mathscr{U} = \{I_u\}_{u=1}^{U} = \{\mathbf{b}_1, \mathbf{b}_2, \ldots, \mathbf{b}_U\}$.

4. MODEL FORMULATION

The main idea of this work is based on achieving semi-supervised learning under the HDP structure. We begin with describing semi-supervised learning with positive and unlabeled data, then propose the correspondence HDP (Corr-HDP), which is an extension of the Corr-LDA model using a hierarchical Dirichlet process instead. Finally we introduce the SSC-HDP model and give the parameter estimation procedure.

4.1 Semi-Supervised Learning with Positive and Unlabeled Data

In many practical applications of the binary classification problem, we encounter such a situation that only one class of labeled data is available, and the unlabeled data may contain both classes. As shown in Figure 2, all the information we have is that the asterisk points are from the positive class, and we do not know which class each of the unlabeled data points (circles) belongs to. The labeled data form the positive data set P, while the unlabeled data form the mixed data set S. Consequently, the dataset which consists of P and S is a partially labeled dataset.

Zhu [30] reviews the problem of learning with positive and unlabeled data. Liu et al. [18] theoretically analyze the binary classification problem using positive and unlabeled data. Given the partially labeled dataset (T, C), where $C \in \{0, 1\}$, and a function f as the classifier, the probability of the classification error is:

$$\begin{aligned}&\Pr[f(T) \neq C]\\ =&\Pr[f(T) = 1 \wedge C = 0] + \Pr[f(T) = 0 \wedge C = 1]\\ =&\Pr[f(T) = 1] - \Pr[C = 1] +\\ &2\Pr[f(T) = 0|C = 1]\Pr[C = 1]. \qquad (1)\end{aligned}$$

Since $\Pr[C = 1]$ is a constant, the method to minimize the classification error is to hold $\Pr[f(T) = 0|C = 1]$ small while minimizing $\Pr[f(T) = 1]$, which is approximately the same as minimizing $\Pr_S[f(T) = 1]$ while holding $\Pr_P[f(T) = 1] \geq 1 - r$ when sufficient data in P and S are available [18]. Here $\Pr_S[f(T) = 1]$ denotes the probability of $f(T) = 1$ in the mixed data set S, $\Pr_P[f(T) = 1]$ denotes the probability of $f(T) = 1$ in the positive data set P, and r is a recall. Liu et al. [18] prove that accurate classifiers can be built with a high probability when P and S are large enough.

The image annotation and retrieval problem has been cast as a multi-label learning problem, which can be solved as M binary classification problems, where M is the total number of the labels. By inference, an accurate model can be built using a large amount of partially annotated images to complete the missing annotations of the training images and to predict the annotations of the new, unannotated images precisely.

4.2 Correspondence HDP Model

We extend the Corr-LDA model introduced by Blei and Jordan [3] to the Corr-HDP model. The graphical models of Corr-LDA and Corr-HDP are shown in Figure 3(a) and (b). The difference between the two models is that in Corr-HDP the prior β is drawn from a stick-breaking distribution, while in Corr-LDA the prior is drawn from a finite Dirichlet distribution. The advantage of Corr-HDP is that it adapts to the number of the latent variables dynamically based on the training set instead of setting the number of the latent variables as a prior.

From the graphical model of Corr-HDP we see that visual words $\mathbf{b}$ and labels $\mathbf{w}$ are both associated with the assignment variable z which is multinomially distributed with the parameter π. The cluster mixing variable π is sampled from a global distribution G_0 with the parameter β. Using the notation of stick-breaking theory, which is an efficient method to establish the Dirichlet process [22], we denote that $\beta \sim Stick(\alpha)$ and $\pi \sim DP(\alpha^{\pi}, \beta)$. For the observed nodes, we set a random variable $y \sim Uniform(1, \ldots, N_i)$ which correlates labels with visual words in the same image. Given an image i, we first generate N_i visual words $b_{i,l}$, $b_{i,l} \sim p(b_{i,l}|z, \phi_z^b)$, which is a multinomial distribution with parameter ϕ_z^b. Then for each of the M_i labels, we use y to select one of the N_i visual words randomly, and draw the corresponding label $w_{i,j}$ conditioned on the latent variable z which generates the selected visual word, $w_{ij} \sim p(w_{i,j}|y_{i,j}, z, \phi_z^w)$, which is a multinomial distribution with parameter ϕ_z^w. The generative process of the Corr-HDP Model is described in Algorithm 1.

Algorithm 1: Generative process of Corr-HDP

```
draw β ~ Stick(α)
for cluster z = 1, 2, ... do
    draw φ_z^b ~ Dir(η)
    draw φ_z^w ~ Dir(ω)
for image i = 1, ..., D do
    draw π_i ~ DP(α^π, β)
    for visual word l = 1, ..., N_i do
        draw z_{i,l} ~ Mult(π_i)
        draw b_{i,l} ~ Mult(φ_{z_{i,l}}^{b_{i,l}}, z_{i,l})
    for label j = 1, ..., M_i do
        draw y_{i,j} ~ Unif(1, ..., N_i)
        draw w_{i,j} ~ Mult(φ_{z_{i,j}}^{w_{i,j}}, y_{i,j}, z_{i·})
```

In practice, we need to truncate β at K to make the parameter estimation feasible [11]. Thus, $\pi \sim DP(\alpha^{\pi}, \beta)$ is approximated as $\pi \sim Dirichlet(\alpha^{\pi}\beta_1, \ldots \alpha^{\pi}\beta_K)$. Note that truncating β at K in the HDP is not equivalent to using a Corr-LDA model with a fixed number of K topics. Using the truncated HDP as a prior adapts to any number of latent variables within K (as the maximum number of the latent variables) based on the training set, while using LDA as a prior would fix the number of latent variables as exactly K.

4.3 SSC-HDP

We now apply the semi-supervised learning scheme with positive and unlabeled data to the Corr-HDP model. Given a partially annotated image training set $\mathscr{D}$, for each label $L_j \in \mathcal{L}$, there exists a pair-set $P_j \times S_j$, where $P_j \subset \mathscr{D}$ denotes a positive set and $S_j \subset \mathscr{D}$ denotes a mixed set; $\forall I_i \in \mathscr{D}$, we claim the following relationship:

$$w_{i,j} = 1 \Longrightarrow I_i \in P_j, \quad w_{i,j} = 0 \Longrightarrow I_i \in S_j$$

Consequently, the training set $\mathscr{D}$ can be represented as a set-pair $P_j \times S_j$ for each $j \in \{1, 2, \ldots, M\}$. Since the training set $\mathscr{D}$ is partially labeled, we note that

$$I_i \in P_j \Rightarrow \Pr[w_{i,j} = 1|\mathbf{b}_i] = 1$$
$$I_i \in S_j \not\Rightarrow \Pr[w_{i,j} = 1|\mathbf{b}_i] = 0$$

$\forall I_i \in S_j$, a more reasonable assumption is that $\Pr[w_{i,j} = 1|\mathbf{b}_i]$ can take any random value in $[0, 1]$.

The graphical model of SSC-HDP is shown in Figure 3(c). Based on the theoretical analysis described in Section 4.1, the main idea of semi-supervised learning here is to update the likelihood $\Pr[w_{k,j} = 1|\mathbf{b}_k]$ for $I_k \in S_j (1 \leq j \leq M)$, while holding $\Pr[w_{i,j} = 1|\mathbf{b}_i] = 1$ for $I_i \in P_j (1 \leq j \leq M)$ under the Corr-HDP structure. The algorithm is described in Algorithm 2. Through updating the likelihood of the labels, the model progressively enhances the correspondence between the labels and the visual words, which ultimately makes the annotations precise and complete.

Algorithm 2: SSC-HDP algorithm

```
Initialize w_{i,j}
    foreach L_j ∈ ℒ do
        foreach I_i ∈ P_j do
            w_{i,j} ← 1;
        foreach I_i ∈ S_j do
            w_{i,j} ← 0;
Build the first Corr-HDP model using the initial w_{i,j}
while parameters of Corr-HDP change do
    foreach L_j ∈ ℒ do
        foreach I_k ∈ S_j do
            Compute Pr[w_{k,j} = 1|b_k] through Corr-HDP;
            w_{k,j} ← Pr[w_{k,j} = 1|b_k] ∈ [0, 1];
        foreach I_i ∈ P_j do
            Pr[w_{i,j} = 1|b_i] ← 1;
            w_{i,j} ← 1;
    foreach I_g ∈ 𝒟 do
        foreach L_j ∈ ℒ do
            if w_{g,j} ≤ e or w_{g,j} in the bottom t% in S_j then
                w_{g,j} ← 0;
    Update the parameters of Corr-HDP model by w_{g,j}
```

Note that even a completely annotated image may only contain a few labels in the whole label vocabulary. We see that $\mathbf{w}_g$ is actually a sparse vector for a given I_g, and most elements of $\mathbf{w}_g$ are zero. Thus, as Algorithm 2 shows, after each element of $\mathbf{w}_g$ for I_g is updated in each iteration, we reserve element $w_{g,j}$ if $w_{g,j} \geq e$, and set other elements to zero. Here e is a threshold, which is selected appropriately to ensure that not only $\mathbf{w}_g$ is a sparse vector, but also the information of the annotations for I_g is lost as least as possible. What is more, in order to avoid adding a large number of labels of one kind into the training set, we also set $w_{g,j} = 0$ if it is in the bottom $t\%$ in the mixed set S_j for each kind of labels.

From Figure 3(c) we note that the information of the unlabeled data can be added seamlessly into the algorithm. After the initial Corr-HDP model is built, we exploit parameters of this initial model to compute the likelihood for each label of each image in the unannotated set $\mathscr{U}$, and allocate all the unannotated images into the mixed set $S_j (1 \leq j \leq M)$. Consequently, the unlabeled data are merged into the mixed set, and are utilized to update the Corr-HDP model in the subsequent iteration.

4.4 Parameter Estimation

In order to maximize the likelihood of the training data for a precise prediction, we adopt the Expectation Maximization (EM) algorithm under the variational framework to learn the parameters of SSC-HDP. Before we list explicitly the estimation steps, the prerequisite knowledge on variational inference is introduced below.

The main idea of variational inference is to select an auxiliary distribution q to approximate the original distribution p through minimizing the KL-divergence $D(q_{\nu}(\mathbf{H})||p(\mathbf{H}|x, \theta))$ in the mean-field framework iteratively and updating the parameters of the latent variables:

$$E_q[\log p(x|\theta)] \geq E_q[\log p(\mathbf{H}, x|\theta)] - E_q[\log q_\nu(\mathbf{H})]. \quad (2)$$

where $\mathbf{H}$ is the set of latent variables, x is the set of observed variables, θ is the set of hyperparameters, and ν is the parameter set of the auxiliary distribution. Herein, $x = \{\mathbf{w}, \mathbf{b}\}$, $\mathbf{H} = \{\beta, \pi, z, y\}$, $\theta = \{\phi_z^w, \phi_z^b\}$, and $\nu = \{\gamma, \phi_n, \lambda_m\}$. We aim to estimate $E_q[\log p(\mathbf{w}, \mathbf{b}|\phi_z^w, \phi_z^b)]$. According to (2) we decompose its lower bound $E_q[\log p(\beta, \pi, z, y, \mathbf{w}, \mathbf{b}|\phi_z^w, \phi_z^b)] - E_q[\log q_\nu(\beta, \pi, z, y)]$ into the algebraic combination of the following ten items and denote this lower bound as $\mathbf{R}$:

$$\begin{aligned}\mathbf{R} \triangleq\ & E_q[\log p(\beta|\alpha)] + E_q[\log p(\pi|\beta)] \\ & + \sum_{n=1}^{N_d} E_q[\log p(z_n|\pi)] + \sum_{n=1}^{N_d} E_q[\log p(b_n|z_n, \phi_{z_n}^b)] \\ & + \sum_{m=1}^{M_d} E_q[\log p(y_m|N_d)] + \sum_{m=1}^{M_d} E_q[\log p(w_m|y_m, \mathbf{z}, \phi_{z_{y_m}}^w)] \\ & - E_q[\log q(\beta)] - E_q[\log q(\pi|\gamma)] \\ & - \sum_{n=1}^{N_d} E_q[\log q(z_n|\phi_n)] - \sum_{m=1}^{M_d} E_q[\log q(y_m|\lambda_m)] \end{aligned} \quad (3)$$

We claim the following relationships of the real distribution p and the auxiliary distribution q:

$$\begin{aligned} \beta|\alpha &\sim_p Stick(\alpha) & & \\ \pi|\beta &\sim_p DP(\alpha^\pi, \beta) & \pi|\gamma &\sim_q Dir(\gamma) \\ z_n|\pi &\sim_p Mult(\pi) & z_n|\phi_n &\sim_q Mult(\phi_n) \\ b_n|z_n, \phi_{z_n}^b &\sim_p Mult(\phi_{z_n}^b) & & \\ y_m|N_d &\sim_p Unif(N_d) & y_m|\lambda_m &\sim_q Mult(\lambda_m) \\ w_m|y_m, \mathbf{z}, \phi_{z_{y_m}}^w &\sim_p Mult(\mathbf{z}, y_m, \phi_{z_{y_m}}^w) & & \end{aligned}$$

As described before, we formulate the estimation steps in four parts. Firstly, in the E-step we derive the updating formulas for parameters $\gamma, \phi_n, \lambda_m$ in the auxiliary distribution q. Secondly, in the M-step we maximize the hyperparameters ϕ_z^w, ϕ_z^b under the smooth and normalization constraints. Thirdly, we update the top level parameter β since there does not exist an analytical form in the above EM steps. Finally, we append the labels to the partially annotated and completely unannotated images based on the likelihood's prediction. After this step, the prior for word $\mathbf{w}_d$ in the next epoch has also been generated. Moreover, we truncate β at K as described in Section 4.2 to make parameter estimation feasible. Thus, $\pi \sim DP(\alpha^\pi, \beta)$ is approximated as $\pi \sim Dirichlet(\alpha^\pi\beta_1, \ldots \alpha^\pi\beta_K)$.

4.4.1 *Updating the parameters $\gamma, \phi_n, \lambda_m$ in q (E-step)*

We denote $q(z_n = i) \triangleq \phi_{n,i}$ and $q(y_m = n) \triangleq \lambda_{m,n}$. Note that omitting $E_q[\log p(\beta|\alpha)]$ and $E_q[\log q(\beta)]$ in (3) does not influence the updating of $\gamma, \phi_n, \lambda_m$, and the term $E_q[\log p(y_m|N_d)]$ in the real distribution p is a constant; therefore, we only estimate the other seven items in (3):

$$\begin{aligned} & E_q[\log p(\pi|\beta)] \\ &= \sum_{i=1}^{K} (\alpha^\pi\beta_i - 1) E_q[\log \pi_i] + \log \frac{\Gamma(\Sigma\alpha^\pi\beta_i)}{\prod_{i=1}^{K}\Gamma(\alpha^\pi\beta_i)} \\ &= \sum_{i=1}^{K} (\alpha^\pi\beta_i - 1)[\Psi(\gamma_i) - \Psi(\Sigma\gamma_i)] + const \end{aligned} \quad (4)$$

The second equation in (4) is due to the logarithm of sufficient statistics being equal to its natural statistics' negative derivative. $\Psi(\cdot)$ is the Digamma function, which is the logarithmic derivative of the gamma function. The following expectation formulas in $\mathbf{R}$ are expanded as formula (4):

$$E_q[\log p(z_n|\pi)] = \sum_{i=1}^{K} \phi_{n,i}[\Psi(\gamma_i) - \Psi(\Sigma\gamma_i)] + const \quad (5)$$

$$E_q[\log p(b_n|z_n, \phi_{z_n}^b)] = \sum_{i=1}^{K} \phi_{n,i} \log p(b_n|z_n = i, \phi_{z_n}^b) \quad (6)$$

$$\begin{aligned} & E_q[\log p(w_m|y_m, \mathbf{z}, \phi_{z_{y_m}}^w)] \\ &= \sum_{m=1}^{M_d}\sum_{i=1}^{K} \phi_{n,i}\lambda_{m,n} \log p(w_m|z_n = i, y_m = n, \phi_{z_{y_m}}^w) \end{aligned} \quad (7)$$

$$\begin{aligned} & E_q[\log q(\pi|\gamma)] \\ &= \sum_{i=1}^{K} (\gamma_i - 1)[\Psi(\gamma_i) - \Psi(\Sigma\gamma_i)] + \log \frac{\Gamma(\Sigma\gamma_i)}{\prod_{i=1}^{K}\Gamma(\gamma_i)} \end{aligned} \quad (8)$$

$$E_q[\log q(z_n|\phi_n)] = \sum_{i=1}^{K} \phi_{n,i} \log \phi_{n,i} + const \quad (9)$$

$$E_q[\log q(y_m|\lambda_m)] = \sum_{m=1}^{M_d} \lambda_{m,n} \log \lambda_{m,n} + const \quad (10)$$

Now $\mathbf{R}$ can be expressed by (4)$\sim$(10). We have found that (4), (5), and (8) are associated with γ. Taking derivative with each γ_i and setting $\frac{\partial \mathbf{R}}{\partial \gamma_i} = 0$, we obtain an estimation of γ_i. Similarly, setting $\frac{\partial \mathbf{R}}{\partial \phi_{n,i}} = 0$ and $\frac{\partial \mathbf{R}}{\partial \lambda_{m,n}} = 0$, we obtain the estimation of $\phi_{n,i}$ and $\lambda_{m,n}$:

$$\gamma_i = \alpha^\pi\beta_i + \sum_{n=1}^{N_d} \phi_{n,i} \quad (11)$$

$$\begin{aligned} \phi_{n,i} \propto\ & p(b_n|z_n = i, \phi_{z_n=i}^b) \exp[\Psi(\gamma_i) - \Psi(\Sigma\gamma_i)] \cdot \\ & \prod_{m=1}^{M_d} [p(w_m|z_n = i, y_m = n, \phi_{z_{y_m}}^w)]^{\lambda_{m,n}} \end{aligned} \quad (12)$$

$$\lambda_{m,n} \propto \prod_{i=1}^{K} [p(w_m|z_n = i, y_m = n, \phi_{z_{y_m}}^w)]^{\phi_{n,i}} \quad (13)$$

4.4.2 *Updating the parameters ϕ_z^b, ϕ_z^w (M-step)*

In the given training set $\mathscr{D}$, we consider ϕ_z^b, ϕ_z^w as multinomial vector parameters of visual words and labels respectively for K latent variables z. In order to avoid overfitting, we smooth the parameters ϕ_z^b and ϕ_z^w by appending the conjugate priors $Dir(\eta, ..., \eta)$ and $Dir(\omega, ..., \omega)$ for the two parameters respectively. We modify $\mathbf{R}$ in (3) by appending normalization constraints on $\phi_{z_n=i}^b$ and $\phi_{z_{y_m}=i}^w$. Applying the method of Lagrange multipliers, we obtain

$$q(\phi_i^{b_j}|\eta_i^j) \propto \exp\{\sum_{d=1}^{D}\sum_{n=1}^{N_d} \phi_{n,i}\mathbf{1}[b_{d,n} \to j] \log \phi_i^{b_j}\} \cdot p(\phi_i^{b_j}|\eta) \quad (14)$$

$$\begin{aligned} q(\phi_i^{w_k}|\omega_i^k) \propto\ & \exp\{\sum_{d=1}^{D}\sum_{n=1}^{N_d}\sum_{m=1}^{M_d} \phi_{n,i}\lambda_{m,n}\mathbf{1}[w_{d,m} \to k] \log \phi_i^{w_k}\} \cdot \\ & p(\phi_i^{w_k}|\omega) \end{aligned} \quad (15)$$

Where $b_{d,n} \to j$ means that $b_{d,n}$ chooses the jth visual word in

$\mathcal{V}$, $w_{d,m} \to k$ means that $w_{d,m}$ chooses the kth label in $\mathcal{L}$, η_i^j and ω_i^k are the updating parameters for $\phi^b_{z_n=i}$ and $\phi^w_{z_{y_m}=i}$ respectively. Thus, through updating the parameters η_i^j and ω_i^k, we achieve the updating of $\phi^b_{z_n=i}$ and $\phi^w_{z_{y_m}=i}$. We obtain:

$$\eta_i^j = \eta + \sum_{d=1}^{D}\sum_{n=1}^{N_d} \phi_{n,i}\mathbf{1}[b_{d,n} \to j] \quad (16)$$

$$\omega_i^k = \omega + \sum_{d=1}^{D}\sum_{n=1}^{N_d}\sum_{m=1}^{M_d} \phi_{n,i}\lambda_{m,n}\mathbf{1}[w_{d,m} \to k] \quad (17)$$

Now that we have assumed that $w_{d,m} = \Pr[w_{d,m} = 1|\mathbf{b}_d]$ is a probability value instead of a Boolean value, we replace $\mathbf{1}[w_{d,m} \to k]$ with $\sum_{w_{d,m}\to k} w_{d,m}$ in (17) and obtain

$$\omega_i^k = \omega + \sum_{d=1}^{D}\sum_{n=1}^{N_d}\sum_{m=1}^{M_d} \phi_{n,i}\lambda_{m,n} \sum_{w_{d,m}\to k} w_{d,m} \quad (18)$$

4.4.3 Updating the top level parameter β

We obtain a target function $\mathbf{L}_\beta$ from $\mathbf{R}$ with the normalization constraint:

$$\mathbf{L}_\beta = E_q[\log GEM(\beta;\alpha)] + E_q[\log Dir(\pi;\alpha^\pi\beta)] + \lambda(\sum_{i=1}^{K}\beta_i - 1) \quad (19)$$

where λ is a Lagrange multiplier. Similar to [17], we compute $\frac{\partial \mathbf{L}_\beta}{\partial \beta_i}$ and use the gradient projection method [21] to find the optimal β.

4.4.4 Updating priors and making predictions

We utilize the updated Corr-HDP model to compute the likelihood and update $\mathbf{w}_d$, which can be considered as a prior of the next iteration and can also be used to make predictions of a new, completely unannotated image after the iteration converges and the SSC-HDP model is established.

$$w_{d,j} = \Pr[w_{d,j} = 1|\mathbf{b}_d] \approx \sum_{n=1}^{N}\sum_{m=1}^{K} p(w_{d,j}|z_m)q(z_m|b_{d,n}) \quad (20)$$

5. EXPERIMENTS

5.1 Data and Parameter Setting

We compare our model with both MoM-HDP and Corr-LDA using the partially annotated images as the training set on three standard datasets: VOC 2010 challenge data [8], NUS-WIDE [6], and the Berkley Drosophila embryo image database [1]. Figure 4 shows examples of the images in the three databases to demonstrate the variety of the images and the complexity of the experiments.

The **VOC 2010** database contains $11,321$ images in 20 categories (labels). For each image in the database, we rescale it for the maximum height of 256 pixels, then slide a window with a 16-pixel interval to divide the image into 16×16 patches. We use the 128-dim SIFT descriptor [20] to extract the features of each patch. Consequently, each image in the database is represented as a collection of SIFT descriptors. Given the collection of SIFT descriptors of each image from the whole database, we cluster them into 400 categories by performing k-means algorithm to learn the visual word vocabulary. Therefore, each image from the database is represented as a bag of visual words and a bag of labels. Each category in the VOC 2010 database contains a different number of images. To keep most of the categories with roughly similar numbers of images and similar frequency distributions, we select $3,876$ images as the partially annotated training set, $1,987$ images as the unlabeled training set, and $2,124$ images as the testing set. Hence, $7,987$ images from the VOC 2010 database are used in the experiment. We consider the original database as the completely annotated data as the ground truth. We randomly remove 30% of the ground truth labels from the images to form the partially annotated training set with the remaining images as the unlabeled data.

Figure 4: Image examples from the three databases: VOC 2010, NUS-WIDE, and BDE.

The **NUS-WIDE** database includes $269,648$ web images and 81 concepts as the ground truth labels. We choose the top 24 concepts from the database as the annotation words and have randomly sampled $10,000$ images for the experiments with $3,500$ images as the partially labeled training set, $4,500$ images as the unlabeled training set, and $2,000$ images as the testing set. In the experiments, we use the 500-D bag of words based on SIFT descriptions provided by the database and randomly remove 30% of the ground truth labels from the images to form the partially labeled training set.

The **Berkeley Drosophila embryo (BDE)** image database contains $36,628$ embryo images classified into different embryo development stages with 227 words as annotations to those images. The images are archived in six different folders with each folder containing images of two to four neighboring development stages. We use one of the folders which contains $5,496$ images and 75 annotation words as the experiment database to evaluate the performance of our model. After removing the low-frequency words in the folder, we keep 53 words and $5,494$ images with $3,846$ images as the partially labeled training set and $1,648$ images as the testing set. There is no unlabeled training set in this database. Following the work in [10], we partition the images into blocks, compute the feature vector for each block, and cluster the feature vectors into 150 categories by k-means. In the experiments we randomly remove 30% of the ground truth labels from the images to form the partially labeled training set.

5.2 Results and Discussions

In order to measure the quality of image annotation by the models, we follow the work in [26] by using the accuracy of the annotations as the performance measure on the annotation prediction and using the completeness of the annotations as the performance measure on the annotation completion. Let W_t be the predicted label set of a given image dataset. Let W_r be the ground truth label set of the given dataset. The accuracy of the predicted annotations is defined as $Acc = \frac{|W_t \cap W_r|}{|W_t|}$. Let W_i be the initial partial label set of the given dataset, which is $\emptyset$ for an unlabeled set. The com-

Table 1: The accuracy and completeness for the testing sets of the three databases using MoM-HDP, Corr-LDA, Corr-HDP, and SSC-HDP, respectively. $M.1$ represents MoM-HDP, $M.2$ represents Corr-LDA, $M.3$ represents Corr-HDP, $M.4$ represents SSC-HDP without the unlabeled data, $M.5$ represents SSC-HDP with the unlabeled data; $M.1 - M.5$ use the partially labeled training set, and $M.6$ represents Corr-HDP using the completely labeled training set.

		$VOC2010$			$NUS-WIDE$			BDE		
		$n=2$	$n=3$	$n=4$	$n=2$	$n=3$	$n=4$	$n=2$	$n=3$	$n=4$
ACC	$M.1$	29.6%	22.7%	19.2%	31.9%	27.3%	23.5%	20.7%	19.5%	19.0%
	$M.2$	30.9%	23.8%	20.2%	32.6%	28.5%	24.7%	21.5%	20.4%	19.9%
	$M.3$	31.7%	24.7%	20.9%	32.9%	28.9%	25.1%	21.9%	20.9%	20.5%
	$M.4$	**33.0%**	25.4%	21.4%	33.5%	29.4%	25.7%	**22.1%**	**21.3%**	**20.8%**
	$M.5$	**33.0%**	**25.7%**	**21.8%**	**33.7%**	**29.8%**	**26.1%**	—	—	—
	$M.6$	**34.5%**	**27.8%**	**24.1%**	**35.1%**	**31.1%**	**27.9%**	**22.8%**	**22.4%**	**21.9%**
COM	$M.1$	36.6%	42.0%	47.4%	36.4%	46.7%	53.7%	11.7%	16.5%	21.4%
	$M.2$	38.2%	44.1%	50.0%	37.2%	48.8%	56.4%	12.1%	17.3%	22.5%
	$M.3$	39.2%	45.7%	51.6%	37.5%	49.5%	57.4%	12.4%	17.7%	23.1%
	$M.4$	**40.8%**	47.0%	52.7%	38.2%	50.3%	58.7%	**12.5%**	**18.0%**	**23.5%**
	$M.5$	**40.8%**	**47.5%**	**53.8%**	**38.4%**	**51.0%**	**59.6%**	—	—	—
	$M.6$	**42.6%**	**51.4%**	**59.4%**	**40.0%**	**53.2%**	**63.8%**	**12.9%**	**19.0%**	**24.7%**

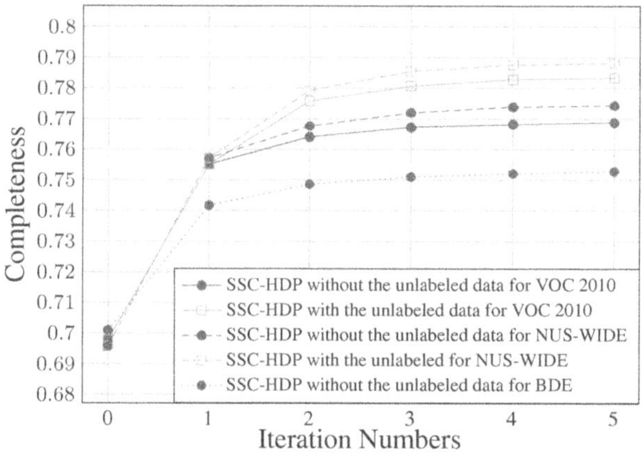

Figure 5: The completeness of the annotations for the partially labeled training set using SSC-HDP.

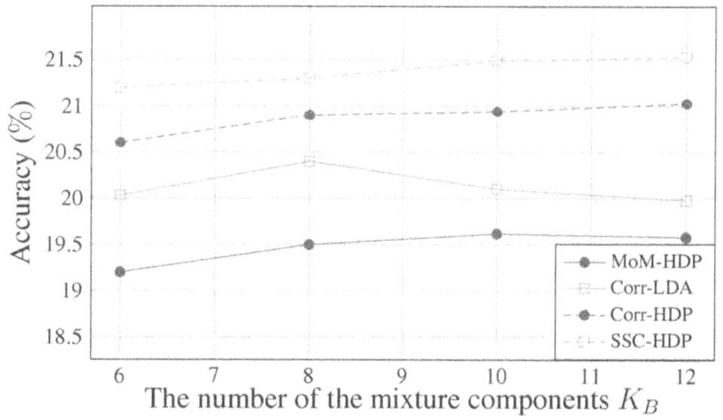

Figure 6: The accuracy for the testing set using MoM-HDP, Corr-LDA, Corr-HDP, and SSC-HDP with the partially labeled training set when $n = 3$ for the BDE image database.

pleteness of the annotations is defined as $Com = \frac{|(W_t \cup W_i) \cap W_r|}{|W_r|}$. For each label, we evaluate the performance of the model on the annotation prediction using the standard performance measures of precision and recall. The precision of a label is the fraction of the images which actually have the predicted label out of all the images predicted with the label. The recall of a label is the fraction of the images which are assigned a given label out of all the images which actually have the label. For the testing set, we choose the predicted label as the new label of a given image if it is within the top n predicted labels.

We describe the completeness of the annotations for the partially annotated training sets of the three databases using SSC-HDP as a function of the iteration in Figure 5. In Table 1, we summarize the prediction accuracy and completeness for the testing sets of the three databases when n is selected as $2, 3, 4$ using MoM-HDP, Corr-LDA, Corr-HDP, and SSC-HDP, respectively. The numbers of the mixture components for the VOC 2010, the NUS-WIDE, and the BDE image databases in Table 1 are chosen as $K_V = 20$, $K_N = 30$, and $K_B = 8$.

We observe from Figure 5 that the completeness increases after the iteration progresses, and the performance of SSC-HDP with the unlabeled data is better than that without the unlabeled data, which shows that the unlabeled data are helpful to improve the performance of the model and that the semi-supervised learning scheme is effective in completing the missing labels of the training set and at the same time in improving the predicted accuracy of the testing set. The curves for the completeness of SSC-HDP in Figure 5 all exhibit their major elevation between the first two iterations, then level off during the subsequent iterations and quickly converge, indicating that SSC-HDP converges fast. Because of the iterations, the complexity of SSC-HDP is four to five times of those of MoM-HDP, Corr-LDA, and Corr-HDP. Although SSC-HDP spends more time in the off-line training process, it is as fast as the other three models when predicting annotations of any new, unannotated image on-line.

From Table 1, we see that our proposed models including Corr-HDP and SSC-HDP perform better than MoM-HDP and Corr-LDA. The performance of SSC-HDP is the closest to that of Corr-HDP using the completely labeled training set which is the baseline, and is better than those of MoM-HDP, Corr-LDA and Corr-HDP using the partially labeled training set, because MoM-HDP, Corr-LDA, and Corr-HDP using the partially labeled training set all consider the training set as the completely labeled set and ignore the missing labels. Corr-HDP using the completely labeled training set as the baseline performs the best, because there is the clearest and the most complete information of the distribution of labels in its train-

Figure 8: Image examples in the six categories in the VOC 2010 database: *aeroplane*, *sheep*, *bus*, *bottle*, *diningtable*, and *tvmonitor* (from left column to right column).

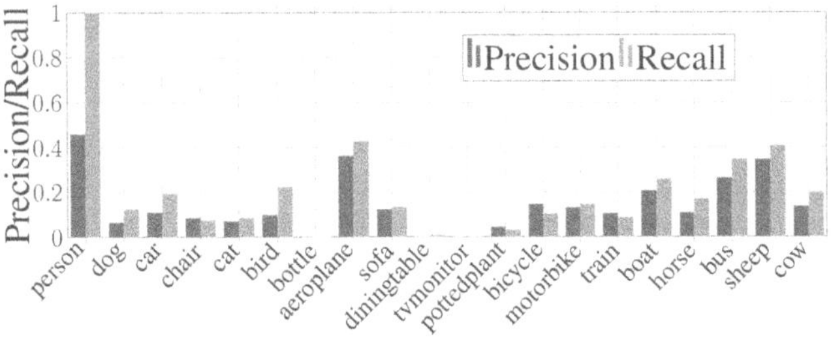

Figure 7: The precision/recall of the 20 labels for SSC-HDP with unlabeled data when n = 3 for the VOC 2010 database.

ing set. Since the performance of SSC-HDP is already close (about 1% to 2%) to that of the baseline which is the best and "ideal" case, the improvement of SSC-HDP over the other models, though small (about 1% to 3%), is still significant. The reason why the baseline has a relatively low performance is related to the fact that the given ground truth labels are far away from being actually complete; this can be seen clearly from the example shown in Figure 1 where the given ground truth, i.e. the "complete" annotation set, only includes *person*, *bottle*, and *TVmonitor*, while many other labels should have been given as part of the ground truth such as microphone and door. This fact further demonstrates the necessity to develop an inductive learning image annotation method based on partially given labels such as SSC-HDP. Also from Table 1 it is further verified that the unlabeled data contribute to the improvement of the SSC-HDP performance. From another perspective, the unlabeled data are considered as the partially annotated data from which 100% of the labels are removed. Although the unlabeled data contain no information about labels, they are useful to make the structure of the distribution of the visual words clearer.

In Figure 6 we describe the accuracy of the predicted annotations when $n = 3$ for the testing set of the BDE image database as a function of the mixture components K_B using MoM-HDP, Corr-LDA, Corr-HDP, and SSC-HDP with the partially labeled training set, respectively. From Figure 6, we see that the performance of Corr-LDA is more sensitive when the number of K_B increases than those of MoM-HDP, Corr-HDP, and SSC-HDP, for the latter three models use the truncated HDP as a prior which adapts to the number of the mixture components dynamically based on the training set. Similar results exist for the other two databases.

Figure 7 shows the precision/recall plots on each label for SSC-HDP with the unlabeled dataset when $n = 3$ for the VOC 2010 database. Since the label *person* occurs most frequently and is contained in 4639 images in the VOC 2010 database, though we try to keep most of the categories roughly the same number of images, the occurrence number of the label *person* is larger than those of other labels. Consequently, most of the visual words establish links to the label *person* during the training process and in Figure 7 the recall and precision of the label *person* are high. Except for the label *person*, labels with the top three highest recalls and precisions are *aeroplane*, *sheep*, and *bus*, and labels with the top three lowest recalls and precisions are *bottle*, *diningtable*, and *tvmonitor*. Figure 8 shows examples of the images in these six categories in the VOC 2010 database, which further reveals an intuitive verification of the SSC-HDP performance that an image with simple semantics results in a high precision and recall.

Further as a case study to demonstrate the superiority of the SSC-HDP performance, Figure 1 is one of the partially labeled training images in the training data of the VOC 2010 database with the given partial labels as *bottle* and *TVmonitor*, and the given ground truth labels to this image as *person*, *bottle*, and *TVmonitor*. After the learning with SSC-HDP, two extra labels are identified and added: one is the missing label *person*; the other is an appropriate label *sofa*, which was even not originally given in the ground truth of the image. This shows that SSC-HDP is an effective inductive learning method to complete all the missing labels in annotations, even in completing the missing labels of the ground truth, as long as those missing labels are in the label vocabulary. Since in the database the given label vocabulary is not actually complete in the ground truth, SSC-HDP is unable to pick up those missing labels that appear in the image of Figure 1 such as microphone and door that are not even included in the label vocabulary.

6. CONCLUSION

This paper studies an important problem in image data mining — mining partially annotated images. We have argued that this problem exists in many real-world applications. We have then presented an effective and promising solution to this problem based on a statistical model we have developed called Semi-Supervised Correspondence Hierarchical Dirichlet Process (SSC-HDP). The novelty of this model is that it uses partially annotated images as the training set to develop an inductive semi-supervised learning statistical model to complete all the missing labels in the given partially labeled training annotations and to predict all the missing labels for the unlabeled and any new, unseen data. We evaluate SSC-HDP on several standard datasets from the related literature in comparison with peer models from the recent literature. Experimental results demonstrate the effectiveness and promise of SSC-HDP as a solution to the problem of mining partially annotated images. The partially labeled problem can be generalized from the image annotation to other multi-label learning problems, and consequently, has a wide range of applications.

7. ACKNOWLEDGMENTS

Zhongfei Zhang is on leave from SUNY Binghamton, USA, and is supported in part by US NSF through grants IIS-0812114 and CCF-1017828. Any opinions, findings, and conclusions or recommendations expressed in this material are those of the authors and do not necessarily reflect the views of the National Science Foundation.

8. REFERENCES

[1] http://www.fruitfly.org/.

[2] K. Barnard, P. Duygulu, D. Forsyth, N. de Freitas, D. M. Blei, and M. I. Jordan. Matching words and pictures. *Journal of Machine Learning Research*, 3:1107–1135, 2003.

[3] D. M. Blei and M. I. Jordan. Modeling annotated data. In *Proceedings of the 26th International ACM SIGIR Conference*, 2003.

[4] D. M. Blei, A. Y. Ng, and M. I. Jordan. Latent dirichlet allocation. *Journal of Machine Learning Research*, 3:993–1022, 2003.

[5] M. R. Boutell, J. Luo, X. Shen, and C. M. Brown. Learning multi-label scene classification. *Pattern Recognition*, 37(9):1757–1771, 2004.

[6] T. S. Chua, J. Tang, R. Hong, H. Li, Z. Luo, and Y. Zheng. Nus-wide: a real-world web image database from national university of singapore. In *Proceedings of the ACM International Conference on Image and Video Retrieval*, pages 1–9, 2009.

[7] R. Datta, D. Joshi, J. Li, and J. Z. Wang. Image retrieval: Ideas, influences, and trends of the new age. *ACM Computing Surveys*, 40:1–60, 2008.

[8] M. Everingham, L. V. Gool, C. Williams, C. K. I., J. Winn, and A. Zisserman. The pascal visual object classes (voc) challenge. *International Journal of Computer Vision*, 88(2):303–338, 2010.

[9] S. Feng, R. Manmatha, and V. Lavrenko. Multiple bernoulli relevance models for image and video annotation. In *Proceedings of International Conference on Computer Vision and Pattern Recognition*, pages 1002–1009, 2004.

[10] Z. Guo, Z. Zhang, E. P. Xing, and C. Faloutsos. Enhanced max margin learning on multimodal data mining in a multimedia database. In *Proceedings of 13th ACM SIGKDD International Conference on Knowledge Discovery and Data Mining*, 2007.

[11] H. Ishwaran and L. F. James. Gibbs sampling methods for stick-breaking priors. *Journal of the American Statistical Association*, 96(453):161–173, 2001.

[12] J. Jeon, V. Lavrenko, and R. Manmatha. Automatic image annotation and retrieval using cross-media relevance models. In *Proceedings of ACM Special Interest Group on Information Retrieval*, pages 119–126, 2003.

[13] V. Lavrenko, R. Manmatha, and J. Jeon. A model for learning the semantics of pictures. In *Proceedings of Neural Information Processing Systems*, 2003.

[14] L.-J. Li and L. Fei-Fei. What, where and who? classifying events by scene and object recognition. In *Proceedings of International Conference Computer Vision*, 2007.

[15] W. Li and M. Sun. Semi-supervised learning for image annotation based on conditional random fields. In *Proceedings of ACM International Conference on Image and Video Retrieval*, pages 463–472, 2006.

[16] Z. Li, J. Liu, X. Zhu, T. Liu, and H. Lu. Image annotation using multi-correlation probabilistic matrix factorization. In *Proceedings of ACM international conference on Multimedia*, pages 1187–1190, 2010.

[17] P. Liang, Petrov, M. I. Jordan, and D. Klein. The infinite pcfg using hierarchical dirichlet processes. In *Proceedings of Empirical Methods in Natural Language Processing*, pages 688–697, 2007.

[18] B. Liu, W. S. Lee, P. S. Yu, and X. Li. Partially supervised classification of text documents. In *Proceedings of the 19th International Conference on Machine Learning*, pages 387–394, 2002.

[19] N. Loeff, A. Farhadi, I. Endres, and D. A. Forsyth. Unlabeled data improves word prediction. In *Proceedings of International Conference Computer Vision*, 2009.

[20] D. G. Lowe. Distinctive image features from scale-invariant keypoints. *International Journal of Computer Vision*, 60(2):91–110, 2004.

[21] D. G. Luenberger and Y. Ye. *Linear and Nonlinear Programming*. Springer, third edition, 2008.

[22] J. Sethuraman. A constructive definition of dirichlet priors. *Statistica Sinica*, 4:639–650, 1994.

[23] A. Sharma, G. Hua, Z. Liu, and Z. Zhang. Meta-tag propagation by co-training an ensemble classifier for improving image search relevance. In *Computer Vision and Pattern Recognition Workshop*, pages 1–6, 2008.

[24] Y.-Y. Sun, Y. Zhang, and Z.-H. Zhou. Multi-label learning with weak label. In *Proceedings of Association for the Advancement of Artificial Intelligence*, pages 593–598, 2010.

[25] Y. W. Teh, M. I. Jordan, M. J. Beal, and D. M. Blei. Hierarchical dirichlet processes. *Journal of the American Statistical Association*, 101:1566–1581, 2004.

[26] O. Yakhnenko and V. Honavar. Annotating images and image objects using a hierarchical dirichlet process model. In *Proceedings of the 9th International Workshop on Multimedia Data Mining*, pages 1–7, 2008.

[27] S.-H. Yang, H. Zha, and B.-G. Hu. Dirichlet-bernoulli alignment: A generative model for multi-class multi-label multi-instance corpora. In *Proceedings of Neural Information Processing Systems*, pages 2143–2150, 2009.

[28] R. Zhang, Z. Zhang, M. Li, W.-Y. Ma, and H.-J. Zhang. A probabilistic semantic model for image annotation and multi-modal image retrieval. In *Proceedings of International Conference Computer Vision*, pages 846–851, 2005.

[29] Z.-H. Zhou and M.-L. Zhang. Multi-instance multilabel learning with application to scene classification. In *Proccedings of Neural Information Processing Systems*, pages 1609–1616, 2007.

[30] X. Zhu. Semi-supervised learning literature survey. Technical report, Computer Sciences TR 1530, University of Wisconsin-Madison, 2005.

Multi-View Transfer Learning with a Large Margin Approach

Dan Zhang
Computer Science Department
Purdue University
West Lafayette, IN
zhang168@cs.purdue.edu

Jingrui He
Machine Learning Group
IBM TJ Watson Research Center
Yorktown Heights, NY
jingruhe@us.ibm.com

Yan Liu
Computer Science Department
University of Southern California
Los Angeles, CA
yanliu.cs@usc.edu

Luo Si
Computer Science Department
Purdue University
West Lafayette, IN
lsi@cs.purdue.edu

Richard D. Lawrence
Machine Learning Group
IBM TJ Watson Research Center
Yorktown Heights, NY
ricklawr@us.ibm.com

ABSTRACT

Transfer learning has been proposed to address the problem of scarcity of labeled data in the target domain by leveraging the data from the source domain. In many real world applications, data is often represented from different perspectives, which correspond to multiple views. For example, a web page can be described by its contents and its associated links. However, most existing transfer learning methods fail to capture the multi-view nature, and might not be best suited for such applications.

To better leverage both the labeled data from the source domain and the features from different views, this paper proposes a general framework: Multi-View Transfer Learning with a Large Margin Approach (MVTL-LM). On one hand, labeled data from the source domain is effectively utilized to construct a large margin classifier; on the other hand, the data from both domains is employed to impose consistencies among multiple views. As an instantiation of this framework, we propose an efficient optimization method, which is guaranteed to converge to ϵ precision in $O(1/\epsilon)$ steps. Furthermore, we analyze its error bound, which improves over existing results of related methods. An extensive set of experiments are conducted to demonstrate the advantages of our proposed method over state-of-the-art techniques.

Categories and Subject Descriptors

I.2.6 [**Artificial Intelligence**]: Learning—*Knowledge acquisition*

General Terms

Algorithms, Performance, Experimentation

Keywords

Multi-View Learning, Transfer Learning, Large Margin Approach

1. INTRODUCTION

Transfer learning has been proposed and commonly used to address the problem of scarcity of labeled data in a particular target domain. It builds a model for the target domain by leveraging the label information from another related domain (source domain), thus avoids the costly process of generating labels for target domain examples. In many real world applications, the examples are often described from different perspectives, which correspond to multiple views. For example, in web mining, a web page can be represented by its contents and in-bound/out-bound links; in image analysis, an image can be described by different types of features, such as, color, texture, and shape. It has been shown that leveraging the consistencies between different views can help improve the learning performance. However, most existing transfer learning methods are designed only for single-view problems. In other words, if applied to problems with multiple views, these methods would fail to utilize the redundancy incurred by the multi-view property. Therefore, they are not ideal for such applications.

Despite its importance, the problem of Multi-View Transfer Learning (MVTL) has received limited attention. Most existing methods integrate the multi-view and transfer learning nature by some heuristics without theoretical analysis, such as the convergence rate of their algorithms, and how the learned model for the target domain can be improved by integrating the characteristics of multi-view features into transfer learning. And researchers tend to put more emphasis on the multi-view side. For example, in [40], the proposed algorithm uses the classifier trained on the source domain to generate the initial seed set, and then applies the co-training [4] algorithm to construct the classifier for the target domain; in [13], the authors explicitly model the view consistency in their objective function without considering the data distribution difference between the source domain and the target domain. Another straightforward method for MVTL is to concatenate the features from multiple views, and apply the transfer learning methods for single-view problems to build the model for the target domain. However, this kind of methods disregard the redundancy incurred by different views. As shown in a lot of previous works [37, 44, 47], without considering the consistencies between different views, the performance of multi-view learning cannot be guaranteed. On the contrary, in MVTL, we utilize the nature of both the transfer learning and the multi-view learning in an unified way.

To achieve this goal, this paper proposes a general framework: Multi-View Transfer Learning with a Large Margin Approach (MVTL-LM). In particular, from the transfer learning perspective, we integrate the nature of the multi-view setting into the transfer learning framework and impose the consistencies among multiple views, which implicitly limits the capacity of the hypothesis class. This is significantly different from previous large margin transfer learning methods [29], which do not consider the problem of multi-view setting. From multi-view learning perspective, the new formulation explicitly models the data distribution difference between the source domain and the target domain, applies the technique of importance sampling [1], and uses weighted labeled data from the source domain to construct a large margin classifier for the target domain. In particular, we propose a novel optimization method based on the bundle method [38, 39], which can solve an instantiation of the MVTL-LM framework in a very efficient way. We further prove that the optimization method can converge to ϵ precision in $O(\frac{1}{\epsilon})$ steps (See Theorem 3.1) and each step takes time $O(sn)$, where s is the average sparsity for features and n is the total number of source domain examples (See Theorem 3.2). Moreover, we analyze the generalized error bound of MVTL-LM in the target domain, which depends on its performance in the source domain and the empirical Rademacher complexity of a related hypothesis class (See Theorem 3.3). The empirical Rademacher complexity is reduced by making use of the multi-view nature. Experimental results demonstrate the advantages of our proposed method over state-of-the-art techniques.

The rest of this paper is organized as follows. The related works are discussed in Section 2. Section 3 introduces the research problem, presents the proposed algorithm and analyzes some properties of the proposed method. Section 4 presents the experimental results. Section 5 concludes the whole paper.

2. RELATED WORKS

This section briefly introduces related works on transfer learning, multi-view learning, MVTL and the bundle method.

2.1 Transfer Learning

As an important technique to address the problem of scarcity of labeled data in the target domain, transfer learning has received much attention recently. A key problem in transfer learning is what kind of knowledge can be transferred from the source domain to the target domain. Roughly speaking, the assumptions introduced in previous transfer learning work can be grouped into four categories:

1. **Feature Representation Transfer.** In [2, 7, 9, 11, 28, 30], the authors assume that there exists a common feature space shared by both the source domain and the target domain, which can be used as a bridge to transfer knowledge.

2. **Parameter Transfer.** In [5, 19], the authors make use of Gaussian Process (GP) models, and assume that the source domain and the target domain have shared parameters / hyper-parameters.

3. **Instance Transfer.** Due to the data distribution difference between the source domain and the target domain, in [8, 42], the authors select or re-weight the examples from the source domain for use in the target domain such that the expectation of the adjusted loss function on the source domain examples can be as close to the expectation of the loss function on the target domain examples as possible. In [23, 24], the authors utilize the data distribution differences between several source domains and the target domain, and propose a method to combine the classifiers from these source domains optimally.

4. **Relation Transfer.** In [10, 25, 26], the authors build the relational map between the source and the target domains, and relax the independently and identically distributed (i.e., iid) assumption in these two domains.

Despite their success on single-view problems, existing transfer learning methods may not work well on MVTL problems since the nature of multiple views are not considered in these works. In contrast, besides transferring knowledge from the source domain to the target domain via instance transfer, our proposed MVTL-LM approach imposes the consistencies between multiple views by explicitly modeling the differences between the outputs from different views, which promises to improve the performance.

2.2 Multi-View Learning

In many real-world applications, examples are represented by multiple views. It has been shown extensively in prior research that leveraging the redundancy among the multiple views can improve the learning performance [12, 17, 20, 31, 36, 44, 45]. For example, the authors of [12] construct a classifier on each view and regulate the consistencies between different views. Furthermore, they show that the Rademacher complexity of the function class can also be greatly reduced by regulating the consistencies.

This idea is further exploited in [20], where the authors incorporate the consistency term into multi-view semi-supervised learning problems, and show a substantial improvement on the classification performance. Similarly, in [44], the authors incorporate this idea into local learning [41] and propose a novel way to define the graph Laplacian. Most existing multi-view learning methods are for the single-domain settings. However, in MVTL problems, the source domain and the target domain do not have the same data distribution. As we will show in the experiments, disregarding the data distribution difference may adversely affect the classification performance. In contrast, besides leveraging the consistency between different views, our proposed MVTL-LM approach also considers the domain difference by an effective re-weighting scheme, so it can achieve better performance in MVTL problems.

2.3 Multi-View Transfer Learning

As mentioned in introduction, existing methods for multi-view transfer learning combine the multi-view learning and transfer learning by some heuristics, and tend to put more emphasis on the multi-view side. For example, the co-adaptation algorithm proposed in [40] uses the labeled examples from the source domain to construct classifiers, which will be used to generate the initial seed set. It then applies the co-training algorithm [4] to construct the classifier for the target domain. Note that in the latter stage, labeled examples from the source domain are not utilized, which may otherwise provide useful insights about consistency between multiple views and the optimal classifier. In [13], the co-regularized loss function consists of the standard regularized log likelihood on multiple views based on the labeled data, as well as the expected Bhattacharyya distance based on the unlabeled data. When applied in MVTL problems, it may fail to capture the data distribution difference between the source domain and the target domain. In contrast, our proposed MVTL-LM approach integrates the multi-view and transfer learning nature in a principled way, and is tailored for MVTL problems. Furthermore, we address some important theoretical problems, such as the convergence rate, time complexity and the generalization error bound, which have not been discussed in previous works for MVTL.

2.4 Bundle Method

The proposed formulation is a convex optimization problem. In this paper, we propose an optimization algorithm based on the bundle method [38, 39], which has shown its superior performances in both efficiency and effectiveness over state-of-the-art methods, to solve this proposed formulation. The basic motivation of the bundle method is to approximate the objective function $J(\mathbf{w})$ through a set of linear functions, where $\mathbf{w}$ is the model parameter. In particular, this objective function is lower bounded as follows:

$$J(\mathbf{w}) \geq \max_{1\leq i\leq t}\{J(\mathbf{w}_{i-1}) + \langle \mathbf{w} - \mathbf{w}_{i-1}, \mathbf{a}_i\rangle\},$$

where $\mathbf{w}_i$ is a set of points picked by the bundle method, and $\mathbf{a}_i$ is the gradient/sub-gradient at point $\mathbf{w}_i$. The bundle method monotonically decreases the gap between $J(\mathbf{w})$ and $\max_{1\leq i\leq t}\{J(\mathbf{w}_{i-1}) + \langle \mathbf{w} - \mathbf{w}_{i-1}, \mathbf{a}_i\rangle\}$ such that the minimal point of $J(\mathbf{w})$ can be approximated by that of the line segments $\max_{1\leq i\leq t}\ \{J(\mathbf{w}_{i-1}) + \langle \mathbf{w} - \mathbf{w}_{i-1}, \mathbf{a}_i\rangle\}$.

Some recent developments in bundle method [39] show that if $J(\mathbf{w})$ contains some regularizers by itself, the bundle method is guaranteed to converge to the precision ϵ in $O(1/\epsilon)$ steps. In MVTL-LM, we adapt the bundle method to solve the proposed problem, which can also be proven to have an efficient convergence rate.

3. MULTI-VIEW TRANSFER LEARNING WITH A LARGE MARGIN APPROACH

In this section, we first introduce the problem statement and some notations for MVTL. Then, a general framework named MVTL-LM is proposed, which integrates the multi-view and transfer learning nature in a principled way. Based on an instantiation of the framework, we propose an optimization method, which is adapted from the bundle method [38, 39]. Towards the end of this section, we analyze some important properties of the proposed method.

3.1 Problem Statement and Notations

Suppose we are given a set of labeled source domain examples from M independent views: $\{(\mathbf{x}_1^{(p)}, y_1^S), \ldots, (\mathbf{x}_n^{(p)}, y_n^S)\}$, $\mathbf{x}_i^{(p)} \in \mathbf{R}^{d_p\times 1}$, $y_i^S \in \{-1, 1\}$, $p \in \{1, 2, \ldots, M\}$, where n is the total number of source domain examples and d_p is the dimensionality of the p-th view. y_i^S is the class label of $\mathbf{x}_i^{(p)}$. Besides the source domain examples, a set of unlabeled target domain examples are also available, and are denoted as: $\{\mathbf{z}_1^{(p)}, \mathbf{z}_2^{(p)}, \ldots, \mathbf{z}_m^{(p)}\}$, $\mathbf{z}_i^{(p)} \in \mathbf{R}^{d_p\times 1}$, $p \in \{1, 2, \ldots, M\}$.

The goal of MVTL is to construct an accurate classifier for the target domain by making use of the labeled examples from the source domain as well as the redundancy incurred by multiple views. In this paper, similar to [15], we assume that $Pr_T(y|\mathbf{x}) = Pr_S(y|\mathbf{x})$. In other words, the conditional probability of the class label given the features is the same for both the source domain and the target domain. This particular case can also be referred to as covariate shift [35]. As claimed in [15], even in some cases when this assumption does not hold, the algorithm, which is based on this assumption, can still perform well.

3.2 MVTL-LM Framework

In this subsection, we propose a general large margin framework for MVTL, which fully exploits the multi-view and transfer learning nature. In this framework, we construct linear classifiers for all of the views, whose weight vectors are obtained via the following optimization problem:

$$\min_{\mathbf{w}^{(1)},\ldots,\mathbf{w}^{(M)}} \sum_{p=1}^{M} \gamma_p \Omega(\mathbf{w}^{(p)}) + \sum_{p=1}^{M} C_p R(Pr_T, l(\mathbf{x}^{(p)}, y, \mathbf{w}^{(p)}))$$
$$+\sum_{p=1}^{M}\sum_{q=1}^{M} C_{p,q} R_c(Pr_T^{(p,q)}, l_c(\mathbf{x}^{(p)}, \mathbf{x}^{(q)}, \mathbf{w}^{(p)}, \mathbf{w}^{(q)})), \quad (1)$$

where $\Omega(\mathbf{w}^{(p)})$ is the regularization term defined on the p-th view weight vector $\mathbf{w}^{(p)}$; $R(Pr_T, l(\mathbf{x}^{(p)}, y, \mathbf{w}^{(p)}))$ is the expected classification loss with respect to the data distribution of the target domain examples (Pr_T), which measures the deviations between the true labels and the predicted labels based on the p-th view; $l(\mathbf{x}^{(p)}, y, \mathbf{w}^{(p)})$ is the classification loss (such as the hinge loss [32]); $R_c(Pr_T^{(p,q)}, l_c(\mathbf{x}^{(p)}, \mathbf{x}^{(q)}, \mathbf{w}^{(p)}, \mathbf{w}^{(q)}))$ measures the expected consistency between the p-th view and the q-th view with respect to their joint distribution in the target domain; $l_c(\mathbf{x}^{(p)}, \mathbf{x}^{(q)}, \mathbf{w}^{(p)}, \mathbf{w}^{(q)})$ is the consistency between the p-th view and the q-th view (such as the squared loss between the predictions on different views); γ_p, C_p, and $C_{p,q}$ are non-negative parameters that balance the relative importance of the three terms in the objective function in Eq.(1).

Notice that when $C_{p,q} = 0$, Eq.(1) is equivalent to training a large margin classifier on each view independently. When $C_{p,q} > 0$, by minimizing Eq.(1), we can obtain large margin classifiers which are also consistent across different views. The final classifier is the average of large margin classifiers on all the views, i.e.,

$$f(\mathbf{x}) = \frac{1}{M}\sum_{p=1}^{M}(\mathbf{w}^{(p)})^T\mathbf{x}^{(\mathbf{p})},$$

where $\mathbf{x} = [(\mathbf{x}^{(1)})^T, \ldots, (\mathbf{x}^{(M)})^T]^T$. Next, we will discuss the loss term and the consistency term respectively.

3.2.1 *Classification Loss*

$R(Pr_T, l(\mathbf{x}^{(p)}, y, \mathbf{w}^{(p)}))$ measures the expected classification loss with respect to the data distribution on the target domain. To be specific, $R(Pr_T, l(\mathbf{x}^{(p)}, y, \mathbf{w}^{(p)})) = \mathbf{E}_{(\mathbf{x},y)\sim Pr_T}[l(\mathbf{x}^{(p)}, y, \mathbf{w}^{(p)})]$. However, in our problem setting, we do not have any labeled examples from the target domain. Therefore, we estimate this term using labeled examples from the source domain as follows:

$$\begin{aligned}
&\mathbf{E}_{(\mathbf{x},y)\sim Pr_T}[l(\mathbf{x}^{(p)}, y, \mathbf{w}^{(p)})]\\
=&\mathbf{E}_{(\mathbf{x},y)\sim Pr_S}[\frac{Pr_T(\mathbf{x}, y)}{Pr_S(\mathbf{x}, y)} l(\mathbf{x}^{(p)}, y, \mathbf{w}^{(p)})]\\
=&\mathbf{E}_{(\mathbf{x},y)\sim Pr_S}[\frac{Pr_T(y|\mathbf{x})Pr_T(\mathbf{x})}{Pr_S(y|\mathbf{x})Pr_S(\mathbf{x})} l(\mathbf{x}^{(p)}, y, \mathbf{w}^{(p)})]\\
=&\mathbf{E}_{(\mathbf{x},y)\sim Pr_S}[\frac{Pr_T(\mathbf{x})}{Pr_S(\mathbf{x})} l(\mathbf{x}^{(p)}, y, \mathbf{w}^{(p)})].\\
=&\mathbf{E}_{(\mathbf{x},y)\sim Pr_S}[\beta(\mathbf{x}) l(\mathbf{x}^{(p)}, y, \mathbf{w}^{(p)})].\\
\approx&\frac{1}{n}\sum_{i=1}^{n}\beta_i l(\mathbf{x}_i^{(p)}, y_i, \mathbf{w}^{(p)}), \qquad (2)
\end{aligned}$$

where Pr_S is the distribution of the source domain, weight function $\beta(\mathbf{x}) := \frac{Pr_T(\mathbf{x})}{Pr_S(\mathbf{x})}$; and $\beta_i = \beta(\mathbf{x}_i)$. Notice that the value of $\beta(\mathbf{x})$ reflects the distribution difference between the source domain and the target domain. If the two distributions are similar, $\beta(\mathbf{x})$ will be close to 1; if the two distributions are dissimilar, under-represented examples in Pr_T will receive a higher weight, whereas over-represented examples will receive a lower weight. In this way, we are able to estimate the classification error for the target domain using labeled examples from the source domain.

There are various ways to estimate β_i, such as Gaussian Mixture Model (GMM) [22], Kernel Density Estimation [34], Kernel Mean Matching [15], etc. In our approach, we concatenate the features on different views together, and measure the probability ratios between source and target domains by using GMM. To be specific, we first estimate the marginal distribution of all the features in the source domain and the target domain using two GMMs respectively. Then, β_i is estimated as the ratio between the two generative probabilities on $\mathbf{x}_i$ given by these two GMMs. Notice that in GMM, we need to specify the number of components. As will be shown in Section 4, the proposed approach is very robust to small perturbations in this number.

3.2.2 *Consistency*

As a consistency term, $R_c(Pr_T^{(p,q)}, l_c(\mathbf{x}^{(p)}, \mathbf{x}^{(q)}, \mathbf{w}^{(p)}, \mathbf{w}^{(q)}))$ regulates that the outputs on individual views should be consistent, and not deviate too much. $l_c(\mathbf{x}^{(p)}, \mathbf{x}^{(q)}, \mathbf{w}^{(p)}, \mathbf{w}^{(q)}))$ is the consistency loss function, which penalizes the deviations between the output of $\mathbf{x}^{(p)}$ and $\mathbf{x}^{(q)}$, under the classifiers $\mathbf{w}^{(p)}$ and $\mathbf{w}^{(q)}$. Similar to Eq.(2), To estimate this term, we use both the labeled examples from the source domain and the unlabeled examples from the target domain as follows:

$$
\begin{aligned}
&R_c(Pr_T^{(p,q)}, l_c(\mathbf{x}^{(p)}, \mathbf{x}^{(q)}, \mathbf{w}^{(p)}, \mathbf{w}^{(q)})) \\
=&\mathbf{E}_{(\mathbf{x}^{(p)},\mathbf{x}^{(q)})\sim Pr_T^{(p,q)}}[l_c(\mathbf{x}^{(p)}, \mathbf{x}^{(q)}, \mathbf{w}^{(p)}, \mathbf{w}^{(q)}))] \\
\approx&\frac{1}{m+n}\left(\sum_{i=1}^{n} \beta_i l_c(\mathbf{x}_i^{(p)}, \mathbf{x}_i^{(q)}, \mathbf{w}^{(p)}, \mathbf{w}^{(q)})\right. \\
&\left.+\sum_{i=1}^{m} l_c(\mathbf{z}_i^{(p)}, \mathbf{z}_i^{(q)}, \mathbf{w}^{(p)}, \mathbf{w}^{(q)})\right). \qquad (3)
\end{aligned}
$$

This term regulates the consistency on both the source domain and target domain examples. Combining this constraint with the standard objective functions for each view yields a multi-view learning algorithm, which was shown to perform better than single view approach on many classification applications.

3.3 Method

In this section, a concrete form of the above framework will be studied. Without loss of generality, we focus on the two view formulation, i.e., M equals 2, which can be easily extended to the case when M is larger than 2. The hinge loss is used to define $l(\mathbf{x}^{(p)}, y, \mathbf{w}^{(p)})$, and the squared loss is used for $l_c(\mathbf{x}^{(p)}, \mathbf{x}^{(q)}, \mathbf{w}^{(p)}, \mathbf{w}^{(q)}))$. 2-norm is used as the regularization term $\Omega(\cdot)$. Then, the concrete form of the Eq.(1) turns to:

$$
\begin{aligned}
\min_{\mathbf{w}^{(1)},\mathbf{w}^{(2)}} &\sum_{p=1}^{2} \frac{\gamma_p}{2}\|\mathbf{w}^{(p)}\|^2 + \sum_{p=1}^{2} C_p \sum_{i=1}^{n} \beta_i \xi_i^{(p)} \qquad (4) \\
&+C(\sum_{i=1}^{n} \beta_i \|\mathbf{w}^{(1)T}\mathbf{x}_i^{(1)} - \mathbf{w}^{(2)T}\mathbf{x}_i^{(2)}\|^2 \\
&+\sum_{i=1}^{m} \|\mathbf{w}^{(1)T}\mathbf{z}_i^{(1)} - \mathbf{w}^{(2)T}\mathbf{z}_i^{(2)}\|^2) \\
s.t.\quad &\forall i \in \{1, 2, \ldots, n\}, \\
&y_i \mathbf{w}^{(1)T}\mathbf{x}_i^{(1)} \geq 1 - \xi_i^{(1)}, y_i \mathbf{w}^{(2)T}\mathbf{x}_i^{(2)} \geq 1 - \xi_i^{(2)}.
\end{aligned}
$$

Here in this proposed method, we have absorbed the scaling components. i.e., $\frac{1}{n}$ and $\frac{1}{m+n}$ into the trade-off parameters C_p and C respectively, for simplicity. The final classification function f : $(\mathcal{X}^{(1)}, \mathcal{X}^{(2)}) \longmapsto \mathbf{R}$ can be specified as: $f(\mathbf{x}) = \frac{\mathbf{w}^{(1)T}\mathbf{x}^{(1)} + \mathbf{w}^{(2)T}\mathbf{x}^{(2)}}{2}$. To simplify this formulation, several concatenate vectors are further introduced:

$$
\begin{aligned}
\widetilde{\mathbf{w}} = [\mathbf{w}_1^T, \mathbf{w}_2^T]^T, \widetilde{\mathbf{x}}_i^{-T} = [\mathbf{x}_i^{(1)T}, -\mathbf{x}_i^{(2)T}]^T \\
\widetilde{\mathbf{x}}_i^{(1)} = [\mathbf{x}_i^{(1)T}, \mathbf{0}]^T, \widetilde{\mathbf{x}}_i^{(2)} = [\mathbf{0}, \mathbf{x}_i^{(2)T}]^T, \qquad (5)
\end{aligned}
$$

where in $\widetilde{\mathbf{x}}_i^{(p)}$, only the $d_{(p-1)} + 1$ to d_p-th elements ($d_0 = 0$) are nonzero and equals $\mathbf{x}_i^{(p)}$. After introducing these notations, Eq.(4) can be simplified to the following form:

$$
\begin{aligned}
\min_{\widetilde{\mathbf{w}}} \quad &\widetilde{\mathbf{w}}^T\mathbf{H}(\beta, C)\widetilde{\mathbf{w}} + \sum_{p=1}^{2}\sum_{i=1}^{n} C_p \beta_i \xi_i^{(p)} \\
s.t. \quad &\forall i \in \{1, 2, \ldots, n\} \\
&y_i \widetilde{\mathbf{w}}^T \widetilde{\mathbf{x}}_i^{(1)} \geq 1 - \xi_i^{(1)}, y_i \widetilde{\mathbf{w}}^T \widetilde{\mathbf{x}}_i^{(2)} \geq 1 - \xi_i^{(2)},
\end{aligned}
$$

where $\mathbf{H}(\beta, C) = \mathbf{I}(\gamma_1, \gamma_2) + C(\sum_{i=1}^{n} \beta_i \widetilde{\mathbf{x}}_i^{-} \widetilde{\mathbf{x}}_i^{-T} + \sum_{i=1}^{m} \widetilde{\mathbf{z}}_i^{-} \widetilde{\mathbf{z}}_i^{-T})$, and $\mathbf{I}(\gamma_1, \gamma_2)$ is a diagonal matrix, with the first d_1 elements being $\frac{\gamma_1}{2}$ and the remaining ones being $\frac{\gamma_2}{2}$. It is clear that this problem is convex, since β_i is given.

There are several alternatives to solve this problem efficiently. Here, an efficient way, which is an adaption of the bundle method, is proposed to solve this optimization problem of the MVTL-LM approach. The concrete procedure is described in Table 1. Here, $R_{emp}(\widetilde{\mathbf{w}}) = \sum_{p=1}^{2}\sum_{i=1}^{n} C_p \beta_i \max\{0, 1 - y_i^S \widetilde{\mathbf{w}}^T \widetilde{\mathbf{x}}_i^{(p)}\}$, $J(\widetilde{\mathbf{w}}) = \widetilde{\mathbf{w}}^T\mathbf{H}(\beta, C)\widetilde{\mathbf{w}} + \sum_{p=1}^{2}\sum_{i=1}^{n} C_p \beta_i \xi_i^{(p)}$ $J_t(\widetilde{\mathbf{w}}) = \widetilde{\mathbf{w}}^T\mathbf{H}(\beta, C)\widetilde{\mathbf{w}} +$

Algorithm: Multi-View Transfer Learning with a Large Margin Approach (MVTL-LM)
Input: 1. Reweighting Ratios for Source Domain Examples: β_i, $i = \{1, 2, \ldots, n\}$ 2. Optimization Parameters: γ_1 and γ_2 for regularizers, and the trade-off parameters C, C_1, C_2 in Eq.(5), $\epsilon = 0.001$. 3. Source Domain Examples: $\{(\mathbf{x}_1^{(i)}, y_1), (\mathbf{x}_2^{(i)}, y_2), \ldots, (\mathbf{x}_n^{(i)}, y_n)\}, i \in \{1, 2, \ldots, M\}$. 4. Target Domain Examples: $\{\mathbf{z}_1^{(i)}, \mathbf{z}_2^{(i)}, \ldots, \mathbf{z}_m^{(i)}\}, i \in \{1, 2, \ldots, M\}$ **Output:** The label assignment $\mathbf{l} = [l_1, l_2, \ldots, l_m]$ for the target domain examples.
1. Initialization $t = 0$, randomly initialize $\widetilde{\mathbf{w}}_0$. 2. Construct $\widetilde{\mathbf{X}}^-$, $\widetilde{\mathbf{X}}^{(1)}$, $\widetilde{\mathbf{X}}^{(2)}$ according to Eq.(5). 3. Construct the matrix $\mathbf{H}(\beta, C)$. 4. repeat 5. $t = t + 1$ 6. Compute the gradient for the empirical loss: $\mathbf{a}_t = \partial_{\widetilde{\mathbf{w}}} R_{emp}(\widetilde{\mathbf{w}}_{t-1})$, and $b_t = R_{emp}(\widetilde{\mathbf{w}}_{t-1}) - < \widetilde{\mathbf{w}}_{t-1}, \mathbf{a}_t >$. 7. Derive the optimization problem: $R_t^{CP} = \max_{1\leq i\leq t} < \widetilde{\mathbf{w}}, \mathbf{a}_i > + b_i$ 8. $\widetilde{\mathbf{w}}_t = \arg\min_{\widetilde{\mathbf{w}}} \widetilde{\mathbf{w}}^T\mathbf{H}(\beta, C)\widetilde{\mathbf{w}} + R_t^{CP}$ 9. $\epsilon_t = min_{0\leq i\leq t} J(\widetilde{\mathbf{w}}_i) - J_t(\widetilde{\mathbf{w}}_t)$ 10. until $\epsilon_t \leq \epsilon$ 11.**Classification Assignment**: for target domain example $\mathbf{z}_i$, if $0.5 \times \widetilde{\mathbf{w}}^T(\widetilde{\mathbf{z}}_i^{(1)} + \widetilde{\mathbf{z}}_i^{(2)}) > 0$, l_i equals 1, and otherwise it equals -1.

Table 1: Algorithm Description: Multi-View Transfer Learning with a Large Margin Approach (MVTL-LM)

$\max_{1 \le i \le t} < \widetilde{\mathbf{w}}, \mathbf{a}_i > +b_i$. Since $R_{emp}(\widetilde{\mathbf{w}})$ is non-smooth, so, when calculating its gradient, we use the sub-gradient instead, which can be calculated as

$$\partial_{\widetilde{\mathbf{w}}} R_{emp}(\widetilde{\mathbf{w}}) = -\sum_{p=1}^{2}\sum_{i=1}^{n} C_p \beta_i I_i^{(p)} y_i^S \widetilde{\mathbf{x}}_i^{(p)},$$

where $I_i^{(p)}$ is set to be 1, if $y_i^S \widetilde{\mathbf{w}}^T \widetilde{\mathbf{x}}_i^{(p)} < 1$, and $I_i^{(p)}$ is set to be 0, otherwise.

3.4 Theoretical Analysis

In this section, we deduct the convergence rate, time complexity as well as the generalized error bound of the proposed method.

3.4.1 Convergence

THEOREM 3.1. *For the convergence rate of the algorithm described in Table 1, Suppose* $R_{max} = \max_{p,i}(C_p\beta_i)\|\widetilde{\mathbf{x}}_i^{(p)}\|$. $\mathbf{A} = C(\sum_{i=1}^{n}\beta_i \widetilde{\mathbf{x}}_i \widetilde{\mathbf{x}}_i^{T} + \sum_{i=1}^{m}\widetilde{\mathbf{z}}_i \widetilde{\mathbf{z}}_i^{T})$, *the corresponding eigenvalues of* $\mathbf{A}$ *are specified as:* $\sigma_1(\mathbf{A}) \ge \sigma_2(\mathbf{A}) \ge \ldots \ge \sigma_{(d_1+d_2)}(\mathbf{A}) \ge 0$. *Assume that* $\beta_i \le B$. *The proposed method converges in* $O(1/\epsilon)$. *In particular,*

- *If* $\epsilon > 16R_{\max}^2/(\min\{\gamma_1,\gamma_2\} + 2\sigma_{(d_1+d_2)}(\mathbf{A}))$, *the proposed method converges to precision* ϵ *after at most* $log_2 \frac{nB(C_1+C_2)(\min\{\gamma_1,\gamma_2\}+2\sigma_{(d_1+d_2)}(\mathbf{A}))}{4R_{\max}^2}$ *steps.*
- *If* $\epsilon \le 16R_{\max}^2/(\min\{\gamma_1,\gamma_2\} + 2\sigma_{(d_1+d_2)}(\mathbf{A}))$, *the proposed method converges to precision* ϵ *after at most* $log_2 \frac{nB(C_1+C_2)(\min\{\gamma_1,\gamma_2\}+2\sigma_{(d_1+d_2)}(\mathbf{A}))}{4R_{\max}^2} + 32R_{\max}^2/(\epsilon(\min \{\gamma_1,\gamma_2\} + 2\sigma_{(d_1+d_2)}(\mathbf{A}))) - 1$ *steps.*

PROOF. We have $J(\widetilde{\mathbf{w}}) = \widetilde{\mathbf{w}}^T\mathbf{H}(\beta,C)\widetilde{\mathbf{w}} + \sum_{p=1}^{2}\sum_{i=1}^{n} C_p\beta_i \xi_i^{(p)}$, $\Omega(\widetilde{\mathbf{w}}) = \widetilde{\mathbf{w}}^T\mathbf{H}(\beta,C)\widetilde{\mathbf{w}}$. $\Omega^*(\mu) = \mu^T\mathbf{H}^{-1}(\beta,C)\mu$ is the Fenchel dual of $\Omega(\widetilde{\mathbf{w}})$. $J(\mathbf{0}) = \sum_{p=1}^{2}\sum_{i=1}^{n} C_p\beta_i \le nB(C_1 + C_2)$. $\|\partial_{\widetilde{\mathbf{w}}} R_{emp}(\widetilde{\mathbf{w}})\| \le R_{max}$. It is clear that $\|\partial_\mu^2 \Omega^*(\mu)\| \le 4/(\min\{\gamma_1,\gamma_2\} + 2\sigma_{(d_1+d_2)}(\mathbf{A}))$. By integrating these inequalities into Theorem 4 of [39], we can get

$$\epsilon_t - \epsilon_{t+1} \ge \frac{\epsilon_t}{2}\min\left(1, \epsilon_t(\min\{\gamma_1,\gamma_2\} + 2\sigma_{(d_1+d_2)}(\mathbf{A}))/16R_{\max}^2\right),$$

where $\epsilon_t = min_{0 \le i \le t} J(\widetilde{\mathbf{w}}_i) - J_t(\widetilde{\mathbf{w}}_t)$. The algorithm will terminate if $\epsilon_t < \epsilon$. So, if $\epsilon > 16R_{\max}^2/(\min\{\gamma_1,\gamma_2\}+2\sigma_{(d_1+d_2)}(\mathbf{A}))$, $\epsilon_t - \epsilon_{t+1} \ge \frac{\epsilon_t}{2}$, and the algorithm will terminate after at most:

$$\begin{aligned} & log_2 \frac{J(\mathbf{0})(\min\{\gamma_1,\gamma_2\} + 2\sigma_{(d_1+d_2)}(\mathbf{A}))}{4R_{\max}^2} \\ \le & log_2 \frac{nB(C_1+C_2)(\min\{\gamma_1,\gamma_2\} + 2\sigma_{(d_1+d_2)}(\mathbf{A}))}{4R_{\max}^2} \end{aligned} \quad (6)$$

steps.

If $\epsilon \le 16R_{\max}^2/(\min\{\gamma_1,\gamma_2\}+2\sigma_{(d_1+d_2)}(\mathbf{A}))$, then, this method needs the above indicated steps to converge to the precision $16R_{\max}^2 /(\min\{\gamma_1,\gamma_2\}+2\sigma_{(d_1+d_2)}(\mathbf{A}))$, then, we should have $\epsilon_t - \epsilon_{t+1} \ge \frac{\epsilon_t^2}{2}(\min\{\gamma_1,\gamma_2\}+2\sigma_{(d_1+d_2)}(\mathbf{A}))/16R_{\max}^2$. It is clear that it needs another $32R_{\max}^2/(\epsilon(\min\{\gamma_1,\gamma_2\} + 2\sigma_{(d_1+d_2)}(\mathbf{A}))) - 1$ steps to converge to the precision ϵ. So, in total, this algorithm converges in

$$\begin{aligned} & log_2 \frac{nB(C_1+C_2)(\min\{\gamma_1,\gamma_2\} + 2\sigma_{(d_1+d_2)}(\mathbf{A}))}{4R_{\max}^2} \\ & +32R_{\max}^2/(\epsilon(\min\{\gamma_1,\gamma_2\} + 2\sigma_{(d_1+d_2)}(\mathbf{A}))) - 1 \end{aligned}$$

steps.

In summary, the algorithm converges in $O(1/\epsilon)$ steps. It is clear that the number of iterations also highly depends on $R_{\max}^2$, which can be viewed as the maximum reweighted norm for the source domain examples. Furthermore, it is clear that increasing the parameter values of C_1 and C_2 will increase the number of iterations. □

3.4.2 Time Complexity

THEOREM 3.2. *For each iteration of the proposed method, it takes time* $O(sn)$.

PROOF. The gradient computation in step 6 takes time $O(sn)$, where s is the average sparsity on both views. Instead of solving the primal quadratic program, one can instead solve the optimization problem in step 8 in the dual form. Setting up the dual for each iteration is dominated by computing the $O(t^2)$ elements of the Hessian, which can be done in $O(t^2 s)$ steps. Since t^2 is normally much smaller than n, it leads to an overall time complexity of $O(sn)$ per iteration. □

This result is similar to the time complexity result per iteration in [16]. However, the total number of iterations in [16] may be as worse as $O(1/\epsilon^2)$, as given by the Lemma 2 of [16]. On the contrary, the number of iterations required in this paper is guaranteed to be in $O(1/\epsilon)$. So, solving the proposed problem by the proposed method is much faster than using the Cutting Plane method [18].

3.4.3 Generalized Error Bound

In this subsection, we assume that $\forall \mathbf{x}$, $\beta(\mathbf{x}) \le B$ if the marginal probabilities in the source domain *or* in the target domain are greater than 0. Let $\mathbf{w}_*^{(1)}$ and $\mathbf{w}_*^{(2)}$ denote the solution of Eq.(4). Similar to [12], we consider the class of functions $\mathcal{F}_{E,D} = \{f | f : \mathbf{x} \to \frac{1}{2}((\mathbf{w}^{(1)})^T\mathbf{x}^{(1)} + (\mathbf{w}^{(2)})^T\mathbf{x}^{(2)})\}$ such that $\|\mathbf{w}^{(1)}\|^2 \le E^2$, $\|\mathbf{w}^{(2)}\|^2 \le E^2$, and with probability at least $1-\delta$,

$$\begin{aligned} & \frac{1}{m+n}\sum_{i=1}^{n}\beta_i\|(\mathbf{w}^{(1)})^T\mathbf{x}_i^{(1)} - (\mathbf{w}^{(2)})^T\mathbf{x}_i^{(2)}\|^2 \\ & + \frac{1}{m+n}\sum_{i=1}^{m}\|(\mathbf{w}^{(1)})^T\mathbf{z}_i^{(1)} - (\mathbf{w}^{(2)})^T\mathbf{z}_i^{(2)}\|^2 \\ \le & \frac{1}{m+n}\sum_{i=1}^{n}\beta_i\|(\mathbf{w}_*^{(1)})^T\mathbf{x}_i^{(1)} - (\mathbf{w}_*^{(2)})^T\mathbf{x}_i^{(2)}\|^2 \\ & + \frac{1}{m+n}\sum_{i=1}^{m}\|(\mathbf{w}_*^{(1)})^T\mathbf{z}_i^{(1)} - (\mathbf{w}_*^{(2)})^T\mathbf{z}_i^{(2)}\|^2 \\ & + \frac{EB}{m+n}\sqrt{\sum_{i=1}^{n}\|\mathbf{x}_i\|^2 + \sum_{i=1}^{m}\|\mathbf{z}_i\|^2} + 3B\sqrt{\frac{\ln(2/\delta)}{2(m+n)}} =: D. \end{aligned}$$

Furthermore, define $\mathcal{F}_{\beta,E,D}$ to be the following class of functions,

$$\mathcal{F}_{\beta,E,D} = \{h | h : (\mathbf{x}, y) \to \beta(\mathbf{x}) \cdot \mathcal{A}(-f(\mathbf{x}) \cdot y), f \in \mathcal{F}_{E,D}\}$$

where $\mathcal{A}(a) = \begin{cases} 1 & \text{if } a > 0 \\ 1+a & \text{if } -1 \le a \le 0 \\ 0 & \text{otherwise} \end{cases}$. Based on these function classes, we have the following theorem with respect to the generalization error of the classifier obtained via the MVTL algorithm.

THEOREM 3.3. *Fix* $\delta \in (0,1)$. *Then, with probability at least* $1-\delta$, *every* $f \in \mathcal{F}_{\beta,E,D}$ *satisfies:*

$$\begin{aligned} & E_{Pr_T}(sign(f(\mathbf{x})) \ne y) \\ \le & \frac{1}{n(C_1+C_2)}\sum_{p=1}^{2} C_p \sum_{i=1}^{n}\beta_i\xi_i^{(p)} + \hat{R}_{S,n}(\mathcal{F}_{\beta,E,D}) + 3B\sqrt{\frac{\ln(2/\delta)}{2n}}, \end{aligned}$$

where $\hat{R}_{S,n}(\mathcal{F}_{\beta,E,D})$ is the empirical Rademacher complexity of $\mathcal{F}_{\beta,E,D}$ in the source domain.

PROOF. Since the conditional probability of y given $\mathbf{x}$ is the same for the source domain and the target domain,

$$E_{Pr_T}(sign(f(\mathbf{x})) \neq y) = E_{Pr_S}(\beta(\mathbf{x}) \cdot sign(f(\mathbf{x})) \neq y).$$

Notice that $\forall h \in \mathcal{F}_{\beta,E,D}$, $h(\mathbf{x}, y) \in [0, B]$. By similar proof as Theorem 4.17 in [33], we obtain that with probability greater than $1 - \delta$,

$$E_{Pr_S}(\beta(\mathbf{x}) \cdot sign(f(\mathbf{x})) \neq y) \leq E_{Pr_S}(\beta(\mathbf{x}) \cdot \mathcal{A}(-f(\mathbf{x}) \cdot y))$$

$$\leq \frac{1}{n(C_1 + C_2)} \sum_{p=1}^{2} C_p \sum_{i=1}^{n} \beta_i \xi_i^{(p)} + \hat{R}_{S,n}(\mathcal{F}_{\beta,E,D}) + 3B\sqrt{\frac{\ln(2/\delta)}{2n}}.$$

□

According to Theorem 3.3, the generalization error bound of any function in $\mathcal{F}_{\beta,E,D}$ depends on the weighted sum of all the slack variables associated with labeled examples in the source domain and the empirical Rademacher complexity of $\mathcal{F}_{\beta,E,D}$ in the source domain (up to a constant). Therefore, from transfer learning perspective, if the data distributions of the source domain and the target domain are similar (B is relatively small), constructing the large margin classifier in the source domain helps improve the generalization error of the classifier in the target domain. More importantly, from multi-view learning perspective, in $\mathcal{F}_{\beta,E,D}$, by leveraging the consistencies among different views, we effectively limit the hypothesis class, thus reduce the empirical Rademacher complexity. As empirically shown in [12], after imposing the consistency on different views, the Rademacher complexity is significantly reduced compared with the single-view correspondents.

This bound improves some existing theoretical results in transfer learning. For example, compared with the bound in Theorem 1 of [3], we make use of the data-dependent convergence measures, which can yield more accurate bounds. In Theorem 5 of [6], the authors also proved a bound for classifiers trained on multiple sources based on empirical Rademacher complexity. However, their bound can not be estimated from the data. For example, it depends on the expected difference between the labeling functions of different domains, which can *not* be estimated in our case where the target domain does *not* have any labeled examples.

Our bound also improves the results in [12], which is a multi-view learning algorithm. First, our bound is proposed for the transfer learning setting, whereas SVM-2K [12] is for the single domain setting. Furthermore, Theorem 3 of [12] can be seen as a special case of our bound when the source domain and the target domain have the same distribution and we do not use the unlabeled data from the target domain. Second, compared with SVM-2K, we make additional use of the unlabeled data from the target domain. If the number of unlabeled examples from the target domain is much larger than the number of labeled examples from the source domain, we tend to decrease the value of D, which is the upper bound on the view consistency. In this way, we reduce the function class, the corresponding Rademacher complexity, and thus improve the bound.

4. EXPERIMENTS

In this section, we present and analyze an extensive set of experimental results, which clearly demonstrate the advantages of the proposed method.

Dataset	Source Domain	Target Domain
comp vs rec	comp.graphics comp.os.ms-windows.misc rec.autos rec.motorcycles	comp.sys.ibm.pc.hardware comp.sys.mac.hardware rec.sport.baseball rec.sport.hockey
comp vs sci	comp.graphics comp.os.ms-windows.misc sci.electronics sci.space	comp.sys.ibm.pc.hardware comp.sys.mac.hardware sci.crypt sci.med
comp vs talk	comp.sys.ibm.pc.hardware comp.sys.mac.hardware talk.politics.guns talk.politics.mideast	comp.graphics comp.os.ms-windows.misc talk.politics.misc
rec vs sci	rec.autos rec.motorcycles sci.electronics sci.space	rec.sport.baseball rec.sport.hockey sci.crypt sci.med
rec vs talk	rec.sport.baseball rec.sport.hockey talk.politics.guns talk.politics.mideast	rec.autos rec.motorcycles talk.politics.misc
sci vs talk	sci.electronics sci.space talk.politics.guns talk.politics.mideast	sci.crypt sci.med talk.politics.misc

Table 2: Descriptions of Six Sub-datasets from 20Newsgroup

4.1 Datasets

4.1.1 20 Newsgroups

20 Newsgroups dataset[1] contains 4 main categories, i.e., 'comp', 'rec', 'sci', 'talk', as well as some small categories, such as 'alt.atheism', 'misc.forsale', etc. The number of examples for each of the four main categories ranges from 3253 to 4881. Each of the four main categories contains some subcategories, which are assigned to different domains. Using the 4 main categories, we create 6 sub-datasets. The detailed descriptions of these sub-datasets are summarized in Table 2. For each sub-dataset, we extract features from 2 views. One view (View 1) corresponds to the original tf-idf content information processed by Principle Component Analysis (PCA), and the other view (View 2) corresponds to the hidden topic information obtained by Probabilistic Latent Semantic Analysis (PLSA)[2] of the binary word features.

4.1.2 Spam Detection

This dataset is from ECML/PKDD Discovery Challenge 2006[3], which focuses on personalized spam filtering and generalization across related learning tasks. In particular, in Task A, we aim to construct spam filters for 3 different users, each of which have 2500 emails. In our experiments, we take the labeled emails from one user as the source domain, and the unlabeled emails from another user as the target domain. The two views are generated using the same way as 20 Newsgroups.

4.1.3 WebKB

This dataset contains web pages from computer science departments of several different universities[4]. They are divided into 7

[1] http://people.csail.mit.edu/jrennie/20Newsgroups/

[2] Actually, PLSA [14] can be considered as a dimensionality reduction method, which maps the documents to some fixed number of hidden topics. The topic distribution for each document can be used as low dimensional representation.

[3] http://www.ecmlpkdd2006.org/challenge.html

[4] http://www.cs.cmu.edu/~webkb/

	20 Newsgroups						WebKB		
	comp vs rec	comp vs sci	comp vs talk	rec vs sci	rec vs talk	sci vs talk	student	course	faculty
SVM-View1	85.4	73.3	95.4	67.2	56.8	81.8	0.595	0.541	0.441
SVM-View2	84.0	70.6	96.4	63.5	65.8	78.3	0.171	0.116	0.236
SVM	86.2	70.9	96.7	64.6	53.6	80.1	0.544	0.562	0.464
SVM-2K	88.5	79.3	97.2	71.0	81.6	**83.1**	0.725	0.512	0.563
CDSC	87.6	72.3	81.3	71.2	80.1	80.4	0.361	0.202	0.291
LLGC	77.5	71.1	92.6	72.6	73.9	81.2	0.167	0.277	0.310
LMTTL	85.8	69.8	96.4	64.5	53.7	78.6	0.546	0.545	0.475
Co-Training	86.9	72.5	97.1	66.7	61.2	81.4	0.495	0.554	0.444
MVTL-LM	**92.9**	**80.1**	**98.3**	**75.3**	**83.4**	83.0	**0.742**	**0.565**	**0.671**

Table 3: Classification Results on 20 Newsgroups and WebKB. For 20 Newsgroups, we report the classification accuracy; for WebKB, we report the F-measure due to the extremely imbalanced nature of this data set. It can be seen that MVTL-LM performs the best in most cases.

categories (i.e., student, faculty, staff, course, project, department and other). We generate three sub-datasets out of them, i.e., student, course and faculty. For each sub-dataset, we pick the corresponding webpages from the four main universities, i.e., Cornell, Washington, Wisconsin, and Texas as the source domain positive examples, and the webpages in 'other' category from these four universities as the source domain negative examples. In the target domain, a similar way is used to extract examples from the other universities. We use the content (View 1) and the link information (View 2) as the two views of this dataset.

4.2 Methods

We compare the proposed method with the following competitors: Support Vector Machines (SVM), which is a supervised classification method; LLGC [46], which is a semi-supervised learning method; SVM-2K [12], which is a multi-view learning method; CDSC [21], LMTTL [29], which are transfer learning methods and have shown state-of-the-art performances. We also adapt the co-training [27] algorithm to work for MVTL problems as follows: we disregard the domain difference, put labeled examples from the source domain and unlabeled examples from the target domain together, and apply the co-training algorithm to construct a classifier for each view of the target domain via SVM. This is similar to the co-adaptation algorithm proposed in [40] except that besides generating the initial seed set, labeled examples from the source domain are also used to construct classifiers for the target domain. Notice that besides SVM-2K and the co-training algorithm, the other baseline methods only work in the single-view settings. Therefore, for the sake of comparison, we first represent each example using a single set of features by concatenating the features from different views, and then apply these methods on this single view. Furthermore, to better understand the benefits brought by the multi-view methods, we also apply SVM on each view and report the performance.

For our proposed method, the re-weighting factors $\beta_i, i = 1, \ldots, n$ are learned by Gaussian Mixture Model, and the numbers of Gaussian components are both set to be 4. We will show later that the performance of MVTL-LM is very robust against small perturbations in the number of Gaussian components. We set $\gamma_1 = \gamma_2 = 1$, and tune the remaining three parameters (C_1, C_2 and C) through five fold cross validation on both the source domain and the target domain. The parameters of SVM-2K are also set in the same way, except that in SVM-2K we do not need to consider the number of Gaussian components. For LLGC, the RBF kernel is used, with its Gaussian variance being determined automatically by local scaling [43]. The parameters of CDSC, SVM, LMTTL and Co-Training are all set through five fold cross validation similarly.

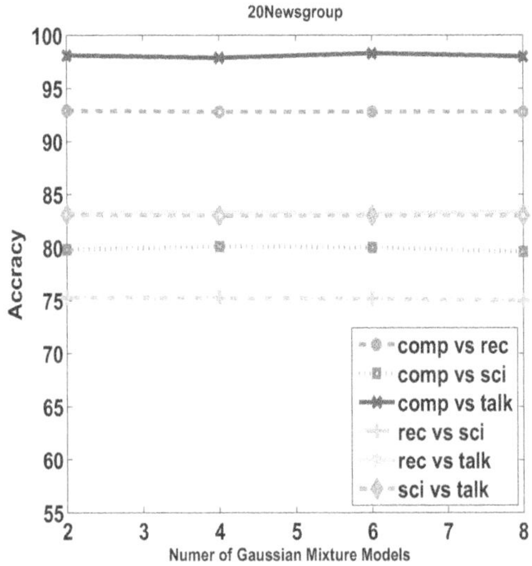

(a)

Figure 1: The impact of changing the number of Gaussian components on the performance of our proposed method. In this evaluation, we are assuming that the numbers of Gaussian components for both the source domain and the target domain are the same. The experiments are conducted by fixing the number of Gaussian components, while tuning the other parameters.

4.3 Results and Analysis

To study the impact of changing the number of Gaussian components on the performance of our proposed method, we vary this number when estimating β_i, and report the classification accuracy on 20 Newsgroups dataset in Fig.1. From these results, we can see that the proposed method is very stable with different numbers of Gaussian components. Similar results have also been observed on WebKB and Spam datasets.

Next we report the comparison results in Tables 3 and 4 respectively. For 20 Newsgroups and Spam datasets, the classification accuracy is reported; whereas for WebKB dataset, the F-measure is reported instead due to the extremely imbalanced nature of this dataset [5]. From these results, we have the following observations.

1. Our proposed method MVTL-LM performs the best in most cases. This is because our method models both the consis-

[5]The number of negative examples is around 6 times more than that of the positive examples.

	user1 vs user2	user1 vs user3	user2 vs user3	user2 vs user1	user3 vs user1	user3 vs user2
SVM-View1	79.7	65.7	83.4	76.7	76.0	80.9
SVM-View2	94.8	97.3	97.4	91.4	89.8	94.2
SVM	94.6	96.9	97.6	92.1	88.7	92.9
SVM-2K	94.1	97.6	97.2	91.8	90.8	94.1
CDSC	84.1	97.2	96.6	90.3	89.1	91.7
LLGC	**97.1**	96.3	93.2	91.7	91.3	93.2
LMTTL	94.9	96.2	97.5	92.0	88.9	93.1
Co-Training	92.5	96.6	96.6	92.2	88.6	93.9
MVTL-LM	95.2	**97.9**	**98.1**	**93.7**	**92.9**	**96.3**

Table 4: Classification Results on Spam dataset. The classification accuracy is reported. It can be seen that MVTL-LM performs the best in most cases.

tency between different views and the domain difference simultaneously, whereas the other methods ignore some useful information (i.e., the data distribution difference between different domains and the redundancy incurred by multiple views).

2. Comparing with multi-view learning methods (SVM-2K and Co-Training), MVTL-LM performs better because it explicitly models the data distribution difference between the source domain and the target domain; whereas the multi-view learning methods simply treat the two domains as a single one.

3. Comparing with transfer learning methods (CDSC and LMTTL), in MVTL-LM, we are able to transfer additional information about view consistency from the source domain to the target domain. We also suspect that these traditional transfer learning methods may not work well in the cases when different kinds of features are merged together. Therefore, MVTL-LM could achieve better performance in most cases.

4. The performance of SVM is worse than SVM-2K in most cases. This is because in SVM, simply concatenating the features from different views together fails to capture the consistency between different views; whereas SVM-2K explicitly models this consistency, which is able to improve the overall performance.

5. Comparing with SVM, SVM-View1, and SVM-View2, we can see that concatenating the features from different views may not necessarily result in an increase in the classification performances although SVM uses more information than SVM-View1 and SVM-View2.

6. As a graph based semi-supervised method, the performance of LLGC is not promising because the basic mainfold assumption in semi-supervised learning does not hold in transfer learning, and concatenating multi-view features together is not well suited in the multi-view learning scenario.

7. The traditional transfer learning methods show very poor performances in WebKB. This is because in the subdatasets of WebKB, the link view contains too much noise as can be seen from the performance of SVM-View2. Concatenating these features together may bring more noise for classification, and therefore could cause a decrease in the classification performance, especially for traditional transfer learning methods.

These observations clearly demonstrate the advantages of the proposed method over state-of-the-art ones. It validates our claims and theoretical analysis that by integrating the multi-view learning and transfer learning together, the classification performance can be greatly improved.

5. CONCLUSIONS

Transfer learning is an important technique for utilizing data in a related source domain for building predictive models in a target domain. Much valuable prior research has been conducted for traditional transfer learning with data from a single view. However, many real world applications often contain data from multiple views, and there is limited work for transfer learning with data from different views. This paper proposes a formal learning framework for Multi-View Transfer Learning with a Large Margin (MVTL-LM) approach. In particular, the weighted labeled data from the source domain is used to construct a large margin classifier for target domain and both the unlabeled data from the target domain and data from source domain are used to ensure the classification consistency between different views. A novel optimization method based on bundle method is proposed to learn model parameters in an efficient manner, which has a theoretical guarantee to generate ϵ-accurate results in $O(1/\epsilon)$ steps. Furthermore, theoretical analysis is provided for the generalization error bound of the proposed method and shows the improved results of the Rademacher complexity. An extensive set of results on three different datasets have been provided to demonstrate the advantages of the proposed method against several other alternatives.

6. ACKNOWLEDGEMENT

We would like to express our sincere thanks to Dr. Zheng Wang (Tsinghua University), Prof. S.V.N. Vishwanathan (Purdue University), and the anonymous reviewers for their valuable comments and suggestions. This research was partially supported by the NSF research grants IIS-0746830, CNS-1012208, IIS-1017837, CCF-0939370.

7. REFERENCES

[1] E. C. Anderson. Monte Carlo Methods and Importance Sampling, 1999.

[2] A. Argyriou, T. Evgeniou, and M. Pontil. Multi-task feature learning. In *NIPS*, page 41. MIT Press, 2007.

[3] S. Ben-David, J. Blitzer, K. Crammer, and F. Pereira. Analysis of representations for domain adaptation. In *NIPS*, pages 137–144, 2006.

[4] A. Blum and T. M. Mitchell. Combining labeled and unlabeled sata with co-training. In *COLT*, pages 92–100, 1998.

[5] E. Bonilla, K. Chai, and C. Williams. Multi-task Gaussian process prediction. *NIPS*, 20:153–160, 2008.

[6] K. Crammer, M. Kearns, and J. Wortman. Learning from multiple sources. *Journal of Machine Learning Research*, 9:1757–1774, 2008.

[7] W. Dai, G.-R. Xue, Q. Yang, and Y. Yu. Co-clustering based classification for out-of-domain documents. In *KDD*, pages 210–219, 2007.

[8] W. Dai, Q. Yang, G. Xue, and Y. Yu. Boosting for transfer learning. In *ICML*, pages 200–207, 2007.

[9] W. Dai, Q. Yang, G. Xue, and Y. Yu. Self-taught clustering. In *ICML*, pages 200–207, 2008.

[10] J. Davis and P. Domingos. Deep transfer via second-order Markov logic. In *ICML*, pages 217–224, 2009.

[11] L. Duan, I. Tsang, D. Xu, and S. Maybank. Domain transfer svm for video concept detection. *CVPR*, pages 1375–1381, 2009.

[12] J. Farquhar, D. Hardoon, H. Meng, J. Shawe-Taylor, and S. Szedmak. Two view learning: SVM-2K, theory and practice. *NIPS*, 18:355, 2006.

[13] K. Ganchev, J. Graça, J. Blitzer, and B. Taskar. Multi-view learning over structured and non-identical outputs. In *UAI*, pages 204–211, 2008.

[14] T. Hofmann. Probabilistic latent semantic indexing. In *SIGIR*, pages 50–57, 1999.

[15] J. Huang, A. Smola, A. Gretton, K. Borgwardt, and B. Scholkopf. Correcting sample selection bias by unlabeled data. *NIPS*, 19:601, 2007.

[16] T. Joachims. Training linear SVMs in linear time. In *KDD*, pages 217–226, 2006.

[17] T. Joachims and N. Cristianini. Composite kernels for hypertext categorisation. In *ICML*, pages 250–257, 2001.

[18] J. Kelley. The cutting plane method for solving convex programs. *Journal of the SIAM*, 8(4):703–712, 1960.

[19] N. Lawrence and J. Platt. Learning to learn with the informative vector machine. In *ICML*, page 65, 2004.

[20] G. Li, S. C. H. Hoi, and K. Chang. Two-view transductive support vector machines. In *SDM*, pages 235–244, 2010.

[21] X. Ling, W. Dai, G.-R. Xue, Q. Yang, and Y. Yu. Spectral domain-transfer learning. In *KDD*, pages 488–496, 2008.

[22] X. Liu, Y. Gong, W. Xu, and S. Zhu. Document clustering with cluster refinement and model selection capabilities. In *SIGIR*, pages 191–198, 2002.

[23] Y. Mansour, M. Mohri, and A. Rostamizadeh. Domain adaptation with multiple sources. In *NIPS*, pages 1041–1048, 2008.

[24] Y. Mansour, M. Mohri, and A. Rostamizadeh. Multiple source adaptation and the rényi divergence. In *UAI*, pages 367–374. AUAI Press, 2009.

[25] L. Mihalkova, T. Huynh, and R. Mooney. Mapping and revising Markov logic networks for transfer learning. In *AAAI*, volume 22, pages 608–613, 2007.

[26] L. Mihalkova and R. Mooney. Transfer learning by mapping with minimal target data. In *Proceedings of the AAAI-08 Workshop on Transfer Learning for Complex Tasks*, 2008.

[27] K. Nigam and R. Ghani. Analyzing the effectiveness and applicability of co-training. In *CIKM*, pages 86–93, 2000.

[28] S. Pan, J. Kwok, and Q. Yang. Transfer learning via dimensionality reduction. In *Proceedings of AAAI*, pages 677–682.

[29] B. Quanz and J. Huan. Large margin transductive transfer learning. In *CIKM*, pages 1327–1336, 2009.

[30] R. Raina, A. Battle, H. Lee, B. Packer, and A. Ng. Self-taught learning: transfer learning from unlabeled data. In *ICML*, pages 766–763, 2007.

[31] D. Rosenberg, V. Sindhwani, P. Bartlett, and P. Niyogi. A Kernel for Semi-Supervised Learning With Multi-View Point Cloud Regularization. *IEEE Signal Processing Magazine*, 2009.

[32] B. Scholkopf and A. Smola. *Learning with kernels*. MIT press Cambridge, Mass, 2002.

[33] J. Shawe-Taylor and N. Cristianini. *Kernel Methods for Pattern Analysis*. Cambridge University Press, New York, NY, USA, 2004.

[34] S. Sheather and M. Jones. A reliable data-based bandwidth selection method for kernel density estimation. *Journal of the Royal Statistical Society. Series B (Methodological)*, 53(3):683–690, 1991.

[35] H. Shimodaira. Improving predictive inference under covariate shift by weighting the log-likelihood function. *Journal of Statistical Planning and Inference*, 90(2):227–244, 2000.

[36] V. Sindhwani and P. Niyogi. A co-regularized approach to semi-supervised learning with multiple views. In *ICML Workshop on Learning with Multiple Views*, 2005.

[37] V. Sindhwani and D. Rosenberg. An RKHS for multi-view learning and manifold co-regularization. In *ICML*, pages 976–983, 2008.

[38] A. Smola, S. Vishwanathan, and Q. Le. Bundle methods for machine learning. *NIPS*, 20, 2008.

[39] C. Teo, S. Vishwanthan, A. Smola, and Q. Le. Bundle methods for regularized risk minimization. *The Journal of Machine Learning Research*, 11:311–365, 2010.

[40] G. Tur. Co-adaptation: Adaptive co-training for semi-supervised learning. In *ICASSP*, 2009.

[41] M. Wu and B. Schölkopf. A local learning approach for clustering. In *NIPS*, pages 1529–1536, 2006.

[42] B. Zadrozny. Learning and evaluating classifiers under sample selection bias. In *ICML*, 2004.

[43] L. Zelnik-Manor and P. Perona. Self-tuning spectral clustering. *NIPS*, 17:1601–1608, 2004.

[44] D. Zhang, F. Wang, C. Zhang, and T. Li. Multi-view local learning. In *AAAI*, pages 752–757, 2008.

[45] T. Zhang, A. Popescul, and B. Dom. Linear prediction models with graph regularization for web-page categorization. In *SIGKDD*, pages 821–826, 2006.

[46] D. Zhou, O. Bousquet, T. N. Lal, J. Weston, and B. Schölkopf. Learning with local and global consistency. In *NIPS*, 2003.

[47] S. Zhu, K. Yu, Y. Chi, and Y. Gong. Combining content and link for classification using matrix factorization. In *SIGIR*, pages 487–494, 2007.

MultiRank: Co-Ranking for Objects and Relations in Multi-Relational Data

Michael K. Ng
Department of Mathematics
Hong Kong Baptist University
Kowloon Tong
Hong Kong
mng@math.hkbu.edu.hk

Xutao Li and Yunming Ye
Department of Computer Science
Shenzhen Graduate School
Harbin Institute of Technology
xutaolee08@gmail.com,yeyunming@hit.edu.cn

ABSTRACT

The main aim of this paper is to design a co-ranking scheme for objects and relations in multi-relational data. It has many important applications in data mining and information retrieval. However, in the literature, there is a lack of a general framework to deal with multi-relational data for co-ranking. The main contribution of this paper is to (i) propose a framework (MultiRank) to determine the importance of both objects and relations simultaneously based on a probability distribution computed from multi-relational data; (ii) show the existence and uniqueness of such probability distribution so that it can be used for co-ranking for objects and relations very effectively; and (iii) develop an efficient iterative algorithm to solve a set of tensor (multivariate polynomial) equations to obtain such probability distribution. Extensive experiments on real-world data suggest that the proposed framework is able to provide a co-ranking scheme for objects and relations successfully. Experimental results have also shown that our algorithm is computationally efficient, and effective for identification of interesting and explainable co-ranking results.

Categories and Subject Descriptors

H.3.3 [**Information Systems**]: Information Search and Retrieval; H.2.8 [**Database Applications**]: Data mining

General Terms

Algorithms

Keywords

Ranking, multi-relational data, transition probability tensors, rectangular tensors, stationary probability distribution

1. INTRODUCTION

Evaluation of object importance or popularity is an important research problem in information retrieval that can assist in many data mining tasks, e.g., ranking query results of search engines, extracting communities in social networks and studying evolution of communities in dynamic networks. In the literature, there are many approaches to evaluating object importance [9, 3, 15, 12, 19, 8]. In these relation analysis methods, a single relation type is focused and studied. For example, both PageRank [19] and HITS [12] consider the structure of web, decompose and study the adjacency matrix that representing the hyperlink structure.

In this paper, we are interested in data with multiple relation types. There are many data mining and information retrieval applications in multi-relational data which objects have interactions with the others based on different relations. For example, researchers cite the other researchers in different conferences, and based on different concepts/topics, papers cite the other papers based on text analysis such as title, abstract, keyword and authorship [14], webpages link to the other webpages through different semantic meanings [13]. A social network [2, 17] where objects are connected via multiple relations, by their organizational structure, communication protocols, etc. This additional link structure can provide a way of incorporating multiple relations among objects into the calculation of object importance or popularity. In Figure 1, we show an example of a multi-relational data set. There are five objects and three relations (R1: green, R2: blue, R3: red) among them. We can also represent such multi-relational data set in a tensor format. A tensor is a multidimensional array. In the figure, a three-way array is used, where each two dimensional slice represents an adjacency matrix for a single relation. The data can be represented as a tensor of size $5 \times 5 \times 3$ where (i, j, k) entry is nonzero if the ith object is connected to the jth object by using the kth relation.

In the literature, there is a lack of a general framework to deal with multi-relational data or the corresponding tensor representation for co-ranking purpose. The main aim of this paper is to propose an algorithm, MultiRank, to determine the importance of both objects and relations simultaneously in multi-relational data. The MultiRank values indicate an importance of a particular object and an importance of a particular relation. In our proposal, the MultiRank of an object depends on the number and MultiRank metric of all objects that have multiple relations to this object, and also the MultiRank values of these multiple relations. An object that is linked via high MultiRank relations by objects with high MultiRanks, receives a high MultiRank itself. Similarly, the MultiRank of a relation depends on which objects

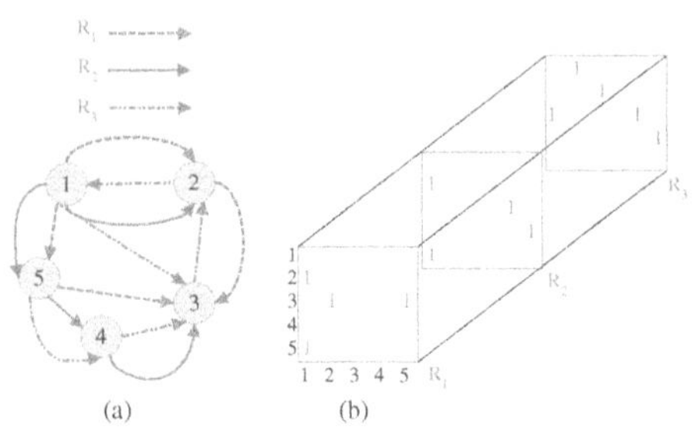

Figure 1: (a) An example of a multi-relational data in a graph representation (left) and (b) the corresponding tensor representation.

to be linked and their MultiRank values. A relation that is linked objects with high MultiRanks, receives a high MultiRank itself.

Similar to PageRank [19], our idea is to imagine infinite random surfers in a multi-relational data/tensor, and consider an equilibrium/stationary probability distribution of objects and relations as evaluation scores for objects and relations respectively. Thus we can consider that MultiRank is a stationary probability distribution that is used to represent the likelihood that we randomly visiting objects and using relations will arrive at any particular object and use any particular relation. However, instead of finding an eigenvector corresponding to the largest eigenvalue of the PageRank matrix [19] under a single relation type, our approach is to solve a set of tensor (multivariate polynomial) equations to determine a stationary probability distribution arising from a tensor that represents multiple relation types among objects.

The main contribution of this paper can be summarized as follows. (i) We propose a framework (MultiRank) to determine the importance of both objects and relations simultaneously based on a stationary probability distribution computed from multi-relational data. (ii) We show the existence and uniqueness of such stationary probability distribution so that it can be used in co-ranking for objects and relations very effectively. (iii) We develop an efficient iterative algorithm to solve a set of tensor equations to obtain such stationary probability distribution. Extensive experiments on real-world data suggest that the proposed framework is able to provide a co-ranking scheme for objects and relations based on stationary probability distribution successfully. Experimental results have also shown that our algorithm is computationally efficient, and effective for identification of interesting and explainable co-ranking results.

The rest of the paper is organized as follows. In Section 2, we describe notations in this paper and some preliminary knowledge. In Section 3, we present the proposed framework. In Section 4, we analyze the proposed methodology. In Section 5, we figure out the differences between the existing work and the proposed one. In Section 6, we show and discuss the experimental results for real-world data sets. In Section 7, we give some concluding remarks and mention some future work.

2. PRELIMINARY

In this section, we describe notations and present some preliminary knowledge on tensors. As we analyze objects under multiple relations and also consider interaction between relations based on objects, we make use of rectangular tensors to represent them.

Let R be the real field. We call $\mathcal{A} = (a_{i_1,i_2,j_1})$ where $a_{i_1,i_2,j_1} \in R$, for $i_k = 1, \cdots, m$, $k = 1, 2$ and $j_1 = 1, \cdots, n$, a real $(2, 1)$th order $(m \times n)$-dimensional rectangular tensor. In this setting, we refer (i_1, i_2) to be the indices for objects and j_1 to be the index for relations. For instance, five objects ($m = 5$) and three relations ($n = 3$) are used in the example in Figure 1. Let $\mathbf{x}$ and $\mathbf{x}'$ be vectors of length m, and $\mathbf{y}$ be a vector of length n. Let $\mathcal{A}\mathbf{xy}$ be a vector in R^m such that

$$(\mathcal{A}\mathbf{xy})_{i_1} = \sum_{i_2=1}^{m} \sum_{j_1=1}^{n} a_{i_1,i_2,j_1} x_{i_2} y_{j_1}, \; i_1 = 1, 2, \cdots, m.$$

Similarly, $\mathcal{A}\mathbf{xx}'$ is a vector in R^n such that

$$(\mathcal{A}\mathbf{xx}')_{j_1} = \sum_{i_1=1}^{m} \sum_{i_2=1}^{m} a_{i_1,i_2,j_1} x_{i_1} x'_{i_2}, \; j_1 = 1, 2, \cdots, n.$$

In addition, $\mathcal{A}$ is called non-negative if $a_{i_1,i_2,j_1} \geq 0$.

As we consider infinite random surfers in a nonnegative rectangular tensor arising from multi-relational data, and study the likelihood that we will arrive at any particular object and use at any particular relation, we can construct two transition probability tensors $\mathcal{O} = (o_{i_1,i_2,j_1})$ and $\mathcal{R} = (r_{i_1,i_2,j_1})$ with respect to objects and relations by normalizing the entries of $\mathcal{A}$ as follows:

$$o_{i_1,i_2,j_1} = \frac{a_{i_1,i_2,j_1}}{\sum_{i=1}^{m} a_{i,i_2,j_1}}, \quad i_1 = 1, 2, \cdots, m,$$

$$r_{i_1,i_2,j_1} = \frac{a_{i_1,i_2,j_1}}{\sum_{j=1}^{n} a_{i_1,i_2,j}}, \quad j_1 = 1, 2, \cdots, n.$$

These numbers gives the estimates of the following conditional probabilities:

$$o_{i_1,i_2,j_1} = \text{Prob}[X_t = i_1 | X_{t-1} = i_2, Y_t = j_1]$$

$$r_{i_1,i_2,j_1} = \text{Prob}[Y_t = j_1 | X_t = i_1, X_{t-1} = i_2]$$

where X_t and Y_t are random variables referring to visit at any particular object and to use at any particular relation respectively at the time t. o_{i_1,i_2,j_1} can be interpreted as the probability of visiting the i_1th object by given that the i_2th object is currently visited and the j_1th relation is used, and r_{i_1,i_2,j_1} can be interpreted as the probability of using the j_1th relation given that the i_1th object is visited from the i_2th object.

We note that if a_{i_1,i_2,j_1} is equal to 0 for all $1 \leq i_1 \leq m$, this is called the dangling node [19], and the values of o_{i_1,i_2,j_1} can be set to $1/m$ (an equal chance to visit any object). Similarly, if a_{i_1,i_2,j_1} is equal to 0 for all $1 \leq j_1 \leq n$, then the values of r_{i_1,i_2,j_1} can be set to $1/n$ (an equal chance to use any relation). With the above construction, we have

$$0 \leq o_{i_1,i_2,j_1} \leq 1, \quad \sum_{i_1=1}^{m} o_{i_1,i_2,j_1} = 1,$$

$$0 \leq r_{i_1,i_2,j_1} \leq 1, \quad \sum_{j_1=1}^{n} r_{i_1,i_2,j_1} = 1.$$

Both $\mathcal{O}$ and $\mathcal{R}$ are nonnegative tensors. We call them transition probability tensors which are high-dimensional analog of transition probability matrices in Markov chains [20].

In addition, it is necessary for us to know the connectivity among the objects and the relations within a tensor. We remark that the concept of irreducibility has been used in the PageRank matrix in order to compute the PageRank vector [19].

Definition 1. *A* $(2,1)$*th order nonnegative rectangular tensor* $\mathcal{A}$ *is called irreducible if* (a_{i_1,i_2,j_1}) *(m-by-m matrices) for fixed* j_1 $(j_1 = 1, 2, \cdots, n)$ *are irreducible. If* $\mathcal{A}$ *is not irreducible, then we call* $\mathcal{A}$ *reducible.*

When $\mathcal{A}$ is irreducible, any two objects in multi-relational data can be connected via some relations. As we would like to determine the importance of both objects and relations simultaneously in multi-relational data, irreducibility is a reasonable assumption that we will use in the following analysis and discussion. It is clear that when $\mathcal{A}$ is irreducible, the two corresponding tensors $\mathcal{O}$ and $\mathcal{R}$ are also irreducible.

3. THE PROPOSED FRAMEWORK

The PageRank matrix can be regarded as a transition probability matrix of a Markov chain in a random walk. Given two transition probability tensors $\mathcal{O}$ and $\mathcal{R}$, we study the following probabilities:

$$\text{Prob}[X_t = i_1] = \sum_{i_2=1}^{m} \sum_{j_1=1}^{n} o_{i_1,i_2,j_1} \times \text{Prob}[X_{t-1} = i_2, Y_t = j_1] \tag{1}$$

$$\text{Prob}[Y_t = j_1] = \sum_{i_1=1}^{m} \sum_{i_2=1}^{m} r_{i_1,i_2,j_1} \times \text{Prob}[X_t = i_1, X_{t-1} = i_2], \tag{2}$$

where $\text{Prob}[X_{t-1} = i_2, Y_t = j_1]$ is the joint probability distribution of X_{t-1} and Y_t, and $\text{Prob}[X_t = i_1, X_{t-1} = i_2]$ is the joint probability distribution of X_t and X_{t-1}. In our approach, we consider an equilibrium/stationary distribution of objects and relations, i.e., we are interested in MultiRank values of objects and relations given by

$$\bar{\mathbf{x}} = [\bar{x}_1, \bar{x}_2, \cdots, \bar{x}_m]^T \quad \text{and} \quad \bar{\mathbf{y}} = [\bar{y}_1, \bar{y}_2, \cdots, \bar{y}_n]^T$$

respectively, with

$$\bar{x}_{i_1} = \lim_{t\to\infty} \text{Prob}[X_t = i_1] \quad \text{and} \quad \bar{y}_{j_1} = \lim_{t\to\infty} \text{Prob}[Y_t = j_1].$$

for $1 \le i_1 \le m$ and $1 \le j_1 \le n$.

In general, it may be difficult to obtain $\bar{x}_{i_1}$ and $\bar{y}_{j_1}$ as (1) and (2) are coupled together and they involves two joint probability distributions. Here we employ a product form of individual probability distributions for joint probability distributions in (1) and (2). More precisely, we assume that

$$\text{Prob}[X_{t-1} = i_2, Y_t = j_1] = \text{Prob}[X_{t-1} = i_2]\text{Prob}[Y_t = j_1] \tag{3}$$

$$\text{Prob}[X_t = i_1, X_{t-1} = i_2] = \text{Prob}[X_t = i_1]\text{Prob}[X_{t-1} = i_2]. \tag{4}$$

Therefore, by using the above assumptions and considering t goes to infinity, (1) and (2) becomes

$$\bar{x}_{i_1} = \sum_{i_2=1}^{m} \sum_{j_1=1}^{n} o_{i_1,i_2,j_1} \bar{x}_{i_2} \bar{y}_{j_1}, \quad i_1 = 1, 2, \cdots, m, \tag{5}$$

$$\bar{y}_{j_1} = \sum_{i_1=1}^{m} \sum_{i_2=1}^{m} r_{i_1,i_2,j_1} \bar{x}_{i_1} \bar{x}_{i_2}; \quad j_1 = 1, 2, \cdots, n. \tag{6}$$

We see from (5) and (6) that the MultiRank of an object depends on the number and MultiRank metric of all objects that have multiple relations to this object, and also the MultiRank values of these multiple relations. Similarly, the MultiRank of a relation depends on which the objects to be linked and their MultiRank values of these objects. It is clear that an object that is linked via high MultiRank relations by objects with high MultiRank, receives a high MultiRank itself. Also a relation that is linked objects with high MultiRank values, receives a high MultiRank itself. Under the tensor operation for (5) and (6), we solve the following tensor (multivariate polynomial) equations:

$$\mathcal{O}\bar{\mathbf{x}}\bar{\mathbf{y}} = \bar{\mathbf{x}} \quad \text{and} \quad \mathcal{R}\bar{\mathbf{x}}^2 = \bar{\mathbf{y}}, \tag{7}$$

with

$$\sum_{i_1=1}^{m} \bar{x}_{i_1} = 1 \quad \text{and} \quad \sum_{j_1=1}^{n} \bar{y}_{j_1} = 1 \tag{8}$$

to obtain the MultiRank values of objects and relations.

We remark that the normalized eigenvector (corresponding to the largest eigenvalue 1) in the PageRank computation can be interpreted as the stationary probability distribution vector of the associated Markov chain [19]. When we consider a single relation type, we can set $\bar{\mathbf{y}}$ to be a vector $\frac{1}{n}\mathbf{1}$ (equal chance of all relations) in (7), and thus we obtain a matrix equation $\mathcal{O}\bar{\mathbf{x}}\frac{1}{n}\mathbf{1} = \bar{\mathbf{x}}$. This is exactly the same as that we solve for the normalized eigenvector to get the PageRank vector. As a summary, the proposed framework MultiRank is a generalization of PageRank to deal with multi-relational data.

3.1 The Algorithm

In this subsection, we present an efficient iterative algorithm to solve the tensor equations in (7) to obtain $\bar{\mathbf{x}}$ and $\bar{\mathbf{y}}$ for the MultiRank values of objects and relations. The MultiRank algorithm is summarized in the following algorithm.

Algorithm 1 The MultiRank Algorithm

Input: Two tensors $\mathcal{O}$ and $\mathcal{R}$, two initial probability distributions $\mathbf{x}_0$ and $\mathbf{y}_0$ ($\sum_{i_1=1}^{m}[\mathbf{x}_0]_{i_1} = 1$ and $\sum_{j_1=1}^{n}[\mathbf{y}_0]_{j_1} = 1$) and the tolerance ϵ

Output: Two stationary probability distributions $\bar{\mathbf{x}}$ and $\bar{\mathbf{y}}$

Procedure:

1: Set $k = 1$;
2: Compute $\mathbf{x}_k = \mathcal{O}\mathbf{x}_{k-1}\mathbf{y}_{k-1}$;
3: Compute $\mathbf{y}_k = \mathcal{R}\mathbf{x}_k^2$;
4: If $||\mathbf{x}_k - \mathbf{x}_{k-1}|| + ||\mathbf{y}_k - \mathbf{y}_{k-1}|| < \epsilon$, then stop, otherwise set $k = k + 1$ and goto Step 2.

In Algorithm 1, the MultiRank computations require several iterations, through the collection to adjust approximate MultiRank values of objects and relations to more closely reflect their theoretical true values (underlying stationary probability distributions). The iterative method is similar to the power method for computing the eigenvector corresponding to the largest eigenvalue of a matrix [19]. The main computational cost of the MultiRank algorithm depends on the cost of performing tensor operations in Steps 2 and 3. Assume that there are $O(N)$ nonzero entries (sparse data) in $\mathcal{O}$ and $\mathcal{R}$, the cost of these tensor calculations are of $O(N)$ arithmetic operations.

4. THEORETICAL ANALYSIS

In this section, we show the existence and uniqueness of stationary probability distributions $\bar{\mathbf{x}}$ and $\bar{\mathbf{y}}$ so that it can be used in co-ranking for objects and relations very effectively. Based on these results, the convergence of MultiRank algorithm can be shown.

We let $\Omega_m = \{\mathbf{x} = (x_1, x_2, \cdots, x_m) \in R^m | x_i \geq 0,\ 1 \leq i \leq m,\ \sum_{i=1}^m x_i = 1\}$ and $\Omega_n = \{\mathbf{y} = (y_1, y_2, \cdots, y_n) \in R^n | y_j \geq 0,\ 1 \leq j \leq n,\ \sum_{j=1}^n y_j = 1\}$. We also set $\Omega = \{[\mathbf{x}, \mathbf{y}] \in R^{m+n} | \mathbf{x} \in \Omega_m, \mathbf{y} \in \Omega_n\}$. We note that Ω_m, Ω_n and Ω are closed convex sets. We call $\mathbf{x}$ and $\mathbf{y}$ to be positive (denoted by $\mathbf{x} > 0$ and $\mathbf{y} > 0$) if all their entries are positive.

It is easy to check that if both $\mathbf{x}$ and $\mathbf{y}$ are probability distributions, then the output $\mathcal{O}\mathbf{x}\mathbf{y}$ and $\mathcal{R}\mathbf{x}^2$ are also probability distributions (the correctness of Steps 2 and 3 in the MultiRank Algorithm).

THEOREM 1. *Suppose $\mathcal{O}$ and $\mathcal{R}$ are constructed in Section 3. For any $\mathbf{x} \in \Omega_m$ and $\mathbf{y} \in \Omega_n$, then $\mathcal{O}\mathbf{x}\mathbf{y} \in \Omega_m$ and $\mathcal{R}\mathbf{x}^2 \in \Omega_n$.*

By using Theorem 1, we show the existence of positive solutions for the set of tensor equations in (7) and (8).

THEOREM 2. *Suppose $\mathcal{O}$ and $\mathcal{R}$ are constructed in Section 3. If $\mathcal{O}$ and $\mathcal{R}$ are irreducible, then there exist $\bar{\mathbf{x}} \in \Omega_m$ and $\bar{\mathbf{y}} \in \Omega_n$ such that $\mathcal{O}\bar{\mathbf{x}}\bar{\mathbf{y}} = \bar{\mathbf{x}}$ and $\mathcal{R}\bar{\mathbf{x}}^2 = \bar{\mathbf{y}}$, and both $\bar{\mathbf{x}}$ and $\bar{\mathbf{y}}$ are positive.*

PROOF. The problem can be reduced to a fixed point problem as follows. We define the following mapping $T : \Omega \to \Omega$ as follows

$$T([\mathbf{x}, \mathbf{y}]) = [\mathcal{O}\mathbf{x}\mathbf{y}, \mathcal{R}\mathbf{x}^2]. \tag{9}$$

It is clear that T is well-defined (i.e., when $[\mathbf{x}, \mathbf{y}] \in \Omega$, $T([\mathbf{x}, \mathbf{y}]) \in \Omega$) and continuous. According to the Brouwer Fixed Point Theorem, there exists $[\bar{\mathbf{x}}, \bar{\mathbf{y}}] \in \Omega$ such that $T([\bar{\mathbf{x}}, \bar{\mathbf{y}}]) = [\bar{\mathbf{x}}, \bar{\mathbf{y}}]$, i.e., $\mathcal{O}\bar{\mathbf{x}}\bar{\mathbf{y}} = \bar{\mathbf{x}}$ and $\mathcal{R}\bar{\mathbf{x}}^2 = \bar{\mathbf{y}}$.

Next we show that $\bar{\mathbf{x}}$ and $\bar{\mathbf{y}}$ are positive. Suppose $\bar{\mathbf{x}}$ and $\bar{\mathbf{y}}$ are not positive, i.e., there exist some entries of $\bar{\mathbf{x}}$ are zero and some entries of $\bar{\mathbf{y}}$ are zero. Let $I = \{i_1 | \bar{x}_{i_1} = 0\}$ and $J = \{j_1 | \bar{y}_{j_1} = 0\}$. It is obvious that I is a proper subset of $\{1, 2, \cdots, m\}$ and J is a proper subset of $\{1, 2, \cdots, n\}$. Let $\delta = \min\{\min\{\bar{x}_{i_1} | i_1 \notin I\}, \min\{\bar{y}_{j_1} | j_1 \notin J\}\}$. We must have $\delta > 0$. Since $\bar{\mathbf{x}}$ and $\bar{\mathbf{y}}$ satisfies $\mathcal{O}\bar{\mathbf{x}}\bar{\mathbf{y}} = \bar{\mathbf{x}}$, we have

$$\sum_{i_2=1}^{m} \sum_{j_1=1}^{n} o_{i_1,i_2,j_1} \bar{x}_{i_2} \bar{y}_{j_1} = \bar{x}_{i_1} = 0, \quad \forall i_1 \in I.$$

Let us consider the following quantity:

$$\begin{aligned} \delta^2 \sum_{i_2 \notin I} \sum_{j_1 \notin J} o_{i_1,i_2,j_1} &\leq \sum_{i_2 \notin I} \sum_{j_1 \notin J} o_{i_1,i_2,j_1} \bar{x}_{i_2} \bar{y}_{j_1} \\ &\leq \sum_{i_2=1}^{m} \sum_{j_1=1}^{n} o_{i_1,i_2,j_1} \bar{x}_{i_2} \bar{y}_{j_1} = 0, \end{aligned}$$

for all $i_1 \in I$. Hence we have $o_{i_1,i_2,j_1} = 0$ for all $i_1 \in I$ and for all $i_2 \notin I$ for any fixed $j_1 \notin J$. Thus the matrices (o_{i_1,i_2,j_1}) (for $j_1 \notin J$) are reducible. It implies that $\mathcal{O}$ is reducible. By using the similar argument and considering the equation $\mathcal{R}\mathbf{x}^2 = \mathbf{y}$, we can find that $\mathcal{R}$ is also reducible. According to these results, we obtain a contradiction. Hence both $\bar{\mathbf{x}}$ and $\bar{\mathbf{y}}$ must be positive. □

In [11], it has been given a general condition which guarantees the uniqueness of the fixed point in the Brouwer Fixed Point Theorem, namely, (i) 1 is not an eigenvalue of the Jacobian matrix of the mapping, and (ii) for each point in the boundary of the domain of the mapping, it is not a fixed point. In our case, we have shown in Theorem 2 that all the fixed points of T are positive when $\mathcal{O}$ and $\mathcal{R}$ are irreducible, i.e., they do not lie on the boundary $\partial\Omega$ of Ω. The Jacobian matrix of T is an $(m+n)$-by-$(m+n)$ matrix:

$$DT([\mathbf{x}, \mathbf{y}]) = \begin{pmatrix} DT_{11}([\mathbf{x}, \mathbf{y}]) & DT_{12}([\mathbf{x}, \mathbf{y}]) \\ DT_{21}([\mathbf{x}, \mathbf{y}]) & 0 \end{pmatrix}, \quad [\mathbf{x}, \mathbf{y}] \in \Omega,$$

where $DT_{11}([\mathbf{x}, \mathbf{y}]) = (\sum_{j_1=1}^n o_{i_1,i_2,j_1} y_{j_1})_{i_1,i_2}$ is an m-by-m matrix corresponding to the derivative of $\mathcal{O}\mathbf{x}\mathbf{y}$ with respect to $\mathbf{x}$, $DT_{12}([\mathbf{x}, \mathbf{y}]) = (\sum_{i_2=1}^m o_{i_1,i_2,j_1} x_{i_2})_{i_1,j_1}$ is an m-by-n matrix corresponding to the derivative of $\mathcal{O}\mathbf{x}\mathbf{y}$ with respect to $\mathbf{y}$, and $DT_{21}([\mathbf{x}, \mathbf{y}]) = (\sum_{i_1=1}^m r_{i_1,i_2,j_1} x_{i_1})_{j_1,i_2} + (\sum_{i_2=1}^m r_{i_1,i_2,j_1} x_{i_2})_{j_1,i_1}$ is an n-by-m matrix corresponding to the derivative of $\mathcal{R}\mathbf{x}^2$ with respect to $\mathbf{x}$. To conclude, we have the following theorem:

THEOREM 3. *Suppose $\mathcal{O}$ and $\mathcal{R}$ are constructed in Section 3, and they are irreducible. If 1 is not the eigenvalue of $DT([\mathbf{x}, \mathbf{y}])$ for all $[\mathbf{x}, \mathbf{y}] \in \Omega / \partial\Omega$, then then the solution vectors $\bar{\mathbf{x}}$ and $\bar{\mathbf{y}}$ in Theorem 2 are unique.*

According to Theorem 3, when $\mathbf{x}_k = \mathbf{x}_{k-1}$ and $\mathbf{y}_k = \mathbf{y}_{k-1}$ in the MultiRank algorithm, then we obtain the unique solution vectors $\bar{\mathbf{x}}$ and $\bar{\mathbf{y}}$ for $\mathcal{O}\mathbf{x}\mathbf{y} = \mathbf{x}$ and $\mathcal{R}\mathbf{x}^2 = \mathbf{y}$. When $\mathbf{x}_k \neq \mathbf{x}_{k-1}$ and $\mathbf{y}_k \neq \mathbf{y}_{k-1}$, there exist a subsequence $[\mathbf{x}_{k_s}, \mathbf{y}_{k_s}]$ converges to $[\bar{\mathbf{x}}, \bar{\mathbf{y}}]$ by using the fact that Ω is compact in R^{m+n}. As we have shown that the solution vectors are unique, it implies that $[\mathbf{x}_k, \mathbf{y}_k]$ converges (up to a subsequence) to $[\bar{\mathbf{x}}, \bar{\mathbf{y}}]$ which are the stationary probability vectors giving MultiRank values of objects and relations respectively for co-ranking purpose effectively.

5. RELATED WORK

Recently, co-ranking has been studied in [7, 26]. In [7], a co-HITS algorithm is proposed to incorporate the bipartite graph with the content information from both sides as well as the constraints of relevance. In [26], a method for co-ranking authors and their publications using several networks is proposed and based on coupling two random walks that separately rank authors and documents following the PageRank paradigm. In these two methods, the score propagation is the mutual reinforcement to boost co-linked entities on the graph only. We see from (5) and (6) that our method involves mutual reinforcement among all the objects and the relations. PopRank [18] uses the PageRank framework by adding popularity to each link pointing to an object. The main challenge of this approach is required to add popularity which is not known in general. The novelty of the proposed method is to provide a framework to determine the weights of relations automatically.

In the literature, tensor factorization is a generalized approach for analyzing multi-way interactions among entities. For instance, Lin et al. [17] proposed a novel relational hypergraph representation for modeling multi-relational and multi-dimensional social data and studied an efficient factorization method for community extraction on a given metagraph. Sun et al. proposed a general and efficient framework for analyzing high-order and high-dimensional stream data [21, 22]. Sun et al. [23] applied a 3-way Tucker decomposition [24] to the analysis of user, query-term and webpage data in order to personalize web search. Acar et al. [1] used various tensor decompositions of user, keyword and time data to separate different streams of conservations in chatroom data. Kolda et al. [14, 13] proposed TOPHITS by adding a third dimension to form an adjacency tensor that incorporates anchor text information, and then to increase the likelihood that the principal singular vectors relate to the query. They also employed a Three-way Parallel Factors (PARAFAC) decomposition [4, 10] to compute the singular vectors for query processing. In these methods, we need to select the number of decompositions (low-rank approximation) in the tensor factorization. The number of decompositions may not be known in advance. On the other hand, the computation of tensor factorization may not be unique as there are several numerical methods (e.g., the alternating least squares procedure) used to compute such factorization and the factorization results depend on the initial guess. There is no detailed algorithmic and mathematical analysis for the convergence of the method. Also the computational cost may be expensive for very large tensors [6]. Different from these methods, we compute stationary probability distributions of tensors for scores of objects and relations to handle the ranking problem. We have shown that such probability distributions can be unique and computed very efficiently.

6. EXPERIMENTAL RESULTS

In this section, we report three experiments to show the effectiveness of the proposed model for co-ranking objects and relations from real-world data sets. We crawled publication information of five conferences (SIGKDD, WWW, SIGIR, SIGMOD, CIKM) from DBLP[1]. Their publication periods are as follows: SIGKDD (1999-2010), WWW (2001-2010), SIGIR (2000-2010), SIGMOD (2000-2010) and CIKM (2000 and 2002-2009) [2]. Publication information includes title, authors, reference list, and classification categories associated with this publication[3]. There are in total 6848 publications, 10305 authors and 617 different categories in the data set. Based on this multi-relational data, we construct different types of tensors in the following three experiments.

[1]http://www.informatik.uni-trier.de/ ley/db/

[2]Missing information for CIKM 2001 is due to fact that DBLP does not provide links to ACM Digital Library.

[3]For each publication, there are several strings indicating the classification categories of this publication, where each string provides the information from the most general concept to the most specific concept. For example, a string may be "H. information systems—>H.3 information storage and retrieval—>H.3.3 information search and retrieval". For each string, we choose the most specific concept as the classification category it indicates for the publication.

6.1 Experiment 1

Tensor construction. In this experiment, we construct a tensor $\mathcal{A}$ based on citations of authors (objects) through different category concepts (relations). In this case there are 10305 objects and 617 relations. The tensor is constructed as follows: If a publication written by the i_2th author cites a publication written by the i_1th author, and the two publications have the same j_1th category concept, then we can add one to the entry a_{i_1,i_2,j_1} of $\mathcal{A}$. By considering all the publications, a_{i_1,i_2,j_1} refers to the number of citations of publications written by the i_2th author to publications written by the i_1th author where these publications have the same j_1th category concept. Here we do not consider any self-citation, i.e., $a_{i_1,i_1,j_1} = 0$ for all $1 \le i_1 \le 10305$ and $1 < j_1 \le 617$. The purpose is to avoid an ambiguous high self-citations in $\mathcal{A}$. The size of $\mathcal{A}$ is $10305 \times 10305 \times 617$ and there are 39851 nonzeros entries in $\mathcal{A}$. The percentage of nonzero entries is $6.08 \times 10^{-5}\%$, and thus $\mathcal{A}$ is sparse. After we construct $\mathcal{A}$, we can generate both transition probability tensors $\mathcal{O}$ and $\mathcal{R}$. The only nonzero entries and their locations are stored in the computational process. It is not necessary to store values $1/m$ or $1/n$ for the dangling nodes in $\mathcal{O}$ and $\mathcal{R}$.

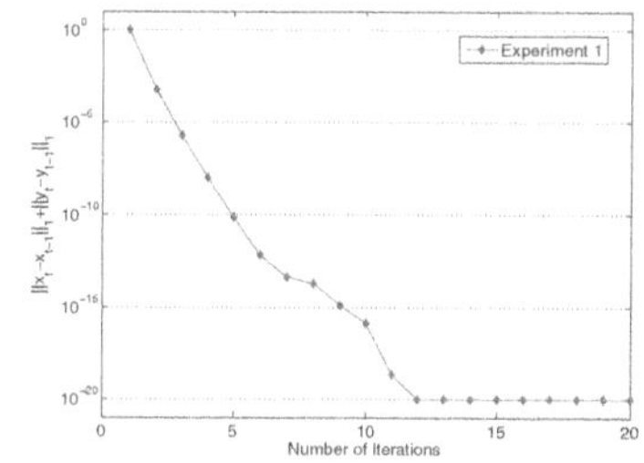

Figure 2: The difference between two successive calculated probability vectors against iterations.

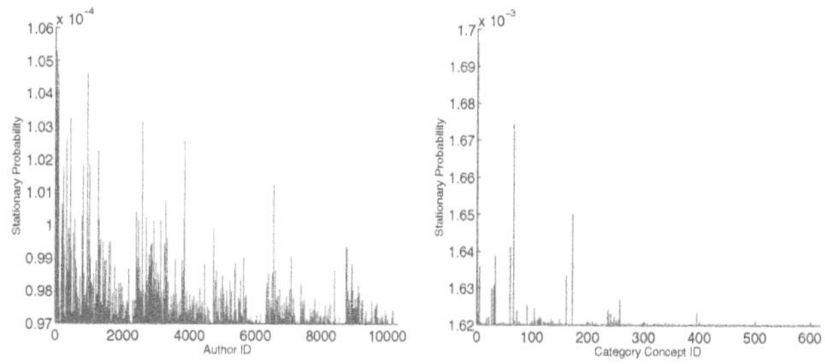

Figure 3: The stationary probability vectors (a) authors; (b) category concepts in Experiment 1.

Results and discussion. Figure 2 shows the convergence of the MultiRank algorithm. We see from the figure that the changes of stationary probabilities for objects and relations, $||\mathbf{x}_k - \mathbf{x}_{k-1}||_1 + ||\mathbf{y}_k - \mathbf{y}_{k-1}||_1$, decreases when iteration number increases, and the successive difference after 12 iterations, is less than 10^{-20} which is small enough for convergence criterion. The computational time is about 114 seconds under the MATLAB implementation in a standard desktop PC. In Figures 3(a)-(b), we show the two resulting stationary probability vectors corresponding to the authors and the category concepts respectively. It is clear in the figures that some authors (relations) have higher stationary probabilities (MultiRank values). These results indicate that some authors (category concepts) are more important (popular) than the others.

ranking	author name	ranking	category concept
1	Bing Liu	1	data mining
2	Pedro Domingos	2	information search and retrieval
3	Wei-Ying Ma	3	retrieval models
4	Jiawei Han	4	search process
5	Philip S. Yu	5	query processing
6	ChengXiang Zhai	6	clustering
7	Thorsten Joachims	7	miscellaneous
8	W. Bruce Croft	8	query formulation
9	Matthew Richardson	9	information filtering
10	Susan T. Dumais	10	performance evaluation

Table 1: The top ten authors (left) and category concepts (right) in Experiment 1.

ranked author/concept	1	2	3	4	5	6	7	8	9	10
1	122	0	0	4	0	2	20	0	14	0
2	180	0	0	0	0	0	0	0	0	0
3	41	111	57	36	0	34	15	0	12	0
4	377	0	0	0	9	0	2	0	0	0
5	138	5	0	10	21	51	0	0	8	0
6	0	151	149	21	0	25	0	0	7	0
7	0	29	65	60	0	0	0	0	0	0
8	0	80	128	2	0	0	0	64	0	4
9	75	39	0	2	0	0	0	0	3	0
10	0	46	0	34	0	0	0	5	13	0

Table 2: The numbers that the top ten authors are cited by the others via the top ten category concepts.

In Table 1, we show the top ten authors and category concepts based on their MultiRank values. As there are two types of conferences in the data set, one is based on data mining like SIGKDD and SIGMOD, and the other is based on information retrieval like WWW, SIGIR and CIKM. Therefore, these two concepts are ranked numbers one and two respectively. In Table 2, we show the numbers that the top ten authors are cited by the others via the top ten category concepts. We find that there are many citations for the cited authors (ranked numbers 1 to 5) via the data mining concept (ranked number 1), and there are many citations for the cited authors (ranked numbers 6 to 10) via the information search and retrieval and retrieval model concepts (ranked numbers 2 and 3). This observation can explain why the first five authors have higher MultiRank values than the last five authors. Also there are more citations based on the first concept for the cited authors (ranked numbers 2, 4 and 5) than for the ranked number one author in Table 2, we find in (7) that his MultiRank value by summing the scores of his linked objects and used relations together, is higher than those of the other cited authors.

Next we compare the MultiRank and PageRank results. In the PageRank algorithm, we aggregate all the citations of different concepts together to construct relations among the authors. In the PageRank results, Philip Yu, Thorsten Joachims and Susan T. Dumais do not appear in the list of the top ten cited authors, and the others still appear. Now they are ranked numbers 14, 29, and 13 respectively. However, there are three new persons: D. R. Mani (rank #8), James Drew (ranked #9) and Andrew Betz (rank #10), who are co-authors of papers cited by Pedro Domingos (rank #1) in the PageRank results. Because Pedro Domingos has the highest PageRank score and cites less papers in the data set, these three persons also receive high PageRank scores even their citations are not many. Because the MultiRank algorithm gives the scores for concepts, it differentiates authors and concepts, and provides a more accurate and comparable ranking results than those by the PageRank algorithm.

6.2 Experiment 2

Tensor construction. In this experiment, we construct a $(2,1)$th order tensor $\mathcal{A}$ based on author-author collaborations through different category concepts. When the i_1th and i_2th authors publish a paper together under the j_1th category concept, we add one to the entries a_{i_1,i_2,j_1} and a_{i_2,i_1,j_1} of $\mathcal{A}$. In this case, $\mathcal{A}$ is symmetric with respect to the index j_1. By considering all the publications, a_{i_1,i_2,j_1} (or a_{i_2,i_1,j_1}) refers to the number of collaborations by the i_1th and the i_2th authors under the j_1th category concept. Again, we do not consider any self-collaboration, i.e., $a_{i_1,i_1,j_1} = 0$ for all $1 \le i_1 \le 10305$ and $1 \le j_1 \le 617$. The size of $\mathcal{A}$ is $10305 \times 10305 \times 617$ and there are 95722 nonzeros entries in $\mathcal{A}$. The percentage of nonzero entries is $1.46 \times 10^{-4}\%$.

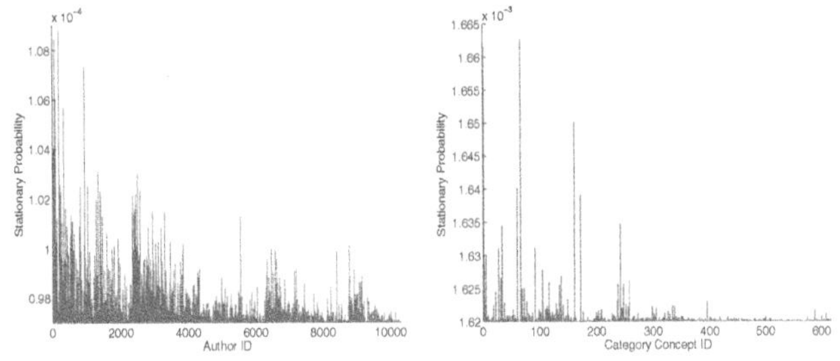

(a) (b)

Figure 4: The stationary probability vectors (a) authors; (b) category concepts in Experiment 2.

ranking	author name	ranking	category concept
1	C. Lee Giles	1	information search and retrieval
2	Philip S. Yu	2	data mining
3	Wei-Ying Ma	3	miscellaneous
4	Zheng Chen	4	search process
5	Jiawei Han	5	retrieval models
6	Christos Faloutsos	6	general
7	Bing Liu	7	query processing
8	Johannes Gehrke	8	web-based services
9	Gerhard Weikum	9	information filtering
10	Elke A. Rundensteiner	10	clustering

Table 3: The top ten authors (left) and category concepts (right) in Experiment 2.

ranked author/concept	1	2	3	4	5	6	7	8	9	10
1	31	5	25	20	17	6	0	5	12	18
2	6	71	3	5	0	8	14	4	7	17
3	38	29	11	54	34	0	0	7	24	27
4	93	11	22	44	22	5	0	8	14	8
5	10	126	7	0	7	18	7	4	2	0
6	0	80	5	11	11	3	4	0	0	2
7	0	38	11	4	9	0	0	4	9	6
8	0	13	6	0	0	6	22	0	0	2
9	8	0	26	19	12	8	1	5	2	0
10	0	5	12	0	0	4	26	0	0	0

Table 4: The numbers that the top ten authors collaborate with the others via the top ten category concepts.

Results and discussion. We apply the MultiRank algorithm to the constructed tensors, and the algorithm converges in 10 iterations. In Figures 4(a) and 4(b), we show the resulting stationary probabilities for the authors and category concepts. Based on the MultiRank values, we show in Table 3 the top ten authors and category concepts. When we compare the results in Experiments 1 and 2, we find that the top ten category concepts changes slightly, i.e., the concepts of query formulation and performance evaluation disappear in Experiment 2 while the concept of general and web-based services appear. This phenomena may suggest the former two concepts are more likely to be used when authors cite the others, while the latter concept are more likely to be used when authors collaborate together. The top ten authors also changes significantly, e.g., Philip S. Yu, Wei-Ying Ma, Jiawei Han and Bing Liu remain in the list of the top ten collaborated authors. This phenomena suggests these four authors not only have high citations via the mostly used concepts, but also have more collaborations via the mostly used concepts in the five conferences. It is clear that the other top cited authors in Table 1(a) have less collaborations in the five conferences. In Table 4, we show the numbers that the top ten authors collaborate with the others via the top ten category concepts. We see from the table that there are many collaborations for the authors (ranked numbers 1 to 5) via the top ten concepts, and there are less collaborations for the authors (ranked numbers 6 to 10) via the top ten concepts.

6.3 Experiment 3

Tensor construction. In this experiment, we co-rank both authors and their papers. We need to construct a $(2,2)$th order tensor for calculating MultiRanks of both authors and papers. Our idea is that if a paper or an author has a high MultiRank value, then the publications or the authors cited by this paper/author have a high chance to obtain high MultiRank values (see the tensor equations in (10)). There are four indices of the entry of $\mathcal{A}$: a_{i_1,i_2,j_1,j_2}. The first two indices (for objects) refer to the authors and the last two indices (for relations) refer to the papers. Here the role of objects and relations can be swapped. We set a_{i_1,i_2,j_1,j_2} to be 1 (or 0) when the j_2th paper written by the i_2th author cite (do not cite) the j_1th paper written by the i_1th author.

The five conferences may have different topics or tasks, e.g., WWW, SIGIR, and CIKM mainly focus on tasks related to information retrieval, while SIGKDD and SIGMOD mainly focus on tasks related data mining or databases. Here we construct three different tensors $\mathcal{A}$ based on the data from (a) all the five conferences; (b) SIGKDD and SIGMOD conferences; and (c) WWW, SIGIR and CIKM conferences. For each case, we construct the tensor as follows. Firstly, we select the top thirty cited authors in Experiment 1, who have at least ten papers in the conferences. For each selected author, we select his/her ten most cited papers by the other papers in the same set of conferences. Again we do not consider any self-citation, i.e., we set $a_{i_1,i_1,j_1,j_2} = 0$ for all i_1, j_1 and j_2. The sizes of $\mathcal{A}$ are $30 \times 30 \times 261 \times 261$, $30 \times 30 \times 252 \times 252$ and $30 \times 30 \times 258 \times 258$ for the cases (a), (b) and (c) respectively. They have different sizes as there are some overlapped papers in the construction. There are 504, 458, 493 nonzeros entries in $\mathcal{A}$ for the case (a), (b) and (c) respectively. The corresponding percentages of nonzero entries are $8.22 \times 10^{-4}\%$, $8.01 \times 10^{-4}\%$ and $8.23 \times 10^{-4}\%$.

In this experiment, we determine the MultiRanks of authors $\bar{\mathbf{x}}$ and papers $\bar{\mathbf{y}}$ by solving the following tensor equations:

$$\mathcal{O}\bar{\mathbf{x}}\bar{\mathbf{y}}^2 = \bar{\mathbf{x}} \quad \text{and} \quad \mathcal{R}\bar{\mathbf{x}}^2\bar{\mathbf{y}} = \bar{\mathbf{y}}, \qquad (10)$$

with $\sum_{i_1=1}^{m} \bar{x}_{i_1} = 1$ and $\sum_{j_1=1}^{n} \bar{y}_{j_1} = 1$. Based on the idea in (7), we can interpret the first equation in (10) by viewing paper-paper citations $\bar{\mathbf{y}}^2$ as relations to give authors' scores $\bar{\mathbf{x}}$ as objects, and the second equation in by viewing author-author citations $\bar{\mathbf{x}}^2$ as relations to give papers' scores $\bar{\mathbf{y}}$ as objects. We can employ the same MultiRank algorithm in Section 4.1 to solve the equations, except we compute $\mathbf{x}_k = \mathcal{O}\mathbf{x}_{k-1}\mathbf{y}_{k-1}^2$ and $\mathbf{y}_k = \mathcal{R}\mathbf{x}_k^2\mathbf{y}_{k-1}$ in the iterative process. By using the similar arguments in Section 5, we can show existence and uniqueness of the solution in (10) and the algorithm can converge to the unique solution.

Results and discussion. We apply the MultiRank algorithm to three different cases, and obtain the stationary probabilities (MultiRanks) of the authors and their papers. The resulting top ten authors and top ten papers for the three cases are shown as in Table 5. We see from the table that there are five top cited authors appearing in both Experiments 3(a) and 3(c), and there are only two top cited authors appearing in both Experiments 3(a) and 3(b). Also there are five top cited papers appearing in both Experiments 3(a) and 3(c), and there is only one top cited paper appearing in both Experiments 3(a) and 3(b). These results suggest that the data set may be imbalanced in the areas of data mining and information retrieval, and it is reasonable to perform co-ranking for two separated cases (b) and (c).

Moreover, we see from the Table 5 that the top ten cited authors and the top ten cited papers are strongly related in the three experiments, i.e., most of the top ten cited authors have papers in the top ten cited papers, and most of the top ten cited papers are written by the top ten cited authors. This phenomena implies that our co-ranking results are reasonable as an author (or a paper) cited by other papers/authors with high MultiRanks, receives a high MultiRank value. To further verify the co-ranking results, we show in Table 6 the numbers that the top ten cited authors (or the top ten cited papers) are cited by the others of different rankings in Experiment 3(a). We see that the authors who are ranked higher usually have either more citations by highly-ranked authors and more citations in total. Similar findings are observed for the top ten cited papers. These observations reflect the design of the MultiRank paradigm by setting equations in (10). Similar observations can also be found in Experiment 3(b) and 3(c).

Experiment 3(a) author				Experiment 3(a) paper			
ranking	(1-10)	(11-20)	(21-30)	ranking	(1-100)	(101-200)	(others)
1	18	24	17	1	16	8	4
2	12	13	2	2	12	8	2
3	13	8	14	3	11	3	6
4	8	13	5	4	9	2	9
5	11	6	13	5	4	6	6
6	18	6	8	6	0	12	0
7	0	19	8	7	6	5	0
8	3	7	9	8	8	8	0
9	8	4	6	9	6	3	2
10	6	12	4	10	3	6	2

Table 6: The numbers that the top ten cited authors (papers) are cited by the other authors (papers) of different rankings in Experiments 3(a).

It is interesting to note that Thorsten Joachims and Jon M. Kleinberg who are ranked number one and number two in Experiment 3(a), disappear in both Experiments 3(b) and 3(c). They are the top cited authors for all five conferences, however, they are not the top cited authors either in data mining conferences or in information retrieval conferences. For Thorsten Joachims, this is because he does not have ten publications either in data mining conferences (Experiment 3(b)) or information retrieval conferences (Experiment

Experiment 3(a)		
ranking	author name	papers
1	Thorsten Joachims	1
2	Jon M. Kleinberg	7
3	Wei-Ying Ma	3, 6, 8
4	Susan T. Dumais	5, 9
5	Zheng Chen	3, 6
6	Ji-Rong Wen	2, 8
7	[illegible]	4
8	W. Bruce Croft	none
9	[illegible]	none
10	Andrew Tomkins	10

Experiment 3(b)		
ranking	author name	papers
1	[illegible]	5
2	Philip S. Yu	1, 2, 9
3	[illegible]	3, 9
4	David J. DeWitt	5, 8
5	Johannes Gehrke	4
6	Mohammed Javeed Zaki	none
7	Jian Pei	3
8	Joseph M. Hellerstein	7
9	Rajeev Rastogi	4
10	Jeffrey F. Naughton	8

Experiment 3(c)		
ranking	author name	papers
1	W. Bruce Croft	6
2	Susan T. Dumais	1, 8
3	Rosie Jones	5
4	Zheng Chen	2, 3
5	ChengXiang Zhai	none
6	Wei-Ying Ma	2, 3, 10
7	Andrew Tomkins	9
8	James P. Callan	none
9	Tie-Yan Liu	2, 7
10	Eugene Agichtein	1, 8

Experiment 3(a)		
ranking	paper title	authors
1	Optimizing search engines using clickthrough data.	1
2	Clustering user queries of a search engine.	6
3	Optimizing web search using web click-through data.	3, 5
4	[illegible]	7
5	Improving web search ranking by incorporating user behavior information.	4
6	A study of relevance propagation for web search.	3, 5
7	Bursty and hierarchical structure in streams.	2
8	Probabilistic query expansion using query logs.	3, 6
9	Learning user interaction models for predicting web search result preferences.	4
10	On the bursty evolution of blogspace.	10

Experiment 3(b)		
ranking	paper title	authors
1	Clustering by pattern similarity in large data sets.	2
2	Mining asynchronous periodic patterns in time series data.	2
3	[illegible]	3, 7
4	Processing complex aggregate queries over data streams.	5, 9
5	Mining high-speed data streams.	1
6	NiagaraCQ: A scalable continuous query system for internet databases.	4
7	Continuously adaptive continuous queries over streams.	8
8	On supporting containment queries in relational database management systems.	4, 10
9	Graph indexing: A frequent structure-based approach.	2, 3
10	Mining association rules with multiple minimum supports.	none

Experiment 3(c)		
ranking	paper title	authors
1	Improving web search ranking by incorporating user behavior information.	2, 10
2	A study of relevance propagation for web search.	4, 6, 9
3	Optimizing web search using web click-through data.	4, 6
4	Clustering user queries of a search engine.	none
5	Generating query substitutions.	3
6	Predicting query performance.	1
7	Adapting ranking SVM to document retrieval.	9
8	Learning user interaction models for predicting web search result preferences.	2, 10
9	Propagation of trust and distrust.	7
10	Learning block importance models for web pages.	6

Table 5: The top ten authors (left) and the top ten papers (right) in Experiment 3(a), 3(b) and 3(c). The column of papers in the left hand side table indicates associated top ten papers. The column of authors in the right hand side table indicates associated top ten authors. The authors who (or papers which) appear in the top ten of both Experiments 3(a) and 3(b) or Experiments 3(a) and 3(c), are indicated with green color (or blue color).

3(c)). When we intentionally add him in Experiment 3(c) and re-run the MultiRank algorithm, he appears in the list of the top ten cited authors, and he is ranked the number three. For Jon M. Kleinberg, even though he has enough publications in Experiment 3(b), he disappears in the list of the top ten cited authors. The main reason is that his high cited paper titled "Bursty and hierarchical structure in streams" published in SIGKDD conference, is more related to information retrieval conferences. Therefore, he does not have many citations from data mining conferences in Experiment 3(b).

7. CONCLUDING REMARKS

In this paper, we have proposed a framework (MultiRank) to determine the importance of both objects and relations simultaneously based on a probability distribution computed from multi-relational data. Both theoretical and experimental results have demonstrated that the proposed algorithm is efficient and effective. Here we give several future research work based on the proposed framework.

(i) In the framework, we assume probability distributions satisfying (3) and (4). It is interesting to employ the other possible forms to set up other tensor equations, compute and analyze stationary probability distributions.

(ii) We consider the (2,1)th and (2,2)th order rectangular transition probability tensors theoretically and numerically in this paper. We can further study and extend to the other types of rectangular transition probability tensors. For instance, (p,q)th order rectangular transition probability tensors can be studied. In this setting, we employ the pth order links among the objects and qth order links among the relations. Such higher-order links have been studied in higher-order Markov chains, see for instance [5]. Based on the proposed framework, we expect to solve the following set of tensor equations:

$$\mathcal{O}\mathbf{x}^{p-1}\mathbf{y}^{q} = \mathbf{x} \quad \text{and} \quad \mathcal{R}\mathbf{x}^{p}\mathbf{y}^{q-1} = \mathbf{y}.$$

In the MultiRank algorithm, we compute $\mathbf{x}_t = \mathcal{O}\mathbf{x}_{t-1}^{p-1}\mathbf{y}_{t-1}^{q}$ and $\mathbf{y}_t = \mathcal{R}\mathbf{x}_t^{p}\mathbf{y}_{t-1}^{q-1}$ in Steps 2 and 3 respectively. By using a similar argument, we expect to show existence and uniqueness of $\mathbf{x}$ and $\mathbf{y}$ in these higher-order links among the objects and relations.

(iii) On the other hand, we can study $(p_1, p_2, \cdots, p_s)$th order rectangular tensors where there are s different kinds of objects/relations to be analyzed. For instance, there are s networks and each network are related to each other based on their objects and relations. In the literature, there are many multiple networks applications and analysis, see for instance [17, 25, 26]. In this setting, we expect to set up a set of tensor equations similar to (7) and (8), and solve it for MultiRank values of objects/relations in these multiple networks.

(iv) We give a generalization of PageRank in this paper. We can study and extend HITS algorithm for computing the scores of hub and authority in multi-relational data. By using the graph structure of hub and authority, we solve a new set of tensor equations to obtain such scores:

$$\mathcal{H}\mathbf{y}\mathbf{z} = \mathbf{x}, \quad \mathcal{A}\mathbf{x}\mathbf{z} = \mathbf{y}, \quad \mathcal{R}\mathbf{x}\mathbf{y} = \mathbf{z},$$

Here three transition probability tensors $\mathcal{H}$, $\mathcal{A}$ and $\mathcal{R}$ corresponds to hubs, authorities and relations, $\mathbf{x}$, $\mathbf{y}$ are the authority and hub scores of objects, and $\mathbf{z}$ are relevance scores of relations. The detailed work can be found in [16].

(v) Theoretically, we need the assumption in Theorem 3 in order to show that $\bar{\mathbf{x}}$ and $\bar{\mathbf{y}}$ are unique. We have tested many different initial probability distributions in the examples in Section 6, the same resulting probability vector is obtained. We conjecture that the assumption in the theorem may be true for irreducible transition probability tensors with some additional properties. We do not have a proof yet, so we leave it as an open problem for future analysis.

Acknowledgments: M. Ng's research supported in part by Centre for Mathematical Imaging and Vision, HKRGC grant and HKBU FRG grant. Y. Ye's research supported in part by NSFC under Grant no.61073195, and Shenzhen Science and Technology Program under Grant no. CXB201005250024A.

8. REFERENCES

[1] E. Acar, S. Camtepe, M. Krishnamoorthy, and B. Yener. Modeling and multiway analysis of chatroom tensors. *Intelligence and Security Informatics*, pages 256–268, 2005.

[2] L. Adamic and E. Adar. How to search a social network. *Social Networks*, 27(3):187–203, 2005.

[3] S. Borgatti. Centrality and network flow. *Social Networks*, 27(1):55–71, 2005.

[4] J. Carroll and J. Chang. Analysis of individual differences in multidimensional scaling via an N-way generalization of "Eckart-Young" decomposition. *Psychometrika*, 35(3):283–319, 1970.

[5] W. Ching, M. Ng, and W. Ching. Markov chains: models, algorithms and applications. International Series on Operations Research and Management Science, 2006.

[6] P. Comon, X. Luciani and A. de Almeida. Tensor decompositions, Alternating least squares and other tales. *Journal of Chemometrics*, 23:393–405, 2009.

[7] H. Deng, M. Lyu, and I. King. A generalized Co-HITS algorithm and its application to bipartite graphs. In *Proceedings of the 15th ACM SIGKDD international conference on Knowledge discovery and data mining*, pages 239–248. ACM, 2009.

[8] C. Ding, X. He, P. Husbands, H. Zha, and H. Simon. PageRank, HITS and a unified framework for link analysis. In *Proceedings of the 25th annual international ACM SIGIR conference on Research and development in information retrieval*, pages 353–354. ACM, 2002.

[9] L. Freeman. A set of measures of centrality based on betweenness. *Sociometry*, 40(1):35–41, 1977.

[10] R. Harshman. Foundations of the PARAFAC procedure: Models and conditions for an" explanatory" multi-modal factor analysis. *UCLA working papers in phonetics*, 16(1):84, 1970.

[11] R. Kellogg, Uniqueness in the Schauder fixed point theorem. *Proceedings of the American Mathematical Society*, 60: 207–210, 1976.

[12] J. Kleinberg. Authoritative sources in a hyperlinked environment. *Journal of the ACM (JACM)*, 46(5):604–632, 1999.

[13] T. Kolda and B. Bader. The TOPHITS model for higher-order web link analysis. In *Workshop on Link Analysis, Counterterrorism and Security*, volume 7, pages 26–29, 2006.

[14] T. Kolda, B. Bader, and J. Kenny. Higher-order web link analysis using multilinear algebra. In *Data Mining, Fifth IEEE International Conference on*, page 8. IEEE, 2005.

[15] V. Latora and M. Marchiori. A measure of centrality based on network efficiency. *New Journal of Physics*, 9:188, 2007.

[16] X. Li, M. Ng and Y. Ye. HAR: hub and authority scores in multi-relational data for query search. preprint, March 2011, http://www.math.hkbu.edu.hk/~mng/tensor-research/har.pdf

[17] Y. Lin, J. Sun, P. Castro, R. Konuru, H. Sundaram, and A. Kelliher. MetaFac: community discovery via relational hypergraph factorization. In *Proceedings of the 15th ACM SIGKDD*, pages 527–536. ACM, 2009.

[18] Z. Nie, Y. Zhang, J. Wen and W. Ma. Object-level ranking: bringing order to web objects, WWW 2005.

[19] L. Page, S. Brin, R. Motwani, and T. Winograd. The pagerank citation ranking: Bringing order to the web. 1998.

[20] S. Ross. *Introduction to probability models*. Academic Pr, 2007.

[21] J. Sun, D. Tao, and C. Faloutsos. Beyond streams and graphs: dynamic tensor analysis. In *Proceedings of the 12th ACM SIGKDD*, pages 374–383. ACM, 2006.

[22] J. Sun, D. Tao, S. Papadimitriou, P. Yu, and C. Faloutsos. Incremental tensor analysis: Theory and applications. *ACM Transactions on Knowledge Discovery from Data (TKDD)*, 2(3):1–37, 2008.

[23] J. Sun, H. Zeng, H. Liu, Y. Lu, and Z. Chen. CubeSVD: a novel approach to personalized Web search. In *Proceedings of the 14th WWW*, pages 382–390. ACM, 2005.

[24] L. Tucker. Some mathematical notes on three-mode factor analysis. *Psychometrika*, 31(3):279–311, 1966.

[25] W. Xi, B. Zhang, Z. Chen, Y. Lu, S. Yan, W. Ma, and E. Fox. Link fusion: a unified link analysis framework for multi-type interrelated data objects. In *Proceedings of the 13th international conference on World Wide Web*, pages 319–327. ACM, 2004.

[26] D. Zhou, S. Orshanskiy, H. Zha, and C. Giles. Co-ranking authors and documents in a heterogeneous network. In *Data Mining, 2007. ICDM 2007. Seventh IEEE International Conference on*, pages 739–744. IEEE, 2008.

On Dynamic Data-Driven Selection of Sensor Streams

Charu C. Aggarwal
IBM T. J. Watson Research Center
Hawthorne, NY, USA
charu@us.ibm.com

Yan Xie
University of Illinois at Chicago
Chicago, IL, USA
yxie8@uic.edu

Philip S. Yu
University of Illinois at Chicago
Chicago, IL, USA
psyu@cs.uic.edu

ABSTRACT

Sensor nodes have limited local storage, computational power, and battery life, as a result of which it is desirable to minimize the storage, processing and communication from these nodes during data collection. The problem is further magnified by the large volumes of data collected. In real applications, sensor streams are often highly correlated with one another or may have other kinds of functional dependencies. For example, a group of sound sensors in a given geographical proximity may pick almost the same set of signals. Clearly, since there are considerable functional dependencies between different sensors, there are huge *redundancies* in the data collected by sensors. These redundancies may also change as the data evolve over time. In this paper, we discuss real time algorithms for reducing the volume of the data collected in sensor networks. The broad idea is to determine the functional dependencies between sensor streams efficiently in real time, and actively collect the data only from a minimal set of sensors. The remaining sensors collect the data passively at low sampling rates in order to detect any changing trends in the underlying data. We present real time algorithms in order to minimize the power consumption in reducing the data collected and show that the resulting data retains almost the same amount of information at a much lower cost.

Categories and Subject Descriptors

H.2.8 [**Database Management**]: Database Applications

General Terms

Algorithms

1. INTRODUCTION

Recent advances in hardware technology have made it feasible to collect large amounts of data from the physical world using small sensor nodes. Details and surveys on sensor networks may be found in [1, 5, 6, 14]. These sensor nodes are often limited by battery power, and therefore limits on battery life can reduce the life time of the sensor network [1, 14]. When the number of sensor nodes is very large, the aggregate amount of data produced may be very large. This creates the dual problems of too much power consumption and information overload.

Sensor networks are inherently redundant, and have a much larger number of nodes than is needed to collect the data necessary to describe the underlying phenomenon. This is often by design in order to avoid loss of information during special circumstances such as node failure. There are two common kinds of redundancies which are built into sensor networks:

- **Direct Redundancies:** In many cases, sensor nodes may collect very similar kinds of data from related sensor nodes. An example is that of audio sensor nodes in geographically proximate locations. Sensors in geographically proximate locations may pick up almost the same signals from multiple nodes, though there may be some differences because of local differences and noise. In some cases, there may be small *lag correlations* in order to account for small temporal differences between different signals.
- **Implicit Redundancies:** In this case, external events may cause different kinds of characteristic behavior in different sensors. Typically, such characteristic behavior may not show up as the same signal on different sensors, but the signal on one sensor can be predicted from the signal on the other. For example, a seismic signal on one sensor may be correlated with an audio signal on another sensor. Typically such signals may show up as *statistical correlations* in the underlying sensor streams.

While the redundancy in data collection is essential, it comes at a huge cost, because of the aggregate power consumption requirements of the network. This increases the costs to maintain the sensor network effectively, and it also increases the complexity of managing the huge information overload from the large number of sensors. Furthermore, heavy power consumption implies frequent maintenance and replacement of the batteries in order to ensure uninterrupted coverage. Therefore, intelligent and selective choice of transmission of data from sensors is essential in maintaining both the robustness and cost-effectiveness of the signal collection process. A further challenge is that the underlying data streams may evolve over time. Therefore, the dependencies in the data streams may also change over time. Therefore,

KDD'11, August 21–24, 2011, San Diego, California, USA.

it is critical to design *dynamic* methods for reducing the power-consumption and information overload issues by sensor selection.

This paper is organized as follows. The remainder of this section is devoted to related work. In the next section, we will discuss the overall formulation of the problem, and the problem of optimizing the redundancies in the underlying sensor stream. In section 3, we will propose the algorithm for dynamic sensor selection. The experimental results are contains in section 4. Section 5 contains the conclusions and summary.

1.1 Related Work

Since sensors are isolated devices which work on batteries, power is one of the most important constraints in their operation. The work in [6] reduces the data size with data reduction techniques at a particular sensor in order to compress the representation. The technique does not however try to use the correlations across different sensor nodes in order to reduce the collected data. The methods in [6] are in fact orthogonal to our work, and can be combined with our methods, if required. The problem of data reduction from correlated data has been widely studied in the conventional database literature, in the context of principal component analysis [11]. We note that this is simply a *data transformation* process which requires input from all the original dimensions in the data. While this is useful in reducing the *size* of the data, it is not useful from the perspective of power-efficiency or cost of collection. This is because, in our application, the reduction can only be in terms of the original dimensions, since this allows us to decide which sensors to keep in activated mode. Furthermore, the relative costs of different sensors are extremely important in making such decisions.

A number of techniques have been designed in recent years in order to determine correlations between multiple streams in real time [17, 18, 20, 21]. The techniques in [17, 18] use statistical measures in order to find lag-correlations and forecast the behavior of the underlying data stream. The works in [2, 8] propose methods for sensor selection with the use of domain-specific linkage knowledge and utility-feedback, respectively. Methods for observation selection are proposed in [12], when the importance of a sensor-set can be *pre-modeled* as a submodular function. Methods for using adaptive models for time-series prediction were proposed in [19]. The works in [3, 4] propose methods for using adaptive querying in the context of pairwise covariances between sensor streams for reducing the communication costs. The method in [20] uses linear regression in order to determine the correlations in the underlying data and use them for forecasting. The technique in [21] proposes general monitoring techniques to determine statistical correlations in the data in real time. While many of these techniques do detect correlations and redundancies with the use of forecasting and regression techniques, they do not propose a method to systematically reduce the collection complexity in a cost-efficient way with these redundancies. In this paper, we will design cost-sensitive senor selection techniques which are able to minimize loss of information.

2. SENSOR SELECTION FORMULATION

One solution to increasing the power-efficiency and complexity of data collection is to "switch-off" the redundant sensor nodes, and collect data only at the non-redundant nodes from which all other data can be predicted. Of course, if we completely switch off the redundant sensor nodes, then we have no way of knowing when the underlying data correlations change, and a different set of nodes become redundant. A solution is that the data collection and transmission rates at most sensor networks are highly adjustable. It is possible to operate most nodes in a very low and power-efficient mode which provides sufficient data in order to keep track of the underlying correlations. This reduces both the information overload and the power consumption for data collection. Based on the analysis from this low-rate of sampled data, it is possible to keep track of the non-redundant nodes. Therefore, we assume two modes of sensor data collection:

- **Power-efficient Mode:** All sensor nodes sample in a *normal mode*, which is a power-efficient and uses a low rate of data collection. We assume that the data streams are collected at multiple sensor nodes which are indexed as $\{1 \dots n\}$. The data at different sensor nodes are received in the form of *ticks*. We assume that the ith tick of the jth sensor is denoted by x_{ij}. Therefore, the values of the ticks in the jth stream are denoted by $x_{1j}, x_{2j} \dots x_{rj} \dots$. For simplicity, we assume that the data collection at different sensors happen at the same rate, and the corresponding ticks are synchronized. We note that the synchronization may not happened at the individual sensor nodes, though a variety of simple imputation techniques can be used to convert the data into synchronized ticks at the centralized server at which the data is received. While this sampling mode is sufficient to determine the relative behavior of different streams, it may not be sufficient to make real-time decisions for the sensor network. We note that the data collected in power-efficient mode is essentially considered *training data* which is used to make decisions on the nature of the redundancy in the different nodes at any given moment in time.

- **Active Mode:** A higher mode of sampling may often be required in order to make effective real time decisions in a sensor network. This is expensive both in terms of power consumption and storage costs. In general, we would like to use the active mode of sampling for *only a small subset of nodes* which minimizes the power consumption, without significantly compromising the total amount of information relative to a network in which all nodes operate in the active mode.

The data from the power-efficient mode (or training data) is used to determine the subset of non-redundant nodes which are actively sampled for the data. By minimizing the number of such nodes, we can reduce both the power consumption and the complexity of storing the underlying data. We assume that the (additional) power costs required to activate the different sensor nodes are denoted by $p_1 \dots p_n$. The different values of p_i are typically not identical, and may vary considerably. This is natural since an audio-sensor would have very different power consumption from a seismic sensor.

A centralized architecture is assumed for the sensor network in which all nodes transmit their signals to a centralized node. We note that we have picked this architecture, since it is the simplest form of organizing the sensor network. The ideas in this paper can also be generalized to networks with arbitrary clusters with a hierarchical structure, since the redundancy reduction algorithms can be applied within a particular cluster of the hierarchy. The data repository is assumed to have the computational power to process and analyze the sensor streams in real time. It is also assumed that the sampling rate of sensor streams can be controlled in an automated way by using signals from the centralized data repository. Therefore, it is critical to continuously monitor and analyze the streams from the centralized data repository in order to minimize the error in estimation. The aim of this paper is to design an effective method for determining the set of sensors which are actively monitored.

Let us denote the set of active sensor nodes by J. We note that the signals from J can be used to estimate approximations on the active (higher frequency) signals from other (power-efficient) low sampled nodes. A variety of techniques such as lag-correlations or the regression-based MUSCLES technique [18, 20] can be used in order to perform this estimation. Let us denote an estimation model by $\mathcal{M}$. The key is that such a model needs to be efficient and real time in order to handle the large volume of data stream, and react to the evolution of the underlying data. Let i be any sensor node which is not included in J. Then, we define the approximation error of the sensor node i as the error in estimation of the tick values with the use of a model $\mathcal{M}$.

DEFINITION 2.1. *Let $\mathcal{M}$ be a model used in order to estimate the signals on inactive nodes from the actively sampled nodes. We denote $E(J, i, \mathcal{M})$ as the error in estimation of the sensor node i from the set J with the use of model $\mathcal{M}$. Specifically, if $Y(J, i, t, \mathcal{M})$ be the estimated value of the tth tick of sensor i with use of model $\mathcal{M}$ and subset J of nodes, then the estimation error $E(J, i, \mathcal{M})$ is defined as the cumulative error over the last window of length w from current time t. Therefore, we have:*

$$E(J, i, \mathcal{M}) = \sum_{r=0}^{w-1} |Y(J, i, t-r, \mathcal{M}) - x_{(t-r)i}| \qquad (1)$$

The corresponding average error over all sensor nodes is defined by $F(J, \mathcal{M}) = \frac{\sum_{i \notin J} E(J,i,\mathcal{M})}{n-|J|}$. Note that the error is defined only over the nodes which are not drawn from J. The key optimization problem is to determine the optimal set J which minimizes the average estimation error over any node which is not in J, subject to a total power consumption constraint on the nodes which are included in J.

PROBLEM 2.1. *For any given model $\mathcal{M}$, determine J so as to find the optimum value of $F(J, \mathcal{M})$, while ensuring that $\sum_{i \in J} p_i \leq P$.*

We note that the quality of the reduction also depends upon the model $\mathcal{M}$ which is picked for forecasting the behavior of the passive nodes. This is especially difficult, since the model $\mathcal{M}$ needs to be a *real time model* which can quickly detect the changing inter-dependencies, and correspondingly adjust the set of non-redundant sensor nodes J.

3. LOCAL REGRESSION CLUSTERING

In this section, we will discuss a *regression-clustering* approach for data reduction. In the regression-clustering approach, we create clusters of the different streams. At any given moment in time, each stream belongs to a particular cluster. These clusters may evolve over time as the underlying stream patterns change. The clustering is constructed in conjunction with a *base of active sensor-stream medoids*, around which the data is appropriately clustered. This is essentially a k-medoid based partitioning approach in which the data is clustered around k medoids [13]. These medoids are the representatives around which the different streams are clustered. This base of sensor-streams is also the set of the sensors J which are kept in active mode in order to collect the underlying data. Therefore, the representatives need to be chosen so that the signals for the passive sensors can be accurately predicted from at least one of the active sensor. The continuous clustering provides us with the real-time assignment of the passive sensors to the active sensors. This assignment is utilized in order to perform a one-to-one regression of the underlying data, and fill in the unsampled data points for the passive sensors. In the clustering process, each of sensor streams are assigned to one of the sensor nodes J with the use of a *regression-error based distance function*. This distance function computes the distance as the regression error of assigning a sensor node to each of these alternative sensor-streams, and computes the distance based on the error of the appropriate prediction. Next, we describe the details of the regression distance function used for similarity computation and analysis. Let us consider to sensors i and j such that j is a passively-sampled sensor, in which the last w passively sampled ticks are given by $z_1(j) \ldots z_w(j)$. The corresponding ticks from the sensor i are given by $z_1(i) \ldots z_w(i)$. We would like to compute the predictability of the signals $z_1(j) \ldots z_w(j)$ from the signals $z_1(i) \ldots z_w(i)$. We assume that a lag of r ticks may be required in order to predict the signals $z_1(j) \ldots z_w(j)$ from the signals $z_1(i) \ldots z_w(i)$. Furthermore, since the sensor j is predicted from sensor i, the lag can only be in one direction for the purpose of predictability i.e. j lags i. It is assumed that the maximum lag allowed in terms of the number of ticks is

Algorithm *MaintainActiveS*(Sensors Streams: $[1 \ldots n]$
  Power Constraint: P);
{ This algorithm describes one iteration of the process
  of maintaining an active set of nodes;}
begin
  J = Randomly sampled set of sensor nodes with
    aggregate power requirement less than P;
  At the next (passively-sampled) tick **do**
  repeat
    Add a sensor to J, which leads to
      maximum decrease in $PError(J)$;
    while J violates the power constraint
    begin
      Drop the sensor from J which leads to
        least increase of $PError(J)$
    end
  until(J did not change in last iteration)
  Collect active ticks for current set J;
  Predict active ticks for all other sensors using
    regression analysis from the current assignment;
end

Figure 1: Dynamically maintaining the active sensor set by local regression clustering

denoted by $maxlag$. For a lag of r ticks, we assume that the regression takes on the following form:

$$z_k(j) = a \cdot z_{k-r}(i) + b \qquad \forall k \in \{r+1 \ldots w\} \qquad (2)$$

Here a and b are constants. We would like to pick a and b, so as to minimize the least squares error of estimation. The total square error $e(i,j,r)$ of predicting j from i is given by the following expression:

$$e(i,j,r) = \sum_{k=r+1}^{w} (a \cdot z_{k-r}(i) + b - z_k(j))^2 \qquad (3)$$

In order to minimize $e(i,j,r)$ we need to pick a and b such $\delta e(i,j,r)/\delta a = 0$ and $\delta e(i,j,r)/\delta b = 0$. This corresponds to the following two relationships:

$$\sum_{k=r+1}^{w} z_{k-r}(i) \cdot (a \cdot z_{k-r}(i) + b - z_k(j)) = 0 \qquad (4)$$

$$\sum_{k=r+1}^{w} (a \cdot z_{k-r}(i) + b - z_k(j)) = 0 \qquad (5)$$

We note that these are linear relationships in a and b, which can be easily solved for the optimal values a^* and b^*. Let $e^*(i,j,r)$ be the minimized value of the error, when we set $a = a^*$ and $b = b^*$ respectively. We note that the value of $e^*(i,j,r)$ over different values of r cannot be compared with one another, since we use different window lengths for computing the different errors. Therefore, we compute the *per-tick optimized error* $E^*(i,j,r)$ by averaging the error over the number of ticks over which it is computed. Therefore, we have:

$$E^*(i,j,r) = e^*(i,j,r)/(w-r) \qquad (6)$$

The distance function $D(i,j)$ between sensors i and j is defined as the minimum value of $E^*(i,j,r)$ over all possible values of the lag $r \in [0, maxlag]$. Therefore, we have:

$$D(i,j) = \min_{r \in [0,maxlag]} E^*(i,j,r) \qquad (7)$$

The optimized value of r denotes the optimal value of the lag at which the sensor signal j can be predicted from the sensor signal i most accurately. This accounts for lag-correlations in the underlying data. Thus, the distance function $D(i,j)$ defines the best predictability of sensor j from sensor i over all possible lag values in the range $[0, maxlag]$. This distance function is used in order to create an effective partition-based clustering algorithm.

3.1 Constructing Regression Clusters

In this section, we will discuss the procedure for constructing regression clusters from the underlying data. We will design a clustering algorithm which uses the regression distance function in order to cluster all sensors around a bunch of representative (active) sensors, so as to maximize predictability. Therefore, we will rely on the class of k-median techniques [10] which utilize a bunch of cluster-representatives which are picked from the original data. The traditional k-median algorithm for clustering uses repeated interchange operations on a set of selected cluster representatives. In our algorithm, this set of cluster representatives is the active set J. The algorithm starts off by setting the active set J using random assignment. Subsequently, the algorithm uses an iterative approach in order to improve the quality of the active set J. We note that the quality of the active set J is defined by the accuracy of the prediction of all other sensor signals from the active set J. This is denoted by $PError(J)$, and is defined by assigning each sensor to its closest sensor in J with the use of the distance function $D(\cdot,\cdot)$. The average error of this assignment is denoted by $PError(J)$. This assignment error is calculated from the set J as follows:

for each pair of sensors $j \in [1,n]$ and
  sensor $i \in J$ compute $D(i,j)$;
Assign j to the sensor with the least value of $D(i,j)$;
Let $PError(J)$ be the corresponding average of the predictability error of the assignment across all sensors;

The overall algorithm for dynamically maintaining the sensor set J is illustrated in Figure 1. This set J serves as the *medoids*, which is also the active sensor set. Typically, k-median algorithms use interchange operations on the medoids in order to compute the representatives from which the cluster partitions are created. However k-median algorithms use a fixed number of representatives, whereas we need to use a power constraint in this case in order to regulate the number of representatives. Therefore, in this case, we separate out the interchange into separate representative addition and deletion operations, and the number of sensors may vary over the course of the algorithm. However, we ensure that the power requirement of the sensors in J is less than the total power constraint P. The algorithm re-computes the active sensor set J after the receipt of each passive tick. This re-computed sensor set is used in order to perform the regression based prediction of the active ticks received between the current passive tick and the next passive tick. Therefore, in each iteration, we first add a sensor to the set J, which minimizes the average assignment error (computed by $D(\cdot,\cdot)$) as much as possible. We note that the addition of this sensor may result in a violation of the power constraint. Therefore, we need to remove some sensors from J, so that the resulting set continues to satisfy the power constraint. To this effect, we remove the sensors, which result in the least increase in prediction error, until the power constraint is satisfied again. We note that it is possible that the same sensor may be removed, which was added during a given iteration. In such a case, the set J does not change. This implies that the current set of active sensors is critical and we can terminate the algorithm. We note that this overall approach is continuously applied in order to maintain the active set J. This set is used in order to make the predictions for the other sensors for which the ticks are not collected actively.

3.2 Speeding up with Ranking Variations

One of the challenges with the use of the technique is that it can sometimes be too slow, when the algorithm requires a large number of iterations. Instead of going through all sensors and finding the one that minimizes the error for every iteration, we only do this process for the first iteration. Subsequently, we rank all the sensor by the errors in terms of regression predictability. In this way, we can get a ranking list of all sensors. From the second iterations, sensors are added sequentially with the use of the ranking list. When there is no change to the active set in a cycle through the ranking list, the process is terminated.

3.3 Leveraging Local-Regression Clusters for Prediction

The prediction of the active ticks from the sensors can be performed in two ways, once the data for the different sensors has been collected:

- For a given sensor j can use a least-squares regression from the sensor $i \in J$ to which the sensor j is assigned in order to predict the corresponding active ticks.
- We can use multi-variate regression on the entire set J in order to predict the active ticks for any sensor i.

We note that the second variation requires more computational power, but can be somewhat more accurate if the remaining sensor set retains information which relates to the prediction effectively. On the other hand, most of the predictive information is encoded in the local sensor node. In such cases, the use of multi-variate regression can add further noise to the predictive process, and in some cases, the quality of multi-variate regression may not be higher. Therefore, it seems like a reasonable tradeoff to use the information in the local sensor node for predictive purposes. In the next section, we will study the experimental effectiveness of the technique over different size of the sensor node sets J. We will see that the local method for prediction turns out to be quite efficient and effective over a wide range of data sets and parameters.

4. EXPERIMENTAL RESULTS

In this section, we will present the experimental evaluation of our algorithm on several real data sets. To be more specific, three real data sets are used for test purposes. The first two are derived from the intel berkeley lab data set [22]. This data set has 54 sensors, and each record includes four values of temperature, humidity, light and voltage. Since the values of light and voltage did not change too much over time, we only used temperature and humidity in our experiments. The third data set is the chlorine data set [16], which is downloadable from [23]. The data set was collected from 166 sensors. In addition, we need to generate a synthetic power requirement for each sensor. In our experiments, the power requirements of the different sensors are uniformly distributed in the range $[0, 1]$.

For each data set, several techniques are adopted to illustrate the effectiveness and efficiency of our proposed approach. The overall approach comprises the process of picking the active sensors and making predictions. The average error in prediction of the sensor values is the key metric, which is used for evaluating the effectiveness of our approach. This section will provide detailed results and is organized as follows. In the first part, we will analyze the effectiveness and accuracy of the technique. In the second part, the efficiency of the algorithm will be analyzed. Finally, we will provide some insights about how the underlying active set of sensors may change over time.

4.1 Accuracy Analysis

In this section, we will provide an accuracy analysis of the sensor data reduction technique. The aim of the approach is to use cluster-based regression techniques to provide a high quality reduction of the sensors over which the data needs to be collected. The best way to measure the effectiveness is to analyze the accuracy of the prediction. To test the effectiveness, we compared the results of several variations of our proposed technique for regression and prediction. In addition, we used a couple of baselines in order to measure the qualitative accuracy. The different algorithms are discussed below, of which the last two are baselines:

- **Univariate Power Efficient Selection(*PES Univariate*):** Note that at the end of the process, each sensor gets assigned to at least one other sensor. The assigned sensor is used for prediction purposes with the use of univariate regression.
- **Multivariate Power Efficient Selection(*PES Multivariate*):** We use multi-variate regression from a subset of the sensors in J in order to make the prediction. For regression purpose, the number of such sensors picked is the minimum of the number of active sensors and $w - maxlag - 2$. In each iteration, the error-minimization criterion is used in order to add sensors to the active set. A multivariate prediction approach is used in conjunction with the selected sensors in order to perform the prediction.
- **Multivariate Power Efficient Selection with Ranking List (*PES Multivariate(RL)*):** In this case, we use the same technique as PES Multivariate for the first iteration. We also obtain a ranking list of sensors as well based on their predictive power. For the remaining iterations within a particular update interval, we do not use the error minimization criterion, but we use the next senor in the ranking list. Multivariate regression is used to perform the prediction.
- **Univariate sampling: Baseline (*Sampled Univariate*):** In this case, we use sampling in order to determine the set of active sensors. The number of sampled sensors is the same as the *PES Univariate* technique. As in the case of the *PES Univariate* technique, we use univariate regression in order to perform the prediction.
- **Multivariate sampling: Baseline (*Sampled Multivariate*):** As in the previous case, we use sampling in order to determine the set of active sensors. The number of sampled sensors is the same as the PES multivariate technique. As in the case of the *PES Multivariate* technique, we use multivariate regression in order to perform the prediction.

We will test the effectiveness of the technique over a wide range of parameters. The most relevant parameter is the power constraint, since it defines the resources which are relevant to the data reduction process. Clearly, a larger power allowance provides greater accuracy for the prediction process, since it allows us to retain a larger number of active sensors. The variations in effectiveness with increasing power constraint for the different data sets are illustrated in Figures 2(a), 2(b) and 2(c) respectively. In the experiment, we use a window size w of 10, a maximum lag $maxlag$ of 5 and an update interval of 5. The power constraint is illustrated on the X-axis, and the error is illustrated on the Y-axis. It is clear that in each case, a larger power constraint provides greater accuracy. The power efficient variations provided much greater accuracy than the sampled variations. An additional observation was that the multivariate versions were significantly more accurate than the univariate prediction techniques. The reason for the greater accuracy of the multivariate prediction techniques was the fact that a larger number of sensors could be used to make more accurate predictions. In each case, the *PES Multivariate technique* provided the greatest accuracy. The ranked technique approximated the *PES Multivariate technique* quite closely. As we will see, this is an excellent practical alternative for the optimal multivariate scheme.

The window size is a parameter related to the number of data points used for regression. The power constraint P was set to 3, the maximum lag $maxlag$ was set to 5, and the update interval was set to 5. With a fixed max lag, a larger window size leads to the use of greater number of data points. Extremely small window sizes leads to lack of robustness in prediction. At the same time, very large window sizes can lead to smoothing of the trends in the data which have predictive power. The results of the three data sets are illustrated in Figures 3(a), 3(b) and 3(c). The window size is illustrated on the X-axis, and the error is illustrated on the Y-axis. It is evident that different window sizes work better with different data sets. In practice, this corresponds to the core periodicity of the different data sets. However, it is also evident that the *effectiveness and efficiency ordering among the different techniques* does not vary across the different ranges of parameters tested.

The choice of update interval is a key parameter which decides the refresh rate for our algorithm. The results are illustrated in Figures 4(a), 4(b) and 4(c). The update interval is illustrated on the X-axis and the error is illustrated on the Y-axis. The value of the power constraint P was 3, the value of the window size w was 3, and the value of the maximum lag $maxlag$ was 5. It is evident that higher update intervals lead to better quality results. This is because higher update intervals lead to the use of less stale data and will therefore naturally lead to more accurate results. On the other hand, a higher update interval also requires more computational processing. This is a natural tradeoff between computational processing and accuracy.

The regression analysis uses a *maximum lag value* to perform the prediction. The larger the value of this maximum lag is, the greater the flexibility of the algorithm is in being able to perform the regression analysis. The results are illustrated in Figures 5(a), 5(b) and 5(c) respectively. The power constraint P was set to 3, the window size w was set to 10, and the update interval was set to 5. The maximum lag is illustrated in the X-axis, and the error is illustrated on the Y-axis. It is clear that the error reduces with the increase in the maximum lag value. The tradeoff is that it results in some delay in the predictive data received from the sensors.

4.2 Computational Efficiency

All experiments were performed on a Microsoft Windows XP machine with Intel Core2 Duo 2.5GHz CPU and 1.5GB main memory. The algorithm was implemented in C++. We will examine the computational complexity of performing each update. Since the sampling techniques do not require such a computational process, they will not be included in this analysis. The running times for updates are mostly determined by the underlying parameter setting. These settings are set to the same values as those used for the effectiveness results. Since the efficiency results for the three data sets were extremely similar, we present the results only on the *intel-humidity* data set.

Before examining each parameter separately, we will provide a brief overview of the relative trends between the different figures. The *PES Multivariate* technique required the greatest amount of time, because it requires an iterative approach in order to determine the optimal set. Furthermore, it requires us to determine the prediction with the use of optimal multivariate analysis. Between *PES Univariate* and *PES Multivariate(RL)*, the two techniques were very close to one another in terms of running time. This is essentially because most of the time was spent in the update process, and the difference between univariate and multivariate analysis was relatively small.

The results with increasing power constraint are illustrated in Figures 6(a). For test purpose, we fixed window size w to be 10, maximum lag to be 5, and update interval to be 5. As the power constraint increases, it is easy to understand that the running time will become longer. This is because the use of a higher power constraint leads to the use of a larger number of sensors. The use of a larger number of sensors naturally increases the running time, because the regression analysis and optimization needs to be performed over a larger number of sensors. However, it is important to note that the running time increases only linearly with the power constraint. This means that the scheme can be implemented fairly efficiently over a large number of sensors.

It is generally expected that a larger window size should increase the running time. However, this is not always the case. The reason is that the running time is also dependent upon the number of iterations required by the algorithm. When the active sensor set changes considerably from one iteration to the other, a larger number of iterations are required. This change over different runs dictates the running time to a greater extent than the window size. The results with increasing window size for the humidity data set are illustrated in Figure 6(b). Here, the power constraint P was 3, the maximum lag $maxlag$ was 5, and the update interval was 5. It is clear that the time is not necessarily monotonically increasing. This will be explained elaborately in similarity analysis. This also means that the scheme can be used over larger window sizes when required without substantially increasing the running time.

The sensitivity of the running time to the maximum lag for regression analysis is illustrated in Figures 6(c). The maximum lag is illustrated on the X-axis and running time is illustrated on the Y-axis in each of the figures. The power constraint P was set to 3, the window size w was set to 10, and the update interval was set to 5. We note that the maximum lag affects the number of possible computations performed by the algorithm. Clearly, a larger lag increases the number of computations, since a larger number of possibilities need to be checked for optimality. While it has been shown that this leads to higher quality results, the corresponding cost is the higher running time. Therefore, the running times also increase with increasing value of the maximum lag. It is evident that the running times increase only modestly with the increase in the maximum lag. Therefore, all the three trend figures on running time show modest scalability with different parameters such as the power constraint, maximum lag, and window size. This suggests good scalability characteristics with increasing data size.

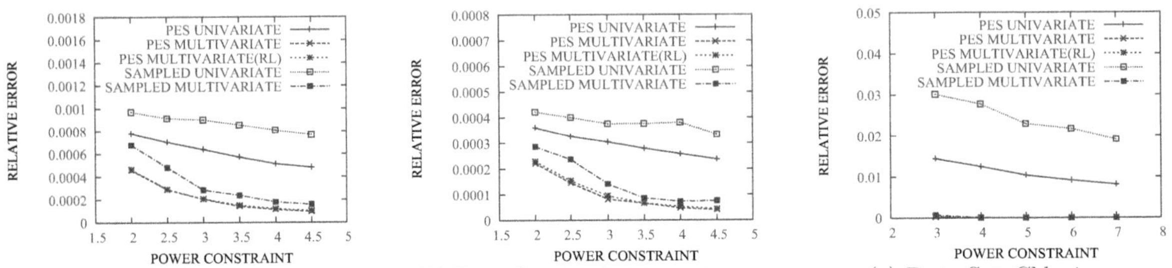

(a) Data Set *intel-humidity* (b) Data Set *intel-temperature* (c) Data Set *Chlorine*

Figure 2: Error Plot on Power Constraint

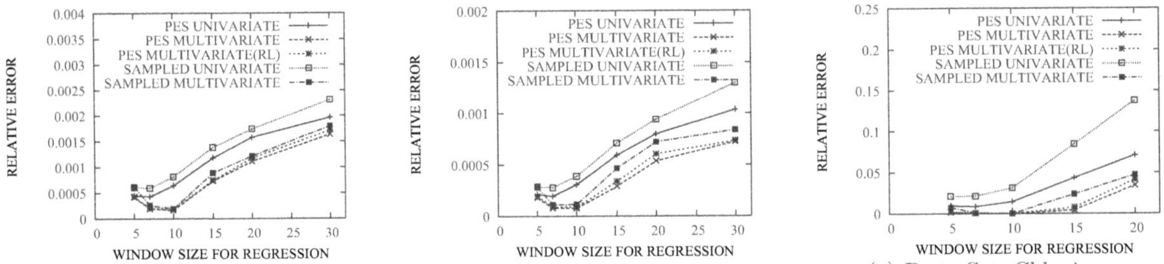

(a) Data Set *intel-humidity* (b) Data Set *intel-temperature* (c) Data Set *Chlorine*

Figure 3: Error Plot on Window Size

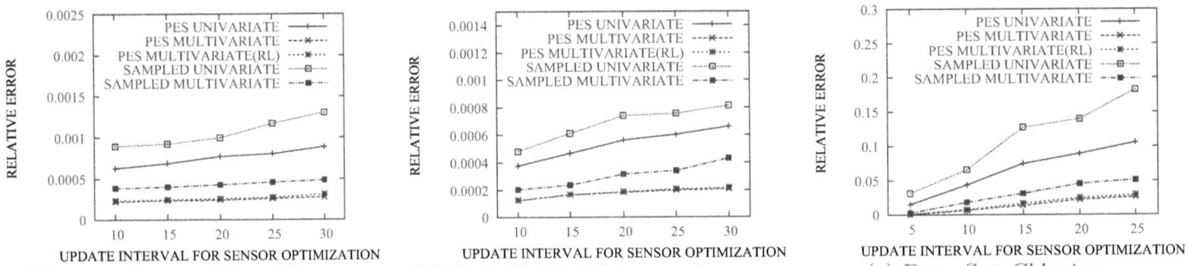

(a) Data Set *intel-humidity* (b) Data Set *intel-temperature* (c) Data Set *Chlorine*

Figure 4: Error Plot on Update Interval

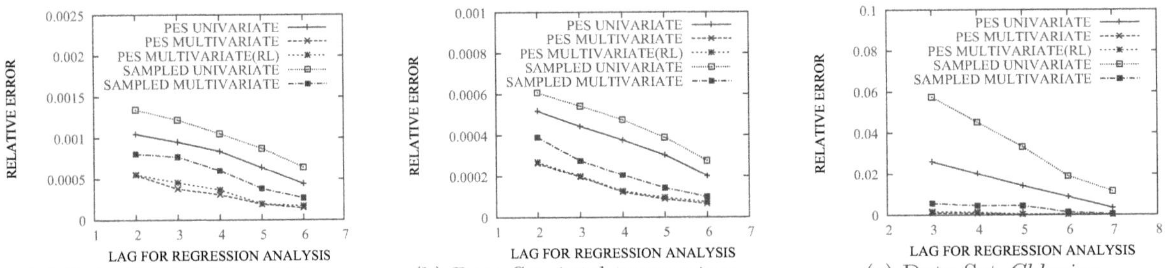

(a) Data Set *intel-humidity* (b) Data Set *intel-temperature* (c) Data Set *Chlorine*

Figure 5: Error Plot on Maximum Lag

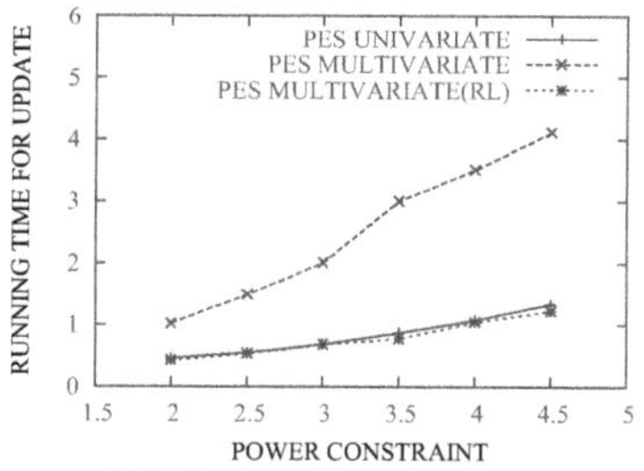

(a) Power Constraint

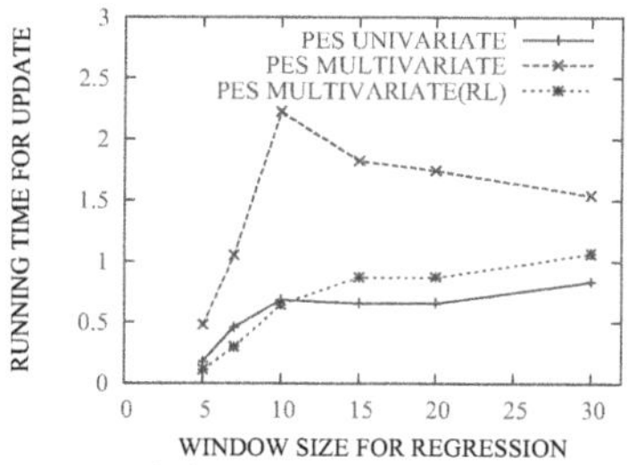

(b) Window Size

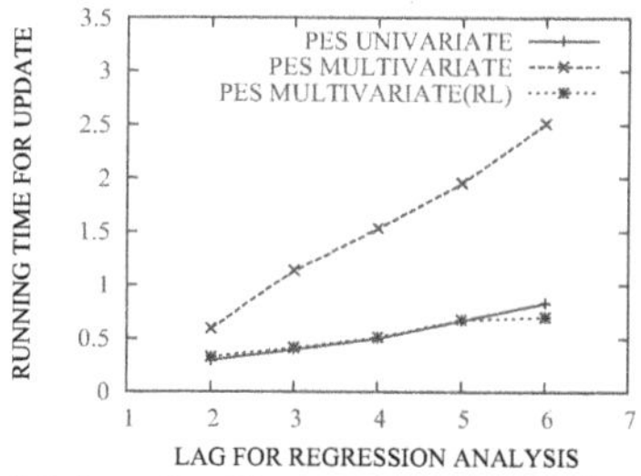

(c) Lag for Regression Analysis

Figure 6: Running Time (Data Set *intel-humidity*)

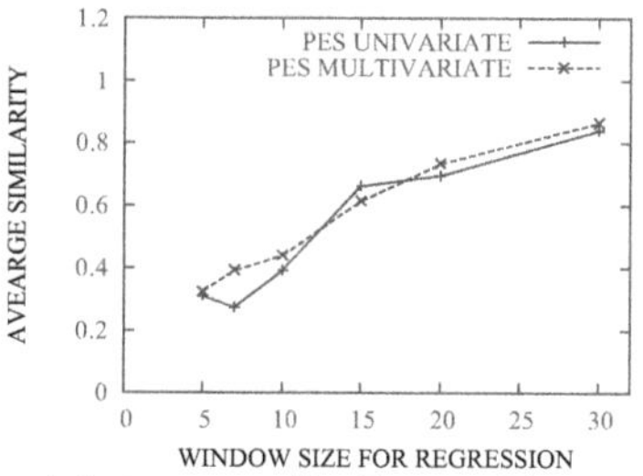

(a) Average Similarity Plot

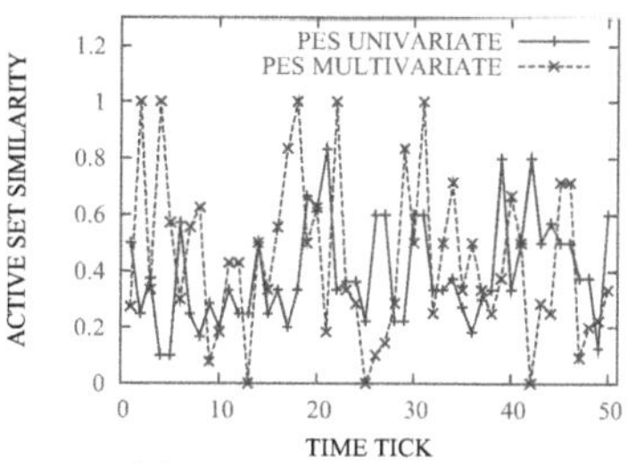

(b) Similarity Plot

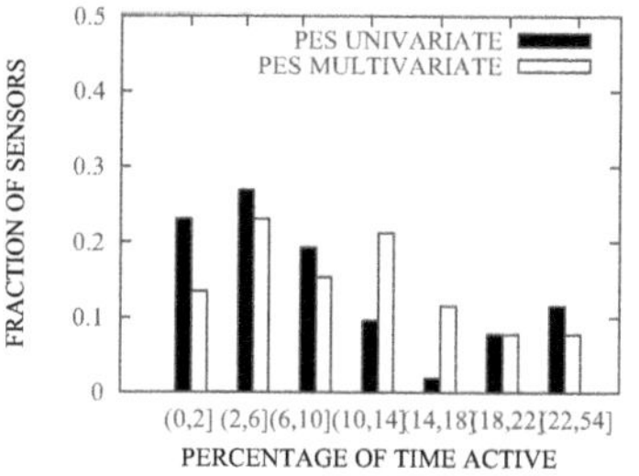

(c) Duration Plot

Figure 7: Sensitivity Analysis (Data Set *intel-humidity*)

4.3 Similarity Analysis

As stated in previous sections, the dependencies between different sensors may change as the data evolves over time. When the active set changes considerably from one iteration to the next, this affects both the prediction errors and the running time. Therefore, it is useful to examine how the sensor set changed during the progression of the algorithm. One way of doing so is to examine the change in the active sensor set from one iteration to the next. To quantify the change of two sets, we adopt the definition of jaccard similarity coefficient between the sensor sets between two iterations. Given two sets A and B, the Jaccard similarity is defined as: $J(A, B) = \frac{|A \bigcap B|}{|A \bigcup B|}$.

According to the previous analysis, the prediction error for different window sizes is influenced by the ability of the system to adapt to changes in the underlying data distribution. Since the prediction error was rather sensitive to window size, we test the average similarity against window size in Figure 7(a). The results clearly show that the average similarity increases with window size. This suggests that the active set changes more slowly with increasing window size. This is because regressions which are based on larger window sizes, tend to change the active set more slowly. As a result the prediction error is better for smaller window sizes, in which the system is able to adjust more rapidly to the changes in the underlying data distribution. This is also the reason for our earlier counterintuitive observation that the execution time is sometimes longer even though we have a smaller window size. If the similarity measure is low, it indicates that it requires more update time to determine the new set.

Figure 7(b) shows the details of the similarity change over time. Here we use a window size of 10 as an example. The results show that the similarity values suddenly drop at specific times. These correspond to the times at which the patterns in the regression stream change a lot, and correspondingly the active set changes. Thus, this figure illustrates the adaptivity of our approach in dynamically changing the sensor set in responses to changes in the underlying sensor stream patterns and correlations.

The other measurement of the change of the active set used in our experiment is the distribution of number of appearances, which is illustrated in Figures 7(c). The X-axis of the histograms is the percentage of time that a particular sensor stays active, while the Y-axis shows the proportion of the sensors whose activity lies within that range. It is clear that most sensors do not stay active for a very long time span. In most cases, they appear to be active only for a few ticks. This suggests that in practical scenarios, it may be possible to use the redundancy inherent in a sensor network and collect most of the relevant information, while keeping only a small fraction of the sensors active at a given time.

5. CONCLUSIONS AND SUMMARY

In this paper, we presented a new power efficient data reduction scheme for sensor networks. The key idea of the technique is to use regression analysis in order to determine a small active set with minimal power requirements. This small active set is used to predict the values on many of the other redundant sensors. We show the effectiveness of using such a technique and show its applicability for a number of different data sets. We present several variations of the scheme and show its efficiency and effectiveness over a number of data sets. The results suggest that it is possible to use a small number of sensors to continuously predict all the streams for the purpose of mining. This allows significant savings in power and storage requirements, while retaining predictive accuracy.

Acknowledgements

The first author's work was sponsored by the Army Research Laboratory and was accomplished under Cooperative Agreement Number W911NF-09-2-0053. The views and conclusions contained in this document are those of the authors and should not be interpreted as representing the official policies, either expressed or implied, of the Army Research Laboratory or the U.S. Government. The U.S. Government is authorized to reproduce and distribute reprints for Government purposes notwithstanding any copyright notation here on.
The work of the second and third authors is supported in part by NSF through grants IIS-0905215, DBI-0960443, OISE-0968341 and OIA-0963278.

6. REFERENCES

[1] C. C. Aggarwal (ed). Data Streams: Models and Algorithms. *Springer*, 2007.

[2] C. C. Aggarwal, A. Bar-Noy, and S. Shamoun. On Sensor Selection in Linked Information Networks. *IEEE DCOSS Conference*, 2011.

[3] C. Anagnostopoulos, N. M. Adams, and D. J. Hand. Streaming Covariance Selection with Applications to Adaptive Querying in Sensor Networks. *The Computer Journal*, 53(9): pp. 1401–1414, 2010.

[4] T. Arici, T. Akgun, and Y. Altunbasak. A prediction error-based hypothesis testing method for sensor data acquisition. *ACM Transactions on Sensor Networks (TOSN)*, Vol. 2, pp. 529–556, 2006.

[5] A. Deligiannakis, Y. Kotidis, and N. Roussopoulos. Compressing Historical Information in Sensor Networks. *ACM SIGMOD Conference* pp. 527–538, 2004.

[6] A. Deligiannakis, and Y. Kotidis. Data Reduction Techniques in Sensor Networks. *IEEE Data Engineering Bulletin* 28(1): pp. 19–25, 2005.

[7] A. Deshpande, C. Guestrin, S. Madden, J. Hellerstein, and W. Hong. Model Driven Data Acquisition for Sensor Networks. *VLDB Conference*, pp. 588–599, 2004.

[8] D. Golovin, M. Faulkner, and A. Krause. Online distributed sensor selection. *IPSN Conference*, pp. 220–231, 2010.

[9] M. Greenwald, and S. Khanna. Power Conserving Computation of Order Statistics over Sensor Networks. *ACM PODS Conference*, pp. 275–285, 2004.

[10] A. Jain, and R. Dubes. *Algorithms for Clustering Data.* Prentice Hall, New Jersey, 1998.

[11] I. T. Jolliffee. Principal Component Analysis. *Springer*, 2002.

[12] A. Krause, and C. Guestrin. Near-optimal observation selection using submodular functions. *AAAI Conference*, pp. 1650–1654, 2007.

[13] R. T. Ng, and J. Han. Efficient and Effective Clustering Methods for Spatial Data Mining. *VLDB Conference*, pp. 144–155, 1994.

[14] G. Kollios, J. Byers, J. Considine, M. Hadjielefttheriou, and F. Li. Robust Aggregation in Sensor Networks. *IEEE Data Engineering Bulletin*, 28(1): pp. 26–32. 2005.

[15] C. Olston, J. Jiang, and J. Widom. Adaptive Filters for Continuous Queries over Distributed Data Streams. *ACM SIGMOD Conference*, pp. 563–574, 2003.

[16] A. Ostfeld(et.al.) The battle of the water sensor networks (BWSN): A design challenge for engineers and algorithms. *Journal of Water Resources Planning and Management*, vol. 134, no. 6, pp. 556–568, 2008. [Online]. Available: `http://link.aip.org/link/?QWR/134/556/1`

[17] S. Papadimitriou, J. Sun, and C. Faloutsos. Dimensionality Reduction and Forecasting of Time-Series Data Streams. *Data Streams: Models and Algorithms, Ed. Charu Aggarwal, Springer*, Chapter 12, pp. 261–288, 2007.

[18] Y. Sakurai, S. Papadimitriou, and C. Faloutsos. BRAID: Stream Mining through Group Lag Correlations. *ACM SIGMOD Conference*, pp. 599–610, 2005.

[19] L. Yann-Ael, S. Santini, and G. Bontempi. Adaptive model selection for time series prediction in wireless sensor networks. *Signal Processing*, Vol. 87, pp. 3010–3020, 2007.

[20] B.-K. Yi, N. Sidiropoulos, T. Johnson, H. V. Jagadish, C. Faloutsos, and A. Biliris. Online Data Mining for Co-Evolving Time Sequences. *ICDE Conference*, pp. 13–22, 2000.

[21] Y. Zhu, and D. Shasha. StatStream: Statistical Monitoring of Thousands of Data Streams in Real Time. *VLDB Conference*, pp. 358–369, 2002.

[22] Available online at: `http://berkeley.intel-research.net/labdata/`

[23] Available online at: `http://www.cs.cmu.edu/afs/cs/project/spirit-1/www/`

On the Privacy of Anonymized Networks

Pedram Pedarsani Matthias Grossglauser *
School of Computer and Communication Sciences
EPFL, Lausanne, Switzerland

ABSTRACT

The proliferation of online social networks, and the concomitant accumulation of user data, give rise to hotly debated issues of privacy, security, and control. One specific challenge is the sharing or public release of *anonymized data* without accidentally leaking personally identifiable information (PII). Unfortunately, it is often difficult to ascertain that sophisticated statistical techniques, potentially employing additional external data sources, are unable to break anonymity.

In this paper, we consider an instance of this problem, where the object of interest is the structure of a social network, i.e., a graph describing users and their links. Recent work demonstrates that anonymizing node identities may not be sufficient to keep the network private: the availability of node and link data from another domain, which is correlated with the anonymized network, has been used to re-identify the anonymized nodes. This paper is about conditions under which such a de-anonymization process is possible.

We attempt to shed light on the following question: can we assume that a sufficiently sparse network is inherently anonymous, in the sense that even with unlimited computational power, de-anonymization is impossible? Our approach is to introduce a random graph model for a version of the de-anonymization problem, which is parameterized by the expected node degree and a similarity parameter that controls the correlation between two graphs over the same vertex set. We find simple conditions on these parameters delineating the boundary of privacy, and show that the mean node degree need only grow slightly faster than $\log n$ with network size n for nodes to be identifiable. Our results have policy implications for sharing of anonymized network information.

Categories and Subject Descriptors

H.1 [**Models and Principles**]: General; G.3 [**Mathematics of Computing**]: Probability and Statistics; K.4.1 [**Computers and Society**]: Public Policy Issues—*Privacy*

*This work has been supported by the Swiss National Science Foundation (SNSF) under grant 200021-116510.

General Terms

Theory, Measurement

Keywords

network privacy, de-anonymization, social networks, random graphs, graph sampling

1. INTRODUCTION

The emergence of online social networks such as Facebook, Twitter, MySpace, Linkedin, etc. with hundreds of millions of users implies that an unprecedented amount of user data is now in the hands of the providers of such services. Not surprisingly, the fair use of this information, the appropriate notions of privacy and security, and the technical and legal tools to control its sharing and dissemination, have become controversial and hotly debated problems in the scientific community and beyond.

There are many reasons why social network data might be shared between organizations, or even released into the public domain. First, this information is very valuable for scientific purposes: the modest number of publicly available datasets has led to a broad variety of research projects and results. For example (and without any claim to exhaustiveness), promising research directions in this area include probabilistic modeling of network properties and dynamics [19], real data measurement and analysis [25, 24, 16, 6], and developing scalable algorithms to navigate and infer data from large-scale networks [18, 20]. Obviously, this requires great care in order to avoid the accidental release of sensitive information about individual users. As AOL's public relations disaster a few years ago [1] illustrates, simply anonymizing user identities may not be sufficient to prevent an attacker from identifying individual users through other means. Second, online social networks are increasingly integrated with other services on the web, which requires a certain amount of sharing between organizations (e.g., facebook third-party applications and the facebook connect function on third-party websites). Third, it has been recognized that social network information has strong potential for marketing purposes (e.g., for churn prediction [32] or for targeted advertisement [12]). In all of these areas lurks the risk of accidental or deliberate violations of user privacy. Several works address the privacy issue in social networks [8, 17], and propose mechanisms to preserve users' privacy [39, 9], or suggest the vulnerability of online social networks to different attacks [15].

In order to protect users' privacy, an established method is replacing their identities with random unique IDs, a process known as *anonymization*. However, recent works have shown methods that are able to infer the true user identities under certain conditions, by relying on side information [28, 3, 38]. We present a more detailed summary of the related work in this field in Section 2. Most of the works in this area focus on proposing *algorithms* and *methods* for de-anonymizing networks, tested on various real datasets of online networks [23, 27]. Papers in this category propose algorithms for either attacking *specific* users in publicly available network data and revealing their identity [3], or de-anonymizing a fraction of all users in a network [38]. A major challenge in all these scenarios is scalability. Recently, algorithms that are applicable for de-anonymizing large networks have also been introduced [28, 27].

What is still lacking in the literature is a thorough understanding of the conditions under which de-anonymization is feasible. We would like to be able to ascertain when a network's anonymity can be guaranteed, given the side information and computational resources available to an attacker. In this paper, we attempt to make a step in this direction. We study a challenging version (from the perspective of an attacker) of the de-anonymization problem, where the attacker has no side information about nodes in the network to be attacked other than network structure, specifically a correlated version of the edge set of that network obtained from other sources.

Contribution. To the best of our knowledge, ours is the first paper to pursue a theoretical treatment of network de-anonymization problem, and in particular, considering its feasibility for *large* networks. Our contributions are three-fold: We explore fundamental limits for de-anonymization regardless of the specific algorithm employed, and investigate the relationship between network parameters and the possibility of guaranteeing anonymity in such networks. Moreover, we introduce a mathematically tractable model that captures the notion of correlated networks, and uses the idea of graph sampling to control the structural similarity of two graphs. This model is based on random graphs, and can be viewed as a generalization of the classical automorphism group problem for random graphs [5, chapter 9]. Finally, we prove that a surprisingly simple and mild condition on the scaling of the expected degree with the number of nodes is sufficient for de-anonymization to be feasible, with strong implications on privacy.

The following important observation is behind our modeling approach: In most real cases, although nodes are anonymized in the released data of social networks, the structure of the graph is preserved, i.e., this is equivalent to having access to an unlabeled graph. We assume that an attacker has access to an auxiliary labeled network, in which user identities are known. Such a network could be obtained for example from public data, or inferred from other sources. This type of attack is also considered in [28].

To give a concrete example, we ask whether it would be safe for an academic institution to release a database of anonymized email or call logs, if an attacker has available to him a correlated but highly incomplete set of likely social links between the staff and students of that institution (e.g., by mining the public web site of groups, departments, and so on)? Could an attacker use this incomplete side information to reverse-engineer the anonymized identities in the database, and therefore the communication pattern of this university? More generally, most of us have many different online identities that are in different hands, and the social links in these different domains are likely not completely identical, but correlated.

It is clear that the availability of additional side information (e.g., class labels for users such as from demographic information, or richer link information such as directed interactions, time stamps) can only further benefit the attacker. Here, we assume that the attacker only has the graph structure for re-identification of nodes.

In this paper we explore the problem of approximate graph matching introduced above. We use the notion of *graph sampling* to develop a model of *similar* or *correlated* graphs. Graph sampling has been used in other contexts, e.g., as a way to estimate node and edge features from the network [35, 11], or to generate different snapshots of an observed network as samples from a hidden underlying graph [31]. The structural similarity we seek is achieved by sampling the two graphs from an underlying *generator* graph. Our key result is that under surprisingly mild conditions on the model parameters, depending on the extent of the overlap between the two graphs, it is possible to establish a perfect mapping between the nodes of the two graphs as the number of nodes grows large.

Our results for approximate graph matching not only exhibit the risk of a privacy breach in the release of even the most basic information about real networks (i.e., only anonymized users and their links), but can have useful applications as well. If matching is feasible, one can combine several "noisy" public (anonymized) versions of social networks obtained from different sources into a more precise, combined network. In another scenario, suppose we have the call graph between all the phone numbers in an organization, and the graph of email exchanges between email addresses in this same organization. One could then establish the correspondence between phone numbers and email addresses solely through the structure of the two social networks (which we expect to be similar but not exactly equal).

We should emphasize that this paper only addresses the *feasibility* of de-anonymization. This amounts to establishing that there exists a cost function over the two graphs, such that minimizing this function finds the correct matching with high probability. We do not address the computational complexity of this process. The recent work of Schmatikov and Narayanan [28] report success in de-anonymizing fairly large networks. However, their work focuses on heuristics for matching, which they evaluate over samples of real social networks, while our focus is to understand the boundaries of anonymity in terms of fundamental network properties.

The remainder of this paper is organized as follows. Section 2 briefly discusses related work. In Section 3, we formally define the de-anonymization problem, and introduce a mathematical model for approximate graph matching of large networks. Section 4 is the core of this paper where we prove that in our model, perfect matching is feasible under mild conditions on the expected degree of the graphs and on their similarity. Section 5 discusses numerical experiments using social network data to justify the assumptions in our model. Finally, Section 6 concludes the paper with a discussion of the implications of the result.

2. RELATED WORK

We briefly summarize related work in network de-anonymization and approximate graph matching. This can be categorized as follows: 1) papers relevant to network modeling with direct application for de-anonymizing users in social networks, 2) papers in the area of graph isomorphism and approximate graph matching, mostly from applications in machine learning and pattern recognition problems.

In the first category, in their recent work [28], Narayanan and Shmatikov propose a novel algorithm for de-anonymizing social networks, based purely on network topology. Their algorithm uses the structural similarity of a target and an auxiliary network. Although the goal and problem definition of our contribution is similar to theirs, we seek insights into the fundamental conditions for de-anonymization to be feasible, while they demonstrate the effectiveness of de-anonymization of a real social network using heuristics.

Backstrom et al. introduce active and passive attacks for de-anonymization of social networks [3]. They show how a target users can be identified in a very large network by identifying a neighborhood subgraph around the user using only network structure. They investigate the effectiveness of these attacks both theoretically and empirically. A limitation of active attacks is the necessity of creating fake (dummy) nodes in the social network before its release (which is of course a strong limitation in practice), while passive attacks are capable of re-identifying only a limited number of users, but without the need for fake nodes. Thus, the method works best for de-anonymization of *specific* users within the network, or a small fraction of all users. A similar attack model is analyzed in [10], where an attacker is allowed to issue queries that reveal a k-hop subgraph around a target node; they analyze the privacy risk to the identity of the target node and to the presence of specific links, both using random graph models and real data.

Finally, a novel de-anonymization attack is introduced by Wondracek et al. [38] that exploits group membership information available on social networking sites. They show that information about the group memberships of a user is often sufficient to uniquely identify this user, or at least to significantly reduce the set of possible candidates, and assess the feasibility of the attack both theoretically and empirically.

In the second category, several works propose different techniques for exact and approximate graph matching, mostly in image processing and pattern recognition. In [30], Cordella et al. propose a so called VF algorithm as a solution for *exact* subgraph matching, or subgraph isomorphism, exhibiting less complexity compared to the famous Ullmann backtracking algorithm [37]. In [36], Tian and Patel suggest an approximate graph matching tool (TALE) through a novel indexing method that incorporates graph structural information in a hybrid index structure. Although the structural information for matching graphs is used, the approximate matching problem in such cases is generally defined as node mismatches or inconsistencies in node attributes, rather than structural difference (in edges) as in our case.

Other works in this area propose different methods such as random walks on graphs [7], using EM algorithm and singular value decomposition [22], and the edit-distance criterion for approximate matching different types of graphs [34, 26]. Because of the complexity of matrix manipulation and computation of probability distributions, such methods are not feasible for application to very large networks.

Our contribution to this existing body of work is to introduce a mathematically tractable, parsimonious model for the problem of matching two similar graphs, and to derive asymptotic bounds in terms of fundamental parameters for network anonymity, independently of specific algorithms.

3. PROBLEM DEFINITION AND MODEL

We define the problem of matching the vertex sets of two graphs, and introduce the $G(n, p; s)$ random graph model, which generates two similar graphs $G_{1,2}$ over the same vertex set. As mentioned before, the goal is to match the vertices of two unlabeled graphs whose edge sets are correlated but not necessarily equal. The motivation for our model is its parsimony and symmetric structure, ingredients for its mathematical tractability.

The model assumes that the observed networks $G_{1,2}$ are incomplete manifestations of a true underlying network G of relationships. For example, the edges of G might represent the true relationships between a set of people, while $G_{1,2}$ capture the observable interactions between these people, such as communications (email, phone calls, proximity, and so on), or "friend"-relationships in a social network. $G_{1,2}$ might alternatively represent observations of the same network at different points in time.

To elaborate on this, let $G = (V, E)$ be a generator graph with vertex set V and edge set E. We assume here that G is an Erdös-Rényi random graph $G(n, p)$ with n nodes, where every edge exists with identical probability p, independently of all the other edges. For a fixed realization of $G = G(n, p)$, we generate two graphs $G_{1,2} = (V, E_{1,2})$ by sampling the vertex set E twice. More precisely, each edge $e \in E$ is in the edge set of $E_{1,2}$ with probability s, independently of everything else. As a result, the sample graphs $G_{1,2}$ are themselves Erdös-Rényi random graph $G(n, ps)$, but their edge sets are correlated, in that the existence of an edge in E_1 implies that the existence of this edge in E_2 is more likely than unconditionally (provided $p < 1$ and $s > 0$) (see Fig. 1). The $G(n, p)$ model has been widely used in the study of complex and social networks [4, 14, 29, 2], which makes it a plausible candidate for the study of the approximate matching problem.

Our goal is to determine whether it is possible to find the correct mapping between the nodes of G_1 and G_2, assuming we only see unlabeled versions of these two graphs (and without access to the generator G). This is equivalent to the assumption that the two graphs have different vertex label sets that contain no information about the graphs, such as random labels allocated in an anonymization procedure. Using this model, our problem can be viewed as the generalization of the classical automorphism group problem in random graphs. We discuss this and also the effect of the choice of other graph models at the end of Section 4 and also in Section 6.

We formally define the graph matching problem as follows. We assume that $G_{1,2}$ are only available in unlabeled form (or equivalently, with two arbitrary and unknown sets of labels). Let π denote a permutation on V, i.e., one way of mapping vertices from G_1 onto G_2. The number of such permutations is $n!$. The identity permutation, denoted by π_0, is the correct mapping between the nodes of G_1 and G_2. We seek an error function over the set of permutations, which succeeds if it is uniquely minimized by π_0.

Therefore, to solve the matching problem, we are interested to show the following:

Among all possible permutations between the two vertex sets, the identity permutation π_0 is the permutation that minimizes an error function, giving the node matching between the two graphs.

The error function should measure to what extent the structures of graphs G_1 and G_2 resemble each other under a given permutation. The structural difference can be viewed as the difference between the corresponding edge sets. This idea has also been investigated in the field of pattern recognition where the *edge-consistency* of two graph patterns (in matching a data graph to a model graph) is used to obtain the correspondence errors [26, 22].

We introduce the error measure for edge-inconsistency, considering only the structures of two graphs $G_1(V, E_1)$ and $G_2(V, E_2)$. The matching error Δ can be generally defined as

$$\Delta_\pi = \sum_{e \in E_1} \mathbf{1}_{\{\pi(e) \notin E_2\}} + \sum_{e \in E_2} \mathbf{1}_{\{\pi^{-1}(e) \notin E_1\}}, \qquad (1)$$

where $\mathbf{1}_{\{A\}}$ denotes the indicator function. In other words, permutation π defines a mapping between the nodes of G_1 and G_2, and Δ counts the number of edges that exist in one graph with the corresponding edges not existing in the other graph under matching π. This is the simplest error function that can be assumed for such a setting when comparing the structures of two graphs. While this cost function is not necessarily optimal (depending on the graph model) nor computationally efficient, it lends itself to probablistic analysis. Specifically, we prove below that if the sampling probability s is beyond some threshold, as n grows large, the identity permutation π_0 minimizes the error function (1).

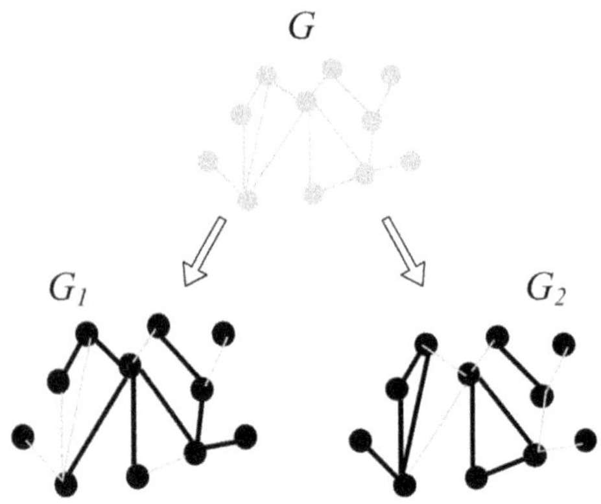

Figure 1: Sampling process applied to the underlying graph G, resulting in the two sampled graphs G_1 and G_2 to be matched.

We reiterate that we do not address the algorithmic aspects of de-anonymization, including the computational complexity of enumerating all mappings and computing their error. Instead, we next show conditions on the model parameters such that minimizing the error function is almost surely equivalent to identifying the correct mapping using only the structures of the two sampled graphs, i.e., we show that *de-anonymization is feasible*, and it is not possible to guarantee anonymity.

4. CONDITIONS FOR PERFECT MATCHING

Following the model introduced in Section 3, we state the main theorem of this paper, followed by its proof.

THEOREM 4.1. *For the $G(n,p;s)$ matching problem with $s = \omega(1/n)$ and $p \to 0$, if*

$$ps\,\frac{s^2}{2-s} = 8\frac{\log n}{n} + \omega(n^{-1}), \tag{2}$$

then the identity permutation π_0 minimizes the error criterion (1) *a.a.s*[1], *yielding perfect matching of the vertex sets of G_1 and G_2.* [2]

PROOF. We denote by Δ_0 the error induced by the identity permutation and Δ_π the error induced by the permutation π. Figure 2 depicts two possible mappings between the same G_1 and G_2 shown in Figure 1 corresponding to the identity mapping π_0 and a permutation π_2 (in which all nodes are fixed except two) respectively, together with their error.

To show the result, we define Π_k on V as the set of all permutations that fix $n-k$ nodes and permute k nodes, calling them an order-k permutation. The number of such permutations, referred to as "rencontre numbers", is as follows [33]:

$$|\Pi_k| = R(n, n-k) = \binom{n}{k} \cdot (!k), \tag{3}$$

where $!k$ is the subfactorial of k, denoting the number of permutations of k objects in which no object appears in its natural place. It is easily verified that $R(n, n-k)$ can be upper-bounded as follows:

$$|\Pi_k| = \binom{n}{k} \cdot (!k) \leq \binom{n}{k} \cdot \left(\frac{k!}{2}\right) \leq n^k. \tag{4}$$

The random variables introduced below are indexed by n, which we omit unless required by the context. We define

$$S_k = \sum_{\pi \in \Pi_k} \mathbf{1}_{\{\Delta_\pi \leq \Delta_0\}}.$$

S_k counts the number of order-k permutations for which the number of matching errors is at most that of the identity permutation. Thus, $S = \sum_{k=2}^{n} S_k$ is the total number of false matches. The expected number of errors can be computed as:

$$\begin{aligned} \mathsf{E}[S] &= \sum_{k=2}^{n} \mathsf{E}[S_k] = \sum_{k=2}^{n} \sum_{\pi \in \Pi_k} \mathsf{E}\left[\mathbf{1}_{\{\Delta_\pi \leq \Delta_0\}}\right] \\ &= \sum_{k=2}^{n} \sum_{\pi \in \Pi_k} \mathsf{P}\{\Delta_\pi - \Delta_0 \leq 0\}, \end{aligned}$$

where the expectation is over $G(n,p;s)$.

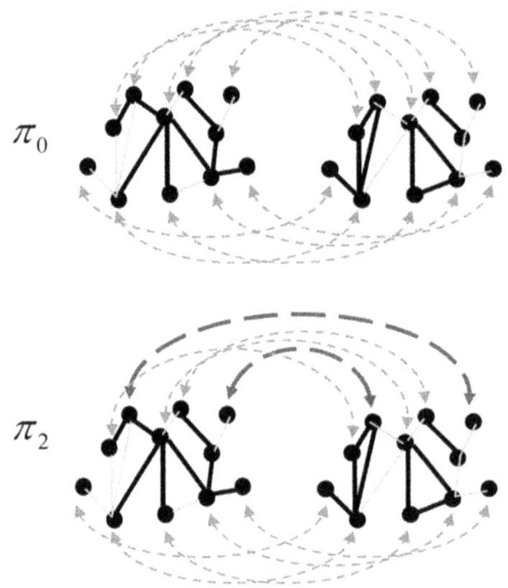

Figure 2: The identity permutation π_0 versus a permutation $\pi_2 \in \Pi_2$ that mismatches $k = 2$ vertices for mapping G_1 to G_2. The error in each case corresponds to the number of edges in one graph with the mapped edge not existing in the other graph. Thus, $\Delta_0 = 8$ and $\Delta_{\pi_2} = 10$, where Δ_0 is the edge difference as a result of the sampling process, and Δ_{π_2} is induced by both the sampling process and the wrong mapping of two nodes in π_2.

S counts the total number of non-identity permutations that minimize the error, and we need to show that with high probability no such permutations exist. By the First Moment Method (following Markov's inequality), since S is a non-negative integer-valued random variable, to show that $\mathsf{P}\{S = 0\} \to 1$, it suffices to show that $E[S] \to 0$.

Using this method and substituting (4) in the above, it is then sufficient to show that

$$\mathsf{E}[S] \leq \sum_{k=2}^{n} n^k \max_{\pi \in \Pi_k} \mathsf{P}\{\Delta_\pi - \Delta_0 \leq 0\} \to 0. \tag{5}$$

[1] a.a.s: asymptotically almost surely, i.e., with probability going to 1 as the number of nodes n goes to infinity. In general, *asymptotic* refers to the behavior for $n \to \infty$.

[2] We use the standard asymptotic notation (o, O, ω, Ω, and θ).

We bound the error probability for a fixed order-k permutation π, i.e., we bound the probability term in (5). For permutation π, let V_π be the set of vertices for which $v \neq \pi(v)$, and let $E_\pi = V_\pi \times V$, i.e., the set of possible edges between one or two vertices mismatched under π. Note that every edge satisfying $e \neq \pi(e)$ is in E_π. The inverse is not true, because transpositions in π (a pair (u, v) such that $\pi(u) = v$ and $\pi(v) = u$) induce invariant edges. The cardinality e_k of E_π is

$$e_k = |E_\pi| = \binom{k}{2} + k(n-k),$$

where the first term is the number of unordered node pairs both in V_π, and the second term is the number of unordered node pairs with one node in V_π.

As every edge e in the complement of E_π (i.e., in $(V \times V) - E_\pi$) is by definition invariant under π, they contribute equally to Δ_0 and Δ_π. Therefore, we can write $\Delta_\pi - \Delta_0 = X_\pi - Y_\pi$, where

$$\begin{aligned} X_\pi &= \sum_{e \in E_\pi} |\mathbf{1}_{\{e \in E_\pi^1\}} - \mathbf{1}_{\{\pi(e) \in E_\pi^2\}}|, \\ Y_\pi &= \sum_{e \in E_\pi} |\mathbf{1}_{\{e \in E_\pi^1\}} - \mathbf{1}_{\{e \in E_\pi^2\}}|, \end{aligned} \quad (6)$$

with $E_\pi^{1,2} = E_\pi \cap E(G_{1,2})$, i.e., the set of edges in $G_{1,2}$ incident to at least one mismatched vertex. Here, Y_π is the number of errors for the identity permutation within the set E_π, i.e., the number of sampling errors within E_π. Note that X_π and Y_π are not independent, because they are functions of the same random sets $E_\pi^{1,2}$.

Y_π counts the number of edges in E_π that are sampled in only one of $G_{1,2}$, i.e., the number of sampling errors under the identity permutation. The probability for each possible edge to be in $E(G)$ and exactly one of $G_{1,2}$ is $2ps(1-s)$. Thus Y_π is binomial with probability $2ps(1-s)$.

For X_π, we need to proceed more carefully. Assume π has $\phi \geq 0$ transpositions. First, note that each transposition in π induces one invariant edge $e = \pi(e) = \pi^{-1}(e)$ in E_π (such an edge contributes to X_π with probability $2ps(1-s)$).

The remaining $e_k - \phi$ edges are not invariant under π. Each pair of such edges $(e, \pi(e))$ contributes 1 to X_π if $e \in G_1$ and $\pi(e) \notin G_2$ or vice versa (cf. (6)). The probability for exactly one of two *different* edges in E_π to be sampled is $2ps(1-ps)$. Note that the terms in (6) are dependent, because conditional on $|\mathbf{1}_{\{e \in E_\pi^1\}} - \mathbf{1}_{\{\pi(e) \in E_\pi^2\}}| = 1$, at least one of e or $\pi(e)$ is present in the generator G. Thus, the conditional probability of an adjacent pair (either $(\pi^{-1}(e), e)$ or $(\pi(e), \pi(\pi(e)))$ contributing 1 to (6) is $s(1-ps)$. We conservatively ignore this positive correlation and stochastically lower-bound X_π by assuming that each pair of edges $(e, \pi(e))$ contributes an i.i.d. Bernoulli with parameter $2ps(1-ps)$ to (6).

Thus, X_π is stochastically lower-bounded by the sum of two independent binomials $\mathsf{Bi}(e_k - \phi, 2ps(1-ps)) + \mathsf{Bi}(\phi, 2ps(1-s))$, where ϕ is the number of transpositions in π. By definition, a transposition can occur only between two vertices that are both in V_π. Hence, $\phi \leq \lfloor k/2 \rfloor \leq k/2$.

Thus, we have

$$X_\pi \overset{(stoch.)}{\geq} \mathsf{Bi}(e_k - \lfloor k/2 \rfloor, 2ps(1-ps)) \quad (7)$$

$$Y_\pi \sim \mathsf{Bi}(e_k, 2ps(1-s)). \quad (8)$$

We upper-bound the probability of the event $\{X_\pi - Y_\pi \leq 0\}$ using the following lemma, which holds regardless of dependence between X_π and Y_π:

LEMMA 4.1. *Let X_1 and X_2 be two binomial random variables with means λ_1 and λ_2, where $\lambda_2 > \lambda_1$. Then,*

$$P\{X_2 - X_1 \leq 0\} \leq 2\exp\left(-\frac{1}{8}\frac{(\lambda_2 - \lambda_1)^2}{\lambda_2 + \lambda_1}\right). \quad (9)$$

PROOF OF LEMMA. Let X_1 and X_2 be two binomial random variables with means λ_1 and λ_2. The probability of the event $\{X_2 - X_1 \leq 0\}$ can be upper-bounded as follows:

$$\mathsf{P}\{X_2 - X_1 \leq 0\} \leq \mathsf{P}\{X_1 \geq x\} + \mathsf{P}\{X_2 \leq x\}, \quad (10)$$

for any x.

We now find an upper-bound for the right-hand side of (10). We use the Chernoff bounds for the binomial random variables X_1 and X_2 using the following theorem [13]:

If $X \in \mathsf{Bi}(n, p)$ and $\lambda = np$, then,

$$P\{X > \lambda + t\} \leq \exp\left(-\frac{t^2}{2(\lambda + t/3)}\right), \quad t \geq 0; \quad (11)$$

$$P\{X < \lambda - t\} \leq \exp\left(-\frac{t^2}{2\lambda}\right), \quad t \geq 0. \quad (12)$$

We upper-bound $\mathsf{P}\{X_1 \geq x\}$ and $\mathsf{P}\{X_2 \leq x\}$ using (11) and (12) (for two arbitrary positive values of t_1 and t_2 respectively). We set $x = (\lambda_1 + \lambda_2)/2$, and thus $t_1 = t_2 = (\lambda_2 - \lambda_1)/2$. Using $\lambda_2 > \lambda_1$ allows to bound the two exponents as follows:

$$\begin{aligned} \mathsf{P}\{X_1 \geq x\} &\leq \exp\left(-\frac{1}{8}\frac{(\lambda_2 - \lambda_1)^2}{\lambda_1 + (\lambda_2 - \lambda_1)/6}\right) \\ &\leq \exp\left(-\frac{1}{8}\frac{(\lambda_2 - \lambda_1)^2}{\lambda_1 + \lambda_2}\right), \end{aligned} \quad (13)$$

and

$$\begin{aligned} \mathsf{P}\{X_2 \leq x\} &\leq \exp\left(-\frac{1}{8}\frac{(\lambda_2 - \lambda_1)^2}{\lambda_2}\right) \\ &\leq \exp\left(-\frac{1}{8}\frac{(\lambda_2 - \lambda_1)^2}{\lambda_1 + \lambda_2}\right). \end{aligned} \quad (14)$$

This completes the proof. □

Now let λ_π and λ_0 denote the means of X_π and Y_π respectively, with values,

$$\lambda_\pi = 2ps(1-ps)(e_k - k/2) \quad (15)$$

$$\lambda_0 = 2pse_k(1-s). \quad (16)$$

Since $0 \leq s \leq 1$, $2 \leq k \leq n$, and $e_k \simeq k(n - k/2)$, to satisfy $\lambda_\pi > \lambda_0$ we need to have,

$$\begin{aligned} 2ps(1-ps)(k(n-k/2) - k/2) &> 2psk(n-k/2)(1-s) \\ \Longrightarrow s &> \left(\tfrac{1-ps}{1-p}\right)\frac{1}{2n-k}, \end{aligned} \quad (17)$$

which will be satisfied for $s = \omega(1/n)$ and $p \to 0$.

Thus, using the above lemma, we obtain,

$$\mathsf{P}\{X_\pi - Y_\pi \leq 0\} \leq 2\exp\left(\underbrace{-\frac{1}{8}\frac{(\lambda_\pi - \lambda_0)^2}{\lambda_\pi + \lambda_0}}_{f(n,p,k)}\right). \quad (18)$$

Substituting (15) and (16) in (18) yields:

$$f(n,p,k) = \frac{1}{8}\frac{(2ps\,((e_k - k/2) - (e_k - e_k s)))^2}{2ps\,((e_k - k/2) + (e_k - e_k s))}$$
$$= \frac{ps}{4}\frac{((k/2)\,((2n-k)s-1))^2}{(k/2)\,((2n-k)(2-s)-1)}$$

For $s = \omega(1/n)$ we have $(2n-k)s = \omega(1)$. Thus,

$$f(n,p,k) \simeq \frac{ps}{4}\frac{(k/2)\,((2n-k)s)^2}{(2n-k)(2-s)}$$
$$\simeq \frac{ps}{4}\frac{s^2}{2-s}k\,(n-k/2)\,. \qquad (19)$$

Using (4), (5), and (19), we have,

$$\mathsf{E}[S] \leq 2\sum_{k=2}^{n} n^k \cdot \exp(-f(n,p,k))$$
$$\stackrel{(a)}{\simeq} 2\sum_{k=2}^{n} n^k \exp\left(-k\left(n-\frac{k}{2}\right)\frac{ps}{4}\cdot\frac{s^2}{2-s}\right)$$
$$\stackrel{(b)}{\leq} 2\sum_{k=2}^{\infty} \exp\left(k\left(\log n - \frac{nps}{8}\cdot\frac{s^2}{2-s}\right)\right), \qquad (20)$$

where (a) is derived using (19), and (b) uses $k \leq n$. The geometric series goes to zero if the first term goes to zero, which is implied by the condition in the statement of the theorem. This completes the proof. □

A more direct approach to prove the result would be to try to condition on a property of the underlying graph G and/or of $G_{1,2}$ that is both asymptotically almost sure, and for which one could show that uniformly over all permutations π, the number of errors is higher than for the identity π_0. It is difficult to identify such a property that would make the second part of the problem tractable. Instead, we show the result using a method commonly employed in the random graph literature [5, 13], which allows us to analyze a fixed permutation π over the full probability space $G(n,p;s)$.

A remarkable aspect of our result is that for fixed similarity parameter s, the condition is $ps = 8c\log n/n$ for some $c(s) > 1$. As expected, $c(s) = (2-s)/s^2$ is monotonically decreasing in $(0,1)$, and $c(1) = 1$. Thus, for an overall edge sampling probability ps of a bit larger than $8\log n/n$, with high probability the identity permutation minimizes the error function and yields the correct mapping. Note that the threshold for connectivity of $G_{1,2} = G(n,ps)$ (and for the disappearance of isolated vertices) is $ps = \log n/n$ [5, 13]. It is obvious that it is impossible to perfectly match a pair of graphs $G_{1,2}$ when at least one of them possesses more than one isolated vertex (as these necessarily give rise to multiple permutations with equal error counts). Therefore, $ps = \log n/n$ is a lower bound for zero-error graph matching using any technique (i.e., any cost function). Our bound for $G(n,p;s)$ matching is therefore tight, up to a constant function of s.

For the case of $s = 1$, the approximate graph matching problem is equivalent to the classical automorphism group problem for random graphs [5]. Specifically, it is known that $G(n,p)$ is asymmetric (has an automorphism group of size one) for $p = \log n/n + \omega(1)$. This suggests that the constant $c(s)$ in our result can be improved upon through more refined bounding techniques. Indeed, we use relatively loose bounds in several places: in particular, we underestimate the mean of X_π quite significantly by ignoring the positive correlation (within each cycle of π) in the terms of (6); also, we assume the worst-case dependence between X_π and Y_π in (10), even though they are in reality positively correlated through the generator G. These bounds are sufficient to show the asymptotic result to within a constant, but more precise techniques akin to those used to show the classical automorphism result may allow to go further. Another obvious extension of our work would employ other generator graph structures such as random regular graphs, small world models, or scale free graphs.

5. NUMERICAL EXPERIMENTS

To be mathematically tractable and parsimonious, our model inevitably embodies several strong assumptions: (i) the underlying graph is a $G = G(n,p)$ random graph, and the edge sets of the "visible" graphs $G_{1,2}$ are sampled (ii) independently and (iii) with identical probability s from G. Despite these assumptions, we believe that our model and our result on anonymity conditions have implications for real networks and scenarios. Although we are unable to explore the validity of our assumptions in full generality, we wish at least to provide some evidence to justify them. First, it is fairly clear that the underlying graph of a social network would possess a structure very different from a $G(n,p)$, as demonstrated in many studies illustrating fascinating properties such as skewed degree distributions and the small-world effect. However, we conjecture that de-anonymizing two networks sampled from a random graph is harder than more "structured" networks. A random graph is in some sense "maximally uniform", and we therefore believe that for other, more realistic hidden graphs G, de-anonymization might in fact be possible under even weaker conditions. This is of course a promising and fascinating area for further research. Second, we consider de-anonymization successful if the error function $\Delta(.)$ has a unique minimum at π_0. We argue that this function is not too sensitive to a non-uniform sampling process over the edge set (i.e., assuming each edge e is sampled with its own sampling rate $s(e)$), provided the sampling process is similar in both graphs, and uncorrelated across edges. This is because the impact of this non-uniformity on X_0 and X_π above would cancel out to a certain extent. On the other hand, if the sampling process to obtain the two samples G_1 and G_2 were very different, then this could make de-anonymization much harder. For example, if the sampling rate over some subset of vertices were atypically large in G_1 compared to the rest, but atypically large for a *different* subset in G_2, then these two high-rate subsets would be likely to be falsely matched. Therefore, it appears that de-anonymization would be quite sensitive to such differences in the sampling process for G_1 and G_2.

While we have not quantified the above argument, it did lead us to explore the stability of the sampling process through some numerical experiments. In order to motivate and illustrate the concept of *similarity* between networks, and also verify the assumption of *independence* in sampling the edges, we present an example of a real social network: an email graph, in which nodes represent email addresses and edges represent message exchanges. The network evolves in time through the observation of new messages that are exchanged.

We consider a dataset of email messages collected at the mail server of EPFL. The dataset includes logs of email exchanges among users on a weekly basis for a period of 75 weeks. In our dataset, the email exchanges *among EPFL users* is considered (i.e., internal EPFL network). The dataset includes snapshots of the network aggregated by week, such that timestamps are in the timescale of weeks (i.e., all messages sent in a particular week have the same timestamp). Using such dataset, we construct the email network of each week for the internal EPFL network.

Having introduced the above, we investigate the similarity between different snapshots of the network, each being a sample of an underlying hidden email network. Note that in order to map real

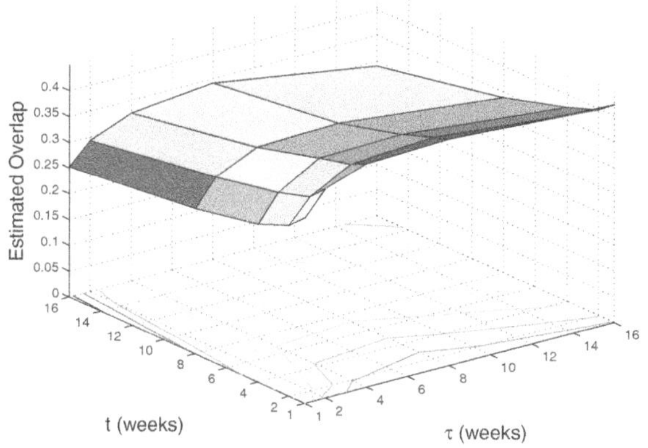

Figure 3: Estimated average edge overlap among overlapped nodes for EPFL internal network, as a function of window size and distance.

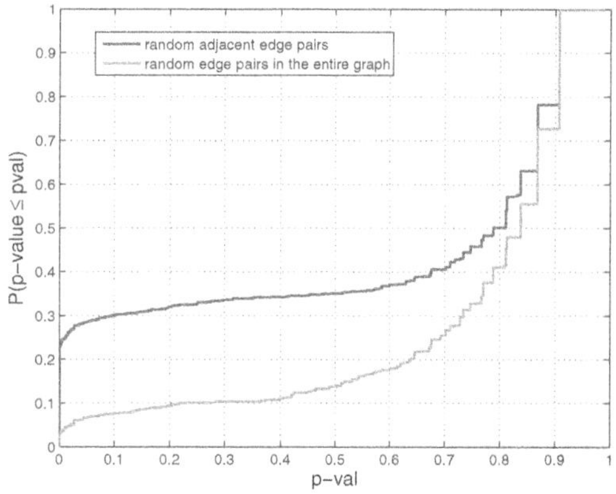

Figure 4: The CDF of the p-values of the Pearson's Chi-Square test for independence, for 1) random adjacent edge pairs (top curve), 2) random edge pairs in the entire graph (bottom curve). Using $\alpha = 0.05$, the test verifies the statistical equivalence of edge pairs in the EPFL dataset.

data to our sampling model, the existence of a hidden underlying graph (including all possible email exchanges over all times) is inevitable - to which we do not have access. However, measuring the amount of *edge overlap* between different snapshots gives us an estimation of the similarity degree between different network samples, or whether the graphs are the outcome of similar sampling processes. Also, since two network snapshots do not contain the same number of nodes necessarily, we estimate the edge overlap as *the proportion of edges among overlapped nodes that exist in both graphs*.

To accomplish the above, we need to pick two networks to be compared. We randomly choose a starting timestamp t_s (week number) in the entire dataset, and construct the first graph starting from t_s accumulated over a window size of τ weeks. For the second graph, we build it starting from timestamp $t_s+\tau+t-1$, again accumulated over a window size of τ, where t denotes the time distance between the two graphs (in weeks). In other words, τ corresponds to the density of the graph (the larger it is, the denser the graph will be), and t implies the time distance between different samples. As an example, $\tau = 1, t = 1$ corresponds to the email network of two consecutive snapshots (each consisting of email exchanges over a one-week period), whereas $\tau = 2, t = 3$ corresponds to two graphs, each consisting of email exchanges over a period of $\tau = 2$ weeks, with a time distance of $t = 3$ weeks. Finally, for each value of τ and t, we repeat the random choice of the networks 30 times and compute the average.

Figure 3 depicts the estimated average edge overlap as a function of the windows size and time distance. It can be observed that the estimated edge overlap is quite significant, and it also exhibits a small increase as τ increases and t decreases, which matches intuition since it is expected that two larger and denser networks have more overlap, and as the samples are farther apart the overlap decreases. However, this change is small over a wide span of the density and distance values. Thus, the graph similarity is fairly robust over different densities and distances. The experiment shows that two graphs sampled from a hidden underlying graph (a hidden overall email network in this case) are similar in structure (even if the sampling processes are non-uniform), with the sampling process being quite stable over different intervals.

Finally, we verify the assumption of independent edge sampling in our model, through looking at the correlation among the edges. In general, the emergence of an edge might correlate with the existence of other edges. In order to investigate how far the independence assumption is from reality, we examine edge correlation in the EPFL internal network. To do so, we choose a random pair of edges from the final accumulated graph (i.e., $\tau = 75$), and examine their joint appearance in 75 weekly snapshots. We use the Chi-Square test for independence to determine whether there is a significant relationship between the appearance of the two edges. We assume a null hypothesis that two randomly chosen edges e_1 and e_2 appear independently, and use the Pearson χ^2 test to decide whether we should reject the null hypothesis, separately for each set of 75 edge pair appearances. We compute the χ^2 test statistics of each sample set of 75 weeks as $X^2 = \sum \frac{(O_{i,j}-E_{i,j})^2}{E_{i,j}}$, $i, j = 0, 1$, where i denotes the existence (1) or non-existence (0) mode of e_1 (similarly $j = 0, 1$ for e_2), $O_{i,j}$ is the observed frequency count of e_1 at mode i and e_2 at mode j, and $E_{i,j} = n_i * n_j/n$, n_i being the total number of sampled observations of e_1 at mode i (similarly n_j for e_2 at mode j) and n being the total number of samples (75). The p-value is calculated as $P\left\{X^2 \leq \chi^2(1)\right\}$, where $\chi^2(1)$ is a Chi-Square random variable with one degree of freedom, as the number of bins for each categorial variable equals 2. We derive the p-value of the test and reject the independence hypothesis if the p-value is smaller than the significance level ($\alpha = 0.05$ in our tests). Repeating this for a large number of random edge pairs (752 in our experiments), we find that 93% of the edge pairs are statistically indistinguishable (p-value $> \alpha = 0.05$).

To strengthen our test even further, we do the same experiment above, by choosing random pairs of *adjacent* edges - i.e., edges incident to the same node - thinking that such edges might express a high correlation. We find that even in this case, most edge pairs (72%) are statistically independent. Figure 4 depicts the CDF of p-values found for each selected pair over 75 weeks, for both experiments. The plot clearly shows that in most cases, p-value is greater than α, as mentioned above.

Finally, we repeat the above experiments for triple edges , i.e. choosing three random edges in the accumulated graph, the null hypothesis being that three randomly chosen edges e_1, e_2 and e_3 appear independently. Again, we consider two cases, one where the edges are chosen randomly in the entire graph, and the other further correlated version where the edges are sampled from the set of 3-chains in the graph, i.e. paths of length 3. Figure 5 depicts the CDF of the p-values for each selected triple over 75 weeks, for

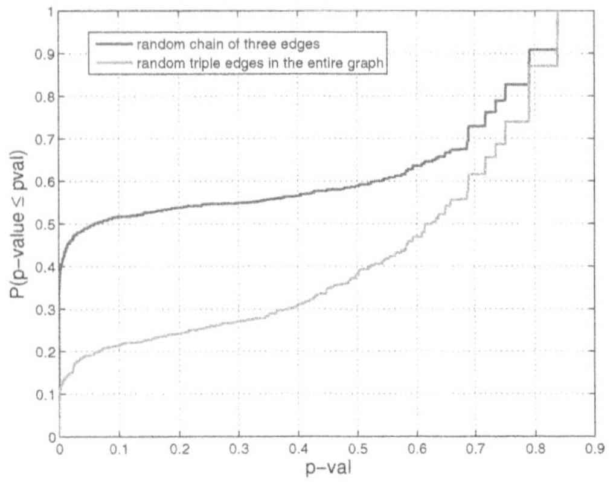

Figure 5: The CDF of the p-values of the Pearson's Chi-Square test for independence, for 1) random chain of three edges (top curve), 2) random triple edges in the entire graph (bottom curve). Using $\alpha = 0.05$, the test verifies the statistical equivalence of triple edges in the EPFL dataset.

both experiments, repeated 1000 times. It is observed that 81% of the random triple edges are independent. Further, for the correlated chain of edges, we observe that 50% of the random 3-chains are statistically indistinguishable. Further experiments show that as the number of randomly chosen edges increases, there will be a higher dependence for their joint appearance, as expected.

Our results suggest that the independence assumption clearly does not hold generally, but many small sets of edges do behave independently. To what extent the i.i.d. assumption built into our model is realistic, in the sense that it would correctly predict the boundary of privacy in real networks, is a subject of further investigation.

6. DISCUSSION AND CONCLUSION

In this paper, we considered the privacy issue in social networks and investigated the possibility of de-anonymization from a mathematical perspective. We defined the problem in the context of approximate graph matching, with the goal of finding the correct mapping between the node sets of two structurally similar graphs. Using ideas from graph sampling in modeling evolution of networks, we proposed a probabilistic model to derive two sampled versions of an underlying graph as "noisy" versions of the networks to be matched. Elaborating our model for the case of random graphs, we proved that using the simplest matching criterion based only on network topology, a perfect matching between the nodes can be established with high probability as the network size grows large, under simple conditions for the sampling process. More specifically, we proved that a surprisingly mild condition on the scaling of the expected degree with the number of nodes is sufficient for de-anonymization to be feasible. For this, we expressed lower bounds for the sampling probability, or more intuitively, the extent of overlap in the edges of two graphs, so that it yields perfect matching.

Two conditions in our theorem are $s = \omega(1/n)$ and $ps \to 0$. How these parameters relate to real networks is of course a crucial and interesting question. Social networks tend to be sparse ($p \to 0$), and a reasonable assumption may be to assume a fixed average node degree ($p = c/n$), as the number of contacts is usually the result of local interactions that should not be influenced by the rest of the network[3]. The scaling of s is more debatable, as it depends on the nature of the two networks. If G_1 and G_2 capture the social interactions between a set of people using different methods (e.g., email and phone calls), then it would make sense to postulate a constant s independent of the size of the network, as the choice of method (i.e., generating a link) would be a purely local one, and therefore not influenced by the rest of the network. However, more cross-domain data should be studied to verify this.

Our result shows that given a specific cost function $\Delta(.)$, a pair of correlated graphs can be perfectly matched under certain conditions. An interesting question would be the converse: can we find conditions such that no cost function could give a match? In the $G(n, p; s)$ model, it is straightforward to show such a converse of the form $ps = o(\log n/n)$, as alluded to before. In this case, G_1 and G_2 would have isolated vertices a.a.s., and obviously no method would be able to determine the correct matching among these. More precise converses, as well as variations of our model (e.g., assuming other generator graphs G) are the topic of future work.

Our work implies the feasibility of de-anonymization of a target network by using the structural similarity of a known auxiliary network, and raises privacy concerns about sharing the simplest topological information of users with partners and third-party applications. One consequence of our work might be guidelines on how to release or share only sampled versions of networks, by enforcing the sparsity constraint to guarantee anonymity. This would be promising provided such a thinned-out network would still provide enough information for the task at hand.

In future, we intend to generalize our approach to a broader class of graphs. As discussed above, we conjecture that in some sense, a random graph as the generator G may be more difficult than a more "structured" graph. On the other hand, the i.i.d. sampling process in our model is an idealistic assumption, and the impact of relaxing it should be explored. Finally, and perhaps most importantly, while this paper proves the *existence* of the perfect matching using the proposed error function, the algorithmic complexity of searching in such a vast space is still an open problem.

Acknowledgments

We are indebted to Mohamed Kafsi and Patrick Thiran for fruitful discussions and feedback on a draft of the manuscript. We gratefully acknowledge financial support for this project from the Swiss National Science Foundation (SNSF).

7. REFERENCES

[1] AOL Search Data Scandal. http://en.wikipedia.org/wiki/AOL_search_data_scandal.

[2] W. Aiello, F. Chung, and L. Lu. A Random Graph Model for Massive Graphs. In *STOC '00*, pages 171–180, 2000.

[3] L. Backstrom, C. Dwork, and J. Kleinberg. Wherefore Art Thou R3579X?: Anonymized Social Networks, Hidden Patterns, and Structural Steganography. In *WWW '07*, pages 181–190, 2007.

[3]Note however that recent work on network densification [21] observes a dependence of the form $p = cn^{\alpha-2}$, for some $\alpha > 1$, i.e., an average degree that grows as $n^{\alpha-1}$ with the size of the network. While the underlying causes of densification are still being debated [31], it is still the case that $p \to 0$. Note that for fixed s, a network densifying in this way would always be non-anonymous, as $n^{\alpha-2} = \omega(\log n/n)$.

[4] S. Boccaletti, V. Latora, Y. Moreno, M. Chavez, and D.-U. Hwang. Complex Networks: Structure and Dynamics. *Physics Reports*, 424(4-5):175–308, 2006.

[5] B. Bollobas. *Random Graphs (2nd edition)*. Cambridge University Press, 2001.

[6] A. Chaintreau, P. Hui, J. Crowcroft, C. Diot, R. Gass, and J. Scott. Impact of Human Mobility on Opportunistic Forwarding Algorithms. *IEEE Transactions on Mobile Computing*, 6:606–620, 2007.

[7] M. Gori, M. Maggini, and L. Sarti. Exact and Approximate Graph Matching Using Random Walks. *IEEE Trans. Pattern Anal. Mach. Intell.*, 27(7):1100–1111, 2005.

[8] R. Gross and A. Acquisti. Information Revelation and Privacy in Online Social Networks. In *WPES '05: Proceedings of the 2005 ACM workshop on Privacy in the electronic society*, pages 71–80, 2005.

[9] S. Guha, K. Tang, and P. Francis. NOYB: Privacy in Online Social Networks. In *WOSN'08: Workshop on Online Social Networks*, 2008.

[10] M. Hay, G. Miklau, D. Jensen, D. Towsley, and C. Li. Resisting Structural Re-Identification in Anonymized Networks. *VLDB Journal*, 19(6), December 2010.

[11] M. R. Henzinger, A. Heydon, M. Mitzenmacher, and M. Najork. On Near-Uniform URL Sampling. In *Proceedings of the 9th international World Wide Web conference on Computer networks*, pages 295–308, 2000.

[12] S. Hill, F. Provost, and C. Volinsky. Network-based Marketing: Identifying Likely Adopters via Consumer Networks. *Statistical Science*, 21:256–276, 2006.

[13] S. Janson, T. Łuczak, and A. Ruciński. *Random Graphs*. Wiley, 2000.

[14] B. Karrer and M. E. J. Newman. Random Graph Models for Directed Acyclic Networks. *Physical review. E*, 2009.

[15] A. Korolova, R. Motwani, S. U. Nabar, and Y. Xu. Link Privacy in Social Networks. In *CIKM '08: Proceeding of the 17th ACM conference on Information and knowledge management*, pages 289–298, 2008.

[16] G. Kossinets, J. Kleinberg, and D. Watts. The Structure of Information Pathways in a Social Communication Network. In *KDD '08*, pages 435–443, 2008.

[17] B. Krishnamurthy and C. Willis. Characterizing Privacy in Online Social Networks. In *WOSN'08: Workshop on Online Social Networks*, 2008.

[18] J. Leskovec, L. Backstrom, and J. Kleinberg. Meme-Tracking and the Dynamics of the News Cycle. In *KDD '09*, pages 497–506, 2009.

[19] J. Leskovec, D. Chakrabarti, J. Kleinberg, C. Faloutsos, and Z. Ghahramani. Kronecker Graphs: An Approach to Modeling Networks. *J. Mach. Learn. Res.*, 11:985–1042, 2010.

[20] J. Leskovec, D. Huttenlocher, and J. Kleinberg. Predicting Positive and Negative Links in Online Social Networks. In *WWW '10*, pages 641–650, 2010.

[21] J. Leskovec, J. Kleinberg, and C. Faloutsos. Graphs over Time: Densification Laws, Shrinking Diameters and Possible Explanations. In *KDD '05*, pages 177–187, 2005.

[22] B. Luo and E. R. Hancock. Structural Graph Matching Using the EM Algorithm and Singular Value Decomposition. *IEEE Trans. Pattern Anal. Mach. Intell.*, 23(10):1120–1136, 2001.

[23] D. Martin and A. Schulman. Deanonymizing Users of the SafeWeb Anonymizing Service. In *Proceedings of the 11th USENIX Security Symposium*, pages 123–137, 2002.

[24] A. Mislove, H. S. Koppula, K. P. Gummadi, P. Druschel, and B. Bhattacharjee. Growth of the Flickr Social Network. In *WOSP '08: Proceedings of the first workshop on Online social networks*, pages 25–30, 2008.

[25] A. Mislove, M. Marcon, K. P. Gummadi, P. Druschel, and B. Bhattacharjee. Measurement and Analysis of Online Social Networks. In *IMC '07: Proceedings of the 7th ACM SIGCOMM conference on Internet measurement*, pages 29–42, 2007.

[26] R. Myers, R. C. Wilson, and E. R. Hancock. Bayesian Graph Edit Distance. *IEEE Trans. Pattern Anal. Mach. Intell.*, 22(6), 2000.

[27] A. Narayanan and V. Shmatikov. Robust De-anonymization of Large Sparse Datasets. In *SP '08: Proceedings of the 2008 IEEE Symposium on Security and Privacy*, pages 111–125, 2008.

[28] A. Narayanan and V. Shmatikov. De-anonymizing Social Networks. *Security and Privacy, IEEE Symposium on*, 0:173–187, 2009.

[29] M. E. J. Newman, D. J. Watts, and S. H. Strogatz. Random graph models of social networks. *Proceedings of the National Academy of Sciences of the United States of America*, 99(Suppl 1):2566–2572, 2002.

[30] L. P. Cordella, P. Foggia, C. Sansone, and M. Vento. A (Sub)Graph Isomorphism Algorithm for Matching Large Graphs. *IEEE Trans. Pattern Anal. Mach. Intell.*, 26(10):1367–1372, 2004.

[31] P. Pedarsani, D. R. Figueiredo, and M. Grossglauser. Densification Arising from Sampling Fixed Graphs. In *SIGMETRICS '08*, pages 205–216, 2008.

[32] Y. Richter, E. Yom-Tov, and N. Slonim. Predicting Customer Churn in Mobile Networks through Analysis of Social Groups. In *Proc. SIAM Int'l Conference on Data Mining (SDM) 2010*, 2010.

[33] J. Riordan. *An Introduction to Combinatorial Analysis*. Wiley, 1958.

[34] A. Sanfeliu and K. Fu. A Distance Measure between Attributed Relational Graphs for Pattern Recognition. *IEEE Transactions On Systems, Man, and Cybernetics*, 13(3):353–362, 1983.

[35] D. Stutzbach, R. Rejaie, N. Duffield, S. Sen, and W. Willinger. On Unbiased Sampling for Unstructured Peer-to-Peer Networks. *IEEE/ACM Trans. Netw.*, 17(2):377–390, 2009.

[36] Y. Tian and J. M. Patel. TALE: A Tool for Approximate Large Graph Matching. *Data Engineering, International Conference on*, 0:963–972, 2008.

[37] J. R. Ullmann. An Algorithm for Subgraph Isomorphism. *J. ACM*, 23(1):31–42, 1976.

[38] G. Wondracek, T. Holz, E. Kirda, and C. Kruegel. A Practical Attack to De-Anonymize Social Network Users. In *IEEE Symposium on Security & Privacy*, 2010.

[39] B. Zhou and J. Pei. Preserving Privacy in Social Networks Against Neighborhood Attacks. In *ICDE '08: Proceedings of the 2008 IEEE 24th International Conference on Data Engineering*, pages 506–515, 2008.

Ontology Enhancement and Concept Granularity Learning: Keeping Yourself Current and Adaptive

Shan Jiang†, Lidong Bing‡, Bai Sun†, Yan Zhang†*, Wai Lam‡

†Department of Machine Intelligence
Peking University
Beijing 100871, China
{jsh, sunbai}@pku.edu.cn
zhy@cis.pku.edu.cn

‡Department of Systems Engineering and Engineering Management
The Chinese University of Hong Kong
Shatin, Hong Kong
{ldbing, wlam}@se.cuhk.edu.hk

ABSTRACT

As a well-known semantic repository, WordNet is widely used in many applications. However, due to costly edit and maintenance, WordNet's capability of keeping up with the emergence of new concepts is poor compared with on-line encyclopedias such as Wikipedia. To keep WordNet current with folk wisdom, we propose a method to enhance WordNet automatically by merging Wikipedia entities into WordNet, and construct an enriched ontology, named as WorkiNet. WorkiNet keeps the desirable structure of WordNet. At the same time, it captures abundant information from Wikipedia. We also propose a learning approach which is able to generate a tailor-made semantic concept collection for a given document collection. The learning process takes the characteristics of the given document collection into consideration and the semantic concepts in the tailor-made collection can be used as new features for document representation. The experimental results show that the adaptively generated feature space can outperform a static one significantly in text mining tasks, and WorkiNet dominates WordNet most of the time due to its high coverage.

Categories and Subject Descriptors

H.3.1 [**Information Storage and Retrieval**]: Content Analysis and Indexing—*Thesauruses, Dictionaries*; I.5.2 [**Pattern Recognition**]: Design Methodology—*Feature evaluation and selection*

General Terms

Algorithms, Design, Experimentation, Performance

Keywords

WorkiNet, Ontology, Tailor-made Concept Representation Learning

*Corresponding author

KDD'11, August 21–24, 2011, San Diego, California, USA.

1. INTRODUCTION

WordNet [7] organizes terms by a variety of relations such as synonymy, antonymy, hyponymy and meronymy. The carefully designed structure and other characteristics make WordNet widely used in many applications [18]. However, maintaining WordNet with updated entries requires costly manual effort, which limits its capability to keep up with the emergence of new concepts. To enhance WordNet and keep it current, we propose a method to merge Wikipedia entities into it and construct an enriched ontology, named as WorkiNet.

As the largest on-line collaborative encyclopedia, Wikipedia[1] provides us a huge amount of knowledge in various domains. The compound annual growth rate of English Wikipedia is 88.4%[2] from 2002 to 2010. 17 million articles (over 3.5 million in English) have been written collaboratively by volunteers around the world. Due to folk wisdom, Wikipedia's ability of covering the newly-minted fact or knowledge is excellent compared with traditional expert-edited ontologies, such as WordNet. Take the term "Bing" as an example. In Wikipedia it may refer to a Web Search Engine from Microsoft, or a soft drink from UK, or others. But in WordNet this term does not even exist. Therefore, it is reasonable and beneficial to enrich WordNet with Wikipedia. Furthermore, it is also expected that the enhanced ontology will perform better in text mining tasks.

Traditionally, text document representation is usually based on the Bag of Words (BOW) approach, which represents the documents with features as weighted occurrence frequencies of individual words. This technique has several drawbacks: first, it breaks a phrase, say "text mining", into independent features. Second, it maps synonymous words into different features. Third, it merges different meanings of a polysemous word into a single feature. These drawbacks make BOW unable to compute document similarity accurately. Methods aiming at overcoming these drawbacks can be categorized into two classes: latent semantic analysis (including LSA [6], PLSA [10] and LDA [17]) and ontology-based methods [12, 21]. In this paper, we focus on the later methodology. It is observed that mapping synonyms into the same dimension can improve the quality of similarity calculation between documents which are described with different terms in the same synset [9]. Another kind of semantically expressive relation is hyponymy, and sibling hyponyms are often tightly related [24]. Therefore, merging these hyponyms can also offer useful hints for determining the similarity between related documents. For example, if we merge "overlip" and "underlip" into their common hypernym "lip", the similar-

[1]http://www.wikipedia.org
[2]http://en.wikipedia.org/wiki/Wikipedia:Size_of_Wikipedia

ity between documents containing these three different words will be increased.

We believe that the decision of the granularity of semantic term representation should be adaptive when dealing with different document collections. For instance, suppose we have two document collections. The first one is associated with coarse granularity categories, such as sports, military, etc, while the second one's granularity is finer, such as football, basketball, etc. In the first collection, "football" and "basketball" should be regarded as related, while in the second one they should be regarded as unrelated. However, most of the existing works are static [12, 29], consequently, these methods cannot handle the above scenarios. To tackle this problem, we propose a Tailor-made Concept Representation Learning (TCRL) model, which can learn a semantic concept collection from an ontology according to the characteristics of a given document collection and represent the documents adaptively.

The remainder of this paper is organized as follows. The details of WorkiNet construction are discussed in Section 2. The TCRL model is proposed in Section 3. Then the experimental results are given in Section 4. The related works are reviewed in Section 5. Finally, we conclude the paper in Section 7.

2. ENHANCED ONTOLOGY: WORKINET

Obviously, expert-edited ontologies are rather static. For example, the maintainers update WordNet once every few years. Ontologies of this kind have poor ability to cover new terms compared with on-line encyclopedias, such as Wikipedia. We propose a method to integrate Wikipedia's entities into WordNet, and construct an enriched ontology, named as WorkiNet.

2.1 Ontology of WordNet

Concepts are the basic components of an ontology, and represented as synonym sets. Among concepts, several semantic relations exist, such as *antonymy*, *hyponymy(is-a)*, *holonymy(part-of)*, etc. From the document representation point of view, synonymy and hyponymy relations are more useful. Thus they are the relations considered in this paper. We give a formal definition of a concept:

Concept: *A semantic concept π is a triple $\langle S, g, H\rangle$, where S is the synonym set, g denotes the gloss, and H is the set of its hyponym concepts. We refer to the items with $\pi.S$, $\pi.g$ and $\pi.H$ respectively. A set of concepts is denoted as Π. If H is empty, π is a leaf concept.*

Organized by hyponymy, the ontology has a Hierarchical Directed Acyclic Graph (HDAG) structure. A fragment of WordNet is shown in Figure 1.

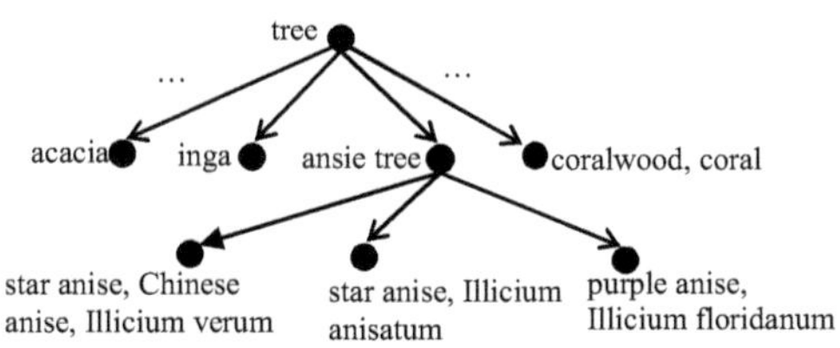

Figure 1: A fragment of WordNet structure. Each node is a concept with its synset attached as the label.

2.2 Wikipedia

Generally speaking, Wikipedia also has a hierarchical structure. However, because of the collaborative manner of editing and the massive number of editors, Wikipedia's structure is much more complicated than that of an expert-edited ontology. Another major difference between Wikipedia and an expert-edited ontology is that the former's categories are quite arbitrarily named, which makes it difficult to match a Wikipedia category with a concept in expert-edited ontologies accurately. To tackle this problem, we propose a concept expansion method to integrate Wikipedia entities into an expert-edited ontology.

For the convenience of describing our method, we first introduce two definitions and one data structure.

Wikipedia Entity: *A Wikipedia entity ϕ is a triple $\langle t, d, C\rangle$ denoting an article in Wikipedia, where t is the title, d denotes the text description, and C is the set of categories that the article belongs to. We refer to the items with $\phi.t$, $\phi.d$ and $\phi.C$ respectively. Each element of C is denoted as c. The entire Wikipedia entity set is denoted as Φ.*

Category Head: *In Wikipedia, each category name can be treated as a noun phrase, and its lemmatized head term is called a category head, denoted as h.*

Index of Entity to Category Head *(IECH): For each ϕ, we construct a forward index: $\phi \rightarrow \{h_{i_1} : f_{i_1}, h_{i_2} : f_{i_2}, \cdots\}$, where f_{i_n} means the frequency of h_{i_n} appearing as a category head in all elements of $\phi.C$. The lemmatized head terms are sorted in descending order according to their frequencies.*

The notations introduced above are summarized in Table 1.

Table 1: Notation used in the paper.

Notation	Meaning
π	A semantic concept in WordNet
$\pi.S$	The synonym set of π
$\pi.g$	The gloss of π
$\pi.H$	The hyponym set of π
ϕ	A Wikipedia entity
$\phi.t$	The title of ϕ
$\phi.d$	The description of ϕ
$\phi.C$	The category set of ϕ
h	A category head of a Wikipedia entity
f_{i_n}	The frequency of h_{i_n} of a Wikipedia entity

2.3 WorkiNet generation

Given a Wikipedia entity ϕ which is not in WordNet, the following procedure is invoked to merge it into WordNet to construct an enhanced ontology, named as WorkiNet. The category information in Wikipedia can be used as clues to discover the higher level concepts. Unfortunately, the category names may not be exactly included in WordNet. We propose a two-phase strategy to generate higher-level concept candidates for a Wikipedia entity. After the candidates are selected, a context matching method is proposed to determine which candidate wins out.

2.3.1 Concept expansion

The design of our concept expansion algorithm is depicted in Algorithm 1. Given an entity ϕ, if $\phi.t$ is not contained by any of the concepts in WordNet, the concept expansion will be performed. First a candidate set Π^c which contains potential higher-level concepts of ϕ is constructed. Then based on the matching score between each candidate and ϕ, the most suitable one from Π^c is chosen as the hypernym of ϕ.

In the generation of Π^c, we employ a two-phase strategy. In the first phase, we retrieve the elements of $\phi.C$ in WordNet. If a certain concept π contains any element of $\phi.C$, π will be put into Π^c. After the first phase, if Π^c is empty, we proceed to the second phase. Utilizing the data structure *IECH*, the set of category heads of ϕ is obtained, denoted as $\{h_{i_1}, h_{i_2}, \cdots\}$. Then we retrieve these category heads in WordNet to compose Π^c. In this method, the original category names of ϕ are our first choice. If the category names are not in WordNet, we make use of the head terms of the categories. For the sake of convenience, we use Π_1^c and Π_2^c to represent the candidate sets generated in Phase 1 and 2 respectively.

We use a running example to illustrate how a Wikipedia entity is processed. Consider the entity $\phi = \langle$"Windows Template Library", "a free software, object-oriented C++ template library ...", {"C++ libraries", "Free development toolkits and libraries", "Free software projects", "Microsoft application programming interfaces", "Object-oriented programming", "Windows-only free software"}$\rangle$[3]. Here $\phi.t$="*Windows Template Library*" is absent in WordNet and no element of $\phi.C$ is in WordNet either. Thus $\Pi_1^c = \emptyset$ in Phase 1. Then we turn to Phase 2. The *IECH* of ϕ is constructed as {library:1, toolkitslibrary:1, project: 1, interface:1, programming:1, software:1}. Among these category heads, "software" is contained by only one WordNet concept. And "project", "programming", "interface", "library" are contained by 2, 2, 4, 5 concepts respectively, while "toolkitslibrary" is absent in WordNet. Therefore, Π_2^c comprises the above 14 concepts.

After Π^c is generated, a matching score is used to determine which candidate is the most suitable one to be the hypernym of ϕ. The matching score between an entity and a concept is defined as

$$match(\phi, \pi_k) = \begin{cases} simT(\phi.d, \pi_k.g) & if\ \pi_k \in \Pi_1^c, \\ \log(f_{i_n}+1) * (simT(\phi.d, \pi_k.g)+1) & if\ \pi_k \in \Pi_2^c, \end{cases} \quad (1)$$

where f_{i_n} is the frequency of h_{i_n} ($h_{i_n} \in \pi_k.S$), and the $simT$ function is used to calculate the similarity between two text fragments, which will be discussed in detail in Section 2.3.2. Here we calculate the similarity between the description of ϕ and the gloss of π_k. The candidate whose matching score dominates others wins out and it is denoted as π^b.

We create a new concept π^ϕ with $\pi^\phi.S$ and $\pi^\phi.g$ setting to be $\{\phi.t\}$ and $\phi.d$ respectively. Finally, if Π_1^c is not empty, π^ϕ is attached under π^b directly. Otherwise, for each category $\phi.c$ whose lemmatized head term is contained in π^b, we create a new concept π^ψ with $\pi^\psi.S = \{c\}$. Then π^ϕ is attached under π^ψ, and π^ψ is added to the hyponym set of π^b.

Returning to the above running example, among the 14 candidates in Π^c, the concept $\pi^b = \langle$\{library, program library, subroutine library\}, "(computing) a collection of standard programs...", $\emptyset\rangle$ in WordNet wins out. Here, "library" is the head term of "C++ libraries" which is one of the categories of ϕ. Therefore, we create a new concept $\pi^\psi = \langle\{\text{C++ libraries}\}, NULL, \{\pi^\phi\}\rangle$, where π^ϕ is generated from ϕ and equals to $\langle$\{Windows Template Library\}, "a free software,...", $\emptyset\rangle$. Here π^ϕ is in the hyponym set of π^ψ, which means π^ϕ is attached under π^ψ. And $\pi^b.H$ becomes $\{\pi^\psi\}$, which means π^ψ is attached under π^b.

In this way, we integrate Wikipedia entities into WordNet and generate the enhanced ontology WorkiNet. As mentioned above, we only integrate the Wikipedia entities whose titles are not in WordNet, thus the terms added into WorkiNet are guaranteed to be new. As for polysemants, different meanings of the same word are demonstrated in different articles with distinct titles in Wikipedia. For example, the computer company "Apple" is demonstrated in the article whose title is "Apple Inc"[4], while the title of the corresponding article of fruit "apple" is "Apple"[5]. Hence, we add new meanings of existing words as well.

2.3.2 *Context based concept similarity*

Leacock and Chodorow [15] propose the following formula to compute semantic similarity between two concepts:

[3]http://en.wikipedia.org/wiki/Windows_Template_Library

[4]http://en.wikipedia.org/wiki/Apple_Inc.

[5]http://en.wikipedia.org/wiki/Apple

Algorithm 1: Concept expansion for WorkiNet generation

input : Wikipedia Φ, WordNet ontology O
output: The enhanced ontology WorkiNet
foreach $\phi \in \{\phi' | \phi' \in \Phi \wedge \nexists \pi(\phi'.t \in \pi.S \wedge \pi \in O)\}$ **do**
  concept set $\Pi_1^c \leftarrow \emptyset$, $\Pi_2^c \leftarrow \emptyset$, $\Pi^b \leftarrow \emptyset$
  / Phase 1 */*
  foreach $c \in \phi.C$ **do**
    $\Pi_1^c \leftarrow \Pi_1^c \bigcup \{\pi | c \in \pi.S \wedge \pi \in O\}$
  / Phase 2 */*
  if $\Pi_1^c = \emptyset$ **then**
    construct $IECH\ idx$ for ϕ
    foreach $h_{i_n} \in idx$ **do**
      $\Pi_2^c \leftarrow \Pi_2^c \bigcup \{\pi | h_{i_n} \in \pi.S \wedge \pi \in O\}$
  foreach $\pi_k \in \Pi_1^c \bigcup \Pi_2^c$ **do**
    calculate $match(\phi, \pi_k)$
  $\pi^b = \arg\max_{\pi_k \in \Pi_1^c \bigcup \Pi_2^c} macth(\phi, \pi_k)$
  create π^ϕ, $\pi^\phi.S \leftarrow \{\phi.t\}$, $\pi^\phi.g \leftarrow \phi.d$
  if $\pi^b \in \Pi_1^c$ **then**
    $\pi^b.H \leftarrow \pi^b.H \bigcup \{\pi^\phi\}$
  else foreach *c whose lemmatized head term is in* π^b **do**
    create π^ψ, $\pi^\psi.S \leftarrow \{c\}$
    $\pi^b.H \leftarrow \pi^b.H \bigcup \{\pi^\psi\}$, $\pi^\psi.H \leftarrow \pi^\psi.H \bigcup \{\pi^\phi\}$

$$sim_{LC}(\pi_1, \pi_2) = -log\frac{len(\pi_1, \pi_2)}{2 \times \max_{\pi \in WordNet} depth(\pi)} \quad (2)$$

where $len(\pi_1, \pi_2)$ is the length of the shortest path between concept π_1 and π_2 in WordNet and $depth(\pi)$ is the length of the path from π to the root. As noted by Sussna [26], sibling-concepts with larger depth appear to be more semantically related than the shallower ones. Based on this observation, we propose the following similarity calculation formula:

$$sim(\pi_1, \pi_2) = \frac{log\frac{len(\pi_1,\pi_2)}{depth(\pi_1)+depth(\pi_1)}}{log\frac{1}{2(\max_{\pi \in WordNet} depth(\pi)+1)}}, \quad (3)$$

where the denominator is for normalization.

Given a text fragment Γ, we use the positive maximum matching method to segment Γ into different terms and each term is included in a certain concept in the ontology. For the words absent in the ontology, we treat each of them as a "pseudo-concept" with itself as synset. Suppose that two text fragments Γ_1 and Γ_2 cover n concepts in all, then they are represented as two n-dimension vectors v_1 and v_2. We design a semantic matrix as follows:

$$SM = \begin{pmatrix} s_{11} & s_{12} & \dots & s_{1n} \\ s_{21} & s_{22} & \dots & s_{2n} \\ \vdots & \vdots & \ddots & \vdots \\ s_{n1} & s_{n2} & \dots & s_{nn} \end{pmatrix}, \quad (4)$$

where $s_{ij} =$

$$\begin{cases} 1 & if(\pi_i = \pi_j) \\ sim(\pi_i, \pi_j) & if((\xi(\pi_i) = 1 \wedge \xi(\pi_j) = 1) \wedge \pi_i \neq \pi_j) \\ 0 & if((\xi(\pi_i) = 0 \vee \xi(\pi_j) = 0) \wedge \pi_i \neq \pi_j) \end{cases}$$

in which $\xi(\pi_i)$ is an indicator, and takes value 1 if $\pi_i \in$ WordNet, otherwise it takes value 0. We calculate similarity between two text fragments Γ_1 and Γ_2 with the following formula:

$$simT(\Gamma_1, \Gamma_2) = \frac{v_1 \cdot SM \cdot v_2^T}{\sqrt{v_1 \cdot SM \cdot v_1^T}\sqrt{v_2 \cdot SM \cdot v_2^T}}. \quad (5)$$

One interesting property is that when SM is set to an identity matrix, $simT(\Gamma_1, \Gamma_2)$ becomes the cosine similarity between v_1 and v_2.

3. TAILOR-MADE CONCEPT REPRESENTATION LEARNING MODEL

We design a Tailor-made Concept Representation Learning (TCR-L) model that can adaptively generate tailor-made semantic concept set for a given document collection. As shown in Figure 2, given a document collection and an ontology such as WordNet or WorkiNet, the algorithm learns which concepts have better capability of discriminating the documents and generates a tailor-made collection $\mathcal{C}$, which is composed of all the concepts denoted by hollow circles. Each concept in $\mathcal{C}$ is generated by aggregating several concepts and part of their descendants. Some of the concepts in $\mathcal{C}$ encapsulate all of the descendants shown in the original ontology graph (located on the dashed line). For example, the terms in π_1 are added into $\pi_a.S$. Then we get a derived concept, π^{d1}, of π_a in the collection. π_2 and π_3 with all the descendants of π_3 in its subtaxonomy are merged into a new concept π^{d2}. The terms in π_4 and π_5 are added into $\pi_b.S$ and form a new concept π^{d3}.

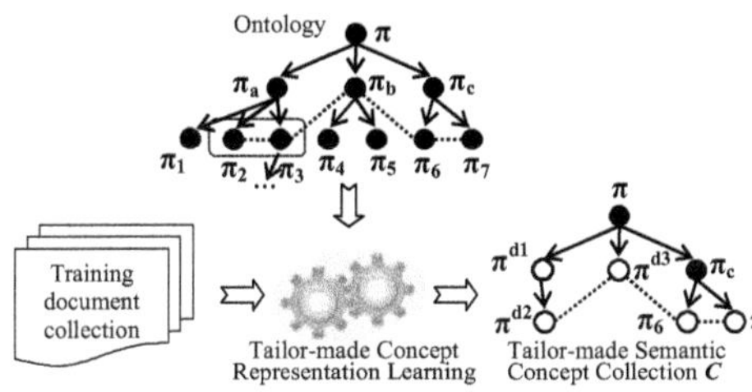

Figure 2: Semantic Concept Representation Learning.

$\mathcal{C}$ represents a semantic summary of the given domains, and it is generated specifically for a given document collection. As a result, each document collection has its own tailor-made semantic concept set. The tailor-made semantic concept set will be used as a new feature space for representing the documents. This new feature space is more effective when a text mining task, such as classification or clustering, is conducted on the corresponding document collection.

3.1 Concept merging

Suppose in the given document collection, the documents have been organized in classes. To select features with good capability of discriminating the documents in different classes, we employ the mutual information (MI) between a term t and a class c_i, denoted as $MI(t, c_i)$, to measure how much information the presence/absence of t contributes to make the correct class prediction on c_i. Formally:

$$MI(t, c_i) = MI(\varepsilon_t, \varepsilon_{c_i}) = \sum_{e_t \in \{0,1\}} \sum_{e_{c_i} \in \{0,1\}} p(\varepsilon_t = e_t, \varepsilon_{c_i} = e_{c_i}) log \frac{p(\varepsilon_t = e_t, \varepsilon_{c_i} = e_{c_i})}{p(\varepsilon_t = e_t) p(\varepsilon_{c_i} = e_{c_i})} \quad (6)$$

where ε_t and ε_{c_i} are two random variables that take the value of 1 or 0. $\varepsilon_t = 1$ denotes the document contains term t and $\varepsilon_t = 0$ denotes the document does not contain term t. Analogously, $\varepsilon_{c_i} = 1$ denotes the document is in class c_i and $\varepsilon_{c_i} = 0$ denotes the document is not in class c_i.

Suppose in the given document collection, there is no pre-defined class information. In this case, we calculate the mutual information between term t and an individual document d_i: $MI(t, d_i) = MI(\varepsilon_t, \varepsilon_{d_i})$. Random variable $\varepsilon_t = 1$ denotes the random selected term is t and random variable $\varepsilon_{d_i} = 1$ denotes the random term is in document d_i.

To generate the tailor-made semantic concept collection, the leaf concepts are merged into their hypernyms recursively, and an indicating function is used to measure whether the merging is profitable. We assume that the more unbalanced the distribution of MI value is, the more plausible it is to add terms into the concept collection. We define the indicating function $I(\pi)$ based on the inequality of the distribution.

3.2 Indicating function

An indicating function is used to indicate whether the merging should be performed, and it is based on the inequality of the distribution of MI values. Any effective method of measurement can be adopted. In this paper, we design two different patterns of the indicating function, namely, Gini coefficient based function and entropy-based function.

3.2.1 Gini indicating function

The Gini [8] coefficient is a measure of the imparity of a distribution which is firstly proposed by Corrado Gini in 1912 and is widely used in various fields such as economics, geography, etc. The Gini coefficient is defined based on the Lorenz curve. Its geometric significance is the proportion of the area between the Lorenz curve of the distribution and the uniform distribution line to the area under the uniform distribution line. The Gini coefficient ranges from 0 to 1, and a lower value indicates a more equal distribution while a higher one implicates more inequality. A number of formulas have been provided for the calculation of the Gini coefficient. In this paper, we take the method proposed by Chotikapanich and Griffiths [5]. Their work suggests an estimator obtained by approximating the Lorenz curve with a series of linear segments.

Supposing that MI values of a particular term set τ have been classified into M groups (for classifying task, each MI value forms an individual group). In the next step, we get the average MI value of each group, then sort them in ascending order. The following information is available for the i-th group:

- The proportion of terms: p_i
- Cumulative proportion of terms: $\varrho_i = p_1 + p_2 + \ldots + p_i$
- The proportion of MI_i: $\vartheta i = \frac{p_i \quad I_i}{\sum_{j=1}^{M} p_j \quad I_j}$

Then the coefficient value can be calculated as:

$$G(\tau, \upsilon) = 1 + \sum_{i=1} \frac{\vartheta i}{p_i} [(1 - \varrho_i)^{\upsilon} - (1 - \varrho_{i-1})^{\upsilon}] \quad (7)$$

where υ is an inequality aversion parameter. $G(\tau, \upsilon)$ is defined for $\upsilon > 1$ and is equal to the original Gini coefficient when $\upsilon = 2$.

The indicating function based on Gini coefficient is defined as:

$$I_{\_Gini}(\pi) = \frac{Gini(\pi)}{\sum_{\pi' \in \pi.H} Gini(\pi') freq(\pi')} \quad (8)$$

where $Gini(\pi)$ is defined as:

$$Gini(\pi) = G(S^g_{\pi}, \upsilon) \quad (9)$$

$S^g_{\pi} = \pi.S \cup_{\pi' \in \Pi^d_{\pi}} \pi'.S$, and Π^d_{π} is the descendant set of π. And $freq(\pi')$ is defined as:

$$freq(\pi') = \frac{count(S^g_{\pi'})}{\sum_{\pi'_i \in \pi.H} count(S^g_{\pi'_i})}, \quad (10)$$

where $count(S^g_{\pi'})$ is the cumulative frequency of π' and all the concepts in its subtaxonomy.

3.2.2 Entropy indicating function

Entropy is another common method to measure the degree of uniformity of a distribution. We define our entropy-based indicating function as follows:

$$I_{\_Entro}(\pi) = \frac{\sum_{\pi' \in \pi.H} entr(\pi') freq(\pi')}{entr(\pi)}, \quad (11)$$

where $entr(\pi)$ is defined as:

$$entr(\pi) = -\sum_{i=1} \widetilde{MI}(S^g_{\pi}, c_i) \cdot log(\widetilde{MI}(S^g_{\pi}, c_i)), \quad (12)$$

Here, $\widetilde{MI}(S^g_\pi, c_i)$ is a normalized MI value:

$$\widetilde{MI}(\pi, c_i) = \frac{MI(\pi, c_i)}{\sum_{j=1} MI(\pi, c_j)}, \tag{13}$$

where M is the number of classes.

For the convenience of explanation, I_{Gini} and I_{Entro} are uniformly referred to as I. The larger $I(\pi)$ is, the less noise is involved when merging the hyponyms of π into π. If $I(\pi) \geqslant \theta$ (a profitable threshold), the merging will be performed.

3.3 Semantic concept representation learning algorithm

The semantic concept representation learning algorithm is summarized in Algorithm 2. The key idea of the algorithm is to recursively merge leaves to their parent node if the merging is profitable. The merged node will be treated as a new leaf.

We introduce a border flag flg for each concept in the ontology. In the beginning, flg is initialized to be $false$ for each concept. Then in each loop, we get the unhandled deepest leaf π^l, that is, the deepest leaf with flg of $false$, and locate its hypernym π.

If the merging process stops in any branch of π, the root of the branch will be recognized as a non-leaf node. If π contains both non-leaf and leaf hyponyms, the merging will not be performed and flg of all the leaf hyponyms of π will be set to be $true$. When all the hyponyms of π are leaves, we will check if the merging is profitable. As long as $I(\pi) \geqslant \theta$, the merging will be performed.

Primarily, we gather leaves sharing high mutual information between each other into the same subset which is known as a "camp" in this paper. The camps and the remaining concepts compose a partition of the set $\pi.H$. Ideally, we should detect the optimal partition with the highest summation of mutual information values in every camp. However, to obtain the optimal solution is very costly due to the exponential number of possible subset partitions. Therefore, a heuristic method is adopted. First for each π'_i in $\pi.H$, $MI(\pi'_i, \pi)$ can be derived from Equation 6 and equals to $MI(\varepsilon_{\pi'_i}, \varepsilon_\pi)$. The random variable $\varepsilon_\pi = 1$ denotes that the document contains at least one term included in $\pi.S$, and $\varepsilon_{\pi'_i}$ is defined analogously. Let $\pi'_m = \arg\max_{\pi'_j \in \pi.H \wedge \pi'_j \neq \pi'_i} MI(\pi'_i, \pi'_j)$. If $MI(\pi'_i, \pi'_m) > MI(\pi'_i, \pi)$, π'_i and π'_m will be put into the same camp. After the camps are built, we pack each camp as a new node with $flg = true$ encapsulating all the concepts in it and their descendants, and attach the node under π. Then we merge the remaining concepts belonging to none of the camps and all of their descendants into π, and set the flg value of π to be $true$.

As a matter of fact, the camps are designed to redivide the concept set so that closely related concepts can be treated as one dimension. It will help the tailor-made semantic concept collection discriminate the documents better. However, if the new nodes generated from the camps are considered as new leaves, in the next loop, π will be recognized as non-leaf nodes and the merging process will stop for all the ancestors of π. To make sure that the merging process go on recursively, in the final step, π with all its child nodes are considered as a virtual leaf with flg=$false$.

If the merging is not profitable, all flg of π's leaf hyponyms will be set to $true$. Then the merging process will stop for all the ancestors of π. To restart the merging process, a non-leaf node whose child nodes are all leaves with $flg = false$ should be found. Finally, $\mathcal{C}$ is composed of all leaves (including the members of virtual leaves) with $flg = true$.

Let us return to the example illustrated in Figure 2. On the condition of $MI(\pi_2, \pi_3) > MI(\pi_2, \pi_a) > MI(\pi_1, \pi_2)$, π_2 and π_3 are put into the same camp. If we get $MI(\pi_1, \pi_3) < MI(\pi_1, \pi_2) < MI(\pi_2, \pi_3) \leqslant MI(\pi_1, \pi_a)$, π_1 will not be included by any camp. Then a new node π^{d2} is generated to encapsulate π_2, π_3 and all the descendants of π_3. The remaining concept π_1 is merged into π_a to form a new concept π^{d1}. π^{d1} and π^{d2} will be treated as a virtual leaf. $MI(\pi_4, \pi_5) \leqslant MI(\pi_4, \pi_b)$ and $MI(\pi_4, \pi_5) \leqslant MI(\pi_5, \pi_b)$, because there is no camp built for π_b, all the three nodes are merged into π^{d3}. The merging is not performed on π_c because $I(\pi_c)$ is less than θ. As a result, in the next loop, π contains the non-leaf hyponym π_c, so the merging process stops. If π_6 and π_7 are merged into π_c, all the child nodes of π will be treated as virtual leaves with flg=$false$. As long as $I(\pi) \geqslant \theta$, the merging will be performed on π recursively.

With an elaborately designed indicating function, a tailor-made concept collection can be selected to construct a better document representation. This selection is adaptive according to different document collections. For example, in our experiments, the concept π^e with synset {blue sky, blue, blue air, wild blue yonder} is merged into its grandparent concept with synset {atmosphere} for one document collection, while it is merged into the parent concept with synset {sky} for another. In the first case, terms in {atmosphere, sky, mackerel sky} $\bigcup \pi^e.S$ are treated as the same dimension. While in the later one, "atmosphere" is separated from others, because the grandparent concept π^g = ⟨atmosphere,"the envelope of gases surrounding any celestial body",{"sky"}⟩ has $I(\pi^g) < \theta$, and the merging is not performed.

3.4 Utilizing semantic concept for document representation

After the tailor-made semantic concept collection $\mathcal{C}$ is generated, we can utilize it to represent a document with a concept-based vector. Suppose t is a term from a particular document. If it is an unambiguous term, we map it to the unique concept in $\mathcal{C}$ that contains t. Otherwise, t is contained by more than one concept, and hence we need to disambiguate it first. For each π_i ($t \in \pi_i.S$) we calculate the similarity between t's context and the gloss of π_i according to Equation 5. t's context is composed of the surrounding sentences of t and denoted as Γ_t, while the gloss of π_i is denoted as $\pi_i.g$. Then the concept

$$\pi^m = \arg\max_{\pi_i} simT(\pi_i.g, \Gamma_t) \tag{14}$$

is selected as the correct concept of t. After the disambiguating, the reconstructed vectors can be applied in traditional vector space model for text mining tasks.

To evaluate the disambiguation approach, we select 60 commonused polysemants. On average, each of them is contained by 6.23 concepts in WordNet. We search these words in Wikipedia and collect the corresponding articles. Each article refers to a particular meaning of the related word. Then one article is randomly selected for each word, and the first sentence that contains the word in the article is extracted as the context of the word.

For instance, the term "orange" appears in 5 concepts in WordNet. It refers to "Orange (fruit)", "Orange (colour)" and "Orange (word)" in Wikipeida[6]. Then if we choose the meaning of orange color, and the context will be "The colour orange occurs between red and yellow in the visible spectrum at a wavelength of about $58 - 620$ nm, and has a hue of 30° in HSV colour space."[7]. After disambiguating as described above, it is mapped to concept ⟨{orange, orangeness}, "orange color or pigment; any of a range of colors between red and yellow", {reddish orange}⟩, which is the correct meaning of the word "orange" in the context. Overall, we achieve a disambiguation precision of 66.67% in our experiment.

[6]http://en.wikipedia.org/wiki/Orange

[7]http://en.wikipedia.org/wiki/Orange_(colour)

Algorithm 2: Semantic Concept Representation Learning Algorithm

input : the HDAG G of an ontology, a document collection
output: tailor-made semantic concept collection $\mathcal{C}$
assign each concept a flag flg with $false$
while *G has leaves with $flg = false$* **do**
  get the deepest leaf π^l with flg=$false$ and its hypernym π
  if *π has non-leaf hyponym concepts* **then**
    set_flag(π)
  else if $I(\pi) \geqslant \theta$ **then**
    merge_descendants(π)
  else *set_flag*(π)
set $\mathcal{C} = \{\pi | flg\ of\ \pi\ is\ true\}$

proc *set_flag*(π)
foreach *π' in $\pi.H$* **do**
  if $|\pi'.H| = 0$ **then**
    set $flg \leftarrow true$ for π'

proc *merge_descendants*(π)
create $Camps$
foreach *π'_i in $\pi.H$* **do**
  $\pi'_m \leftarrow \arg\max_{\pi'_j \in \pi.H \wedge \pi'_j \neq \pi'_i} MI(\pi'_i, \pi'_j)$
  if $MI(\pi'_i, \pi'_m) > MI(\pi'_i, \pi)$ **then**
    if $\exists c(c \in Camps \wedge (\pi'_m \in c \vee \pi'_i \in c))$ **then**
      $c \leftarrow c \bigcup \{\pi'_m, \pi'_i\}$
    else create $c \leftarrow \{\pi'_m, \pi'_i\}$
    $Camps \leftarrow Camps \bigcup \{c\}$
if $Camps \neq \emptyset$ **then**
  foreach *c in $Camps$* **do**
    create π_c with $flg = true$
    foreach *π_k in c* **do**
      $\pi_c.S \leftarrow \pi_c.S \bigcup S^g_{\pi_k}$
      $\pi.H \leftarrow \pi.H - \bigcup\{\pi_k\}$
    $\pi.H \leftarrow \pi.H \bigcup \{\pi_c\}$
foreach $\pi' \in \{\pi'_i | \nexists c(c \in Camps \wedge \pi'_i \in c)\}$ **do**
  $\pi.S \leftarrow \pi.S \bigcup S^g_{\pi'}$
  $\pi.H \leftarrow \pi.H - \bigcup\{\pi'\}$
set $flg \leftarrow true$ for π
pack π and all nodes in $\pi.H$ as a virtual leaf with flg=$false$

4. EXPERIMENTS

4.1 Information about data and resource

We use version 2.1 of WordNet, which contains 89,646 concepts. The Wikipedia data used is a dump in October 2009. After eliminating the articles without category information or valid article content, 2,722,437 articles are collected. Finally, 1,782,276 new leaves are added into 12,888 WordNet concepts. 57,573 of the new leaves are added into WordNet concepts directly and 1,724,703 of them are added into new concepts built from the categories, which are then attached under WordNet concepts containing the head terms of the categories.

4.2 Case study in WorkiNet

Table 2 presents some examples about under which concept a Wikipedia entity is attached. The entities are given in the second column, and their expanded WordNet concepts (denoted by the corresponding synsets) are shown in the fourth column. The third column, "Added Category", denotes the category of the Wikipedia entity. If the cell in "Added Category" is not empty, the Wikipedia entity will be attached directly to category first, and then this category is subsumed by the WordNet concept in the fourth column.

Table 2: Case study 1.

#	Wikipedia Entity	Added Category	WordNet Concept
1	dekopon		citrus, citrus fruit, citrous fruit
2	J2EE application	java platform	platform
3	Proxi		freeware
4	Thenar eminence		hand
5	Yahoo! Meme	real-time web	World Wide Web, WWW, web
6	Conditional entropy	selective information	information, entropy,
7	Standard Template Library	generic programming	program, programme, computer program, computer programme

Table 3: Case study 2.

#	WordNet Concept	Wikipedia Entities and category(if added)	
1	black tea	Golden needle tea; Nepal tea; Nilgiri tea; Tibeti;	
2	thermochemistry	Principle of maximum work; Heat of formation group additivity; Isodesmic reaction; Nernst heat theorem; Exergonic reaction; Endergonic reaction; Van't Hoff equation; Thermochemical equation; Thomsen-Berthelot principle	
3	Supercomputer	NEC supercomputers	SUPER-UX
		IBM supercomputers	PERCS; ACS-1; IBM Roadrunner; Blue Gene; Blue Waters; Cyclops64

We can see that reasonable higher level concepts for the entities are found. "J2EE application" is recognized as a software platform and is subsumed by the WordNet concept ⟨{platform}, "the combination of a particular computer and a particular operating system", $\emptyset$⟩. We create a new hypernym for it from its category, namely "java platform". A Japanese fruit "dekopon", which is a rare term and cannot even be found in many dictionaries, is retrieved as well.

Table 3 gives some examples from another perspective to show the consistency of the semantic meaning of the entities attached under the same concept. In the first example, different kinds of black tea are supplemented. In the second example, chemistry-related phrases are added to "thermochemistry". In the final one, we find 7 examples of supercomputers. All the 6 supercomputers of IBM supercomputers are reasonable, while SUPER-UX is actually the version of the Unix operating system used on NEC SX architecture supercomputers. In spite of some inaccurate information, WorkiNet still digs out quite abundant useful ontology information.

4.3 Quality evaluation of WorkiNet

For evaluation purpose, we define five grades to score the correctness of the semantic relation between a Wikipedia entity and its hypernyms (including the category if added) in WorkiNet. Examples are given in Table 4. In **Excellent** and **Good**, the matching quality is high, and these cases agree with people's general knowledge. In **Fair**, the relation between the entity and the concept is not strong, but still reasonable. If the quality is difficult to judge, we put it into **Neutral**. Finally, the wrong cases are put into **Bad**. Five volunteers have been invited to conduct the evaluation. For a certain case, each volunteer gives a score, then we average all scores and round the average score to its nearest grade as the final result.

Table 4: Evaluation grades.

Grade (Score)	Examples (Wiki entity (⇒ category) ⇒ WordNet concept)
Excellent(5)	Irisbus⇒bus manufacturers⇒manufacturer producer; Guantĺćnamo Bay ⇒ bay, embayment
Good(4)	The Moorcock ⇒ English contract case law⇒ law, practice of law; Helpless Romantic (album) ⇒ Jon B. albums ⇒ album
Fair(3)	Red Fraction ⇒ 2006 singles ⇒ single, bingle Services cricket team ⇒ Military
Neutral(2)	Log-a-Log ⇒ Redwall characters ⇒ character, eccentric, type, case; Stewart v. Abend ⇒ United States Supreme Court cases ⇒ sheath, case
Bad(1)	Dwight Dickinson⇒1916 births⇒birth; Deferiprone ⇒ Chelating agents ⇒ agent, factor, broker

We randomly sample 300 cases and the evaluation result is given in Table 5. The overall average score is 4.26 and 80% of the cases fall into **Excellent** or **Good**. We examine the **Bad** and **Neutral** cases, and find that a main reason for the mis-attaching is that the support of the article's content to the most profitable head term is not dominant. Take "Dwight Dickinson⇒1916 births⇒birth" as an example, "Dwight Dickinson" was a United States diplomat and Navy veteran, but the entity is wrongly categorized into "1916 births" because the matching score of the intended category "officer" (the head term of the original category "United States Navy officers") is lower than that of "birth". Another factor is that $simT$ function does not work well for some cases. "Deferiprone" is a chelating agent, but it is wrongly connected with the concept "agent, factor, broker" because the $simT$ value of this concept is bigger than that of any other concept that contains "agent". Here "agent" is the intended category head, but the WordNet concept selected is not correct.

4.4 WordNet and WorkiNet's performance in text mining

We investigate whether the TCRL model can outperform a static one by conducting experiments on clustering and classification. A previous method denoted as "Hotho" [12] is also implemented for conducting the comparison. In this method, each synonym set, with a fixed number of levels of hypernyms added, is used as one dimension in the vector space. As shown in [12, 13], "Hotho" can dominate BOW approach in different text mining tasks. We also conduct a comparison between WorkiNet and WordNet to see whether WorkiNet can achieve competitive performance or even better under the TCRL model.

4.4.1 Document collections

Two data sets are used in the experiments: 20 Newsgroups (NG20)[8] and TREC 2004 (TREC) data extracted from the document collection Disc 5. All the 20 groups of NG20 are used, while the biggest 10 categories are used in TREC.

4.4.2 Document classification

In this experiment, LibSVM [4] with a linear kernel is employed. The threshold θ is set to 1.2.

Evaluation criteria. Two types of the F-measure scores are computed, namely, macro-average and micro-average [28].

In macro-average, the precision and recall for each category c_i are calculated first, denoted as P_i and R_i. Then F-measure for c_i is: $F_i = \frac{2P_iR_i}{P_i+R_i}$. The macro-averaged F-measure is the average of F-measure for each category: $F^{ma} = \frac{\sum_i F_i}{|C|}$. In micro-averaging, F-measure is computed globally over all category decisions. The global precision and recall are calculated as: $P = \frac{\sum_i TP_i}{\sum_i (TP_i+FP_i)}$, $R = \frac{\sum_i TP_i}{\sum_i (TP_i+FN_i)}$, where TP_i, FP_i and FN_i are true positive, false positive and false negative numbers for category c_i. Micro-averaged F-measure is then computed as: $F^{mi} = \frac{2PR}{P+R}$.

Results. The classification result is given in Table 6. "Gini" and "Entro" denote the performance of TCRL with Gini and entropy indicating function respectively. We can see that TCRL outperforms Hotho under both evaluation metrics, no matter which ontology is used. WorkiNet performs better than WordNet in TREC but a slight decline is found in NG20. One direct cause is that the dimension is over reduced by TCRL when WorkiNet is employed. Too many concepts are merged so that the capability of discriminating documents in the new feature space is weakened. The difference between the performance of WordNet and WorkiNet on NG20 is not significant for both F^{ma} and F^{mi}. It may be due to the insensitivity of NG20 to new words.

Table 5: Evaluation result.

Excellent	Good	Fair	Neutral	Bad
193	47	26	12	22

Table 6: Classification performance comparison.

		WorkiNet		WordNet	
		F^{mi}	F^{ma}	F^{mi}	F^{ma}
NG20	Hotho	.854	.748	.875	.756
	Gini	.881	.771	.893	.764
	Entro	.883	.773	.893	.764
TREC	Hotho	.591	.542	.498	.450
	Gini	.649	.589	.604	.556
	Entro	.648	.588	.603	.555

4.4.3 Document clustering

In this experiment, we run K-Means for three times on each data set to get an average result. The adopted value of θ is 0.6.

Evaluation criteria. The purity measure is employed to evaluate the clustering performance. Let $G = \{g_1, g_2, \cdots\}$ denote the cluster set generated by K-Means, and $C = \{c_1, c_2, \cdots\}$ denote the pre-defined clusters. To compute the purity, each g_k is assigned to the pre-defined cluster c_i which is the most frequent one in g_k, then the purity is measured as:

$$Pur(C, G) = \frac{1}{|D|} \sum_k \max_i |g_k \cap c_i|, \qquad (15)$$

Results. The clustering result is given in Table 7. It can be seen that our adaptive TCRL model works better than the static one significantly. On average, TCRL improves the results by more than 49% for both Gini and entropy indicating function. Moreover, WorkiNet outperforms WordNet.

4.5 Parameter analysis in TCRL

The effects of the threshold θ under different settings are shown in Table 8, Table 9 and Table 10. "AVG" is the average value of the results of TCRL with different θ and "SD(/100)" is the standard deviation between these values divided by 100. We can see that in the classification task, the TCRL model is not sensitive to θ. It is because the number of classes is so small that the distribution is too sparse. In the clustering, the TCRL model is a bit more sensitive, but the difference is still inapparent. For both classification and clustering, performances of Gini and entropy indicating function are similar. From the values of the standard deviation, we can see

[8] http://people.csail.mit.edu/jrennie/20Newsgroups/

Table 7: Clustering performance comparison.

		WorkiNet	WordNet
NG20	Hotho	.601	.696
	Gini	.853	.815
	Entro	.852	.824
TREC	Hotho	.332	.291
	Gini	.543	.509
	Entro	.547	.507

that the performance of Gini indicating function is a bit more stable under different values of θ, especially for classification. Overall, the TCRL model is not sensitive to θ in our experiments.

In general, WorkiNet outperforms WordNet. However, WorkiNet's improvement of classification in NG20 is not significant. It implies that WorkiNet contributes little given an old data set.

Table 8: Parameter θ's effect in classification(Gini indicating function).

θ	NG20				TREC			
	F^{mi}		F^{ma}		F^{mi}		F^{ma}	
	WD	WK	WD	WK	WD	WK	WD	WK
Hotho	.875	.854	.756	.748	.498	.591	.450	.542
0.2	.890	.876	.763	.767	.603	.626	.554	.570
0.4	.890	.876	.763	.767	.602	.628	.553	.571
0.6	.890	.876	.763	.767	.604	.626	.555	.570
0.8	.890	.881	.763	.771	.604	.631	.555	.573
1.0	.890	.881	.763	.771	.602	.649	.554	.589
1.2	.893	.881	.764	.771	.604	.649	.555	.589
AVG	.891	.879	.763	.769	.603	.635	.554	.577
SD(/100)	.122	.274	.041	.219	.098	1.11	.082	.936

Table 9: Parameter θ's effect in classification(entropy indicating function).

θ	NG20				TREC			
	F^{mi}		F^{ma}		F^{mi}		F^{ma}	
	WD	WK	WD	WK	WD	WK	WD	WK
Hotho	.875	.854	.756	.748	.498	.591	.450	.542
0.2	.887	.868	.759	.760	.600	.599	.551	.545
0.4	.887	.868	.759	.760	.600	.599	.551	.545
0.6	.887	.868	.759	.760	.601	.600	.552	.547
0.8	.887	.872	.759	.763	.600	.640	.551	.582
1.0	.893	.876	.764	.767	.603	.644	.554	.585
1.2	.893	.883	.764	.773	.603	.648	.555	.588
AVG	.889	.873	.761	.764	.601	.622	.551	.565
SD(/100)	.310	.606	.258	.527	.147	2.46	.362	2.16

5. RELATED WORK

Researchers have conducted extensive work on automatic ontology generation and enrichment. The work in [2] extends WordNet with syntagmatic information by adding information about the co-occurrence of word meaning in texts. Similar work focusing on WordNet and Wikipedia is reported by Ruiz-Casado et al. [22]. Ponzetto and Navigli [20] present a method to link WikiTaxonomy to WordNet which maximizes the structural overlap between WordNet's taxonomy and Wikipedia's Category by disambiguating with WordNet hierarchy. Ferrández's method [1] presents an algorithm to align FrameNet units to WordNet synsets by exploiting the particular traits of each hierarchy.

In [27] a document-specific hierarchy is automatically extracted from the text and combined with WordNet relations to build an extended WordNet hierarchy, which is trimmed with a disambiguation method. A *head-modifier* relation is used for the hierarchy building. Magnini and Speranza [16] propose an approach to integrate generic and specialized wordnet-like lexical database with *plug-in* relation.

Table 10: Parameter θ's effect in clustering.

θ	Gini				Entropy			
	NG20		TREC		NG20		TREC	
	WD	WK	WD	WK	WD	WK	WD	WK
Hotho	.696	.601	.291	.332	.696	.601	.29	.332
0.2	.818	.852	.511	.548	.815	.852	.502	.539
0.4	.820	.851	.510	.544	.812	.848	.510	.547
0.6	.815	.853	.509	.543	.824	.852	.507	.547
0.8	.802	.855	.508	.542	.813	.850	.509	.541
1.0	.813	.849	.508	.544	.813	.855	.511	.544
1.2	.813	.851	.501	.541	.813	.842	.507	.546
AVG	.814	.852	.508	.544	.815	.850	.508	.544
SD(/100)	.629	.204	.354	.242	.452	.449	.320	.335

YAGO [25] mainly focuses on finding the "individuals" and "facts" from Wikipedia. The authors try to extract 14 kinds of relations, and WordNet is utilized to help them to generate *subClassOf* and *means* relations. In [19], the authors present a method to automatically create an independent lexical ontology based on terms from a semantic network and their ontology has a similar model with WordNet.

As an important semantic bank, WordNet has been used to improve the performance of clustering and classification. Scott and Matwin [23] successfully integrate the WordNet resource for classification. Hotho et al. [11, 12] incorporate synonym and hypernym as background knowledge into document representation. Shehata [24] analyzes each term at sentence-level and improves clustering using terms and the corresponding synonyms and hypernyms. In comparison, both approaches in [12] and [24] provide static feature analyses to all document collections, while ours agilely construct semantic concept collections for different document collections according to their own characteristics. Jing et al. [14] construct a term similarity matrix using WordNet to improve text clustering. Their approach only uses synonyms and hyponyms, but fails to handle polysemy. In Recupero's work [21], two strategies, namely, WordNet lexical categories (WLC) technique and WordNet ontology (WO) technique, are proposed to create a new vector space.

In our previous work [3], we propose two concrete methods, namely, top-down (GBG-g) and bottom-up (GBG-s) algorithms for document presentation. In this paper, we focus on proposing a general framework for concept granularity learning. Compared with merging all the descendants to their roots, the construction of camps helps to redivide the concept set so that the granularity can be learned more precisely and adaptively. With the general framework of merging and redividing, the algorithms can be designed to be more efficient. For instance, the camp building method and the indicating function can be flexibly modified as long as they can help to learn the concept granularity better.

6. ACKNOWLEDGMENT

We thank the anonymous reviewers for their valuable and constructive comments. This work is supported by NSFC with Grant No. 61073081, HGJ with Grant No. 2011ZX01042-001-001, the Research Grant Council of the Hong Kong Special Administrative Region, China (Project Codes: CUHK4128/07 and CUHK413510). This work is also affiliated with the Microsoft-CUHK Joint Laboratory for Human-centric Computing and Interface Technologies.

7. CONCLUSIONS

In this paper, we construct an enhanced ontology, WorkiNet, by integrating the information of Wikipedia into the expert-edited ontology WordNet. In general, the performance of WorkiNet in text mining applications is very encouraging. We have also proposed an adaptive model called TCRL to reconstruct document presentation. The efficacy of the TCRL model is investigated in classification and clustering, and the experimental results show that it outperforms a static one no matter which indicating function is used.

The framework of the TCRL model offers opportunities to further optimize the task of feature selection. Indicating functions can be flexibly modified as long as it is effective to conduct feature selection. In this paper we propose two different types of indicating functions, and both of them perform well. And the camp building algorithm can be further improved as well. Another possible future direction is to further improve the accuracy of WorkiNet generation, and solve the problem of mis-attaching.

8. REFERENCES

[1] Ó. Ferrández, M. Ellsworth, R. Muñoz, and C. F. Baker. Aligning framenet and wordnet based on semantic neighborhoods. In *LREC '10: Proceedings of the 7th Conference on International Language Resources and Evaluation*, pages 310–314, 2010.

[2] L. Bentivogli and E. Pianta. Extending wordnet with syntagmatic information. In *Proceedings of Second Global WordNet Conference*, pages 47–53, 2004.

[3] L. Bing, B. Sun, S. Jiang, Y. Zhang, and W. Lam. Learning ontology resolution for document representation and its applications in text mining. In *CIKM '10: Proceedings of the 19th ACM International Conference on Information and Knowledge Management*, pages 1713–1716, 2010.

[4] C. C. Chang and C.J.Lin. *LIBSVM: a library for support vector machines*. 2001.

[5] D. Chotikapanich and W. Griffiths. On calculation of the extended gini coefficient. *Review of Income and Wealth*, pages 541–547, 2001.

[6] S. Deerwester, S. Dumais, G. Furnas, T.K.Landauer, and R. Harshman. Indexing by latent semantic analysis. *Journal of the American Society for Information Science*, 41(6):391–407, 1990.

[7] C. Fellbaum. *WordNet: An Electronic Lexical Database*. The MIT Press, Cambridge, MA, 1998.

[8] C. Gini. Variabilità e mutabilità. *Bologna: Tipografia di Paolo Cuppini*, 1912.

[9] J. Gonzalo, F. Verdejo, I. Chugur, and J. Cigarrán. Indexing with wordnet synsets can improve text retrieval. In *Proceedings ACL/COLING Workshop on Usage of WordNet for Natural Language Processing*, pages 38–44, 1998.

[10] T. Hofmann. Probabilistic latent semantic indexing. In *SIGIR '99: Proceedings of the 22nd annual international ACM SIGIR conference on Research and Development in Information Retrieval*, pages 50–57, 1999.

[11] A. Hotho, A. Maedche, and S. Staab. Ontology-based text document clustering. *Künstliche Intelligenz*, 4:48–54, 2002.

[12] A. Hotho, S. Staab, and G. Stumme. Wordnet improves text document clustering. In *Proceeding of the SIGIR 2003 Semantic Web Workshop*, 2003.

[13] X. Hu, N. Sun, C. Zhang, and T.-S. Chua. Exploiting internal and external semantics for the clustering of short texts using world knowledge. In *CIKM '09: Proceedings of the 18th International Conference on Information and Knowledge Management*, pages 919–928, 2009.

[14] L. Jing, L. Zhou, M. K. Ng, and J. Z. Huang. Ontology-based distance measure for text clustering. In *Proceedings of the Text Mining Workshop, SIAM International Conference on Data Mining*, 2006.

[15] C. Leacock and M. Chodorow. Combining local context and wordnet similarity for word sense identification. *Christiane Fellbaum, editor, WordNet: An Electronic Lexical Database*, pages 265–283, 1998.

[16] B. Magnini and M. Speranza. Integrating generic and specilized wordnets. In *RANLP: Recent Advances in Natural Language Processing*, pages 149–153, 2001.

[17] D. M.Blei, A. Y. Ng, and M. I. Jordan. Latent dirichlet allocation. *Journal of Machine Learning Research*, 3:993–1022, 2003.

[18] J. Morato, M. Á. Marzal, J. Lloréns, and J. Moreiro. Wordnet applications. In *GWC '04: Proceedings of the Second Global Wordnet Conference*, 2004.

[19] H. G. Oliveira and P. Gomes. Towards the automatic creation of a wordnet from a term-based lexical network. In *TextGraphs-5 Proceedings of the 2010 Workshop on Graph-based Methods for Natural Language Processing*, pages 10–18, 2010.

[20] S. P. Ponzetto and R. Navigli. Large-scale taxonomy mapping for restructuring and integrating wikipedia. In *IJCAI '03: Proceedings of the 21st International Joint Conference on Artificial Intelligence*, pages 2083–2088, 2009.

[21] D. R. Recupero. A new unsupervised method for document clustering by using wordnet lexical and conceptual relations. *Information Retrieval*, 10(6):563–579, 2007.

[22] M. Ruiz-Casado, E. Alfonseca, and P. Castells. Automatic assignment of wikipedia encyclopedic entries to wordnet synsets. In *AWIC '05: Proceedings of Advances in Web Intelligence*, pages 380–386, 2005.

[23] S. Scott and S. Matwin. Text classification using wordnet hypernyms. In *COLING-ACL '98: Workshop on Usage of WordNet in NLP Systems*, pages 45–51, 1998.

[24] S. Shehata. A wordnet-based semantic model for enhancing text clustering. In *ICDMW '09: Proceedings of the IEEE International Conference on Data Mining Workshops*, pages 477–482, 2009.

[25] F. M. Suchanek, G. Kasneci, and G. Weikum. Yago: a core of semantic knowledge. In *WWW '07: Proceedings of the 16th International Conference on World Wide Web*, pages 697–706, 2007.

[26] M. Sussna. Word sense disambiguation for free-text indexing using a massive semantic network. In *CIKM '93: Proceedings of the Second International Conference on Information and Knowledge Management*, pages 67–74, 1993.

[27] P. Vossen. Extending, trimming and fusing wordnet for technical documents. In *NAACL Workshop on WordNet and Other Lexical Resources*, 2001.

[28] Y. Yang and X. Liu. A re-examination of text categorization methods. In *SIGIR '99: Proceedings of the 22nd Annual International ACM SIGIR Conference on Research and Development in Information Retrieval*, pages 42–49, 1999.

[29] I. Yoo, X. Hu, and I.-Y. Song. Integration of semantic-based bipartite graph representation and mutual refinement strategy for biomedical literature clustering. In *KDD '06: Proceedings of the 12th ACM SIGKDD International Conference on Knowledge Discovery and Data Mining*, pages 791–796, 2006.

Personal Privacy vs Population Privacy: Learning to Attack Anonymization

Graham Cormode
AT&T Labs-Research
graham@research.att.com

ABSTRACT

Over the last decade great strides have been made in developing techniques to compute functions privately. In particular, Differential Privacy gives strong promises about conclusions that can be drawn about an individual. In contrast, various syntactic methods for providing privacy (criteria such as k-anonymity and l-diversity) have been criticized for still allowing private information of an individual to be inferred.

In this paper, we consider the ability of an attacker to use data meeting privacy definitions to build an accurate classifier. We demonstrate that even under Differential Privacy, such classifiers can be used to infer "private" attributes accurately in realistic data. We compare this to similar approaches for inference-based attacks on other forms of anonymized data. We show how the efficacy of all these attacks can be measured on the same scale, based on the probability of successfully inferring a private attribute. We observe that the accuracy of inference of private attributes for differentially private data and l-diverse data can be quite similar.

Categories and Subject Descriptors.
H.1[**Models and Principles**]: Miscellaneous—*Privacy*

General Terms. Security

Keywords. Differential Privacy, Anonymization

1. INTRODUCTION

The topic of anonymization and privacy has occupied the computer science research community for over a decade now (with efforts in statistics going back even further). Initial efforts focused on trying to modify microdata, via reducing the precision of data (coarsening values, forming tuples into groups). These generally tried to achieve syntactic requirements: famously, k-anonymization [19], and subsequently an alphabet soup of further definitions (l-diversity [17], t-closeness [16], and so on). However, various attacks have been shown on these models which reduced confidence in their suitability for data release. In this setting, a attack has been defined (de facto) as an analysis of the released data which allows an observer to guess the value of a particular attribute of a tuple. The attack is considered successful when the guess is correct with probability larger than is intended by the anonymizer [21, 9, 14].

In parallel, a more principled approach to privacy has arisen, in the form of differential privacy [6]. In its simplest form, differential privacy releases statistics, by computing the exact value of the statistic, and then adding random noise. The random noise is chosen so that the influence of any individual on the statistic is masked by the noise. This leads to the observation that it is safe to provide one's personal data to a mechanism implementing differential privacy, since the conclusions that can be drawn are (broadly) the same, irrespective of whether or not one's data is collected. Consequently, differential privacy has started to be adopted as a 'gold standard' of privacy, and is becoming widely used.

In this paper, we study an attack on differential privacy, in the sense described above: we demonstrate that it is possible to infer information about an individual with non-trivial accuracy. This does not violate any of the (proven) properties of differential privacy. It leads to the seeming contradiction that regardless of whether an individual contributes or withholds their data to a study (or reports false data), we can nevertheless use observable information about them to infer their private information. The attack is ultimately quite simple, and can be executed with low computational effort.

The main message of this paper is that differential privacy is not a universal salve to privacy concerns. While it is a more robust definition than prior syntactic requirements, data published under differential privacy can still allow an adversary to draw conclusions about an individual. When measuring an attack by the probability of making a correct inference about an individual, we observe that over the same data, this probability can actually be higher for differential privacy than for syntactic anonymizations.

Outline. In Section 2, we focus on Differential Privacy. After defining the model we discuss how to build a simple classifier that can be quite accurate at predicting sensitive information. The experiments in this section quantify this, and we discuss immediate consequences. Section 3 contrasts to similar attacks that have been proposed on other anonymization methods, and argues that, measured in terms of probability of successful inference, the efficacy of all these attacks is quite similar. Finally, Section 4 concludes the paper with further discussion of privacy in the presence of inference.

KDD'11, August 21–24, 2011, San Diego, California, USA.

2. DIFFERENTIAL PRIVACY

2.1 The Model

We adopt the canonical model of data from the initial work on anonymization: the input is a table of tuples T, and each tuple $t \in T$ corresponds to an individual. There is one distinguished attribute that is considered 'sensitive' (stereotypically, a disease suffered by the individual, or their salary band, say). This is commonly referred to as the Sensitive Attribute (SA). The remaining attributes are considered partially identifying: demographic information about the individual, such as their age, gender, approximate location, ethnicity and so on. These are referred to in the literature as quasi-identifiers (QI). Separately, each attribute value applies to a large number of individuals in the data, but taken collectively they are often sufficient to uniquely identify an individual [11].

For syntactic approaches to anonymization, the objective is to modify the input data by various operations so that it achieves a given property. The modifications may be to coarsen attributes (replace exact birth date by only year of birth), suppress some attributes entirely, or form tuples into groups and separate the multiset of sensitive values corresponding to each group. In most prior work, the effect of the data modification results in groups of tuples. The goal may be to ensure that each group has at least k members (k-anonymity [19]); or that each group has at most a $1/l$ fraction of tuples with the same sensitive attribute value (simplified l-diversity [17]); and so on.

The differential privacy approach is different, in that it does not explicitly publish microdata. Instead, a query is posed to the data owner. The data owner computes the exact answer of the query, then perturbs the answer by adding appropriate statistical noise. We focus on the core case when all queries are simply a collection of count queries: to count the number of individuals in the data who satisfy certain predicates. Further, our main construction works when there is only a single round of querying, i.e., asking for various counts. That is, there is no adaptive querying in response to previous results. In the literature, the queries we pose are known as histogram queries or contingency tables, and their privacy analysis is well-understood [2]. Note that we can also interpret this as operating in a publishing model, when the data owner chooses a collection of statistics to publish, and applies the differential privacy mechanism to release them. That is, we can apply the attack to the case when the data owner chooses to publish contingency tables for the data under differential privacy.

For a given query q, we must compute its *sensitivity* s_q, which is the maximum influence that any individual can have on the answer vector. This influence is measured under the L_1 norm. Given a parameter ϵ, the data owner computes the vector of answers and adds iid noise to each entry. This noise may be drawn from a (continuous) Laplace distribution with parameter s_q/ϵ, or from a (discrete) symmetric geometric distribution with parameter $\alpha = \exp(-\epsilon/s_q)$ [10]. This guarantees that, for any individual, the probability of any property holding on the output of the algorithm is within a multiplicative factor of at most $\exp(\epsilon)$ of the probability of the same property holding on the dataset with that individual's data omitted. Less formally, the intent of this definition is that even with substantial knowledge about other individuals in the data, it is still hard to deduce any property of a targeted individual.

Dalenius provided an oft-quoted definition of disclosure resulting from data release: "If the release of the statistic S makes it possible to determine the (microdata) value more accurately than without access to S, a disclosure has taken place..." [5]. Following this definition, we define an *attack* on anonymized data as: given a target individual try to discover their sensitive value. More precisely, given access to the output of the anonymization process, and some knowledge about a targeted individual such as their easily observable characteristics (age, sex, ethnicity: quasi-identifiers), an attack infers their associated sensitive value.

This has been formalized in the literature as attribute (non-)privacy [13]. This definition applies to the earliest linking attack of Sweeney on de-identified data [20]; the homogeneity attack on k-anonymous data [17]; the minimality attack, which conditions on knowledge of the algorithm used to create the anonymized data [21]; and the deFinetti attack (discussed in greater detail in Section 3) [14]. All these attacks demonstrate disclosure, in the sense used by Dalenius. The success of the attack may be characterized by its accuracy: the fraction of input tuples for which the attack gives the correct value. Clearly, this fraction will vary as a function of the data, and of parameters of the anonymization.

2.2 Accurate Differentially Private Classifiers

In line with previous attacks on privacy [14, 3], we describe a method to build an accurate classifier which, given the quasi-identifier of an individual, predicts their sensitive attribute. For simplicity, we initially assume that all attributes in the data are categorical and of relatively low cardinality, and later discuss this assumption.

Many classifiers have been proposed in the machine learning literature, but the simplest is the Naive Bayes (NB) classifier. We will build an NB classifier, which aims to predict the SA value given the evidence of QI values of an individual. On an unanonymized data table T, the classifier is built by computing the conditional distributions of each attribute given the target SA value s, i.e., $\Pr[t_i|s]$ for each of the m QI values t_i. The prediction for the tuple t of QI values is[1]

$$\hat{s}(t) = \arg\max_{s \in SA} \Pr[s] \prod_{i=1}^{m} \Pr[t_i|s]$$

Observe that the parameters of this classifier are easy to learn: given a tuple r, r_i is its ith component, and r_s is its sensitive value. Then we use

$$\Pr[t_i|s] = \frac{\Pr[t_i \cap s]}{\Pr[s]} \approx \frac{|\{r \in T : r_i = t_i \cap r_s = s\}|}{|\{r \in T : r_s = s|\}}$$

That is, to build the classifier, we need the counts of values present in T^i, the ith column of table T:

$$\forall s \in SA, 1 \leq i \leq m, v \in T^i : |\{r \in T : r_i = v \cap r_s = s\}| \quad (1)$$

$$\text{and} \quad \forall s \in SA : |\{r \in T : r_s = s\}|$$

from which we can derive the required conditional probabilities.[2]

[1] This can be normalized so that assignment over the different s values yields a probability distribution.

[2] More correctly, we can draw the parameters for the classifier from a Dirichlet distribution given the observed counts.

Observe that the sensitivity of this query is actually quite low: although there are a moderate number of parameters, the largest L_1 difference that any tuple can make to the answer vector is $m+1$. This is because each individual is counted in at most m joint distributions, plus the marginal distribution of SA values. This is exactly the approach proposed in work on releasing histograms and contingency tables [2]. Thus, the attack proceeds by requesting all counts listed in (1). Some small corrections are required: first, the noise may cause some counts to become negative. These can simply be adjusted up to the smallest feasible value, i.e., 0. Second, due to the noise, there is no guarantee that the sum of the counts for attribute i with SA value s will be equal to the marginal count of s. We remedy this by simply defining

$$\Pr[t_i|s] := \frac{1+\max(0,|\{r \in T : r_i = t_i \cap r_s = s\}|)}{\sum_{t \in T_i} 1+\max(0,|\{r \in T : r_i = t \cap r_s = s\}|)}.$$

Here, the addition of 1 is the standard Laplacian correction. Further, we can use $\Pr[s] =$

$$\frac{\sum_{i=1}^{m}\sum_{t \in T_i} 1+\max(0,|\{r \in T : r_i = t \cap r_s = s\}|)}{\sum_{s' \in SA}\sum_{i=1}^{m}\sum_{t \in T_i} 1+\max(0,|\{r \in T : r_i = t \cap r_s = s'\}|)}$$

and therefore reduce the sensitivity of the query s_q from $m+1$ to m.

This "naive attack" is therefore trying to emulate the corresponding classifier built with exact counts. So we do not expect the attack to predict values better than this noiseless classifier. Rather, the question is to what extent the noise introduced by differential privacy degrades the accuracy of the classifier. Historically, Naive Bayes has been shown to get tolerable accuracy (when compared to other classification methods) with a moderate number of attributes, in the range $m = 3$ to 10, say. The sensitivity, also m, is therefore quite low: for settings of ϵ in the range 1.0 to 0.1, the absolute value of the noise introduced to counts is in the single to double-digit range. While this is enough to mask the contribution of any individual, the crucial issue is that for a large enough dataset (with a large number of individuals, $|T|$), the effect on the derived conditional probabilities is still relatively small, and thus the classifier learns approximately the same correlations. Therefore, while a single individual is dominated by the noise, the noise is in turn dominated by the signal emerging from the whole population.

2.3 Experimental Study

A proof-of-concept version of the "naive attack" was implemented in Python. Tests were performed on two data sets containing demographic data: the 'Adult' and 'Internet' data sets from the UCI Machine Learning repository [1]. The adult data set contains multiple attributes from a census-like survey of adults, while the Internet data set contains details of a survey on Internet usage in 1997. From the adult data set, we selected the attributes workclass, level of education completed, occupation, sex, hours worked per week, and the binary attribute on whether income exceeds \$50K. We bucketized hours worked per week into [0–25], [26–40], [41–60] and 60+. After removing tuples with missing sensitive values, there are a total of 30718 tuples in the adult data set. For the Internet data set, we selected the attributes age (treated as categorical but not bucketized), country, education level, gender, occupation, marital status and household income. The income attribute is partitioned into ranges \$10-20K, \$20-30K, \$30-40K, \$40-50K, \$50-75K, \$75-100K, over \$100K, below \$10K, and 'not given'. There are a total of 10108 tuples in the Internet data set. In neither case did we remove tuples with missing QI values, since the classifier is relatively robust to their presence.

Our classifier was implemented to generate conditional probabilities given counts with geometric noise added as a function of the parameter ϵ. We evaluated the accuracy of the classifier by then providing the quasi-identifiers of each input tuple in turn, and counting the fraction for which the correct sensitive attribute was guessed (based on taking the value deemed most likely by the classifier).

Figure 1 shows the accuracy of the naive attack (fraction of correct predictions) on the adult data set as ϵ is varied. We plot the accuracy when the sensitive attribute is 'occupation' (Figure 1(a)) and when it is 'marital status' (the same attributes are targeted in prior work on attacks [3, 14]). Note that there are fourteen categories of occupation in the data, and the baseline method that simply predicts the most frequent occupation achieves 13% accuracy. There are seven categories of marital status, and the most common one occurs 45% of the time. The classifier is quite successful at learning the target attribute: the plot shows the minimum, maximum and mean accuracy across nine independent iterations (over different draws of the noise on the count queries). When ϵ is high, effectively no noise is being added, so the rightmost points are essentially the result of applying this classifier on the original data. As ϵ is decreased, the accuracy reduces gradually, despite more noise being added. Prior work on differential privacy has mostly used values of ϵ in the range $\epsilon = 0.1$ to 1. Even at $\epsilon = 0.01$, the attack achieves a non-trivial accuracy.

The plots in Figure 1 show the accuracy evaluated over the two parts of the adult data set. On the 'training data', we train the classifier on (noisy) counts, and then evaluate its accuracy on the same training data. On the 'test data', we evaluate the same classifier on a withheld test data set. This shows that the classifier is about as accurate on the withheld data as on the training data.

Figure 2 shows a similar experiment on the Internet usage data set, for the targets of household income and occupation (Figures 2(a) and 2(b) respectively). This data is not explicitly divided into training and test subsets, so we treat the full data as 'training'. Income has nine distinct values, the most frequent of which occurs 18% of the time; Occupation has five distinct values, and the most frequent one occurs 23% of the time. There is a similar trend: the noiseless classifier is quite accurate, and increasing the amount of noise gradually reduces this accuracy.

Observe that the classifier's output on each tuple can be interpreted as a probability distribution over sensitive values. Thus we can focus on those tuples for which the classifier places more of its weight on a particular outcome. Figure 3 shows the accuracy (summarizing nine separate, independent repetitions) when restricted to only those tuples for which the classifier's belief is greater than 0.8. They show that on these tuples, the classifier is indeed quite accurate. In the adult data set, there are a few hundred such tuples on average (around 1% of the data) when the target is occupation, and over 8000 (25%) for marital status. For the occupation attribute in the Internet data, there are around 1700 high confidence tuples (17%), and 300 (3%) for income. In other words, there is an appreciable minority of tuples on

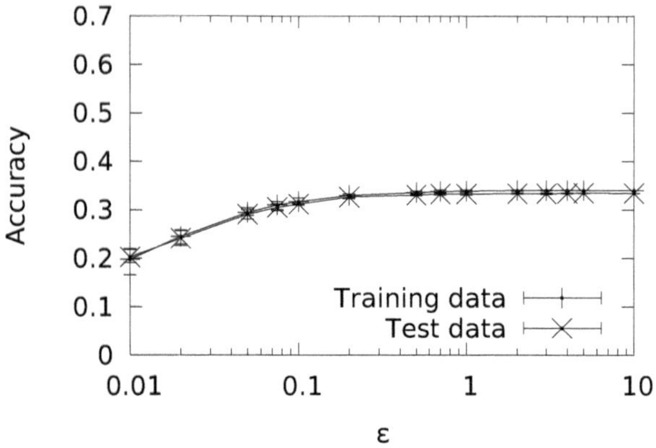

(a) Naive attack on adult-occupation

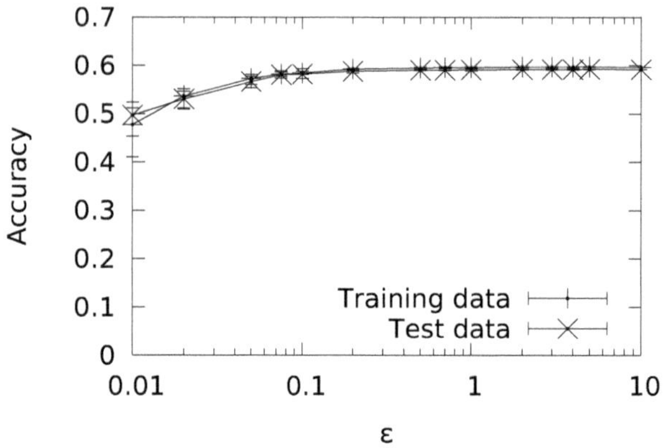

(b) Naive attack on adult-maritalstatus

Figure 1: Naive attack on adult data set

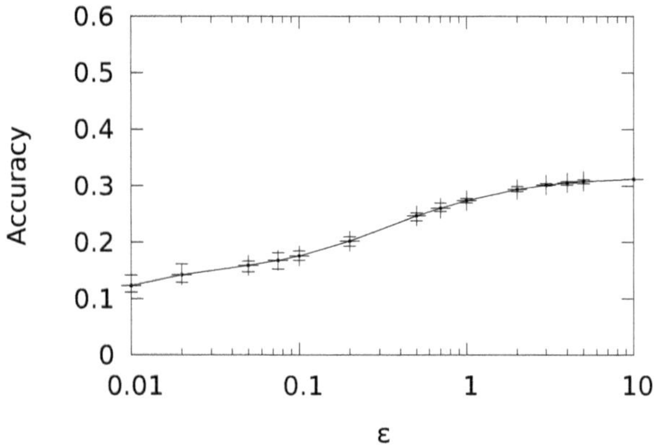

(a) Naive attack on internet-income

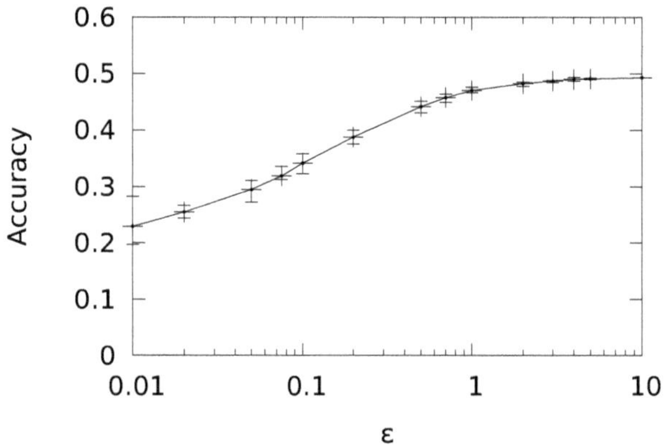

(b) Naive attack on internet-occupation

Figure 2: Naive attack on Internet data set

which the classifier is more confident, and justifiably so: it achieves 85% accuracy on this subset in some cases.

Note that the classifier is quite lightweight to implement. The time to load the data, compute the required counts, add the noise, and apply the classifier to the collection of QI values was about 1 second on the Internet data (10K tuples) and 3 seconds on the adult dataset (32K tuples).

2.4 Discussion

The experiments show that this "attack" can be quite effective: we can learn supposedly private information of an individual with reasonable accuracy. In other words, even under differential privacy, disclosure can take place, in the sense used by Dalenius. Does this contradict the claims for differential privacy? No, in fact it is quite in line with the guarantees of differential privacy. Informally, differential privacy promises that what we can learn from the released data is broadly the same, whether or not any individual contributes their true information, false information, or withholds their information entirely.

This is respected by the attack: rather than directly learning properties of an individual, it is learning properties of a population. The model we learn of the whole population is largely unaffected by any individual's data. However, the potential privacy issue is that this population model is quite accurate at predicting private information at the individual level, given an honest cooperative majority. This is seen most clearly in the experimental study: the classifier is about as accurate on the 'test set' as on the training set. The test set contains individuals who never contributed any information about themselves to building the classifier, yet because they sufficiently resemble the training set, we can still predict their private information.

In fact, this consequence is in some ways anticipated by previous negative results on the possibility of privacy against sufficiently powerful attackers. Dwork [7] illustrates this with the example of an attacker who knows that "Terry Gross is two inches shorter than the average Lithuanian woman": the attacker can learn the average height of the Lithuanian population with high accuracy from a large survey of Lithuanians, and hence learn the individual height of Terry Gross. This example is perhaps easy to dismiss, due to the relative innocuousness of learning anyone's height, and the apparent absurdity of somehow knowing the connection between an individual's height and that of an East European nation. Yet, in our setting, if we replace this knowledge by

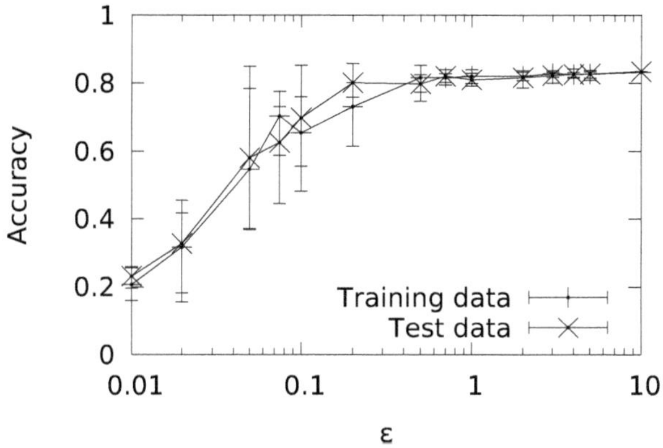

(a) Naive attack with high confidence on adult-occupation

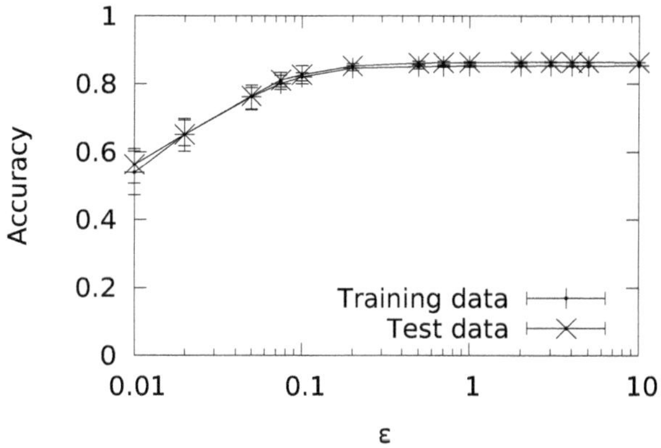

(b) Naive attack with high confidence on adult-maritalstatus

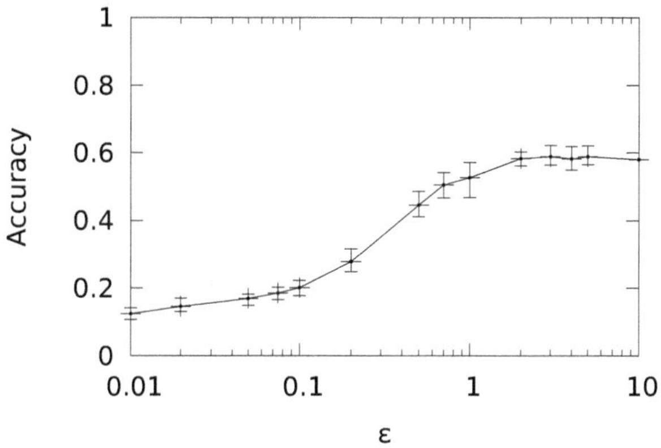

(c) Naive attack with high confidence on internet-income

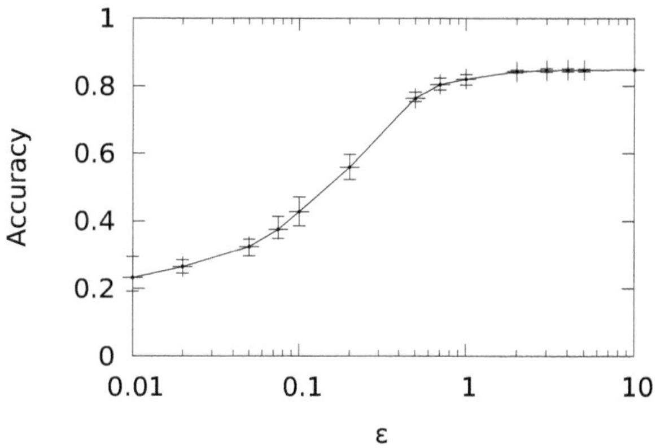

(d) Naive attack with high confidence on internet-occupation

Figure 3: Naive attack restricted to high confidence predictions

the assumption that "Terry Gross' (private) height is correlated with her (observable) age, sex, ethnicity etc., in much the same way as for the population in this survey", then the attack becomes much more plausible. The key differences are that the knowledge of an obscure fact is replaced with a reasonable assumption, and that the correlation can be easily learned from data that meets the differential privacy requirement.

One may still question whether drawing an inference about an individual when they never reveal their private data to anyone is truly an attack in the spirit of the term. We argue that an attack is in the eye of the beholder: if an attacker now believes that he knows an individual's private information with high confidence, then he too is indifferent as to whether the victim contributed to the study that enabled the inference. This is exactly captured by Dalenius' notion of disclosure: this inference would not have been possible without the release of information. Consider the case of a multi-year, many-participant, multi-million dollar genetic study: an attacker would not invest this much effort themself, but can build a very accurate classifier from the released statistics for free. The core issue is that latent properties of a population, when learned, can compromise the privacy of an individual. This example has demonstrated that this is not an academic concern, but can be instantiated easily and cheaply on typical data.

2.5 Variations

Choice of Attributes. In general, adding more attributes to a Naive Bayes classifier improves its accuracy. However, in our setting, each extra attribute increases the sensitivity of the query required, and thus the noise introduced. There is therefore a delicate tradeoff: the increase in classifier accuracy from the increased knowledge of correlations, against the loss in accuracy due to more noise. We leave more detailed discussion of this aspect for future study.

Continuous attributes. Naive Bayes is less effective when treating continuous attributes (such as height in millimetres) as categorical: there is too little evidence for any fixed value to accurately learn the underlying correlation. There are two natural fixes: the first is to model the distribution as, e.g., a Gaussian, and to learn the parameters of the distribution (mean, variance) via appropriate count queries (which remain low sensitivity). The second is to 'bucketize' the attribute based on some natural bucketing scheme to make it categorical: group height into 10cm intervals, for example. This places together values that are semantically similar, so that appropriate correlations can still be determined. The same approach works when an attribute is categorical but has very high cardinality: domain-aware bucketing or coarsening can ensure that each count is sufficiently large to be unaffected by the noise. For example, location data at the street level might be coarsened to the town, state or country level, depending on the detail of the data. We assume that the adversary is able to request data according to the bucketing of their choice.

Other Classifier Choices. We focus on Naive Bayes due to its simplicity, the relatively small number of parameters and the minimal modeling skill needed in its use. Moreover, it is successful in this case because it has a low sensitivity. Naturally, one can also consider other classifiers. A first step is to consider higher-degree correlations: we can remove independence assumptions, e.g., by replacing separate factors of sex and age-range with the joint distribution of sex and age-range conditioned on the SA. This further reduces the sensitivity of the query (and hence the noise), but needs to be approached with care: just as in traditional Naive Bayes, partitioning up the space may lead to too few examples in each category. In our setting, this is further worsened since it increases the *relative* amount of noise added to each count: although the absolute noise on each decreases, the counts themselves are much reduced, so the effect of the noise is greater.

More generally, other classifiers can be built (although these may need multiple rounds of interaction with the data owner, in contrast to the one round for the NB classifier). Indeed, there has been much prior work discussing the suitability of differential privacy for accurate learning [18, 12, 8].[3] The chief concern is to consider the sensitivity of the classifier: extending to Bayesian networks does not substantially alter the sensitivity, which depends only on the number of nodes in the network. Various regression models also have low sensitivity. On the other hand, building a large number of random decision trees has high sensitivity, and requires the data owner to respond interactively to many queries as the classifier determines where to split each node.

3. COMPARISON TO THE DEFINETTI ATTACK

The attack described in the previous section is inspired by the deFinetti attack on syntactically anonymized data, introduced by Kifer [14]. The goal of the deFinetti attack is to build a classifier that, given the quasi-identifiers of a tuple in a group, is able to predict the corresponding sensitive attribute value. In other words, the approach and goal of the deFinetti attack on syntactic anonymization matches that of the above naive attack on differential privacy. Moreover, the instantiation of the attack was also done based on Naive Bayes as the classifier, and the same datasets, meaning that we can compare the methods in more detail.

3.1 The deFinetti Attack

We now briefly summarize our deployment of the deFinetti attack. As in the previous study [14], we fix the method used to anonymize data as Anatomy, and the classifier as Naive Bayes, with the understanding that both of these can be replaced by other methods.

[3]In particular, McSherry and Mironov point to the potential for accurate personalized predictions to compromise the privacy of an individual [18].

Anatomy is a grouping-based anonymization method [22]. Given a parameter l, it partitions the input data of size n into groups of size l (and some of size $l+1$ when l does not divide n), such that in each group there is at most one tuple for any given SA value. The published version of the data includes the multiset of QIs in each group, and the multiset of SAs in each group, but withholds the exact mapping between them. The intent is therefore that a simplistic adversary should believe that any given QI in the group has a uniform chance of being associated with any particular SA in the same group, and thus bounds their belief in any association by at most $1/l$.

Kifer's observation is that there is sufficient correlation in the published group data that a more sophisticated adversary can learn a better set of beliefs (in the form of a classifier). The attack proceeds by guessing an initial random permutation for each group to map each QI value to one SA value. This induces a set of conditional distributions over each quasi-identifier value given a sensitive attribute value, which describes a Naive Bayes classifier. Indeed, this view is present in prior work: Brickell and Shmatikov describe essentially this first step in an earlier paper [3].

The deFinetti attack goes further by using the classifier (built from global information) to assess the relative likelihood of the current permutation in each group. One can then sample other possible permutations, and decide to adopt them in place of the current permutation: deterministically so if they are deemed more likely, and randomly so if they are less likely. The likelihoods are determined by the current classifier. By iterating this process over many steps, the expectation is that the process converges to an accurate classifier.

The classifier can be used in conjunction with information from the anonymized data to make predictions. As originally described, given a QI value within a specific group, its predicted SA value can be that assigned to it based on the current permutation (or a history of recent assignments). This is the version described by Kifer [14], which we refer to as the 'permutation' method. Next, we introduce other ways in which the information computed can be used to predict an SA value. As described above, the current permutation also implies a set of conditional distributions (or marginals) which together yield a Naive Bayes classifier. Given a QI value within a specific group, we can ignore the other values in the group, and directly apply this classifier to it, to obtain a predicted SA value. We call this approach the 'open' method, since it is open to pick any available SA value. Note that the open method should never be appreciably better than the NB classifier built from the original, noiseless data. A third approach extends the open method by using some limited knowledge about the group containing the targeted tuple. Overall, there may be many different possible SA values, but within the group only l are present. In this case, we can condition on this knowledge, and allow the classifier to choose only from those SA values present in the group. We call this the 'group' method. We experimentally compare these three methods—the original 'permutation' method and the new 'group' and 'open' methods.

3.2 Experimental Study

The original study of the deFinetti attack presented experiments with relatively small values of l (2,3,4) on the Adult data set. Starting from Kifer's original implementation, we

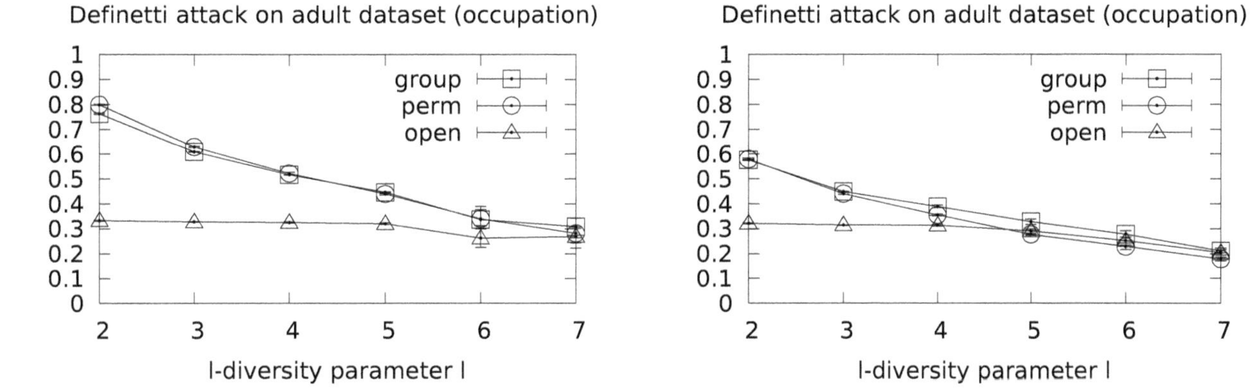

(a) deFinetti attack on adult-occupation (tight groups) (b) deFinetti attack on adult-occupation (larger groups)

Figure 4: deFinetti attack on adult-occupation

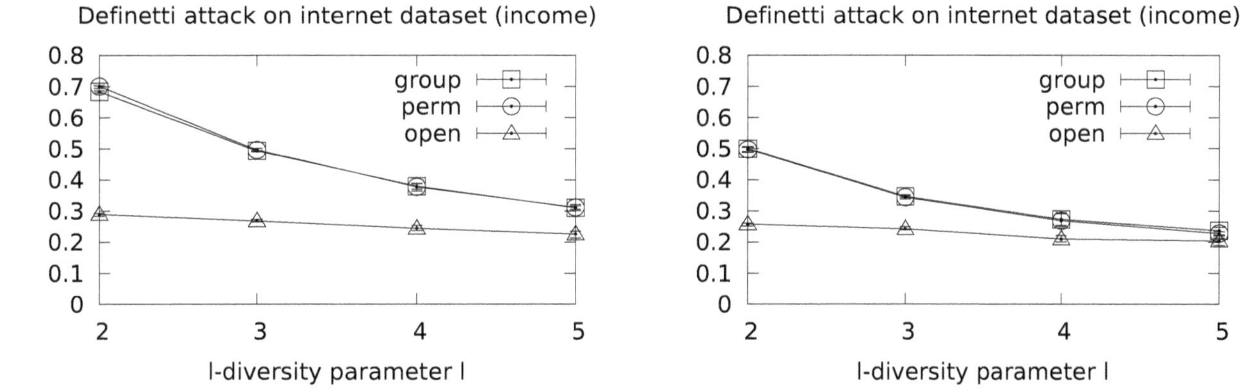

(a) deFinetti attack on Internet-income (tight groups) (b) deFinetti attack on Internet-income (larger groups)

Figure 5: deFinetti attack on Internet-income

extended the method to study its accuracy on larger group sizes, and under the additional prediction methods (group and open, in addition to permutation). We describe our results for the same target, the 'occupation' attribute of the Adult data set. We perform 1000 iterations of the learning process: analyzing the accuracy of the classifier and the L_1 norm between subsequent joint distributions confirms that this is sufficiently many steps for the process to almost converge in most cases. We perform five repetitions of each experiment, and plot the max, min and average accuracy of each of the three methods to predict SA values (permutation, group and open). Note that in many cases, the max, min and average values are so close that they are barely distinguishable on the plots.

Figure 4 shows the effects of the attack for different choices of the parameter l. Note that $l = 7$ is the upper limit for l-diversity on this data set, since there is one occupation which occurs just below $1/7$ of the time. Figure 4(a) shows that our results agree with those reported in [14] for $l = 2, 3, 4$: in fact they show the attack to be more effective due to including tuples with missing QI values (giving more evidence), and choosing a slightly different set of QI attributes (giving a stronger classifier). The observation is that accuracy is clearly better than the trivial bound of $1/l$ when the adversary simply applies a uniform prior over all permutations from QI to SA values in each group, and does not attempt to learn a better classifier. Nevertheless, the trend is for the accuracy to decrease as l increases.

The plot shows that the attack requires locating a target tuple within the published data in order to be truly effective. That is, without applying a constraint to the sensitive attribute (i.e., using the 'open' approach), the accuracy is never better than the corresponding classifier trained on the true counts (see Figure 1(a), for a large ϵ value). Only when the attacker can guarantee finding the target tuple uniquely in the published data can he achieve the higher accuracy via the group or permutation method. For small groups, the permutation method (which conditions on other tuples in the same group) is slightly more accurate, but when the group grows large enough, the group method (which only predicts via the target tuple) becomes more accurate.

While the accuracy in all cases far exceeds $1/l$, at a group size of 7, the impact of the attack is less than that of the naive attack on differential privacy: the accuracy falls below 30%. This implies that the impact of the attack can be reduced by increasing group sizes without changing the level of

l-diversity. Our first set of plots showed the accuracy when the l diverse groups have size exactly l: we call this the *tight groups* case. In the *larger groups* case, we make groups of size $2l$ by taking the output of the Anatomy procedure and merge together pairs of adjacent groups. It follows immediately that the resulting output remains l-diverse, but the groups are now twice as large. The accuracy on these larger groups is shown further in Figure 4(b).

Again, the accuracy exceeds $1/l$, but by a lower amount, and it falls below that of the noiseless classifier for $l = 5$ (group size 10). The permutation method is more clearly dominated by the group method, but both become close to the open method for larger groups. Increasing the size of the groups further decreases the ability of the classifier: when we merge together three groups (not shown), the permutation method degrades to about $1/l$ accuracy.

Similar results are seen on other data sets. Figure 5 shows the results on the Internet data set with 'income' as the SA value. Again, the open approach is never better than the noiseless classifier, and degrades as the group size increases. Being able to identify the target tuple within a group increases the accuracy above $1/l$, although this falls as the group size increases. Merging groups together further reduces the power of the attack: Figure 5(b) shows that the accuracy is the same as that of the noiseless classifier (see Figure 2(a)) when l reaches 4. In larger groups (merging three groups into one), the accuracy is below $1/l$. As in the Differential Privacy case, we can focus in on those predictions in which the classifier places the highest confidence. We omit full details in this presentation, but observe that there are similar trends: under the 'group' definition, on small groups the attack has an appreciable number of individuals with high confidence predictions, which are indeed correct more often than for the rest of the population. As the group size is increased, the number of high confidence predictions dwindles, and the average accuracy falls back to the global level.

3.3 deFinetti and Differential Privacy

Since its introduction, the deFinetti attack has been seen by some as the "last nail in the coffin" of syntactic privacy methods, and used to argue that only differentially private methods should be considered. Certainly, the attack can be potent when applied to data published with very small values of the parameter l and small groups. However, prior work on anonymization has typically used somewhat larger parameters: l in the range 6-10 at least, and group sizes of 10-100 for higher security. In these situations, the attack loses its power: its accuracy reduces to $1/l$ (or worse), the same as simply guessing a value for each tuple uniformly from those in the group. Focusing only on privacy, it seems that the impact of the attack can be mitigated.

Moreover, these experiments show that the deFinetti attack is directly comparable to the above naive attack on differential privacy. Both model the data in the same way, target the same goal and attempt to build the same classifier to predict private information. Most of the effort in the deFinetti attack is expended in building the model of the population, which is trivial under differential privacy. Actually applying the classifier is then quite cheap in comparison.

The potential for the deFinetti attack to reveal more comes from additionally being able to condition on the limited set of possibilities within a group to eliminate or reduce the likelihood of possible values for a given tuple. That is, the 'open' method has (roughly) the accuracy from using properties of the population alone, and the additional power of group/perm comes from the additional information presented by the published data. This is impactful for small group sizes, but the advantage seems to be substantially diminished for larger group sizes. For certain settings of parameters, differential privacy can be *more* susceptible to attack than the corresponding syntactic anonymization: the accuracy of the model of the population built in the latter case is lower than in the former case. Thus neither approach is immune to attacks that build accurate classifiers.

Of course, syntactic anonymization is subject to other criticisms and attacks. But rejecting all such anonymizations because the deFinetti attack exists is erroneous: by the same logic, we should also abandon differential privacy as well. Rather, we need to consider more nuanced threat models: against what adversary do we require the anonymized data to withstand? This should differ depending on whether we are sharing anonymized data with a colleague in another department or releasing a data set publicly on the web. Depending on the perceived threats, and the consequences of a successful attack, it may be appropriate to use any one of deidentification, syntactic privacy, differential privacy, or withholding release entirely.

4. DISCUSSION

The core issue highlighted here is that coarse properties of the population taken together combine to build a model that can be applied to individuals with high accuracy. Existing anonymization methods tend to ignore this issue, and prior work has brushed this aside, assuming that such correlations can be ignored, or are known to all data users already. However, this is not sufficient: in reality, release of (anonymized) data may reveal hitherto unknown population parameters which compromise individual privacy. It seems unlikely that future efforts can satisfactorily resolve this issue, since in some settings, these population statistics may represent exactly the desired *utility* of the data collection and publication. For example, the results of scientific studies are frequently conveyed to the public in the form of simple conditional probabilities ("drinking two glasses of wine each day reduces the chance of heart disease by 50%", say). Allowing individuals to learn these relationships, and modify their behavior accordingly, is seen as a potential benefit of such studies. Meanwhile, the use of such information by a healthcare provider to prioritize patients for treatment may be seen as less desirable for the same individual.

To what extent should the attacks discussed in this paper chill our enthusiasm for differential privacy, or anonymization in general? In part, this depends on how severely we view the disclosure resulting from the attack. Here, the choice of terminology becomes an issue. The term "attack" has been inherited by the privacy world from the area of security. In security, an "attack" is typically understood to be a mechanism that compromises a supposedly secure system and permits access to the system or information within it. For example, a successful attack on an encrypted message typically reveals the cleartext content of the message to the attacker. Critically, our expectation is that a successful instance of an attack on security correctly indicates that it has indeed succeeded: the revealed message is determined to be the message that was sent.

For initial attacks on anonymization systems, it was clear that disclosure had occurred: Sweeney was sure that she had identified the health records belonging to the Governor of Massachusetts [20]. Subsequent attacks are more probabilistic in nature: the minimality attack (as introduced in [21] and analyzed in [4]) and the deFinetti attack [14] give an elevated belief in the association between a private value and an individual, but they do not provide certainty. Although we can empirically determine that these attacks are correct in associating an individual with their true value a large fraction of the time, they do not help to indicate with certainty for which individuals this is a true inference, and for which it is a false positive. The same is true of the naive attack we describe here: the classifier is often right, but we are never fully sure when.

For such probabilistic attacks, we must therefore decide what level of belief we can tolerate. This is naturally a function of the sensitivity of the information being inferred, and the way in which it is being used. For example, a blackmailer threatening to reveal a target's true sexuality to their family can perhaps tolerate making a few false accusations before finding a victim, while a law enforcement organization might require a much higher degree of suspicion before being granted a warrant to investigate further. Note however, as has been elaborated elsewhere, proceeding with an incorrect belief about an individual can be just as damaging to them as a correct belief (e.g., leading to denial of insurance coverage).

Clearly, there are many questions remaining over the use of data and its privacy-respecting dissemination. Recent work in parallel to this also identified ways in which the power of differential privacy has been overstated, and demonstrated that some common informal claims do not in fact hold [15]. One clear message from these studies is that it is not sufficient to naively apply differential privacy to data, and assume that this is sufficient to address all privacy concerns. Instead, much more careful deliberation about the consequences of the data release is needed.

Acknowledgements. Thanks to Divesh Srivastava and Magda Procopiuc for detailed discussions, and to Dan Kifer for sharing his implementation of Anatomy and the deFinetti attack, and comments. Thanks also to Adam Smith, Entong Shen and Michael Hay for comments on earlier drafts. I also acknowledge the comments of anonymous reviewers.

5. REFERENCES

[1] A. Asuncion and D. Newman. UCI ML repository, 2007.

[2] B. Barak, K. Chaudhuri, C. Dwork, S. Kale, F. McSherry, and K. Talwar. Privacy, accuracy, and consistency too: a holistic solution to contingency table release. In *ACM Principles of Database Systems*, 2007.

[3] J. Brickell and V. Shmatikov. The cost of privacy: Destruction of data-mining utility in anonymized data publishing. In *ACM SIGKDD*, 2008.

[4] G. Cormode, N. Li, T. Li, and D. Srivastava. Minimizing minimality and maximizing utility: Analyzing method-based attacks on anonymized data. In *International Conference on Very Large Data Bases*, 2010.

[5] T. Dalenius. Towards a methodology for statistical disclosure control. *Statistik Tidskrift*, 15:429–444, 1977.

[6] C. Dwork. Differential privacy. In *ICALP*, pages 1–12, 2006.

[7] C. Dwork. Differential privacy: A survey of results. In *Theory and Applications of Models of Computation*, 2008.

[8] A. Friedman and A. Schuster. Data mining with differential privacy. In *ACM SIGKDD*, 2010.

[9] S. R. Ganta, S. P. Kasiviswanathan, and A. Smith. Composition attacks and auxiliary information in data privacy. In *ACM SIGKDD*, 2008.

[10] A. Ghosh, T. Roughgarden, and M. Sundararajan. Universally utility-maximizing privacy mechanisms. In *ACM Symposium on Theory of Computing*, 2009.

[11] P. Golle. Revisiting the uniqueness of simple demographics in the us population. In *Workshop On Privacy In The Electronic Society*, 2006.

[12] S. P. Kasiviswanathan, H. K. Lee, K. Nissim, S. Raskhodnikova, and A. Smith. What can we learn privately? In *IEEE Conference on Foundations of Computer Science*, 2008.

[13] S. P. Kasiviswanathan, M. Rudelson, A. Smith, and J. Ullman. The price of privately releasing contingency tables and the spectra of random matrices with correlated rows. In *ACM Symposium on Theory of Computing*, 2010.

[14] D. Kifer. Attacks on privacy and deFinetti's theorem. In *ACM SIGMOD International Conference on Management of Data*, 2009.

[15] D. Kifer and A. Machanavajjhala. No free lunch in data privacy. In *ACM SIGMOD International Conference on Management of Data*, 2011.

[16] N. Li, T. Li, and S. Venkatasubramanian. t-closeness: Privacy beyond k-anonymity and l-diversity. In *IEEE International Conference on Data Engineering*, 2007.

[17] A. Machanavajjhala, J. Gehrke, D. Kifer, and M. Venkitasubramaniam. ℓ-diversity: Privacy beyond k-anonymity. In *IEEE International Conference on Data Engineering*, 2006.

[18] F. McSherry and I. Mironov. Differentially private recommender systems: Building privacy into the netflix prize contenders. In *ACM SIGKDD*, 2009.

[19] P. Samarati and L. Sweeney. Protecting privacy when disclosing information: k-anonymity and its enforcement through generalization and suppression. Technical Report SRI-CSL-98-04, SRI, 1998.

[20] L. Sweeney. k-anonymity: a model for protecting privacy. *International Journal on Uncertainty, Fuzziness and Knowledge-based systems*, 10(5):557–570, 2002.

[21] R. C.-W. Wong, A. W.-C. Fu, K. Wang, and J. Pei. Minimality attack in privacy preserving data publishing. In *International Conference on Very Large Data Bases*, pages 543–554, 2007.

[22] X. Xiao and Y. Tao. Anatomy: Simple and effective privacy preservation. In *International Conference on Very Large Data Bases*, 2006.

Privacy-Preserving Social Network Publication Against Friendship Attacks

Chih-Hua Tai
Dept. of Electrical Engineering
National Taiwan University
hana@arbor.ee.ntu.edu.tw

Philip S. Yu
Dept. of Computer Science
University of Illinois at Chicago
psyu@cs.uic.edu

De-Nian Yang
Inst. of Information Science
Academia Sinica
dnyang@iis.sinica.edu.tw

Ming-Syan Chen
Research Ctr. for Information Tech. Innovation
Academia Sinica
mschen@citi.sinica.edu.tw

ABSTRACT

Due to the rich information in graph data, the technique for privacy protection in published social networks is still in its infancy, as compared to the protection in relational databases. In this paper we identify a new type of attack called a friendship attack. In a friendship attack, an adversary utilizes the degrees of two vertices connected by an edge to re-identify related victims in a published social network data set. To protect against such attacks, we introduce the concept of k^2-degree anonymity, which limits the probability of a vertex being re-identified to $1/k$. For the k^2-degree anonymization problem, we propose an Integer Programming formulation to find optimal solutions in small-scale networks. We also present an efficient heuristic approach for anonymizing large-scale social networks against friendship attacks. The experimental results demonstrate that the proposed approaches can preserve much of the characteristics of social networks.

Categories and Subject Descriptors

H.2.8 [**Database Management**]: Database Applications—*Data Mining*

General Terms

Algorithms

Keywords

privacy, anonymization, social network publication

1. INTRODUCTION

The social relationships and activities shared by individuals in a social network can be modeled as a graph in which each vertex represents an individual, and the social relationships and activities are summarized by the edges. Due to the rapid growth in the number of services and applications that leverage social networks, there is increasing concern about privacy issues in published social networks [8, 15, 20]. The prevention of vertex re-identification is one of the critical privacy issues that have been addressed. The complexity of graph data has motivated various background knowledge attacks [5, 6, 9, 19, 21].

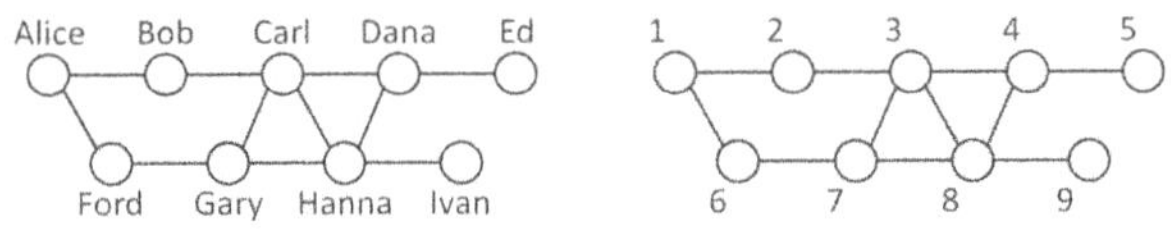

(a) original social network G (b) naïve anonymized $\overline{G}$

Figure 1: An example of the friendship attack.

In this paper, we identify a new type of attack, called a *friendship attack*, based on the vertex degree pair of an edge. Note that in a social networking website, such as Facebook, MySpace or Friendster, an adversary can acquire the number of friends of an individual[1]. Moreover, the adversary can also extract the friendship relation between two individuals from the interaction information publicly available on the website. Therefore, using the vertex degrees of two individuals and their friendship relation, the adversary can issue a friendship attack on the published social network to re-identify the vertices corresponding to an individual and his friend as well as associated vertex information, such as hobbies, activities and religious beliefs. Consider Figure 1 as an example. Suppose that a user's friend count is made publicly available on a social networking website. With the vertex degree information, an adversary cannot uniquely re-identify anyone from the naïve anonymized social network in Figure 1(b). However, if the adversary also knows that Bob and Carl are friends, both Bob and Carl are uniquely identified by the vertex degree pair $(2, 4)$. This example illustrates that it is possible to launch an effective attack and identify individuals as long as the friendship information on the social networking websites can be obtained.

To prevent friendship attacks, we introduce the novel concept of k^2-degree anonymity, which ensures that the prob-

[1]Nowadays the default setting in Facebook is to display all friends of an individual in his/her corresponding profile, in order to encourage users to find common friends.

ability of a vertex identity being revealed is not greater than $1/k$ even if an adversary knows a certain degree pair (d_A, d_B), where A and B are friends and d_A and d_B are their vertex degrees, i.e., the number of friends, respectively. For the k^2-degree anonymization problem, we propose an Integer Programming formulation to find optimal solutions and an efficient heuristic approach for anonymizing large-scale social networks. After that, we also consider a stronger attack based on the degrees of a sequence of friends with length l, and extend the proposed algorithm to achieve the corresponding k^l-degree anonymity. The experimental results show that the social networks anonymized by our approaches preserve the characteristics of the original social networks.

2. RELATED WORK

A number of recent studies have been proposed to protect vertex identities in published social networks against various attacks [5, 6, 9, 13, 19, 21]. In [9], Liu and Terzi consider the attack of vertex degree, and propose k-degree anonymity to protect each individual in a group consisting of at least k vertices of the same degree. For the same attack model, Tai et al. [13] propose k-structural diversity to resist vertex re-identification as well as community re-identification. While the above approaches aim to prevent attacks based on vertex degrees, the objective of this paper is to prevent friendship attacks based on degree pairs.

Zhou and Pei [19] identify the knowledge of the neighborhood configuration and propose a method to prevent 1-neighborhood attacks. Since such attacks focus on the connectivity of a subgraph within the range of one hop to a vertex, the method [19] does not consider the vertex degrees of neighbors; thus, it cannot protect against friendship attacks. For example, the graph in Figure 1(b) satisfies 1-neighborhood anonymity for k set as 2, but the vertex pairs 2 and 3, 6 and 7, 4 and 5, and 8 and 9 can be uniquely re-identified by the degree pairs (2,4), (2,3), (3,1) and (4,1), respectively. Zou et al. [21] propose k-automorphism against subgraph attacks with an arbitrary range to any vertex. However, since any arbitrarily large subgraph must be protected, their approaches need to add many new vertices and adjust many edges of the original graph to make a graph symmetric for anonymization. This decreases the utility of the anonymized graph for some applications. Therefore, unlike [21], we focus on only degree pairs or a limited range of degree sequences that can be specified by users for the corresponding applications. Moreover, in contrast to [19, 21], we preserve the vertex set, i.e., we do not add or delete vertices, to better maintain the data utility of the anonymized graph.

The approaches proposed in [5, 6] also protect against subgraph attacks. However, unlike the above works, [5] groups vertices and then collapses each group of vertices into a single super-vertex for privacy protection, while [6] partitions the graph into local substructures and treats each substructure as a single unit to be anonymized.

Other works focus on the problem of link disclosure [3, 16, 17, 18]. Ying and Wu [16] investigate edge re-identification without considering the background knowledge of an adversary and perform random edge addition, edge deletion and edge swap for anonymization. Zhang et al. [17] assume that an adversary knows some vertex descriptions such as degrees, and propose reducing the probability of the existence of an edge linking two individuals by edge swap and edge deletion. The approach does not consider the resistance to vertex re-identification. Therefore, it is possible that a victim can be uniquely re-identified, even if the probability that an edge links the victim and his/her friend is small. For example, in the social network in Figure 1, an attacker cannot determine whether Bob and Carl are friends from the anonymized graph because the probability of an edge linking a vertex of degree 2 and a vertex of degree 4 is $1/6$. However, if the friendship information is known, both Bob and Carl can be uniquely identified by the degree pair $(2, 4)$. Cheng et al. [3] propose k-isomorphism to protect links as well as vertices against subgraph attacks. Similar to [21], they do not impose restrictions on the size of a subgraph, and they need to add vertices to anonymize a graph such that it becomes symmetric. In addition, the work in [18] considers multiple edge types, and proposes five strategies to protect sensitive edges.

3. PROBLEM FORMULATION

In this paper, we model a social network as a simple graph $G = (V, E)$, where V is the set of vertices corresponding to the individuals, and $E \subseteq V \times V$ is the set of edges representing the relationships between the individuals. Let d_v denote the degree of a vertex v. For a published social network $\overline{G}$ of G, we define a friendship attack as follows.

DEFINITION 1. ***Friendship Attack***. Given a target individual A and the degree pair information $D^2 = (d_1, d_2)$, a friendship attack (D^2, A) exploits D^2 to identify a vertex v_1 corresponding to A in $\overline{G}$, such that v_1 connects to another vertex v_2 in $\overline{G}$ with the degree pair $(d_{v_1}, d_{v_2}) = (d_1, d_2)$.

The published social network $\overline{G}$ may have multiple candidate vertices satisfying the above degree pair requirement. However, it is easier for the adversary to identify A from the candidate vertices when the number of candidate vertices is small. Therefore, to achieve privacy preservation, we define k^2-degree anonymity as follows.

DEFINITION 2. ***k^2-Degree Anonymity***. A graph $\overline{G}$ is k^2-degree anonymous if, for every vertex with an incident edge of degree pair (d_1, d_2) in $\overline{G}$, there exist at least $k - 1$ other vertices, such that each of the $k - 1$ vertices also has an incident edge of the same degree pair.

If $\overline{G}$ has an isolated vertex, i.e., a vertex with degree 0, k^2-degree anonymity requires that at least $k - 1$ other vertices with degree 0 must exist to ensure anonymity. Figure 2 shows examples of different anonymous graphs. The graph in Figure 2(a) has four candidate vertices $\{1, 4, 5, 6\}$ with $D^2 = (1, 3)$, and two candidate vertices $\{2, 3\}$ with $D^2 = (3, 3)$ and $D^2 = (3, 1)$. Therefore, the graph is 2^2-degree anonymous. Similarly, the graph in Figure 2(b) is 3^2-degree anonymous because all three vertices are candidate vertices with $D^2 = (2, 2)$. In contrast, the graph in Figure 2(c) has candidate vertices $\{1, 5\}$ with $D^2 = (1, 2)$, $\{2, 7\}$ with $D^2 = (2, 3)$, $\{6, 7\}$ with $D^2 = (2, 2)$, $\{2, 6\}$ with $D^2 = (2, 1)$, $\{4, 9\}$ with $D^2 = (1, 3)$ and $\{3, 8\}$ with $D^2 = (3, 1)$, $(3, 2)$ and $(3, 3)$. Therefore, the graph is 2^2-degree anonymous. Note that k^2-degree anonymity does not simply identify k edges with degree pair (d_1, d_2) because the k edges in this case are allowed to share some common vertices. Thus, this edge-based approach does not guarantee that at least k vertices will be provided for each degree in (d_1, d_2).

An adversary with the information $D^2 = (d_1, d_2)$ can launch a friendship attack as well as a vertex degree attack, i.e., $D = (d_1)$, to identify a vertex corresponding to A.

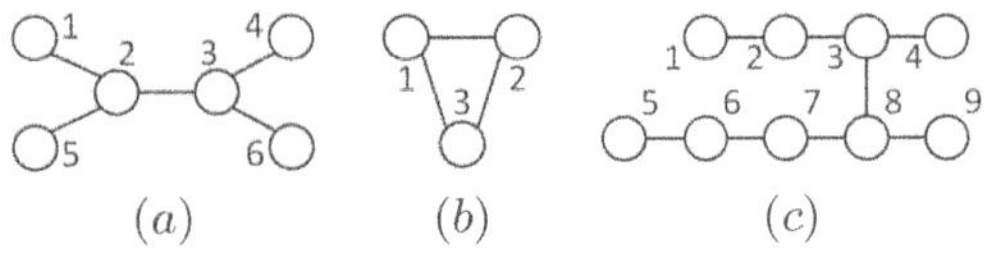

Figure 2: Examples of anonymous graphs: (a) 2^2-degree, (b) 3^2-degree and (c) 2^2-degree.

However, k^2-degree anonymity has the following properties of downward closure protection.

PROPOSITION 1. If a graph $\overline{G}$ is k^2-degree anonymous, $\overline{G}$ is also k-degree anonymous.

PROPOSITION 2. If a graph $\overline{G}$ is k_1^2-degree anonymous, $\overline{G}$ is also k_2^2-degree anonymous for every $k_2 \leq k_1$.

With the above properties, the problem involves anonymizing a graph $G = (V, E)$ to a published version $\overline{G} = (\overline{V}, \overline{E})$ such that $\overline{G}$ is k^2-degree anonymous. To limit the distortion in $\overline{G}$, we preserve the vertex set, i.e., $\overline{V} = V$, and allow only edge addition and deletion operations. Preserving the vertex set prevents the addition or removal of any individual. Since no potential candidates are removed, all possible leaders, influential vertices, and bridge vertices remain. This allows all corresponding behavior patterns to be more easily identified. In contrast, when vertex addition and deletion operations are allowed [3, 21], the information about vertices is likely to be distorted. A similar argument has been pointed out in record anonymization of relational databases, where the deletion or addition of records is considered less desirable than attribute value perturbation or generalization [4].

Based on the above observation, we define the anonymization cost incurred by edge addition and deletion, which are also considered in the anonymization cost of previous works[2] [15, 20].

DEFINITION 3. ***Anonymization Cost.*** Given a weight ω, $0 < \omega < 1$, the cost of anonymizing $G = (V, E)$ to $\overline{G} = (V, \overline{E})$ is

$$Cost(G, \overline{G}) = \omega|\overline{E} \backslash E| + (1 - \omega)\,|E \backslash \overline{E}|.$$

When ω approaches zero, we prefer to preserve the existing edges and generate a super graph $\overline{G}$ of G. In contrast, a larger ω leads to more edge deletions. We compare the solutions with different ω settings in Section 6.4. Next, we define the anonymization problem considered in this paper.

DEFINITION 4. ***Problem k^2-Degree Anonymization.*** Given $G = (V, E)$, a positive integer k, and a weight ω, $0 < \omega < 1$, the problem is to minimize $Cost(G, \overline{G})$ for anonymizing G to $\overline{G} = (V, \overline{E})$ such that $\overline{G}$ is k^2-degree anonymous.

To solve the problem, we propose an Integer Programming formulation in Section 4 to find optimal solutions for small instances. Then, in Section 5, we present an efficient heuristic algorithm for anonymizing large-scale social networks.

4. INTEGER PROGRAMMING

In this section, we propose an Integer Programming formulation for k^2-degree anonymization. The formulation contains the following binary variables. Variable $\alpha_{u,v}$ represents if a new edge (u, v) is added to G, and variable $\delta_{u,v}$ denotes if an existing edge is deleted from G. Variable $\gamma_{u,m}$ indicates if the degree of vertex u is m, where Δ denotes the set of degrees. Variable $\phi_{m,n}$ indicates if $D^2 = (m, n)$ is an anonymous group that needs to be protected from friendship attacks, where Δ^+ denotes the set of positive degrees, i.e., $\Delta = \Delta^+ \cup \{0\}$. Variable $\theta_{m,n,u}$ represents whether vertex u is with degree m and is in an anonymous group $D^2 = (m, n)$, and $\varepsilon_{u,v,n}$ denotes if an edge (u, v) exists in the solution graph $\overline{G}$, with the degree of vertex v as n.

Specifically, the objective function is as follows.

$$\min \omega \sum_{(u,v)\notin E} \alpha_{u,v} + (1 - \omega) \sum_{(u,v)\in E} \delta_{u,v}.$$

The formulation includes the following three categories of constraints to ensure that $\alpha_{u,v}$ and $\delta_{u,v}$ correspond to the solution to k^2-degree anonymization.

1. Degree Constraints

$$\sum_{(u,v)\notin E} \alpha_{u,v} + \sum_{(u,v)\in E} (1 - \delta_{u,v}) = \sum_{m\in\Delta} m \times \gamma_{u,m}, \forall u \in V \quad (1)$$

$$\sum_{m\in\Delta} \gamma_{u,m} = 1, \forall u \in V \quad (2)$$

The two constraints find the degree of each vertex. The left-hand-side (LHS) of constraint (1) is the sum of the number of edges added to G and the number of existing edges that are not deleted. Constraint (2) ensures that only a unique degree is selected for each vertex, and the right-hand-side (RHS) of constraint (1) thereby guarantees that only $\gamma_{u,m}$ with the correct degree is 1 for every vertex u.

2. Anonymization Constraints

$$\gamma_{u,m} + \gamma_{v,n} + \alpha_{u,v} \leq 2 + \phi_{m,n}, \forall (u, v) \notin E, \forall m, n \in \Delta^+ \quad (3)$$

$$\gamma_{u,m} + \gamma_{v,n} - \delta_{u,v} \leq 1 + \phi_{m,n}, \forall (u, v) \in E, \forall m, n \in \Delta^+ \quad (4)$$

$$k \times \phi_{m,n} \leq \sum_{u\in V} \theta_{m,n,u}, \forall m, n \in \Delta^+ \quad (5)$$

$$\theta_{m,n,u} \leq \gamma_{u,m}, \forall m, n \in \Delta^+, \forall u \in V \quad (6)$$

Constraints (3) and (4) identify the anonymous groups that must be protected. Specifically, an anonymous group $D^2 = (m, n)$ needs to be protected if there are two vertices u and v with degrees m and n respectively, and u and v are connected in $\overline{G}$. We consider two cases. First, constraint (3) considers that (u, v) does not exist in G, but is added to the solution. In this case, the LHS of constraint (3) is 3, forcing that $\phi_{m,n}$ on the RHS must be 1. In the second case, if the existing (u, v) is not removed from G, i.e., $\delta_{u,v} = 0$, the LHS of constraint (4) is 2, and $\phi_{m,n}$ on the RHS must be 1. Therefore, the above two constraints guarantee that $\phi_{m,n}$ is 1 for each anonymous group that needs to be protected from friendship attacks. Constraint (5) ensures k^2-degree anonymity by enforcing that there are at least k vertices for each of the two degrees in an anonymous group. Specifically, for each anonymous group $D^2 = (m, n)$ with $\phi_{m,n}$ as 1, the RHS of (5) chooses at least k different vertices in V for m, and $\theta_{m,n,u}$ of each selected vertex u is 1. Meanwhile, constraint (6) guarantees that the degree of each selected vertex u must be m. Note that because edge (u, v) is identical to (v, u), constraints (3) and (4) will implicitly enforce $\phi_{n,m}$ to be 1 if $\phi_{m,n}$ is also set as 1 by these two constraints. Therefore, another k vertices in V are chosen for n in constraint (5), and $\theta_{n,m,v}$ of each chosen vertex v is guaranteed to be 1

[2] However, this paper slightly generalizes the cost model and allows users to specify different weights for edge addition and deletion.

in this case. The degree of each chosen vertex v will be set as n by constraint (6).

3. Enforcement Constraints

$$\theta_{m,n,u} \leq \sum_{v \in V: v \neq u} \varepsilon_{u,v,n}, \forall m,n \in \Delta^+, \forall u \in V \quad (7)$$

$$\varepsilon_{u,v,n} \leq \gamma_{v,n}, \forall u,v \in V, \forall n \in \Delta^+ \quad (8)$$

$$\varepsilon_{u,v,n} \leq \alpha_{u,v}, \forall (u,v) \notin E, \forall n \in \Delta^+ \quad (9)$$

$$\varepsilon_{u,v,n} \leq 1 - \delta_{u,v}, \forall (u,v) \in E, \forall n \in \Delta^+ \quad (10)$$

After the Anonymization Constraints choose the vertices for each anonymous group $D^2 = (m,n)$, the Enforcement Constraints ensure that each chosen vertex u with degree m connects to another vertex with degree n. Specifically, when $\theta_{m,n,u}$ is 1, constraint (7) assigns at least one vertex v with $\varepsilon_{u,v,n}$ as 1, and constraint (8) enforces that the degree of v must be n. Moreover, constraints (9) and (10) require that u and v must be connected by an edge in $\overline{G}$. If the edge does not appear in the input graph G, constraint (9) will add this edge to the solution. On the other hand, constraint (10) enforces that this edge cannot be deleted, i.e., $\delta_{u,v} = 0$, when (u,v) is in G. Therefore, u and v must belong to the same anonymous group with $D^2 = (m,n)$.

Moreover, to consider the isolated vertices with degree 0, we include the following constraint.

$$k \times \gamma_{u,0} \leq \sum_{v \in V} \gamma_{v,0}, \forall u \in V \quad (11)$$

The above constraint states that if any vertex u has degree 0, the solution must have at least k vertices with the same degree to ensure the anonymity of u.

5. SCALABLE APPROACH

In this section, we propose a scalable algorithm, called DEgree SEqence ANonymization (DESEAN), for k^2-degree anonymization of large-scale social networks. Algorithm DESEAN consists of three steps. The first step clusters vertices with similar degrees, selects a target degree for each cluster, and ensures that each cluster contains at least k vertices. In order to achieve the required level of anonymity protection between two clusters, the second step adds or removes edges as necessary. The last step adjusts the edges in the graph such that all the vertices in each cluster meet the target degree selected in step 1. We explain each step in detail below.

STEP 1. DEGREE SEQUENCE ANONYMIZATION.

This step chooses at least k vertices with similar degrees for each cluster. Without loss of generality, we assume that the vertices are sorted in decreasing order of the degrees, i.e., $d_{v_i} \geq d_{v_j}$ for $\forall i \leq j$. The step cuts the sequence into multiple subsequences, each of which will share the same degree with steps 2 and 3 explained later. Specifically, for each v_i and v_j, Formula (12) first evaluates the cost $CluCost(v_i, v_j, d^x)$ of grouping vertices $v_i, ..., v_j$ in the same subsequence with a target degree d^x.

$$CluCost(v_i, v_j, d^x) =$$
$$(1-\omega) \sum_{d_{v_i} \geq d_u > d^x} (d_u - d^x) + \omega \sum_{d^x > d_u \geq d_{v_j}} (d^x - d_u), \quad (12)$$

where the first and second terms are the anonymization costs for edge deletion and addition, respectively. Let $DegCost(v_1, v_j)$ denote the minimum cost of dividing the overall vertex sequence $v_1, ..., v_j$ such that each subsequence contains at least k vertices. We derive $DegCost(v_1, v_j)$ with dynamic programming as follows.

$$DegCost(v_1, v_j) = \min$$
$$\begin{cases} \min_{d^x} CluCost(v_1, v_j, d^x), \\ \min_{k \leq i \leq j-k}(DegCost(v_1, v_i) + \min_{d^x} CluCost(v_{i+1}, v_j, d^x)), \end{cases} \quad (13)$$

where $\min_{d^x} CluCost(v_1, v_j, d^x)$ corresponds to the case that $v_1, ..., v_j$ belong to the same subsequence. To divide $v_1, ..., v_j$ into multiple subsequences, our dynamic programming scheme leverages the existing result $DegCost(v_1, v_i)$ and finds the minimum anonymization cost to move $v_{i+1}, ..., v_j$ to the same subsequence. In other words, given the existing subsequences for $v_1, ..., v_i$, we attach a new subsequence $v_{i+1}, ..., v_j$ to the result. Therefore, $i \geq k$ must hold to ensure that we have at least k vertices in each subsequence from $v_1, ..., v_i$. Similarly, $i \leq j-k$ must hold to ensure that there exist at least k vertices in the new attached subsequence. If no vertex v_i satisfies the above two conditions, we set $DegCost(v_1, v_j)$ as $\min_{d^x} CluCost(v_1, v_j, d^x)$.

The above dynamic programming scheme requires $O(|V|^4)$ time. We devise the following strategies to reduce the complexity to $O(k|V|\log|V|)$ time. The first strategy reduces the time required to find $CluCost(v_i, v_j, d^x)$. We observe that $CluCost(v_i, v_j, d^x)$ first decreases monotonically and then increases monotonically as the target degree d^x varies from d_{v_i} to d_{v_j}. In other words, the function of d^x is convex. Intuitively, as d_x approaches d_{v_i}, the number of vertices required to add edges is significantly more than the number of vertices that are required to remove edges. Therefore, the cost increases accordingly. Similarly, as d_x approaches d_{v_j}, we have much more vertices required to remove edges. Based on the above observation, we propose the following Three-Point Binary Search (TPBS) scheme to find the optimal d^x.

1. Set d_L as d_{v_i} and d_S as d_{v_j}. The optimal d^x must be within the range $[d_{v_i}, d_{v_j}]$, i.e., $d_{v_i} \geq d^x \geq d_{v_j}$.
2. Set d_{Avg} as $\lfloor (d_L + d_S)/2 \rfloor$. Let $C^+ = CluCost(v_i, v_j, d_{Avg}+1)$, $C = CluCost(v_i, v_j, d_{Avg})$, and $C^- = CluCost(v_i, v_j, d_{Avg}-1)$.
3. Consider the three cases in Figure 3: (a) if $C^+ \geq C$ and $C \leq C^-$, return C and d_{Avg}, and terminate the search process; (b) if $C^+ \leq C \leq C^-$, set d_S as d_{Avg} because the optimal $d^x \in [d_L, d_{Avg}]$; or (c) if $C^+ \geq C \geq C^-$, set d_L as d_{Avg} because the optimal $d^x \in [d_{Avg}, d_S]$.
4. Go to 2 and repeat.

The TPBS scheme can reduce the complexity of finding $\min_{d^x} CluCost(v_i, v_j, d^x)$ for each (v_i, v_j) to $O(|V|\log|V|)$ time.

Next, we further reduce the complexity to $O(\log|V|)$ with the proposed Pre-Cumulation (PC) strategy, which determines the cost of decreasing or increasing the degrees in a subsequence to a proper degree d in advance. Specifically, let $LV[d]$ denote the number of vertices with degrees larger than d. First, we determine the following cost of reducing the degrees to ensure that the degrees of all vertices are at most d,

$$Dec2Deg[d] = \sum_{d_u > d} d_u - d \times LV[d]. \quad (14)$$

With $LV[d]$ and $Dec2Deg[d]$, we can derive the cost of decreasing the degrees such that the degrees in a subsequence $v_i, ..., v_j$ are at most d,

$$\sum_{d_{v_i} \geq d_u > d^x} (d_u - d^x)$$

$$= (\sum_{d_u > d^x} d_u - \sum_{d_u > d_{v_i}} d_u) - d^x(LV[d^x] - LV[d_{v_i}])$$

$$= Dec2Deg[d^x] - Dec2Deg[d_{v_i}] - (d_{v_i} - d^x)LV[d_{v_i}]. \quad (15)$$

Therefore, the first part of Formula (12) can be obtained in $O(1)$ time with $LV[d]$ and $Dec2Deg[d]$ derived in $O(|V|)$ time in advance. Similarly, let $SV[d]$ denote the number of vertices with degrees smaller than d. Then, we derive the cost of increasing the degrees such that the degrees of all vertices are at least d,

$$Inc2Deg[d] = d \times SV[d] - \sum_{d_u < d} d_u, \quad (16)$$

where d_u is the degree of vertex u. Next, we find the cost of adjusting the degrees such that the degrees in subsequence $v_i, ..., v_j$ are at least d,

$$\sum_{d^x > d_u \geq d_{v_j}} (d^x - d_u)$$

$$= d^x(SV[d^x] - SV[d_{v_j}]) - (\sum_{d_u < d^x} d_u - \sum_{d_u < d_{v_j}} d_u)$$

$$= Inc2Deg[d^x] - Inc2Deg[d_{v_j}] - (d^x - d_{v_j})SV[d_{v_j}]. \quad (17)$$

Similarly, the second part of Formula (12) can be obtained in $O(1)$ time with $SV[d]$ and $Inc2Deg[d]$ derived in $O(|V|)$ time in advance. Consequently, the complexity of finding $\min_{d^x} CluCost(v_i, v_j, d^x)$ for each (v_i, v_j) is further reduced to $O(\log |V|)$, with an additional storage overhead $O(d_{MAX})$, where d_{MAX} is the maximal vertex degree in the graph for finding LV, $Dec2Deg$, SV and $Inc2Deg$.

The third strategy observes that splitting a subsequence with at least $2k$ vertices into two subsequences with two different target degrees will not increase $DegCost(v_1, v_j)$ in Formula (13). In the extreme case, when $k = 1$, each subsequence should contain only one vertex with the target degree as the degree of the vertex, because no edge needs to be added or deleted in this case. Therefore, the result with more subsequences incurs a smaller anonymization cost. Based on this observation, each time, the strategy only considers $\max(k, j - 2k) < i \leq j - k$ for i in Formula (13), instead of all i in $k \leq i \leq j - k$. With the three strategies, the complexity of the dynamic programming method is thus reduced from $O(|V|^4)$ to $O(k|V| \log |V|)$. On the other hand, the third strategy may generate multiple small subsequences. Therefore, this step also merges the subsequences with the same degree in linear time. In the following, we regard each subsequence of vertices as a cluster.

Example 1. Consider Figure 4(a) as an example of 2^2-degree anonymization with ω set as 0.5, where the vertices are sorted as DEGIBFHJAC in decreasing order of their degrees. DESEAN first generates five clusters {D, E}, {G, I}, {B, F}, {H, J} and {A, C}, and then merges {B, F} and {H, J} because they share the same degree. Therefore, four clusters {D, E}, {G, I}, {B, F, H, J} and {A, C} are returned after step 1 of DESEAN. Figure 4(b) shows the target degree for each vertex obtained in step 1. ■

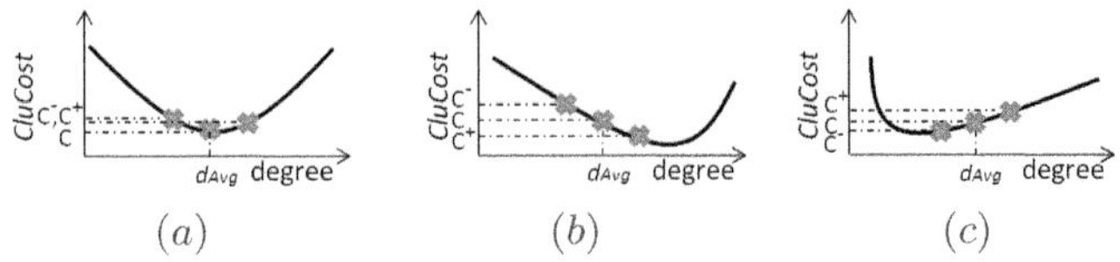

Figure 3: Illustrations of TPBS.

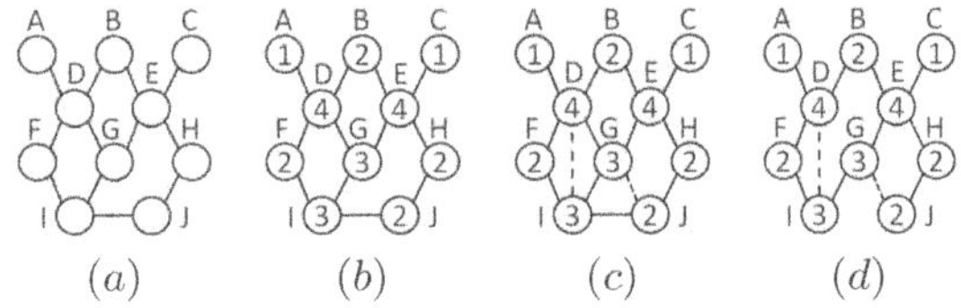

Figure 4: An example of 2^2-degree anonymization.

STEP 2. PRIVACY CONSTRAINT SATISFACTION.

In step 2, we add or remove edges between clusters to ensure that, for every pair of clusters (x, y), the number of vertices in x with edges connecting to the vertices in y is either zero or not less than k. Specifically, table SatTbl$[x][y]$ in DESEAN records the number of vertices in x with edges connecting to the vertices in y, and table DelTbl$[x][y]$ stores the number of edges connecting vertices in x and y. This step builds the two tables in $O(|E|)$ time. We then add or remove edges between x and y to ensure that the two clusters have sufficient edges between them. Specifically, for each pair of clusters (x, y), if $0 <$ SatTbl$[x][y] < k$ or $0 <$ SatTbl$[y][x] < k$, we derive the anonymization cost from edge deletion, i.e., $(1 - \omega)$DelTbl$[x][y]$, and the anonymization cost from edge addition, i.e., $\omega(k - \min($SatTbl$[x][y]$, SatTbl$[y][x]))$. DESEAN removes the edges connecting the vertices in x and y as long as the anonymization cost from edge deletion is less than the anonymization cost from edge addition. After that, SatTbl$[x][y]$, SatTbl$[y][x]$, DelTbl$[x][y]$ and DelTbl$[y][x]$ are set as zero. If it is not that case, we add some edges between clusters x and y. Specifically, we connect vertex u in x and vertex v in y with a new edge if the following conditions hold: 1) vertex u (resp. v) does not connect to any vertex in cluster y (resp. x); 2) u and v are the vertices with the smallest degrees in x and y respectively; 3) the shortest path between u and v is the minimal one among the shortest paths of every two candidate vertices.

By condition 1, our algorithm avoids choosing unnecessary vertices in x or y. For example, if vertex u already has an incident edge connecting to a vertex in y, choosing u for x would not increase the number of vertices that satisfy k^2-degree anonymity in cluster x. Therefore, the minimal number of additional edges required for clusters x and y is $(k - \min($SatTbl$[x][y]$, SatTbl$[y][x]))$. When there are several vertices satisfying condition 1, condition 2 selects the vertex with the smallest degree to avoid increasing the difference between the degrees of the vertices in the same cluster. When there are multiple vertex pairs following the above two conditions, the last condition chooses the pair with the minimal shortest path to reduce the information distortion. Consequently, the above three conditions allow us to achieve k^2-degree anonymity with the minimal anonymization cost and less information distortion.

Example 2. Following Example 1, DESEAN adds or removes some edges between clusters. In Figure 4(b), vertex G can be uniquely identified by the degree pair $(3, 4)$. To protect vertex G, DESEAN adds an edge (D,I) as shown in

Figure 4(c), instead of removing two edges (D,G) and (E,G), when ω is 0.5. Similarly, an edge (G,J) is added to protect vertex I against the degree pair $(3, 2)$. Figure 4(c) shows the resulting graph after step 2 has been executed. ■

STEP 3. ANONYMOUS DEGREE REALIZATION.

The last step scans the vertices in decreasing order of their target degrees determined in step 1 and adjusts the edges to achieve the target degree for each vertex $u \in x$.

Specifically, if the degree of u is smaller than the target degree d^x, we find a subsequent vertex $v \in y$ with the largest degree difference $d^y - d_v$, when SatTbl$[x][y]$ and SatTbl$[y][x]$ are not zero. Note that after step 2, both SatTbl$[x][y]$ and SatTbl$[y][x]$ are either zero or not less than k. Therefore, we can add an edge (u, v) to increase the degree of u without violating k^2-degree anonymity for protecting the pairs of connected vertices in x and y. This process repeats until the degree of u is d^x. Conversely, if the degree of u is larger than d^x, we delete an edge (u, v) to reduce the degree of u if the following three conditions hold: 1) v is a subsequent vertex with the largest degree difference $d_v - d^y$; 2) either SatTbl$[x][y] > k$ holds, or u has more than one edge incident to the vertices in y with SatTbl$[x][y] = k$; and 3) either SatTbl$[y][x] > k$ holds, or v has more than one edge incident to the vertices in x with SatTbl$[y][x] = k$. Once the target degree of a vertex u is achieved, condition 1 ensures that the degree of u would not be changed in the subsequent process. Note that SatTbl$[x][y]$ counts the number of vertices in x with edges connecting to vertices in y. Conditions 2 and 3 guarantee that SatTbl$[x][y] \geq k$ and SatTbl$[y][x] \geq k$ still hold after the deletion of (u, v). Therefore, we can remove the edge (u, v) to reduce the degree of u without violating k^2-degree anonymity for protecting the pairs of connected vertices in x and y. This process repeats until the degree of u is d^x. After all the vertices have been processed to achieve their target degrees, DESEAN outputs the anonymized graph.

Example 3. Following Example 2, DESEAN scans the vertices in the order of DEGIBFHJAC. First, for vertex D with $d_D > 4$, DESEAN removes the edge (D,G) to reduce the degree of D. The edge (D,G) is chosen because G is a subsequent vertex with the largest degree difference among vertices A, B, F and G. In addition, the deletion of (D,G) will not violate 2^2-degree anonymity for protecting the vertices in the clusters {D, E} and {G, I}. Similarly, the edge (I,J) is then deleted to reduce the degree of vertex I. Figure 4(d) shows the resulting 2^2-degree anonymous graph. ■

6. PERFORMANCE STUDIES

In this section, we evaluate the power of friendship attacks and the performance of our approaches on both real and synthetic data sets. The utility of the anonymized graphs is demonstrated from the degree distributions, degree centralities, clustering coefficients, average path lengths and the numbers of edge changes. The programs are implemented in C++. All experiments were performed on a Debian GNU/Linux server with double dual-core 2.4 GHz Opteron processors and 4GB RAM.

6.1 Data Sets

Real data sets: From the DBLP database, we extract two social networks with different scales. One is the PODS09 data set containing 68 authors whose papers were published at the PODS 2009 conference. An edge is added to connect two authors (vertices) if they are co-authors of a paper. There are 107 edges in the PODS09 data set. The other data set is the 20TopConf data set containing the authors who have ever published their papers at 20 top conferences such as KDD, VLDB, ICDM, to name a few. 20TopConf consists of 30,749 vertices representing the paper authors and 78,539 edges representing the co-author relationships.

Synthetic data sets: We use the R-MAT graph model [2] to generate synthetic graphs. The model takes four parameters a, b, c and d as inputs, where $a+b+c+d = 1$. The generated graphs have the power-law degree distributions and small-world properties, which are observed in many real-world social networks. In this work, we use the suggested settings (0.45, 0.15, 0.15 and 0.25) for the four corresponding parameters, and generate two data sets, SD-SG (small dense synthetic graph) and LS-SG (large sparse synthetic graph). SD-SG consists of 20,000 vertices and 150,000 edges, while LS-SG contains 100,000 vertices and 260,000 edges.

Table 1: Percentages of vertices that violate k^2-degree anonymity.

	Original G		k-degree $\overline{G}$	k^2-degree $\overline{G}$
k	**Degree**	**Friendship**	**Friendship**	**Friendship**
5	0.28%	5.37%	2.89%	0.38%
10	0.53%	10.69%	4.65%	1.10%
15	0.73%	14.71%	5.82%	1.43%
20	0.93%	18.44%	7.23%	2.27%

6.2 Privacy Breaches under Friendship Attacks

First, we show that the friendship attack is an important privacy issue in published social networks. We launch both the vertex degree attack and the friendship attack on the original 20TopConf. We also launch the friendship attack on the k-degree anonymous 20TopConf. Table 1 reports the percentages of vertices that could be revealed with a probability greater than $1/k$. We observe that a friendship attack can cause a much more serious privacy breach than a vertex degree attack, and that k-degree anonymity does not provide effective protection against friendship attacks.

Second, the Integer Programming method guarantees to generate k^2-degree anonymous graphs. Similar to other two-phase graph anonymization methods [9], DESEAN may not be able to achieve the target anonymous degrees for a few vertices. Therefore, we also test the power of friendship attacks on 20TopConf anonymized by DESEAN with ω set as 0.5. As shown in Table 1, DESEAN can provide far more effective protection against friendship attacks than k-degree anonymity when an attacker has the precise knowledge of a degree pair (d_1, d_2). If an attacker only knows the degree pair with an uncertainty range of 1, i.e., $(d_1 \pm 1, d_2 \pm 1)$, the percentages of vertices that the attacker can reveal with a probability greater than $1/k$ are reduced to 0.01%, 0.09%, 0.23% and 0.32% for k equal to 5, 10, 15 and 20, respectively.

6.3 Data Utility

In this subsection, we demonstrate that our approaches preserve much of the original graphs from the degree distributions, degree centralities, clustering coefficients, average path lengths and the numbers of edge changes. The test data include two real data sets, PODS09 and 20TopConf,

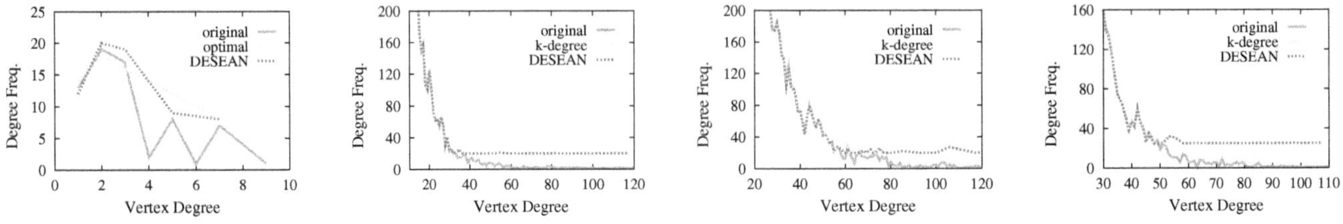

(a) PODS09, $k = 4$ (b) 20TopConf, $k = 20$ (c) SD-SG, $k = 20$ (d) LS-SG, $k = 25$

Figure 5: Degree distributions.

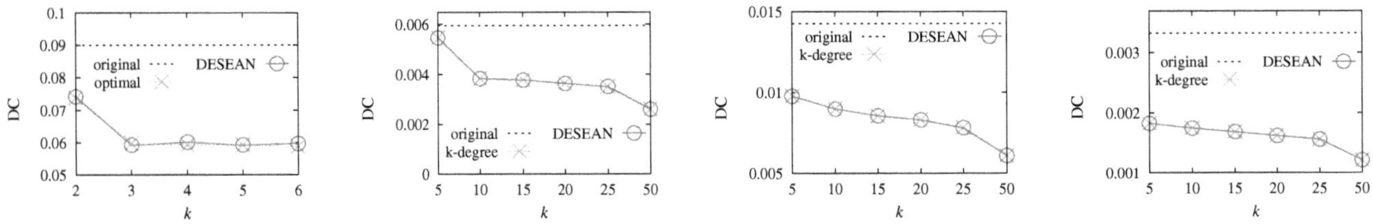

(a) PODS09 (b) 20TopConf (c) SD-SG (d) LS-SG

Figure 6: Degree Centralities.

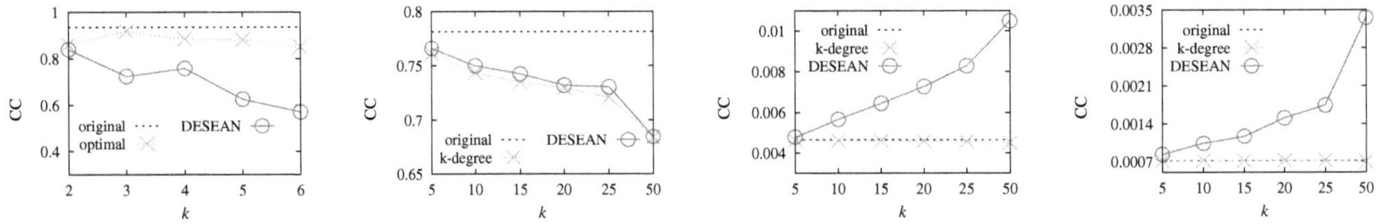

(a) PODS09 (b) 20TopConf (c) SD-SG (d) LS-SG

Figure 7: Clustering coefficients.

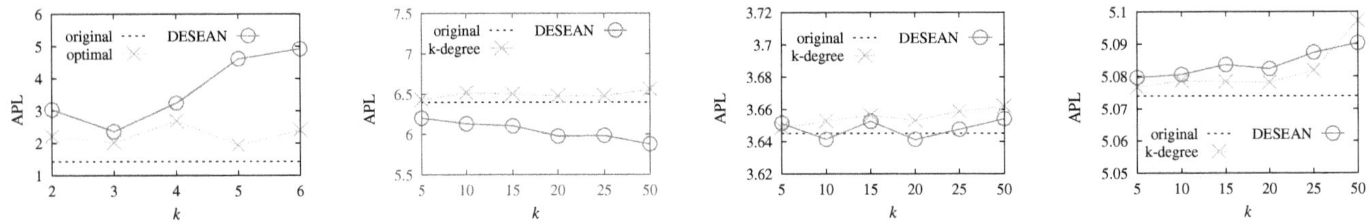

(a) PODS09 (b) 20TopConf (c) SD-SG (d) LS-SG

Figure 8: Average path lengths.

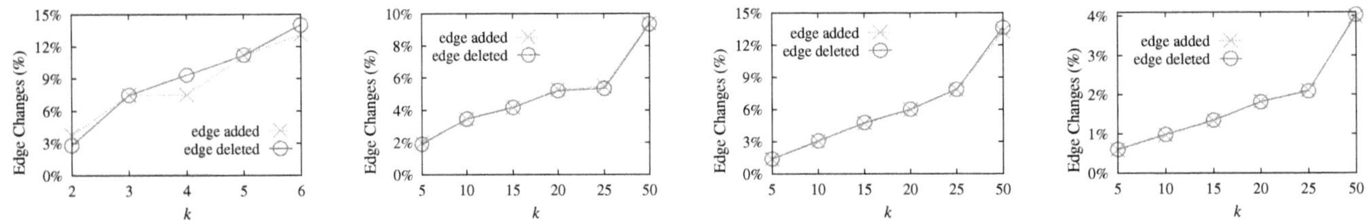

(a) PODS09 (b) 20TopConf (c) SD-SG (d) LS-SG

Figure 9: Number of edge changes.

and two synthetic graphs, SD-SG and LS-SG. All the graphs are anonymized with ω set as 0.5, indicating an equal preference for edge addition and edge deletion. Note that our methods preserve the vertex set. Therefore, in the evaluations, we compare our approaches with a scheme such as [9], which does not perform vertex addition and deletion. Related works such as [3, 21] are not directly comparable since the vertex set has been changed. Specifically, for PODS09, we obtain the optimal solutions with the proposed formulations using CPLEX [7]. We also compare the characteristics of the anonymized graphs produced by Algorithm DESEAN with those of the original graph and the optimal solutions. For the other three data sets, note that finding the optimal solutions on large-scale graphs is computationally infeasible. We compare the characteristics of k^2-degree anonymous graphs generated by DESEAN with those of k-degree anonymous graphs and the original graphs.

Degree Distribution: Figure 5 shows the degree distributions of the anonymized graphs and the original graphs. Accordingly, DESEAN is comparable to the optimal solution and k-degree anonymity in preserving the degree distribution. This is because DESEAN preserves the degree sequences by clustering the vertices with similar degrees in step 1.

Degree Centrality (DC): Figure 6 shows the degree centralities [12, 14] of the anonymized and original graphs as a function of k. For a graph, a large degree centrality indicates the existence of strong leaders and influential vertices. After k^2-degree anonymization, our methods decrease the degree centralities in the same quantity as k-degree anonymization when providing better privacy protection against friendship attacks.

Clustering Coefficient (CC): Figure 7 lists the clustering coefficients of the anonymized graphs as a function of k. The horizontal constant lines represent the CC values of the original graphs, which do not vary with the value of k. In Figure 7(a), the CC values of PODS09 anonymized by the optimal solution approach deviate little from the original CC value as the optimal solution method minimizes the edge editions. DESEAN decreases the CC values of PODS09 a bit more when k is small and reduces the CC values from 0.94 to 0.62 when k is larger than 4. This is because PODS09 has many cliques and DESEAN may connect distant vertices and disconnect vertices in the same cliques for anonymization. When k increases, DESEAN decreases the CC value further as more edge editions are performed. For the other three data sets, Figures 7(b-d) show that the CC values derived by DESEAN do not deviate much from the original values. On 20TopConf, DESEAN even achieves comparable results to k-degree anonymity.

Average Path Length (APL): Figure 8 details the average path lengths between vertex pairs of the anonymized graphs as a function of k. The horizontal constant lines represent the APLs of the original graphs, which do not vary as the value of k increases. First, note that PODS09 has many cliques. Therefore, in Figure 8(a), the optimal solution method increases the APL values of PODS09 by about 1.5 hops because a few vertices in different cliques are connected and a few vertices in the same cliques are disconnected. For the same reason, under Algorithm DESEAN, the APL values of PODS09 deviate a bit more when k is small, and increase from 1.43 to 4.61 with more edge editions when k is larger than 4. For the other three data sets, Figures 8(b-d) show that, under DESEAN, the APL values deviate slightly from the original values and the results are comparable to those of k-degree anonymity.

Number of Edge Changes: Figure 9 reports the ratio of edge editions by DESEAN to the original numbers of edges in the graphs. Accordingly, DESEAN fairly adds edges and deletes edges for anonymization with ω set as 0.5, and the numbers of edge changes increase linearly to the value of k.

All the evaluations on the degree distributions, degree centralities, clustering coefficients, average path lengths and the numbers of edge changes show that both the optimal solution approach and the DESEAN algorithm can preserve much of the original graphs.

6.4 Influence of the Parameters

In this subsection, we evaluate the influence of the preference weight ω between edge addition and edge deletion operations. Figure 10 shows the clustering coefficients (CCs) and average path lengths (APLs) of 20TopConf anonymized by DESEAN as a function of ω. Accordingly, with any ω, both the CC and APL values deviate more for a large k. In addition, for each k, the CC/APL value is best preserved at $\omega = 0.5$, indicating an equal preference for edge addition and edge deletion.

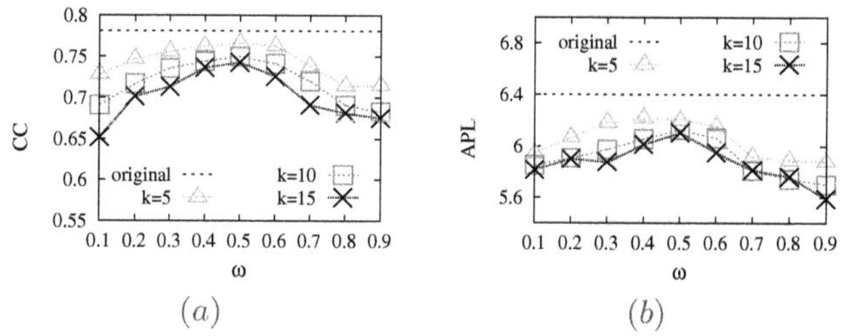

Figure 10: Data utility of 20TopConf w.r.t. ω.

6.5 Algorithm Scalability

Note that the optimal solution method has an exponential execution time. In the experiment, we observed that it takes several hours to find optimal solutions on PODS09 when k is larger than 3. Therefore, in this section, we focus on demonstrating the good scalability of Algorithm DESEAN. Concerning the effects of graph size and graph density, we report the execution time of DESEAN as a function of $|V|$ and $|E|/|V|$ in Figures 11(a) and 11(b), respectively. In Figure 11(a) all the test graphs have the $|E|/|V|$ ratio equal to 2.5, while in Figure 11(b) all the graphs have 100,000 vertices. These results show that the execution time grows linearly with the number of vertices $|V|$ and the graph density.

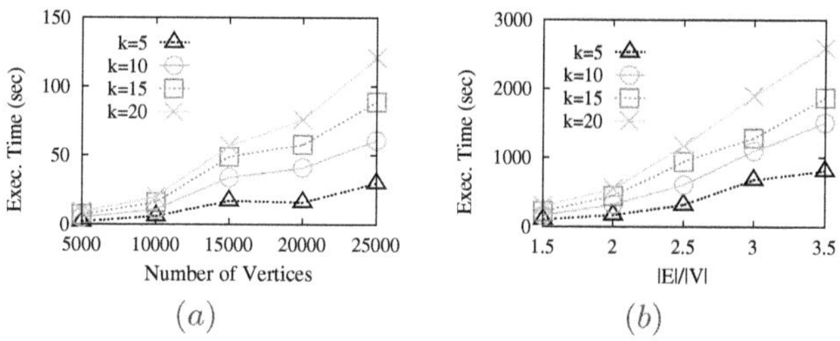

Figure 11: Execution efficiency of DESEAN.

7. GENERAL FRIENDSHIP ATTACKS

In this section, we discuss vertex re-identification under a *general friendship attack*, where an adversary knows a degree sequence of length l, i.e., $D^l = (d_{v_1}, d_{v_2}, ..., d_{v_l})$. Table 2 shows the percentages of vertices that could be re-identified with a probability greater than $1/k$ by D^3, i.e., $D^3 = ((d_A, d_B, d_C), A)$, $D^3 = ((d_A, d_B, d_C), B)$ and $D^3 = ((d_A, d_B, d_C), C)$, in the original/anonymized 20TopConf. Together with those in Table 1, these results demonstrate that the general friendship attack can effectively reveal the vertex identities, and that the power of a friendship attack increases dramatically with the length of the degree sequence.

For privacy protection against a general friendship attack, the definitions of the friendship attack and k^2-degree

Table 2: Percentages of vertices that violate k^3-degree anonymity.

k	Original G	k-degree $\overline{G}$	k^2-degree $\overline{G}$
5	40.67%	38.20%	35.65%
10	56.82%	54.26%	51.01%
15	63.46%	61.35%	59.74%
20	66.80%	66.28%	64.51%

anonymity can be easily modified to accommodate the general friendship attack and k^l-degree anonymity. To solve the problem, we propose the extended DESEAN (E-DESEAN) algorithm. In the following, we describe the concept of E-DESEAN.

E-DESEAN consists of three steps. The first step clusters the vertices with similar degrees such that each cluster contains at least K vertices, where $K \geq k$. Here, we choose another parameter K instead of k. The reason for this substitution is that when l grows, it would be more difficult to satisfy k^l-degree anonymity if for many vertices, there are only $k-1$ other vertices with the same degree in the same cluster. The second step adds and removes edges to ensure that there are sufficient edges between any two clusters required to achieve k^l-degree anonymity. However, for E-DESEAN, when a degree subsequence of length l is considered, the addition of an edge may create new degree subsequences that would need to be processed later. Therefore, the anonymous cost of adding an edge would be different and would vary according to the number of additional edges needed for protecting against the new subsequences. Finally, the third step adjusts the graph such that vertices in the same cluster share the same target degree to ensure that k^l-degree anonymity is achieved.

8. CONCLUSION

In this paper, we have identified the privacy risk in published social networks in terms of a new type of attack, called a friendship attack, and proposed the concept of k^2-degree anonymity to protect against such attacks. For k^2-degree anonymization, we developed an Integer Programming formulation to find optimal solutions. We also designed an efficient heuristic approach for anonymizing large-scale social networks. In addition, we discussed the extension of the heuristic approach to handle the general friendship attack of a degree sequence of length l. The experimental results demonstrate that our approaches can preserve much of the characteristics of social networks.

9. ACKNOWLEDGEMENTS

The work is supported in part by National Science Council of Taiwan under Contract No. NSC 97-2221-E-002-172-MY3, and by US NSF through grants IIS-0914934, OISE-0968341 and OIA-0963278.

10. REFERENCES

[1] L. Backstrom, C. Dwork, and J. M. Kleinberg. Wherefore art thou r3579x?: Anonymized social networks, hidden patterns, and structural steganography. In *Proc. of WWW*, 2007.

[2] D. Chakrabarti, Y. Zhan, and C. Faloutsos. R-mat: A recursive model for graph mining. In *Proc. of SDM*, 2004.

[3] J. Cheng, A. W. Fu, and J. Liu. K-isomorphism: privacy preserving network publication against structural attacks. In *Proc. of SIGMOD*, 2010.

[4] B. C. M. Fung, K. Wang, R. Chen, and P. S. Yu. Privacy-preserving data publishing: A survey on recent developments. *ACM Computing Surveys*, in press.

[5] M. Hay, G. Miklau, D. Jensen, D. F. Towsley, and P. Weis. Resisting structural re-identification in anonymized social networks. In *Proc. of VLDB*, 2008.

[6] X. He, J. Vaidya, B. Shafiq, N. Adam, and V. Atluri. Preserving privacy in social networks: A structure-aware approach. In *Proc. of WI-IAT*, 2009.

[7] IBM. (ILOG CPLEX 12.2, 2010) http://www-01.ibm.com/software/integration/optimization/cplex-optimizer/.

[8] K. Liu, K. Das, T. Grandison, and H. Kargupta. Privacy-preserving data analysis on graphs and social networks. In H. Kargupta, J. Han, P. Yu, R. Motwani, and V. Kumar, editors, *Next Generation Data Mining*. CRC Press, 2008.

[9] K. Liu and E. Terzi. Towards identity anonymization on graphs. In *Proc. of ACM SIGMOD*, 2008.

[10] P. Samarati and L. Sweeney. Generalizing data to provide anonymity when disclosing information. In *Proc. of ACM PODS*, 1998.

[11] L. Sweeney. k-anonymity: A model for protecting privacy. *IJUFKS*, 10(5), 2002.

[12] J. P. Scott. Social network analysis: a handbook. *Sage Publications*, 2nd edition, 2000.

[13] C.-H. Tai, D.-N. Yang, P. S. Yu, and M.-S. Chen. Structural Diversity for Privacy in Publishing Social Networks. In *Proc. of SDM*, 2011.

[14] S. Wasserman, K. Faust, D. Iacobucci, and M. Granovetter. Social network analysis: methods and applications. *Cambridge University Press*, 1994.

[15] X. Wu, X. Ying, K. Liu, and L. Chen. *A Survey of Privacy-Preservation of Graphs and Social Networks*. Springer US, 2010.

[16] X. Ying and X. Wu. Randomizing social networks: a spectrum preserving approach. In *Proc. of SDM*, 2008.

[17] L. Zhang and W. Zhang. Edge anonymity in social network graphs. In *Proc. of CSE*, 2009.

[18] E. Zheleva and L. Getoor. Preserving the privacy of sensitive relationships in graph data. In *Proc. of PinKDD*, 2007.

[19] B. Zhou and J. Pei. Preserving privacy in social networks against neighborhood attacks. In *Proc. of ICDE*, 2008.

[20] B. Zhou, J. Pei, and W. Luk. A brief survey on anonymization techniques for privacy preserving publishing of social network data. *SIGKDD Explorations*, 10(2), 2008.

[21] L. Zou, L. Chen, and M. T. Özsu. K-automorphism: a general framework for privacy preserving network publication. In *Proc. of VLDB*, 2009.

Probabilistic Topic Models with Biased Propagation on Heterogeneous Information Networks

Hongbo Deng, Jiawei Han, Bo Zhao, Yintao Yu, Cindy Xide Lin
Department of Computer Science
University of Illinois at Urbana-Champaign
Urbana, IL 61801, USA
{hbdeng, hanj, bozhao3, yintao, xidelin2}@uiuc.edu

ABSTRACT

With the development of Web applications, textual documents are not only getting richer, but also ubiquitously interconnected with users and other objects in various ways, which brings about text-rich heterogeneous information networks. Topic models have been proposed and shown to be useful for document analysis, and the interactions among multi-typed objects play a key role at disclosing the rich semantics of the network. However, most of topic models only consider the textual information while ignore the network structures or can merely integrate with homogeneous networks. None of them can handle heterogeneous information network well. In this paper, we propose a novel topic model with biased propagation (TMBP) algorithm to directly incorporate heterogeneous information network with topic modeling in a unified way. The underlying intuition is that multi-typed objects should be treated differently along with their inherent textual information and the rich semantics of the heterogeneous information network. A simple and unbiased topic propagation across such a heterogeneous network does not make much sense. Consequently, we investigate and develop two biased propagation frameworks, the biased random walk framework and the biased regularization framework, for the TMBP algorithm from different perspectives, which can discover latent topics and identify clusters of multi-typed objects simultaneously. We extensively evaluate the proposed approach and compare to the state-of-the-art techniques on several datasets. Experimental results demonstrate that the improvement in our proposed approach is consistent and promising.

Categories and Subject Descriptors: H.3.3 [**Information Storage and Retrieval**]: Information Search and Retrieval—*Clustering*; H.2.8 [**Information Systems Applications**]: Database Applications—*Data mining*

General Terms: Algorithm, Experimentation

Keywords: Topic modeling, biased propagation, clustering, heterogeneous information network

KDD'11, August 21–24, 2011, San Diego, California, USA.

1. INTRODUCTION

In this paper, we study the problem of topic modeling and object clustering on text-rich *heterogeneous information networks*. Textual documents, such as web pages, papers and blogs, are ubiquitously interconnected with each other as well as with other objects (e.g., users) in various ways, leading to simultaneous growth of both textual documents and heterogeneous network structures between documents and other objects. Information networks have been popularly used to represent networked systems, and a text-rich heterogeneous information network is formed when the network consists of a large number of text data as well as other objects. Taking bibliographic data as an example, as researchers are regularly publishing papers in various venues (e.g., conferences, journals, etc.), we not only obtain textual information of documents, but also have access to the intersections among multi-typed objects such as documents, authors and venues as shown in Figure 1(a). Figure 1(b) illustrates a simplified and basic heterogeneous information network with two types of objects: the documents D with rich text and the associated users U without explicit text, for example, blogs and bloggers, webpages and online users. There are many other text-rich information network examples that consist of a large number of interacting, multi-typed components accompanying with rich text data.

These examples show that in reality we are dealing with collections of documents as well as other objects in a heterogeneous information network. Therefore, it is important and challenging to examine how text data and heterogeneous information network can mutually enhance each other in topic modeling and other text mining tasks. With multi-typed objects accompanying with text documents, it is highly desirable to analyze how topics propagate from documents to other objects, and how the topics of other objects reinforce topic modeling and object clustering simultaneously.

Many topic models, such as Probabilistic Latent Semantic Analysis (PLSA) [13] and Latent Dirichlet Allocation (LDA) [3], have been proposed and shown to be useful for document analysis, but most of them only consider the textual information while ignore the network structures. Recently, several studies, including NetPLSA [17], Laplacian PLSI [6] and Locally-consistent Topic Model [7], have been proposed for combining topic modeling and network structures. However, these models can merely deal with homogeneous networks, such as document nearest-neighbor graph and co-authorship graph, but not heterogeneous information networks. Although a heterogeneous information network can be transformed into or be regarded as a homogeneous

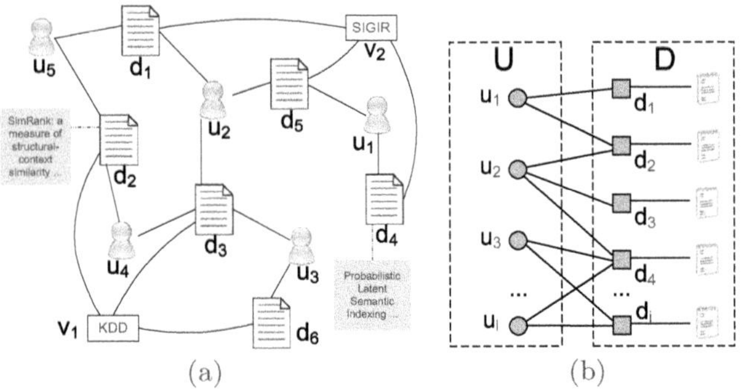

Figure 1: Examples of heterogeneous information networks.

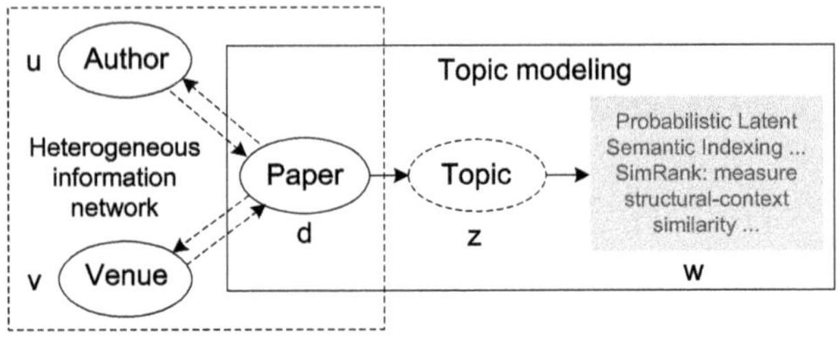

Figure 2: Topic modeling with heterogeneous information network.

information network, this may result in loss of rich semantics of the original network. Moreover, different objects have their own inherent information, which should be treated differently. Therefore, it is reasonable and challenging to directly incorporate the heterogeneous information network with topic modeling in a unified framework.

To address the problem, we propose a novel Topic Model with Biased Propagation algorithm (TMBP in short) which can be used to discover latent semantic topics and reinforce clusters of multi-typed objects simultaneously. Consequently, we investigate two alternative frameworks, i.e., biased random walk framework (TMBP-RW) and biased regularization framework (TMBP-Regu), for incorporating with topic modeling from different views. The basic idea of the biased random walk framework is to propagate the topic probabilities obtained by topic models on the heterogeneous information network via a biased propagation, as illustrated in Figure 2. A simple and unbiased topic propagation across different objects on such a heterogeneous network does not make sense. The underlying intuition is that different objects should be treated differently along with their inherent information. For example, as shown in Figure 1(b), the topic of a document d_i can be identified by mining its text information, while the interest of a user u_l without explicit text information can be characterized simply based on the associated documents which is captured by the heterogeneous network. On the other hand, the estimated interest of a user may affect the topic of a document afterward. In this way, there is a naturally biased topic propagation and consistency across different objects. Furthermore, we develop a joint regularization framework to incorporate a heterogeneous network into topic modeling by regularizing a statistical topic model along with a biased regularization on the heterogeneous information network. The biased regularization framework exploits valuable and reinforced information from heterogeneous network and provides promising constraints of overfitting for topic modeling, which leads to a significant improvement over the baseline method. Finally, we conduct extensive experiments and compare with the state-of-the-art techniques for object clustering and topic modeling tasks using two real-world datasets. Experimental results show that our TMBP-Regu model achieves the best performance.

In a nutshell, our contributions of this paper are: (1) the introduction of the TMBP algorithm to directly incorporate heterogeneous information network instead of homogeneous information network with topic modeling; (2) the investigation of two biased propagation frameworks, including the biased random walk framework and the biased regularization framework, for the TMBP algorithm from different perspectives; (3) the biased regularization term for treating documents with rich text and other objects without explicit text in a different way; and (4) the application of our model for clustering multi-typed objects collaboratively, in which TMBP-Regu achieves the best performance.

The rest of this paper is organized as follows. We first introduce the preliminaries in Section 2. Section 3 briefly describes probabilistic topic models. In Section 4, we systematically present and develop the proposed TMBP algorithm. Extensive experimental results on object clustering and document modeling are reported in Section 5. Finally, we review some related work in Section 6, and present our conclusions and future work in Section 7.

2. PRELIMINARIES

In this section, we formally introduce several related concepts and notations, and define the problem of topic modeling and object clustering in a text-rich heterogeneous information network. We assume that the data to be analyzed consists of both a collection of text documents and an associated heterogeneous network with multi-typed objects.

Definition 1 (Information Network): An information network consists of T types of objects $\mathcal{X} = \{X_t\}_{t=1}^{T}$, where X_t is a set of objects belonging to t_{th} type. Such a network with different types of objects can be denoted as a graph $G = (\mathcal{X}, E)$, where $\mathcal{X}$ is a set of vertices representing objects, i.e., $\mathcal{X} = X_1 \cup X_2 \cup ... \cup X_T$, and E is a set of edges representing the relation between objects. Suppose x is a vertex $x \in \mathcal{X}$, an edge $\langle x_i, x_j \rangle$ is a binary relation between vertices x_i and x_j. Specially, the network is called **homogeneous information network** when $T = 1$; and it becomes **heterogeneous information network** when $T \geq 2$.

A **text-rich heterogeneous information network** is formed when the information network contains a set of text documents $D = \{d_1, d_2, ..., d_N\}$ and several other types of objects, which is denoted as $\mathcal{X} = D \cup \{X_t\}_{t=1}^{T-1}$. Each document is represented as a bag of words, i.e., $d = \{w_1, w_2, ..., w_{|d|}\}$, and we use $n(d_i, w_j)$ to denote the occurrences of word w_j in d_i. For the bibliographic network as shown in Figure 1(a), there are three types of objects (i.e., $T = 3$), including papers D, authors U and venues V. The text-rich information network can be denoted as $G = (D \cup U \cup V, E)$, where E is the set of edges representing the relationships between documents D and objects U, V. For simplicity, in this paper we mainly consider $T = 3$, but the proposed model can be easily extended to incorporate more types of objects.

Now we can formulate our *topic modeling and object clustering* problem as: Given a document collection D and a text-rich information network $G = (D \cup U \cup V, E)$, the task of topic modeling is to model and extract K major topic models $Z = \{z_1, z_2, ..., z_K\}$ associated with multi-typed objects, where K is a user specified parameter. A latent topic model z_k is a probabilistic distribution of words in the vocabulary of collection. The probability of a word w is referred as $P(w|z)$. The task of object clustering is to group different types of objects into proper clusters simultaneously.

3. PROBABILISTIC TOPIC MODELS

Topic modeling has been popularly used for data analysis in various domains [3, 13, 17, 22]. A number of recent approaches [3, 13] to modeling document content are based upon the idea that the probability distribution over words in a document can be expressed as a mixture model of K topics, where each topic is a probability distribution over words. We will describe one of the most well-known and fundamental topic models, Probabilistic Latent Semantic Analysis (PLSA) [13]. In PLSA, an unobserved topic variable $z_k \in \{z_1, ..., z_K\}$ is associated with the occurrence of a word $w_j \in \{w_1, ..., w_M\}$ in a particular document $d_i \in \{d_1, ..., d_N\}$. By summing out the latent variable z, the joint probability of an observed pair (d, w) can be defined as

$$P(d_i, w_j) = P(d_i) \sum_{k=1}^{K} P(w_j|z_k) P(z_k|d_i), \quad (1)$$

where $P(w_j|z_k)$ is the probability of word w_j according to the topic model z_k, and $P(z_k|d_i)$ is the probability of topic z_k for document d_i. Following the likelihood principle, these parameters can be determined by maximizing the log likelihood of a collection C as follows:

$$\mathcal{L}(C) = \sum_{i=1}^{N} \sum_{j=1}^{M} n(d_i, w_j) \log \sum_{k=1}^{K} P(w_j|z_k) P(z_k|d_i). \quad (2)$$

The model parameters $\phi = \{P(w_j|z_k)\}$ and $\theta = \{P(z_k|d_i)\}$ can be estimated by using standard EM algorithm [9].

Thus PLSA provides a simplified solution to model topics of documents in a text-rich information network. However, this model ignores the associated heterogeneous information network as well as other interacted objects, so it cannot model and make use of associated objects simultaneously. Another limitation of PLSA is that there is no constraint on the parameters $\theta = \{P(z_k|d_i)\}$, the number of which grows linearly with the data. Therefore, the model is prone to overfitting the data. To alleviate these problems, we propose the following biased topic propagation algorithm by exploiting the heterogeneous information network.

4. BIASED TOPIC PROPAGATION

In this section, we propose a novel and general biased topic propagation algorithm to incorporate the heterogeneous information network with the textual information for topic modeling, so as to estimate the probabilities of topics for documents as well as other associated objects and improve the performance of topic modeling simultaneously.

4.1 Biased Random Walk Framework

In order to obtain the topics for other objects, a straightforward way is to propagate the topic probabilities from documents to other objects through the heterogeneous information network as shown in the dashed rectangle of Figure 2. The basic criterion is that different objects which are connected with each other should have similar weights of topics. To be more specific, the topic distribution of an object without explicit text information (e.g., u_l in Figure 1(b)) depends on the topic distribution of the documents it connects. For example, the research topic of an author could be characterized by his/her published papers, and the interest of a blogger is highly correlated with the associated blog posts. On the other hand, the topic of a document is also correlated with its authors to some extent, but, most importantly, its topic should be principally determined by its inherent content of the text. Therefore, different objects and interactions reflect distinctive semantics of a heterogeneous network, which should be treated differently. So we propose a biased random walk framework to cope with such a heterogeneous information network.

Let us first take Figure 1(b) as an example and discuss how the topics propagate from documents to neighboring objects. Given the topic probabilities of documents $P(z_k|d_i)$, the probabilities for a user u can be calculated by:

$$P(z_k|u) = \sum_{d_i \in \mathcal{D}_u} P(z_k|d_i) P(d_i|u) = \sum_{d_i \in \mathcal{D}_u} \frac{P(z_k|d_i)}{|\mathcal{D}_u|}, \quad (3)$$

where $\mathcal{D}_u$ is a set of documents that are associated with user u, and $|\mathcal{D}_u|$ is the number of documents (i.e., the degree of user u in the graph). The underlying intuition behind the above equation is that the topic distribution of an object is determined by the average topic distribution of connected documents. Similarly, the probabilities for a venue $v \in \mathcal{V}$ in Figure 1(a) can be defined as:

$$P(z_k|v) = \sum_{d_i \in \mathcal{D}_v} P(z_k|d_i) P(d_i|v) = \sum_{d_i \in \mathcal{D}_v} \frac{P(z_k|d_i)}{|\mathcal{D}_v|}, \quad (4)$$

where $\mathcal{D}_v$ is a set of documents that are published in venue v. Since many objects usually do not have explicit text content for further representation, e.g., users and venues in Figure 1(a), their topic distributions are entirely dependent on the estimated topic distributions of connected documents.

On the other hand, the topic distributions could be propagated from these objects to documents, so as to reinforce the topic distributions of documents. Along with the inherent topic probabilities estimated from the text, we propose the following biased topic propagation

$$P(z_k|d) = \xi P(z_k|d) + \frac{(1-\xi)}{2} \left(\sum_{u \in \mathcal{U}_d} \frac{P(z_k|u)}{|\mathcal{U}_d|} + \sum_{v \in \mathcal{V}_d} \frac{P(z_k|v)}{|\mathcal{V}_d|} \right) \quad (5)$$

where $\mathcal{U}_d$ represents the set of authors of paper d, and $\mathcal{V}_d$ is the venue associated with paper d. Note that ξ is the biased parameter to control the balance between inherent topic distribution $P(z_k|d)$ and the propagated topic distribution. If $\xi = 1$, the topics of documents retain the original ones, while the topics of other objects are determined by their associated documents in one step. We refer this special case as our **baseline** model with PLSA.

According to Eqs. (3), (4) and (5), we formulate the biased random walk framework at the topic level. The final topic probabilities of different objects can be obtained through an iteratively updated process. Here we focus on topic propagation between different objects on heterogeneous networks, but the propagation on homogeneous networks, such as citation graph, can be easily integrated into this framework.

4.2 Biased Regularization Framework

In the previous section, we give a way to biased topic propagation algorithm, but the topic modeling and random walk process are combined as two independent stages, so they can not mutually enhance each other. Here we investigate a joint regularization framework to directly incorporate heterogeneous information network into topic modeling by regularizing a statistical topic model with a biased regularizer on the heterogeneous information network.

In this section, we take bibliographic information network as a concrete example illustrated in Figure 2 to show how this idea works. Let us first discuss the paper-author bipartite graph. Generally, an author $u_l \in \mathcal{U}$ is knowledgeable about a specific topic if author u_l has published papers related to the topic. Similarly, a paper $d_i \in \mathcal{D}$ may be related to a specific topic if its authors have knowledge in that area. Thus, we define a regularization term as:

$$R_U = \frac{1}{2}\sum_{i=1}^{|\mathcal{D}|}\sum_{k=1}^{K}\left(P(z_k|d_i) - \sum_{u_l \in \mathcal{U}_{d_i}} \frac{P(z_k|u_l)}{|U_{d_i}|}\right)^2 + \frac{\tau}{2}\sum_{l=1}^{|\mathcal{U}|}\sum_{k=1}^{K}\left(P(z_k|u_l) - \sum_{d_i \in \mathcal{D}_{u_l}} \frac{P(z_k|d_i)}{|\mathcal{D}_{u_l}|}\right)^2.$$

A natural explanation of minimizing R_U is that authors should have similar topic distribution with their papers, and vice versa. Note that τ is the biased parameter. When $\tau \to \infty$, minimizing R_U will ensure the hypothesis that objects without explicit textual information are completely dependent on the estimated topic distributions of connected documents. Then the objective function R_U can be rewritten as

$$R_U = \frac{1}{2}\sum_{i=1}^{|\mathcal{D}|}\sum_{k=1}^{K}\left(P(z_k|d_i) - \sum_{u_l \in U_{d_i}} \frac{P(z_k|u_l)}{|U_{d_i}|}\right)^2 \quad (6)$$

$$s.t. \quad P(z_k|u_l) - \sum_{d_i \in \mathcal{D}_{u_l}} \frac{P(z_k|d_i)}{|\mathcal{D}_{u_l}|} = 0. \quad (7)$$

Thus we formulate the biased regularization term for treating documents with rich text and other objects without explicit text in a different way.

Similarly, the research topic of a venue could be represented by the published papers of the venue, and the topic of venues will guide relevant papers to be submitted or published in the corresponding venue. Thus, we could define the regularization term between documents and venues as:

$$R_V = \frac{1}{2}\sum_{i=1}^{|D|}\sum_{k=1}^{K}\left(P(z_k|d_i) - \sum_{v_m \in \mathcal{V}_{d_i}} \frac{P(z_k|v_m)}{|\mathcal{V}_{d_i}|}\right)^2 \quad (8)$$

$$s.t. \quad P(z_k|v_m) - \sum_{d_i \in \mathcal{D}_{v_m}} \frac{P(z_k|d_i)}{|\mathcal{D}_{v_m}|} = 0. \quad (9)$$

Minimizing function R_V will smooth the topic distributions between documents and their associated venues, making them more similar.

When a text-rich information network involves several different interactions between multi-typed objects, a joint regularization term $R(G)$ can be defined to combine all these regularization terms together as $R(G) = R_U + R_V$. Intuitively, $R(G)$ measures the difference of the topic models between documents and other objects for each explicit relationship embedded in a heterogeneous network. The more they differ, the larger $R(G)$ would be. So it can be regarded as a "loss function" to help us assess how well the topic distributions on the heterogeneous graph are consistent and correlated semantically. Clearly, we would like the extracted topics to have a small $R(G)$. Actually, the joint regularization term $R(G)$ is very general, which can be straightforwardly extended to consider other graph information.

To incorporate both the textual information and the heterogeneous network, we define a biased regularization framework by adding the regularization term to the log-likelihood

$$\begin{aligned}\mathcal{L} &= L(C) - \lambda R(G), \quad (10)\\ &= \sum_{i=1}^{N}\sum_{j=1}^{M} n(d_i, w_j)\log\sum_{k=1}^{K} P(w_j|z_k)P(z_k|d_i)\\ &\quad -\frac{\lambda}{2}\sum_{i=1}^{|D|}\sum_{k=1}^{K}\left(P(z_k|d_i) - \sum_{u_j \in \mathcal{U}_{d_i}} \frac{P(z_k|u_j)}{|\mathcal{U}_{d_i}|}\right)^2\\ &\quad -\frac{\lambda}{2}\sum_{i=1}^{|D|}\sum_{k=1}^{K}\left(P(z_k|d_i) - \sum_{v_j \in \mathcal{V}_{d_i}} \frac{P(z_k|v_j)}{|\mathcal{V}_{d_i}|}\right)^2,\end{aligned}$$

along with the constraints as defined in Eqs. (7) and (9). In Eq. (10), $L(C)$ measures how likely the data is generated from the topic model based on the collection of documents, and λ is the regularization parameter which is used to control the balance between the data likelihood and the smoothness of topic distributions over the heterogeneous network. It is easy to show that if $\lambda = 0$, the regularized topic model boils down to the standard PLSA. If $\lambda > 0$, the biased regularization model takes into account both the textual information and the heterogeneous relationships across multi-typed objects, which will provide valuable constraints of overfitting for PLSA so as to improve the performance of topic modeling. In the following section, we discuss parameter estimation of the biased regularization framework.

4.3 Model Fitting with Generalized EM

Our parameters include all the topics and the distributions of topics in all objects including documents, authors and venues, which we denote by $\phi = \{P(w_j|z_k)\}$, $\theta = \{P(z_k|d_i)\}$, $\varphi = \{P(z_k|u_l)\}$ and $\psi = \{P(z_k|v_m)\}$. When a probabilistic model involves unobserved latent variables, the standard way for the maximum likelihood estimation of the model is the Expectation Maximization (EM) algorithm [9], which alternates two steps, E-step and M-step.

Let us first consider the special case that $\lambda = 0$. In such a case, the objective function boils down to the log-likelihood function of PLSA with no regularization term. Formally, we have the **E-step** to compute the posterior probabilities $P(z_k|d_i, w_j)$:

$$P(z_k|d_i, w_j) = \frac{P(w_j|z_k)P(z_k|d_i)}{\sum_{k'=1}^{K} P(w_j|z_{k'})P(z_{k'}|d_i)}. \quad (11)$$

In the **M-step**, we maximize the expected complete data log-likelihood for PLSA, which can be derived as:

$$Q_D = \sum_{i=1}^{N}\sum_{j=1}^{M} n(d_i, w_j)\sum_{k=1}^{K} P(z_k|d_i, w_j)\log(P(w_j|z_k)P(z_k|d_i)).$$

There is a closed-form solution to maximize Q_D:

$$P(w_j|z_k) = \frac{\sum_{i=1}^{N} n(d_i, w_j) P(z_k|d_i, w_j)}{\sum_{j'=1}^{M} \sum_{i=1}^{N} n(d_i, w_{j'}) P(z_k|d_i, w_{j'})}, \quad (12)$$

$$P(z_k|d_i) = \frac{\sum_{j=1}^{M} n(d_i, w_j) P(z_k|d_i, w_j)}{\sum_{j'=1}^{M} n(d_i, w_{j'})}. \quad (13)$$

However, there is no closed-form solution in the M-step for the general case $\lambda > 0$ with the complete likelihood function:

$$\mathcal{Q}(\phi, \theta, \varphi, \psi) = Q_D - \lambda R(G).$$

Fortunately, we could use the generalized EM algorithm [19, 17] to maximize the regularized log-likelihood of the model. The major difference between generalized EM and traditional EM is that in the M-step generalized EM finds parameters that only "improve" the expected value of the log-likelihood function rather than maximizing it. It is easy to see that our biased regularization model shares the same hidden variables with PLSA, and has exactly the same E-step as that of PLSA. Since the regularization $R(G)$ does not involve the parameters $P(w_j|z_k)$, we can get the same M-step estimation equation for $P(w_j|z_k)$ as in Eq. (12).

In the following, we discuss how to estimate the parameter values $\theta = \{P(z_k|d_i)\}$ as well as $\varphi = \{P(z_k|u_l)\}$ and $\psi = \{P(z_k|v_m)\}$. Let us first find $\theta_{t+1}^{(1)}$ using Eq. (13) which maximizes Q_D instead of $\mathcal{Q}(\phi, \theta, \varphi, \psi)$. We then try to start from $\theta_{t+1}^{(1)}$ and decrease $R(G)$, which can be done through Newton-Raphson method [20, 6]. Given a function $f(x)$ and the initial value x_t, the Newton-Raphson updating formula to decrease $f(x)$ is defined as $x_{t+1} = x_t - \gamma \frac{f'(x)}{f''(x)}$, where $0 \leq \gamma \leq 1$ is the step parameter. With $\theta_{t+1}^{(1)}$ and put $R(G)$ into the Newton-Raphson formula, we can decrease $R(G)$ by updating $P(z_k|d_i)$ in each step:

$$\begin{aligned} P(z_k|d_i)_{t+1}^{(n+1)} &= (1-\gamma) P(z_k|d_i)_{t+1}^{(n)} \\ &+ \frac{\gamma}{2} \Big(\sum_{u_j \in \mathcal{U}_{d_i}} \frac{P(z_k|u_j)}{|\mathcal{U}_{d_i}|} + \sum_{v_j \in \mathcal{V}_{d_i}} \frac{P(z_k|v_j)}{|\mathcal{V}_{d_i}|} \Big). \end{aligned} \quad (14)$$

In the meantime, $P(z_k|u_l)$ and $P(z_k|v_m)$ are updated as in Eq. (7) and Eq. (9), respectively, for each step. The step parameter γ in Eq. (14) can be interpreted as a controlling factor of smoothing the topic distribution among the neighboring objects. We repeatedly update $\theta_{t+1}^{(n)}$ using Eq. (14) until $\mathcal{Q}(\theta_{t+1}^{(n+1)}) \leq \mathcal{Q}(\theta_{t+1}^{(n)})$. Then we test whether $\mathcal{Q}(\theta_{t+1}^{(n)}) \geq \mathcal{Q}(\theta_t)$. If it is true, re-estimation for θ is done by setting $\theta_{t+1} \leftarrow \theta_{t+1}^{(n)}$. Otherwise, we keep current θ, φ and ψ without updating in the M-step and continue to the next E-step. We summarize the model fitting approach by using generalized EM algorithm in Algorithm 1.

Algorithm 1 Model Fitting for Biased Regularization

Input: A text-rich information network $G = (D \cup U \cup V, E)$ with word occurrences $n(d_i, w_j)$. The number of topics K, Newton step size γ, regularization parameter λ

Output: $\phi = \{P(w_j|z_k)\}$, $\theta = \{P(z_k|d_i)\}$, $\varphi = \{P(z_k|u_l)\}$ and $\psi = \{P(z_k|v_m)\}$.

```
Random initialize the probability distribution φ0 and
  θ0, compute φ0 = {P(zk|u)0} and ψ0 = {P(zk|v)0} as
  in Eq. (7) and Eq. (9), respectively;
t ← 0;
while t < MaxIteration do
  E-step: Compute P(zk|di, wj) as in Eq. (11);
  M-step:
  Re-estimate P(wj|zk)t+1 as in Eq. (12);
  Re-estimate P(zk|di)t+1 as in Eq. (13);
  P(zk|di)(1)t+1 ← P(zk|di)t+1;
  Compute P(zk|di)(2)t+1 (i.e., θ(2)t+1) as in Eq. (14), and
    update P(zk|u)t+1 and P(zk|v)t+1 as in Eq. (7) and
    Eq. (9), respectively;
  while Q(θ(2)t+1) ≥ Q(θ(1)t+1) do
    P(zk|di)(1)t+1 ← P(zk|di)(2)t+1;
    Compute θ(2)t+1, update P(zk|u)t+1 and P(zk|v)t+1;
  end while
  if Q(θ(1)t+1) ≥ Q(θt) then
    P(zk|di)t+1 ← P(zk|di)(1)t+1;
    Update P(zk|u)t+1 and P(zk|v)t+1;
  else
    Keep current θ, φ and ψ.
  end if
  t ← t + 1
end while
```

5. EXPERIMENTS

In this section, we evaluate the effectiveness of our TMBP algorithm, and compare it with the state-of-the-art methods on two data sets through extensive experiments.

5.1 Data Collection

The Digital Bibliography and Library Project (DBLP)[1] is a collection of bibliographic information on major computer science journals and proceedings, which can be used to build a heterogeneous information network with multi-typed objects along with rich text data as Figure 1(a). Each paper is represented by a bag of words that appeared in the abstract and title of the paper. Besides the rich-text documents, we also obtain two other types of objects: author and venue (i.e., conference). In this experiment, we use a subset of the DBLP records[2] that belongs to four areas: *database, data mining, information retrieval* and *artificial intelligence*, and contains 28,569 documents, 28,702 authors and 20 conferences. The abstract is collected for representing each document, and this data collection has 11,771 unique terms. Within the heterogeneous information network, we observe two explicit types of relationships: paper-author and paper-venue, which consist of a total number of 103,201 links. Moreover, we use a labeled data set [24] with 4,057 authors, 100 papers and all 20 conferences for quantitative accuracy evaluation.

The NSF Research Awards Abstracts (NSF-Awards)[3] consists of 129,000 abstracts describing NSF awards for basic research from 1990 to 2003, which are grouped into more than 640 research programs. For each NSF award, we obtain the abstract represented by a bag of words, and the affiliated investigator(s), forming a heterogeneous information network. In our test, we extract a subset of documents

[1]http://www.informatik.uni-trier.de/~ley/db/

[2]http://www.cs.uiuc.edu/~hbdeng/data/kdd2011.htm

[3]http://kdd.ics.uci.edu/databases/nsfabs/nsfawards.data.html

Table 1: Statistics of the DBLP and NSF datasets.

	DBLP	NSF-Awards
# of docs (D)	28,569	16,405
# of authors/PIs (U)	28,702	9,989
# of venues (V)	20	-
# of links (D-U)	74,632	20,717
# of links (D-V)	28,569	-
# of terms	11,771	18,674
# of clusters (K)	4	10

that belong to the largest 10 research programs, such as *applied mathematics, economics* and *geophysics*, thus leaving us with 16,405 documents and 9,989 associated investigators. Within the heterogeneous information network, there are a total of 20,717 links between documents and investigators. Moreover, this data collection has 18,674 unique terms which appear in all the abstracts. Table 1 provides the statistics of these two datasets. Note that we set the number of topics (K) to be 4 and 10 for DBLP and NSF-Awards, respectively.

5.2 Experimental Setup and Metrics

The proposed TMBP algorithm can be applied to different text mining tasks, such as topic modeling and object clustering. We evaluate the performance of our models in two frameworks: the biased random walk framework (TMBP-RW) and biased regularization framework (TMBP-Regu). For further performance comparison, we implemented other state-of-the-art methods as follows:

- Nonnegative Matrix Factorization (NMF) [16]
- Probabilistic Latent Semantic Analysis (PLSA) [13]
- Laplacian Probabilistic Latent Semantic Indexing (LapPLSI) [6]
- Latent Dirichlet allocation (LDA) [3]
- Author-Topic Model (ATM) [22]
- Ranking-based Clustering (NetClus) [24].

Since NMF, PLSA and LDA cannot be directly applied to heterogeneous information networks, only documents are utilized for these models. For LapPLSI, we constructed a homogeneous nearest-neighbor graph, and empirically set the number of nearest neighbors to 10, and the step parameter γ to 0.1. Moreover, the regularization parameter was tuned to produce the best performance among 10, 100 and 1000. For NetClus, we implemented a topic-based NetClus algorithm which utilizes the topic distribution (obtained using PLSA) instead of the word distribution for each document. All the other parameter settings were set to be identical to TMBP.

To quantitatively compare TMBP with these methods, we adopt two popular metrics, accuracy (AC) and normalized mutual information (NMI) [27], to measure the clustering performance. The AC is definded as $AC = \frac{\sum_{i=1}^{n} \delta(a_i, map(l_i))}{n}$, where n denotes the total number of objects, $\delta(x, y)$ is the delta function that equals one if $x = y$ and equals zero otherwise, and $map(l_i)$ is the mapping function [6] that maps each cluster label l_i to the equivalent label from the data corpus. On the other hand, given the two sets of document clusters C and C', their mutual information metric $MI(C, C')$ is defined as: $MI(C, C') = \sum_{c_i \in C, c'_j \in C'} p(c_i, c'_j) \cdot \log_2 \frac{p(c_i, c'_j)}{p(c_i) \cdot p(c'_j)}$, where $p(c_i)$ and $p(c'_j)$ denote the probabilities that a document arbitrarily selected from the corpus belongs to the clusters c_i and c'_j, respectively, and $p(c_i, c'_j)$ denotes the joint probability that arbitrarily selected document belongs to the clusters c_i as well as c'_j at the same time. Suppose $H(C)$ and $H(C')$ are the entropies of C and C', respectively, it reaches the maximum, $\max(H(C), H(C'))$, when the two sets of clusters are identical, whereas it becomes zero when the two sets are independent. In our experiments, we use the normalized mutual information NMI as the $MI(C, C')$ normalized by $\max(H(C), H(C'))$ which ranges from 0 to 1.

5.3 Experimental Results

We consider the question whether our proposed method can boost the performance of topic modeling and object clustering using the biased propagation algorithm. First, the experiments are performed to compare the task of object clustering with quantitative analysis. Then we investigate the parameter setting of our TMBP model. Finally, we analyze the topic modeling with some case studies.

5.3.1 *Quantitative Analysis*

For quantitative evaluation, we apply our models on the task of object clustering using both DBLP and NSF-Awards datasets. The hidden topics extracted by the topic modeling approaches can be regarded as clusters. The estimated conditional probability (e.g., $P(z_k|d_i)$ and $P(z_k|u_l)$) is used to infer the cluster label for each object. The clustering result is evaluated by comparing the cluster label of each object with its label provided by the data corpus.

Table 2 shows the clustering performance of different methods. For each method, 20 test runs were conducted, and the final performance scores were obtained by averaging the scores from the 20 tests. To make the comparison fair, we used the same random starting points for NMF, PLSA, LapPLSI, NetClus and TMBP. The italic results of PLSA in Table 2(a) is obtained by the special case of TMBP-RW with $\xi = 1$, which is set as our **baseline** model.

From Table 2, we observe that PLSA outperforms NMF on paper without using any network information. As expected, LapPLSI outperforms PLSA slightly by incorporating a homogeneous nearest-neighbor graph, and ATM outperforms LDA by considering the paper-author graph. However, both PLSA and LapPLSI fail to outperform TMBP (both TMBP-RW and TMBP-Regu) as well as ATM and NetClus. One reason is that ATM, NetClus and TMBP take into account the heterogeneous information network directly.

For DBLP, our TMBP approach simultaneously clusters all types of objects in different groups by considering both the text information and the heterogeneous information network. As we can see, both TMBP-RW and TMBP-Regu get significantly better performance than **baseline** PLSA, especially on the types of paper and author. Moreover, they can even achieve better results than the state-of-the-art ATM and NetClus algorithms. This shows that by considering the biased propagation on the heterogeneous information network and integrating with topic modeling, TMBP can have better topic modeling power for clustering objects.

For NSF-Awards, we only show the results for documents as there is no available label information for investigators. In general, we can observe similar results as DBLP. The results of TMBP-Regu and ATM are comparable, which outperform all the other methods. Additionally, the improvement of TMBP-Regu over other methods is more significant on the DBLP corpus than the NSF-Awards corpus. One possi-

Table 2: **Object clustering performance of different methods on (a) DBLP and (b) NSF-Awards datasets.**

(a) DBLP

Object	Paper (%)		Author (%)		Venue (%)		Average (%)	
Metric	AC	NMI	AC	NMI	AC	NMI	AC	NMI
NMF	44.55	22.92	-	-	-	-	44.55	22.92
PLSA	59.45	32.75	*65.0*	*37.97*	*80.0*	*74.74*	68.15	48.49
LapPLSI	61.35	33.93	-	-	-	-	60.70	33.37
LDA	47.00	20.48	-	-	-	-	47.00	20.48
ATM	77.00	52.21	74.13	40.67	-	-	75.57	46.44
NetClus	65.00	40.96	70.82	47.43	79.75	76.69	71.86	55.03
TMBP-RW	73.10	53.13	82.59	67.76	81.75	**77.53**	79.15	66.14
TMBP-Regu	**79.15**	**59.16**	**89.81**	**74.25**	**82.75**	76.56	**83.90**	**69.99**

(b) NSF-Awards

Object	Doc (%)	
Metric	AC	NMI
NMF	45.97	40.92
PLSA	63.00	64.48
LapPLSI	63.65	64.58
LDA	65.06	63.36
ATM	65.69	69.58
NetClus	63.51	66.11
TMBP-RW	64.84	68.74
TMBP-Regu	65.15	69.83

ble reason is that the heterogeneous information network of NSF-Awards is much sparser than that of DBLP, in which there are only 1.26 links per document for NSF-Awards, and 3.61 links per document for DBLP. Although the link information is very limited in NSF-Awards, our approach can still improve the performance over baseline methods which confirms its effectiveness.

By comparing the results of TMBP-Regu with TMBP-RW, it is obvious that TMBP-Regu performs better than TMBP-RW. The improvement over the biased random walk method owes to the direct optimization of the heterogeneous information analysis and topic modeling in a unified regularization framework. This observation supports the theoretical analysis of our biased regularization framework that can provide valuable and reinforced information as well as the constraints of overfitting for topic modeling.

5.3.2 Parameter Analysis

In our method, there are two essential parameters, the biased parameter ξ for TMBP-RW and the regularization parameter λ for TMBR-Regu. In this subsection, the effect of parameters ξ and λ is studied and evaluated.

Figure 3 shows how the performance of TMBP-RW varies with the biased parameter ξ. As mentioned before, the biased parameter is used to control the balance between inherent topic distribution and the propagated topic distribution. When $\xi = 1$, it is the **baseline** PLSA model. We can see that the performance is improved over the baseline when incorporating the random walk on the heterogeneous network with $\xi < 1$. The changes are relatively small in Figure 3 (c) and (d) since the topic propagation is constrained by the limited links. With the decrease of ξ, the performance becomes worse, and even worse than the baseline, as the model relies more on the topic consistency while ignores the intrinsic topic of the documents. We empirically set the biased parameter $\xi = 0.9$ in other experiments.

Figure 4 shows how the performance of TMBR-Regu varies with the regularization parameter λ. As mentioned in Section 4.2, the parameter λ is used to control the trade-off between the data likelihood of the topic modeling and the smoothness of topic distributions over the heterogeneous network. When $\lambda = 0$, the regularization framework boils down to be the baseline PLSA model. When $\lambda > 0$, the regularization framework takes into account the topic consistency between documents and their associated objects. As we can see, the TMBP-Regu is relatively stable with respect to the parameter λ, and achieves consistent good performance varying from 400 to 4000. We empirically set the biased parameter $\lambda = 1000$ in other experiments.

Table 3: The representative terms generated by PLSA, ATM and TMBP-Regu models. The terms are selected according to the probability $P(w|z)$.

Topic 1 (DB)	Topic 2 (DM)	Topic 3 (IR)	Topic 4 (AI)
PLSA			
data	data	information	problem
database	mining	retrieval	algorithm
systems	learning	web	paper
query	based	based	reasoning
system	clustering	*learning*	logic
databases	classification	knowledge	based
management	algorithm	text	time
distributed	*image*	search	algorithms
queries	analysis	system	*search*
relational	detection	language	show
ATM			
data	*learning*	information	knowledge
database	data	web	based
query	mining	retrieval	model
systems	algorithm	search	problem
databases	clustering	based	reasoning
queries	based	text	logic
system	classification	language	image
processing	algorithms	user	system
distributed	time	semantic	recognition
management	analysis	document	representation
TMBP-Regu			
data	data	information	learning
database	mining	web	based
query	algorithm	retrieval	knowledge
databases	clustering	search	model
systems	classification	based	problem
queries	based	text	reasoning
system	algorithms	language	system
processing	rules	user	logic
management	analysis	semantic	image
distributed	discovery	document	models

5.3.3 Topic Modeling Analysis and Case Study

In order to visualize the hidden topics and compare different approaches, we extract topics from the data using PLSA, ATM and TMBP-Regu on DBLP dataset. Since the DBLP subset is a mixture of four areas, it is interesting to see whether the extracted topics could automatically reveal this mixture. The most representative terms generated by PLSA, ATM and TMBP-Regu are shown in Table 3. For the first three topics, although different algorithms select slightly different terms, all these terms can describe the corresponding topic to some extent. For Topic 4 (AI), the top keywords like "learning, based, knowledge" derived from TMBP-Regu is obviously more telling than "knowledge, based, model" derived by ATM and "problem, algorithm, paper" derived by PLSA. Similar subtle differ-

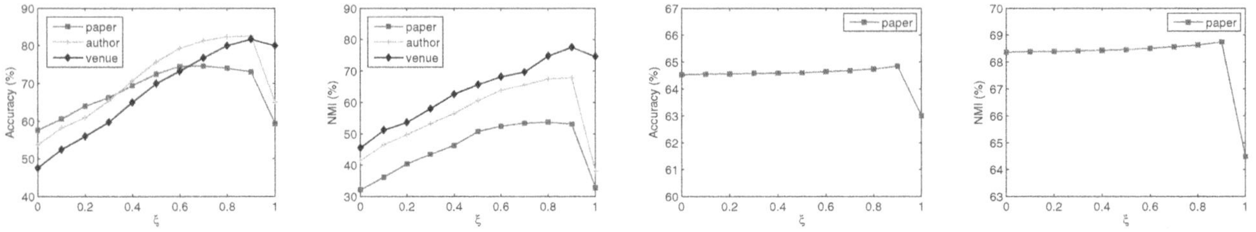

(a) DBLP (b) DBLP (c) NSF-Awards (d) NSF-Awards

Figure 3: The effect of varying parameters ξ in the biased random walk framework (TMBP-RW).

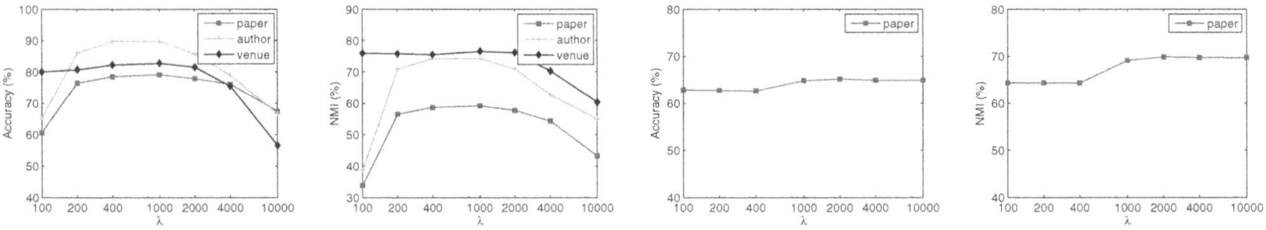

(a) DBLP (b) DBLP (c) NSF-Awards (d) NSF-Awards

Figure 4: The effect of varying parameters λ in the biased regularization framework (TMBP-Regu).

ences can be observed for Topic 2 (DM) as well. Intuitively, TMBP-Regu and ATM select more related terms for each topic than PLSA, which shows the better performance of TMBP-Regu and ATM by considering the heterogeneous information network.

5.3.4 *Summary*

These experimental results demonstrate the effectiveness of our proposed algorithm, which successfully incorporates the heterogeneous information network into topic modeling. Compared with PLSA, TMBP-RW keeps learned topics the same as PLSA, and propagates topic probabilities biasedly between documents and other objects. In contrast, TMBP-Regu results in refined topic-word distribution, and derives the topic probabilities for all types of objects collaboratively in a unified way, leading to better performance as expected. In comparison with ATM, TMBP-Regu is more flexible to deal with all types of objects including authors, and more straightforward to incorporate additional graph information.

6. RELATED WORK

Many topic models have been proposed and shown to be useful for data analysis. There are two principal approaches, PLSA [13] and LDA [3], which have been successfully applied or extended to many problems, including document clustering and classification [6, 7, 14], information retrieval [26, 30], correlated and dynamic topic models [1, 2], geographical topic discovery [28], author-topic modeling [22, 25], and citation and social network analysis [17, 6, 8, 18]. However, most of these models only consider the textual information while ignore network structures. Recently, several studies, including NetPLSA [17], LapPLSI [6], LTM [7] and iTopicModel [23], have been proposed for combining topic modeling with homogeneous networks, such as citation graph and co-authorship graph, but they cannot deal with heterogeneous information network directly. Although there was some research done to model the relationships between different objects, such as Author-Topic Model [22, 25] and collective topic model [12], these models are designed specifically for academic networks or only consider the relationships indirectly through the content information. Our proposed models differs from them as we directly take into account the general heterogeneous information networks with topic propagation techniques.

Link analysis has been a hot topic for a few years since the advent of two distinct methods, HITS [15] and PageRank [5]. Many techniques have been proposed to improve search results [4, 29] and integrate heterogeneous networks [11, 24]. For example, Sun et al. [24] proposed a ranking-based clustering for heterogeneous information networks. Deng et al. [11] developed a generalized Co-HITS algorithm for bipartite graph analysis. However, their algorithms are based on a simple and unbiased propagation method, and ignore the underlying latent topics associated with the network in most cases.

This work is also related to graph-based semi-supervised learning [33, 31, 21, 32], which usually assumes label smoothness over the graph. These types of graph regularization methods have been successfully applied in many data mining tasks [17, 6, 10]. In [10], the authors developed a graph-based re-ranking model by regularizing the smoothness of relevance scores over the latent graph. NetPLSA [17] and LapPLSI [6] explored graph-based regularizers with topic modeling by considering homogeneous networks. Our work is different from theirs, as we focus on heterogeneous information networks and introduce a new biased regularization term, which distinguishes documents with rich text and other objects without explicit text, so as to treat them in a different way.

7. CONCLUSIONS AND FUTURE WORK

We have presented a novel algorithm for topic modeling on text-rich heterogeneous information networks, called Topic Model with Biased Propagation (TMBP). Consequently, we have investigated the biased random walk (TMBP-RW) and biased propagation (TMBP-Regu) frameworks, for incorporating heterogeneous information network into topic modeling directly. As a result, TMBP can make full use of both rich semantics embedded in heterogeneous networks and rich text of documents, which leads to a significant improvement over the baseline topic models. Moreover, TMBP-Regu performs better than TMBP-RW since topic modeling and heterogeneous network analysis can mutually enhance each other in the biased regularization framework. Experimental results on object clustering and topic modeling show that TMBP-Regu achieves the best performance. In future work, the idea of the biased propagation framework can also be naturally incorporated with other topic modeling algorithms, e.g., Latent Dirichlet Allocation. It would be interesting to investigate the performance of our algorithm by varying the weights of different objects besides documents.

8. ACKNOWLEDGMENTS

The work was supported in part by the U.S. National Science Foundation grants IIS-0905215, CNS-0931975, by the U.S. Army Research Laboratory under Cooperative Agreement No. W911NF-09-2-0053 (NS-CTA), and by the U.S. Air Force Office of Scientific Research MURI award FA9550-08-1-0265. The views and conclusions contained in this document are those of the authors and should not be interpreted as representing the official policies, either expressed or implied, of the Army Research Laboratory or the U.S. Government. The U.S. Government is authorized to reproduce and distribute reprints for Government purposes notwithstanding any copyright notation here on.

9. REFERENCES

[1] D. M. Blei and J. D. Lafferty. Correlated topic models. In *NIPS*, 2005.

[2] D. M. Blei and J. D. Lafferty. Dynamic topic models. In *ICML*, pages 113–120, 2006.

[3] D. M. Blei, A. Y. Ng, and M. I. Jordan. Latent dirichlet allocation. *JMLR*, 3:993–1022, 2003.

[4] A. Borodin, G. O. Roberts, J. S. Rosenthal, and P. Tsaparas. Link analysis ranking: algorithms, theory, and experiments. *TOIT*, 5(1):231–297, 2005.

[5] S. Brin and L. Page. The anatomy of a large-scale hypertextual web search engine. *Computer Networks*, 30(1-7):107–117, 1998.

[6] D. Cai, Q. Mei, J. Han, and C. Zhai. Modeling hidden topics on document manifold. In *CIKM*, pages 911–920, 2008.

[7] D. Cai, X. Wang, and X. He. Probabilistic dyadic data analysis with local and global consistency. In *ICML*, page 14, 2009.

[8] D. A. Cohn and T. Hofmann. The missing link - a probabilistic model of document content and hypertext connectivity. In *NIPS*, pages 430–436, 2000.

[9] A. Dempster, N. Laird, D. Rubin, et al. Maximum likelihood from incomplete data via the EM algorithm. *Journal of the Royal Statistical Society. Series B (Methodological)*, 39(1):1–38, 1977.

[10] H. Deng, M. R. Lyu, and I. King. Effective latent space graph-based re-ranking model with global consistency. In *WSDM*, pages 212–221, 2009.

[11] H. Deng, M. R. Lyu, and I. King. A generalized Co-HITS algorithm and its application to bipartite graphs. In *KDD*, pages 239–248, 2009.

[12] H. Deng, B. Zhao, and J. han. Collective topic modeling for heterogeneous networks. In *SIGIR*, 2011.

[13] T. Hofmann. Probabilistic latent semantic indexing. In *SIGIR*, pages 50–57, 1999.

[14] S. Huh and S. E. Fienberg. Discriminative topic modeling based on manifold learning. In *KDD*, pages 653–662, 2010.

[15] J. M. Kleinberg. Authoritative sources in a hyperlinked environment. *Journal of the ACM (JACM)*, 46(5):604–632, 1999.

[16] D. D. Lee and H. S. Seung. Algorithms for non-negative matrix factorization. In *NIPS*, pages 556–562, 2000.

[17] Q. Mei, D. Cai, D. Zhang, and C. Zhai. Topic modeling with network regularization. In *WWW*, pages 101–110, 2008.

[18] R. Nallapati, A. Ahmed, E. P. Xing, and W. Cohen. Joint latent topic models for text and citations. In *KDD*, pages 542–550, 2008.

[19] R. Neal and G. Hinton. A view of the EM algorithm that justifies incremental, sparse, and other variants. *Learning in graphical models*, 89:355–368, 1998.

[20] W. Press, S. Teukolsky, W. Vetterling, and B. Flannery. Numerical Recipes in C: The Art of Scientific Computing, Cambridge, 1992.

[21] A. Smola and R. Kondor. Kernels and regularization on graphs. *COLT*, 2003.

[22] M. Steyvers, P. Smyth, M. Rosen-Zvi, and T. L. Griffiths. Probabilistic author-topic models for information discovery. In *KDD*, pages 306–315, 2004.

[23] Y. Sun, J. Han, J. Gao, and Y. Yu. itopicmodel: Information network-integrated topic modeling. In *ICDM*, pages 493–502, 2009.

[24] Y. Sun, Y. Yu, and J. Han. Ranking-based clustering of heterogeneous information networks with star network schema. In *KDD*, pages 797–806, 2009.

[25] J. Tang, J. Zhang, L. Yao, J. Li, L. Zhang, and Z. Su. Arnetminer: extraction and mining of academic social networks. In *KDD*, pages 990–998, 2008.

[26] X. Wei and W. B. Croft. LDA-based document models for ad-hoc retrieval. In *SIGIR*, pages 178–185, 2006.

[27] W. Xu, X. Liu, and Y. Gong. Document clustering based on non-negative matrix factorization. In *SIGIR*, pages 267–273, 2003.

[28] Z. Yin, L. Cao, J. Han, C. Zhai, and T. S. Huang. Geographical topic discovery and comparison. In *WWW*, pages 247–256, 2011.

[29] B. Zhang, H. Li, Y. Liu, L. Ji, W. Xi, W. Fan, Z. Chen, and W.-Y. Ma. Improving web search results using affinity graph. In *SIGIR*, pages 504–511, 2005.

[30] D. Zhou, J. Bian, S. Zheng, H. Zha, and C. L. Giles. Exploring social annotations for information retrieval. In *WWW*, pages 715–724, 2008.

[31] D. Zhou, O. Bousquet, T. N. Lal, J. Weston, and B. Schölkopf. Learning with local and global consistency. In *NIPS*, 2003.

[32] D. Zhou, B. Schölkopf, and T. Hofmann. Semi-supervised learning on directed graphs. In *NIPS*, 2004.

[33] X. Zhu, Z. Ghahramani, and J. D. Lafferty. Semi-supervised learning using gaussian fields and harmonic functions. In *ICML*, pages 912–919, 2003.

Prominent Streak Discovery in Sequence Data

Xiao Jiang[*]
Shanghai Jiao Tong University
showbufire@gmail.com

Chengkai Li[† ‡]
University of Texas at Arlington
cli@uta.edu

Ping Luo
HP Labs China
ping.luo@hp.com

Min Wang
HP Labs China
min.wang6@hp.com

Yong Yu
Shanghai Jiao Tong University
yyu@cs.sjtu.edu.cn

ABSTRACT

This paper studies the problem of prominent streak discovery in sequence data. Given a sequence of values, a prominent streak is a long consecutive subsequence consisting of only large (small) values. For finding prominent streaks, we make the observation that prominent streaks are skyline points in two dimensions– streak interval length and minimum value in the interval. Our solution thus hinges upon the idea to separate the two steps in prominent streak discovery– candidate streak generation and skyline operation over candidate streaks. For candidate generation, we propose the concept of local prominent streak (LPS). We prove that prominent streaks are a subset of LPSs and the number of LPSs is less than the length of a data sequence, in comparison with the quadratic number of candidates produced by a brute-force baseline method. We develop efficient algorithms based on the concept of LPS. The non-linear LPS-based method (NLPS) considers a superset of LPSs as candidates, and the linear LPS-based method (LLPS) further guarantees to consider only LPSs. The results of experiments using multiple real datasets verified the effectiveness of the proposed methods and showed orders of magnitude performance improvement against the baseline method.

Categories and Subject Descriptors

H.2.8 [**Database Management**]: Database Applications—*data mining*

General Terms

Algorithms, Performance

Keywords

sequence database, time-series database, skyline query

[*]Work performed while the author was visiting HP Labs China.

[†]Work partially performed while the author was visiting HP Labs China.

[‡]This material is based upon work partially supported by NSF Grant IIS-1018865. Any opinions, findings, and conclusions or recommendations expressed in this publication are those of the author(s) and do not necessarily reflect the views of NSF.

KDD'11, August 21–24, 2011, San Diego, California, USA.

1. INTRODUCTION

This paper defines the problem of *prominent streak discovery* in sequence data and presents efficient algorithms for finding prominent streaks. A piece of sequence data is a series of values or events. This includes time-series data, in which the data values or events are often measured at equal time intervals. Sequence and time-series data is produced and accumulated in a rich variety of applications. Examples include stock quotes, sports statistics, temperature measurement, Web usage logs, network traffic logs, Web clickstream, and customer transaction sequence.

Given a sequence of values, a *prominent streak* is a long consecutive subsequence consisting of only large (small) values. Examples of such prominent streaks include consecutive days of high temperature, consecutive trading days of large stock price oscillation, consecutive games of outstanding performance in professional sports, consecutive hours of high volume of TCP traffic, consecutive weeks of high flu activity, and so on. It is insightful to investigate prominent streaks since they intuitively and succinctly capture extraordinary subsequences of data.

Prominent streak discovery can be particularly useful in helping journalists to identify newsworthy stories when data sequences evolve, investigators to find suspicious phenomena, and news anchors and sports commentators to bring out attention-seizing factual statements. Therefore it will be a key enabling technique for *computational journalism* [7]. In fact, we witness the mentioning of prominent steaks in many real-world news articles:

- *"This month the Chinese capital has experienced 10 days with a maximum temperature in around 35 degrees Celsius – the most for the month of July in a decade."* (http://www.chinadaily.com.cn/china/2010-07/27/content_11055675.htm)
- *"The Nikkei 225 closed below 10000 for the 12th consecutive week, the longest such streak since June 2009."* (http://www.bloomberg.com/news/2010-08-06/japanese-stocks-fall-for-second-day-this-week-on-u-s-jobless-claims-yen.html)
- *"He (LeBron James) scored 35 or more points in nine consecutive games and joined Michael Jordan and Kobe Bryant as the only players since 1970 to accomplish the feat."* (http://www.nba.com/cavaliers/news/lbj_mvp_candidate_060419.html)
- *"Only player in NBA history to average at least 20 points, 10 rebounds and 5 assists per game for 6 consecutive seasons. (Kevin Garnett)"* (http://en.wikipedia.org/wiki/Kevin_Garnett)

The examples indicate that general prominent streaks can have a variety of constraints. A streak can be on multiple dimensions (e.g., ⟨point, rebound, assist⟩), its significance can be with regard to a certain period (e.g., "since June 2009") or a certain comparison group (e.g., "the month of July"), and we may be interested in not only the most prominent streaks but also the top-*k* most prominent ones (e.g., "X joined Y and Z as the only players").

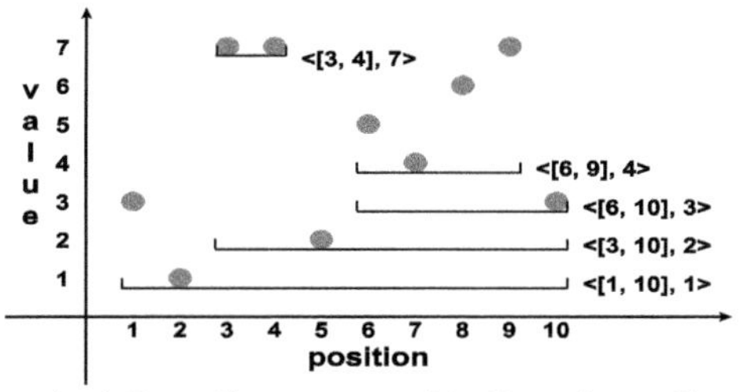

Figure 1: A Data Sequence and its Prominent Streaks.

Given its real-world usefulness and variety, the research on prominent streaks in sequence data opens a spectrum of challenging problems. In this initial effort, we undertake the problem of discovering the simplest kind of prominent streaks, i.e., those without the above constraints. We formally define the concept of prominent streak and our problem as follows.

1.1 Problem Definition

Definition 1 (Streak and Prominent Streak): Given an n-element sequence P=$(p_1, \cdots, p_n)$, a *streak* is an interval-value pair $\langle[l, r], v\rangle$, where $1 \leq l \leq r \leq n$ and v=$\min_{l \leq i \leq r} p_i$.

Consider two streaks s_1=$\langle[l_1, r_1], v_1\rangle$ and s_2=$\langle[l_2, r_2], v_2\rangle$. We say s_1 *dominates* s_2, denoted by $s_1 \succ s_2$ or $s_2 \prec s_1$, if $r_1 - l_1 \geq r_2 - l_2$ and $v_1 > v_2$, or $r_1 - l_1 > r_2 - l_2$ and $v_1 \geq v_2$.

With regard to P=$(p_1, ...p_n)$, the set of all possible streaks is denoted by $\mathcal{S}_P$. A streak $s \in \mathcal{S}_P$ is a *prominent streak* if it is not dominated by any streak in $\mathcal{S}_P$, i.e., $\nexists s'$ s.t. $s' \in \mathcal{S}_P$ and $s' \succ s$. The set of all prominent streaks in P is denoted by $\mathcal{PS}_P$. ∎

Problem Statement: The *prominent streak discovery problem* is to, given a sequence P, produce $\mathcal{PS}_P$.

Figure 1 shows our running example of a 10-value sequence P=$(3, 1, 7, 7, 2, 5, 4, 6, 7, 3)$. There are 5 prominent streaks in P– $\langle[1, 10], 1\rangle$, $\langle[3, 10], 2\rangle$, $\langle[6, 10], 3\rangle$, $\langle[6, 9], 4\rangle$, $\langle[3, 4], 7\rangle$. For instance, $\langle[6, 9], 4\rangle$ is a prominent streak of minimal value 4, whose interval is from p_6 to p_9. $\langle[1, 10], 1\rangle$, the whole data sequence, is also a trivial prominent streak because no other streak can possibly dominate the sequence itself. The streak $\langle[8, 9], 6\rangle$ is an instance of non-prominent streaks because it is dominated by $\langle[3, 4], 7\rangle$.

1.2 Overview of the Solution

A brute-force method for discovering prominent streaks is not appealing. One can enumerate all possible streaks and decide if each streak is prominent by comparing it with every other streak. Given a sequence P with length n, there are $|\mathcal{S}_P|$=$\binom{n+1}{2}$ streaks in total. Thus the number of pair-wise streak comparison would be $\binom{|\mathcal{S}_P|}{2}$=$\frac{n^4+2n^3-n^2-2n}{8}$. Given a sequence of length 10000, the brute-force approach enumerates 10^8 streaks and performs 10^{16} comparisons. Many real-world sequences can be quite long. The sequence of daily closing prices for a stock with 40-year history has about 10000 values. A one-year usage log for a Web site has 8760 values at hourly interval.

Prominent streaks are in fact skyline points [5] in two dimensions– streak interval length $(r - l)$ and minimum value in the interval (v). A streak is a prominent streak (skyline point) if it is not dominated by any point, i.e., there exists no streak that has both longer interval and greater minimum value.

Based on this observation, our solution hinges upon the idea to separate the two steps of prominent streak discovery– *candidate streak generation* and *skyline operation* over candidate streaks. In candidate generation, we prune a large portion of non-prominent streaks without exhaustively considering all possible streaks. For skyline operation, we leverage efficient algorithms from the rich literature on this topic, e.g., [5, 21, 11, 14]. The effectiveness of pruning in the first step is critical to overall performance, because execution time of skyline algorithms increases superlinearly by the number of candidate points [5].

Candidate streak generation: We considered three methods with increasing pruning power in candidate generation– a baseline method, a non-linear LPS (local prominent streak)-based method, and a linear LPS-based method. The baseline method exhaustively enumerates $\mathcal{S}_P$, all possible streaks in a sequence P, by a nested-loop over the values in P. The sketch of this method is in Algorithm 1. It produces quadratic $(\frac{n(n+1)}{2})$ candidate streaks. We then propose the concept of *local prominent streak* (LPS) for substantially reducing the number of candidate streaks (Section 3). The intuition is, given a prominent streak s, there cannot be a super-sequence of s with greater or equal minimal value. In other words, s must be locally prominent as well. Hence we only need to consider LPSs as candidates. The algorithm sequentially scans the data sequence and maintains possible LPSs. We further make the observation that an LPS cannot have a preceding or succeeding data entry that is greater than or equal to its minimal value. Therefore we find the left-end (right-end) of an LPS when we find a data entry that is greater than its preceding (succeeding) entry. The non-linear LPS-based method finds a superset of LPSs as candidates, while the linear LPS-based method guarantees to find only LPSs.

Note that to couple candidate streak generation with skyline operation, Algorithm 1 maintains a dynamic skyline and updates it whenever a new candidate streak is produced. The updating procedure *skyline_update* is in Algorithm 2 and is introduced below.

Algorithm 1: Baseline Method

Input: Data sequence P=$(p_1, ..., p_n)$
Output: Prominent streaks $skyline$

$skyline \leftarrow$ *empty*
for $r = 1$ *to* n **do**
    $min\_value \leftarrow \infty$
    for $l = r$ ***downto*** 1 **do**
        $min\_value \leftarrow \min(p_l, min\_value)$
        $s \leftarrow \langle[l, r], min\_value\rangle$ // candidate streak
        $skyline \leftarrow skyline\_update(skyline, s)$

Algorithm 2: Update Dynamic Skyline ($skyline\_update$)

Input: Dynamic skyline $skyline$, new candidate streak $s = \langle[l, r], v\rangle$
Output: Updated dynamic skyline $skyline$

Find the largest i in $skyline$ s.t. $v_i \leq v$
if $s \prec s_i$ **or** $s \prec s_{i+1}$ **then**
    return $skyline$
while $s \succ s_i$ **and** $i > 0$ **do**
    Delete s_i from $skyline$
    $i \leftarrow i - 1$
Insert s into $skyline$
return $skyline$

Skyline operation: Our focus is not to compare various skyline algorithms. Many existing algorithms can be leveraged. What matters is the number of candidate streaks produced by the candidate generation step. This is also verified by our experiments which show that, under various skyline algorithms, the candidate streak generation methods in Section 3 perform and compare consistently.

We can use a sorting-based method for finding the skyline points in a two-dimensional space [5]. If the candidate streak generation step does not prune streaks effectively, we cannot hold all candidate streaks in memory. The memory overflow can be addressed by external-memory sorting.

Another approach is to progressively update a dynamic skyline with candidate streaks, based on the nested-loop method in [5]. The outline of this approach is shown in Algorithm 2. We use $skyline$ to denote the dynamic skyline. When a new candidate streak s is generated, s is inserted into $skyline$ if it is not dominated by any point in $skyline$. The algorithm also checks if some points in $skyline$ are dominated by s and eliminates them from $skyline$.

The dominance relationship can be efficiently checked, given that the streaks have only two dimensions– interval length $(r - l)$ and minimum value (v). The key idea is that the lengths of streaks monotonically decrease as their minimal values increase (except that there can be identical points, i.e., streaks with equal lengths and equal minimal values.) Hence the streaks in $skyline$ are ordered by v (or by $r - l$). Suppose the candidate streak is $s = \langle [l, r], v \rangle$. We only have to find in $skyline$ a pivoting streak $s_i = \langle [l_i, r_i], v_i \rangle$ such that i is the largest index with $v_i \leq v$, i.e., $v_i \leq v < v_{i+1}$, then check its neighbors to determine the dominance relationship. For quickly finding s_i, we use a balanced binary search tree (BST) on v to store $skyline$. (Thus we call it BST-based skyline method.) We can prove that s is dominated by some points in $skyline$ if and only if s is dominated by s_i or s_{i+1}. Furthermore, if s dominates totally k streaks in $skyline$, then the k streaks are s_i, s_{i-1}, ..., s_{i-k+1}. (We omit the discussion of boundary cases, i.e., i=0 or i=$|skyline|$.)

In comparison with the sorting-based method, the above BST-based skyline method saves both memory space and execution time. It avoids memory overflow because the number of streaks in the dynamic skyline in most cases remains small enough to fit in memory. Hence no streak needs to be read from/written to secondary memory. The small size of dynamic skyline in real data is verified by our experiments in Section 5. After all, prominent streaks (and skyline points in general) are supposed to be minority, otherwise they cannot stand out to warrant further investigation. Furthermore, even if the dynamic skyline grows large, a method such as the block nested-loop based method in [5] can be applied to fall back on secondary memory. The small size of dynamic skyline also means small number of streak comparisons. Intuitively, given c candidate streaks, a fast comparison-based sorting algorithm (say quicksort) requires $O(c \log c)$ comparisons, while the BST-based method only requires $O(c \log s)$ comparisons, where s is the maximal size of the dynamic skyline during computation. Experiments in Section 5 show that s is typically much smaller than c.

1.3 Summary of Contributions and Outline

To summarize, this paper makes the following contributions:

- We defined the problem of prominent streak discovery. The simple concept is useful in many real-world applications. To the best of our knowledge, there has not been study along this line.
- We proposed the solution framework to separate *candidate streak generation* and *skyline operation* during prominent streak discovery. Under this framework, we designed efficient algorithms for candidate streak generation, based on the concept of local prominent streak. Both the non-linear LPS-based method (NLPS) and the linear LPS-based method (LLPS) produce substantially less candidate streaks than the quadratic number of candidates produced by a baseline method. LLPS further guarantees a linear number of candidate streaks.
- We conducted experiments over multiple real datasets. The results verified the effectiveness of our methods and showed orders of magnitude performance improvement over the baseline method. We also showed some insightful prominent streaks discovered from real data, to highlight the practicality of this work.

The rest of the paper is organized as follows. In Section 2 we review related work. Section 3 presents the NLPS and LLPS methods for candidate streak generation. Section 4 discusses how to adapt the algorithms to monitor prominent streaks when data sequence continuously grows. Experiment setup and results are reported in Section 5. Section 6 concludes the paper.

2. RELATED WORK

Data mining on sequence and time-series data has been an active area of research, where many techniques are developed for similarity search and subsequence matching in sequence and time-series databases [1, 8, 2, 26], finding sequential patterns [3, 20, 27, 15, 25], classification and clustering of sequence and time-series data [19, 13, 12, 18], biological sequence analysis [4, 17], etc. However, we are not aware of prior work on the prominent streak discovery problem proposed in this paper.

The skyline of a set of tuples is the subset of tuples that are not dominated by any tuple. A tuple dominates another tuple if it is equally good or better on every attribute and better on at least one attribute. Skyline query has been intensively studied over the last decade. Kung et al. [9] first proposed in-memory algorithms to tackle the skyline problem. Börzsönyi et al. [5] considered the problem in database context and integrated skyline operator into database system. They also invented a block-nested-loop algorithm (BNL) and extended the divide-and-conquer algorithm (DC) from [9]. An improvement of BNL is discussed in [6].

Progressive skyline algorithms optimize the efficiency in returning initial skyline points while producing more results progressively. Various algorithms developed along this line include the bitmap-based algorithm and the index-based algorithm [21], the nearest neighbor search algorithm [11], and the branch-and-bound skyline algorithm (BBS) [14]. Other variants of skyline queries have also been studied, including skyline cube which aims to answer skyline queries over any combination of dimensions [16, 24].

Jiang et al. [10] studied the problem of interval skyline queries on time-series. Given a set of time series and a time interval, they find the time series that are not dominated by others in the interval. A time series dominates another one if its value at every position is at least equal to the corresponding value in the other time series and it is at least larger at one position. The point-by-point equi-length interval comparison is clearly different from our problem.

The plateau of a time series is the time interval in which the vlaues are close to each other (within a given threshold) and are no smaller than the values outside the interval [22]. The plateau problem is not concerned about comparing different intervals.

Our techniques can be useful in disease outbreak detection, by identifying prominent streaks in time series of aggregated disease case counts. Previous works on outbreak detection focus on conventional data mining tasks such as clustering and regression [23]. The concept of prominent streaks has not been studied before.

3. DISCOVERING PROMINENT STREAKS FROM LOCAL PROMINENT STREAKS

For an n-element sequence P, the baseline method (Algorithm 1) produces $\frac{n(n+1)}{2}$ candidate streaks. In this section, based on the concept of *local prominent streak* (LPS) we propose the non-linear LPS-based (NLPS) and linear LPS-based (LLPS) methods. Both dramatically reduce the number of candidate streaks in practice. LLPS further guarantees only a linear number of candidate streaks.

3.1 Local Prominent Streak (LPS)

Definition 2 (Local Prominent Streak): Given a sequence of data values $P = (p_1, \cdots, p_n)$, we say a streak $s = \langle [l, r], v \rangle \in \mathcal{S}_P$ is a *local prominent streak* (LPS) or *locally prominent* if there does not

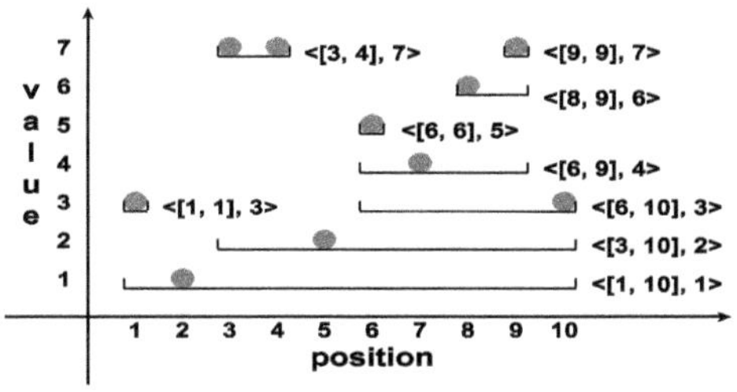

Figure 2: Local Prominent Streaks.

exist any other streak $s' = \langle [l', r'], v' \rangle \in \mathcal{S}_P$ such that $[l', r'] \supset [l, r]$ and $s' \succ s$. (I.e., there does not exist such s' that $[l', r'] \supset [l, r]$ and $v' \geq v$.) The symbol $\supset$ denotes the subsumption check between two intervals, i.e., $[l', r'] \supset [l, r]$ if and only if $l' \leq l \wedge r' > r$ or $l' < l \wedge r' \geq r$. We denote the set of local prominent streaks in sequence P as $\mathcal{LPS}_P$. ■

Figure 2 shows all the local prominent streaks found in our running example. All other streaks are not locally prominent. For example, $\langle [6, 8], 4 \rangle$ is not locally prominent since it is dominated by $\langle [6, 9], 4 \rangle$ and $[6, 9] \supset [6, 8]$. In the following we give several important properties of local prominent streaks.

Property 1: Every prominent streak is also a local prominent streak, i.e., $\mathcal{PS}_P \subseteq \mathcal{LPS}_P$. ■

Proof: Suppose there is a prominent streak that is not locally prominent, i.e., $\exists s \in \mathcal{PS}_P$ s.t. $s \notin \mathcal{LPS}_P$. By Definition 2, there exists some streak s' such that $[l', r'] \supset [l, r]$ and $s' \succ s$. That is contradictory to Definition 1 which says s cannot be dominated by any other streak. Therefore a streak cannot be prominent if it is not even locally prominent. ■

The above Property 1 is illustrated by Figure 2, as all the prominent streaks in Figure 1 also appear in Figure 2. However, the reverse of Property 1 does not hold– local prominent streaks are not necessarily prominent streaks. For example, $\langle [8, 9], 6 \rangle$ is an LPS but is dominated by $\langle [3, 4], 7 \rangle$ and therefore is not in Figure 1.

Lemma 1: Suppose $s = \langle [l, r], v \rangle$ and $s' = \langle [l', r'], v' \rangle$ are two different local prominent streaks in P, i.e., $s, s' \in \mathcal{LPS}_P, l \neq l'$ or $r \neq r'$. For any $k \in argmin_{i \in [l,r]} p_i$ and $k' \in argmin_{i \in [l',r']} p_i$, we have $k \neq k'$. I.e., $argmin_{i \in [l,r]} p_i \cap argmin_{i \in [l',r']} p_i = \phi$. ■

Proof: If $[l, r] \cap [l', r'] = \phi$, i.e., the two intervals do not overlap, it is obvious that $k \neq k'$. Now consider the case when $[l, r] \cap [l', r'] \neq \phi$, i.e., $l \leq l' \leq r$ or $l' \leq l \leq r'$. By definition of $argmin$, $p_k = v = min_{i \in [l,r]} p_i$ and $p_{k'} = v' = min_{i \in [l',r']} p_i$. Suppose there exist such k and k' that $k = k'$. Thus $v = v' = p_k$. By Definition 1, we have $p_i \geq v$ for every $i \in [l, r]$ and every $i \in [l', r']$. Since the two intervals $[l, r]$ and $[l', r']$ overlap, their combined interval corresponds to a new streak $s'' = \langle [l, r] \cup [l', r'], v \rangle$.[1] It is clear $s'' \succ s$ and $s'' \succ s'$. That is a contradiction to the precondition that both s and s' are LPSs. Thus, this lemma holds. ■

Lemma 1 indicates that two different LPSs cannot reach their minimal values at the same position. Therefore each value position in sequence P can correspond to the minimal value of at most one LPS. What immediately follows is that there are at most n LPSs in an n-element sequence. Formally we have the following property.

Property 2: $|\mathcal{LPS}_P| \leq |P|$. ■

From Property 1 we know that $\mathcal{LPS}_P$ is a sufficient candidate set for $\mathcal{PS}_P$, i.e., we can guarantee to find all prominent streaks if we only consider local prominent streaks. Property 2 further shows how small $\mathcal{LPS}_P$ is and thus how good it is as a candidate set. Specifically, the size of $\mathcal{LPS}_P$ is at most $|P|$, the length of the sequence, in contrast to the all $\frac{|P|(|P|+1)}{2}$ possible streaks considered by the baseline method (Algorithm 1). Thus, $\mathcal{LPS}_P$ helps to prune most streaks from further consideration. In the following sections we present efficient algorithms for computing a superset of $\mathcal{LPS}_P$ and $\mathcal{LPS}_P$ itself exactly.

[1]The two intervals can overlap in four different ways. Thus $[l, r] \cup [l', r'] = [l, r]$ or $[l, r']$ or $[l', r]$ or $[l', r']$.

3.2 $\mathcal{LPS}_P^k$ and $\mathcal{LPS}_{P_k}^k$

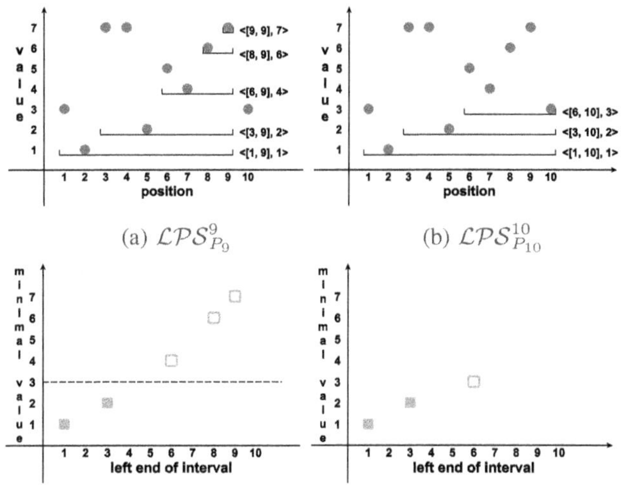

(a) $\mathcal{LPS}_{P_9}^9$ (b) $\mathcal{LPS}_{P_{10}}^{10}$

(c) l-v plot of $\mathcal{LPS}_{P_9}^9$ (d) l-v plot of $\mathcal{LPS}_{P_{10}}^{10}$

Figure 3: From $\mathcal{LPS}_{P_9}^9$ to $\mathcal{LPS}_{P_{10}}^{10}$.

To facilitate our discussion, we first define a new notation, $\mathcal{LPS}_P^k$.

Definition 3: $\mathcal{LPS}_P^k$ is the set of local prominent streaks in P that end at position k, i.e., $\mathcal{LPS}_P^k = \{s | s \in \mathcal{LPS}_P$ and $s = \langle [l, k], v \rangle\}$. ■

There are two key components in the definition of $\mathcal{LPS}_P^k$. The first is the upper script k, which fixes the right end of every interval in the set. It is clear that $\mathcal{LPS}_P^1, \mathcal{LPS}_P^2, \ldots, \mathcal{LPS}_P^{|P|}$ is a natural partition of $\mathcal{LPS}_P$. We use this partition scheme in the design of our algorithms. Specifically, we show how each $\mathcal{LPS}_P^k$ in this partition is calculated in a sequential and progressive way.

The second key component in the definition of $\mathcal{LPS}_P^k$ is the lower script P, which provides the scope for local prominent streaks. By generalizing this component we define $\mathcal{LPS}_{P_k}^k$. We denote the sequence with the first k entries of P as P_k. Then $\mathcal{LPS}_{P_k}$ is the set of local prominent streaks with regard to sequence P_k (instead of P) and $\mathcal{LPS}_{P_k}^k$ are those LPSs in $\mathcal{LPS}_{P_k}$ that end at k. Due to the change of scope, $\mathcal{LPS}_{P_k}^k$ is a superset of $\mathcal{LPS}_P^k$. Formally, we have the following property.

Property 3: $\mathcal{LPS}_P^k \subseteq \mathcal{LPS}_{P_k}^k$. ■

Proof: Consider any streak $s \in \mathcal{LPS}_P^k$. By Definition 3, $s = \langle [l, k], v \rangle$ and $s \in \mathcal{LPS}_P$. Therefore by Definition 2, there does not exist any $s' = \langle [l', r'], v' \rangle$ in P such that $s' \succ s$ and $[l', r'] \supset [l, k]$. Since P_k is a prefix of P, i.e., the first k values in P, it follows that there does not exist any such s' in P_k either. Therefore $s \in \mathcal{LPS}_{P_k}^k$. ■

Consider the running example again. Figure 3(a) shows $\mathcal{LPS}_{P_9}^9$, including $\langle [1, 9], 1 \rangle, \langle [3, 9], 2 \rangle, \langle [6, 9], 4 \rangle, \langle [8, 9], 6 \rangle, \langle [9, 9], 7 \rangle$. As shown in Figure 2, $\mathcal{LPS}_P^9$ contains $\langle [6, 9], 4 \rangle, \langle [8, 9], 6 \rangle, \langle [9, 9], 7 \rangle$. Streaks $\langle [1, 9], 1 \rangle$ and $\langle [3, 9], 2 \rangle$ do not belong to $\mathcal{LPS}_P$, thus do not belong to $\mathcal{LPS}_P^9$, since they are locally dominated by $\langle [1, 10], 1 \rangle$

and $\langle[3,10],2\rangle$, respectively. By contrast, $\langle[1,9],1\rangle$ and $\langle[3,9],2\rangle$ are part of $\mathcal{LPS}^9_{P_9}$ because they are not locally dominated by any streak of P_9, which only contains the first 9 values of P.

3.3 Non-linear LPS Method

By Property 3 and the fact that $\mathcal{LPS}^1_P, \cdots, \mathcal{LPS}^{|P|}_P$ is a partition of $\mathcal{LPS}_P$, we have

$$\mathcal{LPS}_P = \bigcup_{1\le k\le |P|} \mathcal{LPS}^k_P \subseteq \bigcup_{1\le k\le |P|} \mathcal{LPS}^k_{P_k} \quad (1)$$

Thus, we can use $\bigcup_{1\le k\le|P|} \mathcal{LPS}^k_{P_k}$ as our candidate set for prominent streaks. Although its size can be greater than that of $\mathcal{LPS}_P$, in practice it does substantially reduce the size of candidate streaks, verified by the experimental results in Section 5.

Algorithm 3: Non-linear LPS Method (NLPS)

Input: Data sequence $P = (p_1, \cdots, p_n)$
Output: Prominent streaks $skyline$

$skyline \leftarrow empty$
for k = 1 **to** n **do**
  Compute $\mathcal{LPS}^k_{P_k}$ by Algorithm 4
  for each streak s in $\mathcal{LPS}^k_{P_k}$ **do**
    $skyline \leftarrow skyline\_update(skyline, s)$

Algorithm 4: Progressive Computation of $\mathcal{LPS}^k_{P_k}$

Input: $\mathcal{LPS}^{k-1}_{P_{k-1}}$ and p_k
Output: $\mathcal{LPS}^k_{P_k}$
// When it starts, stack lps consists of streaks in $\mathcal{LPS}^{k-1}_{P_{k-1}}$.

$pivot \leftarrow null$
while ! $lps.isempty()$ **do**
  if $lps.top().v < p_k$ **then**
    break
  else
    $pivot \leftarrow lps.pop()$
if $pivot == null$ **then**
  $lps.push(\langle[k,k],p_k\rangle)$
else
  $pivot.v \leftarrow p_k$
  $lps.push(pivot)$
// Now, lps contains all the streaks in $\mathcal{LPS}^k_{P_k}$.

Along this line, Algorithm 3 presents the method to compute candidate streaks. Since the number of candidates may be super-linear to the length of data sequence, we call it the *non-linear LPS method* (NLPS). The algorithm iterates k from 1 to $|P|$, progressively computes $\mathcal{LPS}^k_{P_k}$ from $\mathcal{LPS}^{k-1}_{P_{k-1}}$ when the k-th element p_k is visited, and includes them into candidate streaks. The details of updating from $\mathcal{LPS}^{k-1}_{P_{k-1}}$ to $\mathcal{LPS}^k_{P_k}$ are in Algorithm 4, which is based on the following Lemma 2. For convenience of discussion, we first define the right-end extension of a streak and a streak set.

Definition 4: If $s = \langle[l,r],v\rangle$ is a streak in an n-element data sequence P and $r < n$, the right-end extension of s is streak $\langle[l,r+1],v'\rangle$, where $v' = \min\{v, p_{r+1}\}$. The extension of a streak set S is the set which consists of extensions of all the streaks in S. ■

Lemma 2: If s_1=$\langle[l,k],v_1\rangle \in \mathcal{LPS}^k_{P_k}$ and $l{\neq}k$, then the streak s_2=$\langle[l,k-1],v_2\rangle \in \mathcal{LPS}^{k-1}_{P_{k-1}}$. ■

Proof: First, note that v_2=$\min_{l\le i\le k-1} p_i$ and v_1=$\min\{v_2,p_k\}$. We prove by contradiction. Suppose s_2=$\langle[l_1,k-1],v_2\rangle \notin \mathcal{LPS}^{k-1}_{P_{k-1}}$. By Definition 3, $s_2 \notin \mathcal{LPS}_{P_{k-1}}$. Further by Definition 2, there exists s_3=$\langle[l_3,r_3],v_3\rangle \in \mathcal{S}_{P_{k-1}}$ such that $[l_3,r_3] \supset [l_1,k-1]$ and $s_3 \succ s_2$. Given any s=$\langle[l,r],v\rangle \in \mathcal{S}_{P_{k-1}}$, we have $r \le k-1$. Therefore r_3=$k-1$, $l_3 < l_1$ and $v_3 \ge v_2$. The right-end extension of s_3 is s_4=$\langle[l_3,k],v_4\rangle$, where v_4=$\min\{v_3,p_k\}$$\ge$$\min\{v_2,p_k\}$=$v_1$. Therefore $s_4 \succ s_1$, which contradicts with the pre-condition that $s_1 \in \mathcal{LPS}^k_{P_k}$. The property holds. ■

Lemma 2 indicates that, except $\langle[k,k],p_k\rangle$, for each streak in $\mathcal{LPS}^k_{P_k}$, its prefix streak is in $\mathcal{LPS}^{k-1}_{P_{k-1}}$. Hence, to produce $\mathcal{LPS}^k_{P_k}$, we only need to consider the right-end extension of $\mathcal{LPS}^{k-1}_{P_{k-1}}$. Beyond that, we only need to consider one extra streak $\langle[k,k],p_k\rangle$ since it may belong to $\mathcal{LPS}^k_{P_k}$ as well.

In order to articulate how to derive $\mathcal{LPS}^k_{P_k}$ from $\mathcal{LPS}^{k-1}_{P_{k-1}}$, we partition $\mathcal{LPS}^{k-1}_{P_{k-1}}$ into two disjoint sets, namely,

$$\mathcal{LPS}^{k-1}_{P_{k-1}}{}^{<} = \{s | s = \langle[l,k-1],v\rangle \in \mathcal{LPS}^{k-1}_{P_{k-1}}, v < p_k\}, \quad (2)$$

$$\mathcal{LPS}^{k-1}_{P_{k-1}}{}^{\ge} = \{s | s = \langle[l,k-1],v\rangle \in \mathcal{LPS}^{k-1}_{P_{k-1}}, v \ge p_k\}. \quad (3)$$

It is clear that $\mathcal{LPS}^{k-1}_{P_{k-1}}$ is the disjoint union of these two sets, i.e., $\mathcal{LPS}^{k-1}_{P_{k-1}} = \mathcal{LPS}^{k-1}_{P_{k-1}}{}^{<} \cup \mathcal{LPS}^{k-1}_{P_{k-1}}{}^{\ge}$, and $\mathcal{LPS}^{k-1}_{P_{k-1}}{}^{<} \cap \mathcal{LPS}^{k-1}_{P_{k-1}}{}^{\ge} = \phi$. Use the running example again. For $\mathcal{LPS}^9_{P_9}$ in Figure 3(a), since $p_{10} = 3$, the two sets are $\mathcal{LPS}^9_{P_9}{}^{<} = \{\langle[1,9],1\rangle, \langle[3,9],2\rangle\}$, $\mathcal{LPS}^9_{P_9}{}^{\ge} = \{\langle[6,9],4\rangle, \langle[8,9],6\rangle, \langle[9,9],7\rangle\}$.

We consider how to extend streaks in $\mathcal{LPS}^{k-1}_{P_{k-1}}{}^{<}$ and $\mathcal{LPS}^{k-1}_{P_{k-1}}{}^{\ge}$, respectively. For simplicity of presentation, we omit the formal proofs when we make various statements below.

- $\mathcal{LPS}^{k-1}_{P_{k-1}}{}^{<}$: We use $S1$ to denote the right-end extension of $\mathcal{LPS}^{k-1}_{P_{k-1}}{}^{<}$. Since every streak in $\mathcal{LPS}^{k-1}_{P_{k-1}}{}^{<}$ has a minimal value less than p_k, the corresponding extended new streak has the same minimal value. Hence all the new streaks belong to $\mathcal{LPS}^k_{P_k}$. For the running example, corresponding to $\mathcal{LPS}^9_{P_9}{}^{<}$, we have $S1 = \{\langle[1,10],1\rangle, \langle[3,10],2\rangle\}$.
- $\mathcal{LPS}^{k-1}_{P_{k-1}}{}^{\ge}$: We use $S2$ to denote the right-end extension of $\mathcal{LPS}^{k-1}_{P_{k-1}}{}^{\ge}$. Since every streak in $\mathcal{LPS}^{k-1}_{P_{k-1}}{}^{\ge}$ has a minimal value greater than or equal to p_k, the minimal value of every streak in $S2$ equals p_k. Hence, the longest streak in $S2$, denoted as $S2^*$, dominates all other streaks in $S2$ and it is the only streak in $S2$ that belongs to $\mathcal{LPS}^k_{P_k}$. Furthermore, since every streak in $S2$ has the same r value (the right end of the interval), i.e., k, $S2^*$ is the streak with the minimal l value (the left end of the interval) in $S2$. Clearly there cannot be another streak in $S2$ with the same length. For the running example, corresponding to $\mathcal{LPS}^9_{P_9}{}^{\ge}$, we have $S2 = \{\langle[6,10],3\rangle, \langle[8,10],3\rangle, \langle[9,10],3\rangle\}$. The longest streak in $S2$ is $\langle[6,10],3\rangle$.
- $\mathcal{LPS}^{k-1}_{P_{k-1}}{}^{\ge} = \phi$: If $\mathcal{LPS}^{k-1}_{P_{k-1}}{}^{\ge}$ is empty, a new streak $\langle[k,k],p_k\rangle$ belongs to $\mathcal{LPS}^k_{P_k}$. (Otherwise, it is dominated by $S2^*$.)

The above discussion is captured by the following Property 4.

Property 4: $\mathcal{LPS}^k_{P_k} = S1 \cup \{S2^*\}$ if $S2 \neq \phi$ and $\mathcal{LPS}^k_{P_k} = S1 \cup \{\langle[k,k],p_k\rangle\}$ if $S2 = \phi$. ■

We use Figure 3 to explain the above procedure of producing $\mathcal{LPS}^k_{P_k}$ from $\mathcal{LPS}^{k-1}_{P_{k-1}}$. Figure 3(a) and 3(b) show $\mathcal{LPS}^9_{P_9}$ and $\mathcal{LPS}^{10}_{P_{10}}$, respectively. Figure 3(c) and 3(d) also show $\mathcal{LPS}^9_{P_9}$ and $\mathcal{LPS}^{10}_{P_{10}}$, by using a different presentation– l-v plot. All the streaks $\langle[l,r],v\rangle$ in $\mathcal{LPS}^{k-1}_{P_{k-1}}$ share the same value of r, which is $k-1$. Therefore we plot the streaks by l (x-axis) and v (y-axis). In Figure 3(c), the 5 points represent the 5 streaks in $\mathcal{LPS}^9_{P_9}$: $\langle[1,9],1\rangle$, $\langle[3,9],2\rangle$, $\langle[6,9],4\rangle$, $\langle[8,9],6\rangle$, $\langle[9,9],7\rangle$. The dotted line represents the 10-th data entry $p_{10} = 3$. It bisects $\mathcal{LPS}^9_{P_9}$ into $\mathcal{LPS}^9_{P_9}{}^{\ge}$ (3 hollow points above the line) and $\mathcal{LPS}^9_{P_9}{}^{<}$ (2 filled points below the line). We produce new candidate streaks $\mathcal{LPS}_{P_{10}}^{10}$ by extending the right ends of streaks in $\mathcal{LPS}_{P_9}^{9}$ to 10. The streaks extended from $\mathcal{LPS}_{P_9}^{9}{}^{<}$ all belong to $\mathcal{LPS}_{P_{10}}^{10}$. They are the 2 filled points in Figure 3(d), corresponding to $\langle[1,10],1\rangle$ and $\langle[3,10],2\rangle$. Among the streaks extended from $\mathcal{LPS}_{P_9}^{9}{}^{\geq}$, only the one with the smallest l (the longest one) belongs to $\mathcal{LPS}_{P_{10}}^{10}$. It is the hollow point in Figure 3(d), corresponding to $\langle[6,10],3\rangle$. Hence $\mathcal{LPS}_{P_{10}}^{10}$=$\{\langle[1,10],1\rangle, \langle[3,10],2\rangle, \langle[6,10],3\rangle\}$.

The details of the algorithm are shown in Algorithm 4. We use a stack lps to maintain $\mathcal{LPS}_{P_k}^{k}$. Since the streaks $\langle[l,r],v\rangle$ in $\mathcal{LPS}_{P_k}^{k}$ have the same r value which equals k, we do not need to store r in lps. Hence each item in lps has two data attributes, v and l. The items in the stack are ordered by v (and l, since their v and l values both strictly monotonically increase).[2] In fact, Figure 3(c) and 3(d) visualize all items in lps, before and after p_{10} is encountered, respectively. In each figure, the leftmost point denotes the bottom of the stack (with the smallest v), while the rightmost point denotes the top of the stack (with the largest v). After data entries p_1, ..., p_{k-1} are encountered, lps contains $\mathcal{LPS}_{P_{k-1}}^{k-1}$. Given data entry p_k, we popped from the stack all the streaks whose v values are greater than or equal to p_k. Among the popped streaks, the leftmost one (with the smallest l and v) is pushed back into the stack, with v value replaced by p_k and r extended from $k-1$ to k. (Again, the r value is not explicitly stored in the stack.) If no streak was popped, then $\langle[k,k],p_k\rangle$ is pushed into the stack. The remaining streaks in the original stack are kept, with their v and l values unchanged and r extended from $k-1$ to k.

Algorithm 3 computes candidate streaks for an n-element sequence P. It invokes Algorithm 4 n times.[3] In each invocation, exactly 1 item is pushed into the stack. Therefore in total there are n insertions and thus at most n deletions. Hence, the amortized time complexity of Algorithm 4 is $O(1)$.

In each iteration of Algorithm 3, we compute $\mathcal{LPS}_{P_k}^{k}$ and include them into candidate streaks. Thus, for an n-element sequence, the total number of candidate streaks considered is $\sum_{k=1}^{n}|\mathcal{LPS}_{P_k}^{k}|$. In the worst case, we may have a strictly increasing sequence and the candidate streaks include all possible streaks. This is as bad as the exhaustive baseline method in Algorithm 1. For example, given sequence (10, 20, 30), we have $\mathcal{LPS}_{P_1}^{1}=\{\langle[1,1],10\rangle\}$, $\mathcal{LPS}_{P_2}^{2}=\{\langle[1,2],10\rangle, \langle[2,2],20\rangle\}$ and $\mathcal{LPS}_{P_3}^{3}=\{\langle[1,3],10\rangle, \langle[2,3],20\rangle, \langle[3,3],30\rangle\}$.

3.4 Linear LPS Method

Now we present the linear LPS (LLPS) method (Algorithm 5), which guarantees to produce a linear number of candidate streaks even in the worst case. Similar to Algorithm 3, this method iterates through the data sequence and computes $\mathcal{LPS}_{P_k}^{k}$ from $\mathcal{LPS}_{P_{k-1}}^{k-1}$ when the k-th data entry is encountered, for k from 1 to n. However, different from Algorithm 3, it also computes $\mathcal{LPS}_{P}^{k-1}$ from $\mathcal{LPS}_{P_{k-1}}^{k-1}$. Computation of both $\mathcal{LPS}_{P_k}^{k}$ and $\mathcal{LPS}_{P}^{k-1}$ is done in Algorithm 6, which is a simple extension of Algorithm 4. It is worth noting that, since P_n=P, $\mathcal{LPS}_{P}^{n}$ and $\mathcal{LPS}_{P_n}^{n}$ are identical.

To produce $\mathcal{LPS}_{P}^{k-1}$ from $\mathcal{LPS}_{P_{k-1}}^{k-1}$ given the k-th entry p_k, Algorithm 6 is based on the following Property 5. Due to space limitations, we omit the formal proof, but explain its intuition as follows. Recall that the minimal value of any streak in $\mathcal{LPS}_{P_{k-1}}^{k-1}{}^{\geq}$ (Equation (3)) is not smaller than p_k. It follows that if the minimal value of a streak in $\mathcal{LPS}_{P_{k-1}}^{k-1}{}^{\geq}$ is greater than p_k, the streak cannot grow into a longer local prominent streak without changing the minimal value. Hence, the streak itself is a local prominent streak. To summarize, $\mathcal{LPS}_{P}^{k-1}$ is the same as $\mathcal{LPS}_{P_{k-1}}^{k-1}{}^{\geq}$. The only exception is the longest streak in $\mathcal{LPS}_{P_{k-1}}^{k-1}{}^{\geq}$, i.e., the streak with the smallest l and thus the smallest minimal value v. If its minimal value is equal to p_k, then it does not belong $\mathcal{LPS}_{P}^{k-1}$, because it can be right-extended and included in $\mathcal{LPS}_{P}^{k'}$ for some $k' \geq k$.

Property 5: Given an n-entry sequence P, for any position $1<k\leq n$, $\mathcal{LPS}_{P}^{k-1}=\{s|s=\langle[l,k-1],v\rangle \in \mathcal{LPS}_{P_{k-1}}^{k-1}{}^{\geq}$ and $v>p_k\}$. ■

Continue the running example. We have $\mathcal{LPS}_{P}^{9}=\mathcal{LPS}_{P_9}^{9}{}^{\geq}=\{\langle[6,9],4\rangle, \langle[8,9],6\rangle, \langle[9,9],7\rangle\}$. Note that $\mathcal{LPS}_{P_9}^{9}{}^{\geq}$ and $\mathcal{LPS}_{P}^{9}$ are identical because the minimal values for the streaks in $\mathcal{LPS}_{P_9}^{9}{}^{\geq}$ are all greater than p_{10}.

Similar to Algorithm 4, Algorithm 6 has an amortized time complexity of $O(1)$. However, in LLPS we only need to consider the streaks in $\mathcal{LPS}_{P}^{k-1}$ as candidates. Consequently, LLPS reduces the total number of candidate streaks to $\sum_{k=1}^{n}|\mathcal{LPS}_{P}^{k}|$, i.e., $|\mathcal{LPS}_{P}|$ (Equation (1)). By Property 2, $|\mathcal{LPS}_{P}|$ is n at most, thus LLPS guarantees to produces only a linear number of candidate streaks even in worst case.

Algorithm 5: Linear LPS Method(LLPS)

Input: Data sequence $P=(p_1,\ldots p_n)$
Output: Prominent streaks $skyline$

```
skyline ← empty
for k = 1 to n do
    Compute LPS_P^{k-1} and LPS_{P_k}^k by Algorithm 6
    for each streak s in LPS_P^{k-1} do
        skyline ← skyline_update(skyline, s)
LPS_P^n ← LPS_{P_n}^n
for each streak s in LPS_P^n do
    skyline ← skyline_update(skyline, s)
```

Algorithm 6: Computing $\mathcal{LPS}_{P}^{k-1}$ and $\mathcal{LPS}_{P_k}^{k}$

Input: $\mathcal{LPS}_{P_{k-1}}^{k-1}$ and p_k
Output: $\mathcal{LPS}_{P}^{k-1}$ and $\mathcal{LPS}_{P_k}^{k}$

```
// Insert the following line before Line 1 in Algorithm 4.
LPS_P^{k-1} ← φ
// Insert the following two lines after Line 6 in Algorithm 4, in the
   same else branch as Line 6.
if pivot.v > p_k then
    LPS_P^{k-1} ← LPS_P^{k-1} ∪ {pivot}
```

4. MONITORING PROMINENT STREAKS

One desirable property of a prominent streak discovery algorithm is the capability of monitoring new data entries as the sequence grows continuously and always keeping the prominent streaks up-to-date. For example, a network administrator may check the prominent streaks in the network traffic of a Web server till any particular moment. Formally, given a continuously growing data sequence P (such as a data stream), the k-th data entry that has just come is denoted by p_k and the sequence so far is denoted by P_k. At this moment, if the user requests $\mathcal{PS}_{P_k}$, the prominent streaks of P_k, our method should efficiently discover them.

The BST-based method progressively updates the dynamic skyline with new candidate streaks, thus can be applied for monitoring prominent streaks without modification.

[2] We omit the proof of monotonicity.

[3] With regard to the first data element p_1, $\langle[1,1],p_1\rangle$ is pushed into the stack. It is the only prominent streak and local prominent streak for P_1.

name	length	# prominent streaks	description
Gold	1074	137	Daily morning gold price in US dollars, 01/1985-03/1989.
River	1400	93	Mean daily flow of Saugeen River near Port Elgin, 01/1988-12/1991.
Melb1	3650	55	The daily minimum temperature of Melbourne, Australia, 1981-1990.
Melb2	3650	58	The daily maximum temperature of Melbourne, Australia, 1981-1990.
Wiki1	4896	58	Hourly traffic to `en.wikipedia.org/wiki/Main_page`, 04/2010-10/2010.
Wiki2	4896	51	Hourly traffic to `en.wikipedia.org/wiki/Lady_gaga`, 04/2010-10/2010.
Wiki3	4896	118	Hourly traffic to `en.wikipedia.org/wiki/Inception_(film)`, 04/2010-10/2010.
SP500	10136	497	S&P 500 index, 06/1960-06/2000.
HPQ	12109	232	Closing price of HPQ in NYSE for every trading day, 01/1962-02/2010.
IBM	12109	198	Closing price of IBM in NYSE for every trading day, 01/1962-02/2010.
AOL	132480	127	Number of queries sent to AOL search engine in every minute over three months.
WC98	7603201	286	Number of requests to World Cup 98 web site in every second, 04/1998-07/1998.

Table 1: Data Sequences Used in Experiments.

With regard to candidate streak generation, all three methods (baseline, NLPS, LLPS) use one-pass sequential scan of the data sequence, therefore they all naturally fit into the monitoring scenario. Specifically, the new data point p_k corresponds to the next iteration of the outer loop in Algorithm 1, 3, and 5. The baseline method exhaustively lists all streaks ending at p_k and updates the skyline with these streaks. The NLPS method updates $\mathcal{LPS}^{k-1}_{P_{k-1}}$ to $\mathcal{LPS}^{k}_{P_k}$, and updates the skyline with the streaks in $\mathcal{LPS}^{k}_{P_k}$.

The adaptation of LLPS is a bit more complex, as shown in Algorithm 7. This algorithm records the last position when the user requested the prominent streaks. When p_k arrives, $\mathcal{LPS}^{k-1}_{P}$ and $\mathcal{LPS}^{k}_{P_k}$ are dynamically computed by Algorithms 6. The skyline is updated with the candidate streaks in $\mathcal{LPS}^{k-1}_{P}$, only if $\mathcal{PS}_{P_{k-1}}$ was not requested by the user when p_{k-1} was visited. Note that if $\mathcal{PS}_{P_{k-1}}$ was requested, the skyline has already been updated with the streaks in $\mathcal{LPS}^{k-1}_{P_{k-1}}$. Since $\mathcal{LPS}^{k-1}_{P} \subseteq \mathcal{LPS}^{k-1}_{P_{k-1}}$, we do not need to update the skyline with $\mathcal{LPS}^{k-1}_{P}$ again. Finally, if the user requests $\mathcal{PS}_{P_k}$, the skyline has to be updated with $\mathcal{LPS}^{k}_{P_k}$ since all the local prominent streaks (with regard to P_k) ending at p_k must be considered. In Section 5 we will show the significant superiority of this adaptation of LLPS over other methods.

Note that this algorithm degrades to NLPS (Algorithm 3) if the user requests the prominent streaks at every data entry. On the other hand, if the prominent streaks are only requested at p_n, i.e., the last entry in the sequence, it becomes the same as LLPS (Algorithm 5).

Algorithm 7: Continuous Monitoring of Prominent Streaks

Input: The new data entry p_k

```
Compute LPS_P^{k-1} and LPS_{P_k}^k by Algorithms 6
if last_requested_position < k − 1 then
    for each streak s in LPS_P^{k-1} do
        skyline ← sklyine_update(skyline, s)
if PS_{P_k} is requested then
    for each streak s in LPS_{P_k}^k do
        skyline ← sklyine_update(skyline, s)
    last_requested_position ← k
    // Now, skyline contains all prominent streaks in PS_{P_k}
```

5. EXPERIMENTS

The algorithms were implemented in Java. The experiments were conducted on a computer with 2.26GHz Intel Core 2 Duo CPU under Windows 7. The limit on the heap size of Java Virtual Machine (JVM) was set at 512MB.

We used multiple real-world datasets, including time series data library[4], Wikipedia traffic statistics dataset[5], NYSE exchange data[6], AOL search engine log[7], and FIFA World Cup 98 web site access log[8]. These datasets cover a variety of application scenarios, including meteorology, hydrology, finance, web log, and network traffic. Table 1 shows the information of 12 data sequences from these data sets that we used in experiments. For each data sequence, we list its name, length, and the number of prominent streaks in the sequence. Each data sequence was stored in a data file.

[4]http://robjhyndman.com/TSDL/

[5]http://dammit.lt/wikistats/

[6]http://infochimps.com/datasets/daily-1970-current-open-close-hi-low-and-volume-nyse-exchange-up

	Baseline	NLPS	LLPS
Gold	5.77×10^5	6.04×10^4	1.05×10^3
River	9.81×10^5	2.18×10^4	1.33×10^3
Melb1	6.66×10^6	4.47×10^4	3.50×10^3
Melb2	6.66×10^6	4.28×10^4	3.49×10^3
Wiki1	1.20×10^7	7.16×10^4	4.79×10^3
Wiki2	1.20×10^7	5.77×10^4	4.75×10^3
Wiki3	1.20×10^7	7.31×10^4	4.70×10^3
SP500	5.14×10^7	1.69×10^6	9.98×10^3
HPQ	7.33×10^7	5.24×10^5	1.08×10^4
IBM	7.33×10^7	6.97×10^5	1.13×10^4
AOL	8.78×10^9	3.53×10^6	1.20×10^5
WC98	2.89×10^{13}	1.78×10^8	6.69×10^6

Table 2: Number of Candidate Streaks.

Examples of Interesting Prominent Streaks Discovered: From 1985 to 1989, there had been more than one thousand consecutive trading days with morning gold price greater than $300. During this period, there had been a streak of four hundred days with price more than $400, though the $500 price only lasted two days at most.

In Melbourne, Australia, during the years between 1981 and 1990, the weather had been pleasant. There had been more than two thousand days with minimal temperature above zero, and the streak was not ending. (We do not have data beyond 1990.) The longest streak during which the temperature hit above 35 degrees Celsius is six days. It was in the summer of the year 1981.

More than half of the prominent streaks we found in the traffic data of the Lady Gaga Wikipedia page were around September 12th, when she became a big winner in the MTV Video Music Awards (VMA) 2010. During that time, the page had been visited by at least 2000 people in every hour for almost four days.

Number of Candidate Streaks: The three algorithms for candidate streak generation, namely Baseline (Algorithm 1), NLPS (Algorithm 3), and LLPS (Algorithm 5), differ by the ways they produce candidates and thus the numbers of produced candidates. Table 2 shows the total number of candidate streaks considered by each algorithm on each data sequence. The baseline algorithm produces an extremely large number of candidates since it enumerates all possible streaks, e.g., $\binom{7603202}{2}$=2.89×10^{13} for WC98. By contrast, NLPS only needs to

[7]http://gregsadetsky.com/aol-data/

[8]http://ita.ee.lbl.gov/html/contrib/WorldCup.html

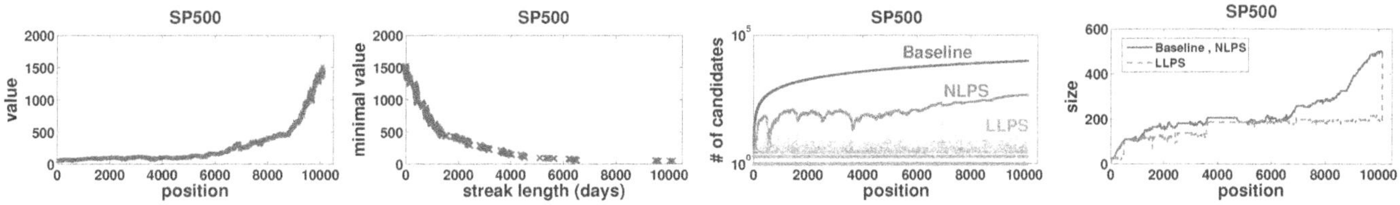

(a) Data Sequence (b) Prominent Streaks (c) Number of Candidate Streaks (d) Size of Dynamic Skyline

Figure 4: Detailed Results on SP500.

data sequence	Baseline	NLPS	LLPS
Gold	78	40	9
River	78	15	3
Melb1	390	22	12
Melb2	387	21	15
Wiki1	711	28	15
Wiki2	711	18	15
Wiki3	689	40	16
SP500	4717	599	21
HPQ	6099	165	18
IBM	5079	209	22
AOL	446622	546	78
WC98	>1 hour	27477	3404

Table 3: Execution Time (in Milliseconds).

consider $\bigcup_{1\leq k\leq |P|} \mathcal{LPS}^k_{P_k}$, which is a superset of the real prominent streaks $\mathcal{PS}_P$ but a much smaller subset of all possible streaks $\mathcal{S}_P$. For instance, the number of candidate streaks by NLPS is 1.78×10^8 for WC98, which is 5 orders of magnitude smaller than what Baseline considers. LLPS further significantly educes the number of candidates by only considering LPSs. For example, there are 6.69×10^6 LPSs in WC98, which is about 30 times smaller than 1.78×10^8. Note that the number of LPSs for LLPS is bounded by sequence length (Property 2), which is verified by Table 2.

Execution Time:

The number of candidate streaks directly determines the efficiency of our algorithms. In Table 3 we report the execution time of our algorithms using the three candidate streak generation methods (Baseline, NLPS, LLPS), for all 12 data sequences. For skyline operation, we implemented the sorting-based, external-memory sorting-based, and BST-based skyline methods mentioned in Section 1. Under these different skyline methods, Baseline, NLPS, and LLPS perform and compare consistently. Therefore in Table 3 we only report the results for implementations based on the BST-based skyline method, due to space limitations. The reported execution time is in milliseconds and is the average of five runs.

We excluded data loading time, i.e., the time spent on just reading each data file. This is because data loading time is dominated by processing time of the algorithms once the data file gets large. In our experiments, WC98 cost 1 second to load while the loading time of all other datasets was below 30ms.

In Table 3 we use '>1 hour' to denote the execution time when an algorithm could not finish within one hour (i.e., 3600000ms). This lower bound is sufficient in showing the performance difference of the various algorithms.

With regard to the comparison of Baseline, NLPS, and LLPS, it is clear from Table 3 that LLPS outperforms NLPS, and both NLPS and LLPS are far more efficient than Baseline. This is exactly due to the large gap in the number of candidate streaks (shown in Table 2), which in turn determines the number of comparisons performed during skyline operations.

A Closer Look:

To have a better understanding of the experimental results, we take a close look at the SP500 data sequence. Similar observations are made on other data sequences, hence we omit the analysis of other sequences. Figure 4(a) shows the data sequence itself. We see that the sequence is almost monotonically increasing at the coarse grain level. Due to that, the number of prominent streaks found in SP500 (497, as shown in Table 1) is the most among all the data sequences. We also visualize the prominent streaks in SP500 in Figure 4(b), where the x-axis is for interval length and the y-axis is for minimal value in the interval.

In Table 2 we have seen the huge difference among Baseline, NLPS and LLPS in total number of candidate streaks. These three algorithms all generate candidates progressively. Therefore in Figure 4(c) we show, for each algorithm, the number of new candidate streaks produced at every value position of the data sequence. The figure clearly shows the superiority of LLPS since it always generates orders of magnitude less candidates at each position.

The BST-based skyline method maintains a dynamic skyline, as a binary search tree, in memory. The size of this tree affects the efficiency of tree operations, such as inserting and deleting a streak. Figure 4(d) shows the size of the dynamic skyline along the sequence of SP500 by each algorithm. The curves for Baseline and NLPS overlap since they both store $\mathcal{PS}_{P_k}$, at every position k, in the dynamic skyline. In contrary, LLPS does not need to store some streaks in $\mathcal{PS}_{P_k}$, hence the tree size is much smaller than that for Baseline/NLPS when the sequence is almost constantly growing in the second half of SP500.

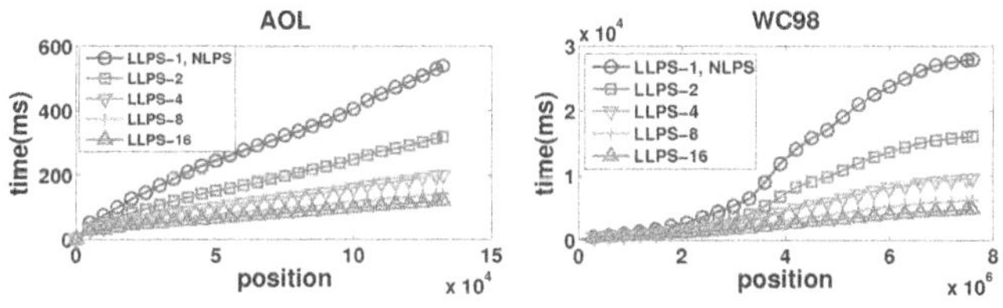

(a) AOL (b) WC98

Figure 5: Cumulative Execution Time at Various Positions, for Different Reporting Frequencies.

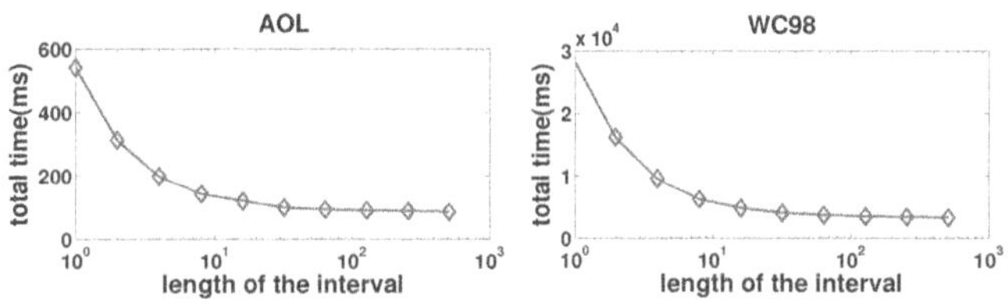

(a) AOL (b) WC98

Figure 6: Total Execution Time by Reporting Frequencies.

Monitoring Prominent Streaks:

In Section 4 we discussed how to monitor the prominent streaks as a data sequence evolves and new data values come. The adaptation of LLPS for monitoring purpose was shown in Algorithm 7. This algorithm can control at which positions the prominent streaks (so far) need to be reported.

Take AOL and WC98 as examples. Figure 5 shows the execution time of Algorithm 7). The x-axis represents the sequence position, and the y-axis is for the total execution time by that position. There are five curves in each figure, corresponding to five different frequencies of reporting prominent streaks. For instance, LLPS-1 means that, whenever a new data entry comes, all the prominent streaks so far are reported; LLPS-16 means the prominent streaks are requested at every 16 data entries. As discussed in Section 4, LLPS-1 is identical to NLPS (Algorithm 3), and LLPS-n is identical to LLPS (Algorithm 5), where n is the sequence length when it does not evolve anymore. Figures 5(a) and 5(b) clearly show that the total execution time of LLPS-i increases as the reporting frequency increases (i.e., reporting interval i decreases). Figures 6(a) and 6(b) further show how the total execution time changes along different reporting intervals. We can see that the execution time drops rapidly at the beginning and quickly reaches near-optimal value even when the frequency is still pretty high (e.g., reporting the prominent streaks at every 16 entries.)

6. CONCLUSION

In this paper, we study the problem of discovering prominent streaks in sequence data. A prominent streak is a long consecutive subsequence consisting of only large (small) values. We propose efficient methods based on the concept of local prominent streak (LPS). We prove that prominent streaks are a subset of LPSs and the number of LPSs is less than the length of a data sequence. Our linear LPS-based method guarantees to consider only local prominent streaks, thus achieving significant reduction in candidate streaks. The results of experiments over multiple real datasets verified the effectiveness of the proposed methods.

Acknowledgements: We thank Jun Yang for discussion of the initial ideas of this paper when Chengkai Li and Jun Yang were both visiting HP Labs in Beijing, China in the summer of 2010.

7. REFERENCES

[1] R. Agrawal, C. Faloutsos, and A. Swami. Efficient similarity search in sequence databases. *Foundations of Data Organization and Algorithms*, pages 69–84, 1993.

[2] R. Agrawal, K. ip Lin, H. S. Sawhney, and K. Shim. Fast similarity search in the presence of noise, scaling, and translation in time-series databases. In *VLDB*, pages 490–501, 1995.

[3] R. Agrawal and R. Srikant. Mining sequential patterns. In *Proceedings of the Eleventh International Conference on Data Engineering*, pages 3–14, 1995.

[4] S. Altschul, W. Gish, W. Miller, E. Myers, and D. Lipman. Basic local alignment search tool. *Journal of molecular biology*, 215(3):403–410, 1990.

[5] S. Börzsönyi, D. Kossmann, and K. Stocker. The skyline operator. In *Proceedings of the 17th International Conference on Data Engineering*, pages 421–430, 2001.

[6] J. Chomicki, P. Godfrey, J. Gryz, and D. Liang. Skyline with presorting. In *Proceedings of the International Conference on Data Engineering*, pages 717–719, 2003.

[7] S. Cohen, C. Li, J. Yang, and C. Yu. Computational journalism: A call to arms to database researchers. In *Proceedings of the 5th Biennial Conference on Innovative Data Systems Research (CIDR)*, pages 148–151, 2011.

[8] C. Faloutsos, M. Ranganathan, and Y. Manolopoulos. Fast subsequence matching in time-series databases. In *SIGMOD*, pages 419–429, 1994.

[9] H.T.Kung, F.Luccio, and F.P.Preparata. On finding the maxima of a set of vectors. *Journal of the ACM*, 22(4):469 – 476, 1975.

[10] B. Jiang and J. Pei. Online interval skyline queries on time series. In *Proceedings of the 25th International Conference on Data Engineering*, pages 1036–1047, 2009.

[11] D. Kossmann, F. Ramsak, and S. Rost. Shooting stars in the sky: an online algorithm for skyline queries. In *Proceedings of the 28th international conference on Very Large Data Bases*, pages 275–286, 2002.

[12] T. W. Liao. Clustering of time series data–a survey. *Pattern Recognition*, 38(11):1857 – 1874, 2005.

[13] T. Oates, L. Firoiu, and P. Cohen. Clustering time series with hidden markov models and dynamic time warping. In *Proceedings of the IJCAI-99 Workshop on Neural, Symbolic and Reinforcement Learning Methods for Sequence Learning*, pages 17–21, 1999.

[14] D. Papadias, Y. Tao, G. Fu, and B. Seeger. Progressive skyline computation in database systems. *ACM Transactions on Database Systems (TODS)*, 30(1):41–82, 2005.

[15] J. Pei, J. Han, B. Mortazavi-Asl, J. Wang, H. Pinto, Q. Chen, U. Dayal, and M.-C. Hsu. Mining sequential patterns by pattern-growth: the prefixspan approach. *IEEE Transactions on Knowledge and Data Engineering*, 16(11):1424–1440, 2004.

[16] J. Pei, Y. Yuan, X. Lin, W. Jin, M. Ester, Q. Liu, W. Wang, Y. Tao, J. X. Yu, and Q. Zhang. Towards multidimensional subspace skyline analysis. *ACM Trans. Database Syst.*, 31(4):1335–1381, 2006.

[17] L. Rabiner. A tutorial on hidden Markov models and selected applications in speech recognition. *Proceedings of the IEEE*, 77(2):257–286, 1989.

[18] Y. Shin and D. Fussell. Parametric kernels for sequence data analysis. In *Proceedings of the 20th international joint conference on Artifical intelligence*, pages 1047–1052, 2007.

[19] P. Smyth. Clustering sequences with hidden Markov models. In *Advances in neural information processing systems*, 1997.

[20] R. Srikant and R. Agrawal. Mining sequential patterns: Generalizations and performance improvements. *Advances in Database Technology (EDBT)*, pages 1–17, 1996.

[21] K.-L. Tan, P.-K. Eng, and B. C. Ooi. Efficient progressive skyline computation. In *Proceedings of the 27th International Conference on Very Large Data Bases*, pages 301–310, 2001.

[22] M. Wang and X. Wang. Finding the plateau in an aggregated time series. In *Advances in Web-Age Information Management (WAIM)*, pages 325–336, 2006.

[23] W.-K. Wong. *Data mining for early disease outbreak detection*. PhD thesis, Pittsburgh, PA, USA, 2004.

[24] T. Xia and D. Zhang. Refreshing the sky: the compressed skycube with efficient support for frequent updates. In *Proceedings of the 2006 ACM SIGMOD international conference on Management of data*, pages 491–502, 2006.

[25] X. Yan, J. Han, and R. Afshar. CloSpan: Mining closed sequential patterns in large datasets. In *Proceedings of SIAM International Conference on Data Mining*, pages 166–177, 2003.

[26] B. Yi, H. Jagadish, and C. Faloutsos. Efficient retrieval of similar time sequences under time warping. In *Proceedings of the 14th International Conference on Data Engineering*, pages 201–208, 1998.

[27] M. Zaki. SPADE: An efficient algorithm for mining frequent sequences. *Machine Learning*, 42(1):31–60, 2001.

Protecting Location Privacy Using Location Semantics *

Byoungyoung Lee[α], Jinoh Oh[α], Hwanjo Yu[α], and Jong Kim[β]
[α]Department of Computer Science and Engineering, [β]Division of IT convergence engineering
Pohang University of Science and Technology (POSTECH)
Pohang, South Korea
{override, kurin, hwanjoyu, jkim}@postech.ac.kr

ABSTRACT

As the use of mobile devices increases, a location-based service (LBS) becomes increasingly popular because it provides more convenient context-aware services. However, LBS introduces problematic issues for location privacy due to the nature of the service. Location privacy protection methods based on k-anonymity and ℓ-diversity have been proposed to provide anonymized use of LBS. However, the k-anonymity and ℓ-diversity methods still can endanger the user's privacy because location *semantic* information could easily be breached while using LBS. This paper presents a novel location privacy protection technique, which protects the location semantics from an adversary. In our scheme, location semantics are first learned from location data. Then, the trusted-anonymization server performs the anonymization using the location semantic information by cloaking with *semantically heterogeneous* locations. Thus, the location *semantic* information is kept secure as the cloaking is done with semantically heterogeneous locations and the true location information is not delivered to the LBS applications. This paper proposes algorithms for learning location semantics and achieving semantically secure cloaking.

Categories and Subject Descriptors

H.2.0 [**Database Management**]: General—*Security, integrity, and protection*; H.2.8 [**Database Management**]: Database Applications—*Spatial databases and GIS*

General Terms

Security, Algorithm, Experimentation

Keywords

Location Privacy, Location Semantics, θ-Secure Cloaking Area

*This research is supported by WCU(World Class University) program (R31-2008-000-10100-0) and Research Grant (KRF-2008-331-D00528), both through the National Research Foundation of Korea funded by the Korean Government.

1. INTRODUCTION

The use of mobile devices has increased dramatically in the last decade. As mobile device technology has developed, context awareness services have become available and mobile devices now support more convenient and user-friendly services. The representative service of context awareness services is a location-based service (LBS). LBS is an information and entertainment service based on the geographical position of the mobile device. There are many different kinds of LBS services, such as navigation services, requesting the nearest business locations, receiving traffic alerts or notifications, and so on.

However, LBS services introduce problematic issues for location privacy due to the nature of the service. The history of certain user's locations could be accumulated, and private information could be exposed if an adversary has access to that history. For example, support for a certain political party, or the whereabouts of a user at a certain time could be handed to adversaries and abused by them. This is a critical problem because most people are reluctant to use LBS services if their location privacy is in danger in spite of its convenience.

In order to protect location privacy, previous research has been done using k-anonymity [23] and ℓ-diversity [19]. A cloaking area, which is an extended area from the exact position of a mobile user, is computed by the anonymization server and the anonymization server delegates the LBS requests for a mobile user. For computing a cloaking area, k-anonymity based location privacy [10, 6, 20, 3, 14, 26, 27] extends a cloaking area until 'k-1' other users are included, and ℓ-diversity based location privacy [1, 24, 28] extends until 'ℓ-1' different locations are included. As a result, an exact position is abstracted with other users (k-anonymity) and other locations (ℓ-diversity), which makes it difficult for an adversary to infer valuable information (see Section 7 for related work).

Although these previous methods guarantee some degree of location privacy, both techniques have a critical limitation. The cloaking area could breach location semantic information, which possibly endangers the user's privacy. To be specific, the cloaking area could include only semantically similar locations even if it is mixed with other users and locations, and the adversary would be able to infer semantic meanings from the extended area. For example, if the extended area only includes an elementary school, high school, and university, then the adversary could infer that a mobile user is doing work related to 'teaching' or 'studying'.

In this paper, we propose a novel location privacy protection technique, which protects the location semantics from an adversary. In our scheme, location semantics are first learned from location data. Then, the trusted-anonymization server performs the anonymization using the location semantic information by cloaking with *semantically heterogeneous* locations. Thus, the location *semantic* information is kept secure as the cloaking is done with semantically heterogeneous locations and the true location information is not delivered to the LBS applications.

Our primary novel contributions are summarized as follows.

- We propose a method for mining location semantics from the perspective of location privacy. A staying duration feature is presented to capture the location semantics from trajectory data, and such mined location semantics are stored in an abstracted graph to be efficiently used.

- We propose a method to obtain a cloaking area which protects location semantic leakages. An adversary's prior and posterior knowledge of location semantics is generally modeled and the adversary's information gain from a cloaking area is restricted below a certain degree. According to the experimental results, our method is much safer at the same cost than k-anonymity and ℓ-diversity based location privacy methods in terms of a semantic heterogeneity.

The remainder of this paper is organized as follows. Section 2 introduces the background of location privacy protection and points out its limitations. Section 3 describes how to obtain location semantic information and Section 4 presents how to compute an extended area with semantically heterogeneous locations. Section 5 shows the evaluation results of our proposed methods. Section 6 discusses the limitations and future work of our method, and Section 7 surveys related work. Section 8 concludes the paper.

2. BACKGROUND AND LIMITATIONS

Many researchers have tried to guarantee location privacy in using LBS, but their attempts have limitations. In this section, we first give the background of location privacy protection techniques and then describe the limitations of such techniques.

2.1 Background: Location Privacy Protection

A primary cause of location privacy breaches in using LBS lies in the fact that the exact position of a mobile device should be used and known to LBS applications. Thus, in order to protect exact position information, location privacy protection techniques use a *cloaking area* instead of exact position information for LBS requests. A *cloaking area* is defined as an area which includes the current position of a mobile device for the purpose of hiding an exact position. Based on using a cloaking area, the adversary cannot easily breach a mobile user's privacy since the exact current position is abstracted. There are largely two approaches for computing the cloaking area, each of which is based on well known data publishing protection techniques, k-anonymity [23] and ℓ-diversity [19]. Depending on which technique has been adopted for location privacy, we refer to as *location k-anonymity* or *location ℓ-diversity*.

The most well known approach is location k-anonymity [10, 6, 20, 3, 14, 26, 27], which provides at least a 'k' anonymity level. In location k-anonymity, the cloaking area is extended until 'k-1' other users are included. This is a good starting point for protecting location privacy because the adversary has to classify each person among 'k' people to identify who actually submitted LBS requests. Similar to k-anonymity, location ℓ-diversity [1, 18, 24, 28] extends a cloaking area until 'ℓ-1' different locations are included. In location ℓ-diversity, the adversary cannot simply tell which location a mobile user actually visited since the cloaking area includes multiple locations.

These location k-anonymity and ℓ-diversity techniques are performed by a trusted-anonymization server for a mobile device and

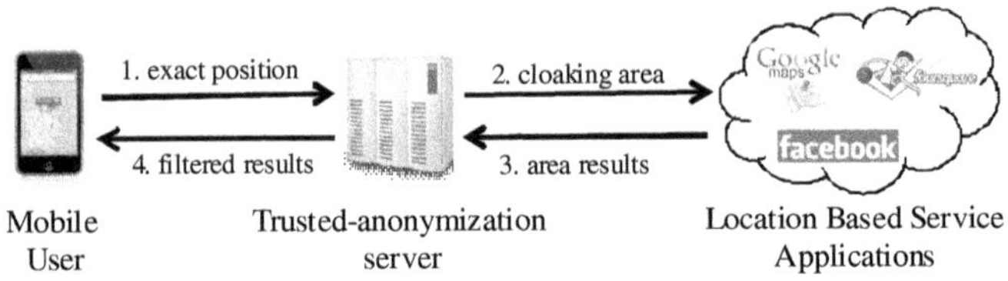

Figure 1: Trusted-anonymization server based location privacy architecture

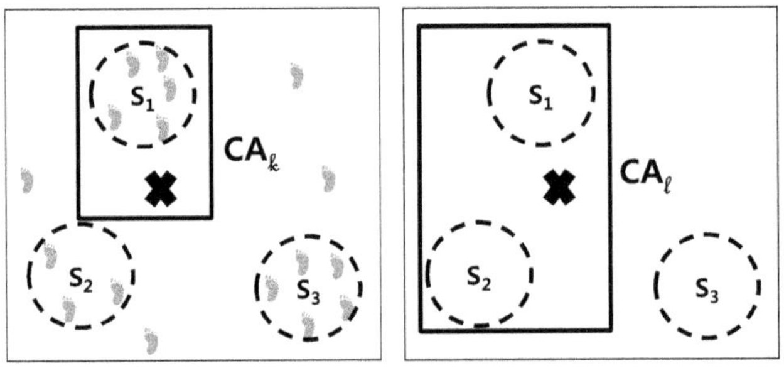

(a) k-anonymity (k=5) (b) ℓ-diversity (ℓ=2)

Figure 2: An example of a location similarity attack against a cloaking area

we call this model a *trusted-anonymization server based model* hereafter. Figure 1 shows a trusted-anonymization server based model. At first, a mobile user requests a service to the trusted-anonymization server (line 1). In this request, the mobile user specifies her exact current position. Then the anonymization server computes the cloaking area using either a number of users (location k-anonymity) or locations (location ℓ-diversity) nearby the user's position. The cloaking area is passed to LBS applications (line 2) and the LBS applications return all results related to the cloaking area (line 3). The anonymization server filters out unnecessary results and gives back the result corresponding to the mobile user's current location (line 4).

As a result, the exact position is not exposed to LBS applications because a cloaking area is used instead of the position. Though the delegating anonymization server knows the exact position of a mobile device, LBS applications only see an abstracted range of an area.

2.2 Limitations of Previous Location Privacy Protection

Though location k-anonymity and ℓ-diversity approaches guarantee some degree of location privacy, both protection schemes are vulnerable to a *location similarity attack* which possibly endangers LBS user's privacy. In other words, a cloaking area CA, which contains n locations denoted as $L(CA) = \{S_1, S_2, ..., S_n\}$, is vulnerable to a location similarity attack if all locations in CA are semantically similar.

Figure 2 shows an example of a *location similarity attack*. Assume that each node from S_1 to S_3 represents a location; S_1 and S_2 are hospitals and S_3 is a library. Note that 'x' marked in the center represents the current location of a mobile user. Based on this setting, two rectangles, CA_k and CA_ℓ, represent the cloaking area under k-anonymity ($k = 5$) and ℓ-diversity ($\ell = 2$) respectively. CA_k in Figure 2-(a) is vulnerable to a location similarity attack since it only includes a single location, S_1. Thus, the mobile user using the cloaking area CA_k for LBS requests would be highly linked to hospitals and can be suspected of having treatment. CA_ℓ

in Figure 2-(b) is also vulnerable because two locations in CA_ℓ are similar in terms of the purpose of its visits. Similarly, a mobile user using CA_ℓ would be suspected for the same reason.

What we actually desire would be to have a cloaking area with semantically heterogeneous locations, which needs to include S_3 in the above example. However, both location k-anonymity and ℓ-diversity methods fail to protect a mobile user from a location similarity attack. Location k-anonymity fails because it picks the users without considering their locations and location l-diversity fails because it picks the locations without considering the semantics of locations.

3. MINING LOCATION SEMANTICS

In order to compute secure cloaking area based on location semantics, we must be aware of *location semantics* beforehand. In this paper, location semantics are interpreted as which type of services are provided at locations. This interpretation makes sense from the perspective of location privacy, because *what people want to secure in location privacy is what they did in a location.*

Based on such an interpretation, this section describes how to obtain location semantics. Locations are identified first (Section 3.1) and features for capturing location semantics are proposed next (Section 3.2). Finally, a location semantic graph which represents semantic relations between locations is constructed (Section 3.3). The location semantic graph will be used to compute the cloaking area with semantically heterogeneous locations (Section 4).

3.1 Identifying Locations

There are several methods for finding a location. The first one is to utilize point of interest (POI) collections, which can be publicly available through OpenStreetMap [11], etc. Since POI collections provide information on locations that people may find useful or interesting, locations including coordinate information can be obtained. The second method, which we use in our experiments, is to analyze trajectory data. The trajectory data contains coordinate information (usually GPS points) and corresponding timestamps. If a trajectory stays in a limited area over a time threshold value, it indicates that someone stayed in that location and did some meaningful job. Thus, locations can be discovered by identifying such a limited area. For interested readers, please refer to [31] for more details.

3.2 Features for Location Semantics

Our proposed method for discovering location semantics is based on the following observations. People visit locations mostly with a reason. We go to restaurants to have food, schools to attend classes, or hospitals to see a doctor. Since we have reasons for a visit, we stay for a while in a location for those reasons. Moreover, we spend a different amount of time depending on these reasons. Motivated by these observations, we propose two quantitative features for extracting location semantics, which are named staying duration, and usage time context.

Staying duration: People spend different amount of time in a location depending on what they do there. We call this amount of time staying duration. Intuitively, having food in a restaurant generally takes one or two hours, whereas students usually stay more than six hours at school. In addition, restaurants themselves have different staying duration distributions according to what they actually serve. For example, eating at a fine dining restaurant takes much longer time than at a fastfood restaurant. Thus visiting purposes of each location can be captured by using the staying duration.

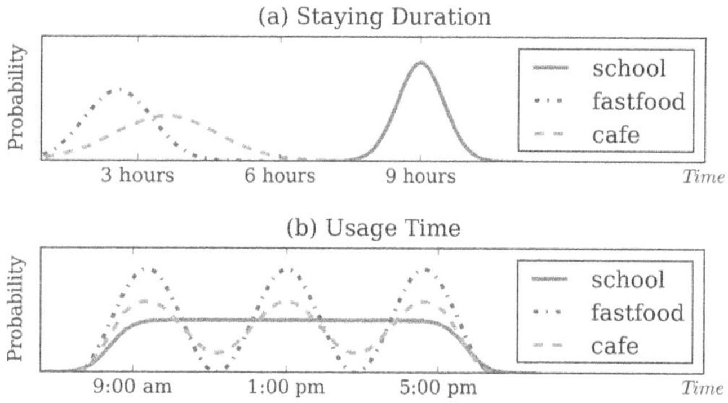

Figure 3: PDF of features for location semantics

Usage time context: It is common to see that places have their own active (popular) times. For example, most restaurants are full of customers during lunch or dinner time. On the contrary, most bars are full during the night but quiet in the morning. Relying on common sense, locations have differences in the distribution of usage times depending on services provided.

The feature data can be acquired via trajectory or survey data which contains such information. From the data, each feature's distribution is computed for each location. For example, hypothetical distributions of each feature are plotted in Figure 3. Distributions for locations such as school, fastfood restaurant, and cafe, are represented according to each location's characteristics. In Figure 3-(a), the x-axis represents staying duration and it reflects the fact that people stay longer at school than a fastfood restaurant or cafe. In Figure 3-(b), the x-axis represents usage time. A fastfood restaurant and cafe are crowded during meal times, but a school is active throughout the daytime.

Though the two features mentioned above can be used to characterize semantics of locations, we choose to use staying duration in our experiments. This is because the usage time context does not capture location semantics in some cases. For instance, a cafeteria and a dining restaurant are difficult to distinguish based on the usage time context because both places have similar crowded times. However, the staying duration feature is able to distinguish such places well because most people spend more time in a dining restaurant than in a cafeteria.

3.3 Constructing Location Semantic Graph

In order to represent location semantics with a simplified data structure, we present a *location semantic graph*. A distance between places (edge-weight) is computed first and a cluster of locations (node) are determined next. Finally, a location semantic graph is built with edges and nodes.

3.3.1 Distance measure

The distance measure should be able to capture the semantic differences between locations. Since all features can be represented in distributions, Kullback-Leibler (KL) divergence could be a reasonable choice to measure the distances between two distributions. KL divergence measures the distances of two distributions P, Q with

$$D_{KL}(P||Q) = \int_{-\infty}^{\infty} p(x) \log \left\{ \frac{p(x)}{q(x)} \right\} dx.$$

However, KL divergence is not an appropriate measure to capture semantic differences, which is explained in the following example.

Figure 4 shows three staying duration distributions P, Q, and R. Intuitively, P is similar to Q than to R. That is, our desired result

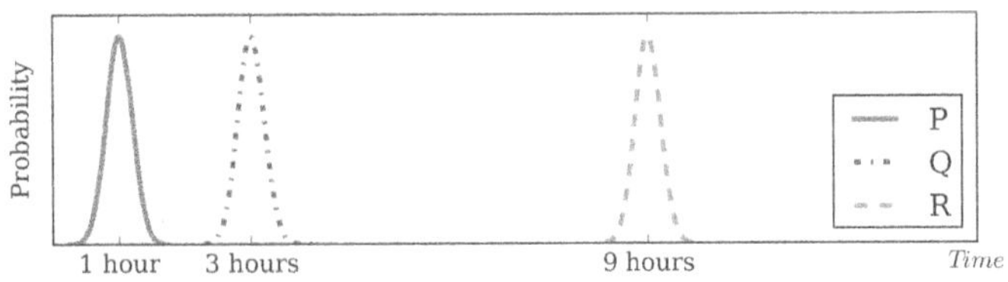

Figure 4: Example of staying duration distribution

is $D(P||Q) < D(P||R)$. However, the actual result from KL divergence is $D_{KL}(P||Q) \approx D_{KL}(P||R)$ because KL divergence cannot capture that the semantic distance between 1 hour and 9 hours is bigger than that between 1 hour and 3 hours is.

In order to overcome this limitation of KL divergence, we use Earth Mover's Distance which has recently been adopted for privacy protection of publishing data [15].

Earth Mover's Distance (EMD):[1] A distribution can be interpreted as an arbitrary arrangement of a mass of particles. In this view, a distribution can be transformed to another distribution by moving particles. EMD captures the minimum costs of transporting particles to equalize two distributions, which can be formally defined using the transportation problem. Suppose P and Q can be represented $P = \{p_1, p_2, \ldots, p_m\}$, $Q = \{q_1, q_2, \ldots, q_m\}$. The workload, needed to make two distribution the same, is defined as follows.

$$\text{WORK}(P, Q, F) = \sum_{i=1}^{m} \sum_{j=1}^{m} f_{ij} d_{ij}$$

with constraints

$$f_{ij} \geq 0, \quad 1 \leq i, j \leq m, \quad p_i - \sum_{j=1}^{m} f_{ij} + \sum_{i=1}^{m} f_{ij} = q_i,$$

$$\sum_{i=1}^{m} \sum_{j=1}^{m} f_{ij} = \sum_{i=1}^{m} p_i = \sum_{j=1}^{m} q_j = 1,$$

where f_{ij} is a flow of mass (the amount of moving particles) from i to j, d_{ij} is a ground distance from i to j, and all flows $F = [f_{ij}]$. From this setting, EMD measures the minimum workload, defined as

$$D_{EMD}(P, Q) = \min_{F} \text{WORK}(P, Q, F).$$

The virtue of EMD is in adjusting ground distance which enables us to capture semantic differences. In our case, the ground distance (d_{ij}) is set to be the normalized difference between staying durations, i.e., the difference of staying duration divided by the maximum difference. Thus, $0 \leq d_{ij} \leq 1$ for all i and j, which results in $0 \leq D_{EMD}(P, Q) \leq 1$ [15]. When revisiting the example in Figure 4, EMD performs $D_{EMD}(P, Q) < D_{EMD}(P, R)$ as desired since EMD sees (1 hour, 3 hours) pair has a much smaller ground distance than (1 hour, 9 hours) pair has. As a result, EMD is a better distance measure than KL divergence for our application and we adopt EMD as the distance measure for location semantic differences.

3.3.2 Location clustering

Based on EMD, locations are grouped into clusters before being structured in a graph. The main reason for performing clustering is that the data which would represent location semantics across all locations is too complicated and huge. Because there are numerous locations which are bases of people activities, computational complexities and exchanging costs with such data would be considerable burdens.

In this respect, k-means clustering is performed by grouping semantically similar locations. Pair-wise distances between locations are represented using EMD and the centroid of each cluster is updated by computing the average of the distributions in the cluster. Detailed explanations for k-means clustering can be found in [12].

3.3.3 Location semantic graph

After having clustered locations, all semantic information is represented by a graph based structure, which we call a *location semantic graph*. In a location semantic graph, a node represents clustered locations and an edge weight represents EMD between corresponding nodes. EMD between cluster nodes is defined as

$$D(C_i, C_j) = \sum_{l_i \in C_i} \frac{1}{|C_i|} \sum_{l_j \in C_j} \frac{D_{EMD}(l_i, l_j)}{|C_j|}$$

where C_i, C_j are clusters, $|C_i|, |C_j|$ are the number of locations in a cluster, and l_i, l_j are the distributions of each location. Note that $D(C_i, C_j)$ is also normalized into [0,1] because $0 \leq D_{EMD}(l_i, l_j) \leq 1$ for all i, j.

Figure 5 shows an example of a location semantic graph. The nodes indicate clustered locations, each of which is a group of semantically similar locations. The edge weight indicates the semantic differences between clusters computed by EMD. The number beside the cluster is the normalized number of locations in the cluster. Since all clusters have one location respectively, all clusters are 0.25.

4. θ-SECURE CLOAKING AREA

Obtaining a privacy preserving cloaking area is difficult because the way of checking the safety of the cloaking area in terms of location semantics is unexplored. In other words, it is difficult to evaluate *how much location semantic information an adversary will gain from the cloaking area*. To handle this, we propose methods for evaluating the safety of cloaking areas (Section 4.1) and obtaining a θ-secure cloaking area (Section 4.2).

4.1 Computing EMD of Cloaking Area

An adversary gains location semantic information from a cloaking area only if it is different from what he/she already knew. In other words, before seeing the cloaking area, the adversary's knowledge is the location semantics of an entire area since he/she has no idea where a mobile user is located (a prior belief). After seeing the cloaking area, the adversary obtains more specific location semantics corresponding to the cloaking area (a posterior belief). Thus, the information gain of the adversary from the cloaking area can be the difference between such prior beliefs and posterior beliefs, which is directly linked to the safety of the cloaking area. Motivated by this observation, we aim at evaluating the differences of the prior belief and the posterior belief.

The prior belief is the location semantic information of an arbitrary area since the adversary has no idea where a mobile user is located. Thus, the prior belief is represented as a location semantic graph in a hypothetically large area. For the posterior belief, the adversary sees a cloaking area which possibly contains more specific semantic information. Thus, the posterior belief is a more elaborated location semantic graph which is built upon the prior belief.

[1] We do not present a detailed description of EMD. Interested readers please refer to [22, 15].

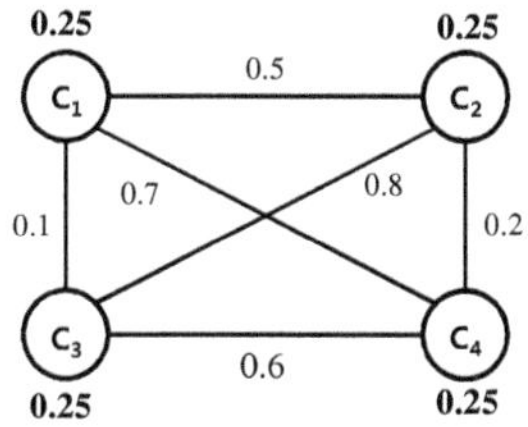

Figure 5: Location semantic graph

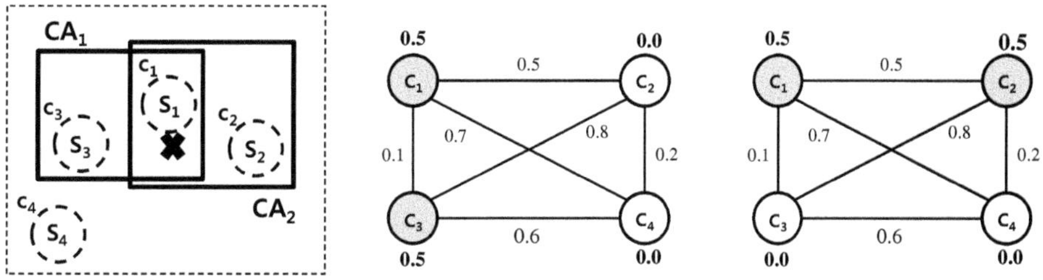

(a) Spatial snapshot of a mobile user

(b1) Location semantic graph of CA_1

(b2) Location semantic graph of CA_2

Figure 6: A spatial snapshot of a mobile user and its location semantic graph

Figure 6 illustrates a spatial snapshot of a mobile user (a) and its location semantic graph (b1) and (b2). Note that the location semantic graph in Figure 5 is constructed based on Figure 6-(a) to be a running example. In Figure 6, locations from S_1 to S_4 are represented with their corresponding cluster labels. A mobile user located at 'x' marked in the center has two choices for the cloaking area, CA_1 and CA_2. The cluster weight of the location semantic graph in (b1) and (b2) is changed because it only considers the cloaking area. For example, (b1) shows 0.5 on C_1, C_3, and 0 on C_2, C_4, because C_1, C_3 have one location respectively but C_2, C_4 have no location.

To measure the safety of a cloaking area by comparing the prior belief and the posterior belief, we compute the EMD of location semantic graphs between before and after seeing the cloaking area. A node (clustered locations) in a location semantic graph is converted into a discrete domain in EMD, and an edge weight (semantic differences) is converted into a ground distance d_{ij}. Numerical computational results of CA_1 and CA_2 are shown below as $D_{EMD}(P_{CA_1}, P_E)$ and $D_{EMD}(P_{CA_2}, P_E)$ respectively.

$$\begin{aligned} D_{EMD}(P_{CA_1}, P_E) &= \min_f \sum_i \sum_j f_{ij} d_{ij} \\ &= f^*_{12}0.5 + f^*_{14}0.7 + f^*_{32}0.8 + f^*_{34}0.6 \\ &= 0.25 \cdot 0.5 + 0 \cdot 0.7 + 0 \cdot 0.8 + 0.25 \cdot 0.6 \\ &= 0.275 \\ D_{EMD}(P_{CA_2}, P_E) &= \min_f \sum_i \sum_j f_{ij} d_{ij} = 0.075 \end{aligned}$$

where P_{CA_k} indicates the posterior belief of cloaking area CA_k, P_E indicates the prior belief. d_{ij} and f_{ij} is a ground distance and a flow between clusters C_i and C_j respectively, and f^*_{ij} is an optimal flow making two beliefs the same (see Section 6 for the discussion on the time complexity of EMD computations). Note that $0 \leq D_{EMD}(P_{CA}, P_E) \leq 1$ is satisfied, because $0 \leq d_{ij} = D(C_i, C_j) \leq 1$ holds.

Based on $D_{EMD}(P_{CA_2}, P_E) < D_{EMD}(P_{CA_1}, P_E)$, we argue that CA_2 is more secure than CA_1. This interpretation makes sense since C_1 and C_2 have bigger semantic distances than C_1 and C_3 have.

4.2 Finding θ-Secure Cloaking Area

Based on the safety measure of the cloaking area, a θ-secure cloaking area is defined below.

Definition 1. ***θ-Secure Cloaking Area.*** If a cloaking area CA satisfies $D_{EMD}(P_{CA}, P_E) \leq \theta$, we denote this cloaking area as a θ-secure cloaking area.

In order to obtain a θ-secure cloaking area, a cloaking area is extended until it satisfies θ-secure cloaking area. Algorithm 1 describes a greedy algorithm for finding a θ-secure cloaking area. Note that all locations are mapped onto a 2^n-by-2^n grid for efficient computation (n is selected by the user).

Algorithm 1. Finding θ-secure cloaking area

```
input : a grid map of location Map, a location semantic
        graph G, a prior belief P_E, a threshold value θ, and
        a maximum number of iterations maxLoop.
output: θ-secure cloaking area

1  CA = getInitialCA();
2  for i=1 to maxLoop do
3      foreach dir ∈ getPossibleDirs(CA, Map) do
4          CA_dir = extendCloakingArea(CA, Map,
           dir);
5          P_CA_dir = computePosteriorBelief(CA, G)
           ;
6          EMD_CA_dir = D_EMD(P_CA_dir, P_E);
7      (p, EMD_min) = findMinEMD();
8      CA = CA_p;
9      if EMD_min ≤ θ then
10         break;
11 return CA;
```

In Algorithm 1, a single cell, which includes a current mobile position, is chosen as an initial cloaking area (line 1). Next, obtain possible directions from {North, East, South, West}, which would make a rectangular form of a cloaking area (line 2). For each direction, the cloaking area is extended (line 4), and a posterior belief and EMD are computed (line 5-6). After iterating over all possible directions, select a cloaking area which has the minimum EMD value (line 7-8). Finally, if the minimum EMD value is less than the threshold θ (line 9), then return the corresponding cloaking area which is a θ-secure cloaking area (line 11).

5. EVALUATION

5.1 Experimental Setting

We extended a traffic simulator [2] to consider the human mobility patterns, which enables us to evaluate the effectiveness and performance of our proposed methods.[2] As described in Section 3, people stay a while in a location according to the location semantics. To be able to reflect such characteristics, the simulator should be able to determine the staying duration of each location. However, to the best of our knowledge, all known traffic simulators do not consider location semantics but simply generate random

[2]All implementations and data sets used for the evaluation are available on the project page, http://hpc.postech.ac.kr/locpriv.

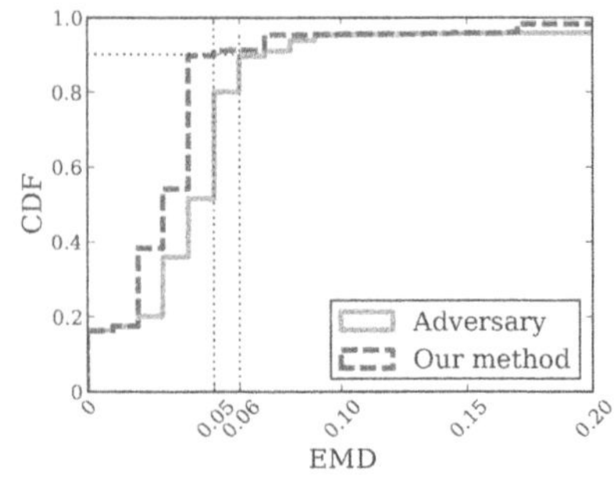

Figure 7: The cumulative distribution function (CDF) of cloaking areas' EMD (θ_t = 0.05)

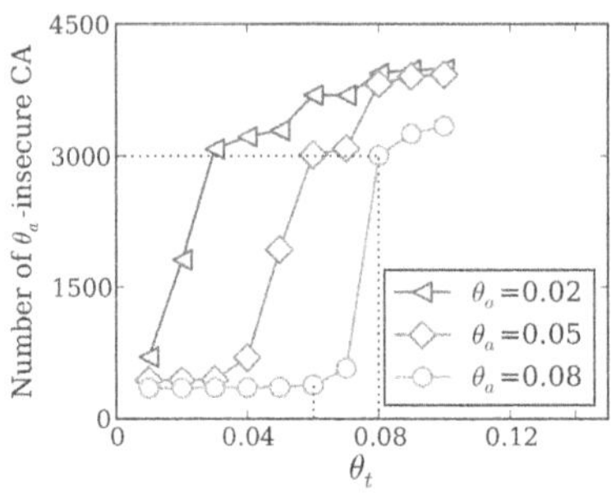

Figure 8: θ_a-insecure cloaking areas

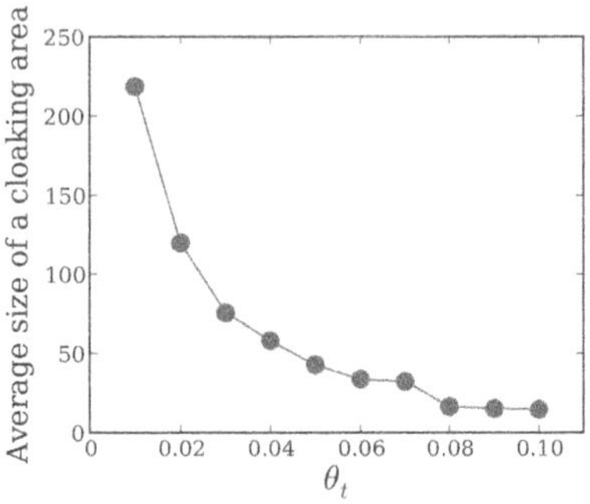

Figure 9: The average size of a cloaking area

Table 1: Parameters for the traffic simulator

Parameters	N_c	$t_{\min}$	$t_{\max}$	N_l	α	β	N_{users}
Values	4	50	400	2000	10	10	4000

movements. Thus, we modify the state of the art traffic simulator, Network-based Generator of Moving Objects [2], in order to reflect realistic human movement patterns.

In our modified simulator, staying duration patterns are modeled relying on the Gaussian distribution with latent variables. First, we sample N_c clusters which represent the group of semantically similar locations. For a cluster C_k, the mean μ_{c_k} and the standard deviation σ_{c_k} of the cluster staying duration pattern are picked from the uniform distributions, $\mu_{c_k} \sim \mathcal{U}(t_{\min}, t_{\max})$ and $\sigma_{c_k} \sim \mathcal{U}(0, \alpha)$, where $t_{\max}$ and $t_{\min}$ represent the maximum and minimum staying duration and α controls the variance of the cluster. Next, N_l locations are sampled from the clusters. For a location l_{ki} from the cluster C_k, the mean $\mu_{l_{ki}}$ and the standard deviation $\sigma_{l_{ki}}$ of a location staying duration pattern are picked from the Gaussian distributions, $\mu_{l_{ki}} \sim \mathcal{N}(\mu_{c_k}, \beta)$ and $\sigma_{l_{ki}} \sim \mathcal{N}(\sigma_{c_k}, \beta)$, where β controls the variance among the locations in each cluster. Once a moving object reaches the location, an actual staying duration t is determined from the Gaussian distribution $t \sim \mathcal{N}(\mu_{l_{ki}}, \sigma_{l_{ki}})$. In addition, a moving object chooses its next destination based on a lévy-flight process that is known to be followed by human mobility patterns according to a recent study [9]. Relying on the lévy-flight process, the probability of visiting nearby locations is higher than those of far away locations.

We generated trajectory data using our modified simulator. N_{users} objects were moved over a real road map of Oldenburg, Germany. The road map contains 6,105 nodes and 7,035 edges, a city about 15×15 km^2, which is presented in a 2^7-by-2^7 grid. Table 1 lists the parameters used for simulating moving objects. It is assumed that a LBS request is sent with a 2% probability from the reported positions. A staying duration pattern for each location is obtained from the trajectory and a location semantic graph is learned from the staying duration patterns. Using the location semantic graph, a θ-secure cloaking area is computed for each LBS request. In order to compare with the proposed method, a cloaking area is also computed based on k-anonymity and ℓ-diversity techniques as described in Section 2.1.

5.2 Experimental Results

5.2.1 *Evaluation on location semantic learning*

From 2000 locations used for generating trajectory data, 1948 locations were identified. Some locations were missing because a small number of moving objects passed by them. Among the identified locations, k-means clustering was performed with a parameter $k = 4$, and the clustering result was close to the perfect; i.e. $F_1 = 0.997$. In order to measure the correctness of the location semantic graph, we measured the normalized edge-weight differences between the modeled location semantic graph (G_M) and learned location semantic graph (G_L) as

$$D(G_M, G_L) = \frac{2}{N_C(N_C-1)} \sum_{i=1}^{N_C} \sum_{j=1}^{i-1} \left| [\mathbf{A}_M]_{ij} - [\mathbf{A}_L]_{ij} \right|,$$

where N_C denote the number of clusters, and $\mathbf{A}_M$ and $\mathbf{A}_L$ denote the weighted adjacency matrix of G_M and G_L respectively. Since the edge-weight is normalized into [0,1], the minimum and maximum of $D(G_M, G_L)$ are 0 and 1. Moreover, to evaluate the goodness of $D(G_M, G_L)$, we randomly created the location semantic graph G_R and the average is obtained from 30 times of running $\overline{D(G_M, G_R)}$. From the experiments, we obtained $D(G_M, G_L) =$ 0.084 and $\overline{D(G_M, G_R)} = 0.281$, which shows much closer results to the modeled location semantic graph.

5.2.2 *Evaluation on θ-secure cloaking area*

Attack models and measures: The adversary is assumed to have location semantic information at best, e.g. the location semantic graph of the model used for generating the trajectory. Consequently, the adversary takes a better position than our method because our method uses the learned location semantic graph which slightly deviates from the actual location semantic graph.

First of all, we checked how much location semantic information the adversary would gain from a cloaking area, which is quantified in EMD of a cloaking area. Since the adversary and our method have a different location semantic graph, EMD computed from the same cloaking area would be different. This implies that the θ-cloaking area returned by our algorithm may not guarantee θ degree of protection from the adversary's view. To be clear, we denote θ_t as a threshold for computing a cloaking area in our algorithm while θ_a is the EMD from the adversary's view.

To evaluate resistance against a location similarity attack launched by the adversary, we measure the number of *θ_a-insecure cloaking areas*. A θ_a-insecure cloaking area is a cloaking area which has EMD higher than θ_a from the adversary's point of view. It implies that the adversary would gain θ_a degree or more of location semantics information from the corresponding cloaking area.

The cost of using a cloaking area is measured by the size of the cloaking area. Since a mobile user uses the cloaking area for the anonymization, he/she needs to spend more network traffic and computing costs proportional to the size of the cloaking area.

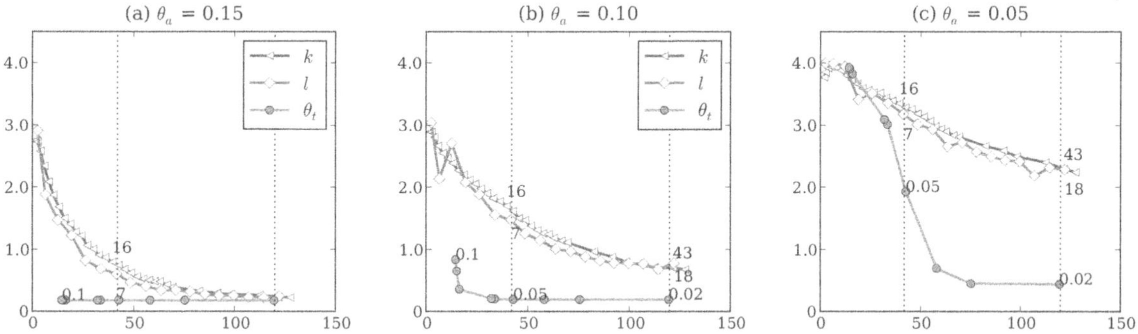

Figure 10: The number of θ_a-insecure cloaking areas by varying k, l, θ_t. X-axis: Average size of cloaking areas; Y-axis: Number of θ_a-insecure cloaking areas ($\times 10^3$).

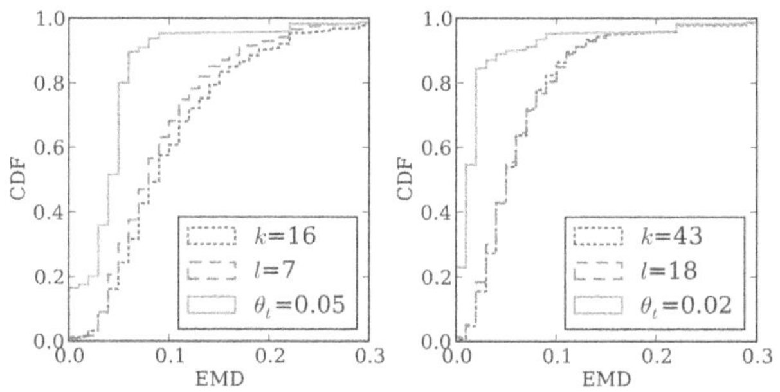

Figure 11: EMD of all cloaking areas by varying k, ℓ, and θ_t

Safety of a θ-secure cloaking area: Figure 7 shows the cumulative distribution function (CDF) of all 4000 cloaking areas' EMD for $\theta_t = 0.05$. When EMD is computed from our algorithm (method's view), 90% of the cloaking areas' EMD is below 0.05, which implies that our algorithm successfully returns θ_t-secure cloaking area in most cases. Some cloaking area's EMD is over 0.05 because our algorithm failed to find θ_t-secure cloaking area under the given number of extending steps. When it comes to the adversary's view, it shows slightly higher EMD value than the method's view. Although computed EMD is different, EMD of most cloaking areas is below 0.06 from the adversary's view, which is close to the model's view.

Figure 8 shows the number of θ_a-insecure cloaking areas while changing θ_t. Overall, as θ_t increases the number of insecure cloaking areas also increases, because a lower privacy level is enforced for higher θ_t. In addition, an actual θ_a degree of anonymity is obtained when $\theta_t < \theta_a$. For example, in 0.08-insecure case ($\theta_a = 0.08$), there are about 3000 insecure cloaking areas when $\theta_t = 0.08$, but fewer than 450 insecure cloaking areas when $\theta_t \leq 0.06$. Since this difference between θ_t and θ_a is a relative difference between the model's view and the adversary's view, we believe this does not indicate a weakness in our method. To achieve θ_a degree of anonymity, a smaller θ_t can be used, e.g. using θ_t=0.06 to achieve θ_a=0.08 degree of anonymity in this case.

Cost of a θ-secure cloaking area: Figure 9 shows the average size of the cloaking area versus θ_t. As θ_t decreases the average size of a cloaking area increases because a small θ_t implies more strict anonymization degree and causes a larger cloaking area. In addition, the curve follows a negative exponential function, which can be interpreted as follows. As θ_t approaches 1 (no location privacy guarantee), the average size would approach zero (the size of an exact position). On the contrary, as θ_t approaches zero (the maximum location privacy guarantee), the average size would approach infinity (the size of the maximum area).

Comparison with k-anonymity and ℓ-diversity: The safety and the costs of our method are compared with baseline methods, location k-anonymity and ℓ-diversity. 4000 requests are anonymized with our method as well as with baseline methods while changing the parameter of each method's privacy requirement (k, l, and θ_t).

Figure 10 plots the number of θ_a-insecure cloaking areas with the average size of cloaking areas for each parameter setting. In most cases, our method shows a lower number of θ_a-insecure the cloaking areas when the average size of cloaking area is similar to the others. For example, in Figure 10-(c), when $k = 43$, $l = 18$, and $\theta_t = 0.02$, the number of insecure cloaking areas of θ_t is much lower than k and ℓ. This signifies that our method provides better safety when the costs for enforcing the location privacy are the same.

Moreover, our method also shows better performances in costs when the provided safety is the same. To be specific, when the number of θ_a-insecure cloaking areas are the same, our method has a lower average size of cloaking areas than the others. Such superiority of our method becomes clearer as a safety requirement gets strict. In other words, as the criteria for insecure cloaking areas (θ_a) decreases, the gap between our method (θ_t) and baseline methods (k and ℓ) remarkably increases as shown from Figure 10-(a) to Figure 10-(c). Thus, a mobile user would get more benefits if location privacy preservation is the primary need.

In order to investigate more details, Figure 11 shows CDF of EMD of all cloaking areas when the costs, the average size of cloaking areas, are similar, e.g. (k=16, ℓ=7, θ_t=0.05) and (k=43, ℓ=18, θ_t=0.02). In both cases, θ_t is always more concentrated to lower EMD than k and l, which implies that our method guarantees better protection of the location semantics against any level of a location similarity attack.

Figure 12 illustrates the two-dimensional distribution of each cloaking area's size and its EMD, when the costs are similar. Overall, the distribution of the cloaking area from our method is concentrated in the bottom but the distributions from baseline methods are dispersed upward, which indicates that our method provides better location semantic protection at the same costs. Moreover, the brightest cell in Figure 12-(b3) is located more left than in Figure 12-(b1) and (b2). As a result, a large portion of the cloaking area in our method has a smaller size. However, since the average size of the cloaking area in these three figures is similar, some cloaking areas of our method would have a bigger size. This suggests that a mobile user using our method would enjoy low costs in most cases, but in some cases would pay relatively high costs.

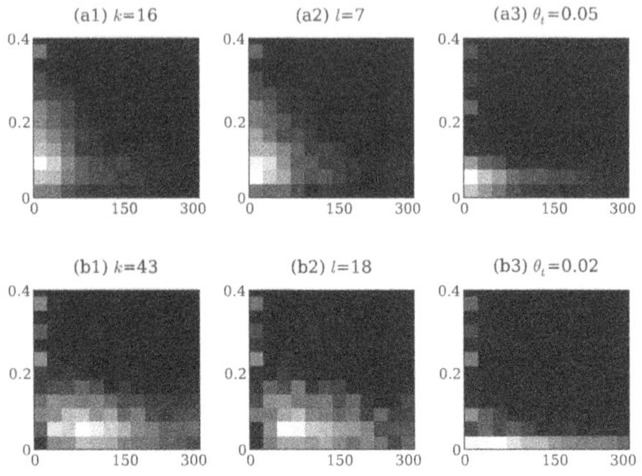

Figure 12: Two-dimensional distribution of each cloaking area's size and its EMD. The brighter the cell is the more frequent the occurrence is. X-axis: Size of a cloaking area; Y-axis: EMD.

6. DISCUSSION

Most previous work guarantees the anonymity and unlinkability based on k-anonymity and ℓ-diversity. Since our work focuses on protecting the location semantics using θ-secure cloaking area, the anonymity and unlinkability could be unprotected in some cases. For resolving this issue, all three parameters, θ-secure cloaking area, k-anonymity, and ℓ-diversity, could be used together, similarly *PrivacyGrid* [1] uses k-anonymity and ℓ-diversity together. In addition, since our method does not have *reciprocity* [14], θ-secure cloaking area may reveal the user location information caused by outliers; i.e. in peripheral areas where there are few semantically related locations, the cloaking area can become quite large and reveal that the user is in that peripheral area. To satisfy the reciprocity property, *HilbertCloak* [14] algorithm could be used.

Furthermore, our method relies on an EMD computation both in an offline step (clustering semantic locations) and an online step (computing a θ-secure cloaking area). Thus, it is vital for our method to be able to efficiently compute EMD, especially in the online stage. The time complexity for computing EMD can be formalized using a minimum cost network problem, and it can be solved in $O(n^3 \log n)$ [22], where n is either the number of locations or clusters in our method. Because the number of clusters would be quite small, we believe this is not the serious load for the online stage. For the offline stage, approximation algorithms can be adopted, which empirically lead to $O(n)$ or $O(n^2 \log n)$ [17, 21] with error bounds. Note that each approximation algorithm requires a specific setting for the ground distance; i.e. L_1 distances [17] or thresholded distances [21]. Since the ground distance in our method is on the non-euclidean space, more investigations should be done to adopt approximation algorithms.

7. RELATED WORK

Anonymization for publishing relational database: In order to protect published relational database data such as medical data, k-anonymity [23] was developed. k-anonymity guarantees the adversary cannot distinguish an individual record from at least 'k-1' other tuples. However, since 'k-1' other tuples may be the same sensitive values, ℓ-diversity [19] was proposed which enforces tuples in the same group have at least 'ℓ-1' diverse sensitive values. Ninghui et al. proposed t-closeness [15] to resolve the semantic breaches of k-anonymity and ℓ-diversity. t-closeness guarantees tuples in the same group are statistically similar to the entire data using EMD.

Anonymization for location based services: Gruteser et al. first proposed location privacy technique based on the k-anonymity concept and trusted-anonymization server [10]. The cloaking area, which is extended until 'k-1' other users are included, is computed through a trusted anonymization server and used for LBS requests instead of exact coordinates. A series of work has improved the computation of a cloaking area under k-anonymity. *Clique-Cloak* [6] and *Casper* [20] proposed personalized location anonymization. CliqueCloak locates a clique in a graph to compute the cloaking area and Casper uses a quadtree-based pyramid data structure for fast computation of the cloaking area. *Probabilistic Cloaking* [3] proposed imprecise LBS requests which yield probabilistic results. The *HilbertCloak* [14] algorithm utilizes Hilbert space-filling curve and its cloaking area is independent of mobile user distribution. To reduce the size of the cloaking area, historical locations of mobile nodes are used for computing the cloaking area instead of the current mobile node's location [26]. Feeling-based location privacy [27] sets 'k' using the location where a mobile user feels safe enough to disclose her location.

Using the k-anonymity based technique, the cloaking area may include only one meaningful location (e.g. a specific hospital or school) and disclose strong relationships to such a location. Thus, *PrivacyGrid* [1] proposed location ℓ-diversity, which extends the cloaking area until 'ℓ-1' different locations are included. *PrivacyGrid* used both location k-anonymity and ℓ-diversity so that the anonymization into different persons and locations can be done together. Similarly, XSTAR [24] attempted to achieve the optimal balance between high query-processing efficiency and robust inference-attack resilience while considering k-anonymity and ℓ-diversity together. Several works [28, 25, 5] have identified semantic breach issues, but impractical assumptions were made to resolve such issues. *Location diversity* [28] assumed that location semantics are pre-labeled and ℓ-diversity is able to protect the semantic breaches, and *PROBE* [5] also assumed the pre-labeled location semantics and requires many profile parameters for each user. *p-sensitivity* [25] assumed that a LBS request is classified into a sensitive or insensitive request.

In architectural perspectives, previous location privacy protection schemes mostly follow the trusted-server-based model in which an anonymization server delegates all LBS requests for mobile users. However, *SpaceTwist* [29] proposes an client-based model which uses a fake location instead of using 'exact location' for computing a cloaking area. [7] also proposes the client-based model based on Private Information Retrieval (PIR) with cryptographic techniques. The peer-to-peer model [4, 8, 13] attempts to remove trusted anonymization server. Based on a decentralized cooperative peer-to-peer model, location information among nearby peers is shared and used for computing the cloaking area.

Location data mining: A recommending system for travelers is proposed in [31, 30]. Trajectory data is analyzed and interesting locations are mined based on visited frequencies on each location. In [16], a similarity between users is mined based on the sequence property of people's movement behaviors, which also enables to identify correlations among locations. To the best of our knowledge, our research is the first to discover location semantics using staying duration and utilize it for computing semantically heterogeneous cloaking areas.

8. CONCLUSION

This paper proposes novel location privacy protecting techniques. Our proposed methods protect the location semantics from the LBS applications by performing the cloaking with *semantically heterogeneous* locations. Experimental results validate our proposed methods.

9. REFERENCES

[1] B. Bamba, L. Liu, P. Pesti, and T. Wang. Supporting anonymous location queries in mobile environments with privacygrid. In *Proceeding of the 17th International Conference on World Wide Web (WWW)*, 2008.

[2] T. Brinkhoff. A framework for generating network-based moving objects. *GeoInformatica*, 6(2):153–180, 2002.

[3] R. Cheng, Y. Zhang, E. Bertino, and S. Prabhakar. Preserving user location privacy in mobile data management infrastructures. In *Privacy Enhancing Technologies (PET)*, 2006.

[4] C.-Y. Chow, M. F. Mokbel, and X. Liu. A peer-to-peer spatial cloaking algorithm for anonymous location-based service. In *Proceedings of the ACM International Symposium on Advances in Geographic Information Systems (GIS)*, 2006.

[5] M. Damiani, E. Bertino, and C. Silvestri. The PROBE Framework for the Personalized Cloaking of Private Locations. *Transactions on Data Privacy*, 3(2):123–148, 2010.

[6] B. Gedik. Location Privacy in Mobile Systems: A Personalized Anonymization Model. In *IEEE International Conference on Distributed Computing Systems (ICDCS)*, 2005.

[7] G. Ghinita, P. Kalnis, A. Khoshgozaran, C. Shahabi, and K.-L. Tan. Private queries in location based services: anonymizers are not necessary. In *Proceedings of the ACM SIGMOD International Conference on Management of Data*, 2008.

[8] G. Ghinita, P. Kalnis, and S. Skiadopoulos. PRIVE: anonymous location-based queries in distributed mobile systems. In *Proceedings of the International Conference on World Wide Web (WWW)*, 2007.

[9] M. C. González, C. a. Hidalgo, and A.-L. Barabási. Understanding individual human mobility patterns. *Nature*, 453(7196):779–82, June 2008.

[10] M. Gruteser and D. Grunwald. Anonymous usage of location-based services through spatial and temporal cloaking. In *Proceedings of the International Conference on Mobile Systems, Applications and Services (MobiSys)*, 2003.

[11] M. M. Haklay and P. Weber. Streetmap: User-generated street maps. *IEEE Pervasive Computing*, 7:12–18, 2008.

[12] J. Han and M. Kamber. *Data mining: concepts and techniques*. Morgan Kaufmann, 2006.

[13] H. Hu and J. Xu. Non-Exposure Location Anonymity. In *IEEE International Conference on Data Engineering (ICDE)*, 2009.

[14] P. Kalnis, G. Ghinita, K. Mouratidis, and D. Papadias. Preventing Location-Based Identity Inference in Anonymous Spatial Queries. *IEEE Transactions on Knowledge and Data Engineering (TKDE)*, 19(12):1719–1733, 2007.

[15] N. Li, T. Li, and S. Venkatasubramanian. t-Closeness: Privacy Beyond k-Anonymity and l-Diversity. In *IEEE International Conference on Data Engineering (ICDE)*, 2007.

[16] Q. Li, Y. Zheng, X. Xie, Y. Chen, W. Liu, and W.-Y. Ma. Mining user similarity based on location history. In *Proceedings of the ACM SIGSPATIAL International Conference on Advances in Geographic Information Systems (GIS)*, 2008.

[17] H. Ling and K. Okada. An efficient Earth Mover's Distance algorithm for robust histogram comparison. *IEEE Transactions on Pattern Analysis and Machine Intelligence (TPAMI)*, 29(5):840–853, 2007.

[18] F. Liu, K. a. Hua, and Y. Cai. Query l-diversity in Location-Based Services. In *International Conference on Mobile Data Management: Systems, Services and Middleware (MDM)*, 2009.

[19] A. Machanavajjhala, D. Kifer, J. Gehrke, and M. Venkitasubramaniam. l-diversity: Privacy Beyond k-Anonymity. *ACM Transactions on Knowledge Discovery from Data (TKDD)*, 1(1):1–52, 2007.

[20] M. Mokbel, C. Chow, and W. Aref. The New Casper: Query Processing for Location Services without compromising privacy. In *Proceedings of the International Conference on Very large data bases (VLDB)*, 2006.

[21] O. Pele and M. Werman. Fast and robust earth mover's distances. In *IEEE International Conference on Computer Vision (ICCV)*, 2009.

[22] Y. Rubner, C. Tomasi, and L. Guibas. The earth mover's distance as a metric for image retrieval. *International Journal of Computer Vision (IJCV)*, 40(2):99–121, 2000.

[23] L. Sweeney. k-anonymity: A model for protecting privacy. *International Journal of Uncertainty Fuzziness and Knowledge Based Systems*, 10(5):557–570, 2002.

[24] T. Wang and L. Liu. Privacy-aware mobile services over road networks. *Proceedings of the VLDB Endowment*, 2(1):1042–1053, 2009.

[25] Z. Xiao, J. Xu, and X. Meng. p-Sensitivity: A Semantic Privacy-Protection Model for Location-based Services. In *International Conference on Mobile Data Management Workshops (MDMW)*, 2008.

[26] T. Xu and Y. Cai. Exploring Historical Location Data for Anonymity Preservation in Location-Based Services. In *IEEE International Conference on Computer Communications (INFOCOM)*, 2008.

[27] T. Xu and Y. Cai. Feeling-based location privacy protection for location-based services. *Proceedings of the ACM conference on Computer and communications security (CCS)*, 2009.

[28] M. Xue, P. Kalnis, and H. Pung. Location Diversity: Enhanced Privacy Protection in Location Based Services. *Location and Context Awareness (LoCA)*, pages 70–87, 2009.

[29] M. Yiu, C. Jensen, X. Huang, and H. Lu. Spacetwist: Managing the trade-offs among location privacy, query performance, and query accuracy in mobile services. In *IEEE International Conference on Data Engineering (ICDE)*, 2008.

[30] V. W. Zheng, Y. Zheng, X. Xie, and Q. Yang. Collaborative location and activity recommendations with GPS history data. In *Proceedings of the International Conference on World Wide Web (WWW)*, 2010.

[31] Y. Zheng, L. Zhang, X. Xie, and W.-Y. Ma. Mining interesting locations and travel sequences from GPS trajectories. In *Proceedings of the International Conference on World Wide Web (WWW)*, 2009.

Ranking-Based Classification of Heterogeneous Information Networks

Ming Ji
Department of Computer Science
University of Illinois at Urbana-Champaign
Urbana, IL, USA
mingji1@illinois.edu

Jiawei Han
Department of Computer Science
University of Illinois at Urbana-Champaign
Urbana, IL, USA
hanj@illinois.edu

Marina Danilevsky
Department of Computer Science
University of Illinois at Urbana-Champaign
Urbana, IL, USA
danilev1@illinois.edu

ABSTRACT

It has been recently recognized that heterogeneous information networks composed of multiple types of nodes and links are prevalent in the real world. Both classification and ranking of the nodes (or data objects) in such networks are essential for network analysis. However, so far these approaches have generally been performed separately. In this paper, we combine ranking and classification in order to perform more accurate analysis of a heterogeneous information network. Our intuition is that highly ranked objects within a class should play more important roles in classification. On the other hand, class membership information is important for determining a quality ranking over a dataset. We believe it is therefore beneficial to integrate classification and ranking in a simultaneous, mutually enhancing process, and to this end, propose a novel ranking-based iterative classification framework, called RankClass. Specifically, we build a graph-based ranking model to iteratively compute the ranking distribution of the objects within each class. At each iteration, according to the current ranking results, the graph structure used in the ranking algorithm is adjusted so that the subnetwork corresponding to the specific class is emphasized, while the rest of the network is weakened. As our experiments show, integrating ranking with classification not only generates more accurate classes than the state-of-art classification methods on networked data, but also provides meaningful ranking of objects within each class, serving as a more informative view of the data than traditional classification.

Categories and Subject Descriptors

H.2.8 [**Database Management**]: Database Applications—*Data Mining*

General Terms

Algorithms

Keywords

heterogeneous information network, ranking, classification

1. INTRODUCTION

Information networks have been found to play increasingly important roles in real life applications. Examples include friendship networks in Facebook[1], co-author networks extracted from bibliographic data, and webpages interconnected by hyperlinks on the Web. Networks and feature vectors are two alternatives to represent the data, and the former is often more natural than the latter in many data sets [8]. Even if the data is naturally represented in a feature space, it is usually helpful to transform the data into a network, or graph structure (for example, by constructing a nearest neighbor graph) to better exploit the intrinsic characteristics of the data. Therefore, learning on networked data is receiving growing attention in recent years [9, 22, 1, 24, 6]. Most of the existing studies [19, 16, 2, 12] about information networks mainly work with homogeneous networks, i.e., networks composed of a single type of object, as mentioned above. However, heterogeneous networks composed of multiple types of objects are more general and prevalent in many real world applications [21, 11, 3]. For example, beyond co-author networks, bibliographic data actually forms a heterogeneous information network consisting of multi-typed objects, such as papers, authors, venues and terms.

Example 1. Bibliographic Information Network. A bibliographic information network generally contains four types of objects: *papers*, *authors*, *venues* (conferences and journals) and *terms*. *Papers* and *authors* are linked by the relation of "written by" and "write". *Papers* and *venues* are linked by "published in" and "publish". *Papers* and *terms* are linked by "contain" and "contained in". ■

In this paper, we study the analysis of heterogeneous information networks. *Classification* and *ranking* are two of the most fundamental analytical techniques. When label information is available for some of the data objects, *classification* makes use of the labeled data as well as the network structure to predict the class membership of the unlabeled data [19, 16]. On the other hand, *ranking* gives a partial ordering to objects in the network by evaluating the node/link properties using some ranking scheme, such as PageRank [2] or HITS [12]. Both classification and ranking have been widely studied and found to be applicable in a wide range of problems.

Traditionally, classification and ranking are regarded as orthogonal approaches, computed independently. However, adhering to such a strict dichotomy has serious downsides. Consider, for instance, an information network of bibliographic data, consisting of some combination of published papers, authors, and conferences. As a concrete example, suppose we wish to classify the conferences in Table 1 into two research areas. We wish to minimize the chance

[1]http://www.facebook.com/

Table 1: Conferences from two research areas

Database	SIGMOD, VLDB, ICDE, EDBT, PODS, ...
Information Retrieval	SIGIR, ECIR, CIKM, WWW, WSDM, ...

Table 2: Top-5 ranked conferences in different settings

Rank	Global Ranking	Within DB	Within IR
1	VLDB	VLDB	SIGIR
2	SIGIR	SIGMOD	ECIR
3	SIGMOD	ICDE	WWW
4	ICDE	PODS	CIKM
5	ECIR	EDBT	WSDM

that the top conferences are misclassified, not only to improve our classification results overall, but also because misclassifying a top conference is very likely to increase errors on many other objects that link to that conference, and are therefore greatly influenced by its label. We would thus like to more heavily penalize classification mistakes made on highly ranked conferences, relative to a workshop of little influence. Providing a ranking of all conferences within a research area can give users a clearer understanding of that field, rather than simply grouping conferences into classes without noting their relative importance. On the other hand, the class membership of each conference is very valuable for characterizing that conference. Ranking all conferences globally without considering any class information can often lead to meaningless results and apples-to-oranges comparisons. For instance, ranking database and information retrieval conferences together may not make much sense since the top conferences in these two fields cannot be reasonably compared, as shown in the second column of Table 2. These kinds of nonsensical ranking results are not caused by the specific ranking approach, but are rather due to the inherent incomparability between the two classes of conferences. Thus we suppose that combining classification with ranking may generate more informative results. The third and fourth columns in Table 2 illustrate this combined approach, showing the more meaningful conference ranking within each class.

In this study, we propose RankClass, a new framework that groups objects into several pre-specified classes, while generating the ranking information for each type of object within each class simultaneously in a heterogeneous information network. More accurate classification of objects increases the quality of the ranking within each class, since there is a higher guarantee that the ranking algorithm used will be comparing only objects of the same class. On the other hand, better ranking scores improve the performance of the classifier, by correctly identifying which objects are more important, and should therefore have a higher influence on the classifier's decisions. We use the ranking distribution of objects to characterize each class, and we treat each object's label information as a prior. By building a graph-based ranking model, different types of objects are ranked simultaneously within each class. Based on these ranking results, we estimate the relative importance or visibility of different parts of the network with regard to each class. In order to generate better within-class ranking, the network structure employed by the ranking model is adjusted so that the sub-network composed of objects ranked high in each specific class is emphasized, while the sub-network of the rest of the class is gradually weakened. Thus, as the network structure of each class becomes clearer, the ranking quality improves. Finally, the posterior probability of each object belonging to each class is estimated to determine each object's optimal class membership. Instead of performing ranking after classification, as facet ranking does [4, 23], RankClass essentially integrates ranking and classification, allowing both approaches to mutually enhance each other. RankClass iterates over this process until converging to a stable state. Experimental results show that RankClass both boosts the overall classification accuracy and constructs within-class rankings, which may be interpreted as meaningful summaries of each class.

The rest of this paper is organized as follows. We briefly review the related work in Section 2. We introduce related concepts and formally define our problem in Section 3. Our ranking-based classification algorithm, RankClass, is introduced in Section 4. Section 5 presents the experimental results, and we conclude this work in Section 6.

2. RELATED WORK

As data sets with inherent network structures become increasingly prevalent, ranking networked objects has received substantial interest in recent years. Two important representative algorithms are PageRank [2] and HITS [12], both of which propagate information throughout the network to compute the ranking score of each object, using different propagation methods corresponding to different ranking rules. These methods mainly work on homogeneous information networks. Recently, PopRank [18] was proposed to rank the popularity of heterogeneous web objects via knowledge propagation throughout the heterogeneous network of web objects. This approach considers that different types of links in a network have different propagation factors, which are trained according to partial ranks given by experts. In contrast, we rank objects according to their importance within each class, rather than within the global set of all objects, and the ranking results in turn facilitate more accurate classification.

Classification is an essential tool in analyzing information networks when some object label information is available [25, 20]. Collective classification [14, 19, 17] has been proposed to employ both the network structure and the feature representation of objects in the classification task. Since local features may not be always available, Macskassy et al. [15] develop a relational neighbor classifier to classify network-only data by iteratively assigning an object to the majority class of its neighbors. This idea is similar to the label propagation scheme in graph-based classification [26]. However, existing algorithms mainly work on homogeneous networks and graphs, and therefore cannot easily distinguish between the type differences among objects in a heterogeneous information network. Recently, the graph-based classification framework has been extended to work on heterogeneous information networks [11]. In this paper, we build on this approach by providing within-class ranking for objects in the information network, which can improve classification results by providing informative summaries of each class.

To enhance the quality of classification, boosting, bagging and ensemble methods have been explored in various studies [10]. In particular, boosting methods such as AdaBoost [5] iteratively learn from their classification mistakes by assigning higher weights to objects which are misclassified in each previous round, until a stable classification state is reached. Like boosting, RankClass also adjusts the relative importance of objects in various rounds of classification. However, RankClass uses within-class ranking to measure the importance of each object with regard to each class, in contrast to boosting, which estimates the global importance of each object based on classification mistakes.

Another relevant algorithm is the newly proposed NetClus [21] method, which uses a ranking-clustering mutual enhancement methodology to cluster objects in heterogeneous information networks. Although this method effectively provides a ranking within each cluster, it has some limitations: (1) it can only work on heterogeneous information networks with a star schema; and (2) it requires a prior distribution specified by several labeled *representative* objects of each cluster, and does not work well with arbitrary labeled objects, which may not be representative. Thus, if we do not know which objects are representative in a data set, NetClus cannot be used. However, for heterogeneous information networks with arbitrary network schema, our proposed RankClass algorithm can make full use of label information available for any data objects to generate accurate classification results and informative rankings.

3. PROBLEM FORMALIZATION

In this section, we introduce several related concepts and notations, and then formally define the problem.

Definition 1. **Heterogeneous information network.** Given m types of data objects, denoted by $\mathcal{X}_1 = \{x_{11}, \ldots, x_{1n_1}\}, \ldots, \mathcal{X}_m = \{x_{m1}, \ldots, x_{mn_m}\}$, a graph $\mathcal{G} = \langle \mathcal{V}, \mathcal{E}, \mathcal{W} \rangle$ is called a heterogeneous information network if $\mathcal{V} = \bigcup_{i=1}^m \mathcal{X}_i$ and $m \geq 2$. $\mathcal{E}$ is the set of links between any two data objects of $\mathcal{V}$, and $\mathcal{W}$ is the set of weight values on the links. When $m = 1$, $\mathcal{G}$ reduces to a homogeneous information network. ■

In the following sections, for convenience, we use $\mathcal{X}_i$ to denote both the set of objects belonging to the i-th type and the type name. We let $\mathcal{W}_{x_{ip}x_{jq}}$ denote the weight of the link between any two objects x_{ip} and x_{jq}, which is represented by $\langle x_{ip}, x_{jq} \rangle$.

In a heterogeneous information network, each type of link relationship between two types of data objects $\mathcal{X}_i$ and $\mathcal{X}_j$ can be represented by a relation graph $\mathcal{G}_{ij}$, $i, j \in \{1, \ldots, m\}$. Note that it is possible for $i = j$. Let $\mathbf{R}_{ij}$ be an $n_i \times n_j$ relation matrix corresponding to graph $\mathcal{G}_{ij}$. The element at the p-th row and q-th column of $\mathbf{R}_{ij}$ is denoted as $R_{ij,pq}$, representing the weight on link $\langle x_{ip}, x_{jq} \rangle$. There are many ways to define the weights on the links, which can also incorporate domain knowledge. A simple definition is as follows:

$$R_{ij,pq} = \begin{cases} 1 & \text{if data objects } x_{ip} \text{ and } x_{jq} \text{ are linked together} \\ 0 & \text{otherwise.} \end{cases}$$

Here we consider undirected relation graphs such that $\mathbf{R}_{ij} = \mathbf{R}_{ji}^T$. In this way, each heterogeneous network $\mathcal{G}$ can be mathematically represented by a set of relation matrices $\mathcal{G} = \{\mathbf{R}_{ij}\}_{i,j=1}^m$.

To naturally generalize classification in homogeneous network data, we define a class in a heterogeneous information network to be a group of multi-typed objects sharing a common topic. For instance, a research community in a bibliographic information network contains not only authors, but also papers, venues and terms belonging to the same research area. Other examples include movie networks in which movies, directors, actors and keywords are tagged with the same genre, and E-commerce networks where sellers, customers, items and tags belong to the same shopping category. The formal definition of a *class* is given below:

Definition 2. **Class.** Given a heterogeneous information network $\mathcal{G} = \langle \mathcal{V}, \mathcal{E}, \mathcal{W} \rangle$, $\mathcal{V} = \bigcup_{i=1}^m \mathcal{X}_i$, a class is defined as $\mathcal{G}' = \langle \mathcal{V}', \mathcal{E}', \mathcal{W}' \rangle$, where $\mathcal{V}' \subseteq \mathcal{V}$, $\mathcal{E}' \subseteq \mathcal{E}$. $\forall e = \langle x_{ip}, x_{jq} \rangle \in \mathcal{E}'$, where $x_{ip} \in \mathcal{V}'$ and $x_{jq} \in \mathcal{V}'$, we have $\mathcal{W}'_{x_{ip}x_{jq}} = \mathcal{W}_{x_{ip}x_{jq}}$. Note here, $\mathcal{V}'$ also consists of multiple types of objects from $\mathcal{X}_1$ to $\mathcal{X}_m$. ■

Definition 2 follows [21] and [11]. Notice that a class in a heterogeneous information network is actually a sub-network containing multi-typed objects that are closely related to each other. In addition to grouping multi-typed objects into the pre-specified K classes, we also aim to generate the ranking distribution of objects within each class k, which can be denoted as $P(x|T(x), k)$, $k = 1, \ldots, K$. $T(x)$ denotes the type of object x. Note that different types of objects cannot be compared in a ranking. For example, it is not meaningful to create a ranking of conferences and authors together in a bibliographic information network. Therefore, each ranking distribution is restricted to a single object type, i.e., $\sum_{p=1}^{n_i} P(x_{ip}|\mathcal{X}_i, k) = 1$.

Now our problem can be formalized as follows: given a heterogeneous information network $\mathcal{G} = \langle \mathcal{V}, \mathcal{E}, \mathcal{W} \rangle$, a subset of data objects $\mathcal{V}' \subseteq \mathcal{V} = \bigcup_{i=1}^m \mathcal{X}_i$, which are labeled with values $\mathcal{Y}$ denoting which of the K pre-specified classes each object belongs to, predict the class labels for all the unlabeled objects $\mathcal{V} - \mathcal{V}'$ as well as the ranking distribution of objects within each class, $P(x|T(x), k)$, $x \in \mathcal{V}$, $k = 1, \ldots, K$.

4. THE RANKCLASS ALGORITHM

In this section we introduce our ranking-based iterative classification method, RankClass. There are two major challenges when working with heterogeneous information networks: (1) how to exploit the links representing the dependency relationships between data objects; and (2) how to model the type differences among objects and links. The intuition behind RankClass is to build a graph-based ranking model that ranks multi-typed objects simultaneously, according to the relative importance of objects within each class. The initial ranking distribution of each class is determined by the labeled data. During each iteration, the ranking results are used to modify the network structure to allow the ranking model to generate higher quality within-class ranking.

4.1 The Framework of RankClass

We first introduce the general framework of RankClass. We will explain each part of the algorithm in detail in the following subsections.

- Step 0: Initialize the ranking distribution within each class according to the labeled data, i.e., $\{P(x|T(x), k)^0\}_{k=1}^K$. Initialize the set of network structures employed in the ranking model, $\{\mathcal{G}_k^0\}_{k=1}^K$, as $\mathcal{G}_k^0 = \mathcal{G}$, $k = 1, \ldots, K$. Initialize $t = 1$.

- Step 1: Using the graph-based ranking model and the current set of network structures $\{\mathcal{G}_k^{t-1}\}_{k=1}^K$, update the ranking distribution within each class k, i.e., $\{P(x|T(x), k)^t\}_{k=1}^K$.

- Step 2: Based on $\{P(x|T(x), k)^t\}_{k=1}^K$, adjust the network structure to favor within-class ranking, i.e., $\{\mathcal{G}_k^t\}_{k=1}^K$.

- Step 3: Repeat steps 1 and 2, setting $t = t + 1$ until convergence, i.e., until $\{P(x|T(x), k)^*\}_{k=1}^K = \{P(x|T(x), k)^t\}_{k=1}^K$ do not change much for all $x \in \mathcal{V}$.

- Step 4: Based on $\{P(x|T(x), k)^*\}_{k=1}^K$, calculate the posterior probability for each object, i.e., $\{P(k|x, T(x))\}_{k=1}^K$. Assign the class label to object x as:

$$C(x) = \arg\max_{1 \leq k \leq K} P(k|x, T(x))$$

4.2 Graph-based Ranking

Ranking is often used to evaluate the relative importance of objects in a collection. In this paper, we propose to rank objects within their own type and within a specific class. The higher an object x is ranked within class k, the more important x is for class k, and the more likely it is that x will be visited in class k. Clearly, within-class ranking is quite different from global ranking, and will vary throughout different classes.

The intuitive idea of our ranking scheme is authority propagation throughout the information network. Taking the bibliographic information network as an example, in a specific research area, it is natural to observe the following ranking rules [21]:

1. Highly ranked conferences publish many high quality papers.
2. High quality papers are often written by highly ranked authors.
3. High quality papers often contain keywords that are highly representative of the papers' areas.

The above authority ranking rules can be summarized as follows: objects which are linked together in a network are more likely to share similar ranking scores. Therefore, the ranking of each object can be iteratively updated by looking at the rankings of its neighbors. The initial ranking distribution within a class k can be specified by the user. When data objects are labeled without ranking information in a general classification scenario, we can initialize the ranking as a uniform distribution over only the labeled data objects:

$$P(x_{ip}|\mathcal{X}_i,k)^0 = \begin{cases} 1/l_{ik} & \text{if } x_{ip} \text{ is labeled to class } k \\ 0 & \text{otherwise.} \end{cases}$$

where l_{ik} denotes the total number of objects of type $\mathcal{X}_i$ labeled to class k.

Suppose the current network structure used to estimate the ranking within class k is mathematically represented by the set of relation matrices: $\mathcal{G}_k^{t-1} = \{\mathbf{R}_{ij}\}_{i,j=1}^m$. For each relation matrix $\mathbf{R}_{ij}$, we define a diagonal matrix $\mathbf{D}_{ij}$ of size $n_i \times n_i$. The (p,p)-th element of $\mathbf{D}_{ij}$ is the sum of the p-th row of $\mathbf{R}_{ij}$. Instead of using the original relation matrices in the authority propagation, we construct the normalized form of the relation matrices as follows:

$$\mathbf{S}_{ij} = \mathbf{D}_{ij}^{(-1/2)}\mathbf{R}_{ij}\mathbf{D}_{ji}^{(-1/2)}, i,j \in \{1,\ldots,m\} \quad (1)$$

This normalization technique is adopted in traditional graph-based learning [26] in order to reduce the impact of node popularity. In other words, we can suppress popular nodes to some extent, to keep them from completely dominating the authority propagation. Notice that the normalization is applied separately to each relation matrix corresponding to each type of link, rather than the whole network. In this way, the type differences between objects and links are well-preserved [11]. At the t-th iteration, the ranking distribution of object x_{ip} with regard to class k is updated as follows:

$$P(x_{ip}|\mathcal{X}_i,k)^t \propto \frac{\sum_{j=1}^m \lambda_{ij} S_{ij,pq} P(x_{jq}|\mathcal{X}_j,k)^{t-1} + \alpha_i P(x_{ip}|\mathcal{X}_i,k)^0}{\sum_{j=1}^m \lambda_{ij} + \alpha_i} \quad (2)$$

The first term of Equation (2) updates the ranking score of object x_{ip} by the summation of the ranking scores of its neighbors x_{jq}, weighted by the link strength $S_{ij,pq}$. The relative importance of neighbors of different types is controlled by $\lambda_{ij} \in [0,1]$. The larger the value of λ_{ij}, the more value is placed on the relationship between object types $\mathcal{X}_i$ and $\mathcal{X}_j$. For example, in a bibliographic information network, if a user believes that the links between *authors* and *papers* are more trustworthy and influential than the links between *conferences* and *papers*, then the λ_{ij} corresponding to the *author-paper* relationship should be set larger than that of *conference-paper*. As a result, the rank of a paper will rely more on the ranks of its authors than the rank of its publication venue. The parameters λ_{ij} can also be thought of as performing feature selection in the heterogeneous information network, i.e., selecting which types of links are important in the ranking process.

The second term learns from the initial ranking distribution encoded in the labels, whose contribution is weighted by $\alpha_i \in [0,1]$. A similar strategy has been adopted in [13, 11] to control the weights between different types of relations and objects. After each iteration, $P(x_{ip}|\mathcal{X}_i,k)^t$ is normalized such that $\sum_{p=1}^{n_i} P(x_{ip}|\mathcal{X}_i,k)^t = 1, \forall i = 1,\ldots,m, k = 1,\ldots,K$, in order to stay consistent with the mathematical definition of a ranking distribution.

We employ the authority propagation scheme in Equation (2) to estimate the ranking distribution instead of other simple measures computed according to the network topology (e.g., the degree of each object). This choice was made since we aim to rank objects with regard to each class by utilizing the current soft classification results. Therefore, if the ranking of an object were merely based on the network topology, it would be the same for all classes. By learning from the label information in the graph-based authority propagation method, the ranking of each object within different classes will be computed differently, which is more suitable for our setting.

Following a similar analysis to [11] and [27], the updating scheme in Equation (2) can be proven to converge to the closed form solution of minimizing the following objective function:

$$\begin{aligned} &J(P(x_{ip}|\mathcal{X}_i,k)) \\ = &\sum_{i,j=1}^m \lambda_{ij} \sum_{p=1}^{n_i}\sum_{q=1}^{n_j} S_{ij,pq}\left(P(x_{ip}|\mathcal{X}_i,k) - P(x_{jq}|\mathcal{X}_j,k)\right)^2 \\ &+ \sum_{i=1}^m \alpha_i \sum_{p=1}^{n_i} (P(x_{ip}|\mathcal{X}_i,k) - P(x_{ip}|\mathcal{X}_i,k)^0)^2 \end{aligned} \quad (3)$$

which shares a similar theoretical foundation with the graph-based regularization framework on heterogeneous information networks [11] that preserves consistency over each relation graph corresponding separately to each link type. However, we extend the graph-based regularization framework to rank objects within each class, which is conceptually different from [11].

4.3 Adjusting the Network

Although graph-based ranking considers class information by incorporating the labeled data, it still ranks all object types in the global network. Instead, a within-class ranking should be performed over the sub-network corresponding to each specific class. The cleaner the network structure, the higher our ranking quality. Therefore, the ranking within each class should be performed over a different sub-network, rather than employing the same global network for every class. The network structure is mathematically represented by the weight values on the links. Thus, extracting the sub-network belonging to class k is equivalent to increasing the weight on the links within the corresponding sub-network, and decreasing the weight on the links in the rest of the network. It is straightforward to verify that multiplying $\mathbf{R}_{ij}$ by any positive constant c will not change the value of $\mathbf{S}_{ij}$. So increasing the weights on the links within a sub-network should be performed relative to the weight on the links of other parts of the network. In other words, we can increase or decrease the absolute values of the weights on the links in the whole network, as long as the weights on the links of the sub-network belonging to class k are larger than those on the links belonging to the rest of the network. Let $\mathcal{G}_k^t = \{\mathbf{R}_{ij}^t(k)\}_{i,j=1}^m$. We propose a simple scheme to update the network structure so as to favor the ranking within each class k, given the current ranking distribution $P(x|T(x), k)^t$:

$$R^t_{ij,pq}(k) = R_{ij,pq} \times \left(r(t) + \sqrt{\frac{P(x_{ip}|\mathcal{X}_i, k)^t}{\max_p P(x_{ip}|\mathcal{X}_i, k)^t} \frac{P(x_{jq}|\mathcal{X}_j, k)^t}{\max_q P(x_{jq}|\mathcal{X}_j, k)^t}} \right) \quad (4)$$

Recall that $\mathbf{R}_{ij}$ is the relation matrix corresponding to the links between object types $\mathcal{X}_i$ and $\mathcal{X}_j$ in the original network. Using the above updating scheme, the weight of each link $\langle x_{ip}, x_{jq} \rangle$ is increased in proportion to the geometric mean of the ranking scores of x_{ip} and x_{jq}, which are scaled to the interval of $[0, 1]$. The higher the rankings of x_{ip} and x_{jq}, the more important the link between them $\langle x_{ip}, x_{jq} \rangle$ is in class k. The weight on that link should therefore be increased. Note that instead of creating hard partitions of the original network into classes, we simply increase the weights on the links that are important to classes k. This is because at any time in the iteration, the current classes represented by the ranking distributions are not very accurate, and the results will be more stable if we consider both the global network structure and the current ranking results. By gently increasing the weights of links in the sub-network of class k, we gradually extract the correct sub-network from the global network, since the weights of links in the rest of the network will decrease to very low values. Note that this adjustment of the network structure still respects the differences among the various types of objects and links.

$r(t)$ is a positive parameter that does not allow the weights of links to drop to 0 in the first several iterations, when the authority scores have not propagated very far throughout the network and $P(x|T(x), k)^t$ are close to 0 in value for many objects. As discussed above, multiplying $\mathbf{R}_{ij}$ by any positive constant will not change the value of $\mathbf{S}_{ij}$. Therefore, it is essentially the ratio between $r(t)$ and $\sqrt{\frac{P(x_{ip}|k)^t}{\max_p P(x_{ip}|k)^t} \times \frac{P(x_{jq}|k)^t}{\max_q P(x_{jq}|k)^t}}$ that determines how much the original network structure and the current ranking distribution, respectively, contribute to the adjusted network $\mathcal{G}^t_k$. Since we hope to progressively extract the sub-network belonging to each class k, and we want to gradually reduce the weights of links that do not belong to class k down to 0, we decrease $r(t)$ exponentially by setting $r(t) = \frac{1}{2^t}$.

Equation (4) is not the only way to gradually increase the weights of links between highly ranked objects in class k. For instance, the geometric mean of $\frac{P(x_{ip}|k)^t}{\max_p P(x_{ip}|k)^t}$ and $\frac{P(x_{jq}|k)^t}{\max_q P(x_{jq}|k)^t}$ can be replaced by the arithmetic mean, and $r(t)$ can be any positive function that decreases with t. We will show in Section 5 that even such simple adjustments as shown above can boost both the classification and ranking performance of RankClass.

4.4 Posterior Probability Calculation

Once the ranking distribution of each class has been computed by the iterative algorithm, we can calculate the posterior probability of each object of type $\mathcal{X}_i$ belonging to class k simply by Bayes' rule:

$$P(k|x_{ip}, \mathcal{X}_i) \propto P(x_{ip}|\mathcal{X}_i, k)P(k|\mathcal{X}_i)$$

where $P(x_{ip}|\mathcal{X}_i, k) = P(x_{ip}|\mathcal{X}_i, k)^*$, and $P(k|\mathcal{X}_i)$ represents the relative size of class k among type $\mathcal{X}_i$, which should also be estimated. We choose the $P(k|\mathcal{X}_i)$ that maximizes the likelihood of generating the set of objects of type $\mathcal{X}_i$:

$$\log L(x_{i1}, \ldots, x_{in_i}|\mathcal{X}_i) = \sum_{p=1}^{n_i} \log P(x_{ip}|\mathcal{X}_i)$$
$$= \sum_{p=1}^{n_i} \log \left(\sum_{k=1}^{K} P(x_{ip}|\mathcal{X}_i, k)P(k|\mathcal{X}_i) \right) \quad (5)$$

By employing the EM algorithm, $P(k|\mathcal{X}_i)$ can be iteratively estimated using the following two equations:

$$P(k|x_{ip}, \mathcal{X}_i)^t \propto P(x_{ip}|\mathcal{X}_i, k)P(k|\mathcal{X}_i)^t$$
$$P(k|\mathcal{X}_i)^t = \sum_{p=1}^{n_i} P(k|x_{ip}, \mathcal{X}_i)^t / n_i$$

where $P(k|\mathcal{X}_i)$ is initialized uniformly as $P(k|\mathcal{X}_i)^0 = 1/K$.

4.5 Computational Complexity Analysis

In this subsection, we analyze the computational complexity of the proposed RankClass algorithm. Let K denote the number of classes, $|V|$ denote the total number of objects, and $|E|$ denote the total number of links in the information network. It takes $O(K|V|)$ time to initialize the ranking distribution in step 0. At each iteration of step 1, we need to process each link twice to update the ranking distribution, once for each object at each end of the link. We also need $O(K|V|)$ time to learn from the initial ranking distribution. So the total time complexity for step 1 at each iteration is $O(K(|E| + |V|))$. In step 2, we need $O(K|E|)$ time to adjust the network structure at each iteration. After the ranking distribution is computed, we need $O(K|V|)$ time at each iteration of the EM algorithm to calculate the posterior probability. Finally, it takes $O(K|V|)$ time to generate the final class prediction in step 4. Hence the total time complexity of the RankClass algorithm is $O\big(N_1 K(|E| + |V|) + N_2 K|V|\big)$, where N_1 is the number of iterations in the computation of the ranking distribution, and N_2 is the number of iterations in the EM algorithm. We will experimentally demonstrate that this algorithm converges in a few iterations. And since the number of classes K is constant, the computational complexity is generally linear in the number of links and objects in the network.

5. EXPERIMENTS

In this section, we apply our proposed ranking-based classification scheme, RankClass, to a real heterogeneous information network extracted from the DBLP[2] database. We try to classify the bibliographic data into research communities, each of which consists of multi-typed objects closely related to the same area. All of the experiments were conducted on a PC with 3.00GHz CPU and 8GB memory. The following five classification methods on information networks are compared:

- Our proposed RankClass algorithm (RankClass).
- Graph-based regularization framework for transductive classification in heterogeneous information networks (GNetMine) [11].
- Learning with Local and Global Consistency (LLGC) [26].
- Weighted-vote Relational Neighbor Classifier (wvRN) [15, 16].
- Network-only Link-based Classification (nLB) [19, 16].

LLGC is a graph-based transductive classification algorithm for homogeneous networks, while GNetMine is its extension, which works on heterogeneous information networks. Weighted-vote relational neighbor classifier and link-based classification are two popular classification methods for networked data. Since a feature representation of nodes is not available for our problem, we use the network-only derivative of the link-based classifier (nLB) [16],

[2] http://www.informatik.uni-trier.de/~ley/db/

Table 3: Comparison of classification accuracy on authors (%)

$(a\%, p\%)$ of authors and papers labeled	nLB (A-A)	nLB (A-C-P-T)	wvRN (A-A)	wvRN (A-C-P-T)	LLGC (A-A)	LLGC (A-C-P-T)	GNetMine (A-C-P-T)	RankClass (A-C-P-T)
(0.1%, 0.1%)	25.4	26.0	40.8	34.1	41.4	61.3	82.9	**85.4**
(0.2%, 0.2%)	28.3	26.0	46.0	41.2	44.7	62.2	83.4	**88.0**
(0.3%, 0.3%)	28.4	27.4	48.6	42.5	48.8	65.7	86.7	**88.5**
(0.4%, 0.4%)	30.7	26.7	46.3	45.6	48.7	66.0	87.2	**88.4**
(0.5%, 0.5%)	29.8	27.3	49.0	51.4	50.6	68.9	87.5	**89.2**
average	28.5	26.7	46.3	43.0	46.8	64.8	85.5	**87.9**

Table 4: Comparison of classification accuracy on papers (%)

$(a\%, p\%)$ of authors and papers labeled	nLB (P-P)	nLB (A-C-P-T)	wvRN (P-P)	wvRN (A-C-P-T)	LLGC (P-P)	LLGC (A-C-P-T)	GNetMine (A-C-P-T)	RankClass (A-C-P-T)
(0.1%, 0.1%)	49.8	31.5	62.0	42.0	67.2	62.7	**79.2**	77.7
(0.2%, 0.2%)	73.1	40.3	71.7	49.7	72.8	65.5	**83.5**	83.0
(0.3%, 0.3%)	77.9	35.4	77.9	54.3	76.8	66.6	83.2	**83.6**
(0.4%, 0.4%)	79.1	38.6	78.1	54.4	77.9	70.5	83.7	**84.7**
(0.5%, 0.5%)	80.7	39.3	77.9	53.5	79.0	73.5	84.1	**84.8**
average	72.1	37.0	73.5	50.8	74.7	67.8	82.7	**82.8**

Table 5: Comparison of classification accuracy on conferences (%)

$(a\%, p\%)$ of authors and papers labeled	nLB (A-C-P-T)	wvRN (A-C-P-T)	LLGC (A-C-P-T)	GNetMine (A-C-P-T)	RankClass (A-C-P-T)
(0.1%, 0.1%)	25.5	43.5	79.0	81.0	**85.0**
(0.2%, 0.2%)	22.5	56.0	83.5	85.0	**85.5**
(0.3%, 0.3%)	25.0	59.0	87.0	87.0	**90.0**
(0.4%, 0.4%)	25.0	57.0	86.5	89.5	**92.0**
(0.5%, 0.5%)	25.0	68.0	90.0	94.0	**95.0**
average	24.6	56.7	85.2	87.3	**89.5**

which creates a feature vector for each node based on neighboring information. Note that LLGC, wvRN and nLB are classifiers which work with homogeneous networks, and cannot be directly applied to heterogeneous information networks. In order to compare all of the above algorithms, we can transform the heterogeneous DBLP network into a homogeneous network in two ways (see Section 5.2): (1) disregard the type differences between objects and treat all objects as the same type; or (2) extract a homogeneous sub-network on one single type of object, if that object type is partially labeled. We try both approaches in the accuracy study. The open-source implementation of NetKit-SRL[3] [16] is employed in our experiments.

5.1 Data Preparation

We extracted a connected sub-network of the DBLP data set on four research areas: database, data mining, information retrieval and artificial intelligence, which naturally form four classes. As previously discussed, this heterogeneous information network is composed of four types of objects: paper, conference, author and term. Among the four types of objects, we have three types of link relationships: paper-conference, paper-author, and paper-term. The data set we used contains 14376 papers, 20 conferences, 14475 authors and 8920 terms, with a total number of 170794 links[4].

For accuracy evaluation, we use a labeled data set of 4057 authors, 100 papers and all 20 conferences. For more details about the labeled data set, please refer to [7, 21]. In the following sections, we randomly choose a subset of labeled objects and use their label information in the learning process. The classification accuracy is evaluated by comparing with manually labeled results on the rest of the labeled objects. Since terms are difficult to label even manually, as many terms may belong to multiple areas, we do not evaluate the accuracy on terms here.

5.2 Accuracy Study

In order to address the label scarcity problem in real life, we randomly choose $(a\%, p\%) = [(0.1\%, 0.1\%), (0.2\%, 0.2\%), \ldots, (0.5\%, 0.5\%)]$ of authors and papers, and use their label information in the classification task. For each $(a\%, p\%)$, we average the performance scores over 10 random selections of the labeled set. We set the parameters of LLGC and GNetMine to optimal values, which were determined experimentally. For our proposed RankClass method, as discussed above, the parameters λ_{ij} are used to select which types of links are important in the ranking process. We consider all types of objects and links to be important in the DBLP network, so we follow [11] and set $\alpha_i = 0.1$, $\lambda_{ij} = 0.2$, $\forall i, j \in \{1, \ldots, m\}$. This may not be the optimal choice, but it is good enough to demonstrate the effectiveness of our algorithm. Since labels are given for selected authors and papers, the results on conferences of wvRN, nLB and LLGC can only be obtained by mining the original heterogeneous information network (denoted by A-C-P-T) and disregarding the type differences between objects and links. While classifying authors and papers, we also tried constructing homogeneous author-author (A-A) and paper-paper (P-P) sub-networks in various ways, where the best results reported for authors are given by the co-author network, and the best results for papers are generated by linking two papers if they are published in the same conference. Note that there is no label information given for conferences, so we cannot build a conference-conference (C-C) sub-network for classification. We show the classification accuracy

[3]http://www.research.rutgers.edu/~sofmac/NetKit.html

[4]The data set is available at www.cs.illinois.edu/homes/mingji1/DBLP_four_area.zip for sharing and experiment repeatability.

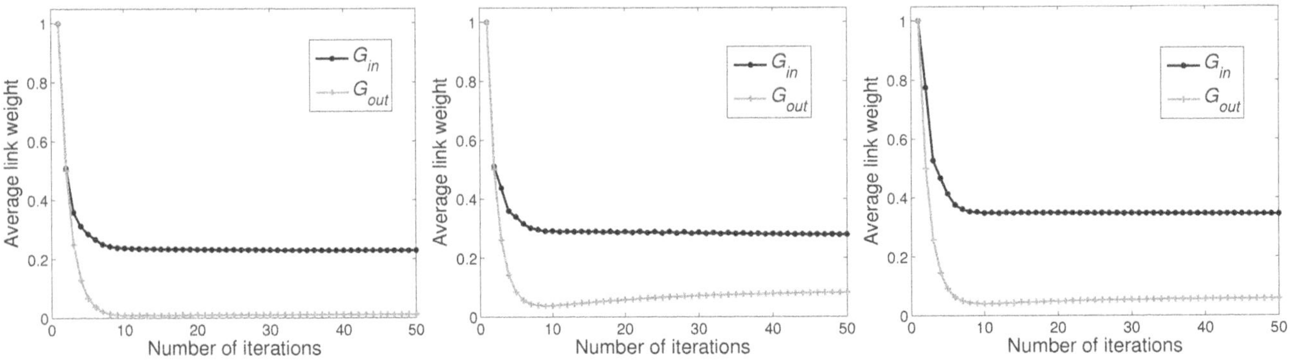

(a) Links connected to authors (b) Links connected to conferences (c) Links connected to papers

Figure 1: Link weight change in 50 iterations

on authors, papers and conferences in Tables 3, 4 and 5, respectively. The last row of each table records the average classification accuracy while varying the percentage of labeled data.

RankClass outperforms all other algorithms when classifying authors, papers and conferences. Note that even though the number of authors is much higher than the number of conferences, RankClass achieves comparable accuracy for both of these types of objects. While classifying authors and papers, it is interesting to note that wvRN and nLB perform better on the *author-author* and *paper-paper* sub-networks than on the whole heterogeneous information network. We observe a similar result when we use LLGC to classify papers. These results serve to verify that homogeneous classifiers like wvRN, nLB and LLGC are more suitable for working with homogeneous data. However, transforming the heterogeneous information network into homogeneous sub-networks inevitably results in information loss. For example, in the *author-author* sub-network, the conferences where each author often publishes papers, and the terms that each author likes to use, are no longer known. Overall, GNetMine performs the second best by explicitly respecting the type differences in links and objects and thus encoding the typed information in the heterogeneous network in an organized way. Compared to GNetMine, RankClass achieves 16.6%, 0.58% and 17.3% relative error reduction in the average classification accuracy when classifying authors, papers and conferences, respectively. Although RankClass has a knowledge propagation framework similar to that of GNetMine, RankClass aims to compute the within-class ranking distribution to characterize each class, and further employs the ranking results to iteratively extract the sub-network corresponding to each specific class. Therefore, the knowledge propagation for each class is more accurate.

We randomly select objects to obtain label information in our experiments. Similar to [21], we observe that if we choose some representative (or highly ranked) objects (e.g., famous authors) to label, the classification performance will be generally slightly better than when using labels of low quality (e.g., authors closely related to multiple fields, or with few publications). However, the difference is not significant. In other words, the initial choice of labeled data does not drastically affect the quality of ranking and classification. This is because our graph-based ranking model in Equation (3) is a summation of two terms, where the first depends on the initial ranking, and the second depends on the network structure which ensures the smoothness of the learner. Even if the quality of the initial ranking distribution is not very high, RankClass can still generate a reasonable ranking distribution and label predictions. This is because RankClass exploits the relationships among objects in the network, iteratively propagating information throughout the network (see the first term of Equation (3)). Therefore, our algorithm is theoretically robust when working with random labels.

5.3 Convergence Study

Since our proposed RankClass algorithm iteratively adjusts the network structure to facilitate within-class ranking, we further explore the changes of the link weights within the network. According to ground truth for each class k, all of the links connected to object type $\mathcal{X}_i$ can be divided into two groups: one contains the links that connect to at least one object of class k (denoted as G_{in}), while the other group does not involve any objects of class k (denoted as G_{out}). Links in G_{in} compose the sub-network corresponding to class k, while links in G_{out} form the sub-network excluding class k. In Figure 1, we show the average weight of the links in G_{in} and G_{out} (averaged over the four classes) connected to authors, conferences and papers, along with the number of iterations, when $(0.5\%, 0.5\%)$ authors and papers are labeled. The link weight changes of G_{in} and G_{out} for each individual class are very similar to Figure 1, and are omitted due to space limitation.

From Figure 1, it can be observed that the average link weight of G_{in} and G_{out} are the same at first, and then decrease at various rates over iterations. During the first several iterations, the ranking scores have not propagated very far throughout the network and are close to 0 in value for many objects. Therefore, the weight of many links decreases almost exponentially as a result of multiplying by $r(t)$. Then the ranking scores of objects within each class k gradually increase, making the average link weight in G_{in} decrease more slowly than that in G_{out}. Within a few iterations, the average link weights in G_{in} and G_{out} converge to relatively stable values. There is also a clear gap between the average link weights of G_{in} and G_{out} (the former being much larger than the latter). Thus, the sub-network corresponding to each class k is well-separated from the rest of the network, and the within-class ranking can be accurately performed within the sub-network, rather than the global network. When the network structure stabilizes, the graph-based ranking scheme can be proven to converge, following a similar analysis to [26, 11].

5.4 Case Study

In this section, we present a simple case study by listing the top ranked data objects within each class. Recall that GNetMine performs the second best in the classification accuracy, and can generate a confidence score for each object related to each class [11]. Thus, we can also rank data objects according to the confidence scores related to each class as the within-class ranking. In Tables 6 and 7, we show the comparison of the ranking lists of confer-

Table 6: Top-5 conferences related to each research area generated by different algorithms

RankClass				GNetMine			
Database	Data Mining	AI	IR	Database	Data Mining	AI	IR
VLDB	KDD	IJCAI	SIGIR	VLDB	SDM	IJCAI	SIGIR
SIGMOD	SDM	AAAI	ECIR	ICDE	KDD	AAAI	ECIR
ICDE	ICDM	ICML	CIKM	SIGMOD	ICDM	ICML	CIKM
PODS	PKDD	CVPR	WWW	PODS	PAKDD	CVPR	IJCAI
EDBT	PAKDD	ECML	WSDM	CIKM	PKDD	ECML	CVPR

Table 7: Top-5 terms related to each research area generated by different algorithms

RankClass				GNetMine			
Database	Data Mining	AI	IR	Database	Data Mining	AI	IR
data	mining	learning	retrieval	interlocking	rare	failing	helps
database	data	knowledge	information	deindexing	extreme	interleaved	specificity
query	clustering	reasoning	search	seed	scan	cognition	sponsored
system	frequent	logic	web	bitemporal	mining	literals	relevance
xml	classification	model	text	debugging	associations	configuration	information

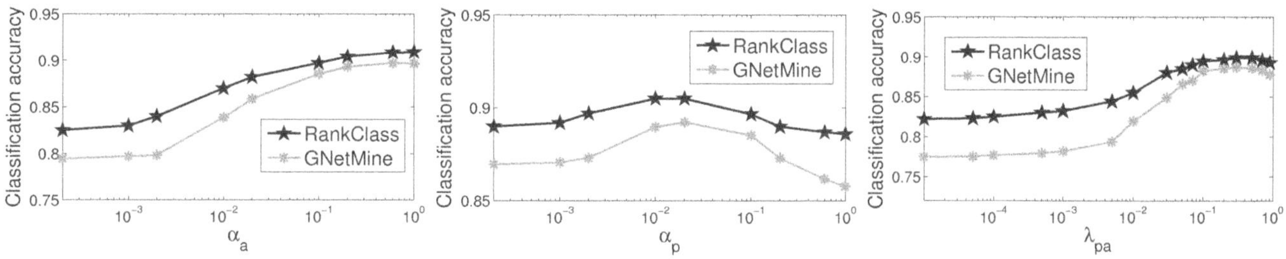

(a) Varying α_a (b) Varying α_p (c) Varying λ_{pa}

Figure 2: Model Selection when (0.5%, 0.5%) of authors and papers are labeled

ences and terms generated by RankClass and GNetMine, respectively, with $(0.5\%, 0.5\%)$ authors and papers labeled.

From comparing the ranking lists of the two types of objects, we can see that RankClass generates more meaningful ranking results than GNetMine. There is a high degree of consensus between the ranking list of conferences generated by RankClass and the top conferences in each research area. Similarly, the highly ranked terms generated by RankClass are in high agreement with the most representative keywords in each field. The reason why GNetMine fails to generate meaningful ranking lists is that the portions of labeled authors and papers are too limited to capture the distribution of the confidence score with regard to each class. In contrast, RankClass boosts the ranking performance by iteratively obtaining the clean sub-network corresponding to each class, which favors the within-class ranking.

5.5 Model Selection

In the graph-based ranking scheme in Equation (2), the α_i's and λ_{ij}'s are essential parameters which control the relative importance of different types of information. In the previous experiments, we empirically set α_i's as 0.1, and λ_{ij}'s as 0.2, $\forall i, j \in \{1, \ldots, m\}$. In this subsection, we study the impact of parameters on the performance of RankClass. Since only several authors and papers are labeled, the α_i associated with authors (denoted by α_a) and papers (denoted by α_p), as well as the λ_{ij} associated with the *author-paper* relationship (denoted by λ_{pa}) are empirically more important than other parameters. Therefore we fix all other parameters and let α_a, α_p and λ_{pa} vary. As GNetMine performs the second best in the classification task, and has been proven to be robust over a large range of parameters [11], we only compare RankClass with GNetMine in this experiment. Note that we also change the corresponding parameters α_a, α_p and λ_{pa} in GNetMine. We show the average classification accuracy on three types of objects (author, paper, conference) as a function of the parameters in Figure 2, with $(a\%, p\%) = (0.5\%, 0.5\%)$ authors and papers labeled.

We observe that over a large range of parameters, RankClass achieves better performance than GNetMine [11]. Since the graph-based ranking scheme in RankClass has a knowledge propagation framework similar to that of GNetMine, the changes in accuracy of the two algorithms over different parameters trend in a similar fashion. However, RankClass generates more accurate and robust results by employing the ranking results to iteratively extract the sub-network corresponding to each class. We therefore conclude that the performance of the RankClass algorithm is generally not very sensitive to the setting of its parameters.

5.6 Time Complexity Study

In this section, we vary the size of the database by randomly selecting connected sub-networks from the original network, and then test the running time of our algorithm. The size of the database is measured by the number of nodes in the network. As can be seen in Figure 3, the time complexity of our method is generally linear with respect to the size of the database, which is consistent with our analysis in Section 4.5.

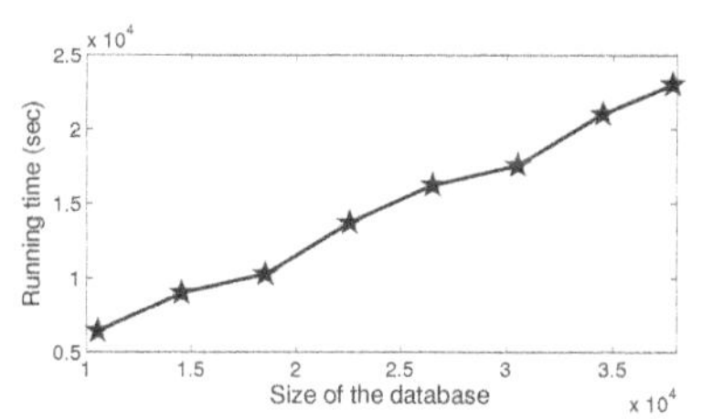

Figure 3: Running time w.r.t. database size

6. CONCLUSIONS

In this paper, we investigate a new problem of classifying data objects in a heterogeneous information network, while simultaneously ranking each object according to its importance within each class, in order to provide informative class summaries. A novel ranking-based classification algorithm called RankClass is proposed to iteratively solve this problem. During each iteration, we calculate the ranking distribution over the nodes of the network by authority propagation. The ranking results are then used to modify the network structure to allow the ranking model to improve the within-class ranking. Thus, we gradually extract the sub-network corresponding to each specific class from the global network. Finally, we calculate the posterior probability of each object belonging to each class to determine each object's optimal class membership.

In the future, we plan to more thoroughly analyze the theoretical foundation behind the ranking-based classification framework to further justify its ability to enhance both classification and ranking. It would also be interesting to study integrating ranking and classification when working with non-networked data.

7. ACKNOWLEDGEMENTS

The work was supported in part by U.S. National Science Foundation grants IIS-0905215, IIS-1017362, and the U.S. Army Research Laboratory under Cooperative Agreement No. W911NF-09-2-0053 (NS-CTA). The views and conclusions contained in this document are those of the authors and should not be interpreted as representing the official policies, either expressed or implied, of the Army Research Laboratory or the U.S. Government. The U.S. Government is authorized to reproduce and distribute reprints for Government purposes notwithstanding any copyright notation here on.

8. REFERENCES

[1] W. Bian and D. Tao. Manifold regularization for sir with rate root-n convergence. In *NIPS 22*, pages 117–125. 2009.

[2] S. Brin and L. Page. The anatomy of a large-scale hypertextual web search engine. *Computer Networks*, 30(1-7):107–117, 1998.

[3] B. Cao, N. N. Liu, and Q. Yang. Transfer learning for collective link prediction in multiple heterogeneous domains. In *ICML*, pages 159–166, 2010.

[4] D. R. Cutting, J. O. Pedersen, D. R. Karger, and J. W. Tukey. Scatter/gather: A cluster-based approach to browsing large document collections. In *SIGIR*, pages 318–329, 1992.

[5] Y. Freund and R. E. Schapire. A decision-theoretic generalization of on-line learning and an application to boosting. *J. Computer and System Sciences*, 55:119–139, 1997.

[6] B. Gao, T.-Y. Liu, Z. Ma, T. Wang, and H. Li. A general markov framework for page importance computation. In *CIKM*, pages 1835–1838, 2009.

[7] J. Gao, F. Liang, W. Fan, Y. Sun, and J. Han. Graph-based consensus maximization among multiple supervised and unsupervised models. In *NIPS 22*, pages 585–593, 2009.

[8] A. Guillory and J. Bilmes. Label selection on graphs. In *NIPS 22*, 2009.

[9] S. Hanneke and E. P. Xing. Network completion and survey sampling. In *AISTAT*, 2009.

[10] T. Hastie, R. Tibshirani, and J. Friedman. *The Elements of Statistical Learning: Data Mining, Inference, and Prediction (2nd ed.)*. Springer-Verlag, 2009.

[11] M. Ji, Y. Sun, M. Danilevsky, J. Han, and J. Gao. Graph regularized transductive classification on heterogeneous information networks. In *ECML/PKDD (1)*, pages 570–586, 2010.

[12] J. M. Kleinberg. Authoritative sources in a hyperlinked environment. *J. ACM*, 46(5):604–632, 1999.

[13] B. Long, Z. M. Zhang, X. Wu, and P. S. Yu. Spectral clustering for multi-type relational data. In *ICML*, pages 585–592, 2006.

[14] Q. Lu and L. Getoor. Link-based classification. In *ICML*, 2003.

[15] S. A. Macskassy and F. Provost. A simple relational classifier. In *MRDM at KDD*, pages 64–76, 2003.

[16] S. A. Macskassy and F. Provost. Classification in networked data: A toolkit and a univariate case study. *J. Mach. Learn. Res.*, 8:935–983, 2007.

[17] J. Neville and D. Jensen. Relational dependency networks. *J. Mach. Learn. Res.*, 8:653–692, 2007.

[18] Z. Nie, Y. Zhang, J.-R. Wen, and W.-Y. Ma. Object-level ranking: bringing order to web objects. In *WWW*, pages 567–574, 2005.

[19] P. Sen and L. Getoor. Link-based classification. Technical Report CS-TR-4858, University of Maryland, February 2007.

[20] L. Sun, S. Ji, and J. Ye. Hypergraph spectral learning for multi-label classification. In *KDD*, pages 668–676, 2008.

[21] Y. Sun, Y. Yu, and J. Han. Ranking-based clustering of heterogeneous information networks with star network schema. In *KDD*, pages 797–806, 2009.

[22] T. Yang, R. Jin, Y. Chi, and S. Zhu. Combining link and content for community detection: a discriminative approach. In *KDD*, pages 927–936, 2009.

[23] O. Zamir and O. Etzioni. Grouper: A dynamic clustering interface to web search results. *Computer Networks*, 31(11-16):1361–1374, 1999.

[24] B. Zhang, H. Li, Y. Liu, L. Ji, W. Xi, W. Fan, Z. Chen, and W.-Y. Ma. Improving web search results using affinity graph. In *SIGIR*, pages 504–511, 2005.

[25] Y. Zhang and Z.-H. Zhou. Non-metric label propagation. In *IJCAI*, pages 1357–1362, 2009.

[26] D. Zhou, O. Bousquet, T. N. Lal, J. Weston, and B. Schölkopf. Learning with local and global consistency. In *NIPS 16*, 2003.

[27] D. Zhou, J. Weston, A. Gretton, O. Bousquet, and B. Schölkopf. Ranking on data manifolds. In *NIPS 16*, 2003.

Real-Time Bidding Algorithms for Performance-Based Display Ad Allocation

Ye Chen
Microsoft
Redmond, WA 98052 USA
yec@microsoft.com

Pavel Berkhin
Microsoft
Redmond, WA 98052 USA
pavelbe@microsoft.com

Bo Anderson
Microsoft
Redmond, WA 98052 USA
brighama@microsoft.com

Nikhil R. Devanur
Microsoft Research
Redmond, WA 98052 USA
nikdev@microsoft.com

ABSTRACT

We describe a real-time bidding algorithm for performance-based display ad allocation. A central issue in performance display advertising is matching campaigns to ad impressions, which can be formulated as a constrained optimization problem that maximizes revenue subject to constraints such as budget limits and inventory availability. The current practice is to solve the optimization problem offline at a tractable level of impression granularity (e.g., the page level), and to serve ads online based on the precomputed static delivery scheme. Although this offline approach takes a global view to achieve optimality, it fails to scale to ad allocation at the individual impression level. Therefore, we propose a real-time bidding algorithm that enables fine-grained impression valuation (e.g., targeting users with real-time conversion data), and adjusts value-based bids according to real-time constraint snapshots (e.g., budget consumption levels). Theoretically, we show that under a linear programming (LP) primal-dual formulation, the simple real-time bidding algorithm is indeed an online solver to the original primal problem by taking the optimal solution to the dual problem as input. In other words, the online algorithm guarantees the offline optimality given the same level of knowledge an offline optimization would have. Empirically, we develop and experiment with two real-time bid adjustment approaches to adapting to the non-stationary nature of the marketplace: one adjusts bids against real-time constraint satisfaction levels using control-theoretic methods, and the other adjusts bids also based on the statistically modeled historical bidding landscape. Finally, we show experimental results with real-world ad delivery data that support our theoretical conclusions.

KDD'11, August 21–24, 2011, San Diego, California, USA.

Categories and Subject Descriptors

F.2.2 [**Nonnumerical Algorithms and Problems**]: Complexity of proof procedures, Computations on discrete structures.

General Terms

Algorithms, Experimentation, Performance

Keywords

Real-time bidding, combinatorial optimization, linear programming, performance display, ad exchange

1. INTRODUCTION

In this paper we consider the problem of performance-based display ad allocation. The goal is to match campaigns (demand-side) to ad impressions (supply-side) such that the total revenue from a publisher's perspective (also referred to as yield) is maximized, while satisfying the constraints primarily imposed by campaign budget and supply inventory availability. In performance-based display advertising, there are two major pricing models, namely cost-per-click (CPC) and cost-per-action (CPA). At an abstract level, advertisers place their bids in the form of CPC or CPA prices on ad impression opportunities from publishers, an ad serving system makes delivery decisions based on advertisers bids, estimated click-through rate (CTR) or conversion rate (CVR), and relevant constraints, and then advertisers only pay publishers for performance-based metrics, i.e., clicks or conversions on their ads. Without loss of generality, we will focus our discussion on an abstract one-sided marketplace of advertisers, with only one publisher and no intermediaries (e.g., ad networks). We further assume that an ad delivery system is optimizing revenue on behalf of the publisher, as well as use CPC campaigns for the purpose of illustration.

Under an unconstrained environment, particularly if advertisers have unlimited budget, the revenue-optimal allocation mechanism is to simply assign each impression to the campaign with highest expected revenue per impression (eCPI = CTR $\times$ CPC). However, it can be trivially shown that this naïve mechanism is suboptimal under a constrained setting where demand-side constraints exist. The current practice is to solve a constrained optimization problem offline (see Section 6 for a formal account), and use the static optimal allocation to guide ad delivery. The constrained optimization is formulated as a linear programming (LP) problem, where the total revenue is maximized with respect to impression allocations subject to linearized constraints. Although an offline optimization takes a global view to achieve revenue optimality at a certain aggregated level, this approach has considerable limitations as follows.

1. An offline global optimization can only be solved at a tractable level of impression granularity. For instance, for one large display network where impressions are allocated at the relatively coarse campaign-placement level, the offline optimization has about 1M decision variables and 0.5M constraints. Impressions within each node of this granularity are treated as homogeneous in terms of valuation; therefore finer-grained impression data cannot be leveraged. Some of these impression-level opportunities are known to be differentiating, such as user historical behavior [5].

2. Even if some constraints are inherently at an aggregated level, such as campaign-level budget constraints and placement-level traffic volume, the offline optimization will quickly become intractable as the number of advertisers and publishers becomes very large, as in ad exchanges [14].

3. Since the offline optimization only creates a static allocation scheme, it lacks a natural way to adapt to marketplace dynamics. In particular, when the distribution from which winning bids are drawn (bidding landscape) changes and the campaign goal is over or under delivered as a consequence, an offline algorithm has no mechanism to adjust accordingly [7].

Motivated by the limitations of the current approach and the emergence of ad exchanges for buying and selling performance display ads [14], we develop a real-time bidding algorithm that enables fine-grained or even individual impression valuation while preserving the offline revenue optimality. The real-time bidding algorithm is not only elegant but also grounded on the duality principle. It turns out that the simple online algorithm solves the original offline optimization problem as the primal by taking the optimal solution to the dual as input, i.e., the bid adjustment term. The dual optimal thus has a natural interpretation, that is, as the shadow price of an extra unit of the primal constraint. With this theoretical foundation from a static perspective, the bidding algorithm requires two key predictive components to account for the dynamic nature of a marketplace.

1. Impression valuation is a function that returns the expected value of an impression to a bidder (advertiser or campaign) given relevant impression-level and demand-side data, which takes the form:

$$\text{eCPI} = \text{CTR} \times \text{CPC}, \tag{1}$$

where eCPI stands for expected cost per impression, and shall be the optimal bid in an unconstrained environment. The CPC price is a constant w.r.t. a given campaign. The critical task is to estimate the click-through rate (CTR):

$$\text{CTR} = p(\text{click}|\text{campaign,impression}), \tag{2}$$

where the impression term encodes relevant impression-level data such as user features, and the campaign term encodes demand-side data such as ad features. The problem of estimating CTR is reasonably well-studied [1, 5, 8]. For a real-time bidding algorithm, a CTR model shall leverage fine-grained and real-time predictor variables, usually high-dimensional and sparse, and perform online prediction efficiently, e.g., in 10s of milliseconds [14]. While we will not focus on building a CTR predictive model, we follow the art and use a regression-based model.

2. Real-time bid adjustment is to adjust the value-based bid according to (1) the bidding landscape so far, and (2) the current constraint satisfaction level. We propose an additive bid adjustment as follows.

$$\text{bid} = \text{eCPI} - \alpha, \tag{3}$$

where α is the bid adjustment term. Intuitively, when the bidding landscape becomes more competitive (i.e., the probability of winning becomes lower given a same bid), and there are more impressions to acquire to satisfy constraints, α should be smaller (or even negative) to bid higher. Theoretically, the additive form can be derived from a primal-dual formulation. Specifically, we develop two real-time bid adjustment approaches (see Section 5 for the update formulae):

   (a) A control-theoretic approach that adjusts the bid using an error function based on constraint satisfaction. We present two forms of optimality control: (1) a proportional-integral controller, and (2) an exponential form.

   (b) A statistical approach that estimates the distribution from which winning bids are drawn, and then derives the bid adjustment to achieve a desired winning probability, also based on the constraint satisfaction level.

We note that the impression valuation function in Eq. (1) is with respect to an advertiser and is not necessarily the same as the revenue function of a publisher (think of a second-price auction). To abstract from the complication of what auction to run, which itself is an open research issue [14], we assume in our discussion a first-price auction run in a one-sided marketplace of advertisers, without loss of generality. In this case, Eq. (1) is equivalent to the revenue function. This simplifying assumption is removed in Section 6 when we develop more general bidding algorithms, e.g., from an ad network point of view and in a second-price auction. Indeed, in a standard auction in a one-sided market as we assume, the revenue equivalence theorem states that first-price, second-price and several other auctions will all yield identical expected revenue in Bayesian equilibrium [10].

2. BACKGROUND

The primary theoretical foundation upon which the online bidding algorithms are grounded is LP duality. We briefly introduce the concepts fundamental to the derivation that follows. The standard form of a LP problem, referred to as a primal problem, is:

$$\begin{aligned} &\max_x \; c^\top x \\ &\text{s.t. } Ax \le b, \\ &\quad x \ge 0. \end{aligned} \tag{4}$$

Here x is a vector of n variables, c is a vector of n coefficients, and $c^\top x$ is the objective function. A is an $m \times n$ matrix of coefficients, b is a vector of m coefficients, and $Ax \leq b$ are the constraints, as well as the non-negative variable constraints. An x is feasible if it satisfies all constraints, and is optimal if it gives the maximal value of the objective function among all feasible solutions.

The standard form can be equivalently converted into an augmented form by introducing a non-negative slack variable for each of the m constraints to replace inequalities with equalities in the constraints. If the optimal value of a slack variable is zero in the augmented form, the corresponding inequality constraint in the standard form becomes tight in its optimal solution.

The primal problem can be converted into a dual problem:

$$\begin{aligned} &\min_y b^\top y \\ &\text{s.t. } A^\top y \geq c, \\ &\quad\;\; y \geq 0. \end{aligned} \tag{5}$$

Here y is a vector of m variables corresponding to the m constraints in the primal, and $A^\top y \geq c$ are the n constraints corresponding to the n primal variables. The weak duality theorem states that the dual problem provides an upper bound to the objective function of the primal, i.e., $c^\top x \leq b^\top y, \forall$ feasible x, y. The strong duality theorem states that if the primal has an optimal solution x^*, then the dual also has an optimal solution y^*, such that $c^\top x^* = b^\top y^*$.

With the primal-dual formulation, we now have a choice of solving either the primal or the dual first (offline), according to the problem structure at hand (e.g., dimensionality and generality); and then derive (possibly online) an optimal solution to one (the primal) when an optimal solution to the other (the dual) is known. There is a very useful necessary condition for optimality that facilitates this idea.

Theorem 1. The complementary slackness theorem states: Suppose that

1. $x = (x_1, \ldots, x_n)^\top$ is a primal feasible,
2. $z = (z_1, \ldots, z_n)^\top$ is the corresponding dual slack,
3. $y = (y_1, \ldots, y_m)^\top$ is a dual feasible, and
4. $w = (w_1, \ldots, w_m)^\top$ is the corresponding primal slack.

Then x and y are optimal for their respective problems if and only if:

1. $x_i z_i = 0, \forall i$, and
2. $y_j w_j = 0, \forall j$.

The complementary slackness condition is a special case of the more general Karush-Kuhn-Tucker (KKT) conditions in convex optimization.

3. PERFORMANCE DISPLAY OPTIMIZATION: A LP FORMULATION

To derive the basic algorithmic form for online bidding, and to establish its optimality, we begin by formulating the basic performance display ad optimization as a LP. In this basic setting, impressions are valuated and allocated individually, and the demand-side constraints (e.g., budget limits) are given in terms of impression delivery goals. This formulation shall capture all theoretical concerns, and practical nuances are discussed in Section 6. Let us first introduce the following notation:

1. i indexes n impressions, and j indexes m campaigns;
2. p_{ij} denotes CTR of impression i assigned to campaign j, q_j denotes CPC for campaign j, and $v_{ij} = p_{ij}q_j$ is the eCPI of such assignment;
3. g_j is the impression delivery goal for campaign j;
4. x_{ij} is the decision variable indicating whether impression i is assigned to campaign j ($x_{ij} = 1$) or not ($x_{ij} = 0$).

We formulate the following LP as the primal:

$$\begin{aligned} &\max_x \sum_{i,j} v_{ij} x_{ij} \\ &\text{s.t. } \forall j, \sum_i x_{ij} \leq g_j, \\ &\quad\;\; \forall i, \sum_j x_{ij} \leq 1, \\ &\quad\;\; x_{ij} \geq 0. \end{aligned} \tag{6}$$

The dual problem is then:

$$\begin{aligned} &\min_{\alpha,\beta} \sum_j g_j \alpha_j + \sum_i \beta_i \\ &\text{s.t. } \forall i, j, \; \alpha_j + \beta_i \geq v_{ij}, \\ &\quad\;\; \alpha_j, \beta_i \geq 0. \end{aligned} \tag{7}$$

It is important to note that since an impression is by nature indivisible, the primal should actually be an integer programming problem, by adding the integer variable constraint $x_{ij} \in \{0, 1\}$. However, as we show more rigorously in Section 4, the optimal solution to the primal LP is indeed integral, given some nice structure of this basic setting, specifically that the constraint matrix is totally unimodular (TU). Even if the LP optimal solution is no longer integral, e.g., using budget constraints directly instead of impression delivery goal, the LP relaxation will not pose any significant problems in practice. For impression i, a fractional optimal x_{ij} can be thought of as a probabilistic assignment, i.e., assign impression i to campaign j with probability x_{ij}. Assume that there is a sufficiently large amount of impressions identical to i (to the extent a practical system can tell), then not only will the probabilistic assignment yield an integral solution, but also one optimal for the LP. As a consequence, we can safely use algorithms to ensure an integral solution.

The dual variables have natural interpretations: α_j is the economic value of acquiring an additional goal impression for campaign j (e.g., by increasing budget), and β_i is the economic value of procuring an additional impression i for the publisher (e.g., by attracting more visits).

We wish to derive an online algorithm to solve the primal LP, thus obtaining a delivery scheme $x_{ij}, \forall i, j$. One may choose to solve the primal directly, as in the current practice of display ad allocation. In this case, the number of variables (x_{ij}) to learn is $n \times m$. On the other hand, solving the dual only requires $n + m$ variables (α_j, β_i), orders of magnitude dimensionality reduction. The Occam's razor principle favors parsimonious models as the dual. The problems remaining are: (1) how to derive an optimal solution to the primal from the optimal solution to the dual, in an online fashion; and (2) how to account for the non-stationary nature of the distribution of impression arrivals. The bidding algorithm in Section 4 addresses the first problem, and the bid adjustment in Section 5 addresses the second problem.

4. A REAL-TIME BIDDING ALGORITHM

Consider an online setting, where each impression i arrives from a stream, and a real-time ad allocation decision needs to be made, i.e., the assignment of $x_{ij}, \forall j$. For each incoming impression i, we will add m decision variables $x_{ij}, \forall j$ and one constraint $\sum_j x_{ij} \leq 1$ to the primal, one decision variable β_i and m constraints $\alpha_j + \beta_i \geq v_{ij}, \forall j$ to the dual. Let us for now assume that the optimal $\alpha_j, \forall j$ are given. The following online algorithm uses the complementary slackness theorem to assign variables such that the offline optimality is preserved.

Algorithm 1: The basic real-time bidding algorithm

Input: $q_j, g_j, \alpha_j, \forall j$
Output: $x_{ij}, \beta_i, \forall i, j$

begin
  $G \leftarrow \emptyset$;
  foreach *impression i from a stream* **do**
    $p_{ij} = p(\text{click}|i, j), \forall j$;
    $v_{ij} \leftarrow p_{ij} q_j, \forall j$;
    $j^* \leftarrow \text{argmax}_{j \notin G}(v_{ij} - \alpha_j)$;
    if $(v_{ij^*} - \alpha_{j^*}) > 0$ **then**
      $x_{ij^*} \leftarrow 1$;
      $x_{ij} \leftarrow 0, \forall j \neq j^*$;
      $\beta_i \leftarrow v_{ij^*} - \alpha_{j^*}$;
      if $\sum_{i'} x_{i'j^*} = g_{j^*}$ **then**
        $G \leftarrow G \cup j^*$;
      end
    end
    $\alpha_j \leftarrow$ `UpdateAlpha`$(\alpha_j), \forall j$;
  end
end

The basic idea conveyed by Algorithm 1 is the following. For an incoming impression i, each campaign j valuates it with $v_{ij} = p(\text{click}|i, j) q_j$, and then bids on it with $v_{ij} - \alpha_j$. The winning bidder with positive bid gets the impression, and campaigns that have reached their goals $j \in G$ will withdraw from future auctions. Here β_i is for bookkeeping the economic value of impression i and is not critical to the auction. The bid adjustment function $\alpha_j \leftarrow \text{UpdateAlpha}(\alpha_j)$ is to adapt α_j's to the current goal delivery level and bidding environment. Under a stationary impression arrival assumption, it reduces to an identity function. We will implement the non-stationary version in Section 5. From an auction perspective, more interestingly, α_j can be interpreted as the minimum profit (revenue minus cost) campaign j requires, and β_i shall be proportional to the floor price demanded by the publisher who sells impression i.

We now establish the offline optimality of this basic online bidding algorithm under a stationary α assumption.

Theorem 2. The optimality of the online bidding algorithm. Given the optimal bid adjustment $\alpha_j, \forall j$, a first-price auction with the following design guarantees the offline optimality.

1. Every campaign j bids on an impression i with the amount $v_{ij} - \alpha_j$;
2. Only active campaigns, i.e., $\sum_{i'} x_{i'j} < g_j$, can participate;
3. The impression is assigned if and only if the highest bid is positive.

Proof. Since a feasible solution exists (e.g., trivially set all variables to zero) and the objective function is bounded, there exist optimal solutions. For each impression i, the winning bidder is $j^* = \text{argmax}_{j \notin G}(v_{ij} - \alpha_j)$.

First, if the highest bid $(v_{ij^*} - \alpha_{j^*}) > 0$, impression i must be assigned; otherwise, the primal constraint $\sum_j x_{ij} < 1$ is slack, and the corresponding dual variable $\beta_i = 0$, thus the dual constraint $\alpha_{j^*} + \beta_i \geq v_{ij^*}$ contradicts. Then assign i to some j', so $x_{ij'} = 1$, and $\alpha_{j'} + \beta_i = v_{ij'}$. If $j' \neq j^*$, $(v_{ij^*} - \alpha_{j^*}) > (v_{ij'} - \alpha_{j'}) = \beta_i$ assuming no ties in bidding, thus the constraint $\alpha_{j^*} + \beta_i \geq v_{ij^*}$ contradicts. Therefore, the optimal solution contains $x_{ij^*} = 1$ and $x_{ij} = 0, \forall j \neq j^*$.

Second, if $(v_{ij^*} - \alpha_{j^*}) < 0$, the impression i should be ignored; otherwise, the tightened dual constraint $\alpha_j + \beta_i = v_{ij}$ corresponding to $x_{ij} = 1$ contradicts, since $\beta_i \geq 0$. If $(v_{ij^*} - \alpha_{j^*}) = 0$, there are multiple optimal solutions.

Third, the constraints $\sum_i x_{ij} \leq g_j, \forall j$ are satisfied by maintaining an active campaign set $\neg G$.

Finally, an impression with a positive highest bid must be all assigned (even in a divisible sense) to the highest bidder j^*; otherwise, if some losing bidder $j' \neq j^*$ gets assigned some non-zero impression (e.g., 0.2 impression), then the corresponding dual constraint tightened $\alpha_{j'} + \beta_i = v_{ij'}$, and hence contradicts the highest-bid proposition $(v_{ij'} - \alpha_{j'}) = \beta_i > (v_{ij^*} - \alpha_{j^*})$ assuming no ties in bidding. More formally, we can rewrite the primal constraints as in Eq. (6) in the standard matrix form:

$$\begin{bmatrix} I_m & I_m & \cdots & I_m \\ U_1 & U_2 & \cdots & U_n \end{bmatrix} \times \begin{bmatrix} x_{11} \\ \vdots \\ x_{1m} \\ x_{21} \\ \vdots \\ x_{nm} \end{bmatrix} \leq \begin{bmatrix} g_1 \\ \vdots \\ g_m \\ 1 \\ \vdots \\ 1 \end{bmatrix}. \tag{8}$$

Here I_m is an $m \times m$ identity matrix, and there are n of them horizontally stacked. $U_i, \forall i$ is an $n \times m$ matrix with ones on the ith row and zeros elsewhere. The constraint matrix A is then an $(n + m) \times (nm)$ matrix. Now we can verify that A is totally unimodular (TU). A unimodular matrix is a square integer matrix with determinant 1 or -1, and a TU matrix is a matrix for which every square non-singular submatrix is unimodular. It is known that if A is TU and b is integral, the LP of the standard form as in Eq. (4) has integral optima. □

5. BID ADJUSTMENT

One simplifying assumption we made in the basic algorithm is that the distribution from which impressions are drawn is stationary, which means given sufficient historical data we can learn the optimal bid adjustment $\alpha_j, \forall j$ a priori by solving the dual offline. In practice, however, since the marketplace is dynamic, impression arrival is non-stationary, e.g., seasonal changes of supply. Additionally, demand-side valuation is a non-stationary process, e.g., old campaigns expire and new campaigns begin. These non-stationarities will violate the complementary slackness condition, and hence the historically-optimal α_j's will not be optimal for future. Our approach is to initialize α_j's with the offline optimal solution to the dual formulated with historical data, and then update α_j's online to accommodate supply-side dynamics and demand-side constraint satisfaction level, through control-theoretic or statistical methods.

5.1 Control-theoretic Bid Adjustment

A simple control design is based on classical control theory. Here we will use a proportional-integral (PI) controller [2], a commonly-used form of the more generic proportional-integral-derivative (PID) controller. It is known that, in the absence of knowledge of the underlying process, a PID controller is the best controller [3]. Formally, let t denote time, $r_j(t)$ and $r'_j(t)$ are the desired and observed probabilities of winning bids, respectively, tracked at time t; and $e_j(t) = r_j(t) - r'_j(t)$ is the error measured at time t. The PI controller takes the following form:

$$\alpha_j(t+1) \leftarrow \alpha_j(t) - k_1 e_j(t) - k_2 \int_0^t e_j(\tau) d\tau. \tag{9}$$

Here k_1 is called proportional gain, and k_2 is called integral gain, both are tuning parameters. In practice, time t does not need to be tracked instantaneously, for both online computational efficiency and the discrete nature of impression arrival. Instead, let $t \in [1, \ldots, T]$ index sufficiently small time intervals, where T is the number of intervals within the entire duration of online bidding; and one only updates α_j's once after each interval.

Another even simpler control approach is inspired by Waterlevel [4], an online and fast approximation algorithm originally designed for resource allocation problems, such as delivering placement-reserved display ads. The Waterlevel-based update formula is:

$$\alpha_j(t+1) \leftarrow \alpha_j(t) \exp\left(\gamma(x_j(t)/g_j - 1/T)\right), \forall j, \tag{10}$$

where $x_j(t)$ denotes the number of impressions won by campaign j during time interval t; and the exponent factor γ is a tuning parameter that controls how fast the algorithm responds to the error measured as $x_j(t)/g_j - 1/T$. If the initial α_j's (e.g., solved from the offline dual) are indeed optimal for future runs, we want γ to be zero. Notice though, in the error term $x_j(t)/g_j - 1/T$ we assume for clarity a uniform impression stream over time intervals. This assumption is not critical since it can be easily removed by adding a time-dependent prior. Moreover, the Waterlevel-based update has a nice chaining property:

$$\begin{aligned} \alpha_j(t+1) &= \alpha_j(t) \exp\left(\gamma(x_j(t)/g_j - 1/T)\right) \\ &= \alpha_j(t-1) \exp\left(\gamma\left(\sum_{\tau=t-1}^{t} x_j(\tau)/g_j - 2/T\right)\right) \\ &= \ldots \\ &= \alpha_j(1) \exp\left(\gamma\left(\sum_{\tau=1}^{t} x_j(\tau)/g_j - t/T\right)\right). \end{aligned} \tag{11}$$

5.2 Model-based Bid Adjustment

The basic idea of our model-based approach is drawn from modern control theory [9], where a mathematical model of the state of the system (the bidding marketplace in our case) is utilized to produce a control signal (the bid adjustment α_j's in our case). More formally, we postulate a parametric distribution $\mathcal{P}$ on the winning bids as follows.

$$w \sim \mathcal{P}(\theta), \tag{12}$$

where θ is the model parameter. We use the generic form since an appropriate parametric choice should be empirically justified by data, and likely domain-dependent. Several reasonable choices are a log-normal distribution [7] and a Gaussian distribution on the square-root of winning bids [13], but neither can handle negative bids naturally. In our additive form of bid adjustment as in Eq. (3), a negative bid $b_{ij} = v_{ij} - \alpha_j < 0$ would mean that the bidder cannot fulfill its minimum profit by acquiring impression i, thus revealing a hidden part of the entire book of the marketplace. We note the PDF as $f(w;\theta)$, the CDF as $F(w;\theta)$, and the inverse CDF as $F^{-1}(p;\theta)$. The MLE of the distribution parameter θ is derived from sufficient statistics of historical winning bids $\{w\}$, which can be readily updated online, e.g., the first and second moments. With this statistical model of the bidding landscape, we can derive the probability of winning by bidding with $b_{ij} = v_{ij} - \alpha_j$:

$$p(w \le b_{ij}) = \int_{-\infty}^{b_{ij}} f(w;\theta) dw = F(b_{ij};\theta). \tag{13}$$

It is unrealistic to assume that the winning bids for all impression i's follow a single distribution (more likely a mixture model), thus we will fit a distribution $\mathcal{P}(\theta)$ for a group of homogeneous impressions, e.g., from a placement. In practice, we align a $\mathcal{P}(\theta)$ with the same impression granularity level as both the supply-side and the demand-side constraints (more on this in Section 6). For now let us focus on homogeneous impressions.

We wish to link the learned winning probability with future bidding behavior to achieve the delivery goal. Suppose that r_j is the expected or desired probability of winning the remaining impressions by campaign j to meet its goal g_j. It is tempting to just bid with $b_{ij} = F^{-1}(r_j;\theta)$ on future impression i's. However, this purely goal-based approach fails to use feedback explicitly to control future bids, thus losing the advantages that a so-called closed-loop controller (e.g., a PID controller) would have, including stability and robustness to model uncertainty. In other words, the purely goal-driven approach does not learn from the errors made by past bidding. We now propose a model-based controller that addresses this limitation, while leveraging the knowledge learned about the bidding landscape. The bid adjustment formula is as follows.

$$\alpha_j(t+1) \leftarrow \alpha_j(t) - \gamma\left(F^{-1}(r_j(t)) - F^{-1}(r'_j(t))\right), \forall j, \tag{14}$$

where $r_j(t)$ and $r'_j(t)$ are desired and observed winning probabilities, respectively, measured at time t. The multiplicative factor γ is a tuning parameter that controls the rate at which an update responds to errors. Compared with classic approaches, a model-based approach does not directly operate on measured errors; instead it transforms an error signal (winning probability error), through a compact model ($\mathcal{P}(\theta)$), to a control signal (updated α_j).

It is also worth noting that in the absence of a good parametric distribution, a non-parametric model can also be used in practice. One needs to maintain an empirical CDF as a two-way lookup table ($F(w;D)$ and $F^{-1}(p;D)$) for online inference.

6. PERFORMANCE DISPLAY OPTIMIZATION: A PRACTICAL FORMULATION

We have developed the basic algorithmic form in Algorithm 1, and established its optimality given the stationary impression arrival assumption. In the basic LP formulation, constraints are encoded as impression delivery goal, and impressions are valuated and assigned individually. We now formulate the LP problem directly with business constraints, primarily demand-side budget limits and supply-side inventory availability; and then discuss major practical aspects that a real-world system shall take into consideration. Let us first update the following notations:

1. i now indexes n impression groups (e.g., placements), impressions within one group are regarded as indistinguishable, and hence yield a same CTR estimation given a campaign;
2. g_j is the budget cap for campaign j;
3. h_i denotes the impression availability constraint or forecast for group i;
4. x_{ij} now denotes the number of impressions from group i allocated to campaign j;
5. w_i denotes the (traffic acquisition) cost per impression from group i, e.g., the second price in a Vickrey auction.

Notice that we make CTR prediction and supply constraint at the same resolution, i.e., per impression group. This is critical to avoid the so-called cream-skimming problem [11]. If CTR prediction is finer-grained than supply constraint for instance, an optimization will always assign impressions to higher-CTR opportunities within each impression group, which is obviously unrealistic. Also, we introduce the cost term w_i to generalize the yield optimization to other players, e.g., an ad network or demand-side platform participating into a second-price auction. The primal LP now becomes:

$$\begin{aligned} \max_x \ & \sum_{i,j} (v_{ij} - w_i) x_{ij} \\ \text{s.t. } \forall j, \ & \sum_i v_{ij} x_{ij} \le g_j, \\ \forall i, \ & \sum_j x_{ij} \le h_i, \\ & x_{ij} \ge 0. \end{aligned} \tag{15}$$

And the dual problem is:

$$\begin{aligned} \min_{\alpha,\beta} \ & \sum_j g_j \alpha_j + \sum_i h_i \beta_i \\ \text{s.t. } \forall i, j, \ & v_{ij}\alpha_j + \beta_i \ge v_{ij} - w_i, \\ & \alpha_j, \beta_i \ge 0. \end{aligned} \tag{16}$$

By a similar derivation as in Section 4, the following auction design would approach offline revenue optimality:

1. Every campaign j bids on an impression from group i with the amount $v_{ij}(1 - \alpha_j)$;
2. Only active campaigns, i.e., $\sum_i v_{ij} x_{ij} < g_j$, can participate;
3. The impression is assigned only if the highest bid is greater than the cost w_i, which is implied if w_i only contains the second price.

The bid adjustment term α_j can now be interpreted as the minimum profit margin (profit divided by revenue) a campaign requires. The cost term w_i is constant with respect to each auction.

Since the primal constraint matrix A in Eq. (15) is no longer TU with the valuation terms v_{ij}'s introduced, the primal optimal is not necessarily integral. As we demonstrated in Section 4, however, the LP relaxation is not a concern in practice. One can solve the primal x^*_{ij}'s, and then stochastically assign impressions from group i to campaign j with probability $x^*_{ij}/\sum_{j'} x^*_{ij'}$, referred to as proportional allocation. Many current practices follow this primal-based approach [4, 6].

As one wishes to valuate impressions at a very fine-grained level, the primal will soon become intractable (recall the cream-skimming problem). We propose a dual-based approach as follows. First, the dual as in Eq. (16) is solved offline using historical data. The offline optimal α_j's are then used as the initial bid adjustment terms for future bidding. In online bidding, a centralized ad delivery system (e.g., owned by the publisher) with perfect information (e.g., the historically optimal α_j's) bids on behalf of all advertisers, and adjusts α_j's near real-time based on observed constraint satisfaction level and bidding landscape, through approaches described in Section 5. The dual has lower dimensionality to start with, i.e., $n + m$ model parameters instead of nm, thus conceived to have a better generality. What we seek from the dual is actually a partial solution, that is, α_j's only, which only causes linear complexity of the offline solver. Furthermore, since we will adjust α_j's dynamically anyway, a good approximation may suffice.

A practical algorithm shall take into consideration the following aspects. First, to avoid multimodality, one distribution density $\mathcal{P}(\theta)$ is estimated for one impression group that exhibits sufficient homogeneity, e.g., a Gaussian distribution on winning bids per group $w \sim \mathcal{N}(\mu_i, \sigma_i^2)$ to allow for negative bids. Since the purpose of the statistical model is to derive a constraint-based bid from the desired winning probability based upon budget limit, the budget constraint g_j needs to be given at the same impression group level at which the distribution is fit. However, constraints such as budget cap are naturally given at the campaign level across all impression groups. This issue can be addressed both offline and online. One can start with distributing offline a campaign-level goal across impression groups with a prior proportion, and then synchronize online these campaign-group level subgoals. More interestingly, the other part of the dual solution, namely β_i's, shall guide this subgoal synchronization. If some β_i becomes positive and larger, the inventory availability from impression group i becomes scarce, which suggests one shall move some delivery subgoals from group i to those with ampler resources and bid less aggressively for group i (think of a reverse auction where impression groups bid for campaigns). Here we focus on pre-distributed campaign-group level goals g_j's.

Second, we consider a fully observed exchange where the winning bid w_i is revealed after each auction. A partially observed setting differs in the penalty for a bidder to learn the distribution of winning bids, i.e., w_i will contain some exploration cost [7].

Third, the algorithm shall be implemented as an online listener, where each impression s arrives from a stream $\mathcal{S}$ one at a time. For online computational efficiency, only minimally required statistics are updated real-time, specifically impression assignments, sample sizes, cumulative valuation, and moments for model parameter θ. Bid adjustment, along with its relevant parameter estimation, is performed near real-time, only once after each time interval t. These near real-time updates may involve expensive computations such as inverting a CDF.

Finally, the estimated CTR p_{sj}, along with eCPI v_{sj} and bid b_{sj}, is made dependent upon individual impressions s. This is only for a bidder to randomize its bids, but not for cream skimming. The expected value of a randomized CTR should still be the group-level CTR, i.e., $\mathbb{E}(p_{sj}) = p_{ij}, \forall s \in i$. Bid randomization has two advantages: (1) bidding ties can be naturally broken (see the optimality theorem and its proof in Section 4), and tie-breaking is especially important in reserved ad allocation where valuations may largely overlap; and (2) one can extend the optimal auction theory [15] to show that the revenue-optimal mechanism for an ad network is to randomize its bids (e.g., by a uniform distribution) within a certain range [14].

7. EXPERIMENTS

In this section, we discuss our empirical evaluation using the application of implicit targeting for performance display advertising [1] with real-world ad delivery data. The goal of implicit targeting is to optimize revenue by leveraging fine-grained impression-level opportunities, such as user signals. Compared with explicit targeting, such as behavioral targeting [5], the audience to target is not explicitly defined, but instead is identified via impression-level valuation. The current approach to performance ad optimization is to solve a LP offline for determining ad assignment at the (placement, campaign) level, and to use a static proportional allocation scheme for online ad delivery. In implicit targeting, we wish to perform the LP optimization at the (placement, user, campaign) level, and to solve it online. Here we define a user as a user-level feature vector that encodes signals relevant to predicting clicks. By distinguishing among users within the same placement, one shall expect higher revenue than if treating them identically. In comparison with the current offline approach, the proposed online bidding algorithm for implicit targeting not only makes impression-level valuation feasible, but also yields substantial computational advantage. Formally, we formulate the problem of implicit targeting as a LP similar to Eq. (15), with the following specializations.

1. Campaign-level budget constraints are given as impression delivery goals g_j's.
2. An impression group i is defined as a (placement, user) tuple, at which level both CTR prediction p_{ij} and inventory control $\sum_j x_{ij} \leq h_i$ are performed.
3. The cost term w_i will be zero, since impressions are from owned inventory.

7.1 Data, Methodology and Metrics

We aim to empirically answer the following questions:

1. Can the online bidding algorithm obtain the offline revenue optimality using the optimal bid adjustment α_j?
2. How do different bid adjustment approaches perform, how well do they approach optimality, and what are their control-theoretic properties?
3. How significant is the initial value of α_j, and is it worthwhile to estimate it using historical data?

A proprietary data set of ad serving for one of the most trafficked placements is obtained from a large display network. There are on average 20M impressions served on each day, and four CPC campaigns involved. The raw log is processed into examples with the schema: (timestamp, placement, user, campaign, clicks, impressions). For each example, let us denote the timestamp as t, the (placement, user) pair as i, the campaign as j, the clicks as $c_{ij}(t)$, and the impressions as $x_{ij}(t)$. When t is tracked instantaneously, an example shall correspond to a single impression assignment. For computational efficiency in our experiments, we trace timestamp in seconds, and hence the composite key (t, i, j) uniquely identifies an example. The impressions $x_{ij}(t), \forall t, i, j$ are the allocation results of the current production system based on a (placement, campaign) level LP optimization, thus aggregating impressions for each campaign j gives the impression delivery goal $g_j = \sum_{t,i} x_{ij}(t)$. The clicks $c_{ij}(t)$ are the ground-truth feedback, thus dividing clicks by impressions gives the empirical CTR. For simulating revenue generated by the proposed approach, we are particularly interested in the empirical CTR for each (placement, user, campaign) tuple marginalized over time, i.e., $p_{ij} = \frac{\sum_t c_{ij}(t)}{\sum_t x_{ij}(t)}$. One may choose to use time-dependent empirical CTR $p_{ij}(t) = \frac{c_{ij}(t)}{x_{ij}(t)}$ to simulate revenue, but that would lead to noisy estimation due to the sparsity of $x_{ij}(t)$. The sum of the products of clicks by CPC q_j is the actual revenue yielded by the current approach $y = \sum_{t,i,j} c_{ij}(t) q_j$.

The online bidding algorithm is implemented as follows, similar to Algorithm 1 but with practical considerations as discussed in Section 6. One first sorts examples by timestamp to form a stream. For each incoming example from the stream, one predicts CTR for each campaign $p'_{ij}, \forall j$, regardless of the actual assigned campaign. Active campaigns then bid with $b_{ij} = p'_{ij} q_j - \alpha_j$, where α_j is initialized as the dual optimal solved from historical data and updated online as bidding runs. The impressions associated with the example are re-assigned to the winning bidder $j^* = \text{argmax}_j (b_{ij})$, i.e., $x'_{ij^*}(t) \leftarrow x_{ij}(t)$ if $b_{ij^*} > 0$; or ignored if $b_{ij^*} \leq 0$,. By so simulating, the impression volume constraints $\forall i, \sum_j x_{ij} \leq h_i$ are naturally satisfied, since all impressions already exist and one only changes the campaign assignments. The campaign-level goals are checked real-time after each auction, while α_j's are updated near real-time once after each hour, i.e., $T = 24$. The algorithm runs on a daily basis, and at the end of each day one will have a simulated impression allocation $x'_{ij}(t), \forall t, i, j$. The simulated revenue is computed as $y' = \sum_{t,i,j} x'_{ij}(t) p_{ij} q_j$, where p_{ij} is the empirical CTR instead of the predicted CTR. To evaluate the performance of different algorithms and bid adjustments, we use revenue lift defined as the ratio of simulated revenue to actual revenue:

$$\text{Revenue lift} = \frac{y'}{y} = \frac{\sum_{t,i,j} x'_{ij}(t) p_{ij} q_j}{\sum_{t,i,j} c_{ij}(t) q_j}. \tag{17}$$

By removing the CPC term, we can also report the overall CTR lift by the proposed approach:

$$\text{CTR lift} = \frac{\text{CTR}'}{\text{CTR}} = \frac{\sum_{t,i,j} x'_{ij}(t) p_{ij} / \sum_{t,i,j} x'_{ij}(t)}{\sum_{t,i,j} c_{ij}(t) / \sum_{t,i,j} x_{ij}(t)}. \tag{18}$$

A sensible implicit targeting algorithm shall have a revenue lift greater than 1, and the offline optimal solution gives an upper-bound lift to any online algorithm.

7.2 Results

Let us start with verifying the optimality of the online bidding algorithm. We take one-day ad serving data, first solve both the primal and the dual LP offline to obtain the offline optimal revenue and α_j's, and then simulate the online bidding on the same data using the optimal α_j's without adjustment. As shown in Table 1, the online algorithm achieves nicely the offline revenue optimality. The small variance is because this particular implementation allocates impressions sharing the same composite key (t, i, j) in batches to save computation, which may violate inventory constraints marginally. Although CTR is not the optimizing objective, the online algorithm yields higher CTR lift than offline. This is because the online algorithm only assigns impressions with positive winning bids, and may disregard perceived non-monetizable ones; while the offline solver does not care as long as the constraints are satisfied.

Table 1: Optimality of Online Bidding

Methods	Revenue lift	CTR lift
Offline optimal	1.4811	1.3180
Online bidding	1.4821	1.4913

We now evaluate different online bid adjustment approaches, specifically the model-based and the Waterlevel-based control mechanisms (shortcut as ModelBidder and WaterlevelBidder). Both use historical optimal α_j's as initial values solved from the day preceding the testing day, and we test on four consecutive days. The rate factor γ is set to 0.01 for ModelBidder, and $0.24 = 0.01T$ for WaterlevelBidder. The results are shown in Table 2.

Table 2: ModelBidder vs. WaterlevelBidder

Revenue lift	Day1	Day2	Day3	Day4
Offline optimal	1.3656	1.4243	1.3652	1.4811
ModelBidder	1.3598	1.3936	1.3683	1.4817
WaterlevelBidder	1.2460	1.3923	1.3675	1.4681

Both bid adjustment methods perform very well in approaching offline revenue optimality, with above 90% offline optimal revenue lift achieved in all cases. The model-based adjustment does slightly better in revenue lift. It is also important to examine the control-theoretic properties of different adjustment algorithms, specifically the stability. Let us define the hourly delivery ratio of a campaign as the hourly winning impressions as a percentage of its daily delivery goal, and the reference ratio as the hourly impression arrivals as a percentage of the total daily impressions. A stable control strategy shall produce delivery ratios close to the reference ratio. We plot the delivery ratios of different adjustment methods against the reference ratio for one top campaign in terms of delivery goal on one day, as shown in Figure 1. The Waterlevel-based method shows superior stability since it directly operates on the error measured against the reference, while the model-based exhibits greater oscillations. On the other hand, using static optimal α_j does not react to the reference.

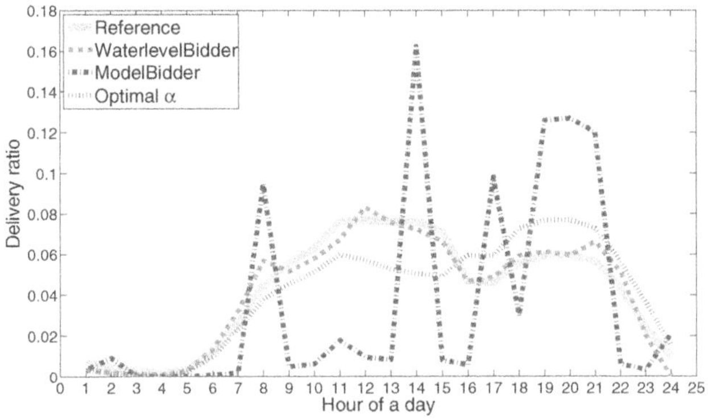

Figure 1: Hourly delivery ratio against reference

To investigate the significance of the initial value of α_j and the merit of solving it offline with historical data, we simulate the Waterlevel-based bid adjustment with different initial α_j values, namely, (1) zero α_j's, (2) historical optimal α_j's, and (3) offline optimal α_j's for the testing day. In reality, one cannot know offline optimal values of α_j's a priori. The results are shown in Table 3.

Table 3: Significance of Initial α_j

Revenue lift	Day1	Day2	Day3	Day4
Offline optimal	1.3656	1.4243	1.3652	1.4811
Zero α_j	1.3652	1.3984	1.3696	1.4819
Historical α_j	1.2460	1.3923	1.3675	1.4681
Optimal α_j	1.3557	1.3973	1.3655	1.4638

Although all different choices approximate offline revenue optimality, varying the initial value of α_j makes no significant difference. We argue that this may be an artifact of offline simulation, where only offline data pre-filtered by the current production system could be obtained. The actual impression allocation in the data has already gone through constraint enforcement by the current delivery system that produces the data; and as a consequence, the delivery goal for the online bidding simulation will not be constraining enough to make α_j significant at the beginning. In fact as empirically shown, all campaigns only exhaust their delivery goals towards the end of a daily run. In reality, when campaign budgets become much more constraining relative to the impressions available from an open exchange, a good initial α_j will matter more.

To test the hypothesis of the pre-selection bias of the offline data and to fully reveal the significance of the initial α_j, we artificially constrain the campaign budget by a factor of $\lambda \in [0, 1]$, thus the campaign delivery goal g_j

derived from the data becomes λg_j. We experiment with $\lambda = 90\%, 75\%, 50\%$ using the Waterlevel-based bid update, and the results support the hypothesis, as shown in Tables 4, 5, and 6. As the campaign budget becomes smaller and the delivery goal becomes more constraining, the performance of the zero-α_j initialization degrades considerably, while the historial or offline optimal α_j largely preserves the offline revenue optimality. When the campaign budget is cut by 50%, a cold start with zero-α_j cannot even recover the revenue yielded by the current approach. These empirical results justify the cost of solving an offline dual LP to obtain a sensible α_j initialization, especially under a constraining budget.

Table 4: Constraining budget by 90%

Revenue lift	Day1	Day2	Day3	Day4
Offline optimal	1.3300	1.3930	1.3652	1.4814
Zero α_j	1.2587	1.2797	1.2562	1.3368
Historical α_j	1.1123	1.3795	1.2536	1.4507
Optimal α_j	1.3269	1.3824	1.3218	1.3406

Table 5: Constraining budget by 75%

Revenue lift	Day1	Day2	Day3	Day4
Offline optimal	1.2858	1.3540	1.3652	1.4813
Zero α_j	1.0796	1.0789	1.0671	1.0953
Historical α_j	1.1092	1.3431	1.3380	1.4599
Optimal α_j	1.2694	1.3526	1.3480	1.3658

Table 6: Constraining budget by 50%

Revenue lift	Day1	Day2	Day3	Day4
Offline optimal	1.2702	1.3248	1.3655	1.4815
Zero α_j	0.7315	0.7076	0.7300	0.7194
Historical α_j	1.2252	1.3181	1.1330	1.4792
Optimal α_j	1.2228	1.1277	1.3555	1.4425

8. CONCLUSIONS

Our contributions are a simple yet well-grounded real-time bidding algorithm for performance display ad allocation, its theoretical revenue optimality guarantee, and practical approaches to adapting bids to market dynamics. We have provided a general framework of bidding in performance-based marketplaces, where both impression valuation and constraints are taken into consideration to compute an optimal bid. Further online experiments are needed to better understand bid adjustment behavior, particularly to investigate the significance of several sources of model uncertainties including impression valuation and bidding landscape distribution. Finally, it will be of great interest to examine the equilibrium properties of the proposed bidding framework at an exchange, and particularly to compare the proposed bidding algorithms with other auction mechanisms with heterogeneous valuations [12, 13].

9. ACKNOWLEDGMENTS

We wish to thank Paul Gorman, Peng Han, Marc Diamond, Asaf Aharoni, and Ishai Oren for inspirational technical discussions; and Padhraic Smyth for scientific guidance.

10. REFERENCES

[1] D. Agarwal, R. Agrawal, R. Khanna, and N. Kota. Estimating rates of rare events with multiple hierarchies through scalable log-linear models. *Proceedings of the 16th ACM SIGKDD International Conference on Knowledge Discovery and Data Mining (KDD 2010)*, pages 213–222, 2010.

[2] K. J. Astrom and R. M. Murray. *Feedback Systems: An Introduction for Scientists and Engineers.* Princeton University Press, 2008.

[3] S. Bennett. *A History of Control Engineering, 1930-1955.* IET, 1993.

[4] D. Charles, M. Chickering, N. R. Devanur, K. Jain, and M. Sanghi. Fast algorithms for finding matchings in lopsided bipartite graphs with applications to display ads. *Proceedings of the 11th ACM Conference on Electronic Commerce (EC 2010)*, 2010.

[5] Y. Chen, D. Pavlov, and J. F. Canny. Large-scale behavioral targeting. *ACM Conference on Knowledge Discovery and Data Mining (KDD 2009)*, pages 209–218, 2009.

[6] U. Feige, N. Immorlica, V. Mirrokni, and H. Nazerzadeh. A combinatorial allocation mechanism with penalties for banner advertising. *Proceeding of the 17th International World Wide Web Conference (WWW 2008)*, 2008.

[7] A. Ghosh, B. I. P. Rubinstein, S. Vassilvitskii, and M. Zinkevich. Adaptive bidding for display advertising. *Proceedings of the 18th International World Wide Web Conference (WWW 2009)*, pages 251–260, 2009.

[8] T. Graepel, J. Q. Candela, T. Borchert, and R. Herbrich. Web-scale Bayesian click-through rate prediction for sponsored search advertising in Microsoft's Bing search engine. *Proceedings of the 27th International Conference on Machine Learning (ICML 2010)*, pages 13–20, 2010.

[9] C. Kilian. *Modern Control Technology.* Delmar Cengage Learning, 2005.

[10] P. Klemperer. Auction theory: a guide to the literature. *Journal of Economic Surveys*, 13(3):227–286, 1999.

[11] J.-J. Laffont and J. Tirole. Optimal bypass and cream skimming. *American Economic Review*, 80(5):1042–1061, 1999.

[12] P. Lu, S. hua Teng, and C. Yu. Truthful auctions with optimal profit. *Workshop on Internet and Network Economics (WINE 2006)*, pages 27–36, 2006.

[13] V. Mirrokni, S. Muthukrishnan, and U. Nadav. Quasi-proportional mechanisms: prior-free revenue maximization. *arXivs*, 2009.

[14] S. Muthukrishnan. Ad exchanges: research issues. *Workshop on Internet and Network Economics (WINE 2009)*, pages 1–12, 2009.

[15] R. B. Myerson. Optimal auction design. *Mathematics of Operations Research*, 6(1):58–73, 1981.

Revisiting Sequential Pattern Hiding to Enhance Utility

Aris Gkoulalas-Divanis
Information Analytics Lab
IBM Research – Zurich
Rüschlikon, Switzerland
agd@zurich.ibm.com

Grigorios Loukides
Health Information Privacy Lab
Vanderbilt University
Nashville, Tennessee, USA
g.loukides@vanderbilt.edu

ABSTRACT

Sequence datasets are encountered in a plethora of applications spanning from web usage analysis to healthcare studies and ubiquitous computing. Disseminating such datasets offers remarkable opportunities for discovering interesting knowledge patterns, but may lead to serious privacy violations if sensitive patterns, such as business secrets, are disclosed. In this work, we consider how to sanitize data to prevent the disclosure of sensitive patterns during sequential pattern mining, while ensuring that the nonsensitive patterns can still be discovered. First, we re-define the problem of sequential pattern hiding to capture the information loss incurred by sanitization in terms of both events' modification (distortion) and lost nonsensitive knowledge patterns (side-effects). Second, we model sequences as graphs and propose two algorithms to solve the problem by operating on the graphs. The first algorithm attempts to sanitize data with minimal distortion, whereas the second focuses on reducing the side-effects. Extensive experiments show that our algorithms outperform the existing solution in terms of data distortion and side-effects and are more efficient.

Categories and Subject Descriptors

H.2.8 [**Database Management**]: Database Applications—*Data Mining*

General Terms

Algorithms, Security, Performance

Keywords

Data privacy, Knowledge hiding, Sequential pattern hiding

1. INTRODUCTION

Sequential data are increasingly collected to support numerous applications in which the sequentiality of events is of primary interest. Examples of such data are web usage logs, which record web page accesses, or mobility data that capture the location of mobile devices at different moments in time [16]. Clearly, sequential data offer remarkable opportunities for discovering interesting behavioral patterns that can be beneficial to a broad community of people. For example, mining user mobility data can reveal interesting patterns that aid traffic engineers and environmentalists in their decisions. Publishing sequential data for data mining purposes, however, may lead to serious privacy violations, if sensitive knowledge patterns are discovered. For instance, the mining of knowledge patterns from mobility datasets may enable intrusive inferences regarding the habits of a portion of the population, or provide the means for unsolicited advertisement and user profiling. Similar concerns have also been raised related to medical data sharing [13,21].

To address these concerns, knowledge hiding methods [5] are necessary. These methods conceal sensitive patterns that can otherwise be mined from published data, without seriously affecting the data and the nonsensitive interesting patterns. Clifton and Marks [12], following D. E. O'Leary [24] who firstly pointed out the privacy breaches that originate from data mining algorithms, indicated the need to consider data mining approaches under the prism of privacy preservation. Since then, several methods emerged to hide knowledge that appears in the form of frequent itemsets and related association rules [19,27,29], or classification rules [11,23].

Unlike these works, this paper considers the problem of hiding sensitive knowledge that appears in the form of frequent sequences and can be disclosed through sequence pattern mining algorithms [6,9]. Sequential pattern hiding is a challenging problem, because sequences have more complex semantics than itemsets, and calls for efficient solutions that offer high utility. To our knowledge, only the work of [3,4] attempts to address this problem, but it may fail to identify high-quality hiding solutions, as we discuss in Section 2.

Our work makes the following contributions:

- We re-define the problem of sequential pattern hiding to capture the utility of released data by considering both the side-effects and the distortion introduced by the hiding process. This allows the production of more useful data for the task they are disseminated for.
- We design two novel sequence hiding algorithms. The first algorithm aims to minimize data distortion, whereas the second focuses on ensuring that the nonsensitive interesting knowledge can still be discovered.
- We extensively evaluate our algorithms, demonstrating that they significantly outperform the existing solution

KDD'11, August 21–24, 2011, San Diego, California, USA.

tid	*events*
1	a b c c d e
2	a b c e
3	a c e b
4	c a b
5	d f g h h
6	d h b
7	d f h h h
8	c d f g
9	f d h f g

(a)

Sensitive seq.
$s_1 =< a, c, e >$
$s_2 =< d, f, g >$
$s_3 =< d, h >$
$s_4 =< f, h >$

(b)

Nonsensitive seq.
$n_1 =< a, b >$
$n_2 =< a, c >$
$n_3 =< a, e >$
$n_4 =< c, e >$
$n_5 =< d, f >$
$n_6 =< d, g >$
$n_7 =< f, g >$
$n_8 =< h >$

(c)

tid	*events*
1	* b c c d e
2	* b c e
3	* c e b
4	c a b
5	d f g h h
6	* h b
7	d f h h h
8	c * f g
9	* * h f g

(d)

tid	*events*
1	* b c c d e
2	a b c e
3	a c e b
4	c a b
5	* * g h h
6	* h b
7	d f h h h
8	c * f g
9	f d h f g

(e)

tid	*events*
1	a b c c d e
2	* b c e
3	a c e b
4	c a b
5	d f g h h
6	* h b
7	d f * * *
8	c * f g
9	f d h f g

(f)

Figure 1: Example of (a) original data, (b) sensitive sequences, (c) nonsensitive sequences (maximal), (d) *HHA* output [4], (e) *DBSH* output, and (f) *SBSH* output (* denotes a suppressed event, $\psi = 3$).

in terms of reducing data distortion and side-effects, while being an order of magnitude more efficient.

The rest of the paper is organized as follows. Related work is in Section 2, where we also discuss the limitations of existing approaches. Section 3 provides the background. In Section 4, we present the hiding strategies used by our algorithms, which are given in Section 5. Section 6 contains the experimental evaluation and Section 7 concludes the paper.

2. RELATED WORK

Approaches for privacy-preserving data sharing fall into two general categories [5]. The first category of approaches attempt to protect the privacy of individuals, whose information is contained in the data, by preventing the disclosure of individuals' identity [28] or sensitive information [8,10,15]. The second category, referred to as *knowledge hiding*, aims to prevent sensitive patterns from being mined from the data, and it is the one our work is related to.

Several hiding algorithms have been proposed with most of the research being conducted along the lines of protecting sensitive association and classification rules. In particular, association rule hiding evolved from efficient heuristic approaches [7,25,29], to border-based approaches [27] and, more recently, to exact hiding approaches that offer stronger quality guarantees at the expense of high computational cost [17,18,22]. Classification rule hiding, on the other hand, evolved around perturbation-based techniques [11] that reduce the confidence of sensitive rules by modifying the values of attributes that support these rules, and reconstruction-based approaches [23] that reconstruct the dataset by using only records supporting nonsensitive rules.

The problem of sequential pattern hiding was recently investigated in [4], where the focus was on hiding the sensitive knowledge in a way that minimally affects the support of the rest of the sequences in the database. The authors proposed *HHA*, a sanitization algorithm that operates as follows. First, for each sequence s of the original database, this algorithm computes the different ways (called *matchings*) in which s supports any sensitive sequence s'. Then, the original sequences are sorted in ascending order with respect to the number of matchings that they contribute to, and the top sequences are selected for sanitization, based on a user-specified disclosure threshold ψ. The sanitization operation eliminates all matches of the sensitive sequences in the sequence s by marking selected events with a special symbol Δ. To sanitize the sequence s, *HHA* finds, for each event e in s, the number of matchings $\delta(e)$ to which e contributes, and marks the events that contribute to most matches, until s no longer supports sensitive sequences. The approach of [4] has three limitations, which we address in this work.

First, the problem formulation adopted by [4] does not focus on side-effects that may be introduced by the hiding process to nonsensitive frequent sequences. As a result, a large number of potentially interesting sequences may be lost in the sanitized dataset. Since the main reason behind publishing sequential data for data mining purposes is to enable the discovery of nonsensitive frequent sequences, the problem formulation of [4] may lead to producing solutions of low data utility. As can be seen in Fig. 1(d), which shows the result of applying the *HHA* algorithm [4] with $\psi = 3$ to the dataset of Fig. 1(a), the nonsensitive frequent sequences n_1, n_2, n_3, n_5 and n_6 are lost. This, however, can be avoided for n_1 and n_5, as shown in Fig. 1(f).

Second, the (global) selection criterion, used by *HHA* to identify sequences for sanitization, often selects sequences that incur high distortion when sanitized. That is, it may mark more events than necessary with Δ. Consider, for example, a sensitive sequence $s' = < a, b, c >$ and the sequences $s_1 = < a, a, a, b, c, c, c >$ and $s_2 = < a, a, b, b, c, c >$. Both s_1 and s_2 contain (i.e., support) s', but s_1 does so with 9 matchings, s_2 with only 8. As a result, *HHA* chooses to sanitize s_2 instead of s_1, assuming that this would incur less distortion. Notice, however, that s_1 should be sanitized instead, since the minimum number of events that should be marked with Δ to sanitize s_1 is 1 (i.e., b should be marked with Δ), whereas 2 events need to be marked with Δ to sanitize s_2 (i.e., both a's, or both b's, or both c's).

Third, *HHA* needs to compute $\delta(e)$ for each event e in every sequence s. As we discuss in Section 5.2.1, our algorithms avoid this costly operation to improve efficiency.

3. BACKGROUND

In this section, we provide the background for the sequence hiding problem and derive the problem statement. Without loss of generality, we follow the work of [4] in that we consider patterns that are simple sequences of symbols (or events). As we discuss in Section 5.2.4, our algorithms can easily be extended to support sequential patterns that follow the classical definition proposed in [6].

Let $\Sigma = \{e_1, e_2, \ldots, e\ \}$ be a set of literals e_i, called *symbols* or *events*, where M denotes the cardinality of the set. A *sequence* s is an ordered list of events from Σ and is represented as $s = < e_1, e_2, \ldots, e_m >$, where $e_i \in \Sigma$, $\forall i \in \{1, \ldots, m\}$. A *transaction* T is an ordered pair (tid, s), where s is a sequence and *tid* a unique identifier used to distinguish among transactions that correspond to the same sequence. Furthermore, a *sequence database* $\mathcal{D}$ is a set of N transactions, carrying different identifiers. We define the *length* or *size* of a sequence s (and denote it by $|s|$) to be the number of events that the sequence contains. Moreover,

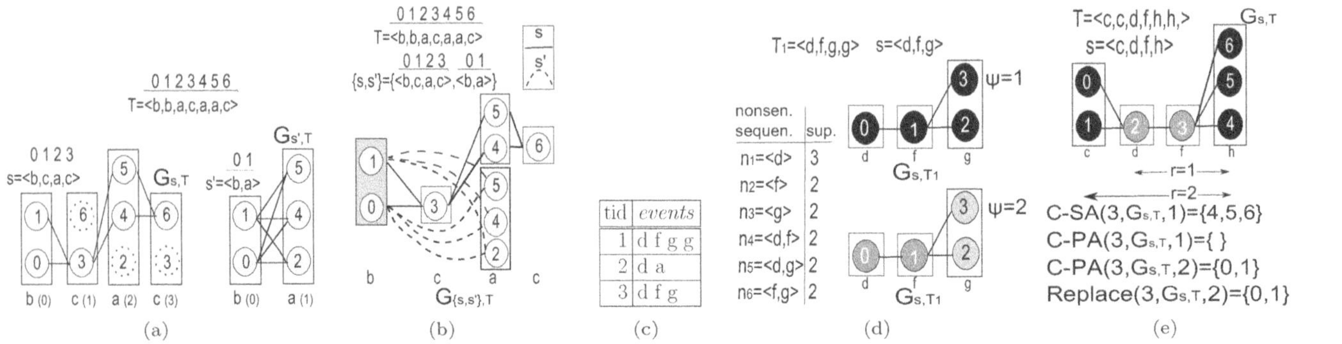

Figure 2: Example of (a) constructing graphs for s, s' and a transaction T, (b) constructing a single graph for $\{s, s'\}$ and T, (c) an original dataset, (d) applying *Annotate*, (e) avoiding side-effects.

we say that a sequence s_1 over Σ is *contained* in (or, equivalently, is a *subsequence* of) a sequence s_2 over Σ, if s_1 can be obtained by deleting ($|s_2|$-$|s_1|$) events from sequence s_2. We use the symbol "$\sqsubseteq$" to denote this type of relationship between two sequences, i.e. $s_1 \sqsubseteq s_2$.

A transaction $T = (tid, s)$ *supports* a sequence s' if $s' \sqsubseteq s$. The *support* of a sequence s in database $\mathcal{D}$ is denoted by $sup(s, \mathcal{D})$, and it is the number of transactions in $\mathcal{D}$ that support s. These transactions are called the *supporting transactions* of sequence s. The sequence s is called *large* or *frequent* in database $\mathcal{D}$, if and only if its support in $\mathcal{D}$ is at least equal to a minimum support threshold ψ, i.e. iff $sup(s, \mathcal{D}) \geq \psi$. Otherwise, s is called *infrequent* in $\mathcal{D}$.

The problem of mining sequential patterns requires, given a sequence database $\mathcal{D}$ and a minimum support threshold ψ, to compute the set of all sequences that are supported by at least ψ transactions in $\mathcal{D}$, which is denoted with $\mathcal{F}_{\mathcal{D},\psi}$. We also formally define the sequence hiding problem below:

PROBLEM 3.1. (Sequence Hiding Problem) *Given a sequence database $\mathcal{D}$, a minimum support threshold ψ, and a set of sensitive sequences $\mathcal{S}$ (selected by data owners among the frequent ones), construct a new, sanitized database $\mathcal{D}'$ from $\mathcal{D}$ such that: (1)* $\mathrm{sup}(s, \mathcal{D}') < \psi$*, for each sensitive sequence $s \in \mathcal{S}$, (2) $\mathcal{F}_{\mathcal{D}',\psi} = \mathcal{F}_{\mathcal{D},\psi} - \mathcal{S}^*$, where $\mathcal{S}^* = \{s^* \in \mathcal{F}_{\mathcal{D},\psi} | s \sqsubseteq s^*, s \in \mathcal{S}\}$ and (3) distance($\mathcal{D}, \mathcal{D}'$), the number of events from $\mathcal{D}$ that are sanitized in $\mathcal{D}'$ is minimum*[1].

The sequence hiding problem requires sanitizing the database $\mathcal{D}$ so that (1) no sensitive sequence can be mined from $\mathcal{D}'$ at a support threshold of ψ or higher, (2) no side-effects are introduced by the hiding process to $\mathcal{D}'$ in terms of (a) sequences in $\mathcal{F}_{\mathcal{D},\psi} - \mathcal{S}^*$ that are infrequent in $\mathcal{D}'$ or (b) infrequent sequences in $\mathcal{D}$ appearing as frequent in $\mathcal{D}'$ (*ghost sequences*), and (3) the least number of events in sequences supported in $\mathcal{D}$ is sanitized (marked or deleted) to derive $\mathcal{D}'$, which implies that $\mathcal{D}'$ should be kept as similar as possible to $\mathcal{D}$. If symbols are marked with Δ when sanitized, then $distance(\mathcal{D}, \mathcal{D}')$ is equal to the number of Δs in $\mathcal{D}'$.

As is proved in [4], the problem of sanitizing a sequence by introducing the least distance is NP-hard. In addition, it is important to observe that the three goals in Problem 3.1 are not of the same importance. That is, a sequence hiding algorithm has to accomplish the first goal to protect all the sensitive knowledge, but needs to prioritize between the second and the third goals, when generating a sanitized database. As we will see shortly, the two algorithms we propose guarantee that the first goal will be satisfied, but each focuses on one of the two other goals. Our first algorithm aims to minimize $distance(\mathcal{D}, \mathcal{D}')$ to incur low distortion, while the second algorithm favors fewer side-effects instead of a smaller distance, a choice adopted by related work in association rule hiding [19]. We also apply only deletions of events to sanitize the sensitive sequences. Thus, no ghost sequences can be introduced by our approach and the second goal can be re-stated as "*minimize the number of nonsensitive frequent sequences that are lost in $\mathcal{D}'$*". Moreover, $distance(\mathcal{D}, \mathcal{D}') = \sum_{\forall T=(tid,s)\in\mathcal{D}} |s| - \sum_{\forall T=(tid,s')\in\mathcal{D}'} |s'|$.

[1]Following related work in frequent itemset hiding [19], we do not consider the loss of a sequence s^* in $\mathcal{F}_{\mathcal{D},\psi}$ that contains a sensitive sequence $s \in \mathcal{S}$ as side-effect, as s^* will be inevitably hidden when we hide s.

4. HIDING STRATEGIES

In this section, we explain how to represent the matchings between sensitive sequences and transactions using multipartite graphs (Section 4.1) and how to hide sequences guided by these graphs (Section 4.2). Strategies to perform these operations in a way that reduces distance and helps prevent side-effects are also discussed (Section 4.3).

4.1 Graph-based sequence representation

Let $\mathcal{S}$ be the set of sensitive sequences from $\mathcal{D}$, $\mathcal{D}_\mathcal{S}$ the transactions in $\mathcal{D}$ that support at least one sensitive sequence, and $\mathcal{D}_{\bar{\mathcal{S}}} = \mathcal{D} - \mathcal{D}_\mathcal{S}$. A nonsensitive frequent sequence is any sequence in $\mathcal{F}_{\mathcal{D}',\psi}$, as defined in Problem 3.1. Given a transaction T, we use T_S to refer to the set of sensitive sequences $S \in \mathcal{S}$ that T supports in $\mathcal{D}$, and T_N to refer to the set of nonsensitive frequent sequences that T supports in $\mathcal{D}$. Given a sequence $s = < e_1, e_2, \ldots, e_m >$, we define the *position* of an event in the sequence: the first event (e_1) is in position 0, ..., the last event (e_m) is in position $(m-1)$. For notational convenience, we refer to a transaction $T = (tid, s)$ as $T_{tid} = s$.

DEFINITION 4.1. *Given a transaction $T \in \mathcal{D}$ and a sensitive sequence s, we define the* **mat hing graph** *$G_{s,T}$ to be a multi-partite graph with the following properties: (a) each position i of s corresponds to a different part (or layer) i in the graph that carries the symbol of s in this position as a label – the layers are positioned consecutively in $G_{s,T}$ in the same order as the symbols of s, (b) for each position in T, a node lies in each layer of the graph that has the same label as the corresponding symbol in T – the node carries a label equal to the position of the corresponding symbol in T,*

(c) an edge between two nodes u, v exists in the graph only if (i) u, v are in adjacent layers, with u preceding v in the graph, and (ii) u, v belong to a path defined as a sequence of nodes $u_1, u_2, \ldots, u_{|s|}$ (based on the corresponding sequence of events in T) for which each node u_i is in the i-th layer of the graph and $label(u_1) < label(u_2) < \ldots < label(u_{|s|})$ - this is called a complete path[2]*, and (d) isolated nodes are removed from $G_{s,T}$.*

Definition 4.1 assumes that $|s| > 1$ (when $|s| = 1$, $G_{s,T}$ contains one node that has a self-loop, forming a complete path by itself). Figure 2(a) presents an example of constructing the matching graph for a transaction T and a sensitive sequence s. Observe that if we assume that, when visited, a node "emits" the symbol of the label of the layer, then traversing a complete path in $G_{s,T}$ corresponds to one occurrence of the sensitive sequence in T. Likewise, the number of complete paths in $G_{s,T}$ represents the different ways that the sensitive sequence is "produced" by T. To sanitize T, all these different matchings have to be removed, which is equivalent to cutting all complete paths in $G_{s,T}$. However, computing the complete paths in the matching graph incurs significant cost [4]. Our algorithms avoid this cost by requiring only the computation of complete paths that pass through a small number of selected nodes, as we show in Section 5. Next, we discuss a graph merging operation that is useful when hiding many sensitive sequences.

DEFINITION 4.2. *Given a transaction $T \in \mathcal{D}$, a set of sensitive sequences $S \subseteq \mathcal{S}$ and the matching graph $G_{s_i,T}$, for each $s_i \in S$, we construct a* **mat hing graph** *$G_{S,T}$* ***for S and*** *by (a) identifying the largest set of nodes V that comprise a single layer in each $G_{s_i,T}$ (breaking ties arbitrarily), (b) for each node in V, constructing a node in $G_{S,T}$ that has the same label, (c) for each node that is not contained in V, constructing a new node in $G_{S,T}$ that has the same label, and (d) for each edge (u, v) in each $G_{s_i,T}$, creating the edge (u, v) in $G_{S,T}$ and annotating it with the identifier i of s_i.*

Constructing the matching graph for a set of sensitive sequences allows our algorithms to find solutions of high quality, as we discuss later. Consider that we want to construct a matching graph $G_{S,T}$ for the set $S = \{s, s'\}$ and the transaction T in Fig. 2(a). The largest set of nodes, which comprise a single layer (i.e., nodes that are contained in a single layer that does not have any other nodes) in both $G_{s,T}$ and $G_{s',T}$, contains the nodes labeled 0 and 1. Thus, for each of the latter nodes, we construct a node in $G_{\{s,s'\},T}$ (i.e., we merge these nodes in $G_{s,T}$ and $G_{s',T}$). Next, we construct a node in $G_{\{s,s'\},T}$, for each node that is not labeled 0 or 1 and is contained in $G_{s,T}$ or $G_{s',T}$, and copy the label of the latter node to the new one. For the edge $(0, 5)$ in $G_{s',T}$, we create an edge $(0, 5)$ in $G_{\{s,s'\},T}$ and annotate this edge as corresponding to s'. Last, we perform the same for each other edge in $G_{s,T}$ and also for $G_{s',T}$ to obtain the matching graph $G_{S,T}$ of Fig. 2(b).

4.2 Sequence hiding

Matching graphs allow tackling the problem of sequence hiding based on a series of graph operations that guide the sanitization of the transactions of $\mathcal{D}$. Specifically, given one transaction T and a set of sensitive sequences S, the sanitization task for T becomes equivalent to applying the minimum number of node deletions in graph $G_{S,T}$, so that all complete paths for the sensitive sequences $s_i \in S$ are cut. As an example, consider the case of sanitizing T so that it no longer supports the sensitive sequence s, shown in Fig. 2(a). This can be achieved by deleting nodes 0 and 1, or 3, or 4 and 5, or 6. Assuming that the criterion we want to optimize is distance (goal 3 in Problem 3.1), deleting any of nodes 3, or 6 will achieve that with a cost of 1.

An important observation follows if we want to sanitize T so that it no longer supports both sensitive sequences, s and s'. If the sanitization is performed separately for s and for s', the hiding algorithm may choose to delete node 3 first, so that s is unsupported by T, and then nodes 0 and 1, so that s' is unsupported by T. This leads to a total distance of 3, and can be avoided if the hiding algorithm operates on the combined graph $G_{\{s,s'\},T}$, shown in Fig. 2(b). In this case, nodes 0 and 1 participate in all complete paths for both s and s', and their removal can lead to the sanitization of T incurring a distance of 2 instead of 3.

Another issue that needs to be addressed is the update of the matching graph after a delete operation. This is accomplished through a function *Update-paths* which, given the transaction $T_{tid} = s$ and the position p in s in which the symbol to be deleted lies, removes the corresponding node from the matching graph and then traverses the graph to delete any edges and nodes that belong to incomplete paths.

4.3 Utility considerations

The hiding of sensitive sequences in $\mathcal{D}$ should be performed in a way that preserves the utility of the database $\mathcal{D}'$ to the highest possible extent. Thus, in this section, we discuss novel strategies that are used by our hiding algorithms to tackle objectives (2) and (3) of Problem 3.1.

Minimizing distance Minimizing distance requires finding the minimum number of events that need to be deleted from a transaction, but this is NP-hard [4]. To deal with this problem, we present *Cost*, which is explained in Algorithm 1. *Cost* begins by iterating over all distinct events contained in at least one sequence in T_S (step 1). For each distinct event e, it constructs the set of sensitive sequences S_e that contain e and assigns the number of occurrences of e to w_e (steps 2-3). Then, *Cost* computes the number of events that need to be deleted from T to sanitize it (steps 4-9). Specifically, it greedily selects the event e with the smallest ratio between w_e and $|S_e|$, and assigns its weight to w (step 7). Next, *Cost* adds w to sc, which is used to count the number of events to be deleted, and S_e to a set S (steps 8-9). This process is repeated until S contains all sequences in T_S. Observe that deleting all occurrences of the selected events from T guarantees that T will be sanitized, because eventually $S = T_S$. Despite its simplicity, *Cost* obtains a tight approximation error of $O(ln(|T_S|))$, as proved in [14].

EXAMPLE 1. *Consider applying* Cost *on T_7 of Fig. 1(a), which supports s_3 and s_4 of Fig. 1(b).* Cost *begins by computing $S_d = \{s_3\}, w_d = 1$, $S_f = \{s_4\}, w_f = 1$, and $S_h = \{s_3, s_4\}, w_h = 3$. Next, it assigns w_d and then w_f to w as $\frac{w_d}{|S_d|} = \frac{w_f}{|S_f|} = 1 < \frac{w_h}{|S_h|} = \frac{3}{2}$, and returns $sc = 2$.*

Minimizing side-effects We present a mechanism that detects events whose deletion does not lead to side-effects.

[2]We use "<", interpreted as "less than", when comparing the labels of two nodes in the graph. In Fig. 2(a), for instance, label(1) < label(3), since b in the first position of T appears before c in the third position.

Algorithm 1 *Cost(T, T_S)*

```
for each (distinct event e in a sequence in T_S)
    S_e ← the sequences in T_S that contain e
    w_e ← the number of occurrences of e in T
sc ← 0
S ← ∅
while (there is a sensitive sequence s ∈ T_S \ S)
    w ← find the weight w_e of the event e with min(w_e / |S_e|)
    sc ← sc + w
    S ← S ∪ S_e
return sc
```

Before doing so, we classify positions of T as follows. A position p is annotated as (i) *black*, if side-effects are not introduced by removing the p-th event of T, (ii) *red* if removing p generates side-effects, or (iii) *gray*, if we cannot be certain whether the removal of p will lead to side-effects.

The annotation of p is performed by *Annotate*, explained in Algorithm 2. After assigning the sequences in T_N that contain the p-th event of T to T_{Np}, *Annotate* checks whether these sequences have a support different than ψ in $\mathcal{D}$, and, in this case, annotates p as *black* (steps 1-3). If there exist sequences with a support of ψ, *Annotate* iterates over them and annotates p as *red*, if at least one of them becomes infrequent after deleting the p-the event from T (steps 5-7). If p has not been marked *red* after examining all sequences in T_{Np}, *Annotate* marks it as *gray* and returns (step 8).

EXAMPLE 2. *Consider applying* Annotate *to the position* 0 *of* T_1 *in Fig. 2(c) using* $\psi = 1$. *Observe in Fig. 2(d) that the node labeled* 0 *in* G_{s,T_1}, *where* $s = < d, f, g >$, *is annotated* black, *because the sequences* n_1 *to* n_6 *are supported by at least* 2 *transactions. Had we used* $\psi = 2$ *instead, this position would be annotated* red, *since the sequences* n_2 *to* n_6 *have a support of* 2, *and* n_4, n_5, *and* n_6 *will be lost if the* 0*-th event is deleted from* T_1.

As explained above, nonsensitive frequent sequences that contain the p-th event of a transaction T will be lost if a *red* position p is deleted. However, this can be avoided if we locate a set of positions in the graph $G_{S,T}$ such that (i) they are all annotated *black*, and (ii) each complete path in $G_{S,T}$ that contains the node labeled p also contains a node labeled with at least one of these positions. We are interested in sets containing positions that appear either *before* or *after* p in T. These types of sets are referred to as *PA* (*Preceding Alternatives*) and *SA* (*Succeeding Alternatives*), respectively. Unfortunately, finding such sets for a position p incurs significant computational overhead, as it may require examining a very large number of positions. To cope with this overhead, we restrict ourselves to considering positions that are reachable from p by following at most r edges in $G_{S,T}$, where (radius) $r \in [1, \max_{j=1,\ldots,|S|} |s_j|]$ is a parameter that controls the part of $G_{S,T}$ to be searched.

Specifically, we find a set *PA* using *C-PA*$(p, G_{S,T}, r)$, a function that traverses $G_{S,T}$ to find a set of positions that satisfy properties (i) and (ii) mentioned above, lie in layers that appear before the layer of node p in $G_{S,T}$, and are reachable from p by traversing at most r edges. *C-PA* starts with positions that are reachable from p by following one edge in $G_{S,T}$ and increases the number of edges that are followed by one in each subsequent iteration. This function stops the first time a set *PA* is found or when the number of edges that are followed exceeds r. A set *SA* for p is found using a function similar to *C-PA*, called *C-SA*.

To find sets of positions in a way that helps reduce both distance and side-effects, we use *Replace*, a function that, given a position p of T, the matching graph $G_{S,T}$, and a specified r, utilizes *C-PA* and *C-SA* and returns the smallest of the sets constructed by them.

EXAMPLE 3. *Consider position* 3 *in* T, *shown in Fig. 2(e), which corresponds to the node labeled* 3 *in the matching graph* $G_{s,T}$, *and is annotated* red. *Applying* Replace *to this position using* $r = 1$ *yields* $\{4, 5, 6\}$, *which implies that the* 4*-th,* 5*-th, and* 6*-th events of* T *can be deleted instead of the* 3*-rd one. Observe that these positions are annotated* black *and* s *is hidden if their corresponding events are deleted. Using* $r = 2$ *instead yields* $\{0, 1\}$, *since the nodes with these labels are reachable from the node labeled* 3 *by following two edges, and the positions they correspond to are fewer than those returned by* C-SA$(3, G_{S,T}, 2)$.

Algorithm 2 Annotate$(p, \mathcal{D}, T_N, \psi)$

```
1. T_Np ← the nonsensitive frequent sequences in T_N
          that contain the p-th event of T
2. if (no sequence n_j ∈ T_Np has sup(n_j, D) = ψ)
3.     return black
4. else
5.     for each (n_j ∈ T_Np such that sup(n_j, D) = ψ)
6.         if (sup(n_j, D) < ψ after deleting the p-th event of T)
7.             return red
8.     return gray
```

5. ALGORITHMS

Sequence hiding involves selecting a number of transactions to sanitize and then deciding which events need to be deleted to perform the sanitization. In this section, we discuss our strategies for these steps and present two novel algorithms to perform the hiding task.

5.1 Selecting transactions to sanitize

As our goal is to release a database $\mathcal{D}'$ in which all sensitive sequences are hidden, we first need to select the transactions from $\mathcal{D}$ that will be sanitized. Clearly, all transactions that do not support any sensitive sequence in $\mathcal{S}$ can safely be disclosed and will be part of $\mathcal{D}'$. Among the transactions supporting sensitive sequences, a set of transactions can be chosen to be part of $\mathcal{D}'$ without being sanitized, as long as the support of each sensitive sequence in $\mathcal{D}'$ remains below ψ. This allows the selection of transactions that support sensitive sequences and incur low distortion when sanitized. To achieve this, we propose *Exclude*, a function that is used by our sanitization algorithms and described in Algorithm 3. *Exclude* begins by computing the number of deletions required to sanitize each transaction in $\mathcal{D}_\mathcal{S}$ using *Cost*, and then sorts these transactions in descending order with respect to this cost (steps 1-3). Next, it iterates over each transaction T in $\mathcal{D}_\mathcal{S}$ and moves the transaction to $\mathcal{D}'$ without sanitizing it only if every sensitive sequence supported by T has been encountered fewer than $(\psi - 1)$ times. The remaining transactions in $\mathcal{D}_\mathcal{S}$ are subsequently sanitized.

5.2 Sanitizing sequences

In what follows, we introduce *DBSH*, an algorithm that employs *Exclude* and *Cost* to minimize distance, and *SBSH* which reduces side-effects by utilizing *Replace*. The differences between these two algorithms and their extension to support itemset sequences, are also discussed.

4. BROADER CONTEXT AND GENERALIZATIONS OF THE FRAMEWORK

4.1 Significant patterns

In recent years, data mining research, and in particular (frequent) pattern mining research (with 'pattern' defined narrowly here), has made increasing use of the notion of a p-value to quantify interest to a data miner (see e.g. [13, 24, 11, 12, 14]. Here, the null hypothesis is taken to be a distribution not unlike our background distribution, representing any prior beliefs the data miner has.

It is easy to see that this approach is a special case of our framework, for a special choice of pattern, with 'pattern' defined in the general way used in the rest of this paper. In particular, choose a test statistic (e.g. the support of a specific itemset), and define a pattern as the fact that this test statistic in the given data is larger than or equal to a certain value (typically its actual support). Then the probability against the background distribution of this pattern being present in the data is, by definition, equal to the p-value associated to the value of the test statistic, with the surrogate background distribution as null hypothesis. Hence, selecting such patterns based on small p-value is equivalent to selecting them based on large self-information.

We believe it has not been fully clear how to iteratively mine for low p-value itemsets, and heuristic approaches have been developed to update the null hypothesis (surrogate background distribution) to take prior selected patterns into account (see e.g. [12]). Interestingly, our framework suggests how it should be done in a theoretically meaningful way, although it must be admitted that it does not guarantee computational feasibility.

4.2 Generalizing the framework

In motivating the choice for conditioning the surrogate background distribution to take a seen pattern into account, we made use of a game-theoretic argument, leading to Eq. (1). We considered patterns that constrain the updated background distribution $P^{*\prime}$ to the set $\mathcal{P}'$ containing distributions that assign probability zero outside some region $\mathcal{X}' \subseteq \mathcal{X}$. For such patterns, the solution of Eq. (1), i.e. the updated surrogate background distribution P', is equal to the initial surrogate background distribution P conditioned on the new domain $\mathcal{X}'$.

However, in information geometry Eq. (1) is studied more generally [15, 3, 1]. In particular, it is known that for any closed convex set $\mathcal{P}'$, the optimum P' of Eq. (1) is the I-projection of P onto $\mathcal{P}'$. Thus, our framework also applies to pattern types that constrain the updated background distribution to any closed convex set of distributions, not just to the set of distributions restricted to a specified domain.

In other words, the conditioning of P in Sec. 2.3 is a special case of an I-projection. We introduced our framework for this special case for reasons of clarity, and also because we believe it is sufficiently general to be applicable to many data mining settings. However, the more general result can be of genuine interest. For example, for computational reasons patterns could be searched for by the algorithm on a subsample of the data, such that they only have a (known) probabilistic relation with the actual data. Interestingly, if this is the case, an I-projection amounts to a Bayes update of the background distribution, rather than a conditioning. Other pattern types could be imagined, with I-projections taking into account the presence of such patterns, possibly amounting to yet different operations on the background distribution.

4.3 Alternative interpretation

We have set up the framework in terms of prior beliefs. Then, patterns are more interesting if they contrast more strongly with these prior beliefs, as quantified using simple information theoretic concepts.

An alternative interpretation of the background distribution P^* is that it models all aspects of the data the data miner is not interested in. A special case of an aspect in which a data miner is not interested is an aspect implied by a prior belief; hence, this alternative interpretation of the background model is in a sense more general.

4.4 Data mining and machine learning

To set out we strongly insisted on distinguishing data mining and machine learning, the former being concerned with identifying interesting patterns, the latter with quantifying predictive performance and designing algorithms that guarantee generalization.

That said, we contend that our framework may be easily integrated with machine learning paradigms—they would simply study different aspects of the same practical problem. For example, we have already highlighted a strong similarity between the description cost (coding length) of a pattern and a regularization cost in machine learning. In fact, all that is needed to add on a learning element would be to make additional statistical assumptions about the data, such as i.i.d.-ness.

5. CONCLUSIONS

In this paper, we introduced a general framework for data mining. It emphatically takes a user perspective, following and modeling the user's state of mind throughout the data mining process, and allowing one to guide the data mining process so as to maximally reduce the data miner's uncertainty and misconceptions about the data. The framework naturally formalizes pattern set mining, iterative data mining, as well as interactive data mining.

By taking a user perspective, fully accounting for any prior beliefs a user may have, we believe our framework is able to capture what is truly of interest to a data miner. Considering the data miner as part of the study object of data mining research, our framework allows to define subjective level of interest of patterns in a formal way.

We argued that various existing methods can be regarded as implementations of this framework, such as PCA, our prior work related to tile mining in binary databases, and our recent work on alternative clustering. We also pointed out that it could be used with great potential in new contexts, such as in subgroup discovery.

We observed that iterative data mining in this framework always amounts to a greedy algorithm for a set coverage type problem attempting to select the best pattern set. However, importantly we did not go into the algorithmic details. As such, our framework is mostly a theoretical ideal, with a few practical instances as indications of its potential. It remains to be investigated if it can be implemented efficiently for more interesting problems. This, and the further development of these ideas for various data mining problems, is subject of our current research.

Acknowledgements

The author is grateful to the anonymous reviewers for useful suggestions, and to Akis Kontonasios, Eirini Spyropoulou and the organizers and participants of the Mining Patterns and Subgroups workshop in Leiden, 2010, for many useful and insightful discussions and critiques related to this work. This work is supported by the EPSRC grant EP/G056447/1.

6. REFERENCES

[1] S.-I. Amari and H. Nagaoka. *Methods of information geometry*. The American Mathematical Society, Oxford University Press, 2000.

[2] E. Bae and J. Bailey. Coala: A novel approach for the extraction of an alternate clustering of high quality and high dissimilarity. In *Proceedings of the International Conference on Data Mining (ICDM)*, 2006.

[3] I. Csiszár and P. C. Shields. *Information theory and statistics: a tutorial*. now Publishers Inc., Delft, The Netherlands, 2004.

[4] T. De Bie. Explicit probabilistic models for databases and networks. Technical report, University of Bristol TR-123931, arXiv:0906.5148v1, 2009.

[5] T. De Bie. Finding interesting itemsets using a probabilistic model for binary databases. Technical report, University of Bristol TR-123930, 2009.

[6] T. De Bie. Maximum entropy models and subjective interestingness: an application to tiles in binary databases. *Data Mining and Knowledge Discovery*, 2010.

[7] T. De Bie. Subjectively interesting alternative clusters. Technical report, University of Bristol TR-133090, 2011.

[8] T. De Bie, K.-N. Kontonasios, and E. Spyropoulou. A framework for mining interesting pattern sets. *SIGKDD Explorations*, 12(2), 2010.

[9] S. Dzeroski. Towards a general framework for data mining. In *Lecture Notes in Computer Science volume 4747*, pages 259–300. springer, 2006.

[10] C. Faloutsos and V. Megalooikonomou. On data mining, compression, and kolmogorov complexity. *Data Mining and Knowledge Discovery*, 15:3–20, 2007.

[11] A. Gallo, T. De Bie, and N. Cristianini. MINI: Mining informative non-redundant itemsets. In *Proceedings of Principles and Practice of Knowledge Discovery in Databases (PKDD)*, 2007.

[12] A. Gallo, A. Mammone, T. De Bie, M. Turchi, and N. Cristianini. From frequent itemsets to informative patterns. Technical report, University of Bristol TR 123936, 2009.

[13] A. Gionis, H. Mannila, T. Mielikäinen, and P. Tsaparas. Assessing data mining results via swap randomization. *ACM Transactions on Knowledge Discovery from Data*, 1(3):14, 2007.

[14] S. Hanhijarvi, M. Ojala, N. Vuokko, K. Puolamäki, N. Tatti, and H. Mannila. Tell me something I don't know: Randomization strategies for iterative data mining. In *Proc. of the 15th ACM SIGKDD International Conference on Knowledge Discovery and Data Mining (KDD09)*, pages 379–388, 2009.

[15] P. Harremoës and F. Topsøe. Maximum entropy fundamentals. *Entropy*, 2001.

[16] H. Hotelling. Analysis of a complex of statistical variables into principal components. *Journal of Educational Psychology*, 24:417–441, 1933.

[17] S. Jaroszewicz and D. A. Simovici. Interestingness of frequent itemsets using bayesian networks as background knowledge. In *Proc. of the 10th ACM SIGKDD International Conference on Knowledge Discovery and Data Mining (KDD04)*, pages 178–186, 2004.

[18] S. Khuller, A. Moss, and J. Naor. The budgeted maximum coverage problem. *Information Processing Letters*, 70, 1999.

[19] J. Kleinberg, C. Papadimitriou, and P. Raghavan. A microeconomic view of data mining. *Data Mining and Knowledge Discovery*, 2(4), 1998.

[20] K.-N. Kontonasios and T. De Bie. An information-theoretic approach to finding informative noisy tiles in binary databases. In *Proceedings of the 2010 SIAM International Conference on Data Mining*, 2010.

[21] H. Mannila. Inductive databases and condensed representations for data mining. In *Proceedings of the 1997 International Symposium on Logic Programming*, pages 21–30, 1997.

[22] H. Mannila. Theoretical frameworks for data mining. *SIGKDD Explorations*, 2000.

[23] H. Mannila. Randomization techniques for data mining methods. In *Proc. of the 12th East European Conference on Advances in Databases and Information Systems (ADBIS08)*, page 1, 2008.

[24] M. Ojala, N. Vuokko, A. Kallio, N. Haiminen, and H. Mannila. Randomization of real-valued matrices for assessing the significance of data mining results. In *Proc. of the 2008 SIAM International Conference on Data Mining (SDM08)*, pages 494–505, 2008.

[25] B. Padmanabhan and A. Tuzhilin. A belief-driven method for discovering unexpected patterns. In *Proc. of the 4th ACM SIGKDD International Conference on Knowledge Discovery and Data Mining (KDD98)*, pages 94–100, 1998.

[26] L. D. Raedt. A perspective on inductive databases. *SIGKDD Explorations*, 4(2):69–77, 2002.

[27] A. Siebes, J. Vreeken, and M. van Leeuwen. Item sets that compress. In *SIAM Conference on Data Mining*, 2006.

[28] A. Silberschatz and A. Tuzhilin. On subjective measures of interestingness in knowledge discovery. In *Proc. of the 1st ACM SIGKDD International Conference on Knowledge Discovery and Data Mining (KDD95)*, pages 275–281, 1995.

[29] N. Tatti. Maximum entropy based significance of itemsets. *Knowledge and Information Systems*, 17(1):57–77, 2008.

[30] L. Valiant. A theory of the learnable. *Communications of the ACM*, 27, 1984.

Tell Me What I Need to Know: Succinctly Summarizing Data with Itemsets

Michael Mampaey Nikolaj Tatti Jilles Vreeken

Department of Mathematics and Computer Science
Universiteit Antwerpen
{firstname.lastname}@ua.ac.be

ABSTRACT

Data analysis is an inherently iterative process. That is, what we know about the data greatly determines our expectations, and hence, what result we would find the most interesting. With this in mind, we introduce a well-founded approach for succinctly summarizing data with a collection of itemsets; using a probabilistic maximum entropy model, we iteratively find the most interesting itemset, and in turn update our model of the data accordingly. As we only include itemsets that are surprising with regard to the current model, the summary is guaranteed to be both descriptive and non-redundant. The algorithm that we present can either mine the top-k most interesting itemsets, or use the Bayesian Information Criterion to automatically identify the model containing only the itemsets most important for describing the data. Or, in other words, it will 'tell you what you need to know'. Experiments on synthetic and benchmark data show that the discovered summaries are succinct, and correctly identify the key patterns in the data. The models they form attain high likelihoods, and inspection shows that they summarize the data well with increasingly specific, yet non-redundant itemsets.

Categories and Subject Descriptors

H.2.8 [**Database management**]: Database applications-*Data mining*

General Terms

Theory, Algorithms, Experimentation

1. INTRODUCTION

Knowledge discovery from data is an inherently iterative process. That is, what we already know about the data greatly determines our expectations, and therefore, which results we would find interesting and/or surprising. Early on in the process of analyzing a database, for instance, we are happy to learn about the generalities underlying the data, while later on we will be more interested in the specifics that build upon these concepts. Essentially, this process comes down to summarization: we want to know what is interesting in the data, and we want this to be reported succinctly and without redundancy.

KDD'11, August 21–24, 2011, San Diego, California, USA.

As a simple example, consider supermarket basket analysis. Say, we just learned that *pasta* and *tomatoes* are very often sold together, and that we already know that many people buy *wine*. Then it is not very interesting to find out that the combination of these three items is also sold frequently. Even if we cannot predict this frequency exactly, we can say that this pattern is redundant. At the same time, at this stage of the analysis we are probably also not interested in highly detailed patterns, e.g., an itemset representing the many ingredients of an elaborate Italian dinner. While its frequency may be surprising, it is also very specific, and may well be better explained by some more general patterns. Still, this itemset might be regarded as highly interesting further on in the discovery process, after we have learned those more general patterns, and if this is the case, we would like it to be reported at that time. Consequently, this is the approach we adopt in this paper; we incrementally adjust our model as we discover new patterns, to obtain a non-redundant summary.

As natural as it may seem to update a knowledge model during the discovery process, few pattern mining techniques actually follow such a dynamic approach of discovering patterns that are surprising with regard to what we have learned so far. That is, while many techniques provide a series of patterns in order of interestingness, most score these patterns using a static model; during this process the model, and hence the itemset scores, are not updated with the knowledge gained from previously discovered patterns. For instance, Tan et al. study 21 of the most well-known interestingness measures, all of which are static, and most of which are based on the independence model [24]. The static approach gives rise to the typical problem of traditional pattern mining: overwhelmingly large and highly redundant collections of patterns.

Our objective is to find a succinct summary of a binary dataset, that is, to obtain a small, yet high-quality set of itemsets that describes key characteristics of the data at hand, in order to gain useful insights. This is motivated by the fact that many existing algorithms often return too large collections of patterns with considerable redundancy, as discussed above. The view that we take in this paper on succinctness and non-redundancy is therefore a fairly strict one.

To model the data, we use the powerful and versatile class of maximum entropy models. We construct a maximum entropy distribution that allows us to directly calculate the expected frequencies of itemsets. Then, at each iteration, we return the itemset that provides the most information, i.e., for which our frequency estimate was most off. We update our model with this new knowledge, and continue the process. The non-redundant model that contains the most important information is thus automatically identified. Therefore, we paraphrase our method as 'tell me what I need to know'.

While solving the maximum entropy model is infeasible in general, we show that in our setting it can be solved efficiently, depending on the amount of overlap between the selected patterns.

Similarly, we give an efficient method for estimating frequencies from the model. Further, we provide an efficient convex heuristic for pruning the search space for the most informative itemsets. This approach allows us to mine our collection of itemsets on the fly, instead of picking them from a larger candidate set which would have to be mined and stored beforehand. Our approach is parameter-free: no maximal error threshold needs to be provided, nor a minimum support or a significance level. The best model can automatically be determined through the Bayesian Information Criterion (BIC); alternatively, we can also mine the top-k most interesting itemsets. Finally, the user can easily infuse background knowledge into the model (in the form of itemset frequencies), to avoid redundancy with regard to what the user already knows.

2. RELATED WORK

Selecting or ranking interesting patterns is a well-studied field in data mining. Existing techniques can roughly be split in two groups.

The first group consists of techniques that measure how *surprising* the support of an itemset is compared against some null hypothesis: the more the observed frequency deviates from the expected value, the more interesting it is. The simplest null hypothesis is the independence model [1,2]. More flexible models have been suggested, for example, Bayesian Networks [14]. The major caveat of these approaches is that the null hypothesis is static and hence we keep rediscovering the same information. As a result, this will lead to pattern collections with high levels of redundancy. The alternative approach is to select itemsets using a dynamic hypothesis. That is, when a new itemset is discovered, the model is updated such that we take the already discovered information into account.

The use of maximum entropy models in pattern mining has been proposed by several authors [15,26,28,30]. Discovering an itemset collection with a good BIC score was suggested by Tatti and Heikinheimo [28]. Alternatively, Tatti [27] samples collections and bases the significance of an itemset on its occurrence in the discovered collections. However, in order to guarantee that the score can be computed, the authors restrict themselves to downward closed and decomposable collections. The method of Tatti [26] uses local models, that is, to compute the support of an itemset X, we are only allowed to use sub-itemsets of X, and it outputs a p-value. A threshold is needed to determine whether X is important. Related, Webb [31] defines itemsets as *self-sufficient*, if their support differs significantly from what can be inferred from their sub- and supersets; therefore such a model is also local. Wang and Parthasarathy [30] incrementally build a maximum entropy model by adding itemsets that deviate more than a given error threshold. The approach ranks and adds itemsets in level-wise batches. This may still, however, lead to redundancy within a batch of itemsets. The method introduced by Kontonasios and De Bie [15] uses row and column margins to construct a maximum entropy model of the data, from which noisy tiles [9] are then discovered, using an MDL-based information score. An important difference, however, is that the data is treated as a single sample from the space of datasets, whereas we consider distributions of transactions.

An alternative approach, called swap randomization, has been suggested by Gionis et al. [10] and Hanhijärvi et al. [13]. The former approach ranks itemsets using a static hypothesis, the latter uses a dynamic hypothesis. Here as well, the authors treat the whole data as a sample from the space of datasets, having the same certain set of statistics, including row and column margins. The authors use an MCMC approach to sample datasets and compute empirical p-values. In both approaches, the framework needs a threshold for deciding which itemsets are significant.

The MINI algorithm by Gallo et al. [7] similarly uses row and column margins to rank itemsets. It first orders all potentially interesting itemsets by computing their p-value according to these margins. Then, as subsequent itemsets are added, the p-values are recomputed, and the itemsets are re-ordered according to their new p-values. This method, however, does not allow querying.

The method of Yan et al. [32] summarizes a collection of itemsets by clustering them, and then representing each cluster as a *profile*. The approach is different from ours, in that it summarizes a given set of patterns, rather than the data itself.

KRIMP, by Siebes et al. [23], employs the MDL principle to select those itemsets that together compress the data best. As such, patterns that essentially describe the same part of the data are rejected. The models it finds are not probabilistic, and therefore cannot easily be used to calculate probabilities. Further, while non-redundant from a compression point of view, many of the patterns it selects are variations of the same theme. Other differences to our method are that KRIMP considers its candidates in a static order, and that it is not trivial to make it consider background knowledge.

It should be noted that in contrast to the algorithm that we propose here, most of the above methods require the user to set one or several parameters, such as a maximum error threshold or a significance level. Many also cannot easily be used to estimate the frequency of an itemset. Further, all of them are two-phase algorithms, i.e., they require that the user provides a collection of candidate (frequent) itemsets to the algorithm, which must be completely mined and stored first, before running the actual algorithm.

3. PRELIMINARIES AND NOTATION

This section provides some preliminaries and the notation that we will use throughout the paper.

By a *transaction* we mean a binary vector of size N generated by some unknown distribution. The ith element in a random transaction corresponds to an *attribute* or an *item* a_i, a Bernoulli random variable. We denote the set of all items by $A = \{a_1, \ldots, a_N\}$. We denote the set of all possible transactions by $\mathcal{T} = \{0,1\}^N$.

The input of our method is a *binary dataset* D, which is simply a sample of $|D|$ (not necessarily distinct) transactions. Given the data D we define an empirical distribution

$$q_D(a_1 = v_1, \ldots, a_N = v_N) = |\{t \in D \mid t = v\}|/|D| \; .$$

An *itemset* X is a subset of A. For notational convenience, given a distribution p, an itemset $X = \{x_1, \ldots, x_L\}$, and a binary vector v of length L, we often use $p(X = v)$ to denote $p(x_1 = v_1, \ldots, x_L = v_L)$. If v consists entirely of 1's, then we use the notation $p(X = 1)$. Given the data D, the *frequency* of an itemset X is defined $fr(X) = q_D(X = 1)$. An *indicator function* $S_X : \mathcal{T} \to \{0,1\}$ of an itemset X maps a transaction t to a binary value such that $S_X(t) = 1$ if and only if t contains X.

The *entropy* of a distribution p over $\mathcal{T}$ is defined as

$$H(p) = -\sum_{t \in \mathcal{T}} p(A = t) \log p(A = t) \; ,$$

where the base of the logarithm is 2, and by convention $0 \log 0 = 0$.

4. IDENTIFYING THE BEST SUMMARY

Our goal is to discover the set of itemsets $\mathcal{C}$ that provides the most important information about the data, while containing as little redundancy as possible. Here, we regard information as whether we are able to reliably predict the data using these itemsets and their frequencies. By non-redundancy, we mean that any subset of $\mathcal{C}$ provides a significantly different description of the data. This is equivalent to requiring that the frequency of an itemset $X \in \mathcal{C}$ should be surprising with respect to $\mathcal{C} \setminus X$. In other words, we do not want $\mathcal{C}$ as a collection to be unnecessarily complex, or capture spurious information. We want it to contain only those itemsets that we really need.

Informally, assume that we have a score $s(\mathcal{C})$ which measures the quality of an itemset collection $\mathcal{C}$. Then our aim is to find that $\mathcal{C}$ with the best score $s(\mathcal{C})$. Analogously, if we only want to know k itemsets, we look for the set $\mathcal{C}$ of size at most k, with the best $s(\mathcal{C})$.

Next, we will detail how we define our models, how we define this score, provide theoretical evidence why it is a good choice, and discuss how to compute it efficiently.

EXAMPLE 1. *As a running example, assume we have a transaction dataset D with eight items, a to h. Furthermore, consider the set of itemsets $\mathcal{C} = \{abc, cd, def\}$ with frequencies 0.5, 0.4 and 0.8, respectively. Assume for the moment that based on $\mathcal{C}$, our method predicts that the frequency of the itemset agh is 0.19. Now, if we observe in the data that $fr(agh) = 0.18$, then we can safely say that agh is redundant because it does not contribute a lot. On the other hand, if $fr(agh) = 0.7$, then the frequency of agh is surprising, and therefore $\mathcal{C} \cup \{agh\}$ would give an improved description of D.*

4.1 Maximum Entropy Model

In our approach we make use of maximum entropy models. This is a class of probabilistic models that are identified by the Maximum Entropy principle [4] as those models that make optimal use of the provided information. That is, they rely only on this information and are fully unbiased otherwise. This property makes these models very suited for identifying good patterns: by using maximum entropy models to measure the quality of a set of patterns, we know that our measurement only relies on the provided frequencies of the patterns, and that it will not be thrown off due to some spurious structure in the data. These models have a number of theoretically appealing properties, which we will discuss after a formal introduction.

Assume that we are given a set of itemsets $\mathcal{C} = \{X_1, \ldots, X_k\}$. Each itemset X_i has a frequency $fr(X_i)$ in the data. We are interested in distributions that satisfy these frequencies, that is, let us consider the following set of distributions

$$\mathcal{P} = \{p \mid p(X_i = 1) = fr(X_i), i = 1, \ldots, k\} .$$

Among these distributions we are interested in only one, namely the unique distribution that maximizes the entropy,

$$p^*_{\mathcal{C}} = \arg\max_p \{H(p) \mid p \in \mathcal{P}\} .$$

For notational convenience we will omit $\mathcal{C}$ from p^* whenever it is clear from the context. Although we restrict ourselves to itemset frequencies here, many other patterns or count statistics that can be expressed as linear combinations of transactions could be used, e.g., transaction lengths [29], association rule confidence, etc. Computing the maximum entropy model, however, is far from trivial, and is treated in Section 4.5.

4.2 Model Scoring

First we discuss how we will measure the quality of a model. A natural first choice would be to directly measure the goodness of fit, using the log-likelihood of the maximum entropy model, that is, $\log p^*(D) = \sum_{t \in D} \log p^*(A = t)$. However, this choice suffers from overfitting: larger collections of itemsets will always provide more information, hence allow for better estimates, and therefore have a better log-likelihood. Consequently, we need to prevent our method from overfitting. Therefore, we use the well-founded Bayesian Information Criterion (BIC), which favors models that fit the data well with few parameters. It has a strong theoretical support in Bayesian model selection [22] as well as through the Minimum Description Length principle [12]. The BIC score of a collection $\mathcal{C}$ is defined as

$$s(\mathcal{C}) = -\log p^*_{\mathcal{C}}(D) + 1/2\, |\mathcal{C}| \log |D| .$$

The smaller this score, the better the model. The first term is simply the negative log-likelihood of the model, while the second term is a penalty on the number of parameters—the number of itemsets in our case. Consequently, the best model is identified as the model that provides a good balance between high likelihood and low complexity. Moreover, we automatically avoid redundancy, since models with redundant itemsets are penalized for being too complex, without sufficiently improving the likelihood.

4.3 Properties of the Model

In this subsection we discuss some properties of the quality measure and the maximum entropy model.

We begin by stating a famous theorem that the maximum entropy model has an exponential form.

THEOREM 2 (THEOREM 3.1 IN [4]). *Given a collection of itemsets $\mathcal{C} = \{X_i\}_{i=1}^k$ with frequencies $fr(X_i)$, let us define $\mathcal{P} = \{p \mid p(X_i = 1) = fr(X_i)\}$. If there is a distribution in $\mathcal{P}$ that has only non-zero entries, then the maximum entropy distribution p^* can be written as*

$$p^*(A = t) = u_0 \prod_{X \in \mathcal{C}} u_X^{S_X(t)} ,$$

where $u_X \in \mathbb{R}$, and u_0 is a normalization factor.

This form will help us to discover the model and compute the likelihood term in the scoring function.

COROLLARY 3 (OF THEOREM 2). *The log-likelihood of the maximum entropy distribution p^* for a set of itemsets $\mathcal{C}$ is equal to*

$$\log p^*(D) = |D|(\log u_0 + \sum_{X \in \mathcal{C}} fr(X) \log u_X) = -|D| H(p^*) .$$

Thus, to calculate the BIC score $s(\mathcal{C})$, it suffices to compute the parameters u_X and u_0 of the distribution p^*.

4.4 Reducing Redundancy

Here we show that our score favors itemset collections with low redundancy, and make a theoretical link with some existing redundancy reduction techniques for pattern mining.

A baseline technique for ranking itemsets is to compare the observed frequency against the expected value of some null hypothesis. The next theorem shows that if the observed frequency of an itemset X agrees with the expected value $p^*(X = 1)$, then X is redundant.

THEOREM 4. *Let $\mathcal{C}$ be a collection of itemsets and let p^* be the corresponding maximum entropy model. Let $X \notin \mathcal{C}$ be an itemset such that $fr(X) = p^*(X = 1)$. Then $s(\mathcal{C} \cup \{X\}) > s(\mathcal{C})$.*

PROOF. We will prove the theorem by showing that the likelihood terms for both collections are equal. Define the collection $\mathcal{C}_1 = \mathcal{C} \cup \{X\}$ and let $\mathcal{P}_1$ be the corresponding set of distributions. Let p_1^* be the distribution maximizing the entropy in $\mathcal{P}_1$. Note that since $\mathcal{C} \subset \mathcal{C}_1$, we have $\mathcal{P}_1 \subseteq \mathcal{P}$ and hence $H(p_1^*) \leq H(p^*)$. On the other hand, the assumption in the theorem implies that $p^* \in \mathcal{P}_1$ and so $H(p^*) \leq H(p_1^*)$. Thus, $H(p^*) = H(p_1^*)$ and since the distribution maximizing the entropy is unique, we have $p^* = p_1^*$. This shows that the likelihood terms in $s(\mathcal{C})$ and $s(\mathcal{C}_1)$ are equal. The BIC penalty term is larger in $s(\mathcal{C}_1)$ which concludes the proof. □

Algorithm 1: ITERATIVESCALING($\mathcal{C}$)

input : itemset collection $\mathcal{C} = \{X_1, \ldots, X_k\}$, frequencies $fr(X_1), \ldots, fr(X_k)$

output: parameters u_X and u_0 of the maximum entropy distribution $p^*_{\mathcal{C}}$ satisfying $p^*_{\mathcal{C}}(X_i) = fr(X_i)$ for all i

1 initialize p;

2 **while** p has not converged **do**

3   **for each** X in $\mathcal{C}$ **do**

4   compute $p(X = 1)$;

5         $u_X \leftarrow u_X \frac{fr(X)}{p(X=1)} \frac{1-p(X=1)}{1-fr(X)}$;

6         $u_0 \leftarrow u_0 \frac{1-fr(X)}{1-p(X=1)}$;

7 **return** p;

Theorem 4 states that adding an itemset X to $\mathcal{C}$ improves the score only if its observed frequency deviates from the expected value. The amount of deviation required is determined by the penalty term. This gives us a convenient advantage over methods that are based solely on deviation, since they require a user-specified threshold.

Two corollaries stated below follow directly from Theorem 4. The first relates our approach to *closed* itemsets [21]. An itemset is closed if all of its supersets have a strictly lower support. An itemset is a *generator* if all of its subsets have a strictly higher support. The second corollary provides a similar relation with *non-derivable* itemsets [3]. An itemset is called derivable if its support can be inferred exactly from the supports of all of its proper subsets.

COROLLARY 5 (OF THEOREM 4). *Let $\mathcal{C}$ be a collection of itemsets. Assume that $X, Y \in \mathcal{C}$ such that $X \subset Y$ and $fr(X) = fr(Y) \neq 0$. Assume that $Z \notin \mathcal{C}$ such that $X \subset Z \subset Y$. Then $s(\mathcal{C} \cup \{Z\}) > s(\mathcal{C})$.*

COROLLARY 6 (OF THEOREM 4). *Let $\mathcal{C}$ be a collection of itemsets. Assume that $X \notin \mathcal{C}$ is a derivable itemset and all sub-itemsets of X are included in $\mathcal{C}$. Then $s(\mathcal{C} \cup \{X\}) > s(\mathcal{C})$.*

Corollaries 5 and 6 connect our approach with popular techniques that losslessly remove redundancy—so-called *condensed representations*. The advantage of our method is that it does not have to be exact. For example, in Corollary 5, $fr(X)$ does not have to equal $fr(Y)$ exactly in order to reject Z from $\mathcal{C}$. This allows us to prune redundancy more aggressively.

4.5 Efficiently Computing the Model

Computing the maximum entropy model comes down to finding the u_0 and u_X parameters from Theorem 2. To achieve this, we use the well-known Iterative Scaling procedure [5], which is given as Algorithm 1. Simply put, it iteratively updates the parameters of the distribution, until it converges to the maximum entropy distribution p^* which satisfies a given set of constraints—itemset frequencies in our case. The distribution is initialized with the uniform distribution, which is done by setting the u_X parameters to 1, and $u_0 = 2^{-N}$ to normalize. Then, for each itemset $X \in \mathcal{C}$, we adjust the corresponding parameter u_X to enforce $p(X = 1) = fr(X)$ (line 5,6). This process is repeated in a round robin fashion until p converges, and it can be shown [5] that p always converges to the maximum entropy distribution p^*. Typically the number of iterations required for convergence is low (usually < 10 in our experiments).

EXAMPLE 7. *In our running example, with $\mathcal{C} = \{abc, cd, def\}$, the maximum entropy model has three parameters u_1, u_2, u_3, and a normalization factor u_0. Initially we set $u_1 = u_2 = u_3 = 1$ and $u_0 = 2^{-N} = 2^{-8}$. Then we iteratively loop over the itemsets and scale the parameters. For instance, for the first itemset abc with frequency 0.5, we first compute its current estimate to be $2^{-3} = 0.125$. Thus, we update the first parameter $u_1 = 1 \cdot (0.5/2^{-3}) \cdot ((1 - 2^{-3})/0.5) = 7$. The normalization factor becomes $u_0 = 2^{-8} \cdot 0.5/(1 - 2^{-3}) \approx 2.2 \cdot 10^{-3}$. Next, we do the same for cd, and so on. After a few iterations, the model parameters converge to $u_1 = 28.5$, $u_2 = 0.12$, $u_3 = 85.4$, and $u_0 = 3 \cdot 10^{-4}$.*

The main bottleneck of this procedure is the inference of an itemset's probability on line 4 of the algorithm,

$$p(X = 1) = \sum_{t \in \mathcal{T}; S_X(t)=1} p(A = t) \ .$$

Since this sum ranges over all possible transactions containing X, it is infeasible to do this in a brute force manner for any non-trivial number of items N. In fact, it has been shown that querying the maximum entropy model is **PP**-hard [25].

Therefore, in order to be able to query the model efficiently, we introduce a partitioning scheme, which makes use of the observation that many transactions have the same probability. Remark that an itemset collection $\mathcal{C}$ partitions $\mathcal{T}$ into blocks of transactions that contain the same set of itemsets. That is, two transactions t_1 and t_2 belong to the same block T if and only if $S_X(t_1) = S_X(t_2)$ for all X in $\mathcal{C}$. Hence, from Theorem 2 we know $p(A = t_1) = p(A = t_2)$. This allows us to define $S_X(T) = S_X(t)$ for any $t \in T$ and $X \in \mathcal{C}$. We denote the partition of $\mathcal{T}$ induced by $\mathcal{C}$ as $\mathcal{T}_\mathcal{C}$. Now we can compute the probability of an itemset as

$$p(X = 1) = \sum_{T \in \mathcal{T}_\mathcal{C}; S_X(T)=1} p(A \in T) \ .$$

The sum has been reduced to a sum over blocks of transactions, and the inference problem has been moved from the transaction space $\mathcal{T}$ to the block space $\mathcal{T}_\mathcal{C}$. In our setting we will see that $|\mathcal{T}_\mathcal{C}| \ll |\mathcal{T}|$, which makes inference a lot more feasible. In the worst case, this partition may contain $2^{|\mathcal{C}|}$ blocks, however, through the interplay of the itemsets, it can be as low as $|\mathcal{C}| + 1$. As explained further on, we can exploit, or even choose to limit, the structure of $\mathcal{C}$, such that practical computation is guaranteed.

All we must do now is obtain the block probabilities $p(A \in T)$. Since all transactions t in a block T have the same probability $p(A = t) = u_0 \prod_{X \in \mathcal{C}} u_X^{S_X(t)}$, it suffices to compute the number of transactions in T to get $p(A \in T)$. So, let us define $e(T)$ to be the number of transactions in T, then

$$p(A \in T) = \sum_{t \in T} p(A = t) = e(T)\, u_0 \prod_{X \in \mathcal{C}} u_X^{S_X(T)} \ .$$

Algorithm 2 describes COMPUTEBLOCKSIZES. In order to compute the block sizes $e(T)$, we introduce a partial order on $\mathcal{T}_\mathcal{C}$. Let

$$sets(T; \mathcal{C}) = \{X \in \mathcal{C} \mid S_X(T) = 1\}$$

be the itemsets in $\mathcal{C}$ that occur in the transactions of T. Note that every block corresponds to a unique subset of $\mathcal{C}$, but conversely not every subset of $\mathcal{C}$ corresponds to a (nonempty) transaction block. We can now define the partial order on $\mathcal{T}_\mathcal{C}$ as follows,

$$T_1 \subseteq T_2 \quad \text{if and only if} \quad sets(T_1; \mathcal{C}) \subseteq sets(T_2; \mathcal{C}) \ .$$

In order to compute the size $e(T)$ of a block, we first compute its *cumulative* size,

$$c(T) = \sum_{T' \supseteq T} e(T') \ ,$$

Algorithm 2: COMPUTEBLOCKSIZES($\mathcal{C}$)

input : itemset collection $\mathcal{C} = \{X_1, \ldots, X_k\}$
output: block sizes $e(T)$ for each T in $\mathcal{T}_\mathcal{C}$

for T in $\mathcal{T}_\mathcal{C}$ **do**
  $I \leftarrow \bigcup\{X \mid X \in sets(T; \mathcal{C})\}$;
  $c(T) \leftarrow 2^{N-|I|}$;
sort the blocks in $\mathcal{T}_\mathcal{C}$;
for T_i in $\mathcal{T}_\mathcal{C}$ **do**
  $e(T_i) \leftarrow c(T_i)$;
  for T_j in $\mathcal{T}_\mathcal{C}$, with $j < i$ **do**
    if $T_i \subset T_j$ **then**
      $e(T_i) \leftarrow e(T_i) - e(T_j)$;
return $\mathcal{T}_\mathcal{C}$;

which is the number of transactions that contain *at least* all the itemsets in $sets(T; \mathcal{C})$. Let $I = \bigcup\{X \mid X \in sets(T; \mathcal{C})\}$. That is, I are the items that occur in all transactions of T. Then it holds that $c(T) = 2^{N-|I|}$, where N is the total number of items. Finally, to extract the block sizes $e(T)$ from the cumulative sizes $c(T)$, we use the inclusion-exclusion principle. To that end, we topologically sort the blocks such that if $T_2 \subset T_1$, then T_1 occurs before T_2 (which can easily be ensured when constructing $\mathcal{T}_\mathcal{C}$). Then we simply iterate over the blocks in reverse, and subtract the sizes of their super-blocks,

$$e(T) = c(T) - \sum_{T' \supsetneq T} e(T') \ .$$

EXAMPLE 8. *Assume again that we have a dataset with eight items (a to h), and an itemset collection containing three itemsets $\mathcal{C} = \{abc, cd, def\}$ with frequencies 0.5, 0.4 and 0.8.*

Table 1 shows the sizes of the transaction blocks. Note that while there are 256 transactions in $\mathcal{T}$, there are only 7 blocks in $\mathcal{T}_\mathcal{C}$, whose sizes and probabilities are to be computed. (The eighth combination, abc and def but not cd, is clearly impossible.)

Let us compute the sizes of the first three blocks. For the first block, $I = abcdef$ and therefore $c(T) = 4$, for the second block $I = abcd$, and for the third block $I = abc$. Since the first block is the maximum with respect to the order $\subseteq$, its cumulative size is simply its size, so $e(T) = 4$. For the second block, we subtract the first block, and obtain $e(T) = 16 - 4 = 12$. From the third block we subtract the first two blocks, and we have $e(T) = 32 - 12 - 4 = 16$. Now, to compute, say, $p(abc = 1)$, we simply need the sizes of the blocks containing abc, and the current model parameters,

$$p(abc = 1) = 4(u_0u_1u_2u_3) + 12(u_0u_1u_2) + 16(u_0u_1).$$

Table 1: Transaction blocks for the running example above, with $X_1 = abc$, $X_2 = cd$, and $X_3 = def$.

X_1	X_2	X_3	$c(T)$	$e(T)$	$p(A = t)$
1	1	1	4	4	$u_0u_1u_2u_3$
1	1	0	16	12	$u_0u_1u_2$
1	0	0	32	16	u_0u_1
0	1	1	16	12	$u_0u_2u_3$
0	1	0	64	36	u_0u_2
0	0	1	32	16	u_0u_3
0	0	0	256	160	u_0

Lastly, the algorithm can be significantly optimized as follows. Assume that we can divide $\mathcal{C}$ into two disjoint groups $\mathcal{C}_1$ and $\mathcal{C}_2$, such that if $X_1 \in \mathcal{C}_1$ and $X_2 \in \mathcal{C}_2$, then $X_1 \cap X_2 = \emptyset$. Let $B = \bigcup \mathcal{C}_1$ be the set of items occurring in $\mathcal{C}_1$. Theorem 2 implies that $p^*(A) = p^*(B)p^*(A \setminus B)$. In other words, the maximum entropy distribution can be factorized into two *independent* distributions, namely $p^*(B)$ and $p^*(A \setminus B)$, more importantly, the factor $p^*(B)$ depends only on $\mathcal{C}_1$. Consequently, if we wish to compute the probability $p^*(X = 1)$ such that $X \in B$, we can ignore all variables outside B and all itemsets outside $\mathcal{C}_1$. The number of computations to perform by COMPUTEBLOCKSIZES can now be greatly reduced, since in the case of independence $|\mathcal{T}_\mathcal{C}| = |\mathcal{T}_{\mathcal{C}_1}| \times |\mathcal{T}_{\mathcal{C}_2}|$, and we can simply compute the block sizes for $\mathcal{T}_{\mathcal{C}_1}$ and $\mathcal{T}_{\mathcal{C}_2}$ separately. Naturally, this decomposition can also be applied when there are more than two of such disjoint groups of itemsets.

Further, in order to *guarantee* that we can apply the above separation, we could reduce the solution space slightly by imposing a limit on the number of items or itemsets per group, such that the number of blocks remains small. Alternatively, we could first partition the items of the dataset into smaller, approximately independent groups [16], and then apply the algorithm for each group separately.

4.6 Including Frequencies of Individual Items

Often it is useful to inspect the frequencies of the individual items (i.e., the column margins) in a dataset, since they supply basic, yet intuitive and easily calculable information about the data. For instance, they say which combinations of items are more (or less) likely to occur together frequently. However, in our method we cannot add the set of all singleton itemsets $\mathcal{I}$ to a collection $\mathcal{C}$, since the number of transaction blocks would become $|\mathcal{T}_{\mathcal{C} \cup \mathcal{I}}| = |\mathcal{T}| = 2^N$, by which we would be back at square one. We sketch (due to space restrictions) how this can be solved easily. Let $\mathcal{C}' = \mathcal{C} \cup \mathcal{I}$. We continue working with $\mathcal{T}_\mathcal{C}$ rather than $\mathcal{T}_{\mathcal{C}'}$. As before, the maximum entropy model has an exponential form: $p^*_{\mathcal{C}'}(A = t) = u_0 \prod_{X \in \mathcal{C}} u_X^{S_X(t)} \prod_{i \in \mathcal{I}} v_i^{S_i(t)}$. The second product defines an independence distribution $v = v_0 \prod_i v_i^{S_i(t)}$. Then $p^*_{\mathcal{C}'}(A \in T) = v(A \in T) \frac{u_0}{v_0} \prod_{X \in \mathcal{C}} u_X^{S_X(T)}$. Thus, we simply need to compute $v(A \in T)$, which is computed very similar to $e(A \in T)$ with COMPUTEBLOCKSIZES—note that $e(A = t)$ is basically the uniform distribution multiplied with 2^N. Hence, we can include the item frequencies at an only marginal additional cost.

4.7 Querying the Model

We have seen how we can efficiently query the probability of an itemset $X \in \mathcal{C}$ when given the maximum entropy distribution p^*. In order to compute the probability of an arbitrary itemset Y that is not a member of $\mathcal{C}$, we do the following. We first set $\mathcal{G} = \mathcal{C} \cup \{Y\}$ and compute the block probabilities $e(T)$ or $v(A \in T)$ for T in $\mathcal{T}_\mathcal{G}$ by calling COMPUTEBLOCKSIZES. Then, we can simply use the parameters of p^* to compute $p^*(Y = 1)$,

$$p^*(Y = 1) = \sum_{\substack{T \in \mathcal{T}_\mathcal{G} \\ S_Y(T) = 1}} v(A \in T) \frac{u_0}{v_0} \prod_{X \in \mathcal{C}} u_X^{S_X(T)} \ .$$

Thus, to obtain the probability of an itemset, it suffices to compute the block probabilities in $\mathcal{T}_\mathcal{G}$, for which we know that $|\mathcal{T}_\mathcal{G}| \leq 2|\mathcal{T}_\mathcal{C}|$.

4.8 Computational Complexity

Let us analyze the complexity of ITERATIVESCALING. To this end, we define $ps(\mathcal{C}) = |\mathcal{T}_\mathcal{C}|$ as the number of blocks in a partition. Note that $ps(\mathcal{C}) \leq \min\left(2^{|\mathcal{C}|}, 2^N\right)$. The computational complexity of COMPUTEBLOCKSIZES is $O(ps(\mathcal{C})^2)$ for a given

Algorithm 3: MTV(D)

input : binary dataset D, background knowledge itemsets $\mathcal{B}$, integer k if mining top-k

output : itemset collection $\mathcal{C}$

$\mathcal{I} \leftarrow$ items in D;
$\mathcal{C} \leftarrow \mathcal{B}$;
while $s(\mathcal{C})$ decreases **and** $|\mathcal{C}| < k$ **do**
    $X \leftarrow$ FINDBESTITEMSET$(\emptyset, \mathcal{I}, \emptyset)$;
    $\mathcal{C} \leftarrow \mathcal{C} \cup \{X\}$;
    $p^*_{\mathcal{C}} \leftarrow$ ITERATIVESCALING$(\mathcal{C})$;
    compute $s(\mathcal{C})$;
return $\mathcal{C}$;

collection $\mathcal{C}$. Assume now that we can partition $\mathcal{C}$ into L disjoint parts $\mathcal{C} = \mathcal{C}_1 \cup \cdots \cup \mathcal{C}_L$, such that if $X \in \mathcal{C}_i$ and $Y \in \mathcal{C}_j$ then $X \cap Y = \emptyset$. As mentioned in Section 4.5, we can now simply compute L independent distributions at a lower total cost. Denoting $B_i = \bigcup_{X \in \mathcal{C}_i} X$, it holds that $ps(\mathcal{C}_i) \leq \min\left(2^{|\mathcal{C}_i|}, 2^{|B_i|}\right)$. If $\mathcal{C}_i$ cannot be partitioned further, this usually means that either $|\mathcal{C}_i|$ is small, or the itemsets in $\mathcal{C}_i$ overlap a lot and $ps(\mathcal{C}_i) \ll 2^{|\mathcal{C}_i|}$. The total execution time of ITERATIVESCALING is $O(K \sum_{i=1}^{L} ps(\mathcal{C}_i)^2)$, where K is the number of iterations, which is usually low. The complexity of estimating the frequency of an itemset requires running COMPUTEBLOCKSIZES once and hence equals $O(\sum_{i=1}^{L} ps(\mathcal{C}_i)^2)$.

5. PROBLEM STATEMENT

In this section we formally state the problem we intend to solve, based on the theory introduced above.

THE PROBLEM. *Given a collection of itemsets $\mathcal{B}$ that represents our background knowledge of a dataset D, a collection of potentially interesting itemsets $\mathcal{F}$, and an integer k, find the subset $\mathcal{C} \subseteq \mathcal{F}$ of size at most k, such that $s(\mathcal{B} \cup \mathcal{C})$ is minimal.*

Note that $\mathcal{F}$ can simply consist of all itemsets, or e.g., be restricted to a collection of frequent itemsets. If we do not wish to constrain the size of $\mathcal{C}$, and essentially disregard k, we can simply set $k = \infty$. Also note that the problem statement does not require $\mathcal{F}$ to be explicitly available beforehand, i.e., it does not have to be mined or materialized in advance (we postpone the details to Section 6.2).

6. MINING SUCCINCT SUMMARIES

In Section 4 we described how to compute the maximum entropy model and its BIC score *given* a set of itemsets. Finding the optimal collection as stated in Section 5, however, is clearly infeasible. The size of the search space is $\sum_{j=0}^{k} \binom{|\mathcal{F}|}{j} \leq 2^{|\mathcal{F}|}$. If we do not restrict the candidate itemsets, then the number of all non-singleton itemsets is $|\mathcal{F}| = 2^N - N - 1$. Moreover, the score function is not monotonic, which prevents us from straightforwardly exploring the search space.

Therefore, we resort to using a heuristic, greedy approach. Starting with a set of itemsets representing our background knowledge—for instance the singletons—we incrementally construct our summary by iteratively adding the itemset that reduces the BIC score the most. The algorithm stops either when k interesting itemsets are found, or when the score no longer decreases. The pseudo-code for our MTV algorithm, which mines Maximally informaTiVe summaries, is given as Algorithm 3.

6.1 A Heuristic for Scoring Itemsets

Finding the best itemset to add to the current collection is practically infeasible, since it involves solving the maximum entropy model for each and every candidate. This remains infeasible even if we restrict the search space (for example, using only frequent itemsets). Therefore, instead of selecting the candidate that optimizes the BIC score directly, we select the candidate that maximizes a heuristic which expresses the divergence between its frequency and its estimate. To derive and motivate this heuristic we first need the following theorem.

THEOREM 9. *Given an itemset collection $\mathcal{C}$, it holds that*

$$\begin{aligned} \arg\min_X s(\mathcal{C} \cup \{X\}) &= \arg\max_X KL(p^*_{\mathcal{C} \cup \{X\}} \,\|\, p^*_{\mathcal{C}}) \\ &= \arg\min_X KL(q_D \,\|\, p^*_{\mathcal{C} \cup \{X\}}) \end{aligned}$$

where KL is the Kullback-Leibler divergence between two distributions, defined as $KL(p \,\|\, q) = \sum_x p(x) \log \frac{p(x)}{q(x)}$, and q_D is the empirical distribution of the data.

PROOF. Let us write $\mathcal{G} = \mathcal{C} \cup \{X\}$. Corollary 3 states that $-\log p^*_{\mathcal{G}}(D) = |D| H(p^*_{\mathcal{G}})$. In addition, we can show with a straightforward calculation that $KL(p^*_{\mathcal{G}} \,\|\, p^*_{\mathcal{C}}) = H(p^*_{\mathcal{C}}) - H(p^*_{\mathcal{G}})$. Therefore, minimizing $s(\mathcal{G})$ is equivalent to maximizing the divergence $KL(p^*_{\mathcal{G}} \,\|\, p^*_{\mathcal{C}})$. The second equality follows similarly. □

Thus, we search for the itemset X such that the new distribution diverges maximally from the previous one, or equivalently, brings us as close to the empirical distribution as possible. The heuristic that we use is an approximation of the KL divergence, where we group the terms containing X in one term, and the terms not containing X into another term. We define $h : [0, 1] \times [0, 1] \rightarrow \mathbb{R}^+$ as

$$h(x, y) = x \log \frac{x}{y} + (1 - x) \log \frac{1 - x}{1 - y} .$$

We then pick the itemset maximizing $h(fr(X), p^*(X = 1))$, which we will denote simply as $h(X)$ when fr and p^* are clear from the context. To compute this heuristic, we only need the frequency of X, and its estimate according to the current p^* distribution. This gives us a measure of the divergence between $fr(X)$ and $p^*(X = 1)$, i.e., its surprisingness given the current model.

The following theorem gives and indication of how KL and h relate to one another.

THEOREM 10. *For an itemset collection $\mathcal{C}$ and itemset X, it holds that*

$$0 \leq h(X) \leq KL(p^*_{\mathcal{C} \cup \{X\}} \,\|\, p^*_{\mathcal{C}}) .$$

Moreover, $h(X) = 0$ if and only if $KL(p^*_{\mathcal{C} \cup \{X\}} \,\|\, p^*_{\mathcal{C}}) = 0$, i.e., when $fr(X) = p^*(X = 1)$.

PROOF. The second inequality follows from the log-sum inequality. The equality to zero is trivially verified. □

6.2 Looking for the Best Itemset

In order to find the itemset maximizing h, we take a depth-first branch-and-bound approach. We exploit the fact that h is convex, and employ the bound introduced by Nijssen et al. [20] to prune large parts of the search space as follows. Say that for a candidate itemset X in the search space, its maximal possible extension in the branch below it is $X \cup Y$ (denoted XY), then for any itemset W such that $X \subseteq W \subseteq XY$, it holds that

$$h(W) \leq \max \{h(fr(X), p^*(XY)), h(fr(XY), p^*(X))\} .$$

If this bound is lower than the best value of h seen so far, we know that no (local) extension W of X can ever become the best itemset with respect to h, and therefore we can safely prune the branch of the search space below X. The algorithm is given in Algorithm 4.

Algorithm 4: FINDBESTITEMSET(X, Y, Z)

input : itemset X, remaining items Y, currently best set Z
output: itemset between X and XY maximizing h, or Z

1 compute $fr(X)$ and $p^*(X)$;
2 **if** $h(X) = h(fr(X), p^*(X)) > h(Z)$ **then**
3 $\quad Z \leftarrow X$;
4 compute $fr(XY)$ and $p^*(XY)$;
5 $b \leftarrow \max\{h(fr(X), p^*(XY)), h(fr(XY), p^*(X))\}$;
6 **if** $b > h(Z)$ **then**
7 $\quad$ **for** $y \in Y$ **do**
8 $\quad\quad Y \leftarrow Y \setminus \{y\}$;
9 $\quad\quad Z \leftarrow$ FINDBESTITEMSET($X \cup \{y\}, Y, Z$);
10 **return** Z;

Table 2: Synthetic and real datasets used in the experiments.

	$\lvert A \rvert$	$\lvert D \rvert$	$minsup$	$\lvert \mathcal{F} \rvert$
Independent	50	100 000	15%	25 110
Markov	20	100 000	5%	8 748
Mosaic	50	100 000	10%	12 256
Abstracts	3 933	859	1%	101 673
Chess (kr-k)	58	28 056	0.1%	19 620
DNA Amplification	391	4 590	0.5%	672 345
Mammals	121	2 183	20%	2 169 624
Mushroom	119	8 124	5%	3 755 512
Paleo	139	124	2%	635 496

An advantage of this approach is that we do not need to collect the frequencies of all candidate itemsets beforehand. Instead, we just compute them on the fly as we need them (line 1). For instance, if we wish to pick itemsets from a collection $\mathcal{F}$ of frequent itemsets for some minimum support threshold, we can integrate the support counting in the depth-first traversal of the algorithm, rather than first mining and storing $\mathcal{F}$ in its entirety. Since mining real datasets with non-trivial minimal support thresholds can easily yield billions of frequent itemsets, this is indubitably a great benefit.

7. EXPERIMENTS

In this section we experimentally evaluate our method and empirically validate the quality of the returned summaries. We implemented a prototype of our algorithm in C++, and provide the source code for research purposes.[1] All experiments were executed on a six-core Intel Xeon machine with 12GB of memory, running Linux.

We evaluate our method on three synthetic datasets, as well as on six real datasets. Their basic characteristics are given in Table 2. The *Independent* data has independent items with random frequencies between 0.2 and 0.8. In the *Markov* dataset each item is a noisy copy of the previous one, with a random copy probability between 0.2 and 0.8. The *Mosaic* dataset is generated by randomly planting five itemsets of size 5 with random frequencies between 0.2 and 0.5, in a database with 1% noise. The *Abstracts* dataset contains the abstracts of all accepted papers at the ICDM conference up to 2007, where words have been stemmed and stop words removed. The *Chess (kr-k)* dataset was obtained from the UCI ML Repository [6], and converted into binary form. The *DNA* data contains information on DNA copy number amplifications. Such copies activate oncogenes and are hallmarks of nearly all advanced tumors [19]. The *Mammals* presence data consists of presence records of European mammals within geographical areas of 50×50 km^2 [17, 18]. The *Mushroom* dataset was obtained from the FIMI dataset repository [11]. Finally, *Paleo* is a dataset of fossil records.

Our method is inherently parameter-free. That is, given enough time, it can select the best set of itemsets from the complete space of possible itemsets. However, although our algorithm is quite efficient, in practice it may not always be feasible to consider *all* itemsets for dense or large datasets. In general, choosing a larger candidate space, yields better models. In our experiments we therefore consider collections of frequent itemsets $\mathcal{F}$ mined at support thresholds as low as feasible. The actual thresholds and corresponding size of $\mathcal{F}$ are depicted in Table 2. Note that the minsup threshold is used to limit the size of $\mathcal{F}$, and is strictly speaking not a parameter of the algorithm itself. For the synthetic datasets, we let the algorithm decide on the best summary size, that is, we set $k = \infty$. As for the real datasets, we do impose a maximum of k itemsets that our algorithm may select. We set k such that the runtime remains within one hour. In all experiments, we initialize $\mathcal{C}$ with the singleton itemsets, i.e., we start from the independence model.

7.1 Model BIC Scores

In Table 3 we give the scores of top-k summaries, the time required to compute them, and for comparison we include the score of the independence model. We see that for most datasets the BIC score (and thus relatedly the negative log-likelihood) decreases a lot, which implies that the summaries we find are of high quality. For very structured datasets, such as *DNA*, this improvement is very large, while it only takes a handful of itemsets to achieve this.

7.2 Summary Evaluation

Here we inspect the discovered data summaries in closer detail.

For the *Independent* dataset we see that the first itemset that the algorithm tries to add immediately increases the BIC score. Therefore, the summary contains only singleton itemsets, which correctly corresponds to the independence model.

With the *Markov* data we notice that the itemsets in the summary are all quite small, and consist of consecutive items. This is in line with expectations, since the items form a Markov chain. The algorithm finds that together with the individual items, a summary of 21 itemsets suffices.

The summary of the *Mosaic* data contains the itemsets that were used to construct the dataset. Figure 1 depicts the evolution of the BIC score. We see that as the five embedded itemsets are discovered, the BIC score is drastically reduced. Afterwards, some additional itemsets are discovered, which contain items from two or more of the generating itemsets. However, they are not noise, and are needed to

Table 3: The BIC scores of the discovered models, compared to the independence model. (Lower scores are better.)

	k	time	$s(\mathcal{C})$	$s(indep)$
Independent	0	10 s	4 494 656	4 494 656
Markov	21	4 834 s	1 826 576	2 000 143
Mosaic	19	686 s	812 792	2 168 276
Abstracts	24	2 774 s	254 974	256 937
Chess (kr-k)	15	3 104 s	774 899	787 078
DNA Amplification	132	3 303 s	91 125	185 499
Mammals	13	1 826 s	107 268	120 132
Mushroom	15	1 817 s	343 367	441 903
Paleo	13	2 307 s	7 787	8 822

[1]http://www.adrem.ua.ac.be/implementations

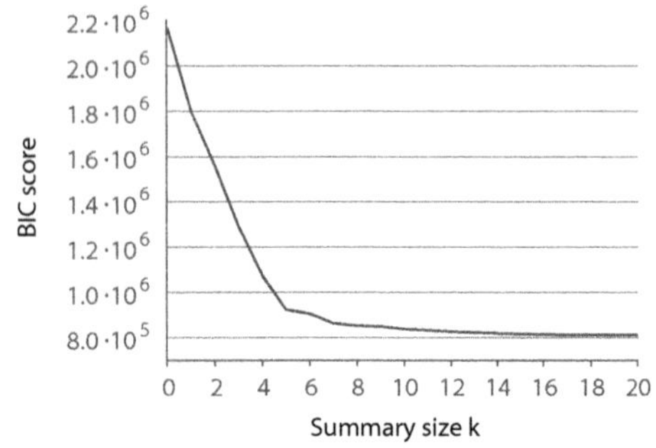

Figure 1: BIC scores for the *Mosaic* dataset for increasing k. The minimum BIC score is attained at $k = 19$.

explain the overlapping behavior of some of the generating itemsets. When k reaches 20, the BIC score increases, and the algorithm stops. (Due to the scale of the plot this is not clearly visible in Figure 1.) Therefore, the algorithm decides that the dataset can be best described with 19 itemsets, of which 5 (the generating itemsets) clearly provide the most information.

The transactions in the *Mammals* data represent geographical areas of 50×50 km^2 in Europe. The itemsets discovered here represent sets of mammals that co-exist in these regions. Investigating the areas where these sets of mammals are present, reveals that many of them form contiguous geographically sound territories, e.g., Scandinavia, the Iberian peninsula, or Eastern Europe. (Pictures are not shown here due to lack of space.)

In the case of the *DNA* data, our algorithm reached more than 100 iterations within one hour. As this dataset is banded, it contains a lot of structure [8]. Our method correctly discovers these bands, i.e., blocks of consecutive items corresponding to related genes, lying on the same chromosomes. The first few dozen sets are large, and describe the general structure of the data. Then, as we continue, we start to encounter smaller itemsets, which describe more detailed nuances in the correlations between the genes. Figure 2 depicts a detail of the *DNA* dataset (note that the figure is transposed), together with a few of the itemsets from the discovered summary.

7.3 Comparison with Other Methods

In Table 4, we give the top-10 itemsets in the *Abstracts* dataset, as discovered by our method (top left), KRIMP [23] (top right), Kontonasios and De Bie's method [15] (bottom left), and Tiling [9] (bottom right). We see that our algorithm discovers recognizable

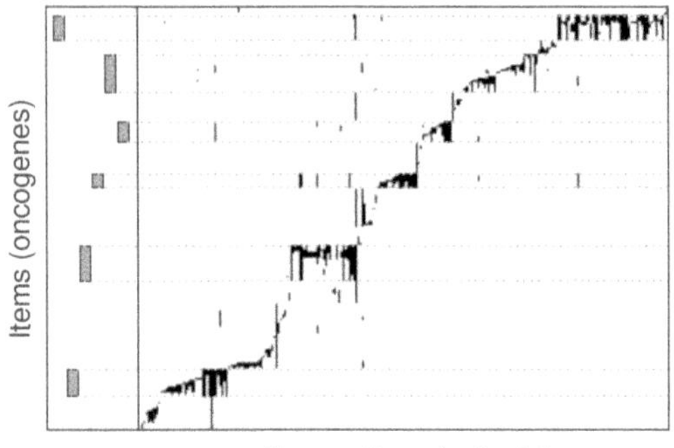

Figure 2: Detail of the *DNA* dataset (right), along with some of the discovered itemsets (left). (Figure is rotated to the left.)

Table 4: Top-10 itemsets of the *Abstracts* dataset for our method (top left), KRIMP [23] (top right), Kontonasios and De Bie [15] (bottom left), and Tiling [9] (bottom right).

machin support svm vector	algorithm experiment result set
associ mine rule	demonstr space
algorithm frequent mine pattern	larg databas
analysi discrimin lda linear	consid problem
algorithm cluster dimension high	knowledg discoveri
nearest neighbor	demonstr experiment
bay naiv	rule mine associ databas
frequent itemset mine	algorithm base approach cluster
analysi compon princip	state art
dimension high real subspac synthet	global local
vector machin support	algorithm mine
discov frequent effici pattern mine algorithm	algorithm base
associ rule database mine algorithm	result set
train learn classifi perform set	approach problem
frequent itemset	method propos
dimensional high cluster mine	result experiment
synthetic real	algorithm perform
seri time	base model
decis tree classifi	set method
experiment propos problem approach result	algorithm gener

data mining topics such as *support vector machines*, *frequent itemset mining* and *principle component analysis*. Further, there is little overlap between the itemsets, and there is no variations-on-the-same-theme type of redundancy present.

For KRIMP we depict the itemsets from the code table which have the highest usage. From a compression point of view, the items in these sets co-occur often, and thus result in small codes for the itemsets. Arguably, this does not necessarily make them the most interesting, however, and we observe that some rather general terms such as *state [of the] art* or *consider problem* are ranked highly. The results of Kontonasios and De Bie's algorithm, based on the Information Ratio of tiles, are different from ours, but seem to be more or less similar in quality for this particular dataset. Finally, for Tiling we provide the top-10 itemsets of size at least two. Without this size restriction, only singletons are returned, which, although having the largest area, are not very informative. Still, the largest discovered tiles are of size two, and contain quite some redundancy, for instance, the top-10 contains only 13 (out of 20) distinct items.

8. DISCUSSION

The approach introduced in this paper fulfills several intuitive expectations one might have about summarization, such as succinctness, providing a characteristic description of the data, and having little redundancy. The experiments show that quantitatively we can achieve good BIC scores with only a handful of itemsets, and that these results are highly qualitative and meaningful; moreover, we can discover them in a relatively short amount of time.

In this paper we consider data mining as an iterative process. By starting off with what we already know, we can identify those patterns that are the most surprising. Simply finding the itemset that is most surprising, is a problem that Hanhijärvi et al. summarize as 'tell me something I don't know'. When we repeat this process, in the end, we will have identified a group of itemsets that 'tell me all there is to know' about the data. Clearly, this group strongly overfits the data. This is where BIC provides a solution, as it automatically identifies the most informative group. Hence, we paraphrase our approach as 'tell me what I need to know'.

The view that we take here on succinctness and non-redundancy is fairly strict. Arguably, there are settings conceivable where limited redundancy (at the cost of brevity) can give some robustness to a technique, or provide alternative insights by restating facts differently. However, this is not the intention of this paper, and we furthermore argue that to this end our method can perfectly be complemented by techniques such as redescription mining [33].

There are a number of possible improvements for our method. We are interested in refining the penalty in our score. Our current score only penalizes the *number* of elements in $\mathcal{C}$, not their complexity (e.g., their size). Such a refinement would make it more strict, and could provide better results. Another problem setting in which our method is applicable, is that of finding the best specialization of a given itemset X. That is, to identify the superset Y of X that provides the best score $s(\mathcal{C} \cup \{Y\})$. This setup allows experts to interactively discover interesting itemsets. As part of future work, we are currently investigating this in practice for finding patterns in proteomics and mass-spectrometry data.

9. CONCLUSION

In this paper we introduced a well-founded method for iteratively mining a non-redundant collection of interesting itemsets from transaction data. We employ the Maximum Entropy principle to build a probabilistic model of the data, use this model to iteratively identify the most surprising itemsets, and then update our model accordingly. As such, unlike static interestingness models, our approach does not return patterns that are redundant with regard to what we have learned, and keeps the result set succinct yet informative.

Experiments show that we discover succinct summaries, which correctly identify important patterns in the data. The resulting models attain high log-likelihoods, and are easy to interpret.

Acknowledgements

Michael Mampaey is supported by the Institute for the Promotion of Innovation through Science and Technology in Flanders (IWT-Vlaanderen), Nikolaj Tatti and Jilles Vreeken are supported by Post-Doctoral Fellowships of the Research Foundation—Flanders (FWO).

10. REFERENCES

[1] C. C. Aggarwal and P. S. Yu. A new framework for itemset generation. In *Proc. PODS'98*, pages 18–24, 1998.

[2] S. Brin, R. Motwani, and C. Silverstein. Beyond market baskets: Generalizing association rules to correlations. In *Proc. ACM SIGMOD'97*, pages 265–276, 1997.

[3] T. Calders and B. Goethals. Non-derivable itemset mining. *Data Min. Knowl. Disc.*, 14(1):171–206, 2007.

[4] I. Csiszár. I-divergence geometry of probability distributions and minimization problems. *The Annals of Probability*, 3(1):146–158, Feb. 1975.

[5] J. Darroch and D. Ratcliff. Generalized iterative scaling for log-linear models. *The Annals of Mathematical Statistics*, 43(5):1470–1480, 1972.

[6] A. Frank and A. Asuncion. UCI machine learning repository. http://archive.ics.uci.edu/ml, 2010.

[7] A. Gallo, N. Cristianini, and T. De Bie. MINI: Mining informative non-redundant itemsets. In *Proc. PKDD'07*, pages 438–445, 2007.

[8] G. C. Garriga, E. Junttila, and H. Mannila. Banded structure in binary matrices. In *Proc. ACM SIGKDD'08*, pages 292–300, 2008.

[9] F. Geerts, B. Goethals, and T. Mielikäinen. Tiling databases. In *Proc. DS'04*, pages 278–289, 2004.

[10] A. Gionis, H. Mannila, T. Mielikäinen, and P. Tsaparas. Assessing data mining results via swap randomization. *Trans. Knowl. Disc. Data*, 1(3), 2007.

[11] B. Goethals and M. Zaki. Frequent itemset mining dataset repository. http://fimi.ua.ac.be/.

[12] P. D. Grünwald. *The Minimum Description Length Principle*. MIT Press, 2007.

[13] S. Hanhijärvi, M. Ojala, N. Vuokko, K. Puolamäki, N. Tatti, and H. Mannila. Tell me something I don't know: randomization strategies for iterative data mining. In *Proc. ACM SIGKDD'09*, pages 379–388, 2009.

[14] S. Jaroszewicz and D. A. Simovici. Interestingness of frequent itemsets using bayesian networks as background knowledge. In *Proc. ACM SIGKDD'04*, pages 178–186, 2004.

[15] K.-N. Kontonasios and T. De Bie. An information-theoretic approach to finding noisy tiles in binary databases. In *Proc. SDM'10*, pages 153–164, 2010.

[16] M. Mampaey and J. Vreeken. Summarising data by clustering items. In *Proc. ECML PKDD'10*, pages 321–336, 2010.

[17] A. Mitchell-Jones, G. Amori, W. Bogdanowicz, B. Krystufek, P. H. Reijnders, F. Spitzenberger, M. Stubbe, J. Thissen, V. Vohralik, and J. Zima. *The Atlas of European Mammals*. Academic Press, 1999.

[18] T. Mitchell-Jones. Societas europaea mammalogica. http://www.european-mammals.org.

[19] S. Myllykangas, J. Himberg, T. Böhling, B. Nagy, J. Hollmén, and S. Knuutila. DNA copy number amplification profiling of human neoplasms. *Oncogene*, 25(55):7324–7332, 2006.

[20] S. Nijssen, T. Guns, and L. De Raedt. Correlated itemset mining in ROC space: a constraint programming approach. In *Proc. ACM SIGKDD'09*, pages 647–656, 2009.

[21] N. Pasquier, Y. Bastide, R. Taouil, and L. Lakhal. Discovering frequent closed itemsets for association rules. In *Proc. ICDT'99*, pages 398–416, 1999.

[22] G. Schwarz. Estimating the dimension of a model. *Annals of Statistics*, 6(2):461–464, 1978.

[23] A. Siebes, J. Vreeken, and M. van Leeuwen. Item sets that compress. In *Proc. SDM'06*, pages 393–404, 2006.

[24] P. Tan, V. Kumar, and J. Srivastava. Selecting the right interestingness measure for association patterns. In *Proc. ACM SIGKDD'02*, pages 32–41. ACM, 2002.

[25] N. Tatti. Computational complexity of queries based on itemsets. *Inf. Proc. Letters*, pages 183–187, 2006.

[26] N. Tatti. Maximum entropy based significance of itemsets. *Knowl. Inf. Sys.*, 17(1):57–77, 2008.

[27] N. Tatti. Probably the best itemsets. In *Proc. ACM SIGKDD'10*, pages 293–302. ACM, 2010.

[28] N. Tatti and H. Heikinheimo. Decomposable families of itemsets. In *Proc. ECMLPKDD'08*, pages 472–487, 2008.

[29] N. Tatti and M. Mampaey. Using background knowledge to rank itemsets. *Data Min. Knowl. Disc.*, 21(2):293–309, 2010.

[30] C. Wang and S. Parthasarathy. Summarizing itemset patterns using probabilistic models. In *Proc. ACM SIGKDD'06*, pages 730–735, 2006.

[31] G. I. Webb. Self-sufficient itemsets: An approach to screening potentially interesting associations between items. *Trans. Knowl. Disc. Data*, 4(1), 2010.

[32] X. Yan, H. Cheng, J. Han, and D. Xin. Summarizing itemset patterns: a profile-based approach. In *Proc. ACM SIGKDD'05*, pages 314–323, 2005.

[33] M. J. Zaki and N. Ramakrishnan. Reasoning about sets using redescription mining. In *Proc. ACM SIGKDD'05*, pages 364–373, New York, NY, USA, 2005. ACM Press.

Direct Local Pattern Sampling by Efficient Two-Step Random Procedures

Mario Boley
Fraunhofer IAIS and
University of Bonn
mario.boley@iais.fhg.de

Claudio Lucchese
I.S.T.I.-C.N.R. Pisa
claudio.lucchese@isti.cnr.it

Daniel Paurat
University of Bonn
daniel.paurat@uni-bonn.de

Thomas Gärtner
Fraunhofer IAIS and
University of Bonn
thomas.gaertner@iais.fhg.de

ABSTRACT

We present several exact and highly scalable local pattern sampling algorithms. They can be used as an alternative to exhaustive local pattern discovery methods (e.g, frequent set mining or optimistic-estimator-based subgroup discovery) and can substantially improve efficiency as well as controllability of pattern discovery processes. While previous sampling approaches mainly rely on the Markov chain Monte Carlo method, our procedures are direct, i.e., non process-simulating, sampling algorithms. The advantages of these direct methods are an almost optimal time complexity per pattern as well as an exactly controlled distribution of the produced patterns. Namely, the proposed algorithms can sample (item-)sets according to frequency, area, squared frequency, and a class discriminativity measure. Experiments demonstrate that these procedures can improve the accuracy of pattern-based models similar to frequent sets and often also lead to substantial gains in terms of scalability.

Categories and Subject Descriptors: H.2.8 [Database Management]: Database Applications—*Data Mining*

General Terms: Algorithms, Theory

Keywords: Local pattern discovery, Sampling, Pattern-based classification, Frequent sets

1. INTRODUCTION

This paper presents simple yet effective procedures for local pattern discovery [20] that attack the task from a different algorithmic angle than the standard search approach—namely, by directly generating individual patterns as the outcome of a random experiment. Local patterns such as association rules [1] or emerging patterns [12] are used in various application contexts from exploratory data analysis where they constitute units of discovered knowledge to predictive model construction where patterns act as binary features [9, 10, 13]. What all applications have in common is that usually only a few patterns can be effectively utilized—either due to the limited attention of a data analyst or because too many features can reduce the comprehensibility and performance of a global model. Standard local pattern discovery algorithms, however, are based on exhaustive search within huge pattern spaces (e.g., frequent set miners [19, 26], or optimistic-estimator-based subgroup and association discovery [17, 23]). Consequently, they tend to either produce a vast amount of output patterns or at least enumerate them internally.

This motivates the invention of algorithms that only sample a representative set of patterns without explicitly searching in the pattern space. Such algorithms exist in the literature [2, 6, 8] but they provide either no control over the distribution of their output or only asymptotic control by simulating a stochastic process on the pattern space using the Markov chain Monte Carlo method (MCMC). In addition to only offering approximate sampling, MCMC methods have a scalability problem: the number of required process simulation steps is often large and, even more critical, individual simulation steps typically involve expensive support counting operations. Hence, these algorithms are often infeasible for large input datasets. Therefore, we present novel pattern generation methods that sample patterns exactly and directly, i.e., without simulating time-consuming stochastic processes. More precisely, given a dataset $\mathcal{D}$ and a number of desired patterns k, the procedures

- produce exactly k patterns each of which is generated exactly according to a distribution proportional to either frequency, squared frequency, area (i.e., frequency times size), or discriminativity (i.e., frequency in positive data portion times negative frequency in negative data portion);
- use time $O(\|\mathcal{D}\| + kn)$ for frequency and area or time $O(\|\mathcal{D}\|^2 + kn)$ for squared frequency and discriminativity, where n denotes the number of items and $\|\mathcal{D}\|$ the size of the dataset, i.e., the sum of all data record sizes[1].

That is, after a linear or quadratic preprocessing phase each pattern is produced in a time linear in the number of items.

[1]This assumes that $\exp(n) > |\mathcal{D}|$; the actual complexities are $O(\|\mathcal{D}\| + k(n + \ln |\mathcal{D}|))$ and $O(\|\mathcal{D}\|^2 + k(n + \ln^2 |\mathcal{D}|))$.

This time complexity appears to be almost optimal, because only reading the data once requires $O(\|\mathcal{D}\|)$ and just printing k patterns without any further computation requires time $O(kn)$.

After giving some more background on the idea of controlled repeated pattern sampling and reviewing other pattern sampling algorithms, the remainder of this paper is structured as follows. We define formal and notational background (Sec. 2) followed by a detailed description of the sampling procedures (Sec 3). Then we report experimental results showing that sampled patterns are equally useful for pattern-based classification as frequent sets and that pattern sampling can easily outperform exhaustive listing on large datasets (Sec. 4). Finally, we give a summarizing discussion of all results (Sec. 5).

1.1 Pattern Sampling

The data mining literature contains several local pattern discovery algorithms that can efficiently produce large output families. Here, efficiency is defined in an output-sensitive way (see, e.g., [16]), that is for instance amortized polynomial time per pattern, which is a useful notion assuming that the produced pattern collections are the final output. When viewed from a global (application-driven) perspective though, the enumerated patterns are usually only an intermediate result, from which a final—often much smaller—pattern collection is selected. That is, enumeration is only one step within a surrounding local pattern discovery process. This two phase approach, which we refer to as "exhaustive search" is illustrated in Figure 1(a): during the enumeration step part of the implicitly defined pattern space is physically constructed—we refer to that part as "enumeration space"—and then, during the selection step, the most valuable patterns from this enumeration space are collected with respect to some interestingness measure.

An example for this paradigm is listing frequent sets of an input dataset, but subsequently using only those sets that provide rules with a large value of some measure that reflects the primary user interest (e.g., lift). A further example is optimistic-estimator-based pruning for subgroup or association discovery. There the enumeration space is the family of all sets having a large enough optimistic estimate of their interestingness, and the patterns that are selected for the result family are those with a large value of the actual interestingness measure. Note that, in this example, enumeration and selection are algorithmically interweaved, i.e., sets are already selected during the enumeration phase. Many more examples emerge from the LeGo approach to data mining [22] where patterns are selected according to their utility for constructing global models.

Two reasons usually motivate this two phase approach: either there is no efficient algorithm that directly optimizes the measure of primary interest or this measure is not known in advance (this happens in exploratory settings where interestingness can be user-specific). In either case, the enumeration step can constitute a severe bottleneck. Even if enumeration is performed by an amortized polynomial time algorithm, its computation time is essentially unpredictable: the size of the enumeration space cannot be directly controlled and its explicit construction takes time at least proportional to that size. On the other hand, if one enforces a maximum computation time by aborting the execution at a certain point, one ends up with an uncontrolled subset of the enumeration space, which depends on the internal search order of the enumeration algorithm.

In contrast, suppose we can access the pattern space $\mathcal{L}$ by an efficient sampling procedure simulating a distribution $\pi : \mathcal{L} \to [0, 1]$ that is defined proportional to some function that either is our primary interestingness measure or a function that correlates with it. Then, for any designated number of patterns (or corresponding designated computation time) it is possible to efficiently generate a collection of exactly that many patterns that is representative of the distribution π. Consequently, since π has a semantic connection to the underlying notion of interestingness, a meaningful allocation of computational resources is guaranteed for any limited time budget.

Figure 1(b) illustrates this alternative approach, which we want to refer to as "controlled repeated pattern sampling". A potentially positive side-effect of this paradigm is that instead of the usual hard constraints it utilizes parameter-free soft constraints [5]. Hence, the user is freed of the often troublesome task of finding appropriate hard threshold parameters such as a minimum frequency threshold.

1.2 Related Work

In contrast to sampling from the input database (see, e.g., [25, 28]), it is a relatively new development in local pattern discovery to sample from the pattern space. In the context of maximal frequent subgraph mining, Chaoji et al. [8] describes a random process that stops after a certain number of steps that is bounded by the maximum number of edges present in an input graph and produces a maximal frequent subgraph. A similar process is already applied in Gunopoulos et al. [18] within a Las Vegas variant of the Dualize and Advance algorithm. More precisely, it is used for the internal randomization of an algorithm with an otherwise deterministic output (all maximal frequent and minimal infrequent sets of a given input database). When applied for the final pattern discovery, however, this random process has the weakness that it provides no control over the generation probabilities of individual patterns.

Several papers propose to overcome this weakness by applying the MCMC method. Boley and Grosskreutz [7] proposes frequent set sampling to approximate the effect of specific minimum frequency thresholds. The proposed algorithm simulates a simple Glauber dynamic on the frequent set lattice: starting with the empty set, in each subsequent time step a single item is either removed or added to the current set. A similar MCMC method is used in Zaki and Al Hasan [2] for generating a representative set of graph patterns. These MCMC methods provide limited control of the generation probabilities, namely of the infinite limit of the state distribution. The worst-case convergence can, however, be exponentially slow in the size of the input database. For sampling from the family of frequent patterns, this problem appears to be inherent: almost uniform frequent pattern sampling can be used for approximate frequent pattern counting, which one can show to be intractable under reasonable complexity assumptions (see [7]). Similar conclusions can be drawn for enumeration spaces defined by linearly scaled versions of the frequency measure such as the standard optimistic estimator for the binomial test quality function in subgroup discovery [27].

In order to avoid this implication of hard-constraint-based pattern discovery (e.g., using a hard frequency threshold),

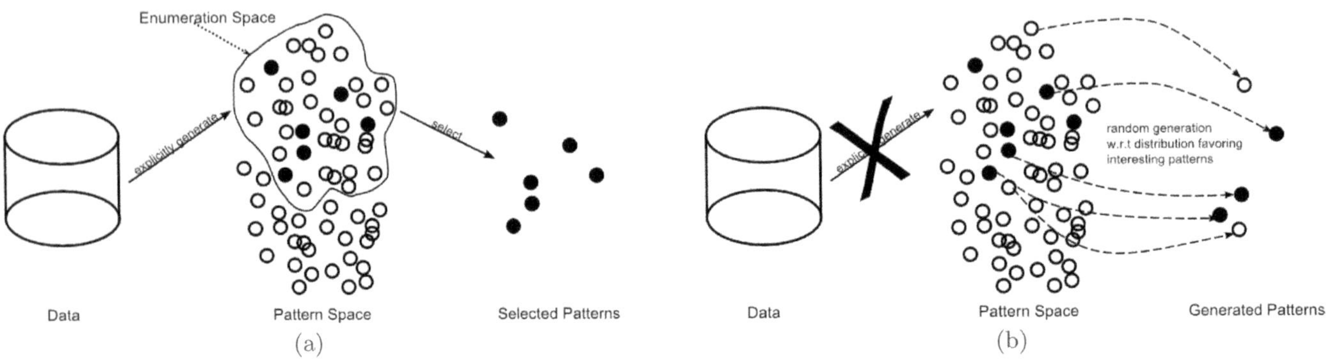

Figure 1: (a) *Exhaustive search*: involves complete generation of an enumeration space guaranteed to contain all interesting patterns; however, size of that space usually has no reasonable bound w.r.t. to input size and is hard to predict. (b) *Controlled pattern sampling*: no explicit construction of uncontrolled, potentially huge, part of pattern space; instead random generation of designated number of patterns; no guarantee of finding patterns satisfying hard interestingness threshold, but control over time, output size, and distribution.

Boley et al. [6] combines pattern space sampling with soft-constraint-based pattern discovery [5]—resulting in the pattern sampling paradigm described in Section 1.1 above. Still, the underlying method is again MCMC-based, and, despite using a more sophisticated chain defined on the closed set lattice of the input database, it shares the practical weaknesses of this technique. The present paper retains the idea of controlled pattern sampling without hard constraints, but proposes novel pattern generation methods that are exact and direct, i.e., they do not involve MCMC process simulation. Consequently, the resulting pattern discovery processes are efficient not only theoretically but also on a wide range of real-world benchmark datasets.

2. PRELIMINARIES

Before going into technical details, we introduce some basic notions and notation. For a finite set X we denote by $\mathcal{P}(X)$ its power set and by $u(X)$ the uniform probability distribution on X. Moreover, for positive weights $w : X \to \mathbb{R}^+$ let $w(X)$ denote the distribution on X arising from normalizing w, i.e., the distribution described by $x \mapsto w(x)/\sum_{x' \in X} w(x)$—assuming that there is an $x \in X$ with $w(x) > 0$.

A binary **dataset** $\mathcal{D}$ over some finite **ground set** E is a bag (multiset) of sets, called **data records**, $D_1, \ldots, D_m$ each of which is a subset of $E = \{e, \ldots, e_n\}$. The **size** of $\mathcal{D}$, denoted by $\|\mathcal{D}\|$, is defined as the sum of all its data record sizes $\sum_{D \in \mathcal{D}} = |D|$. Inspired by the application of market basket analysis the elements of E are often referred to as "items". More generally, one can think of E as a set of binary features describing the data records. In particular, a categorical data table can easily be represented as a binary dataset by choosing the ground set as consisting of all attribute/value equality expressions that can be formed from the table. More precisely, a **categorical data table** T consisting of m data row vectors $d_1, \ldots, d_m$ with $d_i = (d_i(1), \ldots, d_i(n))$ can be represented by the dataset $\mathcal{D}_T = \{D_1, \ldots, D_m\}$ with $D_i = \{(j, v) : d_i(j) = v\}$ over ground set

$$E_T = \{(j, d_i(j)) \colon 1 \leq i \leq m, 1 \leq j \leq n\} \ .$$

For a given dataset $\mathcal{D}$ over E, the **pattern space** (or pattern *language*) $\mathcal{L}(\mathcal{D})$ considered in this paper is the power set $\mathcal{P}(E)$ of the features and its elements are interpreted conjunctively. That is, the *local* data portion described by a set $F \subseteq E$, called the **support (set)** of F in $\mathcal{D}$ and denoted $\mathcal{D}[F]$, is defined as the multiset of all data records from $\mathcal{D}$ that contain *all* elements of F, i.e., $\mathcal{D}[F] = \{D \in \mathcal{D} \colon D \supseteq F\}$.

An **interestingness measure** for a pattern language $\mathcal{L}(\cdot)$ is a function

$$q \colon \{(\mathcal{D}, x) \colon \mathcal{D} \text{ a binary dataset}, x \in \mathcal{L}(\mathcal{D})\} \to \mathbb{R} \ .$$

However, often there is a fixed dataset that is clear from the context. In such cases—and if we want to simplify the notation—we just write q as a unary function $q(\cdot) = q(\mathcal{D}, \cdot)$ and omit the first argument. The most basic measures for set patterns are the **support (count)**, i.e., the size of its support set $q_{\text{supp}}(\mathcal{D}, F) = |\mathcal{D}[F]|$ and the **frequency**, i.e., the relative size of its support with respect to the total number of data records $q_{\text{freq}}(\mathcal{D}, F) = |\mathcal{D}[F]| / |\mathcal{D}|$. For a frequency threshold $t \in [0, 1]$ a set is called **t-frequent** (w.r.t. $\mathcal{D}$) if $q_{\text{freq}}(\mathcal{D}, F) \geq t$. A further measure considered here is the **area function** [15] $q_{\text{area}}(\mathcal{D}, F) = |F| \, |\mathcal{D}[F]|$. Intuitively, the area of a set corresponds to the number of 1 entries of the submatrix (of the binary matrix representation of $\mathcal{D}$) consisting of the columns corresponding to F and the rows corresponding to $\mathcal{D}[F]$.

All measures defined so far are unsupervised measures in the sense that they rely on no further information but the dataset itself. In contrast, there are so-called supervised descriptive rule induction techniques that rely on additional information in the form of **class labels** $l(D) \in C = \{c_1, \ldots, c_k\}$ associated to each data record $D \in \mathcal{D}$. For $c \in C$ we denote by $\mathcal{D}_c$ the data portion labeled c, i.e., $\mathcal{D}_c = \{D \in \mathcal{D} \colon l(D) = c\}$. Examples for this setting are emerging pattern mining [12] and contrast set mining [3], where one is interested in patterns having a high support difference between the positive and the negative portion of the data records, or subgroup discovery [27], where one searches for patterns with a high distributional unusualness of these labels on their support set. An important special case is the case of binary labels, i.e., $C = \{\oplus, \ominus\}$. For this case we consider the following **discriminativity measure**

$$q_{\text{disc}}(F) = |\mathcal{D}_{\oplus}[F]|\,|\mathcal{D}_{\ominus} \setminus \mathcal{D}_{\ominus}[F]| \ .$$

A further measure for the discriminative power of a pattern is the **Fisher score** q_{fish}, which is defined for datasets with arbitrary labels C. Intuitively, it measures the relation of the inter-class variance of a feature to its intra-class variances, i.e.,

$$q_{\text{fish}}(F) = \frac{\sum_{c \in C} |\mathcal{D}_c| \left(q_{\text{freq}}(\mathcal{D}_c, F) - q_{\text{freq}}(\mathcal{D}, F)\right)^2}{\sum_{c \in C} \sum_{D \in \mathcal{D}_c} (\delta(D \supseteq F) - q_{\text{freq}}(\mathcal{D}_c, F))^2}$$

where $\delta(D \supseteq F)$ is 1 if $D \supseteq F$ and 0 otherwise. This paper does not present a sampling algorithm for this measure. However, the Fisher score is used for post-processing generated patterns in the context of constructing global classification models.

3. SAMPLING ALGORITHMS

After the introduction of set patterns and interestingness measures, we can now present our sampling procedures. A naive approach for sampling a pattern according to a distribution π is to generate a list $F_1, \ldots, F_N$ of all patterns with $\pi(F) > 0$, draw an $x \in [0,1]$ uniformly at random, and then return the unique set F_k with $\sum_{i=1}^{k-1} \pi(F_i) \leq x < \sum_{i=1}^{k} \pi(F_i)$. However, the exhaustive enumeration of any non-constant part of the pattern space is precisely what we want to avoid. That is, we are interested in *non-enumerative* sampling algorithms.

Below we give such algorithms for four quality functions: frequency and squared frequency as well as area and discriminativity. The algorithms are inspired by the elementary procedures used in Karp et al. [21] (for estimating the number of satisfying assignments of a DNF formula): in a first step one element of a suitably constructed set of base objects is drawn, and in a second step a sub-object is drawn that is induced by that base object; hence the term "two-step random procedures".

Note that, in contrast to the frequency measures, for the latter two quality functions it is **NP**-hard to find optimal patterns: Finding a set of maximum area for a given input dataset is equivalent to the **NP**-hard problem of computing a biclique with maximum number of edges from a given bipartite graph (see [15]). The same hardness result holds for the discriminativity measure because optimizing area can be linearly reduced to optimizing discriminativity: by setting $\mathcal{D}_{\oplus}$ to $\mathcal{D}$ and $\mathcal{D}_{\ominus}$ to $\{E \setminus \{e\} \colon e \in E\}$ we get

$$q_{\text{disc}}(\mathcal{D}_{\oplus} \cup \mathcal{D}_{\ominus}, F) = |\mathcal{D}[F]|\,(|E| - |E| + |F|) = q_{\text{area}}(\mathcal{D}, F)$$

for all $F \subseteq E$ because with this construction of the negative data portion we have $|\mathcal{D}_{\ominus}[F]| = |E| - |F|$.

3.1 Frequency and Area

Algorithm 1 Frequency-based Sampling

Require: dataset $\mathcal{D}$ over ground set E,
Returns: random set $R \sim q_{\text{freq}}(\mathcal{P}(E)) = q_{\text{supp}}(\mathcal{P}(E))$

1. **let** weights w be defined by $w(D) = 2^{|D|}$ for all $D \in \mathcal{D}$
2. **draw** $D \sim w(\mathcal{D})$
3. **return** $R \sim u(\mathcal{P}(D))$

We start with sampling according to frequency and area, both of which can be achieved by very similar linear time algorithms. The key insight for frequency-based sampling, i.e., $\pi = q_{\text{freq}}(\mathcal{P}(E))$, is that random experiments are good in reproducing frequent events. Namely, if we look at a pattern that is supported by a random data record we are likely to observe a pattern that is supported by many data records altogether. This intuition leads to a two-step non-enumerative sampling routine (see Algorithm 1), which is as fast as it is simple: First select a data record of the input dataset randomly with a probability proportional to the size of its power set. Then return a uniformly sampled subset of that data record. Using the size of the power set in the first step is important, as otherwise the sampling routine would be biased towards sets occurring in small data records. As noted in Proposition 1 below, the random set resulting from combining both steps follows the desired distribution.

Regarding the computational complexity of the sampling algorithm we can observe that it is indeed efficient: if one has knowledge of the numbers $|D|$ for all data records $D \in \mathcal{D}$ and, moreover, has index access to all data records, a single random set can be produced in time $O(\log |\mathcal{D}| + |E|)$ (the two terms correspond to producing a random number for drawing a data record in step 1 and to drawing one of its subsets in step 2, respectively). Both requirements can be achieved via a single initial pass over the dataset. Thus, we have the following proposition.

PROPOSITION 1. *On input dataset $\mathcal{D}$ over E, a family of k realizations of the random set $\boldsymbol{R} \sim q_{\text{freq}}(\mathcal{P}(E))$ can be generated in time $O(\|\mathcal{D}\| + k(|E| + \ln |\mathcal{D}|))$.*

PROOF. Let Z be the normalizing constant $\sum_{F \subseteq E} |\mathcal{D}[F]|$ and $\mathbf{D}$ denote the random data record that is drawn in step 2 of the algorithm. For the probability distribution of the returned random set we have

$$\begin{aligned}\mathbb{P}[\mathbf{R} = R] &= \sum_{D \in \mathcal{D}} \mathbb{P}[\mathbf{R} = R \wedge \mathbf{D} = D] \\ &= \sum_{D \in \mathcal{D}[R]} \frac{1}{2^{|D|}} \frac{2^{|D|}}{Z} \\ &= \frac{|\mathcal{D}[R]|}{Z} = \frac{q_{\text{supp}}(\mathcal{D}, R)}{Z}\end{aligned}$$

with a normalizing $Z = \sum_{D \in \mathcal{D}} 2^{|D|}$ (which is equal to the desired $\sum_{F \subseteq E} |\mathcal{D}[F]|$). □

Algorithm 2 Area-based Sampling

Require: dataset $\mathcal{D}$ over ground set E with $\|\mathcal{D}\| > 0$,
Returns: random set $R \sim q_{\text{area}}(\mathcal{P}(E))$

1. **let** weights w be defined for all $D \in \mathcal{D}$ by
$$w(D) = |D|\, 2^{|D|-1}$$
2. **draw** $D \sim w(\mathcal{D})$
3. **return** $R \sim s(\mathcal{P}(D))$ with $s(F) = |F|$

Sampling according to area, i.e., $\pi = q_{\text{area}}(\mathcal{P}(E))$, can be achieved via a slight modification of frequency-based sampling: in step two, instead of drawing a subset uniformly from a data record, draw a subset with probability proportional to its size. The latter step can be implemented, e.g., by first drawing a size s with probability proportional to $\binom{|D|}{s}$ and then by uniformly drawing from D a subset of size s. As a side effect, this modification affects the normalization constants and in particular the data record weights of step one. Since for the sum of all subset sizes of a data record D we have

$$\sum_{F \subseteq D} |F| = |D| \, 2^{|D|-1} \ ,$$

the data record weights need to be modified accordingly. The resulting pseudo-code is given in Algorithm 2. Again, after all weights have been computed via an initial pass over the data, an arbitrary number of random sets can be produced in time $O(\log |\mathcal{D}| + |E|)$. Hence, with a similar proof as for Proposition 1 we can conclude:

PROPOSITION 2. *On input dataset $\mathcal{D}$ over E, a family of k realizations of the random set $\mathbf{R} \sim q_{\text{area}}(\mathcal{P}(E))$ can be generated in time $O(\|\mathcal{D}\| + k(|E| + \ln |\mathcal{D}|))$.*

It is important to note that area can be replaced by *weighted* area relatively easy without changing the asymptotic complexity—where weighted area is defined as

$$q_{\text{ware}}(F) = \left(\sum_{e \in F} w(e) \right) \left(\sum_{D \in \mathcal{D}[F]} w(D) \right)$$

for a set of positive weights $w \colon (E \cup \mathcal{D}) \to \mathbb{R}_+$. The same holds for weighted frequency. In this paper, however, for the sake of simplicity we only consider the unweighted case.

3.2 Discriminativity and Squared Frequency

Algorithm 3 Discriminativity-based Sampling

Require: binary labeled dataset $\mathcal{D}$ over ground set E such that there is an $F \subseteq E$ with $q_{\text{disc}}(F) > 0$
Returns: random set $R \sim q_{\text{disc}}(\mathcal{P}(E))$

1. **let** weights w be defined by
$$w(D_\oplus, D_\ominus) = (2^{|D_\oplus \setminus D_\ominus|} - 1) 2^{|D_\oplus \cap D_\ominus|}$$
for all $(D_\oplus, D_\ominus) \in \mathcal{D}_\oplus \times \mathcal{D}_\ominus$
2. **draw** $(D_\oplus, D_\ominus) \sim w(\mathcal{D}_\oplus \times \mathcal{D}_\ominus)$
3. **return** $R = (F \cup F')$ with
$$F \sim u(\mathcal{P}(D_\oplus \setminus D_\ominus) \setminus \emptyset) \text{ and } F' \sim u(\mathcal{P}(D_\oplus \cap D_\ominus))$$

In order to design a sampling procedure for discriminativity, i.e., $\pi = q_{\text{disc}}(\mathcal{P}(E))$, we can lift the principle of frequency-based sampling to a random experiment that is a little more complicated and has the following intuition: if we look at a pattern that is supported by a random positive data record and *not* supported by a random negative data record, we are likely to observe a pattern that is altogether supported by many positive data records and only few negative data records, i.e., we are likely to observe a pattern with a relatively high discriminativity score. Again, in order to control the resulting distribution, it is necessary to consider a pair of data records $(D_\oplus, D_\ominus)$ with a probability equal to the number of sets $F \subseteq E$ with $F \subseteq D_\oplus$ and $F \not\subseteq D_\ominus$. This implies that the increased expressivity of discriminativity compared to frequency comes at a price: due to the necessity of weight computation for all pairs of positive and negative data records, we end up with a quadratic preprocessing phase. Algorithm 3 contains all the details of the resulting sampling procedure and leads to the following result.

PROPOSITION 3. *Let $\mathcal{D}$ be a binary labeled input dataset over ground set E such that there is a set $F \subseteq E$ with $q_{\text{disc}}(\mathcal{D}, F) > 0$. A family of k realizations of the random set $\mathbf{R} \sim q_{\text{disc}}(\mathcal{P}(E))$ can be generated in time $O(\|\mathcal{D}\|^2 + k(|E| + \ln^2 |\mathcal{D}|))$.*

PROOF. Let $\mathbf{R}$ denote the random set returned in step 3 of the algorithm and $\mathbf{D}_\oplus$, $\mathbf{D}_\ominus$ the data records drawn in step 2. Moreover, for $D \in \mathcal{D}_\oplus$ and $D' \in \mathcal{D}_\ominus$ let $\delta(D, D')$ denote the family of all sets $F \subseteq E$ that are supported by D but not supported by D'. We can rewrite this definition as

$$\begin{aligned} &\delta(D, D') \\ =&\{F \subseteq E \colon F \subseteq D, F \not\subseteq D'\} \\ =&\{F \cup F' : \emptyset \subset F \subseteq (D \setminus D'), F' \subseteq (D \cap D')\} \ . \end{aligned}$$

This form shows that the weights $w(\cdot, \cdot)$ assigned in step 1 are equivalent to $|\delta(\cdot, \cdot)|$ and, moreover, that $\mathbf{R}$ is a set drawn uniformly from $\delta(\mathbf{D}_\oplus, \mathbf{D}_\ominus)$. With this we can conclude similar to the previous algorithms that

$$\begin{aligned} \mathbb{P}[\mathbf{R} = F] &= \sum_{D \in \mathcal{D}_\oplus} \sum_{D' \in \mathcal{D}_\ominus} \mathbb{P}[\mathbf{R} = F, \mathbf{D}_\oplus = D, \mathbf{D}_\ominus = D'] \\ &= \sum_{D, D' \in \delta^{-1}[F]} \frac{1}{|\delta(D, D')|} \frac{w(D, D')}{Z} \\ &= \frac{1}{Z} \left| \{(D, D') \in \mathcal{D}_\oplus \times \mathcal{D}_\ominus \colon D \supseteq F, D' \not\supseteq F\} \right| \\ &= \frac{1}{Z} |\mathcal{D}_\oplus[F]| \left(|\mathcal{D}_\ominus| - \mathcal{D}_\ominus[F] \right) \end{aligned}$$

with $Z = \sum_{D, D' \in \mathcal{D}_\oplus \times \mathcal{D}_\ominus} |\delta(D, D')| = \sum_{F \subseteq E} q_{\text{disc}}(F)$ as required. □

Algorithm 4 Squared-frequency-based Sampling

Require: dataset $\mathcal{D}$ over ground set E,
Returns: random set $F \sim q^2_{\text{freq}}(\mathcal{P}(E)) = q^2_{\text{supp}}(\mathcal{P}(E))$

1. **let** weights w be defined by
$$w(D_1, D_2) = 2^{|D_1 \cap D_2|}$$
for all $(D_1, D_2) \in \mathcal{D} \times \mathcal{D}$
2. **draw** $(D_1, D_2) \sim w(\mathcal{D} \times \mathcal{D})$
3. **return** $F \sim u(\mathcal{P}(D_1 \cap D_2))$

It is straightforward to see that the approach of drawing two data records can also be used to implement other potentially interesting distributions that can be expressed as the product of two support counts. A basic example is squared frequency. In order to achieve this distribution, one can consider a uniformly[2] drawn subset of two random data records, i.e., a subset of their intersection. The resulting pseudo-code

[2]For sampling according to the squared area function, draw a subset with probabilities proportional to its squared size instead of uniformly.

with appropriate pairwise weights is given in Algorithm 4. Closely following the proof of Proposition 3 this algorithm can be used to show another proposition.

PROPOSITION 4. *On input dataset $\mathcal{D}$ over E, a family of k realizations of the random set $\boldsymbol{R} \sim q^2_{\text{freq}}(\mathcal{P}(E))$ can be generated in time $O(\|\mathcal{D}\|^2 + k(|E| + \ln^2|\mathcal{D}|))$.*

In principle, one can design sampling algorithms for an abitrary power c of the frequency measure by drawing a subset from c random data records. However, the resulting time complexity for computing the weights for each c-tuple of data records gets out of hand quickly.

4. EVALUATION

The sampling procedures presented in the previous section are provably efficient and correct, i.e., their randomized output follows the specified distributions. Beside their practical scalability, it remains to be evaluated how useful these distributions are in the context of local pattern discovery. It is inherently difficult to evaluate pattern discovery methods for exploratory data analysis. There one aims to find *interesting* patterns based on notions of interestingness that are often user-subjective. Hence, a sophisticated experimental design would be required. Here we resort to the other branch of local pattern discovery applications, i.e., pattern-based global model construction, which allows us to simply use Fisher score as primary interestingness measure and accuracy as objective evaluation metric for the overall process.

dataset	class	nm/ct	items	rows	density
autos	7	15/10	135	205	0.190
balance-scale	3	4/0	20	625	0.250
breast-cancer	2	0/9	51	286	0.195
colic	3	7/15	84	366	0.271
credit-a	2	6/9	71	690	0.223
diabetes	2	8/0	40	768	0.225
glass	7	9/0	45	214	0.222
heart-c	5	6/7	49	303	0.285
heart-h	5	6/7	46	294	0.246
heart-statlog	2	13/0	55	270	0.254
hepatitis	2	6/13	55	155	0.344
hypothyroid	4	7/22	78	3772	0.364
iris	3	4/0	20	150	0.250
lymph	4	3/15	57	148	0.333
prim.-tumor	22	0/17	37	339	0.468
sonar	2	60/0	300	208	0.203
tic-tac-toe	2	0/9	27	958	0.370
vehicle	4	18/0	90	846	0.211
zoo	7	1/16	135	101	0.133

Table 1: Benchmark datasets with basic statistics: number of *classes* $|C|$, number of numerical and categorical columns (*nm/ct*), number $|E_T|$ of *items* in corresponding binary dataset, number of *rows*, *density* $|\mathcal{D}_T|\,|E_T|/\|\mathcal{D}_T\|$.

In our experiments we use a variety of databases from the UCI machine learning repository [14] listed in Table 1. In order to apply the pattern discovery algorithms, binary datasets are created from these databases by first converting them into categorical datatables using five bucket frequency discretization of all numeric data columns, and then by considering the corresponding binary datasets (using attribute / value pairs of categorical attributes as items; see Section 2).

Implementations of the sampling algorithms are available in the software section of `http://www-kd.iai.uni-bonn.de`.

4.1 Predictive Performance

We start with experiments evaluating the sampling algorithms in the context of pattern-based classification. Here one aims to improve classification accuracy by enriching given labeled training data with pattern-based features. We closely follow the framework of Cheng et al. [9]. In a nutshell it consists of three basic steps: extraction of a collection of patterns (which are subsequently considered as features of the data records supporting them), feature selection based on Fisher score and pattern redundancy, and classification, for which we use a linear support vector machine.

In more detail, for an input data table T with corresponding binary dataset $\mathcal{D}_T = \mathcal{D}$ and class labels $C = \{1, \ldots, c\}$ we consider **pattern collections** $\mathcal{C}$, $\mathcal{R}_{\text{frq}}$, $\mathcal{R}_{\text{sfr}}$, $\mathcal{R}_{\text{dcr}}$ that are based on deterministic top-k frequent closed sets (these can be efficiently produced, e.g., by the algorithm of Pietracaprina and Vandin [24]) and sampling according to frequency, squared frequency, and discriminativity, respectively. Area-based sampling is not considered here, because it is not designed to provide good features for classification. Each pattern collection $\mathcal{P}$ is the union of c collections $\mathcal{P}_i$ based on the class labels $i \in C$ where the size of $\mathcal{P}_i$ is proportional to the number of training examples of that class, i.e., $|\mathcal{P}_i| = \alpha\,|\mathcal{D}_i|$. Consequently, the size of the complete collection is $\alpha\,|\mathcal{D}|$, which is linear in the input size. The parameter α is set to 32 independently of the method and the dataset. This setting is a compromise between efficiency and stability of the pattern selection process (described below) as captured by the average Fisher score of finally selected features. See Figure 2 for an illustration on three exemplary datasets.

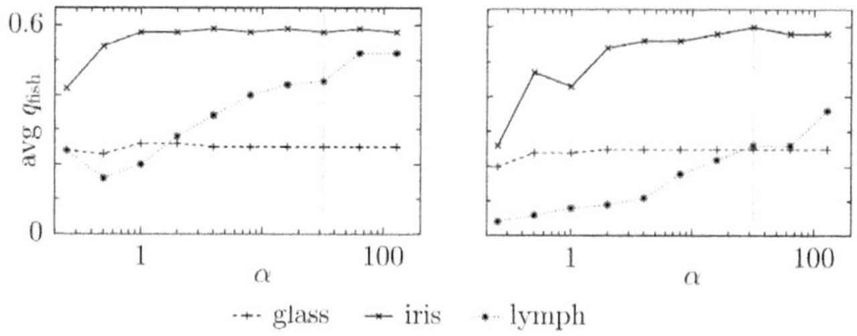

Figure 2: Average Fisher score of collections produced by methods for increasing values of α.

The **feature selection** step for a pattern collection $\mathcal{P}$ is then performed as follows: initialize $\mathcal{P}_0 = \emptyset$ and consider all sets $F_1, \ldots, F_l \in \mathcal{P}$ having $q_{\text{freq}}(\mathcal{D}, \cdot) \geq 0.05$ in descending order of their Fisher score $q_{\text{fish}}(\mathcal{D}, \cdot)$. Select a pattern F_i if the number of previously uncovered data records that it covers is at least 1% of the dataset, i.e.,

$$\left| \mathcal{D}[F_i] \setminus \bigcup_{F \in \mathcal{P}_{i-1}} \mathcal{D}[F] \right| \geq 0.01 \left| \mathcal{D} \right|$$

where $\mathcal{P}_{i-1}$ is the family of sets already selected when considering F_i. The selection process is stopped either after all patterns have been considered or if $\mathcal{P}_i$ covers the dataset completely, i.e., $\bigcup_{F \in \mathcal{P}_i} \mathcal{D}[F] = \mathcal{D}$. This is a very simple instantiation of the framework of Cheng et al. with the condition of 1% coverage improvement acting as binary redundancy measure. A further deviation is that in our case the remaining patterns are not reordered after each selection step. While the original procedure constructs potentially more powerful feature collections, this simplified version is much faster: the time complexity is only linear instead of quadratic in the number of input features. For the final pattern collection $\mathcal{P}'$ the original data table T is then augmented by binary attributes corresponding to the elements of $F_1, \ldots, F_k \in \mathcal{P}'$. That is, the augmented table T' has $n + |\mathcal{P}'|$ columns with rows defined by

$$t'_i(j) = \begin{cases} t_i(j), & \text{if } j \leq n \\ 1, & \text{if } j > n \text{ and } D_i \supseteq F_{j-n} \\ 0, & \text{otherwise} \end{cases}$$

where D_i is the data record of $\mathcal{D}_T$ corresponding the the i-th row of T.

dataset	plain	$\mathcal{C}$	q_{freq}	q^2_{freq}	q_{disc}
autos	76.31	75.79	75.26	74.74	75.79
balance-scale	85.09	85.09	85.09	85.09	85.09
breast-cancer	70.37	**71.48**	**72.59**	**72.22**	**72.96**
colic	65.71	**67.14**	**67.43**	**66.86**	**66.00**
credit-a	85.44	84.56	85.00	85.15	85.00
diabetis	74.40	**75.20**	73.87	73.87	73.87
glass	63.00	**64.00**	**65.50**	**68.00**	**68.50**
heart-c	81.73	79.66	**82.76**	**82.76**	**82.07**
heart-h	82.50	81.79	81.43	81.43	81.79
heart-statlog	81.16	80.39	**83.08**	**83.46**	**82.69**
hepatitis	80.71	80.71	80.71	**85.00**	79.29
hypothyroid	97.55	97.53	97.50	**97.63**	**97.58**
iris	89.29	88.57	**91.43**	**91.43**	**91.43**
lymph	83.08	**85.39**	**85.39**	**83.85**	**84.62**
primary-tumor	40.94	**44.38**	**45.94**	**47.50**	**47.81**
sonar	78.42	77.37	78.42	78.42	78.42
tic-tac-toe	76.28	**92.55**	**96.60**	**96.60**	**94.15**
vehicle	67.95	**70.48**	**69.64**	**69.64**	**70.24**
zoo	91.11	91.11	**93.33**	91.11	**92.22**

Table 2: Accuracy of SVM classification on plain database and with feature enrichment based on frequent sets and sampled pattern collections (bold face indicates outperformed baseline).

The linear SVM of the LIBSVM software is used as **classifier**—wrapped in an optimization layer for its regularization parameter c. That is, the training set is first used to determine the optimal regularization parameter $c \in \{2^i : i = -5, -3, \ldots, 14\}$ using 5-fold cross-validation and then a model is trained with the optimal parameter using the whole training set. The complete workflow is validated using 10-fold cross-validation for all pattern collections simultaneously.

Table 2 contains the **results**. As one can observe, for some of the datasets pattern-based classification provides a substantial accuracy boost compared to the plain SVM baseline ("tic-tac-toe", "primary-tumor", "glass"). For others there is still an improvement but to a lesser extend, or the results are roughly identical. Most importantly, the sampling methods perform stronger than exhaustive top-k mining on a majority of datasets. A Wilcoxon signed ranks test (see [11]) for our $N = 19$ databases reveals that pattern-based classification with each of the random set collections outperforms the plain SVM significantly at the 5%-level (t-values of 42, 28.5, and 45.5 respectively; critical value 46). Moreover, although all random set collections are lying ahead of the frequent set collection on our test databases, it is not significantly outperformed by any of them. We can conclude that pattern-based classification based on all tested sampling algorithms is likely to outperform the plain SVM, and is unlikely to be inferior to standard frequent-pattern-based classification.

4.2 Scalability and Effectivity

Having evaluated the quality of the sampled patterns we now turn to scalability and effectivity studies.[3] The theoretical potential of the direct sampling procedures is already indicated by the guarantees of Propositions 1-4. In particular for frequency and area-based sampling they suggest applicability on larger to large-scale datasets. Below we investigate to what degree this potential can be realized in practice.

The practical advantages of direct pattern sampling over the MCMC pattern sampling algorithms are very clear: while for instance the closed set Markov chain simulation [6] takes seven minutes to sample a closed set from a 30K row subset of the US census dataset, frequency-based direct sampling takes only 0.067 seconds to draw the first sample including preprocessing—afterwards additional samples can be produced in milliseconds.

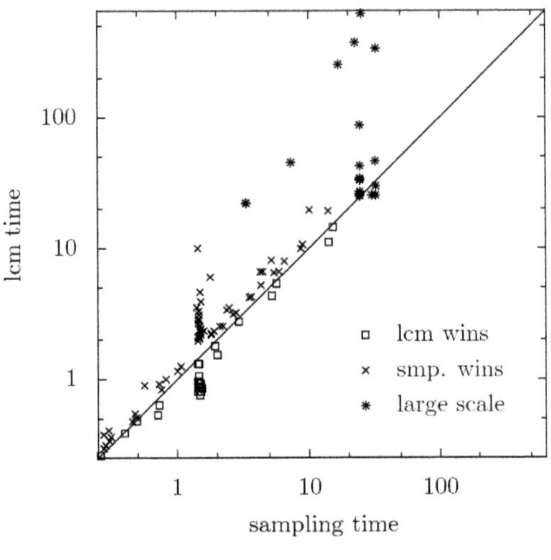

Figure 4: Time of lcm versus time of frequency-based sampling for an identical number of patterns.

For comparing direct sampling to exhaustive search algorithms there is a very large number of possible contenders in the literature, and, in principle, each of them requires an individual comparative study. For this paper we resort to

[3]Used hardware was a 2.67GHz 2 core CPU with 8GB RAM.

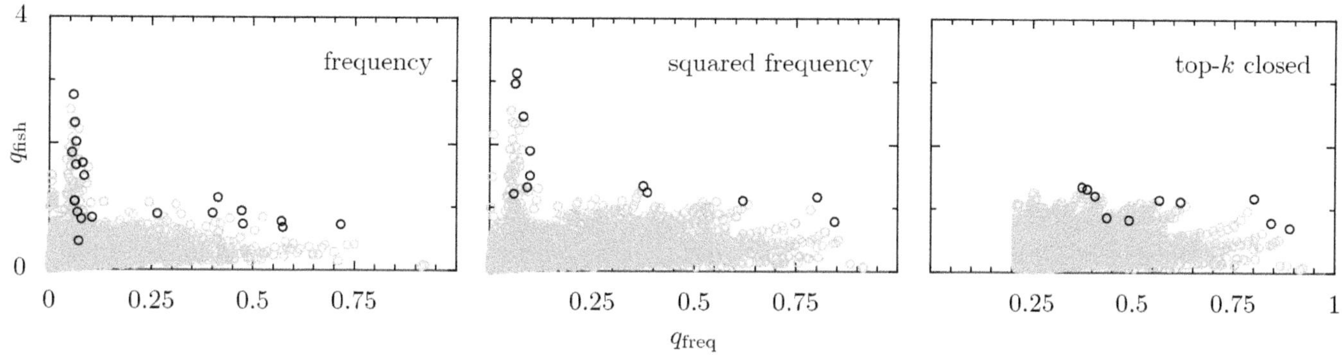

Figure 3: Pattern collections generated for "primary-tumor" by frequency-based sampling, squared-frequency-based sampling, and top-k closed frequent set listing; plotted according to frequency (x-axis) and Fisher score (y-axis); highlighted patterns are selected by feature selection procedure.

a rather general setting: we compare the computation time of the sampling algorithms with that of the linear closed frequent set mining algorithm (lcm) of Uno et al. [26] *per pattern*. For direct sampling this constitutes a worst-case setting because within the group of exhaustive methods frequent set mining algorithms usually produce the largest output per time unit and lcm is known to be among the fastest of them (winner of the FIMI contest [4]). In addition to the datasets used for the predictive performance study, we also consider several of the larger benchmark datasets of the FIMI workshop, including the 1GB sized "webdocs", and a 500MB random dataset.

The results are presented as log/log scatter-plot in Figure 4. One can observe that for most configurations lcm and the frequency-based sampling generate their patterns in approximately equal time with the majority of wins going to the sampling. However, focusing on the configurations with large-scale datasets (star symbol) reveals that the sampling algorithm can substantially outperform lcm. For "webdocs" this includes a speed-up factor of 10, for the random dataset even one of 25. We can conclude that frequency-based sampling can substantially outperform (closed) frequent set listing on large datasets and it performs equally well with slight advantage on small-scale data.

While the time performance of frequency-based sampling is also representative for area-based sampling, this is not true for the two sampling procedures with quadratic time weight computation phase. For almost all of the relatively small datasets of Tab. 1, this weight computation time is only marginal, i.e., less than 0.2 seconds. For large-scale datasets, however, the quadratic complexity is prohibitive; as already indicated on the 3772 row dataset "hypothyroid" where weight computation takes 13 seconds. After data record weights are computed, the performance is essentially equal to frequency-based sampling.

	$\mathcal{C}$	q_{freq}	q^2_{freq}
diabetes	**0.023** (0.066)	**0.023** (0.066)	**0.023** (0.066)
hypo.	0.016 (0.0190)	0.356 (3.613)	**0.414** (5.420)
lymph	**0.446** (0.580)	0.148 (0.352)	0.372 (0.580)
tumor	1.035 (1.270)	1.552 (3.630)	**1.725** (4.336)

Table 3: Average (maximum) Fisher score of features selected from pattern collections.

The scalability experiments above compared computation times for an equal number of generated patterns. This leads to the question of effectivity, i.e., what can be said about the quality per pattern? To this end, we again use the feature selection procedure from Section 4.1 and consider the quality of features within top-k frequent closed sets and random set families of the same size with respect to our measure of primary interest, the Fisher score; again using the setting of $k = 32\|\mathcal{D}\|$. This time we do not split the datasets according to the label, in order to avoid different values for global and local frequency of patterns (hence, we ignore discriminativity, which inherently requires splits). Table 3 shows the results of four datasets that are representative for different constellations: For datasets that contain high-frequency patterns with high discriminative power, as for instance for "lymph", the top-k paradigm is highly effective. Often, however, the patterns with high Fisher score are of relatively low frequency and are hidden (from the perspective of top-k frequent set listing) underneath a large pattern set of high frequency but low discriminativity. Such a constellation can for instance be observed for "primary-tumor" (see also Fig. 3).

5. CONCLUSION

We introduced four simple direct sampling procedures that generate random set patterns distributed according to frequency, squared frequency, area, and a discriminativity measure for binary labels. All procedures come with tight theoretical performance guarantees. Moreover, we described experimental studies demonstrating that the produced patterns are as useful as frequent pattern collections for pattern-based classification, and that direct sampling can compete with and often even outperform the fastest exhaustive mining algorithms when generating an equal number of patterns.

In the context of pattern-based classification there is a large amount of pattern discovery approaches that range from optimistic-estimator-based best-first-search algorithms [23] to methods interweaving model training and pattern discovery [10, 13]. Although such algorithms typically traverse much less patterns per time unit as lcm, their search is more directed towards high quality patterns. This motivates an in-depth comparative study with such methods potentially leading to more sophisticated usage of the sampling algorithms (e.g., applying it within model training just as the cited approaches do with exhaustive mining).

That said, pattern sampling as a paradigm is in no way restricted to pattern-based classification, and should also be evaluated for other in particular unsupervised model construction tasks as well as for exploratory data analysis. This is likely to motivate further variants of pattern sampling procedures. An example is the introduction of column and row weights to the interestingness measure in order to model subjective interest in certain parts of the input data or to decrease the probability of re-discovering redundant patterns.

Acknowledgments

Part of this work was supported by the German Science Foundation (DFG) under 'GA 1615/1-1' as well as by the European Commission under 'ICT-FP7-LIFT-255951' and 'EU-FP7-250527'. The authors would like to thank Andrea Pietracaprina and Fabio Vandin for providing the top-k closed frequent set mining software.

6. REFERENCES

[1] R. Agrawal, H. Mannila, R. Srikant, H. Toivonen, and A. I. Verkamo. Fast discovery of association rules. In *Advances in Knowl. Disc. and Data Min.*, pp. 307–328. 1996.

[2] M. Al Hasan and M. J. Zaki. Output space sampling for graph patterns. *PVLDB*, 2(1):730–741, 2009.

[3] S. D. Bay and M. J. Pazzani. Detecting group differences: Mining contrast sets. *Data Min. Knowl. Discov.*, 5(3):213–246, 2001.

[4] R. Bayardo, B. Goethals, and M. J. Zaki, editors. *Proc. IEEE ICDM Workshop on Frequent Itemset Mining Implementations, 2004*, vol. 126 of *CEUR Workshop Proc.*.

[5] S. Bistarelli and F. Bonchi. Soft constraint based pattern mining. *Data and Knowl. Engineering*, 62(1):118–137, 2007.

[6] M. Boley, T. Gärtner, and H. Grosskreutz. Formal concept sampling for counting and threshold-free local pattern mining. In *Proc. SIAM Int. Conf. on Data Mining (SDM 2010)*, pp. 177–188, 2010.

[7] M. Boley and H. Grosskreutz. Approximating the number of frequent sets in dense data. *Knowl. Inf. Syst.*, 21(1):65–89, 2009.

[8] V. Chaoji, M. A. Hasan, S. Salem, J. Besson, and M. J. Zaki. Origami: A novel and effective approach for mining representative orthogonal graph patterns. *Stat. Anal. Data Min.*, 1(2):67–84, 2008.

[9] H. Cheng, X. Yan, J. Han, and C.-W. Hsu. Discriminative frequent pattern analysis for effective classification. In *Proc. 23rd Int. Conf. on Data Engineering (ICDE 2007)*, pp. 716–725, 2007.

[10] H. Cheng, X. Yan, J. Han, and P. S. Yu. Direct discriminative pattern mining for effective classification. In *Proc. 24th Int. Conf. on Data Engineering (ICDE 2008)*, pp. 169–178, 2008.

[11] J. Demsar. Statistical comparisons of classifiers over multiple data sets. *J. of Mach. Learn. Res.*, 7:1–30, 2006.

[12] G. Dong and J. Li. Efficient mining of emerging patterns: Discovering trends and differences. In *Proc. 5th ACM SIGKDD Int. Conf. on Knowl. Disc. and Data Mining (KDD '99)*, pp. 43–52. ACM, 1999.

[13] W. Fan, K. Zhang, H. Cheng, J. Gao, X. Yan, J. Han, P. S. Yu, and O. Verscheure. Direct mining of discriminative and essential frequent patterns via model-based search tree. In *Proc. 14th Int. Conf. on Knowl. Disc. and Data Mining (KDD '08*, pp. 230–238, 2008.

[14] A. Frank and A. Asuncion. UCI machine learning repository, 2010.

[15] F. Geerts, B. Goethals, and T. Mielikäinen. Tiling databases. In *Proc. 7th Int. Disc. Science Conf.*, vol. 3245 of *LNCS*, pp. 278–289. Springer, 2004.

[16] L. A. Goldberg. *Efficient algorithms for listing combinatorial structures.* Cambridge University Press, New York, NY, USA, 1993.

[17] H. Grosskreutz, S. Rüping, and S. Wrobel. Tight optimistic estimates for fast subgroup discovery. In *Proc. European Conf. on Machine Learning and Knowl. Disc. in Databases (ECML/PKDD 2008), Part I*, vol. 5211 of *LNCS*, pp. 440–456, 2008.

[18] D. Gunopulos, H. Mannila, and S. Saluja. Discovering all most specific sentences by randomized algorithms. In *Proc. 6th Int. Conf. of Database Theory (ICDT '97)*, vol. 1186 of *LNCS*, pp. 215–229, 1997.

[19] J. Han, J. Pei, Y. Yin, and R. Mao. Mining frequent patterns without candidate generation: A frequent-pattern tree approach. *Data Min. Knowl. Discov.*, 8(1):53–87, 2004.

[20] D. J. Hand. Pattern detection and discovery. In *Proc. ESF Workshop on Pattern Detection and Disc.*, vol. 2447 of *LNCS*, pp. 1–12. Springer, 2002.

[21] R. M. Karp, M. Luby, and N. Madras. Monte-carlo approximation algorithms for enumeration problems. *J. Algorithms*, 10(3):429–448, 1989.

[22] A. J. Knobbe, B. Crémilleux, J. Fürnkranz, and M. Scholz. From local patterns to global models: the lego approach to data mining. In *From Local Patterns to Global Models: Proc. ECML/PKDD 2008 Workshop (LEGO '08)*, 2008.

[23] S. Morishita and J. Sese. Traversing itemset lattice with statistical metric pruning. In *Proc. 19th ACM SIGMOD-SIGACT-SIGART Symp. on Principles of Database Systems (PODS)*, pp. 226–236, 2000.

[24] A. Pietracaprina and F. Vandin. Efficient incremental mining of top-k frequent closed itemsets. In *Proc. 10th Int. Disc. Science Conf. (DS 2007)*, pp. 275–280, 2007.

[25] T. Scheffer and S. Wrobel. Finding the most interesting patterns in a database quickly by using sequential sampling. *J. of Mach. Learn. Res.*, 3:833–862, 2002.

[26] T. Uno, T. Asai, Y. Uchida, and H. Arimura. An efficient algorithm for enumerating closed patterns in transaction databases. In *Proc. 7th Int. Disc. Science Conf. (DS 2004)*, vol. 3245 of *LNCS*, pp. 16–31. Springer, 2004.

[27] S. Wrobel. An algorithm for multi-relational discovery of subgroups. In *Proc. 1st Euro. Symp. on Principles of Data Mining and Knowl. Disc. (PKDD '97)*, vol. 1263 of *LNCS*, pp. 78–87. Springer, 1997.

[28] M. J. Zaki, S. Parthasarathy, W. Li, and M. Ogihara. Evaluation of sampling for data mining of association rules. In *Proc. 7th Workshop on Research Issues in Data Engineering (RIDE)*, 1997.

Mining Frequent Closed Graphs on Evolving Data Streams

Albert Bifet, Geoff Holmes, and Bernhard Pfahringer
University of Waikato
Hamilton, New Zealand
{abifet,geoff,bernhard}@cs.waikato.ac.nz

Ricard Gavaldà
LARCA Research Group
UPC-Barcelona Tech
Barcelona, Catalonia
gavalda@lsi.upc.edu

ABSTRACT

Graph mining is a challenging task by itself, and even more so when processing data streams which evolve in real-time. Data stream mining faces hard constraints regarding time and space for processing, and also needs to provide for concept drift detection. In this paper we present a framework for studying graph pattern mining on time-varying streams. Three new methods for mining frequent closed subgraphs are presented. All methods work on coresets of closed subgraphs, compressed representations of graph sets, and maintain these sets in a batch-incremental manner, but use different approaches to address potential concept drift. An evaluation study on datasets comprising up to four million graphs explores the strength and limitations of the proposed methods. To the best of our knowledge this is the first work on mining frequent closed subgraphs in non-stationary data streams.

Categories and Subject Descriptors

H.2.8 [**Database applications**]: Database Applications—*Data Mining*

General Terms

Algorithms

Keywords

Data streams, closed mining, graphs, concept drift

1. INTRODUCTION

Graph mining is a challenging task that extracts novel and useful knowledge from graph data [19, 4]. Due to novel applications in social networks, chemical informatics, bioinformatics, communication networks, computer vision, video indexing and the Web [21], more and more large-scale graphs and sets of graphs are becoming available for analysis. Frequent pattern mining on graphs is one of the ways to obtain useful patterns, e.g. for discriminating graphs in classification and clustering tasks.

Conventional graph mining methods assume that the amount of data is limited and that it is therefore possible to store all data in memory or local secondary storage. There is no limitation on processing time, either. In the *Data Stream* model, we have space and time restrictions. Fundamentally, these restrictions imply the use of incremental techniques. Furthermore, as the data source is not necessarily stationary, methods must be able to adapt to changes over time in the data as well.

As the number of possible subgraphs is exponential, we propose to use *coresets* or compressed representations of the graphs based on closed patterns. Closed patterns are powerful representatives of frequent patterns, since they eliminate redundant information. A frequent pattern is *closed* for a dataset if none of its proper superpatterns has the same support as itself. Other possible definitions of a frequent closed pattern are the following:

- a frequent pattern is closed if it is one of the intersections of all transactions that contain it.
- a frequent pattern is closed if no superpattern is contained in exactly the same transactions as itself.

Generally, there are many fewer frequent closed graphs than frequent ones. In fact, we can obtain all frequent subgraphs with their support from the set of frequent closed subgraphs with their support. So, the set of frequent closed subgraphs maintains the same information as the set of all frequent subgraphs.

There are many methods for computing frequent closed itemsets (see [21]), frequent closed sequences [31, 28], and trees [18, 6, 26, 5], but only two for frequent closed graphs [30, 13], and none for frequent closed graphs on data streams.

We propose the first general methodology to identify closed graphs in a data stream. We develop three closed graph algorithms: IncGraphMiner, an incremental closed graph mining algorithm; WinGraphMiner, a sliding window-based closed graph mining algorithm; and finally AdaGraphMiner, an adaptive closed graph mining algorithm. "Adaptive" means that the model maintains at all times the closed graphs that are frequent in the current state of the data stream, that is, since the latest change in distribution was detected.

The rest of the paper is organised as follows. Sections 2 and 3 give background and present the novel weighted frequent closed pattern setting. Section 4 introduces a new coreset structure and its properties. Section 5 details the handling of concept drift and Section 6 introduces the gen-

KDD'11, August 21–24, 2011, San Diego, California, USA.

eral mining framework. Experimental results are given in Section 7, and conclusions are drawn in Section 8.

1.1 Related Work

There is a large body of work on itemset mining from data streams; see the survey [23] and the references therein. We can divide these data stream methods into two different classes depending on whether they use a landmark window, containing all the examples seen so far, or a sliding window. Only a small fraction of these methods deal with frequent closed mining. *Moment* [17], *CFI-Stream* [24] and *IncMine* [22] are state-of-the-art algorithms for mining frequent closed itemsets over a sliding window. *CFI-Stream* stores only closed itemsets in memory, but maintains all closed itemsets as it does not apply a minimum support threshold, with the corresponding memory penalty. *Moment* stores much more information besides the current frequent closed itemsets, but it has a minimum support threshold to reduce the number of patterns found. *IncMine* proposes a notion of semi-FCIs that increases the minimum support threshold for an itemset as it is retained longer in the window.

For trees, the work in [8] shows a general methodology to identify closed patterns in a data stream, using Galois Lattice Theory. This approach is based on an efficient representation of trees and a low complexity notion of relaxed closed trees, and presents an online strategy and an adaptive sliding window technique for dealing with changes over time. The approach is different to the one presented in this paper, as it does not use coresets, or weighted frequent mining techniques.

In terms of graphs, two main algorithms exist for mining frequent closed graphs:

- CloseGraph [30]: based on gSpan [29], a miner for finding frequent subgraphs, based on depth-first search (DFS)
- MoSS [13]: an extension to MoFa [11] based on breadth-first search (BFS).

Aggarwal et al. [3] present a mining methodology to find frequent and dense patterns in graph streams. Their notion of density is based both on node-occurrence and edge density, and they present an approach based on finding an approximation of the exact method with the use of a min-hash approach.

To the best of our knowledge the work presented here is the first work dealing with mining frequent closed graphs in streaming data that evolve with time.

2. PRELIMINARIES

We are interested in (possibly infinite) sets of graphs, endowed with a partial order relation $\preceq$ among these graphs. The set of all graphs will be denoted by $\mathcal{G}$, but actually all our developments will proceed in some finite subset of $\mathcal{G}$ which will act as our universe of discourse.

Given two graphs g and g', we say that g is a *subgraph* of g', or g' is a *super-graph* of g, if $g \preceq g'$. Two graphs g, g' are said to be *comparable* if $g \preceq g'$ or $g' \preceq g$. Otherwise, they are incomparable. Also we write $g \prec g'$ if g is a proper subgraph of g' (that is, $g \preceq g'$ and $g \neq g'$).

The input to our data mining process is a dataset $\mathcal{D}$ of weighted transactions, where each transaction $s \in \mathcal{D}$ consists of a transaction identifier *tid*, and a graph. The dataset is a finite set in the standard setting, and a potentially infinite sequence in the data stream setting. Tids are supposed to run sequentially from 1 to the size of $\mathcal{D}$.

Following standard usage, we say that a transaction s *supports* a graph g if g is a subgraph of the graph in transaction s. The number of transactions in the dataset $\mathcal{D}$ that support g is called the *support* of the graph g. A subgraph g is called *frequent* if its support is greater than or equal to a given threshold *min_sup*. The frequent subgraph mining problem is to find all frequent subgraphs in a given dataset. Any subgraph of a frequent graph is also frequent and, therefore, any supergraph of a infrequent graph is also infrequent (the *antimonotonicity* property).

We define a graph g to be *closed* (implicitly, w.r.t. to $\mathcal{D}$) if none of its proper supergraphs has the same support as g has in $\mathcal{D}$.

In this paper we focus our examples and experiments on molecular graphs, but our approach is general enough to be applied to any type of graph.

Transaction Id	Graph	Weight
1	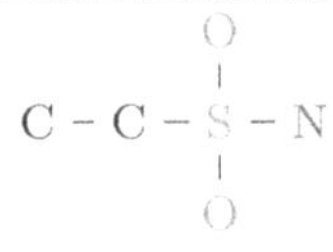	1
2	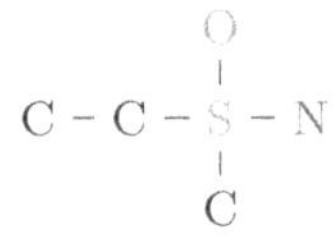	1
3		1
4	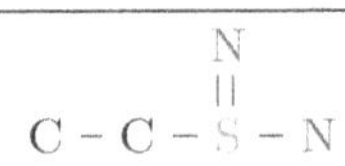	1
5		1
6	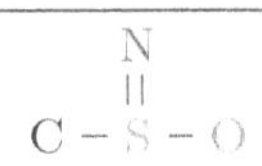	1

Table 1: Example of graph weighted transaction dataset.

3. FREQUENT CLOSED WEIGHTED GRAPH MINING

In this section we introduce an extension to the frequent closed graph mining problem which enables the use of compressed graph representations in our adaptive methods: the frequent *weighted* closed graph mining problem. This problem differs from standard frequent closed graph mining in that each input graph has a weight, and this weight is used to compute its weighted support.

The input into the data mining process is a dataset $\mathcal{D}$ of weighted transactions, where each transaction $s \in \mathcal{D}$ consists of a transaction identifier, *tid*, a graph, and a weight value.

Graph	Relative Support	Support
N	-2	6
C - S	-3	6
C - C - S - N	3	3
O | C - S - N	3	3
N || C - S	3	3
C - S - O	1	4
C - S - N	-1	5

Table 2: Example of a coreset with minimum support 50% and $\delta = 0$ for the transaction dataset of Table 1.

Table 1 shows an example of a weighted dataset with six molecule graphs [11].

The sum of the weights of transactions in the dataset $\mathcal{D}$ that supports g is called the *weighted support* of the graph g. For brevity, weighted support will be abbreviated to just *support*. A subgraph g is called *frequent* if its weighted support is greater than or equal to a given threshold *min_sup*.

We define a graph g to be *closed* if none of its proper supergraphs has the same weighted support as it has. A graph g is *maximal* if none of its proper supergraphs is frequent. All maximal graphs are closed but not necessarily otherwise. We define a graph g to be *δ-tolerance closed* [16, 25] if none of its proper frequent supergraphs has a weighted support larger than or equal to $(1 - \delta) \cdot support(g)$. Note that a maximal graph is a 1-tolerance closed graph, and a closed graph is a 0-tolerance closed graph. Note that, from [8] we have the following propositions:

PROPOSITION 1. *Adding a transaction with pattern g to a dataset of patterns $\mathcal{D}$ where g is closed does not modify the number of closed patterns for $\mathcal{D}$.*

PROPOSITION 2. *Deleting a pattern transaction that is repeated in a dataset of patterns $\mathcal{D}$ does not modify the number of closed patterns for $\mathcal{D}$.*

Using these propositions we can observe that when adding to or removing from the weights of transactions, we are not modifying the number of closed patterns provided they remain frequent.

4. CORESETS OF CLOSED GRAPHS

A *coreset* [2] of a set P with respect to some problem is a small subset that approximates the original set P, in the sense that solving the problem for the coreset provides an approximate solution for the problem on the original set P. This notion was introduced in computational geometry to denote a small subset of points that can be used to obtain approximate solutions with theoretical guarantees.

For example, for clustering [1], a coreset for a set is a small set, such that for any set of cluster centers the clustering cost of the coreset is an approximation for the clustering cost of the original set with small relative error.

Graph	Relative Support	Support
C - C - S - N	3	3
O | C - S - N	3	3
N || C - S	3	3

Table 3: Example of a coreset with minimum support 50% and $\delta = 1$ for the graph dataset of Table 1.

The main advantage of coresets is that we can apply any fast approximation algorithm on the usually much smaller coreset to compute an approximate solution for the original set more efficiently.

Here we use the set of frequent closed subgraphs as a smaller subset of the frequent subgraphs maintaining the same information but using less space. We define the *relative support* of a closed graph as the support of a graph minus the relative support of its closed supergraphs. We define the relative support in this way to exploit the fact that the sum of the closed supergraphs' relative supports of a graph is equal to its own support.

We define a *(s, δ)-coreset* for the problem of computing closed graphs as a weighted multiset of frequent δ-tolerance closed graphs with minimum support s using their relative support as a weight. Table 2 shows a (50%,0)-coreset for the dataset in Table 1 and Table 3 shows a (50%,1)-coreset for the same dataset.

Note that given a graph dataset D, its $(s, 0)$-coreset is the set of frequent closed graphs, and its $(s, 1)$-coreset contains the frequent maximal graphs. As the set of maximal graphs is contained in the set of closed graphs for a minimum support s, the set of graphs in the $(s, 1)$-coreset is also a subset of the graphs in the $(s, 0)$-coreset. For example, the set of graphs in the (50%,1)-coreset of Table 3 is a subset of the graphs in the (50%,0)-coreset of Table 2.

For two minimum supports s_L and s_H where $s_L < s_H$, the set of graphs in its (s_H, δ)-coreset is a subset of the graphs in the (s_L, δ)-coreset.

A coreset is a "compressed representation" of the original dataset. This compression is two-dimensional:

- Minimum support excludes infrequent graphs
- δ-tolerance excludes supergraphs with very similar support

In this paper we focus only on $(s, 0)$-coresets, i.e., frequent closed graphs, as they are the only coresets that can guarantee the recovery of all frequent and frequent closed graphs with minimum support s. To show that this $(s, 0)$-coreset outputs all the frequent subgraphs with minimum support s, we need the following proposition.

PROPOSITION 3. *Let $\mathcal{D}1$ and $\mathcal{D}2$ be two datasets of graphs. Let $C1$ and $C2$ be the $(s, 0)$-coresets of closed graphs for $\mathcal{D}1$ and $\mathcal{D}2$. The set of closed graphs of $C1 \cup C2$ is exactly the set of closed graphs of $\mathcal{D}1 \cup \mathcal{D}2$.*

First, we note that the support of a graph in $C1$ and $C2$ is the same support of a graph in $\mathcal{D}1$ and $\mathcal{D}2$, due to the fact that the support of a graph in $C1$ and $C2$ is the sum of all relative supports. As the support of a closed graph in $\mathcal{D}1$ and $\mathcal{D}2$ is the same support as in $C1$ and $C2$, we can obtain from them the same closed subgraphs, using relative support instead of support.

PROPOSITION 4. *Let $\mathcal{D}1$ and $\mathcal{D}2$ be two datasets of graphs. Let $C1$ and $C2$ be the $(s, 0)$-coresets of closed graphs for $\mathcal{D}1$ and $\mathcal{D}2$. The set of frequent graphs of $C1 \cup C2$ is exactly the set of frequent graphs of $\mathcal{D}1 \cup \mathcal{D}2$.*

To show that we can also obtain the frequent ones, we see that the frequent non-closed graphs have the support of their closure, so we obtain the same frequent graphs.

PROPOSITION 5. *Let $\mathcal{D}1$, $\mathcal{D}2$ and $\mathcal{D}$ be three datasets of graphs with $\mathcal{D} = \mathcal{D}1 \cup \mathcal{D}2$. Let $C1$, $C2$ and C be the $(s, 0)$-coresets of closed graphs for $\mathcal{D}1$, $\mathcal{D}2$ and $\mathcal{D}$. The set of frequent graphs for $C1 = C \backslash C2 = C \cup \overline{C2}$ obtained using relative support for $C1$ and negative relative support for $C2$, is exactly the set of frequent graphs for $\mathcal{D}1 = \mathcal{D} \backslash \mathcal{D}2$.*

As the support of a graph in $C1$ is the support of the graph in C minus its support in $C2$, we can obtain the closed graphs in $C1$ by adding the closed graphs in $C2$, with negated relative support, to C.

In general terms, using $(s, 0)$-coresets we can obtain all frequent, closed and maximal graphs with minimum support s without losing any information. Using (s, δ)-coresets we get more compact representations of the original dataset, and we can still obtain the maximal graphs, but we cannot completely recover all frequent closed graphs of minimum support s.

5. ESTIMATING FREQUENCIES ADAPTIVELY

To deal with concept drift, our methods have to be able to adapt to changes in the input distribution. Keeping a sliding window of recent elements is an option, however, it has the cost of maintaining it in memory. In this paper, we propose to use ADWIN to estimate frequencies of graphs with theoretical guarantees.

ADWIN (ADaptive sliding WINdow) [7] is a change detector and estimation algorithm. It solves, in a well-specified way, the problem of tracking the average of a stream of bits or real-valued numbers. ADWIN keeps a variable-length window of recently seen items, with the property that the window has the maximal length statistically consistent with the hypothesis "there has been no change in the average value inside the window".

More precisely, an older fragment of the window is dropped if and only if there is enough evidence that its average value differs from that of the rest of the window. This has two consequences: one, change is reliably detected whenever the window shrinks; and two, at any time the average over the existing window can be used as a reliable estimate of the current average in the stream (barring a very small or recent change that is not yet statistically significant).

The inputs to ADWIN are a confidence value $\delta \in (0, 1)$ and a (possibly infinite) sequence of real values $x_1, x_2, x_3, \ldots, x_t, \ldots$ The value of x_t is available only at time t. Each x_t is generated according to some distribution D_t, independently for every t. We denote with μ_t the expected value of x_t when it is drawn according to D_t. We assume that x_t is always in $[0, 1]$; rescaling deals with cases where $a \leq x_t \leq b$. No further assumption is being made about the distribution D_t; in particular, μ_t is unknown for all t.

ADWIN is parameter- and assumption-free in the sense that it automatically detects and adapts to the current rate of change. Its only parameter is a confidence bound δ, indicating how confident we want to be in the algorithm's output, inherent to all algorithms dealing with random processes.

It is important to note that ADWIN does not maintain the window explicitly, but compresses it using a variant of the exponential histogram technique [20]. This means that it keeps a window of length W using only $O(\log W)$ memory and $O(\log W)$ processing time per item, rather than the $O(W)$ one expects from a naïve implementation.

The main technical result in [7] about the performance of ADWIN is the following theorem, that provides bounds on the rate of false positives and false negatives:

THEOREM 1. *With ϵ_{cut} defined as*

$$\epsilon_{cut} = \sqrt{\frac{1}{2m} \cdot \ln \frac{4|W|}{\delta}}$$

where for some *partition of W in two parts $W_0 W_1$ (where W_1 contains the most recent items), and m is the harmonic mean of $|W_0|$ and $|W_1|$, at every time step we have:*

1. (False positive rate bound). *If μ_t has remained constant within W, the probability that ADWIN shrinks the window at this step is at most δ.*
2. (False negative rate bound). *Suppose that for* some *partition of W in two parts $W_0 W_1$ we have $|\mu_{W_0} - \mu_{W_1}| > 2\epsilon_{cut}$. Then with probability $1 - \delta$ ADWIN shrinks W to W_1, or shorter.*

6. FREQUENT GRAPH MINING ON DATA STREAMS

In this section we present new graph mining methods for data streams using the results discussed in previous sections. We start by reviewing non-incremental basic methods, and then present the incremental miner INCGRAPHMINER, the sliding-window based miner WINGRAPHMINER, and the adaptive miner ADAGRAPHMINER.

6.1 Non-Incremental Graph Mining

[29, 30] presents two algorithms for computing frequent and closed graphs from a dataset of graphs, in a non incremental way. They represent the potential subgraphs to be checked for, being frequent and closed on the dataset, in such a way that extending them by one single node, in all possible ways, corresponds to a clear and simple operation on the representation. The completeness of the procedure is assured, that is, all graphs can be obtained in this way. This allows them to avoid extending graphs that have already been found to be infrequent.

The pseudocode of CLOSEGRAPH is presented in Figure 1. Note that the first line of the algorithm is a canonical representative check. Such checks are used frequently in tree and graph mining. The use of the right-most extension approach in CLOSEGRAPH, based on depth-first search, guarantees that all possible graphs are reached, but reduces the generation of duplicate graphs. CLOSEGRAPH selects the minimum DFS code based on a DFS lexicographical order as the canonical representative.

In MoSS [12], Borgelt et al. present a different method to perform frequent closed graph mining using breadth-first search instead of using the right-most extension approach.

```
CloseGraph(g, D, min_sup, S)
   Input: A graph g, a graph dataset D, min_sup.
   Output: The frequent graph set S.

if g ≠ Canonical_Representative(g)
   then return S
isClosed ← TRUE
C ← ∅
for each g′ that is a one step right-most
      extension of g
   do if support(g′) ≥ min_sup
         then insert g′ into C
      if support(g′) = support(g)
         then isClosed ← FALSE
if isClosed = TRUE
   then insert g into S
for each g′ in C
   do S ← CloseGraph(g′, D, min_sup, S)
return S
```

Figure 1: The CloseGraph algorithm

```
IncGraphMiner(D, min_sup)
   Input: A graph dataset D, and min_sup.
   Output: The frequent graph set G.

G ← ∅
for every batch b_t of graphs in D
      do C ← Coreset(b_t, min_sup)
         G ← Coreset(G ∪ C, min_sup)
return G

Coreset(b_t, min_sup)
   Input: A graph dataset b_t, and min_sup.
   Output: The coreset C.

C ← CloseGraph(b_t, min_sup)
C ← Compute_Relative_Support(C)
return C
```

Figure 2: The IncGraphMiner algorithm

6.2 Incremental Mining

The incremental setting is different. Suppose that the data arrives in batches of graphs. We consider every batch of graphs b_t as a small finite dataset $\mathcal{D}_b$ of transactions, where each transaction $s \in \mathcal{D}_b$ consists of a transaction identifier, *tid*, a graph and a weight value. We maintain a set of graphs G and we update this set every time a new batch of graphs $\mathcal{D}_b$ arrives. We compute the coreset of the batch b_t, and then we use it to update the graph set G.

Note that using this methodology we can transform non-incremental methods into incremental ones by extending them to use weights and coresets of graphs. Figure 2 shows the pseudocode of IncGraphMiner.

```
WinGraphMiner(D, W, min_sup)
   Input: A graph dataset D, a size window W and min_sup.
   Output: The frequent graph set G.

G ← ∅
for every batch b_t of graphs in D
      do C ← Coreset(b_t, min_sup)
         Store C in sliding window
         if sliding window is full
            then R̄ ← Oldest C stored in sliding window,
                     negate all support values
            else R̄ ← ∅
         G ← Coreset(G ∪ C ∪ R̄, min_sup)
return G
```

Figure 3: The WinGraphMiner algorithm

6.3 Erroneous omission or inclusion bounds

When working on batches of graphs at a time, there is a possibility that the current batch does not contain enough occurrences of a frequent pattern, and it might also contain more than *min_sup* occurrences of an otherwise infrequent pattern. The probabilities for these two types of errors, erroneous omission or inclusion, can be bounded in the following way. Given a fixed batch size n, every *min_sup* value is equivalent to a probability p of finding a specific pattern in any given graph. Then, if the global true probability for some pattern is $p + \Delta$, and if we approximate the binomial distribution with the normal distribution $N(n*(p+\Delta), n*(p+\Delta)*(1-p-\Delta)$, the following bound can be derived:

$$p_{discard}(\Delta, n) \quad \leq \quad \frac{1}{\sqrt{2\pi}} \cdot \int_{-\infty}^{-2\Delta\sqrt{n}} e^{-\frac{t^2}{2}}\, dt \qquad (1)$$

If $\Delta = 0$, then half of the patterns will be missed, but reasonably small values for Δ will already result in acceptable probabilities: if $n = 10000$, then $\Delta = 0.01$ results in less than 5% erroneous omissions or inclusions, and for $\Delta = 0.02$ this percentage is already very close to zero.

This type of argument is a heuristic that can be made formal (at the expense of worse figures) by the use of rigorous Hoeffding bounds, which underlie e.g. the `ADWIN` algorithm.

6.4 Mining with a Sliding Window

We present WinGraphMiner as a learner that maintains a sliding window. Its main important parameter is the size of the window W. The difference to IncGraphMiner lies in the management of the items in the sliding window. We update the recent frequent closed graphs, using the coresets of the new batches that arrive. When the window is full, we delete the oldest batch on the sliding window using negative relative support (Proposition 5).

Figure 3 shows the pseudocode of WinGraphMiner. When a new batch b_t arrives, the method performs as IncGraph-Miner, while the sliding window is not full. Once the window is full, the oldest coreset C is removed. The new coreset for G is computed in one step from the coresets of G and b_t, and C with negated relative support.

AdaGraphMiner(D, $Mode$, min_sup)

Input: A graph dataset D, mode $Mode$ and min_sup.
Output: The frequent graph set G.

```
G ← ∅
Init ADWIN
for every batch b_t of graphs in D
      do C ← Coreset(b_t, min_sup)
         R̄ ← ∅
         if Mode is Sliding Window
            then Store C in sliding window
                 if ADWIN detected change
                    then R̄ ← Batches to remove
                             in sliding window
                             with negative support
         G ← Coreset(G ∪ C ∪ R̄, min_sup)
         if Mode is Sliding Window
            then Insert # closed graphs into ADWIN
            else for every g in G update g's ADWIN
return G
```

Figure 4: The AdaGraphMiner algorithm

6.5 Adaptive Mining

Finally, we present AdaGraphMiner, an extension to the previous methods that is able to adapt to changes on the stream, maintaining only the *currently* frequent closed graphs.

We present two versions of this method. One uses an adaptive sliding window to maintain the batches of graphs. The other uses a separate ADWIN instance for managing the support of every single frequent closed subgraph.

Figure 4 shows the pseudocode of AdaGraphMiner, where the *Sliding Window* test distinguishes between the two methods.

Assume a scenario where at each time t the t-th element of the stream is a graph taken independently from a distribution D_t over a fixed universe $\mathcal{G}$ of graphs. Then, changes in the D_t's over time t are modelling the evolution in the stream. In particular, we say that "the stream is stationary between times $t1$ and $t2$" (for $t1 < t2$) if

$$D_{t1} = D_{t1+1} = \cdots = D_{t2-1} = \cdots = D_{t2}.$$

For a graph g, let $f_t(g)$ be the probability of g under distribution D_t, and $\hat{f}_t(g)$ the observed probability of g at time t (the number of times g has appeared in the window at time t divided by the length of the window). Since $\hat{f}_t(g)$ is our estimate of the current support of t, we would like it to be close enough to $f_t(g)$ to reliably decide whether g is frequent.

We can prove the following theorem:

Theorem 2. *Suppose the* ADWIN*'s in Algorithm* AdaGraphMiner *are initialized with parameter δ. For every time step $t1$, $t2$ such that $t1 < t2$, if the stream is stationary between $t1$ and $t2$, then for every $g \in \mathcal{G}$ we have with probability at least $1 - 2\delta$*

$$|f_{t2}(g) - \hat{f}_{t2}(g)| \leq \sqrt{\frac{1}{t2 - t1} \ln \frac{4W}{\delta}}$$

That is, if the stream remains stationary for T steps, the estimates of graph frequencies tend to the their value at a rate of roughly $O(1/\sqrt{T})$, which tends to 0 as $T \to \infty$. Observe that this is the best convergence rate obtainable by sampling even on a totally stationary stream. That is, the algorithm is able to effectively forget previous history, and converge at an optimal rate on stationary periods. Note that, if instead of ADWIN, we keep a simple sliding window of fixed size W the approximation will not tend to zero, but remain at about $1/\sqrt{W}$. The dependence on $\ln(W)$ in the theorem is to a large extent an artifact of the proof of ADWIN's guarantees, and in practice, slightly increasing the leading constant in the bound suffices for accurate results.

Proof. (Note: this proof uses both the definition of the ADWIN algorithm as well as Theorem 1 stating false positive and false negative ratios; see [7]).

Fix $t1 < t2$. We will show the following statement: For every fixed graph $g \in \mathcal{G}$, with probability at least $1 - 2\delta$ we have

$$|f_{t2}(g) - \hat{f}_{t2}(g)| \leq \sqrt{\frac{1}{t2 - t1} \ln \frac{4W}{\delta}}. \quad (2)$$

Now also fix a graph $g \in \mathcal{G}$. If g is not present in the set G kept by the algorithm, then $\hat{f}_{t2}(g) = 0$ and an application of the Hoeffding bound shows that (2) holds for g. Otherwise, g is in the set G, so it has an associated instance of ADWIN, A. Say that, at time $t2$, A keeps a window of size W. Because the stream is stationary between $t1$ and $t2$, by Theorem 1, part (1), we know that $W \geq t2 - t1$ (i.e., the element gathered at $t1$ has not been cut out from A's window) with probability at least $1 - \delta$.

Let $t0$ be the oldest element present in the window, so that $t0 = t2 - W \leq t1$. Now let $\hat{\mu}_0$ (resp., $\hat{\mu}_1$) be the observed frequence of g in the window $[t0..t1-1]$ (resp., in the window $[t1..t2]$); observe that $E[\mu_1] = f_{t2}(g)$. Observe also that by the definition of ADWIN, if the interval $[t0..t1-1]$ has *not* been cut out from the window, we must have $|\hat{\mu}_0 - \hat{\mu}_1| \leq \epsilon_{cut}$, where

$$\epsilon_{cut} = \sqrt{\frac{1}{2}\left(\frac{1}{t2 - t1} + \frac{1}{t1 - t0}\right) \ln \frac{4W}{\delta}}.$$

The estimate produced by A at time $t2$ is the average of the elements in the window of length W, which is

$$\begin{aligned} \hat{f}_{t2}(g) &= \hat{\mu}_1 \cdot \frac{t2 - t1}{W} + \hat{\mu}_0 \cdot \frac{t1 - t0}{W} \\ &= \hat{\mu}_1 \cdot \frac{t2 - t1}{W} + (\hat{\mu}_1 \pm \epsilon_{cut}) \cdot \frac{t1 - t0}{W} \\ &= \hat{\mu}_1 \pm \epsilon_{cut} \cdot \frac{t1 - t0}{W}. \end{aligned}$$

Now using $W = t2 - t0$ and some simple algebra one can see

$$\begin{aligned} \epsilon_{cut} \cdot \frac{t1 - t0}{W} &\leq \sqrt{\frac{t1 - t0}{2(t2 - t1)(t2 - t0)} \ln \frac{4W}{\delta}} \\ &\leq \sqrt{\frac{1}{2(t2 - t1)} \ln \frac{4W}{\delta}}. \end{aligned}$$

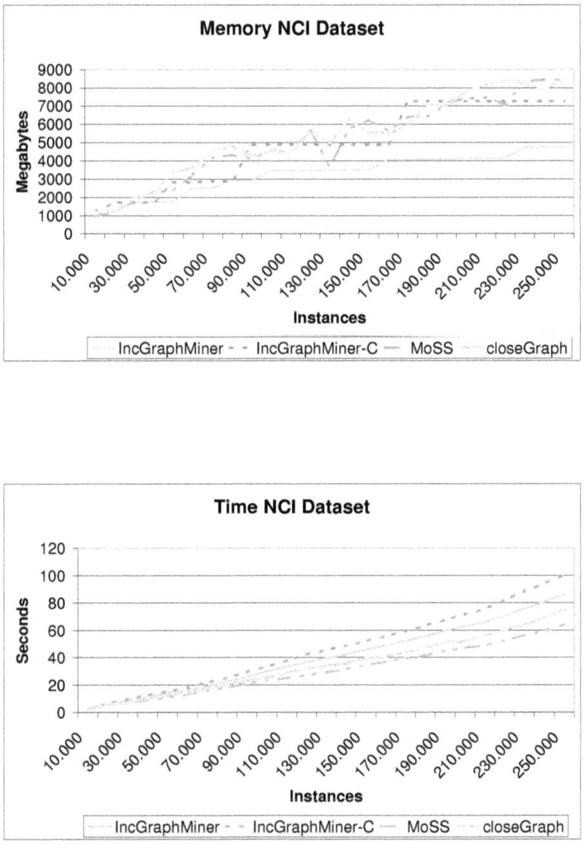

Figure 5: Memory and time used on Open NCI database with minimal support of 40%.

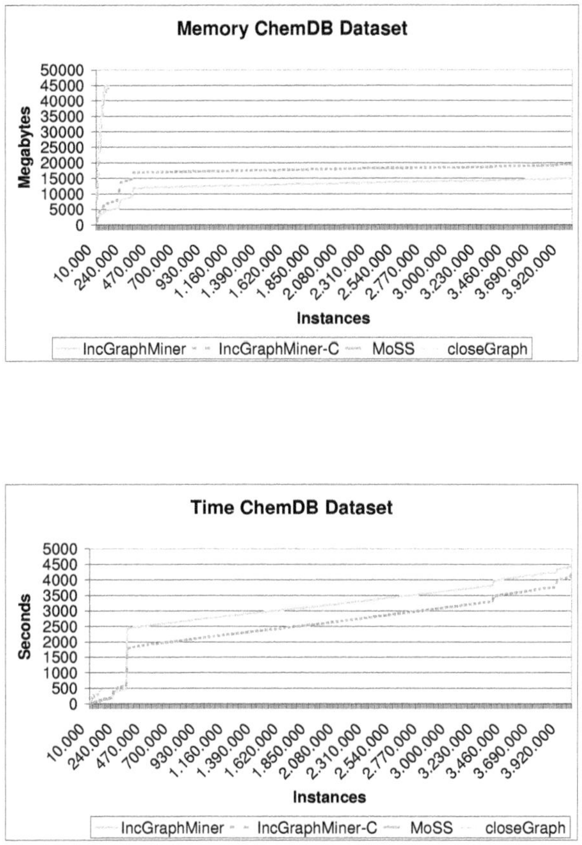

Figure 6: Memory and time used on ChemDB dataset with minimal support of 40%.

and by the Hoeffding bound and $E[\mu_1] = f_{t2}(g)$ we have

$$\Pr\left[|\hat{\mu}_1 - f_{t2}(g)| \leq \sqrt{\frac{1}{2(t2-t1)} \ln \frac{2}{\delta}} \right] \leq \delta.$$

Putting all of this together we conclude that, with probability at least $1 - 2\delta$,

$$\begin{aligned} |f_{t2}(g) - \hat{f}_{t2}(g)| &\leq \sqrt{\frac{1}{2(t2-t1)} \ln \frac{4W}{\delta}} + \\ &\quad \sqrt{\frac{1}{2(t2-t1)} \ln \frac{2}{\delta}} \\ &\leq \sqrt{\frac{1}{t2-t1} \ln \frac{4W}{\delta}}. \end{aligned}$$

as was to be proved. □

7. EXPERIMENTAL EVALUATION

We tested our algorithms on synthetic and real datasets. First, we compare our new incremental strategy with *closeGraph* and *MoSS* as non incremental methods to show the benefits in memory and time. Second, we perform experiments on data streams with synthetic concept drift to show the performance of our adaptive strategy.

We run our experiments extending MOA [10] using MoSS [12]. All experiments were performed on a 2.66 GHz Core 2 Duo machine with 64 GB of memory main memory, running CentOS 5.5.

Massive **O**nline **A**nalysis (MOA) [10] is a framework for online learning from continuous supplies of examples, such as data streams. It comprises online classification and clustering methods as well as tools for both offline and online evaluation.

MoSS is a batch framework for finding frequent molecular substructures and discriminative fragments in a database of molecule descriptions. MoSS is not restricted to molecular data sets, it can mine arbitrary data sets of attributed graphs. Apart from the default MoSS/MoFa algorithm, this framework also contains the gSpan [29] and CloseGraph [30] algorithms as special processing modes.

For our experiments we use the following real datasets:

ChemDB dataset ChemDB [14, 15] is a public dataset of approximately 4 million molecules built using the digital catalogs of over a hundred vendors and other public

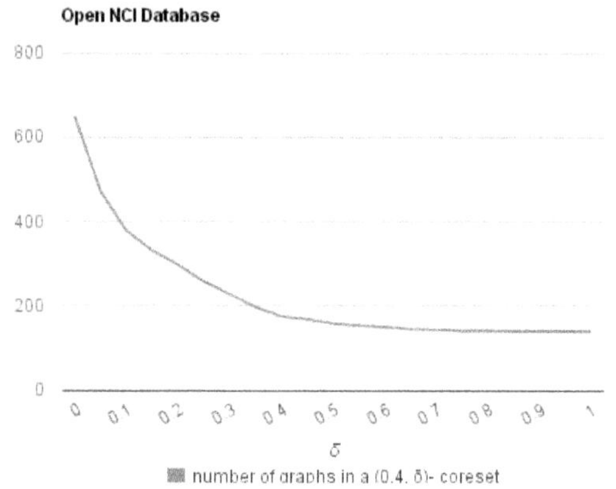

Figure 7: Number of graphs in $(40\%, \delta)$ for NCI.

sources. It is annotated with information derived from these sources as well as from computational methods, such as predicted solubility and 3D structure. It supports multiple molecular formats and is periodically updated, automatically whenever possible. It is maintained by the Institute for Genomics and Bioinformatics at the University of California, Irvine.

Open NCI Database The open National Cancer Institute (NCI) dataset [27] consists of approximately 250,000 structures. It is based on a large NCI database, built using samples from organic synthesis submitted to NCI for testing. While about half of the NCI database is not accessible, the other half of the structural data is free of any disclosure and usage restrictions and therefore termed "open". This data is public domain and often referred to as the "Open NCI Database".

First, we compare the runtime and memory usage of the incremental method IncGraphMiner to the non-incremental ones. As all methods are implemented in Java, the memory shown is the memory allocated by the Java Virtual Machine.

The results of our experiments using batches of 10,000 instances, minimum support of 40%, $\delta = 0$, and 50 Gigabytes of maximum memory are shown in Figures 5 and 6. We test two incremental methods, IncGraphMiner based on MoSS, and IncGraphMiner-C based on closeGraph as batch learners. For the Open NCI database, which is the smaller dataset, we see that our new incremental methods need more time but less memory. However, for the larger ChemDB dataset, the non-incremental methods can only process about 110,000 instances before running out of memory (50 Gigabytes). Surprisingly, the incremental methods also outperform the non-incremental ones both in terms of runtime and memory usage for smaller subsets of ChemDB. Note that in Figure 6 there is a sudden bump in time used, since the graphs in this part of the stream are much larger.

Figure 7 shows the size of the coreset $(40\%, \delta)$ on the Open NCI database. For $\delta = 0$ there are 649 frequent closed graphs, and for $\delta = 1$ there are 140 frequent maximal graphs.

The next experiment shows how the new methods are able to adapt to changes in the distribution of graphs in an evolving stream scenario. Figure 8 shows the number of closed

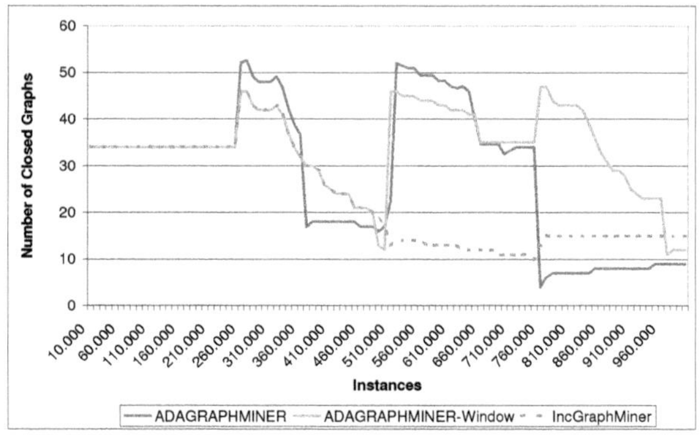

Figure 8: Number of frequent closed graphs on Open NCI database with minimal support of 40% with artificial concept drift.

graphs detected using the incremental method IncGraphMiner, and the two adaptive methods. AdaGraphMiner-Window uses a sliding window monitored only by one `ADWIN` instance, and AdaGraphMiner uses one `ADWIN` instance for each graph to monitor its support. In this experiment, the data stream exhibits artificial concept drift, as it is a concatenation of parts of two different streams. One is the Open NCI database and the other is an artificial data stream with exactly 15 frequent closed graphs generated artificially. Concept drift occurs three times, after 250,000, 500,000, and 750,000 examples, respectively. We follow the methodology in [9] to combine two data streams into one in order to create artificial drift. We observe that the incremental method is the slowest to adapt, as it does not have any forgetting mechanism. Comparing the adaptive ones, we see that AdaGraphMiner-Window, which only maintains one global `ADWIN` instance for change detection, shows a slower response to concept change. AdaGraphMiner, on the hand, can detect and respond to change faster, as it maintains a separate `ADWIN` instance for each graph.

8. CONCLUSIONS

We have presented the first efficient algorithms for mining frequent closed graphs on evolving data streams.

If the distribution of the graph dataset is stationary, the best method to use is IncGraphMiner, as no past transactions need to be forgotten. If the distribution evolves, then a sliding window method is more appropriate. If the right size of the sliding window is known in advance, then WinGraphMineris the method of choice, otherwise AdaGraphMiner is the preferred option.

Future work will analyze the impact of the size of batches and apply these new adaptive frequent mining techniques to discriminative graph feature generation for classification and clustering. Another ambitious direction for future work would be going beyond batch-incremental methods of graph mining, to develop methods that are fully instance-incremental. It is currently unclear how this could be done efficiently.

9. ACKNOWLEDGMENTS

UPC research is partially supported by the Spanish Ministry of Science and Technology TIN-2008-06582-C03-01 (SESAAME), by the Generalitat de Catalunya 2009-SGR-1428 (LARCA), and by the EU PASCAL2 Network of Excellence (FP7-ICT-216886).

The authors would like to thank Christian Borgelt for making his MoSS graph software available and for helpful discussions.

10. REFERENCES

[1] M. R. Ackermann, C. Lammersen, M. Märtens, C. Raupach, C. Sohler, and K. Swierkot. StreamKM++: A Clustering Algorithm for Data Streams. In *Proceedings of the Workshop on Algorithm Engineering and Experiments (ALENEX '10)*, 2010.

[2] P. K. Agarwal, S. Har-Peled, and K. Varadarajan. Geometric approximation via coresets. In J. E. Goodman, J. Pach, and E. Welzl, editors, *Combinatorial and computational geometry*, pages 1–30. Cambridge University Press., 2005.

[3] C. C. Aggarwal, Y. Li, P. S. Yu, and R. Jin. On dense pattern mining in graph streams. *PVLDB*, 3(1):975–984, 2010.

[4] C. C. Aggarwal and H. Wang. *Managing and Mining Graph Data*. Springer Publishing Company, Incorporated, 1st edition, 2010.

[5] H. Arimura and T. Uno. An output-polynomial time algorithm for mining frequent closed attribute trees. In *ILP*, pages 1–19, 2005.

[6] J. L. Balcázar, A. Bifet, and A. Lozano. Mining frequent closed rooted trees. *Machine Learning*, 78(1-2):1–33, 2010.

[7] A. Bifet and R. Gavaldà. Learning from time-changing data with adaptive windowing. In *SIAM International Conference on Data Mining*, 2007.

[8] A. Bifet and R. Gavaldà. Mining adaptively frequent closed unlabeled rooted trees in data streams. In *14th ACM SIGKDD*, pages 34–42, 2008.

[9] A. Bifet, G. Holmes, B. Pfahringer, R. Kirkby, and R. Gavaldà. New ensemble methods for evolving data streams. In *15th ACM SIGKDD*, pages 139–148, 2009.

[10] A. Bifet, G. Holmes, B. Pfahringer, P. Kranen, H. Kremer, T. Jansen, and T. Seidl. MOA: Massive Online Analysis, a Framework for Stream Classification and Clustering. *Journal of Machine Learning Research - Proceedings Track*, 11:44–50, 2010.

[11] C. Borgelt and M. R. Berthold. Mining molecular fragments: Finding relevant substructures of molecules. In ICDM '02, pages 51–, Washington, DC, USA, 2002. IEEE Computer Society.

[12] C. Borgelt, T. Meinl, and M. Berthold. Moss: a program for molecular substructure mining. In OSDM '05, pages 6–15, New York, NY, USA, 2005. ACM.

[13] C. Borgelt, T. Meinl, and M. R. Berthold. Advanced pruning strategies to speed up mining closed molecular fragments. In *IEEE Conf. on Systems, Man and Cybernetics (SMC 2004)*. IEEE Press, 2004.

[14] J. Chen, S. J. J. Swamidass, Y. Dou, J. Bruand, and P. Baldi. ChemDB: a public database of small molecules and related chemoinformatics resources. *Bioinformatics*, September 2005.

[15] J. H. Chen, E. Linstead, S. J. Swamidass, D. Wang, and P. Baldi. ChemDB update full-text search and virtual chemical space. *Bioinformatics*, 23(17):2348–2351, September 2007.

[16] J. Cheng, Y. Ke, W. Ng, and A. Lu. Fg-index: towards verification-free query processing on graph databases. In *SIGMOD Conference*, pages 857–872, 2007.

[17] Y. Chi, H. Wang, P. S. Yu, and R. R. Muntz. Moment: Maintaining closed frequent itemsets over a stream sliding window. In *Proceedings of the 2004 IEEE International Conference on Data Mining (ICDM'04)*, November 2004.

[18] Y. Chi, Y. Xia, Y. Yang, and R. Muntz. Mining closed and maximal frequent subtrees from databases of labeled rooted trees. *Fundamenta Informaticae*, XXI:1001–1038, 2001.

[19] D. J. Cook and L. B. Holder. *Mining Graph Data*. Wiley-Interscience, 2006.

[20] M. Datar, A. Gionis, P. Indyk, and R. Motwani. Maintaining stream statistics over sliding windows. *SIAM Journal on Computing*, 14(1):27–45, 2002.

[21] J. Han, H. Cheng, D. Xin, and X. Yan. Frequent pattern mining: current status and future directions. *Data Mining and Knowledge Discovery*, 15:55–86, 2007.

[22] Y. K. James Cheng and W. Ng. Maintaining frequent closed itemsets over a sliding window. *Journal of Intelligent Information Systems*, 2007.

[23] Y. K. James Cheng and W. Ng. A survey on algorithms for mining frequent itemsets over data streams. *Knowledge and Information Systems*, 2007.

[24] N. Jiang and L. Gruenwald. Cfi-stream: mining closed frequent itemsets in data streams. In *KDD '06*, pages 592–597, New York, NY, USA, 2006. ACM.

[25] I. Takigawa and H. Mamitsuka. Efficiently mining δ-tolerance closed frequent subgraphs. *Machine Learning*, 82(2):95–121, 2011.

[26] A. Termier, M.-C. Rousset, M. Sebag, K. Ohara, T. Washio, and H. Motoda. DryadeParent, an efficient and robust closed attribute tree mining algorithm. *IEEE Trans. Knowl. Data Eng.*, 20(3):300–320, 2008.

[27] J. H. Voigt, B. Bienfait, S. Wang, and M. C. Nicklaus. Comparison of the nci open database with seven large chemical structural databases. *Journal of Chemical Information and Computer Sciences*, 41(3):702–712, 2001.

[28] J. Wang and J. Han. Bide: Efficient mining of frequent closed sequences. In *ICDE*, pages 79–90. IEEE Computer Society, 2004.

[29] X. Yan and J. Han. gSpan: Graph-based substructure pattern mining. In *ICDM '02*, page 721, Washington, DC, USA, 2002. IEEE Computer Society.

[30] X. Yan and J. Han. CloseGraph: mining closed frequent graph patterns. In *KDD '03*, pages 286–295, 2003.

[31] X. Yan, J. Han, and R. Afshar. Clospan: Mining closed sequential patterns in large databases. In *SDM*, 2003.

Latent Topic Feedback for Information Retrieval

David Andrzejewski
Lawrence Livermore National Laboratory
Livermore, CA 94550
andrzejewski1@llnl.gov

David Buttler
Lawrence Livermore National Laboratory
Livermore, CA 94550
buttler1@llnl.gov

ABSTRACT

We consider the problem of a user navigating an unfamiliar corpus of text documents where document metadata is limited or unavailable, the domain is specialized, and the user base is small. These challenging conditions may hold, for example, within an organization such as a business or government agency. We propose to augment standard keyword search with user feedback on latent topics. These topics are automatically learned from the corpus in an unsupervised manner and presented alongside search results. User feedback is then used to reformulate the original query, resulting in improved information retrieval performance in our experiments.

Categories and Subject Descriptors

H.3.3 [**Information Storage and Retrieval**]: Information Search and Retrieval—*query formulation, relevance feedback*

General Terms

Algorithms, Experimentation

Keywords

latent topic models, user feedback

1. INTRODUCTION

This work addresses the problem of ad-hoc information retrieval and text corpus navigation under the following conditions. First, document metadata may be limited, unreliable, or nonexistent. Second, the domain of the text documents is specialized, using vocabulary ill-covered by general web documents or lexical resources such as WordNet [10]. Finally, while the text corpus itself may be large, the set of users accessing the corpus is not. This is an important problem because these conditions can preclude the use of effective information retrieval techniques such as faceted search or query log mining. These conditions are different from those encountered in general web or e-commerce search, but are realistic *within* organizations which are trying make sense of large quantities of text, such as private enterprises or government agencies.

A central problem in ad-hoc information retrieval is that users may not be able to formulate the "right" keyword combination in order to retrieve the most relevant documents. Techniques such as real-time query expansion [34] have been developed to directly attack this problem, but often rely upon a dataset of previously submitted queries, which may be sparse without a large user base. Another approach is to solicit alternative types of user input. Faceted document navigation [29] allows users to select documents based on different attributes (e.g., publication venues or hierarchical subject categories) and has emerged as a powerful complement to traditional keyword search. However, the standard assumption is that the facets are manually defined, and that facet values for each document are known.

Because of the challenging scenario we have defined, it is important to exploit all available data. Latent topic models such as Latent Dirichlet Allocation (LDA) [4] provide a means to take advantage of the statistical structure of the corpus itself. LDA assumes that observed documents have been generated by weighted mixtures of unobserved (latent) topics. These topics are learned from the documents and often correspond to meaningful semantic themes present in the corpus. LDA and its extensions have found interesting applications in fields such as natural language processing, computer vision, and social networks analysis [2].

The contribution of this work is a new method for obtaining and exploiting user feedback at the *latent topic* level. Our approach is to learn latent topics from the corpus and construct meaningful representations of these topics. At query time, we then decide *which* latent topics are potentially relevant and present the appropriate topic representations alongside keyword search results. When a user selects a latent topic, the vocabulary terms most strongly associated with that topic are then used to augment the original query. Our experiments with simulated user feedback show improved information retrieval performance. The presentation of relevant topics alongside search results also has the additional benefit of helping the user to understand corpus themes related to the original keyword query.

KDD'11, August 21–24, 2011, San Diego, California, USA.
Copyright 2011 ACM 978-1-4503-0813-7/11/08 ...$10.00.

Table 1: Example learned topic-word multinomials ϕ from three different datasets (see Table 5). For each topic ϕ_t, the five highest-probability words w are shown.

FT - Topic 1		WSJ - Topic 8		LA - Topic 94	
Word w	$P(w\|z)$	Word w	$P(w\|z)$	Word w	$P(w\|z)$
court	0.080	technology	0.094	gun	0.058
case	0.025	research	0.054	weapons	0.052
legal	0.024	high	0.025	assault	0.034
ruling	0.018	development	0.023	guns	0.029
appeal	0.018	cray	0.020	rifles	0.018

2. RELATED WORK

Our approach is partially motivated by the successes of faceted search [35]. Castanet [29] and related systems [9] aim to *automatically* construct facet hierarchies, but these techniques depend crucially on the existence of a rich lexical resource such as WordNet [10]. While specialized ontologies or controlled vocabularies have been constructed for some domains such as Gene Ontology (GO) [31] and Medical Subject Headings (MeSH) [5], the constraints of our setting prohibit us from assuming the existence of such a resource.

In light of this issue, topic models such as LDA have the advantage of relying upon corpus statistics alone. Indeed, previous analysis [23] of the digital library of the Open Content Alliance (OCA) directly posited the analogy between latent topics and faceted subjects, although specific mechanisms for exploiting this insight were not explored. The Rexa academic search engine[1] also displays relevant latent topics as tags for a given research article, allowing further investigation of the topics themselves. Another interesting topic modeling approach uses seed words to learn facet-oriented topics which can then be used to construct informative summaries [18].

LDA has previously been used in information retrieval for both document language model smoothing [33, 20] and query expansion [27]. These techniques both exploit the dimensionality reduction provided by LDA "behind the scenes" in order to improve performance, but do not leverage explicit user feedback in the way that our approach does. The approach we propose in this work can be viewed as complementary to these existing enhancements.

The BYU Topic Browser [11] provides an environment for rich explorations of learned LDA topics and how they relate to words and documents within a corpus. However, the tasks supported are more appropriate for advanced analysis by a relatively sophisticated user, as opposed to a general search setting.

3. OUR APPROACH

We propose to present automatically learned topics alongside keyword search results, allowing the user to provide feedback at the latent topic level. While it is well-known that we can learn latent topics with LDA, incorporating these topics into an information retrieval system requires us to address several questions. First, how should these topics be presented? Previous user studies [29] have found that users can become frustrated by raw LDA output. Second, which topics should be presented for a given query? To avoid overwhelming the user, we clearly cannot present all latent topics (potentially hundreds or greater) for every query. Furthermore, not all learned topics truly correspond to meaningful semantic concepts, and the presence of these incoherent topics will not be appreciated by users either. Third, how can we incorporate user latent topic feedback into search results? Ideally, the mechanism used should be simple and easy to integrate with existing search technologies. Finally, can this type of feedback improve information retrieval performance, as measured by standard metrics?

We now describe our approach, beginning with a brief review of latent topic modeling concepts and moving on to address the above questions. All examples shown are actual learned topics from the experimental datasets described in Table 5. In Section 4, experimental results demonstrate that our approach can indeed achieve performance gains.

3.1 Latent Dirichlet Allocation (LDA)

In LDA [4], it is assumed that observed words in each document are generated by a document-specific mixture of corpus-wide latent topics. We define our corpus of length N with the flat word vector $\mathbf{w} = w_1 \ldots w_N$. At corpus position i, the element d_i in $\mathbf{d} = d_1 \ldots d_N$ designates the document containing observed word w_i. Similarly, the vector $\mathbf{z} = z_1 \ldots z_N$ defines the hidden topic assignments of each observed word. The number of latent topics is fixed to some T, and each topic $t = 1 \ldots T$ is associated with a topic-word multinomial ϕ_t over the W-word vocabulary. Each ϕ multinomial is generated by a conjugate Dirichlet prior with parameter β. Each document $j = 1 \ldots D$ is associated with a multinomial θ_j over T topics, which is also generated by a conjugate Dirichlet prior with parameter α. The full generative model is then given by

$$P(\mathbf{w}, \mathbf{z}, \phi, \theta \mid \alpha, \beta, \mathbf{d}) \propto \left(\prod_t^T p(\phi_t|\beta)\right) \left(\prod_j^D p(\theta_j|\alpha)\right) \left(\prod_i^N \phi_{z_i}(w_i)\theta_{d_i}(z_i)\right),$$

where $\phi_{z_i}(w_i)$ is the w_i-th element in vector ϕ_{z_i}, and $\theta_{d_i}(z_i)$ is the z_i-th element in vector θ_{d_i}. Given an observed corpus $(\mathbf{w}, \mathbf{d})$ and model hyperparameters (α, β), the typical modeling goal is to infer the latent variables $(\mathbf{z}, \phi, \theta)$.

While exact LDA inference is intractable, a variety of approximate schemes have been developed [24, 4, 30]. In this work, we use Markov Chain Monte Carlo (MCMC) inference, specifically collapsed Gibbs sampling [12]. This approach iteratively re-samples a new value for each latent topic assignment z_i, conditioned on the current values of all

[1]http://rexa.info/

Table 2: Features used to determine "best topic word" labels for each topic. The topic-word posterior $P(z = t|w)$ is computed using Bayes Rule and a uniform prior over topics.

Description	Score
Word probability	$f_1(w) = P(w\|z = t)$
Topic posterior	$f_2(w) = P(z = t\|w)$
PMI	$f_3(w) = \sum_{w' \in W_t \setminus w} PMI(w, w')$
Conditional 1	$f_4(w) = \sum_{w' \in W_t \setminus w} P(w\|w')$
Conditional 2	$f_5(w) = \sum_{w' \in W_t \setminus w} P(w'\|w)$

other z values. After running this chain for a fixed number of iterations, we estimate the topic-word multinomials ϕ and the document-topic mixture weights θ from the final $\mathbf{z}$ sample, using the means of their posteriors given by

$$\phi_t(w) \propto n_{tw} + \beta$$
$$\theta_j(t) \propto n_{jt} + \alpha$$

where n_{tw} is the number of times word w is assigned to topic t, and n_{jt} is the number of times topic t is used in document j, with both counts being taken with respect to the final sample $\mathbf{z}$. The topic-word multinomials ϕ_t for each topic t are our learned topics; each document-topic multinomial θ_d represents the prevalence of topics within document d.

3.2 Topic representation

Typically, each learned topic-word multinomial ϕ_t is presented as a "Top N" list of the most probable words for that topic, as shown for three example learned topics in Table 1. We define the k-argmax operator to yield the k arguments which result in the k largest values for the given function. We use this operator to define the ten most probable words for topic t as W_t, given by the following expression with $k = 10$

$$W_t = \underset{w}{\text{k-argmax}}\, \phi_t(w)$$

We apply techniques from recent topic modeling research to improve on this basic representation. Our post-processing of the learned topics has three components: label generation, n-gram identification, and capitalization recovery.

For topic labeling, we assume the availability of a *reference corpus* containing themes similar to the target retrieval corpus. Since only raw text is required, this should be considerably easier to obtain than a full ontology, even for specialized domains. For example, a user exploring a corpus related infectious disease outbreaks could obtain a suitable reference corpus by crawling web resources from the United States Centers for Disease Control and Prevention. Since our experiments use general newswire corpora for evaluation, we use Wikipedia[2] as our reference corpus.

We label each topic using a simplified variant of the "Best Topic Word" [15] method. For a given topic t, this method selects a single word label from the top ten most probable words W_t, using features designed to test how representative each word is of the topic as a whole. We deviate slightly from Lau et al. to avoid relying upon WordNet, selecting

[2]http://www.wikipedia.org

Table 3: Topic representations for example high-PMI (coherent) and low-PMI (incoherent) topics.

PMI	Label	n-grams
3.09	jurors	Deputy Dist Atty
		cross examination, closing arguments
		trial, jury, case, testified
1.68	Petroleum	state oil company
		North Sea, natural gas
		production, exploration, field, energy
-0.09	things	(no trigrams found)
		pretty good, years ago
		ve, ll, time, don
-0.03	sales	(no trigrams found)
		year earlier, Feb Feb
		December, March, month, rose

the label word by majority vote among five features shown in Table 2 where each feature f_i casts its vote for the highest scoring word and ties are broken arbitrarily. Several of these features are computed from co-occurrence frequencies among words in W_t, counted within ten-word sliding windows taken over the reference corpus. Specifically, we compute the pointwise mutual information (PMI) and conditional occurrence probabilities between each pair of words (w, w') as

$$PMI(w, w') = \log \frac{P(w, w')}{P(w)P(w')}$$
$$P(w|w') = \frac{P(w, w')}{P(w')}$$

where $P(w, w')$ is the probability of jointly observing w and w' within a given sliding window, and $P(w)$ is the probability of observing w within a sliding window. Several example labels can be seen in the "label" column of Table 3.

We then identify statistically significant bigrams and trigrams (e.g., "White House", "President Barack Obama") for each topic using an approach based on the Turbo Topics [3] algorithm. This approach considers adjacent word pairs (w_i, w_{i+1}) occurring in the same document and assigned to the same topic (i.e., $d_i = d_{i+1}$ and $z_i = z_{i+1}$) and identifies pairs which occur much more often than we would expect by chance alone, proceeding similarly for trigrams. For each topic, we show the topic label along with the most significant trigram, the two most significant bigrams and the four most probable unigrams. Example latent topic representations are shown in Table 3.

Finally, we restore capitalization to the topic n-grams before presenting them to the user. As a pre-processing step, all text is converted to lower-case before doing LDA inference. However, the information conveyed by capitalization can ease user interpretation of topics (e.g., by making proper names obvious). For each n-gram, we simply count all occurrences of each possible capitalization occurring in the original documents, and present the most frequent version to the user.

3.3 Topic selection

It will typically be necessary to learn at least hundreds of latent topics in order to get suitably fine-grained topics for user feedback. This makes it impractical to present all topics to the user after every query; we therefore must decide which topics to present.

We use the idea of pseudo-relevance feedback [6] by assuming that the top two documents returned by the original query q, which we call D_q, are relevant. For each of these documents, we consider the top $k = 2$ topics as determined by the topic weights θ to be *enriched* topics for the user query. This constitutes a natural set of candidates for latent topic feedback, and can be defined as

$$E = \bigcup_{d \in D_q} \text{k-argmax}_t \; \theta_d(t).$$

However, we also show the user topics that are *related* to the enriched topic set E, but which may themselves not be present in the highly ranked documents. We identify related topics by looking for topics highly likely to co-occur with the enriched topics E, using the $T \times T$ topic covariance matrix Σ of the estimated $D \times T$ document-topic θ matrix. Letting $\Sigma(t_1, t_2)$ be the covariance between $P(z = t_1|d)$ and $P(z = t_2|d)$ computed over all documents $d = 1, \ldots, D$, we take the $k = 2$ topics with the highest covariance with each of our enriched topics in E. We define this *related* topic set as

$$R = \bigcup_{t \in E} \text{k-argmax}_{t' \notin E} \; \Sigma(t, t').$$

The candidate topics for feedback are the union of the enriched and related topics $E \cup R$, but we perform a final filter before presenting these topics to the user.

One hazard of presenting automatically discovered latent topics to the user is the threat of incoherent "junk" topics which do not seem to have a single clear theme. We filter out these topics using a recently developed topic evaluation method [26, 25] which has been shown to predict human topic quality judgments at nearly the inter-annotator agreement rate. Similar to the topic labeling technique, this method uses PMI values computed over a reference corpus (again, we use Wikipedia), except that we now apply these scores to the topics themselves. We compute the PMI score of a topic t as the average PMI between all pairs of words within the top $k = 10$ most probable words W_t

$$PMI(t) = \frac{1}{k(k-1)} \sum_{(w,w') \in W_t} PMI(w, w').$$

Table 3 shows example high-PMI (coherent) and low-PMI (incoherent) latent topics.

We can use these PMI values to avoid confusing users with incoherent topics. Letting PMI_{25} be the 25th percentile PMI score among all learned topics, we define our set of "dropped" topics D as

$$D = \{t | t \in E \cup R \text{ and } PMI(t) < PMI_{25}\}.$$

We present the topics in $\{E \cup R\} \setminus D$ to the user alongside the returned documents for the original keywords query q. Note that the union operations and final filtering mean that the number of topics actually presented to the user may vary from query to query. Since we consider the top two topics within the top two documents, along with each of their top two related topics, we will present a maximum of $(2 \times 2) + (2 \times 2 \times 2) = 12$ topics, minus set overlaps and PMI-filtered topics.

3.4 Query expansion

If the user selects a topic as relevant, we reformulate the query by combining the top ten most probable words W_t for that topic with the original query q. To preserve the intent of the original query, we use the Indri [22] `#weight()` operator to form a weighted combination of the original query keywords and the highly probable latent topic words. The weight parameter $\gamma \in [0, 1]$ controls the trade-off between the original query keywords and the latent topic words. A larger γ value places more weight on the new latent topic words, while setting $\gamma = 0$ is equivalent to the original keyword query.

Each of the N_q words in the original query is given weight $(1 - \gamma)/N_q$ and each new topic t word w is given weight $\gamma * \tilde{\phi}_t(w)$, where $\tilde{\phi}$ is the re-normalized topic-word probability

$$\tilde{\phi}_t(w) = \frac{\phi_t(w)}{\sum_{w' \in W_t} \phi_t(w')}.$$

While our implementation uses the Indri query language, it would be straightforward to achieve similar results in other information retrieval systems and frameworks (e.g., by using term boosting in Apache Lucene[3]).

3.5 Example

We now walk through an example query for a corpus of news articles from the Financial Times (FT). The query is "euro opposition", and it targets documents discussing opposition to the introduction of the single European currency. The corpus, query, and relevance judgments used here are drawn from our experimental dataset which will be used in Section 4. The number of topics used is $T = 500$.

The *enriched* topics E shown in Table 5a consist of three distinct topics: two topics related to the euro debate within the United Kingdom and Denmark, and a confusing topic vaguely centered around "business" which is *dropped* by our PMI filtering. Within this topic, the interesting trigram "PERSONAL FILE Born" arises from brief biographies sometimes found at the bottom of the articles.

High θ covariance with topics in E is then used to identify the five *related* topics R shown in Table 5b, which deal with various aspects of business and politics. However the appearance of "economic monetary union" and "Europe" in the topic 79 representation appear highly related to the euro currency union, and indeed selecting this topic as feedback improves retrieval results. Selecting topic 79 as user feedback and setting the feedback weight $\gamma = 0.25$, our approach produces an expanded query containing the most probable words from topic 79

```
#weight(0.375 euro, 0.375 opposition,
        0.031 European, ..., 0.015 Emu).
```

[3]http://lucene.apache.org/

Table 4: A detailed example of our approach for the query "euro opposition" on the Financial Times (FT) corpus. The strikethrough topic 466 is not presented to the user due to low PMI coherence score. The bolded topic 79 results in improved information retrieval performance versus the baseline query: NDCG15 increases 0.22, NDCG increases 0.07, and MAP increases 0.02. The prominent term "Emu" appears to be an alternate form of the acronym "EMU" commonly used in Financial Times articles.

Enriched topic	Terms
196 (debate)	Tory Euro sceptics social chapter, Liberal Democrat mps, Labour, bill, Commons
404 (ratification)	ratification Maastricht treaty Poul Schluter, Poul Rasmussen Danish, vote, Denmark, ec
~~466 (business)~~	PERSONAL FILE Born years ago, past years man, time, job, career

(a) Enriched topics E.

Related topic	Terms
79 (Emu)	economic monetary union Maastricht treaty, member states European, Europe, Community, Emu
377 (George)	President George Bush, White House Mr Clinton, administration Democratic, Republican, Washington
115 (powers)	de regulation bill Sunday trading, Queen Speech law, legislation, government, act
446 (years)	chairman chief executive managing director, finance director Sir, board, group, company
431 (cabinet)	Mr John Major prime minister, Mr Major party, tory, government, Conservative

(b) Related topics R.

Using ground truth document relevance judgments, we can see that documents returned by this expanded query have superior performance on standard information retrieval measures as described in the caption of Table 4. Figure 1 shows the receiver operating characteristic (ROC) curves for the baseline query (dotted) and the expanded topic 79 query (solid). Points on the ROC curve correspond to the true positive rates (TPR) and false positive rates (FPR) for sets of documents returned at different ranking thresholds. Here we consider the true positive (TP) set to be the union of relevant documents found within the top 500 documents returned by both queries. This plot visually depicts a clear improvement in the ranking of relevant documents. An additional benefit is that users are given the opportunity to see and explore different aspects of "euro opposition" such as the political dimension with respect to the United Kingdom.

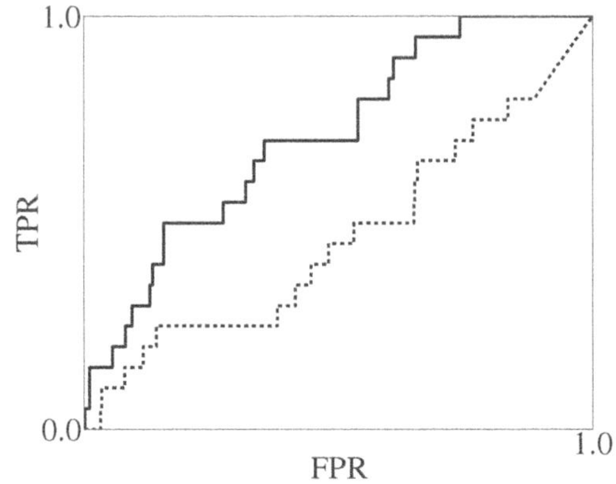

Figure 1: ROC curve of baseline (dashed) versus topic 79 feedback (solid) for the example query "euro opposition".

4. EXPERIMENTS

To our knowledge there has been no attempt to use latent topics as a user feedback mechanism in the way we have described. To determine whether our approach could be genuinely useful in practice, we must answer several questions. First, can query expansion with latent topic feedback improve the results of actual queries? While previous work has found that latent topics align well with existing document subject categories [23], it may be that these categories are more "topically coherent" than the relevant result sets for ad-hoc queries, and therefore more suitable for topic modeling. Second, assuming that for a given query there exists some latent topic which would improve retrieval results, will the topic selection approach described in Section 3.3 present it to the user? Finally, there is a third question which we do not address in this work: if presented with a helpful topic, will a user actually select it? For the following experiments we make the simplifying assumption that the user will always select the most helpful topic (with respect to the information retrieval measure of interest) among those presented. If no topic feedback will improve the set of returned documents, we assume the user will not provide topic feedback.

4.1 Experiment setup

While the ultimate goal of this work is to improve search and navigation under the specialized conditions described in Section 1, we evaluate our approach by conducting information retrieval experiments on several benchmark datasets from the Text REtrieval Conference (TREC) [32], using Wikipedia as a reference corpus. Each datasets consists of a corpus of text documents, a set of queries, and relevance judgments for each query. For each query, the individual words in the the title field are used as the baseline keyword query (e.g., "Industrial Espionage" is broken up into "Industrial", "Espionage"). Table 5 shows dataset details.

For each corpus, we first apply the LDA model to learn a set of latent topics, using the MALLET topic modeling toolkit [21]. We pre-process documents by downcasing, removing numbers and punctuation, applying a standard stopword list, and finally filtering out rarely occurring terms to yield vocabulary sizes of between 10,000 and 20,000 terms. We run parallelized collapsed Gibbs inference for 1,000 samples, re-estimating the document-topic hyperparameter α

Table 5: TREC datasets and queries (known within TREC as "topics") used in experimental evaluations. The number of documents D is given in thousands and Q denotes the number of queries.

Corpus	Abbrev	D	Q	TREC topics
Associated Press	AP	243	100	51-150
Financial Times	FT	210	200	251-450
Los Angeles Times	LA	128	150	301-450
Wall Street Journal	WSJ	173	100	51-100 151-200
Federal Register	FR	37	150	301-450
Foreign Broadcast Information Service	FBIS	127	150	301-450

every 25 samples. We learn $T = 500$ topics for each corpus in our experimental dataset, except $T = 250$ for the significantly smaller Federal Register (FR) corpus.

For all queries, we use the Galago [8] information retrieval system with default settings to retrieve 500 documents. Galago uses a query language and retrieval model based on Indri [22]. For the topic-expanded queries we set $\gamma = 0.25$, based on trial-and-error experimentation on held-aside preliminary development datasets.

4.2 Results

We calculate improvement over the baseline query with respect to three information retrieval measures [8]: mean average precision (MAP), normalized discounted cumulative gain (NDCG), and NDCG calculated with the first 15 results only (NDCG15). These quantitative results are shown in Table 6, along with the average number of feedback candidate topics shown to the user by our topic selection technique (fewer than eight topics per query).

We now return to the experimental questions we had set out to answer. These results demonstrate that latent topic feedback can indeed improve information retrieval results. Across evaluation measures, the results of approximately 40% of queries can be improved by latent topic feedback. However, these gains are irrelevant if we cannot identify potentially helpful topics and present them to the user. Again across measures, we see that our topic selection approach is able present a helpful topic for more than 40% of the queries for which there exists at least one helpful topic. Doing the rough arithmetic, this means that for about 16% of the queries in our experiment the user would be presented with at least one latent topic which would improve the relevance of the returned documents. Furthermore, we stress that even for the "missed" queries where presented topics do not provide quantitative relevance improvement, the corpus theme information conveyed may still be beneficial.

To give a better feel for the nature of these results, Figure 2 shows six queries along with helpful topics which were selected for presentation by our approach. In all cases, the connection between the topic and the query is fairly clear, resulting in gains across retrieval performance measures and visible improvement on ROC curves.

4.3 Analysis

First, we observe that for most queries (roughly 60%), there did not exist a single latent topic for which feedback would enhance information retrieval results. From manual inspection, this can occur because either no learned topic is well-aligned with the relevant documents, or because the results of the original query are good and difficult to improve upon.

Second, for queries where there exists one or more topics which *would* improve results, roughly 60% of the time our topic selection approach fails to select them. Minor variations on our topic selection method (i.e., showing more topics) did not correct this – many of the "missed" topics are not even close to making the cutoff. Manual investigations reveal that, interestingly, these topics often appear to be helpful *because* they are somewhat "distant" from the original query and the top few baseline documents returned. Attempts to predict topic feedback gain using linear or logistic regression and features such as $P(\text{query}|\phi_t)$ were unsuccessful, although more sophisticated approaches or richer features could possibly be applied.

It is also instructive to further examine the impact of two key aspects of our topic selection procedure: the inclusion of related topics and the exclusion of incoherent topics. For simplicity we will discuss NDCG15 measurements, but similar results hold for MAP and NDCG. Our selection approach recovers helpful topics for 133 out of 850 queries (15.6%) while presenting an average of 7.76 topics to the user for each query.

If we do *not* use PMI to filter out topics suspected of being incoherent, the number of topics shown per query rises to 9.79, but the number of queries for which helpful topics are presented only increases to 143 out of 850 (16.8%). The presence of incoherent topics may also impose cognitive burdens on the user, and it is uncertain whether users would be able to successfully identify incoherent topics for feedback.

If we were to omit the related topics R, it would decrease the average number of topics shown to 2.70, but it would decrease substantially the number of queries for which a helpful topic is presented, down to 93 out of 850 (10.9%). Also, we note that the presentation of related topics is potentially useful for exploratory corpus search, giving the user information about corpus themes "adjacent" to the topics present in returned documents.

Taken together, these findings suggest that our topic selection procedure is reasonable. The inclusion of related topics considerably increases the number of queries for which we present helpful topics while presenting novel and possibly interesting corpus themes. The filtering of suspect low-PMI topics does not discard many helpful topics, and should spare users the ordeal of interpreting ill-defined topics.

5. DISCUSSION

In this work we have developed a novel technique for improving text corpus search and navigation in difficult settings where we do not have access to metadata, rich lexical resources, or large user populations. This is an important problem because these conditions make information retrieval more difficult, and are applicable within organizations that have large quantities of *internal* text documents which they wish to explore, analyze, and exploit.

Table 6: Improvement from simulated latent topic feedback calculated only over queries where feedback improves performance. The "avg shown" column indicates the average number of topics actually shown to the user as a result of the topic selection procedure described in Section 3.3. For each query and evaluation measure, the "imprv" column shows the number of queries for which there *exists* at least one latent topic which improves performance, "found" shows the number of queries for which a helpful topic is *actually presented* to the user by our selection scheme, and "avg gain" shows the mean improvement when a helpful topic is presented to the user.

			NCDG15			NCDG			MAP		
Corpus	Q	avg shown	imprv	found	avg gain	imprv	found	avg gain	imprv	found	avg gain
AP	100	7.79	32	16	0.165	32	21	0.093	31	20	0.037
FT	200	7.47	97	43	0.238	138	80	0.134	137	72	0.041
LA	150	8.65	79	27	0.090	81	27	0.070	82	29	0.027
WSJ	100	7.73	29	16	0.205	30	18	0.050	29	18	0.026
FR	150	7.22	26	10	0.131	39	13	0.034	39	11	0.024
FBIS	150	7.78	62	21	0.163	64	25	0.037	67	29	0.024

To enhance search and exploration capabilities in this scenario, we have developed an approach that gives users the ability to provide feedback at the latent topic level. We leverage recent advances in latent topic modeling in order to construct meaningful representations of latent topics while filtering out incoherent "junk topics". We propose a mechanism for deciding on a manageably small set of topics to present to the user, as well as a method for constructing expanded queries based on user topic feedback. Quantitative results on benchmark TREC datasets show that this technique can result in major improvements for a non-trivial proportion of queries. Furthermore, the presentation of enriched and related topics alongside search results can help to deliver insights about corpus themes, which may be beneficial for knowledge discovery as well.

One potential obstacle to this approach is the scalability bottleneck presented by LDA topic inference. However, two factors act to ameliorate these concerns. First, topics can be inferred "offline" in advance; we do not need to do any expensive inference at query-time. Second, there have been significant recent advances along multiple fronts in scalable LDA inference. A distributed system developed at Yahoo! is reported to process 42,000 documents per hour [28]. Alternatively, an online inference algorithm for LDA [13] promises both improved scalability and a principled means of updating topics to reflect new documents. In practice, a hybrid system could update topics in an online fashion as documents are received, periodically performing distributed batch inference to refresh the learned topics.

6. FUTURE WORK

There are several promising directions in which to extend this approach. Two obvious areas for improvement are increasing the proportion of queries for which a helpful topic exists and improving the selection method for presenting helpful topics to the user.

It may be possible to improve the alignment between learned topics and user queries by the use of more sophisticated topic models such as the Pachinko Allocation Model (PAM) [16]. While these models were *not* found to be helpful for document smoothing [36], rich hierarchical topics may be beneficial when combined with the *explicit* user feedback present in our approach. Our approach could also exploit prior information such as predefined concepts by using topic model variants which can incorporate domain knowledge [7, 1].

However, learning finer-grained topics can only increase the importance of carefully choosing which topics to show the user. Here it may be instructive to consider the large body of research on "learning to rank" [19], as well as recent work in facet selection [17, 14].

The query expansion mechanism is another potential target for extension. If our underlying information retrieval system supports phrase search terms (e.g., "White House"), it may be helpful to directly use discovered n-grams as well.

Further work could also compare the use of topics for explicit feedback in this work versus the implicit use of topics to improve document language models in prior work [33]. It may be that the two techniques could be combined profitably, with some topics being more suitable for explicit feedback while others are better used for smoothing.

Finally, another important step is to validate our user model assumptions. One approach may be to directly evaluate information retrieval performance using actual user feedback, for example via Amazon Mechanical Turk [37]. It may also be interesting to explore the relationship between topic presentation (e.g., topic labeling strategies, whether to display n-grams) and user behavior.

7. ACKNOWLEDGMENTS

This work was performed under the auspices of the U.S. Department of Energy by Lawrence Livermore National Laboratory under Contract DE-AC52-07NA27344 (LLNL-CONF-471258).

8. REFERENCES

[1] D. Andrzejewski, X. Zhu, and M. Craven. Incorporating domain knowledge into topic modeling via Dirichlet forest priors. In *ICML*, pages 25–32. Omnipress, 2009.

[2] D. Blei, L. Carin, and D. Dunson. Probabilistic topic models. *Signal Processing Magazine, IEEE*, 27(6):55–65, 2010.

[3] D. Blei and J. Lafferty. Visualizing topics with multi-word expressions. Technical report, 2009. `arXiv:0907.1013v1 [stat.ML]`.

[4] D. Blei, A. Ng, and M. Jordan. Latent Dirichlet allocation. *JMLR*, 3:993–1022, 2003.

FBIS query 426 "law enforcement dogs"
Topic 321 (heroin) seized kg cocaine drug traffickers, kg heroin police, arrested, drugs, marijuana

NDCG15	NDCG	MAP
+0.299	+0.065	+0.046

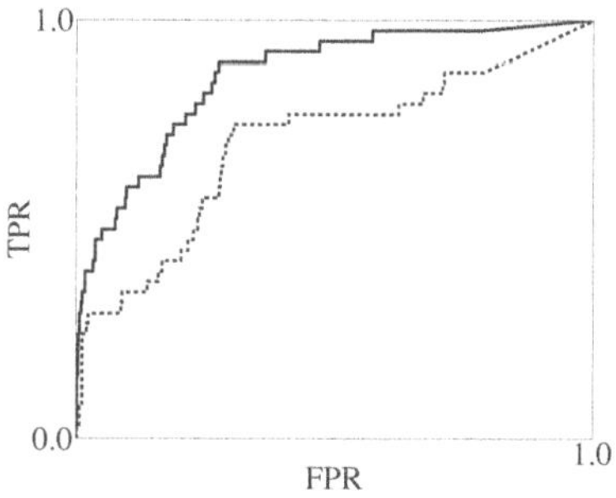

FBIS query 450 "King Hussein, peace"
Topic 293 (Amman) Majesty King Husayn al Aqabah, peace process Jordan, Jordanian, Amman, Arab

NDCG15	NDCG	MAP
+0.708	+0.175	+0.171

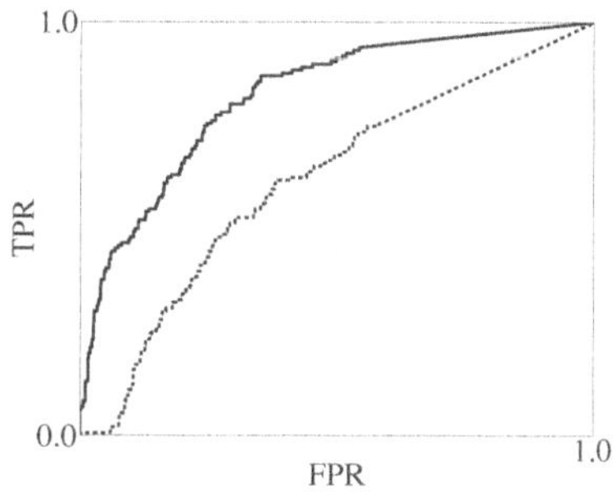

WSJ query 86 "bank failures"
Topic 444 (FDIC) Federal Deposit Insurance William Seidman, Insurance Corp banks, bank, FDIC, banking

NDCG15	NDCG	MAP
+0.602	+0.121	+0.110

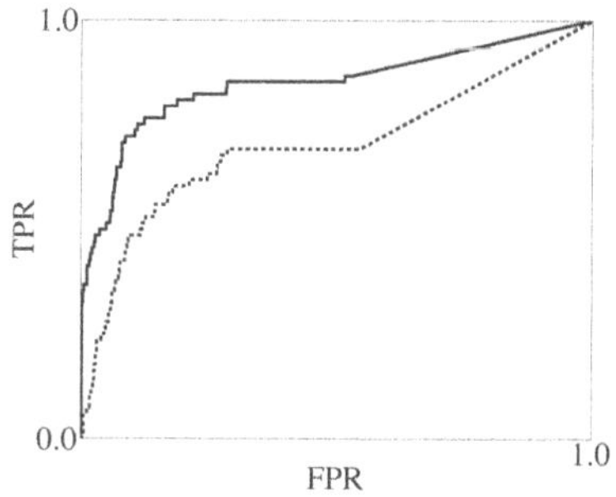

AP query 127 "U.S.-U.S.S.R. Arms Control Agreements"
Topic 232 (missile) Strategic Defense Initiative United States, arms control treaty, nuclear, missiles, range

NDCG15	NDCG	MAP
+0.296	+0.209	+0.105

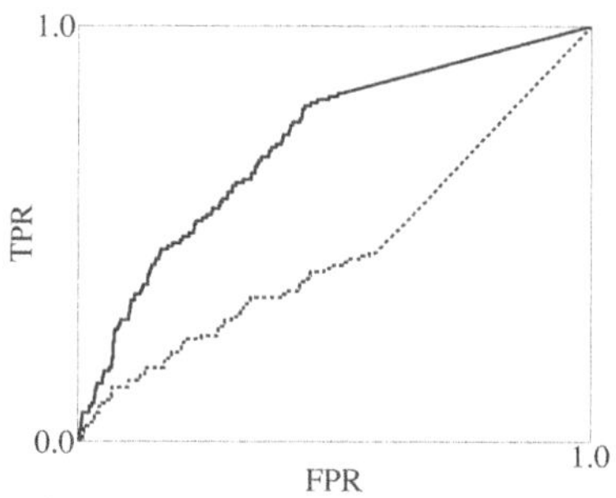

AP query 135 "Possible Contributions of Gene Mapping to Medicine"
Topic 325 (called) British journal Nature immune system, genetically engineered cells, research, researchers, scientists

NDCG15	NDCG	MAP
+0.147	+0.040	+0.019

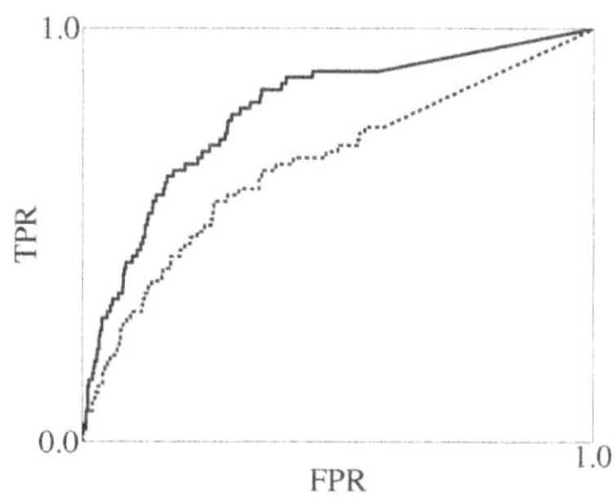

AP query 113 "New Space Satellite Applications"
Topic 237 (communications) European Space Agency Air Force, Cape Canaveral satellite, launch, rocket, satellites

NDCG15	NDCG	MAP
+0.237	+0.033	+0.007

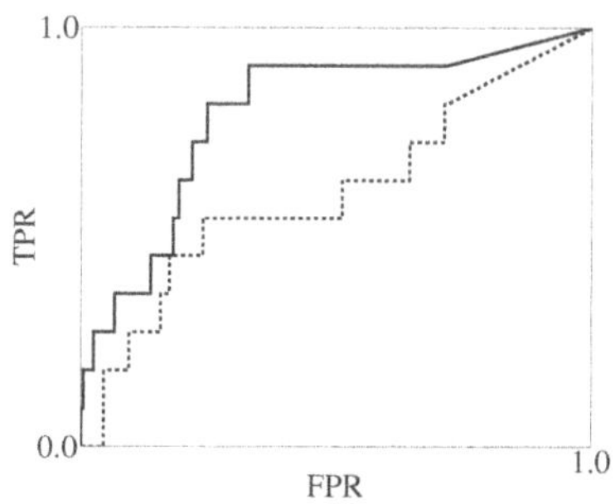

Figure 2: Six example queries with helpful topics and ROC curves. For each ROC curve, the set of true positive (TP) relevant documents is considered to be the union of the relevant documents discovered (i.e., ranked within the top 500) by the baseline query (dashed line) and the expanded query that incorporates latent topic feedback (solid line).

[5] O. Bodenreider. The Unified Medical Language System (UMLS): integrating biomedical terminology. *Nucleic Acids Research*, 32(suppl 1):D267–D270, 2004.

[6] C. Buckley, G. Salton, J. Allan, and A. Singhal. Automatic query expansion using SMART: TREC 3. In *TREC*, pages 69–80. NIST, 1994.

[7] C. Chemudugunta, A. Holloway, P. Smyth, and M. Steyvers. Modeling documents by combining semantic concepts with unsupervised statistical learning. In *ISWC*, pages 229–244. Springer, 2008.

[8] B. Croft, D. Metzler, and T. Strohman. *Search*

Engines: Information Retrieval in Practice. Addison-Wesley, 2010.

[9] W. Dakka, P. G. Ipeirotis, and K. R. Wood. Automatic construction of multifaceted browsing interfaces. In *CIKM*, pages 768–775. ACM, 2005.

[10] C. Fellbaum. *WordNet : an Electronic Lexical Database.* MIT Press, 1998.

[11] M. J. Gardner, J. Lutes, J. Lund, J. Hansen, D. Walker, E. Ringger, and K. Seppi. The topic browser: An interactive tool for browsing topic models. In *NIPS Workshop on Challenges of Data Visualization.* MIT Press, 2010.

[12] T. L. Griffiths and M. Steyvers. Finding scientific topics. *PNAS*, 101(Suppl 1):5228–5235, 2004.

[13] M. Hoffman, D. Blei, and F. Bach. Online learning for latent Dirichlet allocation. In *NIPS*, pages 856–864. MIT Press, 2010.

[14] J. Koren, Y. Zhang, and X. Liu. Personalized interactive faceted search. In *WWW*, pages 477–486, New York, NY, USA, 2008. ACM.

[15] J. H. Lau, D. Newman, S. Karimi, and T. Baldwin. Best topic word selection for topic labelling. In *Coling 2010: Posters*, pages 605–613. Coling 2010 Organizing Committee, 2010.

[16] W. Li and A. McCallum. Pachinko allocation: DAG-structured mixture models of topic correlations. In *ICML*, pages 577–584. ACM, 2006.

[17] S. Liberman and R. Lempel. Approximately optimal facet selection. In *(submission)*, 2011.

[18] X. Ling, Q. Mei, C. Zhai, and B. Schatz. Mining multi-faceted overviews of arbitrary topics in a text collection. In *KDD*, pages 497–505. ACM, 2008.

[19] T.-Y. Liu. Learning to rank for information retrieval. In *SIGIR Tutorials*, page 904, 2010.

[20] Y. Lu, Q. Mei, and C. Zhai. Investigating task performance of probabilistic topic models: an empirical study of PLSA and LDA. *Information Retrieval*, pages 1–26, 2010.

[21] A. K. McCallum. Mallet: A machine learning for language toolkit. http://mallet.cs.umass.edu, 2002.

[22] D. Metzler and W. B. Croft. Combining the language model and inference network approaches to retrieval. *Inf. Process. Manage.*, 40:735–750, 2004.

[23] D. M. Mimno and A. McCallum. Organizing the OCA: learning faceted subjects from a library of digital books. In *JCDL*, pages 376–385. ACM, 2007.

[24] T. Minka and J. Lafferty. Expectation-propagation for the generative aspect model. In *UAI*, pages 352–359. Morgan Kaufmann, 2002.

[25] D. Newman, J. H. Lau, K. Grieser, and T. Baldwin. Automatic evaluation of topic coherence. In *HLT-NAACL*, pages 100–108, Morristown, NJ, USA, 2010. ACL.

[26] D. Newman, Y. Noh, E. Talley, S. Karimi, and T. Baldwin. Evaluating topic models for digital libraries. In *JCDL*, pages 215–224. ACM, 2010.

[27] L. A. Park and K. Ramamohanarao. The sensitivity of latent Dirichlet allocation for information retrieval. In *ECML PKDD*, pages 176–188. Springer-Verlag, 2009.

[28] A. Smola and S. Narayanamurthy. An architecture for parallel topic models. *Proc. VLDB Endow.*, 3:703–710, 2010.

[29] E. Stoica, M. Hearst, and M. Richardson. Automating creation of hierarchical faceted metadata structures. In *HLT-NAACL*, pages 244–251, Rochester, New York, April 2007. ACL.

[30] Y. W. Teh, D. Newman, and M. Welling. A collapsed variational Bayesian inference algorithm for latent Dirichlet allocation. In *In NIPS*. MIT Press, 2007.

[31] The Gene Ontology Consortium. Gene Ontology: Tool for the unification of biology. *Nature Genetics*, 25:25–29, 2000.

[32] E. M. Voorhees and D. K. Harman. *TREC: Experiment and Evaluation in Information Retrieval.* MIT Press, 2005.

[33] X. Wei and W. B. Croft. LDA-based document models for ad-hoc retrieval. In *SIGIR*, pages 178–185. ACM, 2006.

[34] R. W. White and G. Marchionini. Examining the effectiveness of real-time query expansion. *Inf. Process. Manage.*, 43:685–704, 2007.

[35] K.-P. Yee, K. Swearingen, K. Li, and M. Hearst. Faceted metadata for image search and browsing. In *CHI*, pages 401–408. ACM, 2003.

[36] X. Yi and J. Allan. A comparative study of utilizing topic models for information retrieval. In *ECIR*, pages 29–41. Springer-Verlag, 2009.

[37] L. Zhang and Y. Zhang. Interactive retrieval based on faceted feedback. In *SIGIR*, pages 363–370. ACM, 2010.

Localized Factor Models for Multi-Context Recommendation

Deepak Agarwal, Bee-Chung Chen and Bo Long
Yahoo! Labs
Sunnyvale, CA
{dagarwal,beechun,bolong}@yahoo-inc.com

ABSTRACT

Combining correlated information from multiple contexts can significantly improve predictive accuracy in recommender problems. Such information from multiple contexts is often available in the form of several incomplete matrices spanning a set of entities like users, items, features, and so on. Existing methods simultaneously factorize these matrices by sharing a single set of factors for entities across all contexts. We show that such a strategy may introduce significant bias in estimates and propose a new model that ameliorates this issue by positing *local*, context-specific factors for entities. To avoid over-fitting in contexts with sparse data, the local factors are connected through a *shared* global model. This sharing of parameters allows information to flow across contexts through multivariate regressions among local factors, instead of enforcing exactly the same factors for an entity, everywhere. Model fitting is done in an EM framework, we show that the E-step can be fitted through a fast multi-resolution Kalman filter algorithm that ensures scalability. Experiments on benchmark and real-world Yahoo! datasets clearly illustrate the usefulness of our approach. Our model significantly improves predictive accuracy, especially in cold-start scenarios.

Categories and Subject Descriptors

H.3.3 [**Information Search and Retrieval**]: Information filtering; G.3 [**Mathematics of Computing**]: Probability and Statistics

General Terms

Algorithms, Design, Experimentation

1. INTRODUCTION

Amalgamating information from multiple related contexts to improve predictive accuracy is important in several large scale recommender problems, especially those where severe data sparsity is typical. For instance, user affinity to different kinds of news categories inferred from prior visits to Yahoo! News may help in improving article recommendation when users visit the Yahoo! Front Page and vice-versa. User activity on different Yahoo! verticals like Sports, MyYahoo!, Finance, and others can potentially be combined to improve content recommendation on every single page that the user visits on Yahoo! . A content module on the Yahoo! Front Page maybe syndicated and displayed in other contexts like MyYahoo! Yahoo! Mail — interchanging the role of users and items, one can potentially leverage enormous amounts of feedback received on Front Page module articles to improve performance of the same module on MyYahoo! which is a significantly lower volume site with a different user population. Similar issues arise in other recommender applications like movie recommendation, advertising, and so on.

Abstractly, multi-context data in recommender problems consists of the following: (1) user-item interaction matrices in different contexts (e.g. Yahoo! Front Page, Yahoo! News) measuring some response (clicks, ratings, etc), where the response is typically available only for a small subset of all possible user-item pairs; (2) user-feature and item-feature matrices in different contexts, some features are declared (e.g. user age, movie genre, zip code, etc) while others are inferred (user affinity to news type). For the inferred features, associating different weights to capture uncertainty is important. It is routine to see matrices with different degrees of data sparsity and different user (item) populations across contexts. Users (items) that have no or little data (cold-start) in the prediction context of interest may have data in other contexts that could be leveraged to improve performance.

Loosely speaking, predicting user-item response in a context of interest could improve if information available from other contexts are used as *predictors* (especially in cold-start and small sample size scenarios.) While true, constructing such predictors is a challenging task in recommender problems due to several reasons. Interaction and feature matrices are often noisy and highly incomplete. Entries are often not missing at random since occurrence distribution of items served in a recommender systems tends to be heavy-tailed; hence, imputation is difficult. The amount of overlap in user (item) population for different contexts may vary, and the amount of data in different contexts can have large variation. If predictors are not constructed and used appropriately, there is a danger of high volume contexts having excessive influence and even deteriorating predictions in sparse contexts.

KDD'11, August 21–24, 2011, San Diego, California, USA.

For the sake of concreteness, consider a scenario with data from three contexts: (1) user-item response matrix from a module on Yahoo! Front Page, (2) user-item response matrix on Yahoo! News, and (3) user-category inferred feature matrix based on articles read by users in the past. There is no overlap in the items for these contexts; the only overlap that exists is for users. A natural approach to deal with missing entries and noise in such scenarios is to extract sufficient statistics that capture user-item interactions in each context. Matrix factorization is a popular approach whereby the incomplete matrix Y_k in context k is approximated as $f(Z_k B_k')$, where Z_k and B_k are dense user and item factors respectively, and f is some function (linear or non-linear) depending on the response type. Given user factors in all three contexts, one can build regression models to predict factors in each context by using the estimated factors in the other two contexts as predictors (or features) for the common user population. For example, Z_1 may be predicted by using Z_2 and Z_3 as predictors. If such a regression relationship (or correlation) is strong among contexts, we can obtain a better estimate of Z_1 by exploiting the information in Z_2 and Z_3, especially when the response matrix in context 1 is sparse, because the data in contexts 2 and 3 is implicitly used to *smooth* the estimate of Z_1. This is the main idea of our localized matrix factorization (LMF) approach — we produce *local* factors in each context that are *smoothed* by borrowing strength from factor estimates in other contexts. However, regressions to share factor information across contexts cannot be learnt using point estimates of factors since these are subject to different degrees of uncertainty; this may lead to biased regression estimates due to measurement error in the predictors [12]. To see this, consider a simple linear regression $y = a + bx + \text{error}$, where $x = z + \text{error}$. When predictor x is subject to error, performing a linear regression of y on a noisy version of the true predictor z leads to downward bias in the estimate of b. It is easy to visualize this geometrically, a relatively tight straight line of y on z incurs more scatter when z is measured with error through x and the slope shrinks towards zero. Incorporating the measurement error in z through a model reduces this bias in estimating b. Figure 1 shows an illustration. Further, the set of users in different contexts have different degrees of overlaps. A naive regression approach using estimated factors may not be suitable for combining information, especially when the number of contexts is large. Hence we borrow information across contexts through a multi-level hierarchical model where the observed response matrix in a context is generated from a distribution centered around a context-specific local factorization, and the latent context-specific local factors are assumed to be drawn from a common prior distribution. Such sharing of local factors induces factor correlations that are estimated from the data, which facilitates information sharing that depends on the strength of inter-context correlations. Other than reducing bias due to measurement error in the factors, joint modeling also helps in utilizing overlaps across multiple contexts in a principled way to improve the estimates of all local factors. For instance, assume there are users in context 1 that overlap with users in context 2 but not with the users in context 3. Then estimation of Z_1 can naturally benefit from data in context 2 because of the overlap. Furthermore, if users in context 2 overlap with some users in context 3, the estimation of Z_1 can also benefit from data in context 3, even if there is no direct overlap between contexts 1 and 3. Such transitivity becomes important in the presence of many contexts that are correlated; naive regressions on estimated factors do not have the flexibility to fully utilize such information.

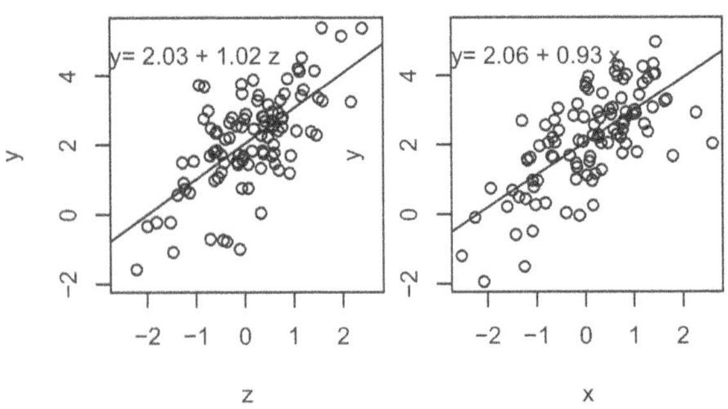

Figure 1: *Attenuation bias in estimating regression line with measurement error in predictor. Data simulated using $y = 2.0 + 1.0x + error$, left panel is regression fit from exact predictor, right panel has error in the predictor.*

Existing approaches in the literature do not posit local factors; instead, they are too constrained and assume same factors per user (item) across contexts. We shall refer to this as collective matrix factorization (CMF) as in [40]. In our example, this approach assumes a common global user factor matrix Z for all contexts, which gets estimated by optimizing the joint multi-context likelihood (with suitably regularized factors). Since the likelihood of contexts with large amounts of data would have more influence on global factor estimates, such an approach may introduce significant bias for sparse and skewed contexts. To mitigate this issue, a weighted geometric mean of the likelihoods that balance the information entering in estimating the common global factors is used. Such an approach requires careful tweaking of the geometric weights that gets difficult and formidable with a large number of contexts. Also, separate tweakings of weights may have to be done for each prediction task. This makes it an unattractive approach compared to our LMF mode that provides a relaxation of factors locally and eliminates the need to tweak influence of information from different contexts.

Although LMF provides additional flexibility through factor localization, scalable model-fitting is an important consideration. As typical with most multi-level hierarchical models, fitting can be done through an EM algorithm. In our case, we show the E-step can be computed through a fast multi-resolution Kalman filter [23, 13, 22] algorithm, this makes the fitting procedure scalable to large applications.

Our **contributions** are as follows. We propose a novel method LMF to enhance predictions in multi-context recommender problems through a localized latent factor model. Our method posits local user (item) factors in each context, and then borrows strength across contexts by positing a second stage prior which assumes local factors are centered around a global factor with some variance. In fact, our second stage prior can be interpreted as performing a multivariate regression for all local factors through a reduced-rank model; one could also interpret this as estimating local factor covariances parametrized through outer products of low-rank matrices. Our LMF approach removes several deficiencies of existing approaches that learn from different contexts by using the same factors for each entity. We illustrate the deficiencies of CMF and the flexibility of LMF on benchmark data sets and a new Yahoo! multi-context data set from Yahoo! Front Page and Yahoo! News.

2. MODEL

We provide modeling details for the localized matrix factorization model (LMF). Although the model is general and can combine information for both items and users that are common across contexts, we make some simplifying assumptions for ease of exposition and to avoid notational clutter. We assume only user-ids have possible overlaps across contexts, item populations are distinct with no overlaps. Hence, we only describe the joint learning of user factors, joint learning of both user and/or item factors follow a straightforward generalization. We begin with notations.

Notations: We consider K different contexts, each of which may represent a recommendation application or a collection of features. Let $\mathcal{I}$ denote the set of all users from the union of all contexts. We use y_{ijk} to denote the rating that user i gives to item j in context k, or user i's feature value on feature j in context k. Since features play the same role as ratings in the model, to simplify notations and terms, we call a feature an item, and call a rating and a feature value the response. As stated before, we assume each context has a different set of items for simplicity. Let $\mathcal{K}_i$ denote the set of contexts that include data of user i. Let $\mathcal{J}_{ik}$ denote the set of items in context k with response from user i. Note that some users do not have any observed response in some contexts. Our goal is to simultaneously *impute* the missing response values for all (or some selected) contexts of interest.

Localized matrix factorization model (LMF): We assume that the response y_{ijk} of a (user i, item j) pair in context k is generated according to a *local latent profile* vector $\boldsymbol{z}_{ik}$. (Recall that we use the term "response" to refer to both user's ratings and features.) Then, the distribution of response conditional on latent factors is denoted by

$$p(y_{ijk}|f(\boldsymbol{z}_{ik})),$$

where $f(.)$ is a known function, and p is a generic symbol used to denote probability distributions. For computational ease, we assume $f(.)$ is a linear function of latent factor $\boldsymbol{z}_{ik}$. We consider two response distributions — normal distribution for continuous response and Bernoulli distribution for binary response. Hence we have the following two response distributions conditional on latent factors.

$$y_{ijk} \,|\, \boldsymbol{z}_{ik} \sim N(\boldsymbol{\beta}'_{jk}\boldsymbol{z}_{ik} + \alpha_{jk},\ \sigma^2_{y,k}w_{ijk}),\ \text{or}$$
$$y_{ijk} \,|\, \boldsymbol{z}_{ik} \sim \text{Bernoulli}((1+\exp\{-(\boldsymbol{\beta}'_{jk}\boldsymbol{z}_{ik}+\alpha_{jk})\})^{-1})$$

Note that:

- $\boldsymbol{\beta}_{jk}$ and α_{jk} are the regression weight vector and the bias term for item j in context k, respectively.
- w_{ijk} is a known weight attached to response y_{ijk}, in many scenarios $w_{ijk} = 1$ for each response. One can also set w_{ijk} based on the known uncertainty associated with each response.
- $\sigma^2_{y,k}$ is the variance of the response in context k, which will be estimated from data.

To transfer knowledge cross different contexts, we assume the local profiles of user i are generated according to a *global latent profile* vector $\boldsymbol{u}_i$, which captures a user's deeper taste across multiple contexts. The conditional distribution capturing this is denoted by

$$p(\boldsymbol{z}_{ik}|g(\boldsymbol{u}_i)),$$

where $g(.)$ is a known function. Again, for computational ease, we assume $g(.)$ is a linear function of $\boldsymbol{u}_i$ and the conditional distribution of local factors $\boldsymbol{z}_{ik}$ is normal. Furthermore, we assume standard normal distribution for the global latent user profile $\boldsymbol{u}_i$. The complete specification of the generative model for latent user profiles is given as

$$\boldsymbol{z}_{ik} \,|\, \boldsymbol{u}_i \sim N(A_k\boldsymbol{u}_i,\ \sigma^2_{z,k}I)$$
$$\boldsymbol{u}_i \sim N(\mathbf{0},\ I).$$

Note that:

- A_k is a linear transformation matrix that transform the global profile to the local profile in context k. A_k will be learnt from data.
- $\sigma^2_{z,k}$ is the variance that determines the strength of correlation between local and global factors for context k. $\sigma^2_{z,k}$ will also be estimated from data.

For ease of exposition, we use the following notations:

- $\mathbf{y} = \{y_{ijk}\}_{\forall i\in\mathcal{I},k\in\mathcal{K}_i,j\in\mathcal{J}_{ik}}$ denotes all observed response.
- $\mathbf{z} = \{\boldsymbol{z}_{ik}\}_{\forall i\in\mathcal{I},k\in\mathcal{K}_i}$ denotes all local profile vectors.
- $\mathbf{u} = \{\boldsymbol{u}_i\}$ denotes all global profile vectors.
- $\mathbf{y}_k$ and $\mathbf{z}_k$ denote response and factors for context k.
- B_k denotes the matrix created by stacking the β_{jk}s together for items in application k.
- Let $\boldsymbol{\Theta} = (\boldsymbol{\alpha}, \boldsymbol{\beta}, \mathbf{A}, \boldsymbol{\sigma}^2)$, where $\boldsymbol{\alpha} = \{\alpha_{jk}\}$, $\boldsymbol{\beta} = \{\boldsymbol{\beta}_{jk}\}$, $\mathbf{A} = \{A_k\}$, and $\boldsymbol{\sigma}^2 = \{\sigma^2_{\cdot,k}\}$ denote all the model parameters that needs to be estimated from data.

Our goal is to obtain $E[y_{ijk}\,|\,\mathbf{y}]$, for (i,j,k) triples such that $k \notin \mathcal{K}_i$ or $j \notin \mathcal{J}_{ik}$.

Discussion: Our multi-level hierarchical model LMF provides a number of advantages over existing methods. To simplify discussion, assume two contexts, i.e., $K = 2$. Existing methods assume $z_{i1} = z_{i2} = z_i$ for each i. We note that this is a special case of our LMF that arises by assuming $A_1 = A_2 = I$ and $\sigma^2_{z,k} = 0$. To see this, consider a Gaussian response, then negative log-likelihood of $\mathbf{y}$ is (ignoring regularization terms)

$$|\mathbf{y}_1 - B_1Z|^2/\sigma^2_{y,1} + |\mathbf{y}_2 - B_2Z|^2/\sigma^2_{y,2} + const \qquad (1)$$

The common user factor matrix Z is obtained by minimizing the loss function in Equation 1 (after adding L_2 regularizers for B_1, B_2, Z). This is referred to as collective matrix factorization in the literature [40], we shall call this CMF. However in CMF, the weighting attached to loss functions in different contexts are assumed known and in general obtained through cross-validation, in our case the weights $\sigma^2_{y,k}$s are obtained through an EM algorithm. This is attractive and necessary for large K where it gets unwieldy to determine a large number of such parameters through cross-validation. One of the datasets on Epinions we analyze in section 4.4 has 10 contexts, automatic estimation of weights attached to likelihood of different contexts is essential in such scenarios.

However, estimating such weighting parameters automatically when common factors are shared across contexts may cause problems. For instance, if the first context is a sparse response matrix that needs to be predicted and the second context is a dense matrix represents user feature vectors, the sparse response matrix will force the common user factors to be influenced more by features and may result in inferior performance. By assuming $Z_1 \neq Z_2$ in LMF but rather correlated, we avoid this problem inherent in CMF. In fact, it is easy to see that a-priori, the covariance matrix Σ_{12} of (z_{i1}, z_{i2}) is given by

$$\Sigma_{12} = \begin{pmatrix} A_1A_1' + \sigma_{z,1}^2 I & A_1A_2' \\ A_2A_1' & A_2A_2' + \sigma_{z,2}^2 I \end{pmatrix}$$

Thus, LMF provides more flexibility by assuming local factors per context but avoids over-fitting by connecting the parameters through a joint multivariate normal distribution with covariance estimated through a reduced rank structure. For Gaussian response, the posterior distribution is also Gaussian and hence the local factors across contexts are smoothed through cross-context global covariance. If a user is new in context 1 but have been seen in context 2, one could predict the local factor z_1 through the conditional posterior of $z_1|z_2$. This is how LMF transfers information from one context to the other without getting overly influenced by contexts merely due to large sample size. The simpler approach of performing factorization separately in each context and then using the estimated factors as features does not account for the uncertainty in estimated factors. By obtaining a joint posterior, our LMF provides a principled way of learning across contexts.

To provide further intuition on how LMF learns across contexts, consider the Gaussian model and our two-context example. Then, the predicted rating for a new user-item pair (i, j) in context k is given as $\beta_{jk}'\hat{z}_{ik}$, where $\hat{z}_{ik}$ is the estimated posterior mean. For two contexts, the posterior mean estimate is obtained from the joint posterior as $E_{z_{i2}}[E(z_{i1}|z_{i2})]$, i.e., we average out the conditional expectation of $z_{i1}|z_{i2}$ w.r.t. the marginal distribution of z_{i2}. This is referred to as Rao-Blackwellization in the literature [7] and is known to reduce variance in estimators. Hence our LMF can also be thought of as a Rao-Blackwellization procedure to obtain low-variance estimates by leveraging data across contexts.

3. FITTING ALGORITHM

We take an *empirical bayes* approach to model fitting by treating $\mathbf{\Theta} = (\boldsymbol{\alpha}, \boldsymbol{\beta}, \mathbf{A}, \boldsymbol{\sigma}^2)$ as model parameters, and $\mathbf{u}$ and $\mathbf{z}$ as hidden variables. Our goal is to first obtain the maximum likelihood estimate of $\mathbf{\Theta}$; i.e.,

$$\hat{\mathbf{\Theta}} = \arg\max_{\mathbf{\Theta}} \Pr[\mathbf{y} \,|\, \mathbf{\Theta}] = \arg\max_{\mathbf{\Theta}} \int \Pr[\mathbf{y}, \mathbf{u}, \mathbf{z} \,|\, \mathbf{\Theta}] \, d\mathbf{u} \, d\mathbf{z},$$

and then obtain the posterior distribution of the hidden variables. Because all the distributions are normal, the marginal distribution is available in closed form, but quite complicated. In the following, we provide the details for the Gaussian model. For the Logistic model, we use variational approximation [25]. This approximation converts the logistic into a weighted Gaussian by obtaining a quadratic approximation to the logistic loss.

EM algorithm: Iteratively, we can solve the problem using the EM algorithm [19]. Let q_k and r denote the lengths of vectors $\boldsymbol{z}_{ik}$ and $\boldsymbol{u}_i$ respectively. Let n denote the total number of users. The complete data (including the hidden variables) log likelihood is $L(\mathbf{\Theta}, \mathbf{u}, \mathbf{z}; \mathbf{y})$, given in Table 1. Let $\hat{\mathbf{\Theta}}_t$ denote the current estimated value of $\mathbf{\Theta}$ at the beginning of the tth iteration. In the tth iteration, the EM algorithm update $\mathbf{\Theta}$ to get a new estimate

$$\hat{\mathbf{\Theta}}_{t+1} = \arg\max_{\mathbf{\Theta}} E_{(\mathbf{u}, \mathbf{z} \,|\, \mathbf{y}, \hat{\mathbf{\Theta}}_t)}[L(\mathbf{\Theta}, \mathbf{u}, \mathbf{z}; \mathbf{y})], \quad (2)$$

where $\hat{\mathbf{\Theta}}_t$ is constant; $\mathbf{\Theta}$ is the variable to optimize; $\mathbf{u}$ and $\mathbf{z}$ are the random variables to take expectation over; and the expectation is taken over the posterior distribution of $(\mathbf{u}, \mathbf{v} \,|\, \mathbf{y}, \hat{\mathbf{\Theta}}_t)$, which is Gaussian; and $E_{(\mathbf{u}, \mathbf{z} \,|\, \mathbf{y}, \hat{\mathbf{\Theta}}_t)}[L(\mathbf{\Theta}, \mathbf{u}, \mathbf{z}; \mathbf{y})]$ is given in Table 1. Note that, in the rest of this section, we consider the computation in a single EM iteration, thus dropping subscript t in the following notations: Let $\hat{\boldsymbol{u}}_i = E[\boldsymbol{u}_i \,|\, \mathbf{y}, \hat{\mathbf{\Theta}}_t]$, $\hat{\boldsymbol{z}}_{ik} = E[\boldsymbol{z}_{ik} \,|\, \mathbf{y}, \hat{\mathbf{\Theta}}_t]$, $\hat{V}[\boldsymbol{u}_i] = Var[\boldsymbol{u}_i \,|\, \mathbf{y}, \hat{\mathbf{\Theta}}_t]$, $\hat{V}[\boldsymbol{z}_{ik}] = Var[\boldsymbol{z}_i \,|\, \mathbf{y}, \hat{\mathbf{\Theta}}_t]$ and $\hat{V}[\boldsymbol{z}_{ik}, \boldsymbol{u}_i] = Cov[\boldsymbol{z}_{ik}, \boldsymbol{u}_i \,|\, \mathbf{y}, \hat{\mathbf{\Theta}}_t]$. Let $A_{k,\ell}$ denote the ℓth row of A_k.

3.1 E-step

In the E-step, we compute $\hat{\boldsymbol{u}}_i$, $\hat{\boldsymbol{z}}_{ik}$, $\hat{V}[\boldsymbol{u}_i]$, $\hat{V}[\boldsymbol{z}_{ik}]$ and $\hat{V}[\boldsymbol{z}_{ik}, \boldsymbol{u}_i]$ using the multi-resolution Kalman filter algorithm. It is safe to skip this section without loss of continuity but it is crucial to understand the implementation of fitting algorithm. The Kalman filter algorithm provides an essentially linear time algorithm (for small number of latent factors) to obtain state estimates that are connected linearly in a hierarchical fashion (see [23, 13] for more discussion). As such, it is important to scale our fitting to large datasets. At a high-level, the algorithm consists of two steps: (1) **Bottom-up filtering** where information is transmitted from observed data to local factors $\boldsymbol{z}_{ik}$, and from local factors $\boldsymbol{z}_{ik}$ to the global factors $\boldsymbol{u}_i$. (2) **Top-down smoothing** which transmits information from global factors to the local factors and facilitates cross-context learning. Detailed derivation of formulas for a general hierarchical linear state-space model is provided in [23]; we provide the details in the context of our model. For ease of exposition, if $\boldsymbol{a}_1, ..., \boldsymbol{a}_n$ are n column vectors, each has length m, then $[\boldsymbol{a}_1, ..., \boldsymbol{a}_n]$ denotes a $m \times n$ matrix that binds them together. We use (HC Eq n) to denote Equation n in [23], and the following notation.

$$\begin{aligned}
\boldsymbol{d}_{ik}' &= [(y_{ijk} - \alpha_{jk}) \,:\, \forall j \in \boldsymbol{\mathcal{J}}_{ik}] \\
C_{ik}' &= [\boldsymbol{\beta}_{jk} \,:\, \forall j \in \boldsymbol{\mathcal{J}}_{ik}] \\
D_{ik} &= \text{diag}([\sigma_{y,k}^2 w_{ijk} \,:\, \forall j \in \boldsymbol{\mathcal{J}}_{ik}]) \\
\Sigma_{ik} &= Var[\boldsymbol{z}_{ik}] = \sigma_u^2 A_k A_k' + \sigma_{z,k}^2 I \quad \text{(independent of } i\text{)} \\
E_{ik} &= C_{ik}\Sigma_{ik}C_{ik}' + D_{ik} \\
F_{ik} &= \Sigma_{ik}^{-1} + C_{ik}' D_{ik}^{-1} C_{ik} \\
H_{ik} &= \sigma_u^2 A_k' \Sigma_{ik}^{-1} \\
R_{ik} &= \sigma_u^2 I - \sigma_u^4 A_k' \Sigma_{ik}^{-1} A_k
\end{aligned}$$

Note that with this notation, we have

$$\boldsymbol{d}_{ik} \,|\, \boldsymbol{z}_{ik} \sim N(C_{ik}\boldsymbol{z}_{ik}, D_{ik})$$

$$\text{Marginally, } \boldsymbol{d}_{ik} \sim N(\mathbf{0}, E_{ik}) \quad \text{(they are not } iid\text{)}$$

$$E_{ik}^{-1} = D_{ik}^{-1} - D_{ik}^{-1} C_{ik} F_{ik}^{-1} C_{ik}' D_{ik}^{-1}$$

$$\boldsymbol{u}_i = H_{ik}\boldsymbol{z}_{ik} + \boldsymbol{\xi}_{ik}, \quad \boldsymbol{\xi}_{ik} \sim N(\mathbf{0}, R_{ik})$$

Filtering: By (HC Eq 1.4) and (HC Eq 1.5), we obtain

Complete data log-likelihood: $L(\Theta, \mathbf{u}, \mathbf{z}; \mathbf{y}) = \Pr[\mathbf{u}, \mathbf{z}, \mathbf{y} \mid \Theta] = $ some constant
$-\frac{1}{2}\sum_i \sum_{k\in\mathcal{K}_i^y} \sum_{j\in\mathcal{J}_{ik}} \left(\log\sigma_{y,k}^2 + \frac{(y_{ijk} - \boldsymbol{\beta}'_{jk}\boldsymbol{z}_{ik} - \alpha_{jk})^2}{\sigma_{y,k}^2 w_{ijk}}\right) - \frac{1}{2}\sum_i \sum_{k\in\mathcal{K}_i}\left(q_k \log\sigma_{z,k}^2 + \frac{\lVert\boldsymbol{z}_{ik} - A_k\boldsymbol{u}_i\rVert^2}{\sigma_{z,k}^2}\right) - \frac{1}{2}\sum_i \frac{\lVert\boldsymbol{u}_i\rVert^2}{\sigma_u^2} - \frac{1}{2}nr\log\sigma_u^2$
Expected log-likelihood: $E_{(\mathbf{u},\mathbf{z}\mid\mathbf{y},\hat{\Theta}_t)}[L(\Theta, \mathbf{u}, \mathbf{z}; \mathbf{y})] = $ some constant
$-\frac{1}{2}\sum_i \sum_{k\in\mathcal{K}_i^y} \sum_{j\in\mathcal{J}_{ik}} \left(\log\sigma_{y,k}^2 + \frac{(y_{ijk} - \boldsymbol{\beta}'_{jk}\hat{\boldsymbol{z}}_{ik} - \alpha_{jk})^2 + \boldsymbol{\beta}'_{jk}\hat{V}[\boldsymbol{z}_{ik}]\boldsymbol{\beta}_{jk}}{\sigma_{y,k}^2 w_{ijk}}\right) - \frac{1}{2}\sum_i\sum_\ell \frac{\hat{u}_{i,\ell}^2 + \hat{V}[u_{i,\ell}]}{\sigma_u^2} - \frac{1}{2}nr\log\sigma_u^2$
$-\frac{1}{2}\sum_i \sum_{k\in\mathcal{K}_i}\left(q_k\log\sigma_{z,k}^2 + \sum_\ell \frac{(\hat{z}_{ik,\ell} - A_{k,\ell}\hat{\boldsymbol{u}}_i)^2 + A_{k,\ell}\hat{V}[\boldsymbol{u}_i]A'_{k,\ell} - 2A_{k,\ell}\hat{V}[z_{ik,\ell}, \boldsymbol{u}_i] + \hat{V}[z_{ik,\ell}]}{\sigma_{z,k}^2}\right)$

Note that $A_{k,\ell}$ denotes the ℓth rows of A_k; $\hat{a}$ and $\hat{V}[a]$ denote the posterior mean and variance of variable a.

Table 1: Log likelihood formulas

$$\begin{aligned}\hat{\boldsymbol{z}}_{ik\mid ik} &= E[\boldsymbol{z}_{ik} \mid \boldsymbol{d}_{ik}] = \gamma_{ik}\Sigma_{ik}C'_{ik}E_{ik}^{-1}\boldsymbol{d}_{ik}\\ &= \gamma_{ik}(\Sigma_{ik}C'_{ik}D_{ik}^{-1}\boldsymbol{d}_{ik} - \Sigma_{ik}C'_{ik}D_{ik}^{-1}C_{ik}F_{ik}^{-1}C'_{ik}D_{ik}^{-1}\boldsymbol{d}_{ik}),\\ \Gamma_{ik\mid ik} &= Var[\boldsymbol{z}_{ik} \mid \boldsymbol{d}_{ik}] = \Sigma_{ik} - \gamma_{ik}\Sigma_{ik}C'_{ik}E_{ik}^{-1}C_{ik}\Sigma_{ik}\\ &= \Sigma_{ik} - \gamma_{ik}(\Sigma_{ik}C'_{ik}D_{ik}^{-1}C_{ik}\Sigma_{ik}\\ &\quad - \Sigma_{ik}C'_{ik}D_{ik}^{-1}C_{ik}F_{ik}^{-1}C'_{ik}D_{ik}^{-1}C_{ik}\Sigma_{ik}),\end{aligned}$$

where $\gamma_{ik} = 1$ if $k \in \mathcal{K}_i$; otherwise, $\gamma_{ik} = 0$. Here, $\hat{\boldsymbol{z}}_{ik|ik}$ and $\Gamma_{ik|ik}$ are the posterior mean and covariances of $\boldsymbol{z}_{ik}$ for user i using data only in context k. Letting $\boldsymbol{d}_i = \{\boldsymbol{d}_{ik}\}_{\forall k}$, by (HC Eq 1.8) and (HC Eq 1.9), we obtain

$$\begin{aligned}\hat{\boldsymbol{u}}_i &= E[\boldsymbol{u}_i \mid \boldsymbol{d}_i] = \hat{V}[\boldsymbol{u}_i]\sum_k \Gamma_{i|ik}^{-1}H_{ik}\hat{\boldsymbol{z}}_{ik|ik}\\ \hat{V}[\boldsymbol{u}_i] &= Var[\boldsymbol{u}_i \mid \boldsymbol{d}_i] = \left(I/\sigma_u^2 + \sum_k(\Gamma_{i|ik}^{-1} - I/\sigma_u^2)\right)^{-1}\\ \Gamma_{i|ik} &= \hat{V}[\boldsymbol{u}_i|z_{ik}] = H_{ik}\Gamma_{ik|ik}H'_{ik} + R_{ik}\end{aligned}$$

Here, the global factors are estimated by combining information across all contexts through local factors, the weighting depends crucially on $\Gamma_{i|ik}$, posterior covariance of global factor when one uses information only from context k. Note the summation $\sum_k$ in the above formulas. We consider two options: (1) $\sum_{k\in\mathcal{K}_i}$; (2) $\sum_{k\in \text{ all applications}}$ (as Huang and Cressie suggest).

Smoothing: Finally, by (HC Eq 1.13) and (HC Eq 1.14), we obtain

$$\begin{aligned}\hat{\boldsymbol{z}}_{ik} &= E[\boldsymbol{z}_{ik} \mid \boldsymbol{d}_i]\\ &= \hat{\boldsymbol{z}}_{ik|ik} + \Gamma_{ik|ik}H'_{ik}\Gamma_{i|ik}^{-1}(\hat{\boldsymbol{u}}_i - H_{ik}\hat{\boldsymbol{z}}_{ik|ik})\\ \hat{V}[\boldsymbol{z}_{ik}] &= Var[\boldsymbol{z}_{ik} \mid \boldsymbol{d}_i]\\ &= \Gamma_{ik|ik} + \Gamma_{ik|ik}H'_{ik}\Gamma_{i|ik}^{-1}(\hat{V}[\boldsymbol{u}_i] - \Gamma_{i|ik})\Gamma_{i|ik}^{-1}H_{ik}\Gamma_{ik|ik}\\ \hat{V}[\boldsymbol{z}_{ik}, \boldsymbol{u}_i] &= Cov[\boldsymbol{z}_{ik}, \boldsymbol{u}_i \mid \boldsymbol{d}_i] = \Gamma_{ik|ik}H'_{ik}\Gamma_{i|ik}^{-1}\hat{V}[\boldsymbol{u}_i]\end{aligned}$$

Notice how information collected by the global factors from all contexts are now being transmitted to each individual local factors to facilitate cross-context learning. Such learning depends crucially on the matrices H_{ik} that are functions of the global correlation model parameters A_ks.

3.2 M-step

In the M-step, we compute $\hat{\Theta}_{t+1}$. In fact, we solve two instances of the following optimization problem:

$$\begin{aligned}&\text{Let loss}(\boldsymbol{\eta}; o, \boldsymbol{s}, V, \boldsymbol{v}, w, c, \boldsymbol{\mathcal{I}})\\ &= \textstyle\sum_{i\in\mathcal{I}} \frac{(o_i - \boldsymbol{\eta}'\boldsymbol{s}_i)^2 + \boldsymbol{\eta}'V_i\boldsymbol{\eta} - 2\boldsymbol{\eta}'\boldsymbol{v}_i + c_i}{w_i}\\ &= \boldsymbol{\eta}'\left(\textstyle\sum_i \frac{V_i + \boldsymbol{s}_i\boldsymbol{s}'_i}{w_i}\right)\boldsymbol{\eta} - 2\left(\textstyle\sum_i \frac{\boldsymbol{s}_i o_i + \boldsymbol{v}_i}{w_i}\right)\boldsymbol{\eta} + \textstyle\sum_i \frac{o_i^2 + c_i}{w_i}\\ \hat{\boldsymbol{\eta}} &= \arg\min_{\boldsymbol{\eta}}\ \text{loss}(\boldsymbol{\eta}; o, \boldsymbol{s}, V, \boldsymbol{v}, w, c, \boldsymbol{\mathcal{I}})\\ &= \left(\textstyle\sum_i \frac{V_i + \boldsymbol{s}_i\boldsymbol{s}'_i}{w_i}\right)^{-1}\left(\textstyle\sum_i \frac{\boldsymbol{s}_i o_i + \boldsymbol{v}_i}{w_i}\right),\end{aligned}$$

Estimating A_k and $\sigma_{z,k}^2$: For each context k and each row ℓ of A_k, solve the regression problem by letting $\boldsymbol{\eta}' = A_{k,\ell}$, $\boldsymbol{s}_i = \hat{\boldsymbol{u}}_i$, $o_i = \hat{z}_{ik,\ell}$, $V_i = \hat{V}[\boldsymbol{u}_i]$, $\boldsymbol{v}_i = \hat{V}[z_{ik,\ell}, \boldsymbol{u}_i]$, $w_i = 1$, $c_i = \hat{V}[z_{ik,\ell}]$ and $\boldsymbol{\mathcal{I}} = \{i : k \in \mathcal{K}_i\}$. Let $\text{loss}_{k,\ell}$ denote the corresponding loss. Then, for each k,

$$\hat{\sigma}_{z,k} = \frac{\sum_\ell \text{loss}_{k,\ell}}{q_k \cdot |\{i : k\in\mathcal{K}_i\}|}.$$

Estimating α_{jk}, $\boldsymbol{\beta}_{jk}$ and $\sigma_{y,k}^2$: For each context k and each item j, solve the regression problem by letting $\boldsymbol{\eta}' = [\alpha_{jk}, \boldsymbol{\beta}_{jk}]$, $\boldsymbol{s}'_i = [1, \hat{\boldsymbol{z}}'_{ik}]$, $o_i = y_{ijk}$, $V_i = I_0(\hat{V}[\boldsymbol{z}_{ik}])$, $\boldsymbol{v}_i = 0$, $w_i = w_{ijk}$, $c_i = 0$ and $\boldsymbol{\mathcal{I}} = \{i : k \in \mathcal{K}_i \text{ and } j \in \mathcal{J}_{ik}\}$. Note that $I_0(X)$ is a function that adds a row and a column of all zeros to matrix X; the added row and column are the first row and first column of $I_0(X)$. Let $\text{loss}_{j,k}$ denote the corresponding loss. Then, for each k,

$$\hat{\sigma}_{y,k} = \frac{\sum_j \text{loss}_{j,k}}{\sum_j |\{i : k\in\mathcal{K}_i \text{ and } j\in\mathcal{J}_{ik}\}|}.$$

4. EXPERIMENTS

We begin with an example that shows how LMF can be used to perform linear/logistic regression when features have missing values for a large fraction of records. Although not directly related to recommender problems, it is interesting to note that this is a special case of LMF. It also provides an interesting benchmark dataset for future research in this area.

4.1 UCI Ad data

To illustrate the use of LMF for correcting the effects of missing feature values in regression, we use the Ad data available from the UCI repository. This dataset represents a set of possible advertisements on Internet pages. The features encode the geometry of the image (if available) as well as phrases occuring in the URL, the image's URL and alt text, the anchor text, and words occuring near the anchor text. The task is to predict whether an image is an advertisement ("ad") or not ("nonad"). Previous approach to this problem using C4.5 achieved more than 97% accuracy [29], so this is a relatively simple classification problem. There are 3279 instances, of which 458 are ads. We build a logistic regression by using only 3 continuous attributes — height, width and aspect ratio. There are about 28% missing attribute values, so a correction for missing attribute values may lead to good results. In addition to 3 attributes, we also include 3 second order interactions among the variables. The vanilla logistic regression is run by encoding missing values for an attribute as a separate binary indicator (missing or not), we fit LMF by assuming the response matrix has one item and each record is a user. In other words, $y_{i1} \sim \text{logistic}(\beta' z_i)$ and features $x_{ij} \sim N(Bz_i, \sigma_x^2)$, $j = 1, \cdots, 6$. Since this is a regression problem, it makes sense to assume a common factor for both feature and response.Thus, $z_i \sim MVN(\mathbf{0}, \sigma_z^2 I)$. We fit this model with 6 factors, note that factorization on the feature matrix is possible with missing values. To compare the performance of LMF with vanilla logistic regression, we report area under the ROC curve (AUC) based on leave-one-out model fitting. This involves fitting LMF 3279 times, which is fast due to our Kalman filtering based model fitting procedure. The AUC for vanilla logistic regression is 82% but LMF obtains an AUC of 99%. This is remarkable since we are able to achieve such high accuracy by using only 3 features through corrections on missing attribute values.

Next, we illustrate the difference between CMF and LMF in the presence of additional feature information in recommender problems. In particular, we show that using the same user factors both for the response and feature matrices can lead to biased estimates, relaxing the factors to be local and using feature information through multivariate regression in the latent space leads to better performance. In fact, the flexibility provided by locality prevents the user factors from being overwhelmed by information in other contexts when response information is sparse.

4.2 Movielens Data

We experiment with the benchmark Movielens dataset, Netflix was not considered since it did not have user features. Our goal here is to compare the behavior of CMF and LMF on response (movie rating) prediction in the presence of different amounts of feature information. In this experiment, we study the impact on predictive performance for different models in the presence of weak and noisy features. To facilitate such a comparison, we consider the top 100 out of approximately 5k movies. The pruned dataset has 6040 users and approximately 182k ratings. We do a 75:25 split sorted by event timestamp into training and test sets respectively. The test set has approximately 900 new users (not seen in the training set), roughly 25% of test set ratings belong to these new users. We construct a feature matrix for users using their gender, age-groups, occupation and first two digits of zipcode. Each level of these categorical variables are considered as separate binary predictors, this gives us a total of 129 distinct binary features.

We fit both CMF and LMF by varying the amount of feature information available during the training period. In fact, we randomly sample features of f% users where f varies from 0 (no feature) to 1 (consider all user features). Since

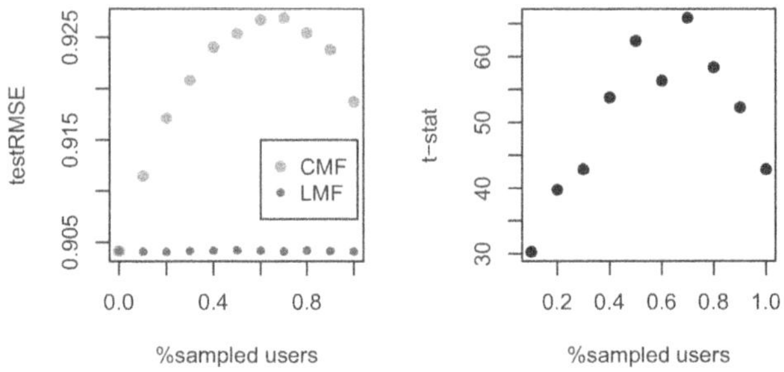

(a) Mean test RMSE (b) t-statistic

Figure 2: Performance of CMF and LMF with varying amount of feature information. A t-statistics > 3 is highly significant.

the model performance depends on initial parameter values, we perform 100 replications of our model fitting procedure for each value of f. Note that both CMF and LMF are fitted on a simulated dataset for a given f in each replication. In Figure 2(a), we show the mean value of test RMSE across different replications for each value of f; we also plotted the two-sample t-test statistic between CMF and LMF for each f using 100 replications(see Figure 2(b)). Both figures clearly show the performance of CMF deteriorates with increase in number of sampled users with feature information. However, after a certain threshold (approximately .75) there is an interesting point of inflexion where the deterioration gets smaller. Further inspection revealed that this happens due to the presence of a large number of cold-start users, obtaining feature information for these users through a factorization slightly improves performance. However, performance of LMF does not deteriorate with addition of features, in fact it improves slightly. For this application, the feature information is noisy and does not help much in improving predictive performance, but CMF gets impacted by noise while LMF is able to learn the weak correlation of features with response and avoids getting affected.

4.3 Yahoo! Warm Start Data

We now illustrate the bias problem of CMF on a proprietary Yahoo! data. We study the impact on predictive performance when one of the contexts has sparse response while others have relatively large amounts of data. This dataset also illustrates the use of our model on binary response through variational approximation.

The task is to predict click-rates (CTR) on two content modules: (1) The today module on Yahoo! Front Page [2] and (2) the top stories module that display links to articles on the top-right when a user is reading some news article on Yahoo! News. The goal of the Top stories module is to prolong the stay of a user on Yahoo! News and increase engagement. For instance, a user may click on a news link about "Egyptian revolution" somewhere outside Yahoo! News and get routed to the main article page of the topic on Yahoo! News. The Top stories module on this article page may show an article about Obama which the user may click and end up reading another news story. We collected click event stream for a subset of heavy users on Today module and Top stories for a period of 6 weeks. Overall there were 10k users in the dataset we used for this experiment, there was 55% overlap in the News and Front Page user population. In addition, we constructed profile features for users in News by using all the News pages they read during the time period under study. Each news article was classified into a topic category and a user topic profile is defined as affinity to different categories. Our data had 460 news categories, the procedure for estimating user-category affinity is described below.

Profile construction: Let n_{ij} denote the number of articles read by user i in category j ($i = 1, \cdots, N, j = 1, \cdots, M$). Let p_{+j} denote the overall probability of reading articles in category j in the heavy user population in News, we estimate this as $\hat{p}_{+j} = n_{+j}/n_{++}$, the "pluses" in the suffix denote marginalization over the corresponding dimension. Then user affinity λ_{ij} is estimated from the following model

$$n_{ij} \sim \text{Poisson}(n_{i+}\hat{p}_{+j}\lambda_{ij}) \quad (3)$$
$$\lambda_{ij} \sim \text{Gamma}(\text{mean} = 1, \text{var} = 1/a)$$

The parameter a can be interpreted as additional psuedo clicks added to the cells. For this Gamma-Poisson model one could obtain a method-of-moments estimator of a given as

$$\hat{a} = (\bar{e_{ij}}/(\mathcal{X}^2 - 1))$$

where $e_{ij} = n_{i+}\hat{p}_{+j}$ is the expected number of reads under baseline model of no affinity and

$$\mathcal{X}^2 = \text{mean}(n_{ij} - e_{ij})^2/e_{ij}.$$

Higher values of $\mathcal{X}^2$ indicates more deviation from baseline (and stronger affinity signal), when $\mathcal{X}^2 < 1$ we assume $\hat{a} = \inf$ and hence there is no affinity in the data. For our data, we obtained $\hat{a} = 0.22$ which indicates high variation in data. Given $\hat{a}$, the posterior of $\lambda_{ij} \sim \text{Gamma}(\text{mean} = \hat{\lambda}_{ij} = (n_{ij} + \hat{a})/(e_{ij} + \hat{a}), \text{var} = \hat{\lambda}_{ij}/(e_{ij} + \hat{a}))$. To work with a Guassian predictor in our framework we consider $\ell\lambda_{ij} = log(\lambda_{ij})$ with approximate mean and variance given by given by $\ell\hat{\lambda}_{ij} = log(\lambda_{ij})$ and $w_{ij} = 1/(e_{ij} + \hat{a})$ respectively(from second order Taylor series expansion). To reduce noise we only retain observations with z-statistic $(|\ell\hat{\lambda}_{ij}|/\sqrt{w_{ij}})$ exceeding the threshold of 1.

Prediction task: For both today module and top stories clickstream our prediction task is based on splitting the data at the item level. In fact we sort the events for each item by timestamp and perform a training-test split. Although this is not exactly the scenario in our actual system where the set of articles in the content pool change over time, it is a realistic setting to study the predictive power of different methods that play an important role in determining the quality of our recommendations. We consider the task of predicting test set response for both today module and top stories by utilizing user feature information available from pages read by users on News. We performed a 25:75 and and 75:25 training-test split on today module and top stories clickstream respectively. For today module this gave us a training set with 171K events, the test set had 514k events. For top stories the training data consisted of 2.16M events while the test set contained 719K events. The feature matrix in News contained 1.47M feature values for roughly 9.6K users. Our goal here is to study the impact CMF has on predictions in today module in the presence of large amounts of data on top stories compared to today module. Such asymmetric data distributions are common in context specific learning for recommender problems, large amounts of additional data from different contexts should not bias predictions for response in a smaller context.

Method	News	Today
CMF (Feature)	.757	.614
CMF (No Feature)	.708	.662
LMF (Feature)	.753	.661
LMF (No Feature)	.709	.664
SMF (No Feature)	.703	.666

Table 2: AUC on different model variations for Yahoo! warm start data.

Table 2 shows the area under the ROC curves (AUC) for three different methods:

- CMF (Feature, No Feature) shares same user factors for all three matrices (for the Feature case) or two matrices (for the No Feature case).
- SMF (separate matrix factorization) fits two models, one for today module and the other for News, separately.
- LMF (Feature, No Feauture) fits localized factors for all three or two matrices jointly.

Since there is little cold-start in this data, matrix factorization done separately has comparable performance to LMF on the today module. On the top stories module, adding feature matrix improves performance significantly for both CMF and LMF, this is because the category affinity of users are strongly correlated to click-rates on top stories articles. However, using CMF deteriorates performance on today module significantly due to the bias induced on user factors. Since the amount of data available on top stories is significantly larger, the user factors are swamped by it and this leads to inferior performance on today module. On the other hand, LMF does not suffer from this problem due to the flexibility of having local user factors in each application, it is able to exploit information from all three sources to obtain good performance on both today module and top stories. Further scrutiny on both lift due to category features and deterioration in today module performance was done by splitting the user population in test according to the total clicks in the training period. Both improvement and deterioration was uniform across all user populations. This clearly shows the ability of LMF to exploit large amounts of additional data from other contexts to improve performance everywhere, even in contexts that are sparse where CMF suffers.

4.4 Epinions Data

We now use the Epinions dataset [34] to show the superior performance of LMF over CMF and the baseline method SMF (separate matrix factorization). This dataset consists of ratings that users of epinions.com gave to reviews in several different verticals on the site. We take the top 10 verticals (each of which contains more than 0.5M ratings) as 10 contexts. Here we consider a user recommendation problem — we want to recommend review authors for users to follow. Thus each (vertical, author) pair is an item. We only consider items that received at least 100 ratings and users

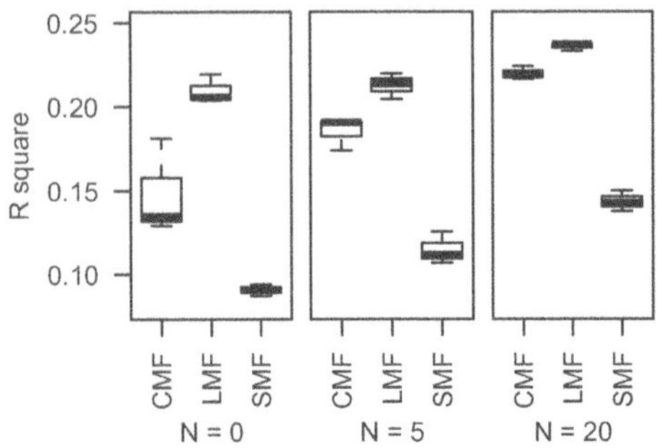

Figure 3: Accuracy of different models on the Epinions dataset with different levels of sparseness

who rated at least 30 items. We compare different methods using R^2 as the accuracy measure; a higher R^2 number means better performance. Five-fold cross validation is used to compute the R^2 of each method. In particular, we use one fold to select the best number of user factors for each method and report the R^2 numbers of the other four folds. The selected numbers of factors are 3 for LMF, 3 for CMF, and 1 for SMF. Instead of averaging the R^2 numbers for each method, we show a boxplot. To understand how different methods perform in cold start, when we compute the R^2 numbers, we only consider the test-set (user,context) pairs, each of which receives $\leq N$ ratings in the training set. We show R^2 of different methods for $N = 0, 5, 20$ in Figure 3. As expected, all the methods perform better in warm start ($N = 20$) than in cold start ($N = 0$). In all three scenarios ($N = 0, 5, 20$) LMF is significantly better than CMF which is significantly better than SMF. Notice that no boxes overlap in any boxplot. The difference between LMF and CMF shrinks as N goes up. Interestingly the $R^2$of LMF for $N = 0$ is still comparable to that of CMF for $N = 20$. This shows the strong performance of LMF over CMF.

5. RELATED WORK

In this section, we discuss related work and describe how LMF is different from prior work.

Matrix factorization: One major motivation for LMF is to perform collaborative filtering in multiple contexts. In recent years, matrix factorization (MF) has gained great popularity since it usually outperforms more traditional methods [21, 42] It has achieved the state-of-the-art performance particularly on large scale recommendation tasks [28]. However, most MF approaches focus on learning latent factors from a single rating matrix. A few recent work extends MF to jointly modeling multiple matrices [1, 41, 40]. Specifically, in [1, 41], user and item feature matrices are used to improve the factorization of the rating matrix. The major difference between [1, 41] and LMF is that the former assumes the features are all known withouth any uncertainty, while LMF allows the feature values to be uncertain or missing. Collective matrix factorization (CMF) [40] jointly factorizes the rating matrix and other feature matrices by assuming user factors are the same in both the rating and feature matrices. The main advantage of LMF over CMF is that LMF defines a different user factor vectors for each matrix and then connects these factors through a regression prior.

Multi-task learning: Multi-context recommendation is closely related to the field of multi-task learning [37], which learns multiple related tasks simultaneously to take advantage of knowledge transfer cross the tasks. Multi-task learning can be broadly summarized into four classes. First class of multi-task learning approaches aims to uncover the common (latent) features that can benefit each individual task [9, 38, 33, 14, 3, 4, 5, 31, 40]. Those methods are most related to our approaches; however they have again follow the spirit of collective matrix factorization where some shared factors are assumed to be the same across different tasks. The second class of of multi-task learning approaches are based on parameter-sharing [39, 30, 20, 11, 44, 45], which assumes that the source tasks and the target tasks share some parameters or priors of their models. Of those methods, hierarchial Bayesian approaches, such as [44], are close to our LMF approach in the sense of multi-level structure, however they do not learn low-dimensional local and global latent factors, which are critical for multi-context recommendation. The third and fourth classes of multi-task learning based on instance re-weighting [6, 26, 15, 32, 8, 24, 17, 43, 16] and relational knowledge transfer [36, 18, 35], individually. Those two classes of approaches are not as relevant as first two class of approaches to our approach.

Multi-view learning: Another related field is multiple view learning introduced by [10] and [27] in the semi-supervised setting. They propose the co-training approach to train a classifier from two representations with both labeled and unlabeled instances. The idea of the co-training approach is to train one learner on each view of the labeled instances and then to iteratively let each learner label the unlabeled instances it predicts with the highest confidence. Given independence between the learners, newly labeled examples from one learner may give the other learner new information to improve its model. In our approach, we assume dependence among different contexts, that is crucial for learning across contexts.

6. CONCLUSION

Learning from multiple contexts is an effective strategy to ameliorate cold-start problems in recommender systems. In this paper, we presented a new methodology called LMF that provides a flexible modeling framework to estimate cross-context correlations and use them to enhance local factor estimates across all contexts. We clearly illustrated the pitfalls of using the current practice of sharing exactly the same factors across contexts for each entity. On a large benchmark dataset we clearly showed the superior performance of LMF, especially for cold-start scenarios.

Our LMF assumes local factors are linear functions of a global factor a-priori, this is equivalent to assuming a low-rank covariance matrix for local factors. Relaxing this assumption to incorporate richer class of covariance functions is an interesting research direction. Moving away from the low rank structure would require new computational fitting algorithms that are scalable since the multi-resolution Kalman filter fails to work in the absence of linearity.

7. REFERENCES

[1] D. Agarwal and B.-C. Chen. Regression-based latent factor models. In *KDD*, 2009.

[2] D. Agarwal and B.-C. Chen, et al. Online models for content optimization. In *NIPS*, 2008.

[3] R. Ando and T. Zhang. A high-performance semi-supervised learning method for text chunking. In *ACL*, 2005.
[4] A. Argyriou, T. Evgeniou, and M. Pontil. Multi-task feature learning. In *NIPS*, 2007.
[5] A. Argyriou, C. Micchelli, M. Pontil, and Y. Ying. A spectral regularization framework for multi-task structure learning. *NIPS*, 2008.
[6] S. Bickel, M. Brückner, and T. Scheffer. Discriminative learning for differing training and test distributions. In *ICML*, 2007.
[7] D. Blackwell. Conditional expectation and unbiased sequential estimation. *Annals of Math. Stat.*, 1947.
[8] J. Blitzer, K. Crammer, A. Kulesza, F. Pereira, and J. Wortman. Learning bounds for domain adaptation. *NIPS*, 2008.
[9] J. Blitzer, R. McDonald, and F. Pereira. Domain adaptation with structural correspondence learning. In *EMNLP*, 2006.
[10] A. Blum and T. Mitchell. Combining labeled and unlabeled data with co-training. In *COLT*, 1998.
[11] E. Bonilla, K. Chai, and C. Williams. Multi-task gaussian process prediction. *NIPS*, 2007.
[12] R. Carroll, D. Ruppert, L. Stefanski, and C. Crainiceanu. *Measurement Error in Nonlinear Models*. Chapman and Hall, 2008.
[13] K. C. Chou, A. S. Willsky, and R. Nikoukhah. Multiscale systems, Kalman filters, and Ricatti equations. *IEEE Trans. on Automatic Control*, 1994.
[14] W. Dai, G. Xue, Q. Yang, and Y. Yu. Co-clustering based classification for out-of-domain documents. In *KDD*, 2007.
[15] W. Dai, Q. Yang, G. Xue, and Y. Yu. Boosting for transfer learning. In *ICML*, 2007.
[16] H. Daumé. Cross-task knowledge-constrained self training. In *EMNLP*, 2008.
[17] H. Daume III and D. Marcu. Domain adaptation for statistical classifiers. *Journal of Artificial Intelligence Research*, 2006.
[18] J. Davis and P. Domingos. Deep transfer via second-order markov logic. In *AAAI Workshop on Transfer Learning for Complex Tasks*, 2008.
[19] A. P. Dempster, N. M. Laird, and D. B. Rubin. Maximum likelihood from incomplete data via the EM algorithm. *J. of the Royal Statistical Society, Series B*, 1977.
[20] T. Evgeniou and M. Pontil. Regularized multi-task learning. In *KDD*, 2004.
[21] J. L. Herlocker, J. A. Konstan, A. Borchers, and J. Riedl. An algorithmic framework for performing collaborative filtering. In *SIGIR*, 1999.
[22] H. Huang and N. Cressie. Fast spatial prediction of global processes from satellite data. *SIAM J. on Scientific Computing*, 2000.
[23] H. Huang and N. Cressie. Multiscale graphical modeling in space: Applications to command and control. In *Spatial Statistics Workshop*, 2000.
[24] J. Huang, A. Smola, A. Gretton, K. Borgwardt, and B. Scholkopf. Correcting sample selection bias by unlabeled data. *NIPS*, 2007.
[25] T. Jaakkola and M. Jordan. Bayesian logistic regression: a variational approach. *Statistics and Computing*, 2000.
[26] J. Jiang and C. Zhai. Instance weighting for domain adaptation in NLP. In *ACL*, 2007.
[27] H. Kaji and Y. Morimoto. Unsupervised word sense disambiguation using bilingual comparable corpora. In *COLIN*, 2002.
[28] Y. Koren, R. Bell, and C. Volinsky. Matrix factorization techniques for recommender systems. *Computer*, 2009.
[29] N. Kushmerick. Learning to remove internet advertisements. In *Int. Conf. Autonomous Agents*, 1999.
[30] N. Lawrence and J. Platt. Learning to learn with the informative vector machine. In *ICML*, 2004.
[31] S. Lee, V. Chatalbashev, D. Vickrey, and D. Koller. Learning a meta-level prior for feature relevance from multiple related tasks. In *ICML*, 2007.
[32] X. Liao, Y. Xue, and L. Carin. Logistic regression with an auxiliary data source. In *ICML*, 2005.
[33] X. Ling, W. Dai, G.-R. Xue, Q. Yang, and Y. Yu. Spectral domain-transfer learning. In *KDD*, 2008.
[34] P. Massa and P. Avesani. Trust metrics in recommender systems. In *Computing with Social Trust*, 2009.
[35] L. Mihalkova, T. Huynh, and R. Mooney. Mapping and revising markov logic networks for transfer learning. In *AAAI*, 2007.
[36] L. Mihalkova and R. Mooney. Transfer learning by mapping with minimal target data. In *AAAI Workshop on Transfer Learning for Complex Tasks*, 2008.
[37] S. J. Pan and Q. Yang. A survey on transfer learning. Technical Report HKUST-CS08-08, Hong Kong University of Science and Technology, 2008.
[38] R. Raina, A. Battle, H. Lee, B. Packer, and A. Ng. Self-taught learning: Transfer learning from unlabeled data. In *ICML*, 2007.
[39] A. Schwaighofer, V. Tresp, and K. Yu. Learning Gaussian process kernels via hierarchical Bayes. *NIPS*, 2005.
[40] A. P. Singh and G. J. Gordon. Relational learning via collective matrix factorization. In *KDD*, 2008.
[41] D. H. Stern, R. Herbrich, and T. Graepel. Matchbox: large scale online bayesian recommendations. In *WWW*, 2009.
[42] X. Su and T. M. Khoshgoftaar. A survey of collaborative filtering techniques. *Adv. in Artif. Intell.*, 2009.
[43] M. Sugiyama, S. Nakajima, H. Kashima, P. von Bunau, and M. Kawanabe. Direct importance estimation with model selection and its application to covariate shift adaptation. *NIPS*, 2008.
[44] K. Yu and V. Tresp. Learning to learn and collaborative filtering. In *In NIPS Workshop on Inductive Transfer: 10 Years Later*, 2005.
[45] S. Yu, K. Yu, V. Tresp, and H.-P. Kriegel. Collaborative ordinal regression. In *ICML*, 2006.

Latent Aspect Rating Analysis without Aspect Keyword Supervision

Hongning Wang, Yue Lu, ChengXiang Zhai
Department of Computer Science
University of Illinois at Urbana-Champaign
Urbana IL, 61801 USA
{wang296, yuelu2, czhai}@cs.uiuc.edu

ABSTRACT

Mining detailed opinions buried in the vast amount of review text data is an important, yet quite challenging task with widespread applications in multiple domains. *Latent Aspect Rating Analysis* (LARA) refers to the task of inferring both opinion ratings on topical aspects (e.g., location, service of a hotel) and the relative weights reviewers have placed on each aspect based on review content and the associated overall ratings. A major limitation of previous work on LARA is the assumption of pre-specified aspects by keywords. However, the aspect information is not always available, and it may be difficult to pre-define appropriate aspects without a good knowledge about what aspects are actually commented on in the reviews.

In this paper, we propose a unified generative model for LARA, which does not need pre-specified aspect keywords and simultaneously mines 1) latent topical aspects, 2) ratings on each identified aspect, and 3) weights placed on different aspects by a reviewer. Experiment results on two different review data sets demonstrate that the proposed model can effectively perform the *Latent Aspect Rating Analysis* task without the supervision of aspect keywords. Because of its generality, the proposed model can be applied to explore all kinds of opinionated text data containing overall sentiment judgments and support a wide range of interesting application tasks, such as aspect-based opinion summarization, personalized entity ranking and recommendation, and reviewer behavior analysis.

Categories and Subject Descriptors

H.3.3 [**Information Search and Retrieval**]: Text Mining

General Terms

Algorithms, Experimentation

Keywords

Aspect Identification, Latent Rating Analysis, Review Mining

KDD'11, August 21–24, 2011, San Diego, California, USA.

1. INTRODUCTION

In the era of Web 2.0, more and more people express their opinions on all kinds of entities, including products and services, which in turn help not only customers make informed decisions but also merchants improve their services. The rapid growth of such opinionated text data on the web, such as user reviews, raises interesting new challenges for text mining communities and leads to many studies on extracting information from reviews [4, 20, 17], sentiment analysis [19, 18, 11] and opinion summarization [6, 8, 14].

To help users efficiently and accurately digest a large number of online reviews about a particular entity (e.g., mp3 player), it is necessary to reveal detailed opinions on multiple topical aspects of the entity (e.g., battery life of mp3 player). To this end, recent work on opinion mining has attempted to perform fine-grained sentiment analysis: in most work (e.g., [21, 25, 6, 7]), the proposed algorithms are able to identify sentiment orientation or ratings on specific topical aspects, leading to useful detailed opinion summaries.

However, decomposing an overall rating into ratings on specific aspects is still not informative enough from a user's perspective. For example, a hotel with a five-star rating on the "*value*" aspect may actually be quite expensive by common standard if the reviewer emphasizes much more on the "*service*" of the hotel than the "*value*" (e.g., for a business trip), though it could also be indeed cheap if the reviewer really cares much more about the price than about other aspects of a hotel (e.g., for a casual vacation).

Figure 1: A sample output of LARA.

To further differentiate such different meanings of the same aspect rating, in our previous work [23], we went beyond aspect rating prediction to also infer the relative emphasis placed by a reviewer on different aspects, and introduced a new opinion mining problem named *Latent Aspect Rating Analysis* (LARA). The task of LARA is to take as input a set of review text documents about an entity with overall ratings and generate as output 1) ratings on a set of predefined aspects of the entity, and 2) relative weights placed by a reviewer on each aspect when writing the review.

For example, Figure 1 shows a sample result of LARA on a hotel review where we see that LARA not only decomposes the overall rating into ratings on each of the four topical aspects (e.g., three stars on "*value*" and two stars on "*room*"), but also infers that the reviewer has placed a much higher weight on "*value*" than other aspects (thus the actual price of this hotel is likely indeed cheap). The inferred aspect weights of reviewers can be very useful. For example, to help a current user who also cares much about "*room*", we could selectively emphasize more on the reviews written by reviewers who have a similar taste to the current user (i.e., also placing a very high weight on "*room*") to recommend hotels, achieving personalized ranking of hotels. The inferred weights can also be used to analyze the rating behavior of reviewers with applications in business intelligence as shown in [23].

However, a major limitation of [23] is that the aspects must be given through keywords specified by users, restricting its usefulness in applications. Indeed, such supervision of specifying aspects with keywords requires manual work and is not always available. More importantly, in many cases, it is often unclear what are the aspects actually commented on in the reviews, thus it is very difficult, if not impossible, to pre-specify the aspects beforehand.

To address this limitation and enable LARA on arbitrary review data without explicit aspect keyword supervision, in this paper, we propose a unified generative Latent Aspect Rating Analysis Model (LARAM), which simultaneously identifies: 1) latent topical aspects, 2) ratings on each identified aspect, and 3) weights placed on different aspects by a reviewer. LARAM is a fully generative model for both the review text and the companion overall rating. Specifically, it is assumed that the text content describing a particular aspect is generated by sampling words from a topic model (i.e., a multinomial word distribution) corresponding to the latent aspect, the latent rating on an aspect is determined based on the words describing each aspect with latent sentiment polarities, and the overall rating is generated based on a weighted combination of aspect ratings where the (latent) weights reflect the relative emphasis on each aspect by the reviewer.

LARAM can be regarded as an extension of the Latent Rating Regression (LRR) model proposed in [23] to perform both aspect segmentation and aspect rating prediction in a unified framework (in contrast, the two tasks were performed separately in [23] with segmentation done based on user-provided keywords).

Experiment results on a hotel review data set crawled from TripAdvisor (`www.tripadvisor.com`) and a product review data set crawled from Amazon (`www.amazon.com`) show that the proposed LARAM can effectively perform Latent Aspect Rating Analysis task without requiring the supervision of aspect keywords. Since LARAM is a general framework, it can be applied to analyze any kind of review text data with overall sentiment judgment to discover opinionated latent topical aspects, decompose overall opinion into sentiment specific topical aspects, and infer relative weights placed by reviewers on different topical aspects; such detailed opinion analysis can support many interesting applications such as aspect-based opinion summarization, personalized opinion-based ranking of entities, and reviewer behavior analysis.

2. RELATED WORK

The closest work to this study is our previous work [23], which introduced the problem of Latent Aspect Rating Analysis (LARA) and proposed a two-stage approach: in the first stage, keywords specified by users are used in a bootstrapping algorithm to identify the aspects and segment the review content; in the second stage, a generative Latent Rating Regression (LRR) model is applied to infer aspect ratings and weights in a review. However, this previous work requires a user to specify aspect keywords in advance, which requires manual work and is often very hard to achieve without knowing well about the opinions buried in the target review text. In this paper, we overcome this limitation, and propose a new generative model (i.e., LARAM) that can be regarded as an extension of LRR to perform aspect segmentation and aspect rating prediction simultaneously in a unified framework, thus enabling LARA without needing keyword specification from users.

The proposed LARAM is a hybrid generative model containing both aspect modeling and rating prediction, thus it is also related to the work of using topic modeling techniques to extract aspects and associated opinions. Mei et al. incorporated two additional sentiment language models into topic models to extract the facets and positive/negative opinions in weblogs [16]. Later, some work further introduced aspect-specific sentiment models in different ways, e.g., using supervision from sentiment priors [12, 9] or supervision from labeled sentences [24]. In [21], Titov and McDonald extended their multi-grain topic model [22] to discover topics that are representative of ratable aspects. Their regression module requires "ground truth" user ratings on the pre-defined aspects, which are not always available. In contrast, the proposed LARAM does not require aspect ratings from users and can decompose overall ratings into the ratings on the discovered aspects. More importantly, none of the work in this line is able to identify a reviewer's relative emphasis on different aspects, which is required for accurate interpretation of aspect ratings as we discussed in Section 1.

Other work on finer granularity analysis of opinions expressed in review text content is mostly to analyze the aspect-level opinion orientations [25, 6, 7, 20, 4, 15]. However, these methods can only identify the opinions associated with each individual aspect, but they cannot infer the reviewer's relative emphasis on different aspects, which the proposed LARAM is designed to achieve.

3. LATENT ASPECT RATING ANALYSIS

As a text mining problem, Latent Aspect Rating Analysis (LARA) [23] is to take as input a set of reviews of some interesting entities with companion overall ratings, and discover: 1) latent topical aspects that are commented on in the reviews; 2) ratings on each individual latent aspects; and 3) relative weights placed on different aspects by a reviewer when generating the overall rating.

Formally, the input can be represented as $D = \{d_1, d_2, \cdots, d_{|D|}\}$, a set of review text documents for a particular entity, where each review $d \in D$ is associated with a numerical overall rating r. A review d is modeled as a bag of words $\mathbf{W}$ in a fixed vocabulary $V = \{v_1, v_2, \ldots, v_{|V|}\}$.

The desired output of LARA consists of the following three kinds of detailed information about opinions buried in the reviews: 1) k topical aspects that are frequently commented on in all the review data: $\{A_1, A_2, \ldots, A_k\}$, where each aspect A_i is characterized by a topic model, i.e., multinomial word distribution $p(w|A_i)$, where $w \in V$; 2) for each review d, a k dimensional aspect rating vector $\mathbf{s}$, where $\mathbf{s}_i$ is the predicted rating for aspect A_i in the review; and 3) for each review d, an aspect weight vector α, where α_i is the relative weight (emphasis) placed by the reviewer on aspect A_i when writing the review. In the following discussions, we will use "aspect" and "topic" interchangeably unless noted otherwise.

Note that a main difference between our definition of LARA here and that in our previous work [23] is that in the previous definition, all the aspects are explicitly specified with keywords provided by a user, thus while the aspect ratings are latent, the aspects are not really latent, whereas here, both aspect ratings and the aspects themselves are latent, which we need to infer from the data. Naturally, such a definition of the problem is more challenging, but it is also more general. If we can solve such a problem setup, it would enable a much wider scope of future applications.

Because the aspects are assumed to be latent, the previously proposed Latent Rating Regression (LRR) model cannot solve the new problem setup directly. Below, we present an extension of the LRR model that can simultaneously discover latent aspects, decompose overall ratings into aspect ratings, and infer weights on different aspects.

4. A GENERATIVE MODEL FOR LARA

A main challenge in solving LARA without the aspect keywords supervision is to properly associate the words with those meaningful aspects corresponding to the major opinions. To address this challenge, our basic idea is to use topic modeling techniques which provide a convenient way of segmenting the review contents by exploiting the word co-occurrence patterns in the data. The main technical contribution of this work is to incorporate topic modeling technique into the Latent Rating Regression (LRR) model proposed in [23] to obtain a more "complete" generative model called Latent Aspect Rating Analysis Model (LARAM), which can model the generation of both text data and the overall ratings in a unified framework. As a result, by fitting LARAM to the review data, we can identify latent topical aspects from the review contents as well as discover the latent ratings and weights for each aspect in a review.

The basic assumption in LARAM is that the latent aspects of a particular entity are characterized by a set of coherent topics, which are shared across different reviews discussing the same entity (e.g., "*service*" and "*location*" for a hotel). The topics can be used to identify aspect text segments which contribute to the observed overall ratings in each review via the latent aspect ratings and weights. Along this line, we propose a fully generative framework to capture such dependency between the review contents and overall sentiment ratings.

Based on the notations in Section 3, our generative assumption of a reviewer's rating behavior is as follows: to generate an opinionated review d, the reviewer would first decide the set of aspects $\{A_i\}$ she wants to comment on, and then for each aspect, the reviewer would choose the words with appropriate sentiment polarities to reflect her opinions on the aspects which are characterized by the aspect ratings $\mathbf{s}$. Finally the reviewer would assign an overall rating r based on a weighted sum of all the aspect ratings in her mind, where the weight α reflects the relative emphasis she has placed on each aspect.

According to this generative assumption, we define and combine two components: 1) an aspect modeling module based on statistical topic modeling is introduced to discover the topical aspects from the review contents, and 2) a rating analysis module similar to the Latent Rating Regression Model (LRR) used in [23], is employed to infer the latent aspect ratings and weights based on the aspect segmented review contents.

In the aspect modeling part, we assume an aspect A_i is characterized by a multinomial word distribution $Mul(\epsilon_i)$ over the vocabulary V. The proportion of aspects θ being discussed in each review d is drawn from a Dirichlet distribution $Dir(\gamma)$, where γ postulates the prior distribution of aspects in the whole corpus. Then, a review is treated as a mixture over the latent aspects, and the joint probability of observed word contents $\mathbf{W}$, latent aspect assignments $\{z_n\}_{n=1}^{|d|}$ and aspect proportion θ is defined as follows:

$$p(\mathbf{W}, \mathbf{z}, \theta|\gamma, \epsilon) = p(\theta|\gamma) \prod_{n=1}^{|d|} p(w_n|z_n, \epsilon)p(z_n|\theta) \qquad (1)$$

where z_n is an indicator variable representing the latent aspect from which the word w_n is drawn.

In the rating analysis part, aspect rating $\mathbf{s}_i$ is assumed to be determined by the aggregated sentiment over the text segments discussing aspect A_i:

$$\mathbf{s}_i = \sum_{n=1}^{|d|} \beta_{ij} \mathbf{\Delta}[w_n = v_j, z_n = i] \qquad (2)$$

where $\beta_{ij} \in \Re$ represents the word j's sentiment polarity on aspect A_i, and $\mathbf{\Delta}[w_n = v_j, z_n = i]$ is an indicator function representing the nth word in review d, which is the jth entry in vocabulary V, is discussing aspect A_i. When we have each aspect's rating, the overall rating r is assumed to be drawn from a Normal distribution with fixed variance δ^2 and mean value as the weighted sum of aspect ratings, i.e., $\alpha^T\mathbf{s} = \sum_{i=1}^{k} \alpha_i \mathbf{s}_i$. Plugging in $\mathbf{s}_i$ defined in Eq (2), we have:

$$r \sim N(\sum_{i=1}^{k} \alpha_i \sum_{n=1}^{|d|} \beta_{ij} \mathbf{\Delta}[w_n = v_j, z_n = i], \delta^2) \qquad (3)$$

In order to further capture the diversity of different reviewers' preferences over different aspects and the dependency among the aspects, we employ a multivariate Normal distribution as the prior for aspect weight α, i.e., $\alpha \sim N(\mu, \mathbf{\Sigma})$. As a whole, the probability of observing the overall rating r and aspect weight α given the aspect segments in review d is defined as:

$$\begin{aligned} &p(r, \alpha|\mathbf{W}, \mu, \mathbf{\Sigma}, \delta^2) \qquad (4)\\ =&p(\alpha|\mu, \mathbf{\Sigma})p(r|\sum_{i=1}^{k} \alpha_i \sum_{n=1}^{|d|} \beta_{ij} \mathbf{\Delta}[w_n = v_j, z_n = i], \delta^2) \end{aligned}$$

We can find from the above description of the two components that the dependency between review text content

$\mathbf{W}$ and the latent aspect ratings $\mathbf{s}$ is bridged by the aspect assignment $\{z_n\}_{n=1}^{|d|}$. More specifically, we introduce the latent aspect assignments to associate the appropriate word descriptions with the corresponding aspect, so that the rating regression model can exploit such association to infer the latent aspect ratings/weights. Compared with the previous two-stage approach in [23], where a bootstrapping algorithm is used to generate a hard association, in the unified model, such correspondence is determined by the probabilistic aspect assignments.

Combining the two components, the joint probability of the observed text content $\mathbf{W}$ and overall rating r in a given review d can thus be defined as:

$$\begin{aligned}&P(r, \mathbf{W}|\epsilon, \gamma, \beta, \mu, \mathbf{\Sigma}, \delta^2) \quad (5)\\ =&P(\mathbf{W}|\epsilon, \gamma) \times P(r|\mathbf{W}, \beta, \mu, \mathbf{\Sigma}, \delta^2)\\ =&\iint \prod_{n=1}^{|d|} \sum_{z_n=1}^{k} p(w_n|z_n)p(z_n|\theta)p(\theta|\gamma)d\theta \times\\ &p(r|\sum_{i=1}^{k} \alpha_i \sum_{n=1}^{|d|} \beta_{ij}\mathbf{\Delta}[w_n = v_j, z_n = i], \delta^2)p(\alpha|\mu, \Sigma)d\alpha\end{aligned}$$

where we denote $\mathbf{\Theta} = (\epsilon, \gamma, \beta, \mu, \mathbf{\Sigma}, \delta^2)$ as the set of *corpus-level* model parameters, which do not depend on individual reviews. A graphical model illustration of the unified LARAM is shown in Figure 2.

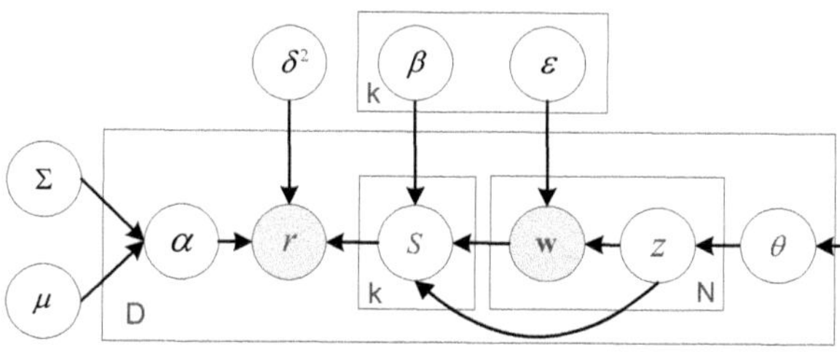

Figure 2: Graphical model representation of LARAM. The outer box represents reviews, while the inner box represents the composition of latent aspect rating regression and word generation within a review.

As illustrated in Figure 2, the word usage patterns embedded in the review text collection are captured by the aspect modeling part; the latent aspect assignments $\{z_n\}_{n=1}^{|d|}$ associate such word clusters with the corresponding aspect, and based on such probabilistic aspect segmentations, the latent aspect ratings and weights are discovered accordingly. We want to emphasize that the aim of the proposed LARAM is not to predict the overall ratings; instead, we are more interested in leveraging the observed general sentiment polarities from overall ratings to identify the opinions in each detailed latent aspect.

We should also note the proposed LARAM is not a trivial replacement of previous keyword-based bootstrapping method in [23] with topic models. Instead, it naturally bridges the gap between the aspect segmentation and sentiment analysis procedure in the previously used two-stage approach. There are two important factors distinguishing the proposed LARAM from the previous LRR model. First, in the current model, the latent aspect rating is a random variable, or more specifically, sum of a set of random variables (because each word's aspect assignment is a probability distribution over all the aspects), while in LRR model, it is treated as a fixed response variable of a rating regression module based on the given aspect segments. This difference enables us to model the uncertainty from the aspect segmentation part as well. Second, the latent rating analysis part provides informative feedback for the aspect segmentation part in the new model. Intuitively, in LARAM, we should assign the word w_j to a proper aspect A_i, in which the word's sentiment orientation β_{ij} is the most consistent with the identified orientation $\mathbf{s}_i$, or in other words, to be consistent with other words in its segment. In the previous LRR model, such segmentation is fixed once the set of aspect keywords is determined.

It would be also interesting to compare LARAM with sLDA introduced in [2]. sLDA is a topic modeling based regression method, which aims at modeling the labeled data in the projected latent topic space. One obvious difference between LARAM and sLDA is that sLDA is designed to predict the overall response for the given input; it can not discover the latent aspect ratings, since it assumes the observed overall response is directly generated from the weighted combination of the latent topic factors. Our LARAM further assumes that the overall rating is determined based on a set of latent ratings over different topical aspects, naturally modeling the latent aspect ratings.

4.1 Posterior Inference

Given the model parameters $\mathbf{\Theta} = (\epsilon, \gamma, \beta, \mu, \mathbf{\Sigma}, \delta^2)$, the key step of applying the proposed LARAM is to infer the posterior distribution of the latent aspect assignment $\{z_n\}_{n=1}^{|d|}$ and aspect weight α in a given review d. Once this is done, the aspect ratings can be easily derived from Eq (2). In this work, we use the variational inference method [10] due to its computational efficiency. The key idea behind variational approximation is to optimize the free parameters of a distribution over the latent variables so that the approximated distribution is close to the true posterior by Kullback-Leibler divergence.

More specifically, we introduce a family of factorized variational distribution for the hidden variables (z, θ, α) in each review d,

$$q(\mathbf{z}, \theta, \alpha|\phi, \eta, \lambda, \sigma^2) = q(\theta|\eta) \prod_n q(z_n|\phi_n)q(\alpha|\lambda, \sigma^2) \quad (6)$$

where the aspect assignment z for each word in d is specified by a k-dimensional multinomial distribution $Mul(\phi)$, aspect proportion θ is governed by a k-dimensional Dirichlet distribution $Dir(\eta)$, and aspect weight α is determined by a k-dimensional multivariate Normal distribution $N(\lambda, \sigma^2)$ with a diagonal covariance matrix to simplify the computation.

Based on the introduced variational distribution, the lower bound of the log-likelihood in review d can be approximated as follows:

$$\begin{aligned}&\log p(r, \mathbf{W}|\epsilon, \gamma, \beta, \mu, \mathbf{\Sigma}, \delta^2) \quad (7)\\ =&\log p(\mathbf{W}|\epsilon, \gamma) + \log p(r|\mathbf{W}, \beta, \mu, \mathbf{\Sigma}, \delta^2)\\ \geq& E_q[\log p(\mathbf{z}, \theta, \mathbf{W}|\epsilon, \gamma)] - E_q[\log q(\mathbf{z}, \theta|\phi, \eta)]\\ &+E_q\big[\log p(r, \alpha, \mathbf{z}|\mathbf{W}, \beta, \mu, \mathbf{\Sigma}, \delta^2)\big] - E_q[\log q(\alpha, \mathbf{z}|\epsilon, \gamma, \phi, \eta)]\end{aligned}$$

where the bound is derived from the Jensen's inequality for convex function. In the following discussions, we will use

$\mathcal{L}_d(\phi, \eta, \lambda, \sigma^2)$ to represent the lower bound defined by a set of variational parameters $(\phi, \eta, \lambda, \sigma^2)$ in review d.

The explanation for this lower bound is quite intuitive: the first part of $\mathcal{L}_d(\phi, \eta, \lambda, \sigma^2)$ represents the objective of aspect modeling module, which aims at finding the optimal aspect assignments $\{z_n\}_{n=1}^{|d|}$ and the corresponding aspect proportion θ for the observed review contents; the second part explains the objective of rating analysis module, which tunes both $\{z_n\}_{n=1}^{|d|}$ and α to fit the overall ratings. These two parts are not independently separated but connected by the common aspect assignments $\{z_n\}_{n=1}^{|d|}$. Both parts attempt to allocate proper aspect assignments to better accommodate the observed text contents and overall rating, respectively.

Details for calculating the expectation of the first part can be found in [3]. The expectation of the complete-data log-likelihood function for the rating analysis module under the variational distribution is derived as:

$$E_q\left[\log p(r, \alpha, \mathbf{z}|\mathbf{W}, \beta, \mu, \mathbf{\Sigma}, \delta^2)\right]$$
$$= -\frac{(\lambda^T\bar{\mathbf{s}} - r)^2}{2\delta^2} - \frac{1}{2\delta^2}\sum_{i=1}^{k}\left\{(\lambda_i^2 + \sigma_i^2)Var[\mathbf{s}_i] + \sigma_i^2\bar{\mathbf{s}}_i^2\right\}$$
$$-\frac{1}{2}(\lambda - \mu)^T\Sigma^{-1}(\lambda - \mu) - \frac{1}{2}Tr\left(diag(\sigma^2)\Sigma^{-1}\right) - \frac{1}{2}\log\delta^2 - \frac{1}{2}\log|\Sigma|$$

where $\bar{\mathbf{s}}_i = \sum_{n=1}^{|d|}\beta_{ij}w_n^j\phi_{ni}$, $Var[\mathbf{s}_i] = \sum_{n=1}^{|d|}(\beta_{ij}w_n^j)^2\phi_{ni}(1-\phi_{ni})$ (w_n^j is a short for the indicator function $\mathbf{\Delta}[w_n = j]$).

Once the expectations in $\mathcal{L}_d(\phi, \eta, \lambda, \sigma^2)$ are analytically determined, an iterative fixed-point method is employed to find the set of variational parameters $(\phi, \eta, \lambda, \sigma^2)$ in order to maximize the lower bound of the original log-likelihood, which in turn would minimize the KL divergency between the variational posterior and true posterior in each review. In particular, we compute the derivative of $\mathcal{L}_d(\phi, \eta, \lambda, \sigma^2)$ with respect to the variational parameters accordingly, and use them to find the optimal setting for each variational parameter.

In the aspect modeling part, the variational parameter η can be easily estimated as

$$\hat{\eta}_i = \gamma_i + \sum_{n=1}^{|d|}\phi_{ni} \tag{8}$$

Due to the involvement of rating analysis part, it is hard for us to get a closed-form solution for ϕ as in [3]. Therefore, we appeal to the gradient-based optimization procedure to obtain the optimal solution:

$$\hat{\phi}_n = \arg\max_{\phi_n}\sum_{i=1}^{k}w_n^j\phi_{ni}\left[\psi(\eta_i) - \psi(\sum_{j=1}^{k}\eta_j) + w_n^j\log\epsilon_{ij} - \log\phi_{ni}\right]$$
$$-\frac{1}{2\delta^2}(\lambda^T\bar{\mathbf{s}} - r)^2 - \frac{1}{2\delta^2}\sum_{i=1}^{k}\left[(\lambda_i^2 + \sigma_i^2)Var[\mathbf{s}_i] + \sigma_i^2\bar{\mathbf{s}}_i^2\right] \tag{9}$$

s.t. $\forall$ i, $0 \leq \phi_{ni} \leq 1$ and $\sum_{i=1}^{k}\phi_{ni} = 1$

In the rating analysis part, to make it comparable across different aspects within the same review, we need to force the aspect weight α to satisfy the constraint that $\forall$ i, $0 \leq \alpha_i \leq 1$ and $\sum_{i=1}^{k}\alpha_i = 1$. This would postulate additional constraints on the optimization procedures for $\mathcal{L}_d(\phi, \eta, \lambda, \sigma^2)$ with respect to variational parameter λ. We use posterior constrained expectation maximization [5] to address this problem. Gradient-based searching algorithm is utilized to find the optimal solution:

$$\hat{\lambda} = \arg\min_{\lambda}\left\{\frac{1}{2\delta^2}\left[\sum_{i=1}^{k}\lambda_i^2Var[\mathbf{s}_i] + (\lambda^T\bar{\mathbf{s}} - r)^2\right] + \frac{1}{2}(\lambda - \mu)^T\Sigma^{-1}(\lambda - \mu)\right\} \tag{10}$$

s.t. $\forall$ i, $0 \leq \lambda_i \leq 1$ and $\sum_i^k\lambda_i = 1$.

Finally, σ^2 could be easily calculated as,

$$\sigma_i^2 = \frac{\delta^2}{Var[\mathbf{s}_i] + \bar{\mathbf{s}}_i^2 + \delta^2\Sigma_{ii}^{-1}} \tag{11}$$

The interaction between the aspect modeling module and latent rating analysis module is now clearly stated in the above inference procedures: an optimal aspect assignments $\{z_n\}_{n=1}^{|d|}$ should not only fit the observed review contents as much as possible, but also minimize the overall rating prediction error and the variance of each aspect rating prediction; in other words, the rating prediction part can be considered as a regularization factor for the aspect assignments. Meanwhile, the rating analysis part should also consider the variance of each inferred aspect rating, i.e., we should not put too much emphasis on any single aspect, which is highly uncertain.

4.2 Model Estimation

In the previous section, we have discussed how to infer the latent aspect assignments $\{z_n\}_{n=1}^{|d|}$ and aspect weight α in each review d when given the model $\mathbf{\Theta} = (\epsilon, \gamma, \beta, \mu, \mathbf{\Sigma}, \delta^2)$. In this section, we discuss how to estimate these *corpus-level* parameters using the Expectation Maximization (EM) algorithm by maximizing the expectation of observing review contents and the overall ratings in a given review document collection.

As defined in Eq (7), we can approximate the log-likelihood in each individual review d by the introduced variational distribution $q(z, \theta, \alpha|\phi, \eta, \lambda, \sigma^2)$. Since the variational inference is carried out independently for each review in the collection, the log-likelihood over the whole collection D is simply a summation over the lower bound of each review:

$$\mathcal{L}(D) = \sum_{d \in D}\mathcal{L}_d(\phi, \eta, \lambda, \sigma^2) \tag{12}$$

Following similar procedures used in Section 4.1, we maximize Eq (12) by finding the optimal *corpus-level* model parameters $\mathbf{\Theta} = (\epsilon, \gamma, \beta, \mu, \mathbf{\Sigma}, \delta^2)$.

The detailed procedures for updating the parameters in the aspect modeling part is the same as derived in [3], so we only list them here:

$$\epsilon_{ij} \propto \sum_{d}^{D}\sum_{n}^{N_d}\phi_{dni}w_{dn}^j \tag{13}$$

$$\frac{\partial\mathcal{L}(\gamma)}{\partial\gamma_i} = D\left[\psi(\sum_j\gamma_j) - \psi(\gamma_i)\right] + \sum_{d}^{D}\left[\psi(\eta_{di}) - \psi(\sum_j\eta_{dj})\right] \tag{14}$$

$$\frac{\partial^2\mathcal{L}(\gamma)}{\partial\gamma_i\partial\gamma_j} = D\left[\psi'(\sum_j\gamma_j) - \sigma(i,j)\psi'(\gamma_i)\right] \tag{15}$$

The updating equations for the aspect weight prior $(\mu, \mathbf{\Sigma})$, and overall rating prediction variance δ^2 in the rating analysis part can be easily obtained from their sufficient statistics accordingly:

$$\hat{\mu} = \frac{1}{D}\sum_{d=1}^{D}\lambda_d \tag{16}$$

$$\hat{\Sigma} = \frac{1}{D}\sum_{d=1}^{D}\left[(\lambda_d - \hat{\mu})(\lambda_d - \hat{\mu})^T + diag(\sigma_d^2)\right] \tag{17}$$

$$\hat{\delta}^2 = \frac{1}{D}\sum_{d=1}^{D}\left\{(r_d - \lambda_d^T\bar{\mathbf{s}}_d)^2 + \sum_{i=1}^{k}\left[(\lambda_{di}^2 + \sigma_{di}^2)Var[\mathbf{s}_{di}] + \sigma_{di}^2\bar{\mathbf{s}}_{di}^2\right]\right\} \tag{18}$$

However a closed-form updating formula for the term weight matrix β is hard to write out:

$$\hat{\beta} = \arg\min_{\beta}\sum_{d}^{D}\left\{(\lambda_d^T\bar{\mathbf{s}}_d - r_d)^2 + \sum_{i=1}^{k}\left[(\lambda_{di}^2 + \sigma_i^2)Var[\mathbf{s}_{di}] + \sigma_{di}^2\bar{\mathbf{s}}_{di}^2\right]\right\} \tag{19}$$

We apply the gradient-based optimization technique to find the optimal solution of β with the following gradients:

$$\frac{\partial\mathcal{L}(\beta_i)}{\partial\beta_{ij}} = \sum_{d}^{D}\Big[(\lambda_d^T\bar{\mathbf{s}}_d - r_d)\lambda_{di} + \sigma_{di}^2\bar{\mathbf{s}}_{di} + (\lambda_{di}^2 + \sigma_{reviewi}^2)\beta_{ij}w_{dn}^j(1 - \phi_{dni})\Big]\phi_{dni}w_{dn}^j$$

From the above equation, we can find another evidence of the interaction between aspect modeling module and rating analysis module: an optimal word sentiment polarity setting should not only ensure the sentiment orientation expressed in the review content consist with the observed overall sentiment judgment, but also reduce the uncertainty on each latent aspect's opinion prediction, which would help the model allocate the aspect assignment for each word more accurately.

All the parameters are first randomly initialized to obtain $\Theta_{(0)}$ (subscript indicates the iteration step) and then the following EM algorithm is applied to iteratively update and improve the parameters by alternatively executing the *E-step* and *M-step* in each iteration until the log-likelihood defined in Eq (12) converges.

E-Step: For each review d in the corpus, infer aspect weight α and topic assignments $\{z_n\}_{n=1}^{|d|}$ based on the current parameter $\Theta_{(t)}$ by using Eq (8) to Eq (11) and compute aspect rating $\mathbf{s}$ by Eq (2).

M-Step: Given the sufficient statistics collected from each review in ***E-Step***, find the updated model parameters $\Theta_{(t+1)}$ by using Eq (13) to Eq (19).

5. EXPERIMENT RESULTS

In this section, we first describe the review data sets we used for evaluation purpose, and then discuss both qualitative and quantitative experiment results.

5.1 Data Sets and Preprocessing

We include two review data sets in our experiments: a hotel review data set originally used in [23], and an MP3 player review data set crawled from `www.amazon.com`. In the hotel data, in addition to the overall ratings, reviewers are also asked to provide ratings on 7 pre-defined aspects in each review: *value, room, location, cleanliness, check in/front desk, service, business service* ranging from 1 star to 5 stars. This can serve as the ground-truth for quantitative evaluation of both aspect identification and latent aspect rating prediction. In the MP3 data set, there is only one overall rating in each review, ranging from 1 star to 5 stars. Both data sets are available at `http://timan.cs.uiuc.edu/downloads.html`.

Table 1: Statistics of data sets

	#Item	#Review	#Reviewer	Avg Len	Rating
Hotel	2,232	37,181	34,187	96.5	3.92±1.23
MP3	686	16,680	15,004	87.3	3.76±1.41

Table 2: Topical aspects learned on MP3 reviews

Low Overall Ratings			High Overall Ratings		
unit	jack	service	files	player	vision
usb	headphone	charge	format	music	video
battery	warranty	problem	included	download	player
charger	replacement	support	easy	headphones	quality
reset	problem	hours	convert	button	great
time	player	months	mp3	set	product
hours	back	weeks	videos	hours	sound
work	months	back	file	buds	radio
thing	buy	customer	wall	volume	accessory
wall	amazon	time	hours	ear	fm

We first perform simple pre-processing on these two data sets: 1) remove the reviews with any missing aspect rating or document length less than 50 words (to keep the content coverage of all possible aspects); 2) convert all the words into lower cases; and 3) removing punctuations, stop words defined in [1], and the terms occurring in less than 10 reviews in the collection. After the pre-processing, we have 37,181 hotel reviews and 16,680 MP3 reviews; the detailed statistics are listed in Table 1.

5.2 Aspect Identification

Automatic Adaptation of Aspects: In Amazon reviews, the reviewers are only asked to give an overall rating, so they would have more freedom, or less guidance to write the comments. In this case, it is *very difficult* to pre-specify aspects in keywords. Here, we will qualitatively demonstrate that our unified model, LARAM, can automatically identify meaningful aspects based on the data characteristics. We separate the reviews into two subsets, one with low overall ratings (at most 3 stars) and the other with high overall ratings (at least 4 stars), and run LARAM to extract 20 aspects on each subset. It is expected that users usually comment on different aspects in positive reviews and negative reviews. In Table 2, we show the top 10 words of the highest generation probability for the three aspects with the highest aspect weight prior μ which can be considered as contributing most to the overall ratings. We can see that LARAM automatically adapts to such different data characteristics: in the negative reviews, the most complained aspects are about warranty and service while positive reviews emphasize the good product features such as flexible file format and great video quality.

Next, we quantitatively compare our model with existing methods on the quality of identified topical aspects.

Algorithms for Comparison: Since we depend on the topic modeling techniques to discover the aspects, we compare LARAM with two different topic models: unsupervised **LDA** model and supervised **sLDA** model. LDA behaves similarly as our aspect modeling module, but it can only fit the word co-occurrence patterns in the review content. sLDA extends LDA by adding a regression module to model the observed overall response, so that it uses the same input as our model. However, since sLDA and LARAM employ

Table 3: KL divergence between the align aspects

	LDA	sLDA	LARAM
7 topics	**5.675**	14.878	5.827
14 topics	8.819	19.074	**8.356**
21 topics	12.745	22.411	**11.167**

different generation assumption for the overall response, it would be interesting to compare these two models.

Measure: In the hotel data set, since TripAdvisor asks reviewers to rate the predefined 7 aspects, it is reasonable to assume those are the major aspects most reviewers comment about. Thus, we use the full set of keywords (in total 309 words) generated by the bootstrapping method used in [23] as a prior to train a LDA model on this data set, and treat the learned topics as the "ground-truth" aspect descriptions. Then we train all the three models *without* any supervision of aspect keywords, find the optimal alignment between the learned topics with "ground-truth" aspects by Kuhn-Munkres algorithm [13] and quantitatively measure the quality of the identified aspects using KL divergence:

$$D(p||q) = \sum_x p(x) \log \frac{p(x)}{q(x)}$$

where p(x) is the "ground-truth" word distribution, and q(x) is the word distribution learned by a given model.

Result Analysis: We train these three models with 7, 14 and 21 topics (since we already know there are 7 aspects) on the hotel data set separately and list the results in Table 3. From the results, we can find that compared with the unsupervised LDA model, the aspects identified by LARAM are closer to the ground-truth aspects when we have more topics (i.e., smaller KL divergence); sLDA's performance is the worst, even though it has additional information from the overall ratings. From the comparison we can see that the inferred aspect ratings from LARAM help the aspect model to better allocate the words across different aspects, which would not be easily distinguished solely from the co-occurrence patterns (LARAM versus LDA). The sLDA model assumes that the topics (aspects) directly characterize the overall ratings, rather than the words' sentiment polarities in the specific aspects as we assumed in LARAM, so it prefers rating sentiment sensitive words than those general content words. As a result, the word distribution under each topic learned by sLDA is quite different from the keyword specified aspects. Besides, we can observe that when we use more topics, KL divergence gets larger. The reason is that with more topics, all the models will then have more freedom to distinguish the aspects in a finer granularity, which is not covered by the predefined aspect keywords.

5.3 Aspect Rating Prediction

Although LARAM is designed to infer ratings on any discovered topical aspects, we can only quantitatively evaluate the predicted ratings on the collection where we have ground-truth aspect ratings from the users. In this experiment, we use the hotel review data set as the testing corpus. In order to ensure our discovered aspects are aligned with the pre-defined aspects, we use the full set of keywords as prior to guide the aspect modeling part.

Algorithms for Comparison: As an alternative method to the proposed unified method **LARAM**, we can take a two-stage approach: apply topic models (e.g., LDA or sLDA) or bootstrapping to identify the aspect segments and then apply LRR to predict aspect ratings. Therefore we include three methods for the comparison purpose, i.e., **LDA+LRR**, **sLDA+LRR**, and **Bootstrap+LRR**.

Table 4: Aspect rating prediction performance on reviews

	LDA+LRR	sLDA+LRR	LARAM
MSE	2.130	2.360	**1.234**
ρ_{aspect}	0.080	0.079	**0.228**
Mis_{aspect}	0.439	0.439	**0.387**
$nDCG_{aspect}$	0.860	0.886	**0.901**
ρ_{hotel}	0.558	0.450	**0.622**
$MAP_{hotel}@10$	0.427	**0.437**	0.436

Measures: We quantitatively evaluate the algorithms using six different measures, including: (1) Mean Square Error (MSE_{aspect}) of the predicted aspect ratings compared with the ground-truth aspect ratings; (2) Pearson correlation inside reviews (ρ_{aspect}) measures how well the predicted aspect ratings can preserve the relative order of aspects within a review given by their ground-truth ratings; (3) percentage of mis-ordered aspects inside reviews (Mis_{aspect}) measures the cases when the predicted aspect ratings confuse the best and worst aspects within reviews (if they are different as in ground-truth); (4) nDCG of aspect ranking inside reviews ($nDCG_{aspect}$) evaluates the model's ranking accuracy of aspects inside reviews, where the ground truth aspect ratings are used as the graded relevance in the measure; (5) Pearson correlation across hotels (ρ_{hotel}) measures how well the predicted aspect ratings (average over the predicted aspect ratings of all the reviews commenting on this hotel) can preserve the relative order of hotels by their ground-truth ratings; and (6) Mean Average Precision ($MAP_{hotel}@10$) evaluates the model's ranking accuracy of hotels. We treat each aspect as a query, the top 10% of hotels ranked by the ground-truth aspect ratings as the relevant answers, and test whether we would be able to rank these top 10 hotels on the top, if we use the predicted aspect ratings to rank them. Those measurements can be categorized into two different groups: aspect-level evaluation, including the first four metrics, which are averaged over all the reviews, and hotel-level evaluation, including the last two metrics, which are averaged over all the aspects.

Result Analysis (1): Since we are only interested in predicting the latent aspect ratings, we used all the data for both training and testing. We report the performance of running different models on individual reviews in Table 4, where we highlight the best performance in each metric. We did not include Bootstrap+LRR in this table, because only a small subset of reviews can be tagged with all 7 aspects using the bootstrapping method, but the second-stage LRR requires all reviews to be tagged with 7 aspects as input.

In general, LARAM outperforms other methods in all measures except that its $MAP_{hotel}@10$ performance is basically the same as sLDA+LRR. The top part of the table shows MSE, which directly measures the difference between the predicted aspect ratings and ground truth ratings. The middle part shows the performance of ranking different aspects inside reviews. The absolute values of ρ_{aspect} are generally low because this measure is over-penalizing all numerical regression methods which produce ratings in real value while ground-truth ratings are all integers. This bias is eliminated in $nDCG_{aspect}$ which also measures the aspect ranking accuracy but handles the integer tie cases well. Mis_{aspect} only looks at the most confident cases where reviewers show explicit preference of one aspect to another. All three measures show superior performance of the proposed unified model in aspect ranking inside reviews which can answer questions like "Do the reviewer like the *location* better than *cleanliness* of hotel XXX?". Finally, the bottom part of the table demonstrates the model's ranking capability of hotels based on the predicted aspect ratings. Since we average the aspect ratings from individual reviews to get aspect ratings for the same hotel, which are in real value, there is no bias in the ρ_{hotel} measure.

Table 5: Aspect rating prediction performance on h-reviews

	Bootstrap+LRR	LARAM	LARAM+LRR
MSE	1.617	1.589	**0.947**
ρ_{aspect}	0.322	0.197	**0.445**
Mis_{aspect}	0.298	0.318	**0.239**
$nDCG_{aspect}$	0.889	0.905	**0.947**
ρ_{hotel}	0.697	**0.767**	0.764
$MAP_{hotel}@10$	0.599	**0.627**	0.590

Result Analysis (2): In order to compare with Bootstrap+LRR, we perform another set of experiments where we concatenate all the reviews commenting on the same hotel together as a new review (we call it "h-review") and average the overall/aspect ratings over them as the ground-truth ratings for this hotel.

The results are shown in Table 5. We observe mixed results when comparing Bootstrap+LRR with our unified LARAM model: LARAM is worse in the middle part which measures the aspect ranking performance within reviews while better in MSE_{aspect} (top part) and hotel ranking (bottom part). To explain this behavior, we analyzed the results from aspect modeling component of LARAM and found that the bag-of-words assumption affected the aspect tagging results of general sentiment words a lot[1]. For example, if a word like "nice" appears in a review, LARAM can hardly associate it with the correct aspect with regard to the local context, or mistakenly assign it to a fixed aspect only because they co-occur more often. And the situation gets even worse when we concatenate different reviews together. In contrast, by considering the adjacency of words or sentence boundaries, we will know that "nice" should contribute to the aspect "*location*" if they are in the same sentence. To test this hypothesis, we first use the topics learned using LARAM to annotate sentences and then apply LRR on the tagged sentences. We call this method LARAM+LRR and show its performance on the last column in Table 5, where the highlighted numbers are the best results on each measure. We can see that by tagging each whole sentence with one aspect, LARAM+LRR provides the best performance in almost all measures. It also validates that the topical aspects discovery by LARAM are effective.

[1]A sample annotation result can be found in `http://sifaka.cs.uiuc.edu/~wang296/Data/annotation.html`

5.4 Aspect Weights Prediction

As we discussed before, a significant advantage of our unified model over existing joint models of aspect and sentiment is that we can infer the relative wights that reviewers have placed on different aspects, i.e., α. Unfortunately, it is infeasible to evaluate the inferred aspect weights directly because we cannot obtain the ground-truth weights from the reviewers. As a result, we choose to evaluate the weights indirectly through clustering the reviewers based on their weights on different aspects.

More specifically, we apply k-means on the aggregated aspect weights of each reviewer over all her reviews to get 10 clusters, where reviewers in the same cluster are expected to share similar taste if the clustering based on the inferred weights is meaningful. In other words, we assume reviewers who share similar aspect preference tend to give the same entity (hotel/MP3 player) similar overall ratings. We test this hypothesis by looking at two sets of standard deviations of ground-truth overall ratings: the first set is for reviewers in the same cluster who also reviewed the same entity while the second control set is for all the reviewers who reviewed the same entity. To make the comparison stable and accurate, we filter out the entities with less than 10 reviews and get 884 hotels with 23,870 reviews and 222 MP3 players with 11,012 reviews in the testing set.

In Figure 3, we show the scatter plot of the two sets of standard deviations. It is clear that most standard deviations of the first set (reviewers from the same cluster on the same entity) are smaller than those of the second control set (all the reviewers on the same entity). Furthermore, two-sample Kolmogorov-Smirnov (KS) test of the samples in the two sets of standard deviations indicates that the difference between the two groups is statistically significant with p-value of e^{-10} for both data sets. This means that reviewers clustered together based on similar aspect weights tend to give more similar overall ratings to the same entity. It also indirectly suggests that the aspect weights learned by our unified model capture the taste of different reviewers.

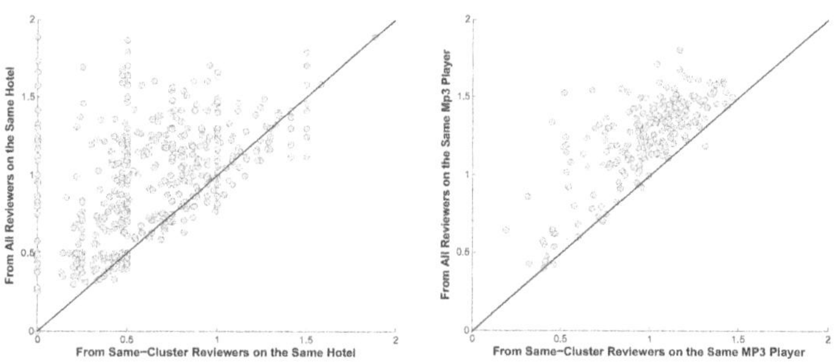

(a) Hotel (b) MP3

Figure 3: Scatter plot of standard deviations of overall ratings

6. CONCLUSIONS

In this paper, we propose a unified generative Latent Aspect Rating Analysis Model (LARAM) which can explore review text data with companion overall ratings to simultaneously discover: 1) latent topical aspects, 2) latent ratings on each identified aspect, and 3) latent weights placed on different aspects by a reviewer. It is a fully generative model for both the review text and the overall rating, and enables LARA task on arbitrary review data without needing aspect keyword supervision. Our empirical experiments on a hotel review data set and an MP3 player review data set show that the proposed LARAM can effectively solve the problem of LARA, including automatically identifying meaningful topical aspects, inferring interesting differences in aspect ratings within reviews, and modeling users' preferences with the inferred relative emphasis on different aspects. Such detailed analysis of opinions at the level of topical aspects enabled by LARAM can support multiple application tasks, including aspect opinion summarization, ranking of entities based on aspect ratings, and analysis of reviewers rating behavior.

As we have observed in the detailed experiment results, the bag-of-words assumption seriously hampers the model's aspect segmentation capability, which provides inaccurate segments for the later rating analysis part. For our future work, we are interested in restricting the naive bag-of-words assumption by adding sentence boundary and proximity information into the model for better associating general sentiment words with the appropriate aspect, which will lead to better aspect rating prediction performance. Also, it would be interesting to study how to alleviate the data sparseness problem because reviewers usually do not comment on all the aspects for a given entity. In this situation, borrowing some ideas from the collaborative filtering problem would be beneficial.

7. ACKNOWLEDGMENTS

This material is based upon work supported by the National Science Foundation under Grant Numbers IIS-0713581 and CNS 1028381, and by an AFOSR MURI Grant FA9550-08-1-0265.

8. REFERENCES

[1] Onix text retrieval toolkit stopword list. `http://www.lextek.com/manuals/onix/stopwords1.html`.

[2] D. Blei and J. McAuliffe. Supervised topic models. *Advances in Neural Information Processing Systems*, 20:121–128, 2008.

[3] D. Blei, A. Ng, and M. Jordan. Latent dirichlet allocation. *The Journal of Machine Learning Research*, 3:993–1022, 2003.

[4] X. Ding, B. Liu, and L. Zhang. Entity discovery and assignment for opinion mining applications. In *Proceedings of the 15th KDD*, pages 1125–1134. ACM, 2009.

[5] J. Graça, K. Ganchev, and B. Taskar. Expectation maximization and posterior constraints. In *Advances in Neural Information Processing Systems*, volume 20. MIT Press, 2007.

[6] M. Hu and B. Liu. Mining and summarizing customer reviews. In *Proceedings of the 10th KDD*, pages 168–177. ACM, 2004.

[7] M. Hu and B. Liu. Mining opinion features in customer reviews. In *AAAI*, pages 755–760. AAAI Press / The MIT Press, 2004.

[8] N. Jindal and B. Liu. Identifying comparative sentences in text documents. In *Proceedings of 29th SIGIR*, 2006.

[9] Y. Jo and A. H. Oh. Aspect and sentiment unification model for online review analysis. In *Proceedings of the fourth ACM international conference on Web search and data mining*, 2011.

[10] M. Jordan, Z. Ghahramani, T. Jaakkola, and L. Saul. An introduction to variational methods for graphical models. *Machine learning*, 37(2):183–233, 1999.

[11] S. Kim and E. Hovy. Determining the sentiment of opinions. In *Proceedings of the 20th international conference on Computational Linguistics*, pages 1367–1373. Association for Computational Linguistics, 2004.

[12] C. Lin and Y. He. Joint sentiment/topic model for sentiment analysis. In *Proceeding of the 18th CIKM*, pages 375–384, New York, NY, USA, 2009. ACM.

[13] L. Lovász and M. Plummer. *Matching theory*. Elsevier Science Ltd, 1986.

[14] Y. Lu and C. Zhai. Opinion integration through semi-supervised topic modeling. In *Proceeding of the 17th WWW*, pages 121–130. ACM, 2008.

[15] Y. Lu, C. Zhai, and N. Sundaresan. Rated aspect summarization of short comments. In *Proceedings of the 18th WWW*, pages 131–140, 2009.

[16] Q. Mei, X. Ling, M. Wondra, H. Su, and C. Zhai. Topic sentiment mixture: modeling facets and opinions in weblogs. In *Proceedings of the 16th WWW*, pages 171–180. ACM, 2007.

[17] S. Morinaga, K. Yamanishi, K. Tateishi, and T. Fukushima. Mining product reputations on the web. In *Proceeding of the 8th KDD*, pages 341–349, 2002.

[18] B. Pang and L. Lee. Seeing stars: Exploiting class relationships for sentiment categorization with respect to rating scales. In *Proceedings of the 43rd ACL*, pages 115–124, 2005.

[19] B. Pang, L. Lee, and S. Vaithyanathan. Thumbs up? Sentiment classification using machine learning techniques. In *Proceedings of the 2002 Conference on Empirical Methods in Natural Language Processing*, pages 79–86, 2002.

[20] A.-M. Popescu and O. Etzioni. Extracting product features and opinions from reviews. In *HLT '05*, pages 339–346, Morristown, NJ, USA, 2005.

[21] I. Titov and R. T. McDonald. A joint model of text and aspect ratings for sentiment summarization. In *Proceedings of the 46th ACL*, pages 308–316, 2008.

[22] I. Titov and R. T. McDonald. Modeling online reviews with multi-grain topic models. In *Proceeding of the 17th WWW*, pages 111–120, 2008.

[23] H. Wang, Y. Lu, and C. Zhai. Latent aspect rating analysis on review text data: a rating regression approach. In *Proceedings of the 16th KDD*, pages 783–792. ACM, 2010.

[24] W. X. Zhao, J. Jiang, H. Yan, and X. Li. Jointly modeling aspects and opinions with a maxent-lda hybrid. In *Proceedings of the 2010 Conference on Empirical Methods in Natural Language Processing*, EMNLP '10, 2010.

[25] L. Zhuang, F. Jing, and X.-Y. Zhu. Movie review mining and summarization. In *Proceedings of the 15th ACM international conference on Information and knowledge management*, 2006.

Density Estimation Trees

Parikshit Ram
Georgia Institute of Technology
Atlanta GA, 30332
p.ram@gatech.edu

Alexander G. Gray
Georgia Institute of Technology
Atlanta GA, 30332
agray@cc.gatech.edu

ABSTRACT

In this paper we develop *density estimation trees* (DETs), the natural analog of classification trees and regression trees, for the task of density estimation. We consider the estimation of a joint probability density function of a d-dimensional random vector X and define a piecewise constant estimator structured as a decision tree. The integrated squared error is minimized to learn the tree. We show that the method is nonparametric: under standard conditions of nonparametric density estimation, DETs are shown to be asymptotically consistent. In addition, being decision trees, DETs perform automatic feature selection. They empirically exhibit the interpretability, adaptability and feature selection properties of supervised decision trees while incurring slight loss in accuracy over other nonparametric density estimators. Hence they might be able to avoid the curse of dimensionality if the true density is sparse in dimensions. We believe that density estimation trees provide a new tool for exploratory data analysis with unique capabilities.

Categories and Subject Descriptors

I.5 [**Pattern Recognition**]: Models; G.3 [**Probability and Statistics**]: Nonparametric statistics

General Terms

Algorithms, Experimentation

Keywords

Decision trees, density estimation, data analysis

1. INTRODUCTION

Three most fundamental tasks of machine learning are classification, regression, and density estimation. Classification and regression are instances of supervised data analysis where a training set of examples is provided. The learning task is to estimate a function using the training set which also performs well on a test set. The third task, density estimation, is an instance of unsupervised learning. This is generally harder because one does not have any instance of the ground truth regarding the quantity being estimated. Decision trees [1] have been widely used in the supervised setting for classification and regression. *In this paper we introduce, derive, and explore the natural analog of classification trees and regression trees for the unsupervised task of density estimation.* To our knowledge this analogy has never been explored rigorously, though several other ideas for density estimation involving hierarchical schemes have been proposed. Our hope is that the unique advantages of decision trees in the supervised setting will transfer to the unsupervised setting, to give rise to a new nonparametric density estimation method with interesting capabilities.

Density estimation. The problem of density estimation can be defined as estimating an unknown distribution f on $\mathcal{X}$[1] with a close approximation $\hat{f}\colon \mathcal{X} \to \mathbb{R}_+$ given a set of N IID (independent and identically distributed) observations $\{X_1, X_2, \ldots, X_N\} \subset \mathcal{X}$ drawn from f. Estimating the probability density of the given data is a fundamental task in multivariate statistics. It often appears as a subroutine in other inference – for example, in classification, one is required to find $\hat{P}(C|X) = \frac{\hat{p}(X|C)P(C)}{\hat{p}(X)}$, where C is one of the possible K classes and $\hat{p}(X|C)$ is the class-conditional density of the data X [2, 3, 4]. It is also widely used for conducting exploratory analyses such as outlier or cluster detection.

Decision trees. Decision trees [1] were developed for classification [5] and regression [6]. They are primarily used for the purpose of supervised learning and have been widely and successfully used in nonparametric classification and regression. The piecewise constant estimators and the simplistic model of univariate binary splits of the data in decision trees lead to relatively *less accurate* estimators with unknown convergence rates [7]. Techniques such as bagging are used to boost this accuracy. More sophisticated methods with better accuracies and clearer asymptotic properties such as local linear regression [8] and support vector machines [9] exist for regression and classification respectively.

Nonetheless, anecdotally, decision trees remain one of the more widely used methods in practice [7], possibly even the most widely used. This is due to the inherent *intuitiveness*, *adaptability* and *interpretability* of the models learned. Moreover, they are capable of dealing with *mixed* categorical, discrete and continuous variables within one unified framework. They also perform *feature selection* and are easy to implement. These properties come at the cost of accuracy in prediction but still make decision trees very desirable and

[1]If all the attributes of the data are continuous then $\mathcal{X} \subset \mathbb{R}^d$

KDD'11, August 21–24, 2011, San Diego, California, USA.

Table 1: Characteristics of Methods for Density Estimation

METHODS	np	Accuracy	Interpretability			Adaptability		Speed	
			COD	VI	Rules	ABD	AWD	Training	Query
MoG	×	low	✓	×	×	×	×	fast EM algorithm	very fast $O(d^2)$
Histogram	✓	low	×	×	×	×	×	fast $O(MdN)$	very fast $O(d)$
KDE (FBW)	✓	medium	×	×	×	×	×	slow $O(HdN^2)$	slow $O(dN)$
KDE* (FBW)	✓	medium	×	×	×	×	×	fast $O(HdN)$	medium $O(d \log N)$
KDE (VBW)	✓	highest	×	×	×	✓	✓	very slow $O(H^d dN)/q$	slow $O(dN)$
KDE* (VBW)	✓	high	×	×	×	✓	✓	slow $O(H^d d \log N)/q$	medium $O(d \log N)$
local r-KDE	✓	very high	×	×	×	✓	✓	fast CV step/q	slow $O(dN)$
global r-KDE	✓	medium/high	×	×	×	✓	×	t fast CV steps	slow $O(dN)$
DET	✓	medium	✓	✓	✓	✓	✓	slow LOO-CV	fast $O(D_T)$

practical. Another advantage of decision trees is the *efficient test querying* once the model (in this case a tree) has been trained.

Decision trees trade some accuracy for a simple, interpretable model. Considering that density estimation is widely used in exploratory analysis, giving up accuracy (which is not a useful concept in the absence of the ground truth) for understanding is acceptable.

1.1 Nonparametric Density Estimators

Histograms and kernel density estimators (KDEs) [10] are simpler nonparametric (np) techniques, whereas variants of KDEs such as rodeo-KDEs [11] and wavelet based methods [8] are more complex nonparametric estimators. A number of nonparametric Bayesian methods have also been developed for the task of density estimation [12]. Mixtures of Gaussians (MoGs) are widely used parametric density estimators. Even though the nonparametric methods have been shown to be significantly more accurate than the parametric methods and require fewer assumptions on the data than parametric methods, MoGs are widely used because of their interpretability as clusters (as well as their simple implementation).

Adaptability and Speed. Adaptability has two implications in density estimation: (1) *adaptable between dimensions (ABD)* – the estimation process should treat dimensions differently depending on their influence on the density (for example, addition of unimportant dimensions of uniform noise should not affect the estimator) (2) *adaptable within a dimension (AWD)* – determining regions of interest for a given dimension and adjusting the estimator to the local behavior of the density in that dimension (for example, regions with fast changing density vs. regions with flat densities).

MoGs are not known to adapt between or within dimensions. Fixed-bandwidth KDEs (FBW) are accurate nonparametric estimators but are not adaptable between or within dimensions because of the restriction of using a multivariate kernel with the same bandwidth in every dimension (spherical kernel) for every point. The bandwidth is chosen through leave-one-out cross-validation (LOO-CV) by picking the one with the best CV loss among the H different values tried. A significantly high value of H is required to obtain accurate results. LOO-CV for the naïve implementation of KDE takes $O(HdN^2)$. Spatial partitioning tree data structures have been used for fast-approximate computation of KDEs (KDE*s) [13, 14]. For cover-trees [15], this process requires $O(HdN)$ time [16].

Various KDEs with adaptive bandwidths have been developed but are complicated in practice. The nearest-neighbor KDEs [10] are locally adaptive by choosing bandwidths based on their k^{th}-nearest-neighbor distance. However, they are not adaptive over dimensions since they still use a spherical multivariate kernel. Moreover, the estimate does not represent a probability density function (pdf), and is discontinuous and heavy tailed. A truly adaptive (ABD) KDE would require an optimal bandwidth for each dimension (VBW). This means the kernel used would be elliptical, adapting to the density of the data. This makes the VBW-KDEs adaptable between dimensions. If H bandwidths are tried in *each* dimension, the training time required for the naïve implementation of KDEs would be $O(H^d dN)$. To make this locally adaptive for each dimension(AWD), the bandwidth estimation would be required for each query q. Even the faster methods (KDE*) would require $O(H^d d \log N)$ training time for each query. This makes the computational cost of CV for VBW-KDEs intractable even in medium dimensions.

A recent algorithm [11] uses *rodeo* [17] to greedily select adaptive bandwidths for a KDE in each dimension. Under certain sparsity conditions on the unknown density function, the resulting estimator is shown to empirically perform well and obtain near optimal convergence rate for KDEs. The local version (local r-KDE) of this estimator computes the optimal bandwidth in every dimension for every query point. The paper demonstrates rodeo's adaptability – implicitly identifying the dimensions of interest during the process of bandwidth selection as well as identifying regions of interest within a single dimension, selecting smaller bandwidths where the density varies more rapidly. However, this technique is expensive, requiring a rodeo step for every single query. The rodeo step is iterative and we are not aware of its runtime bound. However, it is empirically faster than LOO-CV for VBW-KDEs. The global-rodeo [11] (global r-KDE) improves efficiency by using a fixed bandwidth within each dimension, and estimating it by averaging the estimated bandwidths for t training points in every dimension. Hence, the resulting estimator loses local adaptability within a dimension (property 2 of adaptability). The training time now involves t rodeo steps instead of a rodeo step for each query. The accuracy of the estimate obviously depends on the t (larger number training queries imply more accurate estimates and slower training).

KDEs can be made adaptable, however, at the cost of computational complexity. Moreover, given the estimated bandwidths, the time taken for a single query using the naïve implementation of a KDE is $O(dN)$. The cover-tree data structure provides an approximate estimate in $O(d \log N)$ query time. For $O(N)$ queries, the query cost can be amortized over the queries using a tree-data-structure over the queries, requiring a total time of $O(dN)$ [16][2].

Decision trees are known for their adaptability over the data (over features by implicit feature selection and within dimensions by choosing different leaf size in different regions). In this paper, we will demonstrate their adaptability for the task of density estimation. However, training decision trees using LOO-CV is an expensive step involving the growing of the tree, and the subsequent cost-complexity pruning [1, 7]. However this cost is amortized over the multiple empirically efficient queries. The query time for a decision tree estimator is $O(D_T)$ where D_T is the depth of a decision tree T. The worst case upper bound for D_T is $O(N)$, but is empirically seen to be much tighter in practice (much more closer to $O(\log N)$). Hence decision trees also bring efficiency to nonparametric density estimation at the cost of some accuracy. Histograms are also fast nonparametric estimators during training as well as query time. They require $O(MdN)$ training time for trying M different bin-widths and choosing the one with the best CV error. The query time is a blazing $O(d)$. However, they lack the adaptability of decision trees, and become prohibitively inaccurate as the number of dimensions increases.

Interpretability. We also propose the use of decision trees for density estimation to introduce interpretability in the nonparametric setting. The decision trees provide an interesting overlap between the accuracy of nonparametric methods and the simplicity and interpretability of parametric methods. Interpretability in density estimation can be useful in the providing the following information about the density of the data: (1) *detecting clusters and outliers (COD)* (2) *providing relative variable/dimension importance (VI)* – identifying dimensions that significantly affect the density (3) *providing simple univariate rules* – these simple rules can be used, for example, for directly specifying some chunk of a huge data set which sits on a DBMS database. In the case of a DET, this chunk might represent a cluster.

MoGs are known to detect clusters but are incapable of imparting any interpretability regarding the dimensions. The aforementioned method using rodeo [11] implicitly does identify dimensions of interest. However, it is hard to obtain relative importance of dimensions by just looking at the values of the estimated bandwidths. Moreover, cluster and outlier detection is complicated with KDEs – an exhaustive scan of the whole space provides regions of high (clusters) and low density (outliers). So KDEs are not interpretable density estimators. When accuracy is required with no concern over computation time, adaptive-KDEs are the method of choice. However, they might be too costly for exploratory analysis.

We attempt to achieve the properties of interpretability, while retaining adaptability, by using the CART-style univariate splits which gives rise to the uniquely readable rule structure of decision trees. This key property is not shared by the several other methods for density estimation involving hierarchical schemes which have been proposed over the years. Determining dimensions of interest is a direct by-product of the decision tree framework via the measure of *relative importance* of predictor variables [1][3]. While linear models such as linear regression and linear SVMs yield such

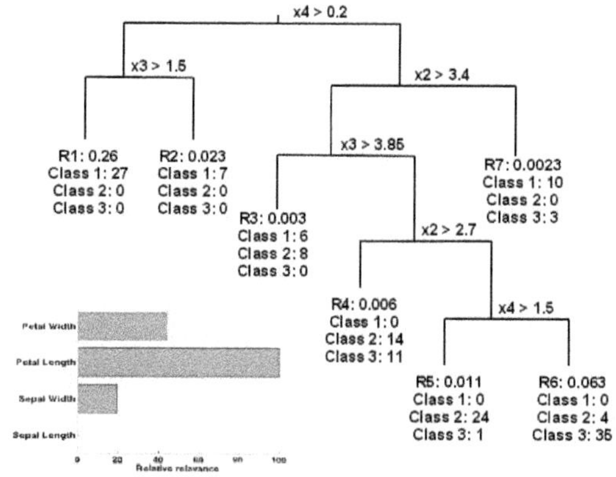

Figure 1: Density estimate in form of a decision tree and the relative variable importance.

a capability via examination of the linear coefficients, this capability is harder to find in nonparametric methods. A sorted list of the leaves of a DET can easily identify the clusters and the outliers in the data.

All the aforementioned properties of these estimators are summarized in Table 1. We further motivate the desirability of interpretability of a decision tree in the following example:

Motivating example. Consider the density estimates for the **Iris** data set (150×4)[4] as a set of rules depicted in Figure 1. Each leaf node contains the piecewise constant density estimate. More explicitly, $\hat{f}(x) = 0.026\ \forall x \in R_1$ (say). Here the leaf $R_1 = \{x \colon x_4 \leq 0.2\ \&\ x_3 \leq 1.5\}$. We have also listed the class memberships of the points in the leaf nodes[5]. This figure also presents the relative importance of the attributes.

The tree representation lets us easily find regions of relatively high (R_1) and low densities (R_3). The subtree corresponding to the regions R_1 and R_2 contains purely class 1, representing the well-known linearly separable class in the Iris data. The chart containing the relative importance of the predictor variables implies that the *petal length* has the highest importance with regards to the density, whereas, the *sepal length* has no influence on the density (example of feature deletion).

Thus we see that density estimation in the decision tree framework provides much more information about the data than just the density estimates. There are several other cases where it would be useful to get this kind of information about the data: (1)*Astronomy* – performing density estimation on quasar data is a common task in astronomy [18]. Common features in the data are colors. The feature-importance analysis corresponding to the density will indicate the unimportant color features. This information can be useful in deciding which filters are useful in future analyses, thereby, conserving resources. (2)*Bioinformatics* – consider a metabolomics data set containing pa-

[2]It is important to note that the spatial partitioning tree building has a one-time cost of $O(dN \log N)$.

[3]We will define this measure in the technical section of the paper.

[4]We will continue to represent the size of data sets with N point with d attributes/dimensions in the form $(N \times d)$ throughout this paper.

[5]We intend to perform density estimation only on the points in the unsupervised setting. However, we provide class memberships of the points in the node to motivate a well known property of the Iris data set.

tient information with over 20000 features, where the task is to differentiate cancer patients from healthy patients [19]. Density estimation performed over all patients' profiles can reveal which features are responsible for the main variation within, say, cancer patients, or within healthy patients. This is different from feature selection for classification which would select features which most differentiate the patients with cancer from the rest. In addition, cluster and outlier detection performed on this data set will produce interesting and possibly crucial information.

Moreover, a representative partition of the state space by itself sheds light on the underlying structure of the distribution. Such information is particularly valuable in high dimensional problems where direct visualization of the data is difficult.

Remark. DETs are similar to variable bin-width histograms, but are restricted only to a hierarchical partitioning of the data (hence possibly having lower accuracy than the best possible variable bin-width histogram, although our experiments suggest otherwise).

1.2 Overview

The focus of this paper is to develop a rigorous decision-tree-structured density estimator and demonstrate the usefulness and interpretability of the same.

In Section 2, we discuss existing connections between density estimation and decision trees. In the following section, we define an estimator based on the decision tree and apply the decision-tree framework for density estimation using this estimator. We also provide certain asymptotic properties of the decision-tree-structured estimator. Section 4 contains experimental results displaying the performance of DETs with some comparisons with histograms and KDEs. The adaptability of DETs is demonstrated by using some synthetic data sets. High dimensional image data sets are used to demonstrate the DETs' interpretability and their application to classification. Training and querying time of DETs are compared with the fastest training and querying method for KDEs (KDE*s). In the final section, conclusions are discussed along with certain open questions.

2. FURTHER RELATED WORK

Decision trees have been used alongside density estimation in earlier works. For example, Kohavi, 1996 [20] and Smyth et al., 1995 [21] use decision trees for the supervised task of classification, and density estimation (with naïve Bayes classifiers and KDEs respectively) is used solely for the purpose of obtaining a smoother and more accurate classification and class-conditional probabilities in contrast to the piecewise constant non-smooth estimates of the standard classification trees. Decision trees been used for the task of diagnosing extrapolation [22] by building a classification tree differentiating the given data set from a random sample from a uniform distribution in the support of the data set. This tree provides a way to compute a measure for extrapolation. This measure can be indirectly used to compute the density, but the tree still performs classification. Decision trees have also been used in the supervised setting for estimating the joint probability (of the data and the label of the training examples) [23] for censored data by replacing the standard loss function (for example 0-1 loss or Gini-index) with the negative loglikelihood of the joint density.

The idea of having a nested hierarchy of partitions of the support of the data has been used for dicretization of univariate data [24]. The set of observations are partitioned on the basis of the density using the loglikelihood loss function. But the focus is solely on univariate data. Decision trees have also been used in an unsupervised setting to perform hierarchical clustering [25] but do not trivially translate to density estimation. Siedl et al., 2009 [26] propose a novel method for indexing the density model in the form of a tree (called Bayes tree) for fast access with desired level of accuracy. This tree is grown bottom-up from the estimate of a KDE for the whole data set. The Bayes tree uses MoGs to index the density at the intermediate levels (increasing the number of Gaussians with the depth). This tree successfully locates clusters in the data. However, being a MoG, it fails to determine relative relevance of the dimensions. Pólya trees [27] are hierarchical spatial partitioning trees but used as a prior for probability measures over the data space. Density estimation is done either by computing the posterior mean density given this prior or "learning" a fixed tree topology and computing the piecewise constant estimate conditional on this topology.

DETs are related in spirit, however, they will be learned by directly minimizing the density estimation loss and the estimates are finally obtained directly from the tree. Moreover, the aforementioned methods, though hierarchical in nature, do not share the interpretability and feature selection properties of decision trees, which are based on univariate splits.

3. DENSITY ESTIMATION TREE

This section provides the road map to perform density estimation using decision trees. We define an estimator and the corresponding loss function to be minimized during the training of the decision tree for continuous and mixed data. Following that, we explain the process of learning the optimal decision tree over the given sample and provide an asymptotic property of the DET.

3.1 Continuous Features

Definition 1. *The piecewise constant density estimate of the decision tree T built on a set $\mathcal{S}$ of N observations in $\mathbb{R}^d$ is defined as*

$$\hat{f}_N(x) = \sum_{l \in \tilde{T}} \frac{|l|}{NV_l} \mathbb{I}(x \in l) \tag{1}$$

where $\tilde{T}$ is the set of leaves of the decision tree T representing the partitions of the data space, $|l|$ is the number of observations of $\mathcal{S}$ in the leaf l, V_l is the volume of the leaf l within the d dimensional bounding box of $\mathcal{S}$ and $\mathbb{I}(\cdot)$ is the indicator function.

A decision tree T requires a notion of a loss function $R(T)$ which is minimized using a greedy algorithm to construct a tree on the set of observations. For the unsupervised task of density estimation, we consider the Integrated Squared Error (ISE) loss function [10]. The ISE gives a notion of overall distance between the estimated and the true density and is a favored choice in nonparametric density estimation for its inherent robustness in comparison to maximum-likelihood-based loss functions [8]. However, other distance functions such as the KL-divergence can be used as the loss function. We will explore this in the longer version of the paper.

The task of learning a DET would involve solving the following optimization problem:

$$\min_{\hat{f}_N \in \mathcal{F}_N} \int_{\mathcal{X}} \left(\hat{f}_N(x) - f(x)\right)^2 dx \tag{2}$$

where $\mathcal{F}_N$ is the class of estimators of form in Definition 1 that can learned with any set of N observations. After expanding the square and the following Monte-Carlo substitution $\int_{\mathcal{X}} \hat{f}_N(x) f(x) dx \approx \frac{1}{N}\sum_{i=1}^N \hat{f}_N(X_i)$ (where $\{X_i\}_{i=1}^N$ is the training set), the objective function in Eq. 2 is replaced by the following consistent plug-in estimator of the ISE [10][6]:

$$\min_{\hat{f}_N \in \mathcal{F}_N} \left\{ \int_{\mathcal{X}} \left(\hat{f}_N(x)\right)^2 dx - \frac{2}{N}\sum_{i=1}^N \hat{f}_N(X_i) \right\} \tag{3}$$

Using the piecewise constant estimator from Definition 1 (which is constant within each leaf l), the objective function in Eq. 3 is replaced with the following:

$$\sum_{l \in \tilde{T}} \left\{ \int_l \left(\frac{|l|}{NV_l}\right)^2 dx - \frac{2}{N}\frac{|l|}{NV_l} \cdot |l| \right\} \tag{4}$$

by substituting

$$\hat{f}_N^2(x) = \sum_{l \in \tilde{T}} \left(\frac{|l|}{NV_l}\right)^2 \mathbb{I}(x \in l)$$

(since the cross terms in the expansion of $\hat{f}_N^2(x)$ vanish because of the indicator function) and simple calculation shows that

$$\sum_{i=1}^N \hat{f}_N(X_i) = \sum_{i=1}^N \sum_{l \in \tilde{T}} \frac{|l|}{NV_l} \cdot \mathbb{I}(X_i \in l) = \sum_{l \in \tilde{T}} \frac{|l|}{NV_l} \cdot |l|$$

By making the following substitution

$$\int_l \left(\frac{|l|}{NV_l}\right)^2 dx = \left(\frac{|l|}{NV_l}\right)^2 \int_l dx = \left(\frac{|l|}{NV_l}\right)^2 \cdot V_l,$$

the estimator of the ISE for DET has the following form:

$$\sum_{l \in \tilde{T}} \left\{ -\frac{|l|^2}{N^2 V_l} \right\} \tag{5}$$

Defining Eq. 5 as the error $R(T)$ of the tree, the greedy surrogate of the error for any node t (internal or otherwise) can be defined as

$$R(t) = -\frac{|t|^2}{N^2 V_t}. \tag{6}$$

The tree is grown in a top down manner by maximizing the reduction in this greedy surrogate of the error over the given observations.

3.2 Mixed Features

For density estimation over data with mixed features, we define a novel density estimator and a loss function involving ordinal and categorical data along with continuous data that can be used to learn DETs with mixed data:

[6]The term $\int_{\mathcal{X}} (f(x))^2 dx$ is removed from the objective function since it is independent of the estimate and hence doesn't affect the optimum.

Definition 2. *Let $\mathcal{S} \subset \mathbb{R}^d \times \mathbb{Z}^{d'} \times \mathbb{C}^{d''}$ with d real features, d' ordinal features and d'' categorical features. The piecewise constant density estimator of the decision tree T built on $\mathcal{S}$ is defined as*

$$\hat{f}_N(x) = \sum_{l \in \tilde{T}} \frac{|l| \cdot \mathbb{I}(x \in l)}{N \cdot V_{l_d} \cdot \prod_{j=1}^{d'_l} R_{l_j} \cdot \prod_{i=1}^{d''_l} M_{l_i}} \tag{7}$$

where V_{l_d} is the volume of the leaf l within the d dimensional bounding box of the real part of $\mathcal{S}$, R_{l_j} is the range of the ordinal values in the jth of the d'_l ordinal dimensions present in l and M_{l_i} is the number of categories present in l for the ith of the d''_l categorical dimensions present in l.

The error at a node t corresponding to the ISE is then obtained as

$$R(t) = -\frac{|t|^2}{N^2 \cdot V_{t_d} \cdot \prod_{j=1}^{d'_t} R_{t_j} \cdot \prod_{i=1}^{d''_t} M_{t_i}} \tag{8}$$

where V_{t_d} is the volume of the node t in the d real dimensions, R_{t_j} is the range of the ordinal values in the jth of the d'_t ordinal dimensions present in t and M_{t_i} is the number of categories present in t for the ith of the d''_t categorical dimensions present in t.

3.3 Tree Construction

We use the tree learning algorithm presented in Breiman, et al.,1984 [1]. The splitting, pruning and the cross-validation procedures are modified to work with this new loss function and for the unsupervised task of density estimation.

Splitting. For growing the tree, each node is split into two children. Let S be the set of all univariate splits.

Definition 3. *[1] The best split s^* of a node t is the split in the set of splits S which maximally reduces $R(T)$.*

This is done by greedily reducing $R(t)$ for all the terminal nodes t of the current tree. Hence, for any currently terminal node, we need to find a split s^* for a node t into t_L and t_R such that

$$s^* = \arg\max_{s \in S}\{R(t) - R(t_L) - R(t_R)\} \tag{9}$$

where $|t| = |t_L| + |t_R|$. For continuous and ordinal dimensions, this optimization is performed by trying every $|t| - 1$ possible splits of the data in each of the dimensions. For categorical dimensions, the splits are performed in the manner similar to the CART model [1]. The splitting is stopped when the node size $|t|$ goes below a certain threshold (say $N_{\min}$).

Pruning. To avoid overfitting, we use the minimal cost-complexity pruning [1]. The regularized error of a subtree rooted at a node t is defined as

$$R_\alpha(t) = R(\tilde{t}) + \alpha \cdot |\tilde{t}| \tag{10}$$

where α is a regularization parameter (to be estimated through cross-validation) and $\tilde{t}$ is the set of leaves in the subtree rooted at t. The value of α is gradually increased and a subtree rooted at t is pruned for the value of α where $R_\alpha(t) = R_\alpha(\{t\})$, the regularized error of the pruned subtree. Since the size of the initial tree constructed by the splitting algorithm described previously is finite, the number of possible values of α at which a prune occurs is finite and can be calculated efficiently. Hence we only need to select the optimal α from a finite set of values (See Section 3.3 in Breiman, et al., 1984 [1] for complete details).

Cross-validation. The leave-one-out cross-validation (LOO-CV) estimator of the density estimation loss function in Eq. 3 is given by

$$\hat{J}(\alpha) = \int_X \left(\hat{f}_N^\alpha(x)\right)^2 dx - \frac{2}{N}\sum_{i=1}^{N} \hat{f}_{(-i)}^\alpha(X_i) \qquad (11)$$

where $\hat{f}_N^\alpha$ is the estimator with the decision tree T pruned with a regularization parameter α, and $\hat{f}_{(-i)}^\alpha$ is the estimator with the decision tree $T_{(-i)}$ built without the training example X_i pruned with the regularization parameter α. This LOO-CV estimator is obtained from Silverman, 1986 [10] by switching the regularization parameter (replacing the bandwidth with α). The best sized tree is the tree T pruned with the parameter α^* such that:

$$\alpha^* = \arg\min_\alpha \hat{J}(\alpha) \qquad (12)$$

3.4 Asymptotic Properties

We show that the method is *nonparametric* – it is consistent under mild assumptions on the model class of the input distribution f. Consistency is typically shown [28] for a nonparametric estimator $\hat{f}_N$ obtained from a set of N observations by showing that

$$\Pr\left(\lim_{N\to\infty} \int_X \left(\hat{f}_N(x) - f(x)\right)^2 dx = 0\right) = 1. \qquad (13)$$

We prove the consistency of DETs on data with continuous features. The proof of consistency of the density estimator proposed in Definition 1 follows arguments similar to those used to show the consistency of regression trees [1] .

THEOREM 1. *The estimator $\hat{f}_N$ defined in Definition 1 satisfies Eq. 13.*

PROOF. Given a fixed positive integer d_1, let $\mathcal{B}$ denote the collection of all sets $t \subset X$ that can be described as the solution set to a system of d_1 inequalities, each of the form $b^T x \leq c$ for $b \in \mathbb{R}^d$ and $c \in \mathbb{R}$. Now in a decision tree T, every leaf $l \in \tilde{T}$ is the solution set of a system of d_1 inequalities of the form $b^T x \leq c$ with $b \in \mathbb{R}^d$ with just one entry equal to 1 and the rest of the entries equal to 0. Therefore, $\tilde{T} \subset \mathcal{B}$.

Let X_n, $n \geq 1$, be a random sample from a density function f on X. For $N \geq 1$, let $\hat{F}_N$ denote the empirical distribution of $X_n, 1 \leq n \leq N$, defined on a set $t \subset X$ by

$$\hat{F}_N(t) = \frac{1}{N}\sum_{n=1}^{N} \mathbb{I}(X_n \in t) = \frac{|t|}{N} = \int_t \hat{f}_N(x)dx \qquad (14)$$

where $|t|$ is the number of random samples in the set $t \cap \{X_n\}_{n=1}^N$ and $\hat{f}_N(x)$ is the estimator given in Definition 1.

According to a general version of the Glivenko-Cantelli theorem [29],

$$\Pr\left(\lim_{N\to\infty} \sup_{t\in\mathcal{B}} |\hat{F}_N(t) - \int_t f(x)dx| = 0\right) = 1. \qquad (15)$$

By Eq.14 and 15, we get

$$\Pr\left(\lim_{N\to\infty} \sup_{t\in\mathcal{B}} |\int_t \hat{f}_N(x)dx - \int_t f(x)dx| = 0\right) = 1$$

$$\Rightarrow \Pr\left(\lim_{N\to\infty} \sup_{t\in\mathcal{B}} \int_t |\hat{f}_N(x) - f(x)|dx \geq 0\right) = 1.$$

Assuming that $\lim_{N\to\infty} \Pr(\text{diameter}(t) \geq \epsilon) = 0$, hence $\Pr\left(\lim_{N\to\infty} \int_t dx = 0\right) = 1$, we get the following with probability 1

$$\begin{aligned} \lim_{N\to\infty} \sup_{t\in\mathcal{B}} \int_t |\hat{f}_N(x) - f(x)|dx &\leq \\ \lim_{N\to\infty} |\hat{f}_N(x') - f(x')| \cdot \int_t dx \text{ for some } x' \in t &= 0 \end{aligned}$$

This assumption is commonly used for the consistency of data-partitioning estimators [30] and is justified since as $N \to \infty$, the diameter of any leaf node would become smaller and smaller since the leaf node can only have a bounded number of points. Hence

$$\Pr\left(\lim_{N\to\infty} \sup_{t\in\mathcal{B}} \int_t |\hat{f}_N(x) - f(x)|dx = 0\right) = 1$$

$$\Rightarrow \Pr\left(\lim_{N\to\infty} \int_X \left(\hat{f}_N(x) - f(x)\right)^2 dx = 0\right) = 1.$$

Hence $\hat{f}_N$ satisfies Eq. 13. □

4. EXPERIMENTS

In this section, we demonstrate the performance of DETs under different conditions using synthetic and real data sets. Estimation accuracies of DETs are compared with existing nonparametric estimators. We exhibit the interpretability of DETs with two real data sets. Furthermore, density estimates of DETs are applied to classification and subsequent labelling accuracies are presented. Finally, the speed of training and querying DETs are presented on several real data sets and compared with an existing method. We only consider continuous and ordinal data in this paper for the lack of space. Experiments with categorical and mixed data will be presented in the longer version of the paper.

4.1 Estimation Accuracy: Synthetic Examples

For the unsupervised task of density estimation, estimation accuracy can only be computed on synthetic data sets. We choose the best-sized tree through LOO-CV. To compute estimation error on synthetic data for density queries, we use 2 measures: *Root Mean Squared Error* (RMSE) and *Hellinger Distance* (HD). We compare DETs only with other nonparametric density estimators since parametric estimators would involve choosing the model class (like choosing the number of Gaussians in MoGs). We report the comparison between DETs, histograms (bin-width selected by LOO-CV) and KDEs (using the Gaussian kernel) with the bandwidth selected by unbiased LOO-CV using the ISE criterion (FBW) and by local rodeo (local r-KDE) (VBW) on synthetic data sets.

Example 1. (Strongly skewed distribution in one dimension) This distribution is defined as

$$X \sim \sum_{i=0}^{7} \frac{1}{8}\mathcal{N}\left(3\left(\left(\frac{2}{3}\right)^i - 1\right), \left(\frac{2}{3}\right)^{2i}\right).$$

Figure 2 shows the estimated density functions by a DET, a histogram and two KDEs for a sample size $N = 1000$. Because of the high skewness of the density function, the KDE (FBW) and the histogram fail to fit the very smooth

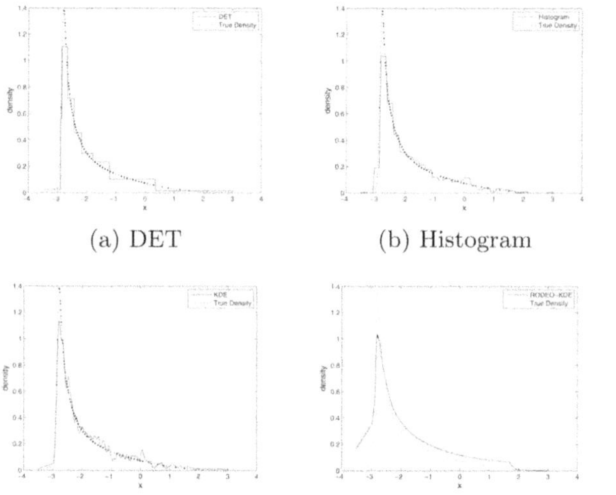

(a) DET (b) Histogram

(c) KDE (FBW) (d) local r-KDE

Figure 2: The density estimates obtained with 1000 points for Example 1 using DET, Histogram and KDEs compared to the true density.

Table 2: Estimation errors for Histograms, KDEs and DETs with increasing number of observations

Type	N	Hist	KDE(FBW)	local r-KDE	DET
RMSE	10^2	0.2213	0.1748	0.1318	0.2548
	10^3	0.1158	0.0949	0.1339	0.1090
	10^4	0.0565	0.0235	0.0596	0.0527
HD	10^2	0.1292	0.2365	0.0967	0.1187
	10^3	0.0832	0.0684	0.2343	0.0278
	10^4	0.01	0.0130	0.1634	0.0072

tail. The fixed bandwidth/binwidth results in a highly wiggly estimate of the very smooth tail. The DET provides a piecewise constant estimate, but it adjusts to the different parts of the density function by varying the leaf size – the tree has small leaves closer to the spike where the density function changes rapidly, having larger leaves where the density function does not change rapidly. This demonstrates the adaptability of DETs within the same dimension. The local r-KDE exhibits the same adaptability by obtaining different bandwidths at different regions, hence capturing the smooth tail of the true density.

Table 2 provides the estimation errors with increasing sample sizes for the different methods. The RMSE values are fairly close and the HD values for the DETs are in fact better than that of KDE using unbiased LOO-CV. This can be attributed to the adaptive nature of DET with respect to the leaf sizes. The error values of local r-KDE are better than DET when the data set size is small (in case of larger data sets, the local method might be overfitting over this instance of the data set). The accuracies of the histogram estimators and DETs are comparable in this univariate example. But we will demonstrate in the next example that the performance of histograms decline with increasing dimensions.

Example 2. (Two dimensional data – Mixture of Beta distributions in one dimension, uniform in the other dimension) We create a (600×2) data set by sampling one dimension as a mixture of Beta distributions and the other dimension as a uniform distribution

$$X_1 \sim \frac{2}{3}\mathcal{B}(1,2) + \frac{1}{3}\mathcal{B}(10,10); X_2 \sim \mathcal{U}(0,1).$$

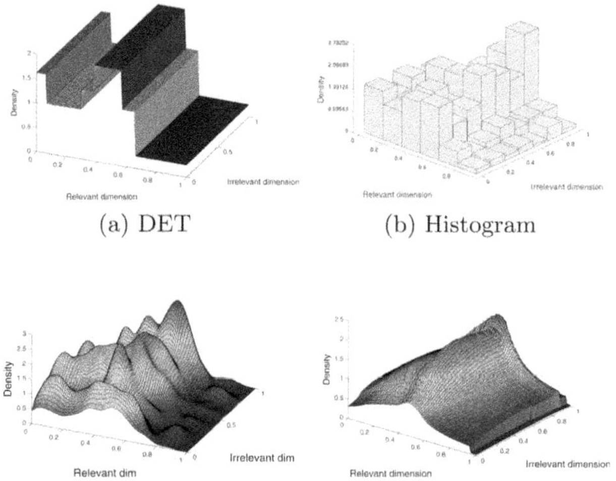

(a) DET (b) Histogram

(c) KDE (FBW) (d) local r-KDE

Figure 3: Perspective plots of the density estimates for a DET, a Histogram and two KDEs on the data set in Example 2.

Figure 3 shows the 2-dimensional density estimates of a DET, a histogram and two KDEs. The DET fits the irrelevant uniform dimension perfectly, while closely approximating the mixture of Beta distributions in the relevant dimension. The KDE with fixed bandwidth and the histogram estimator completely fail to fit the irrelevant dimension. The local r-KDE does a better job of fitting the irrelevant dimension compared to the KDE (FBW), but still does not entirely capture the uniform density.

4.2 Interpretability: Variable Importance

The decision-tree framework defines a *measure of relevance* for each of the predictor variables [1] as following:

DEFINITION 4. *The measure of relevance $\mathcal{I}_d(T)$ for each attribute X_d (the dth attribute) in a decision tree T is defined as*

$$\mathcal{I}_d(T) = \sum_{t=1}^{|\tilde{T}|-1} \hat{\iota}_t^2 \mathbb{I}(d(t) = d) \qquad (16)$$

where the summation is over the $|\tilde{T}| - 1$ internal nodes of the tree T, and the attribute $d(t)$ used to partition node t obtains $\hat{\iota}_t^2$ improvement in squared error over the constant fit in node t.

We use this measure to present the interpretability of the DETs on two real data sets.

Example 3. (Iris data set) We perform density estimation on this 4 dimensional data set and compute variable importance for each of the dimensions. Figure 1 displays the tree and the relative variable importance. The interpretation has been explained in Section 1.1.

Example 4. (MNIST digits – image data) Each image has 28-by-28 pixels providing a 784-dimensional data set. We perform density estimation on the 5851 images of the digit 8 (left panel of Figure 4). This is also an instance of performing density estimation with *ordinal data* since the pixel values are discrete. We compute the variable importance of each of the dimensions (pixels in this case). The right panel of Figure 4 displays the results obtained. The black pixels indicate pixels with zero variable importance in density

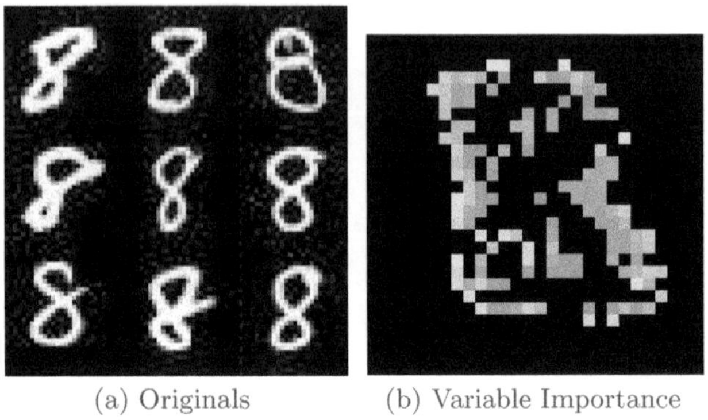

Figure 4: Relative importance of the predictor variables (pixels in this case) in density estimation for images of digit 8.

Table 3: Classification Accuracy: r-KDE vs. DET

Case	# Train	# Test	r-KDE	DET
1v7	240	121	0.93	0.91
2v7	237	119	0.97	0.87
3v8	238	119	0.81	0.81
5v8	237	119	0.86	0.72
8v9	236	118	0.75	0.77
All	1347	450	0.70	0.73

estimation. For the pixels with non-zero variable importance, the color transitions for green (indicating low relative variable importance) to red (indicating high relative variable importance). The marginal densities of many pixels are close to point masses. Hence the density does not vary at all in those dimensions, and the relative variable importance depicted in Figure 4 indicates that the DET is capable of capturing this property of the data.

4.3 Classification

As mentioned earlier, density estimation is a common subroutine in classification where the class-conditional density $\hat{p}(x|C)$ is to be estimated for the query point x using the training set X. The estimated class $\hat{C}(x) = \arg\max_C P(x|C) \cdot P(C)$. We compare the accuracy of classification between the density estimates computed by DETs and local r-KDEs.

Example 5. (Opt-digits – image data (1797×64) [31]) We conduct binary as well as multi-class classification. For binary classification, we consider the following cases: 1 vs. 7, 2 vs. 7, 3 vs. 8, 5 vs. 8, 8 vs. 9. We perform multi-class classification using all the classes (0-9). Table 3 lists the classification accuracies for the different tasks. In most cases, the accuracies are close for the two methods of density estimation, with the r-KDEs being more accurate than the DETs. But in the last two cases, the DETs outperform the r-KDEs. Moreover, the whole experiment (training and testing) with the DETs is much faster than the one using the local r-KDEs. For example, in the last experiment performing multi-class classification required ~ 8 seconds using DETs and ~ 500 seconds using r-KDEs[7].

4.4 Speed

We compare DETs to KDE*s(FBW) using the fast approximate dual-tree algorithm [32] with *kd*-trees. We use LOO-CV to estimate the optimal bandwidth for the KDE*s

[7]The DET is implemented in C++ and the rodeo-KDE is implemented using MATLAB on the same machine.

Table 4: Timings (in seconds) for training(T) and all queries(Q) with KDE*s and DETs

Data set	T(KDE*)	T(DET)	Q(KDE*)	Q(DET)
SJ2	93.77	485.77	11.79	0.0026
Colors	101.68	427.02	12.11	0.0022
Bio	421.22	1213.84	5.7	0.0069
Pall7	1240.75	1719.26	10.67	0.0046
PSF	18039.27	32456.43	77.48	0.975

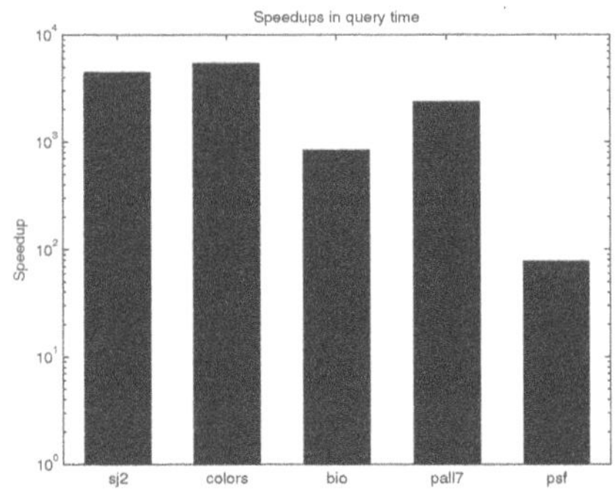

Figure 5: Query Time speedup for the DTE over the KDE. Note that the KDE is faster than the DTE in case of training.

(FBW). Real world data sets drawn from the SDSS repository [33] (SJ2 (50000×2), PSF (3000000×2)) and the UCI Machine Learning Repository [31] (Colors (50000×2), dimension reduced version of the Bio dataset (100000×5), Pall7 (100000×7)) are used. The query set is same as the training set in all the experiments and the KDE*s provide the leave-one-out estimates.

For the KDE*, we use around $H \approx 10$ bandwidths and chose the one with the best CV error. Usually, a much larger number of bandwidths are tried and the training times scale linearly with H. For the DETs, we use 10-fold cross-validation since we were not able to find an efficient way to conduct LOO-CV with decision trees and it would require prohibitively long time for these large data sets. This is one major limitation of this method. However, for sufficiently large data sets, our experiments indicate that DETs trained with LOO-CV are only slightly more accurate than those with 10-fold CV.

The absolute timing values (in seconds) for training(T) and querying(Q) are given in Table 4. The speedups of the DETs over the KDE*s in test/query time are shown in Figure 5. As can be seen from the results, the training time for the decision tree algorithm is significantly larger than the LOO-CV for the KDE*s, but the DETs provide up to 3.5 orders of magnitude speedup in query time. The KDE*s are fast to train, but their work comes at test time. This experiment demonstrates the efficient querying of decision trees while also indicating that the task of training decision trees using LOO-CV is quite challenging.

5. DISCUSSION AND CONCLUSIONS

This framework of decision-tree-structured density estimation provides a new way to estimate the density of a given set of observations in the form of a simple set of rules which are inherently intuitive and interpretable. This framework has the capability of easily dealing with categorical, discrete as well as continuous variables and performs automatic feature selection. On having these rules, the density of a new test point can be computed cheaply. All these features stem from the fact that the density estimation is performed in the form of a decision tree. Along with that, the DETs are easily implementable like supervised decision trees. Although these advantages come with the loss of accuracy, the DETs are shown to be consistent, and hence are quite reliable in the presence of enough data.

Future directions of improvement include the reduction of the discontinuities in the density estimate because of the piecewise constant estimator and the boundary bias since the DETs put no mass outside the span of the data. Boundary bias is a common problem for almost all density estimators. One possible remedy is to use a normalized KDE at each of the leaves instead of using the piecewise constant estimator (similar to the approach in Smyth et.al. [21].

An analysis of the convergence rate of the DETs would quantify the amount of loss of accuracy to account for the simplicity of the estimator. Being effectively a variable bin-width histogram, we conjecture that the convergence rate for the DETs would be $o(N^{-2/3})$ for univariate data and better than histograms in higher dimensions since we demonstrate that the DETs can effectively model uninformative dimensions easily without requiring that extra number of points as imposed by the curse of dimensionality. Moreover, we are actively working on obtaining density dependent bounds on the depth of the DETs to quantify the runtimes for training and test query.

Overall, this method for density estimation has immediate application to various fields of data analysis (for example, outlier and anomaly detection)[8] and machine learning due to its simple and interpretable solution to the fundamental task of density estimation.

6. REFERENCES

[1] L. Breiman, J. H. Friedman, R. A. Olshen, and C. J. Stone. *Classification and Regression Trees.* Wadsworth, 1984.

[2] C. Bishop. *Neural Networks for Pattern Recognition.* Oxford University Press, 1995.

[3] C. M. Bishop. *Pattern recognition and machine learning.* Springer, 2006.

[4] R. O. Duda and P. E. Hart. *Pattern Classification and Scene Analysis.* Wiley New York, 1973.

[5] J. H. Friedman. A Recursive Partitioning Decision Rule for Nonparametric Classification. *Transactions on Computers*, 1977.

[6] J. H. Friedman. A tree-structured approach to nonparametric multiple regression. *Smoothing Techniques for Curve Estimation*, 1979.

[7] T. Hastie, R. Tibshirani, and J. Friedman. *The Elements of Statistical Learning: Data Mining, Inference, and Prediction.* Springer, 2001.

[8] L. Wasserman. *All of Nonparametric Statistics.* Physica-Verlag, 2006.

[9] C. Cortes and V. N. Vapnik. Support vector networks. *Machine Learning*, 1995.

[10] B. W. Silverman. *Density Estimation for Statistics and Data Analysis.* Chapman & Hall/CRC, 1986.

[11] H. Liu, J. Lafferty, and L. Wasserman. Sparse Nonparametric Density Estimation in High Dimensions Using the Rodeo. In *AISTATS*, 2007.

[12] P. Müller and F.A. Quintana. Nonparametric Bayesian data analysis. *Statistical Science*, 2004.

[13] A. G. Gray and A. W. Moore. Nonparametric density estimation: Toward computational tractability. In *SIAM Data Mining*, 2003.

[14] D. Lee and A. G. Gray. Fast high-dimensional kernel summations using the monte carlo multipole method. In *Advances in NIPS*, 2008.

[15] A. Beygelzimer, S. Kakade, and J.C. Langford. Cover Trees for Nearest Neighbor. *ICML*, 2006.

[16] P. Ram, D. Lee, W. March, and A. Gray. Linear-time algorithms for pairwise statistical problems. In *Advances in NIPS*. 2009.

[17] J. Lafferty and L. Wasserman. Rodeo: Sparse Nonparametric Regression in High Dimensions. *Arxiv preprint math.ST/0506342*, 2005.

[18] R. Riegel, A. G. Gray, and G. Richards. Massive-Scale Kernel Discriminant Analysis: Mining for Quasars. In *SIAM Data Mining (SDM)*, 2008.

[19] W. Guan, M. Zhou, C. Y. Hampton, B. B. Benigno, L. D. Walker, A. G. Gray, J. F. McDonald, and F. M. Fernandez. Ovarian Cancer Detection from Metabolomic Liquid Chromatography/Mass Spectrometry Data by Support Vector Machines. *BMC Bioinformatics Journal*, 2009.

[20] R. Kohavi. Scaling up the accuracy of naive-Bayes classifiers: A decision-tree hybrid. In *KDD*, 1996.

[21] P. Smyth, A. G. Gray, and U. M. Fayyad. Retrofitting decision tree classifiers using kernel density estimation. In *ICML*, 1995.

[22] G. Hooker. Diagnosing extrapolation: Tree-based density estimation. In *SIGKDD*, 2004.

[23] A.M. Molinaro, S. Dudoit, and M.J. Van der Laan. Tree-based multivariate regression and density estimation with right-censored data. *Journal of Multivariate Analysis*, 2004.

[24] G. Schmidberger and E. Frank. Unsupervised discretization using tree-based density estimation. *Lecture Notes in Computer Science*, 2005.

[25] J. Basak and R. Krishnapuram. Interpretable hierarchical clustering by constructing an unsupervised decision tree. *IEEE transactions on knowledge and data engineering*, 2005.

[26] T. Seidl, I. Assent, P. Kranen, R. Krieger, and J. Herrmann. Indexing density models for incremental learning and anytime classification on data streams. In *ICEDT: Advances in Database Technology*, 2009.

[27] W.H. Wong and L. Ma. Optional Pólya tree and Bayesian inference. *The Annals of Statistics*, 2010.

[28] E. Parzen. On the estimation of a probability density function and mode. *Annals of Mathematical Statistics*, pages 1065–1076, 1962.

[29] V. N. Vapnik and A. Y. Chervonenkis. On the uniform convergence of relative frequencies of events to their probabilities. *Theory of Probability and its Applications*, 1971.

[30] L. Devroye, L. Györfi, and G. Lugosi. *A probabilistic theory of pattern recognition.* Springer Verlag, 1996.

[31] C.L. Blake and C.J. Merz. UCI repository of machine learning databases. 1998.

[32] A. G. Gray and A. W. Moore. 'n-body' problems in statistical learning. In *Advances in NIPS*, 2000.

[33] R. Lupton, J.E. Gunn, Z. Ivezic, G.R. Knapp, S. Kent, and N. Yasuda. The SDSS Imaging Pipelines. *Arxiv preprint astro-ph/0101420*, 2001.

[8]We will demonstrate these applications in the longer version of the paper.

Unsupervised Clustering of Multidimensional Distributions using Earth Mover Distance

David Applegate
david@research.att.com

Tamraparni Dasu
tamr@research.att.com

Shankar Krishnan
krishnas@research.att.com

Simon Urbanek
urbanek@research.att.com

AT&T Labs - Research
180 Park Ave
Florham Park, NJ 07932

ABSTRACT

Multidimensional distributions are often used in data mining to describe and summarize different features of large datasets. It is natural to look for distinct classes in such datasets by clustering the data. A common approach entails the use of methods like k-means clustering. However, the k-means method inherently relies on the Euclidean metric in the embedded space and does not account for additional topology underlying the distribution.

In this paper, we propose using Earth Mover Distance (EMD) to compare multidimensional distributions. For a n-bin histogram, the EMD is based on a solution to the transportation problem with time complexity $O(n^3 \log n)$. To mitigate the high computational cost of EMD, we propose an approximation that reduces the cost to linear time. Given the large size of our dataset a fast approximation is crucial for this application.

Other notions of distances such as the information theoretic Kullback-Leibler divergence and statistical χ^2 distance, account only for the correspondence between bins with the same index, and do not use information across bins, and are sensitive to bin size. A cross-bin distance measure like EMD is not affected by binning differences and meaningfully matches the perceptual notion of "nearness".

Our technique is simple, efficient and practical for clustering distributions. We demonstrate the use of EMD on a real-world application of analyzing 411,550 anonymous mobility usage patterns which are defined as distributions over a manifold. EMD allows us to represent inherent relationships in this space, and enables us to successfully cluster even sparse signatures.

Categories and Subject Descriptors

I.5.3 [**Pattern Recognition**]: Clustering

General Terms

Algorithms, Similarity measures

Keywords

Earth mover distance (EMD), clustering, signatures, distributions

1. INTRODUCTION

Massive data sets are often summarized using *signatures* that capture important characteristics of the data. Signatures are compact representations that can be used for further mining tasks such as clustering and anomaly detection. For example, Cortes *et al* [3] discuss the use of signatures for mining massive telecommunications data to find communities of interest, and for detecting fraud. In [19], Wong *et al* demonstrate the use of data signatures for visualizing complex scientific data sets.

In many instances, signatures are multidimensional distributions that represent the distribution of probability mass over a manifold. An important data mining task involves measuring distances between such distributions, which are then used for subsequent tasks such as clustering, change detection or alerting. For instance, clustering usage signatures of telecommunications customers identifies canonical patterns of usage that can be used to provide better service and for network load balancing tasks.

While clustering algorithms like k-means are frequently used to cluster distributions, they can lead to misleading results. Consider the following example of a population of cell phone users with different types of usage behavior. Figure 1 shows examples of different usage signatures. We defer a detailed explanation to Section 5.1, but for now let us treat them as heat maps that show the density of usage for voice calls and text messages aggregated over two months across "hour of the day" (rows in the heat map) by "day of the week" (columns). The signature in Figure 1 (left) is representative of users with a moderately high volume of calls and texts, distributed across the bins corresponding to working days. The signature in Figure 1 (right), on the other hand, is representative of users with lower usage. Such users generate very few calls or text messages, their signatures are quite sparse, typically consisting of isolated spikes. Any method that relies on a distance that treats bins separately is bound to fail on such data. To demonstrate, we applied a k-means clustering algorithm to a sample of 5,000 signatures from the bottom quartile of the usage distribution. The centers of the resulting 8 clusters are shown in Figure 2. Regardless of the choice of the number of clusters, k, the clustering scheme always resulted in one large cluster and many small clusters consisting entirely of individual bins from the

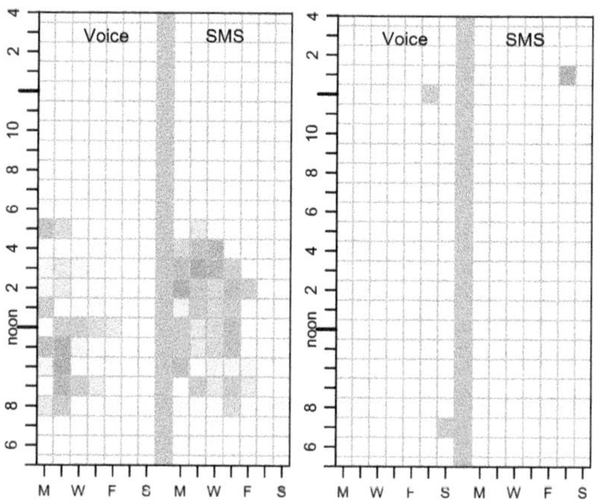

Figure 1: Two examples of a mobile usage distributions created by binning usage by hour of day, day of the week and type of activity. Color scale of the counts in bins ranges from light yellow (zero) to red (high density). Columns of each matrix correspond to days of week, rows correspond to hours of day. Left: Moderately high usage, mostly during work hours on working days. Right: Sparse usage. For privacy reasons the examples do not match any actual, individual user's signature in the data.

distribution. The location of those small clusters is determined by the initial seeds of cluster centers, quite unrelated to any underlying structure in the data and therefore conveys no meaningful information. This is an example of a real world application where k-means would result in arbitrary clusters. For comparison purposes, Figure 3 shows the clustering obtained with EMD as the underlying similarity measure. Even with very sparse signatures, EMD is capable of separating them into coherent groups such as weekday (Clusters 1-5) weekend (Clusters 6-8), or time of the day (Clusters 2,3).

The reason for such odd clusters is that the k-means method inherently relies on the Euclidean metric in the embedded space and does not take into account any additional topology of the bins. This is not surprising, because in such a high-dimensional space, all sparse signatures are roughly equidistant from each other. Distributions lie on the probability simplex, and the right distance metric must be applied to the clustering framework to find meaningful clusters. More specifically, in order to cluster distributions, we need a notion of similarity or distance between distributions.

1.1 Distance Between Distributions

There are numerous *statistical distances* that measure the distance between distributions. Many of them are not true metrics because they violate one or more of the three requirements of a metric, that of non-negativity, symmetry and triangular inequality. We briefly describe some well know distances below.

A prominent class of distances known as f-divergences, is based on the expected value of a convex function of the ratio of the two distributions. If P and Q are two probability distributions over $\mathbb{R}^d$ such that P and Q are continuous with respect to each other, and f is a convex function such that

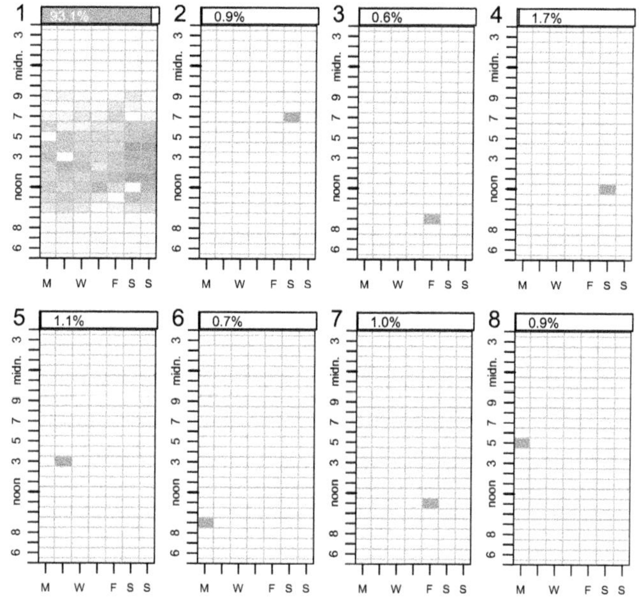

Figure 2: Cluster centers of low voice usage signatures using k-means clustering for $k = 8$. The bold number on top represents cluster number (id), top bar represents relative cluster size. Regardless of the value of k, the number of clusters, the method is unable to separate any clusters other than individual bins of the histogram. The location of the bins is random, based entirely on the initial cluster seeds.

$f(1) = 0$, then the f-divergence is given by:

$$D_f(P,Q) = E_Q\left(f\left(\frac{P}{Q}\right)\right) \tag{1}$$

where the subscript Q refers to the expectation E taken over the distribution Q. This class of distributions is known by the names Csiszar's f-divergence [4], Csiszar-Morimoto divergences or Ali-Silvey family of distances [1]. Depending on the form of f, distances in this family include the Kullback Leibler distance, Hellinger distance, total variational divergence, χ^2 divergence and alpha-divergence. Gibbs *et al.* [5] provide an overview of choosing appropriate probability metrics, including whether the metric has an interpretation with respect to the problem at hand. This is critical, since the results of clustering are heavily dependent on the choice of the metric. Liese *et al.* [11] describe a novel approach characterizing distances and their relationships, and the derivation of new properties with respect to desirable statistical properties like sufficiency.

Other popular distributional distances include Jensen Shannon divergence which is a symmetricized version of KL-divergence, Bhattacharya distance used to measure separability of classes, and Wasserstein's metric.

In this paper, we focus on Wasserstein's metric, popularized in computer vision and image retrieval community by the name Earth Mover Distance or EMD. The major drawback of the Kullback-Leibler divergence and statistical χ^2 distance is that they account only for the correspondence between bins with the same index, and do not use infor-

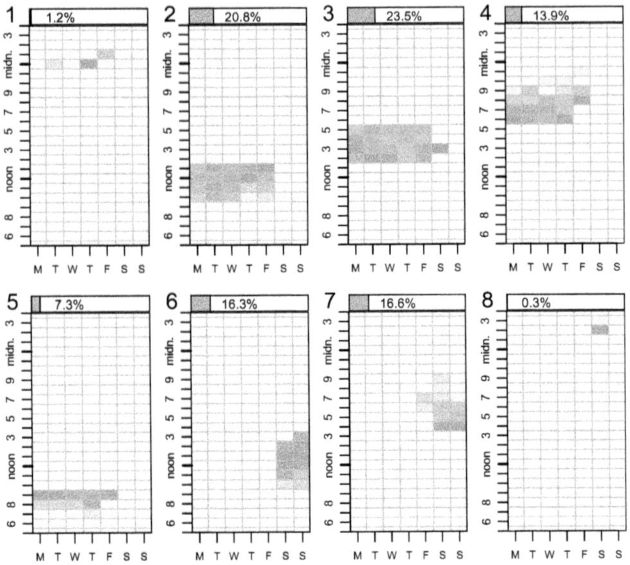

Figure 3: Cluster centers of the same low voice usage signature data as Figure 2, but using hierarchical clustering with EMD. Even with very sparse signatures, EMD is capable of separating them into coherent groups such as weekday (Clusters 1-5) weekend (Clusters 6-8), or time of the day (Clusters 2,3).

mation across bins, or distributions with different binning schemes. They are also sensitive to bin size. A binning that is too coarse will not have sufficient discriminative power, while a binning that is too fine will place similar features in different bins which will never be matched. EMD is a cross-bin distance and is not affected by binning differences. It meaningfully matches the perceptual notion of "nearness" and hence its popularity in image matching and retrieval.

EMD has not found widespread application outside the computer vision community due to its prohibitive computational cost. A lone exception has been the work of Zhou *et al.* [20], who propose the use of Mallows distance for comparing clusters.

By generalizing the wavelet approximation proposed in [17] to any general manifold we create a fast approximation to EMD that is applicable in any general domain. This allows us to apply it specifically to signatures that are defined on a manifold, not limited to flat feature spaces.

The rest of the paper is organized as follows. We define the problem, outline our approach and describe our contributions in Section 2. In Section 3 we discuss the Earth Mover Distance and its relationship to other distances like the Mallows distance. Section 4 describes an efficient, linear time approximation to EMD, which makes it feasible on very large data. In Section 5, we conduct experiments on a massive real-world application involving anonymized mobility data. Finally, we present our conclusions and outline directions for future research in Section 6.

2. OUR APPROACH

In this paper, we address the problem of clustering distributional signatures derived from massive multidimensional data. Extant approaches typically rely on methods such as k-means that are based on the Euclidean distance. However, signatures are not mere points in a metric space, they are defined over a distinct topology of the underlying domain. While well known distributional divergences can be used for clustering distributions, the advantages of EMD discussed in Section 3 make it an ideal candidate for clustering distributional signatures. EMD has not found widespread use due to its computational cost. Our approximation makes it feasible, and to the best of our knowledge, we introduce the notion of EMD for data mining.

We make three contributions.

- While wavelet-based approximations to EMD have been proposed for Euclidean spaces, we generalize it to any manifold, thus making it widely applicable to topologies that include probability distributions on manifolds. This novel generalization allows us to apply EMD to distributional signatures, and on a previously infeasible scale.
- We use the Earth Mover Distance for the unsupervised clustering of multi-dimensional data distributions.
- We demonstrate the efficacy of the method and showcase its properties using a compelling real world application of mobility data patterns.

We start with a brief introduction to EMD in the next section.

3. EARTH MOVER DISTANCE

Rubner *et al.* [15, 16] introduced EMD to the computer vision community as a technique for image retrieval. It is also known as the Mallows distance [10] or Wasserstein distance in statistical literature. EMD is a distance measure between two distributions. We start by introducing some terminology to define EMD.

Distributions can generally be described as functions over an underlying (feature) domain. In the rest of the paper, we will assume that multidimensional distributions are defined as histograms by partitioning the underlying domain into bins with a mass associated with each bin. Defining a distance between two distributions requires a notion of distance between points in the underlying domain defining the distributions. This distance is called the *ground distance*. EMD is a natural and intuitive metric between histograms if we think of them as piles of sand sitting on the ground (underlying domain). Each grain of sand is an observed sample. To quantify the difference between two distributions, we measure how far the grains of sand have to be moved so that the two distributions coincide exactly. EMD is the minimal total ground distance travelled weighted by the amount of sand moved (called flow). For perceptually meaningful ground distances, EMD agrees with perceptual dissimilarity better than other measures [16, 17]. Further, if the ground distance is a metric and the distributions all have the same mass (this is true in the case of probability distributions), EMD is a metric as well. There are several advantages of using EMD over other distribution dissimilarity measures. For example, it does not suffer from arbitrary quantization problems due to rigid binning strategies. Therefore, it is robust to errors in transformation that take raw data into feature space.

We provide a formal definition for EMD by using the same notation as proposed in Rubner *et al.* [16]. Let $\mathcal{F}$ be the underlying (feature) space over which the distributions are defined, endowed with a distance function $d : \mathcal{F} \times \mathcal{F} \rightarrow \mathbb{R}^+$. Rubner *et al.* describe a distribution using *signatures* - a sparse representation of a histogram. Specifically, a signature is defined as a vector of tuples, $P = \{< \mathbf{p}_1, w_{p_1} >, < \mathbf{p}_2, w_{p_2} >, \ldots, < \mathbf{p}_m, w_{p_m} >\}$, where $\mathbf{p} \in \mathcal{F}$ is a point in the feature space and w_p is the weight. Let P and Q be two distributions of the form

$$P = \{(\mathbf{p}_1, w_{p_1}), (\mathbf{p}_2, w_{p_2}), \ldots, (\mathbf{p}_m, w_{p_m})\} \quad (2)$$

$$Q = \{(\mathbf{q}_1, w_{q_1}), (\mathbf{q}_2, w_{q_2}), \ldots, (\mathbf{q}_n, w_{q_n})\}, \quad (3)$$

and let $D = [d_{ij}]$ be the ground distance between points $\mathbf{p}_i$ and $\mathbf{q}_j$. We want to find a flow, $F = [f_{ij}]$, where f_{ij} is the flow between points $\mathbf{p}_i$ and $\mathbf{q}_j$, that minimizes the overall cost

$$W(P, Q, F) = \sum_{i=1}^{m} \sum_{j=1}^{n} f_{ij} d_{ij} \quad (4)$$

The flow f_{ij} must satisfy the following linear constraints:

$$f_{ij} \geq 0, \qquad \forall i \in 1, \ldots, m, j \in 1, \ldots, n \quad (5)$$

$$\sum_{j=1}^{n} f_{ij} \leq w_{p_i} \qquad \forall i \in 1, \ldots, m \quad (6)$$

$$\sum_{i=1}^{n} f_{ij} \leq w_{q_j} \qquad \forall j \in 1, \ldots, n \quad (7)$$

$$\sum_{i=1}^{m} \sum_{j=1}^{n} f_{ij} = min\left(\sum_{i=1}^{m} w_{p_i}, \sum_{j=1}^{n} w_{q_j}\right) \quad (8)$$

The first constraint limits the flow to move from P to Q and not the other way around. The next two constraints limit the flow from exceeding the weights in the corresponding bins, and the final constraint sets a lower bound on the flow. Let $[f^*_{ij}]$ be the optimal flow that minimizes Equation 4. Then, the Earth Mover Distance is defined to be

$$EMD(P, Q) = \frac{\sum_{i=1}^{m} \sum_{j=1}^{n} {f^*}_{ij} d_{ij}}{\sum_{i=1}^{m} \sum_{j=1}^{n} {f^*}_{ij}} \quad (9)$$

The optimization problem above is essentially a linear program. However, it can be formulated as an uncapacitated minimum cost flow problem and can be solved optimally by using Orlin's algorithm [9] in $O(n^3 \log n)$, where n is the number of bins in the two histograms. The biggest drawback of using EMD for clustering distributions is its high computational complexity. When dealing with large datasets (with each distribution potentially having a large number of bins) as in our case, the exact computation of EMD becomes impractical. To alleviate this problem, we propose a modified version of an algorithm proposed by Shirdhonkar *et al.* [17] that works on arbitrary ground spaces.

4. APPROXIMATION TO EMD

In order to mitigate the high computational cost of EMD, several approximation schemes have been proposed in the literature. Ling and Okada [12] empirically showed that EMD could be computed in $O(n^2)$ time if an L_1 ground distance is used instead of the usual Euclidean distance. Indyk and Thaper [7] use a randomized multiscale embedding of histograms into a space equipped with the L_1 norm. The multiscale hierarchy is obtained by a series of random shifting and dyadic merging of bins. The histogram levels are weighted by powers of 2, with more weight at the coarser levels. They show that the L_1 norm computed in this space, averaged over all random shifts, is equivalent to the EMD. Their approach runs in roughly $O(ndk)$ time, where d is the histogram dimension and k is the number of times randomized embedding is performed. Shirdhonkar and Jacobs [17] present a linear time algorithm for approximating the EMD for low dimensional histograms using the sum of absolute values of the weighted wavelet coefficients of the difference histogram. The weighted wavelet transform is computed in time linear in the number of histogram bins. One main restriction in the methods of Indyk *et al.* and Shirdhonkar *et al.* is that the underlying (feature) space must be flat (for example, Euclidean).

In the context of our work, the distributions are embedded in a manifold-like space. In these cases, the above approximation strategies are not applicable. Inspired by the work of Shirdhonkar *et al.*, we modify their approach to extend it to the case where manifolds can be the underlying space. We model manifolds as weighted graphs and apply wavelets on these graphs using spectral graph theory [6].

We start our description of the approximate EMD computation by describing the theory behind the approach of Shirdhonkar *et al.*. The connection becomes apparent when we look at the continuous version of the EMD problem known as the Kantorovich-Rubinstein transshipment problem. Let $S \subset \mathbb{R}^d$ be a compact space, and let P_1 and P_2 be probability distributions with densities p_1 and p_2, respectively, defined on S, endowed with a continuous cost function $d : S \times S \rightarrow \mathbb{R}^+$. Let $0 < s \leq 1$ be a fixed parameter. Then the transshipment problem is to find

$$\mu_d = \inf_q \int d(x, y)^s q(x, y) dx dy,$$

where the infimum is over all joint probability densities q on $S \times S$. q is analogous to the flow in the discrete setting. The joint distribution must satisfy a mass conservation constraint of the form

$$p_1(u) - p_2(u) = \int q(u, y) dy - \int q(x, u) dx$$

Here $p := p_1 - p_2$ is the difference distribution with the property that $\int p = 0$. The Kantorovich-Rubinstein theorem states that the above problem admits a dual representation

$$\mu_d = \sup_f \int f(x) p(x) dx \quad (10)$$

The supremum is over all bounded continuous functions f on S satisfying the order s Hölder continuity condition $f(x) - f(y) \leq d(x, y)^s$, for all $x, y \in S$. In the special case of $S = \mathbb{R}^d$, and $d(x, y) = \| x - y \|$, Shirdhonkar *et al.* observed that the dual objective function is the maximum inner product between the potential function and the difference histogram, which can be easily represented in the wavelet domain (since orthonormal wavelets preserve inner products). Their formulation in the wavelet domain has the explicit solution:

$$\mu^*(p_1, p_2) = \sum_{\lambda} 2^{-j(1+n/2)} |p_\lambda|, \quad (11)$$

where p is the n-dimensional difference histogram and p_λ are its wavelet coefficients. The main result of their paper states that, depending on the wavelet used, there exist constants C_L and C_U such that $C_L\mu^* \leq \mu_d \leq C_U\mu^*$. We refer the reader to their paper for more details.

Diffusion wavelets [13, 18] generalize classical wavelets, allowing for multiscale analysis on general structures, such as manifolds, graphs and point clouds in Euclidean space. They allow us to perform signal processing tasks on functions on these spaces. We are interested in preserving dot products; hence we rely on orthonormal wavelets. The diffusion wavelets were designed specifically to be orthonormal, and applicable to smooth manifolds as well as graphs. Their construction interacts with the underlying graph or manifold space through repeated applications of a diffusion operator T (like the heat operator on graphs). The orthogonality of the wavelets is achieved by running a localized orthogonalization procedure after applying dyadic powers of T at each scale to yield nested approximation spaces. Wavelets are then produced by locally orthogonalizing vectors spanning the difference of these approximation spaces.

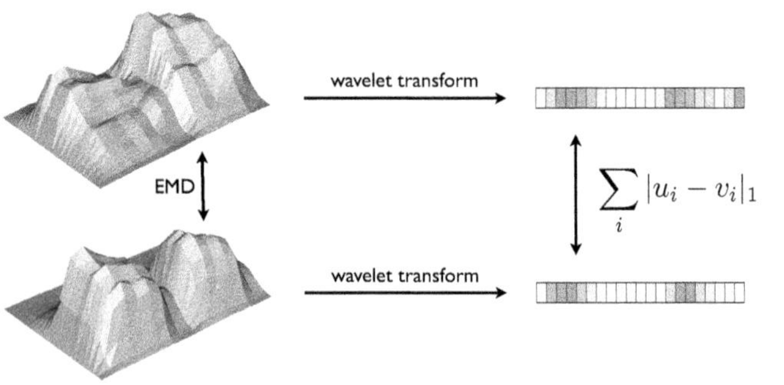

Figure 4: Illustration of the EMD approximation process

We generate a weighted graph to reflect the underlying topology of our space (a product space of a torus and real line), and perform the wavelet computation once. This wavelet replaces the simpler wavelets used by Shirdhonkar *et al.*. All the results directly extend to this wavelet except for the specific values of C_L and C_U. The rest of the computation remains exactly the same. In order to perform the approximate computation, we compute the weighted wavelet transform (as in Equation 11) of each distribution independently. Once the coefficients are obtained as a sparse vector, the approximate EMD is essentially the L_1 norm of the difference of transform coefficients. Figure 4 illustrates the process of approximating EMD using wavelet transforms on a simple domain and the main steps of the algorithm are described in Algorithm 1.

4.1 Accuracy and Performance of Approximate EMD

We compare the results of exact EMD and our approximation on a simulated example and real data. For the simulation, we generate uniformly distributed vectors of size 16^3 using a sparsity factor ρ. From this vector we generate two histograms: one with all positive entries and one with absolute values of only the negative entries. We then compute the EMD between those histograms using exact computation (using the code provided by Rubner[16]) and our approximation. We repeat this process 1000 times varying ρ linearly between 0 and 1. The resulting scatterplot of the exact values vs approximations is shown in Figure 5(a).

Algorithm 1: Approximate EMD(p_1, p_2)

Input: Two distributions p_1 and p_2 over a compact space $S \subset \mathbb{R}^d$

Output: ApproxEMD(p_1, p_2)

Discretize the compact space S by sampling bin locations
Construct a weighted graph G reflecting manifold metric
Construct diffusion wavelets for G (Maggioni *et al.* [13])
Let wd_1 (wd_2) be the weighted diffusion wavelet descriptor (Eq. 11) of p_1 (p_2)
$D^* = L_1\text{-dist}(wd_1, wd_2)$
return D^*

We also used data from the application described in section 5.1 to perform the same comparison. Here, we calculated the EMD of a random non-sparse signature from 5,000 random signatures. The result is shown in Figure 5(b). Our experiments validate the theoretical guarantees provided by the algorithm.

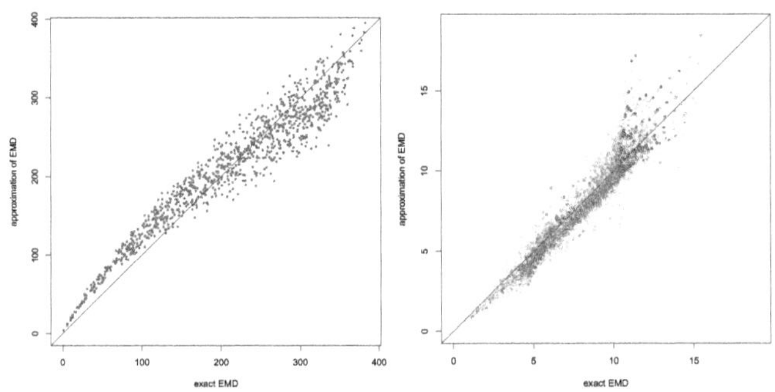

(a) simulated vectors (b) mobility application

Figure 5: Comparison of EMD distances based on exact EMD (x−axis) vs wavelet approximation (y−axis).

In order to measure the performance of the approximate algorithm we picked 50 histogram sizes varying from 25 to 1600. For each histogram size, we generated 25 random histograms and performed pairwise distance computations between them. The timing reported is the average over the 300 distance computations for each histogram size. Figure 6 shows the performance of our algorithm with respect to the exact method. The timing measurements were performed on a Linux machine with 2.27GHz Intel Xeon CPU with 12GB of RAM.

5. A REAL WORLD APPLICATION

In this section, we demonstrate the use of EMD based clustering of signatures of cell phone usage data, and compare conventional clustering based on Euclidean distances with clusters derived using the EMD. We hypothesize that while k-means might provide a reasonable approximation in situations where the signature distributions are fairly smooth, it will struggle when the distributions have spikes e.g. when the density is concentrated in a few bins such as when the signatures are sparse as shown in Figure 1 (right). We have already discussed in Section 1 that k-means results in ar-

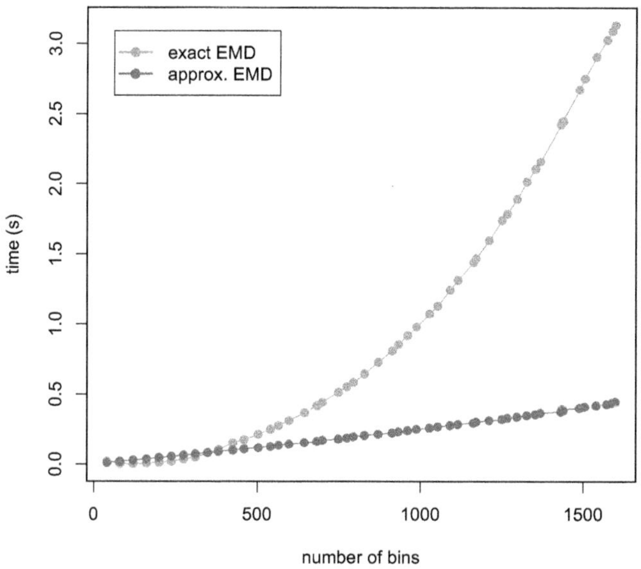

Figure 6: Timing comparison of the exact EMD algorithm (red) vs our approximate algorithm (blue). The timing measurements were performed on a Linux machine with 2.27GHz Intel Xeon CPU with 12GB of RAM.

bitrary clusters determined entirely by the initial seeds, illustrated by cluster centers shown in Figure 2. We will see in Section 5.1 that such extreme situations do arise in real world data making it imperative that the proper distance metric be used for clustering distributional signatures.

5.1 Mobility Usage Signatures

Given the ubiquity of cellphones and their constant use, cell phone calling patterns have been used extensively to study the location and movements of large numbers of people for urban planning, event management and traffic monitoring. In addition, aggregated cell phone usage data find application for traditional network management and monitoring tasks. Isaacman *et al* [8] show by using anonymized, aggregated statistics based on hundreds of thousands of cell phone calls in New York and Los Angeles, that the commuting patterns, travel distances and times are very different for New Yorkers and Los Angelenos. Similarly, by clustering anonymized aggregates of cell phone calls in a small town, Becker *et al* [2] identify interesting clusters of users with distinct behavior such as commuters and students.

In general, we are interested in analyzing mobile phone usage signatures in order to find common patterns, detect outliers, and identify trouble spots in the network. We describe below our experiments with the use of EMD for clustering mobile usage signatures. There exist many more applications of EMD to signatures, like clustering network traffic patterns and detecting changes in traffic distributions, but for the purpose of this paper, we confine ourselves to clustering usage signatures.

5.2 Data Description

The data consisted of 411,550 unique handsets that generated around 15 million voice calls and 26 million text messages collected over a 60 day period from 35 cell towers located within a radius of 5 miles.

Given the sensitivity of the data, we took several steps to ensure the privacy of individuals. First, only anonymous records were used in this study. The data was collected and anonymized by a third party not involved in the data analysis. We worked only on usage aggregates by hour and day of week. Second, all our results are presented as aggregates. That is, no individual anonymous identifier was singled out for the study. By observing and reporting only on the aggregates, we protect the privacy of individuals.

For each user, we aggregated the calls and text messages separately over the 24×7 grid of "hour of day" vs. "day of the week" resulting in 168 bins. We had two such grids, one for voice and one for text message activity. The voice minutes and text message counts were made comparable by normalizing them so that they have the same global mean, resulting in one SMS corresponding to approximately 1.5 minutes of a voice call. The two usage vectors for each handset were concatenated to form one vector of $2 \times 24 \times 7 = 336$ elements. This vector was further normalized to have a total sum of one. The distribution of cell phone usage across 336 bins defines our signature. Examples of such distributions were presented in Figure 1, visualized as heat maps of the underlying voice and SMS matrices each consisting of 24 rows and 7 columns.

5.3 Clustering the Signatures

The size of our data set consists of 411,550 signatures which poses a challenge for clustering algorithms. Distance-based methods typically require a distance matrix consisting of $(n^2 - n)/2$ entries, which in our case implies more than 84 billion distances. Although our proposed EMD approximation algorithm reduces the computational cost to linear time, the estimated duration for the computation of the 8.4×10^{10} distances was 6 days, therefore we decided to use a random sample of 50,000 signatures to perform the clustering. We can then use EMD to compute distances from cluster centers to the entire data set, allowing for both outlier detection and cluster assignment. The computation of EMD distances to each of the cluster centers for the entire large set is highly feasible and is completed in a matter of minutes.

A major advantage of using our novel approximation to EMD is that it allows us to define a topology on the bins, and introduce the notion of nearness of bins. Since the boundaries of bins by hour are in a sense arbitrary, we would consider neighboring bins in time as 'close'. For example, we would consider users exhibiting activities at 12:45pm and 1:15pm more similar than those active at 7am and 11pm. Also typically human activities follow a daily cycle, so that there is a certain similarity between different days of the week at the same time. Finally, we have two types of activities – voice and SMS – which are distinct, so we model them as being at a constant distance from each other over the space of time. EMD allows us to specify such complex relationship between the bins.

To model the "time of day" and "day of week" relationship, we use a torus as the underlying geometry for the time and day of week space since the torus is defined as the product of two circles. By using a uniform helix on the torus we have a structure that wraps around at the end from one day to another and also from the end of the week to the beginning

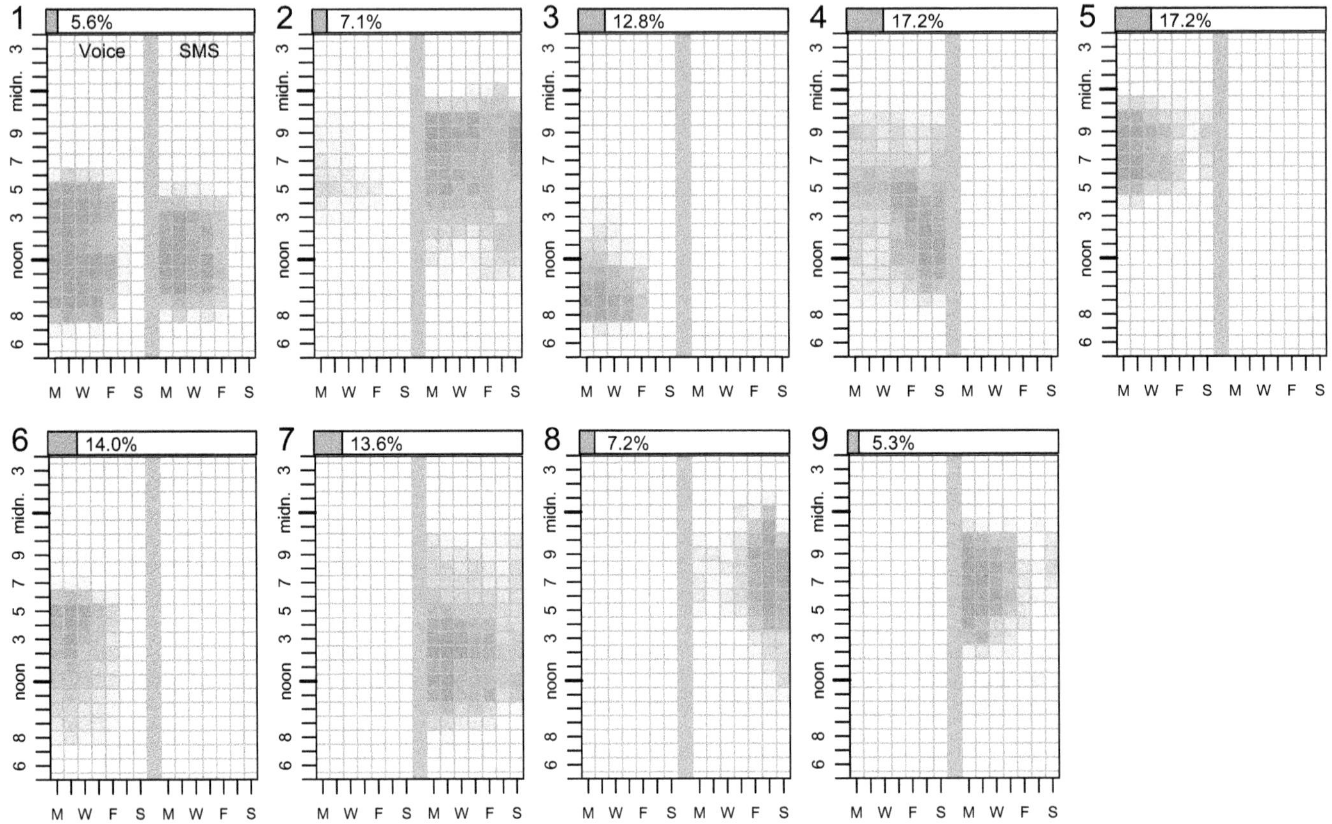

Figure 7: Aggregate usage per cluster for clusters obtained using hierarchical clustering with EMD on a random sample of 50,000 signatures drawn from the full range of signatures including sparse ones, . The clusters capture distinct patterns, such as mixed activity during work hours (Cluster 1), morning voice call activity (Cluster 3), or exclusive texting (Clusters 8 and 9).

of the week. Finally we add the activity type as a product with ℝ.

In our experiments, we used *complete linkage hierarchical clustering*[14] given Earth Mover Distances. Figure 7 shows the result of the clustering. It was run on a random sample of 50,000 cases from the dataset, including a large portion of low usage signatures. We plot the aggregate signatures based on all members in each cluster. The cluster number is at the top left corner of each plot. The blue bar on top of each signature represents the relative size of the cluster. Since we are interested in detection of general patterns, the exact number of clusters is not critical for our application. We selected the number of clusters taking into account within-cluster variance and cluster size.

The EMD clusters show distinct patterns. Cluster 1 corresponds to a mixed usage of both voice and SMS, predominantly during working hours. In contrast, Cluster 2 represents mostly SMS usage on evenings and into the weekend. Similar structure but limited to voice calls can be seen in Cluster 4. Clusters 3-6 separate signatures with almost no SMS activity whereas Clusters 7-9 have predominantly SMS usage. The clustering allows us to identify groups with similar usage patterns and their relative sizes, which can be used in many applications such as optimization of the operation of the cellular network, or on a local scale, to help in urban planning by identifying spatial groupings.

Once the clusters have been formed, their signature distribution can be used to compute EMD for new data. This operation is computationally far less expensive than computing a full pairwise distance matrix. This is useful for several purposes. We can compare the resulting distances with the within-cluster distances to find outliers with respect to the existing data and clusters. In addition, we can use this information to assign new data into clusters.

Figure 8 shows cluster signatures based on the entire dataset. We assigned each of the 411,550 signatures into clusters by taking the cluster with the closest center as determined by EMD. We see only a slight shift of the cluster size distribution between clusters compared to the clustering result on the subset of 50,000. The resulting signatures are consistent with the cluster centers, with some patterns standing out even more sharply. Weekends are more strongly represented in Clusters 4 and 8, and Cluster 7 is more clearly focused on SMS during working hours. This allows us to extend our identification of patterns to the entire dataset.

In the same way that we used cluster signatures for comparison, any set of target distributions could be used, allowing supervised clustering applications on a large scale as well. In our example, we used a fixed time frame, but if new data are obtained periodically, it allows for comparison of cluster evolution over time.

Alternatively, it is also possible to compare the evolution

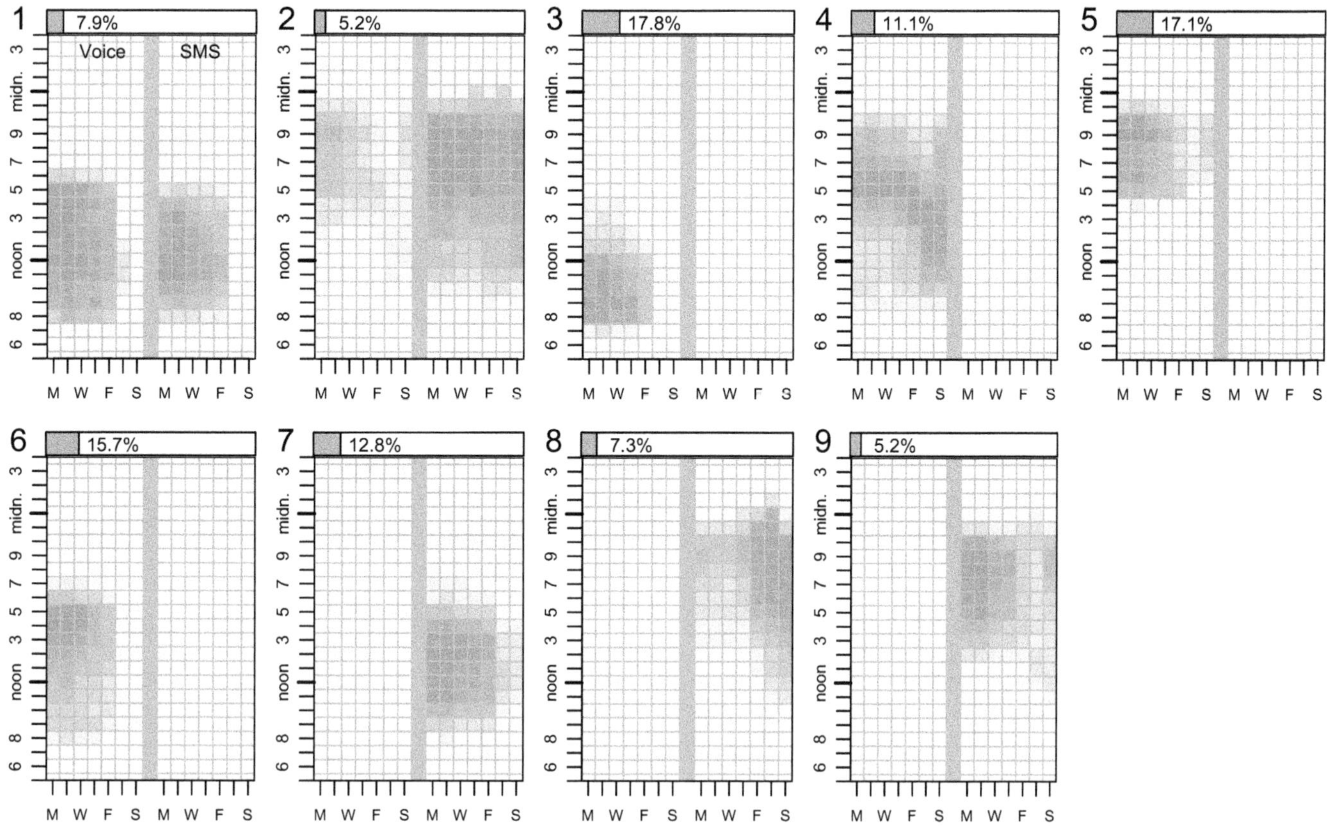

Figure 8: Aggregate signatures of clusters for all 411,550 data points. Cases are assigned to clusters according to their proximity to cluster centers derived using EMD on a random sample of 50,000 signatures.

of signatures in linear time using our proposed EMD approximation by measuring the distance between distributions of subsequent signature in time. There are numerous application for EMD based analysis in change detection and spatio-temporal clustering.

6. CONCLUSION

In this paper, we proposed the use of the Earth Mover Distance for clustering distributions and signatures. EMD is inherently meaningful since it takes into account the underlying topology of the distributions unlike clustering methods like k-means that simply use the Euclidean metric defined over the point space. It allows for cross-bin comparisons creating a similarity measure that matches the perceptual notion of nearness and is tolerant to heterogeneous binning strategies.

EMD runs in $O(n^3 \log n)$ time, but we proposed a novel generalization of a well-known wavelet-based approximation algorithm that enables us to apply EMD to massive data for general topologies including distributional signatures.

We applied EMD based clustering to a massive real world mobile phone usage data set of 411,550 users by computing full pairwise distances, clustering a sample subset of 50,000, and extending the results to the entire population by assigning to clusters using EMD. The results of EMD based clustering are meaningful in every part of the usage distribution while k-means fails in clustering sparsely populated signatures.

6.1 Future Research

An interesting problem for further research involves clustering multivariate time series. Existing techniques represent time series as signatures and cluster them as was done in this paper, or impose artificial windows that capture slices of the time series and treat them as multi-dimensional vectors that are clustered in a routine way. While we ignore the temporal aspect in signatures, EMD can be used to cluster multivariate time series by defining similarity on the time space. Because of its notion of 'nearness' in the time domain, it recognizes small shifts in the time series as being similar enough to belong to the same cluster.

The wavelet-based approximation transforms the calculation of EMD into a computation of the L_1 norm between vectors in a sparse high-dimensional space. This space lends itself to dimensionality reduction techniques like locality sensitive hashing to further optimize the clustering algorithm without the need to compute the complete distance matrix.

7. REFERENCES

[1] S. M. Ali and S. D. Silvey. A general class of coefficients of divergence of one distribution from another. *Journal of the Royal Statistical Society. Series B (Methodological)*, 28(1):131–142, 1966.

[2] R. Becker, R. Cáceres, K. Hanson, J. M. Loh, S. Urbanek, A. Vasharsvky, and C. Volinsky. A tale of one city: Using cellular network data for urban planning. *In Review*, 2011.

[3] C. Cortes and D. Pregibon. Signature-based methods for data streams. *Data Mining and Knowledge Discovery*, 5(3):167–182, 2001-07-01.

[4] I. Csiszar. Information-type measures of difference of probability distributions and indirect observations. *Studia Sci. Math. Hungar.*, 2:299–318, 1967.

[5] A. L. Gibbs and F. E. Su. On choosing and bounding probability metrics. *International Statistical Review*, 70(3):419–435, 2002.

[6] D. K. Hammond, P. Vandergheynst, and R. Gribonval. Wavelets on graphs via spectral graph theory. Dec. 2009.

[7] P. Indyk and N. Thaper. Fast image retrieval via embeddings. In *3rd International Workshop on Statistical and Computational Theories of Vision*. ICCV, 2003.

[8] S. Isaacman, R. Becker, R. Cáceres, S. Kobourov, J. Rowland, and A. Varshavsky. Ranges of human mobility in los angeles and new york. In *Proc. of 8th International Workshop on Managing Ubiquitous Communications and Services (MUCS)*, 2011.

[9] B. Korte and J. Vygen. *Combinatorial Optimization: Theory and Algorithms*. Springer Publishing Company, Incorporated, 4th edition, 2007.

[10] E. Levina and P. Bickel. The earth mover's distance is the mallows distance: Some insights from statistics. In *ICCV 2001*, pages 251–256, 2001.

[11] F. Liese and I. Vajda. On divergences and informations in statistics and information theory. *Information Theory, IEEE Transactions on*, 52(10):4394 -4412, October 2006.

[12] H. Ling and K. Okada. An efficient earth mover's distance algorithm for robust histogram comparison. *IEEE Trans. Pattern Anal. Mach. Intell.*, 29:840–853, May 2007.

[13] M. Maggioni, J. C. Bremer, R. R. Coifman, and A. D. Szlam. Biorthogonal diffusion wavelets for multiscale representations on manifolds and graphs. volume 5914. Proc. SPIE Wavelet XI, 2005.

[14] F. Murtagh. Multidimensional clustering algorithms. In *COMPSTAT Lectures 4*, Wuerzburg, 1985. Physica-Verlag.

[15] Y. Rubner, C. Tomasi, and L. J. Guibas. A metric for distributions with applications to image databases. In *Proceedings of the Sixth International Conference on Computer Vision*, ICCV '98, pages 59–, Washington, DC, USA, 1998. IEEE Computer Society.

[16] Y. Rubner, C. Tomasi, and L. J. Guibas. The earth mover's distance as a metric for image retrieval. *Int. J. Comput. Vision*, 40:99–121, November 2000.

[17] S. Shirdhonkar and D. W. Jacobs. Approximate earth mover's distance in linear time. *Computer Vision and Pattern Recognition, IEEE Computer Society Conference on*, 0:1–8, 2008.

[18] A. D. Szlam, M. Maggioni, R. R. Coifman, and J. C. Bremer. Diffusion-driven multiscale analysis on manifolds and graphs: top-down and bottom-up constructions. volume 5914, 2005.

[19] P. C. Wong, H. Foote, R. Leung, D. Adams, and J. Thomas. Data signatures and visualization of scientific data sets. *IEEE Computer Graphics and Applications*, 20:12–15, 2000.

[20] D. Zhou, J. Li, and H. Zha. A new mallows distance based metric for comparing clusterings. In *Proceedings of the 22nd international conference on Machine learning*, ICML '05, pages 1028–1035, New York, NY, USA, 2005. ACM.

Online Heterogeneous Mixture Modeling with Marginal and Copula Selection

Ryohei Fujimaki
NEC Laboratories America
Media Analytics Department
NEC Laboratories America
rfujimaki@sv.nec-labs.com

Yasuhiro Sogawa*
The Institute of Scientific and Industrial Research
Osaka University
sogawa@ar.sanken.osaka-u.ac.jp

Satoshi Morinaga
Information and Media Processing Research Labs.
NEC Corporation
morinaga@cw.jp.nec.com

ABSTRACT

This paper proposes an online mixture modeling methodology in which individual components can have different marginal distributions and dependency structures. Mixture models have been widely studied and applied to various application areas, including density estimation, fraud/failure detection, image segmentation, etc. Previous research has been almost exclusively focused on mixture models having components of a single type (e.g., a Gaussian mixture model.) However, recent growing needs for complicated data modeling necessitate the use of more flexible mixture models (e.g., a mixture of a lognormal distribution for medical costs and a Gaussian distribution for blood pressure, for medical analytics.) Our key ideas include: 1) separating marginal distributions and their dependencies using copulas and 2) online extension of a recently-developed "expectation minimization of description length," which enable us to efficiently learn types of both marginal distributions and copulas as well as their parameters. The proposed method provides not only good performance in applications, but also scalable, automatic model selection, which greatly reduces the intensive modeling costs in data mining processes. We show that the proposed method outperforms state-of-the-art methods in application to density estimation and to anomaly detection.

Categories and Subject Descriptors

H.2.8 [**Database Management**]: Database applications—*Data Mining*; I.2.6 [**Artificial Intelligence**]: Learning

General Terms

Algorithms

*Under internship program of NEC Corporation.

1. INTRODUCTION

Mixture models have been widely studied and applied in a variety of areas, including topic analysis [15], fraud detection [27], image segmentation [25], and speech recognition [20]. Previous research has been almost exclusively focused on mixture models having single types of distributions (e.g., a Gaussian mixture model, a Bernoulli mixture model, etc.) However, in many real applications, the assumption that all variables have the same distribution type will not be satisfied, and the estimation/prediction performance of such models will consequently degrade. In medical analytics [6], for examples medical costs and blood pressure usually have, respectively, a log normal distribution (or a mixture of lognormal and normal distributions) and a (skewed) normal distribution.

Fig. 1 presents the concept of the issue dealt with in this paper. "Component 1" has (lognormal, Gaussian) marginal distributions, and they have negative dependency. "Component 2" has (Gaussian, Gaussian) marginal distributions, and they have positive dependency. The learning problem with such models includes selection of the number of components and types of marginal distributions and their dependency structures as well as parameter estimation. A brute-force search with such classical statistical information criteria as Akaike's information criterion [1] or the minimum description length principle (MDL) [21] might be expected to suffer from a combinatorial scalability problem with respect to types of components.

Recently, Fujimaki et al. [9] have proposed the concept of "heterogeneous mixture models," in which individual components can have different types. The algorithm, "expectation minimization of description length (EMDL)," addresses the model selection issue for heterogeneous mixture models in which types of components, as well as the number of components and their parameters, are optimized. Their model and EMDL have two limitations w.r.t. our problem: Limitation 1) it is difficult to define joint distributions for individual components having different types of marginal distributions[1], and Limitation 2) the number of component candidates will become prohibitively large with increasing data dimensionality D if we allow different variables to have different types of marginal distributions[2].

[1]Let us consider the case where random variables X_1 and X_2 have different types of marginal distributions. The pdf $p(X_1|X_2)$ or $P(X_2|X_1)$ will not generally be obvious.
[2]Let us assume that we have two marginal candidates,

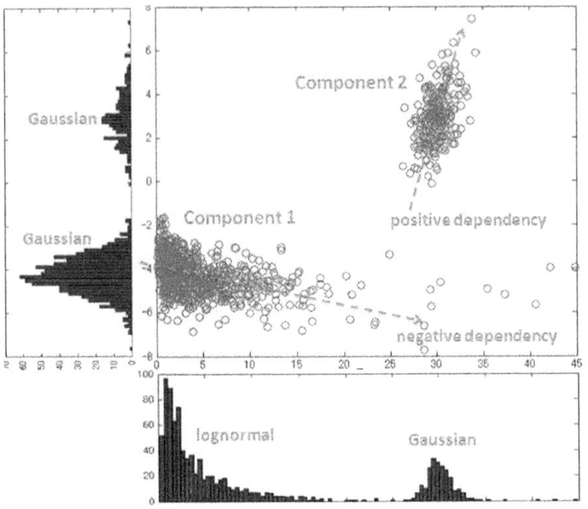

Figure 1: Concept of our problem. The goal is to specify all of the number of components, types of marginal distributions, dependency structures, and their parameters.

The goal of this study is to construct a mixture modeling methodology for the simultaneous model selection and parameter estimation described above. In addition to achievement of good estimation/prediction performance using a flexible model, we address computational scalability and modeling automation issues, which are essential for reduction of the total cost of data mining processes.

Our key ideas and contributions may be summarized as:

Heterogeneous Marginals and Copulas.
We separate, for individual components, marginal distributions and their dependency structures using copulas [17] to address Limitation 1. Our model here, which we refer to as a "mixture model with heterogeneous marginals and copulas" (MHMC), allows us to use both heterogeneous types of marginal distributions and heterogeneous types of dependencies among variables (i.e., copulas), and it provides a powerful tool of modeling complicated data. From the viewpoint of computational and modeling costs, this direct incorporation of copulas into the heterogeneous mixture model actually contributes importantly to the efficiency of our learning algorithm (we can separately optimize individual marginal distributions and copulas.)

Online Model Selection Algorithm.
We propose an online EMDL algorithm for MHMC which automatically optimizes the number of components, types of marginal distributions, types of copulas, and their parameters. By combining MHMC and (online) EMDL, we can avoid the combinatorial scalability issue involved in selecting marginal and copula types (Limitation 2). Further, MHMC with online EMDL, which we abbreviate as OMHMC, addresses the scalability issue for large datasets, and it is also expected to have good convergence properties, on the basis of an analogy with the EM algorithm [5] and the incremental EM algorithm[3] [16].

Gaussian and lognormal. Then we have 2^D candidates for marginal combinations for each component: i.e., (Gaussian, Gaussian), (Gaussian, lognormal), (lognormal, Gaussian), (lognormal, lognormal) for $D = 2$.

	Batch	Online	Nonstationary
Parameter	EM algorithm[5]	incremental EM[16]	Sequential Discounting EM[27]
Component Number	Variational Bayes Model Selection[4] Dirichlet Process Mixture[12,18] AIC[1], MDL[21] Cross Validation	Online VB Model Selection[22]	Dynamic Model Selection[15,28]
Component Type	EMDL[9]	**OMHMC**	
Marginal and Copula Type			

Figure 2: Related work

To the best of our knowledge, OMHMC is the first online model selection algorithm which is capable of optimizing types of components (further, OMHMC is capable of optimizing marginal distributions and copulas for individual components.) Fig.2 lists a number of studies for parameter estimation and model selection of the number of component algorithms [1, 4, 5, 12, 18, 21] and their online/nonstationary learning extensions [16, 15, 22, 27, 28], including OMHMC.

We summarize the notation in Section 6. It is rather complicated because we must distinguish a large number of variables and parameters (marginal distributions of individual variables, copulas for individual components, and their parameters.)

2. MIXTURE MODEL WITH HETEROGENEOUS MARGINALS AND COPULAS

2.1 Copulas

Copulas [17] separate a dependency structure among variables from their marginal distributions. Intuitively speaking, their joint distribution can be represented as the product of the marginals of individual variables and a copula. Historically, copulas have been actively studied in financial engineering [13, 17] in order to model dependencies among different types of risks. Recently, data mining and machine learning communities have also noticed their powerful and useful properties, and a number of studies have been conducted [7, 26].

Let $X = (X_1, \ldots, X_D)$ be a random variable. Let $F(x) = P(X_1 \leq x_1, \ldots, X_D \leq x_D)$ and $F_d(x_d) = P_d(X_d \leq x_d)$ be cumulative distribution functions (cdfs), respectively.

A copula function is formally defined as follows:

Definition 1 (Copula). *Let $U = (U_1, \ldots, U_D)$ and $u = (u_1, \ldots, u_D)$ be, respectively, random variables uniformly distributed on $[0, 1]^D$ and its realization. Copula function $Q : [0, 1]^D \to [0, 1]$ is a joint distribution function represented as follows:*

$$Q(u) = P(U_1 \leq u_1, \ldots, U_D \leq u_D). \quad (1)$$

Sklar's theorem [24] provides theoretical support of copulas:

[3]We were unable to confirm that our online EMDL had better convergence than the batch EMDL because a numerical error resulted in non-convergence of the batch algorithm. Briefly, $x \neq \zeta^{-1}(\zeta(x))$, where ζ and ζ^{-1} are, respectively, a cumulative distribution function and its inverse.

THEOREM 1 (SKLAR'S THEOREM). *There exists a copula function such that*

$$F(x) = Q(F_1(x_1), \ldots, F_D(x_D)). \quad (2)$$

If $F_1, \ldots, F_D$ are all continuous, then Q is unique.

Let us denote joint and marginal probabilistic density functions (pdfs) as $f(X) = \frac{\partial^D F(X)}{\partial X_1 \cdots \partial X_D}$ and $f_d(X_d) = \frac{\partial F_d(X_d)}{\partial X_d}$, respectively. Then, using the chain rule, we have,

$$\begin{aligned} f(X) &= \frac{\partial^D Q(F_1(X_1), \ldots, F_D(X_D))}{\partial F_1(X_1) \cdots \partial F_D(X_D)} \prod_{d=1}^{D} f_d(X_d) \\ &= q(F_1(X_1), \ldots, F_D(X_D)) \prod_{d=1}^{D} f_d(X_d), \end{aligned} \quad (3)$$

where $q(F_1(X_1), \ldots, F_D(X_D))$ is referred to as the "copula density function."

2.2 Heterogeneous Mixture Modeling

Let us define "component candidates" as $\mathcal{S} = \{\mathcal{S}_j | j = 1, \ldots, |\mathcal{S}|\}$, where $|\circ|$ represents the number of elements in a set $\circ$. If $\mathcal{S}_j$ is Gaussian, $p(X; \phi(\mathcal{S}_j), \mathcal{S}_j)$ is the Gaussian distribution having parameter $\phi(\mathcal{S}_j)$. For notational simplicity, we denote $\phi(\mathcal{S}_j)$ as ϕ alone, so long as there is no fear of confusion.

For given component candidates $\mathcal{S}$, a heterogeneous mixture model is defined as follows [9]:

$$p(X; \boldsymbol{\theta}, \boldsymbol{S}, C) = \sum_{c=1}^{C} \alpha_c p_c(X; \boldsymbol{\phi}_c, S_c). \quad (4)$$

We denote the number of components, types of components, and parameters of components as C, $\boldsymbol{S} = (S_1, \ldots, S_C)$ ($S_c \in \mathcal{S}$) and $\boldsymbol{\theta} = (\boldsymbol{\alpha}, \phi_1, \ldots, \phi_C)$, respectively. $\boldsymbol{\alpha} = (\alpha_1, \ldots, \alpha_C)$ is the mixture coefficient.

This paper proposes a mixture model with heterogeneous marginals and copulas (MHMC) in order to address Limitations 1) and 2) for (4). Let us define "marginal candidates" and "copula candidates" as $\mathcal{M} = \{\mathcal{M}_j | j = 1, \ldots, |\mathcal{M}|\}$ and $\mathcal{Q} = \{\mathcal{Q}_j | j = 1, \ldots, |\mathcal{Q}|\}$, respectively. MHMC is defined by replacing the pdf of each component in (4) with the product of marginal distributions and a copula as follows:

$$p_c(X; \boldsymbol{\phi}_c, S_c) = q_c(\boldsymbol{\psi}_c; \boldsymbol{\xi}_c, Q_c) \prod_{d=1}^{D} p_{cd}(X_d; \boldsymbol{\phi}_{cd}, M_{cd}). \quad (5)$$

$p_{cd}(X_d; \boldsymbol{\phi}_{cd}, M_{cd})$ and $\boldsymbol{\phi}_{cd}$ are the marginal distribution and its parameter[4] specified by $M_{cd} \in \mathcal{M}$. $\psi_{cd} = F_{cd}(X_d)$ is the cdf. of $p_{cd}(X_d; \boldsymbol{\phi}_{cd}, M_{cd})$ where $\boldsymbol{\psi}_c = (\psi_{c1}, \ldots, \psi_{cD})$. $q_c(\boldsymbol{\psi}_c; \boldsymbol{\xi}_c, Q_c)$ and $\boldsymbol{\xi}_c$ are, respectively, the copula density function and its parameter[5] specified by $Q_c \in \mathcal{Q}$. We redefine the component types and the parameter in (4) as $S_c = (M_{c1}, \ldots, M_{cD}, Q_c)$ and $\boldsymbol{\theta} = (\boldsymbol{\alpha}, \phi_{11}, \ldots, \phi_{CD}, \boldsymbol{\xi}_1, \ldots, \boldsymbol{\xi}_C)$, respectively.

A copula plugged into each component naturally addresses Limitation 1). In addition, by separating the marginal distributions and dependencies among them using copulas, we can avoid the combinatorial issue (Limitation 2)) and can efficiently learn the model.

[4]For example, if M_{cd} is Gaussian, p_{cd} is a one dimensional Gaussian distribution and $\boldsymbol{\phi}_{cd}$ is mean and variance.

[5]For example, if Q_c is Gaussian, q is a Gaussian copula and $\boldsymbol{\xi}_c$ is a correlation matrix.

3. ONLINE MIXTURE MODELING

3.1 Expectation Minimization of Description Length

For MHMC, we must specify the number of components C, the types of marginal distributions M_{cd}, and the types of copulas Q_c as well as their parameters $\boldsymbol{\theta}$. This is a issue of "model selection for heterogeneous models," and an efficient batch learning framework, "expectation minimization of description length" (EMDL), has been proposed [9].

Let $\boldsymbol{x}^N = \boldsymbol{x}_1, \ldots, \boldsymbol{x}_N$ be N observed data of X. Let us denote latent variables as $\boldsymbol{z}^N = \boldsymbol{z}_1, \ldots, \boldsymbol{z}_N$, where $\boldsymbol{z}_n = (z_{n1}, \ldots, z_{nC})$. $\boldsymbol{z}_n$ indicates the component assignment of $\boldsymbol{x}_n$ and $z_{nc} = 1$ if $\boldsymbol{x}_n$ is generated from the c-th component and $z_{nc} = 0$ otherwise. A pair $(\boldsymbol{x}^N, \boldsymbol{z}^N)$ is called "complete data" while $\boldsymbol{x}^N$ by itself is called "incomplete data."

Like the EM algorithm [5], for the fixed number of components C, EMDL iterates the EM steps by optimizing the types of components S_c and their parameter $\boldsymbol{\theta}_c = (\alpha_c, \boldsymbol{\phi}_{c1}, \ldots, \boldsymbol{\phi}_{cD}, \boldsymbol{\xi}_C)$ for $\forall c$. This procedure for MHMC is described below. In the t-th E step, we calculate the posterior of latent variables as follows:

$$\begin{aligned} p(z_{nc} | \boldsymbol{x}^N, \boldsymbol{\theta}_c^{(t-1)}, S_c^{(t-1)}) &\propto \alpha_c^{(t-1)} \prod_{d=1}^{D} p_{cd}(x_{nd}; \boldsymbol{\phi}_{cd}^{(t-1)}, M_{cd}^{(t-1)}) \\ &\times q_c(\boldsymbol{\psi}_c^{(t-1)}; \boldsymbol{\xi}_c^{(t-1)}, Q_c^{(t-1)}), \end{aligned} \quad (6)$$

where superscription (t) represents the t-th EM step. Then, in the t-th M step, for individual components, we optimize S_c and $\boldsymbol{\phi}_c$ as follows:

$$S_c^{(t)}, \boldsymbol{\theta}_c^{(t)} = \arg\min_{S_c, \boldsymbol{\theta}_c} E_Z^{(t)}\Big[J(\boldsymbol{x}^N, \boldsymbol{z}^N; \alpha_c, \boldsymbol{\phi}_c, S_c)\Big], \quad (7)$$

$$\begin{aligned} J(\boldsymbol{x}^N, \boldsymbol{z}^N; \boldsymbol{\theta}_c, S_c) &= \sum_{n=1}^{N} -z_{nc}\Big(\sum_{d=1}^{D} \log p_{cd}(x_{nd}; \boldsymbol{\phi}_{cd}, M_{cd}) \\ &+ \log q_c(\boldsymbol{\psi}_{nc}; \boldsymbol{\xi}_c, Q_c) + \log \alpha_c\Big) \\ &+ \frac{\sum_{d=1}^{D} \beta(M_{cd}) + \beta(Q_c)}{2} \log\Big(\sum_{n=1}^{N} z_{nc}\Big), \end{aligned}$$

where $\boldsymbol{\psi}_{nc} = (\psi_{nc1}, \ldots, \psi_{ncD})$, $\psi_{ncd} = F_{cd}(x_{nd})$ and $\boldsymbol{\phi}_c = (\phi_{c1}, \ldots, \phi_{cD}, \boldsymbol{\xi}_c)$. The objective $J(\boldsymbol{x}^N, \boldsymbol{z}^N; \boldsymbol{\theta}_c, S_c)$ is the expected description length of complete data w.r.t. the c-th component. $E_Z^{(t)}[\bullet]$ is the expectation of $\bullet$ w.r.t. the posterior (6). $\beta(\bullet)$ is the dimensionality of $\bullet$, i.e., $\beta(M_{cd}) = 2$ if M_{cd} is Gaussian.

Fujimaki et al. [9] show that it is possible to efficiently calculate the second order approximation[6] of $E_Z^{(t)}[\log(\sum_{n=1}^{N} z_{nc})]$ for the last term in (7) as follows:

$$\begin{aligned} E_Z^{(t)}[\log(\sum_{n=1}^{N} z_{nc})] &\approx \log\Big(\sum_{n=1}^{N} E_Z^{(t)}[z_{nc}]\Big) \\ &- \frac{\sum_{n=1}^{N} E_Z^{(t)}[z_{nc}] - \sum_{n=1}^{N} (E_Z^{(t)}[z_{nc}])^2}{2(\sum_{n=1}^{N} E_Z^{(t)}[z_{nc}])^2}. \end{aligned} \quad (8)$$

The number of components is determined on the basis of

[6]We can calculate the higher order approximations with $\mathcal{O}(N)$ computational cost.

MDL [21] as follows:

$$\hat{C} = \arg\min_{C}\Big\{-\sum_{n=1}^{N}\log p(\boldsymbol{x}_n;\hat{\boldsymbol{\theta}},\hat{\boldsymbol{S}},C)+\frac{\beta(\boldsymbol{S})+C-1}{2}\log N\Big\}, \tag{9}$$

where $\hat{\boldsymbol{\theta}}$ and $\hat{\boldsymbol{S}}$ are the estimated parameters and the component types for C through the EM procedure.

The key to MHMC in EMDL is that the M step can be separated into optimizations of individual marginals and copulas for individual components, and therefore we can avoid the combinatorial issue for component types. Otherwise, a naive modeling of the joint distribution of each component would suffer from a drastic increase in the number of component candidates (i.e., the combination of marginal distributions.) even if we made use of EMDL for Limitation 2). Further, in order to address the scalability issue for large scale data, we next propose our online learning algorithm.

3.2 Online EMDL for MHMC

We design the online EMDL with reference to two existing algorithms: an incremental EM algorithm [16] and an inference functions for marginals (IFM) [10]. The incremental EM algorithm estimates a mixture model by incrementally updating sufficient statistics with respect to complete data. Neal and Hinton [16] show that incremental learning provides faster convergence than the standard batch EM algorithm. For a joint distribution having a single component, IFM estimates the marginal parameters first and then estimates the copula parameter among them because the simultaneous estimation of marginals and a copula is generally prohibitively difficult.

3.2.1 Online Update Procedure

Let us assume that the number of components C is fixed (C is optimized in (21).) The online EMDL sequentially updates the model and sufficient statistics on the basis of input dataset $\mathcal{X}_t = \boldsymbol{x}_{K_0+K(t-1)+1},\ldots,\boldsymbol{x}_{K_0+Kt}$, where K_0 and K are the numbers of initial data $\mathcal{X}_0$ and sequential dataset $\mathcal{X}_t$ ($\mathcal{X}_0 = \boldsymbol{x}_1,\ldots,\boldsymbol{x}_{K_0}$.) Though the cases $K=1$ and $K>1$ are usually called "online" and "mini-batch", respectively, we do not distinguish them.

The update procedure for each component consists of the four steps summarized below. Let us redefine the superscription (t) as the notation of the t-th online update.

Latent Variable Update.

The latent variable update corresponds to the E step in EMDL. First, we calculate the posterior expectation of the latent variable $E_Z^{(t)}[z_{nc}]$ ($n = K_0+K(t-1)+1,\ldots,K_0+Kt$), which calculation is identical to that of the posterior distribution of z_{nc}, as follows:

$$E_Z^{(t)}[z_{nc}] = \frac{\alpha_c^{(t-1)}p_c(\boldsymbol{x}_n;\boldsymbol{\phi}_c^{(t-1)},S_c^{(t-1)})}{\sum_{c=1}^{C}\alpha_c^{(t-1)}p_c(\boldsymbol{x}_n;\boldsymbol{\phi}_c^{(t-1)},S_c^{(t-1)})}. \tag{10}$$

For sufficient statistics, we update the r-th order moment of latent variables as follows:

$$\mathcal{U}_{rc}^{(t)} = \mathcal{U}_{rc}^{(t-1)} + \sum_{n=K_0+K(t-1)+1}^{K_0+Kt}(E_Z^{(t)}[z_{nc}])^r \quad (r=1,\ldots,R_z), \tag{11}$$

where R_z is set[7] to $R_z=2$. The first order moment is used in (19) and (12), and moments of higher order than one are used in (12). We can calculate the complexity term of the c-th component in the t-th update as follows:

$$\mathcal{E}_c^{(t)} = \log(\mathcal{U}_{1c}^{(t)}) - (\mathcal{U}_{1c}^{(t)} - \mathcal{U}_{2c}^{(t)})/2(\mathcal{U}_{1c}^{(t)})^2, \tag{12}$$

where $\mathcal{E}_c^{(t)}$ is used in (15) and (18).

Marginal Update.

This update step, corresponding to the M step of EMDL, updates moments of individual marginal distributions and optimizes types of marginals and their parameters. As for sufficient statistics, we update the r-th order moment of observed variables as follows:

$$\mathcal{V}_{rcd}^{(t)} = \mathcal{V}_{rcd}^{(t-1)} + \sum_{n=K_0+K(t-1)+1}^{K_0+Kt}E_Z^{(t)}[z_{nc}](x_{nd})^r \quad (r=1,\ldots,R_x). \tag{13}$$

For a given marginal candidate $\bar{\mathcal{M}} \in \mathcal{M}$, we obtain the moment-matching estimator[8] $\bar{\phi}_{cd}(\bar{\mathcal{M}},\mathcal{V}_{cd}^{(t)})$ of ϕ_{cd}, where $\mathcal{V}_{cd}^{(t)} = (\mathcal{V}_{1cd}^{(t)},\ldots,\mathcal{V}_{Rcd})$. Using moment-matching estimation, we need to memorize only moments. This is an advantage over other estimation methods, such as maximum likelihood estimation, which memorizes parameters for all marginal candidates. We set R_x to a value sufficient for moment-matching estimation (Here, $R_x=2$. See the next section for more detail.)

We then update the (negative) expected complete likelihood of the marginal distribution $\bar{\mathcal{M}}$ as follows:

$$\mathcal{I}_{cd}^{(t)}(\bar{\mathcal{M}},\mathcal{V}_{cd}^{(t)}) = \mathcal{I}_{cd}^{(t-1)}(\bar{\mathcal{M}},\mathcal{V}_{cd}^{(t-1)}) - \sum_{n=K_0+K(t-1)+1}^{K_0+Kt}E_Z^{(t)}[z_{nc}]\log p_{cd}\Big(x_{cd};\bar{\phi}_{cd}(\bar{\mathcal{M}},\mathcal{V}_{cd}^{(t)}),\bar{\mathcal{M}}\Big), \tag{14}$$

using the moment-matching estimator $\bar{\phi}_{cd}(\bar{\mathcal{M}},\mathcal{V}_{cd}^{(t)})$. The optimal types of marginals and their parameters are obtained by solving the following optimization problem:

$$M_{cd}^{(t)},\phi_{cd}^{(t)} = \arg\min_{\bar{\mathcal{M}}\in\mathcal{M},\bar{\phi}_{cd}}\Big\{\mathcal{I}_{cd}^{(t)}(\bar{\mathcal{M}},\mathcal{V}_{cd}^{(t)}) + \frac{\beta(\bar{\mathcal{M}})}{2}\mathcal{E}_c^{(t)}\Big\}. \tag{15}$$

Copula Update.

This update step, updating moments of copulas and optimizing types and parameters of copulas, also corresponds to the M step in EMDL. As with IFM, the types and parameters of marginals are fixed in this step. In order to avoid notational confusion, we here explain the update procedure for the Gaussian type of copulas which this paper implements (Section 4.) Other types of copulas, such as t-copulas and Archimedean copulas [17], can be implemented in a similar manner.

[7]To obtain more accurate approximation than (8), we could set a higher value of R_z but this would scarcely have a practical impact.

[8]For a Gaussian distribution, the first and second order moment-matching estimator is consistent with the maximum likelihood estimator. The same holds for the first order moment-matching estimator in an exponential distribution.

For sufficient statistics, we update the moment for copulas as follows:

$$\mathcal{W}_c^{(t)} = \mathcal{W}_c^{(t-1)} + \sum_{n=K_0+K(t-1)+1}^{K_0+Kt} E_Z^{(t)}[z_{nc}]\zeta^{-1}(\boldsymbol{\psi}_{nc}^{(t)})\zeta^{-1}(\boldsymbol{\psi}_{nc}^{(t)})^{\dagger}, \quad (16)$$

where $\zeta^{-1}(\boldsymbol{\psi}_{nc}) = (\zeta^{-1}(\psi_{nc1}), \dots, \zeta^{-1}(\psi_{ncD}))$. ζ^{-1} is the inverse cdf of the standard Gaussian distribution. The superscription $\dagger$ represents the vector/matrix transpose operation.

We then update the (negative) expected complete likelihood of the copula $\bar{\mathcal{Q}}$ as follows:

$$\mathcal{J}_c^{(t)}(\bar{\mathcal{Q}}, \mathcal{W}_c^{(t)}) = \mathcal{J}_c^{(t-1)}(\bar{\mathcal{Q}}, \mathcal{W}_c^{(t-1)}) - \sum_{n=K_0+K(t-1)+1}^{K_0+Kt} E_Z^{(t)}[z_{nc}] \log q_c(\boldsymbol{\psi}_{nc}^{(t)}; \boldsymbol{\xi}_c(\mathcal{W}_c^{(t)}, \bar{\mathcal{Q}}), \bar{\mathcal{Q}}), \quad (17)$$

where $\bar{\mathcal{Q}} \in \mathcal{Q}$. We use the moment-matching estimator $\boldsymbol{\xi}_c(\mathcal{W}_c^{(t)}$ of $\boldsymbol{\xi}_c$ as in the case of the marginal update. The optimal types of copulas and their parameters are obtained by solving the following optimization problem:

$$Q_c^{(t)}, \boldsymbol{\xi}_c^{(t)} = \arg \min_{\bar{\mathcal{Q}} \in \mathcal{Q}, \bar{\boldsymbol{\xi}}_c} \left\{ \mathcal{J}_c^{(t)}(\bar{\mathcal{Q}}, \mathcal{W}_c^{(t)}) + \frac{\beta(\bar{\mathcal{Q}})}{2} \mathcal{E}_c^{(t)} \right\}. \quad (18)$$

In the marginal update and the copula update, we can separately optimize the individual marginal distributions and copulas for individual components, and therefore can address the combinatorial scalability issue (Limitation 2). This is an important advantage in our modeling, in which the joint distributions of individual components are divided into marginal distributions and copulas (5).

Other Updates.

At the end of the t-th update procedure, we update the number of data, the mixture ratio, and the negative incomplete likelihood as follows:

$$N^{(t)} = N^{(t-1)} + K, \quad \alpha_c^{(t)} = \mathcal{U}_{1c}^{(t)}/N^{(t)}, \quad (19)$$

$$\mathcal{L}^{(t)}(C) = \mathcal{L}^{(t-1)}(C) - \sum_{n=K_0+K(t-1)+1}^{K_0+Kt} \log p(\boldsymbol{x}_n; \boldsymbol{\theta}^{(t)}, \boldsymbol{S}^{(t)}, C), \quad (20)$$

where both $\boldsymbol{\theta}^{(t)}$ and $\boldsymbol{S}^{(t)}$ are functions of C. We can then select the number of components which will minimize the value of MDL as follows:

$$C^{(t)} = \arg \min_{1 \le C \le C_{\max}} \left\{ \mathcal{L}^{(t)}(C) + \frac{\beta(\boldsymbol{S}^{(t)}) + C - 1}{2} \log N^{(t)} \right\}, \quad (21)$$

where $C_{\max}$ is the predetermined maximum component size. Through these online update procedures, we optimize the number of components (21), types and parameters of marginal distributions (15), and types and parameters of copulas (18).

3.2.2 *Initialization Procedure*

For the initialization ($t = 0$), we randomly set $E_Z^{(0)}[z_{nc}]$ ($n = 1, \dots, K_0$). Then we execute the same procedure with (11)-(21), where the terms having superscription $(t-1)$ are set to zero.

3.2.3 *Whole Algorithm Description*

The whole process of Online EMDL for MHMC (OMHMC) is described in Algorithms 1 and 2. Let us define $\mathcal{A}$ as

Algorithm 1 Online EMDL for MHMC

input : $\{\mathcal{X}_0, \mathcal{X}_1, \dots, \mathcal{X}_T\}$, $C_{\max}$, $\mathcal{M}$, $\mathcal{Q}$
output : $C^{(T)}$, $\boldsymbol{S}^{(T)}$, $\hat{\boldsymbol{\theta}}^{(T)}$, $\mathcal{A}^{(T)}$

1: **for** $C = 1, \dots, C_{\max}$ **do**
2: $\quad(\boldsymbol{S}^{(0)}, \boldsymbol{\theta}^{(0)}, \mathcal{A}^{(0)}) = \mathit{Initialization}(\mathcal{X}_0, C, \mathcal{M}, \mathcal{Q})$
3: **end for**
4: **for** $t = 1, \dots, T$ **do**
5: $\quad$**for** $C = 1, \dots, C_{\max}$ **do**
6: $\quad\quad(\boldsymbol{S}^{(t)}, \boldsymbol{\theta}^{(t)}, \mathcal{A}^{(t)}) = \mathit{updateModel}(\mathcal{X}_t, C, \mathcal{M}, \mathcal{Q}, \boldsymbol{S}^{(t-1)}, \boldsymbol{\theta}^{(t-1)}, \mathcal{A}^{(t-1)})$
7: $\quad$**end for**
8: $\quad$Select $C^{(t)}$, $\boldsymbol{S}^{(t)}$, $\boldsymbol{\theta}^{(t)}$ by solving (21)
9: **end for**

Algorithm 2 updateModel

input : $\mathcal{X}_t$, C, $\mathcal{M}$, $\mathcal{Q}$, $\boldsymbol{S}^{(t-1)}, \boldsymbol{\theta}^{(t-1)}, \mathcal{A}^{(t-1)}$
output : $\boldsymbol{S}^{(t)}, \boldsymbol{\theta}^{(t)}, \mathcal{A}^{(t)}$

1: Calculate $E_Z^{(t)}[z_nc]$ and update $\mathcal{U}_{rc}^{(t)}$ and $\mathcal{E}_c^{(t)}$ ((10)-(12))
2: **for** $c = 1 \dots C$ **do**
3: $\quad$**for** $d = 1 \dots D$ **do**
4: $\quad\quad$Update $\mathcal{V}_{rcd}^{(t)}$ based on (13)
5: $\quad\quad$**for** $\bar{\mathcal{M}} \in \mathcal{M}$ **do**
6: $\quad\quad\quad$Calculate $\bar{\phi}_{cd}^{(t)}(\bar{\mathcal{M}}, \mathcal{V}_{cd}^{(t)})$ using the moment-matching method for $\bar{\mathcal{M}}$
7: $\quad\quad\quad$Update $\mathcal{I}_{cd}^{(t)}(\bar{\mathcal{M}}, \mathcal{V}_{cd}^{(t)})$ (14)
8: $\quad\quad$**end for**
9: $\quad\quad$Select $M_{cd}^{(t)}$ and $\phi_{cd}^{(t)}$ based on (15)
10: $\quad$**end for**
11: $\quad$Update $\mathcal{W}_c^{(t)}$ based on (16)
12: $\quad$**for** $\bar{\mathcal{Q}} \in \mathcal{W}$ **do**
13: $\quad\quad$Calculate $\boldsymbol{\xi}_c(\mathcal{W}_c^{(t)}, \bar{\mathcal{Q}})$
14: $\quad\quad$Update $\mathcal{J}_c^{(t)}(\bar{\mathcal{Q}}, \mathcal{W}_c^{(t)})$ based on (17)
15: $\quad$**end for**
16: $\quad$Select $Q_c^{(t)}$ and $\boldsymbol{\xi}_c^{(t)}$ based on (18)
17: **end for**

all moments $\mathcal{A} = \mathcal{U}_{rc}, \mathcal{V}_{qcd}, \mathcal{W}_c, \mathcal{I}_{cd}, \mathcal{J}_c, \mathcal{L}, N$ (for all $c = 1, \dots, C, d = 1, \dots, D, r = 1, \dots, R_z, q = 1, \dots, R_x$.)

First, the initialization (steps 1-3 in Algorithm 1) is executed for each component on the basis of the initialization procedure described in Section 3.2.2. For the t-th update with the fixed number of components C (steps 4-9 in Algorithm 1), we update the corresponding model on the basis of Algorithm 2. In Algorithm 2, we first execute the latent variable update (step 1). Then, for each component, marginal updates (step 3-10) and a copula update (steps 11-16) are executed, and we obtain the updated model and parameters $\boldsymbol{S}^{(t)}, \boldsymbol{\theta}^{(t)}, \mathcal{A}^{(t)}$. In step 8 of Algorithm 1, we select the number of components $C^{(t)}$.

3.3 Implemented Model

In this paper, we implement MHMCs in which $\mathcal{M}$ is a set of (Gaussian, exponential, lognormal) and $\mathcal{Q}$ is a set of sparse Gaussian copulas.

Gaussian Marginal.

The Gaussian marginal distribution described as

$$p_{cd}(X_d; \phi_{cd}, M_{cd}) = \frac{1}{\sqrt{2\pi(\sigma_{cd})^2}} \exp\left(\frac{-(X_d - \mu_{cd})^2}{2(\sigma_{cd})^2}\right) \quad (22)$$

has two parameters, mean μ_{cd} and variance $(\sigma_{cd})^2$, and the moment-matching estimator is obtained as follows:

$$\bar{\phi}_{cd}^{(t)} = (\bar{\mu}_{cd}^{(t)}, (\sigma_{cd}^{(t)})^2) = (\mathcal{V}_{1cd}^{(t)}/\mathcal{U}_{1c}^{(t)}, (\mathcal{V}_{2cd}^{(t)} - (\mathcal{V}_{1cd}^{(t)})^2)/\mathcal{U}_{1c}^{(t)}), \tag{23}$$

The parameter dimensionality $\beta(M_{cd})$ is 2.

Exponential Marginal.

The exponential marginal distribution described as

$$p_{cd}(X_d; \phi_{cd}, M_{cd}) = \frac{1}{\lambda_{cd}} \exp(-X_d/\lambda_{cd}) \tag{24}$$

has one scale parameter, λ_{cd}, and the moment-matching estimator is obtained as follows:

$$\bar{\phi}_{cd}^{(t)} = (\bar{\lambda}_{cd}^{(t)}) = (\mathcal{V}_{1cd}^{(t)}/\mathcal{U}_{1c}^{(t)}), \tag{25}$$

The parameter dimensionality $\beta(M_{cd})$ is 1.

Lognormal Marginal.

The lognormal marginal distribution described as

$$p_{cd}(X_d; \phi_{cd}, M_{cd}) = \frac{1}{\sqrt{2\pi(\rho_{cd})^2}X_d} \exp\Big(\frac{-(\log(X_d) - \nu_{cd})^2}{2(\rho_{cd})^2}\Big) \tag{26}$$

has two parameters, log-mean ν_{cd} and log-variance $(\rho_{cd})^2$, and the moment-matching estimator is obtained as follows:

$$\begin{aligned}\bar{\phi}_{cd}^{(t)} &= (\bar{\nu}_{cd}^{(t)}, (\rho_{cd}^{(t)})^2) \qquad (27)\\ &= (\log(\mathcal{V}_{1cd}^{(t)}) - (\sigma_{cd}^{(t)})^2/2, 1 + \log(\mathcal{V}_{2cd}^{(t)}/(\mathcal{V}_{1cd}^{(t)})^2) - 1),\end{aligned}$$

The parameter dimensionality $\beta(M_{cd})$ is 2.

Sparse Gaussian Copula.

The sparse Gaussian copula, having sparse correlation parameter $\boldsymbol{\xi}_c = \boldsymbol{\Sigma}_c(\tau)$, is described as:

$$q_c(\boldsymbol{\psi}_c; \boldsymbol{\xi}_c, Q_c) = \frac{\mathcal{N}(\boldsymbol{\psi}_c; \mathbf{0}, \boldsymbol{\Sigma}_c(\tau_c))}{\prod_{d=1}^{D} \mathcal{N}(\psi_{cd}; 0, 1)}, \tag{28}$$

where $\mathbf{0}$ is a zero vector and $\mathcal{N}(\bullet; *, \star)$ is the multivariate Gaussian distribution of $\bullet$ with mean $*$ and correlation $\star$ (diagonal elements of $\star$ are one). The moment-matching estimator is obtained as follows:

$$[\bar{\boldsymbol{\xi}}_c^{(t)}]_{ij} = [\bar{\boldsymbol{\Sigma}}_c(\tau_c)]_{ij} = \begin{cases} 1 & \text{if } i = j \\ c_{ij}^{(t)} & \text{if } i \neq j \quad |c_{ij}^{(t)}| > \tau_c \\ 0 & \text{if } i \neq j \quad |c_{ij}^{(t)}| \leq \tau_c \end{cases} \tag{29}$$

$$c_{ij} = [\mathcal{W}_c^{(t)}]_{ij}/\sqrt{[\mathcal{W}_c^{(t)}]_{ii}[\mathcal{W}_c^{(t)}]_{jj}}, \tag{30}$$

where $[\bullet]_{ij}$ represents the (i,j)-th element of a matrix $\bullet$. If τ_c is 0, the sparse Gaussian copula will be consistent with the regular Gaussian copula. Candidates for sparse Gaussian copulas can be defined as those having different values of τ. The parameter dimensionality $\beta(Q_c)$ is the number of non-diagonal, non-zero elements divided by two.

4. EXPERIMENTS AND DISCUSSION

We conducted experiments with respect to two basic investigations and two applications. The former consisted of evaluations of 1) model selection performance and 2) scalability and update scheduling. The applications were 3) density estimation and 4) anomaly detection, both of which are important applications for mixture modeling.

For OMHMC, the hyperparameters are set to $C_{\max} = 10$, $\mathcal{M} = \{gaussian, lognormal, exponetial\}$, $\mathcal{Q} = \{\tau = 0, \tau = 0.05, \tau = 0.1, \tau = 0.2\}$, $K_0 = 10, T = 100$ (therefore, K takes different values for different data). All results represent the averages of ten runs (or ten-fold cross validation.) In Tables 1 and 2, the best value for each dataset is highlighted in boldface.

4.1 Model Selection

In this evaluation, we investigated the basic model selection performance of OMHMC, especially focusing on selection of marginal and copulas types. Hereafter, superscription $*$ represents the true model.

Experimental Settings.

We first evaluated marginal selection error and copula selection error, which are calculated[9] as:

$$ERR_M = \frac{1}{C^* D} \sum_{c=1}^{C^*} \sum_{d=1}^{D} (M_{cd}^* \neq M_{cd}^{(T)}), \tag{31}$$

$$ERR_C = \frac{1}{C^* D(D-1)} \sum_{c=1}^{C^*} ||B(\boldsymbol{\xi}_c^*) - B(\boldsymbol{\xi}_c^{(T)})||_F, \tag{32}$$

where $[B(\bullet)]_{ij} = 0$ if $[\bullet]_{ij} = 0$, and $[B(\bullet)]_{ij} = 1$ otherwise. $|\bullet|_F$ is the Frobenius norm of $\bullet$. ERR_C is the ratio of non-diagonal elements of $[B(\boldsymbol{\xi}_c^*)]_{ij} \neq [B(\boldsymbol{\xi}_c^{(T)})]_{ij}$. Note that both ERR_M and ERR_C are zero if $M_{cd}^* = M_{cd}^{(T)}$ and $\boldsymbol{\xi}_c^* = \boldsymbol{\xi}_c^{(T)}$ for all c and d. Since there is no previously-reported algorithm which can optimize marginal and copula types, we only evaluated them for OMHMC.

We also evaluated the Kullback-Leibler (KL) divergence between the true pdf and the estimated pdf, which was approximated as[10]:

$$KL = \sum_{n=1}^{N_{KL}} p(\boldsymbol{x}_n^{KL}; \boldsymbol{\theta}^*, \boldsymbol{S}^*, C^*) \log \frac{p(\boldsymbol{x}_n^{KL}; \boldsymbol{\theta}^*, \boldsymbol{S}^*, C^*)}{p(\boldsymbol{x}_n^{KL}; \boldsymbol{\theta}^{(T)}, \boldsymbol{S}^{(T)}, C^{(T)})},$$

where $\boldsymbol{x}_n^{KL}$ are samples for the KL calculation. We compared OMHMC with a state-of-the-art variational Dirichlet process Gaussian mixture model[11] [12] (VDPGMM).

We artificially generated the true model on the basis of Algorithm 3. Here we only explain the results for $C^* = 5$ because of space limitations (in fact, results show that the value of C^* scarcely affected basic behaviors.) In step 1, parameters for marginal distributions were sampled from $\mu_{cd}^* \sim [-5, 5]$, $(\sigma_{cd}^*)^2 \sim [0.5, 1.5]$, $\lambda_{cd}^* \sim (0, 1]$, $\nu_{cd}^* \sim (0, 1.5]$ and $(\rho_{cd}^*)^2 \sim [0.5, 1.0]$. In step 2, τ_c^* was sampled from $[0, 0.5]$ and $\boldsymbol{\xi}_c^*$ were generated using the "gallery" function in MATLAB. In step 3, α_c^* was sampled from $(0, 1]$.

Results and Discussion.

Fig. 3 presents ERR_M and ERR_C over the number of data and the data dimensionality. The marginal selection

[9]We had to identify the correspondence between the estimated components and the true components. For this purpose, we calculated Kullback-Leibler divergences between all component pairs and determined the correspondence which minimizes the sum of KL divergence.

[10]We set $N_{KL} = 10000$ in our experiments.

[11]We used the implementation of Kenichi Kurihara at `http://sites.google.com/site/kenichikurihara/`, and also used the default hyperparameter values in the software.

Algorithm 3 Data Generation Recipe

input : C^* and D

1: Randomly select M^*_{cd} from (Gaussian, lognormal, exponential), and set their parameters ϕ^*_{cd}.

2: Randomly set τ^*_c for Q^*_c and generate correlation matrices $\boldsymbol{\xi}^*_c$. The non-diagonal elements of $\boldsymbol{\xi}^*_c$ smaller than τ^*_c are set to be zero.

3: Randomly set α^*_c. Normalize α^*_c so that $\sum_{c=1}^{C^*} \alpha^*_c = 1$.

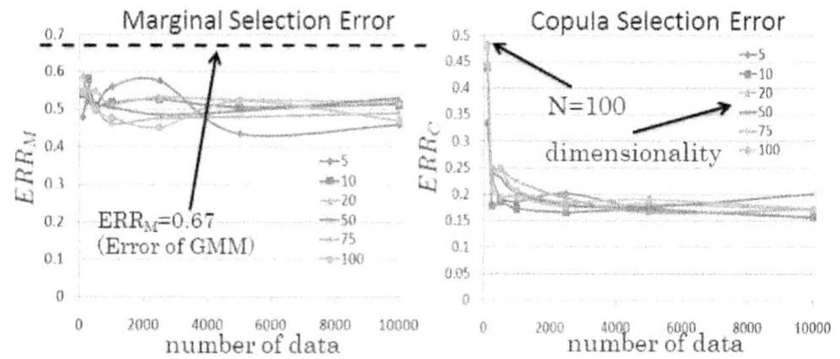

Figure 3: Marginal selection error (left) and copula selection error (right) for OMHMC.

errors are distributed around $ERR_M = 0.5$ and are better than the marginal error of the usual Gaussian mixture model[12] (GMM). Because there are parameter ranges for which it is difficult (or unnecessary) to distinguish (Gaussian, lognormal, exponential) distributions, ERR_M did not decrease over N (in the other settings, we observed that ERR_M decreased over N.) The copula selection errors EMM_C converged over N around $EMM_C = 0.2$, and OMHMC succeeded in its sparse dependency discovery. Since the correlation between different types of marginal distributions is no longer "linear," this results indicate that OMHMC can discover nonlinear dependency structures among variables (further, different components can have different nonlinearities[13].) With respect to both ERR_M and ERR_C, the data dimensionality ($D = 5 \sim 100$) scarcely affected the model selection performance, while it will degrade in higher dimensional spaces due to the curse of dimensionality.

Fig. 4 presents a comparison of the KL between OMHMC and VDPGMM. The KL of OMHMC (left) decreased over N, while the KL of VDPGMM did not markedly decrease. At high dimensionality ($D = 50, 75, 100$), OMHMC greatly outperformed VDPGMM.

4.2 Scalability and Update Scheduling

OMHMC has two important predetermined parameters: initial data size K_0 and the number of updates T (or size of mini-batch data $\mathcal{X}_t$, i.e., $K = (N^{(T)} - K_0)/T$.) These update-scheduling parameters determine the scalability and stability of OMHMC.

To investigate the behavior of OMHMC over K_0 and T, we evaluated: 1) CPU time (scalability), and 2) MDL value per data item, $\mathcal{L}^{(T)}/N^{(T)}$ (convergence and stability). Here, we employed the KDDCUP99 network intrusion dataset, which has 976158 data in total (see Section 4.4 for more detail.)

[12]Since we randomly selected M^*_{cd} from (Gaussian, exponential, lognormal), ERR_M of GMM is 0.67.

[13]For example, the correlation between Gaussian and lognormal distributions has different nonlinearity from that of the correlation between two lognormal distributions.

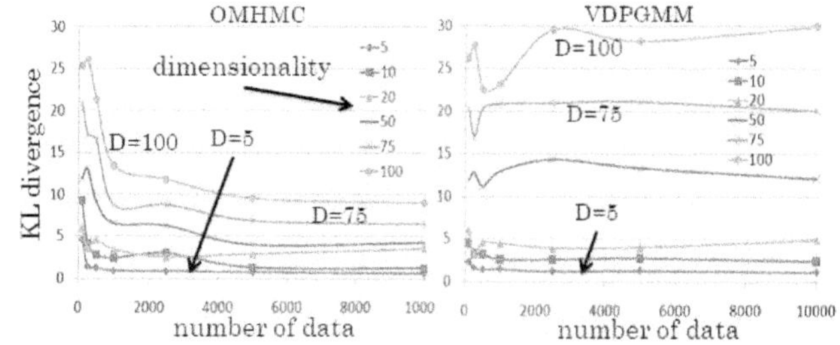

Figure 4: KL divergences between the true model and the estimated model (left: OMHMC, right: VDPGMM).

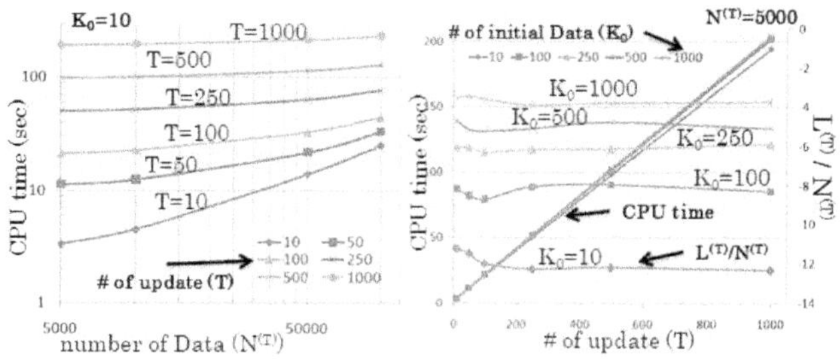

Figure 5: CPU time and $\mathcal{L}^{(T)}/N^{(T)}$. The left figure ($K_0 = 10$) shows CPU time over $N^{(T)}$ (double log plot). The right figure ($N^{(T)} = 5000$) shows CPU time (left axis) and $\mathcal{L}^{(T)}/N^{(T)}$ (right axis) over T.

First, we observed that the impact of $N^{(T)}$ on CPU time was only linear (Fig. 5, left.) In fact, the difference between the cases of $N^{(T)} = 5000$ and $N^{(T)} = 100000$ is only about 20 sec, with little relation to T. Second, with $T = 100$, $\mathcal{L}^{(T)}/N^{(T)}$ nearly converged, with little relation to K_0 (Fig. 5, right.) On the other hand, CPU time grew linearly with T. We have obtained the significant insight that the choice of a relatively small value of T has a great advantage in scalability, with little performance degradation. We further observed that the smaller value of K_0 showed better performance w.r.t. $\mathcal{L}^{(T)}/N^{(T)}$. All components were initialized to closely similar values of moments and parameters when K_0 was large, and they had little difference through the updates in OMHMC. On the other hand, a small value of K_0 generated differences among components. In summary, both T and K_0 will preferrably be set to small values to obtain both good scalability and performance. The CPU time for all data ($N^{(T)} = 976158, K_0 = 10, T = 100$) was 242.6 sec in total.

4.3 Density Estimation

Density estimation is the most basic and significant application of mixture modeling, and a number of unsupervised methods, such as topic modeling [15], image segmentation [25], and speech recognition [20], are based on it.

We compared OMHMC with VDPGMM on the basis of the predictive likelihood (likelihood of test data) per data item. We used the seven datasets from the UCI data repository [8] that are shown in Table 1.

As Table 1 shows, for the well-known iris data, VDPGMM outperformed OMHMC, partly because iris data can be well modeled by a Gaussian mixture (therefore OMHMC is likely

Table 1: Predictive likelihood per data.

Data[14]	N	D	OMHMC	VDPGMM
iris	150	4	-4.60±3.41	**-2.00 ± 0.99**
FF	466	11	**-21.51 ± 2.90**	-24.78 ± 0.23
yeast	1255	8	**31.77 ± 3.49**	2.081 ± 2.91
YQ	5848	11	**-3.76 ± 0.66**	-5.68 ± 1.73
CT	61236	16	**16.16 ± 0.90**	15.50 ± 0.86
CM	68040	9	-7.51 ± 0.62	**-7.45 ± 0.64**
YPMSD	463811	12	**13.59 ± 0.09**	**13.59 ± 0.12**

to be overfitted), and partly because $N = 150$ is too small for the online learning algorithm. With increasing N, OMHMC outperformed VDPGMM, except for the Color Moment data. This result indicates that the "Gaussian assumption" is not satisfied with real data, which our modeling with heterogeneous marginal distributions and copulas fit well. Since VDPGMM also has strong expressiveness, the density estimation performance of the two methods was competitive for large scale data (YPMSD).

4.4 Anomaly Detection

Anomaly detection is also a significant application. On the basis of the assumption that the number of anomaly data is much smaller than that of normal data, mixture-model-based anomaly detectors [27] are used to detect anomalous data having low log-likelihood (or high negative log-likelihood.) We employed datasets from the Rätsch's benchmark repository [19] (Dataset 1) and the KDDCUP99 network intrusion dataset[15]. The sample size and data dimensionality of each dataset are shown in Table 2.

For each dataset in Dataset 1, to satisfy the small sample size assumption for anomaly data, we randomly selected 10% of the anomaly data in each run. Further, for KDDCUP99, we generated normal (normal access) and anomaly (intrusion success) data on the basis of generation recipe in [27]. Briefly, we chose (duration, src_bytes, dst_bytes) attributes and picked up all 972781 normal samples and 3377 intrusions whose logged_in attributes were positive. Then, for each run, we randomly selected 50% of the samples.

We compared OMHMC-based anomaly detection with state-of-the-art anomaly detectors: VDPGMM [12], i-forest [14], and one-class support vector machine (OSVM) [23] with a Gaussian kernel[16] and local outlier factor (LOF) [2]. For a comparison with another mixture modeling method, we applied VDPGMM on the basis of "log-likelihood" scoring, as with OMHMC, while the original VDPGMM has not been applied to anomaly detection. The performance was measured using Area Under the ROC Curve (AUC), which is widely used in the domain of anomaly detection.

Table 2 shows a comparison of AUCs. OMHMC, VDPGMM, and i-forest worked in large scale datasets where OSVM and LOF were not available because of computational time/memory issues. OMHMC and i-forest outperformed the others, and their performance was similar (both of them took first place for four datasets.) Since estimation performance increases with an increased number of data, OMHMC has tended to perform well with comparatively large datasets. OSVM and LOF were sensitive to parameter changes, and we do not have systematic ways to choose their parameters (cross validation is not available in anomaly detection.)

[14] FF:forest fire, WQ: wine quality, CT: Cooc Texture, CM: Color Moment

[15] `http://www.sigkdd.org/kddcup/index.php`

[16] We use the libsvm [3] for implementation of OSVM.

5. SUMMARY

This paper has addressed the data mining issue for mixture modeling with complicated data having heterogeneous marginal distributions and dependencies among variables. The proposed OMHMC provides a powerful, scalable model selection tool that can execute fully-automatic model selection of types of marginal distributions and copulas as well as parameter estimations. Our experimental results confirm the scalability and performance of OMHMC in application to density estimation and anomaly detection.

We have two challenges for future study. First, as seen in Fig. 2, a nonstationary extension of OMHMC remains as an open problem. It should be addressed by incorporating a time-discounting concept into OMHMC. Second, mixture models have been employed for classification/regression problems (e.g., a mixture of experts [11]), and OMHMC might be usable for help in their model selections.

6. NOTATION

We summarize here the notations used in this paper.

c : component number
n : data number
d : dimension number
r : the order of the indexed moment
t : update number
$*$: true model
N : data size
D : data dimensionality
X and $\boldsymbol{x}_n$: random variable in $\mathbb{R}^D$ and its observation
$\boldsymbol{z}_n$: latent variable of $\boldsymbol{x}_n$
p : pdf of whole model
p_c : pdf of component
p_{cd} : pdf of marginal
q_c : pdf of copula
$\mathcal{M}$: possible candidates of marginal distribionts
$\mathcal{Q}$: possible candidates of copulas
C : # of component
M_{cd} : type of marginal distribution
Q_c : type of copula
$\boldsymbol{\alpha}$: mixture ratio
ϕ_{cd} : parameter of M_{cd}
ψ_{cd} : cdf. corresponding to $p_{cd}(\bullet; \phi_{cd}, M_{cd})$
$\boldsymbol{\xi}_c$: parameter of Q_c
S_c : $(M_{c1}, \ldots, M_{cD}, Q_c)$
$\boldsymbol{\theta}$: $(\boldsymbol{\alpha}, \boldsymbol{\phi}_{11}, \ldots, \boldsymbol{\phi}_{CD}, \boldsymbol{\xi}_1, \ldots, \boldsymbol{\xi}_C))$
$\boldsymbol{\theta}_c$: $(\alpha_c, \boldsymbol{\phi}_c, \boldsymbol{\xi}_C)$ and $\boldsymbol{\phi}_c = (\phi_{c1}, \ldots, \phi_{cD})$
$\mathcal{U}_{rc}$: the r-th order momnent of latent variables
$\mathcal{V}_{rcd}$: the r-th order moment of observed variables
$\mathcal{V}_{cd}$: $(\mathcal{V}_{1cd}, \ldots, \mathcal{V}_{R_x cd})$
$\mathcal{W}_c$: moment for copula
T : the number of update
K_0 : initial data size
K : mini-batch data size
$\beta(\bullet)$: dimensionality of $\bullet$
$E_Z[\bullet]$: expectation of $\bullet$ w.r.t. latent variables' posterior
$[\bullet]_{ij}$: the (i,j)-th element of $\bullet$

Table 2: AUC values (N/A represents "not available" because of computational time/memory issues.)

Dataset	# of normal / total anomalies	dim D	OMHMC	VDPGMM	i-forest	OSVM	LOF $k=5$	LOF $k=30$
bcancer	186/77	9	0.61 ± 0.09	$\mathbf{0.70 \pm 0.10}$	$\mathbf{0.70 \pm 0.07}$	0.61 ± 0.05	0.53 ± 0.08	0.67 ± 0.01
heart	150/120	13	0.78 ± 0.07	0.73 ± 0.05	$\mathbf{0.83 \pm 0.05}$	0.56 ± 0.03	0.47 ± 0.10	0.76 ± 0.06
diabetis	500/268	8	$\mathbf{0.73 \pm 0.03}$	0.68 ± 0.04	0.72 ± 0.04	0.67 ± 0.05	0.60 ± 0.05	0.67 ± 0.05
twonorm	3697/3703	20	$\mathbf{0.87 \pm 0.01}$	0.73 ± 0.01	0.84 ± 0.01	0.57 ± 0.01	0.56 ± 0.02	0.62 ± 0.02
ringnorm	3736/3664	20	$\mathbf{1.00 \pm 0.00}$	$\mathbf{1.00 \pm 0.00}$	$\mathbf{1.00 \pm 0.00}$	0.80 ± 0.00	$\mathbf{1.00 \pm 0.00}$	$\mathbf{1.00 \pm 0.00}$
shuttle	45586/3511	9	0.99 ± 0.00	0.99 ± 0.00	$\mathbf{1.00 \pm 0.01}$	0.78 ± 0.01	N/A	N/A
KDDCUP	972781/3377	3	$\mathbf{0.89 \pm 0.02}$	0.87 ± 0.04	0.85 ± 0.00	N/A	N/A	N/A

7. REFERENCES

[1] H. Akaike. Information theory and an extension of the maximum likelihood principle. In B. N. Petrov and F. Caski, editors, *Proceedings of the 2nd International Symposium on Information Theory*, pages 267–281, 1973.

[2] M. M. Breunig, H. P. Kriegel, R. T. Ng, and J. Sander. LOF: identifying density-based local outliers. *Sigmod Record*, 29(2):93–104, 2000.

[3] C.-C. Chang and C.-J. Lin. LIBSVM: a library for support vector machines. `http://www.csie.ntu.edu.tw/~cjlin/libsvm`, 2001.

[4] A. Corduneanu and C. Bishop. Variational bayesian model selection for mixture distributions. In *Proceedings of the Eighth International Workshop on Artificial Intelligence and Statistics*, 2001.

[5] A. P. Dempster, N. M. Laird, and D. B. Rubin. Maximum likelihood from imcomplete data via the em algorithm. *Journal of the Royal Statistical Society*, B39(1):1–38, 1977.

[6] P. Diehr, D. Yanez, A. S. Ash, M. Hornbrook, , and D. Y. Lin. Methods for analyzing health care utilization and costs. *Annual Review of Public Health*, 20:125–144, 1999.

[7] G. Elidan. Copula bayesian networks. In *Advances in Neural Information Processing Systems 23*, pages 559–567, 2010.

[8] A. Frank and A. Asuncion. UCI machine learning repository. `http://archive.ics.uci.edu/ml`, 2010. University of California, Irvine, School of Information and Computer Sciences.

[9] R. Fujimaki, S. Morinaga, M. Momma, K. Aoki, and T. Nakata. Linear time model selection for mixture of heterogeneous components. In *Proceedings of the 1st Asian Conference on Machine Learning*, pages 82–97, 2009.

[10] H. Joe, editor. *Multivariate Models and Dependence Concepts*. Chapman & Hall, 1997.

[11] M. I. Jordan and R. A. Jacobs. Hierarchical mixtures of experts and the EM algorithm. *Neural Computation*, 6:181–214, 1994.

[12] K. Kurihara, M. Welling, and N. Vlassis. Accelerated variational dirichlet mixture models. In *Advances in Neural Information Processing Systems 19*, pages 761–768. MIT Press, 2006.

[13] D. X. Li. On default correlation: A copula function approach. *Journal of Fixed Income*, 9(4):43–54, 1999.

[14] F. T. Liu, K. M. Ting, and Z. H. Zhou. Isolation Forest. In *Proceedings of the 2008 Eighth IEEE International Conference on Data Mining*, pages 413–422, 2008.

[15] S. Morinaga and K. Yamanishi. Tracking dynamics of topic trends using a finite mixture model. In *Proceedings of the tenth ACM SIGKDD international conference on Knowledge discovery and data mining*, pages 811–816. ACM Press, 2004.

[16] R. Neal and G. E. Hinton. A view of the EM algorithm that justifies incremental, sparse, and other variants. In *Learning in Graphical Models*, pages 355–368, 1998.

[17] R. B. Nelsen, editor. *An Introduction to Copulas*. Springer Series in Statistics, 2006.

[18] C. E. Rasmussen. The infinite gaussian mixture model. In *In Advances in Neural Information Processing Systems 12*, pages 554–560, 2000.

[19] G. Rätsch, T. Onoda, and K. Müller. Soft margins for AdaBoost. *Machine Learning*, 42(3):287–320, 2001.

[20] D. A. Reynolds, T. F. Quatieri, and R. B. Dunn. Speaker verification using adapted gaussian mixture models. *Digital Signal Processing*, 10(1):19–41, 2000.

[21] J. Rissanen. Modeling by shortest data description. *Automatica*, 14:465–471, 1978.

[22] M. Sato. On-line model selection based on the variational bayes. *Neural Computation*, 13:1649–1681, 2001.

[23] B. Scholkopf, J. C. Platt, J. Shawe-Taylor, A. J. Smola, and R. C. Williamson. Estimating the support of a high-dimensional distribution. *Neural computation*, 13(7):1443–1471, 2001.

[24] A. Sklar. Fonctions de repartition a n dimensions et leurs marges. Technical report, Publications de l'Institut de Statistique de L'Universite de Paris, 1959.

[25] C. Stauffer and W. E. L. Grimson. Adaptive background mixture models for real-time tracking. In *IEEE Computer Society Conference on Computer Vision and Pattern Recognition*, pages 246–252, 1999.

[26] A. Wilson and Z. Ghahramani. Copula processes. In *Advances in Neural Information Processing Systems 23*, pages 2460–2468, 2010.

[27] K. Yamanishi, J. ichi Takeuchi, G. Williams, and P. Milne. On-line unsupervised outlier detection using finite mixtures with discounting learning algorithms. *Data Mining and Knowledge Discovery*, 8(3):275–300, 2004.

[28] K. Yamanishi and Y. Maruyama. Dynamic model selection with its applications to novelty detection. *IEEE Transactions on Information Theory*, 53:2180–2189, 2007.

Dual Active Feature and Sample Selection for Graph Classification

Xiangnan Kong
University of Illinois at Chicago
Chicago, IL, USA
xkong4@uic.edu

Wei Fan
IBM T. J. Watson Research
Hawthorn, NY, USA
weifan@us.ibm.com

Philip S. Yu
University of Illinois at Chicago
Chicago, IL, USA
psyu@cs.uic.edu

ABSTRACT

Graph classification has become an important and active research topic in the last decade. Current research on graph classification focuses on mining discriminative subgraph features under supervised settings. The basic assumption is that a large number of labeled graphs are available. However, labeling graph data is quite expensive and time consuming for many real-world applications. In order to reduce the labeling cost for graph data, we address the problem of how to select the most important graph to query for the label. This problem is challenging and different from conventional active learning problems because there is no predefined feature vector. Moreover, the subgraph enumeration problem is NP-hard. The active sample selection problem and the feature selection problem are *correlated* for graph data. Before we can solve the active sample selection problem, we need to find a set of optimal subgraph features. To address this challenge, we demonstrate how one can simultaneously estimate the usefulness of a query graph and a set of subgraph features. The idea is to maximize the dependency between subgraph features and graph labels using an active learning framework. We propose a branch-and-bound algorithm to search for the optimal query graph and optimal features simultaneously. Empirical studies on nine real-world tasks demonstrate that the proposed method can obtain better accuracy on graph data than alternative approaches.

Categories and Subject Descriptors

H.2.8 [**Database Management**]: Database Applications-Data Mining

General Terms

Algorithm, Experimentation, Performance

Keywords

Active Learning, Feature Selection, Graph Classification, Subgraph Pattern, Data Mining, Feature Construction

1. INTRODUCTION

Graphs arise naturally in a wide range of application domains. Examples include chemical compounds, XML documents and program flows. There is a great need for building models to classify graph objects. For example, in chemoinformatics, researchers would like to predict the anticancer activities of chemical compounds in order to find new drugs for cancer or chronic diseases [26, 17]; in software engineering, researchers are interested in studying how to automatically identify bugs in program flows [5]. Motivated by these challenges, *graph classification* has received considerable attention in the last decade.

Graph classification has been studied extensively in the literature [18, 24, 3]. Conventional approaches focus on mining discriminative subgraph features [28] under supervised settings. They assume explicitly or implicitly that a large number of labeled graphs are available. However, in many real-world applications, labeling graph data can be very expensive and time consuming. For example, in molecular medicine, it is very expensive to test the anticancer activity by preclinical studies and clinical trials; in software engineering, human experts have to examine a program flow carefully in order to find software bugs. The labeling cost for graph data can be significantly reduced by training a model that can select the most important graph to query for the label. This setting is also known as *active learning* or *active query selection*. It aims to exploit unlabeled data effectively by selecting important examples to query for labels. Thus, active learning approaches can usually achieve performance comparable to supervised approaches, while using less labeled data. Active learning has been shown to be useful in many real-world applications [25, 29].

Formally, the active learning problem for graph data corresponds to learning a model to select important graphs to obtain class labels. Active learning is particularly challenging in graph data. Conventional active learning approaches estimate the importance of unlabeled examples, and assume that all useful features are given. However, in graph data the useful features are not available. Thus, additional steps of subgraph feature mining and selection are required to estimate the usefulness of subgraphs. What makes this problem even more interesting and challenging is that subgraph enumeration and graph isomorphism testing problems are NP-

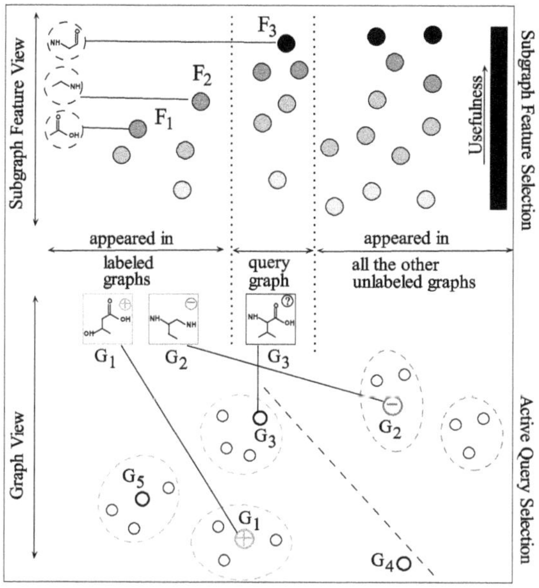

Figure 1: An example of dual active feature and sample selection in graph data.

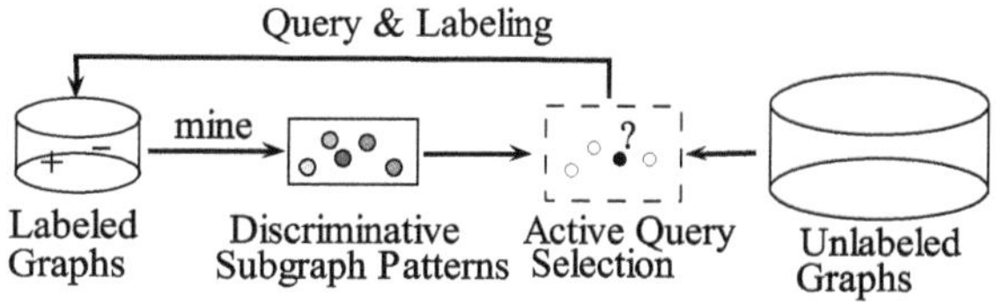

Figure 2: Two-stage active learning in graph data

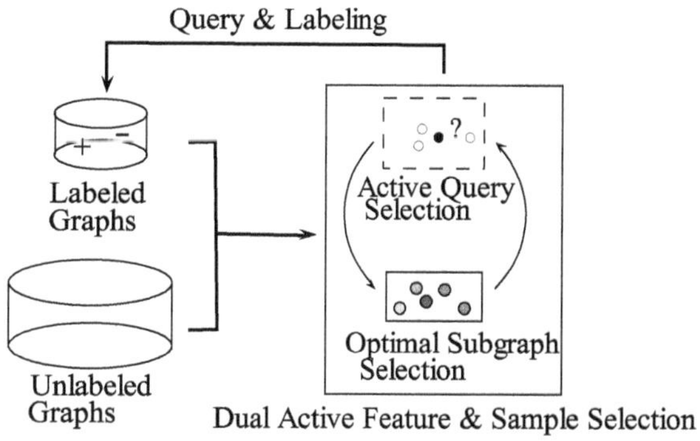

Figure 3: Dual active feature and sample selection

complete. Thus, it is impossible to enumerate all subgraph features and adopt existing approaches for active learning.

In active learning for graph data, the active query selection problem and the subgraph feature selection problem are closely related to each other. The reasons are summarized as follows:

- In active query selection, we need to estimate the importance of each unlabeled graph in order to select the most important graph to query for the label. However, before the most important graph can be determined, we need to find a set of useful subgraph features. Graph data are not directly represented in a meaningful feature space. The performance of the active sample selection directly depends on the quality of the subgraph features mined from the graph dataset. For example, in Figure 1, G_3 is the most important graph which we want to query for the label. G_3 is close to the class boundary like graph G_4. Moreover, G_3 is representative of a cluster of unlabeled graphs. However, the informativeness and representativeness of a graph object depends on which feature set is used. The better the feature set we use, the better we will be able to estimate the importance of the query graphs.

- In the subgraph feature selection problem, we also need to select a set of important subgraph features for the graph classification task. Conventional feature selection approaches for graph data focus on supervised settings [26, 17]. The feature evaluation strategies strictly follow the assumption that a large number of labeled graphs are available. However, in the active learning settings, we can only afford to query a small number of unlabeled graphs and obtain their labels. The performance of the feature selection process depends strongly on the quality of the queried graphs in the active sample selection process. For example, in Figure 1, suppose we are given two labeled graphs (G_1 and G_2). Only a small number of the useful subgraph features (F_1 and F_2) appear in the labeled graphs. If we query the graph G_3 that is both representative and informative, we are more likely to find new features like F_3. The process of query selection can assist the process of feature selection in finding useful subgraph features. In other words, the better the query graph we select, the more effectively we can discover the useful subgraph features.

Thus, the active sample selection problem and the subgraph feature selection problem are correlated and should be considered simultaneously. The combined problem is referred to as *dual active feature and sample selection for graph classification*. This problem can be summarized as follows: in order to minimize the labeling cost in graph classification, we need to determine how one can actively select the most important graph to obtain the class label.

To the best of our knowledge, the dual active feature and sample selection for graph classification has not been studied in this context. A straightforward solution to this problem would be the two-stage active learning framework as shown in Figure 2. In this framework, the feature selection problem and the active sample selection problem are considered in two separate steps. In the first step, we select a set of subgraph features based upon the labeled graphs. In the second step, we estimate the importance of query graphs based upon the feature set selected in the first step. Obviously, only the subgraph features that appear in the label graphs can be found in the first step. The useful features that only appear in the unlabeled graphs can not be found. Thus, when we only use the features found in the first step, the estimation of the importance of query graphs will not be accurate.

In this paper we introduce a novel framework for the above problems by exploiting useful subgraph features and optimal query graphs simultaneously. Our framework is illustrated

Table 1: Important Notations.

Symbol	Definition
$\mathcal{D} = \{G_1, \cdots, G_n\}$	given graph dataset, G_i denotes the i-th graph in the dataset.
n_ℓ, n_a and n_u	number of labeled graphs, unlabeled graphs including and excluding the query graph in $\mathcal{D}$
$l = \{1, \cdots, n_\ell\}$	index set for labeled graphs in $\mathcal{D}$
s and u	index of selected graph and the index set of the other unlabeled candidate graphs in $\mathcal{D}$.
$a = \{n_\ell + 1, \cdots, n\}$	index set for all unlabeled graphs in the pool including the selected graph. $a = \{s\} \cup u$
$\mathbf{y} = [y_1, \cdots, y_n]^\top$	class label vector for graphs in $\mathcal{D}$, $y_i \in \{+1, -1, 0\}$
$\mathcal{S} = \{g_1, \cdots, g_m\}$	set of all subgraph patterns in the graph dataset $\mathcal{D}$.
$\mathbf{x}_i = [x_i^1, \cdots, x_i^m]^\top$	binary vector for G_i using subgraph features in $\mathcal{S}$, $x_i^k \in \{0, 1\}$ and $x_i^k = 1$ iff $g_k \subseteq G_i$
$\mathbf{f}_i = [f_i^1, \cdots, f_i^n]^\top$	binary vector for subgraph pattern g_i in the $\mathcal{D}$
$X = [X_{ij}]_{(m \times n)}$	matrix of all binary feature vectors in the dataset, $X = [\mathbf{x}_1, \cdots, \mathbf{x}_n] = [\mathbf{f}_1, \cdots, \mathbf{f}_m]^\top$
$\mathcal{T}$	set of selected subgraph patterns, $\mathcal{T} \subset \mathcal{S}$
$\mathbf{K}(\mathcal{T}) = [K_{ij}]_{(n \times n)}$	kernel matrix of all graphs using the selected subgraph features $\mathcal{T}$
$\mathbf{L}(y_s, \mathbf{y}_\ell) = [L_{ij}]_{(n \times n)}$	label kernel matrix of all graphs based upon the class labels
$\mathbf{H} = [H_{ij}]_{(n \times n)}$	centering matrix, $H_{ij} = \delta_{ij} - n^{-1}$. ($\delta_{ij} = 1$ iff $i = j$, otherwise 0)
$D_\mathcal{T}$	an $m \times m$ diagonal matrix indicating which features are selected from $\mathcal{S}$ into $\mathcal{T}$
Π_ℓ, Π_u and Π_s	mapping matrices, $\Pi_\ell \in \{0,1\}^{(n_\ell \times n)}$, $\Pi_s \in \{0,1\}^{(1 \times n)}$, $\Pi_u \in \{0,1\}^{(n_u \times n)}$ and $[\Pi_\ell^\top, \Pi_s^\top, \Pi_u^\top] = \mathbf{I}_n$

in Figure 3. Unlike the two-stage active learning method, the proposed approach, called gActive, can estimate the usefulness of a query graph and effectiveness of subgraph features simultaneously. The gActive method maximizes the dependence between subgraph features and graph labels based upon an active learning framework. Furthermore, we propose a branch-and-bound algorithm to search for optimal features efficiently by pruning the subgraph search space. Empirical studies on real-world tasks demonstrate that the proposed method can obtain promising results using fewer labeled graphs than alternative approaches.

2. PROBLEM FORMULATION

Suppose we are given a graph dataset $\mathcal{D} = \{G_1, \cdots, G_n\}$ that consists of n graphs. $\mathbf{y} = [y_1, \cdots, y_n]^\top$ denotes the vector of labels, where $y_i \in \{+1, 0, -1\}$ is the label of G_i. $y_i = 0$ implies that G_i is unlabeled. Active learning in graph data is the task of selecting one graph G_s from the pool of unlabeled graphs to query for its label. For convenience, we partition the graph dataset into three parts: the labeled graphs $\mathcal{D}_\ell$, the query graph G_s, and the remaining unlabeled graphs D_u. $\mathcal{D}_a = \mathcal{D}_u \cup \{G_s\}$ denotes all unlabeled graphs. The vector $\mathbf{y}$ is partitioned as follows:

$$\mathbf{y} = \begin{bmatrix} \mathbf{y}_\ell \\ y_s \\ \mathbf{y}_u \end{bmatrix} = \begin{bmatrix} \mathbf{y}_\ell \\ \mathbf{y}_a \end{bmatrix} \quad \text{and} \quad \mathbf{y}_a = \begin{bmatrix} y_s \\ \mathbf{y}_u \end{bmatrix}$$

where $\mathbf{y}_\ell$, y_s and $\mathbf{y}_u$ represent the class labels assigned to the graphs in $\mathcal{D}_\ell$, $\{G_s\}$ and $\mathcal{D}_u$ respectively. We denote the number of labeled graphs by n_ℓ. n_u is the number of unlabeled graphs excluding the query graph, and n_a is the number of all unlabeled graphs. $n_a = n_u + 1$. We assume the first n_ℓ graphs in the dataset $\mathcal{D}$ are labeled.

Definition 1 (Graph). *A graph is represented as $G = (\mathcal{V}, E, \mathcal{L}, l)$. $\mathcal{V}$ is the set of vertices, and $\mathcal{V} = \{v_1, \cdots, v_{n_v}\}$. $E \subseteq \mathcal{V} \times \mathcal{V}$ is the set of edges. $\mathcal{L}$ is the set of labels for the vertices and edges. $l : \mathcal{V} \cup E \to \mathcal{L}$ is the function assigning labels to the vertices and edges.*

We focus on using subgraph patterns to define the feature space of graph classification. It is assumed that a graph object G_i is represented as a binary vector $\mathbf{x}_i = [x_i^1, \cdots, x_i^m]^\top$ associated with a set of subgraph patterns $\{g_1, \cdots, g_m\}$. Here, $x_i^k \in \{0, 1\}$ is the binary feature of G_i corresponding to the subgraph pattern g_k. $x_i^k = 1$ iff g_k is a subgraph of G_i. Now suppose the full set of subgraph features in the graph dataset $\mathcal{D}$ is $\mathcal{S} = \{g_1, \cdots, g_m\}$, which we use to predict the class labels of the graph objects. The full feature set $\mathcal{S}$ is very large. Only a subset of the features ($\mathcal{T} \subseteq \mathcal{S}$) is relevant to the graph classification task. Let X denote the matrix consisting of the binary feature vectors based on $\mathcal{S}$ to represent the graph dataset $\mathcal{D}$. $X = [\mathbf{x}_1, \mathbf{x}_2, \cdots, \mathbf{x}_n] = [\mathbf{f}_1, \mathbf{f}_2, \cdots, \mathbf{f}_m]^\top \in \{0, 1\}^{m \times n}$, where $X = [X_{ij}]_{m \times n}$, $X_{ij} = 1$ iff $g_i \subseteq G_j$. We briefly summarize the notations used in this paper in Table 1.

Definition 2 (Subgraph). *Let $G' = (\mathcal{V}', E', \mathcal{L}', l')$ and $G = (\mathcal{V}, E, \mathcal{L}, l)$ be graphs. G' is a subgraph of G ($G' \subseteq G$) iff there exists an injective function $\psi : \mathcal{V}' \to \mathcal{V}$. $\forall v \in \mathcal{V}'$, $l'(v) = l(\psi(v))$. $\forall (u, v) \in E'$, $(\psi(u), \psi(v)) \in E$ and $l'(u, v) = l(\psi(u), \psi(v))$. If G' is a subgraph of G, then G is a supergraph of G'.*

The key issue of *dual active feature and sample selection* is to find the most important query graph and a set of optimal subgraph patterns simultaneously. The problems studied in this paper are as follows:

1) How can one estimate the importance of a query graph among unlabeled graphs?
2) How can one estimate the usefulness of a set of features for the graph classification task?
3) How can one determine the optimal subgraph features within a reasonable amount of time, and avoid the exhaustive enumeration of all features?

2.1 Optimization Framework

We propose an optimization framework to select the optimal query graph by maximizing the minimum score of an evaluation function.

$$G_s^* = \arg\max_{G_s \in \mathcal{D}_a} \min_{y_s \in \{\pm 1\}} \mathcal{E}(G_s, y_s, \mathcal{D}, \mathbf{y}_\ell) \tag{1}$$

where $\mathcal{D}_a$ denotes the pool of all unlabeled graphs. $\mathcal{E}$ denotes the evaluation function for querying a graph G_s in $\mathcal{D}_a$. Because the label of the selected graph G_s can be either 1 or -1, we need to consider both alternatives and select the worst case to maximize. In this max-min view of active learning, it guarantees that the selected graph G_s will lead to a large value for the function $\mathcal{E}(G_s, y_s, \mathcal{D}, \mathbf{y}_\ell)$.

Note that in graph data the useful features are not given. We need to make use of the label information to select a subset of optimal subgraph features. If we know the class label

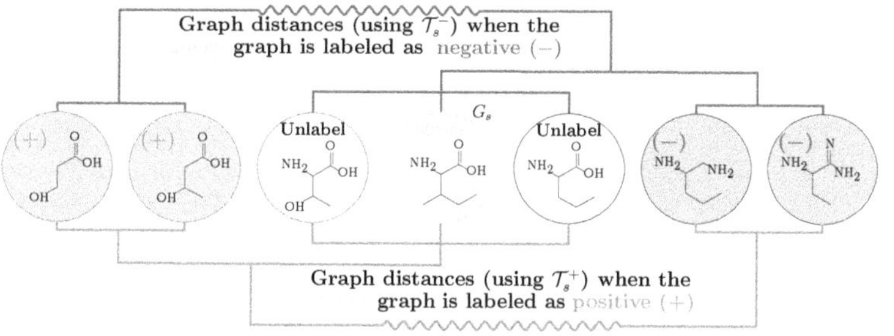

Figure 4: Graph distances using two optimal feature sets ($\mathcal{T}_s^+$ and $\mathcal{T}_s^-$) respectively depending on the label of the query graph.

of the selected query graph G_s, we can select the optimal feature set by maximizing the following function.

$$\mathcal{E}(G_s, y_s, \mathcal{D}, \mathbf{y}_\ell) = \max_{\mathcal{T}\subseteq \mathcal{S}, |\mathcal{T}|=t} J(G_s, y_s, \mathcal{D}, \mathbf{y}_\ell, \mathcal{T}) \quad (2)$$

We select a subset of subgraph features $\mathcal{T}$ from $\mathcal{S}$, such that the feature selection evaluation function $J(G_s, y_s, \mathcal{D}, \mathbf{y}_\ell, \mathcal{T})$ is maximized.

2.1.1 *The Intuition*

Now, we show the key ideas of this paper from the following views.

Query Selection View: from the active query selection view, we assume that the optimal query graph should satisfy the following properties:

(a) Dependence maximization: based upon a feature set $\mathcal{T}$, the query graph G_s should be able to maximize the dependence between features of graphs and labels in a max-min view as in Eq. 1.

(b) Informative and representative: the selected query graph should be both informative and representative among the pool of unlabeled graphs. The query graph G_s should be close to some of the unlabeled graphs in the dataset, such that G_s is likely to be representative of a group of unlabeled graphs instead of being an outlier. The query graph G_s should also be far from the labeled graphs in $\mathcal{D}_\ell$, such that the label of G_s is unlikely to be redundant.

Feature Selection View: from the subgraph feature selection view, the optimal feature set can be very different depending on which graph we query, and what class label we get from the domain expert. For example, in Figure 4, we have a graph dataset with seven graph objects. Suppose the selected query graph is G_s. We denote the optimal feature set as $\mathcal{T}_s^+$, when G_s is positive. $\mathcal{T}_s^-$ represents the optimal feature set, when G_s is negative. From the feature selection perspective, the optimal subgraph features should also satisfy the following properties:

(a) Dependence maximization: graphs with the same class labels should have similar subgraph features, and be close to each other; while graphs with different labels should have different features and be far away from each other.

(b) Informative and representative: the query graph G_s should be close to the other unlabeled graphs, and be far from the existing labeled graphs.

2.1.2 *The Solution*

Many criteria can be used to evaluate the dependence between subgraph features and graph labels. In this paper we adopt the Hilbert-Schmidt Independence Criterion (HSIC) [12] for subgraph evaluation. HSIC measures the dependence between two variables (X, Y) in the kernel space. We briefly review the definition of HSIC. Suppose we have two reproducing kernel Hilbert spaces (RKHS) of functions $\mathcal{G}$ and $\mathcal{F}$. Let a covariance operator be

$$C = \mathrm{E}\left\{[p(X) - \mathrm{E}(p(X))][q(Y) - \mathrm{E}(q(Y))]\right\}, \ \forall p \in \mathcal{G}, q \in \mathcal{F}$$

Then the HSIC is defined as the Hilbert-Schmidt norm of the operator C, *i.e.*, $\|C\|_{HS}^2$. Given a data sample, HSIC has an empirical estimator HSIC = tr($\mathbf{K}$ $\mathbf{H}$ $\mathbf{L}$ $\mathbf{H}$). Here, tr$(\cdot)$ is the trace of a matrix. $\mathbf{H} = [H_{ij}]_{n\times n}$, where $H_{ij} = \delta_{ij} - 1/n$. δ_{ij} is the indicator function. $\delta_{ij} = 1$ i ffi $= j$, otherwise $\delta_{ij} = 0$. $\mathbf{K}$ and $\mathbf{L}$ are kernel matrices on the samples.

Based upon the HSIC measure, we propose the following evaluation function for active feature selection:

$$\begin{aligned} J(G_s, y_s, \mathcal{D}, \mathbf{y}_\ell, \mathcal{T}) =& \mathrm{tr}\left[\, \mathbf{K}(\mathcal{T})\ \mathbf{H}\ \mathbf{L}(y_s, \mathbf{y}_\ell)\ \mathbf{H}\,\right] \\ &+ \alpha\frac{\mathbf{1}^\top\mathbf{K}_{u,s}(\mathcal{T})}{n_u} - \beta\frac{\mathbf{1}^\top\mathbf{K}_{l,s}(\mathcal{T})}{n_\ell} \end{aligned} \quad (3)$$

where $\mathbf{K}(\mathcal{T}) = [K_{ij}]_{(n\times n)}$ denotes the kernel matrix of graphs based upon a subgraph feature $\mathcal{T}$. $K_{ij} = \langle D_\mathcal{T}\mathbf{x}_i, D_\mathcal{T}\mathbf{x}_j\rangle$. $D_\mathcal{T} = diag(\mathbf{d}_\mathcal{T})$ is a diagonal matrix, where $\mathbf{d}_\mathcal{T} = [d(\mathcal{T})_i]_{(m\times 1)}$ and $d(\mathcal{T})_i = I(g_i \in \mathcal{T}) \in \{0, 1\}$. $\mathbf{L}(y_s, \mathbf{y}_\ell) = [L_{ij}]_{(n\times n)} = \mathbf{y}\mathbf{y}^\top$ denotes the kernel matrix based on the labels of the graphs, where $\mathbf{y} = [\ \mathbf{y}_\ell^\top, y_s, \mathbf{y}_u^\top\ ]^\top$. $L_{ij} = \langle y_i, y_j\rangle$ is used in our current implementation. Other kernels can also be directly used in this formulation. α and β are two parameters that control the weights of the three terms in the evaluation function. The first term denotes the dependence between the features and labels of the graphs. The second term represents the average similarity between the query graph and the unlabeled graphs. The third term represents the average similarity between the query graph and the labeled graphs.

The evaluation function in Eq. 3 can be simplified as follows:

$$\begin{aligned} \mathrm{tr}\left(\mathbf{K}(\mathcal{T})\mathbf{H}\mathbf{y}\mathbf{y}^\top\mathbf{H}\right) &= \mathrm{tr}\left(X^\top D_\mathcal{T} D_\mathcal{T} X\ \mathbf{H}\ \mathbf{y}\mathbf{y}^\top\ \mathbf{H}\right) \\ &= \mathrm{tr}\left(D_\mathcal{T} X\ \mathbf{H}\ \mathbf{y}\mathbf{y}^\top\ \mathbf{H}\ X^\top D_\mathcal{T}\right) \\ &= \sum_{g_i\in\mathcal{T}}\left(\mathbf{f}_i^\top\mathbf{H}\ \mathbf{y}\mathbf{y}^\top\ \mathbf{H}\ \mathbf{f}_i\right) \end{aligned}$$

Input:
$\mathcal{D}$: the graph dataset $\{G_1, \cdots, G_n\}$ $\quad$ t: the maximum number of features.
$\mathbf{y}_\ell$: the vector of class labels for labeled graphs, $\quad$ *min_sup*: the minimum frequency.

Initialize:

- Construct the feature evaluation functions $h(g, \mathbf{M})$ and initialize candidate feature lists:
  1. Calculate $2 \times n_a$ matrices using Eq. 4 by considering each case for G_s and y_s as follows:
     $\mathbf{M}_i^+ = \mathbf{H}\ \mathbf{L}(y_i = +1, \mathbf{y}_\ell)\ \mathbf{H}\ + \frac{\alpha}{n_u}\ \Pi_i \mathbf{1}^\top \Pi_u^\top - \frac{\beta}{n_\ell}\ \Pi_i \mathbf{1}^\top \Pi_\ell^\top,\ (\forall\ i,\ n_\ell < i \leq n)$
     $\mathbf{M}_i^- = \mathbf{H}\ \mathbf{L}(y_i = -1, \mathbf{y}_\ell)\ \mathbf{H}\ + \frac{\alpha}{n_u}\ \Pi_i \mathbf{1}^\top \Pi_u^\top - \frac{\beta}{n_\ell}\ \Pi_i \mathbf{1}^\top \Pi_\ell^\top,\ (\forall\ i,\ n_\ell < i \leq n)$
  2. Initialize $2 \times n_a$ empty lists for candidate subgraph features as follows:
     $\forall\ i\ (n_\ell < i \leq n)$, let $\mathcal{T}_i^+ = \mathcal{T}_i^- = \emptyset$ with maximum size t, and pruning thresholds $\theta_i^+ = \theta_i^- = -\infty$

Recursive Feature Mining:

- Depth-first search the gSpan's code tree and update the feature lists as follows:
  1. Update each of the candidate feature lists using the current subgraph feature g_c:
     $\forall\ i$, if $h(g_c, \mathbf{M}_i^+)$ is larger than the worst feature in $\mathcal{T}_i^+$, replace it and update $\theta_i^+ = \min_{g \in \mathcal{T}_i^+} h(g, \mathbf{M}_i^+)$
     $\forall\ i$, if $h(g_c, \mathbf{M}_i^-)$ is larger than the worst feature in $\mathcal{T}_i^-$, replace it and update $\theta_i^- = \min_{g \in \mathcal{T}_i^-} h(g, \mathbf{M}_i^-)$
  2. Test pruning criteria for the sub-tree rooted from node g as follows:
     if $freq(g_c) < min\_sup$, prune the sub-tree of g_c
     if $\forall\ i\ (n_\ell < i \leq n)$, $\widetilde{h}(g_c, \mathbf{M}_i^+) \leq \theta_i^+$ and $\widetilde{h}(g_c, \mathbf{M}_i^-) \leq \theta_i^-$, prune the sub-tree of g_c
  3. Recursion: Depth-first search the sub-tree rooted from node g_c

Active Query Selection:

- Select the query graph using Eq. 5

Output:
G_s: The selected query graph.
$\mathcal{T}_s^+$: the optimal subgraph features if G_s is labeled as a positive graph.
$\mathcal{T}_s^-$: the optimal subgraph features if G_s is labeled as a negative graph.

Figure 5: The gActive algorithm

We can rewrite $J(G_s, y_s, \mathcal{D}, \mathbf{y}_\ell, \mathcal{T})$ in Eq. 2 as

$$J(G_s, y_s, \mathcal{D}, \mathbf{y}_\ell, \mathcal{T})$$
$$= \sum_{g_i \in \mathcal{T}} \mathbf{f}_i^\top \left(\mathbf{H}\ \mathbf{y}\mathbf{y}^\top\ \mathbf{H}\ + \frac{\alpha}{n_u}\ \Pi_s \mathbf{1}^\top \Pi_u^\top - \frac{\beta}{n_\ell}\ \Pi_s \mathbf{1}^\top \Pi_\ell^\top\right) \mathbf{f}_i$$
$$= \sum_{g_i \in \mathcal{T}} \mathbf{f}_i^\top\ \mathbf{M}\ \mathbf{f}_i$$

whereΠ_ℓ andΠ_u are projection matrices. $X_\ell = X\Pi_\ell$, $X_u = X\Pi_u$ and $\mathbf{x}_s = X\Pi_s$.

$$\mathbf{M} = \mathbf{H}\ \mathbf{y}\mathbf{y}^\top\ \mathbf{H}\ + \frac{\alpha}{n_u}\ \Pi_s \mathbf{1}^\top \Pi_u^\top - \frac{\beta}{n_\ell}\ \Pi_s \mathbf{1}^\top \Pi_\ell^\top \qquad (4)$$

Given the evaluation function $h(g_i, G_s, y_s, \mathcal{D}, \mathbf{y}_\ell) = \mathbf{f}_i^\top\ \mathbf{M}\ \mathbf{f}_i$, we can define the optimization problem of dual active feature and sample selection as follows:

$$G_s^* = \arg\max_{G_s \in \mathcal{D}_a}\ \min_{y_s \in \{\pm 1\}}\ \max_{\mathcal{T} \subseteq \mathcal{S}, |\mathcal{T}| = t} \sum_{g_i \in \mathcal{T}} h(g_i, G_s, y_s, \mathcal{D}, \mathbf{y}_\ell) \qquad (5)$$

Definition 3 (gFScore). *Let $\mathcal{D} = \{G_1, \cdots, G_n\}$ denote a graph dataset, with first n_ℓ graphs labeled as $y_1, \cdots, y_{n_\ell}$. Suppose we have a query graph G_s with its potential label y_s. We define a quality criterion $h(g_i, G_s, y_s, \mathcal{D}, \mathbf{y}_\ell) = h(g_i, \mathbf{M}) = \mathbf{f}_i^\top\ \mathbf{M}\ \mathbf{f}_i$, called gFScore, for a subgraph feature g_i. $\mathbf{M}$ is a matrix defined in Eq. 4.*

The optimal solution to Eq. 5 can be found by the following method: we go through each unlabeled graph one by one. Suppose G_s is the currently selected graph. We need to go through a positive case ($y_s = 1$) and a negative case ($y_s = -1$). In each case, we mine the top-t best subgraph features according to the gFScore. As shown in Figure 6, we need to mine $2 \times n_a$ optimal feature sets from the graph dataset. $\mathcal{T}_i^+$ denotes the optimal feature set, when the i-th graph is queried and labeled as a positive graph. $\mathcal{T}_i^-$ denotes the optimal feature set, when G_i is queried and labeled as negative. Then, we can directly use Eq. 5 to find the optimal query graph.

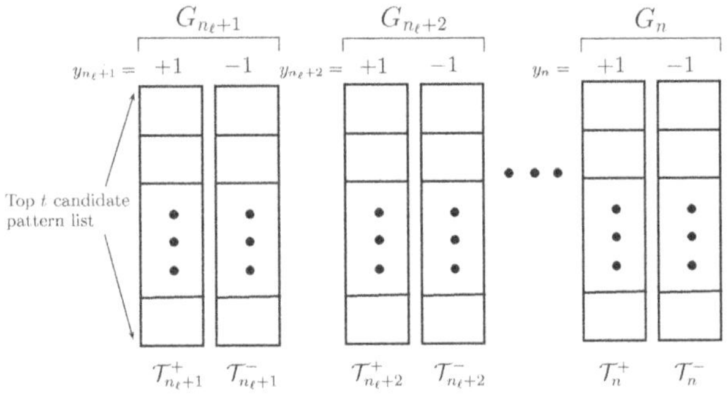

Figure 6: Candidate subgraph pattern lists

2.1.3 Upper Bound of gFScore

Now we address the problem on how to mine the optimal feature sets without exhaustive enumeration of all subgraphs. Note that the number of subgraphs in a graph dataset can be extremely large. It grows at an exponential rate as the size of the graphs increases. Thus, it is computationally intractable to enumerate all subgraphs in the graph dataset.

Some recent graph classification approaches [26, 24, 18] incorporate constraints to prune the search space of gSpan [27]. In this paper we derive a new constraint to prune the search space in the DFS-code tree. A straightforward upper-bound of gFScore is defined as follows:

Theorem 1 (Upper bound of gFScore). *Suppose we have two subgraph patterns $g_i, g_j \in \mathcal{S}$, and g_j is a supergraph of g_i*

$(g_j \supseteq g_i)$. *The gFScore value of* g_j *is bounded by* $\widetilde{h}(g_i, \mathbf{M})$ *, i.e.,* $h(g_j, \mathbf{M}) \leq \widetilde{h}(g_i, \mathbf{M})$. $\widetilde{h}(g_i, \mathbf{M})$ *is defined as follows:*

$$\widetilde{h}(g_i, \mathbf{M}) \triangleq \mathbf{f}_i^\top \widetilde{\mathbf{M}} \mathbf{f}_i \tag{6}$$

where the matrix $\widetilde{\mathbf{M}}$ *is defined as* $\widetilde{M}_{pq} \triangleq \max(0, M_{pq})$.

PROOF.

$$h(g_j, \mathbf{M}) = \mathbf{f}_j^\top \mathbf{M} \mathbf{f}_j = \sum_{p,q: G_p, G_q \in \mathcal{D}(g_j)} M_{pq} \tag{7}$$

where $\mathcal{D}(g_j) \triangleq \{G_k | g_j \subseteq G_k, 1 \leq k \leq n\}$. Since g_j is a supergraph of g_i $(g_j \supseteq g_i)$, we have $\mathcal{D}(g_j) \subseteq \mathcal{D}(g_i)$ according to the anti-monotonic property. $\widetilde{M}_{pq} \triangleq \max(0, M_{pq})$. We have $\widetilde{M}_{pq} \geq M_{pq}$ and $\widetilde{M}_{pq} \geq 0$. Thus,

$$\begin{aligned} h(g_j, \mathbf{M}) &= \sum_{p,q: G_p, G_q \in \mathcal{D}(g_j)} M_{pq} \leq \sum_{p,q: G_p, G_q \in \mathcal{D}(g_j)} \widetilde{M}_{pq} \\ &\leq \sum_{p,q: G_p, G_q \in \mathcal{D}(g_i)} \widetilde{M}_{pq} = \widetilde{h}(g_i, \mathbf{M}) \end{aligned} \tag{8}$$

For any $g_j \supseteq g_i$, $h(g_j, \mathbf{M}) \leq \widetilde{h}(g_i, \mathbf{M})$. □

We now utilize the upper bound to prune the DFS-code tree in gSpan by the branch-and-bound pruning. The top-t best features are maintained in $2 \times n_a$ candidate lists. Figure 6 shows an example of the candidate lists. During the course of the subgraph pattern mining, we calculate the upper-bound of each subgraph pattern in the search tree. If a subgraph pattern node with its children nodes cannot update any of the candidate feature lists, we can prune the subtree of gSpan rooted from this node. It is guaranteed by the upper-bound that we will not miss any better features for any of the candidate feature lists. Thus, the subgraph feature mining process can be speeded up without loss of performance. The algorithm of gActive is summarized in Figure 5.

3. EXPERIMENTS

Data Collection: in order to evaluate the performance of the proposed approach for graph classification, we tested our algorithm on nine real-world datasets as summarized in Table 2.

1) *Anti-cancer activity prediction (NCI)*: the first eight benchmark datasets are collected from the *PubChem* website[1]. The datasets contain records of anticancer activities for more than 20,000 chemical compounds against eight types of cancer. Each chemical compound is represented as a graph. We collected eight graph data sets with *active* and *inactive* labels from the *PubChem* website. The original datasets are unbalanced, where the percentage of positive compounds is around 5%. We randomly sampled 500 inactive compounds and 500 active compounds from each dataset for performance evaluation.

2) *AIDS anti-virus prediction (HIV)*: the last benchmark dataset is collected from the AIDS anti-viral screening program[2]. The dataset consists of screening records of more than 7700 chemical compounds. Each compound is described by its activity against HIV, which is one of the following categories: confirmed active (CA), confirmed moderately active (CM) and confirmed inactive (CI). We treat CA+CM as the *positive* label, and CI as the *negative* label. This is the same setting used in [9]. The original data set is unbalanced, where the percentage of positive compounds is around 3%. We randomly sampled 266 inactive compounds and used the original 266 active compounds for performance evaluation.

[1] http://pubchem.ncbi.nlm.nih.gov
[2] http://dtp.nci.nih.gov/

Table 2: Summary of experimental datasets. "# Pos" denotes the number of active graphs in the dataset.

Dataset	# Pos	# Graph	Details
NCI1	2040	40526	Lung Cancer
NCI33	1636	40209	Melanoma
NCI41	1561	27585	Prostate Cancer
NCI47	2011	40447	Central Nerve System
NCI81	1396	40700	Colon Cancer
NCI83	2276	27992	Breast Cancer
NCI123	3112	40152	Leukemia
NCI145	1940	40164	Renal Cancer
AIDS	266	7781	HIV Anti-virus

Comparative Methods: in order to demonstrate the effectiveness of the proposed approach, we compare our method against four baseline methods. These baseline methods include both supervised and unsupervised feature selection approaches combined with active sample selection approaches. The compared methods are summarized as follows:

- *Dual Active Feature and Sample Selection (gActive)*: the proposed method in this paper. The default parameter setting for the gActive method is $\alpha = \beta = 10^{-3}$.

- *Supervised Feature Selection + Random Sampling (IG + Random)*: we compare with a supervised feature selection method combined with random sampling. A set of frequent subgraphs within the graph dataset is first mined. Then a supervised feature selection method based upon Information Gain (IG) is used to select a subset of discriminative features from the frequent subgraphs. We randomly select query graphs from the pool. Note that discriminative features are recomputed after each iteration of feature and graph selection.

- *Supervised Feature Selection + Margin (IG + Margin)*: we compare with a two-stage active learning approach. A supervised feature selection method is combined with a margin-based active learning method. In this approach, a set of frequent subgraphs within the graph dataset are first mined. Then we iteratively use information gain to select a subset of discriminative features from the frequent subgraphs. We use a margin-based active learning approach [25] to select informative graphs to query for labels.

- *Unsupervised Feature Selection + Random Sampling (Top-k + Random)*: we compare with an unsupervised feature selection method combined with random sampling. In this approach, we use the top-k frequent subgraph features in the pool dataset. Then we randomly select query graphs from the pool.

- *Unsupervised Feature Selection + Margin (Top-k + Margin)*: we compare with an unsupervised feature selection method combined with a margin-based active

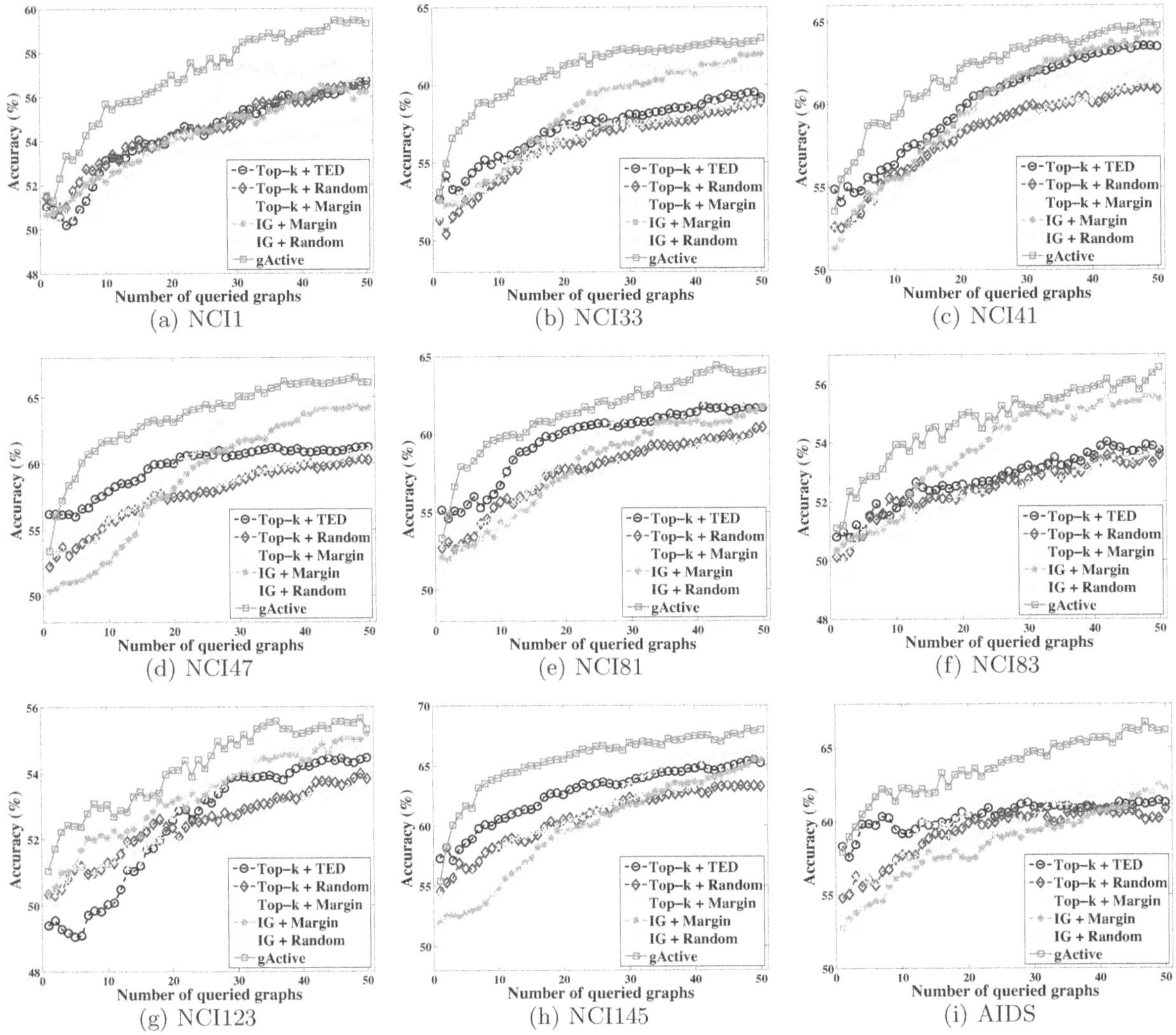

Figure 7: Graph classification accuracy after different number of graphs being queried.

learning method. In this approach, we use the top-k most frequent subgraphs in the pool dataset. Then margin-based active learning is used to select informative graphs to query.

- *Unsupervised Feature Selection + Sequential TED (Top-k + TED)*: we compare with an unsupervised feature selection method combined with experimental designs. In this approach, we use the top-k most frequent subgraphs in the pool dataset. Then the sequential transductive experimental design [30] is used to select representative graphs from the pool dataset.

All experiments are conducted on machines with Intel Xeon^{TM} Quad-Core CPUs of 2.27 GHz and 24 GB RAM. LibSVM [4] with the linear kernel is used as the base classifier for all compared methods. min_sup =10% in the gSpan. The default number of selected features in all compared methods is set as 500.

3.1 Performance on Graph Classification

In our experiments, we first randomly sample two labeled graphs, *i.e.*, one positive and one negative graph. They are used as the initial training set. Then we partition the remaining graphs into two groups with equal size: one group is used as the pool dataset; the other group is used as the testing dataset for performance evaluation. In each iteration, the active learner selects one unlabeled graph in the pool dataset and queries the label. Then, the queried graph is put into the training set, and the base classifier is trained to classify the testing graphs. We report the average results of 50 runs on randomly sampled graph datasets.

The results of all compared methods are summarized in Figure 7. We run each of the methods for 50 iterations and compare the learning curves. In all datasets, the proposed dual active feature and sample selection algorithm (gActive) consistently outperforms other baseline methods. Note that in the NCI33 and NCI145 datasets, all the baselines with margin-based active learning (IG + Margin and Top-k + Margin) are unable to achieve better performance than randomized baselines (IG + Random and Top-k + Random). However, our method can achieve substantially better performance than other baselines. This result supports the intuition of this paper: the feature selection problem and the active query selection problem are correlated, and should be considered simultaneously. Moreover, we notice that in the NCI41 dataset, all the baselines using margin-based active learning can improve the performance over randomized baselines. In this dataset, the improvements by the proposed gActive method can be even more significant.

3.2 Parameter Settings

In the proposed model, different weights can be assigned to the three terms in Equation 3. If we use different settings for the two parameters, α and β, we can perform the dual active feature and sample selection with different weights for the three constraints: *dependence maximization*, *representativeness* and *informativeness*. To be precise, α represents how much we weight the *representativeness*, and β denotes how much we weight the *informativeness*. The larger the value of α is, the closer the query graph is with other unlabeled graphs. The larger the value of β is, the further away the query graph is from the other labeled graphs. We test α and β with values among $\{100, 10, 1, 0.1, 0.01, 0.001, 0\}$ separately. The average results for our model in the first 50 iterations are reported. As shown in Figure 8, the performance of our model using α and β with similar values is often better than other settings. In these real-world graph classification tasks, the constraints for *informativeness* and *representativeness* are equally important for our active feature and sample selection problem.

In Figure 8(a), we find that the best parameter setting for NCI47 dataset is $\alpha = 0.001$, $\beta = 0.001$, and the accuracy is 63.5%. This setting is the same as our default parameter setting. The best parameter setting for NCI145 dataset is $\alpha = 0$, $\beta = 0.001$, and the resulting accuracy is 65.5%. Under our default setting, the accuracy is 65.4%. We find that the performance of our gActive model with the default setting is satisfactory. If we try to optimize the selection of α and β values, the accuracy improvement over other baselines will be even larger.

We also compare gActive models with and without pruning in the subgraph search space as summarized in Figure 9. The average CPU time with different *min_sup* during the first iteration is reported. gActive can improve the efficiencies by pruning the subgraph search space.

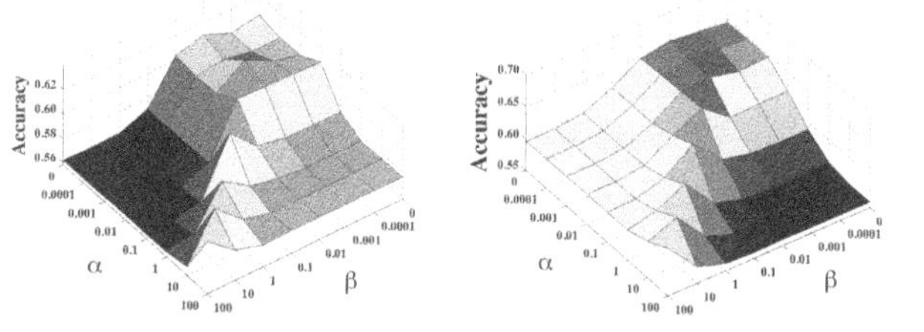

(a) NCI47 (b) NCI145

Figure 8: gActive accuracies with different α and β.

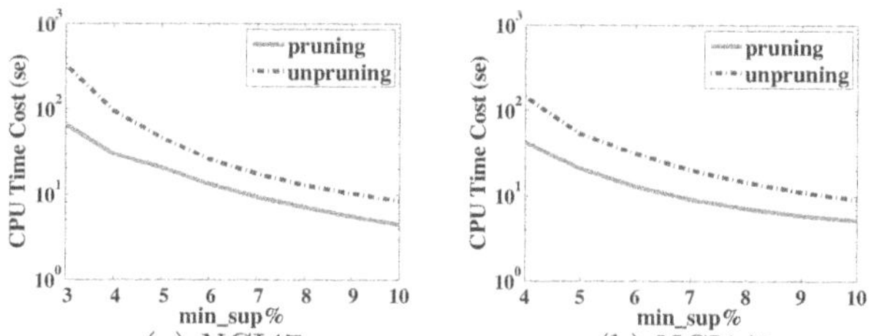

(a) NCI47 (b) NCI145

Figure 9: CPU time with/without pruning.

4. RELATED WORK

In this section, we discuss some related work. Active learning aims at reducing the labeling cost by querying the most informative example. Many methods have been proposed based upon different active learning settings. Please see [23] for a detailed survey. Conventional active learning approaches focus on data in vector space. One approach is to query the most informative instance. The active learners select the uncertain instances based upon a single classifier [25, 1] or a committee of classifiers [6, 10, 22]. The problems with this approach are that it can be sensitive to outliers or noise, and can not exploit the structures of unlabeled data. The alternative approach is to query the most representative instance. The active learners exploit the structure of unlabeled data using clustering methods [20, 7] or optimal experimental design approaches [30]. The major problems are that this approach is unsupervised and can not use the labeled data. Some work has also been done to combine informativeness and representativeness measures to find the optimal query examples [8, 15].

Mining subgraph features from graph data has also been studied in recent years [19]. The aim of these approaches is to extract useful subgraph features from a set of graphs by adopting some filtering criteria. Depending on if the label information is considered in the feature mining process, the existing methods can roughly be classified into two types: unsupervised and supervised. In the unsupervised setting, the frequency of each subgraph is used as the criterion for feature selection. To discover frequent subgraphs, Yan and Han developed a depth-first search algorithm, gSpan [27], which builds a lexicographic order among graphs, and maps each graph to a unique minimum DFS code as its canonical label. The gSpan algorithm adopts a depth-first search in the DFS code tree to mine frequent subgraphs efficiently. There are also many other frequent subgraph feature mining approaches that have been developed recently, *e.g.*, AGM [16], FSG [19], MoFa [2], FFSM [14], and Gaston [21]. Supervised subgraph feature mining approaches have also been proposed in the literature, such as LEAP [26], CORK [24] and MbT [9], where the focus is on discovering discriminative features for graph classifications. In addition, gSSC [18] addresses the problem of feature selection for graph classification under semi-supervised settings. Some other graph classification approaches based upon graph kernels have also been proposed [11, 13].

5. CONCLUSIONS

In this paper we studied the dual active feature and sample selection problem for graph classification. The objective was to minimize the labeling efforts in graph classification. We demonstrated how to find a useful query graph and a set of optimal features simultaneously. We proposed to maximize the dependence between subgraph features and labels based upon an active learning framework. Our approach can find the most representative and informative graph and an optimal feature set. Then a branch-and-bound algorithm was proposed to prune the subgraph search space efficiently.

6. ACKNOWLEDGEMENTS

The work is supported in part by NSF through grants IIS-0905215, DBI-0960443, OISE-0968341 and OIA-0963278.

7. REFERENCES

[1] M. F. Balcan, A. Z. Broder, and T. Zhang. Margin based active learning. In *COLT*, pages 35–50, 2007.

[2] C. Borgelt and M. Berthold. Mining molecular fragments: Finding relevant substructures of molecules. In *ICDM*, pages 211–218, 2002.

[3] K. M. Borgwardt. *Graph Kernels*. PhD thesis, Ludwig-Maximilians-University Munich, 2007.

[4] C.-C. Chang and C.-J. Lin. *LIBSVM: a library for support vector machines*, 2001. Software available at `http://www.csie.ntu.edu.tw/~cjlin/libsvm`.

[5] H. Cheng, D. Lo, Y. Zhou, X. Wang, and X. Yan. Identifying bug signatures using discrimative graph mining. In *ISSTA*, pages 141–152, 2009.

[6] I. Dagan and S. P. Engenlson. Committee-based sampling for training probabilistic classifiers. In *ICML*, pages 150–157, 1995.

[7] S. Dasgupta and D. Hsu. Hierarchical sampling for active learning. In *ICML*, pages 208–215, 2008.

[8] P. Donmez, J. G. Carbonell, and P. N. Bennett. Dual strategy active learning. In *ECML*, pages 116–127, 2007.

[9] W. Fan, K. Zhang, H. Cheng, J. Gao, X. Yan, J. Han, P. S. Yu, and O. Verscheure. Direct mining of discriminative and essential frequent patterns via model-based search tree. In *KDD*, pages 230–238, 2008.

[10] Y. Freund, E. S. H. S. Seung, and N. Tishby. Selective sampling using the query by committee algorithm. *Machine Learning*, 28(2-3):133–168, 1997.

[11] T. Gärtner, P. A. Flach, and S. Wrobel. On graph kernels: Hardness results and efficient alternatives. In *COLT/Kernel*, 2003.

[12] A. Gretton, O. Bousquet, A. Smola, and B. Schölkopf. Measuring statistical dependence with Hilbert-Schmidt norms. In *ALT*, pages 63–77, Singapore, 2005.

[13] T. Horvath, T. Gärtner, and S. Wrobel. Cyclic pattern kernels for predictive graph mining. In *KDD*, 2004.

[14] J. Huan, W. Wang, and J. Prins. Efficient mining of frequent subgraph in the presence of isomorphism. In *ICDM*, pages 549–552, 2003.

[15] S.-J. Huang, R. Jin, and Z.-H. Zhou. Active learning by querying informative and representative examples. In *NIPS*. 2011.

[16] A. Inokuchi, T. Washio, and H. Motoda. An apriori-based algorithm for mining frequent substructures from graph data. In *PKDD*, pages 13–23, 2000.

[17] N. Jin, C. Young, and W. Wang. GAIA: graph classification using evolutionary computation. In *SIGMOD*, pages 879–890, 2010.

[18] X. Kong and P. S. Yu. Semi-supervised feature selection for graph classification. In *KDD*, pages 793–802, 2010.

[19] M. Kuramochi and G. Karypis. Frequent subgraph discovery. In *ICDM*, pages 313–320, 2001.

[20] H. T. Nguyen and A. W. M. . Smeulders. Active learning using pre-cluster. In *ICML*, pages 623–630, 2004.

[21] S. Nijssen and J. Kok. A quickstart in frequent structure mining can make a difference. In *KDD*, pages 647–652, 2004.

[22] M. Opper, H. S. Seung, and H. Sompolinsky. Query by committee. In *COLT*, pages 287–294, 1992.

[23] B. Settles. Active learning literature survey. Computer Sciences Technical Report 1648, University of Wisconsin–Madison, 2009.

[24] M. Thoma, H. Cheng, A. Gretton, J. Han, H. Kriegel, A. Smola, L. Song, P. Yu, X. Yan, and K. Borgwardt. Near-optimal supervised feature selection among frequent subgraphs. In *SDM*, pages 1075–1086, 2009.

[25] S. Tong and D. Koller. Support vector machine active learning with applications to text classification. In *ICML*, pages 999–1006, 2000.

[26] X. Yan, H. Cheng, J. Han, and P. Yu. Mining significant graph patterns by leap search. In *SIGMOD*, pages 433–444, 2008.

[27] X. Yan and J. Han. gSpan: Graph-based substructure pattern mining. In *ICDM*, pages 721–724, 2002.

[28] X. Yan, P. S. Yu, and J. Han. Graph indexing based on discriminative frequent struture analysis. *ACM Transactions on Database Systems*, 30(4):960–993, 2005.

[29] B. Yang, J. Sun, T. Wang, and Z. Chen. Effective multi-label active learning for text classification. In *KDD*, pages 917–926, 2009.

[30] K. Yu, J. Bi, and V. Tresp. Active learning via transductive experimental design. In *ICML*, pages 1081–1088, 2006.

It's Who You Know: Graph Mining Using Recursive Structural Features

Keith Henderson
Lawrence Livermore Lab
keith@llnl.gov

Brian Gallagher
Lawrence Livermore Lab
bgallagher@llnl.gov

Lei Li & Leman Akoglu
Carnegie Mellon University
{leili,lakoglu}@cs.cmu.edu

Tina Eliassi-Rad
Rutgers University
eliassi@cs.rutgers.edu

Hanghang Tong
IBM Watson
htong@us.ibm.com

Christos Faloutsos
Carnegie Mellon University
christos@cs.cmu.edu

ABSTRACT

Given a graph, how can we extract good features for the nodes? For example, given two large graphs from the same domain, how can we use information in one to do classification in the other (i.e., perform across-network classification or transfer learning on graphs)? Also, if one of the graphs is anonymized, how can we use information in one to de-anonymize the other? The key step in all such graph mining tasks is to find effective node features. We propose ReFeX (Recursive Feature eXtraction), a novel algorithm, that recursively combines local (node-based) features with neighborhood (egonet-based) features; and outputs regional features – capturing "behavioral" information. We demonstrate how these powerful regional features can be used in within-network and across-network classification and de-anonymization tasks – without relying on homophily, or the availability of class labels. The contributions of our work are as follows: (a) ReFeX is scalable and (b) it is effective, capturing regional ("behavioral") information in large graphs. We report experiments on real graphs from various domains with over 1M edges, where ReFeX outperforms its competitors on typical graph mining tasks like network classification and de-anonymization.

Categories and Subject Descriptors

H.2.8 [**Database Applications**]: Data mining; E.1 [**Data Structures**]: Graphs and networks

General Terms

Algorithms, Design, Performance, Experimentation.

Keywords

Graph mining, feature extraction, network classification, identity resolution

1. INTRODUCTION

Extracting effective features for nodes of a given graph is a key step for many data mining tasks, such as outlier detection (i.e., nodes with strange feature combinations), or mining across different graphs from the same domain. For example, given IP communication graphs from different days or different enterprise networks, can we train a classifier on one day (say Monday) and use the same classifier to accurately predict traffic on another day (say Thursday) without any labels on the latter graph? Here, the key step is to extract effective and transferrable features from each node that would best capture node characteristics, so that we can distinguish and classify the nodes (or edges). Another example is the following: given an anonymized social network (say Twitter's who-follows-whom graph) and a non-anonymized communication graph (say Twitter's who-mentions-whom graph), can we find node features that will help de-anonymize (or re-identify) the people in the social network?

Here, we propose a novel solution, *ReFeX* (Recursive Feature eXtraction) to these graph mining tasks. *ReFeX* recursively combines local (node-based) features, with neighborhood (egonet-based) features, and outputs regional features that capture "behavioral" information. These regional features represent the *kind* of nodes to which a given node is connected (e.g., connected to rich people), as opposed to the *identity* of those nodes (e.g., connected to Bill Gates) – i.e., it is who you know at the type-level that matters in mining across different graphs. In empirical studies, we demonstrate how these powerful regional features can be used in within- and across-network classification and de-anonymization tasks – without relying on homophily, or the availability of class labels.

Thus, the problem is defined as follows. Given a graph G, compute a node-feature matrix F with the following properties:

- *Structural*: The construction of F should not require additional attribute information on nodes or links.
- *Effective*: Good node-features should (1) help us predict node attributes, when such attributes are available (as in the case of IP traffic that we discuss next), and (2) be transferable across graphs (e.g., when the graph changes over time).

The ideal features should help with data mining tasks. Typical tasks include node classification (after we are given some labels), de-anonymization of the nodes of a graph, and transfer learning.

Figure 1 gives a quick overview of (a) the intuition behind *ReFeX* and (b) a preview of its classification accuracy. In (a), we show egonets of nodes from different days in an IP network, where node size and edge size are proportional to the traffic. The main point is that the characteristics of the neighbors are valuable and help us characterize the center node (manually labeled as 'web', 'dns-server' and 'p2p', respectively for each column). Figure 1(b) shows the classification accuracy of *ReFeX* (in blue bars) vs competitors - higher is better; *ReFeX* wins consistently.

KDD'11, August 21–24, 2011, San Diego, California, USA.

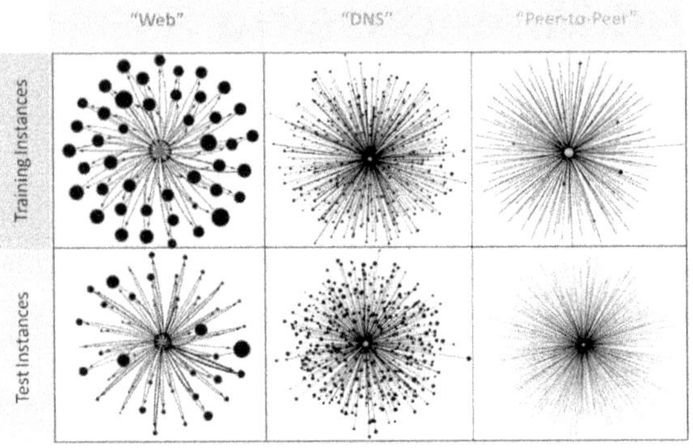

(a) Intuition (neighbors matter)

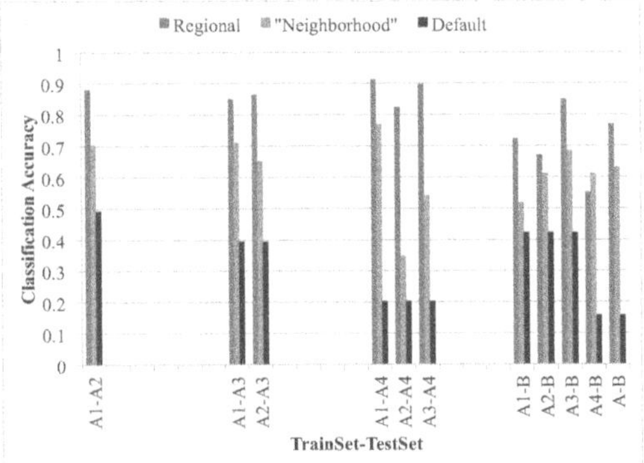

(b) Performance preview (blue bars: highest - win)

Figure 1: (a) Intuition behind *ReFeX*: Six IP hosts from different days of an enterprise network trace and (manually) labeled by their primary traffic type. Node and edge size indicate communication volume relative to the central node in each frame. Regional structure, i.e. the *types* of neighbors that a given host connects to, are vital. (b) classification accuracy of *ReFeX* with respect to transfer learning, in blue bars (higher is better) - see Figure (4) for more details.

The contributions of our work are as follows:

- *Novel Design*: We propose *ReFeX*, a scalable algorithm that computes regional features capturing "behavioral" information on large graphs.
- *Effectiveness*: *ReFeX*'s regional features perform well for several graph mining tasks, like transfer learning (across-network classification) and node de-anonymization on large graphs.

The rest of the paper is organized as follows: the proposed strategies are presented in Section 2; the experiments are presented in Sections 3 and 4. In Section 5, we review the related work; and we conclude the paper in Section 6.

2. PROPOSED ALGORITHM

Our algorithm *ReFeX* aggregates existing feature values of a node and uses them to generate new *recursive* features. The initial set of features used to seed the recursive feature generation can be structural information from the network or attributes from an external source. Here, we focus on tasks where only structural information is available. We separate structural attributes into three types: *local*, *egonet*, and *recursive* features. Local and egonet features together are called *neighborhood* features, and all three together are called *regional* features.

2.1 Neighborhood Features

The base features that seed the recursive *ReFeX* process are *local* and *egonet* features. These can be computed quickly for a given node. We call the set of local and egonet features together *neighborhood* features.

Local features are all essentially measures of the node degree. If the graph is directed, they include in- and out-degree as well as total degree. For weighted graphs, they contain weighted versions of each local feature.

Egonet features are computed for each node based on the node's ego network (a.k.a. egonet). The egonet includes the node, its neighbors, and any edges in the induced subgraph on these nodes. Egonet features include the number of within-egonet edges, as well as the number of edges entering and leaving the egonet. Strictly speaking, the latter are not in the egonet but they can be counted without looking at non-egonet nodes. As with local features, we compute directed and/or weighted versions of these features if the edges are directed and/or weighted.

2.2 Recursive Features

We broadly define a recursive feature as any aggregate computed over a feature value among a node's neighbors.

2.2.1 Generating Recursive Features

Currently *ReFeX* collects two types of recursive features: means and sums.[1] As a typical example, one recursive feature is defined as the mean value of the feature *unweighted degree* among all neighbors of a node. The features that can be aggregated are not restricted to neighborbood features, or even to structural features. The aggregates can be computed over any real-valued feature (including other recursive features). We compute the means and sums of all feature values. Moreover, when applicable, we compute these for incoming and outgoing edges separately.

2.2.2 Pruning Recursive Features

Clearly, the number of possible recursive features is infinite and grows exponentially with each recursive iteration. To reduce the number of generated features, a variety of pruning techniques can be employed. A simple example is to look for pairs of features that are highly correlated. In this example case, the pruning strategy is to eliminate one of the features whenever two features are correlated above a user-defined threshold.

For computational reasons, *ReFeX* uses a simplified version of this approach. Specifically, feature values are mapped to small integers via *vertical logarithmic binning*, then *ReFeX* looks for pairs of features whose values never disagree by more than a threshold. For details on the threshold, see Section 2.3 below.

First, each feature's values are transformed into *vertical logarithmic bins* of size p (where $0 < p < 1$). The process is as

[1]We selected sum and mean as aggregate functions heuristically. These simple measures capture the dominant trends among a node's neighbors w.r.t. each feature. Other functions, such as maximum, minimum, and variance could easily be added to *ReFeX*. In our experiments, sum and mean were sufficient to provide good empirical performance on data mining tasks with a reasonable runtime.

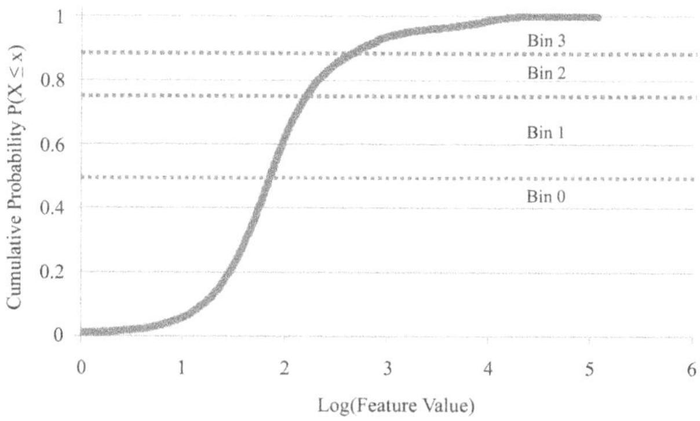

Figure 2: Vertical logarithmic binning of a feature value.

follows. For feature f_i, the $p|V|$ nodes with the lowest f_i value are reassigned f_i value 0. If there are ties, it may be necessary to include more than $p|V|$ nodes. Next, p fraction of the remaining nodes are assigned f_i value 1, and p of the remaining nodes after this are assigned value 2. This is repeated until all f_i values have been replaced by integer values between 0 and $log_{p^{-1}}(|V|)$ (see Figure 2).

We choose logarithmic binning for all features based on the observation that many graph properties exhibit power law distributions [1]. In particular, logarithmic binning always places most of the discriminatory power among sets of nodes with large feature values. This is reasonable, given that we expect to be able to make better predictions about active nodes for which we have many observations than nodes for which we only have a few.

Once a set of features has been generated and binned, *ReFeX* looks for pairs of features that do *not* disagree at any vertex by more than a threshold s. We call such a pair of features s-friends. To eliminate redundant features, we construct a *feature-graph*, whose nodes are features and whose links are s-friend relations. Each connected component of this graph is replaced by a single feature. When possible, we retain "simpler" features, i.e. features generated using fewer recursive iterations.[2]

If a recursive iteration results in no retained features, *ReFeX* halts and reports the retained feature values from each of the previous iterations. Note that a feature retained in iteration k may not be retained in iteration $k+1$, due to recursive features connecting them in the feature-graph. In this case, we still record and output the feature because it was retained at some iteration.

2.3 Parameters

ReFeX requires two parameters: p, which is the fraction of nodes placed in each logarithmic bin, and s, which is the feature similarity threshold.

The parameter p takes a value between 0 and 1, inclusive. Increasing p too close to 1 reduces the number of bins and increases the effective pruning aggressiveness, which can lead to a loss of discriminatory power. Decreasing p to near 0 can generate many bins and retain many features during pruning, which can increase runtime significantly. In our experiments, we found $p = 0.5$ to be a sensible choice – with each bin containing the bottom half of the remaining nodes. We also found that the results were not sensitive to the value of p as long as its value was not near 0 or 1.

For s, *ReFeX* uses *relaxation* at each iteration. For small graphs ($\leq 100K$ nodes), *ReFeX* uses $s = 0$ for the initial iteration (to generate neighborhood features). This effectively retains any feature that does not totally agree with another feature in logarithmic bin values. For larger graphs ($> 100K$ nodes), the initial value of s may be increased if computational resources are insufficient to generate the full set. On each subsequent iteration, *ReFeX* increased s by 1. This ensures that the process will halt after no more than $log_{p^{-1}}(|V|)$ iterations, since the maximum value of any feature is s at that point.

2.4 Computational Complexity

Let n be the number of nodes, m be number of edges, M = maximum degree, f = number of features, and d_i = degree of node i. Computational complexity of *ReFeX* can be divided into two steps: (1) computation of neighborhood features, and (2) computation at each subsequent iteration. Computation of neighborhood features is expected to take $O(n)$ for real-world graphs. See Lemma 1 for details. At each subsequent iteration, *ReFeX* takes $O(f(m+nf))$ time, where $f \ll n$. The space requirement is $O(m+nf)$.

Lemma 1. The computation of neighborhood features takes $O(nM^{\epsilon})$.

Proof. For brevity, we only give a sketch of the proof:
$\sum_{(u \to v) \in E} degree(u) \approx \int_1^M n * d_i^{(\epsilon-1)} \partial d_i \approx nM^{\epsilon}$.
$\epsilon = 3 - \alpha$ for real-world graph with power-law degree distributions with exponent α. However, since α is typically in the range $2 < \alpha < 3$ for real-world graphs [3], $0 < \epsilon < 1$. ■

3. FEATURE EFFECTIVENESS ON NETWORK CLASSIFICATION

We describe experiments on within- and across-network classification using features from *ReFeX*.

3.1 Data

IP-A and IP-B are real network-trace data sets collected roughly one year apart on separate enterprise networks. The nodes are IP addresses and the links are communications between the IPs. The IP-A trace begins at midnight on day 1 and continues up to 12pm on day 5. The IP-B trace begins at midnight on day 1 and continues up to ≈5pm on day 6.

For days 1-4 of the IP-A dataset (IP-A1 to IP-A4), we extract flows in the period from 12pm-1pm. We exclude day 5 because the trace ended at 12pm. For IP-B, we extract flows from 12pm-1pm for day 3 only. We then label all flows using a payload signature-based classification tool. Once network flows are labeled, we transfer labels to hosts by selecting the most frequent class labels from among the host's flows. The payload classifier can distinguish between over 15 classes of traffic (e.g., Web, DNS, SMTP, P2P). However, since we found that 3 classes (namely, Web, DNS, and P2P) made up the dominant traffic type for over 90% of the labeled hosts, we remove all other labels and focus on the 3-class classification problem. Table 1 summarizes the data that we extracted.

3.2 Classifiers

To test the predictive ability of *ReFeX*'s features, we use the log-Forest model described by Gallagher et al. [11]. The logForest is a bagged model, composed of a set of logistic regression (LR) clas-

[2]It may be the case that two features are not similar enough to be joined in the feature graph, but reside in the same component because of a chain of similar features between them. We examined feature graphs for a number of data sets and found that this does occur. However, any other choice of criterion for joining features (cliques, community discovery algorithms, etc.) would be similarly heuristic and probably include outside cases that are unsatisfactory. Any of these criteria could be used in place of the connected-components criterion, however; we use connectedness for its simplicity and ease of computation.

	IP-A1	IP-A2	IP-A3	IP-A4	IP-B
Nodes	81450	57415	154103	206704	181267
(labeled)	29868	16112	30955	67944	27649
Links	968138	432797	1266341	1756082	1945215
(unique)	206112	137822	358851	465869	397925
Web	32%	38%	38%	18%	42%
DNS	36%	49%	39%	20%	42%
P2P	32%	12%	23%	62%	16%

Table 1: Extracted data

sifiers, where each is given a subset of $\log(f) + 1$ of the f total features. For our experiments, we use a logForest of 500 LR classifiers. Like Gallagher et al. [11], we found that the overall performance of logForest was superior to standard logistic regression. In addition, as a baseline, we include a standard homophily-based relational neighbor classifier: wvRN (short for weighted-vote Relational Neighbor) [23]. The wvRN classifier has been shown to have excellent performance across a range of tasks. The classifiers we compare are:

- *wnRN+RL* - a relational neighbor model, which uses wvRN and relaxation labeling for collective classification
- *Neighborhood* - a logForest model, which uses the neighborhood features only
- *Regional* - a logForest model, which uses the regional features (i.e., neighborhood + recursive)

3.3 Feature Effectiveness on Within-Network Classification

3.3.1 Methodology

Each data set contains a set of core nodes for which we have ground-truth (i.e., we know the true class labels). In all cases, classifiers have access to the entire data graph during both training and testing.[3] However, not all of the core nodes are labeled. We vary the proportion of labeled core nodes from 10% to 90%. Classifiers are trained on all labeled core nodes and evaluated on all unlabeled core nodes.

Our methodology is as follows. For each proportion of core nodes labeled, we run 10 trials and report the average performance. For each trial and proportion labeled, we choose a class-stratified random-sample containing (1.0 - proportion labeled)% of the core instances as the test set and the remaining core instances become the training set. Note that proportion labeled less than 0.9 (or greater than 10 trials) means that a single instance will necessarily appear in multiple test sets. The test sets cannot be made to be independent because of this overlap. However, we carefully choose the test sets to ensure that each instance in our data set occurs in the same number of test sets over the course of our experiments. This ensures that each instance carries the same weight in the overall evaluation regardless of the proportion labeled. Labels are kept on the training instances and removed from the test instances. We use identical train/test splits for each classifier. Our experimental framework sits on top of the open source Weka system [28]. We implement our own network data representation and experimental code, which handles tasks such as splitting the data into training and test sets, labeling and unlabeling of data, and converting network fragments into a Weka-compatible form. We rely on Weka for the implementation of logistic regression and for measuring classifier performance on individual training/test trials.

[3]This is the norm in within-network classification.

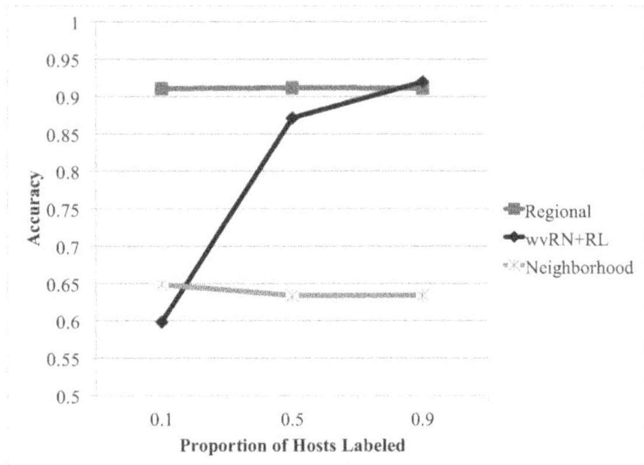

Figure 3: Within-network classification with wvRN+RL, neighborhood, and regional classifiers. The regional classifier dominates when labels are sparse.

3.3.2 Results

Figure 3 demonstrates the performance of the *wnRN+RL*, *Neighborhood* and *Regional* classifiers on a within-network classification task on the IP-A3 data set. We repeated this task on each of the IP-A data sets with essentially equivalent results. The within-network classification setting is the sweet spot for homophily-based models like wvRN. So, it is no surprise that wvRN+RL performs well on this task with 90% of nodes in the network labeled. However, the performance of wvRN+RL degrades quickly as labels become more sparse. The Regional and Neighborhood classifiers are less sensitive to the availability of labeled data since they do not rely on labeled neighbors to make accurate classifications. As a result, the Regional classifier outperforms wvRN+RL when labeled data are sparse. The dramatic difference in performance between Neighborhood and Regional demonstrates that the recursive feature generation process leads to more expressive features that are able to represent important concepts that cannot be captured by the neighborhood features alone.

3.4 Feature Effectiveness on Across-Network Transfer Learning

3.4.1 Methodology

For each experiment, the training graph has all known labels available. The test graph is *completely* unlabeled. Each classifier is evaluated on all known ground truth labels in the test graph. We use an identical set of features for all data sets. This set of features comes from running *ReFeX* on the IP-A1 data set. Table 2 summarizes the across-network experiments.

3.4.2 Results

Figure 4 demonstrates the performance of *Neighborhood* and *Regional* on a series of across-network transfer learning tasks. Here, we train on one network, where all known labels are available, and test on a separate network that is completely unlabeled. We emphasize the difficulty of these tasks given the (sometime extreme) differences in class distributions between data sets (see Table 1). The performance of the *Default* classifier is a good indicator of the difficulty of each task since this model makes predictions based

Train Graph	Test Graph: IP-A2	IP-A3	IP-A4	IP-B
IP-A1	✓	✓	✓	✓
IP-A2		✓	✓	✓
IP-A3			✓	✓
IP-A4				✓
IP-A1 to IP-A4				✓

Table 2: Across-network experiments performed

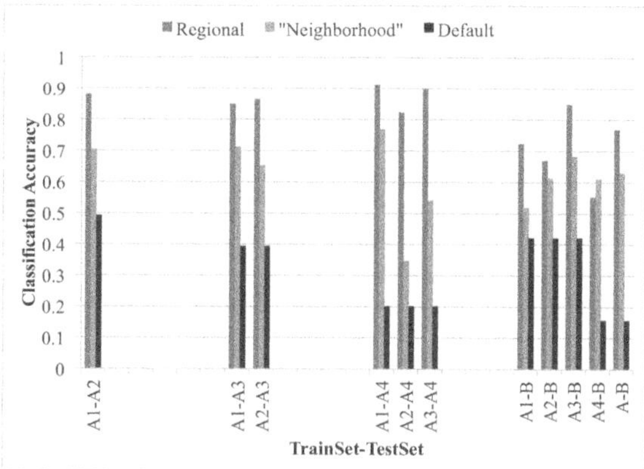

Figure 4: Across-network transfer learning with neighborhood and regional features. Regional demonstrates consistently high accuracy on difficult transfer learning tasks.

solely on the most frequent class from the training set. We also note that *wnRN+RL* is not applicable for these tasks since it relies on the availability of some known class labels to seed the inference process.

As in the within-network setting, the Regional classifier is the best overall performer on the across-network tasks, achieving 82% - 91% accuracy training and testing on separate days of IP-A and 77% accuracy training on all days of IP-A and testing on IP-B. The performance of Regional applied to IP-A4 is particularly impressive, given the extreme differences in class distribution between IP-A4 and the other data sets (see Table 1). We note that Regional is somewhat less successful training on IP-A4. In fact, training on IP-A4 and testing on IP-B is the one case where Regional underperforms Neighborhood. However, the difference in performance is small (<5%). Finally, and not surprisingly, we see a benefit to training on a number of diverse data sets instead of a single data set. Specifically, we achieve 77% training on all of the IP-A data sets and testing on IP-B, whereas we see a lot of variation (55% - 85%) training on individual days from IP-A.

4. FEATURE EFFECTIVENESS ON IDENTITY RESOLUTION

To demonstrate that regional features capture meaningful and informative behaviors of nodes, we present a collection of identity resolution tasks. In each task, we compute a set of regional features on a pair of networks whose node-sets overlap. Our hypothesis is that a node's feature values will be similar across graphs. We present an experimental framework that allows us to test this empirically. In our experiments, we will demonstrate how this method can be used to perform "de-anonymization"on social network datasets when external non-anonymized data is available.

4.1 Problem Statement

For a pair of graphs whose node-sets overlap, but whose edge-sets can be distinct (or even represent a totally different type of observation), can we use network structure alone to map nodes in one network to nodes in the other? More realistically, can we reduce the entropy associated with each node in one graph, with respect to its possible identity among nodes in the second graph? For a given method, we will measure success at this task by counting how many "incorrect" nodes the method guesses before it finds the correct node in the second graph.

4.2 Methodology

We are given two graphs, G_{target} and $G_{reference}$, and a vertex v_{test} which exists in both graphs. To test a given identity resolution strategy, we allow the strategy to guess reference vertices $\langle v_1^{guess}, v_2^{guess}, \ldots, v_k^{guess} \rangle$ until it correctly guesses v_{test}. The score associated with this strategy is k, the number of guesses required to find the node. The baseline method is to guess at random; for this strategy we assume the expected score $|V_{reference}|/2$.

The strategies we test experimentally use structural features to compute guesses. We present results for (1) Local features only, (2) Neighborhood features only, and (3) Regional features. The features are computed using *ReFeX* on G_{target}. The same features are then computed on $G_{reference}$. For a given strategy, the guesses are generated in order of increasing Euclidian distance from V_{target} in feature space. Our hypothesis is that Regional will score lower (i.e. better) than Local or Neighborhood.

To compare the overall performances of strategies, we compute scores across a set $S_{overlap}$ of all vertices that exist in both graphs. When it is not computationally feasible to analyze every node in $S_{overlap}$, we select a set of vertices $S_{test} \subset S_{overlap}$ and report all scores for nodes in S_{test}. In these experiments, we select S_{test} by taking the 1000 vertices in V_{target} with the highest degree, and keeping only those vertices that are also in $S_{overlap}$.

There are a number of ways to compare performance on a given test set. For example, the mean score across all target instances is a measure of success, with lower mean scores indicating better performance. We can also compute the fraction of target instances that score less than a given threshold; here a larger fraction is better. For example, we can report the fraction of target vertices whose score is less than 1% of $|V_{reference}|$.[4]

4.3 Data

Table 3 outlines the data sets used in this set of experiments. The first is a pair of Twitter networks from 2008, including a who-follows-whom network and a who-mentions-whom network. The second is an SMS communication network. The third is a collection of 28 days of Yahoo IM events. The fourth is IP traffic on two separate enterprise networks, observed at several different times. We described the IP network in details in Section 3.1.

Yahoo! IM Networks. Each graph here is a collection of IM

[4]If we combine the latter across all thresholds, we can treat it as the cumulative distribution function of $p(score(x))$, the empirical probability distribution over scores for this strategy. This presentation is harder to interpret, however, since one strategy may perform better in some regions and worse in others, and we are generally concerned with the lowest possible scores.

Data Graph	Source	# Nodes	# Edges	Weighted?	Directed?	# Local Features	# Nbrhood Features	# Regional Features	# Recursive Iterations
Twitter (T)	Who-follows-whom	465K	845K	Yes	No	3	8	45	6
Twitter (R)	Who-mentions-whom-1st	840K	1.4M	Yes	No	3	8	45	–
SMS (T)	04/01/2008	144K	580K	Yes	Yes	7	21	53	3
SMS (R)	04/02/2008	128K	505K	Yes	Yes	7	21	53	–
Yahoo! IM (T)	Day 1	50K	123K	Yes	Yes	3	12	79	5
Yahoo! IM (R)	Day 2-28	29K-100K	80K-280K	Yes	Yes	3	12	79	–
IP Comm. (T)	IP-A1	81K	206K	Yes	Yes	7	22	373	4
IP Comm. (R)	IP-A2, -A3, -A4, IP-B	57K-206K	137K-466K	Yes	Yes	7	22	373	–

Table 3: Data sets used in the identity resolution task. (R) refers to the Reference Graph. (T) refers to the Target Graph. The features are generated on the Target Graph are used to compute feature values in the Reference Graph.

events taken from one of 28 days of observation.[5] Each node is an IM user, and each link is a communication event on a given day. In some cases, multiple events are reported for a given pair of users on a given day; when this happens the links are given weights according to how many events are reported.

We use the IMs from day 1 as G_{target}, and compute scores for the other days (2 - 28) as $G_{reference}$. The task here is to take an IM user from day 1 and locate him in later days. Figure 5 shows that the similarity in node-sets and edge-sets with G_{target} is low for all $G_{reference}$ graphs. However, in most cases there is a significant overlap with the 1000 nodes in the test set S_{test}.

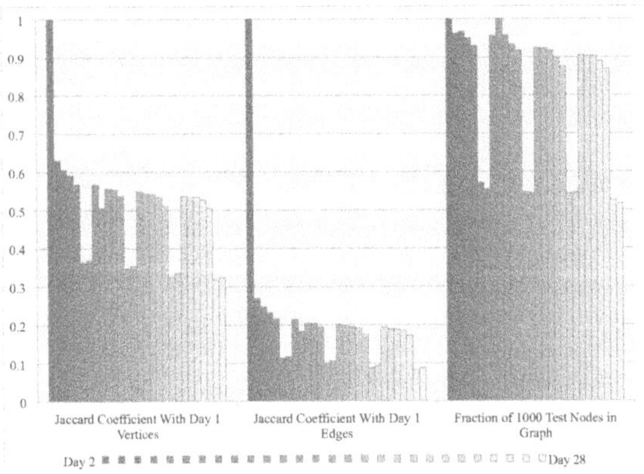

Figure 5: Yahoo! IM graphs across 28 days. The similarity between G_{target} on Day 1 and $G_{reference}$ on Days 2 to 28 is low but there is significant overlap in most cases with the test nodes.

Enterprise Network Traces. We describe these IP networks in detail in Section 3.1. The target graph comes from IP-A1. There are four reference graphs total: IP-A2, IP-A3, IP-A4, and IP-B. The task is to identify an external IP address from one day to the next or one IP network to the next. A potential application of this task is to de-anonymize a network trace where the IP addresses are hidden; one could observe a non-anonymized enterprise trace and use structural information to guess the identities of the anonymized IPs.

Twitter Relationships. This dataset consists of two graphs taken from Twitter in 2008.[6] One is a social "who-follows-whom" network that was generated by starting with a few seed users (all famous people with verified accounts) and crawling "follows" links for a few iterations. The other is taken from actual tweets observed during a year. The users whose tweets are observed are the same as the users in the social network.

To construct a graph from tweets, we generate "mentions-first" edges. That is, if a tweet by $user1$ contains a username (e.g. @$user2$), we add a link between $user1$ and $user2$ in the network, but only if $user2$ is the first user mentioned in the tweet. We do not include self-mentions.

For this experiment, we use the social network as G_{target} and the mentioning network as $G_{reference}$. Success at this task indicates that one could de-anonymize a social network by using publicly available text data, so long as usernames can be parsed from the text. This has important implications with respect to privacy of users in published "anonymized" social networks.

SMS Messages. SMS-Message dataset is constructed from short messages in a mobile phone operator at Asia. Each node corresponds to a mobile phone client. The reference and the target graphs encode the number of short messages among those nodes, extracted at two different days. We also eliminate those pairs of less active users with only one message exchange between them.

4.4 Feature Effectiveness Results

We present results for each of the four datasets. The first three demonstrate the effectiveness of regional features for identity resolution, and the fourth serves as a practitioner's note regarding test-set selection.

Yahoo! IM Networks. Figure 6 shows the average score for each of the 27 reference graphs, as a percentage of the expected score in the baseline strategy (recall that the baseline strategy scores $\frac{|V_{reference}|}{2}$ on average). All feature-based strategies outperform the baseline strategy, but performance of all strategies suffers on weekends when the graphs are significantly different. In general, expected scores are much better (lower) for Neighborhood than Local, and somewhat better for Regional than Neighborhood.

Figure 7 provides another view of the performance. Each data point here shows the fraction of test nodes that scored better than 1% of the maximum possible score $|V_{reference}|$. A higher fraction here indicates better performance, as the distribution of scores is higher near the minimum score 1. Again, Regional outperforms the other strategies in most instances. This improvement decreases on the weekends, and in one case (Day 27) Regional does no better than Local.

Poor performance on the weekends is not unexpected, and strength-

[5] http://sandbox.yahoo.com/

[6] http://www.public.asu.edu/ mdechoud/datasets.html

ported results are fractions of $|S_{test}|$. Even though the traces were collected from separate networks, common external nodes (e.g., google.com) will be included in both.

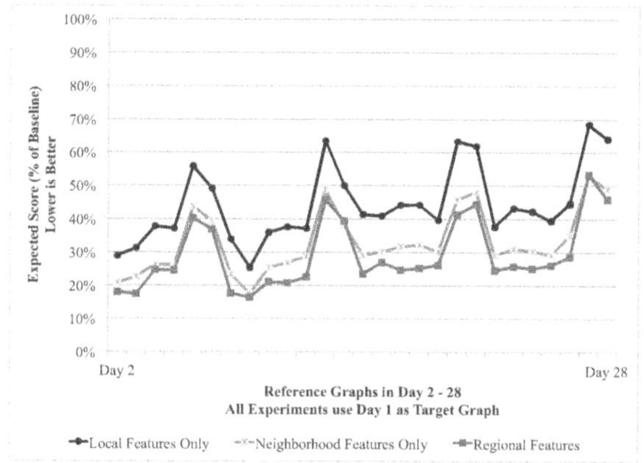

Figure 6: Yahoo! IM: Regional is consistently better (lower average score) at tracking test nodes across several weeks of IM traffic.

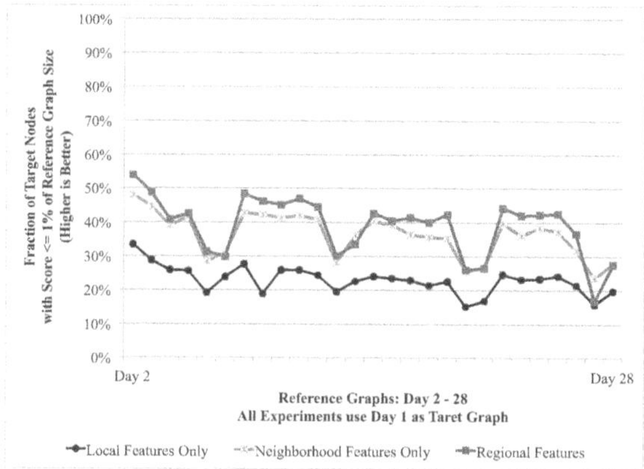

Figure 7: Yahoo! IM: Regional is consistently able to identify more test nodes within the first 1% of guesses (higher is better). It dips in performance corresponding to weekends, when the graph structure is very different.

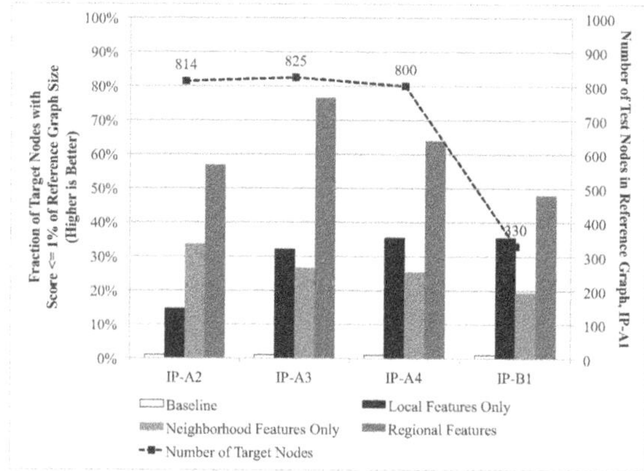

Figure 8: IP Communication: Regional is the best strategy for tracking IP addresses (higher is better). Even in the IP-B1 graph, which was observed on a different enterprise network, Regional locates nearly 50% of test nodes in the first 1% of its guesses.

ens our belief that structural features are capturing behavior. Recall from Figure 5 that the set of active users is significantly different on the weekends, as is the set of observed communications. Intuitively, it is an obvious fact that many users behave differently both in general and specifically with respect to IM communication on the weekend than during the weekdays. Regional is especially susceptible to errors in this case, because these changes in behavior are amplified during recursive feature generation.

Enterprise Network Traces. Regional is very effective at tracking external IP addresses over time, as seen Figure 8. It dominates the performance of Local and Neighborhood in all tests, with over 45% of S_{test} scoring in the top 1% of possible scores even a year after the communications in G_{target} are observed. Note that S_{test} is significantly smaller after a year due to decreased overlap; the reported results are fractions of $|S_{test}|$.

In this task, average scores were inconsistent, with Local outperforming Regional in some instances. Analysis of the distributions of scores here shows that Regional outperforms Local for a majority of the test instances, but there is a small subset of test nodes for which Regional performs extremely poorly (near baseline).

Twitter Relationships. This experiment is the "hardest", in that G_{target} and $G_{reference}$ are generated by different processes altogether. G_{target} is a social network of users following other users, while $G_{reference}$ is generated by users mentioning each other in tweets. Surprisingly, our method is still able to do well at resolving some users here.

For this experiment, we applied each strategy to several different test sets, rather than just taking the top 1000 nodes by degree. In particular, we tested separately on each vertical logarithmic bin (see Section 2.2.2). For bins with over 1000 users, we sampled 1000 users uniformly at random.

Figure 9 shows the expected scores of each strategy. The ten highest-degree bins, taken together, correspond roughly to the top 1000 nodes by degree. Regional features outperform other strategies in this range, although their performance drops off in the lower degree bins.

All three strategies perform less well on these graphs than on the other datasets, but they are still able to reduce the entropy significantly for the most active users. For example, the highest degree user is BarackObama, and Regional achieved a score of 5 on that instance (the four wrong guesses were AddToAny, MrTweet, tferriss, and THE_REAL_SHAQ). Local and Neighborhood each scored 24 for BarackObama.

For the lowest-degree nodes, all methods perform worse than baseline. This drop-off is expected; less active nodes are harder to identify because (1) they have fewer observed behaviors to leverage and (2) there are more nodes that are very similar to them.

SMS Messages. This dataset serves to point out a case in which Regional does not perform best, but also a practitioner's note that

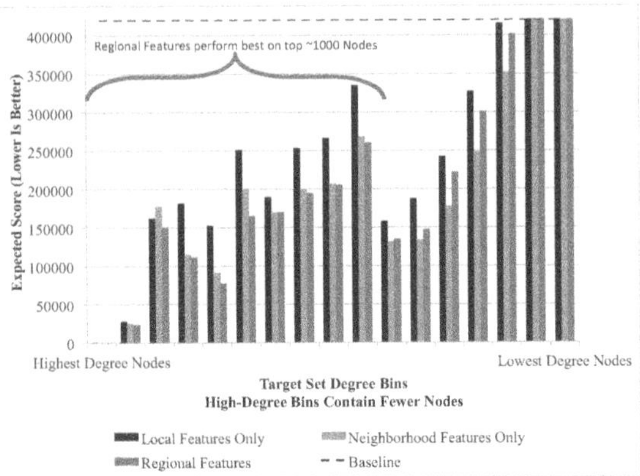

Figure 9: Twitter: Regional features are able to de-anonymize more active nodes (lower is better).

often allows for improved results when performing identity resolution outside of an experimental setting.

Figure 10 shows that the performance with respect to nodes scoring better than 1% of $|V_{reference}|$ can depend on the elements of S_{test}. When S_{test} consists of the top 1000 nodes by degree, each method scores better than 1% on $60-65\%$ of the test nodes, and Regional performs worst. However, if each strategy is allowed to "hand-pick" a test set by taking the top 1000 nodes by feature-vector magnitude (in that strategy's feature space), performance improves across the board. Regional improves the most, and is the top performer in this case.

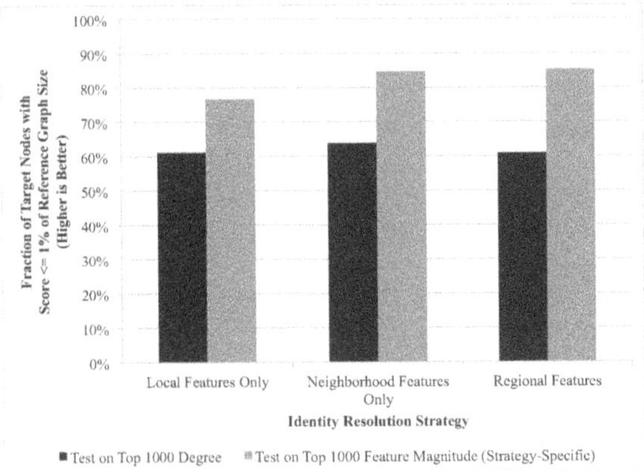

Figure 10: SMS: When allowed to suggest test nodes, Neighborhood and Regional locate near 85% of test nodes in the top 1% of guesses. Without test set selection, all strategies perform equally well.

By allowing each strategy to select its test set, we leverage the fact that a high-degree node may be less distinctive than a low-degree node that has other large feature values. However, as an experiment to compare strategies this approach is not "fair" because the set of test instances is different for each strategy.

We tested the other datasets to determine whether feature magnitude is always better than degree for selecting test nodes. While this is true in general, there are cases in which performance degrades when using feature magnitudes. This is often due to different sizes in the overlap between the 1000 proposed test nodes and $V_{reference}$.

With respect to runtime, our largest graph (Twitter Mentions graph with 840K nodes and 1.4M edges) ran in about 5 hours on a commodity processor. Graphs with fewer than 100K nodes run in an hour or less.

5. RELATED WORK

Feature Engineering in Graph data. There has been comprehensive work studying both global and local structural features of real graphs. For example, at global scale, graph diameter has been observed to be small [2] and to shrink over time [20]. It has also been reported that the number of edges in a time-varying graph grows super-linearly with the number of nodes, following a power-law relation [20]. Moreover, the principal (largest) eigenvalue of the graph is shown to be informative as a vulnerability measure of the graph [27]. Other local and community-level observations show that degree distributions in many graphs follow power-laws [5, 7, 17, 24] and that graphs exhibit modular structure, with nodes forming groups, and groups within groups [9, 14]. This body of work has informed our selection of a set of neighborhood features, upon which we then build recursive features.

Feature Extraction for Data Mining. There also exists related work which exploits feature extraction from graphs for several data mining tasks. One study approaches link prediction as a supervised learning problem [21]. They extract topological features for node pairs and show that the features boost prediction performance and that the supervised approach outperforms unsupervised methods. Another recent study [16] develops a multi-level framework to detect anomalies in time-varying graphs based on graph, subgraph, and node level features. The algorithms rely on extracting graph-level (global) features and tracking these metrics over time. The time points identified as interesting or suspicious are passed to finer levels where more complex tools inspect node and community features to spot regions of interests and flag abnormal nodes. Another study extracts egonet features and patterns in order to detect anomalous nodes in weighted graphs[1]. There has also been work on using local and global structural features to improve the performance of network classifiers[10]. In our work, we introduce methods for *recursive feature extraction.* Our results show that recursive features yield better performance in several data mining tasks, such as transfer learning and identity resolution, compared to their non-recursive counterparts.

Another body of related work uses frequent sub-graphs as structural features for classification of graphs [18, 8] and anomaly detection [26, 22]. These methods, however, assume that the nodes in given graphs have labels. On the other hand, our feature extraction procedures exploit the structure of the graphs, without any assumption on the availability of labels.

Transfer Learning. Transfer learning (i.e., domain adaption) has been a very active research area in recent years. Representative work includes multi-label text classification [30, 13], cross-domain sentiment prediction [4, 6, 15], intrusion detection [12], verb argument classification [19], cross-lingual classification [25], and cross-domain relation extraction [29]. In all of these scenarios, the features are *given* as the input of their algorithms (e.g. the word frequency of the documents) and the goal is to leverage the given features to boost performance in the target domain. In this paper, we aim to answer an orthogonal question: *what kind of features are effective in transferring the knowledge from the source domain to the target domain?* Our case studies show that the proposed recursive features are indeed effective for across-network classification and identity resolution, especially when there are few or no labels in the target domain, or homophily among class labels does not hold. We expect the proposed recursive features to have wide applicability for transfer learning tasks.

6. CONCLUSIONS

We described a novel algorithm *ReFeX*, which extracts regional features from nodes based on their neighborhood connectivity. These regional features capture behavior in terms of the the kind of nodes to which a given node is connected as opposed to the identity of those nodes. We showed that *ReFeX* was scalable and effective in various graph mining tasks including within- and across-network classification and identity resolution tasks.

Future work includes using the regional features generated by *ReFeX* for other mining tasks such as clustering, anomaly detection, and network comparison.

7. ACKNOWLEDGEMENTS

We thank Danai Koutra for all her help on this paper. This work was performed under the auspices of the U.S. Department of Energy by Lawrence Livermore National Laboratory under Contract No. DE-AC52-07NA27344 (LLNL-CONF-479453) and partially supported by Army Research Laboratory (ARL) under Cooperative Agreement No. W911NF-09-2-0053. The U.S. Government is authorized to reproduce and distribute reprints for Government purposes notwithstanding any copyright annotation thereon. The views and conclusions contained herein are those of the authors and should not be interpreted as necessarily representing the official policies or endorsements, either expressed or implied, of ARL or the U.S. Government.

8. REFERENCES

[1] L. Akoglu, M. McGlohon, and C. Faloutsos. Oddball: Spotting anomalies in weighted graphs. In *PAKDD*, pages 410–421, 2010.

[2] R. Albert, H. Jeong, and A.-L. Barabasi. Diameter of the world wide web. *Nature*, (401):130–131, 1999.

[3] A.-L. Barabasi, R. Albert, and H. Jeong. Scale-free characteristics of random networks: the topology of the world-wide web. *Physica A: Statistical Mechanics and its Applications*, 281(1-4):69 – 77, 2000.

[4] J. Blitzer, M. Dredze, and F. Pereira. Biographies, bollywood, boom-boxes and blenders: Domain adaptation for sentiment classification. In *ACL*, 2007.

[5] D. Chakrabarti, Y. Zhan, and C. Faloutsos. R-MAT: A recursive model for graph mining. In *SDM*, Apr. 2004.

[6] W. Dai, Q. Yang, G.-R. Xue, and Y. Yu. Boosting for transfer learning. In *ICML*, pages 193–200, 2007.

[7] M. Faloutsos, P. Faloutsos, and C. Faloutsos. On power-law relationships of the internet topology. *SIGCOMM*, pages 251–262, Aug-Sept. 1999.

[8] H. Fei and J. Huan. Structure feature selection for graph classification. In *CIKM*, pages 991–1000, 2008.

[9] G. Flake, S. Lawrence, C. L. Giles, and F. Coetzee. Self-organization and identification of web communities. *IEEE Computer*, 35(3), Mar. 2002.

[10] B. Gallagher and T. Eliassi-Rad. Leveraging label-independent features for classification in sparsely labeled networks: An empirical study. *Lecture Notes in Computer Science*, 5498:1–19, 2010.

[11] B. Gallagher, H. Tong, T. Eliassi-Rad, and C. Faloutsos. Using ghost edges for classification in sparsely labeled networks. In *KDD*, pages 256–264, 2008.

[12] J. Gao, W. Fan, J. Jiang, and J. Han. Knowledge transfer via multiple model local structure mapping. In *KDD*, pages 283–291, 2008.

[13] N. Ghamrawi and A. McCallum. Collective multi-label classification. In *CIKM*, pages 195–200, 2005.

[14] M. Girvan and M. E. J. Newman. Community structure in social and biological networks. *PNAS*, 99:7821, 2002.

[15] J. He, Y. Liu, and R. D. Lawrence. Graph-based transfer learning. In *CIKM*, pages 937–946, 2009.

[16] K. Henderson, T. Eliassi-Rad, C. Faloutsos, L. Akoglu, L. Li, K. Maruhashi, B. A. Prakash, and H. Tong. Metric forensics: a multi-level approach for mining volatile graphs. In *KDD*, pages 163–172, 2010.

[17] J. M. Kleinberg, R. Kumar, P. Raghavan, S. Rajagopalan, and A. S. Tomkins. The Web as a graph: Measurements, models and methods. *Lecture Notes in Computer Science*, 1627:1–17, 1999.

[18] X. Kong and P. S. Yu. Multi-label feature selection for graph classification. In *ICDM*, pages 274–283, 2010.

[19] S.-I. Lee, V. Chatalbashev, D. Vickrey, and D. Koller. Learning a meta-level prior for feature relevance from multiple related tasks. In *ICML*, pages 489–496, 2007.

[20] J. Leskovec, J. Kleinberg, and C. Faloutsos. Graphs over time: densification laws, shrinking diameters and possible explanations. In *KDD*, pages 177–187, 2005.

[21] R. N. Lichtenwalter, J. T. Lussier, and N. V. Chawla. New perspectives and methods in link prediction. In *KDD*, pages 243–252, 2010.

[22] C. Liu, X. Yan, H. Yu, J. Han, and P. S. Yu. Mining behavior graphs for "backtrace" of noncrashing bugs. In *SDM*, 2005.

[23] S. A. Macskassy and F. Provost. A simple relational classifier. In *Proc. of the 2nd Workshop on Multi-Relational Data Mining (MRDM) at KDD*, pages 64–76, 2003.

[24] M. E. J. Newman. Power laws, Pareto distributions and Zipf's law. *Contemporary Physics*, 46:323–351, 2005.

[25] X. Ni, J.-T. Sun, J. Hu, and Z. Chen. Cross lingual text classification by mining multilingual topics from wikipedia. In *WSDM*, pages 375–384, 2011.

[26] C. C. Noble and D. J. Cook. Graph-based anomaly detection. In *KDD*, pages 631–636, 2003.

[27] H. Tong, B. A. Prakash, C. E. Tsourakakis, T. Eliassi-Rad, C. Faloutsos, and D. H. Chau. On the vulnerability of large graphs. In *ICDM*, pages 1091–1096, 2010.

[28] I. H. Witten and E. Frank. *Data Mining: Practical Machine Learning Tools and Techniques, Second Edition (Morgan Kaufmann Series in Data Management Systems)*. Morgan Kaufmann Publishers Inc., San Francisco, CA, USA, 2005.

[29] L. Yao, S. Riedel, and A. McCallum. Collective cross-document relation extraction without labelled data. In *EMNLP*, pages 1013–1023, 2010.

[30] J. Zhang, Z. Ghahramani, and Y. Yang. Learning multiple related tasks using latent independent component analysis. In *NIPS*, 2005.

Triangle Listing in Massive Networks and Its Applications

Shumo Chu
Nanyang Technological University, Singapore
shumo.chu@acm.org

James Cheng
Nanyang Technological University, Singapore
j.cheng@acm.org

ABSTRACT

Triangle listing is one of the fundamental algorithmic problems whose solution has numerous applications especially in the analysis of complex networks, such as the computation of clustering coefficient, transitivity, triangular connectivity, etc. Existing algorithms for triangle listing are mainly in-memory algorithms, whose performance cannot scale with the massive volume of today's fast growing networks. When the input graph cannot fit into main memory, triangle listing requires random disk accesses that can incur prohibitively large I/O cost. Some streaming and sampling algorithms have been proposed but these are approximation algorithms. We propose an I/O-efficient algorithm for triangle listing. Our algorithm is exact and avoids random disk access. Our results show that our algorithm is scalable and outperforms the state-of-the-art local triangle estimation algorithm.

Categories and Subject Descriptors

H.2.8 [**DATABASE MANAGEMENT**]: Database Applications—*Data mining*
; G.2.2 [**DISCRETE MATHEMATICS**]: Graph Theory—*Graph algorithms*

General Terms

Algorithms, Experimentation, Performance

Keywords

Triangle Listing, Triangle Counting, Clustering Coefficient, Large Graphs, Massive Networks

1. INTRODUCTION

We study the problem of **triangle listing** in a simple undirected graph G, that is, *listing all triangles in* G. Our focus is to design efficient algorithm for triangle listing when G is too large to fit into main memory and is disk-resident.

Triangles are one of the fundamental types of small subgraphs most commonly used in the analysis of complex graphs/networks. In particular, a triangle is also the shortest non-trivial cycle (i.e., a cycle of length 3) and the smallest non-trivial clique (i.e., a clique of size 3). The concept of triangle is at the heart of the definition of many important measures for network analysis, such as the clustering coefficient (of a single vertex and of the entire network) [36], transitivity [35, 28], triangular connectivity [8], etc. All these measures can be directly computed from the result of triangle listing.

The aforementioned triangle-centered measures have a large number of important applications. In addition, triangle listing also has a broad range of applications in other areas such as in the discovery of dense subgraphs [34], in the detection of spamming activities [9], in the study of motif occurrences [27], in the uncovering of hidden thematic relationships in the Web [15], etc. In all these applications, triangle listing plays a vital role in their computation.

Although many algorithms have been proposed for triangle listing, these existing algorithms [22, 23, 4, 7, 30, 29, 26, 16] all fall into the category of *in-memory algorithms*. The best existing in-memory algorithms require space that is asymptotically linear in the size of the input graph. Unfortunately, many real-world networks have grown exceedingly large in recent years and are continuing to grow at a steady rate. For example, the Web graph has over 1 trillion webpages (by Google in 2008), most social networks (e.g., Facebook, MSN) have millions to billions of users, many citation networks (e.g., DBLP, Citeseer) have millions of publications, other networks such as phone-call networks, email networks, stock-market networks, etc., are also massively large.

For handling large graphs that cannot fit into main memory, a number of approximation algorithms have been proposed [3, 6, 14, 10, 9, 33]. However, all these algorithms are restricted to approximation of *triangle counting*, i.e., estimating the number of triangles in a graph or that formed at each vertex. Algorithms for estimating the total number of triangles in a graph only are more accurate [3, 6, 14, 10, 33], but their applications are also much more limited than those of triangle listing. Algorithms for estimating the number of triangles formed at each vertex in a graph, also called *local triangle counting*, have a wider range of applications but the state-of-the-art algorithm [9] is still not accurate enough. Moreover, the set of applications of triangle counting is only a small subset of that of triangle listing, as the result of triangle counting is directly obtainable from that of triangle listing.

We propose an I/O-efficient algorithm for exact triangle listing. Designing such an algorithm is difficult because triangle listing requires to access the neighbors of the neighbor of a vertex, which may appear arbitrarily in any position in the graph. Thus, random access to the graph stored on disk is required, which incurs huge I/O cost.

Our algorithm iteratively partitions the input graph G into a set of subgraphs that fit into memory and processes triangle listing in

KDD'11, August 21–24, 2011, San Diego, California, USA.

each local subgraph. To ensure the correctness and completeness of the final result computed iteratively from the local subgraphs, we categorize the triangles into three types. We devise an mechanism that lists all Type 1 and Type 2 triangles, and then converts the remaining Type 3 triangles into Types 1 and 2 by a new partition at the next iteration. To limit the total number of iterations, we show that we can remove all edges in each subgraph at the end of each iteration, thus shrinking G until it becomes empty. We propose two effective algorithms for graph partitioning for the task of triangle listing in our framework, one achieving high efficiency in practice while the other giving theoretical bound on the total number of iterations (also efficient in practice).

We evaluate our algorithm on large real datasets with up to 106 million vertices and 1,877 million edges, by comparing with the state-of-the-art in-memory algorithm [26] and the most related approximation algorithm [9]. Our algorithm achieves comparable performance with the in-memory algorithm when the graph can fit into memory. For large graphs that cannot fit into memory, the error rate of the approximation algorithm [9] can be as large as 95% to 133% while ours returns exact result, with comparable running time and memory. When we attempt to attain a lower error rate, e.g., at 50%, the approximation algorithm is already orders of magnitude slower than our exact algorithm.

Paper Organization. Section 2 gives the notations and problem definition. Section 3 describes an in-memory algorithm. Section 4 discusses our main algorithm. Section 5 presents two applications of our algorithm. Section 6 reports the experimental results. Section 7 gives the related work. Section 8 concludes the paper.

2. NOTATIONS AND PROBLEM DEFINITION

Let $G = (V_G, E_G)$ be a simple undirected graph, where V_G is the set of vertices and E_G is the set of edges. We define the set of *adjacent vertices* (or *neighbors*) of a vertex v in G as $adj_G(v) = \{u : (u, v) \in E_G\}$, and the *degree* of v in G as $deg_G(v) = |adj_G(v)|$. We assume that the graph is stored in the adjacency list representation, with vertices ordered according to their ID.

Given three distinct vertices, $u, v, w \in V_G$, we say that u, v and w form a *triangle* in G if $(u, v), (u, w), (v, w) \in E_G$. We use $\triangle_{uvw}$ to denote the triangle formed by the vertices u, v and w.

The set of triangles that consist of a vertex v, denoted by $\triangle(v)$, is defined as

$$\triangle(v) = \{\triangle_{uvw} : u, w \in adj_G(v), (u, w) \in E_G\}. \quad (1)$$

The *triangle number* of v, denoted by $N_\triangle(v)$, is defined as $N_\triangle(v) = |\triangle(v)|$.

Let $\triangle(G)$ be the set of all triangles in G. Then, $\triangle(G)$ is given by

$$\triangle(G) = \bigcup_{v \in V_G} \triangle(v). \quad (2)$$

The number of triangles in G, denoted by $N_\triangle(G)$, is defined as $N_\triangle(G) = |\triangle(G)|$, which is also given as follows

$$N_\triangle(G) = \frac{1}{3} \sum_{v \in V_G} N_\triangle(v). \quad (3)$$

Equation 3 holds because every triangle $\triangle_{uvw}$ is counted three times for the three vertices u, v and w.

Given a vertex $v \in V_G$, we say that u, v and w form an *open triangle* centered at v if $u, w \in adj_G(v)$. An open triangle is considered as a potential triangle. A triangle $\triangle_{uvw}$ may be regarded as a *closed triangle* and by definition, $\triangle_{uvw}$ contains three open triangles, centered at u, v, and w, respectively.

Table 1: Notations

Symbol	Description
$G = (V_G, E_G)$	A simple undirected graph
$adj_G(v)$	The set of adjacent vertices of v in G
$deg_G(v)$	Degree of v in G
$\triangle_{uvw}$	A triangle formed by u, v and w
$\triangle(v)$	The set of triangles that contains v (Eq. 1)
$N_\triangle(v)$	The triangle number of v, $N_\triangle(v) = \|\triangle(v)\|$
$\triangle(G)$	The set of all triangles in G (Eq. 2)
$N_\triangle(G)$	The number of triangles in G (Eq. 3)
$N_\vee(v)$	The number of open triangles centered at v (Eq. 4)
M	Available main memory size
B	Disk block size
$scan(N)$	$\Theta(N/B)$ I/Os
$sort(N)$	$\Theta(\frac{N}{B} \log_{M/B} \frac{N}{B})$ I/Os

The number of open triangles centered at v, denoted by $N_\vee(v)$, is defined as

$$N_\vee(v) = \frac{1}{2} deg_G(v)(deg_G(v) - 1). \quad (4)$$

Intuitively, $N_\vee(v)$ defines the maximum number of triangles that can be potentially formed from v.

The following example illustrates the concepts.

Example 1. Let G be the graph given in Figure 1. Consider the vertices b and e, we have $\triangle(b) = \{\triangle_{abc}, \triangle_{bcg}, \triangle_{bgi}\}$ and $\triangle(e) = \{\triangle_{dej}, \triangle_{efh}\}$. Thus, $N_\triangle(b) = 3$ and $N_\triangle(e) = 2$. By Equation 4, $N_\vee(b) = 6$ and $N_\vee(e) = 6$ since $deg_G(b) = 4$ and $deg_G(e) = 4$. We can also easy find $\triangle(G) = \{\triangle_{abc}, \triangle_{bcg}, \triangle_{bgi}, \triangle_{dej}, \triangle_{efh}, \triangle_{jkl}\}$ and $N_\triangle(G) = |\triangle(G)| = 6$. □

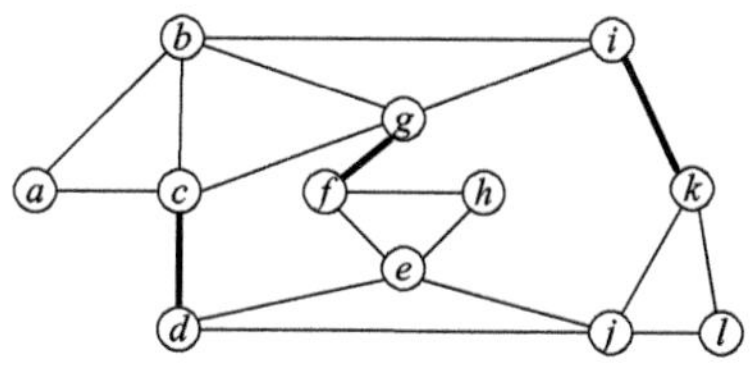

Figure 1: A Graph G

Problem Definition. This paper studies the problem of **triangle listing** defined as follows. Given a graph $G = (V_G, E_G)$, output $\triangle(G)$. In particular, we design I/O-efficient algorithms when G cannot fit into main memory, i.e., $(|V_G| + |E_G|) > M$, where M is the size of available main memory.

For the complexity analysis of I/O-efficient algorithms, we use the standard I/O model [2] with the following parameters: M is the available main memory size and B is the disk block size, where $1 \ll B \leq M/2$.

We also use the following standard I/O complexity notations: $scan(N)=\Theta(N/B)$ I/Os and $sort(N)=\Theta(\frac{N}{B} \log_{M/B} \frac{N}{B})$ I/Os, where N is the amount of data being read or written from/to disk.

Table 1 gives the frequently-used notations in the paper.

3. IN-MEMORY TRIANGLE LISTING

In this section, we first present an in-memory algorithm for triangle listing and use it to highlight the difficulty for triangle listing when main memory is insufficient.

We sketch the algorithm in Algorithm 1. Assume that the input graph G is in its adjacency-list representation and the vertices are

Algorithm 1 *In-Memory Triangle Listing*

Input: A graph $G = (V_G, E_G)$
Output: $\triangle(G)$

```
1. △(G) ← ∅;
2. for each u ∈ V_G do
3.     for each v ∈ adj_G(u), where v > u, do
4.         for each w ∈ (adj_G(u) ∩ adj_G(v)), where w > v, do
5.             △(G) ← (△(G) ∪ {△_uvw});
6. return △(G);
```

ordered in ascending order of their vertex ID, which is the most common format used for graph storage. The algorithm intersects the adjacency-list of each vertex u with the adjacency-list of u's neighbor v. Clearly, each vertex w as the result of the intersection is a neighbor of both u and v, and as u and v are also neighbors, we obtain a triangle $\triangle_{uvw}$.

A naive algorithm for triangle listing processes every neighbor v in $adj_G(u)$, and intersects the entire $adj_G(u)$ and $adj_G(v)$. This involves much redundant processing. In Algorithm 1, we only process a neighbor v that is ordered after u (Line 3), because if v is ordered before u, i.e., $v < u$, then v has been processed before u and hence the triangle $\triangle_{vuw}$ must have been already listed (note that $\triangle_{vuw} = \triangle_{uvw}$). For the intersection between $adj_G(u)$ and $adj_G(v)$ (Line 4), we also skip those vertices that are ordered before v (hence also u) in $adj_G(u)$ and $adj_G(v)$. The above process is similar to the state-of-the-art in-memory algorithm for triangle listing [26], except that their work orders the vertices in non-increasing order of their degree, which requires pre-processing.

When G cannot fit into main memory, however, the I/O cost becomes a bottleneck. Most existing in-memory algorithms [22, 23, 4, 7, 29, 26, 16] require random access to each $adj_G(v)$ for each $v \in adj_G(u)$ (as in Line 4 for the intersection). Note that each $adj_G(u)$ in Algorithm 1 is read sequentially as we read G, but $adj_G(v)$ can be in an arbitrary position on disk where G is stored. Others [30] use an additional array for each vertex in G and the total size of these arrays is in the order of the size of the input graph; thus these arrays need to be stored on disk and random access is again inevitable.

When G cannot fit into main memory, Algorithm 1 requires $O(|E_G| \cdot scan(d_{max}))$ I/Os in the worst case, where d_{max} is the maximum vertex degree in G, since we need to randomly access $adj_G(v)$ for each edge $(u, v) \in E_G$ and $deg_G(v) = O(d_{max})$. This I/O cost can be prohibitively large especially when G is large.

4. I/O-EFFICIENT TRIANGLE LISTING

In this section, we first sketch the framework of our algorithm and then present the details of the algorithm.

4.1 Algorithm Framework

When the input graph G cannot fit into memory, we could only load a portion (i.e., a subgraph) of G that can fit into memory each time. Thus, our algorithm iteratively performs triangle listing in a subgraph of G that fits in memory. We outline the framework of our algorithm as follows.

- Each iteration:
  - Partition G into a set of subgraphs, $\mathcal{P} = \{G_1, \ldots, G_i, \ldots, G_p\}$, such that each G_i can fit into memory;
  - Load each G_i into memory and perform triangle listing in G_i;
  - Remove from G those edges of G_i that can no longer contribute to triangle listing.
- Repeat the above iteration until G becomes empty.

The main idea of our algorithm is to iteratively partition the graph and perform triangle listing in each local subgraph G_i separately, as to avoid random access to arbitrary vertices (and their adjacency-list) in the graph.

The concept is simple but there are a number of challenging technical issues: (1) ensuring the correctness and completeness of the final result obtained from the iterative local computations; (2) an effective and efficient partitioning algorithm for triangle listing; and (3) bounding the overall I/O complexity of the algorithm (i.e., the I/O complexity at each step and the number of iterations). We discuss the above three issues in each of the following subsections.

4.2 Correctness and Global-Completeness of Local Triangle Listing

We first propose an algorithm that ensures the correctness of triangle listing in each local subgraph of G as well as the completeness of the global result obtained from all local computations.

The design of our algorithm is based on the following Lemma.

LEMMA 1. *Let $\mathcal{P} = \{G_1, \ldots, G_i, \ldots, G_p\}$ be a partition of G, where $\cup_{1 \le i \le p} V_{G_i} = V_G$ and $V_{G_i} \cap V_{G_j} = \emptyset$ for $1 \le i < j \le p$. Then, $\triangle(G) = \triangle 1 \cup \triangle 2 \cup \triangle 3$, where $\triangle 1$, $\triangle 2$, and $\triangle 3$ are disjoint sets defined as follows.*

- $\triangle 1 = \cup_{1 \le i \le p}\{\triangle_{uvw} : u, v, w \in V_{G_i}\}$.
- $\triangle 2 = \cup_{1 \le i,j \le p \,\wedge\, i \ne j}\{\triangle_{uvw} : u, v \in V_{G_i}, w \in V_{G_j}\}$.
- $\triangle 3 = \cup_{1 \le i < j < k \le p}\{\triangle_{uvw} : u \in V_{G_i}, v \in V_{G_j}, w \in V_{G_k}\}$.

PROOF. First, $(\triangle 1 \cup \triangle 2 \cup \triangle 3) \subseteq \triangle(G)$, since the elements in $\triangle 1$, $\triangle 2$, and $\triangle 3$ are triangles in G.

Next we show $\triangle(G) \subseteq (\triangle 1 \cup \triangle 2 \cup \triangle 3)$. For any triangle $\triangle_{uvw} \in \triangle(G)$, there are only three cases where u, v, and w can be located: (1) they are all in the same subgraph G_i; (2) two of them are in the same subgraph G_i while the other in another different subgraph G_j (WLOG, we may assume that $u, v \in V_{G_i}, w \in V_{G_j}, i \ne j$); (3) they are in three different subgraphs G_i, G_j, and G_k (WLOG, we may assume that $u \in V_{G_i}, v \in V_{G_j}, w \in V_{G_k}, i < j < k$). The three cases correspond to the three types $\triangle 1$, $\triangle 2$, and $\triangle 3$, and thus $\triangle(G) \subseteq (\triangle 1 \cup \triangle 2 \cup \triangle 3)$. □

We call triangles in $\triangle 1$, $\triangle 2$, and $\triangle 3$, *Type 1*, *Type 2*, and *Type 3* triangles. The following example illustrates the concept of the three types of triangles.

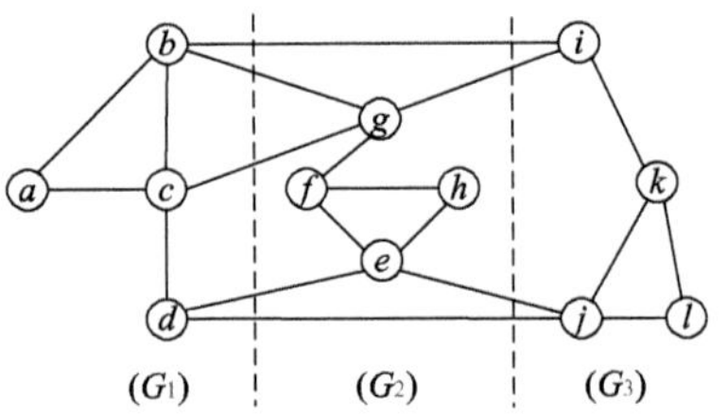

Figure 2: A partition of G in Figure 1: $\mathcal{P} = \{G_1, G_2, G_3\}$

Example 2. Figure 2 shows a partition, $\mathcal{P} = \{G_1, G_2, G_3\}$, of the graph shown in Figure 1. In the figure, $\triangle_{abc}$, $\triangle_{efh}$ and $\triangle_{jkl}$

are Type 1 triangles because all the three vertices of each triangle are in the same subgraph. We only have one Type 2 triangle, $\triangle_{bcg}$, because its vertices are in two subgraphs in $\mathcal{P}$. We have two Type 3 triangles, $\triangle_{bgi}$ and $\triangle_{dej}$, because all the three vertices of each triangle are in three different subgraphs in $\mathcal{P}$. □

According to Lemma 1, a triangle $\triangle_{uvw}$ can be listed by searching any subgraph G_i alone only if u, v and w are all in G_i (i.e., Type 1 triangles). However, the number of Type 1 triangles may be limited. More critically, we cannot remove any edge (and hence any vertex) of G_i from G even after we list all Type 1 triangles, because an edge (u, v) in $\triangle_{uvw}$ may form another triangle $\triangle_{uvx}$ with a vertex x in another subgraph G_j.

To enable the removal of edges after all triangles containing these edges are listed, and at same time to ensure the completeness of the global result, we introduce the notion of *extended subgraph*.

Definition 1 (EXTENDED SUBGRAPH). *Let $H = (V_H, E_H)$ be a subgraph of G. An* extended subgraph *of H in G, denoted by H^+, is a* directed *subgraph defined as $H^+ = (V_{H^+}, E_{H^+})$, where $V_{H^+} = V_H \cup \{v : u \in V_H, v \in V_G \backslash V_H, (u,v) \in E_G\}$ and $E_{H^+} = \{(u,v) : (u,v) \in E_G, u \in V_H\}$.*

Intuitively, an extended subgraph of H is a subgraph obtained by adding (to H) those directed edges from the vertices in H to those vertices not in H. In this paper, we assume that if $V_H = \{v\}$, for any $v \in V$, then the corresponding H^+ fits into memory. We give an example of extended subgraph as follows.

Example 3. Figure 3 depicts the extended subgraphs of G_1, G_2, and G_3 in Figure 2. The shaded vertices are the vertices in each G_i, while the directed edges show the extension to vertices outside each G_i. □

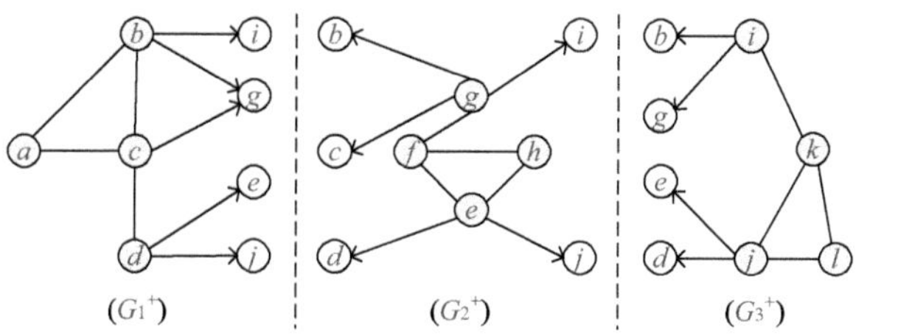

Figure 3: The extended subgraphs of G_1, G_2, G_3 in Figure 2

Based on Definition 1, we have the following lemma for triangle listing in an extended subgraph.

LEMMA 2. *Let H^+ be an extended subgraph of a subgraph H of G. Then:*

- *Let $\triangle 1(H^+) = \{\triangle_{uvw} : \triangle_{uvw} \in \triangle 1,\ u,v,w \in V_H\}$. Then, $\forall \triangle_{uvw} \in \triangle 1(H^+)$, $\triangle_{uvw}$ can be listed by searching H^+ alone.*
- *Let $\triangle 2(H^+) = \{\triangle_{uvw} : \triangle_{uvw} \in \triangle 2,\ u,v \in V_H\}$. Then, $\forall \triangle_{uvw} \in \triangle 2(H^+)$, $\triangle_{uvw}$ can be listed by searching H^+ alone.*

In addition, for any edge $(u,v) \in E_H$, (u,v) does not exist in any triangle in $\triangle(G) \backslash (\triangle 1(H^+) \cup \triangle 2(H^+))$.

PROOF. First, $\forall \triangle_{uvw} \in \triangle 1(H^+)$, $\triangle_{uvw}$ can be listed by searching H^+ alone because all the three edges (u,v) (u,w), and (v,w) of $\triangle_{uvw}$ are in H and hence also in H^+. Second, $\forall \triangle_{uvw} \in \triangle 2(H^+)$, $\triangle_{uvw}$ can be listed by searching H^+ alone because $u, v \in V_H$, $w \in adj_{H^+}(u)$, $w \in adj_{H^+}(v)$, and $\triangle_{uvw}$ can be found by intersecting $adj_{H^+}(u)$ and $adj_{H^+}(v)$.

Finally, for any edge $(u,v) \in E_H$, (u,v) does not exist in any triangle in $\triangle(G) \backslash (\triangle 1(H^+) \cup \triangle 2(H^+))$ because any triangle containing (u,v) must be in either $\triangle 1(H^+)$ or $\triangle 2(H^+)$. □

Algorithm 2 *I/O-Efficient Triangle Listing*

Input: A graph $G = (V_G, E_G)$
Output: A listing of $\triangle(G)$

```
1. while(G is not empty)
2.     Partition G into P = {G_1, ..., G_i, ..., G_p};
3.     for each extended subgraph G_i^+ of G_i ∈ P do
4.         List all triangles in △1(G_i^+) and △2(G_i^+) (by Algorithm 3);
5.         Remove all edges in G_i from G;
```

Algorithm 3 *Triangle Listing in Extended Subgraph*

Input: An extended subgraph $H^+ = (V_{H^+}, E_{H^+})$
Output: A listing of $\triangle 1(H^+)$ and $\triangle 2(H^+)$

```
for each u ∈ V_H do
    for each v ∈ adj_H(u), where v > u, do
        for each w ∈ (adj_{H+}(u) ∩ adj_{H+}(v)) do
            if(w > v or w ∉ V_H)
                List △_uvw;
```

Lemma 2 implies that we can list all Type 1 and Type 2 triangles from the extended subgraph G_i^+ of each subgraph G_i in the partition $\mathcal{P}$ of G. More importantly, after listing the two types of triangles in each G_i^+, we can remove all edges in G_i (i.e., those bi-directed edges in G_i^+), since all triangles containing these edges have been already listed.

The above scheme lists all Type 1 and Type 2 triangles but still misses all Type 3 triangles. We devise an efficient algorithm that iteratively converts Type 3 triangles into Type 1 and Type 2 triangles so that all triangles can be listed, while at the same time reducing the size of the graph to reduce the I/O cost. We outline our algorithm in Algorithm 2.

Algorithm 2 is essentially an iterative computation of $\triangle 1(G_i^+)$ and $\triangle 2(G_i^+)$ from the extended subgraph G_i^+ of each $G_i \in \mathcal{P}$, as defined in Lemma 2, where $\mathcal{P}$ is the new partition of G at each iteration. (G_i^+ can be easily obtained along with the computation of $\mathcal{P}$, which we discuss in Section 4.3.)

At the end of each iteration, we remove all edges in each G_i in the current $\mathcal{P}$ and obtain a shrunk new graph. Then, at the beginning of the next iteration, we re-partition the new shrunk graph. The new partition $\mathcal{P}$ defines new sets of $\triangle 1(G_i^+)$ and $\triangle 2(G_i^+)$ for the G_i^+ of each $G_i \in \mathcal{P}$. Thus, Algorithm 2 iteratively converts the old set of Type 3 triangles in the previous iteration into Type 1 and Type 2 triangles with respect to the new partition at the current iteration. This process continues until all edges in G are removed.

Note that another purpose of graph partition is to make sure that each subgraph in $\mathcal{P}$ is small enough to fit into main memory, so as to avoid random disk access for triangle listing. Meanwhile, we also want to take full utilization of the available memory and hence each $G_i \in \mathcal{P}$ should be as big as possible under the condition that $(|V_{G_i}| + |E_{G_i}|) \leq M$. Thus, if G at any iteration is small enough to fit into memory, Step 2 of Algorithm 2 computes a partition consisting of only one element, i.e., $\mathcal{P} = \{G\}$, after which the algorithm terminates since all edges in G will be removed at the end of the iteration.

Step 4 of Algorithm 2 invokes Algorithm 3 to compute $\triangle 1(G_i^+)$

and $\triangle 2(G_i^+)$ from G_i^+, i.e., H^+ in Algorithm 3. Algorithm 3 is an in-memory algorithm similar to Algorithm 1. The only difference is that the extended graph H^+ contains two sets of vertices, V_H and $V_{H^+} \backslash V_H$. Algorithm 3 only intersects the adjacency-lists of those vertices in V_H. Let w be a vertex found in $(adj_{H^+}(u) \cap adj_{H^+}(v))$, where $u, v \in V_H$. If $w \in V_H$, we also require $w > v$ (and hence also $w > u$) in order to avoid duplicate listing of the triangle $\triangle_{uvw}$. If $w \notin V_H$, then we simply list $\triangle_{uvw}$ since it cannot be listed elsewhere.

We now prove the correctness and completeness of Algorithm 2.

THEOREM 1. *Given a graph $G = (V_G, E_G)$, Algorithm 2 lists all triangles in G and no false or duplicate triangle is listed.*

PROOF. Lemma 2 ensures that (1) all triangles containing a removed edge are listed, (2) all edges of any triangle not yet listed are still in the current G, and (3) the already listed triangles will not be listed again in future iterations because at least one of their edges has been removed from G. By (1) and (2), all triangles in G are listed because G becomes empty when Algorithm 2 terminates. Since Algorithm 3 does not list any duplicate triangle due to the enforced vertex ordering, by (3) Algorithm 2 does not list any duplicate triangle. Finally, since all triangles listed by Algorithm 3 are real triangles in G, Algorithm 2 does not list any false triangle. □

4.3 Graph Partitioning for Triangle Listing

The objectives of graph partitioning for the task of triangle listing are: (1) each subgraph in the partition should fill the available memory as much as possible; and (2) each subgraph should contain as many intra-partition edges (i.e., edges within the same subgraph) as possible. The first objective is to fully utilize memory, while the second objective is to remove as many edge as possible at each iteration of Algorithm 2 in order to reduce the number of total iterations.

Graph partitioning that fulfills the above two objectives, however, is known to be APX-hard [5] when the number of subgraphs in the partition is more than 2. There have been a number of approximation algorithms proposed [25, 19, 24, 17, 18, 1], but they are in-memory algorithms that are not suitable for triangle listing in massive networks that cannot fit into memory. Instead, we need an efficient algorithm that partitions a large graph with limited memory consumption. We devise two efficient graph partitioning algorithms that require only one scan or two scans of the input graph and has linear CPU time complexity.

4.3.1 Sequential Graph Partitioning

Sequential graph partitioning is a simple but very efficient algorithm, which works as follows: we sequentially read the input graph G from disk, whenever the available memory is filled up, the portion of G being read in memory forms a subgraph in the partition. Note that this subgraph is actually an extended subgraph, because each vertex v being read is associated with its adjacency-list $adj_G(v)$.

After we scan G once, we obtain a partition with approximately $(|V_G|+|E_G|)/M$ subgraphs in it. Since the algorithm scans G only once, it requires only $O(scan(|V_G| + |E_G|))$ I/Os and $O(|V_G| + |E_G|)$ CPU time. Furthermore, since the subgraphs in the partition is obtained sequentially one after another as we read G, it allows pipelining such that we can process triangle listing for each subgraph as soon as it is produced, rather than starting triangle listing until the entire partitioning process finishes.

Sequential graph partitioning is effective when graphs exhibit high locality, i.e., vertices are naturally clustered according to the sequential order by which the graph is stored. For example, in a road network proximate vertices are assigned consecutive vertex IDs and they are stored sequentially in nearby positions in the adjacency-list graph representation. In social network graphs, local communities may also be stored together.

Procedure 4 *DominatingSet(G)*

1. Create a bit array A of size $|V_G|$ and set each bit to 0;
2. **for each** v in G, where $A[v] = 0$, **do**
3. Add v to D and mark v and all v's neighbors as 1 in A;
4. **return** D;

Algorithm 5 *Dominating-Set-based Graph Partitioning*

Input: A graph $G = (V_G, E_G)$
Output: A partition of G, $\mathcal{P} = \{G_1, \ldots, G_i, \ldots, G_p\}$

1. Compute a dominating set D of G by invoking *DominatingSet(G)*;
2. Divide D into p disjoint subsets of roughly the same size;
3. Create p subgraphs for $\mathcal{P}$ out of the p subsets of D;
4. **for each** $v \in V_G$, where $v \notin D$, **do**
5. Add v (and $adj_G(v)$) to the smallest subgraph in $\mathcal{P}$ that has at least $(deg_{\mathcal{P}}(v)/p)$ neighbors of v;
6. **return** $\mathcal{P}$;

4.3.2 Dominating-Set-based Graph Partitioning

Sequential graph partitioning may be efficient in practice but it gives no guarantee on the number of iterations Algorithm 2 may take. To this end, we propose another graph partitioning algorithm based on the concept of *dominating set*.

A dominating set of a graph G is a subset of vertices $D \subseteq V_G$ such that every vertex in G is either in D or a neighbor of some vertex in D. Computing the minimum dominating set is known to be NP-hard. However, for our purpose of graph partitioning, we do not require a minimum dominating set. More specifically, we devise a one-pass algorithm to compute a dominating set for G as shown in Procedure 4.

In Procedure 4, we first initialize a bit array A of size $|V_G|$ and set each bit to 0. Then, we read G from disk sequentially and for each vertex v (together with $adj_G(v)$) read, we add v to D only if $A[v] = 0$. If v is added to D, then we also set v and all v's neighbors to 1 in A. Thus, all vertices in $V_G \backslash D$ are neighbors of some vertex in D.

We then use D to compute a partition of G, as outlined in Algorithm 5. For triangle listing, we want the vertices in the same subgraph in the partition to be highly connected with each other. We divide D into $p = O((|V_G| + |E_G|)/M)$ subsets and create p initial subgraphs in $\mathcal{P}$. Then, we use the dominating vertices in each subset as seeds to grow each of the p subgraphs by attracting their neighbors. Again, we read G sequentially from disk. For each vertex v (together with $adj_G(v)$) read, let $deg_{\mathcal{P}}(v)$ be the *current* total number of neighbors of v in all the subgraphs in the *current* $\mathcal{P}$, which can be easily obtained by scanning $adj_G(v)$. We choose the subgraph that has at least $(deg_{\mathcal{P}}(v)/p)$ neighbors of v currently, and add v to that subgraph. If there are more than one such subgraph, we add v to the subgraph with the smallest size so far. Upon adding v, we also add $adj_G(v)$ to the subgraph, so that the resultant subgraph is an extended subgraph ready for triangle listing in Algorithm 2.

Whenever the size of a subgraph becomes greater than B (i.e., the block size), we write a block of the subgraph to disk. Thus, we need extra I/Os to first write all subgraphs in $\mathcal{P}$ to disk and then read each subgraph in $\mathcal{P}$ into memory for triangle listing in Algorithm 2. However, the asymptotic I/O complexity of Algorithm 5 is still $O(scan(|V_G| + |E_G|))$. The CPU time complexity is $O(|V_G| + |E_G|)$ since we only need to scan $adj_G(v)$ for each v. But to compute $deg_{\mathcal{P}}(v)$ efficiently we need a look-up table of size $(|V_G| \log_2 p)$ bits. However, in this case, the algorithm is considered as a semi-external-memory algorithm.

Dominating-set-based graph partitioning not only groups neighborhood vertices together, but more importantly it gives a lower bound on the number of intra-partition edges, i.e., edges that can be removed at the end of each iteration of Algorithm 2.

LEMMA 3. *Let $\mathcal{P} = \{G_1, \ldots, G_i, \ldots, G_p\}$ be a partition of G computed by Algorithm 5. Then, the number of intra-partition edges of $\mathcal{P}$ (i.e., edges that are incident on vertices within the same subgraph in $\mathcal{P}$) is at least $|E_G|/p$.*

PROOF. Let $P_{t(v)}$ be the current partition P at the time when a vertex v is added to P at Step 5 of Algorithm 5. For each vertex v, v is added to the smallest subgraph in $\mathcal{P}_{t(v)}$ that has at least $(deg_{\mathcal{P}(v)_{t(v)}}/p)$ neighbors of v. First, there must exist such a subgraph in $\mathcal{P}_{t(v)}$ when v is being added, because v is the neighbor of at least one vertex in D. Thus, the total number of intra-partition edges is at least $\sum_{v \in V_G \setminus D}(deg_{\mathcal{P}_{t(v)}}(v)/p)$. We have $\sum_{v \in V_G \setminus D} deg_{\mathcal{P}_{t(v)}}(v) = |E_G|$ because each edge is counted once by one of its end vertices and no edge exists between any two vertices in D according to Procedure 4. The result thus follows. □

We further show that Lemma 3 implies an upper bound on the total number of iterations required for Algorithm 2 in Lemma 4 in the following subsection.

4.4 Bounding I/O Complexity

We now analyze the overall complexity of our algorithm. As discussed in Section 4.3, graph partitioning at each iteration of Algorithm 2 requires $O(scan(|V_G|+|E_G|))$ I/Os. For triangle listing at each iteration, we only read once the extended subgraph of each subgraph in the partition into memory. Thus, the overall I/O complexity for each iteration is $O(scan(|V_G|+|E_G|))$ (for a shrinking G). Note that both partitioning algorithms in Section 4.3 actually output the extended subgraphs.

From the above analysis, the overall I/O complexity of Algorithm 2 depends on the total number of iterations needed. If we use sequential graph partitioning, the number of iterations depends largely on the locality of the graph data, which varies for different datasets. If we use dominating-set-based graph partitioning, then we can obtain an upper bound on the number of iterations (but require $|V_G| \log_2 p$ bits of memory) for Algorithm 2 as follows.

LEMMA 4. *If Algorithm 2 partitions G by Algorithm 5, then the number of iterations in Algorithm 2 is $O(|E_G|/M)$.*

PROOF. According to Lemma 3, the number of intra-partition edges of $\mathcal{P}$ is at least $|E_G|/p$, which means that at least $|E_G|/p \approx |E_G|/(|E_G|/M) = M$ edges can be removed at the end of each iteration since $p = O((|V_G|+|E_G|)/M) \approx |E_G|/M$. Thus, the total number of iterations in Algorithm 2 is approximately $|E_G|/M$. □

THEOREM 2. *If Algorithm 2 partitions G by Algorithm 5, then Algorithm 2 requires $O(\frac{|E_G|}{M} scan(|V_G| + |E_G|) - (\frac{|E_G|}{M})^2 M)$ I/Os, where $(|V_G|+|E_G|)$ is the original size of the input graph G.*

PROOF. According to Lemma 4, at least M edges are removed from G at the end of each iteration of Algorithm 2. Thus, at the start of the i-th iteration, $(i-1)M$ edges have been removed from the original G. Summing up, the overall complexity of Algorithm 2 is $O(\sum_{i=1}^{|E_G|/M}(scan(|V_G| + |E_G|) - (i-1)M)) = O(\frac{|E_G|}{M} scan(|V_G|+|E_G|) - (\frac{|E_G|}{M})^2 M)$. □

Algorithm 6 *Triangle Counting, Clustering Coeff., and Transitivity*

Input: A graph $G = (V_G, E_G)$
Output: $N_\triangle(v)$ and $\mathcal{C}(v)$ for each $v \in V_G$, $\mathcal{C}(G)$, and $\mathcal{T}(G)$

1. $\forall v \in V_G, N_\triangle(v) \leftarrow 0$;
2. $\mathcal{C}(G) \leftarrow 0$; $N_\triangle(G) \leftarrow 0$; $N_\vee(G) \leftarrow 0$;
3. **for each** triangle $\triangle_{uvw}$ listed by Algorithm 2 **do**
4. $\quad N_\triangle(x) \leftarrow N_\triangle(x) + 1$, for $x \in \{u, v, w\}$;
5. **for each** $v \in V_G$ **do**
6. $\quad \mathcal{C}(v) \leftarrow 2N_\triangle(v)/deg_G(v)(deg_G(v) - 1)$;
7. $\quad \mathcal{C}(G) \leftarrow \mathcal{C}(G) + \mathcal{C}(v)$;
8. $\quad N_\triangle(G) \leftarrow N_\triangle(G) + N_\triangle(v)$;
9. $\quad N_\vee(G) \leftarrow N_\vee(G) + deg_G(v)(deg_G(v) - 1)/2$;
10. $\mathcal{C}(G) \leftarrow \mathcal{C}(G)/|V_G|$;
11. $\mathcal{T}(G) \leftarrow 3N_\triangle(G)/N_\vee(G)$;

Finally, we remark that the CPU time complexity for triangle listing at each iteration of Algorithm 2 is the same as that of the counter-part in-memory algorithm with the same input graph. We thus refer the readers to the related work [26] for details.

5. APPLICATIONS OF TRIANGLE LISTING

Triangle listing has many important applications. Here, we focus on a few popular ones and demonstrate how our algorithm can be applied to benefit these applications in massive networks that cannot fit into main memory.

5.1 Triangle Counting, Clustering Coefficients, and Transitivity

Our algorithm can be readily applied to compute triangle counting, clustering coefficients, and transitivity. For completeness, we first give the definition of the concepts.

Clustering coefficient [36], which is a popular index for network analysis, is defined as follows.

Definition 2 (CLUSTERING COEFFICIENT). *The clustering coefficient of a vertex $v \in V_G$, where $deg_G(v) > 1$, denoted by $\mathcal{C}(v)$, is defined as*

$$\mathcal{C}(v) = \frac{N_\triangle(v)}{N_\vee(v)}. \tag{5}$$

When $deg_G(v) \leq 1$, we define $\mathcal{C}(v) = 0$.
The clustering coefficient of G, denoted by $\mathcal{C}(G)$, is defined as

$$\mathcal{C}(G) = \frac{1}{|V_G|} \sum_{v \in V_G} \mathcal{C}(v). \tag{6}$$

Transitivity [35, 28] is defined as follows.

Definition 3 (TRANSITIVITY). *The transitivity of a graph G, denoted by $\mathcal{C}(G)$, is defined as*

$$\mathcal{T}(G) = \frac{N_\triangle(G)}{\frac{1}{3}\sum_{v \in V_G} N_\vee(v)}. \tag{7}$$

Instead of first computing all triangles and performing a post-processing, our algorithm can be pipelined to compute all the above measures as shown in Algorithm 6. The algorithm is self-explanatory.

Lines 5-9 of Algorithm 6 requires another scan of G, but the asymptotic I/O complexity of the algorithm is the same as Algorithm 2. Updating $N_\triangle(v)$ for all $v \in V_G$ may require $O(|V_G|)$ space, but this can be avoided by writing $N_\triangle(v)$ after processing each extended subgraph and then merging the results of all extended subgraphs. The asymptotic I/O complexity still remains the same since the size of $N_\triangle(v)$ for all v in an extended subgraph is bounded by the size of the subgraph.

5.2 Triangular Vertex Connectivity

Triangular vertex connectivity (also called *3-gonal connectivity*) defines stronger connectivity in a network than single link connectivity, since edges that are in short cyclic component (e.g., triangles) are considered as strong ties [21, 8]. Triangular vertex connectivity is formally defined as follows [29].

Definition 4 (TRIANGULAR-VERTEX-CONNECTIVITY). *Two vertices* u *and* v *are* triangularly vertex connected *if there exists a sequence of triangles* $\langle \triangle_1, \ldots, \triangle_n \rangle$ *such that* u *is in* $\triangle_1$, v *is in* $\triangle_n$, *and either (1)* $n = 1$, *or (2) for* $1 \leq i < n$, $\triangle_i$ *and* $\triangle_{i+1}$ *share at least one common vertex.*

Intuitively, if u and v are connected by a single path, then they become disconnected if any edge on the path is removed. On the contrary, if u and v are connected by a sequence of triangles, then removing any edge does not disconnect them.

Triangular vertex connectivity is important in many applications [15, 20, 32, 36]. It defines an equivalence relation $\mathcal{V}^{\triangle}$ on V_G. Two vertices u and v belong to the same equivalence class if they are triangularly vertex connected. The following example further explains the concept.

Example 4. In the graph in Figure 1, there are two equivalence classes defined by triangular vertex connectivity, $\{a, b, c, g, i\}$ and $\{d, e, f, h, j, k, l\}$, which can be obtained by removing the three edges (in bold lines) that are not part of any triangle. Removing any edge from the induced subgraph by any class does not disconnect the vertices in the class, which shows a stronger connectivity. □

The existing algorithm for computing the equivalence classes of $\mathcal{V}^{\triangle}$ is based on triangle listing [8]. However, the algorithm requires random disk access when the graph is stored in disk.

The result of Algorithm 2 can be easily pipelined to compute the equivalence classes of $\mathcal{V}^{\triangle}$. Upon processing each extended subgraph, we first mark the directed edges (u, v), (u, w), (v, w), where $u < v < w$, for each triangle $\triangle_{uvw}$ listed. Then, we write these marked edges to disk. When Algorithm 2 terminates, we read the marked edges one by one to find which equivalent class each $v \in V_G$ belongs to. This can be done by using two lookup tables, C and A, where $C[j] = i$ indicates that i is the smallest class ID that Class j is connected to, and $A[v] = i$ indicates v belongs to Class i. Initially, $C[i] = i$ and $A[v] = \infty$. We keep a counter c which is initialized to 0. For each marked edge (u, v) read, we do the following: (1) if $A[u] = A[v] = \infty$, we set $A[u] = A[v] = c$ and increment c; (2) if $A[u] \neq A[v]$, WLOG assuming $A[u] < A[v]$, we set $C[A[v]] = min(C[A[v]], A[u])$ and $A[v] = A[u]$; (3) otherwise, do nothing. Finally, we scan C once to update each $C[i]$ to the small class ID that Class i is connected to, and update $A[v] = C[A[v]]$, which indicates the class v belongs to.

Since the number of marked edges written to disk for each extended subgraph cannot exceed the size of the subgraph, the asymptotic I/O complexity of computing the equivalence classes of $\mathcal{V}^{\triangle}$ by the above algorithm is the same as Algorithm 2.

6. EXPERIMENTAL RESULTS

We compare our algorithms with the semi-streaming local triangle estimating algorithm (denoted by **Semi-stream**) [9] and the state-of-the-art in-memory triangle listing algorithm (denoted by **In-mem**) [26]. We run the experiments on a machine with an Intel Xeno 2.67GHz CPU and 4GB RAM, and we use g++ 4.4.5 compiler on CentOS 5.4.

Dataset. We use four real datasets: *LiveJournal* (**LJ**), *U.S. road network* (**USRD**), *World Wide Web of UK* (**WebUK**), and *Billion Triple Challenge* (**BTC**). LJ is a social network (http://www.livejournal.com, http://snap.stanford.edu), where vertices are members and edges represent friendship between members. USRD is the road network of United States, where vertices represent intersections and endpoints, and edges represent the roads connecting these intersections or road endpoints. WebUK is obtained from the YAHOO webspam dataset (http://barcelona.research.yahoo.net), where vertices are pages and edges are hyperlinks. BTC is a semantic graph converted from the Billion Triple Challenge 2009 RDF dataset (http://vmlion25.deri.ie), where each vertex represents an object such as a person, a document, and an event, and each edge represents the relationship between two vertices such as "has-author", "links-to", and "has-title". We give the number of vertices and edges, and the storage size on disk, of the datasets in Table 2.

Table 2: Datasets

	LJ	USRD	WebUK	BTC
$\lvert V_G \rvert$	4.8M	24M	106M	165M
$\lvert E_G \rvert$	69M	58M	1,877M	773M
Disk size	809.1MB	969.6MB	20.3GB	10.0GB

6.1 Effectiveness of Partitioning Algorithms

We first show the effectiveness of two graph partitioning algorithms, *sequential graph partitioning* (**Seq**) and *dominating-set-based graph partitioning* (**DS**). We set the available memory size M for partitioning to be $512MB$, $1GB$, $2GB$, and $4GB$, respectively. Table 3 reports the number of iterations Algorithm 2 takes by adopting Seq or DS, on the two large datasets BTC and WebUK. The theoretical upper bound on the number of iterations by adopting DS is also shown.

Table 3: Number of Iterations of Algorithm 2

	M=512MB	M=1GB	M=2GB	M=4GB
BTC (Seq)	$\rightarrow \infty$	7	2	1
BTC (DS)	6	3	2	1
BTC (Theoretical)	19	10	5	3
WebUK (Seq)	3	2	2	1
WebUK (DS)	3	2	2	1
WebUK (Theoretical)	29	15	7	4

The result shows that Seq is effective in practice. The number of iterations of Algorithm 2 by adopting Seq is as small as that by adopting DS in most cases, but as shown in Table 4 in Section 6.2 adopting Seq is more efficient than adopting DS since DS requires two more scans of G at each iteration of Algorithm 2.

However, when the available memory becomes smaller (M = 512MB), adopting Seq does not terminate since there is a point that all triangles are Type 3 triangles w.r.t. the partition; thus no more edges can be removed. Such a situation may also happen to other datasets that exhibit low locality. In this case, DS shows its advantage as it gives a guaranteed upper bound on the number of iterations, while our result shows that it indeed has consistent performance. The result also shows that in all cases, the actual number of iterations needed by adopting DS is always less than its theoretical upper bound.

6.2 Triangle Listing

We now report the performance of Algorithm 2 by adopting Seq (denoted by **TL-Seq**) and by adopting DS (denoted by **TL-DS**), compared with In-mem and Semi-stream. We set the available memory size to be 2GB.

Table 4 reports the running time of the different algorithms. We do not report the memory consumption since the smaller datasets

LJ and USRD can fit in memory and all algorithms use roughly the same memory (less than 1GB), while our algorithms and Semi-stream use all available memory for BTC and WebUK. In-mem runs out of memory for BTC and WebUK (BTC and WebUK requires about 10GB and 20GB of memory).

Table 4: Running time (wall-clock time in seconds)

	LJ	USRD	BTC	WebUK
TL-Seq	29.63	6.24	350	2411
TL-DS	29.43	12.46	412	2503
In-mem	32.98	6.68	N.A.	N.A.
Semi-stream ($\overline{\sigma}(N_\triangle(v)) \approx 0.8$)	306	321	3402	7032
Semi-stream ($\overline{\sigma}(N_\triangle(v)) \approx 0.5$)	1275	1683	13711	34722

The result shows that the performance of our algorithms is very competitive. When the graphs can fit into memory, our algorithms have comparable performance compared with In-mem. When the graphs are too large to fit into memory, our algorithms demonstrate great advantage over Semi-stream, which makes multiple passes over the data as do our algorithms.

Let $\overline{\sigma}(N_\triangle(v))$ be the *average approximation error rate* for $N_\triangle(v)$, defined as (|approximate value − exact value|/exact value) averaged over all vertices. We find that Semi-stream takes prohibitively long time to obtain a low $\overline{\sigma}(N_\triangle(v))$. Table 4 reports the running time for Semi-stream by setting $\overline{\sigma}(N_\triangle(v)) \approx 0.8$ and $\overline{\sigma}(N_\triangle(v)) \approx 0.5$. The result shows that Semi-stream is many times slower than both our algorithms for $\overline{\sigma}(N_\triangle(v)) \approx 0.8$ and up to orders of magnitude slower for $\overline{\sigma}(N_\triangle(v)) \approx 0.5$.

From another angle of comparison, if we choose a setting for Semi-stream that it takes slightly longer time than our algorithm TL-Seq, we also report its error rate in Table 5. The result shows that at comparable time, the error rate $\overline{\sigma}(N_\triangle(v))$ of Semi-stream increases significantly.

Table 5: Error rate of Semi-stream at comparable time as TL-Seq

LJ	USRD	BTC	WebUK
97.6%	133.6%	115.4%	95.0%

6.3 Performance on Applications

When the graphs are too large to fit into memory, our algorithm shows significant advantages over approximation algorithms. Table 6 reports the error rate of clustering coefficient of a network and of transitivity approximated by Semi-stream, denoted by $\sigma(\mathcal{C}(G))$ and $\sigma(\mathcal{T}(G))$, respectively. The result shows that, although the error rate of Semi-stream is not too large for those global measures, we obtain exact results at comparable time.

Table 6: Error rate of Semi-stream for $\sigma(\mathcal{C}(G))$ and $\sigma(\mathcal{T}(G))$

BTC ($\sigma(\mathcal{C}(G))$)	**BTC** ($\sigma(\mathcal{T}(G))$)	**WebUK** ($\sigma(\mathcal{C}(G))$)	**WebUK** ($\sigma(\mathcal{T}(G))$)
26.5%	40.2%	12.7%	15.3%

We also assess the performance of using our algorithm for computing triangular-vertex-connectivity-based equivalence classes, compared with the state-of-the-art in-memory algorithm [8] (also denoted by **In-mem** here for simplicity).

Table 7 shows that the running time of our algorithm is comparable with In-mem for LJ and USRD. But for the larger datasets, BTC and WebUK, In-mem runs out of memory while our algorithm still records high efficiency. The result again demonstrates our algorithms are I/O-efficient for processing large graphs.

Table 7: Triangular Vertex Connectivity

	LJ	USRD	BTC	WebUK
TL-Seq	173.1	11.5	380.2	3670.3
In-mem	138.1	9.0	N.A.	N.A.

7. RELATED WORK

The algorithms for triangle listing or counting can be categorized into *exact* algorithms and *approximation* algorithms.

The first non-trivial exact algorithm was a spanning-tree-based algorithm [22, 23], which achieves a running time of $O(|E_G|^{1.5})$. The asymptotic complexity of in-memory exact triangle listing has not been improved since then. However, a number of practical fast algorithms have been proposed that use vertex ordering and efficient data structures such as lookup tables to facilitate the intersection of the adjacency-lists of the neighboring vertices [30, 29, 26]. For triangle counting, the number of triangles can be counted in $O(|E_G|^{1.41})$ time with a fast matrix multiplication algorithm [4]. The basic triangle listing algorithm was also extended to count triads (directed subgraph with three vertices) in directed graph [7]. Maintaining the number of triangles in a dynamic graph was discussed in [16]. All the aforementioned algorithms are in-memory algorithm and require at least $O(|V_G| + |E_G|)$ space.

Approximation algorithms have been proposed for triangle counting in large graphs that cannot fit in memory. Accurate streaming algorithms [3, 6, 14, 10] and sampling algorithm [33] have been proposed to estimate the total number of triangles in a graph. More closely related to estimate the number of triangles formed locally at each vertex in a graph. All these algorithms, however, cannot handle triangle listing, which has a broader range of applications.

Very recently, a parallel algorithm for triangle counting using MapReduce framework [31] has been proposed. Their algorithm is exact and do not require to keep the entire input graph in memory at each individual machine. Algorithms for listing more complex subgraphs are also studied in [13, 12].

8. CONCLUSIONS

We propose an I/O-efficient algorithm for exact triangle listing. To avoid random disk access, we partition the input graph and only process one subgraph in the partition each time. By carefully extracting the subgraphs, we prove that triangle listing in those local subgraphs gives globally correct and complete result. We devise two effective partitioning strategies, one achieving high efficiency in practice while the other bounding the I/O complexity theoretically. Our experimental results on large graphs with up to 106 million vertices and 1,877 million edges show that our algorithm is significantly more efficient than the state-of-the-art approximation algorithm for local triangle counting [9]: at comparable running time and memory, their algorithm records a very high error rate while ours returns the exact result. We also demonstrate the efficiency of applying our algorithm on computing various network measures such as clustering coefficients and transitivity, as well as equivalence classes of the graph based on triangular vertex connectivity. Thus, we believe that our work can benefit many other applications in processing large graphs.

For future work, we plan to study the relationship between the triangles and the k-cores [11] for analyzing massive networks.

Acknowledgment

The authors would like to thank the reviewers for their constructive comments. This research is supported in part by the AcRF Tier-1 Grant (M52020092) from Ministry of Education of Singapore.

9. REFERENCES

[1] A. Abou-Rjeili and G. Karypis. Multilevel algorithms for partitioning power-law graphs. In *IPDPS*, 2006.

[2] A. Aggarwal and S. Vitter, Jeffrey. The input/output complexity of sorting and related problems. *Commun. ACM*, 31(9):1116–1127, 1988.

[3] N. Alon, Y. Matias, and M. Szegedy. The space complexity of approximating the frequency moments. *J. Comput. Syst. Sci.*, 58(1):137–147, 1999.

[4] N. Alon, R. Yuster, and U. Zwick. Finding and counting given length cycles. *Algorithmica*, 17(3):354–364, 1997.

[5] K. Andreev and H. Racke. Balanced graph partitioning. In *SPAA*, pages 120–124, 2004.

[6] Z. Bar-Yossef, K. Hildrum, and F. Wu. Incentive-compatible online auctions for digital goods. In *SODA*, pages 964–970, 2002.

[7] V. Batagelj and A. Mrvar. A subquadratic triad census algorithm for large sparse networks with small maximum degree. *Social Networks*, 23(3):237–243, 2001.

[8] V. Batagelj and M. Zaveršnik. Short cycle connectivity. *Discrete Mathematics*, 307(3-5):310 - 318, 2007.

[9] L. Becchetti, P. Boldi, C. Castillo, and A. Gionis. Efficient semi-streaming algorithms for local triangle counting in massive graphs. In *KDD*, pages 16–24, 2008.

[10] L. S. Buriol, G. Frahling, S. Leonardi, A. Marchetti-Spaccamela, and C. Sohler. Counting triangles in data streams. In *PODS*, pages 253–262, 2006.

[11] J. Cheng, Y. Ke, S. Chu, and M. T. Özsu. Efficient core decomposition in massive networks. In *ICDE*, pages 51–62, 2011.

[12] J. Cheng, Y. Ke, A. W.-C. Fu, J. X. Yu, and L. Zhu. Finding maximal cliques in massive networks. *ACM Transactions on Database Systems*.

[13] J. Cheng, Y. Ke, A. W.-C. Fu, J. X. Yu, and L. Zhu. Finding maximal cliques in massive networks by h*-graph. In *SIGMOD Conference*, pages 447–458, 2010.

[14] D. Coppersmith and R. Kumar. An improved data stream algorithm for frequency moments. In *SODA*, pages 151–156, 2004.

[15] J.-P. Eckmann and E. Moses. Curvature of co-links uncovers hidden thematic layers in the world wide web. *PNAS*, 99:5825–5829, 2002.

[16] D. Eppstein and E. S. Spiro. The *h*-index of a graph and its application to dynamic subgraph statistics. In *WADS*, pages 278–289, 2009.

[17] U. Feige and R. Krauthgamer. A polylogarithmic approximation of the minimum bisection. In *FOCS*, pages 105–115, 2000.

[18] U. Feige, R. Krauthgamer, and K. Nissim. Approximating the minimum bisection size (extended abstract). In *STOC*, pages 530–536, 2000.

[19] C. M. Fiduccia and R. M. Mattheyses. A linear time heuristic for improving network partitions. In *IEEE Design Automation Conference*, 1982.

[20] B. Fritzke. A self-organizing network for unsupervised learning. *TR-03-026*, 42, 1993.

[21] M. Granovetter. The strength of weak ties. *American Journal of Sociology*, 78(6):1360–1380, 1973.

[22] A. Itai and M. Rodeh. Finding a minimum circuit in a graph. In *STOC*, pages 1–10, 1977.

[23] A. Itai and M. Rodeh. Finding a minimum circuit in a graph. *SIAM J. Comput.*, 7(4):413–423, 1978.

[24] G. Karypis and V. Kumar. Parallel multilevel k-way partitioning for irregular graphs. *SIAM Review*, 41(2):278–300, 1999.

[25] B. W. Kernigham and S. Lin. An efficient heuristic procedure for partitioning graphs. *Bell System Technical Journal*, pages 291–308, 1970.

[26] M. Latapy. Main-memory triangle computations for very large (sparse (power-law)) graphs. *Theor. Comput. Sci.*, 407(1-3):458–473, 2008.

[27] R. Milo, S. Shen-Orr, S. Itzkovitz, N. Kashtan, D. Chklovskii, and U. Alon. Network Motifs: Simple Building Blocks of Complex Networks. *Science*, 298(5594):824–827, 2002.

[28] M. E. J. Newman, D. J. Watts, and S. H. Strogatz. Random graph models of social networks. *PNAS*, 99:2566–2572, 2002.

[29] T. Schank. Algorithmic aspects of triangle-based network analysis. *Ph.D. Dissertation, Universität Karlsruhe, Fakultät für Informatik*, 2007.

[30] T. Schank and D. Wagner. Finding, counting and listing all triangles in large graphs, an experimental study. In *WEA*, pages 606–609, 2005.

[31] S. Suri and S. Vassilvitskii. Counting triangles and the curse of the last reducer. In *WWW*, pages 607–614, 2011.

[32] G. Taubin and J. Rossignac. Geometric compression through topological surgery. *ACM Trans. Graph.*, 17(2):84–115, 1998.

[33] C. E. Tsourakakis, U. Kang, G. L. Miller, and C. Faloutsos. Doulion: counting triangles in massive graphs with a coin. In *KDD*, pages 837–846, 2009.

[34] N. Wang, J. Zhang, K.-L. Tan, and A. K. H. Tung. On triangulation-based dense neighborhood graphs discovery. *PVLDB*, 4(2):58–68, 2010.

[35] S. Wasserman and K. Faust. Social network analysis: Methods and applications. *Cambridge University Press*, 1994.

[36] D. J. Watts and S. H. Strogatz. Collective dynamics of 'small-world' networks. *Nature*, 393(6684):440–442, 1998.

Fast Clustering using MapReduce*

(Extended Abstract)†

Alina Ene‡
University of Illinois
Urbana, IL, USA
ene1@illinois.edu

Sungjin Im§
University of Illinois
Urbana, IL, USA
im3@illinois.edu

Benjamin Moseley¶
University of Illinois
Urbana, IL, USA
bmosele2@illinois.edu

ABSTRACT

Clustering problems have numerous applications and are becoming more challenging as the size of the data increases. In this paper, we consider designing clustering algorithms that can be used in MapReduce, the most popular programming environment for processing large datasets. We focus on the practical and popular clustering problems, k-center and k-median. We develop fast clustering algorithms with constant factor approximation guarantees. From a theoretical perspective, we give the first analysis that shows several clustering algorithms are in $\mathcal{MRC}^0$, a theoretical MapReduce class introduced by Karloff et al. [26]. Our algorithms use sampling to decrease the data size and they run a time consuming clustering algorithm such as local search or Lloyd's algorithm on the resulting data set. Our algorithms have sufficient flexibility to be used in practice since they run in a constant number of MapReduce rounds. We complement these results by performing experiments using our algorithms. We compare the empirical performance of our algorithms to several sequential and parallel algorithms for the k-median problem. The experiments show that our algorithms' solutions are similar to or better than the other algorithms' solutions. Furthermore, on data sets that are sufficiently large, our algorithms are faster than the other parallel algorithms that we tested.

Categories and Subject Descriptors

F.2.2 [**Analysis of Algorithms and Problem Complexity**]: Nonnumerical Algorithms and Problems

General Terms

Algorithms, Theory, Experimentation

Keywords

Clustering Algorithms, Approximation Algorithms, Parallel Algorithms, MapReduce, k-center, k-median

*All authors are first authors.

†This is an extended abstract without proofs. A full version of the paper will be made available on arXiv.

‡Partially supported by NSF grants CCF-0728782 and CCF-1016684.

§Partially supported by NSF grants CCF-0728782, CCF-1016684, and a Samsung Fellowship.

¶Partially supported by NSF grants CCF-0728782 and CCF-1016684.

1. INTRODUCTION

Clustering data is a fundamental problem in a variety of areas of computer science and related fields. Machine learning, data mining, pattern recognition, networking, and bioinformatics use clustering for data analysis. Consequently, there is a vast amount of research focused on the topic [3, 29, 14, 13, 4, 32, 10, 17, 9, 31]. In the clustering problems that we consider in this paper, the goal is to partition the data into subsets, called clusters, such that the data points assigned to the same cluster are similar according to some metric.

In several applications, it is of interest to classify or group web pages according to their content or cluster users based on their online behavior. One such example is finding communities in social networks. Communities consist of individuals that are closely related according to some relationship criteria. Finding these communities is of interest for applications such as predicting buying behavior or designing targeted marking plans and is an ideal application for clustering. However, the size of the web graph and social network graphs can be quite large; for instance, the web graph consists of a trillion edges [30]. When the amount of data is this large, it is difficult or even impossible for the data to be stored on a single machine, which renders sequential algorithms unusable. In situations where the amount of data is prohibitively large, the MapReduce [16] programming paradigm is used to overcome this obstacle. MapReduce and its open source counterpart Hadoop [33] are distributed computing frameworks designed to process massive data sets.

The MapReduce model is quite novel, since it interleaves sequential and parallel computation. Succinctly, MapReduce consists of several *rounds* of computation. There is a set of machines, each of which has a certain amount of memory available. The memory on each machine is limited, and there is no communication between the machines during a round. In each round, the data is distributed among the machines. The data assigned to a single machine is constrained to be sub-linear in the input size. This restriction is motivated by the fact that the input size is assumed to be very large [26, 15]. After the data is distributed, each of the machines performs some computation on the data that is available to them. The output of these computations is either the final result or it becomes the input of another MapReduce round. A more precise overview of the MapReduce model is given in Section 1.1.

Problems: In this paper, we are concerned with designing clustering algorithms that can be implemented using MapReduce. In particular, we focus on two well-studied problems: metric k-median and k-center. In both of these problems, we are given a set V of n points, together with the distances between any pair of points; we give a precise description of the input representation below. The goal is to choose k of the points. Each of the k chosen points represents a cluster and is referred to as a *center*. Every data point is assigned to the closest center and all of the points assigned to a given point form a cluster. In the k-center problem, the goal is to choose the centers such that the maximum distance between a center and a point assigned to it is minimized. In the k-median problem the objective is to minimize the sum of the distances from the centers to each of the points assigned to the centers. Both of the problems are known to be NP-Hard. Thus previous work has focused on finding approximation algorithms [23, 5, 12, 11, 4, 21, 8]. Many of the existing algorithms are inherently sequential and, with the exception of the algorithms of [8, 20], they are difficult to adapt to a parallel computing setting. We discuss the algorithms of [20] in more detail later.

Input Representation: Let $d : V \times V \rightarrow \mathbb{R}_+$ denote the distance function. The distance function d is a metric, i.e., it has the following properties: (1) $d(x, y) = 0$ if and only if $x = y$, (2) $d(x, y) = d(y, x)$ for all x, y, and (3) $d(x, z) \leq d(x, y) + d(y, z)$ for all x, y, z. The third property is called the triangle inequality; we note that our algorithms only rely on the fact that the distances between points satisfy the triangle inequality.

Now we discuss how the distance function is given to our algorithms. In some settings, the distance function has an implicit compact representation; for example, if the distances between points are shortest path distances in a sparse graph, the graph represents the distance function compactly. However, currently there does not exist a MapReduce algorithm that computes shortest paths in a constant number of rounds, even if the graph is unweighted. This motivates the assumption that we are given the distance function *explicitly* as a set of $\Theta(n^2)$ distances, one for each pair of points, or we are given access to an *oracle* that takes as input two points and returns the distance between them. Throughout this paper, we assume that the distance function is given explicitly. More precisely, we assume that the input is a *weighted complete graph* $G = (V, E)$ that has an edge xy between any two points in V, and the weight of the edge xy is $d(x, y)$[1]. Moreover, we assume that k is at most $O(n^{1-\delta})$ for some constant $\delta > 0$, and the distance between any pair of points is upper bounded by some polynomial in n. These assumptions are justified in part by the fact that the number of points is very large, and by the memory constraints of the MapReduce model; we discuss the MapReduce model in more detail in Section 1.1.

Contributions: We introduce the *first* approximate metric k-median and k-center algorithms designed to run on MapReduce. More precisely, we show the following results.

THEOREM 1.1. *There is a randomized constant approximation algorithm for the k-center problem that, with high probability, runs in $O(\frac{1}{\delta})$ MapReduce rounds and uses memory at most $O(k^2 n^\delta)$ on each of the machines for any constant $\delta > 0$.*

[1]We note that some of the techniques in this paper extend to the setting in which the distance function is given as an oracle.

THEOREM 1.2. *There is a randomized constant approximation algorithm for the k-median problem that, with high probability, runs in $O(\frac{1}{\delta})$ MapReduce rounds and uses memory at most $O(k^2 n^\delta)$ on each of the machines for any constant $\delta > 0$.*

To complement these results, we run our algorithms on randomly generated data sets. For the k-median problem we compare our algorithm to a parallelized implementation of Lloyd's algorithm [28, 7, 1], arguably the most popular clustering algorithm used in practice (see [2, 22] for example), the local search algorithm [4, 21], the best known approximation algorithm for the k-median problem and a partitioning based algorithm that can parallelize any sequential clustering algorithm (see Section 4). Our algorithms achieve a speed-up of 1000x over the local search algorithm and 20x over the parallelized Lloyd's algorithm, a significant improvement in running time. Further, our algorithm's objective is similar to Lloyd's algorithm and the local search algorithm. For the partitioning based algorithm, we show that our algorithm achieves faster running time when the number of points is large. Thus for the k-median problem our algorithms are fast with a small loss in performance. For the k-center problem we compare our algorithm to the well known algorithm of [17, 19], which is the best approximation algorithm for the problem and is quite efficient. Unfortunately, for the k-center problem our algorithm's objective is a factor four worse in some cases. This is due to the sensitivity of the k-center objective to sampling.

Our algorithms show that the k-center and k-median problem belong to the theoretical MapReduce class $\mathcal{MRC}^0$ that was introduced by Karloff et al. [26][2]. Let N denote the total size of the input, and let $0 < \epsilon < 1$ be a fixed constant. A problem is in the MapReduce class $\mathcal{MRC}^0$ if it can be solved using a constant number of rounds and an $O(N^{1-\epsilon})$ number of machines, where each machine has $O(N^{1-\epsilon})$ memory available [26]. Differently said, the problem has an algorithm that uses a sub-linear amount of memory on each machine and a sub-linear number of machines. One of the main motivations for these restrictions is that a typical MapReduce input is very large and it might not be possible to store the entire input on a single machine. Moreover, the size of the input might be much larger than the number of machines available. We discuss the theoretical MapReduce model in Section 1.1. Our assumptions on the size of k and the point distances are needed in order to show that the memory that our algorithms use on each machine is sub-linear in the total input size. For instance, without the assumption on k, we will not be able to fit k points in the memory available on a machine.

Adapting Existing Algorithms to MapReduce: Previous work on designing algorithms for MapReduce are generally based on the following approach. Partition the input and assign each partition to a unique machine. On each machine, we perform some computation that eliminates a large fraction of the input. We collect the results of this computations on a single machine, which can store the data since the data has been sparsified. On this machine, we perform some computation and we return the final solution. We can use a similar approach for the k-center and k-median problems. We partition the points across the machines. We cluster each of the partitions. We select one point from each cluster and put all of the selected points on a single machine. We cluster these points and output the solution. Indeed, a similar algorithm was considered by Guha et al. [20] for the k-median problem in the streaming model. We give the details of how to implement this algorithm in

[2]Recall that we only consider instances of the problems in which k is sub-linear in the number of points, and the distances between points are upper bounded by some polynomial in n.

MapReduce in Section 4 along with an analysis of the algorithm's approximation guarantees. Unfortunately, the total running time for the algorithm can be quite large, since it runs a costly clustering algorithm on $\Omega(k\sqrt{n/k})$ points. Further, this algorithm requires $\Omega(kn)$ memory on each of the machines.

Another strategy for developing algorithms for k-center and k-median that run in MapReduce is to try to adapt existing parallel algorithms. To the best of our knowledge, the only parallel algorithms known with provable guarantees were given by Blelloch and Tangwongsan [8]; Blelloch and Tangwongsan [8] give the first PRAM algorithms for k-center and k-median. Unfortunately, these algorithms assume that the number of machines available is $\Omega(N^2)$, where N is the total input size, and there is some memory available in the system that can be accessed by all of the machines. These assumptions are too strong for the algorithms to be in used in MapReduce. Indeed, the requirements that the machines have a limited amount of memory and that there is no communication between the machines is what differentiates the MapReduce model from standard parallel computing models. Another approach is to try to adapt algorithms that were designed for the streaming model. Guha et al. [20] have given a k-median algorithm for the streaming model; with some work, we can adapt one of the algorithms in [20] to the MapReduce model. However, this algorithm's approximation ratio degrades exponentially in the number of rounds.

Related Work: There has been a large amount of work on the metric k-median and k-center problems. Due to space constraints, we focus only on closely related work that we have not already mentioned. Both problems are known to be NP-Hard. Bartal [6, 5] gave an algorithm for the k-median problem that achieves an $O(\log n \log\log n)$ approximation ratio. Later Charikar et al. gave the first constant factor approximation of $6+\frac{2}{3}$ [12]. This approach was based on LP rounding techniques. The best known approximation algorithm achieves a $3+\frac{2}{c}$ approximation in $O(n^c)$ time [4, 21]; this algorithm is based on the local search technique. On the other hand, Jain et al. [24] have shown that there does not exist an $1+(2/e)$ approximation for the k-median problem unless NP $\subseteq$ DTIME$(n^{O(\log\log n)})$. For the k-center problem, two simple algorithms are known which achieve a 2-approximation [23, 17, 19] and this approximation ratio is tight assuming that P $\neq$ NP.

MapReduce has received a significant amount of attention recently. Most previous work has been on designing practical heuristics to solve large scale problems [25, 27]. Recent papers [26, 18] have focused on developing computational models that abstract the power and limitations of MapReduce. Finally, there has been work on developing algorithms and approximation algorithms that fit into the MapReduce model [26, 15]. This line of work has shown that problems such as minimum spanning tree, maximum coverage, and connectivity can be solved efficiently using MapReduce.

1.1 MapReduce Overview

In this section we give a high-level overview of the MapReduce model; for a more detailed description, see [26]. The data is represented as $\langle key; value\rangle$ pairs. The key acts as an address of the machine to which the $value$ needs to be sent to. A MapReduce round consists of three stages: map, shuffle, and reduce. The map phase processes the data as follows. The algorithm designer specifies a map function μ, which we refer to as a *mapper*. The mapper takes as input a $\langle key; value\rangle$ pair, and it outputs a sequence of $\langle key; value\rangle$ pairs. Intuitively, the mapper maps the data stored in the $\langle key; value\rangle$ pair to a machine. In the map phase, the map function is applied to all $\langle key; value\rangle$ pairs. In the shuffle phase, all $\langle key; value\rangle$ pairs with a given key are sent to the same machine; this is done automatically by the underlying system. The reduce phase processes the $\langle key; value\rangle$ pairs created in the map phase as follows. The algorithm designer specifies a reduce function ρ, which we refer to as a *reducer*. The reducer takes as input all the $\langle key; value\rangle$ pairs that have the same key, and it outputs a sequence of $\langle key; value\rangle$ pairs which have the same key as the input pairs; these pairs are either the final output, or they become the input of the next MapReduce round. Intuitively, the reducer performs some sequential computation on all the data that is stored on a machine. The mappers and reducers are constrained to run in time that is polynomial in the size of the initial input, and not their input.

The theoretical $\mathcal{MRC}$ class was introduced in [26]. The class is designed to capture the practical restrictions of MapReduce as faithfully as possible; a detailed justification of the model can be found in [26]. In addition to the constraints on the mappers and reducers, there are three types of restrictions in $\mathcal{MRC}$: constraints on the number of machines used, on the memory available on each of the machines, and on the number of rounds of computation. If the input to a problem is of size N then an algorithm is in $\mathcal{MRC}$ if it uses at most $N^{1-\epsilon}$ machines, each with at most $N^{1-\epsilon}$ memory for some constant $\epsilon > 0$[3]. Notice that this implies that the total memory available is $O(N^{2-2\epsilon})$. Thus the difficulty of designing algorithms for the MapReduce model does not come from the lack of total memory. Rather, it stems from the fact that the memory available on each machine is limited; in particular, the entire input does not fit on a single machine. Not allowing the entire input to be placed on a single machine makes designing algorithms difficult, since a machine is only aware of a subset of the input. Indeed, because of this restriction, it is currently not known whether fundamental graph problems such as shortest paths or maximum matchings can be computed in a constant number of rounds, even if the graphs are unweighted.

In the following, we state the precise restrictions on the resources available to an algorithm for a problem in the class $\mathcal{MRC}^0$.

- **Memory**: The total memory used on a specific machine is at most $O(N^{1-\epsilon})$.
- **Machines**: The total number of machines used is $O(N^{1-\epsilon})$.
- **Rounds**: The number of rounds is constant.

2. ALGORITHMS

In this section we describe our clustering algorithms `MapReduce-kCenter` and `MapReduce-kMedian`. For both of our algorithms, we will parameterize the amount of memory needed on a machine. For the MapReduce setting, the amount of memory our algorithms require on each of the machines is parameterized by $\delta > 0$ and we assume that the memory is $\Omega(k^2 n^\delta)$. It is further assumed that the number of machines is large enough to store all of the input data across the machines. Both algorithms use `Iterative-Sample` as a subroutine which uses sampling ideas from [32]. The role of `Iterative-Sample` is to get a substantially smaller subset of points that represents all of the points well. To achieve this, `Iterative-Sample` performs the following computation iteratively: in each iteration, it adds a small sample of points to the final sample, it determines which points are "well represented" by the sample, and it recursively considers only the points that are not well represented. More precisely, after sampling, `Iterative-Sample` discards most points that are close to the current sample, and it recurses on the remaining (unsampled) points. The algorithm repeats this procedure until the number of points that are still unrepresented is small and all such points are added to the sample. Once we have a good sample, we

[3] The algorithm designer can choose ϵ.

run a clustering algorithm on just the sampled points. Knowing that the sampling represents all unsampled points well, a good clustering of the sampled points will also be a good clustering of all of the points. Here the clustering algorithm used will depend on the problem considered. In the following section, we show how `Iterative-Sample` can be implemented in the sequential setting to highlight the high level ideas. Then we show how to extend the algorithms to the MapReduce setting.

2.1 Sampling Sequentially

In this section, the sequential version of the sampling algorithm is discussed. When we mention the distance of a point x to a set S, we mean the minimum distance between x and any point in S. Our algorithm is parameterized by a constant $0 < \epsilon < \frac{\delta}{2}$ whose value can be changed depending on the system specifications. Simply, the value of ϵ determines the sample size. For each of our algorithms there is a natural trade-off between the sample size and the running time of the algorithm.

Algorithm 1 `Iterative-Sample`(V, E, k, ϵ):

1: Set $S \leftarrow \emptyset$, $R \leftarrow V$.
2: **while** $|R| > \frac{4}{\epsilon} kn^{\epsilon} \log n$ **do**
3: Add each point in R with probability $\frac{9kn^{\epsilon}}{|R|} \log n$ independently to S.
4: Add each point in R with probability $\frac{4n^{\epsilon}}{|R|} \log n$ independently to H.
5: $v \leftarrow$ `Select`(H, S)
6: Find the distance of each point $x \in R$ to S. Remove x from R if this distance is smaller than the distance of v to S.
7: **end while**
8: Output $C := S \cup R$

Algorithm 2 `Select`(H, S):

1: For each point $x \in H$, find the distance of x to S.
2: Order the points in H according to their distance to S from farthest to smallest.
3: Let v be the point that is in the $8 \log n$th position in the ordering.
4: Return v.

The algorithm `Iterative-Sample` maintains a set of sampled points S and a set of points R that contains the set of points that are not well represented by the current sample. The algorithm repeately adds new points to the sample. By adding more points to the sample, S will represent more points well. More points are added to S until the number of remaining points decreases below the threshold given in line 2. The point v chosen in line 5 serves as the pivot to determine which points are well represented: if a point x is closer to the sample S than the pivot v, the point x is considered to be well represented by S and dropped from R. Finally, `Iterative-Sample` returns the union of S and R. Note that R must be returned since R is not well represented by S even at the end of the while loop.

2.2 MapReduce Algorithms

First we show a MapReduce version of `Iterative-Sample` and then we give MapReduce algorithms for the k-center and k-median problems. For these algorithms we assume that for any set S and parameter η, the set S can be arbitrarily partitioned into sets of size $|S|/\eta$ by the mappers. To see that this is the case, we refer the reader to [26].

Algorithm 3 `MapReduce-Iterative-Sample`(V, E, k, ϵ):

1: Set $S \leftarrow \emptyset$, $R \leftarrow V$.
2: **while** $|R| > \frac{4}{\epsilon} kn^{\epsilon} \log n$ **do**
3: The mappers arbitrarily partition R into $\lceil |R|/n^{\epsilon} \rceil$ sets of size at most $\lceil n^{\epsilon} \rceil$. Each of these sets is mapped to a unique reducer.
4: For a reducer i, let R^i denote the points assigned to the reducer. Reducer i adds each point in R^i to a set S^i independently with probability $\frac{9kn^{\epsilon}}{|R|} \log n$ and also adds each point in R^i to a set H^i independently with probability $\frac{4n^{\epsilon}}{|R|} \log n$.
5: Let $H := \bigcup_{1 \le i \le \lceil n^{\epsilon} \rceil} H^i$ and $S := S \cup (\bigcup_{1 \le i \le \lceil n^{\epsilon} \rceil} S^i)$. The mappers assign H and S to a single machine along with all edge distances from each point in H to each point in S.
6: The reducer whose input is H and S sets $v \leftarrow$ `Select`(H, S).
7: The mappers arbitrarily partition the points in R into $\lceil n^{1-\epsilon} \rceil$ subsets, each of size at most $\lceil |R|/n^{1-\epsilon} \rceil$. Let R^i for $1 \le i \le \lceil n^{1-\epsilon} \rceil$ denote these sets. Let v, R^i, S, the distances between each point in R^i and each point in S be assigned to reducer i.
8: Reducer i finds the distance of each point $x \in R^i$ to S. The point x is removed from R^i if this distance is smaller than the distance of v to S.
9: Let $R := \bigcup_{i \in [\eta]} R^i$.
10: **end while**
11: Output $C := S \cup R$

The following propositions give the theoretical guarantees of the algorithm; these propositions can also serve as a guide for choosing an appropriate value for the parameter ϵ. If the probability of an event is $1 - O(1/n)$, we say that the event occurs with high probability, which we abbreviate as w.h.p. The first two propositions follow from the fact that, w.h.p., each iteration of `Iterative-Sample` decreases the number of remaining points — i.e., the size of the set R — by a factor of $\Theta(n^{\epsilon})$. We give the proofs of these propositions in the next section. Note that the propositions imply that our algorithm belongs to $\mathcal{MRC}^0$.

PROPOSITION 2.1. *The number of iterations of the while loop of* `Iterative-Sample` *is at most* $O(\frac{1}{\epsilon})$ *w.h.p.*

PROPOSITION 2.2. *The set returned by* `Iterative-Sample` *has size* $O(\frac{1}{\epsilon} kn^{\epsilon} \log n)$ *w.h.p.*

PROPOSITION 2.3. `MapReduce-Iterative-Sample` *is a MapReduce algorithm that requires* $O(\frac{1}{\epsilon})$ *rounds when machines have memory* $O(kn^{\delta})$ *for a constant* $\delta > 2\epsilon$ *w.h.p.*

PROOF. Consider a single iteration of the while loop. Each iteration takes a constant number of MapReduce rounds. By Proposition 2.1, the number of iterations of this loop is $O(\frac{1}{\epsilon})$, and therefore the number of rounds is $O(\frac{1}{\epsilon})$. The memory needed on a machine is dominated by the memory required by Step (7). The size of S is $O(\frac{1}{\epsilon} kn^{\epsilon} \log n)$ by Proposition 2.2. Further, the size of R^i is at most $n/n^{1-\epsilon} = n^{\epsilon}$. Let η be the maximum number of bits needed to represent the distance from one point to another. Thus the total memory needed on a machine is $O(\frac{1}{\epsilon} kn^{\epsilon} \log n \cdot n^{\epsilon} \cdot \eta)$, the memory needed to store the distances from points in R^i to points in S. By assumption $\eta = O(\log n)$, thus the total memory needed on a machine is upper bounded by $O(\frac{1}{\epsilon} kn^{2\epsilon} \log^2 n)$. By setting δ to be a constant slightly larger than 2ϵ, the proposition follows. □

Once we have this sampling algorithm, our algorithm `MapReduce-kCenter` for the k-center problem is fairly straightforward. This is the algorithm considered in Theorem 1.1. The memory needed by the algorithm is dominated by storing the pairwise distances between points in C on a single machine. By Proposition 2.2 and the assumption that the maximum distance between any two points can be represented using $O(\log n)$ bits, w.h.p. the memory needed is $O((\frac{1}{\epsilon}kn^{\epsilon}\log n)^2 \cdot \log n) = O(n^{\delta}k^2)$, where δ is a constant greater than 2ϵ.

Algorithm 4 `MapReduce-kCenter`(V, E, k, ϵ):

Let $C \leftarrow$ `Iterative-Sample`(V, E, k, ϵ).
Map C and all of pairwise distances between points in C to a reducer.
The reducer runs a k-center clustering algorithm $\mathcal{A}$ on C.
Return the set constructed by $\mathcal{A}$.

However, for the k-median problem, the sample must contain more information than just the set of sampled points. This is because the k-median objective considers the sum of the distances to the centers. To ensure that we can map a good solution for the points in the sample to a good solution for all of the points, for each unsampled point x, we select the sampled point that is closest to x (if there are several points that are closest to x, we pick one arbitrarily). Additionally, we assign a weight to each sampled point y that is equal to the number of unsampled points that picked y as its closest point. This is done so that, when we cluster the sampled points on a single machine, we can take into account the effect of the unsampled points on the objective. For a point x and a set of points A, let $d(x, A)$ denote the minimum distance from the point $x \in V$ to a point in A, i.e., $d(x, A) = \min_{y \in A} d(x, y)$. The algorithm `MapReduce-kMedian` is the following.

Algorithm 5 `MapReduce-kMedian`(V, E, k, ϵ):

Let $C \leftarrow$ `MapReduce-Iterative-Sample`(V, E, k, ϵ)
The mappers arbitrarily partition V into $\lceil n^{1-\epsilon} \rceil$ sets of size at most $\lceil n^{\epsilon} \rceil$. Let V^i for $1 \le i \le \lceil n^{1-\epsilon} \rceil$ be the partitioning.
The mappers assign V^i, C and all distances between points in V^i and C to reducer i for all $1 \le i \le \lceil n^{1-\epsilon} \rceil$.
Each reducer i, for each $y \in C$, computes $w^i(y) = |\{x \in V^i \setminus C \mid d(x, y) = d(x, C)\}|$.
Map all of the weights $w^i(\cdot)$, C and the pairwise distances between all points in C to a single reducer.
The reducer computes $w(y) = \sum_{i \in [m]} w^i(y) + 1$ for all $y \in C$.
The reducer runs a weighted k-median clustering algorithm $\mathcal{A}$ on that machine with $\langle C, w, k \rangle$ as input.
Return the set constructed by $\mathcal{A}$.

The `MapReduce-kMedian` algorithm performs additional rounds to give a weight to each point in the sample C. We remark that these additional rounds can be easily removed by gradually performing this operation in each iteration of `MapReduce-Iterative-Sample`. The maximum memory used by a machine in `MapReduce-kMedian` is bounded similarly as `MapReduce-kCenter`. The proof of all propositions and theorems will be given in the next section. The algorithm `MapReduce-kMedian` is the algorithm considered in Theorem 1.2. Notice that both `MapReduce-kMedian` and `MapReduce-kCenter` use some clustering algorithm as a subroutine. The running times of these clustering algorithms depend on the size of the sample and therefore there is a trade-off between the running times of these algorithms and the number of MapReduce rounds.

3. ANALYSIS

3.1 Subroutine: Iterative-Sample

This section is devoted to the analysis of `Iterative-Sample`, the main subroutine of our clustering algorithms. Before we give the analysis, we introduce some notation. Let S^* denote any set. We will show several lemmas and theorems that hold for any set S^*, and in the final step, we will set S^* to be the optimal set of centers. The reader may read the lemmas and theorems assuming that S^* is the optimal set of centers. We assign each point $x \in V$ to its closest point in S^*, breaking ties arbitrarily but consistently. Let x^{S^*} be the point in S^* to which x is assigned; if x is in S^*, we assign x to itself. Let $S^*(x)$ be the set of all points assigned to $x \in S^*$.

We say that a point x is *satisfied* by S with respect to S^* if $d(S, x^{S^*}) \le d(x, x^{S^*})$. If S and S^* are clear from the context, we will simply say that x is satisfied. We say that x is *unsatisfied* if it is not satisfied. Throughout the analysis, for any point x in V and any subset $S \subseteq V$, we will let x^S denote the point in S that is closest to x.

We now explain the intuition behind the definition of "satisfied". Our sampling subroutine's output C may not include each center in S^*. However, a point x could be "satisfied", even though $x^{S^*} \notin C$, by including a point in C that is closer to x than x^{S^*}. Intuitively, if all points are satisfied, our sampling algorithm returned a very representative sample of all points, and our clustering algorithms will perform well. However, we cannot guarantee that all points are satisfied. Instead, we will show that the number of unsatisfied points is small and their contribution to the clustering cost is negligible compared to the satisfied points' contribution. This will allow us to upper bound the distance between the unsatisfied points and the final solution constructed by our algorithm by the cost of the optimal solution.

Since the sets described in `Iterative-Sample` change in each iteration, for the purpose of the analysis, we let R_ℓ, S_ℓ, and H_ℓ denote the sets R, S, and H at the beginning of iteration ℓ. Note that $R_1 = V$ and $S_1 = \emptyset$. Let D_ℓ denote the set of points that are removed (deleted) during iteration ℓ. Note that $R_{\ell+1} = R_\ell - D_\ell$. Let U_ℓ denote the set of points in R_ℓ that are not satisfied by $S_{\ell+1}$ with respect to S^*. Let C denote the set of points that `Iterative-Sample` returns. Let U denote the set of all unsatisfied points by C with respect to S^*. If one point is satisfied by S_ℓ with respect to S^* then it is also satisfied by C with respect to S^*, and therefore $U \subseteq \bigcup_{\ell \ge 1} U_\ell$.

We start by upper bounding $|U_\ell|$, the number of unsatisfied points at the end of iteration ℓ.

LEMMA 3.1. *Let S^* be any set with no more than k points. Consider iteration ℓ of `Iterative-Sample`, where $\ell \ge 1$. Then* $\textbf{Pr}\left[|U_\ell| \ge \frac{|R_\ell|}{3n^{\epsilon}}\right] \le \frac{1}{n^2}$.

Recall that we selected a threshold point v to discard the points that are well represented by the current sample S. Let $\texttt{rank}_{R_\ell}(v)$ denote the number of points x in R_ℓ such that the distance from x to S is greater than the distance from v to S. The proof of the following lemma follows easily from the Chernoff inequality.

LEMMA 3.2. *Let S^* be any set with no more than k points. Consider any ℓ-th iteration of the while loop of*

`Iterative-Sample`. *Let v_ℓ denote the threshold in the current iteration, i.e. the $(8\log n)$-th farthest point in H_ℓ from $S_{\ell+1}$. Then we have* $\mathbf{Pr}[\frac{|R_\ell|}{n^\epsilon} \leq \mathtt{rank}(v_\ell) \leq \frac{4|R_\ell|}{n^\epsilon}] \geq 1 - \frac{2}{n^2}$.

COROLLARY 3.3. *Consider any ℓ-th iteration of the while loop of* `Iterative-Sample`. *Then* $\mathbf{Pr}[\frac{|R_\ell|}{n^\epsilon} \leq |R_{\ell+1}| \leq \frac{4|R_\ell|}{n^\epsilon}] \geq 1 - \frac{2}{n^2}$.

The above corollary immediately implies Proposition 2.1 and 2.2. Now we show how to map each unsatisfied point to a satisfied point such that no two unsatisfied points are mapped to the same satisfied point; that is, the map is injective. Such a mapping will allow us to bound the cost of unsatisfied points by the cost of the optimal solution. The following theorem is the core of our analysis. The theorem defines a mapping $p : U \rightarrow V$; for each point x, we refer to $p(x)$ as the *proxy* point of x.

THEOREM 3.4. *Consider any set $S^* \subseteq V$. Let C be the set of points returned by* `Iterative-Sample`. *Let U be the set of all points in $V - C$ that are unsatisfied by C with respect to S^*. Then w.h.p., there exists an injective function $p : U \rightarrow V \setminus U$ such that, for any $x \in U$, $d(p(x), S^*) \geq d(x, C)$.*

3.2 MapReduce-KCenter

This section is devoted to proving Theorem 1.1. For the sake of analysis, we will consider the following variant of the k-center problem. In the `kCenter`(V, T) problem, we are given two sets V and $T \subseteq V$ of points in a metric space, and we want to select a subset $S^* \subseteq T$ such that $|S^*| \leq k$ and S^* minimizes $\max_{x \in V} d(x, S)$ among all sets $S \subseteq T$ with at most k points. For notational simplicity, we let $\mathrm{OPT}(V, T)$ denote the optimal solution for the problem `kCenter`(V, T). Depending on the context, $\mathrm{OPT}(V, T)$ may denote the cost of the solution. Since we are interested eventually in $\mathrm{OPT}(V, V)$, we let $\mathrm{OPT} := \mathrm{OPT}(V, V)$.

PROPOSITION 3.5. *Let C be the set of centers returned by* `Iterative-Sample`. *Then w.h.p. we have that for any $x \in V$, $d(x, C) \leq 2\mathrm{OPT}$.*

PROPOSITION 3.6. *Let C be the set of centers returned by* `Iterative-Sample`. *Then w.h.p. we have $\mathrm{OPT}(C, C) \leq \mathrm{OPT}(V, C) \leq \mathrm{OPT}$.*

THEOREM 3.7. *If $\mathcal{A}$ is an algorithm that achieves an α-approximation for the k center problem, then w.h.p. the algorithm* `MapReduce-kCenter` *achieves a $(4\alpha + 2)$-approximation for the k center problem.*

By setting the algorithm $\mathcal{A}$ to be the 2-approximation of [17, 19], we complete the proof Theorem 1.1.

3.3 MapReduce-KMedian

In the following, we will consider the following variants of the k-median problem similar to the variant of the k-center problem considered in the previous section. In the `kMedian`(V, T) problem, we are given two sets V and $T \subseteq V$ of points in a metric space, and we want to select a subset $S^* \subseteq T$ such that $|S^*| \leq k$ and S^* minimizes $\sum_{x \in V} d(x, S)$ among all sets $S \subseteq T$ with at most k points. We let $\mathrm{OPT}(V, T)$ denote a fixed optimal solution for `kMedian`(V, T) or the optimal cost depending on the context. Note that we are interested in obtaining a solution that is comparable to $\mathrm{OPT}(V, V)$. Hence, for notational simplicity, we let $\mathrm{OPT} := \mathrm{OPT}(V, V)$. In the `Weighted-kMedian`$(V, w)$ problem, we are given a set V of points in a metric space such that each point x has a weight $w(x)$, and we want to select a subset $S^* \subseteq V$ such that $|S^*| \leq k$ and S^* minimizes $\sum_{x \in V} w(x) d(x, S)$ among all sets $S \subseteq V$ with at most k points. Let $\mathrm{OPT}^w(V, w)$ denote a fixed optimal solution for a `Weighted-kMedian`(V, w).

Recall that `MapReduce-kMedian` computes an approximate k-medians on C with each point x in C having a weight $w(x)$. Hence we first show that we can obtain a good approximate k-medians using only the points in C.

PROPOSITION 3.8. *Let $S^* := \mathrm{OPT}$. Let C be the set of centers returned by* `Iterative-Sample`. *Then w.h.p., we have that $\sum_{x \in V} d(x, C) \leq 3\mathrm{OPT}$.*

PROPOSITION 3.9. *Let C be the set returned by* `Iterative-Sample`. *Then w.h.p., $\mathrm{OPT}(V, C) \leq 5\mathrm{OPT}$.*

So far we have shown that we can obtain a good approximate solution for the `kMedian`(V, V) even when we are restricted to C. However, we need a stronger argument, since `MapReduce-kMedian` only sees the weighted points in C and not the entire point set V.

PROPOSITION 3.10. *Consider any subset of points $C \subseteq V$. For each point $y \in C$, let $w(y) = |\{x \in V - C \mid x^C = y\}| + 1$. Then we have $\mathrm{OPT}^w(C, w) \leq 2\mathrm{OPT}(V, C)$.*

THEOREM 3.11. *If $\mathcal{A}$ is an algorithm that achieves an α-approximation for* `Weighted-kMedian`, *w.h.p. the algorithm* `MapReduce-kMedian` *achieves a $(10\alpha + 3)$-approximation for* `kMedian`.

Recall that there is a $(3 + 2/c)$ approximation algorithm for k-median that runs in $O(n^c)$ time [4, 21]. In order to complete the proof of Theorem 1.2, we pick a constant c and we use the $(3 + 2/c)$-approximation algorithm.

4. EXPERIMENTS

In this section we give an experimental study of the algorithms introduced in this paper. The focus for this section is on the k-median objective because this is where our algorithm gives the largest increase in performance. Unfortunately, our sampling algorithm does not perform well for the k-center metric. This is because the k-center objective is quite sensitive to sampling. Since the maximum distance from a point to a center is considered in the objective, if the sampling algorithm misses even one important point then the objective can substantially increase. From now on, we only consider the k-median problem. In the following, we describe the algorithms we tested and we give an overview of the experiments and the results.

4.1 Implemented Algorithms

We compare our algorithm `MapReduce-kMedian` to several algorithms. Recall that `MapReduce-kMedian` uses `Iterative-Sample` as a sub-procedure and we have shown that `MapReduce-kMedian` gives a constant approximation when the local search algorithm [4, 21] is applied on the sample that was obtained by `Iterative-Sample`. We also consider Lloyd's algorithm together with the sampling procedure `Iterative-Sample`; that is, in `MapReduce-kMedian`, the algorithm $\mathcal{A}$ is Lloyd's algorithm and it takes as input the sample constructed by `Iterative-Sample`. Note that Lloyd's algorithm does not give an approximation guarantee. However, it is the most popular algorithm for clustering in practice and therefore it is worth testing its performance. We will use

	Number of points	10,000	20,000	40,000	100,000	200,000	400,000	1,000,000
cost	Parallel-Lloyd	1.000	1.000	1.000	1.000	1.000	1.000	1.000
	Divide-Lloyd	1.030	1.088	1.132	1.033	1.051	0.994	1.023
	Divide-LocalSearch	0.999	1.024	1.006	0.999	1.008	0.999	1.010
	Sampling-Lloyd	1.086	1.165	1.051	1.138	1.068	1.095	1.132
	Sampling-LocalSearch	1.018	1.019	1.011	1.006	1.024	1.025	1.029
	LocalSearch	0.948	0.964	0.958	N/A	N/A	N/A	N/A
time	Parallel-Lloyd	0.0	3.3	6.0	18.0	29.3	52.7	205.7
	Divide-Lloyd	0.0	0.3	0.3	1.3	1.0	1.0	2.7
	Divide-LocalSearch	5.0	5.0	5.0	6.0	9.0	19.0	70.7
	Sampling-Lloyd	0.3	0.0	0.3	0.7	1.3	3.0	4.0
	Sampling-LocalSearch	1.7	2.3	3.0	4.3	6.0	8.3	11.0
	LocalSearch	666.7	943.0	2569.3	N/A	N/A	N/A	N/A

Figure 1: The relative cost and running time of clustering algorithms when the number of points is not too large. The costs are normalized to that of `Parallel-Lloyd`. The running time is given in seconds.

	Number of points	2,000,000	5,000,000	10,000,000
cost	Parallel-Lloyd	1.000	1.000	1.000
	Divide-Lloyd	1.018	1.036	1.000
	Sampling-Lloyd	1.064	1.106	1.073
	Sampling-LocalSearch	1.027	1.019	1.015
time	Parallel-Lloyd	458.0	1333.3	702.3
	Divide-Lloyd	8.3	24.7	50.7
	Sampling-Lloyd	8.0	18.3	38.0
	Sampling-LocalSearch	16.3	29.3	86.3

Figure 2: The relative cost and running time of the scalable algorithms when the number of points are large. The costs were normalized to that of `Parallel-Lloyd`. The running time is given in seconds.

`Sampling-LocalSearch` to refer to `MapReduce-kMedian` with the local search algorithm as $\mathcal{A}$ and we will use `Sampling-Lloyd` to refer to `MapReduce-kMedian` with Lloyd's algorithm as $\mathcal{A}$. Note that the only difference between `Sampling-LocalSearch` and `Sampling-Lloyd` is the clustering algorithm chosen as $\mathcal{A}$ in `MapReduce-kMedian`.

We also implement the local search algorithm and Lloyd's algorithm without sampling. The local search algorithm, denoted as `LocalSearch`, is the only sequential algorithm among all algorithms that we implemented [4, 21]. We implement a parallelized version of Lloyd's algorithm, `Parallel-Lloyd` [28, 7, 1]. This implementation of Lloyd's algorithm parallelizes a sub-procedure of the sequential Lloyd's algorithm. The parallel version of Lloyd's gives the same solution as the sequential version of Lloyd's; the only difference between the two implementations is the parallelization. We give a more formal description of the parallel Lloyd's algorithm below.

Finally, we implement clustering algorithms based on a simple partitioning scheme used to adapt sequential algorithms to the parallel setting. In the partition scheme `MapReduce-Divide-kMedian` we consider, points are partitioned into ℓ sets of size $\lceil \frac{n}{\ell} \rceil$. In parallel, centers are computed for each of the partitions. Then all of the centers computed are combined into a single set and the centers are clustered. We formalize this in the algorithm `MapReduce-Divide-kMedian`. We evaluated the local search algorithm and Lloyd's algorithm coupled with this partition scheme. Throughout this section, we use `Divide-LocalSearch` for the local search together with this partition scheme. We call Lloyd's algorithm coupled with the partition scheme as `Divide-Lloyd`. We give the details of the partition framework `MapReduce-Divide-kMedian` shortly.

The following is a summary of the algorithms we implemented:

- `LocalSearch`: Local Search
- `Parallel-Lloyd`: Parallel Lloyd's
- `Sampling-LocalSearch`: Sampling and Local Search
- `Sampling-Lloyd`: Sampling and Lloyd's
- `Divide-LocalSearch`: Partition and Local Search
- `Divide-Lloyd`: Partition and Lloyd's

A careful reader may note that Lloyd's algorithm is generally used for the k-means objective and not for k-median. Lloyd's algorithm is more commonly used for k-means, but it can be used for k-median as well, and it is one of the most popular clustering algorithms in practice. We note that the parallelized version of Lloyd's algorithm we introduce only works with points in Euclidean space.

Parallel Lloyd's Algorithm: We give a sketch of parallelized implementation of Lloyd's algorithm used in the experiments. More details can be found in [7, 1]. The algorithm begins by partitioning the points evenly across the machines and these points will remain on the machines. The algorithm initializes the k centers to an arbitrary set of points. In each iteration, the algorithm improves the centers as follows. The mapper sends the k centers to each of the machines. On each machine, the reducer clusters the points on the machine by assigning each point to its closest center. For each cluster, the average[4] of the points in the cluster is computed along with the number of points assigned to the center. The mappers map all this information to a single machine. For each center, the mappers aggregate the points assigned to the center over all partitions along with the centers, and then the reducers update the center to be the average of these points. It is important to note that the solution

[4]Recall that the input to Lloyd's algorithm is a set of points in Euclidean space. The average of the points is the point in Euclidean space whose coordinates are the average of the coordinates of the points.

computed by the algorithm is the same as the sequential version of Lloyd's algorithm.

Partitioning Based Scheme: We describe the partition scheme `MapReduce-Divide-kMedian` that is used for the `Divide-LocalSearch` and `Divide-Lloyd` algorithms. The algorithm `MapReduce-Divide-kMedian` is a partitioning-based parallelization of any arbitrary sequential clustering algorithm. We note that this algorithm and the following analysis have also been considered by Guha et al. [20] in the streaming model.

Algorithm 6 `MapReduce-Divide-kMedian`(V, E, k, ℓ):

1: Let $n = |V|$.
2: The mappers arbitrarily partition V into disjoint sets $S_1, \cdots, S_\ell$, each of size $\Theta(n/\ell)$.
3: **for** $i = 1$ to ℓ **do**
4: The mapper assigns S_i and all the distances between points in S_i to reducer i.
5: Reducer i runs a k-median clustering algorithm $\mathcal{A}$ with $\langle S_i, k\rangle$ as input to find a set $C_i \subseteq S_i$ of k centers.
6: Reducer i computes, for each $y \in C_i$, $w(y) = |\{x \in S^i \setminus C_i \mid d(x, y) = d(x, C_i)\}| + 1$.
7: **end for**
8: Let $C = \bigcup_{i=1}^{\ell} C_i$.
9: The mapper sends C, the pairwise distances between points in C and the numbers $w(\cdot)$ to a single reducer.
10: The reducer runs a `Weighted-kMedian` algorithm $\mathcal{A}$ with $\langle C, w, k\rangle$ as input.
11: Return the set constructed by $\mathcal{A}$.

It is straightforward to verify that setting $\ell = \sqrt{n/k}$ minimizes the maximum memory needed on a machine; in the following, we assume that $\ell = \sqrt{n/k}$. The total memory used by the algorithm is $O(kn \log n)$. (Recall that we assume that the distance between two points can be represented using $O(\log n)$ bits.) Additionally, the memory needed is also $\Omega(kn)$, since in Step (9), $\Theta(\sqrt{n/k})$ sets of k points are sent to a single machine along with their pairwise distances. The following proposition follows from the algorithm description.

PROPOSITION 4.1. *`MapReduce-Divide-kMedian` runs in $O(1)$ MapReduce rounds.*

From the analysis given in [20], we have the following theorem which can be used to bound the approximation factor of `MapReduce-Divide-kMedian`.

THEOREM 4.2 (THEOREM 2.2 IN [20]). *Consider any set of n points arbitrarily partitioned into disjoint sets $S_1, \cdots, S_\ell$. The sum of the optimum solution values for the k-median problem on the ℓ sets of points is at most twice the cost of the optimum k-median problem solution for all n points, for any $\ell > 0$.*

COROLLARY 4.3 ([20]). *If the algorithm $\mathcal{A}$ achieves an α-approximation for the k-median problem, the algorithm `MapReduce-Divide-kMedian` achieves a 3α-approximation for the k-median problem.*

By this Corollary, note that `Divide-LocalSearch` is a constant factor approximation.

4.2 Experiment Overview

We generate a random set of points in $\mathbb{R}^3$. Our data set consists of k centers and randomly generated points around the centers to create clusters. The k centers are randomly positioned in a unit cube. The number of points generated within a cluster is sampled from a Zipf distribution. More precisely, let $\{C_i\}_{1 \le i \le k}$ be the set of clusters. Given a fixed number of points, a unique point is assigned to the cluster C_i with probability $i^\alpha / \sum_{i=1}^{k} i^\alpha$ where α is the parameter of the Zipf distribution. Notice that when $\alpha = 0$, all clusters will have almost the same size and, as α grows, the sizes of the clusters become more non-uniform. The distance between a point and its center is sampled from a normal distribution with a fixed global standard deviation σ. Each experiment with the same parameter set was repeated three times and the average was calculated. When running the local search or Lloyd's algorithm, the seed centers were chosen arbitrarily.

All experiments were performed on a single machine. When running MapReduce algorithms, we simulated each machine used by the algorithm. For a given round, we recorded the time it takes for the machine that ran the longest in the round. Then we summed this time over all the rounds to get the final running time of the parallel algorithms. In these experiments, the communication cost was ignored. More precisely, we ignored the time needed to move data to a different machine. The specifications of the machine were Intel(R) Core(TM) i7 CPU 870 @ 2.93GHz and the memory available was 8GB. We used the standard `clock()` function to measure the time for each experiment. All parallel algorithms were simulated assuming that there are 100 machines. For the algorithm `MapReduce-kMedian` the value of ϵ was set to .1 for the sampling probability.

4.3 Results

Because of the space constraints, we only give a brief summary of our results. The data can be found in Figures 1 and 2. For the data in the figures, the number of points is the only variable, and other parameters are fixed: $\sigma = 0.1$, $\alpha = 0$ and $k = 25$. The cost of the algorithms' objectives is normalized to the cost of `Parallel-Lloyd` in the figures. Figure 1 summarizes the results of the experiments on data sets with at most 10^6 points, and Figure 2 summarizes the results of the experiments on data sets with at most 10^7 points.

Our experiments show that `Sampling-Lloyd` and `Sampling-LocalSearch` achieve a significant speedup over `Parallel-Lloyd` (about 20x), a speedup of more than ten times over `Divide-LocalSearch` and a significant speedup over `LocalSearch` (over 1000x) as seen in Figure 1. The speedup increases very fast as the number of points increases. Further, this speedup is achieved with negligible loss in performance; our algorithm's objective performs close to the `Parallel-Lloyd` and `LocalSearch` when the number of points is sufficiently large.

Finally, we compare the performance of `Sampling-LocalSearch` and `Sampling-Lloyd` with the performance of `Divide-Lloyd` on the largest data sets; the results are summarized in Figure 2. These algorithms were chosen because they are the most scalable and perform well; as shown in Figure 1, `LocalSearch` is far from scalable. Although `Divide-LocalSearch`'s running times are similar to `Parallel-Lloyd`'s, we were not able to run additional experiments with `Divide-LocalSearch` because it takes a very long time to simulate on a single machine. These additional experiments show that, for data sets consisting of 5×10^6 points, the running time of `Sampling-LocalSearch` is slightly larger than `Divide-Lloyd`'s and the clustering cost of `Sampling-LocalSearch` is similar to the cost of `Divide-Lloyd`. The algorithm `Sampling-Lloyd` achieves a speedup of about 25% over `Divide-Lloyd` when the number of points is 10^7. Overall the experiments show that, when coupled with Lloyd's algorithm, our sampling algorithm runs faster than any previously known algorithm that we considered, and this speedup is achieved at a very small loss in performance. We also ran experiments with different settings for the parameters α, k, and σ, and the results were similar; we omit these results from this version of the paper.

5. CONCLUSION

In this paper we give the first approximation algorithms for the k-center and k-median problems that run in a constant number of MapReduce rounds. We note that we have preliminary evidence that the analysis used for the k-median problem can be extended to the k-means problem in Euclidean space; for this problem, our analysis also gives a MapReduce algorithm that runs in a constant number of rounds and achieves a constant factor approximation.

Acknowledgments: We thank Kyle Fox for his help with the implementation of the algorithms and several discussions. We thank Chandra Chekuri for helpful comments on an earlier draft of this paper. We thank Ravi Kumar and Sergei Vassilvitskii for helpful comments on the problems considered. We thank Jeff Erickson for his advice on how to improve the presentation.

6. REFERENCES

[1] Google: Cluster computing and mapreduce. *http://code.google.com/edu/submissions/mapreduce-minilecture/listing.html.*

[2] P. K. Agarwal and N. H. Mustafa. k-means projective clustering. In *PODS*, pages 155–165, 2004.

[3] D. Arthur and S. Vassilvitskii. k-means++: the advantages of careful seeding. In *SODA*, pages 1027–1035, 2007.

[4] V. Arya, N. Garg, R. Khandekar, A. Meyerson, K. Munagala, and V. Pandit. Local search heuristics for k-median and facility location problems. *SIAM J. Comput.*, 33(3):544–562, 2004.

[5] Y. Bartal. Probabilistic approximations of metric spaces and its algorithmic applications. In *FOCS*, pages 184–193, 1996.

[6] Y. Bartal. On approximating arbitrary metrices by tree metrics. In *STOC*, pages 161–168, 1998.

[7] M. Berry. Mapreduce and k-means clustering. *http://blog.data-miners.com/2008/02/mapreduce-and-k-means-clustering.html*, 2008.

[8] G. E. Blelloch and K. Tangwongsan. Parallel approximation algorithms for facility-location problems. In *SPAA*, pages 315–324, 2010.

[9] M. Charikar, C. Chekuri, T. Feder, and R. Motwani. Incremental clustering and dynamic information retrieval. *SIAM J. Comput.*, 33(6):1417–1440, 2004.

[10] M. Charikar, C. Chekuri, A. Goel, and S. Guha. Rounding via trees: Deterministic approximation algorithms for group steiner trees and k-median. In *STOC*, pages 114–123, 1998.

[11] M. Charikar and S. Guha. Improved combinatorial algorithms for the facility location and k-median problems. In *FOCS*, pages 378–388, 1999.

[12] M. Charikar, S. Guha, É. Tardos, and D. B. Shmoys. A constant-factor approximation algorithm for the k-median problem. *J. Comput. Syst. Sci.*, 65(1):129–149, 2002.

[13] K. Chen. On k-median clustering in high dimensions. In *SODA*, pages 1177–1185, 2006.

[14] K. Chen. A constant factor approximation algorithm for k-median clustering with outliers. In *SODA*, pages 826–835, 2008.

[15] F. Chierichetti, R. Kumar, and A. Tomkins. Max-cover in map-reduce. In *WWW*, pages 231–240, 2010.

[16] J. Dean and S. Ghemawat. MapReduce: Simplified data processing on large clusters. In *Proceedings of OSDI*, pages 137–150, 2004.

[17] M. E. Dyer and A. M. Frieze. A simple heuristic for the p-centre problem. *Operations Research Letters*, 3(6):285 – 288, 1985.

[18] J. Feldman, S. Muthukrishnan, A. Sidiropoulos, C. Stein, and Z. Svitkina. On distributing symmetric streaming computations. *ACM Transactions on Algorithms*, 6(4), 2010.

[19] T. F. Gonzalez. Clustering to minimize the maximum intercluster distance. *Theoretical Computer Science*, 38:293 – 306, 1985.

[20] S. Guha, A. Meyerson, N. Mishra, R. Motwani, and L. O'Callaghan. Clustering data streams: Theory and practice. *IEEE Trans. Knowl. Data Eng.*, 15(3):515–528, 2003.

[21] A. Gupta and K. Tangwongsan. Simpler analyses of local search algorithms for facility location. *CoRR*, abs/0809.2554, 2008.

[22] R. Herwig, A. J. Poustka, C. Müller, C. Bull, H. Lehrach, and J. O'Brien. Large-Scale Clustering of cDNA-Fingerprinting Data. *Genome Research*, 9(11):1093–1105, November 1999.

[23] D. S. Hochbaum and D. B. Shmoys. A best possible heuristic for the k-center problem. *Mathematics of Operations Research*, 10(2):180–184, May 1985.

[24] K. Jain, M. Mahdian, and A. Saberi. A new greedy approach for facility location problems. In *STOC*, pages 731–740. ACM, 2002.

[25] U. Kang, C. Tsourakakis, A. P. Appel, C. Faloutsos, and J. Leskovec. Hadi: Fast diameter estimation and mining in massive graphs with hadoop. Technical report, School of Computer Science, Carnegie Mellon University Pittsburgh, December 2008.

[26] H. J. Karloff, S. Suri, and S. Vassilvitskii. A model of computation for mapreduce. In *SODA*, pages 938–948, 2010.

[27] J. Lin and C. Dyer. *Data-Intensive Text Processing with MapReduce*. Synthesis Lectures on Human Language Technologies. Morgan & Claypool Publishers, 2010.

[28] S. P. Lloyd. Least squares quantization in PCM. *IEEE Transactions on Information Theory*, 28(2):129–136, 1982.

[29] A. Ma and I. K. Sethi. Distributed k-median clustering with application to image clustering. In *PRIS*, pages 215–220, 2007.

[30] G. Malewicz, M. H. Austern, A. J. C. Bik, J. C. Dehnert, I. Horn, N. Leiser, and G. Czajkowski. Pregel: a system for large-scale graph processing. In *SIGMOD Conference*, pages 135–146, 2010.

[31] R. M. McCutchen and S. Khuller. Streaming algorithms for k-center clustering with outliers and with anonymity. In *APPROX-RANDOM*, pages 165–178, 2008.

[32] M. Thorup. Quick k-median, k-center, and facility location for sparse graphs. *SIAM J. Comput.*, 34(2):405–432, 2004.

[33] T. White. *Hadoop: The Definitive Guide*. O'Reilly Media, 2009.

Clustering Very Large Multi-dimensional Datasets with MapReduce*

Robson L. F. Cordeiro
CS Department - ICMC,
University of São Paulo - Brazil
robson@icmc.usp.br

Caetano Traina Jr.
CS Department - ICMC,
University of São Paulo - Brazil
caetano@icmc.usp.br

Agma J. M. Traina
CS Department - ICMC,
University of São Paulo - Brazil
agma@icmc.usp.br

Julio López
SCS, Carnegie Mellon
University - USA
jclopez@andrew.cmu.edu

U Kang
SCS, Carnegie Mellon
University - USA
ukang@cs.cmu.edu

Christos Faloutsos
SCS, Carnegie Mellon
University - USA
christos@cs.cmu.edu

ABSTRACT

Given a *very large* moderate-to-high dimensionality dataset, how could one cluster its points? For datasets that don't fit even on a single disk, parallelism is a first class option. In this paper we explore `MapReduce` for clustering this kind of data. The main questions are (a) how to minimize the I/O cost, taking into account the *already existing* data partition (e.g., on disks), and (b) how to minimize the network cost among processing nodes. Either of them may be a bottleneck. Thus, we propose the ***Best of both Worlds*** – *BoW* method, that automatically spots the bottleneck and chooses a good strategy. Our main contributions are: (1) We propose *BoW* and carefully derive its cost functions, which dynamically choose the best strategy; (2) We show that *BoW* has numerous desirable features: it can work with most serial clustering methods as a plugged-in clustering subroutine, it balances the cost for disk accesses and network accesses, achieving a very good tradeoff between the two, it uses no user-defined parameters (thanks to our reasonable defaults), it matches the clustering quality of the serial algorithm, and it has near-linear scale-up; and finally, (3) We report experiments on real and synthetic data with *billions* of points, using up to $1,024$ cores in parallel. To the best of our knowledge, our *Yahoo! web* is the *largest real dataset ever reported* in the database *subspace clustering* literature. Spanning 0.2 TB of multi-dimensional data, it took only 8 minutes to be clustered, using 128 cores.

Categories and Subject Descriptors

H.2.8 [**Database Applications**]: Data mining; D.1.3 [**Concurrent Programming**]: Parallel programming

General Terms

Algorithms, Design, Performance, Experimentation.

* Work performed during Mr. Cordeiro's visit to the Carnegie Mellon University.

KDD'11, August 21–24, 2011, San Diego, California, USA.

1. INTRODUCTION

Given a *very large* dataset of moderate-to-high dimensional elements, how could one cluster them? Numerous successful, serial *subspace clustering* algorithms for data in five or more dimensions exist in literature. See [14] for a recent survey. However, the existing algorithms are impractical for datasets spanning Terabytes and Petabytes (e.g., Twitter crawl: $>$ 12 TB, Yahoo! operational data: 5 *Petabytes* [10]). In such cases, the data are *already* stored on multiple disks, since the largest modern disks are 1-2TB. Just to read a single Terabyte of data (at 5GB/min on a single modern eSATA disk) one takes more than 3 hours! Thus, parallelism is not another option – it is by far the best choice. Nevertheless, good, serial clustering algorithms and strategies are still extremely valuable, because we can (and should) use them as 'plug-ins' for parallel clustering. Naturally, the best algorithm is the one that combines (a) a fast, scalable serial algorithm and (b) makes it run efficiently in parallel. This is exactly what our proposed method does.

Examples of applications with Terabytes of data in five or more dimensions abound: weather monitoring systems and climate change models, where we want to record wind speed, temperature, rain, humidity, pollutants, etc; social networks like Facebook TM, with millions of nodes, and several attributes per node (gender, age, number of friends, etc); astrophysics data, such as the SDSS (Sloan Digital Sky Survey), with billions of galaxies and attributes like red-shift, diameter, spectrum, etc.

This paper focuses on the problem of finding *subspace clusters* in *very large* moderate-to-high dimensional data, that is, having typically more than 5 axes. Our method uses `MapReduce`, and can treat as plug-in most of the serial clustering methods. The major research challenges addressed are (a) how to minimize the I/O cost, taking into account the *already existing* data partition (e.g., on disks), and (b) how to minimize the network cost among processing nodes. Any of them may be a bottleneck. So, we propose the ***Best of both Worlds*** – *BoW* method, that automatically spots the bottleneck and picks a good strategy. Our main contributions are:

1. *Algorithm design and analysis*: we propose *BoW*, a novel, adaptive method to automatically pick the best of two strategies and proper parameters for it, one of the strategies uses a novel *sampling-and-ignore* idea to shrink the network traffic;
2. *Effectiveness, scalability and generality*: we show that *BoW* can work with most serial clustering methods as a plugged-in clustering subroutine, it balances the cost for disk accesses and network accesses, achieving a very good tradeoff between the two, it uses no user defined parameters (thanks

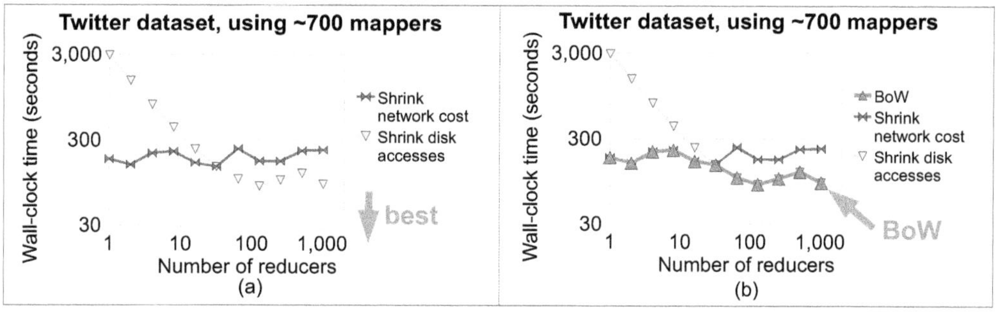

Figure 1: Results on real data from Twitter. Time vs. # of machines (`MapReduce` reducers), in log-log scale. $\sim$ 700 `MapReduce` mappers used for all runs. Left: the upcoming *ParC* (yellow down-triangles) and *SnI* (dark-green butterflies) approaches. The latter uses our *sampling-and-ignore* idea; Right: the same, *including BoW* (in red up-triangles). *BoW* uses cost-based optimization to pick the winning method and proper parameters for it, and thus practically over-writes the respective curve on the graph.

to our defaults), and it maintains the serial clustering quality, with near-linear scale-up;

3. *Experiments*: we report experiments on real and synthetic data of *billions* of points, using up to $1,024$ cores in parallel.

Figure 1 shows an example of *BoW*'s results on real data. It plots the wall-clock-time versus the number of machines (`MapReduce` reducers), in log-log scales. The data consists of the top 10 eigenvectors of the adjacency matrix of the Twitter (http://twitter.com/) graph, which represents ~ 62 million users and their relationships. The eigenvectors span $\sim 14GB$. The full details are in Section 5. Figure 1(a) shows the results for two of the best approaches we studied: the first, in yellow down-triangles, processes the whole dataset, while the second, in dark-green 'butterfly' glyphs, uses our proposed *sampling-and-ignore* idea. Notice that there is no universal winner, with a cross-over point at about 30 machines for this setting. Figure 1(b) shows exactly the same results, this time *including* the wall-clock time of our *BoW*, in red up-triangles. Notice that *BoW* locks onto the best of the two alternatives, hence its name *'Best of both Worlds'*. This is due to our upcoming cost-estimation formulas (Eq. (4) and (5)), which help *BoW* to pick the best alternative and set proper parameters for the chosen environment, while requiring nimble computational effort. Furthermore, notice that the two curves in Figure 1(a) intersect at a narrow angle, which means that the optimal curve has a *smooth plateau*, and thus the cost is rather *robust* wrt small variations of the environment parameters (like effective network bandwidth, disk transfer rate, file size, etc.).

We report experiments on real and synthetic, large datasets, including the *Yahoo! web* one.[1] To the best of our knowledge, the Yahoo! web is the largest real dataset for which results have ever been reported in the database clustering literature for data in five or more axes. Although spanning 0.2 TB of multi-dimensional data, *BoW* took only 8 minutes to cluster it, using 128 cores. We also report experiments using $1,024$ cores, the highest such number in the clustering literature for moderate-to-high dimensional data.

Notice that *BoW* is *tailored to subspace clustering* and can handle most serial algorithms as plug-ins, since the only required API is that the serial algorithm should return clusters of points in hyper-rectangles, which we shall refer to as β-clusters. Subspace clustering methods spot clusters that exist only in subspaces of the original, d-dimensional space (i.e., spaces formed by subsets of the original axes or linear combinations thereof). Thus, the *natural* shape of the clusters in the original space facilitates their representation with hyper-rectangles, as the points of each cluster spread linearly through several irrelevant axes (original axes or linear combinations thereof) in the original space. For that reason, many serial, subspace clustering methods (e.g., CLIQUE [5], FPC/CFPC [19], MrCC [8], P3C [17] and STATPC [16]) return clusters in hyper-rectangles, and adapting others to work with *BoW* tends to be facilitated by the clusters' natural shape. Nevertheless, besides focusing on subspace clustering and moderate-to-high dimensional data, *BoW* also works with traditional clustering methods and low dimensional data, if the plug-in returns clusters in hyper-rectangles.

The remaining of the paper comprises: related work (Section 2); proposed techniques (Sections 3 and 4); experiments (Section 5) and conclusions (Section 6). Table 1 lists the used symbols.

Table 1: Table of symbols.

Symbols	Definitions
${}^dS$	A d-dimensional dataset.
d	Dimensionality of dataset ${}^dS$.
η	Cardinality of dataset ${}^dS$. $\eta = \lvert {}^dS \rvert$
k	Number of clusters in dataset ${}^dS$.
r	Number of reducers for parallel run.
m	Number of mappers for parallel run.
F_s	Database file size in bytes.
D_s	Disk transfer rate in bytes/sec.
N_s	Network transfer rate in bytes/sec.
D_r	Dispersion ratio.
R_r	Reduction ratio.
S_r	Sampling ratio.
$start\_up\_cost(t)$	Start-up cost for t `MapReduce` tasks.
$plug\_in\_cost(s)$	Serial clustering cost wrt the data size s.

2. RELATED WORK

2.1 Subspace Clustering

Clustering methods for data in five or more dimensions, known as *subspace clustering* methods, usually follow one of two approaches: density-based and k-means-based. A recent survey is found in [14]. Density-based methods assume that a cluster is a data space region in which the element distribution is dense. Each region may have an arbitrary shape and the elements inside it may be arbitrarily distributed. A cluster is separated from the others by regions of low density, whose points are considered as noise. The algorithms use own heuristics to identify dense and non-dense regions, usually relying on user-defined density thresholds. Examples of such algorithms are CLIQUE [5], COPAC [1], P3C [17], 4C [6], FIRES [13], FPC/CFPC [19], STATPC [16] and MrCC [8].

[1] Provided by Yahoo! Research (www.yahoo.com).

Methods like k-means start by picking k space positions as clusters centroids, selected either by own heuristics or randomly. Clustering is achieved by an iterative process that assigns each point to its closest center, constantly improving the centers according to the points assigned to each cluster. The process stops when a quality criterion is satisfied or when a maximum number of iterations is achieved. Some of these methods are: PROCLUS [4], ORCLUS [3], PkM [2], CURLER [18] and LWC/CLWC [7].

Despite the several desirable properties found in existent methods, currently no *subspace clustering* algorithm is able to handle *very large* datasets in feasible time, and interesting datasets span way over the existing method's limits (e.g., Twitter crawl: $>$ 12 TB, Yahoo! operational data: 5 *Petabytes* [10]). For data that do not fit even on a single disk, parallelism is mandatory, and thus we must re-think, re-design and re-implement existing serial algorithms in order to allow for parallel processing.

2.2 MapReduce

`MapReduce` is a programming framework [9] to process large-scale data in a massively parallel way. `MapReduce` has two major advantages: the programmer is oblivious of the details related to the data storage, distribution, replication, load balancing, etc.; and furthermore, it adopts the familiar concept of functional programming. The programmer must specify only two functions, a *map* and a *reduce*. The typical framework is as follows [15]: (a) the *map* stage passes over the input file and outputs (key, value) pairs; (b) the *shuffling* stage transfers the mappers' output to the reducers based on the key; (c) the *reduce* stage processes the received pairs and outputs the final result. Due to its scalability, simplicity and the low cost to build large clouds of computers, `MapReduce` is a very promising tool for large scale data analysis, something already reflected in academia (see [12] [11] for examples).

3. PROPOSED MAIN IDEAS – REDUCING BOTTLENECKS

The major research problems for clustering *very large* datasets with `MapReduce` are: (a) how to minimize the I/O cost, and (b) how to minimize the network cost among processing nodes. *Should we split the data points at random, across machines? What should each node do, and how should we combine the results? Do we lose accuracy (if any), compared to a serial algorithm on a huge-memory machine?*

Our proposed method answers all these questions, by careful design and by adaptively trading-off disk delay and network delay.

In a nutshell, our proposed method *BoW* is a hybrid between two methods that we propose next: the *ParC* method and the *SnI*. The former does data partitioning and merges the results; the latter does some sampling first, to reduce communication cost at the expense of higher I/O cost. Next, we describe each proposal in detail.

3.1 Parallel Clustering – ParC

The *ParC* algorithm has three steps: (1) appropriately partition the input data and assign each data partition to one machine, (2) each machine finds clusters in its assigned partition, named as β-clusters, and, (3) merge the β-clusters found to get the final clusters.

We considered three options for data partitioning, shortly described as follows due to space limitations: (a) *random data partitioning*: elements are assigned to machines at random, striving for load balance; (b) *address-space data partitioning*: eventually, nearby elements in the data space often end up in the same machine, trading-off load balance to achieve better merging of the β-clusters; and (c) *arrival order or 'file-based' data partitioning*: the first several elements in the collection go to one machine, the next batch goes to the second, and so on, achieving perfect load balance. The rationale is that it may *also* facilitate the merging of the β-clusters, because data elements that are stored consecutively on the disk, may also be nearby in address space, due to locality: For example, galaxy records from the Sloan Digital Sky Survey (SDSS) are scanned every night with smooth moves of the telescope, and thus galaxies close in (2-d) address space, often result in records that are stored in nearby locations on the disk.

Notice one observation: we performed an extensive experimental evaluation of the three partitioning approaches, which is omitted here due to space limitations. The *file-based data partitioning* was the fastest approach in our evaluation, still providing highly accurate results. Thus, the *file-based* approach is considered and used as the default strategy for the rest of this paper. Notice, however, that our methods work with the three partitioning approaches described, and, *potentially*, work with any user-defined partitioning strategy.

As described in Section 2.2, a `MapReduce`-based application has at least two modules: the map and the reduce. Our *ParC* method partitions the data through `MapReduce` mappers and does the clustering in `MapReduce` reducers. The final merging is performed serially, since it only processes the clusters descriptions, which consist of a tiny amount of data and processing. Figure 2a (2b will be explained latter) illustrates the process. It starts in phase **P1** with m mappers reading the data in parallel from the `MapReduce` distributed file system. In this phase, each mapper receives a data element at a time, computes its key, according to the data partition strategy used, and outputs a pair $\langle key, point \rangle$. All elements with the same key are forwarded in phase **P2** to be processed together, by the same reducer, and the elements with distinct keys are processed apart, by distinct reducers.

In phase **P3**, each reducer receives its assigned set of elements and normalizes them to a unitary hyper-cube. Each reducer then applies the plugged-in serial clustering algorithm over the normalized elements, aiming to spot β-clusters. For each β-cluster found, the reducer outputs, in phase **P4**, a pair $\langle key, cluster\_description \rangle$. The key concatenates the reducer identification and a cluster identification. The reducer identification is the input key. The cluster identification is a sequential number according to the order in which the β-cluster was found in the corresponding reducer. A β-cluster description consists of the unnormalized minimum/maximum bounds of the cluster in each dimension, defining a hyper-rectangle in the data space. Notice that this is a tiny amount of data, amounting to two float values per axis, per β-cluster.

The final phase **P5** is performed serially, as it processes only the tiny amount of data (β-clusters' bounds) received from phase **P4**, and *not* the data elements themselves. Phase **P5** merges all β-clusters pairs that overlap in the data space. Checking if two β-clusters overlap refers to checking if two hyper-rectangles overlap in a d-dimensional space.

3.2 Sample-and-Ignore – SnI

The first algorithm, ParC, reads the dataset once, aimed at minimizing disk accesses, which is the most common strategy used by serial algorithms to shrink computational costs. However, this strategy does not address the issue of minimizing the network traffic: in the shuffle phase of the *ParC* algorithm (phase **P2** of Figure 2a), almost all of the records have to be shipped over the network, to the appropriate reducer. *How can we reduce this network traffic?*

Our main idea is to exploit the skewed distribution of cluster sizes that typically appears in real datasets: Most of the elements usually belong to a few large clusters, and these are exactly the elements that we try to *avoid* processing. Thus, we propose *SnI*, a

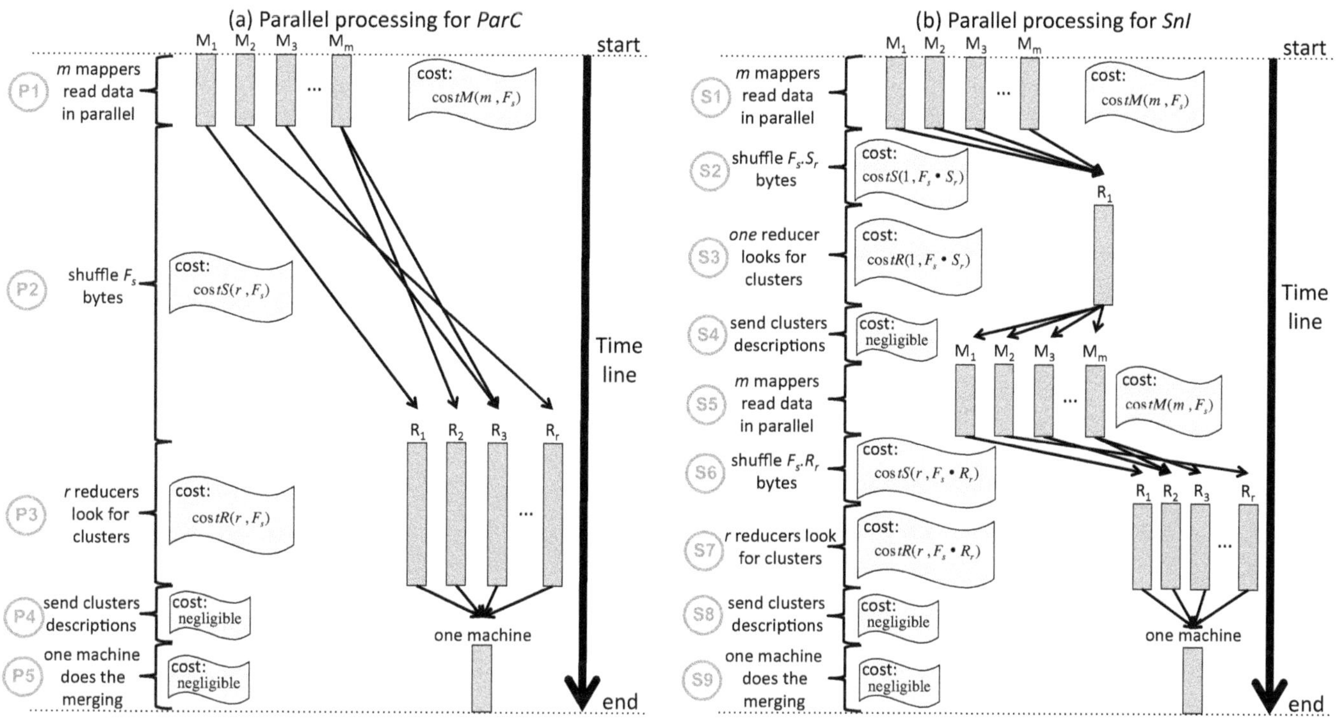

Figure 2: *Which one is best?* **Parallel run overview for *ParC* (left) and *SnI* (right - with sampling). *ParC* executes the map (*P1*), shuffle (*P2*) and reduce (*P3*) phases once, on the full dataset. *SnI* uses sampling (phases *S1-S4*) to get rough cluster estimates and then uses phases *S5-S9* to cluster the remaining points (see section 3.2 for details). Their clustering qualities are similar (see Section 5). The winning approach depends on the environment; *BoW* uses cost-based optimization to automatically pick the best.**

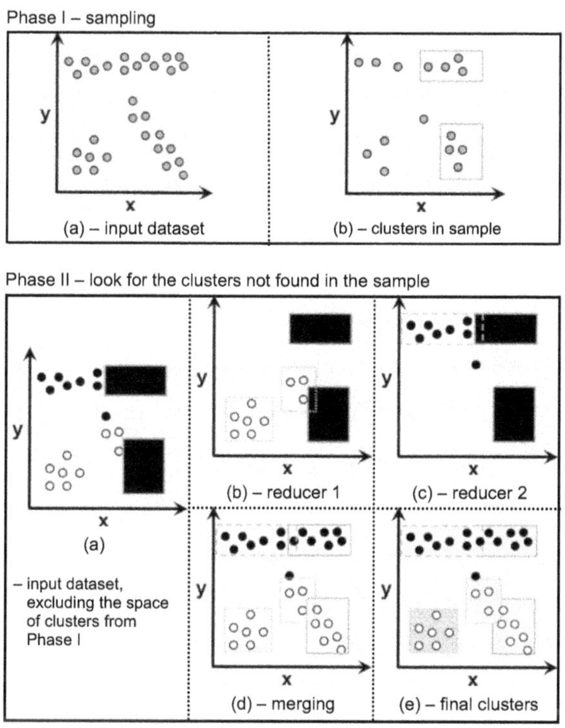

Figure 3: Multi-phase Sample-and-Ignore (SnI) Method. Phase-I finds clusters on a sample of the input data. Phase-II ignores elements that fall within any previously found cluster and finds clusters using the remaining elements only.

parallel clustering algorithm that consists of: (a) a novel *sample-and-ignore* preprocessing step; and (b) the *ParC* algorithm from Section 3.1. The *sample-and-ignore* step works on a small dataset sample, spots the major clusters and ignores their members in the follow-up steps. It significantly reduces the amount of data moved in the shuffling phases of *SnI*, with consequent savings for the network traffic, as well as the I/O cost for the intermediate results and processing cost for the receiving reduce tasks. Notice one point: the proposed *sample-and-ignore* idea is an alternative general strategy that can improve many clustering methods, and not only *ParC*.

The *SnI* method is defined in Algorithm 1 and the process is illustrated in Figure 2b. At a high-level, in Phase I (steps **S1-S4** in the figure, and lines **1-3** in the algorithm) the method *samples* the input data and builds an initial set of clusters. In the second phase (steps **S5-S9** in the figure, and lines **4-8** in the algorithm) , the input data is filtered, so that we only include *unclassified* elements, that is, those that do not belong to any of the clusters found in Phase I. These unclassified elements are then clustered using *ParC*.

Figure 3 illustrates the *SnI* approach over a toy dataset, assuming that we have $r = 2$ reducers available for parallel processing. The top part of the figure shows Phase-I. First, in Phase-I (a) the input dataset is read in parallel by m map tasks, each mapper passes the input elements to the same reducer with some probability, for example, 0.5 for the case shown in the figure. A single reducer builds clusters using the sample elements in Phase-I (b). In this case two clusters were found and are denoted by the gray boxes around the elements. The summary descriptors of the clusters found in Phase-I, i.e., the minimum/maximum limits of the clusters wrt each dimension, are passed to Phase-II. In Phase-II (a), m mappers perform a second pass over the data, this time filtering out elements that fall in the clusters found in Phase-I, which are denoted by the black boxes. The elements that do not fall into clusters are passed to the two reducers available, as shown in Phase-II (b) and (c), in which we assume that the used partitioning strategy divided the elements into 'black points' and 'white points'. Each reducer finds new clusters, denoted by the points surrounded by dotted boxes. In Phase-II (d), the clusters found by the reducers are merged with the clusters from the sampling phase using the same merging strategies used in *ParC*. The global set of clusters, with three clusters represented in Phase-II (e) by distinct gray levels, is the final output.

The main benefit of the *SnI* approach is realized in the shuffle/reduce stages. In Phases **S2** and **S3** of Figure 2b, only a small sample is shuffled and processed by a receiving reducer. In Phases **S6** and **S7** of Figure 2b, only the *non-ignored* elements may need to be shuffled through the network to other machines and processed. This means that most elements belonging to the major clusters spotted in the sample are ignored, *never* being shuffled through the network nor processed by a reducer. Compared to the *ParC* algorithm, *SnI* significantly minimizes the network cost and the reducers processing, at the cost of reading the whole dataset twice. In other words, *ParC* does a single pass over the data, but almost all of the records have to be shipped over the network (phase **P2** of Figure 2a), to the appropriate reducer. On the other hand, *SnI* minimizes the shuffle/reduce cost, at the expense of reading the data one extra time. *What approach is the best?* The answer is given in Section 4.

Algorithm 1 : Multi-phase Sample-and-Ignore (SnI) Method.

Input: dataset ${}^dS$; sampling ratio S_r;
Output: $clusters$;
1: // Phase 1 – Sample
2: m mappers read the data and send the elements to one reducer with probability S_r;
3: one reducer uses plug-in to find clusters in $\sim \eta.S_r$ received elements, and passes clusters descriptions to m mappers;
4: // Phase 2 – Ignore
5: m mappers read the data, ignore the elements from the clusters found in the sample and send the rest to r reducers, according to the data partition approach used;
6: r reducers use the plug-in to find clusters in the received elements, and send the clusters descriptions to one machine;
7: one machine merges the clusters received and the ones from the sample, let the merged result be $clusters$;
8: **return** $clusters$

4. PROPOSED COST-BASED OPTIMIZATION

We propose an adaptive, hybrid method named *BoW (Best of both Worlds)* that exploits the advantages of the previously described approaches, *ParC* and *SnI*, taking the best of them. There is no universal winner, since it depends on the environment and on the data characteristics. See Figure 1 and Section 5 for a complete explanation. Therefore, the main question here is: *When should our sampling-and-ignore idea be used and when should it be avoided?* *ParC* runs the map, shuffle and reduce phases only once on the whole dataset. *SnI* reduces the amount of data to be shipped to and processed by the reducers, at the cost of a second pass on the input data (in the map phase). We propose a cost-based optimization that uses analytics models to estimate the running time of each clustering strategy. *BoW* picks the one with the lowest estimated cost.

The environmental parameters required by *BoW* are presented in Table 2. They describe the hardware characteristics (i.e., the specs of the available MapReduce cluster), the total amount of data to be processed, and the cost estimate for the plugged-in serial clustering method. Setting the value for F_s is straightforward. D_s, N_s and $start\_up\_cost(t)$ are inferred by analyzing the cloud of computers' logs, while $plug\_in\_cost(s)$ is defined based on the plugged-in method's original time complexity analysis and/or experiments, or measured by the user in a simple experiment. Notice: each machine in the cloud may run many MapReduce tasks (mappers and/or reducers) in parallel, *sharing* the machine's disks and network connection. So, N_s and D_s are expected to be *smaller* than the effective network bandwidth and disk transfer rate respectively.

Table 2: Environmental parameters

Parameter	Meaning	Explanation
F_s	data file size (bytes)	Size of the dataset to be clustered.
D_s	disk speed (bytes/sec.)	Average bytes/sec. that a MapReduce task (mapper or reducer) can read from local disks.
N_s	network speed (bytes/sec.)	Average bytes/sec. that a MapReduce task (mapper or reducer) can read from other computers in the cloud.
$start\_up\_cost(t)$	start-up cost (seconds)	Average time to start-up t MapReduce tasks (mappers or reducers).
$plug\_in\_cost(s)$	plug-in cost (seconds)	Average time to run the plugged-in serial method over s data bytes on a standard computer in the cloud.

Two other parameters are used, shown in Table 3. We provide reasonable default values for them based on empirical evaluation. Notice one *important* observation: As is the common knowledge in database query optimization, at the cross-over point of two strategies, the wall-clock-time performances usually create *flat plateaus*, being not much sensitive to parameter variations. This occurs in our setting, and the results in Figures 1a, 7a and 7d exemplify it (notice the log-log scale). Thus, tuning exact values to our parameters barely affects *BoW*'s results and the suggested values are expected to work well in most cases.

Table 3: Other parameters

Param.	Meaning	Explanation	Our defaults
D_r	dispersion ratio	Ratio of data transferred in the shuffling through the network relative to the total amount of data involved.	0.5
R_r	reduction ratio	Ratio of data that does not belong to the major clusters found in the sampling phase of *SnI* relative to the full data size F_s.	0.1

The following lemmas and proofs define the equations of our cost-based optimization. First, we give the expected costs for the map, shuffle and reduce phases wrt the number of mappers and/or reducers available and to the data size involved. Then, we infer the costs for: *ParC*, that minimizes disk accesses, and; *SnI*, that aims at shrinking the network cost. For clarity, consider again Figure 2 that provides a graphical overview of the parallel execution of both methods, as well as their expected cost equations.

LEMMA 1. *Map Cost – the expected cost for the map phase of the parallel clustering approaches is a function of the number of mappers m used and the involved data size s, given by:*

$$costM(m, s) = start\_up\_cost(m) + \frac{s}{m}.\frac{1}{D_s} \quad (1)$$

PROOF. In the map phase, m mappers are started-up at the cost of $start\_up\_cost(m)$. The majority of the extra time spent is related to reading the input data from disk. s bytes of data will be read in parallel by m mappers, which are able to read D_s bytes per second each. Thus, the total reading time is given by: $\frac{s}{m}.\frac{1}{D_s}$. □

LEMMA 2. *Shuffle Cost – the expected shuffle cost is a function of the number of reducers r to receive the data and the amount of data to be shuffled s, which is given by:*

$$costS(r, s) = \frac{s.D_r}{r}.\frac{1}{N_s} \quad (2)$$

PROOF. The majority of the shuffling cost is related to shipping the data between distinct machines through the network. Whenever possible, `MapReduce` minimizes this cost by assigning reduce tasks to the machines that already have the required data in local disks. D_r is the ratio of data actually shipped between distinct machines relative to the total amount of data processed. Thus, the total amount of data to be shipped is $s.D_r$ bytes. The data will be received in parallel by r reducers, each one receiving in average N_s bytes per second. Thus, the total cost is given by: $\frac{s.D_r}{r}.\frac{1}{N_s}$. □

LEMMA 3. *Reduce Cost – the expected cost for the reduce phase is a function of the number of reducers r used for parallel processing and the size s of the data involved, which is given by:*

$$costR(r, s) = start\_up\_cost(r) + \frac{s}{r}.\frac{1}{D_s} + plug\_in\_cost(\frac{s}{r}) \quad (3)$$

PROOF. In the reduce phase, r reducers are started-up at cost $start\_up\_cost(r)$. After the start-up process, the reducers will read from disk s bytes in parallel at the individual cost of D_s bytes per second. Thus, the total reading time is $\frac{s}{r}.\frac{1}{D_s}$. Finally, the plugged-in serial clustering method will be executed in parallel over partitions of the data, whose average sizes are $\frac{s}{r}$. Therefore, the approximate clustering cost is $plug\_in\_cost(\frac{s}{r})$. □

LEMMA 4. *ParC Cost – the expected cost for* ParC *is:*

$$costC = costM(m, F_s) + costS(r, F_s) + costR(r, F_s) \quad (4)$$

PROOF. The parallel processing for *ParC* is: (i) m mappers process F_s bytes of data in the map phase; (ii) F_s bytes of data are shuffled to r reducers in the shuffling phase; (iii) F_s bytes of data are analyzed in the reduce phase by r reducers, and; (iv) a single machine merges all the β-clusters found. The last step has negligible cost, as it performs simple computations over data amounting to two float values per β-cluster, per dimension. Thus, summing the costs of the three initial phases leads to the expected cost. □

LEMMA 5. *SnI Cost – the expected cost for* SnI *is:*

$$costCs = 2 \,.\, costM(m, F_s) + costS(1, F_s.S_r) + costR(1, F_s.S_r) + costS(r, F_s.R_r) + costR(r, F_s.R_r) \quad (5)$$

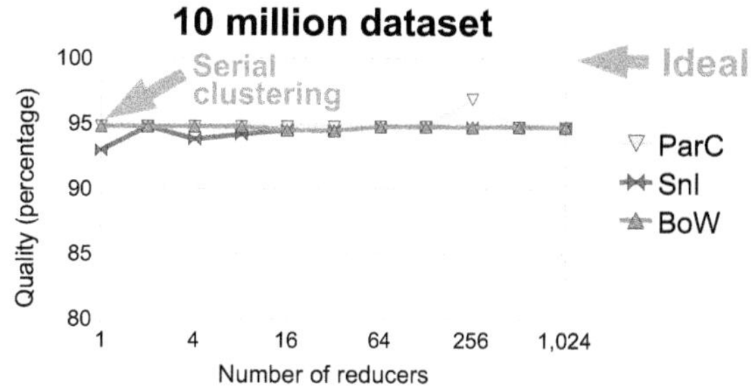

Figure 4: All our variants give top quality results. 10 million dataset; quality vs. number r of reducers, for *ParC*, *SnI* and *BoW*. All methods match the quality of the serial clustering method (top left), for all values of r, like $1,024$.

PROOF. *SnI* runs two complete map, shuffle and reduce phases. In both map phases, the full dataset is processed by m mappers, at combined cost: $2 \,.\, costM(m, F_s)$. In the first shuffle phase, a data sample of size $F_s.S_r$ bytes is shuffled to a single reducer, at cost $costS(1, F_s.S_r)$. The reduce cost to process this sample is: $costR(1, F_s.S_r)$. R_r is the ratio of data that does not belong to the major clusters, the ones found in the sampling phase, relative to F_s. That is, $F_s.(1 - R_r)$ bytes are *ignored* in the Second Phase of *SnI*, while $F_s.R_r$ bytes of data are *not ignored*, being processed after clustering the sample. Also, both second shuffle and reduce phases involve r reducers. Thus, their combined costs are: $costS(r, F_s.R_r) + costR(r, F_s.R_r)$. The costs for shipping and processing β-clusters descriptions is negligible, since the involved amount of data and processing is extremely small. □

Notice one observation: when our algorithms are executed, the number of distinct key values to be sorted by the `MapReduce` framework is tiny; it is *always* the number r of reducers used only. Each reducer handles a single key, so it does not need to do sorting. Thus, the sorting cost is negligible for our approaches. The I/O and network costs are the real bottlenecks. The wall-clock time results in all of our experiments (see Section 5) confirm this assertion.

Algorithm 2 describes the main steps of *BoW*. In summary, *ParC* executes the map, shuffle and reduce phases once, involving the full dataset. *SnI* runs these phases twice, but involving less data. *What is the fastest approach?* It depends on your environment. *BoW* takes the environment description as input and uses cost-based optimization to automatically choose the fastest, prior to the real execution. Provided that the clustering accuracies are similar for both approaches (see Section 5 for a complete explanation), *BoW* actually picks the *'Best of both Worlds'*.

Algorithm 2 : The ***Best of both Worlds – BoW*** method.

Input: dataset ${}^dS$; environmental parameters (Table 2); other parameters (Table 3); number of reducers r; number of mappers m; sampling ratio S_r;
Output: $clusters$;
compute $costC$ from Equation 4;
compute $costCs$ from Equation 5;
if $costC > costCs$ **then**
  $clusters$ = result of *SnI* for ${}^dS$; // use *sampling-and-ignore*
else $clusters$ = result of *ParC* for ${}^dS$; // use no sampling
end if
return $clusters$

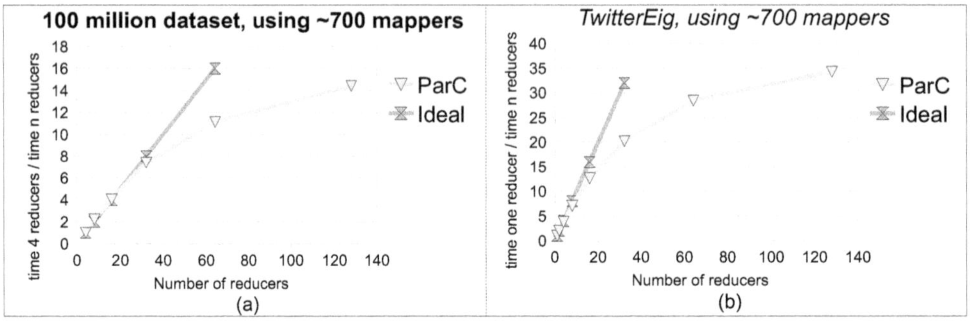

Figure 5: Near-linear scale-up wrt the number of reducers. Expected behavior: our method starts with near-linear scale-up, and then flattens. 100 **million dataset (left);** `TwitterEig` **(right). X-axes: # of reducers, Y-axes: the relative performance with r reducers compared to that with** 1 **reducer (right) or** 4 **reducers (left).** $r = 1$ **in the left case needs prohibitively long time.** $\sim$ 700 **mappers used.**

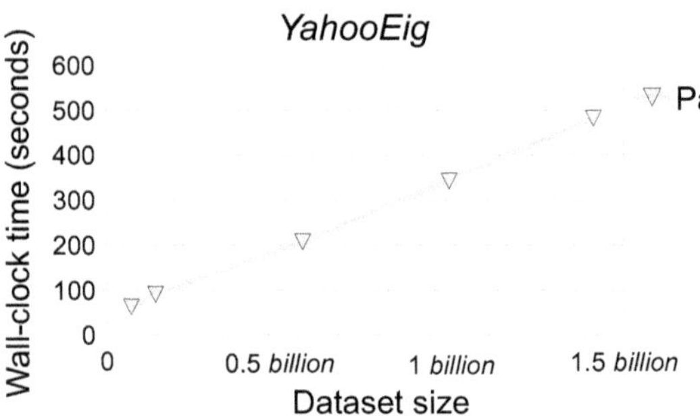

Figure 6: Linear scale-up on db size: wall-clock time vs. data size. Random samples from `YahooEig`**, up to** 1.4 *billion* **points. Fixed numbers of reducers** (128) **and mappers** ($\sim$ 700)**.**

5. EXPERIMENTAL RESULTS

In this section, we describe the experiments performed. We aimed at answering the following questions:

Q1 How much (if at all) parallelism affects the cluster's quality?

Q2 How does our method scale-up?

Q3 How accurate are our cost-based optimization equations?

All experiments were done using the `Hadoop`[2] implementation for the `MapReduce` framework, on two `Hadoop` clusters: M45 by Yahoo! and DISC/Cloud by Parallel Data Lab in CMU. M45 is one of the top 50 supercomputers in the world totaling 400 machines (3, 200 cores), 1.5 PB of storage and 3.5 TB of main memory. DISC/Cloud has 512 cores, distributed in 64 machines, 1TB of RAM and 256 TB of raw disk storage. We used the real and synthetic datasets described in Table 4, which are detailed as follows.

- `YahooEig`: The top 6 eigenvectors from the adjacency matrix of one of the largest web graphs. The web graph was crawled by Yahoo! [3] in 2002 and contains 1.4 *billion* nodes and 6.6 *billion* edges. The eigenvectors amount to 0.2 *TB*.
- `TwitterEig`: The top 10 eigenvectors from the adjacency matrix of the Twitter [4] graph, that represents 62 million users and their relationships. Eigenvectors amount to 0.014 TB.
- `Synthetic`: A group of datasets with sizes varying from 100 thousand up to 100 million 15-dimensional points, containing 10 clusters each. We created clusters following standard procedures used by most of the clustering algorithms cited in Section 2, including the plugged-in serial method used in our experiments. All clusters follow normal distributions with random means and random standard deviations in at least 50% of the axes, spreading through at most 15% of these axes domains. In other axes, all clusters have uniform distribution, spreading through the whole axes domains.

[2] www.hadoop.com

[3] www.yahoo.com

[4] http://twitter.com/

Table 4: Summary of datasets. TB: TeraBytes

Dataset	# of Points	# of Axes	File Size
`YahooEig`	1.4 *billion*	6	0.2 *TB*
`TwitterEig`	62 million	10	0.014 TB
`Synthetic`	up to 100 million	15	up to 0.014 TB

As our real world datasets have 6 and 10 axes, we chose the MrCC algorithm as the serial clustering method for the plug-in in all experiments. MrCC is one state-of-the-art clustering method for medium-dimensionality data. Its original code was used.

Notice one observation: to evaluate how much (if at all) parallelism affects the serial clustering quality, the ideal strategy is to use as ground truth the clustering results obtained by running the plugged-in algorithm serially on any dataset, synthetic or real, and to compare these results to the ones obtained with parallel processing. But, for most of our large datasets, to run a serial algorithm (MrCC or, potentially, any other clustering method for moderate-to-high dimensionality data) is an impractical task – it would require impractical amounts of main memory and/or take a very long time. Thus, in practice, the `Synthetic` datasets are the only ones from which we have clustering ground truth, and they were used to evaluate the quality of all tested techniques in all experiments.

For a fair comparison with the plugged-in serial algorithm, the quality is computed following the same procedure used in its original publication. That is, the quality is computed by comparing the results provided by a technique to the ground truth, based on the averaged precision and recall of all clusters.

The *file-based data partitioning* strategy used may provide distinct quality results wrt the order in which the input data is physically stored. Obviously, the best results appear when the data is totally ordered, i.e., the elements of each cluster are sequentially stored in the data file. On the other hand, when the elements are randomly positioned in the file, the qualities are similar to the ones obtained when using the *random data partitioning*. For a fair analysis, we built each dataset from the `Synthetic` group considering an average case, i.e., 50% of the elements from the totally ordered case were randomly repositioned throughout the data file.

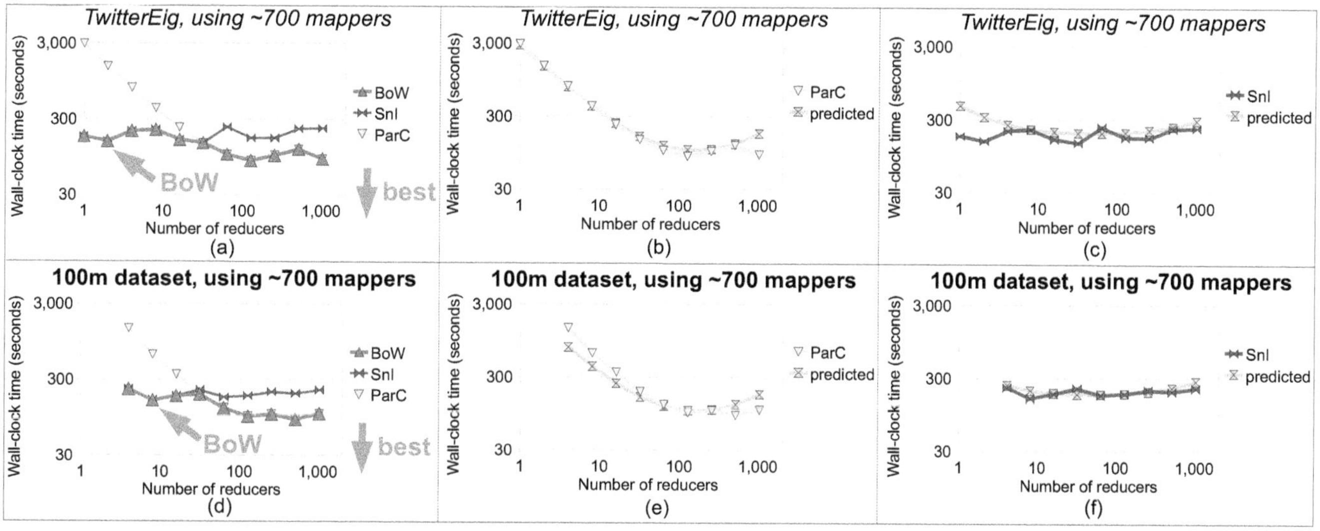

Figure 7: Top: `TwitterEig`; Bottom: `Synthetic`, 100 million. Time vs. # of reducers, in log-log scale. $\sim$ 700 mappers always. Left column: *BoW*'s ability to pick the winner, among *ParC* (yellow down-triangles) and *SnI* (dark-green butterflies). *BoW* (red up-triangles) gets the best of both, always picks the winning strategy, and thus practically over-writes the winner's curve. Middle/right columns: accuracy of our Equations 4 and 5; In all cases, the light-green hour-glass shapes stand for our formulas; Notice how close they are to the actual measurements (*ParC* in yellow triangles and *SnI* in dark-green butterflies).

The following values were used for the environmental parameters: F_s: the data file size; D_s: $40MB/sec$; N_s: $20MB/sec$; $start\_up\_cost(t)$: $0.1t$; $plug\_in\_cost(s)$: $1.4E^{-7}s$. They were measured by experiments on the M45 machines and on the serial plug-in to represent the environment employed. Details on this procedure are not shown due to space limitation. All experiments involving *BoW* used these parameters and the M45 machines.

The results on quality and wall-clock time shown for all experiments are averages of 10 *distinct runs*. All experiments used a sample size of ~ 1 *million*, i.e., $S_r = \frac{1\ million}{\eta}$, and, in all cases, the number of mappers m used was automatically chosen by `Hadoop`.

5.1 Quality of results

This section intends to answer question $Q1$: How much (if at all) does the parallelism affect the clustering quality? Figure 4 shows the quality results obtained by *ParC*, *SnI* and *BoW* over our `Synthetic` dataset with 10 million elements. All tested methods presented top quality, even for large numbers of reducers, like $1,024$. Notice, that the serial execution quality of the plugged-in clustering method is the one obtained when using a single reducer ($r = 1$, extreme left in the plot). Similar results were observed with the other `Synthetic` datasets, not shown for brevity.

An interesting observation is that the quality may decrease for small datasets, when using a large number of reducers. The obvious reason is that, in those cases, we are partitioning a small amount of data through a large number of reducers, which actually receive too little data, not enough to represent the main data patterns. This fact was confirmed in all our experiments, and they lead us to recommend at least $\sim 150k$ points per reducer in average, i.e., $r \leq \frac{\eta}{150k}$.

Thus, based on our experiments, the answer to question $Q1$ is: as long as you have enough data, parallelism barely affects the accuracy, even for large numbers of reducers, like $1,024$. *BoW* found top quality clusters in little time from all our *very large* datasets.

5.2 Scale-up results

This section intends to answer question $Q2$: How does our method scale-up? Scale-up results with different numbers of reducers are in Figure 5. Here we used the `TwitterEig` eigenvectors and the `Synthetic` dataset with 100 million points. The plots show X-axes as the number of reducers r, and the Y-axes as the relative performance with n reducers compared to that with 1 reducer (`TwitterEig`) or 4 reducers (`Synthetic`). A fixed number of mappers $m =\sim 700$ was used. The results shown are the average of 10 distinct runs. We picked 4 reducers for our `Synthetic` dataset, as the running time for one reducer was impractical. Notice that our method achieves near-linear scale-up.

The scale-up results with different data sizes are in Figure 6. The `YahooEig` dataset is used. Random samples of the data with increasing sizes, up to the full dataset (1.4 *billion* elements) were generated to perform this experiment. We plot wall clock time vs. data size. The wall-clock time shown is the average time of 10 distinct runs. Fixed numbers of reducers and mappers ($r = 128$ and $m =\sim 700$) were used. As shown, our method has desired scalability, scaling-up linearly with the data size.

It took only $\sim$ 8 *minutes* to cluster the full dataset, which amounts to 0.2 *TB*! Let's provide some context to this result by characterizing the time taken at different stages in the process: (a) the mappers took 47 seconds to read the data from disks; (b) 65 seconds were taken to shuffle the data; and (c) the reduce stage took 330 seconds. To estimate the time taken by the serial method in item (c), we clustered a random sample of the `YahooEig` dataset, of size $\frac{F_s}{r} = \frac{0.2\ TB}{128}$, by running the plug-in on a single machine (one core), similar to the ones of the used cloud of computes. The serial clustering time was 192 seconds. This indicates that the plug-in took $\sim 43\%$ of the total time, being the main bottleneck.

Similar scale-up results were obtained for all other datasets, not shown here due to the space limitation.

5.3 Accuracy of our cost equations

Here we refer to question Q3, by checking *BoW*'s ability to pick the correct alternative and the accuracy of our cost formulas, (Eq. (4) and (5)) from Section 4. The results for the `TwitterEig` and `Synthetic` (with 100 million points) datasets are shown in the top and bottom lines of Figure 7, respectively. The six plots give the wall-clock time (average of 10 runs) versus the number of reducers r, in log-log scales. The left column ((a) and (d)) shows that *BoW*, in red up-triangles, consistently picks the winning strategy among the two alternatives: *ParC* (yellow down-triangles) and *SnI* (dark-green butterflies), that uses our *sample-and-ignore* idea. For both datasets, *BoW* gives results so close to the winner, that its curve practically overwrites the winner's curve; the only overhead of *BoW* is the CPU time required to run the cost equations, which is negligible. The next two columns of Figure 7 illustrate the accuracy of our cost formulas. Light-green hour-glasses refer to our theoretical prediction; yellow triangles stand for *ParC* (middle column), and dark-green butterflies stand for *SnI* (right column). Notice: the theory and the measurements usually agree very well. All other datasets gave similar results, omitted for brevity.

6. CONCLUSIONS

Given a *very large* moderate-to-high dimensionality dataset, how could one cluster its points? For data that don't fit even on a single disk, parallelism is mandatory. The bottlenecks are then: I/O cost and network cost. Our main contributions are:

1. *Algorithm design and analysis*: We proposed *BoW* and carefully derived its cost functions that allow the automatic, dynamic trade-off between disk delay and network delay;
2. *Effectiveness, scalability and generality*: We showed that *BoW* has many desirable features: it can work with most serial methods as a plugged-in clustering subroutine (the only API: clusters described by hyper-rectangles), it balances the cost for disk accesses and network accesses, achieving a very good tradeoff between the two, it uses no user defined parameters (thanks to our defaults) and it matches the serial algorithm's clustering accuracy with near-linear scale-up;
3. *Experiments*: We report experiments on real and synthetic data of *billions* of points, using up to $1,024$ cores in parallel.

To the best of our knowledge, the *Yahoo! web* is the *largest real dataset ever reported* in the database *subspace clustering* literature. *BoW* clustered its $0.2TB$ in only 8 minutes, with 128 cores!

Finally, notice that *BoW* is a hard-clustering method and, as well as any other method of this type, it may not be the best solution for data with many overlapping clusters. So, we report an idea for future work: to extend *BoW*'s merging stage to return soft-clustering results, allowing any data point to belong to two or more clusters. In our opinion, soft-clustering is a promising idea, but there are several issues involved, which are out of the scope of this paper.

7. ACKNOWLEDGMENTS

This material is based upon work supported by FAPESP (São Paulo State Research Foundation), CAPES (Brazilian Coordination for Improvement of Higher Level Personnel), CNPq (Brazilian National Council for Supporting Research), Microsoft Research, the National Science Foundation (NSF), under award CCF-1019104, the Qatar National Fund, under award NPRP 09-1114-1-172 in the QCloud project, the Gordon and Betty Moore Foundation, in the eScience project, the Defense Threat Reduction Agency, accomplished under contract No. HDTRA1-10-1-0120, and the Army Research Laboratory, accomplished under Cooperative Agreement Number W911NF-09-2-0053. The views and conclusions contained in this document are those of the authors and should not be interpreted as representing the official policies, either expressed or implied, of the Army Research Laboratory, the U.S. Government, the National Science Foundation, or other funding parties. The U.S. Government is authorized to reproduce and distribute reprints for Government purposes notwithstanding any copyright notation here on. We also thank the member companies of the PDL Consortium (including APC, EMC, Facebook, Google, HP Labs, Hitachi, IBM, Intel, Microsoft Research, NEC Labs, NetApp, Oracle, Panasas, Riverbed, Samsung, Seagate, STEC, Symantec, and VMware) for their interest, insights, feedback, and support.

8. REFERENCES

[1] E. Achtert, C. Böhm, H.-P. Kriegel, P. Kröger, and A. Zimek. Robust, complete, and efficient correlation clustering. In *SDM, USA*, 2007.

[2] P. K. Agarwal and N. H. Mustafa. k-means projective clustering. In *PODS*, pages 155–165, Paris, France, 2004. ACM.

[3] C. Aggarwal and P. Yu. Redefining clustering for high-dimensional applications. *IEEE TKDE*, 14(2):210–225, 2002.

[4] C. C. Aggarwal, J. L. Wolf, P. S. Yu, C. Procopiuc, and J. S. Park. Fast algorithms for projected clustering. *SIGMOD Rec.*, 28(2):61–72, 1999.

[5] R. Agrawal, J. Gehrke, D. Gunopulos, and P. Raghavan. Automatic subspace clustering of high dimensional data for data mining applications. *SIGMOD Rec.*, 27(2):94–105, 1998.

[6] C. Böhm, K. Kailing, P. Kröger, and A. Zimek. Computing clusters of correlation connected objects. In *SIGMOD*, pages 455–466, NY, USA, 2004.

[7] H. Cheng, K. A. Hua, and K. Vu. Constrained locally weighted clustering. *PVLDB*, 1(1):90–101, 2008.

[8] R. L. F. Cordeiro, A. J. M. Traina, C. Faloutsos, and C. Traina Jr. Finding clusters in subspaces of very large, multi-dimensional datasets. In *ICDE*, pages 625–636, 2010.

[9] J. Dean and S. Ghemawat. Mapreduce: Simplified data processing on large clusters. *OSDI*, 2004.

[10] U. Fayyad. A data miner's story – getting to know the grand challenges. In *Invited Innovation Talk, KDD*, 2007: Slide 61. Available at: http://videolectures.net/kdd07_fayyad_dms/.

[11] U. Kang, C. Tsourakakis, A. P. Appel, C. Faloutsos, and J. Leskovec. Radius plots for mining tera-byte scale graphs: Algorithms, patterns, and observations. *SDM*, 2010.

[12] U. Kang, C. Tsourakakis, and C. Faloutsos. Pegasus: A peta-scale graph mining system - implementation and observations. *ICDM*, 2009.

[13] H.-P. Kriegel, P. Kröger, M. Renz, and S. Wurst. A generic framework for efficient subspace clustering of high-dimensional data. In *ICDM*, pages 250–257, USA, 2005.

[14] H.-P. Kriegel, P. Kröger, and A. Zimek. Clustering high-dimensional data: A survey on subspace clustering, pattern-based clustering, and correlation clustering. *ACM TKDD*, 3(1):1–58, 2009.

[15] R. Lämmel. Google's mapreduce programming model – revisited. *Science of Computer Programming*, 70:1–30, 2008.

[16] G. Moise and J. Sander. Finding non-redundant, statistically significant regions in high dimensional data: a novel approach to projected and subspace clustering. In *KDD*, pages 533–541, 2008.

[17] G. Moise, J. Sander, and M. Ester. Robust projected clustering. *Knowl. Inf. Syst.*, 14(3):273–298, 2008.

[18] A. K. H. Tung, X. Xu, and B. C. Ooi. Curler: finding and visualizing nonlinear correlation clusters. In *SIGMOD*, pages 467–478, New York, NY, USA, 2005.

[19] M. L. Yiu and N. Mamoulis. Iterative projected clustering by subspace mining. *IEEE TKDE*, 17(2):176–189, Feb. 2005.

Selective Block Minimization for Faster Convergence of Limited Memory Large-Scale Linear Models

Kai-Wei Chang and Dan Roth
Dept. of Computer Science
University of Illinois at Urbana-Champaign, IL USA
{kchang10, danr}@illinois.edu

ABSTRACT

As the size of data sets used to build classifiers steadily increases, training a linear model efficiently with limited memory becomes essential. Several techniques deal with this problem by loading blocks of data from disk one at a time, but usually take a considerable number of iterations to converge to a reasonable model. Even the best block minimization techniques [1] require many block loads since they treat all training examples uniformly. As disk I/O is expensive, reducing the amount of disk access can dramatically decrease the training time.

This paper introduces a selective block minimization (SBM) algorithm, a block minimization method that makes use of selective sampling. At each step, SBM updates the model using data consisting of two parts: (1) new data loaded from disk and (2) a set of informative samples already in memory from previous steps. We prove that, by updating the linear model in the dual form, the proposed method fully utilizes the data in memory and converges to a globally optimal solution on the entire data. Experiments show that the SBM algorithm dramatically reduces the number of blocks loaded from disk and consequently obtains an accurate and stable model quickly on both binary and multi-class classification.

Categories and Subject Descriptors

I.5.2 [**Pattern Recognition**]: Design Methodology—*Classifier design and evaluation*

General Terms

Algorithms, Performance, Experimentation

1. INTRODUCTION

In the past few years, the size of data sets used to build classifiers has steadily increased. Significantly larger amounts of annotated data are available now (e.g., for web applications such as spam filtering), and it has been argued that using more samples and adding more features (e.g, using n-gram in a bag-of-words model) actually boosts performance [2]. In some applications, unlimited amounts of annotated data can be generated (e.g., see Sec. 7). Linear classification models have been shown to handle large amounts of data well, and several optimization techniques (e.g., [3, 4, 5]) have been applied to efficiently train linear models. However, when the data cannot fit into memory, batch learners, which load the entire data during the training process, suffer severely due to disk swapping [1]. In these cases, training techniques that deal well with memory limitations become crucial.

A popular scheme that addresses the memory problem processes the data in an online fashion in multiple rounds (e.g., [6, 7, 4, 8]). However, an online learner, which performs a simple weight update over a single training example at a time, usually requires a large number of iterations to converge. Therefore, when an online learner loads data from disk at each step, disk I/O overhead becomes the bottleneck of the training process. Sec. 7 shows an example where the online learner MIRA [9] takes more than one hour loading data but spends less than one minute updating the model. As discussed in [1], training time consists of (1) the time used to update the model's parameters given the data in memory and (2) the time needed to load data from disk. The machine learning literature focuses on the first issue and neglects the second. Consequently, most algorithms aim at reducing CPU time and the number of passes over the data required to obtain an accurate model (e.g, [4, 5]). However, the cost of disk access could be orders of magnitude higher. *In this paper, we focus on the second issue – saving I/O time by reducing disk access.* To our knowledge, this is the first work that targets minimizing disk access when training a linear model.

There are two ways to reduce the expensive I/O overhead. One is by applying data compression to reduce loading time. The other, orthogonal direction, is algorithmic. It suggests placing more effort on learning from data that is already in memory (e.g, [7, 8]). Recently, [1] proposed a block minimization framework which makes progress in both directions. Their solver splits the data into blocks and stores them in compressed files. By loading and training on a block of samples at a time, it employs a better weight update scheme and achieves faster convergence than online algorithms. However, they assume that all training samples are equally important and treat them uniformly. Consequently, their proposed block minimization method still requires a considerable number of iterations to converge to a reasonable model.

KDD'11, August 21–24, 2011, San Diego, CA, USA.

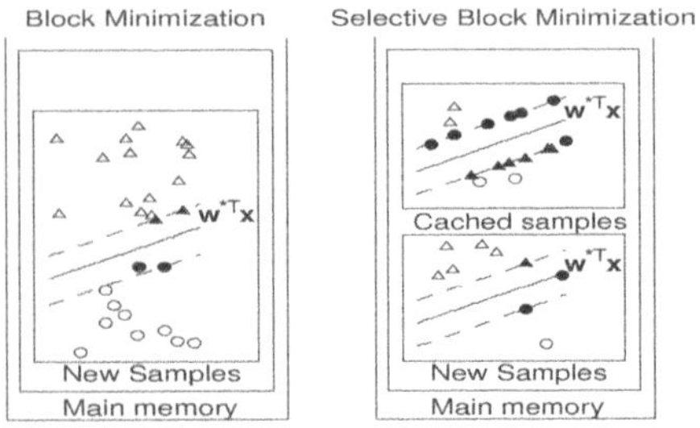

Figure 1: The figure illustrates how a block minimization method wastes resources by considering a lot of unimportant samples (blank circles/triangles), while the selective block minimization (SBM) algorithm focuses on training on informative samples (solid circles/triangles) by caching. The circles/triangles represent the samples drawn from the entire data set. We treat samples closer to the final separator ($\boldsymbol{w}^*$) as more informative (see Sec. 2.2).

This paper develops the selective block minimization (SBM) algorithm, which is shown to significantly improve the I/O cost. SBM can be applied to various linear models, such as SVM and Logistic Regression, when the model can be learned in the dual form. At each step, the proposed algorithm solves the minimization problem on a block of data consisting of new samples loaded from disk along with samples that are already stored in memory, selected from previous steps. The cached samples are selected based on gradient information computed while solving the sub-problem. Figure 1 illustrates the comparison between the proposed algorithm and the block minimization framework (details are given in Sec. (2)). By caching informative samples in memory, the selective block minimization algorithm fully utilizes the memory capacity. The proposed method enjoys the following properties:

- SBM caches informative samples in memory, thus requiring fewer data loads before reaching a given level of performance relative to existing approaches. For example, in one document classification experiment (Sec. 7.2), SBM obtained a model that was as accurate as the optimal one with just a single pass over the data set. For the same data, the current best method [1] requires loading the data from disk 10 times to reach the same performance. That is, SBM saves I/O access by reducing the number of required iterations.
- SBM caches data selectively and thus treats samples non-uniformly, but it still keeps the convergence properties of the block minimization approach.

We present experimental results that exhibit the dramatic reduction in training time achieved by SBM when solving large binary and multi-class problems with limited memory. Moreover, when SBM is required to load each sample into memory once, it is shown to outperform online learners.

The rest of this paper is organized as follows. The selective block minimization algorithm is presented in Sec. 2. Extensions to multi-class classification and streaming data are discussed in Sec. 3 and 4. We address implementation issues in Sec. 5 and analyze SBM's relations with other algorithms for learning with large scale data in Sec. 6. Experimental results are presented in Sec. 7, and Sec. 8 concludes with some discussion. Proofs, additional experiments, and code can be found at
`http://cogcomp.cs.illinois.edu/page/publication_view/660.`

Algorithm 1 A Selective Block Minimization Algorithm for Linear Classification

1. Split data D into subsets $B_j, j = 1 \dots m$.
2. Initialize $\boldsymbol{\alpha} = \mathbf{0}$.
3. Set cache set $\Omega^{1,1} = \emptyset$.
4. For $t = 1, 2, \dots$ (outer iteration)
   For $j = 1, \dots, m$ (inner iteration)
   (a) Read $B_j = (\boldsymbol{x}_i, y_i)_{i=1\dots m_D}$ from disk.
   (b) Obtain $d^{t,j}$ by exactly or loosely solving (3) on $W^{t,j} = B_j \cup \Omega^{t,j}$, where $\Omega^{t,j}$ is cache.
   (c) Update $\boldsymbol{\alpha}$ by (4).
   (d) *Select cached data $\Omega^{t,j+1}$ for next round from $W^{t,j}$ (see Sec. 2.2).*

2. SELECTIVE BLOCK MINIMIZATION

In this section, we describe the selective block minimization method by exemplifying it in the context of a L1-loss linear SVM for binary classification. Given a sequence of data $D = \{(\boldsymbol{x}_i, y_i)\}_{i=1}^{l}, \boldsymbol{x}_i \in R^n, y_i = \{1, -1\}$, linear SVM considers the following minimization problem:

$$\min_{\boldsymbol{w}} 1/2\|\boldsymbol{w}\|^2 + C\sum_{i=1}^{l} \max(1 - y_i \boldsymbol{w}^T \boldsymbol{x}_i, 0), \quad (1)$$

where $C > 0$ is a penalty parameter. Instead of solving (1), in this paper we solve its equivalent dual problem:

$$\begin{aligned} \min_{\boldsymbol{\alpha}} \quad & f(\boldsymbol{\alpha}) = (1/2)\boldsymbol{\alpha}^T Q \boldsymbol{\alpha} - \boldsymbol{e}^T \boldsymbol{\alpha} \\ \text{subject to} \quad & 0 \le \alpha_i \le C, i = 1, \dots, l, \end{aligned} \quad (2)$$

where $\boldsymbol{e} = [1, \dots, 1]^T$ and $Q_{ij} = y_i y_j \boldsymbol{x}_i^T \boldsymbol{x}_j$. Eq. (2) is a box constraint optimization problem, and each variable corresponds to one training instance. Let $\boldsymbol{\alpha}^*$ be the optimal solution of (2). We call an instance $(\boldsymbol{x}_i, y_i)$ a support vector if the corresponding parameter satisfies $\alpha_i^* > 0$, and an instance i is an unbounded support vector if $0 < \alpha_i^* < C$. We show in Sec. 2.2 that unbounded support vectors are more important during the training process.

With abundant memory, one can load the entire data set and solve (1) or (2) with a batch learner. However, when memory is limited, only part of the data can be considered at a given time. [1] applies a block minimization technique to deal with this situation. We first introduce their method for solving (2). In [1] the data is split into subsets $B_j, j = 1 \dots m$, and a two-level iterative procedure is considered, as follows. Initializing $\boldsymbol{\alpha}$ to zero vectors, the block minimization algorithm generates a sequence of solutions $\{\boldsymbol{\alpha}^{t,j}\}_{t=1\dots\infty, j=1\dots m}$. We refer to the step from $\boldsymbol{\alpha}^t = \boldsymbol{\alpha}^{t,1}$ to $\boldsymbol{\alpha}^{t+1} = \boldsymbol{\alpha}^{t,m+1}$ as an *outer* iteration, and $\boldsymbol{\alpha}^{t,j}$ to $\boldsymbol{\alpha}^{t,j+1}$ as an *inner* iteration. For updating from $\boldsymbol{\alpha}^{t,j}$ to $\boldsymbol{\alpha}^{t,j+1}$, [1] considers solving a sub-problem on B_j. After the sub-problem is solved, they update the models and removed all the samples $i, i \in B_j$ from memory, and then load another block into it. As each sample only appears in one B_j, their process treats all the samples equally. Since informative samples are likely to be present in different blocks, the solver wastes time on unimportant samples.

Intuitively, we should select only informative samples and use them to update the model. However, trying to select only informative samples and using only them in training may be too sensitive to noise and initialization and does not yield the appropriate convergence result we show later. Instead, we propose a selective block minimization algorithm. On one hand, as we show, our method maintains the convergence property of block minimization by loading a block of new data B_j from disk at each iteration. On the other hand, it maintains a cache set $\Omega^{t,j}$, such that informative samples are kept in memory. At each inner iteration, SBM solves the following sub-problem in the dual on $W^{t,j} = B_j \cup \Omega^{t,j}$:

$$\begin{aligned} \boldsymbol{d}^{j,t} &= \arg\min_{\boldsymbol{d}} \; f(\boldsymbol{\alpha}+\boldsymbol{d}) \\ &\text{subject to } \boldsymbol{d}_{\bar{W}^{t,j}} = 0, 0 \le \alpha_i + d_i \le C, \forall i, \end{aligned} \tag{3}$$

where $\bar{W}^{t,j} = \{1 \dots l\} \setminus W^{t,j}$. Then it updates the model by

$$\boldsymbol{\alpha}^{t,j+1} = \boldsymbol{\alpha}^{t,j} + \boldsymbol{d}^{t,j}. \tag{4}$$

In other words, it updates α_W, while fixing $\alpha_{\bar{W}}$. [1] shows that, by maintaining a temporary vector $\boldsymbol{w} \in R^n$, solving equation (3) only involves the training samples in $W^{t,j}$. After updating the model, SBM selects samples from $W^{t,j}$ to the cache $\Omega^{t,j+1}$ for the next round.

We discuss the cache selection in Sec. 2.2 and show that by solving the sub-problem mentioned above with coordinate descent methods, SBM reduces to a dual coordinate descent method [3] and converges to the global solution of (2), regardless of the cache selection strategy. Note that the samples in cache $\Omega^{t,j+1}$ are only chosen from $W^{t,j}$ and are already in memory. If a sample is important, though, it may stay in the cache for many rounds, as $\Omega^{t,j} \subset W^{t,j}$. Algorithm 1 summarizes the procedure.

We assume here that the cache size and the data partition are fixed. One can adjust the ratio between $|\Omega|$ and $|W|$ during the training procedure. However, if the partition varies during training, we lose the advantage of storing B_j in a compressed file. In the rest of this section, we discuss the design details of the selective block minimization method.

2.1 Solving using Dual Coordinate Decent

While [1] considers solving the linear SVM both in the primal and in the dual forms, here we only consider solving it in the dual form. The reason is that primal methods directly update $\boldsymbol{w}$, which corresponds to the entire data set [4], so they usually assume that samples are treated uniformly. In Algorithm 1, a cached sample appears in several sub-problems within an outer iteration. Therefore, primal methods cannot directly apply to our model. In the dual, on the other hand, each α_i corresponds to a sample. Therefore, it allows us to put emphasis on informative samples, and train the corresponding α_i.

Following the discussion in [1], we use LIBLINEAR [10] as the solver for the sub-problem. LIBLINEAR implements a dual coordinate descent method [3], which iteratively updates variables in $W^{t,j}$ to solve (3) until the stopping condition is satisfied. The following theorem shows the convergence of $\{\boldsymbol{\alpha}^{t,j}\}$ in Algorithm 1:

Theorem 1
Assume that a coordinate descent method is applied to solving (3). For each inner iteration (t,j) assume that

- *the number of updates, $\{t^{t,j}\}$, used in solving the sub-problem is uniformly bounded, and*
- *each α_i, $for i \in W^{t,j}$, is updated at least once.*

Then, the vector $\{\boldsymbol{\alpha}^{t,j}\}$ generated by algorithm 1 globally converges to an optimal solution $\boldsymbol{\alpha}^*$ at a linear rate or better. That is, there exist $0 < \mu < 1$ and k_0 such that

$$f(\boldsymbol{\alpha}^{k+1}) - f(\boldsymbol{\alpha}^*) \le \mu\left(f(\boldsymbol{\alpha}^{k}) - f(\boldsymbol{\alpha}^*)\right), \forall k \ge k_0.$$

The proof can be modified from [1, Theorem 1].

Sec. 3.1 and Sec. 3.2 in [1] show that the sub-problem can be solved tightly until the gradient-based stopping condition holds, or solved loosely by going through the samples in $W^{t,j}$ a fixed number of rounds. Either way, the first condition in Theorem 1 holds (see [1, Theorem 2]). Moreover, as LIBLINEAR goes through all the data at least once at its first iteration, the second condition is satisfied too. Therefore, Theorem 1 implies the convergence of Algorithm 1. Notice that Theorem 1 holds regardless of the cache selection strategy used.

2.2 Selecting Cached Data

The idea of training on only informative samples appears in the selective sampling literature [11], in active set methods for non-linear SVM (see Sec. 6), and in shrinking techniques in optimization [12]. In this section we discuss our strategy for selecting $\Omega^{t,j}$ from $W^{t,j}$.

During the training, some α_is may stay on the boundary ($\alpha_i = 0$ or $\alpha_i = C$) until the end of the optimization process. Shrinking techniques consider fixing such α_is, thus solving a problem with fewer variables. In the following, we show that those unbounded support vectors with $0 < \alpha_i^* < C$ are more important during the training process. We first show in the following theorem that, if we have an oracle of support vectors, solving a sub-problem using only the support vectors provides the same result as if training is done on the entire data.

Theorem 2
Let $\boldsymbol{\alpha}^*$ be the optimal solution of (2), $V = \{i \mid \alpha_i^* = 0\}$ and $\bar{V} = \{1 \dots l\} \setminus V$. If $\boldsymbol{\alpha}'$ is the optimal solution of the following problem:

$$\begin{aligned} &\min_{\boldsymbol{\alpha}} \; (1/2)\boldsymbol{\alpha}^T Q \boldsymbol{\alpha} - \boldsymbol{e}^T \boldsymbol{\alpha} \\ &\textit{subject to } \boldsymbol{\alpha}_{\bar{V}} = 0, 0 \le \alpha_i \le C, i = 1, \dots, l, \end{aligned}$$

then $f(\boldsymbol{\alpha}') = f(\boldsymbol{\alpha}^*)$ and $\boldsymbol{\alpha}'$ is an optimal solution of (2).

The proof is omitted due to space limitations. Similarly, if we know in advance that $\alpha_i^* = C$, we can solve a smaller problem by fixing $\alpha_i = C$. Therefore, those unbounded support vectors are more important and should be kept in memory. However, we do not know the unbounded support vectors before we solve (2). Therefore, we consider caching unbounded variables ($0 < \alpha_i < C$), which are more likely to eventually be unbounded support vectors.

In dual coordinate descent, α_i is updated in the direction of $-\nabla_i f(\boldsymbol{\alpha})$. Therefore, if $\alpha_i = 0$ and $\nabla_i f(\boldsymbol{\alpha}) > 0$ or if $\alpha_i = C$, and $\nabla_i f(\boldsymbol{\alpha}) < 0$, then α_i is updated toward the boundary. Theorem 2 in [3] implies such α_i will probably stay on the boundary until convergence.

Based on the shrinking strategy proposed in [3], we define the following score to indicate such situations:

$$g(\alpha_i) = \begin{cases} -\nabla_i f(\boldsymbol{\alpha}) & \alpha_i = 0, \nabla_i f(\boldsymbol{\alpha}) > 0, \\ \nabla_i f(\boldsymbol{\alpha}) & \alpha_i = C, \nabla_i f(\boldsymbol{\alpha}) < 0, \\ 0 & \text{Otherwise.} \end{cases}$$

$g(\alpha_i)$ is a non-positive score with the property that the lower its value is, the higher the probability is that the corresponding α_i stays on the boundary. We calculate $g(\alpha_i)$ for each sample i, and select the l_c samples with the higher scores into $\Omega^{t,j+1}$, where l_c is the cache size.

In some situations, there are many unbounded variables, so we further select those with the higher gradient value:

$$g(\alpha_i) = \begin{cases} -\nabla_i f(\alpha) & \alpha_i = 0, \\ \nabla_i f(\alpha) & \alpha_i = C \\ |\nabla_i f(\alpha)| & \text{Otherwise.} \end{cases}$$

To our knowledge, this is the first work that applies a shrinking strategy at the disk level. Our experimental results indicate that our selection strategy significantly improves the performance of a block minimization framework.

3. MULTI-CLASS CLASSIFICATION

Multi-class classification is important in a large number of applications. A multi-class problem can be solved by either training several binary classifiers or by directly optimizing a multi-class formulation [13]. One-versus-all takes the first approach and trains a classifier $\boldsymbol{w}^i$ for each class i to separate it from the union of the other labels. To minimize disk access, [1] proposed an implementation that updates $\boldsymbol{w}^1, \boldsymbol{w}^2 \dots \boldsymbol{w}^k$ simultaneously when B_j is loaded into memory. With a similar technique, Algorithm 1 can be adapted to multi-class problems and maintain separate caches $\Omega_u, u = 1 \dots k$ for each sub-problem. In one-versus-all, the k binary classifiers are trained independently and the training process can be easily parallelized in a multi-core machine. However, in this case there is no shared information among the k binary classifiers so the solver has little global information when selecting the cache. In the following, we investigate an approach that applies SBM in solving a direct multi-class formulation [14] in the dual:

$$\begin{aligned} \min_{\boldsymbol{\alpha}} \quad & f_M(\boldsymbol{\alpha}) = 1/2 \sum\nolimits_{u=1}^{k} \|\boldsymbol{w}^u\|^2 + \sum\nolimits_{i=1}^{l} \sum\nolimits_{u=1}^{k} e_i^u \alpha_i^u \\ \text{subject to} \quad & \sum\nolimits_{u=1}^{k} \alpha_i^u = 0, \forall i = 1, \dots, l \qquad (5) \\ & \alpha_i^u \leq C_{y_i}^u, \forall i = 1, \dots, l, u = 1, \dots, k, \text{ where} \end{aligned}$$

$$\boldsymbol{w}^u = \sum\nolimits_{i=1}^{l} \alpha_i^u \boldsymbol{x}_i, \; C_{y_i}^u = \begin{cases} 0 & \text{if } y_i \neq u, \\ C & \text{if } y_i = u, \end{cases} \; e_i^u = \begin{cases} 1 & \text{if } y_i \neq u, \\ 0 & \text{if } y_i = u. \end{cases}$$

The decision function is

$$\arg\max_{u=1,\dots,k} (\boldsymbol{w}^u)^T \boldsymbol{x}.$$

The superscript u denotes the class label, and the underscript i represents the sample index. Each sample corresponds to k variables $\alpha_i^1 \dots \alpha_i^k$, and each $\boldsymbol{w}^u$ corresponds to one class. Similar to Algorithm 1, we first split data into m blocks. Then, at each step, we load a data block B_j and train a sub-problem on $W^{t,j} = B_j \cup \Omega^{t,j}$

$$\begin{aligned} \min_{\boldsymbol{d}} \quad & f(\boldsymbol{\alpha} + \boldsymbol{d}) \\ \text{subject to} \quad & \sum\nolimits_{u=1}^{k} (\alpha_i^u + d_i^u) = 0, \; (\alpha_i^u + d_i^u) \leq C_{y_i}^u, \forall i, u \\ & d_i^u = 0, \text{ if } i \notin W^{t,j}, \qquad (6) \end{aligned}$$

and update the $\boldsymbol{\alpha}$ by

$$\boldsymbol{\alpha} \leftarrow \boldsymbol{\alpha} + \boldsymbol{d},$$

To apply SBM, we need to solve (6) only with the data block $W^{t,j}$. [15] proposed a sequential dual method to solve (5). The method sequentially picks a sample i and solves for the corresponding k variables $\alpha_i^u, u = 1, 2, \dots, k$. In their update, i is the only sample needed. Therefore, their methods can be applied in SBM. We use the implementation of [15] in LIBLINEAR.

In Sec. 2.2, we mentioned the relationship between shrinking and cache selection. For multi-class SBM, [10, Appendix E.5] describes a shrinking technique implemented in LIBLINEAR. If α_i^u is on the boundary (i.e., $\alpha_i^u = C_i^u$) and satisfies certain conditions, then it is shrunken. To select a cache set, we consider a sample 'informative' if a small fraction of its corresponding variables $\alpha_i^u, u = 1, 2, \dots, k$ are shrunken. We keep such samples in the cache $\Omega^{t,j}$. Sec. 7 demonstrates the performance of SBM in solving (5).

4. LEARNING FROM STREAMING DATA

Learning over streaming data is important in many applications when the amount of data is just too large to keep in memory; in these cases, it is difficult to process the data in multiple passes and it is often treated as a stream that the algorithm needs to process in an online manner. However, online learners make use of a simple update rule, and a single pass over the samples is typically insufficient to obtain a good model. In the following, we introduce a variant of SBM that considers Algorithm 1 with only one iteration. Unlike existing approaches, we accumulate the incoming samples as a block, and solve the optimization problem one data block at a time. This strategy allows SBM to fully utilize its resources (learning time and memory capacity) and to obtain a significantly more accurate model than in standard techniques that load each sample from disk only once.

When SBM collects a block of samples B from the incoming data, it sets the corresponding $\alpha_i, i \in B$ to 0. Then, as in Algorithm 1, it updates the model by solving (3) on $W = B \cup \Omega$, where Ω is the cache set collected from the previous step. In Sec. 2, we described SBM as processing the data multiple times to solve Eq. (2) exactly. This required maintaining the whole $\boldsymbol{\alpha}$. When the number of instances is large, storing $\boldsymbol{\alpha}$ becomes a problem (see Sec. 5.2). However, when dealing with streaming data each sample is loaded once. Therefore, if a sample i is removed from memory, the corresponding α_i will not be updated later, and keeping $\alpha_i, i \in W$ is sufficient. Without the need to store the whole $\boldsymbol{\alpha}$, the solver is able to keep more data in memory.

The SBM for streaming data thus obtains a feasible solution that approximately solves (2). Compared to other approaches for streaming data, SBM has two advantages:

- By adjusting the cache size and the tightness of solving the sub-problems, we can obtain models with different accuracy levels. Therefore, the solver can adjust to the available resources.
- As we update the model on both a set of incoming samples and a set of cached samples, the model is more stable than the model learned by other online learners.

We study its performance experimentally in Sec. 7.2.

5. IMPLEMENTATION ISSUES

[1] introduces several techniques to speed up block minimization algorithms. Some techniques such as data compression and loading blocks in a random order can also be applied to Algorithm 1. In the following, we further discuss implementation issues that are relevant to SBM.

5.1 Storing Cached Samples in Memory

In Step 4(d) of Algorithm 1, we update the cache set $\Omega^{t,j}$ to $\Omega^{t,j+1}$ by selecting samples from $W^{t,j}$. As memory is limited, non-cached samples $i \notin \Omega^{t,j+1}$ are removed from memory. If data is stored in a continuous array[1] we need a careful design to avoid duplicating samples.

Assume that $W^{t,j}$ is stored in a continuous memory chunk MEM_W. The lower part of MEM_W, MEM_Ω, stores the samples in $\Omega^{t,j}$, and the higher part stores B_j. In the following we discuss a way to update the samples in MEM_Ω from $W^{t,j} = \Omega^{t,j} \cup B_j$ to $W^{t,j+1} = \Omega^{t,j+1} \cup B_{j+1}$ without using extra memory. We want to update MEM_W and store

[1]This operation can be performed easily if the data is stored in a linked list. However, accessing data in a linked list is slower than in an array.

$\Omega^{t,j+1}$ in its lower part. However, as $\Omega^{t,j+1}$ is selected from $\Omega^{t,j} \cup B_j$, which is currently in Mem_W, we need to move the samples in such an order that the values of samples in $\Omega^{t,j+1}$ will not be covered. Moreover, as data is stored in a sparse format, the memory consumption for storing each sample is different. We cannot directly swap the samples in memory. To deal with this problem, we first sort the samples in $\Omega^{t,j+1}$ by their memory location. Then, we sequentially move each sample in $\Omega^{t,j+1}$ to a lower address of MEM_W and cover those non-cached samples. This way, we form a continuous memory chunk $\Omega^{t,j+1}$. Finally, we load B_{j+1} after the last cached sample in $\Omega^{t,j+1}$; MEM_W stores $W^{t,j+1}$ now.

5.2 Dealing with a Large α

When the number of examples is huge, storing $\boldsymbol{\alpha}$ becomes a problem. This is especially the case in multi-class classification, as the size of $\boldsymbol{\alpha}$ grows rapidly since each sample corresponds to k elements in $\boldsymbol{\alpha}$. In the following we introduce two approaches to cope with this situation.

1. Storing $\alpha_i, i \notin W$ in a hash table: In real world applications, the number of support vectors is sometimes much less than the number of samples. In these situations, many α_is will stay at 0 during the whole training process. Therefore, we can store the α_is in a sparse format. That is, we store non-zero $\alpha_i > 0$ in a hash table. We can keep a copy of the current working $\alpha_i, i \in W$ in an array, as accessing data from a hash table is slower than from an array. The hash strategy is widely used in developing large scale learning systems. For example, VW uses a hash table to store the model $\boldsymbol{w}$ when n is huge.

2. Storing $\alpha_i, i \notin W$ in disk: In solving a sub-problem, $\alpha_i, i \notin W^{t,j}$ are fixed. Therefore, we can store them in disk and load them when the corresponding samples $B_j, i \in B_j$ are loaded. We maintain m files to save those α_is which are not involved in the current sub-problem. Then, we save the α_i to the jth file when the corresponding sample $i \in B_j$ is removed from memory. To minimize disk access, the α_is can be stored in a sparse format, and only the α_is with non-zero value are stored.

6. RELATIONS WITH OTHER METHODS

In Sec. 1 and Sec. 2 we discussed the differences between the block minimization framework and our Algorithm 1. In the following, we review other approaches to large scale classification and their relations to Algorithm 1.

Online learning: Online learning is a popular approach to learning from huge data sets. An online learner iteratively goes over the entire data and updates the model as it goes. A commonly held view was that online learners efficiently deal with large data sets due to their simplicity. In the following, we show that the issues are different when the data does not fit in memory. At each step, an online learner performs a simple update on a single data instance. The update done by an online learner is usually cheaper than the one done by a batch learner (e.g., Newton-type method). Therefore, even though an online learner takes a large number of iterations to converge, it could obtain a reasonable model quickly [16, 17]. However, when the data cannot fit into memory, we need to access each sample from disk again every round. An online method thus requires large I/O due to the large number of iterations required. One may consider a block of data at a time to reduce the number of iterations.

Some online learning algorithms have considered solving a block of data at a time. For example, Pegasos [4] allows a block-size update when solving (1) with projected stochastic gradient descent. However, as they assume data points are randomly drawn from the entire data, they cannot do multiple updates on one block. Therefore, it still cannot fully utilize the data in memory. Some online learning methods have considered a caching technique. [18] suggested periodically updating the model on samples the model gets wrong. However, their caching technique is ad-hoc and has no convergence guarantees. To our knowledge, SBM is the first method that uses caching and *provably converges* to (1).

Parallelizing batch algorithm: Although parallel algorithms such as [19, 20] can scale up to huge problems, the communication across machines still incurs a large overhead. Moreover, the aforementioned algorithms still require that training is done on a single machine, so we do not consider parallel solutions in this work. Recently there have been proposals for solving large problems by parallelizing online methods using multi-core machines [21]. However, these methods only shorten the learning time and do not solve the I/O problem.

Reducing data size: Sub-sampling and feature pruning techniques as in [22, 23] reduce the size of the data. In some situations, training on a subset of the data is sufficient to generate a reasonable model. But in other situations, the huge amount of data is already preprocessed and further pruning may degrade the performance. In fact, in SBM we start from a model trained on a randomly drawn data block, and iteratively improve the model by loading other sample blocks. Therefore, its performance should be at least as good as random sub-sampling.

Bagging models trained on a subset of the data: Bagging [24] is an algorithm that improves test performance by combining models trained on subsets of data. To train on large data, a bagging algorithm randomly picks k-subsets of the entire data, and trains k models $\{w^1, w^2, \ldots, w^k\}$ separately on each subset. The final model is obtained by averaging the k models. Some analysis was provided recently in [25]. Although a bagging algorithm can sometimes learn a good model, it does not solve Eq. (1). Therefore, in practice, it is not clear if a bagging model can obtain as good a classifier as obtained by solving (1).

Selective sampling: Selective sampling and active learning methods select informative samples for learning a model [26, 27]. Even though their goal is different, these methods can be applied when training on large data sets (See Sec. 6 in [22]). Starting from a subset of the data, selective sampling methods iteratively select the samples that are close to the current margin, and update the model on those samples. To compute the margin accurately, a selective sub-sampling method may require access to the entire data from disk, which is expensive. In contrast, SBM loads a data block not only for selection but also for training. It selects samples into the cache only if they are already in memory. Therefore, it suffers a very small overhead when selecting samples. Moreover, selective sampling is not guaranteed to converge to (1), while SBM converges linearly.

Related methods for non-linear models: In solving non-linear models, data is usually mapped into a high dimensional feature space via a kernel trick. When the kernel matrix goes beyond memory capacity, an active set method (e.g., [28, 29, 30]) maintains an active set A and updates only the variables $\alpha_i, i \in A$ each time. If $|A|$ is small, the

Table 1: Data statistics: We assume data is stored in a sparse representation. Each feature with non-zero value takes 16 bytes on a 64-bit machine due to data structure alignment. l, n, and #nonzeros are number of instances, features, and non-zero values in each training set, respectively. l_t is the number of instances in the test set. Memory is the memory consumption needed to store the entire data. #nBSV shows the number of unbounded support vectors ($0 < \alpha_i < C$) in the optimal solution. #classes is the number of class labels.

Data set	l	l_t	n	#nonzeros	Memory (Bytes)	C	#nBSV	#classes
webspam	280,000	70,000	16,609,143	1,043,792,623	16,700,681,968	64	7071	2
kddcup10	19,264,093	748,401	29,890,095	566,345,790	9,061,532,640	0.1	2,775,946	2
prep	60,000,000	5,710,649	11,148,531	918,704,364	14,699,269,824	0.1	-	10

corresponding kernel entries can be stored in memory and the active set method yields fast training. Active set methods are related to our work as they also select samples during training. However, the memory problem of dealing with non-linear models is different from the one we face. Non-linear solvers usually assume that samples are stored in memory, while the entire kernel cannot be stored. Therefore, there is no restriction on accessing data. In our case, the samples can only be loaded sequentially from disk.

Another algorithm, Forgetron [31], is related to our work. However, the focus there is different. When training a model with a non-linear kernel, the model is represented by some samples (support vectors). When they have too many samples to store in memory, Forgetron selects the samples which can represent the current model best. In the linear case, $\boldsymbol{w}$ can be directly stored. In our case, on the other hand, the selection process is done in order to speed up the training rather than to just represent the model more concisely.

7. EXPERIMENTAL STUDY

In this section, we first show that SBM provides an improvement over the block minimization algorithm (BMD) in [1]. Then, we demonstrate that SBM converges faster than an online learner. Finally, we investigate the setting in which each sample is loaded from disk only once and show that SBM deals better with streaming data.

We consider two large binary classification data sets, webspam and kddcup10, and one multi-class data set, prep. webspam is a document collection; kddcup10 is taken from educational applications and has been used in the data mining challenge.[2] prep is a 10-classes classification task, aiming at predicting the correct preposition in an English sentence with a bag-of-words model [32].[3] In kddcup10 and webspam, the feature vectors are scaled to unit length, so that $\forall i, \|\boldsymbol{x}_i\| = 1$. prep takes binary features, and we prune the features which appear less than 5 times in all samples. Table 1 lists the data statistics. As shown in [33], applying sub-sampling or bagging downgrades the test performance on kddcup10 and webspam. Each data set is stored as an ASCII file before the training process.

We tune the penalty parameter C using a five-fold cross-validation on the training data and report the performance of solving (2) with the best parameter. This setting allows SBM for linear SVM to be compared with other learning packages such as VW. The implementation of BMD and SBM is in C/C++[4] with double precision in a 64-bit machine. We restrict each process to use at most 2GB memory.

7.1 Training Time and Testing Accuracy

Comparison between SBM and BMD: We compare SBM with the block minimization algorithm in the dual (BMD) [1], as both the algorithms consider a block of data at a time. For a fair comparison, we take the largest block size ($|D_{\text{BM}}| = \max_j |B_j|$) in BMD as a reference, and adjust SBM to use the same amount of memory during training. We consider three variants of Algorithm 1: SBM-1/2, SBM-1/3, and SBM-1/2-rand. SBM-1/2 and SBM-1/2-rand load half the memory with new data and the rest is kept for the cache ($|B_j| = |\Omega| = 1/2|D_{\text{BM}}|$). SBM-1/3 reserves 1/3 of the memory capacity for cache and loads the rest with new data ($|\Omega| = 1/3|D_{\text{BM}}|$ and $|B_j| = 2|\Omega|$). Both SBM-1/2 and SBM-1/3 select the cached sample using the gradient information as described in Sec. 2.2 and 3. SBM-1/2-rand selects the cached sample by picking randomly from the samples in memory (W). All sub-problems in BMD and SBM-* are solved by a dual coordinate method with 10 rounds ($t^{i,j} = 10$). We split both webspam and kddcup10 into 12 blocks ($m = 12$)[5] and split prep into 15 blocks in BMD. The cache size and block size of SBM-* are adjusted according to BMD. Each block is stored in a compressed file. The compression introduces additional cost in storing compressed files but it reduces the load time of each block (see [1, Sec. 5.1]). We report the *wall clock* time in all experiments including the initial time to generate the compressed files (the time to read data from an ASCII file, split it, and store the compressed data in disk.)

The number of α_i^us in prep is 600 million. Therefore, storing all α_i^u takes 4.8GB memory which exceeds the memory restriction. Following the discussion in Sec. 5.2, we store the unused α_i^u in files for BMD and SBM-*.

To check the convergence speed of each method, we compare the relative difference between the dual objective function value (2) and the optimum ($f(\boldsymbol{\alpha}^*)$),

$$|(f(\boldsymbol{\alpha}) - f(\boldsymbol{\alpha}^*))/f(\boldsymbol{\alpha})|, \tag{7}$$

over time. We are also interested in the time it takes each method to obtain a reasonable and stable model. Therefore, we compare the difference between the performance of the current model ($\text{acc}(\boldsymbol{w})$) and the best test accuracy among all methods (acc^*)

$$(\text{acc}^* - \text{acc}(\boldsymbol{w}))\%. \tag{8}$$

Note that tightly solving (1) is not guaranteed to have the best test performance. Some solvers may reach a higher accuracy before the model converges.

[2] kddcup10 is preprocessed from the second data set in KDD Cup 2010. webspam and kddcup10 can be downloaded at `http://www.csie.ntu.edu.tw/~cjlin/libsvmtools/datasets/`.

[3] prep is extracted from Wikipedia and New York Times. As the annotation can be automatically generated from articles (assuming the given text is correct), the supervised data can be very large.

[4] The experimental code is modified from [1] `http://www.csie.ntu.edu.tw/~cjlin/liblinear/exp.html`.

[5] Although the data size of webspam is larger than kddcup10. kddcup10 has a huge number of samples and features, and it takes about 500MB to store the model.

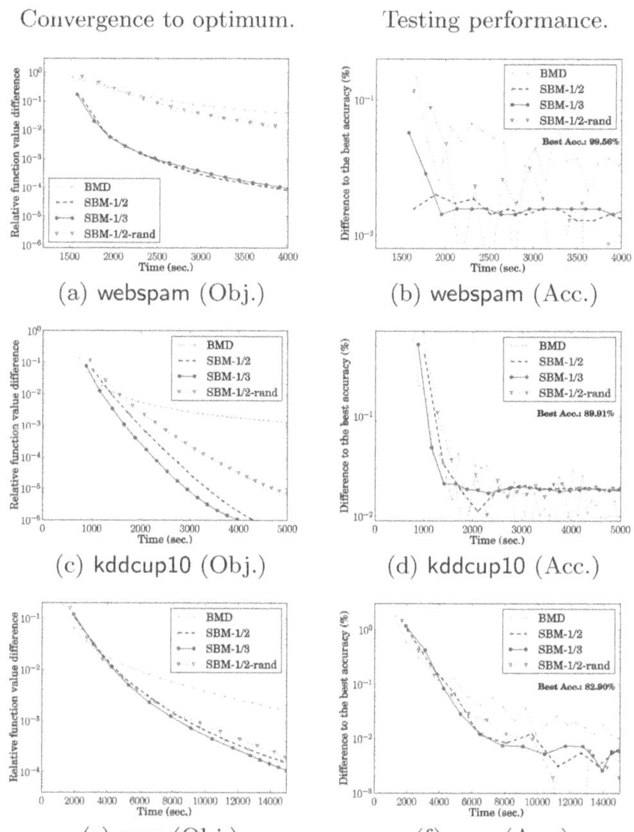

(a) webspam (Obj.) (b) webspam (Acc.)

(c) kddcup10 (Obj.) (d) kddcup10 (Acc.)

(e) prep (Obj.) (f) prep (Acc.)

Figure 2: Comparison between the proposed methods (SBM-*) and the block minimization algorithm (BMD) [1]. Left column: the relative function value difference (7) to the minimum of (2). Right column: the test accuracy difference (8) from the best achievable accuracy. Time is in seconds, and the y-axis is in log-scale. Each marker indicates one outer iteration. As all the solvers access all samples from disk once at each outer iteration, the markers indicate the amount of disk access. It is shown that SBM-* converges faster and obtains a more accurate and stabler model quickly.

Figure 2 shows that all the SBM-* outperform BMD significantly. By selecting cached samples using the gradient information, our key methods, SBM-1/2 and SBM-1/3 perform even better. In particular, when the unbounded support vectors can fit into memory, SBM-1/2 and SBM-1/3 keep most of them in cache during the training process and thus enjoy fast convergence.[6] Consequently, the models generated are more stable in test. The performance of SBM-1/2 and SBM-1/3 are similar. This indicates that the model is not sensitive to the ratio between block size and cache size. Note that SBM is more general than BMD, as it is reduced to BMD when the cache size is zero.

It's interesting to note that even when the cached set is selected randomly, SBM-1/2-rand is still faster than BMD. One possible reason is that partitioning the data affects the performance of the solver. BMD uses a fixed partition $B_j, \forall j$, throughout the training process. For SBM, although, $\forall j$, B_j is fixed as well, the cached set Ω varies at each iteration.

[6]E.g., in figure 2(a), more than 98% of the unbounded support vectors are stored in cache after 2 iterations.

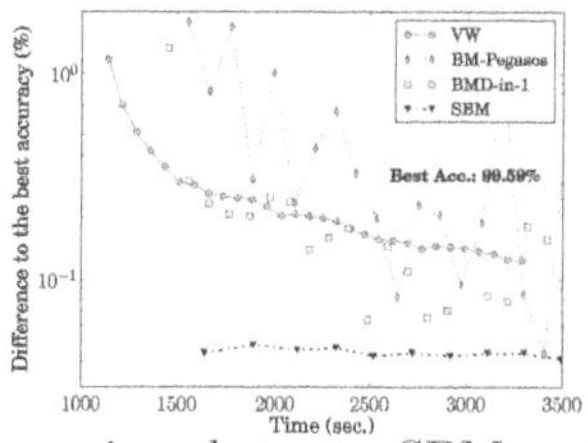

Figure 3: A comparison between SBM and online learning algorithms on webspam. We show the difference between test performance and the best accuracy achievable (8). Time is in seconds. The markers indicate the time it takes each solver to access data from disk once. Except for VW, each solver takes about 90 sec. in each round to load data from the compressed files.

Therefore, SBM avoids wasting time on a bad data block. When the number of bounded support vectors is large, the selection of Ω is less important since drawing a sample randomly already has a high probability of including bounded support vectors in the cache (see figure 2(c)). SBM-* works better in binary classification than in multi-class classification, as sub-problems of the multi-class formulation take more learning time. Thus, the I/O overhead plays a smaller role at training time.

Comparison between SBM and online learners: In Sec. 6, we mentioned that people in the community believe that online learners are fast for large data sets since they make use of a simple update rule. However, as we show, online learners use more I/O time when the data is not in memory. We compare the following solvers:

- VW[7]: an online learning package (version 5.1).[8] It implements a stochastic gradient descent method [34].
- BM-Pegasos: A version of Pegasos implemented under a block minimization framework [1, 4].
- BMD-in-1: Similar to BMD but the inner solver goes through the samples in each sub-problem only once.
- SBM: The same as SBM-1/2 in the previous experiment.

We implemented Pegasos under the block minimization framework such that it saves considerable I/O time by loading data from a compressed file. Although VW also considers a hinge loss function, it does not converge to (2). Therefore, its final accuracy is different from that of the others. Except for SBM, all the methods update the model on each sample once per outer iteration. BMD-in-1 takes the same update rule as the passive-aggressive online algorithm [9], but it keeps $\boldsymbol{\alpha}$ and its solution converges to (2). Except for VW, all methods take about 90 seconds to access each sample from the compressed files. VW has a faster implementation[9] for loading data and takes about 70 seconds per outer iteration.

Figure 3 shows the test performance over time (8) on webspam. SBM converges faster than other online methods to the final performance. *The reason is that an online learner spends most of its time loading data instead of learning a*

[7] `https://github.com/JohnLangford/vowpal_wabbit`

[8]We use the latest version 5.1, and set the parameter as -b 24 --loss_function hinge --initial_t 80000 --power_t 0.5 -l 1000 --compressed as the author suggested.

[9] VW uses single floating point precision while our implementations use double precision. Although using single precision reduces the training time, numerical inaccuracy may occur. In addition, VW is a multi-threaded program. It uses one thread for loading data and another thread for learning.

Table 2: Training time (*wall clock time*) and testing accuracy for each solver *when each sample is loaded into memory only once*. We show both the loading time (the time to read data from an ASCII file) and the learning time. The reference model is obtained by solving (1) until it converges (see text). We show that by updating the model on one data block at a time, SBM obtains an accurate model for streaming data. Note that the time reported here is different from the time required to finish the first iteration in Figure 2 (see text). Some entries in the table are missing. BM-Pegasos and VW do not support multi-class classification. Also, it is difficult to access the I/O and learning time of VW since it is a multi-threaded program. The top three methods are implemented in Java, and the rest are in C/C++.

Method	webspam				kddcup10				prep			
	Training Time (sec.)			Acc.	Training Time (sec.)			Acc.	Training Time (sec.)			Acc.
	I/O	Learning	Total		I/O	Learning	Total		I/O	Learning	Total	
Perceptron	5078	31	5108	98.66	1403	42	1448	84.93	1843	903	2753	76.10
MIRA [9]	5392	27	5419	98.73	1265	44	1312	86.14	1829	816	2652	76.81
CW [8, 35]	4698	59	4757	99.49	1439	99	1535	89.07	1820	1121	2949	77.70
VW	-	-	507	98.42	-	-	223	85.25	-	-	-	-
BM-Pegasos	470	9	479	97.87	187	20	207	87.48	-	-	-	-
BMD	472	60	532	99.48	181	201	382	88.62	265	649	914	80.06
SBM-in-3	484	81	565	**99.55**	181	151	332	89.54	321	778	1099	81.61
SBM	473	177	650	**99.55**	180	442	634	**89.67**	354	1956	2310	**81.80**
Reference	-	-	-	99.55	-	-	-	89.90	-	-	-	82.90

model (see Sec. 6). For example, BM-Pegasos spends only 15 seconds updating the model. Therefore, it spends 85% of the training time loading data. In contrast, the learning time per iteration in SBM is 180 seconds. Thus, SBM uses 2/3 of the training time to update the model and consequently converges faster.

7.2 Experiments on Streaming Data

In Sec. 4, we introduced a variation of SBM that deals with streaming data. Now we investigate its performance.

In addition to the solvers BMD, SBM, BM-Pegasos and VW introduced in previous experiments, we further compare them to the implementations in [35].[10] The package currently supports the following solvers for data streams:

- MIRA: an online learning algorithm proposed in [9].
- CW: a confidences weighted online algorithm [8, 35].
- Perceptron: an online learning algorithm.

In addition, we consider a setting of SBM, SBM-in-3, in which we only allow 3 rounds when solving each sub-problem (the general setting allows 10 rounds). The training time of this version of SBM is similar to the training time of BMD. Note that MIRA, CW and Perceptron are implemented in JAVA, and the rest of the solvers are implemented in C/C++. For multi-class problems, we used the top-1 approach [35] in MIRA, CW and Perceptron.

Table 2 lists the training time and test accuracy when each sample is loaded from disk only once. To see if loading data once can achieve a result similar to running over the data multiple times, we show a reference model in the table, which solves Eq. (1) until the model converges. We provide both the time to load data from an ASCII file (I/O) and the update time of the model (Learning). For each solver we focus on the ratio of loading to learning time rather than on comparing the absolute times across different solvers. Note that the time reported in Table 2 is different from the time to complete the first round in Figure 2. Figure 2 includes the time it takes to generate compressed files from an ASCII file. However, for streaming data, each sample is loaded into memory once and there is no need to store data in compressed files, resulting in shorter I/O time.

The results show that SBM is able to utilize the memory capacity and spend more learning time to achieve an accurate model. It even achieves a model that is almost as accurate as the reference model on webspam. As the I/O is expensive, for all the methods, the loading time takes a large fraction of the total training time. Online methods such as MIRA and Perceptron use a simple update rule. Their learning time is indeed small, but the model learned with a single pass over the samples is far from converging. CW uses a better update rule and achieves a more accurate model, but the performance is still limited. In contrast, both SBM and BMD are able to update on a data block at a time, thus taking more information into account. Therefore, they achieve a better result. Comparing SBM-in-3 to BMD we see that SBM-in-3 has a similar training time to that of BMD, but learns a model with better accuracy. As shown, by keeping informative samples in memory, SBM utilizes the memory storage better. When the resources are limited, users can adjust the test performance of SBM by adjusting the memory usage and the accuracy level of solving the sub-problems.

8. DISCUSSION AND CONCLUSION

In summary, we presented a selective block minimization algorithm for training large-scale linear classifiers under memory restrictions. We also analyzed the proposed algorithm and provided extensive experimental results. To reduce the amount of disk access, we suggested caching informative samples in memory and updating the model on the important data more frequently. We show that, even though the proposed method treats data points non-uniformly, it provably converges to the global optimum on the entire data. Our experimental results on binary, multi-class and streaming data, show the significant advantage of SBM over block minimization and online algorithms. SBM converges quicker to a more accurate and stable model.

We note that these methods can be applied more broadly. For example, it can be applied for solving L2-loss SVM, regularized least square problems, and logistic regression, by

[10] `http://www.cs.jhu.edu/~mdredze/`. The original package takes a very long time to train on the webspam data set. It might be due to the deep class hierarchy in the package. We fixed the problem and sped up the package.

applying the corresponding dual solvers [3, 36]. Moreover, note that in this work we considered sparse data stored in row format. Therefore, we could split the data into blocks and access particular instances. When data is stored in a column format, splitting can only be done feature by feature. It would be interesting to investigate how to extend our method to this scenario.

Acknowledgments This research is supported by the Defense Advanced Research Projects Agency (DARPA) Machine Reading Program under Air Force Research Laboratory (AFRL) prime contract no. FA8750-09-C-0181 and by the DARPA under the Bootstrap Learning Program. Any opinions, findings, and conclusion or recommendations expressed in this material are those of the author(s) and do not necessarily reflect the view of the DARPA, AFRL, ARL or the US government.

9. REFERENCES

[1] H.-F. Yu, C.-J. Hsieh, K.-W. Chang, and C.-J. Lin, "Large linear classification when data cannot fit in memory," in *ACM KDD*, 2010.

[2] G. Loosli, S. Canu, and L. Bottou, "Training invariant support vector machines using selective sampling," in *Large Scale Kernel Machines* (L. Bottou, O. Chapelle, D. DeCoste, and J. Weston, eds.), pp. 301–320, Cambridge, MA.: MIT Press, 2007.

[3] C.-J. Hsieh, K.-W. Chang, C.-J. Lin, S. S. Keerthi, and S. Sundararajan, "A dual coordinate descent method for large-scale linear SVM," in *ICML*, 2008.

[4] S. Shalev-Shwartz, Y. Singer, and N. Srebro, "Pegasos: primal estimated sub-gradient solver for SVM," in *ICML*, 2007.

[5] T. Joachims, "Training linear SVMs in linear time," in *ACM KDD*, 2006.

[6] J. Langford, L. Li, and T. Zhang, "Sparse online learning via truncated gradient," *JMLR*, vol. 10, pp. 771–801, 2009.

[7] P. Rai, H. Daumé III, and S. Venkatasubramanian, "Streamed learning: One-pass SVMs," in *IJCAI*, 2009.

[8] M. Dredze, K. Crammer, and F. Pereira, "Confidence-weighted linear classification," in *ICML*, 2008.

[9] K. Crammer, O. Dekel, J. Keshet, S. Shalev-Shwartz, and Y. Singer, "Online passive-aggressive algorithms," *JMLR*, 2006.

[10] R.-E. Fan, K.-W. Chang, C.-J. Hsieh, X.-R. Wang, and C.-J. Lin, "LIBLINEAR: A library for large linear classification," *JMLR*, vol. 9, pp. 1871–1874, 2008.

[11] G. Loosli, S. Canu, and L. Bottou, "Training invariant support vector machines using selective sampling," in *Large Scale Kernel Machines*, pp. 301–320, Cambridge, MA.: MIT Press, 2007.

[12] T. Joachims, "Making large-scale SVM learning practical," in *Advances in Kernel Methods - Support Vector Learning*, MIT Press, 1998.

[13] S. Har-Peled, D. Roth, and D. Zimak, "Constraint classification for multiclass classification and ranking," in *NIPS*, 2003.

[14] K. Crammer and Y. Singer, "On the learnability and design of output codes for multiclass problems," in *COLT*, 2000.

[15] S. S. Keerthi, S. Sundararajan, K.-W. Chang, C.-J. Hsieh, and C.-J. Lin, "A sequential dual method for large scale multi-class linear SVMs," in *ACM KDD*, 2008.

[16] L. Bottou and Y. L. Cun, "Large scale online learning," in *NIPS*, 2004.

[17] S. Shalev-Shwartz and N. Srebro, "SVM optimization: inverse dependence on training set size," in *ICML*, 2008.

[18] M. Collins and B. Roark, "Incremental parsing with the perceptron algorithm," in *ACL*, 2004.

[19] K. Woodsend and J. Gondzio, "Hybrid mpi/openmp parallel linear support vector machine training," *JMLR*, vol. 10, pp. 1937–1953, 2009.

[20] E. Chang, K. Zhu, H. Wang, H. Bai, J. Li, Z. Qiu, and H. Cui, "Parallelizing support vector machines on distributed computers," in *NIPS*, 2007.

[21] J. Langford, A. J. Smola, and M. Zinkevich, "Slow learners are fast," in *NIPS*, 2009.

[22] H. Yu, J. Yang, and J. Han, "Classifying large data sets using SVMs with hierarchical clusters," in *ACM KDD*, 2003.

[23] J. L. Balcázar, Y. Dai, and O. Watanabe, "A random sampling technique for training support vector machines," in *ALT*, 2001.

[24] L. Breiman, "Bagging predictors," *Machine Learning*, vol. 24, pp. 123–140, August 1996.

[25] M. Zinkevich, M. Weimer, A. Smola, and L. Li, "Parallelized stochastic gradient descent," in *NIPS*, 2010.

[26] F. Pérez-Cruz, A. R. Figueiras-Vidal, and A. Artés-Rodríguez, "Double chunking for solving SVMs for very large datasets," in *Proceedings of Learning 2004, Spain*, 2004.

[27] S. Tong and D. Koller, "Support vector machine active learning with applications to text classification," *JMLR*, vol. 2, pp. 45–66, 2002.

[28] S. V. N. Vishwanathan, A. J. Smola, and M. N. Murty, "Simplesvm," in *ICML*, 2003.

[29] K. Scheinberg, "An efficient implementation of an active set method for svms," *JMLR*, vol. 7, pp. 2237–2257, 2006.

[30] A. Bordes, S. Ertekin, J. Weston, and L. Bottou, "Fast kernel classifiers with online and active learning," *JMLR*, vol. 6, pp. 1579–1619, 2005.

[31] O. Dekel, S. Shalev-Shwartz, and Y. Singer, "The forgetron: A kernel-based perceptron on a budget," *SIAM Journal on Computing*, vol. 37, pp. 1342–1372, January 2008.

[32] A. Rozovskaya and D. Roth, "Generating confusion sets for context-sensitive error correction," in *EMNLP*, 2010.

[33] H.-F. Yu, C.-J. Hsieh, K.-W. Chang, and C.-J. Lin, "Large linear classification when data cannot fit in memory," tech. rep., National Taiwan University, 2011. `http://www.csie.ntu.edu.tw/~r96050/papers/bm.pdf`.

[34] Y. Freund, R. E. Schapire, Y. Singer, and M. K. Warmuth, "Using and combining predictors that specialize," in *STOC*, 1997.

[35] K. Crammer, M. Dredze, and A. Kulesza, "Multi-class confidence weighted algorithms," in *EMNLP*, 2009.

[36] H.-F. Yu, F.-L. Huang, and C.-J. Lin, "Dual coordinate descent methods for logistic regression and maximum entropy models," *Machine Learning*, 2011. To appear.

Bounded Coordinate-Descent for Biological Sequence Classification in High Dimensional Predictor Space

Georgiana Ifrim
Cork Constraint Computation Centre (4C)
University College Cork
Cork, Ireland
g.ifrim@4c.ucc.ie

Carsten Wiuf
Bioinformatics Research Centre (BiRC)
C.F. Møllers Allé 8
DK-8000 Aarhus C, Denmark
wiuf@cs.au.dk

ABSTRACT

We present a framework for discriminative sequence classification where linear classifiers work directly in the explicit high-dimensional predictor space of all subsequences in the training set (as opposed to kernel-induced spaces). This is made feasible by employing a gradient-bounded coordinate-descent algorithm for efficiently selecting discriminative subsequences without having to expand the whole space. Our framework can be applied to a wide range of loss functions, including binomial log-likelihood loss of logistic regression and squared hinge loss of support vector machines. When applied to protein remote homology detection and remote fold recognition, our framework achieves comparable performance to the state-of-the-art (e.g., kernel support vector machines). In contrast to state-of-the-art sequence classifiers, our models are simply lists of weighted discriminative subsequences and can thus be interpreted and related to the biological problem – a crucial requirement for the bioinformatics and medical communities.

Categories and Subject Descriptors

H.3 [**Information Storage and Retrieval**]: Content Analysis and Indexing; I.2.6 [**Artificial Intelligence**]: Learning

General Terms

Algorithms, Performance, Experimentation

Keywords

Greedy Coordinate-Descent, Sequence Classification, String Classification, Logistic Regression, Support Vector Machines

1. INTRODUCTION

Many problems in biology today require accurate computational prediction of properties. For example, the primary DNA sequence is a main determinant of functional and structural protein properties, yet little is known about this relationship and we must therefore turn to computational prediction for advancing our understanding. Likewise, accurate gene and motif prediction is of crucial importance for the annotation of recently sequenced genomes. To achieve this goal, we need machine learning techniques that are fast, highly scalable and preferably treat feature selection as an integral part of the learning algorithm. The latter requirement means that neither time nor expertise is invested in pre-processing the original data (e.g., for defining features) and no potentially hard to validate assumptions are made about data distribution. Recent advances in developing efficient machine learning tools such as fast logistic regression [7, 27, 28] and support vector machines [16, 9, 36, 35] enable learning of classifiers in very large predictor spaces, thus reducing the need for pre-processing the data. Nevertheless, most of these techniques are typically designed to exploit the sparsity of the training set (i.e., many features occur sparsely in the training data) which holds for many applications, such as text categorization [27, 9]. This assumption unfortunately does not hold for biological sequences, where many subsequences often occur very frequently.

We present an efficient coordinate-descent algorithm for optimizing regularized fitting of classification loss in high dimensional predictor space. Our approach does not rely on feature sparsity assumptions. In our framework, the feature space is spanned by all subsequences present in the training set. Furthermore, the features can have a flexible number of wildcard matches, which allows us to model complex biological processes such as substitutions, insertions and deletions. The optimization proceeds coordinate-wise by iteratively selecting the feature with maximum (absolute) gradient value, following the Gauss-Southwell rule [30, 37]. In order to select the best features quickly, we provide bounds on the gradient value of any subsequence based on its prefix. This drastically reduces the search space. We discuss the tightness of the proposed bounds as well as the convergence of the algorithm.

Our learning technique is applicable to both unregularized and regularized loss functions. In this paper we show bounds for the more complex case of *elastic-net* regularized loss [10]. By adding an explicit elastic-net penalty (a convex combination of $l1$ and $l2$ regularizers) to the loss function, we allow the user to directly trade-off $l1$-regularization (encouraging model sparsity) for $l2$-regularization (correcting for correlations) [8, 10, 6]. As can be observed in our experiments this positively affects the prediction quality. We present applications of our learning algorithm to protein remote homology detection and fold recognition. In order to

KDD'11, August 21–24, 2011, San Diego, California, USA.

compare to previously published results, we work with standard protein benchmarks. For homology detection we use SCOP1.59 [15, 22, 24, 19], and for fold recognition we use the challenging dataset of [3]. The classification problems associated with these datasets are hard and the training data is rather small scale (2,800 and 300 sequences respectively). In order to further analyse the scalability of our technique, we present a large scale experiment on the latest version of the Silva-LSUPARC102 database (150,000 unique sequences). We compare our algorithm to state-of-the-art sequence classifiers, support vector machines with spectrum kernel [24], mismatch kernel [22, 21], and the recent sparse spatial sample kernel [19, 20]. Besides being fast and highly accurate, our classification models are easily interpretable, an important advantage for the bioinformatics and medical communities.

The remainder of this paper proceeds as follows. Section 2 addresses related work. Section 3 presents our learning framework. Section 4 and 5 analyse the experimental setup and results. We conclude with pointers to future work in Section 6.

2. RELATED WORK

Working in high dimensional predictor space and regularizing is statistically preferable to a two-step procedure of first reducing the dimension, then fitting a model in the reduced space [32]. Recently, efficient regularized learning algorithms for logistic regression and support vector machines (SVM) were proposed for fitting classifiers in high dimensional predictor space [27, 9]. In order to scale, most of these techniques restrict the allowed features (i.e., use k-mers, for fixed and reasonably small k) and exploit the feature space sparsity. For some applications, such as text categorization, where the features occur sparsely in the training instances, existing techniques perform very well [12]. However, this is not the case for applications involving biological sequence classification where the feature space is dense (i.e., many subsequences occur in many of the training sequences), thus challenging the running time and memory requirements of existing methods.

Recent work on efficiently computing string kernels for SVM [22, 24, 19, 33, 36] addressed some of the computational challenges associated with this type of techniques. Nevertheless, the kernels proposed still restrict the set of features to subsequences of certain length (e.g, $k = 10$) or format (e.g., allowing some mismatches) in order to scale. In this paper we work with the space of all (unrestricted-length) subsequences in the training set and allow wildcard matches.

A popular class of models used for sequence classification is the generative classifier family, such as profile Hidden Markov Models [4]. Generative models only learn from positive training examples, while discriminative techniques (such as SVM and those proposed in this paper) directly focus on separating the positive and negative training examples. Previous work has shown that discriminative approaches outperform generative approaches for sequence classification [2, 22, 17].

In this paper we propose learning linear classifiers directly in the explicit high dimensional feature space rather than using an implicit mapping via a string kernel as in kernel-SVM. The computational trick in our algorithm is to use coordinate descent coupled with bounding the search for the best coordinate. The idea of using branch-and-bound to efficiently search the feature space has been proposed for graph boosting [18]. Boosting approximately minimizes its l1-regularized loss criterion [32]. Our generic algorithm can be used for *exact* regularized fitting of a range of classification loss functions, such as exponential loss, binomial log-likelihood loss of logistic regression, gaussian loss and the squared hinge-loss of SVM [8]. This work is an extension of [14] which focused on (unregularized) logistic regression applied to text categorization. Here, we extend the bounds of [14] to a class of regularized loss functions, discuss the tightness of the proposed bounds and focus on the aspect of dense feature spaces characteristic of biological applications.

3. METHOD PROPOSED

In this section we present our generic learning algorithm and its concrete implementation for logistic regression and support vector machines.

3.1 Preliminaries and Basic Notation

We first introduce the theoretical framework and some basic notation. Assume we have a training set of instance-label pairs $\{x_i, y_i\}_{i=1}^N$, with $y_i \in \{-1, +1\}$. The training instances x_i are sequences, e.g., biological sequences $x_i = AGTCAACTGGAA....$, text sequences $x_i = ABCD...$, sequences of rankings $x_i = A < B < C < D < \ldots$, sequences of tasks $x_i = ABCD\ldots.$ Let d be the number of distinct subsequences in the feature space. We formally represent the training sequences as binary vectors in the space of all subsequences of the training set: $x_i = (x_{i1}, \ldots x_{ij}, \ldots x_{id})^T$, $x_{ij} \in \{0,1\}$, $i = \overline{1, N}$. Let $\beta = (\beta_1, \ldots, \beta_j, \ldots, \beta_d)$ be a parameter vector (defining a linear classifier).

The goal is to learn a mapping, also called classification model, $f : X \to \{-1, +1\}$ from the given training set such that given a new sample $x \in X$, we can predict a label $y \in \{-1, +1\}$.

Let

$$L(\beta) = \sum_{i=1}^{N} \xi(y_i, x_i, \beta) + CR_\alpha(\beta) \tag{1}$$

be the regularized classification loss criterion. Here, $\xi(y_i, x_i, \beta)$ is a classification loss function, C is a constant and $R_\alpha(\beta)$ is a regularizer. Learning a classification model is achieved by finding the parameter vector β that minimizes the regularized classification loss on the training set

$$\hat{\beta} = \text{argmin}_\beta L(\beta).$$

In Equations (2)–(5) we list a few examples of commonly used classification loss functions.

$$\textit{Exponential loss} : \xi(y_i, x_i, \beta) = e^{-y_i \beta^t x_i} \tag{2}$$

$$\textit{Binomial loglikelihood loss} : \xi(y_i, x_i, \beta) = \log(1 + e^{-y_i \beta^t x_i}) \tag{3}$$

$$\textit{Squared hinge loss} : \xi(y_i, x_i, \beta) = \max(1 - y_i \beta^t x_i, 0)^2 \tag{4}$$

$$\textit{Gaussian loss}^1 : \xi(y_i, x_i, \beta) = \log \frac{1}{\Phi(y_i \beta^t x_i)} \tag{5}$$

The penalty weight $C \geq 0$ controls the amount of regularization of the parameter vector β. A large C means more

[1] Φ is the cdf of the standard normal distribution.

penalty on the β parameters. The regularization term can take various forms, the most common being the $l1$ and the $l2$ (Equation (6)). In our work $R_\alpha(\beta)$ is the elastic-net regularizer [10, 6] (defined in Equation (7)), which is a compromise between the $l2$ ($\alpha = 0$) and the $l1$ ($\alpha = 1$).

$$l1 = \sum_{j=1}^{d} |\beta_j|, \qquad l2 = \frac{1}{2}\sum_{j=1}^{d} \beta_j^2 \tag{6}$$

$$R_\alpha(\beta) = \alpha \sum_{j=1}^{d} |\beta_j| + (1-\alpha)\frac{1}{2}\sum_{j=1}^{d} \beta_j^2 \tag{7}$$

Depending on the type of regularization, increasing the weight C of the penalty term results in many zero β_j (for $l1$-regularization) or shrinking the coefficients β_j of correlated predictors (for $l2$-regularization). The elastic-net regularizer allows balancing the two effects.

3.2 Gradient-Bounded Coordinate-Descent Algorithm

In this section we describe our learning algorithm and characterize the properties of loss functions to which it can be applied. Assume the following properties for the loss function:

1. ξ depends on y_i, x_i and β only through the classification margin $m_i = y_i\beta^t x_i$. Note that x_i is correctly classified if the margin m_i is positive and the higher the margin the higher the classification confidence. We write $\xi(y, x, \beta) = \xi(m)$.
2. ξ is a monotone decreasing function of the margin: $\xi'(m) \leq 0$.
3. ξ is convex and continuously differentiable.

Properties 1-2 are required for the bounding strategy (Theorem 1), while property 3 is required for the convergence result (Theorem 2). The gradient of $L(\beta)$ (defined in Equation (1)) with respect to a coordinate β_j is

$$\frac{\partial L}{\partial \beta_j}(\beta) = \sum_{i=1}^{N} y_i x_{ij} \xi'(y_i \beta^t x_i) + C[\alpha \operatorname{sign}(\beta_j) + (1-\alpha)\beta_j]$$

or using the margin notation

$$\frac{\partial L}{\partial \beta_j}(\beta) = \sum_{i=1}^{N} y_i x_{ij} \xi'(m_i) + C R'_\alpha(\beta_j).$$

If $R_\alpha(\beta)$ is not differentiable in $\beta = 0$ we use the left-right derivatives. We proceed minimizing $L(\beta)$ by coordinate-wise gradient descent in the feature space of all subsequences. In each iteration we update only the coordinate corresponding to the subsequence with the largest gradient magnitude, following the Gauss-Southwell rule [30]:

$$j = \operatorname{argmax}_l \left| \frac{\partial L}{\partial \beta_l}(\beta) \right|$$

This results in a greedy advance towards the optimum of the objective function, without having to explicitly generate the full space of subsequences. All we need is an efficient way to find the best coordinate (i.e., feature) in each iteration. We summarize the steps of our generic coordinate-descent algorithm in Algorithm 1. The core part of the algorithm

Algorithm 1 Generic coordinate-descent algorithm

1. Set $\beta^{(0)} = 0$
2. For t=1:T
   (a) Find $j_t = \operatorname{argmax}_j \left| \frac{\partial L}{\partial \beta_{j_t}}(\beta^{(t-1)}) \right|$ (using Theorem 1)
   (b) Use line search to set the step length ϵ_t for coordinate j_t
   (c) Set $\beta_{j_t}^{(t)} = \beta_{j_t}^{(t-1)} - \epsilon_t \frac{\partial L}{\partial \beta_{j_t}}(\beta^{(t-1)})$ and $\beta_k^{(t)} = \beta_k^{(t-1)}, k \neq j_t$

is a search routine (line 2(a) in Algorithm 1) that quickly returns the best feature in each iteration. The search procedure relies on bounding the gradient value of any subsequence early on, by only looking at its prefix. This looks difficult at first glance since the prefix may be a poor feature, while its extension can be highly discriminative. The intuition behind our bound is based on two observations: the gradient is determined by class-wise feature frequency and the subsequence space has structure (that we can exploit to bound the per-class frequency). More concretely, a feature has high gradient value if its frequent in one class and infrequent in the other. Per class, the frequency of a given feature is bounded by the frequency of its prefix. Thus, class-wise, we can bound the gradient of a given subsequence based on its prefix, and then build a global bound from the class-wise bounds. Using this bound we can discard large parts of the search space during the search for the best subsequence, making the whole search process efficient, both time-wise (fast running time) and space-wise (low memory). Once we found the best feature, we do an adapted Armijo rule line search [37, 12] to compute the feature weight and guarantee convergence.

Let j be a coordinate corresponding to a given subsequence s_j, and l be a coordinate corresponding to a super sequence of s_j, s_l, i.e. s_j is a prefix of s_l. We write $s_j \in x_i$ to denote $x_{ij} \neq 0$.

The following theorem gives a *tight* upper bound on the gradient value of any subsequence.

THEOREM 1. *For any loss function ξ satisfying properties 1-2 and any subsequence $s_l \supseteq s_j$, $j = 1, \ldots, d$,*

$$\left|\frac{\partial L}{\partial \beta_l}(\beta)\right| \leq \max \left\{ \left| \sum_{\{i | \mathbf{s_j} \in \mathbf{x_i}, y_i = +1\}} \xi'(m_i) + C R'_\alpha(\beta_l) \right|, \right. \tag{8}$$
$$\left. \left| \sum_{\{i | \mathbf{s_j} \in \mathbf{x_i}, y_i = -1\}} -\xi'(m_i) + C R'_\alpha(\beta_l) \right| \right\}.$$

PROOF. *We split the analysis in two parts, the first part focuses on deriving a bound within the negative class, and the second part focuses on the positive class. Recall that*

$\xi'(m) \le 0$. *Then,*

$$\begin{aligned}\frac{\partial L}{\partial \beta_l}(\beta) &= \sum_{\{i|s_l \in x_i\}} y_i x_{il} \xi'(m_i) + CR'_\alpha(\beta_l) \quad (9)\\ &\le \sum_{\{i|s_l \in x_i, y_i=-1\}} y_i x_{il} \xi'(m_i) + CR'_\alpha(\beta_l)\\ &\le \sum_{\{i|s_j \in x_i, y_i=-1\}} y_i x_{ij} \xi'(m_i) + CR'_\alpha(\beta_l)\\ &= \sum_{\{i|s_j \in x_i, y_i=-1\}} -\xi'(m_i) + CR'_\alpha(\beta_l)\end{aligned}$$

The last inequality in Equation (9) holds because of the anti-monotonicity property $\{i|s_l \in x_i, y_i = -1\} \subseteq \{i|s_j \in x_i, y_i = -1\}$. *Similarly, we can show for the positive class that*

$$\frac{\partial L}{\partial \beta_l}(\beta) \ge \sum_{\{i|s_j \in x_i, y_i=+1\}} \xi'(m_i) + CR'_\alpha(\beta_l)$$

Thus we obtain the lower and upper bounds

$$\begin{aligned}\sum_{\{i|s_j \in x_i, y_i=+1\}} \xi'(m_i) + CR'_\alpha(\beta_l) \le \frac{\partial L}{\partial \beta_l}(\beta) \quad (10)\\ \le \sum_{\{i|s_j \in x_i, y_i=-1\}} -\xi'(m_i) + CR'_\alpha(\beta_l).\end{aligned}$$

We are interested in an upper bound on the absolute magnitude of the gradient at a given coordinate, thus we write more conveniently

$$\left|\frac{\partial L}{\partial \beta_l}(\beta)\right| \le \max \left\{ \left| \sum_{\{i|s_j \in x_i, y_i=+1\}} \xi'(m_i) + CR'_\alpha(\beta_l) \right|, \left| \sum_{\{i|s_j \in x_i, y_i=-1\}} -\xi'(m_i) + CR'_\alpha(\beta_l) \right| \right\}.$$

□

The main property on which Theorem 1 relies on (last inequality in Equation (9)) is *anti-monotonicity*: the prefix frequency is higher than that of its extension subsequence. This means that the same bound holds for *any* weight x_j as long as $x_j \ge x_l$. This observation is useful for example if we want to integrate prior biological knowledge about the target problem, such as the fact that some amino acids in protein sequences are more useful than others. We could encode this information by giving weights $w_a \in (0,1)$ to individual amino acids and still have the property that $x_j = \Pi_a w_a \ge x_l$.

As we can observe from Equation (8), without explicit regularization of the loss function, the upper bound on the gradient of a subsequence s_l solely depends on the frequency of its prefix s_j. This means that we can decide not to expand the s_j prefix further, without inspecting the longer feature s_l. If we use a regularizer, we have the term β_l in the bound which depends on the longer subsequence, rather than the prefix alone. Thus, we have to take care to compute the correct bound whenever $\beta_l \ne 0$. Since at start all β_j are zero, during the iterations we only need to check those features that have non-zero β_l because they were selected in the model in previous iterations. In practice, as supported by our experiments, this part is fairly fast due to the sparsity of the final model learned by this algorithm.

The bound presented in Theorem 1 is tight since we can construct examples for which the inequality is an equality. Consider the simple case of a training set with positive examples of the type $AAAAAAA$, and negative examples of the type $BBBBBB$. Whenever the subsequence set of occurrences is the same as that of its prefix, the inequality becomes equality.

The iterates generated by Algorithm 1 converge to the optimal solution of the objective function given in Equation (1). Based on results from [37] characterizing the convergence of iterates generated by coordinate-descent using the Gauss-Southwell rule for l1-regularized convex minimization we have:

THEOREM 2. *Let* $\beta^{(t)}$ *be a sequence of iterates generated by Algorithm 1. Then* $\beta^{(t)}$ *converges to the optimal solution of (1).*

In the next subsections we describe the specific bounds used to design learning algorithms in the style of Algorithm 1 for logistic regression and support vector machines. We choose these popular classifiers for concrete implementations because their loss functions satisfy the properties 1-3 and they are margin maximizing [32]. The latter property typically translates into good generalization ability in practice.

3.3 Logistic Regression

Let

$$L(\beta) = \sum_{i=1}^{N} \log(1 + e^{-y_i \beta^t x_i}) + CR_\alpha(\beta)$$

be the elastic-net-regularized binomial log-likelihood loss [8]. The gradient of $L(\beta)$ with respect to a coordinate j at a given parameter vector β is:

$$\frac{\partial L}{\partial \beta_j}(\beta) = \sum_{i=1}^{N} y_i x_{ij} \underbrace{\left(\frac{-1}{1 + e^{y_i \beta^t x_i}}\right)}_{\xi'(m_i)} + CR'_\alpha(\beta_l)$$

COROLLARY 1. *For binomial log-likelihood loss and any subsequence* $s_l \supseteq s_j$, $j = 1, \ldots, d$,

$$\left|\frac{\partial L}{\partial \beta_l}(\beta)\right| \le \max \left\{ \left| \sum_{\{i|s_j \in x_i, y_i=+1\}} \frac{-1}{1 + e^{\beta^t x_i}} + CR'_\alpha(\beta_l) \right|, \left| \sum_{\{i|s_j \in x_i, y_i=-1\}} \frac{1}{1 + e^{-\beta^t x_i}} + CR'_\alpha(\beta_l) \right| \right\}.$$

3.4 Support Vector Machines

Let

$$L(\beta) = \sum_{i=1}^{N} \max(1 - y_i \beta^t x_i, 0)^2 + CR_\alpha(\beta)$$

be the elastic-net-regularized squared hinge loss [1]. We can rewrite $L(\beta)$ in the equivalent form

$$L(\beta) = \sum_{\{i|1 - y_i \beta^t x_i > 0\}} (1 - y_i \beta^t x_i)^2 + CR_\alpha(\beta)$$

The gradient of $L(\beta)$ with respect to a coordinate j at a given parameter vector β is:

$$\frac{\partial L}{\partial \beta_j}(\beta) = \sum_{\{i|1 - y_i \beta^t x_i > 0\}} y_i x_{ij} \underbrace{2(y_i \beta^t x_i - 1)}_{\xi'(m_i)} + CR'_\alpha(\beta_l)$$

COROLLARY 2. *For squared hinge loss and any subsequence $s_l \supseteq s_j$, $j = 1, \ldots, d$,*

$$\left|\frac{\partial L}{\partial \beta_l}(\beta)\right| \leq \max\left\{\left|\sum_{\{i|s_j \in x_i, 1-\beta^t x_i>0, y_i=+1\}} 2(\beta^t x_i - 1) + CR'_\alpha(\beta_l)\right|, \left|\sum_{\{i|s_j \in x_i, 1+\beta^t x_i>0, y_i=-1\}} 2(1 + \beta^t x_i) + CR'_\alpha(\beta_l)\right|\right\}.$$

3.5 Algorithmic Details

In this section we give some details on using the bound of Theorem 1 to prune the search space.

Before starting the optimization iterations we build an inverted index on all the distinct unigrams in the training set, i.e., a list of document ids and positions of occurrence for each unigram. In each iteration we start the process of searching for the best feature from the level of unigrams.

We implement two strategies of prefix-expansion. The breadth-first-search (BFS) expands all unigrams to bi-grams, then all bi-grams to tri-grams, etc. For each unigram, we compute the gradient value, we keep track of the best gradient/feature seen so far and we compare the bound to the current best gradient. If the bound is lower than the current best gradient value, no subsequence starting with this unigram can improve the current optimum and we prune this part of the search space (i.e., we discard this prefix). Then we move on to the next level of expansion, and repeat this process. The depth-first-search (DFS) strategy expands the unigram to its longest subsequence until the pruning condition is met, and it then backtracks to the longest valid prefix and re-attempts to expand. Depending on the sequence tokenization used, word-level or character-level, the two strategies have different benefits. For word-level tokenization, such as in text categorization, short subsequences are more likely to be useful than long ones (e.g., phrases of 2-3 words are typically good discriminators), and therefore BFS may be a better expansion strategy. For character-level tokenization, such as for biological sequences, longer subsequences tend to be more useful than shorter ones (e.g., subsequences of length 3 or less may occur in all the sequences), so DFS is a better expansion choice. For the experiments in this paper we have used DFS. In order to keep track of the occurrences of all active prefixes (e.g., subsequences that could not be pruned using Theorem 1), we expand the inverted index on-demand. The inverted index does not grow excessively due to the effectiveness of the bound. After selecting the feature with the best gradient in a given iteration, we do a line search to compute the final feature weight [12]. We stop the optimization iterations based on a threshold on the change of predicted scores [12].

The worst-case complexity of each iteration is $O(dN)$, where d is the number of features and N is the number of training samples. In practice, our algorithm drastically prunes the search space and is thus very fast. For example, for the classification task *Scorpion-toxin like* (presented in detail in Section 5) we have observed the following behaviour. There are 23 distinct unigrams in the training set (22 amino acids and we add the wildcard as an additional unigram). The longest sequence in the training set has length 892, and the average sequence lenght is ~ 50. Even if we were to restrict the maximum k-mer size to $k = 50$, the number of features d is $O(23^{50})$ (all the subsequences up to size $k = 50$ created using the 23 unigrams; in practice, there are 6.5 million such features in the training set). For finding the best feature in the first iteration using SVM loss and unrestricted k, our algorithm checks the pruning bound 1,113 times, and prunes the space 1,104 times (i.e., discards 1,104 prefixes out of the total 1,113 analysed). The algorithm stops in 3 seconds, after 77 iterations. In the last iteration, it checks the bound 14,077 times and prunes the space 13,952 times. Thus, the bound in Theorem 1 efficiently prunes the huge search space. For future work we will focus on quantitative measures of index growth as a function of the alphabet size and number of training examples.

For simplifying the implementation we currently prune the space using a prefix-expansion strategy. Theorem 1 however can be used for pruning all features that contain a given subsequence, not necessarily in the start position as a prefix. This observation could be used to further speed up the training process.

4. EXPERIMENTS

We implement the generic coordinate-descent algorithm in our machine learning tool SEQL (**SEQ**uence **L**earner), available from `http://www.daimi.au.dk/~ifrim/seql` (v2.0). For now, SEQL implements the two elastic-net-regularized classifiers presented in the previous section: logistic regression and support vector machines. In this section we describe the datasets, the techniques compared and the methodology for designing experiments.

4.1 Datasets

In order to compare our results to the state-of-the-art we compare directly to published results and perform experiments on the same benchmarks.

For **protein remote homology detection** we use the benchmark SCOP1.59 [22, 24, 38, 19]. This is an expert-curated database of protein domains organized heirarchically into folds, superfamilies and families. Protein sequences belonging to different families, but the same superfamily, are considered to be remote homologs in SCOP. This dataset contains 2,862 labeled sequences organized into 54 binary classification problems simulating homology detection by predicting the super-family using a hold-one-family-out strategy. No pair of sequences shares more than 95% identity. The positive training sets are quite small and the learning task is challenging. For more details on this benchmark see [15, 24, 38].

For **protein remote fold recognition** we use the benchmark published by [3]. This dataset consists of sequences from 27 folds divided into two independent sets such that the training and test sequences share less than 35% sequence identities and within the training set, no sequences share more than 40% sequence identities. There are 311 training sequences and 383 test sequences.

In order to analyze the **scalability** of our method in a large scale experiment, we have downloaded the latest **ribosomal RNA** (rRNA) database Silva-LSUParc[2] [31], version 102 (released in February 2010.) The LSUParc102 database contains 180,344 rRNA sequences. After removing duplicate sequences we obtain a dataset of 150,780 unique sequences organized in 3 (one-vs-all) binary classification tasks

[2]Silva-LSUParc database: http://www.arb-silva.de/documentation/background/release-102/.

according to the Bacteria, Archaea and Eukarya domains. The distribution by domain is dominated by Eukarya with 141,601 sequences, followed by Bacteria with 8,967 and Archaea with 212 sequences. All datasets are available from `http://www.daimi.au.dk/~ifrim/seql/data`.

4.2 Techniques Compared

Previous studies have shown that discriminative approaches for sequence classification (such as kernel-SVM) outperform generative approaches (such as profile HMM) by a large margin [2, 17, 22, 26].

We compare our algorithms to the latest sequence kernels for SVM: the spectrum kernel, the mismatch kernel [22, 24, 29], and the recent sparse spatial sample kernel (SSSK) [20, 19]. All these methods aim at computing similarity for all pairs of sequences (the kernel matrix) in a particular feature space. Due to computational challenges, these techniques typically restrict the length and expressive power of the subsequences used as features. For example, the spectrum-k kernel [23] implicitly compares sequences in the space of all k-mers, where the length k of subsequence-features is a parameter of the model. The mismatch kernel [22] generalizes the spectrum-k kernel by allowing up to m mismatches or substitutions to accomodate mutations. The sparse spatial sample kernel (SSSK) further generalizes the mismatch kernel by sampling the sequences at different resolutions and comparing the resulting spectra [19]. SSSK has 3 parameters, (k, t, d), where k is the probe size, t is the number of probes and d is the number of *maximum* allowed positions between the probes. Our learning algorithm SEQL uses all (unrestricted-length) subsequences in the training set as features. Furthermore, we also allow mismatches or so called wildcard matches, by a parameter that controls the *maximum* number of *consecutive* wildcards allowed. This allows us to model complex biological processes such as substitutions, insertions and deletions. Figure 1 gives examples of the types of features implicitly used by the above described kernels, as compared to the features used by our technique.

One advantage of kernel techniques is their ability to integrate unlabeled data during kernel computation to relax labeled data requirements [19]. However, computing all-pair similarities for large datasets (resulting from the addition of unlabeled sequences) remains computationally very challenging for kernel methods both time and memory-wise. For example, we couldn't apply any of the above mentioned kernel methods on our large dataset (150,000 sequences) since this would require more than 90GByte memory. In contrast, by exploiting the feature space structure, SEQL can use more expresive features and still be able to scale.

For completion we also report the results of a technique published by [26] which applies SVM using an empirical kernel map based on pairwise Smith-Waterman sequence alignment scores (SVM-pairwise in Table1).

We use SEQL-LR and SEQL-SVM to denote the logistic regression and support vector machines implementations of our generic learning algorithm.

4.3 Methodology

Previous studies on biological sequence classification have extensively used the AUC (area under the ROC curve) and AUC50 for evaluation [5, 24, 34]. AUC describes the ranking of prediction scores rather then being dependent on a fixed classification threshold. The ROC curve is obtained by plotting the fraction of true positives versus the fraction of false positives for a binary classifier as its discrimination threshold is varied [5]. A common aggregate measure is to report the area under the ROC curve (AUC) where an area of 1 represents a perfect ranking of all positives above all negatives and an area close to 0.5 represents a random classifier. The AUC50 focuses on top ranked examples and is defined as the normalized area under the ROC curve computed for up to 50 true negatives [34]. It is typically used to evaluate classifiers on datasets where the number of positives is much lower than the number of negatives. While for a complete test set the AUC is betwen 0.5 and 1, the AUC values for truncated top lists are between 0 and 1. The shorter the top list is, the smaller the AUC values [34]. In some studies instead of AUC or AUC50 only the balanced-error-rate (BER) is reported. To compare our results to the state-of-the-art, we also show the balanced-error (Equation (11)) which measures the average of the errors on each class for a fixed classification threshold. It can equivalently be interpreted in terms of Specificity and Sensitivity [25].

$$BER = \frac{1}{2}\left(\underbrace{\frac{FN}{TP+FN}}_{1-\text{Sensitivity}} + \underbrace{\frac{FP}{FP+TN}}_{1-\text{Specificity}}\right) \quad (11)$$

The benchmarks for remote homology detection and fold recognition have pre-defined training and test splits. We use the same data for experiments for all methods compared, and for the prior techniques *we report directly the results published in the original papers*. For the large scale experiment on ribosomal RNA, we show 5-fold cross-validation results on the full dataset. Since the prior techniques required more than the available memory, for the large dataset we only report results using our method.

All experiments were run on a Linux laptop with 2.5GByte memory and 2.8GHz Intel CPU.

5. RESULTS AND DISCUSSION

In this section we present the results of applying SEQL-LR and SEQL-SVM to protein remote homology detection and fold recognition. Furthermore, to evaluate the scalability of our approach, we present a large-scale experiment on the latest release of the Silva-LSUParc database [31].

5.1 Comparison to State-of-the-Art

We first compare the performance of SEQL-LR and SEQL-SVM to that of kernel-SVM techniques on two protein classification tasks.

5.1.1 Protein remote homology detection

In Table 1 we show results on the SCOP1.59 benchmark for all compared methods. The numbers in brackets next to the name of each method refer to their explicit parameters as discussed in the previous section (e.g., length k of subsequences used as features or maximum number of wildcards). The results are averaged over all 54 binary classification tasks which correspond to superfamilies.

For SEQL-LR and SEQL-SVM we do grid search to set d (the maximum allowed number of consecutive wildcards, $d \in \{0, 1, 2, .., 5\}$), and the regularization parameters C and α of the elastic-net penalty ($C \in \{0, 0.001, 0.01, .., 100\}$, $\alpha \in \{0, 0.1, 0.2, .., 1\}$). We show the most accurate results across

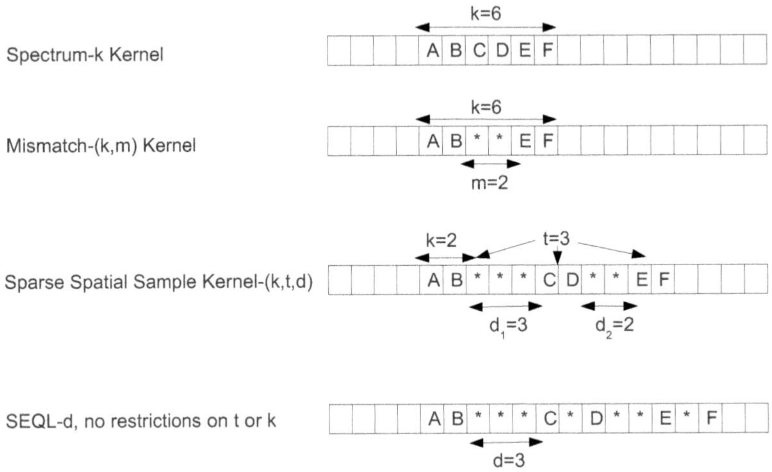

Figure 1: Features employed by state-of-the-art kernels versus our method SEQL. Spectrum-k Kernel, k is the length of features. Mismatch-(k,m) Kernel, k is the length of features, m is the maximum number of mismatches. Sparse Spatial Sample-(k,t,d) Kernel, k is the probe size, t is the number of probes and d is the number of maximum allowed positions between the probes. SEQL-d, d is the maximum number of consecutive wildcards.

Method	AUC	AUC50	BER
SVM-SPECTRUM(2)	0.8581	0.3583	-
SVM-SPECTRUM(3)	0.8723	0.4037	-
SVM-MISMATCH(5,1)	0.8749	0.4167	-
SVM-SSSK(1,2,5)	0.8901	0.4629	-
SVM-SSSK(1,3,3)	0.9148	0.5118	-
SVM-pairwise	0.8930	0.4340	-
SEQL-LR(5)	**0.9155**	**0.5184**	**0.4477**
SEQL-SVM(5)	**0.9220**	**0.5237**	**0.4158**

Table 1: Remote homology detection on the Scop1.59 dataset. The average AUC, AUC50 and BER scores over the 54 target superfamilies. Results for kernel-SVM methods cited directly from [24, 19]. SEQL-LR and SEQL-SVM are the methods proposed in this paper.

the parameter values tried. We observe that our techniques are comparable to the state-of-the-art methods regarding classification quality. We believe it is important to allow flexible features, (e.g., allowing wildcards and not restricting the feature lenght in advance), although here the training sets are quite small and the gain is not large. We note that SEQL-SVM has slightly better AUC and AUC50 than SEQL-LR. Learning SEQL classifiers on this dataset took a few seconds per topic and about 80MByte memory. The computational requirements of SEQL are mainly influenced by the maximum allowed number of consecutive wildcards.

Figure 2 shows a graphic comparison of some of the methods (for which we had access to published per class AUC50 scores) by plotting the total number of superfamilies above an AUC50 score threshold, as a function of the threshold value. The threshold is changed so as to generate the next AUC50 value in the ranked list of AUC50 scores of the respective method. The numerical integral of this cumulative

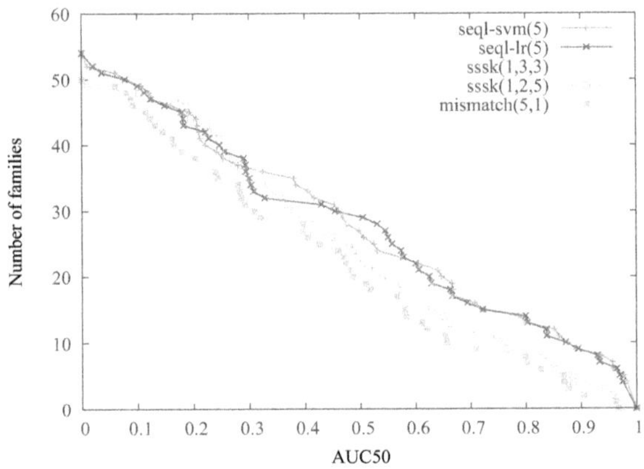

Figure 2: Comparison of mismatch-SVM, SSSK-SVM, SEQL-LR and SEQL-SVM on SCOP1.59. The total number of superfamilies for which a given method exceeds an AUC50 score threshold.

AUC50 curve is the arithmetic average of the AUC50 values shown in Table 1 [34]. SVM with sparse-sample-spatial kernel (SSSK-SVM) behaves best among the prior techniques. Even though the features employed by SSSK-SVM are quite flexible (see Figure 1), we observe we can gain some performance by imposing less restrictions on features.

[19] analyzed the biological relevance of features learned by SSSK-SVM taking the *Scorpion toxin-like* superfamily as an example. This classification task has 16 members of this superfamily as positive training examples, 1067 non-members as negative examples and the *short-chain scorpion toxin* family as a test case. SSSK-SVM(1,2,5) achieved an AUC50 of 0.7661 for this task [19]. In their work [19] present the schematic representation of the *short-chain scorpion toxin*

family obtained from PROSITE [11]. The PROSITE database consists of a large collection of manually-curated biologically meaningful signatures that are described as patterns or profiles [11]. In Figure 3 we show the PROSITE representation. The scheme shows that these type of toxins contain six

```
       +---------------------+
       |                     |
       |     xxxxxxxxxxxxxxxxxxxxxxx
*******C*****C***C***********C****C*C***
             |   |                | |
             |   +----------------|-+
             +--------------------+

'C': conserved cysteine involved in a disulfide bond.
'x': position of the consensus pattern
```

Figure 3: Schematic representation of the *short-chain scorpion toxins* family from PROSITE.

conserved cysteines (C) residues involved in disulfide bonds. PROSITE also lists a consensus pattern present in all the members of this family shown as well in Figure 3 (marked with 'X'). We focus here on the same superfamily and look at the features learned by SEQL-SVM(5). In Table 2 we show

Positive Features	
Weight	Feature
0.0460	SG*C
0.0450	N**C***C
0.0415	C*C**L
0.0410	C***C***G
0.0340	C*C
0.0329	G**G*C
0.0326	C*****C***C
0.0308	GYC
0.0308	C***C
0.0307	G***G*C

Negative Features	
Weight	Feature
-0.0329	G
-0.0313	A
-0.0292	S
-0.0541	Q
-0.0502	E
-0.0462	A*****K
-0.0217	K
-0.0216	CP
-0.0206	C**G
-0.0205	C**C

Table 2: Top-10 positive and negative SEQL-SVM features on the SCOP.1.59 Scorpion-toxin-like superfamily.

the top-10 positive and top-10 negative features selected by SEQL-SVM on this superfamily.

SEQL-SVM(5) has an AUC50 of 0.9573 on this task. [19] analyzed the support vectors of their method and observed that the feature C***C had the highest weight. Similarly, SEQL-SVM(5) selects the feature C***C in top-10, but ranks features such as SG*C and N**C***C higher. In order to understand the effect of these features on the AUC50 score, we took a closer look at the quality of some of the selected features. We observed that although C***C occurs in all positive examples, it is also present in many negatives and is thus less useful than SG*C, which occurs in most positive examples, but in very few negative examples.

5.1.2 *Protein remote fold recognition*

In this section we show an application of SEQL-LR and SEQL-SVM to protein remote fold recognition on the dataset published by [3]. They proposed a technique based on building an SVM classifier using features deemed biologically relevant for this problem, such as percentage composition of the 20 amino acids, predicted secondary structure, polarity. In Table 3 we show results comparing the technique of [3], denoted by SVM(D&D), with published results of kernel-SVM methods and with our SEQL-LR and SEQL-SVM algorithms. Recall that lower BER means better classification quality.

Method	AUC	AUC50	BER
SVM (D&D)	-	-	0.5650
SVM-MISMATCH(5,1)	-	-	0.5322
SVM-SSSK(1,2,5)	-	-	0.4619
SVM-SSSK(1,3.3)	-	-	0.4499
SEQL-LR(5)	**0.7882**	**0.3551**	**0.4412**
SEQL-SVM(5)	**0.7982**	**0.3742**	**0.4222**

Table 3: Remote fold recognition on the D&D dataset. The average AUC, AUC50 and BER over the 27 target folds. Results for SVM(D&D) and other kernel-SVM methods cited from [3, 19].

Even if we don't use any domain-specific knowledge in this experiment, we observe that our techniques have better classification quality than the method of [3] which relies on deep biological insight. We believe this advantage results from having feature selection as a part of the learning algorithm and allowing for a large degree of flexibility in the features. SEQL-LR and SEQL-SVM outperform the state-of-the-art techniques in terms of balanced-error-rate on this benchmark.

5.2 Large-Scale Experiment

In this section we analyze the scalability of our method on a ribosomal RNA (rRNA) domain-prediction task.

5.2.1 *Ribosomal RNA Domain-Prediction*

The dataset used for this task contains 150,780 unique rRNA sequences. It is estimated that based on the new capacity for cheap and rapid sequencing there is a steady flow of about 10,000 rRNA sequences per month into the public sequence databases [31]. Furthermore, many sequences are derived from cultivation independent biodiversity surveys, which rely on rapid pattern- or clone-based approaches that often generate partial rRNA sequences [31] (problematic for sequence alignment).

We show the average results of SEQL-LR and SEQL-SVM over 5-fold cross-validation splits for fixed parameter values. We set the amount of regularization $C = 1.0$, we balance $l1$ and $l2$ regularization by setting $\alpha = 0.5$ and allow no wildcards by setting the maximum number of consecutive wildcards $d = 0$.

In Table 4 we show classification quality, training time and memory resources required by SEQL-LR and SEQL-SVM. We

Method	AUC	AUC50	BER	Time	Memory
SEQL-LR	0.9992	0.9745	0.0095	30 min	2GByte
SEQL-SVM	0.9986	0.9744	0.0118	25 min	2GByte

Table 4: Ribosomal RNA domain-prediction on Silva-LSUParc102.

note that both SEQL-based techniques have high classification quality. Additionally, they only take about half-an-hour running-time and a reasonable 2GByte memory instead of 90GByte required by a kernel matrix computation. Instead of building sequence classifiers by costly multiple sequence alignment as currently done for sequence retrieval in this database, we could directly learn domain SEQL-classifiers from the original input sequences in the respective domains.

6. CONCLUSION

In this paper we present a new learning algorithm for sequence classification in high dimensional predictor space. Our framework has at its core a gradient-bounded coordinate-descent strategy to quickly retrieve high quality features. The generic learning algorithm works with a wide range of loss functions, including that of logistic regression and support vector machines. When applied to protein remote homology detection and fold recognition, as well as large-scale domain-prediction for ribosomal RNA, our techniques are comparable to the state-of-the-art in terms of classification quality. In addition, the techniques presented are highly scalable and the resulting classification models can easily be interpreted and connected to biologically relevant facts. Furthermore, the same gradient-bounding strategy can be used for tackling sequence regression [13]. Finally, our algorithm can be applied to more complex structured data such as trees and graphs which follow the anti-monotonicity property required by our theoretical framework. We plan to investigate these research directions in our future work.

7. ACKNOWLEDGMENTS

This work was supported by the Danish Cancer Society and Science Foundation Ireland Grant 10/IN.1/I303.

8. REFERENCES

[1] K.-W. Chang, C.-J. Hsieh, and C.-J. Lin. Coordinate descent method for large-scale l2-loss linear support vector machines. *J. Mach. Learn. Res.*, 9:1369–1398, 2008.

[2] J. Cheng and P. Baldi. A machine learning information retrieval approach to protein fold recognition. *Bioinformatics*, 22(12):1456–1463, 2006.

[3] C. H. Ding and I. Dubchak. Multi-class protein fold recognition using support vector machines and neural networks . *Bioinformatics*, 17(4):349–358, 2001.

[4] S. R. Eddy. Profile hidden markov models. *Bioinformatics*, 14(9):755–763, 1998.

[5] T. Fawcett. Roc graphs: Notes and practical considerations for researchers, 2004.

[6] J. H. Friedman, T. Hastie, and R. Tibshirani. Regularization paths for generalized linear models via coordinate descent. *Journal of Stat. Soft.*, 33(1):1–22, 2010.

[7] A. Genkin, D. Lewis, , and D. Madigan. Large-scale bayesian logistic regression for text categorization. *Technometrics*, 49(3):291–304, 2007.

[8] T. Hastie, R. Tibshirani, and J. Friedman. *The Elements of Statistical Learning.* Springer Series in Statistics, 2003.

[9] C.-J. Hsieh, K.-W. Chang, C.-J. Lin, S. S. Keerthi, and S. Sundararajan. A dual coordinate descent method for large-scale linear SVM. In *ICML*, 2008.

[10] Z. Hui and T. Hastie. Regularization and variable selection via the elastic net. *Journal of the Royal Stat. Soc. Series*, 67(2):301–320, 2005.

[11] N. Hulo, A. Bairoch, V. Bulliard, L. Cerutti, E. De Castro, P. S. Langendijk-Genevaux, M. Pagni, and C. J. A. Sigrist. The prosite database. *Nucl. Acids Res.*, 34(1):227–230, 2006.

[12] G. Ifrim. *Statistical Learning Techniques for Text Categorization with Sparse Labeled Data.* PhD thesis, Universität des Saarlandes, 2009.

[13] G. Ifrim. Gradient-bounded coordinate-descent for sequence regression. www.4c.ucc.ie/ ifrim/seql/data, 2010.

[14] G. Ifrim, G. Bakir, and G. Weikum. Fast logistic regression for text categorization with variable-length n-grams. In *KDD*, pages 354–362, USA, 2008.

[15] T. Jaakkola, M. Diekhans, and D. Haussler. Using the fisher kernel method to detect remote protein homologies. In *ICISMB*, pages 149–158. AAAI Press, 1999.

[16] T. Joachims. Training linear SVMs in linear time. In *KDD*, pages 217–226, USA, 2006. ACM Press.

[17] R. Kuang, E. Ie, K. Wang, K. Wang, M. Siddiqi, Y. Freund, and C. Leslie. Profile-based string kernels for remote homology detection and motif extraction. In *CSBC*, pages 152–160, USA, 2004. IEEE Computer Society.

[18] T. Kudo, E. Maeda and Y. Matsumoto. An Application of Boosting to Graph Classification. In *NIPS*, 2004.

[19] P. Kuksa, P. H. Huang, and V. Pavlovic. A fast, semi-supervised learning method for protein sequence classification. In *International Workshop on Data Mining in Bioinformatics*, pages 29–37, 2008.

[20] P. Kuksa, P. H. Huang, and V. Pavlovic. Scalable algorithms for string kernels with inexact matching. In *NIPS*, 2008.

[21] C. Leslie, E. Eskin, A. Cohen, J. Weston, and W. S. Noble. Mismatch string kernels for discriminative protein classification. *Bioinformatics*, 20(4):467–476, 2004.

[22] C. Leslie, E. Eskin, and W. Noble. Mismatch string kernels for svm protein classification. In *NIPS*, 2002.

[23] C. Leslie, E. Eskin, and W. Noble. The spectrum kernel: a string kernel for svm protein classification. In *Pacific Biocomputing Symposium*, pages 564–575, 2002.

[24] C. Leslie and R. Kuang. Fast string kernels using inexact matching for protein sequences. *J. Mach. Learn. Res.*, 5:1435–1455, 2004.

[25] I. Levner, V. Bulitko, and G. Lin. Feature extraction for classification of proteomic mass spectra: A comparative study. *Studies in Fuzziness and Soft Computing*, 207:607–624, 2006.

[26] L. Liao and W. S. Noble. Combining pairwise sequence similarity and support vector machines for remote protein homology detection. In *ICCB*, pages 225–232, USA, 2002.

[27] C.-J. Lin, R. C. Weng, and S. S. Keerthi. Trust region Newton method for large-scale logistic regression. *J. Mach. Learn. Res.*, 9:627–650, 2008.

[28] J. Liu, J. Chen, and J. Ye. Large-scale sparse logistic regression. In *KDD*, pages 547–556, USA, 2009.

[29] H. Lodhi, C. Saunders, J. Shawe-Taylor, N. Cristianini, and C. Watkins. Text classification using string kernels. *J. Mach. Learn. Res.*, 2:419–444, 2002.

[30] D. Luenberger. *Linear and Nonlinear Programming.* Addison-Wesley Publishing Co.: Reading Mass, 1984.

[31] E. Pruesse, C. Quast, K. Knittel, B. M. Fuchs, W. Ludwig, J. Peplies, and F. O. Glockner. SILVA: a comprehensive online resource for quality checked and aligned ribosomal RNA sequence data compatible with ARB. *Nucl. Acids Res.*, 35(21):7188–7196, 2007.

[32] S. Rosset, J. Zhu, and T. Hastie. Boosting as a regularized path to a maximum margin classifier. *J. Mach. Learn. Res.*, 5:941–973, 2004.

[33] Q. Shi, J. Petterson, G. Dror, J. Langford, A. Smola, and S. Vishwanathan. Hash kernels for structured data. *J. Mach. Learn. Res.*, 10:2615–2637, 2009.

[34] P. Sonego, A. Kocsor, and S. Pongor. ROC analysis: applications to the classification of biological sequences and 3D structures. *Brief. in Bioinf.*, 9(3):198–209, 2008.

[35] S. Sonnenburg and V. Franc. Coffin : A computational framework for linear svms. In *ICML*, 2010.

[36] S. Sonnenburg, G. Rätsch, S. Henschel, C. Widmer, J. Behr, A. Zien, F. de Bona, A. Binder, C. Gehl, and V. Franc. The SHOGUN machine learning toolbox. *J. Mach. Learn. Res.*, 11:1799–1802, 2010.

[37] P. Tseng and S. Yun. A coordinate gradient descent method for nonsmooth separable minimization. *Mathematical Programming*, 117:387–423, 2009.

[38] J. Weston, C. Leslie, E. Ie, D. Zhou, A. Elisseeff, and W. S. Noble. Semi-supervised protein classification using cluster kernels. *Bioinformatics*, 21(15):3241–3247, 2005.

Multi-Source Domain Adaptation and Its Application to Early Detection of Fatigue

Rita Chattopadhyay [1], Jieping Ye [1,2], Sethuraman Panchanathan [1], Wei Fan [3], Ian Davidson [4]
[1]Computer Science and Engineering, Arizona State University, AZ 85287
[2]Center for Evolutionary Medicine and Informatics, The Biodesign Institute, Arizona State University, AZ 85287
[3]IBM T.J.Watson Research, Hawthorne, NY 10532
[4]Department of Computer Science, University of California, Davis, CA 95616

ABSTRACT

We consider the characterization of muscle fatigue through noninvasive sensing mechanism such as surface electromyography (SEMG). While changes in the properties of SEMG signals with respect to muscle fatigue have been reported in the literature, the large variation in these signals across different individuals makes the task of modeling and classification of SEMG signals challenging. Indeed, the variation in SEMG parameters from subject to subject creates differences in the data distribution. In this paper, we propose a transfer learning framework based on the multi-source domain adaptation methodology for detecting different stages of fatigue using SEMG signals, that addresses the distribution differences. In the proposed framework, the SEMG data of a subject represent a domain; data from multiple subjects in the training set form the multiple source domains and the test subject data form the target domain. SEMG signals are predominantly different in conditional probability distribution across subjects. The key feature of the proposed framework is a novel weighting scheme that addresses the conditional probability distribution differences across multiple domains (subjects). We have validated the proposed framework on Surface Electromyogram signals collected from 8 people during a fatigue-causing repetitive gripping activity. Comprehensive experiments on the SEMG data set demonstrate that the proposed method improves the classification accuracy by 20% to 30% over the cases without any domain adaptation method and by 13% to 30% over the existing state-of-the-art domain adaptation methods.

Categories and Subject Descriptors

H.2.8 [**Database Management**]: Database Applications - Data Mining

General Terms

Algorithm

Keywords

Multi-source domain adaption, transfer learning, surface electromyogram, subject based variability

1. INTRODUCTION

Daily life activities such as typing on the keyboard, dusting, brooming, ironing, as well as the use of hand tools such as scissors and knives, repetitive work in assembly lines, repetitive lifting, involve repetitive movements of the different parts of the body. It has been proved that repetitive task makes work particularly hazardous, as it is the primary cause of muscle fatigue [28, 13, 30]. According to the US Bureau of Labor Statistics, in 2002, there were more than 345,000 on the job back injuries, due to muscle fatigue, which required time off from work. According to the Bureau of Labor Statistics (2004), annual direct cost of occupational injuries due to slip and fall caused due to muscle fatigue is expected to exceed $43.8 billion by the year 2020 in the US.

These accidents and the consequential loss in work hours and lifes, besides the high medical cost, can be avoided if one can intervene such fatigue inducing repetitive activities at an early stage by intelligent devices having the capability for detecting different stages of fatigue. Technologies for detecting muscle fatigue at an early stage can also be used to remove the cause of fatigue by altering the environmental ergonomics where possible [1].

There are a number of techniques that can be used to objectively determine the level of fatigue in a subject. Electromyography (EMG) is a method for biosignal recording of skeletal muscle activity. Surface Electromyography (SEMG) allows for noninvasive recording of these biosignals. Researchers have observed that certain aspects of SEMG signals change as a muscle becomes fatigued. Localized muscle fatigue has been correlated with a shift in the power spectral density of SEMG signals, root mean square (rms), instantaneous frequency, zero crossing rate, mean-frequency, median-frequency, etc. However, there is a large variation in the values of these measures across different subjects, due to variances in their SEMG power spectrum and their shifts. These generally unpredictable and wide variations make the task of modeling SEMG difficult, and the task of automating the process of signal classification as a generalized tool challenging. The variation in SEMG parameters from subject to subject creates differences in the data distribution. Figure 1 shows the distribution of the data over four stages of a fatigue-causing activity, done with varying speed, for three different subjects (subjects 1, 2, 4). The data distribution shown in Figure 1 is of factor scores obtained as a

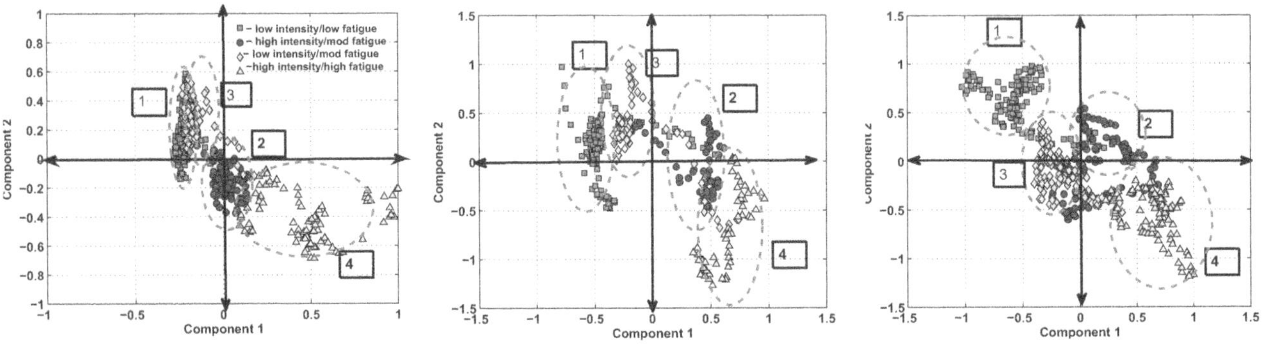

(a) Subject 1 (b) Subject 2 (c) Subject 4

Figure 1: Three sample subjects (subjects 1, 2, 4) with four classes (four physiological stages) in our SEMG data set: SEMG signals are predominantly different in conditional probability distribution across subjects.

result of factor analysis [2] applied on the twelve dimensional feature vectors derived from raw SEMG signals[1]. The four physiological stages corresponding to four classes, shown in the figure, are (1) *low intensity of activity and low fatigue*, (2) *high intensity of activity and moderate fatigue*, (3) *low intensity of activity and moderate fatigue* and (4) *high intensity of activity and high fatigue*. We observe that the data distribution during each stage or class varies from subject to subject. This variation leads to predominantly conditional probability differences across subjects.

Traditional data mining algorithms assume that training data and test data are drawn from the same distribution, and they may not be effective if the assumption is violated as in the case of SEMG data over multiple subjects. One effective approach is domain adaptation which enables transfer of knowledge between the source and target domains [22]. It has been applied successfully in various applications [6, 11, 10, 20] including text classification (parts of speech tagging, webpage tagging, etc), video concept detection across different TV channels, sentiment analysis (identifying positive and negative reviews across domains), WiFi Localization (locating device location depending upon the signal strengths from various access points.

In this paper we present a successful case study of application of multi-source domain adaptation techniques for detecting different stages of fatigue based on the Surface Electromyogram signals across multiple subjects. The proposed framework addresses the subject based variability, predominantly the distribution differences in conditional probabilities in Surface Electromyogram signals. Specifically, a classifier is learnt to distinguish the four classes as shown in Figure 1 on the basis of some labeled and unlabeled data from the target domain (or subject). The unlabeled data are labeled using a weighting scheme that measures the similarities in conditional probabilities between the source and target domain data; the key of the proposed weighting scheme is a joint optimization framework based on smoothness assumption on the probability distribution of the target domain data. To the best of our knowledge, this is the first systematic analysis of subject based variability in SEMG signals. We have applied the proposed algorithm to Surface Electromyogram signals collected from 8 people during a fatigue-causing repetitive gripping activity. Our extensive experiments on the SEMG data set demonstrate that the proposed method improves the subject independent classification accuracy by 20% to 30% over the cases without any domain adaptation method and by 13% to 30% over the existing state-of-the-art domain adaptation methods.

[1]More details on the twelve features derived, the factor analysis results and a real time deployment of fatigue grading framework can be found in our earlier papers [8, 9].

2. PROPOSED FRAMEWORK

The proposed domain adaptation framework focuses on learning from multiple auxiliary sources related to the target data, e.g., multiple subject data having different distributions, collected under similar physiological conditions. Specifically, we consider the problem of detecting different stages of fatigue in a subject for whom we have very few labeled samples available in the training data. The training data also includes data from many other subjects collected under similar physiological conditions. The test subject data forms target domain data and the multiple subject data in the training domain form multiple auxiliary sources.

2.1 Problem Setting and Motivation

Assume that there are k subjects in the source domain. The s-th subject in the source domain is characterized by a sample set $D^s = (x_i^s, y_i^s)|_{i=1}^{n_s}$, where x_i^s is the feature vector, y_i^s is the corresponding label, and n_s is the total number of samples for the subject s. The target domain consists of a few labeled data $D_l^T = (x_i^T, y_i^T)|_{i=1}^{n_l}$ and plenty of unlabeled data $D_u^T = x_i^T|_{i=n_l+1}^{n_l+n_u}$ where n_l and n_u are numbers of labeled and unlabeled target domain samples respectively, $D^T = D_l^T \bigcup D_u^T$, and $n_T = n_l + n_u$. The goal is to develop a target classifier f^T that can predict the labels of the unlabeled data in the target domain, using the multi-source domain data and a few labeled target domain data.

One simple approach for predicting the labels of the target domain data is to combine the training samples from all subjects and build a single classifier based on the pooled training samples. However, this simple approach will not work well in our application as there are significant conditional probability differences across subjects in the SEMG data. A better alternative is to learn individual models for each subject in the source domain, and then combine the hypothesis generated by each of these source models, on the basis of some similarity measures between the source and target domains. The similarity measures are commonly computed by considering each source domain data separately. This procedure has two potential limitations. First, it minimizes the loss with respect to the probability distribution $P_s(x, y|D^s)$ on the source domain which will not generally coincide with the minimal loss on the distribution $P_T(x, y|D^T)$ on the target domain. Second, it assumes all sources are independent when computing the similarity measures, thus it does not fully exploit the interaction among multiple sources.

Thus one of the important issues is to choose the right similarity measure between the source and target domains depending upon the nature of differences in the distribution. There are predominantly conditional probability differences in our multi-subject SEMG data as shown in Figure 1. In addition, we observe from the figure that different classes vary differently over subjects. For example, subjects 1 and 2 have similar data distributions of classes 1 and 3, and subjects 1 and 4 have similar data distributions of class 4. Hence computing a single similarity measure for an auxiliary source with respect to target data does not capture the differences at the class level. The proposed approach presented below addresses all these challenges.

2.2 Proposed Approach

We learn a classifier f^T for the target domain data, using a few labeled samples and a large number of unlabeled samples from the target domain. The key of our proposed approach is a novel weighting scheme that integrates multiple source domain data using a set of weights, one for each source domain. We use these weights to compute the labels of the unlabeled target domain data, called "pseudo labels". The target domain prediction model is then learnt from both labeled and pseudo labeled target domain samples in a regularized framework. Specifically, the proposed multi-source domain adaptation framework is given as follows:

$$\min_{f^T \in H_K} \gamma_A \|f^T\|_K^2 + \frac{1}{n_l} \sum_{i=1}^{n_l} V(x_i, y_i, f^T) + \Omega_r(f_u^T) + \Omega_m(f^T) \quad (1)$$

The first term controls the complexity of the classifier f^T in the Reproducing Kernel Hilbert Space (RKHS) H_K, γ_A controls the penalty factor, the second term is the empirical error of the target classifier f^T on the few labeled target domain data D_l^T, and n_l is the number of labeled target domain data. The empirical error on the unlabeled target data, labeled using a conditional probability based weighting scheme, forms the third term. This regularizer enforces the target classifier f^T to have similar decision values to the auxiliary source which has similar conditional probability distribution, explained in detail in Subsection 2.3. The fourth term is a manifold based regularizer based on the smoothness assumption [4] on target domain data: if two points x_i and x_j are close to each other in the intrinsic geometry of marginal distribution then they are most likely to have similar conditional probabilities, i.e., $f^T(x_i)$ should be similar to $f^T(x_j)$. The *manifold based regularizer* is defined as in [4]:

$$\Omega_m(f^T) = \frac{\gamma_I}{n_T^2} f^{T'} L f^T. \quad (2)$$

where L is the graph Laplacian matrix constructed on D^T, $f^T = [f^T(x_1), \cdots, f^T(x_{n_T})]$, γ_I controls the complexity of the function f^T in the intrinsic geometry of the marginal probability of x and the normalizing coefficient $\frac{1}{n_T^2}$ is the natural scale factor for the empirical estimate of the Laplace operator, and the symbol $'$ is used to represent the matrix or vector *transpose* operation.

2.3 Multi-Source Weighting

Let $f_u^T = [f_{n_l+1}^T \cdots f_{n_T}^T]'$ be the decision values of the target classifier f^T for the unlabeled target domain data and let $f_u^s = [f_{n_l+1}^s \cdots f_{n_T}^s]'$ be the decision values of the s-th auxiliary classifier for the same unlabeled target domain data. Let γ_s be the measure of relevance or similarity between the distributions of the s-th source and the target data, and let $f_j^T = f^T(x_j)$ be the decision value of target classifier on the target domain data x_j and $f_j^s = f^s(x_j)$ be the decision value of the s-th auxiliary source classifier on x_j. We use a weighted combination of the k source domain classifiers f^s to estimate the target classifier. Specifically, the estimated label $(\hat{y}_j)$ of the unlabeled target data x_j based on the k source domain classifiers f^s is given by

$$\hat{y}_j = \sum_{s=1}^{k} \gamma_s f_j^s, \quad (3)$$

where $\gamma_s > 0$ is the weight for the s-th source. We assume that the weights are normalized, that is, $\sum_s \gamma_s = 1$. The auxiliary classifier f^s for the s-th source is pre-computed based on its respective data. The auxiliary classifiers f^s and the target classifier f^T can be trained using different kernels or even different learning methods. The resulting regularizer, $\Omega_r(f_u^T)$, named as *relevance based regularizer* measures the difference between the target classifier decision value and the estimation based on multiple source data, and is defined as follows:

$$\Omega_r(f_u^T) = \frac{\theta}{2} \sum_{j=n_l+1}^{n_T} \|f_j^T - \sum_{s=1}^{k} \gamma_s f_j^s\|^2, \quad (4)$$

where $\theta > 0$ is a constant.

The weight γ_s which provides a measure of relevance between the s-th auxiliary source domain and the target domain is computed on the basis of a *Conditional Probability based Weighting Scheme*, which evaluates the similarities in distributions between the source and target domains predominantly based on conditional probability differences.

Next, we show how to estimate the weights γ_s's. The proposed weighting scheme evaluates the similarities between auxiliary source data and the target domain data considering the similarities in their conditional probabilities.

Let $F_i^S = [f_i^1 \cdots f_i^k]$ be the $1 \times k$ vector of predicted labels of k auxiliary source models for the i-th sample of target domain data. Let $\gamma = [\gamma_1 \cdots \gamma_k]^T$ be the $k \times 1$ weight vector, where γ_s is the weight corresponding to the s-th auxiliary source. Following (3), the predicted label for the i-th sample of target domain data is

$$\hat{y}_i = \sum_{s=1}^{k} \gamma_s f_i^s = F_i^S \gamma. \quad (5)$$

This motivates us to estimate the weight vector γ based on the smoothness assumption on the conditional probability distribution: we compute the optimal weight vector γ by minimizing the difference in predicted labels between two nearby points in the target domain. Specifically, the proposed weighting framework solves the following problem:

$$\min_{\gamma:\gamma' e=1,\gamma\geq 0} \sum_{i,j=n_l+1}^{n_l+n_u} (F_i^S\gamma - F_j^S\gamma)^2 W_{ij} \tag{6}$$

where $F_i^S\gamma$ and $F_j^S\gamma$ are the predicted labels for i-th and j-th samples of target domain data and W_{ij} is the edge weight between the two samples. We can rewrite the minimization problem as follows:

$$\min_{\gamma:\gamma' e=1,\gamma\geq 0} \gamma' \left(F^S\right)' L_u F^S \gamma \tag{7}$$

where F^S is an $n_u \times k$ matrix with each row of F^S being the $1 \times k$ vector of k predicted labels for a sample of target domain data and L_u is graph Laplacian associated with the target domain data D_u^T, given by $L_u = D - W$, where W is the adjacency graph defining edge weights between the samples in the target domain data, and D is the diagonal matrix given by $D_{ii} = \sum_{j=1}^{n} W_{ij}$.

The minimization problem in (7) is a standard quadratic problem and can be solved by applying many existing solvers. We simply use the 'quadprog' function in MATLAB. With the computed weights, the labels for the unlabeled target domain data, called *psuedo labels*, are computed using (3), and are substituted into the regulariser in (4).

Intuitively, by enforcing that nearby points in the marginal distribution of the target data have similar class labels (or conditional probability) via the optimization in (7), the proposed weighting scheme is likely to give higher weights to those sources with the conditional probability distribution similar to the target data. This is verified in our empirical study on both SEMG and synthetic data. If a source has a conflicting conditional distribution as the target, it is likely to get a low or even zero weight. In addition, different from many existing weight schemes which compute the weights by considering each source independently, the proposed weighting scheme computes the optimal value of γ or the optimal weights of all the k sources simultaneously, thus taking the potential interaction among multiple subjects in the source domain into account.

2.4 Proposed Algorithm

Using the least square error and substituting the regularizers we can rewrite (1) as follows:

$$\min_{f^T\in H_K} \gamma_A \|f^T\|_K^2 + \frac{1}{n_l}\sum_{i=1}^{n_l}(f_i^T - y_i^T)^2$$
$$+\frac{\theta}{2}\sum_{j=n_l+1}^{n_T}\|f_j^T - \sum_{s=1}^{k}\gamma_s f_j^s\|^2 + \frac{\gamma_I}{n_T^2} f^{T'} L f^T \tag{8}$$

By the Representer theorem [24], we can find an optimal solution of (8), which is a linear expansion of the kernel function K, over both the labeled D_l^T and the pseudo labeled target domain data D_u^T given as follows:

$$f^T(x) = \sum_{i=1}^{n_l+n_u} \alpha_i K(x_i, x). \tag{9}$$

Substituting this into (8), we can obtain the optimal $\alpha = [\alpha_1 \cdots\cdots\cdots \alpha_{n_l+n_u}]^T$ by solving the following optimization problem:

$$\min_{\alpha} \frac{1}{n_l + \theta n_u}(Y - K\alpha)' J(Y - K\alpha)$$
$$+\gamma_A \alpha' K\alpha + \frac{\gamma_I}{(n_u + n_l)^2}\alpha' KLK\alpha \tag{10}$$

where K is the $(n_l+n_u)\times(n_l+n_u)$ kernel Gram matrix over the target domain data, Y is the label vector over labeled and pseudo labeled target domain data points given by:

$$\left[y_1 \cdots y_{n_l} \sum_s \gamma_{s(n_l+1)} f_{(n_l+1)}^s \cdots \sum_s \gamma_{s(n_l+n_u)} f_{(n_l+n_u)}^s\right] \tag{11}$$

L is the graph Laplacian defined over labeled and pseudo labeled target domain data, and J is a diagonal matrix of size $(n_l + n_u) \times (n_l + n_u)$ given by $J = diag(1, \cdots 1, \theta, \cdots \theta)$ with the first n_l diagonal entries as 1 and the rest as θ. θ is assigned a number between 0 and 1, thus the pseudo labels of the target domain data get smaller weights compared to the labels of the labeled target domain data. From (10), the optimal α^* is given by:

$$\alpha^* = \left(JK + \gamma_A(n_l + \theta n_u)I + \frac{\gamma_I(n_l + \theta n_u)}{(n_u + n_l)^2} LK\right)^{-1} JY.$$

With the computed α^*, the prediction of any unseen test data x is given by:

$$f^T(x) = \sum_{i=1}^{n_l+n_u} \alpha_i^* K(x_i, x). \tag{12}$$

Since the proposed domain adaptation framework is based on multiple sources whose similarities to target domain data or weights are computed based on a conditional probability based weighting scheme, we refer the proposed framework as *Conditional Probability based Multi-Source Domain Adaptation (CP-MDA)*.

3. RELATED WORK

Most of the existing methods measure the similarity between a particular source and the target domain based on the similarity of their marginal probabilities. Shimodaira *et al.* [27] biased the training samples by their test-to-training ratio to match the marginal distribution of the test data. Sugiyama *et al.* [29] proposed to reduce the gap in marginal probabilities by minimizing the KL-divergence between test and weighted training data and Bickel *et al.* [5] discriminated training against test data with a probabilistic model that accounts for the marginal probability difference between training and test distribution. There are several other methods which are also based on marginal probability differences using Maximum Mean Discrepancy [7] as a measure such as Kernel Mean Matching [14] and Transfer Component Analysis [20]. The proposed domain adaptation framework CP-MDA, differs from all these methods in two ways: (1) it is predominantly based on conditional probability differences, and (2) it is based on multiple source domains.

Several algorithms have been developed in past to combine knowledge from multiple sources. Luo *et al.* used consensus maximization as the basis of combining multiple source data [18]. Mansour *et al.* based the transferability of knowledge on a distribution weighted combination of the hypothesis generated by the independent sources [19]. The theoretical proof of both frameworks are based on strong assumptions on the predictive power of the individual source domains on the target domain data. In [26], a clustering based knowledge transfer was proposed for applications with different class labels across source and target domains, unlike the application addressed in this paper.

The proposed framework is related to two multi-source domain adaptation frameworks including Domain Adaptation Machine (DAM) [11] and Locally Weighted Ensemble (LWE) [12]. The proposed framework differs from DAM in the way the weights are computed for different auxiliary sources. In DAM, the weight assigned to each auxiliary source is obtained by measuring the marginal probability distribution difference between the target domain and the particular auxiliary source only, using an empirical estimate of the difference based on the Maximum Mean Discrepancy measure [7]. The proposed framework however computes weights for the auxiliary source data considering predominantly conditional probability distribution of the target data. The weights for all sources are computed in a joint optimization framework, which takes the interaction among multiple auxiliary sources into account.

The proposed framework differs from LWE [12] in that in LWE, the label y of an unlabeled target domain data x is computed using a local weighting ensemble (LWE) scheme:

$$P(y|x) = \sum_{i=1}^{k} w_{M_i,x} P(y|M_i, x) \tag{13}$$

where $P(y|M_i, x)$ is the prediction made by one of the k models M_i for target data point x and $w_{M_i,x}$ is the weight of the model M_i at point x computed by comparing the similarity graphs of the source and target data around point x. Different from the proposed weighting scheme where we compute all weights in a joint framework, the weight for each auxiliary classifier is computed independently [12].

We also compare our framework with representative single-source domain adaptation algorithms such as Kernel Mean Matching (KMM) proposed by Huang *et al.* [14], Transfer Component Analysis (TCA) proposed by Pan *et al.* [21] and KMapEnsemble (KE) proposed by Zhong *et al.* [31]. KMM re-weights the samples in the source domain so as to minimize the marginal probability difference between the source and target domain using Maximum Mean Discrepancy (MMD) as the measure. TCA is based on feature mapping so as to reduce the marginal probability differences between the source and target distributions again using MMD as the measure. KE differs from the first two algorithms, in which it addresses the conditional probability differences by sample selection after performing a feature mapping step to reduce the marginal probability differences.

There was some classification work dealing with physiological signals using neural networks [17] and linear discriminant analysis [15]; they achieved moderate generalization performance across subjects. To the best of our knowledge we report the first systematic empirical analysis of domain adaptation methods to address the distribution differences due to the subject based variability in physiological signals.

4. EXPERIMENTS

The proposed algorithm has been evaluated on a synthetic dataset and on real-world SEMG data collected from 8 different subjects during a fatigue-causing exercise.

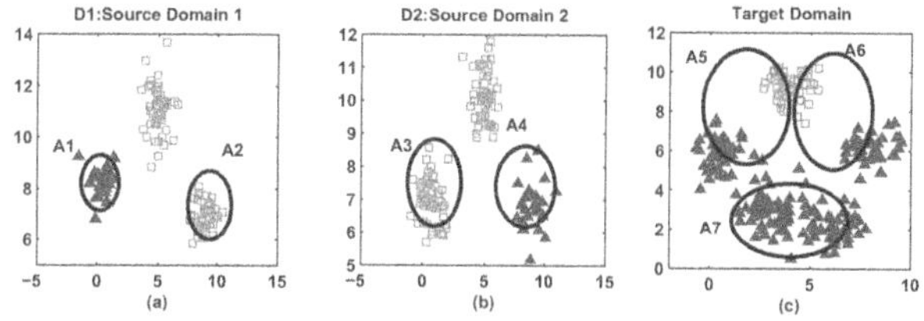

Figure 2: The synthetic dataset includes two source domains (D1 and D2) and one target domain with conflicting conditional probabilities.

4.1 Experimental Setup

4.1.1 Synthetic data

The synthetic data set consisting of two source domains D1 and D2 and a target domain as shown in Figure 2, are generated from several Gaussian distributions with different mean and variances. Source domain D1 has 20 positive and 90 negative examples and source domain D2 has 25 positive and 100 negative examples. There are conflicting conditional probabilities between D1 and D2 as shown in four regions (A1, A2, A3 and A4) in Figure 2. The target domain has 180 positive and 60 negative examples. Region A5 of the target domain is similar to D1, while region A6 is similar to D2. Thus the data exhibits conflicting and varied difference in conditional probability between the source domains and the target domain.

4.1.2 SEMG data

The SEMG data was collected during a repetitive gripping action performed by the forearm. Figure 3 shows the subject with surface EMG differential electrodes on the extensor carpi radialis muscle to record the SEMG signal. The subject performs a cycle of flexion-extension of forearm as shown in Figure 3 at two different speeds, i.e., low speed (1 cycles/sec) and high speed (2 cycles/sec) repetitively for about 4 minutes. The cycles of low and high speed are alternated after every minute to form four phases (or classes) as discussed in the introduction.

The raw SEMG activity was recorded by Grass Model 8-16C at 1000Hz and passed through a band pass filter of 20Hz to 500Hz. The data was collected and saved by the LabView software (from National Instruments) running on a PC. Data of the order of 1.92 Million samples ($1000 \times 4 \times 60 \times 8$), was collected from 8 subjects including male and female of the age group of 25 years to 45 years. A set of twelve amplitude and frequency domain features including mean frequency, median frequency, spectral energy, spectral entropy, root mean square, number of zero crossings, to mention a few are derived from running windows of 1000 time samples with 50% overlap [16].

Each subject data consists of around 280 to 400 samples of 12 dimensional feature vectors, belonging to four classes with around 70 to 100 samples per class (some subjects who got fatigued sooner and hence could not maintain the required uniform speed for 1 minute the time period was reduced to 30 to 45 secs per phase, hence the number of samples varies between different subjects).

4.1.3 Experimental Procedure

To evaluate the effectiveness of the proposed method, we compare the results with four baseline methods, including

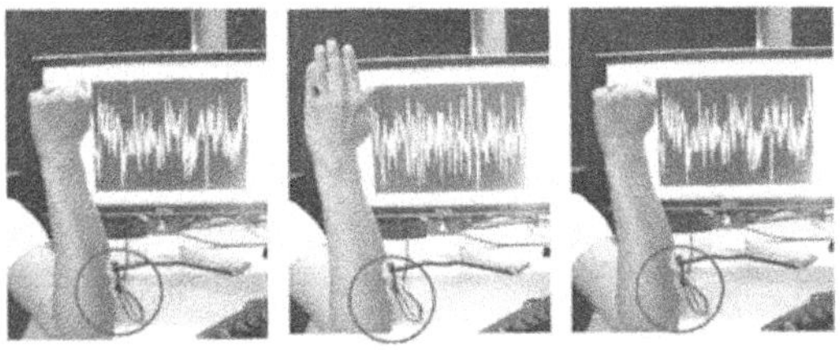

Figure 3: SEMG data collection during a repetitive gripping activity

SVM-C, SVM-M, SMA, and TSVM (Transductive SVM), and two recently proposed multi-source learning methods, including Locally Weighted Ensemble (LWE) [12] and Domain Adaptation Machine (DAM) [11]. More details on LWE and DAM are given in Section 3.

SVM-C refers to *all but one* method where the training data comprises of data from seven subjects and the test data is the data from the remaining subject. SVM-M, refers to the *majority voting* based ensemble framework. The class y assigned to each unlabeled test data x is $\max_y NV(y|x)$ where $NV(y|x)$ is the number of votes given for class y for a particular test sample x by the seven auxiliary sources. SMA refers to *simple model averaging*, which provides equal weight to all the classifiers learned on each auxiliary source domain in an weighted ensemble framework used to generate the label for the target domain data. TSVM refers to Transductive SVM [3] implemented in the svmlight package. It is a semi-supervised method where the training data consists of labeled data from all seven subjects from the source domain and unlabeled data from the target subject.

We vary the number of labeled samples per class in the target domain. DAM(1) and DAM(7) refer to the DAM framework with 1 and 7 target domain labeled samples per class respectively. The proposed CP-MDA method is also implemented using 1 and 7 labeled data from target domain, referred as CP-MDA(1) and CP-MDA(7) respectively. For both cases the unlabeled data from the target domain, is fixed at 10% of the target domain data. The weights of the auxiliary sources computed by the proposed method are also based on this 10% unlabeled target domain data. The rest of the target domain data is treated as unseen target domain data. All the methods are tested on the same pool of *unseen* unlabeled target domain data. The accuracies are computed in a subject independent manner.

We mention here briefly some of the parameters used in implementing the existing and the proposed method. The values of γ_A and γ_I were kept as 0.014 and 0.01 respectively, as suggested in [4]. The Laplacian graph matrix used in calculating the weights was set as 'binary' type based on the N nearest neighbors with $N = 10$. The value of Θ was estimated via 5-fold cross validation on the set $\{i10^{-2}|i = 0, 1, \cdots, 100\}$.

4.2 Results and Analysis

4.2.1 Synthetic data

Figure 4 shows the classification accuracies of different methods on the synthetic dataset. The classification accuracies on the target domain data when the SVM classifier is applied on the source data D1 or D2 without using any transfer learning methodologies are 62.97% and 72.61%, respectively.

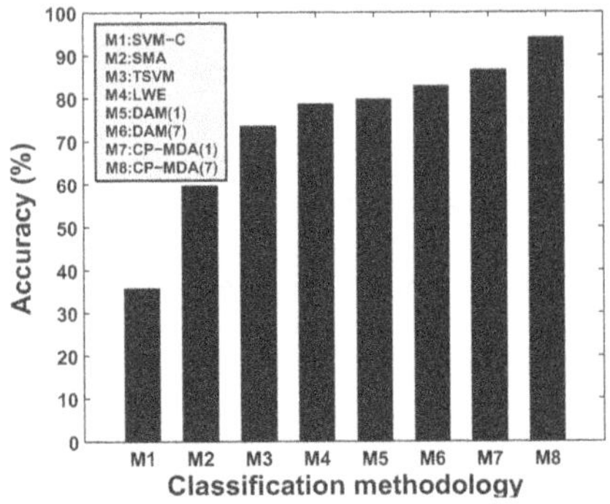

Figure 4: Comparative performance of different methods on the synthetic data - Accuracy (%)

We observe that SVM-C and SMA perform poorly. This may be attributed to the conflicting conditional probabilities between the two training sets, that degrade the performance of the classifier when learned on the combined data. In addition, there is a conditional probability difference with the test data, hence the brute-force use of knowledge without evaluating similarities between the source and the target data degrades the performance of the classifier in the target domain [25] related to *negative transfer* [23].

We also observe that CP-MDA(1) improves the classification accuracy by 20% to 50% over the baseline methods without any transfer learning and by 11% over LWE. We also observe that CP-MDA(1) outperforms DAM(7). Since the target classifier is learned using some labeled and some pseudo labeled data, which is labeled using the proposed weighting scheme, hence higher classification accuracy verifies the effectiveness of the proposed weighting scheme in Section 2.3.

To further evaluate the effectiveness of the proposed weighting scheme, we compared three different weighting schemes using the weighted ensemble methodology of LWE in (13). MMD-WE refers to the method when weights are computed based on MMD, and CP-MDA-WE refers to the method when weights are computed based on the proposed framework in (7). The accuracies using LWE, MMD-WE, and CP-MDA-WE are 78.6%, 72.75%, and 80.54%, respectively. To examine why the proposed method outperforms the other two, we report the predictive power of each of the two source data (D1, D2) as well as the weights obtained by different methods. The classification accuracies obtained using the source data D1 and D2 individually are 62.97% and 72.61%, respectively. The weights for D1 and D2 obtained by MMD-WE are 0.93 and 0.06, respectively; the weights for D1 and D2 obtained by CP-MDA-WE are 0.08 and 0.91, respectively. Thus, the weights obtained by the proposed method match the predictive powers of the source data better than MMD-WE.

4.2.2 SEMG data

We compare different methods including SVM-C, SVM-M, SMA, TSVM, LWE, DAM and the proposed CP-MDA. The results are summarized in Table 1. The first column of the table indicates the subject data under test (target domain). The training data (source domain) consists of the data from the remaining seven subjects. Similar to the results obtained in the case of synthetic data we see that

Table 1: Comparative performance of different methods on SEMG data - Accuracy (%)

Test Sub	SVM-C	SVM-M	SMA	TSVM	LWE	DAM(1)	DAM(7)	CP-MDA(1)	CP-MDA(7)
1	70.76	33.9	44.96	49.09	67.44	74.83	77.43	81.93	85.25
2	43.69	50.76	44.61	55.68	77.54	81.36	83.35	84.73	87.7
3	50.11	56.85	56.84	65.09	75.55	74.77	78.99	82.45	85.06
4	59.65	47.93	49.67	56.98	81.22	80.63	84.32	81.27	86.4
5	40.37	44.79	50.15	62.5	52.48	76.74	81.14	80.74	86.62
6	59.21	61.45	60.33	71.32	65.77	59.21	74.28	83.12	88.09
7	47.13	46.91	45.76	60.73	60.32	74.27	83.31	81.57	86.4
8	69.85	64.53	74.46	68.55	72.81	84.55	86.6	88.5	90.56
Average	55.09	50.85	53.34	61.24	69.14	75.79	81.18	**83.04**	**87.01**

Table 2: Comparison of SVM-T, DAM, and CP-MDA on Subject 6 (top) and Subject 7 (bottom) in terms of accuracy (%) when the number of labeled target domain data per class varies.

	Number of labeled data per class					
Method	1	2	3	4	6	7
SVM-T	4.26	4.26	49.09	73.63	84.69	85.67
DAM	59.12	59.21	59.35	59.59	65.03	74.28
CP-MDA	**83.12**	83.12	85.45	87.58	87.77	88.09
SVM-T	10.59	45.5	77.79	83.25	85.48	84.97
DAM	74.27	75.11	79.10	81.19	82.43	83.3
CP-MDA	**81.57**	83.99	85.81	86.24	86.32	86.4

SVM-C, SVM-M, SMA, and TSVM perform very poorly. We observe significant improvement in classification accuracy when domain adaptation methodologies are employed. The proposed method CP-MDA(1) provides a 20% to 30% improvement over the baseline methods including SVM-C, SVM-M, SMA and TSVM. The classification accuracies of the proposed method are in average 13% higher than LWE. It is also observed as in the case of synthetic data that CP-MDA(1) performs not only better than DAM(1) but also better than DAM(7) in 5 out of 8 cases. These results verify the effectiveness of the proposed method.

Next, we evaluate the performance of CP-MDA when the number of labeled target domain data varies. We compare CP-MDA with DAM and SVM-T. SVM-T refers to an SVM classifier trained on the labeled target domain data. The results for two subjects are summarized in Table 2; we obtain similar results for the other six subjects and the results are omitted. We can observe from the table that when the number of labeled target domain data per class is small, e.g., 1 to 4 samples per class, both domain adaptation methods perform much better than SVM-T. But with an increasing number of labeled data from the target domain the accuracies become comparable. However the proposed method always performs better than the other two methods. This result demonstrates that domain adaption is especially useful when the amount of labeled target domain data is small.

Similar to the synthetic data case, we compare the performance of the weighting schemes used in LWE, DAM and CP-MDA. Table 3 summarizes the results for different test cases. We observe that CP-MDA-WE performs better than the other methods in 6 out of 8 cases, and LWE performs better in the remaining 2 cases. Recall that like CP-MDA-WE, LWE computes weights for the auxiliary source domain based on the conditional probability differences between the source and target domains, while MMD-WE computes the weights based on the marginal probability differences only. Since SEMG data has significant conditional probability differences, CP-MDA-WE and LWE are expected to outperform DAM-WE.

Table 3: Comparison of different weighting schemes for different test subjects - Accuracy (%).

Test Sub	LWE	MMD-WE	CP-MDA-WE
1	67.44	68.27	75.12
2	77.54	69.48	83.23
3	75.55	71.84	75.68
4	81.22	62.65	81.09
5	52.48	68.32	78.16
6	65.77	58.91	76.11
7	60.32	67.75	75.07
8	72.81	66.11	78.71
Average	69.14%	66.66%	**77.89**%

The proposed algorithm CP-MDA computes weights for each class for each of the auxiliary source domain data, thus exploiting the similarities and dissimilarities at the class level. Table 4 shows the weights for four different classes assigned to each training subject in the source domain for test subject 1 in the target domain. We observe that the proposed weighting scheme assigns different weights to different auxiliary source domain data (subject data) for different classes. Subjects 5 and 8 get higher weights for class 1, subject 7 gets a higher weight for class 2, subject 5 gets a higher weight for class 3, and for class 4 subject 4 gets a higher weight. We observe from Figure 1 that the data distribution of class 4 of subject 1 is very similar to that of class 4 of subject 4.

Table 4: Weights computed by CP-MDA for four different classes for each of the source domain subjects 2-8 for test target subject 1.

Class	Target subject						
	2	3	4	5	6	7	8
1	0	0	0.02	0.50	0.48	0	0
2	0	0.01	0.03	0	0.11	0.74	0.11
3	0	0.02	0.12	0.75	0	0.01	0.11
4	0.09	0.02	0.66	0.11	0.11	0.01	0

One of the key advantage of the proposed algorithm is that it exploits the information from multiple source domains for classifying the target data. It will be interesting to study how the number of sources used in the training set affects the classification. Figure 5 presents the error rates

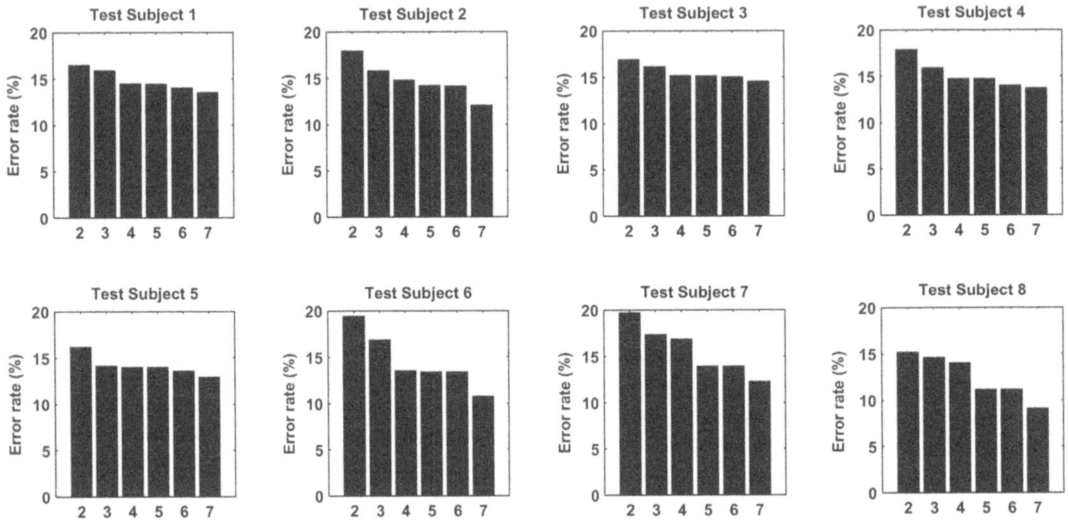

Figure 5: The effect of the number of auxiliary source domains (horizontal axis) in the training set on the proposed CP-MDA algorithm in terms of the classification error rates (%) for all eight subjects.

obtained for each test subject when the number of subjects in the source domain varies (from 1 to 7); we simply keep adding subjects to the training set in increasing order of the subject number. We observe that for all subjects, the error rate decreases monotonically when the number of subjects increases. These results demonstrate the effectiveness of the proposed algorithm for extracting useful information from multiple sources.

Table 5: Comparison of CP-MDA with three single source domain adaptation algorithms (KMM, TCA, and KE) - Accuracy(%).

Test Sub	CP-MDA(7)	KMM	TCA	KE
1	85.25	65.15	45.15	71.85
2	87.7	46.96	68.93	74.62
3	85.06	59.55	56.78	74.79
4	86.4	73.38	52.68	69.35
5	86.62	45.31	60.15	73.44
6	88.09	70.62	76.92	83.92
7	86.4	51.13	55.64	77.97
8	90.56	42.79	67.24	79.48
Average	**87.01**	56.86	53.84	75.67

To evaluate the benefit of a multi-source domain adaption framework for addressing subject based variability, we compare the proposed algorithm with three representative single-source domain adaption algorithms discussed in Section 3. Table 5 summarizes the classification accuracies obtained by different methods for each of the test subjects. The target data is from the subject shown in column 1 and the source data consists of the combined data from the remaining seven subject. Classification results were averaged over 10 runs with different sets of randomly selected 7 labeled samples per class from the target domain data. We can observe from the table that combining all the subject data and forming a single domain degrades the performance. We also observe that among the three single domain adaption algorithms, KMM or TCA which consider the marginal probability differences only perform worse than KE. These results are expected as SEMG data has significant conditional probability differences. Our results demonstrate the effectiveness of the proposed multi-domain framework for dealing with subject based variability in SEMG data.

5. CONCLUSION

We consider the characterization of muscle fatigue through noninvasive sensing mechanism such as surface electromyography (SEMG). The variation in SEMG parameters from subject to subject creates a difference in the data distribution, thus traditional data mining algorithms may not be effective. In this paper, we propose a transfer learning framework based on the multi-source domain adaptation methodology for detecting different stages of fatigue using SEMG signals. The proposed CP-MDA framework differs from most existing work in domain adaption in that it addresses the conditional probability distribution differences across domains based on a novel weighting scheme. We have validated the proposed framework using a synthetic dataset and real-world SEMG data collected from eight different subjects during a fatiguing exercise. Our comprehensive experiments demonstrate the effectiveness of the proposed framework and suggest that it is possible to develop a generalized framework with SEMG data. This increases the scope of application of SEMG data for fatigue detection in a larger scale beyond training and rehabilitation settings for monitoring during daily life and industrial work, as it alleviates the need for subject specific calibration for assessing the physiological state across subjects.

We plan to extend the proposed framework to applications involving other types of physiological signals for developing generalized models across subjects for emotion and health monitoring in everyday life, industrial work and geriatric care [17, 15]. In addition, we plan to study the generalization performance of the proposed framework.

6. ACKNOWLEDGEMENTS

We acknowledge Dr. Arthur Gretton, Dr. Yishay Mansour, Dr. Lixin Duan, Dr. Jing Gao, Dr. Erheng Zhong, Dr. Luo Ping, Dr. Sinno Jialin Pan, and Dr. Masashi Sugiyama for providing codes and other supporting materials. This research is sponsored in part by NSF IIS-0953662, CCF-1025177, and ONR N00014-11-1-0108.

7. REFERENCES

[1] `http://www.environmental-ergonomics.org/`.

[2] `http://en.wikipedia.org/wiki/Factor_analysis`.

[3] http://svmlight.joachims.org/.

[4] M. Belkin, P. Niyogi, and V. Sindhwani. Manifold regularization: A geometric framework for learning from labeled and unlabeled examples. *JMLR*, 7:2399–2434, 2006.

[5] S. Bickel, M. Brückner, and T. Scheffer. Discriminative learning under covariate shift. *JMLR*, 10:2137–2155, 2009.

[6] J. Blitzer, M.Dredze, and F. Pereira. Biographies, bollywood, boom-boxes and blenders: Domain adaptation for sentiment classification. In *ACL*, 2007.

[7] K. Borgwardt, A. Gretton, M. Rasch, H. Kriegel, Schölkopf, and A. J. Smola. Integrating structured biological data by kernel maximum mean discrepancy. *Bioinformatics*, 22(14):49–57, 2006.

[8] R. Chattopadhyay, P. Gaurav, and P. Sethuraman. A generalized machine learning framework for continuous monitoring of physiological conditions based on fatigue and intensity of activity in daily living. In *WIML, NIPS*, 2009.

[9] R. Chattopadhyay, P. Sethuraman, and P. Gaurav. Towards fatigue and intensity measurement framework during continuous repetitive activities. In *I2MTC*, 2010.

[10] H. Daumé III. Frustratingly easy domain adaptation. In *ACL*, 2007.

[11] L. Duan, I. W. Tsang, D. Xu, and T. S. Chua. Domain adaptation from multiple sources via auxiliary classifiers. In *ICML*, pages 289–296, 2009.

[12] J. Gao, W. Fan, J. Jiang, and J. Han. Knowledge transfer via multiple model local structure mapping. In *KDD*, pages 283–291, 2008.

[13] P. Higgs. Upper extremity impairment in workers performing repetitive tasks. *Plastic and reconstructive surgery*, 90:614, 1992.

[14] J. Huang, A. J. Smola, A. Gretton, K. Borgwardt, and B. Schölkopf. Correcting sample selection bias by unlabeled data. In *NIPS*, 2007.

[15] J. Kim and E. Andre. Emotion recognition based on physiological changes in music listening. *IEEE Transactions on Pattern Analysis and Machine Intelligence*, 30(12):2067–2083, 2008.

[16] M. Knaflitz and P. Bonato. Time-frequency methods applied to muscle fatigue assessment during dynamic contractions. 9(5):337–350, Oct. 1999.

[17] E. Leon, G. Clarke, V. Callaghan, and F. Sepulveda. A user independent real time emotion recognition system for software agents in domestic environment. *Engineering Applications of Artificial Intelligence*, 20(3):337–345, 2007.

[18] P. Luo, F. Zhuang, H. Xiong, Y. Xiong, and Q. He. Transfer learning from multiple source domains via consensus regularization. In *CIKM*, 2008.

[19] Y. Mansour, M. Mohri, and A. Rostamizadeh. Domain adaptation with multiple sources. In *NIPS*, 2009.

[20] S. J. Pan, J. T. Kwok, and Q. Yang. Transfer learning via dimensionality reduction. In *AAAI*, 2008.

[21] S. J. Pan, I. W. Tsang, J. T. Kwok, and Q. Yang. Domain adaptation via transfer component analysis. In *IJCAI*, 2009.

[22] S. J. Pan and Q. Yang. A survey on transfer learning. *IEEE Transactions on Knowledge and Data Engineering*, 2009.

[23] M. Rosenstein, Z. Marx, and L. Kaelbling. To transfer or not to transfer. In *NIPS 2005 Workshop on Inductive Transfer: 10 Years Later*, 2005.

[24] B. Schölkopf and A. J. Smola. *Learning with Kernels Support Vector Machines, Regularization, Optimization and Beyond*. The MIT Press, 2002.

[25] G. Schweikert, C. Widmer, B. Schölkopf, and G. Rätsch. An empirical analysis of domain adaptation algorithms for genomic sequence analysis. In *NIPS*, 2009.

[26] X. Shi, W. Fan, Q. Yang, and J. Ren. Relaxed transfer of different classes via spectral partition. In *KDD*, 2009.

[27] H. Shimodaira. Improving predictive inference under covariate shift by weighting the log-likelihood function. In *JSPI*, 2000.

[28] B. Silverstein, L. Fine, and T. Armstrong. Hand wrist cumulative trauma disorders in industry [1351-0711]. *Occupational and Environmental Medicine*, 43:779, 1986.

[29] M. Sugiyama, S. Nakajima, H. Kashima, P. V. Buenau, and M. Kawanabe. Direct importance estimation with model selection and its application to covariate shift adaptation. In *NIPS*, 2008.

[30] V. L. Young, M. K. Seaton, C. A. Feely, C. Arfken, D. F. Edwards, C. M. Baum, and S. Logan. Detecting cumulative trauma disorders in workers performing repetitive tasks. In *AJIM*, 1995.

[31] E. Zhong, W. Fan, J. Peng, K. Zhang, J. Ren, D. Turaga, and O. Verscheure. Cross domain distribution adaptation via kernel mapping. In *KDD*, 2009.

Author Index

Abdulhayoglu, Melih 222
Achlioptas, Panagiotis 726
Agarwal, Deepak 123, 132, 141, 609, 1361
Aggarwal, Charu C. 992, 1226
Agrawal, Rakesh 351, 404
Ahmed, Amr 114
Akoglu, Leman 663
Almeida, Virgílio 150
Alqadah, Faris 795
Aly, Mohamed 114
Anand, Anushka 6
Anderson, Bo 1307
Andrzejewski, David 600
Aoyama, Kazuo 1055
Applegate, David 636
Atkinson, Martin 749
Attenberg, Josh 186
Balac, Natasha 747
Banerjee, Arindam 956, 1163
Barabási, Albert-László 1100
Barbier, Geoffrey 511
Batista, Gustavo 761
Bekkerman, Ron 231
Belkin, Mikhail 877
Berger-Wolf, Tanya Y. 105
Berkhin, Pavel 1307
Bhadra, Sahely 1406
Bhaduri, Kanishka 859
Bhatnagar, Raj 795
Bhattacharyya, Chiranjib 78
Bifet, Albert 591, 868
Bilenko, Mikhail 413
Bing, Lidong 1244
Blei, David M. 448
Böhm, Christian 1127
Boire, Richard 785
Boley, Daniel 956
Boley, Mario 582
Bonchi, Francesco 529
Borgwardt, Karsten M. 726
Botvinick, Matthew 940
Boyd, Stephen 1
Briffa-Mirabella, Susan 301
Brückner, Michael 547
Butler, Patrick 360
Buttler, David 600
Calais Guerra, Pedro H. 150
Capra, Licia 1181
Castillo, Carlos 529
Cerrato, Dean 343
Chaki, Sagar 15
Chakrabarti, Soumen 78
Chang, Kai-Wei 699
Chattopadhyay, Rita 717
Chau, Duen Horng 739
Chawla, Sanjay 1010
Chen, Bee-Chung 132, 159, 609
Chen, Feilong 386
Chen, Feng 240
Chen, Jian 735, 983
Chen, Jianhui 42
Chen, Kewei 931
Chen, Ming-Syan 1262
Chen, Ning 475
Chen, Rui 493
Chen, Shu-Ching 283
Chen, Weizhu 1388
Chen, Ye 1307
Cheng, James 672
Chitrapura, Krishna-Prasad 141
Chitta, Radha 895
Cho, Eunjoon 1082
Chu, Shumo 672
Chu, Wei 195
Cicotti, Pietro 747
Cohen, Cory 15
Cook, Diane J. 904
Cordeiro, Robson L. F. 690
Cormode, Graham 1253
Cotter, Andrew 805
Crammer, Koby 24
Cristianini, Nello 466
Cui, Ying 265
Cule, Boris 1172
Dai, Jing 240
Dalvi, Nilesh 1325
Danilevsky, Marina 1298
Das, Gautam 538
Das, Mahashweta 538
Das, Puja 1163
Dasgupta, Anirban 1073
Dasu, Tamraparni 636
Davidson, Ian 717, 1136
Davison, Brian D. 484
De Bie, Tijl 466, 564
Delporte, Julien 377
Deng, Guishi 292
Deng, Hongbo 1271

Devanur, Nikhil R. 1307
Dhillon, Inderjit S. 1064
Dhurandhar, Amit 1118
Djuric, Nemanja 24
Dom, Byron 832
Dror, Gideon 1109
Dubey, Avinava 78
Dufau-Joel, Frédéric 377
Dumais, Susan 457
Ebadollahi, Shahram 395
Elango, Pradheep 132
El-Arini, Khalid 439
Elder, IV, John F. 786
Eliassi-Rad, Tina 663
Ene, Alina 681
Faloutsos, Christos .. 663, 690, 739, 1091, 1370
Fan, Jian 743
Fan, Quanfu 307
Fan, Wei 654, 717, 1001
Fei, Hongliang 886
Fernandez Martinez, Felipe 780
Fleisher, Adam 931
Fogelman-Soulié, Françoise 377
Fujimaki, Ryohei 645
Fung, Benjamin C. M. 493
Fuxman, Ariel 404
Fyson, Nick 466
Gabbur, Prasad 307
Gallagher, Brian 663
Gao, Bin 96
Gao, Bo 769
Gao, Byron J. 177
Garcia-Molina, Hector 1019
Garg, Sachin 141
Gärtner, Thomas 582
Gavaldà, Ricard 591
Gavish, Matan 231
Ge, Yong 735, 983
Gemulla, Rainer 69
Getoor, Lise 87
Ghani, Rayid 325
Gherman, Sorin 213
Ghoting, Amol 334
Giannella, Chris R. 859
Giannotti, Fosca 1100, 1190
Gilpin, Sean 1136
Gionis, Aristides 529
Givoni, Inmar E. 404
Gkoulalas-Divanis, Aris 1316
Gleich, David F. 60
Goethals, Bart 757
Gray, Alexander G. 627
Grossglauser, Matthias 1235
Guérif, Sébastien 377
Guestrin, Carlos 439
Gundecha, Pritam 511
Guo, Jian 159, 484
Guo, Li 177
Guo, Yanhong 292
Gupta, Avinash 343
Gupta, Umesh 222
Gurfinkel, Arie 15
Gurumurthy, Siva 832
Haas, Peter J. 69
Hainsworth, John 274
Han, Jiawei 753, 1271, 1298
Hanauer, David A. 360
Hartikainen, Aleksi 965
Haussler, David 3
Havens, Timothy C. 895
He, Jingrui 1028, 1208
Henderson, Keith 663
Hinkka, Atte 965
Ho, Chia-Hua 33
Holmes, Geoff 591, 868
Hong, Hui 922
Hong, Jason I. 739
Hong, Liangjie 484, 832
Hristidis, Vagelis 538
Hseuh, Pei-yun 1145
Hsieh, Cho-Jui 1064
Hsu, Tai 783
Hu, Jianying 395
Huan, Jun 886
Huang, Shuai 931
Ieong, Samuel 351
Ifrim, Georgiana 708
Im, Sungjin 681
Imberman, Susan P. 301
Inchiosa, Mario E. 778
Jack, Jr., Clifford R. 369
Jain, Anil K. 895
Janowicz, Krzysztof 520
Jansen, Timm 868
Ji, Ming 1298
Jiang, Long 1397
Jiang, Ruoyi 886
Jiang, Shan 1244
Jiang, Xiao 1280
Jin, Rong 204, 895
Jin, Ruoming 922, 992
Jin, Xin 753
Jones, Rosie 343
Jonna, Kishore 773

Joshi, Parag 743
Josifovski, Vanja 114
Kambadur, Prabhanjan 334
Kang, U 690, 1091
Kannan, Anitha 404
Kannan, P V 779
Kannan, Ramakrishnan 334
Karras, Panagiotis 1334
Kashyap, Shrikant 1334
Kataria, Saurabh S. 1037
Kaufman, Shachar 556
Keller, Benjamin J. 360
Keogh, Eamonn 761, 1154
Keshet, Joseph 805
Kim, Jong 1289
Kittur, Aniket 739
Kohn, Martin S. 395
Kok, Stanley 87
Kong, Xiangnan 654
Konuru, Ravi 1028
Koren, Yehuda 913, 1109
Kota, Nagaraj 141, 1361
Kranen, Philipp 868
Kremer, Hardy 868
Kress, Michael E. 301
Krishna, P. Radha 773
Krishnamurthy, Prabhakar 1019
Krishnan, Shankar 636
Kumar, Krishnan S. 1037
Kumar, Mohit 325
Kumar, Ravi 1073, 1325
Kumar, Vipin 823
Kushnir, Igor 301
Lam, Wai 1244
Lane, Terran 841
Lao, Ni 475
Laserson, Jonathan 395
Lathia, Neal 1181
Lawrence, Richard D. 1208
Lawrence, Rick 1145
Lee, Byoungyoung 1289
Lee, Lillian 1397
Lee, Victor E. 922
Lee, Wang-Chien 520
Leskovec, Jure 1082
Lewis, Randall A. 1019
Li, Chengkai 1280
Li, Cheng-Te 765
Li, Hang 96
Li, Jing 931
Li, Jun 177
Li, Lei 663, 1370
Li, Lexin 258
Li, Lihong 195
Li, Peter W. 369, 823
Li, Ping 1397
Li, Tao 222, 283
Li, Wei 265
Li, Xutao 1217
Liang, Chieh-Jan Mike 1370
Liberty, Edo 913
Lim, Lek-Heng 60
Lim, Suk Hwan 743
Lin, Chih-Jen 33
Lin, Ching-Yung 1028, 1091
Lin, Cindy Xide 1271
Lin, Jimmy 422
Lin, Shou-De 765
Liu, Chuanren 735
Liu, Eric Yi 947
Liu, Huan 511
Liu, Jerry 743
Liu, Jie 1370
Liu, Jun 814
Liu, Lin 992
Liu, Qi 983
Liu, Sam 743
Liu, Tie-Yan 96
Liu, Wei 1010
Liu, Yan 1145, 1208, 1343
Long, Bo 609
López, Julio 690
Loukides, Grigorios 1316
Low, Yucheng 114
Low, Yucheng 123
Lu, Chang-Tien 240
Lu, Yue 618
Lucchese, Claudio 582
Luis, Steve 283
Luo, Chunyu 292
Luo, Jiebo 753
Luo, Ping 743, 1280
Luong, Binh Thanh 502
Maarek, Yoelle 913, 1109
Machanavajjhala, Ashwin 1325
Mafra Neto, Agenor 761
Maiya, Arun S. 105
Malbasa, Vuk 1352
Mampaey, Michael 573
Manning, Christopher D. 457
Mao, Jianchang 265
Mascolo, Cecilia 1046
Mathioudakis, Michael 529
Matthews, Bryan L. 859

McCloskey, Dan P. 301
McCue, Colleen 782
Meira Jr., Wagner 150
Meliksetian, Steve 1145
Menon, Aditya Krishna 141
Mesterharm, Chris 850
Metwally, Ahmed 249
Miettinen, Pauli 51
Moens, Sandy 757
Mohammed, Noman 493
Moore, Cristopher 841
Morgan, William 422
Morinaga, Satoshi 645
Moseley, Benjamin 681
Mueen, Abdullah 1154
Mukerjee, Kunal 213
Myers, Seth A. 1082
Namata, Galileo Mark 87
Nanni, Mirco 1190
Naphade, Milind 240
Nath, Suman 1370
Neuvirth, Hani 395
Ng, Michaek K. 1217
Nijkamp, Erik 69
Norton, David 784
Norvig, Peter 2
Noulas, Anastasios 1046
Ntoulas, Alexandros 168
Oh, Jinoh 1289
Ohashi, Orlando 787
Otey, Matthew Eric 274
Ozery-Flato, Michal 395
Paduano, Matt 249
Panchanathan, Sethuraman 717
Pankanti, Sharath 307
Papadimitriou, Panagiotis 1019
Parida, Laxmi 360
Patnaik, Debprakash 360
Paurat, Daniel 582
Pazzani, Michael J. 850
Pearl, Judea 5
Pedarsani, Pedram 1235
Pednault, Edwin 334
Pedreschi, Dino 1100
Pei, Jian 1379
Pennacchiotti, Marco 430
Pereira, Francisco 940
Perlich, Claudia 556, 1145
Pfahringer, Bernhard 591, 868
Pinelli, Fabio 1190
Piskorski, Jakub 749
Plant, Claudia 1127
Pohl, Michael 274
Popescu, Ana-Maria 430
Porter, Todd 213
Pradel, Bruno 377
Provost, Foster 186
Qi, Zhongang 1199
Rai, Harikrishna G. N. 773
Raïssi, Chedy 1379
Ram, Parikshit 627
Ramage, Daniel 457
Ramakrishnan, Naren 360
Ranjan, Supranamaya 386
Rashidi, Parisa 904
Rastogi, Rajeev 1037, 1406
Rastogi, Vibhor 1325
Reiley, David H. 777, 1019
Reiman, Eric 931
Rejto, Paul 781
Richardson, Matthew 413
Rodriguez, Paul 747
Rosen-Zvi, Michal 395
Rosset, Saharon 556
Roth, Dan 699, 974
Rouquier, Jean-Baptiste 841
Rouveirol, Céline 377
Rowton, Edgar 761
Ruggieri, Salvatore 502
Sahu, Sambit 240
Saito, Kazumi 1055
Sandler, Roman 913
Sarlós, Tamas 1073
Satpal, Sandeepkumar 1406
Sawada, Hiroshi 1055
Scellato, Salvatore 1046
Scheffer, Tobias 547
Schölkopf, Bernhard 726
Sculley, D. 274
Sean, Savaneary 377
Seidl, Thomas 868
Sen, Prithviraj 1037, 1406
Sengamedu, Srinivasan H. 1037
Shao, Xuhui 258
Shen, Chao 283
Shi, Xiaoxiao 1001
Shou, Dong 520
Si, Luo 1208, 1343
Simon, György J. 369, 823
Sinkovits, Robert S. 747
Sismanis, Yannis 69
Smola, Alexander J. 114, 123
Snow, Rion 422
Snowsill, Tristan 466

Sogawa, Yasuhiro 645
Song, Chaoming 1100
Spitznagel, Bridget 274
Srebro, Nathan 805
Srebro, Nathan 877
Steinberg, Dan 780
Strande, Shawn 747
Sun, Bai 1244
Sun, Guangzhong 316
Sun, Jimeng 1091
Sundararajan, S. 1406
Szpektor, Idan 1109
Tai, Chih-Hua 1262
Tan, Chenhao 1397
Tan, Pang-Ning 386
Tang, Jie 769, 1397
Tang, Liang 283
Tas, Egemen 222
Tatineni, Mahidhar 747
Tatti, Nikolaj 573, 1172
Terzi, Evimaria 168
Terzis, Andreas 1370
Thomas, Achint 195
Toivonen, Hannu 965
Tong, Hanghang 663, 1028, 1091
Torgo, Luis 787
Traina, Agma J. M. 690
Traina, Jr., Caetano 690
Trasarti, Roberto 1190
Trinh, Hoang 307
Tsaparas, Panayiotis 168
Tseng, Belle 159
Tseng, Belle 195
Tsioutsiouliklis, Kostas 832
Tuan, Dang Nhon 6
Turini, Franco 502
Tuzhilin, Alexander 983
Ueda, Naonori 1055
Ukkonen, Antti 529
Urbanek, Simon 636
Usunier, Nicolas 377
Valizadegan, Hamed 204
Veen, Alejandro 1145
Veloso, Adriano 150
Velu, Raja 351
Vemuri, Prashanthi 369
Vijayaraghavan, Ravi 779
Vreeken, Jilles 51, 573, 757
Vucetic, Slobodan 24, 1352
Vydiswaran, V.G.Vinod 974
Wan, Yang 769
Wang, Bingsheng 240
Wang, Chi 753
Wang, Chong 448
Wang, Dashun 1100
Wang, Dong 1388
Wang, Hongning 618
Wang, Huahua 956
Wang, Min 1280
Wang, Peng 177
Wang, Shijun 204
Wang, Taifeng 96
Wang, Wei 947
Wang, Xuanhui 132
Wang, Zhuang 24
Wei, Wei 96
Wen, Zhen 1028
Wilkinson, Leland 6
Wiuf, Carsten 708
Wolter, Nicole 747
Wu, Sen 769
Wu, Teresa 931
Xie, Xing 316
Xie, Yan 1226
Xing, Eric P. 475
Xing, Xie 1010
Xiong, Hui 292, 735, 983
Yan, Xiaoran 841
Yang, De-Nian 1262
Yang, Jie 159
Yang, Ming 1199
Yang, Qiang 1388
Ye, Jieping 42, 717, 814, 931
Ye, Mao 520
Ye, Yanfang 222
Ye, Yunming 1217
Yin, Dawei 484
Yin, Peifeng 520
Young, Neal 1154
Yu, Hwanjo 1289
Yu, Philip S. 493, 654, 1001, 1226, 1262
Yu, Xiao 753
Yu, Yintao 1271
Yu, Yong 1280
Yuan, Guo-Xun 33
Yuan, Jing 316, 1010
Yuan, Lei 814
Zhai, ChengXiang 618, 974
Zhang, Dan 1208, 1343
Zhang, Jianping 1001
Zhang, Peng 177
Zhang, Ruofei 265
Zhang, Yan 1244
Zhang, Yuchen 1388

Zhang, Zhaojun 947
Zhang, Zhengyou 1199
Zhang, Zhongfei (Mark) 1199
Zhao, Bo 1271
Zheng, Li 283
Zheng, Yu 316, 1010
Zhou, Fang 965
Zhou, Jiayu 42, 814
Zhou, Ming 1397
Zhou, Wenjun 292
Zhou, Xueyuan 877
Zhou, Yunkai 274
Zhu, Jun 475
Zhu, Shenghuo 222
Zhu, Xingquan 177
Zhu, Yaojia 841
Zhuang, Weiwei 222
Zinkevich, Martin 195

www.ingramcontent.com/pod-product-compliance
Ingram Content Group UK Ltd.
Pitfield, Milton Keynes, MK11 3LW, UK
UKHW051240300926
15471UKWH00015B/1209

9 781450 312585